WHO WAS WHO AMONG ENGLISH AND EUROPEAN AUTHORS 1931-1949

Based on Entries Which First Appeared in
"The Author's and Writer's Who's Who & Reference Guide,"
Originally Compiled by Edward Martell and L. G. Pine,
and in "Who's Who Among Living Authors of Older Nations,"
Originally Compiled by Alberta Lawrence

Volume 2
G-M

An Omnigraphics Book

Gale Composite Biographical Dictionary Series
Number 2

**GALE RESEARCH COMPANY
BOOK TOWER
DETROIT, MICHIGAN 48226**

Bibliographic Note

The 23,000 entries in the present work represent the latest sketches on substantially all the individuals included in the original series, *The Author's & Writer's Who's Who & Reference Guide.* The series, edited by Edward Martell, and later by L. G. Pine, was published from 1934 through 1949 by Shaw Publishing Company, London, England. In addition, *Who's Who Among Living Authors of Older Nations,* edited by Alberta Lawrence, first published in 1931 by Golden Syndicate Publishing Company, Los Angeles, California, and reprinted in 1966 by Gale Research Company, was used for entries which did not appear in the British work.

Copyright © 1978 by Omnigraphics

Library of Congress Catalog Card Number 77-280
ISBN 0-8103-0040-7

G. B. See BOAS, Guy.

"G. J." (pen name): see Jackson, George.

"G. K. C." (pseudonym): see Chesterton, Gilbert Keith.

GABAIN, Marjorie. *b*: Le Hâvre, France. *e*: Lycée de Jeunes Filles du Hâvre, Godolphin Sc Salisbury, Höhere Töchter Schule Düsseldorf & Newnham, Cam. *Publ*: (Eng trans) Language and Thought of the Child; The Child's Conception of Causality; The Moral Judgment of the Child (Prof J. Piaget). *c.t*: Criterion. *s.s*: Philos & psychology. *c*: Arts Theatre *a*: 23 Taviton St, W.C.1. *t*: Museum 1938.

GABELENTZ, HANS von der: author; *b*. Münchenbernsdorf, Germany, April 10, 1872; *s*. Albert and Margarete (von Carlowitz) von der Gabelentz; *educ*. Gymnasium of Weimar and Jena, Univs. of Lausanne, Munich, Berlin. DEGREES: Dr. Phil. AUTHOR: Zur Geschichte der oberdeutschen Miniaturmalerei im 16. Jahrhundert, 1899; Mittelälterliche Plastik in Venedig, 1903; Die kirchliche Kunst im Italienischen Mittelalter, 1907; Führer durch das Grossherzogliche Museum in Weimar, 1910; Die Biblia pauperum der Grossherzoglichen Bibliothek zu Weimar, 1912; Zeichnungen alter Meister im Museum zu Weimar, 1913; Die Bartolommeo und die Florentiner Renaissance, 1922; Ahnentafel und Stammtafeln der Familie von der Gabelentz, 1922. Contributor to Zeitschrift für bildende Kunst, Repertorium für Kunstwissenschaft. General character of writing: history of art, family history. Religion, Evangelical. HOME: Lemnitz bei Triptis, Thüringen, Germany.

GABRIEL, Ralph Henry, M.A., Ph.D. *b*: Reading, N.Y. 1890. *e*: Starkey Semin, Watkins Glen Hgh Sch, Yale Univ. *m*: Christine Davis Gabriel. *s*: 2. *d*: 1. Sterling Prof of American History Yale, Mem Mass Hist Soc. *n.a*: New England Quarterly 1939—41. *Publ*: The Course of American Democratic Thought; Elias Boudinot, Cherokee, & His America; Main Currents in American History; The Evolution of Long Island; Gen-Ed The Pageant of America, 15 Vols. *Ctr*: Amer Hist Rev, Virginia Quart Rev, Amer Polit Sci Rev. *s.s*: Intellectual History of the U.S. *Rec*: Hiking, swimming, boating, fishing. *c*: Graduate's. *w.s*: World War I A.E.F., World War II Mem of Faculty & Lect War Dept Sch of Mil Government. *a*: 127 Verit St, New Haven, Connecticut, U.S.A. *T*: 6-7198.

GABRIEL, William Maurice, M.R.C.S., L.D.S. *b*: Lon 1863. *e*: U.C.Sc, St Bart's Hosp, Roy Dental Hosp, & N.Y., U.S.A. *m*: Leah Piza. *s*: 1. *d*: 2. Dental Surgeon. *n.a*: Ed Dental Surgeon 1904–14, Chm Ed Cmt Publ Dental Service Gazette '29–. *Publ*: Co-Trans with Dr Elgar Neumann of Witkowski's "Tightening of Loose Teeth"; Trans of Mamlok's "Filling of Teeth with Porcelain." *c.t*: Times, Dental Record, B. D. Journ, Brit Journ of Dental Science, etc. *s.s*: Dental Surgery. *Rec*: Golf. *c*: Mem B.D.A. *a*: 5 Wardrobe Pl, E.C.4, & 41 Compayne Gdns, N.W.6. *t*: City 8317.

GADD, Henry Wippell. *b*: Lon 1869. Barrister-at-Law. *Publ*: A Synopsis of the British Pharmacopœia (12 eds); Drugs: Their Production, Preparation & Properties; Notes on the Poisons & Pharmacy Act; A Guide to the Nat Ins Act. *s.s*: Law regarding pharmacy & poisons. *a*: 32 St Leonard's Rd, Exeter, Devon. *t*: 4571.

GADDUM, John Henry, F.R.S. *b*: Hale, Cheshire 1900. *e*: Rugby Sch, Camb Univ, Coll Hosp Lond. *m*: Iris Mary Harmer. *d*: 3. Prof of Pharmacology Edin. *Publ*: Pharmacology; Gefasserweiternde Stoffe Der Gewebe; Med Research Counc Reports 128 & 183. *Ctr*: Journ of Physiology, Brit Journ of Pharmacology, Biochemical Journ, Nature. *s.s*: Pharmacology. *c*: Savage. *a*: Dunraven, Lasswade, Midlothian. *T*: Lasswade 2209.

GAEHDE, CHRISTIAN: professor, author; *b*. Schwerin i. Mecklenburg, Germany, April, 1875; *s*. Julius and Franziska (Franzen) G.; *educ*. Three-Kings-School of Dresden, Realgymnasium, Univ. Leipzig. DEGREES: Dr. Phil., Professor; married. AUTHOR: David Garrick als Shakespearedarsteller, 1904; Das Theater, 1908 (3rd edit. 1921). Edited: Shakespeare's Werke (with biography and introduction), 1928 (2nd edit. 1929); Adolf Hern, 12 years dramatic critic at Dresden, 1909; Sheridan, Die Lästerschule, 1911; Emil Rosenow (dramatic collections), 1912; Heinrich von Kleist, Prinz Friedrich von Hamburg, 1922. General character of writing: essays, dramatic criticism. Religion, Lutheran. ADDRESS: Sedanstrasse 29, Dresden, Germany.

GAEKWAR III, HIS HIGHNESS MAHARAJA, SIR SAYAJI RAO: Sena Khas Khel, Samsher Bahadur, Farzand - i - Khas-i-Daulat-i-Englishia, G.C.S.I., G.C.I.E.; ruler of the State of Baroda, India; *b*. Kavlana (India), March 10, 1863; *s*. Kashirao Gaekwar (adopted by H. H. Maharaja Khanderao Gaekwar); *educ*. Maharaja's school, Baroda; DEGREE: LL.D., Benares Hindu University; *m*. (1) Chimnabai Maharani I, 1880 (d. 1885); (2), Her Highness Maharani Chimnabai II. C. I., Dec. 28, 1885. Author of Position of Women in Indian Life. AUTHOR: From Caesar to Sultan; Famine Notes. Religion: Hindu. HOME: Laxmi, Vilas Palace, Baroda, India.

GAFFNEY, Gertrude. Journalist. *n.a*: Ed Woman's Page, Feature, Gossip & Travel Writer for Irish Independent 1920–. *Publ*: Towards the Dawn. *a*: 23 Upper O'Connell St, Dublin. *t*: 44083.

GAFFNEY, Rev. Michael H., M.A., Ph.D. *b*: Kilkenny 1895. *e*: Nat Univ, Eng Coll Lisbon & the Angelic Coll Rome. *Publ*: Church & Stage; The Sorrow of the Stars (poems); Sweet Miracle (from the Portuguese); Tristram Lloyd, A Novel (with Canon Sheehan); Boys of Ben Eadar. *Ctr*: Studies, Blackfriars, Catholic World, etc. *s.s*: Revival of Christian Theatre. *a*: Black Abbey, Kilkenny.

GAIGER, S. H. Professor of Animal Path L'pool Univ; Pres Roy Col Vety Surgeons. *Publ*: Veterinary Pathology & Bacteriology. *a*: Dept of Vety Pathology, University, L'pool.

GAINFORD, Lord Joseph Albert, P.C., M.A., F.R.G.S. Dir Elec & Coal Coys. *c.t*: Trade Press. *a*: Headlam, Gainford. *t*: 7.

GAINSBOROUGH, Hugh, M.D., F.R.C.P. Physician. *c.t*: Med & Biochem Journs. *a*: 6 Park Cres, W.1. *t*: Welbeck 1519.

GAIRDNER, Alan Campbell. Surgeon. *c.t*: Post Grad Med Journ. *a*: St George in the East Hosp, Wapping, E.1. *t*: Royal 8449.

GAIT, Sir E. A., K.C.S.I., C.I.E., Kt of Grace St John of Jerusalem. *Publ*: History of Assam; Five Indian Census Reports. *c.t*: Research journs. *a*: The Croft, Park Hill, Ealing, W.5.

GALANOS, SPYROS: professor, writer; *b*. Athens, Greece, Dec., 1896; *s*. Demetrius and Tsapekou G.; *educ*. Athens Univ.; Berlin Univ.; Polytechnic Sch. of Berlin; Munich Univ.; Polytechnic Sch. of Munich; DEGREES: Doctor

Athens Univ.; chemist's diploma of foodstuffs of Berlin; m. Totomi, July 7, 1925. AUTHOR: Study of Greek Butters, 1918; Beitrag zur Kreatininbestimmung, 1922; The Greek Olives, 1922; The Greek Olive Oils, 1922; Search on the substance of Cocoa and its shell, 1924; The Vitamins, 1924; The Grease of the shell of the Cocoa Seed, 1924; Beitrage zur Kakaountersuchung, 1924; Ueber Kakaoshalenfett, 1924; Object and Importance of Chemistry of Foodstuffs, 1925; The Ouzo, 1925; Optische Untersuchungen uber die Schwefligsäure und ihre Alkalisalre, insbersondere das Kalium und Ammoniumpyrosulft., 1925; Citric acid and its presence in the Greek must., 1925; The Alcoholic Beverages, 1926; Ueber den Citronensauregehalt der Griechischen Moste, 1926; Introduction in the analysis of foodstuffs, 1926; Coffee, Tea, Cocoa, 1927. Collaborator of the Great Greek Ency.; and Encyclopedic Dictionary. Contributor to Scientific Echo; Pharmaceutical Archives; Zeitschrift fur Untersuchung der Lebensmittel (Berlin); Zeitschrift fur Elektrochemie (Leipzig). General character of writing: searching and instructive. Has made a study in general of the agricultural and cattle-raising products of Greece in every respect. Prof. of chemistry of foodstuffs, Athens Univ.; dir. of the university's Chemical Laboratory of Foodstuffs; technical adviser of Central Current Organization; mem. of High Chemical Council of the State. Relig. denom., Greek Church. CLUBS: Parnassos; Club of Men of Science. OFFICE: Chemical Laboratory, Athens University. HOME: 44 Cypress St., Athens, Greece.

GALANTIERE, Lewis. *b*: Chicago, Ill, U.S.A. 1895. *m*: Nancy Norris Davis. Ed, Translator. *Publ*: France is Full of Frenchmen. Ed & Trans: The Goncourt Journals 1851—70; The Viking Portable Maupassant; A Basic Voltaire; Kabloona. Adaptor: Antigone. Trans: Several works by well-known German & French Writers. *Ctr*: Various in U.S.A. & France. *s.s*: French Lit, Political Science & Monetary Questions. *Rec*: Conversation, music. *c*: Century, Coffee House (New York). *a*: Century Club, New York, U.S.A.

GALASSO, F., B.Sc., Sc.D., M.D., D.P.H. *Publ*: Ricerche sull 'apparecchio velenifero della Muraena h.L.; Nuova ipotesi sul Sonno Fisiologico; Höffding. Saggio di una Psicologia basata sull esperienza (trans); Tigellimus' Dictatorship; Booklets of " Il Comento " No. 1. *a*: 21 Frith St, Shaftesbury Ave, London, W.1; & 2 Sheriff Rd, London, N.W.6. *T*: Maida Vale 7522.

GALBRAITH, Dr. S. Nicol. Med Officer of Health S.W.Kent. *Publ*: Supervision of Hop-Pickers; articles on tuberculous milk; vaccination; etc. *c.t*: National & Medical press. Fel Roy Inst of Public Health. Ex-Capt R.A.M.C. *a*: Public Health Offices, The Castle, Tonbridge, Kent.

GALE, Arthur James Victor, M.A.(Cantab). *b*: London 1895. *e*: Latymer Upper Sch Hammersmith, Selwyn Coll Camb. *m*: Gwendoline Veysey. *s*: 1. *d*: 1. Editor. *n.a*: Assist-Ed Nature 1920—38, Jt-Ed '39—. *a*: c/o Macmillan & Co Ltd, St Martin's St, London, W.C.2. *T*: Whitehall 8831.

GALE, Frederick, Robert, M.B.E. *b*: Kensington 1877. *e*: Harlow. *m*: Emily Frances Tapply. *s*: 3. *d*: 1. Journalist. *n.a*: Acting Ed ('33) India Rubber Journal. *Publ*: Seaford of the Past (Jt Author); Some Unpublished Letters of George Canning. *c.t*: Various. *s.s*: Canning's Family Connections. War Service '14-19. *Rec*: Genealogical Research. *c*: Press. *a*: Orchewood, Gerrards Cross, Bucks. *t*: 457.

GALE, Rev. (James Randolph) Courtenay, M.A., O.B.E. *b*: Tavistock 1857. *e*: Priv & St John's Col Cam. *m*: May Simpson Jago (dec). *s*: 1 (dec). *d*: 4 (1 dec). *Publ*: Songs of Hope, An Anglican Appendix of Hymns & Hymn Tunes, Courses of Lectures on Music & Poetry, Songs, etc. *s.s*: Poetry, music. C.F. 1900-21. *Rec*: Travel. *a*: Christ Church Vicarage, Sutton, Surrey. *t*: 260.

GALE, N. *a*: Barganny, Brassey Rd, Bexhill-on-Sea.

GALE, Walter Keith Vernon, F.R.Hist.S. *b*: West Bromwich 1913. *e*: West Brom Gr Sch. *m*: Edith Anne Lambe. Engineer. *Publ*: Soho Foundry, A Summary of its History. *Ctr*: Engineer, Hardware Trades Journ, Steam Engineer, Ironmonger, Engineering, Newcomen Society Transactions. *s.s*: Histories of: Steam Engines, Midland Iron & Birmingham Trades, Cornish Mining & Engineering. *Rec*: Motoring, metal-working. *a*: 3 Halton Rd, Boldmere, Sutton Coldfield, Warwicks. *T*: Sutton 2614.

GALE, William Daniel. *b*: Johannesburg 1906. *e*: Boksburg Hgh Sch Transvaal. *m*: Kathleen Margaret Davidson. *d*: 2. Acting Director Pub Relations Dept Sth Rhodesia. *n.a*: Rand Dly Mail & S. Times 1926—28, The Star (Johannesburg) '28—30, Rhodesia Herald '30. Cape Argus '34, News Ed Rhodesia Herald '37—38. *Publ*: One Man's Vision: The Story of Rhodesia; The Hundred Wagons. *s.s*: History & Development of Southern Rhodesia. *Rec*: Golf, shooting. *c*: Salisbury. *a*: Public Relations Dept, P.O Box 1150, Salisbury, Southern Rhodesia. *T*: Office: Salisbury 2171 & 5546, Home: Salisbury 4124.

GALE, Zona. Author. *Publ*: Miss Lulu Bett; Faint Perfume; Mister Pitt; Preface to a Life; Yellow Gentians & Blue. *a*: c/o D. Appleton & Co, 34 Bedford St, W.C.

GALL, Douglas C., F.Inst.P., M.I.E.E. Mfr Sci Instruments. *Publ*: A.C. & D.C. Potentiometer Measurements; etc. *a*: Werndee Hall, Sth Norwood, London, S.E.25. *T*: Addiscombe 1400.

GALLACHER, William, M.P. *b*: Paisley 1881. *e*: Elem. *m*: Jean Roy. M.P. (Com) West Fife 1935—, Chrm Clyde Worker's Cttee '14—18 & Mem of Communist Party & International '20—. *Publ*: Revolt on the Clyde; Marxism & The Working Class; The Chosen Few. *Ctr*: Dly Worker, various Brit & Amer journs. *s.s*: Political Econ & Marxian Dialectics. *Rec*: Communist Party Demonstration. *a*: 68 Rowan St, Paisley.

GALLAGHER, Frank. Foundation Ed Irish Press 1931—35, Deputy Director of Broadcasting '35—39, Director of Gov. Inf Bureau '39—47. *Publ*: Days of Fear; Short Stories.

GALLARD, Joseph Adams Levitt. *b*: Greens Norton 1878. *e*: Towcester Sc & Roan Sc (Greenwich). Financial Journalist. *n.a*: Mining Ed Financial Times 1902—19, Mem Finan Staff Daily Mail '20—. *Publ*: Mines & the Speculative Investor ('20); Tin: Salient Facts & Opinions (with Dr. Murray Stuart, '29). *s.s*: Mining finance. *c*: Mining & Metallurgical. *a*: 31 Morley Rd, Lewisham, S.E.13. *t*: Lee Green 1525.

GALLE, ANDREAS WILHELM GOTTFRIED: professor (retired), author; b. Breslau, Germany, June, 1858; s. Johann Gottfried and Marie (Regenbrecht) G.; educ. Gymnasium of Breslau, Univs. of Göttingen, Berlin and Breslau. DEGREES: Dr. Phil., Professor, Privy Counselor; m. Clara Petsch, 1894 (died), AUTHOR: Geodäsie (collection Schubert XXIII), 1907; Mathematische Instrumente; Lotabweichungen im Harz und in seiner weiteren Umgebung, 1908; Das Geoid im Harz, 1914; Uber die geodäsischen Arbeiten von Gauss (Carl Friedrich Gauss works, 11 vols.), 1924 to -929. Contributor to Astronomische Nachrichten, Zeitschrift für Instrumentenkunde, Weltall, Deutsche Revue, Astronomische Vierteljahrsschrift, Braunschweiger Monatsschrift, Deutsche Literaturleitung, Forschungen und Fortschritte, Zeitschrift des deutschen Markscheider-Vereins, Zeitschrift für Vermessungswesen, Deutsche Uhrmacherzeitung, Zeitschrift für angewandte Mathematik und Mechanik, and others. General character of writing: scientific; astronomic-geodetic observations and measurements. CLUBS: Imperial Leopold German Academy of Natural Scientists at Halle, Astronomical Society, Society of Geology of Berlin, Society of Literature of Potsdam. Religion, Evangelical. ADDRESS: Neue Königsstrasse 103, Potsdam, Prussia, Germany.

GALLETLY, Alexander, M.C. *b*: Scot 1888. *e*: Edin. Gynæ & Obstetric Surg. *n.a*: Gynæ Appts held at Lon Special Women's & Gen Hosps. *c.t*: Med Journ's etc. *s.s*: Gynæ & obstetrics. *Rec*: Golf. *a*: 20 Harley St, W.1. *t*: Langham 2185.

GALLICHAN, Walter Matthew. *b*: St Helier 1861. *e*: Priv. *m*: Norah Kathleen Mutch. Author. *n.a*: Asst-Ed Free Review 1904—07, Special Comm Daily Mail '15 & '27. *Publ*: The Psychology of Marriage; Pitfalls of Marriage; The Great Unmarried; Our Hidden Selves; The Religion of Kindness; The Story of Seville; Sterilization of the Unfit; etc. *c.t*: Daily Mail, Daily Express, Star, News-Chronicle. M/C Guardian, Strand, Glasgow News, etc. *s.s*: Psychology, diet, hygiene Founded Conglomerates Supper Club. Thirty pen-names in press. *Rec*: Fly-fishing, gardening. *c*: Savage, Gaiety Luncheon, Soc of Authors. *a*: Savage Club, Adelphi, Lon, W.C.

GALLOP, Rev. Ernest Harold, H.C.F. *b*: Tottenham 1876. *e*: Marlborough, Keble & Cuddesdon Colls. *m*: Mary Parkinson. *d*: 2. *Publ*: In a Large Room ; Music; Missa Liberorum Dei; Benedicite Omnia Opera; Why Support Missions Overseas; For Better: For Worse. *a*: Bobbingworth Rectory, Ongar. *T*: Moreton 216.

GALLOP, Rodney Alexander. *b*: Folkestone 1901. *e*: Harrow and King's Coll Camb. *m*: Marjorie D. C. Bell. *s*: 2. Foreign Service, Broadcaster in seven languages, Hon Mem Danish Resistance Movement for services during the occupation. *Publ*: A Book of the Basques ; Portugal—a land of folk ways; Mexican Mosaic; The Traditional Dance (with Miss Violet Alford); Cantares Do Povo Portugues (in Portuguese). *Ctr*: Geog Mag, Cornhill, N.Y. Musical Quarterly, Times, etc. *s.s*: Travel, Folklore, Music & Dances. *Rec*: Travel, music. *c*: United Univ. *a*: 709 Nelson Hse, Dolphin Sq, London, S.W.1.

GALLOWAY, Andrew Fleming, M.D., ChM. (Glas). *b*: Bothwell 1873. *e*: H.S. & Univ Glas. Physician. *Publ*: Moveable Kidney. *c.t*: Glas Med Journ. *s.s*: Sickness & accident claims. Capt R.A.M.C (1918-19). *Rec*: Golf. *c*: R.A.C, Glas Univ. *a*: 87 Clarence Gate Gdns, N.W.1, & Little Barn, Crowlink, Friston, Sussex. *t*: Paddington 0185.

GALLOWAY, GEORGE: principal and professor; b. Stenton, Fifeshire (Scotland); s. of John G.; educ. Madras Coll., St. Andrews (Scotland), Univs. St. Andrews and Edinburgh (Scotland), Göttingen and Berlin (Germany); DEGREES: M.A., B.D., D.Phil., D.D. Officier de l'Instrution Publique; m. Lucy Lockhart Black. AUTHOR: Studies in the Philosophy of Religion, 1904; Principles of Religious Development, 1909; The Philosophy of Religion, 1914; The Idea of Immortality, 1919; Modern Thought and Religion, 1922; Faith and Reason in Religion, 1927; Religion and the Transcendent (London University Lectures), 1930. General character of writing: philosophical and theological aspects of religion. Delivered lectures on Baird Foundation, Glasgow, 1917; principal St. Mary's Theol. Coll. (Univ. St. Andrews) and occupant of chair of Systematic Theology. Relig. denom., Presbyterian. CLUB: University (Edinburgh). OFFICE: St. Mary's College, St. Andrews, Scotland.

GALLOWAY, James Forbes, M.D., M.R.C.S., L.R.C.P., D.P.H. *c.t*: Lancet. *a*: Arnold Hse, Chester. *t*: 217.

GALLOWAY, Maj. Gen. Rudolf William, C.B., C.B.E., D.S.O., M.B., Ch.B. *b*: Aberdeen 1891. *e*: Aberdeen Gr Sch, Aberdeen Univ. *m*: Lois Mary Leaning. *d*: 1. Maj Gen (late R.A.M.C.) Hygiene Specialist Army Sch of P.T. (Aldershot). *Publ*: Anatomy & Physiology of Physical Training. *s.s*: P.T., Physiology, Hygiene. *Rec*: Shooting, fishing, golf, swimming, tennis. *w.s*: A.D.M.S. 51st Div Alamein, D.D.M.S. Tripolitania, D.M.S. Italy, Chief M.O. Supreme H.Q., A.E.F. 1942 —44. *a*: c/o Messrs. Glyn Mills & Co, Kirkland Hse, Whitehall, London, S.W.1.

GALPIN, Canon Francis William, B.A., M.A. *b*: Dorchester 1858. *e*: Sherborne & Trinity Col Cam. *m*: Mary Maude Hawkins. *s*: 3. *d*: 1. Clerk in Holy Orders (ret). Hon Chapter Clerk Dio. Chelmsford 1922-33. Hon Sec Dio Synod '23. Hon Freeman of Worshipful Coy of Musicians '05. Pres Essex Archæological Soc '21-26. F.L.S. 1887. H.C.F. Hon Canon Chelmsford Cath. *Publ*: The Music of the Bible (Rev ed 1914); Old English Instruments of Music (3 eds); The Church Plate of Essex (Jt Author). *c.t*: Times Lit Supp, Roy Asiatic Soc's Journal, Music & Letters, Musical Times, Scientific American, The Antiquary, etc. *s.s*: Botany, archæology & hist & ethnology of musical instruments. *Rec*: Cycling, field work in botany & archæology, collection of musical instruments. *a*: Stanmore, 164 New Rd, Richmond, Surrey. *t*: 2063.

GALPIN, Stanley Ingram. *b*: London 1873. *e*: Sherborne Sch. *m*: Gertrude Dorothy Thomas. *n.a*: Hon-Ed Dorset Year Book (12 yrs). *Ctr*: Sporting Times, Shooting Times, Winning Post, T.P's Weekly, Dorset Year Book, etc. *Publ*: Author & Composer of Children's Songs; Upstairs to Fairyland; Little Brown Legs; Little Brown Stockings; etc. *Rec*: Golf. *c*: Willingdon Golf, Berkeley. *a*: 40-43 Fleet St, London, E.C.4. *T*: Central 8211.

GALSTER, KARL PAUL HANS: sea officer, Vice-Admiral; b. Stettin, Germany, November, 1851; s. Karl Christian and Pauline (Schulze) G.; educ. Oberrealschule St. Peter (Danzig), Marine School and Marine Academy (Kiel); m. Helene Geissel, Nov. 6, 1864. AUTHOR: Schiffs-und Küstengeschütze der deutschen Marine, 1876; Pulver und Munition der deutschen Marineartillerie, 1884; Welche Seekriegsrüstung braucht Deutschland? 1907. Contributor to Berliner Tageblatt, Frankfurter Zeitung, Zeitschrift für Politik, Preussische Jahrbücher, and others. General character of writing: marine-political and historical. Religion, Evangelical Reformed. ADDRESS: Adolfallee 21, Wiesbaden, Germany.

GALSWORTHY, JOHN, O. M.: a u t h o r; b. Coombe, Surrey, Eng., Aug. 14, 1867; s. John and Blanche Bailey (Bartleet) G.; educ. Harrow, 1881-86; New College (Oxford), 1886-89; DEGREES: M.A. (in Law, Honour degree, Oxford), Hon. LL.D. (St. Andrew's Univ.), D. Litt. (Manchester Univ.); Cambridge; Dublin; Sheffield, Princeton, U.S.A.; m. Ada Cooper, 1905. AUTHOR: From the Four Winds, 1897; Jocelyn, 1898; Villa Rubein, 1900; A Man of Devon, 1901; The Island Pharisees, 1904; The Man of Property, 1906; The Country House, 1907; A Commentary, 1908; Fraternity, 1909; A Motley, 1910; The Patrician, 1911; Moods, Songs and Doggerels, 1911; The Inn of Tranquility, 1912; The Dark Flower, 1913; The Little Man and Other Satires, 1915; The Freelands, 1915; A Sheaf (vol. I), 1916; Beyond, 1917; Five Tales, 1918; A Sheaf (vol. II), 1919; Saints' Progress, 1919; Addresses in America, 1919; Tatterdemalion, 1920; In Chancery, 1920; Awakening, 1920; To Let, 1921; The Forsyte Saga, 1922; Captures, 1923; The White Monkey, 1924; Caravan, 1925; The Silver Spoon, 1926; Verses, New and Old, 1926; Castles in Spain, 1927; Swan Song, 1928; A Modern Comedy, 1929; On Forsyte 'Change, 1930; Maid in

Waiting, 1931. Plays: The Silver Box, 1906; Joy, 1907; Strife, 1909; Justice, 1910; The Little Dream, 1911; The Pigeon, 1912; The Eldest Son, 1912; The Fugitive, 1913; The Mob, 1914; A Bit o' Love, 1915; The Foundations, 1916; The Skin Game, 1920; Six Short Plays, 1921; A Family Man, 1921; Loyalties, 1922; Windows, 1922; The Forest, 1924; Old English, 1924; The Show, 1925; Escape, 1926; Exiled, 1929; The Roof, 1929. General character of writing: novels, essays, plays, poems. CLUB: Athenaeum (London). A DDRESS: Bury House, N. Pulborough, Sussex, Eng.

GALT, A. *a*: c/o Clydesdale Bank, Melville Pl, Edinburgh.

GALT, Dr. H. M. Pathologist. *Publ*: Microscopy of the Starches. Medico-legal Examiner for the Crown for Glasgow & Lanarkshire. *a*: Chantemerle, Beaumont, Jersey, C.I.

GALTON, Frank W. *e*: Elem. Mem Roy Comm on Transport. *n.a*: Ed Volunteer Gazette 1914—18, Ed Municipal Journ '18—20. *Publ*: The Tailoring Trade; Workers on their Industries; etc. *Ctr*: Various political journs. *s.s*: Economics, Politics. *a*: Bleak Hse, Bassingbourn, Royston, Herts. *T*: Steeple Morden 254.

GALTREY, Sidney ("Hotspur"). *n.a*: "Rapier" of the Sporting & Dramatic. *a*: 135 Fleet St, E.C.4.

GAMBIER-PARRY, Thomas Robert, M.A., F.R.HistS. *b*: Lon 1883. *e*: Eton, Magdalen Col Oxf. Keeper of Oriental Dept Bodleian Library Oxf. Ed for the Oxf Records Soc 1931-32. *Publ*: A Catalogue of Sanskrit MS purchased for the admin's of the Max Muller Meml Fund ('22); A Collection of Charters relating to Goring, Streatley & the neighbourhood 1181—1546. *c.t*: Eng Hist Review, Bodleian Quarterly Record. *s.s*: Sanskrit lang, Western liturgies. *Rec*: Botany, numismatics. *c*: Athenæum. *a*: 5a King Edward St, Oxf & Highnam Ct, Glos.

GAMBLE, JOHN: canon of Bristol Cathedral; *b*. Northern Ireland, Feb. 20, 1859; *s*. Arthur and Agnes (Macartney) G.; educ. abroad and Trinity Coll. (Dublin); DEGREES: M.A., B.D.; unmarried. AUTHOR: St. Paul (Dent's Bible Handbooks), 1904; Christ and Criticism, 1904; Spiritual Sequence of the Bible, 1912; Christian Faith and Worship, 1912; Baptism, Confirmation and the Eucharist, 1913; Newman's Apologia, first edition, with preliminary pamphlets; edited with Introduction, 1918; Wordsworth's Other Essays (by James Rawley), edited with Preface, 1927; Traditional Idea of God, 1928. Contributor of article on Christian Symbolism, Haskell's Dictionary of Religion and Ethics. Contributor to Quarterly Rev., Contemporary Rev., Hibbert Journal, Expositor, Times, Modern Churchman, Journ. Biblical Literature (U. S. A.). General character of writing: religious criticism and research. Relig. denom., Church of England. CLUBS: Reform, Clifton. (*)

GAMBRELL, Horace William, F.R.S.A. *b*: Rugby 1898. *e*: Rugby Col of Technology & Arts. *m*: Elsie Mabel Church. *Publ*: Charging for Profit: A Handbook on the Efficient Operation of Charging Stations. *c.t*: Journal of Inst of Wireless Technology, etc. *s.s*: Radio & electrical eng. *Rec*: Fishing, yachting. Mem Inst of Wireless Technology & Inst of Radio Engineers. *a*: Stanford, Lincoln Close, Lincoln Rd, N. Harrow, Middx.

GAMMANS, Leonard David, M.P. *b*: East Cosham, Hants 1895. *e*: Portsmouth Gr Sch, Lond Univ. *m*: Muriel Paul. M.P. (C) Hornsey, Colonial Service (Brit Malaya) 1920—34, M.O.I. '39—41. *Ctr*: Times, Telegraph, Dly Mail, Sun Times, Dly Despatch, Ev News, Ev Standard, Spectator, Time & Tide, Everybody's. *s.s*: Colonial & Foreign Affairs. *c*: Roy Auto, Roy Emp. *w.s*: Roy Field Artillery 1914—18. *a*: 19 Buckingham Palace Mans, S.W.1. *T*: Sloane 4463.

GAMMIE, Alexander. Author. *Publ*: Dr Archibald Fleming of St Columba's; Dr John White; Dr Geo H. Morrison; From Pit to Palace; John McNeill. *a*: 15 Fleurs Av, Dumbreck, Glasgow.

GAMMIE, John Douglas Lumsden. *b*: Aberdeen 1908. *m*: Caroline R. Dutton. *s*: 1. *n.a*: Ed John Bull 1945—, Formerly Sub-Ed & Film Critic The Bulletin Glasgow '30, Review-Ed '31 & Assoc-Ed '33—37, Film Weekly, Ed Woman '37—40. *w.s*: 1940—45 R.A.F. *a*: c/o Odham's Press Ltd, 186 High Holborn, London, W.C.1. *T*: Temple Bar 2468.

GAMMON, Reginald William. *b*: Petersfield 1894. *e*: Churchers Coll Petersfield. *m*: Bessie Knight. *s*: 2. Dairy Farmer, Artist & Writer. *Ctr*: C.T.C. Gazette, Scout, Boys Own Paper. *s.s*: Walking, Cycling, Camping. *a*: Carney Farm, Llanthony, Abergavenny Mon.

GAMON, Hugh Reece Percival. *b*: Chester 1880. *e*: Hartford Hse Hartley Wintney, Harrow Sch, Exeter Coll Oxf. *m*: Eleanor Margaret Lloyd. *s*: 1. *d*: 3. County Court Judge. *Publ*: The London Police Court To-day & To-morrow. *a*: The Lodge, 21 Front St, Acomb, York. *T*: York 78304.

GAMOW, George. *b*: Odessa 1904. *e*: Univ of Leningrad. *m*: Loubov R. Vokhminzeva. *s*: 1. Prof of Physics. *Publ*: Constitution of Atomic Nuclei & Radioactivity; Structure of Atomic Nuclei & Nucl. Trans; Theory of At Nucleus & Nucl. Energy Sources; Mr Tompkins in Wonderland; Mr Tompkins Explores the Atom; Atomic Energy in Cosmic & Human Life; The Birth & Death of the Sun; Biography of the Earth; One, Two, Three... Infinity. *Ctr*: Various Sci Journs. *s.s*: Theory of Relativity, Nuclear Physics, Cosmology & Ostrophysics. *Rec*: Travel. *a*: 19 Thoreau Drive, Bethesda, Md., U.S.A. *T*: OL 5416.

GAMPELL, Sydney, M.Sc. *b*: Manchester 1904. Financial Ed (Reuters). *s.s*: International Economic Affairs, Industry, Stock Exchanges, Wheat, Cotton & other Raw Materials, Foodstuffs. *a*: Chiswick Hse, Ditton Rd, Surbiton, Surrey.

GANDER, Leonard Marsland. *b*: London 1902 *e*: City of Lond Coll. *m*: Hilda Mabel Ellen Rowley. *s*: 2. Journalist. *n.a*: Times of India Bombay 1924—26, Daily Telegraph Radio Corr '26, War Corr five campaigns '41—45, Radio Corr '46. *Publ*: Atlantic Battle; Long Road to Leros. *Ctr*: N.Y. Times, Times of India, etc. *s.s*: Radio. *Rec*: Chess, gardening, golf. *a*: 11 Beverley Close, Barnes.

GANDHI, M. P., M.A.(Benares). *b*: Junagad 1901. *m*: Rambha Sukalal. *n.a*: Ed Indian Cotton Textile Industry & Indian Sugar Industry Annuals 1935—. *Publ*: The Indian Cotton Textile Industry (& Annual); Future of Handloom Weaving in India; The Indian Sugar Industry (& Annual); Problems of Sugar Industry in India, Scope & Prospects in Post-War Period. *Ctr*: Times of India, Commerce, Indian Finance. *s.s*: Economics of Industry (Cotton & Sugar). *Rec*: Tennis, badminton, billiards. *c*: B.P. Radio & Hindu Gymkhana. *a*: Jan Mansion, Sir Pherozeshah Menta Rd, Fort, Bombay 1, India. *T*: 25961.

GANDON, Yvet Pierre Louis. *b*: Blois (Loire-et-Cher) 1899. *n*:. *d*: 3. Homme de Lettres et Journaliste. *n.a*: L'Intransigeant 1931—39, Nouvelles Litteraires '29—39, Minerve '45—, etc. *Publ*: Le Dernier Blanc; Amanda; Le Grand Depart; Le Pavillon des delices regrettes ; Mascarades Litteraires ; Usage de Faux, etc *Ctr* : France-Illustration, Plaisir de France. *s.s* : Critique Litteraire & Dramatique, Romancier. *a* : 180 rue Blomet, Paris 15. *T* : Lecourbe 8179.

GANDRUP, Richardt. *b* : Aggersborg, Jylland 1885. *e* : State Training Coll of Ranum. *m* : Julie Bro. *s* : 1. Author & Editor. *Publ* : Det Ode Land ; Tomme Steder ; Orknens Hyl ; Morket ; De Blinde Spor ; Jeftas Datter ; Jordens Kreds ; etc. *Ctr* : Politiken, Danish Outlook, In Words & Pictures, etc. *s.s* : Lit & Pictorial Art. *Rec* : Chorus Leader. *a* : Aarhus, Denmark. *T* : Aarhus 2071.

GANDY, Eric Worsley, V.D., O.B.E. *b* : Lon 1879. *e* : Tottenham's Sc, St Leonards & Emanuel Col Cam. *m* : Edith Margaret Kenyon. *s* : 1. *d* : 3. Med Pract. *c.t* : Journ of Obstetrics & Gynæ, etc. *s.s* : Anæsthetics. War Service 4½ y. Officier Legion d'Honneur. *Rec* : Book collecting, golf. *c* : Arthur's. *a* : The Hill Top, Gipsy Hill, S.E.19. *t* : Sydenham 0243.

GANDY, Mabel, M.R.S.T. *b* : Penketh. *m* : Wallace Gandy. *s* : 3. *d* : 1. *Publ* : Her Adopted Father ; The Tenth Arch ; Strange Goods ; The Shrieking Hands ; A Modern Sheba ; A Monograph on Instinct and Intelligence. *c.t* : Daily Mail, Daily Express, etc. *s.s* : Folk-lore, comparative religion & philosophy. *Rec* : Woodland gardening. *a* : Belmont, Duncombe Hill, S.E.23.

GANDY, Wallace, M.R.S.T., L.C.P. *b* : Warrington 1884. *e* : Lon Univ. *m* : Mabel Soderland. *s* : 3. *d* : 1. Teacher & Lect. *n.a* : Advertiser's Annual 1915—16, Advertiser's Weekly '15—18. *Publ* : When Lionheart was King ; A Persian Hero ; The Wanderings of Rama ; Lancashire Oath Rolls of 1696 ; American Oath Rolls 1696 ; John Bull, Mystic ; The Pandar Princes ; etc. *c.t* : Educ & Advtg press. *s.s* : Psych, salesmanship, advertising. *c* : Suffolk Inst of Archæ, etc. *a* : Belmont, Duncombe Hill, S.E.23.

GANE, Crofton Endres. *b* : Bristol 1878. *e* : Wycliffe Coll Stonehouse Glos. *m* : Grace Osborne. *s* : 1. *d* : 1. *Ctr* : Bristol Ev Post. *s.s* : The Human Factor in Industry, Modern Design in Furniture. *Rec* : Travel, cycling, gardening. *a* : 24 Downs Park W., Bristol 6. *T* : 67287.

GANE, Percival Carlton, K.C., M.A., LL.B. *b* : Nth Walsham, Eng 1874 *e* : Kingswood Sch Bath, Jesus Coll Oxf. *m* : Emma Gladys Caldecott. *s* : 3. *d* : 3. Judge of Supreme Court of Sth Africa (ret). *Publ* : Trans from Ulric Huber's Jurisprudence. *Ctr* : Sth African Law Journ. *s.s* : Lit of Roman & Dutch Law. *c* : Grahamstown & Roy Port Alfred Golf. *a* : 18 Park Rd, Grahamstown, Cape Province. *T* : 194.

GANGE, Edwin Stanley, J.P. *b* : Bristol 1871. *e* : Priv. *m* : Alice Maud Denning. *s* : 2. Merchant. Chm Bristol Evening Post. M.P. N. Bristol 1918–22; J.P. since '16; Sheriff of Bristol '31–32; Dir several other Coy. *Rec* : Reading, golf. *c* : Bristol & Constitutional. *a* : Clifton, Bristol. *t* : 56001.

GANGE, Dr. F. W. *a* : 40 Court St, Faversham, Kent.

GANGULEE, Nagendra Nath, C.I.E., M.Sc., Ph.D Author. *n.a* : India 1946, Asian Horizon '47. *Pub.*; Teachings of Sun Yat-Sen ; Guiseppe Mazzini ; Russian Horizon ; Mind & Face of Nazi Germany ; Alexander Hertzen ; Reflections of Russia's Destiny ; India—What Now ? ; Constituent Assembly for India ; Indians in the Empire Overseas ; Making of Federal India ;

Indian Peasant & His Environment ; Bibliography of Nutrition in India ; What to Eat & Why ; Health & Nutrition in India ; Red Tortoise & Other Tales of Rural India ; Thomas Paine. *s.s* : Economics & Politics. *a* : Royal Empire Society, London, W.C.2. *T* : Ambassador 5234.

GANGULI, Suprakash. *b* : Calcutta 1886. *e* : Doveton Col Calcutta. *m* : Tanujabala Devi. Curator Baroda Museum & Picture Gallery Baroda, India. *n.a* : Archæological Survey of India 1912—18, Eastern Circle (Bengal, Behar, Assam, Orissa & Chota-Nagpur). *Publ* : Descriptive Guide to the Baroda Museum & Picture Gallery. *c.t* : Times of India (Bombay), Statesman (Calcutta), Rupam. *s.s* : Persian, Moghal, Rajput & Kangra Paintings of the early scs, Oriental Textiles, Old Ivory & Wood Carvings, Chinese & Japanese Porcelain & Pottery, etc. *Rec* : Golf, badminton, photography. *c* : F.R.S.A.(Lon), Mem W. Indian Auto Assoc, Indian Soc of Oriental Art. *a* : Pushpabag, Baroda, India. *t* : 331.

GANN, Thomas, J.P., M.R.C.S., L.R.C.P., F.R.G.S., F.R.A.I. Author, *Publ* : Mystery Cities ; In an Unknown Land ; Ancient Lands & Modern Tribes ; Maya Cities ; Discoveries & Adventures in Central America ; The History of the Maya ; Indians of Northern Honduras & Southern Yucatan. Lecturer on Central American Archæology L'pool Univ. In charge Brit Museum Exped to Pusilha. Hon Assoc Tulane Univ. *a* : The Shrubbery, La Rocque, Jersey, C.I.

GANPAT. See Gompertz, M. L. A.

GANS, Richard. *b* : Hamburg 1880. *e* : Wilhelm-Gymnasium, Hamburg, Technische Hochschule Hannover, Universitat Strassburg. *m* : Leonie Buttmann. *s* : 2. Dir of II Physikalisches Institut, Königsberg Univ. *Publ* : Einführung in die Theorie des Magnetismus (1908); Repertorium der Physik '15–16; Vektoranalysis (6th edn '29; Eng & Spanish edns '29 & '32). *c.t* : Encyclopædia der mathem, Wissenschaften, Handbuch der Experimental-physik, Physikalische Zeitschrift, etc. *s.s* : Magnetism & optics. *c* : Mem Gelehrte Gesellschaft Königsberg, Mem Deutsche Physikalische Gesellschaft. *a*: Königsberg (Preussen), Cäcilien-Alle 13. *t* : 33437.

GANZ, Charles J. W. A. *b* : Lon 1866. *e* : Univ Col Sc, Univ Col, Roy Col of Music London & Frankfort, Germany. *m* : Elizabeth K. Deeley. Prof of Music (ret) & author. *n.a* : Ed Aldeburgh Times, Suffolk 1899–1912. *Publ* : A FitzGerald Medley (1933); The Popular Guide to Aldeburgh, Suffolk (6 ed); George Crabbe Celebration Souvenir ('05). *s.s* : Edward Fitzgerald, George Crabbe. Dir of Musical Entertainments in Aldeburgh, Broadstairs & in Bexhill. *Rec* : Gardening. *c* : Vice Chm Bexhill Lect Soc, Bexhill on sea. *a* : Brownboys, Peartree Lane, Bexhill on sea, Sussex.

GARAI, Bert. *b* : Budapest 1891. *e* : Budapest Sc & Budapest Univ. *m* : Alice Rose. *s* : 3. Journalist & Coy Dir. *n.a* : Budapest 1910, N.Y. '14–15, Mang Dir Keystone Press Agency. *Publ* : Guide to N.Y. (in Hungarian). *c.t* : English, American & Foreign dailies & periodicals. Interviewed every crowned head in Europe (except King George) & foremost statesmen. *Rec* : Philately. *c* : Press. *a* : 48 Chiltern Drive, Surbiton, Surrey. *t* : Elmbridge 4607.

GARBEDIAN, H. Gordon. *b* : Cairo 1905. *e* : Sc of Journalism, Columbia Univ. (Pulitzer Prize Scholar). *n.a* : Edit Staff of the New York Times 1928–. *Publ* : Major Mysteries of Science; Epic of

Mankind. *c.t*: The New York Times Mag, The New York Times Book Review, Scribner's Mag, Harper's Mag. *s.s*: Science, history. *Rec*: Tennis, golf, theatre, etc. *a*: 11 William St. East Williston, N.Y., U.S.A.

GARBETT, Sir Colin Campbell, K.C.I.E., C.S.I., C.M.G., B.A., LL.B., F.R.G.S., F.R.E.S. *b*: Dalhousie, India 1881. *e*: King William's Coll I.O.M. & Jesus Coll Camb. *m*: Marjorie Josephine Maynard. *d*: 1. Indian Civil Service (ret), formerly Regional Food Commissioner Nth India, Minister of Agric & Land Revenue (Bhopal State), O.St.J. *Publ*: Friend of Friend; The Hundred Years, etc. *s.s*: Administration in India, Land Revenue, Settlement, Tenancy Law & Agriculture. *Rec*: Rowing, tennis. *c*: Overseas, E. India & Sports. *a*: Wishingpool Hse, Woodcote Green, Wallington, Surrey. *T*: Wallington 7586.

GARBETT, Most Rev. and Rt. Hon. Cyril Forster, P.C., D.D., D.L. *b*: 1875. *e*: Portsmouth Gr Sch, Keble Coll & Cuddesdon Coll Oxf. Archbishop of York 1942—, Bishop of Winchester '32—42. *Publ*: The Church & Modern Problems; The Challenge of the King; The Work of a Great Parish; After the War; Secularism & Christian Unity; In the Heart of South London; A Call to Christians; The Church & Social Problems; What is Man?; We Would See Jesus; Physician, Heal Thyself; The Burge Memorial Lecture. *a*: Bishopthorpe, York.

GARBUTT, Miss E., B.A. *a*: 8 Alan Rd, Withington, M/C.

GARBUTT, William Henry. *b*: Worcester 1855. *e*: Roy G.S. Worcester. *m*: F. M. Burgess. *s*: 2 (1 dec). *d*: 1. Journalist. *n.a*: Derbys Times 1879, Limerick Chron '79, Evesham Journ '80, Birm Post '83, etc. 1st Pres Midland Esperantist Fed 1908–09, etc. *Rec*: Music, chess. *a*: 16 Wentworth Gate, Harborne, Birm 17.

GARCIA, Juan C. *b*: Socorro, Santander, Colombia 1883. *e*: Colegio de Colon, Collegio de San Bartolome, Seminario Conciliar de Bogota. Vice-Chancellor to the Archbishop of Bogota, Ecclesiastical Judge, Prof of Humanities, Writer, Fellow-Member Sociedad Colombiana de Ciencias Naturales. *Publ*: Sintesis de Historia Universal; Nociones de Literatura; Guia historica de la Catedral de Bogota; Oraciones sagradas y profanas; Seleccion de escritos; Tratado de epigrafia latina; Totius latinitatis exempla; Guia de las iglesias bogotanus. *Ctr*: Boletin del Instit Caro y Cuervo, Revista Javeriana, Revista del Colegio del Rosario, Revista de Estudios eclesiasticos, Revista Moderna, Revista Pedagogica, Revista de Historia y Antiguedad, America Espanola, Santafe y Bogota, etc. *s.s*: Fine Arts, Folk Lore, Colombian Literature & History. *Rec*: Drawing, paleontological collections. *a*: Calle 14, No 14–46, Bogota, Colombia, Sth America.

GARD, John Stanley Fabian, M.Sc.(Dunelm), F.R.I.C., M.Inst.F., F.C.S. *b*: Southsea 1888. *e*: Priv & Armstrong Coll (now King's) Newcastle-on-Tyne. *m*: Eliza Ainsley. *s*: 2. Industrial Chemist, Fuel Technologist. *Ctr*: Journs of Soc. of Chem Industry, Inst of Fuel, Pharmaceutical Conference, Elec Power Engineers Assoc, Ceramic Soc, etc. *s.s*: Manufacture & Application of Magnesium Compounds, Thermal Insulation. *Rec*: Motoring. *c*: Newcastle Chemical Industry. *a*: 2 Station Rd, Washington, Co Durham. *T*: Washington 183.

GARDE, Axel. *b*: Denmark 1876. *m*: Agnes Thyregod. *s*: 1. Founder of Kulturslind Royal Theatre. *n.a*: Tilskiseren 1932–39. *Publ*: Hendes Drommelir; Dansk Aand; Hamlet; Bag Forharget, etc. *Ctr*: Berlingske Tidende, Politiken, Nationaltidende, etc. *s.s*: Essays on Literature & Philosophy. *a*: Thavraldsensvej 17 111, Kobenharn, V, Denmark. *T*: Ein 7830.

GARDHAM, Arthur John, M.S., F.R.C.S. *Publ*: Burns & Scalds; Radium Burns (Sections of Choyce's System of Surgery). *c.t*: Brit Journ of Surgery, Lancet, etc. *a*: 40 Harley St W.1. *t*: Langham 3662.

GARDINER, Alan Henderson, D.Litt, M.A., F.B.A., F.S.A. *b*: Eltham 1879. *e*: Charterhouse, Sorbonne, Paris & Queen's Col Oxf. *m*: Hedwig von Rosen. *s*: 2. *d*: 1. Egyptologist. *n.a*: Ed Journ of Egyptian Archæology 1916–21, '34–. *Publ*: The Inscription of Mes ('05); Egyptian Hieratic Texts; Egyptian Grammar; The Chester Beatty Papyri, No 1; The Theory of Speech & Language ('32); etc; In collab, Theban Ostraca; Tarkhan I, Memphis V; The Tomb of Amenemhet; Egyptian Letters to the Dead. *c.t*: Journ Egyptian Archæology, Zeitschrift für Ägyptische Sprache und Altertumskunde, Ency Brit, etc. *s.s*: Ancient Egyptian philology. Discovered origin of the alphabet '15. Research Prof of Egyptology in Univ of Chicago. *Rec*: Tennis. *c*: Oxf & Cam, Burlington Fine Arts. *a*: 9 Lansdown Rd, Holland Pk, W.11. *t*: Park 5109.

GARDINER, Alfred G., J.P. *b*: 1865. Journalist. Editor, Author. *Publ*: Prophets, Priests, and King's; Pillars of Society; The War Lords; Certain People of Importance: Life of Geo Cadbury, etc. *c.t*: Various. Pres Institute of Journalists 1915. Ed Daily News '02–19. *a*: The Spinney, Whiteleaf, Princes Risborough.

GARDINER, Dorothea Frances (Theodore Frank). *b*: Clifton 1879. *e*: Cheltenham Ladies' Coll. *m*: C. I. Gardiner. *Publ*: The Prison House; Another Night; Another Day; The Lifted Latch; The Beguiling Shore; Murder at a Dog Show, etc. *s.s*: Breeding & Showing Dogs, Farming. *a*: Shaw Green Cottage, Prestbury, Glos. *T*: Cheltenham 7338.

GARDINER, Dorothy, J.P. *b*: London 1873. *e*: Francis Holland Sch, Lady Margaret Hall Oxford. *m*: Canon Thory Gage Gardiner (dec'd). Writer, Social Worker, Chrm Canterbury Archæological Soc, Chrm of Governors Simon Langton Gr Schs Canterbury. *Publ*: English Girlhood at School; The Oxinden Letters; Companion into Kent; Mary in the Wood; Six little plays from Canterbury History; Story of Lambeth Palace; Companion into Dorset; The Oxinden & Seyton Letters; Canterbury Lyrics, etc. *Ctr*: Review of English Studies. *s.s*: History, Topography, Education. *c*: Univ Women's. *a*: Cogan Hse, 53 St Peter's St, Canterbury. *T*: Canterbury 2587.

GARDINER, Ernest Alexander, M.A. *b*: Bretherton 1880. *e*: Preston G.S. & Keble Col Oxf. *m*: Norah Fannie Watt. *d*: 1. Headmaster of K. Edward VI Sc, Louth. *n.a*: Sr Sci Master Plymouth Col 1903–12 & Berkhamsted Sc '12–17, Headmaster Louth '17–. *Publ*: First Year Course of Natural Science; The Life & Teaching of Christ; Acts of the Apostles; etc. *s.s*: Nat Sci. *Rec*: Cricket & tennis. *c*: I.A.H.M., S.M.A. *a*: Greenways, Louth, Lincs. *t*: 289.

GARDINER, FREDERICK GEORGE: legal; b. London, Eng., Apr., 1874; s. Edward Bennett and Sidonie A.F.A. (von Doeringk) G.; educ. Diocesan Coll. (Cape of Good Hope); Keble Coll. (Oxford); DEGREES: B.A. (Cape of Good Hope); B.A. (Oxford); m. Julia Stella Clare Brailey, 1901. AUTHOR: South African Criminal Law and Procedure, 1918 (3rd edit. 1930) (with C. W. H. Lansdown). Contributor to Cape Law Journal, Law Quarterly Review. Relig. denom., Church of England. CLUBS: Civil Service, Cape University. OFFICE: Supreme Court, Cape Town, South Africa.

GARDINER, Frederick Keith, J.P. *b*: Plumstead, Kent. *m*: Ruth Dixon. *s*: 2. Ed Sheffield Telegraph & Daily Independent. *n.a*: Reporter & Sub-Ed Southern

Publishing Co, Dep Chief Sub-Ed Northern Echo Darlington, Chief Sub-Ed Yorkshire Herald, Chief Sub-Ed Oxford Mail, Asst-Ed Daily Independent, Ed (March 1931). *Rec*: Golf. *c*: St James, Hallamshire Golfers, Sheffield. *a*: 8 Canterbury Ave, Fulwood, Sheffield 10. *T*: 31996.

GARDINER, Harold. *Publ*: Anatomy & Physiology. *a*: St Osyth, Queensmere Rd, Wimbledon. *t*: 3590.

GARDINER, Harold Charles, M.A., S.T.L., Ph.D. *b*: Washington D.C. 1904. *e*: High Sch Washington D.C., St Andrews-on-Hudson, Poughkeepsie, Woodstock Coll, Maryland, Camb Univ. Roman Catholic Priest, Member of the Society of Jesus, Literary Ed. *n.a*: Literary Ed of America, National Catholic Weekly 1940. *Publ*: Mysteries End ; Tenets for Readers & Reviewers. *Ctr*: America, Steren, Survey Graphic, Catholic Sch Journ, Catholic Book Club Newsletter. *s.s*: Medieval Religious Drama, Modern Eng Literature. *a*: 329 West 108 St, New York, N.Y. *T*: Academy 2-4636.

GARDINER, John Stanley, M.A., F.R.S., F.L.S., F.R.G.S. Prof of Zoology. *Publ*: The Fauna & Geography of the Maldives and Laccadives (1903); The Percy Sladen Expedition to the Indian Ocean '06–32; The Natural History of Wicken Fen; Coral Reefs & Atolls ('32). *c.t*: Journs of Science Socs. *a*: Bredon Hse, Selwyn Gdns, Cambridge. *t*: 2442.

GARDINER, Linda (Ethelind). *b*: Gorleston. *e*: Priv. Sec Roy Soc for Protection of Birds 1900–. *n.a*: Ed Bird Notes & News '03–. *Publ*: Sylvia in Flowerland; etc. *c.t*: Various in n/ps & periodicals, Org & Cond of Bird & Tree Scheme of Nature Study in Scs. *a*: 82 Victoria St, S.W.1.

GARDINER, Robert Strachan. F.S.I., F.L.A.S., M.R.A.S.E., J.P. *b*: Cards. *e*: Aberystwyth G.S. & Univ Col of Wales & Agricultural Col Aspatria. Married. *s*: 1. *d*: 1. Secretary. *n.a*: Ed The C.L.A. Journ. *Publ*: The Agricultural Landowners' Handbook on Taxes, Rates, Tithe Rent Charge & the Death Duties; The Farmers' Guide to Ownership of Land. *c.t*: Various. *s.s*: Taxation of land, land management. *c*: Farmers. *a*: Central Landowners Assoc, 7 Charles St, St James's Sq, S.W.1. *t*: Whitehall 4068.

GARDINER, W., M.A.(Aber). *a*: Aberdeen Press & Journal, Aberdeen.

GARDINER, Wm. Chetwynd, M.A. *b*: Croydon 1876. Schoolmaster & Games Master (ret). *Publ*: A Running Commentary; Team Games for Schoolgirls; the only book of its kind containing all six games in one cheap book. *s.s*: Cricket, hockey, tennis. Well-known in Lon & elsewhere as highly successful amateur games coach. 20 y games master at C.o.L. Sc. *Rec*: Rock-climbing, coaching games. *a*: Moss Ghyll, King's Drive, Eastbourne. *t*: 3659.

GARDNER, Hon. Mrs. Alan (Nora Beatrice). *b*: Lon . *m*: Col Alan Gardner (dec). *s*: 2. *d*: 1. *Publ*: Life in Somalu Land; etc. *c.t*: Country Life, Field, Queen, Daily Telegraph. *s.s*: Big game shooting. Extensive travel, exploring where no white woman has been before. *Rec*: Gardening, sketching. *a*: The Old Malt Hse, Worplesdon, Surrey. *t*: 8.

GARDNER, Arthur, M.A., F.S.A. *b*: 1878. *e*: Harrow, King's Col Cam. *Publ*: Medieval Sculpture in France; Peaks, Lochs & Coasts of the Western Highlands; Sun, Cloud & Snow in the Western Highlands; Medieval Figure Sculpture in England (with late Prof E. S. Prior). *c.t*: Archæ Journ, S.M.T. Mag. *s.s*: History of medieval Archit & Sculpture. *Rec*: Walking, photog. *c*: Fellow Soc of Antiquaries. *a*: Oakhurst, Mount Pk, Harrow-on-the-Hill.

GARDNER, Arthur Duncan, M.A., D.M., B.Ch., F.R.C.S. *b*: Rugeley, Staffs 1884. *e*: Rugby Sch, Univ Coll Oxf, St Thomas's Hosp. *m*: Violet Mary Newsam. *s*: 1. *d*: 1. Prof of Bacteriology Oxf Univ. *Publ*: Microbes & Ultramicrobes ; Bacteriology for Medical Students & Practitioners. *Ctr*: Various in Med Journs. *s.s*: Bacteriology. *a*: Chilswell Edge, Hinksey Hill, Oxford. *T*: 85397.

GARDNER, Rev. Charles, M.A. *b*: Crouch End 1874. *e*: Highgate Sc & T.C.D. *m*: Monica Beatrice Macdona. *d*: 1. *Publ*: Inner Life of George Eliot (1912); Vision & Vesture; Redemption of Religion; William Blake, the Man; Romance of Eternal Life; In Defence of the Faith. *c.t*: Challenge, Spectator, Church Quarterly, Atlantic Monthly, Hibbert Journal, etc. *s.s*: Lecturing. *Rec*: Motoring. *a*: Dyke Lodge, Brighton. *t*: Preston 3901.

GARDNER, Charles, O.B.E. *b*: 1912. *m*: Eve Fletcher. *s*: 2. *d*: 1. B.B.C. Air Correspondent 1936—. *Publ*: A.A.S.F.; The Gen Book. *Ctr*: Brit, Amer & Overseas Aviation Mags. *s.s*: Aviation *Rec*: Cricket, golf. *c*: Savage, Roy Aero *w.s*: 1939–40 War Corres & '40–45 Pilot R.A.F. *a*: c/o B.B.C., London, W.1.

GARDNER, Diana. *b*: Sutton, Surrey 1913. *e*: Priv & Bedford High Sch. *Publ*: Halfway Down the Cliff. *Ctr*: Horizon, Life & Letters, New English Wkly, English Story, Modern Reading, New Statesman, Tribune, Writing To-day, Selected Writing. *s.s*: Short Stories. *Rec*: Gardening, Russian literature, travel. *a*: Thatched Cottage, Rodmell, Sussex.

GARDNER, Dorothy Ellen Marion, M.A. *b*: Secunderabad, India 1900. *e*: Cheltenham Ladies Coll, Univ of Leeds. Head of Dept of Child Development Univ of Lond Inst of Educ, Vice-Chrm Nursery Sch Assoc of Gt Brit. *Publ*: Testing Results in the Infant Schools; The Children's Play Centre. *s.s*: Psychology & Educ of Children. *a*: Lindfield, Shalford Rd, Guildford, Surrey; Univ of Lond Inst of Educ, Dept of Child Development, Malet St, London, W.C.1. *T*: Museum 5525.

GARDNER, Edmund Garratt, LittD.(Cantab). *b*: Lon 1869. *e*: Beaumont Gonville & Caius Col Cam. Prof of Italian (ret). *Publ*: Dante's Ten Heavens ('98); Dukes & Poets in Ferrara; St Catherine of Siena; Dante & the Mystics; The Arthurian Legend in Italian Literature (1930); etc. *s.s*: Italian hist & lit. Fell Brit Acad. Commendatore of Order of Crown of Italy. *Rec*: Ornithology. *a*: 5 Ruskin Close, Meadway, N.W.11. *t*: Speedwell 3933

GARDNER, Erle Stanley. (See **FAIR, A. A.**) *b*: Malden, Mass 1889. *e*: High Sch. *m*: Natalie Talbert. *d*: 1. Lawyer, Writer, Mem American Bar Assoc, Amer Jurdic Soc, Authors' League of America, Calif Bar Soc. *Publ*: The Case of the Lucky Legs; The Case of the Lazy Lover; The Case of the Fan-Dancer's Horse, & 27 other books featuring Perry Mason; 8 books in the "D.A." Series; The "Gramp Wiggins" books: The Case of the Turning Tide & The Case of the Smoking Chimney; The "Terry Clane" books: Murder Up My Sleeve; The Case of the Backward Mule. *Ctr*: Hearst Newsps, This Week, Toronto Star, Chatelaine, Sat Ev Post, Liberty, Atlantic Monthly, etc. *s.s*: Mystery Stories, Travel Articles & Books, Chinese Background Stories. *Rec*: Travel, archery, hunting & fishing, photography. *c*: Adventurers'. *a*: Ranchio de Paisano, Temecula, California, U.S.A.

GARDNER, Ernest Arthur, LittD.(Cantab), Hon LittD.. T.C.D. *b*: Lon 1862. *e*: City of Lon Sc &

Cam Univ. Married. *s*: 1. *d*: 2. Emeritus Prof of Arch, Univ of Lon. *n.a*: Jt Ed Journ of Hellenic Studies '97-1933, Vice-Chancellor Univ of Lon '23-25. *Publ*: Handbook of Greek Sculpture (1896-7); Ancient Athens (1902); The Art of Greece ('24); Poet & Artist in Greece ('33). War Service. Greek Order of Redeemer. Gold Cross. *a*: Recess, Boyn Hill, Maidenhead. *t*: 1124.

GARDNER, Harold Bellamy, M.R.C.S.(Eng), L.R.C.P.(Lon). *b*: Lon. *e*: Merchant Taylors Sc & Charing X Hosp. Married. *s*: 2. Anæsthetist. *Publ*: A Manual of Surgical Anæsthesia (2nd edn 1916). *c.t*: Lancet, Times, Connoisseur, Antique Collector. *s.s*: Anæsthetics Vice-Pres Eng Ceramic Circle '28-. *Rec*: Collecting Chelsea Porcelain. *c*: F.R.S.M. *a*: 91 Clarence Gate Gdns, N.W.1. *t*: Paddington 9839.

GARDNER, John Addyman. *b*: Bradford 1868. *e*: Bradford G.S., Magdalen Col Oxf & Heidel. *m*. Mrs Henrietta White (dec). Reader in Physiolog Chem, Lon Univ. *Publ*: Sections on Blood-Hæmoglobin & its derivations (with Dr Buckmaster) in Allan's Commercial Analysis (Edn IV & V); etc. *c.t*: Lancet, B.M.J., Practitioner, Proc Roy Soc, Biochem Journ, etc. *s.s*: Biochem. Hon Treas Biochem Soc 1913-. *Rec*: Fishing. *c*: Savile. *a*: 24 Palace Mansions, Kensington, W.14. *t*: Fulham 5853.

GARDNER, (JOHN) EDMUND G(ARRATT): professor of Italian; *b*. London, Eng., May 12, 1869; *s*. John and Amy Vernon (Garratt) G.; *educ*. Beaumont; Univ. Coll. (London); Gonville and Caius Coll. (Cambridge); DEGREES: M.A. (Cambridge), Litt.D. (Cambridge); Fellow of British Acad.; Commendatore of the Order of the Crown of Italy; unmarried. AUTHOR: Dante's Ten Heavens, 1898; A Dante Primer, 1900; The Story of Florence, 1900; The Story of Siena and San Gimignano, 1902; Dukes and Poets in Ferrara, 1904; The King of Court Poets, 1905; St. Catherine of Siena, 1907; The Painters of the School of Ferrara, 1911; Dante and the Mystics, 1913; The Book of St. Bernard on the Love of God, 1916; The National Idea in Italian Literature, 1921; Tommaso Campanella and his Poetry, 1923; Dante, 1923; Italian Literature, 1927; The Arthurian Legend in Italian Literature, 1930. Virgil in Italian Poetry (in press). Contributor to Modern Language Review. Professor of Italian in Univ. of London. Relig. denom., Roman Catholic. CLUBS: Royal Societies; University of London. OFFICE: University College. HOME: 5 Ruskin Close, Meadway, N. W. 11, London, Eng.

GARDNER, Mary Campbell, M.A. Lect in Classics Ambleside 1919—36. *Publ*: A Latin Book for Beginners. *s.s*: Classics (Latin & Greek). *a*: Ascham Hse, Gosforth, Newcastle-on-Tyne 3. *T*: Gosforth 51619.

GARDNER, Percy. *b*: Lon 1846. *e*: C.o.L. Sc & Christ's Col Cam. *m*. Agnes Reid. Emeritus Prof of Class Archæ, Oxf 1887-1924. *n.a*: Ed Journ Hellenic Studies 1881-96. *Publ*: British Museum Catalogue of Greek Coins (1873); Types of Greek Coins; Manual of Greek Antiquities; Principles of Greek Art; Practical Basis of Christian Belief; Modernism in the English Church (1925); etc. *c.t*: Quarterly Review, Hibbert Journ, Modern Churchman, etc. *s.s*: Greek Art, Ancient Athletics. Corr Mem French Inst & Acads of Prussia & Göttingen. Fell Brit Acad. *Rec*: Golf. *a*: 12 Canterbury Rd, Oxf. *t*: 2030.

GARDNER, Robert Cotton Bruce. *b*: Conington Hall, Camb 1889. *e*: Oundle & Caius Coll Camb. *m*: Olive Muriel Holmes. *s*: 2. *Ctr*: Times, Morning Post, Spectator, Chamber's Journ, John O'London's Qrtly, Journ of Forestry, Country Life, Field, Fishing Gazette, etc. *s.s*: Forestry & Arboriculture, Topography, Touring Articles, etc. *Rec*: Fly fishing, motoring, photography.

c: Flyfishers, Union Soc, Camb. *w.s*: R.G.A. 1914—18, '39—45. *a*: Royal Forestry Society of England & Wales, 49 Russell Square, London, W.C.1. *T*: Museum 4892.

GARDNER, WALTER M.: college principal, retired; *b*. Leeds, Eng., July, 1861; *s*. John Myers and Jane (Wilson) G.; DEGREES: M.Sc., F. I. C.; *m*. Blanche Atkinson, July 9, 1890, 1 s., 1 d. (*m*. W. H. Moberly, Q. V.). AUTHOR: Wool Dyeing, 1890; Wool Dyeing, 1897; A Dictionary of Dyes (with C. Rawson), 1901; The British Coal-tar Industry, 1915. Co-editor of Journal of the Society of Dyers and Colourists, 1895-1925; editor, from 1925. Contributor to Thorpe's Dictionary of Applied Chemistry and Allen's Commercial Organic Analysis; Nature, Journal of Chemical Soc., and others. Victoria Univ. Extension Lecturer, 1892-1897; prof. of chemistry Bradford Technical Coll., 1895-1905; Chmn. Yorkshire section, Soc. of Chemical Industry, 1908-10; principal, Bradford Technical Coll., 1905-1921. ADDRESS: care of Westminster Bank, Ltd., Bradford, Eng.

GARDNER-SMITH, Rev. Percival. *b*: Lincs 1888. *e*: Jesus Coll Camb. *m*: Sophia Dorothy Leeke. Clerk in Holy Orders, Dean of Jesus Coll, Univ Lect. *Publ*: The Narratives of the Resurrection; The Church's Faith; The Church in the Roman Empire; The Christ of the Gospels; St John & the Synoptic Gospels. *Ctr*: Ency Brit, Chambers's Ency, The Modern Churchman. *s.s*: Eccles Hist & New Testament. *Rec*: Golf, motoring, photography. *a*: Jesus Coll, Cambridge. *T*: 4621 & 9341.

GARIS, Howard R. Author. *Publ*: Tam of the Fire Cave; The Uncle Wiggily Book; Tuftoo the Clown. *a*: c/o D. Appleton & Co, 34 Bedford St, London, W.C.

GARLAND, Claude Malory. *b*: Bowlingreen, Ky 1880. *e*: Grafe Sch, Private, Univ. *m*: Fage Ellen Sims. Mem American Tech Mech Engineers & American Inst Elec Engineers. *Publ*: Washington & His Portraits; Depressions & their Solution; The Great American Fraud. *Ctr*: Various to Engineering publs. *s.s*: Engineering. *Rec*: Hunting, farming, painting, collecting paintings & sculptures. *a*: 3850 Dearborn St, Chicago 3, Ill. *T*: State 8576.

GARLAND, DAVID JOHN (pen name: Joseph Mede): priest, Church of England; *b*. Dublin, Ireland, Oct., 1864; *s*. James and Mary (Saunders) G.; *educ*. privately; *m*. Mary Hadfield. AUTHOR: Religious Instruction in State Schools, 1913. Editor of Ithaca Church News, 1922. Contributor to various Australian papers. General character of writing: historical, ecclesiastical. Canon, St. John's Cathedral, Brisbane; rector, Ithaca parish, Brisbane; justice of peace; formerly Archdeacon of North Queensland; chaplain in Australian Army. Knight of the Holy Sepulchre, Jerusalem; order of merit, King Charles, the Martyr; dir. of Immigration for Church of Eng. in Queensland; pres. New Settlers' League, Queensland; founder and dir., Soldiers' Ch. of Eng. Help Soc., Queensland; Hon. organizing sec. for recruiting, Queensland, during Great War. Introduced religious instruction into state schools of West Australia in 1893; into Queensland. 1910. Relig. denom., Church of England. OFFICE: Riviera, North Quay. HOME: St. Barnabas' Rectory, Brisbane, Queensland, Australia.

GARLAND, H. G., M.D. *Publ*: Uveo-Parotid Tuberculosis; Tuberculoma Cerebri; etc. Physician to the Leeds Public Dispensary & Hosp. *a*: 32 Park Sq, Leeds.

GARLAND, John K. *b*: Leicester 1895. *e*: Wyggeston G.S. Leicester. Journalist. *n.a*: Sporting Chronicle, M/C 5 y till 1926. Press

Assoc, Lon '26—. Mem N.U.J. '24—. *s.s*: Racing. Was Football Corr (" Touch-Line ") & " Racecourse Commissioner " of The Racing World. *a*: 2 Red Bull Wharf, Upper Thames St, E.C.4.

GARLAND, Mrs. Madge. *a*: Vogue, 1 New Bond St, W.

GARLAND, Peter. *b*: N.Y., U.S.A. *Publ*: Plays—The Eternal Spring; Made in Heaven; An Evening on Dartmoor; Eine Vollkommen Frau. *s.s*: Drama. *a*: Ronceval, Claygate, Surrey. *t*: Esher 885.

GARMENT, Colin Stafford. *b*: Bow, City of Lon 1887. *e*: Coopers Coy G.S. *m*: Daisy Clare Savage. Mang Dir Photographic Press Agency. *a*: 26–29 Poppins Ct, Fleet St, E.C.4.

GARNEAU, Adolphe. *b*: St Stanislas, Champlain 1874. *e*: Commercial Acad, Quebec Semin & Laval Univ. Prof Ecole des Beaux Arts, Chaplain Maison de Bethanie. *Publ*: Precis de Geographie; Christmas Stories & Short Novels; Geographical Notes; Latin Notes. *Ctr*: Le Canada Francais, Bulletin de Geographie, L'Enseignement Secondaire, L'Action Catholique. *s.s*: Fine Arts, History & Geography, Boy Scouts. *Rec*: Summer camps for boys. *a*: 5 Christie St, Quebec, P.Q., & 14 Couillard St, Quebec. *T*: 2–6555.

GARNEAU, Hector, LL.B., F.R.S.C. *b*: Ottawa, Ontario 1871. *e*: Ottawa Coll & Univ of Montreal. *m*: Blanche Pillet. *s*: 2. Lawyer & Journalist, Lect French Canadian Literature, Mem Soc des Ecrivains Canadiens. *n.a*: Political Corres Le Soleil Quebec, Ed Paris & Montreal editions of F. X. Garneau's Histoire du Canada. *Ctr*: Les Nouvelles, Revue Nationale, Canadian Bookman, Montreal Gazette, Le Canada, Le Devoir, etc. *s.s*: History of Canada. *Rec*: Reading. *c*: Canadian. *a*: 1374 Sherbrooke St West, Montreal, Quebec. *T*: Ma.6528.

GARNER, Frederic Horace, O.B.E., Ph.D., M.I.A.E. M.I.Chem.E., F.R.I.C. Assoc Ed Science of Petroleum; Ed Trans of English Ceramic Circle; Modern Road Emulsions. *a*: The University, Edgbaston, Birmingham.

GARNER, Miss Katherine Minta. *n.a*: Sec & Advtg Mang Newark Advertiser. *Publ*: Verse & plays. *a*: 6 Spring Gdns, Newark.

GARNET, FRANCES: see Wolseley, Viscountess.

GARNETT, Alice, B.A., Ph.D. *b*: London 1903. *e*: U.C.L. Univ Lect in Geography 1924—, Hon Sec Geographical Assoc. *Publ*: Insolation & Relief; The Geographical Interpretation of Topographical Maps; Time & Place (with Prof Lyde), etc. *Ctr*: Geog periodicals. *s.s*: Microclimatology, Alpine & Balkan Regions. *a*: Dept of Geog, The University, Sheffield. *T*: 61142.

GARNETT, Constance. *b*: Brighton 1861. *e*: High Sc & Newnham Col, Camb. *m*: Edward Garnett. *s*: 1. *Publ*: Translations of Works of :—Turgenev; Tolstoy; Dostoevsky; Tchekov; Gogol; Herzen. *s.s*: Russian Language & literature. *Rec*: Gardening. *a*: The Cearne, Edenbridge, Kent. *t*: Limpsfield Chart 62.

GARNETT, David. *b*: Brighton 1892. *e*: Roy Coll of Sci. *m*: (1) Rachel Marshall (*s*: 2); (2) Angelica Bell (*d*: 4). Author & Dir of Rupert Hart-Davis Ltd Publishers. *Publ*: Lady into Fox; Go She Must; No Love; A Rabbit in the Air; Pocahontas, etc. *Rec*: Fishing, shooting. *a*: Hilton Hall, Huntingdon. *T*: Papworth 23.

GARNETT, Edward. *b*: Lon 1868. *m*: Constance Clara Black. *s*: 1. Lit Critic. *Publ*: Friday Nights: The Trial of Jeanne d'Arc; & Other Plays; Letters from Conrad 1895—1924; Letters from W. H. Hudson '01—22; Letters from John Galsworthy 1900—32. Translator of Turgenev, Tolstoy, Dostoevsky, Tchekov, Gogol. First literary friend of Joseph Conrad & D. H. Lawrence, & backer of W. H. Hudson, C. M. Doughty & John Galsworthy. *a*: 19 Pond Pl, Chelsea, S.W.3.

GARNETT, James Clerk Maxwell, C.B.E., Sc.D. *b*: Cambridge 1880. *e*: Marlborough Coll, St Paul's Sch & Trin Coll Camb. *m*: Margaret Lucy Poulton. *s*: 3. *d*: 3. Barrister, Prin Coll of Technology Manch & Dean of Faculty of Technology Manch Univ 1912—20, Sec of the League of Nations Union '20—38. *Publ*: Education & World Citizenship; The World We Mean to Make; Knowledge & Character; A Lasting Peace (with H. F. Koeppler); World Loyalty; The Dawn of World Order (with Nowell Charles Smith). *Ctr*: Contemp Rev, Hibbert Journal, Philosophy, Journal of Educ, etc. *s.s*: Education, World Affairs. *Rec*: Walking, sailing. *c*: Athenæum, Leander. *a*: 37 Park Town, Oxford. *T*: 4100.

GARNETT, LUCY MARY JANE: author; b. Sheffield, Yorkshire, Eng.; d. Thomas and Lucy Sarah (Roberts) G.; unmarried. AUTHOR: Greek Folkpoesy, 1885 (2nd edit. 1888; 3rd, in 2 vols., 1896); The Women and Folklore of Turkey: Christian Women, 1890, (vol. 2, Jewish and Moslem Women, 1891; Turkish Life in Town and Country, 1895; The Turkish People, 1909; Turkey of the Ottomans, 1911; Mysticism and Magic in Turkey, 1912; Greek Wonder Tales, 1913; Ottoman Wonder Tales, 1915; Balkan Home Life, 1917. Contributor to Nineteenth Century, Fortnightly Review; The Nation (New York). Has travelled and resided many years both in the Near and Far East, has written extensively on Oriental manners, customs and folklore. Was awarded Civil List Pension in 1893 for her services to literature. CLUBS: London Folklore Society. ADDRESS care of Messrs. Thos. Cook and Son, Florence, Italy.

GARNETT, Martha. *b*: Lon 1869. *e*: Queen's Col Sc, Harley St & Priv Sc. *m*: Robert Singleton Garnett (dec). *s*: 2. *d*: 3. *Publ*: (Novels) The Infamous John Friend; Amor Vincit; Samuel Butler & his Family Relations; Unrecorded (1930). *Rec*: Gardening. *a*: Hardown, Morcombelake, Bridport, Dorset.

GARNETT. WILLIAM: retired; b. Portsea, Eng., Dec., 1850; s. William and Selina (Webb) G.; educ. City of London; DEGREES: M.A. (Cambridge); Hon. D.C.L. (Durham); m. Rebecca Samways, Aug. 21, 1879. AUTHOR: Elementary Dynamics, 1875; Elementary Treatise on Heat, 1877; Elementary Mechanics. 1878; Life of James Clerk Maxwell, 1882; Heroes of Science, Physicists, 1886; A Little Book on Map Projection, 1914; A Little Book on Water Supply, 1922. Editor of Clerk Maxwell's Elementary Treatise on Electricity: of London Technical Education Gazette. 1894-1904. Contributor to Ency. Britannica, Electrician, Nature and other technical papers. General character of writing: scientific biography and school and university text books. Has been demonstrator and lecturer in Univ. of Cambridge; fellow of St. John's Coll.; prof. in Univ. Coll., Nottingham; prof. of math. in Univ. of Durham, and prin. of Durham Coll. of Science, Newcastle-on-Tyne; mem. of Royal Comm. for exhibition of 1851; sec. of technical educ. brd. and educ. adviser for London County Council; Hon. life mem. of Institution of Mining Engineers. Relig. denom., Congregational. HOME: Sea View, Isle of Wight, Eng.

GARNONS WILLIAMS, Basil Hugh. *b*: New Radnor 1906. *e*: Winchester Coll & Hertford Coll Oxf. *m*: Margaret Olive Shearme. *s*: 1. *d*: 1. Schoolmaster. *Publ*: Part III (Rome) in W. N. Weech's History of the World. *Ctr*: Classical Quarterly, Greece & Rome. *a*: Headmaster's Hse, Plymouth Coll, Devon. *T*: Plymouth 3353.

GARNSEY, Edward Rock, B.A. Barrister-at-Law. *Publ*: A Translation & Exposition of the Odes of Horace; Students' Edition of the Odes of Horace; Epilegomena on Horace. *c.t*: Classical Rev, Melbourne Argus, etc. *a*: c/o High Commissioner for Australia, Australia Hse, Lon, W.C.2.

GARRAD, Barry, B.Litt(Oxon), PhD.(Lon). *a*: College of St Mark & St John, Chelsea.

GARRARD, Major A. Ed Practical Motoring. *Publ*: Gas; Oil; Petrol Engines; etc. *a*: c/o Waverley Book Co, 96/7 Farringdon St, E.C.4.

GARRARD, Charles Cornfield, PhD., M.I.E.E., A.Am.I.E.E. *b*: Lon 1877. *e*: Cent Foundation Scs Lon, Finsbury Tech Col, Univ of Göttingen. *m*: Kate Mary Brett. *s*: 2. *d*: 1. Elec Eng. *Publ*: Electric Switch and Controlling Gear; A Short way with Unemployment. *c.t*: Times Engineering Supplement, Elec Review, Accountant, Engineering Review, Western Mail & S. Wales News. *s.s*: Electric Control gear. Mem of Counc Birm Chamber of Comm. *Rec*: Gardening. *c*: Devonshire, Engineers Birm. *a*: Dennington, Somerville Rd, Sutton Coldfield, nr B'ham. *t*: Sut 2087.

GARRATT, Geoffrey Theodore, J.P. *b*: Little Tew 1888. *e*: Rugby Sc, Hertford Coll Oxf. *m*: Anne Beryl Benthall. I.C.S. 1913—23. *Publ*: Hundred Acre Farm; The Mugwumps and the Labour Party; The Rise & Fulfilment of British Rule in India (with Edward Thompson); Lord Brougham; The Organisation of Farming; etc. *c.t*: New Statesman. *s.s*: India & agriculture. *Rec*: Travel, gardening, tennis. Political Sec Round Table Conf. *c*: Authors'. *a*: Bishopsteignton House, nr Teignmouth. S. Devon. *t*: Bishopsteignton 30.

GARRETT, Christina Hallowell, M.A. *b*: 1876. *e*: Bryn Mawr Coll & Harvard Univ. Historical Research. *Publ*: The Marian Exiles. *Ctr*: Journ of Mod Hist, Church Quart Rev, The Library. *s.s*: Early Reformation in England. *a*: c/o Barclay's Bank, Banbury Rd Branch, Oxford, & c/o The Merchant's National Bank, State St, Boston, U.S.A.

GARRETT, Edmund William, M.A., J.P. *b*: Ire 1850. *e*: Shrewsbury Sc & St John's Col Cam. *m*: Frances Andrews. *s*: 1. *d*: 1. Met Police Magis (ret). *Publ*: Law of Nuisances; Wanted. *a*: Ardeevin, Epsom.

GARRETT, F/O. John Ellis, R.A.F.V.R. *b*: London 1915. *e*: Purley Gr Sch. *n.a*: Surrey County Herald 1933—34, Corres The Times, Lond Ev News, Various Technical Journs '34—40, Ed Diversion '34—35, President Inst of Authors '37—38, Ed The Drogue (South Africa) '44. *Publ*: The Business Side of Writing; etc. *Ctr*: Times, Ev News, Cape Times (South Africa), Globe & Mail (Toronto), Various South African, British, Canadian & American nwsprs & mags. *s.s*: Fiction. *a*: c/o Lloyds Bank, Croydon, England.

GARRETT, John Walter Percy. *b*: Trowbridge 1902. *e*: Trowbridge Hgh Sch & Exeter Coll Oxf. Head Bristol Gr Sch. *Publ*: The Poet's Tongue (with W. H. Auden); Scenes from School Life; Four vols for King's Treasuries. *Ctr*: New Statesman & Nation, Spectator, Times Educ Suppl, Observer, Eng Rev. *s.s*: Shakespeare, the Elizabethan Theatre, Modern Drama. *Rec*: Gardening. *a*: Bristol Grammar School, Bristol 8. *T*: 36006.

GARRETT, Margaret Frances, B.A. *b*: Newcastle-under-Lyme 1917. *e*: Beauchamp Hall Leamington & Lady Margaret Hall Oxf. *m*: Ronald Garrett (dec'd). Journalist. *n.a*: i/c Mag Section Farmer & Stock Breeder 1946—. *s.s*: General Country Interests. *Rec*: Books, music, swimming, art, films & the theatre. *c*: Farmer's & Women's Press. *a*: 162 Chelsea Cloisters, London, S.W.3.

GARRETT, Philip Leslie. *b*: London 1888. *e*: Highgate Sch. *m*: Phyllis Kathleen Medland. *s*: 2. *d*: 1. Ed The Ironmonger, Mem Law Soc. *n.a*: Staff Ironmonger 1914, Asst Ed '25, Ed '34. *Ctr*: Various newspapers & periodicals. *Rec*: Reading, travel, ornithology. *a*: 28 Essex St, Strand, London, W.C.2. *T*: Central 6565.

GARRETT, William, K.C., B.A., LL.B.(Cantab), LL.B.(Glas). *b*: Coatbridge 1890. *e*: Fettes Coll & Camb & Glas Univs. *m*: Mary McNaught. *s*: 1. *d*: 1. Advocate, Sheriff-Substitute for Ayrshire. *Publ*; Novels—St Anthony's Grove; The Secret of the Hills; Doctor Ricardo; Treasure Royal; The Multitude; From Dusk till Dawn; The Man in the Mirror, etc. *Ctr*: Various. *s.s*: Scots Law, Internat Private Law. *Rec*: Golf, badminton. *a*: 37 Heriot Row, Edinburgh. *T*: 26454.

GARROD, Sir Archibald Edward, K.C.M.G., M.D., M.A.(Oxon), HonLL.D.(Glas & Aberdeen), HonM.D.(Dub)., F.R.C.P., F.R.S. *b*: Lon 1857. *e*: Marlborough, Christ Ch Oxf & Bart's Hosp. *m*: Laura Elizabeth Smith. *g*: 1. Physician & Prof of Medicine (ret). *Publ*: Inborn Errors of Metabolism (1909); The Inborn Factors in Disease; A Treatise on Rheumatism (1890); Jt Ed Diseases of Child. *c.t*: Med Jnls. Col late A.M.S. *a*: 1 Huntingdon Rd, Cambridge. *t*: 2660.

GARROD, Lawrence Paul, M.D., B.Ch., F.R.C.P. *b*: London 1895. *e*: Sidcot Sch, King's Coll Camb, St Bart's Hosp. *m*: Marjorie Pierce. *s*: 3. *d*: 1. Bacteriologist St Bart's Hosp & City of Lond, Prof Bact Univ Lond, Mem B.M.A. *Publ*: Recent Advances in Pathology (with G. Hadfield). *Ctr*: Various Med Journs brit Brit, France, U.S.A., etc. *s.s*: Bacteriology. *Rec*: Music, gardening, golf. *w.s*: Surg Sub Lt R.N.V.R. 1917—18. *a*: 19 Douglas Rd, Harpenden, Herts. *T*: 230.

GARROOD, Dr. J. R. *c.t*: Proc Zool Soc, 1924, Antiquaries' Journal, Trans C. & H.A.S., etc. Hon Sec Cambs & Hunts Arch Soc; Local Sec Soc Antiq Lon; Hon Curator Huntingdon Museum. *a*: Alconbury Hill, Huntingdon.

GARROTT, Hal. *b*: Chicago 1877. *e*: Univ of Chic, Amer Conservatory of Music. *m*: Marion Caplin. *n.a*: Drama & Music Ed Monterey Peninsular Herald. *Publ*: Snythergen; Squiffer; First Aide to Santa Claus. *Ctr*: Various. *s.s*: Literary Fantasy, Musical & Dramatic Criticism. *Rec*: Music, piano-playing, gardening. *a*: P.O. Box 1344, Carmel, California. *T*: Carmel 652.

GARROW, James, F.Z.S. *b*: New York. *m*: Alice Emily Pillans. *s*: 2. *d*: 1. Playwright, actor & jnlst. *n.a*: Ed British Fancier 1897, Fanciers Review '98—1900, Stock-keeper, '26—34. *Publ*: Plays: Auld Robin Gray, Rollicking Barney; Eileen Alannah; Laughing Water; Only a Coster's Daughter. *c.t*: Fur & Feather, Poultry Wld, Glasgow Dly Record, Scotsman, Hutchinson's Dog Encyclopædia, etc. *s.s*: Dogs, small live-stock, sport, folk-lore. Internat Dog & Poultry Judge. Officiated at all leading shows in Britain, Ireland & Continent. Managed theatres & dramatic companies for 25 yrs. Played Rob Roy every night for 13 months, a record. *Rec:* Reading, walking. *a:* Edmalee, Loanhead, Midlothian. *t:* Loanhead 65.

GARSIA, Lt.-Col. Willoughby Clive, D.S.O., M.C. *b:* Nelson, N.Z. 1881. *e:* New Zealand. Author, ret Army Officer. *Publ:* Key to Victory; Planning the War; Tenacity (pseudonym Guy Cottar). *s.s:* International Affairs. *Rec:* Gardening. *c:* Army & Navy. *a:* Ashley Rd, Epsom. *T:* 9722.

GARSIDE, Bernard, M.A., B.Sc., F.R.Hist.S. *b:* Skipton-in-Craven, Yorks 1898. *e:* Leeds Univ & U.C.L. *m:* Edith May Preston, B.A. Grammar School Master. *Publ:* The History of Hampton School 1556—1700; Series of Monographs on Hampton-on-Thames History & Records, etc. *Ctr:* Various. *s.s:* Local History & Records. *Rec:* Hill-climbing. *w.s:* 1914—18 & '39—45 R.A.S.C. *a:* 74 Ormond Ave, Hampton-on-Thames, Mddx. *T:* Molesey 3133.

GARSTANG, BASIL (pen name): see **Brereton, John LeGay.**

GARSTANG, John, M.A., D.Sc., B.Litt., Hon.LL.D., F.S.A. *b:* Blackburn 1876. *e:* Blackburn Gr Sch, Jesus Coll Oxf. *m:* Marie Louise Bergès. *s:* 1. *d:* 1. Archæologist, Emeritus Prof Univ of L'pool. *Publ:* The Foundations of Bible History: Joshua, Judges; The Heritage of Solomon; The Third Egyptian Dynasty; Burial Customs of Ancient Egypt; The Land of the Hittites; The Hittite Empire; Reports on Excavations at Mersin, Jericho, Abydos, etc. *Ctr:* Times, Dly Telegraph, Observer, American Journ of Archæology, Journ of Near Eastern Studies. *s.s:* Archæology, Turkey. *Rec:* Fishing, exploration. *c:* L'pool Univ, Formby Golf. *a:* Thornbury, Formby, Lancs. *T:* Formby 303.

GARSTANG, Walter, M.A., D.Sc., F.L.S., F.Z.S. *Publ:* inc Songs of the Birds; The Theory of Re-capitulation; The Siphonophora; etc. *a:* 18 Apsley Rd, Oxford.

GARSTIN, Edward John Langford, M.C. *b:* Lon 1893. *e:* Charterhouse & Cam Univ. *Publ:* Theurgy; The Secret Fire; The Book of the Master of the Hidden Places. *c.t:* London Forum, etc. *s.s:* Religion, philosophy, psychology. War Service '14—20. *Rec:* Tennis, swimming. *a:* 53 Bassett Rd, W.10. *t:* Park 6415.

GARTNER, Paul William, B.Sc. *b:* Junction City, Kansas 1908. *e:* Kansas State Col, Manhattan. Writer. *n.a:* Mang Sports Publicity, Kansas State Col '28—35. *Publ:* First Aid Afield. *c.t:* Field & Stream, Outdoor Life, National Sportsman, Hunting & Fishing, Sports Afield, The Sportsman, Modern Mechanics & Inventions, Popular Mechanics, Fur-Fish Game, Pacific Sportsman, Angling Success. *s.s:* Angling, shooting, first aid, lifesaving, outdoor sports. Instructor of lifesaving methods for the American Red Cross. *Rec:* Swimming, camping, running, fishing. *c:* Kappa Sigma, Sigma Delta Chi. *c:* 324 Tenth St, Santa Monica, California, U.S.A. *t:* Santa Monica 28673.

GARTON, Maj. James Archibald, M.C. *b:* Shepton Mallet 1891. *e:* Eton. *m:* Dora Marjorie Cuvelier *d:* 2. Farmer, Landowner. *Publ:* The Bowman; The Guest. *s.s:* Somerset dialect, history, tradition, etc. Vice Chm Shepton Mallet R.D.C., Broadcasting, etc. *a:* Pylle Manor, Shepton Mallet, Somerset. *t:* Ditcheat 2.

GARTON, John Charles. *b:* Boston 1893. *e:* Chr Ch Newark, Clapton Col Lon. *m:* Isobella Mackenley. *s:* 2. *d:* 1. Journalist. *n.a:* Chf Sub-Ed Lincs Echo 1930, Newcastle Chronicle, Asst Ed Whitley Bay Observer '19—22, Ed Pudsey Advtr & Arnley & Wortley News '22—28, Yorks Post, Sub-Ed Hull Evening News '29—30. War Service '16—19. Salvation Army Officer '12—15. *Rec:* Music, poetry, book collecting. *c:* N.U.J. *a:* Mountford, Newark Rd, Lincoln.

GARVIE, Rev. Alfred Ernest, M.A.(Oxon), D.D.(Glas), D.D.(Lon), D.Th(Berlin). *b:* Poland 1861. *e:* German Sc in Poland, George Watson's Col Edin & Univs of Edin, Glas & Oxf. *m:* Agnes Gordon (dec). *s:* 1. (dec). *d:* 2. Cong Min. Prof of Theo. Princ Emeritus of Hackney & New Col, '08—33. Chm Cong Un Scot 1902—03, & of Cong Un Eng & Wales '19—20. Pres Nat F.C.C. '23—24. Moderator of Fed Counc of F. Ch's '27—28. Dep Chm Lausanne Con on Faith & Order '27. Chm Chr Soc Counc of Eng '28—. Pres World Alliance (Br Counc). *Publ:* The Ritschlian Theology; Commentary on Romans (Century Bible); The Christian Certainty & the Modern Perplexity; The Christian Doctrine of the Godhead; The Christian Ideal for Human Society; The Christian Belief in God; Can Christ Save Society?; Revelation in History and Experience; etc. *c.t:* Contemporary Review, Free Churchman, British Weekly, Sociological Review, Philosophy, etc. *s.s:* Philos, ethics, sociology, theology. In business in Glas 1880—84. *Rec:* Reading, walking. *a:* 34 Sevington Rd, Hendon, N.W.4. *t:* 6834.

GARVIN, James Louis, HonLittD.(Durham). *n.a:* Ed The Outlook 1905—6, Ed Pall Mall Gazette '12—15, Ed Ency Britannica (14th edn) '26—29, Ed The Observer '08—. *Publ:* The Economic Foundations of Peace; The Life of Joseph Chamberlain, Vol I 1836—85, & Vol II '85—95 & Vol III 1895—1901. *c.t:* Ency Britannica, National Review, Fortnightly Review, Quarterly, etc. *c:* Athenæum, Garrick. *a:* Gregories, Beaconsfield Bucks.

GARVIN, Viola Gerard. *b:* Newcastle-on-Tyne 1898. *e:* S. Hampstead H.S. & Oxf Univ. Journalist. *n.a:* Lit Ed The Observer 1926—34. *Publ:* Dedication (verse); Trans: Life of Solomon; Fanny & Jane; Recaptured; The Last of Cheri (all from French); etc. *a:* 28 Shepherd St, W.1.

GASCOIGNE, Hubert Claude Victor, A.R.A.M. Prof & Examiner Roy Acad of Music. *c.t:* Musical Opinion, R.A.M. Club Mag. *a:* 89 Hamlet Gdns, W.6.

GASCOYNE, David Emery. *b:* Harrow 1916. *e:* Salisbury Cathedral Choir Sc Regent St Polytech. *Publ:* Opening Day '33. *c.t:* New Verse, New English Weekly, Bookman, Listener. *s.s:* Poetry, French lit, contemporary art. Cont to Mrs Harold Monro's Anthology, Recent poetry '32—33. *Rec:* Music, swimming. *a:* 402 Richmond Rd, East Twickenham, Middx.

GASCOYNE-CECIL, Lord Hugh Richard Heathcote, P.C., M.P. *Publ:* Conservatism; Liberty & Authority; Nationalism & Catholicism. *a:* 21 Arlington St, S.W.1. *t:* Regent 0501.

GASELEE, Sir Stephen, K.C.M.G., C.B.E., HonD.Litt.(L'pool). *b:* London, 1882 *e:* Eton, Cam. *m:* May Evelyn Hulme. *d:* 3. Librarian and Keeper of the Papers at Foreign Office. *n.a:* Ed The Cambridge Review '08—09.

Publ: Oxford Book of Mediæval Latin Verse; Anthology of Mediæval Latin; The Codex Tragusiensis of Petronius; Stories from the Christian East; Achilles Tatius. *c.t*: Times Lit Supplement, Classical Review, Jnl of Theological Studies. *s.s*: Mediæval & late Latin, Coptic, Portuguese, literature of music. *Rec*: Shooting. Fell Magdalene Col Cam. Commdr of the Order of St John of Jerusalem. *c*: Athenæum, Carlton, Beefsteak. *a*: 24 Ashburn Pl, S.W.7. *t*: Frobisher 4218.

GASK, Arthur. Author. *Publ*: The Judgment of Larose; etc. *a*: c/o Herbert Jenkins Ltd, 3 York St, S.W.1.

GASK, Norman. *b*: Beckenham 1879. *m*: Gwladys Tattersall Jones. Journalist. *n.a*: Dly Express Lond 1908—, N.Y. Tribune '01—'07, Lond Dly Mail '07—08. *Publ*: Old Silver Spoons of England. *Ctr*: Connoisseur, Apollo, Country Life, Fine Arts, etc. *a*: The Daily Express, Shoe Lane, E.C.4.

GASKELL, Dr. H. S. *Publ*: With Lord Methuen in South Africa; Pot Pourri (Poems). *a*: The Corner House, Stowmarket.

GASKELL, Dr. J. F., M.A., M.D.(Cantab), F.R.C.P. (Lon). *Publ*: (Jtly) Cerebro-spinal fever; The Evolution of the Vertebral Column. Hon Physician to Addenbrooke's Hosp, Cambridge. Late Beit Memorial Research Fellow. *a*: The Uplands, Gt Shelford, nr Cambridge.

GASKOIN, Charles Jacinth Bellairs. *b*: Ealing. *e*: Fitzwilliam Hall & Jesus Coll Camb (1st Cl Hist Tripos, Senior Univ Tripos). Formerly Univ Examiner Lecturer Camb & Lond, Head of Code Sects Postal & Telegraph Censorships London, Liverpool & Bermuda World Wars I & II. *Publ*: Alcuin; The Hanovarians; Britain in the Modern World. *Ctr*: Brit Year Book of Internat Law, Chamber's Journal, Camb Rev, etc. *s.s*: History, especially Anglo-American relations. *Rec*: Amateur Drama. *c*: Athenæum. *a*: The Athenæum Club, Pall Mall, London, S.W.1. *T*: Whitehall 4843.

GASS, John Bradshaw, F.R.I.B.A. Architect. *Publ*: Some American Methods; Some Travel Sketches; etc. *c.t*: Various. *a*: Silverwell St, Bolton. *t*: 1746.

GASS, JOSEPH: canon of the Cathedral of Strasbourg; b. Mutzig, May 24, 1864; s. Gregoire and Catherine (Schickelé); educ. Grand Seminary of Strasbourg, Univs. of Munich and Wurzburg. DEGREE: D.D. AUTHOR: Mutzig in der Revolutionszeit, 1902; Die Bibliothek des Strassburger Prieterseminars, 1902; Strassburgs Bibliotheken, 1902; Strassburger Dominikanerinnen, 1905; La Cathédrale de Strasbourg, 1907; Alte Bücher und Papiere aus dem Kloster Alspach, 1907; Die Franziskaner in Mutzig-Hermolsheim, 1908; Album Mutzig, 1910; Album Molsheim, 1911; Das Strassburger Priesterseminar während der Revolution, 1914; Der Adel in Mutzig, 1915; Konstitutionelle Professoren am Strassburger Priesterseminar, 1916; Strassburger Theologen im Aufklärungszeitalter, 1917; Vergilbte Blätter, 1918; Elsässische Jesuiten, 1918; Chanoine Stoeffler, 1920; Vom konstitutionellen Kultus und Klerus, 1921; Studien zur elässischen Kirchengeschichte (vol. I), 1924 (vol. II), 1926; Imitation de Jésus-Christ en Alsace, 1929. Editor: Bulletin ecclésiastique du Diocèse de Strasbourg, Revue Catholique d'Alsace. General character of writing: historical. CLUBS: Membre correspondant du Ministere de l'Instruction publique, Président des Amis de la Cathédrale, Vice-Président de la Société des Monuments historiques d'Alsace. Religion, Catholic. ADDRESS: Grand Seminaire, 2 rue des Freres, Strassburg, France.

GASSNER, GUSTAV: college professor; b. Berlin, Germany, Jan. 17, 1881; s. Georg and Luise (Voigt) G.; educ. Friedrich Gymnasium (Berlin), Univs. of Halle, Berlin, and technical college of Charlottenburg. DEGREES: Dr. Phil., Professor; m. Lily Fassler-Farnkopf, April 27, 1910. Co-Editor: Phytopathologische Zeitschrift. Contributor to Berichte der deutschen botanischen Gesellschaft, Zeitschrift für Botanik, Angewandte Botanik, die Gartenbauwissenschaft, Phytopathologische Zeitschrift, Arbeiten aus der Biologischen Reichsanstalt für Land und Forstwirtschaft, Jahrbücher für wissenschaftliche Botanik, Blumen-und Pflanzenbau, Zeitschrift für angewandte Chemie. General character of writing: botanic-physiology and botanic-pathology. CLUBS: German Botanical Society, Club of Applied Botany, Society for the Advancement of German Botany. Religion, Protestant. OFFICE: Humboldtstrasse 1, Braunschweig. HOME: An der Wabe 23, Braunschweig-Gliesmarode, Germany.

GASSON George. Journalist. *n.a*: Eastbourne Chronicle (61 y). Official shorthand writer to Eastbourne & Lewes Bankrupcty Courts (52 y). *a*: 2a Station Parade, Eastbourne.

GASTER, Moses, PhD. *b*: Bucharest 1856. *e*: Bucharest, Breslau & Leipzig. *m*. Lucy Friedlander. *s*: 7. *d*: 6. Late Chf Rabbi Sephardies, late Lect Bucharest Univ & Oxf. *Publ*: Roumanian Chestomathy; History of Roumanian Popular Literature; The Samaritans; The Titled Bible; Sephardie Prayer Book; etc. *c.t*: Journ Roy Asiatic Soc, Folklore, Gipsy Lore, Jewish Forum, etc. *s.s*: Roumanian, Samaritan, Hebrew folklore. *Rec*: Books. *a*: 193 Maida Vale, W.9.

GATE, William Sidney. *b*: Liverpool 1887. *e*: Nelson Gr Sch, Wigton, Cumb. *m*: Amy Bowler. *s*: 1. Journalist. *n.a*: Glas Herald Parl Corr, West Cumberland Times 10 yrs, St Anne's Visitor, Rossendale Free Press, West Herts & Watford Observer, Chief Rep Streatham News. *s.s*: Politics. *Rec*: Bowls. *c*: Press. *a*: 58 Mitcham Lane, S.W.16.

GATENBY, James Bronte, M.A., Ph.D., D.Sc., D.Phil. *b*: Wanganui, N.Z. 1892. *m*: Enid Kathleen Meade. *s*: 2. *d*: 2. Foundation Universitaire Lecturer, Louvain, Brussels, Ghent, Theresa Seessel Fellow Yale Univ. *n.a*: Sub Ed Science Progress, Ed Bd Journal Roy Microscopical Soc, Ed Microtomists' Vademecum. *Ctr*: Encyc Brit, Chambers's Encycl & various scientific journals. *s.s*: Zoology, Cytology. *Rec*: Motoring, fishing. *a*: Scratnagh Hse, Arklow, Ireland, & Zoology Dept, Trinity Coll, Dublin. *T*: 62061.

GATES, Reginald Ruggles, M.A., D.Sc., LL.D., Ph.D., F.R.S. *b*: Middleton, Nova Scotia. *e*: Univs of Mt Allison, McGill, Chic, Lond. Biologist, Emeritus Prof Univ of London. *n.a*: Jt-Ed, Journ Roy Micros Soc, formerly Jt-Ed Brit Journ Egypt Biology & Annals of Eugenics. *Publ*: Human Genetics; Heredity in Man; Human Ancestry; Heredity & Eugenics; A Botanist in the Amazon Valley; The Mutation Factor in Evolution. *Ctr*: Nature, Science, Eugenics Rev, Times, Ev Standard, Man, etc. *s.s*: Human Genetics, Blood Groups, Race Crossing, Cytology & Plant Breeding, Anthropology, Mutations. *Rec*: Travel. *c*: Athenæum. *a*: Biological Laboratories, Harvard University, Cambridge, Mass, U.S.A.

GATES, Roy. *Publ*: Animal Diseases, Cures; Lyrics; Racing stories. *s.s*: Agric. *a*: 6 Glynde Ave, Hampden Park, Eastbourne.

GATEY, Kenneth, B.A., M.C. *b*: Barnes 1886. *e*: Marlboro' & Hertford Col Oxf. *m*: Margery, daughter of Sir James & Lady Owen.

d: 2. Dir, Gen Mang & Ed Western Times Group of Papers. *n.a*: Dir Western Times 1920, Ed Football Express '20, Mang Ed Devon & Exeter Gazette '31. Sheriff Exeter '25—26, Mayor Exeter '32—33. *c*: Devon & Exeter, Exeter & County. *a*: Kelston, Exeter. *t*: 2197.

GATFIELD, Albert William. Publisher. Jnt Mang Dir Chapman & Hall Ltd. *a*: 11 Henrietta St, W.C.2. *t*: Temple Bar 5762.

GATHORNE-HARDY, Geoffrey Malcolm, M.C., Ph.D. (Oslo). *e*: Eton & New Coll Oxf. Barrister (ret). *Publ*: A Short History of International Affairs; Norway; The Norse Discoverers of America. *s.s*: Norway, Internat Affairs. *a*: Donnington Priory, Newbury. *T*: 241.

GATHORNE-HARDY, Hon R. *Publ*: Village Symphony & Other Poems; The House by the Bay; Other Seas; etc. *a*: The Mill House, Stanford, Dingley, nr Reading.

GATLEY, Clement Carpenter, M.A., D.C.L. (Oxon), LL.D.(Dublin). *b*: Lon 1881. *e*: Westminster Sc & Exeter Col Oxf. Married. *s*: 1. *d*: 3. Barrister-t-Law, Inner Temple. S.E. Circuit. *Publ*: The Law & Practice of Libel & Slander (1st ed 1924, 2nd '29). *c.t*: Ency Britannica, etc. *Rec*: Fly-fishing. *a*: 3 Brick Ct, Temple, E.C.4, & 18 High St, Marylebone, W. *t*: Cent 4613 & Welbeck 3397.

GATTERMAN, EUGEN LUDWIG (pen names: Eugen Alban Corvin; A. M. Renner): author, composer; b. Quedlinburg, Germany, Oct. 12, 1886; s. Ludwig and Eugenie Gattermann; educ. Gymnasium (Quedlinburg), Journalisten College (Berlin), Univs. of Tübingen and Berlin; unmarried AUTHOR: Über die Heide, 1910; Wenn die Schatten steigen, 1913; Das Sühnopfer, 1917; Der bittere Weg, 1918; Einer unter Euch, 1919; Die Erlösung der Freunde, 1920; Feuer des Eros, 1920; Ein Haus brennt, 1921; Der Spiesserspiegel, 1921; Das Nachtgesicht, 1922; Die Teufelsschmiede, 1922; Anna Maria (with A. H. Huber), 1923. Editor, composer: Der Lustige Wald, 1921; Beardsley, Das Haus der tausend Freuden, 1921; A.M.v. Thümmel, Das heilige Strumpfband, 1928. General character of writing: novels, plays, poems. CLUBS: Schutsverband deutscher Schriftseller. ADDRESS: Heinrichstrasse 10, Quedlinburg, Germany.

GATTI, Cmdr. Attilio. *b*: Voghera, Italy 1896. *e*: Modena Mil Acad, Cavalry Superior Sch of Pinerolo. *m*: Ellen Morgan Wadill. Author & Writer, Organised & Led several scientific expeditions to South & Central Africa. *n.a*: Spec Corr Fawcett Pubs, for Toronto Star Weekly, etc. *Publ*: Great Mother Forest; Saranga the Pygmy; Tom-Toms in the Night; Kamada; Killers All; South of the Sahara; The Wrath of Moto; Black Mist. *Ctr*: Illus Lond News, Passing Show, Observer, Dly Mail, etc, Sat Ev Post, Collier's, Life, etc. *s.s*: African Natives, Witchcraft, Big-Game, Prehistory, Belgian Congo, Sth Africa, Pygmies, Giant Gorilla, Okapi. *Rec*: Horse riding, high jumping, short-wave radio, helicopter flying. *c*: Adventurers (N.Y.). *w.s*: 1914—18. *a*: Glenbrook Hse, Derby Line Vermont, U.S.A. *T*: Rock Island 353.

GATTY, Rev. Edmund Percival, M.A.(Cantab). *b*: Accrington 1866. *e*: Harrow & St John's Cam. *m*: Mabel Wellwood Ker. *s*: 1. *d*: 1. *Publ*: History of Offley & Its Church. Vicar of Offley, Herts 1900-25. *Rec*: Shooting, cricket. *c*: Junior Constitutional. *a*: Downgate, Wadhurst, Sussex. *t*: 164.

GAUBA, Khalid Latif, B.A., LL.B. *b*: Lahore 1899. *e*: Govt Coll Lahore & Downing Coll Camb. *m*: (1) Husnara Aziz Ahmed, (2) Sarwar Sultana. *s*: 1. *d*: 2. Barrister, Senior Advocate Federal Court of India, Pres Punjab Journalist's Assoc 1928. *Publ*: Uncle Shem, a reply to Mother India; His Highness; The Prophet of the Desert; The Rebel Minister; Consequences of Pakistan; Verdict on England; etc. *Ctr*: Civil & Mil Gazette, Hindustan Times, Tribune, Hindu, etc. *s.s*: Political & Legal. *Rec*: Tennis, walking. *c*: Rotary, Bar Assoc. *a*: The Mall, Lahore, Pakistan. *T*: 4052.

GAUHAR, Harbakhshsingh. *b*: Gurjranwala 1912. *e*: Khalsa Col, Amritsar & Punjab Univ. Journalist. *n.a*: Ed The Paras, The Tiryaq, The Akali, Chief Ed The Beema. *Publ*: Dalkash Afsanc (Pt 1 & 2); Love Stories of Great Men (in Urdu). *c.t*: Adab, Lucknow, Riyasat, Delhi Film Stage, Lahore, etc. *s.s*: Translation, short stories. Sec Journalist Assoc. *Rec*: Trans. *a*: Ramnagar (Dish), Gujranwala, Punjab, India.

GAULLE, Gen. Charles Andre Joseph Marie de. *Publ*: inc La Discorde chez l'Ennemi; Vers L'Armée de Metier; La France et son Armee. *a*: Paris.

GAULTIER, Paul Louis Victor. *b*: Paris 1872. *m*: Marthe Gouël. Director, Commandeur de la Legion d'Honneur. *n.a*: Revue Bleue, Revue Scientifique, Synthèse (Revue Médicale), Bibliotheque de Philosophie Scientifique, etc. *Publ*: Le Rire et la Caricature; L'Ideal Moderne; Les Maladies Sociales; Les Leçons Morales de la Guerre; L' Avenir de la France; Les Moeurs de Temps; Le Leçon des Moeurs Contemporaines; Reflets d'Histoire; Les Maitres de la Pensee Contemporairee; L'Ame Française; Le Sens de l'Art; La Barbarie Allemande; etc. *Ctr*: Revue de Deux Mondes, Revue de Paris, Correspondant, Revue Philosophique, Le Temps, etc. *s.s*: Philosophy. *c*: des Cent. *a*: 4 Avenue de Villiers, Paris XVII. *T*: Wagram 9762.

GAUNT, Arthur, F.R.G.S., M.J.I. *Publ*: Exploring Historic Britain; Collecting for Pleasure & Profit; Pennine Ways. *s.s*: Snapshooting Articles & Features, Outdoor Articles, Fiction for Boys. *a*: 45 Haworth Rd, Heaton, Bradford, Yorkshire.

GAUNT, Admiral Sir Guy Reginald Archer, K.C.M.G., C.B. *b*: Ballarat, Aust 1869. *e*: Melbourne Gr Sch. *m*: Sybil Joseph. *d*: 2. M.P. (C) Buckrose Div of Yorkshire 1922—26. *Publ*: Yield of the Years. *Ctr*: Stories of Adventure. *a*: United Service Club, Fall Mall, London, S.W.1.

GAUNT, Mary. *b*: Victoria, Australia. *e*: Grenville Col Ballarat, Australia. *m*: Hubert Lindsay Miller, (dec). Author. *Publ*: Dave's Sweetheart; Harmony; Joan of the Pilchard; Reflection in Jamaica; Alone in West Africa; A Woman in China; Where the Twain Meet, etc. *c.t*: Morning Post, Times, Daily Chronicle, Pearson's, Sphere, Brittania, A.P. *s.s*: Travel articles. *Rec*: Travel, bridge. *a*: Villa Camilla, Bordighera, Italia.

GAUNT, William, M.A. *b*: Hull 1900. *e*: Hull Gr Sch, Worcester Coll Oxford. *m*: Mary Catherine O'Reilly. Writer & Painter. *n.a*: Art Critic Ev Standard. *Publ*: The Pre-Raphaelite Tragedy; The Aesthetic Adventure; Bandits in a Landscape; London Promenade. *s.s*: Visual Arts & Literature. *a*: Ockham Cottage, Kingsley, Bordon, Hants.

GAUTIER-SMITH, Dr. C. E. *a*: Grantchester, Chessel Ave, Bournemouth.

GAUTREY, Rev. Robert Moffat. *b*: Peterboro' 1872. *e*: Richmond Col Surrey. *m*: (1) Kate Gertrude Moxon, (2) Mabel Rosewarne Bradford. *s*: 2. *d*: 1. Meth Minister. *n.a*: Corr North Cambs Echo '90-92. *Publ*: The Chivalry of Jesus; The Sacrament of

Liberty; The Eternal Optimist; The Glory of Going On; This Tremendous Lover; The Burning Cataracts of Christ. *c.t*: Religious Press. *s.s*: Theological & devotional literature. Nat Press of B'hood Movement '11–12, Pres Metrop F. of Free Chs '26–27, Preacher & Lect Canada & America. *Rec*: Golf, gardening. *a*: Wakefield, Wellswood Av, Torquay. *t*: 3507.

GAUVAIN, Sir Henry John. M.A., M.D., M.Chir, F.R.C.S., J.P. *Publ*: Index of Treatment; Recent Progress in Medicine & Surgery; etc. Contrib to Modern Operative Surgery. *c.t*: Lancet, B.M.J., etc. *a*: Alton, Hants, & 125 Harley St, W.1. *t*: Alton 39 & Welbeck 1514.

GAVIN, William, C.B.E., M.A. *b*: Lon 1886. *e*: Uppingham, T.C. Camb. *m*: Lilian M. F. Forteath. *s*: 2. *c.t*: Morning Post, Times, Financial News, Country Life, Field, Farmer & Stockbreeder, Review of Reviews, etc. *s.s*: Agr. Gold Med for Research, Roy Agr Soc 1912, War Service R.N.V.R., Sec of Dep Dir Army Cattle Cmt '17, Dir Land Reclam, Min of Agr '19, Dir of Strutt & Parker (Farms) Ltd & The Agr Mortgage Corp Ltd. *c*: United Univ. *a*: Luctows, West Hoathly, Sussex. *t*: Sharpthorne 66.

GAW, Harry. *b*: Bangor 1890. *m*: Mabel Kathleen Irwin. *s*: 2. N/p Editor. *n.a*: Apprentice & Reporter Co Down Spectator Bangor 1904–20, Ed North Down Herald Bangor '20–26, Ed Co Down Spectator Bangor '29–. Ex-Chm Ulster Dis Inst of Journalists. *Rec*: Golf, bowls (Irish Internat Bowls Team 2 y). *a*: Clevedon, 56 Ballyholme Rd, Bangor, Co Down, Ulster. *t*: Bangor 488.

GAWALOWSKI, KARL WILHELM: Director of the Styrian National Library; b. Zubri, Moravia, June 30, 1861; s. Wilhelm and Aurelia (Ferles) G.; educ. High Sch. in Kaaden and Brüx, Univs. of Prague, Leipzig and Graz. DEGREE: Court Counselor; m. Anna Erhart, Sept. 10, 1884. AUTHOR: Lieder (songs), 1881; Egerberg, 1884; Ramphold Gorenz, 1885 (2nd edit. 1892); Steiermärkisches Dichterbuch (anthology), 1887; Im heiligen deutschen Osten (poems), 1894; Wie der Weihnachtsbaum in die Welt kam (tale), 1900; Friedrich Marx (biography), 1907; Steiermark, 1911; Brüx in seiner Vergangenheit und Gegenwart, 1911; Karl Lacher (biography), 1911. Edited: Deutschnationaler Kalender, 1886-1890; Südmark Kalender, 1898-1921; Balder, deutscher Jugendkalender, 1903; Steiermark, Hand- und Reisebuch, 1914 (2nd edit. 1926). Contributed: Brümmer Franz, Lexikon deutscher Dichter des 19. Jahrhunderts. Kosch Wilhelm, Deutsche Literatur Lexikon; Die K.W.G. betitelten Essays von W. Rott in "Der politische Bezirk Podersam", 1902; Karl Vallazza in den Wiener literarischen Mitteilungen, 1909; Franz Wastian in den Freien Bildungsblättern, 1911. General character of writing: novels, essays, poems. CLUBS: German Authors Club. ADDRESS: Plabutscherstrasse 206, Gösting near Graz (Steiermark), Austria.

GAWLER, J. H. Classics Master. *a*: L'pool Col Sc, Shaw St, Liverpool.

GAWSWORTH, John (T. I.Fytton Armstrong), F.R.S.L. *b*: Kensington 1912. *e*: Merchant Taylors Sch. *m*: Barbara Kentish. Poet, Man of Letters, Bibliographer, Gen Ed Mellifont Press, Benson Medallist, Freeman of the City of London & Merchant Taylors' Co, Del Gen de la Soc d'Ecrivans de L'Afrique du Nord, Dir The Twyn Barlwm Press 1931—32, Ed English Digest '39—41. *Publ*: (poems): New Poems; The Mind of Man; Marlow Hill; Legacy to Love; Snow & Sand; Blow No Bugles; also (Ed) Poems of M. P. Shiel, Havelock Ellis, Edwardian Poetry, Fifty Years of Modern Verse; etc. (Prose): Above the River Backwaters; Apes Japes & Hitlerism, a Study of P. Wyndham Lewis; The Invisible Voices (with M. P. Shiel); The Dowson Legend; also Ed of several works by Wilfrid Ewart; (Bibliographies): Ten Contemporaries; Annotations on Some Minor Writings of T. E. Lawrence.

GAWSWORTH. Mrs. John, (Mrs. T. I. Fytton Armstrong). *n.a*: Social Editress Daily Mail. *a*: Daily Mail, Northcliffe House, Tudor St, E.C.4 & 33 Gt James St, Bedford Row, W.C. *t*: Holborn 7086.

GAY, Arthur. *b*: Rhondda 1877. Widower. *d*: 1. Journalist. *c.t*: Lon & prov n/ps & periodicals. *s.s*: Welsh coal ind. *a*: 3 North Rd, Pontypridd, Glam. *t*: 458.

GAY, Maisie. *e*: Germany & Lon Collegiate. Actress. *Publ*: Laughing Through Life. *a*: c/o Messrs. Brown, Shipley & Co, 123 Pall Mall, S.W.1.

GAYE, Phoebe Fenwick. *b*: Boston Spa 1905. *e*: Putney Hgh Sch. *m*: F. L. S. Pickard. *s*: 1. Asst-Ed Time & Tide 1931—35. *Publ*: Vivandiere; Good Sir John; New Heaven, New Earth; The French Prisoner; Louisa Vandervoord; (poem) Lowesater; (biog) John Gay. *Ctr*: Time & Tide, Britannia & Eve, Woman's Journal, Poetry Rev, Listener. *s.s*: 19th-Cent Hist, Flowers & Gardens. *Rec*: Painting & gardening. *a*: Devon Cottage, Ardleigh, Colchester, Essex. *T*: Ardleigh 320.

GAYER, Arthur David. M.A., D.Ph. *b*: Poona, India 1903. *e*: St Paul's Sch Lond, Lincoln Coll Oxf. *m*: Muriel Stirling Cafeman. *s*: 1. Prof of Econs Queen's Univ N.Y. *Publ*: Monetary Policy & Economic Stabilisation; Ed, The Lessons of Monetary Experience, Essays in Honour of Irving Fisher; In collab: The Sugar Economy of Puerto Rico; etc. *Ctr*: American Journ of Econs. *a*: 456 Riverside Drive, New York City, N.Y., U.S.A.

GAYFORD, Rev. Sydney Charles. *b*: Essex 1871. *e*: Felsted Sc, Exeter Col Oxf & Cuddesdon Theo Col. *m*: Agnes Eileen Milner. *s*: 2. Rector of Little Waltham, Essex. *Publ*: The Future State; Sacrifice & Priesthood; Leviticus & Hebrews in The New Commentary on Holy Scripture; etc. *c.t*: Guardian, Ch Times, Hastings' Dictionary of Bible. *s.s*: Theo & philos. Vice-Princ Cuddesdon Col 1899—1909. Vice-Princ Bishops' Col Cheshunt '09—14. *Rec*: Wood-sawing. *a*: Little Waltham Rectory, Chelmsford. *t*: Little Waltham 241.

GAYLOR, John Baxter. M.A., B.Sc., M.B., Ch.B., F.R.F.P.S.G., F.R.S.M. *b*: Sanquhar, Dumfriesshire 1904. *e*: Greenock Hgh Sch, Univs of Glasgow, Utrecht, Munich & Pennsylvania. *m*: Elizabeth Stewart. *s*: 1. *d*: 3. Lect in Medical Neurology Univ of Glas 1947, Neurologist Dept of Health Scotland & Western Inf Glas. *Publ*: Neurological Section, Textbook of Medical Treatment; St Andrew's Ambulance Handbook (with E. G. Gerstenberg). *Ctr*: Brain, Speech, Clinical Science, Journ of Neurology & Psychiatry. *s.s*: Diseases & Physiology of the Nervous System. *Rec*: Golf, music. *c*: College (Glas Univ) & Roy Scot Automobile. *a*: 9 University Gdns, Glasgow, W.2. *T*: Western 2414.

GAYNOR, Joseph Alfred, Surgeon. *c.t*: Journ of Newfoundland Med Assoc, B.M.J., etc. *a*: Fiveways, Hope Rd, Shanklin, I.O.W. *t*: Shanklin 77.

GAYRE, George Robert. M.A., D.Ph., D.Sc., D.Pol.Sc. *b*: Ireland 1907. *e*: Exeter Coll Oxf, Edin Univ. *m*: Nina Mary Terry. *s*: 1. Author & Company Dir. *Publ*: Teuton & Slav on the Polish Frontier; Italy in Transition; La Posizione della Sicilia Nel Compleso Etnologico Europeo, Palumbo, Palermo. *Ctr*: Tablet, Internat Affairs, Times, Cornish Times. *s.s*: Racial Problems of European People, Heredity & Educ, Eugenics, Old English Wines, Sicily & Southern Italy, Beekeeping. *Rec*: Riding, shooting. *w.s*: Lt-Col 1939—44. *a*: Norhyrst, Battle, Sussex. *T*: 419.

GAYTON, Catherine. *b*: London. *e*: P.N.E.U. Sch. Novelist & Short Story Writer. *Publ*: Those Sinning Girls; That Merry Affair; Young Person. *Ctr*: Woman & Home; My Home; Woman's Weekly; Woman's Pictorial; Ill Lond News. *s.s*: Fiction of early Victorian period. *Rec*: Sketching. *a*: 65 Palace Ct, London, W.2. *T*: Bayswater 0220.

GAYTON, Charles Edgar. Journalist. *n.a*: Various News Ed & Parl Lobby Corr Evening News, Political & Indust Corr Sunday Times. *s.s*: Politics, Economics. *a*: Kemsley Hse, London, W.C.1. *T*: Terminus 1234.

GEARY, Francis J. *b*: Kilkenny. *e*: Irish Christian Bros. Journalist & Reporter. *n.a*: Kilkenny People, Midland Tribune, Carlow Nationalist, Irish Independent 1922. Sub-Ed & Dep Chief Sub-Editor, Asst Ed '32, Special Staff Corr with Irish Delegations to Denmark, Italy, etc, & accompanied Pres Cosgrave on U.S.-Canadian Tour '27–28. *a*: Dublin.

GEARY, Frank J. *n.a*: Ed Irish Independent Dublin. *a*: c/o Irish Independent, Dublin.

GEARY, Sir William N. Montgomerie, Bt. Barrister. *Publ*: Law of Marriage & Family Relations; Nigeria Under British Rule; A Lawyer's Wife (novel). *a*: 2 Plowden Bldgs, Temple, E.C.4, & Oxon Heath, Tonbridge. *t*: Central 5762 & Hadlow 32.

GEBAUER, JOHANNES: educational council, state archives; b. Wilsnack, Prince of Brandenburg, Aug. 8, 1868; s. Johannes and Luise (Gantzer) G.; educ. Gymnasium, Univs. of Berlin and Halle. DEGREE: Dr. Phil.; m. Gertrud Reichel, April 4, 1903. AUTHOR: Die Publizistik über den böhmischen Aufstand von 1618, 1892; Kurbrandenburg : in der Krisis des Jahres 1627, 1896; Kurbrandenburg und das Restitutionsedikt von 1629, 1899; Christian August, Herzog von Schleswig-Holstein, 1910; Herzog Friedrich VIII. von Schleswig-Holstein, 1912; Geschichte der Stadt Hildesheim, 1922 (2nd vol. 1924). Editor: Alt-Hildesheim, Zeitschrift für Stadt und Stift Hildesheim. Contributes to many historical magazines. General character of writing: historical. CLUBS: Historical Commission of Nether-Saxony. Relig. denom., Lutheran. OFFICE: Stadtarchiv (Rathaus) Hildesheim. HOME: Langelinienwall 17, Hildesheim, Germany.

GEBLER, Ernest. *b*: Dublin 1915. Playwright & Novelist. *Publ*: He Had My Heart Scalded. *s.s*: 15th-Cent Ireland, The Pilgrim Fathers, Contemporary Irish, English Theatre. *a*: 3 Cabra Grove, Cabra Rd, Dublin, Ireland; & c/o Sampson Low, 25 Gilbert St, London, W.1. *T*: Mayfair 9771.

GEDDES, PATRICK: university professor (retired), author; b. Aberdeenshire, Scotland, Oct. 2, 1854; s. Capt. Alexander and Janet (Stevenson) G.; educ. Perth Acad. (Scotland), Royal Coll. of Mines (London), Univ. Coll. (London), Sorbonne (Paris), Univ. Edinburgh (Scotland); m. (1) Anna Morton, 1886; (2) Lilian Brown, 1928. AUTHOR: Evolution of Sex (jointly with Prof. J. A. Thomson), 1889; The Life and Work of Sir Jagadis Bose, F.R.S., 1920; Biology, Sex and Evolution (3 vols. with Prof. Thomson), 1920, 1925, 1926; Chapters in Modern Botany, City Development, Evolution of Cities, Town Planning and City Development, Classification of Statistics, Analysis of the Principles of Economic and numerous similar treatises, between 1881-1928; (with Sir Arthur Thomson): Life: Outlines of General Biology, 1931. Editor (with V. V. Branford): The Making of the Future Series. Contributor to Sociological Rev. (1905-29). General character of writing: scientific, biological, sociological. Subject of a sketch by Amelia Defries, "The Interpreter: Geddes and His Gospel." President of Sociological Institutes of Edinburgh, London and Montpellier; Hon. Member American Sociological Society. ADDRESSES: College des Ecossais, Montpellier, France, and Outlook Tower, Edinburgh, Scotland.

GEDDES, W. H. *b*: Dundee 1875. *e*: Alyth, Perthshire, & Dundee. *m*: Janet Thomson. *d*: 2. Journalist. *n.a*: John Leng & Co's (Dundee) publs 1890–99, Asst Ed Scot Weekly Record '99-1905, Ed Forfar Herald '08, Sub-Ed Times '17–21, Sub-Ed Sunday Times '22–23, Bexley Heath Observer '22–34. *c.t*: Various. *s.s*: Empire migration, serial writing. *a*: 100 Olyffe Av, Welling, Kent. *t*: Bexley Heath 715.

GEDDIE, John Liddell, M.A. *b*: Edinburgh 1881. *e*; Daniel Stewart's Coll, Edin Univ. *m*: Agnes Mary Muller (dec'd). Pres Scot P.E.N. 1938—44, Hon Ed Scot Polish Soc, Chrm Scot-Czechoslovak Soc, Legion d'Honneur '36. *n.a*: Asst-Ed Cape Times 1906—10, Asst-Ed Everyman '13—14, Joined Edit Staff W. & R. Chambers Journal, Ed Chambers's Twentieth Century Dictionary & Biographical Dictionary. *Ctr*: Scotsman, Glas Herald, Cape Times, etc. *s.s*: French & Eng Lit, Sth Africa. *Rec*: Golf. *c*: Scot Arts, Scot P.E.N., Internat Hse. *a*: 11 Thistle St, Edinburgh. *T*: 26163.

GEDEN, Rev. A. S. *a*: Royapettah, Harpenden, Herts

GEDYE, George Eric Rowe, M.B.E., F.J.I. Author & Journalist, Central European Staff N.Y. Times. *Publ*: inc Fallen Bastions; Heirs to the Hapsburgs; (trans) George London's Red Russia. *a*: Moscow.

GEE, Herbert Leslie. *b*: Bridlington 1901. *e*: Bridlington Gr Sch & Leeds Tr Coll. Journalist. *n.a*: S. Post (Scotland), Thomson's Wkly New, Methodist Recorder, etc. *Publ*: Romance of the Yorkshire Coast; The Cheerful Day; The Shining Highway; Winter Journey; The Pilgrim; Pleasant People; Friendly Folk; Nodding Wold; The Sunny Room; The Friendly Year; Wartime Pilgrimage; Caravan Joe; Immortal Few (verse); etc. *s.s*: Yorkshire History & Topography, Educ, Humour. *a*: Eynsford, Harland Rd, Bridlington, Yorks.

GEE, Philip. Public Relations Cttee Scotch Whisky Assoc. *n.a*: Times, Dly Mail, Pall Mall Gazette, etc. *Publ*: Industrial Year Book; Employers Year Book; Who's Who in the New Parliament; 100 Questions & Answers About Coal; etc. *s.s*: Coal, Heavy Industries, Economics. Formerly Chrm Economical League. *a*: 67 New Cavendish St, London, W.1. *T*: Langham 2434.

GEER, Walter, A.M., LL.M. *b*: Williamstown, Mass 1857. *e*: Williams Col, Law Sc Nat Univ (Washington). *m*: (1) Mary Potter; (2) Beatrice MacWilliams Parslow. *s*: 3. *d*: 1. Lawyer, Author. *Publ*: Story of Terra Cotta (1919); Napoleon the First; The French Revolution; Napoleon & Marie-Louise; Campaigns of the Civil War; Napoleon & His Family (3 vols); etc. *s.s*: Hist, biog. *Rec*: Golf, chess, bridge. Founder Nat Terra Cotta Soc '11. *a*: 1088 Park Av, N.Y. *t*: Atwater 9-0036.

GEFFEN, Dennis H., M.D., B.S., M.R.C.S., L.R.C.P., F.R.San.I., D.P.H. *b*: London 1898. *e*: U.C.S., U.C. & U.C.H. Lond. M.O.H. St Pancras, Lect in Hygiene to Lond Sch of Hygiene & Trop Med, Chm Nat Baby Welfare Counc. *n.a*: Ed Public Health & Hygiene, Mothering Manual B.R.C.S. *Publ*: (jtly) Social Services; Child Welfare Manual. *Ctr*: Various. *s.s*: Public Health & Hygiene, Sch Med Service & Maternal & Child Welfare. *a*: 168 Oakwood Ct, Kensington, London, W.14. *T*: Western 5660.

GEIGER, George Raymond, A.B., M.S., B.Lit., Ph.D. *b*: New York, N.Y. 1903. *e*: Columbia Univ, New Coll Oxf. *m*: Louise Jarratt. Prof of Philosophy. *n.a*: Staff N.Y. Times 1925—28, Ed American Journ of Econs & Sociology, & of The Antioch Review. *Publ*: Philosophy & the Social Order; The Philosophy of Henry George; The Theory of the Land Question; Towards an Objective Ethics; The Philosophy of John Dewey. *Ctr*: Journ of Philosophy, etc. *s.s*: Philosophy & the Social Order. *Rec*: Amateur Acting. *a*: 131 W. Center College St, Yellow Springs, Ohio, U.S.A. *T*: 5381.

GEIGER, WILHELM: univ. professor; b. Nuremberg, Bavaria, Germany, July 21, 1856; s. Johannes and Emma (Paur) G.; educ. Gymnasium Nuremberg; Univs. of Erlangen, Bonn and Berlin. DEGREES: Ph.D., Privy Counselor, Corresp. Fellow of British Academy, London, and of the Bavarian Academy of Science; honorary member of the American Oriental Society; m. Magdalene Grobe, 1917. AUTHOR: Handbuch der Awestasprache, 1879; Ostiranische Kultur im Altertum, 1882; Du Gamirgebiche, 1887; Ceylon, Reiseerinnerungen und Tagebuchblätter, 1897; Literatur und Sprache der Singhalesen, 1900; Dipavamsa und Mahavamsa und die geschichtliche Überlieferung in Ceylon, 1905; The Mahavamsa, edited Tali Text Society, 1908; The Mahavamsa or the Great Chronicle of Ceylon (translated), 1912; Tali, Literatur und Sprache, 1916; Elementarbuch des Sanskrit (3rd edit.), 1923; Samyutta Nikaya (ins Deutsche übertragen, vol. 2), 1925; Eularamsa (being the more recent part of the Mahavamsa), (edited vol. 1), 1925 (vol. 2), 1927); Die singhalesische Literatur (Handbuch der Literaturwissenschaft), 1928; Culavamsa (translted vol. 1), 1929 (vol. 2, 1930). Editor: Zeitschrift für Indologie und Tranistik-Grundriss der Tranischen Thilologie, 1896-1904. Contributor to Zeitschrift der D. Morgent-Gesellschaft, Sitzungsberichte und Abhandlungen der Bayrischen Akademie der Wissenschaft, Orientalistische Literaturzeitung, Indian Historical Quarterly. General character of writing: scientific, ancient languages. Religion, Protestant. OFFICE: University of Munich. HOME: Neubiberg near Munich, Bavaria, Germany.

GEIKIE, Mary Dorothea. *b*: Edinburgh. *e*: Edinburgh & France. *Publ*: Phantasie; Sleeve o' Silk; Reeds in the River; etc. *Rec*: Gardening, breeding Airedales. *a*: 83 Colinton Rd, Edinburgh. *T*: 61545.

GEIKIE-COBB, Ivo, M.D., M.R.C.S., L.R.C.P. (see WEYMOUTH, Anthony). *b*: Addlestone, Surrey 1887. *e*: West Downs Winchester, Loretto, St Thomas's Hosp & Brussels. *m*: Audrey de Poix. *s*: 1. *d*: 2. Formerly Ed The New Health Soc Bulletin. *Publ*: The Glands of Destiny; The Organs of Internal Secretion; Aids to Organtherapy. *s.s*: Health, Internal Secretions, Psychology, Nervous Disorders. *Rec*: Reading, writing, motoring. *w.s*: 1914—18 R.A.M.C. (Capt), '39—45 B.B.C. Broadcaster. *a*: 30 Harley Hse, London, N.W.1. *T*: Welbeck 9343.

GEIKIE-COBB, Rev. William Frederick. *b*: Danbury 1857. *e*: T.C.D. Married. *s*: 2. *d*: 1. Rector of St Ethelburga's Bishopsgate, E.C.2. *n.a*: Church Times 1890-98. *Publ*: Mysticism & the Creed; Theology, Old & New; The Path of the Soul; St Ethelburga's Leaflet (11 vols). *c.t*: Nineteenth Century, Times. *s.s*: Philos & psychology teacher 1880-1934. Asst Sec of Eng Ch Un '90-98. Chm Marriage Law Reform League '31—. Sec Indian Ch Aid Assoc '99-1907. *Rec*: Reading, teaching. *c*: St Andrews. *a*: 26 Drayton Ct, S.W.10. *t*: Kensington 4881.

GEIRINGER, Karl J., Ph.D. *b*: Vienna 1899. *e*: Univs of Berlin & Vienna. *m*: Irene Steckel. *s*: 2. Prof of the Theory & Hist of Music Boston Univ Coll of Music 1941—, Vis Prof Roy Coll of Music Lond '39—40, Hamilton, Coll Clinton N.Y. '40—41. *Publ*: Johannes Brahms, His Life & Work; Musical Instruments, Their History from the Stone Age to the Present Day; Joseph Haydn, A Creative Life in Music. *Ctr*: Musical Quarterly, Musical Times, Musical America, Monthly Musical Record, Musical Opinion. *s.s*: Haydn, Brahms, Musical Instruments, Austrian Music of the Early 17th Century. *Rec*: Mountain climbing, swimming, ski-ing, stamp collecting. *a*: 32 Norwood Ave, Newton Centre, Mass, U.S.A. *T*: Boston Mass, Bigelow 9835.

GEISE, DR. OTTO: see Homberg, Otto von.

GEISSLER, MAX: author; b. Grossenhain, Saxony, Germany, Apr. 4, 1868; s. Ernest Fuerchtegott and Johanna (Mueller) G.; m. Mathilda Lauterbach, June 1, 1900. AUTHOR: Das Moordorf, 1904; Inseln im Winde, 1905; Die Herrgottswiege, 1906; Die Rose von Schottland, 1908; Das Tristanlied, 1911; Der Erlkoenig, 1915; Schollentreue, 1928; Die Fahrt Zur Unsterblichkeit, ein Roman um van Gogh, 1929. General character of writing: novels, juveniles, plays, nature books, poems. HOME: Marina Grande di Capri, Italy.

GELDER, George Stuart. Journalist. *n.a*: Nott'm Journ, Nott'm Evening News 1927—34, News-Chronicle '34. *Publ*: Early Life of D. H. Lawrence (with Ada Lawrence); The Chinese Communists. *a*: c/o News-Chronicle, Fleet St, E.C.4.

GELL, Hon. Mrs. Edith. *b*: Lon 1860. *e*: Priv. *m*: Philip Lyttelton Gell. *Publ*: The Happy Warriors; The New Crusaders; Under Three Reigns; Ways & Sign Posts; Live Gloriously; The Spirit of the Home; The More Excellent Way; The Empire's Honour; Look before you Leap; Silver Jubilee Masque; etc. *c.t*: Nat Review, 19th Cent, etc. *s.s*: Music, choral training. Pres Women's Cmt in defence of Ch in Wales, Women's Emigration Cmt to Rhodesia. etc. *c*: Derbys Ladies. *a*: Hopton Hall, Wirksworth, Derbys & Mapleton, Gt Missenden.

GELL, Dr. H. W., O.B.E., M.B.(Oxon). *a*: Wickstead, nr Leamington, Warwicks.

GELLAN, A. T. *n.a*: London Rep, Huddersfield Examiner. *a*: 173 Fleet St, E.C.4.

GELLERT, Leon. *b*: Adelaide Sth Australia 1892. *e*: Adelaide Hgh Sch & Univ. *m*: Kathleen Saunders. *d*: 1. Ed The Home, Lit Ed Sydney Morning Herald. *Publ*: Songs of a Campaign; The Isle of San; Desparate Measures; These Beastley Australians. *Rec*: Rowing, boxing. *c*: N.S.W. Amateur Sports. *w.s*: 1915—18. *a*: Sydney Morning Herald, Hunter St, Sydney, N.S.W., Australia.

GELLIBRAND, Edward Thomas. *b*: Onega, Russia 1879. *e*: Priv. *Publ*: The End of a Cigarette; Windblow; Trans—The Key (Aldanov); Anna Pavlova (Dandre); Trans of Jesus Manifest by Korsky. *s.s*: Russian. *a*: 30 W. Cromwell Rd, S.W.5.

GEMMELL Dr. A. A., M.C., T.D. *c.t*: Med Journs. *a*: 31 Rodney St, Liverpool.

GEMMELL, G. H., F.I.C. Analytical Chemist & Public Analyst, Lect in Chemistry Roy Col Edin. *Publ*: Chemical Notes & Equations; Public Health, Laboratory Notes. *c.t*: Various. *a*: Chemical Lab, 4 Lindsay Pl, Edin. *t*: 22921.

GEMÜND, WILHELM: professor; b. Niederbreisig, Germany, May, 1873; s. Wilhelm and Ida (Linden) G.; educ. Universities of Wuerzburg,

Strassburg, Munich and Kiel; DEGREES: M.D.; m. Emma Henrici, 1900. AUTHOR: Bodenfrage und Bodenpolitik, 1911; Die Grundlagen zur Besserung der Staedtischen Wohnverhaeltnisse, 1914; Die Kommunen als Grundbesitzerinnen, 1914; Leben und Anpassung, 1925; Liebe und Ahnenerbe, 1928; Wesen und Entstehung der Krebsdisposition, 1930. General character of writing: scientific. CLUBS: Kantgesellschaft. Relig., Catholic. ADDRESS: Ruetscherstrasse 43, Aix-la-Chapelle, Germany.

GENDERS, William Roy. *b*: Sheffield 1914. *e*: King's. Sch Ely & St John's Coll Camb. Farmer, Timber Merchant, Greyhound Breeder & Mushroom Grower. *Publ*: Modern Greyhound Racing; I Buy A Farm; Money From Your Garden; Mushroom Growing for Profit; Chrysanthemums for Pleasure & Profit; Dog Breeding for Pleasure & Profit; Holiday in Dublin; The Profitable Smallholding; etc. *s.s*: Dog-Breeding, Gardening. *Rec*: Watching assoc football, greyhound racing, reading country books & playing county cricket (Worcestershire). *a*: Fanshawe Gate Hall Farm, Holmesfield, nr Sheffield.

GENGENBACH, Adolf. *b*: Mannheim 1873. *m*: Maria Leopold. *s*: 2. *d*: 3. *Publ*: Author. *Publ*: Aus Deutschlands Grosser Zeit (Anthology). *s.s*: Aphorisms, leading articles. *Rec*: Piano, photography. *c*: German N/p Publishers', etc. *a*: Mannheim, Tageblatthaus, H. 2, 3. Germany.

GENT, David Robert. *b*: Llandovery 1883. *e*: Swansea G.S. Married. *d*: 2. Schoolmaster. *Publ*: British Sports Library; Rugby Football; Contributed Sections to—Football: The Rugby Union Game, Modern Rugby Football, etc. *c.t*: Sun Times, Eng Review & 19th Cent. *Rec*: Golf. *c*: Richmond, Press. *a*: 43a Blackwater Rd, Eastbourne.

GENT, Gerard Edward James, D.S.O., M.C. *b*: Kingston-on-Thames 1895. *e*: King's Sc Canterbury & Trinity Col Oxf. *m*: Gwendolen Mary Wyeth. *s*: 2. *d*: 2. Civil Servant, Colonial Office. *n.a*: Ed Col Office List 1924-25, Ed Dominions Office & Col Office List '26–. *a*: Yondover, Orchard Gate, Esher, Surrey. *t*: Emberbrook 1215.

GENTLE, Sir W. B., J.P. *Publ*: Guide to Children's Art. *a*: Croxton Pk, Norfolk. *t*: Thetford 111.

GENTRY, W. G., J.P. Dist Reporter, St Helens, Lancs.

GEOGHEGAN, Joseph, M.D., F.R.C.S. *b*: Edinburgh 1888. *e*: Geo Watson's Coll Edin & Edin Univ. *m*: Muriel Kerr-Brown. *s*: 1. *d*: 1. Consultant Roy Hosp Richmond. *Publ*: Poems & Sonnets; etc. *Ctr*: Med Journs. *c*: R.A.F., Roy Soc Med. *a*: 22 Wimpole St, W.1. *T*: Langham 1216.

GEORGE, E. F. Free-lance jnlst. *Publ*: Many technical articles, etc. *a*: 43 Charlotte St, Devonport, Plymouth, Devon.

GEORGE, Mary Dorothy, M.A., LittD., F.R.Hist Soc. *b*: Lon. *e*: St Leonard's Sc, St Andrews, Girton, Lon Sc of Econ. *m*: Eric George. Hist Research & Writing. *Publ*: English Social Life in the Eighteenth Century (1923); England in Johnson's Day; England in Transition ('31); etc. *c.t*: English Hist Review, Journal of Roy Econ Soc, etc. War Office (Intelligence) '15-19. *a*: 51 Paulton's Sq, Chelsea, S.W.3. *t*: Flaxman 9019.

GERAGHTY, Thomas, M.C. *b*: Hull 1890. Journalist. *n.a*: Chief Sub-Ed Hull Daily Mail 1922—. *a*: Daily Mail, Jameson St, Hull.

GERAUD, Charles Joseph Andre. *n.a*: For Ed L'Echo de Paris 1917—38, Ed l'Europe Nouvelle '38—40. *Publ*: incl Les Fossoyeurs. *a*: 91 rue de l'Université Paris.

GERBAULT, Alain. *b*: France. *Publ*: Fight of the Firecrest; Gospel of the Sun; Sailing Alone Across the Atlantic; In Quest of the Sun. *a*: c/o Messrs Christy & Moore Ltd, 222 Strand, W.C.2. *t*: Central 5394.

GERDES, Finn, M.A. *b*: Horsens, Denmark 1914. *e*: Univ of Copenhagen. *m*: Jytte Gerdes. *s*: 3. Author. *Publ*: The Blue Curtains; Black Angels. *Ctr*: Politiken, Berlingske Tidende, Social-Demokraten, etc. *a*: Hvidbjerghus pr. Borkop, Denmark. *T*: Gaarslev 70.

GERHARDI, William Alexander, O.B.E., M.A., B.Litt. *b*: St Petersburg 1895 of English parents. *e*: St Annen-Schule & Reformierte-Schule, St Petersburg & Worcester Coll Oxf. Novelist, B.B.C. (European Service) 1942—45. *Publ*: Futility, a novel on Russian Themes; Anton Chehov, a Critical Study; The Polyglots; My Sinful Earth; Pending Heaven; Memoirs of a Polygeot; The Memoirs of Satan (in collab with Brian Lunn); Resurrection; Donna Quixote, a Comedy in 3 Acts; The Casanova Fable (with Hugh Kingsmill); Of Mortal Love; Meet Yourself (with Prince Leopold Loewenstein); My Wife's the Least of It; The Romanovs; Biography; etc. *Ctr*: Various periodicals. *s.s*: Music, Lit, Eng, Russian, German & French Literary & Dramatic Criticism. *w.s*: World War I 5th Res Cav. with Mil Attaché Brit Embassy Petrogad 1917—18, Brit Mil Missn to Siberia '18—20, Capt. *a*: Rossetti Hse, 106 Hallam St, Portland Pl, W.1. *T*: Welbeck 1878.

GERHART, Walter. See Gurian, Waldemar.

GERLACHE de GOMERY, BARON de: directeur général (Marine Dépt.); *b*. Hasselt, Belgium, August, 1866; *s*. Auguste de Gerlache de Gomery and Emma (Biscops) de G.; educ École Polytechnique, Brussels Univ.; *m*. Elisabeth (Höjer. AUTHOR: Quiuze Mois dans l'Antarctique, 1902; La Belgique et les Belges pendant la guerre (transl. into Norwegian, Swedish, Spanish and English), 1917; The Unconquerable Soul (Belgium in War Time), 1918. Promoter and chief of the Belgian Antarctic Expedition with the "Belgica", 1897-1899. (The "Belgica" was the first ship to winter in the anarctic pack-ice); Scientific expedition into Persian Gulf, 1900; Captain of the "Belgica" during her cruises into arctic waters, 1905, 1907, 1909. Twice (1905 and 1909) farthest north across the east Greenland pack-ice. CLUBS: Cercle Artistique et Littéraire; Société Royale des Beaux-Arts, Société Royale de Géographie (Brussels); Geographical Society (Philadelphia, U.S.A.). HOME: 123 Chaussée de Vleurgat, Brussels, Belgium.

GERMAN, Sir Edward. *b*: 1862. Composer. Wrote Incidental Music to "Henry VIII"; Merrie England; Tom Jones; etc. Composed March for King George's Coronation. Mem Council Inc Soc of Authors, Playwrights & Composers. *a*: 5 Bidulph Rd, W.9.

GERMAN, Richard William ("Dick German"). *b*: Swansea 1880. *e*: Day Sc & Swansea Art Sc. *m*: Maria Ann Knill. *s*: 1. Cartoonist & humorous illustrator. *n.a*: Staff cartoonist S. Wales Daily Post Swansea 1907-21, Cartoonist & Picture Ed S. Wales News, & S. Wales Echo Cardiff '21-30. Ed Ilford Recorder, Romford Recorder, various Lon periodicals. *s.s*: Sport, humour. War Service. Prize Best Humorous Drawing, Passing Show (Brit Humour Campaign) '20-21. *Rec*: Reading. *a*: 40 Purbeck Rd, Romford, Essex.

GERRIE, Reginald Kirsop. *b*: Newcastle-on-Tyne 1913. *e*: Barnard Castle Sc. Dis Reporter. *n.a*: Jnr Dis Reporter with Newcastle Chronicle Ltd publ's at N. Shields 1929, Whitley Bay & Monkseaton '33. *c.t*: Newcastle Chronicle Ltd. *Rec*: Books, swimming. *a*: c/o West Dene Hse, 67 Linskill Terr, N. Shields, Northumberland.

GERVASE-LANG, John, F.Z.S., M.R.S.L. *b*: London 1891. Major Royal Fusiliers (ret), Mem East India Assoc, Vice-Chm United Nations Assoc City of London, Freeman of the City of London. *n.a*: Beaux Arts Journ Paris 1936. *Publ*: Ireland, Where to Go, What to See, What to Do; Old Glass & How to Collect It; Indian States from Within. *s.s*: Zoology, India, Ceramic Art, Indian States, Art. *Rec*: Golf, motoring. *c*: Golfer's, Unit Services, Sussex Motor Yacht. *a*: 58 Grosvenor St, Mayfair, London, W.1. *T*: Mayfair 3311.

GESELL, Arnold, Ph.D., B.Ph., M.D., Hon.Sc.D. *b*: Alma Wisconsin 1880. *e*: Univs of Wisconsin, Clark & Yale. *m*: Beatrice Chandler. *s*: 1. Pediatrician, Dir of Clinic of Child Development Sch of Med Yale Univ New Haven Connecticut. *n.a*: Cons Ed Journ Genetic Psychology (Provincetown Mass), Brit Journ Educational Psychology (Birmingham England). *Publ*: Developmental Diagnosis; Mental Growth of the Pre-School Child; Embryology of Behavior; Feeding Behavior of Infants; Infant Behavior, its Genesis & Growth; Infant & Child in the Culture of To-Day; The Child from Five to Ten; An Atlas of Infant Behavior. *s.s*: Child Development, Child Psychiatry, Cinematograph. *Rec*: Sailing, skating. *c*: Graduates New Haven, Yale Club of New York. *a*: 185 Edwards St, New Haven, Connecticut. *T*: 7-2567.

GESSLER, Jean. *b*: Maeseyek 1878. *e*: Maeseyek Coll, St Cloud, Univ of Louvain. *m*: Louise Chennaux. *s*: 1. Professor Univ of Louvain Belgium, Ed Volkskunda. *Publ*: Le Livre des Mettiers; La Maniere du Language & other books on the history of teaching French in England; etc. *Ctr*: Muree Belge, Antiquite Classique, Revue Belge Philol et Histoire, etc. *s.s*: History of Pedagogy, Folklore. *Rec*: English Novels & Films. *a*: 31 Boulevard Leon Schreurs, Louvain.

GETTY, Robert John, M.A. *b*: Co. Londonderry 1908. *e*: Acad Inst Coleraine L'derry, Queen's Univ Belfast & St John's Coll Camb. *m*: Margaret Wood. Prof of Latin Univ of Toronto, Asst to Regius Prof Humanity Univ of Aberdeen 1930—34, Lect in Latin Univ of L'pool '34 —37, Fell & Lect in Classics St John's Coll Camb '37—47, Foreign Off '40—45. *Publ*: The Lost St Gall MS of Valerius Flaccus. *Ctr*: Classical Quarterly, American Journ of Philology, Classical Philology, Journ of Roman Studies *s.s*: Latin Literature. *Rec*: Walking. *a*: University College, Toronto 5, Canada.

GEYL, Pieter. *b*: Dordrecht 1887. *e*: Hague Gymnasium, Leyden Univ. *m*: Cjarberline Kremer. *s*: 1. *d*: 1. Prof of Modern Hist in the Univ of Utrecht. *n.a*: Lond Corr N.R.C. 1914—19, Ed Bd Leiding '30—31, & other Reviews '38—. *Publ*: Oranje en Stuart; Vryheid; Trans: A Beautiful Play of Lancelot of Denmark; The Tale of Beatrice. *Ctr*: Various in Holland, England & America. *s.s*: History *Rec*: Bicycling. *a*: Willem, Barentz Straat 5, Utrecht *T*: 18617.

GHARPUREY, Lt-Col. Khanderad Ganpatrao, B.A., L.R.C.P.S., L.R.F.P.S., F.R.G.S., F.Z.S., F.R.S.A. *b*: Wardha, C.P., India 1880. *e*: Calcutta, Edin & Glas. *m*:. *s*: 2. *d*: 2. I.M.S. (ret). *Publ*: Snakes of India; (Marathi) Animal Life & Health; Snakes in Maharashtra. *Ctr*: Journ of Bombay Nat Hist Soc, Indian Med Gazette, Bombay Med Journ, etc. *s.s*: Snakes of India. *Rec*: Tennis, billiards, cricket, hockey, etc. *c*: Deccan Gymkhana. *w.s*: 1909 Somaliland, '15—16 Brit & German East Africa, '18 Persian Gulf. *a*: Deccan Gymkhana Colony, Poona 4, Bombay Presidency.

GHASWALA, Soli Kaikobad, B.E., F.R.S.A. *b*: Bombay 1919. *e*: St Xavier's Coll Bombay Univ. Civil & Structural Engineer, Fell Roy Meteor Soc & Mem of many Scientific & Eng Socs. *n.a*: Ed-Collab Science & Culture 1945—, Ed-Corres Engineer's Digest '47—, Pt-Ed Journ of Institute of Metals '47—. *Ctr*: Science & Culture, Indian & Eastern Engineer, Engineering (Lond), Times of India, Jame-Jamshed, Mumbai Vartaman, etc. *s.s*: Light Alloy Technology, Structural Engineering, Civil Engineering & Construction. *Rec*: Tennis, skating, swimming & rowing. *a*: Edena, Queen's Rd, Fort, Bombay, India. *T*: Bombay 34534 & 34370.

GHATAK, Jyotish Chandra, M.A. *b*: Bhowanipur, Calcutta 1891. *e*: Lond Missns Soc Inst Calcutta, Bangabasi Coll, Calcutta Univ. *m*: Hem Lata Devi. *s*: 1. Prof of Sanskrit, Pali & Bengali in Surendra Nath Coll. Homeopathic Physician, Prof of Astrology, Palmistry, Physiognomy, Numerology & Tantras. *Publ*: The Dramas of Bhasa; Social Life in Ancient India; The Legend of Elephant-Snake-Tortoise as bearing the Earth in the Light of Modern Science; Nine Plants & Nine Plants; The Tattvas & Cosmology; etc. *Ctr*: Journ of the Roy Asiatic Soc of Bengal, Indian Culture, The Astrological Mag, Modern Astrology, Basumati, Hindu Patrika, etc. *s.s*: Indology, Sanskrit, Pali, Astrology, Music, Medicine, The Tantras & Philology. *Rec*: Music, gardening, boating. *a*: 4 Boloram Bose Ghat Rd, P.O. Bhowanipur, Calcutta 25, Bengal, India.

GHEY, Miss F. L., M.A. Headmistress of Public Sc for Girls. *Publ*: Articles & verse. *a*: St Mary's Hall, Kemp Town, Brighton.

GHOSH, Birendra Nath, M.B.E., F.R.F.P.S.(Glas), L.M. (Dubl), F.R.S.(Edin), F.R.S.M.(Lond). *b*: Calcutta 1882. *e*: Calcutta, Dublin, Glasgow. Married. *s*: 3. *d*: 1. Author, Prof of Pharmacology Carmichael Med Coll Calcutta, Fell of Calcutta Univ. *Publ*: Pharmacology; Materia Medica & Therapeutics; Treatise on Hygiene & Public Health, with special reference to the Tropics. *Ctr*: B.M.J., Therapeutic Gazette (U.S.A.), Indian Med Gazette, etc. *s.s*: Pharmacology, Public Health. *a*: Carmichael Medical College, Calcutta, India. *T*: P.K. 3030.

GHOSH, Kali Pala, B.Sc.(Calcutta). *b*: Calcutta 1905 *m*: Paula Wiking. Journalist, Sec-Treas Indian Journalist's Assoc (G.B). *n.a*: London Ed United Press of India 1945 & Jt-Ed Swadhinata '28—30. *Ctr*: Forward, Ny Dag, Folkviljan, Mandira, Irish Review, etc. *s.s*: Current politics, Indian Affairs & Far East. *Rec*: Gardening. *a*: 21a Teignmouth Rd, London, N.W.2. *T*: Gladstone 8508.

GHYKA, MATILA C.: navy, and diplomatic service; b. Jassy, Roumania, Sept. 13, 1881; educ. College in Paris and Jersey (Jesuits), then French Naval Sch. DEGREE: LL.D.; m. Eileen O'Conor, 1918. AUTHOR: L'Esthetique des Proportions dans la Nature et dans les Arts, 1927; Le Nombre d'Or (2 vols.), vol. I: Les Rythmes; vol. II: Les Rites, 1931. General character of writing: theory of esthetics. CLUBS: Cercle de l'Union (Paris), Jockey Club (Bucharest). Religion, Roman Catholic. OFFICE: Roumanian Legation. HOME: Rue Henri Heine, Paris XVIe, France.

GIBB, Sir Alexander, G.B.E., C.B., LL.D., F.R.S., M.Inst.C.E., M.I.Mech.E., F.R.G.S., F.S.A. *b*: Broughty Ferry, Scotland 1872. *e*: Rugby & Univ Coll Lond. *m*: Norah Isobel Monteith (dec'd). *s*: 3. Cons & Chartered Civil Engineer, Past-Pres Inst of Civil Engineers, Lond Chamber of Commerce, Inst of Welding, Inst of Chem Engineers, Inst of Engineers-in-charge, etc. *Publ*: The Story of Telford—The Rise of Civil Engineering. *s.s*: Engineering subjects. *Rec*: Shooting, fishing & hunting. *c*: Athenæum, Carlton, Roy Auto, Roy Clyde Yacht, Travellers' etc. *w.s*: Chief Engineer Ports Construction, Dep Dir of Docks B.E.F. France, Civil Eng in Chief Admiralty 1914—19. *a*: Queen Anne's Lodge, Westminster, London, S.W.1. *T*: Whitehall 9700.

GIBB, Andrew Dewar, M.B.E., K.C. *b*: Paisley 1888. *e*: Glenalmond & Glasgow Univ. *m*: Margaret Isabel Walker Downie. *s*: 1. *d*: 2. Advocate & Barrister, Regius Prof of Law, Univ of Glasgow. *Publ*: Scottish Empire; Scotland in Eclipse; International Law of Jurisdiction; Law of Collisions on Land; Scottish Judicial Dictionary; With Winston Churchill at the Front; A Preface to Scots Law; etc. *Ctr*: Various. *s.s*: Law, Scottish National Questions. *Rec*: Sailing. *a*: 1 The College, Glasgow.

GIBB, Cassidy de Wet, F.R.C.S.E. Aurist &, Laryngologist. *c.t*: Lancet, S. African Med Record B.M.J., Journ of Laryngology, Otology. *a*: Onslow Lodge, Babbacombe Rd, Torquay. *t*: 4176.

GIBB, Hamilton Alexander Rosskeen, F.B.A. *e*: Edin & Lond Univs. Professor. *Publ*: Arabic Literature; Damascus Chronicle of the Crusades; Travels of Ibn Battuta; Modern Trends in Islam. *s.s*: Arabic, Islamic Culture. *a*: St John's College, Oxford.

GIBBENS, F. *n.a*: Mang Northcliffe N/ps. *a*: Carmelite House, E.C.4.

GIBBERD, Frederick, F.R.I.B.A., A.M.T.P.I. *e*: King Henry VIII Sch Coventry & B'ham Sch of Architecture. Architect. *Publ*: The Architecture of England; The Modern Flat (jt author). *Ctr*: Architectural Review, Architect's Journ, Architect & Building News, Country Life, etc. *s.s*: Town Planning. *a*: 35 Gordon Sq, London, W.C.1. *T*: Euston 7795.

GIBBINGS, Robert. *e*: Univ Coll Cork, Slade Sch & Central Sch of Arts & Crafts London Author & Artist. *Publ*: Sweet Thames Run Softly; Coming Down the Wye; Lovely is the Lee. *a*: c/o J. M. Dent & Son, 10 Bedford St, London, W.C.2.

GIBBON, Helena, F.R.S.A. *b*: Lancaster. *e*: Priv. Asst Curator Harris Museum & Art Gallery, Preston, Lect for Lancs County Education & Women's Institutes. *Ctr*: Times, Nthrn Dly Telegraph, Antique Collector Lancs Dly Post. *s.s*: 19th Century Costume, Art Criticism. *Rec*: Collecting antique china. *a*: 1 Oak Grove, Garstang, Preston, Lancs. *T*: Preston 3989.

GIBBON, Sir Ioan Gwilym, Kt., C.B., D.Sc. *e*: Lond Sch Econ & Polit Sch. Civil Servant (ret). *Publ*: Reconstruction & Town & Country Planning; History of the London County Council (with R. W. Bell). *Ctr*: Various. *s.s*: Government Town & Country Planning. *a*: Reform Club, Pall Mall, London, S.W.1.

GIBBON, J. B. L. *a*: 139 Queen's Rd, Ashford, Kent.

GIBBON, JAMES MORGAN: minister; b. South Wales, educ. New Castle Sch., Emlyn (Wales), Presbyterian Coll. (Caermathen); m. Nino Lewis. AUTHOR: Commentary on the Epistle of St. John; In the Days of Youth; Lectures on Galatians; several other religious volumes. Contributor to the World, British Weekly. General character of writing: religious essays. Mem. Royal Comm. for dealing with Established Church in Wales. Chairman of Conj. Union, Eng. and Wales. Relig. denom., Congregationalist. CLUBS: National Liberal, Eclectic, The Galeb. HOME: 7 Springfield, Claptodn, London, Eng.

GIBBON, John Murray. *b*: Ceylon 1875. *e*: King's Coll, Aber & Ch-Ch Oxf. *m*: Anne Fox. *s*: 3. *d*: 1. Canadian Pacific Rly. *Publ*: Scots in Canada (historical); (Novels) Drums Afar; The Conquering Hero; Pagan Love; etc. Canadian Folk Songs Old & New; Magic of Melody; Canadian Mosaic; Three Centuries of Canadian Nursing; Our Old Montreal; etc. *Ctr*: Numerous mags. *s.s*: Folk Songs, Canada. *Rec*: Riding, trout fishing. *a*: St Anne de Bellevue, Province of Quebec, Canada. *T*: St Anne's 714.

GIBBON, Monk. *b*: Dublin 1896. *e*: St Columba's Rathfarnham & Oxf Univ. *m*: Winifred Dingwall. *s*: 1. *d*: 1. Poet. *Publ*: The Tremulous String; The Branch of Hawthorn Tree; For Daws to Peck at; Seventeen Sonnets (1932); The Seals. *c.t*: Fortnightly Review, Spectator, Life & Letters, etc. War Service France & Ireland, invalided out. Farmed in the Channel Islands. Taught in Switzerland. Wandered in Italy, Greece, Egypt, Palestine & Denmark. Awarded the Silver Medal for Poetry at the Tailteann Games Dublin '27. *Rec*: Digging. *a*: Dundrum, Co Dublin, Ireland.

GIBBONS, John. Author. *Publ*: Afoot in Portugal; London to Sarajevo; Afoot in Italy. *a*: c/o G. Newnes Ltd, 8—11 Southampton St, W.C.2.

GIBBONS, M. Morgan. Barrister, author, Bard of Welsh Gorsedd. *Publ*: And Others Came; Justin Keyes; The Albatross; No. 7 Paradise; Curious Fool. *a*: 5 Pump Court, Temple, London, E.C.4. *T*: Central 2532.

GIBBONS, Reginald Herbert. *b*: Bath 1888. *m*: *s*: 1. *d*: 1. Journalist. *n.a*: Surrey Times 1906—07, Surrey & Hants News '07—08, Woking News & Mail '08—. *a*: Engleberg, Holyoake Ave, Horsell, Woking.

GIBBONS, Stella. *b*: London 1902. *m*: Allan Bourne Webb. *d*: 1. *Publ*: The Mountain Beast & Other Poems; Cold Comfort Farm (Femina Vie Heureuse Prize '33); Bassett; The Priestess & Other Poems; Enbury Heath; Miss Linsey & Pa; Nightingale Wood; Roaring Tower & Other Stories; The Untidy Gnome; My American; The Rich House; The Lowland Venus & Other Poems; Christmas at Cold Comfort Farm & Other Stories; Ticky; The Bachelor; Westwood; The Gentle Powers. *a*: 19 Oakeshott Ave, London, N.6.

GIBBS, ANTHONY: author; b. Lancashire, Eng., March, 1902; s. of Sir Philip Gibbs (K.B.E.) and Agnes (Rowland) G.; educ. Stonyhurst, Oxford Univ.; m. Maisie Martin, 1928. AUTHOR: Little Peter Vacuum, 1925; The Elder Brother, 1926; High Endeavor, 1927; Enter—a Greek, 1928. Contributor to Cosmopolitan (U.S.A.). General character of writing: fiction. CLUB: R.A.C. HOME: 2 Cheltenham Terrace, Chelsea, London. S. W. 3, Eng.

GIBBS, Jeanette Phillips. *m*: A. Hamilton Gibbs. *Publ*: Portia Marries; Café Noir; Copy for Mother. *a*: c/o A. M. Heath & Co Ltd, Princes Hse, Jermyn St, London, S.W.1.

GIBBS, Leonard Angas. *b*: London 1855. *e*: Private & abroad. *Publ*: Miscellaneous Writings; Plays For Amateurs; The Nom de Plume; Notes From A Diary. *e*: Caledonian, Authors, The Club, (Bournemouth). *a*: Hawthorn's Hotel & The Club, Bournemouth. *t*: 1911.

GIBBS, Sir Philip, K.C.B.E. *b*: London 1877. *e*: Priv. *m*: Agnes Rowland. *s*: 1. Author, Chevalier Légion d'Honneur. *n.a*: Formerly on Ed Staffs of: Dly Mail, Dly Chron, etc, Ex-Ed Review of Reviews. *Publ*: Novels—The Street of Adventure; Back to Life; The Middle of the Road; The Age of Reason; Darkened Rooms; The Golden Years; The Cross of Peace; etc. Historical—Realities of War; The Day

After To-morrow; Since Then; Ways of Escape; Sons of the Others; The Amazing Summer; The Battle Within; The Long Alert; Through the Storm; The Hopeful Heart; The Pageant of the Years; etc. *Rec*: Painting, gardening. *c*: Reform, R.A.C. *a*: Dibdene, Shamley Green, Surrey.

GIBBS, Robt A. Journalist. *n.a*: Chief Reporter Oxf Mail, Oxf Times. *a*: Norland, Apsley Rd, Oxford. *T*: Oxford 5434.

GIBBS-SMITH, Charles Harvard, M.A. *b*: Teddington, Middx 1909. *e*: Westminster & Harvard Univ. Keeper of Museum Extension, Victoria & Albert Museum, London, 1932, Assoc Mem Inst of Journalists, Organiser & Classifier of Photographic Libraries for M.O.I., Press Censorship, Admiralty Press Div, U.S. Office of War Inf, Counc of Indust Design, Hulton Press; B.B.C Broadcasts on History of Aeronautics & Crime. *n.a*: London Art Critic, Liverpool Post, '32—37. *Publ*: Basic Aircraft Recognition; The Aircraft Recognition Manual; German Aircraft; Ballooning. *Ctr*: Country Life, Picture Post, Lilliput, Listener, Dly Telegraph, Yorks Post, L'pool Post, John O' London's Weekly. *s.s*: History of Aeronautics, Photo Classification, Crime (Historical), Early Photography. *Rec*: Fencing, travel, classification. *c*: Roy Aero, Harvard (London). *a*. 720 Kensington Close, London, W.8. *T*: Western 8170.

GIBBS-SMITH, Edward Gibbs, M.D., D.P.H., L.R.C.P.I., L.S.A. *c.t*: Lancet, Jnl State Med. *a*: 32 Scarsdale Villas, Kensington, W.8. *t*: Western 2538.

GIBERNE. Agnes. *b*: India 1845. *e*: Priv & Abroad. *Publ*: Maude Grenville (for children) '64; Detained in France; The Mists of the Valley; Sun, Moon and Stars; The World's Foundations (On Geol); The Ocean of Air; The Romance of the Mighty Deep; Under Puritan Rule; etc. *c.t*: Various mags. *s.s*: Astron, geol, meteorology. Started writing at age of 7 y. Family originally "de Giberne" of France. *Rec*: Art. *a*: 14 Enys Rd, Eastbourne, & c/o Messrs. Barclay & Co, Bankers, 115 Terminus Rd, Eastbourne.

GIBSON, A. M., M.A. *e*: M/C G.S. Gonville & Caius Col Cam. *m*: Isabel Martin. *s*: 2. *d*: 1. Headmaster L'pool Col Sc. *n.a*: Gen Ed Modern Language Texts. *Publ*: Several vols (French & German) in Bill's Modern Language Texts. *c.t*: Times Educ Suppl, Journ of Educ, Education. *s.s*: Modern langs, hist, music, educ. War Service. *Rec*: Walking, gardening, golf. *a*: 70 Knowsley Rd, Cressington Pk, L'pool. *t*: Garston 518.

GIBSON, Alexander Boyce, M.A. *b*: London 1900. *e*: Melbourne Gr Sch & Univ, Balliol Coll Oxf. *m*: Kathleen Grace Durham. *d*: 1. Univ Prof. *Publ*: The Philosophy of Wescarles; Should Philosophers be Kings?; Thinking at Work (with A. A. Phillips). *Ctr*: Australian Journ of Philosophy & other Philosophical journs. etc. *s.s*: Philosophy, especially Political Theory of Æsthetics. *a*: 747 Canterbury Rd, Mount Albert E.10, Melbourne, Australia. *T*: WX3157.

GIBSON, Alexander George. *b*: Hull 1875. *e*: Univ Col Aberystwyth, Ch Ch Oxf & St Thomas's Hosp Lon. *m*: Constance Muriel Jones. *s*: 2. *d*: 1. Cons Phys. *n.a*: Sec to Ed Bd Quarterly Journ of Med 1907–. *Publ*: Handbook for the Post-Mortem Room (1914); The Radcliffe Infirmary; The Physician's Art ('33); etc. *a*: 27 Banbury Rd, Oxf. *t*: 3228.

GIBSON, Arnold Hartley, D.Sc., LL.D. *b*: Sowerby Bridge, Yorks 1878. *e*: Rishworth Gr Sch & Manch Univ. *m*: Amy Quarmby. *s*: 3. Prof of Engineering Manch Univ, formerly St Andrews 1910—20, Mem Severn Barrage Cttee & Other Govt Scientific Cttees. *Publ*: Hydraulics & Its Applications; Hydro-Electric Engineering; Report on The Severn Barrage; Water Hammer in Long Pipe Lines; Natural Sources of Energy; The Circular Arc Bow Girder. *Ctr*: Ency Brit. *s.s*: Hydraulic Engineering. *a*: Beech Hse, Alderly Edge, Cheshire. *T*: Alderley 2358.

GIBSON, Arthur J. *b*: Wellingborough 1888. Married. *s*: 1. *d*: 1. Journalist (Acting Ed). *n.a*: N. Western Daily Mail (Barrow) '07–11, Derbyshire Times (Chesterfield) '11–19, Lancaster Observer '19–. *a*: 5 Hubert Pl, Lancaster. *t*: 717.

GIBSON, CHARLES R(OBERT): manufacturer, author; *b*. Glasgow, Scotland, Oct., 1870; *s*. Thomas Bowe and Jane Ramsey (Orr) G.; *educ*. Albany Acad., Glasgow Acad.; DEGREES: (Hon.) LL.D. (Glasgow), F.R.S. (Edinburgh); *m*. Jean Faulds Dobbie, 1899. AUTHOR: Romance of Modern Electricity, 1905; Romance of Modern Photography, 1907; Electricity of Today, 1908; Scientific Ideas of Today, 1908; How Telegraphs and Telephones Work, 1908; Romance of Modern Manufacture, 1909; Heroes of the Scientific World, 1912; Autobiography of an Electron (now What is Electricity?), 1912; Twentieth Century Inventions, 1913; Romance of Scientific Discovery, 1913; The Great Ball on which we live, 1914; Our Good Slave Electricity, 1914; The Stars and their Mysteries, 1915; War Inventions and How They were Invented, 1916; Ships that saved the Empire, 1917; The Engine Book, 1919; Wireless of Today (part-author), 1923; Radium and What it Tells; The Oceans of Air and Water; Photography and its Mysteries, 1924; Electrical Amusements and Experiments, 1924; Scientific Amusements and Experiments, 1925; Electricity as a Messenger, 1925; The Mysterious Ocean of Aether, 1925; Telephones and Gramophones, 1925; Wireless, 1925; How we harness Electricity, 1926; How Photography Came About, 1926; Machines and How they Work, 1926; Chemical Amusements and Experiments, 1927; The Story of the Motor Car, 1927; Romance of Great Inventors, 1928; Discoveries in Chemistry, 1929; About Coal and Oil, 1929; Engineering and its Mysteries, 1929; Electricity as a Wizard. Contributor of more than 100 articles to mags. and scientific jrnls. General character of writing: popular science. All literary work done between 5 a. m. and breakfast. Books have been transl. into German, Dutch, Italian, Hungarian, Spanish, Arabic, Japanese, Estonian. Relig. denom., Presbyterian. CLUB: Royal Scottish Automobile. OFFICE: Pollokshaws. HOME: Mansewood, by Pollokshaws, Glasgow, Scotland.

GIBSON, Charles Stanley, O.B.E., M.A., Sc.D., F.R.S. Prof of Chem. *Publ*: Chemistry of Dental Materials; Essential Principles of Organic Chemistry. *Ctr*. Nature, Chem & Ind, Proc Roy Soc, Journ Chem Soc. *a*: Greenaway, Warren Drive, Kingswood, Surrey. *T*: Mogador 2414.

GIBSON, Donovan. Free-lance Journalist 1933—. *n.a*: Sub-Ed Reuter's 1926—27, Asst-Ed The New Way '30—32. *Publ*: Golden House on High. *Ctr*: Leading Nat Newsps. *s.s*: Foreign Affairs, Fluent Russian, German, French, Turkish. *a*: Salisbury Sq Hse, London, E.C.4, & 21 Bride Lane, London, E.C.4.

GIBSON, Douglas Charles. *b*: Belmont 1910. *e*: Barrow Hedges Sch Carshalton. *m*: Dorothy Gibson. *s*: 1. *d*: 1. *Ctr*: Star, John O'London, Man of the World, Picturegoer, Lond Opinion, Blighty, Lady, Reveille, Irish Tatler & Sketch, Good Humour Annual, etc. *Publ*: Winter Journey & Other Poems. *s.s*: Poetry, Film-Writing. *Rec*: Walking, cricket, tennis, lazing. *a*: 47 Mildmay Grove, Islington, London, N.1.

GIBSON, E. Reporter, Northern Echo, Darlington.

GIBSON, GEORGE ALEXANDER: professor emeritus of mathematics; b. Greenlaw, Berwickshire, Scotland, Apr. 19, 1858; s. Robert and Jean (Gibson) G.; educ. Free Church Sch. (Greenlaw); DEGREES: M.A. (Glasgow); LL.D. (Edinburgh and Glasgow); m. Nellie Stenhouse, Hunter, Apr. 18, 1890. AUTHOR: An Elementary Treatise on the Calculus, 1901 (reprinted, 1903, 1910, 1916, 1926); An Elementary Treatise on Graphs, 1904 (frequently reprinted, with additions, up to present time); An Introduction to the Calculus, 1904 (very frequently reprinted, with additions); Elements of Analytical Geometry (with Dr. Pinkerton). General character of writing: text-books. Has had long experience as an educator. Relig. denom., Presbyterian. HOME: 166 Southbrae Drive, Glasgow, W. 3, Scotland.

GIBSON, Harold Edward, M.A., M.D.(Oxon). b: Madras 1881. e: Newton Abbot, Queen's Col Oxf & King's Col Hosp. m: Lucie Lonsdale Gibson. s: 1. Med Pract. c.t: B.M.J., Lancet, King's Col Hosp Gazette. s.s: Electro-Therapeutic Treatment. War Service R.A.M.C. 1914–18. Rec: Cricket. c: M.C.C., R.A.C., B.M.A. a: Homewood, S. Godstone, Surrey. t: 24.

GIBSON, Prof. J., M.A., D.Litt. Emeritus Prof of Philos at Univ of Wales, Bangor. Publ: Locke's Theory of Knowledge and its Historical Relations. a: Bron Hwfa, Bangor.

GIBSON, John Ashley. Journalist & Author of The Twilight Drummers; Postscript to Adventure; Ceylon; Children of the Lion; etc. a: Spectator, 585 Finchley Rd, London, N.W.3.

GIBSON, Rev. John Paul Stewart Riddell, M.A.(Cantab), F.I.A. b: Paris 1880. e: Kingswood Sch Bath, Sidney Coll Camb. m: Kathleen May Armitage. s: 3. d: 2. Clerk in Holy Orders, Princ Training Colony Ceylon 1914—27, Princ Ridley Hall Camb '27–45. Publ: Shakespeare's Use of the Supernatural; Highway of the Cross; The Wonder of Christian Discipleship; Christ & the Renewal of the Church; Reported Dead; Intercommunion; Quietness, Confidence, Strength. Ctr: Internat Review of Missions, Record. s.s: Theology. a: c/o C.M.S. Box 56, Kampala. T: Kampala 394.

GIBSON, Dr. P. C. Physician to the Torbay Hosp. Ctr: Lancet, Med Press Circ. Publ: The Technique of Blood Transfusion; The Silent Gap in Auscultatory Estimations of Blood Pressure; The Importance of Estimation of Blood Pressure. a: Muntham, Barrington, Rd, Torquay.

GIBSON. Dr. R.. M.D., ChB. Dermatologist. Hon Physician M/C & Salford Skin Hosp. Clinical Lect Dermatology M/C Univ. Visiting Dermatologist M/C Munic Hosps. a: Winter's Buildings, 30 St Anne St, M/C.

GIBSON, Rowland Routledge, F.R.S.A. b: Lon 1876. e: Radley Col & R.M.C. Sandhurst. m: Jane Crawford. d: 2. Artist, ex-Army Officer. Publ: Forces Mining & Undermining China; Patsy in Willowpat Land 1916; Patsy, Midland Theatre Manchester 1916; Mandalay, Q. Theature 1928. s.s: Far East, art, coloured labour. Entered Army 1897. W. Africa, Burma, Russia, China, Brit Guiana, European War, wounded, command Chinese Labour Group in France. Chinese Striped Tiger, 4th class. c: Garrick, F.R.S.A., Liveryman Skinners Co. Rec: Bridge, golf, tennis. a: Flat 4, 25 Roland Gardens, S.W.7. t: Ken 4939.

GIBSON, S. Cameron, M.I.E.E., F.R.S.A. m: Mary Valentine Watt. d: 3. Elec Eng. c.t: Elec Review, Elec Times. War Service R.N.V.R. Rec: Golf, photography. a: Elec Works, Coton Rd, Nuneaton. t: 601.

GIBSON, Strickland, M.A. b: Oxf 1877. e: New Col Sc & St Catherine Soc Oxf. m: Margaret Clinkard. s: 1. d: 1. Librarian & Archivist. Publ: Early Oxford bindings; Some Oxford Libraries; Statuta Antiqua Universitatis Oxoniensis (ed '31). c.t: Proc Oxf Bibliog Soc, Bodleian Quart Record, etc. s.s: Oxf univ hist. a: 34 Hill Top Rd, Oxf.

GIBSON, Walcot, F.R.S., F.G.S. Civil Servant (ret). Publ: Geology of Coal & Mining; Coal in Great Britain; etc. c.t: Scientific Journs. a: Pathway, Fairlight Rd, Hythe, Kent.

GIBSON, Wilfrid. b: Hexham 1878. Publ: Collected Poems, 1905—1925; The Alert; The Searchlights; The Outpost; Solway Ford (a selection); Coldknuckles. a: Greenway, Yaverland, Sandown, I.O.W.

GIBSON, WILLIAM RALPH BOYCE: university teacher of philosophy; b. Paris, France, Mar., 1869; s. William and Helen Wilhelmina (Boyce) G.; educ Ecole Monge, Paris, Woodhouse Grove, Leeds, Kingswood Sch., Bath; Queen's Coll. (Oxford), and at the Universities of Paris, Jena and Glasgow. DEGREES: M.A., D.Sc. (Oxon) (Oxford); m. Lucy Judge Peacock, Sept. 8, 1898. AUTHOR: The Problem of Freedom in relation to Psychology, 1902; A Philosophical Introduction to Ethics, 1904; Rudolf Eucken's Philosophy of Life, 1906; The Problem of Logic (with Augusta Klein), 1908; God with Us, 1909; various translations of Eucken's Works (with others); Ideas; An Introduction to Pure Phenomenology (a translation of Husserl's 'Ideen'), 1931. Contributor to Mind, The British Journal of Philosophical Studies, The Hibbert Journal, Quest, Australasian Journal of Psychology and Philosophy, Life (Melbourne), Revue de Métaphysique et de Morale. General character of writing: philosophical. OFFICE: University of Melbourne, Carlton, Vic. HOME: 2 Tower St., Surrey Hills, Melbourne, Victoria, Australia.

GIDDEN, Harry William, M.A., D.Ph. b: S'hampton 1865. e: K. Edward's Sc S'hampton, Univ Col & Lon Univ. m: Fanny Elizabeth Longland. s: 1. d: 3. n.a: Jt Gen Ed of S'hampton Record Soc 1905-. Publ: The Charters of Southampton (2 vols); The Letters Patent & Sign Manuals of same (2 vols); The Book of Remembrance of Southampton 1303–1620 (3 vols); The Growth & Municipal Government in Southampton. c.t: S'hampton Advtr. s.s: Records of S'hampton. For 43 y Classical Master at K. Edward's Sc S'hampton. a: Heathfield Lodge, Shirley Rd, S'hampton. t: 71534.

GIDDINGS, William John Peter, F.J.I. b: N. Adelaide 1861. e: St Peter's Col. m: Aurora Killicoat. Journalist. n.a: Advertiser, Adelaide 1879-89, Ed & Proprietor The Silver Age, Broken Hill '89-94, News Tamworth '94, Golden Age Coolgardie '95, Brit Australasian '96-97, Ed Faulding's Journ '99-1913, Ed Standard Adelaide '13-18, Advertiser Adelaide '18-. s.s: Interviews, biographies. 1st Australian to be elected Fellow Inst Journalists, Eng '06. Rec: Motoring. c: Authors, Press. a: Talunga, Glenelg, S. Australia.

GIDE, Andre Paul Guillaume. Author of Amyntas; Oscar Wilde; La Symphonie Pastorale; L'Ecole des femmes, Montaigne; etc; Translations of works by William Blake, Walt Whitman, Joseph Conrad, etc.

GIDE, CHARLES: professor of law; b. Uzès, France, June 29, 1847; s. Tancréde and Clémence (Granier) G.; educ. Univ. of Paris. DEGREE: LL.D.; m. Anna M. Thurn. AUTHOR: Principes d'Economie, 1884 (24th edit. 1923; transl. into Czech, 1922; into Spanish, 1911;

into Polish, 1916; into English, into Finnish, 1904; into German, 1928; into Italian, 1909; into Turkish, 1909; into Dutch, 1920; into Swedish, 1915; into Russian, 1916; into Greek, into Japanese, 1918; into Georgian, 1919; into Chinese, 1916; Braille edition, 18 vols. (1921-22); Les Sociétés coopératives de consommation (5th edit.), 1918 (8 transls.); Premiers Notions d'Économie Politique, 1921 (11 translations); Le Juste Prix par la Coopération, 1921-22; Fourier, Precurseur de la Coopération, 1921-22; La Coopération, Conférences de Propogande (4th edit.), 1922; Histoire des Doctrines economiques depuis les Physiocrates jusqu'a nos jours (5th edit.), 1922; Le Profit et la Coopération, 1922-23; Les Association Coopératives de Production, 1922-23; La Programme coopératiste, 1923-24; La Question du Logement et la coopération, 1923-24; LaLutte contre La Cherte et la Cooperation, 1924-25; Les Associations Coopératives Agricoles, 1924-25; La Cooperation a l'Étranger, 1925-26; L'École de Nîmes, 1925-26; La Coopération dans les Pays Latins, 1926-27; La Coopération française durant la Guerre, 1926-27. Editor: Revue d'Économie Politique. Contributor: Emancipation, Revue de Christianisme social, and others. ASSOCIATIONS: Mem. American Economic Assn., Corres. of Royal Economic Soc., Mem. Academy of Brussels, Rome, Naples, Madrid, and Budapest. Relig. denom., Reformed Protestant (Calvinist). OFFICE: Collège de France. HOME: 2 rue Decamps, Paris, France.

GIELGUD, Lieut.-Col. Lewis Evelyn, M.B.E., M.A. *b*: London 1894. *e*: Eton & Magdalen Coll Oxf. *m*: Zita Gordon. *d*: 1. Official Inter-Allied Reparation Agency, Under Sec-Gen League of Red Cross Societies 1927—39. *Publ*: About It & About; Red Soil; The Wise Child. (Plays with Naomi Mitchison) As it Was in the Beginning; The Price of Freedom. (Poems from the Polish) Mist Before the Dawn; First & Last Poems. The Story of The Red Cross (from the French). *s.s*: Verse Translations. *Rec*: Travel, reading, writing. *w.s*: '14—19 & '40—44 British Army. *a*: 3 Rue Belle Vue, Brussels.

GIELGUD, Val Henry. *b*: London 1900. *e*: Rugby & Trin Coll Oxf. *m*: Barbara Dillon. *s*: 1. Dramatic Dir B.B.C. *Publ*: Black Gallantry; Gathering of Eagles; Imperial Treasure; The Broken Men; Gravelhanger (with Hart Marvell); Under London; Death at Broadcasting House (last 2 with Holt Marvel); How to Write Broadcast Plays; Death as an Extra; The Red Account; Confident Morning; Radio Theatre, Years of Locust. *Ctr*: Dly Mail, Dly Express, Dly Herald, Tatler, Dly Mirror, etc. *s.s*: Broadcast Drama, M. Hist. *Rec*: Reading, travel. *c*: Savile. *a*: 4/127 Long Acre, London, W.C. *T*: Temple Bar 2744.

GIEROW, Karl Ragnar. *b*: Helsingborg, Sweden 1904. *e*: Lond Univ. *m*: Karin Hellmer. *n.a*: Norstedt & Sons Publ '30—37, Radiotjanst (Swed Broadcast Corp) '37—46, Lit Ed Svenska Dagbladet since '46. *Publ*: Plays:—The Beast of Prey; A Saint's Saga; The Ferry; To Your Heart's Content. Poems:— Odletid; Vid Askens Rotter. *a*: Storgatan 29, Stockholm, Sweden. *T*: 61 20 13.

GIEVE, John E. *a*: 75 Ferme Park Rd, Hornsey, N.8.

GIFFARD, Evelyn. *b*: London. *e*: Priv. *m*: Edward Walter Giffard. *Publ*: The Charm of Innocence. *c.t*: Sketch, Queen, Woman's Magazine, etc. *c*: Ladies Army & Navy. *a*: Charts Edge, Westerham, Kent. *t*: 41.

GIFFORD, Dr. G. T. *c.t*: Lancet. *a*: Ellesmere, Crowthorne, Berks.

GIGLIOLI, George, M.D., M.R.C.P., D.T.M. & H.(Eng). *b*: Naples 1897. *e*: Univs of Pisa Italy & Lon. *m*: Gina Perret. *s*: 2. Physician. *Publ*: Malarial Nephritis (1930). *c.t*: Med journs. *s.s*: Trop med. Med Supt Davson S.C.'s Estates, Berbice B. Guiana. *Rec*: Shooting. *a*: Blairmont, Brit Guiana, S. America.

GILBERT, George William. *b*: Brightlingsea 1887. *e*: Priv. *m*: Ethel Florence Lewis. Motor Ins Mang & Solicitor. *Publ*: How to Answer Questions on Motor Ins; Motor Ins. *c.t*: Post Mag, Policy, Ins Record. *Rec*: Golf. *a*: 38 Donnington Rd, Brondesbury Park, N.W. 10. *t*: Willesden 7000.

GILBERT, John Charles George, F.R.S.A., A.R.P.S. *b*: London 1908. *e*: Westminster City Sch, Univ Coll, Regent Street Polytech. *m*: Marian Miles. *s*: 1. *d*: 1. Lecturer & Consultant, Lect in Telecommunication Northern Polytech Holloway Rd '33—47. *n.a*: Tech Ed Music Trades Review 1936—. *Publ*: Radio Engineering (in collab). *Ctr*: Wireless World, Electronic Engineering, Dly Express, Music Trades Review, *s.s*: Radio, Television, Electronics, Sound Recording. *Rec*: Motor Racing, photography, music. *c*: R.A.C. *w.s*: Tech Officer M.A.P. Radar '40—45. *a*: Glenmayne, 7 Corkran Rd, Surbiton, Surrey. *T*: Elmbridge 2359.

GILBERT, Sir John William, K.B.E., B.A., LL.D. *b*: Lon 1871. *e*: St Joseph's Col Clapham & Tooting & Lon Univ. Secretary. *n.a*: Ed The Shield 1903-08. *Publ*: Monsignor Gilbert: a memoir; Present position of Catholic Schools; Relation of the State to Religious Education England & Wales—R.C. point of view (in educational year book, international training of teachers Col, Columbia Univ '32). *c.t*: Daily Telegraph, 19th Cent & After, Dublin Review, Catholic Times, etc. *s.s*: Educ & Catholic matters. Alderman L.C.C. '10 & '20-21. L.C.C. Educ Cmt '13-, '17 & '28-32. Mem Lon Passenger Transp Bd '33-. Papal Decor K.C.S.G., K.S.S. *a*: 79 Grove Park, Denmark Hill, S.E.5, & 15 George St, Mansion Hse, E.C.4. *t*: 7527.

GILBERT, Stuart. *Publ*: James Joyce's Ulysses (a study). *c*: Mem Translators' Gld. *a*: 7 Rue Jean du Bellay, Paris IV.

GILBERT-CARTER, Humphrey, M.B., ChB., M.A. Dir Cam Univ Botanic Garden. *Publ*: Genera of Brit Plants; Guide to Univ Botanic Garden; Catkin-bearing Plants. *c.t*: Cam Review. *a*: University Botanic Garden, Cambridge. *t*: 101.

GILBERTSON, George Waters, Maj. *b*: Caithness 1860. *e*: Edin Univ. *m*: Marion Ada Price. *s*: 1. *d*: 3. Indian Army (ret). *Publ*: Assembly of Mirth (Trans from Hindi); Indian Events; First Pakhato Book; The Balochi Language; Balochi Colloquial Dictionary. The Pakhato Idiom. *s.s*: Eastern languages, Pakhato, Balochi, Kurdish, Urdu, etc. 8 Medals, 10 Mentions. *a*: 373 Holmesdale Rd, South Norwood, S.E.25.

GILBEY, Geoffrey, M.C. *m*:. *d*: 2. *n.a*: Racing Corr & Racing Ed Sporting Record. *Ctr*: Town & Country. *Publ*: Pass it On; One More Chance; It Isn't; The Way Out; She's & Ski's; Not Really Rude. *a*: 27 Ormonde Gate, S.W.3. *T*: Flaxman 5470.

GILBEY, Jack Newman. *b*: St John's, Beaumont Coll, Stronghurst Coll, Sandhurst. Author, Poet. *Publ*: In Loving Memory & Other Poems; Come to Me All Ye & Other Poems; Haven & Other Poems; Milestones & Other Poems; In All the Signs & Other Poems; Snowdrops at Dusk & Other Poems; Collected Poems 1935—46.

Ctr: Universe, Catholic Fireside, Catholic Gaz. *s.s*: Religious Poems, Hymns, Country Poems, Poems About Children. *c*: Army & Navy, Lord's. *w.s*: Black Watch France '14—18. *a*: Glan Avon, Harlow, Essex. *T*: Potter St, 7.

GILCHRIST, Marion. LL.A. *b*: Bothwell Park Farm. *e*: Bothwell Sch, Hamilton Acad, Glas Univ. *Ctr*: Glasgow Herald & Articles to various Med Journs. *Rec*: Walking, travel, motoring. *a*: 5 Buckingham Terr, Glasgow, W.2. *T*: W797.

GILCHRIST, Mary Lyle. M.O.H.(Asst). *c.t*: Glas Med Journ, Archives of Diseases of Children. *a*: 75 Cambridge Park, Wanstead, Lon, E.11. *t*: 3605.

GILCHRIST, Robert Niven, C.I.E., M.A. *b*: Aberdeenshire 1888. *e*: Aberdeen Univ. *m*: Winifred Buyers. Late Ind Educ Serv, Head of Polit Philos, Pres Coll Calcutta 1911—16, Princ & Prof Economics & Polit Philo Brishagar Coll Bengal '16—22, etc. *Publ*: Principles of Political Science; Indian Nationality; Conciliation & Arbitration; The Payment of Wages & Profit Sharing; The Executive & Judicial. *s.s*: Pol Science, India, Labour Problems. *c*: East India & Sports. *a*: East India & Sports Club, 16 St James's Sq, London, S.W.1. *T*: Whitehall 1000.

"GILCRAFT." *Publ*: Spare Time Activities; Scouting Out-of-Doors; Wolf Cubs; Knotting, Boy Scouts; Exploring; Preparing the Way; Pioneering; Wide Games; Rover Scouts; Training in Tracking; How to Run a Pack; Scout Games; Cub Games; etc. *s.s*: Scouting interests. *a*: The Boy Scouts' Assoc, 25 Buckingham Palace Rd, London, S.W.1.

GILDER, Rosamond. *b*: Marion, Mass. *e*: Brearly Sch New York City. Ed & Dramatic Critic Theatre Arts. *n.a*: Theatre Arts 1924, Assoc Ed & Dramatic Critic '38, Ed-in-Chief '45, Sec New York Drama Critics Circle '45—, Sec American Nat Theatre &'Academy '45—. *Publ*: John Gielgud's Hamlet, A Record Performance; Enter the Actress, The First Women in the Theatre; A Theatre Library, A Bibliography of One Hundred Books Relating to the Theatre; Ed: Letters of Richard Watson Gilder; In collab: Theatre Collections in Libraries & Museums, An International Handbook; Trans: My Life, By Emma Calve. *Ctr*: Theatre Arts, New York Times. *s.s*: Theatre & Allied Subjects. *Rec*: Gardening. *c*: Cosmopolitan, N.Y. *a*: 24 Gramercy Park, New York 3, N.Y., & 130 West 56th St, New York 19, N.Y. *T*: Circle 6-9492.

GILDER, T. H. *n.a*: Ed Staff I. of W. County Press. *a*: 99 Trafalgar Rd, Newport, I.o.W.

GILDING, Henry Percy. *b*: Nott'm 1895. *e*: St John's Col Oxf, St Bart's Hosp Lon. *m*: Violet Mary Frances Margaret Teresa Hazlitt-Brett. *d*: 3. Prof of Physiology. *c.t*: Journ Experimental Med, Brit Journ of Experimental Pathology, Quarterly Journ of Experimental Phys, etc. *s.s*: Phys. Snr Demonstrator St Bart's Hosp. Fell Rockefeller Inst. Reader in Experimental Phys U.C.L. *Rec*: Music, tennis. *a*: Shelfield Hse, nr Alcester, Warwicks & The Univ, Edmund St, Birm. *t*: Gt Alne 50.

GILES, Arthur Edward, M.D., B.Sc(Lon), M.B., ChB.(M/C), F.R.C.S.Ed, M.R.C.P.Lon. *b*: Bombay 1864. *e*: Lycée du Havre, City of Lon Sc, M/C G.S. & Owen's Col M/C. *m*: May Hartree Tindall. Surgeon. *n.a*: Jt Ed Owen's College Mag 1886-88, Jt Ed British Gynæcological Journal '98-1902. *Publ*: Moral Pathology; Diseases of Women (with Sir John Bland-Sutton); Gynæcological Nursing; The After-Results of Abdominal Operations (based on 1000 cases); Sterility in Women; etc; A Fantasy of the Seasons & other verses. *c.t*: Trans of the Obstetrical Soc, & of Roy Soc of Med, Lancet, B.M.J., Med Press & Circular etc. *s.s*: Gynæcology. Ex-Pres Section of Obstetrics & Gynæcology, Roy Soc of Med. Past Master Worshipful Coy of Drapers. Brev Major R.A.M.C. *a*: The Elms, Welwyn, Herts.

GILES, C. Parliamentary Journalist (ret). *a*: 3 Cautley Ave, Clapham, S.W.4.

GILES, Carl Prausnitz. *b*: Hamburg, Germany 1876. *e*: Raalgymnasium, Hamburg, Tech Hgh Sch Darmstadt, Univs of Leipzig, Kiel, Breslau. *m*: Margot Bruck. *s*: 2, *d*: 1. Late Univ Prof, Mem Ventnor U.D.C. *Publ*: Grundzuge der Hygiene (in collab); Investigations on Respiratory Dust Disease in Operation in the Cotton Industry; The Teaching of Preventive Medicine in Europe. *s.s*: Bacteriology, Asthma, Hayfever. *c*: Medical Research. *a*: Kingseat, Ventnor, I.O.W. *T*: 140.

GILES, Charles Tyrrell, M.A., K.C., J.P., D.L. *b*: Regent's Park 1850. *e*: Harrow, King's Coll Cam. *m*: Isabella Colman. *d*: 1. *Publ*: 3rd Ed Cunningham on Elections. *c.t*: Times, Field, Country Life, etc. *s.s*: Cricket, shooting, fishing. M.P. North Cambs 1895-1900. Chm of Wimbledon & Putney Commons 1892-. High Sheriff of Surrey 1915-16. Kt of Grace of Order of St John. Surrey C.C. Ald '07-25. *a*: Copse Hill Hse, Wimbledon. *t*: 0150.

GILES, D. R. C. *n.a*: Chief Reporter Daily Mail. *a*: Jameson St, Hull.

GILES, George Marr, M.A. *b*: Udny 1882. *e*: Aberdeen Gr Sch, Aberdeen Univ. *m*: Margaret Cantlay. Journalist, Hon Mem Inst of Journalists. *n.a*: Aberdeen Free Press, Sub Ed 1903—04; Pioneer (Allahabad) Lond Sub Ed '04—15, Reuter's Telegram Co Ltd '15. *Ctr*: Saturday Review, Field. *Rec*: Golf. *a*: 9 Wilton Grove, New Malden, Surrey. *T*: Malden 1760.

GILES, JOANNA ELDER: see Magill, Marcus.

GILES, Lionel, M.A., D.Litt. *b*: Sutton 1875. *e*: Coll St Servais Liege & Stella Matutina, Feldkirch Austria, Aberd Univ & Wadham Col, Oxf. *m*: Phyllis Isabel Coughtrie. *s*: 1. *d*: 1. Dep Keeper Dept of Oriental Printed Books & MSS Brit Museum. *Publ*: Sayings of Lao Tzu; Sayings of Confucius; Taoist Teachings; Sun Tzu on the Art of War; The Analects of Confucius; Six Centuries at Tunhuang; Book of Mencuis. *Ctr*: Journ Roy Asiatic Soc, Bulletin School of Oriental Studies, Toung Pao, Aryan Path. *s.s*: Chinese Lang, Hist & Lit. *Rec*: Lawn tennis. *a*: The Knoll, Abbots Rd, Abbots Langley, Herts.

GILES, Rev. Robbie Abney, M.A., B.Litt.(Oxon), J.P. *b*: Victoria, Australia 1888. *e*: St Aidan's Coll Victoria, Keble Coll Oxford and Trinity Coll Dublin. *m*: Maud Lillian McConagby. *s*: 2. Clerk in Holy Orders. *Publ*: Constitutional History of the Australian Church. *s.s*: Municipal & Local Government. *Rec*: Shooting. *a*: Sheriffhales Vicarage, nr Shifnal, Salop. *T*: Shifnal 51.

GILFORD, Hastings, F.R.C.S. *b*: Melton Mowbray 1861. *m*: Private. *m*: Lilian Adele Hope. *s*: 2. *d*: 2. Surgeon. *Publ*: Disorders of Postnatal Growth and Development; Tumours & Cancers; Cancer: Civilization: Degeneration; The Cancer Problem and its Solution. *c.t*: The Lancet, British Medical Jnl. *s.s*: Cancer, disorders of postnatal development, infantilism. *Rec*: Tennis. Fellow Royal Soc Medicine. Former Hunterian Prof Roy Col Surg. *a*: 47 Cressingham Rd, Reading.

GILKES, Antony Newcombe. *b:* Dulwich 1900. *e:* Dulwich Coll & Christ Church Oxf. *m:* Ruby Agatha Shaw. *s:* 3. Headmaster. *Publ:* Selections From the Old Testament; Selections From the New Testament. *Ctr:* Church Guardian, The Literary Guide. *s.s:* Education, Religion. *Rec:* Music, cricket, travel. *a:* Dean Close School, Cheltenham. *T:* 52537.

GILKYSON, Walter, A.M., LL.B. *b:* Phœnixville, Pa 1880. *e:* Swarthmore Coll, Univ of Penn. *m:* Beatrice Kenyon. Writer, American Sec Internat Mil Tribunal Nuremberg Germany 1946. *Publ:* Towards What Bright Land; The Lost Adventurer; Oil; Lights of Fame; Tomorrow Never Comes. *Ctr:* Atlantic Monthly, Harper's Mag, Colliers, Scribner's Mag, Woman's Home Companion, Pictorial Review, Forum, Story Mag. *s.s:* Novels & Short Stories. *c:* The Coffee House, N.Y. City. *w.s:* Major U.S. Army World War I. *a:* Appleby, New Hartford, Conn, U.S.A. *T:* Winstead 2052 ring 12.

GILL, Alexander Wilson, M.D., F.R.C.P. *b:* Edinburgh 1888. *e:* Roy High Sch & Univ of Edinburgh *m:* Edith Mary Johnson. Senior Physician Nth Staffs Roy Infirmary, Ex-Pres Nth Staffs Med Soc & Staffs Branch B.M.A. *Publ:* Seale-Hayne Neurological Studies (Asst-Ed). *Ctr:* Lancet, B.M.J., etc. *s.s:* Psychiatry & Cardiology. *Rec:* Fishing. *w.s:* 1914—18 R.A.M.C. (Capt). *a:* The Limes, Barlaston, Stoke-on-Trent. *T:* Barlaston 60, & 16 King St, Newcastle, Staffs. *T:* Newcastle 67184.

GILL, Bessie. *b:* Chard. *e:* Chard H.S. *Publ:* Zider an' Bread an' Cheese; Two Toil Worn Hands (songs). *c.t:* Somerset County Yr Book, Schoolmistress, Chatterbox, Poets' Guild, Bristol Observer, etc. *s.s:* Song-writing. Won the silver cup in Poets' Guild for poetry '32. Copy of Two Toil Worn Hands accepted by Queen Mary. *Rec:* Gardening, handicrafts. *c:* Life Mem Brit Song Soc, The Imp Writers' Circle. *a:* Clayhanger, Wadeford, Chard, Som.

GILL, Enid. *b:* Bulawayo, S. Africa. Journalist. *n.a:* Morning Post, Asst to Woman's Page Ed 1928—29, Newcastle Evening World, Feature Dept '29—30, Modern Home Sub Ed '30—34. *Publ:* Writing for a Living. *a:* c/o C. Arthur Pearson Ltd, 18 Henrietta St, Strand, W.C.2. *t:* Temple Bar 3521.

GILL, Eric Franklin, A.M.I.Mech.E. *b:* Harrow, Middlx 1893. *e:* Wealdstone Elem Sch, Regent Street Polytech, Sch of Mech Engineering. *m:* Mabel Corbett. *d:* 3. Chartered Mech Eng. *Ctr:* Mechanical World, Practical Engineer, Modern Refrigeration, Daily Telegraph. *s.s:* Mech Eng (Thermo Dynamics, Fluid Flow). *w.s:* R.F.C. 1914—19, H.G. (6th Glos) '41—45. *a:* 7 Elmcroft Drive, Surbiton, Surrey. *T:* Elmbridge 3460.

GILL, Ernest Walter Brudenell, O.B.E., M.A., B.Sc. *b:* London 1883. *e:* Bristol Gr Sch & Christ Church Oxf. *m:* Mary Beatrice Harriss. *s:* 3. *d:* 1. Fellow & Bursar Merton Coll Oxf. *Publ:* War, Wireless & Wangles. *Ctr:* Scientific Papers in Philosophical Magazine. *s.s:* Electricity. *Rec:* Travel. *w.s:* World Wars I & II. *a:* Larkfield, Boar's Hill, Oxford. *T:* 85368.

GILL, Rev. Frederick Cyril, M.A. *b:* London 1898. *e* Cheltenham Gr Sch, Didsbury Coll, Univs of Manch & L'pool. *m:* Margaret Frankland Harrison. Minister St John's Methodist Church Colwyn Bay. *Publ:* The Romantic Movement & Methodism; New Horizons; The Light on the Moor. *Ctr:* Lond Quarterly, Brit Weekly, Methodist Recorder, John O'London's, T.P's Weekly, Methodist Mag, Youth Christian World. *s.s:* Essays, Literary Critic, Book Reviews, General Articles & Short Stories. *w.s:* 1916—19. *a:* Tranby, Colwyn Bay. *T:* 2589.

GILL, HENRY VINCENT: Roman Catholic priest; b. Dublin, Ireland, July 8, 1872; s. Henry Joseph and Mary Julia (Keating) G.; educ. St. Gall's Cath. Univ. Sch., Clongowes Wood Coll., Univ. Coll. (Dublin), Univ. Cambridge, Downing Coll., Cavendish Laboratory. DEGREES: M.A. (Cambridge), M.A., M.Sc (Nat. Univ. of Ireland). Contributor of scientific papers to Amer. Journ. Science, Proceeding Royal Soc., Royal Dublin Soc., Philosophical Mag., Nineteenth Century, Studies, Thought, Irish Ecclesiastical Record. General character of writing: religious, scientific. Service as Chaplain, 2nd Royal Irish Rifles, during Great War, 1914-18, on Western Front, in Belgium. Orders conferred: D.S.O., M.C., "de la Reconnaissance Francaise". Relig. denom., Roman Catholic. HOME: Belvedere College, Dublin, Ireland.

GILL, Hubert Alexander. *b:* Redhill 1881. *e:* Yorkshire Col Leeds, Queen's Col Cam. Married. *s:* 1. *d:* 3. Chrtd Patent Agent. *s.s:* Patents. *c:* Athenæum, City Livery. *a:* 51-2 Chancery Lane, W.C.2. *t:* Holborn 7764.

GILL, J. *s.s:* Polit, econ. *a:* Transport Hse, Smith Square, S.W.1.

GILL, Thomas Harvey, B.A., M.F. *b:* Philadelphia, Pa 1891. *e:* Univ of Penn, Yale Forest Sch. *m:* Vivian Perry. Author, Forester, Sen Mem Soc of American Foresters. *Publ:* Gay Bandit of the Border; Tropical Forests of the Caribbean; Guardians of the Desert; Death Rides the Mesa; Starlight Pass; Red Earth; Heartwood; Firebrand; Gentlemen of the Jungle; Wildcat; North to Danger; Jungle Harvest; No Place for Women; (With L. Pack) Forests & Mankind; Forest Facts for Schools. *s.s:* Forestry. *c:* Cosmos (Wash D.C.), Univ (Wash D.C.), Explorers (N.Y.). *v:* 2800 Jenifer St, N.W. Washington 15, D.C., & 1214 Sixteenth St, N.W. Washington, 6, D.C. *T:* District 3258.

GILLAM, JOHN GRAHAM: writer; b. Brighton, Eng., Dec. 22, 1883; s. George William and Prudence (Wallis) G.; educ. Brighton and Slough Schls.; m. Sheilah Graham, Apr. 18, 1925. AUTHOR: A Gallipoli Diary, 1918. Contributor to Daily Mail, Daily Express (both London), and to many mags. General character of writing: historical, essays, fiction. Saw service in Great War; promoted from gunner to major; twice mentioned in dispatches; awarded D.S.O. Relig. denom., Nonconformist. CLUB: R.A.C. (Royal Automobile Club) (London). HOME: 128 Wigmore St., London, W. 1, Eng.

GILLAN, Sir (James) Angus, K.B.E., C.M.G. *b:* Aberdeen 1885. *e:* Edin Acad & Magdalen Coll Oxf. *m:* Margaret Douglas Ord-Mackenzie. *s:* 1. Controller Overseas Dvn A The British Council, Order of Nile (Egypt) 2nd Class. *Ctr:* Sudan Notes & Records, Commonwealth & Empire Review & Journs of various Socs. *s.s:* Anglo-Egyptian Sudan, Commonwealth & Empire Affairs, International Cultural Relations, Rowing. *w.s:* 1940—41 Princ Off Nth Midland C.D. *Rec:* Shooting, tennis, golf. *c:* Conservative, Leander, Roy Empire Soc, Overseas League, etc. *a:* How Hatch, Chipstead, Surrey. *T:* Downland 444.

GILLAN, Percival Milne. *b:* Buckie 1905. *e:* Buckie Sec Sc, Robert Gordon's Col Aber & Aber Univ. Teacher of Modern Langs Robert Gordon's Col Aber '28-33, George Heriot's Sc Edin '33-, etc. *Publ:* Beginner's German Reader. *s.s:* French & German. *Rec:* Tennis, music. *a:* 39 Mardale Cresc, Edin.

GILLESPIE, Rev. Francis Charles, M.A. *b:* Lon 1875. *e:* Ellesmere Col Salop, Keble Col Oxf. *m:* Florence Boffin (dec). Schoolmaster. *Publ:* Worked Examples in Elementary Geometry; Latin Lists & Notes for Examination

Purposes; Their Sound Goeth Forth, a Missionary Play; Songs—The Greengrocer; Not Exactly Original; Papers; Come On; Belgium. *c.t*: Everyman, The New Clarion, Evening Standard, Daily Mirror. *s.s*: Cross-Word Construction. *Rec*: Hockey, cricket. *a*: 35 Warnborough Rd, Oxford. *T*: 3316.

GILLESPIE, Henry Winterstein, M.D., D.M.R., F.R.S.M. *b*: Bostock 1910. *e*: Switzerland, Univs of Lond & Innsbruck. *m*: Anne Frances Roden Buxton. *d*: 1. *Ctr*: Brit Journ of Radiology, St George's Hosp Gaz, & other Radiological & Med Journs. *s.s*: Radiology & Medicine, Spine, Midgets & Dwarfs. *Rec*: Ski-ing & Riding. *c*: Authors. *a*: Fishers Hill, Hook Heath, Woking, Surrey. *T*: 1030.

GILLESPIE, Dr. Isabella Anne, M.B., ChB., D.P.M. *Publ*: Treatment of Post-Enceptialitis. *c.t*: Journ of Mental Sci. Dep Med Supt Co Mental Hosp Chester. *a*: Co Mental Hosp, Chester.

GILLESPIE, John, L.R.I.B.A., F.R.I.A.S., F.R.S.A., F.S.A.(Scot). *b*: Scottish Borders 1897. *e*: Pollokshields Publ Sch, Albert Rd Acad & Roy Tech Coll Glas. Chief Staff Architect with Greenock Corp. *Ctr*: Poetry to Mags, periodicals Home & Overseas. *s.s*: Lit & Verse of Scot Borderland. *Rec*: Sketching, yachting. *a*: 56 Kenmure St, Pollokshields, Glas.

GILLESPIE, John Richard, M.A., M.D., B.Ch,. B.A.O., D.P.H. *b*: Newry, Co Down 1871. *e*: Newry & Queens Coll Belfast, R.U.I. *m*: Catherine Robinson Hunter. *s*: 1. *d*: 1. Chief Tuberculosis Med Officer Co Down 1912—47 (ret), Fell Soc of M.O.H., Ulster Med Soc, Mem Ulster Tuberculosis Assoc, B.M.A., etc *Publ*: The Use & Misuse of Tuberculin in the Treatment of Pulmonary Tuberculosis; Rational Method of Using Tuberculin in the Treatment of Pulmonary Tuberculosis; Use of Tuberculin in Diagnosis & Treatment of Tuberculosis *Ctr*: B.M.J., etc. *s.s*: Tuberculosis. *a*: 28 Knockdene Park South, Belfast, Nth Ireland. *T*: Belfast 53162.

GILLESPIE, Noel Alexander, B.A., M.A., B.M., B.Ch, M.R.S.M., F.Z.S. *b*: Sydenham 1904. *e*: Perse Sc Cam & New Coll Oxf. Anæsthetist. *Publ*: Revision of Technical Terms; More from the Primeval Forest by Albert Schweitser. *c.t*: Toc H Journ, B.M.J., E. Anglian Daily Times, etc. *s.s* Anæsthetics. Hse Surg Roy S. Hants & S'hampton Hosp '32. Senr Res Anæsthetist Lon Hosp '33. *Rec*: Toc H, scouting & golf. *c*: Roy Soc. *a*: 3 Langham Mans, Earls Ct Sq, S.W.5. *t*: Fla 8850.

GILLESPIE, Robert Dick, M.D., F.R.C.P., D.P.M. *Publ*: Hypochondria; Sleep: & the Treatment of its Disorders; Textbook of Psychiatry (with D. K. Henderson, 3rd edit 1932); Mind in Daily Life ('33). *c.t*: Lancet, Brit Journ Neurology & Psychopathology, Journ Ment Sci, Guy's Hosp Reports, Acta Pediatrica, etc. *a*: 49 Wimpole St, W.1. *t*: Welbeck 5220.

GILLESPIE, Susan. *b*: Lancs 1904. *e*: Priv & Paris. *m*: G/Capt J. H. Tutton-Jones. *Publ*: The Rajah's Guests; Cantonment; Government House; Take My Youth; The Man He Was; They Went to Karathia; The Promotion of Fools; North From Bombay; Himalayan View. *Ctr*: Vogue, Good Housekeeping. *s.s*: Travel Articles on the Far East & India, Br Emp & Eng Speaking Peoples, Polish Hist & Place in Europe. *w.s*: Civilian Cypher Officer H.Q.F.C. '40, Att M.O.I. '43—45. *a*: c/o A. P. Watt & Son, Hasting Hse, Norfolk St, London, W.C.2.

GILLESPIE, Thomas Haining. *b*: Dumfries 1876. *e*: Priv & Edin Univ. *m*: Mary Elizabeth Gamble. Solicitor. Founder & Sec Zool Soc of Scotland & Dir Scot Nat Zool Park 1913—. *Publ*: A Book of King Penguins; Is it Cruel? A Study of the Conditions of Captive & Performing Animals; Zoo Ways & Whys; More Zoo Ways; The Way of a Serpent; Zoo Tales; Animal Stories. *s.s*: Animal Life & Behaviour. *Rec*: Reading, writing, photography, music. *c*: Overseas League, Scottish Arts Edin. *a*: Corstorphine Hill Ho, Edinburgh 12. *T*: 66110.

GILLESPIE, William Reid. *b*: Aberdeen 1899. *e*: Walker Rd Publ Sc & Central Evg Sc Aber. *m*: Ethel May Manning. *s*: 1. Journalist. *n.a*: Asst Sub-Ed Aberdeen Evening Express 1913—17, Senr Reporter Clacton News '20—22, Dis Reporter Surrey Times, Guildford '22—24, Second Reporter Grantham Journal '24—35, Ed '35—. *c.t*: Lon dailies & prov papers, trade periodicals, etc. *s.s*: Book reviews, football. War Service. *Rec*: Reading, radio. *a*: 56 Castlegate, Grantham. *t*: 80.

GILLESPY, George Thomas, A.M.I.Mech.E., M.I.Mar.E., F.R.S.A. *b*: Tonbridge 1872. *e*: Priv & F.T.C Married twice. *s*: 2. *d*: 2. Chrtd Mech Eng, Dir of Inst Internat Corres Schs Lond. *Ctr*: Mechanical World, I.C.S. periodicals, etc. *s.s*: Tech Educ 50 yrs practical cons & teaching experience in engineering. *a*: Brooklyn, The Grove, Ferring, Sussex.

GILLET, Eric Walkey, M.A. *b*: Bowdon 1893. *e*: Radley & Lincoln Colls, Oxford. Author, Lecturer, Broadcaster, Journalist, Literary Adviser Longmans, Green, Warden of Chancellors Hall B'ham Univ, Johors Professor of English Literature Raffles Coll Singapore 1927—31. *n.a*: Ed St Martin's Rev '40—46, Ed Books of To-day '41—42. *Publ*: The Literature of England A.D 500—1945 (with W. J. Entwistle); Elizabeth Ham; Maria Jane Jewsbury; Poets of our Time; Books & Writers; Junior Film Annual '46—47; Eric Gillet's Film Book. Film Fairyland. *Ctr*: Sun Times, Times, Times Lit Sup, Sun Exp, Time & Tide, Fortnightly Rev, Manch Gdn, Leader, Dly Telegraph. *s.s*: Contemporary Literature, Films (Children's angle), Malaya. *c*: United Univ, M.C.C., R.A.C. *a*: 65 Earl's Court Sq, London, S.W.5. *T*: Flaxman 6733.

GILLETT, Rev. George Gabriel Scott. *b*: Hawley, Hants 1873. *e*: Westminster Sch & Keble Coll Oxf. Clerk in Holy Orders. *n.a*: Ed-Sec S.P.G. 1926—83, Lit-Ed Christendom '33, Read to Ch Lit Assoc '33—, Ed Report of Anglo-Cath Cent Congress '33. *Publ*: The Claims & Promise of the Church (with William Scott Palmer); Politics & Religion; Revolution, Christian or Pagan?; A Garden of Song; The Rector explains his position. *Ctr*: Church Times, Christendom, etc. *a*: 75 Pevensey Rd West, St Leonards-on-Sea. *T*: Hastings 4039.

GILLETT, Henry Martin Francis, B.A. *b*: Andover 1902. *e*: Blundell's Sc, Devonshire, St Chad's Col, Durham, Univ of the South, U.S.A. & Philadelphia U.S.A. Writer, lecturer. *Publ*: St Bede the Venerable; Walsingham & Its Shrine; Story of the Relics of the Passion; Story of the London Oratory Church; Folklore of Andover & Neighbourhood. *c.t*: Daily Telegraph, Tablet, Universe, Catholic Times & Herald, Blackfriars, etc. *s.s*: History, topography. *Rec*: Walking, climbing, camping, swimming. Elected Mem, Sigma Upsilon American National Univ Literary fraternity '25. Awarded Univ of the South special prize for versification. *a*: 10a Red Lion Passage, Holborn, W.C.1. *t*: Holborn 3894.

GILLIATT, George. Journalist. *n.a*: Asst Ed Daily Express. *a*: Daily Express, Fleet St. E.C.4.

GILLIES, Arthur Suttie. F.R.S.A. *b*: Broughty Ferry, Scotland 1901. *e*: Grove Acad Broughty Ferry, Dundee Inst of Art & Technology. *m*: Daisy Grant. *s*: 1.

Textile Technologist, Mang of the Jute Technological Research Labs of the Indian Govt. *Ctr*: I.C.J.C. Bulletin, Indian Farming, Journ of the Textile Inst of Gt Brit. *s.s*: Textile Technology, Treatment of Bast Fibres. *Rec*: Tennis, golf. *c*: Calcutta Swimming, Roy Calcutta Golf. *a*: 12 Regent Park, Tollygunge, PO, S, Calcutta. *T*: South 1474.

GILLIES, Marshall Macdonald, M.A.(Cantab), Ph.D. (Edin). *b*: Lesmahagow, Lanarks 1901. *e*: Eton, King's Coll Camb, Univ of Edin, Univ of Vienna, New Coll Oxf. Prof of Classics University Coll Hull. *Publ*: Appolonios Rhodius Argonautica III. *Ctr*: Classical Review, Classical Quarterly, Liverpool Annals of Archæology. *s.s*: Classics Alexandrine Literature. *a*: 131 Westbourne Ave, Hull. *T*: 7085.

GILLIES, W. King, M.A., F.R.S.E., LL.D. Schoolmaster. *Publ*: Latin of the Empire; A Latin Leader; A Latin Grammar (all jt). *a*: 12 Suffolk Rd, Edin. *t*: 42468.

GILLIGAN, A. E. R. *n.a*: Cricket Corr News-Chron. *a*: Chronicle Hse, 72—78 Fleet St, E.C.4.

GILLILAND, Adam Raymond, M.A., Ph.D., LL.D. *b*: Reinersville, Ohio 1887. *m*: Rachel Flaherty. *s*: 1. *d*: 1. Professor. *Publ*: Genetic Psychology; Psychology of Individual Differences (with Clark); General Psychology (with Morgan & Stevens); Introduction to Psychology (with Morgan). *Ctr*: Numerous Psychol journs. *s.s*: Psychology. *Rec*: Golf, hunting, fishing. *c*: University (Evanston). *a*: 2426 Marcy Ave, Evanston, Illinois, U.S.A. *T*: Uni 5238.

GILLIN, John Lewis, M.A., LL.D., B.D., Ph.D. *b*: Hudson, Iowa 1871. *e*: Grinnell Coll, Columbia Univ, Union Theol Sem. *m*: (1) Etta Shaffner, (2) Mary W. McCutcheon. *s*: 1. *d*: 1. Prof of Sociology (Emeritus 1941—). *Publ*: Poverty & Dependency; Taming the Criminal; Criminology & Penology; The Wisconsin Criminal; A History of Legislation for the Relief of the Poor in Iowa; Social Pathology; Wholesome Citizens & Spare Time; (in collab) Outlines of Sociology; An Introduction to Sociology; Social Problems; The Madison Community. *Ctr*: Amer Journ of Sociology, Journ of Criminal Law & Criminology, Marriage Hygiene, etc. *s.s*: Criminology, Penology, Social Pathology, etc. *Rec*: Gardening, golf, photography, travel. *c*: Univ & Rotary, Madison. *a*: Sterling Hall, Univ of Wisconsin, Madison 6, Wis. *T*: B 580 Ext 85.

GILLMAN, F. R. *b*: Devizes 1893. *e*: Priv. *m*: *s*: 2. Ed Evening Despatch Birm. *a*: Newspaper Hse, Corporation St, Birmingham. *T*: Central 8461.

GILLMAN, Frederick Charles. *b*: York 1898. *e*: Sidcot Sch Somerset. *m*: Constance Mary Walton. *d*: 2. Journalist. *n.a*: Northern Echo 1915—16 & '19—25, Westminster Gazette '25—28, Starmer Group Chief Reporter Lond Office '29—30, Yorks Post Lond Office '30—, Parliamentary Corr Yorks Post & Lobby Corr Leeds Mercury '35—39, Press Super B.O.A.C. '45—. *Rec*: Reading, music. *w.s*: Public Relations (R.A.F.) 1939—45. *a*: 70 East Sheen Ave, London, S.W.14. *T*: Prospect 6953.

GILMOUR, Cyril Jackson. *b*: London 1917. *e*: Sec, Edin Univ. Journalist, Public Relations Adviser & Ghost & Radio-script Writer, Mem N.U.J., Roy Inst of Internat Affairs. *n.a*: Lond Ed Hollywood Filmograph, Lond Film Corr Southern Newspapers Ltd, Features Staff Dly Sketch. *Ctr*: Various Brit & American publs. *s.s*: Films, Radio/Television. *Rec*: Study of Comparative Religions. *a*: 37 Connaught Sq, London, W.1. *T*: Paddington 8860.

GILMOUR, Elizabeth Hervey. *b*: Edin. *m*: T. Lennox Gilmour. *s*: 2. *d*: 1. *Publ*: Sons of God & Sons of Men; The Woman at the Altar; The Modern Revival & Jesus Christ. *c.t*: Forum, Seeker, etc. *s.s*: Chr psych. *c*: Sesame Imp. *a*: 49 Grosvenor St, W.1.

GILMOUR, James Pinkerton. *b*: Glas 1860. *e*: Andersonian Col Glas & Glas Sc of Pharmacy. *m*: Annie Smith Forrester. *d*: 1. Pharmacist (ret). *n.a*: Ed Chemists' & Druggists' Year Book for Scotland 1911—16, Ed Pharmaceutical Journal & Pharmacist '16—33. *Publ*: Gen Ed Champion of Liberty—Charles Bradlaugh ('33); Chapters on Dyestuffs & Photographic Chemicals in The Raw Materials of Commerce. *c.t*: Chemist & Druggist, The American Pharmaceutical Journal, The Australasian Pharmaceutical Journal, Literary Guide. *s.s*: Hist of pharmacy, anthropology. *Rec*: Boating, travel. *a*: 96 Hillway, Highgate, N.6. *t*: Mountview 1436.

GILMOUR, John Scott Lennox, M.A., F.L.S. *b*: London, 1906. *e*: Uppingham & Clare Coll Camb. *m*: Molly Berkley. *d*: 2. Dir. R.H.S. Gardens Wisley, Joint-Ed New Naturalist Series since 1942, Asst-Dir Kew Gardens '31—46 (seconded Min of Fuel & Power '40—45). *Publ*: British Botanists (Britain in Pictures); Wild Flowers of the Chalk. *Ctr*: Botanical journals. *s.s*: Botany. *Rec*: Music & book collecting. *c*: Reform, Oxford & Cambridge Musical. *a*: Director's Hse, R.H.S. Gardens, Wisley, Ripley, Surrey. *T*: Byfleet 265.

GILSON, A. Chief Sub-Ed United Metropolitan Press Group. *a*: 113 Torriano Ave, Kentish Town, N.W.5.

GILSON, Charles James Louis. *b*: Dedham 1878. *e*: Dulwich Col. *m*: Barbara Marian Ashwin. *s*: 1. *Publ*: Novels—Wild Metal; Barry Royle; The Cat & the Curate; That Woman Venus; Memoirs—Chances & Mischances; Books for Boys—The Lost Island, Treasure of Kings; The Realm of the Wizard King; etc. *c.t*: Blackwood's, Adventure (U.S.A.), Chambers's, Frontier Stories (U.S.A.), and boys' mags throughout the world. S. African War (Wounded, Des). Gt War R. Naval Div (Des). *Rec*: Golf, cricket, rugby. *a*: Palma de Mallorca

GILTINAN, Donal J. *b*: Cork 1908. Officer of Customs & Excise, Mem Authors' & Composers' Soc, Irish P.E.N., Writers' Actors, Artists & Musicians Assoc (Ireland). *n.a*: Ed Monthly Mag (Cork) '31—33, Columnist Cork Wkly Examiner '33—37, Ed Puck Fare '43. *Publ*: Plays: Bitter Rue; This Book is Banned; Mixed Blood; Revues: Anything May Happen; Trouble in Harlem; Operetta; The Impresario (with D. Macmurrough). *Ctr*: Irish Independent, Times Pictorial, Ev Herald, People, Irish Digest, Cuisle Na Tire An Cosantoir. *s.s*: Irish Theatre, Juvenile Delinquency. *Rec*: Bridge, golf, film-going. *a*: Glan-Na-Shee, Killiney Rd, Killiney, County Dublin. *T*: Dublin 84375.

GIMBLETT, Charles Leonard, M.A., M.D., M.R.C.P., F.R.C.S. Ophthalmic Surg. *Publ*: Principles & Practice of Surgery. *c.t*: Med Journs. *a*: 12 Devonshire Pl, W.1. *t*: Welbeck 1763.

GINN, J. C. *a*: Gazette Office, Palmers Green, N.13.

GINNER, Ruby. *b*: Cannes, France 1886. *e*: Priv. *m*: Alexander Kidd Dyer. Dancer, Lecturer & Teacher of Stage Arts, Founder & Pres Greek Dance Arts. *Publ*: The Revived Greek Dance. *Ctr*: Dancing Times, Dance Journ, etc. *s.s*: Ancient Greek Dance & Drama: the reconstruction of these arts for modern educ & stage art. *Rec*: Study of the arts of ancient civilization, reading, photography. *a*: St Corentin, Boscastle, Cornwall.

GINSBERG, Morris, M.A., D.Litt. Prof of Sociology Lon Sc of Econ. *n.a*: Jt Ed Sociological Review. *Publ*: Psychology of Society; Studies in Sociology; The Material Culture & Social Institutions of the Simpler Peoples, etc. *a*: Three Oaks, Birdshill Rd, Oxshott, Surrey.

GINSBURG, BENEDICT WILLIAM: barrister-at-law; b. Liverpool, Eng., Oct., 1859; s. Christian David (LL.D.), and Margaret Ryley (Crosfield) G.; educ. Charterhouse, St. Catharine's Coll. (Cambridge), Inner Temple (London); DEGREES: B.A. (1880), M.A., L.L.M. (1885), LL.D. (1894), all Cambridge; unmarried. AUTHOR: Hints on the Legal Duties of Shipmasters (4th edit.); War Speeches, 1914-1917. Editor: Journ. Royal Statistical Soc., 1898-1904; Royal Navy Journ., 1908-10. Contributor to Encyclop. Brit. (10th and 11th edits.); Dict. Nat. Biography; serials on legal and shipping topics. General character of writing: technical-legal. Worked in War Trade Intelligence Dept., 1915-18; memb. Northern Circuit since 1883. Relig. denom., Church of England. CLUBS: Devonshire, Ranelagh, Pegasus. OFFICE: 12 King's Bench Walk, Temple, E. C. 4. HOME: 6 Gledhow Gardens, S. W. 5, London, Eng.

GIPSON, Lawrence Henry, B.A.(Oxon), Ph.D., Hon.D. Litt(Temple Univ), F.R.Hist.S. *b*: Greeley, Col 1880. *e*: Idaho Univ, Oxf Univ (Rhodes Scholar), Yale Univ (Farnham Fellow), Chicago Univ. *m*: Jeannette Reed. Research Prof of History Lehigh Univ Bethlehem, Pa Pres Pennsylvania Hist Assoc 1939—42. *Publ*: The British Empire before the American Revolution, Vols I-VI; Jared Ingersoll; Lewis Evans; The Moravian White River Indian Mission; Studies in Connecticut Colonial Taxation; etc. *Ctr*: Amer Hist Review, Journ of Modern Hist, Penn Hist, N.Y. Times Book-Rev, Amer Oxonian, etc. *s.s*: The Old British Empire 1750 —1775. *Rec*: Hiking, gardening. *c*: Franklin Inn (Philadelphia). *a*: Rotha, Panther Rd, Rydal, Pennsylvania. *T*: Ogontz 3125.

GIRALDO-JARAMILLO, Gabriel. *b*: Manizales, Colombia 1916. *e*: Nat Univ Bogota. *m*: Julia Arciniegas. *s*: 1. General Consul of Colombia in Switzerland, Mem of Nat Acad of Hist, Bogota. *Publ*: La Printura en Colombia; La Minitura en Colombia; Los Tratados De Montevideo de 1904; Gregorio Vasquez Ceballos; Las Acuarelas De La Comision Corografica; Derecho Diplomatico. *Ctr*: El Tiempo, Cromos, America Indigena, Boletin De La Acad De Historia. *s.s*: Art, Internat Law. *c*: Rotary. *a*: Geneva: 29 Avenue de Miremont. *T*: 5-7494.

GIRALDUS. See **O'Driscoll, Gerald John.**

GIRDLESTONE, Cuthbert Morton, M.A., Lic.-es-L. (Paris). *b*: Bovey Tracey, Devon 1895. *e*: Southey Hall, Worthing, Ecole de L'Immaculée Conception Pau, Lycée Bernadotte Pau, Sorbonne Paris, Trin Coll Camb. *m*: Anne Marie Micheletti. *d*: 2. Prof of French Durham Univ, King's Coll Newcastle-upon-Tyne. *Publ*. Dreamer & Striver, The Poetry of Frédéric Mistral; Mozart et ses concertos pour piano. *Ctr*: Monthly Musical Record, Music & Letters, Durham Univ Journal, Archæological Journal, Listener. *a*: King's College, University of Durham, Newcastle-upon-Tyne 1.

GIRDLESTONE, Rev. F. S. P. L. *a*: Old Church Vicarage, Smethwick, Birm.

GIRDLESTONE, Gathorne Robert, M.A., B.M., B.Ch, F.R.C.S. Consulting Orthopædic Surg. *Publ*: The Care & Cure of Crippled Children (with Mrs. Hey Groves); The Care & Cure of Crippled Children (2nd edn); Tuberculosis of the Hip. *c.t*: Brit Journ of Surgery, B.M.J., Lancet, Journ of Bone & Joint Surg, Amer Journ of Surg, etc. *a*: The Red Hse, Old Rd, Headington, Oxf. *t*: 6800.

GIRVIN, Brenda. *b*: London. *e*: Wycombe Abbey Sch. Playwright & Author. Plays produced (in collaboration with Miss Monica Cosens) Madame Plays Nap; The Red Umbrella; Miss Black's Son; Wee Men. *Ctr*. All principal London newspapers & periodicals. *Rec*: Gardening, swimming, photography. *a*: Venice Yard Hse, Smith Sq, London, S.W.1; & Cock Rock, Croyde, Nth Devon.

GISSING, A. *a*: Bloxham, nr Banbury, Oxf.

GITTINGS, Dr. F. C. B. Ophthalmic Surgeon, Surgeon Capt R.N. (ret). *c.t*: R.N. Med Journ & Journ of Hygiene, etc. *a*: 15 Brading Ave, Southsea.

GITTINS, Anthony. Writer. *c.t*: Tatler, Sketch, Evening Standard, etc. *a*: c/o Robert Sommerville, Granville Hse, Arundel St, W.C.2. *t*: Temple Bar 8951.

GIUSEPPI, Montague Spencer, I.S.O., F.S.A. *b*: Hammersmith 1869. *e*: Kensington & King's Coll Schs, Priv. *m*: Emilie Louise Hardinge. *s*: 2. *d*: 1. Asst Keeper Public Records (ret). *n.a*: Ed of the Calendar of Scottish State Papers in the Public Record Office & Brit Museum. *Publ*: Guide to the manuscripts preserved in the Public Record Office, Vol I Legal, Vol II State Papers & Departmental; Calendar of Patent Rolls, Philip & Mary, 4 Vols; Calendar of Salisbury MSS; Guide to Surrey Records in the Public Record Office; History of Surrey Industries. *Ctr*: Publs of Roy Hist Soc, Antiquaries, Archæological Inst, etc. *s.s*: Historical & Antiquarian Research (espec Archives). *c*: Cocked Hat. *a*: 72 Burlington Ave, Kew Gdns, Surrey. *T*: 2749.

GIUSEPPI, Paul Eugene Hedwige, M.B., C.M.(Edin), F.R.E.S. *b*: St Joseph, Trinidad B.W.I. 1868. *e*: St Thomas's Sch, St Mary's Coll Port-of-Spain Trinidad, Sch of Med of Roy Colls of Edin, Edin Univ. *m*: (1) Grace Mann-Mackinnon, (2) Sybil Wyatt. *s*: 1. *d*: 1. Journalist, Lecturer, Writer. *Publ*: Who Made God?; Trinidad in Retrospect; Let's Talk This Over; How the Virgin Became a Mother. *Ctr*: Passing Show, Chambers's Journ, Wkly Scotsman. *s.s*: Philosophy & Science. *Rec*: Reading, research. *c*: Roy Emp Soc. *a*: Shangrila, 86 Moring Rd, Upper Tooting, London, S.W.17. *T*: Balham 5430.

GIUSEPPI, Paul Leon, M.D., F.R.C.S. *c.t*: Bulletin of Alpine Garden Soc, B.M.J., Clinical Journ, Bulletin of Roy Soc of Med, etc. *a*: Trevose, Felixstowe, Suffolk. *t*: 123.

GIVEN, Dr. D. H. C. Surgeon-Capt R.N. (ret). Fell Roy Soc Med, late Res Med Supt Norwood Sanatorium for treatment of Inebriety & Drug Addiction. *a*: 16 Sundridge Ave, Bromley, Kent.

GIVEN, E. C., C.B.E., M.InstC.E., M.I.MechE. Cons Engineer. *c.t*: Various n/ps & periodicals. *a*: Heatherleigh, Pelworth Rd, S.W.16.

GLADSTONE, ARTHUR (pen name: Arthur Stone): merchant, author; b. Edgbastion, Eng., April, 1861; s. Thomas and Mary Gibbon (Whitfield) G.; educ. Lancaster, Owen's Coll. (Manchester); m. Mary Louisa Stokes. AUTHOR: Poems, 1924; Poems, 1925; Charity Ball, Aunt's Will, 1925-26; Dialogue in Dabs, 1925-26; The Girdle of Narcissus, 1925-26; Poems, 1926, Parts I and II; The Letters of a Society Woman, 1927. Contributor to Home and Abroad; Writer's Own Mag., Poet's Scroll, Amer. Poetry Mag., Poetry Rev., Peverel Monthly. General character of writing: poems, essays, fiction. Began first book of verse March, 1923, and completed same before Christmas. Has been writing at same rate ever since. Life Mem. Soc. Academique d'Histoire International, Paris. Relig. denom., Unitarian. OFFICE: 90 Dale End, Birmingham. HOME: Eastcote Grange, Hampton-in-Arden, Warwickshire. Eng.

GLADSTONE, Gareth Page, M.B., B.S., M.R.C.S., L.R.C.P. *c.t*: Brit Journ Experimental Path. *a*: 14 Casewick Rd, W. Norwood, S.E.27.

GLADSTONE, H. B., M.D., C.M. *Publ*: Clinical Observations on Infant Feeding & Nutrition. *a*: 109 Mayow Rd, Sydenham, S.E.26.

GLADSTONE, VISCOUNT HERBERT J O H N: Privy Councillor; b. 12 Downing St., Whitehall (London), Eng., June 7, 1856; s. W. E. and Catherine (Glynne) G.; educ. Eton Coll., Univ. Coll. (Oxford); DEGREES: M.A. (Oxford), L.L.D. (South African Univ.); m. Dorothy Mary Paget, Nov. 2, 1901. AUTHOR: W. E. Gladstone, 1918; After Thirty Years, 1928. General character of writing: biographical. Relig. denom., Church of England. CLUBS: Reform, National Liberal (both Bath, Eng.). HOME: 4 Cleveland Square, St. James, London and Dane End, Ware, Hertfordshire, Eng.

GLADSTONE, Sir Hugh, J.P., D.L., M.A.(Cantab), F.Z.S., F.R.S.E. *b*: London 1877. *e*: Eton & Camb. *m*: Cecil Talbot. *s*: 3. *d*: 1. *Publ*: Birds of Dumfriesshire ; The Fauna of Dumfriesshire ; Record Bags & Shooting Records ; Shooting with Surtees. *Ctr*: British Birds Mag, Scottish Naturalist. *s.s*: Ornithology. *Rec*: Shooting. *c*: Bath, New (Edinburgh). *a*: Capenoch, Penpont, Dumfries. *T*: Thornhill 261.

GLADSTONE, Reginald John, M.D., F.R.C.S., D.P.H. Recorder, Anatomical Soc of G.B. & Ire. *c.t*: Annals of Surgery, Archives of Middx Hosp, etc. *a*: 22 Court Lane Gdns, Dulwich, S.E.21. *t*: Sydenham 6774.

GLAISE von HORSTENAU, Edmund. *b*: Braunau am Inn Austria 1882. *e*: Military Sc & Vienna Univ. Keeper of Archives. *Publ*: Heimkehr Tirols 1914; Erzherzog Franz Ferdinand '22; Die Katastrophe ('23) (Eng & Italian Eds); Oesterreichs-Ungarns letzter Kreig '14-18 (7 vols). *c.t*: Neue Österr Rundschau, Berliner Monatshefte zur Erforschung der Kriegsursachen, Mil Tech press. *s.s*: History, politics, military. *Rec*: Riding, swimming. *c*: Katholische Akademikergeme inschaft Pres '32-34. Verein der katholischen Edelleute. *a*: Stiftgasse 2, Vienna VII. *t*: B. 34-5-36.

GLAISTER, J. Norman. *s.s*: Psychology & educ. *a*: 2 Devonshire Pl, W.1.

GLAISTER, John, M.D., D.Sc, F.R.S.E., J.P. *b*: Glas 1892. *e*: Glas H.S. & Glas Univ. *m*: Isobel R. Lindsay. *d*: 2. Regius Prof of Forensic Med Glas Univ. & Medico-Legal Exam in Crown Cases Glas & W. of Scotland. *Publ*: Co-Author, Recent Advances in Forensic Medicine; Hairs of Mammalia (Egyptian Govt); Manual of Legal Medicine; etc. *s.s*: Scientific Aspects of Criminology. Formerly Prof of Forensic Med, The Univ of Egypt, Cairo. Medico-Legal Cons to Egyptian Govt. *a*: 5 Kew Terr, Glas, W.2. *t*: W. 5733.

GLANVILLE, Edythe Mary, B.A., LL.B., C.B.E. *b*: 1876. *e*: Alexandra Col Dublin. *m*: Frank Henry Glarville. *s*: 1. *Publ*: The Pinnacle (1926); many short stories. *s.s*: Hist, const law. 1st woman to be Vice-Chm Metro Div Nat Unionist Assoc. *Rec*: Travel, gardening. *c*: Dickens Fell, Soc of Authors. *a*: 8 Newton Gve, Bedford Pk, W.4.

GLANVILLE, Stephen Ranulph Kingdon, M.B.E., F.B.A. *b*: London 1900. *e*: Marlborough & Lincoln Coll Oxf. *m*: Ethel Mary Chubb. *d*: 2. Herbert Thompson Prof Egyptology Camb Univ. *Publ*: Catalogue of Demotic Papyri in the British Museum I ; (in collab) Mural Painting of El Amarneh ; Daily Life in Ancient Egypt ; The Legacy of Egypt (ed & ctr) ; Studies presented to F. Griffith (ed & ctr); The Egyptians. *Ctr*: Journ of Egyptian Archæology, Journ of Royal Asiatic Soc, Nature, Antiquity, etc. *s.s*: Egyptology. *Rec*: Bird watching, etc. *c*: Athenæum. *a*: King's College Cambridge. *T*: 55011.

GLAS, Norbert, M.D., L.R.C.P., M.R.C.S. *b*: Vienna 1897. *e*: Univ of Vienna. *Publ*: Formensprache Des Gesichtes; Kinderkrankheiten als Entwicklungesstufeudes Menschen ; Adolescence & Diseases of Puberty ; Five Commentaries to Grimm's Fairy Tales. *a*: San Remo, Grange Rd, Gloucester. *T*: 2354.

GLASGOW, Ellen Anderson. *b*: Virginia 1874. *e*: Priv. Author. *Publ*: The Descendant (1897); The Voice of the People (1900); The Freeman, & Other Poems; The Deliverance; They Stooped to Folly; The Romance of a Plain Man; Virginia; Life & Gabrielle; The Builders; Shadowy Third; Barren Ground; The Sheltered Life ('32); etc. Mem Phi Beta Kappa. Mem Nat Inst Arts & Letters. Doctor of Lit N. Carolina Univ. *a*: Richmond, Virginia, U.S.A.

GLASGOW, George, B.A. *b*: Bolton 1891. *e*: Bolton Gr Sch & Manch Univ. *m*: Una Geraldine Ridgeway. *n.a*: Diplomatic Corr Observer 1920—42, Asst-Ed The New Europe '16—20, Author Foreign Affairs section Contemporary Rev '23—, Spec Corr Manch Guardian '20—28, l'Europe Nouvelle '20—26, Prager Presse '21—38. *Publ*: The Minoans ; Ronald Burrows, a Memoir ; MacDonald as Diplomatist ; From Dawse to Locarno ; The Scottish Investment Trust Companies ; Continental Statesmen ; The Dupe as Hero ; The English Investment Trust Companies ; General Strikes & Road Transport ; Glasgow's Guide to Investment Trust Companies ; Peace with Gangsters ? ; Diplomacy & God ; etc. *Ctr*: Cath Times, New Republic, Neue Freie Presse, Vienna, 13th & 14th Ency Brit. *s.s*: Diplomacy, Finance. *a*: 12 Bessborough Rd, Roehampton, London, S.W.15. *T*: Putney 1365.

GLASGOW AND GALLOWAY, Bishop of, (See HOW, Rt. Rev. John Charles Halland, Hon.D.D.(Glas)).
GLASGOW, Edwin. *b*: Liverpool. *e*: Wadham Coll Oxf. *m*: Eva C. Postance. *s*: 1. *d*: 2. Late Keeper National Gallery. *Publ*: Sketches of Wadham College, Oxford ; Sketches of Magdalen College, Oxford ; The Painters' Eye. *a*: Charlbury, Oxford. *T*: Charlbury 49.

GLASPELL, Susan. *b*: Davenport, Iowa 1882. *e*: Davenport Public Schs, Drake & Chicago Univs. *m*: George Cram Cook. Writer. *Publ*: Brook Evans ; The Morning is Near Us ; Judd Rankin's Daughter ; Ambrose Holt & Family; Fidelity ; The Glory of the Conquered ; The Road to the Temple (Biog) ; (Plays) Alison's House ; Inheritors ; The Verge ; Trifles. *a*: Provincetown, Massachusetts, U.S.A.

GLASS, E. J. G., F.R.C.S. Surgeon. *n.a*: Abstracting Staff Journ of Laryngology. *a*: 36 Regent St, Nottingham.

GLASS, Frederick Charles. *b*: Enfield, London 1871. *e*: Orsett Col; City of London Middle Cl Sc. *m*: Fanny Crawley. *s*: 5. *d*: 2. Bible Soc agent. *Publ*: Through the Heart of Brazil ; A Thousand Miles in a Dog-Cart ; Adventures with the Bible in Brazil ; Through Brazilian Jungleland. *c.t*: Wide Wld, S. Amer, The Christian. *s.s*: The Bible in Brazil; The Indians of Brazil. Started with Dly Chronicle when 16. Assayer on chief gold mine in Brazil. Mem of the 1913 Putumayo Expedition to the N.W. Indians. *Rec*: Gardening, chess, motoring. *a*: Garanhuns, Pernambuco, Brazil.

GLASSER, Otto. *b*: Saarbrücken, Germany 1895. *e*: Heidelberg & Freiburg Univs. *m*: Emmy von Ehrenberg. *d*: 1. Dir dept Radiation Research, Cleveland Clinic Foundation. *n.a*: Staff Strahlentherapie Berlin 1929, Assoc Ed Radiology St Paul '31, Staff Radiologische Rundschau Berlin '33, Ed The Science of Radiology Springfield '33. *Publ*: Wilhelm Conrad Röntgen und die Geschichte der Roentgenstrahlen ('31); Wilhelm Conrad Röntgen and the Early History of the Roentgen Rays ('33); The Genealogy of the Roentgen Rays ('33); etc. *c.t*: Strahlentherapie Berlin, American Journ of Roentgenology, Radiology, Journ Optical Soc of America, Proc Nat Academy of Sciences Washington, etc. *s.s*: Biophysical research. Biophysicist Howard Kelly Hosp Baltimore '22-24, Asst Prof of Biophysics N.Y. Post-Grad Med Sc '25-27. Naturalized American. War Service (German). *c*: Fel American Assoc for Advancement of Sci, Mem American Roentgen Soc, etc. *Rec*: Book collecting, swimming. *a*: 2040 East 93rd St, Cleveland Clinic Foundation, Cleveland, Ohio, U.S.A. *t*: Cedar 6800.

GLASSTONE, Samuel, D.Sc, PhD.(Lon). *b*: Lon 1897. *e*: Cent Foundation Sc & Lon Univ. *m*: Violette Frederica Collingwood, B.A.(Oxon). Lecturer. *Publ*: Chemistry in Daily Life; The Electrochemistry of Solutions; Recent Advances in Physical Chemistry. *s.s*: Popular Sci, Phys Chem, Electrochem. *c*: F.InstChem, F.ChemSoc, Mem Faraday Soc. *a*: 15 Northumberland Rd, Sheffield 10. *t*: 62243.

GLAUERT, Hermann, F.R.S., F.R.AeS., M.A. *b*: Sheffield 1892. *e*: K. E. VII Sc, Sheffield & Trin Col Cam. *m*: Muriel Barker, B.Sc, M.A. *s*: 2. *d*: 1. Princ Sci Officer Roy Aircraft Establishment, Farnboro'. *Publ*: Elements of Aerofoil & Airscrew Theory. *s.s*: Aeronautics. *a*: Glenhurst, 6 Reading Rd, Farnboro', Hants. *t*: 369.

GLAYEBROOK, Sir Richard Tetley, K.C.B., K.C.V.O., F.R.S. Dir Nat Physical Lab (ret). *Publ*: Text Book of Practical Physics (with Sir W. N. Shaw); Text Book of Physical Optics; Text Books Mechanics, Heat, Optics & Electricity; (Ed) Dictionary Appied Physics; Clerk Maxwell & Modern Physics. *c.t*: Nature, Philos Mag, Times, etc. *a*: Ballards Oak, Limpsfield, Surrey. *t*: 114.

GLAZEBROOK, Sir R. T. Chm Aeronautical Research Cmt, Dir Dept Aeronautics Imperial Col Technology. *c.t*: Ency Britannica. *a*: c/o Ency Britannica Co Ltd, 80-86 Regent St, W.1.

GLEAVE, Walter Stanley. *b*: Southport 1895. *e*: Christ Church Southport. *n.a*: Chief Reporter Southport Guardian. *s.s*: Sport, floriculture. *a*: 19 Cobden Rd, Southport. *t*: 4867.

GLEAVE, William Arthur. *b*: Warrington. Mang Dir & Ed-in-Chief Southern Newspapers Ltd. *Rec*. Golf & motoring. *c*: Lon Press, Roy Southampton Yacht. Mem Counc N/p Soc. *a*: 70 Westwood Rd, Southampton.

GLEDHILL, Frank Alfred. *b*: York 1898. *e*: Mun Sc Scarboro'. *m*: Edith Eleanor Nelson. *d*: 1. Journalist. *n.a*: Reporter, Scarboro' & Dist n/p Co Ltd 1914-32, Scarboro' & Dist Repres Northern Echo '32–. *s.s*: Sport. War Service R.A.F. *c*: Dir Scarboro' F.C. *a*: 12 Av Rd, Scarboro'. *t*: 1175.

GLEESON, Gertrude, B.A. *b*: Aberdeen 1900. *e*: Leytonstone High Sc & U.C.L. Writer & Journalist.

Publ: The Zoological Gardens; A Zoo Holiday. *c.t*: Scotsman, Evening News, Evening Standard, Glas Evening Times, The Queen, Daily Telegraph, Daily Express, Birm Mail, Morning Post, Glasgow Herald, etc. *s.s*: Humorous sketches, articles about animals, articles on engineering, building & allied topics, boys' adventure stories, popular scientific articles, fiction. *Rec*: Lawn tennis, badminton, swimming, music. *c*: Mem Soc of Authors, Artists & Playwrights. *a*: Room 54, 12 & 13 Henrietta St, Covent Garden, W.C.2.

GLEGG, Alexander Lindsay, J.P., A.M.I.E.E., A.C.G.I. *b*: Lond 1883. *e*: Dulwich Col, City & Guilds Institute. *m*: Lilian Grace Kilvington Olney. *s*: 2. Engineer. *Publ*: Life with a Capital L; Youth with a Capital Why. *s.s*: Religion. Chm, Messrs. Masson Scott & Co Ltd. Director, The Linoleum Manufacturing Co Ltd, The Barry & Staines Linoleum Co Ltd. *Rec*: Golf, tennis. Ex-Pres National Sunday School Union. Hon Supt Down Lodge Hall Mission, Wandsworth. *a*: Birchstone, Coombe Park, Kingston Hill, Surrey. *t*: Kingston 5983.

GLEICHEN, Major Gen. Lord Edward, K.C.V.O., C.B., C.M.G., D.S.O. Major-Gen (ret). *Publ*: With the Camel Corps up the Nile; With the Mission to Menelik; London's Open-Air Statuary; The Doings of the 15th Inf'y Brigade; Chronology of the War; A Guardsman's Memories. *c.t*: Times, Contemporary, Blackwood's Mag, Chambers's Mag, etc. *a*: 35 Catherine St, Buckingham Gate, S.W.1. *t*: Victoria 2815.

GLEN, Alexander Richard, D.S.C. & Bar. *b*: Glasgow 1912. *e*: Fettes & Balliol Oxford. *m*: Baroness Zora de Collaert. Poland Med, (Clasp Arctic 1935—36), Knt of St Olav, Norwegian War Cross, Czecho-Slovak Mil Cross. *Publ*: Young Man in the Arctic; Under the Pole Star. *Ctr*: Times, Weekly Illustrated press. *s.s*: Polar Exploration, European Politics. *Rec*: Ski-ing, sailing. *c*: Travellers, Junior Carlton, Explorers New York. *a*: 6 Trevor Place, London, S.W. *T*: Kensington 5593.

GLEN, William. Editor and proprietor. *Publ*: Thistle Guide to Highlands; Grangemouth Directory. *a*: Advertiser Office, Grangemouth.

GLENDAY, Roy, M.C., M.A., LL.B. *b*: Sutton Coldfield 1889. *e*: Brighton Coll & Emmanual Coll Camb. *m*: Pamela Rogers. *d*: 1. Barrister, Econ Adv & Dir Fed of Brit Industries, Mem Counc Roy Stats Soc. *Publ*: Passing of Free Trade; Economic Consequences of Progress; Future of Economic Society. *Ctr*: Times, etc. *s.s*: Economic & Social Questions of all kinds. *Rec*: Ski-ing, golf. *c*: United Univs, Authors. *a*: Lawyers Cott, Magpie Lane, Coleshill, Amersham, Bucks. *T*: Amersham 1262.

GLENISTER, R. A. *n.a*: Ed West Herts Post. *a*: Sunnycroft, Hampermill Lne, Watford.

GLENN, Isa. *b*: Atlanta, Georgia, U.S.A. 1888. *e*: Priv. *m*: Brig-Gen S. J. Bayard Schindel (decd). *s*: 1. Novelist and short story writer. *Publ*: Heat (1926); Little Pitchers; Transport; East of Eden; Mr. Darlington's Dangerous Age ('33). *c.t*: Scribner's Mag, Century Mag, Harper's Bazaar, etc. *s.s*: Fiction. *Rec*: Reading detective stories. *a*: c/o Brandt & Brandt, Washington, D.C., U.S.A.

GLENNIE, Donald. *b*: London 1919. *e*: Lindisfarne Coll. Free-lance Journalist 1939. *n.a*: Features Dept London General Press 1937—38, Feature Writer World Service Ltd '38. *Ctr*: Various Nat & Prov. *s.s*: Criminology & Penology, Educ, Social & Hist Research. *Rec*: Motoring, tennis, lecturing. *a*: 6 Winton Ave, Westcliff, Southend-on-Sea. *T*: Southen 45990.

GLENTOFT, Valborg Emilie. *b*: Copenhagen, Denmark 1889. *m*: Carl Glentoft. *s*: 1. *d*: 2. *Publ*: En Stribe Soli Morket; Altid paa Stikkerne; Kun en Fattigtos Foljeton i Social-Demokraten; etc. *Ctr*: Various. *a*: Vendersgade 21, 1 Sal, Copenhagen K, Danmark. *T*: Byen 206y.

GLICK, Carl Cannon, B.S. *b*: Marshalltown, Iowa 1890 *e*: North Western Univ Evanston Ill. *m*: Sue Ann Wilson. Writer, Community Theatre Dir, Teacher of of English & Drama. *n.a*: Springfield (Mass) Republican 1931—40, Book Reviewer, New York Times & Philadelphia Inquirer '46—47. *Publ*: Shake Hands with the Dragon; Double Ten; Three Times I Bow; The Laughing Buddha; (in collab) Swords of Silence; Curtains Going up; (Juvenile) Oswald's Pet Dragon; Micky, the Horse that Volunteered. *Ctr*: Reader's Digest, Coronet, Esquire, Collier's, This Week, Your Life, China Monthly, The Bookman, Smart Set, etc. *s.s*: The Chinese in America. *Rec*: Music, books. *a*: 21 Bethune St, New York 14, N.Y., U.S.A. *T*: Watkins 9-3344.

GLOAG, John. *b*: Lon 1896. *e*: Self-ed. *m*: Gertrude Mary Ward. *s*: 1. *d*: 1. Art Dir F. C. Pritchard Wood & Partners Ltd. *n.a*: Art Ed The Cabinet Maker, 1922—26. Ed 1927. Ed Year Books of Design & Industs Assoc '22—27. *Publ*: Simple Furnishing & Arrangement ('21); Time, Taste & Furniture ('25); Men & Buildings ('31); English Furniture ('34); etc.; Home Life in History, in collab with C. Walker ('27); Tomorrow's Yesterday ('32); The New Pleasure ('33); Board Room Ballads ('33); Winter's Youth ('34); Industrial Art Explained ('34). *c.t*: Architectural Review, Architect's Journal, etc. *s.s*: Indus, design, archit, typography. Talks from B.B.C. on Indus Design, & architecture. *c*: Mem Archit Assoc; The Arts. *Rec*: Walking. *a*: The Mall, Sheen Common, S.W.14. *t*: Prospect 4530.

GLOVER, Archie. Journalist. *n.a*: Shipley Express 1895, Bradford Telegraph & Argus 1901, Ch Rep Leeds Daily News '02, Yorkshire Evening Post '04, News Ed Yorkshire Evening Post '29. Mem Counc J.I. *a*: Albion Hse, Spencer Pl, Leeds. *t*: Leeds 41367.

GLOVER, Denis James Matthews, D.S.C., B.A. *b*: Dunedin, N.Z. 1912. *e*: Christ's Coll, Canterbury Univ Coll. *m*: Mary Granville. *s*: 1. Printer & Publisher. *Publ*: The Wind & the Sand (Poems); Cold Tongue (Poems); D. Day; Thirteen Poems; The Arraignment of Paris; Three Short Stories. *Ctr*: New Writing, Tomorrow, Landfall. *s.s*: Typography. *Rec*: Yachting, books. *c*: Canterbury Officers. *w.s*: Lieut R.N.Z.N.V.R. '39—45. *a*: 10 Aranoni Track, Clifton, Christchurch, N.Z.

GLOVER, Edward. *b*: Lesmahagow, Scotland 1888, *e*: Lesmahagow, Glas Univ & Berlin. Dir Psychopathic Clinic Lond, Formerly Dir of Research Lond Clinic of Psycho-analysis. *n.a*: Ed Research Monographs, Internat Journ of Psycho-analysis. *Publ*: War, Sadism & Pacifism; Psycho-analysis; Investigation of the Technique of Psycho-analysis; The Technique of Psychoanalysis; The Dangers of Being Human; The Psychology of Fear & Courage; The Diagnosis & Treatment of Delinquency; Basic Mental Concepts. *Ctr*: Internat Journ of Psycho-analysis, Brit Journ of Med Psychology, Psycho Analytic Quarterly, Horizon, World Rev, Listener, B.M.J., Lancet, etc. *s.s*: Psycho-analysis, Social Psychology, Sociology, War Delinquency. *a*: 18 Wimpole St, London, W.1. *T*: Langham 4146.

GLOVER, Sir Harold Matthew. Kt. *e*: Worcester Roy Gr Sch & Magdalen Coll Oxf. Indian Forest Service (ret). *Publ*: Erosion in the Punjab—Its causes & Cure; Soil Erosion. *Ctr*: Many Forestry journs. *s.s*: Forestry. *a*: Ombersley, Worcestershire. *T*: 292.

GLOVER, J. A., O.B.E., M.D., F.R.C.P., D.P.H. Senr Med Officer Bd of Educ. *Publ*: Official Reports on Cerebro-spinal fever, rheumatism; Articles on Scarlet fever; Tonsilitis; etc. *a*: 51 Netherhall Gardens, N.W.3.

GLOVER, James, M.A.(Cantab), M.InstC.E. *b*: L'pool 1859. *e*: L'pool Collegiate, Corpus Christi Col Cam (Math Tripos). *m*: Charlotte Elizabeth Cooper. *s*: 1 (dec). *d*: 2. Civil Engineer. I/c of Construction of large public works Contracts. Railways, Waterworks, Docks, etc. *Publ*: Formulæ for Railway Crossings and Switches; Income Tax Reform: a Simple, Practical and Scientific Income Tax. Transition Curves for Railways (Proceedings Inst of Civil Engineers). *c.t*: Various. *s.s*: The Church of England. Basic and Essential Agriculture. Former Mem National Church Assem. Former Mem of the Lancs County Counc. *Rec*: Yachting, music, etc. *c*: Royal Mersey Yacht, The Farmers (Lon). *a*: Lowton House, Lowton, Lancs.

GLOVER, JIMMY (James Mackey Glover): musical composer and author; b. Dublin, Ireland, June, 1861; s. James Mackey and Mary Glover (added Glover to surname, 1880); educ. Trinity Coll. (Dublin), Belvidere Coll. (Catholic Univ.), Lycée, Caen (France); m. Kitty Collins. AUTHOR: Jimmy Glover, His Book, 1911; Jimmy Glover, His Friends, 1913; Hims, Ancient and Modern, Being the third book of Jimmy Glover, 1926; The Theatrical Manager's Handbook; author of hundreds of songs, dances, ballet music, etc. Editor: Theatrical Managers' Journal, The Concert World. Contributor to Daily Mail, Daily Telegraph (both London); music critic on Sun, Evening News (London); on staff Liverpool Express, The Stage (oLndon). General character of writing: music and on musical matters. Relig. denom., Roman Catholic. CLUBS: National Liberal, Eccentric (both London). OFFICE: 52 Shaftesbury Ave., London. HOME: The Albany, Hanstings, Eng.

GLOVER, John Halcott. *b*: Cambridge 1877. Author. *Publ*: (Plays) Three Comedies; Wat Tyler & Other plays; The Second Round; (Novels) Both Sides of the Blanket; Louise & Mr. Tudor; Louise in London; Morning Pride; Dead Man's House. *a*: c/o Curtis Brown Ltd, 6 Henrietta St, London, W.C.2.

GLOVER, Terrot Reaveley. Lecturer St John's Col Camb. *n.a*: Weekly Articles in Daily News 1922-28. *Publ*: Life & Letters in the Fourth Century; The Conflict of Religions in the Early Roman Empire; Greek Byways. *a*: 67 Glisson Rd Cambridge. *t*: 125.

GLUCK, Sheldon, A.M., LL.M., Ph.D. *b*: Poland 1896. *e*: Georgetown Univ Law Sch, George Washington Univ, Harvard. *m*: Eleanor Touroff. *d*: 1. Prof Criminal Law & Criminology Harvard Univ. *n.a*: Ed Bd Journ of Crim Law & Criminology, Mental Hygiene, Federal Probation. *Publ*: Mental Disorder & the Criminal Law; War Criminals: Their Prosecution & Punishment; The Nuremberg Trial & Aggressive War; Crime & Justice; (with E. T. Glueck) Five Hundred Criminal Careers; One Thousand Juvenile Delinquents; Five Hundred Delinquent Women; After-Conduct of Discharged Prisoners. *Ctr*: Harvard Law Rev, Amer Law Rev, Yale Law Journ, etc. *s.s*: Criminology, etc. *Rec*: Foreign travel. *c*: Harvard, Harvard Faculty. *a*: Continental Hotel, 25 Garden St, Cambridge, Mass, U.S.A. *T*: Trowbridge 4666.

GLYDER, John. *b*: Croydon. *Publ*: Compulsory Wife; Compulsory Husband; Rising Generation; Sleeping Beauty; Adam & Eve; Jill in the Box; Half Horse; Any Port; Unlucky Dip; Lady in the Moon; Mixed Infant; Midsummer Night; Wet & Windy; Ungentle Guest; etc. *Ctr*: Strand. *s.s*: Humorous Novels & Short Stories. *Rec*: Writing. *a*: 17 York Rd, Weybridge. *T*: Weybridge 3561.

GLYN, Elinor. See Clayton Glyn, Elinor.

GLYN, Margaret Henrietta. *b*: Ewell 1865. Music & Lit. *Publ*: The Rhythmic Conception of Music (1907); Editions of Virginal Music (for piano) '22–28; Theory of Musical Evolution (in prep, '34). *c.t*: N.Y. Musical Courier, The Beacon, The Musical Standard. *s.s*: Tudor virginal & organ music; exec artist on old keyboard instruments. *c*: Pioneer. *a*: The Well Hse, Ewell, Surrey.

GOAD, H. E., M.A. Dir British Inst Florence. *Publ*: The Making of the Corporate State. *a*: c/o Messrs Christophers, 22 Berners St, W.1.

GODBER, Amy Joyce, M.A., F.R.Hist.S. *b*: Kempston, Beds 1906. *e*: Bedford H Sch, Univs of Oxf & Munich. County Archivist to Beds County Council. *n.a*: Hon Ed Beds Hist Record Soc 1946—. *Publ*: The Cartulary of Bushmead Priory (with G. H. Fowler). *Ctr*: Beds Times, Beds Mag. *s.s*: Local Hist of Beds. *a*: Willington Manor, Bedford. *T*: Cardington 249.

GODBER, Noël Lambert. *b*: Nottingham 1881. *e*: Ellesmere Coll. *m*: Betty Brunsdon. *s*: 1. *Publ*: Amazing Spectacles; Keep it Dark; Twin Bedsteads; Don't do it Doctor; How dare you Sir; Miss Barelegs *a*: 25 Rivermead Court, Hurlingham, London, S.W.6. *T*: Renown 4761.

GODDARD, Rev. Edward Hungerford, F.S.A. *b*: Wilts 1854. *e*: Winchester Col & B.N.C. Oxf. *m*: Elizabeth Annica Bradford. *s*: 1. *d*: 2. Vicar of Clyffe Pypard, Wilts. *n.a*: Hon Sec Wilts Arch & Nat Hist Soc, & Ed Wilts Arch Mag '90—. *Publ*: Wiltshire Words: A Glossary of Words Used in the County of Wiltshire (Jt Author with G. E. Dartnell '93); Wiltshire Bibliography. *c.t*: Wilts Arch Mag, papers on Wilts antiquities, etc. *s.s*: Archaeology, topography, botany, etc. *Rec*: Gardening. *a*: Clyffe Vicarage, Swindon, Wilts. *t*: Broad Hinton 14.

GODDARD, Ernest Hope, C.B.E. *b*: Lon 1879. *e*: City of Lon. Editor & Journalist. *n.a*: Asst Ed Illustrated Lon News 1909–, Asst Ed The Sketch '05–, Acting Ed of both papers '16–18, Ed Advisor Illus Sporting & Dramatic News '23–33, Ed Ministry Journalism. War Work Min of Information (C.B.E.) & News Dept, Foreign Office. Formerly Officer in H.Q.C.D. Metro Special. Medal with bar (desp). *c*: Savage, Roy Aut, F.I.J. *a*: Greenhow, Champion Hill, S.E.5.

GODDARD, Canon Frederick George, M.A., B.D., H.C.F. *Publ*: Life, Death & After (2nd edn). *c.t*: Various ch papers & periodicals. *a*: Jesmond Vicarage, Newcastle-on-Tyne 2. *t*: 180.

GODDARD, Gerald Hamilton, D.S.O., M.R.C.S., L.R.C.P. *c.t*: B.M.J., R.A.M.C. Journ. *a*: Buena Vista, Barneshall Av, Worcester. *t*: 866.

GODDARD, Roy Hamilton, F.C.A.(Aust). *b*: Petersham N.S.W. 1888. *e*: The King's Sch, Sydney Univ. *m*: Helen Noel Keep. *s*: 1. *d*: 1. Chartered Accountant, Mem Scientific Expedition to Carnarvons 1939. *Publ*: Aboriginal Sculpture; Aboriginal Rock Carvings in the Carnarvons; Captain Raine & the Surry; Yachting in Australia; A Century of Yachting. *Ctr*: Journs-Oceania, Mankind, Roy Geog Soc, Victorian Naturalist, Sydney Morning Herald, etc. *s.s*: Anthropology & Australian Hist. *Rec*: Yachting, Anthropological Research. *c*: Union Sydney, Naval Officers. *a*: The Royal Exchange, 54A Pitt St, Sydney, Australia. *T*: B1503.

GODDARD, T. N., M.B.E., B.A.(Oxon). Asst Colonial Sec Sierra Leone. *Publ*: The Handbook of Sierra Leone. *a*: c/o Grant Richards Ltd.

GODDEN, Rumer. *b*: Sussex 1907. *e*: Moira Hse Eastbourne. *m*: L. S. Forster. *d*: 2. *Publ*: Black Narcissus; Breakfast with the Nikolides; Fugue in Time; The River; Rungli-Rungliot. *Ctr*: Various in U.S.A. & U.K. *Rec*: Ballet, gardening, sailing. *a*: Home Farm Hse, Dale Park, Sussex.

GODFREY, Cecil Gordon. *b*: Lon 1889. *e*: Mercer's Sc Holborn. Journalist, Artist, Display Expert. *n.a*: Daily Chron, Asst Art Ed 1922, News Chron, Art Ed '30, Bristol Evening World Advt Lay-out Specialist & Writer. *s.s*: Illus display, art, advtg. *Rec*: Yachting. *a*: 64 Devonshire Rd, Bristol 6.

GODFREY, Sir Dan, F.R.C.M., HonR.A.M., L.R.A.M. Dir Mun Orchestra Bournemouth. *Publ*: Memoirs & Music (1924). *c.t*: Various n/ps & periodicals. *a*: Dannholme, Alumhurst Rd, Bournemouth. *t*: 4045.

GODFREY, E. G. Mang-Ed & Author, Jt Mang-Dir Geo Philip & Son Ltd. *a*: 32 Fleet St, London, E.C.4. *T*: Central 3651.

GODFREY, Emmeline Stuart. *b*: Cookstown, Tyrone 1861. *e*: Abercorn Ladies' Col, Dublin, Landavia Col, Rheinpfalz. *m*: Ernest H. Godfrey. *s*: 2. *d*: 1. Ottawa Journ, Montreal Gazette, Canadian Churchman, Quebec Chronicle, Vancouver Daily Province, Gloucestershire Standard (during the past thirty ys), etc. Travelled extensively. *Rec*: Gardening, music. *a*: The Cottage, Carlton, Bedford. *t*: Harrold 242.

GODFREY, Ernest Henry. *b*: Northampton 1862. *e*: Northampton G.S. & Priv. *m*: Emmeline Stuart Lindesay. *s*: 2. *d*: 1. Civil Servant (ret). Life Fell Roy Stat Soc. Mem Internat Stat Inst 1910–. Sec Cent & Assoc Chambers of Agric 1898–1901. *n.a*: Asst Ed Roy Agric Soc of Eng, & Sec Nat Agric Exam Bd '01–07; Ed Journ of Roy Agric Soc '05–06; Ed Census & Stat Office Canada '07–20; Ed Canada Year Book '12–19; Chief Agric Br Dominion Bureau of Stat Canada '20–28. *c.t*: Ency Britannica, Ency Americana, Journals of Roy Agric Soc, Yorkshire Post, Nottingham Guardian, etc. *s.s*: Agric econ & statistics. *Rec*: Gardening, lawn tennis. *a*: Carlton, Bedford. *t*: Harrold 242.

GODFREY, Gordon. *n.a*: Editorial Dir George Philip & Son Ltd. *s.s*: Hist, geography, educational practice. *a*: Heath Drive, Potters Bar.

GODFREY, Philip. *b*: Lon 1895. Dramatist & Actor. *Publ*: Back Stage (1933). *a*: 121 Adelaide Rd, Hampstead, N.W.3. *t*: Primrose 6337.

GODFREY, Robert Samuel, C.B.E., F.F.A.S., M.InstB.E. *b*: Gedling 1876. *e*: Public Sc & Univ Col. *m*: Mildred Eleanor Price. Registered Architect & Surveyor. *Publ*: Short History of Lincoln Cathedral & the Special Repairs 1922—1932; Half an Hour at Lincoln Cathedral. *s.s*: Ancient monuments, architecture. Surveyor & Clerk of Works Dean & Chapter, Lincoln Cathedral. *Rec*: Gardening. *c*: Lincs Architectural & Archaeological Soc, Lincoln Record Soc, Ancient Monuments Soc. *a*: 3 Priory Gate, Minster Yd, Lincoln. *t*: 237.

GODFREY, Walter Hindes, F.S.A., F.R.I.B.A. b: Lon 1881. e: Whitgift Sc Croydon. m: Gertrude Mary Warren. s: 1. d: 3. Architect. Hon Sec Roy Archæol Inst G.B. & I. (1928–30), Chm of Counc & Hon Ed of the Lon Topographical Soc & the Lon Survey Cmt, Chm Counc Sussex Record Soc. Publ: The Work of George Devey, Architect ('07); The Hist of the English Staircase; The Parish of Chelsea, 4 Vols ('09–27); The Book of John Rowe ('28); The Story of Architecture in England, 2 Vols ('28–31); Official Guide to Lewes ('33); Swakeleys Middx ('33); etc. c.t: Architecture, Topographical & Antiquarian Journals, etc. s.s: Architecture, topography of Lon & Sussex. a: 203 High St, Lewes, Sussex. t: 268.

GODFREY, Most Rev Monsignor William, D.Ph., D.Th. b: Liverpool 1889. e: Ushaw Coll Durham, Venerable Eng Coll Rome. Apostolic Del to Gt Brit, Malta & Gibraltar, Titular Arch/Bp of Cius Publ: The Young Apostle; God & Ourselves & pamphlets. Ctr: Tablet & various Cath mags. s.s: Religion & Social Problems. Rec: Music. c: Athenæum. a: Apostolic Delegation, 54 Parkside, Wimbledon, London, S.W.19. T: Wimbledon 1410.

GODLEY, Gen. Sir Alexander, G.C.B., K.C.M.G. b: Chatham 1867. e: Haileybury, United Services Coll & Roy Mil Coll Sandhurst. m: Louisa Fowler. Publ: Life of an Irish Soldier; British Military History in Sth America. Ctr: Times, Military & Empire mags. c: Guards, Turf. a: Boxford Farm Ho, Newbury, Berks. T: Gt Shefford 7.

GODLEY, Eveline Charlotte, F.R.Hist.S. b: London 1874. e: Priv. Publ: The Great Condé; Charles XII of Sweden; The Trial of Count Konigsmark. n.a: Dramatic critic Nat Rev 1904—05, Annual Register '10—15. Ctr: Longman's Mag, Nat Rev, Annual Register, Dict Nat Biog. s.s: Hist (17th & 18th Cent), Drama. c: Kent Co Cricket. a: Durrants Court, High Halden, Ashford, Kent. T: High Halden 210.

GODWIN, Rev. Charles Hy. Sellwood, M.A. (Cantab). b: West Knoyle, Bath 1866 e: Golspie Hse, Warminster (Prep), Priv & St John's Col Cam. Publ: Critical & Exegetical Notes on Obscure & Corrupt Passages in the Hebrew Text (of the Psalms) in the Light of Modern Knowledge; Vol I The Anglican Proper Psalms, with Preface by the Rev. Prof A. H. Sayce, D.D. s.s: Textual criticism (Bibl); liturgiology & ceremonial & pastoral work. Trav extensively in Europe, Asia, Africa & N. America. Founded New Parish of St Aidan's Middlesbro' 1898. Built the Ch by Voluntary Labour of 80 skilled working men, as Meml of Thanksgiving for deliverance from the great Smallpox Plague '98. Created Patron of St Aidan's Middlesbro' by Order of the King in Council 1901. Hon Chap to Most Hon The Marquis of Zetland, K.T. '02. Vicar of St Aidan's Middlesbrough '01—34. Rector of Nunburnholme York '34—. Rec: Motoring. c: Roy Socs, Chap Lady Margaret Lodge F.M. a: The Rectory, Nunburnholme, York, & Roy Socs Club, St James's St, S.W.1. t: Pocklington 012.

GODWIN, Ernest John. b: Swindon 1892. e: H.S. Swindon. m: Dora Winifred Heynes. Journalist. n.a: Nth Wilts Herald 1907—12, Register Adelaide Aust '12, Times & Directory Bournemouth '21—20, Salisbury Times '23—26, Western Gazette '26—. a: 49 Victoria Ave, Winton, Bournemouth. T: Winton 1421.

GODWIN, George. Barrister & Writer. Publ: The Eternal Forest; Why Stay We Here?; Empty Victory; Cain; (all novels) Columbia; Queen Mary College—A History; Priest or Physician; The Land Our Larder; Our Woods in War; When We Build Again (part author); Peter Kuerten; Japan's New Order; The Great Mystics; Marconi—A War Record; Vancouver; A Life; Discovery; Anna Berger (novel); The Disciple (play). Ctr: English daily, weekly & monthly press. c: Savage. a: 20 Old Buildings, Lincoln's Inn, London, W.C. T: Holborn 1531.

GODWIN, Harry. Univ Lecturer in Botany. n.a: Jt Ed New Phytologist 1931. Publ: Plant Biology. Rec: Plant ecology. a: Clare Col, Cambridge.

GODWIN-AUSTEN, Sir Alfred Reade, K.C.S.I., C.B., O.B.E., M.C. b: Frensham, Surrey 1889. e: St Lawrence Coll, R.M.C. Sandhurst & Staff Coll Camberley, Chm S.E. Div Nat Coal Board. Publ: The Staff & the Staff College. Ctr: Army Review, Fighting Forces, Cavalry Journal, etc. s.s: Military. Rec: Walking gardening. c: United Service. a: Many Trees, Cefn-Coed Rd, Cardiff.

GODWIN SALT, Miss L., O.B.E., M.A. Publ: English Patriotic Poetry. s.s: Educ. a: 32 Ch Lane, Handsworth Wood, Birm.

GOERING, General Hermann. Publ: Germany Reborn. a: c/o Elkin Mathews & Marrot Ltd, 44 Essex St, W.C.2.

GOERTZ, Arthémise Anna, B.A. b: New Orleans 1903. e: Newcomb Memorial Coll, Tulane Univ New Orleans, Internat Students' Inst Tokyo. m: Hector A. Alfonso. Author. Publ: South of the Border; Give Us Our Dream. Ctr: Sat Even Post, Amer Mercury, Lond Illus News, Amer Hist Rev, Women's Mags, etc. s.s: Languages—French, Spanish, Japanese, Internat Cultural Relations. Rec: Music, travel. a: Mandeville, Louisiana.

GOETTE, John. b: Philadelphia, Penn 1896. e: Law Sch, Temple Univ, Phila, Pa. Foreign Corr, Author, Lecturer. n.a: Europe & Far East, Internat News Service 1924—41, China, Lond Dly Express '27—40. Publ: Jade Lore; Japan Fights for Asia. Ctr: Sat Rev of Lit, China Monthly, Free World, Tomorrow. s.s: Far Eastern Affairs, Chinese Jade, Book Reviewer. c: Peking (China), Nat Press (Wash, D.C.), Overseas Press of America (N.Y.). w.s: U.S. Navy World War I. a: 340 East 63rd St, New York 21, N.Y., U.S.A.

GOETZ, Herman. Ph.D.(Mun). b: Karlsruhe 1898. e: Univs of Iena, Berlin, Munich. m: Anne Marie Bartels. Curator Baroda State Museum & Picture Gallery, Mem R.A.S.B., A.O.S., P.E.N. n.a: Annual Bibliog of Indian Arch Ed Bd 1947, Founder-Ed Journ of Indian Museums '44—, Ed Bd of Marg Bombay '46—, Corres Nieuwe Rotterdamsche Courant '37—39. Publ: Indian Book Painting (Jahangir's Album); Bilderatlas zur Kulturgeschichte Indiens; Epochen der Indischen Kultur; Commonwealth of Tomorrow; Geschichte der Indischen Miniatur-Malerei; Crisis of Indian Civilization; Gedichte aus der Indischens Mystik des Mittelalters; Art of Y. K. Shukla. Ctr: Aryan Path, New Review, Asia, Burlington Mag, Ostasiatische Zeitschrift, Gazette des Beaux Arts. s.s: European & Asiatic (esp Indian) Art, Modern Political & Cultural Problems (East-Western Relations). Rec: Travelling & Music. a: Sitaram, Racecourse Rd, Baroda, India.

GOFF, Rev. Eric Noel Porter, M.A. b: Dublin 1902. e: T.C.D. m: Barbara Denman Hodgson. s: 2. Provost of Portsmouth & Chap to P'mouth Corp. Publ: The Christian & the Next War; Successful Living. Ctr: Dly Herald, Church Times, Guardian, Ch of Eng newspapers. s.s: Internat Affairs, Anglo-American Relations. Rec: Travel. c: Nat Lib & Roy Naval Portsmouth. a: Provost's Hse, Portsmouth. T: 74050.

GOFF, Thomas Theodore, B.Sc. b: New Eldorado Springs, Mo. 1882. e: Okla.

Texas, Wisconsin Univs. *m*: Myrta Louise Hixson. *d*: 1. Hd of Dept of Comm Mathematics, State Teachers' Col, Whitewater, Wis. *Publ*: Self-Proving Business Arithmetic (2 vols); jntly: Modern Life Arithmetics (3 vols); Practical Arithmetic Work Books. *s.s*: Mathematics. *Rec*: Golf, tennis. *c*: Nat Educational Assoc, Nat Comm Teachers' Fed. *a*: 802 Main St, Whitewater, Wisconsin. *t*: 78.

GOFFE, Ernest George Leopold, M.D., B.S.(Lond), F.R.S.M. *b*: Jamaica 1867. *e*: York Castle H.S. Jamaica & Univ of Lond. *m*: Edna Powell. *s*: 4. Med Ref Legal & Gen Life Ass & Gresham Life Ass, Mem B.M.A. *Ctr*: Ency Med 1st Edn, Proc Roy Soc Med, etc. *s.s*: Surgery. *Rec*: Sailing, golf, photography. *a*: 10 High St, Kingston-on-Thames, & The Red Hse, 76 Kingston Hill. *T*: Kingston 1771 & 0781.

GOITEIN, Hugh, LL.D. *b*: London 1896. *e*: City of Lond Sch & Univ Coll Lond. *m*: Freda Archer Goodman. *s*: 1. *d*: 1. Barrister. *Publ*: The Law as to C.I.F. Contracts; Smith's Mercantile Law; Company Law. *s.s*: Commercial & International Law. *a*: 11 King's Bench Walk, Temple, London, E.C.4. *T*: Central 2484

GOKAK, Vinayak Krishna, M.A. *b*: Savanur Dist. Dharwar 1909. *e*: Bombay & Oxf Univs. *m*: Sharada Betadur. *s*: 1. *d*: 3. Princ & Prof of English M.N. Coll Visnagar, Mem Advisory Board Manpara Grantha Nala since 1934, Mem Exec Cttee All-India P.E.N. *Publ*: Ijjodu; Yugantara; Samudrageetagula; Sahitya-Pragatri; Abhyuday; The Songs of Life. *Rec*: Tennis. *a*: Principal M.N. College, Visnagar (N.G.) Baroda State.

GOLDENWEISER, Alexander G., A.B., A.M., Ph.D.(Columbia). *b*: Kiev, Russia 1889. *e*: Kiev Gymnasium, Harvard Col, Columbia Univ. *m*: Ethel Cantor Goldenweiser. *d*: 1. Prof of Thought & Culture, Oregon Univ, Extension; Visiting Prof of Sociology, Reed Col, Portland, Oregon. *n.a*: Ed staff, Encyclopædia of Social Sciences, '27–29. *Publ*: Totemism, An Analytical Study; Early civilisation; Robots or Gods: History, Psychology and Culture; Sex and Civilisation; The Making of Man. *c.t*: The Nation, The New Republic, Century, Sat Review of Lit. *s.s*: Sociology, anthropology, psycho-analysis, education. *Rec*:] Billiards, chess, tennis. *c*: Amer Anthropological Assoc, Amer Folklore Soc, Amer Socological Soc. *a*: 2744 Talbot Rd, Portland, Oregon. *t*: Be 9860.

GOLDIE, W. Cockburn. *n.a*: Ed Glasgow Ev News, Sub Ed Scotsman (Edinburgh), Dundee Advertiser (London Office), Dly Mail, Chief Sub Ed The Sunday Mail. *s.s*: Topical Verse, Bard of Ayrshire Pageant 1934. *a*: Kemsley Hse, 67 Hope St, Glasgow. *T*: City 7000

GOLDING, Cecil Edward, LL.D., F.C.I.I., F.C.I.B., F.S.S F.I.L., F.R.S.A. *b*: Hinckley 1882. *e*: King Edward VI Sch Chelmsford, Univ of London. Reinsurance Broker. *Publ*: Law & Practice of Reinsurance; Burglary Insurance; Personal Accident Insurance; Workmen's Compensation Insurance. *s.s*: Reinsurance. *c*: Constitutional, Devonshire. *a*: Farleigh Hse, Lawrence Lne, London, E.C.2. *T*: Metropolitan 0766.

GOLDING, Edward William, M.Sc.Tech., M.I.E.E. Mem.A.I.E.E., M.I.B.A.E. *b*: Northwich 1902. *e*: Sir John Deane's G.S. Northwich & Coll of Tech Manch. *m*: Eleanor Mary Owen. Head of Rural Electrification Sect Elec Res Assoc, Lect Elec Eng Univ Coll Nott'm 1926–45. *Publ*: Electrical Measurements & Measuring Instruments; Elementary Prac Mathematics (with H. G. Green, M.A.); The Electrification of Agriculture & Rural Districts. *Ctr*: Whittaker's Elec Eng Pocket Book, Elec Eng'r Ref Book, Elec Educator, Ency Brit, E.R.A. Tech Rep on Rural Electrific'tn, Electrician, Elec Times, Journ Inst Elec Eng'rs, etc. *s.s*: Rural Electrification, Elec Measurements & Measuring. *Rec*: Golf, tennis. *a*: Electrical Research Assoc, 15 Savoy St, London, W.C.2. *T*: Temple Bar 7907.

GOLDING, Harry, F.R.G.S. *b*: Lon. Married. *s*: 1. *d*: 1. *n.a*: Ed Windsor Mag 1927—. Gen Ed Ward Lock Guide Books, Wonder Books for Boys & Girls, etc. *Publ*: Many guide books, children's books, novels. *Rec*: Golf, walking, travel. *a*: Mariposa, 16 Millway, Mill Hill, N.W.7. *t*: 1704.

GOLDING, John, D.S.O., F.I.C. *b*: Plaxtol 1871. *e*: Q. Elizabeth's G.S. Sevenoaks & Pharmaceutical Lab's Lon. *m*: Florence Mundella. Head of Chem Dept The Nat Inst for Research in Dairying, Shinfield. *c.t*: Journ of Biochem Soc, Journ of Soc of Chemical Ind, Standard Cyclopedia of Modern Agric, etc. *s.s*: Dairy chem, research work on the vitamin requirements of pigs, factors influencing the composition of milk, etc. War Service '15–19. San Officer. Agric Officer. Des, twice. *Rec*: Motoring. *c*: Farmers, Roy Agric Soc, Chem Soc, American Chem Soc, etc. Chevalier du Mérite Agricole. *a*: Lyndhurst Grange, Shinfield, nr Reading, Berks. *t*: Spencers Wood 67.

GOLDING, Louis, M.A. *b*: Manchester 1895. *e*: Manch Gr Sch & Queen's Coll Oxf. Author. *Publ*: Sorrow of War (poems); Forward From Babylon; Shepherd Singing Ragtime (poems); Seacoast of Bohemia; Sicilian Noon (travel); Store of Ladies; Give Up Your Lovers; Adventures in Living Dangerously; Magnolia Street; James Joyce; Letter to Hitler; Five Silver Daughters; The Doomington Wanderer; The Camberwell Beauty; In the Steps of Moses the Lawgiver (travel); In the Steps of Moses the Conqueror (travel); The Dance Goes On; Mr. Emmanuel; Who's There Within; No News from Helen; The Glory of Elsie Silver; Three Jolly Gentlemen; & various films incl Freedom Radio; Mr Emmanuel; Theirs is the Glory; etc. *Ctr*: Manch Guardian, Yale Rev, Time & Tide, Dly Express, Ev Standard, Ev News, N.Y. Herald Tribune, Dly Mail, Spectator, etc. *c*: Savage. *a*: c/o Curtis Brown, 6 Henrietta St, London, W.C.2.

GOLDING, William Gerald. *b*: Newquay Cornwall 1911. *e*: Marlborough G.S. & Brasenose Col, Oxford. *Publ*: Various Poems: Proserpine. *Rec*: Parody, music, walking, sailing. *a*: 29 The Green, Marlborough.

GOLDING-BIRD, Cuthbert Hilton. *b*: Lon 1848. *e*: King's Col Lon & Univ of Paris. *m*: Florence Marion Baber. Cons Surg to Guy's Hosp. *Publ*: History of the United Hospitals Club of Guy's & St Thomas' (2 eds); Story of the Village of Meopham. *c.t*: Learned socs & professional pubs. *s.s*: Surgery. *a*: Pitfield, Meopham, Kent. *t*: 26.

GOLDMAN, Raymond Leslie. *b*: St Louis, Missouri 1895. *e*: Smith Acad, Miss & Columbia Univs. *m*: (1) Helen Heineman (dec'd); (2) Bernice Anderson. *s*: 1. Author. *Publ*: Stay Young; The Sunday Lady; Bing, Bang, Boom; The Hartwell Case; The Murder of Harvey Blake; The Good Fight; Judge Robinson Murdered; Murder without Motive; Death Plays Solitaire; Out on Bail; The Snatch; Murder Behind the Mike; The Purple Shells; Even the Night. *Ctr*: Periodicals in United States & England. *s.s*: Fiction, Essays, General Articles, Motion Pictures, Radio. *c*: Writers (Hollywood), Author's League of America, Author's Guild. *a*: c/o Curtis Brown Ltd, 6 Henrietta St, London, W.C.2.

GOLDMAN, Victor, L.R.C.P., M.R.C.S., D.A.(R.C.P. & S.) *b*: Birmingham 1903. *e*: King Edward's Sch B'ham, Univ of B'ham. Lt-Col R.A.M.C, Mem B.M.A. & Assoc of Anæsthetists of Gt Brit & Ireland. *n.a* : Reviewer of Anæsthetic & allied books for The Medical Press, Abstracter (Anæsthetic Section) Excerpta Medica. *Publ* : Aids to Anæsthesia. *Ctr* : Proc Roy Soc Med, B.M.J., Medical Press, Indian Journ of Surgery. *s.s* : Anæsthesia, Blood Transfusions, Oxygen Therapy, Resuscitation. *Rec* : Motoring, photography. *c* : Savage. *a* : 235 Sussex Gardens, London, W.2. *T* : Paddington 5558.

GOLDMAN, William. *b* : London 1911. *e* : Elem Sch. Author. *Publ* : The Forgotten Word ; East End My Cradle ; A Start in Life ; A Tent of Blue ; Some Blind Hand ; The Light in the Dust ; In England & in English. *Ctr* : New Writing, English Story, Fortnightly Rev, Modern Reading, Jewish Chron, New Life, Lilliput, Harper's Bazaar, etc. *Rec* : Tramping London's streets, conversation. *a* : 7 Doughty St, London, W.C.1. *T* : Holborn 1843.

GOLDRING, Douglas. *b* : Greenwich 1887. *e* : Felsted Oxf. *m* : Malin Nordstrom. *s* : 1. Writer. *n.a* : Sub-Ed Country Life 1908, English Review '09, Ed The Tramp '10, Mang & Lit Adviser to Max Goschen Ltd '12—14, Lecturer in Eng at Univ Coll of Comm Gothenburg Sweden '25—27. *Publ* : inc, in addition to numerous novels & travel books, Odd Man Out (autobiog) ; Facing the Odds ; The Nineteen Twenties ; Marching with the Times ; South Lodge ; Journeys in the Sun ; The Last Pre-Raphaelite ; Life Interests ; etc. *s.s* : Foreign Affairs, Georgian Archit & Mod Art. *Rec* : Travel. *a* : Stonar Hse, Middle St, Deal. *T* : 825.

GOLDS, Lionel Barton Swan, F.R.S.A., M.I.E.E. *b* : Brasted, Kent 1903. *e* : Tonbridge Sch. *m* : Sheila Joan Sandy. Chartered Electrical Engineer, Asst Eng Shanghai Municipal Elec Dept '26—35, Chief Instrument Engineer Edmundsons Elec Corpn Ltd '36—. *Publ* : A Modern Earth Fault Relay Equipment for Use on Systems Protected by Petersen Coils. *Ctr* : Electrical Times, Electrical Review. *s.s* : Elec & Scientific Instruments, Elec Meters & Protective Devices. *Rec* : Music, tennis, rowing, etc. *a* : Pinecrest, Homefield Rd, Warlingham, Surrey. *T* : Upper Warlingham 430.

GOLDSACK, R. E., M.J.I. Journalist. Mang Dover & Canterbury Branch Offices Kent Messenger. *a* : 2 Market Square, Dover, & 43 High St, Canterbury *t* : Canterbury 1111.

GOLDSBROUGH, Rev. Albert, M.A.(Edin). *b* : Wilts 1858. *e* : Priv Scs, Edin Univ, Yorks Independent Col Bradford. *Publ* : Memorials of the Goldesborough Family ; History of the Independent Church, Pickering, Yorks. *s.s* : Genealogy. Chm Yorks Con Un 1918–. *a* : Avondale, Station Rd, Ilfracombe, Devon.

GOLDSCHMIDT, HERMANN (pen names: Hermann Faber; Goldschmidt-Faber): author; b. Frankfurt a. M., Germany, July 18, 1860; s. Moritz and Luise (St. Goar) G.; educ. Gymnasium (Frankfurt a. M.), Univs. of Heidelberg, Leipzig, Marburg. DEGREE: Dr. Juris; m. Lili Kupfer, Sept. 22, 1909. AUTHOR: Ein Weg zum Frieden (novel), 1890; plays: Fortuna (produced), 1890; Der freie Wille (produced), 1891; Goldene Lüge (produced), 1892; Hans der Träumer (produced), 1895; Ewige Liebe (produced), 1897; Ein glückliches Paar (produced), 1899; Frau Lili (produced), 1901; Maria und Eva (produced), 1903; Ein Jungeseile, 1906; Der dramatische Dichter und unsere Zeit (scientific), 1909; Sterben und Werden des liberalen Bürgertums (scientific), 1919; Brutus und Coriolan (novel), 1919. Contributor: Frankfurter Zeitung, Über Land und Meer, Preussische Jahrbücher, Die Woche, Jugend, Die Hilfe. General character of writing: plays, novels and essays. CLUBS: P. E. N. Club, Verband deutscher Bühnenschriftsteller und Bühnenkomponisten, Schutzverband deutscher Schriftsteller. ADDRESS: Hohenzollerndamm 198, Berlin-wilmersdorf, Germany.

GOLDSCHMIDT, Richard. *b* : Frankfurt 1878. *e* : Univs of Heidelberg & Munich. *m* : Else Kahnbein. *s* : 1. *d* : 1. Prof of Zoology. *Publ* : Physiological Theory of Heredity ; The Mechanism & Physiology of Sex Determination ; The Material Basis of Evolution ; Physiological Genetics ; The Sex Inter-grades ; Introduction to Genetics ; etc. *Ctr* : Various. *s.s* : Genetics & Evolution. *a* : Dept of Zoology, Univ of Calif, Berkeley, California, U.S.A.

GOLDSCHMIDT, Lt.-Col. Sidney George, T.D. *b* : Rusholme 1869. *e* : Priv, Manch Sch of Tech & Engineering Apprenticeship. *m* : Jane Maud Grieve Thorburn. *s* : 2. *d* : 2. E. India Merchant, Vice-Pres Manch Babies Hosp Counc, Nat Pony Soc. *Publ* : Bridle Wise ; Stable Wise ; The Fellowship of the Horse ; An Eye for a Horse. *Ctr* : Country Life, Polo Monthly, Polo (U.S.A.), Dly Dispatch, B.B.C., Horse Breeding Journ (India), etc. *s s* : Horses & Old Eng Furniture. *Rec* : Golf. *c* : Devons, St James's, Clarendon Manch. *a* : Ollerton, nr Knutsford. *T* : Knutsford 371.

GOLDSMID, Louis Lionel, B.A!., F.J.I. *b* : Birm, Eng 1876. *e* : K.E. G.S. Birm & Univs of Sydney, Capetown *m* : Ada Solomon. *s* : 2. *n.a* : Ed Bulawayo Owl 1897, Die Stellanlander '98, Observer '99, Transvaal Critic '99, S.A. Jewish Chron 1902, S.A'. Property Owners' Review '33. *Publ* : Life & Works of Lord Beaconsfield ; Three Heroes of the Saxon Period ; Zionism—What it is & What it Might be. *c.t* : Cape Times, Cape Argus, Sunday Times, Daily Express Lon, Die Volkstem, The Star Johannesburg, etc. *s.s* : Jewish activities in hist of Johannesburg. 1898 Reuter's Corr & Special Commssr in Bechuanaland '99—1900. War Corr Boer War '03. Counc of Nat Cmt opposing withdrawal constitution of the Cape Colony (services specially recognised by Prime Min). Mem 1st Jewish Bd of Deputies, Cape Colony. J.P. Witwatersrand, S. Africa '05. Commssr of Oaths '26. *Rec* Riding, hurdling, golf, tennis. *c* : Sci & Tech & French, Johannesburg & Brit Emp & Authors Lon. *a* : 90—3 Permanent Bldgs, Harrison St, Johannesburg, & Aida Mansions, cor Leyds & Wanderers Sts, Johannesburg. *t* : 33—1933.

GOLDSMITH, Charles Thomas. *b* : Kettering 1876. *e* : Ampthill Rd & Harpur Trust. *m* : A. R. Reed. Journalism. *n.a* : Chief Reporter & Sports Ed Beds Times & Indep. *s.s* : Local gov. *Rec* : Cycling, gardening. *a* : Howardville, Putnoe Lane, Bedford. *t* : 2783.

GOLDSMITH, Margaret, M.A *b* : U.S.A. 1897. Writer, Journalist & Economist, Biographies, Novels & Translations, Mem N.U.J., Roy Inst of Internat Affairs, Roy Empire Soc, 1939—45 For Research & Press Service Balliol Coll Oxf, European Service B.B.C. Lond. *Publ* : Frederick the Great ; Maria Theresa of Austria ; Christina of Sweden ; Mesmer ; Madame de Stael ; Women at War ; etc. *a* : 1 Granville Sq, Wharton St London, W.C.1. *T* : Terminus 7249.

GOLDSMITH, Septimus Jesse. Medical. *c.t* : Calcutta Med Journ, B.M.J. *a* : 3 York Terr, Cheltenham.

GOLDSMITH, William Noel, M.D., F.R.C.P., F.R.S.M. *b* : London 1893. *e* : Camb Univ Coll Hosp Med Sch, Phys in Charge Skin Dept Univ Coll Hosp. *n.a* : Ed Brit Journ of Dermatology & Syphilis 1939—. *Publ* : Recent Advances in Dermatology. *Ctr* : Ency of Medical Practice, various Med Journs. *s.s* : Dermatology. *Rec* : Music, photography. *c* : Public Schs, Hurlingham. *a* : 6 Upper Wimpole St. London, W.1. *T* : Welbeck 5814.

GOLDSTON, William (Will). *b* : Liverpool 1877. *m* : Lee Laurie. Magician. *n.a* : Ed The Magician 1904—14, Mag of Magic '14—34; Goldston's Magical Quarterly. *Publ:* Exclusive Magical Secrets; Further Exclusive Magical Secrets; Modern Card Tricks; Sensational Tales of Mystery Men; Secrets of Famous Illusionists; A Magician's Swansong; etc. *c.t:* Pearson's Mag, Capt, Sphinx, Everybody's Weekly, Sunday Express, Empire News, Daily Sketch, etc. *s.s:* Magic & spiritualism. Founder & past Pres of the Magicians' Club. Ex-performing Magician. entertained Royalty, taught several members of the Royal Family magic. War Service. *Rec:* Gardening. *a:* "Magic," Willow Crescent East, Willowbank Village, Denham, Bucks. *t:* Whitehall 3304.

GOLDSWORTHY, Frank Edward. *b:* Darlington 1912. *e:* Priv & Darlington Gr Sch. Reporter. *n.a:* N. Echo & N. Despatch '28—34, Daily Express Leeds '35—41, Manchester '46—47, London since '47. *w.s:* R.N. 1941—45. *T:* Central 8000.

GOLDTHORP, Leslie Mallinson, M.A., F.R.Hist.S., F.R.S.A. *b:* Heckmondwike, Yorks 1909. *e:* Heckmondwike Gr Sch, Leeds Univ. *m:* Olive Swan. *d:* 1. Schoolmaster Hebden Bridge Gr Sch Yorks 1946—. *Ctr:* Yorkshire Archæological Journ. *s.s:* The Orders of Friars in Yorkshire. *Rec:* Music, tennis. *w.s:* 1941—46. *a:* 27 Central St, Hebden Bridge, Yorks.

GOLLANCZ, ISRAEL: university professor; b. London, Eng., July, 1863; s. The Rev. Samuel Marcus and Johanna (Koppel) G.; educ. City of London Sch.; Univ. Coll. (London); Christ's Coll. (Cambridge); DEGREES: M.A., Litt.D. (Cambridge); m. Alide Goldschmidt (painter), July 5, 1910. AUTHOR: Pearl, 1891; (Red Cross edit. 1918), (new edit. 1921); Hamlet in Iceland, 1898; The Sources of Hamlet, 1926. Editor of Cynewulf's Christ, 1892; Exeter Book of Anglo-Saxon Poetry, 1895; Temple Shakespeare, 1894-96; Lamb's Specimens of Elizabethan Dramatists, 1893; The Parliament of the Three Ages, 1897. Critical editions of Mediaeval alliterative poems: Patience, Cleanness, Winner and Wuster, St. Erkenwald, and others; Boccaccio's Olympia. Editor of The Temple Classics; The King's Library, The Mediaeval Library; The Caedmon Manuscript of Anglo-Saxon Biblical Poetry, 1927; The Book of Homage to Shakespeare and others. Fellow and sec. of British Academy since its foundation, 1902; prof. of Eng. language and literature in Univ. of London since 1903; hon. director of the Early Eng. Text Soc.; hon. sec. of Shakespeare Tercentenary Comm.; English student and lecturer, Univ. Coll., 1892-95; Univ. lecturer in Eng., Cambridge, 1896-1906. Relig. denom., Jewish. CLUBS: Athenaeum; Savage; University of London. (*)

GOLLANCZ, Victor. *Publ:* inc The Betrayal of Left; What Burchenwald Really Means; Leaving The to Their Fate; Our Threatened Values; etc. Brimpton. Berkshire.

GOLLOCK, Georgina Anne. *b:* Kinsale, Co Cork 1861. *e:* Priv. Journalist. *n.a:* Ed Internat Review of Missns 1912—26. *Publ:* Sons of Africa; Daughters of Africa; Heroes of Health; At the Sign of the Flying Angel; etc. *s.s:* Inter-racial problems, African anthropology. *c:* Roy Empire Soc. *a:* 3 Sloane Ct, S.W.3. *t:* 7856.

GOLLOMB, Joseph. *b:* Russia 1881. *e:* Coll of City of New York, Columbia Univ. Writer, Mem N.Y. Acad of Sci; Amer Soc for Res in Psychosomatic Probs. *n.a:* N.Y. Ev World 1912—13, Sun World '19—25, A.P. '22—23 (Europe,) Newspaper Enterprises Assoc '23—25. *Publ:* Scotland Yard; Unquiet; Portrait Invisible; That Year at Lincoln High; What's Democracy to You?; Armies of Spies; Tiger at City High; Window on the World. *Ctr:* Observer, Strand, Twentieth Cent,

New Yorker, U.S.A., Collier's, Reader's Digest, etc. *s.s:* Fiction, Politics, Psychology. *Rec:* Sports, music, chess. *a:* 214 East 17th St, New York 3, U.S.A. *T:* Orchard 3-0189.

GOMES, Rev. Edwin Herbert, B.A., M.A. *b:* Sarawak 1862. *e:* Forest Sc Walthamstow & St John's Col Cam. *m:* Ella Mabel Mole. *s:* 1. *Publ:* The Sea Dyaks of Borneo; Seventeen Years Among the Sea Dyaks of Borneo; Children of Borneo. *a:* 276 Beulah Hill, Norwood, S.E.19. *t:* Streatham 4619.

GOMES, William Ignatius, M.J.I. *b:* Brit Guiana 1907. *n.a:* Special Repres New Daily Chron 1934, Asst Sub-Ed Daily Chron '31—33, Special Repres '28—33, Asst Ed Sporting Times '26, Ed New Sporting Times '27, Ed Demerara Sportsman '25. *c.t:* Daily Mail, Universe, Chr Sci Monitor, Trinidad Guardian, Catholic Standard. *s.s:* Brit Guiana agric & mining. Mem Counc B. Guiana F.A. '27–. Mem Counc Assoc Football Referees B. Guiana & Bd of Examiners. *Rec:* Football, walking. *c:* Demerara Un, Catholic Guild, etc. *a:* 69 Main St, Georgetown, Demerara, B. Guiana, S. America. *t:* Central 632.

GOMME, Arnold Wycombe, M.A., F.B.A. *b:* London 1886. *e:* Merchant Taylors' Sch, Trin Coll Camb. *m:* Phyllis Kate Emmerson. *s:* 1. *d:* 1. Prof of Greek Univ of Glas. *Publ:* Historical Commentary on Thucydides (Vol I); Essays in Greek History & Literature; The Population of Athens in the Fifth & Fourth Centuries B.C.; Sections on The Greeks & the Roman Republic in Eyre's European Civilization; Greece. *Ctr:* Classical Periodicals in Britain & America. *s.s:* Ancient & Modern Greece. *w.s:* Army 1914—19. *a:* 1 Melrose St, Glasgow, C.4, & Long Crendon, Aylesbury, Bucks. *T:* Douglas 4610 & Long Credon 235.

GONGGRIJP, G(EORGE) (LODEWIJK): professor of economics; b. Njalindoeng, Java, Oct. 17, 1885; s. George Lodewijk and Agnes Charlotte (van der Valk) G.; educ. Higher Burgess School; University of Leyden; m. Pauline Nennstiehl, Aug. 15, 1923. AUTHOR: Asoka (drama in vier bedrijven), 1921; Winstdeeling bij de suckerindustrie op Java (Profit-sharing in the sugar industry of Java), 1921; Het arbeidsvraagstuk in Nederl.—Indië (The labour question in the Netherlands Indies), 1925; Schets eener economische geschisdenis van Nederlandsch—Indië (Economic History of the Netherlands Indies), 1928. Editor: Koloniaal Tijdschrift. Contributes to Koloniaal Tijdschrift Economisch-Statistische Berichten. General character of writing: Colonial Economics, plays, science, history. Religion, Protestant. HOME: Palmboomstraat 32, The Hague, Holland.

GONIN, Lucy Maud. *b:* London. *e:* Governess, Simon Langton, Canterbury, Art Sch Beckenham. Author-Artist. *Publ:* Frolic & His Friends. *Ctr:* Kemsley Papers, Woman's Mag, Sussex County Mag, Parents, Nursery World, Playways, etc. *s.s:* Verse, Juvenile Stories, Drawings & Designs in Black & White & Colour. *Rec:* Piano, horse riding, gardening, country walks. *a:* The Gables, Kingswood Rd, Shortlands, Kent. *T:* Ravensbourne 4181.

GONSALVES, Victor Paschal, M.D., L.R.C.P., L.R.C.S.(Edin). *b:* Mangalore, India 1873. Married. *Publ:* India; etc. *s.s:* Science & religion. Barrister-at-Law, Inner Temple. *Rec:* Cricket, tennis. *a:* 6 Prince of Wales' Mansions, Battersea Pk, S.W.11. *t:* Macaulay 2148.

GONZALEZ LLUBERA, Ignacio M., D.enL. (Madrid), M.A.(Belfast). *b:* Barcelona 1893. *e:* Univs of Barcelona, Madrid & the Sorbonne. *m:* Jeanne Georgette Montrouge. *d:* 2. Prof of Spanish Lang & Lit Queen's Univ Belfast. *Publ:* Santob de Carrión, Proverbios Morales (edit with Intro); Coplas de Jocef (poem); etc. *Ctr*: Spanish, British & Am Journals. *s.s*: Mediæval Sp Philosophy & Lit, Med Hebred Lit. *a*: 90 Balmoral Ave, Belfast. *T*: 66060.

GOOCH, Edward Horace. *b*: London 1898. *e*: Priv. *m*: (1) Mabel Jessie Purkis; (2) Hilda Waters. *d*: 1. Art Dealer & Editor. *n.a*: Ed Staff George Newnes Ltd 1912—29, Press Illustrator '29—38, Art Staff Dly Mail '40, Picture Staff Picture Post '41—43, Art Ed S. Chron '43—44, Art Ed Dly Sketch '44—45. *Ctr*: Various Scientific & Photographic Journs. *s.s*: Historical Portraits, Prints & Art subjects. *Rec*: Fishing, photography. *a*: 36 Marine Parade, Brighton, Sussex. *T*: 1917.

GOOCH, Edwin George, C.B.E., M.P., J.P. *b*: Wymondham 1889. *e*: Norwich Munic Sec Sch. *m*: Ethel Banham. *s*: 1. M.P. (Lab) North Norfolk since 1945, Alderman & Vice-Chm of Norfolk County Council, Vice-Chm Norfolk Education Cttee. *n.a*: Sub Ed Norwich Mercury Series. *Rec*: Bowls, gardening. *a*: Rydal Mt, Wymondham, Norfolk. *T*: Wymondham 3179.

GOOCH, George Peabody, C.H., Hon.D.Litt., F.B.A. Jt-Ed Contemporary Review, British Documents on the Origins of the War, 1898—1914. *Publ*: inc Annals of Politics & Culture; Franco-German Relations 1871—1914; Recent Revelations of European Diplomacy; etc. *a*: Upway Corner, Chalfont St Peter, Bucks.

GOOCH, Henry Martyn, M.B.E., F.R.H.S. *b*: Falmouth 1874. *e*: Priv & Stanley Hse Sc Cliftonville. *m*: Adrienne May Punnett. Gen Sec World's Evangelical Alliance. *n.a*: Ed Evangelical Christendom 1904-. *Publ*: Wm Fuller Gooch: a Tribute & Testimony; (Ed) Universal Standard Stamp Catalogue (first edn, 1898). *c.t*: Various Brit & Amer papers. *s.s*: Horticulture & philately. *Rec*: Garden. *c*: Swiss Alpine. *a*: Green Wood, Manor Rd South, Esher, Surrey. *t*: Emberbrook 2238.

GOOD, Edward (Moysheh Oyved) *b*: Poland 1885. Antique Jeweller. *Publ*: Out of Chaos (Yiddish & Eng Edns); Songs of Life (Yiddish); Gems & Life (Eng & Amer Edns); The Book of Affinity (Illus by Jacob Epstein); etc. *c*: P.E.N., Anglo-Palestinian. *a*: 1 New Oxford St, W.C.1. *t*: Holborn 8230.

GOOD, Edward Thompson. *b*: Hull 1876. *e*: St Paul's Hull. *m*: Ada Wibberley. *s*: 2. F.L. 40 y. Trade Un br Official at 16, Del (local) at 19. Writer Labour & Socialist Press 17. *Publ*: Pamphlets—Real Case for Tariff Reform; Truth About U.S. Steel Trust; Trade Unions (jtly with Sir George B. Hunter, K.B.E.); etc. *c.t*: Times, Standard, Morning Post, Financial Times, Economist, Investor's Chron, Westminster Review, Eng Review, Engineer, etc. *s.s*: Labour, rlys, steel, shipbuilding, etc. Abandoned by both parents when a baby. Spent some time in workhouse. Taken on barge & sloop by grandparents. Original proposer of Unemployed Ins. The scheme taken up by Lloyd George. Wrote hundreds of articles advocating the measure & showing from workers' point of view how it could be worked before it was carried. Steel Works & Shipyard Workman till 30 y of age. On canal barges & coasting sloop from early infancy till 12 y of age, then few months at school. *Rec*: Gardening. *a*: 50 Norfolk Rd, Sheffield.

GOOD, Dr. J. P. *c.t*: Journ Anat & Physiol, B.M.J. Late Capt (Temp Acting Major) R.A.M.C. *a*: 27 Farquhar Rd, Edgbaston, Birmingham 15. *t*: Edgbaston 1915.

GOOD, Meyrick George Bruton. *b*: Wilton 1877. *m*: Amy Millie Trussell. *s*: 1. Journalist. *n.a*: Sporting Life '97—. *c.t*: Sporting Life. *s.s*: Racing. *Rec*: Golf, riding. *a*: Pentridge, Shewood Pk Rd, Sutton, Surrey. *t*: 836.

GOOD, R. *Publ*: Plants & Human Economics; Botanical Memoirs on Plant Geography; etc. Head of Dept of Botany, Univ Col Hull. *a*: Univ Col, Hull.

GOOD, Rankine, M.D., F.R.F.P.S., D.P.M. *b*: Hamilton, Lanarks 1912. *e*: Hamilton Acad, Glas Univ. *m*: Isobel Young Ross. Dep Med Supt Lanark District Asylum. *Ctr*: B.M.J., Journ of Mental Science, Brit Journ of Medical Psychology. *s.s*: Psychiatry & Psychological Med. *Rec*: Golf, swimming, linguistics, anthropology. *w.s*: Major R.A.M.C. 2nd World War. *a*: Ashgrove, Hartwood, Shotts, Lanarks. *T*: Shotts 110.

GOOD, Thomas Saxty, M.A.(Oxon), O.B.E., L.R.C.P., M.R.C.S. *b*: Lon 1870. *e*: Priv & St George's Hosp. *m*: Constance E. Colbeck. *s*: 1. *d*: 1. Psychiatrist & Psychotherapist. *c.t*: Journ of Mental Science, Trans Ophthamol Soc, Brit Journ of Med Psychology, Lancet, Practitioner, etc. *s.s*: Psychotherapy & psychiatry. Pres R.M.P.A. 1930-31. Med Supt Oxf County & City Mental Hosp. Mem of Board of Control Mental Deficiency Standing Cmt. Lon Sc Econ & Polit Science Mem of Consult Cmt. Mem of Nat Counc Ment Hygiene of Counc, Eugenics Soc, of Soc for Study of Inebriety & of Inst for Scientific Treatment of Delinquency, etc. *Rec*: Fishing, shooting. *c*: United Sports. Mem & Past Pres Oxf Med Soc, etc. *a*: Littlemore Hosp, nr Oxf. *t*: Cowley-Oxf 7079.

GOODACRE, Hugh George, J.P. *b*: Wilby 1865. *e*: Marlboro Col. *m*: Mabel Paton. *s*: 1. Boy Scout Commssr for Leics. High Sheriff Leics 1917-18. *Publ*: The Bronze Coinage of the Late Roman Empire; Handbook of the Coinage of the Byzantine Empire; Parson Paul & Other Poems; Justice Byrd, a Historical Romance. *c*: County Club Leicester, Roy Numismatic Soc (Fell), Mem Counc Boy Scout Assoc. *a*: Ullesthorpe Ct, nr Rugby. *t*: Lutterworth 3X5.

GOODALL, A. Physician. *n.a*: Ed Ency Medica. *Publ*: The Blood; Aids to Histology. *c.t*: Med journs. *a*: 14 Walker St, Edin. *t*: 23596.

GOODALL, Constance K. V. *b*: Leeds 1904. *m*: Thomas Goodall. *s*: 1. *d*: 2. Editor Womans Mag, Girl's Own Paper, Playways. *n.a*: Ed Armley & Wortley News, Ed Christian Endeavour Times. *Ctr*: Star. *c*: Women's Press. *a*: c/o Lutterworth Periodicals Ltd, Doran Court, Reigate Rd, Redhill, Surrey. *T*: Redhill 431 & 1003.

GOODALL, Frederick Charles. *n.a*: Mang Ed British Trade Review. Hon Sec Sound Currency Assoc. *Publ*: Foreign Trade. *c*: Nat Liberal. *a*: 1—3 St Paul's Churchyard, Lon E.C.4. *t*: City 2665.

GOODALL, G. Carto Ed Geo Philips & Son Ltd. *a*: 98 Victoria Rd, Willesden, London, N.W.10. *T*: Elgar 7431.

GOODALL, J. Strickland, M.B., M.S.A.(Lon), F.R.C.S., F.R.S.(Edin). *b*: 1874. *e*: Middx Hosp Edin, & Paris. *m*: Amelia Hunt. *s*: 1. Consulting Cardiologist. Physician Nat Hosp for Diseases of Heart Lon. Late Lecturer on Physiology, Middx

Hosp. c.t: B.M.J., Lancet, Med Journ & Record. Rec: Yachting. c: R.T.Y.C. & R.M.Y.C. a: 136 Harley St, W.1. t: Welbeck 2291.

GOODALL, Thomas. b: Bradford 1903. e: Pudsey G.S. m: Constance K. V. Powers. s: 1. d: 1. Journalist & Organiser. n.a: Reporter Armley & Wortley News series '20–27, Org to Nat " Safety First " Assoc, N. Midland Area '27–. c.t: Northern n/ps. s.s: Traffic problems, politics. T. Counc '28–. a: 21 Uppermoor, Pudsey, Yorks. t: Stanningley 71551.

GOODALL, Mrs. Thomas. b: Leeds 1904. m: Thomas Goodall. s: 1. d: 1. Journalist. n.a: Reporter Armley & Wortley News series '24–30, Ed Armley & Wortley News & Pudsey Advertiser '30–31. a: 21 Uppermoor, Pudsey, Yorks. t: Stanningley 71551.

GOODBAR, Joseph Ernest, B.A.(Ark.), LL.B.(Boston), b: St Louis, Miss 1890. e: Univs of Arkansas, Boston & Harvard. m: Octavia Walton. Lawyer. n.a: Student-Ed B.U. Law Review 1928–30. Publ: Managing the People's Money. Ctr: N.Y. Times Sunday Mag, Current Hist Mag, Made in America Mag. s.s: Economics, Law, Law of Corporation Finance. Rec: Travel, research, study of international conditions, causes & remedies. c: R.A.C. (Lond), Harvard (Boston & N.Y.), Cosmos (Wash), etc. a: 645 Congress St, Portland, Maine, U.S.A.

GOODCHILD, George. b: Kingston-on-Thames 1888. m: Dora Mary Hill. s: 1. d: 2. Author. Publ: Colorado Jim; McLean of Scotland Yard; Monster of Grammont; Jack o' Lantern; Quest of Nigel Rix; The Black Orchid; Emperor of Hallelujah Island; Safety Last; Behind That Door; Cauldron Bubble; etc. Ctr: Dly Mail, Sat Rev, Everyman, Answers, etc. s.s: Music, Spiritualism, Riviera. Rec: Golf, fishing, travel. c: Savage. a: Woodlands, The Great Quarry, Guildford, Surrey. T: 2555.

GOODCHILD, George Richard. b: Tottenham 1891. e: Priv & Reedham, Purley, Surrey. m: Effie Smith. d: 1. Journalist. n.a: Commercial Press Ag Bradford 1906–16, Ed Staff Halifax Guardian '19, Ed Staff Bradford Office Yorkshire Post & allied papers '19, i/c Bradford Ed Staff of Yorkshire Post & allied papers '32. s.s: Industry, sport. War Service '16–18, M.S.M. & Despatches. Hon Sec 10th Bn Duke of Wellington's Regt O.C.A. '33. Rec: Tennis, table tennis, swimming. c: Bradford & County Conservative. a: Yorkshire Post, 16 Market St, Bradford, & 991 Leeds Rd, Thornbury, Bradford, Yorks. t: 6904-5, 8307-8, 6417.

GOODCHILD, John. b: Cowley (Mx) 1878. m: Lily Ethel Newis. s: 1. Ed Western Gazette Yeovil, Pres S.W. Fed Newspaper Owners 1927-'37-'38, Mem Counc Newspaper Soc '28—, of Exec Cttee '33—44, Jun Vice-Pres '38, Senior Vice-Pres '39, Chm Wyndham Museum Yeovil '26—. n.a: Various appts in Midlands & Eastern Counties till 1906, when joined staff of Western Gazette, Apptd Ed Western Gazette & Pullman's Weekly News 1922. Publ: Outline of History of Yeovil Parish Church. Ctr: Proc Som Archæ Soc, County Yr Books, etc. s.s: Mediæval Hist. Rec: Golf. a: Covelei, Preston Rd, Yeovil. T: 253.

GOODE, Clarence Shirley. b: Hinckley 1894. e: St Peter's Dominican Priory. m: Hilda Abbott. d: 2. Radio Engineer. c.t: Radio Times, Wireless Trader, Music Seller, Leicester Evening Mail, Leicester Mercury, Morning Post. s.s: Radio & broadcasting. Controlled Wireless communications important in theatre of War. Inaugurator & Dir of B.B.C. Station 2 y. Rec: Fox hunting, golf, swimming. c: R.S.A. & Constitutional. a: Abbotsford, Hinckley, Leics. t: 44.

GOODE, Dr. H. N., M.C. Publ: Method of Providing Baths For Soldiers in the Field. c.t: Lancet, R.A.M.C. Journ. Medical officer, Military Hospital, York. a: 4 Clifton, York.

GOODE, Kenneth M. Author. Publ: Modern Advertising Makes Money; What About Advertising?; a: c/o Harper & Brothers, 90 Gt Russell St, W.C.1.

GOODENOUGH, Sir Francis (William), C.B.E. b: Newton Abbot 1872. e: Priv & Torquay Publ Col. m: Ellen Rees. Sales Mang Dir. Publ: Business Principles & Practice. c.t: Various n/ps & Technical Journs. s.s: Salesmanship, education for commerce & principle of commerce. Pres Incor Sales Mang Assoc 1929—1934. Pres Nat Assoc Trade Protection Soc. Pres Incor Soc Brit Advertisers. Chm Brit Assoc for Comm & Industrial Education. Chm Brit Commercial Gas Assoc. Rec: Golf & fishing. c: Marlborough, Ranelagh, Reform & City Livery. a: 28 Grosvenor Gdns, S.W.1. t: Sloane 8226.

GOODENOUGH, Frederick Craufurd, D.C.L. (Oxon). b: Calcutta 1866. e: Charterhouse. m: Maeve Macnamara. s: 3. d: 2 (1 dec). Bank Chm. Mem India Counc 1918–30. Chm Barclays Bank '17–. Rec: Farming. c: Brooks's, Athenæum. a: Filkins Hall, Lechlade, Glos & Kinnaird Hse, 1 Pall Mall E, Lon.

GOODHART, Arthur Lehman, K.C., M.A., LL.D., D.C.L. b: N.Y. City 1891. e: Yale & Trinity Coll Camb. m: Cecily Carter. s: 2. Prof of Jurisprudence Oxf Univ. n.a: Ed Law Quarterly Review. Publ: Poland & The Minority Races; Precedent in English & Continental Law; etc. Ctr: Prince Law Periodicals. s.s: Law. Rec: Tennis. c: Athenæum, Oxf & Camb, Savile. a: Univ Coll. Oxford.

GOODHART, Arthur Murray, M.A., MusB. Asst Master Eton 1889–1924, Master in Col 1894–1904, Hse Master '04–24 (ret). Publ: Musical Compositions —Choral Works; Piano Solos; Songs; Organ Solos; Instrumental Solos; Works for Orchestra; etc. a: 99 Montpellier Rd, Brighton.

GOODHART-RENDEL, Harry Stuart, M.A. b: Cambridge 1887. e: Eton, Trin Coll Camb. Architect, Slade Prof Oxf Univ 1933—36. Publ: Fine Art; Vitruvian Nights; How Architecture is Made. Ctr: Nineteenth Century & After, Spectator, Time & Tide, etc, The Architect & Architectural Press in general. s.s: Architecture, Aesthetics. c: Guards', Travellers, Turf. a: Hatchards, Guildford, Surrey.

GOODHEAD, Alfred, M.J.I. b: Derby 1893. e: Diocesan Sc Derby. m: Maggie Simnett. s: 1. Chief Sub Ed. n.a: Chief Sub Ed Yorks Evening News 1933, before with W. Lancs Evening Gazette, etc. Mem N.U.J. '20. s.s: Russia. Lived in Russia '10–17. Russian Interpreter with the N. Russian Expeditionary Force. Rec: Reviewing books, cinema & theatre. c: Brit Russia. a: Yorks Evening News, Leeds. t: 27341 & Headingley 52053.

GOODIER, Most Rev. Alban, B.A.(Lon). b: Gt Harwood 1869. e: Stonyhurst & Lon. Publ: The Prince of Peace; The School of Love; Jesus Christ Model of of Manhood; The Public Life of Our Lord Jesus Christ (2 vols); The Passion & Death of Our Lord Jesus Christ; The Inner Life of the Catholic; etc. c.t: Various reviews. Mem Adv Cmt for Educ in Colonies '30. a: St Scholastica's Abbey, Teignmouth, S. Devon.

GOODLAND, Roger, F.R.A.I. b: Taunton 1880. e: Taunton Sc (ret). Publ: A Bibliography of Sex Rites & Customs (1931). Extensive travel, Priv Sec to Curator of European Archæ at Harvard Univ '13—24. War Service. c: Appalachian Mountain & Field & Forest (Boston, U.S.A.), Universala Esperanto-Asocio (Geneva). a: c/o Westminster Bank Ltd., Stuckey's Bank, Taunton. Som.

GOODMAN, Colonel A. W., M.P. a: Old Dean Hall, Camberley, Surrey.

GOODMAN, Rev. Arthur Worthington, M.A., B.D., F.S.A., F.R.Hist.S. b: Chapel-en-le-Frith 1871. e: Newcastle H.S. Staffs & Christ's Coll Camb. m: Florence R. Merriott. Hon Canon Winchester Cathedral. Publ: A Little History of St Botolph's Cambridge; Winchester Cathedral Statutes (with Dr Hutton); Winchester Cathedral, Chartulary, etc. s.s: Ecclesiastical Records. c: Hampshire. a: Dormy Cottage, 49 Saint Cross Rd, Winchester. T: 4187.

GOODMAN, Frank Charles. b: Kettering 1911. m: Mildred Florence Dixon. d: 1. Editor. n.a: Northamptonshire Even Telegraph 1928, Chf-Rep Biggleswade Chron & Bedfordshire Gazette '34, Dep-Ed '45 & Editor '47. s.s: Horticulture. Rec: Music, reading, serving on many cttees. w.s: 1940—45 R.A.F. a: Cytringan, Banks Rd, Biggleswade, Beds. T: 2122. Pa 1899. e: Public Schs in Phila, Univ of Penn. m: Julia Nusbaum. d: 1. Writer, Free-lance Journalist. Publ: Benjamin Rush, Physician & Citizen; A Benjamin Franklin Reader; Benjamin Franklin's Own Story; The Ingenious Dr Franklin; Diplomatic Relations between England & Spain 1597—1603; (with R. P. Coffman) Famous Authors for Young People; Famous Explorers for Young People; Famous Pioneers for Young People; Famous Generals and Admirals for Young People; etc. Ctr: Baltimore Sunday Sun, Phila Ev Bulletin, N.Y. Times Book Review, etc. s.s: American History & Biography. Rec: Hiking, searching out hist places. a: 301 W. Schoolhouse Lane, Philadelphia 44, Pa.

GOODMAN, George. b: Lon 1866. e: Bishop Stortford, Windsor & Germany. m: Margaret Glasgow. s: 1. Solicitor. Publ: What to Teach & How to Reach the Young; Seventy Best Bible Stories; Great Truths Simply Stated; The Spirit-Led Life; Sunday Sc Lessons. c.t: Christian, Witness. s.s: Bible exposition, child welfare. c: Nat. a: 13 Calverley Pk, Tunbridge Wells. t: 446.

GOODMAN, John, M.I.C.E. b: Royston, Herts 1862. e: Priv Scs & Univ Col Lon. Civil Eng. Publ: Mechanics Applied to Engineering (2 vols); Proc of Institutions of Civil Engineers, & Mech Engineers. s.s: Friction, lubrication, hydraulics. Prof of Eng Leeds Univ '90-1922. War Service R.A.F. Rec: Gardening. a: Beamsley, Bolton Abbey, Skipton.

GOODMAN, Nathan G., A.M., Ph.D. b: Philadelphia, s.s: School & Adventure Stories, Rural Plays, Sporting Novels. Rec: Village drama production, watching football & cricket. a: Wintergleam, Wheatcroft, Scarborough. T: 2211.

GOODMAN, Paul, F.R.Hist.S. b: Dorpat, Estonia 1875. m: Romana Manczyk. s: 2. d: 1. Jewish Historian. n.a: Ed Zionist Review 1920—. Publ: The Synagogue & The Church; History of the Jews; Moses Montefiore; Think & Thank; Zionism: Problems & Views; Zionism in England; The Jewish National Home; Chaim Weizmann; B'nai B'rith; Die Liebestätigkeit im Judentum. Ctr: Encyclopedias, Jewish periodicals & general press in England & abroad. s.s: Jewish History. Theology & Politics. Rec: Reading, walking. a: Hatikvah, The Ridgeway, Golders Green, London, N.W.11. T: Speedwell 0587.

GOODMAN, Philip Charles. b: Beckenham, Kent 1907. e: Croydon & priv. m: Marion Dorothy Kynaston. Journalist. n.a: Beckenham Journal (Kent) 1926—28, Evening Times & Echo Bristol '29—'32, Art Ed & Sub-Ed Daily Independent Sheffield '32—35. Sub-Ed Daily Telegraph, London. c.t: Motor, film & stage journals. s.s: Motoring, flying, engineering, films. Mem N.U.J. a: 15 The Avenue, Orpington, Kent.

GOODMAN, Richard Willis, F.J.I. b: Reading 1864. e: Christ's Hosp. n.a: Surrey Advertiser '90, Dis Mang (Chertsey). a: Homelands, Pretoria Rd, Chertsey, Surrey.

GOODRICH, Carter. B.A., Ph.D. b: Plainfield, New Jersey 1897. e: Amherst, Mass Coll & Univ of Chicago. m: Florence Perry Nielsen. s: 1. d: 2. Prof of Economics Columb Univ. Publ: Migration & Economic Opportunity (collab); The Frontier of Control; The Miner's Freedom; Migration & Planes of Living (collab). Ctr: Ency of Social Sciences, etc. s.s: Econ Hist, Labour Problems, Population. c: Century, Adirondack Mountain. a: 445 Riverside Drive, New York 27, New York, U.S.A. T: Monument 2-3015.

GOODRICH, EDWIN STEPHEN: zoologist; b. 1868; DEGREES: M.A., D.Sc., Hon. L.L.D.; F.R.S., 1905; Fellow of Merton Coll. (Oxford); m. Helen Lucia Mary Pixell. AUTHOR: Vertebrata Craniata, 1909; Living Organisms, 1924; Studies in the Structure and Development of Vertebrates, 1930; and other works in zoology. Editor of Quarterly Jnl. of Microscopical Science. OFFICE: University Museum, Oxford, Eng.

GOODRICH, Rev. Canon Harold Spencer, M.A. b: Sheffield 1892. e: Sheffield & St John's Coll Camb. m: Gertrude Alice Hornby. s: 1. d: 2. Rector of Irnham with Corby Lincoln, Canon of Lincoln, Rural Dean of Beltisloe. Publ: Thomas Field, D.D., A Memoir. Ctr: Schoolmaster, Teacher's World, Nottingham Guardian, Sheffield Telegraph, Men's Mag, Stamford Mercury, D Telegraph, C. of E. Newsp. a: Corby Vicarage, Grantham. T: Corby Glen 63.

GOODRICH, Capt. Louis, M.B.E. b: Sandhurst. e: Oxf Mil Col. m: Beatrice Kathleen Huggins. Actor, Playwright & Author. Publ: (Plays) Keep Calm; July the Fifth; Ann & Harold; The Old & The Young; Three Rags. c.t: Blackwood's. Rec: Dry-fly fishing. c: Garrick & Green Room. a: 166 Clarence Gate Gdns, Regent's Park, N.W. 1. t: Paddington 2381.

GOODRICH, Luther Carrington. A.M., Ph.D.(Columbia). b: Tungchou, China 1894. m: Anne Perkins Swann. s: 3. d: 2. Professor of Chinese, Mem Amer Oriental Soc. Publ: The Literary Inquisition of Ch'ien Lung; Short History of the Chinese People; Syllabus of the History of Chinese Civilization & Culture. Ctr: Journ of Amer Oriental Soc, Far Eastern Quarterly, Pacific Affairs, etc. s.s: Chinese History & Literature. Rec: Tennis, swimming. c: Columb Univ Men's Faculty, Riverdale Yacht, N.Y. Oriental. a: 640 West 238 St. New York 63, New York, U.S.A. T: Kingsbridge 3-3589.

GOODRIDGE, W. L. T., M.D., M.R.C.S., L.R.C.P., D.P.H. Cons Phys. Publ: Sidelights on Cancer: Its Biologic Ontogeny Reviewed 1929; Pre-Cancerous Plasmotrophic Changes '30; etc. c.t: Various Med Journs. a: Les Chenolles, St John's, Jersey, C.I.

GOODSELL, Frederick William. Ed Hasting & St Leonards Observer 1940—. a: 17 Glen Rd, St Leonards-on-Sea.

GOODWAY, George Albert. Hon.F.G.I. Editor. *Publ:* Imprisonment for Debt; Military Tribunals; Trade Organization. Formerly Milk Reporter to Ministry of Agriculture, Asst Food Commissioner (Midland Div), Sec to Grocery Trade, Dairy Trade, Licensed Trade, Laundry Trade, etc. *a:* Editorial Offices, Eckington West, Worcester.

GOODWIN, Albert, F.R.Hist.S. *b:* Sheffield 1906. *e:* King Edward VII Sch Sheffield, Jesus Coll Oxf & Sorbonne Paris. *m:* Mary Ethelwyn. *s:* 2. *d:* 1. *Publ:* The Battle of Britain (A.M. pamph); The Abbey of St Edmundsbury. *Ctr:* Eng Hist Rev, History, French Studies, Oxford Mag. *s.s:* French & European History, 18th & 19th Centuries partic French Revolution, History of R.A.F. partic Coastal & Fighter Commands, Brit Econ Hist since 1760. *Rec:* Cricket, golf, badminton, modern art. *c:* Oxf Union. *w.s:* 1940—45 R.A.F., A.M. *a:* 196 Iffley Rd, Oxford; & Jesus College, Oxford. *T:* 48191.

GOODWIN, H. S. *b:* Manchester 1893. *e:* Manchester Gr Sch. *m:* Florence Waggott. *s:* 1. Journalist, Sec Economic Research Counc. *n.a:* Ed Musical News & Herald 1924, Ed Music Teacher & Music Student '26—34, Staff News-Chronicle '32—34, Ed the Pianoforte Teacher '34—39, Ed Consol Classics (Aust Consolidated Press), Jt-Ed Economic Digest '47—. *Publ:* with Rodney Bennett) Let's Get Up a Concert; Through the Eyes of the Times. *s.s:* Politics, Economics. *Rec:* Photography. *a:* 42 Bushey Grove Rd, Bushey, Herts. *T:* Grosvenor 4581 & Watford 5276.

GOODWIN, Helen Barton. *b:* Magnolia Plantation, La. U.S.A. 1896. *e:* Publ H.S. Chicago Art Inst, George Washington Univ Wash, D.C. & Columbia Univ N.Y. *m:* Douglas Goodwin. *d:* 1. F.L. Journalist of Barton Art Interiors, Wash, D.C. *n.a:* Ex-Mang Dir Barton Art Interiors, Wash, D.C. Spec Corr Washington Post on Interior Decoration & Design 1923—4. *c.t:* Washington Post, Edin Evening Dispatch, Evening News, Birm Gazette, Town and Country Review, etc. *s.s:* Art interior decoration, gardening news, film subjects, the art of cooking, short stories, features, interviews, short biographies. *c:* Writers Club Columbia Univ. *a:* Belfort, Woodlands Rd, Surbiton, Surrey. *t:* Elmbridge 2041.

GOODWIN, John. Author. *Publ:* King's Elm Mystery; Blackmail; Without Mercy; Jennifer; Helen of London. *a:* c/o H. Jenkins Ltd, 3 York St, St James's, S.W.1.

GOODWIN, Capt. John Cuthbert. *b:* L'pool 1891. *e:* L'pool Col & Keble Col Oxf. Capt King's Own Roy Regt 1912—20 (ret). *n.a:* Staff A.P. '28—31, H.M. Insp of Taxes '21—23 (resigned). *Publ:* Practical Musketry Instruction ('15); The Visual Training of the Soldier; Sidelights on Criminal Matters; Insanity & the Criminal; The Soul of a Criminal; Queer Fish; Crook Pie; The Zig-Zag Man; Diamonds & Hearts ('27); The Rainbox; One of the Crowd. *c.t:* Chambers's Journ, Cornhill Mag, Time & Tide, John o' London's, Regent Mag, Gaiety, Woman's Pictorial, Sovereign Mag, Wheatsheaf, Detective Mag, News-Chronicle, Daily Express Daily Mail, Criminologist, Dactylography, Premier Mag.. *s.s:* Short stories. War Service B.E.F. France '14—15. Mil Repres Birm '15. Lect in Mil Law N. Command. Adjutant N. Command Sc for Officers '16. Staff Capt 112th Infantry Brigade '17. Commanded Training Battn R.A.M.C. Dept '17. A.P.M. Mil Police & Special Service '17—20. Has lect on Short-story writing & Journalism & trained pupils. *Rec:* Boxing, gardening. *a:* c/o J. B. Pinker & Son, Talbot Hse, Arundel St, W.C.2.

GOODWIN, W. *a:* Brougham House, Wye, Kent.

GOODYEAR, Robert Arthur Hanson. *b:* Barnsley 1877. *e:* Archbishop Holgate's Gr Sch Barnsley. *m:* Jessie Jackson Crawshaw (dec'd). Author & Dramatist. *Publ:* Forge of Foxenby; Hope of His House; Isle of Sheer Delight; Tringle of Harlech; Our Bessie; The Old Golds; etc. *Ctr:* Yorks newspapers & Nth Country mags.

GOODYEAR, S. H. Editor. *a:* Darlington & Stockton Times, Darlington.

GOOLD WALKER, George, D.S.O., M.C., F.R.HistS. Sec Hon Artillery Coy. *Publ:* The Honourable Artillery Company (1926). War Service. *c:* Roy Utd Service Inst, Soc for Army Hist Research. *a:* Armoury House, E.C.1.

GOOLDEN, Barbara. *e:* Priv Scs. Novelist. *Publ:* Children of the Peace; The Waking Bird; The Toils of Law; Thin Ice; Sugared Grief; Separate Paths; Eros; Slings & Arrows; etc. *Rec:* Theatre. *c:* P.E.N. *a:* 28 Nevern Mansions, S.W.5.

GOOSEMAN, E. Sports Editor, Journalist. *n.a:* Allied Northern N/ps (new Evening at Reading). *s.s:* Sport, wireless, television. *a:* 3 Monksway, Southcote Lne, Reading.

GOOSEMAN, Eric S. *b:* Grimsby. Ed The Star Sheffield. *a:* 101 Bents Rd, Sheffield 11. *T:* 72192.

GORDIS, Robert, Ph.D. *b:* Brooklyn N.Y. 1908. *e:* Coll of City of N.Y., Dropsic Coll of Philadelphia. *m:* Fannie Jacobson Gordis. *s:* 3. Rabbi & Professor of Bible. *Publ:* Conservative Judaism, An American Philosophy; The Wisdom of Ecclesiastes; The Jew Faces a New World; The Biblical Text in the Making, A Study of The Kethib-Qere. *Ctr:* Hadoar, Jewish Quarterly Rev, Journs of Near Eastern Studies, Amer Oriental Soc, Biblical Literature, Theological Studies, etc. *a:* 153 Beach 133 St, Rockaway Beach, Long Island, New York, U.S.A. *T:* Belle Harbor 5-1269.

GORDON, Alan. See Hynes, Samuel Gordon.

GORDON, Alec Knyvett, M.A., M.B., B.Chir(Cantab). *b:* Quebec 1870. *e:* Clifton Coll, King's Coll Camb, St Mary's Hosp Lond. *m:* Gertrude Archer. *s:* 1. *d:* 1. *Publ:* Health in the Home; Haematology in General Practice; Systemic Infections. *Ctr:* Lancet, B.M.J., Med Press & Circular. *s.s:* Pathology. *a:* King's College, Cambridge.

GORDON, Caroline, B.A., Litt.D. *b:* Todd County, Kentucky 1895. *e:* Bethany Coll. *m:* Allen Tate. *d:* 1. Novelist, Short Story Writer & Lecturer. *Publ:* Penhally; Aleck Maury; None Shall Look Back; The Garden of Adonis; Green Centuries; The Women on the Porch; The Forest of the South. *Ctr:* Harper's Mag, Scribner's Mag, Yale Review, etc. *s.s:* History of the Southern United States. *Rec:* Painting & mycology. *a:* c/o Charles Scribner's, 597 Fifth Ave, New York 17, N.Y., U.S.A.

GORDON, Cora Josephine, R.B.A. *b:* Buxton. *e:* Slade Sch of Art & Atelier Colarossi Paris. *m:* Jan Gordon. Painter, Wood Engraver, Lecturer & Musician. *n.a:* Art Critic Studio Mag & Ch Sci Monitor. *Publ:* (with Jan Gordon) Misadventures with a Donkey in Spain; On Wandering Wheels; Star Dust in Hollywood; Poor Folk in Spain; The Two Vagabond Series; Portuguese

Somersault; etc. *Ctr*: New Witness, Blackwoods, etc. *s.s*: Vagabond Travelling, Folk Music. *Rec*: Spanish lute. *a*: 48b Clanricarde Gdns, London, W.2. *T*: Bayswater 3534.

GORDON, Dorothy K., M.A. *Publ*: A Junior History of Europe; The House of History. *a*: c/o T. Nelson & Sons Ltd, 35–6 Paternoster Row, E.C.4.

GORDON, Eric Valentine, M.A.(Oxon). *b*: Canada 1896. *e*: Victoria Col, B.C., McGill Univ & Oxf Univ. *m*: Ida Lilian Pickles. *s*: 1. *d*: 1. Prof of Eng Lang & Germanic Philol. *Publ*: Sir Gawain & the Green Knight (with J. R. R. Tolkien, 1923); An Introduction to Old Norse ('27). *c.t*: Acta Philologica Scandinavica, Proc Philological Soc, etc. *s.s*: Eng & Germanic philology, Icelandic lang & lit. Icelandic Kt of the Falcon. Hon Fell Icelandic Lit Soc. *Rec*: Fives, tennis. *a*: Hollygirt, Marple Bridge, via Stockport *t*: Marple 449.

GORDON, George, M.A., LL.D. President, Magdalen College, Oxf.

GORDON, George, M.B. *b*: Helmsdale, Sutherland. *e*: West Public Sc Helmsdale & Glas Univ. Phys & Surg. *c.t*: B.M.J., Scotsman, People's Journ. War Service. *Rec*: Fishing, horticulture. Mem B.M.A. *a*: Lennox Villa, 91 Friern Barnet Rd, New Southgate, N.11.

GORDON, Hampden, C.B. *b*: London 1885. *e*: Haileybury & Hertford Coll Oxf. *m*: (2nd) Mary Eileen Llewelyn. *s*: 1 (1st m). Civil Servant, Chev Leg d'Honneur. *n.a*: Ed Isis 1907. *Publ*: The War Office; Through the Enchanted Wood; The Golden Keys; The Lost Princess; Paradoc to the Rescue. *Ctr*: Various. *s.s*: Old English Furniture, Light Verse. *Rec*: Writing. *c*: Oxf Un, Roy Thames Yacht. *a*: 4 Motcomb St, London, S.W.1. *T*: Sloane 2526.

GORDON, Harold Sidney. Manchester 1893. *e*: Manchester G.S. *m*: Florence Waggott. *s*: 1. Journalist. *n.a*: Ed Musical News & Herald 1924, Ed Music Teacher & Music Student '26–34, Staff News-Chronicle '32–34, Ed the Pianoforte Teacher. *s.s*: Music. *Rec*: Photography. *a*: The Spinney, W. Drive, Harrow Weald, Middx.

GORDON, Helen Cameron, (Lady Russell), F.R.G.S. *b*: South India. *m*: Sir Alison Russell. *Publ*: A Woman in the Sahara; Loves Island; Spain as it Is; My Tour of Portugal; The Sunwheel; Syria as it Is; West Indian Scenes.

GORDON, Sir Home, Bt. *b*: Brigh on 1871. *e*: Eton. *Publ*: Memorial Biography of W. G. Grace; Reminiscences of an Irish Land Agent; Cricket Form at a Glance for Sixty Years; Background of Cricket; Eton v Harrow at Lords; Leaders of Men. *Ctr*: Quarterly Rev, Fortnightly, Nat Rev, Ency Brit, The Cricketer, etc. *s.s*: Cricket, Conservative Politics. *Rec*: Cricket, golf, music, chess. *c*: Carlton (Lond), Union (Brighton). *a*: Carlton Club, St James's St, London, S.W.1.

GORDON, Ian Alistair, M.A., Ph.D. *b*: Edinburgh 1908. *e*: Roy Hgh Sch & Univ of Edin. *m*: Mary A. M. Fullerton. *s*: 1. *d*: 3. V-Chancellor Univ of New Zealand, Professor of English. *Publ*: John Skelton, Poet Laureate; The Teaching of English, A Study in Secondary Education; Edinburgh Essays in Scottish Literature (pt-author); The University & The Community (pt-author). *Ctr*: Rev of English Studies, Mod Lang Rev, Modern Lang Notes, Listener (N.Z.), etc. *s.s*: Renaissance Literature, 18th-Century Lit, University Education, Teaching of English. *Rec*: Ski-ing. *c*: Norwegian Ski, P.E.N. *a*: 91 Messines Rd, Wellington, New Zealand.

GORDON, J. *b*: Brierley Hill 1872. Married. *s*: 2. *d*: 1. Journalist. *n.a*: County Express Stourbridge 87–. Mem Brierley Hill Fire Brigade 32 y. Mem Brierley Hill U.D.C. 30 y. *a*: 53 Heath St, Stourbridge.

GORDON, J. R. *n.a*: Ed Sunday Express. *a*: Sunday Express, Fleet St, E.C.4.

GORDON, Jan. *b*: Reading 1882. *e*: Marlborough Col, Truro Sc of Mines, & Lon Sc of Art. *m*: Cora Josephine Turner. Painter, Etcher, Art Critic, Lecturer & Musician. *Publ*: (with Cora Gordon) Poor Folk in Spain; Misadventures with a Donkey in Spain; The Two Vagabond series (4 vols); Star Dust in Hollywood; The London Roundabout; On a Paris Roundabout; A Stepladder to Painting; Piping George; Beans Spilt in Spain; etc. *c.t*: New Witness, Athenæum, Blackwoods, etc. *s.s*: Vagabond trav, folk music, poetry. *Rec*: Guitar. *c*: Savage. *a*: 50 Clanricarde Gdns, W.2.

GORDON, James. *b*: London 1912. *e*: L.C.C. Elem & Central Schs. *m*: Anne Richards. *d*: 1. Publisher. *Publ*: Of Our Time; Take Her Up Tenderly; London Peasants. *Ctr*: Selected Writing, Bugle Blast, Tribune, B.B.C., Worlds Press News, D Telegraph. *s.s*: The Short Story, London. *Rec*: Printing, carpentering. *a*: 32 Regent's Park Rd, London, N.W.1. *T*: Gulliver 4960.

GORDON, Rt. Rev. James Geoffrey *b*: Lon 1881. *e*: Eton, Trinity Col Cam & Cuddesdon Col. *m*: Martha Sabrina Brinton. *Publ*: An Interpreter of War; Papers from Picardy; Completeness in Christ. *Rec*: Boy Scouts. C.F. 1916–19. Pres Cam Union. *a*: Bishop of Jarrow, The Col, Durham. *t*: 57.

GORDON, Jane. *n.a*: Mem of Staff News Chronicle. *Publ*: Home Beauty Treatment; A Book for Mothers. *s.s*: Fashion, beauty, children. *a*: 70 Gloucester Place, W.1. *t*: Welbeck 1405 & 6.

GORDON, John. *n.a*: Ed Sunday Express. *a*: Sunday Express, Fleet St, London, E.C.4.

GORDON, John William, K.C. *b*: Lon 1853. *Publ*: Monopolies by Patents; Compulsory Licences Under the Patent Acts; etc. *s.s*: Patent Law, Optics, Mechanics. *c*: M.R.I., F.R.G.S. *a*: 113 Broadhurst Gdns, N.W.6. *t*: Maida Vale 5203.

GORDON, Leland James. M.A., B.S., Ph.D.(Penns). *b*: Janesville, Minn 1897. *m*: Doris Mellor Gilbert. *s*: 1. *d*: 1. Prof & Head of Dept of Economics Denison Univ Granville Ohio. *n.a*: Ed-Bd Social Science. *Publ*: Economics for Consumers; American Relations with Turkey; Consumers in Wartime. *Ctr*: Social Science, The Annals, Christian Century. *s.s*: Consumer & Internat Economics. *a*: Granville, Ohio. *T*: 84652.

GORDON, Mary L., L.R.C.P., L.R.C.S., L.F.P.S. *Publ*: Penal Discipline. *c*: Brit Med Assoc. *a*: Hank Wood, Crowborough, Sussex. *t*: 413.

GORDON, Mervyn Henry, C.M.G., C.B.E., F.R.S., M.D. *b*: Harting 1872. *e*: Marlborough & Oxf. *m*: Mildred Olive Power. Experimental Pathologist. *c.t*: Medical & Scientific Press. *s.s*: Pathology of Infectious Diseases. Consulting Bacteriologist to War Office for Cerebrospinal Fever 1915–18. *Rec*: Archæology. *a*: Holly Lodge, East Molesey, Surrey.

GORDON, Molyneux L., K.C. b: Toronto, Ontario, Canada 1884. e: Toronto Ch Sch, Dover Coll England, Trinity Coll Toronto, Osgood Hall. m: J. Bernice Britton. d: 4. Publ: Digest of Income Tax Cases. Ctr: Financial Post, Canadian Bar Rev, Accountant's Mag, etc. s.s: Taxation. Rec: Hunting, sailing. c: Roy Canadian Yacht. a: 259 Dunvegan Rd, Toronto 12, Canada. T: Hy 9214.

GORDON, Percy, MusBac(Oxon), L.R.A.M.(Hons). b: Glas 1877. e: Glas & Leipzig. m: Amy Helen Heaven. d: 1. Music Critic & Lect. n.a: Music Critic Glasgow Herald 1922. c: I.J., Inc Soc of Musicians, R.S.T., Glas Art. a: 18 Southpark Av, Glas. W.2.

GORDON, Dr. R. G., M.D., D.Sc., F.R.C.P.S. Physician Roy United Hosp Bath. a: 9 Circus, Bath.

GORDON, R. M., B.A., M.D., D.T.M., D.P.H. c.t: Med Journs. a: School of Tropical Medicine, Pembroke Place, L'pool, Sir A. L. Jones Research Laboratory, Freetown, Sierra Leone, W. Africa.

GORDON, Ronald Grey. b: Monifieth, N.B. 1889. e: Charterhouse & Edin Univ. m: Agnes Theodora Henderson. s: 2. Publ: The Philosophy of a Scientist; Neurotic Personality; Chronic Rheumatic Diseases (with F. G. Thomson); Paralysis in Children (with M. F. Brown); Abnormal Behaviour. Ctr: B.M.J., Lancet, etc. s.s: Neurology, Psychiatry. Rec: Gardening. c: Caledonian. w.s: World War I Capt R.A.M.C., World War II Col R.A.M.C. a: 23 Queen's Sq, Bath (T: 2390); & Woodex, Limpley Stoke, Bath (T: Limpley Stoke 3296).

GORDON, Seton, C.B.E., B.A. e: Oxford Univ. Author. Publ: Highways & Byways in the Western Highlands; The Immortal Isles; Hebridean Memories; Highways & Byways in the Central Highlands; A Highland Year; etc. a: Upper Duntuilm, Isle of Skye.

GORDON, SETON (PAUL): author and nature photographer: b. Aberdeen, Scotland, April, 1886; s. William (LL.D., O.B.E.) and Ella Mary (Paul) G.; educ. Oxford Univ. and privately; DEGREES: B.A. (Honors, Natural Science); Diploma, rural economy; m. Evelyn Audrey Pease, Aug., 1915. AUTHOR: Birds of Loch and Mountain, 1907; The Charm of the Hills, 1912; Hill Birds of Scotland, 1915; Land of the Hills and Glens, 1920; Wanderings o' a Naturalist, 1921; Amid Snowy Wastes, 1922; Hebridean Memories, 1923; The Cairngorm Hills of Scotland, 1925; Immortal Isles, 1926; Days with the Golden Eagle, 1927; The Charm of Skye, 1929; In the Highlands (in press). Contributor to London Times, National Review, Contemporary Review; English, 19th Century, Empire reviews; Country Life, The Field, The Graphic, Scotsman, Glasgow Herald. General character of writing: natural history and descriptive; special subject: the Highlands and Islands of Scotland, their folk-lore, history and legends. Highland pipe player; acts as judge of piping events at most of highland gatherings in Scotland; naturalist; lecturer on nature and the Highlands and Islands of Scotland; photographer of nature, bird and animal life. Relig. denom.: United Church of Scotland. CLUBS: Conservative (London), Vincent's (Oxford). HOME: Achantoul, Aviemore, Inverness-shire, Scotland.

GORDON, W. T., M.A., D.Sc, F.R.S.E., F.L.S. Sec G.S. Prof of Geology. c.t: Scientific Journs. a: Geological Dept, King's Col, Strand, W.C.2.

GORDON, W. T. N. n.a: Ed Surrey Weekly Press Guildford. Publ: Over 200 short stories. a: 2 The Quarry, York Road, Guildford.

GORDON, WILLIAM: physician; b. Strabane, Ireland, July, 1863; s. George and Martha (Ramsay) G.; educ. private schools; Trinity Coll. (Cambridge); Heidelberg; Univ. Coll. Hospital (London); DEGREES: M.A., M.D. (Cambridge); F.R.C.P. (London). AUTHOR: The Influence of Strong, Prevalent, Rain-bearing Winds on the prevalence of Phthisis, 1910; The Place of Climatology in Medicine, 1913. Contributor of various papers on medical subjects in numerous medical journals. First class, prt. I, Nat. So. Tripos, Cambridge, 1884; 1st class, Prt. II, 1885; chmn. of sub-comm. of British Medical Assn. on Army Medical Reform, 1896-98; pres. of sec. of medicine, annual meeting of British Medical Assn., 1907; pres. of sec. of Balneology and Climatology, Roy. Soc. of Medicine, 1915-17; Hyde lecturer on the Place of Climatology in Medicine, 1918; v. pres. of sec. of medicine, R.S.M., 1921-24; medical officer No. 1, temporary hospital, Exeter, Oct., 1914. to Feb., 1918; consulting physician of Royal Devon. and Exeter Hospital and to West of England Eye Infirmary. *

GORDON-BARRETT, Richard Regis, F.R.G.S., M.J.I. b: Hornsey 1889. e: Oakfield Col Highgate & Lon Univ. m: Yvonne Bonnard de l'Aage. Journalist (Free Lance). Publ: Motoring in France; Motoring in Italy; etc. c.t: The Field, The Autocar, Tee Topics, The Morris Owner, Modern Motoring, The Motor World, etc. s.s: Travel, motoring & publicity. Rec: Photography. a: 14 Rue Nicolo, Paris XVI & 71 Sandgate Rd, Folkestone. t: Auteuil 68:45 & Folkestone 4507.

GORDON-CANNING, Capt. Robert, M.C. b: 1888. e: Eton. Late 10th Royal Hussars. Publ: The Death of Akbar (poems); Ypres & Empire (essays); Saviours of England (play); Boabdil (historical dramatic poem); Political Articles. a: 16 Cadogan Sq, London, S.W.1.

GORDON-LENNOX, Victor C. H. b: Lond 189". e: Priv. m: Diana Kingsmill. s: 1. Journalist. n.a: Polit Corres D Mail 1922—29, Peterboro' D Telegraph '29—34, Dip Corres D Telegraph '34—. s.s: Internat Politics, Represented Daily Telegraph Ottawa Conf 1932 & World Econ Conf Lond '33. Rec: Golf, lawn tennis, motoring. c: White's, Carlton, Pratt's. a: Carlton Club, 94 Pall Mall, London, S.W.1.

GORDON-TAYLOR, Sir Gordon, K.B.E., C.B., M.A., LL.D., (Hon) M.S., B.Sc., F.R.C.S., F.R.A.C.S., F.A.C.S.(Hon), I.R.C.S.(Hon). b: Aberdeen 1878. e: Gordons Coll Aberdeen, Aberdeen Univ & Middlesex Hosp Lond. m: Florence Mary Pegrume. Consulting Surgeon to The Middlesex Hospital & The Royal Navy. Publ: The Fourth Army, B.E.F. 1918; The Dramatic in Surgery; The Abdominal Injuries of War. Ctr: Medical Journs. s.s: Cancer & Abdominal Surgery. a: 40 Portland Pl, London, W.1. T: Langham 3232.

GORDON-WALKER, Patrick Christien, M.P. b: Worthing 1907. e: Wellington & Christ Church Oxf. m: Audrey Muriel. s: 2. d: 3. Broadcaster, Chief Ed Radio Luxemburg 1944—6. Publ: Sixteenth & Seventeenth Centuries; Outline of Man's History; The Lid Lifts. Ctr: B.B.C. Home, European & Overseas Service. a: 6 Linnell Close, London, N.W.11.

GORE, CHARLES: Bishop (retired), preacher, author; b. Wimbledon, Eng., Jan. 22, 1853; s. The Hon. Charles Gore and Augusta Ponsonby (Countess of erry) G.; educ. Harrow and Balliol Coll., Oxford. DEGREES: D.D. (Oxon), Hon. D.D. (Durham and Edinburgh), Hon. D.ch., Hon. LL.D. (Cambridge and Birmingham), Ph.D. (Athens); unmarried. AUTHOR: Church and Ministry, 1888 (new edit. 1919); Roman Catholic Claims, 1889 (11th edit. 1919); Leo the Great, 1889; Incarnation of the Son of God (Bampton Lectures), 1891; The Mission of the Church, 1891; Roman Thoughts on Religion, 1895; Dissertations, 1896; The Sermon on the Mount, 1897; The Body of Christ, 1901; The

Reconstruction of Belief, 1921-24; Can We then Believe? 1926; Birth Prevention, 1927; The Lambeth Conference and Contraception, 1930; Christ and Society, 1928; The Philosophy of the Good Life (Gifford's Lecture), 1930. Editor: Lux Mundi, 1889; Essays on Church Reform, 1898; Property, 1914; Commentary on Holy Scripture, 1928. Relig. denom., Anglican. HOME: 27 Eaton Terrace, London, S.W.1, Eng.

GORE, James, ChM., F.R.C.S. *c.t*: Med World, Queens Med Mag Birm, Birm Med Review *a*: 43 Paget Rd, Wolverhampton. *t*: 21835.

GORE, John Francis, C.V.O., T.D., J.P. *b*: Wimbledon 1885. *e*: Radley & Trin Coll Oxf. *m*: Lady Janet Campbell. *s*: 1. *d*: 2. Barrister, Author & Journalist (pen name, Old Stager). *Publ*: King George V—A Personal Memoir; Creevey's Life & Times; Nelson's Hardy & his Wife; Sydney Holland, Lord Knutsford; Charles Gore—Father & Son; Creevey. *Ctr*: (Pen name, Old Stager) Sun Times, D Telegraph, Ev Standard, Sphere. *s.s*: Biog, 19th-Cent Memoirs. *Rec*: Shooting. *c*: Travellers, M.C.C., I.Z. *a*: Fyning Combe, Rogate (Petersfield), Sussex. *T*: Rogate 70.

GORE, Narayan Anant, M.A. *b*: Devgad Ratnagiri 1911. *e*: Bombay Univ. *m*: Vimal Harihar Moghe. *s*: 1. *d*: 2. Sen Prof of Sanskrit MM Arts Coll Bombay, Mem Indian P.E.N. *n.a*: Ed Poona Orientalist. *Publ*: Bibliography of the Ramayana; Malatimadhavakatha-Rijulaghvi; Aryashatak of Appayyadiksita; Svapnavasavadatta of Bhasa; Paumacariya of Vimalasuri; Vetalapacavimsati; Sringarakallolo. *Ctr*: Poona Orientalist, Pracya Vani, Indian P.E.N., Aryan Path, Journ of Bombay Univ, etc. *s.s*: Sanskrit, Prep of Bibliographies & Indexes, Study of Lit on Lit Science. *Rec*: Practice of Yogic Asanas. *a*: Dr Moghe's Bungalow, Linking Rd, Khar, Bombay No 21, India.

GORE-BROWNE, Robert, O.B.E. *b*: London 1893. *e*: Harrow, New Coll Oxford. *m*: Agnes Margaret Elias. Barrister, Writer of Plays & Film Scenarios. *Publ*: (Novels) The Crater; An Imperfect Lover; Death on Delivery; (Plays) Can We Tell?; These Mortals (jnt); Cynara (jnt); King Queen Knave (jnt); The Key (jnt); Lord Bothwell (biog). *Ctr*: Sat Review. *s.s*: The Stage, the Cinema, Cent African Subjects, Travel in Europe, Africa, Amer. *c*: Brooks's, Garrick. *w.s*: World War I R.F.A., Admiralty; World War II Roy Sigs. *a*: 17 Hamilton Terr, London, N.W.8. *T*: Cunningham 5579.

GORELL, Lord, C.B.E., M.C., M.A. *b*: 1884. *e*: Harrow & Balliol Col Oxf. Publisher & Author. *Publ*: Plush; Devils' Drum; Gauntlet; Elizabeth Star; etc. Ex-Chairman & Mem Counc Soc of Authors. Ed Cornhill Magazine 1933. Under Sec of State for Air '21—22. Chm & Treas King's Col Hosp. *a*: 31 Kensington Sq, W.S. *t*: Western 1678.

GORELL, 3rd Baron, Ronald Gorell Barnes, C.B.E., M.C., M.A. Author of many books inc Poetry, Fact & Fiction; formerly Editorial Staff The Times. *a*: 31 Kensington Sq, London, W.8.

GORHAM, Maurice A. C. *b*: London 1902. *e*: Stonyhurst Coll & Balliol Coll Oxf. Journalist, Head of Television Service B.B.C. since 1946. *n.a*: Wkly Westminster 1923, Westminster Gazette '26, The Radio Times '26—41 (Art Ed '28, Ed '33—41). *Publ*: The Local. *c*: Univ Dublin. *a*: 16 Ashley Gdns, London, S.W.1.

GORJAN, Zlatko. *b*: Mitrovica 1901. *e*: Univ of Vienna. Journalist. *n.a*: Novosti, Morgenblatt, Zagreb. *Publ*: Plays :—Egoizam d.d.; The Affairs of Fortunato; Anna looks for justice; The Burning Bush (anthology of modern German poetry); Kroatische Dichtung (Anthology of Croat poets in German language), etc. *s.s*: Translations from English, German & French into Croatian. Exhibitions of water-colours in Zagreb 1928 & '34. *a*: Zagreb, Jurjevska St 37a, Yugoslavia.

GORKI, Maxim. *b*: 1868. Author. *Publ*: The Orloff Couple; Malva; Twenty-Six Men & a Girl; The Spy; Reminiscences of Leonid Andreyev; The Outcast; Comrades. Imprisoned as political offender Tsarist régime. *a*: Sorrento, Italy.

GORMAN, John, F.J.I. *b*: Dublin. *m*: Annie Lyst. *s*: 3 (1 dec). *n.a*: Editorial staff B'ham Post 1907, successively Asst Ed & Ed Indian Daily Telegraph (Lucknow) '05-07, Asst Ed Bombay Gazette '99-1905, previously n/p Lancs & Cumberland. *s.s*: India. *c*: Press. *a*: 105 Pershore Rd, Edgbaston, B'ham. *t*: Calthorpe 1479.

GORMAN, Samuel. *b*: Belfast 1906. *e*: Elem Sch & Municipal Coll of Tech Belfast. *m*: Marjorie Elizabeth Manning. *s*: 1. *d*: 2. Min of Religion & Lect of Elim Bible Coll London, Mem Exec-Counc Elim Churches of Brit Isles & Guernsey 1937 & Trs '47—48, Mem Elim Missionary Counc '44—. *Publ*: The Coming World Ruler; Christ & The Created; If Jesus Rules; Christ's Glorious Supremacy; Christ, the Infallible Exemplar; Britain Awake; Two Phases or One? *Ctr*: Elim Evangel. *s.s*: Theology, Sociology. *a*: 12 Cowslip Hill, Letchworth, Herts. *T*: Letchworth 755.

GORST, Harold Edward. *b*: London 1868. *e*: Sherborne, Eton, Germany. *m*: (1) Nina Kennedy, (2) Dorothy Isobel Bevan. *s*: 3. *d*: 4. Author. *n.a*: Sat Review 1896, Rev of the Week (ed) 1899, Ev Standard 1901, Standard '04, Ed Free Food League '04, Westminster Gazette '12. *Publ*: China; The Earl of Beaconsfield; The Curse of Education; The Fourth Party; The Proof of Christ's Deity; Much of Life is Laughter. *Ctr*: Times, Blackwoods Mag, Chambers's Journ, Fortnightly Rev, 19th Century Rev, North Amer Rev, Nash's. *s.s*: Education. *Rec*: Music. *a*: Walberton, Arundel. *T*: Eastergate 262.

GOSNELL, Harold Foote, A.B.(Roch), Ph.D.(Chic). *b*: Lockport N.Y. 1896. *m*: Florence Fake. *s*: 2. Research Consultant Div of Historical Policy Research, Dept of State. *Publ*: Democracy, Threshold of Freedom; Negro Politicians; Machine Politics; Grass Roots Politics; Boss Platt & His New York Machine; Why Europe Votes; The American Party System (co-author); Getting Out the Vote; Non-Voting. *Ctr*: Amer Polit Sc Rev, Polit Sc Quarterly, Public Opinion Quart, etc. *s.s*: Amer Politics, Comparative Political Parties, etc. *a*: 5618 Wilson Lane, Bethesda 14, Maryland, U.S.A. *T*: Wisconsin 0657.

GOSS, Charles W. F., F.S.A. *b*: Lon. Librarian. *Publ*: History of Crosby Hall, London; Descriptive Bibliography of the Writings of George Jacob Holyoake; Bibliography of London Directories 1677—1855; Methods of Producing and Preserving Prints; etc. *c.t*: Various. *s.s*: History of London, bibliography, engraving. *Rec*: Print & stamp collecting. *c*: Pepys. *a*: Childs, Kevingtown, nr St Mary Cray, Kent. *t*: Bishopsgate 2254.

GOSS, Madeleine B. *b*: Chicago, Illinois. *e*: St Mary's Sch Knoxville, Switzerland, Italy, Dresden, Paris. *m*: Joseph Marien Goss (dec'd). *s*: 1. *d*: 1. *Publ*: Beethoven, Master Musician; Deep-Flowing Brook, The Story of Johann Sebastian Bach; Unfinished Symphony, The Story of Franz Schubert; Bolero, The Life of Maurice Ravel; Brahms the Master. *s.s*: Biogs of Musicians. *Rec*: Raising Chinchillas, swimming, ranching. *a*: Woodnvale, Arcadia, California. *T*: Monrovia 8323.

GOSS-CUSTARD, Reginald, F.R.C.O. *b*: St Leonards-on-Sea 1877. *e*: Priv. *m*: Lilian Mary Jones. *d*: 1. Musician. *Publ*: 35 original compositions for Organ; numerous arrangements from Orchestral & Piano Works for Organ; numerous compositions recorded for H.M.V. *Rec*: Motoring, gardening, fishing. Mem Inc Soc of Musicians. Mem Counc Lon Soc of Organists 1934. *a*: 12 Methuen Pk, Muswell Hill, N.10. *t*: Tudor 2014.

GOSSE, A. Hope. *b*: South Australia 1882. *e*: St. Peter's Coll Adelaide & Caius Coll Camb, Cons Phys to St Mary's & Brompton Hosps, Ed St Mary's Hosp Gazette 1912—13. *Ctr*: Practitioner, Clinical Journ, Quarterly Journ of Med, etc. *s.s*: Diseases of the Chest & Heart. *Rec*: Golf. *c*: United Univ. *w.s*: R.A.M.C., T.A. Col (Despatches 3 times). *a*: 119, Harley St, London, W.1. *T*: Welbeck 1218.

GOSSE, Jeanne. *b*: New York. *m*: . *d*: 3. Writer. *n.a*: Book reviews, Indian Mirror 1916. *Publ*: St Felix; Alsatian Vignettes; etc. *s.s*: Books dealing with France. *Rec*: Gardening & writing. *a*: Sunspot, Banks Rd, Sandbanks, Dorset.

GOSSE, Philip, M.D., M.R.C.S., L.R.C.P., F.R.S.L. *b*: London 1879. *e*: Haileybury & St Bart's. *m*: Anna Gordon Keown. *d*: 2. Writer, Naturalist to Fitzgerald Expedition to the Andes. *Publ*: Natural History of the Aconcagua Valleys; My Pirate Library; Bibliography of the Works of Capt Charles Johnson; Pirate's Who's Who; History of Piracy; Memoirs of a Camp Follower; Go to the Country; Traveller's Rest; St Helena; The Squire of Walton Hall; An Apple a Day. *Rec*: Foreign trav & book collecting. *c*: Savile, M.C.C., Fountain. *w.s*: World War I France & India. *a*: 256 Hills Rd, Cambridge. *T*: 87089.

GOSSIP, Rev. Arthur John, M.A.(Edin), D.D.(Edin), LL.D.(Glas). *b*: Glasgow 1873. *e*: George Watson's Coll, Edin Univ. *m*: Nina H. Carslaw (dec'd). *s*: 3. *d*: 2. Minister of the Church of Scotland, formerly Prof Glas Univ. *Publ*: From the Edge of the Crowd; In Christ's Stead; The Galilean Accent; The Hero in Thy Soul; Experience Worketh Hope; In the Secret Place of The Most High. *s.s*: Pastoral Theology, Christian Ethics, Buddhism. *Rec*: Gardening, cycling, walking, reading. *a*: Inverton, Kingussie, Invernessshire.

GOSSIP, Mr. Broadbent. See **Thompson, Noel Henry**

GOTCH, John Alfred, M.A., F.S.A., F.R.I.B.A., J.P. *b*: Kettering 1852. *e*: Priv Sc, Kettering G.S. & Zurich Univ. *m*: Annie Perry. *s*: 1 (dec). *d*: 1. Archt. *Publ*: The Buildings of Sir Thomas Tresham (1883); Early Renaissance Architecture in England; The English Home from Charles I to George IV; Old English Houses; Inigo Jones (1928); etc. *c.t*: Archt publs. *s.s*: Hist of Eng domestic archt. Pres Archt Assoc 1886-87. Pres R.I.B.A. 1923-25. Pres Northants Assoc of Archts '11-22. Chm Quarter Sessions Northants '26-34. *Rec*: Sketching. *c*: Arts, etc. *a*: Weekley Rise, Kettering. *t*: 86.

GOTT, Sir Charles, M.InstC.E. *b*: Bradford 1866. *e*: Priv. *m*: Annie Docksey. Chrtd Surveyor & Civil Eng. *Publ*: Ed The Practical Surveyor; Auctioneer & Estate Agent. *c.t*: Tech Pr. *Rec*: Music. *c*: Authors' Bradford, Vice-Pres Chrtd Surveyor's Assoc, Fell Geological Soc. *a*: Linden Lea, Pinner, Middx. *t*: 372.

GOTTSCHALK, Louis, M.A., Ph.D. *b*: Brooklyn, N.Y. 1899. *e*: Brooklyn Boy's Hgh Sch & Cornell Univ. *m*: Fruma Kasdan. *s*: 2. Prof of Modern History Univ of Chicago. *n.a*: Asst-Ed Journ of Modern History 1929 —45. *Publ*: Life & Times of Lafayette; Jean Paul Marat, A Study in Radicalism; Era of the French Revolution; Use of the Personal Document in History, Anthropology & Sociology (in collab). *Ctr*: Journ of Mod Hist, Amer Hist Rev, Annales Historiques de la Revolution Francaise, etc. *s.s*: 18th & 19th-Century French Hist, Franco-American Diplomatic & Cultural Relations. *Rec*: Tennis. *c*: Quadrangle (Chic). *a*: 5551 University Ave, Chicago, Illinois, U.S.A. *T*: Hyde Park 1143.

GOUDGE, Elizabeth de Beauchamp. *b*: Wells 1900. *e*: Grassendale Sch, Southbourne Art Sch, Reading Univ. Novelist, Winner M.G.M. Prize in U.S.A., Winner Carnegie Medal (1946) for children's book. *Publ*: Island Magic; The Middle Window; A City of Bells; Towers in the Mist; The Bird in the Tree; The Castle on the Hill; Green Dolphin Country; The Pedlar's Pack; The Golden Skylark; The Ikon on the Wall; Smoky House; Henrietta's House; The Little White House. *a*: Providence Cott, Westerland, nr Paignton.

GOUDGE, Rev. Henry Leighton, M.A., D.D. (Oxon). *b*: Lon 1866. *e*: Blackheath Prop Sc & Univ Col Oxf. *m*: Ida de Beauchamp Collenette. *d*: 1. Canon of Ch Ch & Regius Prof of Divinity, Oxf Univ. *n.a*: Jt Ed & pt author with Dr Gore & the Rev A. Guillaume of A New Commentary on Holy Scripture. *Publ*: A Commentary on the First Epistle to the Corinthians; The Pastoral Teaching of St Paul; The Church & the Bible; etc. *Rec*: Cycling, golf. *a*: Christ Church, Oxf.

GOUDIE, William John, D.Sc, M.I.MechE., M.A.S.M.E.(Amer), A.M.InstC.E. *b*: Girvan 1868. *e*: Girvan Parish Sc, Kilmarnock Acad & Univ of Glas. *m*: Elizabeth MacLean. Prof of Heat Engines, Glas Univ. *Publ*: Steam Turbines; Ripper's Steam Engine Theory and Practice. *c.t*: Leading eng journs. *s.s*: Theory & practice of heat engine prime movers. 1st Occupant of the James Watt Chair on Theory & Practice of Heat Engines 1921-. *Rec*: Music. *a*: 1 Kay Pk Terr, Kilmarnock. *t*: 501.

GOUGAUD, DOM LOUIS, O.S.B: monk of the Order of St. Benedict; b. Malestroit, Morbihan, France, June, 1877; s. Louis and Desirée (Nouvel) G.; educ. St. Vincent's Coll. (Rennes); Univ. of Rennes; DEGREES: Licencié en droit; D. Litt Celt. (hon. Causa), (Nat. Univ. of Ireland). AUTHOR: Les Chrétientés Celtiques, 1911; Gaelic Pioneers of Christianity, 1923; Confessions de Saint Augustin: Traduction nouvelle. 1923; Devotions et Pratiques ascetiques du Moyen Age, 1925; Devotional and Ascetic Practices in the Middle Ages, 1927; Ermites et Reclus, 1928; Modern Research, with special reference to early Irish Ecclesiastical History, 1929; Anciennes contumes claustrales, 1930. Contributor to Revue d' historire ecclésiastique, Jahrbuch für Liturgiewissenschaft. Relig. denom., Roman Catholic. HOME: St. Michael's Abbey, Farnborough. Hants. Eng.

GOUGH, ALFRED WILLIAM: prebendary of St. Paul's; b. Hartshill, Staffordshire. Eng., Dec., 1862; s. Rev. Howard England Tunnicliffe and Julia Mead (Cave-Browne-Cave) G.; educ. Merchant Taylors' Sch. (London); DEGREES: M.A. (Oxford), F.R.S.L.; married. AUTHOR: Life of Christ, 1906; Service and Sacrament. 1909; God's Strong People; Repentance and Strength, 1916; The Saving of Democracy, 1919; The Fight for Man, 1924; The Lure of Simplicity, 1929. Contributor to English Mag., Nat. rev. and other mags. General character of writing: religious and social survey treatises. Relig. denom., Church of England. CLUB: The Wellington. HOMES: Brompton Vicarage, London, S. W., and Gorse Cliff, Nevin, North Wales.

GOUGH, Herbert John, C.B., M.B.E., D.Sc., Ph.D. M.I.Mech.E., F.R.S. *e*: Univ Coll Sch & Lond Univ. *m*: Sybil Homes. *s*: 1. *d*: 1. Eng-in-Chief Lever Bros. & Unilever Ltd 1945—, Dir of Research W.O. '38, DirGen Sc Research & Development Min of Supply '38—45. *Publ*: The Fatigue of Metals. *Ctr*: Many scientific &

technical papers in England, U.S.A., Sweden, Holland, France, etc. *s.s*: Strength & Properties of Construction Materials, etc. *Rec*: Golf, swimming, tennis. *c*: Athenæum. *w.s*: 1914—19 R.E's, B.E.F. *a*: 46 Clarence Rd, Teddington, Mddx. *T*: Kingston 3880.

GOUGH, Rev. Percival. *b*: Oxford 1880. *e*: Oxf Univ. Rector of Acton. *Publ*: Outspoken Addresses. *c.t*: Contemporary Review, Quest. *s.s*: Comparative religion. *Rec*: Cricket. *a*: The Rectory, Acton, W.3. *t*: Acorn 0630.

GOULBURN, Bishop of (see **BURGMANN, Rt. Rev. Ernest Henry,** M.A., Th.D.).

GOULD, Frederick James, L.C.P. *b*: Brighton 1855. *e*: St George's Chapel Sc Windsor Castle. *m*: M. E. Lash. *s*: 1 (dec). *d*: 2 (1 dec). Teacher, Educationist. *Publ*: Concise History of Religion; Life of Hyndman, Prophet of Socialism; Youth's Noble Path; This England; Bright Lamps of History; Life-Story of a Humanist; etc. *c.t*: Literary Guide, School, Guardian, Eastern Times (Lahore), etc. *s.s*: Educ, humanism, L.o.N. *a*: Armorel, Woodfield Av, Ealing W.5. *t*: Per 5424.

GOULD, Gerald, M.A. *b*: Scarboro' 1885. *e*: Bracondale & Oxf & Lon Univs. *m*: Barbara Ayrton. *s*: 1. Author & Journalist. *Publ*: The Happy Tree, & Other Poems (1919); Beauty the Pilgrim, & Other Poems; Democritus, or the Future of Laughter; All About Women; Essays & Parodies; Isabel (Novel); Refuge from Nightmare, & Other Essays ('33); etc. *c.t*: Observer, News-Chronicle, etc. *s.s*: Belles-lettres. *a*: 1 Hamilton Terr, N.W.8. *t*: Cunningham 1544.

GOULD, Howard Ernest, M.A. *b*: London 1898. *e*: City of Lond Sch & Univ of Lond. *m*: Marjorie Macbeth *s*: 1. *d*: 1. Schoolmaster, Mem Classical Assoc. *Publ*: Lucian; New Latin Course for Schools (with J. L. Whiteley); Modern School Classics. *a*: 238 Chamberlayne Rd, London, N.W.10. *T*: Willesden 2848.

GOULD, John Alexander, M.C., F.R.S.A., M.I.Gas.E. M.I.Mech.E. *b*: London 1894. *m*: Doris Kathleen Gough (dec'd). Chartered Gas Engineer, Mem Soc for Army Hist Research. *Publ*: Short History of 19th County of London Bn Home Guard. *Ctr*: Gas Journ & World, various newsps on military hist, etc. *s.s*: Gas Distribution & Supply. *Rec*: Lawn tennis, fencing, swimming, British Legion work. *c*: Junior Army & Navy, Rifle Bgde. *w.s*: 1914—19 Rifle Bgde, '40—45 c.o. 19th Cty of Lond Bttn H.G. (Lt-Col). *a*: Hurst, Woodland Way, West Wickham, Kent. *T*: Springpark 2057.

GOULD, Commander R. T. Author. *Publ*: The Loch Ness Monster; Oddities; The Case for the Sea-Serpent. *a*: c/o G. Bles Ltd, 2 Manchester Sq. W.1.

GOULDEN, Charles Bernard, O.B.E., M.A., M.D., M.Chir., F.R.C.S. *b*: Canterbury. *e*: St Edmund's Coll, Old Hall, Downing Coll Camb. *m*: Norah O'Brien. Surg-Oculist to Household of H.M. Queen Mary, Cons Ophth Surg Queen Alexandra Mil Hosp Milbank, Sen Ophth Surg & Lect in Opthalmology in Med Sch of London Hosp, etc. *Publ*: The Refraction of the Eye; Koby's Slit Lamp Microscopy of the Living Eye (trans with Clara Harris). *Ctr*: Medical journals, etc. *s.s*: Ophthalmology. *Rec*: Music, walking. *c*: Athenæum. *a*: 29 Harley St, London, W.1. *T*: Langham 3147.

GOULDEN, Mark. *b*: Clifton 1897. *e*: Priv. Managing Ed. *n.a*: Camb Dly News 1912, Managing Ed Eastern Morning News Hull '24, & Yorks Evening News Leeds '30—32, & Sunday Referee '32, & Argus Press, Director Macfarden Mags, Illus Nwsprs '35—39, Managing Director W. H. Allen Publishers '40. *Ctr*: All Trade Journs. *c*: London Press. *Rec*: Golf, flying, riding. *a*: 43 Melbury Ct, London, W.8. *T*: Western 4734.

GOULDER, George Frederick. *e*: City of Lon Sc. Journalist. *n.a*: Editor & Founder Newsagent-Booksellers' Review 1889—. *a*: 37 Strand, W.C.2. *t*: Temple Bar 5761.

GOULDESBROUGH, Claude, M.A., M.B., B.Ch (Oxon), M.R.C.S., L.R.C.P. Radiologist. *a*: 56 Welbeck St, W.1. *t*: Welbeck 9071.

GOULDING, Vincent. *b*: Burton 1904. *e*: Downfield Sc, Stroud. *m*: Gladys Bendall. *d*: 1. Joint Chief Reporter Citizen Gloucester. *s.s*: Court & church council work. *Rec*: Tennis, gardening. *a*: c/o The Citizen, Gloucester, & Mayfair, Waverley Rd, Gloucester. *t*: Gloucester 3006.

GOUR, Sir Hari Singh, Kt., M.A., D.Litt., D.C.L., LL.D. *b*: Saugor 1866. *m*: Grace Olvia. *s*: 1. *d*: 4. Barrister. *Publ*: Law of Transfer; The Spirit of Buddism; His Only Love; The Hindu Law; The Indian Penal Code. *Ctr*: Various. *s.s*: Political, Philosophical & Law. *c*: Saugor. *a*: Saugor Univ, 21 The Mall, University Hse, Saugor.

GOVAN, Christine (Mary Allerton) (J. N. Darby). *b*: New York 1898. *e*: High Sch. *m*: Gilbert E. Govan. *s*: 1. *d*: 2. Writer. *Publ*: Jennifer's House; The Shadow & the Web; Those Phimmer Children; Judy & Chris; Narcissus & the Children; The House with the Echo; Fine at Ashes Field; Carolina Caravan; Sweet Poosom Valley; Murder on the Mountain; Plantation Murder; Murder in the House with the Blue Eyes. *Ctr*: Chattanooga Times. *c*: Hamilton County League of Women Voters. *a*: 4517 Alabama Ave, Chattanooga 9, Tennessee, U.S.A. *T*: 3-1523.

GOVER, John Eric Bruce. *b*: Chelsea 1895. *e*: Rugby, Emmanuel Col Cam. Asst Ed Eng Placename Soc. *Publ*: The Place Names of Middlesex; (with A. Mawer & F. M. Stenton) The Place Names of Devon; The Place Names of Northamptonshire; The Place Names of Surrey. *s.s*: Philology, hist. *Rec*: Riding, swimming. *c*: Eng-Speaking Union. *a*: Univ Col, London.

GOW, Alexander Edward, M.D., B.S. (Lond), F.R.C.P. *e*: King Edward Sch Stratford-on-Avon, St Bart's Hosp Med Coll, Berlin, Munich & Freiburg. *m*: Helen Gordon Rannie. *s*: 2. *d*: 1. *Publ*: Essentials of Medical Diagnosis (with Lord Horder). *Ctr*: Price's Textbooks, St Bart's Hosp Journ, Quarterly Journ of Med, B.M.J., etc. *s.s*: Diseases of Blood Forming Organs, Lymphadenopathy, Infections. *a*: Robinwood Cottage, Kingston Vale, London, S.W.15. *T*: Kingston 2556, & 149 Harley St, London, W.1. *T*: Welbeck 4444.

GOW, Rev. Henry, HonM.A.(Oxon), D.D.(Meadville, U.S.A.). *b*: Cheltenham 1861. *e*: Owen's Col M/C & M/C Col Lon. *m*: (1) Edith Beard; (2) Joyce Cobb. *s*: 1 (dec). *d*: 1. Vice-Princ M/C Col, Oxf '24-31. *Publ*: The Alchemy of Sorrow, & Other Sermons; Out of the Heart of the Storm, & other Sermons; The Unitarians. *c.t*: Hibbert Journ, etc. *s.s*: New Testament, ornithology. *Rec*: Nat hist. *c*: Nat Lib, Eng Speaking Un. *a*: Holywell, 2 Hove Pk Rd, Brighton. *t*: Preston 3428.

GOW, Ronald, B.Sc. *b*: Heaton Moor 1897. *e*: Gr Sch Altrincham, Manch Univ. Dramatist. *Publ*: (plays) Gallows Glorius; Love on the Dole; Tess of the D'Urbevilles (adapt); & several Film Scripts & Radio Plays. *a*: Stratton Rd, Beaconsfield. *T*: 788.

GOWAR, Dr. F. J. S. *Publ*: Works on Acute Aseptic Meningitis. *c.t*: Lancet. *a*: St Oswald's, South Mimms, Middlx.

GOWEN, Emmett. *b*: Lavergne, Tenn 1902. *e*: Lavergne Public Sch, Watkins Inst, Columb Univ. *m*: Claire Loeb. Novelist. *n.a*: Ed The Fourth Estate (N.Y) 1926—27. *Publ*: Mountain Born; Dark Moon of March; Old Hell; Racketeers, An Expose. *Ctr*: Atlantic Monthly, Yale Rev, True, Scribner's, Esquire, etc. *s.s*: Politics, Economy, Lit Criticism, Farming, Fishing. *Rec*: Fishing. *c*: Author's League. *a*: Lavergne, Tennessee, U.S.A.

GOWER, Charles. *b*: Toorak, Victoria, Australia. *e*: Private. *Publ*: Cordis Flamma (verse). *c.t*: Bookfellow, Sydney, N.S.W. Sometime teacher Eng, languages, science. *Rec*: Aust bush botany, lit, music, painting. *c*: Incorporated Soc of Authors, Playwrights & Composers. *a*: c/o Mrs Weatherston, 10 Green St, East St. Kilda, S.2. Victoria, Australia.

GOWER, Pauline Mary de Peauly. *b*: Tunbridge Wells 1910. *e*: Sacred Heart Convent Tunbridge Wells & Paris. Pilot to Air Trips Ltd. *Publ*: Piffling Poems for Pilots. *c.t*: Popular Flying, Roy Pictorial, Sunday Mercury, Girls' Own Paper, Australian Women's Mirror, etc. *s.s*: Aviation. 1st woman to start air travel business in partnership with another woman. Taken up more passengers than any other woman. *Rec*: Riding, music. *c*: Ladies' Carlton, Forum, Mem Women's Engineering Soc. *a*: Sandown Ct, Tunbridge Wells, Kent; 204 Ashley Gdns, S.W.1. *t*: Tunbridge Wells 593; Victoria 2274.

GOWER, SIR ROBERT: author, statesman; b. Tunbridge Wells, Eng., Nov. 10, 1880; s. Joshua Robert (J. P.) and Kate (Fagge) G.; educ. privately; DEGREES: F.R.G.S., F.S.G., Law Society's Honorman (Eng.); m. Dorothy Wills, June 29, 1907. AUTHOR: The National Insurance Act; How it affects Friendly Societies, 1909; The Perils of Socialism, 1910. Contributor to Times, Daily Telegraph, Morning Post, Nat. Rev., Journ. Soc. of Internat. Affairs, Kent and Sussex Courier, and many other mags. and papers. General character of writing: political, social reviews. Chairman Royal Soc. for Prevention Cruelty to Animals (Eng.); chmn. Nat. Canine Defense League (Eng.); M. P. for Central Hackney since 1924; memb. Kent county council for 15 yrs.; Alderman, Hon. Freeman, Ex-Mayor Borough Royal Tunbridge Wells; Freeman City of London; memb. Royal Inst. Internat. Affairs and of Internat Law Assn.; past-Pres. Nat. Soc. for Prevention and Relief of Cancer. Knighted, 1919; O.B.E., 1919. Relig. denom., Church of England. CLUBS: Carlton, Jr. Carlton, St. Stephens, Kent County, Tunbridge Wells, Counties. HOME: Sandown Court, Tunbridge Wells, Kent, and 205 Ashley Gardens, Westminster, London, S. W. 1, Eng.

GOWING, Venerable Ellis Norman, M.A., L.Th. *b*: Sydney, N.S.W. 1883. *e*: Sydney & Aust Coll of Theol. *m*: Dorothy Mary Watts-Ditchfield. *s*: 2. Vicar of Prittlewell 1917, Rural Dean Canewdon & Southend 1918, Archdeacon of Southend '38. *Publ*: John Edwin Watts-Ditchfield, 1st Bishop of Chelmsford; The Story of Prittlewell Church. *a*: The Vicarage, Prittlewell, Southend-on-Sea. *T*: 3470.

GOWLAND, T. B. *n.a*: Sub-Ed M/C Guardian. *a*: Westbourne, Rochdale Rd, Middleton, nr M/C.

GOWLLAND, Lt.-Col. E. L., D.S.O., M.B.(Lon), T.D. *Publ*: After-Treatment of Paraplegia following Spinal Injuries, and Disseminated Sclerosis. Commandant Star & Garter Homes for disabled sailors and soldiers, Richmond & Sandgate. *a*: Star & Garter Home, Richmond, Surrey.

GOWNES, Arthur Trenam. *n.a*: Sub Ed Yorks Evening Post (Doncaster Ed) 1929—. *s.s*: Sport. *a*: 12 Albany Rd, Doncaster. *t*: Doncaster 1012.

"**Gpc**" (pseudonym): see Panconcelli-Calzia, Guilio.

GRACE, Edward Nathaniel, M.C. *b*: London 1914. *e*: Westminster Sch & Montana Coll of Languages, Switzerland. *m*: Ivy Henderson. Solictor. *Publ*: The Promise of the Years; Africa Saga. *Ctr*: The Field, Country Life, The Lady. *s.s*: Travel & Photography. *Rec*: Photography, music, cricket, acting & producing. *c*: P.E.N., Richmond Arts & Literary. *w.s*: Queens Own Cameron Hgldrs. *a*: 50 Beechwood Ave, Kew Gardens, Surrey. *T*: Prospect 2011.

GRACE, Harvey, F.R.C.O., MusDoc. *b*: Romsey 1874. *m*: Dorothy Kirby. *s*: 1. *d*: 1. Musician & Journalist. *n.a*: Ed Musical Times 1918—. *Publ*: Organ Works of Bach; Beethoven; A' Musician at Large; The Complete Organist; etc. Organist & Choir Dir Chichester Cathedral '30—. *a*: The Treasury, Chichester.

GRACE, John, B.A., Ph.D., F.R.S.A. *e*: Univs of B. Columbia, Paris & Cambridge. University Teacher, Advisory Mem Wartime Information Bd Ottawa 1944—45. *Publ*: Boulainvilliers, Historian & Philosopher. *Ctr*: Canadian Geog Journ, Internat & Canadian Affairs. *s.s*: Internat Affairs. *Rec*: Cruising. *c*: University Cruising. *w.s*: World War II Westminster Regt (Col). *a*: 5 Kent Hse, Sussex St, Cambridge.

GRACE, William Francis Forster, M.A., Ph.D., F.R.Hist.S. Schoolmaster. *Publ*: Great Britain & the Polish Question in 1863; The Congress Policy of British History. *Ctr*: Cambridge Hist Journ. *s.s*: Catholicism in England 1485—1850. Anglo-Polish Relations in the Nineteenth Century. *Rec*: Gardening. *a*: Thornfield, Huyton, nr Liverpool.

GRACEY, George Frederick Handel, D.S.O. *b*: Belfast 1879. *e*: Prof O'Neil's Mil Law & Training Col. *m*: Amelia Turnley Coulter. *s*: 2. *d*: 2. Secretary. Overseas Delegate Save the Children Fund. *c.t*: Contemporary Review, Outward Bound, Missionary Mags, etc. *s.s*: Armenians, Assyrians & Turks. Missionary Urfa Turkey 1904—14. Mem of Amer Relief Commission to Caucasus to assist 250,000 Armenian refugees who fled from Turkey to Russia in '15 Piloted the evacuation of 25,000 refugees (Armen) from Van to Igdir single-handed '16. Intelligence staff officer attached Brit Mil Mission Tiflis '17. Raised large numbers of Armens, Russians, Georgians to hold position evacuated by Russian troops. Captured by Bolsheviks & imprisoned in Valadikarkaz & Moscow for 9 mths. Exchanged by Brit Gov, returned to Eng '19. Russian Order of St Anne 2nd Class. Order of St Gregory the Illuminator 1st Class. *Rec*: Riding. *c*: Roy Inst of Internat Affairs, Roy Auto, etc. *a*: 40 Gordon Sq, Lon, W.C.1. *t*: Museum 5204.

GRACEY, HUGH KIRKWOOD: Indian civil servant (retired); b. London, Eng., 1868; s. David and Mary Nelson (Bigge) G.; educ. City of London Sch., St. Katherine's Coll. (Cambridge). DEGREE: B.A.; widower. AUTHOR: Rhyming Legends of India, 1892; The Zuff Ballads, 1901. Contributor to many papers and mags. of India and Gt. Britain. General character of writing: poems, articles, fiction. Service of 35 yrs. in

India. Last 8 yrs. Comm. (chief administrative office) of the Gopakhpur division (pop. 7,000,000); received O.B.E.; mentioned in dispatches for war work. CLUB: R.A.C. (London). HOME: Keppel Cottage, La Roque, Jersey, Channel Islands, Eng.

GRACEY, Dr. Ivan. *c.t*: B.M.J., Malayan M.J., etc. *a*: Verduge, Rockingham Rd, Kettering.

GRAFLY, Dorothy, B.A. *b*: Paris 1896. *e*: Priv, Wellesley Col & Harvard Univ. Writer, Journalist & Lecturer. *n.a*: Reporter, Art & Feature Writer Philadelphia N. American 1920–25, Art Ed & Feature Writer Public Ledger '25–34, Evening Public Ledger '34, etc. *Publ*: History of the Philadelphia Print Club ('29). *c.t*: Theatre Guild Mag, Amer Mag of Art, Art & Archæ, Boston Transcript, etc. *s.s*: Amer art & artists, European & Amer sculpt. Backed 1st art show of Disney Cartoons in Amer. Lecturer on contemp art. In charge of collections, Drexel Inst '34. *Rec*: Philately, theatre, trav. *c*: Mem-at-large Pi Gamma Mu Zeta Alpha (Wellesley), Phil Art Alliance, Phil Chapter Nat Assoc Altrusa Club, Wellesley Col Alumnal Assoc, etc. *a*: 131 N. 20th St, Phila, Pa, U.S.A. & 1233 Washington St, Gloucester, Mass. *t*: Locust 1684.

GRAEME, Bruce, (See JEFFRIES, Graham Montague). *Publ*: inc The Story of Buckingham Palace; The Story of Windsor Castle; The Trail of the White Knight; A Murder of Some Importance; Dead Pigs at Hungry Farm; etc; also The Return of Blackshirt & other Volumes in the same series. *a*: Bourne Farm, Aldington Frith, nr Ashford, Kent.

GRAHAM, Alan Philps, M.A. *b*: Newport 1904. *e*: Mill Hill Sch & Sydney Sussex Coll Camb. Biology Master Clifton Coll Bristol, Head Biol Dep King Edward VII's Sch Sheffield. *Publ*: Elements of Practical Biology; Botany for Beginners (with E. J. Holmyard); Biology (with Prof B. J. Marples). *s.s*: Biology. *a*: 78 Clarkegrove Rd, Sheffield. *T*: 61037.

GRAHAM, David. *b*: Falkirk 1854. *e*: Falkirk, St And, Edin. *m*: Sophie Mary Thomson. *s*: 2. *d*: 1. Author. *Publ*: Grammar of Philosophy; Religion & Intellect; etc Plays—Rizzio; Darnley; etc. *c*: Authors'. *a*: The Chalet, Gipsy Lane, Putney, S.W.

GRAHAM, David Alan. *b*: Whitehaven 1912. *e*: Elmfield Col York. Journalist. *n.a*: Newark Herald '31–33, Peterborough Standard '33–34, Chief Reporter & Sports Ed Huntingdonshire Post '34. *c.t*: Daily Mail, Daily Express, Daily Telegraph & Daily Herald. *s.s*: Sport, humour, film & dramatic criticism. *Rec*: Athletics. *a*: 13 Ingram St, Huntingdon. *t*: 79.

GRAHAM, Dorothy. *b*: New Rochelle, New York. *e*: Priv & at Lausanne & Florence. *m*: James W. Bennett. Writer. *Publ*: Chinese Gardens; Wind Across the World; The Chinese Venture; Candles in the Sun; The French Wife; Lotus of the Dusk; Through the Moon Door—A Study of Peking; Brush Stroke on the Fan of a Courtesan Verse (in collab). *Ctr*: Asia, N.Y. Times, N.Y. Herald-Tribune, Tomorrow, etc. *s.s*: Far East History, Aesthetics, Human Relations. *Rec*: Travel, photography. *a*: 12 East 97th St, New York, N.Y. *T*: Atwater 9-0136.

GRAHAM, Dorothy Kathleen. *b*: Lancashire. *e*: Cheltenham Ladies Col, King's Col for Women, Univ of Lond. Author, Writer, Examiner for the General Nursing Council for England & Wales, Hospital Examiner. *Publ*: Hygiene for Probationer Nurses; Bacteriology for Probationer Nurses; Chemistry of Food & Sick Room Cookery; Outline of Medicine & Medical Nursing '35. *c.t*: Nursing Mirror.

British Journ of Nursing; The Public Assistance Journ. *a*: 2 Holders Hill Gdns, Hendon, N.W.4. *t*: Hendon 8074.

GRAHAM, Dr. G. F., M.B., F.R.C.S.I., Lt-Col I.M.S. (ret). Mem B.M.A. *a*: Wyndham Lodge, Milford, Nr Godalming, Surrey.

GRAHAM, George. *b*: Petrograd, Russia, 1910. *e*: Heath Mount & St Paul's Scs, & Pozzo Col, St Cloud, France. *n.a*: Ed, "Skating Times," '32—; Ed, "Swimming & Bathing Pool Review " '34; on staff, British-Continental Press, Ltd. *c.t*: Morning Post, the Field, The Star, The Music Lover, etc. *s.s*: Winter sports, skating, ice hockey, & swimming. *Rec*: Skating & swimming. *a*: 80, Fleet St, E.C.4 & 10 North Hill Ct, North Hill, Highgate Village, N.6. *t*: Central 4878.

GRAHAM, George, M.D., F.R.C.P. *Publ*: Pathology & Treatment of Diabetes Mellitus. Part-Ed (with V. H. Mottram) Hutchinson's Food & the Principles of Dietetics, 9 & 10th edns. *Ctr*: Various. *a*: 149 Harley St, London, W.1. *T*: Welbeck 4444.

GRAHAM, Gerald. *b*: Middleton 1885. *e*: Bootham, York. *m*: Mabel Firth. *d*: 2. N/p Reporter. *n.a*: Saddleworth Rep Oldham Chronicle 1931–. Mem N.U.J. '21–. Ed Daily Phœnix, Saskatoon, Canada '15–16. Comm Chamber of Commerce Saskatoon '16–20. Reporter Oldham Chronicle '21–28. Sub Ed Cardiff Evening Express '29. Sub Ed Leicester Evening Mail '30. *s.s*: Music, chess. *a*: Spring Bank, Uppermill, nr Oldham. *t*: Saddleworth 119.

GRAHAM, Gerald Sandford, M.A., Ph.D., F.R.Hist.S. *b*: Sudbury, Ontario 1903. *e*: Queen's Univ Kingston Ont. *m*: Winifred Emily Ware. *s*: 1. *Publ*: Sea Power & British North America 1783–1820; British Policy & Canada 1774–91; Britain & Canada; etc. *Ctr*: Canadian Hist Rev, Canadian Defence Quarterly, New England & Queen's Quarterlies. *s.s*: British Imperial & Naval History, Colonial Policy. *Rec*: Walking, travel. *c*: Roy Empire. *w.s*: 1942–44 Inst Lieut-Cmmdr R.C.N. Coll, '44–46 Historical Section Canadian Army Overseas. *a*: Birkbeck College, University of London, London.

GRAHAM, Harry Jocelyn Clive. *b*: Lon 1874. *e*: Eton & R.M.C. Sandhurst. *m*: Dorothy Villiers. *d*: 1. Author & Playwright. Trustee Brit Museum. *Publ*: Ruthless Rhymes for Heartless Homes; Departmental Ditties; The Bolster Book; The Perfect Gentleman; The World We Laugh in; etc. Plays produced :—By Candle Light; White Horse Inn; Sybil; Land of Smiles; etc. Service S. African & European Wars. Was Private Sec to late Lord Rosebery. *Rec*: Golf. *c*: Garrick & Beefsteak. *a*: 5 Montagu Sq, W.1. *t*: Welbeck 8381.

GRAHAM, Rev. Canon Henry Burrans. *b*: Lockwood, Yorks 1909. *e*: King James Gr Sch Almondsbury. Clerk in Holy Orders, Diocesan Secretary, Hon Chap to Bishop of St Edmundsbury Surrogate. *n.a*: Ed St Edmundsbury & Ipswich Diocesan Directory. *Publ*: Music in Church; The Christian Privilege of Almsgiving. *Ctr*: Ch Times, East Anglian Dly Times. *s.s*: Church Music. *Rec*: Walking, motoring. *a*: Diocesan Hse, Ipswich. *T*: 2530.

GRAHAM, Henry Tucker. *b*: Winchester, Va, U.S.A. 1865. *e*: Sydney Coll, Union Theol Sem Va. *m*: Lilian Gordon Baskerville. *d*: 1. Minister, for 5 yrs Missionary in Japan. *n.a*: Hampden-Sydney Mag 1885—86, Florence (S.C.) Morn News 1914—19. *Publ*: Men of Might; An Old Manse & Other Sermons; The

Praying Christ; Greatest Book in the World; etc. *Ctr*: Christian Observer, Presbyterian Journ. *s.s*: History, Theology. *a*: c/o F.M.C., Red Springs, N.C. *T*: 357-1.

GRAHAM, James Gibson, M.D., F.R.F.P.S.G. *b*: Glasgow 1897. *e*: Glas Acad & Univ. *m*: Elizabeth Waddell. *s*: 1. *d*: 1. Asst-Phys Western Infirmary Glasgow. *Publ*: (Part-author) The Case of Rudolph Hesse. *Ctr*: Various Sc journs. *Rec*: Golf, fishing. *w.s*: 1939—45 R.A.M.C. (Lieut-Col). *a*: 17 Westbourne Gardens, Glasgow, W.2. *T*: Western 1547.

GRAHAM, Lt.-Col. John Henry Porteus, M.R.C.S., L.R.C.P. *c.t*: Lancet. *a*: Hastingleigh, Ashford, Kent. *t*: Elmsted 44.

GRAHAM, John Lancelot. *b*: India 1908. *m*: Joan Elizabeth Stericker. *s*: 1. *d*: 1. Writer. *Publ*: Good Merchant (novel '34). *a*: High St, Winchelsea.

GRAHAM, JOHN WILLIAM: College Principal (retired); b. Preston, Lanc., Eng., July, 1859; s. Michael and Ann (Harrison) G.; educ. Friends Sch. (Ackworth and Kendal, Eng.), Flounders Inst., Univ. Coll. (London), King's Coll. (Cambridge); DEGREES B.A. (London), M.A. (Cambridge), (Hon.) Litt.D., Swarthmore Coll. (U.S.A.); m. Margaret Brockbank, 1891; 2 sons, 3 daughters. AUTHOR: The Destruction of Daylight, 1907; Evolution and Empire, 1912; William Penn, Founder of Pennsylvania, 1916; War From a Quaker Point of View, 1916; The Harvest of Ruskin, 1920; The Faith of a Quaker, 1920; Conscription and Conscience, 1922; The Quaker Ministry, 1925; The Divinity in Man, 1927; Britain and America (Merttens Lecture), 1930. Editor (formerly) The British Friend. Contributor to Manchester Guardian, Hibbert Journ., Friend, Friends' Intelligencer and other mags. Principal Dalton Hall, Univ. Manchester, 1897-1924; Lecturer and Fellow Woodbrooke, 1924-25; Prof. Swarthmore Coll. Penna., U.S.A.), 1925-26; lectured at Univs. and Coll. of India, 1927-28; Exten. Lecturer Manchester Univ. Frequent speaker in behalf Soc. of Friends and on Internat. Peace and allied subjects. Chmn. Smoke Abatement League, Gt. Britain, for 16 yrs. Relig. denom., Society of Friends. HOME: 149 Huntingdon Road, Cambridge, Eng.

GRAHAM, Malcolm. *b*: Wolverhampton 1901. *e*: Tettenhall Coll. *m*: Mollie Evans. *s*: 2. *d*: 2. Newspaper Proprietor, Dir Press Assoc Ltd 1941. *n.a*: Asst-Mgr Express & Star '23 & Gen Mgr '27, Mang-Dir Midlands News Assoc Ltd '44, Dir Reuters '44, Pres West Midlands Newsp Soc '47. *Rec*: Golf, lawn tennis, shooting. *a*: Cottage Piece, Wightwick, Wolverhampton.

GRAHAM, Molly. *b*: Quorn, Leics 1910. *e*: Heathfield, St Clothilde Paris. Journalist, mem N.U.J. *Ctr*: Loughborough Echo, Leicester Mercury, Dly Sketch, Newcastle Chron, Woman's Mag, Queen, Lady, John Bull, Dly Mail, Sat Ev Post. *s.s*: Cookery, Housecraft & Child Welfare, Maritime Research. *Rec*: Sailing, sports, tennis, squash, badminton. *c*: Women's Press, Soc of Women Journalists, etc. *a*: 58 Gower St, London, W.C.1. *T*: Museum 9058.

GRAHAM, Norval Bantock. J.P. :*b*: Wolverhampton 1870. *e*: Tettenhall Col. *m*: Ethel Esther Bratt. *d*: 1. *n.a*: Ex-Pres Newspaper Soc, Mem Mang Cmt P.A., Mem Bd of Reuter's. *Rec*: Hunting. Chm Roy Hosp Wolverhampton & Midland News Assoc. *c*: Reform, Royal Thames Yacht. *a*: End Hall, Compton, Wolverhampton. *t*: Tettenhall 51077.

GRAHAM, Philip, Ph.D. *b*: Comanche, Texas 1898. *e*: Univ of Chicago. *m*: Lila White. *s*: 1. Univ Prof. *Publ*: Life & Poems of Mirabeau B. Lamar; Complete Works of Sidney Lanier; Early Texas Verse; (With J. J. Jones) Concordance to the Poems of Sidney Lanier. *Ctr*: Southwest Rev, Sewanee Rev, Amer Lit, etc. *s.s*: American Novels & Novelists, The South & its Writers. Negro Lit. *a*: 1007 Gaston Ave, Austin, Texas. *T*: 22162.

GRAHAM, Stanley Galbraith. *b*: Ontario, Canada 1895. *e*: Univ of Toronto. *m*: Grace Hay Anderson. *s*: 2. Prof of Child Health Univ of Glasgow. *Publ*: Acidosis & Alkalosis; Diseases of Nutrition in Diseases of Children; etc. *Ctr*: Various Med journs. *s.s*: Diseases of Children. *a*: 18 Woodside Pl, Glasgow, C.3. *T*: Douglas 5201.

GRAHAM, Stephen. *b*: 1884. Novelist & Essayist, B.B.C. (Foreign Service, Slavonic). *Publ*: A Vagabond in the Caucasus; The Way of Martha & The Way of Mary; The Lay Confessor; New York Nights; The Death of Yesterday; Life of Peter the Great; St Vitus' Day; A Private in the Guards; The Challenge of the Dead; Under London; In Search of El Dorado; Alexander of Yugoslavia; Life of Ivan the Terrible; Life of Stalin; Lost Battle; Balkan Monastery; The Moving Tent. *s.s*: Russia. *a*: 60 Frith St, London, W.1.

GRAHAM, THOMAS OTTIWELL: physician, surgeon; b. Great Malvern, Eng., Jan. 25, 1883; s. Christopher and Rachel (Moore) G.; educ. St. Faith's, Perse Sch. (both Cambridge), Smyth's Sch. (Southsea), Trinity Coll. (Dublin), Vienna (Austria), Heidelberg, Freiberg (both Germany). DEGREES: B.A. (Senior Moderator and Gold Medallist), M.B., B.Ch., (Step cond), B.A.O., M.D. (Dublin Hosp.), D.P.H., F.R.C.S.I., L.M. (Rotunda Hosp.); m. Susan Eva Sanctuary, June 13, 1918. Contributor to Brit. Med. Journ., Irish Journ. Med. Science, Taylor's Operative Surgery. General character of writing: scientific, medical. Consulting Surg. and Surg. for Dr. Stevens Hosp., Royal Victoria Eye and Ear Hosp., Royal City of Dublin Hosp., Ministry of Pensions Hosp., Monkstown Hosp. (all eye, nose, ear, throat). Expres. Dublin Univ. Biol. Ass'n. Recd. Mil. Cross for war service. Relig. faith, Protestant. CLUBS: Dublin Biol. Club, Malahide Island Golf Club, Brit. Med. Ass'n., Fellow Royal Acad. Med., Ireland. HOME: 61 Fitzwilliam Sq., Dublin, Ireland.

GRAHAM, Virginia Margaret. *b*: London 1910. *e*: Notting Hill Hgh Sch. *m*: Antony Thesiger. *Publ*: Heather Mixture; Consider the Years. *Ctr*: Punch, Spectator, Country Life, Sun Times. *s.s*: Light Verse. *Rec*: Piano, reading, theatre. *a*: 32 Cambridge Sq, London, W.2. *T*: Paddington 9942.

GRAHAM, Walter Armstrong. Farmer. *Publ*: The French Roman Catholic Mission in Siam (Bangkok 1903); Kelantan, A State of the Malay Peninsula (Glas); Siam, London (3rd edn '24). *c.t*: Journ Roy Geog Soc, Journ Roy Cent Asian Soc, Asiatic Quarterly Review, etc. Kt Grand Cross, White Elephant of Siam. *a*: Plush Manor, Piddletrenthide, Dorset. *t*: 22.

GRAHAM, WILLIAM: journalist; b. Peebles, Scotland, July, 1887; s. George and Jessie (Newton) G.; educ. Peebles Pub. Sch., George Herlot's Sch. (Edinburgh); DEGREES: M.A. (Honors in Econ. Science), LL.B., (Hon.) LL.D. (Edinburgh); m. Ethel Margaret Dobson, Oct. 14, 1919. AUTHOR: The Wages of Labour, 1920. Contributor to many newspapers and monthly publications of Gt. Britain. General character of writing: economic subjects. An expert in problems of public finance, social and industrial questions, etc.; memb. House of Commons; privy councillor; financial sec'y. to Brit. Treasury in the Labour Govt., 1924; chmn. Pub.

Accts. Com., House of Commons; President of the Board of Trade, 1929. Relig. faith, Protestant. HOME: 29 Sunningfields Road, Hendon, London, N. W. 4, Eng.

GRAHAM, Winifred. See Cory, Winifred Muriel.

GRAHAM, Winston. *b*: Manchester. *m*: . *s*: 1. *d*: 1. Author & Scriptwriter. *Publ*: Ross Poldark; Demelza; The Forgotten Story; The Merciless Ladies; Take My Life. *s.s*: 18th Century Cornwall. *Rec*: Tennis & beachcombing. *a*: Perranporth, Cornwall & Hallam St, London, W.1.

GRAHAM-BONNALIE, Dr. F. E. *a*: 17 Forth Ave, Hove, Sussex.

GRAHAM-DOW, Catherine Irvine, M.A., Ph.D., F.R.Hist.S. *b*: Aberdeen 1907. *e*: Albyn Sc, Univ of Aberdeen. *m*: Walter Graham-Dow. Lecturer in History, Univ of Glasgow. *Publ*: Louis Philippe. *c.t*: Glasgow Herald, Bulletin, Evening News, Evening Times, Scottish Daily Express, Time & Tide. *s.s*: History, foreign politics, French literature. *Rec*: Reading, writing, riding. *c*: College, Glasgow. *a*: 8 Queen Margaret Rd, Glasgow, N.W. *c*: Maryhill 747.

GRAHAM HODGSON, Harold Kingston, C.V.O., M.R.C.P., M.B., B.S., D.M.R.E. *b*: L'pool 1890. *e*: Mulgrave, St Edward's Sc Oxf & Clare Col Cam. *m*: Winifred Elizabeth Jenkins. *s*: 1. *d*: 1. Physician. *c.t*: Yr Book of Radiology, B.M.J., Practitioner, Brit Journ of Radiology, etc. *s.s*: Radiology. War Service, despatch rider 1914; Major '18. *Rec*: Hunting, fishing. *a*: 55 Upper Brook St, Grosvenor Sq, W.1. *t*: Mayfair 3100.

GRAHAM-SMITH, George Stuart, M.A., M.D., D.P.H., F.R.S. *b*: India 1875. *e*: Clifton Coll, Pembroke Coll Camb & Guy's Hosp. *m*: Elena Violet Leith-Ross. *s*: 1. Lect in Hygiene & Reader in Preventive Medicine Camb Univ 1908–40. *n.a*: Ed Journ of Hygiene '39–. *Publ*: The Bacteriology of Diptheria; Flies in Relation to Disease. *Ctr*: Various Sc & Med journs. *s.s*: Medical Bacteriology, Transmission of Diseases by Insects, esp Flies. *Rec*: Cricket, golf. *a*: Forvie, Hills Rd, Cherryhinton & Pathological Laboratory. Cambridge. *T*: Cambridge 87118.

GRAHAM-STEWART, Alexander, M.B., ChB. Physician. *c.t*: Practitioner, etc. *a*: 26 Ulster Pl, U. Harley St. W.1. *t*: Welbeck 1204.

GRAHAME-PARKER, Jack M.J.I., B.A. Married. *s*: 1. *d*: 1. Asst City Ed Financial Times. *n.a*: Financial News, Daily Mail, Evening News, Daily Express. *Rec*: Sport. *a*: 5 Sherwood Rd. Hendon. N.W.4.

GRAHAME-WHITE, Claude. *b*: Burseldon 1879. *e*: Crondall Hse Sch & Bedford Gr Sch. *m*: Phœbe Lee. Real Estate. *Publ*: The Aeroplane; With the Airmen; The Aeroplane Past, Present & Future; The Aeroplane in War; Aviation—Learning to Fly; Aircraft in the Great War; Air Power; Our First Airways—Their Organisation; Flying, an Epitome & Forecast; etc. *Ctr*: Various newspapers & periodicals. *s.s*: Aeroautics. *w.s*: R.N.A.S. 1914—18. *a*: 20 Rossmore Court, Park Rd, London, N.W.1. Upper Ribsden, Windlesham, Surrey, & 9419 Sunset Boulevard, Beverly Hills, California, U.S.A. *T*: Paddington 2995.

"GRAMIADES" (pen name): see Horton-Smith, Lionel Graham Horton.

GRAMLING, Oliver. *b*: Tallahassee, Florida 1904. *e*: Oglethorpe & Columbia Univs. Asst Gen Mang Associated Press. *Publ*: AP—The Story of News; Free Men Are Fighting. *Ctr*: Various. *s.s*: Biography, News Subjects. *Rec*: Horseshoe pitching. *a*: 444 East 52nd St, New York, N.Y. *T*: Eldorado 5-6457.

GRAN, HAAKEN HASBERG: professor; b. Toensberg, Norway, April, 1870; s. Capt. August Gran (in the Navy) and Agnes (Hasberg) G.; educ. Cathedral Sch. of Oslo (Norway), Univ. Oslo, Univ. Leipzig (Germany); DEGREE: Ph. D. (Oslo, 1902; m. Margrethe Holm, Aug. 26, 1927. AUTHOR: Das Plankton des Norwegishen Nordmeeres, 1902; Diatomeen, in Nordische Plankton, 1905; Pelagic Plant Life in Murray and Hjort, Depths of the Ocean, 1912; The Plankton Production of the North European Waters in the spring of 1912, 1915; Investigation of the Production of Plankton outside the Romsdals-Fjord 1926-1927, 1929; Quantitative Plankton Investigations carried out during the Expedition with the "Michael Sars", July-Sept., 1924, 1929; The Spring Growth of the Plankton at Moere in 1928-29 and at Lofoten in 1929 in Relation to its limiting Factors, 1930; Plankton Diatoms of Puget Sound (with E. C. Angst), 1931. Contributor to Morgenbladet, Samtidon. General character of writing: scientific (botany, agriculture, fisheries). Professor of Botany: director Botanical Lab., Univ. Oslo, since 1905. Student of marine biology; mem. expeditions for Norwegian gov't. Made expedition in Atlantic, 1910, under leadership Sir John Murray and Dr. John Hjort. Visiting prof. at Univ. of Washington (Seattle, U.S.A.), 1928-1930. Relig. denom., Lutheran. OFFICE: University Botanical Laboratory. HOME: Slemdal, by Oslo, Norway.

GRAND, Sarah. *b*: Donaghadee, Ireland. *e*: Roy Naval Sc for Officers' Daughters. *m*: Brig-Surg Lt-Col D. Chambers McFall, A.M.D. *s*: 1. Authoress. *Publ*: The Heavenly Twins; The Beth Book; A Domestic Experiment; Babs the Impossible; The Winged Victory; Adnam's Orchard; etc. *a*: 7 Sion Hill Pl, Bath, Som.

GRANGE, C. D'O., O.B.E., F.R.C.S. Surg. *a*: 2 Lancaster Rd, Harrogate.

GRANGE, Capt. G. W., M.C. Journalist. *n.a*: Lon Corr Times of Ceylon 1930–. Del to Fourth Imp Press Conf '30. *s.s*: Tea, rubber & matters general or political connected with Ceylon. War Service, Despatches. *a*: Blackfriars Hse, E.C.4.

GRANGE, Cyril, F.B.S.A., F.R.H.S. *b*: March 1900. Married. Agricultural & Poultry Journalist & Photographer. *Publ*: Bottling & Canning; Home Doctoring of Poultry; (& other Agric Books). *Ctr*: Leading Poultry journs, Leading Ladies' journs & dailies. *s.s*: Preservation of Fruit & Vegetables, Poultry-keeping, Dog-breeding. *Rec*: Tennis, motoring, fishing, gardening. *c*: Farmers. *a*: West Hill Hse, Bury St Edmunds, Suffolk. *T*: Bury St Edmunds 1030

GRANGER, Frank Stephen, A.R.I.B.A., D.Lit. *b*: Nott'm 1864. *e*: Nott'm H.S. *m*: Annie Ball Burton. *s*: 1. *d*: 1. Prof of Class, Univ Col Nott'm. *Publ*: Worship of the Romans ('95); Historical Sociology (1910); Via Romana ('15); Vitruvius, De Architectura, Vol I ('30); Vol II ('34); etc. *c.t*: Class Review, Journ Theo Studies, Expositor, Journ R.I.B.A., etc. *Rec*: Golf. *a*: 37 Lucknow Driv, Nott'm. *t*: 64343.

GRANT, Arthur James, M.A., D.Litt. *b*: Farlesthorpe, Lincs 1862. *e*: Boston Gr Sch, King's Coll Camb. *m*: Edith Alice Radford. Emeritus Professor. *Publ*: History of Europe; Outlines of European History; French Monarchy; Europe in the Nineteenth &

Twentieth Centuries (with Dr Temperley); Europe in the Sixteenth Century; The Huguenots; Scott; English Historians. *s.s*: French & Italian History. *a*: 4 Oak Bank, Leeds 6.

GRANT, Rev. Cecil, M.A. *b*: Linton, Kent 1870. *e*: Sutton Valence Sc & Wadham Col Oxf (Open Classical Scholar). *m*: Lucy Thompson. Headmaster St George's Sc Harpenden 1907—. *Publ*: A School's Life (sermons); English Education & Dr Montessori; The Case for Co-education (with Norman Hodgson); Abridged edn of Clutton Brock's What is the Kingdom of Heaven (with Francis House); The School of Prayer & the St George's Hymnal. *c.t*: Various. *s.s*: Religious teaching. *Rec*: Golf. *c*: Authors'. *a*: St George's Sc, Harpenden.

GRANT, D. W. Journalist. *n.a*: Ed Sunday Pictorial. *a*: Geraldine Hse, Fetter Lane, E.C.4. *t*: Holborn 4321.

GRANT, Donald, J.P. *a*: Grant Educational Co Ltd, 91 & 93 Union St, Glasgow.

GRANT, Duncan. Mang dir & editor. *n.a*: Jt Mang Dir & Ed Highland News. *c*: Inverness Rotary, Vice-Pres Scottish Liberal Fed. Chm Inverness-shire Liberal Assoc. *a*: Highland News Office, Inverness.

GRANT, E. Donald. *n.a*: Birm Corr Practical Bldg. *s.s*: Bldg, films & fiction. *a*: Roseland, 79 Wychall Lane, King's Norton, Birmingham.

GRANT, Sir Francis James, K.C.V.O., LL.D.(Aberdeen). *b*: 1863. *e*: Roy Hgh Sch Edin & Edin Univ. *m*: (1) Anne Irvine Cruickshank (dec'd—*d*: 2); (2) Violet Madeline Bourne Murphy. Lord Lyon King of Arms in Scotland, Sec Order of the Thistle 1929—45, Albany Herald '45—, Pres Old Edinburgh Club & Scottish Record Soc, Treas Scottish Text Soc. *Publ*: Zetland County Families; Catalogue of Heraldic Exhibition Edinburgh 1891; Grants of Corrimony; Zetland Family Histories; Manual of Heraldry; co-author History of Society of Writers to the Signet; etc. *Ctr*: Scots Peerage, Ed (joint) Fasti Ecclesiæ Scoticanæ (New Ed), Indexes to Commissarial Registers of Edinburgh, etc (for Scottish Record Soc). *a*: 18 George Sq, Edinburgh. *T*: 44224.

GRANT, Rev. Frederick Clifton, Th.D. *b*: Beloit, Wisconsin 1891. *e*: Lawrence Coll, Nashotah House, General & Western Theol Semins. *m*: Helen McQueen Hardie. *s*: 1. *d*: 1. Clerk in Holy Orders. *n.a*: Ed-in-Chief Anglican Theol Rev 1924—, Chm-Ed-Bd The Witness '41—47. *Publ*: Economic Background of the Gospels; The Earliest Gospel; The Gospel of the Kingdom; New Horizons of the Christian Faith; Can We Still Believe in Immortality?; The Practice of Religion; Various translations. *Ctr*: Anglican Theol Rev, Journ of Religion, Religion in Life, etc. *s.s*: Theology, Biblical Study, New Testament Text & Translation. *Rec*: Travel, music. *a*: 606 W. 122 St, New York, 27, N.Y., U.S.A. *T*: Mo 2-7100.

GRANT, Isabel F. *b*: Scotland. *e*: Priv. Founder of Highland Folk Mus. *Publ*: Everday Life on an Old Highland Farm; Social & Economic Development of Scotland; In the Tracks of Montrose; The Lordship of the Isles. *s.s*: Scots Social Hstory. *a*: Am Fasgadh, Kingussie. *T*: 107.

GRANT, Joan, (Mrs. Charles Beatty). *b*: London 1907. *e*: Priv. *m*: (1) Arthur Leslie Grant, (2) Charles Robert Longfield Beatty. *d*: 1. Author. *Publ*: (Hist Novels) Winged Pharaoh; Life as Carola; Eyes of Horus; Lord of the Horizon; Scarlet Feather; Return to Elysium. (Children's) The Scarlet Fish; Redskin Morning. (Travel)Vague Vacation. *a*: Trelydan Hall, Welshpool, Montgomeryshire. *T*: 89.

GRANT, John Charles Boileau, M.C. *b*: Edinburgh 1886. *e*: High Sch Nottingham, Univ of Edin. *m*: Catriona Anne Christie. Prof of Anatomy Univ of Toronto. *Publ*: A Method of Anatomy; An Atlas of Anatomy; Anthropometry of Chipewyan Indians; Anthropometry of Beaver, Sekani & Carrier Indians; (With H. A. Cates) A Handbook for Dissectors; etc. *Ctr*: Morris Human Anatomy, Cunningham's Textbook of Anatomy. *s.s*: Human Anatomy. *c*: Toronto Skating. *a*: 46 Bedford Rd, Toronto 5, Canada. *T*: Mi 3194.

GRANT, Julius, Ph.D., M.Sc.(Lond), F.R.I.C. *b*: London 1901. *e*: Strand Sch, King's Coll & Lond Univ. *m*: Selina Levy. *s*: 1. *d*: 1. Scientist. *n.a*: On Staffs of Bureau of Chem Abstracts 1926—, Analyst '26—, Ed Chemical News '27—31, Ed Chemical Dictionary. *Publ*: The Measurement of Hydrogen Ion Concentration; Fluorescence Analysis in Ultra Violet Light; Science for the Prosecution; Books & Documents; Laboratory Handbook of Pulp & Paper Manufacture; Wood Pulp & Allied Products. *Ctr*: Tech Scientific Publ. *s.s*: Popular & Tech Science. *Rec*: Trav, sailing. *c*: Chemical. *a*: 109 Pencisely Rd, Cardiff, Glam. *T*: Llandaff 475.

GRANT, K. *a*: Evening Chronicle, Newcastle.

GRANT, Malcolm, B.A. *b*: Argentina 1904. *e*: Winchester & Ch Ch Oxf. *Publ*: A New Argument for God & Survival & A Solution to the Problem of Supernatural Events. *s.s*: Nat Theo, Psych research. *Rec*: Shooting, fishing, sailing. *a*: c/o Lloyd's Bank, 39 Piccadilly, W.1.

GRANT, Maurice Harold. *b*: London 1872. *e*: Harrow & Sandhurst. Colonel (ret). *Publ*: History of the English Landscape; Catalogue of British Medals; Words by An Eye-witness; Mechanism of War; Makers of Black Basaltes; Book of the Snipe. *Ctr*: Blackwood's, Spectator, Times, etc. *s.s*: British Art. *Rec*: All Sports & games. *w.s*: 1899—1902, '14—20 & '40—45. *a*: c/o Lloyd's Bank, Pall Mall, London, S.W.1.

GRANT, Neil Forbes, C.B.E., M.A. *b*: Forres 1882. *e*: Edin Univ & B.N.C. Oxf. *m*: Nancy Elizabeth Puckett. Journalist & Dramatist. *n.a*: Staff Morning Post 1907, Ed Wireless & Cable Section '17, Foreign Ed '18—25, Lon Ed Cape Times, Rand Daily Mail, Natal Mercury, Sunday Times of Johannesburg '25—. *Publ*: Possessions; Getting Mother Married; Petticoat Influence; The Nelson Touch; etc. Officer of the Order of the Crown of Belgium. *Rec*: Lawn tennis. *c*: Un Univ. *a*: 81 Chiltern Ct, Clarence Gate, Regent's Park, N.W.1. *t*: Welbeck 5544 (Ex 81).

GRANT, R. A., M.B., ChB., F.R.C.S.(Edin). Med Supt Birkenhead Munic Hosp. *c.t*: B.M.J. *a*: Craigellachie, Bryanton Rd, Prenton, Birkenhead.

GRANT, Robert. *a*: Messrs John Grant, 31 George IV Bridge, Edinburgh.

GRANT, T. C., M.C. Journalist. *b*: Worcester 1879. *e*: St Martin's Sc. *n.a*: Asst Ed Newcastle Journal. *Publ*: Pt Author, History of Northumberland Hussars. War Service S. Africa & Gt War. *a*: 14 Cherryburn Gdns, Fenham, Newcastle-on-Tyne. *t*: 33763.

GRANT, William, M.A., LL.D. *b*: Elgin 1863. *e*: Elgin Acad, Aberdeen Univ. *m*: Janet C. R. Holm. Teacher. *Publ*: What Still Remains to be Done for the Scottish Dialects; Phonetic Tests for Scottish Dialects; Pronunciation of English in Scotland; Speech Training for Scottish Students (Jt Author); Transactions of the Scottish Dialects Committee I–IV; Scottish National Dictionary Parts I, II, III; etc. Lect on Eng Lang Aber Univ 1916–20. Summer Lect on Phonetics in Smith Col, Mass, U.S.A. '26. Convener Scot Dialects Cmt '07–28. Ed Scot Nat Dictionary & Sec Scot Nat Dictionary Assoc 28–. *a*: Ashfield, Cults, Aberdeen. *t*: Cults 133.

GRANT, William McBain. *e*: George Heriot's Sch. *n.a*: Sports Sub Ed Edinburgh Evening News. *a*: 67 Pilton Place, Edinburgh.

GRANT-ALLAN, Anne (Nance) Davidson, J.P. *b*: Adelaide Sth Australia 1887. *e*: Miss Gillis Girl's Sch Adelaide, Ch of Eng Girl's Sch Sth Yarra Victoria, Adelaide Univ. Secretary, Pres Fed Assoc Aust Housewives. *n.a*: Ed The Housewife 1943–. *Ctr*: Boomerang, The Housewife. *s.s*: Articles on Current Topics, Serial & Short Stories, Broadcasts. *Rec*: Reading, bridge & politics. *c*: Epworth Christian, Liberal. *a*: 97 Cremorne St, Unley, Sth Australia. *T*: U.3195.

GRANT DUFF, Hon Mrs. Ursula. *Publ*: The Life Work of Lord Avebury; A Mere Woman's Notebook. *c.t*: Eugenics Review. *s.s*: Eugenics, education. *a*: 16 Mulberry Walk, Chelsea. *t*: Flaxman 3401.

GRANT WATSON, Elliot Lovegood, B.A. *b*: 1885. *e*: Trinity Coll Camb. *m*: Katarine Hannay. *d*: 2. Author. *Publ*: But to What Purpose; The Nun & the Bandit; The Partners; Walking with Fancy; The Leaves Return; Priest Island; The Desert Horizon; The Contrasting Circle. *Ctr*: Lond Mercury, New Statesman, Eng Rev, Observer, Criterion, News Chronicle Dly Exp, Country Life, etc. *s.s*: Biology & Psychology. *Rec*: Gardening. *a*: West Melville, Northam, Devon. *T*: Northam 192.

GRANTHAM, A. E. *b*: Wiesbaden 1867. *e*: Oxford & Cambridge. Writing. *Publ*: Hills of Blue; The Wisdom of Akhnaton; A Manchu Monarch; The Twilight Hour of Yung Kuei Fei; The Temple of Heaven; Mater Dolorosa; etc. *c.t*: Sinica, China Journal of Science & Arts, La Politique de Pekin. *s.s*: History, poetry. *Rec*. Music. *a*: Banna Boo, Farnham Common, Bucks. *t*: 284.

GRANTHAM, William Wilson, K.C., V.D. *Publ*: Stoolball Illustrated & How to Play It (1919, 2nd edn '31); List of the Wardens of the Grocers' Coy from 1345 to 1907 with M.S. Notes; Pt Author, Will Adams The Pilot-Major of Gillingham ('34). *c.t*: Times, Morning Post, Sussex n/ps. *a*: 6 Crown Office Row, Temple, E.C.4, & Balneath Manor, nr Lewes. *t*: Central 2682.

GRANVILLE-BARKER, Harley, HonLL.D. (Edin), F.R.S.L. *b*: Lon 1877. *Publ*: Prunella (with Lawrence Housman, 1906); The Madras House ('10); The Red Cross in France ('16); An English Version of Sacha Guitry's Deburau; The Harlequinade (with Dion Clayton Calthrop '18); The Secret Life ('23); Doctor Knock (from the French by Jules Romains); His Majesty ('28); On Dramatic Method ('31, the Clark Lectures for 30); A National Theatre (with William Archer '07); Three Plays ('09); Anatol (a paraphrase from German of A. Schnitzler); Soulson Fifth ('16); Three Short Plays ('17); The Exemplary Theatre ('22); Prefaces to Shakespeare (commenced '29); His Majesty ('28); Ed with B. B. Harrison A Companion to Shakespeare Studies ('38); Study of Drama (lecture at Cambridge '34); versions of Spanish plays by G. Martinez, Siezza, Joaquim & Serafin Alvarez Quintezo, with Helen Granville-Barker; also various plays & English versions of Spanish plays; etc. *c*: Garrick, Athenæum, Travellers (Paris). *a*: 18 Place des Etats-Unis, Paris, XVIe. *t*: Kleber 4138.

GRAS, Norman Scott Brien, A.M., Ph.D. *b*: Toronto, Canada 1884. *e*: Univ of Western Ontario, Harvard Univ. *m*: Ethel G. Culbert. *s*: 3. Prof of Business History Harvard Univ 1927–. *n.a*: Ed Harvard Studies in Business History 1931–. *Publ*: Evolution of the English Corn Market; Business & Capitalism; Are You Writing a Business History; Shifts in Public Relations; (In collab) Economic & Social History of an English Village; Casebook on American Business History. *Ctr*: Bulletin of the Business Hist Soc. *s.s*: Hist of Business. *Rec*: Walking & Boating. *a*: 20 Craigie St, Cambridge 38, Mass, U.S.A. *T*: Kir 9736.

GRASBY, Ernest Dudley Yarnold, M.D., B.S., M.R.C.O.G. *b*: Teignmouth 1903. *e*: Lond Univ, Guy's Hosp & Gray's Inn. *m*: Margaret Elizabeth Coldicott. *d*: 1. *Publ*: Wenda I Wonder (play). *Ctr*: B.M.J., Guy's Hosp Gazette. *Rec*: Golf, tennis. *c*: Medico Legal Soc. *a*: Pembury, Kent. *T*: 263.

GRATTAN, Clinton Hartley, B.A. *b*: Wakefield, Mass. 1902. *e*: Clark Coll Worcester Mass. *m*: Marjorie Campbell. *s*: 1. *d*: 3. Free-lance Writer. *n.a*: Contrib-Ed Harper's Mag 1943–. *Publ*: Introducing Australia; Why We Fought; The Three Jameses, A Family of Minds; etc. *Ctr*: Barron's, Liberty, N.Y. Times, etc. *s.s*: Australian Affairs. Economic & Social Developments in U.K., Political & Economic Affairs in U.S.A. *a*: 9 Bedford Rd, Katonah, N.Y., U.S.A. *T*: Katonah 436 J.

GRATTAN, John Henry Grafton. *b*: Croydon 1878. *e*: Whitgift Gr Sch Croydon, Univ Coll Lond & Berlin Univ. Fell Univ Coll Lond, Emeritus Prof L'pool Univ. *Publ*: Our Living Language (with P. Gurrey). *Ctr*: Mod Lang Rev, Review of English Studies, Eng Assoc Essays & Studies. *s.s*: Eng Hist Gram, Philol & Mediæval Textual Criticism. *Rec*: Walking. *c*: Univ (L'pool). *a*: The University, Liverpool.

GRATWICKE, Ainslie, M.J.I. *b*: Exeter 1912. Journalist. *n.a*: Reporter Devon & Exeter Gazette '27–31, Dis Reporter Western Morning News '31–33. Mem N.U.J. '21–. *c.t*: Western Morning News, Western Weekly News, Western Evening Herald. *a*: Hetmere, Topsham, Devon.

GRAVELY, Frederic Henry, D.Sc. *b*: Wellingborough 1885. *e*: Friends Schs at Ackworth Yorks & Bootham, Manch Univ. *m*: Laura Balling. *s*: 1. *d*: 1. Supt Govt Museum Madras (ret). *Publ*: Oriental Passaledæ; Passaldiæ of the World; Outline of Indian Temple Architecture; Shells & Other Animal Remains of the Madras Beach. *Ctr*: Records & Memoirs of the Indian Museum, Bulletin of the Madras Government Museum. *Rec*: Walking. *a*: 52 London Rd, Reading. *T*: 61570.

GRAVES, ALFRED PERCIVAL: author, Gov't. Inspector of Schools; b. Dublin, Ireland, July 22, 1846; s. Charles Graves, Lord Bishop of Limerick, and Selina (Cheyne) G.; educ. Windemere Coll., Dublin Univ.; DEGREES: B.S., M.A., Litt.D. (Dublin); m. (1) Jane Cooper (died), 1874; (2) Amalie von Ranke, 1891. AUTHOR: Songs of Killarney, 1872; The Elementary School Manager, 1875; Irish Songs and Ballads, 1879; Songs of Old Ireland, and Irish Songs and Ballads (with Charles Villiers Stanford), 1882–1892; Satires: Blarney Ballads and the Green above the Red, 1883; Songs of Irish Wit and Humor, 1894; The Irish Song Book, 1894; Irish Folk Songs (with Dr. Charles

Wood); Songs of Erin (with Sir C. Stanford); Roseen Dhu (dramatic monologue); The Postbag, a lesson in Irish (operetta, with Michael Esposito), 1901; English Lyrics (with Sir Hubert Parry); Spring Songs (with Sir Alexander Mackenzie); Welsh Melodies (with Dr. Arthur Somervell and Dr. Lloyd Williams), 1907; The Absentee (play), 1908; Songs of the Gael, 1908; Irish Countryside Songs and Ballads, 1908; Welsh Poetry, Old and New, in English Verse, 1912; Irish Countryside Songs and Ballads (with Dr. C. Wood); Irish Literary and Musical Studies: The Reciter's Treasury of Prose and Verse (with Guy Pertwee), 1915; The Book of Irish Poetry (anthology), 1915; A Celtic Psaltery (trans. Irish, Scotch-gaelic, Welsh religious poems); (poems): Irish Doric in Song and Story; The Celtic Song-Book (being English verse versions of the songs of the Celtic Nations with music, and of Ceiriog Hughes, the Welsh Burns). Collaborated with Mary Carmichael, Lisa Lehmann, Mrs. Needham, Norman Demuth and Joseph Holbrooke over various groups of songs. Is best known as author of "Father O'Flynn" and is at present engaged with Maureen O'Moor upon a Talkie Musical Play, " Father O'Flynn and His Friends", an opera, "Beatrice", founded on Le Fanu's Poem (with Dr. Annio Patterson), and Morality Plays on the Creation, Nativity and the Life of St. Patrick. Contributor to Contemporary Rev., Cornhill Mag., Dublin Quarterly, Morning Post, Daily Mail, Manchester Guardian, Cambridge News, Boston Pilot, Providence Journal, and many other mags. and papers. General character of writing: poetry, translations, anthologies. Organized the Harlech Historical pageants and wrote main portions of the books. CLUBS: Athenaeum, Savage, Sesame; SOCIETIES: Irish Literary Society, Royal Literary, Folk-Song, Irish and Welsh Folk-Song, Authors', Dublin Univ. Philosophical Soc. HOME: Erinfa, Harlech, North Wales.

GRAVES, ARNOLD FELIX: barrister-at-law; b. Dublin, Ireland, Nov., 1847; s. Charles, Lord Bishop of Limerick, and Selina (Cheyne) G.; educ. Windermere Coll., Univ. Dublin; DEGREE: B.A. (Trinity Coll., Dublin); married. AUTHOR: Prince Patrick, A Fairy Tale; Clytemnestra; Helen of Troy; The Long Retreat; The Turn of the Tide; Healthy, Wealthy and Wise; Jonathan Swift (play); Cross Purposes (play); Private Wire (play); O Water Cure (play); The Cat (play). Contributor to Daily Express. General character of writing: plays, poems, fantasies. Apptd. Secy. to Commnr. of Education for Ireland, 1897; Secy. to Charity Commnr. (Ireland), 1885; Hon. Secy. for following organizations, all of which he was instrumental in founding: City of Dublin Tech. Schls., Tech. Education Assn., Pembroke Tech Schs. Relig. denom., Church of England. HOME: Sunny Cottage, West Hampstead, Herts, Eng.

GRAVES, Charles, M.A. b: Wimbledon 1899. e: Charterhouse & Oxf Univ. Writer. n.a: Dly Express 1921, News Ed Sunday Express '23—24, Columnist Daily Mail '27—31, rejoined '37—41. Publ: And the Greeks; Gone Abroad; Gone Abroad Again; The Price of Pleasure; Panorama; Deanville Taxi; Other People's Money; War Over Pence; Off the Record; The Avengers; Londoner's Life; The Home Gd of Britain; Black Beret; Great Days; Five Survive; Drive for Freedom; Pride of the Morning; The Thin Red Line; Dusk to Dawn; etc. Rec: Golf, gin rummy. a: 15 Berkeley Ct, London, N.W.1. T: Welbeck 1405.

GRAVES, Charles. m: Gertude Norah Lindsay Keyes. Journalist. n.a: Leamington Spa Courier 1912, Glasgow Ev Citizen '20, The Scotsman '21. Publ: The Wood of Time; The Bamboo Grove & Other Poems; Selected Poems of Pierre de Ronsard (trans). Ctr: Various. s.s: English, Modern Scottish & Irish Poetry, The Theatre. Rec: Golf, chess. c: Scottish Arts. a: 34 Buckingham Terr, Edinburgh 4. T: 23728.

GRAVES, CHARLES LARCOM: journalist and author; b. Dublin, Ireland, Dec., 1856; s. Charles, Lord Bishop of Limerick, and Selina (Cheyne) G.; educ. Marlborough Coll.; DEGREE: M.A. (Oxford); m. Alice Grey, 1889. AUTHOR: The Hawarden Horace, 1894-96; Life of Sir George Grove, 1903; Diversions of a Music Lover, 1904; Post-Victorian Music, 1911; Mr. Punch's History of the Great War, 1919; Mr. Punch's History of Modern England, 1921-22; Odes of Horace (Book V), English version, with Rudyard Kipling; Eight vols. of Light Verse, 1886-1927; (in collab. with E. V. Lucas, the following): Wisdom While You Wait, Hustled History, Signs of the Times. Assistant-editor of The Spectator, 1899-1917; ass'.-editor of Punch since 1928. Contributor to Cornhill Mag., Quarterly Rev., Edinburgh Rev., Chambers' Journ., Music and Letters, Spectator, Punch. General character of writing: poems, biography, musical criticism, historical prose. Relig. faith: Protestant. CLUB: Athenaeum. OFFICE: "Punch" Editorial Office. HOME: 3 Palmer St., Westminster, London, S. W., Eng.

GRAVES, CLOTILDE INEZ AUGUSTA MARY: see Dehan, Richard.

GRAVES, Francis. b: Bedford. e: Bedford Modern Sch, Strand Sch, King's Coll Lond. m: Winifred Allen. d: 1. Newspaper Editor. n.a: Ed Northampton Daily Echo & Northampton Mercury 1924—32, Ed Windsor, Eton & Slough Express '33. a: 25 Clarence Rd., Windsor.

GRAVES, Frank Pierrepoint. b: Brooklyn, N.Y. 1869. m: (1) Helen Hope Wadsworth (dec'd), (2) Jessie Chase Malcolm. s: 2. d: 2. Educator, Lawyer. Publ: Burial Customs of the Greeks; Edition of Philoctetes of Sophocles; First Book in Greek; Histories of Education (1) Before & (2) During the Middle Ages; Great Education of Three Centuries; Pater Remus & The Educational Reformation; A History of Education in Modern Times; What Did Jesus Teach?; A Student's History of Education; Administration of American Education; etc. Ctr: Introduction to Revised & Re-codified Law on Education. s.s: Education. Law. Rec: Hiking, tennis, rowing, swimming. c: Univs & Columb Univ. a: 303 Woodlawn Ave,, & 120 State St, Albany, New York, U.S.A. T: 2-7351 & 3-2510.

GRAVES, John, M.A. b: Wimbledon 1903. e: Copthorne, Charterhouse & St John's Col Oxf. Schoolmaster. Publ: The Boys' Book of Association Football ('31); Tales of the Three Musketeers; The Great Cham; Herbert Chapman on Football ('34); etc. c.t: Daily Express, Morning Post, B.O.P., various Annuals, etc. s.s: Association football, cricket & teaching of Eng. Rec: Golf, winter sports. a: Sandroyd, Cobham, Surrey. t: 460.

GRAVES, Dr. K. A. H. Med Pract. c.t: Lancet. a: Rubery Hill, Birmingham.

GRAVES, Philip Perceval. b: 1876. Married. d: 1. Journalist. n.a: The Times 1906. Publ: The Land of Three Faiths; The Pursuit (poetical); The Question of the Straits. a: c/o The Times, Printing Hse Sq, E.C.4.

GRAVES, Robert. b: London 1895. e: Charterhouse, St John's Oxf. Poet & Writer, Hawthorden Prize & James Tait Black Memorial Award 1935, Femina Vie Heureuse Prize '39. Publ: Lawrence & the Arabs; Goodbye to All That; I, Claudius; Claudius the God; Antigua Penny Puce; T. E. Lawrence to His Biography; Count Belisarius; Collected Poems; The Long Week End (with Alan Hodge); Sergeant Lamb of the Ninth; Proceed Sergeant Lamb; Wife to Mr Milton; The Reader Over Your Shoulder (with Alan Hodge); The Golden Fleece; King Jesus; Collected Poems, 1926, 1938, 1947; White Goddess; etc. a: c/o Messrs J. B. Pinker & Son, Lit Agents, Talbot Hse, Arundel St, London, W.C.

GRAVES, Dr. T. C. c.t: Journ Mental Sci. a: Rubery Hill, Birmingham.

GRAY, Alan, MusDoc(Cantab), Hon Fellow Trin Col. Publ: Various Musical Compositions. s.s: Eng lit. a: 10 Chaucer Rd, Cambridge.

GRAY, Albert Alexander., b: Glas 1868. e: Friends' Scs, Bootham Sc York. m: Mabel Henderson. s: 2. Aural Surgeon, Pathologist. Publ: The Labyrinth of Animals (2 vols); Textbook of Diseases of the Ear; The Mechanism of the Cochlea (collab George Wilkinson Atlas of Orology, 2 vols); etc. s.s: Anatomy, physiology & pathology of the ear. a: 5 Hammersmith Terr, W.6.

GRAY, Albert Edward, F.R.S.A. b: Brightlingsea 1871. e: Priv. Widower. s: 1. d: 2. Pottery Manufr (Founded Gray's Pottery 1907). s.s: Industrial art. Mem Gorell Cmt on Art & Industry. Chm Art & Designs Cmt Brit Pottery Manufrs Fed. Chm Ceramic Art Soc. Mem F.B.I. Industrial Art Cmt. Rec Golf. a: 40 Kingsway West, Newcastle, Staffs. t: 67116.

GRAY, Sir Alexander, C.B.E., M.A. b: Dundee 1882. e: Dundee Hgh Sch, Univs of Edinburgh, Gottingen, Paris. m: Alice Gunn. s: 1. d: 3. Prof of Polit Econ Edin Univ, formerly Civil Servant 1905—21 & Prof Polit Econ Aberdeen Univ '21—34. Publ: The Socialist Tradition ; The Development of Economic Doctrine ; The Scottish Staple at Veere (jointly) ; Vols of Poetry, etc. c: Univ (Edinburgh). a: 8 Abbotsford Park, Edinburgh, 10. T: 56027.

GRAY, Sir Archibald Montague Henry, Kt., C.B.E., M.D.(Lond), F.R.C.P., F.R.C.S. b: Ottery St Mary, Devon 1880. e: Cheltenham Coll & U.C.H. m: Elsie Cooper. s: 1. d: 1. Formerly Phys-in-Charge Skin Dept U.C.H. & Hosp for Sick Children Great Ormond Street, etc. n.a: Ed British Journ of Dermatology & Syphilology 1916—29. Ctr: Articles on Skin Diseases to Official Hist of 1914—18 War & various Medical journs. s.s: Dermatology. c: Athenæum. w.s: Cons Dermatologist to B.E.F. 1914—18 & R.A.F. '20—46. a: 39 Devonshire Place, London, W.1. T: Welbeck 7493, & 12 Maresfield Gdns, London, N.W.3. T: Hampstead 3614.

GRAY, Rev. Arthur Herbert, D.D.(Glas). b: Edinburgh 1868. e: Leys Sch Camb & Edin Univ. m: Mary Christian Dods. s: 2. d: 3. Presbyterian Min, Chrm Natural Marriage Guidance Council. Publ: As Tommy Sees Us ; Men, Women & God ; Finding God ; Sex Relations without Marriage ; About People ; Successful Marriage ; The Secret of Inward Peace ; etc. Ctr: St Martin's Review. s.s: Social Reconstruction. Rec: Fishing, gardening. a: 56 Kingsley Way, London, N.2. T: Speedwell 7408.

GRAY, Cecil. b: Edinburgh 1895. e: Haileybury Coll, Edin Univ. m: Margery Mary Binner. d: 2. Writer of Books on Music, Composer. Publ: Music Critic to The Nation & Athenæum, Dly Telegraph, Manch Guardian. Publ: History of Music ; Survey of Contemporary Music ; Sibelius ; Peter Warlock ; Predicaments ; Bach's Fortyeight Preludes & Fugues ; Contingencies ; Carlo Gesualdo (with P. Heseltine); The Bed, on Clinophile's Vade Medcum (with Margery Gray); Gilles de Rais (play); Ctr : Observer, Radio Times, Listener, Manch Guardian. Dly Telegraph, Music & Letters, Nation & Athenæum, Music Review, Musical Times, Sackbut, New Age, etc. a: C.3 Albany, London, W.1, & The Mill, West Chiltington, Sussex.

GRAY, Edward Francis. b: Alwalton 1871. e: Haileybury & Oriel Col Oxf. m: Diana N. Smyth. d: 2. H.M. Consular Service (ret). Publ: Leif Eriksson, Discoverer of America. s.s: Local county archæology. Brit Pro Consul Christiana, Norway 1896, Vice-Consul 1900; trans to Caracas, Venezuela '05; to Bergen, Norway '06; H.M. Consul Christiania '10; H.M. Consul-Gen Boston, U.S.A. '22 (ret '31). Rec: Gardening. c: Eng Speaking Un, R.A.C., A.A., etc. a: Ripple Hall, Tewkesbury. t: Upton-on-Severn 86.

GRAY, Ethel Lilian. b: England. e: Normal Coll Pretoria. m: James Gray. s: 1. d: 1. Publ: (in collab with J. Gray) Payable Gold ; History of the Discovery of the Witwatersrand Goldfields. s.s: South African Goldfield Discoveries. a: 73 Houghton Drive, Johannesburg. T: 43.3480.

GRAY, Frances Ralph, O.B.E. b: Roscrea. e: Plymouth H.S. & Newnham Col Cam. High Mistress of St Paul's Girls' Sc 1903-27. Publ: Gladly Wolde He Lerne & Gladly Teche. c.t: N/ps & periodicals. s.s: Educ Foundations. J.P. Co of Lon '20. Pres Assoc of Univ Women Teachers '21–22. Pres Assoc of Head Mistresses '23–25. Rec: Reading, travel. a: Church Side, Grayshott, Hindhead. t: Hindhead 469.

GRAY, FRANCIS W(ILLIAM): university lecturer in chemistry; b. Aberdeen, Scotland, March, 1874; s. Francis William and Jane (Horn) G.; educ. Robert Gordon's Coll. (Aberdeen), Aberdeen Grammar Sch., University of Aberdeen; DEGREES: M.A., Sc.D.; unmarried. AUTHOR: A Manual of Practical Physical Chemistry, 1914; The Chemistry Tangle Unravelled, 1923. Contributor to Journ. of Chemical Soc. (London), The Philosophical Mag. (London). General character of writing: scientific, text books, chemical research. Later research work has been done along lines of Magneto-chemistry. Relig. denom., Presbyterian. OFFICE: Chemistry Dept., Aberdeen University. HOME: 31 Hamilton Place, Aberdeen, Scotland.

GRAY, Frank. b: Oxf 1880. Solicitor (ret). n.a: Dir Oxford Times, Oxford Mail & N. Berks Herald 1927-. Publ: Confessions of a Private ; Confessions of a Candidate; My Two African Journeys; The Tramp. Solicitor '03-16. War Service '16-19. Special n/p Corr Poland, Germany, Ireland '19–22. M.P. '22–24. Travel in W. & C. Africa '24–26. Vagrancy Work in Casual Wards & Hostels '26–33. Rec: Motoring, travel. c: Reform. a: Shipton Manor, Oxf. t: Woodstock 14.

GRAY, George Milne, M.A., M.B., ChB., F.R.C.S. Surgeon. c.t: Lancet, Brit Journ of Surgery. a: 11 Gloucester Rd, Weymouth. t: 784.

GRAY, Harold St. George, F.S.A. b: Lichfield 1872. e: Ilfracombe G.S. & Priv. m: Florence Harriett Young. Museum Curator & Sec Arch Soc. Publ: On The Excavations at Arbor Low, 1901-2 (1903); Report on Excavations at Wick Barrow, Somt; On the Stone Circles of East Cornwall (Archæologia); Five Reports on Excavations at Avebury (Brit Assoc); The Glastonbury Lake Village, 1892-1907 (jointly with Dr A. Bulleid; Vol I '11, Vol II '17); Excavations at Kingsdown Camp, Som 1927-29 (Archæologia '31). c.t: Times, Connoisseur, etc. s.s: Archæologia. Pres S.W. Group of Museums & Art Galleries '33–34. Curator Som County Museum '01-. Rec: Motoring. a: Taunton Castle, Taunton, Som. t: 429.

GRAY, HERBERT BRANSTON: author; b. Putney, London, Eng., Apr. 22, 1851; s. of Thomas and Emily Mary Gray; educ. Winchester Coll., Queen's Coll. (Oxford); DEGREES: D.D., M.A.; m. Selina Marriott, 1882. AUTHOR: Modern Laodiceans, 1883; Men of Like Passions, 1896; The Public Schools and the Empire, 1913; Eclipse of Empire, 1916; America at School and at Work, 1918; Autobiography, 1929. Contributor (occasionally) to Quarterly Rev. General character of writing: religious, educational, industrial. Warden and chmn. Council and Headmaster Bradfield Coll. (Berkshire), 1880-1910. Originated idea of an experimental ranch, in

Canada, where British youths, sent from Engineering course of Bradfield Sch., might become proficient in ranch management; scheme flourished until 1914 when Great War ended it. Excavated and built first open-air Greek theatre in Europe since downfall of Attic stage, 400 B. C.; this theatre plan has been extensively copied. Relig. denom., Church of England. CLUB: Connaught (London). HOME: The Vicarage, Lynton, North Devon. Eng.

GRAY, Hester Alice, M.A. *e*: Girton Coll Camb. *n.a*: Corr Manch Guardian 1912—22. *Publ*: Key to Progress (part); Political India (part); Education of Girls in India; Modern India and The West (part). *Ctr*: Times, Times of India, etc. *s.s*: Education, India. *a*: 36 Well Walk, London, N.W.3. *T*: Hampstead 2758.

GRAY, J., M.C., ScD., F.R.S. Reader in Exper Zoology Cam. *n.a*: Ed Journ of Exper Biology 1923–. *Publ*: Experimental Cytology. *a*: King's Field, West Rd, Cam. *t*: 1439.

GRAY, James, F.R.I.C. *b*: Cape Town. *e*: Roy Tech Coll Glas. *m*: Ethel Lilian Anderton. *s*: 1. *d*: 1. Analytical & Cons Chemist. *Publ*: (in collab with E. L. Gray) Payable Gold; History of the Discovery of the Witwatersrand Goldfields. *s.s*: South African Gold Discoveries. *c*: Rand, Country, etc. *a*: 73 Houghton Drive, Johannesburg. *T*: 43-3480.

GRAY, James Andrew. *n.a*: Ed South Africa 1934—, Man-Ed African World '45—, Ed Pretoria News '24—32, formerly Mem of Staff The Scotsman & The Times. *a*: 653 Salisbury Hse, London Wall, E.C.2. *T*: Clerkenwell 5264.

GRAY, James C. *n.a*: Ed National Guardian. *a*: 111 Union St, Glasgow.

GRAY, James Gordon, D.Sc, M.I.E.E. *b*: Glas 1876. *e*: Glas Univ. Prof of Applied Physics Glas Univ. *Publ*: Treatise in Dynamics (with the late Prof Andrew Gray LL.D., F.R.S.). *c.t*: Proc of Socs & Tech Journs. *s.s*: Applied physics & sc of gyrostatics. *Rec*: Billiards. *c*: Roy Socs, etc. *a*: La Mancha, Dowanhill, Glas. *t*: Western 2166.

GRAY, Janet Milner Campbell, L.R.C.P., L.R.C.S., L.R.C.P.& S. Med Missionary. *c.t*: Mag Lon Sc of Med, Brit Weekly, News Chron, etc. *a*: 6 Elliot Park, S.E.13.

GRAY, JOSEPH HENRY: Scholar in Holy Orders; *b*. Douglas, Isle of Man, July 26, 1856; *s*. Joseph Henry and Emilie Jane (Awdry) G.; educ. King William's Coll. (Isle of Man); DEGREES: M.A.; m. Ada Frances Amos, 1887 (died 1923). AUTHOR: History of the Queen's College, 1898 (new edit. 1926). Editor of T. M. Plauti: Epidicus, 1893, Asinaria, 1894, Trinummus, 1897 (3rd edit. 1923); P. Terenti: Hauton Timorumenos, 1895. Contributor of occasional articles in classical and other periodicals. Fellow and vice-pres., formerly dean, tutor and classical lecturer, of Queen's Coll., Cambridge. Honorary canon of Peterborough; Justice of Peace; pres. Cambridge Univ. Rugby Union Football Club. OFFICE: Queen's College. HOME: The Close, Upper Cumberland Walk, Tunbridge Wells, Eng.

GRAY, Kenneth Andrew Gordon. *b*: Glasgow, Scotland 1915. *e*: Boissevain Hgh Sch Canada, Glas Hgh Sch, Glas Univ. *m*: Mona Durham. *s*: 1. Author & Journalist. *n.a*: Entertainment Ed Weekly Sporting Review 1946—. *Publ*: Who's Who in Variety; British Television 1947—48. *Ctr*: Film Industry, Picturegoer, Film Illust Monthly, World Review, Nuit et Journ, etc. *s.s*: Entertainment. *Rec*: Golf. *c*: Middlx Regt Officers. *w.s*: Middlx Regt World War II. *a*: 41 Wembley Park Drive, Wembley, Middlx. *T*: Wembley 3741.

GRAY, Nicolette Mary. *b*: 1911. *e*: St Paul's Girls Sch & Lady Margaret Hall Oxf. *m*: Basil Gray. *s*: 2. *d*: 3. Housewife. *Publ*: Rosetti, Dante & Ourselves; 19th-Century Ornamented Types & Title Pages. *Ctr*: Papers of Brit Sch at Rome, Burlington Mag, Architectural Review, Times Litt Supp, Catholic Herald, Signature. *s.s*: The Dark Ages (Lombard, Italy), 19th-Cent Eng Art & Typography, Modern Art. *a*: 9 Essex Villas, London, W.8.

GRAY, Peter, PhD.(Lond), A.R.C.S., D.I.C. *b*: Lon 1908. *e*: Chelsea Poly, Roy Col of Science. *m*: Freda Dolman. Lect in Vertebrate Embryology to the Dept of Zoology, Edin Univ. *Publ*: French Grammar for Science Students. *c.t*: Quarterly Journ of Microscop Science, Parasitology, Museums Journ, Brit Journ of Photog, etc. *s.s*: Zoology, embryology, microscopy. Zoologist to Norwich Castle Museum '28–31. *Rec*: Tennis. *a*: 9 Crawford Rd, Edin.

GRAY, R. *a*: 8 River Bank, East Molesey, Surrey.

GRAY, Tina. *b*: Helensburgh 1884. *e*: Priv & Glasgow Univ. Asst-Surg E.M.S. 1943—47. *Publ*: Hospital Days in Rouen. *Ctr*: Various medical & general publs *s.s*: Surgery, Descriptive articles. *Rec*: Gardening. *a*: 27 Munro Rd, Glasgow, W.3. *T*: Scotstoun 1060.

GRAY, W. C. Schoolmaster. *a*: Foundling Hosp, Redhill, Surrey.

GRAY, William Forbes, F.R.S.(Edin), F.S.A.(Scot). *Publ*: inc The Poets Laureate of England—Their History & Their Odes; Historic Churches of Edinburgh; A Short History of Haddington; etc. *Ctr*: Dict of Nat Biog, etc. *a*: 8 Mansionhouse Rd, Edinburgh.

GRAYSON, Rupert Stanley Harrington. *b*: Oxton. *e*: Harrow. Novelist & Publisher. *Publ*: Scarlet Livery; Gun Cotton; Gun Cotton, Adventurer; Gun Cotton, Secret Agent; Death Rides the Forest; Escape with Gun Cotton. *c.t*: Sketch, Evening News, Evening Standard, Tatler, Bystander, News Chron. *s.s*: Secret service & intelligence stories. Irish Guards 1915—18. twice wounded. Knight of Holy Sepulchre. *c*: Guards. *a*: 66 Curzon St, Mayfair.

GRAZEBROOK, Owen Francis, M.A., J.P. *b*: Dudley 1884. *e*: Marlborough, Caius Coll Camb. *m*: M. A. Rostron. *d*: 2. *Publ*: Nicanor of Athens; Socrates Among his Peers; The Pilgrimage of a Thousand Years; Cruise 45. *Rec*: Bridge, travel. *c*: Arts, Carlton. *a*: Stourton Castle, West Stourbridge, Worcs. *T*: Kinver 22.

GREALISH, John T. *b*: Galway 1906. *e*: St Joseph's Seminary Galway. Journalist. *n.a*: Connacht Tribune, Irish Press, Asst News Ed '33—. Mem N.U.J. & Press Fund. *a*: Irish Press Offices, Dublin. *t*: 45196.

GREATOREX, Clifford Willey ("Norma Twydale" & "Frank C. Willey"), F.Z.S. *b*: Worksop 1896. *e*: Priv, Sec Sc Worksop. *m*: Lilian E. M. Hughes. *s*: 1. F/L Journalist & Author. *n.a*: Local Corr World's Press News 1932—, Practical Building '33—. *Publ*: The Wild Animals of Ireland, Living & Extinct; The Secret of the Diamonds. *c.t*: Various n/ps & periodicals G.B. & overseas. *s.s*: Nat study, occultism, short stories. R.S.P.C.A. War Service. Corr Mem Derbys Entomological Soc. *Rec*: Keeping cats & fancy mice. *a*: 66 Gateford Rd, Worksop, Notts.

GREATWICH, Frank Bernard. *b*: Wednesbury 1906. *e*: King Edward VI Sch Stourbridge. Journalist. *n.a*: County Express Stourbridge 1922—31, Kidderminster Times '31—35, Ed Geo Williams Press Ltd Worcester Weekly Group '35—37, Ed Berrow's Worcester Journ & Mag-Ed Berrow's Newspapers Ltd., Worcester Weekly Group '37—. *a*: Donington, Beckett Close, Worcester. *T*: 3882.

GREAVES, Edwin. *b*: London 1854. *m*: Emma Sansom. *s*. 2. *d*: 3. Missionary (India). *Publ*: Hindi Grammar; Notes on the Grammar of The Ramayan; Short History of Hindi Literature; Handbook of Benares; Several books in Hindi. *c.t*: Various. *s.s*: Hindi language. Missionary in India 1881-1919. *a*: The Limes, Malvern.

GREAVES, H. R. G., B.Sc.(Econ). *b*: Naples 1907., *e*: Priv, Lond & Geneva Univs. Univ Teacher. *n.a*: Asst-Ed Politica. *Publ*: The League Committees & World Order; The Spanish Constitution; The British Constitution; Federal Union in Practice. *Ctr*: Polit Quarterly, Economica. *s.s*: Political Science & International Affairs. *a*: Lond Sch of Economics, Aldwych, London, W.C.2.

GREAVES, Leonard, F.R.S.A. *b*: London 1918. *e*: Westminster City School, Chelsea Sch of Art & Univ of London. *m*: Baroness Henriette Pereira-Arnstein. Painter & Critic of Art, Assoc Lect Nat Gallery 1937—39. *Ctr*: Burlington Mag, Architectural Design & Construction, Architects' Journ, Fortnightly, Listener, Antique Collector, Counterpoint, etc. *s.s*: History of Art, British Painting, etc. *Rec*: Travel. *c*: Chelsea Arts. *a*: 25 Danvers St, Paulton's Sq, London, S.W.3. *T*: Flaxman 0755.

GREAVES, Robert William, M.A., D.Phil., F.R.Hist.S. *b*: Leicester 1909. *e*: Alderman Newton's Sch Leicester & Merton Coll Oxf. Lect in Hist Bedford Coll Lond. *Publ*: The Corporation of Leicester 1689—1836. *Ctr*: Leicestershire Archæ Soc Transactions, Eng Hist Review, Theology, Transactions of Roy Hist Soc. *s.s*: Modern Eng Hist, Municipal, Economic, Administrative, Church History. *Rec*: Books, music, company, countryside. *a*: 19 Craven Hill Gdns, London, W.2.

GREEN, A. J. B., M.A. *a*: Roy G.S., Guildford, Surrey.

GREEN, A. L. B., D.S.O., M.R.C.S. (Eng), L.R.C.P.(Lon). Medical Practitioner. Police Surgeon. *a*: The New Hse, Ross-on-Wye, Herefordshire.

GREEN, Anna Katharine, A.B. *b*: Brooklyn 1846. *e*: Female Col, Poultney Vermont. *m*: Charles Rohlfs. *s*: 1. Author. *Publ*: The Leavenworth Case ('78); The Step on the Stair (1923); etc. *c*: 20th Century. *a*: 156 Park St, Buffalo, N.Y., U.S.A. *t*: Grant 3691.

GREEN, Anthony, M.B., Ch.B., F.R.C.S., D.M.R.E. (Camb). *m*: Susan Unthank. *s*: 1. *d*: 2. Mem B.M.A., etc. *Publ*: Radium Beam Therapy; Subfertility; Cancer of the Breast. *s.s*: Cancer, Radiotherapy. *Rec*: Iris hybridising. *c*: Jun Carlton. *a*: 86 Harley St, London, W.1. *T*: Langham 3623.

GREEN, Archibald Charles. Ed & Comm Rep Gloucestershire Echo, Tewkesbury.

GREEN, Arthur George, F.R.S., M.Sc, F.I.C. Research Chemist & Chemical Engineer. *Publ*: Survey of the Organic Colouring Matter; Analysis of Dystuffs. *c.t*: Journ of Chemical Soc, Journ of Soc of Chemical Industry, Ency Brit, etc. *a*: Conarth, Ashley Drive. Walton-on-Thames, Surrey. *t*: Walton 523.

GREEN, Arthur Robert, F.S.A. *b*: Bromsgrove 1865. *e*: Bromsgrove Sc. Med Pract (ret). *Publ*: Sundials, Incised Dials or Mass Clocks. *c.t*: Antiquaries Journ, Proc Hants Archæological Soc. *s.s*: Archæology, Anglo-Saxon sundials. *Rec*: Photography. *a*: Croyland, nr Romsey.

GREEN, Rt. Rev. Charles Alfred Howell, M.A., D.D. *b*: Llanelly 1864. *e*: Charterhouse Oxf. *m*: Hon Katharine Mary Lewis. Counc of Univ Col of N. Wales. *Publ*: Notes on Churches in the Diocese of Bangor; Jt Cont to Episcopacy, Ancient & Modern. *c.t*: Yr Haul, Ch Quarterly Review. *s.s*: Ancient endowments of the Ch, const of the Ch. Librarian '86 & Pres '87 of the Oxf Un Soc. *c*: Oxf & Cam. *a*: Bishopscourt, Bangor, Caerns.

GREEN, Charles Arthur Freer, M.A., LL.D. *b*: Bucks 1870. *e*: Oakham Sc & T.C.D. *m*: Silvia Ruth Elderton. *s*: 2. *d*: 2. Schoolmaster. *Publ*: Test Examinations in Latin; First Stages in Latin. *Rec*: Lit, music. Mem Classical Assoc. *a*: Normanton, Longton Av, Sydenham, S.E. 26.

GREEN, F. C. *n.a*: Sub-Ed Eastern Dly Press. *a*: London St, Norwich.

GREEN, Francis Henry Knethell, M.D.(Lond), F.R.C.P. (Lond). *b*: London 1900. *e*: Highgate Sch & St Bart's Hosp Lond. *m*: Elsie Joyce Hinde. Admin Staff Med Research Council. *Publ*: ("Frank Egan") Through the Hollow Oak; Mary in Beastie Island. *Ctr*: Sci journs (own name). *a*: 129 Nether St, Nth Finchley, London, N.12.

GREEN, Frederick Lawrence. *b*: Portsmouth. *e*: Salesian Coll Farnborough. *m*: Margaret Edwards. Novelist. *Publ*: On the Night of the Fire; The Sound of Winter; Give Us The World; Music in the Park; A Song for the Angels; On the Edge of the Sea; Odd Man Out; A Flask for the Journey; Odd Man Out (screen play, with Carol Reed); A Fragment of Glass; Mist on the Waters. *Rec*: Painting, collecting pictures, music. *c*: Ulster Arts. *a*: c/o Pearn Pollinger & Higham Ltd, 39-40 Bedford St, Strand, London, W.C.2.

GREEN, G. Grafton. *b*: Birkenhead. *m*: Constance Rangeley. *n.a*: Exchange Telegraph Co, M/C Evening News '27, News Ed '31, Lon Ed. *a*: 4 Green Walk, N.W.4. *t*: Hendon 6225.

GREEN, Geo. Alfred Lawrence. *b*: Portsmouth, Hants 1868. *e*: P'mouth Diocesan Gr Sch. *m*: Katharine Muriel Bell. *s*: 1. *d*: 2. Journalist (ret 1946). *n.a*: Ed & Ed-in-Chief Cape Argus Cape Town 1910—46, formerly Portsmouth Times & E. Mail 1883—'90, Allahabad Pioneer (London Office) '90—94, Cape Times '94—98, Diamond Fields Advertiser '98—1910. *Publ*: Siege of Kimberley; An Editor Looks Back. *s.s*: South African Politics. *Rec*: Walking. *a*: Ardencote, Cumner Ave, Kenilworth, Cape Town, South Africa.

GREEN, George H., B.Sc, Ph.D.(Lon), M.A. (Wales), B.Litt(Oxon), M.R.S.T., M.C.P. *b*: I.o.W. *e*: Southampton Univ Col & Exeter Col Oxf. *m*: Lena Sophia Beatrice Pritchard. Lecturer Wales Univ Col Aberys. *Publ*: Psychoanalysis in the Classroom; The Daydream; The Terror Dream; The Child's Religion (trans of Le Sentiment Religieux by Pierre Bovet);

Education for Intercultural Understanding. *c.t*: Nat n/ps, Journ of Careers, Mother & Child, Schoolmaster, Teachers World, etc. *s.s*: Psychology, educ. Dir of New Educ Fellowship Ltd. *c*: Mem of Court of Governors, Wales Univ Col, Soc of Authors. *a*: 8 Marine Terr, Aberys & 52 Moreland Court, Finchley Rd, Lon. N.W.2. *t*: Hampstead 6425.

GREEN, H. L. H. H., M.A., M.R.C.S. Fell Sidney Sussex Col Cam, Lecturer in Anatomy Cam Univ. *Publ*: Ed Gadow's Evolution of the Vertebral Column (jt). *c.t*: Journ of Anatomy. *a*: Sidney Sussex College, Cam.

GREEN, Harry Norman. Physician. *c.t*: B.M.J., Lancet, Biochem Journ, Roy Soc Med, etc. *s.s*: Med research. *a*: 631 London Rd, Sheffield.

GREEN, Sir J. Formerly Dir Rural Inds at Min of Agric. *a*: 2 Belmont Park, Lewisham, S.E.13.

GREEN, Dr. J. Dixon, M.B.E., M.D., D.P.H. *a*: Hanslope, 47 Wimborne Rd, Bournemouth.

GREEN, James Maurice Spurgeon, M.B.E., B.A. *e*: Rugby & Univ Coll Oxf. *n.a*: Financial & Industrial Ed The Times 1938—, Ed The Financial News '34—38. *a*: 1 Hyde Park St, London, W.2.

GREEN, John Dennis Fowler, B.A. *b*: 1909. *e*: Cheltenham Coll & Peterhouse Camb. Barrister. *Publ*: Mr Baldwin. *Rec*: Hunting, shooting. *c*: Cons. *a*: Chedworth Manor, Gloucestershire.

GREEN, JOSEPH FREDERICK: on staff of Conservative Central Office; b. London, Eng., July, 1855; s. Joseph Edwin and Hannah Rosa (How) G.; educ. Islington Proprietary Sch.; Oriel Coll. (Oxford); m. Eliza Emma Claydon, 1899. AUTHOR: The Wisdom of Life: An Anthology, 1925. Was sec. of Internat. Arbitration and Peace Assn., 1886-1917; clerk in Holy Orders, 1880-86. Relig. denom., Positivist. CLUBS: Johnson. HOME: 32 Upper Mall, London, W. 6, Eng.

GREEN, L. DUNTON (pen name): (Louis John Herman Grein): musical critic; b. Amsterdam, Holland, Dec. 22, 1872; s. Jacob Herman and Frances (Davids) Grein; educ. various schools and universities abroad. AUTHOR: Musical Inspiration, 1929. Sub-editor of the Chesterian. Contributor to Chesterian (London); Revue Musicale (Paris); Die Musik (Berlin); La Rassegna Musicale (Torino); Morning Post (London); Musical Quarterly (New York). General character of writing: musical criticism. OFFICE: 11 Park Lane, London, W. I, Eng.

GREEN, Lawrence George. *n.a*: Ed Staff Cape Argus Sth Africa. *Publ*: The Coast of Treasure; Great African Mysteries; Secret Africa; Strange Africa; Old Africa Untamed; Authors, Post-War Guide. *Ctr*: Cape Argus, London & New York newspapers & mags, Sat Ev Post, Strand, Blackwoods. *s.s*: Africa. *Rec*: Seafaring, travel. *a*: Editorial Dept, The Cape Argus, Cape Town, South Africa.

GREEN, Louis Joseph. *b*: Lon 1898. *e*: Cent Foundation Sc. Registered Med Pract. *c.t*: Lancet, B.M.J. *s.s*: Ophth. *a*: 45 Litchfield Way, N.W. 11. *t*: Speedwell 3344.

GREEN, Maurice. Ed, Financial News. *a*: 20 Bishopsgate, E.C.2.

GREEN, Owen Mortimer. *b*: Southampton 1876. *e*: Lancing & Caius Coll Camb. *m*: Catherine Ferris Mortimer. *d*: 2. Journalist. *n.a*: North China Dly News Shanghai, Asst-Ed 1907—10, Ed '10—30, Reuter's London Staff '33—, Specialist in Far Eastern affairs, Observer '44. *Publ*: China's Struggle with the Dictators; The Foreigner in China; The Story of China's Revolution; Discovering China. *Ctr*: Fortnightly Rev, Yorks Post, Scotsman, Manch Guardian, Manch Ev News, etc. *s.s*: Far East. *Rec*: Gardening, photography. *a*: Greenway Cott, Wentworth, Virginia Water. *T*: Wentworth 2382.

GREEN, Paul Eliot, A.B. *b*: Lillington, North Carolina 1894. *e*: Buies (N.C.) Acad, Univ of N.C. *m*: Elizabeth Atkinson Lay. *s*: 1. *d*: 3. Writer & Teacher. *n.a*: Ed The Reviewer 1925. *Publ*: Drama: In Abraham's Bosom & the Field God (Pulitzer Prize 1927); The House of Connelly & Other Plays; Johnny Johnson; The Lost Colony; The Common Glory; Roll Sweet Chariot; Hymn to the Rising Sun; (Novel): This Body the Earth; (Essays): The Hawthorn Tree; (Short Stories): Salvation on a String. *Rec*: Farming, baseball, tennis. *a*: Chapel Hill, North Carolina, U.S.A. *T*: 8431.

GREEN, Rev. Canon Peter, M.A. ("Artifex" of The Manchester Guardian). *b*: Southampton 1871. *e*: Cranleigh Sc & Cam Univ. Clergyman. Canon of M/C. Chap to H.M. the King. Rural Dean of Salford. *Publ*: How to Deal with Lads (1910); Studies in Popular Theology ('13); Studies in the Cross ('14); The Problem of Evil ('20); Betting & Gambling ('24); Parochial Missions To-day ('28); The Problem of Right Conduct ('31); The Holy Ghost, the Comforter ('33); etc. *s.s*: Evangelistic Missns. *c.t*: Ecclesiastical weeklies & monthly reviews, Manchester Guardian, 1910-. Pres Cam Un 1893. Mem Missn of Help to S. Africa 1904. Lect in Pastoral Theol at Cam & King's Col, Lon '14-. *a*: 6 Encombe Pl, Salford 3, Lancs. *t*: Blackfriars 4945.

GREEN, Dr. R. *a*: Woodside, Slad, nr Stroud, Gloucs.

GREEN, Roger Lancelyn, M.A., B.Litt. *b*: Norwich 1918. *e*: Merton Coll Oxf. College Librarian. *Publ*: Andrew Lang, A Critical Biography; Tellers of Tales; The Searching Satyrs; The Singing Rose & Other Poems; The Lost July & Other Poems. *Ctr*: English, Scots Mag, Everybody's, Notes & Queries, Times Lit Supp, etc. *s.s*: Children's Books, Later Victorian Literature & Literary Biography. *Rec*: Amusing children & climbing trees, writing & producing lyric drama. *c*: Univs. *a*: Merton College, Oxford, & Poulton-Lancelyn, Bebington, Wirral. *T*: Bromborough 57.

GREEN, Roland, F.R.S.A. *b*: Rainham, Kent 1896. *e*: Mathematical Sch Rochester. Artist, Lectures on Bird Life illustrated by sketches, Hon Life Fell Roy Soc Protection of Birds, Mem Brit Ornith Un. *Publ*: Wing Tips (Author & Artist); Birds One should Know; Birds in Flight; Birds & their Young. *Ctr*: Various sci & popular mags & books. *s.s*: Painting of Birds, Ornithology. *a*: The Studio, Hickling Broad, Norwich, Norfolk.

GREEN, Russell. *b*: 1893. *e*: Queen's Col, Oxford. Civil Servant. *Publ*: Prophet without Honour; Wilderness Blossoms; Dreamers in Venice (in prep.); Translations:—Foch Talks; The Paris Front. *c.t*: Spectator, John O'London's, Observer, M/c Guardian, Sunday Times. *s.s*: Fiction critiques, classical plays, reading for publishers, translations from French. Newdigate Prizeman, Chancellor's English Essayist. Honour Mods & Final English Honours. *a*: c/o J. B. Pinker & Co., Talbot House, Arundel Street, W.C.

GREEN, Thomas, F.R.S.A. *b*: Halifax. *e*: Halifax Tech Coll & Manch Univ. *m*: Frances Maud Sutcliffe.

Journalist. *n.a*: Ed Printing Review 1938— & Home Owner '45—, Ed Three Ridings Journal '29—40. *Publ*: From a Pennine Window; Unconsidered Trifles; History of Printing in Yorkshire; A Greater Power (Play); Country Walks round Halifax; Pageant of Methodism. *Ctr*: Yorks Post, Yorks Observer, Sun Dispatch, Yorks Ev Post, Yorks Ev News, Fleet Street Annual, Halifax Courier, Forward View, Queue, Caxton Mag, B.B.C. Talks. *s.s*: Walking in British Isles, Literary Characters, Printing, etc., Historical Buildings. *Rec*: Walking, swimming, tennis, poultry rearing, reading. *a*: Newlands Hse, Warley, Halifax, Yorks. *T*: Halifax 61605.

GREEN, Vincent, M.D., C.M. *b*: Hampstead 1870. *e*: St Paul's Sc & Edin Univ. *m*: (1) Helen Kemp Welch; (2) Muriel Holmes. *d*: 2. Medical Practitioner. *c.t*: Homœopathic Journ. *s.s*: Oto-Laryngology. Ex-Pres British Homœopathic Soc. *Rec*: Tennis, gardening. *c*: Hunterian Soc. *a*: 1 Belvedere Drive, Wimbledon. *t*: 1323.

GREEN, Rev. Vivian Hubert Howard, M.A., B.D., F.R.Hist.S. *b*: Wembley 1915. *e*: Bradfield Coll Berks & Trinity Hall Camb. Chaplain & Hist Master Sherborne Sch Dorset 1942—. *Publ*: Reginald Pecock, a study in ecclesiastical history & thought. *Ctr*: Theology, Ch Quart Rev. *s.s*: Church History, History (Sch). *Rec*: Walking. *c*: Cambridge Union. *a*: Sherborne School, Dorset, & Danesmoor, Woodcombe, Minehead, Somerset. *T*: Minehead 662.

GREEN, Walter Robert. *b*: Long Buckby 1914. *e*: Elem Sch, Bennett Coll Sheffield. *m*: Gladys Lottie Hillyard. Journalist. *n.a*: Rep Rugby Advertiser 1940, Northampton Chron & Echo '44, Founded Daventry & District Weekly Express newspaper '46, Mang Dir Weekly Express Printing Co Ltd. *Ctr*: Leading London Daily, Ev & Sunday newspapers. *Rec*: Cricket, brass band playing. *a*: Hylgrene, Watson Rd, Long Buckby, nr Rugby. *T*: Long Buckby 278, Daventry 290.

GREEN-ARMYTAGE, Vivian Bartley. *b*: Clifton & Thick Hollins, Yorks 1882. *e*: Clifton Coll, Univ of Bristol & Roy Inf Paris. *Publ*: Tropical Gynæcology & Tropical Midwifery; Management & Treatment of Diseases of Children in India. *Ctr*: Various surgical, obst & gynæ journs. *s.s*: Gynæcology. *w.s*: Croix de Chev de Legion d'Honneur, Order of White Eagle of Serbia, 1914 —18 (3 mentions). *Rec*: Riding, bridge. *c*: Oriental & Reform. *a*: 140 Harley St, London, W.1. *T*: Langham 3611.

GREENBAUM, Harry Jacob. M.J.I. *a*: 2 William St, Cannon Street Rd, E.1.

GREENBERG, Ivan Marion. *b*: West Hampstead, Mddx 1896. *e*: Univ Coll Sch & Brussels. *m*: Doris Rosalie Sandground. *d*: 1. Journalist, Mem N.U.J. *n.a*: Asst-Ed 1925—35, Ed '36—46 Jewish Chron Lond, Dramatic Critic '29—46. *s.s*: Internat Affairs, Zionism, Politics of Palestine & the Middle East, Dramatic & Lit Criticism, Economics. *Rec*: Theatre, cycling. *a*: 71 Chatsworth Rd, Brondesbury, London, N.W.2. *T*: Willesden 3857.

GREENE, Dr. A. Sen Ophthalmic Surg. *Publ*: Works on Ophthalmia. *c.t*: B.M.J., Med Press, Brit Journ Opthalmology, etc. Sen Ophthalmic Surg Norfolk & Norwich Eye Infm. *a*: 4 Theatre St, Norwich. *t*: 840.

GREENE, B. C. *b*: Newmilns, Ayrshire 1902. *e*: Newmilns Publ Sc & Galston Hr Gr Sc. *n.a*: Irvine Valley News, Newmilns '18, succeeded to Editorship on death of father '22, Ed Galston Weekly Supp. *c.t*: Glas & prov daily & weekly. *Rec*: Golf. *a*: Norrelbank, Darvel Rd, Newmilns, Ayrshire. *t*: 27.

GREENE, Graham. *b*: Berkhamsted 1904. *e*: Berkhamsted Sch & Balliol Oxf. *m*: Vivien Dayrell Browning. *s*: 1. *d*: 1. Author, Foreign Office 1941—44, Special Duties in West Africa '42—43. *n.a*: Sub-Ed Times 1926—30, Lit-Ed Spectator '40—41. *Publ*: The Man Within; The Name of Action; Rumour at Nightfall; Stamboul Train; It's a Battlefield; The Old School (ed); The Bear Fell Free; England Made Me; The Basement Room (short stories); A Gun for Sale; Brighton Rock; The Lawless Roads; Mexican Journey; The Confidential Agent; The Power & the Glory (Hawthornden Prize 1940); British Dramatists; The Ministry of Fear; Journey without Maps (account of journey through Liberia); Nineteen Stories. *Ctr*: Spectator. *s.s*: Restoration Lit, West Africa. *a*: 15 Bedford St, Strand, London, W.C.2.

GREENE Harry Plunket. *b*: Dublin 1865. *e*: Dublin, Clifton Col, Stuttgart. *m*: Gwendolen Maud Parry. *s*: 2. *d*: 1. Prof Singer. *Publ*: Interpretation in Song; Where the Bright Waters Meet; Pilot; From Blue Danube to Shannon; Life of Charles Villiers Stanford; etc. *c.t*: Music & Letters, Times, etc. *c*: Savile, Flyfishers. *a*: 65 Holland Park Rd, W.14. *t*: Western 3125.

GREENE, Hugh Carleton. *b*: Berkhamsted, Herts 1910. *e*: Berkhamsted & Merton Coll Oxf. *m*: Helga Guinness. *s*: 2. Controller of Broadcasting in the Br Zone Germany, formerly Asst Berlin Corr Dly Telegraph 1934—38, Chief Berlin Corr Dly Telegraph '38—39, Chief of B.B.C. German Service '40—46. *a*: Broadcasting Sect, I.S.C. Branch, Zonal Exec Offices, C.C.G. Hamburg, 63 H.Q., C.C.G., B.A.O.R.

GREENE, John Arthur. Organiser & Dir Med Centre Brit Industries Hse. *Publ*: Ed Treatise on Brit Mineral Oil; Patent Smokeless & Semi-Smokeless Fuels. Fell Chem Soc, Fell Soc Chem Industry. *a*: The Old Hse, Alexandra Gdns, Hounslow. *t*: 3959.

GREENE, Raymond, M.A., D.M., M.R.C.P. *b*: Berkhamsted 1901. *e*: Berkhamsted Sch, Pembroke Coll Oxf. *m*: Elanor Gamble. *s*: 1. *d*: 1. *n.a*: Founded & Ed Oxf & Camb Mountaineering 1921, Ed Climbers' Club Journ '23. *Publ*: Medical Aspects of High Climbing, in F. S. Smythe's Kamet Conquered. *Ctr*: Spectator, Saturday Rev, Climbers' Club Journ, Lancet, etc. *Rec*: Mountain Climbing, travel. *a*: Quaker Barn, Whitchurch, Bucks; 16 Woodfall St, London, S.W.3; 148 Harley St, London, W.1.

GREENE, William Chase, M.A., Ph.D. *b*: Brookline, Mass 1890. *e*: Harvard & Oxford Univs. *m*: Margaret W. Schfeldt. *s*: 1. *d*: 1. Prof of Greek & Latin Harvard Univ. *n.a*: Formerly Ed Harvard Studies in Classical Philol & Publs of Amer Acad of Arts & Sciences. *Publ*: Moira, Fate, Good & Evil in Greek Thought; Scholia Platonica (ed); etc. *Ctr*: Amer Journ of Philol, Classical Philol, Classical Journ, etc. *s.s*: Classical Literature, Greek Poetry & Philosophy. *Rec*: Music, gardening, golf. *c*: Harvard Faculty. *a*: 60 Sheperd St, Cambridge 38, Massachusetts, U.S.A. *T*: Kirkland 4250.

GREENE, William Herbert. *b*: Berkhamsted 1898. *e*: Marlborough. *m*: Audrey Blanche Nutting. Journalist. *n.a*: Lon Corr Times of Brazil. *c.t*: Times, etc. *s.s*: South America, Africa. *Rec*: Lawn tennis, cricket. *c*: Queen's. *a*: 89 Comeragh Rd, Baron's Court. *t*: Fulham 7037.

GREENFIELD, Eric Viole, M.A. *b*: Williamstown, N.Y. 1881. *e*: Harvard, Univs of Marburg, Grenoble & Madrid. *m*: (1) Gudrida Buck. *s*: 1. (2) Elizabeth Storrie. *s*: 1. University Professor, Mem Amer Soc of Univ Profs. *Publ*: Outline of Spanish Grammar; Outline of German Grammar; Brief Summary of French Grammar; Outline of Portuguese Grammar; Technical & Scientific German; Chemical German; Spain Progresses; Parmi les Conteurs Modernes. *s.s*: Modern languages. *Rec*: Swimming, volley ball. *a*: 316 Forest Hills Rd, West La Fayette, Indiana, U.S.A. *T*: 6461.

GREENFIELD, Joseph Godwin, M.D., F.R.C.P., F.R.S.M. *b*: Edinburgh 1884. *e*: Merchiston Castle Sch Edin, Edin Univ. *m*: Florence Mary Jaeger. *s*: 1. *d*: 2. Neuropathologist. *n.a*: Asst-Ed Brain 1929—. *Publ*: Pathology of the Nervous System (with E. F. Buzzard); Cerebro-Spinal Fluid (with E. A. Carmichael). *Ctr*: Ency Brit, numerous articles on neuropathology in med papers. *s.s*: Neuropathology. *w.s*: R.A.M.C. 1914—18. *a*: The Nationa lHosp, Queen Sq, London, W.C.1. *T*: Terminus 7721.

GREENHALGH, H. S. Journalist. *n.a*: Editorial Staff Times Trade & Eng Supp. *s.s*: Trade, music, wireless. *a*: 4 Mitre Ct, E.C.4. *t*: Cen 4340.

GREENIDGE, Terence, B.A. *b*: Oxford 1902. *e*: Rugby Sc & Oxf Univ. *m*: Nora Pfeil. Actor & Author. *n.a*: Asst Ed The Socialist Review '31–34. *Publ*: Degenerate Oxford?; The Magnificent; Brass & Paint. *c.t*: The Morning Post, The New Clarion, The Era, The Sackbut, Amateur Films. *s.s*: Drama, films. Started play producing societies at preparatory Sc & at Rugby & a film-producing society at Oxford in '24. *a*: Afterwards, 14 Rudyard Grove, Mill Hill, N.W.7. *t*: Mill Hill 2467.

GREENLAND, Rev. William Kingscote. *b*: Brierley Hill 1868. *e*: Coventry G.S., Kingswood Bath, & Handsworth Col B'ham. *m*: Gertrude Evelyn Mutch. *d*: 1. Meth Min, Editor, Lecturer & Author. *n.a*: Asst Ed Meth Times & Leader, Ed of The Young Man, Good Times Organ of Commercial Travel Assoc. *Publ*: (Novels) Heavens of Brass; Behind the Granite Gateway; The Seekers; The Price of Life; God's Englishman; The Victorious Child; Life of Raymond Preston; etc. *c.t*: Sun Companion, Home Messenger, British Weekly, Chambers's Journ, etc. *s.s*: Children's books & lectures & penal reform. C.F. France & Germany. *Rec*: Travel. *c*: Nat Lib. *a*: Meth Times, Temple Hse, E.C.4, & Tanglewood, Burkham, Guildford, Surrey. *t*: Central 1140.

GREENLEY, A. *a*: 26 St George's Rd, Cullercoats, Whitley Bay.

GREENLY, Henry. *b*: B'head 1876. *e*: St Andrew's Sc B'head & Regent St Poly Lon. *m*: Lilley M. Richardson. *s*: 2. *d*: 1. Journalist & Cons Eng. *n.a*: Sub-Ed Model Engineer 1901–07, Owner Ed Model Rlys & Locomotives '06-19, Asst Ed Everyday Sci '19–23. *Publ*: The Model Locomotive ('04); Model Electric Locos; Model Electric Locos & Railways; Model Rly Planning; Model Rly Signals & Signalling; Walscheart's Valve Year of Models ('34); etc. *c.t*: Boys Own Paper, Hobbies, English Mechanics, etc. *s.s*: Miniature rly construction. Installed miniature rlys at Geneva, Rhyl, Southport, Nancy, Brussels, Vienna, Margate. *Rec*: Model making, travel. *c*: Soc of Mod & Experimental Engineers, etc. *a*: 66 Heaton Rd, Heston, Hounslow, Middx.

GREENSHIELDS, Robert Scott. *b*: Singapore 1858. *e*: Birkenhead Sc. I.C.S. (ret). *Publ*: Persian Texts & Trans. *c*: E. India Utd Service & Hurlingham, Roy Asiatic Soc, Roy Geog Soc. *a*: 35 Clarges St, W.1.

GREENSTONE, Julius H., A.B., Ph.D., Hon.L.H.D. *b*: Lithuania 1873. *e*: N.Y. City Coll, Jewish Theol Coll & Univ of Penns. *m*: Ray Abeles. *d*: 3. Principal Emeritus Gratz Coll Philadelphia. *n.a*: Contributing-Ed Jewish Exponent 1925—44. *Publ*: Numbers with Commentary; The Jewish Religion; The Messiah Idea in Jewish History; Jewish Feasts & Fasts; The Religion of Israel. *Ctr*: Jewish Ency, Quarterly Rev & Year Book, etc. *s.s*: Jewish Religion & Bible. *a*: 6429 Nth 16 St, Philadelphia 26, Pa, U.S.A. *T*: Li 9-4737.

GREENUP, Rev. Albert William, M.A., D.D., Litt.D., M.R.A.S. *b*: London 1866. *e*: St John's Col Cam. *m*: Evelyn Heron. *s*: 1. *d*: 2. *Publ*: Yalkut Machiri on the Minor Prophets; R. Meyuchas on Genesis & Exodus; Megillath Taanith; Yalkut Shimeoni on Jonah; New Testament, Revised Version, with Fuller References (with Dr J. H. Moulton); etc. *c.t*: The Record, The Churchman, Jewish Quarterly Review, etc. *s.s*: Theology & Semitic languages. *a*: St John's Cottage, Heath End, Basingstoke. *t*: Heath End 16.

GREENWALL, Henry James, M.J.I. *b*: Lon. *e*: Univ Col Sc & Hanover. *m*: Annette Josephine Riehl. *d*: 1. *n.a*: Asst Paris Corr Standard 1910, N.Y. World '10, Continental Daily Mail staff '11—14, Daily Express '14—34. *Publ*: Paris Calling; Underworld of Paris; Mirrors of Moscow, Storm over India; etc. *c.t*: Many n/ps & periodicals. *s.s*: Foreign polit. Was 1st Brit Corr Berlin after signature of Armistice Nov '18, 1st Brit Corr Russia, after break of diplomatic relations. *Rec*: Golf, tennis. *c*: Authors', Press, R.A.C., etc. *a*: c/o Lloyds Bank, 43 Boulevard des Capucines, Paris.

GREENWELL, Hubert. *b*: N. Shields 1878. *e*: Newcastle G.S. Editor. *n.a*: Newcastle Daily Chronicle 1896–1900, Colliery Guardian 1900, Ed (Joint) '12, Ed '29–, Ed (Joint) Water & Quarry '12–29. *Publ*: Various dealing with Coal Mining. *c.t*: Times, etc. *s.s*: Coal mining. Mem of S.W. Inst of Engineers. War Service '15–19. *a*: 30-31 Furnival St, Holborn, Lon, E.C.4. *t*: 7141-2.

GREENWOOD, A. Y., M.D.(Edin). *b*: Mysore, S. India 1873.. *e*: Kingswood Sc Bath & Edin Univ. *m*: Clara Woolley. *s*: 1. *d*: 4. Regional M.O. Mins of Health. *c.t*: B.M.J. Fell Dermatological Soc of Lon. Life-Mem & Exam St John's A.A. *Rec*: Rowing. *a*: Min of Health, Q. Anne's Chambers, Dean Farrar St, S.W.1 & 45 Redcliffe Sq, S.W.10. *t*: Flaxman 6546.

GREENWOOD, Alfred, M.D., ChB., B.Sc, D.P.H., L.R.C.P., L.R.C.S. Married. *s*: 1. *d*: 2. *Publ*: Annual Health Reports for the last 35 years, for Crewe, Blackburn, & Kent; School Medical Annual Reports for 35 years; Underfeeding in School Children, etc. *c.t*: Daily Telegraph, Times, Lancet, B.M.J., Journ Roy Inst of Publ Health, etc. *a*: Sessions Hse, Maidstone. *t*: 2378.

GREENWOOD, Rt. Hon. Arthur, P.C., C.H., M.P. *Publ*: inc The Education of the Citizen; Juvenile Labour Exchanges & After Care; (pt author) The War & Democracy; An Introduction to the Study of International Relationship; etc. *a*: Transport Hse, Smith Sq, London, S.W.1.

GREENWOOD, E. J., F.R.C.S.(Eng). *a*: 14 Star Hill, Rochester, Kent.

GREENWOOD, G. D., C.B.E. *n.a*: Chrm & Man Dir Trade & Travel Publications. *a*: Trade & Travel Publications Ltd, 14 Leadenhall St, London, E.C.3.

GREENWOOD, George. *n.a*: Golf Corr Daily Telegraph. *a*: Fleet St, E.C.4.

GREENWOOD, SIR GEORGE (pen name); (Granville George Greenwood): barrister and M. P.; *b*. London, Eng., Jan., 1850; *s*. John and Fanny

Harriet (Welsh) G.; educ. Eton; Trinity Coll. (Cambridge); DEGREES: 11 classic in Ripos; m. Laurentia Trent Cumberbalch, 1878. AUTHOR: The Shakespeare Problem Restated, 1908; In re Shakespeare, 1909; The Vindicators of Shakespeare, 1911; Is there a Shakespeare Problem? 1916; Shakespeare's Law and Latin, 1916; The Faith of an Agnostic, 1919; Shakespeare's Law, 1920; Shakespeare's Handwriting, 1920; Ben Johnson's Shakespeare, 1921; See Shakespeare, a Tertium Quid, 1923; The Powers and the Turk, 1923; The Stratford Bust and the Doreshout Engraving, 1923; The Shakespeare Signatures and Sir Thomas More, 1924; Poems: Xennes Koenoe, 1925. Contributor to The Times, Daily News, Westminster Gazette, Athenaeum, Bookman and many humanitarian papers and magazines. Became barrister in 1876; original mem. of Eighty Club; contested Peterborough, 1886; Central Hull, 1900. Relig. denom., Church of England. CLUBS: Pall Mall; United Universities Club. (*)

GREENWOOD, George Arthur. *b*: Batley 1893. *e*: Heckmondwike H.S. & Priv. Publicist & Journalist. *n.a*: Reporter series. Batley & Dewsbury, then on S. Wales Voice, Western Mail 1915—20, Daily News '20—23, Daily Chron '27—30, Daily Herald '31—33. Mem N.U.J. '10—. *Publ*: Civilisation in the Melting Pot ('15); England To-Day ('22, revised edn '26); Solo (novel, '28). *c.t*: Times, Observer, Radio Times, Yorks Post, Western Mail, etc. *s.s*: Biog sketches. *Rec*: Reading, theatre-going. *a*: The White Hse, Stanmore, Middx & 10 Devereux Bldgs, Devereux Ct, Strand, W.C.2. *t*: Stanmore 408 & Central 8328—9.

GREENWOOD, H. H., F.R.C.S. Cons Surg to the G. W. R. Hosp & British Legion. *Publ*: Scientific publications on surgery, etc. *a*: 34 Victoria Rd, Swindon.

GREENWOOD, Leonard Hugh Graham. Univ Lecturer in Classics & Fellow of Emmanuel Col Cam. *Publ*: Aristotle, Nicomachean Ethics (Book VI); Cicero, Verrine Orations. *a*: Emmanuel Col, Cam.

GREENWOOD, MAJOR: university professor; *b*. London, Eng., Aug., 1880; *s*. Major and Annie (Burchell) G.; educ. Merchant Taylors'; London Hospital Medical Coll.; Univ. Coll. (London); DEGREES: D. Sc. (London); F.R.S., F.R.C.P.; m. Rosa Baur, 1908. AUTHOR: The Physiology of the Special Senses, 1910; The Health of the Industrial Worker (with Prof. Collis), 1921. Joint-editor of Jnl. of Royal Statistical Soc. Contributor to Biometrika; Jnl. of Royal Statistical Soc.; Proc. of Royal Soc. of London. General character of writing: scientific. Has written numerous papers on physiological, statistical and epidemiological topics; served as medical officer in the British Ministry of Health; univ. prof. in Sch. of Hygiene and Tropical Medicine, Univ. of London. OFFICE: London School of Hygiene and Tropical Medicine. HOME: Loughton, Essex, Eng.

GREENWOOD, R. *n.a*: Hanley Evening Sentinel, Hanley, Staffs.

GREENWOOD, Robert. *b*: Crosshills, Yorks 1897. *m*: Alice Ross. Local Govt Officer. *Publ*: Mr. Bunting; Mr. Bunting at War; The Squad Goes Out. *C*: Short Stories to all leading mags. *a*: York Cott, Landsowne Rd, Felixstowe, Suffolk. *T*: Felixstowe 1000.

GREENWOOD, Walter. *b*: Salford 1903. *e*: Elem Counc Sch. *Publ*: (Novels) Love on the Dole; Tale of the Two Cities; His Worship the Mayor; The Secret Kingdom; Only Mugs Work; Something in my Heart. (Plays) Love on the Dole; The Cure for Love; So Brief the Spring; (Films) Where's George?; Isle of Man. *Ctr*: Storyteller, Time & Tide, Clarion Manch Guardian, Allied Newspapers, Lond Mercury, etc. *s.s*: Sociology, Economics, etc. *Rec*: Riding, rowing, etc. *c*: Savile. *a*: Brent Hse, Polperro, Looe, Cornwall. *T*: Polperro 96.

GREENWOOD, Rev. William Osborne, M.D. (Leeds), M.B., B.S.(Lon), F.R.S.E. *b*: Halifax. *e*: Halifax Hr Gr Sc, Durham Univ & Leeds Univ. *m*: Hilda Louise Coleman. *d*: 1. Obstetrician. Hon Curate St Peter's Ch Harrogate 1932. Obstetric Phys Harrogate Gen Hosp '33. *Publ*: What Science is Doing for Religion; Handbook of Midwifery for C.M.B. Students; etc. *c.t*: Relationship between science & religion. Lect Lit, Scientific & Learned Socs. *Rec*: Nat hist. *a*: 19 Ripon Rd, Harrogate, Yorks. *t*: 2712.

GREEVER, (Gustavus) Garland, A.M., Ph.D. *b*: Lead Hill, Arkansas 1883. *e*: Cent Coll, Duke Univ, Harvard Univ. *m*: May St Clair Stocking. *s*: 1. Prof of English Univ of Southern California 1930—. *Publ*: (Ed) Tiger-Lilies & Southern Prose; A Wiltshire Parson & His Friends; (in collab) The Century Handbook of Writing; The Century Collegiate Handbook; Facts & Background of Literature, English & American; The Century Book of Selections. *Ctr*: The Personalist (Univ of Sth Calif) & various other mags and newspapers. *s.s*: American Lit, Confederate Hist. *a*: 4132 Creed Ave, Los Angeles 43, Calif, U.S.A. *T*: Axminster 7738.

GREG, Walter Wilson, Litt.D.(Cantab), Hon.D.Litt. (Oxon), Hon.LL.D.(Edin). *Publ*: inc Capell's Shakespeariana; The Editorial Problem in Shakespeare; A Bibliography of the English Printed Drama to the Restoration; etc. *a*: River Cott, Petworth, Sussex.

GREGG, Arthur Leslie, M.D., M.Ch., D.T.M.& H. *b*: Belfast 1893. *e*: Campbell Coll & Dublin Univ. *m*: Norah Pilkington. *s*: 1. *d*: 1. Cons Phys Colonial Office & Chrm Adv-Cttee, Diseases of Bees (M.O.A.). *Publ*: Tropical Nursing; etc. *Ctr*: Brit Journ of Surgery, Trans of Roy Soc of Trop Med. *s.s*: Tropical Medicine, Bees. *Rec*: Golf. *a*: 149 Harley St, London, W.1. *T*: Welbeck 4444.

GREGG, Cecil Freeman. *b*: London 1898. *e*: St Augustine's Sch Kilburn. *m*: Muriel Flora Thomson. *d*: 1. Chartd Sec & Inc Acct *Publ*: Inspector Higgins Sees it Through; The Body Behind the Bar; Inspector Higgins Hurries; The Rutland Mystery; The Brazen Confession; The Three Daggers; The Murdered Manservant; Execution of Diamond Deutsch; The Ten Black Pearls; The Old Manor; Exit Harlequin; Expert Evidence; Justice; Who Dialled 999?; The Fatal Error; The Return of Henry Prince; etc. *s.s*: Detective Stories. *Rec*: Bowls. *a*: 161 Carlton Ave East, Wembley, Middx. *T*: Arnold 1658.

GREGG, John Allen Fitzgerald. *b*: North Cerney, Gloucestershire 1873. *e*: Bedford Sch, Christ's Coll Camb. *m*: (1) A. A. Jennings (dec'd). *d*: 2. (2) Lesley McEndoo. Archbishop of Armagh, Archbishop King's Prof of Divinity, Trin Coll Dublin 1911—15, Hon Fell Christ's Coll Cambridge, Archbishop of Dublin '20—38. *Publ*: Decian Persecution; Wisdom of Solomon. *Ctr*: Journal of Theological Studies, Expository Times. *s.s*: Hellenistic Greek. *c*: Athenæum, Ulster, Belfast University, Dublin. *a*: The Palace, Armagh, Ireland. *T*: Armagh 151.

GREGORY, Alyse. *b*: Connecticut. *e*: America & Paris. *m*: Llewelyn Powys. *n.a*: Mang Ed The Dial Mag 1923—25. *Publ*: She Shall Have Music; King Log & Lady Lea; Hester Craddock (novels); Wheels on Gravel; Essays; The Day is Gone (autobiog). *Ctr*: Nineteenth Century & After, John O'London's, etc. *s.s*: Lit Criticism, Belles Lettres. *a*: Chydyok, Chaldon Herring, Dorchester, Dorset.

GREGORY, AUGUSTA (pen name): see Gregory, Lady Isabella.

GREGORY, Rev. Benjamin, D.Litt. *b*: Torrington 1875. *e*: Kingswood Bath. *m*: Edith Mary Crossley Helme. *s*: 1. Meth Min. *n.a*: Ed Methodist Times & Leader. *Publ*: Heroes of the Free Churches. *Rec*: Golf. *c*: Nat Lib. *a*: Temple Hse, Temple Ave, E.C.4; Hill Crest, Arkley, Barnet, Herts, & Brightside, Selsey, Sussex. *t*: Cent 1140, Barnet 3384 & Selsey 57.

GREGORY, Edward William. *b*: Derby 1871. Journalist. *n.a*: Ed The Cabinetmaker. *Publ*: The Furniture Collector; Old English Inns (in collab); etc. *c.t*: Leading Eng & Amer journ's. *s.s*: Decorative & furnishing art. *c*: Nat Lib. *a*: 11 Hillside Rd, Sevenoaks.

GREGORY, Edwin, Ph.D. M.Sc(Lon), F.I.C., A.Met(Sheffield). *b*: Stannington, nr Sheffield 1894. *e*: Sheffield Cent Sec Sc & Sheffield Univ. *m*: Edith M. Starr. *s*: 2. Univ Lect in Metallurgy & Metallurgical Chém. *Publ*: Metallurgy; Non-ferrous Metallurgy (in prep). *c.t*: Ind & Tech Buyer, Quality, Metal Industry, Iron & Steel Industry. *s.s*: Metallography, chemistry, metallurgical analysis. Considered expert on the manufr of steel in elec arc furnaces. *Rec*: Golf, billiards. *a*: 46 Armthorpe Rd, Nether Green, Sheffield, 11.

GREGORY, LADY ISABELLA AUGUSTA: author, b. Roxborough, Co. Galway, Ireland; d. Dudley and Frances (Barris) Persse. AUTHOR: Poets and Dreamers; The Kiltartan History Book; The Kiltartan Wonder Book; Ideals in Ireland; Autobiography of Sir William Gregory; Mr. Gregory's Letter Box; Our Irish Theatre; The Kiltartan Poetry Book; Visions and Beliefs in the West of Ireland; Three Wonder Plays; Mirandolina (La Locandiera); Cuchulain of Muerthemne; Gods and Fighting Men; Saints and Wonders; The Golden Apple; Hugh Lane's Life and Achievements; (plays): Kinoora; The White Cockade; Dervorgilla; The Canavans; The Deliverer; Grania; (comedies): Coats; The Full Moon; The Bogie Men; Damer's Gold; McDonough's Wife; (short plays): Spreading the News; Hyacinth Halvey; The Rising of the Moon; The Jackdaw; The Workhouse Ward; The Travelling Man; The Gaol Gate; The Image; The Wren; Shanwalla; Hanrahan's Oath. General character of writing: drama, biography, history. Relig. denom., Church of Ireland. OFFICE: Abbey Theatre, Dublin. HOME: Coole Park, Gort Co., Galway, Ireland.

GREGORY, Jackson. Author. *Publ*: The First Case of Mr. Paul Savoy; The Second Case of Mr Paul Savoy; The Third Case of Mr Paul Savoy; etc. *a*: c/o Hodder & Stoughton Ltd, Warwick Sq, E.C.4.

GREGORY, John Duncan, C.B., C.M.G. *b*: London 1878. *e*: Eton. *m*: Gwendolen Lind Maude. *d*: 2. Formerly Asst Under Sec of State Foreign Affairs. *Publ*: On the Edge of Diplomacy; Dolfuss & His Times. *Ctr*: Weekly Review, Everybody's Weekly. *a*: Ireland Hse, Ashburton, S. Devon.

GREGORY, Joshua Craven, B.Sc.(Lond), F.R.I.C., F.C.S. *b*: Leeds 1875. *e*: Craigmount Ho Sch Edinburgh, Heriot Watt Coll Edinburgh, Yorkshire Coll Leeds. Hon Lect in the Hist of Science Leeds Univ (ret), Membre Correspondant de l'Academie Internationale d'Histoire des Sciences. *Publ*: The Nature of Laughter; A Text Book of Inorganic Chemistry (with Mrs Burr); The Scientific Achievements of Sir Humphry Davy; A Short History of Atomism; Combustion from Heracleitos to Lavoisier. *Ctr*: Various Phil & Scientific periodicals *s.s*: Hist of Science. *Rec*: Walking, reading. *a*: Mount Hotel, Clarendon Rd, Leeds 2. *T*: 239071.

GREGORY, Mrs. Octavia. *b*: L'pool. *e*: Priv. *m*: Rev James Walter Gregory (dec). *Publ*: A Garden Enclosed; Apples of Gold; Dreams of Arcady; The Magic Garden; Sweet Lavender; Love Unforgetting. *c.t*: Aviculture Mag. *s.s*: Aviculture, 18th century letters. *a*: Melville, Parkstone, Dorset.

GREGORY, Padriac, LL.D., F.R.S.L., F.R.I.B.A., Mem Roy Inst Arch of Ireland, M.I.Struct.E., Mem Roy Sanitary Inst., etc. *b*: Belfast 1886. *e*: U.S.A., Christian Brothers & Priv. *m*: (1) Madeline Crothers (dec'd), (2) Sara McKeown. *s*: 5. *d*: 5. Poet, Dramatist, Folklorist, Architect, Vice-Pres Cath Poetry Soc of Eng, formerly Lit Ed Cath Monthly Rev 1926—27. *Publ*: The Ulster Folk; Old World Ballads; Love Sonnets; Ireland: A Song of Hope; Ulster Songs & Ballads; Selected Poems for Use in Schools; Selected National Ballads; Complete Collected Ballads; Poets of the Insurrection (with Rev Geo O'Neill & Prof Arthur Clery); When Painting Was in Glory; also 4 Sacred Dramas & 2 vols of Folk Songs. *Rec*: Chess, angling, motoring, etc. *c*: Co Antrim Yacht, Whitehead. *a*: 25 Gresham St, Belfast, & The Cottage, Killough, Co Down. *T*: Belfast 26548.

GREGORY, Sir Richard Arman, Bt., F.R.S., F.R.A.S., F.R.Met.Soc., F.Inst.P., Hon.D.Sc., Hon.LL.D. *b*: Bristol 1864. *e*: Primary Sch, Ev Classes, Clifton Coll Bristol & Roy Coll of Sci London. *m*: (1) Kate Florence Dugan (dec'd), (2) Dorothy Mary Page. *s*: 1. *d*: 1. Scientist, Author & Editor. *n.a*: Asst-Ed Nature 1895—1919 & Ed '19—39, Jt-Ed The School World & Journ of Educ 1899—1939. *Publ*: Discovery, or The Spirit & Service of Science; Religion in Science & Civilization; The Vault of Heaven; many Textbooks on Physiography, General & Exprimental Sciences. *s.s*: Physics, Astronomy, Meteorology, Social Science. *Rec*: Gardening, reading. *c*: Athenæum. *a*: The Manor Hse, Middleton-on-Sea, Sussex. *T*: 153.

GREGORY, Stephen Mesrope, L.M. *b*: Persia 1863. *e*: Armenian Philanthropic Acad & St Zavier's Col Calcutta. Civil Servant (ret). *Publ*: The Land of Ararat & Translation in Classical Armenian of Milton's Samson Agonistes. *c.t*: Sion, Pazmaveb, etc. *s.s*: Earliest hist of Armenia & her people. Ret as Chief Auditor Fed Malay States Railways 1913. *a*: Bedford Hotel, S'hampton Row, W.C.1. *t*: Terminus 3655.

GREGORY, Rev. Thomas, M.A., D.D. Min Emeritus. *Publ*: Memories; Mercy & Faithfulness; Studies in Gospel of John; Epistles of St Paul (Ellerton's Prize Essay Oxf 1883). *a*: Kilmacolm, Renfrews.

GREGORY, William King, M.A., D.Sc., Ph.D. *b*: New York 1876. *e*: Trinity Sch N.Y., Columb Coll, Univs of Columb & Witwatersrand. *m*: (1) Laura Grace Foote. (2) Anglea DuBois. Curator Dept of Fisheries 1925—44, Emeritus '44—. *Publ*: Evolution Emerging; On the Structure & Relations of Northarctus; Origin & Evolution of the Human Dentition; Man's Place Among the Anthropoids; A Half Century of Trituberculy, the Cope-Osborn Theory of Dental Evolution; Our Face From Fish to Man; In Quest of Gorillas; The Orders of Mammals. *Ctr*: Various Scientific journs. *s.s*: Evolution of Vertebrates, Locomotor & Masticatory Apparatus. *Rec*: Conchology. *a*: 235 West 76 St, New York 23, U.S.A.

GREGSON, Arthur Herbert. *Publ*: Hope for the Consumptive. *c.t*: B.M.J. *a*: The Poplars, Wilpshire, Blackburn. *t*: 48102.

GREGSON, James Gilroy. *b*: L'pool 1874. *e*: Catholic Inst L'pool. *m*: Annie Goodwin. *s*: 1. *d*: 3. Journalist. *n.a*: Reporter L'pool Daily Post & Echo '91. Pres N.U.J. 1932—33, Ex-Pres L'pool Press Club, Pres St Nicholas's Perpetual Benefit Bldg Soc L'pool. *c*: Press, L'pool. *a*: 16 Onslow Rd, Fairfield, L'pool 6.

GREGSON, James Richard. *b*: Brighouse 1889. *e*: Victoria & Rastrick Common Board Schs Brighouse. *m*: Florence Hine. *d*: 1. Actor, Producer, Dramatist & Journalist, B.B.C. North Region Drama Producer. *Publ*: Plays—Young Imeson; Liddy; Melchisedek; The Devil a Saint; Saint Mary Ellen; A Family Fugue; High Dudgeon; T'Marsdens; Sar'Alice; Robert Owen; Dead Reckoning; Portrait of a Lady; The Rochdale Pioneers; Mate in Two; etc. *Ctr*: Manch Guardian, News Chronicle, Yorks Post, Leeds Mercury, etc. *s.s*: Play Production & Yorks Character Sketches. *Rec*: Garden. *a*: Riverside Cottage, Lintan Falls, Skipton-in-Craven, Yorks. *T*: Grassington 9.

GREIDANUS, Tjardus. *b*: Holland 1890. *m*: Johanna Van Den Briel. *s*: 2. *d*: 1. Banker. *Publ*: De Waarde der Ruilmiddelen (1918); The Value of Money ('32). *c.t*: De Economist. *s.s*: Economics *a*: Oranje Nassaulaan 42, Amsterdam. *t*: 26574.

GREIG, David Middleton, T.D., LL.D. *Publ*: Clinical Observations on the Surgical Pathology of Bone (1931). *c.t*: Brit Journs. *a*: Roy Col of Surgeons, Edin.

GREIG, Ian Borthwick, M.C. *b*: Lon 1892. *e*: Marlboro', Bonn Univ Germany. *m*: Ailsa McLean. *s*: 1. *Publ*: The King's Club Murder; The Tragedy of the Chinese Mine; Baxter's Second Death; False Scent; The Inspector Swinton Murder Omnibus; Murder at Lintercombe; etc. *a*: 45 Eaton Terr, S.W.1. *t*: Sloane 3692.

GREIG, Rt. Rev. John Harold, 1st Bishop of Guildford, B.A., M.A., B.D., D.D.(Cantab). *b*: Lon 1865. *e*: Pembroke Col Cam. *m*: Lilian S. Robinson. *s*: 2. *d*: 1. Hon Canon of Worcester 1907–21, Canon Missnr & Archdeacon, Hon Canon of Coventry '10–27, Bishop of Gibraltar '21–27. Sub Prelate Order St John of Jerusalem. *c*: Athenæum. *a*: Farnham Castle, Surrey.

GREIG, John Russell, PhD., M.R.C.V.S., F.R.S.E. *b*: Leith 1889. *e*: Roy H.S. Edin, Roy (Dick) Vet Col Edin. *m*: Margaret Christe Smart. *s*: 2. Dir Moredun Inst, Animal Diseases Research Assoc, Gilmerton, Midlothian. Hon Research Prof in Animal Pathology Roy (Dick) Vet Col Edin. *Publ*: Wallis Hoare's Veterinary Materia Medica & Therapeutics, 4th & 5th edn's. *s.s*: Vet science. *Rec*: Fishing, gardening. *a*: Wedderlie, Kirk Brae, Liberton, Edin. *t*: Liberton 79194.

GREIG, John Young Thomson, M.A., D.Litt. ("John Carruthers"). *b*: Ch'ang Ch'un, Manchuria 1891. *e*: Collegiate Sch Greenock, Glas Acad, Glas Univ. *m*: Margaret Theresa Thomson. *s*: 1. *d*: 1. Prof of English Lang & Lit. *n.a*: Glasgow Herald 1912–14. *Publ*: The Psychology of Laughter & Comedy; David Hume (Biog); Letters of David Hume (Ed); Language at Work; Breaking Priscians Head. ("John Carruthers") The Virgin Wife; A Man Beset; Scheherazade, or the Future of the English Novel. *s.s*: English Lit, Philosophy *Rec*: Tennis, swimming, skating. *w.s*: 1914–19. *a*: University of the Witwatersrand, Johannesburg, South Africa. *T*: 44-3781.

GREIG, Maysie. *b*: Sydney Aus. *m*: Delano Ames. *Publ*: Cake Without Icing; Jasmine—Take Care; Parents Are a Problem; Lovely Clay; Satin Straps; Ragamuffin; Laughing Cavalier; This Way to Happiness; etc. *a*: 25 Market St, Mayfair, W.1. & Yew Tree Hse, St Mary Bourne, nr Andover. *t*: Grosvenor 3358.

GREIN, James Thomas. *b*: Amsterdam 1862. *e*: Amsterdam, Bremen, Antwerp. *m*: Alex Augusta Greeven. Dram Critic & Consul Gen of Liberia. *n.a*: Weekly Sketch 1923, Illus Lon News '21. Consul of the Congo '10. Consul Gen Liberia '11–. *Publ*: 5 Vols Dramatic Criticism 1898–1903; 2 Vols World of the Theatre ('21–22, '23–24); A Dream of Charity ('05); etc. *c.t*: Sunday Times, Illus Lon News, Dutch, French, German papers, etc. Longest service as Dramatic Critic in the World, began 1879 in Antwerp. Founder Independent Theatre '91, German Theatre 1901–14, French Theatre '15–, People's Theatre '31–32, Cosmopolitan Theatre '25–, Lon Marionette Theatre Gld '34 & many other similar enterprises. Kt of St Olaf, Norway. Officier de l'Instruction Publique. *Rec*: Reading. *c*: R.A.C., etc. *a*: 4 Cambridge Pl, Kensington, W.8. *t*: Western 0477.

GREIN, LOUIS JOHN HERMAN: see Green, L. Dunton.

GRENARD, Claud Kenneth. *b*: Ipswich 1907. *e*: Rutlish, Merton. *m*: Mildred Ellen Harris, Journalist. *n.a*: Rep Surrey Comet '26–29, Sub-Ed Yorkshire Post '29–. *c.t*: Daily & evening papers. *a*: 7 Henconner Cresc, Chapel Allerton, Leeds 7.

GRENFELL, Elsie Winifred. *b*: Lon 1901. *e*: Clapham County Sec Sc. *m*: Ferdinand Erricker Grenfell. *d*: 1. Editor. *n.a*: Sub Ed Lady's Companion '23–25, Ed'25–. Ed Lady's Companion Knitting Series, & Household Series. Leach's New Cookery Series, Leach's Wonder Value Book of Mothercraft. *s.s*: Knitting, mothercraft. *Rec*: Gardening, yachting. *c*: I.J. *a*: 32 Battlefield Rd, St Albans, Herts. *t*: 1599.

GRENFELL, Sir Wilfred Thomason, K.C.M.G., F.R.C.S., M.D. *b*: Parkgate, Cheshire 1865. *e*: Marlborough Oxf. *m*: Anne MacClanahan. *s*: 2. *d*: 1. Supt Internat Gren Assoc. *Publ*: Forty Years for Labrador; A Labrador Doctor; Yourself & Your Body; Labrador Looks at the Orient; Adrift on an Ice-Pan; Down North on the Labrador; The Romance of Labrador. Lord Rec St Andrews Univ 1929. *Rec*: Fishing. *a*: c/o Grenfell Assoc, 66 Victoria St., S.W.1.

GRENSTED, Rev. Lawrence William, B.A, M.A., B.D., D.D., F.R.E.S. *b*: Blundellsands 1884. *e*: Mch'nt Taylor's Sch Crosby, Univ Coll Oxford & Egerton Hall. *m*: Norah Frances Knott. *s*: 2. Nolloth Prof Philos Chr Religion Oxf & Canon Emeritus of L'pool, Exam Chap to Bishop of Rochester, Prin Egerton Hall 1919—24. *Publ*: Introduction to the Books of the New Testament (with W. C. Allen); Psychology & God; The Natural History of the Oxf District; The Making of Character; The Person of Christ; This Business of Living; Jesus & Our Need. *s.s*: Psychotherapy. *w.s*: C.F. 1915—19. *Rec*: Nat history, sketching. *a*: 32 Charlbury Rd, Oxf, & Oriel Coll, Oxford. *T*: 5570.

GRENYER, Frederick Ruthven. *b*: Calcutta 1893. *e*: Victoria Sc Kurseong India & La Martiniere Col Calcutta. *m*: Jessie Catherine Graham Watson. Comm Journalist. *n.a*: Ed Bengal Nagpur Rly Mag 1928 & the Commercial & Technical Journ '32 & Mang Ed Indian Engineering '34. *c.t*: Various n/ps & periodicals. *s.s*: Rly life in India & model yachting. Govt of India Mil Accounts Dep '12. War Service '14–18. Acct King Hamilton & Co, Calcutta (Bankers) '19, Lloyds Bank '23, Amer Mfg Co '25. Acting Sec B.T.H. Co Ltd Calcutta '26. Sec Aluminium Mfg Co Ltd Calcutta '26. *Rec*: Golf, tennis, bridge. *c*: Barrackpore Golf, Calcutta Model Yacht & Dalhousie Athletic. *a*: 26 Chowringher, Calcutta, India. *t*: 3130.

GREPON, Marguerite. *b*: Souillac, Lot 1899. *e*: Lycee de Toulouse. Romanciere-Conferencier. *Publ*: Introduction a une Histoire de l'Amour; La Voyages Nue; Poursuites; Ruptures; Comme Tout Serait Simple; Contributions Indirectes; Les Femmes et la Liberte; Vie-en-Vrac. *Ctr*: Gavroche, Paysage,

Femmes, etc. *s.s*: l'Evolution Feminine & Travers l'Histoire Etudes sur Eve et Lilith. Sex Psychology. *Rec*: Peinture Decorative, voyages, etudes de psychotechnie. *c*: P.E.N., Soc des Gens des Lettres. *a*: 147 rue de Rennes, Paris 6e.

GRESLEY, Rev. Roger St. John. *b*: Ashby-de-la Zouch 1853. *e*: Repton & St Edward's Oxf. *Publ*: In the Ship of the Church. *a*: The Hermitage, Butleigh, Glastonbury.

GRESSWELL, Ronald Kay, M.A., F.R.S.A., F.R.G.S., F.G.S. *b*: Southport 1905. *e*: Tutors & Univ of L'pool. *m*: Freda Hooper. Geomorphologist, Demonstrator Dept of Geography Univ of Liverpool. *Ctr*: Meccano Mag, Nature, Geographical Journ, Journ of Geomorphology, Reps of Brit Assoc for Advancement of Sci, Congres Internat de Geographie Amsterdam, Southport Sci Soc. *s.s*: Geomorphology (physical geography). *a*: 28 Albert Rd, Southport, Lancs. *T*: 4410.

GRESTY, Sidney. Journalist. *n.a*: Ed Lloyd's List & Shipping Gazette 1926—(founded 1734 & the oldest London n/p published daily). *s.s*: Shipping. *a*: Lloyd's, Lon, E.C.3.

GRETTON, George Hermann, M.A., D.Ph. *b*: Ilford, Essex 1906. *e*: Oxf & Hamburg. *m*: Wanda Alma Elisabeth Jahn. *s*: 3. *d*: 1. Asst Dir B.B.C. German Service. *Publ*: Victory Begins at Home; German By Yourself (with W. Gretton). *Ctr*: Spectator, Brit Weekly, Toronto Dly Star, & newspapers in Latin America, Sth Africa, Switzerland, etc. *s.s*: Germany, Sociological & Economic Subjects, Post-war Reconstruction. *Rec*: Translating, cricket, children's stories, athletics. *a*: 47 Hampstead Way, London, N.W.11. *T*: Speedwell 3745.

GRETTON, Mrs. R. H., J.P., D.Litt. *m*: Richard Henry Gretton, M.A.(Oxon). Author. *Publ*: Corner of the Cotswolds; Burford Past & Present; Oxfordshire Justices of the Peace in the 17th Century; Perkin Warbeck's Wife; etc. *c.t*: Contemporary Review, Internat Journ of Ethics, M/C Guardian, Westminster Gazette, etc. *s.s*: Rural hist. *a*: Calendars, Burford, & 17 St Giles, Oxf.

GRETTON, Mary Sturge, J.P., B.Litt. *e*: Mount Sch York, Mason Coll, Oxf Univ. *m*: R. H. Gretton (dec'd). Author & Lecturer. *Publ*: A Corner of the Cotswolds Through the 19th Century; A Calendar of the War, 1914—18; Burford Past & Present; Writings & Life of George Meredith; Crumplin; 17th Century Oxfordshire Quarter Sessions Records. *Ctr*: Various. *s.s*: Hist Records (Rural Oxfordshire). *a*: Montserrat, Bradmore Rd, Oxford, & Calendars, Burford, Oxon. *T*: Oxford 2394.

GREUSEL, John Hubert, B.Litt. *b*: Detroit, Mich 1866. *e*: Univ Mich. *m*: Stella Tolsma. Journalist, Biographer, Historian. *n.a*: Staff N.Y. World 1892-98, N.Y. Herald, Collier's Weekly, Detroit Free Press, Detroit News, McClure's Syndicate, N/p Ad Assoc, San Francisco Chron, Los Angeles Times, 1910-34 travel. *Publ*: Blood & Iron (study of Bismarck); Origins of Democracy; Life of Thos A. Edison; Mystery of Cadillac's Lost Grave; etc. *s.s*: Interviewing. *Rec*: Golf, chess, travel. For 5 y 250-word ed daily feature, 6 per week Time & Tide to 30 U.S.A. Mems. *c*: Sons of American Revolution. *a*: 6061 Hollywood Blvd, Hollywood, Calif, U.S.A. *t*: HE 2873.

GREW, E. S., M.A. *b*: Derby 1868. *e*: Christ's Col Cam. *m*: Marian Ethel Tuckwell, F.R.HistS. Journalist. *n.a*: Ed Illus Scientific News, Ed Knowledge, & Asst Ed Daily Graphic. *Publ*: The Growth of a Planet; with M. E. Grew: The Court of William III; The Court in Exile. *c.t*: Morning Post, Observer, Field. *s.s*: Science, sport. *Rec*: Golf. *c*: Albemarle. *a*: 47 Oakley St, S.W.3.

GREW, Eva Mary. *b*: Birm. *m*: Sydney Grew. Essayist & Journalist. *n.a*: Asst Ed The British Musician. *Publ*: Franz Schubert (a sequence of sonnets & prose anthology). *c.t*: Musical Quarterly, Daily Telegraph, Musical Opinion, The British Musician, etc. *s.s*: Music, poetry. *Rec*: Cycling, walking. *a*: 53 Barclay Rd, Warley Woods, Birm.

GREW, Sydney. *b*: Birmingham 1879. *m*: Eva Mary Instone. Musicologist. *n.a*: Daily Mail 1910-12. *Publ*: Art of the Player Piano ('22); A Book of English Metre; Masters of Music; Makers of Music; etc. *c.t*: Leading lit monthlies, quarterlies, etc. *s.s*: Music & poetry. *Rec*: Swimming. *a*: 53 Barclay Rd, Warley Woods, Birmingham.

GREX, Leo. See **Gribble, Leonard Reginald.**

GREY, Brenda. See **Mackinlay, Leila S.**

GREY, Charles Grey. *b*: London 1875. *e*: Belvedere Ho Norwood, Erasmus Smith Sch Dublin, Crystal Palace Sch of Engineering. *m*: Margaret Sumner Marriner. *s*: 1. *d*: 1. *n.a*: The Cycle & Motor Trade Rev 1905—09, The Aero (founder), The Aeroplane (founder & Ed '11—39), All the World's Aircraft, Ed '16—41 & Partner since '16 etc, Air Corr Yorkshire Evening News, Lancashire Daily Post, The Edinburgh Evening News '39—. *Publ*: A History of the Air Ministry; The History of Combat Airplanes (U.S.C.); British Fighter Planes; Bombers; Sea Flyers; The Luftwaffe; The Civil Air War. *Ctr*: The A.T.C. Gazette (now Air Reserve Gazette), Aeronautics, Meccano Mag. *s.s*: Air Affairs & Technicalities. *Rec*: Reading & motoring. *c*: Roy Aero Soc (Founder Member); Roy Aero. *a*: Coombe Hill Lodge, New Malden, Surrey. *T*: Kingston 0213.

GREY, Sir George Duncan, LL.D. *b*: Olney, Bucks 1868. *e*: Bristol G.S. *m*: Mary Elizabeth Spence. *s*: 2. *d*: 1. Solicitor. County Alderman 1925—. *Publ*: A Venture in Variety: The Joyous Journey; Secret Riches. *c.t*: Punch, Poetry Review, Saturday Review, Morning Post, etc. *s.s*: Light verse, lit essays. *Rec*: Sport, collecting old prints & antique furniture. *c*: Carlton. *a*: Windgarth, Weston-super-Mare. *t*: 265.

GREY, J. *n.a*: North Mail & Newcastle Daily Chronicle.

GREY, John. *n.a*: Ed North Mail & Newcastle Daily Chron. *a*: Westgate Rd, Newcastle-on-Tyne.

GREY, Louis. See **Gribble, Leonard Reginald.**

GREY, Zane, M.Litt. *b*: Zanesville, Ohio 1875. *e*: Univ of Pennsylvania. *m*: Luia Elise Roth. *s*: 2. *d*: 1. Novelist, Sportsman. *Publ*: Betty Zane (1904); Riders of the Purple Sage; The Lone Star Ranger; The Rainbow Trail; The Desert of Wheat; The Mysterious Rider; The Thundering Herd; Wild Horse Mesa; The Hash Knife Outfit ('33); The Code of the West ('34); etc; (Juveniles) The Young Forester; Ken Ward in the Jungle; etc. *c.t*: Collier's, Ladies' Home Journ, McCall's, Cosmopolitan, etc. *s.s*: Western romances, fishing. *c*: Authors League & Club. *a*: Box 26, Altadena, Calif, & 3680 Beverly Blvd, Los Angeles, Calif. *t*: Federal 1321.

GREY, OF FALLODON: see **Edward, Viscount Grey of Fallodon.**

GREY ROWLAND (pen name); (Lilian Rowland-Brown): author; b. London, Eng., Sept., 1863; d. Henry Rowland-Brown and Catherine (Woodgates) Rowland-Brown; educ. Cambridge; Fontainbleau, France; unmarried. AUTHOR: In Sunny Switzerland, 1885; Lindenblumen, 1887; By Virtue of His Office, 1889; Jacob's Letter, 1889; Her One Ambition, 1891; Story of Chris, 1892; Myself When Young, 1894; The Unexpected, 1894; The Power of the Dog, 1896; The Craftsman, 1900; Green Cliffs, 1905; Surrender, 1909; La Belle Alliance, 1918; Life of L. S. Gilbert (with Sidney Dark), 1923; (American edition, 1924). Contributor to Nineteenth Century, Fortnightly Review, Cornhill Mag.; Dublin Review, Times, Bookman, Church Times and many newspapers and other magazines. Relig. denom., Anglo-Catholic. CLUB: Pioneer. ADDRESS: Pioneer Club, 12 Cavendish Place, London, Eng.

GREYS-EDWARDS, Rev. Alfred Howell, M.A. b: Llaninorwic 1861. e: Worc Cathedral Sc, Friars Sc Bangor, Hertford Col Oxf. m: Florence Scott Lester. s: 2. Publ: A Great Missionary: John Thomas of Tinnevelly S. India; A Great Heart: Life of Canon Major Lester of Liverpool; Church Reform (Clericus). c.t: Welsh Religious Press. Former Organising Sec C.M.S. in S. Wales & Mons '97-1907. Chap to the Welsh Church Chester 1887-'97. Rec: Fishing, gardening. a: The Rectory, Halfway Bridge, Bangor, N.W.

GRIBBIN, Henry Thomas. Barrister-at-Law. n.a: Literary Ed, Leader-Writer & Legal Adviser Liverpool Echo. Mem N.U.J. & N/p Press Fund. a: 41 Hereford Rd, Southport.

GRIBBIN, Rev. Thomas Mangnall, B.A., M.A. n.a: Ed M/C Diocesan Leaflet 1930, etc. a: St Chad's Rectory, Withington, M/C t: Didsbury 1185.

GRIBBLE, Francis Henry. b: Barnstaple 1862. e: Oxf. Widower. c.t: Edinburgh Review, Fortnightly Review, National Review, Nineteenth Century, Times, Saturday Review, Daily Graphic. c: Authors. a: 68 W. Kensington Mans, W.14. t: Fulham 4134.

GRIBBLE, Leonard. b: London. m: Nancy Mason. d: 1. Author & Literary Adviser to several Lond Publs. Publ: Superintendent Slade crime novels & altogether about 60 books under own name & pseudonyms, also for Radio & Films. Ed Best Children's Stories of the Year. Ctr: Nat Press & various periodicals. s.s: Criminology. a: Cynlanen, Purley Downs Rd, Sanderstead, Surrey. T: 2457.

GRIBBON, Fanny Rinder. b: Stourbridge, Worcs. c.t: Progress. Lived in Aust 1879—'85, S. America '12—15. Rec: The theatre, walking, etc. c: Anthroposophical Soc in G.B., Halcyon, Eng Speaking U. a: Halcyon Club, Cork St. W.1.

GRICE, Thomas Ward. b: Malton, Yorks. Journalist. n.a: National Trade Press Ltd, Ed Draper's Organiser & Drapers Organiser Overseas until end of 1945, then Features Ed for Group. a: 32 Sinclair Grove, Golders Green, London, N.W.11. T: Speedwell 1911.

GRID LEAK. See Kidd, Charles David.

GRIER, Mary Lynda Dorothea, M.A. b: Rugeley, Staffs 1880. e: Newnham Coll Camb. Late Principal Lady Margaret Hall Oxf. Publ: Life of Winifred Mercier; Investigations into the Substitution of Men by Women in Industry. Ctr: Economic Journ & various other economic & educational papers. s.s: Social Services, Education. Rec: Bird & picture gazing. c: Univ Women's & Roy Empire Soc. a: Whittall, King's Sutton, Banbury. T: King's Sutton 58.

GRIER, William James, B.A. b: Ramelton, Co Donegal 1902. e: Foyle Coll, Londonderry Queen's Univ Belfast. m: Catherine Robinson Gillespie. s: 1. Minister of Religion. n.a: Ed Irish Evangelical 1928—. Publ: The Momentous Event; The Origin & Witness of the Irish Evangelical Church. Ctr: Evangelical Quarterly, Presbyterian Guardian, Peace & Truth. s.s: Church Hist, Theology, Greek New Testament. a: 28 Knockdene Park South, Belfast. T: Belfast 53162.

GRIERSON, Elizabeth Wilson. b: Hawick. e: Edin & Germany. Author & Social Worker. Publ: The Children's Book of Edinburgh (1906); The Scottish Fairy Book; Life of St Paul for Young People; Things Seen in Florence; The Story of St Francis of Assisi; Our Scottish Heritage ('17); Tales of Scottish Keeps & Castles; Tales of English Castles & Manors ('28); Tales of the Covenanters ('32) etc. a: Whitchesters, Hawick, Scotland.

GRIERSON, Francis. e: St Dunstan's Coll & Priv. m: Elinor Abraham. d: 1. Publ: More than 40 detective novels, including: Out of the Ashes; Entertaining Murder; Thrice Judas; etc, also The Compleat Crook in France (official account of Paris C.I.D.) & other Tech works. Ctr: Punch, various mags, journals & Daily newspapers. s.s: Crime. a: c/o National Liberal Club, Whitehall Pl, S.W.1.

GRIERSON, Sir George Abraham, C.I.E., K.C.I.E., O.M., PhD.(Halle), LittD.(Dublin), LL.D. (Cantab), D.Litt(Oxon). b: Glenageary, Co Dublin 1851. e: St Bees, Shrewsbury, T.C.D. m: Lucy Elizabeth Jean Collis. I.C.S. (ret). Prix Volney Académie Française 1905. Gold Medal Roy Asiatic Soc. Gold Medal Brit Acad. Sir W. Jones Gold Medal Asiatic Soc of Bengal. Publ: Seven Grammars of the Bihar Dialects; Bihar Peasant Life; The Modern Vernacular Literature of Hindustan; Dictionary of the Kashmiri Language; Ishkashmi, Zebaki, & Yazghulami; The Torwali Language; etc. s.s: Oriental lang's. Rec: Philology, music. c: Old Salopians, Roy Socs, Fell Brit Acad. a: Rathfarnham, Camberley, Surrey. t: 43.

GRIERSON, H. A. c.t: Lancet a: H.M. Prison, Brixton, S.W.2. t: Tulse Hill 1905.

GRIERSON, Herbert John Clifford, LL.D., Litt.D. e: King's Col, Aberdeen, Christ Church Oxford. Publ: The Poems of John Donne; Cross Currents in the Literature of the 17th Century; Background of English Literature; etc. a: 12 Regent Terr, Edinburgh. t: 20596.

GRIERSON, John. b: Liverpool 1909. e: Charterhouse, R.A.F. Coll Cranwell. m: Frances Hellyer. s: 1. d: 1. Test Pilot & Writer. n.a: This Modern Age 1946—47, Special Corresp Times '46. Publ: Jet Flight; High Failure; Through Russia by Air. Ctr: Times, Flight, Aeroplane. s.s: Aviation, Test Flying, Arctic & Antarctic Exploratory Work. Rec: Rowing & Riding a: Royal Aero Club, 119 Piccadilly, London. W.

GRIERSON, Philip, F.R.Hist.S., F.S.A., F.R.N.S. b: Dublin 1910. e: Marlborough Coll & Camb. Univ. Fellow & Librarian Gonville & Caius Coll, University Lecturer in History. n.a: Lit-Director Roy Hist Soc 1945. Publ: Les Annales de Saint-Pierre de Gand et de Saint-Amand; Books on Soviet Russia 1917—42. Ctr: Eng Hist Rev, Slavonic Rev, Revue Benedictine, Revue Belge de Philologie et d'Histoire, Le Moyen Age, Revue du Nord. s.s: Mediæval History, esp France & the Low Countries, Mediæval Numismatics. Rec: Numismatics, walking, squash. a: Gonville & Caius College, Cambridge.

GRIESSEN, Albert Edouard Pierre, F.R.S.A., F.R.H.S., A.T.P.I. *b*: Lon 1875. *e*: Paris, Versailles & Lon. *m*: M. E. M. Wagon. *d*: 1. Dep Dir Agric Dept U.P. India (ret). *Publ*: Horticulture in France ('98); Indian Town Planning Notes (Muttra, 1918); 2nd edn of Influence of Parks & Gardens & Open Spaces in Civic Developments; Rural Arboriculture with Vernacular Translations; De L'Adaptation de Certaines Espèces; The Evolution of the Moghul Gardens of the Plains of India; Quelques Arbres a Fleurs de l'Inde; De la Distribution de Certaines Espèces sur le Globe Terrestre ('33); Causerie Sur Les Palmiers des Indes; etc. *s.s*: Hortic, town planning. Restoration of the Moghul Gardens of India '00—13. Exec Officer Coronation Assemblage Delhi '02—03, Roy Durbar Delhi '12. Exec Officer New Capital Works Delhi '13—22. Dep Dir Agric Dept U.P. Reorganisation of Garden Circle '22—28. K.-i.-H. for Publ Service in India, R.U.M. *a*: 11 Park Rd, Craven Pk, N.W.10. *t*: Willesden 2923.

GRIEVE, Christopher Murray, J.P., (Hugh Macdiarmid). *b*: Langholm 1892. *m*: Valda Trevlyn. *s*: 1. Author & Journalist. *n.a*: Ed Scottish Chapbook, Scottish Nation, Northern Review, '25—27. Ed Vox or the Radio Critic, '29. Publicity Off L'pool Organisation, '30—31. *Publ*: Essays—Contemporary Scottish Studies: At the Sign of the Thistle; Albyn, or Scotland and the Future; poetry—Stony Limits; A Drunk Man Looks at a Thistle; Penny Wheep; First Hymn to Lenin; etc. *c.t*: Spectator, Modern Scot, Criterion, Scottish Educational Journ, New English Wkly, etc. *s.s*: Scottish arts & affairs, foreign lit, Communism. Translator from Russian, German, French, Spanish & Scottish Gaelic. One of Founders of Scottish Nationalist Party. *c*: Founder of Scottish P.E.N. Centre. *a*: c/o Scots Free Press, 1 India Bldgs, Victoria St, Edinburgh.

GRIEVE, Harry Bernard, F.F.I., F.C.I.I. *b*: Lon. *e*: King's Col. Married. *d*: 2. Gen Sec Gld of Ins Officials. *c.t*: Insurance Gld Journ. *a*: Gld of Ins Officials, 79 Queen St, E.C.4. *t*: City 3709.

GRIEVE, Mrs. Maud, F.R.H.S. *m*: Sommerville Grieve (dec). *Publ*: Modern Herbal; Culinary Herbs (1st edn); Bulbs & Tubers Used in Medicine & Commerce; Fungi as Food & in Medicine; etc. *c.t*: Star, Daily Express, etc. *s.s*: Med work. *a*: Whins Cottage, Chalfont St Peter, Gerrard's Cross, Bucks. *t*: Chalfont St Giles 104.

GRIEVE, Peter. *n.a*: Sub Ed London Office M/c Guardian. Travelled extensively. *a*: 43 Fleet St, E.C.4.

GRIFFIN, Dr. A. J. B. *a*: Public Health Dept, Guildhall, Worcester.

GRIFFIN, Arthur Harold. *b*: Liverpool 1911. *e*: Barrow G.S. Reporter. *n.a*: Barrow Guardian, Lancs Daily Post. *s.s*: Lake dist. *Rec*: Music, swimming. *c*: Fell & Rock Climbing of the English Lake Dist. *a*: Gordonville, Black Bull Lane, Broughton, Preston & 127 Fishergate, Preston. *t*: 4841.

GRIFFIN, Rev. Bernard. M.A. *b*: Ealing 1892. *e*: Roy G.S. High Wycombe & St Chad's Col Durham. *m*: Angela Eileen Donaldoh Pugh. *d*: 2. Dir of the Lon Diocesan Counc for Youth. *Publ*: A Good Warfare & The Apostles Creed. *c.t*: Indian Daily Telegraph & Ch Teacher. *s.s*: Religious educ. War Service 1914-20 with 1/10th Middx Regt T.F. as a Combatant Officer. Rank, Maj, Staff Appointments G.S.O. 11 & D.A.A.G. 8th (Lucknow) Div. *Rec*: Yachting & tennis. *a*: St Margaret's Rectory, Ironmonger Lane, E.C.2. *t*: Metropolitan 7796.

GRIFFIN, ERNEST HARRISON: physician; *b*. London, Eng., Oct., 1877; *s*. John and Miriam G.; educ. St. Peter's Coll. (Cambridge); Guy's Hospital (London); DEGREES: M.D., M.A.; unmarried. AUTHOR: Letters of a Wanderer, 1912; Adventures in Tripoli, 1924; A Doctor in the Desert, 1924. Contributor to many newspapers of articles on Eastern politics and affairs. Military distinctions: D.S.O.; M.C.; Order of the Liberator (Venzuela); Order of the Medjedie (Turkey). Relig. denom., Methodist Episcopal. CLUBS: Connaught; Royal Automobile. OFFICE: 48 Upper Berkeley St., London, W. I, Eng.

GRIFFIN, Frederic William Waudby, M.A., M.D., B.C., M.R.C.S., L.R.C.P. *b*: Weymouth 1881. *e*: Weymouth Col, Cam Univ. Journalist. *n.a*: B.M.J. Sub-Ed 1923-30, Ed Scouter '30-, Med Corr Morning Post '31-32. T.B. Officer Co of Surrey. *Publ*: Quest of the Boy; Rover Scouting; Always a Scout; Practical Pathology. *s.s*: Psych, psychotherapy. Asst County Commssr Lon Boy Scouts. *Rec*: Golf. *c*: Overseas *a*: 38 Gunterstone Rd, W.14. *t*: Fulham 5317.

GRIFFIN, Gerald. *b*: Galway 1888. *m*: Josephine Doyer. *d*: 1. Translator & jnlst. *n.a*: Chief Sub-Ed Evening Herald, Dublin, Sub-Ed Daily Telegraph. *Publ*: Gabrielle D Annunzio; Translator of:—From Seraievo to the Rhine (German); Balbo's Air Armada (Italian); Among Congo Pigmies (German); Christ Rescued (German); etc. *c.t*: Daily Telegraph, Irish Independent, Evening Herald, etc. *s.s*: Languages. *Rec*: Sailing. *a*: c/o John Hackney, 6 John St, Adelphi, W.C.2. *t*: Temple Bar 8908.

GRIFFIN, Harold John. *b*: Lon 1912. *e*: Brixton Sr Commercial. *m*: Hilda Maude Josephine Haylmore. *n.a*: 1928—30 Apprenticeship Finchley Press & Crystal Palace Dist Advtr editorials '30, Central News (London) Lon Editorial '31, Regina (Sask Canada) Leader Post editorial '32, Vancouver (B.C. Canada) Province feature writer, columnist Vancouver (B.C.) News '32, '33—34, Ed & publ N. Toronto Times-Echo, Mang Ed & Publisher Radio—The Modern Weekly '34—, Ed The Greeters' Guide—Travel '34—35. *c.t*: N/p World, Daily Province, Evening News & foreign press. *s.s*: Canadian Northland, Amer Esquimaux. Trav extensively. Overseas Mem B.I.J. *Rec*: Mountaineering, golf, tennis, fishing, hunting. *a*: c/o Mag Section, Daily Province, Vancouver, B.C., & 307 Skelly Bldg, Pender St. W, Vancouver, B.C.

GRIFFIN, Watson, F.R.G.S., F.R.S.A. *b*: Hamilton, Ontario 1860. *e*: Hamilton Collegiate Inst, Toronto Univ, Private. Journalist, Special Commissioner, The Canadian Government, Chief Government Intelligence Service. *Publ*: The Gulf of Years; Turok; Canada, The Country of Twentieth Century; Protection Prices; The Provinces the States, a disenssion of Economic Relationship of Canada & The United States; An Irish Evolution; Natural Resources of Canada. *Ctr*: North American Review, Mag of Amer Hist, Empire Review, Canadian Mag, etc. *s.s*: Development & Natural Resources of Canada, Scientific Problems. *a*: 196 Jameson Ave, Toronto, Ontario, Canada. *T*: 1860.

GRIFFITH, Dudley David. A.B., Ph.D. *b*: Evanstown, Ill 1882. *e*: Simpson Coll & Univ of Chicago. *m*: Ann Hewitt Moran. *s*: 1. Prof of English Univ of Washington. *n.a*: Ed Modern Language Quarterly 1940—. *Publ*: Bibliography of Chaucer; Origin of the Griselda Story. *Ctr*: Modern Language Quarterly. *s.s*: Technique of Fiction, Mediæval Story. *Rec*: Golf, gardening. *c*: Faculty (Univ of Wash). *a*: 5810 Cowen Pl, Seattle 5, Washington. *T*: VE 1055.

GRIFFITH, Edward Fyfe, M.R.C.S., L.R.C.P. *b*: Los Angeles, Cal 1896. *e*: England & Lausanne, St Mary's Hosp Lond. *m*: Mary Leigh Trafford. *s*: 1. *d*: 1. *Publ*: Modern Marriage ; The Road to Maturity ; Sex & Citizenship ; Morals in the Melting Pot ; The Childless Marriage ; Sex in Everyday Life. *Ctr*: Practitioner, Lancet. *s.s*: Marriage Consultant. *c*: Lansdowne. *a*: 25 Park Cresc, London, W.1. *T*: Welbeck 7144.

GRIFFITH, Ernest Stacey, A.B., Ph.D. *b*: Utica, New York 1896. *e*: Hamilton Coll & Oxf Univ. *m*: Margaret Dyckman Davenport. *s*: 2. *d*: 3. Dir Legislative Reference Service, Library of Congress Wash 25 D.C. *Publ*: Modern Development of City Government in United Kingdom & United States ; Current Municipal Problems ; History of City Government—The Colonial Period ; The Impasse of Democracy ; The Modern Government in Action. *s.s*: Political Theory, Comparative & Municipal Government. *Rec*: Basket ball, tennis, hiking. *c*: Authors. *a*: 1941 Parkside Drive, N.W. Washington 12, D.C. *T*: Randolph 5335.

GRIFFITH, **Helen Sherman.** *b*: Iowa. *e*: Priv Scs. *m*: William Oglesby Griffith. *s*: 2. *d*: 2. Writer. *Publ*: The Letty Books (10 vols) ; The Virginia Series (6 vols) ; Her Wilful Way ; Rosemary for Remembrance ; The Lane ; etc. Over 30 one-act (a few 2- or 3-act) plays for amateur production. *c.t*: Various mags. *s.s*: Books for girls. *Rec*: Motoring, walking gardening. *c*: Authors League America, The Boston Authors, League American Penwomen, The Art Alliance. *a*: 500 E. Evergreen Ave, Chestnut Hill, Philadelphia, Pa, & The Clearing, Saunderstown, Rhode Island. *t*: Chestnut Hill 3000 & Wickford 102-R.

GRIFFITH, Hubert Freeling. *b*: London 1896. *e*: St Paul's Sch & Berlin. Dramatic Critic Journalist & Playwright. *n.a*: Chief Dramatic Critic Dly Chronicle 1923—27, Oberserver '25, Ev Standard '27—30, Chief Dramatic Critic Sun Graphic, & New English Review '46, Chief Lit Critic, Dly Express '27—29, Theatre Corres Observer '32—39. *Publ*: Tunnel Trench ; The Tragic Muse ; Red Sunday ; Youth at the Helm ; Seeing Soviet Russia ; European Encounters ; Playtime in Russia ; R.A.F. Occasions ; R.A.F. in Russia ; This is Russia ; Several three-act Plays ; etc. *Ctr*: Manch Guardian, Dly Chronicle, New Statesman, Nineteenth Century, etc. *s.s*: Drama, Travel. *Rec*: Hunting, sailing. *c*: Arts Theatre. *w.s*: World Wars I & II. *a*: 37 Panetons Sq, Chelsea. *T*: Flaxman 5066.

GRIFFITH, Rev. Leopold David, F.R.S.A. *b*: London 1883. *e*: Malmesbury Ho Sch, Aske Schs & St Pauls Coll Burgh Lincs. *m*: Sarah Pearce. *s*: 2. *d*: 4. C. of E. Clergyman, Vicar of Tunstead 1936—. *Publ*: Paradox, or Perfect Reproduction ; etc. *Ctr*: Church Guardian, Church Record, C. of E. Newspaper, Manch Guardian, Gramophone, Bacup Times & local papers. *s.s*: Church Matters, Prayer Book Revision, Divorce, Education, etc, Gramophones & Recorded Music. *a*: Tunstead Vicarage, Stacksteads, Bacup, Lancs. *T*: Bacup 508.

GRIFFITH, **Llewelyn Wyn.** *b*: Llandrillo-yn-Rhos 1890. *e*: Dolgelley G.S. *m*: Winifred Frimston. *s*: 2. Civil Servant. *Publ*: Up to Mametz. *c.t*: Listener, World Radio, Observer. *s.s*: Poetry & early music. *a*: Crawford Cottage, Berkhamsted. *t*: Berkhamsted 235.

GRIFFITH, **Percy,** M.I.C.E., M.I.MechE., F.G.S., F.R.SanI. Cons Water Engineer. *Publ*: The Law Relating to Small Waterworks ; A Synthetic Psychology. *c.t*: Trans Soc of Engineers (Inc), Inst of Water Engs, Inst of San Engs. *a*: 39 Victoria St, S.W.1. *t*: Victoria 1703.

GRIFFITH, Reginald Harvey, M.A., Litt.D., Ph.D. *b*: Charlotte, Carolina 1873. *e*: Furman Johns Hopkins & Chicago Univs. *m* :. *d*: 2. Graduate Prof of English Univ of Texas. *Publ*: Alex Pope, A Bibliography ; Descriptive Catalogue of MSS & Books by Lord Byron ; Sir Percival of Galles, A Study of the Sources. *Ctr*: Athenæum, Times Lit Supp, N.Y. Times, Modern Philology, etc. *s.s*: English Lit 1640—1840, Lit Criticism, Bibliography. *Rec*: Reading, philosophy & mathematics. *c*: Univ, Fortnightly, etc. *a*: M.B. 1702, University of Texas, Austin 12, Texas, U.S.A.

GRIFFITH, Richard Clewin, M.I.M.M. *b*: Lon 1872. *e*: Charterhouse & Royal Sc of Mines. *m*: Edith Adelaide Gwynn. *s*: 3 (1 dec). *d*: 2. Metallurgical Chem. *n.a*: Chess Ed Daily Mail, Ed British Chess Mag 1919–. Counc Hampstead Boro' Counc. *Publ*: Modern Chess Openings (5th ed). *s.s*: Chess. British Chess Champion '12. *Rec*: Cricket, tennis, golf, billiards. *a*: 18 Wedderburn Rd, N.W.3. *T*: Hampstead 2000.

GRIFFITH, **Capt Richard Glyn,** M.R.A.S. *b*: Allahabad U.P., India 1892. *e*: Imp Services Col. *m*: Eleanor Gertrude Knatchbull (dec). *d*: 2. Author & Journalist. Late of the Political Service in the Near East. *Publ*: (Co-Author with Commdr Worsley, D.S.O.) The Romance of Lloyd's ; Hangman's Isle (novel). *c.t*: N/p in Lon, Provs & Empire. *s.s*: Nr East & Africa. Late Wilts Regt. *Rec*: Fishing, motoring. *c*: Overseas. *a*: Empire Service, 4—7 Red Lion Court, Fleet St, E.C.4. *t*: Central 9417 & 8.

GRIFFITH, **Robert.** Missionary Sec 1915–. *Publ*: Madagascar, a Century of Adventure ; Chwedl a Hanes (Welsh) ; Stracon Gwerin Affrica (Welsh) ; Crist Yng Nghynnwrf y Byd ; Hanes a Chan O lawer Gwlad ; etc. *a*: Livingstone Hse, Broadway, Westminster. *t*: Victoria 5057.

GRIFFITH, **Robert Arthur.** *b*: Carnarvon 1860. *e*: Liverpool Inst & Univ Col of Wales, Aberystwyth. Stipendiary Magistrate Merthyr Tydfil & Aberdare. *Publ*: Murmuron Menai ; O Fôr i Fynydd ; Y Bardd a'r Cerddor ; The Welsh Pulpit (Jt) ; etc. *a*: Abernant, Lake Rd E., Cardiff.

GRIFFITH, Rev. Robert Gladstone, M.A. *b*: Llandaff 1885. *e*: Llandaff Cathedral Sch, Clifton Coll, Emanuel Coll Camb & Wells Theo Coll. *m*: Esme Vera Whatley. *d*: 1. S.P.G. Services 1913—16 North China, Chefoo, Shantung & with Chinese Labourers War Area France. *n.a*: Ed Modern Churchmen's Union Pamphlets & Papers 1929—31. *Publ*: The Gospel History Examined ; The Necessity of Modernism ; Jesus for Every-Child. *Ctr*: Modern Churchman, Religions. *s.s*: Lit & Hist Criticism of the Four Gospels. *Rec*: Golf, Hon Sec V-Chm Modern Churchmen's Union. *c*: Authors. *a*: Steeple Claydon Vicarage, Bletchby, Bucks. *T*: S.C.35.

GRIFFITH, **Sir William Brandford,** K.B., C.B.E. *b*: Stone 1858. *e*: Oxenford Hse Jersey, Harrison Col Barbados & Univ Col Lon. Widower. *s*: 1. *d*: 1. Barrister-at-Law, Legal Adviser Min of Pensions. *Publ*: Revised & compiled Ordinances of Gold Coast Colony 1898 & 1903 ; Digest of Gold Coast Law Reports '34. Chief Justice G.C. 1895. Admin Govt of Lagos '96. Deputy for Gov of G.C. '97 (ret 1911). Pres Special Court for trial of Human Leopards in Sierra Leone '12. Special Constable '14—20. *Rec*: Tramping. *c*: Const, Roy Empire, African, & Swiss Alpine. *a*: 56 Russell Sq, W.C.1, & 2 Essex Ct, Temple, E.C.4. *t*: Museum 2210.

GRIFFITH, Wyn. *b*: Glanwydden 1890. P.R.O. Bd of Inland Revenue, Hon Ed The Hon Soc of Cymmrodonon, Mem P.E.N. *Publ*: Up to Manctz; Spring of Youth; The Wooden Spoon; The Way Lies West; The Barren Tree & other Poems; The Welsh & Their Country; The Voice of Wales; etc. *Ctr*: Listener, Welsh Rev, etc. *a*: Board of Inland Rev, Somerset Hse, London.

GRIFFITH-BOSCAWEN, Rt. Hon. Sir A. S. T. *b*: N. Wales 1865. *e*: Rugby & Queen's Col Oxf. *m*: (1) Edith Sarah Williams; (2) Phyllis Maude Dereham. *d*: 1. *Publ*: Fourteen Years in Parliament; Memories. *c.t*: National Review, Quarterly. *s.s*: Church affairs, agriculture, housing, transport. M.P. 1892–1922. Cabinet Minister '21–23. Chm Roy Comm on Transport '28–31. *Rec*: Shooting, travel, motoring. *c*: Carlton. *a*: Pangbourne Lodge, Berks. *t*: 55.

GRIFFITH-JONES, Rev. Ebenezer, B.A., D.D. *b*: Merthyr Tydfil 1860. *e*: Emlyn G.S., Newcastle Emlyn, S. Wales, Presby Col Carmarthen, New Col & U.C.L. *m*: Carita Stoner. *s*: 1. *d*: 1. Cong Min, Princ & Prof Yorks Utd Col 1907–32. *Publ*: The Ascent Through Christ (1898); The Master & His Method; Faith & Verification; The Unspeakable Gift; Divine & Human Providence (2 vols); etc. *c.t*: Brit Weekly, Cong Quarterly, Great Thoughts, Yorkshire Observer, Sunday Companion, etc. *s.s*: Relation of Science & Religion. Chm C.U.E. & W. 1918–19. Pres N.F.C.C. '31–32. *Rec*: Golf, photography, chess. *a*: Bryn, Manordilo, Llandilo, S. Wales.

GRIFFITH-JONES, J. C. *b*: Caernarvons 1895. *e*: Dolgelley G.S., M/C Col of Tech, external Univ Studies. *m*: Edith Rees. *d*: 2. Journalist & Publicist. *n.a*: Special Corr, Feature Writer. Sub-Ed. Leader Writer Western Mail & S. Wales Echo 1928–33. Special Corr & Feature Writer for Wales for News Chronicle '34—. Wales Corr for Trav & Industrial Development Assoc of Gt Brit & Ire '30—. for New Brit, News Chronicle, Everyman, Radio Times, World Radio, Welsh & Amer Press, The Writer, etc. *s.s*: Trav & Wales. Welfare Officer Baldwins Ltd (W. Wales) '20—27. Broadcast talks B.B.C. '24—. War Service Gallipoli & France '15—17. Author of series of travel & industrial talks on Wales broadcast abroad. *Rec*: Writing. *a*: 205 Cathedral Rd, Cardiff. *t*: 4888.

GRIFFITHS, Bernard Binstead. *b*: Long Eaton 1910. *e*: Secondary. Incorporated Accountant. *Publ*: (Plays) A Matter of Form; Who's Who; Misguided Genius; The Rehearsal: etc. *s.s*: Plays & poetry. *Rec*: Amateur Theatricals. *a*: 50 Victoria St, Long Eaton, N'ham.

GRIFFITHS, Constance Annie Elizabeth. *b*: Lon 1902. *e*: Eldon Col & Priv. Journalist. *n.a*: Graphic '21, Sunday Dispatch '32—. *c.t*: Daily Mail, Sketch, Graphic, Bystander, Sunday Dispatch, Yorks Evening News, Edin Evening News. *s.s*: Travel, dramatic criticism, gossip. *Rec*: Theatre, motoring, golf. *a*: 39 Wimpole St. W.1. *t*: Welbeck 2555.

GRIFFITHS, Ezer, D.Sc, F.InstP., F.R.S. *b*: Aberdare 1889. *e*: Aberdare C.Sc & Cardiff Univ Col. Princ Scientific Officer Nat Phys Lab Teddington. *Publ*: Methods of Measuring Temperature; Pyrometry; etc. *c.t*: Proc Roy Soc, Phys Soc, Proc Brit Assoc of Refrigeration, Internat Congresses of Refrigeration, Soc of Chemical Industry, etc. Business Sec of the Phys Soc, Sec of Section A of the Brit Assoc. *a*: 139 Ch Rd, Teddington, Middx.

GRIFFITHS, Gilbert Henry Colling St. George. *b*: Umballa, India 1888. *e*: Priv & Bristol Univ. *m*: Rebecca Jones. *s*: 1. *Publ*: Contract Bridge Self Taught. *Ctr*: Lancet. *Rec*: Cricket, rowing, collecting antiques, philatelist. *w.s*: Surg-Lt R.N. 1914—18 & R.N. '39—. *a*: H.M.S. Raleigh, Surg-Lt Comdr, Q.O. R.N.V.R. *T*: 4691 Colwyn Bay.

GRIFFITHS, Gwenvron M. Physician. *c.t*: Lancet, etc. *a*: 50 Wimpole St, W.1.

GRIFFITHS, Ivor. *b*: 1890. *n.a*: Chm Berrow's Newsps Ltd, Press Alliances Ltd, formerly Deputy Ed-in-Chief Daily Chronicle & Sunday News. *c*: Reform, Press. *a*: The Trinity, Worcester.

GRIFFITHS, Jenkyn, B.Sc, F.C.S., P.A., Inst W.E. *b*: Aberdare 1896. *e*: Cardiff Univ. *m*: Daisy Harrington-Lilley. *s*: 1. Ed. *n.a*: Ed 1919– Water & Water Engineering, Quarry & Road-Making, Colliery Guardian Co, Baths & Bath Engineering. *Publ*: Analyses of British Coals & Coke; Analysis of Coal & its Bye Products. *s.s*: Chemical engineering. *Rec*: Golf & rowing. *a*: 30–31 Furnival St, Holborn. *t*: 7141/2.

GRIFFITHS, John Gwyn, M.A. *b*: Porth, Rhondda 1911. *e*: Univs of Wales, Liverpool & Oxford. *m*: Kate Bosse. *s*: 2. Lect in Classics. *n.a*: Co-Ed Y Fflam 1946. *Publ*: Yr Efengyl Dywyll; Anarchistiaeth; Dyneiddiaeth mewn Byd Technolegol. *Ctr*: Greece & Rome, Classical Review, Journ of Egyptian Archæology, Man, Expository Times, Chambers's Ency (Egyptian Religion), Welsh Journs. *s.s*: Egyptian Religion & Religions in General. *a*: University College, Swansea.

GRIFFITHS, Leonard, A.M.I.E.E., M.I.Mech.E. *b*: Coventry 1894. *e*: Bablake Sch Coventry. Elec Eng. *Publ*: Automobile Electrical Equipment (with A. P. Young). *Ctr*: Tech & Sci Journs. *s.s*: Ignition Apparatus. *a*: Kennington, Biggin Hall Cresc, Coventry. *T*: 2430.

GRIFFITHS, Maurice. *b*: London 1902. *e*: Elizabeth's Ipswich. Ed Naval Architect, 1927. *n.a*: Ed The Yacht 1925—26, Yachting Monthly '27. *Publ*: The Magic of the Swatchways; The Sands of Sylt; Post War Yachting. *Ctr*: Various. *s.s*: Yacht Designing, Assoc Inst Naval Architects. *Rec*: Yacht cruising, motoring. *c*: Roy Harwich Yacht. *a*: 3 & 4 Clements Inn, London, W.C.2. *T*: Holborn 5327.

GRIFFITHS, Michael Henderson. *b*: Deganwy, Nth Wales 1916. *e*: Epsom Coll. *m*: Brenda Davies. *s*: 1. Art Editor. *n.a*: Good Housekeeping, Asst Art Ed 1937, Art Ed '47—. *Rec*: Motor-cycling. *a*: 76 Charlwood St, London, S.W.1. *T*: Victoria 2965.

GRIFFITHS, Oswald, M.A., LL.B. *b*: Merthyr Tydfil 1896. *e*: Wales Univ Col Aberystwyth, Trin Col Cam & Lincoln's Inn. *m*: Margaret Hannah Davies. *d*: 1. Barrister-at-Law. *Publ*: Principles of Bankruptcy Law & Deeds of Arrangement; Law Relating to Bankruptcy, Deeds of Arrangement, Receiverships & Trustees; Principles of Partnership Law; Law of Arbitrations & Awards; Summary of Executorship Law; etc. *c.t*: Various legal journs. *s.s*: Coy law, bankruptcy. *a*: The Croft, Torver Rd, Harrow, Middx. *t*: 1764.

GRIFFITHS, Sir Percival Joseph, Kt., C.I.E., B.A., B.Sc. *b*: London 1899. *e*: Central Foundation Sch Lond & Peterhouse Camb. *m*: Kathleen Mary Wilkes. *s*: 3. I.C.S. (ret). Adviser to India Burma Assoc. *Publ*: The British in India. *Ctr*: Various. *s.s*: India. *c*: Oriental. *a*: St Christopher, Bickerly Park Rd, Bickley, Kent. *T*: Imperial 2007.

GRIFFITHS, Rev. Rees, B.A., M.A., B.D., PhD. Cong Min. *Publ*: God in Idea & Experience; The Reserves of the Soul. *c.t*: Western Mail & S. Wales News, Expository Times, Y Dysgedydd, Scottish Congregationalist, etc. *a*: 34 Llanedeyrn Rd, Penylan, Cardiff.

GRIFFITHS, Thomas. *b*: Afan Valley. Journalist. *n.a*: Bridgend Chronicle 1890, Glam County Times '96, S. Wales News 1904, S. Wales Argus '29. *c.t*: Farmer & Stockbreeder, Daily Mail, Daily Herald, Daily Express, Shoe Leather Record, etc. *s.s*: Agric & Welsh. *c*: N.U.J. (Ex-Pres S. Wales Branch). *a*: Arfryn Queen's Hill Cresc, Newport, Mon.

GRIGG, Sir Edward William MacLeay, K.C.M.G., K.C.V.O., D.S.O., M.C., M.P. *b*: 1879. *e*: Winchester & New Col Oxf. *m*: Hon. Joan Poynder. *s*: 2. *d*: 1. *n.a*: Ed Staff Times 1903, Asst Ed Outlook '05–06, Ed Staff Times '08–13, Mil Sec to Prince of Wales, Canada '19, Aus & N.Z. Priv Sec to Mr. Lloyd George '21–22, M.P. (N.L.) Oldham '22–25, Sec Rhodes Trustees '23–25, Gov & Commander-in-Chief & High Commssr for Trans Kenya Col '25–31, Chm Milk Reorganisation Comm '32, M.P. (C.) for Altrincham '33–. *Publ*: The Greatest Experiment in History ('24); Three Parties or Two ('31). War Service Gren Guards. *a*: 113 Eaton Sq, S.W.1 & Tormarton Ct, Badminton, Glos. *t*: Sloane 1735.

GRIGG-SMITH, Rev. Canon Thomas, M.A. *b*: King's Norton, Worcs 1884. *e*: Gonville & Caius Coll Camb. *m*: Emma Freeman. Canon Residentiary Portsmouth Cathedral, Dir Religious Education Diocese of Portsmouth. *Publ*: The Child's Knowledge of God; The Use of the Voice; For Youth & the Years; Editor 12 Vols of Training in Faith, Worship & Service; Prayers for Day & Sunday School; Revised Handbook of Christian Teaching. *Ctr*: Various. *s.s*: Religious Education. *Rec*: Walking, golf, tennis, fishing, riding. *c*: Authors'. *a*: Diocesan Hse, 60 High St, Portsmouth. *T*: 73279.

GRIGGS, George Philip, B.A. *b*: Ewell, Surrey 1919. *e*: Nevill Holt Prep Sch, Nautical Coll Pangbourne, New Coll Oxf. Author. *n.a*: Asst Ed The Isis 1945—46. *Publ*: The Readiness is All; Destroyer at War. *Ctr*: Spectator. *s.s*: Naval & Naval Hist. *Rec*: Yachting, cricket. *c*: Savile, United Service, R.N. *w.s*: 1939—44 R.N. & S.H.A.E.F. *a*: Dart Bank, Dartmouth, Devon, & 123 Cheyne Walk, London, S.W.10. *T*: Dartmouth 38.

GRIGGS, Rev. S. R. Rural Dean of Canterbury. *Publ*: The Mystic Flock; The Splendour of God. *a*: Harbledown Rectory, Canterbury.

GRIGSBY, Joan. *b*: Portsmouth 1909. *e*: Milton Mount Coll & Bedford Coll Lond. *m*: Sqdrn Ldr G. M. Bryer, O.B.E., A.F.C. Journalist. *Publ*: Longshore & Down Channel; An Island Rooing. *Ctr*: News Chron, Dly Telegraph, Manch Guardian, Lond Ev News, etc. *s.s*: Sailing Ships, Children's Stories. *Rec*: Sailing, music. *a*: Messrs Heath Cranton, 6 Fleet St, London, E.C.4, or Overseas Club, Park Pl, St James's, London, W.

GRIGSON, Geoffrey. Journalist & critic. *n.a*: Asst Lit Ed Morning Post. Ed New Verse. *Publ*: Arts To-day. *s.s*: Modern art & poetry. *a*: 4a Keats Grove, N.W.3.

GRILLO, ERNESTO: professor; *b*. Italy, Dec. 2, 1877; s. Don Vincenzo and Sonna Maria (Ripandell); educ. Italy, Switzerland, Germany, England; DEGREES: M.A. (Urbino), Litt. D. (Royal Inst. of Superior Studies, Florence); LL.D. (Perugia); Hon. M.A. (Glasgow); married. AUTHOR: Lezioni d' Inglese, 1903; Lezioni di tedesco, 1904; Chaucer and Boccaccio, 1903; De Luci Acci Vita et Scriptis, 1907; De Joanne Cassiano, 1910; Italy and the War, 1914; The Italian Poets, 1917; The Italian Prose Writers, 1917; A New Italian Grammar, 1918; La Dolce Favella, 1918; The Teaching of English, 1918; Fiume: The Only Possible Solution, 1919; Pre-Dante Poetical Schools, 1919; The Dawn of Italian Prose, 1920; a new Italian Dictionary, 1921; Dante, the Prophet, 1921; The University of Padua, 1922; The University of Naples, 1924; The University of Pavia, 1925; Girolamo Savonarola, 1925; Shakespeare in Italy, 1925; Machiavelli, 1928; Foscolo, 1928; Gemme e Fior, 1928; Studies in Modern Italian Literature, 1930; poems and short articles. Editor of Tasso's Aminta, with an essay on pastoral poetry and prose translation, 1923. Prof. of Italian studies (Glasgow); dir. Italian Dept., Commercial Coll. (Glasgow); examiner to Royal Soc. of Arts; ass't. exam. to Civil Service Comm.; lecturer for many societies, literary and political. CLUBS: Savage. OFFICE: Stevenson Professor of Italian Language and Literature, Glasgow University. HOME: 1 Westbank Quartrant, W. 1, Glasgow, Scotland, and Casa Grillo, S. Angelo Lombardi, South Italy.

GRIME, Arthur. *b*: Blackpool. N/p Dir. *n.a*: Ed Yorkshire Evening Post, Gen Mang Yorkshire Post & allied papers, now Jt Govg Dir Evening Gazette, Blackpool Press Newspaper Soc. *a*: Evening Gazette, Blackpool. *t*: 1782.

GRIME, Harold Riley. *n.a*: Ed West Lancs Evening Gazette & Blackpool Gazette & Herald. *a*: Temple Street Press, Blackpool.

GRIME, John Favell. *b*: Leeds 1904. *e*: Leeds G.S. & Haileybury Col. *m*: Olive M. Joyner. Journalist & Author. *n.a*: Blackpool Gazette & Herald, M/C Evening News, Daily News (Lon), Daily Mail (Lon), Malay Mail (F.M.S.), res May 1934 Daily Express (Lon) '34—. Mem N.U.J. '25—. *Publ*: No One Walked; Personal Column; etc. *c.t*: Britannia & Eve, Amer Mags. *s.s*: Fiction, travel. *Rec*: Golf. *a*: c/o Curtis Brown Ltd, Henrietta St, W.C.2.

GRIMES, Rev. Charles Hugh Duffy, M.A., F.R.Hist.S., F.R.G.S. *b*: Stanton on Hine Heath, Salop 1874. *e*: Portsmouth Gr Sch, King's Sch Chester. Clerk in Holy Orders, Rector of Newton Ferrers, H.C.F. *Publ*: In the Steps of William the Conqueror; History of Hitcham; History of English Colony of Bordeaux; History of English Colony of Barcelona; History of Newton Ferrers. *Ctr*: Times, Church Times, Record, Home Words, C. of E. Newsps, Church Standard, Western Morning News, West Australian. *s.s*: Local History & Antiquarian Subjects. *Rec*: Tennis, swimming. *a*: The Rectory, Newton Ferrers, Sth Devon. *T*: 296.

GRIMES, Harold Hutchings. *b*: Brighton 1888. *e*: Castle Gate Sch Lewes. *m*: Leonora Alice Carter. *s*: 2. *d*: 2. Journalist. *n.a*: Sussex Express 1903, Seaford Telegraph '09, Hastings Mail & Times '11, Sussex Dly News '11, Derby Dly Express '18, Nottingham Journ '19—. *w.s*: 1916—18. *s.s*: Sport. *Rec*: Walking. *a*: 81 Kennick Rd, Mapperley, Nottingham. *T*: Nottingham 45911.

GRIMLEY, Rev. Bernard, D.D., PhD. *b*: Shepshed 1898. *e*: Gregorian Univ, Rome. Catholic Priest *n.a*: Ed Catholic Gazette 1925–, & Catholic Times '33–. Lect & Writer. *Publ*: The Atonement; The Church, Six Sacraments, Moral Principles & Practice, etc. *s.s*: Catholic defence work. Preacher in New York Lent '31. *Rec*: The Sea—on it, and in it, and by the shores of it. *a*: The Missn Hse, Brondesbury Pk, N.W.6. *t*: Willesden 0682.

GRIMLEY, Montague Cyril, M.J.I. b: Lon 1905. e: Xaverian Col Brighton. m: Margaret Teresa Gilmartin. d: 2. Reporter. n.a: Allied N/ps Ltd M/C. Reader '24—25, Asst Librarian '25—26, Reporter '26—34, Blackpool Ed Rep '34—. s.s: Ecclesiastical & maritime. R.N.V.R. '24—31. Rec: Golf, cricket, rowing. c: N.U.J., N/p Press Fund. a: 15 Dryburgh Ave, Marton, Blackpool. t: 177.

GRIMLEY, Vivian Edmund, M.J.I. n.a: Circulation Mang Machinery 1911, Sub-Ed Pathé Cinema Journ '13, T.P.'s Weekly '14, Asst Mang & Reader Herbert Jenkins Ltd '16, Staff Writer Picture Show '19—34, Sub-Ed Boys' Cinema '34. Publ: Compiler Picture Show's Who's Who on the Screen '31—34. c.t: Boy's Cinema, Modern Boy, Daily Mirror, etc. s.s: Films. a: 13 Gerda Rd, New Eltham, S.E.9. t: Cen 8080.

GRIMMER, George Kerr, M.D.(Edin), B.A., F.R.C.S.(Edin), C.M. b: St Andrews, New Brunswick, Canada 1866. e: New Brunswick & Edin Univs. m: Lilian Florence Nash Selwyn. s: 1. d: 1. Late Asst Surg Met Ear, Nose & Throat Hosp W.1. 1924—30. Late Oculist L.C.C. Sc Clinic Tooting S.W. '16—34. Ophthalmic Surg to Western Dispensary S.W.1. (L.C.C. Eye Clinic) '34—. c.t: Archives of Otology N.Y., Reports Edin R.C.P. Lab. s.s: Eye, ear, nose & throat. a: 28 St Nicholas Rd, Lon, S.W.17. t: Battersea 3717.

GRIMSDALE, Elsie, F.R.S.A. b: Lon 1898. e: County Sc Putney, Fulham T.C., & Anti-Socialist Un. Married. d: 1. Polit Org, Speaker & Sec for Cons Party. c.t: Morning Post, Daily Telegraph, Wandsworth Boro' News, S. Poplar Local Press. s.s: Politics, social welfare. Mem Reg Inst of Women Sec (Assoc Chrtd Inst of Book-keepers). Mem C.o. Lon Conservative Assoc & Primrose League. a: 54 Ringford Rd, W. Hill, S.W.18.

GRIMSDITCH, Herbert Borthwick, M.A. b: Liverpool 1898. e: Priv Sch, Univ of Liverpool. Writer & Journalist, Mem N.U.J. n.a: Asst Ed The Studio 1923—29, Asst Ed The Artist '36—38, B.B.C. Dly Digest '42—45, Illustrated '45—47, Chambers Ency '47. Publ: Character & Environment in the Novels of Thomas Hardy; Vathek (Trans); Pitfalls in Everyday French; (Pt-Author): Dictionary of National Biography, Supplement; Cambridge Bibliography of English Literature; British Authors of the Nineteenth Century; Twentieth Century Authors. Ctr: Various Trans of books on Art to the Studio, Lond Mercury, Art Review, Manch Guardian, Nation, John Bull, Observer, etc. s.s: Art, English Lit, Biogs. Rec: Cycling, sculling, painting. a: 15 Steele's Rd, Hampstead, London, N.W.3. T: Primrose 6381.

GRIMSHAW, Beatrice. Author. Publ: Helen of Man o' War Island; The Wreck of the Redwing; etc. a: c/o C. A. Pearson Ltd, Henrietta St, W.C.2.

GRIMSHAW, Beatrice Ethel. b: Nth Ireland. e: Bedford Coll (Lond), Queen's Univ Belfast, Ecole Retaillaud, Caen France. Author. Publ: When the Red Gods Call; My Lady of the Islands; The Sorcerer's Stone; My Lady Far Away; The Sands of Oro; The Star in the Dust; Kris-Girl; Queen Vaiti; Nobody's Island; The Coral Palace; Rita Regina; Eyes in the Corner; The Long Beaches; Isles of Adventure; South Sea Sarah; Lost Child; Pieces of Gold; etc. s.s: Pacific Islands & New Guinea (Cannibal & Headhunting Tribes). Rec: Travel. a: Box 29, Oberon, N.S.W., Australia.

GRIMSHAW, Percy Hall, I.S.O., F.R.S.E., F.R.E.S. b: Leeds 1869. e: Leeds Ch Sc. m: Jeanie Blair White. d: 1. Keeper Nat Hist Dept, Roy Scot Museum. Ed Scot Naturalist. c.t: The Scotsman, The Field, the Scottish Naturalist. s.s: Entomology. Diptera. Vice-Pres Roy Phys Soc (Edin). Rec: Botany & music. a: 49 Lygon Rd, Edin. t: 42867 & 24488.

GRIMSTEAD, Hettie. b: Manchester 1903. e: Priv. Author & Journalist. n.a: Woman Ed Northern News Agency 1926—29, Asst Ed Controversialist '29. Publ: Painted Virgin; Stolen Heavens. Ctr: Leading Nat & Prov Newspapers & various periodicals. s.s: Theatrical Celebrities, Home Furnishing & Decorating. Rec: Singing, cookery. c: Arts Theatre. a: Charlwood St, London, S.W.1. T: Victoria 6023.

GRIMWADE, H. C. n.a: Dir & Sec Forest of Dean Newspapers Ltd. Hon Sec Three Shires Newspaper Soc. a: Longmead, Libertus Rd, Cheltenham.

GRIMWADE, H. J. n.a: Asst Art Ed Times 1922—. E. Anglian Daily Times, Surrey Advertiser, Halifax Guardian, Sheffield Daily Telegraph, Daily Sketch. a: 101 Cassiobury Park Ave, Watford, Herts.

GRINBLAT, Nathan. b: Weds, Russia 1887. e: Jewish Coll & Univ Kowna. m: Nechama Dimitrowsky. s: 1. d: 1. Teacher & Writer. n.a: Dawar, Hapoel-Hazair, Mozhaim, Gazith, Gilionth, Haolam. Ed Am W. Ssefer. Publ: Fivoush; Bamidron; Bathjachen; Bashalecheth; Lina; Criticisms, etc. s.s: Criticism. c: Hebrew Writer's. a: 30 Pansker St, Tel-Aviv, Palestine.

GRINFIELD, Charles Theodore. e: Private Schools. n.a: The Era, The Stage 1900—. c.t: London & Provincial Press. s.s: Pianoforte, orchestral conducting, composer, organist. etc a: 10 Ellenborough Park South, Weston-super-Mare, Som. t: 719.

GRINSTEAD, Roger. b: Birmingham 1914. e: Elem. m: Leah Gough. s: 1. d: 1. Publ: Some Talk of Alexander; They Dug A Hole. s.s: Left Wing Political Activity, Gardening. a: 18 Lacey Ave, Wilmslow, nr Manchester.

GRINSTED, W. F. Harrison, A.R.C.M., L.R.A.M., M.R.S.T. n.a: W. Sussex Gazette. s.s: Music, art, archit. a: 7 Gaisford Rd, Worthing.

GRISCOM, Ludlow. M.A. b: New York 1890. e: Private Schs, Univs of Columbia & Cornell. m: Edith Sumner Sloan. s: 1. d: 2. Ornithologist, Editor, Conservationist, Museum Trustee. n.a: Asst-Ed Rhodora 1929—39, Assoc-Ed Bull of Mass Audubon Soc '40—, Ed Bd Audubon Mag, New York '37—, Ed Bd Audubon Field Notes '47—. Publ: Birds of the New York City Region; Distribution of the Birds of Guatemala; Birds of Dutchess Co, N.Y.; Modern Bird Study; Birds of Nantucket. Ctr: Over 400 articles on ornithology, fish, botany, conservation & techniques of field study of living birds in technical journs, popular magazines & in newspapers. s.s: Birds. Rec: Music & travel. c: Union & Century N.Y., Cosmos, (Wash), Union & Harvard, Faculty, Cambridge, Colonial Soc of Mass. a: 21 Fayerweather St, Cambridge, Mass. T: Kirkland 5222.

GROENEWEGEN, HERMAN YSBRAND: professor of ethics and philosophy of religion, Univ. of Amsterdam; b. Amsterdam, Holland, Jan., 1862; s. John Henry and Johanna Margarete (Rogge) G.; educ. Gymnasium at Amsterdam; Univ. of Amsterdam; Univ. of Leiden; DEGREES: D.D.; m. Henrietta Antonio Kollewyn, 1887. AUTHOR: Paulus van Hemert, Theologian and Philosopher, 1889; Two Problems of the Philosophy of Religion, 1891; The Ethics of Abr. Kuenen, 1893; A Religious People, 1897; Sermons, 1899; Pulpit Studies, 1901; The Theology and his Philosophy, 1904; History of Remonstrantism in Rotterdam, 1906; Jacobus Arminius, 1909; The Remonstrance in its original form. facsimile, copy, explanatory study, 1910;

On Aesthetical Education, 1910; Students' Life and Religion, 1915; The Dark Problem of Sexual Ethics, 1923; Lectures on Sexual Ethics, 1925. Contributor to Theologisch Yydschrift, Nieuw Theol. Tydschrift, De Gids, De Tydspiegel, Kantstudien, Proc. of Congresses of Religious Liberals, Jubilee of Calvin; and others; newspapers: Handelsblad, Telegraaf, De Hervorming and others. Minister of Remonstrant Soc., 1887-1902; prof. of Remonstrant Sem., with Leiden Univ., 1902-1916; prof. of ethics and philosophy of religion, Univ. of Amsterdam, since 1916; preacher in different religious congregations; lecturer on religious, theological, ethical, philosophical, literary subjects. Relig. denom., Remonstrant. CLUBS: Hon. mem. of Kant-Gesellschaft (Berlin). OFFICE: University of Amsterdam. HOME: Huister Heide (U), Rembrandloan, 28, Netherlands.

GROMER, Belle Burns. *b*: Tacoma, Washington 1890. *e*: St Helen's Hall Portland Oregon, Washington Coll. *m*: J. G. B. Gromer (dec'd). *Publ*: Young Navy Man. *Ctr*: Cosmopolitan, Colliers, American, Chicago Tribune, Unity Weekly, etc. *c*: P.E.N. (Los Angeles). *a*: 1138 Shenandoah St, Los Angeles 35, California, U.S.A. *T*: CR 6-4015.

GRONBACK, Fred. Trade & Tech Journalist. *Ctr*: Business Journs. *a*: 7 Staplands Rd, Broad Green, Liverpool 14. *T*: Stoneycroft 1873.

GRONDAHL, Illit. *b*: New Cross 1882. *e*: Eng & Norweg Sch Oslo, Caen & Lond Univ. Lect in Norwegian Lang & Lit Univ of Lond 1918—48. *Publ*: Henry Drummond: Menneskets Skabelse (The Ascent of Man)—trans & adapt for Norwegian public, Oslo; Mot Solrenning (Selections from Edward Carpenter with Introduction); Chapters in Norwegian Literature (with Ola Raknes); Henrik Wergeland; Poems (with G. M. Gathorne-Hardy & J. Bithell); contributed a Norwegian Appreciation to Edward Carpenter, ed by Gilbert Beith; Landmarks of English Literature; A First Norwegian Reader. *Ctr*: W. W. Hall—Recorded Illuminates, B. Wayler—Towards a Philosophy of Faith. *s.s*: Mysticism in Literature. *Rec*: Tramping, ski-ing, swimming. *c*: Univ of Lond, Norwegian Club (Lond). *a*: Yddebu, Heggenes, Norway.

GROOM, Arthur. *b*: Hove, Sussex 1898. *e*: Whitgift Sch Croydon. *m*: Marjorie Helen Grimsley. *d*: 1. Author, Journalist, Lecturer. *n.a*: T.O.T. (Underground Rlys) Staff Mag Working Ed 1929, Inst of Journ. *Publ*: Edward the Eighth—Our King; Writing for Children; The Power of Public Speaking; The Ghost of Gordon Gregory; The Adventure at Marston Manor; Scouting in Europe; Etiquette for Everyone; The Kidnapped Form; The Money Box. *Ctr*: Dly Mirror, John Bull, Ch Sc Monitor, Home Chat, Ev News, Sun Pict, Manch Ev News, Dly Express, Tit-Bits, Sun Dispatch. *s.s*: Children, Public Speaking, Scouting, Nat Savings, Youth in General. *w.s*: Capt R.A.P.C. 1940—45. *Rec*: Motoring, reading, collecting things in miniature. *a*: Sea Home, Sea Meads, Praa Sands, Marazion, Cornwall. *T*: Germoe 3127.

GROOM, Bernard. M.A.(Oxon), M.A.(Lon). *b*: Lon 1892. *e*: Stationers' Co's Sc, Lon; Univ Col. Lon; Magdalen Col, Oxford. Senior English Master, Clifton College. *Publ*: A Literary History of England; A Short History of English Words; Poems. *s.s*: English literature & language. *a*: 15 Clifton Park, Bristol 8.

GROOM, Gladys Laurence. *Publ*: inc A Sentimental Journey through Greece; (Poems) The Ship of Destiny; Poems 1936—46; etc. *a*: 65a Eresson St, Athens, Greece.

GROOM, SIR LITTLETON ERNEST: barrister, M. P.; b. Toowoomba, Queensland (N. S. W.), April 22, 1867; s. Hon. William Henry and Grace (Littleton) G.; educ. Toowoomba Grammar Sch, Melbourne Univ., Ormond Coll. DEGREES: M.A., M.L.; m. Jessie Jane Bell, July, 1894 AUTHOR: Real Property Acts (with G. W. River), 1901; The Judicial Power of the Commonwealth of Australia (with Sir John Quick), 1902. Editor (jointly): Torrens Digest, 1899; Queensland Supreme Court Reports (5 vols), 1900-1902. General character of writing: technical, judicial. Relig. denom., Church of England. CLUB: Johnsonian (Brisbane). HOME: Unara, Toowoomba, Queensland, New South Wales.

GROOT, ALBERT WILLEM de: univ. prof.; b. Groningen, Holland, Jan. 13, 1892; s. Folkert de Groot and Alberdina ten (Cate) De G.; educ. Lagere Sch. and Gymnasium (Groningen), Univs. of Groningen, Munster in Westfalen, and Basel (Switzerland). DEGREE: Dr. of Philology; m. Ida Kitty Fanny Nelly de Geus, Dec. 30, 1919. AUTHOR: Untersuchungen zum byzantinischen Prosarnythmus (Procopios von Cäsarea), 1918; Handbook of Antique Prose Rhythm I, 1918; De numero oratorio latino, 1919; Die Anaptyxe im Lateinischen, 1921; Verouderde denkwÿzen en nieuwe problemen in de latÿnsche taalwetenschap, 1921; Der antike Prosarnythmus, I, 1921; La prose métrique des anciens, 1926; Instrumental Phonetics, its value for linguists, 1928. Contributor to Classical Quarterly; Philologische Wochenschrift; Museum; Gnomon; Revue des études latines; Rheinisches Museum; Neophilologus. General character of writing: scientific. OFFICE: Univ. of Amsterdam. HOME: Zandvoortsche Laan 174, Aerdenhout, Holland.

GROPIUS, Walter Adolf. M.A. *b*: Berlin, Germany 1883. *e*: Humanistisches Gymnasium Berlin, Technische Hochschule Munich & Berlin. *m*: (1) Alma Mahoer, (2) Ise Frank. *d*: 2. Chm Dept of Archt Harvard Univ. *Publ*: The New Architecture & the Bauhaus; Bauhaus 1919—28. *Ctr*: Various. *s.s*: Architecture. *a*: Baker Bridge Rd, Lincoln, Mass, U.S.A. *T*: Lincoln 0098.

GROS, ETIENNE: professor in liberal arts in Univ. of Aix; b. Marseille, France, Feb. 2, 1882; s. Valentin and Marie (Védlèr) E. DEGREE: Litt. D., Licentiate of Letters. AUTHOR: Philippe Quinault, sa vie et son oeuvre, 1926. Editor: La Mère coquette (by Philippe Quinault), 1926. Contributor to Revue d'Histoire litteraire de la France. General character of writing: literary criticism. Religion, Catholic. OFFICE: Faculté des Lettres d'Aix. HOME: 104 cours Lieutaud, Marseille, France.

GROSE, Helena. *b*: Lon 1904. *e*: Various Scs & King's Col Lon. *m*: Reginald Grose (dec). Novelist & Journalist. *n.a*: Daily Express & Sunday Express 1927—31, gen reporter, rising to sub-ed, then humour-columnist, children's ed, gen articles, etc. *Publ*: When Women Whisper; The Stork Called Twice; It Was Wonderful; Then Came Sally; The Marrying Kind; Dearest; They Meant to Marry; Young Bride; Secret Honeymoon; Marriage Shy; etc. *c.t*: Daily & Sunday Express, Amal Press Ltd, D. C. Thomson publications, Evening Standard, Tit-Bits, various mags, etc. *s.s*: Romance, mystery stories, women's interests. *Rec*: Travel, motoring. *c*: St Andrews. *a*: 27 Queensberry Hse, Richmond, Surrey. *t*: 0733.

GROSE-HODGE, Humfrey, M.A., F.S.A. *b*: Anningsley Park, Ottershaw 1891. *e*: Marlborough Coll & Pembroke Coll Camb. *m*: Pamela Moresby. *s*: 2. Head Master Bedford School, I.C.S. 1914—18, Asst-Master Charterhouse '20—28. *Publ*: Roman Panorama; Cicero (four speeches trans); Murder at Larinum; Verres in Sicily. *s.s*: Education, The Classics. *c*: St James's, Head Masters' Conference. *w.s*: Served with Q.V.O. Corps of Guides I.A. in India, Mespot & Palestine 1916—18. *a*: School Hse, Bedford. *T*: 2919.

GROSER, Horace George. *m*: Mary Louise Banbury. *s*: 1. *d*: 2. *Publ*: Life of Field-Marshal Lord Roberts; Life of Lord Kitchener; Out with the Old Voyagers; Atlantis (poems); etc. *Ctr*: Various. *s.s*: Hist. *Rec*: Tramping, gardening. *a*: Wychwood, Fitzjohn Ave, Barnet, Herts. *T*: Barnet 2914.

GROSER, Rev. Thomas Sidney. *b*: Adelaide, Sth Australia 1886. *e*: Australia & Canterbury Coll England. *m*: Mary Ann Lacey. Clerk in Holy Orders, Vicar of Scientific Monthly, Delineator, McCall's, etc. *Rec*: Travel, reading, walking. *a*: 418 Central Park West, New York 25, N.Y., U.S.A. *T*: Academy 2-7670.

GROSS, Dr. M. *a*: Town Hall, Hemel Hempstead, Herts.

GROSSMAN, Reuben, B.A. *b*: Chicago 1905. *e*: New York Univ. *m*: Anna Shaffer. *s*: 2. Instructor English Language & Author. *Publ*: Collected Poems; Palestinian Idylls; Father & Daughter; Hebrew Anthology of English Verse; Compendious Hebrew-English Dictionary; Many translations: Tagone, Zangwill, Shakespeare, Poe, Lewisohn, London. *Ctr*: Hatekufah, Knesseth, Moznayim, Jilyonoth, Heb Writers Miscell, American Heb Year Books, Hadoar, Hapoel Watzair, Heidim, etc. *s.s*: Poetry, Literary Essays. *Rec*: Music & the theatre. *c*: P.E.N., Hebrews Writers Assoc, Exec Habimah Circle. *a*: 103 Rothschild Boulevard, Tel Aviv, Palestine.

GROSVENOR, Caroline Susan Theodora, C.B.E. *m*: Hon Norman de l'Aigle Grosvenor. *d*: 2. *Publ*: The First Lady Wharncliffe and Her Family (1779—1856); Novels—The Bands of Orion; The Thornton Device; Laura. *s.s*: Emigration for educated women. Chm Counc Women's Farm and Garden Assoc. *c*: Ladies Empire. *a*: 2 U. Grosvenor St, W.1. *t*: Grosvenor 1071.

GROSVENOR, Ernest. *b*: Bow 1884. *e*: Priv. Married *s*: 2. *d*: 2. *n.a*: Mang W. H. S. Walsall 1914–. *c*: Rotary (Walsall). *a*: Seymour Hse, Townsend St, Walsall. *t*: 3055.

GROSVENOR, Gilbert (Hovey), A.M., LL.D., Litt.D., Sc.D. *b*: Istanbul, Turkey 1875. *e*: Robert Coll Istanbul, Worcester (Mass) Acad, Amherst Coll. *m*: Elsie May Bell. *s*: 1. *d*: 5. Geographer, Ed, Writer, Dir Nat Geographic Soc 1899—, Pres 1920—. *n.a*: Asst-Ed Nat Geographic Mag 1899—1900, Mang-Ed 1900—02, Ed-in-Chief '03—. *Publ*: Book of Birds; Insignia & Decorations of the United States Armed Forces; History of the National Geographic Society; Scenes from Every Land. *Ctr*: Flags of the World, The Hawaiian Islands, Discovery & Exploration, A Maryland Pilgrimage. *s.s*: Geography. *Rec*: Golf, yachting. *c*: Cosmos, Nat Press. *a*: National Geographic Soc, 1146 Sixteenth St, N.W., Washington, D.C. *T*: District 3330.

GROSVENOR-GILL, Hilda May. *b*: Mortimer, Berks. *e*: Private. Journalist. *s.s*: Foreign news, etc. *a*: 162a Strand, W.C.2. *t*: Temple Bar 3962.

GROTRIAN, Edgar. Mang Dir Hull & Grimsby n/p's Ltd. *a*: Daily Mail, Jameson St, Hull.

GROUSSET, Rene. *Publ*: inc Bilan de l'histoire; Histoire des Croisades; In the Footsteps of the Buddha; Histoire de l'Asie; etc. *a*: 7 Avenue Velasquez, Musee Cernuschi, Paris.

GROVER, Frederick Shaftain. *b*: Lon 1884. Sub Ed The Guardian. *n.a*: Started Journalism on The Echo. *c.t*: Passing Show, Daily Herald, Westminster Gazette. War Service M.S.M. *a*: 12 Hazeldene Rd, Goodmayes, Essex.

GROVES, E. W. H., F.R.C.S., M.S., D.Sc. Cons Surgeon. *n.a*: Ed Brit Journ of Surgery 1918–. *Publ*: Synopsis of Surgery; Modern Method of Treating Fractures; etc. *c.t*: Brit Journ of Surgery, B.M.J., Lancet, etc. *a*: 25 Victoria Sq, Clifton, Bristol. *t*: 35570.

GROVES, Ernest Thomas, A.I.A.A. *b*: Lon 1905. *e*: Priv & Roy Acad. *m*: Sheila Bassett. Dramatic Critic, Reporter & Architect. *n.a*: Lewisham N/p Coy '32. *s.s*: Politics. Articles with Gunton & Gunton F.F.R.I.B.A. '21–23. Asst Architect '23–26. Work on period domestic design & restoration. '26–32. *Rec*: Golf & garden. *a*: Tilemans Field, Farningham, Kent. *t*: Lee Green 0437.

GROVES, Brig.-Gen. Percy Robert Clifford, C.B., C.M.G., D.S.O. *e*: Bedford. Officer Royal Air Force (Ret). *n.a*: Ed Monthly Mag "Air" '27—29. *Publ*: Behind The Smoke Screen; Our Future in the Air. *c.t*: Times, Telegraph, Observer, Sunday Dispatch, Daily Mail, Daily Express, Various British Reviews & Mags, The Atlantic Monthly, National Geographic. Strand (under Pseudonym C. Benbow). *s.s*: Aviation, international affairs. Served in South African War & Gt. War in France, the Dardanelles, Egypt, Palestine & Manchuria. Director of Flying Operations Air Ministry 1918, British Air Adviser to Supreme Council at Peace Conference & British Air Representative at Geneva '19—22. Hon Sec General Air League of the British Empire '27—29. *Rec*: Swimming, fishing, motoring. Commandant, Legion of Honour, Order of White Eagle of Serbia. *c*: United Services, Royal Institute of International Affairs, Royal Aeronautical Society. *a*: 49 Avenue Rd, N.W.8. *t*: Primrose 1948.

GROVES, Reg. *b*: London 1908. *e*: Elem. *m*: Daisy Cox. *d*: 2. Film Scenarist. *n.a*: Ed World Film News 1936—38, Lond Corr New York New Leader Weekly '38—41. *Publ*: The Mystery of Victor Grayson; But We Shall Rise Again; Rebels Oak; The Peasants Revolt (with Philip Lindsay); Chelsea; Jesse James. *Ctr*: World Film News, New Leader, Leeds Weekly Citizen. *s.s*: Hist, especially Labour, Assoc Football, Films. *a*: 2 Granard Rd, London, S.W.12. *T*: Battersea 7799.

GROVES, William Charles. *b*: Ballarat, Victoria, Australia 1898. *e*: Ballarat State Hgh Sch, Univs of Melbourne & Sydney. *m*: Doris F. Kathleen Smith. *s*: 1. *d*: 2. Dir of Education Territory of Papua-New Guinea. *Publ*: Native Education & Culture-Contact in New Guinea; Tabor To-day. *Ctr*: Melbourne-Herald, Age, Argus, Walkabout, Life, Sydney-Mankind, Oceania, etc. *s.s*: Pacific Affairs, Race Relations, Internat Affairs, Social Anthropology, Travel, Education, Colonial Administration. *Rec*: Reading, human relations. *w.s*: A.I.F. 1915—19; '42—45. *a*: Dir of Educ, Administration H.Q., Territory of Papua-New Guinea, Port Moresby, Papua, via Australia.

GROVES-WHITE, Dr. J. H. *a*: Dyer Ct, Cirencester.

GROZIER HERBERTSON, Agnes. *b*: Oslo Norway. *e*: Priv. Author. *Publ*: Novels:—The Summit; Deborah; Patience Dean. Poetry:—The Quiet Heart. For Children:—Book of Happy Games; Cap-o-Yellow; The Spindle Tree; Ponsonby and His Friends. *c.t*: Strand Magazine, Grand Magazine, Modern Woman, Windsor Magazine; Truth, Manchester

Guardian, Queen, etc. *s.s*: Short stories. *Rec*: Reading, walking, golf. *c*: Lon Lyceum. *a*: 87 St Mark's Rd. W.10. *t*: Park 3380.

GRUBB, Edward, M.A. *b*: Sudbury 1854. *e*: Friends' Scs, Sidcot & Bootham, Founders Inst Ackworth & Lon Univ Col. *m*: Emma Maria Horsnaill. *s*: 2. *d*: 3. Editor, Author & Lecturer. *n.a*: Prop & Ed of British Friend (monthly) 1901-13. *Publ*: Authority and the Light Within ('08); The True Way of Life (3rd edn, '15); What is Quakerism? (3rd edn, '29); The Bible, Its Nature & Inspiration (4th edn, '34); The Worth of Prayer ('30); Flowers of the Inner Life ('33); etc. *c.t*: The Cong Quarterly, The Contemporary Review, The Friend's Quarterly Examiner, Amer Quaker, etc. *s.s*: Rel & ethics. Sec of Howard Assoc (for Penal reform) '01-06. *Rec*: Garden. *a*: 9 Sollershott West, Letchworth, Herts. *t*: 583.

GRUBB, Miss Isabel, M.A.(Lon). *Publ*: Quakers in Ireland; J. Ernest Grubb; Quakerism and Industry; Quaker Homespuns (1933). *a*: Seskin, Carrick-on-Suir, Co Tipperary, I.F.S.

GRUBB, Kenneth George, C.M.G. *b*: Oxton, Notts 1900. *e*: Marlborough Coll. *m*: Nancy Mary Arundel. *s*: 3. *d*: 1. Company Director, Controller of Overseas Publicity M.O.I. 1941—46, Pres Church Missionary Soc '44—, Dir Commission of the Churches on International Affairs '46—, Man-Dir British Weekly '46. *Ctr*: British Weekly, Economist, Spectator, etc. *s.s*: Latin America, Church Affairs, Publicity & Propaganda. *Rec*: Gardening. *c*: Authors. *a*: 36 Shepherds Hill, London, N.6. *T*: Mountview 4391.

GRUBER, Rudolph. *b*: Vienna 1868. *e*: Univ of Vienna. *m*: Dorothy Hariot Brock. Ophth Surg. *n.a*: Cons Ophth Surg German Hosp 1928. *c.t*: Cræfes Archiv für Ophthalmologie, Archiv für Augenheilkunde. Ex-Lect on Ophth Univ of Vienna, etc. *Rec*: Ornithology. *a*: 81 Harley St, W.1, & Joyden Crest, Bexley, Kent. *t*: Welbeck 6486.

GRUCHY, Harold. *b*: Jersey 1905. *n.a*: Rep Morning News Jersey '21-24, Kent Messenger '24-25, B'ham News '25-31, Ed B'ham Town Crier '31-32, rep Streatham News '34. Sec B'ham N.U.J. '29-32. *c*: N.U.J. *a*: 131 Norbury Cresc, S.W.16.

GRUENBERG, Benjamin Charles, *b*: 1875. *e*: Univs of Minnesota, Columb & N.Y., N.Y. Botanical Gardens, Coll of Phys & Surgeons. *m*: Sidonie Matsner. *s*: 3. *d*: 1. Educator, Scientist, Consultant, Writer. *Publ*: (collab) Biology & Man; Science in Our Lives; Science & the Public Mind; Parents, Children & Money; The Story of Evolution; (Ed & co-Author) Modern Science & People's Health; Biology & Human Life; High Schools & Sex Education; etc. *Ctr*: Atlantic Monthly, to India; Fuel for the Fire; Should the Modern Papacy Receive a New Evaluation?; (co-author) Luther's Works in English. *Ctr*: Sun Sch Times, Lutheran Standard, Lutheran Ch Quarterly, Columb Theol Mag. *s.s*: Church History. *Rec*: Gardening, hunting. *a*: Willow Hill, Flagerstown, Maryland, Route 3, U.S.A. *T*: Flagerstown 792.W.4.

GRUFFYDD, William John, M.A.(Oxon), Hon.D.Litt., M.P. *b*: Llanddeiniolen 1881. *e*: Caernarvon Intermed Sch, Jesus Coll Oxf. *m*: . *s*: 1. M.P. (Univ of Wales), Mem Fleming Cttee on Public Schools, Pres Counc of Roy Nat Eisteddfod of Wales. *n.a*: Founder & Ed Lienor Welsh Critical Quarterly 1921. *Publ*: (Poetry) Telynegion; Ynys yr Hud; Caniadau; etc; (Drama) Beddau's Proffwydi; etc; (Criticism) Hanes Llenyddiæth Cymru, I Poetry, II Prose; etc. *Ctr*: Nation, Manch Guardian, Ency Brit, etc. *s.s*: Welsh Lit, Arthurian Legend. *w.s*: R.N.V.R. *c*: Athenæum. *a*: Athenæum Club, London, S.W.1.

GRUMMITT, John Halliday. *b*: Anerley, Surrey 1901. *e*: Cheltenham Coll, Caius Coll Camb. *m*: Mary Christine Bennett. *s*: 2. *d*: 2. Schoolmaster. *Publ*: The Sacrament of Life. *s.s*: Education. *Rec*: Sailing, golf. *a*: Maryville, 135 Malone Rd, Belfast, Nth Ireland. *T*: 67452.

GRUNDY, Cecil Reginald. *b*: L'pool 1870. *e*: H.S. L'pool Inst & L'pool Sc of Art. *m*: Clara Beatrice Eliza Rawlings-Smith. *d*: 1. Author & Journalist. *n.a*: Jd Staff Connoisseur 1910, Ed '14-32, Mang Dir '26-32. *Publ*: Life of James Ward, R.A. ('09); Local War Museums: a Suggestion; English Art in the 18th Century; Lessons from America in Museum Organisation & Upkeep; The Sacristy of Westminster Abbey ('30); A Catalogue of the Pictures & Drawings in the collection of Frederick John Nettlefold (vol 1, '33); etc. *c.t*: Numerous n/ps & periodicals. *s.s*: Art, hist & criticism. Lectured on Art at leading Univs & Museums in U.S.A., etc. *Rec*: Chess. *c*: Devonshire, Walpole Soc, Roy Soc of Miniature Painters, etc. *a*: 12 De Vere Gdns, Kensington, W.8. *t*: Western 5994.

GRUNDY, G. B., D.Litt(Oxon). *b*: Wallasea 1861. *e*: Oxf Univ. Formerly Fell & Tutor of Corpus Christi Coll Oxf. *Publ*: The Great Persian War; Thucydides & the History of his Age; A History of the Greek & Roman World; The Battles & Battlefields of Plataea & Leuctra; Fifty-five Years at Oxford (autob). *Ctr*: Hellenic Journ, Journ of Philology, Class Rev, etc. *s.s*: Greek & Roman History, English Archæology. *a*: Corpus Christi College, Oxford. *T*: Oxford 4205.

GRUNDY, John Brownsdon Clowes, M.A., PhD. Schoolmaster. *n.a*: Asst Ed The Connoisseur 1928-29. *Publ*: Tieck and Runge: A Study of the Relationship of Literature and Art in the Romantic Period; Brush up Your German; etc. *c.t*: Modern Languages, Sight & Sound, etc. *a*: The Schools, Shrewsbury.

GRUNDY, Rupert Francis Brooks, B.Sc, A.M. Inst.C.E., etc. *b*: Lon 1903. *e*: Emanuel Sc, S.W., U.C.L. Chartered Civil Eng. *Publ*: Builders' Materials. *Rec*: Bridge. *a*: 10 Polworth Rd, Streatham, S.W.16.

GRUNDY, Wilfred Walker. *b*: Prestwich 1884. *e*: Repton & King's Col Cam. *m*: Jane Hilda Jones. *n.a*: Ed Reptonian 1902—03. *Publ*: Not Worth Reading. *c.t*: Western Mail, South Wales News, M/C Guardian, Granta, Hermathena, etc. *s.s*: Classics. Prof of Latin Univ Cardiff. Deputy Principal Univ of Cardiff. *Rec*: Motoring, golf. *c*: A.A., R.A.C., Authors, Fortnightly (Cardiff). *a*: Lerryn, Rhiwbina, nr Cardiff. *t*: Whitchurch 355.

GRUNER, Oskar Cameron. *b*: Altrincham, Cheshire 1877. *e*: M/C G.S., Owen's Col M/C & Univ Col Hosp Lon. *m*: Alice Nightingale. *s*: 2 (1 dec). *Publ*: Biology of the Blood Cells; etc. *s.s*: Cancer Research. *Rec*: Oriental lit. *a*: c/o Bank of Montreal, Peel St, Montreal, Quebec.

GRUNWELL, G. W. *b*: Middlesborough. *e*: Priv & Hugh Bell Hgh Sch M'boro. Journalist. *n.a*: Chief Reporter North Star, Deputy Sports-Ed, Sports-Ed N.E. Daily Gazette. *Ctr*: Nat newsps & periodicals. *s.s*: Iron & Steel Trade, Sport. *Rec*: Angling, bowls. *a*: 69 Kensington Rd, Middlesborough. *T*: 89693.

GRUNWELL, Richard Edgar. *b*: Middlesbrough 1888. *e*: Hugh Bell H.S. *m*: Sarah Jane Crisp. *s*: 1. *d*: 1. F.L. *s.s*: Iron & steel trade, sport. *Rec*: Motoring, fishing, bowls. *a*: 25 Kensington Rd, Middlesbrough. *t*: Linthorpe 8678.

GRY, LÉON P. F.: rector of the Catholic University of the West; b. Rennes, France, Oct. 1, 1879; s. Eugène and Marie (Delaunay) G.; educ. Institution St. Martin (Rennes), Univs. of Angers and Fribourg, Commission Biblique (Rome), École Bibliques et d'archiologie St. Etienne (Jerusalem). DEGREES: D.D., Doctor of Holy Scriptures. AUTHOR: Le Millénarisme dans ses origines et son développement, 1904; Les Paraboles d'Hénoch et leur Messianisme, 1910; Séjours et habitats divins d'après les Apocryphes de l'Ancien Testament, 1910. Contributor to Muséon, Revue biblique, Revue des question historiques et philosophiques, Revue des facultés Catholiques de l'Ouest. General character of writing: theological. Interested in Semitic philology. Does research work in the Old Testament and in Jewish documents. Prepares critical editions of texts. CLUBS: Royal Asiatic Society of Great Britain, American Oriental Society, Deutsche Morgenländische Gesellschaft, Vorderasiatische Gesellschaft. Religion, Catholic. OFFICE: Catholic University of the West, Angers. HOME: 10 rue La Fontaine, Angers,

GRYLLS. R. Glynn. See **Mander, Mrs. G. Le M.**

GUBBINS, Nathaniel. Journalist. *n.a*: Humourist on Sunday Express. *Publ*: The Diary of a Worm; A Roll in the Hay. *a*: c/o Sunday Express, Fleet St, E.C.4. *T*: Central 8000.

GUBSKY, Nicholas. *b*: Leningrad 1890. *e*: Pushkin's Lytsey & Leningrad Univ. *m*: Nadine Azanchevsky. *s*: 1. *d*: 1. Novelist, Russian Vice-Consul in England 1919—20, B.B.C. European Service. *Publ*: The Gladiator; The Greatest of These; Foreign Bodies; Its Silly Face; Mathews Passion; Mara the Gypsy; Surprise Item; Angry Dust; My Double & I. *s.s*: Russian & German Lit. *Rec*: Reading. *a*: 23 Clavering Ave, London, S.W.13. *T*: Riverside 3846.

GUDENIAN, Haig Krikor. *b*: Kensington Lond 1918. *e*: Univ Coll Sch. Journalist. *n.a*: Chief Sub-Ed John Bull 1946—. *a*: 452 Watford Way, London, N.W.7. *T*: Hendon 6675.

GUDMUNDSSON, Kristmann. *b*: Lundareykjadal, Iceland 1902. Author. *n.a*: Former Ed Hugrun. *Publ*: Morning of Life; The Holy Mountain; Winged Citadel; The Early Spring; The Blue Shore; The Bridal Gown; The Lamp; etc. & various Trans. *a*: Hveragerdi, Iceland.

GUEDALLA, Philip J.P., M.A. *b*: Lon 1889. *e*: Rugby & Balliol Oxf. *m*: Nellie Maude Reitlinger. Hon Dir Ibero-American Inst of Gt Brit. *Publ*: Ignes Fatui, A Book of Parodies (1911); The Partition of Europe, 1715—1815; Supers & Supermen; The Industrial Future; The Second Empire; Independence Day; Conquistador ('27); Bonnet & Shawl; Gladstone & Palmerston; The Missing Muse; The Duke; Argentine Tango ('32); The Queen & Mr Gladstone ('33); The Hundred Days ('34). *c*: Athenæum, Beefsteak, Garrick. *a*: 5 Hyde Pk St, W.2. *t*: Paddington 3378.

GUERIN, Raymond. *b*: Paris 1905. *m*: Sonia Benjacob. Writer. *n.a*: Litt Crit Juin 1946. *Publ*: Zobain; Quand Vient La Fin; Quand Vient la Fin suivi de Apres la Fin; l'Apprenti; La Confession de Diogene; La Main Passe. *Ctr*: Juin, Nouvelle Revue Francais, L'Arche, Valeurs, Le Scribe Egyptien, La France Libre. *s.s*: Romans et Essais. *Rec*: Travel, motoring, swimming, ski-ing, etc. *c*: P.E.N., Comite Nat des Ecrivains francaise. *a*: 65 rue Frantz Despagnet a Bordeaux (Gironda), France. *T*: 21-50.

GUEST, Val. *b*: Hollywood, Calif. *c*: Eng & Amer. Writer, Author, Composer. *n.a*: Lon Ed Hollywood Reporter. Lon Ed Zits Motion Picture Review. *c.t*: Los Angeles Times, Photoplay, Screen Play, Screenland, Motion Picture, Amal Press, Odham's, Newnes, Pearson's etc. *s.s*: Film personnel. Author & Composer of Let's Go, Broadway Musical Comedy. Writer of Popular Music, Cuban Love Song, Star of Araby, You, etc. *a*: 32 Winchester Rd, N.W.3.

GUGAN. A. Dennison. *n.a*: Asst Ed Sunday Dispatch. *a*: 4 Orchard Rise, Coombe Hill, Surrey. *t*: Kingston 2767.

GUGGENHEIM, Edward Armand. *b*: M/C 1901. *e*: Charterhouse & Gonville & Caius Col Cam. Univ Lecturer & Scientist. *Publ*: Modern Thermodynamics *c.t*: Various scientific journs. *s.s*: Physics, chemistry. *a*: The University, Reading & Pendyke, Lewes.

GUHA, Satisa Chandra. *b*: Saptagram-Barisal, Bengal 1889. *e*: Bengal National Coll. *m*: Nalinikadevi Vasuduhita. *s*: 1. *d*: 2. Curator Kalabhabhana (Art Museum & Sch) Visvabharati International Univ, Santiniketan, India. *n.a*: Mang 1907 & Asst-Ed '08 The Dawn Mag Calcutta, Mang & Asst-Ed C.M.C. Mag Benares '15, Ed & Publ Indiana Benares '36, Asst-Ed Journ of Benares Hindu Univ, Ed Nandana '46. *Publ*: Prachya - Vargikarana - Paddhati; Gandhi - mahatmya; Gandhi-kirtana. *Ctr*: The Dawn Mag & Modern Rev, Calcutta, The Indian Rev, Aryan Path, Bombay, etc. *s.s*: Bibliography, Library-Science, Sociology & Art Criticism. *Rec*: Swimming, cooking, bookbinding. *a*: Gandhigram, Benares, India.

GUHDES, Conrad Bruno, M.A., Litt.D. *b*: Wangerin, Pomerania, Germany 1866. *e*: Dramburg, Pomerania & Columb Univ, Ohio. *m*: Clara L. Fleiser. *s*: 3. *d*: 3. Prof of History 1912—45 (ret). *n.a*: Ed Lutheran Youth 1912—. *Publ*: Biography of John Schwartz, the Apostle Laneast Truro 1939—. *Publ*: The Lure of the Golden West; The Dream Flower; The Ocean Hell; Boys of Back o' Beyond; Short History of the Parish of Whitworth. *Ctr*: Jarrow Guardian, Swan Express (Aus), Sunderland Echo, Northern Echo. *s.s*: Travel, Early Australian History, Convicts, Aborigines, etc. *Rec*: Chess, swimming, cricket, football & gardening. *a*: Laneast Vicarage, Launceston, Cornwall. *T*: Pipers Pool 227.

GUIBARA, Ignacio Lopez. *b*: Glasgow 1871. *e*: St Aloysius Col, Glasgow. Teacher of Languages. *Publ*: A Businesslike Spanish Course (Parts I & II). *c.t*: Middx Cty Times. *s.s*: Spanish, French, & English (tuition). Has lived & travelled in Mexico many ys. *c*. Anglo-Spanish Soc. *a*: 37 Gordon Rd, Ealing, W.5. *t*: Perivale 4734.

GUICHARD, Beatrice Catherine. *b*: Chatham, Kent 1878. *e*: Priv. *m*: Eugene Guichard. *n.a*: N.Y. World Corr Russia & Balkan 1911—14 & Rome '14—31, Dly Telegraph Corr Rome '33—40, Yorks Post Corr Rome '40. *Publ*: The Polish Jew; Taras Bulba (Russian); Their Yesterday; When Summer Comes Again; Baldwin's Kingdom; Love & Sacrifice; Passover; The Enchanted Garden; What Next O Dove? (with Elliot Monk); By Whose Hand; The Amethyst Button; The St Clous Affair. *Ctr*: Various. *s.s*: Politics, Travel, etc. *Rec*: Walking. *a*: Old Barn, Sorgues sur Ouveze, Vaucluse, France.

GUILD, David Alexander. *b*: Edinburgh 1884. *e*: Edin Acad, Edin Univ. *m*: Maggie Clark Ritchie. *s*: 1. *d*: 1. Mem of the Faculty of Advocates Edin. *Publ*: Law of Arbitration in Scotland. *Ctr*: Green's Ency of Scots Law. *Rec*: Motoring, golf, trout fishing. *c*: Scot Cons (Edin), Roy Scot Auto (Glas). *a*: Ardchoille, Commonhead, Airdrie, Lanarkshire. *T*: Airdrie 3308.

GUILDFORD, John. See Hunter, Bluebell Matilda.

GUILFORD, Edward, O.B.E., C.I.E., K.I.H. with Bar. *b*: Portsea 1853. *e*: Brighton, Ch Missny Col. *m*: (1) Louisa C. Chase; (2) Elizabeth Rose Grimwood. *s*: 1. *d*: 3. Missny C.M.S. (ret). *Publ*: Streaks of Light in the Mabjha Country; Vook of Common Prayer in Punjabi; Revision of the Bible in Punjabi; etc. *c.t*: Spectator, Morning Post, Times. *s.s*: Indian subjects. 30 y Chm Tarn Taran Munic, Punjab. War Service, Capt Indian Army (Victory Medal). *Rec*: Cricket, football, lawn tennis. *c*: Overseas, etc. *a*: The Anchorage, Cottesmore, Oakham, Rutland. *t*: Cottesmore 2.

GUILLAN, Sydney Charles. *b*: London 1895. *e*: St Dunstan's Coll. Sec of Inst of Metals & Ed of its publs. *n.a*: Ed Metallurgical Abstracts, Monographs 1937—. *s.s*: Metallurgy—non-ferrous. *Rec*: Golf. *c*: R.A.C. *w.s*: Norfolk Regt 1914—19, R.A. '39—46. *a*: 4 Grosvenor Gdns, London, S.W.1. *T*: Sloane 6233.

GUILLAUME, Alfred. M.A., D.D. *b*: London, 1888 *e*: Wadham Coll Oxf. *m*: Margaret Leadbitter. *s*: 2. *d*: 2. Prof of Arabic Univ of London. *Publ*: The Traditions of Islam; The Influence of Islam on Judaism (in the legacy of Israel); The Summa Philosophica of all Shahrastani; Prophecy & Divination; etc. *Ctr*: Journ Roy Asiatic Soc, Moslem World, Palestine Exploration Quarterly, etc. *d.s*: Old Testament & Islamic Studies. *Rec*: Tennis, walking. *c*: Athenæum. *w.s*: 1914—18. *a*: Ridges Farm, Clifton Hampden.

GUILLAUME, CHARLES, EDOUARD: director of the International Bureau of Paris and Meture; *b.* Fleurier, Switzerland, Feb. 15, 1861; *s.* Edouard and Emilie (Lebet) G.; *educ.* Ecole de Fleurier, Académie de Neuchâtel, Ecole Polytechnique de Zurich. DEGREES: Sc.D., Professor; *m.* Anne-Marie Tauflieb, Oct. 30, 1888. AUTHOR: Études thermométriques, 1886; Formules pratiques pour la transformation des coefficients thermiques, 1888; Traité pratique de thermométrie de Precision, 1888; Unités et Étalons, 1893; Les applications des Aciers au nickel, 1894; Mètres prototypes. vol. X., Travaux et Mémoires du Bureau international des Poids et Mesures (in collaboration with J. R. Benoit), 1894; Mètres prototypes et Étalons vol. XI, Travaux et Mémoires du Bureau international des Poids et Mesures (in collaboration with J. R. Benoit), 1895; Nouvelle détermination des metres étalons: vol. XII., Travaux et Mémoires du Bureau international des Poids et Mesures (in collaboration with J. R. Benoit), 1895; Les Rayons X, 1896; Mètres à Bouts: vol. XII., Travaux et Mémoires du Bureau international des Poids et Mesures (in collaboration with J. R. Benoit), 1902; Étalonnage des Échelles divisées: vol.XIII., Travaux et Mémoires du Bureau international des Poids et Mesures, 1907; Initiation à la Mecanique, 1909; Les récents Progrès du Systeme Métrique, 1907, 1913, 1921; Determination du volume du kilogramme d'eau: vol. XIV., Travaux et Mémoires du Bureau international des Poids et Mesures, 1910; Le premier quart de siècle de la Tour Eiffel, 1912; Première détermination des étalons à bouts, vol. XV., Travaux et Mémoires du Bureau internationale des Poids et Mesures, 1913; La mesure rapide des bases géodésiques (5th edit.), 1917; La compensation des horloges et des montres, 1921; Esquisse de ma Vie, 1929; Récherches métrologiques sur les aciers au Nickel: vol. XVII., Traxaux et Mémoires du Bureau international des Poids et Mesures. Contributor: Archives de Genéve, La Nature, La Revue Générale des Sciences, La Revue générale d'Electricite L'Industrie Electrique, Bulletin de la Société Français des Electriciens, and others. General character of writing: scientific, technical. Particular field of interest is the measurement of time, space, and temperature. In relation to time, experiments with acid, nickel and iron combinations to determine expansion rates. As a result of these experiments, was awarded the Nobel Prize in physics in 1920. Is also interested in the energy of the spectrum and in X-rays. Is Doctor honoris causa of the Univs. of Geneva and Neuchatel. CLUBS: Société de Physique de Londres (honorary member), British Association for the Advancement of Science, Société Helvétique des Sciences Naturelles (honorary member), Sociétés de Geneve, de Lausanne et de Neuchatel, l'Institut Générois, l'Institut de France (correspondant), l'Académie des Sciences de Russie Autour du Monde. OFFICE: Bureau international de Poids et Mesures, Sèvres. HOME: Pavillon de Breteuil, Sèrves, France.

GUILLEBAUD, Claude William, C.B.E. *b*: Yatesbury 1890. *e*: Repton Sch, Manch Univ, St John's Coll Camb. *m*: M. T. Prunner. *d*: 2. Univ Lect, Fell & Tutor St John's Coll Camb, Girdlers' Lect in Econ at Camb. *Publ*: The Works Council: A German Experiment in Industrial Democracy; The Economic Recovery of Germany 1933—38; The Social Policy of Nazi Germany. *Ctr*: Econ Journal, The Times. *s.s*: Economic Matters. *a*: St John's College, Cambridge. *T*: 5052.

GUINNESS, Bryan Walter, (See MOYNE, 2nd Baron of Bury St Edmunds). *Publ*: Under the Eyelid; & 23 Other Poems; Singing Out of Tune; Landscapes With Figures; A Week by the Sea; Lady Crushwell; The Children in the Desert; Johnny & Jemima. *a*: Biddesden Hse, Andover. *T*: Ludgershall (Wilts) 37.

GUINNESS, Paul Grattan, B.Sc., B.D. *b*: Hastings 1908. *e*: Christ's Hosp, Northwestern Univ Evanstown Ill, Dallas Theol Sem. *m*: Jean Elliot. *s*: 1. *d*: 1. Minister of Religion. *n.a*: Responsible for certain Internat Publs of the World's Cttee of Y.M.C.A. *Publ*: We Pledge Our Lives; The Christ of all Nations. *a*: World's Ctte, Y.M.C.A., 37 Quat Wilson, Geneva.

GUIREC, Jean. *b*: Bordeaux, Gironde 1898. *e*: Prytanee Militaire de la Fleche. *m*: Jeanne Mercier. *s*: 1. Writer & S/Dir to the Ministry of War, Chevalier de la Legion d'Honneur, Croix de Guerre. *Publ*: La Maison au bord du Monde; L'Enchantement de la Nuit; Le Crime des Indifferents; La Port Ouverte; La Couronne d'Ombre; La Carrefour des Anges; Allegres; Danger de Mort. *Ctr*: Paris-Soir, Le Petit Parisien, L'Eclaireur de Nice et du Sud-Est, L'Intransigeant. *s.s*: Roman Psychologique. *c*: P.E.N. *a*: 40 rue de Seine, Paris VI, France. *T*: Odeon 35-34.

GUISE-MOORES, Maj.-Gen. Sir Samuel, K.C.B., K.C.V.O., C.M.G., M.R.C.S., L.R.C.P., D.P.H. *Publ*: Manual of Hygiene & Sanitation. *c.t*: B.M.J., Journ of R.A.M.C., etc. *a*: 1 Elysee Mns, Kingsnorth Gdns, Folkestone.

GUITRY, Sacha. *b*: 1885. Author. *Publ*: Plays—La Clef; Beau Mariage; Beranger; Le Grand Duc; Mozart; Desiré; etc. *a*: Paris.

GULABDAS, Broker, B.A. *b*: Porhandar, India 1909. *e*: Elphinstone Coll Bombay. *m*: Suman S. Kapadia. *s*: 2. *d*: 2. Author. *Publ*: (in Gujarati) On the Main Street; Vasundhara & Other Stories; Lata & Other Stories; etc. *Ctr*: Prasthan, Kaumudi, Manasi, Sanskriti, etc. *s.s*: Short Stories. *Rec*: Tennis, indoor games, walking. *c*: P.E.N. & Silverfish. *a*: Ghodbunder Rd, Vale Parle (West), Bombay 24, India. *T*: 86428.

GULL, Edward Manico, M.A. *b*: Rio de Janeiro 1883. *e*: Trin Cam. Sec China Assoc. *Publ*: Facets of the Chinese Question. *c.t*: Times, M/C Guard, Nineteenth Century, etc. *s.s*: Far Eastern affairs. Ex-Chinese Maritime Customs Service. *c*: Utd Univ, Roy Cent Asian Soc (Hon Sec). *a*: 104 Oakwood Ct. Kensington. *t*: Western 7804.

GULLAN, Archibald Gordon, T.D., M.D., F.R.C.S., M.R.C.P. *b*: Swansea 1871. *e*: Birkenhead Sc & Univ Col L'pool. *m*: Louisa Bowman. Cons Physician. Cons Phys L'pool Stanley Hosp, Waterloo & Dist Hosp. Ex Phys L'pool Stanley Hosp 1900–31. Lecturer & Examiner Clinical Med L'pool Univ. *c.t*: B.M.J., etc. *s.s*: Gen Med. War Service, Lt-Col R.A.M.C.T. France '16, O.C. Mil Hosp Gibraltar '18. *Rec*: Golf. *c*: L'pool Med Inst. *a*: 37 Rodney St, L'pool, & Homestead, Blundellsands, L'pool 23. *t*: Roy 2425.

GULLAN, Marjorie Isabel Morton. *b*: Reading. *e*: Hutchesons' Girls' Gr Sch Glasgow. Lect on Speech Training & Verse Speaking, Pres Speech Fellowship Lond, Lect in Speech Training & Choral Speaking Lond Univ Inst of Educ, formerly Head Speech Dept Regent St Polytechnic. *Publ*: Spoken Poetry in the School; Poetry Speaking for Children; Choral Speaking; Speech Training in the School; The Poet Speaks. *s.s*: Spoken English, Choral Speaking, Speech & Voice Training, The Speaking of Verse. *Rec*: Swimming. *a*: 61A Heathcroft Golders Green, London, N.W.11. *T*: Speedwell 7219,

GULLAND, George Lovell, C.M.G., LL.D. *b*: Edin 1862. *e*: Roy H.S. Edin & Edin Univ. *m*. Helen Masson. *s*: 1. *d*: 1. Phys. Prof Emeritus of Med & Clin Med Univ of Edin. *Publ*: Diseases of the Blood; Pernicious Anæmia. *c.t*: numerous. *s.s*: Diseases of the blood. War Service Col A.M.S. Ex-Pres R.C.P. (Edin). *Rec*: Golf, fishing, sketching. *a*: 11 Chester St, Edin. *t*: 22328.

GULLAND, John Masson, M.A.(Oxon), D.Sc (Edin), PhD.(St And), F.R.S.E. *b*: Edin 1898. *e*: Edin Acad, Univs of Edin, St And & M/C. *m*: Ruth Madeline Ida Russell. *d*: 2. Reader in Biochem, Lon Univ. Snr Asst in Biochem Lister Inst. Hon Sec Chem Soc. *c.t*: Scientific journ's. *s.s*: Chem, biochem. War Service R.E. *Rec*: Golf, fishing, walking. *a*: 2 Ernle Rd, Wimbledon, S.W.20.

GULLBERG, Hjalmer Robert. *b*: Malmo 1898. *e*: Univ of Lund. Literary Adviser of the Royal Dramatic Theatre, Stockholm. *Publ*: Andliga ovningar, 1932 (poems); Dramatic translations from Euripides and Aristophanes, etc. *s.s*: Greek tragedy & comedy. *Rec*: Travel, music. *c*: Pen, Swedish Assoc of Authors. *a*: Vestergatan II, Lund, Sweden.

GULLICK, Norman. Translator. *a*: 14 Sherwood Park Rd, Sutton, Surrey. *t*: Sutton 5311.

GUMBLEY, George S. Walter, O.P., F.R.Hist.S. *b*: Aston Manor, Birmingham 1887. *e*: Dominican Theol Coll Hawkesyard Rugeley Staffs & Louvain Univ. Prior of St Sebastion's Salford 1933—36 & of Blackfriars Oxford '42—45. *Publ*: The Cambridge Dominicans; Parish Priests Amongst the Saints; Life of Mother Margaret Hallahan, O.P.; (Revision of) Christian Schools & Scholars; English Dominicans; Patron Saints by Whale etc. *Ctr*: English Hist Rev, Tablet, Irish Ecclesiastical Rec, The Month, & many other journs on the Continent & America. *s.s*: Mediæval Hist. *a*: St Domonic's Priory, Southampton Rd, London, N.W.5. *T*: Gulliver 5491.

GUN, William Townsend Jackson, F.R.HistS. *b*: M/C 1876. *e*: Harrow, Trin Cam. *m*: Ethel Winifrid Young. Writer. *Publ*: Studies in Hereditary Ability. Ed Harrow School Register 1571–1800. *s.s*: Genealogical & eugenic research. *c*: Bath, Soc of Genealogists & Eugenics. *a*: 43 Horton Ct, W.8. *t*: Western 2176.

GUN-MUNRO, J. F.R.G.S. *Publ*: Short stories & travel articles (Europe & Asia). Formerly Ed Malay Mail. Deputy chief Sub-Ed Chronicle and Echo, Northampton.

GUNN, Battiscombe George, F.B.A., M.A. *b*: London 1883. *e*: Westminster & Bedales. Prof of Egyptology Univ of Oxf 1934—. *Publ*: The Instruction of Ptahhotep; Harageh (in collab); Studies in Egyptian Syntax; Excavations at Sakkara; Teti Pyramid Cemeteries (in collab). *Ctr*: Various Archæological journs. *a*: Queen's Coll, Oxford. *T*: 3356.

GUNN, Herbert Smith. *b*: Gravesend 1904. Ed Evening Standard. *n.a*: Manch Ev News 1925—27, Ev News Lond '27—29, Evening Standard '29—34, Ed Dly Express Manch '36—38, Man Ed Dly Express Lond '38—45, Ed Ev Standard '45—. *a*: 39 Flood St, Chelsea, London, S.W.3; Heron's March, Ockley, Surrey.

GUNN, James, C.B.E., M.A., M.D., D.Sc., F.R.C.P. *b*: Kirkwall 1882. *e*: Edin Univ. *m*: Annie M. Gunn. *s*: 3. *d*: 1. Prof Emeritus Oxf Univ, Fell Balliol Coll, Chm Pharmacopœia Revision Commssn. *n.a*: Ed Journ of Pharmacology & Experimental Therapeutics, Assoc-Ed Archives Internationales de Pharmacodynamie. *Publ*: Introduction to Pharmacology; Cushny Textbook of Pharmacology. *Ctr*: Sci & Med Journs, Dictionary of Nat Biog. *s.s*: Action of Drugs & Poisons. *Rec*: Golf, fishing. *c*: Authors. *a*: 59 Banbury Rd, Oxford.

GUNN, JOHN WILLIAM CORMACK: professor of pharmacology; b. Kirkwall, Scotland, Jan. 1889; s. John Robertson Gunn (deceased); educ. Kirkwall Burgh Sch., Univ. Edinburgh. DEGREES: M.A., M.B., Ch.B., F.R.S.S. Af.; m. Marian Lambe, 1916. Contributor to Journ. of Pharmacology and Experimental Therapeutics, Trans. Royal Soc. of S. Africa and other mags. General character of writing: scientific, medical. OFFICE: University of Cape Town. HOME: 35 Rosemead Ave., Cape Town, South Africa.

GUNN, John William Miller. H.M. Inspector of Schools. *Publ*: A Geometry for Advanced Division Central & Secondary Scs; Trigonometry Tests. *a*: Hillview Terr, Corstorphine, Edinburgh 12.

GUNN, Neil M. *b*: Caithness 1891. *Publ*: The Grey Coast; Hidden Doors; Morning Tide; The Lost Glen; Sun Circle; Butcher's Broom; Highland River; Off in a Boat; Wild Geese Overhead; Second Sight; The Silver Darlings; Young Art & Old Hector; The Serpent; The Green Isle of the Great Deep; The Key of the Chest; The Drinking Well; Whisky & Scotland. *s.s*: Scottish Affairs. *a*: Brae, Dingwall, Scotland.

GUNN, William, M.A., M.B., Ch.B., F.R.C.P., F.R.S.M. D.P.H. *b*: Caithness 1897. *e*: Aberdeen Univ. Physician Supt North-Western Hospital (L.C.C.), Fell Roy Soc Med, Soc Med Officers of Health, B.M.A. *Ctr*: B.M.J., Lancet, Practitioner, Journ of Hygiene, Medical Press, Brit Journ of Children's Diseases, Ency Brit. *s.s*: Infectious Diseases & Epidemiology. *Rec*: Golf, ski-ing, cinematography. *a*: Bartram Lodge, Fleet Rd, Hampstead, N.W.3. *T*: Primrose 2212.

GUNN, Winifred Eleanor. *b*: Peebles 1888. *e*: Edin. *Publ*: Scott of Abbotsford (play); A Crime Will Do (play). *Ctr*: Spectator, Cornhill, John o'London's Wkly, Scotsman, Glasgow Herald, Yorkshire Post. *a*: 5 York Place, Edinburgh.

GUNNARSON, Gunnar, Ph.D. *b*: Valpjofsstadur 1889. *m*: Franzisca Josephine Antonie Jorgensen. *s*: 2. Author & Farmer, Mem P.E.N., Mark Twain Internat, Icelandic Literary & Icelandic Student Socs. *Publ*: Ships in the Sky; The Night & The Dream; Guest, the One Eyed; The Sworn-Brothers; The Good Shepherd; etc. *a*: Skriduklaustur, Iceland. *T*: Bessastadir 2.

GUNNING, Hugh. *b*: Glas 1902. Rep, Sub Ed & Art Ed. *n.a*: Served on n/ps in these capacities Glas, Hull, M/C & Lon '20—. *a*: 35 Pickwick Rd, Dulwich Village, S.E.21. *t*: Brixton 3731.

GUNSON, Dr. C. H. *a*: Crescent Hse, Wisbech.

GUNSTON, J. *m*:. *s*: 1. Farm Manager (Nat Diplomas in Farming & Dairying) Earl of Leicester's estates. *Publ*: To be a Farmer; Farming Month by Month; Farm Friends & Foes; How to Run a Small Farm; The Reason Why of Farming. *Ctr*: Leading agricultural & allied publications. *s.s*: Agriculture, Allied Sciences, Marketing, Coastal Erosion, etc, Norfolk & Fenland Problems & History. *Rec*: Writing, bird watching, natural history. *a*: c/o Cecil Hunt, Lit Agent, 11 Poultry, Cheapside, London, E.C.2.

GUNTHER, Eustace Rolfe. Zoologist. *n.a*: Zoologist on staff *Discovery* Investigations 1924—. *Publ*: Notes & Sketches Made During Two Years on the *Discovery* Expedition ('25–27). *c t*: Caian, Draconian, Nature, Polar Record, Journ Exper Biol. *a*: Eastcot, Ember Lane, Esher.

GUNTHER, John. *Publ*: inc The Red Pavilion; Inside Europe; D-Day; Inside U.S.A.; Inside Latin-America; The Golden Fleece; etc. *a*: 40 East 49th St, New York City, U.S.A.

GUNTHER, Robert Theodore, HonLL.D. *b*: Surbiton. *e*: Univ Col Sc Lon, Univ Col, Magdalen Col Oxf & Freiburg Univ. *m*: Amy Neville-Rolfe. *s*: 2. Museum Curator. *Publ*: Early Science in Oxford (9 vols); Astrolabes of the World (2 vols); The Greek Herbal of Dioscorides; The Oxford Country. *c.t*: Nature. *s.s*: Hist of nat sci & med. *a*: Old Ashmolean Bldg, Oxf.

GUNZBURG, ISIDORE: physician; *b*. Riga, Latvia, December, 1875; *s*. Sylvain and Amélie (Zeitlin) G.; educ. Athénée Royal d'Anvers, Univ. of Brussels. DEGREE: M.D.; *m*. Ella (Kirschen). AUTHOR: Studie der Schoolziekten, 1903; Sexuelle Gezondheidsleer, 1904; School Hygiene, 1904; De Hedenaagsege toest and der evolutieleer, 1905; Over achtярlyke Meisjes, 1906; La question des enfants anormaux en Belgique, 1916; Cours de Physiologie donné à la Croix Rouge de Belgique, 1917; Sommaire du Cours de Physiologie à la Croix Rouge (2nd edit.), 1917; Stof en Energie wisseling in het levend lichaam, 1918; Assimilation de l'energie par l'organisme vivant: No. 3-4, Revue Université Libre de Bruxelles, 1922; Action de l'émanation sur le Muscle strié, 1926; Traitment physiothérapiquées Algies du membre superieur, 1928. Editor: Annales de Médecine physique. Contributor to: Annales de Médecine physique, Revue de l'Université de Bruxelles, Pædologisch Jaarbok, Revue de Physiologie, and others. General character of writing: medical. Founder and president of the International Congress of physiotherapie. Lecturer at the University of Utrecht. CLUBS: Club Universitaire, Société de physiotherapie Belge, Société Royale de Médecine. OFFICE: 1 rue des Escrimeurs, Antwerp. HOME: 3 rue Bex, Antwerp, Belgium.

GUPPY, Henry, C.B.E., M.A., D.Phil et Lit., Litt.D. *b*: London 1861. *e*: London, etc. *m*: Matilda Bumby. *s*: 1. *d*: 2. Librarian John Ryland's Library Manchester. *n.a*: Ed Record 1899—1903 & Bulletin of John Ryland's Library '03—. *Publ*: The History of the Transmission of the Bible; History of the First Folio of Shakespeare; The Reconstruction of the Library of the University of Louvain; Stepping Stones to the Art of Typography; Seventy-Five Years of Public Library Development 1850 —1925; The Art of Reading; Beginnings of Printed Book Illustration to 1500; The French Journals of Mrs Thrale & Dr Johnson; etc. *Ctr*: Various. *s.s*: Bibliographical, Historical & Literary. *Rec*: Walking & work. *a*: Sunwick, Lansdowne Rd, Buxton, Derbys. *T*: 260.

GUPPY, Mrs Septima Robinson. *e*: Queen's Col, Harley St. Married. Writer, lecturer. *Publ*: Life's Mysteries; Poems & Reflections on Cruelty. Plays:—Justice versus Crime, etc. Film:—1st Anti-vivisection film. Foxtrot:—Be Happy, also sacred songs. *c.t*: Various. *s.s*: Anti-vivisection, vegetarianism, horses. Well-known resister of Mr Lloyd George's Health Insurance Tax on Servants, which led to her name being introduced in the play "Who Killed that Fly" at the Alhambra. *Rec*: Motoring. *a*: Morley Towers, Wimbledon Pk, S.W.19. *t*: Putney 5213.

GUPTA, Hari Ram, M.A., Ph.D., D.Litt. *b*: Ambala 1905. *e*: Univ of Lahore. *m*: Lajjavati. *s*: 4. *d*: 5. Teaching, Head of Dept of History Aitchison Coll Lahore 1945—. *Publ*: History of the Sikhs 1739—1799; Studies in later Mughal History of the Punjab; Life & Work of Mahan Lal Kashmiri, Indian Diplomat of 19th. Century. *Ctr*: Journ of Indian Hist, Islamic Culture, Calcutta Rev, Hindustan Rev, etc. *s.s*: Sikh History, History of Punjab & Delhi. *Rec*: Gardening, nature study. *a*: Aitchison College, Lahore, India. *T*: 4940.

GUPTA, Jayanta Kumar Das, M.A., Ph.D. *b*: Barisal Bengal 1901. *e*: Calcutta & Lond Univs. *m*: Induprabha Roy. *s*: 3. *d*: 3. Vice-Princ & Head of the Dept of English Darbar Coll Rewa Central India. *n.a*: Lond Corr of Advance 1931—33. *Publ*: Life & Novels of Bankim Chandra Chatterjee; Various Text-books for Coll & Univ Students. *Ctr*: Calcutta Rev, Indian Rev, Madras, Calcutta-Bharatvarsha, etc. *s.s*: Eng & Bengali Lit, Educ & Cultural subjects. *Rec*: Reading, tennis, newspaper cutting. *c*: Venkat, Rewa, C.I., Indian P.E.N. *a*: Vice-Princ, Darbar Coll, Rewa, Rewa State, Central India.

GUPTA, Shyam Ratna, M.A. *b*: Najibadad (U.P.) India 1919. *e*: Lucknow Univ. Author & Journalist. *n.a*: Ed Bharat Mag 1943—46, Cine-critic Mysindia '44—46. *Publ*: Modern Writing, Indian Arts & Letters. *Ctr*: World's Press News, Prince Albert Herald (Can), Daily News (Chatham Ont), Port William (Ont), B.B.C. Eastern Serv & various Indian newsps. *s.s*: Indian Arts & Letters, Films, etc, Prog Dir All India Radio 1942—43, Film Comment All India Radio '45—46. *Rec*: Sketching, photography. *c*: P.E.N. (All India & Internat). *a*: Najibadad (United Provinces), India.

GURBUTT, Fred. Ed-Mang. *n.a*: Ed Mang Louth & North Lincolnshire Advertiser Series. *s.s*: Agriculture. *a*: 105 High Holme Rd, Louth. *t*: 107.

GURDON, John Everard. *b*: Lon 1898. *e*: Tonbridge Sc & Roy Mil Col Sandhurst. *m*: Florence Mary Fleming. *s*: 3. Writing. *Publ*: Over and Above; Feeding the Wind; The German Air Force in the Great War (trans from the German by Major Georg Paul Newmann); The Sky Trackers; etc. *c.t*: Times, Evening News, Weekly Telegraph, Strand Mag, etc. *s.s*: Aviation, archæ & medical hist. Invalided out of regular army 1919, began writing during long spells in Hosp. *Rec*: Reading, music. *a*: Uley, Gloucester.

GURIAN, Waldemar, D.Phil. *b*: St Petersburg 1902. *e*: Gymnasium Düsseldorf, Universitäten Breslau, München, Köln. *m*: Edith Schwarzer. *d*: 1. Journalist. *Publ*: Der Bolschewismus; Der Integrale Nationalismus in Frankreich; Der Katholische Publizist; Um des Reiches Zukunft ('32) (" Walter Gerhart "); etc. *c.t*: Hochland, Kilnische Volkszeitung, Germania. *s.s*: Bolshevism. *a*: Bad Godesberg am Rhein, Viktoria str 13.

GURNER, S. R. K. *b*: Lon 1890. *e*: Merchant Taylors & St John's Col Oxf. *m*: Rosalie Leila Romer. *s*: 1. Schoolmaster. *Publ*: The Day Boy; For Sons of Gentlemen; The Riven Pall; Pass Guard at Ypres; Reconstruction; Day Schools of England; etc. *Rec*: Motoring, golf. *c*: Authors. *a*: 40 Beechwood Rd, Sanderstead. *t*: 1933.

GURNEY, Alexander George. *b*: Portsmouth, England 1902. *e*: Hobart State Sch Tasmania. *m*: Junee Grover. *s*: 1. *d*: 3. Cartoonist. *n.a*: Cartoonist on Sydney Telegraph, "The World" Sydney, The News Adelaide, The Herald Melbourne. *Publ*: Bluey & Curley Annual 1941—47. *Rec*: Fishing, hunting. *w.s*: War Corres Pacific 1942—45. *a*: 7 Merton Ave, Elwood, S.3, Melbourne, Australia. *T*: XM 1437 Melbourne.

GURNEY, Alfred Henry. Editor. *n.a*: Ed Hunts Post '08—. *a*: 27 High St, Huntingdon. *t*: 79.

GURNEY, John. B.A., B.Sc., F.C.S., J.P. *e*: Eton Col, Oxford Univ. Publisher. Managing Director Medici Society Ltd. *a*: Grafton St, W.1. *t*: Mayfair 5676.

GURNEY, Maj-Gen. Russell, C.B. (ret). *b*: Swanage 1890. *e*: Clifton Coll. *m*: Margaret Emily Thorp. *s*: 2. *Publ*: History of the Northamptonshire Regiment. *Rec*: Fishing, golf. *c*: United Service. *a*: Hayne Hse, Seaton, Devon. *T*: Seaton 51.

GURNEY, S. Gamzu, M.B.E. *b*: Blackburn. *e*: Blackburn & Somerville Coll Oxf. *m*: Robert Gurney, M.A., D.Sc. *s*: 1. *Publ*: Totem Magic; Children of the Wilderness & other books for scouts & children. *s.s*: Educ of Children, Archæology, Nature Study & Gardening. *Rec*: Travel. *a*: Bayworth Corner, Boar's Hill, Oxf. *T*: 85282.

GURNEY-SALTER, EMMA: author; b. London, Eng., Jan. 16, 1875; d. William Henry Gurney and Jane (Reyner) Salter; educ. Notting Hill High Sch., Girton College (Cambridge); DEGREES: M.A., Litt. D. (Dublin); Classical Tripos (Cambridge, 1896); unmarried. AUTHOR: Franciscan Legends in Italian Art, 1905; Nature in Italian Art, 1912; Translations: The Legend of the Three Companions; Life of St. Francis (by Sr. Bonaventura); The Coming of the Friars Minor to England and Germany, 1926; Early Tracts on Poor Relief (by J. L. Vives), 1926; The Vision of God (by Nicholas of Cusa), 1928. Assistant Editor (until recently) of The Contemporary Review. Contributor to Edinburgh Rev., Fortnightly Rev., Nineteenth Century, Cornhill, World's Work, Discovery, Times, Punch, Spectator, Guardian, Pall Mall Gazette, Westminster Gazette, Author, Saturday Rev., and other mags. General character of writing: historical, art, poetry. Lecturer (occasionally) on Art and Literary subjects; Mem. Com. of British Soc. of Franciscan Studies and of Stockwell Training Coll. for Teachers; Mem. Children's Care Com. and other Social work. On staff Admiralty Intelligence during Great War. Relig. denom., Anglican. CLUB: Albermarle. HOME: 66 Ladbrook Road, Holland Park, London, W. 11, Eng.

GURR, Thomas Stuart. *b*: Bombay 1877. *e*: Priv. *m*: Ann Elizabeth Johnson. *s*: 2. *d*: 1. Sec & Author. *n.a*: Advert Mang N.Z. Herald Auckland Weekly 1913—16, Herald & Weekly Times Melbourne, '16—19, Gen Mang Sunday Times Newspaper Agency Sydney '19—22, Mang Ed Later Day '23—25, Sec N.S.W. Newspaper Proprietor Assoc '25, Sec Audit Museum of Lit Sydney '34—. *Publ*: The Third String; White Man, Brown Woman; (with T. L. Richards); Jungle Vagabonds; The Valley of the Lost Trail; Castaways. *Ctr*: Sydney—Sun & Sunday Sun, Pocket Book Weekly, Sun Telegraph, World News; Melbourne—The Sun Pictorial, The Leader, The Sun Mail, etc. *s.s*: Short Stories & Juvenile Books. *Rec*: Gardening. *a*: 39 Raglan St., Mosman, Sydney, Australia. *T*: XM 1659.

GURREY, P., B.A., Ph.D. *e*: Lond Univ. Reader in Education. *Publ*: (in collab) Our Living Language; Our Language, Book 1; Notes on Our Language; Poetry Speaking (parts 1 & 2); The Appreciation of Poetry; (in collab) Grammar at Work (parts 1 & 3). *s.s*: Educ, Eng Lit & Linguistics. *w.s*: 1914—19, '40—44 R.A.F. *a*: Halcyon, Ewell Downs Rd., Ewell, Surrey. *T*: 1717.

GURTON, Denis Leonard, N.U.J. *b*: London 1922. *e*: London Univ. Journalist. *n.a*: Rep Drapers' Record 1942—43, Asst Ed Men's Wear '43—45, Ed Man & His Clothes '45—46, European Corres Women's Wear News, Man & His Clothes '47. *Ctr*: Man & His Clothes, Women's Wear News, Tailor & Cutter, Children's Outfitter, World Window. *s.s*: Textiles, Eng & Continental, Men's Women's Fashions, Brit & Continental, Fabrics, Design, Display Merchantising, Retail & Wholesale Dist, Foreign Textile, Methods & Processes. *Rec*: Travel, foreign languages, reading, chess, recorded music. *a*: 66 Nethuen Ave, Gaywood, King's Lynn, Norfolk.

GURU, Rameshwar, M.Sc. *b*: Jubbulpore, C.P. 1914. *e*: Univ of Allahabad. *m*: Shanti Dube. *s*: 2. *d*: 2; Senior Science & Maths Master Christ Church Boy's Sch. *n.a*: Amrita Bazar Patrika '45—, Indian News Chron, New India & Azad Hind '47, Khilaima '38, Oriental Temple of Literature & Knowledge. *Publ*: Book of General Knowledge; Midnight; Colour on the Map; Ruins; Heroine of Gujrat; Diary of a Police Officer; Biographical Sketches; Collection of Poems. *Ctr*: Balsakha, Khilauna, Sentinel, Madhuri, Veena, Karmaveer, etc. *s.s*: Mathematics, Poetry, Essays, Biographical Sketches, etc. *Rec*: Walking, picnics, correspondence, collecting ancient & rare books. *c*: Progressive Writer's & Book. *a*: 289 Jawargunj Jubbulpore, C.P., India. *T*: 142.

GURUMURTI, D., M.A., Ph.D. *b*: Cuddalore 1893. *m*: Srimati Lakshmi. Prof Hon Reader in Madras Univ. *Publ*: Ed Saptapadarthi; Idealism & Theism; God & Progress. *Ctr*: Aryan Path. *s.s*: Philosophy, Religion, Educ, Art, Literature. *a*: 39 East Kottapeta, Mandanapalle, India.

GUSTAF-JANSON, Gosta. *b*: Duvnæs 1902. *e*: Univ of Munich, Univ of Stockholm. *m*: Karin Ernmark. *s*: 1. *Publ*: Rydsholm; Lindbom Paa Saevlunda; Tvaa Herrar; Krisaar; Kapitulation?—Nej; Gubben Kommer; (Eng trans under title of Old Man Coming); Stora Famnen. *c*: P.E.N. Club of Sweden. *a*: Vartavagen 37, Stockholm. *T*: 602595.

GUTHRIE, Archibald Cowan Guthrie, M.B. (Edin). *b*: Ayr. *e*: Ayr Acad & Edin Univ. Married. *s*: 3. *d*: 1. Consult Phys. *s.s*: Pneumonia & tuberculosis. *Publ*: Research work on Pneumococci & their Enzymes in Pneumonia. *Rec*: Golf. *c*: F.R.E.S. *a*: 56 Harley St., W.1. *t*: Langham 1497.

GUTHRIE, Douglas, M.D., F.R.C.S.E., F.R.S.E. *b*: 1885. *e*: Edinburgh, Jena & Paris. *m*: Helen Stark. Lect History of Medicine Edin Univ, Cons Surg Ear Nose & Throat Dept Edin Roy Hosp Sick Children. *n.a*: Asst-Ed Journ of Laryngology. *Publ*: Speech in Childhood (with G. Seth); History of Medicine; etc. *Rec*: Travel, photography, book-hunting. *w.s*: R.A.M.C. (2 years), later Commandant R.A.F. Officers' Hosp. *a*: 21 Clarendon Cres., Edinburgh 4. *T*: 21095.

GUTHRIE, Duncan Dunbar. *b*: London 1911. *e*: Malvern & abroad. *m*: Prunella Holloway. Asst Reg Dir Arts Council of Gt Brit, Traveller, Actor. *Publ*: Jungle Diary. *s.s*: Geography Central America, Art, Theatre, History. *w.s*: Army (with the Maquis) '44, behind Japanese lines in Burma '45. *a*: Wistaria Cottage, Amberley, Sussex.

GUTHRIE, George Calderwood. *e*: Ardrossan Acad, George Watson's Edinburgh. Publisher & Editor. *n.a*: Ed Ardrossan & Saltcoats Herald 1924—. *Publ*: In Days of Peace, In Times of War. (Poems). *a*: Dunaber, Ardrossan, Saltcoats.

GUTHRIE, George Davidson. *e*: Ardrossan Acad, Glasgow Hgh Sch. Publisher & Ed. *n.a*: Ardrossan & Saltcoats Herald series of papers 1944. *a*: Burnbrae, Sorbie Rd., Ardrossan.

GUTHRIE, James. *b*: Glasgow 1874. *e*: Priv. *m*: Marion Stewart Craig. *s*: 3. Author, Artist & Printer of Fine Books. *Publ*: Vols of Essays & Verse & Illus Books. *c.t*: Various on Art & Technique of Printing. *s.s*: Hand press printing from type & plates, bookplates. *Rec*: Walking, cycling. *a*: Flanshan, nr Bognor Regis.

GUTHRIE, Rev. Malcolm. Ph.D., B.Sc., F.R.S.M., A.R.S.M. *m*: Margaret Helen Near. Reader in Bantu Languages Univ of London. *Publ*: Grammaier et Dictionaire de Lingala; The Classification of the Bantu Languages. *Ctr*: Africa, Bulletin of Sch of Oriental & African Studies. *s.s*: Bantu Languages & African Linguistics. *a*: School of Oriental & African Studies, University of London, W.C.1. *T*: Museum 2023.

GUTHRIE, RAMSAY (pen name): see Bowran, John George.

GUTHRIE, T. R. Sec Stirlingshire Br N.U.J. *a*: c/o Ritchie, 36 Oswald Av, Grangemouth.

GUTHRIE, William Keith Chambers. *b*: London 1906. *e*: Dulwich Coll & Trin Coll Camb. *m*: Adele Marion Ogilvy. *s*: 1. *d*: 1. Univ Lect & Fell Peterhouse Camb, Public Orator of Univ. *Publ*: Jt Ed Monumenta Asiae Minoris Antiqua; Orpheus & Greek Religion; Aristotle De Caelo. *Ctr*: Classical Quarterly, Classical Review, Greece & Rome. *s.s*: Classics. *a*: Peterhouse, Cambridge. *T*: 4256.

GUTHRIE, William Tyrone, M.A.(Oxon). *b*: Tunbridge Wells 1900. *e*: Wellington Coll & St John's Coll Oxf. *m*: Judith Bretherton. Theatrical Producer. *Publ*: Squirrel's Cage & other Radio Plays; Theatre Prospect. *s.s*: Acting & the Theatre. *a*: Annagh Ma, Kerrig, Doohat-Newbliss, County Monaghan, Eire. *T*: Newbliss 3.

GUTKIND, E. A. *b*: Berlin 1886. *m*:. *s*: 1. *d*: 1. Architect & Town Planner, Adviser to Control Comm for Germany on Physical Planning & Reconstruction. *Publ*: Creation & ———; Man & Environment; Revolution & Environment; Modern Architecture. *s.s*: Architecture, Town & Country Planning, Sociology. *Rec*: Geography. *a*: 103 Corringham Rd, London, N.W.11. *T*: Speedway 0484.

GUTMAN-NATHAN, Adele, A.B. *b*: Baltimore, Maryland. *e*: Goucher Coll, Peabody Inst, Johns Hopkins Univ Baltimore. Writer, Theatrical Dir. *n.a*: Music Crit Baltimore Post, For. Corres Baltimore Post 1924—25, '29, Columnist '24—32, Feature Ed St Nicholas Mag N.Y. *Publ*: The Iron Horse; The Farmer Sows His Wheat; Let's Play Garden; Youth United. *Ctr*: Baltimore Post, Atlantic Monthly, Theatre Arts Mag, Ency Americana, etc, also articles in How to Speak & Write for Radio, A New Children's Theatre, The Little Theatre in the United States, etc. *s.s*: Little Theatre, Transportation, History of Communications, Mechanized Farming, Gilbert & Sullivan, Pageantry. *Rec*: Gardening, music, theatre, collecting historical railroad memorabilia. *c*: Woman Pays, Overseas Press, American Woman's Univ, Paris, France Authors' Guild N.Y. *a*: 157 West 57th St, New York 19, N.Y., U.S.A. *T*: Circle 6-7491.

GUTTERIDGE, Harold Cooke, K.C., LL.D. *b*: Naples 1876. *e*: Leys Sch Camb & King's Coll Camb. *m*: Mary Jackson. *s*: 1. *d*: 1. Emeritus Prof Comparative Law Cambridge. *n.a*: Jt-Ed Journ Comparative Legislation & Cambridge Series of Studies in International & Comparative Law. *Publ*: Comparative Law, Bankers Commercial Credits; Nelson & the Neapolitan Jacobins. *Ctr*: Law Quarterly Rev, Cambridge Law Journ, Hist Rev, Modern Law Rev, various foreign legal reviews, etc. *s.s*: Comparative Law. *w.s*: 1914—18 Brit Salonika Force. *c*: Roy Societies. *a*: Trinity Hall, Cambridge.

GUY, DOUGLAS SHERWOOD: clergyman; b. Hampton Wick, Middlesex, Eng., May 14, 1855; s. John and Sarah (Vernon) G.; educ. Tonbridge; Trinity Coll. (Cambridge). m. Mary (Owen) G.; AUTHOR: Steps Towards Intercommunion; Sacrifice in Holy Communion, 1921; Was Holy Communion Instituted by Jesus? a candid inquiry; with foreword by Bishop (Strong) of Ripon, 1924; Personality and Holy Communion; with introduction by Archbishop (Temple) of York, 1931. General character of writing: theological. Honorary Canon of Ripon Cathedral. Relig. denom., Church of England. HOME: Sherwood, Warwick's Bench, Guildford, Surrey, Eng.

GUY, William, F.R.S.E., L.L.D.(Penn), F.R.C.S., L.D.S.(Edin). *b*: Biddenden 1859. *e*: Norwich G.S. & Edin. *m*: Helen Beatrice Smith. *Publ*: Hygiene of the Mouth & Teeth (in collab); etc. *c.t*: Brit Dental Journ, Edin Med Journ, Edin Evening Despatch, etc. *s.s*: Dental educ, anæsthesia. Lect on Dental matters. 34 y Dean of Edin Dental Hosp. Brevet-Major, ret R.A.M.C., T.A. Pres Brit Dental Assoc 1914. Vice-Pres Internat Dental Fed. *Rec*: Shooting, writing verses. *c*: Scot Cons, Pen & Pencil. *a*: 11 Wemyss Pl, Edin. *t*: 20568.

GWALIA, ALFRED (pen name: see Thomas, Alfred.

GWIAZDOWSKI, Alexander P., M.E. *b*: Poland 1883. *e*: Classical Gymnasium, Poland & Columbia Univ, N.Y. *m*: Agnes Gradalska. *s*: 1. *d*: 2. Assoc Prof of Machine Production. *n.a*: Chief Ed Mvsl 1909-10, Mechanik, tech monthly mag '17-21. *Publ*: Machine Shop Practice Laboratory Manual; Economics of Tool Engineering; Machine Shop Engineering; etc. *c.t*: Machinery (N.Y.), Journ of Soc for Promotion of Eng Educ, etc. *s.s*: Production eng. Organized machine tool industry for Republic of Poland & tech sc which serves as model for other scs of this type. Cross of Independence, Poland Republic. *Rec*: Swimming, travel, visiting industries. *c*: Amer Soc of Mech Eng, Soc for Promotion of Eng Educ, Amer Soc of Tool Eng. *a*: Case Sc of Applied Sci, Cleveland, Ohio, U.S.A.

GWYNN, Dennis, D.Litt., F.R.Hist. S., M.R.I.A. *b*: 1893 *e*: Nat Univ of Ireland. Prof Mod Irish Hist Univ Coll Cork. *n.a*: Ed Nat Press Agency 1919—20, Lond Corr Freemans Journal '24, Leader Writer Westminster Gazette '25, Lit Dir Burns Oates & Washbourne Ltd '33—39, & Ed Dublin Review. *Publ*: Life of John Redmond; Life & Death of Roger Casement; Edward Martyn & the Irish Revival; The Struggle for Catholic Emancipation; The Second Spring 1818—52; Lord Shrewsbury, Pugin & the Catholic Revival. *a*: 4 Lower Montenotte, Cork, Eire.

GWYNN, EDWARD JOHN: Provost of Trinity College; b. Ramelton, Co. Donegal, Ireland, April, 1868; s. John and Lucy Josephine (O'Brien) G.; educ. St. Columba's Coll. (Dublin); DEGREES: M.A., Litt. D. (Dublin); (Hon.) Litt. D. (Oxford and Wales); (Hon.) LL.D. (Glasgow); (Hon.) D. Litt. Celt. (Nat. Univ. of Ireland); m. Olive Mary Ponsonby, Aug. 23, 1906. AUTHOR:: The Metrical Dindshenchas (vol. 1), 1903; (vol. 2), 1906; (vol. 3),

1913; (vol. 4), 1924); (vol. 5), in preparation; The Monestry of Tallaght (in collob. with W. J. Purton), 1911; Catalogue of Irish MSS. in the Library of Trinity College, Dublin (jointly with T. . Abbott), 1921; The Rule of Tallaght, 1927. Contributor to Eriu (journ. of School of Irish Learning), Hermathena (learned periodical pub. by Trinity Coll.), English Historical Rev., Irish Church Quarterly, and other periodicals. General character of writing: technical (philological), critical. Has done extensive research in Irish MSS. and has edited some texts in Old and Middle Irish previously unpublished. Relig. denom., Church of Ireland. CLUB: University (Dublin). HOME: Provost's House, Trinity College, Dublin, Irish Free State.

GWYNN, John Tudor. *b*: Donegal 1881. *e*: St Columba's Coll, Trin Coll Dublin. *m*: Joan Katherine Sedding. *s*: 1. *d*: 2. Indian Civil Service (ret). *Publ*: Indian Politics. *Ctr*: Manch Guardian. *a*: Baymount, Dollymount, Dublin.

GWYNN, Stephen. *b*: 1864. *e*: Ireland & Brasenose Col Oxf. Author. *Publ*: For Second Reading; Ireland (Kitbag Travel Books); Thomas Moore; The Letters & Friendships of Sir Cecil Spring Rice; The Charm of Ireland; etc. *a*: c/o Harrap & Co, 39-41 Parker St, Kingsway, W.C.

GWYNN, Stephen (Lucius). Author of many novels, verses, essays, & translations. *a*: Temple Hill, Terenure, Dublin, Eire.

GWYNN, Ursula Grace. *b*: Plymouth 1886. *e*: Priv. *m*: Kenneth H. Gwynn. *s*: 3. Novelist. *Publ*: The Green Hill; The Purple Shawl; The Four Miss Ramsays; If This Be Love; (under Ursula Leigh) Chinook; Give Me My Robe. *a*: Strangeways, Bury St, Ruislip, Middx. *t*: 788.

GWYNNE, ERSKINE: writer, publisher; b. Paris, France, November, 1898; s. Edward Erskine and Helen (Steele) G.; educ. E c o l e Brazilier (France); Bilton Grange (England); Cathedral School (Washington, D.C., U.S.A.), and Uppingham (England); m. Josephine Armstrong, June 6, 1926. Editor: The Boulevardier (in English). Contributor to many of the smaller mags. in the U.S.A. and England, and also writes in French for the French mags. Started as reporter on the San Francisco Bulletin (U.S.A.); then 4 yrs. on Le Journal of Paris. Subsequently corres. for the American Weekly. In 1927 started the Paris American Mag., "The Boulevardier". OFFICE: 65-67 Champs Elysee. HOME: 41 Rue Copernic, Paris, France.

GWYNNE, H. A. *b*: 1866. Journalist. *n.a.*: War & Foreign Corr The Times & Reuter's, Ed Standard 1904—11, Ed Morning Post '11. *a*: Mawlyns, Little Easton, Dunmow, Essex. *T*: Dunmow 25.

GWYNNE-VAUGHAN, HELEN CHARLOTTE ISABELLA: professor of botany, Univ. of London; b. London, Eng., Jan., 1879; d. Capt. the Hon. Arthur Hay David and Lucy Jane (Ferguson) Fraser; educ. King's Coll. (Univ. of London); DEGREES: D.Sc. (London), (Hon.) LL.D. (Glasgow); m. Professor D. T. Gwynne-Vaughan (deceased), 1911. AUTHOR: Fungi (Ascomycetes, Ustilaginales, Uredinales), 1922; The Structure and Development of the Fungi, 1927 (jointly, with Dr. B. Barnes; reprint with additions, 1930). General character of writing: technical, scientific. Pres. Section K. British Assn. for the Advancement of Science, 1928; Pres. British Mycological Soc., 1928. Author of a number of scientific papers in Annals of Botany and other publications. CLUB: Univ. of London, Ex-Service Women's. OFFICE: Birkbeck College, Univ. of London. HOME: 93 Bedford Court Mansions, W. C. 1, London, Eng.

"H. C. H. C. (occasional pseudonym):: see **Candy, Hugh Charles Herbert.**

"H. J. M." (pen name): see **Massingham, Harold John**

H. W. See **Williams, Harold.**

HAAFF, Katherine Maurine. *b*: Spencer Co., Indiana, 1902. *e*: Chrisney High Sc, Lockyear's Business Col. *m*: George W. Haaff. *c.t*: Psychology, Junior Home, The Editor, Writer's Markets & Methods, American Author, The Camera, Home & Abroad, The American Poet, The Prism, The Lariat, The Poetess, The Poet's Scroll, Poetry Studies, The Oracle Anthology, Poems of America, etc. *s.s*: Psychological articles and poems. *c*: Indiana Poetry Scc. *a*: 2184 N. Riley Ave, Indianapolis, Indiana, U.S.A. *t*: Cherry 6117—R.

HAAGNER, Alwin Karl, Hon.D.Sc.(Pitts.). *b*: Hankey, Cape Province 1880. *m*: Gwendoline Allen. *s*: 1. *d*: 1. Zoologist (ret), Accountants Clerk & Auditor. *Publ*: Sketches of South African Bird Life; A Short Manual of South African Mammals. *Ctr*: Ostrich, Farmer's Weekly, The Farmer, The Outspan, Pax Mag, etc. *s.s*: Natural History, Preservation of South African Wild Life. *Rec*: Motoring & fishing, singing. *a*: P.O. Box 451, Pietermaritzburg, Natal, Union of South Africa. *T*: 4103.

HAAN, J. A. BIERENS de: university lecturer; b. Haarlem, Holland, March, 1883; s. Jan Bierens de Haun and Lonide van (Leeuden) De H.; educ. Gymnasium (Haarlem), Univ. (Utrecht). DEGREE: D.Sc.; unmarried. AUTHOR: Animal Psychology for Biologists, 1929. General character of writing: scientific. Work is in Experimental Zoology, Animal Sense Physiology and Animal Psychology. Religion, Protestant. OFFICE: Zoological Laboratory. HOME: 26 Minerva Caan, Amsterdam, Holland.

HAARHOFF, Thedore Johannes, F.R.S.A. *b*: Paarl, S.A. 1892. *e*: S.A. Coll Sch, Cape Town, Univs of Oxf, Lond, Berlin, Amsterdam. *m*: Jessie Kilburn Davis. *s*: 2. Univ Prof, Mem S.A. Acad, Vice-Pres of Afrikaans & English P.E.N. Centre. *n.a*: Dir & Assoc Ed The Forum (Joh'burg) since 1937, Dir Suid-Afrika since '40. *Publ*: The Stranger at the Gate; Vergil in the Experience of Sth Africa; The ABC of Afrikaans; Schools of Gaul; Life & Thought in the Greek & Roman World (with Prof Carey); Harvest Home (trans of Van den Heeven's novel); Tria Corda; Die Wefde van Catullus; Briewe aan Reinhard; Short Stories of the Greeks & Romans. *Ctr*: Forum, Suid-Afrika, Star (S.A.), Classical Review. *s.s*: Interpretations of Greek & Roman Lit in both official langs of the Union, Afrikaans Lang & Lit. *Rec*: Cricket, walking. *a*: 6 Rhodes Ave, Parktown West, Johannesburg, Sth. Africa. *T*: 44/6250.

HAAS, ARTHUR: professor; b. Bruenn, Germany, Apr. 30, 1884; s. Gustav and Gabriele (Strakosch) H.; educ. grammar school (Bruenn), Univs. of Berlin and Goettingen. DEGREE: Ph.D.; m. Emma Beatrice Huber, Sept. 8, 1924. AUTHOR: Die Entwicklungsgeschichte des Satzes von der Erhaltung der Kraft, 1909; Der Geist des Hellenentums in der modernen Physik, 1914 (Greek transl.: To Pneuma tou Hellenismou en te neotera Physike, 1922); Die Grundgleichungen der Mechanik, 1914; Einführung in die theoretische Physik, 2 vols., 1920-21 (2nd edit. 1921; 3rd edit. 1923; 4th edit. 1924; 5th and 6th edits. 1930; English transl. Introduction to Theoretical Physics, 2 vols., 1924-25; 2nd edit. 1928-29), Vektoranalysis, 1922 (2nd edit. 1930); Das Naturbild der neuen Physik, 1920 (2nd edit. 1924; English transl.: The New Physics, 1923; 2nd edit. 1924; 3rd edit. 1930; Swedish transl.: Naturen Enligt den moderna Fysiken, 1924); Atomtherorie, 1924 (2nd edit. 1929; English transl.: Atomic Theory, 1927); Mechanik der Massenpunkte und der starren Körper, 1926; Materiewellen und Quantenmechanik, 1928 (2nd edit. 1929; 3rd edit. 1930; English transl.: Wave Mechanics and the New Quantum Theory, 1928); Die Grundlagen der Quantenchemie, 1929 (English transl.: Quantum Chemistry, 1930; French transl.: Mecanique ondulatoire, 1929). Editor: Commentary on the Works of J. Willard Gibbs (by order of Yale Univ.). Contributor to Physikalische Zeitschrift, Zeitschrift für Physik, Sitzungsberichte der Akademie der Wissenschaften in Wien, Monatshefte für Mathematik und Physik, Monatshefte für Chemie, Naturwissenschaften Science, Scientific Monthly, Archiv für die Geschichte der Naturwissenschaften, Archiv für Geschichte der Philosophie, and others. General character of writing: theoretical physics. Lecturer at Univ. of Vienna, 1912; Professor at Univ. of Leipzig, 1913; Professor at Univ. of Vienna, 1923; Lectured at the University College in London, 1924; visiting Lecturer in several American Universities, 1927. CLUBS: Deutsche Physikalische Gesellschaft, Chemisch-Physikalische Gesellschaft (Vienna); Comité international des Sciences (Paris), America-Austria Society (Vienna). Relig. denom., Protestant. OFFICE: Physikalisches Institut, Boltzmanngasse 5, Vienna IX. HOME: Baumgartenstrasse 58, Vienna XIII, Austria.

HAAS, P, D.Sc, PhD. *Publ*: Laboratory Notes on Organic Chemistry for Medical Students; The Chemistry of Plant Products (with T. G. Hill). Reader in Plant Chem Lon Univ. *a*: 11 Westbourne Park Rd, W.2.

HAASE, JULIUS: author; b. Elze, Hannover, Germany, Oct. 16, 1858; s. Senator Heinrich and Louise (Sievero) Haase; educ. Gymnasium, Technische Hochschule, Hannover. DEGREES: Dr.Ing.,Geheimer Baurat; m. Marie Windhorn, June 1, 1889. AUTHOR: Die Bauhütten des Späten Mittelalters, ihre Organisation, Triangulatur Methode und Zahlen-Symbolik, 1919; Der siebenarmige Leuchter des Alten Bundes, seine Geschichte und Symbolik, 1922. Contributor to: Abhandlungen über Proportionen in der Baukunst in der "Zeitschrift für Geschichte der Architektur", Heidelberg (Winter); Zeitschrift "Das Reich"—Süddeutsche Bauzeitung, Munich; Zeitschrift für Architektur und Ingenieure Hannover. General character of writing: historical, art history. CLUBS: Arch. und Ing. Verein (Berlin and Munich); Verein zur Erforschung der Proportionen in der bildenden Kunst, Munich. Relig. denom., Evangelical-Lutheran. OFFICE: Geheimer Baurat, Munich. HOME: Friedrich-Strasse 9.11., Munich, Bayern, Germany.

HABERLING, WILHELM: professor of the history of medicine; b. Liegnitz, Germany, Feb. 14, 1871; s. Konrad and Emma (Hüttner) H.; educ. Gymnasium (Bromberg), Univs. of Breslau, Königsberg, Marburg. DEGREE: M.D.; m. Elseluise Meyer-Becherer, Dec. 22, 1915. AUTHOR: Die Altrömischen Militärärzte, 1910; Sonnenbäder, 1912; Das Dirnenwesen in den Heeren und seine Bekämpfung, 1914; Die Verwundetenfürsorge in den Heldenliedern des Mittelalters, 1917; Die Entwicklung der Kriegsbeschädigtenfürsorge von den ältesten Zeiten bis zur Gegenwart, 1918; Johannes Müller. Das Leben des rheinischen Naturforschers, 1924; Alexander von Suchten, ein Danziger Arzt und Dichter des 16. Jahrhunderts, 1929. Editor: Mitteilungen zur Geschichte der Medizin und der Naturwissenschaften. Contributor to Militärärztliche Zeitschrift, Deutsche Medizinische Wochenschrift, Medizinische Welt, Therapeutische Berichte, Archiv für Geschichte der Medizin, Archiv für Geschichte der Mathematik und der Naturwissenschaften und der Technik, Medical Life, etc. General character of writing: biographical, medical-historical. Before the war, was occupied with the history of military medicine. After the war, began to write biographies of celebrated doctors. In 1926 received the gold medal of the great medical-historical exposition. Edits the magazine, Mitteilungen zur Geschichte der Medizin und Naturwissenschaften, the only one in the world to give a general view of the contributions of all peoples in the field of medicine and science. CLUBS: Deutsche Gesellschaft für Geschichte der Medizin und der Naturwissenschaften, Rheinische Gesellschaft für Geschichte Naturwissenschaften, der Medizin und der Technik, Goethe Gesellschaft. Relig. denom., Catholic. ADDRESS: Alexanderplatz 1, Düsseldorf, Germany.

HABICHTS, V. C.: art historian; b. Oberstein-Nahe, Germany, May, 1883; s. Hermann and Lina (Hoffmann) H.; educ. Ludwig-Georgs-Gymnasium (Darmstadt), Univs. of Kiel and Heidelberg. DEGREE: Ph.D., 1911, Professor, 1918, Extraordinary Professor, 1922; m. Mally Lohmann, 1913. AUTHOR: Hannover, 1914; Die niedersächsischen mittelalterlichen Chorgestühle, 1915; Die mittelalterliche Plastik Hildesheims, 1917; Die mittelalterliche Malerei Niedersachsens, 1919; Der Roland zu Bremen, 1922; Der heilige Bernward von Hildesheim Kunstwerke, 1922; Die goldne Tafel der St. Michaelskirche zu Lüneburg, 1922; Hanseatische Malerei und Plastik in Skandinavien, 1926; Maria, 1926; Celle und Wienhausen, 1929; Der niedersächsischen Kunstkreise, 1929. General character of writing: history of art. From 1914 to 1922 was assistant in the Technical High School at Hannover; since 1922 has been Lecturer on lower Saxon and modern art. CLUBS: Schutzverband deutscher Schriftsteller. Relig. denom., Evangelical. ADDRESS: Almersstrasse 8 III, Hannover, Prussia, Germany.

HABULANDT, ARTHUR: museum director; b. Vienna, Austria, March, 1889; s. Michael and Lolo (Malovich) H.; educ. Mittelschule, University (Univ. of Vienna); m. Marie Weiss. AUTHOR: Kulturwissenschaftliche Beiträge zur Volkskunde von Albanien, Montenegro, und Serbien, 1917; Volkskunst der Balkanländer. Contributor to Burchaus Illustrierte Völkerkunde. Character of writing: comparative ethnography. Relig. denom., Protestant. OFFICE: Landangasse 15-19, Vienna VIII. HOME: Sieveranzerstrasse 5, Vienna XIX, Austria.

HACCIUS, Jacqueline Lucy. b: London 1903. e: Priv & Lausanne. m: R. A. Haccius. s: 1. Publ: Listening Hands (also French trans); The Play of a Lifetime; The Flapdoodle Who Always Knew Best (illustrated by the author). s.s: Reincarnation, the Psychic, Other World in General, Folklore, Children's Stories, Book Illustration (colour & line work), Woodcuts. Rec: Music, painting, reading. a: 19 Boileau Rd, London, W.5. T: Perivale 6135.

HACHISUKA, MASAUJI: naturalist; b. Tokyo, Japan, Feb., 1903; s. Marquis Hasaaki and Fudeko (Tokugawa) H.; educ. Peer's Sch. (Tokyo), Magdalen Coll. (Cambridge, Eng.); unmarried. AUTHOR: A Comparative Hand List of the Birds of Japan and the British Isles, 1925; Birds of Egypt (in Japanese), 1926; A Handbook of the Birds of Iceland, 1927; Contributions to the Birds of Philippines No. 1, 1929; No. 2, 1930. Editor Bulletin of the Biogeographical Soc. of Japan. Contributor to Tori (Bul. of the Ornithological Soc. of Japan), Ibis (Brit. Ornith. Union), L'oisseau (La Societe National d'aclimation de France). General character of writing: scientific, about birds. Religion, Buddhist. CLUB: Peers (Tokyo). HOME: Mita, Shiba, Tokyo, Japan.

HACKER, Louis Morton, M.A. b: New York City 1899. e: Columbia Coll. m: Lillian Lewis Hacker. s: 1. d: 1. University Professor, Writer & Editor. n.a: New Internat Ency & Year Book, Ency of Social Sciences, Columbia Ency. Publ: Triumph of American Capitalism; Shaping of the American Tradition; The United States, A Graphic History; United States since 1865; The Farmer is Doomed; Short History of the New Deal; American Problems of To-day; the United States & its Place in World Affairs. Ctr: N.Y. Times Book Rev, N.Y. Herald-Tribune Book Rev, Fortune, Nation, etc. s.s: American Economic & Political History. Rec: Cycling, bridge. a: 106 Morningside Drive, New York 27, N.Y., U.S.A. T: Monument 2-4800.

HACKETT, Rev. B. Cong Min. n.a: Ed Ch Mag. Publ: Early Sunset; Memories of a Ministry. a: Roachdale Clent, Stourbridge.

HACKETT, E. J. Fox. n.a: Chief Reporter Morecambe Visitor. s.s: Sports. a: 16 Leyster St, Morecambe.

HACKETT, Francis. b: Kilkenny, Ireland 1883. e: Clongowes Wood Col, Co. Kildare. m: Signe Toksvig. Writer. n.a: Literary Ed Chicago Evening Post '06—11, Co Ed New Republic, New York '14—22, Correspondent New York World '22—3, McClure Syndicate '22—3. Publ: Horizons; Ireland; Invisible Censor; Essays; Story of the Irish Nation; That Nice Young Couple; Henry the Eighth; Francis the Frst. c.t: Harper's; Atlantic Mthly, Saturday Evening Post; Forum, Survey(N.Y.), Nash's, Dublin Mag, Sunday Times, Mercury (N.Y.), Politiken. c: P.E.N. a: Killadreenan House, Newtownmountkennedy, Co. Wicklow, Ireland.

HACKETT, J. D. Publ: Labor Management. a: c/o D. Appleton & Co, 34 Bedford St, W.C.

HACKETT, M. T. n.a: Ed North-Western Daily Mail. a: Barrow-in-Furness.

HACKETT, Walter. b: California 1876. Dramatist. Plays—The Freedom of the Seas; Ambrose Applejohn's Adventure; Other Men's Wives; etc. a: Stratton House, Piccadilly, W.1. t: Grosvenor 2034.

HACKFORD, John. b: Boston 1859. m: Annie E. Wigfall. n.a: Chief Rep Express & Star '86-94, Sub-Ed Nott'm Evening Post '94-1921. a: 14 Burford Rd, Nott'm.

HACKFORTH, Reginald, F.B.A. b: London 1887. e: Westminster Sch & T.C.C. Prof of Ancient Philosophy Camb since 1939, Fell Sidney-Sussex Coll. n.a: Ed Classical Quarterly '26. Publ: The Authorship of the Platonic Epistles; The Composition of Plato's Apology; Plato's Examination of Pleasure. Ctr: Classical Rev, Classical Quarterly, Philosophy. a: Sidney-Sussex College, Cambridge. T: 5027.

HACKFORTH-JONES, Gilbert. b: Arkley, Herts 1900. e: R.N. Colls Osborne & Dartmouth. m: Margaret Eardley-Howard. s: 1. Retired Naval Commander, R.N. '14—36. Publ: The Prize was High; Sixteen Bells; The Questing Hound; Rough Passage; Submarine Alone; One, One, One; Submarine Flotilla; No Less Renowned; etc. Ctr: Blackwood's, Sketch, Britannia & Eve, Ev News, Esquire (U.S.A.), Toronto Star, Sydney Sun, Illus Lond News, etc. s.s: Stories of the Royal Navy, Radio Plays & Features. Rec: Yachting. c: United Services & Roy Lymington Yacht, etc. w.s: 1st & 2nd World Wars. a: 14 High St., Lymington, Hants. T: 514.

HACKING, The Ven. E. a: Hill House, Southwell, Notts.

HACKING, Sidney Cochrane. *e*: Mexboro' Gr. Sch & King's Coll London. *m*: Ethel Hoyland. *s*: 2. Editor South Yorkshire Times 1935—, Council Mem Guild of British Newsp Editors, Mem Jt Ed Cttee of Newsp Soc. *s.s*: Sport. *a*: Kinglands, Cemetery Rd., Mexborough, Yorks. *T*: 2327.

HACKMANN, HEINRICH FRIEDRICH: professor; *b*. Osnabrück, Germany, Aug., 1864; *s*. Ernst and Clara (Koch) H.; educ. Rats-Gymnasium, Osnabrück, Universities of Leipsig and Göttingen; DEGREES: Licentiate of Theo., Göttingen, Hon. D.D., Basel, Switzerland; member of the Royal Academy of Sciences of Netherlands; m. Gabriele Elisabeth Vogler, 1898. AUTHOR: Die Zukunfts-Erwartung des Jesaia, 1893; Chinesische Schriftzeichen, 1900; Vom Omi bis Bhamo. Wanderungen an den Grenzen von China, Tibet und Birma, 1905; Der Buddhismus, 1906; Psalmen des Westens, 1907; Am Strand der Zeit (Predigten), 3 vol., 1909-11-14; Die Entwicklung der deutsch-evangelischen Kirchengemeinde von Denmark, 1910; Buddhism as a Religion; Its Historical Development and Its Present Conditions, 1910; Welt des Ostens, 1912; Religionen und heilige Schriften, 1914; A German Scholar in the East, 1914; Der Charakter der Chinesischen Philosophie, 1917; Alphabetisches Verzeichnis zum Kao Seng Chuan, 1923; Laien-Buddhismus in China. Das Lung shu Ching tu wen des Wang Tih hsiu, 1924; Chinesische Philosophie, 1927; Der Zusammenhang zwischen Schrift und Kultur in China, 1928; Chineesche denkers, I, 1929; II, 1930. Editor of Nieuw Theologisch Tydschrift. Contributor to Die Christliche Welt, Toung Pao, Acta Orientalia, Nieuw Theologisch Tydschrift, Theologische Literaturzeitung, Zeitschrift für Missionskunde und Religionswissenschaft, Der Ostasiatische Lloyd, Der ferne Osten, Jahresberichte der Geschichtswissenschaft, Westermanns Monatshefte, Weserzeitung, Berliner Tageblatt, Gartenlaube, Geist des Ostens, Tägliche Rundschau, Preussische Jahrbücher, Kreuzzeitung, Ostasiatische Zeitschrift, Mensch en Maatschappy, China, Mitteilungen des Seminars für Orientalische Sprachen zu Berlin, Festschrift für Friedrich Hirth zu seinem 75. Geburtstag, Die Religion in Geschichte und Gegenwart. General character of writing: religious, scientific and historical; poems and books on travel. Traveled in eastern and central Asia for investigation of historical and anthropological questions; deputed by the University of Amsterdam to the University of Jerusalem at its opening in 1925; pastor of a German congregation in Shanghai, 1894-1901, and in London, 1904-1913. Relig. denom.: Lutheran. ADDRESS: Hoofdweg 34, Amsterdam, Holland.

HACKNEY, John. *b*: Lyminge, Kent, 1905. *m*: Sheila Griffin. *Publ*: Short stories; Ed The Grayson Books. *a*: 6 John St, Adelphi, W.C.2. *t*: Temple Bar 8908.

HADATH, Gunby, M.A.(Cantab), F.R.S.A. *b*: Owersby, Lincs. *e*: St Edmunds Sch Canterbury, Peterhouse Camb. *m*: Florence Annie Webber. Author, Citoyen d'Honneur of St Gervais-les-Bains, Director of the Performing Right Soc. *Publ*: Author of numerous popular works for youth in Gt Brit, U.S.A. & (in translation) in France & Scandinavia, also transposed several works into Braille in Gt Brit & U.S.A. *Ctr*: Several works, periodicals, etc, in Gt Brit & Italy. *s.s*: Fiction. *Rec*: Climbing. *a*: 39 Chichele Rd, London, N.W.2. *T*: Gladstone 6998.

HADCOCK, Richard Neville, F.S.A., F.R.S.A. *b*: Newcastle-on-Tyne 1895. *e*: Marlborough Coll & Hertford Coll Oxf. *m*: Jeanne Le Pajolec *s*: 3. *d*: 1. Farmer. *Publ*: Tynemouth Priory; Official Guides to Bradfield & Newbury Districts. *Ctr*: Archæologia Aeliana, La Revue Moderne, Trans of Newbury Field Club, etc. *s.s*: Archæology & Mediæval Building. *Rec*: Painting & etching. *w.s*: 1914—18 R.F.A. (Despatches). *a*: Winchcombe Farm, Bucklebury, Reading. *T*: Thatcham 3287.

HADDOCK, Rev. Josiah, M.A. *b*: Castle Hamilton, Co Cavan 1888. *e*: Roy Coll of Science Dublin, Trinity Coll Dublin. *m*: Fannie J. Andrews. Rector of Donaghcloney, Waringstown, Co Down. *Publ*: The Gospel of Common Things; Thoughts on the Epistles; Short History of Donaghcloney Parish. *Ctr*: Spectator, Lit Reviews, B.B.C. talks & recordings. *s.s*: Science, Music. *Rec*: Music & gardening. *a*: The Rectory, Waringstown, Co Down, N. Ireland. *T*: Waringstown 218.

HADDON, Archibald. *b*: Ironbridge 1871. *e*: Old Hall, Wellington, Salop & Birkenhead Sc. *m*: (1) Lily Jones, (2) Johanna Simonsen. *s*: 1. *d*: 3. Journalist & Dramatic Critic. *n.a*: Dramatic Critic B.B.C. 1923 & '24 & '33, Dramatic Critic Daily Express '02—22, Sunday Express '18—22, etc. *Publ*: Green Room Gossip '22; Hullo, Playgoers (book of broadcast theatre talks '24; Story of the Music Hall '35. *c.t*: Times, Daily Telegraph, Observer, Radio Times, etc. *s.s*: Theatre & music hall. *a*: 39 Kensington Hall Gdns, W.14. *t*: Fulham 6478.

HADDON, James Douglas, B.Sc, A.F.R.AeS. *b*: Wellington 1897. *e*: Roy Masonic Sc, Bristol Univ. *m*: Gladys Mildred Verran. *s*: 2. Educ Officer R.A.F. *Publ*: Intro to Aeronautical Engineering (Vol II, Structures; Vol III: Properties & Strength of Materials). *c.t*: Flight. *s.s*: Aero eng. War Service. *Rec*: Tennis, amateur dramatics. *a*: Edgecumbe, Miswell Lane, Tring.

HADDON, R. W. *n.a*: Mang Dir Farmer & Stock-breeder. *a*: Dorset Hse, Stamford St, S.E.1. *t*: Hop 3333.

HADDOW, Hugh Paterson, M.C. *b*: Renfrewshire 1896. *e*: Greenock H.S. & Lon Univ. Mang Ed. *n.a*: Reporter Greenock Telegraph 1914, Glasgow Herald '22—24, Finan Sub Ed Glasgow Evening Times '25—27, Sub Ed B.M.J. '28, Chief Sub Ed Northcliffe N/p's Lon Office '29—32, Mang Ed Lincolnshire Echo, Lincoln '32—33, Mang Ed Evening Telegraph, & Saturday Telegraph, Grimsby '33—. *s.s*: Economics. War Service '14—19; M.C. *Rec*: Travel. *a*: Grimsby Telegraph, 80 Cleethorpe Rd, Grimsby. *t*: 6610.

HADEN GUEST, Carmel. *b*: Belfast. *e*: R.A.M. & R.A.D.A. *m*: Leslie Haden Guest. *s*: 2. *d*: 1. Novelist & Free Lance Journalist. *n.a*: Westminster Gazette. *Publ*: Mary in Mermaidland; Children of the Fog; The Yellow Pigeon ('28); Scent of Magnolia ('34); Ed Marie José's Children's Book; The Proselyte (play '34). *c.t*: John o' London, Punch, Windsor Mag, etc. *c*. P.E.N. *a*: 192 Sloane St, S.W.1. *t*: Vic 0278.

HADER, Berta Hoerner. *b*: San Pedro, Chihuahua, Mo. *e*: Univ of Wash & Calif Sch of Design. *m*: Elmer Stanley Hader. Illustrator & Writer of Children's Books. *Publ*: Spunky; Picture Book of Mother Goose; What'll You Do When You Grow Up?; Lions, Tigers & Elephants Too. *Ctr*: Chris Sc Monitor, McCall's Mag, Pictorial Rev, Good Housekeeping. *s.s*: Portraits (miniature on ivory). *Rec*: Gardening, sketching, cooking, dress designing. *a*: 55 River Rd, Grand View on Hudson, New York. *T*: Nyack 769.

HADER, Elmer Stanley. *b*: Pajaro, Calif 1889. *e*: Calif Sch of Design, Julian Acad & Paris. *m*: Berta Hoerner. Illustrator & Writer of Children's Books 1925—. *Publ*: Spunky; Picture Book of Mother Goose; What'll You Do When You Grow Up?; Lions, Tigers & Elephants Too. *Ctr*: Christ Sc Monitor,

McCall's Mag, Pictorial Rev, Good Housekeeping. *s.s*: Writing & Illustrating Children's Books. *Rec*: Oil & water-colour sketching, piano playing, house building. *a*: 55 River Rd, Grand View on Hudson, New York, U.S.A. *T*: Nyack 769.

HADFIELD, Charles Frederick, M.B.E., M.A., M.D.(Cantab), M.R.C.S., L.R.C.P. *b*: Birkenhead 1875. *e*: Leys Sc Cam, Trinity Col Cam & St Bart's Hosp. Married. *s*: 2. *d*: 1. Anæsthetist. *Publ*: Practical Anæsthetics; Anæsthetics in Rose & Carless' Text Book of Surgery. *c.t*: Proc Roy Soc Medicine, B.M.J., Brit Journal of Anæsthesia, Medical Press & Circular, Clinical Journal. *s.s*: Anæsthetics. Hon Sec Jt Anæsthetics Cmt of Med Research Counc & Roy Soc of Med. Ex-Pres Section of Anæsthetics Roy Soc Med. *Rec*: Mountaineering. *c*: Alpine, French Alpine. Fell & Rock Climbing (Ex-Pres). *a*: 47 Queen Anne St, W.1., & The Dove Hse, Dunmow, Essex. *t*: Welbeck 1035.

HADFIELD, Geoffrey, M.D.(Lond), F.R.C.P.(Lond). *b*: Manchester 1889. *e*: St Bart's Hosp. *m*: Eileen Irvine. *s*: 2. *d*: 1. Prof of Pathology Lond Univ. *Publ*: Recent Advances in Pathology. *Ctr*: B.M.J. *s.s*: Pathology. *a*: St Bartholomew's Hospital, London. *T*: Clerkenwell 1141.

HADFIELD, James Arthur, M.A., M.B., Ch.B. *Publ*: inc Psychology & Morals; War Neuroses; Psychology & Mental Health; etc. *a*: 4 Upper Harley St, London, N.W.1.

HADFIELD, John Charles Heywood. *b*: Birmingham 1907. *e*: Bradfield. *m*: Phyllis Anna McMullen. *s*: 1. Dir National Book League, joined Messrs J. M. Dent & Sons 1928, Ed '35—42, Book Officer for Brit Council Middle East '42—44. *Publ*: Ed of Modern Stories of the Open Air; Modern Short Stories; The Christmas Companion. *s.s*: Lit & the Book World. *Rec*: Books, pictures, cricket. *c*: Savile. *a*: Sadleirs End, Preston, Hitchin, Herts. *T*: Hitchin 1157.

HADFIELD, Rev. Percival, M.A., B.D., F.R.A.I. *b*: Ashton Preston 1903. *e*: Priv. *m*:. *s*: 1. *d*: 2. Vicar of Youlgreave nr Bakewell, Examiner in Scripture Northern Univ '47. *Publ*: The Savage & His Totem. *s.s*: Anthropology, botany, langs. *Rec*: Walking, gardening. *a*: The Vicarage, Youlgreave, nr Bakewell.

HADFIELD, Sir Robert A., Bt, F.R.S., J.P., HonD.Sc(Oxon & Leeds), M.InstC.E., HonM.I. MechE., M.I.E.E., Mem I.S.I., F.PhysS., F.I.C., F.C.S., F.InstP. *b*: 1858. *m*: Frances Belt, C.B.E. Coy Dir & Chm. *Publ*: Metallurgy & Its Influence on Modern Progress; Faraday & His Metallurgical Researches; etc. Freeman City of Lon. Vice-Pres & Mang Roy Inst 1932-33. Vice-Pres Fed of Brit Ind's, R.S.A., Brit Science Gld. Membre Correspondant de l'Institut de France. Foreign Assoc Nat Acad of Science Washington, etc. Bessemer Gold Medal Iron & Steel Inst; Howard Prize & Premium Inst C.E.; Inst of Transport Gold Medal; American Franklin Inst John Fritz Gold Medal; Napoleon III Bronze Medal; etc. Officier Legion d'Honneur. Japanese Order of Sacred Treasure. Commendatore Order Crown of Italy. Inventor of manganese steel, silicon steel, etc. Extensive travel. *Rec*: *c*: Athenæum, Reform, R.A.C., etc. *a*: 22 Carlton House Terr, S.W.1., & Parkhead House, nr Sheffield. *t*: Whitehall 7107 & Sheffield 70900.

HADFIELD, Walton John, C.B.E., M.InstC.E. *b*: Norton 1871. *e*: Roy G.S. Sheffield. Civil Eng, City Eng of Sheffield. *Publ*: Highways & Their Maintenance. *c.t*: Various tech journ's. *s.s*: Highways, main drainage, town planning. *a*: 2 The Mount, Newbould Lane, Sheffield. *t*: Broomhill 61566.

HADFIELD-PEAT, Leslie John ("Peter Hadfield"). *b*: M/C 1906. *e*: Rishworth & William Ellis Scs. Journalist. *n.a*: Press Assoc '24—26, Chief Reporter N. Lon Recorder '26—27, News Ed '27—29, Coventry Standard Reporter '30, Palmer's Green & Southgate Gazette Reporter & Sports Ed '33—. *c.t*: Various. *s.s*: Motoring, flying. Mem N.U.J. *Rec*: Cricket, rugby. *a*: Conservative Cottage, Bucknall's Lane, Garston, Watford.

HADGKISS, Herbert. *b*: Brierley Hill, Staffs, 1871. *e*: Board Sc. *m*: Prudence Lyndon. *d*: 2. Jnlst. *n.a*: Ed County Advertiser, '07—14, Ed & Dir County Express for Worcs & Staffs '26—. Dist Corr B'ham Post. *Rec* Cycling. *c*: Rotary. *a*: Appiegarth, Red Hill, Stourbridge, Worcs. *t*: 57290.

HADLEY, Cecil Montague. *b*: Lon 1886. Sports Ed. *n.a*: Star 1905—24, The People '24. *s.s*: All sport (except rugby football), cockney characters & wireless. *Rec*: Golf. *a*: The People. 93 Long Acre, W.C.2. *t*: Temple Bar 2468.

HADLEY, Laurence Percival. F.J.I. *b*: Birm 1875. *e*: King VI Sc Birm. *m*: Nora Katharine Alabaster. *s*: 1. *d*: 1. Asst Ed Birm Post. *n.a*: Ed Midland Counties Herald, Lit Ed Birm Post, Leader-Writer & Chief Asst Ed 1910—. *s.s*: Polit, Eng lit. *Rec*: Fishing, photography. *c*: Birm Press, Post & Mail Sports (Chm). *a*: 102 Anderton Pk Rd, Moseley, Birm. *t*: S.2248.

HADLEY, W. W. Ed, Sunday Times. *a*: Sunday Times, Daily Telegraph Blgs, 135 Fleet St, E.C.4. *t*: Central 4242.

HADLEY, Wilfred James, F.R.C.S., M.D. *n.a*: Writer of Diseases of Respiration 2-3 yrs, Wright's Medical Annual. *Publ*: Fibroid Diseases of Lung; Nursing General, Medical & Surgical. *c.t*: Med papers. *a*: Parkside, Reigate, Surrey. *t*: 45.

HADOW, Grace Eleanor. *b*: S. Cerney 1875. *e*: Truro H.S., Germany & Somerville Oxf. Prine Soc Oxf Home-Students. *Publ*: Trans of Litzmann's Life of Madame Schumann; The Oxford Treasury of English Literature (with W. H. Hadow); Chaucer & His Times. *c.t*: Various n/p's & periodicals. *s.s*: Rural life. Vice-Chm Nat Fed of Women's Insts. *Rec*: Gardening. *c*: Univ Women's. *a*: 1 Jowett Walk, Oxf. *t*: 2880.

HADOW, Sir William Henry, C.B.E., J.P., D.Mus, LL.D., D.C.L. *b*: Ebrington, Glos 1859. *e*: Malvern Col & Worcester Col Oxf. *m*: Edith Troutbeck. Ex-Vice Chancellor Sheffield. *Publ*: Studies in Modern Music (1st & 2nd series); Oxford Treasury of English Literature (with G. E. Hadow); Citizenship; Collected Essays; Richard Wagner. *s.s*: Music, educ. *Rec* Travel. *c*: Athenæum.

HADRILL, Geoffrey Frederick. *b*: London 1904. *e*: Pitman's Coll. Free Lance Journalist, sometime Hon Sec W. Lond N.U.J. *n.a*: Bucks Examiner Chesham '19—35, Ev Gazette Reading '35—38, M.O.I. for Dly Sketch '38—39, Dly Mirror '39—42. *Publ*: Experiences of Chesham Boy Scouts Abroad. *Ctr*: Leading Lond dailies & wklys, agencies & evs. *s.s*: Scouting, Social Welfare. *Rec*: Tennis, photography. *w.s*: In charge of E.N.S.A.'s publicity Far East. *a*: Hazeldene, Higher Denham, Bucks. *T*: Denham 2107.

HAENSEL, Paul, M.A., B.Comm., Ph.D., LL.D. *b*: Moscow 1879. *e*. Moscow Acad. of Commerce & University. *m*: Nina von Tugenhold. *s*: 3. Prof Mary Washington Coll Va 1943—. *Publ*: Many books & several hundred articles in 8 languages including:— (Russian) Inheritance Tax; Local Taxation; Finance Reform in Russia; (English) The Economic Policy of Soviet Russia; American Federal State & Local Tax Problems; Public Finance of U.S.S.R.; Illinois Tax Reform; etc. *Ctr*: Russian, American & foreign newsps & periodicals, etc. *s.s*: Public Finance & Taxation, European & Soviet Economics. *a*: 406 Amelia St, Fredericksburg, Virginia, U.S.A., & Clarendon Hills, Illinois, U.S.A.

HAERING, THEODOR L.: univ. professor; b. Stuttgart, Germany, April 22, 1884; s. Theodor Johannes and Emma (Chevalier) H.; educ. Gymnasium Gœttingen and Tübingen), Univs. of Tübingen, Berlin, Bonn, Halle. DEGREE: Ph.D. (Tübingen), Professor of Philosophy (Tübingen). AUTHOR: Der Duisburg'sche Kantnachlass und Kants Kritizismus um 1775, 1910; Untersuchungen zur Psychologie der Wertung (on experimental bases), 1913; Die Materialisierung des Geistes, 1919; Die Struktur der Weltgeschichte, 1920; Philosophie der Naturwissenschaft, 1923; Hauptprobleme der Geschichtsphilosophie, 1925; Individualität in Natur und Geisteswissenschaft, 1927; Hegel. Sein Wollen und Sein Werk, 1929. Relig. denom., Evangelical. ADDRESS: Neckarhalde 31, Tübingen, Württemberg, Germany.

HAFEN, Leroy R., Ph.D., Hon.Litt.D. *b*: Bunkerville, Nevada 1893. *e*: Brigham Young & Calif Univs. *m*: Ann Woodbury Hafen. *s*: 1. *d*: 1. Historian & Professor Univ of Denver 1940—. *n.a*: Ed Colorado Mag '25—, Exec Dir & State Historian '43—, Hist State Hist Soc of Col '24—. *Publ*: Colorado, the Story of a Western Commonwealth; The Overland Mail; (collab) Western America; Fort Laramie & the Pageant of the West; Colorado, a Story of the State & its People; Broken Hand, Life of Thomas Fitzpatrick; Ed of several vols dealing with Colorado gold rush. *Ctr*: Various historical reviews, etc. *s.s*: Colorado & Western American History. *a*: 1986 South Fillmore St, Denver, Colorado, U.S.A. *T*: Sp. 3160.

HAFF, CARL: professor; b. April 9, 1879; s. Max and Caroline (Joersen) H.; educ. Gymnasium (Kempten, Bayern), Univs. of München, Würzburg, Berlin. DEGREE: Juris Dr.; Professor; m. Gertrud Dahm. AUTHOR: Geschichte einer ostalemannischen Gemeinlandsverfassung, 1903; Dänische Gemeinderechte, Hartsgenossenschaft I, 1908; Feldgemeinschaft, 1909; Bauernbefreiung und Stand des Bodengiusrechtes in Bayern, 1908, 1910; Die Alp- und Weidegenossen in Bayern, 1910; Wasserkraftrechte, 1910; Gesetze der Willensbildung bei Genossenschaft und Staat, 1915; Institutionen des Personlichkeitsrechtes und des Körperschaftsrechts, 1918; Studien zum Waadtländer Stadtrecht, 1918; Rechtspsychologie, 1924; Institutionen des deutschen Privatrechts, I, 1927; Rechtsgeschichte und Sociologie, 1929. Contributor to Archiv für Rechts- und Wirtschaftsphilosophie, Vierteljahrschrift für Sozial- und Wirtschaftsgeschichte, Zeitschrift der Savignystiftung für Rechtsgeschichte, Juristische Wochenschrift. General character of writing: history of jurisprudence and sociology. Interest chiefly in the sociology of the old German law. CLUBS: Archiv für Rechts- und Wirtschaftsphilosophie. Relig. denom., Protestant. OFFICE: University of Hamburg. HOME: Carlstrasse 16, Hamburg, Germany.

HAFFKINE, WALDEMAR MORDECAI WOLFF: bacteriologist; b. Odessa, So. Russia, Mar. 15, 1860; s. Aaron and Rasalie (Landesberg) H.; educ. District Sch., Berdiansk, So. Russia, 1870-71; Classical Gymnasium, Berdiansk, 1872-78; Faculty of Science, Univ. of Odessa, 1879-1883; DEGREES: Sc.D.; unmarried. AUTHOR: Anti-cholera Inoculation, 1895; Report on the Epidemic of Plague in Lower Damaon (Portuguese, India) and on the effect of preventative inoculation there (Surgeon Major Lyons, I.M.S.), 1898; Experiment on protective inoculation in the Epidemic of Plague at Undhera (Taluka Baroda), 1898; Preventative inoculation against plague, 1898; Report on preventative inoculation against plague in the Khoja Community of Bombay during the epidemic of 1897-8, 1898; On the present condition of manufacturing the plague prophylactic, 1900; On the inoculation statistics as reported from large towns, 1901; On Health of the Inoculated, 1901; La vaccination contre la cholera, las peste bubonique et la fievre typhoide, et les experiences de bacteriotherapic, 1909; Protective Inoculation against cholera, 1913; Concerning inoculation against plague and pneumonia, and experimental study of curative methods, 1915; De levenskracht van het joodschevolk, 1923. Contributor to Memoirs of the Soc. of Naturalists (Odessa); Annales d' Histoire Naturelle (Zoologie) (Paris); Annals de l'Institut Pasteur (Paris); Comptes rendus de des seances de la Societe de Biologie (Paris); British Medical Jnl. (London); Lancet (London); Indian Medical Gazette (Calcutta); trans. of 1st Indian Medical Congress (Calcutta); proc. of Royal Soc. (London); the Science Monthly (New York); Menorah Jnl. (New York). General character of writing, scientific research in Microbiology and epidemiology; essays on Jews. Research in Microbiology, Odessa, 1883-88; asst. to Prof. Moritz Schiff, Physiological Laboratory, Medical Sch., Geneva, Switzerland, 1888-9; Asst. and research in bacteriology, Pasteur Inst., Paris, 1889-93; Study of Anti-cholera inoculation in Man, British India, 1893-96; Studies in anti-plague inoculation in British India, 1896-1904; Foundation of the Plague Research Laboratory, now the Haffkine Inst., Bombay, India. Bacteriologist with the Government of India, 1904-15. Religion, Jew. HOME: 17 Avenue Victor-Hugo. Boulogne-sur-Seine. France.

HAFTER. ERNST: univ. professor; b. Zürich, Switzerland, December, 1876; e d u c. public schools, high schools, Univs. of Zürich, Berlin, Strassburg, Berne. DEGREES: LL.D., Dr.h.c., Univ. of Padua; m. Magdalene Springer. 1903. AUTHOR: Delikts-und Straffähigkeit der Personenverbände, 1903; Kommentar zum schweizer Zivilgesetzbuch, Personenrecht (2nd edit.), 1919; Vorentwurf zu einem schweizerischen Militär-Strafgesetzbuch, 1916; Lehrbuch des schweizerischen Strafrechts, Allgemeiner Teil, 1926. Co-editor: Schweizerische Zeitschrift für Strafrecht. General character of writing: scientific. Judge of the supreme martial court of Switzerland. ADDRESS: Kilchberg near Zürich, Switzerland.

HAGALIN, Guomundur Gislason. *b*: Iceland, 1898. *m*: Kristin Jonsdottir. *s*: 1. *d*: 1. Librarian. *n.a*: Jnlst Daily Frettir Reykjavik 1918, Ed Conservative Weekly in Seyoisfjorour 1919—23, Daily Althyoublaoio, Reykjavik, '28, Ed Nyjar Kvoldvokur 1932. *Publ*: Kristrun i Hamravik; Gue og lukkan; Einn af postullunum; Veour oll valynd; Strandbuar; Vestan ur Fjoreum; Brennumenn. *c.t*: Eimreioin, Odinn, Freyr, Reykjavik, Norsk Aarbok, Bergen, Bygd och folk, Stockholm, Nyjar Kvoldvokur, Akureyri, Dansk islandsk Aarbog Kobenhavn. *s.s*: Literary Essays. Written articles on literature and accounts of travellings for Icelandic & Norwegian N/ps. Lectured in Norway '24—27. Mem Icelandic Labour Party from '32. Mem Town Council Isafjorour from '34. President '35. *a*: Isafjorour, Iceland.

HAGEDORN, Hermann. *b*: New York 1882. *e*: Harvard. *m*: Dorothy Oakley. *s*: 1. *d*: 2. Writer. *Publ*: The Bomb that fell on America; Prophet in the Wilderness, the Story of Albert Schweitzer; Leonard Wood; Combat at Midnight (poems); The Book of Courage; Americans; etc. *a*: 28 East 20th St, New York 3, N.Y., U.S.A. *T*: Alg 4-1700.

HAGEN, JOHANN GEORG, S. J.; astronomy, mathematics; b. March 6, 1847; s. Martin and Theresia (Schick) H.; educ. Feldkirch, "Stella

Matutina", Univs. of Munster (Westfales), Bonn (a|Rh.); DEGREE: Dr. L. C. (Philosophy and Theology). AUTHOR: Synopsis der Höheren Mathematik (vol. I), 1891; (vol. II.), 1894; (vol. III), 1905; (vol. IV), 1930; Atlas Stellarum Variabilium (series I), 1899; (series II), 1899; (series III), 1900; (series IV), 1906; (series V), 1907; (series VI), 1908; (series VII), 1927; Rotation de la Terre, ses preuves mecaniques, 1911; Die Veränderlichen Sterne, 1921. General character of writing: scientific. Rediscovered W. Herschel's nebulosities; made record of the heavens of cosmic nebular clouds. Religion, Catholic. (*)

HAGEN, Louis. *b*: Potsdam, Germany 1916. Journalist. *n.a*: Phœnix Mag '45—46, Sunday Express '46, John Bull '47. *Publ*: Arnhem Lift; Indian Route March. *Ctr*: News Chron, etc. *s.s*: Airborne Fighting, India, Germany. *Rec*: Sailing, swimming. *a*: c/o L. Mohrenwitz, 1 Airlie Gardens, Campden Hill Rd, London, W.8.

HAGER, Alice Rogers. A.B. *b*: Peoria, Illinois. *e*: Stanford & Columb Univs. Reporter, Fell Amer Geog Soc, Mem Women's Nat Press & Overseas Press, etc. *n.a*: Los Angeles Herald 1924, Aviation Rep N. American Newsp Alliance '34—40, Skyways Mag '42—. *Publ*: Wings for the Dragon; Wings over the Americas; Frontier by Air, Brazil takes the Skyroad; Brazil, Giant to the South; Wings to Wear; Big Loop & Little, the Story of the American Cowboy; etc. *Ctr*: N.Y. Times, Washington Star, etc. *s.s*: Aviation. *Rec*: Riding, swimming. *w.s*: War Corres Skyways Mag '42—, China, Burma, India. *a*: 1095 National Press Building, Washington, D.C., U.S.A. *T*: District 5834.

HAGER, KARL: director of the Bavarian state craft institution of Nuremberg; b. Mainz, Germany, Jan. 17, 1868; s. Theodor and Marie (Mayer) H.; educ. Gymnasium of Darmstadt, Dresden and Munich; technical college. DEGREES: Professor; m. Elsa Halm, May 18, 1897. AUTHOR: Berechnung rechteckiger Platten mittels trigonometrischer Reihen, 1911; Vorlesungen über die Theorie des Eisenbetons, 1916; Technischer Wortschatz, 1917. Contributor to Armierter Beton; Zeitschrift Beton; Beton und Eisen; Deutsche Bauzeitung; Der Bau-Ingenieur; Zentralblatt der Bauverwaltung. General character of writing: technical. Was first professor for reinforced concrete construction at Munich; member of technical college; Deutscher Ausschuss für Eisenbeton; Beratendes Mitglied des Deutschen Betonvereins. CLUBS: Architekten- und Ingenieur Verein; Verein deutscher Ingenieure; Gesellschaft der Bauingenieure. Religion, Protestant. OFFICE: Bayerische Landesgewerbeanstalt, Nuremberg. HOME: Gewerbemuseumplatz 2, Nuremberg, Germany.

HAGERTY, Andrew Millar, B.A. *b*: Ballymena Antrim 1877. *m*: (1) Janet Marguerite Brice; (2) Doris Anne Trevor. *s*: 4. *d*: 3. Author, Journalist, Lecturer. *n.a*: Life Mag (Melbourne), The Churchman (Melbourne), Redditch Indicator, Rugby Advertiser, Belfast Telegraph, Counties Press, etc; now F.L. *Publ*: Little Business Books; Fairy Wake & Other Poems; Moral Law in Industry; etc. *c.t*: Leading Lon dailies. Early life Aust. Entered Civil Service. Sec Labour Commssrs & Mines Accident Relief Bd. Princ Gunyah Hse G.S. Sydney, N.S.W. & Head Master Roy Savoy Choir Sc. Dir Ind Research Nat Alliance Employers & Employed (Lon). Asst Dir Publicity Ulster Assoc, etc. *Rec*: Riding, golf. *a*: Ruskin, 182 Herne Hill Rd, Herne Hill, S.E.24, & 33 & 34 Craven St, Strand.

HAGGAR, Reginald George, A.R.C.A. *b*: Ipswich 1905. *e*: Ipswich Sch of Art, Royal Coll of Art. *m*: Dorothy Frances Wood. Artist & Writer, Art Director Minton's Ltd '30—35, Headmaster Stoke-on-Trent Art Sch '34—41, Headmaster Burslem Art Sch '41—45. *Publ*: Recent Ceramic Sculpture in Gt Brit; English Pottery Figures 1660—1860. *Ctr*: Pottery & Glass. *s.s*: English Sculpture, Pottery & Industrial Design. *Rec*: Walking. *a*: Ronson, 337 Stone Rd, Hanford, Stoke-on-Trent. *T*: Trentham 49365.

HAGREEN, Mrs. Philip, B.A. (See Aileen Mary Clegg.) *b*: London 1888. *e*: London Univ & Bedford Coll Lond. *m*: Philip Hagreen. *s*: 1. *d*: 2. Writer. *Publ*: Lourdes; St Bernadette. *Ctr*: Universe, Blackfriars, Catholic Times, etc. *s.s*: Travel, Music. *a*: 1 The Spinney, Ferndale Rd, Burgess Hill, Sussex.

HAGUE, Frances Dorothy. *b*: Sheffield 1882. *e*: Priv. *Publ*: Candied Fruits (short stories); Octave; Poems. *Ctr*: Poetry of To-day, Teacher's World, Weekly Telegraph. *Rec*: Chess. *a*: Fircroft, Devenish Rd, Sunningdale, Berks.

HAHN, E. Adelaide, M.A., Ph.D. *b*: New York 1893. *e*: Hunter Coll & Columb Univ. Prof of Latin & Greek, Chm of Classic Dept Hunter Coll. *Publ*: Co-ordination of Non-Co-ordinate Elements in Virgil. *Ctr*: Various classical journs. *s.s*: Classics, Linguistics. *Rec*: Walking, novel reading, theatre. *a*: 640 Riverside Drive, New York 31, U.S.A. *T*: Wadsworth 6-8071.

HAIG, Sir (Thomas) Wolseley, K.C.I.E., C.S.I., C.M.G., C.B.E., M.A.(T.C.D.). *b*: Woolwich 1865. *e*: Wellington Col Sandhurst. *m*: Beatrice Ferrar (dec). *s*: 1. *d*: 2. Retired. *n.a*: An Ed of Cam Hist of India. *Publ*: Historic Landmarks of the Deccan. *s.s*: Oriental hist & langs. Asst Sec to Govt of India, Foreign Dept 1907. Polit Ag Alwar '07—08. Officiating Polit A.D.C. to Sec of State for India '09—10. H.B.M.'s Consul Kerinan '10. Consul-Gen Meshed '14—16. Consul-Gen Ispahan '16. March Pursuivant '23. Albany Herald '27. Ex-Prof Arabic, Persian & Hindustani, T.C.D. *a*: 34 Gledstanes Rd, W.14.

HAIGH, Douglas. *b*: Goole 1894. *e*: Priv. Married. *s*: 2. Chartered Sec. *n.a*: Ed of Unity 1931. *c.t*: Various tech & other journs. *s.s*: Industrial relations & welfare. *Rec*: Motoring. *c*: R.A.C., etc. *a*: 18 Windermere Av, Wembley, Mddx. *t*: Arnold 4417.

HAIGH, H. *n.a*: Yorkshire Post 1927—47, Bradford Telegraph & Argus '47—. *w.s*: '40—46 R.A.F. *a*: Birchwood Hse, Birchwood Rd, Utley, Keighley, Yorks.

HAIGH, Holden. *b*: Shawforth 1865. L'pool Rep of Shipping World. *n.a*: Reporter Salford Chronicle 1886, Warrington Guardian '89, Liverpool Courier '92, Shipping World '98–. *s.s*: Shipping. *a*: 21 Dale St, L'pool.

HAIKERWAL, B. S. *b*: Lucknow, India 1904. *e*: M.C. Coll Allahabad, Lucknow Univ. *Publ*: Social & Economic Aspects of Crime in India. *Ctr*: I.D.T. (Lucknow), Leader (Allahabad). *s.s*: Criminology, Penology. *Rec*: Tennis, riding. *a*: District Inspector of Schools, Kanpur, U.P., India.

HAILEY, 1st Baron, of Shahpur, Punjab, and Newport Pagnell, Bucks, William Malcolm Hailey, G.C.S.I., G.C.M.G., G.C.I.E., Hon.D.C.L. *b*: Newport Pagnell, Bucks 1872. *e*: Merchant Taylor's Sch & Corpus Christi Coll Oxf. Indian Civil Service (ret). *Publ*: An African Survey; Britain & Her Dependencies; The Future of Colonial Peoples. *s.s*: Empire, particularly Indian & Colonial. *c*: Athenæum. *a*: 16 York Hse, Kensington Church St, London, W.8. *T*: Western 3849.

HAILSHAM, 1st Viscount of, Douglas McGarel Hogg, P.C., K.C., D.C.L., LL.D., Hon.D.Litt. *b*: 1872. *e*:

Eton. *m*: (1) Elizabeth Trimble Brown. *s*: 2. (2) Mildred Parker Dew. Attorney-General 1922—24 & '24—28, Lord Chancellor '28—29 & '35—38, Secretary of State for War & Leader of House of Lords '31—35, K.C. '17, P.C. '22, M.P. (Con) St Marylebone '22—28, Pres Old Etonians' Assoc '28, Sussex C.C.C. '31 & M.C.C. '33, Chm British Empire Cancer Campaign '36—, V-Pres & V-Chm The Polytechnic '02 (founded by his father). *Publ*: Editor Hailsham Edition of Halsbury's Laws of England. *Rec*: Travel. *c*: Athenæum, Carlton, M.C.C. *w.s*: Sth African War 19th Yeomanry, '14—19 County of London Volunteer Regt (Capt & Group Adj), Hon Col Inns of Court Regt 1932—47. *a*: Carter's Corner Place, Hailsham, Sussex. *T*: Hurstmonceux 3119.

HAILSTONE, Jane, S.R.N. *b*: Southsea 1898. *e*: Cheltenham Ladies' Col. *Publ*: Helen Waterfield (1933). *a*: Dean Hse, Newnham, Glos. *t*: 41.

HAIME, John Warren, B.A.(Lond), M.R.S.T., Mem Class Assoc. *b*: Cardiff 1892. *e*: Cardiff H. Sch & Univ Coll of Wales, Aberystwyth. *m*: D. Roberts. Personnel Officer B.O.A.C. *n.a*: Asst Ed 1913 & Ed The Dragon Mag Univ Coll Wales '14. *Ctr*: A.M.A., Journ of Educ Greece & Rome. *Rec*: Gardening. *a*: 22 Heron Rd, Hoylake, Wirral. *T*: 595. The Marxist Philosophy & the Sciences; Science & Everyday Life; Keeping Cool & other Essays; Science in Peace & War; New Paths in Genetics; A Banned Broadcast; Science Advances; etc. *Ctr*: Journ of Physiology, Biochemical Journ, Journ of Genetics, Dly Herald, Dly Express, News Chronicle, etc. *s.s*: Biochemistry, Genetics, etc. *w.s*: '14—19. *Rec*: Gardening, etc. *a*: University College, London. *T*: Museum 8494.

HAINES, Florence Mary. *b*: Ulverston. *e*: Ladies Col Daltongate, Ulverston. G.F.S. Diocesan Head of Dept for Candidates from Institutions & Orphanages (Carlisle 1908-21). G.F.S. Central Head of Candidates '24-25. Dist Commissioner Girl Guides Morecambe, N.W. Lancs '20-27. Mem of Diocesan Counc M/C '21, Blackburn '26-30. *Publ*: The Changing Tear ('18); The G.F.S. Worker's Vade Mecum ('15); Concerning a Blotter ('29). *c.t*: Mothers' U.J., The G.F.S. Mag, The Parents' Review, Jack & Jill, etc. *s.s*: Educ, child study & nat hist. *a*: Croftlands, Lancaster. *t*: 491.

HAINISCH, MICHAEL: writer; b. Aug. 15, 1858; s| Michael and Marianne (Terger) H.; educ. High Sch. (Vienna), Univs. of Leipzig and Vienna. DEGREE: LL.D.; m. Emily Figdor. AUTHOR: Zukunft der Deutsch-Österreicher, 1892; Zur österreichischen Wahlreform, 1895; D. Kampf ums Dasein u. d. Entstehung des Kapitalzinses, 1907; Einige Neue Zahlen z. Statistik d. Deutsch-Österreicher, 1909; Ist der Kapitalzins berechtigt? 1919; D. Landflucht, 1924. Religion: Roman Catholic. HOME: Peratergasse 17, Vienna XIX, Germany.

HAINWORTH, Dr. E. M., M.B.E. *a*: 18 Albion St, Hull.

HAIRE, John E., M.A., M.P. *b*: Portadown, N. Ireland 1908. *e*: Queen's Univ Belfast, Trinity, Dublin, London. *m*: Suzanne Kemeny. *s*: 1. M.P. (Lab) Wycombe Div Bucks since '45, Journalist. *Ctr*: News Chronicle, Observer, News of the World, New Statesman & Nation. *s.s*: Foreign Affairs, esp E. European & Hungarian Parliamentary Affairs, Shakespearean Criticism, European Hist, etc. *Rec*: Tennis, golf, squash, gardening, motoring. *c*: R.A.C. *w.s*: F/Lt R.A.F. Costl Commd, Air Liaison Officer to Admlty, Air Historian to A.M. *a*: 3 Cheyne Gardens, Chelsea, London, S.W.3, & The Platt, Bourne End, Bucks. *T*: Flaxman 6846.

HAIRE, Norman, Ch.M., J.P. (See **Terriss, Wykeham.**) *b*: Sydney 1892. *e*: Fort St Sch, Sydney Univ & Inst of Sexual Science Berlin. Sexologist, Gynæcologist, Obstetrician, Lecturer & Writer, Mem B.M.A., Pres Sex Educ Soc. *n.a*: Ed Marriage Hygiene (England), Co-Ed Sexus, Internat Bd of Eds Anthropos, Ed Cttee Le Probleme Sexuel. *Publ*: Sex Talks; Sex Problems of To-day; Encyclopædia of Sexual Knowledge; Birth Control Methods; Hymen, the Future of Marriage; More Medical Views on Birth Control; Rejuvenation; etc. *Ctr*: Med Sc, lay papers & periodicals. *s.s*: Sexology, Birth Control, Abortion, Sterilisation. *c*: City Livery (Lond) etc. *a*: 127 Harley St, London, W.1. *T*: Welbeck 7840.

HALAS, Frantisek. *b*: Brno 1901. *e*: Higher Elem Sch Brno. *m*: Dr Libuse Rejlova. *s*: 2. Poet, Chief of Publications Dept M.O.I., Chm of Synd of Czech Writers since '45, Mem of Provisional Nat Assembly '45—46, Mem Czech Acad of Sci & Art (Lit Sect) since '45, Asst Ed Plan, Pasmo, Kvart, Doba, Chief Ed. Rozhledy '36—37, Fronta '28, Orbis, Prague '26—45. *Publ*: Poetry, Wide Open; The Cock Defies Death; The Face; Tuning; Hope's Torso; Old Women; The Cuttle Fish; Our Bozena Nemcova. *Ctr*: Kriticky, Mesicnik, Kvart, Doba, Zivot. *s.s*: Poetry. *Rec*: Art & book collecting. *a*: Na Stahlavce 5, Prague XIX, Czechoslovakia. *T*: 621-85.

HALDANE, Charlotte. *b*: Lon. *m*: Prof J. B. S. Haldane, F.R.S. *s*: 1. Writer. *n.a*: Daily Express ed staff '21—25. *Publ*: Man's World; Brother to Bert; I Bring Not Peace; Youth is a Crime; trans from the German Prof Lange's Crime as Destiny. *c.t*: Nat newspapers, periodicals, etc. *Rec*: Music, horticulture. *a*: 16 Pk Village E, N.W.1.

HALDANE, Elizabeth Sanderson, C.H., LL.D., J.P. *b*: Edin 1862. *e*: Priv. *Publ*: Life of Descartes; The British Nurse in Peace & War; Life of George Eliot; The Scotland of Our Fathers, etc. *c.t*: Hastings' Ency of Ethics & Religion, Nineteenth Century, Dictionary of National Biography, etc. Gov of Birkbeck Col, Sc of Econ (Lon Univ). Ex P.C. Rep Gen Nursing Counc. Mem Q.A.I.N. Counc. Pres Perthshire Musical Festival. *Rec*: Reading. *a*: 29 Ashley Pl, S.W.1., & Cloan, Auchterarder, Perthshire. *t*: Vic 5193.

HALDANE, General Sir J. Aylmer L., G.C.M.G., K.C.B., D.S.O. *b*: Edinburgh 1862. *e*: Edin Acad, Wimbledon Sch & R.M.C. Sandhurst. Army (ret), Grand Officer de l'Ordre de la Coronne (Belge), Comm Legion of Honour, Croix de Guerre (French & Belgian), etc. *Publ*: How We Escaped from Pretoria; A Brigade of the Old Army; The Insurrection in Mesopotamia; The Haldanes of Gleneagles. *Rec*: Golf, travel, deer-stalking. *c*: Naval & Military. *w.s*: Sth Africa, Gordon Hgldrs 1914—19 (Despatches 9 times), Gen Off C-in-C Mesopotamia '20—22, '39—45. *a*: 107 Westbourne Ter, London, W.2. *T*: Paddington 0522.

HALDANE, John Burdon Sanderson, F.R.S. *b*: Oxf 1892. *e*: New Coll Oxf & Eton. *m*: Helen Spurway. Prof of Biometry Lond Univ Coll. *n.a*: Chm Ed Bd Dly Worker, Ed Journ of Genetics 1933. *Publ*: Dædalus or Science & the Future; Possible Worlds; Science & Ethics; Enzymes; The Causes of Evolution; The Inequality of Man; Fact & Faith; Heredity & Politics;

HALDANE, John Scott, C.H., M.D., F.R.S., HonLL.D.(Birm & Edin), HonD.Sc(Oxon, Leeds & Witwatersrand), HonScD.(Cam & Dublin). *b*: Edin 1860. *e*: Edin Acad, Edin Univ & Abroad. *m*: Louisa Kathleen Trotter. *s*: 1. *d*: 1. Physiologist & Univ Prof. Dir Mining Research Lab, Birm Univ & Gas Referee Bd of Trade. *n.a*: Jt Ed Journal of Hygiene 1900—. *Publ*: Essays in Philosophical Criticism (Jt Author); Methods of Air Analysis; Mechanism, Life & Personality; Respiration; The Philosophical Basis of Biology; Materialism; The Philosophy of a Biologist; etc. *c.t*: Trans & Proc Roy Soc, Journ of Physiology, Journ of Hygiene, etc. *s.s*: Physiology & Ind Hygiene. Specially Interested in deep diving, high balloon ascents, & everything related to the health & safety of miners. Fell New Col Oxf. *c*: Athenæum. *a*: Cherwell, Oxf. *t*: 5745.

HALDEN, Leon Gilbert, M.A.(Texas). *b*: Austin, Texas 1893. *m*: Sallie Fellman. *s*: 1. Prof Univ of Houston. *Publ*: Japan, Colossus of the Far East; The Currency Problem; Current Problems in Government; Ethiopian Crisis; Red Facism. *Ctr*: Houston Post & Press, Dallas News, South-western Quarterly. *s.s*: Government, Internat Law & Relations. *Rec*: Golf, fishing. *a*: 1801 Rosedale, Houston, Texas, U.S.A. *T*: L.4016.

HALDIN-DAVIS, Hal David. *b*: Blackheath. *e*: Charterhouse, Balliol Col Oxf & Bart's Hosp. *m*: Lily Samuel. Dermatologist. *Publ*: Skin Diseases in General Practice 1922, 2nd Edition; Modern Skin Therapy '31. *c*: Reform. *a*: 52 Harley St, W.1. *t*: Langham 2214.

HALE, A. E. *a*: Dorland Advertising, 14 Regent St, W.1.

HALE, H. R. *n.a*: Dir Hutchinson & Co (Publishers) Ltd., Jarrolds (Publishers) London Ltd, John Long Ltd, Selwyn & Blount Ltd. *a*: Paternoster House, Paternoster Row, E.C.4.

HALE, Lionel. *b*: London 1909. *e*: Charterhouse & Balliol Coll Oxf. Journalist, Dramatist & B.B.C. Broadcaster. *n.a*: Dramatic Critic Daily Mail '45—. *Publ*: (Plays) She Passed Through Lorraine; The Mocking Bird; Festival Time. *a*: Flat 3, 13–16 Embankment Gardens, London, S.W.3. *T*: Flaxman 1957.

HALE, Oron James, M.A., Ph.D. *b*: Goldendale, Washington 1902. *e*: Wash & Penns Univs. *m*: Annette van Winkle. Prof of European History Univ of Va 1929—, Fell Social Sc Research Counc, Mem Amer Hist & Virginia Social Sc Assocs, etc. *Publ*: Germany & the Diplomatic Revolution, a Study in Diplomacy & the Press; The Shadow of War; Publicity & Diplomacy 1890–1914. *Ctr*: Amer Hist Rev, Journ of Mod Hist, Social Forces, Va Quarterly Rev, Annals of Amer Acad, etc. *s.s*: Newspaper Press History, Social Control & Communication by Radio, Military History. *c*: Colonnade, etc. *w.s*: '42–46 Mil Intell Dvn, W.D. General Staff. *a*: Department of History, University of Virginia, Charlottesville, Virginia, U.S.A.

HALE, Sidney Harold. *b*: Apperley 1902. *m*: Rene Niblett. Journalist. *n.a*: Jt Chief Reporter The Citizen Gloucester. *s.s*: Football, cricket, council & court work. *Rec*: Tennis. *a*: Deerhurst, Sisson Rd, Gloucester.

HALE-WHITE, Sir William, K.B.E., M.D. *b*: London 1857. *e*: Framlingham & Guy's Hosp. *m*: Edith Jane Spencer Fripp. *s*: 1. Physician Guy's Hosp. *Publ*: Materia Medica; Great Doctors of the Nineteenth Century; Keats as Doctor & Patient. *Ctr*: Various med journs. *s.s*: Medicine. *c*: Athenæum & Savile. *a*: 24 Warnborough Rd, Oxford. *T*: 4232.

HALECKI, Oscar, Ph.D. *b*: Vienna 1891. *e*: Univs of Cracow, Lyons, Montreal & De Paul. *m*: Helen Sulima Szarlowska. Prof of History Univ of Montreal 1944— *n.a*: Polish Review of Heraldry & Genealogy '30–39, Co-Ed Cambridge History of Poland '36—, etc. *Publ*: History of the Polish-Lithuanian Union 1385–1569; Un Empereur de Byzance à Rome; La Pologne de 963 à 1914: History of Poland: The Crusade of Varna;

The League of Nations; etc. *Ctr*: Various. *s.s*: Central & European History. *a*: Château Lorraine 5 E, Scarsdale, New York, U.S.A. *T*: Sc 3-6032.

HALER, David Henry, M.B., B.S.(Hons)Lon, L.M.S.S.A. *b*: Tottenham 1906. *e*: Bancroft's Sc, Woodford, Essex, King's Col Lon & King's Col Hosp. *m*: Doris Emily Butters. Cons Pathologist. Path The Infants' Hosp '32–, Path Battersea Gen Hosp '31–. *Publ*: Aids to Pathological Technique ('33). *c.t*: Med Press & Circular, Archives of Disease in Childhood, etc. *s.s*: Pathology. B.M.A. Prize Essay on Epidemic Encephalitis '28. *Rec*: Bridge. *c*: B.M.A. Roy Soc Med. *a*: 4 Deauville Mansions, Clapham Pk, S.W.4. *t*: Brixton 1648 & Sloane 4554.

HALER, Percy James, M.B.E., M.Sc(Leeds), B.Sc(Vict), M.I.MechE, Mem Am Soc M.E. *b*: Leeds 1876. *e*: Cent H.S. & Leeds Univ. *m*: Edith Haler. *s*: 2. Princ, Tech Col. *Publ*: 1st Course & 2nd Course Technical Mathematics; 1st & 2nd Course Engineering Science; Text Book on Physics. *c.t*: Proc Amer Soc Mech Engs, Jnr Inst Engs, Amer Machinist, Mech World, Practical Engineering. *s.s*: Engineering, educ. *a*: Tech Col, Leyton, E.10. *t*: Leytonstone 1211.

HALES, A. G. Author. *Publ*: McGlusky, M.P.; Moon of the Devil's Own; Snowey & McGlusky; The Great White Wolf; Ginger & Joan; McGlusky the Trail Blazer; McGlusky's Great Adventure; President McGlusky; etc. *a*: c/o Wright & Brown, 4 Farringdon Ave, E.C.4.

HALES, Ada Matilda Mary. *b*: Brighton. *e*: St Hugh's Coll Oxf. Mem P.E.N. *Publ*: Stories from Chaucer; Leslie; The Puritan's Progress; The Hamlet on the Hill; The Story of Ben-Ban. *c*: Lyceum. *a*: 1 Roman's Place, Writtle, Essex. *T*: Writtle 218.

HALES, D. W. Journalist *a*: 65 Cavendish Ave, Eastbourne.

HALES, Harold Keates. Merchant & Shipper. *Publ*: Harold's Adventures. *c.t*: Rangoon Gazette, Penang Gazette, Straits Times, Statesman, etc. *a*: Selahdale, 6 W. Heath Av, Golder's Green, N.W.11. *t*: Speedwell 1456.

HALÉVY, ÉLIE. French historian, professor in the School of Political Science, Paris; *b*. Etretat, France, Sept. 6, 1870; *s*. Ludovic and Louise (Breguet) H.; educ. Lycée Condorcet, Faculty of Letters of the Univ. of Paris, Ecole Normale Supérieure. DEGREES: Fellow in Philosophy, Litt.D., Hon. Litt.D. (Oxon.), m. Florence Noufflard, 1901. AUTHOR: La Théorie Platonicienne des Sciences, 1890; La Formation du Radicalisme Philosophique (3 vols), 1899-1904 (Eng. transl. under title: The Growth of Philosophic Radicalism, 1928); Histoire du Peuple Anglais au XIX Siècle (3 vols.), 1924-1927; Epilogue (1895-1914), 1926; (vol. 2), 1926; (vol. 3), 1927 (Eng. translations. General character of writing: history. ADDRESS: La maison blanche, Sucy-en-Brie, Seine-et-Oise, France.

HALEY, William John. *b*: Jersey 1901. Journalist. *n.a*: Mang Ed Manchester Evening News, Dir Manchester Guardian, Evening News Ltd. *a*: Manchester Evening News, 3 Cross St, Manchester. *t*: Blackfriars 2345.

HALFORD, Jeannette, O.B.E. *b*: London 1870. *e*: Notting Hill H. Sch Lond & Germany. Hon Sec Nat Assoc of Maternity & Child Welfare Centres for 28 years. *Publ*: Bachelor Girls' Cookery Book. *Rec*: Gardening. *a*: Cottesloe, Cookham, Berks. *T*: Bourne End 739.

HALFORD, Victor Albert, M.J.I. *b*: Lon 1875. *e*: Lon & Heidelberg. *m*: Cecile Black. *s*: 2. *d*: 2. Journalist. *n.a*: Ed Business Adviser 1908-09, Mang Canada '09-18, Dir & Mang Canadian Gazette '18-32. *c.t*: Canadian press. *s.s*: Canada. *Rec*: Reading, chess, theatre, crime, angling. *c*: Canada. *a*: Mellow Rd, Staines, Middx. *t*: Staines 131 & Whitehall 3087.

HALFPENNY, Thomas. *b*: S. Bank 1914. *e*: St Mary's Col, Linthorpe, Middlesborough. Reporter. *n.a*: Cleveland & Middlesbrough Standard Series. *c.t*: London Evening News, World's Press News, Stratford Express, etc. *s.s*: Soccer & tennis. *a*: 11 Costa Rd, S. Bank, Yorkshire. *t*: Redcar 128.

HALL, A., F.I.C.S. *b*: Tulse Hill 1885. *e*: Wesleyan Sc Brixton Hill, Aske's Hatcham Sc. Married. *s*: 1. Chrtd Shipbroker. *Publ*: Handy Guide to Shipping. *s.s*: Shipping & Wireless. *a*: 25 Coombe Gdns, New Malden, Surrey. *t*: Malden 1241.

HALL, Rev. Alfred, M.A., B.D., D.D. (Meadville Theol Sch U.S.A.). *b*: Boston 1873. *e*: Boston Gr Sch, Owen's Coll Manch, Unitarian Coll Manch, St Catherine's & Manch Coll Oxf, Berlin Univ. *m*: Amy Mary Sudbery. *s*: 1. *d*: 4. Unitarian Min Lincoln Unitarian Chapel 1939—, Pres Manch Coll Oxf '45—. *Publ*: The Beliefs of a Unitarian; Jesus & Christianity in the Twentieth Century; Religious Problems of Laymen; James Martineau; Aspects of Modern Unitarianism (ed & jt author). *Ctr*: The Inquirer. *s.s*: Theology. *Rec*: Gardening. *a*: 82 Yarborough Cres, Lincoln. *T*: 10001.

HALL, Sir Alfred Daniel, K.C.B., F.R.S., Hon LL.D.(Cam, Aber), Hon D.Sc(Oxf). *b*: Rochdale 1864. *e*: M/C G.S., Balliol Col Oxf. *m*: Ida Scott Audsley Beaver. *s*: 1. Dir John Innes Horticultural Inst, Chief Scientific Adviser Ministry of Agriculture. *Publ*: The Soil; Pilgrimage of British Farming; The Book of the Tulip; Digressions of a Man of Science; etc. *c.t*: Times, Saturday Review, New Statesman, Observer. *s.s*: Agriculture & horticulture. *Rec*: Fishing, oriental art. *c*: Athenæum, Savile. *a*: The Manor House, Merton, S.W.20. *t*: Lib 3769.

HALL, Sir Arthur Edward, Kt., K.B.E., C.B., C.St.J. *b*: Swindon 1885. *e*: Roy Coll of Science London. *m*: Constance Martha Gibbens. *s*: 1. *d*: 1. Instructor Rear-Admiral R.N. Dir, Educ Dept Admlty 1936—45, Dir of Studies & Dean R.N. Coll Greenwich since '46, Vice-Chm R.N. War Library. *Publ*: Ed Phœnix (Imp Coll Sci) '07, '09—15 & of Scientific & Service publications. *Ctr*: The Academy, Times & Engineering Supplement, Mariners' Mirror. *s.s*: Education. *Rec*: Travel, music. *c*: Authors, Junior United Service. *a*: 10 Liskeard Gardens, London, S.E.3. *T*: Greenwich 2263.

HALL, Arthur Henry, C.B.E., M.I.C.E., F.R.AeS. *b*: Clifton 1876. *e*: Clifton Col & Trinity Hall Cam. *m*: Maud Henrietta Webster. *s*: 2. Mech Eng. *c.t*: Photographic Journals, Country Life, Illus London News, Gardening papers, etc. *s.s*: Photography, ornithology, dry fly-fishing. Now Chief Supt Roy Aircraft Est, Farnboro'. Dir Mine & Torpedo Production Admiralty '17 till Armistice. Later Controller various sections of Disposal Bd. *Rec*: Fishing, ornithology, photography, gardening. *c*: Authors. *a*: Woodlands, Farnboro,' Hants.

HALL, Arthur J., M.A., M.D., D.Sc, F.R.C.P. *Publ*: Epidemic Encephalitis. *a*: 342 Glossop Rd, Sheffield.

HALL, Rev. Arthur Vine. *b*: Luddendfoot, Yorks 1862. *e*: Hastings & Cheshunt Coll Cambridge. *m*: (1) Constance Pate; (2) Kate van Cappelle. *d*: 1. Clerk in Holy Orders. *Publ*: South Africa & Other Poems; Katrina & Other Poems; Table Mountain & Other Poems; Round the Camp Fire in East Africa; Poems of a South African; Childland; Fruit from an Old Tree; etc. *s.s*: Poetry. *Rec*: Billiards. *a*: Tecoma, Bowwood Rd, Claremont, Cape Town, South Africa.

HALL, C. G. *b*: Middlesbro' 1900. *e*: Middlesbro' H.S. Reporter. *n.a*: N.E. Daily Gazette, Middlesbro' '16, Newcastle Chron Publ's '26, N.E. Press Services, Newcastle (F. L. Agency) '31, Daily Express '33. *s.s*: Ind & Crime. *a*: 28 Clayton St W., Newcastle-on-Tyne. *t*: 27021.

HALL, Rev. Charles Albert. *b*: Peterborough 1872. *e*: Deacon's Sch, Peterborough & New Church Coll. *m*: Annie Unwin. *s*: 2. Minister of Religion & Author, Fell Roy Micros Soc. *n.a*: Ed New Church Herald 1920—42. *Publ*: Plant Life; Wild Flowers in their Haunts; Open Book of Nature; Ants, Bees & Wasps; British Birds' Eggs & Nests; How to Use the Microscope; etc. *Ctr*: Amateur Gardening. *s.s*: Plant Life & General Nature Study, Photography of Wild Plants. *Rec*: Gardening, photography. *a*: Clynder, 71 Lansdowne Rd, Worthing, Sussex. *T*: Worthing 1133.

HALL, Rev. Charles William. *b*: Lon 1877. *m*: Christine B. J. Pottinger. *s*: 2. *d*: 1. *n.a*: Liskeard & District Free Churchman 1905–10. *Publ*: Old End & New Beginnings; etc. *c.t*: Bucks Advertiser, Herts & Essex Observer, Daily News & Chronicle, occas Daily Herald '29–31 as The Labour Organiser. Ex-Parl Cand. 3 y in Army, 10 y R.A.F. with equivalent rank of Major. Mang Elem Sc Hadham Herts '31–. *Rec*: Golf. *c*: Past Prov Grand Chap Freemasons (Bucks). *a*: The Manse, Briston, Melton Constable, Norfolk.

HALL, Cyril. *b*: London 1884. *e*: Whitgift Gr Sch. *m*: Hilda Clare Partridge. Author & Publisher's Ed. *Publ*: Conquests of Engineering; Treasures of the Earth; The Sea & its Wonders; Round the Great World; Everyday Science; The Green Earth; Living in Boats; Leave to Presume the Death. *s.s*: Horticulture & Popular Science. *Rec*: Gardening. *a*: Old Farm, Wootton, New Milton, Hants.

HALL, DANIEL GEORGE EDWARD: university professor of history; b. Offey, Hitchin, Eng., Nov. 17, 1891; s. Daniel and Elinor Ann (Field) H.; educ. Hitchin Grammar Sch., King's Coll., London Sch. of Economics, Inst. of Historical Research (all Univ. of London); DEGREES: M. A. (London); m. Helen Eugenie Banks, Aug. 6, 1919. AUTHOR: Imperialism in Modern History, 1923; A Brief Survey of English Constitutional History, 1925; The League of Nations (a Handbook for Teachers in India and Ceylon), 1926; Early English Intercourse with Burma, 1587-1743, 1928. At present engaged in editing correspondence of Lord Dalhousie with Sir Arthur Phayre, 1852-1856. Contributor to History (Quarterly journ. Hist. Assn.), Journ. of the Burma Research Soc., Rangoon Gazette. General character of writing: historical research. Mem. Burma Legislature council, 1923-24; Prof. of History, Univ. Rangoon, since 1921; corres. mem. Indian Hist. Records Comm. since 1925. Fellow Royal Hist. Soc. Relig. denom., Congregationalist. CLUB: Rangoon Boat. OFFICE: University College. HOME: University Estate, **Rangoon, Burma, India.**

HALL, Donald John. *b*: Oxford 1903. *e*: Shrewsbury Sc & Corpus Christi Col Camb. *m*: Isabel Compton. *s*: 1. *d*: 1. Author. *Publ*: Enchanted Sand—A New Mexican Pilgrimage; Romanian Furrow. *c.t*: Various. *s.s*: Travel. *Rec*: Travelling. *a*: c/o A. D. Peters, 4 & 5 Adam St, Adelphia, W.C.1.

HALL, Eleanor Dunbar. *b*: Bury, Lancs. *e*: Bury Girls' Gr Sch. *m*: Thomas Clough. Journalist, Novelist

& Short Story Writer. *n.a*: Manch Ev Chron, Dly Dispatch, Dly Express. *Publ*: Alliance; Winter's Night; The Acceptable Woman; The Changing Three; Six Rays to the Rising Sun; High Romance; Tambour Terrace; Dauntless Needle. *s.s*: Magazine Stories. *Ctr*: Woman's Journ & Pictorial. *c*: Women's Press & S.W.J. *a*: 20 Wellington Rd, Bury, Lancs.

HALL, Evans Spencer. *b*: Fort Adams, Mississippi 1889. *e*: Pub Scs, Comm Col & Tulane Univ. *m*: Violet Mildred Ashley. *d*: 1. Novelist *Publ*: Love Fetish; The No-Nation Girl; Danger; River God: etc. *c.t*: McClure's Mag, People's Home Journal, The Echo, Telling Tales, The Modern Thinker, etc. *s.s*: Psychology. *Rec*: Shooting, fishing, swimming, etc. *a*: 432 Calhoun St, New Orleans, Louisiana, U.S.A.

HALL, Frederick James Simkin. M.B., B.S., F.R.C.S., M.R.C.S., L.R.C.P. Surgeon. *c.t*: B.M.J. *a*: Courtlands, Walmer, Kent. *t*: Deal 404.

HALL, Geoffrey Fowler. C.I.E., M.C., A.C.G.I. *b*: Surbiton 1888. *e*: Marlborough Coll & Cent Tech Coll of Lond Univ. *m*: Nellie Kate Pidduck. *s*: 1. Indian Service of Eng (ret), Commissioned R.E. Sp Res & Reg Army Res of Off 1910—38. *Publ*: Moths Round the Flame; The Guru's Ring & Other Stories; The Dragon & the Twisted Stick; A Parisienne's Notebook (trs). *Ctr*: Statesman, Ill Weekly of India, Onlooker, New Horizons, Patiala Post. *Rec*: Golf. *c*: Junior Army & Navy. *a*: c/o Imperial Bank of India, 25 Old Broad St, London, E.C.2.

HALL, George Rome. M.S., M.D. *b*: Birtley, Northumberland 1864. *e*: Durham Sc, Sc of Medicine Univ of Durham. *m*: Margaret Jane Woods. *s*: 3. *d*: 2. Med practitioner. *Publ*: Pamphlet—The Atom, the Etherion & the Beyond. *c.t*: Med World, Medical Press & Circular, Journ of Tropical Medicine, West Africa, Masonic Record, Psychic Science. *s.s*: Biology, the early stages of disease, archæology, primitive hist. *Rec*: Natural hist, West African Med Staff 1893—1903, R. A. F. Med Staff '23—26. *c*: Fell Royal Empire Soc, Fell Royal Inst of Public Health, Mem United Services Sect of Royal Soc of Medicine. *a*: c/o Royal Empire Society, Northumberland Ave, W.C.2.

HALL, Gladys Mary, M.A. *a*: c/o The Penn Club, 9 Tavistock Sq, W.C.1.

HALL, Henry Lindsay, M.A., DipEd. Teacher. *Publ*: Victoria's Part in the Australia Federation Movement. *a*: 7 Cambridge Rd, S.W.11.

HALL, Henry Noble, C.B.E. *b*: Penge 1872. *e*: King's Sch Canterbury, Victoria Coll Jersey & Sorbonne Paris. *m*: (1) Suzanne Arot (dec'd); (2) Jean Oertel. Journalist, Writer, Lecturer, Off Leg d'Honn (France), Kt of Order of Leopold (Belge), Free-lance in U.S.A. since 1941. *n.a*: Paris Corres Cyclist, Ed & Prop The Pioneer Trinidad '03, Ed Broadway News N.Y. '06, Diplomatic Corres N.Y. World '09, Washington Corres The Times' 17. *Publ*: I Took the Isthmus; Why Palestine; & various translations. *s.s*: Editing English Books for American Market, Internat, Finan, Econ, Social & Polit Affairs. *c*: O'seas Press, Adventurer's, Dutch Treat. *a*: 150 East 49th St, New York, N.Y., U.S.A. *T*: Plaza 5-8862.

HALL, Herbert Leslie. Director William Heinemann Ltd, William Heinemann (Med Books) Ltd, Heinemann Holdings Ltd, Peter Davies Ltd, Heinemann & Zsolnay,

The World's Work Ltd. *Publ*: The Four Horsemen Ride. *a*: Manton, Walton-on-the-Hill.

HALL, Ion Simson, M.B., Ch.B., F.R.C.P.E., F.R.C.S.E. *b*: Glasgow 1896. *e*: George Watson's Coll, Univs of Edinburgh & Paris. *m*: Kathleen Scott Troup, B.Sc. Hon Surgeon Roy Infirmary Edinburgh, B.M.A. (Counc Member). *Publ*: Diseases of Nose, Throat & Ear & Sections on same to Miles & Thomson's Manual & Index of Treatment. *Ctr*: Journ of Laryngology & Otology, B.M.J., Edin M.J., Practitioner, Procs of Roy Soc of Med. *s.s*: Diseases of Nose, Throat & Ear (Oto-Rhino-Laryngology). *Rec*: Golf, fishing, shooting, ski-ing, gardening. *c*: University & Hon Co of Edinburgh Golfers. *a*: 14 Moray Pl, Edinburgh. *T*: 77476.

HALL, Isaac Walker, M.D. *b*: Lincoln. *e*: Victoria Univ. *m*: Anna Maria Carlson. *d*: 1. Dir Preventive Med Dept, Bristol Univ; Ex-Prof Pathology, Bristol Univ. *Publ*: Purin Bodies; Methods of Morbid Histology; Ed, Metabolism & Practical Medicine. *c.t*: Journal of Pathology & med journals. *s.s*: Pathology, Bio-Chem. *Rec*: Gardening. *a*: Shortwood Lodge, Pucklechurch, Glos & 218 Redland Rd, Bristol. *t*: Fishponds 176 & Bristol 34324.

HALL, John Arrowsmith. *b*: Fenny Stratford 1897. *e*: Alexander Hse Broadstairs & Northampton Sc. *m*: Dorothy Irene Botten. Bank Clerk. *Publ*: Hikes in Kent & Sussex; Rambles From Chichester. *c.t*: Articles in health magazines, short stories. *s.s*: Health & walking tours. *Rec*: Hiking, swimming, gardening. *a*: "Heyton", Salisbury Ave, Broadstairs, Kent.

HALL, John Herbert, M.A., LL.M. *b*: Southland N.Z. 1897. *e*: Gore H. Sch New Zealand, Canterbury Coll & Univ of Otago. *m*: Ina McKenzie. *s*: 1. *d*: 1. Journalist. *n.a*: Rep Southland Times, Parl Rep The Sun Christchurch, Cable Sub-Ed The Press Christchurch, Ed Hawera Star, Ed The Sun Christchurch, Ed The Dominion Wellington, War Corres & P.R.O. to N.Z.E.F., Supervisor of Talks N.Z. Broadcasting Service. *s.s*: New Zealand Econs & Polits, Farming, Broadcasting. *a*: New Zealand Broadcasting Service, Wellington, N.Z.

HALL, Julian Henry, B.A.(Oxon). *b*: Orchard Siding, Cape Province S.A. 1907. *e*: Eton Coll & Balliol Coll Oxf. Author, Ed Colour '31—32. *Publ*: The Senior Commoner; Laura Seaborne; Two Exiles; Alma Mater, or the Future of Oxford & Cambridge. *w.s*: Intell Corps '39—45. *a*: Garrick Club, Garrick St, London, W.C.2.

HALL, Manly Palmer. *b*: Peterboro, Canada 1901. *e*: Hgh Sch. Author & Lecturer. *Publ*: Encyclopædic Outline of Masonic, Hermetic, Cabalistic & Rosicrucian Symbolical Philosophy; Lectures on Ancient Philosophy; Man, the Grand Symbol of the Universe; Lost Keys of Masonry; The Phœnix; Healing, the Divine Art; Journey in Truth; First Principles of Philosophy. *s.s*: Comparative Religion, Philosophy. *Rec*: Philately. *a*: 3341 Griffith Park Boulevard, Los Angeles 27, California, U.S.A. *T*: Morningside 1-2222.

HALL, Marie. Violinist. *c.t*: Articles on Music. *a*: Inveresk, Cheltenham. *t*: 2303.

HALL, P. E. Asst-Ed Daily Herald. *a*: Wilson St, Long Acre, London, W.C.2.

HALL, Radclyffe. *b*: Bournemouth. *e*: Lon Univ. Novelist. Formerly on Counc of Soc for Psychical Research. *Publ*: The Forge (1924); The Unlit Lamp; A Saturday Life; Adam's Breed ('26); The Well of Loneliness ('28); The Master of the House; Miss Ogilvy

Finds Herself ('34); etc. Received for Adam's Breed, James Tait Black Meml Prize, Femina Vie Heureuse Prize, Eichelberger Gold Humane Award. *Rec*: Collecting old oak, breeding, showing & judging pedigree dogs. *a*: The Forecastle, The Huckstepps, Rye, Sussex.

HALL, Richard Watson. *b*: Cockermouth 1882. *e*: Bootham Sch York. *m*: Frances Lilian Brooker. *d*: 1. *Publ*: On Cumbrian Fells; The Art of Mountain Tramping. *Ctr*: Whitehaven News, W. Cumberland News, Everyman, The Hiker & Camper, Mountaineering Journ, etc. *s.s*: Climbing, Camping, Canoeing. *c*: P.E.N., Fell & Rock Climbing. *w.s*: Friends' Ambulance Unit. *a*: 7 Castlegate Drive, Cockermouth.

HALL, Robert, F.R.S., F.L.S., C.M.Z.S. *b*: Lal Lal, Victoria, Australia 1867. *e*: Scotch Coll Melbourne, Univ of Tasmania. *m*: Edith Mary Giblin. Naturalist *Publ*: Key to the Birds of Australia; Useful Birds of South Australia; Insectivorous Birds of Victoria; Australian Bird Maps. *Rec*: Gardening. *a*: Little Grange, Sandy Bay Rd, Hobart, Tasmania, Australia. *T*: 4105.

HALL, Robert Lowe. *b*: Tenterfield, N.S.W. 1901. *e*: Ipswich Gr Sch, Univ of Queensland & Magdalen Coll Oxf. *m*: Laura Margaret Linfoot. *d*: 2. Director Econ Section Cabinet Office. *Publ*: The Economic System in a Socialist State; Earning & Spending. *Ctr*: Econ Journ, Oxford Econ Papers. *s.s*: Economics. *Rec*: Walking, chess. *c*: Reform. *a*: Trinity College, Oxford. *T*: 3116.

HALL, Stephen Barton, M.D., Ch.B., D.P.M. Physician, Cons Psychiatrist. *c.t*: Lancet, B.M.J., Practitioner, etc. *a*: 8 Rodney St, L'pool 1. *t*: Royal 3993.

HALL, T. *n.a*: Sports Ed Newcastle Evening Chron & Sunday Sun Newcastle. *a*: 26 Ivanhoe, Monkseaton, Northumberland.

HALL, T. Walter, HonM.A.(Sheffield), F.S.A., F.R.HistS., F.S.G. *b*: Sheffield 1862. *e*: Sheffield. Solicitor (ret). *Publ*: Sheffield Pedigrees (vol i, 1909); Jackson Collection at Sheffield ('14); Sheffield & Rotherham Charters; Wincobank Charters; Brooke-Taylor Collection; Hawksyard ('22); Sheffield Manorial Records (vol i); Waldershelf Manor ('30); The Aula in Hallam; The Fairbanks of Sheffield; Elton; (edtd 5 vols) Sheffield Parish Register '18–27; etc. *c.t*: Book reviews for the Soc of Genealogists. *s.s*: The trans & publication of ancient hist records relating to the city of Sheffield & outlying districts. *c*: Sheffield & Jr Constitutional. *a*: 6 Gladstone Rd, Ranmoor, Sheffield 10.

HALL, Rev. Thomas Schoales, B.A., B.D. *b*: Enniskillen, Ireland 1860. *e*: T.C.D. *m*: Mary M. Potter. *s*: 3. *d*: 1. *Publ*: South America & the South American Missionary Society, for S.A.M.S.; Is Infant Baptism Scriptural?; Ask What I Shall Give Thee. Vice-Pres S.A.M.S. *a*: 1 Wellington Pk Terr, Belfast.

HALL, Thomas Smith. *b*: Northampton 1896. *e*: Counc Schs. *m*: Catherine Beatrice Stewart. *s*: 2. *d*: 1. Civil Servant, Founder Glasgow & W. Scotland Fed of Ramblers. *n.a*: Ed Wayfaring Year Book 1929—. *Publ*: Citizen Rambles, Glasgow; Rambles near Glasgow; Rambles near Falkirk; Tramping in Arran; Firth of Clyde Holiday Haunts; Tramping Holidays in Scotland; Walking Tours in England & Wales; etc. *Ctr*: Weekly Scotsman, etc. *s.s*: Tramping, Building Mountain Indicators, Camp Organisation. *Rec*: Travel & mountaineering. *a*: 4 Heugh St, Falkirk, Scotland. *T*: 1408.

HALL, Thomas William. F.R.P.S.L., F.R.E.S. *e*: Collegiate, Sheffield. Solicitor. *n.a*: Ed The London Philatelist '17—. *Publ*: Stamps of Venezuela. *c.t*: Various Philatelic Journs. *s.s*: Philately, Entomology. *c*: Pres Roy Philatelic Soc (6 y), & Chm Expert Com. *a*: 61 West Smithfield, London. *t*: National 0855.

HALL, W. Arnold. *n.a*: Ed One & All. *a*: 30 Bloomsbury St, London, W.C.1. *T*: Museum 1056.

HALL, W. Glenvil. *b*: Almeley, Herefords 1887. *m*: Rachel Bury Sanderson. *s*: 1. *d*: 1. Barrister-at-Law. *n.a*: Dir John Quill Ltd, Lit, Lect & Dramatic Agents. *Publ*: The Green Triangle. *c.t*: Numerous daily & weekly publ's. War Service 1914–19; wounded; despatches. M.P. Cent Portsmouth '29–31. *c*: Paternosters. *a*: 78 Eaton Terr, S.W.1. *t*: Sloane 6514.

HALL, William. *b*: Fleetwood Lancs 1908. *e*: Poulton le Fylde. Journalist. *n.a*: Preston Herald ('26), Lancaster Observer ('27), Lancashire Daily Post ('29). Hon Sec Preston & Dist Br of N.U.J. *Rec*: Golf & swimming. *c*: Preston Guildhall, Conservative. *a*: 127 Fishergate Preston, Lancs. *t*: 4841.

HALL, William Winslow, M.B., C.M., M.D., M.R.C.S. Ret. *Publ*: Human Verses (1895); Applied Religion; The Clodhopper, A Development in Verse; The Prayer Quest; A Physiological Extension; Metred Playlets; The Peacemaker; A Retrospective Forecast; Corfe Castle Ballads (1927); The Seven Chines; etc. *a*: 50 Seaward Av, Bournemouth, Hants.

HALLACK, Cecily. *b*: Sussex 1898. *e*: Alice Otley Sc Worcester. *Publ*: Beardless Counsellors; Swordblade of Michael; Candlelight Attic; The Sunny Wall; Miss Becky O'Toole. (Books for children)— For the Smallest Person; Having an Angel Guardian; The Small Person's Confession & Communion Book; etc. *s.s*: Choosing writers & artists for children's books.

HALLAR, Soeren, M.Sc., Ph.D. *b*: Thisted, Jutland 1887. *e*: Univs of Copenhagen, Paris & Rome. *m*: Kirsten Andersen. *d*: 2. Librarian Univ & Drama Library Copenhagen. *Publ*: Books About Modern Danish Authors, Sophus Claussen — Tom Kristensen — Jacob Paludan — Leck Fischer; Beyond the Ocean; East of Suez; Two Plays; Two Radio Plays; Poems; etc. *Ctr*: Various articles & reviews. *s.s*: Modern Danish Literature. *Rec*: Travel, gardening. *c*: Danish Authors. *a*: Tordenskjoldsgade 21, Copenhagen K, Denmark, or University Library, I, Copenhagen. *T*: Palae 4503 & Byen 409.

HALLETT, C. G. H., M.A.(Cantab), M.I.H.V.E. *Publ*: Articles on electric heating, etc. Lt-Com R.N. (ret). *a*: Airlie, Littleworth Ave, Esher, Surrey.

HALLETT, Harold Foster, M.A., D.Litt. *b*: 1886. *e*: B'ton Sec Sch & Tech Coll, Lond Univ, Edin Univ. Prof of Philos in Lond Univ & Head of Dept of Philos at King's Coll Lond 1931—, Mem Delegacy K.C.L. '45—, Chm of Exam in Philos Lond Univ '38—. *Publ*: Aeternitas. *Ctr*: Mind, Proc Aristotleian Soc, Philosophy, Récherches Philosophiques, Septimana Spinozana, etc. *s.s*: Philos of Spinoza, Ethics, Epistemology, Metaphysics. *Rec*: Painting, walking, golf. *a*: King's Coll, Strand, London, W.C.2.

HALLETT, Rt. Rev. Mgr. Philip Edward, B.A.(Lond). *b*: London 1884. *e*: St Mary's Coll Woolhampton, St John's Seminary Wonersh & Univ of Innsbruck. Catholic Priest, Rector of St John's Seminary Wonersh 1924—47, Domestic Prelate to H.H. the Pope '29,

Protonotary Apostolic '39. *n.a*: Vice-Chm Catholic Truth Soc. *Publ*: A Son a Priest; Trans of the Life & Illustrious Martyrdom of Sir Thomas More (from Latin of Thos Stapleton); Trans of Spiritual Exercises & Devotions of Blessed Robert Southwell, S.J.; Trans St John Fisher's Defence of the Priesthood; Edited Sir Thomas More's Utopia, Dialogue of Comfort & History of Passion. *Ctr*: Dublin Rev, Tablet, Catholic Med Guardian, Clergy Rev, Univ, Cath Herald, Cath Times, etc. *s.s*: Cath Moral Sci, Lives & Writings of Sir Thomas More & Cardinal Fisher of Rochester. *a*: The Grange, Ashtead, Surrey. *T*: Ashtead 78.

HALLETT, R. C. J. *n.a*: Clapham Observer. *a*: May Blossom, Picardy Manor Way, Belvedere, Kent.

HALLEWELL, H. G. Leveson. *n.a*: Ed Torquay Standard. *s.s*: Politics. *a*: 38 Fleet St, Torquay.

HALLIBURTON, Richard, B.A.(Princeton). *b*: Memphis, Tennessee 1900. *e*: Lawrenceville Prep Sc, Princeton Univ. *Publ*: The Royal Road to Romance; The Glorious Adventure; New Worlds to Conquer; The Flying Carpet; Seven League Boots. *c.t*: American mags & N/ps. *s.s*: Travel, adventure. Swam the Panama Canal from Atlantic to Pacific '28. Flew in Flying Carpet to Timbuctoo & Borneo '31. Rode own elephant over the Alps (Gt St Bernard Pass) to retrace the military march of Hannibal ('35). Foreign Corr & Feature Writer for N/p Syndicates. *Rec*: Flying, swimming. *a*: c/o Geoffrey Bles, 2 Manchester Square, W.1.

HALLIDAY, Brett. *Publ*: Michael Shayne Investigates; Michael Shayne Takes a Hand; Michael Shayne's Long Chance, etc. *a*: c/o A. M. Heath & Co Ltd, Princes Hse, Jermyn St, London, S.W.1.

HALLIDAY, James Lorimer, M.D., D.P.H. *b*: Dumfries 1897. *e*: Dumfries Acad & Glasgow Univ. *m*: Beryl Grieve. *d*: 2. *Publ*: Psychosocial Medicine; etc. *Ctr*: B.M.J., Lancet, Brit Journ of Med Psychology, etc. *s.s*: Psychosomatic Medicine & Emotional Aspects of Bodily Illnesses, Rheumatism. *a*: Airlie, Thornliebank, Glasgow. *T*: Giffnock 1365.

HALLIDAY, John. Exam in Craftwork Oxf Locals Del, late Organiser of Handwork. *Publ*: Bookbinding as a Handwork Subject; Upholstery in Schools (collab); Modern Teaching (pt vols); Practical Senior Teacher (pt); etc. *Ctr*: Teachers' World, Schoolmaster, Schoolmistress, Education Outlook. *s.s*: Crafts, Teaching & Lect on Design & Colour. *a*: 29 Capel Close, Oxford.

HALLIDAY, Lieut. Sydney, R.N.V.R., F.R.S.A. *b*: Redhill, Surrey 1919. *e*: Privately. *m*: Betty Matilda Dorothy Martin. *s*: 2. Technical Representative. *Publ*: 500 Questions & Answers for Sailors & Sea Cadets. *Ctr*: London Opinion, Gas World, Drapers' Record, Nursing Mirror, Animal Ways, France, The Légionaire. *s.s*: Nautical Subjects. *Rec*: Gardening, travel, flying. *a*: 18 Thorncroft Rd, Portsmouth, Hants.

HALLIDAY, Thomas Symington, F.R.S.A. *b*: Thornhill, Dumfriesshire 1902. *e*: Carronbridge, Ayr Acad & Glasgow Sch of Art. *m*: Agnes Morris Barr. Sculptor & Painter, Teacher, Mem Soc of Scottish Artists & New Art Club. *Publ*: Scottish Sculpture; British Birds; Scottish Castles. *Ctr*: Scottish Field, Scotsman, Life & Work, Scots Mag. *s.s*: Art & Nature. *Rec*: Walking, bird watching. *c*: R.A.S.C. *a*: 9 Hill Cres, Wormit, Dundee. *T*: Wormit 2152.

HALLIDAY, Wilfrid Joseph, M.A. *b*: Pudsey 1889. *e*: City of Leeds Sc & Leeds Univ. *m*: Winifred Kirkwood. *s*: 1. Second Master, Pudsey G.S. *n.a*: Editorial Sec Yorks Dialect Soc. *Publ*: Soldier Poets (1916); Pro Patria; Refining Fires; The Shoemaker's Holiday; The Gentle Craft; Minor Poems of John Milton; etc. *c.t*: Yorks Evening Post, Observer, News-Chron, etc. *s.s*: Dialect & folklore. *Rec*: Tennis, cross-words. *a*: Gavrelle, Armley Grange Drive, Leeds 12.

HALLIDAY, William Reginald, M.A., B.Litt, Hon LL.D.(Glas). Princ King's Col Lon. *Publ*: Greek Divination; The Growth of the City State; Indo-European Folk Tales and Greek Legend; etc. *c.t*: Cam Ancient Hist, Encyclopædia Britannica, Folklore, etc. *a*: 2 Upper Phillimore Gdns, W.8. *t*: Western 5556.

HALLIS, Frederick. *b*: Sth Africa 1901. *e*: Balliol Coll Oxf. *m*: Helga Stang. Barrister. *Publ*: Corporate Personality, a Study in Jurisprudence; The Law & Obscenity. *s.s*: Jurisprudence, Political Philosophy. *Rec*: Fishing, travel, yachting. *a*: 6 Crown Office Row, Inner Temple, London, E.C.4. *T*: Central 2729.

HALLIWELL, Arthur Clare, B.A., M.B., B.Ch (Cantab), F.R.C.S.(Eng). *b*: Lees 1896. *e*: Cam & St Thomas's Hosp. *m*: Winifred Dorothea Goode. *s*: 2. *d*: 1. Surgeon. *c.t*: Brit Journ of Surgery, B.M.J., Clin Journ, etc. *s.s*: Insects. Surg Probationer R.N.V.R., Surg-Lieut R.N. 1916–19, Ex-Res Asst Surg St Thomas's Hosp. *Rec*: Nat hist. *c*: Fell Roy Ent Soc, Mem B.M.A. *a*: 1 Cæsarea Pl, Jersey, C.I. *t*: 1434.

HALLOWES, Rev. Kenneth Knight, M.A., F.G.S., A.R.S.M., A.InstM.M., F.R.M.S., F.InstP., M.R.S.L. *b*: Barnsley 1879. *e*: K.E. VI G.S. Birm, Gonville & Caius Cols Cam. *m*: Augusta Manly. Vicar of Lingen. Govt Geologist H.M. Geol Survey of India 1905–26. *Publ*: The Poetry of Geology (1933); Songs of War & Patriotism (2nd edn '20); Poems of Science, or Pages of Indian Earth History ('23); Chimes from Leighton's Church Tower ('33); etc. *c.r*: Westmorland Gazette, Hunts Post, Hereford Times, Times, etc. *s.s*: Poetry of sci, religion. Founder with Sir Ronald Ross, New Sc of Poetry, The Poetry of Sci '28–31. Vicar of Pempesford, Cam '28–31. Vicar of Leighton-Bromswold, Hunts '31–33. *Rec*: Rowing, fishing. *c*: Huntingdon County. *a*: Lingen Vicarage, Bucknell, Salop.

HALLOWS, Ralph Watson, T.D., M.A., M.I.E.E. *b*: Doncaster. *e*: Felsted Sch & Magdalene Coll Camb. *m*: Muriel Smith. *s*: 3. Author. *Publ*: Radar; Radiolocation Simply Explained; Television; Wireless Simply Explained; etc. *Ctr*: Wireless World & other Tech Journs in Gt Britain, France & U.S.A. *s.s*: Wireless. *Rec*: Shooting, salmon & trout fishing. *c*: Constitutional. *a*: 70 Cross Oak Rd, Berkhamsted, Herts. *T*: 156.

HALLPIKE, C. S., M.R.C.P.(Lon). Foulerton Student of Roy Soc, Ferens Inst Otology Middlesex Hosp, Late Rockefeller Travelling Fell. *a*: 6 Vaughan Ave, Chiswick. W.6.

HALLS, Leonard. *b*: Leytonstone 1893. *e*: Cann Hall Sch, West Ham Tech Inst. *m*: Hilda May Harvey. *d*: 1. Author & Journalist, Editor. Mem N.U.J. *n.a*: Ed Boy's Own Paper 1942—, former Sub-Ed A.P. '10–16, '19—29 & Ed '30—33. *s.s*: Fiction for Women, Adaptations from Films & Novels. *Rec*: Reading, photography. *a*: Atcroft, 36 Bunns Lne, Mill Hill, London, N.W.7. *T*: Mill Hill 3850.

HALLS, Wm. John. *b*: Bristol 1869. Married. *s*: 2. *d*: 2. Journalist. *n.a*: N. Devon Journ Barnstaple 50 y, Chief Rep & Acting Ed 30 y. First Chm N.

Devon Br N.U.J. 1912–25. Resigned post on becoming a Dir of N. Devon Journ Ltd, but since continued to be (voluntarily) an hon mem of N.U.J. Also a Dir of Barnstaple Freehold Land Soc, one of the oldest & most influential insts of its kind in W. of Eng. *Rec*: Chess. *c*: Barnstaple Lib, Pres '29–33. *a*: 2 Kingsley's, Landkey Rd, Barnstaple, N. Devon.

HALLSWORTH, Harry Mainwaring, M.A., M.ComB.Sc., C.B.E.(civ), O.B.E.(Mil). *b*: Oldham 1876. *e*: Manchester Univ. David Dale Prof of Econ, Armstrong Col, Newcastle-on-Tyne. *Publ*: Unemployment in Lancs, with Sir Sydney Chapman ('09); Elements of Railway Operating; An Industrial Survey of the N.E. Coast Area (Ed) ('32). *c.t*: Various. *Rec*: Tennis, golf, walking. *c*: Pen & Palette. *a*: 3 Collingwood Terr, Newcastle-on-Tyne. *t*: Jesmond 83.

HALPIN, Lawrence Michael. *b*: L'pool 1888. *e*: Catholic Inst, L'pool & St Mary's Col, Hammersmith. *m*: Helena Mathews. *s*: 1. *d*: 3. Schoolmaster. *Publ*: Art in the Classroom. *s.s*: Art, music. War Service 1916–19. *Rec*: Football, cricket, golf. *a*: 16 Irby Av, Wallasey, Cheshire.

HALSTEAD, DAVID: manufacturer (retired); b. Haslingden, Lancashire, Eng., March, 1861; s. Richard and Susannah (Anderton) H.; educ. St. James Sch. (Haslingden), Stanley St. Acad. (Accrington, Eng.); m. (1) Esther Lindsay (died); (2) Louisa Duckworth. AUTHOR: Annals of Haslingden, Lancashire, 1915; Papers on the Geology cf Rossendale; History 5th Battalion East Lancashire Regiment; Sketches in Lancashire Dialect; History of St. James' Parish Church, Haslingden; History of Haslingden, 1929. Contributor to Haslingden and Accrington Observer, Haslingden Guardian. General character of writing: historical research, poems. M.P. (Conservative) for Rossendale, 1922-23; J.P., F.S.A., T.D., D.L., M.S.P. Relig. denom., Church of England. HOMES: Highfield, Haslingden, Lancashire, and Martin Croft, Macclesfield, Cheshire, Eng.

HALSTEAD, Ivor. *n.a*: Reporter Eastern Morning News, 1913–14, Asst Ed Chatham Observer '21–23, Reporter Daily Mail '26–27, Daily Sketch '27–34. Now specialist in publicity Daily Sketch. *s.s*: Cricket, rugby, publicity. *a*: Glengarry, Clarence Rd, Clapham Park, S.W.4.

HALSTEAD, John. Author. *Publ*: The Black Templar; The Black Nat; The Black Arab; The Black Fear. *a*: c/o S. Paul & Co Ltd, Paternoster Hse, E.C.4.

HALTON, Charles. *b*: Liverpool 1910. P.R.O. Kent County Council. *n.a*: Yorkshire Post 1930–48. *a*: County Hall, Maidstone, Kent. *T*: Maidstone 4321.

HALTON, Ernest Gladstone. *e*: U.C.S. Man Dir Hulton & Co Ltd. *n.a*: Asst-Ed Art Journ 1895—1900, Studio '05—23. *Ctr*: Art Journ, Studio, Connoisseur. *s.s*: Fine & Applied Art. *a*: 18 Okehampton Close, London, N.12. *T*: Hillside 6943.

HALUGALLE, Haj. Dir Assoc Newspapers of Ceylon Ltd, Ceylon Delegate Empire Press Conference Lond 1946. *n.a*: Ed Ceylon Dly News since 1931. *a*: Lake Hse, Colombo, Ceylon.

HAM, Bertie Burnett, M.D., M.R.C.S., L.R.C.P., D.P.H. *b*: Ballarat, Victoria, Australia 1866. *e*: Wesley Coll & Univ of Melbourne, Guy's Hosp. *m*:. *d*: 1. Former Perm Hd of Health Dept & Chm of State Bd of Health Victoria Australia, D.C.M.S. Min of Nat Service & Pensions. *Publ*: Handbook of Sanitary Law for Candidates for Public Health Qualifications; Synopsis Chart of Skin Diseases; Handbook, Nervous Diseases, Organic; Plague, Queensland 1900—09; Venereal Disease, Victoria '10—12; Know Thyself. *Ctr*: B.M.J., etc. *Rec*: Cricket, golf, painting, modelling. *a*: 87 Kensington Gardens Sq, London, W.2. *T*: Bayswater 5115.

"HAMBLETONIAN" (pen name): see Fairfax-Blakeborough, John.

HAMBLETT, Charles. *b*: Newton-in-Makerfield, Lancs 1919. *e*: Vienna. *m*: Susan Scott. *d*: 1. Journalist. *n.a*: Dly Herald Editorial '44—45, Illustrated Staff Feature Writer '46—. *Publ*: Fifteen Poems; The Cactus Harvest. *Ctr*: Tribune, New Statesman, Listener, etc. *s.s*: The Play & Film. *Rec*: Boxing, riding. *w.s*: 1939—42 R.A.F. *a*: c/o John Lane, The Bodley Head, 8 Bury Place, London, W.C.1.

HAMBLY, Edmund Henry Tregothwyn, F.R.C.S. *b*: Port Isaac, Cornwall 1914. *e*: Blundell's Sch, Tiverton & St Bart's Hosp E.C.1. *m*: Elizabeth Mary Cadbury, M.R.C.S., L.R.C.P. *s*: 3. *d*: 1. Cons Orthopædic Surgeon Prince of Wales General Hosp, Acton Hosp, Royal Hosp, Richmond & Staines Hosp, Mem Quaker (Soc of Friends) Med Soc, Mem L.C.C. '46—. *Publ*: History of Family of Hamley & Hambly; Homeland Guide to North Cornwall, etc. *Ctr*: B.M.J., Lancet, Med Press & Circular, Brit Journ of Surg, etc. *s.s*: Orthopædic Surgery, Genealogy, Town-planning. *Rec*: Ornithology, music, Cornish language, family life. *a*: Treeharrock, Seer Green, Bucks, & 130 Harley St, London, W.1. *T*: Beaconsfield 1265.

HAMBLY, Wilfred Dyson, D.Sc. *b*: Clayton, Yorks 1886. *e*: Hartley Coll Southampton & Jesus Coll Oxf. *m*: Annie Elizabeth Larkin. *d*: 1. Anthropologist. *Publ*: Source Book for African Anthropology; Ethnology of the Ovimbundu of Angola; Cultural Areas of Nigeria; Origins of Education; Tattooing; Tribal Dancing; Serpent Worship in Africa; etc. *Ctr*: Illus Lond News, Hibbert Journ, etc. *s.s*: Anthropology, esp African Ethnology. *Rec*: Sailing, swimming, bridge, billiards. *a*: 5338 Harper Ave, Chicago, Illinois, & Chicago Natural History Museum, U.S.A. *T*: Dorchester 0796.

HAMBOURG, Mark. *b*: Bogotchar, South Russia 1879. *e*: Moscow Conservatory of Music, London & Vienna. *m*: The Hon Dorothea Frances Hambourg. *d*: 4. Pianist. *Publ*: From Piano to Forte, Autobiography; How to Play the Piano. *Ctr*: Strand Mag, London Mag, Literary Digest, Musical Opinion, Musical Courier, The Etude, etc. *Rec*: Golf, bridge, collecting antiques. *c*: Savage. *a*: 5 Langford Close, St John's Wood, London, N.W.8.

HAMBROOK, Rev. Arthur. *b*: Betshanger 1878. *m*: Margaret Page. *s*: 1. *d*: 2. *Publ*: The Perfect Offering. *s.s*: History & theology. *Rec*: Gardening. *a*: Week's Mary Rectory, Holsworthy, N. Devon.

HAMEL, Frank. Author, Publisher & Antiquarian Bookseller, Assoc Mem Arts Theatre. *n.a*: Proprietor The Library World. *Publ*: Famous French Salons; The Dauphines of France; A Lady of the Garter; Jean de la Fontaine; The Lady of Beauty; Agnes Sorel; Human Animals; Tiger Wolves; Trust to Boyd; etc. *Ctr*: Various. *s.s*: French History, Biography & Fiction. *Rec*: Drama, films. *c*: Forum. *a*: Coptic Hse, 51 Great Russell St, London, W.C.1. *T*: Holborn 6050.

HAMER, Rev. Charles John. *b*: Lon 1856. *e*: Priv, Lon Col of Divinity, Pembroke Col Oxf. *m*: Margaret Winn. *s*:1. *d*: 4. Clergyman. *n.a*: Ed Bradford Diocesan Year Book 1920–. *Publ*: Old & New Testament Histories for Young Students; Notes on St Matthew; etc. Hon Canon of Newcastle-on-Tyne '04–20, & of Bradford '22–. *a*: The Vicarage, Ilkley, Yorks. *t*: 468.

HAMER, Frederick Edward, J.P. b: Newtown Mont 1866. Journalist, Dir. n.a: Ed Montgomeryshire Express '90—93, Ed Edition for Wales Manchester Guardian '93—16, Editorial Staff Benn Bros & Dir '16—35, Pres N.U.J. '13—14, Executive Inst of Journalists '18—20, Sec The New Commonwealth '33. Publ: The Personal Papers of Lord Rendel ('32). Rec: Gardening. a: 25 Wilmington Av, Chiswick W.4. t: Chiswick 1925.

HAMERTON, Albert Ernest Hillary, C.M.G., D.S.O., M.R.C.S., L.R.C.P. b: Stalybridge 1873. Brevet Col R.A.M.C. (ret). c.t: Medical & Scientific. a: c/o Messrs. Glyn Mills & Co, Whitehall, S.W.1.

HAMID, Abdul. b: Lahore 1892. e: Govt Coll Lahore, Fitzwilliam Hall Oxf. m: (1) Jessie E. Chalk ; (2) Razia Begum. s: 3. d: 2. Journalist. n.a: Paisa Akhbar Daily 1918—20, Ed Khatijn Bombay '35—40, The Dly Eastern Times '41—47. Publ: Guide to Advertising in India ; Pakistan Series (Nos 1 & 2) ; & several books Urou. s.s: New Thought, Muslim Culture. Rec ; Reading mags, physical culture. w.s: World War I. a: Paisa Akhbar St, Lahore, Pakistan. T: 2085.

HAMILL, J. M., O.B.E., M.A., M.D., D.Sc. Sen Med Officer Ministry of Health. Publ: Articles on Nutrition. c.t: Official publications. a: 28 Bramham Gardens. S.W.5.

HAMILTON, Lt.-Col. Arthur Francis, M.B., F.R.C.S., C.I.E. Indian Med Service. c.t: Indian Med Gazette, Times of India. Rec: Racing, music. a Eastlands, Ashley Rise, Walton-on-Thames. t: 620.

HAMILTON, Arthur Kirkham, F.R.S.A. b: Crowle, Lincs 1878. e: Bradford Gr Sch & Inner Temple. m: (1) Violet Madeleine Roberts (dec'd) ; (2) Miriam Tolerton. s: 1. Prof of Public Speaking, Lecturer, Writer, Organiser, Barrister. Publ: Marriage & Divorce. Ctr: Many humorous papers, including Punch. s.s: Public Speaking & Speeches, Humour & Wit. Rec: Music, opera. c: The English Assoc, Savage. a: Abbey Hse, London, S.W.1. T: Abbey 3605 & Welbeck 4947.

HAMILTON, Bruce. Teacher. Publ: Pro, Traitor's Way ; Rex v Rhodes ; The Spring Term. a: c/o A. M. Heath & Co Ltd, Princes Hse, Jermyn St, London, S.W.1.

HAMILTON, Catherine James. b: 1841. e Priv. Publ: Marriage Bonds ; True to the Core; Notable Irishwomen ; Famous Love Matches; Rupert's Wife ; etc. c.t: Graphic, St James's Gazette, Queen, Our Homes, etc. c: Women Writers. a: The Cottage, Freckenham, Bury St Edmunds, Suffolk.

HAMILTON, Cicely. b: Lon 1872. e: Priv Scs Eng & Germany. Author, Journalist, Dramatist—formerly Actress. n.a: Dir Time & Tide. Publ: Marriage as a Trade ; Lest Ye Die; Full Stop ; Modern Germanies ; Modern Italy; Modern France ; Modern Russia ; etc. The Old Adam ; The Beggar Prince ; etc. (Plays) c.t: Leading n/p's & periodicals. Rec: Walking. a: 44 Glebe Pl, Chelsea, S.W.3. t: Flaxman 4605.

HAMILTON, Cosmo. Novelist & playwright. Edited The World. Captain Legion of Frontiersmen ; Sub Lieut R.N.V.R. 1914. a c/o Hutchinson & Co., Paternoster Row, E.C.4.

HAMILTON, 14th Duke of & 11th Duke of Brandon, Sir Douglas Douglas-Hamilton, P.C., G.C.V.O., A.F.C., LL.D.(St Andrews), F.R.G.S. b: London 1903. e: Eton, Balliol Coll Oxf. m: Lady Elizabeth Percy. s: 3. Dir Scottish Aviation Ltd, Norwich Union Insurance Socs. Publ: Pilot's Book of Everest (with Group Cptn McIntyre). Rec: Boxing, gliding, ski-ing, swimming. c: Bath, Roy Aero, etc. w.s: R.A.F. a: Dungavel, Strathaven, Lanarkshire, Scotland. T: Drumclog 234.

HAMILTON, Eben Stuart Burt, M.C., M.B., ChB., F.R.C.S., F.R.S.M. b: Co Donegal 1886. e: Campbell Col, Belfast, Queen's Univ Belfast, Edin Univ. m: Marjory Kathleen Bird. s: 3. Ear, Nose & Throat Surgeon. c.t: Journ of Laryngology, B.M.J., etc. s.s: Diseases of ear, nose & throat. Major R.A.M.C. Hon Surgeon M/C Hosp for Chest & Throat. Stretford Meml Hosp, etc. Rec: Badminton, tennis. c: Fell Roy Soc Med, Mem B.M.A., Constitutional M/C. a: 30 St Ann St, M/C. t: Blackfriars 5791.

HAMILTON, Eric Ronald, M.A.(Cantab), B.Sc.(Lond). b: London 1893. e: Clapham H. Sch, Univ Coll Lond & Trin Coll Camb. m: Alys Janet Wood. d: 2. Princ Boro' Rd Coll Isleworth, Teacher in Sec Schs 1920—22, Lect in Educ Univ Coll of Nth Wales. Publ: The Art of Interrogation ; Geometry ; Fundamental Geometry ; Air Navigation ; The Teacher on the Threshold. Ctr: Educ Research, Math Gazette, Teacher's World, Educ Times, Times Educ Supp, The New Era, etc. s.s: Educ, Psych, Maths. Rec: Reading, writing. w.s: Instr Lieut R.N. '15—20. a: The Lodge, Boro' Rd Coll, Isleworth, Middx. T: Hounslow 5646.

HAMILTON, Esme Violet. b: Burbury Hill, Winchcombe, Glos 1912. e: Priv. Publ: Speedy, the Story of an Irish Pony. Rec: Riding, sailing, travel. c: Kildare St Club Dublin. w.s: A.T.S. '39—44. a: Hamwood, Dunboyne, Co Meath, Eire. T: Dunboyne 10.

HAMILTON, GEORGE HALL: astronomer; b. London, Eng., Jan. 31, 1884; s. J. McLure and Clara Augusta (Raiguel) H.; educ. Trinity Coll., Cambridge, Eng.; DEGREES: B.A., M.A.; m. Elizabeth L. Williams, June 2, 1922. AUTHOR: Mars at its Nearest, 1925. Contributor to Popular Astronomy, Pan-American Geologist, Scientific Monthly, Journ. of the Astronomical Soc. of the Pacific; Journ. of the British Astronomical Assn., The Observatory, Comptes Randues. General character of writing: scientific, particularly in astronomy; has been occupied in building astronomical instruments for own observatory. HOME: The Hamilton Observatory, Mandeville, Jamaica, B.W.I.

HAMILTON, George Rostrevor. b: London 1888. e: Bradfield, Exeter Coll Oxf. m: Marion Hermine Coghlan. s: 1. Poet, Writer, Civil Servant, Special Commissioner of Income Tax since 1934, Fell & Mem of Council Roy Soc of Lit. Publ: Selected Poems & Epigrams ; Death in April ; Crazy Gaunt & Other Dramatic Sketches ; Bergson & Future Philosophy ; Poetry & Contemplation ; The Latin Portrait ; The Greek Portrait ; etc. Ctr: Various. Rec: Walking, bird-watching, entomology. c: Athenæum. a: Swan Hse, Chiswick Mall, London, W.4. T: Chiswick 3170.

HAMILTON, Gerald Stafford. b: Leeds 1906. e: Durham Sch. m: Audrey Sylvain Lewis. s: 1. d: 1. Chartered Accountant, Sec to Whitbread & Co Ltd. Publ: Brewery Income Tax ; Brewery Accounting. Ctr: Brewing Trade Review, Accountant, Taxation. s.s: Brewing & Licensed Trade matters, Taxation, Accountancy. Rec: Squash racquets, literature. c: R.A.C. a: Andersley Hse, Spring Terrace Rd, Burton-on-Trent. T: Burton 3696.

HAMILTON, Hamish, M.A., LL.B. b: Glasgow 1900. e: Rugby & Caius Coll Camb. m: Countess Yvonne Pallavicino. s: 1. Barrister, Publisher, Mang Dir Hamish Hamilton Ltd, Lond Ed Harper's Mag, European Rep Harper & Bros N.Y. Ctr: Ev News, Cambridge Review, Times, Observer. s.s: Sport, Publishing, Anglo-American Relations. Rec: Music, theatre, flying, squash racquets, ski-ing, rowing. *c*: Garrick, Bath, Leander, Hawks (Camb), Thames Rowing. *w.s*: Army 1939—41, seconded Amer Div M.o.I. '41—45. *a*: 90 Gt Russell St, London, W.C.1, & 34 Hereford Hse, North Row, London, W.1. *T*: Museum 0828 & Mayfair 1900.

HAMILTON, Sir Ian. *Publ*: Now & Then. *a*: c/o Methuen & Co Ltd, 36 Essex St, W.C.2.

HAMILTON, Ian Ayliffe, M.B.B.S., F.R.C.S., F.R.A.C.S. *b*: Glenelg, Sth Australia 1901. *e*: St Peter's Coll Adelaide, Univ of Adelaide. *m*: Irene Scholefield Mildred. *s*: 1. *d*: 2. Viticulturist & Farmer, Mem of Hon Surgical Staff of Roy Adelaide Hosp '31—. *Ctr*: Med Journ of Australia, Australian & New Zealand Journ of Surgery, etc. *s.s*: General Surgery. *Rec*: Viticultural & farming work, golf, tennis. *c*: Amateur Sports of Sth Australia. *w.s*: Major (Surg Specialist) 1939—45. *a*: 251 Payneham Rd, Joslin, Adelaide, Sth Australia. *T*: F 1367.

HAMILTON, John Bruce. *b*: Hobart 1901. *e*: Tasmania, Sydney & Oxford Univs. *m*: Dora Jessie Grant. *s*: 1. *d*: 1. *n.a*: Co-Ed (Australia) Internat Journ of Ophthalmology, Assoc-Ed Ophthalmic Literature, Co-Ed Trans of Ophthal Soc of Australia. *Ctr*: Various English & Australian Med Journs. *s.s*: Ophthalmic Surgical Literature. *Rec*: Travel. *w.s*: A.I.F., 8th Army (Major). *a*: 174 Macquarie St, Hobart, Tasmania, Australia. *T*: 3347.

HAMILTON, Mary Agnes. *Publ*: inc (Novels) Life Sentence; The Last Fortnight; Murder in the House of Commons; (Biog) Margaret Bondfield; J. Ramsay MacDonald; Sidney & Beatrice Webb; etc. *a*: 15 Mulberry Close, Chelsea, London, S.W.

HAMILTON, Mildred. See Dicker, Mrs. R. M. H.

HAMILTON, Major Owen Philip. *b*: India 1889. *e*: Wellington Coll & R.M.C. Sandhurst. *Publ*: Dreamers & Doers; The Old Shepherd; Leaves of Life; Tyrolean Summer; Hebridean Holiday; Poems 1930—36; Heart of Hertfordshire; Lincolnshire Landscape; Temple of Nanda Devi. *Ctr*: Cornhill Mag, Chambers's Journ, Adelphi, Lady, Queen, Country Life, Field, Countryman, etc. *s.s*: Travel Books, Fiction, Poetry. *Rec*: Travel. *c*: Utd Service. *w.s*: 21 yrs India, Egypt & China. *a*: c/o Lloyds Bank Ltd (Cox's Br), 6 Pall Mall, London, S.W.1.

HAMILTON, Patrick. Author. *Publ*: Monday Morning; Craven House; Twopence Coloured; The Midnight Bell; The Siege of Pleasure; The Plains of Cement; Twenty Thousand Streets under the Sky (a trilogy); Hangover Square; The Slaves of Solitude; (Plays) Rope; Gaslight; The Duke in Darkness; The Governess. *a*: c/o Constable & Co Ltd, 10 Orange St, London, W.C.2.

HAMILTON, Patrick Macfarlan, M.A., B.Litt., Dip.Ed. *b*: Stratford, Victoria Aust 1892. *e*: Scotch Coll Melbourne, Univ of Melbourne, Balliol Coll Oxf. *m*: Dulcie Seymour Shepherd. *s*: 1. *d*: 1. Schoolmaster. Princ Brisbane Boys Coll 1931—46. *n.a*: Ed Reports of the New Education Fellowship Conf '43 & '44 Brisbane Queensland. *Publ*: Australia & the United Nations; Our Australian Heritage; Method in the Study of History. *Ctr*: The Courier, Mail & The Telegraph Brisbane. *s.s*: Internat Affairs, The United Nations, The League of Nations, Education. *w.s*: A.I.F. 1915—19. *a*: 40 Thanet St, Malvern, Melbourne, Victoria, Aust. *T*: U 3642.

HAMILTON, Robert. *b*: London 1908. *e*: Westminster Cathedral. *m*: Margaret Sheridan. *s*: 2. *Publ*: Hilaire Belloc—An Introduction to his Spirit & Work; W. H. Hudson—The Vision of Earth. *Ctr*: Quarterly Rev, Nineteenth Cent, Horizon, Adelphi, Contemporary Rev, Tablet, etc. *s.s*: Critical Biography. *a*: 141A Kensington High St, London, W.8.

HAMILTON, The Hon. Robert Alexander Benjamin, F.R.G.S., F.R.C.A.S. *b*: Rajputana, India 1903. *e*: Eton & R.M.C. Sandhurst. *Publ*: The Old House. *s.s*: S.W. Arabia. *Rec*: Sporting. *a*: Wishaw Hse, Wishaw, Scotland. *T*: 161.

HAMILTON, Sir Robert William, M.P., M.A., F.R.G.S., F.S.A. M.P.(Lib), Orkney & Shetland ('22–). *Publ*: East Africa Law Reports. *a*: 161 Oakwood Ct, Kensington, W.14. *t*: Western 0362.

HAMILTON, Stanley Baines, M.Sc., A.R.C.S., M.I.Struct.E., A.M.I.C.E., F.R.S.A. *b*: Lowestoft 1889. *e*: Royal Coll of Science London. *m*: Christina Bruce MacFarlane. *s*: 2. *d*: 1. Principal Scientific Officer Building Research Station of the D.S.I.R. *Ctr*: Transactions of Newcomen Soc, Structural Engineer, State Service, D.S.I.R. publications. *s.s*: Hist of Technology, particularly Structural Engineering & Building, Ancient & Modern. *w.s*: R.G.A. & R.E. 1914—19. *a*: Building Research Station, Garston, Watford, Herts. *T*: Garston (Watford) 2246.

HAMILTON, Walter, M.A. *b*: Lon 1908. *e*: St Dunstan's & Trin Col Cam. Class Teaching & Research. *c.t*: Classical Quarterly, Classical Review. *s.s*: Greek Philos. Asst Lect in Classics Victoria Univ, M/C 1931–32. Asst Master Eton Col '33–34. Fell Trin Col Cam. *a*: Trinity Col, Cam.

HAMILTON, Rev. William H., M.A., D.D. *b*: Barnhill, Dundee 1886. *e*: Broughty Ferry Collegiate Sch, Dundee Hgh S St Andrews Univ, Trin Coll Glas. *m*: Annie Seivwright. *d*: 2. Minister of Church of Scotland & Gen Sec World Alliance of Presbyterian & Reformed Churches. *n.a*: Greatheart (Church of Scotland Young People's Mag) 1921—29 (Ed), Presbyterian Register '27— (Ed). *Publ*: Murray's Scarlet Gown; Gauldry & other Verses; John Masefield; The Desire of the Moth & other poems; Holyrood—A Garland of Modern Scots Verse; Children Praising with H. Wiseman). *Ctr*: Scotsman, Glas Herald, Lond Mercury, Scots Mag, The Quest, etc. *s.s*: Poetry, Musical & Lit Criticism, Presbyterian Church Hist. *Rec*: Poetry, music, rural life, foreign travel. *a*: 12 Oxford Terr, Edinburgh 4. *T*: 20885.

HAMILTON, Prof. William James, M.D., D.Sc., F.R.S.Ed. *b*: Islandmagee, Co Antrim 1903. *e*: Queen's Univ Belfast. *m*: Mamie C. Young. *s*: 4. *d*: 1. Regius Prof of Anatomy Univ of Glasgow, Ed Board Journal of Anatomy. *Publ*: Human Embryology; Surface & Radiological Anatomy. *Ctr*: Many scientific journals. *s.s*: Embryology, Anatomy. *Rec*: Golf. *a*: Anatomy Dept, The University, Glasgow, W.2; (priv) Tara, Wolsey Rd, Moor Park, Northwood, Middlesex. *T*: Northwood 2258.

HAMILTON JENKIN, Alfred Kenneth, M.A., B.Litt(Oxon). *b*: Redruth. *e*: Clifton Col & Univ Col Oxf. *m*: Luned Jacobs. *d*: 2. Author, Journalist, Broadcaster, Lect. *Publ*: The Cornish Miner; Cornish Seafarers; Cornish Homes & Customs; A Short History of Cornwall; etc. *c.t*: M/C Guard, Daily Herald, Contemp Rev, Radio Times, Western Morn News, etc. *s.s*: Cornwall, industry. Vice-Pres of Fed of Old Cornwall Soc. *Rec*: Climbing. *a*: Bostenner, St Ive's, Cornwall.

HAMILTON-PATERSON, James Lee, F.R.S.M. *b*: Grimsby 1908. *e*: Barnard Castle Sch Durham & U.C.H. London. *m*: Doris Bunyard. *s*: 1. Mem Pathol Soc of Gt Britain. *Publ*: Penicillin in General Practice; Anatomy & Physiology for Nurses; Sternal Puncture (with A. Piney). *Ctr*: Lancet, B.M.J., Biochemical Journ, Brit Heart Journ, Brit Journ of Ophthalmology, etc. *s.s*: Hæmatology. *Rec*: Philately. *a*: 45 Cavendish Drive, Edgware, Mddx. *T*: 8181.

HAMLEY, Herbert Russell, M.A., M.Sc, PhD. Prof of Educ. *n.a*: Ed Teaching, Bombay. *Publ*: Relational & Functional Thinking in Mathematics; School Discipline; The Teaching of Arithmetic. *c.t*: Times of India. *a*: Inst of Educ, Southampton Row, W.C.1. *t*: Hol 5918.

HAMLYN, Rev. Frederick Conrad. *b*: Paignton 1890. *e*: St John's Sch Leatherhead & Hatfield Hall Durham. *m*: Iris Gertrude Linsell. *d*: 2. Vicar of Everton with Tabworth Ely, Vicar of Morwenstowe 1927—32. *Publ*: Morwenstowe since Stuart Times; Pilgrim's Way at Morwenstowe; Church Histories of Long Bennington & Everton. *s.s*: Local History. *a*: Everton Vicarage, Sandy, Beds. *T*: Sandy 138.

HAMMARLING, Vilgot. *b*: Sweden 1892. *m*: Beatrix Moore. *s*: 2. Press Attaché Swedish Embassy London 1938. *n.a*: Foreign News Ed & Foreign Corr Dagens Nyheter Stockholm 1921—38. *s.s*: Internat Affairs, Anglo-Swedish Trans. *a*: Swedish Embassy, 27 Portland Pl, London, W.1.

HAMMERSLEY, S. S., M.A., M.P. *Publ*: Industrial Leadership. *c.t*: Daily Dispatch, M/C Guardian, Allied Press. *a*: Stroods, Uckfield, Sussex. *t*: Crowboro' 312.

HAMMERTON, Sir John Alexander, Kt. *b*: Alexandria, Dumbartonshire 1871; *e*: Alexander's Sch Glasgow. *m*: Rhoda Lawrence. Editor & Author. *n.a*: Edited newsps in Bolton '94, Blackpool '95, Nottingham '96 —97, B'ham '97—1900, Lond Mag 1905—07, War Illustrated '14—19, '39—47, Second Great War '39—47, Founded World Digest May '39, still Ed-in-Chief, Man-Ed El Diccionario Enciclopedico Hispáno-Americano Buenos Aires '12—13. *Publ*: The Actor's Act; Stevensoniana; The Argentine Through English Eyes; Wrack of War; George Meredith : His Life & Art; Barrie : The Story of a Genius; With Northcliffe in Fleet Street; Books & Myself : an autobiography; Child of Wonder : A Biography of Arthur Mee; Ed of The Universal Encyclopedia; Universal History of the World; Wonders of the Past; New Book of Knowledge; etc. *s.s*: Literary, Biography. *Rec*: Reading, travel. *c*: Savage, Reform. *a*: World Digest, John Carpenter Hse, Whitefriars, London, E.C.4, & De Walden Lodge, Eastbourne, Sussex. *T*: Central 8080 & Eastbourne 3416.

HAMMETT, Samuel Dashiell. *b*: Maryland, U.S.A. 1894. *e*: Public Scs, Baltimore. *m*: Josephine Dolan. *d*: 2. Novelist. *Publ*: The Thin Man; The Maltese Falcon; The Glass Key; Red Harvest; The Dain Curse; Creeps by Night (edited). *s.s*: Detective Stories. *a*: Beverly Hills, California, U.S.A.

HAMMOND, A. W., M.C. *n.a*: News Ed Sunday Graphic. *a*: 37 Church Crescent, Church End, Finchley, N.3.

HAMMOND, Aileen Vera. *b*: Rickmansworth 1895. *e*: Priv. *m*: Capt E. F. E. Hammond. *s*: 2. F. L. Livestock Journalist & Breeder. *c.t*: Cage Bird Fancy, Fur & Feather, Smallholder, Pet Expert Home Notes, Pet Expert Hertfordshire Mercury, etc. *s.s*: Breeding & exhibiting of fancy stock. Claims to be practically the only journalist writing on these subjects who is a specialist in so many varieties. *a*: Sootfield Green, Preston, nr Hitchin, Herts.

HAMMOND, Albert Edward. *b*: Wheathampstead 1896. *e*: Village Sch. *m*: Winifred Elizabeth Willis. *s*: 1. *d*: 3. Technical Journalist & Author. *Publ*: Store Interior Planning & Display; Self-Service Trading; The Fruit Shop of To-morrow; Multiple Shop Organisation; Practical Aids to Retail Selling; Shopfitting & Display; (Ed) Footwear Display; Men's Wear Display. *Ctr*: Times Rev of Industry, Grocers' Gazette, Fruit Trade Journ, Shoe & Leather Record, Hardware Trade Journ, Packaging, Display, etc. *s.s*: Shopfitting & Display, Mechanical Handling, Lighting & Heating, Packaging, Store & Factory Equipment. *Rec*: Gardening, walking, architectural study. *w.s*: 1914—18. *a*: Eaton Lodge, Eaton Rd, Sutton, Surrey. *T*: Vigilant 5397.

HAMMOND, Arthur, A.R.P.S. *n.a*: Assoc Ed American Photography; *Publ*: Pictorial Composition in Photography. *a*: c/o Chapman & Hall Ltd, Henrietta St, W.C.2.

HAMMOND, G. H. *n.a*: Manager & Sec The Evening Citizen Glasgow. *a*: St Vincent Pl, Glasgow, C.1.

HAMMOND, George Peter, M.A., Ph.D. *b*: Hutchinson, Minnesota 1896. *e*: Univ of Calif. *m*: Carrie Nelson. *s*: 2. *d*: 2. Historian. *n.a*: Mang-Ed & Co-Founder The Quivira Society 1929—, Ed Coronado Hist Series '40— & The Historian '38—46. *Publ*: Don Juan de Chate & the Founding of New Mexico, Santa Fe; Expedition into New Mexico; (collab) Narratives of the Coronado Expedition; The Story of New Mexico; Adventures of Don Francisco Vasquez de Coronado; New Mexico in 1602; Obregon's History of 16th Century Exploration in Western America. *Ctr*: New Mexico Hist Rev, etc. *s.s*: South-western History & Mexico. *Rec*: Gardening. *a*: 810 Contra Costa Ave, Berkeley 7, California, U.S.A.

HAMMOND, Hector Richmond Granville, LL.B. *b*: Haverfordwest 1900. *e*: H'west Gr Sch, Univ Coll of Aberystwyth. Barrister, Journalist. *n.a*: Chief Sub-Ed West Wales Guardian '28—. *Rec*: Badminton, golf, swimming. *a*: 18 Market St, Haverfordwest, Pembs. *T*: 57.

HAMMOND, J. L. Author. *Publ*: C. P. Scott. *a*: c/o G. Bell & Sons Ltd, York House, Portugal St W.C.2.

HAMMOND, John, M.A., Hon.D.Sc., F.R.S. *b*: Briston, Norfolk 1889. *e*: Greshams Sch, Holt & Downing Coll, Camb Univ. *m*: Frances Mercy Goulder. *s*: 3. Reader in Agricultural Physiology Camb Univ, Fellow of Downing Coll Camb, Served on Livestock Cttees of Post-War Allied Rehabilitation Cttees & UNRRA 1942—45, Livestock officer UNRRA Missions to Poland, Czechoslovakia, Austria, Italy '46. *n.a*: Mem Ed Board of Journal Agricultural Sc '43, Empire Journal Experimental Agriculture '39, British Journal of Nutrition '47. *Publ*: Growth & Development of Mutton Qualities in the Sheep; Reproduction in the Cow; Reproduction in the Rabbit; Farm Animals; Artificial Insemination of Cattle. *Ctr*: Scientific journals, Agricultural press & journals. *s.s*: Science of Animal Production. *c*: Athenæum, Farmers. *a*: 1 Luard Rd, Cambridge. *T*: 87506.

HAMMOND, John Lawrence Le Breton, Hon.D.Litt(Oxon & Manch), F.B.A. *b*: Drighlington nr Bradford 1872. *e*: Bradford Gr Sch, St John's Coll Oxf. *m*: Lucy Barbara Bradby. Journalist, Hon Fellow of St John's Coll Oxf. *n.a*: Editorial Staff Manchester Guardian 1939—, Special Corr Manchester Guardian at Peace Conference '18—19. *Publ*: Gladstone & the Irish Nation; C. P. Scott; Charles James Fox; also other books with L. B. Hammond. *Rec*: Walking. *c*: Reform. *a*: Oatfield, Piccotts End, Hemel Hempstead, Herts. *T*: Boxmoor 316.

HAMMOND, Lucy Barbara, Hon. Fellow of Lady Margaret Hall, D.Litt.Oxon. *b*: Haileybury 1873. *e*: St. Leonards' Coll. *m*: J. L. Hammond. *Publ*: (with J. L. Hammond) The Rise of Modern Industry; The Village Labourer (1760—1832); The Town Labourer (ditto); The Skilled Labourer (ditto); Lord Shaftesbury; The Age of the Chartists; The Black Age. *Ctr*: Manch Guardian. *Rec*: Gardening, walking. *a*: Oatfield, Piccotts End, Hemel Hempstead, Herts. *T*: Boxmoor 316.

HAMMOND, Rev. Thomas Chatterton, M.A., Th.D. *b*: Cork 1877. *e*: Nat Sch & T.C.D. *m*: Margaret McNay. *s*: 3. *d*: 1. Principal Theol Coll 1936—. *Publ*: In Understanding, Be Men; Perfect Freedom; Reassuring Faults; Concerning Penal Laws; Authority in the Church; Fading Light; Age-long Questions. *Ctr*: Evangelical Quart, Nineteenth Century & After, Irish Theol Quart. *s.s*: Theology & Apologetics. *Rec*: Chess, croquet, tennis. *a*: Moore Theological College, Newtown, New South Wales. *T*: L.A.1243.

HAMMOND, William James. *b*: Worcester 1887. *e*: King Charles I Sc Kidderminster. *m*: Annie Stalker Brown. *s*: 1. *d*: 1. Journalist. *n.a*: Kidderminster Times & Allied N/ps 1902—. *c.t*: Various. *Rec*: Cricket. Hon Mem Kidderminster Ch of Comm Kidderminster Rotary Club. Chm Worcester Branch N.U.J. *c*: Kidderminster Club & Inst. *a*: The Cottage, 171 Chester Rd, Kidderminster, Worcs. *t*: 145.

HAMMOND-RYAN, Miss Nell. *Publ*: My Years at the Austrian Court. *c.t*: Thomsons, A.P., Pearsons, True Story, etc. *s.s*: Life stories of celebrities, articles on unusual customs & people met on extensive travels. *c*: Cowdray. *a*: Westfield Lodge, Elmfield, I.o.W.

HAMOND, Rev. E. W. *Publ*: A Short Religious History of Israel; The Eighth Century Prophets; The Seventh & Sixth Century Prophets. *a*: Whilton Rectory, Daventry.

HAMOR, William Allen, M.A., Hon.D.Sc., Hon.LL.D. *b*: Du Bois, Pa 1887. *e*: Univ of Pittsburgh. Chemist & Author. *n.a*: Science Hist of the Universe 1909—10, Journ of Industrial & Engineering Chemistry '12—14, Contributing-Ed Pitt Quarterly '39—, Ed-Adviser Nutritional Observatory '40—. *Publ*: History of Chemistry; (co-author) The American Petroleum Industry; Examination of Petroleum; American Fuels; Science in Action; Glances at Industrial Research. *Ctr*: Ency Brit, Britannica Yearbooks, Amer Annuals, Chemistry Journs, etc. *a*: Author's, Chemists & Rotarian, etc. *a*: Mellon Institute of Industrial Research, University of Pittsburgh, Pittsburgh 13, Pa, U.S.A.

HAMPDEN, John, M.A., M.R.S.T. *b*: Folkestone 1898. *e*: Oxford. *m*: Rosalind Vallance. Head of Lit Group Brit Counc, English Master Guildford Gr Sch, Lect in and later Prof of English Lit Queen's Coll Lond. *n.a*: Gen-Ed Thomas Nelson & Sons Ltd. *Publ*: An Eighteenth Century Journal; The King Decides; Mrs Adis; Over the Garden Wall; etc; Ed of many Anthologies, Plays & Short Stories for Everyman's Library, Penguin Books, Nelson Classics, etc. *Ctr*: Times Lit Supp, John O'London's Weekly, Britain Today, Drama, etc. *s.s*: Anthony Trollope (Life & Work), The Short Story, R. L. Stevenson, English Drama & Theatre, Drama in Educ. *Rec*: Walking, talking. *c*: P.E.N. *a*: Kenilworth, Park Hill, Carshalton, Surrey.

HAMPSHIRE, Charles Herbert, M.B., B.S., B.Sc., F.R.I.C., M.R.C.P., L.R.C.P., Ph.C., F.R.S.M. *b*: Ilkley, Yorks 1885. *e*: Ilkley Gr Sch, Lond Univ. *m*: Grace Mary Taylor. *d*: 1. Sec Brit Pharmacopoeia Commssn Pharmaceutical Conf 1933 & '34. *n.a*: Ed Quarterly Journ of Pharmacy & Pharmacology. *Publ*: Manual of Volumetric Analysis. *Ctr*: Med & Tech Journs. *s.s*: Med & Sci Research. *a*: 44 Hallam St, London, W.1.

HAMPSON, Ethel Mary, M.A., Ph.D. *b*: Southport, Lancs 1896. *e*: Gr Sch Southport, Liverpool Univ, Lond Sch of Econs, Newnham Coll Camb. Lect in Econ Hist Univ of Aberdeen 1946—. *Publ*: The Treatment of Poverty in Cambridgeshire 1597—1834; Victoria County History of Cambridgeshire. *Ctr*: Econ Hist Rev, Cambridge Hist Journ, etc. *s.s*: Econ Hist, Local Govt, Historical Biog. *Rec*: Walking, sketching. *a*: King's Coll, Aberdeen, & 6 Craigie Loanings, Aberdeen. *T*: 4524.

HAMPSON, SIR GEORGE FRANCIS, Bt.: naturalist; *b.* London, Eng., Jan. 14, 1860; *s.* William Seymour and Julia Jane (Franks) H.; educ. Charterhouse (London), Exeter Coll. (Oxford); DEGREE: B.A. (Oxford); m. Minnie Frances Clark-Kennedy, June 1, 1894. AUTHOR: Lepidoptera in the British Museum, Part VIII, Nilgiri District, India (16 plates), and Part IX, 1891; Lepidoptera Heterocero of Ceylon (19 plates), 1893; Fauna of British India, Ceylon and Burma (vols. 1, 2, 3, 4), 1892-1896; Catalogue of the Lepidoptera Phalaenae in the British Museum (vols. 1-13), 1898-1913; Supplementary (vols. 1, 2, 3), 1914-1926. Contributor of numerous papers in Transactions of Asiatic Soc., of Bengal, Bombay Nat. Hist. Soc., Proc. Zoological Soc. of London, Entomological Soc. of London, Novitates Zoologicae of Tring, Herts (Eng.). General character of writing: natural history, scientific. Religion: Evolutionist. HOME: Thurnham Court, Maidston, Kent, Eng.

HAMPSON, John. *b*: Birmingham. *m*: Therese Giehse. *Publ*: Saturday Night at the Greyhound; O Providence; Strip Jack Naked; Family Curse; The Larches (with L. A. Pavey); Care of " The Grand "; The English at Table. *Ctr*: Spectator, Dly Herald, Ev Standard, Life & Letters, New Writing, Strand Mag, Modern Reading, Story, etc. *s.s*: Food, Fiction, Reviewing. *a*: Four Ashes, Dorridge, nr Birmingham. *T*: Knowle 2011.

HAMSON, Harry T. *b*: Northampton. 1868 *e*: British & Gr Schs Northampton. Journalist. *n.a*: Ed Middlesex Advertiser for 40 yrs, V-Pres Guild of Editors. *s.s*: Local Government Rating, Town Planning. *Rec*: Walking, music. *a*: County Gazette Office, Uxbridge, Middlesex.

HAMSUN, Knut. *b*: 1859. Author. *Publ*: Growth of the Soil; Pan; The Woman at the Pump, August, etc. Nobel Prize (Lit) 1920. *a*: Norway.

HANBURY, Frederick Janson, F.L.S., F.R.E.S., V.M.H. *b*: Stoke Newington. *e*: Friends Sc. *m*: (1) Mary Jane Scarborough King; (2) Mary Ethel Lancaster Satow. *s*: 3. *d*: 3. Chm Allen & Hanburys Ltd. *Publ*: Flora of Kent; The London Catalogue of British Plants. *c.t*: Journ of Botany, Entomol, Entomological Monthly Mag. *s.s*: British Botany & entomology, gardening, esp orchids, alpines, etc. Rep for the Diocese of Chichester in Ch Assembly. *Rec*: Hortic. *c*: Carlton. *a*: Brockhurst, E. Grinstead. *t*: 20.

HANBURY, Harold Greville. *b*: Kineton, Warwick 1898. *e*: Charterhouse & Brasenose Coll Oxf. *m*: Anna Margaret Dreyer. Sub-Rector & Senior Tutor of Lincoln Coll Oxf, Barrister. *Publ*: Modern Equity; English Courts of Law; Essays in Equity. *Ctr*: Law Quarterly Rev, Univ of Toronto Law Rev. *s.s*: Law. *Rec*: Literature, film & drama, cricket. *a*: 31 Belsyre Court, Oxford. *T*: 2445.

HANBURY-SPARROW, Lt.-Col. Arthur Alan, D.S.O. (bar), M.C. *b*: Wolverhampton 1892. *e*: Winchester, Sandhurst. *m*: Ileen Margaret Aitken Gray. *s*: 3. *d*: 2. Poultry Farmer, Reserve of Officers. *Publ*: The Landlocked Lake. *c.t*: Anthroposophy. *s.s*: Economics, politics, anthroposophy. France '14-18, Persia '20. *Rec*: Lit. *c*: Shropshire. *a*: The Yeld, Church Stretton, Salop. *t*: 122.

HANBURY-WILLIAMS, Major-Gen. Sir J., G.C.V.O., K.C.B., C.M.G. H.M. Marshal Diplomatic Corps. *Publ*: The Emperor Nicholas as I knew him. *a*: Henry III Tower, Windsor Castle.

HANBY, H. W. Editor. *n.a*: Ed Bromley & West Kent Mercury. *a*: Bromley & West Kent Mercury. 240 High St, Bromley, Kent.

HANCOCK, A. C., M.B., B.S., D.P.M., M.R.C.S., L.R.C.P., D.P.H. Med Supt Kent Cnty Ment Hosp Maidstone, Hon Phys W. Kent Gen Hosp. Late Maj R.A.M.C. Fel Roy Soc Med. *c.t*: B.M.J., Journ Ment Science, Proc Roy Soc Med. *a*: Barming Heath. Maidstone.

HANCOCK, A. M. *a*: 6 Flavia Terrace, South Shields.

HANCOCK, Rev. Arthur. *b*: Withiel 1855. *e*: Dobwalls Acad, Shebbear Col. *m*: Jennie Holden. *s*: 4. *d*: 3. *Publ*: Why We Are Nonconformists; The Deity of Christ; etc. *c.t*: Bible Christian (Meth) Mag. Pres of Meth Bible Chr Conf. Supt Lon, Plymouth, Sheffield Dis Synods. *Rec*: Angling. *a*: Hylands, Fermoy Rd, Thrope Bay.

HANCOCK, Rev. Bernard Matthew, B.A., L.Th. *b*: Lon 1870. *e*: Melbourne C.E. G.S. & Durham Univ. *m*: Mabel Edith Marriot. *s*: 1. *d*: 2. *Publ*: The Christian Patriot; Fellowship is Life; Preparation for Holy Matrimony; Free Bondmen; A Certain Priest; etc. *s.s*: Book of Common Prayer. *Rec*: Theatre. *a*: Rectory of Monksilver, Taunton.

HANCOCK, Elsie, B.A., M.A. *b*: M/C 1895. *e*: M/C H.S. for Girls, Victoria Univ M/C, Cam T.C. for Women. Snr Classics Mistress, Barrs Hill Sec Sc Coventry. *c.t*: Classical Quart. *s.s*: Latin, Greek Classics Mistress City of Cardiff H.S. for Girls '18–25. Classics Mistress Withington Girls' Sc Fallowfield, M/C '25–27. *Rec*: Travel, reading, archæ. *a*: Silverdale, Osborne Rd, Levenshulme, M/C.

HANCOCK, G. C. F/L & Feature Writer. *n.a*: Reporter Leominster News. *a*: 11 Caswell Rd, Leominster, Herefords.

HANCOCK, Rev. H., M.A., F.R.A.S. Chaplain to the Queen Alexandra Hosp Home for disabled Ex-service men Worthing. *Publ*: Mechanics & Hydrostatics; Stokesby W. Herringbey; also author of sev plays & poems. *a*: 88 Heene Rd, Worthing. *T*: 5212.

HANCOCK, Henry Mason. M.R.S.T. *b*: Nottingham 1864. *e*: Elem. *m*: Mary Hannah Miller (dec). *s*: 1. *d*: 1. Teacher (ret). *c.t*: Schoolmaster, Nottingham Guardian, Nottingham Journ, Mansfield Reporter, Mansfield Advertiser, Everyman, Melody & London Anthology, Poetry of To-day, Poet's Guild, Western Morning News. *s.s*: Poetry, criticism, education. Science Lecturer Kettering & Nottingham, Peripatetic Science Demonstrator in Nottingham, Teacher in Student Teachers Classes Nottingham. *Rec*: Reading, writing, walking, architecture, art. *c*: Mem Sunday Sc Union Counc, Pres-elec Notts Congregational Union, Lay Preacher, Asst Sec Mansfield Branch of League of Nations Union, Poetry Soc, Poets Guild, Poetry Circle, Pen, etc. *a*: 2 Stella St, Mansfield, Notts.

HANCOCK, Reginald Mark. *b*: Worksop 1907. *e*: Sec Sch. *m*: Jessie Banham. *d*: 1. Journalist, Mem N.U.J. *n.a*: Reporter Retford, Gainsborough & Worksop Times '22–28, Derbyshire Times Bakewell '28–31, Staff Rep Doncaster Gazette & Yorks E. News '44–47, Doncaster Chron & Yorks E. Post '47—. *Rec*: Gardening, tennis. *a*: 24 Pamela Drive, Warmsworth, nr Doncaster, Yorks. *T*: (Office) Doncaster 4001.

HANCOCK, Walter Charles, B.A., F.I.C. Cons Chemist. *c.t*: Tech & Sci Journs. *a*: 10 Upper Chadwell St Myddelton Sq, E.C.1.

HANCOCK, William Keith. *b*: Melbourne, Australia 1898. *e*: Melbourne Univ, Balliol Coll Oxf. *m*: Theaden Brocklebank. Fell All Souls' Coll, Chichele Professor of Economic History. *Publ*: Survey of British Commonwealth Affairs (2 Vols); Ricasoli & the Risorgimento in Tuscany; Australia; Argument of Empire; Politics in Pitcairn. *Ctr*: Various. *s.s*: Modern History. *Rec*: Fishing, walking. *c*: United Univ. *a*: All Souls' College, Oxford.

HANCOX, Edward Richard Henry, F.S.A. *b*: 1863. *e*: Priv. Priv Sec (ret). *Publ*: Romance of the Penny. *c.t*: Various. *s.s*: Prehistoric archæology, numismatics, old pewter. *Rec*: Music. *a*: Nacton, Ipswich.

HAND, Gerald. *b*: Liverpool, 1874. *e*: St Francis Xavier's Col Liverpool, Ampleforth Col. *m*: Constance Ball. *s*: 1. *d*: 2. Newspaper manager. *n.a*: 30 y association with the Catholic Press. *c.t*: Catholic Herald, George Newnes' periodicals, Liverpool Daily Press, Irish Press. *s.s*: Catholic matters, short stories, light articles. Travelled extensively. *a*: The Bungolow, Southern Crescent, Davenport, Stockport. *t*: Bramhall 885.

HANDFIELD-JONES, Ranald Montagu, M.C., M.S., F.R.C.S., F.R.E.S. *b*: London 1892. *e*: Epsom Coll, St Mary's Hosp Med Sch, Univ Lond. *m*: Lilian Dilys. *s*: 3. *d*: 1. Pres United Hosp C.C. & St Mary's Hosp C.C. *Publ*: Essentials of Modern Surgery (with A. E. Porritt); Surgery of the Hand; Ctr to Fleming's "Penicillin." *Ctr*: Brit Journ of Surgery, Lancet, Practitioner. *s.s*: Surgery. *Rec*: Cricket, ski-ing, squash rackets, golf, photography. *a*: 149 Harley St, London, W.1. *T*: Welbeck 4444.

HANDFORD, Stanley Alexander. Lect in Classics King's Col Lon. Prof of Classics Queen's Col Lon. *Publ*: Revision & Completion of L. W. Hunter's Xenophon, Anabasis III & IV; Aeneas on Siegecraft. *a*: 57 Wembley Park Drive, Wembley, Middx. *t*: 3837.

HANDFORD, Wilfred James. *b*: Barnstaple 1900. *m*: Olive Mary Edwards. *n.a*: North Devon Journ, Salisbury Times, Salisbury & Winchester Journ, Westmorland Gazette, Chief rep Salisbury & Winchester Journ 1926—. Formerly of the Inst of Shorthand Writers practising in Supreme Court of Judicature, London. Correspondent to London dailies & weeklies. *s.s*: Church, archæological & historical; Legal shorthand note taking. *Rec*: Photography. Army Service Russia & Ireland. Ex-Chm Salisbury branch N.U.T. & Cmt Mem Wessex area Newspaper Press Fund. *a*: 19 Ashley Rd, Salisbury, Wilts. *t*: 10.

HANDLEY, Wm. Sampson, M.S., F.R.C.S., Hon.F.A.C.S. *b*: Loughborough 1872. *e*: Loughborough Sch, Guy's Hosp. *m*: Muriel Rigby. *s*: 4. *d*: 1. *n.a*: Late Ed Middx Hosp Archives, formerly Lond Assoc Ed Annals of Surgery. *Publ*: Cancer of the Breast; The Genesis of Cancer. *s.s*: Abdominal & Cancer Surgery. *a*: Park Hse, Debden, Saffron Walden, & 35a Welbeck St, London, W.1. *T*: Newport (Essex) 136, & Langham 1237.

HANDLEY-TAYLOR, Geoffrey, F.R.S.A. *b*: Horsforth, Yorks 1920. Author, Biographer, Publisher, Ballet Critic, Founder York Theatre Club 1945, Jt Dir William Tyndale Poetry Series, Man Dir Cope & Fenwick Ltd Publishers, Chm Lotus Press, Head Cultural Mission to Italy '45–46. Studied Ballet '46. *Publ*: Narrow

Escape; On a Post-War Plan; Cornish Barnstormer; The Valuation of Silver & Plate; Lichfield's Doctor Johnson 1709—1784; Random Palms; Mona Inglesby, Ballerina & Choreographer; Italian Ballet Today; Riding Through the Ridings (Jt-Ed). *Ctr*: Brit Ballet, Ballet Today, etc. *Rec*: Ballet dancing, travel, sailing. *c*: P.E.N., Economic Reform. *w.s*: 1939—41. *a*: c/o Grindlay & Co Ltd, 54 Parliament St, London, S.W.1.

HANDSAKER, Gene, B.A. *b*: Davenport, Wash 1909. *e*: S. California Univ. *m*: Frances Hoffmann. *s*: 2. Reporter & Hollywood Columnist for A.P. *n.a*: Rep: San Diego Sun 1932—33, Los Angeles Post-Record '34—35, Los Angeles Ev Herald-Express '36—42, Associated Press since Dec. '42. *Rec*: Amateur radio. *a*: 4710 Mascot St, Los Angeles 6, Calif, U.S.A. *T*: Whitney 2126.

HANFORD, Kenneth James. *b*: Peterborough 1921. *e*: King's Sch Peterborough. *m*: Gwendolyn Sybil Thorpe. Journalist. *n.a*: Rep Peterborough Advertiser from '38—41, Sub-Ed from '46—47, Sub-Ed Lynn News & Advertiser from August '47. *Rec*: Tennis, table tennis, golf, swimming. *w.s*: R.A.F. '41—46. *a*: 137 Gaywood Rd, Kings Lynn, Norfolk.

HANFORTH, T. W., Mus.B. *Publ*: Musical Compositions. *a*: Clarendon Rd, Fulwood Pk, Sheffield. *t*: Broomhill 31761.

HANISON, Bernard. *b*: London 1923. *e*: Secondary, Evening Classes. Director of Ace Books Ltd, Mem N.U.J. *n.a*: Sub-Ed Soviet Weekly 1946. *s.s*: Socialist Literature. *a*: 22 Cedra Ct, Cazenove Rd, London, N.16. *T*: Stamford 6941.

HANITSCH, Karl Richard, PhD. Late Dir, Raffles Museum, Singapore. *Publ*: Guide to the Raffles Museum, Singapore; etc. *a*: 99 Woodstock Rd, Oxf.

HANKEY, Rev. Cyril Patrick. *b*: Folkestone 1886. *e*: Haileybury, Pembroke Coll Camb, Ely Theological Coll. *m*: Frances Mary Harris. *s*: 1. *d*: 1. Vicar of St Paul's Bedford. *Publ*: A Confession of My Faith; The Young Priest; Lives of the Serbian Saints (trans). *s.s*: Theological & Devotional. *a*: St Paul's Vicarage, Bedford. *T*: Bedford 2314.

HANKIN, Ernest Hanbury, M.A., Sc.D. *b*: Ware, Herts 1865. *e*: Merchant Taylors Sc Lon. Late Fellow of St John's Col Cam. Govt Service in India (ret). *Publ*: The Cause & Prevention of Cholera; Cholera in Indian Cantonments; Animal Flight; Common Sense & Its Cultivation; etc. *a*: c/o Lloyds Bank, Greenford, Middx.

HANKINS, Frank Hamilton, A.B., Ph.D. *b*: Willshire, Ohio 1877. *e*: Baker & Columb Univs. *m*: Anna Keeling Hankins. *s*: 2. *d*: 1. Prof of Sociology Univ of Penns 1946—48. *n.a*: Ed Amer Sociological Rev '36—37. *Publ*: The Racial Basis of Civilization; An Introduction to the Study of Society; Adolphe Quetelet as Statistician; (collab) Political Theories; Recent Times; History & Prospects of the Social Sciences; Biology in Human Affairs; Contemporary Social Theory; Dictionary of Sociology. *Ctr*: Amer Sociol Rev & Journ of Sociol, Social Forces, etc. *s.s*: Population, Eugenics, Social Theory. *Rec*: Golf, gardening. *a*: 197 Elm St, Northampton, Mass, U.S.A. *T*: 2255M.

HANKINSON, CHARLES JAMES: see **Holland Clive.**

HANKINSON, Cyril F. J. *b*: Bournemouth 1895. *e*: Queen Elizabeth's Gr Sch Wimborne. *m*: Lillian Louise Read. *s*: 1. *n.a*: Asst-Ed Debrett's Peerage 1921—35 & Ed '35—. *Ctr*: London & American Press. *s.s*: Genealogy, Heraldry, Court, Society. *a*: 22 Welsby Ct, Eaton Rise, Ealing, London, W.5. *T*: Perivale 5018.

HANKS, Rev. William Parker, M.A., HonD.D., HonC.F., F.R.S.L. *b*: Lon 1869. *e*: Forest Sc, King's Col, Glasgow Univ. *m*: Agnes Lermitte Coles. *s*: 2. *d*: 2. *Publ*: The Eternal Witness. *c.t*: Church Times, Guardian, Sunday Times, Glasgow Herald, etc. *s.s*: Philosophy, theology, criminology. *Rec*: Gardening, golf, angling, shooting. Formerly Vicar of St Peter's Bayswater. Travelled extensively. *a*: Grimsbury Manor, Banbury, Oxon. *t*: Banbury 151.

HANLEY, James. Author. *Publ*: Drift; Boy; Men in Darkness; Captain Bottell; Ebb & Flood; The Furys; Hallow Sea; No Directions; Sailors' Song; Crilley. *a*: c/o Pearn, Pollinger & Higham, 39-40 Bedford St, London, W.C.2.

HANLEY, James Alec. *b*: Hemsworth 1886. *e*: Wakefield Gr Sch, Roy Coll of Sci Lond, Univ of Munich. Former Prof of Agriculture, Min of Agr Research Scholarship. *Publ*: Grassland (with Sir R. Stapledon); Essay in Agriculture in the Twentieth Century. *Ctr*: Various, relating to agriculture. *s.s*: Agriculture, Grassland, Soils. *Rec*: Fishing. *a*: Applethwaite, Keswick.

HANMER, Hassal, M.A., B.D.(Edinburgh). *b*: Liverpool 1889. *e*: Wallasey G.S., Yorks Independent Col, Edinburgh Univ. *m*: Margaret Campbell Murray. *s*: 2. *d*: 2. Minister, Sec Scottish Temperance Alliance. *n.a*: Ed Scottish Temperance Reformer, Ed The Adviser. *s.s*: Alcoholism & temperance reform. *Rec*: Angling, philately. War Service '14—19. *c*: Mem Peterhead Town Counc '23—24, Mem Aberdeenshire Education Authority '22—24. *a*: St Leonards, Lenzie, Glasgow; 226 West George St, Glasgow, C.2. *t*: Douglas 4095.

HANNA, Evelyn Isla. *b*: Thomaston, Georgia. *e*: Wesleyan Coll Georgia, Agnes Scott Coll, Emory Univ. *m*: Robert L. Sommerville. Writer. *n.a*: Lond Corres Atalanta Constitution 1945—. *Publ*: Blackberry Winter; Sugar in the Gourd; History of Upson County, Georgia; etc. *Ctr*: Atalanta Journ. *s.s*: Hist of Georgia. *c*: Women's Press (Lond). *a*: Thomaston, Georgia, U.S.A. & 6 Maiden Lne, Covent Garden, London, W.C.2. *T*: Temple Bar 0224.

HANNA, Dr. W. *Publ*: Studies in Smallpox & Vaccination; Industrial Hygiene & Medicine (Jt). Late Deputy M.O.H. City & Port L'pool. *a*: 10 Hill Rd, Birkenhead.

HANNAFORD, C., R.B.A. Artist. *a*: The Lodge, South Walsham, Norfolk.

HANNAH, Cameron. F/L Journalist. *s.s*: Films, health. Short stories. *a*: 69 Elgin Crescent, Notting Hill, W.11.

HANNAH, Ian Campbell. *b*: Brighton 1874. *e*: Winchester Col, Trin Col Cam. *m*: Edith Browning Brand. *s*: 3. Univ Lect. *Publ*: Eastern Asia: A History; Berwick & Lothian Coast; Capitals of the Northlands; Arms & the Map; Quaker Born; Story of Scotland in Stone; etc. *c.t*: Sussex Archæ Collections, Antiquaries Journ, Art & Archæ, etc. *s.s*: Archæ, hist. Master of Eng Sc Tientsin. Pres King's Col Nova Scotia. Prof of Ch Hist Oberlin Col. *Rec*: Cycling. *a*: Whim, Lamancha, Peeblesshire & Fernroyd, Forest Row, Sussex. *t*: Lamancha 2.

HANNAN, Canon Thomas, M.A., HonC.F. *b*: Edin. *e*: Priv & Glas Univ. *m*: Gertrude

Charteris. d: 3. Rector S. Peter's Ch Musselburgh. Publ: The Beautiful Isle of Mull (1926); Iona & some Satellites; Famous Scottish Houses —Lowlands ('28). c.t: Scotsman, Daily Telegraph, Morning Post, Nineteenth Century, Fortnightly Review, Chambers's Journal, & others. s.s: Education, antiquities & ch hist. Rec: Travel, shooting, fishing, photography. Mem Midlothian Ed Cmt. a: The Rectory, Musselburgh, Midlothian. t: 113.

HANNAY, Alexander Howard. b: Lon 1889. e: Winchester & Balliol Col Oxf. m: (1) Winifred Lynton; (2) Leonora Lockhart. s: 3. Civil Servant. n.a: Art Critic Lon Mercury 1920-33, Hon Sec & Ed Aristotelian Soc '24–. c.t: Lon Mercury, etc. s.s: Art & philosophy. a: 17 Charlotte St, Lon, W.1. t: 1889.

HANNAY, J. C. W. Author, Dir of Hannay Brothers Inc. Publ: The Thirteenth Floor; Gin & Ginger; Flight of an Angel; Rebels Triumph. a: Cotton Exchange, Dallas, Texas, U.S.A.

HANNAY, Rev. James Owen, Hon.Litt.D.(Dublin), (See BIRMINGHAM, G. A.). b: Belfast 1865. e: Haileybury & T.C.D. m: Adelaide Susan Wynne (dec'd). s: 2. d: 2. c: Athenæum, Garrick. a: 187 Queen's Gate, London, S.W.7. T: Kensington 3340.

HANNEFORD-SMITH, William, F.R.S.(Edin), Hon. A.R.I.B.A., Assoc.Inst.C.E., M.Inst.Met. e: Aske's Sch Lond & City of Lond Coll. Engineer & Metallurgist. Publ: Kempe's Engineer's Year Book (36 Editions); Metallurgical Manual; Life & Work of Sir Banister Fletcher. s.s: Architecture & Building. a: 15 North Audley St, London, W.1. T: Mayfair 4361.

HANNIGAN, M. T., J.P. b: Rutherglen 1874. e: Elem Scs. Married. s: 4. d: 4. N/p Mang. n.a: Hamilton Herald '94, Cambuslang Pilot '96, W. Lothian Courier '98, Dundee Catholic Herald 1901–. Town Counc 18 y. Pres N.U.J. 3 terms. Ex-Magis. c.t: Daily & weekly press. Rec: Gardening, photography. a: 82 Bell St, Dundee & Cambuscathie, Monifieth, Angus, Scot. t: Dundee 2655 & Monifieth 52.

HANNUM, Alberta Pierson. b: Condit, Ohio 1906. e: Columbus Sch, Univs of Ohio & Columbia. m: Robert Fuiton Hannum. d: 2. Author, Lecturer for W. Colston Leigh Agency N.Y. Publ: Spin A Silver Dollar; The Mountain People in the Great Smokies & the Blue Ridge; Thursday April; The Hills Step Lightly; The Gods & One. Ctr: Story Mag, Collier's, Woman's Journ, Reader's Digest, Reader's Scope, etc. s.s: The Southern Applachian Mountain People & The Navahos. Rec: Golf, tennis, swimming, riding, gardening. c: Fort Henry, Wheeling Country, Moundsville Country. a: Waynesburg Pike, Moundsville, West Virginia, U.S.A. T: Moundsville 916 R.

HANRATTY, Christopher James. b: Dublin 1877. e: McGill Univ Montreal. m: Mary Catherine McCrory. Journalist. n.a: Montreal Star '94, Montreal Gaz 1902, City Ed Montreal Star '11, Canadian Daily Record (Canadian Corps Daily) '18, Montreal Gaz '20. Canadian National Railways (Can Nat Rlys Mag) '24. s.s: Railway Transport in Canada. War Service 4 y Canadian Exped Force. Rec: Golf. c: Press (London) R.A.C. a: 17 Cockspur St, S.W.1. t: Whitehall 2150.

HANS, Nicholas, Ph.D., D.Lit. b: Odessa 1888. e: King's Coll Lond. m: Grace Florence. Reader in Comparative Educ Univ of Lond King's Coll. Jt-Ed of the Year Book of Education. Publ: The Principles of Educational Policy; History of Russian Educational Policy; Educational Policy in Soviet Russia; Educational Traditions in the English-Speaking Countries Ctr: Year Book of Educ, Ency Brit, Internat Rev of Educ, Amer Bulletin of Educ Research, Adult Educ. s.s: Comparative Educ. a: 17 Elmcroft Cresc, London N.W.11. T: Speedwell 4550.

HANSARD, Gillian Elizabeth. b: Lon 1916. e: France. Publ: Old Books for the New Young. Rec: Sports, music, pictures. c: Girl Guide. a: Lou Miracle, Mougins, France. t: 35.

HANSEL, Carl William. b: Leicester 1886. e: Alderman Newton's Sch, Leicester Imp Coll of Science & Technology. m: Annie Elizabeth Green. s: 3. d: 2. Retired Schoolmaster. Publ: Numerical Physics—Heat—Light—Sound; Introductory Electricity & Magnetism; Calculations Made Easy; (Ed) The Construmag. Ctr: Phil Mag, Sch Sci Rev, Pract Engineering, Journ of Educ, Biology & Human Affairs, Nature, Mathematical Assoc, Trans Soc of Engineers. s.s: Mathematics, Physics, Education. Rec: Walking. a: 103 Bromham Rd, Bedford. T: Bedford 2218.

HANSEN, Aase. b: Frederiksvark 1893. Author, Mem P.E.N. & Internat Fed of Univ Women. Publ: En Kvinde Kommer Hjem; De Rode Baand; Tordenluft; Vraggods; Drommen Om I Gaar; Et Par Huse Om En Station. a: 25 Langebrogade, Copenhagen K, Denmark. T: Amager 7197.

HANSEN, Alvin Harvey, B.A., Ph.D. b: Viborg, Sth Dakota 1887. m: Mabel Lewis Hansen. d: 2. Littaner Prof of Economics Harvard Univ. n.a: Ed-Bd Quart Journ of Econ 1937—, Rev of Econ Statistics '37—, Inter-American Affairs '47—. Publ: Fiscal Policy & Business Cycle; American Role in the World Economy; Economic Policy & Full Employment; Business Cycle Theory. Ctr: Quart Journ of Econ, etc. s.s: Fiscal Policy, Full Employment, Business Cycles. a: 56 Juniper Rd, Belmont, Mass, U.S.A. T: Belmont 4721.

HANSEN, Robert. b: Copenhagen 1883. m:. s: 1. Author. Publ: (Pen name: Jens Onker): Djaevlakloen; Der er en Morder; Saadan straffer Jeg; En Mand i Taagen; To Dode Maend; Du Maa Ikke Ihjelslaa!; For Aabent Taeppe. Ctr: Litteraturen, Bog-Anmelderen, etc. s.s: Detective novels & short stories. a: Harsdorffsvej, 10A, 3 Sal.

HANSHEW, Hazel Phillips. b: Brooklyn, N.Y. m: Arnold Hackney. d: 1. Publ: Murder in the Hotel; Riddle of the Winged Death; etc. Ctr: Various Women's Publications. a: c/o Messrs Pearn, Pollinger & Higham Ltd, 39-40 Bedford St, Strand, London, W.C.2.

HANSI (see J. Jacques Waltz). b: Colmar 1873. e: Lycee de Colmar, Ecole des Beaux Arts à Lyon. Artist, Painter, Writer, Curator of Colmar Museum, Officier de la Légion d'honneur, Croix de Guerre. n.a: l'Illustration le Figaro, Le Matin, Le Rire. Publ: Professor Knatschke; L'Histoire d'Alsace; Mon Village; Le Paradis Tricolore; L'Alsace heureuse; Le bon St Florentin; Cloches dans les Vignes; Au pied de la Montagne St Ovile; Colmar-en-France; A Travers les lignes ennemies (with M. Tonnelaz); Alsace; L'Art heraldique en Alsace; etc. s.s: Heraldry, Hist of Alsace, Maintenance of French spirit in Alsace. a: 9 Bd du Champs-de-Mars, Colmar (Ht Rh) France.

HANWORTH OF HANWORTH, Baron (Ernest Murray), K.B.E., K.C. b: Wimbledon 1861. e: Charterhouse Trin Col Cam. m: Laura Helen Salt. s: 1. (dec). d: 1. Barrister 1885. Solicitor Gen 1919. Attorney Gen 1922. Master of the Rolls '23. High Steward of Stratford-on-Avon. Dep High Steward of Cam Univ. Freeman of Warwick & of Leamington. Trustee of Brit Mus. Mem Standing Comm on Museums. J.P. Herts. Gov Wellington Col & of Charterhouse, & Mem Govg Body Charterhouse Sc.

Who Was Who Among English and European Authors

Chm Roy Comm on Hist MSS. Pres Dugdale Soc of Brit Record Assoc. *Publ*: Memoir of Lord Chief Baron Pollock ('29). Officer Legion of Honour & of St Maurice & Lazarus (Italy). M.P. for Warwick & Leamington '10–18, Warwick & Leamington Div of Warwicks '18–23. P.C. '22. *Rec*: Shooting, fishing. *c*: Oxf & Cam, Carlton, Athenæum. *a*: 2 Lygon Pl, S.W.1. *t*: Sloane 4277.

HAPGOOD, Norman, A.B., LL.B., A.M. *b*: Chicago 1868. *e*: Harvard Col & Law Sc. *m*: (1) Emilie Bigelow; (2) Elizabeth Reynolds. *s*: 2. *d*: 2. Author. *n.a*: Ed Collier's Weekly 1903–12, Harper's Weekly '13–16 & Hearst's Internat '23–25, Drama Critic Bookman 1897–1902, Norman Hapgood page, Leslie's Weekly '18–19, etc. *Publ*: Literary Statesmen (1897); George Washington; The Advancing Hour; Up From the City Streets (1928, with H. Muskowitz); The Stage in America; The Changing Years ('30); etc. *s.s*: Public affairs. Chm N.Y. Fusion Cmt '13. League of Free Nations Assoc '18. Min to Denmark '19. Lect on econ & polit problems Calif Univ '34, etc. *c*: Cent Assoc N.Y. *a*: 139 E. 66th St, N.Y. City. *t*: Regent 7-8030.

HAPPOLD, Frederick Crossfield, D.S.O., M.A., Hon. LL.D. *b*: Lancaster 1893. *e*: Rydal Sch & Peterhouse Camb. *m*: Dorothy Vectis Halbach. *s*: 1. Headmaster Bishop Wordworth's Sch Salisbury. *Publ*: Towards a New Aristocracy; Citizens in the Making; The Adventure of Man; This Modern Age; The Finding of the King. *Ctr*: Times Educ Supp, Journ of Educ, Spectator. *s.s*: History, Educ, Sociology. *Rec*: Walking, gardening, reading. *a*: Gales, Bouverie Ave South, Salisbury. *T*: 2833.

HARBAGE, Alfred Bennett, A.B., M.A., Ph.D. (Pennsylvania). *b*: Philadelphia, 1901. *e*: Univ of Pennsylvania. *m*: Eliza Price Finnesey. *s*: 1. *d*: 2. Instructor in English, Univ of Pennsylvania. *Publ*: Thomas Killigrew, Cavalier Dramatist; Sir William Davenant, Poet Venturer. *c.t*: Studies in Philology, Modern Language Notes, Modern Language Assoc. *s.s*: English literary history & biography. *Rec*: Water sports. *c*: Modern Language Assoc of America. *a*: 335 E. Hortter St, Philadelphia, Penn., U.S.A.

HARBERTON, VISCOUNT (Ernest Arthur George Pomeroy): author; *b*. London, Eng., Dec. 1, 1867; *s*. 6th Viscount Harberton and Florence (Legge) Pomeroy; educ. Charterhouse (London), Trinity Coll. (Cambridge); unmarried. AUTHOR: How to Lengthen Our Ears, 1917; Worse than Scripture, or the Truth About Science, 1924. Served in S. African campaigns, awarded medal. HOME: Cottage Castelli, Ville-et-Martin, St. Nazaire, Brittany, France.

HARBORD, Maurice Assheton. *b*: Blackheath 1874. *e*: Prep Sch Blackheath, Haileybury Coll. *m*: Ethel Florence Goldsmith. *s*: 2. *Publ*: Froth and Bubble. *a*: Morden Hse, 138 Parker Rd, Hastings.

HARBORD, Victor H., M.J.I. (Overseas). *b*: Fermoy Ireland 1872. *e*: Bath Col, Priv & Germany. *m*: Janet Gordon Anderson. *s*: 5; *d*: 5. Journalist. *n.a*: Vancouver World 1918–20, Vancouver Sun '20–21, World '22–23, F/L '21–22, Vancouver Daily Province '23–, Ed Writer Surrey Gazette, Cloverdale, B.C. '29–, Ed B.C. Co-operator '29–30. B.C. Civil Service '12–17, Acting Govt Agent, Nicola '17. *c.t*: Toronto Weekly Star, Montreal Herald & Weekly Star, etc. *s.s*: Agric, Christmas stories & poetry (" Justin Wilson "), early hist of B.C. Trop products planter Ceylon, N. Guinea & F.M.S. 1893–1911. Syndicates " Sunny Tales " descriptive of Ceylon, N. Guinea & S. Seas, n/p stories for boys. Mem B.C. I.J. *Rec*: Fishing, writing poetry. *c*: Overseas Author's. *a*: 614 Sixth Av, N. Westminster, B.C. Canada. *t*: 1604.

HARBRON, George Dudley, F.R.I.B.A. *b*: Hull 1880. *e*: Eastbourne Col. Architect. Lect Architectural Sc, City of Hull Col of Art. Ex-Pres York & E. York Architectural Soc. Ex-Mem Counc R.I.B.A. 1929–33. *Publ*: Amphion or the Nineteenth Century. *c.t*: The Builder, Architecture, The Architect, Everyman's Encyclopædia, Arcnt Review, Nation, Outlook, *s.s*: Architectural hist & criticism, biography. *Rec*: Water-colour sketching. *a*: 32 George St, Hull. *t*: 31155.

HARBY, Herbert Leslie, B.Sc., F.R.S.A., M.In.R.A. *b*: London 1901. *e*: Lond Univ. *m*: Doris Fomroy. *d*: 1. Hd of Dept Training College. *Publ*: Science & Handicrafts. *Ctr*: Practical Education. *s.s*: Physics, Mathematics, Technology. *Rec*: Tennis, golf, swimming. *a*: Tutor's Residences, College Rd, Carmarthen. *T*: 442.

HARCOURT, Cyril. Playwright. *Publ*: In the Night; A Pair of Silk Stockings; The Reformer; Wanted—A Husband. *a*: Samuel French Ltd, 26 Southampton St, W.C.2.

HARCOURT, Guy Elliot. *b*: St Heliers, Jersey 1869. *e*: Elizabeth Col Guernsey. Married. *s*: 2. Sailor & Soldier. *Publ*: Fay, A Memory (short stories); Passing Shadows; Queer Passengers: Lying Tongues. *s.s*: Sea & fiction. War Medals S. African & Gt Wars. *a*: c/o Messrs Tylee & Co, 14 Essex St. W.C.2, & 2 Branksome Eastern Parade, Southsea.

HARCOURT, HENRY: barrister-at-law; *b*. Essex, Eng., Sept., 1873; *s*. Frederick and Caroline H.; educ. Merchant Taylors' Sch. (London), Pembroke Coll. (Oxford); DEGREE: M.A.; *m*. Elsie Mary Knight, Oct. 21, 1913. AUTHOR: Sidelights on the Crisis in India, 1924. General character of writing: political. Official service of 25 yrs. in India. Relig. denom., Church of England. CLUB: National Liberal. OFFICE: Free Court, Temple, E. C. 4. HOME: 119 Gipsy Hill, S. E. 19, London, Eng.

HARD, Arnold. Managing Ed :—Tailor & Cutter & Women's Wear, Hatters Gazette, Textile Review & British Millinery & Apparel Production, Founder & Man-Ed :—The Maker-up, The Manufacturing Clothier. *Publ*: The Story of Rayon; The Rayon Dictionary. *a*: 42 Gerrard St, London, W.1 (*T*: Gerrard 5353); & 24 Bride Lane, Fleet St, London, E.C.4 (*T*: Central 3172).

HARDACRE, Geoffrey Ronald. *b*: Poppleton, nr York 1900. *e*: Archbishop Holgate's G.S. *m*: Doris Bartley. Journalist. *n.a*: York Herald & York Evening Press '25–29, Chief Sub-Ed Oxford Mail '29–. *c.t*: Birm Evening Despatch, Darlington Despatch, Evening Advertiser (Swindon). *s.s*: Light verse. R.A.F. '18–19. *a*: 4 Lonsdale Rd, Oxford.

HARDAKER, Charles. *b*: Darlington 1885. *m*. Margaret Underwood. *s*: 3. *d*: 1. Dir & Gen Mang Birmingham Gazette Ltd. *a*: 82 Russell Rd, Moseley, B'ham. *t*: South 3003.

HARDCASTLE, Douglas Noel, M.R.C.S., L.R.C.P., D.P.M.(Cantab), F.R.S.M.M.B., M.A. *b*: Brighton *e*: Taunton Hse Sc Brighton & St Mary's Hosp Paddington. *m*: Dorothy Hilda Timmis. Psychiatrist. Med Dir Fulham Child Guidance Clinic 1933, Psychiatrist St Albans Nerve Clinic Hillend Hosp for Mental & Nervous Diseases '34–, Clinical Asst Paddington Green Children's Hosp '33–. *c.t*: Journ of Neurology & Psychopathology, Journ of Mental Sc. Child Guidance Clinic in Amer; Brit Journ of Med Psychology; *s.s*: Psychological disorders of childhood. Capt R.A.M.C.T.F. '15–20, France, Salonica & Palestine. *c*: Roy Medico Psychological Assoc, Brit Psychological Assoc, Amer Ortho Psychiatric Assoc. *a:* 102 FitzJohn's Av, N.W.3. *t:* Ham 4761.

HARDEN, Arthur, LLD.(honM/C), D.Sc(M/C), PhD., F.R.S. *b:* M/C 1865. *e:* Victoria Pk Sc M/C, Tettenhall Col Staffs, Owen's Col M/C & Univ of Erlangen. *m:* Georgina Sydney Bridge. Emeritus Prof of Biochem Lon Univ. *n.a:* Jt Ed The Biochemical Journal 1913–. *Publ:* Alcoholic Fermentation; Inorganic Chemistry for Advanced Students; Elementary Course of Practical Organic Chemistry (with Dr F. C. Garrett); etc. *c.t:* Scientific journals. *s.s* Biochem. Nobel Laureate in Chem '29. Mem Govg Bodies of Lister Inst & Sir John Cass Tech Inst. *a:* Sunnyholme, Bourne End, Bucks. *t:* 276.

HARDERN, Leslie, B.A., F.R.S.A. *b:* Barrow-in-Furness 1903. *e:* Barrow Gr Sch & St John's Coll Camb. *m:* Elsie Fishwick. *s:* 2. P.R.O., Gas Light & Coke Coy. *Publ:* Physical Planning. *Ctr:* Architectural Press, Art & Industry, Smokeless Air. *s.s:* Planning, Design of Domestic Equipment, Housing, Smoke Abatement, Fuels, Gastronomy. *Rec:* Reading, farming, foreign travel. *a:* Stanbridge Farm, Handcross, Sussex. *T:* Handcross 264.

HARDIE, John Jackson. *b:* Troon, Scotland 1894. *e:* Troon Sch & Irvine Roy Acad. *m:* Marguerite Daly. Executive Graziers Co-operative Shearing Co Ltd, Tech Adv Gaumont British Instructional Films & Internat Wool Secretariat. *Publ:* Pastoral Symphony; Cattle Camp; Bridle Track; Lantana; Wool Classing & Shed Management (Bulletin). *Ctr:* Bulletin (Sydney), Pastoral Review. *s.s:* Wool, Sheep, Cattle & Horses. *Rec:* Tennis, surfing. *c:* P.E.N. *a:* 1 Lindsay St, Neutral Bay, Sydney, N.S.W. *T:* XA 1677.

HARDIE, John Lipp, M.A., Ed.B. *b:* Coatbridge 1893. *e:* Hutchesons Boys Gr Sch Glas, Univ of Glas. *m:* Mary McKinlay. *s:* 1. *d:* 1. Dir of Studies Aberdeen Training Coll. *n.a:* Ed The Outpost (mag of 17th H.L.I. 1915—16). *Publ:* The Craft of Composition (three books); Education & the Community; Ed Verse of Valour, an Anthology; Tales of Tusitala; Twenty-Two Strange Stories; The Bookshelf Classics; etc. *Ctr:* Brit Journ of Psychology, Journ of Educ, Aberdeen Univ Rev, etc. *s.s:* English Lit, Educ, Psychology. *Rec:* Fishing, walking. *c:* Univ (Aberdeen), Roy Scots (Edin). *a:* La Perouse, Fochabers, Morayshire. *T:* Fochabers 278.

HARDIMAN, John Percy, C.B.E. *b:* Kidderminster 1874. *e:* Malvern Col, Oriel Col Oxf & Lincolns Inn. Married. *d:* 2. I.C.S. (ret). *Publ:* Gazetteer of Upper Burma (with Sir J. George Scott); Report of Original Revenue Settlement of the Lower Chindwin District, Upper Burma; Gazetteer of the Lower Chindwin District, Upper Burma. Controller of Munitions, Burma 1917. Comm of the Tenasserim Div Burma '19. *Rec:* Ornithology. *a:* Hyrons Cottage, Woodside Lane, Amersham. *t:* 367.

HARDING, A. J., C.M.G., C.B.E. *n.a:* Co-Ed Dominions Office & Colonial Office List. Dir of Colonial Audit. *a:* Colonial Audit Dept, Queen Anne's Chambers, S.W.1.

HARDING, AUSTIN (pen name): see **Lendon, Alfred Austin.**

HARDING, Colin, C.M.G., D.S.O. *b:* Montacute, Som 1863. *e:* Priv. *m:* Margaret Porter. *d:* 1. Lt-Col (ret). Vice-Pres Berks C.C. of Brit Legion. Vice-Pres S. African Veterans Assoc, Reading Br. *Publ:* In Remotest Barotseland; Far Bugles (1933), foreword by the Rt Hon. Neville Chamberlain, M.P.). *s.s:* Travel, S. African affairs, Gold Coast Colony. Ex-Mem Legislative Counc Gold Coast Colony, Prov Comm Gold Coast Colony, Commandant of Northern Rhodesia Police, Inst of B.S.A. Police. War Service Mashonaland & Matabele Rebellion 1896–97 & European War '14–17. *Rec:* Hunting. *c:* White's, Eng Speaking Un, Authors'. *a:* Gaye Hse, Highmoor Rd, Caversham, Reading, & White's Club. *t:* 72536.

HARDING, Dolores Charlotte Frederica. *b:* Lon. 1889. *e:* Queen's Col Lon. Married. *d:* 2. Novelist & Playwright. *Publ:* Oranges & Lemons; Daughters of Lear; Dark Halo; etc. *c.t:* Vanity Fair, Land Mag, Cassells, etc. *Rec:* Gardening & needlework. *c:* P.E.N., Arts Theatre & Lansdowne House Club. *a:* 19 Park Pl Villas. W.2. *t:* Paddington 3037.

HARDING, Harold Edward, B.A., D.M., B.Ch. *b:* London 1899. *e:* St Olave's Gr Sch, Oriel Coll Oxf & Guy's Hosp. *m:* Mavis K. Thomas. *s:* 2. *d:* 1. Senior Lecturer in Pathology. *Ctr:* Lancet, Brit Journ of Surgery & other medical scientific journs. *s.s:* Pneumoconiosis, Morbid Anatomy & Physiology. *Rec:* Territorial Army. *c:* Artist's Rifles. *a:* Dept of Pathology, The University, Sheffield 10. *T:* 27451.

HARDING, Jane. *b:* Lon 1889. *e:* Priv. *Publ:* The Puppet; Margaret's Mead; The House of Memory. *a:* The Doorway, Ringwood, Hants. *t:* Ringwood 147.

HARDING, John W., M.I.J. *b:* London 1864. Editor & Author. *n.a:* Galignani's Messenger Paris Ed-in-Chief 1892—94, Foreign Ed N.Y. Recorder '94—96, Ed Staff N.Y. Times' 97—1907, Proprietor & Ed of Discovery '07, Ed People's Magazine '09—10, rejoined N.Y. Times '13, Corr Dly Chron Lond '17—29. *Publ:* An Art Failure; The Strolling Piper of Brittany; The Gate of the Kiss; etc; Novels Adapted from the Plays—Paid in Full; The Chorus Lady; etc; Trans—Facing the Flag (Jules Verne); Memoirs (Victor Hugo); Sacrifice of Silence (Edouard Rod); & author of many mag stories. *c:* The Pilgrims, St George's Soc, etc. *a:* 1722 Undercliff Ave, New York 53, N.Y.; Office N.Y. Times, N.Y.

HARDING, Joseph. *b:* Kimberley, Sth Africa 1913. *e:* Boy's Hgh Sch Kimberley. *m:* Elise Mary Bronn. *n.a:* Ed/Sec On the Road 1944—, former Ed Public Works of South Africa '39—41, & Licensed Victualler's Gazette '41—42. *a:* c/o South African Commercial Traveller's Association, P.O. Box 828, Cape Town, South Africa. *T:* 26804.

HARDING, M. Esther, M.D., B.S., M.R.C.P. *b:* Shrewsbury 1888. *e:* Shrewsbury H. Sch for Girls, Lond Univ. *Publ:* The Way of All Women; Woman's Mysteries, Ancient & Modern. *s.s:* Analytical Psychology, Psychic Energy—Its Source & Goal. *a:* 108 East 38th St, New York. *T:* Lexington 2, 6044.

HARDING, Margaret Snodgrass, A.M.(Indiana). *b:* Chicago, Ill 1885. *m:* Samuel Bannister Harding. *s:* 1. *d:* 2. Editor & Publisher. *n.a:* Ed-Dir Univ of Minnesota Press 1927. *Publ:* (With S. B. Harding) New Mediæval & Modern History; Old World Background to American History; Story of Europe. *Ctr:* Publisher's Weekly, Current Biography, etc. *s.s:* History, Education. *a:* 58 Orlin Ave, S.E., Minneapolis 14, Minnesota, U.S.A. *T:* Gladston 5655.

HARDING, Robert. *b:* Watford, 1897. *e:* Dorchester Boys' Sch, Weymouth Sec Sch. *m:* Evelyn M. Wernham. Author, Mem N.U.J. *n.a:* Ed Boy's Own Paper 1935—41. *Publ:* Dallenger of the Police; The Keys of Freedom; Pioneer Jack; The Riddle of the Frontier; Tales of the Frontiers; Songs of Camp & Trail (Verses); etc. *s.s:* All leading juvenile publications. *s.s:* India & Arabia. *Rec:* Golf, cricket, tramping, swimming, reading Kipling. *w.s:* World War I 1914—19 Dorset Terr, World War II '42—45 Mil Police. *a:* 57 Burnham Rd, Leigh-on-Sea, Essex.

HARDING, Walter Ambrose Heath, M.A. (Cantab)., F.L.S., F.Z.S. *b*: Leeds 1870. *e*: Cheltenham & Peterhouse Cam. *m*: Ethel Adela Hirst. *s*: 1. *d*: 1. *Publ*: (pt Author of Vol) Hirudinea in The Fauna of British India series (1927); edited with notes, Waterton's Wanderings in South America ('03). *c.t*: Trans of Linnean Soc, Proc of Zoological Soc, Mems of the Indian Museum. Victoria Hist of County of Hunts, etc. *s.s*: Zoology & nat hist. *Rec*: Trav & book collecting. *c*: Carlton. *a*: Madingley Hall, Cam. *t*: Madlingley 2.

HARDING NEWMAN, Maj.-Gen. John Cartwright, C.B., C.M.G. *Publ*: Military Law (1905); Modern Military Administration, Organisation & Transportation; Letters of a Self-made General to his Son. *c.t*: Army & Navy Gazette. *a*: 2 Cam Rd, Colchester. *t*: 2871.

HARDINGE, Lady Alexandra. *a*: The Halsteads, 3 Fife Rd, East Sheen. *t*: Prospect 4544.

HARDINGE, Rex. *b*: Poona, India 1904. *e*: Wellington Col, Berks. *m*: Ellen Hanson. *s*: 2. *d*: 1. Author. *n.a*: Bombay Rep for Pioneer & Civil & Military Gazette '28. *Publ*: Gambia & Beyond (travel); Beyond the Skyline (novel); Motley (verse). *c.t*: Times of India, Illustrated Wkly, Novel Mag, Pearson's Mag, Answers, Chums, Sexton Blake Library, Detective Wkly, Dixon Hawke Library, Adventure, World Radio. *s.s*: Detective fiction, adventure, juvenile thrillers, travel & short stories. Travelled in Canada, South Africa, West Africa, India. *a*: 8 King St, Emsworth, Hants.

HARDMAN, David Rennie, M.A., LL.B., J.P., M.P. *b*: London 1901. *e*: Coleraine Academical Inst N. Ireland, Christ's Coll Camb. *m*: Barbara Pauline Lambert. *d*: 1. Parl Sec Min of Educ, Chm Cambridgeshire Educ Cttee 1946, Leader U.K. Delegations U.N.E.S.C.O. (Paris '46, Mexico '47), Pres Shaw Soc '47. *Publ*: What About Shakespeare. *s.s*: Shakespeare. *Rec*: Gardening, mountaineering, swimming. *c*: Savile. *a*: Little Ote Hall, Wivelsfield, Sussex.

HARDWICK, Rev. John Charlton. *b*: Bournemouth 1885. *e*: Wadham Coll Oxf. Clergyman (Church of England). *Publ*: No Casual Creed; What to Believe; A Professional Christian; Conquest of Disability; Letter to an Archbishop. *s.s*: Relations between Religion & Science. *a*: The Vicarage, Partington, Manchester. *T*: Irlam 220.

HARDWICK, Walter Osborn. *b*: Earls Barton 1877. *e*: Wellingborough. G.S. *n.a*: Northampton Echo (1892–99), S. Wales Argus, Newport 1900–. *a*: 44, West Hill, Tredegar, Mon.

HARDWICKE, Sir Cedric Webster. *b*: Stourbridge 1893. *e*: Bridgenorth, Salop. *m*: Helena Pickard. *s*: 1. Actor. *Publ*: Let's Pretend. *a*: 10 Chester Pl, N.W.1. *t*: Welbeck 2848.

HARDY, Alfred Cecil, B.Sc., F.R.G.S., A.M.I.M.E., M.I.N.A., M.Inst.Pet. *b*: Cromer 1898. *e*: Priv & Durham Univ. *m*: Nina M. Gaskins. *s*: 1. Naval Architect & Marine Consultant. *n.a*: Journ of Commerce & Lloyd's List, Ed Motorship (N.Y.) 1924–28, Tech Ed The Marine Engineer. Sen Tech Mem Tripartite Naval Commssn Berlin '45, Dep Command-Constructor Officer B.N. C-in-C Germany, Personal Tech Asst to Chief Combined Ops 1st Quebec Conf '43. *Publ*: Merchant Ship Types; Motorships; From Slip to Sea; American Ship Types; Motorships of the World; Oil Ships; Brit Ships & Shipping Illustrated; Diesels & the Fishing Industry; World Shipping; Bulk Cargoes; Warships at Work; Sea Transport; You & Your Ships; Sky Ships; Seafood Ships; Ships at Work; Inland Waterway & Harbour Craft; Merchant Ships Identification (B.R. 115); Allied Navies Official Handbook. *Ctr*: Scandinavian Shipping Gaz, Shipping World, Fishing News, Dagblad Scheepvaart, The Harbour. *s.s*: Types & Construction of Ships, Diesel Machinery & Electric Drive, the Fishing Industry. *a*: Roundway Hse, Rustington, Sussex, & 110 Fenchurch St, London, E.C.3. *T*: Rustington 884, & Royal 5204/5.

HARDY, Eric. *b*: Liverpool. *e*: Holt Hgh Sch & L'pool City Tech Sch. *m*:. *s*: 1. *d*: 1. Editor, Naturalist, Nature-writer, Lecturer & Broadcaster. *n.a*: Ed Wild Birds Mag, Staff Liverpool Dly Post & Echo. 1930–33. *Ctr*: Leading pubs at home & abroad. *Publ*: Birds of Liverpool Area; Birds of Palestine; etc. *s.s*: Birds & Nature, Angling, Dogs, Short Stories, etc. *w.s*: Roy Sigs & Army Pigeon Svce. *a*: 47 Woodsorrel Rd, Liverpool 15. *T*: Childwall 2819.

HARDY, Evan Alan, M.S.(Iowa). *b*: Sioux City, Iowa 1890. *m*: Lois A. Hicks. *d*: 3. Prof of Agricultural Engineering. *Publ*: Gasoline Ignition; Maintenance & Overhaul of the Farm Tractor; Engine Lubrication; Engine Fuels; Ploughs & Ploughing; The Header & Header Barge; Maintenance & Operation of the Plough & the One Way Disc; Farm Shop Work; Automobile & Farm Lighting Plant Storage Batteries; Binder Adjustments; Water & Disposal Systems. *Ctr*: Various. *s.s*: Farm Power & Machinery, the Mechanisation of Agriculture in Western Canada. *Rec*: Rugby football, boating, fishing. *c*: Canadian, etc. *a*: 1037 Aird St, Saskatoon, Sask, Canada. *T*: 97510.

HARDY, F., M.B.E., J.P. *Publ*: Letters from South & South Central Africa. *a*: Oakhurst, Mansfield. Notts.

HARDY, Henry Harrison, C.B.E., M.B.E.(Mil). *b*: Allahabad, India 1882. *e*: Rugby, New Coll Oxf. *m*: (1) Eleanor Mary Colbeck (dec'd). *d*: 2; (2) Edith Jocelyn Dugdale. *s*: 3. Dir of Studies R.M.A. Sandhurst since 1946, Chmn Roy Coll for the Blind, Headmaster Cheltenham Coll '19–32 & Shrewsbury Sch '32–44, Late Major Rifle Bde. *Publ*: History of Rugby School; The Shorter Aeneid; The Shorter Iliad. *Ctr*: The Tramp, Brit Overseas, The Fighting Forces, The Alpine Journ. *c*: Naval & Military, Athenæum, Alpine. *a*: Old Farm, Bishops Cleeve, Gloucester. *T*: Cleeve Hill 89.

HARDY, Jocelyn Lee, D.S.O., M.C. With Bar. *b*: Lon 1894. *e*: Berkhamsted Sc & R.M.C. Sandhurst. *m*: Kathleen Isabel Hutton-Potts. Farmer. *Publ*: I Escape (1927); The Key (with Robert Gore-Browne, at the St Martin's Theatre) '33; Everything is Thunder. *c.t*: Sunday Chronicle, Nash's, London Mercury. Escaped prisoner-of-war invalided out with loss of leg. Served with forces in Ireland. *a*: Rougham, Kings Lynn, Norfolk. *t*: Rougham 2.

HARDY, Norman Felix. Benedictine Monk. *n.a*: Ampleforth Journ ('28–). *a*: Ampleforth Abbey, York.

HARDY, Dr. Percy, B.A., M.B., B.Ch(Camb), M.R.C.S., L.R.C.P. *a*: 1 Magdala Rd, Nottingham.

HARDING, Revel. *b*: Ashford, Kent. Novelist & Journalist. *Publ*: Aftermath (22nd thous); Rooks Build Low. *c.t*: Nat, prov & col n/ps & periodicals. *s.s*: Botany, ornithology. *a*: c/o Skeffington & Son Ltd, 34 Paternoster Row, E.C.4. & c/o J. H. Sears, Inc, N.Y.

HARDY, Richard. *b*: Ilford, Essex. P.R.O. West Ham Stadium. *n.a*: Asst Ed Advertisers Weekly, Rep Athletic News Agency, Sports News Asst, Palmers Green & Southgate Gazette. *Ctr*: Various Sporting periodicals. *a*: West Ham Stadium, London, E.16. *T*: Albert Dock 2441 & Uplands 3383.

HARDY, Roy. *b*: London. Advtg & Journalism, Ex Chmn Bureau of Advtg Facts, Chm 1926—27 Publicity Club Lond. *Ctr*: Advertiser's Weekly, World's Press News, The Announcer, Ev News, Recorder, Cinema, Era, etc. *s.s*: Advtg, Comm Art, Personalities, Gossip, Humour, Advt Man Cologne Post 1919—20 with Army of Occupation. *c*: Lond Sketch, Publicity of London, Cercle de la Maison de France, Poor Richard (Phil Pa), Regent Advertising. *a*: 35 King St, Covent Gdn, London, W.C.2. *T*: Temple Bar 6446.

HARDY, THOMAS: poet, novelist; *b*. Dorset, Eng., June 2, 1840; s. of Thomas Hardy; educ. Dorchester and King's College (London). DEGREES: D.Litt.; Litt.D.; Hon. Fellow Queen's College (Oxford); Hon. Fellow Magdalen College, Cambridge; m. Florence Emily Dugdale. AUTHOR: Desperate Remedies, 1871; Under the Greenwood Tree or the Mellstock Quire, 1872; A Pair of Blue Eyes, 1872-73; Far From the Maddening Crowd, 1874; Hand of Ethelberta, 1876; Return of the Native, 1878; The Trumpet-Major, 1879; A Laodicean, 1880-81; Two on a Tower, 1882; The Life and Death of the Mayor of Casterbridge, 1884-85; The Woodlanders, 1886-87; Wessex Tales, 1888; A Group of Noble Dames, 1891; Tess of the D'Urbervilles, 1891; Life's Little Ironies, 1894; Jude the Obscure, 1895; The Well-Beloved, 1897; A Changed Man, etc. (collected), 1913; Verse: Wessex Poems, 1865-98; Poems of the Past and the Present, 1901; The Dynasts (epic drama), 1903-1908; Select Poems of William Barnes, with Preface, 1908; Time's Laughing Stock, 1909; Satires of Circumstances, 1911-14; Selected Poems, 1916; Moments of Vision, 1917; Complete Political Works (2 vols.), 1919; Late Lyrics, 1922; Queen of Cornwall (play), 1923; Human Shows, 1925. General character of writing: poetry and novels. Studied architecture and was, in early life, articled to an architect. (Submitted by Thomas Hardy before his death for publication in this work, and included in Introductory Volume published 1928.—Editor). (*)

HARDY, Rev. Thomas John, M.A. *b*: Oldham 1868. *e*: Magnus Sc Newark-on-Trent & Cam Univ. *m*: Olive Margaret Shaw-Stewart. *Publ*: The Gospel of Pain; The Religious Instinct; Christianity Misunderstood; The Secret of Progress; Books on the Shelf; The Year with Christ. *c.t*: Times, Hibbert Journal, Guardian, Downside Review, etc. *s.s*: Theology, literary criticism. *a*: Benet Wood, Torquay, Devon.

HARDY, William Edwin. *b*: Sheffield 1899. *n.a*: Ed Management of Hatton Press. *Ctr*: Times Trade & Eng Supp, Star, Dly Express, etc. *s.s*: Sci Instruments, Optics. *c*: Various Sci & Soc. *a*: 72/78 Fleet St, London, E.C.4. *T*: Central 6652/3.

HARDY, William George, M.A., Ph.D. *b*: Oakwood, Ont, Canada 1895. *e*: Toronto Univ, Chicago Univ. *m*: Llewella Sonley. *s*: 1. *d*: 2. Prof & Head Dept of Classics Univ of Alberta, Vice-Pres Internat Ice Hockey Assoc. *Publ*: All the Trumpets Sounded; Father Abraham; Turn Back the River. *Ctr*: Collier's, Maclean's Mag, Can Home Journ, Strand Mag, Tomorrow Mag, Classical Philology, etc. *s.s*: Classical Education, Relationship between the U.K & Canada, Stories with an Archæological background. *Rec*: Tennis, golf. *w.s*: 1914—18. *a*: University of Alberta, Edmonton, Alberta, Canada. *T*: 22131.

HARDYMAN, Dr. G., M.B., F.R.C.S.(Eng), F.R.MedS. *Publ*: Four Rare Forms of Dislocation, Lancet 1887; Shadow Test in Retiniscopy, B.M.J.

1912. *Rec*: Croquet. *a*: Perrymead Court, & 9 Paura Pl, Bath.

HARE, Amy, F.R.A.M. Pianist & Composer. *a*: 205 Oakwood Ct, W.14. *t*: Wes 6557.

HARE, Cyril. (See **CLARK, Alfred Alexander Gordon**.
HARE, Kenneth, M.A. *b*: Twickenham 1888. *e*: St Paul's, Wadham Coll Oxf, abroad. *m*: Mary Lee Bennett. *d*: 1. Author. *Publ*: Verse—Green Fields; Sir Gawayne & the Green Knight; New Poems; Prose—London's Latin Quarter; Our Cockney Ancestors; Roads & Vagabonds; No Quarrel with Fate; Gloucestershire; etc. *Ctr*: Truth, New English Rev, Wine & Food, Oxford Mag, Cambridge Rev, Quarterly Rev, Chamber's Journ, etc. *c*: Authors. *w.s*: World War I. *a*: Bussage, nr Stroud, Glos.

HARE, Kenneth, M.A. *b*: Twickenham 1888. *e*: St Paul's Sc & Oxf Univ. *m*: Mary Maud Lee-Bennett. *d*: 1. Author. *n.a*: Dramatic Critic to Hearth & Home & Vanity Fair, under Editorship of late Mr. Frank Harris. Curator of Photographs in the collection made by order of the War Cabinet (Imp War Museum). *Publ*: Verse: Green Fields (1911); etc. Prose—Guide to Bruges (5th ed, '25); Archers' Chronicle & Greenwood Companion ('29); Roads & Vagabonds ('30); etc. *c.t*: Various. Poets' Club Gold Medallist '25. War Service 1914-18. *Rec*: Visiting picture galleries, & theatre. *c*: Authors', Poets', Soc of St Sebastian (Archery Club, Bruges). *a*: Three Beeches, Bussage, Stroud, Glos.

HARE, Lloyd C. M., LL.B.(Calif). *b*: Berkeley, California 1893. *e*: Univ of California. *m*: Brizaide C. M. Giannugnani. Lawyer, Mem Adv Staff Amer Hist Co Inc N.Y. *n.a*: Ed Staff California Law Review 1924—25, Asst Ed California Decisions '27—28, Asst Ed California Appellate Decisions '27—28, Mem Ed Staff Official Reports of Supreme Court of California & of Dist Courts of Appeal of California '23—29. *Publ*: Thomas Mayhew: Patriarch to the Indians; The Greatest American Woman—Lucretia Mott. *Ctr*: The Dictionary of American Biography, Americana. *s.s*: Anglo-American Colonial Hist. *c*: California Writers'. *w.s*: Sergt Army T'port Service 1918, Co-ordinator Civil Defence '41. *a*: 617 San Carlos Ave, Berkeley, California, U.S.A. *T*: Thornwall 2155.

HARE, Hon. Richard, Laming Fell Queen's Coll Oxf. *b*: London 1907. *e*: Balliol Coll Oxf & abroad. *m*: Dora Gordine. Author & Lecturer, formerly H.M. Diplomatic Service & Dir of Russian Div M.o.I. *Publ*: Russian Literature from Pushkin to the Present Day; (trans) Selected Works of Ivan Turgenev; Prose Works of Lermontov; Selected Stories of Ivan Bunin. *s.s*: Russian Literature, History & Art. *a*: Dorich Hse, Kingston Vale, London, S.W.15. *T*: Kingston 4254.

HARE, Robert. See **Hutchinson, Robert Hare**.

HARE, Ronald, M.B., B.S. Bacteriologist. *c.t*: Lancet, Brit Journ of Experimental Pathology, etc *a*: Bernhard Baron Meml Research Laboratories, Q. Charlotte's Hosp. W.6. *t*: Riverside 6081.

HARE, T. Leman. *a*: Apollo, Field Hse, Breams Bldgs, Chancery Lane, W.C.2.

HARES, Ven. Archdeacon Walter Pullin, M.B.E., B.A. *b*: Alcester 1877. *e*: Durham Univ. *m*: Marion Pullin. *s*: 2. Archdeacon of Sind & Baluchistan 1946—. *Publ*: Church History of the First Six Centuries; Story of a Canal Colony; Teaching & Practice of the Church of Rome in India; English-Punjabi Dictionary; 900 Punjabi Proverbs; The Supremacy of St Peter; The One Holy Catholic & Apostolic Church. *Ctr*: The Record, various missionary mags. *s.s*: Punjab.

Languages, Church History. *w.s*: 1940—46 Indian Army, Staff Major, C.L.O. *a*: 753 Lawrence Rd, Karachi, Pakistan, India.

HARFITT, Rev. Frederick H. E., F.R.S.A., F.R.G.S., M.R.S.L. *b*: New Sarum 1888. *e*: Bishop's Sch Salisbury, King's Coll Lond. *m*: Lillian Gill. *s*: 2. Rector of St Mary-at-Hill E.C., Chm Philosphical Soc of Eng 1946, Mem Court of Governors Sion Coll Lond. *Publ*: The Truth Series. *Ctr*: Various. *s.s*: Christian Apologetics. *Rec*: Motoring, open-air work. *a*: The Rectory, St Mary-at-Hill, London, E.C. *T*: Mansion House 4184.

HARFORD, Rev. Dundas, M.A. *b*: Keswick 1858. *e*: Repton, Trin Col & Ridley Hall Cam. *m*: Enid Howell. *s*: 2. *d*: 2. *n.a*: Ed The Shewings of Lady Julian of Norwich, A.D. 1373; etc. *Publ*: Memoir of Canon T. D. Harford-Battersby (Jt Author); etc. *c.t*: Norfolk archæ, etc. *s.s*: Middle Eng mystics & lit. Ret 1926. *Rec*: Skating. *a*: Sandpit Cottage, Seaford. *t*: 179.

HARFORD, Rev. J. W. *Publ*: Comrades of Christ; Pamphlets. *c.t*: Christian World Pulpit. *a*: All Saints Vicarage, 5 Larkhall Rise, S.W.4. *t*: Macaulay 2906.

HARFORD, JOHN BATTERSBY: clergyman, canon on Ripon Cathedral; b. Keswick, Cumberland, Eng., June, 1857; s. Thomas Dundas and Mary (Forbes) Harford-Battersby; educ. Repton Sch., Trinity College, Cambridge; DEGREES: B.A. (1880) (First Class Theological Tripos); M.A. (1883), B.D. (1927); m. Edith Rachel Pelly (deceased), Oct. 5, 1887. AUTHOR: Letters and Poems of Bishop Moule (edited), 1921; Life of Handley Moule, Bishop of Durham, 1922; Since Wellhausen, 1926; Altars and Sanctuaries in the Old Testament, 1929. Articles in Expositor and in Expository Times. General character of writing: biographical, biblical criticism. Vice-prin. Ridley Hall, Cambridge, 1898-1900; prin. Midland Clergy Coll., 1900-1902; prin. Ripon Coll., 1902-12; Canon of Ripon Cathedral since 1911. Examining chaplain (for 25 yrs.) to four Bishops of Ripon. Relig. denom., Church of England. HOME: 8 The Crescent, Ripon, Eng.

HARGRAVE, John Gordon, F.R.S.A. *b*: Midhurst 1894. *e*: Wordsworth's Hawkshead. *m*: Ruth Clark. *s*: 1. Artist, Writer, Organiser & Leader, Founder & Leader Social Credit Party. *n.a*: Staff C. Arthur Pearson Ltd 1914, Art Mang '17—29. *Publ*: At Suvla Bay; Harbottle; Young Winkle; And Then Came Spring; The Pfenniger Failing; The Imitation Man; Summer Time Ends; Professor Skinner; Words Win Wars; Social Credit Clearly Explained. *Ctr*: New Age. *Rec*: Camping. *a*: Wayside, King's Langley, Herts. *T*: 7344.

HARGREAVES, Eric Lyde, M.A., Ph.D. *b*: London 1898. *e*: St Pauls Sch Lond, Corpus Christi Coll Oxf. Tutor & Lect, Fell of Oriel Coll Oxf, Official Historian Civil Hist of the War 1942—. *Publ*: The National Debt; Restoring Currency Standards. *s.s*: Economics & Econ Hist. *w.s*: 1917—18. *a*: Oriel Coll, Oxford. *T*: 3135.

HARGREAVES, Sir Gerald de la Pryme. *b*: Southport, Lancs 1881. *e*: Eton & Magdalen Coll Oxf. County Court Judge. *Publ*: Deeds of Arrangement. *Rec*: Lawn tennis, music. *c*: Carlton, Stoke Poges Golf. *w.s*: 1914—19. *a*: 59 Sloane St, London, S.W.1. *T*: Sloane 6855.

HARGREAVES, J. *a*: Lancs Daily Post, Clitheroe.

HARGREAVES, Reginald, M.C. *b*: London 1888. *e*: Cheltenham. Military Historian. *Publ*: John Bull from Hanover; The Enemy at the Gate; Women at Arms; Mr Crofts the King's Bastard (with Lewis Melville); Famous Duels & Assassinations (with Lewis Melville); etc. *Ctr*: Blackwoods, Army Quarterly, Chambers, Nat Rev, Cavalry Journ, Cornhill, Cavalry Journ (U.S.A.), Dly Telegraph, Wine & Food Quarterly. *s.s*: Mil Hist, Mil Biog, Hist of Uniform, Arms & Armour. *Rec*: Gardening, painting, reading, music. *a*: Beech Cottage, Wootton St Lawrence, nr Basingstoke.

HARI-KARI. See Browning, Robert.

HARINGTON, Charles Robert, M.A., Ph.D.(Edin), F.R.S. *b*: Llanerfyl, Nth Wales 1897. *e*: Malvern Coll, Magdalene Coll Camb, Edin Univ. *m*: Jessie McCririe Craig. *s*: 1. *d*: 2. Dir Nat Institute for Med Research Lond, Croonian Lect & Roy Medallist of Roy Soc 1944, Hon Fellow of Magdalene Coll Camb '44, Dr (Honoris Causa) Paris '45. *n.a*: Ed Biochem Journ 1930—42. *Publ*: The Thyroid Gland, Its Chemistry & Physiology. *Ctr*: Biochem Journ, Lancet, B.M.J., Nature, etc. *s.s*: Organic Chem, Biochem, Immunochem. *c*: Athenæum. *a*: Mount Vernon Hse, Hampstead, London, N.W.3. *T*: Hampstead 2037.

HARINGTON, D. L. *n.a*: "Tobacco", Industrial Newspapers Ltd. *a*: 49 Wellington St, W.C.2.

HARKER, Alfred, M.A.(Cantab), LL.D.(Edin & McGill), F.R.S. *b*: Hull 1859. *e*: Cam. Emeritus Reader in Petrology Cam. *Publ*: Petrology for Students; The Natural History of Igneous Rocks; Metamorphism (1932); etc. *c.t*: Geological Socs & Journs. *s.s*: Geology. *a*: St John's Col, Cam.

HARKER, L. ALLEN: author; b. Gloucester, Eng., d. William and Elizabeth Matson (Ferguson) Watson; educ. Cheltenham Ladies' Coll.; m. J. James Allen-Harker (died). AUTHOR: Concerning Paul and Fiammetta, 1906; A Romance of the Nursery, 1907; Miss Esperance and Mr. Wycherly, 1908; Master and Maid, 1909; The Ffolliots of Redmarley, 1910; Mr. Wycherly's Wards, 1911; Allegra, 1915; Jan and Her Job, 1916; Montagu Wycherly, 1919; The Vagaries of Tod and Peter, 1920; The Bridge Across, 1921; Children of the Dear Cotswolds, 1923; The Broken Bow, 1924; The Really Romantic Age, 1925; Hilda Ware, 1928; Black Jack House. Contributor to Pearson's, Scribner's, Century, Cornhill, Woman's Home Companion, Atlantic Monthly, Outlook, Daily Chronicle, Woman at Home, Good Housekeeping, Daily News and other papers and mags. General character of writing: novels, plays. Relig. denom., Church of England. CLUBS: P.E.N., Lyceum. HOME: The Old House, Cirencester, Gloucester, Eng.

HARLAND, James Penrose, M.A., Ph.D. *b*: Wenonah, N.J. 1891. *e*: Univs of Princeton, Bonn, Uppsala & American Sch at Athens. *m*: Agnes Westerlund. Professor of Archæology. *n.a*: Cont-Ed Amer Journ of Archæol 1940—. *Publ*: The Peloponnesus in the Bronze Age; Prehistoric Aigina; etc. *Ctr*: Various. *s.s*: Helladic Civilisation, Hellenic Alphabet, Horticulture, Philately. *c*: Archæological, etc. *w.s*: 1917—19 U.S.N. *a*: 1 Brierbridge Lne, Chapel Hill, North Carolina, U.S.A. *T*: Chapel Hill 5736.

HARLER, Christopher Cranfield. *b*: Somerset 1906. *e*: Elem Sc. *m*: Edna Grace Grandfield. Journalist. *n.a*: Apprentice Western Chronicle Yeovil 1920-25, Improver Tunbridge Wells Advertiser & Tonbridge Free Press '25-6, Reporter Brentwood Gazette & Mid Essex Recorder '26-9, Dist Reporter Bromley & West Kent Mercury '29. *c.t*: Correspondent to Nat Dailies. Hon Treas S.E. Lon Branch N.U.J. '32. *Rec*: Walking, photog. *a*: 7 Bramley Way, West Wickham, Kent. *t*: Spring Park 1401.

HARLEY, CATHERINE WINIFRED: ..schoolteacher, writer; b. Birmingham, Eng., Dec. 9, 1895; d. John and Mary Jane S. (Anderson)H.; educ. Moseley Coll. (Birmingham), Maria Grey Coll. (London); unmarried. Contributor to Junior Home Mag., Childhood Education, Child Health Bulletin. Wrote: English and American Nursery School Contrasted (in New Era, Nov.) 1930; Health Education for Preschool Children (in Public Health Nurse, May), 1931; Children's Play (with Suggestions for Summer Time Activity): First Steps in Christian Nurture, 1931. General character of writing: educational, development of childhood. Holder Nat. Froebel Union Higher certificate; organizer of one of first nursery schls. to obtain grant under Education Act 1918 in London, (Union Jack, N.S.); 6 yrs. at Merrill-Palmer Sch.: organized Child Development center, Dartington Hall, Totnes, Devon. 1930. Relig. denom., Episcopalian. OFFICE: Merrill-Palmer School. HOME: 61 Southway, Hampstead, London, Eng.

HARLEY, John Eugene, A.B., J.D.(Southern California), M.A.(Harvard). b: Mount Vernon, Missouri, U.S.A., 1892. e: Univs of Southern California and Harvard, L'Institut de Hautes Etudes Internationales Geneva, Univ of Southern California Law Sc. Prof of political science, Univ of S. California. Publ: The League of Nations and the New International Law; International Understanding: Agencies Educating for a New World; Documentary Textbook on International Relations. c.t: American Jnl of Internat Law, World Affairs Interpreter, Annals of the American Academy of Political and Social Science, etc. s.s: Internat law, League of Nations, disarmament, world peace. Rec: Tennis, mountaineering, volley ball, fishing. Carnegie Fell in internat law Harvard Univ, '18—20. c: Pres Counc on Internat Relations Los Angeles, American Soc of Internat Law, American Political Science Assoc, Foreign Policy Assoc, etc. a: 1227 West 39th St, Los Angeles, California, U.S.A.

HARLEY, John Hunter, M.A., F.R.Hist.S., F.R.G.S. Publ: inc The New Social Democracy; Colonel Beck; Towards a Free Europe; etc. a: 59 Parliament Hill, Hampstead, London, N.W.3.

HARLEY, M. R. a: Wembley News, 12 Neeld Parade, Wembley.

HARLING, Robert. b: 1910. Editor. n.a: Ed Typography 1936—39, Ed Alphabet & Image from '46. Publ: The Steep Atlantick Stream; Amateur Sailor; Home: A Victorian Vignette; The London Miscellany. a: The Mill Hse, Wiston, Nayland, Suffolk.

HARLOW, Frank Wilson, M.B., B.S., F.R.C.S. b: Newcastle-on-Tyne 1893. e: Univ of Durham. Surgeon to Roy I.o.W. County Hosp, Roy Nat Hosp for Diseases of the Chest, H.M. Prison Parkhurst. Publ: Modern Surgery for Nurses. Ctr: Lancet, Medical World, Medical Press & Circular, etc. s.s: Surgery. Rec: Tennis, literature. w.s: R.A.M.C. 1914—22 & Surg E.M.S. '40—45. a: Lynwood, St John's Park, Ryde, I.o.W. T: Ryde 2652.

HARLOW, Frederick James, M.B.E., PhD., B.Sc, A.R.C.S., D.I.C., F.InstP. b: Whitstable 1886. e: Simon Langton Sc Canterbury & Roy Col Sci Lon. m: Isabel Elsie Pettman. s: 1. d: 1. Princ Chelsea Polytech Lon 1928-. c.t: Proc Phys Soc Lon, Proc Far Soc, Bull Inst Min & Met, Journ Inst Elec Eng; etc. s.s: Educ, physics. X-ray & Electromed Physicist Army Med Dept War Office '15—19. Princ Wigan & Dis College of Art & Tech Col '25—28. Hon Sec Assoc of Princ's of Tech Inst's '31—34. Vice-Chm '34—35, etc. a: 62 Harwood Av, Bromley, Kent. t: Ravensbourne 0562.

HARMAN, Arthur Jympson. b: Hastings 1891. m: s: 1. Journalist. n.a: Reporter, News Sub-Ed & Feature Page the Ev News 1914—. Publ: Good Films; How to Enjoy Them. s.s: Films. Rec: Reading & tramping. a: The Ev News, Carmelite Hse, London, E.C.4. T: Central 6000 & Balham 3511.

HARLOW, Vincent Todd, M.A., F.R.Hist.S., D.Litt. b: Newcastle-on-Tyne 1898. e: Durham Sch & Brasenose Coll Oxf. m: Margretta Badcock. Rhodes Prof of Imperial History Univ of London. Publ: A History of Barbados; A Life of Christopher Codrington; Critical Edition of Sir Walter Ralegh's Discovery of Guiana; Ralegh's Last Voyage; The British Colonies; etc. Ctr: Sunday Times. s.s: History & Current Affairs of British Commonwealth & Empire. Rec: Walking, gardening. c: Athenæum. a: 32 Queen Court, Queen Sq, London, W.C.1. T: Terminus 1726; & Fir Tree Hse, Old Marston, Oxford. T: 3872.

HARLOW, Rex Francis. b: Winfield, Mo 1892. Editor, Author, etc. n.a: Ed The Public Relations Journ, Publics, etc. Publ: Public Relations in War & Peace; Practical Public Relations; etc. Ctr: N.Y. Times, Journ of Higher Education, Public Opinion Quarterly, School & Society, etc. a: 365 Guinda St, Palo Alto, California, U.S.A. T: 7384.

HARMAN, Rev. Canon Christopher Francis, M.A., L.Th. b: Swansea, Glam 1890. e: King's Sch Gloucester, Lond Coll of Divinity, St John's Coll. Durham Univ. Clerk in Holy Orders, Hon Canon of Bristol Cathedral. Publ: Christ in the Press. Ctr: Bristol Ev Post, Swindon Ev Advertiser, North Wilts Herald & Advertiser. s.s: Russian Religious Philosophy, Christian Sociology, Christianity & World Peace. Rec: Walking, music, drama. a: South Marston Vicarage, Swindon, Wilts. T: Stratton St Margaret 326.

HARMAN, Ian Denys Anthony. b: Lewisham 1911. e: Hutchin's Sch, Hobart, Tasmania. m: Winifred Gahagan. d: 1. Free-lance Journalist. Publ: Ponds & Aquariums. Ctr: Various. s.s: Natural History, Cinema, Children. Rec: Entomology, cycling. a: 150 Hither Green Lne, Lewisham, London, S.E.13.

HARMAN, Richard. b: Lon 1900. e: County Sc Cam. Publisher & Journalist. c.t: Display, Signs, Hotel & Boarding Hse, etc. s.s: Sales promotion & window display. a: 43 Blandford St, Lon W.1. t: Welbeck 7456.

HARMER, Sir Sidney Frederic, K.B.E., F.R.S., ScD. b: Norwich 1862. e: U.C.L. & King's Col Cam. m: Laura Russell. s: 2. d: 1. Ret Civil Servant. Publ: Jt Ed The Cam Nat Hist. c.t: Quarterly Journ of Microscop Soc, etc. s.s: Zoology. Ex-Asst Tutor King's Col Cam & Supt Univ Museum of Zool. Rec: Gardening. c: Athenæum. a: The Old Manor Hse, Melbourn, nr Royston, Herts. t: Melbourn, 8.

HARMER, W. Scotford. N/p Ed. n.a: Mang Dir Cirencester N/p Co Ltd. a: River Court, Cirencester. t: 211.

HARMSWORTH, 1st Baron of Egham, Cecil Bisshopp Harmsworth, M.A., LL.D.(D.U.). e: St Marylebone Gr Sch, T.C.D. m: Emilie Alberta Maffett. s: 2. d: 1. M.P. (L) Droitwich 1906—10, S. Beds (Luton) '11—22, Under Sec of State for For Affairs '19—22. n.a: Ex Dir A.P. Ltd & Assoc Newspapers Ltd. Publ: Pleasure & Problem in Sth Africa; Immortals at First Hand; A Little Fishing Book. Rec: Flyfishing. c: Reform, Nat Lib, Univ Dublin. a: 13 Hyde Park Gardens, London, W.2. T: Paddington 6860.

HARMSWORTH, Hon. Esmond Cecil. e: Eton. n.a: Dir Assoc N/ps Ltd, etc. c: White's. a:

Warwick Hse. St James's S.W.1. *t:* Whitehall 1175.

HARMSWORTH, Geoffrey. *b:* London. *e:* Harrow. *n.a:* Ed The Queen 1929—33, Dir Field Press Ltd '33, Dir Western Morning News Co Ltd '34. *Publ:* The Maid of the Mountains; Her Story (with J. Collins); Abyssinian Adventure; I Like America. *Rec:* Golf, Christie's. *c:* R.A.C. *w.s:* War Corr 1939—40, Sqdr-Ldr R.A.F. '41—45. *a:* 1 Mount Vernon, Hampstead, London, N.W.3.

HARMSWORTH, Sir Harold Cecil. *b:* London 1897. *e:* Westminster Sch & Christ Church Oxf. *n.a:* Chm Western Morning News Co, Field Press Ltd. *c:* Oxf & Camb Univ. *a:* 7 Ilchester Place, London, W.14; & Worstead Hall, Norwich, Norfolk.

HARMSWORTH, Sir Hildebrand Alfred, Bt. *b:* Lon 1901. *e:* Harrow. *m:* Ellen Billensen. *s:* 1. *d:* 1. N/p Dir. *n.a:* Dly Mirror ('29), Dir Continental Dly Mail. *s.s:* N/p org & finance. *a:* 4 Kensington Palace Gdns, W.S.

HARMSWORTH, Sir Robert Leicester. *b:* 1870. *e:* Marylebone G.S. *m:* Annie Scott. *s:* 3. *d:* 3. *n.a:* N/p Dir. *c:* Reform. *a:* Moray Lodge, Campden Hill, W.S.

HARNAMAN, Daniel Goronwy. *b:* Denbigh. Journalist. *n.a:* Sub Ed Cambrian News, Aberystwyth 1919—24. Potteries Rep Staffs Advtr '24—. *s.s:* Pottery, Celtic subjects, Archæology. Mem Inst of Journalists, Chm North Staffs N.U.J. *a:* 93 York St, Basford, Stoke-on-Trent. *t:* Hanley 5241.

HARPER, Ethel Isabel. *b:* Northampton 1898. *e:* County Hgh Sch Wellingboro', Training Coll of Domestic Subjects, Battersea Poly. *n.a:* Housecraft 1947—. *s.s:* Homecraft. *a:* 29 Gordon Sq, London, W.C.1. *T:* Euston 2475.

HARPER, Harry. *b:* London 1880. *e:* Priv. *m:* Beatrice Mary Tebbutt. Journalist & Author, Original Air Correspondent Daily Mail 1906—26. *Publ:* The Aeroplane, Past, Present & Future; The Aeroplane in War; The Evolution of the Flying Machine; Air Power, Naval, Military, Commercial; Our First Airways, their Organisation, Equipment & Finance; Dawn of the Space Age (non-technical exposition of atomic-driven space flight possibilities). *Ctr:* World reviews, mags & newsp. over 30 years. *s.s:* Aviation, Astronautics & Interplanetary Communication. *Rec:* Collecting all Historical Data relating to Aeronautics & Astronautics. *a:* Hatherton, Worple Rd, Epsom, Surrey. *T:* Epsom 9453.

HARPER, Rev. James Walker. *b:* Daviot 1859. *e:* G. S. Aberdeen, King's Col Aberd & Edin Theological Col. *m:* Edith Honora Michell. *s:* 1. *d:* 3. Curator of Dunimarle & Chaplain Dean of St Andrews. *n.a:* The Scottish Standard-Bearer, The Year Bk of the Episcopal Ch in Scotland, Ch Kalendar, etc. *c.t:* The Scottish Guardian, The Scottish Churchman. *s.s:* History & biography. *a:* Dunimarle, Culross, Dunfermline. *t:* Newmills 29.

HARPER, John. *b:* Banff. *e:* Banff Acad. *n.a:* News Ed Sunday Mail, Glas. *a:* 67 Hope St, Glas.

HARPER, John Ernest Troyte, C.B., M.V.O. *b:* Christchurch, N. Zealand 1874. *e:* Christ's Coll N. Zealand, H.M.S. Britannia. *m:* Dorothy Meldrum. *s:* 1. Vice-Admiral, Nautical Assessor House of Lords 1934—46. *Publ:* The Truth About Jutland; The Riddle of Jutland (with L. Gibson); The Royal Navy at War. *Ctr:* Various on Naval matters. *s.s:* Naval subjects. *c:* United Service. *a:* Ilam, Hawkhurst, Kent. *T:* 110.

HARRADEN, BEATRICE: author; b. Hampstead, London, Eng., Jan. 24, 1864; d. Samuel and Rosalie (Lindstedt) H.; educ. Cheltenham Ladies Coll., Bedford Coll. (Univ. London); DEGREE: B.A. (London); unmarried. AUTHOR: Things Will Take a Turn, 1891; Ships That Pass in the Night, 1893; In Varying Moods, 1894; Hilda Strafford, 1897; Untold Tales of the Past, 1897; The Fowler, 1899; Katherine Frensham, 1903; The Scholar's Daughter, 1906; Interplay, 1908; Out of the Wreck I Rise, 1912; The Guiding Thread, 1916; Where Your Treasure is, 1918; Spring Shall Plant, 1920; Thirteen All Told, 1921; Patuffa, 1923; Youth Calling, 1924; Rachel, 1926; Search Will Find it Out, 1928. Contributor to Blackwood's, Cornhill, Century, Windsor, Story Teller, Times, Country Life, Illustrated London News, Graphic, Manchester Guardian, Time and Tide and many mags. General character of writing: novels. Member of many societies for social reform; with Save-the-Children Fund; with League of Nations Union; with numerous library assns. and educnl. organizations. Mem. Women's Internat. University Federation. Worker for Woman Suffrage and other reforms connected with woman movement. Recreations: traveling, and music. Librarian Mil. Hosp., Endell St. (London), during Great War. CLUBS: Halcyon, 13 Cork St., London, W., Eng.

HARRIES, D. A. Travel Ed Stock Exchange Gazette, 330 Gresham Hse, E.C.2.

HARRIES, Frederick James. *b:* Haverfordwest. *e:* Merthyr Tydfil G.S. *m:* Mary Lloyd. N/p Ed & Prop. *n.a:* Merthyr Express (1881), Western Mail ('90), Glamorgan County Times (1900), Barry & Dist News ('31). *Publ:* Shakespeare & the Welsh; Famous Writers & Wales; Shakespeare & the Scots. *Rec:* Walking, lecturing & research work. *a:* 19 Plymouth Rd, Penarth (Glam). *t:* Barry 378.

HARRINGTON, Frank Tandy. *b:* Newport, Mon 1891. *e:* Taunton & Guy's Hosp. *m:* Mary Fogarty. *s:* 2. *Publ:* Treatment of Asthma. *Ctr:* Clinical Medicine & Surgery, Lancet, B.M.J. *s.s:* Asthma. *Rec:* Music, rugby football, tennis, billiards, shooting, bridge. *c:* Bengal, Calcutta & Union, Malta. *w.s:* Commanded 43rd Indian Gen Hosp 1942—46. *a:* c/o Lloyds Bank, Baker St, London.

HARRINGTON, John Charles. *n.a:* Ed The Miller, The Leather Trades' Review. *a:* 24 Southdean Gdns, S.W.19.

HARRINGTON, Karl Pomeroy, M.A., D.Mus. *b:* Somersworth, N.H. 1861. *e:* Wesleyan, Yale & Berlin Univs. *m:* Jennie Eliza Canfirld. *d:* 1. Emeritus Prof of Latin, Organist & Choir Director. *Publ:* The Roman Elegiac Poets; Third Year Latin (collab); Selections from Latin Prose & Poetry (collab); Catullus; Richard Alsop, a Hartford Wit; Walks & Climbs in the White Mountains; Mediæval Latin; Live Issues in Classical Study; Education in Church Music; etc. *Ctr:* N.Y. Times, Classical Journ & Weekly, etc. *s.s:* Mediæval Latin, Roman Elegiac Poets, Church Music. *Rec:* Mountaineering, music. *c:* Conversational, etc. *a:* 163 High St, Middletown, Connecticut, U.S.A. *T:* 2731.

HARRINGTON, Dr. S. H. N., J.P. *Publ:* The Engraved Work of Sir Francis Seymour Haden, F.R.E. (1910); various articles on Art. *a:* 90 Park Rd S, Birkenhead.

HARRINGTON, T. R., F.J.I. *b*: Berehaven, Co Cork 1869. *e*: Presentation Col, Cork. *m*: Katherine Collins. *s*: 4. *d*: 3. Mang Ed Irish Independent 1904-31. *n.a*: News Ed Irish Daily Independent '00-04. Dir Independent N/ps Ltd, Dublin '29-. *a*: Derreen, Lindsay Rd, Glasnevin, Dublin, N.W. *t*: Drumcondra 66.

HARRIS, Dr. A. Butler. *c.t*: Med papers. *s.s*: Vaccine Therapy, M.O.H., Chigwell U.D.C., Lt-Col R.A.M.C., D.L.(Essex), County Controller V.A. Detachments. *a*: The Shrubbery, Loughton, Essex.

HARRIS, Abram Lincoln, M.A., B.S., Ph.D. *b*: Richmond, Va 1899. *e*: Univs of Va Union, Pittsburgh & Columb. *m*: Callie McGuinn. Assoc Prof of Econ The College Univ of Chicago. *Publ*: The Black Worker (collab); The Negro as Capitalist. *Ctr*: The Nation, New Republic, etc. *s.s*: Labour & Current Econ Problems. *Rec*: Billiards. *a*: Box 268, Faculty Exchange, University of Chicago 37, Illinois, U.S.A. *T*: Midway 0800, Ext 1135.

HARRIS, Alan Martin. *b*: Wimbledon 1899. *e*: Rugby & Balliol Col Oxf. *m*: Angelica Messarosh. Publisher. *n.a*: Ed Staff Daily News 1922-24, Lect in Classics U.C.L. '25-27, Staff G. Bell & Sons '27-31, Gerald Duckworth & Co '31-. *Publ*: (Trans) England the Unknown Isle; The Spirit of France; Is God a Frenchman?; The Open Door; Germany, Prepare for War; etc. *c.t*: Times Lit Supp, XIXth Cent, Listener, etc. *s.s*: Class Lit, Philos, Eng Lit of XIXth Century. War Service. *Rec*: Mountaineering, curio-hunting. *c*: Savile. *a*: 15a Gower St, W.C.1. *t*: Museum 6392.

HARRIS, Arthur James Meredith, B.A. *b*: Highgate 1908. *e*: Sherborne, Christ Ch Oxford. *m*: Helena Felton. Jnlst. *n.a*: Sub-Ed The Laundry World '33, Associate Ed Industria Britanica '33. Asst Ed The Independent '33—35. Associate Ed Industria Britanica '35—. *Rec*: Tennis, drawing, painting, etc. Called to the Bar by Inner Temple '32. *a*: 10 Cyril Mansions, S.W.11. *t*: Macaulay 4855.

HARRIS, Dr. C. J. J. Late Major R.G.A. Served in Boer War & Great War. Cnty Commn Scouts. Officer St John's Ambulance Brig. *a*: Moresby Hall, Whitehaven.

HARRIS, Preb. Charles, D.D. *b*: Barnsbury 1865. *e*: St Olave's Southwark, Wadham Col Oxf. *m*: Emily Mary Smith. *s*: 2 (1 dec). Chm Lit Cmt of Ch Un 1923-. *Publ*: Pro Fide ('06, 4th edn revised & enlarged '30); First Steps in the Philosophy of Religion; Asst Ed of & cont to Liturgy & Worship ('32); Jt Ed Northern Catholicism ('33); Promoter of & cont to A New Commentary on Holy Scripture ('28); etc. *c.t*: Theology, Hastings's Ency of R. & E., Murray's Dictionary of the Bible ('08), Commentary ('09), etc. *s.s*: Dogmatic theo, metaphysics. Composer of the tune " The Supreme Sacrifice " sung at the burial of the Unknown Warrior & at nat meml services throughout the Empire & U.S.A., etc. Mem Convocation & of Ch Assembly '23-. Preb Hereford Cath '27-. *Rec*: Music. *a*: Rosemary, Eynsham, Oxon.

HARRIS, Sir Charles Alexander, K.C.M.G., C.B., C.V.O. *b*: Wrexham 1855. *e*: Spondon Hse Prep Sc, Richmond Sc Yorks, Christ's Col Cam. *m*: Constance Shute. *s*: 2. *d*: 1. Qualified as Barrister. Formerly of Colonial Office & Gov of Newfoundland. *Publ*: Harcourt's Voyage to Guiana; Cambridge History of the British Empire (Chapters on Newfoundland); etc. *c.t*: Westminster Review, Empire Review, Edin Review, Quarterly Review, Dictionary of Nat Biog, Dictionary of Polit Econ, etc. *s.s*: Economics. Extensive travel. Boundary Cases on behalf of Brit Guiana. *Rec*: Nat hist. *c*: Gov New England Co. *a*: Greenhill Brow, Farnham, Surrey. *t*: 27.

HARRIS, Charles Edward S., M.B., ChB. *b*: N.Z. 1877. *e*: Edin Univ. *m*: Muriel Davenport. Surgeon. *Publ*: From the Deep of the Sea. *c t*: The Cunarder N.Y., Sea Stories Mag N.Y., B.M.J. *s.s*: Sea tales. Temp Surg S. African Field Force 1900-02. Lieut Army Motor Reserve '05-10. Temp Surg-Lieut R.N. '14-19. Cunard Steam Ship Coy '20. *Rec*: Model making, bridge. *a*: c/o Cunard Steam Ship Co, L'pool.

HARRIS, Charles Reginald Schiller, M.A., D.Phil(Oxon), PhD.(Princeton). *b*: Wimbledon 1876. *e*: Clifton Col, Corpus Christi Col Oxf. *m*: Lucia de Pitinga. Journalist. *n.a*: Ed 19th Century & Atter 1930-, Mem Staff Times '25-. *Publ*: Duns Scotus (2 vols). *s.s*: Finance & econ. Fell All Souls' Col. *Rec*: Fishing. *c*: Athenæum. *a*: Foulis Terr, Onslow Gdns, S.W.7. *t*: Kensington 4332.

HARRIS, Charles Wesley Edgar. *b*: Walsall 1887. *e*: Walsall Tech Sc. Dist Reporter. *n.a*: Wolverhampton Express & Star '08—. *s.s*: Sport. *c*: N.U.J. *a*: 29 Station St, Walsall. *t*: 2101.

HARRIS, Clifford. *Publ*: A Broken Doll; Lyrics in " The Maid of the Mountains." *s.s*: Lyrics. Mem P.R.S. *a*: 16 Camden Sq, N.W.1.

HARRIS, Rev. Clifford Ashleigh, M.A., H.C.F. *b*: Bristol 1891. *e*: St Chad's Hostel, Hooton Pagnall & Durham Univ. *Publ*: On Hearing Confessions. *s.s*: Mediæval educ. C.F. Mesopotamia 1919-20. *Rec*: Golf. *a*: St Augustine's Clergy Hse, Settles St, Stepney, E.1. *t*: Bishopsgate 4133.

HARRIS, D. T., M.D., D.Sc, F.InstP. *Publ*: Ultra-violet Radiology (1932); Practical Histology; Experimental Physiology (3rd ed '34). *a*: 40 Alexandra Grove. N. Finchley, N.12.

HARRIS, David Robert, M.A. *b*: Merthyr Tydfil. *e*: U.C.W. & St John's Coll Camb. *m*: Evelyn Elizabeth Kempster, B.Sc. *s*: 2. *d*: 1. Principal N. Wales Teachers' Coll Bangor 1905—33. *n.a*: Prop & Ed Police Review 1918—, Chmn Police Review Publishing Co. *a*: Wood Edge, Copthorne Rd, Croxley Green, Herts. *T*: Rickmansworth 4496.

HARRIS, E. A. *b*: Finedon. *e*: Wellingboro'. Journalist. *n.a*: Nott'm Guardian Group. *s.s*: Hosiery, lace, mining. *a*: 16 Mapperley Hall Drive, Nott'm.

HARRIS, Edna Edith ("Estrith Mansfield"). *b*: Bampton 1893. *e*: Priv. *m*: Major E. Clifford Harris. *s*: 1. *d*: 1. *Publ*: The Flaming Flower; Wind-Bound; Morning Rainbow; The Mascot of the School. *c.t*: Oxford Mail, Oxford Times, Kentish Express, Girl's Own Paper, etc. *s.s*: Historical fiction & essays, architecture. *Rec*: Photography, gardening, breeds Great Danes. *c*: Canterbury Archæological Soc, Oxfordshire Folklore Group. *a*: Lullingstone House, Castle St, Canterbury. *t*: 549.

HARRIS, Ernest Howard, M.A. *b*: Swansea 1876. *e*: Univ Coll Aberystwyth, Queen's Univ Belfast. *m*: Ailie Chegwidden, Gr Sch Master (ret). *Publ*: Welsh Regional Verse: An Exile's Lute; The Harp of Hiraeth; Songs in Shot Silk; Singing Seas; Song

Cycle at the Worm; Kantele Larin Kyosti; Literature in Estonia. *Ctr*: Baltic & Scandinavian Countries, Mark Twain Quarterly (U.S.A.), Manch Quarterly, Sth. Wales Ev Post (Swansea), Western Mail (Cardiff), etc. *s.s*: Baltic Lit. *Rec*: Reading. *c*: P.E.N., R.S.L. *a*: Inglenook, Woodlands Ter, Swansea.

HARRIS, F. E. Jt Hon Sec Exeter & Dis N.U.J. *a*: 226 High St, Exeter.

HARRIS, Frank L. M. *b*: Hereford 1897. *e*: Abingdon G.S. Married. Jnlst. *n.a*: Ed, Car Illustrated '21—23. Ed, Light Car '24—33. Founder-Ed, The Caravan '33. Founder-Ed, The Sports Car '35. *Publ*: The A.B.C. of Caravanning. *c.t*: Trade & tech press, Woman's Journ, Field. *s.s*: Motoring, engineering, camping, caravans. *Rec*: Caravanning. War Service. *a*: 12 Holborn, E.C.1. *t*: Holborn 6621—2.

HARRIS, Franklin Stewart, B.S., Ph.D., LL.D. *b*: Benjamin, Utah 1884. *e*: Guarez State Acad Mo, Univs of Brigham Young, Cornell & Paris. *m*: Estella Spilsbury. *s*: 2. *d*: 4. *n.a*: Assoc-Ed Utah Farmer 1912—21, For Corres Desert News '26—27. *Publ*: The Principle of Agronomy; The Sugar Beet in America; Soil Alkali; Scientific Research & Human Welfare; The Fruits of Mormonism; The Young Man & His Vocation. *Ctr*: The Improvement Era, Salt Lake Tribune, N.Y. Times, etc. *s.s*: Agriculture, Irrigation, Foreign Affairs, etc. *Rec*: Travel, outdoor life. *c*: Rotary, Knife & Fork, etc. *a*: Utah State Agricultural College, Logan, Utah, U.S.A. *T*: 100.

HARRIS, George ("**Gobannium**" & "**Aristarchus the Scribe**"). *b*: Otley. Journalist. *n.a*: Ed Abergavenny Chron, Repres Western Mail, Hereford Times, etc. *Rec*: Bowls. *a*: Glanville Ave Rd, Abergavenny. *T*: 137.

HARRIS, Rev. George Herbert, M.A.(Oxon). *b*: Slough 1865. *e*: U.C.Sc & Oxf. *m*: (1) Emelia Moore; (2) Ethel White. *Publ*: The Faroe Islands. *s.s*: Theology, botany. Ox '99, Oxf 3 y & took Orders. Diocese of Birm 1902—31, ret '31. *Rec*: Travel. *c*: Cam Univ Union. *a*: 9 Huntingdon Rd, Cam. *t*: 2600.

HARRIS, George Montagu, O.B.E.,M.A. *b*: Torquay 1868. *e*: Newton Coll, Winchester, New Coll Oxf. *m*: Violet Estelle Martineau. *d*: 1. Pres Internat Union of Local Authorities 1936—, formerly Sec of County Councils Assoc, Head of Intell Div Min of Health, Barrister. *n.a*: Ed Co Councils Assoc Gazette 1908—19, Local Govt Abroad '27—30, Local Govt Admin '35—38. *Publ*: Local Government in Many Lands; Municipal Self-Government in Britain; Westward to the East; The Garden City Movement; Problems of Local Government. *s.s*: Local Govt, Town Planning. *c*: Eng Speaking Un. *a*: Sorel, Meadfoot Rd, Torquay. *T*: 4758.

HARRIS, Dr. H. A. C. *a*: Chesterton, Hassocks, Sussex.

HARRIS, H. Gordon. *s.s*: Philately, Gr Mythol. *c*: Old Alleynian; Merchant Navy. *a*: 87 Emmanuel Rd, Streatham Hill, S.W.12.

HARRIS, Harold Lark, M.A., LL.B. *b*: Sydney, N.S.W. 1889. *e*: Burwood Publ Sch, Teacher's Coll & Univ of Sydney. *m*: Elsie Mildred Cavell. *s*: 2. Director of Youth Welfare Dept of Labour & Industry N.S.W. *Publ*: Australia in the Making; Australia's National Interests & Policy; The Economic Resources of Australia; The Teaching of History in Secondary Schools; Doing Our Best for Our Children. *Ctr*: Harmsworth's New Universal Ency. *s.s*: Australian Affairs. *Rec*: Tennis. *a*: 61 Wentworth Rd, Vaucluse, Sydney, New South Wales. *T*: F.U.9165.

HARRIS, Harold M. *b*: London 1915. *e*: St Paul's Sch & abroad. *m*: Josephine Byford. Editor, Mem N.U.J. *n.a*: Golders Green Gazette 1933—36, Ed Fish Traders Weekly '36—38, Tobacco '39 & '46—, Confectioner Baker & Restaurateur '46—. *a*: 5 Palmer St, Westminster, London, S.W.1. *T*: Whitehall 0344.

HARRIS, Henry Kingsford, M.A., A.M.I.E.E., F.R.G.S. *b*: Hythe 1867. *e*: Trin Col Cam. *m*: Cecile Blanche Simms. *s*: 1. *d*: 1. Chartered Elec Engineer. *c.t*: Country Life, Illus Lon News, Engineering, etc. *s.s*: Publicity telegraphs. 18 y Rector of Runwell, Essex. Many y on the Dist Counc. Commissioner of the Levels of Canvey Isle, etc. Later ret through illness. Specialised in the Publicity Telegraph, an invention which transmits a message in a telegraph code & announces it at a distance as arranged, in letters formed instantly from a few inches to sev feet in height without the use of elec lamps by day or night to form the letters. The only invention that can do this & applicable to many uses. Trav extensively. *Rec*: Photography, science & archæology. *a*: 58 Madrid Rd, Lon, S.W.13. *t*: Riverside 0659.

HARRIS, Henry Wilson, M.P. *b*: Plymouth 1883. *e*: Plymouth Coll & St John's Coll Camb. *m*: Florence Cash. *d*: 1. Journalist, M.P. (Ind) Camb Univ 1945—. *n.a*: News-Ed Leader Writer, Diplomatic Corres & Special Writer Daily News 1909—34, Ed Spectator '32—. *Publ*: President Wilson, His Problems & His Policy; What the League of Nations Is; The Future of Europe; 99 Gower Street; The Daily Press; Problems of the Peace; Caroline Fox; J. A. Spender. *s.s*: Internat Affairs. *c*: Reform. *a*: 13 Park Village West, London, N.W.1. *T*: Euston 6973.

HARRIS, Herbert. *b*: London 1911. *e*: Clapham Coll. *m*: Bonney Genn. Journalist-Publicist, Free-lance, Mem N.U.J. *n.a*: World's Press News 1929, Press Officer N.A.A.F.I. '41—46, Press Officer Lond Music Festival etc '47—. *Ctr*: Punch, B.B.C., & numerous newspapers & periodicals. *s.s*: Entertainment, Films, Radio, Music, Fiction, Humour, etc. *c*: Press. *a*: 30 Fleet St, London, E.C.4. & 13 St Phillips Rd, Surbiton, Surrey. *T*: Central 5887 & Elmbridge 7423.

HARRIS, Isaac. *Publ*: The Significance of Existence; Race & Civilization; Immortality; High Blood Pressure; Diet & High Blood Pressure; The Woof of Life; Studies in Hypertony; Diseases of the Heart. *Ctr*: Lancet, B.M.J., Edin Med Journ, Practitioner, Med Press & Circ, Liverpool Med Journ, etc. *a*: 72a Rodney St, Liverpool 1. *T*: Royal 4505.

HARRIS, Sir John. *b*: Wantage, Berks 1874. *m*: Alice Seeley. *s*: 2. *d*: 2. *Publ*: Several Books upon Foreign & Colonial Affairs. *c.t*: New Statesman, Listener, Times, Nation, Manchester Guardian, Daily News, Daily Telegraph, etc. *s.s*: Foreign & colonial questions, native races, slavery, etc. Trav extensively. *Rec*: Gardening. *c*: Nat Lib. *a*: Nat Lib Club & Stonelands, Frome, Som.

HARRIS, Kathleen Mary. Artist. *n.a*: Ed The Embroideress. *s.s*: Design, embroidery. *a*: The Nab, Ducks Hill, Northwood. *t*: 886.

HARRIS, Lancelot Stephen. *b*: Wigton 1902. Housemaster. *Publ*: The Nature of English Poetry. *c.t*: Yorks Post, Western Morn News, Western Dly Press. *s.s*: Poetry. *a*: Wellington Sc, Somerset. *t*: 168.

HARRIS, Leslie J., D.Sc., Ph.D., F.R.I.C. *b*: Liverpool 1898. *e*: Liverpool Coll, Univ of Manch, Emmanuel Coll Camb. *m*: Rose Snowman. *s*: 2. Dunn Nutritional Lab (Univ of Camb & Med Research Counc). *Publ*: Vitamins in Theory & Practice; Vitamins & Vitamin Deficiencies. *Ctr*: Brit Ency of Med Practice, Thorpe's Dict of Pure & Applied Chem, Annual Review of Biochem, Annual Review of the Chem Soc, etc. *s.s*: Vitamins, Nutrition, Medical & Biochemical Research. *a*: 22 Newton Rd, Cambridge. *T*: 4866.

HARRIS, Mary O'Brien, D.Sc., J.P. *b*: Holywood, Co Down 1865. *e*: Univ Col of Wales, Aberystwyth & Somerville Col, Oxford. *m*: J. Theodore Harris. *Publ*: Towards Freedom (educational); A Seasonal Botany; jnt author of :—Professional Women; Industrial Co-Operation, etc. *c.t*: The Friend, Examiner, etc. *s.s*: Education, Socialism, esperanto. Mem L.C.C. for Central Hackney (Labour) 1934. *e*: Mem Women's Internat League, New Educ Fellowship & Nat Assoc of Labour Teachers, etc. *a*: 9 Queensdown Rd, E.5. *t*: Amherst 1535.

HARRIS, Noel Gordon, M.D., P.R.C.P. *b*: Worcester Park, Surrey 1897. *e*: Westminster Sch & St Thomas's Hosp, London. *m*: Hon Thelma Eirene Kitson. *s*: 1. *d*: 3. Former Physician for Psychological Medicine Mddx Hosp, Examiner in Psychol Med Univ of London. *Publ*: Introduction to Psychological Medicine; Modern Psychotherapy. *Ctr*: Various med journs. *a*: 2 Devonshire Pl, London, W.1, & Finchley Cottage, East End Road, London, N.2. *T*: Tudor 3119.

HARRIS, Norman Avery. *b*: Herne Hill 1898. *e*: St John's, Beckenham & Southend-on-Sea. *m*: Alice May Vinten. *s*: 1. *d*: 1. Sporting Journl. *c.t*: Sunday Times, Observer (London), Sporting Life, Exchange Telegraph Co Ltd, etc. *s.s*: Yachting, football, tennis, boxing. *Rec*: Walking, sailing. *a*: 239 Fairfax Drive, Westcliff-on-Sea & 136 Westcliff Park Drive, Westcliff-on-Sea.

HARRIS, Rt. Hon. Sir Percy Alfred, Bt., P.C. *b*: London 1876. *e*: Harrow, Trin Hall Camb. *m*: Frieda Bloxam. *s*: 2. Mem L.C.C., M.P. (L) Harborough Div Leicestershire 1916—18, M.P. (L) South Western Bethnal Green '22—45. *Publ*: Forty Years In & Out of Parliament; London & Its Government; New Zealand & Its Politics. *Ctr*: Contemporary Review, Fortnightly, Star. *s.s*: London. *c*: Reform. *a*: Morton Hse, Chiswick Mall, London, W.4. *T*: Chiswick 2230.

HARRIS, Peter. *b*: Surbiton, Surrey 1923. *e*: St Paul's. *m*: Winifred Mary Peach. Journalist, Short Story Writer, Mem N.U.J. *n.a*: West Middx Gazette '40—41, Sub-Ed Ev Gazette Middlesbrough '41—42 & '47—. *Ctr*: Tribune, Country Life, Modern Reading. *s.s*: Politics, Rural Affairs, Forestry. *Rec*: Lawn tennis, walking. *a*: c/o 146 Argyle Rd, London, W.13, & Kemsley Hse, Middlesborough. *T*: Perivale 6789.

HARRIS, Rev. Silas Morgan, M.A. *b*: Vaynor, Brecon 1888. *e*: Merthyr Cty Sch, St David's Coll, Lampeter & Keble Coll Oxf. Priest. *n.a*: Founder & Ed (1916—18) The Faith in Wales. *Publ*: Saint David in the Liturgy; What Do the Celtic Churches Say?; The First Ten Years. *Ctr*: The Faith in Wales, Wales, Ch Times, Bulletin des Missions, Laudate, etc. *s.s*: Liturgy, Hagiology (esp Welsh), Hymnology, Catholic Reunion. *a*: Egmanton Vicarage, Newark, Notts.

HARRIS, Stephen Bruce. *b*: Londonderry. *e*: Middlesbro H.S. *m*: Hannah Dennington. *s*: 1. Journalist. *n.a*: Sports Writer Evening Standard. Mem N.U.J. 1909—. *Publ*: Jardine Justified ('33). *s.s*: Sport. *Rec*: Lawn tennis. *c*: Chiswick Pk & W. Middx Lawn Tennis. *a*: 192 Gunnersbury Av, W.3. *t*: Acorn 3677.

HARRIS, Sydney Taylor, M.B., M.R.C.S., L.R.C.P. *b*: Leicester 1886. *e*: Bd Sch Leicester, King's Coll London, Charing Cross Hosp. *m*: Dorothy Joan Symondson. *n.a*: Musical Critic Leicester Pioneer 1918—19. *Publ*: Six Sea Shanties; Seven Seas Shanty Book (with J. Sampson). *Ctr*: Brain, Charing Cross Hosp Gazette. *s.s*: Folk Music, Obstet. *Rec*: Riding, bridge. *a*: 162 Kingston Rd, London, S.W.19. *T*: Liberty 1625.

HARRIS, Thomas Alexander Britten, M.B., B.S. Anæsthetist. *c.t*: B.M.A., etc. *a*: 10 Rowan Rd, W.6. *t*: Riverside 3800.

HARRIS, Thomas Noel Cleather, M.C., B.A. (Oxon). *b*: Tunbridge Wells 1890. *e*: Tonbridge Sc Kent & Univ Col Oxf. *m*: Aggie Nita Charles. *s*: 1. *d*: 1. Civil Servant, Lit Adv, Fourth Estate. *c.t*: Theatre World, Daily Sketch, Sunday Times, Old Vic Mag. *s.s*: Eng & French, dramatic criticism. Lit Adv to G. P. Putnam's Sons, Ltd 1919—30, Thornton Butterworth Ltd '26—27 & Herbert Jenkins Ltd. '33—. Clerk in Dept Overseas Trade. Mem Critics Circle. *Rec*: Cricket, lawn tennis. *a*: 82 Barons Ct Rd, W. Kensington, W.14. *t*: Whitehall 9040.

HARRIS, W. H. Dramatic critic. *a*: Esterel, Woodmansterne Rd, Carshalton Beeches, Surrey.

HARRIS, Wilfred, M.D., F.R.C.P. *b*: India 1869. *e*: Sherborne, Univ Col, Caius Col Cam. *m*: Mabel Mayne. *s*: 2. *d*: 1. Neurologist. *Publ*: Neuritis & Neuralgia. *c.t*: Brain, Lancet, B.M.J. *s.s*: Neurology. *Rec*: Golf. *c*: Oxf & Cam. *a*: 56 Wimpole St, W.1. *t*: Welbeck 2708.

HARRIS, Rev. William Gregory. *b*: Tavistock 1865. *e*: Tavistock G.S., Queen's Col Taunton & Richmond Theo Col. *m*: Anna Elizabeth Hockin (dec). *d*: 2. Methodist Minister (ret). Vice-Pres Bath Shakespeare Soc. Vice-Pres Devonian Soc. Hosp Chap (under Bath Corp). *Publ*: Sketches of the West Countree; Zummerset Volk and Devonshire Diversions; Trengwith: Cornish Novel (Preface by "Q"); Old Words and Old Ways (West Country Ballads and Poems). *c.t*: The Devon Year Book, Methodist Magazine, West Morning News, Bath Chronicle, etc. *s.s*: West Country dialects, Chatterton, Browning, Coleridge. In Active Ministry of the Wesleyan Meth Church 35 y. Chief Ministerial Appoints, Nott'm, Bristol, Torquay, Taunton, Kingston-on-Thames, Weston-super-Mare, Brixham & Dartmouth. *Rec*: Books, verse writing, music. *a*: 26 Coome Park, Bath. *t*: 7405 Weston Bath.

HARRIS, Rev. William Henry, M.A., B.Litt(Oxon). *b*: Pantysgallog, Dowlais 1884. *e*: Merthyr County Sch, St David's Coll Lampeter, Jesus Coll Oxf. *m*: Dorothy Clough. *d*: 2. Prof of Welsh, Precentor & Sen Tutor St David's Coll Lampeter, Canon of St David's Cathedral. *Publ*: Amos; Jonah & Micah; Joel & Malachi; Obediah, Nahum, Habaccuc & Zephaniah; Welsh Compline. Lit Ed Welsh Church Hymnal. *Ctr*: Welsh Biblical Dictionary. *s.s*: Theology, Celtic Langs, Esperanto, Church Music, Ch Hist. *a*: St David's Coll, Lampeter, Cards. *T*: Lampeter 42.

HARRIS, Rev. William Melville, M.A. *n.a*: Jt Ed Teachers & Taught 1914-18. *Publ*: The Unsealed Book; The Purpose of Prayer; Our Sunday Schools; The Founders of New England; John Milton, Puritan, Patriot, Poet; David Livingstone. *c.t*: Various. *a*: Wilderness, St Boniface Rd, Ventnor, I.O.W.

HARRISON, A. *n.a*: Ed Evening Post. *a*: 2 Charles St, St Helier's, Jersey.

HARRISON, A. C.   n.a: Gt Yarmouth Mercury (1930–34), Norwich Eastern Daily Press ('34–).

HARRISON, Rev. Archibald Walter, M.C., B.A., B.Sc, D.D.(Lon). b: Swindon 1882. e: Loughboro' G.S., Univ Col Notts & Didsbury Col M/C. m: Grace Elizabeth Simon. s: 1. d: 2. Princ T.C. for Teachers. Publ: The Beginnings of Arminianism; Christianity & the League of Nations; Christianity & Universal Peace; The Church of Twenty Centuries. c.t: Methodist Recorder, History, Hibbert Journ. s.s: Hist. War Service as Chap. Rec: Walking. a: Westminster Col, 130 Horseferry Rd, S.W.1. t: Victoria 4475.

HARRISON, Cedric Evan.   e: Public Sc. Bookseller, Publisher & Printer. a: The Ancient Hse. Ipswich. t: 3401.

HARRISON, Sir Edward Richard, Kt. b: 1872. m: Elsie Green. Barrister. Publ: Digest & Index of the Official Reports of Tax Cases; Harrison of Ightham; History & Records of Ightham Church. a: Old Stones, Ightham, Kent. T: Boro' Green 14.

HARRISON, Ernest, M.A. b: 1877. e: St Paul's Sc & Trinity Col Cam. Registrary Univ of Cam. n.a: Jt Ed Classical Review 1923–, Ed Cam Univ Reporter '26–. Publ: Studies in Theognis. a: Trinity Col, Cam.

HARRISON, Ernest John. b: M/C 1873. e: York Model Sc. Deansgate H.G. & Priv. m: Eirene Scott-Oldfield. d: 1. Journalist & Author. n.a: Numerous in Canada, Calif, Japan, Siberia, Russia, etc. Tokyo Corr Daily Mail, Russo-Japanese War, Asst Corr Times, Petrograd 1914–18, also N.Y. Herald in Japan, Sec Brit Missn to Baltic States '19. Brit Vice-Consul Kaunas, Kovno & Vilna '19–21. Publ: Peace or War East of Baikal ('10); The Fighting Spirit of Japan; Lithuania, Past & Present; The Red Camarilla; Rasprava; Lithuania, a Review; The Art of Jiu-jutsu ('32); The Art of Wrestling ('34); Jt—Physical Culture for Men; Physical Culture for Women; Physical Culture for Juveniles (all '35); etc. s.s: Japanese art of jiu-jutsu, Lithuania, hist, Russian lang. Trav Widely in Far East. War Service '14–18, Chinese Labour Corps at Tsangkou, China, France & Mil Intelligence. N. Russia. Lithuanian Order of Grand Duke Gediminas. Holder of 3rd degree (Sandan) in Japanese art of Judo. With Lithuanian Del to Genoa Conf '22 & Brit Parl Del to Lithuania '23. Probably only English Mem of Slavonic sporting & polit org known as "Sokol" (Falcon). Rec: Judo, Swimming, skating, travel. c: Authors & Budokwai, Lon. a: 42 Upper Mall, Hammersmith, W.6. t: Riverside 4247.

HARRISON, Rev. Chancellor Frederick, M.A.(Cantab). b: Macclesfield 1884. e: King Edward VI's Sch Macclesfield, King's Coll Camb. m: Helen Wilson. s: 1. Canon-Residentiary. Chancellor & Librarian of York Minster. Publ: The Painted Glass of York Minster; York Minster; English Illuminated MSS of the Fourteenth Century; A Book About Books; The Medieval Man & His Notions; The Bible in Britain; The Main Stream of European History. Ctr: Times, Yorkshire Post, Guardian, Yorkshire Archæol Journ, Trans of York Archæol Soc, etc. s.s: Medieval Painted Glass, The Medieval Records of York Minster, Medieval Illuminated MSS, Medieval Books. Rec: Walking, researches into medieval life. a: The Chancery, York. T: York 2866.

HARRISON, G. A., M.D. Chem Pathologist to St Bart's Hosp. Publ: Chemical Methods in Clinical Medicine.

s.s: Chemical Pathology.   a: St Bart's Hosp, London, E.C.1.

HARRISON, George Bagshawe, M.A.(Cantab), Ph.D. (Lond). b: Hove 1894. e: Brighton Coll & Queens' Coll Camb. m: Dorothy Barker. s: 1. d: 1. Prof & Head of Dept of English Queens' Univ Kingston Ont Canada, Reader in Eng Lit Univ of Lond 1929–, Ed Penguin Skakespeare (21 Vols). Publ: An Elizabethan Journal, 1591–94; A Second Elizabethan Journal 1595–98; A Last Elizabethan Journal, 1599–1603; A Jacobean Journal, 1603—06; Shakespeare at Work; etc. Ed The Church Book of Bunyan Meeting; The Trial of the Lancaster Witches; The Bodley Head Quartos (15 vols); A Companion to Shakespeare Studies (jt); Elizabethan Plays & Players; etc. Ctr: London Mercury, Observer, Times Lit Supp, Review of English Studies, Library, etc. s.s: Shakespearian & Elizabethan Studies. Hon Sec Shakespeare Assoc. a: Birchanger, nr Bishops Stortford. T: Stansted 38.

HARRISON, George Kent, M.D., F.R.C.S. b: London, Canada 1907. e: Univ of Toronto. m: Mary Marryat. s: 2. d: 1. Thoracic Surgeon to Papworth Village Settlement & Addenbrooks Hosp Camb. Ctr: Lancet, B.M.J. s.s: Thoracic Surgery. Rec: Tennis, squash. w.s: '41–46 R.A.M.C. a: Papworth Village Settlement, Papworth, Cambridge.

HARRISON, Guy Hardy. b: Chiswick 1911. e: King's Sc Worcester. m: Enid Audrey Mitchell. Journalist. n.a: Press Assoc '29–33. Sub-Ed Lon off Yorkshire Post '33–34, Sub-Ed Western Morning News '34, Sub-Ed Press Assoc '35—. s.s: Railways, wireless. Rec: Tennis, walking. a: 11 Kent Court, Queen's Drive, Ealing, W.5.

HARRISON, Dr. H., M.B., C.H.B., D.P.H. c.t: Lancet, The Possible Existence in this Country of Disease due to Infection with Brucella Abortus. Medical Referee Wes & Gen Assur Co. a: 284 Whalley Range, Blackburn, Lancs.

HARRISON, H. D., M.C., M.Com. b: Walsall 1898. e: Queen Mary's Walsall, B'ham Univ. m: Marjorie Watson Dewsbury. d: 1. n.a: Belgrade Correspondent: Morning Post '24–29. Manchester Guardian '25–29, Reuter '29–, N.Y.T. '35—. Publ: Industrial Psychology & the Production of Wealth (1925). s.s: Balkan affairs. a: Milutina Bojica 7, Belgrade, Jugoslavia. t: 23598.

HARRISON, HERBERT ERIC: editor; b. London, Eng., April, 1899; s. Kingsley and Annie Kate (Ingram) H.; educ. Ellerslie Rd. Sch. (London); m. Vivian Mary Baker, June 19, 1926. Sub-editor Kent and Sussex Courier. General character of writing: on political and social topics. Relig. denom., Baptist. CLUB: Tunbridge Wells, Rotary. OFFICE: Great Hall Buildings. HOME: 20 Cambridge St., Tunbridge Wells, Kent, Eng.

HARRISON, Herschel Roads, LL.B. b: Brit Columbia, Canada 1896. e: Santa Barbara Acad, Corrig Coll. Law S.B.C. & California. m: Valine Kenmoath Henry. s: 1. d: 2. Barrister. Publ: Some Early Legal Writers; Interesting Characters in Legal History; Great Sages of the Law; Illustrious Men of the Law; etc. Ctr: Saturday Mag, Vancouver Dly Province etc. s.s: Shakespearian & Elizabethan, Anglo-American Constitutional Legal History. Rec: Hiking, motoring. c: Adventurer's, Anglo-American, etc. a: Kent Pl, R.R.1. Duncan, British Columbia, Canada.

HARRISON, Hubert. Journalist. n.a: Derbyshire Courier, Derbyshire Times, Sheffield Independent,

Sheffield Mail, Evening Advertiser (Ed 1930–). Mem N.U.J. & N/p Press Fund. War Service. *a*: 13 Grovelands Av, Swindon, Wilts.

HARRISON, James Austin, M.D., D.P.H. *b*: Corkstown, Tyrone, Ireland 1889. *e*: Blackrock Coll, Univs of Queens Belfast & Harvard. *m*: Sheelagh Macsherry. *s*: 2. County M.O.H. Dublin. *Publ*: Bacterial Food Poisoning. *Ctr*: The Med Officer, Public Health, Journ of State Medicine, etc. *s.s*: Public Health. *Rec*: Golf. *a*: 6 Parnell Sq, Dublin. *T*: 71721.

HARRISON, James Maurice, D.S.C. *b*: London 1892. *e*: Malvern Coll Woodbridge, St Thomas's Hosp London. *m*: Rita Graham. *s*: 2. Late Surgeon-Lieut R.N., Admiralty Surgeon & Agent. *Publ*: Handbook of the Birds of Sevenoaks or Western District of Kent; etc. *Ctr*: B.M.J., Ibis, British Birds, Vogelzug, etc. *s.s*: Ornithology, Endocrinology, Biology, Birds of Balkan Peninsula, etc. *Rec*: Travel, shooting, trap-drumming. *a*: Bowerwood Hse, St Botolph's Rd, Sevenoaks, Kent. *T*: Sevenoaks 3814.

HARRISON, John A. Ed The Coventry Ev Telegraph. *a*: Quinton Rd, Coventry. *T*: 5011.

HARRISON, John Henry. *b*: Carlisle 1883. *e*: Penrith Wesleyan Sch & Evening Sch. *m*: A. E. Todhunter. *s*: 1. *d*: 1. Journalist, Mem N.U.J. *n.a*: Reporter 1907 & Ed '29 Penrith Observer, Lake District Press Representative '35—. *Ctr*: Yorks Post, Manch Guardian, Liverpool Dly Post, Newcastle Chron, Scotsman, Glas Herald, Cumberland News, Westmorland Gazette. *s.s*: General News, Lake District Sports, etc. Natural History & Agriculture. *Rec*: Nature study, bowls. *a*: 64 Croft Ave, Penrith, Cumberland. *T*: Penrith 2178.

HARRISON, John Smith, A.B., Ph.D. *b*: Orange, N.J. 1877. *e*: Columb Univ. *m*: Elizabeth S. Southworth. *s*: 3. *d*: 1. Prof of English (ret), Mem Modern Language Assoc of America. *Publ*: Platonism in English Poetry; The Teachers of Emerson; The Vital Interpretation of English Literature; Types of English Poetry. *s.s*: Philosophical backgrounds of English Literature, esp Greek. *Rec*: Fishing, reading. *c*: Indianapolis Literary. *a*: 347 N. Audubon Rd., Indianapolis 19, Indiana. *T*: In 3792.

HARRISON, Joseph Le Roy. *b*: North Adams, Mass 1882. *e*: Drury Acad, Cascadilla Sch & Univs of Cornell & Heidelberg. Librarian Forbes Library Northampton Mass 1912—. *Publ*: The Great Bore, Souvenir of Hoosac Tunnel; Guide to the Study of James Abbott McNeill Whistler (collab). Ed Fisherman's Verse; Winter Sports Verse. *c*: Lake Placid, Adirondack Camp & Trail. *a*: Northampton, Massachusetts, U.S.A.

HARRISON Julius, Hon.R.A.M., F.B.S.M. *b*: Stourport-on-Severn 1885. *e*: Queen Elizabeth Sch Hartlebury. *m*: Dorothie Helen Day. *s*: 1. *d*: 1. Musical Composer, Author & Conductor, Dir Elgar Festival Malvern. *Publ*: Brahms & His Four Symphonies. *Ctr*: Musical Companion, Antonin Dvorak, His Achievement; New Musical Educator. *s.s*: Musical Criticism. *Rec*: History, poetry, drama, the Fine Arts generally, gardening, cricket. *a*: The Greenwood, Ox Lane, Harpenden, Herts. *T*: 478.

HARRISON, Lawrence Whitaker, C.B., D.S.O. *b*: Haslingden, Lancs 1876. *e*: Manch Gr Sch, Glasgow Univ, Roy Army Med Coll & St Thomas's Hosp London. *m*: Mabel Alice Fairland. *s*: 2. *d*: 2. R.A.M.C. 1899 —1919, Adviser in Venereal Diseases M.O.H. '19—46. *n.a*: Co-Ed Brit Journ of Venereal Diseases 1925—42. *Publ*: The Diagnosis & Treatment of Venereal Diseases in General Practice; A Manual of Venereal Diseases for Students; The Modern Diagnosis & Treatment of Syphilis, Chancroid & Gonorrhœa. *Ctr*: B.M.J., Lancet, Med Press & Circ, Practitioner, etc. *s.s*: Venereal Diseases. *Rec*: Gardening. *c*: Army & Navy. *w.s*:

1899—1902 (Despatches), 1914—18 (Despatches, D.S.O.). *a*: 63 Eccleston Sq, London, S.W.1. *T*: Victoria 7435.

HARRISON, Leslie Ivor. *e*: Public Sc. Publisher & Bookseller. *a*: The Ancient Hse, Ipswich. *t*: 3401.

HARRISON, Lewis, A.Mus.T.C.L., F.Ph.S., F.R.S.A., M.R.S.L., M.S.P. *b*: Rochester, Kent 1889. *e*: Gillingham Higher Grade Sch, Medway Tech Coll. L.A.M. *m*: Clara Ada Weatherly. *s*: 1. Professor of Music, Lect on Literature, Organist & Precentor Chatham Pres Church 1903—46, Local Sec Trin Coll of Music from '27. *Publ*: What's in a Name; How to Play Scales; "Romance in F" for Organ; Chanson Humoristique; An Old World Garden. *Ctr*: Philosopher, Dickensian etc., *s.s*: Nomenclature, Literature, Music, Philosophy. *Rec*: Music, walking, amateur theatricals. *a*: Budleigh, Queen's Rd, Hersham, Walton-on-Thames. *T*: Walton-on-Thames 2526.

HARRISON, Marjorie, M.B.E. *b*: Haverfordwest. *e*: Priv. Author & Journalist, Broadcaster for Affairs & Women's Interests 1939—46. *n.a*: Rep Morning Post 1925, Special Corres War Graves of Gallipoli & Salonica Dly Express '26 also Egypt & Palestine '27, Special Corres Canada '28, Editress Women & Home Page Morning Post '30, Fashion Editress '32. *Publ*: Go West Go Wise—Canadian Revelation; Saints Run Mad; A Criticism of the Oxford Group Movement. *Ctr*: Dly Express, S. Times, Manch Guardian, Time & Tide, N.Y. Times. *s.s*: Women's Interests, Travel. *Rec*: Fishing. *a*: 200 Rivermead Court, Hurlingham, London, S.W.6. *T*: Renown 2988.

HARRISON, MARY ST. LEGER: see Malet, Lucas.

HARRISON, Maude. Journalist. *n.a*: Reporter London News Agency, Daily Herald, Lloyd's News, Asst Ed & Ed Woman's Page, Daily Chronicle, Sunday News, Ed Woman's Features, London Newspaper Services Ltd., Provincial N/ps Ltd. *Publ*: Between Friends; Good Company. *s.s*: Leader articles, etc. *c*: M.J.I., National Union of Jnlsts, N/p Press Fund. *a*: 10 Elgin Ct, W.9. *t*: Abercorn 3723.

HARRISON, Maj. Michael Charles Cooper, D.S.O., M.C. *b*: 1888. *e*: Malvern, Bradfield & R.M.C. Camberley. *m*: Lucy Kathleen Hansell. Army. *Publ*: Within Four Walls; Escapers All (both jt). *c*: Naval & Military. *a*: Garryowen, Parkstone, Dorset.

HARRISON, Ronald J. K. *b*: Walton-on-Thames 1903. *e*: Priv & U.C.L. *m*: Frances Bradford. *s*: 1. Rep Allied N/p '31 onwards. *n.a*: Rep Morn Post '25-27, Edu Section B.B.C. '27-28, Ed Industrial Daily News & Cinema Construction '29, Rep Daily Sketch '29-31. Mem N.U.J. '25. Organised large scale provincial meetings & demonstrations of wireless in schools for the B.B.C. *Rec*: Piano, golf. *a*: 200 Gray's Inn Rd, W.C.1. *t*: Museum 9841.

HARRISON, Sam. *b*: Birmingham 1879. *e*: Birmingham Secondary. *m*: Mabel Marlow. *s*: 1. *d*: 1. Sec Birmingham Boy Scouts' Assoc. *n.a*: Ed Scouting. *Publ*: Scouts' Own Hymnal; Some Scout Secrets. *c.t*: Various. *s.s*: Scouts. *Rec*: Golf, reading. *a*: The Nook, Stanmore Rd, Edgbaston, Birmingham. *t*: Edgbaston 0804.

HARRISON, Suzanne Eleanor. *b*: Leeds. *e*: St Winefride's Sc Swansea & France. Lady Ed. *n.a*: S. Wales Evening Post 1930-31, Leicester Evening

Mail '31–. *Rec:* Golf, bridge & tennis. *a:* 164 Upper New Walk, Leicester, & Leicester Evening Mail, Leics. *t:* 205901 & 20411.

HARRISON, Sydney H. *n.a:* Ed Scottish Field 1946. *a:* 82 Mitchell St., Glasgow.

HARRISON, William John, T.D. Surgeon. *c.t:* B.M.J., Practitioner, Journ Otology & Laryngology. *a:* 20 Jesmond Rd, Newcastle-on-Tyne. *t:* Jesmond 823.

HARRISON-NAYLOR, E. *Publ:* Red Caswell's Women; Hussy. *a:* Walnut Tree Hse, Hampton Wick, Kingston-on-Thames, Surrey. *T:* Kingston 5913.

HARRISSON, Tom, D.S.O., F.R.G.S., F.R.Econ.S., F.R.A.I. *b:* Buenos Aires 1911. *e:* Harrow & Camb. Married. *s:* 2. Sociologist. *n.a:* Ed-in-Chief Mass-Observation '37—47, Radio Critic Observer '40—44. *Publ:* Letter to Oxford; The Great Crested Grebe Census; Savage Civilisation; Borneo Jungle; Mass-Observation; & numerous volumes of Mass-Observation Results. *Ctr:* New Statesman, Observer, S. Express, Ev Standard, Spectator, News Chronicle, Manch Guardian, Political Quarterly. *s.s:* Mass-Observation, Anthropology, Opinion, Birds. *Rec:* Collecting early English China, exploration, parachuting. *c:* Reform, Special Forces *a:* 82 Ladbroke Rd, London, W.11. *T:* Park 6517.

HARROD, Frances. *b:* London. *e:* France & Italy. *m:* Henry Dawes Harrod. Author. *Publ:* The Devil's Pronoun; The Hidden Model; What We Dream; The Taming of the Brute; The Horrible Man; The Wanton; The Triumphant Rider; Lovers; Trespass; Stained Wings; Temperament; etc. *Ctr:* Times, Times Litt Supp, Westminster Gazette. *a:* 51 Campden Hill Sq., London, W.8.

HARROD, Henry Roy Forbes, F.B.A. *b:* London 1900. *e:* Westminster Sch (Scholar), New Coll Oxf (Scholar). *m:* Wilhelmine Margaret Eve Creswell. *s:* 2. Student of Christ Church Oxf, Pres F. Section British Assoc 1938, Served in Mr Churchill's Private Statistical Dept '40—42. *n.a:* Jt Ed Economic Journal since 1945. *Publ:* International Economics: Trade Cycle; Britain's Future Population; A Page of British Folly; Are These Hardships Necessary. *Ctr:* Economic Journ, Quarterly Journ of Economics, Economics, Mind, etc. *s.s:* Economics. *c:* Athenæum. *a:* Christ Church, Oxford. *T:* Oxford 4256.

HARROD, Leonard Montague. *b:* 1905. Librarian. *Publ:* Lending Library Methods; Librarians' Glossary of Terms Used in Librarianship & the Book Crafts. *Ctr:* Times Educ Supp, Journ of Educ, Municipal Journ, etc. *s.s:* Libraries & Adult Education. *a:* 41 Milton Rd, Harpenden, Herts.

HARROD, Roy Forbes. *b:* Lon 1900. *e:* Westminster Sc & New Col Oxf. Student Ch Ch Oxf. *Publ:* International Economics (Cam Econ Handbook) 33. *c.t:* Econ Journ, Economica, Quarterly Journ of Econ. *s.s:* Econ. Jnr Censor of Ch Ch '27—29, Senr Censor '30—31, Mem Hebdomadal Counc Oxf Univ '29–. *c:* Athenæum. *a:* Christ Ch, Oxf.

HARROP, Angus John, M.A.(N.Z.), Ph.D.(Cantab), Litt.D.(N.Z.). *b:* New Zealand 1900. *e:* Waitaki N.Z. & N.Z. & Camb Univs. *m:* Hilda Mary Valentine. *s:* 1. *d:* 1. Journalist, Author, Mem P.E.N. *n.a:* The Press Christchurch N.Z. 1921—22, Dly Mail Lond '24—28, S. Dispatch '28—32, Ed New Zealand News Lond '27—, News Ed Sydney Dly Mirror Cable Service '41—, Rep in Eng of N.Z. Univ '31—43. *Publ:* The Romance of Westland; England & New Zealand Chapters of the Cambridge History of the British Empire; Touring in New Zealand; England & the Maori Wars; My New Zealand; New Zealand After Five Wars. *s.s:* N.Z. History. *Rec:* Squash rackets, gardening. *c:* Roy Empire Soc, Press. *a:* Otria, 7 Northiam, London, N.12. *T:* Hillside 3539.

HARROW, Benjamin, Ph.D. *b:* London 1888. *e:* Finsbury Coll London & Columb Univ. *m:* Carolyn Solis. *d:* 1. Prof of Chemistry. *Publ:* Textbook of Biochemistry; Romance of the Atom; Chemistry in the Making; Eminent Chemists of Our Times; Chemistry of the Hormones (collab); Organic Chemistry (collab); Ed Contemp Science. *Ctr:* Nation, N.Y. Times. *s.s:* Chemistry, Biochemistry. *Rec:* Walking. *a:* 333 Central Park West, New York 25, N.Y., U.S.A. *T:* Riverside 9-2246.

HARROWBY, Earl of. *a:* Sundon Hall, Stafford.

HARROWER, Alexander Bede. *b:* 1890. *e:* King Edward's Sch Birmingham & Worcester Coll Oxf. *m:* Dorothea Simpson. Publicity Mang The Brit Oxygen Co Ltd & Asst Ed Industrial Gases, Barrister. *n.a:* Asst Ed The Arena 1912, Sub-Ed The Bystander '13—14, Asst-Ed '19—20. *Publ:* Oxy-Acetylene Welding & Metal Cutting; Within the British Empire; Handbook for Oxy-Acetylene Welders, etc. *Ctr:* Dly Graphic, Ev Standard, Chambers's Journ, etc. *s.s:* Metal Cutting, Printing & Commercial Art. *Rec:* Golf, swimming, riding. *c:* Gray's Inn Golfing. *w.s:* 1914—18. *a:* Inzievar Cottage, Hook Heath, Woking, Surrey. *T:* 277.

HARRY, Philip Anthony, M.D., D.P.H.(Edin). *b:* Jamaica 1880. *e:* Edin & Lon. *m:* Isabel Smith. *s:* 1. *d:* 1. Ophthalmic & Aural Surgeon. *c.t:* Prescriber, Medical Times. *s.s:* Ophthalmology, otology. *Rec:* Motoring, fishing. *c:* Roy Soc of Medicine. *a:* Grosvenor Mount, Middleton Rd, M/C. *t:* 2726 Rochdale.

HART, Bernard, C.B.E., M.D., F.R.C.P. *b:* London 1879. *e:* Univs Coll & Hosp London. *m:* Mabel E. Spark. *Publ:* Psychology of Insanity; Psychopathology. *Ctr:* Various Med & Psychol Journs. *s.s:* Psychiatry & Psychology. *c:* Athenæum. *a:* 77 Harley St., London, W.1. *T:* Langham 3170.

HART, Rev. Charles, B.A., M.R.S.T. *b:* Chorley 1861. *e:* Ushaw Col Durham. Master at St Cuthbert's G.S. Newcastle-on-Tyne 40 y, P.P. St Mary's Whittingham. *Publ:* Intermediate English Grammar; Manual of Bible History (Old Testament); Shorter Bible History (Old & New Test in one vol); Student's Church (vols 1 & 2); etc. *a:* St Mary's, Whittingham, Northumberland.

HART, Frances Noyes. *b:* Silver Spring, Maryland 1890. *e:* Chicago Latin Sc, Florence, The Sorbonne, College de France, Columbia Univ, New York City. *m:* Edward Henry Hart. *d:* 2. Writer. *Publ:* The Bellamy Trial; The Crooked Lane; Hide in the Dark; Pigs in Clover; Contact; My A.E.F.; Mark. *c.t:* Saturday Evening Post, McCall's, Ladies Home Journal, Pictorial Review, Scribner's. *s.s:* Criminology, child psychology, economics. Naval Intelligence Bureau '17, Canteen work for Y.M.C.A. '18—19. *Rec:* Gardening, microscopy, music, book collecting, travel. *c:* Colony New York, Women's National Country Club of Washington, D.C., Author's League of America, etc. *a:* 1757 N. Street, Washington, D.C. & Rancho Santa Fe, California. *t:* Rancho Santa Fe 2131.

HART, Frank. *b:* Brighton. Free-lance Artist-Writer, Lecturer, Exhib R.A. & R.I. *Publ:* The Animals Do Their Bit; Andrew; Master Toby's Hunt (with Arthur O. Fisher); Every Horse; etc. *Ctr:* Punch, Country Life Books, Graphic, Men Only, Sussex County Mag, etc.

Rec: Nature study, swimming, travel. *c*: Chelsea Arts. *a*: Mill Gap Cottage, Eastbourne.

HART, George Henry, F.R.S.A. *b*: London 1882. *e*: Epping, Essex. *m*: Edith Haines. *s*: 2. Goldsmith, Artist Craftsman. *Publ*: Metalwork for Craftsmen. *s.s*: Ecclesiastical Gold & Silver Work. *Rec*: Sport. *a*: Campden, Glos.

HART, G/Capt. Ivor B., O.B.E., Ph.D., B.Sc. *b*: London 1889. *e*: Earlsmead, Queen Mary's Coll & U.C.L. *m*: Deborah Anidijar Romain. *s*: 1. R.A.F. (Educational Branch), Princ Deputy Dir Educ Services, A.M. *Publ*: The Mechanical Investigation of Leonardo da Vinci; Makers of Science; The Great Engineers; Introduction to Physical Science; A Student's Heat; Elementary Experimental Statics; Elementary Aeronautical Science (with W. Laddler); The Great Physicists; Introduction to Advanced Heat; James Watt & the Story of Steam Power. *Ctr*: Aryan Path, Journ of Educ, Sci Progress etc. *s.s*: Hist of Science. *a*: 5 Waverley Way, Carshalton Beeches, Surrey. *T*: Wallington 7252.

HART, John Hamilton, M.R.C.S., L.R.C.P. *c.t*: Lancet, Med World. *a*: 27 The Avenue, Worcester Pk, Surrey. *t*: Malden 0880.

HART, Rev. John Wesley. *b*: Wisbech 1866. *e*: Coll Sch Peterborough & Headingly Coll Leeds. *m*: Frances Elizabeth Turner. *s*: 1. *Publ*: In the Iron Time; Castle Hampstead; The Secret Lady of Escott; Where the Heart Is; The Man in Corduroy; etc. *Ctr*: Methodist Mag & Times. *s.s*: Hist Fiction. *Rec*: Art, cricket. *a*: Clovelly, Meadow Way, Letchworth. *T*: Letchworth 970.

HART, L. E. (Miss). *n.a*: Fiction Ed Daily Sketch. *a*: c/o Daily Sketch, 200 Gray's Inn Rd, W.C.1.

HART, Madge. *b*: London. *e*: Somerville Coll Oxf. *Publ*: Eating & Drinking (a miscellany); Utopias, Old & New. *a*: 27 King's Court North, London, S.W.3.

HART, GENERAL SIR REGINALD CLARE, V.C., K.C.B., K.C.V.D.: Army officer (retired); *b*. Scariff, County Clare, Ireland, June 11, 1848; *s*. Lieut.-Gen. Henry George and Frances Alicia (Okes) H.; educ. Marlborough Coll., Cheltenham Coll., Royal Military Academy, Staff College; *m*. Charlotte Augusta Synnot, Aug. 6, 1872. AUTHOR: Reflections on the Art of War, 1894 (3rd edit. 1901). Contributor to Hibbert Journ., Nineteenth Century and After, My Magazine. General character of writing: military and scientific science. Relig. faith, Protestant. HOME: 39 West Cliff Road, Bournemouth, Hampshire, Eng.

HART, Robert Edward. *b*: Mauritius 1891. *e*: Priv. Head Librarian & Curator Mauritius Inst. *Publ*: (poetry) Le Destin de Sapho (1923); Interlude Mélodique; Poëmes Anglais; Poëmes Choisis; (prose) Le Cycle de Pierre Flandre (1, 2 & 3 edns '32); etc. *c.t*: Mercure de France, La Revue Bleue, La Vie, L'universite de Paris, etc. *s.s*: Poetry & mesmerism, etc. Literary, musical & scientific lecturer, Mem La Société des Gens de Lettres de France, L'Académie de la Réunion, etc. *Rec*: Music, drawing, trav. *a*: The Mauritius Inst, Port Louis, Mauritius, S. Africa.

HART, Robert Walter. *b*: London 1895. *e*: Priv & Croydon Hgh Sch. Married. *s*: 1. Publicity Manager, Journalist, Book Critic, Assoc Ed Author's & Writer's Who's Who, formerly Lit Staff Dly Herald, Ed Staff Burke's Peerage & Landed Gentry, Pub & Press Off Johnson, Matthey & Co Ltd. *Publ*: The Precious Metals in Industry. *Ctr*: Times, Dly Telegraph, N.A.G. Journ, J'wlr & Metalworker, etc. *s.s*: Publicity, Precious Metals, Books. *Rec*: Sport, music. *w.s*: 1915—19, C.D. (E.M.S.) '39—44. *a*: 39a Kenton Park Parade, Kenton Rd, Harrow, Middlesex.

HART, Walter G., LL.D. *Publ*: The Old School Lists of Tonbridge School. *a*: c/o G. Allen & Unwin Ltd, Museum St, W.C.1.

HARTE, Rev. Frederick Edward, M.A.(Q.U.B.). *b*: Belfast 1872. *e*: Wes Col Dublin, Theo Training Meth Col Belfast, R.U.I. & Q.U.B. *m*: Mary Letitia Martin. *s*: 3. *d*: 1. Meth Min. *Publ*: The Philosophical Treatment of Divine Personality from Spinoza to Hermann Lotze; This Dreamer (studies in the life of Joseph). *c.t*: Irish Chr Advocate, N.Y. Chr Advocate. *s.s*: Philos. Pres Meth Ch in Ireland 1931-32. Now Min Donegall Sq Ch. *Rec*: Golf, chess. *a*: 11 Chlorine Gdns, Belfast *t*: Malone 1023.

HARTE, Walter James. *b*: Wells, Somerset 1866. *e*: Bath Coll & Worcester Coll Oxf. *m*: Christina Eliza Christian Bennett. *s*: 1. Former Professor of History University College Exeter. *Publ*: John Hooker's History of Exeter; Drake; etc. *Ctr*: History, Trans of Devonshire Assoc, Devon & Cornwall Notes & Queries, etc. *s.s*: History. *a*: Windsor Hotel, Exeter. *T*: 388311.

HARTERT, ERNST J. O.: zoologist; *b*. Hamburg, Germany, Oct., 1859; *s*. Carl and Betty H. educ. German high schls. and universits.; DEGREE: Ph.D. (Hon.); *m*. Claudia Endris, 1891. AUTHOR: Many books and essays upon subjects of zoology, geography, travel. Contributor of hundreds of articles to ornithological journals and bulletins. Co-Editor of Novitates Zoologicae (Tring). General character of writing: natural history. Was Director Zoological (Rothschild) Museum, Triang, from 1892 to 1930. Relig. faith, Lutheran. HOME: Berlin, Germany.

HARTFORD, Richard Randall, M.A., B.D., M.R.I.A. *b*: Abbeyleix, Ireland 1904. *e*: Kilkenny Coll, Monntjoy Sch & Trinity Coll Dublin. *m*: Diana Mary Barton. Canon of St Patrick's Cath, Univ Prof (Theology), Univ Lecturer in Philosophy. *Publ*: Godfrey Day, Missionary, Pastor & Primate; John Scotus Erigena; Edward Synge. *Ctr*: Hermathena, Theology. *s.s*: Theology, Philosophy. *Rec*: Walking, golf. *a*: Churchtown Lodge, Co. Dublin, & 39 Trinity Coll, Dublin. *T*: Dublin 96970.

HARTILL, Rev. Isaac, D.D., D.Litt. *b*: Gornal 1863. *e*: Hackney Theo Col & Lon Univ. *m*: Lizzie Squire. *Publ*: Life of Sir Isaac Newton; House of Memories; Sermons on the Ascension; Autobiography; etc. *s.s*: Lit, philos. Fell, Exam & Vice-Pres Philos Soc of Eng. *a*: Newton Lodge, Salisbury Av, St Albans. Herts.

HARTILL, Ven Percy, M.A., B.D.(Oxon). *b*: Willenhall, Staffs 1892. *e*: Priv, New Coll Oxf, Cuddesdon Theol Coll. Rector & Archdeacon of Stoke-on-Trent, Chm Anglican Pacifist Fellowship since 1939. *Publ*: The Necessity of Redemption; Revealing Christ; Pacifism & Christian Common-sense; Faith & Truth (with Rev F. H. Brabant); Ed & Ctr—Into the Way of Peace; On Earth Peace; *Ctr*: The Christian Life. *s.s*: Theology, with special emphasis on Philosophy of Religion. *Rec*: Lawn tennis, walking. *a*: The Rectory, Stoke-on-Trent. *T* 48778.

HARTLAND, William. *b*: 1866. *Publ*: Newton Spa, Porthcawl (St John's). *Ctr*: Western Mail Cardiff. *s.s*: Church Orientation & Discovery of the Lost Dedications of the Reformation Churches. *Rec*: Swimming & fishing. *a*: The Poplars, Porthcawl, Glamorgan. *T*: 159.

HARTLETT, F. T. *n.a*: Wolverhampton Express, Bournemouth Echo, Leicester Mail, Nott'm Guardian. *a*: 23 Harrington Drive, Nott'm.

HARTLEY, Harold Osborne. *b*: London 1888. *m*: Grace Horsefield. *d*: 2. Journalist. *n.a*: Sth Eastern Press Ltd Greenwich, Ed & Dir 1912, Ed Oxford Times '26—. *Ctr*: Times, Dly Telegraph, etc. *a*: 44 Lonsdale Rd., Oxford. *T*: 5664.

HARTLEY, Dr. J. B., Jnr. *a*: 2 Palatine Crescent, Withington, M/C.

HARTLEY, James, F.R.S.L., M.J.I. *b*: Stalybridge 1878. *e*: Priv. *m*: Betty Hatton. *s*: 3. *d*: 1. Journalist. *n.a*: Ed the Manxman I.O.M., Preston Herald, Scarbro' Gazette, Darwen Gazette. Sec Preston & Dis Bowling League, etc. *Publ*: The Housing Problem: Its Modern Solution; Industrial Germany; How to Play Bowls Scientifically; Preston Municipal Year Book; etc. *c.t*: Daily Express, News of the World, News-Chron, Cigar & Tobacco World, Lancs Daily Post, Shoe & Leather Record, etc. *s.s*: Trade subjects. Foundation Mem M/C Centre Printers, Mangs & Overseers Assoc. A Founder of Macclesfield Swimming Club, etc. Life Mem Nat Life Saving Soc. *Rec*: Bowls. *a*: Claremont, 160 Addison Rd, Ashton-on-Ribble, Preston.

HARTLEY, Leslie Poles. *b*: Whittlesey, Cambs 1895. *e*: Harrow Sch, Balliol Coll Oxf. Author. *Publ*: The Shrimp & the Anemone; The Sixth Heaven; Eustace & Hilda; Simonetta Perkins; The Killing Bottle; Night Fears. *Ctr*: Weekly Sketch, Observer, Week-end Review, Time & Tide, Spectator. *s.s*: Reviewing of Fiction. *Rec*: Rowing, swimming, walking. *c*: Athenæum. *a*: Avondale, Bathford Somerset.

HARTLEY, Miss Olga. *b*: London. *e*: Priv Sch & Bedford Coll. *Publ*: Anne; The Malaret Mystery; The Witch of Chelsea; The Gentle Art of Cookery (with Mrs. C. Leyel); Lucullus; Meatless Meals; Women & the Catholic Church. *Ctr*: Various newspapers & periodicals. *a*: St. Annes, Chipping Campden, Glos.

HARTLEY, Sir Percival Horton-Smith, Kt., C.V.O., M.A., M.D., F.R.C.P. *b*: London 1867. *e*: Marlborough, St John's Coll Camb, Paris, Vienna. *m*: Lucy Josephine Hartley. *s*: 1. *d*: 1. Cons Physician to St Bart's & Brompton Hosps, K. St. J. *Publ*: The Typhoid Bacillus & Typhoid Fever; Diseases of the Lungs (jtly). *Ctr*: Journ of Physiology, B.M.J., etc. *s.s*: Diseases of the Chest, Hist of Med. *Rec*: Gardening, travel. *c*: Athenæum. *a*: Adkins, Ingatestone, Essex. *T*: 143.

HARTMAN, Herbert, B.A., Ph.D.(Yale). *b*: Lancaster, Penn., 1901. *e*: Laurenceville Sc, Yale Univ. *m*: Cornelia V. R. Stanwood. Asst prof of English, Bowdoin Col. *Publ*: Imperial Fiddlesticks; Hartley Coleridge: Poet's Son and Poet; Ed Surrey's Fourth Book of Virgil. *c.t*: Modern Language Notes, Review of English Studies, Modern Language Assoc. *s.s*: English literature. Instructor Bowdoin Col '29—31. Asst prof Bowdoin Col since '31. *c*: Yale Club, Shakespeare Assoc of America, Modern Language Assoc. *a*: 17 Belmont St, Brunswick, Maine, U.S.A. *t*: 12W.

HARTMANN, Cyril Hughes. M.A., B.Litt. *b*: Thames Ditton 1896. *e*: Charterhouse, Univ Col Oxf & Univ de Neuchâtel. *m*: Marguerite Marie-Louise Alcoforado. *s*: 1. Author. *Publ*: La Belle Stuart; The Cavalier Spirit; The Vagabond Duchess; The Magnificent Montmorency: Ed: Memoirs of the Comte de Gramont, Memoirs of Captain Carleton; The Temperate Zone (play); Charles II and Madame; etc. *c*: Roy Socs. *a*: 78 Palace Gardens Terr. W.8.

HARTNESS, Mrs. Belle Harpster. *b*: Ohio 1867. *e*: Ohio Northern Univ. Univ of Lon etc. *m*: John Anton Hartness. Company Dir-Sec. *c.t*: The American Register & Anglo Colonial World, The New York Tribune, N.Y., Herald Paris, Washington Post, Springfield Reporter, Lima Times. *s.s*: Chemistry, Astronomy & Greek Mythology. Has lectured on Astronomy in U.S.A. & England. Has represented several states at Internat Congress. Representative in London of the League of American Pen Women for a number of years. Was Hon Sec of the American Circle of Lyceum Club. *Rec*: Motoring & Theatre *c*: Fellow Roy Soc Arts, Soc of Chem Ind, Lyceum. *a*: Excelsior Hse, 8 Gordon St, W.C.1. *t*: Museum 7769.

HARTOG, Lady (Mabel Helene), B.Sc.(Lond). *b*: London. *e*: Univ Coll Lond. *m*: Sir Philip Hartog, K.B.E., C.I.E. *s*: 3. *Publ*: Living India; India in Outline; India (Nelson's Practical Work Books). *a*: 5 Inverness Gdns, London, W.8.

HARTOG, Sir Philip Joseph, K.B.E., C.I.E., LL.D. *Publ*: The Writing of English; Examinations & Their Relation to Culture & Efficiency. *c.t*: M/C Guardian. *a*: 5 Inverness Gdns, W.8. *t*: Bayswater 4294.

HARTRICK, Archibald Standish, R.W.S. *b*: Bangalore, India 1864. *e*: Fettes Coll Edin, Edin Univ, Slade Sch of Fine Art, Julian's & Atelier Cormon Paris. *m*: Lily Blatherwick. Painter, Lithographer. *Publ*: A Painter's Pilgrimage through 50 years; Drawing; Recording Britain. *Ctr*: (Illustrations) Borrow's Wild Wales, Kipling's Soldier Tales. *s.s*: Lithography as a Fine Art. *Rec*: Looking for ancient painted glass in old churches. *c*: Chelsea Arts. *a*: 75 Clancarty Rd, Fulham, London, S.W.6.

HARTRIDGE, Hamilton, M.A., M.D., Sc.D., M.R.C.P., F.R.S. *b*: London. *e*: Harrow Sch, King's Coll Camb, St George's Hosp. *m*: Kathleen Adele Wilson. *s*: 1. *d*: 3. Prof of Physiology. *n.a*: Ed of Bainbridge & Menzies Essentials of Physiology since 1930. *Publ*: Histology for Medical Students (with F. Haynes). *Ctr*: Procs of Roy Soc, Journ of Physiology, Nature, B.M.J. *s.s*: Vision & Hearing. *Rec*: Sketching, metal working, short story writing. *w.s*: Experimental Officer R.A.F. 1915—18. *a*: 21 Frithwood Ave, Northwood, Middx. *T*: 1844.

HARTSHORNE, Charles, A.B., Ph.D.(Harvard). *b*: Kittanning, Penn 1897. *e*: Haverford Coll, Germany & France. *m*: Dorothy Eleanore Cooper. *d*: 1. University Instructor. *Publ*: The Philosophy & Psychology of Sensation; Ed The Collected Papers of Charles Peirce 6 vols; Beyond Humanism; Man's Vision of God & the Logic of Theism. *Ctr*: New Humanist, Internat Journ of Ethics, Journ of Philos, Philos of Science, The Monist, Philos Rev, New Frontier, Journ of Religion, Hibbert Journ, etc. *s.s*: Aesthetics, Metaphysics, Philosophy of Religion. *Rec*: Ornithology. *a*: Faculty Exchange, The Univ of Chicago, Chicago, Ill. *T*: Fairfax 5656.

HARTWIG, Thora. *b*: Haderslev, North Sleswick. *e*: Haderslev Hgh Sch & Univs of Munich, Berlin & Copenhagen. Author & Broadcaster. *Publ*: Die Traumerin von Helleby (Novel); Von Strassen und Garten des Lebens (Short Stories); Aus Marchenlanden (Tales); Kraft aus der Höhe, etc. *Ctr*: Leading German periodicals. *s.s*: Corsica. *c*: Assoc of Danish Authors. *a*: Haderslev, North-Sleswick, Denmark.

HARVEY, A. J. *n.a*: Ed of Young Chronicle *s.s*: Australia. *a*: Burrowa St, Young, N.S. Wales, Australia.

HARVEY, F. W. *n.a*: Ed Bromsgrove, Droitwich & Redditch Messenger. *a*: Wyncroft, New Rd, Bromsgrove, Worcs.

HARVEY, Frank ("Keystone"). *n.a*: Racing Corr Sunday Dispatch. *a*: Northcliffe Hse, London, E.C.4.

HARVEY, Lt-Col. Frederic, M.R.C.S., L.R.C.P., D.P.H. *b*: Glasgow 1872. *e*: Brighton Coll, St Bart's Hosp, R.A.M.C. Coll Millbank. R.A.M.C. (ret), O.St.J., Barrister, Mem Hon Soc Middle Temple. *n.a*: Black & White, Our Military Correspondent 1899—1902, Brochure Writer Danish Tourist Bureau '39. *Publ*: Health Legislation; The Modern Home Doctor; etc. *Ctr*: Sheffield Independent, Yorks Post, Leeds Mercury, Leominster News, Times Lit Supp, Contemp Rev. *s.s*: Public Health, Social Welfare & Nutrition. *Rec*: Travel & motoring. *c*: Overseas League. *w.s*: 1914—18 (Despatches). *a*: 24 Amberley Ct, Worthing, Sussex. *T*: Worthing 6069.

HARVEY, Frederic Bright. *b*: Rochester 1886. *e*: Sir Joseph Williamson's Sc Rochester. Married. *s*: 1. *d*: 1. Journalist. Picture Ed Daily Express. *n.a*: Daily Dispatch '11, Daily Chronicle '12, Sunday Dispatch '26, Daily Express '28—. *Rec*: Riding & Golf. *a*: 8 Princeton Mans, Red Lion Sq, W.C.1. *t*: Holborn 6855.

HARVEY, Rev. Frederick Brompton. *b*: Castle Donington 1883. *e*: Loughboro' Gr Sch, Univ Coll Nott'm, Didsbury Coll Manch. *m*: Alice Margaret Horton. *s*: 1. *d*: 1. Chaplain Wycliffe Coll 1939—45. *Publ*: Should Germany Be Forgiven; The Necessity of the New Birth; Church State & Letters; Short Life Sketch of Dr. A. W. Harrison, Thrills of Bookland. *Ctr*: Times Lit Supp, Nineteenth Century & After, Contemporary Review, Meth Recorder, Lond Quarterly Review. *s.s*: History. *a*: 36 Marmion Rd, Liverpool 17. *T*: Lark Lane 1872.

HARVEY, George. *b*: Glas. *Publ*: Guide Books to Belgium, Paris & Scotland. *a*: 10 South Hill Park Gdns, N.W.3. *t*: Hampstead 3788.

HARVEY, Godfrey Eric. *b*: London 1889. *e*: Aldenham & Exeter Schs, Lond Univ. *m*: Stella Hope Garratt. *s*: 1. *d*: 1. Lecturer in Burmese Oxf Univ 1935—40, I.C.S. '12—35. *Publ*: History of Burma; British Rule in Burma. *Ctr*: Cambridge History of India. *s.s*: S.E. Asia, Buddhism, Comparative Religion. *a*: 13 St Margaret's Rd, Oxford. *T*: 2679.

HARVEY, Herbert Frost. *b*: Hertford 1875. *e*: Hertford Sc. *m*: Adeline Hulme. *s*: 2, *d*: 1. *n.a*: Herts Guardian, Coventry Herald, Birmingham Post, Manchester Dispatch, Ed Birmingham Mail 1907—. Chm Roy Cripples Hosp Birm. *Rec*: Horticulture, golf. *c*: Midland, Birm, Birm Press, Moseley Golf, R.A.C. *a*: Redditch Rd, Kings Norton, Birm. *t*: Kings Norton 1076.

HARVEY, Rev. J., D.D. *a*: 7 Western Terrace, Edinburgh.

HARVEY, John Henry. *b*: Nott'm 1891. *e*: Storrey's Col, Nott'm, Nott'm Univ Col & L'pool Univ. Schoolmaster. *Publ*: The Arithmetic of Commerce. *c.t*: Tech Journ & Journ of Educ. *s.s*: Comm & economics. *Rec*: Riding, swimming, etc. *a*: Bedford Ct Hotel, Brixton Hill, S.W.2. *t*: 2536.

HARVEY, John Wilfred. Prof of Philos Leeds Univ. *Publ*: Pt Author, Competition (1917); Christianity & the Present Moral Unrest; Poems; Trans of Das Heilige (by R. Otto); The Naturalness of Religion; The Nine Nicks ('29) (under pseudonym "John Farndale"). *a*: 6 Claremont Rd, Headingley, Leeds. *t*: 52925.

HARVEY, Kenneth. *c.t*: Various. *s.s*: Co-operation, Agriculture & Horticulture, Transport (road & rail), Political. F/l trade correspondent & photographer. Also lecturing. *a*: 68 Ommaney Rd, S.E.14.

HARVEY, Thomas Edmund, Hon.LL.D.(Leeds). *b*: Leeds 1875. *e*: Bootham Sch York, Yorkshire Coll, Christ Church Oxf, Univs Berlin & Paris. *m*: Alice Irene Thompson. Retired, formerly Asst Brit Mus, Deputy Warden & Warden Toynbee Hall, M.P. (L) West Leeds 1910—18, Dewsbury '23—24, & (Ind) Combined Eng Univs '37—45. *Publ*: The Rise of the Quakers; St Aelred of Rievaulx; A Wayfarer's Faith; The Christian Church & the Prisoner; Stolen Aureoles; Songs in the Night. *Ctr*: Nation, Contem Rev, etc. *Rec*: Country walks. *c*: Nat Lib. *a*: Rydal Hse, Grosvenor Rd, Leeds 6.

HARVEY, Lt.-Col. W. F., C.I.E. Medical. *n.a*: Sectional Ed Tropical Diseases Bulletin 1925. *c.t*: B.M.J., Indian Journ of Med Research, Biometrika, Edin Med Journ, Journ of Hygiene, Protozoology. *a*: 56 Garscube Terr, Edin. *t*: 62701.

HARVEY, William, J.P., F.S.A.Scot. *b*: Stirling 1874. *e*: Stirling & Priv. *m*: Marjorie Mackay (dec). *s*: 1. Journalist & Author. *n.a*: Asst Ed People's Journ 1906, Lit Ed Dundee Advertiser '08—12, Dundee Fiction Ed Messrs John Leng & Co Ltd '12—. *Publ*: Scottish Life & Character in Anecdote & Story; Irish Life & Humour; Robert Burns in Stirlingshire; Robert Burns as a Freemason; Manual of Freemasonry; The Stirling Repository; etc. *c.t*: People's Friend, People's Journ, Sunday Post, Dundee Courier & Advertiser. *s.s*: Robert Burns, local hist (Scot). Chm Dundee Ins Cmt. Ex-Pres Scot Assoc of Ins Cmts. Ex-Pres Scot Foresters' Fed. *Rec*: Book-collecting. *a*: Nethercrag, Blackness Av, Dundee.

HARVEY, William Clunie, M.D., Ch.B., D.P.H., (see **SCOTT, Sutherland.**) *b*: Glasgow 1900. *e*: Bellahouston Acad & Univ of Glasgow. *m*: Winifred May Brown. *s*: 2. *d*: 1. M.O.H. Borough of Southgate, Fell M.O.H., Roy San Inst & Roy Inst of Public Health & Hygiene, Mem B.M.A. *Publ*: Milk Production & Control; Milk Products; Insect Pests; (Fiction) Murder Abroad; Death's Treasure Hunt. *Ctr*: B.M.J., Lancet, Better Health, Public Health, Journ of Hygiene, etc. *s.s*: Public Health. *Rec*: Bridge, writing. *w.s*: 1943—46 R.A.M.C. (Lt-Col). *a*: The Garth, Wolves Lane, Palmers Green, London, N.13. *T*: Bowes Park 3104.

HARVEY, William Fryea, M.A., M.B. *b*: Leeds 1885. *e*: Bootham Sc York & Oxf Univ. *m*: Margaret Muir Henderson. *s*: 1. *d*: 1. Doctor (ret). Awarded Albert Medal 1918. *Publ*: Midnight House & other Tales (Dent) '10; The Beast with Five Fingers ('27); Moods & Tenses ('33); etc. *c.t*: Cornhill, Tatler, Red Mag, Yorks Wkly Post, Evening Standard, etc. *s.s*: Tales of the supernatural. *c*: Nat Lib. *a*: Firth Hse, Oatlands Close, Weybridge.

HARVEY-GIBSON, ROBERT JOHN: professor (emeritus) of botany; b. Rhu, Dumbartonshire, Scotland, Nov., 1860; s. Rev. Robert Gibson and Jane Isabel (Harvey) G.; educ. Grammar Sch., Aberdeen (Scotland), Univs. Aberdeen, Edinburgh, Strasburg (Germany). DEGREES: M.A., D.Sc. (Univ. Aberdeen); m. Eda Lawrie, March, 1887. AUTHOR: Primer of Biology, 1905; Outlines of the History of Botany, 1919; Derivations of Plant Names, 1922; Short History of Botany, 1924; The Master Thinkers, 1928; (in the press): New World of Plants; Two Thousand Years of Science; The Wonder of Common Things; Elements of Botany. Contributor to Chamber's Journ., T. P.'s Weekly, Chamber's Encyclopedia, Annals of Botany, Linnean Soc., Proceedings and trans. Royal Soc. of Eng., Journ of Botany and many other scientific publications. General character of writing: scientific, technical, historical. Served in War (lieut.-Col.), decorated, C.B.E.; Retired from university work, 1921, after 37 yrs. service. Fellow Royal Soc. Edinburgh. HOME: 30 Huntly Gardens, Glasgow W. 2. Scotland .

HARVIE, William, F.R.G.S. *e*: St John's G.S. Hamilton, Financial Secretary. *n.a*: Ed Investments '33; etc. *Publ*: The Investor's Assistant. *s.s*: Finance. *a*: 17 Fore St, E.C.2. *t*: Metropolitan 1994.

HARWOOD, Dr. Basil, M.A., MusDoc(Oxon). *b*: Woodhouse, Glos 1859. *e*: Chaterhouse & Trin Col Oxf. *m*: Mabel Ada Jennings. *s*: 2. Musical Composer. Organist St Barnabas, Pimlico 1883-87, Ely Cath '87-92, Ch Ch Cath, Oxf '92-1909, Precentor Keble Col Oxf '92-1903, Choragus of the Univ of Oxf '00-09. *Publ*: As By the Streams of Babylon (1907); Concerto for Organ & Orchestra in D, Op 24 (three Choirs Festival, Glos; Song on May Morning (Leeds Mus Festival; The Choirs of New Jerusalem (3 Choirs Festival, Clos '28); etc. Musical Ed The Oxf Hymn Book '08. *c*: Authors. *a*: Woodhouse, Almondsbury, nr Bristol.

HARWOOD, Frank Courtney, B.Sc., F.R.I.C., M.I.Chem.E., F.T.I., F.R.S.A. *b*: Torcross, Devon 1897. *e*: Kingsbridge Gr Sch Devon, Univ Coll Lond. *m*: Marguerite Mary Fenn. *s*: 2. *d*: 1. Dir of Research. *Ctr*: Trans of Chem Soc & Inst of Chem Engineers, Chem & Industry, Journ of the Textile Inst, Journ of the Inst of Brit Launderers, etc. *s.s*: Chemical Engineering, Physical Chemistry, Technical Education, Laundry Technology. *Rec*: Motoring, gardening, sailing, walking, lecturing. *a*: Broad Oak, 28 Parkside, Mill Hill, London, N.W.7. *T*: Mill Hill 3072.

HARWOOD, H. M. Playwright. *Publ*: Billeted (with F. Tennyson Jesse); The Confederates; Cynara (with R. F. Gore-Brown); Please Help Emily; Girl's Best Friend; The Grain of Mustard Seed; Honour Thy Father; How to be Healthy though Married; King Queen Knave (with R. F. Gore-Brown); The Man in Possession; The Mask; The Pelican (with F. Tennyson Jesse); So Far & No Farther; A Social Convenience; The Supplanters; The Transit of Venus; The Old Folks at Home. *a*: 11, Melina Place, London, N.W.8.

HARWOOD, Henry Cecil. *b*: Boston 1893. *e*: Shrewsbury & Balliol Coll Oxf. *m*: Dorothy Blackledge. Reviewer & Publisher's Reader. *Publ*: Judgement Eve. *Ctr*: Manch Guardian, Quarterly Rev, 19th Century, Nation, New Statesman, Spectator, Sat Rev, Dly Herald, etc. *s.s*: Fiction, Hist. *Rec*: Travel. *c*: Savage. *a*: 57 Ladbroke Gr, London, W.1. *T*: Park 5424.

HARWOOD, Henry William. *b*: Halifax 1885. Journalist. *n.a*: Yorks Observer. *s.s*: Dialect, folklore. Chm W. Riding dis n/p Press Fund, 1931-2. *Rec*: Reading, walking. *a*: Newstead Hse, Halifax, Yorks. *t*: 61140.

HARWOOD, John Edward Godfrey, B.A., M.A. *b*: Oxf 1900. *e*: Charterhouse & Christ Ch Oxf. *m*: Winifred Chapman. Engineer. *n.a*: Ass Ed Motor Cycling '27-29. *Publ*: Speed, & how to obtain it. *c.t*: Motor Cycling, The Motor Cycle, The Motor Boat, The Yachting World. *s.s*: Internal combustion engines. *Rec*: Motor cruising. *c*: Authors' Bristol, Mem Inst Brit Eng & Inst Motor Trade. *a*: Woodhouse, Almondsbury, nr Bristol.

HASAN, S(YED) Z(AFAR-UL), Prof. Dr.: professor of Philosophy, Aligarh Muslim University, United Provinces, India; *b*. Multan, India, Feb., 1885; *s*. K. S. Syad Diwan Mohd; educ. Arabic School, Delhi, and Aligarh College, Aligarh (India). DEGREES: B.A., LL.B., M.A. (Allahabad Univ.); Dr. Phil. (Erlangen), D. Phil. (Oxford); married. AUTHOR: Realism, 1927; Monismus Spinoza, 1929; Philosophy of Kant; Outline of Moral Philosophy; Philosophy of Religion; A Lecture on Philosophy and Education, 1929; Die historischen Anfänge des neuzeitlichen Realismus, 1931. General character of writing: philosophical—also some essays and poems. Relig. faith, Mohammedan. CLUBS: Kant gessellschaft (Berlin), Mind Association (E n g.). HOME: Kharar, Dist. of Ambala, India.

HASELDEN, William Kerridge. *b*: Seville 1872. *n.a*: Dly Mirror 1904, Punch '06—. *Publ*: Daily Mirror Reflections (Annual); The Adventures of Big & Little Willie. *a*: Aldeburgh, Suffolk.

HASENCHEVER, Pamela Glwadys Hope. *b*: Preston 1911. *e*: Park Sc Preston. *s.s*: Short stories, poems. *Rec*: Tennis, amateur theatricals. *a*: 59 St Andrews Avenue, Ashton-on-Ribble, Preston, Lancashire.

HASHIMI, Naseeruddin. *b*: Hyderabad, Deccan 1895. *e*: Madarsai Darul-Uloom Hyderabad Deccan. *m*: Zubeda Begum. *s*: 1. *d*: 3. City Registrar Registration Office. *Publ*: Deccan me Urdu; Madras me Urdu; Europe me Deccani Manscripts; Makhalatay Hashmi; Khawateen i Deccan ki Urdu Khidmat; Khawateen i Ahad i Osmani; Ahad Asafi ki Khadim Taleem; Tazkeray Darululloom; etc. *Ctr*: Humayun Lahore, Musannif Aligarh, Sakhi Delhi, Ismat Delhi, Shab Hyderabad, etc. *s.s*: History & comment of Urdu Lit; Educ & Lit Hist of Deccan. *Rec*: Cinema, travel. *c*: P.E.N. *a*: Mumtaz Mention Rd, Khairtabad, Hyderabad, Deccan, India.

HASKELL, Arnold Lionel, M.A., F.R.S.A. *b*: London 1903. *e*: Westminster, Trinity Hall Camb. *m*: Vera Saitzoff. *s*: 2. *d*: 1. Author, Lecturer, Dir of Sadlers Wells Sch 1946, Trustee Sadlers Wells Ballet Benevolent Fund 1943, Joint Dir Royal Acad of Dancing Teachers Training Course '46, V-Pres Royal Acad of Dancing '46. *Publ*: Balletomania; Diaghileff; Ballet a Guide to Appreciation; Waltzing Matilda; The Australians; The Sculptor Speaks; Ballet Panorama; The National Ballet. *Ctr*: On Ballet to papers all over the World. *s.s*: Ballet. *Rec*: Travel, collecting Victoriana & paintings, also material relating to Walter Scott. *a*: 34 Walton St, London, S.W.3. *T*: Kensington 5063.

HASKINS, Caryl Parker, Ph.D. *b*: Schenectady, N.Y. 1908. *e*: Albany Acad, Univs of Yale & Harvard. *m*: Edna Ferrell. Research Scientist, Administrator. *Publ*: Of Ants & Men; The Amazon. *Ctr*: Excursions in Science, A Treasury in Science, The Book of Naturalists, American Thought, Foreign Affairs, Atlantic Monthly, etc. *s.s*: Science, American Foreign Policy. *Rec*: Hiking, canoeing, etc. *c*: Century, Chemist's, Cosmos, etc. *a*: Green Acre Lane, Westport, Conn, U.S.A.

HASKINS, Minnie Louise. *b*: Warmley, Glos 1875. *e*: Priv & Univ of London. Tutor Social Science Dept Sch of Econ Lond Univ (ret). *Publ*: Through Beds of Stone; Gate of The Year; Smoking Flax (Verse); A Few People. *Ctr*: Various. *s.s*: Sociology, Social Philosophy. *Rec*: Gardening. *a*: Brooklands, Crowborough, Sussex. *T*: Crowborough 299.

HASLAM, James. *b*: Lancashire 1868. *n.a*: Founder & Ed People's Year Book, Northern Weekly '94, L'pool Courier '99, Co-op News 1908, C.W.S. publ '16, Cotton Factory Times '33, Ed The Journalist '24—. *Publ*: (novel) Handloom Weaver's Daughter; 3 Co-operative Histories. *c.t*: Various n/ps & periodicals.

s.s: Social & industrial, etc. Ex-Pres N.U.J. c: M/C Chamber of Commerce, M/C & L'pool Press, etc. a: 31 Mauldeth Rd, W., Withington, M/C. t: 2054.

HASLAM, Robert Heywood. b: Bolton. e: Sedbergh & Bedales. m: Dolores Lomax. n.a: Founder & Controller What's on, 1907–18. c.t: British Architect, Vanity Fair, The Builder, The Studio. Ministry of Information during War. Rec: Bowls, fishing, travel. c: Reform, Arts, Art Worker's Guild. a: Wonersh Park, nr Guildford, & Bowderdale, Wastwater, Cumberland. t: Bramley 34.

HASLEHURST, Rev. Richard Stafford Tyndale, B.D. (Durham & Cantab). b: West Felton Salop. e: Trin Coll Camb. Clerk in Holy Orders, Examiner for Cambridge Locals, Mem of Author's Soc. Publ: Works of Fastidius; Penitential Discipline of the Early Church; Church of England Doctrines; How to read the Bible aloud; Clerical Etiquette. Ctr: Ch Quarterly, Theology. s.s: Theology. Rec: Billiards, bowls, bridge. a: Clun Vicarage, Salop. T: Clun 216.

HASLETT, Dame Caroline, D.B.E. Dir Electrical Assoc for Women. n.a: Ed The Electrical Age. Publ: Electrical Handbook for Women; Housing Digest; Teach Yourself Household Electricity. a: 35 Grosvenor Pl, London, S.W.1. T: Sloane 0401.

HASLIP, Joan. b: 1911. Author, News Ed B.B.C. European Service 1942–46. Publ: Lady Hester Stanhope; Grandfather's Steps; Out of Focus; Parnell; Portrait of Pamela; Balkan Fairy Stories; etc. a: 208 Carrington Hse, Hertford St, London, & Le Belvedere Settignano, Italy. T: Mayfair 6232.

HASLUCK, Eugene Lewis, M.A.(Lond), F.R.Hist.S., D.P.A.(Lond). b: London 1889. e: St Paul's Sch, Univ Coll Lond. m: Edwina Cushion. s: 1. Author & Lecturer, Mem Herne Bay U.D.C. 1930–38, Mem K.C.C. '38–46, Mem Library Assoc Council '39–45. Publ: Foreign Affairs 1919–37; Local Government in England; The Teaching of History; Modern Europe; The Second World War. Ctr: Local Gov Service. s.s: Local Gov, Current Affairs. Rec: Motoring, gardening, philately. w.s: '14–18 R.N. (Minesweeper Flotilla of Grand Fleet), '39–45 Lecturer to H.M. Forces (Current Affairs & Public Administration). a: Heathfield, Western Ave, Herne Bay, Kent. T: Herne Bay 375.

HASLUCK, Margaret Masson, M.A.(Aber), B.A.(Cam). b: Aberdeen 1885. e: Elgin Acad, Aberdeen, Cambridge & Berlin Univs. m: F. W. Hasluck M.A. (dec). n.a: Albanian Corr for Near East & India 1932–. Publ: Albanian English Reader '32; Ed Athos & Its Monasteries; Letters on Religion & Folklore; Christianity & Islam under the Sultans. c.t: Times, M/C Guardian, Fortnightly Review, Near East & India, Folk Lore, etc. s.s: Folklore. Rec: Travel, riding, sewing. a: Elbasan, Albania, & c/o Mrs Hunter, 295 Boston Rd, Hanwell, W.7.

HASLUCK, Paul, M.A. b: Fremantle 1905. e: Univ of Western Australia. m: A. A. M. Darker. s: 2. Historian & Journalist. n.a: Lit Staff West Australian, Perth 1923–29. Publ: Black Australians; Into the Desert; Workshop of Security. Ctr: " Political & Social " Sect in Official History of Australia in the War. s.s: Australian History & Politics, International Affairs. a: 2 Adams Rd, Claremont, Western Australia.

HASSALL, Christopher Vernon, F.R.S.L. b: London 1912. e: St Michael's Coll Tenbury, Brighton Coll, Wadham Coll Oxf. m: Evelyn Helena Chapman. s: 1. d: 1. Author, Dir of Voice Old Vic Sch. Publ: Penthesperon; Christ's Comet; Crisis; Devil's Dyke; Poems of the Years; S.O.S. Ludlow. s.s: Music, Poetry, Drama. Rec: Musical composition. a: The Manor Hse, Old Woking, Surrey. T: Woking 2623.

HASSON, Dr. James. b: Alexandria 1892. e: Pub Schs & Univs Edin, Paris, Geneva. m: Olive Olga Phyllis Ionide. Medaille d'Honn. Military Medicine, Distinguished Officer Australian Red Cross. Publ: History of Leprosy; Biology Medical. s.s: Skin Diseases. Rec: Fishing, gardening. a: 76 Gloucester Terr, London, W.2. T: Paddington 4990; & Shenfield Mill, Theale, nr Reading, Berks. T: Theale 73.

HASSARD-SHORT, Adrian Hugh, O.B.E. b: Lee, Kent 1879. e: H.M.S. Britannia Dartmouth. m: Amelia Eliza Renouf. s: 1. Secretary Poor Persons Cttee The Law Society. Publ: The Practice in Poor Persons Cases. Ctr: Various. s.s: Legal Aid & Divorce. a: 2 Princess Ct, Queensway, London, W.2. T: Bayswater 5589.

HASTE, Lilian Florence Thomson, LL.A. b: London. e: London & St Andrews Univs. m: Harry Court, B.Sc(Econ). Writer. Publ: Voice Production, Normal Press; Civil Service Arithmetic Gregg; In collab with H. Court, B.Sc: Story of British Government; Our Empire, Parts 1, 2 & 3; History for the Senior School Parts 1, 2 & 3 (In collab with H. Court, B.Sc); Teaching of History to Juniors (Vols 1, 2); Modern Teaching. c.t: Teachers' World, Sunday Dispatch. s.s: Education. Rec: Music, reading. a: Glen Mavis, Decoy Drive, Eastbourne, Sussex, & Silverdale Hotel, Eastbourne, Sussex.

HASTE, W. F. b: Teignmouth 1898. e: Highweek Sch, Newton Abbot. m: E. M. Hatch. s: 2. Journalist. n.a: Cornish & Devon Post, Langport & Somerton Herald & Launceston Wkly News, Lond dailies, P.A. & Exchange Telegraph Co Ltd, sports corr Western Morning News. Ctr: Western Independent. s.s: Sport. a: Wooda, Launceston, Cornwall.

HASTESKO HEPORAUTA, Elsa Matilda. b: Puumala, Finland 1883. m: Dr. F. A. Heporauta. s: 3. Authoress. Publ: Suuri Yo; Ursula Keivaara I–III; Maa vai Taivas; Temu Hulivili; Huli ja Mies; Hiljainen aani Katveessa; Lintu Loi Ruutuun; Helena Saarlahti; Kohtalonsa Vaalikki; Saaren Juhannus; Hulkan Emannan; Elamani Kaarisilta; etc. Ctr: Various newsps & periodicals. s.s: Psychology. c: P.E.N., Authors' Assoc of Finland. a: Temppelik, 19 Helsinki, Finland. T: 46.089.

HASTINGS, Anne Wilson, M.A. b: Kinneff, Kincardineshire. e: Leeds Girls' Hgh Sch, Aberdeen Univ. m: Leonard John Page. H.M. Supt Insp of Factories. n.a: Jt-Ed Expository Times 1922—. a: 11 Kings Gate, Aberdeen, & 30 Cleveland Rd, West Ealing, London, W.13. T: Aberdeen 2805, & Perivale 1959.

HASTINGS, Archibald Charles Gardiner. b: London 1878. e: Private, Charterhouse & Abroad. m Marguerite Elizabeth Harrison. Colonial Administrative Service (ret). Publ: Nigerian Days (also in Braille); The Voyage of the Dayspring; Novels:—Beyond the Hill; Hoodman Blind; Gone Native; Venom (also as serials in England). c.t: Blackwood, Nat Review, Chambers's Journ, Empire Review, Truth, Spectator, M/c Guardian, Crown Colonist, Yorkshire Weekly Post, West Africa, etc. s.s: Africa (West Coast & Morocco particularly). Served in Imperial Yeomanry, S. Africa 1900 & '01, Consular Service, Fez, Morocco '02—05. Administrative service, Nigeria '06—24. c: Sports Club, P.E.N., Thursday. a: Kensington Palace Mans, De Vere Gdns, W.8. t: Western 8121.

HASTINGS, Rev. Edward, M.A. e: Aber Univ & New Coll Edin. Editor. n.a: Jt Ed Expository Times. Publ: The Local Colour of the Bible; The Speaker's Bible. a: 11 King's Gate, Aberdeen, Scotland. T: Aberdeen 2805.

HASTINGS, Rev. Frederick. *b*: Thorne 1838. *e*: Cong Col. *m*: Emily Brightman. *s*: 3. *d*: 2. *n.a*: Ed The Homiletic Mag & of Nisbet's Theological Library 8 y. *Publ*: Background of Sacred Story; Back Streets & London Slums; Phases of a Joyous Life; " Don't Worry "; Spins of the Cycling Parson; etc. *c.t*: Windsor Mag, Sunday At Home, Cassell's Mag, Quiver, etc. *Rec*: Sketching, music. *a*: 3 Spencer Rd, Eastbourne.

HASTINGS, Graham. *b*: Lon 1898. *e*: Priv & R.M.C. Sandhurst. *n.a*: Ed Scot Country Life. *Rec*: Sport, travel. *a*: The Manor Hse, Earnley, Chichester.

HASTINGS, Harold Charles. *b*: Lon 1908. *e*: Lon & Scot. Journalist & Press Agent. *n.a*: Ex Editorial Services Ltd, Wembley Stadium Ltd (Press Repres). *c.t*: News of the World, Sunday Express, Reynolds, Evening Standard, News Chronicle. *s.s*: Speedway & Greyhound Racing, Football & all sports. *Rec*: Cricket. *a*: Rookery Hse, Riverside Rd, Watford, Herts. *t*: Watford 2549.

HASTINGS, Hubert de Cronin. *m*: Hazel Rickman Garrard. *s*: 1. *d*: 1. *n.a*: Ed Architectural Review 1927, Architect's Journ '32, Contact Publications '32—. *Rec*: Hunting, palmistry, shooting. *a*: 9-13 Queen Anne's Gate, London, S.W.1. *T*: Whitehall 0611.

HASTINGS, Sir Patrick, Kt. *Publ*: (plays) inc The River ; Escort ; etc. *a*: Thurston Hall, Framfield, Sussex.

HASTINGS, S., M.B., M.S., F.R.C.S., L.C.C. *Publ*: Summer Flowers of the High Alps; Toadstools at Home; First Aid for the Trenches; etc. *c.t*: Spectator, Daily Herald, New Clarion, Lancet. *a*: 43 Devonshire St, Portland Pl, W.1. *t*: Welbeck 8035.

HASTINGS, Somerville, M.B., M.S., F.R.C.S., M.P. *Publ*: inc Wild Flowers at Home ; Toadstools at Home ; Alpine Plants at Home ; etc. *a*: Brackenfell, Kingswood, Oxon.

HASUND, S(IGVALD MATIAS): agriculturist; *b*. Ulstein, Norway, March, 1868; *s*. Sivert Hasund and Ingeborg (Skeide) *h.; educ*. Higher Public Sch. (Volda); the State Agricultural Coll. (Aas); *m*. Johanne Margrete Raanes, 1894. AUTHOR: Landhusholdningens okonomi, 1895; Smorstel hjemme og paa sae teren, 1902; Myrdyrkning, 1910; Det norske landbruks historie (i Landbruksboken av N. Ødegaard), 1919; Driftslaere (i Landbruksboken), 1919; Rydningsmaend, 1913; Landbrukets historie, 1916; Arbeidsliv og idealitet, 1918; Ikring mannedauden, 1920; Jordbrukslaere av N. Ødegaard (Omarb. av M. Langballe, K. Vik og S. H.), 1922; Bonder og stat under naturalsystemet, 1924; Norges landbruk 1875-1925, (I "Lantbruket i Norden", Goteborg), 1925. Some bulletins of field experiments and historical researches. Contributor to: Tidsskrift for det norske landbruk (Oslo); Nordisk Jordbruksforskning (Kjobenhavn); Syn og Segn (Oslo); Meldinger fra Norges Landbrukshoiskole (Aas); Beretning om Norges Landbrukshoiskole (Aas). General character of writing: popular scientific, historical. In 1890, teacher in rural public schools and agricultural schools;; 1898, in agric. extension serv. Bratsbery county; 1907, teacher by the State Agric. Coll. (Aas) (Agric. economy, soil culture and agric. history); 1914, professor (Aas); 1919, Prof. Agric. history; February, 1928, Minister of Church and Education. During this time published many short articles of agricultural matters in mags. and the press. CLUBS: Det kgl. Selskap for Norges Vel, Det norske Videnskaps-akademi i Oslo, Hon. Mem. of Finska Lanthushallningssels kapet. Relig. denom., Lutheran. OFFICE: P. t. Kirkedepartementet, Oslo. HOME: Hegdehaugsveien 15, Oslo, Norway.

HATCH, Edith Beatrice. *b*: Croydon. *e*: Old Palace, Croydon. *m*: Thomas James Hatch. Chm Croydon Times Group. *n.a*: Croydon Times 1861. *c.t*: Sutton Times & Cheam Mail; Wallington & Carshalton Times; Caterham Times; etc. *a*: 104 High St, Croydon. *t*: 3434.

HATCH, Evelyn Maud. *b*: Oxford. *e*: Baker St Hgh Sch Lond, St Hugh's Coll Oxf. Compiler of Hist Reports War Office 1916—22. *Publ*: Burgundy Past & Present ; The Letters of Lewis Carroll to his Child-Friends ; (trans) Eastward in Eden. *a*: 52 Sheffield Terr, London, W.8.

HATCH, Herbert Andrew, B.Sc(Geol). *b*: Halifax 1875. *e*: Leeds Univ. *m*: Agnes Emma Peacock. Teacher of Geography. *Publ*: Observational Geography of the British Isles; Outdoor Geography. *c.t*: Times Educational Supp, The Scout, etc. *s.s*: Geography, geology, astronomy. *Rec*: Field work in geology. *a*: Thornton Hse, 58 Hibson Rd, Nelson, Lancs.
HAUGH, Irene, B.A. *b*: Dublin 1905. Jnlst. *n.a*: Sec & Asst to E. Irish Statesman '28—29. *Publ*: The Valley of the Bells. *c.t*: The Spectator, The Sunday Times, The Commonweal, The Saturday Review, Poetry Mag, Irish Statesman, Irish Independent, The Irish Times, The Irish Monthly, The Standard. *s.s*: Poetry. *a*: 31 Northumberland Rd, Dublin. *t*: Ballsbridge 250.

HATCH, Richard Warren, M.A., B.S. *b*: Framingham Mass 1898. *e*: Univ of Pennsylvania, Columbia Univ. *m*: Ruth Dunwoody Selser. *s*: 2. Teacher. *n.a*: Philadelphia Public Ledger 1920—21. *Publ*: The Fugitive ; Lift Up the Glory ; This Bright Summer ; Leave the Salt Earth ; Into The Wind ; All Aboard the Whale ; The Curious Lobster ; The Curious Lobster's Island. *Ctr*: Field & Stream, etc. *Rec*: Fishing, gunning, small boats, wrought iron. *w.s*: U.S. Navy 1918, '42—45. *a*: Deerfield, Mass, U.S.A.

HATCH, Thomas James. *b*: Croydon. *m*: E. B. Purnell. Mang Dir Croydon Times Group. *n.a*: Croydon Times 1861. *a*: 104 High St, Croydon. *t*: 3434.

HATCH, Rev. William Henry Paine, A.M., Ph.D., D.D., D.Theol. *b*: Camden, N.J. 1875. *e*: Harvard Univ. *m*: Marion Louise Townsend. *s*: 1. Clergyman & Prof Emeritus, Epis Theol Sch Cambridge Mass, Fell Amer Acad of Arts, Oriental Soc, etc. *Publ*: The Pauline Idea of Faith ; Gospel MSS of General Theol Seminary (collab) ; Greek & Syrian Miniatures in Jerusalem ; Greek MSS of New Testament, (1) at Mount Sinai & (2) in Jerusalem ; The Western Text of the Gospels ; Principal Uncial MSS of the New Testament ; Album of Dated Syrian MSS. *Ctr*: Hibbert Journ, Classical Philology, Journ of Theol Studies, etc. *s.s*: New Testament, Greek & Syriac Palæography, Coptic Studies. *Rec*: Walking, motoring. *c*: Faculty, etc. *a*: Randolph, New Hampshire, U.S.A.

HATFIELD, C(HARLES) W(ILLIAM) : civil servant, literary research work; *b*. Sheffield, Eng., Jan., 1877. Editor: The Complete Poems of Annie Brontë (now for the first time collected), with a Bibliographical Introduction, 1920; The Complete Poems of Charlotte Brontë (now for the first time collected, with Bibliography and Notes, 1923; The Complete Poems of Emily Jane Brontë (arranged and collected), with Bibliography and Notes, 1923, (in this edition facsimiles of the handwriting of the four Brontës are included); The Twelve Adventures and Other Stories by Charlotte Brontë (extracted and arranged from the early MSS. of Charlotte Brontë). Contributor to Brontë Society Publications; writer of introductions to various Brontë pamphlets. Vice-President of Brontë Society. HOME: Kidderminster, Eng.

HATFIELD, W. Wilbur, A.B., Hon.D.Lit. b : Pittsfield, Ill 1882. e : Illinois Coll, Univs of Chicago & Columb. m : Grace Chamberlain. d : 2. Editor. n.a : Asst-Ed English Journ 1918—20 & Ed '21—, Ed College English '39—. Publ : (co-author) English in Service; Introductory Studies in Literature; Spirit of America in Literature; English Activities; Senior English Activities; Grammar of Living English. Ctr : Various. a : 211 West 68th St, Chicago 1, Illinois, U.S.A. T : Aberdeen 3744.

HATFIELD, William. b : Nottingham 1892. e : Nott'ham Hgh Sch, Nott'ham Univ Coll. m : Janet G. Fulton. s : 1. d : 1. Author. Publ : Sheepmates; Desert Saga; Ginger Murdoch; Black Waterlily; Big Timber; I Find Australia (Autobiog); Australia Through the Windscreen; Australia Reclaimed (Econ). Ctr : Sydney : Morning Herald, Mail, Bulletin, Sun, & Australian Journ. s.s : Australian Outback Life, Central Australian Aborigines, Soil Conservation, Forestry & Irrigation. Rec : Shooting, Boating, Fishing. a : Mooney Mooney, N.S.W., Aust.

HATHORNE, Dr. E. S., F.R.C.S., L.R.C.P., D.P.H., F.R.I.P.H. M.O.H. Barnard Castle & Startforth R.D.C. Publ: Infectious Nature of Rheumatic Fever; Vaccination in Early Stages of Smallpox. Ex-Capt R.A.M.C., B.E.F. 1914. a: Ronaldkirk, Yorks.

HATHWAY, Cecil. b : Bristo' 1887. e : Bishop Rd Sc Bristol. m: Marjorie Hulin. s : 1. Journalist, Chief Reporter Evening World. n.a : Exchange Tel Coy Ltd 1905-20, Western Daily Press Bristol '20-29, Evening World '29-. Ex-Chm Bristol Br N.U.J. Rec : Cricket. c: Hon Sec Bristol & W. of Eng N/p Press Fund. a: Northcliffe Hse, Colston Av, Bristol. t: 44863.

HATTERSLEY, Alan Frederick, M.A. b : Leeds 1893. e : Leeds Gr Sch, Downing Coll Camb. Prof of Hist Natal Univ Coll, Lecturing tour in U.K. 1946—47. Publ : Portrait of a Colony; Western Civilisation; Short History of Democracy; More Annals of Natal; Later Annals of Natal. Ctr : History, Dict of Nat Biography, Canadian Hist Review. s.s : Brit Colonial Hist—Emigration—Colonisation—Overseas Empire, Sth Africa, Scouting in overseas Dominions. Rec : Boy Scout movement. c : Authors (Lond). a : Natal Univ Coll, Pietermaritzburg, Sth Africa. T : 2725.

HATTON, Charles. b : Stourbridge 1905. m : Gladys I. Hatton. d : 1. Author, Journalist, Mem Soc of Authors. Publ : They Can't Hang Me; Mr. Everyman; Black Country Folk; Radio Plays & How to Write Them. Ctr : Radio Times, Television, Radio Pictorial, Leader, Cinema, Dly Telegraph, etc. s.s : Theatre, Films, Broadcasting, Television (non-technical). Rec : Walking, reading, listening, cricket. a : 24 Yeovil Close, Orpington, Kent. T : Orpington 5906.

HATZIDAKIS, NICHOLAS (pen name: Zéfiros Vradinnos): professor of mathematics; b. Berlin, Germany, May, 1872; s. John and Penelope (Lakonos) H.; educ. Univs. of Athens, Paris, Göttingen and Berlin. DEGREE: D.Sc. AUTHOR: Néo Zoe (New Life), a literary calendar, 1905; Eisagoge eis ten Theorian ton Epphaneion (theory of surfaces), 1912; Theoretiké Mechaniké (Theoretical Mechnics), 1916; Kinetiké Geometria (Cinematical Geometry), 1919; Sphairiké Trigonometria (Spherical Trigonometry), 1926; Sméne kai Sumalégmata Kampulon kai epiphaneion (Congruency and Complexes of curves and surfaces), 1929. Contributes to Nea Hastia, 1928 (under pen name, "Zéfiros Bradinos); Numas, 1919-20 (under pen name, "Zéfiros Vradinos"). General character of writing: novels and poems. One of the founders of the "Greek Mathematical Society" and its president during seven years. Member of: Société Mathématique Suisse (Switzerland); Deutsche Mathematische Vereinigung (Germany), and the Circolo Matematico di Palermo (Italy). Professor of theoretical mechanics at the Military School, 1900-1904; Ord. Professor of higher mathematics at the University of Athens since 1904. Relig. denom., Greek Orthodox. OFFICE: University of Athens (Mathem. Seminary). HOME: Aristomenos Street 55, Athens, Greece.

HAUGBOLL, Charles. b : Kobenhavn 1902. e : Autodidach. m : Gurli Stoltze. Author. Publ : Voergelos; Sabotor; Del er Miz der er Morderen. Ctr : Land iz Folk, Polisken, Berlingske Tidende, Social-Demokraten (Danish), Arbeiderbiddet (Norway), Ny Dag (Stockholm). s.s : Psychological & Social Short Stories. Rec : Topography. a : Ahornkrogen 6, Bagsvaard, Denmark. T : Bagsvaard 22.

HAUGE, Yngvar, M A. b : Olso 1899. e : Sec Sch & Univ. m : Lolla J. Johannesen. s : 1. Author. Publ : Carl Johan ; Slottet og Byen ; Pa Ytterste Post; Fra Herregarden og fra Bruket etc. Ctr : (Oslo) Morgenbladet, St Hallvard, Vi Selv og vare Hjem, Samtiden (Trondhjem) Nidaros, Adresseavissen etc., s.s : Historical Biographies. c : Arkeologisk Selskap, Norsk Historisk forening og Den Norske Forfatterforening. a : Ullevolsvelen 67, Oslo, Norway. T : 694164.

HAUGH, Irene, B.A. b : Dublin 1906. Journalist. n.a : Sec & Asst to A.E. Irish Statesman 1928—29. Book reviewer (Radio). Publ : The Valley of the Bells. Ctr : Spectator, Sun Times, Commonweal, Sat Rev, Poetry Mag, Irish Statesman, Irish Independent, Irish Times, etc. s.s : Poetry. a : 31 Northumberland Rd, Dublin. T : Ballsbridge 61865.

HAUGHTON, C. V. n.a: Principality Press, Wrexham. a: Rhyhygaled, Mold, Flints.

HAUGHTON, Rev. Walter Wigley. b : Clapham 1862. e : Southboro' Col Sc & Handsworth Col Birm. Widower. s : 1. d : 1. Publ : Thomas Dean s Lost Money; Parson Hardwork's Nut & How He Cracked It; Mr Sam & His Talkative Clock; Twentieth Century Miracles; Is the Church Dying? c.t: Meth Recorder, Meth Times. a: Holmcroft, Ponsford Rd, Minehead, Som.

HAUGSTED, EJLER: librarian, historian; b. Vester Skerninge, Denmark, Oct. 1, 1875; s. Peter Emil and Anna (Farrer) H.; educ. Herlufsholm, 1887-1893; Univ. of Copenhagen, 1893-1899. DEGREES: Candidatus Magisterii, 1899 (in History, English and Latin); m. Augusta Jessen, June 25, 1901. AUTHOR: Forsvarssagens 40 Aars Kampe (with E. Fog), 1907; Ungravningerne paa Bispetorvet, 1923; Aarhusegnens historiske Minder, 1925; Udgravningerne Nord for Domkirken, 1927. Contributed 13 monographs of Danish manors in the collection, "Danske Herregaarde", 1919-1922. Has also contributed largely to books of historical societies. Contributor to daily newspapers. General character of writing: archaeology, topography and librarian matters. Teacher of preparatory schools, 1899-1906; Librarian of the Danish State Library at Aarhus, 1906—. Editor of the Year-Book of the Historical Society of the Diocese of Aarhus, 1908— (President, 1916—); Director of Aarhus Museum, Historical Department, 1910—; President of the Section of Alliance Francaise at Aarhus, 1921—. Is interested in the archaeology and history of East Jutland, working on same in connection with the Historical Society and Museum of AArhus. Lecturer. Active in rearranging the Museum of Northern Antiquities of Aarhus, and works with the regional survey (in collaboration with Lektor Regnar Knudsen), Relig. denom., Lutheran. OFFICE: Staatsbibliotek (State Library). HOME: St. Paul Kirkeplads, Aarhus, Denmark.

HAULTAIN, William Francis Theodore, O.B.E., M.C., B.A., M.B., B.Ch., F.R.C.P.E., F.R.C.S.E., F.R.C.O.G. b : Edinburgh 1893. e : Edin Acad, Univs of Edin & Camb. m : Winifred Outram. s : 2. d : 1. Cons

Gynæcologist Roy Infirmary Edin, Gynæcologist to Leith Hosp, Ministry of Pensions & E.M.S. Hosp Bangour West Lothian, Pres Edin Obstetrical Soc, R.A.M.C. (Lt-Col). *Publ*: Practical Handbook of Midwifery & Gynecology; Ante Natal Care. *Ctr*: B.M.J. & other med journs. *s.s*: Obstetrics, Gynæcology. *Rec*: Golf, bridge, rugby football. *c*: Caledonian United Services, R.S.A.C. *a*: 2 Eglinton Cresc, Edinburgh. *T*: 22378.

HAUPTMANN, Gerhart. *b*: Silesia 1862. Poet & Playwright. *Publ*: Reconciliation; Lonely Lives; The Sunken Bell; Hannele; The Weavers; etc. Nobel Prize (Lit) 1912. *a*: Germany.

HAUSSER, FRIEDRICH: civil engineer; b. Neustadt a.d. Haarot, Germany, Sept. 29, 1875; s. Martin and Mathilde (Flach) H.; educ. Oberrealschule Nuremberg, technical college of Munich. DEGREES: Dr. Engineer, Professor; m. Elisabeth Steigelmann. AUTHOR: Gesammelte Untersuchungen über die Verbrennlichkeit von Hüttenkoks in technischen Körungen, 1926 (The technical synthesis of nitric acid by means of gaseous explosions). Author and publisher: Mitteilungen über Fortschritte in der Kohlenauswertung. Contributor to: Zeitschrift des Vereins deutscher Ingenieure; Mitteilungen über Forschungsarbeiten auf dem Gebiet des Ingenieurwesens; Stahl und Eisen; Verhandlungen des Vereins zur Beförderung des Gewerbefleisses in Preussen; The Chemical Age; Journal of the Society of Chemical Industry. General character of writing: scientific, technical. CLUBS: Verein deutscher Ingenieure; Verein deutscher Eisenhüttenleute; Verein deutscher Chemiker; Deutsche Chemische Gesellschaft. Relig. denom., Evangelical. ADDRESS: An der Hörder Bäumen 21, Dortmund, Germany.

HAVARD, Robert Emlyn, M.A., M.D. *c.t*: Journ of Physiology, Journ of Biochemistry, Journ of Experimental Pathology, etc. *a*: 28 Sandfield Rd, Headington, Oxf.

HAVELL, ERNEST B.; artist, author; b. Reading, Eng., Sept. 16, 1861; s. Charles R. and Charlotte Amelia (Lord) H.; educ. Reading Schls., Royal Coll. of Art, and in Paris Studios. DEGREE: Associate Royal Coll. of Art; m. Lili Jacobson, 1894. AUTHOR: A Handbook to Agra and the Taj; Benares: the Sacred City; Indian Sculpture and Painting; The Ideals of Indian Art; Indian Architecture: its Psychology, Structure and History; Essays on Indian Art, Industry and Education; The Basis for the Artistic and Industrial Revival of India; The Ancient and Medieval Architecture of India, 1915; History of Aryan Rule in India, 1918; A Handbook of Indian Art, 1920; The Himalayas in Indian Art, 1924; Essays on Indian Art, Industry and Education, 1927; A Short History of India from the Earliest Times to the Present Day, 1928. Contributor to Nineteenth Century and After, Asia Asiatica, Studio, Rupam, Burlington Mag., Asiatic Rev., Indian Rev., Calcutta Rev., House and Garden (U.S.A.). General character of writing: historical, art, architecture, etc. Joined Indian Educnl. Service, 1884; Principal Govt. Sch. of Art (Calcutta), 1895-1908; a founder of New Calcutta Sch. of Painting on Indian lines; initiated movement for revival of Indian handloom weaving; a founder of the Indian Soc. of London. HOME: Hvide Hus, Headlington Hill, Oxford, Eng.

HAVELOCK, Thomas Henry, M.A., D.Sc, F.R.S. Prof of Maths. *c.t*: Sci Journs. *a*: 8 Westfield Drive, Gosforth, Newcastle-on-Tyne. *t*: 52393.

HAVERFORD, John, J.P. *b*: Langum 1879. *e*: Langum Nat Sc & Skerry's Civil Service Col. *m*: Constance Williams. *s*: 2. *d*: 2. Jnlst & N/p proprietor. *n.a*: Reporter, Western Chron, '01—04. Ed & Proprietor, Western Telegraph, '16—. *Rec*: Golf, boating, motoring. *c*: Haverfordwest Liberal. *a*: St Kennox, Albert Town, Haverfordwest, Pembrokeshire. *t*: 186.

HAVIGHURST, Walter, M.A. *b*: Appleton, Wisconsin 1901. *e*: Univs of Denver & Columbia. *m*: Marion Boyd. Writer, Professor of English. *Publ*: Land of Promise, Story of the Northwest Territory; The Long Ships Passing; Story of the Great Lakes; Upper Mississippi, a Wilderness Saga; The Winds of Spring; The Quiet Shore, Pier 17; No Homeward Course; Masters of the Modern Short Story. *Ctr*: Sat Ev Post, Collier's, Sat Rev of Lit, etc. *Rec*: Tennis, swimming, water-colour, photography. *a*: Shadowy Hills Rd, Oxford, Ohio, U.S.A. *T*: 421.

HAVILAND, H., M.B., M.R.C.S. *a*: Langleys, Woodside Av, Finchley, N.12.

HAVILAND-TAYLOR, Katharine. *b*: Mankato Minnesota U.S.A. *e*: Priv. Writer. *Publ*: Cecilia of the Pink Roses; Barbara of Baltimore; Natalie Page; Real Stuff; Cross Currents; The Youngest One; Pablito; When Men A-Wooing Go; Boulevard; Yellow Soap; The Second Mrs Clay; A Modern Trio in an Old Town; Tony from America; Stanley John's Wife; The Secret of the Little Gods; Nine Hundred Block; etc. Plays—Keeping Him Home; The Taming of the Crew; A Mother's Influence; Mix Well and Stir; Rest and Quiet; Who Can Cook?; etc. *c.t*: Over 400 short stories in England, U.S., Australia, New Zealand, Holland, Denmark, Norway, Sweden, Finland, Spain & S. Africa. 221 Articles, 87 poems, 25 syndicates, 3 Motion Picture Plays. *Rec* Gardening, travel. *c*: Authors League of America. *a*: York, Pennsylvania, U.S.A.

HAWARD, Edwin. *b*: Bungay 1884. *e*: Stamford & Reading Schs, Lond Univ. Sec India Burma Assoc 1942—; Liveryman in Stationers & Newspaper Makers Coy. *n.a*: Civil & Military Gaz (Lahore) 1909, Mang '16, Mang & Ed '20, Corr The Times & Pioneer Simla/Delhi '21—26, Ed Pioneer '26—28, Ed Nth China Dly News '30—38, Information Officer India Office '28—30, Brit Mem Information Dept League of Nations Geneva '39—40, Adv Indian Affairs Far Eastern Bureau Min Information Singapore '40—41. *Publ*: Manchurian Medley; Last Rebellion, A Picture of India. *c*: Authors. *a*: India Burma Assoc, 222 Strand, London, W.C.2.

HAWARD, Sir Harry Edwin, K.B., B.A.(Lon). *b*: Lon 1863. *e*: Univ Col Sc. *m*: (1) Alice Bates; (2) Edith Thomas; (3) Vera Hopper. *s*: 1. *d*: 3. Publ Official (ret). *Publ*: The London County Council from Within. *s.s*: Local govt finance. Vice-Chm Elec Comm 1920-30. *Rec*: Golf. *c*: Nat. *a*: 3 West Hse, Campden Hill Rd, W.8. *t*: Park 0958.

HAWARD, Lawrence Warrington, M.A. *b*: Lon 1878. *e*: Uppingham & Cam Univ. *m*: Suzanne Courvoisier. *s*: 2. *d*: 1. *n.a*: Times 1906-14. Curator M/C Corp Art Galleries '14–. *Publ*: Bibliography of Walter Headlam ('10); Art's Opportunity; The Function of Art Museums; The Problems of Provincial Galleries & Art Museums ('22); etc. *c.t*: Times, Manchester Guardian, Edinburgh Review, Grove's Dictionary of Music. *s.s*: Art, music. Trustee on Nat Loan Collection Trust '17—. *c*: Athenæum. *a*: 9 Moorfield Rd, W. Didsbury, M/C.

HAWE, Philip, ChM., F.R.C.S. Surgeon. *c.t*: Lancet, B.M.J., L'pool Medico Chirurgical Journal, Clinical Journal, Surgeon Northern Hosp L'pool, Roy L'pool Children's Hosp, Ormskirk Gen Hosp, etc. *c*: L'pool Medico-Literary Soc. *a*: 31 Rodney St, L'pool.

HAWES, Harry Bartow. *b*: Kentucky 1869. *e*: Law Sc, Washington Univ, St Louis, Mo. *m*: E. Eppes Osborne Robinson. *d*: 2. Lawyer. *Publ*: Philippine Uncertainty; My Friend the Black Bass; etc. *c.t*: Sporting mags, etc. *s.s*: Conservation & restoration of wild life, fish & game, Philippine Indep. Pres St Louis Police Bd 5 y. Mem all leading hunting & fishing organisations. Major World War; Mem Missouri Legislature; Mem Hse of Reps & U.S. Senate; resigned from Senate Feb 3 1933; awarded Distinguished Gold Medal for outstanding accomplishments in conservation of wild life in 1933. *Rec*: Fishing, hunting, yachting. *a*: 711 Transportation Bldg, & 2443 Kalorama Rd, N.W., Washington, D.C. *t*: National 8451 & Decatur 2346.

HAWGOOD, John Arkas. Ed Adviser to New Democracy Books & Ed Dir to Europa Publications Ltd. *Publ*: inc The Citizen & Government; The Tragedy of German-America; etc. *a*: The Knoll, Kemerton, Tewkesbury, Glos.

HAWK, Philip Bovier, M.S.(Yale), Ph.D.(Columb). *b*: New York State 1874. *m*: Gladys Taylor. *s*: 1. *d*: 1. Chemist, Food Research. *Publ*: Practical Physiological Chemistry; What We Eat & What Happens to It; Streamline for Health; Off the Racket; etc. *s.s*: Foods & Nutrition. *Rec*: Tennis, cards. *a*: 750 West 50th St, Miama Beach, Florida, U.S.A. *T*: 6-2956.

HAWKE, Baron. Chm Oxo Coy. *Publ*: Recollections & Reminiscences. *a*: 10 Belgrave Sq, S.W.1. *t*: Sloane 5244.

HAWKE, Jack. *b*: Lon 1904. *m*: Minnie Duffield. Parliamentary Sketch Writer, Irish Times. *n.a*: Devon & Exeter Gazette, '24, Kentish Independent '28–29, Northern Whig (Belfast) '29–30, Irish Times '31–. *s.s*: Irish politics. Free-lance Canada & U.S.A. '30, toured Russia '32. Chm Dublin Branch N.U.J. *Rec*: Books, theatres, travels. *a*: 351 Griffith Av, Whitehall, Dublin.

HAWKE, JOHN: literary research; *b*. Eng., 1846; *s*. John and Sarah Anne (Brown) H.; educ. Christ's Hosp. (London); *m*. Caroline Simpson. Editor: Poems and Songs (anthology); The Grasmere Wordsworth, 1925 (2nd edit. 1927). General character of writing: critical essays. Spent 5 yrs. in prep. of "Grasmere" Wordsworth. HOME: Ravensfield, New Barnet, Eng.

HAWKE, Montague, M.R.C.S., L.R.C.P, L.M.S. S.A. Physician & Surg. *c.t*: B.M.J., etc. *a*: 273 Lon Rd, Westcliff-on-Sea. *t*: Southend 3477.

HAWKES, Arthur John, F.S.A., A.L.A. *b*: Bournemouth 1885. *m*: Anne Elizabeth Hirst. *s*: 1. Borough Librarian Wigan 1919–, Mem Council Library Assoc '24–45, Pres N.W. Branch '45–46, Pres Lancs & Cheshire Antiquarian Soc '44–45. *Publ*: Degradation of Womanhood; Bibliography of Robert Owen; Best Books of '14; Lancashire Printed Books: A Bibliography to 1800; Annotated Catalogue of Early Mining Literature; Wigan's Part in the Civil War, 1639–1651; Outline History of Wigan; Find it Yourself; Wigan Grammar School 1596–1936; Sir Roger Bradshaigh of Haigh 1628–1684. *Ctr*: Various. *s.s*: Bibliography, Antiquities. *a*: Central Library, Wigan. *T*: 3181.

HAWKES, Charles Francis Christopher. *Publ*: Various archæological works inc The Prehistoric Foundations of Europe; (in collab) Camulodunum: the Excavations at Colchester; Prehistoric Britain; etc. *a*: Keble College, Oxford.

HAWKES, Lt.-Col. Charles Pascoe, M.A. *b*: Edgbaston, Birmingham 1877. *e*: Dulwich Coll & Trin Coll Camb. *m*: Eleanor Victoria Cobb. *s*: 1. *d*: 1. A Registrar in the High Court 1925–. *n.a*: Polit Cartoonist Graphic 1907. *Publ*: The London Comedy; Bench & Bar in the Saddle; Heydays, A Salad of Memories & Impressions; Authors at Arms; The Soldiering of Three Great Writers; etc. *Ctr*: Punch, Times, Sunday Times, Cornhill Mag, Ev News, etc. *s.s*: London, Islam, Morocco, Algeria. *Rec*: Travel, amateur acting. *c*: Oxf & Camb, Garrick, Beefsteak, etc. *a*: 17 Campden Hill Sq, London, W.8. *T*: Park 4828.

HAWKES, Howard Ivon. *b*: Birmingham 1880. *e*: Elemen Sch. *m*: Emily Alice Rogan. *s*: 2. *d*: 1. *n.a*: Staff Photographer Derby E. Telegraph 1928–32, Commssn Photographer Derbys Advertiser, Supplies Free-lance Photos to Sport & Gen Press Agency. *a*: 19 Chestnut Ave, Derby.

HAWKES-CORNOCK, Elsa. *b*: Walmer 1877. *e*: Priv. *m*: John Hawkes-Cornock. *c.t*: Over 1570 stories to Pearson's, The Quiver, Leisure Hour, The Queen, Home Chat, etc ("E. Burrowes"). *a*: Moneens, Budleigh Salterton Devon. *t*: 158.

HAWKIN, Richard (York). *b*: York. *e*: Private Sch. Journalist & Lecturer, Ex Pres Darwen Lit Soc. *n.a*: Ed Sheffield Guardian 1912–16, Ed Huddersfield Worker '19–21. *Publ*: Tales of York Streets; Historical Notices of Helmshore & Musbury; The Pageant of Darwen; Walks Round Huddersfield; The Cockerill Family of Haslingden; Mysterious Darwen; Art of York Minster. *s.s*: Local Hist, Architecture, Municipal matters, Public Health, Economics. *Rec*: Walking. *a*: 70 Duckworth St, Darwen, Lancs.

HAWKING, Ernest. *b*: Holsworthy 1871. Museum Curator (L.C.C. Geffrye Museum). *c.t*: Connoisseur, Builder, Cabinet Maker. *s.s*: Antique furniture. *Rec*: Painting in water & oil colour. *a*: 2 Riverview Gve, Chiswick, W.4.

HAWKINS, Alec Desmond. *n.a*: Lit Ed Purpose. *c.t*: Time & Tide, Listener, Criterion, New Statesman, Bookman. *a*: 46 Bernard St, W.C.1. *t*: Terminus 4691.

HAWKINS, Arthur William. *b*: 1903. Author. *c.t*: Weekly periodicals. *s.s*: Stories for the workingclass reader. *a*: 3 King Edward Rd, New Barnet, Herts.

HAWKINS, Rev. C. V. *Publ*: War of the Schools (collab E. H. Visiak). *a*: York Hse School, 1 Crediton Hill, N.W.6.

HAWKINS, Francis Henry, LL.B. *b*: Handsworth 1863. *e*: K.E. Sc Birm, Univ Col Lon. *m*: Frances Lydia Ingall. *s*: 2. Solicitor. Ex-Foreign Sec Lon Missny Soc. *Publ*: Through Lands that were Dark. *c.t*: Internat Review of Missns, Missny Mags, Christian World. *s.s*: Foreign missny matters. Dir & Foreign Sec Lon Missny Soc 42 y. Extensive travel in China, Africa, Madagascar, & Canada. Chm Conf Brit Missny Socs. Chm Eng Con Un N. Wales. *a*: 90 Burbage Rd, S.E.24.

HAWKINS, George Leslie, M.C., F.R.P.S., F.I.B.P., F.R.S.A. *b*: Sidcup, Kent 1897. *e*: Priv. *m*: Betty Damonde Hocken. *s*: 2. *d*: 3. *Publ*: Pigment Printing. *Ctr*: Numerous illustrated publications. *s.s*: Pictorial Photography. *Rec*: Photography, walking, reading. *a*: Beaconsfield, North Hill, Minehead, Somerset.

HAWKINS, Herbert Leader, D.Sc.(Manch), F.R.S. F.G.S. *b*: Reading 1887. *e*: Reading, Stramogate, Kendal & Manch Univs. *m*: Amy Mitchell. *s*: 2. *d*: 1. Prof of Geology Reading Univ. *Publ*:

Invertebrate Palæontology; The Restless Earth. *Ctr*: Phil Trans Roy Soc, Quarterly Journ Geol Soc, Proc Zool Soc, Proc Geol Assoc, etc. *s.s*: Geology, Palæontology. *a*: Ballintrae, 68 Elmhurst Rd, Reading, & The University, Reading.

HAWKINS, Herbert Walter. *b*: Bristol 1874. Married. *s*: 1. *d*: 2. Journalist. *n.a*: Mang Dir Bristol Times Mirror & Bristol Evening Times & Echo, Mang Dir Bristol Evening Post Ltd 1932. *a*: Downs Edge, Stoke Bishop, Bristol.

HAWKINS, W. A., A.C.A., M.J.I. *n.a*: Sec Bristol Evening Post. *a*: Silver Street, Broadmead. Bristol.

HAWKINS, Rev. Walter. *b*: Brixton Hill 1857. *e*: Binfield Hse Sc Clapham & Didsbury Theo Col. *m*: Annie White. *s*: 2. *d*: 4. *Publ*: Old John Brown; Life of Alfred the Great (collab with Rev. E. Thornton Smith). *c.t*: Various n/p's & periodicals. *s.s*: Sport. Pres Meth Sports Assoc since its foundation 1904. *c*: Surrey C.C. *a*: Clifton Lodge, St John's Pk Rd, Blackheath, S.E.3.

HAWKS, Ellison, F.R.A.S. *b*: Hull 1890. *e*: Hulme Gr Sch. *m*: Edna Fawcett. *s*: 1. *d*: 2. Advert Mang Meccano Ltd. *n.a*: Sometime Gen Ed Amalgamated Press, Ed The Dog Owner. *Publ*: The Book of Air & Water Wonders; The Earth Shown to the Children; Romance of Astronomy; The Microscope Shown to the Children; Wonders of Speed; Pioneers of Plant Study; Wonders of Engineering; My Book of Trains; Romance of the Merchant Ship; Book of Natural Wonders; The Starry Heavens; Electricity for Boys; The Choice of a Career; How it Works & How it is Done; Marvels & Mysteries of Science; Everyday Things & their Story; Britain's Wonderful Fighting Forces; The War in the Air; Fighters; More Fighters; Bombers; British Seaplanes Triumph in the Schneider Trophy Contests; This Wonderful World; etc. *Ctr*: Manch Guardian, Yorks Ev Post, Children's Zoo, etc. *Rec*: Philately, photography, Irish setters. *c*: Authors, Roy Aero. *a*: Dovercourt, Ainsdale, Southport, Lancs. *T*: Ainsdale 7549.

HAWKS, Dr. F. S. *a*: 45 Rodney St, Liverpool.

HAWORTH, David H. *b*: Bacup 1874. *n.a*: Reporter Eccles Telegraph, Swinton & Pendlebury Telegraph, Burnley Gazette, Sub-Ed Bacup Times & Ed 1913, Ed Preston Herald 1918, Rossendale Free Press series. *a*: Woodlea Rd, Waterfoot, Rossendale, Lancs. *t*: Rossendale 10.

HAWORTH, Sir Norman, Sc.D., LL.D., F.R.S. *b*: Chorley, Lancs 1883. *e*: Univs of Manchester & Gottingen. *m*: Violet C. Dobbie. *s*: 2. V-Princ & Prof of Chem Birmingham Univ. *Publ*: The Constitution of Sugars. *Ctr*: Journ of Chem Soc, etc. *s.s*: Research on Chemistry of Natural Products, esp Carbohydrates & Vitamin C. *a*: The University, Edgbaston, Birmingham.

HAWORTH, Peter, M.A., B.Litt., Ph.D. *b*: Manchester 1891. *e*: Manch Univ, Innsbruck Univ, Oxf Univ. *m*: May Cumberbirch. *d*: 1. Prof of English Rhodes Univ Coll. *Publ*: English Hymns & Ballads; Humorous Readings from Charles Dickens; Before Scotland Yard; The Elizabethan Story-book; etc. *s.s*: English Language & Belles Lettres. *a*: Rhodes Univ Coll, Grahamstown, Africa.

HAWORTH, Walter Norman, F.R.S. *b*: Chorley, Lancs 1883. *e*: Univs of M/C & Göttingen. *m*: Violet C. Dobbie. *s*: 2. Prof of Chem, Birm Univ. *Publ*: The Constitution of Sugars. *c.t*: Journ of Chem Soc, etc. *s.s*: Researches on the chem of natural products. *a*: The Univ, Edgbaston, Birm.

HAWORTH, Wilfrid George, F.R.S.A. *b*: Gosport 1885. *e*: Priv. *m*: Kathleen Vera Hurley. *s*: 1. Artist in Photography. *c.t*: Weekly Scotsman. etc. *s.s*: Exhibition photography, Lake district climbing, original portraiture, Landscapes of the Lakes. W.S. 1915—19. *Rec*: Cycling, music. *a*: Derwent Gallery, Keswick, Cumberland.

HAWORTH-BOOTH, Maude. *b*: East Yorks 1871. *e*: Sandwell & Paris. *m*: Digby Clifton Haworth-Booth. *s*: 4. *d*: 2. *Publ*: My Garden Diary. *Ctr*: Eastern Morning News, Gentlewoman, Queen, Gardening Illustrated, Chris Sci Monitor. *s.s*: Gardening. *c*: Womens Inst. *a*: The Mill Hse, Balcombe, Sussex. *T*: 240

HAWTHORN, Joseph, M.J.I. *n.a*: Liverpool Post & Echo. *a*: Sidlaws, London Rd, Appleton, Cheshire.

HAWTHORNE, Hildegarde. *b*: N.Y. *e*: Priv. *m*: John M. Oskison. Author. *Publ*: Romantic Rebel; The Story of Nathaniel Hawthorne; Wheels Toward the West: A Tale of the Covered Waggon; Open Range; Riders of the Royal Road; Tabitha of Lonely House: A Story of Old Concord; Corsica & other books of travel; etc. *c.t*: Various n/p's & periodicals. *s.s*: Biog, travel, western books based on careful research of Amer pioneer & settlement days. *Rec*: Swimming, gardening. Granddaughter of Nathaniel Hawthorne. *c*: Authors League, P.E.N., Calif Writers, MacDonnell (N.Y.). *a*: 1801-B Spruce St, Berkeley, Calif, U.S.A. *t*: Ashberry 5116.

HAWTON, Hector. *b*: Plymouth 1901. *e*: Plymouth Coll. Author. *n.a*: Western Morning News 1917—20, Nat Press Agency '20—22, Empire News '22—25. *Publ*: Murder at H.Q.; Murder Most Foul; Unnatural Causes; (Aviation) Men Who Fly; Night Bombing; Air Transport; (Philosophy) The Flight from Reality; Men Without Gods; Philosophy for Pleasure. *s.s*: Aviation, Philosophy. *c*: Press. *a*: c/o John Farquharson, 8 Halsey Hse, Red Lion Sq, London, W.C.1.

HAWTREY, Ralph George. *b*: Slough 1879. *e*: Eton & Trin Coll Camb. *m*: Hortense Emilia D'Aranyi. Late Asst Sec H.M. Treasury. *Publ*: Good & Bad Trade; Currency & Credit; Monetary Reconstruction; The Economic Problem; The Gold Standard in Theory & Practice; Economic Aspects of Sovereignty; Trade Depression & the Way Out; The Art of Central Banking; Capital & Employment; A Century of Bank Rate; Economic Destiny; Economic Rebirth; Bretton Woods for Better or Worse. *s.s*: Econ & Monetary Theory. *c*: Utd Univ. *a*: 29 Argyll Rd, London, W.8. *T*: Western 3805.

HAXON, Thomas. *m*: Kathleen Story. *d*: 1. Hosp Nurse. *Publ*: Glimpses of The Past (in collab); Radio Plays—The Tilted Chair; The Prince Confesses; By Special Request; etc. *c.t*: Various n/p's & periodicals. *s.s*: Adaptation. Programme Critic to Newcastle Station of B.B.C. 1925—27. *Rec*: Auto-engines. *a*: Fourstones, Tynedale Ave, Wallsend Hall, Northumberland.

HAXTON, Herbert Alexander, B.Sc., M.D., Ch.M., F.R.C.S. *b*: St Andrews 1913. *e*: Madras Coll & Univ of St Andrews. *m*: Muriel Horstead. *d*: 2. Cons Surgeon Crumpsall Hosp Manchester, Mem B.M.A. & Manch Med Soc. *Ctr*: Brit Journ of Surgery, B.M.J., Journ of Physiology, Lancet, Surgery—Gynæcology & Obstetrics & Anatomical Record (U.S.A.), Journ of Anatomy, Ulster Med Journ. *s.s*: Neurovascular

Surgery, Action of Muscles. *Rec*: Golf, gardening. *c*: Bramhall Park & Didsbury Golf. *a*: The Grange, Cheadle Hulme, Cheshire. *T*: 1647.

HAY, Denys, M.A. *b*: Gosforth, Newcastle 1915. *e*: Newcastle Roy Gr Sch & Balliol Coll Oxf. *m*: Gwyneth Morley. *s*: 1. *d*: 1. Lecturer in European & Mediæval History Univ of Edinburgh, Official Historian M.O.S. 1942—46. *Ctr*: English Hist Rev. *a*: 6 Gilmour Rd, Edinburgh 9. *T*: 42886.

HAY, Henry Hanby, F.R.S.L. *b*: Douglas 1848. *e*: Collegiate Sc & America. *m*: Sophia Booth Rodney. Professor, English Master, Author, Poet. Senior Master of Girard Col. Pa., 1876—1916. *Publ*: Plays:—Created Gold; Trumpets and Shawms; The Great Elizabeth (a poetic drama); As Shakespeare Was (a drama in verse); The Fanatic (an Elizabethan Tragedy); Collected Poems; Leonardo, Lord of Expression (a dramatic poem). *s.s*: Poetry, English literature & composition. *c*: No Name, Hon Mem Society of the Sons of St George, & Literary societies. *a*: 3 Albert Terrace, Douglas, I.O.M.

" **HAY, Ian** " (**Major-Gen. John Hay Beith**), C.B.E., M.C. *b*: 1876. *e*: Fettes & St John's Coll Camb. Author & Playwright. *Publ*: Pip; The " First Hundred Thousand "; Carrying On; The Last Million; A Safety Match; Happy-go-Lucky; A Knight on Wheels; Paid, with Thanks; The Poor Gentleman; David & Destiny; The King's Service; Little Ladyship; The Unconquered Isle; etc; Plays—Tilly of Bloomsbury; A Safety Match; Good Luck (with Seymour Hicks); The Sport of Kings; The Middle Watch; The Midshipmaid; Admiral's All (with Stephen King-Hall); The Frog; Housemaster; etc. *a*: 49 Hill St, London, W.1. *T*: Grosvenor 4533.

HAY, John, M.D., F.R.C.P., D.L. *b*: Birkenhead 1873. *e*: Liverpool Institute, Liverpool Univ. *m*: Agnes Margaret Duncan. *s*: 2. *d*: 2. Emeritus Prof of Med Univ of Liverpool, Bradshaw Lecturer 1923, St Cyres Lecturer '33, J. Strickland Goodall Lecturer '36. *Publ*: Graphic Methods in Heart Disease. *Ctr*: Lancet, B.M.J., etc. *s.s*: Cardiology. *Rec*: Golf, gardening, painting. *c*: Univ L'pool. *a*: 12 Rodney St Liverpool, & Underfell, Bowness-on-Windermere. *T*: Royal Liverpool 1167; Windermere 503.

HAY, Malcolm Vivian. *Publ*: Wounded and a Prisoner of War; A Chain of Error in Scottish Hist; The Blairs Papers 1603-1660; The Jesuits and the Popish Plot; Winston Churchill & James II. *c*: Travellers. *a*: Seaton Hse, Aberdeen. *t*: 1417.

HAY, Lt.-Col. Sir William Rupert, K.C.I.E., C.S.I. *b*: Bridport, Dorset 1893. *e*: Bradfield, Univ Coll Oxf. *m*: Sybil Ethel Abram. *s*: 3. *d*: 2. Indian Political Service. *Publ*: Two Years in Kurdistan. *Ctr*: Roy Geog Soc Journ. *Rec*: Tennis, shooting. *a*: c/o Messrs Lloyds Bank, Cox & King's Branch, 6 Pall Mall, London, S.W.1.

HAY DRUMMOND-HAY, Lady Grace Marguerite, M.J.I. *b*: L'pool. *m*: Sir Robert Hay Drummond-Hay (dec). Journalist. *n.a*: Special Corr Daily Express 1924-26; F.L. '26-. *c.t*: Britannia & Eve, Times of India, La Nacion of S. America, N.Y. Times, etc. *s.s*: Internat politics,, aviation. Only woman aboard Graf Zeppelin on its pioneer trans-Atlantic flight '28, & on Round-the-World flight '29. On pioneer flight to S. America '30. Attached journalistically to Dornier 12-motor Do.X on initial flights '30, etc. Pres Women s Internat Assoc of Aeronautics. *Rec*: Flying " A " pilot's licence, own personal aeroplane), Lang. *c*: R.AeroC., Heston Flying, Cinque Ports, Internat Adventurers, Overseas. *a*: 76 Strand, W.C.2. *t*: Temple Bar 7440 & Primrose 1794 (Sec).

HAYATA, BUNZO: professor of botany; *b*. Kamomachi, Echigo, Japan, Dec., 1874; *s*. Shinkichi and Shinkichi H.; educ. 1st Higher Sch. Tokyo; Coll. of Science, Imperial Univ. of Tokyo. DEGREES: D.Sc. (Rigakuhakushi); *m*. Kuni Amaya, Dec. 14, 1907. AUTHOR: The Natural Classifications of Plants, according to the Dynamic System, 1921; Le système dynamique des plantes fondé sur la théorie de la participation, Comptes rendus des séances de l'Académie des Sciences, Paris, 1931. Contributes to Botanical Mag. (Tokyo); Berichte der Deutschen Botanischen Gesellschaft (Berlin); Flora oder Allgemeine Botanische Zeitung (Jena). General character of writing: botanical or systematic. Relig. denom., The Nichiren Sect (a sect in Buddhism). OFFICE: Botanical Institute, Botanic Gardens, Koishikawa. HOME: No. 133, Haramachi, Koishikawa-ku, Tokyo, Japan.

HAYAVANDANA, Rao, C., B.A., B.L. *e*: Presidency Col & Christian Col Madras & Madras Univ. Married. *s*: 3. *d*: 1. Founder Ed & Prop Mysore Economic Journ & Sec Bangalore Printing & Publishing Co, Ltd. *n.a*: Madras Mail 1900-10, Ed Leader (Allahabad U.P.) '10, Asst Ed & Ed Madras Times '10-14, Ed Mysore Economic Journ '15. *Publ*: Indian Biographical Dictionary ('15); Mysore Gazetteer in 5 Vols issued for Mysore Government ('30 edn); Indian Caste System; Guide to Pictures in Government House & Lalita Mahal Mysore ('34); etc. *c.t*: Madras Mail, Hindustan Review, Indian Review, etc. *s.s*: Indian ethnology & ethnography, etc. Titles conferred: Rao Sahib & Rajacharitavi Sharada. Fellow Mysore Univ. Vice-Pres Prov Co-operative Apex Bank Bangalore. *Rec*: Walking. *a*: 19 Gundopunt Bldgs, Bangalore City P.O.

HAYCRAFT, William Clifford. *b*: Lon 1904. *e*: St Paul's Sc Kensington, Eastbourne Col. Tech Journalist & Draughtsman. *n.a*: 3 y in drawing office Messrs Short Bros, Rochester (Aviation), Ed Asst Tech Dept of Messrs Sir Isaac Pitman & Sons Ltd '27—29. *Publ*: The Book of the A.J.S.; The Book of the P. & M.; The Book of the Matchless; The Book of the Norton; The Book of the Ariel (5th edn); The Book of the Rudge ('35 edn). *c.t*: Modern Motor Cycles, Motor Cycle, Model Engineer, Garage Workers' Handbooks, Modern Motor Repair, etc. *s.s*: Motor-cycling, aviation, model engineering. Served in Infantry Battn of H.A.C. '24—28. Awarded efficiency cup. Awarded " Lockhart " Silver Cup (£12) & Silver Medal at Model Engineer Exhib for " workmanship & perfection of detail " with a true scale Halberstadt Fighter Model. For same model also awarded prize by Princess Arthur of Connaught at another exhib. At 1933 M.E. Exhib awarded Diploma for drawings of motorcycle engine parts. *Rec*: Swimming, golf. *a*: 43 Woodstock Rd, Bedford Pk, W.4.

HAYDEN, Arthur. *b*: 1868. Civil Servant (ret). Late Senior Auditor Air Min. *Publ*: Royal Copenhagen Porcelain; Spode & his Successors; Old English Porcelain (The Lady Ludlow Collection); Chats series for Collectors (following vol); English China; Old Furniture; Old Prints; Old Clocks; etc. *c.t*: Eng & foreign Art Journs. *s.s*: Antiques. Knight's Cross of Order of Dannebrog. *a*: 11 St Alban's Villas, Highgate Rd, Lon, N.W.5. *t*: Gulliver 2914.

HAYDEN, Ernest George, M.J.I. *b*: Kildare 1871. *e*: Vic Sc Tunbridge Wells. *m*: Lois Clarke. *s*: 1. Ed of the Mid-Sussex Times, Haywards Heath & a Dir of Chas Clarke (Haywards Heath) Ltd. *n.a*: On the Cmt Brighton Branch of the N/P Press Fund. *s.s*: Graphology & phrenology. *Rec*: Lawn mowing & starting young people with Savings bank books. *a*: Kildare, Balcombe Rd, Haywards Heath, Sussex.

HAYDEN, John Patrick. *b*: Roscommon 1863. *e*: Priv & Sec Schs Roscommon. *m*: Harriett Scott. *s*: 1.

Journalist & Newspaper Proprietor. *n.a*: Founder & Ed Westmeath Examiner 1882—. *Ctr*: Various. *s.s*: Politics, Irish Questions, Local Government Administration. *a*: Bishopsgate St, Mullingar, Co Westmeath, Ireland.

HAYDN, Hiram, M.A., Ph.D. *b*: Cleveland, Ohio 1907. *e*: Amherst Coll, Western Reserve & Columb Univs. *m*: Mary Wescott Tuttle. *s*: 1. *d*: 1. Author & Editor. *n.a*: The American Scholar 1944— & Assoc-Ed Crown Publishers '45—, Staff Books & Things, N.Y. Herald-Tribune '47—. *Publ*: By Nature Free; Manhattan Furlough; The Portable Elizabethan Reader; (Co-Ed) A World of Great Stories; Explorations in Living. *Ctr*: N.Y. Times Sunday Mag, Collier's, Reader's Digest, etc. *a*: 178 Sullivan St, New York 12, N.Y., U.S.A. *T*: Gramercy 7-0486.

HAYDON, Arthur Lincoln. *b*: London 1872. *e*: Woodhouse Grove Yorks. Author & Journalist, Late Asst Dir of Studies Lond Sch of Journalism. *n.a*: W. T. Stead Ltd, B.O.P., Lady's World, Our Home. *Publ*: The Book of the V.C.; The Riders of the Plains; The Trooper Police of Australia; Stand Fast Wymondham; The Skipper of the Team; Pole for Cock House; The Book of Robin Hood; etc. *Ctr*: Various. *s.s*: School Stories. *a*: 57 Gordon Sq, London, W.C.1.

HAYDON, Eric, D.C.M. *b*: London 1894. Author & Lyric Writer. *Publ*: Rosanna: The Romance of a Spy in Erin; One Act Play:— Honor's Last Act; Song Lyrics including The Menin Gate; Short Stories; Verse. *c.t*: Various Boys' Journals. *s.s*: Humorous verse. War Service. *Rec*: Amateur acting. *a*: 91 Fitzjohn's Ave, Hampstead, N.W.3. *t*: Hampstead 6596.

HAYDON, Percy Montague, M.C. *b*: London 1895. *n.a*: Controlling Ed, A.P. Group, Juvenile periodicals, annuals & libraries 1925—. *a*: Fleetway Hse, Farringdon St, London, E.C.4. *T*: Central 8080.

HAYDON, Walter. F/l. *a*: 42 Maison Dieu Rd, Dover. *t*: Dover 816 & 817.

HAYEK, von, Friedrich August, F.B.A. *b*: Vienna 1899. *e*: Vienna Univ. Tooke Prof of Econ Sci & Statistics Lond Univ. *Publ*: Prices & Production; Monetary Theory & the Trade Cycle (trans from German); Monetary Nationalism & International Stability; Profits, Interest & Investment; The Pure Theory of Capital; The Road to Serfdom. *s.s*: Economics. *a*: 8 Turner Close, London, N.W.11. *T*: Speedwell 4413.

HAYES, Alexander Henry, F.C.S., F;F.Sc., A.M.Inst.E. *b*: Scarborough, Yorks 1884. Tech Ed & Consultant. *n.a*: Ed The Foundry Trade Journ 1905—19, Tech Sub-Ed The Iron & Coal Trades Review '05—14, Ed Oil Engineering & Technology '26—28, Ed The Fuel Economist '34, Ed The South African Engineers' Diary, Ed The Architects' Desk Diary. *Publ*: Steam for Process & Industrial Heating; Steam-raising Boilers for Industrial Purposes; Approach to Therapeutic & Child Psychology; Reformer, Walk Warily. *Ctr*: Tech periodicals. *s.s*: Fuels, Combustion, Steam-raising & Power, Steam-heating in Industry. *c*: Roy Soc. *w.s*: Capt (tech) R.A.F. 1916—19. *a*: Helan Brae, Winifred Rd, Coulsdon, Surrey, & 24 Buckingham St, London, W.C.2. *T*: Purley 2969; Temple Bar 6368.

HAYES, ALFRED: principal Midland Institute, Birmingham, Eng.; b. Wolverhampton, Staffordshire, Eng., Aug., 1857; s. Edwin John and Fanny (Puddicombe) H.; educ. Wolverhampton Grammar Sch., King Edward's Sch. (Birmingham), New Coll. (Oxford), (Hon.) M.A., Birmingham; m. Edith Mary Chattock (died), 1885. AUTHOR: The Death of St. Louis, 1885; The Last Crusade and Other Poems, 1886; David Westren, 1887; The March of Man, 1891; The Vale of Arden and Other Poems, 1895; The Cup of Quietness, 1911; Simon de Montfort, A Drama in five acts, 1918; Boris Goodounov, a Drama (trans. from the Russian of Pushkin), 1918; Czar Feodor Ioannovich, a Drama (trans. from the Russian of Alexis Tolstoi), 1924; The Death of Ivan the Terrible, a Drama (trans. from the Russian of Alexis Tolstoi), 1926. General character of writing: poems, plays. Schoolmaster (1881-89), King Edward's Sch. (Birmingham); Secy. Midland Institute, 1889-1912, principal since 1912. Relig. denom., Church of England. OFFICE: Midland Institute. HOME: 54 Wheeleys Road, Edgbaston, Birmingham, Eng.

HAYES, Chris (Christopher Daniel), N.U.J., Mem Roy Art Assoc. *b*: Tooting, London 1916. *e*: Cormont Rd Sch Camberwell. *m*: Madeleine Emily Lyons. Journalist. *n.a*: Melody Maker, Editorial Staff Reptr since 1934. *Publ*: Stairway to the Stars. *Ctr*: Melody Maker, Rhythm, Band Wagon, Ev News, Everybodys. *s.s*: Entertainment. *Rec*: Cricket, football. *c*: British Legion. *w.s*: World War II. *a*: 4 Stonehall Ave, Ilford, Essex.

HAYES, Edmund Duncan Tranchell. *b*: S. Africa 1891. *e*: Dio Col Rondebosch, Cape Town, T.C.D. & Vienna. *m*: Mabel Gertrude Beauchamp. Med Pract. *Publ*: Principles & Practice of Psychiatry (with A. Cannon); Principles & Practice of Neurology (with A. Cannon); etc. *c.t*: Med Journs. *s.s*: Nervous & mental diseases. Capt R.A.M.C. 1915-19. Twice wounded. P.o.W. (Desp). Asst M.O. Croydon Mental Hosp '20-26. Dep Med Supt Mental Hosp, Berry Wood, Northampton '26—. *Rec*: Shooting. *c*: Jnr Const, Roy Soc Med, Roy Medico-Psych Assoc, etc. *a*: Berry Wood, Northampton. *t*: Duston 58.

HAYES, Ernest Henry. *b*: London 1881. Married. *s*: 1. *d*: 1. Author & Publisher, Mang Ed Religious Education Press & Carwal Publications. *n.a*: Sub-Ed Sunday Circle, etc 1906—11, Sub-Ed Cassell's Penny Mag, etc '11—14, Publs Mang Lond Missny Soc '18—25, Ed Nat S.S.U. '25—31, Ed Meth Youth Educ Dept '31—, Ed Teacher of Today. *Publ*: The Child in the Midst, Pioneer series, etc; Founder Concise Guides Lesson Helps); Christianity Goes into Action; Jesus & the Kingdom; etc. *Ctr*: News Chron. *s.s*: Religious Educ. *Rec*: Motoring. *c*: Nat Lib. *a*: 210 Woodcote Rd, Wallington, Surrey. *T*: 5386.

HAYES, Gerald Ravenscourt. *b*: London 1889. *e*: Cranleigh. *m*:Mary Winifred Yule. *s*: 1. Civil Servant. *n.a*: Founder & first Ed of The Consort. *Publ*: Anthony Munday's Romances of Chivalry; The Preparation of an Admiralty Chart; The Treatment of Instrumental Music; The Viols & other Bowed Instruments. *c.t*: Articles in periodicals & dly press on early music & bibliography. *s.s*: Early musical instruments & romances of chivalry. Hon Sec & co-founder of The Dolmetsch Foundation. Mem Biblio Soc; Soc of Genealogists. *c*: Athenæum, Arts. *a*: 177 Holland Park Ave, W.11. *t*: Park 7647.

HAYES, Gertrude, A.R.E. (Mrs. A. Kedington Morgan). *s.s*: Archæ & crafts, etching & oil & w.c. painting. Roy Soc of Painter Etchers. Late Head of Art Centre Forest Hill. Asst Art Teacher Rugby Sc & Exhibitor R.A. & W.A.G. etc. *a*: The Church Hse, Buttenhall, Coventry.

HAYES, Rev. Henry Beaumont, F.R.Econ.S. *b*: Stretford, Lancs 1881. *e*: Manchester Gr Sch & Banker's Inst. *m*: Dora Bedford. Clerk in Holy Orders. *Publ*: Extracts from the Old Altar Book in Denmark (trans). *s.s*: Lutheran, Old Catholic & Eastern Church Liturgies. *Rec*: 18th century English & 19th century Russian literature, Armenian & Arabic languages. *a*: Wilby Rectory, Northants. *T*: Wellingborough 2677.

HAYES, James George, L.R.C.P. & S. *b*: Dublin 1879. *e*: Clongowes Wood Col & Castleknock Col. *m*: Josephine Mary Cheyers. *s*: 1. *d*: 1. Surgeon & Physician. *c.t*: B.M.J. *s.s*: Surgery, gynæcology. R.A.M.C. 1914-18. *Rec*: Tennis, travel. *c*: Hove. B.M.A. Brighton & Sussex Medico-Chirurgical Soc. *a*: 47 Norton Rd, Hove. *t*: 2756.

HAYES, Rev. James Gordon, M.A., F.R.G.S. *b*: Worcester 1877. *e*: Worcester G.S. Corpus Christi Col. *m*: Mabel Rickard. *Publ*: Antarctica 1928; Robert Edwin Peary; Institutional Christianity; The Conquest of the South Pole ('32); etc. *s.s*: Polar exploration, religious subjects. Civil Engineer 1896-1906. *Rec*: Fruit growing, trophies. *c*: Roy Soc, Roy Geog Soc. *a*: Storridge Vicarage, Malvern, Worcs. *t*: Ridgeway Cross 23.

HAYES, Lionel Charles Maclean, B.A., M.S.M. *b*: Nailsea 1885. *e*: King Edward VI Sc, Retford, Melle Col Belgium & Ghent, Erlangen Univ, Bavaria. *m*: Margaret Holden. Schoolmaster. *Publ*: La Composition Libre d'après la Méthode Directe; German Free Composition; Aids to French Composition; A German Course. *c.t*: Journ of Educ & French Review. *s.s*: French & German. War Service 1914-19 (Desp twice), M.S.M. & Croix de Guerre (palms), etc. *a*: 9 Coronation Drive, Gt Crosby, L'pool, 23.

HAYES, Marjorie. *b*: Newton Center, Mass. *e*: Newton Mass & Bradford Junior Coll. Teacher & Writer. *Publ*: The Little House on Wheels; Wampum & Sixpence; Alice-Albert Elephant; The Little House on Runners; The Young Patriots; Green Peace; Homer's Hill. *Ctr*: Boston Herald, C.S. Monitor, Instructor, Child Life. *s.s*: Historical Fiction for Young People, New England Background. *a*: 209 Middlesex Rd, Chestnut Hill, Massachusetts, U.S.A. *T*: Longwood 4135.

HAYES, Patrick Maguire. *b*: Glasgow 1903. *e*: Sec Sch. *m*: Robina Tweedie Leghorn. Journalist *n.a*: Rep Arbroath Guide 1930—, Corr for Edin, Glas & Lond newspapers. *Rec*: Golf, cycling. *a*: 18 Culloden Terr, Arbroath Angus. *T*: 3361.

HAYES, Richard, D.Litt. Film Censor for Eire, Dir of the Abbey Theatre Dublin. *Publ*: Ireland & Irishmen in the French Revolution; The Last Invasion of Ireland; Irish Swordsmen of France; Old Irish Links with France. *a*: Woodlands, Kill-o-Grange, Blackrock, Co Dublin.

HAYES, WILL: clergyman; b. Whinfell, Westmoreland, Eng., Jan. 26, 1890; s. William and Agnes (Armistead) H.; educ. Friends Sch., Kendal and Manchester Coll., Oxford; m. Dorothy Manners, August, 1914. AUTHOR: The Cure of Souls, 1921; The Gospel According to Thomas, 1921; Walt Whitman: the Prophet of the New Era, 1921; A Book of Twelve Services, 1924; The Larger Bible, 1925; My Buddha, 1928; The Man Who Had Never Seen a Woman, 1929; The Man Who Emptied Hell, 1929; Men and Mountains, 1929; Leaves from the Larger Bible, 1929; The Book of the Cow, 1930; After the Great Companions, 1930; Sweet Calamus, 1931; Water from the Old Wells, 1931; Indian Bibles, 1931. Editor: Calamus (Quarterly Journ. of the Order of the Great Companions) (Dublin), since 1929. Minister of the Unitarian Church, Chatham, since 1921; leader of the Free Religious Movement, Lindsey Hall, The Mall, Notting Hill Gate, London. HOME: **5 Maidstone Rd., Chatham, Eng.**

HAYLEN, Leslie Clement. *b*: Amungula, Canberra, Australia 1902. *m*: Sylvia Gordon-Rogers. *s*: 2. Journalist, Author, M.P. *n.a*: Found Ed Standard 1943—, Asst-Ed Australian Women's Weekly '32—43. *Publ*: Brown Boy Singing; The Game Darrells; Brierley Rose; Plays—Blood on the Battle; Two Minutes Silence; Freedom has a Beard; Change of Policy. *Rec*: Golf, Australian research. *a*: 130 The Boulevard, Strathfield, New South Wales, & Parliament Hse, Canberra, Australia.

HAYLER, Guy. *b*: Battle, Sussex 1850. *e*: Hastings. *m*: Ann Elizabeth Harriss. *s*: 4. *d*: 4. Sec & Editor. *n.a*: Band of Hope Advocate 1875-78, Sunday Closing News '82, Good Templars Guide '86-89, Houghton le Spring Reformer '92. Temperance Witness '90-1906, Northern Temperance Year Book '94-97, International Record '17-. *Publ*: George Proctor (novel); Famous Fanatics; Temperance Outlook Throughout the World; Joseph Malins—An Appreciation; etc. *c.t*: Various. *s.s*: Temp & prohibition. *Rec*: Chess, reading (has one of most complete private libraries of temperance books in Eng). *a*: Courtfield, S. Norwood Pk, S.E.25. *t*: Livingstone 2833.

HAYLES, Alfred Arthur. *b*: London 1887. *e*: London & Paris. *m*: S. A. Copeland. Ed & Mang Dir The Madras Mail. *n.a*: Madras Times Sub Ed 1912; Madras Mail Asst Ed '21; Ed '28. *s.s*: Indian Affairs. *Rec*: Sailing, swimming, billiards, tennis, travel. *c*: Mem Madras City Counc, Mem Madras Chamber of Commerce, Mem Madras Port Trust etc, Madras Club, Madras Gymkhana, Madras Boat, Roy Madras Yacht. *a*: Sunnyside, White's Rd, Madras, India. *t*: 3725.

HAYNE, Coe Smith, A.B., Litt.D. *b*: Tecumseh, Michigan 1875. *e*: Kalamazoo Coll, U. of C. *s*: 2. *d*: 2. *Publ*: Vanguard of the Caravans; Redmen on the Big Horn; Cry Dance; Race Grit; They Came Seeking; Old Trails & New; For a New America; By-paths to Forgotten Folks. *Ctr*: Missions Mag. *s.s*: History & Fiction, Church Expansion & Missionary History. *Rec*: Gardening. *a*: Route 2, Box 219, St Joseph, Michigan, U.S.A. *T*: 3-7303.

HAYNES, Doris Victoria. *b*: Market Overton. *e*: Banbury Munic Sc. *m*: Leslie Starkey Haynes. *s*: 1. *d*: 2. Freelance. *c.t*: Sunday Mercury, Dundee Courier, Hampshire Telegraph, Nottingham Journal, Modern Home, Daily Mail, etc. *s.s*: Psych. *c*: Nott'm Writers'. *a*: 189 Coppice Rd, Mapperley, Nott'm.

HAYNES, Frederic Harry, F.R.C.P., M.D.Lond. Physician. *c.t*: B.M.J., Med Press & Circular. Late Magistrate Boro' of Leamington Spa. *a*: 17 Clarendon St, Leamington Spa. *t*: 635.

HAYNES, George Henry. *b*: Stamford. *a*: Maiden Lane, Stamford. *t*: 161.

HAYNES, George Secretan, M.D., F.R.C.P. *b*: Maidstone 1872. *e*: Maidstone Gr Sch, King's Coll Camb, St Bart's Hosp. *m*: Lily Edmundson Daville Atkinson. *s*: 2. *d*: 2. Chm Recruiting Bd Min of Labour & Nat Service 1939—47 (Cambridge). *Publ*: Notes on Medical Case-Taking. *Ctr*: B.M.J., Med Press & Circular, Practitioner, St Bart's Hosp Journ. *s.s*: Medicine. *Rec*: Motoring. *w.s*: R.A.M.C.T. 1914—19. *a*: Corner Hse, 1 Trumpington St, Cambridge. *T*: 5222.

HAYNES, Lt.-Col. Horace Guy Lankester. Physician. *Publ*: Ed With 2/2 London Field Ambulance in France. *c.t*: Westminster Hosp Gazette. *a*: Littleton Hall, Brentwood, Essex. *t*: 45.

HAYNES, Nathan Gallup Williams, D.Sc. *b*: Detroit, Mich 1886. *e*: Cutler Sch, N.Y. City & Johns Hopkins Univ. *m*: (1) Elizabeth Bown Batchelor; (2) Dorothy Wilson Farrand. *d*: 3. Author, Consult Chemical Economist. *n.a*: Ed Field & Fancy 1906—07, Spec European Corres N.Y. Sun & Springfield Republican

'11—16, Ed-Dir D. O. Haynes & Co '16—20 & Pres Haynes & George Co Trade & Tech Publs '20—40. *Publ*: American Chemical Industry, a History; This Chemical Age; The Stone that Burns; Men, Money & Molecules; Southern Horizons; Chemical Economics; Practical Dog Breeding & Practical Dog Keeping. *Ctr*: Various. *s.s*: Chemistry for Laymen, History. *Rec*: Breeding & showing smooth fox-terriers, herb gardening, photography. *a*: 161-63 Water St, & Stonecrop Farm, Stonington, Connecticut, U.S.A.

HAYNES, Sydney Walter, M.D., C.M. *b*: 1858. *c.t*: B.M.J., Birm Mail. *a*: 75 Harborne Rd, Edgbaston, & 96 Newhall St, Birm. *t*: Edg 0531 & Central 5827.

HAYNES, Thomas Watson, A.C.A. *b*: Melbourne 1878. *m*: Ethel Timmins. *s*: 2. *d*: 4. Managing director & chartered accountant. *Publ*: Our Daily Bread. *c.t*: Bulletin, Sydney, Argus, Melbourne. *s.s*: Novels of serious nature. *Rec*: Golf, bridge, travel, reading. *c*: Melbourne, Australian, Royal Melbourne Golf. *a*: Hamurana, Murrumbeena, Victoria, Australia. *t*: Um 2372.

HAYNES, W. J. *n.a*: Chief Sub-Ed Western Evening Herald. Formerly Parly staff Western Daily Mercury. Twice Chm Plymouth Branch N.U.J. *a*: 28 Endsleigh Park Rd, Peverell, Plymouth.

HAYSOM, Derrick Harold. *e*: Cheam Sec Sch & Pitmans. Journalist. *n.a*: Amalgamated Press 1944, National Trade Press '45, British Kinematography '46—47. *Ctr*: Brit Journ Photography, Film Industry. *s.s*: Kinematography. *a*: 183 Coulsdon Rd, Caterham, Surrey.

HAYWARD, A. G. *n.a*: I/c Belper News, Dist reporter Derbyshire Times. *a*: Welcombe, Marsh Lane, Belper.

HAYWARD, Arthur Lawrence. *b*: Croydon. Journalist, Book Editor. *n.a*: Ed Cassell & Co Ltd. *Publ*: Days of Dickens; Dickens Encyclopædia; Treason; (Ed) Ward's London Spy; Mme de Sevigne's Letters; Johnson's History of Pirates; Smith's Highwaymen; Tom Brown's Amusements, Serious & Comical; etc. *Ctr*: Chambers Journ, Spectator, Listener, etc. *s.s*: London, Dickens, Lexicography. *a*: Crutches Cottage, Jordans, Beaconsfield, Bucks. *T*: Jordans 2171.

HAYWARD, Charles Harold. *b*: London 1898. *e*: Westminster City Sch. Editor. *Publ*: English Furniture at a Glance; English Rooms & their Decoration. *a*: Handicrafts Ltd, Weedington Rd, Kentish Town, London, N.W.5. *T*: Gulliver 4451, Ext 6.

HAYWARD, John (Davy), M.D., F.R.C.S., M.R.C.P. Book Reviewer & Editor of various poetical works, anthologies, etc. *a*: 19 Carlyle Mansions, Cheyne Walk, Chelsea, London, S.W.3.

HAYWARD, Richard. *b*: Larne, Ireland. *e*: Larne. Gr Sch. *m*:. *s*: 2. Film Producer & Dir, Author *Publ*: The Jew's Fiddle-play; Love in Ulster; Ulster Songs & Ballads (poems); Sugarhouse Entry (novel); Travel books—In Praise of Ulster; Where the River Shannon Flows; The Corrib Country; The Kingdom of Kerry; Irish & Proud of it; In the Footsteps of St Patrick; Anna Liffey Goes to Dublin; Films—Luck of the Irish; Early Bird; Shipmates of Mine; & many B.B.C. plays. *s.s*: Ulster Balladry & Folklore. *Rec*: Golf, music, antiquities. *c*: Un Arts, Irish P.E.N., Belfast Field. *a*: 7 Bedford St, Belfast. *T*: 26343.

HAYWOOD, Miss A. *a*: Ingleside, Morley Rd, Farnham, Surrey.

HAYWOOD, Colonel Austin Hubert Wightwick, C.M.G., C.B.E., D.S.O. *b*: Ranikhet, India 1878. *e*: Abroad & R.M.A. Woolwich. *m*: Isabella Rosamond Walters. *s*: 1. Military Knight of Windsor 1936—, Colonel R.A. (ret). *Publ*: Through Timbuctu & Across the Great Sahara; Sport & Service in Africa; English-Hausa Vocabulary. *c*: Junior United Services. *a*: 10 Castle Yd, Windsor Castle. *T*: Windsor 789.

HAYWOOD, Helen Riviere. *b*: South Hampstead: London 1907. *e*: Priv, Lansdown Sch of Art. Children's Writer & Illustrator. *Publ*: The Peter's Friends Books; The Helen Haywood Colour Book; (in collab) Figgles Frog; Dawdles Duckling; Sandy's Seven Tails; Barty Bantam; Clarrie Coot; Basil Bumblebee; Hermione Hen; Monte Mongoose; Corne Coon; Winnie Wombat; Henry Penn; Penny Pullett; Miss Emma of Dustbin Alley; Hedgehog's Holiday (in collab). *s.s*: Animal Characters, Nat History. *Rec*: Reading, country walks, etc. *a*: Summerfield, 58 Princess Rd, Bournemouth, Hants. *T*: Westbourne 63766.

HAZARD, PAUL: professor; b. Noordpeere, Nord, France, August, 1878; s. Gustav and Marie (Looten) H.; educ. École Normale Supérieure. DEGREES: Fellow of the Univ., Litt.D.; married. AUTHOR: La Revolution française et les lettres italiennes, 1910; Journal de guiguère, 1910; Discours sur la langue française, 1913; Giacomo Leopardi, 1913; L'Italie vivante, 1921; Histoire illustrée de la littérature française (with Joseph Bedier), 1923; Lamartine, 1925; Vie de Stendhal, 1927 (Amer. transl., 1929). Editor: Revue de littérature comparée. Contributor to Revue des Deux Mondes, Revues d'histoire littéraire de la France. General character of writing: literary history. ADDRESS: 101 rue de Bar, Paris, France.

HAZAREESINGH, Kissoonsingh. *b*: Mauritius 1909. *e*: Verdun C. of E. Aided Sch, London Sch of Econ & Middle Temple. *m*: Coolwantee Gorburdhun. *s*: 1. Asst Public Assistance Commissioner, Mem P.E.N., R.S.A., E. India Assoc, etc. *Publ*: History of Indians in Mauritius; Story of the Present War; Bacon n'est pas Shakespeare; (Ed) Poemes Vediques of R. E. Hart; History of 1945 Cyclones in Mauritius. *Ctr*: Crown Colonist, Edin Ev News, Indian Cultural Rev, Advance (Mauritius). *s.s*: Sociology, Colonial Administration & Social Services. *Rec*: Gardening. *a*: Phoenix, Mauritius. *T*: Vacoas 224.

HAZEL, Edward John, M.J.I. *b*: Lon 1866. *e*: Hastings G.S. Married. *d*: 3. *n.a*: Pupil Hastings & S. Leonard's Times, Hastings Dist rep Sussex Daily News, Evening Argus & Southern Weekly News '87–96, Sub-Ed Sx Daily News '96–99, Mang Ed Hastings issue Argus '99–1901, Ed Mang Hastings Mail & Times '01–03, Ed Yarmouth Evening Standard '03–05, Sub-Ed Railway Times '05–13, Sub-Ed Transport World. *Publ*: The Complete Territorial ('12). *s.s*: Rail & road traction. Specialist in training pupils, 30 y service Vol & T.F. K. Edward service medal, Gt War 2 medals. Ed yearly Gazette of 4th City of Lon Bn Roy Fusiliers. Assisted late Col McHugh with Vol & Territorial notes for Daily Telegraph. *a*: 68 Ingram Rd, Thornton Heath, Surrey.

HAZELL, W., J.P. *b*: London 1890. *e*: Counc Sch. *m*:. *s*: 4. *d*: 2. Sec Miners' Inst & Journalist. *Ctr*: Producer, Co-operative Review, New Dawn, Scottish Co-operator & other Co-operative Journs. *s.s*: Co-operation, Trade Unionism & Gen Lit. *a*: 24 Clive Ter-Ynysbwl. *T*: 8.

HAZELL, W. HOWARD: printer; b. London, Eng., Aug., 1869; s. Walter and Sarah Anne H.; educ. Dulwich Coll., Paris Schls.; m. Mary L. Inman, Oct. 28, 1905. AUTHOR: Federation of Master Printer's Cost-Finding System, 1914; Estimating for Printers, 1916; Office Organization for Printers, 1917; Costing for Manufacturers, 1921; Labour and Capital in Alliance, 1926. Contributor to Times Trade Supplement, Nineteenth Century, British Colonial Printer and other trade papers. General character of writing: technical, text-books. Memb. Royal Comm. controlling paper supplies during great War; Past-Pres. Federation of Master Printers. Relig. denom., Church of England. CLUB: Reform. (*)

HAZELTINE, Harold Dexter, F.B.A., L.H.D. *b*: Warren, Penna 1871. *e*: Brown, Berlin & Paris Univs, Harvard Law Sch. *m*: Hope Graves. *d*: 1. Downing Prof of Law Univ of Cambridge Mass (ret), Barrister of Inner Temple. *Publ*: Geschichte des Englischen Pfandrechts; The Law of the Air; etc. *Ctr*: Cambridge Mediæval Hist, Harvard Law Rev, Law Quarterly Rev, etc. *s.s*: Legal History. *Rec*: Travel. *a*: Harvard Law School, Cambridge, Massachusetts, U.S.A.

HEAD, Alice Maud. *b*: London. *e*: N. Lond Coll. Journalist, Dir Country Life Ltd, Mang Dir National Mag Co 1924—39. *n.a*: Ed Woman at Home 1909, Asst Ed Nash's '18. *Rec*: Theatre, travel. *c*: P.E.N. *a*: 22 Whitelands Hse, Chelsea, London, S.W.3. *T*: Sloane 1967.

HEAD, Cecil. *b*: Lon 1906. *e*: North Hse Sc Crawley. *m*: Alexandrina Stopani. *s*: 1. Journalist. *n.a*: Fairchild Publ's, Lon '26—27, Publ's Fairchild, Paris '28—32, Exec Ed Fashion Age, News Ed Women's Wear News, Exec Ed Textile Journals News Service. *c.t*: Women's Wear Daily, N.Y., Man & His Clothes, Lon, N.Y. Herald, Paris, Paris Times, Daily Express, Lon, etc. *s.s*: Retail distribution, dept store org, aviation. *Rec*: Writing. *a*: 59 Leinster Sq, W.2.

HEAD, Charles Octavius, D.S.O. *b*: Birr, Ireland 1869. *e*: Private & R.M.A. Woolwich. *m*: Alice Margaret Threlfall. *s*: 1. *d*: 2. Army Officer (ret). *Publ*: Napoleon & Wellington; No Great Shakes; A Glance at Gallipoli. *s.s*: Military Hist. *c*: Cavalry, Naval & Military, Shropshire. *a*: Hinton Hall, Shrewsbury.

HEAD, June. *b*: London. *Publ*: Star Gazing 1931. *s.s*: Trans from the German. *c*: P.E.N. *a*: 14 Grosvenor St, W.1. *t*: Mayfair 3065.

HEAD, Walter Lionel. *b*: Congleton 1894. *e*: King's Sch & Denstone Coll. *m*: Doris Titley. *d*: 2. Newspaper Proprietor & Editor. *n.a*: Ed Congleton Chron & Series 1926—. *a*: 15 Moody Terr, Congleton, Cheshire. *T*: 599.

HEADLAM, Cecil. *b*: Lon 1872. *e*: Rugby & Oxf. *m*: Mary May Fraser. Author. *n.a*: Ed State Papers of the Colonial Office. *Publ*: The Milner Papers (Lord Milner's S. African Papers); The Story of Nuremberg; The Story of Naples; History of France; Friends That Fail Not; Red Screes; etc. *c.t*: Times, Sphere, Cam History of the Brit Empire. *s.s*: Hist, topography, biography, belles lettres. *a*: Broadmead, Charing, Kent. *t*: 47.

HEADLAM, Rt. Hon. Sir Cuthbert M., Bt., P.C., D.S.O., O.B.E., T.D., D.L., J.P., M.P. Barrister, M.P. (C) North Newcastle since 1940. *Publ*: History of Guards' Division in the Great War; Letters of Lady Harriot Eliot; A Strange Delilah; Knight Reluctant. *Ctr*: Quarterly Review, Army Quarterly, Nat Review, Eng Review, etc. *a*: Holywell Hall, Durham, & Travellers Club, Pall Mall, London.

HEADLAM, Sir Edward James, Kt, C.S.I., C.M.G., D.S.O. Capt R.I.N. (ret). *a*: Lloyds Bank Ltd, King's Branch, 6 Pall Mall, S.W.1.

HEADLEY, Lord (Rowland George Allanson Winn, Baron Allanson & Winn), B.A. Civil Engineer. *n.a*: Ed Salisbury Journ 2y. *Publ*: Boxing; Western Awakening to Islam; The Affinity between the Original Church of Jesus Christ & Islam; etc. *c.t*: L'pool Journ of Commerce, Daily Graphic, Yorks Post, Times, Irish Times, Morning Post, etc. *a*: 98 Portland Pl, W.1. *t*: Welbeck 7322.

HEADRIDGE, David, L.D.S., R.C.S.(Eng). *b*: M/C 1869. *e*: M/C G.S. & Owens Col M/C. *m*: Gertrude Banning. *s*: 2. *d*: 1. Dental Surg. *Publ*: Dental Anatomy. *c.t*: Dental Journ's. *s.s*: Dental educ. Exam under Dental Bd. Exam M/C Leeds & L'pool Univs. Hon Dental Surg M/C Dental Hosp. Ex-Lect in Dental Anatomy & Physiol & Dental Histol, M/C Univ. Ex-Pres E. Lane & Ches Br Brit Dental Assoc, M/C Odentological Soc, etc. *Rec*: Gardening. *c*: Athenæum. *a*: 323 Oxford Rd, M/C, & Daleside, Rose Hill, Marple. *t*: Ard 3598 & Marple 94.

HEAF, Frederick Roland George, M.A., M.D., F.R.C.P. *b*: Desborough, Northants 1894. *e*: Oundle, Camb & St Thomas's Hosp. *m*: Madeleine Denison. *s*: 2. *d*: 1. Pres Tuberculosis Assoc, Senior Med Off L.C.C., Hon Med Dir Brit Legion, Cons Phys Papworth Village Settlement. *Publ*: Rehabilitation of the Tuberculous. *Ctr*: Lancet, B.M.J., Tubercle, etc. *s.s*: Tuberculosis & Diseases of the Chest. *Rec*: Sketching, gardening, geology. *a*: Stone Hse, Potten End, Berkhamsted.

HEAL, Sir Ambrose, F.S.A., R.D.I. *b*: London N. 1872. *e*: Marlborough Coll & France. *m*: Edith Digby Todhunter (dec'd). *s*: 2. *d*: 1. Chm & Mang-Dir Heal & Son Ltd, Vice-Pres of D.I.A. Counc of Vic & Alb Museum. *Publ*: London Tradesmen's Cards of the Eighteenth Century; English Writing Masters & their Copy Books 1570—1800; The London Goldsmiths 1200 —1800; The Signboards of Old London Shops. *Ctr*: Notes & Queries, Country Life, Connoisseur. *s.s*: London Tradesmen's Cards & Shop Signs, Eighteenth-Century Cabinet Makers. *Rec*: Collections of trade-cards & shop signs, squash, collection of modern press books. *a*: Baylins Farm, Knotty Green, Beaconsfield, Bucks. *T*: Beaconsfield 188.

HEAL, Jeanne Reynolds. *e*: Benenden Sch & France. *s*: 1. *d*: 1. *Publ*: Interior Decorating—Your Career. *Ctr*: Various. *s.s*: Furnishing & Decorating. *Rec*: Cooking, converting junk furniture. *a*: 7 Park Village West, London, N.W.1. *T*: Euston 7107.

HEALD, Andrew. *b*: Chorley. *m*: Hannah Ada Pickles. *s*: 2. Foundation Mem N.U.J. Southport. *n.a*: Chorley Standard, Salford Reporter, Wharfedale Observer, as reporter, Southport Guardian 1904, Ch-rep '13—26, Ed Southport Journ '26—40, Ed Southport Visitor '36—40, now Free-lance. *Ctr*: Various agencies, daily, wkly & trade press. *a*: 23 Bengarth Rd, Southport, Lancs. *T*: 87012.

HEALD, Edith Shackleton. Journalist. *n.a*: Formerly Leader Writer & Dramatic Critic Ev Standard, now Freelance, Book reviewer for Lady, Observer, Britain To-day, etc. *a*: The Chantry Hse, Steyning, Sussex. *T*: Steyning 3163.

HEALD, Fredk. Arnold. *b*: Southport 1920. *e*: King George V Sch Southport. *n.a*: Southport Journ, now Rep Southport Guardian 1948—. *Ctr*: Various. *s.s*: Music, Films, Gramophone, Sport (Rugby, Tennis, Golf). *a*: 23 Bengarth Rd, Southport, Lancs. *T*: 87012.

HEALD, Frederick De Forest, B.S., M.S.(Wisconsin), Ph.D.(Leipzig). *b*: Midland City, Michigan, 1872. *e*: Univs of Wisconsin & Leipzig. *m*: Nellie Towney. *s*: 1. *d*: 2. Plant pathologist, Heald Dept of Plant Pathology, Washington State Col, Pullman, Wis. *n.a*: Assoc Ed, Phytopathology, '11—16, '19— 21, '31—33. *Publ*: Manual of Plant Diseases; etc. *c.t*: Botanical Gazette, Plant World, Phytopathology, Mycologia, Annual Report of the

Nebraska Experimental Station, Newspaper Bulletin, Washington Agricultural Experimental Station Bulletin, American Jnl of Botany, The Book of Rural Life, Webester's New International Dictionary, etc. *s.s*: Plant pathology, mycology. *Rec*: Gardening, lawn tennis. *a*: College Station, Pullman, Wisconsin, and State College of Washington, Pullman, Wisconsin, U.S.A. *t*: 578.

HEALD, Nora Shackleton. Journalist. *n.a*: Ed of The Lady, ex-Ed of the Queen, ex-Dramatic Critic of the Daily Mail, appointments held on Daily Chron, Daily Herald, Dispatch, etc. *a*: 39 Bedford St, W.C.2; & The Chantry Hse, Steyning, Sussex.

HEALEY, Dennis. *b*: Faversham, Kent 1907. Information Officer H.M. Forestry Commission. *n.a*: Kent Messenger Series, Press Officer Min of Health. *a*: 25 Savile Row, London, W.1. *T*: Regent 0221.

HEALY, Cahir, M.P. *b*: Donegal. *m*: *s*: 2. *d*: 1. Retired Insurance Official, M.P. Northern Parliament since 1925. *Publ*: The Mutilation of a Nation. *Ctr*: Irish Press, Irish News, Catholic Herald. *s.s*: Political, Literary & Topical Articles. *a*: Enniskillen, Ireland.

HEALY, JOHN: Archdeacon of Meath (retired); b. Limerick, Ireland, Jan., 1850; s. George and Margaret (Bradley) H.; educ. privately. DEGREE: LL.D. (Trinity Coll., Dublin); m. (1) Eunice Suzanne Lelievre; (2) Mary Thornton. AUTHOR: Ancient Irish Church, 1895; Art Teaching of the Irsh Church, 1896; St. Patrick, 1897; The Vikings in Ireland; History of the Diocese of Meath (2 vols.), 1908. General character of writing: historical. Secy. for many yrs. of Diocese of Meath; representative Canon (for Meath), St. Patrick's Cathedral, Dublin. Relig. denom., Church of Ireland. HOME: Thormanby, Howth, Ireland.

HEANLEY, Charles Montague, M.B.(Lon), D.P.H., D.T.M.H. *b*: Croft, Lincs 1877. *e*: Marlborough Col, Portsmouth G.S. & St George's Hosp. *m*: Mary Morella Tassell. *s*: 2. *c.t*: B.M.J., Lancet, Bulletin Geol Soc of China. *Rec*: Anthropology, geology. *a*: Kymer House, nr Hassocks, Sussex. *t*: 246.

HEAP, Harry. *b*: Burnley 1901. *e*: Burnley G.Sc, Burnley Munic Col of Art. N/p Cartoonist. *n.a*: Burnley Express 1921-28, Yorkshire Telegraph & Star Sheffield '28. *c.t*: Burnley Express, Yorkshire Telegraph & Star, Sheffield Dly Telegraph, Sports Special, A Wandering Minstrel by Sir Henry Lytton. *s.s*: Sport, General Cartooning, Caricature. Won Daily Mail prize for Advt Design 1927. Joined N.U.J. '21. *Rec*: Golf. *c*: Dore & Totley Golf. *a*: 22 Linscott Rd, Sheffield & Yorkshire Telegraph & Star Offices, Sheffield.

HEAP, Rev. William Henry. *b*: Bradford 1869. *e*: Bradford Tech Col, & Headingley Col. *m*: Gertrude Byrom. *s*: 1. *d*: 5. Cham Meth Ch throughout E. Anglia. *n.a*: Ed Joyful News & Meth Chron 1933-. *c.t*: Meth Recorder, Meth Times & Leader. *s.s*: Educ, temp. *c*: Nat Lib, Exec Nat F.C.C., Fed of F.C.'s. *a*: 6 Park Rd, Cromer, Norfolk. *t*: 78.

HEAPE, Robert Grundy. *b*: Manchester 1874. *e*: Manch Gr Sch, Victoria Univ. *m*: Dorothy Ogden. Architect (ret), Fellow of Manch Soc of Architects. *Publ*: Salisbury: An Architectural Study; Georgian York; The Soul of Bath: An Architectural Study; Buxton Under the Dukes of Devonshire. *s.s*: Architectural Illustration, Biography. *a*: Nithen Cott, Buxton, Derbyshire. *T*: Buxton 64.

HEAPY, Harold Ernest, M.C., M.D. *b*: Birkenhead 1880. *e*: Wirral Col, Birkenhead Inst, & L'pool Univ. *m*: Florence Elizabeth Thomas. Physician. War Service. Late Captain in R.A.M.C., M.O. i/c 100th Brigade R.F.A. (Des). *Rec*: Tennis, motoring. *a*: 15 Blake Lane, Birm 9. *t*: Victoria 0333.

HEARD, Henry FitzGerald. *b*: London 1889. *e*: Sherborne, Caius Coll Camb. Journalist. *n.a*: Lit-Ed The Realist 1929. *Publ*: Narcissus; The Social Substance of Religion; The Emergence of Man; This Surprising World; These Hurrying Years; The Ascent of Humanity; Science in the Making; The Stratosphere; Third Morality; Pain, Sex & Time; Man the Master; Preface to Prayer; Taste for Honey; Reply Paid; Great Fog; etc. *Ctr*: Week-end Review, Spectator, Sunday Times, Fortnightly Review, etc. *s.s*: Hist of Sci, Broadcasting popular talks on Science & Discovery 1930—34. *a*: Trabuco Ranch, Trabuco Canyon, P.O. California.

HEARN, George. *b*: Stowmarket 1884. *e*: Elem. *m*: Alice Perry. Cinema Operator. *Publ*: Strange Happenings in Wild Life; True Dramas of Wild Life. *c.t*: Animal World, Sunday at Home, British Birds, The Countryman, Woman's Mag, Country Life, etc. *s.s*: Wild birds, photography. *c*: B.E.N.A. *a*: 5 Townfield Rd, Chelmsford, Essex.

HEARN, Colonel Sir Gordon Risley, Kt., C.I.E., D.S.O. *b*: 1871. *e*: Winchester Coll (Scholar), R.M.A. Woolwich. Colonel Royal Engineers (ret), Mang Eastern Bengal Railway 1923—26. *Publ*: Seven Cities of Delhi; Murray's Handbook to India, Burma & Ceylon (Ed 15 & 16 Editions); Permanent Way; Surveying; Railway Engineer's Field Book; Railway Plans. *Ctr*: India's Past Revealed. *s.s*: India—Railway Engineering & Transport. *c*: Roy Empire Soc, Author's Soc. *a*: 52 Woodbourne Ave, London, S.W.16. *T*: Streatham 6680.

HEARNSHAW, Fossey John Cobb, M.A.(Lon), M.A., LlM.(Cam), LlD.(Dub). *b*: Birmingham 1869. *e*: Q. Mary's Sc Walsall & Manchester G.S. & Cam & Lon & Dub Univ. *m*: Dorothea Mabel Spencer. *s*: 1. *d*: 1. Prof of Hist. *Publ*: King Alfred the Great ('01); Life of Sir Henry Vane; History of Southampton; First Book of English History; Freedom in Service; Democracy & Labour ('24); Main Currents of European History ('29); Conservatism in England ('33). *s.s*: Hist & Pol Theory. *c*: Roy Empire Soc. *a*: King's Col Lon & Hammerwood Oxted.

HEARSON, Harry J. S., F.R.Hort.S., M.J.I. *b*: Uttoxeter 1907. *e*: Uttoxeter Gr Sch, Wycliffe Coll. *m*: Olive Andrew. *s*: 1. *d*: 2. Journalist, Mem Soil Assoc. *n.a*: Rep Nth Devon Journ & Dover Standard, Sub-Ed Coventry Herald, Feature-Ed Midland Dly Telegraph, Art Ed Wkly Illustrated, Prod-Ed John Bull, Asst Lit-Ed Illustrated Lond News, Asst-Ed The Sketch. *Ctr*: Britannia & Eve, The Sketch, Homes & Gardens, Modern Reading, Help Yourself Annual, John Bull, Illustrated & Mags in Canada, Sth Africa, India, Australia, etc. *s.s*: Short Stories & Articles on Country Life & Horticulture, etc. *Rec*: Gardening & writing fiction. *a*: Boode Hse, Honister Heights, Purley, Surrey. *T*: Uplands 3025.

HEARST, William Randolph. *b*: San Francisco 1863. N/p Proprietor & Editor. Owner of New York American, San Francisco Examiner, Los Angeles Examiner, etc. *a*: The Clarendon, 86th Street, New York.

HEATH, Ambrose. *b*: London 1891. Culinary Journalist & Broadcaster. *n.a*: Formerly Cookery Corr Morning Post, Cookery Corr The Queen. *Publ*: More than 40 books on Cookery including: Good Food; Madame Prunier's Fish Cookery Book; Good Potato Dishes; Good Drinks; Dining Out; Meat Dishes without Joints; Good Fish Dishes; Good Food for Children; Good Food in Wartime; How to Cook in Wartime; Good Dishes from Tinned Foods; Simple American Dishes; Good

Cheese Dishes; Good Cooking on Rings. *Ctr*: The Queen, Ideal Home, Housewife, Dly Mirror, Ev Standard, etc. *s.s*: Food & Wine. *a*: c/o Faber & Faber, 24 Russell Sq, London, W.C.1.

HEATH, Arthur Douglas, M.D., F.R.C.P. *c.t*: Brit Journ of Dermatology, B.M.J., etc. *a*: 41 Newhall St, Birm. *t*: Central 1665.

HEATH, Carl. *b*: Epsom 1869. *e*: Epsom, Ecole Alsacienne, Paris & Brussels. *m*: Effie Margaret Holden. *Publ*: Religion & Public Life (Swarthmore Lecture); The Ikon of the Invisible God; The Free Spirit; The Challenge of Karl Barth; Religion & Dictatorship. *s.s*: Internat problems, religious & missny matters, peace & penological matters. Sec of the Nat Peace Counc 1909-20, Sec of the Soc of Friends internat work 20. Travelled Europe, Nr East & America. *a*: Friends Hse, Euston Rd, N.W.1.

HEATH, Rev. Charles Herbert, M.A. *b*: Lon 1865. *e*: City of Lon Sc, St John's Col Cam. *m*: Mabel Rickett. *d*: 1. (dec) Schoolmaster. *Publ*: Service Record of King Edward's School in the Great War (Ed); etc. *s.s*: Classics, Eng hist. 10 y Highgate Sc. 30½ y K.E. Sc Birm. *Rec*: Rugby football, cycling, photography. *c*: Old Edwardians Assoc, Class Assoc, etc. *a*: 224 Hagley Rd, Birm, 16. *t*: Edgbaston 0291.

HEATH, Sir H. Frank, G.B.E., K.C.B., Hon A.R.I.B.A. Civil Servant (ret). *n.a*: Ed of Modern Language Quarterly 1897/1903. *Publ*: Chapters on English & Scottish Literature to 1509, in Traill's Social England; (Ed) Special Reports on Educational Subjects (Bd of Educ) '03-15; Article: The Organisation of Intellectual Co-operation by the League of Nations; The Year Book of Education '33; Life of Sir Wm S. McCormick (in the Dictionary of National Biography); Lord Haldane: his Influence on Higher Education & Administration—in Viscount Haldane of Cloan: The Man & his Work: a symposium published by the Institute of Public Administration ('28); etc. *c.t*: Times, Transactions Philol Soc. *a*: 5 Milbourne Lane, Esher, Surrey, & Brown Tiles, Guiestling, Sussex.

HEATH, Harry Cecil, B.A. *b*: Wolstanton, Staffs 1898. *e*: Newport Gr Sch, Pembroke Coll Oxf, Inner Temple. *m*: (1) Margaret Harvey (dec'd), (2) Muriel G. Adams. *d*: 2. Barrister. *n.a*: Ed Alliance News since 1933, Ed Alliance Year Book '47. *Publ*: The Control of a Dangerous Trade; Alcohol & World Traffic Safety; Magisterial Practice in Regard to Occasional Licences; Alcohol & Democracy; The Case Against the Public Ownership of the Drink Trade. *Ctr*: Various newspapers & mags at home & overseas. *s.s*: Drink Problem, Licensing Law, Gambling Problem. *Rec*: Mem of the magic circle. *a*: 62 Becmead Ave, Streatham, London, S.W.16. *T*: Streatham 6649.

HEATH, Irene. *b*: Beds 1905. *e*: Bedford H.S. *m*: James Crooks. Artist & Writer. *Publ*: Heard by a Mouse; A Birthday Book for Children; The Book of Little Bill & Elizabeth; A.B.C. of Irene Heath; Sugar & Spice. *c.t*: Various. *s.s*: Children's books and verses. All books own illus. *Rec*: Travel. *a*: 19 Westbourne St, Sloane Sq, Lon. *t*: Sloane 5630.

HEATH, Sidney Herbert Samuel. *b*: Lon 1872. *e*: King Edward VI Sc Birm, Maison de Melle Belgium, Birm Sc of Art. *m*: Ethel Mary Mabey. *s*: 2. *d*: 1. Author & Artist. *Publ*: (with own illustrations) Songs for the Children; A First Book for Little Ones; Dorset Manor Houses; Old English Houses of Alms; The South Devon and Dorset Coasts; Our Homeland Churches; The Homes and Buildings of Other Days; etc. *c.t*: Builder, Architects Journ, Carpenter & Builder, Young England, etc. *s.s*: Old buildings, ancient hist & customs. English Master at Weymouth & Art Master Plymouth Col. Double Medallist of S. Kensington for design & book illustration. *Rec*: Cricket, fishing. *c*: Conservative Plymouth. *a*: Sparkwell, Plympton, S. Devon.

HEATH, Sir Thomas Little, K.C.B., K.C.V.O., ScD.(Cantab), Hon D.Sc(Oxon), Hon LittD.(Dublin), F.R.S., F.B.A. *b*: Barnetby-le-Wold 1861. *e*: Caistor G.S., Clifton Col & Cam Univ. *m*: Ada Mary Thomas. *s*: 1. *d*: 1. Civil Servant. Jt Permanent Sec to Treasury 1913-19; Comptroller Gen of Nat Debt Office '19-26. *Publ*: Diophantus of Alexandria: A Study in the History of Greek Algebra (1885); Apollonius of Perga, Treatise on Conic Sections ('96); The "Method" of Archimedes ('12); A History of Greek Mathematics, etc (2 vols) '21; Manual of Greek Mathematics ('31); Greek Astronomy (in Library of Greek thought) ('32); etc. *c.t*: Mathematical Gazette, Classical Review, Journal of Hellenic Studies, Nineteenth Century & After, etc. *s.s*: Greek maths & astronomy. Mem Roy Comm on Museums & Galleries. *Rec*: Music. *c*: Athenæum, United Univ. *a*: 64 Bedford Gdns, Kensington, W.8. *t*: Park 0083.

HEATH, W. SHAW (pen name): see Williamson, William Henry.

HEATH-STUBBS, John Francis Alexander. *b*: London 1918. *e*: Queen's Coll Oxf. *Publ*: Wounded Thammuz; Beauty & the Beast; The Divided Ways; Poems from Giacomo Leopardi. *Ctr*: Time & Tide, Spectator, New English Review, New English Wkly, New Writing, Windmill, Poetry (Lond), Poetry Quarterly, etc. *s.s*: Lit, esp Eng Poetry of 18th & 19th Cents. *a*: 18 Kingdon Rd, London, N.W.6. *T*: Hampstead 5178.

HEATHCOTE, John Norman. *b*: Lon 1863. *e*: Eton & Cam *Publ*: St Kilda (1900). *Rec*: Shooting & Yachting. High Sheriff & County Ald Hunts. *a*: Conington Castle, Peterborough. *t*: Sawtry 32.

HEATHCOTE, Joseph Clee, F.R.Hist.S. *b*: Birchover 1874. *e*: Hunt Bridge House & Tor House Matlock. *m*: Mary Hartle. *s*: 2. *d*: 1. Postmaster, Mem Counc Derbyshire Archæological Soc. *Publ*: The Arbor Low Stone Circle; Birchover Church & Cratcliffe Hermitage. *Ctr*: Derbyshire Times, High Peak News. *s.s*: Archæology & Prehistory. *a*: Birchover, Matlock, Derbyshire. *T*: Winster 218.

HEATHER, HENRY JAMES SHEDLOCK: engineer; *b*. London, Eng., May, 1863; *s*. James and Frances (Shedlock) H.; *educ*. St. Paul's Sch. (London); DEGREE: B.A. (Oxon) *m*. Ethel Kate Wilson (died), April 1, 1894. AUTHOR: Electrical Engineering for Mechanical and Mining Engineers, 1912. Contributor of various technical papers to Proceedings Institute Civil Engineers, Electrician, World Power (both London), Inst. Mining and Metallurgy (London), Inst. Electrical Engineers, Natal (S. Africa) Mercury, and many other papers. General character of writing: technical. Memb. Inst. Civil Engineers; Memb. Inst. Elect. Engineers; Electrical Eng. with Central Mining and Investment Corp., 1904-13; prof. Electrotechnics, S. Africa Sch. of Mines (later Univ. of Witwatersrand), 1914-24. Relig. denom., Church of England. CLUBS: Rand (Johannesburg, S. A.), Royal Societies (London). OFFICE: Margate, South Coast, Natal, S. A.

HEATLEY, David Playfair, M.A. *b*: Northumberland 1867. *e*: Roy H.S. Edin & Edin Univ. Reader in Political Science & Lecturer in Modern Hist, Univ of Edin. *Publ*: Studies in British History & Politics (1913); Diplomacy & the Study of International Relations ('19). *c.t*: The Juridical Review, The Law Quarterly Review, The Scotsman, The Glas Herald, etc. *s.s*: The hist of mod political thought, Brit statesmen of the 18th cent, present day internat relations. Official Adviser of Studies in the Faculty of Arts, Univ of Edin '07-15. *Rec*: Fishing & golf. *c*: Scottish Arts. *a*: 28 Minto St, Edinburgh.

HEATON. *n.a:* Mang Ledbury Reporter. *a:* Bank Cres, Ledbury, Herefordshire.

HEATON, Harold. *b:* Didsbury 1894. *m:* Agnes Stockton. *d:* 1. Newspaper Correspondent. *n.a:* Lytham Times 1911, Crewe Observer 1913—27, Reading Mercury '27—. *Ctr:* Nat dailies & agencies. *Rec:* Football. *c:* Maidenhead Cons. *w.s:* 1914—18. *a:* Sylton, Forlease Rd, Maidenhead. *T:* 798.

HEATON, Noel, Hon.A.R.I.B.A., B.Sc(Lon). *b:* Watford. *e:* Univ Col Lon. *m:* Edith Annie Wright. Tech Chemist. *Publ:* Outlines of Paint Technology; Volatile Solvents & Thinners. *c.t:* Times, R.I.B.A. Journ, Chemistry & Industry, Journ of Decorative Art, etc. *s.s:* Chemistry of painting. *Rec:* Archæology, stained glass work. *c:* Brit Soc of Master Glass Painters. (Hon Fell), Savage, Oil & Colour Chem Assoc (Pres 1931–33), Chem Soc, Soc of Chem Ind, Art Workers Guild, Soc for Protection Ancient Bldgs (Hon Chem Adviser). *a:* Kittyghyll, Chislehurst Rd, Orpington, Kent. *t:* 795.

HEATON, Rose Henniker. Author. *Publ:* Cruising with James; Dinner with James; Chez James; Contract with James. *a:* c/o Elkin Mathews & Marrot Ltd, 44 Essex St. W.C.2.

HEAWOOD, Edward. *b:* Newport Salop 1863. *e:* Queen Elizabeth Sch Ipswich, Gonville & Caius Coll. Camb. *m:* Lucy Eleanor Cookson. *s:* 2. Librarian Roy Geog Soc 1901—34. *Publ:* Geographical Discovery in the 17th & 18th Centuries; Geography of Africa. *Ctr:* Geog Journ, The Library (Bibliographical Soc). *s.s:* Hist of Exploration, Hist of Cartography, Watermarks in Old Paper. *Rec:* Gardening, pile rug making. *a:* Briarfield, Church Hill, Merstham, Surrey. *T:* 2348.

HEAWOOD, Geoffrey Leonard. *b:* Durham 1893. *e:* Wells House Malvern Wells, Blundells, Wadham Coll Oxf. *m:* Norah Buchanan Inskip. *s:* 1. *d:* 1. Headmaster Cheltenham Gr School. *Publ:* Religion in School. *a:* Red Gables, Charlton Lane, Cheltenham. *T:* 2453.

HEAWOOD, Percy John, HonD.C.L. Prof of Maths Durham Univ. *c.t:* Proc Lon Math Soc & other math & theo journs. *a:* High Close, Durham.

HEBBLETHWAITE, Dr. A. G., D.S.O. Lt-Col R.A.M.C. (Ret). Hon Consulting Surgeon Keighley Victoria Hosp. *a:* Westworth, Seascale, Cumberland.

HEBER, Adolph Reeve. *b:* London 1883. *e:* Silesia Col Barnet, Württemberg & Univ of Bristol. *m:* Kathleen Mary Cole. *s:* 1. *d:* 2. Physician and Surgeon. *Publ:* In Himalayan Thibet. *c.t:* Lancet. Gold Medallist Univ of Bristol. *Rec:* Golf & tennis. *a:* St Agnes, Caterham-on-the-Hill, Surrey. *t:* 77.

HEBERDEN, Doris Irene (Doris Thompson). *b:* Durban, S.A. *e:* Johannesburg. *m:* Reginald Fitzgeorge Heberden. *s:* 1. *Publ:* Foolish Fire; Come Into the Sun; Youth's Manuscript; Joy Cometh; The House of Concorde. *c.t:* The Star, Rand Daily Mail, The Outspan and Woman's magazines. *s.s:* Romantic stories of domestic life. *Rec:* Golf, tennis. *c:* Country Club, Johannesburg. *a:* Eldorado Estate, Duivelskloof, N. Transvaal, S. Africa. *t:* 402.

HEBERT, Rev. Arthur Gabriel, M.A. *b:* Silloth 1886. *e:* Harrow & New Coll Oxf. Tutor Kelham Theo Coll- *Publ:* Intercommunion; Liturgy & Society (Ed); The Parish Communion; The Throne of David; The Form of the Church; Scripture & the Faith; The Authority of the Old Testament. *a:* House of the Sacred Mission, Kelham, Newark, Notts.

HECHT, Charles E., M.A., HonM.C.A. Hon Sec Food Educ Soc. *Publ:* Ed The Gateway to Health; Rearing an Imperial Race; etc. *a:* c/o The Food Education Soc, 29 Gordon Sq, W.C.1.

HECKER, Julius F., PhD. Author. *Publ:* Russian Sociology; Moscow Dialogues; Religion & Communism. *a:* c/o Chapman & Hall Ltd, Henrietta St, W.C.2.

HECKSTALL-SMITH, Major Brooke. *b:* Hove 1869. Married. *s:* 1. *d:* 1. Journalist. *n.a:* Yachting Ed Field 1900–28, Yachting Corr Daily Telegraph '28–, Ed Yachting World '29–. Sec Yacht Racing Assoc '06–. Sec Internat Yacht Racing Un. *Publ:* Manual of Yacht & Boat Sailing & Yacht Architecture (9th, 10th & 11th edns); The Complete Yachtsman (6 edns); The Helmsman's Handbook; The Rule of the Road in Yacht Racing; Britannia & Her Contemporaries; Yacht Racing: a Text Book on the Sport (2 edns) the standard work on the rules of yacht racing, dedicated to H.M. the King, by permission; etc. *c.t:* Daily Telegraph, Yachting World. *s.s:* Yachting. Proposed the foundation of an Internat Un of Nations to consolidate the Yacht Measurement Rules & Racing Rules of all nations. Internat Yacht Racing Un formed Lon & Paris at Confs held in '06–07. 21 Nations now belong to it. In '30 in N.Y. with W. N. Clark-Neill acted as repres of G.B. & reached an agreement with Amer Yachtsmen of the N.Y. Yacht Club whereby uniform Rules of Yacht Racing were attained between European nations & America. Agreement consolidated complete friendliness between Yachting Nations. *Rec:* Angling, shooting. *c:* Roy Victoria, R.T.Y.C., etc. Late R.A.S.C. & R.A.M.C.(T.). *a:* Rowlands Manor, St Mary Cray, Kent. *t:* Orpington 176.

HEDDERWICK, Arthur Stuart, B.A., LL.B. *b:* Glasgow 1885. *e:* Rossall Sc & Cam & Glas Univs. *m:* Vera Sophia Elizabeth MacBrayne. Advocate (Scottish Bar). *n.a:* Editor Glasgow Evening Citizen 1922—. War Service 1914—19 (Des twice). *Rec:* Yachting. *c:* R. Scottish A.C. *a:* Citizen Office, St Vincent Place, Glasgow. *t:* 7000 Central.

HEDDLE, Eric William Masson, M.C., M.A., B.Sc., A.R.P.S., F.R.S.A. *b:* Laurencekirk, Kincardineshire. *e:* The Acad Hamilton & Univs of Glasgow & London. *m:* Winifred Mary Orr, B.Sc. *s:* 1. Senior Lecturer in Physics. *n.a:* Ed The Science Mag Glas Univ. *Ctr:* Various scientific & popular journs. *s.s:* Photography, Visual Aids to Education, Film Strips, Broadcasting. *Rec:* Swimming, tennis, golf, photography. *a:* 20 Danehurst Gdns, Ilford, Essex, & S.E. Essex; Technical College, Dagenham. *T:* Seven Kings 3766.

HEDDLE, William. *n.a:* Ed Bulletin & Scots Pictorial. *a:* 65 Buchanan St, Glas, C.1.

HEDDY, W. R. H., M.R.C.S., L.R.C.P., D.P.H. Barrister at Law. *c.t:* Various. *a:* Public Health Department, Middlesex Guildhall, Westminster.

HEDGCOCK, Frank Arthur, M.A. *b:* Brighton 1875. *e:* Brighton Hgh Sch & Gr Sch, Paris Univ. *m:* Georgette De Mendiri. *s:* 2. Former Insp of Modern Langs, L.C.C. Lect at Paris & Birmingham Univs. *Publ:* Thomas Hardy, Penseur et Artiste; David Garrick & His French Friends; Active French Course; Le Chemin du Français; Modern Constructive French; L'Année Française et Vacances Françaises; La Gerbe D'Or. *Ctr:* Revue Francaise, Times Educ Supp, Modern Langs, etc. *s.s:* Modern Langs. *Rec:* Bridge, billiards. *a:* 21 Onslow Ct, East Worthing, Sussex. *T:* Worthing 3199.

HEDGES, F. A. Mitchell, F.L.S., F.R.G.S., F.Z.S. Author. *Publ:* Battles with Giant Fish;

Land of Wonder & Fear; The White Tiger. *a*: c/o G. Duckworth & Co Ltd, 3 Henrietta St, W.C.2.

HEDGES, John. *b*: Aston Abbotts. *e*: Hayes. Married. *s*: 3. *d*: 1. *c.t*: Various n/p's. *s.s*: Agric. *a*: Ditton Mt, Ditton Ct Rd, Westcliff-on-Sea, Essex, & Stockall, Stewkley, Bucks.

HEDGES, Killingworth, M.I.C.E. *b*: Streatham. *m*: Ivy Frances Hewetson. *s*: 1. Civil Eng. Hon Sec The Lightning Research Cmt 1908–10. Jt Author with Sir Oliver Lodge of Cmt's Rules. With Sir John Gavey, started the collection of early Elec Lighting Generators & appliances now exhib at Science Museum. S. Kensington. *Publ*: Improved Street Lighting; Gas v. The Electric Light; American Electric Street Railways; Modern Lighting Conductors; etc. *c.t*: Brit Assoc, Engineer, Elec Review, Inst of Civil Eng's. *s.s*: Protection of Bldgs from Lightning. Asst Eng for Construction of Denver & Rio Grande Rly, designed the Aerated Bread Coy's plant, suggested the first teashop, opened 1878. Dir Lambeth Waterworks until taken over by the Metro Water Bd. Cons Eng for installation of air to earth system of Lightning Conductors at St Paul's Cath, & Westminster Abbey '90–. *a*: St Stephen's Club, Westminster, S.W.1.

HEDGES, Robert Yorke, LL.D. *b*: Manchester 1903. *e*: Victoria Univ Manchester, Harvard Univ & Inst of Internat Studies Geneva. Chief Justice of Sarawak, Prof of Law Univ of Queensland 1936—45. *Publ*: International Organisation; Law Relating to Restraint of Trade; Legal History of Trade Unionism (collab). *Ctr*: British Year Book & American Journ of International Law. *s.s*: Law, International Affairs. *Rec*: Travel. *a*: Chief Justice's Chambers, Kuching, Sarawak. *T*: Kuching 196.

HEDGES, Sidney George. *b*: Bicester 1897. *e*: Elem. *m*: Mary Dixon. *s*: 1. Author. *Publ*: Over 80 books on Swimming, Games, Youth Club Work, also Juvenile Tales & Novels. *Ctr*: Leading English & American journals. *Rec*: Swimming, travel, Sunday Sch work, skating, music. *c*: Authors. *a*: Rialto, Buckingham Rd, Bicester, Oxon.

HEDIN, Sven Anders, B.A.(Uppsala), Ph.D.(Halle), Hon.M.D., Hon.LL.D. *b*: Stockholm 1865. Explorer, Mem many Scientific Acads & Socs, Scientific Expeditions Persia, Khorasan & Turkestan, Central Asia, Tibet, Gobi Desert, etc. *Publ*: Through Asia; Central Asia & Tibet; Overland to India; From Pole to Pole; Bagdad, Babylon, Ninive; Till Jerusalem; Southern Tibet; Mount Everest; Across the Gobi Desert; Jehol, City of Emperors; A Conquest of Tibet; My Life as an Explorer; The Silk Road; The Wandering Lake; Chiang Kai-shek; History of the Expedition in Asia 1927—35; etc. *a*: Statens Etnografiska Museum, Stockholm, 0.

HEDLEY, John Prescott, F.R.S.M. *b*: Middlesbrough 1876. *e*: Uppingham Sc, King's Col Cam, St Thomas's Hosp. *m*: Kathleen Halliday. *s*: 5. *d*: 1 Prof. Obstetric Physician. *c.t*: B.M.J., Journal of Obstetrics & Gynæcology, Lancet, etc. *s.s*: Obstetrics & gynæcology. Fell Med Soc Lon. *a*: 65 Harley St, W.1. *t*: Langham 3432.

HEDWORTH, Barbara. *b*: London 1904. *e*: Roermond Holland. *m*: Cedric Pearson. Novelist & Journalist. *Publ*: Just being a Woman; After September; Husband to Aima; A Love was Born; Jewelled Heels; Prelude to Happiness; The Song Goes On; The Women in Possession. *Ctr*: Ev News, Dly Herald, Dly Mirror, Dly Sketch, princ women's mags. *Rec*: Theatre, cinema, reading. *a*: Florodora, Hassacks, Sussex. *T*: 556.

HEDWORTH-WHITTY, Reginald George, M.A.(Lond), Ph.D.(Lond), F.R.Hist.S. *b*: Wimbledon 1899. *e*: Rutlish Sch Merton, King's Coll Lond. *m*: Olyve Ruth

Wells. *s*: 1. *Publ*: The Court of Taunton. *s.s*: Local History. *Rec*: Swimming, music, etc. *a*: Thone, Staplegrove Rd, Taunton, Somerset. *T*: 3804.

HEEKES, John William. Surgeon. *c.t*: B.M.J. *a*: Grange Corner, Church Rd, Barnes, S.W.13. *t*: Riverside 0325.

HEELEY, Maureen. Author. *Publ*: Flame of the Desert; The Isle of Revenge; The Desert of Lies; Favourites Sometimes Win. *a*: c/o Mills & Boon, 50 Grafton St, W.1.

HEFFER, E. W. *s.s*: Higher education. *a*: c/o W. Heffer & Sons Ltd, 3/4 Petty Cury, Cambridge.

HEFFERMAN, Leslie William, M.D., F.R.C.S., D.R.C.O.G. *b*: 1895. *e*: Epsom Coll & Middx Hosp Med Sch Lond. *m*: Bronwen Evans. *s*: 1. *d*: 4. Asst Commsn St John's Ambulance Brig Swansea. *Ctr*: Medical World, Brit Med Journ, Indian Med Gaz. *s.s*: Domiciliary Obstetrics. *Rec*: Tennis, swimming, motoring. *w.s*: Border Regt 1914—18. *a*: Granville Hse, 1 Ysgol St, St Thomas, Swansea, Glam. *T*: Swansea 3560.

HEFFERNAN, Patrick, M.D. *b*: Cuckoo Hill, Tipperary 1878. *e*: Rockwell, Blackrock & U.C.D. *m*: Winifred Wakefield. *s*: 2. I.M.S. Major (ret), former R.M.O. 1st Bengal Lancers. *Publ*: The Heffernans & Their Times; Random Rhymes; The Indian Lunacy Manual. *Ctr*: B.M.J., Public Health, Discovery, The Field, Indian Med Gazette, Tubercle, etc. *s.s*: Industrial Diseases of the Chest, Irish Local & Family History, Anglo-Irish & Irish-American Verse. *Rec*: Rugby football, cricket, lawn tennis, jackal hunting, polo, etc. *a*: Hop Garden Ct, Westgate, Chichester, Sussex. *T*: Eastergate 264.

HEGLAND, Martin, M.A., Ph.D. *b*: Steele Co Minn 1880. *e*: St Olaf Coll, Univ of Minnesota, Columb Univ. *m*: Georgina E. Dieson. *d*: 1. Teaching at St Olaf Coll. *n.a*: Ed various Coll & Church publs. *Publ*: The Danish Peoples High School; The Secrets of a Happy Life; Things That See; Walking With God; Problems of Young Christians; Aspirations: Getting Acquainted With the Bible; In the Holy Land (with G. Dieson); For His Name's Sake. *s.s*: Religion & Education. *Rec*: Gardening, motoring. *a*: 1114 St Olaf Ave, Northfield, Minn, U.S.A. *T*: 293 L.

HEHIR, Maj.-Gen. Sir Patrick, M.D., F.R.C.P.E., F.R.C.S.E., F.R.S.E., D.P.H. (Cantab), D.T.M.(Liv Univ), K.C.I.E., C.B., C.M.G. *b*: Templemore, Ireland 1859. *e*: India, Guy's Hosp Lon & Edin. Married. *d*: 1. I.M.S. (ret). *Publ*: Malaria in India; Medical Jurisprudence for India (6 edns with J. D. B. Gribble, I.C.S.); Hygiene & Diseases of India (3 edns); Sanitation for Indian Schools (3 edns); etc. *c.t*: Lancet, B.M.J., Indian Med Gazette, Pioneer (India), etc. *s.s*: Malaria, mil med admin. 7 campaigns Gt War, 1914 Star, Victory Medal, G.S. Medal, etc. Afghan War '19; wounded. I.G.S. Medal. 7 times Des. Kt St John of Jerusalem '15, Life Saving Medal St John of Jerusalem '05. Med Adv B.R.C.S. Greece, Macedonian '23. Delhi Durbar Medals '02, '11. *a*: 2a, Brunswick Pl, Hove, Sussex. *t*: 5375.

HEIGHWAY, Arthur James. *b*: Gerringong, N.S.W. Australia. *e*: Otago Univ & London Sch of Econ. Journalist. *n.a*: Ed World's Press News 1940—, Founder-Ed N Z. Dairy Exporter 1925—33 & N.Z. Radio Record '26—40. *Publ*: Inky Way Annual. *Ctr*: B.B.C. *s.s*: Empire Development & Press Activities. *Rec*: Philately. *a*: World's Press News, 20 Tudor St, London, E.C.4. *T*: Central 4040.

HEIJERMANS, LOUIS: director health department; b. Rotterdam, Holland; s. Herman Heyermons and Mathilda M. (Spiers) H.; educ. Lyceum; Univ. (Amsterdam). DEGREES: M.D.; m. Maria Bastiana Filaroki, Dec. 12, 1902. AUTHOR: Hygiene for labourer (Dutch); Communal hygiene (Dutch); A series of articles in the daily press, medical reviews, etc. Instructor at the Univ. of Amsterdam. General character of writing: scientific and popular books, and articles on social hygiene. OFFICE: N. Achtergraeut 100. HOME: Lomanstraat, Amsterdam, Holland.

HEILBRON, Sir Ian Morris, Kt., D.S.O., D.Sc., LL.D., F.R.S. b: Glasgow 1886. e: High Sch Glas, Roy Tech Coll Glas, Leipzig Univ. m: Elda Marguerite Davis. s: 2. Prof Organic Chemistry Univ Lond, Ed-in-Chief Dictionary of Organic Compounds, Chm Editorial Board Thorpe's Dictionary of Applied Chemistry. Ctr: Various chemical journals. s.s: Scientific. w.s: World War I, Greek Order of the Redeemer, Medaille d'honneur. Rec: Golf, music. c: Athenæum, Liphook Golf. a: 145 Oakwood Ct, London, W.14.

HEILSKOV, Christian Petersen. b: Gerslev, Sealand 1873. e: Univ of Copenhagen. m: (1) Frida Sophie Schmidt, (2) Sigrid Ebba Johanne Holmstrom, (3) Gerda Vera Johanne Heimann. d: 2. Librarian (ret). n.a: Ed Dimmalaetting 1901—02, Esperanto Raporto '17—18, Theosophia '23—27. Publ: Dansk Provinstopografi; Baelum sogn gennem syv sekler, Aalborg; Life & Works of Hans Christian Andersen; From Skaw to Skallingen; Memorial Leaves of Gerhard Faye, Prefect & Poet; Northern Names. Ctr: Jydske Samlinger, Fra Randers Amt, Fra Viborg Amt, Berlingske Tidende, Nationaltidende, etc. s.s: Historical Topography & Personal History of Denmark. a: Addit, Denmark.

HEIMANN, Franz Anton, M.D., L.R.C.P.&S.E., L.R.F.P.S.G. b: Katowice 1898. e: Gr Sch Breslau, Univs of Breslau & Munich, Med Sch St George's Hosp Lond. m: Susanne Besson. Publ: Deutsche Kinderfibel. Ctr: Times Educ Supp, B.M.J., Fabian Quarterly, etc. s.s: Serology-Bacteriology, Infectious Diseases, Social Medicine. Rec: Walking. a: 436 Christchurch Rd, Bournemouth. T: Boscombe 2419.

HEIMANN, Heidi, Ph.D. b: Berlin. e: Westend Gym Berlin, Univs of Freiburg, Berlin, Bonn & Hamburg. Journalist & Research Worker, formerly Lect in Mediæval Art, Sorbonne Paris, Mem Brit Fed Univ Women. n.a: Picture Post 1944—. Ctr: Journ of Warburg Inst, Lilliput, Burlington Mag, etc. s.s: Hist of Art. Rec: Music, walking. a: 28 Westmorland Rd, Barnes, London, S.W.13. T: Riverside 4956.

HEINRICH, Herbert William. b: Bennington, Vermont, U.S.A., 1886. e: Pub scs and private tuition. m Virginia E. King. d: 1. Insurance engineer. Publ: Industrial Accident Prevention —A Scientific Approach. c.t: Travellers Standard & Protection, National Safety News, Safety Engineering, The Eastern Underwriter. s.s: Accident prevention, industrial, traffic and home. Rec Golf. War service in U.S. Navy. c: Mem A.I.E.E., American Welding Soc, Underwriters Laboratories, Hartford Engineers Club. a: 819 Burnside Ave, East Hartford, Conn, U.S.A. t: East Hartford 8—4250.

HEITLAND, Margaret, F.J.I. b: Cam 1860. e: Highfield Sc Hendon & Heidelberg. m: W. E. Heitland, M.A. Journalist (ret). n.a: Many years Ed Women's Employment Dept of the Queen N/p until 1919. Publ: Professional Women Upon their Professions. c.t: Various n/ps & periodicals. s.s: The polit & econ position of women. a: Carmefield, Wordsworth Grove, Cambridge.

HEITNER, Jesse. b: Long Buckby 1898. Journalist. n.a: Editor Sphere, Britannia & Eve, Dir British National Newsps Ltd. Ctr: Tatler, Sphere, etc. Rec: Chess, flying, book-binding. c: Devonshire. a: 21 Carlisle Mans, London, S.W.1, & 1 New Oxford St, London, W.C.1. T: Victoria 1932, & Holborn 6955.

HELE, John Warwick, M.R.C.S., L.R.C.P., L.D.S.(Eng), J.P., T.D. Dental Surg. c.t: Brit Dental Journ, etc. a: 11 Portland Sq, Carlisle. t: 26.

HELLEWELL, Richard Alexander, M.R.S.L. b: Bradford 1895. e: Hanson High Sch Bradford, Sheffield City Coll. Ctr: Spectator, Sun Times, Notes & Queries, Travel Log (W.T.A.) & local press. s.s: Bibliography, Bibliophily, French & English Lit. Rec: Reading & research, travelling. a: 3 Greenhill St, Bradford.

HELLIER, Francis Findlay, M.A., M.D., M.R.C.P. Physician. n.a: Co-Ed Leeds Univ Medical Mag 1933—. c.t: Lancet, Brit Journ of Pathology, etc. a: 5 Bank View, Stainbeck Lane, Leeds. t: 41380.

HELLMAN, Geoffrey Theodore. b: New York City 1907. e: Taft Sch, Yale. m: Daphne Van Beuren Bayne. d: 1. Writer, Assoc Historian Office of Strategic Services 1944—45. n.a: Staff Writer The New Yorker Mag. Publ: How to Disappear for an Hour. Ctr: The New Yorker, Life Mag, Fortune Mag, Promenade Mag, Sat Review of Lit, etc. s.s: Biography, Satire. Rec: Amateur lepidopterist. c: Yale, Dutch Treat, Coffee House, P.E.N., Nat Press, etc. a: 228 East 61 St, New York City.

HELLMAN, George Sidney, M.A. b: New York City 1878. e: Columb Univ. m: (1) Hilda E. Josephthal, (2) Irene Schuman. s: 1. d: 1. Author, former Staff Reviewer N.Y. Times & The Bookman. Publ: Peacock Feather; Washington Irving Esquire; The True Stevenson; The Hudson & Other Poems; Benjamin A. Cardozo, American Judge; Persian Conqueror; Lane of Memory; Original Drawings of the Old Masters. Ctr: Atlantic Monthly, Harper's, Century, Sat Ev Post, The Nation, N.Y. Times, N.Y. Herald Tribune, etc. s.s: Unpublished Writings of Famous Authors. Rec: Reading, cards, tennis, swimming. a: Monsey, N.Y., U.S.A. T: Suffern 764.

HELLMAN, Lillian. b: New Orleans 1905. e: Univs of New York & Columbia. Writer. Publ: The Children's Hour; Days to Come; Watch on the Rhine; The Little Foxes; The Searching Wind; Another Part of the Forest (Plays); Plays adapted for motion pictures: The Dark Angel; These Three; Dead End; The North Star; The Little Foxes. Ctr: Various. a: Hardscrabble Farm, Pleasantville, New York, U.S.A.

HELM, John Richard. b: Scarboro' 1913. e: Scarboro' Boys' H.S. Reporter. n.a: Scarboro' Evening News & Mercury '29. c.t: Yorkshire Evening Post (golf notes). s.s: Golf. Rec: Golf, tennis, skating. c: Scarboro' North Cliff Golf. a: 197 Prospect Rd, Scarboro'.

HELM, William Henry. b: Worcester 1860. e: Bradfield Col. m: Ada Emmeline Physick. s: 1. d: 1. Author, Journalist & Lecturer. n.a: Lit Ed Morning Post 1889-1906. Asst Ed 1906-10. Publ: Studies in Style ('00); The Blue Fox; Vigée-Lebrun; Homes of the Past ('21); etc. Rec: Outdoor life. c: Authors'. a: Northanger, Felixstowe. t: 288.

HELME, Eleanor E. b: Cobham 1887. e: Priv. Jnlst & author of children's books. n.a: Woman Golf correspondent Morning Post '19. Golf Ed Bystander '32. Tatler, Britannia & Eve. Publ: Down the Stream; Five Thorns Farm; The Perfect Friend (a children's life of Christ). Jt with Nance Paul:—Jerry; The Joker; Seek There; Roddy, Scuttle. c.t: Sporting & Dramatic, Yorkshire Post, etc. s.s: Women's golf, children's books. Rec: Riding, sketching. Semi Finalist in Ladies' Open Golf Championship '24. Played golf for England '11, '12, '13, '20. *c*: Women's Automobile & Sports Assoc, F.Z.S. *a*: 20 Kensington Gardens Sq, W.2. *t*: Bayswater 4150.

HELMORE, William, C.B.E., Ph.D., M.Sc.(Cantab), F.C.S., F.R.Ae.S. *b*: 1894. *e*: Blundell's Sch, R.M.A. Woolwich, Christ's Coll Camb. *m*: Enid Sylvia Capes. Hon Air Commodore (R.A.F.), Dir-Gen Aluminium Dev Assoc, Dir C. C. Wakefield & Co Ltd, MP (C) Watford Div of Herts 1943—45, Asst Sci Adviser Chief of Air Staff '39, Tech Adviser Min of Aircraft Production '41—45, Broadcaster on R.A.F. and Official air events since '26. *Publ*: Cavalry of the Air; Air Commentary; Numerous sci works on fuels, engines & aeronautical subjects. *Rec*: Fishing, sailing. *c*: Athenæun, R.A.F. *w.s*: R.F.C. 1916, later with R.A.F., R.A.F. War Commentator '41—43. *a*: Shotover, Coombe Lane, Kingston Hill, Surrey.

HELSBY, Richard Gordon. *b*: Denbigh 1894. *e*: Ruthin G.S. *m*: Dorothea Palmer. Journalist. *n.a*: Daily Express (London) Crime Reporter, Asst Ed Northern Edition Daily Express M/C, Northern News Ed Daily Mail, Assoc Ed Daily Herald. *Rec*: Tennis. *a*: York House, Queen's Rd, Teddington, Middlesex. *t*: Molesey 1809.

HELSTROM, Erik Gustaf, M.A., Hon.Ph.D. *b*: Kristianstad 1882. *e*: Univ of Lund. *m*: Britt Helen. Author. *n.a*: Foreign Corr Dagens Nyheter London 1907—10 & '27—35, Paris '10—19 & U.S.A. '19—22. *Publ*: Snormakare Lekholmhar Enide; Carl Heribrert Malmos; Storm over Tjuro; En Man Utanhumor; Kustar; Ett Rekommendationsbrev; Kring en Kvinna; Fren Redingot till Kavaj Kojyym. *Ctr*: Dagens Vyheter, etc. *Rec*: Walking. *a*: Eriksbergsgatan 5, Stockholm, Sweden. *T*: 20-46-99.

HELTBERG, Grethe, M.A. *b*: Horsens, Jutland 1911. *m*: Niels Heltberg. *s*: 1. *d*: 1. Shorthand Writer in the Parliament 1930—40, Mem Danish Soc of Authors. *Publ*: Testament; Portrait of a Girl; Death & Spring; Eternal Fire; A Gentleman Arrived & Left; Cauli's Love; Purple Darkness. *Ctr*: Politiken, Nationaltidende, Berlingske Tidende, Aarhuus Stiftstidende, etc. *s.s*: Modern Psychology, Sociology. *Rec*: Reading, music, theatre, travel. *a*: C. F. Richsvej 122, Copenhagen, Denmark. *T*: Godthaab 4935.

HEMING, Jack. *m*: Eileen Marsh. *s*: 3. *d*: 2. *n.a*: Mang-Ed Jersey Morning News. *Publ*: The Scoop (Play 1933, Film '34); Air Spies; Voyage of the Dauntless; Air Treasure Hunt; etc. *s.s*: B.B.C. Plays & Talks, Articles & Sport. *Rec*: Flying, sailing, motoring. *c*: Press. *w.s*: R.N.A.S. 1914—18, R.N.V.R. (Comdr) '39—45. *a*: Le Petit Jardin, St Mary, Jersey, C.I. *T*: St Peter 122.

HEMINGWAY, Ernest. *Publ*: inc For Whom the Bell Tolls; To Have & Have Not; Fiesta; A Farewell to Arms; etc. *a*: 4-Place de la Concorde, Paris.

HEMINGWAY REES, Mary Isabel, M.B., ChB. (Edin), M.R.C.S., L.R.C.P. *b*: Melton Mowbray. *e*: Cheltenham Ladies Col, Edin, Glas & Birm Univs. *m*: John Rawlings Rees, M.A., M.D., D.P.H. *d*: 1. *c.t*: Nursing Mirror. *s.s*: Psychotherapy. *Rec*: Nature study, travel. *c*: Pioneer, B.M.A., Med Women's Fed, Brit Psychological Soc. *a*: 14 Wimpole St, W.1. *t*: Langham 4064.

HEMMERDE, Edward George, K.C. *b*: Teckham 1871. *e*: Winchester & Univ Coll Oxf. *m*: Lucy Elinor Colley. *d*: 1. Recorder of L'pool 1909—, M.P. (L) East Denbighs '06—10, N.W. Norfolk '12—18, M.P. (Lab) Crewe Div of Cheshire '22—24. *Publ*: (Plays) A Butterfly on the Wheel (in collab); Proud Maisie; The Cardinal's Romance; etc. *Rec*: Travel, music. *a*: 1 Hare Ct, Temple, London. E.C.4. *T*: Central 4640.

HEMMING, Francis, C.B.E. *Publ*: The Generic Names of the British Rhopalocera. *c.t*: Trans Roy Ent Soc of Lon, Stylops, Annals & Mag of Nat Hist, The Entomologist, etc. *a*: 18 Glebe Pl, S.W.3.

HEMMINGWAY, Henry Cartwright. *b*: Sheffield 1858. *n.a*: Weekly Post Sheff 1873, Jr Rep Sheffield Daily Telegraph '75 connection still retained, also Yorks Telegraph & Star other publ of firm, dist office of Sheffield Telegraph Retford, '79, etc. 60 y n/p work. Original mem of I.J., Fellow '98. Ret 1930 receiving due commendation for service, etc. *Rec*: Photography *a*: 12 Tooker Rd, Rotherham.

HEMSTED, Dr. E. S., *a*: Notrees, Kintbury, Newbury, Berks.

HENDERSON, Rev. Alexander. *b*: Coldstream 1865. *e*: Berwick Gr Sch, Gregorian Univ, Rome. *m*: Mary Frances Waugh. *d*: 1. Clerk in Holy Orders. *Publ*: A Ladder of Meditation & Devotion; The Lesson of the Catacombs; Sketches of Primitive Christianity; The Wheel of Life; A Study of Palingenesis; A Historical Survey of Christian Missions (pt author); Pagan & Christian Symbols; Wanted—A Philosophy. *Ctr*: Churchman, Mod Churchman, Eastern Dly Press, Theology, etc. *s.s*: Philosophy, Theology. *a*: 3 Kimbolton Ave, Bedford.

HENDERSON, Alexander John. *b*: Romford 1910 *e*: Univ Col Sc & Lon Univ. Journalist. *n.a*: Foreign Sub-Ed Reuters, Ltd 1930. Mem N.U.J. '30—. *Publ*: Founder & Ed '32, of David: An Internat Review of Politics & Lit. *s.s*: Foreign Affairs, especially Jugoslavia & the Balkans. Chm Lon Young P.E.N. Club. Del to Eleventh Internat Congress of P.E.N. Club at Dubrovnik, Jugoslavia '33. *c*: P.E.N. *a*: 5 Guilford St, W.C.1. *t*: Holborn 3285.

HENDERSON, Rt. Hon. Arthur, P.C., K.C., M.A., LL.B. *b*: Newcastle-on-Tyne 1893. *e*: Cent Sch Darlington, Queen's Coll Taunton, Trinity Hall Camb. Minister of State, Commonwealth Relations, M.P. (Lab) Kingswinford Div of Staffs since 1935, M.P. Cardiff S. '23—24 & '29—31, Parl Priv Sec to H.M. Attorney-Gen '29—31, Joint Parl Under-Sec of State for War '42, Financial Sec to War Office Feb '43—May '45, Parl Under Sec of State for India & Burma Aug '45—47. *Publ*: Trade Unions & the Law; (Jtly) Industrial Law; Housing Law. *a*: 402 Collingwood Hse, Dolphin Sq, London S.W.1, & 6 Pump Court, Temple, London, E.C.4. *T*: Victoria 3800 & Central 6187.

HENDERSON, Arthur Edward, F.S.A., F.R.I.B.A., R.B.A. *b*: Aberdeen. *e*: Aberdeen. *m*: Susanna More. *s*: 1. Architect & Artist. *Publ*: Chapters & Drawings in Excavation at Ephesus, Brit Museum; Then & Now Series; Abbeys, Tintern, Glastonbury, Melrose, Fountains, Westminster, some Yorkshire Abbeys, etc., St Paul's Cathedral, Canterbury Cathedral. *Ctr*: Builder, Country Life, Ill Lond News, Sphere, etc. *a*: The Rosery, Crawley Down, Sussex. *T*: Copthorne 258.

HENDERSON, Bernard Lionel Kinghorn, M.A., D.Lit(Lon). *b*: Hornsey 1873. *e*: Sir George Monoux G.S. King's Col & Lon Sc of Econ. Lect & Examiner in English. *Publ*: Series of Folk-Lore Tales; The English Way; A Mirror of English; Monographs on Romney & Morland; Days of History; A Guide to Correspondence for Bankers and other Business Men; Schoolmasters All, or Thirty Years Hard; Schoolboys of Other Days; etc. *s.s*: English. *Rec*: Golf, tennis, swimming. *c*: Authors'. *a*: Spinney Cottage, Balcombe Rd, Horley, Surrey. *t*: 205.

HENDERSON, Daniel MacIntyre. *b*: Baltimore, Md. 1880. *e*: Public Schs. *m*: Ernestine Rauch. *d*: 1. Author & Editor. *n.a*: McClure's Mag 1915—21, N.Y.

Ev Post '21—22, McClure's Mag & People's Home Journ '22—24, Hearst Mags since '24. *Publ*: Frontiers; From the Volga to the Yukon; Yankee Ships in China Seas; A Crown for Carlotta; The Crimson Queen; A Harp in the Wind; Life's Minstrel; Children of the Tide; Reveille (Ed). *Ctr*: Sat Rev of Literature, Harper's Mag, Sat Ev Post, Good Housekeeping, Poetry Rev of London. *s.s*: Biography, History. *Rec*: Farm life, travel, reading. *c*: Coffee House, Authors. *a*: 333 West 57 St., New York 19, New York. *T*: CI 6-6721.

HENDERSON, David, D.D., M.R.S.L. *b*: Glasgow 1874. *e*: Tech Coll, Bible Training Inst, Glasgow Trin & Baptist Colls Dublin. *m*: Elizabeth Gaston. Baptist Minister, Tutor in the Baptist Bible Sch on Homiletics, Ex-Pres Baptist Union of Ireland. *Publ*: A Well Furnished Life; The Bible & Science; Notable Utterances of Great Men; Life at its Best. *Rec*: Reading. *a*: 59 South Parade, Belfast.

HENDERSON, David Kennedy. *b*: Dumfries 1884. *e*: Dumfries Acad, Roy H Sch Edin, Edin Univ, New York, Baltimore, Munich. *m*: Margaret Mabon. *d*: 3. Professor of Psychiatry Edin Univ, Physician-Superintendent Roy Edin Hosp for Nervous and Mental Diseases. *Publ*: Text Book of Psychiatry (with late R. D. Gillespie); Psychopathic States. *s.s*: Psychiatry. *Rec*: Tennis, fishing. *c*: Univ Edin, Union Lond. *a*: Tipperlinn Hse, Edinburgh, Scotland. *T*: 51391.

HENDERSON, E. L. & W. T. G. Experts in Oriental Works of Art. *c.t*: Antique Collector, Apollo, Connoisseur, Bazaar. *s.s*: Japanese & Chinese Art. Pen names, Pat Graham, Esther McLees & Esther Henderson. *a*: Aviemore, 55 Holmdene Av, N. Harrow, Middx.

HENDERSON, GEORGE COCKBURN: emeritus professor of history; b. Hamilton, New South Wales, May 1, 1870; *s*. Richard Turnbull and Annie (Robinson) H.; educ. Univ. Sydney (N. S. W.), Balliol Coll. (Oxford); DEGREES: M.A. (Oxford), B.A. (Sydney); m. 1922. AUTHOR: Sir George Grey, Pioneer of Empire in Southern Lands, 1904; Reflections on the War, 1914; The British Navy at War, 1916; Fiji and the Fijians, 1931. General character of writing: historical. essays. Professor History, Adelaide (S. Australia), 1902-24; founder Archives of S. Australia; at present engaged in research into early history Fijan Archipelago. CLUBS: Authors, British Empire (London), Adelaide (S. Australia). OFFICE: Mitchell Library, Sydney. HOME: Anelstom, Dora Creek, New South Wales.

HENDERSON, Col. Harry Dalton, C.B., D.S.O., V.D., T.D., D.L. Civil Servant (ret). *n.a*: Scot Corr The Record 1893-1914. *Publ*: The Episcopal Church in Scotland; The Official Guide to Perth (4 edns 1924-33). *c.t*: Record, Lon Cham of Comm Journ, Scot Country Life, Glas Weekly Herald, Perthshire Advertiser. *a*: The Orchard, Perth, Scot. *t*: 617.

HENDERSON, Sir Hubert Douglas, Kt. *b*: Beckenham, Kent 1890. *e*: Aberdeen Gr Sch, Rugby Sch, Emmanuel Coll Camb. *m*: Faith Bagenal. *s*: 1. *d*: 2. Professor of Political Economy Oxf Univ, Mem West India Roy Commission 1938—39, Economic Adviser to H.M Treasury '40—44, Chm of Roy Commission on Population '44. *n.a*: Ed the Nation & Athenæum '23—30. *Publ*: The Cotton Control Board; Supply & Demand. *s.s*: Economics. *a*: 5 South Parks Rd, Oxford. *T*: 2862.

HENDERSON, Prof. Sir J. B., D.Sc., LL.D., M.I.E.E., F.I.P., AssocI.N.A. *b*: Glas 1871. *e*: Glas & Berlin Univs. *m*: Annie Margaret Henderson. Engineer & Physicist. *Publ*: Transactions of the Institutions of Electrical Engineers & Naval Archs; Philos Proceedings of R.S. *s.s*: Gunnery & gyroscopics. Order of Sacred Treasure of Japan. Lecturer on Electrical Eng Glas Univ 1901-05, Prof of Applied Mech R.N. C. Gwich '05-20, Adviser to Admiralty on gyroscopic equipment '20-25. Inv improvements in Gunnery in Brit Navy, *Rec*: Golf, skating, hunting. *c*: R.A.C. & Roy Inst. *a*: 38 Blackheath Park, S.E.3. *t*: Lee Green 2748.

HENDERSON, James, M.A. *b*: 1889. *e*: Methodist Coll Belfast, Dublin Univ. Company Director, Delegate to Imp Press Con 1920, Pres Newspaper Soc '36—37, Pres Golfing Union of Ireland '46—47, Pres Trin Coll (Dub) Assoc of Northern Ireland since '46. *n.a*: Actg Ed Dub D Express, Belfast News Letter, Joint Man Dir Belfast News Letter since '28, Dir of Portsmouth & Sunderland Newspapers Ltd, Dir Press Assoc Ltd '35—47, Dir Reuters Ltd '36—42, Trustee Reuters Ltd *Ctr*: Belfast News Letter, Dublin D Express, Times, D Mail, Irish Life. *s.s*: Golf. *Rec*: Golf & gardening. *w.s*: R.A.S.C. World War I. *a*: 36 Windsor Park, Belfast. *T*: Belfast 67508.

HENDERSON, James Samuel. *b*: Dublin 1866. *e*: Merchant Taylors Sc. Married. *s*: 2. *d*: 1. News Ed. *n.a*: Ed-Reporter Roscommon Constitutionalist 1887, Rep Staff Waterford News, Waterford Standard, King's County Chronicle, Chief Reporter Evening Echo, Dublin '91, Reporter Staff Irish Times, Dublin Daily Express & Evening Mail, Ed Colwyn Bay Sentinel, Reporter Staff Warrington Examiner, Wharfedale Observer, Worcester Evening Echo, Burnley Express '15-24, Sub-Ed Bristol Evening News, Daily News (M/C), Derby Daily Express, News-Ed Northern Constitution, Coleraine Co Derry '24. *c.t*: Various n/ps & periodicals. *s.s*: Reviews, dramatic criticism. M.J.I. 1893-, N.U.J. 1912-. Chm N. Ireland Br N.U.J. '33, '34. *Rec*: Fishing, golf. *a*: Portstewart, N. Ireland.

HENDERSON, John, M.D., Ch.B., F.R.F.P.S.(Glas). *b*: Glasgow 1876. *e*: Allan Glen's & H Schs & Glas Univ. *m*: Jenny H. G. Martin. *s*: 1. *d*: 1. Formerly Pres of Royal Faculty of Physicians & Surgeons Glasgow. *n.a*: Part Ed Glas Med Journ. *Publ*: Handbook of Medicine; Medicine-Catechism Series. *Ctr*: B.M.J., Glas Med Journ, Amer Med Journ of Clinical Research, Nurses' League Journ, etc., etc. *Rec*: Golf. *c*: Royal Scot Auto Glas, Palette. *a*: 6 Newton Pl, Glasgow, C.3. *T*: Douglas 5035.

HENDERSON, Rev. Joseph Graham. *b*: Newcastle-on-Tyne 1861. *e*: Armstrong Sc Newcastle-on-Tyne & Cheshunt Col Cam. *m*: Emily Alice Arter. *s*: 2. *d*: 1. Congregational Minister. *n.a*. Leader-Writer for Shields Daily Gazette 1885-91, Northern Daily & Weekly Leader '85-88. *Publ*: Memoir of Rev G. H. R. Garcia. *c.t*: Christian World & Newcastle Weekly Chronicle. *s.s*: Tyneside hist. *Rec*: Tennis, cricket. *c*: Lon Missionary Soc (Dir). *a*: Spenholme, Marriott Rd, Barnet.

HENDERSON, Keith, O.B.E., R.W.S., R.S.W., R.O.I. *b*: London 1883. *e*: Marlborough & Paris. *m*: Helen Knox-Shaw. Artist & Author. *Publ*: Written & Illustrated: Burns by Himself; Prehistoric Man; Palm Groves & Humming Birds; Letters to Helen; also illustrated Conquest of Mexico; Green Mansions; etc. *a*: Coirechoille, Spean Bridge, Inverness-shire. *T*: Spean Bridge 56.

HENDERSON, Norman Percy. Consulting Radiologist. *Publ*: History of the 600 City of London Bombing Squadron. *c.t*: Times & News of the World. *a*: 7 Harley St, W.1. *t*: Langham 3430.

HENDERSON, Patrick Hagart, D.S.O., K.H.P., M.B., ChB., D.P.H. *b*: Perthshire 1876. *e*: Dollar Acad & Edin Univ. *m*: Alice Ethel Thompson. Major-Gen Army Med Services. Dir of Hygiene War Office 1930-. *c.t*: Journal of R.A.M.C., Proc Roy Soc of Med, Nat Playing Fields Journal, etc. *s.s*: Preventive medicine, physical educ. *Rec*: Hunting, golf, shooting, fishing. *c*: Army & Navy, Hurlingham, Edin Univ, Lon, & Ski Club of G.B. *a*: 50 Coleherne Ct, S.W.5. *t*: Flaxman 7836.

HENDERSON, Philip Prichard. *b*: London 1906. *e*: Bradfield. Poet & Critic. *n.a*: Asst Ed Everyman's Library 1929—31, Literary Ed New Britain '33—34, Ed British Counc Pubs Dept (Brit Book News) '43—46. *Publ*: And Morning in His Eyes; The Complete Poems of John Skelton; The Poet & Society; Emily Brontë: Selected Poems; George Crabbe: Selected Poems; First Poems; The Novel To-Day; Literature & a Changing Civilization; Events in the Early Life of Anthony Price; Various volumes in Everyman's Library. *Ctr*: Spectator, Listener, New Statesman, John O'London's Wkly, World Review, British Book News, etc. *s.s*: Elizabethan Drama, Brontë Literature, Modern Poetry. *a*: c/o Barclays Bank, 208 Regent St, London, W.1.

HENDERSON, Ralph Bushill, M.A., B.D. *b*: Coventry 1880. *e*: King Henry VIII's Sch Coventry, Bristol Gr Sch, Oxf Univ. *m*: Elizabeth Beatrice Mansfield. *s*: 1. Master Rugby Sch 1902—11, Headmaster Strand Sch '11—20, Alleyn's Sch Dulwich '20—40, Bristol Gr Sch '42 (ret). *Publ*: The Scaley Winged; The School Liturgy; Mediterranean Civilisation; The Four Witnesses; The Modern Meaning of the Bible; A Modern Handbook to the Old Testament. *Ctr*: Ch Quarterly, New Education, Inquirer & Modern Churchman, Blackwood's Mag. *s.s*: Divinity, Greek History. *Rec*: Rock-climbing & music. *w.s*: 1916—19. *a*: Prior's Close, Bradford-on-Avon. *T*: 2122.

HENDERSON, Thomas, B.Sc, F.E.I.S. *b*: Stirling. *e*: Stirling H.S. & Glas & Lon Univs. *m*: Emma Drummond. Gen Sec Educ Inst of Scot. *n.a*: Ed Scottish Educ Journ. *Publ*: Findhorn, the River of Beauty. *s.s*:—Scottish cultural subjects. *Rec*: Golf, walking. *c*: Nat Lib, Scottish Arts, Roy Scots, St Andrews Lon. *a*: 2 Hillview Terr, Corstorphine, Edin. *t*: 86379.

HENDERSON, W. E., M.A., M.B., ChB., D.P.H. *Publ*: Epidemic Poliomyelitis (article). Co M.O. Westmorland. *a*: Public Health Dept, Lowther House, Kendal.

HENDERSON-HOWAT, Rev. Rudolph, L.D. *b*: Le Vesinet, Paris 1896. *e*: St David's Coll Lampeter & Manch Univ. *m*: Agatha Mary Dorothea Cooke. *s*: 2. *d*: 1. Rector of All Souls' Invergowrie. *n.a*: Assoc-Ed Scottish Guardian 1935—39, Ed '39—. *Publ*: Co-Reviser of The Succession of the Scottish Bishops. *w.s*: King's Regt 1914—19. *a*: The Rectory, Invergowrie, by Dundee Angus. *T*: Invergowrie 245 & Dundee 4636.

HENDRICK, James, B.Sc. Strathcona Fordyce Professor of Agric, Aber Univ. *Publ*: The Farmers Raw Materials; Gen Ed Scot Series of Jnr Agric Textbooks; Sections Agric Ency, etc. *c.t*: Medical & Agric Press. *a*: Marischal Col, Aber. *t*: 1046.

HENDRY, Capt. F.C. ("Shalimar"), O.B.E., M.C. Author. *Publ*: Around the Horn & Home Again; The Yomak—& After; Four Frames; Adown the Tigris I was Borne; From All the Seas; A Windjammer's Half-Deck; One Monsoon Night; Mingled Yarn; The Peaceful Wanderer; True Tales of Sail & Steam; Sail Ho!; etc. *a*: Shalimar, Grantown-on-Spey, Scotland.

HENDRY, Harold Clifford. *e*: Private. Lecturer, actor. *Publ*: Plays:—Marriage of Inconvenience; Heaven Exploited; The Human Touch. *c.t*: Various magazines & N/p. *s.s*: English literature. Collaborates in plays with Alec Stansbury Higgs. *a*: 100a Western Rd, Hove. *t*: 4919.

HENDRY, James Findlay. *b*: Glasgow 1912. *e*: Univs of Glas, Paris & Vienna. *m*: Dorothy Stainton. *s*: 2. *d*: 1. Foreign Office. *Publ*: The Fernie Brae; The Bridal Tree; Bombed Happiness; Orchestral Mountain; Blackbird of Ospo. Ed: Scottish Short Stories; The White Horseman. *Ctr*: Life & Letters Today, Scottish Art & Letters, Poetry (Chicago), etc. *s.s*: Lit Criticism, Translations. *Rec*: Chess, music, boxing, looking at paintings. *a*: Cartcraigs Hse, Kennishead Read, Pollokshaws (West), Glasgow.

HENDRY, W.J. *b*: Rayne, Aberdeenshire 1890. P.R.O. Central Electricity Bd. *n.a*: Rep & Sub Ed Aberdeen Free Press 1908—12, Lond Office Glasgow Herald '12—33 (Parl Press Gallery '14—27). *a*: Trafalgar Bldgs, 1 Charing Cross Rd, London, S.W.1. *T*: Whitehall 2121.

HENDY, Ernest William, B.A.(Oxon). *b*: Wilts. *e*: Blundell's Sch & Balliol Coll Oxf. *m*: Hannah Mary Ramsbottom. Solictor (ret), Author & Journalist, V-Pres Devon Birdwatching & Preservation Soc, Mem Wild Birds Protection Cttee Somerset, B.B.C. Broadcaster on Bird Watching. *Publ*: The Lure of Bird Watching; Wild Exmoor Through the Year; Here & There With Birds; Selworthy & Other Poems; Somerset Birds & Some Other Folk. *Ctr*: Birds of Britain, West Country Mag, Sunday Times, Western Morning News, Field, etc. *s.s*: Birds, Natural History, Country Life. *Rec*: Bird watching, gardening, fruit growing. *a*: Holt Antiss, Porlock, Somerset. *T*: Porlock 29.

HENDY, Philip. *Publ*: inc Matthew Smith; Giovanni Bellini; Spanish Painting; & several other volumes dealing with paintings & drawings. Director of National Gallery since 1946.

HENHAM, Ernest George ("John Trevena"). *b*: Lower Norwood, Surrey 1870. *e*: St Edward's Oxf & Manitoba, Univ. Canada. *m*: Rose Macdonald. Novelist & General Author. *Publ*: A Pixy in Petticoats; Arminal & the West; Heather; Adventures among Wild Flowers; The Vanished Moor; Typet's Treasure. *c*: Cornhill Mag, Contemporary Review, Fortnightly, Century Mag, Argosy, Land & Water, etc. *s.s*: Botany & folklore. *Rec*: Garden designing. *a*: The Nook, Verwood, Dorset.

HENLEY, Herbert James. *b*: Kemsing, nr Sevenoaks 1882. *m*: Eva Phillips. *s*: 1. Journalist (Dramatic criticism & sporting subjects). *n.a*: St James Gazette 1902—03, Sporting Life '03—14, Evening News '14 (Dramatic Critic), Daily Mail '19—34 (Dramatic & Sport Critic, Sunday Graphic & Dly Sketch '34—35. Mem I.J. '26—. *Publ*: Test Match Souvenir ('21); The Oval Cricket Guide ('23). *s.s*: Drama, cricket, rugby football. War Service. *Rec*: Reading, cricket. *c*: Press & Surrey, Middx & Essex C.C. Clubs. *a*: 11 Wavertree Ct, Streatham Hill, S.W.2. *t*: Tulse Hill 6737.

HENN, Thomas Rice, C.B.E. *b*: Sligo, Ireland. *e*: Aldenham Sch & St Catharine's Coll Camb. *m*: Mary Enid Roberts. *s*: 1. *d*: 1. Fellow & Senior Tutor St Catharine's Coll, Univ Lect in English. *Publ*: Longinus & English Criticism. *Ctr*: Bookman, Cambridge Rev, Essays of the Year. *s.s*: Lit Criticism, Shakespearean Studies. *w.s*: (1940—45) Brig Gen Staff; Legion of Merit, Dispatches. *a*: 32 Millington Rd, Cambridge, & St Catharine's College, Cambridge. *T*: 1176.

HENNESSY, Maurice Noel, F.R.S.A. *b*: Co Cork, Ireland. *e*: St Joseph Coll Roscrea Eire, St Mary's Coll Dublin. *m*: Olive Thompson. Army Officer. *Ctr*: Cork Examiner, Sunday Independant, Irish Digest, Irish Travel, Tipperary Star, etc. *s.s*: Irish Biography & Research, West African Hist & Research. *Rec*: Polo, shooting. *c*: United Hunts. *a*: Norton Manor Camp, Taunton, Som. *T*: Taunton 4432.

HENNESSY, Peter, F.R.S.A., F.R.P.S. *b*: Bickleigh 1916. *e*: Private, Rugby Sch. *m*: Jean Irving Anderson. Cinematographer, Cameraman & Stile Photographer, Free-lance Photographic Journalism. *Ctr*: Photographic Press '35—47. *s.s*: Pictorial Photography. *c*: Camera. *a*: 4 Bathurst Mews, Hyde Park, London, W.2. *T*: Paddington 5546.

HENNESSY, Richard. *b*: Paris 1876. *e*: H.M.S. Worcester & Wellington Coll Berks. *m*: Ethel Frederica Selmes (dec'd). *s*: 2. *d*: 2. Army Officer (ret). *Publ*: Leaves From the Log of Mona. *s.s*: Yachting Subjects. *Rec*: Shooting. *c*: Army & Navy, Roy Yacht Sqdn, Roy Auto, etc. *w.s*: 1914—18 Belgian Croix de Guerre & Palms. *a*: Denton Lodge, Harleston, Norfolk. *T*: Homersfield 206.

HENNIKER-HEATON, Raymond, F.S.A. *b*: London. *m*: Faith Heaton. *s*: 1. *d*: 1. Writer on Art & Psychology, Mem Cons Cttees, Burlington Mag & Old Masters' Drawings. *n.a*: Dir Newsp Features Ltd. *Publ*: Official Catalogue of British Government Exhibitions of War Paintings & Drawings; Monograph on a Titian; The Goal (Play); Perplexes & Complexes; Drifting with Direction; Sexes & Sevens. *Ctr*: Art in America, D Telegraph, Dly Herald, etc. *s.s*: Art & Psychology. *c*: R.A.C. *a*: 214 Nell Gwynn Hse, Sloane Ave, London, S.W.3. *T*: Kensington 8862.

HENRIKSEN, Agner Damgaard. *b*: Aarhus 1896. *m*: Berthe Mazar de la Garde. *s*: 1. Archivist, Author. *n.a*: Fremad 1920—21, Film-Kurer '30—31. *Publ*: Lidt om Boeger; Lidt om Exlibris; Danske Laege-Exlibris; Digte I Udvalg Gennem Femogtyve Aar; Bogen, En Sonetkrans; & various translations. *Ctr*: Hvem Skrev Hvad, Philobiblon, Exlibris Tidsskrift. *s.s*: Books about Books & Book Plates, etc. *c*: Danish Authors' Union. *a*: Ordrup Jagtvej 44 C, Charlottenlund, Copenhagen Denmark. *T*: Ordrup 1357.

HENRIQUES, Basil Lucas Quixano, M.A., J.P., *b*: London 1890. *e*: Harrow, Univ Coll Oxf. *m*: Rose Loewe. Social Worker. *Publ*: Club Leadership; The Indiscretions of a Warden. *Ctr*: Star, Standard, The Boy, Jewish Outlook. *s.s*: Youth, Juvenile Delinquency, Jewish Problems. *Rec*: Travel. *c*: Reform. *a*: The Bernhard Baron Settlement, Berners St, London, E.1. *T*: Royal 5526.

HENRIQUES, Col. Robert David Quixano, M.B.E. *Publ*: inc The Journey Home; No Arms No Armour; etc. *a*: E2 Albany, London, W.1.

HENRY, AUGUSTIN: professor of forestry; b. July 2, 1857; educ. Queen's Colleges: Galway and Belfast (both Ireland); DEGREES: M.A. (Cambridge), Queen's Univ. (Ireland), L.R.C.P. (Edinburgh), F.L.S.; m. Alice Helen Brunton, 1908. AUTHOR: Trees of Great Britain and Ireland (in collab. with H. J. Elwes), 1906-1913; Forests and Trees in Relation to Hygiene, 1919. Contributor to Gardener's Chronicle, Kew Bulletin and other technical mags. General character writing: scientific, forestry. Officer of Chinese Imperial Maratime Customs, 1891-1900. Explored flora in China, discovered one thousand species of plants new to science, many of which are now growing in European and American gardens; produced hybrid Populus Genciora and introduced Lilium Henryi into Occident. Studied Forestry at Nancy (France) and researched extensively in forests of North Amer., Algeria, Corsica, Italy, Spain, Balkans, France, Switzerland, Poland, Czecho-Slovakia and Scandinavia. Reader, Coll. of Forestry, Cambridge Univ., 1907-13; apptd. Prof. Forestry, Royal Coll. (Dublin), 1913; Univ. Coll. (Dublin). Corr. memb. Pharm. Soc., London. OFFICE: Science Buildings, Merrion St. HOME: 5 Sandford Terrace, Dublin, Ireland.

HENRY, C. Bowdler, M.R.C.S., L.R.C.P., L.D.S., R.C.S. Surg & Dentist. *Publ*: Tomes's Dental Anatomy (8th edn with A. W. Marrett-Tims). *c.t*: Lancet, B. Dental Journ, etc. *a*: 62 Harley St, W.1. *t*: Langham 2758.

HENRY, Robert Mitchell, M.A., B.A'., LittD. Prof of Latin, Queen's Univ Belfast. *n.a*: Dir Irish Statesman 1922—30. *Publ*: Livy Book XXVI (ed with intro & commentary) ('05); Selections from Livy; An Irish Corpus Astronomiæ (with F. W. O'Connell); The Evolution of Sinn Fein ('25); Cicero Tusc Disp III—IV (Ed with intro, jt); etc. *c.t*: Classical Review & Ency Brit. *a*: Crosshill, Windsor Ave, Belfast. *t*: Malone 241.

HENRY, Sydney Alexander, M.A., M.D., M.R.C.S., F.R.C.P., D.P.H., D.T.M. *b*: Rochdale, Lancs 1880. *e*: Rossall, Trin Coll Camb, St Thomas's Hosp Lond. H.M. Med Insp of Factories, Home Office then Min of Labour 1920—44. *Publ*: Cancer of the Scrotum in Relation to Occupation; Ed: Industrial Maladies. *Ctr*: Brit Med Bulletin, Brit Journ of Radiology, Journ of Dermatology, etc. *s.s*: Cutaneous Cancer in Relation to Occupation, Industrial Diseases. *c*: Un Univ. *a*: 61 Overstrand Mansions, Battersea Park, S.W.11. *T*: Macaulay 1391.

HENRY, Thomas Anderson, D.Sc. *b*: Dundee. *e*: Barrow Gr Sch, Pharmaceutical Soc Sch & Lond Univ. *m*: Jane Holmes, B.A., B.Sc. Dir Wellcome Chem Research Labs (ret), former Supt of Labs Imperial Inst. *Publ*: Plant Alkaloids. *Ctr*: Thorpe's Dictionary of Applied Chem, Ency Brit, Nature, etc. *s.s*: Chemistry of Natural Products. *Rec*: Walking. *a*: 70 Doneraile St, London. S.W.6. *T*: Putney 7191.

HENRY, Thomas Edward. *b*: Derby 1910. *e*: Bemrose Sch Derby & Ratcliffe Coll Leics. *m*: Dorothy Marcia Allen. *s*: 2. *d*: 1. *n.a*: Ed Manchester E. News, formerly Derbyshire Advertiser '28, Derby E. Express '30, Worthing Herald '32, Leicester E. Mail '34, Manch E. News '37. *Rec*: Violin. *a*: Manchester Evening News, 3 Cross St, Manchester 2. *T*: Blackfriars 2345.

HENSCHEL, Sir G., Mus Doc (Edin). *Publ*: Personal Recollections of Brahms; Musings & Memories of a Musician; Articulation in Singing. *a*: Alltnacriche, Aviemore, Scotland, & 15 Stafford Terr, W.8.

HENSHAW, Laurence Carlyle. *b*: London 1917. *e*: Priv & Southend Art Sch. *m*: L. V. Roebuck. Journalist. *n.a*: Ed Brit & Colonial Printer & Stationer '42—45, Feature Writer & Rep Melody Maker Odhams Press. *Ctr*: Odhams, periodicals, Band Waggon, Dly Mirror. *s.s*: Jazz, Swing, Dance Music, Dancing, Record Reviewing & Allied Subjects. *Rec*: Music, reading newspapers & periodicals, golf. *c*: Muswell Hill Golf. *a*: 110 Sloane St, London, S.W.1. *T*: Sloane 7715.

HENSLOW, T. Geoffrey, M.A., F.R.H.S. Author. *Publ*: Suburban Gardens; Cottage Gardens; Gardening Do's & Do Not's; etc. *a*: c/o Rich & Cowan Ltd, 27 Maiden Lane, W.C.2.

HENSLOWE, Leonard. *Publ*: Quite Well, Thanks; How to Keep Slim & Fit; How to Motor on Ten Shillings per Week. *a*: c/o Hutchinson & Co Ltd, 34-36 Paternoster Row, E.C.4.

HENSON, Bertram, M.A., LL.B. *b*: Lon 1899. *e*: Univ Col Sch & Downing Col, Cam. Press Agent. *a*: 7 New Ct, Lincoln's Inn, W.C.2. *t*: Hol 1311.

HENSON, Very Rev. Herbert Hensley, Bishop of Durham, D.D.(Oxon), HonD.D.(Glas & Durham), HonLL.D., F.R.H.S., F.R.L.S., F.R.S.A. *b*: Lon 1863. *e*: Priv & Oxf. *m*: Isabella Caroline Dennistoun. *Publ*: Apostolic Christianity ('98); Moral Discipline in the Christian Church (1905); The Creed in the Pulpit ('12); Notes on Spiritual Healing ('25); Church & Parson in England ('27); Disestablishment ('29); etc. *s.s*: Ecclesiastical hist & moral theology. Canon of Westminster & Rector of St Margaret's Westminster '00-12, Dean of Durham '13-18, Bishop of Hereford 1918-1920, Bishop of Durham '20-. *Rec*: Walking. *c*: Athenæum. *a*: Auckland Castle, Bishop Auckland, Co Durham.

HENSON, Leslie. Comedian. *Publ*: Well! Well! Well!. *a*: c/o Hutchinson & Co Ltd, 34-36 Paternoster Row, E.C.4.

HENSON, Leslie Lincoln. *b*: London 1891. *e*: Cliftonville Coll Margate, Emanuel Sch Lond. Actor-Manager. *Publ*: My Laugh Story; Yours Faithfully. *Rec*: Golf, cinematography. *c*: Green Room, Savage. *a*: Harrow Weald Hse Farm, 40 Elms Rd, Harrow Weald, Middlesex.

HENSTOCK, Herbert, M.Sc(M/C), PhD. (Zürich), F.I.C., F.C.S., F.R.S.A. *b*: Bonsall 1876. *e*: Rossall, M/C & Zürich Univs. *m*: Florence Frow. *d*: 1. Teacher of Chem, & Chem Research Worker. *c.t*: Trans of Faraday Soc, Journ of Soc of Chem Ind, etc. *s.s*: Organic & Colloid Chem. Research Fell M/C Univ. *Rec*: Entomology. *c*: Mem Faraday Soc, etc. *a*: Chem Dept Univ Col, Perry Rd, Exeter & Theta, Radden Stile Lane, Exmouth, Devon.

HENSTOCK, J. H. *n.a*: Ed Ashbourne Telegraph. *a*: Ashbourne Telegraph, Derbyshire. *T*: Ashbourne 34.

HEPPELL, Rev. Thomas. *b*: Corbridge-on-Tyne 1876. *e*: Westminster T.C. *Publ*: The Divine Refuge & Other Sermons. *Rec*: Golf. *a*: 50 Clarendon Park Rd, Leicester. *t*: 7342.

HEPPLE, Anne. *b*: Widdington. *e*: Morpeth Sc & Cronberg im Taunus, Germ. *m*: William Bain Dickinson. *s*: 1. *d*: 1. Ed, Novelist & Short Story Writer. *n.a*: Ed Woman's Mag '31. *Publ*: Jemima Rides ('28); Gay go Up; Scotch Broth; The Old Woman Speaks; etc. *c.t*: Woman's Mag, Quiver, Time & Tide, Country Life, Daily Mirror, & Sunday Times. *s.s*: The Border Country. *c*. Writers & New Century. *a*: Broadmeadows, nr Berwick-on-Tweed.

HEPPLESTON, Alfred Gordon. *b*: Crewe 1915. *e*: Manch Gr Sch, Faculty of Medicine Victoria Univ of Manch. *m*: Eleanor Rix Tebbutt. *s*: 2. Asst Lect in Pathology Welsh Nat Sch of Med 1944—. *Ctr*: Journ of Pathology & Bacteriology, Brit Journ of Industrial Med, etc. *s.s*: Pathology. *Rec*: Religion, fell walking, literature. *a*: 1 Thistle Way, Llandaff, Cardiff. *T*: Llandaff 1358.

HEPPNER, Sam. *b*: Lon 1913. *e*: L.C.C. F.L. Journalist. *c.t*: Daily Express, Sunday Express, Sunday Graphic, Film Weekly, Everybody's Weekly, Winner, Pearson's Weekly, Modern Weekly, Home Notes, Film Pictorial, Picture Show, Popular Motoring, Words & Music, etc. *s.s*: Competitions, theatre, films, radio. *Rec*: Music, swimming. *c*: Press, Stage. *a*: 18 Oakleigh Ct, Edgware. *t*: Colindale 7704.

HEPWORTH, H. M. *a*: Lincombe, North Hill Rd, Headingley, Leeds.

HER, ERICH (pen name): see Paetel, Erich.

HERAS, Rev. Henry, S.J., M.A., D.D. *b*: Barcelona, Spain 1888. Dir & Founder Indian Historical Research Inst St Xavier's Coll Bombay. *Publ*: History of the Manchu Dynasty of China (in Spanish); The Writing of History; The Aravidu Dynasty of Vijayanagara; Beginnings of Vijayanagara History; The Pallava Geneology; The Conversion Policy of the Jesuits in India; Studies in Palava History. *Ctr*: Various to the leading journs of India. *s.s*: Ancient Indian Culture. *a*: St Xavier's Coll, Bombay 1, India.

HERBERT, A. H. *n.a*: Mang Ed Hythe Reporter & Southern Chron. *a*: Great Conduit St, Hythe.

HERBERT, Agnes, O.B.E. *b*: Pendlebury, Lancs. *e*: Privately. *m*: Comdr A. T. Stewart, O.B.E., R.N. *d*: 1. Author. *n.a*: Ed Writers & Artists Year Book 1920—29, Vice-Chm Soc of Women Journalists '29—33, Vice Pres Soc of Women Journalists '39. *Publ*: Two Dianas in Somaliland; Two Dianas in Alaska; The Isle of Man; The Life Story of a Lion; Casuals in the Caucasus; The Moose; Her Mighty Youth; The Elephant; Northumberland; Korea; etc. *Ctr*: Various newspapers & periodicals. *s.s*: Big Game, Animals, Alaska, Somaliland. *a*: National Provincial Bank Ltd., 208-9 Piccadilly, London, W.1. *T*: Lab 1614.

HERBERT, Sir Alan Patrick, Kt., M.P. *b*: 1890. *e*: Winchester & New Coll Oxf. Barrister, Author, Dramatist, Trustee Nat Maritime Mus 1947, M.P. (Ind) for Oxford Univ since '35. *n.a*: Punch, Sun Graphic. *Publ*: The Bomber Gipsy; The Secret Battle; Wisdom for the Wise; Misleading Cases in the Common Law; Honeybubble & Co; No Boats on the River; Holy Deadlock; The Water Gypsies; Trials of Topsy (verse); The Wherefore & the Why; Tinker, Tailor; Topsy; M.P.; Laughing Ann; etc; Plays—Helen; Derby Day; Tantivy Towers; Home & Beauty; Big Ben; Bless the Bride; Perseverance, etc. *w.s*: R.N.D. 1914—17, R.E.S. & R.N.A.P. '39—45. *a*: 12 Hammersmith Terr, W.6. *T*: Riverside 1627.

HERBERT, Rev. Arthur Gabriel. *b*: 1886. *e*: Harrow, New Coll Oxf. Clerk in Holy Orders. *Publ*: Liturgy & Society; The Throne of David; The Form of the Church; The Authority of the Old Testament; Scripture & the Faith; An Essay in Baptismal Revision. *a*: Hse of the Sacred Mission, Kelham, Newark, Notts.

HERBERT, Arthur Stanley, O.B.E. Physician. *Publ*: The Hot Springs of New Zealand; Mineral Waters & Spas of New Zealand; Military Physical Orthopædics. *a*: 14 Argyll Rd, Kensington, W.8. *t*: Western 1772.

HERBERT, Rt. Hon. Sir Dennis H., P.C., K.B.E., M.P. *b*: Hemingford Abbots 1869. *e*: King's Sc Ely, Wadham Col Oxf. *m*: Mary Græme Bell. *s*: 3. Solicitor. Hon Fell Wadham Col. *Publ*: The Law As to Solicitors. *a*: Clarendon Lodge, Watford.

HERBERT, Edward Hugh. *b*: Hampstead 1881. *e*: Priv & King's Sc Rochester. Mang Dir Cent News Ltd. *n.a*: Cent News Finan Ed 1907, Advtg Dir '25, Mang Dir '27—. *a*: 5 New Bridge St, E.C.4.

HERBERT, Elizabeth Hamilton. Author. *Publ*: Sold for a Song; Happy Sinner; House of Wives. *a*: c/o Mills & Boon, 50 Grafton St, London, W.1.

HERBERT, Evelyn. *b*: Nantyglo 1904. *e*: St.; Margaret's Burnham Som. *Publ*: Anna Priestly, The White Peony. (Plays) Exit Mrs Rose; Hannah Davydd; The Dark Curtain. *w.s*: 1941—46 W.R.N.S. *a*: Dewi Hse, Brynmawr, Brecon.

HERBERT, Gerald, F.R.C.S.(Eng), L.R.C.P.(Lon), B.A.(Cantab). *c.t*: Lancet. *a*: 20 Clifton Rd, Rugby. *t*: 599.

HERBERT, Lt.-Col. H. Late Prof of Ophthal Bombay Univ. *Publ*: Cataract Extraction. *c.t*: British Journ of Ophthal, Trans Ophthal Soc U.K., Proc Roy Soc of Med, etc. *s.s*: Ophth surg in cataract & glaucoma, research on the origin of glaucoma. *a*: c/o Messrs Thomas & Cook, Berkeley St, W.1.

HERBERT, Joan. *b*: Folkestone 1902. *e*: Roedean. *n.a*: Ed The Guide '26—30, Asst Ed The Merry-go-Round '31—32, Ed & Publisher The Merry-go-Round '33—34. *Publ*: Pages for Patrol Leaders; Lorna's First Term; With Best Intentions; etc. *c.t*: Girls' Own Paper, The Guide, Annuals, etc. *s.s*: Children's stories. *c*: English-Speaking Union. *a*: 22 Manor Rd, Folkestone. *t*: 3475.

HERBERT, John Alexander, B.A., F.S.A. *b*: Gateshead 1862. *e*: Roy G.S., Newcastle-on-Tyne & St John's Col Cam. *m*: Alice Low. *d*: 1. Civil Servant (ret). Formerly Dep Keeper of MSS in the Brit Museum. *Publ*: Titus & Vespasian (1905); Illuminated MSS ('11); Part III of the Guide to Exhibited MSS, Brit Mus ('12, '23); Schools of Illumination, parts I–VI ('14–30); Sherborne Missal ('20); etc. *c.t*: Library, Walpole Socs Annual, Burlington Mag, etc. *s.s*: Palæography & mediæval romances. *Rec*: Chess. *a*: 29a Brook Green, W.6. *t*: Riverside 1287.

HERBERT, S. Mervyn. *b*: 1912. *e*: Ryde Sch. *m*: *d*: 1. Journalist. *n.a*: Foreign Ed News Chron '46—, former Head of European Information Dept F.O. '46, Morning Post '36—37, News Chron '38—41. *Publ*: Britain's Health. *c*: Travellers'. *a*: c/o News Chronicle, Bouverie St, London, E.C.4.

HERBERT, Solomon, J.P., M.D.(Vienna), M.R. C.S., L.R.C.P.(Lon). *b*: Austria 1874. *e*: Vienna & M/C Univs. *m*: Lily Tiano. *d*: 2. Psycho-Therapist. *Publ*: First Principles of Heredity (1910–); Fundamentals in Sexual Ethics ('20); The Unconscious Mind ('23); The Unconscious in Life & Art ('32); etc. *s.s*: Pyscho-analysis. *Rec*: Music, lit. *a*: 2 St Peter's Sq, M/C. *t*: Cent 0254.

HERBERT, Thomas Arnold, K.C. (ret). *Publ*: Law of Prescription. *c.t*: Various. *a*: 12 Kensington Pk Gdns, W.11. *t*: Pk 7189.

HERBERT, Walter Elmes, L.R.C.P. *b*: Egham, Surrey 1902. *e*: Queen's Coll Taunton, Guy's Hosp Dental & Med Schs, Northwestern Univ. *m*: Joyce Mary Griffith Clogg. *s*: 1. *d*: 1. Dir of Dept of Conservative Dental Surg Guy's Hosp Dental Sch' 31—Lect in Operative Dental Surg '33—. *Publ*: Operative Dental Surgery (with J. B. Parfitt). *Ctr*: Proc Roy Soc Med, Brit Dental Journ, Guy's Hosp Reports. *s.s*: Dental Surgery. *Rec*: Mountaineering. *c*: Alpine. *a*: Newlands, 28 Worcester Rd., Sutton, Surrey. *T*: Vigilant 6284.

HERBERTSON, Agnes Grozier. *b*: Oslo. *e*: Priv. Author. *Publ*: (Novels) The Summit; Deborah; Patience Dean; We Know Each Other's Faces. (Poetry) The Quiet Heart; This is the Hour; Here is My Signature. (Children) Book of Happy Gnomes; Cap-o-Yellow; The Spindle Tree; Ponsonby & His Friends. *Ctr*: Strand Mag, Grand Mag, Modern Woman; Windsor Mag, Truth, Manch Guardian, Queen, etc. *s.s*: Short Stories. *Rec*: Reading, walking, golf. *c*: Lyceum. *a*: Dreynes Bungalow, nr St Cleer, Liskeard, Cornwall.

HERBERTSON, Jessie Leckie. *b*: Glasgow. Author. *Publ*: The Stigma; Mortal Men; Young Life; Treasure of Drummer's Head; The House of Surprises; Schooldays at Beverley; A Disagreeable Girl; A Family From Nowhere; Crofton's Daughter; etc. *Ctr*: Various short stories & articles to periodicals & annuals. *a*: Dreynes, nr St Cleer, Liskeard, Cornwall.

HERBST, Josephine Frey, A.B. *b*: Sioux City, Iowa 1897. *e*: Univ of California. Writer. *Publ*: Somewhere the Tempest Fell; Pity is Not Enough; The Executioner Waits; Rope of Gold; A Triology; Nothing is Sacred; Satan's Sergeants; Money for Love. *a*: Erwinna, Buck's County, Penn, U.S.A.

HERD, Dr. D. A. Designer & Inventor of:—Combined Radium Needle, Inserter & Probe, Pliable Rule, Double Test Tube-Holder & other instruments. *a*: Woodvale, 24 Coronation Drive, Gt Crosby, Lancs.

HERD, Harold. *b*: 1893. *m*: Kate Lancaster. *d*: 1. Author & Journalist. *n.a*: Ed Fleet Street Annual, Princ The Regent Inst. *Publ*: Effective Sales Letters; Watch Your English; Bigger Results from Advertising; The Writer's Guide; The Making of Modern Journalism; An English Prose Treasury; The Newspaper of To-morrow; Panorama; (play) Roman Road. *Ctr*: Various newspapers, periodicals & business journals, Ed English Collection, Writer's Library & Outline Series of Modern Reading Courses, Ex-Ed To-day & To-morrow, The Magazine of To-day, etc. *s.s*: Journalism, English, advertising. *Rec*: Travel, reading, walking. *a*: 1 Prince Arthur Rd, Hampstead, London, N.W.3. *T*: Hampstead 2916.

HERD, Henry, M.A., M.B., ChB., D.P.H. Chief School M.O. Manchester. *Publ*: Diagnosis of Mental Deficiency; Chapter on Mental Defect in "The Chances of Morbid Inheritance"; Chapter on Intelligence Tests in "Clinical Interpretation of Aids to Diagnosis"; Chapter on Symptoms in "Children in Early Mental Diseases." *c.t*: Lancet. *a*: 51 Derby Rd, Heaton Moor, Stockport. *t*: Heaton Moor 2960.

HERD, Muriel. *b*: L'pool. *e*: Priv. *m*: E. H. Smart. *Publ*: Gill & the Others; Pageant Play—From Darkness to Light. *Rec*: Music, reading. *a*: Amberley, Dunoon Rd, Forest Hill, S.E.23. *t*: Forest Hill 5717.

HERDAL, Harald. *b*: Copenhagen 1900. *e*: Elem Sch. *m*: Edith Cederstrand. *s*: 1. *d*: 1. Author. *n.a*: Periodical Asst Politiken, Land & Folk, Ekstrabladet. *Publ*: You Are Forced to Live; Log; A Part of the Country; Self-Biography; etc. *a*: Frydenlundsvej 81, Trorod pr Vedbœck, Denmark. *T*: Trorod 184.

HERDMAN, Ramona. *b*: Greenwich, N.Y. 1902. *e*: Univs of Syracuse & Columb. *m*: John Lewis Craddock. Publicity Director Harper & Bros Publishers, former Director of Health Education City of Syracuse '27—29. *n.a*: Feature Writer Syracuse Herald '22—27, N.Y. Sunday World '29—30. *Publ*: A Time for Love; Five O'Clock Whistle; To-day is Forever. *Rec*: Reading. *a*: Harper & Brothers, 49 East 33rd St, New York, N.Y., U.S.A. *T*: Murray Hill 3-1900.

HERFORD, CHARLES HAROLD: professor of English (retired); b. Manchester, Eng., Feb., 1863; s. Charles James and Mary (Robbards) H.; educ. private Sch. (Lancaster), Owens Coll. (Manchester), Trinity Coll. (Cambridge); DEGREES: Litt.D. (Cambridge), (Hon.) Litt.D. (Manchester, Wales, New York State); m. Marie Betge, 1888. AUTHOR: Studies in the Literary Relations of England and Germany in the 16th Century, 1886; Ibsen's Brand (translated) (in the Original Metres, with Notes and Introduction), 1893; The Age of Wordsworth, 1897; Is

There a Poetic View of the World? (Warton lecture to the British Acad.), 1916; Shakespeare's Treatment of Love and Marriage, and Other Essays, 1921; The Mind of Post-War Germany, 1926; Warwick Library and Warwick Shakespeare; Belles Lettres Series (critical section). Edited: "Eversley" Shakespeare (10 vols.), with Introductions and Notes, 1899; Ibsen's Love's Comedy (transl. in the original metres), 1900; English Tales in Verse, 1900; Browning, 1904; Memoirs of W. H. Herford, 1911; Lectures on Germany in the 19th Century, 1911; Shakespeare, 1912; Goethe, 1913. Contributor of articles on Ben Jonson, Middleton and others to Dictionary of National Biography. General character of writing: literary criticism and history, biography. Chief interest is in English and comparative literature. (*)

HERFORD, Rev. Robert Travers, B.A., D.D. *Publ*: Christianity in Talmud & Midrash (1903); Pharisaism, its Aim & its Method; Pirkē Aboth (Ed, 2nd edn '30); Talmud & Apocrypha ('32); etc. *a*: Summertrees, Kelsall, nr Chester. *t*: Kelsall 21.

HERFORD BRAUNHOLTZ, Mrs. M., M.A. *Publ*: Handbook of Greek Vase Painting. *c.t*: Journal of Hellenic Studies, Manchester Guardian, etc. *a*: 22 Old Rd, Headington, Oxford.

HERGESHEIMER, Joseph. *b*: Philadelphia 1880. Author. *Publ*: The Lay Anthony; Mountain Blood; The Three Black Pennys; Java Head; The Happy End; Cytherea; The Limestone Tree; The Party Dress; The Bright Shawl; Quiet Cities; Tampico; Swords & Roses; Balisand; From an Old House; Love in the United States; Linda Condon; San Cristobal de la Habana; Berlin; Tropical Winter; etc. *a*: The Dower House, West Chester, Chester Co, Penn, U.S.A.

HERING, Henry A. *b*: Shipley Yorks 1864. *e*: Bradford G.S. *m*: Clare McLandsborough. *d*: 1. *Publ*: Platonia; The Burglars' Club; Further Chronicles of the Burglars' Club; Hunt the Tiger (play broadcast and filmed); Adventures & Fantasy; Major Butterfield's Adventure (play broadcast); etc. *c.t*: Cassell's **Mag**, Strand, Windsor, Pearson's, Sketch, Story-Teller, Nash's Everyman, etc. *c*: Authors'. *a*: Gray Gables, Pashley Rd, Eastbourne. *t*: 2068.

HERING, James Arthur, M.J.I. *b*: Lon 1915. *e*: Dover Col. Journalist. *n.a*: A.P. '30–32, World's Press News '32, Wireless Trader '33–. *c.t*: Advertiser's Weekly, The Cinema, Newspaper World, The Performer, Daily Film Renter, The Writer, World's Press News, etc. *s.s*: Theatrical & film journalism, press & publ campaigns for private individuals, lit ag's, work. *Rec*: Hockey, tennis, fives. *a*: 12 Trebovir Rd, Earl's Ct, S.W.5. *t*: Frobisher 4835.

HERJE, Emil. *b*: Grip 1894. *e*: Teachers' Training Coll. *m*: Margit Mathisen. *s*: 1. *d*: 3. Headmaster. *Publ*: Varden pa Ukstein; Mot og Vilje; Da minen sprang; Eventyret i Villmarken; Et Herrens vaer; Jamboree; To gutter til havs; Fedrelandet kaller; etc. *Ctr*: Nidaros, Norsk ped. tidsskr, Speideren etc. *c*: Norwegian Authors' Union. *a*: Breidablikk, Trondheim, Norway.

HERKLOTS, Rev. Bernard, M.A. *b*: Guernsey 1873. *e*: Bedford Sc, Corpus Ch Col & Ridley Hall Cam. *m*: Emily Frances Bazeley. *s*: 2. *d*: 2. *Publ*: Revelatio Dei; The Future of the Evangelical Party; A Portraiture of Christ; The Challenge to the Church. *Rec*: Cycling, climbing, word cutting. *a*: The Rectory, Pool, Dorset.

HERKLOTS, Rev. Hugh Gerard Gibson, M.A. *b*: Sikandra, India. *e*: Trent Coll, Trin Hall Camb. *m*: Helen Beveridge Murgoci. *s*: 2. *d*: 2. Dir of Religious Educ Diocese of Sheffield, Hon Canon Sheffield Cathedral, Canon St John's Cathedral Winnipeg & Prof St John's Coll 1930—36, Mem Youth Advisory Counc M. of Educ '42—45. *Publ*: The Epistle to the Philippians; These Denominations; For Such A Time as This; Pilgrimage to Amsterdam; The New Universities; Paper Aeroplanes. *Ctr*: Times, Guardian, Record, Expository Times, Churchman, Sheffield Telegraph. *s.s*: New Testament, Youth, The Ecumenical Movement. *a*: 10 Claremont Pl, Sheffield 10. *T*: Sheffield 629394.

HERLIHY, Martin. *b*: Cork 1897. *e*: Belvedere Col Dublin & City of Lon Sc. *m*: Nellie Kerin. *d*: 2. Journalist. *n.a*: Parl Staffs of Central News, Press Assoc, M/C Guardian & Reuters 1919–33, Ed i/c Reuters '33–. *s.s*: Foreign Affairs. Chm Parl Press Gallery '33–34. Called to the Bar, Gray's Inn '21. *c*: Press. *a*: 24 Manville Rd, S.W.17. *t*: Streatham 7681.

HERMANNSSON, Halldor, Ph.D. *b*: Iceland 1878. *e*: Coll of Iceland, Univ of Copenhagen. Prof Emeritus Scandinavian Lang & Lit Cornell Univ U.S.A. *Publ*: Icelandic Illuminated Manuscripts of the Middle Ages; Icelandic Manuscripts; The Cartography of Iceland; Two Cartographers; Modern Icelandic; Catalogues of the Fiske Icelandic Collection; Bibliographies of Icelandic Literature; etc. *s.s*: Icelandic Lit, Mediæval & Mod. *a*: 700 Stewart Ave, Ithaca, N.Y., U.S.A.

HERMON-HODGE, Harry Baldwin. *b*: Wyfold Ct 1885. *e*: Winchs & Magdalen Col Oxf. Res Ilorin, Nigeria (ret). *Publ*: Up Against it in Nigeria (Langa-Langa); Gazetteer of Ilorin. *c.t*: Blackwood's Mag, West Africa, etc. W.S. W. African Field Force. *Rec*: Polo, tennis, shooting, hunting. *c*: Carlton. *a*: Abbot's Thatch, Runfold, Farnham, Surrey.

HERNAMAN-JOHNSON, Francis, M.D., F.F.R. *b*: Crosby, Lancs 1879. *e*: Merchant Taylor's Sch, Univ of Aberdeen, St Bart's Hosp. *m*: Janet Eleanor Townend. *s*: 1. *d*: 1. *Publ*: Radiology in relation to General Medicine; Play (in collab)—Accident. *Ctr*: B.M.J. Lancet, Ev Standard, etc. *s.s*: Rheumatism. *Rec*: Sailing. *c*: Arts Theatre. *a*: Weymouth St, London, W.1. *T*: Welbeck 1264.

HEROD, Frank, M.R.SanI., A.I.S.E. *b*: Hyde 1879. Ed & Advertising Man. *Publ*: (Ed) Heating & Ventilating; Sewage Disposal for Isolated Districts; The Use of Copper in Plumbing. *a*: 9 Albert Sq, Manchester 2. *t*: Blackfriars 5379.

HEROLD, Don, A.B. *b*: Bloomfield, Indiana 1889. *e*: Indiana Univ, Chicago Art Inst. *m*: Katherine Porter Brown. *d*: 2. Writer-Cartoonist. *n.a*: Indianapolis Star 1914—16, Life Mag '16—30. *Publ*: Doing Europe & Vice Versa; Strange Bed Fellows; There Ought to be a Law; Bigger & Better; Companionate Goldfish; So Human. *Ctr*: Judge, Readers Digest, Colliers, etc. *s.s*: Humour. *Rec*: Golf. *a*: 103 East 86th St, New York City. *T*: Atwater 9-3372.

HERON, Albert. *b*: Lon 1876. *n.a*: Financial Times 1893–. *a*: 44 Crowborough Rd, S.W.17.

HERON, Edward Thomas, J.P. *b*: Lon 1867. *e*: Haberdashers Sc. *m*: May Baldrey. *s*: 2. Printer & Publisher. *n.a*: Originator Kinematograph Weekly, Talking Machine News, The Advertiser (W. Lon), Balloooning. *c.t*: Local & prov papers. Chm Melina Estates Ltd, & Turner Advtg Service. Mang Dir Maxclif Pubg Co Ltd. Ex-Mayor St Pancras. *Rec*: Golf. *a*: Silver End, St Leonards-on-Sea. *t*: Hastings 235.

HERON-ALLEN, Edward, F.R.S. *b*: Lon 1861. *e*: Harrow. *m*: Edith Pepler. *d*: 2 (1 dec). Scientist. *Publ*: Three pages of the British Museum Catalogue. *c.t*: Scientific journals, etc. *s.s*: Persian lit. *Rec*: Archæological research. *c*: Garrick, R.A.C. *a*: Large Acres, Selsey Bill, Sussex. *t*: Selsey 19.

HERRICK, Marvin Theodore, A.B., Ph.D. (Cornell), A.M.(Harvard). *b*: Mocksville, Nth Carolina, 1899. *e*: Cornell & Harvard Univs. *m* Nigel Hill. *d*: 1. Teacher. *Publ*: The Poetics of Aristotle in England. *c.t*: Classical Wkly, Modern Lang Notes, Philological Quarterly, American Jnl of Philology, American Speech, Pittsburgh Record, English Journal. *s.s*: Criticism, drama. *Rec*: Tennis, golf. *c*: Modern Lang Assoc of America. *a*: Trinity Col, Hartford, Conn., U.S.A. *t*: 7—0249.

HERRICK, Robert, A.B. *b*: Cambridge, U.S.A. 1868. *e*: Cam Latin Sc & Harvard Col. *m*: Harriet Emery. *s*: 1. Writer & Novelist. Govt Sec to Virgin Is '35—. Formerly Prof Eng Chicago Univ. *Publ*: Gospel of Freedom; The Web of Life; Master of the Inn; The Healer; A Life for a Life; Waste; Wanderings; Sometime; End of Desire ('31); etc. *c.t*: Various magazines. *s.s*: Contemporary Amer life. *a*: St Thomas, U.I. U.S.A. *t*: York 14.

HERRING, George Herbert. *b*: Sandford 1873. *e*: Oxf Wesleyan H.G. Sc & Oxf H.S. *m*: Louise Baker. *d*: 2. Journalist. *n.a*: Oxf Chronicle '89-99, Chief Rep & Sub-Ed Surrey Times '99-1909, Sub-Ed Essex Weekly Series '09—. Charter Mem Inst Journ, Fell '27. Mem Counc, Hon Vice-Pres '25. Life Mem of N/p Press Fund. *a*: Newlands, Queen's Rd, Chelmsford. *t*: 203.

HERRING, H. T., O.B.E., M.B., B.S. *s.s*: Cremation. Mang Dir Woking & Golders Green Crematoria, Hon Sec Cremation Soc, Hon Sec Nat Counc Disposition of the Dead. *a*: 50 Harley St, W.1.

HERRING, Paul. *b*: Nottingham. *Publ*: Dragon's Silk; Hoodman Grey; Christian ("David Raeburn"); Bold Bendigo; Sir Toby and the Regent; The Murder of Margot Midnight; The Midnight Murder; etc. *c.t*: Amalgamated Press, Newnes', Pearsons' publications, & Nottinghamshire Weekly Guardian. *a*: "Lynne Holme," 2 Robinson Rd, Mapperley, Nottingham.

HERRING, Percy Theodore. *b*: Yorks 1872. *e*: Christ's Col N.Z., Otago & Edin Univs. *m*: Mary Marshall Callender. *d*: 4. Chandos Prof of Physiology, Univ of St And. *c.t*: Physiological Journ's. *a*: Linton, St Andrews, Fife. *t*: 488.

HERRINGTON, John Montague. *b*: Reading. *e*: Reading & Christ's Hosp. Journalist. *n.a*: Chief Asst-Ed The Field, former Ed Western Weekly News 1937—39 Senior Sub-Ed Western Morning News '27—37, Chief Sub Whig Belfast '23—27. *a*: The Field, 8 Stratton St, London, W.1.

HERRIOT, Edouard. *b*: 1872. Maire de Lyon, Depute du Rhone, Pres de l'Assemblee Nationale. *Publ*: Vie de Beethoven; Dans la Foret Normande; Sous l'Olivier; La Porte Oceane; Orient; Sanctuaires; Lyon n'est plus; Mme Recamier et ses amis. *a*: 1 Cours d'Herbouville, Lyon, France. *T*: B. 06-55.

HERROD-HEMPSALL, J. *n.a*: Ed British Bee Journal. *a*: British Bee-Keeper's Association, 23 Bedford St, W.C.2. *t*: Temple Bar 0027.

HERRON, Vennette. *b*: Ohio. *e*: Private. *m*: Johannes Jacobus van der Leeuw, Writer, Actress. *Publ*: Peacocks, Stories of Java; Italian Love; PlayGods; Perfume & Poison—Poems. *Ctr*: Nash's, Pearson's, Bystander, etc. *s.s*: Fiction, Travel, Plays. *a*: 817 Vistabula St, Lakeland, Florida, U.S.A.

HERSEY, Mrs. Mayo D., A.B., Litt.D. (See **WARNER, Frances Lester**), *b*: Putnam, Conn 1888. *e*: Mount Holyoke Coll. *m*: Mayo Dyer Hersey. Writer, Lecturer, Head of Dept of English New England Conservatory of Music 1946. *n.a*: Atlantic Monthly 1921—22. *s.s*: Family Life Essays, Amateur Music, Country & Seashore. *Rec*: Music, Cooking, Travel. *c*: Boston Author's. *a*: Monument Beach, Massachusetts, U.S.A. *T*: Buzzards Bay 601.

HERST, Norbert N. ("Alertus"), M.J.I. *b*: Baden 1887. *e*: Royal Col Bruchsal Germany. F.L., Pol & Econ. *c.t*: English, German, American n/ps. *c*: Constitutional, etc. *a*: 55 Belsize Pd Gdns, N.W.3. *t*: Primrose 0634.

HERTSLET, Rev. E. L. A. *b*: Richmond 1878. *e*: Kings Sc Canterbury, Jesus Col Cam, Wells Theol Col. Vicar St Mary Redcliffe, Hon Canon Bristol. *Publ*: The Cup and the Sacrifice; God's Embassy; Vox Mundi, Vox Dei; Wrought in the Silence of God; etc. *s.s*: Theol. Res Chap to Archbishop Canterbury, Lord Davidson 1909-14. Vicar of Ramsgate '14—28. Six Preacher Canterbury Cathedral. *c*: Athenæum & Roy Socs. *a*: St Mary Redcliffe Vicarage, Bristol. *t*: Bristol 20917.

HERTZ, Frederick Otto. *b*: Vienna 1878. *e*: Vienna, Munich & London Univs. *m*: Edith Hirsch. *s*: 1. *d*: 1. Author, Dr Ec, former Univ Prof of Sociology & Economics, former Ministerial Counsellor Austrian Chancellery. *Publ*: Nationality in History & Politics; Nationalgeist und Politik; Race & Civilisation; The Economic Problem of the Danubian States; Die agrarischen Fragen im Verhaeltnis zum Sozialismus; Die Produktionsgrundlagen der oesterreichischen Industrie; Recht und Unrecht im Burenkrieg. *Ctr*: Contemporary Rev, Sociological Rev. *s.s*: History & Sociology of Nationalism & Internationalism, History of Foreign Relations, etc. *a*: 37 Corringham Rd, London, N.W.11. *T*: Speedwell 0379.

HERTZ, Very Rev. J. H. *b*: 1872. Chief Rabbi. *Publ*: Book of Jewish Thoughts; Affirmations of Judaism; Pentateuch & Haftorahs. *a*: 48 Hamilton Terr, N.W.8.

HERTZ, William Axel. *b*: Burma 1859. *e*: St Xavier's Col Calcutta C.S.I. I.C.S. (ret). *c.t*: Asia (N.Y.), Graphic, Field, Pioneer (India), Rangoon Gazette (Burma), Journ Roy Asiatic Soc, etc. *s.s*: Reminiscences of Service in Burma & amongst wild tribes on the Burma-China frontier. Mem Viceroy of India's Counc 1919, ret '20. Lect in Burmese Cam Univ & Sc of Oriental Studies, Lon '20. *Rec*: Gardening. *a*: Thornfield, Mason's Bridge, nr Red Hill, Surrey.

HERTZIAN, David. See **Kidd, Charles David.**

HERVEY, George F. F/l & Card specialist. *n.a*: Cards Ed Sunday Referee 1931—34. *Publ*: Auction Bridge Informatory Doubles (with A. E. Manning-Foster); Auction Bridge (with Mrs. A. M. Taylor); Advanced Auction Bridge (do); Headlights of Contract Bridge; Modern Contract Bridge; Contract Bridge Dictionary. *a*: 52 George St, W.1.

HERZFELD, Gertrude, M.B., ChB., F.R.C.S. *c.t*: Lancet, B.M.J., etc. *a*: 16 Great Stuart St, Edin. *t*: 22649.

HESELTINE, George Coulehan. *b*: Hull, Yorks 1895. *Publ*: The Change; Kalendar & Compost of Shepherds (trans & ed 1931); William of Wykeham; Great Yorkshiremen; Town to Country; The Fire of Love, R. Rolle, trans; etc. *c.t*: Mags & periodicals in Gt Britain, Colonies & U.S.A. *s.s*: Biography, agricultural development, mediæval lit. *c*: Press. *a*: Press Club, Lon, E.C.4.

HESILRIGE, Arthur George Maynard. *b*: Bourne, Lincs 1863. *e*: Wellington Coll Berks. *m*: Amy Florence Myers. *d*: 3. Editor. *n.a*: Ed Debrett's Peerage, Baronetage, Knightage & Companionage, & Debrett's House of Commons & Judicial Bench 1887—1935, & Paper Makers Dir of all Nations 1900—1935. *Publ*: Debrett's Coronation Guide; Debrett's Heraldry; Debrett's City of London Book; Debrett's British Empire Book; Debrett's West End Book. *s.s*: Biographical Publs. *Rec*: Tennis & badminton. *a*: Grantleigh Hotel, Inverness Ter, London, W.2.

HESLOP, Harold. *b*: Hunwick, Co Durham 1898. *e*: H. Grange Coun S., Bishop Auckland G.S., Lon Labour Col. *m*: Phyllis Hannah Varndell. *d*: 1. Advertisement Mang. *Publ*: The Gate of a Strange Field; Journey Beyond; The Crime of Peter Ropner; Goaf. *c.t*: Various. *s.s*: Mining, economics, short-story writing, etc. *Rec*: Hiking. *a*: c/o Wishart & Co, 9 John St, Adelphi, W.C.2. *t*: Tem Bar 5411.

HESLOP, Harry Hunter. *b*: Beckenham 1905. *e*: Shrewsbury H.S. *m*: Annette Montague. *d*: 1. Chief Reporter Buxton Advertiser & High Peak News 1929—42, Mem N.U.J. '27— (N.E.C. '45—). *n.a*: Reporter Shrewsbury Chron 1925—29, Sub-Ed Sheffield Telegraph since '42. *a*: 16 Dover Rd, Sheffield 11.

HESLOP, J. See **Park, Fanny Heslop.**

HESLOP-HARRISON, John William, D.Sc., F.R.S., F.R.S.E. *b*: Birtley 1881. *e*: Rutherford Coll Newcastle-upon-Tyne, Armstrong Coll Durham. *m*: Christian Watson-Henderson. *s*: 2. *d*: 1. Emeritus Prof of Botany King's Coll Durham. *n.a*: Asst Ed Entomologist, Ed Vasculum & Trans of Northern Naturalists Union. *Ctr*: Proc Roy Soc, Annals of Botany, Journ of Genetics, Entomologist, etc. *s.s*: Botany, Entomology, Genetics. *Rec*: Rock-gardening. *a*: Gavarnie, The Avenue, Birtley, Co Durham.

HESS, Fjeril, A.B., Hon.L.H.D. *b*: Omaha, Nebraska 1892. *e*: MacMurray Coll Jacksonville. Editor & Writer. *n.a*: Ed Woman's Press Mag 1921—24, Dir Publs Dept Girl Scouts of the U.S.A. 1930—. *Publ*: The Mounted Falcon; The House of Many Tongues; Castle Camp; Social Aspects of the Schools in Prague; Buckaroo; Sandra's Cellar; Handkerchief Holiday; Fly Away Home; Wacs at Work. *s.s*: Fiction for Young People based on Factual Material. *Rec*: Gardening, carpentry, printing, reading, sketching, riding, camping. *a*: 400 East 49th St, New York 17, N.Y., U.S.A. *T*: Eldorado 5-4765.

HESS, Victor Francis, Sc.D., Ph.D. *b*: Waldstein, Austria 1883. *e*: Univs of Graz & Vienna. *m*: Mary Bertha Breisky. *s*: 1. *d*: 1. Prof of Physics Fordham Univ New York. *Publ*: The Electric Conductivity of the Atmosphere & Its Causes; Atmospheric Electricity (collab); The Ionization Balance of the Atmosphere; Biological Action of Cosmic Rays (collab). *Ctr*: Phys Rev, Journ of Terrestial Magnetism & Electricity, etc. *s.s*: Physics, esp Geophysics. *Rec*: Motoring. *a*: 20 William St, Mount Vernon, New York. *T*: MO 8-3513.

HESSELAA, Peder. *b*: Over Saustrup, Holstebro 1900. *m*: Anna Olesen. Author, Translator. *n.a*: Literary Advisor Jespersen & Pio Publishers, Ed De Nye Bager 1931—44. *Publ*: Marie Bregendahl; En Nat i November; Leo Tolstoy; Vor Tids Digtere; Essays; Sommervandringer. *Ctr*: Nordisk Tidskrift, Den Nye Litteratur, Social-Demokraten, Hojskoleblad. *s.s*: Modern Scandinavian Literature. *Rec*: Travel. *a*: 116 Emdrupvej, Copenhagen NV, Denmark. *T*: Soborg 1946.

HESSEY, James Dodson. Physician. *Publ*: The Use of Colour in the Treatment of Disease. *c.t*: Practitioner. *a*: 8 Weymouth St, Lon, W.1. *t*: Welbeck 8232.

HESSION, Rev. Brian, M.A. Vicar of Holy Trinity Aylesbury & Chm Dawn Trust & Bible Films, Lect & Journalist. *Publ*: Film Scripts: An Undergraduate Affair; More than a Prophet; Sailing. *s.s*: Films, Photography & Colour Photography. *Rec*: Religious visual educ, sailing. *a*: Holy Trinity Vicarage, Aylesbury, & Goathorn Cottage, Poole Harbour, Dorset

HETHERINGTON, Arthur Lonsdale, C.B.E., M.A. *b*: London 1881. *e*: Highgate Sch & Trinity Coll Cambridge. *m*: Doris P. Sells. *s*: 4. *d*: 2. Civil Servant (ret). *Publ*: Industrial Research & Development (with Sir Frank Heath); Early Ceramic Wares of China; Chinese Ceramic Glazes; Art of the Chinese Potter (with R. L. Hobson). *s.s*: Chinese Ceramics, Industrial Research, Turning. *Rec*: Chinese ceramics & turning. *c*: Oxf & Camb, Savile. *a*: 5 Roland Houses, London, S.W.7. *T*: Freemantle 0737.

HETHERINGTON, John Aikman. *b*: Melbourne, Vic, Australia 1907. *e*: All Saints Gr Sch St Kilda Vic. *m*: Olive Meacher. Journalist. *n.a*: Rep Ev Sun Melbourne 1924, Rep & Feature Writer Mel Herald '25—35, Sub-Ed Australian News Cable Service & Australian A.P. Lond & Rep Sunday Dispatch Lond '35—37, Sub-Ed Australian A.P. New York '37, Feature Ed Melbourne Herald '38—39, War Correspondent Middle East '40—43, Western Europe '44—45, Ed in Chief News Ltd '45. *Publ*: Airborne Invasion; Australian Soldier; The Winds Are Still (Sydney Morning Herald £1,000 prize). *Rec*: Amer Argosy, Esquire, Sat Ev Post, etc. *Rec*: Reading, unscientific fishing. *a*: 223 Stanley St, North Adelaide, Sth Australia. *T*: Central 3242.

HETHERINGTON, Joseph. *b*: Bishop Auckland 1900. *e*: Elem & Sec. *m*: Stella Winifred Downer. *d*: 2. Journalist. *n.a*: Bishop Auckland staff Northern Echo & Auckland Chronicle 1923—29, Chief Ed Repres Northern Echo & Durham County News, for S.W. Durham & Weardale area '29—. *Rec*: Swimming, tennis. *a*: Glen Esk, Hestobel Gdns, Bishop Auckland, Co Durham. *t*: 348.

HETHERWICK, Rev. Alexander, C.B.E., D.D., M.A. Missny Emeritus, Ch of Scotland. *Publ*: Letters of Robert Hellier Napier (Ed); Scott's Nyanja Dictionary (Ed); The Building of Blantyre Church; The Romance of Blantyre; The Gospel & the African. Croall Lecturer. *c.t*: Life & Work. *a*: 62 Beaconsfield Place, Aberdeen. *t*: 2185.

HETT, Francis Paget, M.B.E. *b*: Victoria, B.C. 1878. *e*: Upper Canada Coll Toronto. *m*: Alice Helena Talbot (dec'd). High Sheriff of Surrey, D.L. *Publ*: The Memoirs of Susan Sibbald; The Memoirs of Robert Sibbald; Georgina, Study of Early Settlement & Church Building in Upper Canada. *s.s*: Oriental. *a*: Littleworth, Esher, Surrey. *T*: Esher 221.

HETT, W. S., M.A. *Publ*: Short History of Greece, Greek Reader. Translator Loeb Library. *a*: Brighton College, Brighton.

HEUNER, E. H. *s.s*: Econ & Internat trade. *a*: Bouverie Hse, Fleet St, E.C.4.

HEWAT, Aubrey Middleton, M.D., D.P.H. Sen M.O. L.C.C. *c.t*: Med & Public Health Journs. *a*: 28 St John's Rd, Putney, S.W.18.

HEWAT, Elizabeth Glendinning Kirkwood, M.A., B.D., Ph.D. *b*: Prestwick, Ayrshire 1895. *e*: Wellington Sch Ayr, Univ & New Coll Edinburgh. Missionary Professor, Missionary Manchuria 1927—32, Asst North Merchiston Church Edin '33—34. *n.a*: Editorial Asst Internat Review of Missions 1920—21. *Publ*: (Jt-Author) Introduction to Missionary Service; Adventures for God in China; China. *Ctr*: Scotsman, Scots Observer, Greatheart, Other Lands, Nat Christian Counc Rev (India). *s.s*: Theology, Religious Educational, Missions. *Rec*: Country dancing, swimming, tennis, sketching. *a*: 33 Palmerston Place, Edinburgh, & Wilson College, Bombay. *T*: Edinburgh 30202.

HEWER, Christopher Langton, M.B., B.S., M.R.C.P., D.A., R.C.P. & S. *b*: London 1896. *e*: U.C.S. & St. Bart's Hosp. *m*: Doris Phœbe Hewer. *s*: 2. *d*: 1. *n.a*: Ed Anæsthesia. *Publ*: Recent Advances in Anæsthesia. *s.s*: Anæsthetics. *a*: Redmayes, Marshalswick Lane, St Albans, Herts. *T*: St. Albans 632

HEWER, Evelyn Everard, D.Sc. Univ Lect. *Publ*: An Introduction to the Study of the Nervous System (2nd edn 1933); med books. *c.t*: Journ of Physiology, Journ of Anatomy, Lancet, B.M.J., Physiological Abstracts, etc. *s.s*: Histology. *a*: Lon (Roy Free Hosp) Sc of Med for Women, Hunter St, W.C.1.

HEWES, John Vernon. *b*: London 1912. Author. *Publ*: The High Courts of Heaven; The Herald of God; Lord of the Eagle. *Ctr*: Highways, Bridges & Aerodromes, Contractor's Record & Municipal Engineering. *s.s*: Aviation, Motoring, History of Middle Ages. *Rec*: Motor racing. *c*: Roy Aero. *a*: 102 High St, Tenterden, Kent.

HEWETT, Peter, B.A. *b*: London 1914. *e*: Latymer Sch Hammersmith & Christ Church Oxf. *m*: Diana Spikes. *d*: 1. Schoolmaster. *Publ*: Poems; Poets of To-morrow I; Bridge over Chaos. *Ctr*: Our Time, Schoolmaster, Modern Education, New Writing. *s.s*: Poetry, Criticism, Politics, Education. *Rec*: Camping, music, painting, gardening. *a*: 44 Lee Park, Blackheath, London, S.E.3. *T*: Lee Green 2493.

HEWITT, Arthur W., M.J.I. Journalist & Lecturer. Authority on European travel, walking tours, camping. *n.a*: Ed Oldham Rucksack Club Journ 1932—35. *c.t*: Oldham Wkly Chronicle ("Skipper"), M/C Guardian ("A. W. H."), News Chronicle, Daily Express etc. *s.s*: Tramping & Pedestrian camping in Britain & W. Europe. Vice Pres Ramblers' Fed M/C '31—35, Exec Mem, Nat Counc Ramblers' Feds. Fndr, & Pres Oldham Rucksack Club, Nat Ramblers' witness before H.M. Nat Parks Comm '30. *Rec*: Walking-tours & camping in little-known corners of Brit & Western Europe. *c*: Oldham Rucksack. *a*: 105 Kirkbank St, Oldham, Lancs.

HEWITT, Francis Vernon. *b*: Leicester 1888. *e*: Queens Col Taunton. *m*: Mary Mabel Partridge. N/p Chm & Dir. *Rec*: Dairy farming. *a*: Buddon Lodge, Herstmonceux, Sussex. *t*: 80.

HEWITT, John Theodore, F.R.S., O.B.E., M.A. PhD., D.Sc. *e*: Hartley Inst, Southampton, Roy Col of Science & St John's Col Camb, Berlin Univs, Heidelberg & Lon. Consulting Chemist, formerly Prof of Chemistry, (Emeritus) E. Lon Col. *Publ*: Organic Chemical Manipulation; Dyestuffs derived from Pyridine, Quinoline, Acridine & Xanthene. *c.t*: Journ of the Chemical Soc, Berichte der deutschen chemischen Gesellschaft, etc. *s.s*: Chemistry. *c*: Athenæum & Savage. *a*: Hurst, nr Reading, Berks.

HEWITT, Kathleen. *b*: Darjeeling, India. Author. *Publ*: Strange Salvation; Mardi; Fetish; A Pattern in Yellow; Comedian; Decoration; Return to the River; The House by the Canal; The Golden Milestone; No Time to Play; Stand-in for Danger; Lady Gone Astray; The Mice are not Amused; Plenty Under the Counter; Thanks for the Apple; The Only Paradise (autobiography); African Shadows (play). *Ctr*: Various. *a*: 29 Forest Court, London, W.2. *T*: Paddington 0233.

HEWITT, Laurence Beamish. *b*: Bath 1882. *e*: K.E. Sch Bath. Musical & Dramatic Critic Bath Chronicle, Mem I.J. 1928—, Fdr Bath Br Gilbert & Sullivan Soc. *n.a*: Bath Herald 1905—07, Bath Chronicle '08—26 & '33—. *Ctr*: Kinematograph Wkly. *s.s*: Music, Dramatic Criticism, Poetry. *Rec*: Cycling, music, verse-making. *a*: 60 Lower Oldfield Park, Bath. *T*: 3583.

HEWITT, Reginald Mainwaring. Prof of English. *Publ*: George Borrow; Sonnets for Helen & other Poems. *c.t*: Slavonic Review, Journ of Gypsy Lore Soc. *a*: The Small House, Beeston.

HEWITT, William Graily, B.A., LL.B. *Publ*: Several works on handwriting & illuminating inc Lettering; Handwriting: Everyman's Craft; Pen to Pantograph; etc. *a*: Steward's Stodham, Liss, Hants.

HEWITT-MYRING, Philip. *b*: Paris 1900. *e*: Eton. Journalist. *n.a*: Asst Lit Ed Daily News '19—20, Leader Page Ed '24—27, staffs of various Amer papers as holder of the Walter Hines Page Fellowship in Journalism '27—28, Chief Foreign Sub-Ed Daily News '28—29, Ed Lon Bureau Assoc Press of Amer '29—32. *c.t*: Sunday Times, News Chron, Spectator, Landmark. *s.s*: Lit criticism, ships & maritime affairs, travel. 2nd Lieut Grenadier Guards (S.R.) '29. *Rec*: Yachting, bridge. *a*: Authors' Club, 2 Whitehall Ct, S.W.1. *t*: Victoria 3160.

HEWLETT, A. E. May. *b*: Sutton-on-Hull, Yorks 1887. *e*: Bedford Coll & London Day Training Coll. *m*: Arthur Hewlett. *s*: 3. *n.a*: Feature Columnist Saskatchewan Farmer 1929—46. *Ctr*: Canadian Farm Mags, Western Dailies & Sunday School Publs; (England) Times, Spectator, Empire Rev, Dly Mail, Farmer's Weekly, Woman's Companion, Housewife, etc; (U.S.A.) Letter. *s.s*: Prairie Farm Life & Local Pioneer History. *Rec*: Writing, travel. *c*: Canadian Women's Press. *a*: Cannington Manor, Saskatchewan, Canada.

HEWLETT, E. F. J. *a*: Holcombe, Vole Way, Mansfield.

HEWLETT, Richard Tanner, M.D.(Lon),F.R.C.P., D.P.H. *b*: Lon. *e*: King's Col Sc & Hosp. *m*: (1) L. M. Stratton; (2) G. Lilian F. Collins. *s*: 6. *d*: 2. *Publ*: Manual of Bacteriology; Manual of Pathology; Serum and Vaccine Therapy; etc. *c.t*: Nature & Med Jnls. *s.s*: Bacteriology & microscopy. Emeritus Prof of Bacteriology Univ of Lon, F. King's Col. Hon Sec Roy Microscopical Socy. *a*: 11 Crooms Hill, Greenwich, S.E.10.

HEWSON, Irene Dale, (see **ROSS, Jean.**) *b*: Dundee, Angus 1907. *e*: Froebel Educ Inst, Roehampton & R.A.D.A. London. *m*: George Robert Dale-Hewson. *s*: 1. *d*: 1. Author & Playwright, Mem Soc of Authors, Playwrights & Composers. *Rec*: Travel, theatre, literature, gardening, the occult. *a*: White Lodge, Crawley Rd, Newport Pagnell, Bucks. *T*: Newport Pagnell 230.

HEWSON, Lionel Lloyd, M.V.O. *b*: Bantry 1874. *e*: Ardvreck Sc Crieff & U.S. Col, Westward Ho! *m*: E. F. Hewson. Ed Irish Golf (Proprietor). *n.a*: Irish Times Golf 1907-11, Ed Irish Life '10-14. *Publ*: Irish Golf Directory. *s.s*: Golf, Irish affairs. War Service, S. African & Gt War. *c*: Roy Irish Auto. *a*: Gathorne, Portmarnock, Co Dublin. *t*: 20.

HEY, Wilson Harold, F.R.C.S. Consulting Surgeon. *a*: 16 St John St, Manchester. *t*: Blackfriars 8028.

HEYER, Georgette. *b*: Wimbledon 1902. *m*: G. R. Rougier. *s*: 1. Novelist. *Publ*: The Black Moth; Beauvallet; Devil's Cub; The Unfinished Clue; An Infamous Army; Royal Escape; The Spanish Bride; Friday's Child; The Reluctant Widow; etc. *s.s*: Costume & Detective Novels. *c*: Empress. *a*: Albany, London, W.1.

HEYER, Gustav Richard. *b*: Kreûznach A.N 1890. *m*: Friederika Zobel. *s*: 1. Doctor of Medicine, Psycho-Analyst. *Publ*: Seelen führung (1929); Der nervöse mensch; Hypnose u. Hynotherapie; The Organism of the Mind ('33); etc. *Rec*: Shooting. W.S. (Iron Cross 1st Cl.) *c*: Psychological, Zurich, Internat Soc for Psychotherapy. *a*: München (Bavaria), Kaûlbachstr. 28. *t*: 21296.

HEYGATE, John. *b*: Eton. *e*: Eton, Balliol Coll Oxf. *m*:. *s*: 2. Author, Asst News Ed B.B.C. 1926—29, Supervisor English versions of films with UFA Berlin '32—33 & '35. *Publ*: Decent Fellows; A House for Joanna; Motor Tramp; Talking Picture; White Angel; These Germans; Love & Death. *Ctr*: Dly Express. *s.s*: Germany. *a*: Bellarena, Co Londonderry, Nth Ireland.

HEYGATE, Sir John Edward Nourse, Bt. (See HEYGATE, John.)

HEYLIN, Henry Brougham, O.B.E. *b*: Worsley 1870 *m*: Annie Elizabeth Ball. Brit Textile Authority. Insp & Adv Textiles Brit War Office 1913-33. Head of Textile Dept Salford Roy Tech Inst '00—05. Mill Mang Dir '05—11. *Publ*: Cotton-Weaver's Handbook; Buyers & Sellers in the Cotton Trade; Visions Amidst the Strands of Web; etc. *s.s*: Textile Manufrs. Inventor of Porosity-test machine for fabrics. Designed a special texture of cotton tent duck for Brit War Office, also new form of Hosp Tent Marquee. Fell Textile Inst. *Rec*: Nature studies. *a*: The Fibres, Clevedon Rd, Tilehurst-on-Thames, Reading.

HEYM, Stefan, M.A.(Chicago). *b*: Chemnitz, Germany 1913. *m*: Gertrude Heym. Author, Mem Authors' Guild. *n.a*: Ed Deutsches Volksecho '37—39. *Publ*: Hostages; Of Smiling Peace; Nazis in U.S.A.; etc. *Ctr*: N.Y. Times Mag. *s.s*: Fiction. *ws.*: 1943—45 U.S. Army, Field & Assoc-Ed U.S. Army Press. *a*: c/o Little, Brown & Co, 34 Beacon St, Boston, Mass, U.S.A.

HEYMANSON, Sydney Rendall, M.A. *b*: Melbourne 1904. *e*: Univs of Melbourne & London. Journalist, Lecturer, Political Science, Science & Economics. *n.a*: City Ed Australian Newsps Cable Service. *Publ*: World Economic Conference Handbook. *Ctr*: English, Australian & American Newsps. *s.s*: Finance & Politics, Aviation, Travel. *Rec*: Reading. *a*: 67–69 Chancery Lne, London, W.C.2. *T*: Central 3160.

HEYNEMAN, Julie Helen. *b*: San Francisco 1878. *e*: Art Scs, Paris, San Francisco, & John S. Sargent, London. Portrait Painter, Journalist, Author. *Publ*: Desert Cactus (Biography of a Sculptor); Headline Stuff; The Pioneer Police Woman; Woman at the Cross Roads. *c.t*: Observer, Landmark, Pall Mall Mag,

Harper's Mag, The Smart Set (U.S.A.), San Francisco Chronicle, etc. *s.s*: Art, criticism, book reviews. War Diplomas Red Cross, Medal R.C. Mem Elizabeth of Belgium. *Rec*: Travel. *c*: English Speaking Union. *a*: 56 Lansdowne Rd, W.11. *t*: Park 1261.

HEYNES, Amy Elizabeth. *b*: Kenilworth 1860. *e*: Montpellier Hse, Kenilworth. *Publ*: Stray Rhymes; The Red Valley; The Dance of Flowers; Thoughts & Dreams; Chimney Corner Shivers. *c.t*: Leamington Chronicle, Local papers, Home & Abroad, Poetry Quarterly, etc. *s.s*: Poems & short stories. *a*: 9 Cross Rd, Milverton, Leamington Spa.

HEYST, Axel, Ph.D. *b*: 1903. Married. *d*: 1. Writer & Political Publicist, Mem Internat P.E.N. & Un of Journalists. *n.a*: Worked for Cent European papers & broadcasting systems. *Publ*: After Hitler; Wanted, A New Vision; Words & Darkness; There Shall be No Victory. *Ctr*: 19th Century & After, Nat Rev, Empire Rev, Time & Tide. *s.s*: Internat Affairs, Psychoanalysis. *Rec*: Ski-ing, tennis, rock climbing. *c*: R.A.C., Allied Circle. *w.s*: British War Corres & Lecturer 41—44. *a*: 105 Hallam St, London, W.1.

HEYWARD, Du Bose, LittD.(Hon). *b*: Charleston 1885. *e*: Pub Sc. *m*: Dorothy Hartzell Kuhns. *d*: 1. Writer. *Publ*: Carolina Chansons (with Hervey Allen) Poems (1922); Angel —a Novel; Porgy—a Play, with Dorothy Heyward; Brass Ankle—a Play; Jasbo Brown & collected Poems; Mambra's Daughters— a Novel ('29); Peter Ashley—a Novel ('33). *c.t*: Atlantic Mthly, American Outlook, American Mercury, Lon Mercury, etc. *s.s*: The primitive American negro. *c*: Authors' League of America, Poetry Soc of America, etc. *a*: Summer-Dawn Hill, Hendersonville N.C., U.S.A. Winter—Follywood, Folly Beach S.C., U.S.A. *t*: 484J—Summer only.

HEYWOOD, Rt. Rev. Bernard Oliver Francis, M.A., D.D. *b*: Swinton, Lancs 1871. *e*: Harrow & Trin Coll Camb. *m*: Marion Maude Lempriere. *s*: 5. *d*: 2. Canon of St Albans Cathedral & Assistant Bishop to Bishop of St Albans since 1942. *Publ*: This is Our Faith; About the Lambeth Conference; The Bible Day by Day; Seeking God; Memoir of Bishop Harry Wollcombe (Ed). *Ctr*: Manch Guardian, Yorks Post, Hull Dly Mail, C. of E. Newsp, Church Times, etc. *Rec*: Motoring. *c*: Church Hse. *a*: 34 Lancaster Rd, St Albans, Herts. *T*: 251.

HEYWOOD, Harry Norval. *b*: Oldham. Journalist. *n.a*: Dir & Chief Lond Ed Kemsley Newspapers Ltd. *a*: Kemsley Newspapers Ltd, Kemsley Ho; 200 Gray's Inn Rd, London, W.C.1, & 92 Princes Pk Ave, Golders Green, London, N.W.11. *T*: Terminus 1234 & Speedwell 4500.

HEYWOOD, Jean Schofield. *b*: Middleton 1915. *e*: Manchester Hgh Sch for Girls & Manch Univ. Hospital Almoner. *Publ*: St Peter's Fields, the Story of Peterloo. *Ctr*: Middleton Guardian, The Serpent. *s.s*: Lancashire Life & Character in Early 19th Century. *Rec*: Singing & bee-keeping. *a*: Denehurst, Archer Park, Middleton, Lancs. *T*: Middleton 3279.

HEYWOOD, Thomas Taylor. *b*: Rochdale 1892. *e*: Rochdale Parish Church Sc. *m*: Gladys Turner. *s*: 1. Journalist. *Publ*: New Annals of Rochdale. *s.s*: Sport. Engaged writing a History of Rochdale. War Service 1914-19. Mem Rochdale Town Counc. *Rec*: Golf, public work. *c*: Manchester Golf Club, Rochdale Conservative Club, Rochdale Bowling Club, British Legion (Rochdale Branch). *a*: 11 Geneva Terrace, Rochdale, Lancs. *t*: 3069.

HEYWOOD, Valentine. Deputy Ed Sunday Times. *n.a*: Mang Ed Yorkshire Observer 1919, Ed Sheffield Independent '20—25, Asst Ed The Star '26—30 & Mang Ed The Sunday News '30—32, News Ed Sun Times '33—44, Asst Ed '44—46. *a*: Birch Hanger, Chalfont St Giles, Bucks. *T*: 256.

HEZLET, Maj.-Gen. R. K., C.B.E., D.S.O. Army Officer. *Publ*: Nomography. *a*: c/o Lloyd's Bank, Cox & King's Branch, 6 Pall Mall, S.W.1.

HIBBART-GILSON, Marcus Mervyn Tobias. *b*: Lon 1899. *e*: Priv. *m*: Ethel Constance Wilkinson. *d*: 1. *n.a*: Ed Mossel Bay Advertiser (Cape Province) 1921—22. *Publ*: Uninspired Verse; The Hidden Splendour; Beyond a Dream's Domain; The Unaccepted Death (novel); Dinner Din (play); Songs of a Mood; etc. *c.t*: Bookman, John o' London, Yorkshire Post, Sunday Referee, etc. *s.s*: Lit criticism, book production. Publ's Reader '16—. Lect on Lit Subjects in Johannesburg '21—23. *Rec*: Swimming, chess. *c*: Nat Lib. *a*: Nat Lib Club, Whitehall Pl, S.W.1. *t*: Whitehall 9871.

HIBBERT, Walter. Physico-Chemist & Electrician. *Publ*: Life & Energy; Electric Ignition; Magneto & Electric Ignition. *c.t*: Ency Brit. *a*: Cainford, nr Darlington, Co. Durham

HIBBERT, William Nembhard, LL.D. *b*: W. Norwood 1873. *e*: Dulwich Col & King's Col Lon. *m*: Alice Mary Ball. *d*: 1. Barrister-at-Law. Lect & Recognised Teacher in Jurisprudence, Evidence & Procedure & Conflict of Laws at King's Col '98–1933. *Publ*: Law of Evidence; Law of Procedure; International Private Law; History of the Worshipful Company of Founders, London; etc. *s.s*: Conflict of laws. Sometime Dean of Faculty of Laws at Univ of Lon & King's Col Lon. Fell King's Col. *Rec*: Billiards. *a*: Arthur Seat, Harvey Rd, Guildford, Surrey & 1 Garden Ct, Temple, E.C.4. *t*: Central 8649.

HIBBS, Ben, A.B., Litt.D. *b*: Fontana, Kansas 1901. *e*: Public Schs of Kansas, Univ of Kansas. *m*: Edith K. Doty. *s*: 1. Ed Sat Ev Post '42—, Dir Curtis Publ Co. *n.a*: News Ed Fort Morgan (Colo) Times '23, Pratt (Kan) Tribune '24, Ed & Mang Goodland (Kan) News-Republic '26—27, Ed Mang Ed Arkansas City (Kan), Traveller '27—29, Assoc Ed Country Gentleman Phila, Pa '29—40. *Ctr*: Sat Ev Post, Country Gentleman, Reader's Digest, etc. *a*: 713 Braeburn Lane, Penn Valley, Narberth, Penn.

HIBERNIA (pen name): see **Potten, Henry Thomas.**

HICHENS, Robert Smythe, F.R.S.L. *b*: 1864. *e*: Clifton. Journalist & Author. *Publ*: The Green Carnation; Flames; Tongues of Conscience; The Woman with the Fan; Bella Donna; The Garden of Allah; The Paradine Case; The Prophet of Berkeley Square; Felix; Barbary Sheep; The Way of Ambition; On the Screen; Doctor Artz; Snake Bite; Mortimer Brice; The Call of the Blood; The Fruitful Vine; The Dweller on the Threshold; A New Way of Life; Veils; Harps in the Wind; etc; (plays) The Garden of Allah; The Real Woman; etc. *c*: Athenæum, R.A.C. *a*: Muralto, Zurich, Switzerland.

HICK, John. *b*: York 1897. *e*: St George's R.C. Sc York. *m*: Mary Ginley. *d*: 2. Sub-Ed. *n.a*: Reporter Yorks Herald 1911–23, Yorks Evening Argus '23-25, Yorks Post '26–29, Sub-Ed Yorks Observer '29–. *s.s*: Agric, rugby. War Service. Cmt York & Dis Rugby League. Chm Bradford Br N.U.J. '31. Sec '33. *a*: 4 Spring Terrace, Shipley, Yorks.

HICKEY, Theodosia Frances Wynne, B.A. *b*: Westport, Ireland 1895. *e*: Alexandra Col, Dublin & T.C.D. *m*: Jeremy Hickey. *s*: 1. *d*: 1. *Publ*: Semi-detached; Easter Week; The Birthday Party. *Rec*: Golf, bridge. *a*: c/o Messrs A. P. Watt, 10 Norfolk St, Strand, W.C.2.

HICKINGBOTHAM, Harry. *e*: Lincoln Sc. Jnlst. *n.a*: Ed Folkestone Express '15—. *a*: 96 Radnor Park Rd, Folkestone. *t*: 2834.

HICKLING, Arthur, J.P. County Councillor for Westmorland. *n.a*: Mang Carlisle Journ 1916—23, Mang Whitehaven News & W. Cumberland News '18—23, Mang Ed Durham Co Advertiser & Durham Chron '23—30. *Publ*: The Ritual Explained; Northumberland & Durham Coals & Coke; The Scottish Coalfields. *a*: Ruskin Hse, Ambleside, Westmorland. *T*: Ambleside 200.

HICKMAN, Moreland. *b*: Stepney 1864. *e*: St John's Col Battersea. *m*: Ellen Ottaway. *s*: 2. Journalist & Master Printer. *n.a*: Daily Telegraph (F.L. 50 y), South London Press, Battersea & Wandsworth Times, etc. *c.t*: Lon & prov press. *a*: Old Station Rd, Loughton, Essex. *t*: 231.

HICKMAN-SMITH, Arthur Ernest. *b*: Birm 1876. *e*: Masons Col, Municipal Sc of Art & Inst Sc of Music Birm. *m*: Marie Westcott. *d*: 1. Author-Composer. *Publ*: Tales from the Trenches; Yiddisher Yarns; Fishy Fishing Fables; Wee Draps O' Scotch; Twenty-Six Monologues; Twelve Recitations for Ladies; Have you heard These; etc. *c.t*: Musical News, Musical Standard, Musical Courier, The Melody, Lancs Advertiser & many Provincial N/ps. *s.s*: Music, verse, humour. Exhibited paintings in many exhibitions. War Capt Scottish Rifles (Cameronians). Conductor of Battalion Orchestra. Wrote the Battalion March " Shoulder to Shoulder." Pres " National Music Circle." *Rec*: Fishing, painting, singing. *a*: Highbury Quadrant, N.5.

HICKS, Sir Cedric Stanton, Kt.Bach, M.D., M.Sc., Ph.D., F.R.I.C., O.St.J. *b*: Mosgiel, N.Z. 1892. *e*: Otago Boys' Hgh Sch & Univ, Trinity Coll Camb & Univs of Freiburg, Zurich & Vienna. *m*: Florence Haggitt. *s*: 2. Prof of Human Physiology & Pharmacology Univ of Adelaide. Co-Ed Aust Journ of Experimental Biology & Med Science, Mem Ed-Bd Excerpta Medica, Amsterdam. *Publ*: Soil, Food & Life; Nutrition for the Australian People. *Ctr*: Various Sc Journs. *s.s*: Physiology, Pharmacology, Chemistry, Pathology, Nutrition as National Problem of Food Production & Soil Management. *Rec*: Gardening & fruit farm. *c*: Roy Socs, Naval & Military. *w.s*: Founder & Cmmdr Australian Army Catering Corps 1942—45. *a*: Woodley, Glen Osmond, Sth Australia. *T*: U.4108.

HICKS, E. *b*: Cornwall 1878. *e*: Llandovery Col. Widower. *s*: 1. *d*: 2. Ed. *Publ*: Sir Thomas Malory: His Turbulent Career. *c*: Rotary, Leamington. *a*: Leamington Courier, Leamington. *t*: 972.

HICKS, Sir (Edward) Seymour. *Publ*: inc Vintage Years; Me & My Missus; Acting : A Book for Amateurs; Twenty-four Years of an Actor's Life; etc.

HICKS, Ernest George. *b*: Vernham Dean 1879. *e*: Elem Sc & Polytechnic. *m*: Kate Louisa Bennett. *s*: 1. *d*: 1. Gen Sec Amal Union Bldg Trade Workers. *Publ*: Poverty from Plenty; The Struggle for Socialism; The Chaos Produced by Capitalism; The Future of the Workers' Clubs; etc. *c.t*: Daily Herald, Clarion, Woolwich Citizen, etc. *s.s*: Trade unionism, econ, etc. *Rec*: Cricket. *c*: Nat Labour, Nat Trade Union, etc. *a*: The Builders, Cresc Grove, S. Side, Clapham Common, S.W.4. *t*: Macaulay 2442.

HICKS, Rt. Rev. F. C. N., Lord Bishop of Lincoln. *Publ*: The Fullness of Sacrifice (1930). *a*: Old Palace, Lincoln. *t*: 1430.

HICKS, G. Dawes, M.A., PhD., LittD., F.B.A. *b*: Shrewsbury 1862. *e*: Roy G.S. Guildford, Owen's Col M/C, M/C Col Oxf, Leipzig Univ. Married twice. Emeritus Prof of Philos U.C.L. *n.a*: Asst Ed Hibbert Journ 1902-. Pres Aristotelian Soc '13–14. Hibbert Lect '31. Upton Lect '33–34. Essex Hall Lect '34. *Publ*: Die Begriffe Phanomeron & Nommenon bei Kant (1897); English Philosophy in the 19th Century; Ways Towards the Spiritual Life; Berkeley (Leaders of Philosophy, series); Human Personality & Future Life (1934). *c.t*: Proc Aristotelian Soc, Mind, Brit Journ Psych, Inquirer, etc. *s.s*: Philos, Psych. Many y Chm Bd Philos Studies Lon Univ. *Rec*: Gardening. *c*: Savile, etc. *a*: 9 Cranmer Rd, Cam.

HICKS, John Donald, M.A.(North-western), Ph.D.(Wis). *b*: Pickering, Mo 1890. *m*: Lucile Curtis Hicks. *d*: 3. Morrison Prof of History Univ of Calif 1942—. *Publ*: The Populist Revolt; The Federal Union; The American Nation; Short History of American Democracy. *Ctr*: Various Historical Journs. *s.s*: Recent & Western U.S. History. *a*: University of California, Berkeley 4. California, U.S.A. *T*: Ash. 3-8516.

HICKS, Seymour. *Publ*: Difficulties; Hullo, Australians; If I Were Your Father. *a*: c/o G. Duckworth & Co Ltd, 3 Henrietta St, W.C.2.

HICKS, Rev. Walter Percy, B.D., F.J.I. *b*: Witney 1868. *e*: Blue Coat Sc. *m*: Augusta Saunders Smith. *s*: 1. *d*: 1. Bapt Min & Ed Christian Herald. *n.a*: 8 y Assoc Ed Christian Herald 1894—1902, 32 y Ed 1902—34. Pastorates:—Chigwell, Essex '05—10, Woodford '10—13, Stratford '13—22. *Publ*: Life of Dr. Talmage (2 edns); The World's Present Crisis (2nd edn); The World's Saturday Night (15th edn); The Antichrist To-day (3rd edn); What is the Oxford Group Movement; numerous articles; etc. *s.s*: Eschatology, evangelism. *Rec*: Gardening. *a*: Dunrovin, 23 Fitzjames Av, Addiscombe, Croydon. *t*: Addiscombe 2993.

HICKS, William John. *b*: Launceston 1912. *e*: Howell G.S. Launceston. Jnlst. *n.a*: Cornish & Devon Post '28—32; Peterborough Standard '32—33; Eastern Daily Press, Norwich, '33. *s.s*: Table tennis, cricket, travel. *Rec*: Cricket, table tennis, swimming, travel. *c*: N.U.J., Toc H. *a*: 4 Park Rd, Dereham, Norfolk. *t*: 124.

HICKS, William Mitchinson, ScD.(Cantab), D.Sc(Sheff), F.R.S. *b*: Launceston 1850. *e*: Priv Sc & St John's Col Cam. *m*: Ellen Perrin. *s*: 2. Emer Prof of Physics Sheff. *Publ*: Elementary Dynamics 1879; The Analysis of Spectra (1922), etc. *c.t*: Proc & Transaction Roy Soc, Philos Mag, etc. *s.s*: Phys Sc. Princ of Firth Col 1883, 1st Vice-Chanc Sheff Univ 1905, Prof of Physics Sheff Univ '05, Pres of Sect A at Ipswich meeting of Brit Assoc 1895. *a*: The Crowhurst Hotel, Crowhurst, Sx. *t*: 56.

HICKS BEACH, Susan. *b*: Dumbleton. *m*: W. F. Hicks Beach. *Publ*: A Cotswold Family; Shuttered Doors; Blackmarston; Cousin Georgina; A Cardinal of the Medici; Anabel & Mary Verena. *Ctr*: Yellow Book, Nineteenth Century, Blackwood. *a*: Mawley Ho, Quenington, Glos. *T*: Coln St Aldwyn 33.

HICKSON, Sydney John, F.R.S., M.A., D.Sc(Lon & M/C), LL.D.(Edin). *b*: Lon 1859. *e*: Mansion G.S. Leatherhead, Univ Col Sc & Univ Col Lon, St Bart's Hosp & Downing Col Cam. *m*: A. Fletcher. *s*: 1. *d*: 1. Prof of Zool (ret); Dr Zool Gröningen. *Publ*: A Naturalist in North Celebes ('89); The Fauna of the Deep Sea; The Story of Life in the Seas; An Introduction to the Study of Recent Corals (1924). *c.t*: Scientific Journals, Manchester Guardian, Nature, etc. *s.s*: Corals. Trav in Malay Archipelago, in Mexico & U.S.A. Beyer Prof of Zool in M/C Univ 1894-1926. Prof Emeritus in '26 & Hon Fell Downing Col Cam. *a*: 26 Barton Rd, Cam. *t*: 1869.

HIGBY, Chester Penn, M.A.(Bucknell), LL.D., Ph.D.(Columb). *b*: nr Ottawa, Ill 1885. *m*: Jane McKinner. *s*: 1. Prof of History Univ of Wisconsin, Mem Amer Hist Assoc. *n.a*: Ed-Bd Journ of Modern Hist 1935—38, Book Reviewer Greensboro Dly News '23—27. *Publ*: Religious Policy of Bavarian Government during Napoleonic Period; Present Status of Modern European History in the U.S.; History of Europe '42—45; Motley (Jt-Author); Growth of European Civilisation '42—45. *Ctr*: Milwaukee Journ, Journ of Modern Hist, Amer Hist & Political Sc Revs. *s.s*: Modern European History. *Rec*: Golf. *c*: Univ & Blackhawk Country. *a*: 1829 Van Hise Ave, Madison 5, Wisconsin, U.S.A. *T*: Gifford 1728.

HIGGIN, J. Reporter Accrington dis, Lancs Daily Post & Preston Guardian 1922-. Treas E. Lancs Br N.U.J. '19-. Treas N. Counc N.U.J. '28-. Sec Modern Lang Club, Accrington '22-23-24. Sec Accrington Billiards Championship '20-21-22, etc. C.Q.M.S. 8th Bn York & Lancaster Regt. *a*: 115 Avenue Parade, Accrington. *t*: 2109.

HIGGINBOTHAM, J. *n.a*: Art Ed Evening Post, Jersey. *s.s*: Press photography, cartoons, process engraving, etching. *a*: c/o Evening Post, Charles St, St Helier, Jersey.

HIGGINBOTTOM, Frederick James. *b*: Accrington 1859. *e*: Priv Sc. *m*: Anne Elizabeth Neville (dec). Journalist (ret). *n.a*: Southport Daily News '75—78, Ed Southport Critic '78—80, Press Assoc Special Corr & Ed '81—91, Nat Press Dublin Lon Corr '91—92, Pall Mall Gazette Polit Corr Mang Ed & Ed '92—1915, Daily Chron Polit & Parl Corr '18—30. *Publ*: The Vivid Life: A Journalist's Career ('34); House of Commons Handbook 1895—1911; Islington Year Book (1898). Ed Pall Mall Gazette during Parl Bill Controversy '09—11, Mem Del of Brit Eds to Sweden '06 & to Germany '07. Took part in world tour of Empire Press Un to Melbourne Conf '25. Fell & Hon Vice-Pres I.J. & Chm of its Provident & Convalescent Funds. Hon Treas Women's Utd Services League '18. Life Gov Roy N. Hosp Lon. *c*: Press. *a*: The Lawn, Briston, Melton Constable, Norfolk.

HIGGINS, Alexander Pearce, C.B.E., K.C., LL.D., F.B.A. *b*: Worcester 1865. *e*: Worcester Cath (King's) Sc, Downing Col Cam. *m*: Mina MacLennan. *s*: 2. Prof of Internat Law Cam. Lect on Maritime Internat Law R.N. War & Staff Cols Greenwich. *n.a*: Jt-Ed Brit Yr Book of Internat Law. *Publ*: The Hague Peace Conferences; War & the Private Citizen; The Binding Force of International Law; Studies in International Law & Relations; Ed 7th & 8th edns of W. E. Hall's International Law. *c.t*: Law Quarterly, Juridical Review, etc. *a*: Trin Col Cam & 52 Bateman St, Cam. *t*: 1756.

HIGGINS, James Hart, N.U.J. *b*: Sth Norwood 1911. *e*: Sth Norwood Elem Sch, John Ruskin Cent Sch Croydon. *m*: Marjorie Clark. *d*: 1. Author & Journalist. *n.a*: Free-lance fiction writer for main periodical houses '37—40, at present Editorial Writer in Press Dept of R.K.O. Pictures Ltd. *Ctr*: Adventure, Rover, Skipper, Wizard, Triumph, Boy's Cinema, Buzzer, Flying, Peg's Paper, Miracle, Red Star Weekly, Oracle, etc. *s.s*: Boys Fiction, Film matters. *Rec*:

Music, motor-cycling, reading. *c*: Trade Union. *w.s*: Army '40—45. *a*: 12 Thornton Hill, Wimbledon, London, S.W.19.

HIGGINS, John T. *b*: Grenoside 1875. *e*: Independ Endowed Sc & Old Firth Col. Married. *s*: 1. *d*: 1. Journalist. *n.a*: Chief Rep Sheffield Independ & Sheffield Mail 1919, etc, Special Corr, original Sheffield Mail 1908, etc, at present, and for some years Commercial Ed Daily Independ, Ed & Founder Industrial Supplement (Annual), Daily Independ, Housing Supplement, etc. Formerly Ed of Weekly Independent. *c.t*: Continental, S. Africa & Amer n/ps (formerly). *s.s*: Sheffield industrialism & the coalfield of the three counties. Nominated by the first Minister of Labour to write Industrial Sketches for Daily Citizen, etc. *Rec*: Various. *a*: 5 May Rd, Hillsboro', Sheffield.

HIGGINSON, Alexander Henry. *b*: Boston U.S.A. 1876. *e*: Harvard Univ. *m*: Mary Newcomb. *s*: 1. *Publ*: Hunting in the U.S. & Canada; Letters of an Old Sportsman to a Young One; As Hounds Ran; Try Back. *c.t*: The Times, The Morning Post, The Field, The Sportsman (U.S.A.), Polo. *s.s*: Hunting & Hounds. Forty years an M.F.H. *Rec*: Hunting. *a*: Cattistock, Dorchester, Dorset. *t*: Maiden Newton 7.

HIGGINSON, Ella. *b*: Kansas, U.S.A. *e*: High Scs & privately. *m*: Russell Carden Higginson (dec). Poet Laureate Washington State. *n.a*: Conducted literary dept Seattle Times 1900—05. *Publ*: Stories:—The Flower that Grew in the Sand; From the Land of the Snow Pearls; A Forest Orchid; poems:—When the Birds go North Again; The Voice of April-Land; The Vanishing Race; novel:—Mariella of Outwest; travel:—Alaska, The Great Country. *c.t*: Collier's, Scribner's, McClure's, Sippincott's, Success, Harper's, Leslie's etc. *s.s*: Fiction, poetry. *c*: Hon Mem Washington State Fed of Women's Clubs, etc. *a*: 605 High St, Bellingham, Washington State, U.S.A. *t*: 4160.

HIGGINSON, Tom. *b*: Hambleton, nr Blackpool 1904. *e*: Baines's G.S., Poulton-le-Fylde. Journalist. *n.a*: Blackpool, Burton-on-Trent, Northern Daily Telegraph ('29). *Rec*: Angling. Mem N.U.J. *a*: 7 Osborne St, Preston. *t*: 56187.

HIGGS, Alec Stansbury ("Alec Stansbury"). *b*: Lon 1890. *e*: Westcliff Col Ramsgate. Author, Playwright & Journalist. *Publ*: Searchlight; Charred Wood; Cupid Painted Blind; Cocoon; Othello's Visage; etc. Plays in collab with W. H. Clifford Hendry:—Marriage of Inconvenience; When You've said that You've said All. *a*: 59 New Church Rd, Hove, Sussex. *t*: 3452.

HIGGS, H. *a*: Fairlight, Kew Road, Richmond, Surrey.

HIGGS, Mary, HonM.A. *b*: Devizes 1854. *e*: Girton. *m*: Rev Thomas Kilpin Higgs. *s*: 1. *d*: 3. Social Worker. *n.a*: Pioneer of Beautiful Oldham Soc 1902, 1st Sec of Oldham Counc of Social Service, Northern Sec Nat Women's Lodging Hse Assoc, etc. *Publ*: Glimpses into the Abyss: Five Days & Nights as a Tramp; How to Deal with the Unemployed; Mother Wareing; Where Shall She Live?; Where Shall He Live?; An Octave of Song; The Way to the Joyous Life; etc. *c.t*: M/C Guardian, Oldham Chronicle, Friend, etc. *s.s*: Vagrancy, city beautification, maternity welfare. See 20th Cent New Testament Coy. Pioneered Casual Ward Reform. Witness before Cmt on Vagrancy, Wage-earning Children & Vagrancy Reform. Garden Cities & Housing Reform, etc. *Rec*: Country. *a*: Bent Hse, Oldham, & Greenacres, Shepton Mallet. *t*: Oldham 4370 (Main).

HIGGS-WALKER, James Arthur, M.A.(Oxon). *b*: Clent, Worcs 1892. *e*: Repton Sch, St John's Coll Oxf. *m*: Muriel Jessie Smith. *d*: 1. Headmaster Sevenoaks Sch, Mem Headmasters' Conference. *Publ*: European History 1789—1915; Introduction to French Society in the Eighteenth Century. *Ctr*: History. *s.s*: History. *Rec*: Cricket, riding, travel. *w.s*: Capt Worcs Regt 1914—18. *a*: Sevenoaks School, Kent.

HIGHAM, Sir Charles. *b*: Lon 1876. *e*: Priv. (Divorced). *s*: 1. *d*: 1. Author & Publicist. M.P. 1918—22. *Publ*: Scientific Distribution ('16); Looking Forward ('21); Advertising ('26). *c.t*: Various n/ps. *s.s*: Politics, business. Dir of Publicity War Savings Cmt '16—17. Org War Shrines (with Mr. Sydney Walton C.B.E.) '17—18. Chm Coalition Publicity Cmt '18. Writer of Appeals of Men & Money '14—18. Rejected for Army Service '14—15. Freeman City of Lon. *c*: Carlton, Devons, Advertising, City Livery. *a*: Africa Hse, Kingsway, Lon. *t*: Holborn 9471.

HIGHAM, Thomas Farrant. *b*: Kasauli, India 1890. *e*: Clifton Coll & Trin Coll Oxf. *m*: Mary Elizabeth Rogers. *s*: 1. *d*: 1. Public Orator Oxf Univ, Fell, Senior Tutor, Tutor in Classics Trin Coll Oxf. *Publ*: (co-editor) The Mind of Rome; The Oxford Book of Greek Verse; The Oxford Book of Greek Verse in Translation; From the Greek. *Ctr*: Classical Rev, Classical Quarterly; Greece & Rome. *s.s*: Classics, Translations, Modern Uses of Latin. *Rec*: Conchology. *w.s*: Attached G.S.I. Brit Salonika Force 1916—19, For Off 1940—45. *a*: Trinity College & 26 Northmoor Rd, Oxford. *T*: 3116 & 5588.

HIGHFIELD, George. *b*: Bradford 1884. *e*: Hartley Coll Southampton. *m*: Alexandra Kozlova. *s*: 1. Parliamentary Journalist (ret). *n.a*: Ed Vladivostok 1918—19, N China D News Shanghai '19—20, Ed Central China Post Hankow '20—26, Central Press '27—40. *Ctr*: Newcastle Journ, Nott'm Guardian, Financial News. *s.s*: Parliamentary Sketches, Far East, etc. *Rec*: Gardening. *c*: Press, I.J. *w.s*: 1914—18 Eng Instructor Imp Russian Naval Cadet Corps. *a*: 7 Spencer Rd, East Molesey, Surrey.

HIGSON, Kit. *b*: Blackburn. *n.a*: Clarion, B.B.C., Red Mag. *Publ*: The Law Allows; That Surprising Boy Spinks; The Dull House. *s.s*: Novels, sketches, plays, short stories. *a*: Mid Oaks, Horns Cross, Northiam, Sussex.

HILDEBRAND, Karl Gustaf H., Ph.D. *b*: Stockholm 1911. *e*: Uppsala Univ. *m*: Majstina Rydh. *s*: 1. *d*: 1. Historian Uppsala Univ. *n.a*: Ed Religious Sect Nu 34—'36, Ed Var Losen '38—40. *Publ*: Falu stads historia; Vardagjamning; Nodvarn; Kristna perspektiv; Medan natter vanar; etc. *Ctr*: Svenska Dagbladet, Svensk Tidskrift. *s.s*: Econ Hist, Religious Questions, Poetry. *a*: Norrlandsgaten 28, Uppsala, Sweden. *T*: 36785.

HILDESLEY, His Hon. Judge, K.C., M.A., J.P. *b*: M/C 1873. *e*: Priv & Pembroke Col Oxf. *m*: Cicely Ayliffe Glynn (dec). *s*: 3. *d*: 1. Judge of County Courts. *Publ*: The Press Gang ('25); Konstam & Hildesley on Rates & Taxes; Ed of Butterworth's Digest of Leading Cases in Workmen's Compensation ('33), etc. *c.t*: Prov n/ps, etc. *s.s*: Legal hist, antiquities. Chm of E. Suffolk Quarter Sessions '33—. *Rec*: Bibliog, fly-fishing, etc. *c*: Oxf & Cam. *a*: Onehouse Lodge, Stowmarket, Suffolk. *t*: 120.

HILDESLEY, P. T., F.R.S.A., F.I.B.D. Archit, Interior Designer, Artist. *Publ:* English Furniture Designs. *a:* 73 Grosvenor St, W.1.

HILDYARD, Mrs. Ida Jane ("Ida Lemon"). *b:* Lon 1867. *e:* Notting Hill H.S. & Priv. *m:* Canon William Hildyard. *s:* 2. *d:* 1 (dec). *Publ:* A Divided Duty; A Pair of Lovers; Matthew Furth; etc. *c.t:* Girl's Own Paper, Sunday at Home, Leisure Hour, Cornhill & Argosy. Church Army Gazette. *c:* Lon Lyceum. *a:* Rowley Rectory, Little Weighton, nr Hull. E. Yorks. *t:* Kirkella 46401.

HILEY, Albert Edward. *b:* Gainsborough 1905. *e:* Gainsborough Sch. *m:* Miss Morrison. *s:* 2. *d:* 1. Journalist, Sec East Midland Guild of Newsp Eds. *n.a:* Ed Retford, Worksop, Isle of Axholme, Gainsborough News & Gainsborough Ev News. *Rec:* Golf. *c:* Gainsborough. *a:* 42 Market Pl, Gainsborough. *T:* 155.

HILL, Adrian Keith Graham, R.B.A., R.O.I., R.I. *b:* Charlton, Kent. *e:* Dulwich Coll, Roy Coll of Art. *m:* Dorothy Whitley. *s:* 1. Artist, Life Master & Sect Anatomy Westminster Sch of Art 1934—37, Official War Artist '14—18. *Publ:* Art versus Illness; On Drawing & Painting Trees; On the Mastery of Painting in Water Colours. *Ctr:* The Studio, Artist, Times, Strand, etc. *s.s:* Art Therapy, Art in the Home. *a:* Old Laundry Cottage, Midhurst, Sussex. *T:* Midhurst 18.

HILL, Archibald Vivian, F.R.S., *b:* Bristol 1886. *e:* Blundell's Sch & Trinity Coll Camb. *m:* Margaret Neville Keynes. *s:* 2. *d:* 2. Foulerton Research Prof of Roy Soc. *Publ:* Living Machinery; Muscular Activity; Muscular Movement in Man; Adventures in Biophysics; Chemical Wave Transmission in Nerve. *Ctr:* Journ of Physiology, Proc Roy Soc, etc. *s.s:* Biophysics. *a:* 16 Bishopswood Rd, Highgate, London, N.6, & University College, London.

HILL, Lady Arthur. Musician. Composer of—In the Gloaming; O Perfect Love; Holiday Songs for Children; etc. *a:* 3 Chesham St, S.W.1.

HILL, Rev. Arthur Cooke, D.D. *b:* Leicester. *e:* Belfast. *m:* Edith Taylor. *d:* 3. Congregational Minister (ret). *Publ:* Christian Imperialism; Democratic Realism; Man & the Multitude; The Tragic Faith. *Rec:* Golf, fishing. *a:* Achnacoille, Grantown-on-Spey, N.B.

HILL, Rev. Arthur DuBoulay, M.A.(Oxon). *b:* Torquay 1850. *e:* Winchester & Magdalen Coll Oxf. *m:* Gertrude Esther Palmer. *n.a:* Ed Trans of Thoroton Soc (Notts) 1918—26, late Rector E. Bridgford Notts (ret). *Publ:* East Bridgford: The Story of an English Village ('32). *c.t:* Roy Archæ Journ, Wilts Arch Soc Journ, etc. *s.s:* Archæology. Asst Master Winchester Col 1874—82. Vicar of Downton with Nunton '82—98. eRctor of East Bridgford Notts '98—1927. Rural Dean of Bingham '16—26. Founder of Winchester Diocesan Guild of Ringers. *a:* St Winnow, Dudswell, Berkhamsted, Herts.

HILL, Sir Arthur William, C.M.G., K.C.M.G., F.R.S., ScD., D.Sc(Adelaide). *b:* Greenhill, Harrow 1875. *e:* Marlboro & King's Col Cam. Dir Roy Botanic Gdns Kew. *Publ:* Memoir of Canon H. N. Ellacombe. *c.t:* Annals of Botany, Kew Bulletin Journ of Linn Soc, Phil Trans Roy Soc, Nature. *s.s:* Botanical research. *c:* Athenæum. Extensively travelled. *a:* The Roy Gdns, Kew.

HILL, Beatrice Birkbeck, M.A. *b:* Oxford 1897. *e:* Belvedere Sc L'pool, Somerville Col Oxf, Bedford Col for Women Lon. Organising Sec. *Publ:* Drovers Bridge (novel). *s.s:* Fiction. Sec fund for advancement of Officers children. L'pool & Lon War Risks Ins Assoc 1924. *a:* 9 Elsworthy Rd, London, N.W.3.

HILL, Brian. *b:* Hampstead 1896. *e:* Mer Taylors' Sch, Wadham Coll Oxf. Publicity journalist Brit Gas Council. *n.a:* Reviewer Crime Fiction Bookman 1933—34, Times '37—40. *Publ:* Hide & I'll Find You (filmed); (poems) Take All Colours; The Sheltering Tree; Wild Geese; (play, with Laura Wildig) Ever So Long Ago; Who Shall Hang?; & other detec novels under the name of Marcus Magill; (Ed with Geoffrey Keynes) Letters Between Samuel Butler and Miss E. M. A. Savage. *Ctr:* Newspaper & mag press. *s.s:* Crime Fiction, Book Reviewing. *Rec:* Theatre, gardening, collecting antiques. *c:* Savile. *a:* 31 Kensington Pl, Campden Hill, London, W.8. *T:* Park 8147.

HILL, Charles, M.A., M.D., D.P.H. *b:* London 1904. *e:* St Olave's Sch, Trin Coll Camb, Lond Hosp. *m:* Marion Spencer Wallace. *s:* 2. *d:* 3. Sec B.M.A., Broadcasts as "Radio Doctor." *Publ:* The Way to Better Health; Your Body; Good Health, Children; Your Aches & Pains; What is Osteopathy? (with H. A. Clegg); etc. *Ctr:* Leading daily newspapers, Woman's Pictorial, etc. *s.s:* Health. *Rec:* Golf, walking. *c:* Reform. *a:* 26 Milton Rd, Harpenden, Herts. *T:* 1024.

HILL, David Beatty. *b:* London 1918. *e:* Priv. Journalist, Mem N.U.J., Free-Lance 1936—39. *n.a:* Rep Kentish Times 1945—47, Executive Ed Outfitter Export '47—. *Ctr:* Dly Mail, Dly Express, Dly Mirror, Ev Standard. *s.s:* General Features. *c:* Press. *w.s:* 1939—45. *a:* 46 Chessington Ave, Bexley Heath, Kent.

HILL, Dorothy Elizabeth. *m:* George Alexander Hill. Author & Journalist. *Publ:* The Big Spy Plot; The Little Blue Man. *Ctr:* D Sketch, Manch Guardian, Leader, Travel, John O' London's, etc. *Rec:* Travel. *a:* The Hut, Coleman's Hatch, Sussex. *T:* 80.

HILL, George Alexander, Brigadier, D.S.O., O.B.E., M.C. *b:* London 1893. Author & Playwright, On Staff of High Com to S. Russia, Coy Dir, Foreign Mang Maurice Browne Ltd 1929—31, Dep Gen Mang Charles B. Cochran '32, Tech Adv for films. *Publ:* Go Spy the Land; It is the Law; (play) Dreaded Hour. *Ctr:* Sun Times. *s.s:* Aviation, Russia, Balkans, Cent Europe. *Rec:* Theatre, travel. *c:* Roy Socs. *w.s:* Spec Forces 1941—45. *a:* The Hut, Coleman's Hatch, Sussex. *T:* 80.

HILL, George Douglas. *b:* Leicester 1902. *e:* Elem & Gr Sch. Journalist, Mem N.U.J. *n.a:* Reporter Leicester Ev Mail 1946—, Hinckley Times & Guardian '24—31, Bromley & West Kent Mercury '31—35, Kentish Independent '35—41, Clapham Observer '41 & Leics Ev Mail '41—46. *a:* 19 St Mary's Ave, Scraptoft Lane, Leicester.

HILL, Sir George Francis, K.C.B., D.C.L.(Oxon), Litt.D.(Cantab & Manch), LL.D.(Edin), F.B.A., F.S.A., Hon.F.S.A.Scot., Fell Univ Coll Lond. *b:* Berhampore, Bengal, 1867. *e:* Univ Coll Sch & Univ Coll Lond, Merton Coll Oxf. *m:* Mary Paul (dec'd). Dir & Prin Librarian Brit Mus 1930—36, Medallist Roy Numismatic Soc & the American & French Numismatic Socs, Vice-Pres Hellenic & Roman Soc. *n.a:* Ed Journ of Hellenic Studies 1898—1912, Ed Numismatic Chron '12—30. *Publ:* Pisanello; Development of Arabic Numerals in Europe; Corpus of Italian Medals of the Renaissance; Treasure Trove in Law & Practice; A History of Cyprus; (Vols I—III) Catalogue of Greek Coins in Brit Mus (6 vols). *Ctr:* Journ Hellenic Studies, Roman Studies, Numismatic Chronicle & various for numismatic periodicals. *a:* 23 Whitehall Ct, London, S.W.1.

HILL, Mrs. Grace Livingston. *b:* Wellsville N.Y. 1865. *m:* Rev Thomas Franklin Hill. *d:* 2. Author & Public Speaker. *Publ:* Rainbow Cottage; The Beloved Stranger, Happiness Hill; Silver Wings; The Gold Shoe; Ladybird; Blue

Who Was Who Among English and European Authors

Ruin; Crimson Roses; The Tryst, Cloudy Jewel; The Enchanted Barn; The Finding of Jasper Holt; The Best Man; Dawn of the Morning; Phoebe Deaner; The Girl from Montana; Amorelle; The Christmas Bride; Matched Pearls; Kerry; The White Flower; Marcia Schuyler; The Witness; Beauty for Ashes; etc. *c.t*: Revelation, etc. *a*: 215 Cornell Av, Swarthmore, Pa. *t*: 464.

HILL, Rev. Henry Erskine, M.A., D.D. *Publ*: The Seven Parables of the Kingdom; The Parables of the Advent; The Parables of Redemption; The Master Teacher; Studies in St John's Gospel; Guide to Faith & Worship. *c.t*: Expositor & Search. *a*: The Vicarage, Monk Hopton, Bridgnorth.

HILL, Colonel Henry Warburton, C.M.G., D.S.O. *b*: London 1877. *e*: Bradfield Coll, Roy Mil Acad Woolwich. *m*: Ellinor Walters. *s*: 1. *d*: 1. Retired Army Officer, late Royal Artillery, Croix de Guerre, Lefroy Gold Medal. *Publ*: Rowland Hill & the Fight for Penny Post; Rowland Hill & his Great Postal Reforms. *Ctr*: R.A. Journal & other mil pubs, Philatelist & other philatelic mags. *s.s*: Postal History. *Rec*: Golf, bridge, ivory turning & instrument making. *c*: Army & Navy. *w.s*: S Africa 1899—1902, 1914—18. *a*: Avalon, Oban, Argyll. *T*: Oban 2352.

HILL, Herbert. Journalist. *n.a*: Joint Gen-Mang Financial Times, Man Investors' Chron, The Banker. *a*: 72 Coleman St, London, E.C.2. *T*: Monarch 8833.

HILL, Herbert, M.A. *b*: Wakefield 1901. *e*: Wakefield Gr. Sch. Sheffield Univ. *m*: Lena Kaye. *s*: 1. University Lecturer. *Ctr*: Classical Review, Classical Quarterly, Classical Philology (U.S.A.), American Journ of Philology. *s.s*: Classics & Ancient History. *Rec*: Gardening. *a*: 15 Cae Bryn Ave, Sketty, Swansea. *T*: 87147.

HILL, J. Arthur. *Publ*: inc New Evidences in Psychical Research; Spiritualism, its History, Phenomena & Doctrine; From Agnosticism to Belief; etc. *a*: Claremont, Thornton, Bradford

HILL, James William Francis, M.A., LL.M.(Cantab) F.S.A., F.R.Hist.S. *b*: Lincoln 1899. *e*: City Sch Lincoln, Trin Coll Camb. Solicitor & Company Dir, Mayor of Lincoln 1945—46. *Publ*: Medieval Lincoln. *Ctr*: Lincolnshire Arch Soc Reports & Papers. *s.s*: Local Government, Legal & Local Hist. *w.s*: 2nd-Lt K.R.R.C. 1918. *a*: 2 Lindum Terr, Lincoln. *T*: 1184 & 1759.

HILL, John Charles, M.A. Minister of Church of Scotland. *Publ*: Sun Dial Sayings; The Life and Work of Robert Burns in Irvine (illus). *c.t*: Irvine Herald, Irvine & Fullarton Times, Lennox Herald. *c*: Mem of Irvine Burns. *a*: Mure Manse, Irvine, Ayrshire.

HILL, SIR LEONARD ERSKINE: physiologist; *b*. Tottenham, Eng., June 7, 1866; *s*. Birkbeck and Annie (Scott) H.; educ. Haileybury, Univ. Coll. (London). DEGREES: M.B.; *m*. Janet Alexander, 1891. AUTHOR: The Physiology and Pathology of the Cerebral Circulation; Manual of Physiology for Beginners; Sunshine and Open Air, 1924 (2nd edit. 1925); Health and Environment (with A. Campbell); Science of Ventilation and Open Air Treatment; Common Colds, 1929; The Monkey Man Back (fairy stories). Editor Recent and Further Advances of Physiology. Contributor to scientific publications on hygiene and physiology. General character of writing: text books, medical fairy stories. F.R.S., M.R.C.S., L.R.C.P. OFFICE: London Light and Electrical Clinic, London, N. W. 3. HOME: Nicholls Wood, Chalfant St. Peter, Bucks, Eng.

HILL, Lorna, B.A. *b*: Durham City 1902. *e*: Durham Univ. *m*: Rev Victor Rowland Hill, M.A. *d*: 1. *Publ*: Marjorie & Co. *s.s*: Children's Fiction. *Rec*: Music, ballet, sketching. *a*: The Vicarage, Matfen, Newcastle-on-Tyne. *T*: Stamfordham 201.

HILL, Mabel. *b*: Lowell, Mass 1867. *e*: Howe Sch Billerica, Bradford Acad & Radcliffe Coll. *Publ*: Liberty Document; Lesson for a Junior Citizen; Teaching Civics; Joy & The Church; Wise Men Worship; Living at Our Best; Civics for New Americans; etc. *Ctr*: Various poems, essays & stories in mags & newsps. *a*: 42 Mansur St, Lowell, Massachusetts, U.S.A.

HILL, Matthew Davenport. *b*: Lon 1872. *e*: Eton, New Col Oxf. Master at Eton Col '96-1927. *Publ*: Eton Nature Study; Eton & Elsewhere. *c.t*: Quarterly Journal of Microscopical Science, Nature, Natural Science, etc. Founder Science Masters Assoc. *Rec*: Farming, gardening, shooting. *c*: Travellers. *a*: Uplands, nr Ledbury, Herefords. *t*: 60.

HILL, Mildred. *b*: Norwich 1878. *Publ*: His Little Bit o' Garden (1912); Michael's Quest; Princess Daisyflower ('23); Wings of the Morning (poems, '28); Green Withs ('29); etc. *c.t*: Dawn, Home Words, etc. *s.s*: Parable stories. *Rec*: Cello piano. *a*: 23 St Stephen's Gates, Norwich.

HILL, Muriel ("Erskine Macdonald"), M.A., *e*: Glas H.S. for Girls & Glas Univ. Research Student. *Publ*: Wimple Wing & other poems; Rebels for the Kirk. *c.t*: Scots Mag, Glas Herald, Palette, Greatheart, Record of the Church of Scotland. *s.s*: Literary criticism, Scots hist & lit, Scots Ch hist. *a*: St Vigeans, Giffnock, by Glasgow. *t*: 101.

HILL, Norman Hammond. Physician. *c.t*: B.M.J., Lancet, Clin Journ, Med Press & Circular. *a*: 136 Harley St, W.1. *t*: Welbeck 6397.

HILL, Rev. Percival Oakley. *b*: Glos 1857. *e*: Chipping Campden G.S. & Lon Col of Div. *m*: Annie Eliza Coulthard. *s*: 3. *d*: 3. *Publ*: A Temple of the Sun; A History of Upton, Norfolk; Echoes from the Past Life of Burgate, Suffolk. *a*: All Saints' Vicarage, Stoke Newington, 207 Green Lanes, N.4. *t*: Stamford Hill 4936.

HILL, Rev. Percy William, L.Th. *b*: Jersey 1890. *e*: Priv & St Boniface Coll Warminster. *m*: Mary Burn. *s*: 3. *d*: 1. Mem all leading Anglo-Catholic Socs. *Publ*: Stories of the Saints of East & West; Peace Be Unto You; Revised the devotional writings of Dorothy Reynalds. *Ctr*: Symbol Mag. *s.s*: Poetry, Philos Ch Hist Theology (general). *Rec*: Walking. *w.s*: Y.M.C.A. huts in England & Church Army overseas 1914—18. *a*: Brede Rectory, Sussex. *T*: Brede 17.

HILL, Polly. *b*: Cambridge 1914. *e*: Newnham Coll Camb. *Publ*: Through the Dark Wood; The Unemployment Services. *a*: 28 Lawn Road Flats, London, N.W.3. *T*: Primrose 0290.

HILL, Prudence Mifanwy. *b*: Farnborough, Hants 1921. *e*: Dragon Sch Oxf, St Swithau's Sch Winchester, Central Sch of Speech Training & Dramatic Art. Teacher. *Publ*: Wind & Weather Permitting. *Rec*: Exploring London, mending things, drawing. *a*: c/o Grindlay's Bank Ltd, 54 Parliament St, London, S.W.1.

HILL, Ralph. *b*: Watford 1900. *e*: Latymer Upper Sch. *m*: Ida Bryce. Music Critic, Editor, Author, Broadcaster & Lecturer. *n.a*: Dly Mail Asst Music Critic 1933—39 & Chief Music Critic '45, Music Ed Radio Times '35—45, Music Critic Liverpool Post (London)

'44—, Ed Penguin Music Mag '46—. *Publ*: An Outline of Musical History; Life of Liszt; Life of Brahms; Challenges; Listening Without Fears. *Rec*: Reading & talking. *c*: Authors', Press & Critics' Circle. *w.s*: 1918. *a*: 39 Hazlewell Rd, Putney, London, S.W.15. *T*: Putney 3891.

HILL, Reginald Harrison, M.A., F.L.A. *b*: Oxford 1894. *e*: City of Oxford Sch & Oxf Univ. *m*: Winifred Irene Langford. *s*: 1. Librarian & Sec to Trustees Nat Central Library. *n.a*: Ed Bodleian Quarterly Record 1914—17 & '19—31. *Publ*: The Shelley Correspondence in the Bodleian Library; Bibliotheca Osleriana (with Dr. W. W. Francis & Dr. T. A. Malloch). *Ctr*: Library Assoc Record, etc. *s.s*: Libraries & Library Co-operation. *Rec*: Bibliography, gardening. *a*: 6 Kensington Mans, Trebovir Rd, Earls Ct, London, S.W.5. *T*: Frobisher 3020.

HILL, Richard Athelstane Parker. Physician. *Publ*: The Interregnum; The British Revolution. *c.t*: Various Med Journs. *a*: Palmeira, Courtland Rd, Paignton, S. Devon. *t*: 5081.

HILL, Robert Henry. *b*: Wellingboro' 1900. *e*: E. Anglian Sc, St Edmundsbury & Oxf Univ. *m*: Edith Mary Soper. Parliamentary Journalist. *a*: 6 Castlegate, Richmond, Surrey. *t*: 3979.

HILL, Robert Henry, B.A. *b*: London 1910. *e*: Kilburn Gr Sch & King's Coll, Univ of Lond. *m*: Margery Horler. *s*: 1. *d*: 1. Editor. *n.a*: Assoc-Ed World Digest '39— & New Universal Ency '44—, Dly Express Ency '33, Ency Dept Amal Press '34—36, Asst-Ed Hutchinson's Pict Ency '36—37, Asst-Ed Amal Press Book of Knowledge '37—38, etc. *Publ*: Jarrold's Dictionary of Difficult Words. *s.s*: Language, Phonetics, etc, Popular Science & Medicine, Modern Literature. *a*: 9 Donnington Rd, London, N.W.10. *T*: Willesden 1922.

HILL, Rosalind, M.T., M.A., B.Litt(Oxon), F.R.Hist.S., F.S.A. *b*: Neston, Cheshire 1908. *e*: The Downs Sch Seaford, St Hilda's Coll Oxf. University Lecturer. *Publ*: The Rolls & Register of Oliver Sutton, Bishop of Lincoln. *Ctr*: Eng Hist Review, Trans of Leicestershire, Berkshire, Bristol & Glos Archæol Socs, The Liberal Forward. *s.s*: Medieval History. *Rec*: Mountaineering. *c*: Pinnacle. *a*: Westfield College, London, N.W.3. *T*: Hampstead 7601.

HILL, Roscoe R., A.B., Litt.D., Ph.D. *b*: Illinois 1880. *e*: Eureka Coll Ill & Univs of Chicago & Columb. *m*: Edith Irene Rowell. *d*: 3. Historian, Archivist. *n.a*: Ed-Bd, Hispanic Amer Hist Rev 1936—, Advisory Ed The Americas '45—. *Publ*: Descriptive Catalogue of Documents relating to History of U.S. in Papeles Procedentes de Cuba; Fiscal Intervention in Nicaragua; National Archives of Latin America. *Ctr*: Political Sc Quarterly, Veritas, Amer Archivist, Books Abroad, etc. *s.s*: Latin American History & Affairs, Archivology. *Rec*: Motoring. *a*: 4500 47th St, N.W., Washington, D.C., U.S.A. *T*: WO. 0553.

HILL, T. G. Prof of Plant Physiology in Lon Univ. *Publ*: The Chemistry of Plant Products (with Dr. P. Haas); The Essentials of Illustration. *c.t*: Various Sci Periodicals. *a*: Hambledon, Godalming.

HILL, Thomas Rowland. *b*: Kent 1903. *e*: Univ of London & Guy's Hosp. *m*: Sybil Janet Cumming. Physician West End Hospital of Nervous Diseases. *Publ*: Various Medical Books. *Ctr*: Med journs, etc. *s.s*: Neurology. *Rec*: Sailing. *c*: Reform & Nat Lib. *w.s*: World War II R.A.M.C. (Major). *a*: 14 Wimpole St, London, W.1. *T*: Langham 1711.

HILL, Thomas Walter, M.B., ChB.(Glas), D.P.H., M.D.(Glas). *b*: Glas 1902. *e*: Darlington G.S. & Glas Univ. Deputy M.O.H. *Publ*: The Health of England. *c.t*: The Medical Officer, Public Health, Mother & Child, etc. *s.s*: Public health administration, child hygiene, eugenics. *c*: Mem Soc of M.O.H., Mem Roy Sanitary Inst, etc. *a*: 51a Longridge Rd, S.W.5. *t*: Flaxman 8945.

HILL, Thomas William. *b*: W. Bromwich 1866. *e*: Priv & King's Col. *m*: Alice Marian Atkinson. *d*: 2. Sec. *Publ*: Open Air Statues in London 1910. *c.t*: Daily Express, Times, Evening News, Architectural Review, etc. *s.s*: Archæ, Dickens. Sec Herbert Spencer's Trustees '24. Ed Descriptive Sociology '24—. Ch Organist for 40 y. *Rec*: Music, photog. *c*: Savage, Whitefriars, City Pickwick & Musicians. *a*: Hillsden, Bromley, Kent. *t*: Ravensbourne 2614.

HILL, W. A. *b*: Crewe 1902. P.R.O. National Farmers' Union. *n.a*: Warrington Guardian Series, Northcliffe Newsps, P.R.O. Milk Marketing Bd. *a*: 45 Bedford Sq, London, W.C.1. *T*: Museum 7525.

HILL, W. H. Ed, Dorset Daily Echo. *a*: 57 St Thomas St, Weymouth.

HILL, W. Leonard. *b*: Gateshead-on-Tyne 1894. *m*: E. M. Burgess. N/p Proprietor. *n.a*: Nat Trade Press 1919—22, Benn Bros '22—24. *Publ*: Various. *c.t*: Publishing, Advertising Press, etc. *s.s*: Industrial publishing. War Service R.F.C. *Rec*: Golf, ski-ing, fishing. *c*: R.A.F., Sports. *a*: 2 West Hill Ct, N.6. *t*: Mountview 3551.

HILL, Warren. See Standring, Willie.

HILL, William Kirkpatrick, B.A.(Lon). *b*: Edmonton 1862. *e*: Sc for Sons of Missnys, Blackheath & U.C.S. *m*: Eleanor Margaret Childs. *d*: 1. Author & Artist. *n.a*: Ex-Ed Educational Review, Ex-Corr The School Review Chicago, Ex-Sec to Finance Cmt of Lon Univ. *Publ*: William Henry Widgery, Schoolmaster (biog); Under Three Kings (hist romance); Edwin Trafford, Altruist (1908). *c.t*: Contemporary Review, Westminster Review, Journ of Educ, Educ Review of America, etc. *Rec*: Music, painting. *a*: 14 Downshire Hill, Hampstead, N.W.3. *t*: Hampstead 2284.

HILL, William Thomson, F.J.I. *b*: Peterborough 1875. *e*: King's Sch Peterboro. *m*: Edith Gertrude Jackson. Journalist The Times since '43. *n.a*: Ed Sunday Graphic & Illd Sun Herald '26—31, formerly acting Ed Dly Sketch & on editorial staffs Ev Standard, Dly Mail, Manch Dly Dispatch, Manch Ev Chron, etc. *Publ*: Nurse Cavell. *Ctr*: Leading dailies & reviews. *w.s*: 1917—19 2/5 the Buffs, Lieut R.N.V.R., Capt R.A.F. *a*: 27 Willett, Close, Petts Wood, Orpington, Kent.

HILL, William Wills. *b*: Castle Donnington 1881. *e*: Page Green Sch Tottenham, Upper May Coll East Lond, Westminster Training Coll. *m*: Mary Frances Dixon. *s*: 2. Journalist, Headmaster Hinckley Council Sch 1918—33, Pres of N.U.T. '28. *n.a*: Ed of Schoolmaster 1933—46. *Ctr*: Various daily & weekly journals. *s.s*: Education. *a*: 45 Queens Ave, Muswell Hill, London, N.10. *T*: Tudor 2885.

HILL-BRAMWELL, William, F.R.G.S., M.J.I., F.Z.S. *b*: Stratton St Margaret. Journalist & Author, Special Cont Lond & Prov Journs & Swindon Press, Ex-Past Chn & Mem Swindon Br N.U.J., Special week-end preaching & Lect in Free Ch's & Meth Ch's, Widely known as platform speaker in Sth & West of Eng, Area representative B.B.C. & Poll of Public Opinion. *Ctr*: Dly Express, News Chron, Bristol Ev World, Bath Herald, Meth Recorder, Christian World, Nth Wilts Herald, etc.

s.s: Methodism, Folklore. *Rec*: Cricket, football, lecturing. *a*: Oxford Rd, Stratton St Margaret, Swindon, Wilts. *T*: Stratton St Margaret 43 & 316.

HILLARD, Rev. A. E., D.D. *Publ*: Joint Author of North & Hillard's Latin Prose, & Greek Prose; etc. *a*: Braeside, Dormans Park, E. Grinstead. *t*: Dorman's Park 212.

HILLAS, E. F. *n.a*: Sub-Ed of Yorkshire Observer. *a*: 17 Bank Crest, Baildon, Yorks.

HILLAS, Julian. See Dashwood, Robert Julian.

HILLELS, Shloma. *b*: Russia 1873. *m*: Fanny Bromberg. Teacher & Author. *Publ*: Har Ha Kramin; B'himot Aratz; Tahat Shmei Biserabia; Artzah, etc. *Ctr*: Davar, Havlom, Hiratz, Memelitz, etc. *s.s*: Belles lettres. *a*: Tel-Aviv, Zemenhof 42, Palestine. *T*: 3751.

HILLIAR, William, F.J.I. *b*: Milborne Port 1849. *e*: British Sc. *m*: Annie Abbott. *s*: 2. *d*: 1. N/p Reporter (ret). *n.a*: Oxf Times, Oxf & Cam Undergraduates Journ 1874-81, Essex County Telegraph '81-1903, Ilford Recorder '03-22. *a*: 76 Seymour Gdns, Ilford, Essex.

HILLIARD, Edward, M.A., B.C.L. Barrister-at-Law *Publ*: The Balliol Col Register. *a*: Woodlawns, Bunch Lane, Haslemere.

HILLIARD, Harvey, C.B.E., M.D., M.R.S.C., L.R.C.P., D.P.H. *b*: London 1874. *e*: Epsom Coll, Charing Cross & St George's Hosps. *m*: (1) Charlotte R. Hazell, (2) Margaret R. Hemsted. *s*: 2. Former Registrar i/c Ceylon Medical College & Asst P.C.M.O. *Publ*: Anæsthetics in Dental Surgery (with F. Coleman). *Ctr*: Practitioner, Dental Record, Lancet, Brit Dental Journ, etc. *s.s*: Anæsthetics. *Rec*: Fly fishing & gardening. *c*: R.A.F. *a*: 1 Gardens Cresc, Lilliput, Parkstone, Dorset. *T*: Canford Cliffs 817.

HILLIER, George Lacy. *b*: Sydenham 1856. *e*: Priv. Stock Broker. *n.a*: Ed The Tricyclist '82, Wheel World '82–, Bycycling News '83–. *Publ*: The Art of Ease in Cycling; Training; etc. *c.t*: Cyclist, Sporting Life, etc. *s.s*: Cycling. Won all Amateur Cycling Championships 1881. *c*: Nat Cyclists Un, etc. *a*: 4 Q. Victoria St, E.C.4. *t*: City 5456.

HILLMAN, H. *c.t*: Various Mags articles. *a*: 38 Westbourne Gardens, W.2.

HILLMAN, Oscar Stanley, M.B., B.S., M.S., F.R.C.S., M R.C.S., L.R.C.P. Cons Surg. *Publ*: Operative Surgery for Nurses. *c.t*: Lancet, B.M.J., Proc Roy Soc Med. *a*: 4 South Parade, Southsea, Hants. *t*: Portsmouth 73682.

HILLMAN, William, B.A. *b*: New York City 1895. *e*: Columbia College, Columbia Univ. *m*: Angela Sermolino. *s*: 1. Journalist. *n.a*: Lon, Paris, Berlin & Cent Eur corr Hearst Newspapers, Assoc Press, N.Y. Evening Post. Executive Rep British Isles King Features Syndicate. *a*: 78 Fleet Street, E.C.4. *t*: Central 1453—1454.

HILLS, Alban. *n.a*: Ed Hardware Trade Journal. *a*: Bouverie Hse, 154-160 Fleet St, London, E.C.4.

HILLS, JOHN WALLER: member of Parliament; *b*. London, Eng., Jan. 2, 1867; *s*. Herbert Augustus and Anna (Grove) H.; educ. Balliol Coll. (Oxford); DEGREES: B.A. (Oxford); D.C.L. (Durham); *m*. Stella Duckworth (died), 1897. AUTHOR: Poor Law Reform, 1911; A History of Flyfishing for Trout, 1921; The Golden River, 1922; A Summer on the Test, 1924; The Finance of Government, 1926. Contributor to London Mercury, Salmon and Trout Mag., Observer, Evening News and others. General character of writing: finance, political, sport. Relig. denom., Church of England. CLUBS: Brooke's, Flyfishers'. OFFICE: 20 Bishopsgate E. C. London Flat, 98 Mount Street, London. HOME: Highhead Castle, Carlisle, Eng.

HILLS, Stanley M. A.M.I.E.E. *n.a*: Ed Electrical Industries. *a*: 15 Fisher St, W.C. *t*: Holborn 5171.

HILLYARD, Fabienne Laura Evelyn Caroline. *b*: St Sever, France 1901. *e*: France. *m*: (1) Vicomte P. de Carvalhæs, (2) J. M. Hillyard. *s*: 1. Author. *Publ*: I Do Betray; Margot; Painted Toys (with Elizabeth Heygate); The Varleys of the New Forest; In Loving Thee; (French poems) Chansons Triste; La Coupe d'Albatre; Sous les Etoiles; (Trans) Sonnets of Lord Alfred Douglas. *Rec*: Tennis, golf, parties. *a*: 104 Cheyne Walk, Chelsea, London. *T*: Flaxman 7716.

HILLYER, Robert Silliman, A.B. *b*: East Orange, N.J. 1895. *e*: Kent Sch, Harvard Coll & Univ of Copenhagen. *m*: (1) Dorothy Stewart Mott, (2) Dorothy Hancock Tilton. *s*: 1. Poet, Novelist, Critic, Prof of Rhetoric & Oratory Harvard 1937—44. *Publ*: (Poems) Sonnets & Other Lyrics; Book of Danish Verse; The Coming Forth By Day; The Seventh Hill; In Time of Mistrust; etc; (Novels) Riverhead; My Heart for Hostage. *Ctr*: Various. *s.s*: English, American, French & Classic Literature, Ancient Egypt, History, Music, Philosophy. *Rec*: Sailing & music. *c*: Harvard. *a*: Warwick Towers, Greenwich, Connecticut. U.S.A.

HILTON, Harold H. *b*: 1869. *e*: Norfolk County Sc. Editor & Author. *n.a*: Editor Golf Illustrated. *Publ*: My Golfing Reminiscences; etc. Winner Amateur Golf Championship 1901, '11, '13, Open Championship, 1892, '97, American Championship 1911. *a*: Manor Golf Club, Ashford.

HILTON, James, M.A. *b*: Leigh, Lancs 1900. *e*: Leys Sch & Christ's Coll Camb. Author, Awarded Hawthornden Prize 1934 & Hollywood Motion Picture Acad Writing Award '42. *Publ*: Catherine Herself; Contango; Knight Without Armour; Murder at School (Glen Trevor); Lost Horizon; Good-by Mr. Chips; We Are Not Alone; Random Harvest; The Story of Dr. Wassell; So Well Remembered, Nothing So Strange. *Rec*: Music, Travel. *a*: c/o Macmillan & Co. Ltd, 10-15 St Martin's St, Strand, London, W.C.2.

HILTON, John, M.A. *b*: Bolton 1880. *e*: Publ Elem Scs, Bolton G.S. & Evening Tech Classes. Married. *s.1*. *d*: 2. Prof of Industrial Relations Cam Univ 1931–. *Publ*: Reports on Investigations into Unemployment, etc; Memoranda presented to Royal Commission & Committees on Unemployment; Cost of Living; etc. *c.t*: Econ Journ, News Chronicle, Listener, Spectator, Political Quart, etc. *s.s*: Industrial relations, trusts & combines, unemployment. Apprenticed mill mechanic 1896. Fitter, turner & later foreman & mang of engineering works. Lect & tech journalist 1908-12. Acting Sec of Garton Foundation '12-18. Asst Sec & Director Statistics Min of Labour '19-31. *Rec*: Drama, manual work. *a*: 24 De Freville Av, Cambridge. *T*: 2273.

HILTON, Michael. *b*: 1913. *e*: Marlborough Coll. *n.a*: Dly Telegraph 46—. *a*: '24 Main Way, Chorley Wood, Herts. *T*: 686.

HILTON, R. *Publ*: Researches on Treatment of Pulmonary Tuberculosis; Physiological Principles in Treatment, 7th Edit. Gold Medallist in Medicine. Brit Research Fellow, Physician St Thomas's Hosp. Copeman Medallist. *a*: 39 West Heath Drive, Golders Gn, N.W.11.

HILTON-SIMPSON, Melville William. *b*: Albury 1881. *e*: Wellington Col, Exeter Col Oxf. *m*: Helen Dorothy Mackenzie. *s*: 1. *d*: 1. Ethnologist. *Publ*: Algiers & Beyond; Land & Peoples of the Kasai; Arab Medicine & Surgery; Among the Hill-Folk of Algeria. *s.s*: Ethn. Chev Legion of Honour France, & of Roy Order of the Lion, Belgium. *Rec*: Travel, shooting. *c*: Athenæum. *a*: Sole St Hse, nr Faversham, Kent. *t*: 9.

HILTON YOUNG, Sir Edward, P.C., G.B.E., D.S.O., D.S.C. *b*: 1879. *e*: Eton, Trin Col Cam. *m*: Lady Scott. *s*: 1. Min of Health. *Publ*: Foreign Companies & Other Corporations; A Muse at Sea; By Sea & Land; etc. *c*: Brooks's. *a*: Leinster Corner, W.2. *t*: Paddington 3886.

HIMA, LUDWIG: author; b. Vienna, Austria, Jan. 18, 1872; s. Ludwig and Marie (Wawra) Hima; educ. Volksschule Olmütz, Militärunterrealschule, Kaschau (Ungarn), Militäroberrealschule, Mährisch-Weisskirchen, Militärakademie, Wiener-Neustadt. DEGREES: First Lieutenant; m. Greta Huna Hraba, 1894. AUTHOR: Offiziere, 1911; Monna Beatrice, 1913; Der Friedensverein, 1914; Die Harmonien im Hause Sylvanus, 1915; Der Wolf in Purpur, 1919; Die Stiere von Rom, 1920; Der Stern des Orsini, 1921; Das Mädchen von Nettuno, 1922 (the three last novels compose the Borgia-Trilogie); Der Kampf um Gott, 1923; Wieland der Schmied, 1924; Die Verschwörung der Pazzi, 1925; Walther von der Vogelweide, 1926; Granada in Flammen, 1927; Hexenfahrt, 1928; Der Goldschmied von Segovia, 1929; Wunder am See (in preparation). General character of writing: historical novels. Saw active duty in the Austrian army, Borgia-Trilogie has been translated into three languages. CLUBS: Deutscher Schriftstellerverband, Vienna; Heinischer Schriftstellerbund, Grax. Relig. denom., Evangelical. OFFICE: St. Gallen, Steuermark. HOME: Vienna, Niederostenweig, Austria.

HIMBURY, Sir William H. *a*: 333/350 Royal Exchange, M/C.

HIMSWORTH, Joseph Beeston, F.R.S.A., F.S.A.Scot. *b*: Beeston, Notts 1874 ; *e* : Sheffield Coll of Arts & Crafts. *m*: Dora Elizabeth Gill. *d*: 1. Manufacturing Cutler & Silversmith. *Publ* : A History of Cutlery ; From Flint to Stainless Steel. *Ctr*: Master Glass Painters' Journ, etc. *s.s*: Cutlery History, Old Stained Glass, Archæology & Pre-History. *Rec*: Research in archæological field work. *a*: 31 Chelsea Rd, Sheffield 11. *T*: 50375 & 23563.

HINCHLIFFE, Stanley Taylor. *b*: Great Yarmouth 1909. *e*: Hemsworth Gr Sch. Journalist, Mem N.U.J. *n.a*: South Elmsall & Hemsworth Express 1926—33 & '45—, Skyrack Express '34—43. *Ctr*: Nat & Prov Press. *c*: Hemsworth Rotary. *a*: 3 Mount Ave, Hemsworth, Yorks. *T*: 84.

HINCKS, Cyril Malcolm. *b*: London 1881. *e*: Priv. *m*: Adelaide Thompson. *s*: 3. *d*: 2. Author & Journalist. *n.a*: Staff of C. Arthur Pearson 6 yrs. *Publ* : A Commutation of Sentence ; Pincher in Peace & War ; The Iron Way. *Ctr*: Eng & Amer press. *s.s*: Domestic Serials & Short Stories. *a*: Mt Pleasant, The Common, Cranbrook. Kent.

HIND, Arthur M., O.B.E., M.A., LL.D., F.S.A. *b*: Burton-on-Trent 1880. *e*: City of Lond Sch & Emmanuel Coll Camb. *m*: The Hon Dorothy Pakington. *d*: 3. Historian of Art, Landscape Painter. *Publ*: History of Engraving & Etching; History of Woodcut; Rembrandt's Etchings ; Early Italian Engraving ; Drawings by Dutch & Flemish Artists—the Brit Mus (4 vols); Rembrandt; etc. *s.s*: The History of Engraving, Old Master Drawings. *Rec*: Music (esp string quartet playing). *c*: The Athenæum. *a*: Saragossa Hse, Henley-on-Thames. *T*: Henley 33.

HIND, H. Lloyd, B.Sc, F.I.C. *n.a*: Ed Brewing Journal. *Publ*: The Problem of Fermentation. *a*: c/o Chapman & Hall, Henrietta St, W.C.2.

HIND, John R., M.R.S.T., A.T.I. *b* : Farsley 1896 *m* : Evelyn Wood. *d*: 1. *Publ*: Worsted Carding & Combing (1932) ; Woollen & Worsted Raw Materials ('34). *s.s*: Wool & textile. *a*: 93 Kaye Lane, Almondbury, Huddersfield.

HIND, Rev. William Arthur. *b*: Gateshead-on-Tyne 1872. *e*: St Paul's Sc W. Kensington & Bishop's Hostel Lincoln. *m*: E. Carpenter. *Publ*: Browning Teaching on Faith, Life & Love (1912). *s.s*: Eng lit. *a*: The Vicarage, Sutton-on-Sea, Lincs.

HINDE, Preb. H. W. *Publ*: The Life of Love. *a*: Oak Hill Col, Southgate, N.14.

HINDE, Ida Emily Lucy. *b* : Plymouth 1883. *e* : Priv. Teacher of Singing & Dramatic Art, Bristol Scholar Singing R.C.M. 1901—05. *Publ*: At the Edge of Dream ; The Maxims of a Fairy Godmother ; The Treasure of Life. *Ctr*: Poetry of To-day. *s.s*: Poetry. *a* : 22 Elliston Rd, Redland, Bristol 6. *T*: 38107.

HINDEN, Rita, B.Sc., Ph.D. *b* : Capetown, Sth Africa 1909. *e* : Good Hope Semin, Cape Town, London Sch of Econ & Lond Univ. *m*: Elchon Hinden. *s*: 1. *d*: 1. Sec Fabian Colonial Bureau. *n.a*: Ed Empire '41—, Ed-Bd Socialist Commentary '46—. *Publ*: Plan for Africa; (Ed) Fabian Colonial Essays; Co-operation in the Colonies. *Ctr*: New Statesman, Economist, Tribune, etc. *s.s*: Colonial Affairs. *c*: Roy Empire Soc, etc. *a*: 134 Greenhill, London, N.W.3. *T*: Hampstead 6278.

HINDENACH, J. C. R., M.D., ChB. Surgeon. *n.a*: Otago Univ Review Mang 1925-6-7—. *c.t*: Journ of Anatomy, B.M.J. *a*: c/o The High Commssr for N.Z. *t*: Holborn 2452.

HINDES, Gwendolen, M.Sc., M.P.S. *b*: Grantham 1896. *e*: Trinity Hall Southport & M/C Univ. Pharmacist, Asst Warden of Univ Students' Hostel. *Publ*: Materia Medica & Pharmacology for Nurses. *c.t*: Nursing Times, Chemist & Druggist, Pharm Journ, Modern Woman, The Tourist, Health Logic, Church Mthly, Red Cross Review, etc. *s.s*: Health, travel, & technical articles. Sec Nat Assoc of Women Pharmacists. Mem British Assn of Chemists. V.A.D. Officer during War. *Rec*: Travel. *c*: Mem of V.A.D. Ladies. *a*: 58 Queensborough Terr W.2. *t*: Bayswater 0320.

HINDLE, Edward, Sc.D.(Cantab), Ph.D., F.R.S. *b*: Sheffield 1886. *e*: Magdalene Coll Camb, King's Coll & Roy Coll of Science Lond, Univ of California Berkeley. *m*: (1) Irene M. Twist (dec'd), (2) Ellen M. T. Boyen. Scientific Dir Zoo Soc of Lond, Holder of Belgian Croix Civique (1st class), Regius Prof Zoology Univ Glas 1935 —43. *n.a*: Ed Zoo Life '46—, Assoc-Ed various scientific publications. *Publ*: Flies & Disease—Bloodsucking Flies. *Ctr*: Numerous scientific journals. *s.s*: Zoology. *Rec*: Music, travel. *c*: Athenæum, Savile. *a*: Elleray, 91a King Henry's Rd, Hampstead, London, N.W.3. *T*: Primrose 0080.

HINDLE, Wilfrid Hope, M.A. *b*: Barrow-in-Furness 1903. *e*: Local G.S. & Oxf Univ. *m*: Annette Zeiss. *d*: 2. Journalist. *n.a*: Leader-Writer Yorks Post 1926, Foreign Dept Times '27—34, Ed Review of Reviews '33—. The Londoner of the Evening Standard '34—. Ed Songs for New Soldiers & Is This Man's Aim? *c.t*: Statesman's Year Book, Times, Observer, Sunday Times, Spectator, Nineteenth Century, Fortnightly Review, etc. *s.s*: Foreign affairs, cinema. Travelled widely America, Russia & Europe. Broadcast Lect on Balkan travel, Russian folk-songs, etc. *Rec*: Sailing & work. *c*: P.E.N., Savage. *a*: 2 Hammersmith Terr, W.6. *t*: Riverside 1778.

HINDLEY-SMITH, James Dury, M.A.(Cantab), B.Ch. M.R.C.S., F.R.S.M., L.R.C.P., M.R.I. *b*: Newton-le-Willows 1894. *e*: Aysgarth, Uppingham & Camb Univ. *m*: Mary Ethel Josephine McMaster. *s*: 2. Mem Senate Camb Univ 1923—. *Publ*: Chronic Rheumatism & the Pre-Rheumatic State. *Ctr*: Journ Phys Med, Brit Journ Children's Diseases, St George's Hosp Gazette, B.M.J. *s.s*: Chronic Toxæmia & Rheumatism. *Rec*: Golf, music. *c*: Wyndham. *w.s*: World War II, France & Flanders 1914—19. *a*: 45 Welbeck St,. London, W.1. *T*: Welbeck 8167 & 3066.

HINDMARSH, Albert Edward, A.M., Ph.D. *b*: Nanaimo, B.C., Canada 1902. *e*: Univ of Washington, Harvard. *m*: Merrill Pearson. *s*: 1. *d*: 2. Educator & Naval Officer, Former Lect & Prof Dir U.S. Naval Intelligence Sch Washington D.C. '45—. *Publ*: Force in Peace; Basis of Japanese Foreign Policy; La Paix en Asie. *Ctr*: Amer Journ of Internat Law, Foreign Affairs, Amer Journ of Educ. *s.s*: Japan & the Far East, Naval Intelligence. *Rec*: Foreign langs. *a*: 401 Woodland Terr, Alexandria, Virginia, U.S.A. *T*: Temple 1746.

HINE, Reginald Leslie, F.S.A., F.R.Hist.S. *b*: Newnham Hall, Herts 1883. *e*: Priv & Leys Sch Camb. *m*: Florence Lee Pyman. *d*: 1. Solicitor & Historian. *n.a*: Reviewer Times Lit Supp. *Publ*: Confessions of an Un-Common Attorney; The History of Hitchin; Hitchin Worthies; The Cream of Curiosity; Dreams & The Way of Dreams. *s.s*: Biography, Law & History of Hertfordshire. *Rec*: Hertfordshire. *a*: Willian Bury, Letchworth, Herts. *T*: Letchworth 532.

HINGSTON, Lt.-Col. C. A. F., C.I.E., O.B.E. *b*: India 1877. *e*: Priv, Middx Hosp Lon Univ. *m*: Gladys Violet Scroggie. *s*: 2. *d*: 1. Lt-Col I.M.S. (ret). Now Cons Gynæcologist Madras India. *c.t*: Indian med journs, etc. *s.s*: Midwifery, gynæcology. Ex-Supt & 1st Obstet Surg & Gynæcologist Women & Children's Hosp Madras, etc. *Rec*: Riding, golf. *c*: Madras, E. India Utd Service, Jnr Army & Navy. *a*: c/o Grindlay & Co, 54 Parliament St, S.W.1.

HINGSTON, Richard William George, M.C., M.B., B.Ch., F.R.G.S., F.Z.S., F.L.S., F.R.E.S. *b*: London 1887. *e*: Mer Taylors' Sch & Nat Univ Ire. *m*: Mary Kennedy. *s*: 1. *d*: 2. Major Indian Medical Service (ret), Med Officer & Naturalist to Mount Everest Expedition 1924, Surg-Naturalist to the Roy Indian Marine, 2nd in Command Oxf Univ Expedition to Greenland '28, Organiser & Leader of Oxf Univ Expedition to Brit Guiana '29. *Publ*: A Naturalist in Himalaya; Problems of Instinct & Intelligence; A Naturalist in the Guiana Forest; The Meaning of Animal Colour & Adornment; Darwin; etc. *s.s*: Nat Hist & Exploration. *c*: Alpine. *a*: c/o Lloyds Bank, 6 Pall Mall, London, S.W.1.

HINKS, Arthur Robert, M.A., F.R.S., C.B.E. *b*: Lon 1873. *e*: Whitgift G.S. Croydon & Trinity Col Cam. *m*: Lily Mary Packman (dec). Sec Roy Geog Soc 1915- & Gresham Lecturer in Astronomy. *Publ*: Astronomy (Home Univ Library '11); Maps & Survey ('13, '23, '33). *c.t*: Edin Review, Nineteenth Century & After, Geographical Journ, etc. *s.s*: Solar & Stellar parallax, stereogrammetric survey, cartography, map projections. Formerly Astronomer at Cam Observ 1895-1913. Gold Medal Roy Astronomical Soc '12. Cam Univ Lecturer in Surveying & Cartography '08-13. *c*: Trav. *a*: The White Cottage, Royston, Herts. *t*: 140.

HINRICHS, AUGUST: novelist; *b.* Oldenburg, Germany, Apr. 18, 1879; *s.* Herman Diehl and Helene (Tiemen) H.; *educ.* Sawyers School; *m.* Helene Hanken, 1906. AUTHOR: Lish den Helmah, 1920; Nest in der Heide, 1921; Wanderer ohne Weg, 1923; Die Hartjes, 1924; Gerwandis, 1927; Volk am Meer, 1929. CLUBS: Schutsverland deutscher Schriftsteller. Religion, evangelical. ADDRESS: Oldenburg 1 Old, Germany.

HINSHELWOOD, Cyril Norman, M.A., D.Sc., F.R.S. *b*: London 1897. *e*: Westminster City Sch, Balliol Coll Oxf. Dr Lee's Prof of Chem Oxf Univ. *Publ*: Kinetics of Chemical Change; Chemical Kinetics of the Bacterial Cell; The Reaction Between Hydrogen & Oxygen (with A. T. Williamson); Thermodynamics for Students of Chemistry. *Ctr*: Proc of Roy Soc & Other Scientific Journs. *s.s*: Physical Chem. *a*: Exeter Coll, Oxford.

HINTON, Herbert, M.B.E. *b*: Birmingham 1881. *e*: Priv. *m*: Olive J. King. *s*: 2. Late Officer of Supreme Court of Judicature. *Publ*: Evidence & Service Abroad; Yearly Practice of Supreme Court (Jt Ed); Chitty's King's Bench Forms (Asst Ed). *s.s*: Law. *Rec*: Rifle shooting. *a*: 27 Chaucer Rd, Ashford, Middlesex. *T*: 2120.

HINTON, Phyllis. *b*: Clifton, Bristol 1900. *m*:. *s*: 1. *d*: 1. Journalist. *n.a*: Ed-Staff Horse & Hound 1944—47, Country Life & Riding '41—44, Ev Standard '31—33. *Publ*: Showing Your Horse. *Ctr*: The Lady, Sport & Country, News Rev, Riding, etc. *s.s*: Riding. *Rec*: Riding, ballet, opera, country walks, reading essays. *a*: 6 Mansel Rd, Wimbledon, London, S.W.19. *T*: Wimbledon 5628.

HINTON, Rex. See **Butler, R. H.**

HIORNS, Edward Ainge. *b*: Ragley, Warwickshire, 1898. *e*: Bablake Secondary Sc Coventry. *m*: Ethel Maud Kendall. *d*: 1. Commercial traveiler. *n.a*: Hon Ed, Coventry Engineering Soc Journ, '21—. *a*: Sunnyside, Duggins Lne, Tile Hill, Coventry. *t*: 66184.

HIRD, Dr A. E. W., Surg-Capt R.N.V.R. *Publ*: Articles on Apparatus for Admin of Continuous Saline. *a*: 106 Hagley Rd, 126 Monument Rd, & 34 City Rd, Birm.

HIRD, A. F. *b*: Lon. *n.a*: Daily Graphic, M/C Courier, Times, Daily Mail (Asst News Ed). *a*: 46 Boreham Rd, Wood Green, N.22. *t*: Bowes Pk 4087.

HIRD, Benjamin Whitworth, F.J.I. Press Consultant. *a*: 12 Whitehall, S.W.1. *t*: 1873.

HIRD, Frank, O.B.E. Author. *Publ*: H. M. Stanley, The Authorized Life; The Fourth Road; Clipped Hedges; The Golden Crystal. *a*: c/o S. Paul & Co Ltd, Paternoster Hse, E.C.4.

HIRD, Norman Leslie, J.P. *b*: Woodford 1886. *e*: Lon Univ. *m*: Mabel M. Fuller. Gen Mang & Dir Union Bank of Scot, Glas. *c.t*: Glas Herald, Times, Scottish Bankers Mags. *s.s*: Banking, econ. Vice-Pres Brit Bankers Assoc, Ex-Vice-Pres Glas Cham of

Comm. *Rec*: Ski-ing, tennis, mountaineering. *c*: Conservative, Western, Glas Univ, Edin. *a*: Beechwood Hse, Stirling. *t*: 738.

HIRSCH, Nathaniel D. M., A.B., Ph.D.(Harvard), A.M.(Columbia). *b*: Nashville, Tennessee, 1897. *e*: Harvard & Columbia Univs. *m*: Nancy Ruth Maddy. Psychologist. *Publ*: A Study of Natio-Racial Mental Differences; An Experimental Study of the East Kentucky Mountaineers; Twins: Heredity and Environment; An Experimental Study of 300 Children Over a Period of Six Years; Genius and Creative Intelligence. *s.s*: Clinical psychology, social psychology, differential psychology, abnormal psychology. *c*: American Psychological Assoc, Nat Geographic Soc, Nat Council on Religion in Higher Education. *a*: 2 Park View Apartments, Nashville, Tennessee, U.S.A.

HIRSCH, Paul Adolf. *b*: Frankfurt, A/M 1881. *e*: Stadt Gymnasium (Munic Coll) Frankfurt. *m*: Olga A. H. Ladenburg. *s*: 2. *d*: 2, Musical Research Worker, Music Library was on loan 1936 to '46 at Univ Library Camb, now acquired for the Nation & housed at the Brit Mus. *Publ*: Katalog der Musik—Bibliothek Paul Hirsch, 4 vols (with Kathi Meyer); Katalog einer Mozart-Biliothek; Ed Veroffentlichungen der Musikbiblioth Paul Hirsch, 12 vols. *Ctr*: Music & Letters, Music Review, etc. *s.s*: Musicology, Bibliography & Typography. *Rec*: Music, collecting books, golf. *c*: Reform. *a*: 10 Adams Rd, Cambridge. *T*: 5288.

HIRST, Arthur, F.R.S.A. *b*: Patea, N.Z. 1883. *e*: N.Z. Schools. *m*: Ada Temple Layton. Pianist & Lecturer. *c.t*: Various. *s.s*: Music, painting, languages. War Service (Navy). *Rec*: Bridge. Fell Roy Empire Soc. *a*: Brackenhirst, Roehampton, S.W.15. *t*: Putney 2027.

HIRST, Edmund Langley. M.A., D.Sc., F.R.I.C., F.R.S. *b*: Preston 1898. *e*: Northgate Sch Ipswich, Madras Coll, St Andrews, Univ of St Andrews. Prof of Chemistry, Lect & Reader in Chem Univ of Birm, Prof of Organic Chem-Biliothek, Prof of Chem & Dir of the Chem Labs Univ of Manch, Forbes Prof of Organic Chem in Univ of Edin. *Ctr*: Journ of the Chem Soc, Trans of Faraday Soc, Biochem Journ, Nature, Chemistry & Industry. *s.s*: Organic Chem. *a*: The University, King's Bldgs, Edinburgh.

HIRST, Edward Wales, M.A.(Lon), B.Sc(Oxon). *b*: Dewsbury 1870. *e*: Dewsbury G.S. & Edin, Lon & Oxf Univs. *m*: Frances Sanderson. Theo Lect. Lect in Christian Ethics in M/C Univ, Lect in Christian Ethics & Moral Philos in M/C Meth Cols. *Publ*: Self & Neighbour (1919); Ethical Love ('28). *c.t*: Mind, Internat Journ of Ethics, Philos. *s.s*: Christian ethics & moral philos. *Rec*: Orchestral music. *a*: Lynton, The Firs, Bowdon, Altrincham, Cheshire. *t*: 125.

HIRST, Francis W. Author & Economist. *Publ*: Money; Biographies of Adam Smith —John Morley—Thomas Jefferson. *a*: Dunford Hse, Midhurst, Sussex.

HIRST, Leonard Fabian, M.D. *b*: Prestwich, Lancs 1882. *e*: Merchant Taylors' Sch, U.C.L. & U.C. Med Sch. *m*: Kathleen Heffernan. Member League of Nations Expert Commission on Plague Research 1927, F.R.S.M., Roy Soc of Trop Med & Hygiene. *Publ*: Researches on the Parasitology of Plague; etc. *Ctr*: B.M.J., Lancet, Ceylon Journ of Science, Journ of Hygiene, Brit Ency of Med Practice, etc. *s.s*: Plague, Epidemiology, Bacteriology, Parasitology. *Rec*: County walks, travel, theatre. *c*: Roy Empire. *a*: Stanwood, Begbroke, Oxford. *T*: Kidlington 138.

HIRST, Margaret Esther, M.A. *e*: Newnham Cam. Univ Lect. *Publ*: Life of Friedrich List (1907); The Story of Trusts; The Quakers in Peace & War ('23). *c.t*: Classical Review, etc. *c*: Cowdray. *a*: 114a Gough Rd, Edgbaston, Birm.

HIRST, Stuart A. *b*: Leeds 1877. *e*: Leeds Hgh Sch & Univ. *m*:. *s*: 1. Journalist & Publicist, Fell Inc Adv Cons & Agent Dir of Publ to C. E. Fulford Ltd of Leeds, Sydney, Calcutta & Toronto, Chm Stuart Hirst Agency. *Publ*: How to Find Where You Fit; The Basic Principles of Success; Inspiration; Lectures & Essays on Advertising; Aircraft in Peace & War; Story of the Leeds Tercentenary; Christianity Awake; Yorkshire Yarns of Yore; How Advertising is Done. *Ctr*: Various. *s.s*: Advtg & Salesmanship, Music Advertising, Aviation. *Rec*: Literature & Philos Research. *a*: Oak Lea Hall, Adel, Leeds 6. *T*: Leeds 22779 & 73179.

HIRST, Wilfred. Journalist. *n.a*: Sports Ed Evening Sentinel Hanley, Stoke-on-Trent. *s.s*: Cricket, assoc & rugby football. *a*: 115 The Avenue, Harpfield, Newcastle, Staffs. *t*: N/c-under-Lyme 67253.

HIRST, William Alfred. *b*: Huddersfield 1870. *e*: Clifton Col, Worcester Col Oxf. *m*: Kathleen Pauline Thompson. *s*: 1. Author. *Publ*: A Survey of Ethics (1903); Short History of India; Argentina ('10); Handbook of South America; Rambles in the Home Counties; Real Self-Government for India ('33); etc. *c.t*: Quarterly Review, English Review, etc. *s.s*: Lit, topography. War Service. *Rec*: Travel, chess. *c*: New Univ. *a*: 19 Upper Park Rd, Hampstead, N.W.3.

HISCOCKS, Dr. H. F. *Publ*: Adenoma of the Liver with Malignant Changes associated with Infantilism, B.M.J. *a*: Newlyn, The Cliffs, Westcliff-on-Sea, Essex.

HISCOX, Ralph Edwin. *b*: Northampton 1879. *m*: (1) Alice Lavinia Wood; (2) Olive Marian Binning. *s*: 4. *d*: 2. Journalist (Sub-Ed). *n.a*: Western Daily Press & Bristol Evening News '94, Bristol Times & Mirror & Bristol Evening Times 1904, Bristol Evening Post '32. *a*: 5 Wentworth Rd, Bishopston, Bristol.

HISKETT, William Robert. *b*: St Albans 1885. Married. *s*: 1. Rly Acc. *Publ*: The Tyranny of Gold. *c.t*: British Trade Review; Rly Service Journ. *s.s*: Economics, monetary questions. *a*: 8 Clarence Rd, St Albans, Herts.

HISLOP, James Andrew, M.D., D.P.H., L.R.C.P. & S. *Publ*: Annual Reports on the Health of the County Borough of Tynemouth 1909-29-. *c.t*: B.M.J., Public Health. *a*: Hartsop, Patterdale, nr Penrith.

HISS, Philip Hanson. *b*: Brooklyn, N.Y. 1910. *e*: Priv Schs & Tutors. *m*: Marjorie Boothe. *s*: 1. *d*: 1. Author, Lecturer, Photographer, Explorer. *Publ*: Bali; Netherlands America; Selective Guide to the English Literature on the Netherlands West Indies; Immortal Verse (Jt-Ed). *Ctr*: Various. *s.s*: Anthropology, Sociology, Photography, Exploration, Colonial Government, South East Asia. *Rec*: Sailing, tennis, mountain climbing, cruising. *c*: Explorers', etc. *a*: Cedarcrest, New Canaan, Connecticut, U.S.A. *T*: New Canaan 9-1058.

HISTON, H. W. F/l. Hon Sec Notts Chess Assoc. *a*: 47 Florence Rd, Thorneywood, Notts.

HITCHCOCK, Edward Baring. *b*: Amherst, Mass 1884. *e*: Cornell Univ. *m*: Myrna Sharlow. *s*: 1. Journalist, White Lion of Prague. *n.a*: For Corres Chicago Dly News, For Desk Christian Sci Monitor 1933–37, European Ed Man in London '37–39. *Publ*: Memoirs of Minnie Hauk; I Built a Temple for Peace—The Life of

Eduard Benes; Benes, The Man & the Statesman. *Ctr*: Various American newsps. *s.s*: Internat Affairs & Biography. *a*: 1724 North Quinn St, Arlington, Va, U.S.A., & 58 Seelye St, Amherst, Mass, U.S.A.

HITCHCOCK, Elsie Vaughan, B.A., Ph.D., D.Lit. *b*: Streatham. *e*: Univ Col, Lon. Lecturer in English, Univ Col, Lon. *Publ*: Critical Editions of Pecock's Donet; Pecock's Folewer to the Donet; Harpsfield's Life of More; Roper's Life of More (for E.E.T.S.); Index to Chambers' Thomas More. *s.s*: Reginald Pecock, Sir Thomas More, History of English Language. *Rec*: Reading, walking. *c*: Fel of Univ Col, Lon. *a*: 67 Selborne Rd, Southgate, N.14.

HITCHCOCK, Rev. Francis Ryan Montgomery, D.D. *b*: 1867. *e*: Trin Coll Dublin. *m*: (1) K. Ingram. (2) Mrs A. I. Traill. *s*: 2. Rector of Tolleshunt Knights, Donnellan Lecturer T.C.D. 1912, Rector of Kinnitty King's Co '03—24, Examining Chaplain to the Bishop of Killaloe '18—24. *Publ*: The Atonement & Modern Thought; Irenæus of Lugdunum; Fresh Study of the Fourth Gospel; Celtic Types of Life & Art; Midland Sepis & the Pale; St Patrick & His Gallic Friends; The Holy Communion in the New Testament; Gospel Miracles; Harvest Thoughts; The Reformation in England & Ireland; The Mystery of the Cross; Christ & His Critics, etc. *Ctr*: Various Ecclesiastical Journals. *Rec*: Swimming, walking, Latin verse. *a*: The Rectory, Tolleshunt Knights, Maldon, Essex. *T*: Tiptree 12.

HITCHINGS, Winifred Mary. *b*: Plymouth 1878. *e*: Priv. Sec Book-keeper. *Publ*: Seagull Billy. *Rec*: Foreign travel. *a*: Hinton Martel, Nr Wimborne, Dorset.

HITCHINS, Courtenay Eden. *b*: Jamaica, B.W.I. 1905. *e*: Queen's Roy Col Port of Spain, Columbia Univ. N.Y., U.S.A. Asst Ed Trinidad Guardian. *n.a*: Chief Sub-Ed Trinidad Guardian 1930, Asst Ed '33. *c.t*: Various n/ps & periodicals. *s.s*: Polit, travel. Ex-Acct & Business Mang. *Rec*: Tennis, swimming. *a*: 55 Mucurapo Rd, Pt of Spain, Trinidad, B.W.I. *t*: 2000.

HITCHON, Dr. H. H. I. Pres Lancs Co & M/C C.C. *a*: Bamford Lodge, Heywood, Lancs.

HITTI, Philip Khuri, B.A.(Beirut), Ph.D.(Columb). *b*: Shimlan, Lebanon 1886. *m*: Mary Elizabeth George. *d*: 1. Chm Dept of Oriental Languages & Literature Princeton 1944. *Publ*: History of the Arabs; The Arabs; An Arab-Syrian Gentleman & Warrior in the Period of the Crusades; The Origins of the Islamic State; The Orgins of the Druze People & Religion; Characteristics of Moslem Sects; The Syrians in America. *Ctr*: Ency of Soc Sciences, Ency Americana, etc. *s.s*: Mediæval Arab & Moslem History & Civilization, Modern Arab World, etc. *Rec*: Walking, tennis, mountain climbing. *c*: Intercollegiate, etc. *a*: 106 Fitzrandolph Rd, Princeton, New Jersey, U.S.A. *T*: 1127.

HOAR, Charles Herapath. *b*: London 1890. *e*: St Paul's Jersey. *m*: Eva Minnie Nicolle. *s*: 1. *d*: 2. Journalist, M.J.I., Sec The Times & Times Book Club. *n.a*: Jersey Morning News 1909, The Times '17. *Ctr*: The Times. *Rec*: Tennis, gardening. *a*: Chez Nous, 11 Westmoreland Rd, Barnes. *T*: Riverside 6252.

HOARE, Albert George. *n.a*: Chepstow Rep. South Wales Argus. *a*: Argus Off, Chepstow.

HOARE, Alfred. *b*: 1850. *e*: Eton & Cam. Widower. *s*: 1. *d*: 4. Banker (ret). *Publ*: An Italian Dictionary; Modern Italian & English Dictionary; etc. *Rec*: Bridge. *a*: Charlwood, E. Grinstead. *t*: Sharpthorn 21.

HOARE, B. S. Publisher. *s.s*: Accountancy, business economics, banking, foreign exchange, general literature. *a*: c/o Macdonald & Evans, 8 John St, Bedford Row, W.C.1.

HOARE, George Henry, J.P. *b*: Pontypool 1806. *e*: West Mon Gr Sch. *m*: Anne Betterton. *s*: 1. Dir & Mang Ed South Wales Argus & Weekly Argus Series. *n.a*: Sth Wales News & Sth Wales Echo 1915—19, Chief Rep Sth Wales Argus '19—27, Asst Ed '27, Ed '39. Mang Ed '45, Dir '47. *Rec*: Music, drama, public work. *c*: Press, Nat Lib, Monmouthshire County. *a*: Cilsanws, Newport, Mon. *T*: 3496.

HOARE, Henry, J.P. *b*: Lon 1866. *e*: Eton & Trin Col Cam. *m*: Lady Geraldine Hervey. *s*: 2. *d*: 1. Banker. *Publ*: Flowering Trees & Shrubs; Spadework. War Service. *Rec*: Gardening, travel, golf. *c*: Marlborough, Leander, Addington Golf. *a*: Ellisfield Manor, Basingstoke. *t*: Herriard 9.

HOARE, Lionel Richard. *b*: Highgate 1915. *m*: Joyce Russell. *d*: 1. Chief Film Ed Entertainment Shorts Paths Pictures. *a*: 35 Gladsmuir Rd, Highgate, London, N.19.

HOARE, Percy C. *n.a*: Streatham News Series. *a*: 14 Falkland Park Avenue, South Norwood, London, S.E.25.

HOARE, Robert Rawdon, D.S.O., M.C. *b*: Underhill, Surrey 1897. *e*: Beaumont Coll Windsor. Dir Economic League. *Publ*: Rhodesian Mosaic; This, Our Country. *Ctr*: Blackwood's Contemp Rev, Cornhill Mag, Times, Sun Dispatch, Dly Mail, etc. *s.s*: Social Work for Ex-Servicemen Hospitals. *Rec*: Travel, golf, tennis. *c*: Cavalry, Buck's, Union, Manchester. *w.s*: 1938—45 C.M.F. 8th Army, Chief Artillery Adviser Brit Mil Mission to Egyptian Army '44. *a*: Arlington Chambers, 5 Dover St, London, W.1. *T*: Regent 5950.

HOARE, Rt. Hon. Sir Samuel, M.P. *Publ*: The Fourth Seal; A Flying Visit to the Middle East. *a*: c/o W. Heinemann Ltd, 99 Gt Russell St, W.C.1.

HOBART, Alice Nourse Tisdale. *b*: Lockport, N.Y. State 1882. *e*: Univ of Chicago. *m*: Earle Tisdale Hobart. Novelist, Mem Internat P.E.N. *Publ*: Oil for the Lamps of China; The Peacock Sheds His Tail; Yang & Yin; River Supreme; The Cup & The Sword; Their Own Country; Within The Walls of Shanking; Pioneering Where the World is Old; By the City of the Long Sand. *Ctr*: Harpers Mag, Nat Geographic Asia, Sat Rev of Lit, Chic Sun, Atlantic Monthly, Century. *s.s*: Internat Understanding. *a*: 6017 Margarido Drive, Oakland, California, U.S.A. *T*: Olympic 0967.

HOBBS, Grace Mary Noel. *b*: Ludlow 1888. *e*: Whitelands Col Sec Sc, Whiteland Training Col & King's Col, Lon Univ. L.C.C. Head Mistress. *Publ*: Reading & Scissor Work for Infants & Juniors (Books 1 & 2); Raffia Work for Juniors. *s.s*: Eng, botany & handicraft. Lecturer L.C.C. Teachers' World Classes & Mem L.C.C. Advisory Text Book Panel. *Rec*: Music, photography, golf. *c*: Forum. *a*: 35 Graham St, Eaton Sq, S.W.1. *t*: Sloane 1418.

HOBDAY, FREDERICK: consulting veterinary surgeon. DEGREES: C.M.G., F.R.C.V.S., F. R. S. E. AUTHOR: Anaesthesia of Animals and Birds; Surgical Diseases of the Dog and Cat; Courtenay's Veterinary Medicine; Castration and Ovariatomy of Animals; Canine Surgery; Veterinary Medicine; Atlas of the Anatomy of the Dog. Editor of The Veterinary Jnl. General character of writing: scientific, surgical. Hon. Veterinary Surgeon to His Majesty, the King; prin. of Royal Veterinary Coll., London; Hon. Fellow of American Veterinary Medical Assn.;

Hon. Fellow, Hunterian Soc. of London; Hon. Fellow of Harveian Soc. of London; Officer du Mèrite Agricole (France); Cavaliere del S. S. Maurizio e Lazzaro (Italy). CLUBS: Savage, Knights of the Round Table. ADDRESS: Royal Veterinary College, London, N. W. 1, Eng.

HOBHOUSE, LEONARD TRELAWNY: professor of Sociology, Univ. of London; b. Cornwall, Eng., Sept. 8, 1864; s. (Archdeacon) Reginald and Caroline (Trelawny) H.; educ. Exmouth; Marlborough; Corpus Christi Coll. (Oxford); DEGREES: M.A. Oxon., 1887; Hon. D.Litt. (Durham, 1930); Hon. LL.D. (St. Andrews, 1919); m. Nora Hadwen, Apr. 9, 1891. AUTHOR: Labour Movement, 1893-1912; Theory of Knowledge, 1896-1920; Mind and Evolution, 1901-26; Social Evolution and Political Theory, 1911; Development and Purpose, 1913-27; The Metaphysical Theory of the State, 1919; Rational Good, 1920; Elements of Social Justice, 1920; Social Development, 1924. Contributor to Mind, Internat'l. Jnl. of Ethics and others. Served on editorial staff of Manchester Guardian, later on the Tribune; sec. of Free Trade Union. CLUBS: National Liberal (London). (*)

HOBHOUSE, Neill, M.D.(Oxon), F.R.C.P.(Lond). b: Oxford 1888. e: Winchester, New Coll Oxf & St Thomas's Hosp. Married. d: 2. Publ: Nervous Disorder in Infancy & Childhood. Ctr: Lancet & other Med Journs. s.s: Nervous Diseases. c: Athenæum. a: 18 Harley St, London, W.1, & Upper Cheyne Row, London, S.W.3.

HOBHOUSE, Rosa Waugh, M.R.S.T., J.P. b: Old Southgate N. 1882. e: Priv & Slade Sch of Art. m: Stephen Hobhouse, M.A. Art Teacher & Author, Christian Socialist & Pacifist. Publ: Life of Benjamin Waugh, Founder of the N.S.P.C.C.; Life of Christian Samuel Hahnemann, Founder of Homœopathy; Story Making, Poems; etc. Ctr: Educ Outlook, Child Educ, The Sch Mistress, King's Treasury Series, etc. s.s: Youth Work for Senior Boys, The Spread of Homœopathy. a: 20 St Catherine's, Broxbourne, Herts.

HOBHOUSE, Stephen Henry, M.A. b: Pitcombe, Somerset 1881. e: Eton Coll, Balliol Coll Oxf, Germany. m: Rosa Waugh. Author, Examiner under Board of Educ Whitehall 1905—12, War Relief Work in Turkey & Bulgaria '12—13, Chm Soc of Friends Emergency Cmt for Enemy Aliens & Prisoners '14—16, '16—18 Prison Experiences C.O., Jt Sec of Prison System Enquiry Cmt '18—22. Publ: English Prisons To-day (with A. F. Brockway): An English Prison from within; William Law & 18th Century Quakerism; Selected Mystical Writings of William Law; Joseph Sturge; Margaret Hobhouse & Her Family; Christ & Our Enemies (with Archbishop Temple); & various other War-time Pamphs. a: 20 St Catherine's, Broxbourne, Herts.

HOBLEY, G. F. a: 2 Elm Terrace, Penrith.

HOBMAN, D. L. (Mrs. Daisy Lucie Hobman, née Adler): author; b. 1891; educ. Roedean Sch.; St. Hilda's Coll., Oxford; diploma in Economics. AUTHOR: Zion, 1924. Translated Winter (by Griese), from the German. Contributor to Westminster Gazette, Daily News, Contemporary Review, Jewish Chronicle and others. General character of writing: fiction and social problems. Public speaker; late Hon. Sec. Women's Internat. Zionist Organization. CLUBS: Women's University; P.E.N. HOME: Shelley Barn, Pilt Down, Sussex, Eng.

HOBMAN, JOSEPH BURTON (pen name: **The Man from the North**): political journalist; b. Sheffield, Eng., May, 1872; s. Joseph and Annie Marie (Burton) H.; educ. Wesley Coll. (Sheffield); m. Daisy Lucie Adler. Editor of Birmingham Gazette, 1912-21; of Westminster Gazette, 1921-8. Contributor to Yorkshire Observer, Sheffield Independent, Northern Echo, Birmingham Gazette, Nottingham Jnl. General character of writing: political and literary. Candidate British House of Commons (Sheffield), July, 1928; for (No. Bradford, Yorkshire), May 1929. Executive P.E.N. Club (London). Relig. denom., Free Churchman. CLUBS: Reform, National, Liberal, P.E.N. OFFICE: Newspaper House, Fleet St., London. HOME: Shelley Barn, Pilt Down, Sussex, Eng.

HOBSON, A. D., M.A. (Cantab), F.R.S.E., Prof of Zool at Armstrong Col Durham Univ 1932-. c.t: Proc Roy Soc of Edin, Journ Experimental Biol. s.s: Cytology. a: 33 Eldon Pl, Newcastle-on-Tyne.

HOBSON, Eric. b: Doncaster 1918. e: Doncaster Tech Coll. m: Dorothy Jean Hobson. Journalist, Sec Sth Yorkshire Branch N.U.J. n.a: Yorkshire Ev Post (Doncaster edn) '36, Doncaster Chronicle '36, Deputy News Ed '46. Rec: Motoring, tennis. w.s: 1939—45 Sgt R.A.F. a: 32 Hampton Rd, Town Moor, Doncaster, Yorkshire.

HOBSON, Oscar Rudolf, M.A. b: Cambridge 1886. e: Aldenham Sch & Camb Univ. m: Frances Josephine Atkinson. n.a: Finan Ed Manchester Guardian 1920—29, Ed-in-Chief Financial News '29—34, City Ed News Chron since '35 & The Star since '41. Publ: How the City Works; Does Money Matter?; Can We Afford It? Talks with a Banker. a: Roughwood Farmhouse, Chalfont St Giles, Bucks. T: 254.

HOBSON, Robert Lockhart, B.A., C.B. b: Lisburn Ire 1872. e: St John's Sc Leatherhead & Cam Univ. m: Daisy Denison. s: 4. d: 1. Civil Servant. Keeper of Dept Oriental Antiquities & of Ethnography, Brit Museum. Publ: Catalogue of English Pottery in the British Museum (1903); Catalogue of English Porcelain in the British Museum ('05); Chinese Pottery & Porcelain ('15); The Art of the Chinese Potter ('23); Guide to the Pottery & Porcelain of the Far East in British Museum ('24); The Later Ceramic Wares of China ('25); Guide to the Islamic Pottery of the Near East in the British Museum ('32). c.t: Burlington Mag, etc. s.s: Ceramics & Chinese art. Rec: Golf & tennis. c: Athenæum. a: Widecombe, Rosslyn Rd, Watford. t: 3207.

HOBY, John Charles James, M.B.E., MusDoc (Oxon), A.R.C.M., L.R.A.M. b: Lon. e: Priv. m: Ishbael McKay McLeay Fraser. s: 2. Prof & Exam R.C.M. Lon. Publ: Pronunciation for Singers (Juta); Lecture on Wind-Bands & Music. c.t: Musical Times, Musical Progress, Musical Mail. s.s: Music & archæology. Rec: Photography, foreign travel. c: Assoc of Retired Naval Officers, Overseas, etc. a: 30 Gledstanes Rd, W.14. t: Fulham 0782.

HOCHWALT, Albert Frederick, D.Litt. b: Ohio 1869. e: Dayton Univ, Ohio. m: Adele M. Butz. s: 4. (1 dec). Writer, Author & Publisher. n.a: Associate Ed Sportsmen's Review 1905-15, American Field '15-, Outdoor Life '28-. Publ: Arrows of Ambition (novel, '07); The Pointer and the Setter in America ('11); The Modern Pointer ('17, 2nd edn, '23); Dogcraft ('07); Dog Keeping for the Amateur ('20); The Airedale for Work & Show ('21); The Farmer's Dog ('21); Beagles & Beagling ('21); Makers of Bird Dog History ('27); Greymist ('25); etc. c.t: Amer Field, Sportsman, Dayton Daily News, St Louis Post Dispatch, Ency Brit, etc. s.s: Dogs & hunting. Extensive travel. Rec: Fishing, riding. c: Hon Mem Princ Amer Field Trial Clubs. a: 542 Forest Av, Dayton, Ohio. t: Fulton 5583.

HOCKABY, Stephen Michael. b: Oxford 1901. Publ: Marsh Hay; Seven Stars & Orion; Gabriel's Hold; Grand Master; Shallow Brown. s.s: Athletics, Boxing, Children, etc. a: c/o Curtis Brown Ltd, 6 Henrietta St London, W.C.2.

HOCKETT, Homer Carey, B.Litt., Ph.D. *b*: Martinville, Ohio 1875. *e*: Earlham Coll, Univs of Indiana & Wis. *m*: Amy Francisco. Emeritus Prof of History Ohio State Univ, Writer. *Publ*: Constitutional History of the United States ; Political & Social Growth of the American People ; Introduction to Research in American History ; Land of the Free ; Western Influences on Political Parties to 1825. *Ctr*: Miss Valley Hist Rev, Amer Hist Rev, Polit Sci Quart, Lawyers' Guild Rev, Social Studies, etc. *s.s*: Constitutional History of the U.S. *Rec*: Walking, swimming, touring. *a*: 202 West Valerio St, Santa Barbara, California, U.S.A.

HOCKIN, John (J. G. Wall). *Publ*: Britain's Folly; The Lesson of Ceylon (foreword by The Rt Hon the Viscount Rothermere). *c.t*: Many publ in Gt Britain & the Empire. *s.s*: The East. *a*: c/o Raymond Savage Ltd, Princes Hse, 39 Jermyn St, W.1.

HOCKING, Frederick Denison Maurice, M.B., B.S., M.Sc, F.I.C. Cons Pathologist & Biochemist. *c.t*: Lancet, Journ of Clinical Research, Medical News, etc. *a*: 140 Harley St, Lon W.1. *t*: Welbeck 2795.

HOCKING, Joseph. *b*: St Stephens 1861. *e*: St Stephens G.S. & Owen's Col M/C. *m*: Annie Brown. *s*: 1. *d*: 4. Novelist. Held various ministerial apptmts. *Publ*: The Woman of Babylon; The Man Who Rose Again ; The Eternal Challenge ; Rosemary Carew ; etc. *c.t*: Brit Weekly, Sunday Companion, etc. *s.s*: Religious questions. Mem C'wall C.C. 1931—34. The Cuthbertson Prize. *Rec*: Golf. *c*: Reform, Whitefriars. *a*: Bodvean, Perranporth, C'wall. *t*: 106.

HOCKING, (Mona Naomi) Anne. *b*: London. *e*: Sidcot Sc & Roy Holloway Col. Novelist. *Publ*: Cats Paw ; Death Duel ; Walk into my Parlour ; The Hunt is Up ; Without the Option. *s.s*: History. Daughter of Joseph Hocking, Niece of Silas Hocking. *Rec* Motoring, swimming. *a*: Gibraltar, The Common, Tunbridge Wells. *t*: 2089.

HOCKING, Silas Kitto. *b*: St Stephens 1850. *m*: Esther Mary Lloyd. *s*: 2. *d*: 2. *n.a*: Founded & Edited Temple Mag '96 & Family Circle '94-95. *Publ*: Her Benny (1st book & nearly 100 others, Gerry Storm latest). *c.t*: Various n/ps & periodicals. *s.s*: Autobiog & trav. With Walter Besant established Atlantic Union, now The English Speaking Union (Vice-Pres). Vice-Pres of Nat Counc of Free Chs. *Rec*: Golf, bowls, etc. *c*: Whitefriars. *a*: 10 Avenue Rd, Highgate, N.6. *t*: Mountview 0437.

HOCKLIFFE, Ernest, M.A., J.P. Ex Master at Uppingham Sc. *Publ*: Ed for Roy Hist Soc; Diary of Ralph Jocelyn; pt author with John Sargeant: The History of Bedford School; author of some poems in: A Rhymers Ring. *a*: Barrow Ct Farm, Tickenham, Somerset. *t*: Nailsea 86X.

HOCKLY, Harod Edward, B.A., LL.B. *b*: King Williamstown, S.A. 1897. *e*: Dale Coll King Williamstown, Rhodes Univ Coll Grahamstown, Univ of Cape Town. *m*: Katherine Maria Bester. *s*: 1. *d*: 1. Barrister. *Publ*: The Story of the British Settlers of 1820 in South Africa ; The Insolvency Law of South Africa ; Students' Guide to the Insolvency Law. *s.s*: Africana, Insolvency, Industrial & Commercial Law in Sth Africa. *Rec*: Golf, riding, tennis. *c*: City & Owl, Cape Town. *w.s*: 1916—18. *a*: Eikenhof, Greenfield Rd, Kenilworth, Cape Town, S.A. *T*: 7-4808.

HODDER, Thomas Knowles, M.J.I. *n.a*: Sports Ed Morning Post. *a*: 16 Gt James St, W.C.1.

HODESS, Jacob. *e*: England & Abroad. *n.a*: Ed New Judea 1924—, Ed Palcor News Agency '34. *Ctr*: Leading English & Foreign publs. *s.s*: Lit, Politics, Zionism, Jewish Affairs. *a*: 24 Hillfield Ct, N.W.3. *T*: Primrose 4817.

HODGE, Albert Ernest. *b*: Lon 1877. *e*: Harlesden Col. Ed The Aquarist & Pond-Keeper. *n.a*: Reporting Staff Press Assoc 10 y, Daily Chronicle 8 y, subsequently " Zoo " corr. *Publ*: Vivarium & Aquarium Keeping for Amateurs; Goldfish Culture for Amateurs; Tropical Aquarium Fishes; Garden Ponds & Pools; Peeps at the " Zoo " Aquarium; Young Collector's Guide to Butterfly & Moth Collecting. *c.t*: Daily Chronicle, Daily Express, Evening News, etc. *s.s*: Animal life, pisciculture, aquarium keeping & reptilian pets. Founder & First Pres Brit Aquarist's Assoc. *Rec*: Nature study, photography. *a*: 14 Astonville St, Southfields, S.W.18.

HODGE, Charles. *b*: Plymouth 1907. *e*: Montpellier Univ, France. *m*: Iris Cole. Schoolmaster & Author. *Publ*: The Raven's Causeway ; The House of the Winds. *s.s*: Boys' Stories ; Railways ; Cornwall. *Rec*: Travel, reading, folklore. *a*: c/o Messrs A. P. Watt & Sons, Norfolk St, Strand, London, W.C.

HODGE, Dorothy Maude. *b*: Rugby. *m*: Henry Hodge. *s*: 1. Jnlst. *s.s*: Women's interests. *c*: Soroptimist, B'ham. *a*: 63 Holly Lane, Erdington, Birmingham. *t*: Erdington 0701.

HODGE, Frederick Webb, LL.D., Lit.D, D.Sc. *b*: Plymouth 1864. *e*: Univs of Columb, New Mexico & Southern Calif. *m*: (1) Margaret Whitehead Magill (dec'd). *s*: 1. *d*: 2. (2) Zahrah E. Preble (dec'd). (3) Gene P. Meany. Archæologist & Ethnologist. *Publ*: Coronado's Route from Culiacan to Quivira ; History of Hawikuh ; & many others. Editor of several learned & historical publs. *a*: South West Museum, Highland Park, Los Angeles 42, California, U.S.A.

HODGE, H. S. Vere, M.A. *Publ*: Verse; Pantoia; Half Way (1920). *a*: Hightrees, Tonbridge, Kent.

HODGE, Harry. *b*: Edin 1872. *e*: Glas Acad, Glas Univ & Leipzig Univ. *m*: Agnes Hunter Moffatt. *s*: 1. *d*: 2. Publisher. *n.a*: Gen Ed Notable British Trials Series (60 volumes) 1905-, Ed Scottish Law Review, etc. *Publ*: Pianoforte Composition. *s.s*: Music, criminology. *Rec*: Travel, music, crime. *c*: P.E.N., Savage, Constitutional, Royal Automobile, Scottish Conservative, Musicians, Arts, Edinburgh, Royal Scottish Automobile, Palette, Conservative, Glasgow. *a*: 58 Murrayfield Av, Edinburgh. *t*: 62185.

HODGE, Harold. *b*: Lon 1862. *e*: Islington Proprietary Sc, St Paul's & Pembroke Col Oxf. Barrister-at-Law. *n.a*: Edited Saturday Review 1897-1913. *Publ*: In the Wake of the War; Parliament or Imperial Government. *c.t*: Nineteenth Century, Fortnightly Review. *c*: Travellers. *a*: 9 Highbury Place, Lon, N.5.

HODGE, Horace Emerton (Merton Hodge). Dramatist. *Publ*: inc The Wind & the Rain ; Men in White ; To Whom We Belong ; etc. *a*: 48 Ebury St, London, S.W.1.

HODGE, James H. *b*: Edinburgh 1906. *e*: Edin Acad, Edin Univ. *m*: Anne Essex Leslie. *d*: 1. Publisher Ed Scott Law Rev 1947—, Gen Ed Notable Brit Trials, Ass Gen Ed War Crimes Trials. *s.s*: Criminology. *Rec*: Reading, music. *c*: R.A.F. *w.s*: World War II (Des). *a*: 14 Ramsay Gdn, Edinburgh. *T*: 33591.

HODGE, Merton. *b*: Gisborne, New Zealand 1903. *e*: Otago Univ, Dunedin, N.Z., Edinburgh Univ. Medical Practitioner, Dramatist. *Publ*:

Plays:—The Wind and the Rain; Grief Goes Over. s.s: Drama, films. Rec: Motoring, theatre-going. c: Brit Med Assoc. a: c/o A. D. Peters, 4 & 5 Adam St, Adelphi, W.C.2. t: Temple Bar 3794.

HODGES, Arthur. b: Philadelphia, U.S.A. 1868. e: Public Scs. m: Pauline Chapin. s: 2. d: 1. Publ: Lord Kitchener; Man of Substance; The Glittering Hour; The Bounder; Spendthrift Town; Pincus Hood; The Essential Thing; The Body in the Car; The Embassy Murder. a: 27 Chesham Place, S.W.1. t: Sloane 7545.

HODGES, Cyril Evelyn, M.A. (" Uncle Peter " of the Evening News). b: Leicester 1881. e. Wyggeston Sc & Cam Univ (Christ's Col). m: Clare Hodges Humphreys. d: 2. Mang Dir of Community Service Ltd, Lecturer, Educationist, Author. Formerly Organiser of Children's Hr B.B.C. n.a: Lon Evening News 1929—. Various offices in connection with Local Administrative & Soc Welfare organisations. Publ: The Empire Day Book of Patriotism; The School Hymn Book. c.t: Leading Lon & Prov Publs. s.s: Classics, modern langs, instruction & entertainment of children, production & distribution of scientific, educational & travel films. Rec: Music, tennis, golf, swimming & badminton. a: 1 Montague St, Lon, W.C.1. t: Museum 3413.

HODGES, Harold Winter, M.A., F.R.Hist.S. e: Malvern Coll, Lincoln Coll Oxf. Head of History & Eng Dept R.N.C. Dartmouth (ret). Publ: Select Naval Documents (with E. A. Hughes); Modern Hist. s.s: Naval History. a: Windmill Hse, Wingrave, Bucks. T: Aston Abbots 244.

HODGES, Herbert Arthur. b: Sheffield 1905. e: Elem Sch, King Edward VII Sch Sheffield, Balliol & Magdalen Colls Oxf. m: Vera Joan Willis. s: 2. Prof of Philos Univ of Reading. Publ: Wilhelm Dilthey, an Introduction. s.s: Philosophy. Rec: Cycling, music. a: 8 Mansfield Rd, Reading, Berks. T: 3560.

HODGES, John Cunyus, M.A., Ph.D. b: Cotton Valley, Louisiana 1892. e: Meridian Coll, Univs of Tulane & Harvard. m: Lilian Nelson. s: 1. Prof of English Univ of Tenn. Publ: William Congreve, the Man; Harbrace College Handbook; Harbrace Handbook of English; English Manual for Teachers; Basic Writing & Reading; Harbrace Omnibus (collab); Manual of Instructions for Freshman English. Ctr: Revue Celtique, Mod Philology, Mod Lang Notes, etc. s.s: Literary & Biographical Research in 18th Century England, Problems in the Teaching of English. Rec: Golf, music. a: 1908 White Ave, Knoxville 16, Tennessee, U.S.A. T: 2-0878.

HODGES, Rev. Joseph Percy, M.A. b: Rodbourne Cheney, Wilts 1899. e: Downing Coll Camb. m: Dorothy Amelia Carter. Clerk in Holy Orders, Hon Canon of Truro Cathedral. n.a: Ed Youth Series, Bible Reading Fellowship Notes since 1941. Publ: Influence & Implications of the Reformation; Riches of Our Frayer Book; The Glory of God; Various books of Sunday School Lessons. Ctr: Echo, The Modern Churchman, The Parade. s.s: History & Theology. Rec: Gardening. a: The Rectory, Falmouth, Cornwall. T: Falmouth 76.

HODGES, Maj. Phelps, M.C. b: Mass 1894. e: Sherborne Sc Dorset & R.M.A. Woolwich. m: Madeleine Fayou. d: 1. Advisory Accountant & Army (ret). Publ: Britmis (British Military Mission, 1931). War Service '14–18, severely wounded (desp). Escaped from Bolsheviks across Central Asia '20. Twice round the world. a: Jnr Untd Service Club, St James's, S.W.1.

HODGKIN, Curwen Eliot. b: Purley, nr Reading 1905. m: Maria Clara Franceschi. s: 1. Painter & Writer. Publ: Fashion Dawing; She Closed the Door. a: 23 Jubilee Pl, London, S.W.3. T: Flaxman 6036.

HODGKIN. L.V. (Pen-name of HOLDSWORTH, Lucy Violet.)

HODGKIN, Mary. b: Darlington 1882. e: Oaklands Ilkley, Polam Hall Darlington & Westfield Coll. Hon Sec Darlington Town Mission since 1929, Officer Univ Women's Camps for Schoolgirls '05—07, Officer Student Chr Movement Summer Confs '06—07. n.a: Founder & 1st Ed By Kent & Skerne (Polam Hall Mag '01—05), Ed Our Missions (Quart Rev of Friends For Missn Assoc) '06—07. Publ: A Diary for the Thankfulhearted (9 edns); The Way Home (2 edns). s.s: Bible Study, World Travel. Rec: Gardening. a: Ridge Ways, Darlington. T: 5502.

HODGKINSON, Frederick. b: Cheadle 1866. e: Tettenhall Col Wolv'ton & Owen's Col M/C. m: Agnes Sharples. d: 3. Cotton Manufacturer (ret). c.t: M/C Guardian, N. Daily Telegraph. s.s: Cotton-growing (Empire). Indian Cotton Comt 1917–18. c: Empire Cotton-growing Corp, Brit Cotton-growing Assoc, Blackburn Chamber of Commerce. a: Higher Feniscowles Hall, Pleasington, Blackburn. t: 48.

HODGKINSON, Mary Clemence. b: Manchester 1917. e: Culcheth Hall Bowden, Salt Hgh Sch Shipley, King's Coll, Univ of Lond. Journalist. n.a: Rep Yorks Observer & Bradford Telegraph & Argus '40—, Agricultural Corr '46—. Ctr: Yorks Observer, Telegraph & Argus, Time & Tide, Northern Rev, The Y.M.C.A. Ambassador, etc. s.s: Poetry, Books, Urban Life. Rec: Books, films, plays, country walks, etc. a: 6 Crossfield Rd, Hale, Altrincham, Cheshire.

HODGKINSON, William Richard. b: Sheffield 1851. e: Edward VI G.S. Sheffield, Roy Col Chem, Lon Univ. m: C. D. Limpach. s: 2. d: 2. Ex-Prof R.C.C., later at Mil Col of Sci (Ex-Ordnance Col Woolwich). c.t: Science journs. s.s: War materiel. c: Chem. a: 89 Shooter's Hill Rd, S.E.3. t: Greenwich 2676.

HODGSON, Geraldine, B.A., M.A.(Cantab), B.A., LittD.(T.C.D.). b: Brighton 1865. e: Priv & Newnham Col Cam, Cobden Scholar '87—89. Lect & Writer. Temporary Factory Insp. Head of Sec Training Dept Bristol Univ 1902—19 Vice-Princ Ripon, Wakefield, Bradford Diocesan Training Col '17—22, etc. Publ: The Teacher's Rabelais; The Teacher's Montaigne; Studies in French Education; Rationalist Eng Educators; English Mystics; Richard Rolle's Form of Perfect Living; The Sanity of Mysticism, Sometime in Vision; Nature and Illumination; etc. c.t: Ch Quar Review, Theology, Dublin Review, Science Progress, The Quest, Contemporary Review, Ch Times, etc. s.s: Literature & mysticism. Mem of House of Laity Diocese of Ripon in Ch Assembly '20—29. c: Authors' Soc. a: 17 Sion Hill, Clifton, Bristol 8.

HODGSON, Herbert Henry, M.A., B.Sc., Ph.D., F.R.I.C. b: Bradford 1883. e: Bradford Gr Sch, Trin Coll Camb, Zurich Poly, Heidelberg Univ. m: Annie Gertrude Procter. d: 1. Head of Dept of Chemistry & Colour Chemistry Tech Coll Huddersfield, Mem of Council the Royal Institute of Chemistry since 1927, Vice-Pres '34—37. Publ: The Theory & Practice of Enamelling on Iron & Steel (Trans from German by Grünwald); The Chemistry of Colloids (Trans from Pöschl); Celluloid (Trans from French by Masselon), etc. Ctr: Journal of Chemical Soc, Trans Faraday Soc, etc. s.s: Chemistry, Physical Science. Rec: Languages. a: 136 Paley Rd, Bradford, Yorks, & Tech Coll, Huddersfield. T: Huddersfield 5260-1.

HODGSON, Irvin. *s.s*: Hist and biog sketches. *a*: 68 Taylor St, Middleton, M/C.

HODGSON, John Stuart, B.A. (Oxon.) *b*: Rochdale 1877. *e*: Richmond, Yorks & Brecon Sth Wales, Oxford Univ. *m*: Emily Storr Best. *d*: 1. Journalist. *n.a*: Leader Writer Lancs Dly Post '01, Morning Leader '03, Daily News '12 & Ed '21—31, Leader Writer News Chron '32—. *Publ*: Portraits & Reflections; The Liberal Policy for Industry, a Summary of the Liberal Yellow Book; etc. *Ctr*: Nineteenth Century, Contemp Rev, John O' London, To-day & To-morrow, Lord Halifax, a Study. *s.s*: Politics, Hist, For. Languages. *Rec*: Chess. *a*: 98 Croydon Rd, Beckenham, Kent. *T*: 0677.

HODGSON, Rev. Joseph Trousdale. *b*: Nott'm 1889. *e*: E. Lon Tech Col. *m*: Alice Gertrude Burgess. *s*: 2. *Publ*: The Companion of the Lonely; The Unknown Steersman. *c.t*: Allied Press, Religious Press, N.E. Daily Gazette, A.P., etc. Broadcast Preacher (N. & Midland Regional). *Rec*: Tennis, cricket. *c*: Reform, Nott'm. *a*: 2 Mapperley Park Drive, Nott'm. *t*: 6310.

HODGSON, Rev. Leonard, M.A., Hon.D.D., Hon.D.C.L. *b*: London 1889. *e*: St Paul's Sch, Hertford Coll Oxf & St Michael's Coll Llandaff. *m*: Ethel Margaret Du Plat Archer. *s*: 1. *d*: 1. Clerk in Holy Orders, Regius Prof of Divinity & Canon of Christ Church Oxf. *n.a*: Lit Ed of the Living Church (Milwaukee U.S.A.) 1926—31. *Publ*: The Place of Reason in Christian Apologetics; And Was Made Man; Essays in Christian Philosophy; Eugenics; The Grace of God; Towards a Christian Philosophy; The Doctrine of the Trinity. *s.s*: Theology. *a*: Christ Church, Oxford. *T*: Oxford 3091.

HODGSON, Dr. N. *a*: 6 Windsor Terrace, Newcastle-on-Tyne.

HODGSON, Ralph. Poet. *Publ*: Poems; Last Blackbird; and other Verse. *a*: c/o Macmillan & Co, Ltd, St Martin's St, London, W.C.2.

HODGSON, Rev. Randolph Llewelyn, B.A. *b*: Playford Parsonage, Suffolk 1870. *e*: Private, Heversham Sch Westmorland, Queens' Coll Camb. *m*: Nora Conway Marsh. Clerk in Holy Orders (ret), Curate of Campsea Ashe Suffolk 1905—06, Ashill Norfolk '06—08, Curate-in-Charge Bashley New Milton Hants '08—12, Curate St Paul's Ave Road South Hampstead '12—13, Vicar of South Baddesley Lymington Hants '17—46, Also writes under the Pen Name of " A Country Vicar ". *n.a*: Ed The New Forest Magazine '38—46. *Publ*: Elma Trevor (in Collab with Florence, Countess of Darnley); On Plain & Peak; Wanderings Through Unknown Austria. *Ctr*: The Cricketer. *s.s*: Cricket, Natural History, History of the Church of England. *Rec*: Nature study, shooting, watching cricket. *a*: 23 Howitt Rd, Belsize Park, London, N.W.3.

HODGSON, Richard Arthur, B.Com.(Lond). *b*: London 1904. *e*: Hackney Downs Sch & Lond Sch of Econ. *m*: Phyllis Bertha Holt. *s*: 1. *d*: 2. Lect in Econ Univ Coll Southampton, Diploma in Public Administration (Lond). *Publ*: An Introduction to International Trade & Tariffs. *Ctr*: New Eng Wkly, Economist, Erasmus. *s.s*: Soc Hist & Lit of 19th Cent. *Rec*: Poetry, fives. *a*: 25 Welbeck Ave, Southampton.

HODGSON, Rose Marie. *b*: Leeds 1910. *e*: Thoresby High Sc, Leeds, Somerville Col, Oxford. *n.a*: Ed, Lysistrata '34. *Publ*: Rosy Fingered Dawn. *Rec* Theatre, cinema, art galleries. *a*: St. Mark's Sc House, Woodhousemoor, Leeds 6.

HODGSON, Miss Ursula, B.A. *s.s*: Classical lit & language. *a*: 20 Corder Rd, Ipswich.

HODGSON, WILLIAM ARCHER; (pen name: Thearcher): dental surgeon; b. London, Eng., June, 1887; s. Frederick and Caroline Elizabeth (Archer) H.; educ. Wilson's Grammar Sch.; Guy's Hospital Dental Sch.; DEGREES: L.O.S., R.C.S. (England); m. Gladys Martha Hyde, 1916. AUTHOR: Chronic Suppurative Periodontitis section of Norman Bennett's Science and Practice of Dental Surgery; Hush, (a play), Fellow of the Royal Soc. of Medicine. CLUBS: Overseas. OFFICE: 7 Cavendish Place, Cavendish Square, W. 1. HOME: Torrington Lodge, Claygate, Surrey, London, Eng.

HODGSON, Willoughby (Mrs). *b*: Delcombe Manor, Dorset. *e*: Private & St Hilda's Coll St John's Wood. *m*: (1) E. C. Gay-Roberts (dec'd); (2) J. Willoughby Hodgson (dec'd). *s*: 1. *d*: 1. Author & Journalist. *Publ*: How to Identify Old China; How to Identify Old Chinese Porcelain; Old English China; The Quest of the Antique. *Ctr*: Times, Ev Standard, Dly Sketch, Connoisseur, Ladies' Field, Queen, Lady, Gentlewoman, Pottery & Glass Record, etc. *s.s*: Antiques. *Rec*: Archery, croquet. *a*: Lloyds Bank, Exmouth.

HODSON, Arnold Wienholt. *Publ*: Seven Years in Southern Abyssinia; Where Lion Reigns; also plays & poetry. *c.t*: Field, Badminton, Times. *s.s*: Sport, travel. *a*: Travellers' Club, Pall Mall.

HODSON, Ernest William. *b*: Cranford, St John 1885. *m*: Leonie Josephine Allen. Newspaper Ed. *n.a*: Ed Hertfordshire Express 1916—. *a*: The Little Ho, Wymondley Rd, Hitchin, Herts. *T*: 93.

HODSON, Geoffrey. Author. *Publ*: American Lectures; The Angelic Hosts; Brotherhood of Angels and of Men; Fairies at Work and at Play; etc.

HODSON, Harold. *b*: Warrington 1903. *s.s*: Sociology. *a*: 100 Thelwall Rd, Thelwall, nr Warrington. *t*: 79.

HODSON, Henry Vincent. *b*: London 1906. *e*: Gresham's Sch, Holt & Balliol Coll Oxf. *m*: Margaret Elizabeth Honey. *s*: 3. Journalist. *n.a*: Staff Economist '28—30, Asst-Ed The Round Table '31—34, Ed '34—45, Asst-Ed Sunday Times '46. *Publ*: Economics of a Changing World; Slump & Recovery; (Ed) British Commonwealth & The World. *Ctr*: Manch Guardian, Christian Sc Mon, Sydney Morning Herald, Foreign Affairs, etc. *s.s*: Economic & Imperial Affairs, Broadcasts on Internat Affairs. *c*: Athenæum, Brooks's. *a*: 26 Mount St, London, W.1. *T*: Grosvenor 2489.

HODSON, James Lansdale, O.B.E. *b*: Hazelhurst, Lancs 1891. *e*: Various Schs. *m*: Elizabeth Rickleton. *s*: 1. *d*: 2. Author & Journalist. *n.a*: Dly Mail '13—24, News Ed Nth Edition Dly Mail '24—28, Spec Writer Dly News & News Chron '28—35, Scenario Writer London Films '36, Spec Writer & War Corr Kemsley Newspapers '38—42, Writer on Official Films & Books '42—45. *Publ*: Novels:—Grey Dawn-Red Night Harvest in the North; Carnival at Blackport; Jonathan North; English Family. War Diaries:— Through the Dark Night; War in the Sun; And Yet I Like America; The Sea & the Land; etc. Plays:— Red Night; Nelson; These Fathers; Before Trafalgar; Farewell Emma; The Back Way. *Rec*: Golf, sketching. *e*: Savile. *w.s*: 1914—18. *a*: 6 Vineyard Hill Rd, Wimbledon, London, S.W.19. *T*: Wimbledon 4125.

HODSON, Rev. Joseph J., M.A. Meth Min. *n.a*: Archæ Corr of Ripon Advertiser 1930—32. *Publ*: Outlines of P.M. Church History & Polity; Jonah the Rebel Prophet. *c.t*: Meth papers & mags. *a*: Manse, Blackberry Lane, Halesowen, Birm.

HOEL, ADOLF: geologist, arctic explorer; b. Sorum, Norway, May, 1879; s. Martin Hoel and Anne (Iversen) H.; educ. Univ. of Oslo, Academy of Sciences (Leningrad), Univ. of Lausanne. DEGREE: M.Sc. (Univ. Oslo); m. Elisabet Birgitte Fredrikke Thomson, Dec. 25, 1916. AUTHOR: Exploration du Nord-Ouest du Spitsberg entreprise sous les auspices de S. A. S. le Prince de Monaco par la Mission Isachsen (III Partie, Geologie, in Result. Camp. Sc., fasc. XLII), 1914; Nouvelles observations sur le district volcanique du Spitsberg du Nord (in Vid Selsk Skr. I, No. 9), 1914; Observations sur la vitesse d'ecoulement et sur l'ablation du Glacier Lilliehöök au Spitsberg (in Vid Selsk. Skr. I, No. 4), 1916; Hints to explorers in Spitsbergen (in Brouwer, H. A.), Practical Hints to scientific travellers (vol. II), 1924; the coal deposits and coal mining of Svalbard (Spitsbergen and Bear Island), in Resultater av de norske statsunderstottede Spitsbergenekspeditioner, B. I., No. 6), 1925; Les nappes de lave, les volcans et les sources thermales dans les environs de la Baie Wood au Spitsberg (in Vid. Selsk. Skr. I, No. 8; with O. Holtedahl), 1911; Exploration du Nord-Ouest du Spitsberg entreprise sous les auspices de S. A. S. le Prince de Monaco par la Mission Isachsen (II Partie; in Result. Camp. Sc., fasc. XLI; with Gunnar Isachsen); Nephelin-bearing pegmatic dykes in Seiland-in Festskrift til professor Amund Helland pa hans 70 ars fodselsdag (with J. Schetelig) Bjornoya (with A. Kvalheim and Claus Schive), 1918. Editor: Norges Svalbard- og Ishavs-Undersokelser. Skrifter om Svalbard og Ishavet, Norges Svalbard- og Ishavs- Undersokelser. (Meddelelser). General character of writing: scientific. First geological works in Norway were researches of the great glacier regions, Frostisen and Okstindene. From 1907 worked in Spitsbergen and the Arctic Ocean. Since 1911 has been the leader of the Norwegian Government Expeditions at these places; in 1928, motivated erection of a central institution for the exploration of the Polar regions; was director of same. The results of these expeditions are published in two series named: Norges Svalbaru-og Ishavs-undersokelser, Skrifter om Svalbard og Ishavet, and: Norges Svalbard- og Ishave-undersokelser. Edits publication issued by Norges Svalbard "og Ishavs-undersokelser" (Norwegian Scientific Exploration of Svalbard and the Polar Regions). Relig. denom., Lutheran. OFFICE: Bygdo Alle 34. HOME: Professor Dahls gate 32, Oslo, Norway.

HOFF, Harry Summerfield. b: Crewe 1907. e: Crewe & Cam. Schoolmaster. Publ: Trina; Rhéa. (1st two novels of a trilogy called Three Girls). a: 13 Sandown Rd, Leicester.

HOFF, HUBERT: professor, Polytechnic Academy; b. Essen, Germany, February, 1870; s. Adolf and Maria Katharina (Greveler) H.; educ. Polytechnic Academy at Aix-le-Chapelle. DEGREES: B.A.; m. Paula Stuckmann, 1911. Contributor to Stahl und Eisen, Zeitschrift des Vereins Deutscher Ingenieure. General character of writing: technical. CLUBS: Verein Deutscher Ingenieure, Verein Deutscher Eisenhuetteleute. ADDRESS: Vaelserstrasse 82, Aix-la-Chapelle, Germany.

HÖFFDING, HAROLD: professor emeritus of the University of Copenhagen; b. Copenhagen, Denmark, March 11, 1843; s. Niels Frederik and Martha (Rasmine) H.; educ. Metropolitan School, Copenhagen. DEGREES: Doctor: Univs. of Copenhagen, Oxford, Cambridge, St. Andrew, Aberdeen, Dublin, Geneva; m. (1) Emma Pape, 1870 (died 1877); (2) Greta Guckern, 1924. AUTHOR: Psychology, 1882; Ethics, 1887; History of Modern Philosophy, 1895; Philosophy of Religion, 1901; Human Thought, 1910; The Great Humour, 1918; Autobiography, 1928. (The dates are of the Danish editions. Several of the books have been translated into English, French, German, Spanish, etc.). Several essays on Epistemology and on History of Philosophy, in the papers of the Royal Academy of Copenhagen. General character of writing: essays, scientific, text books. (Died May 31, 1931).

HOFFE, Monckton. Dramatist. Publ: Cristilinda; etc. a: c/o Samuel French Ltd, 26 Southampton St. W.C.2.

HOFFMAN, Philip Christopher. b: Essex 1878. e: Cooper's Sc Stepney, Warehousemen, Clerks & Drapers Sc. m: Annie Mary Morgan. d: 2. T.U. Official. c.t: Shop Assistant, Drapery Times, Le Jura (France). s.s: Distribution trades. Dep Chm L.C.C. Adv Cmt on Distributive Training. M.P. 1923-4, '29-31. Rec: Gardening. a: 38 Oakwood Rd, Hampstead Garden Suburb, N.W.11 & Dilke Hse, Malet St, W.C.1. t: Museum 2103.

HOFFMAN, Ross John S., M.A., Ph.D., Litt.D., LL.D. b: Harrisburg, Pa 1902. e: Lafayette Coll, Univs of Columb & Penna. m: Hannah McCruden. d: 1. Prof of History & Chm of Dept Fordham Univ Graduate Sch. Publ: Great Britain & The German Trade Rivalry; Restoration; The Organic State; Tradition & Progress; The Great Republic; The Will to Freedom; Origins of the Second World War; Durable Peace. Ctr: Thought, The Sign, Amer Rev, Journ of Modern Hist, Catholic Hist Rev. a: Hix Park, Rye, N.Y., U.S.A. T: Rye 955-J.

HOFMAN-BANG, Inge. b: Kobenhavn 1875. e: Priv. Author. n.a: Ed Israelsmissionen. Publ: En Borbroint Praest; Fru Annes Til Helminge; F. Ulvetalene; Bag Morke Bjoerge; Jonas; etc. Ctr: Nationaltidenden. s.s: Jewish Problems, Nat Hist & Ethical Subjects. a: Hofsmansgave, pr. Otterup, Danmark. T: Otterup 6.

HOFMEYR, Rt. Hon. Jan Hendrik, P.C., M.A.(Cape), M.P. b: Capetown 1894. e: Sth Africa Coll Sch Capetown, Sth Africa Coll Capetown, Balliol Coll Oxf. Min of Finance & Educ, M.P. (Jo'burg Nth) since 1919, six times Acting P.M. (Sth Africa), Cabinet Min '33–38, '39—, Administrator of Transvaal Province '24–29, Princ Univ of Witwatersrand Jo'burg '19–24, Rhodes Scholar '13–16, Hon Fellow of Balliol Coll Oxf, Hon Bencher of Grays Inn London. n.a: Chm The Forum (Pty) Ltd, Chm Wallacks Printing & Publishing Coy. Publ: South Africa; The Life of Jan Hendrik Hofmeyr; History & Control of National Debts; The Open Horizon. Ctr: The Forum. Rec: Cricket, tennis. c: Rand Jo'burg, Pretoria, Western Province Sports, Cape. a: 743 Schoeman St, Pretoria, Union of South Africa. T: Pretoria 2-7862.

HOFPREDIGER, JOHANNES MARTIN VOGEL: see under pen name Vogel, Dr. Johannes.

HOGAN, Herbert Thomas. b: Lon 1871. e: Priv. m: Edith Ruth Johns. Journalist. n.a: Asst Sub Ed The Record, Sub Ed, Asst Ed 1892-1925, Ed '25–. s.s: Eccles Journalism. a: 16 Pollards Hill E, Norbury, S.W.16. t: Pollards 1426.

HOGAN, J. P. b: Manchester 1904. P.R.O. Friends Relief Service. n.a: Former Asst Publ The Friend, Contemporary Review. Ctr: Adelphi, Manch Guardian, Aryan Path, New English Weekly, Twentieth Century, Everyman, New Britain, etc. a: Friends Hse, Euston Rd, London, N.W.1. T: Euston 8551.

HOGARTH, Alfred Moore, F.R.E.S., F.I.S.A. b: Darlington 1876. e: Priv & Pitman's Col Lon. m: Agnes Palmer. s: 6. d: 1. Entomologist & Bacteriologist. Publ: The Rat (Preface by Lord Horder); British Mosquitoes (Preface by Sir Wm Simpson, F.R.C.P.). c.t: John Bull, Daily Express, T.P.'s Weekly. s.s: Entomological & Zoological Research. Chm Inst of Micro-Biology (Inc). c: Jnr Army & Navy. a: 143 Golder's Green Rd, N.W.11. t: Speedwell 1061.

699

HOGARTH, Basil. *b*: M/c 1908. *e*: Priv & Univ of Glasgow. Jnlst. *n.a*: Music Critic to Reynolds News '34—. *Publ*: An Anthology of Musical Criticism; The Technique of Novel writing; Sir Thomas Beecham: A Study; How to write Plays; Perfect Memory; Trial of Robert Wood; Music as a Profession; How to Write a Thriller. *c.t*: English Review, Reynolds News, Gramophone, Musical Times, Daily Record, Glasgow Evening News, Musical Mirror, etc. *s.s*: Music, musical criticism, ballets, criminology, psycho-analysis. Prizeman in Law, Glasgow Univ. *a*: 11 Reynolds Ave, Chadwell Heath. Essex.

HOGARTH, Rev. Henry, B.A. Meth Minister. *Publ*: A Method of Affirmation; More Life & Fuller; Old Testament Characters. *c.t*: Lon Quart Review, Meth Recorder, Chr World Pulpit, etc. *a*: Nantwyn, Holyrood Av, Old Colwyn, Denbighshire. *t*: Old Colwyn 5612.

HOGARTH, Miss M. I. *a*: Littlewick Green, Maidenhead, Berks.

HOGARTH, Robert George, C.B.E., F.R.C.S., HonLLD.(Edin). *b*: Eccles Tofts 1868. *e*: Felsted, St Bart's. *m*: Mabel Lynam. *s*: 1. Surgeon. *s.s*: Hosp's & their future. Ex-Pres B.M.A. *Rec*: Shooting, golf, cricket. *c*: Notts County (Ex-Pres), Boodles. *a*: The Ropewalk, Nott'm. *t*: 41385.

HOGBEN, Lancelot. *b*: Southsea 1895. *e*: Trin Coll Camb. *m*: Enid Charles, M.A. *s*: 2. *d*: 2. Prof Med Statistics Birmingham Univ, former Regius Prof Nat Hist Aberdeen. *Publ*: Comparative Physiology; Principals of Animal Biology; Nature & Nurture; Mathematics for the Million; Science for the Citizen; Dangerous Thoughts; Interglossa. *Ctr*: Time & Tide, Nature, Athenæum, etc. *s.s*: Biol, Genetics. *a*: 40 Store St, London, W.C.1.

HOGBIN, H. Ian, M.A., Ph.D., F.R.A.I. *b*: Bawtry, Yorks 1904. *e*: Univs of Sydney & Lond. Anthropologist. *n.a*: Asst-Ed Oceania '31—32, '35—. *Publ*: Experiments in Civilization; Law & Order in Polynesia; Peoples of the South-West Pacific; Development & Welfare in the Western Pacific. *Ctr*: Journ of Roy Anthrop Inst & Polynesian Soc, American Anthropologist, Geographical Mag, National Geographic. *s.s*: Anthropology of the Pacific. *w.s*: Advr Native Problems to Mil Gov of Solomons '43 & Australian Army (Lt-Col) '44—46. *a*: c/o Bank of N.S.W., George St, Sydney, Australia.

HOGG, Alexander Frederick, M.A. Princ of Woolwich Polytechnic (ret). *c.t*: Various n/ps & periodicals. *a*: The Pines, Tadworth, Surrey.

HOGG, Miss M. T. ("Corisande"). *n.a*: Fashion & Society Ed Evening Standard. *a*: The Evening Standard, 46—7 Shoe Lane, E.C.4.

HOGG, Brigadier Oliver Frederick Gillilan, C.B.E., P.A.C., F.S.A., F.R.S.A., F.R.G.S., F.R.Hist.S. *b*: 1887. *e*: Bedford Sch & R.M.A. Woolwich. *m*: Ella Harold Hallam. *s*: 1. Dir Military Administration M.O.S. 1941—46 (ret), Mem Soc of Genealogists & Soc for Army Historical Research, Order of Polonia Restituta 3rd Class. *Ctr*: R.A. Journ, Journ of Soc for Army Hist Research, Army Ordnance (U.S.A). *s.s*: Tech Military subjects, Early Army Administration, History & Development of Weapons, Genealogy. *c*: United Services. *a*: 4 Dial Sq, Royal Arsenal, Woolwich, London, S.E.18. *T*: Woolwich 2044, Ext 150.

HOGG, Hon. Quintin McGarel, M.P. *b*: London 1907. *e*: Eton & Christ Ch Oxf. *m*: Mary Evelyn Martin. M.P. (Nat Con) Oxford City since '38, Under-Sec of State for Air '45, Pres Oxf Un '29, Fell of All Souls' Coll Oxf. *Publ*: The Law of Arbitration; One Year's Work; The Law & Employers' Liability; The Times We Live In; Making Peace; The Left Was Never Right; The Purpose of Parliament; The Case for Conservatism. *Ctr*: Dly Express, Dly Mail, Sun Chronicle, Ev News, Ev Standard, Spectator, Time & Tide, Nineteenth Century, etc. *s.s*: Politics, Philos, Ancient & Mod Hist. *Rec*: Mountaineering, shooting. *c*: Carlton, Alpine. *w.s*: Commissioned Rifle Brigade '39, wounded '41. *a*: Corner Hse, Heathview Gdns, Putney Heath, London S.W.15. *T*: Putney 4177.

HOLBORN, Hajo, M.A., Ph.D. *b*: Berlin 1902. *e*: Roy Gymnasium Berlin, Univ of Berlin. *m*: Anne Marie Bettman. *s*: 1. *d*: 1. Randolph W. Townsend Jr Prof of Hist Yale Univ, Consultant Dept of State '47—. *n.a*: Ed Bd Journ Mod Hist '43, Journ Hist of Ideas '42. *Publ*: Hutten & the German Reformation; Germany & Turkey; Erasmus, Collected Works; American Military Government: Its Organisation & Policies. *Ctr*: American Hist Review, Military Affairs, Social Research, etc. *s.s*: Mod European Hist (Hist of Reformation), 19th & 20th Century Diplomacy, Philos of Hist. *a*: 233, Santa Fe Ave, Hamden, Conn, U.S.A. *T*: New Haven 2-1904.

HOLBOURN, Stanley Vernon. *b*: Newry, Ireland 1890. *e*: St Mary's H.G. *m*: Kathleen Margaret Gilbert. Journalist. *n.a*: Folkestone Herald 1905—14, Chief Rep Windsor Slough & Eton Express '14—. *Ctr*: Dly Express, Dly Chron & Westminster Gaz. *s.s*: Football. *Rec*: Lawn tennis, chess. *a*: Abbotsley, Orchard Ave, Windsor.

HOLBROOK, Col. Sir Arthur Richard, K.B.E., V.D., D.L., J.P. *b*: Bath 1850. *e*: Portsmouth. *m*: Amelia Mary Parks. *s*: 6 (alive). *d*: 3. N/p Owner. *n.a*: Joined Staff of Portsmouth Times '66, Est Southern Daily Mail at Portsmouth. 44 y Army Service '60—1904, War Service 1914—19, Sons Served in Great War (V.C.). *c*: Carlton, Constitutional, & Savage. *a*: 52 Westbourne Terr, W.2. *t*: Padd 7126.

HOLBROOKE, Joseph Charles. *b*: Croydon 1878. *e*: Private. *m*: Dorothy Hadfield. *s*: 2. *d*: 3. Musician & Writer, formerly Music Hall Pianist. *Publ*: Josef Holbrooke; Contemporary British Composers; Holbrooke—Appreciations; Musical Adventures; British Music. *Ctr*: English Rev, Saturday Rev, Apollo, Nat Magazine, etc. *s.s*: Br Music & Performers. *Rec*: Gardening, walking. *c*: Authors. *a*: Authors' Club, Whitehall Ct, London, S.W.

HOLBURN, James. M.A. *b*: Glas 1900. *e*: Harris Acad Dundee, Glas Univ. *m*: Elizabeth Margaret McConnachie. *s*: 1. Journalist. *n.a*: Sub-Ed Glas Herald '21, Dep Chief Sub-Ed '29—31, Leader-Writer '32—34, Foreign room Times '34. *c.t*: Glas Herald. *s.s*: Imp & foreign politics. R.A.F. '18—19. *Rec*: Golf, travel. *c*: I.J.

HOLCOMBE, Albert Richard. *b*: Chudleigh 1871. Married. *d*: 2. Printer & Stationer, Mem News Exec Lond Soc of Compositors. *n.a*: Prop & Ed Sth Devon Wkly Express. *c*: Conservative, Sporting. *a*: South Devon Weekly Express, Chudleigh, Devon. *T*: 3137.

HOLCOMBE, Arthur Norman, A.B., Ph.D. *b*: Winchester, Mass 1884. *e*: Harvard, Berlin & Paris Univs. Carolyn Crossett. *s*: 3. *d*: 2. University Prof. *Publ*: The Middle Classes in American Politics; The Chinese Revolution; Foundation of the Modern Commonwealth; State Government in the United States; The Political Parties of Today; The New Party Politics; Government in a Planned Democracy; Dependent Areas in the Post-War World. *Ctr*: American Political Science & Econ Revs, Journ of Econ, Current History Mag, etc. *a*: 20 Berkley St, Cambridge, Mass, U.S.A. *T*: Tro 4466.

HOLDEN, 3rd Baron of Alston, Sir Angus William Eden Holden, Bt. *b*: Scarborough 1898. *e*: Eton & Magdalen Coll Oxf. Author. *Publ*: Uncle Leopold, a Life of the First King of the Belgians; Ceylon; Four Generations of Our Royal Family; Elegant Modes in the 19th Century; The Land of France (with Ralph Dutton); English Country Houses open to the Public (with R. Dutton); French Chateaux open to the Public (with R. Dutton); *s.s*: 19th-Century History, Architecture, Costume. *c*: St James's, R.N.V.R. *a*: 6 Wilton St, London, S.W.1. *T*: Sloane 4210.

HOLDEN, Arnold. *b*: Darwen 1881. *m*: Mary Margaret Haworth. *d*: 3. Sub Ed. *n.a*: Reporter Darwen News (5 y), Sub Ed Northern Daily Telegraph Blackburn (7 y), Sub Ed Daily News (N. Ed) (10 y), Sub Ed Daily Mail (N. Ed) (16 y), Foundation Mem N.U.J., Mem of Cmt for M/C of the n/p Press Fund. *Rec*: Golf. *a*: 57 Ashbourne Grove, Higher Broughton, Manch.

HOLDEN, Inez. *b*: Warwickshire 1906. Novelist, Short Story Writer, Script Writer for Films & B.B.C. *Publ*: Born Old—Died Young; Friend of the Family; Death in High Society; Night Shift; There's no Story There; It Was Different at the Time; To the Boating. *Ctr*: Best Short Stories, Harper's Bazaar, Ev Standard, Horizon, New Writing, News Chron, Observer, etc. *a*: 106 George St, London, W.1. *T*: Welbeck 7592.

HOLDEN, Rev. John Stuart, M.A.(Cantab), HonD.D. (Westminster Mo). *b*: Liverpool 1874. *e*: Liverpool Col, Corpus Chr Col Cam. *m*: Jessie Findlay Galloway. *n.a*: Ed The Christian 1915-21, Ed The Home Messenger 1922–. *Publ*: Supposition of Certainty; The Price of Power; The Gospel of Second Chance; etc. *c.t*: British Wkly; Christian Advocate (U.S.A). *s.s*: Theology. Vicar of St Paul's Portman Sq, W.1, 1905–. Freeman Glazier Co, Freeman City of Lon. *c*: Brooks's, M.C.C., Fly Fisher's, Univ Club (N.Y.). *a*: The Old Pound House, Wimbledon Common, S.W.19.

HOLDEN, Oscar Madeley. *b*: India 1885. *e*: Dean Close Sc Cheltenham. *m*: Constance Anne Adams. M.O.H. *n.a*: Sc M.O. Gen Med Supt of Corporation Hosp's, County Boro' of Croydon. *c.t*: Various n/ps & periodicals. *s.s*: Publ health. M.O.H. Blackburn, Dewsbury, Dep M.O.H. Swansea, Asst M.O.H., T.B. Officer, etc, Southampton. *Rec*: Gardening. *c*: F.R.S.I., F.R.I.H., etc. *a*: 23 Warham Rd, S. Croydon. *t*: 3254.

HOLDEN, T. S. *n.a*: Ed Sunderland Echo. *Publ*: Where Ships are Born—Sunderland 1346–1946 (jt author). *a*: Bridge St, Sunderland. *T*: 56261.

HOLDER, Thomas Henry. *b*: Co Durham. *m*: Rose May Prior. *s*: 2. *d*: 2. *c.t*: Daily Mail, Daily Express, Daily Mirror, North Mail, Sunday Chron, Sunday Sun, Sunday Mercury (B'ham). *s.s*: Northern mining life. *a*: Woodlawn, Villas, Thornley, Co Durham.

HOLDERNESS, George William. *b*: Spilsby, Lincs. *n.a*: Ed & Proprietor, Ilfracombe Chron & North Devon News. *a*: Southwold, Ilfracombe. *t*: 99.

HOLDSWORTH, Ernest Thornton. *b*: Bradford 1877. *e*: Bradford G.S. & City of Bradford Tech Col. *m*: Edith Annie Gill. *s*: 2. Dir of Brit Cotton & Wool Dyers Assoc Ltd. *s.s*: Textile industries. Vice-Pres of Soc Dyers & Colourists. Freeman of C.L. Fel Textile Inst. *c*: Chemical, Bradford Liberal. *a*: Park Gate, Guiseley, via Leeds. *t*: 213.

HOLDSWORTH, GLADYS BRONWYN: see (pen name) G. B. Stern.

HOLDSWORTH, Lucy Violet. *b*: Newcastle-on-Tyne 1869. *e*: Priv. *m*: John Holdsworth. Swarthmore Lect 1919. *Publ*: A Book of Quaker Saints; Silent Worship the Way of Wonder; A Quaker Saint of Cornwall: Lovedav-Hambly & her Guests; The Romance of the Inward Light; Anima; Daybook of Epistles of George Fox; Shoemaker of Dover; In Quietness; Gulielma, Wife of William Penn; etc. *s.s*: Early Quaker Hist. *Rec*: Water-colour drawing, gardening. *a*: Bareppa Hse, nr Falmouth. *T*: Mawnan Smith 210.

HOLDSWORTH, Sir W. S., K.C., D.C.L. Prof Law. *Publ*: History of English Law; Charles Dickens as a Legal Historian; The Histories of Anglo-American Law; Historical Intro to Land Law; etc. *c.t*: Law Review, etc. *a*: All Souls Col, Oxf. *t*: 2043.

HOLDSWORTH, Rev. Wm West, M.A., B.D. *b*: Jamaica 1859. *e*: Kingswood Oakham & Sidney Sussex Col Cam. *m*: Mary Clarke Osborn. *s*: 2. *d*: 3. *Publ*: Christ and the Gospels; The Life of Faith; Gospel Origins; The Life Indeed; History of Methodist Missionary Society (in part). *Rec*: Wood-carving, bee-keeping. *a*: Gorse Wick, Crowborough. *t*: 181.

HOLE, Rev. Donald, A.K.C. *b*: I.O.W. 1867. *e*: King's Col Sc & King's Col Lon. *m*: Dulcie Sydney-Anderson. *s*: 1. *d*: 3. Chap St James's Home, Fulham. *Publ*: Love & Death with Intro by Sir Wm Barrett, F.R.S.; Bill's Book; Bill's Adventure; Spiritualism in relation to Science & Religion; The Church & "The Church of England" with preface by Lord Halifax, etc. Founder & Hon Sec of The Actor's Ch Union. Mem Soc Psych Research. *a*: St James's Lodge, Fulham, S.W.6. *t*: Fulham 0440.

HOLE, Lt.-Col. Hugh Marshall, C.M.G., B.A., F.R.E.S. *b*: Tiverton 1865. *e*: Blundell's Sc & Balliol Col. *m*: (1) Ethel Rickman; (2) Olive Mary Torin. *d*: 1 (dec). Comp Dir. *Publ*: Joint Author (with late Earl Grey) Native Disturbances in Rhodesia 1897; The Making of Rhodesia (1926); Old Rhodesian Days; Lobengula; The Jameson Raid; The Passing of the Black Kings. *c.t*: Times, Daily Telegraph, Morning Post, Nat Review, etc. *s.s*: Hist of Rhodesia & Sth Central Africa. *Rec*: Travel. On Staff Brit Sth Africa Co 1890. Priv Sec to Administrator (Dr L. S. Jameson) Rhodesia '91. Many pub offices in Govt service of Rhodesia. Sec for Matabeleland. Civil Commissioner of Bulawayo. Chief Sec for Sth Rhodesia. Acted Administrator of N.W. Rhodesia. Joined Lon Office of B.S.A. Co 1913. Mem of Executive Cmt & Sec of the Company '23–28. Memb of Headquarter Counc of British Empire Service League. Accompanied Earl Haig to Canada '25. *c*: Authors, Salisbury, Rhodesia, Memb of African Soc, etc. *a*: Authors' Club, 2 Whitehall Court, S.W.1. *t*: Whitehall 3160.

HOLE, Philippa. *e*: L.H.M. Soulsby. Ed Decachord, a mag of poetry. *c.t*: Poetry Review, Queen, Lady. *Rec*: Riding, tennis. *c*: P.E.N. *a*: 49 Earl's Ct Sq, S.W.5.

HOLE, W. G. *Publ*: Poems Lyrical & Dramatic (1902): Queen Elizabeth, An Historical Drama ('04); The Chained Titan (Poems); The Master (Play); Queen Elizabeth, new ed ('28; produced Everyman Theatre); Gates of Ur '32; (Play, produced Arts Theatre); Listenings-In (Poems) ('34); etc. *c.t*: Fortnightly Review, Contemporary Review, Spectator. *Rec*: Tramping. *c*: P.E.N. *a*: 49 Earls Ct Sq, S.W.5. *t*: Flaxman 8674.

HOLFORD, William Graham. *b*: Johannesburg, Sth Africa 1907. *e*: Diocesan Coll Capetown, Univ of L'pool, British Sch at Rome. *m*: Marjorie Brooks. Architect & Town Planning Consultant, Univ Prof, Consultant on reconstruction of City of London. *Publ*: The Future of Merseyside. *Ctr*: The Listener, R.I.B.A. Journal, Town Planning Inst Journal. *s.s*: Architecture & Town Planning. *Rec*: Travel. *a*: 80 Bedford St, Liverpool, & 1 Bank Bldgs, Princes St, London, E.C.2.

HOLKER, Harold. *b*: Eccles, Lancs 1885. *e*: Municipal Sch of Technology Manch. *m*: Mary A. Johnson. *s*: 1. *d*: 1. Editor. *n.a*: Reporter Eccles & Patricroft Journ, Kentish Express, Dist Rep Kentish Express, Kent Messenger, Ed Diss Express 1928—. *s.s*: Agriculture. *Rec*: Grandfather clocks. *w.s*: '14—19. *a*: Caxton Cott. Diss, Norfolk. *T*: 143.

HOLKER, John, M.D., D.Sc, ChB. Cons Physician. *c.t*: Journ of Pathology and Bacteriology, Biochemical Journ, etc. *c*: Brit Med Assoc. *a*: 342 Oxford Rd, Manchester. *t*: M/C Ardwick 1508.

HOLLAMBY, H. J. Journalist, F.J.I., Chief Librarian Kemsley Newsps Manchester. *n.a*: Features Sub-Ed Manch Ev Chron 1935—42, Asst to Mang-Ed Kemsley Newsps Manch '42—46, formerly L'pool Courier & Ev Express, Dly Dispatch Manch, Sun News, Yorks Post Leeds, Sun Chron. *a*: Shirley, 15 Hilltop Ave, Cheadle Hulme, Stockport.

HOLLAND, A. K. *b*: Lon 1894. *e*: Christ's Hosp & Lon Univ. Music Critic. *n.a*: L'pool Daily Post 1921—. Lit Ed L'pool Daily Post '25-8. *Publ*: Henry Purcell ('32). *c.t*: Musical Times, Chesterian, Music Teacher, etc. *s.s*: English music. *Rec*: Reading. *c*: Sandon Studios Soc. *a*: 24 Aigburth Drive, L'pool. *t*: Lark Lane 684.

HOLLAND, Charles Thurstan, D.L., T.D., F.R.C.S., M.Ch, L.R.C.P. Lect on Radiology (& Head of Dept) The Univ, L'pool 1920-31. *a*: 43 Rodney St, L'pool.

HOLLAND, Clive, M.B.E. *b*: Bournemouth 1866. *e*: Mill Hill Sch & Priv. *m*: Violet Downs (dec'd). *s*: 4. *d*: 3. Novelist & Author, Hon M. J.I., Mem Inter Cttee Inst Journ, Kt Roy Order of Dannebrog, Chev de' l'O de la Couronne (Belgium), Med du Roi Albert. *Publ*: My Japanese Wife (novel); The Lovers of Mademoiselle; Thomas Hardy, O.M.; Wessex; Unknown Hampshire; & many travel books. *n.a*: Ed Brit Congregationalist 1914, Travel Ed several ill papers '18 onwards. *Ctr*: Sphere, Bookman, Ill Lond News, etc. *s.s*: Literary & Travel. *Rec*: Photography, book collecting. *a*: 10A Woodville Gdns, Ealing, London, W.5. *T*: Perivale 7725.

HOLLAND, F. G. *b*: London 1895. P.R.O. Erith Borough Council. *Ctr*: Erith Borough Bulletin, etc. *a*: Council Offices, Erith, Kent. *T*: Erith 3040/9.

HOLLAND, George Frederick. *b*: Sowerby Bridge, Yorks 1882. *e*: St John's Coll York, Lond Univ. *m*: Lucy Gammack. Lecturer on Drama, Literature, History of Art. *n.a*: Asst Dramatic Critic The Sketch 1923—38, Illus Lond News '25—38, Co-Ed The Curtain '24—31. *Publ*: Drama in Youth Organisations; (in collab) Ships & Men; (adaptations) The Storm; Bargains in Brides. *Ctr*: New York Theatre Mag, Christian Sci Mon, The Queen, etc. *s.s*: Drama, General Lit, Hist of Shipping & Ships. *a*: Bay Tree Cott, Freshwater, I.O.W. *T*: 241.

HOLLAND, Leicester Bodine, B.S., M.A., Ph.D. *b*: Louisville, Ky 1882. *e*: William Penn Charter Sch & Univ of Penn. *m*: Louise W. Adams. *s*: 1. *d*: 2. Educator & Archaeologist, Prof of Fine Arts Univ of Penn 1928—46. *Publ*: The Garden Blue Book; Ready Written Specifications (collab). *Ctr*: Amer Journ of Archæol. *s.s*: Architecture, Archæology. *Rec*: Primitive Roof Construction. *a*: 415 West Price St, Philadelphia 44, Pennsylvania, U.S.A. *T*: Germantown 8-0518.

HOLLAND, Hon. Lionel, B.A., L.L.B., J.P. *b*: Lon 1865. *e*: Harrow & King's Col Cam. *n.a*: Jt Founder (with Mr Murray Guthrie) of The Granta, Ex-Ed The English Illus Mag. *Publ*: The Notebooks of a Spinster Lady. *c*: Nat Review, Saturday Review. War & Victory Medals. *c*: Athenæum, Brooks's, Beefsteak. *a*: 14 Buckingham St, Adelphi, W.C.2. *t*: Temple Bar 5260.

HOLLAND, Otho Lloyd. *b*: Lon 1856. *e*: A. F. Westmacott's Sc, Clifton Col & Oriel Oxf (Schol). *m*: Mary Edna Chave Winter. *s*: 2. *d*: 1. Greek Translator. *Publ*: The Antigone of Sophocles (trans according to the metres of the original 1931). Has endeavoured with success to discover the rhythm of Greek prose & trans into corresponding Eng. Only son of Horace Lloyd, Q.C. 1829–74; grandson of John Horatio Lloyd 1798-1884, barrister, deviser of Lloyd's Bonds. *a*: 31 Chatsworth Rd, Bournemouth.

HOLLAND, Robert Henry Code, B.A. *b*: M/C 1904. *e*: Newport H.S. & U.C.L. *m*: Eveline Mary Bonnett. *d*: 2. Ed. *n.a*: Ed Butterworth & Co Ltd '24—31, Ed Staff Justice of the Peace '26—29. Law Journal '30—31, Legal Ed Sir Isaac Pitman & Sons Ltd '31—. Ed The Solicitor '34—. *Publ*: Slater's Mercantile Law (Jt Ed 7th '31 & 8th '33 ed); Poley's Law & Practice of the Stock Exchange (Jt Ed 5th '32 ed). *a*: Highclere, Kemsing, Sevenoaks.

HOLLAND, Robert Wolstenholme, O.B.E., M.A., M.Sc., F.R.S.A., LL.D. *b*: Romiley, Cheshire 1880. *e*: Owens Coll Victoria, Univ of Manch. *m*: (1) Annie Glover Code, (2) Bertha Mills. *s*: 3. *d*: 1. Barrister, Dep Mang Dir of Sir Isaac Pitman & Sons Ltd, Chrm Book Centre Ltd & Simpkin Marshal Ltd, Mem of Management Royal Masonic Institution for Boys. *n.a*: Occasional Literary & Dramatic Critic Manch City News 1909—13. *Publ*: The Child, its Education Employment & Protection; Partnership Law & Accounts; Guide to Company Law; Law of Contract; Banking Law; Business Statistics; Business Organisation & Personnel; Course in Bookkeeping. *Ctr*: Manch City News. *s.s*: Commercial Education. *a*: 2 Vermont Rd, Upper Norwood, London, S.E.19. *T*: Livingstone 2659.

HOLLAND, Rupert Sargent, A.B., LL.B. *b*: Louisville, Ky 1878. *e*: William Penn Charter Sch, Harvard Coll & Univ of Penn Law Sch. *m*: Margaret Currier Lyon. *s*: 2. *d*: 1. Lawyer, Writer. *Publ*: Builders of United Italy; William Penn; Lafayette for Young Americans; Boy Scouts of Birch-Bark Island; Historic Boyhoods; Knights of the Golden Spur; Drake's Lad; Yankee Ships in Pirate Waters. *Ctr*: Woman's Home Companion, The American Girl, Ladies' Home Journ, etc. *s.s*: History, Geography. *Rec*: Golf. *a*: 216 Walnut Ave, Wayne, Pennsylvania U.S.A. *T*: Wayne 0763 W.

HOLLAND, Sir Thomas Henry, K.C.S.I., K.C.I.E., D.L., F.R.S., D.Sc., LL.D., Princ & Vice-Chancellor Univ of Edin 1929—. *Publ*: Memoirs on Geology, Mineralogy, Anthropology & Education. *a*: The Univ, Edin.

HOLLAND, Rev. William Edward Sladen, M.A. *b*: Leeds 1873. *e*: Loretto (King's Scholar) Durham, Magdalen Coll Oxf, Wycliffe Hall Oxf. *m*: (1) Muriel Ardill Maxwell (dec'd). *d*: 2. (2) Cicely Dillworth. *s*: 1. *d*: 1. Rector St Mary Woolnoth 1933—, Chaplain to Lord Mayor Lond '33—34, '33—39, '42—43, High Sheriff's Chaplain '40—41, '44—45 Commissary to the Bishop of Lucknow since '34. *Publ*: The Call of the World; The Goal of India; The Indian Outlook. *Rec*: Tennis & fives. *a*: Hurstmead, Chislehurst, Kent (*T*: Imperial 743); St Mary Woolnoth, Lombard St, London, E.C.3. *T*: Mansion House 9701.

HOLLANDER, BERNARD: physician for nervous and mental disorders; b. Vienna, Austria, June, 1864; educ. King's Coll. (London Univ.); Universities of Freiburg and Vienna; DEGREES: M.D., M.R.C.S.; L.R.C.P.; mem. Royal Academy of Medicine, Madrid; m. Louise Vogel, 1906. AUTHOR: Die Psychischen Thaligkeiten des Gehirns, 1900; The Mental Function of the Brain, 1901; Scientific Phrenology, 1902; The Mental Symptoms of Brain Disease, 1910; Hypnotism and Suggestion, 1910; The First Signs of Insanity, 1912; Nervous Disorders of Men, 1916; Nervous Disorders of Women, 1916; Abnormal Children, 1916; The Search of the Soul and the Mechanism of Human Thought, Emotion and Conduct, 1920; Psychology of Misconduct, Vice and Crime, 1922; Methods and Uses of Hypnosis and Self-Hypnosis, 1928. Editor of Ethnological Journal since 1904. Contributor to many magazines and newspapers of articles on psychological subjects. Known for his research in mental functions of brain, and one of exponents of Psychotherapy; founder of Ethnological Soc., 1904. Relig. denom., Rationalist. CLUBS: Royal Automobile. OFFICE: 57 Wimpole St., London, W. 1, Eng.

HOLLICK, Dr. J. O., M.B.(Durham), M.R.C.S. (Eng), L.R.C.P.(Lon). *c.t*: Med journs. *a*: Dorridge, Knowle, Warwicks.

HOLLIDAY, George, M.B., C.M.(Edin). *b*: Carlisle 1874. *e*: Priv, Heriot-Watt Col Edin, Edin Univ, W. Lon Hosp. *m*: Mary Margaretta Rees. *d*: 2. Physician & Surg. *Publ*: Ed Life of Sam Bough, R.S.A. *c.t*: B.M.J., Times, Univ mags. *s.s*: Hist med research, art. *Rec*: Cubbing, shooting, photography. *c*: Edin Univ, etc. *a*: 10 Tollington Pk, N.4. *t*: Archway 2121.

HOLLINGWORTH, Gertrude Eleanor, M.A., B.A. *b*: Lon 1892. *e*: N. Polytech Sec Sc, E. Lon Col, Lon Univ. *Publ*: Primer of Literary Criticism; Pt Author—Matriculation English Course; Modern English Literature; Ed—Drake, The World Encompassed; etc. *a*: 315 Milton Rd, Cambridge.

HOLLINS, Dr. A. S. *c.t*: B.M.J. *a*: Lime Grove, Thames Ditton, Surrey.

HOLLINS, Thomas John. Med Pract. *c.t*: Practitioner, B.M.J. *a*: 2 Frognal, Hampstead, N.W.3. *t*: 5427.

HOLLIS, Sir (Alfred) Claud, G.C.M.G., C.B.E., J.P. *b*: Highgate 1874. *e*: Priv & Switzerland, Germany. *m*: Enid Mabel Longman (dec'd). *d*: 2. Colonial Civil Servant (ret). *Publ*: The Masai, their language & folklore; The Nandi, their language and folklore; A Brief History of Trinidad under the Spanish Crown. *c*: East India & Sports. *a*: Bishops, Widdington, nr Saffron Walden, Essex. *T*: Newport Essex 10.

HOLLIS, Rev. Frederick James, D.D. *b*: Highgate 1878. *e*: Cholmeley Sch Highgate, King's Coll Lond. *m*: Christina Mary Hanbury. *s*: 2. Clerk in Holy Orders, Rector of Widford. *Publ*: Archæology of Herod's Temple. *Ctr*: The Story of the Bible, Myth & Ritual. *s.s*: Old Testament Literature & Langs. *Rec*: Light Literature. *c*: Church Imperial, Univ of Lond. *a*: Widford Rectory, Ware, Herts. *T*: Much Hadham 93.

HOLLIS, Gertrude. *b*: Newborough. *e*: Priv. Church Worker. *Publ*: That Land & This; The Romance of the Bible; How the Prayer Book Came to Us; The Children's Church Kalendar Book; Our Wonderful Cathedrals (2 vols); The Place Where Two Ways Met; etc. *s.s*: Ch hist. *Rec*: Gardening, painting. *c*: Peterboro' Dio Conf. *a*: 98 Kingsley Pk Terr, Northampton.

HOLLIS, Henry Park. *b*: N. Lon 1858. *e*: Westminster, Jesus Col Cam. *m*: Clara Susannah Clark (dec). *s*: 2. *d*: 1. Asst in Roy Observatory, Greenwich '81–1920. *n.a*: Ed Observatory Mag 1893-1912. *c.t*: Eng Mechanic, Times. *s.s*: Astron. *a*: 65 Tranquil Vale, Blackheath, S.E.3. *t*: Lee Green 0132.

HOLLIS, Maurice Christopher, B.A., M.P. *b*: Axbridge 1902. *e*: Eton & Balliol Coll Oxf. *m*: Margaret Madeleine King. *s*: 3. *d*: 1. M.P. (C) Devizes Div of Wiltshire, Dir Tablet & Hollis & Carter Ltd. *Publ*: Glastonbury & England; American Heresy; Dr Johnson; Monstrous Regiment; St Ignatius; Erasmus; Dryden; Breakdown of Money; Sir Thomas More; Death of a Gentleman; Fossetts Memory; Letters to a Sister; Foreigners Aren't Fools; We Aren't So Dumb; The Rise & Fall of the Ex-Socialist Government. *Ctr*: Various. *s.s*: Hist, Econ. *Rec*: Cricket, squash racquets. *a*: Claveys, Mells, nr Frome, Somerset.

HOLLOWAY, Charles Philip. *b*: Portsmouth. Married. *d*: 3. Journalist. *n.a*: City Ed Pall Mall Gazette '16—21, City Ed Daily Sketch '25—. *c.t*: Lon n/ps & journs. *s.s*: Finance. *a*: 64 Brightwell Av, Westcliff-on-Sea, Essex.

HOLLOWAY, Emory, M.A., LL.D. *b*: Marshall, Missouri 1885. *e*: Hendrix Coll, Univ of Texas. *m*: Ella Brooks Harris. *s*: 1. *d*: 1. College Prof. *n.a*: Assoc Ed 1939—42, Adv Bd '42—, American Literature. *Publ*: Uncollected Poetry & Prose of Walt Whitman; Whitman, an Interpretation in Narrative; Leaves of Grass; I Sit & Look Out (with V. Schwarz); New York Dissected (with R. Adimari); The Hoosier Schoolmaster; Janice in To-morrow-land; etc. *Ctr*: Amer Mercury, Studies in Philosophy, N.Y. Times Books Review, etc. *s.s*: American Lit, Walt Whitman, Edward Eggleston. *Rec*: Travel, fishing. *a*: 1013 East 26th St, Brooklyn 10, New York.

HOLLOWAY, Frederick William, F.R.C.O. *b*: St Ives, Hunts 1873. Widower. *s*: 2. Organist, Teacher, Composer. *Publ*: Organ Music; Church Music; Songs; Pianoforte Music. *s.s*: Voice production. *Rec*: Gardening. Closely assoc with Crystal Palace 1892–. *a*: 61 Palace Rd, S.W.2. *t*: Tulse Hill 7102.

HOLLOWAY, Rev. Henry, M.A., D.D. *b*: Hanley, Stoke-on-Trent 1876. *e*: Queens Univ of Belfast, Univ of Durham. Clerk in Holy Orders. *Publ*: The Reformation in Ireland; A Study of the Byzantine Liturgy; The Norwegian Rite. *Ctr*: Laudate, The Guardian, Scottish Guardian. *s.s*: Liturgiology. *c*: Hampden. *a*: 29 Riversdale Gr, Edinburgh 12.

HOLLOWAY, John Gifford Everett, B.A. *b*: Freshwater 1894. *e*: Westminster Sc & Queen's Col Oxf. *m*: Irene May Tofts. Editor & Journalist. *n.a*: F.L. Journalist 1919-24, Assoc Ed The Decorator '24-28, Ed '28—. *c.t*: Tatler, Truth, Passing Show, Pearson's, Tech Press, etc. *s.s*: Decoration. War Service '14-19. *Rec*: Golf, riding. *a*: 13 Tudor Gdns, Leigh-on-Sea, Essex.

HOLLOWELL, Clifford George. *b*: New Barnet, Herts 1918. *e*: Borden Gr Sch Sittingbourne, Medway Coll of Art Rochester. *m*: Joan Erica Battersby. *s*: 2. *d*: 1. Publicity & Advertising Manager, Mem Assoc Roy Aeronautical Soc. *Publ*: Air Travel Digest (pt author). *s.s*: Aircraft, Air Travel, Aircraft Eng'g, Civil Aviation. *Rec*: Golf, tennis. *a*: Diamond Cott, Drewton Dale, South Cave, East Yorks. *T*: Brough 10x.

HOLLOWOOD, Albert Bernard, M.Sc. *b*: Burslem, Staffs 1910. *e*: Hanley Hgh Sch & London Univ. *m*: Marjorie Duncan Lawrie. *d*: 2. Journalist, Author, Broadcaster. *n.a*: Editor Pottery & Glass '44—, Assoc-Ed Contact Pubis, Ed Staff Economist '44—45. *Publ*: An Innocent at Large; Scowle & Other Papers; Money is No Expense; Pottery & Glass; Direct Economics. *Ctr*: Punch, Contact. *s.s*: Economics, Pottery, Cricket. *Rec*: Cricket, music, chess. *c*: P.E.P. *a*: Coneyhurst-on-the-Hill, Ewhurst, Surrey. *T*: Ewhurst 35.

HOLM, H. H. FRITS VILHELM, prince, duke of Kolachine (pen name: Duke of Xensi): explorer, author; b. Charlottenlund, Denmary, July 23, 1881; elder son of Consul-General Frederik Peter Holm and Emma G. M. (Bording) H.; educ. private and govt. Latin Schs. and Danish Royal Navy College. DEGREES: LL.D. (Lincoln Memorial Univ., U.S.A.); D.C. L. (Susquehanna Univ., U.S.A.), Litt. D. (Thiel Coll); G.C.G., G.C.O.D., G.C.C.M.; titular professor in National Museum of Mexico; bvt. lieut-general; hon. minister plenipotentiary; chamberlain to His Royal Highness the Count of Caserta; m. Marguerite Macdonaugh Green, Lady of Grace of the Constantinian Order of St. George, 1919. AUTHOR: The Nestorial Adventures in China, 1923, 1924; His Majesty's Secret Service: Memoirs of the Duke of Xensi, 1929. Former co-editor of Records of the Past. Contributor to Putnam's Mag., Open Court, Travel, N. Y. Times Book Review, Chambers's Journal, Ex Libris, Gad's Danish Mag., Petermann's Mitteilungen, Leslie's Weekly, and to numerous newspapers, includ. Sunday magazines, all over the word (notably his war-abolition plan of 1928). As a young man went to the Far East as war-corres. for Danish and Amer papers during Russo-Japanese conflict; engaged in special journalistic wirk in London under the Earl of Kintore, Sir William Ramsay, Sir Rider Haggard, and others, 1905-7; represented the Associated Press at Interparliamentary Conf. in House of Lords, 1906. Organized and commanded a scientific mission into the far interior of China at 25 yrs. of age. Sponsored an outstanding archaeological achievement of the Holm-Nestorian Expedition to Sian-Fu (1907-1908), which covered by caravan and native houseboat more than 2500 miles of little-travelled ground, and brought to western civilization the only existing two-ton, nine-foot, monolithic Replica of the famed Nestorian Monument of A. D. 781, which rested from 1908-16 in the Metropolitan Museum of New York, and since then permanently in the Lateran, Rome; bringing the Stela from America to Italy across the submarine zone, formally presenting the monument at the first of his private audiences with H. H. Pope Benedict XV, 1916. From 1910-27 presented fourteen nine-foot casts of the Replica to fourteen countries: Athens, Berlin, Calcutta, Copenhagen, Hanoi, Kioto, Madrid, Mexico City, Montreal, New Haven, Paris, and Rome as cities in their respective countries. Decorations: Grand Cross with Collar of the Constantinian Order of St. George and of the Orthodox Order of the Holy Sepulchre; forty-nine other decorations from Belgium, France, Greece, Japan, Montenegro, Persia, Portugal, Russia, Spain, Austria, Bulgaria, Cuba, etc., since 1902. ASSOCIATIONS: Member of 35 scientific or humane societies and royal academies in 14 countries; in many cases, Vice-president, honorary, corresponding or life member. CLUB: Royal Yacht, Copenhagen. (*)

HOLMAN, Prof. B. W., O.B.E. *s.s*: Articles on science and social service. *a*: Royal School of Mines, S.W.7.

HOLMAN, Dennis Idris, B.A. *b*: Lahore, India 1915. *e*: St George's Coll Mussoorie India, Punjab Univ India. Journalist. *n.a*: John Bull (Odham's Press) since 1946. *Publ*: Radio Play; Nocturne Macabre. *Ctr*: John Bull & various other British & American magazines. *s.s*: Personality Stories of Celebrities, Film & Show Business Articles, Fiction, Radio, Drama. *Rec*: Talking. *a*: 3 Highclere, Old Hill, Chislehurst, Kent. *T*: Imperial 3230.

HOLMAN, John Northcott Gordon, Croix de Guerre (France). *b*: Willesden 1904. *e*: Fulham Cent Sec Sch

m Annie Lilian Fairweather. *s*: 2. Journalist & Author, first war corr to sail with Commandos (Lofoten) representing world press, only war corr to meet Mr. Winston Churchill on the Normandy beaches. *n.a*: Dly Chron 1927, Egypt '29, Ex Tel Co '30, Ev Std '42. *Publ*: Commando Attack; The Little Ships; Stand By to Beach; The King's Cruisers. *s.s*: Naval & Shipping. *Rec*: Tennis & walking. *a*: c/o Christy & Moore Ltd, The Ride Annexe, Gerrards Cross, Bucks. *T*: Putney 3565.

HOLMAN, Robert N. *b*: Midlothian 1879. *e*: General. *m*: Rankin C. Forbes. Journalist. *Publ*: Character Studies of Fife Miners; History of Cowdenbeath; Scottish Sketches, Comedy & Romance for B.B.C. *s.s*: Coal Mining Life, Habits of Coal Miners, Social, Domestic, Recreations. *Rec*: Photography, golf, rifle shooting. *a*: 101 High St, Cowdenbeath, Fife. *T*: 2143.

HOLME, Charles Geoffrey, M.B.E., F.R.S.A. *b*: Hampstead 1887. *e*: Abbotsholme. *m*: Margaret Nina Bolton. *s*: 2. *d*: 2. Ed The Studio. *n.a*: Most of the Studio Publ's 1919—. *Rec*: Sailing. *a*: Feeringhill Hse, Kelvedon, Essex.

HOLME, Constance (Mrs. F. B. Punchard). *Publ*: Eight novels. *a*: The Gables, Kirby Lonsdale Westmorland.

HOLME, Hugh Christopher, B.A. *b*: Thyetmyo, Burma 1907. *e*: Rugby Sch, Oriel Coll Oxf. *m*: Anthea Musman. *s*: 1. *d*: 1. Ed & Internat Affairs Specialist, Reuters—Berlin, Abyssinia, Spain, Vienna, Anschluss, etc., '31—39, Ed Observer Foreign News Service '46—47, Dir of Information Services, Chatham House '47—. *Ctr*: Various, B.B.C., etc. *s.s*: Palestine & Middle East, Germany. *Rec*: Pure Mathematics, music. *a*: 12 Upper Berkeley St, Portman Sq, London, W.1. *T*: Ambassador 1712.

HOLMES, Arthur, A.M., Th.D., LL.D. *b*: Cincinnati, Ohio 1872. Prof of Psychology of Religion Butler Univ 1934—. *Publ*: Conservation of the Child; Principles of Character-Making; Backward Children; Controlled Power; Mind of St Paul; Special Class & Backward Children; Eugenics; Masters of Advertising Copy. *Ctr*: Various. *a*: 245 West 38th St, Indianapolis, Ind, U.S.A.

HOLMES, Arthur, D.Sc., F.R.S., F.R.S.E., F.G.S. *b*: Hebburn-on-Tyne 1890. *e*: Imp Coll of Sci & Tech London. *m*: Doris Livesey Reynolds. *s*: 1. Regius Prof of Geology Univ of Edin, Explorer in Mozambique 1910—11, Prof of Geology Durham Univ '24—43, Demonstrator in Geology Imp Coll Lond '11—20. *n.a*: Ed Proc of the Geologists' Assoc '17—21, (Jt-Ed) Trans of the Geological Soc Edin since '46. *Publ*: Principles of Physical Geology; The Age of the Earth; Nomenclature of Petrology, Petrographic Methods & Calculations. *Ctr*: Nature, Endeavour, Geological Magazine, Geographical Journal, etc. *s.s*: Geology, Petrology, Physical Geology. *Rec*: Geological field work, music. *a*: Grangestone, 7 West Mains Rd, Edinburgh 9, & Grant Institute of Geology, West Mains Rd, Edinburgh 9. *T*: Edinburgh 44106.

HOLMES, Burton. *b*: Chicago 1870. *e*: Allen Acad, Harvard Sch, Chicago. *m*: Margaret Oliver. Travel Lecturer, Travel Film Producer. *Publ*: The Traveller's Russia; School Readers—China, Japan, Egypt & Mexico; etc. *Ctr*: Various. *Rec*: Travel, photography. *c*: Explorers', Chicago, etc. *a*: 2020, Grace Ave Hollywood 28, California. *T*: Granite 6382.

HOLMES, Sir C. J., K.C.V.O., D.Litt, R.W.S., etc. Painter. *n.a*: Ed Burlington Magazine 1903-9, Dir Nat Gallery '16-28. *Publ*: Numerous books and articles on painting and the fine arts. *a*: 19 Pembridge Gdns, W.2.

HOLMES, Charles Henry, M.C., F.R.G.S. *b*: Victoria, Australia 1891. *e*: Balwyn Victoria. *m*: Malvina Pooley. *s*: 1. Business Manager & Editor, Manager Australian Geog Soc 1946—. *n.a*: Gen-Man Australian Nat Publicity Assoc '29—, Mang-Ed Aust Geog Mag Walkabout '34—. *Publ*: A Passport Round the World; We Find Australia. *s.s*: Topical Geography of Australia. *Rec*: Angling, golf. *a*: Charles St, Mount Eliza, Victoria, Australia. *T*: Mount Eliza 339.

HOLMES, Dr. E. G. Lect in Biochem, Univ of Cam. *Publ*: Papers dealing wth the Metabolism of the Central Nervous System. *c.t*: B.M.J., Annual Review of Biochem. Fell & Tutor Downing Col. *a*: Biochem Laboratory, Cam.

HOLMES, Edmond Gore Alexander. *b*: Westmeath, Ireland 1850. *e*: Merchant Taylors Sc & St John's Col Oxf. *m*: Florence Mary Syme. *s*: 1. *d*: 2. H.M. Insp of Scs (ret). *c.t*: Nineteenth Century & After, Hibbert Journal, The Quest. *s.s*: Philosophy. *c*: Athenæum & Alpine. *a*: 5 Phené St, Chelsea, S.W.3. *t*: Flaxman 2560.

HOLMES, Ernest, M.J.I. *b*: London 1884. *e*: Priv. *m*: Gertrude Alice Robinson. *d*: 2. Journalist. *n.a*: Worcestershire Advertiser, Assoc-Ed Uxbridge Recorder, Corr Dly Express & Dly Mail, Corr Hairdressers' Weekly (Uncle Ernie). *Ctr*: Home Companion, Violet Mag, etc. *s.s*: Early Patents, Verses & Poems. *Rec*: Swimming, cricket, rowing, music. *a*: Locking Rd, Worle, Weston-super-Mare.

HOLMES, Frank Hubert Worrall, M.M. *b*: Walsall 1897. *e*: King's Sch Pontefract. *m*: Doris Maude Clarke. *s*: 1. *d*: 1. *n.a*: Editor Printer & Proprietor Pontefract Advertiser 1920—37. *Ctr*: Various. *Rec*: Gardening, photography, carpentry. *w.s*: 1915—19 R.E's. *a*: The Priory Hse, Pontefract. *T*: 99.

HOLMES, Frederick Noel. *b*: Streatham 1905. *e*: St Olave's G.S. Tower Bridge S.E.1 & St Bride's Inst Fleet St, Cam Univ Press. *c.t*: Sunday Times, Cam Library Record, Northern Wkly Gazette, etc. *s.s*: Poetry, literary criticism, typography. Counc Brit Literary Assoc '27—. *Rec*: Cricket, tennis, boating. *c*: L.N.U. *a*: 6 Brooklands Av, Cam.

HOLMES, Canon G. E. W. *a*: All Saints' Parsonage, Edin.

HOLMES, George John. *b*: Lon 1876. *e*: City of Lon Col & Caterham. Married. *s*: 3. *d*: 2. Ed & jnlst. *n.a*: Founder Investors Chron & Money Market Review 1899, Mang Ed 1914—. *s.s*: Economics, finance, business. *Rec*: Yachting, travel, politics. *a*: Wickford Hall, Wickford, Essex. *t*: Avenue 7543.

HOLMES, Gordon, C.M.G., C.B.E., M.D., F.R.C.P., D.Sc.(Dub), F.R.S. *b*: Dublin 1876. *e*: Dublin Univ, Berlin & Frankfort. Married. *d*: 3. *n.a*: Ed Brain 1922—. *Ctr*: Brain & others on med & neurological subjects. *s.s*: Neurology, Consltg Physician Charing X Hosp & Nat Hosp for Nervous Diseases. *c*: Athenæum. *a*: 11 Harley St, London, W.1. *T*: Welbeck 2567.

HOLMES, H. R. *b*: London 1896. P.R.O. Royal Philatelic Soc Lond. *n.a*: Ed Philatelic Journ of Great Britain 1935—45. *Publ*: Postage Stamps of Geneva; Bypost Postage Stamps of Norway; Postage Stamps of Tibet. *Ctr*: Philatelic Journs. *a*: 41 Devonshire Pl, London, W.1. *T*: Welbeck 8004.

HOLMES, Henry Alfred, M.A., Ph.D. *b*: Alfred, Maine 1883. *e*: Wesleyan Univ, Univs of Columbia, Buenos Aires, Mexico, Sorbonne. *m*: Lula E. Thomas. *s*: 1. *d*: 2. Title Prof of Romance Languages & Literature Coll of the City of New York. *n.a*: Mem Ed Bd Revista Ibero Americana 1943—45. *Publ*: Martin Fierro, An Epic of the Argentine; Spanish America in Song & Story; Contemporary Spanish Americans; A Prose Translation of Martin Fierro; Vicente Huidobro & Creationism; (in collab) Spanish America at Work; Tierra; As Protestant Spanish America Sees It. *Ctr*: Various. *s.s*: Spanish America, Spanish American Lit. *Rec*: Walking, swimming, motoring. *a*: 460 Riverside Drive, New York 27, N.Y. *T*: UN 4-1890.

HOLMES, John Maurice, F.R.S.A., Hon.F.I.B.D. *b*: Derby 1893. *e*: London Univ, Slade Sch of Fine Art. *m*: Vera Cathleen Taylor. *d*: 1. Prnc. Manchester Municipal Sch of Art, Dip Fine Art (London) etc, Vice-Pres Design & Industries Assoc, Assoc of Arts Insts, Soc for Art Education, etc, Westminster. *Publ*: Colour in Interior Decoration; Architectural Shadow Projection; Applied Perspective; Psychology of Interior Decoration. *Ctr*: Architect's Journ, Architectural Rev, Journ of Decorative Art. *s.s*: Architecture, Industrial Design, Colour, Perspective, Interior Design, Art & Design Education. *c*: Manch Luncheon etc. *a*: 30 Brunswick Rd, Withington, Manchester 20.

HOLMES, Marjorie Marion, B.A. *b*: Hove, Sussex 1911. *e*: Clapham Hgh Sch, Roy Holloway Coll, Lond Univ. *m*: Bernard Francis Voss. *s*: 1. Journalist. *n.a*: Asst Ed Transport World 1941—, Traveller & Tourist '46—, Office Mang Black Star Photos '40—41, Ed Asst Everybody's '36—40, Provincial Newspapers Ltd '34—36. *a*: 10 Seymour Mews, Albion Ave, London, S.W.8. *T*: Macaulay 3891.

HOLMES, Oswald Gurnie. *n.a*: 10 years with Pontefract Advertiser. 8 years F/l. Photographer. *a*: 11a Market Place, Pontefract.

HOLMES, Lt.-Col. R. G. A., C.M.G., O.B.E. *s.s*: Educational subjects. *c.t*: Various. *a*: The Ship Sc, Redhill, Surrey.

HOLMES, Richard Ellis, B.A., M.A. *b*: Pontefract 1863. *e*: Wakefield Q. Elizabeth's Sc & Trinity Col Oxf. *m*: Laura Mary Coulson. *d*: 1. Vicar of Bywell St Peter. *Publ*: A Tyneside Parish (Holy Trin, S. Shields); Tynemouth & its Priory; etc. During 25 y curate & vicar of Holy Trin, S. Shields. 17 y Vicar of Tynemouth. Hon Canon of Newcastle. *a*: Bywell Vicarage, Stocksfield, Northumberland.

HOLMES, Robert. Police Ct Miss (ret). *Publ*: My Police Court Friends with the Colours; Walter Greenway, Spy & Hero; Sister Mattie & Company; Chance Acquaintance; Them That Fall. *c.t*: Blackwood's Mag. *a*: 14 Montgomery Rd, Sheffield.

HOLMES, THOMAS RICE: author; b. Ireland, May 24, 1855; s. Robert and Jane (Henn) H.; educ. Merchant Taylor's Sch. (London), Christ Church (Oxford); DEGREES: B.A. (Oxon), (Hon.) Litt.D. (Dublin), (Hon.) D.Litt. (Oxon). m. Eliza Isabel Isaacs, Aug. 14, 1888. AUTHOR: History of the Indian Mutiny, 1883 (subsequent edits. revised, 1885, 1888, 1891, 1898, 1904, 1913); Four Famous Soldiers, 1889; Caesar's Conquest of Gaul, 1899 (2nd edit. revised, 1911); Ancient Britain and the Invasions of Julius Caesar, 1907; Caesar's Commentaries on the Gallic War, translated into English, 1908; A complete edition of the Bellum Gallicum and (for schools) separate editions of Books I-VII, 1914; The Roman Republic and the Founder of the Empire, 1923; Sir Charles Nepier, 1925; Chapter on "The War Craft of the Romans" in Harmsworth's Universal History; the chapter entitled "The Mutiny," written by request for The Cambridge History of India in 1926 (not yet published). The Architect of the Roman Empire (44-27 B. C.), 1928; The Architect of the Roman Empire (vol. II, 27 B. C.-A. D. 14), 1931. Contributor to Nat. Rev., Macmillan's Mag., The Times, Classical Quarterly, Classical Rev. and other mags. General character of writing: historical. Elected (1925), Fellow Brit. Acad. CLUB: Old Pauline (hon. life mem.). HOME: 1 Akehurst St., Roehampton, S. W. 15, London, Eng.

HOLMES, Urban Tigner, Jr., M.A., Ph.D., Litt.D. *b*: Washington, D.C. 1900. *e*: Danville Sch, Univ of Penn, Harvard & Paris Univs. *m*: Margaret Allen Gemmell. *s*: 1. *d*: 2. Univ Prof. *n.a*: Assoc Ed Language 1939—41, Speculum '37—40, Romance Philology '47—, Studies in Philology '25—, American Speech '47—. *Publ*: A History of Old French Literature ; At the Crossroad on the Hill ; (Ed) Adenet le Roi's Berte aus grans pies ; (in collab) The Life & Works of Guillaume du Bartas ; A Bibliography of French Literature ; etc. *Ctr*: Mod Philology, French Rev, Speculum, Language, Studies in Philology, etc. *s.s*: Mediæval French Lit & Civilisation, Romance & Comparative Linguistics. *Rec*: Music, gen science. *a*: 202 Coolidge St, Chapel Hill, N.C. *T*: 3876.

HOLMES, William Kersley. *b*: Harbourne. *e*: Dollar Acad. *n.a*: Ed-Staff Messrs Blackie & Son Ltd. *Publ*: Ballads of Field & Billet ; In the Open ; A Pocketful of Rhymes ; The Stolen Trophy ; Tramping Scottish Hills. *Ctr*: Punch, Glas Herald, Edin Ev News, Glas Walking, sketching. *c*: Glasgow Literary. *w.s*: 1914—19. *a*: Tod's Field, Dollar, Scotland.

HOLMES, Winifred. *b*: London 1903. *e*: Hobart & Surrey. *m*: John Bruce Holmes. Writer. *n.a*: F.L. *Publ*: Variations on a Metaphysic Theme, and other poems ('33). *c.t*: Observer, Evening Standard, Times, Daily Express, Mod Woman, New Britain, etc. *s.s*: Poetry, socialism, travel. Lect on books & travel in America in '30, Washington & Boston. Publicity work in '32 for L'Hermitage & Kasbeck Restaurants, also a F.L. *Rec*: Music, theatre, swimming. *c*: Gargoyle. *a*: 75 Pelham Court, S.W.3. *t*: Kensington 8395.

HOLMYARD, Eric John, M.A.(Cantab), M.Sc., Litt.D., F.R.I.C. *b*: Midsomer Norton 1891. *e*: Sexey's Sch, Bruton & Sidney Sussex Coll Camb. *m*: Ethel Elizabeth Britten. *s*: 2. Author & Editor, V-Pres Brit Soc for Hist of Science, Mem Roy Asiatic Soc, Soc of Chem Ind, etc. *n.a*: Sci-Ed Everyman's Ency, Gen-Ed Dent's Modern Science Series, Educ Film Ed I.C.I. & Ed Endeavour 1941—. *Publ*: A Higher School Certificate Inorganic Chemistry ; British Scientists' Chemistry ; Chemistry to the Time of Dalton ; Makers of Chemistry ; A Junior Chemistry ; & several mediæval Arabic works on chemistry. *Ctr*: Science Progress, Discovery, The Aryan Path, Manch Guardian, Sun Times, etc. *s.s*: Alchemy, Early Science, Arabic. *Rec*: Travel, Oriental languages. *c*: Athenæum, Clevedon Golf. *a*: 5 Lanchester Rd, Highgate, London, N.6. *T*: Tudor 4683.

HOLROYD, George Henry, M.A. *b*: Bradford 1904. *e*: Hanson H. Sch Bradford, Dalton Hall Manchester, Leeds T.C. & Univ. *m*: Edith Seller. *s*: 1. *d*: 1. Schoolmaster. *n.a*: Late Chief Ed & Educational Adviser E. J. Arnold & Co. *Publ*: Education for Leisure ; The Baker Twins ; Organisation of School Societies & Other Activities ; Drama in School. *Ctr*: Educ Handwork, New Era, The Boy, Practical Senior School Teacher, Schoolmaster, etc. *s.s*: Drama, Biog, Welfare Work, Education. *Rec*: Gardening, music. *a*: 7 Hartley Cresc, Birkdale, Southport. *T*: 68123.

HOLROYD, Michael, F.R.G.S. *Publ*: Chapters on Greek & Roman Art in Martial; Art & Civilisation. *c.t*: Journ Roman Studies, Journ Hellenic Studies, etc. *a*: Brasenose Col, Oxf.

HOLROYD-REECE, John. *Publ*: inc English translations of Keyserling, Meier-Graefe, etc. *a*: 13 New Sq, Lincoln's Inn, London, W.C.2.

HOLST, AXEL: professor of medicine; b. Oslo, Norway, September, 1860; s. Axel and Anna Charlotte Mathilde (Flemming) H.; educ. The Cathedral School (Oslo); The University (Oslo). DEGREE: M.D.; m. Anna Midelfart, Dec. 29, 1886. AUTHOR: Synopsis of Bacteriology, 1891 (2nd edit. 1901). Chief articles on ship-beriberi were published in the English Journal on Hygiene, 1907; and the German "Zentralblatt fuer Bakteriologie", 1918 (vol. 87). Articles on experimental scurvy were published in Norsk Magazin for Logevidenskapen, 1907 and 1910; Journal of Hygiene, 1907; and Zeitschrift fuer Hygiene und Infectionskrankheiten, 1912. General character of writing: in connection with the Norwegian ship-beriberi, and experimental scurvy. The latter has been carried on with Professor Frölich, of Oslo. Has recently written on the antique history of medicine. Relig. denom., Protestant. HOME: Oscarsgate 21, Oslo, Norway.

HOLT, Anne Durning, M.A. *b*: Liverpool 1899. *e*: St Paul's Girl's Sch, St Hugh's Coll Oxf. Engaged in Historical Research. *n.a*: Ed Unitarian, Hist Soc Trans 1934—46. *Publ*: Life of Joseph Priestley ; A Ministry to the Poor ; Walking Together ; William Ellery Channing. *s.s*: Parl Hist & Insts, Protestant Nonconformity, Liverpool Hist. *c*: Univ Women. *a*: Oakfield, Penny Lane, Liverpool 15.

HOLT, Edgar, B.A. *b*: Burnley 1900. *e*: St Bees Sc & Ch Ch Oxf. Journalist. *n.a*: Reporter Daily Dispatch '24—27, Asst Ed Yorks Post '28—30, Asst News Ed B.B.C. '30—32, News Ed B.B.C. '32—33, Dep Ed World Radio '33—35, Dep Ed The Listener '35—. *Publ*: (novel) Quick Work ('33). *c.t*: The Bookman, Whitaker's Almanack & The Yorks Post, etc. *s.s*: Drama, broadcasting & foreign lit. *Rec*: Tennis & squash rackets. *a*: 25 Stanhope Gdns, Lon, S.W.7. *t*: Kensington 1860.

HOLT, Harald Christian. *b*: Copenhagen 1892. *e*: Ostersogades Gymnasium & Copenhagen Univ. *m*: Eli Olesen. *s*: 2. *d*: 2. Ed Kristeligt Dagblad. *n.a*: Kristeligt Dagblad 1930, Ed '32, Ed Vaebneren '22—29. *Publ*: With G. Ipsen—Patruljesystemet ; Handbook Use of Y.M.C.A. Scouts. *s.s*: Ch & sc. Pres Y.M.C.A. Scouts of Denmark, Mem Exec Cmt Kirkeligt Forbund '33. Min in Danish Lutheran Ch to '30. *a*: 3 Sonderborggade, Copenhagen, O. *t*: Obro 8864.

HOLT, Harry Mainwaring, T.D., M.B., Ch.B., D.P.H. *b*: Norton, Malton, Yorks 1891. *e*: Epsom Coll, Univ of Leeds. *m*: Susan Isabel Holt. *s*: 2. *d*: 1. M.o.H. *Ctr*: New English Rev, Yorks Post, Yorks Illus, Med Officer, Journ of State Med, Better Health. *s.s*: Top Med, Subjects of Antiquarian interest confined to Yorks. *Rec*: Reading & book collecting. *a*: Lowfield Hse, Town Hall Sq, Keighley, Yorks. *T*: 2244/5.

HOLT, Henry. *Publ*: Calling All Cars ; The Midnight Mail ; Murderer's Luck ; The Ace of Spades ; The Mayfair Mystery ; The Wolf's Claw ; etc. *s.s*: Mystery thrillers.

HOLT, MARVELL: (pen name): see Maschwitz, Eric.

HOLT, Paul. Journalist. *n.a*: Columnist Daily Express, formerly film critic. *a*: 94 Troy Court, Kensington, London. *T*: Western 5955.

HOLT, William. *b*: Todmorden 1897. *m*: Florence Holt. *s*: 1. *d*: 3. Author, Broadcaster, Film Commentator. *n.a*: Ed Todmorden Gazette 1933—34.

Publ: Backwaters ; I was a Prisoner ; Under a Japanese Parasol ; The Price of Adventure ; I Haven't Unpacked. *Ctr* : Dly Dispatch, Everyman, Left Rev, New Challenge, Strand Mag, Picture Post, Listener, etc. *s.s* : Descriptive Travel Articles, Illustrations. *Rec* : Riding, painting. *c* : Savage. *a* : Higher Kilnhurst, Todmorden, Yorks, & 3 Devonshire Terr, London, W.1. *T* : Todmorden 582 & Welbeck 1090.

HOLT-JACKSON, William. *b* : M/C 1898. *m* : Norah Noné Heighway. *d* : 1. Dir Holt-Jackson Book Coy Ltd. *Publ*: The Hustling Hobo ; Camping & Hiking for All ; Coast & Bush Life in West Africa ; etc. *c.t*: Illus Sporting & Dramatic News, Weekly Scotsman, Young England, etc. *s.s*: Camping, travel. War Service Artists Rifles & Coldstream Guards. *Rec*: Cricket. *a*: Montauban Chambers, St Annes-on-Sea, Lancs. *t*: 575.

HOLT-WILSON, Brigadier Sir Eric E. B., C.M.G., D.S.O. *b* : Norwich 1875. *e* : Harrow & R.M.A. Woolwich. *m* : (1) Susannah Mary Shaw ; (2) Audrey Stirling. *s* : 1. *d* : 3. Roy Eng (ret), Commandant War Dept Constabulary since 1942, Legion of Honour, Crown of Belgium, Sec Lord Chancellor's Sub Cttee Cttee of Imp Def '24—38, Brit Commssr for Police & Security Duties in Occupied Rhineland '19. *Publ*: Field Entrenchments ; Manual of Field Engineering ; etc. *Ctr* : R.E. Journ, Police Journ. *s.s* : Police Intelligence Systems & Work in War, War Legislation & Martial Law. *Rec* : Shooting, ski running, Pres Ski Club of G.B. 1934—35. *c* : Army & Navy. *a* : Spye Arch Hse, Lacock, Wilts.

HOLTBY, Rev. William Henry, M.A., B.D. Supt Meth Min. *c.t*: Teacher's Mag, Religious mags, etc. *a*: 81 Waldegrave Rd, Brighton, Sussex.

HOLTBY, Winifred, M.A. *b* : Rudstone 1898. *e* : Q. Margaret's Scarboro' & Oxf Univ (Somerville Col). Writer & Journalist. *n.a* : Dir Time & Tide 1926—. *Publ*: Mandoa, Mandoa! ; Women ; The Land of Green Ginger ; Truth is not Sober (short stories) ; Virginia Woolf (criticism) ; etc. *c.t*: Time & Tide, Manchester Guardian, Radio Times, Yorks Post, News-Chronicle, & Sunday Times, etc. *s.s*: Politics, education, literary criticism & S. Africa. Univ Ext Lecturer on Mod Hist for Oxf Extra Mural Delegacy. For sev yrs Regular Lecturer for League of Nations Union, for which trav in Europe & Africa. Till '26 was a P.T. Teacher in G.S's. Worked on Care Cmt & Sc Management boards in Bethnal Green. Brought up on farm in Yorks. War Service Q.M.A.A.C. France '17. *a* : 19 Glebe Pl, Lon, S.W.3, & Bainesse, Cottingham, E. Yorks. *t*: Flaxman 7714.

HOLTZ, Alfred Christian Carlsen. *b* : Melbourne, Australia 1874. *e* : Univ of Melbourne. *m* : Susan Ann Thompson. *s* : 1. *d* : 2. *n.a* : Gen-Mang The Argus (ret), Foundation Dir Australian Assoc Press, Ed Southern Congregationalist 1944—. *Ctr* : Various. *Rec*: Literature, horticulture, philately, motoring. *c* : Roy Auto, Rotary, Overseas League, etc. *a* : 25 Grange Rd, Kew, Melbourne, E.4, Victoria, Australia. *T* : Haw 6446.

HOLZ, NICOLAUS: professor, Polytechnic Academy, Aix-la-Chapelle; b. Koeln-Muelheim, Germany, Nov., 1868; s. Christian and Margaretha (Hasslacher) H.; educ. Kaiser Wilhelm's Gymnasium, Cologne, Polytechnic Academy at Aix-la-Chapelle; DEGREES: C.E.; m. Elisabeth Intze. AUTHOR: Wasserkraftverhaeltnisse in Scandinavien und im Alpengebiet, 1901; Bericht ueber die Wasserverhaeltnisse der Provinz Westpreussen, 1902; Bericht ueber die Wasserverhaeltnisse der Provinz Pommern, 1902; Bericht ueber die Wasserverhaeltnisse der Provinz Posen, 1907. Contributor to: Zeitschrift fuer Bauwesen, Zentralblatt der Bauverwaltung, Handwoerterbuch des Kaufmann's. General character of writing: technical and economic. Civil engineering projects in Germany, Sweden and Norway. CLUBS: Verein Deutscher Ingenieure, Norsk Ingenlör Forening. ADDRESS: Ruetscherstrasse 41, Aix-la-Chapelle, Germany.

HOMAN, Paul Thomas, A.B., Ph.D. *b* : Indianola, Iowa 1893. *e* : Williamethe Univ, Oxf Univ. *m* : Christine Cluthenden. Economist, Prof of Econ Cornell Univ 1927—46. *n.a* : Mang Ed American Economic Review 1941—. *Publ*: Contemporary Economic Thought ; (co-author) The National Recovery Administration ; Government & Economic Life ; The Sugar Economy of Puerto Rico ; American Marches of Social Science. *Ctr* : Quarterly Journ of Econs, etc. *s.s* : Econ Theory & Policy, Public Control of Business. *Rec*: Tennis, golf. *a* : 1705 21st St, N.W. Washington 9, D.C. *T* : Adams 8514.

HOMBERG, OTTO von (pen name); (Dr. Otto Geise): author; b. Naumburg, June, 1857; s. Carl Casimir and Amalie (Kannegiesser) Geise; educ. Gymnasiums of Meiningen and Corbach; Univs. of Leipzig and Kiel. DEGREES: Doctor; m. Anna Schmalfeld, Oct. 18, 1929. AUTHOR: Die moralische Wirkung, 1900; Tage und Nächte, 1903; Aprilregen, 1903; Jahresring, 1904. General character of writing: essays, poems. ADDRESS: Staatsrat, Viktorienstrasse 10, Lübeck, Germany.

HOME, Ethel, M.A. *b* : London. *e* : Girls Pub Day Schs, Newnham Coll Camb. Music Lecturer. *Publ*: Short History of Music ; Music as a Language ; Improvising ; Transposition ; Ear Training. *s.s* : Music, mathematics. *Rec*: Travelling. *a* : 50 Bullingham Mansions, Church St, Kensington, London, W.8. *T* : Western 1034.

HOME, Gordon Cochrane, F.S.A.(Scot). Editor of Dent's Cathedral Series. *Publ*: inc What to see in England ; The Romance of London ; Roman London ; Canterbury of our Grandfathers ; The Charm of Surrey ; York Minster ; The History & Antiquities of Cyprus ; etc. *a* : Langhaugh Hse, Galashields, Selkirkshire.

HOME, Michael. *b* : Heathley 1885. *e* : Thetford Gr Sch & King's Coll. *Publ*: God & the Rabbit ; In this Valley ; The Place of Little Birds ; Autumn Fields ; The Strange Prisoner ; etc. *Ctr* : (short stories) Ev News, Ev Standard, Good Housekeeping, etc. *s.s* : Country life. *Rec*: Golf, bridge, gardening. *w.s* : 1914—18, '39—45 (Maj Roy Norfolk Regt). *a* : c/o Christy & Moore, The Ride Annexe, Gerrards Cross, Bucks. *T* : Gerrards Cross 2387.

HOME-GALL, William Bolingbroke. *b* : Charlton 1894. *e* : Hampton Gr Sch. *m* : Kathleen Maria Charlton. *s* : 2. *d* : 1. Editor. *n.a* : Air Mail 1947, Ed Chums Annual '39, Amalg Press '12—39. *c* : Press. *w.s* : 1914—18 Roy Fus, '40—45 R.A.F. *a* : Air Mail, R.A.F.A. Publishing Co, 14 Park Cres, London, W.1. *T* : Welbeck 1156.

HONE, Lt.-Col. P. F., D.S.O.(& Bar), M.C. (& 2 Bars). Civil Service. *Publ*: Southern Rhodesia. *a*: Little Wix. W. Horsley, Surrey. *t*: E. Horsley 92.

HONEY, William Bowyer. *b* : London 1889. *e* : Sir Walter St John's Sch Battersea Lond. *m* : Helen Julie Neild. *s* : 2. Keeper Dept of Ceramics Victoria & Albert Museum. *Publ*: Ceramic Art of China ; The Art of the Potter ; Dresden China ; Brought Out in Evidence (autobiog by William Bowyer) ; Gardening Heresies & Devotions ; Science & the Creative Art. *Ctr* : Burlington Mag, Connoisseur, Apollo, Pantheon, Spectator, etc. *s.s* : Pottery, Porcelain, Glass. *Rec*: Gardening. *a* : The White Hse, Jordans, Bucks.

HONEYMAN, Tom John, M.B., Ch.B., F.R.F.P.S. *b*: Glasgow 1891. *e*: Glasgow Univ. *m*: Victoria Catherine Burnett. *s*: 2. *d*: 1. Dir Glasgow Art Gallery, Hon Lect History of Painting Glas Univ. *n.a*: Ed Scottish Art Review. *Publ*: Introducing Leslie Hunter. *Ctr*: The Studio, The Artist, & various Scottish newsps. *s.s*: History of Art, Art Appreciation. *Rec*: Theatre, antiphilistinism. *c*: Glasgow Art. *w.s*: World War I R.A.M.C. (Capt). *a*: The Art Gallery, Glasgow. *T*: Kelvin 1134.

HONIGMANN, Georg F. W., PhD. *b*: Wiesbaden 1903. *e*: Univs of Prague, Breslau, Berlin, Giessen. *m*: Ruth H. Bachert. Journalist. *n.a*: Finan Corr of the Vossische Zeitung in Lon. *c.t*: Papers of the Ullstein Pubg Coy Berlin. *s.s*: German lit. *a*: 91c Lexham Gdns, W.8. *t*: Western 7988.

HONZIKOVA, Marie (see **PRUSAKOVA, Marie**). *b*: Praha 1903. *e*: Gymnasium & Univ. *m*: Karel Honzik, *d*: 1. Writer, Mem Synd of Czechoslovak Writers & P.E.N. *a*: Praha 11, Opletalova 19, Czechoslovakia. *T*: 298-96.

HOOD, Rev. Canon Archibald Frederic, M.A. *b*: Bridgend 1895. *e*: Univ Coll Oxf. Princ Pusey House, Canon of Monmouth, Select Preacher Oxf 1946—48. *Publ*: The Christ of St Mark; Union of Christendom (contrib Catholic sermons); Darwell Stone; The Language of the Faith. *Rec*: Travelling. *c*: Athenæum, Bath, Oxf, Carlton, Dublin Univ. *a*: Pusey Hse, Oxford. *T*: 2332.

HOOD, Christobel Mary, F.R.Hist.S., J.P. *b*: London 1886. *e*: Priv. *m*: Capt the Rev Charles Ivo Sinclair Hood, C.F. (killed in action 1918). *n.a*: Ed Norfolk Archæology 1923—35. *Publ*: The History of an East Anglian Soke; The Choreography of Norfolk; Records of a Norfolk Village; Sequestered Loyalists & Bartholomew Sufferers; The Book of Robert Southwell. *s.s*: Norfolk History & Topography. *c*: Norfolk County. *a*: Sidestrand, Cromer, Norfolk. *T*: Overstrand 244.

HOOD, Hon. Dorothy Violet. *b*: London 1877. *e*: Priv. Writer. *Publ*: The Admirals Hood; London is Invincible; Looking Back on London. *Ctr*: Good Housekeeping, Ev News, Dly Mail, News Chron. *s.s*: London. *Rec*: Reading, games. *a*: Little Water Farm, Stogursey, Bridgwater, Som.

HOOD, Harold. *b*: Middlesbrough 1871. *e*: Coatham Sc. *m*: Clara Smith. *s*: 2. Engraver & Printer. *c.t*: British Printer, Printing Review, Printers Plant, Amateur Photographer, To-Day, Daily News. *s.s*: Colour photog. Fellow of Roy Photographic Soc. Pres Tees-side Assoc of B.M.P. Fed. *Rec*: Tennis, gardening. *a*: Nunthorpe, North Yorks. *t*: 56151.

HOOD, John. *b*: Adelaide, South Australia 1904. *e*: Hutchins Sc Hobart, Univ of Tasmania & Magdalen Col Oxf. *m*: Margaret MacLeod. Jnlst. *n.a*: Reporter Hobart News 1925—26. Imperial & Foreign Dept The Times '29—. *s.s*: Australian, New Zealand & Pacific affairs. *a*: 45 St Peters Sq, W.6. *t*: Riverside 1163.

HOOD, Rev. John Charles Fulton, M.A.(Cantab), D.D.(Durham), O.C.F. *b*: Stockport 1884. *e*: Leatherhead, Christ Coll Camb. *m*: Patuffa Kennedy-Fraser. *d*: 2. Rector Moulton, Suffolk. *Publ*: Icelandic Church Saga; Breastplate for a Soldier; Handbooks to Norway & Iceland; Accounts of St Mary's Church Nottingham; Garstang & Keighley Parish Churches. *n.a*: Founder & Ed "Midnight Sun" Forces newspaper. *Ctr*: Times, Yorkshire Post, My Garden, etc. *s.s*: Ecclesiastical History & Antiquarian, Gardening. *Rec*: Gardening. *w.s*: Chaplain in World Wars I & II. *a*: Moulton, Suffolk. *T*: Kentford 233.

HOOD-PHILLIPS, Jack, M.A. *b*: 1902. Univ Officer. *Publ*: Hurrying Feet. *Ctr*: Various newspapers & periodicals. *s.s*: Educ, Youth Service. *c*: Arts Theatre. *a*: 4 Hunter Rd, London, S.W.20.

HOOK, Sidney, M.A., Ph.D. *b*: N.Y. City 1902. *e*: Columb Univ. *m*: Ann E. Zinken. *s*: 2. *d*: 1. Prof of Philosophy. *n.a*: Assoc & Cont Ed Modern Monthly, New Leader, Modern Review. *Publ*: The Hero in History; The Metaphysics of Pragmatism; Reason, Social Myths & Democracy; From Hegel to Marx; Towards the Understanding of Karl Marx; Education for Modern Man. *Ctr*: Partisan Rev, Journ of Philos, N.Y. Times, Ethics, Commentary, etc. *s.s*: Philosophy, Social Criticism, Historical Analysis. *Rec*: Gardening. *a*: New York University, 100 Washington Sq, East, N.Y.C.3, U.S.A. *T*: Sp. 7-2000.

HOOKE, Samuel Henry. M.A., B.D., F.S.A. *b*: Cirencester 1874. *e*: St Mark's Windsor & Jesus Coll Oxf. Prof Emeritus Old Testament Studies Univ of Lond. *n.a*: Ed Palestine Exploration Fund Quarterly Statement. *Publ*: Christ & the Kingdom of God; Christianity in the Making; New Year's Day; Myth & Ritual; The Labyrinth; In the Beginning; What is the Bible? *Ctr*: Hastings Dict Apostolic Christy. *s.s*: Archæology, Semitic Studies. *a*: 28 Oxford Gdns, Strawberry Hill, Middx.

HOOKER, Chas. Wm. Ross, O.B.E., M.A., B.Sc. *b*: Lon 1884. *e*: Bancroft's Sc, Univ Col Lon & Clare Col Cam. *m*: Mary Ruth Whittle. *s*: 1. *d*: 1. *n.a*: Ed Lady Clare Mag Cam 1903—04, Code & Cryptographic expert to Intelligence Service during War '15—19. *Publ*: What is the Fourth Dimension?; Textbook of Chemistry (with H. A. Wootton). *c.t*: The Police Journ, Harmsworth Business Ency, etc. *s.s*: Popular science, codes & cryptography. *a*: "Little Rock", Hillside Rd, Harpenden. *t*: 544.

HOOLE-JACKSON, Percy ("P.H.J."). *b*: Prestwich. 1894. *e*: Priv & Lichfield Cadet Schs. *m*: Elizabeth Jacka Harry. *s*: 3. *d*: 1. Author & Editor. *n.a*: Ed Manch Group Periodicals & Newspapers 1927—28—29, resigned for authorship & F/L owing to ill-health & war-disabilities. *Publ*: Maid o' the Moors; Thanksgiving (poems); Behind the News (wireless plays); We Must Get That Boat; Old Soldiers. *Ctr*: Manch Guardian, Daily Herald, English Review, Times, Pearson's Mag, Good Housekeeping, Radio Times, etc. *s.s*: Short & Serial Stories, Poetry, Radio Plays. *Rec*: Sea-fishing, swimming, nat hist. *c*: Press. *w.s*: 1914—19. *a*: c/o Guild of Newspaper Editors, Salisbury Sq Hse, London, E.C.4, & 30 Bay View Terr, Penzance.

HOOPER, Alfred, M.A. *b*: London 1894. *e*: Durham. Writer & Lecturer. *Publ*: A Mathematics Refresher; The River Mathematics; An Arithmetic Refresher; Makers of Mathematics; A Modern Course in Trigonometry (with A. L. Griswold). *s.s*: Mathematics. *a*: Hillcot, Pownal, Vermont, U.S.A. *T*: Pownal 3851.

HOOPER, David, LL.D.(McMaster, Toronto), F.I.C., F.C.S., F.R.H.S. *b*: Redhill 1858. *e*: Chelmsford, Lon, The Hague, Holland. Late Govt Quinologist, Madras. Late Curator Econ & Art Section Indian Museum, Calcutta. Late Econ Botanist to Govt of India. *Publ*: Jt Author:—Pharmacographia Indica (1892—93); Materia Medica of Madras ('93); Materia Medica for India ('98); Chinese Drugs (Malay States Bulletin 1928); Persian Drugs (Kew Bulletin, '31). *s.s*: Medicinal & econ products. Hanbury Gold Medallist '07. Pres Brit Pharmaceutical Conf '16. *Rec*: Travel. *a*: 151 Highbury New Pk, N.5.

HOOPER, F. H. American Ed Ency Britannica. Ed Century Dictionary. *a*: c/o Ency Britannica Co Ltd, 80—86 Regent St, W.1.

HOOPER, Reginald Stewart, B.A.(Oxon). *b*: Solihull 1889. *e*: Uppingham Sc & Oxf Univ. *m*: Marjorie Isabella Rose (dec). *s*: 1. *d*: 2. Journalist. *n.a*: Sub-Ed Tatler 1913—14. Asst Ed Eve '19—29. Art Ed Britannia & Eve. Ed Bystander '31—. *Publ*: And the Next?; One At a Time. *s.s*: Dramatic criticism. *Rec*: Golf. *c*: United Univ & Stoke Poges. *a*:

HOOPER, Sydney Ernest. *b*: Liss 1880. *e*: St John's Coll Highbury, Univ Coll Durham & U.C.L. *m*: Frances Gramina Lindesay Brine. *s*: 1. *d*: 1. Dir of Brit Inst of Philos. *n.a*: Ed Philosophy, concerned with founding of Roy Inst of Philos & Journ, Philosophy 1924—25. *Ctr*: Psych & philos journs. *s.s*: Philos & Psych. *Rec*: Gardening. *a*: Redlayne, Cookham Dean, Berks.

HOOPER, Rev. Willmore. *b*: Sheffield 1854. *e*: Rossall Sc & Durham Univ. *m*: Mildred B. Leaton-Blenkinsopp. *s*: 2. *d*: 1. *Publ*: Sketches of Academic Life (1886). *a*: Coneysthorpe. York.

HOOPINGTON, AMBROSE (pen name): see **Binney, Cecil**

HOORNAERT, Rev. Rodolphe Louis. *b*: Courtrai 1886. *e*: Bruges & Louvain Univs. Catholic Priest. *Publ*: Pour la Patrie (1919); Les Béguines de Bruges; Le Beguinage de Bruges; Collaboration a la Traduction des Œuvres de St Jean de la Croix; etc. *c.t*: Les Etudes, Revue Générale, Annales de la Sociétéd'Emulation, Revue Carmélitaine, etc. *s.s*: Liturgy, mysticism. *a*: Curé du Béguinage, Princier de la Vigne, 119 Place de la Vigne, Bruges. *t*: K 682.

HOOTON, Earnest Albert, A.B., B.Litt., Ph.D. *b*: Clemansville, Wisconsin 1887. *e*: Lawrence Coll, Univ of Wisconsin, Univ of Oxf. *m*: Mary Camp. *s*: 2. *d*: 1. Prof of Anthropology Harvard Univ. *Publ*: Up from the Ape; The American Criminal; Crime & the Man; The Indians of Peces Pueblo; The Ancient Inhabitants of the Canary Islands; Man's Poor Relations; Apes, Men & Morons; Twilight on Man; Why Men Behave like Apes & Vice Versa; Young Man You Are Normal. *Ctr*: Colliers, Atlantic Monthly, Good Housekeeping, etc. *s.s*: Anthropology, Human Evolution, etc. *Rec*: Golf, drawing, water colours, light verse. *a*: 13 Buckingham St, Cambridge, Mass, U.S.A. *T*: Tro 1162.

HOOTON, Rev. Walter Stewart, M.A.(Camb), B.D.(Durham). *b*: London 1870. *e*: Highgate Sch & St John's Coll & Ridley Hall Camb. *m*: M. Gertrude Barber. *d*: 3. Clergyman C. of E. (ret). *Publ*: Problems of Faith & Conduct; The Missionary Campaign; Turning Points in the Primitive Church; etc. *Ctr*: The Christian, The Life of Faith, etc. *s.s*: Expository & Devotional. *c*: Fellowship of Evangelical Churchmen. *a*: 6 Sunset View, Barnet, Herts. *T*: Barnet 4213.

HOOVER, Calvin Bryce, A.B., Ph.D. *b*: Berwick, Ill 1897. *e*: Monmouth Coll & Univ of Wisconsin. *m*: Faith Miriam Sprole. *d*: 2. Prof of Econ Duke Univ 1925—. *Publ*: The Economic Life of Soviet Russia; Germany Enters the Third Reich; Dictators & Democracies; International Trade & Domestic Employment. *c*: N.Y. Times, Foreign Affairs, Harpers, Econ Journ, Journ of Polit Econ, Washington Post, etc. *s.s*: Economic Theory, Internat Trade, Russia, Germany, Econ Systems. *w.s*: 1917—19 U.S. Army. *a*: 1702 Duke University Rd, Durham, North Carolina, U.S.A.

HOOVER, Herbert. *Publ*: inc Agricola de Re Metallica; The Challenge to Liberty; America's First Crusade: The Problem of Lasting Peace; etc. *a*: Palo Alto, California, U.S.A.

HOPCRAFT, Joseph. *b*: Lon 1884. *m*: Jessie Louisa Souter. *s*: 2. *d*: 1. *n.a*: Sports Ed News of the World 1919—. *a*: 34 Dovedale Rd, Honor Oak, S.E.22.

HOPE. Camilla. See Thompson, Grace Elsie.

HOPE, E. W., Coppice, Caldy, Cheshire.

HOPE, Dr. E. W., O.B.E., Univ Sc of Hygiene L'pool.

HOPE, Frances Essex Theodora ("Essex Smith"). *b*: Hereford. *e*: Cheltenham Coll & St Hilda's Hall Oxf. *m*: William Hope. *Publ*: Wind on the Heath; Shepherdless Sheep; Revolving Fates;. If Ye Break Faith; The Wye Valley Mystery; Turned Adrift; Garry (U.S.A.); I Have Come Home; etc. *Ctr*: Dly Mail, Ev News, Occult Review, etc. *a*: Monnington, West Ave, Worthing. *T*: 1836.

HOPE. Helen. See Thorogood, Helen Roy.

HOPE, R. A. Sec York Br N.U.J. 34 Sycamore Terr, Bootham, York.

HOPEWELL-ASH, Edwin, M.D.(Lond). *e*: Univ Coll Sch, St Mary's Hosp Lond. *Publ*: Problem of Nervous Breakdown; Hypnotism & Suggestion; Therapy of Personal Influence; Notes on the Nervous System; Mental Nurses' Dictionary. *Ctr*: Former medical corres Dly Telegraph. *s.s*: Medicopsychology. *a*: 8 Harley St, London, W.1.

HOPF, Rev. Constantin Ludwig Adolph Rudolph, D.Phil.(Oxf). *b*: Schloss Wettin, Halle, S. Germany 1911. *e*: Lubeck & Univs of Goettingen, Koenigsberg, Tartu (Estonia), Ridley Hall Camb & Oxf Univ. *m*: Hilda Linde. *s*: 1. Asst Priest St Michael's Tilehurst Reading. *Publ*: Martin Bucer & the English Reformation. *Ctr*: Journ of Theological Studies. *s.s*: 16th Century (Reformation). *Rec*: Hist of arts, literature, swimming. *w.s*: Chap to Women Internees Holloway Prison 1940—41, Off Chap to H.M. Forces '45—. *a*: The Rectory, Tilehurst, Reading, Berks. *T*: Reading 67331

HOPF, LUDWIG: professor; b. Nuremberg, Germany, Oct. 23, 1884; s. Hans and Elise (Josephthal) St. Hopf; educ. Gymnasium Nuremberg; Univs. of Munich, Berlin, Paris and Zürich. DEGREES: Ph.D.; m. Alice Goldschmidt, Sept. 1, 1912. AUTHOR: Aerodynamik (with R. Fuchs), 1922; Mechanik (with Th. von Kármán, im Jahrbuch der technischen Physik), 1924; Zähe Flüssigkeiten (im Handbuch der Physik) 1927. Editor: Hydrodynamische Theorie der Schmiermittelreibung (Ostwalds Klassiker No. 218). Contributes to: Annalen der Physik; Zeitschrift für ang. Mathematik und Mechanik; Zeitschrift für Flugtechnik und Motorluftschiffahrt; Naturwissenschaften. General character of writing: scientific, mathematics, physics, mechanics. CLUBS: Deutsche physikalische Gesellschaft; Gesellschaft für technische Physik; Deutsche Mathematiker Vereinigung; Gesellschaft für ang. Mathematik und Mechanik; Wissenschaftliche Gesellschaft für Luftfahrt. ADDRESS: Technical College, Eupenerstrasse 129, Aachen, Germany.

HOPKINS, Arthur Frederick. Sub-Editor. *n.a*: Sub-Ed Oxford Mail. *a*: Newspaper Hse, Oxford.

HOPKINS, Cyril John, A.C.G.I., A.M.I.E.E., F.R.S.A. *b*: Leighton Buzzard, Beds. *e*: Berkhamsted Gr Sch, City & Guilds Central Tech Coll London. *m*: Marjorie

Newton Gilbert. s: 1. d: 2. Chartered Electrical Engineer, Editor of many tech publs on electric tools 1920—47. Ctr: Amer Elec Rev, Amer Elec Rly Journ, Times Eng Supp, Zeitschrift des Vereins der A.E.G., etc. s.s: Railway Electrifications, Technical German, Ball Bearings, Electric Tools, Foot Arch Supports. Rec: Tennis, swimming. c: Bedford & Riverside Lawn Tennis. a: 19 Cauldwell St, Bedford. T: 3000.

HOPKINS, Gerard Walter Sturgis, M.C. b: London 1892. e: Marlborough, Balliol Coll Oxf. Publisher, Reviewer, Novelist, Translator. Publ: Seeing's Believing; An Angel in the Room; Nor Fish, Nor Flesh; Madame Bovary (translation); The Novels of Francois Mauriac (translation); Men of Goodwill (translation). Ctr: Time & Tide. Rec: Walking. c: Garrick. a: 10c Ashburn Pl, London, S.W.7. T: Frobisher 3084.

HOPKINS, Guy S. b: Hampton Court 1912. e: Wolsey Hall Oxf & Sec Scs. F/L. Journalist. n.a: Lon & Suburban News Agency. c.t: Writer, Nat Newsagent, Wimbledon Free Press, etc. s.s: Films, trade specialists. Rec: Motor cycling, rowing, billiards. a: 10 Penn Rd, Holloway N.7.

HOPKINS, Harry. b: Preston, Lancs 1913. e: Preston Gr Sch, Merton Coll Oxf. Journalist. n.a: Asst Ed Birm Gazette 1936—38, Special Writer Favourite Weekly (defunct '38), Ed Contact, British troops newspaper India Command & India Army Observer '43—45, Diplomatic Corres Manchester Ev News '46, Special Writer John Bull. a: 162 Watchfield, London, W.4. T: Chiswick 0729.

HOPKINS, Kenneth. b: Bournemouth 1914. Writer & Journalist. n.a: Brit Corres Book Collector's Packet, Chic & Imprimatur Cincinnatti. Publ: Love & Elizabeth; The English Lyric; Miscellany Poems; etc. Ctr: Argosy, Lilliput, Time & Tide, John O' London's, Ev Standard, New Statesman, Lit Digest, Tribune, etc. s.s: English Lit. a: 104 Cambridge Gardens, London, W.10. T: Ladbroke 4117.

HOPKINS, Miss M. A. n.a: Ed Somerset Guardian & Radstock Observer, Sub-Ed Bath & Wilts Chron & Herald. a: 12 Seymour Road, Bath, Somerset.

HOPKINS, Reginald Haydn, D.Sc., F.R.I.C., F.C.S. b: Birmingham 1891. e: King Edward's Gr Sch & the Univ Birmingham. m: Ruth Storer. s: 1. Prof of Brewing & Industrial Fermentation Univ of Birm'ham 1931—, Research Supervisor Inst of Brewing '34—47. Publ: Textbook, Biochemistry Applied to Malting & Brewing. Ctr: Biochem Journ, Journ of Inst of Brewing, etc. s.s: Malting, Brewing, Indust Fermentation. Rec: Music. a: The Univ, Edgbaston, Birmingham, & 90 Fitzroy Ave, Harborne, Birmingham 17. T: Selly Oak 1181.

HOPKINS, Robert Thurston. b: Bury St Edmunds 1883. e: Thetford Gr Sch Norfolk & U.C.L. m: Sybil Bately. s: 1. n.a: Lit Ed London Internat Press, Founder & V-Pres Soc of Sussex Downsmen. Publ: Rudyard Kipling, his Life & Work; Thomas Hardy's Dorset; H. G. Wells; This London; Small Sailing Craft; The Man Who Was Sussex; The Romance of the Bank of England; Life & Death at the Old Bailey; English Moated Houses; Valentine Vaughan; Adventures with Phantoms; The Amber Girl; Corpses can Walk. Ctr: Ev News, Answers, Pearsons, N.Y. Times, Bookman, Times of India, Dly Sketch, etc. s.s: Old & New London, Windmills & Watermills, Old English Inns. Rec: Ghost hunting. c: Savage, Sussex Yacht. w.s: 1916—20. a: 11 Richmond St, Brighton, Sussex.

HOPKINS, Roy. e: Spalding Gr Sch. m: Maude Knott. d: 1. Journalist. n.a: Formerly Asst Ed of the Economist, Dir Empire Service, Dir Photopress Ltd, Founder & Ed Newspaper Finance Annual, Old London Mag. Publ: Reform & Control of the Bank of England.

Ctr: Newspapers throughout the world. s.s: Econs, Finance. Rec: Golf. a: 51 Chepstow Pl, London, W.2. T: Bayswater 4743.

HOPKINS, Rev. Wilfred Morley. Publ: The Tabernacle & Its Teaching; Thoughts in His Presence; Pearls from The Ocean. c.t: English Churchman, Bible League Quarterly. a: Christ Church Hse, Leamington Spa.

HOPKINSON, Rev. Arthur Wells. b: Manchester 1874. e: Dulwich Coll, Univ Coll Oxf, Wells Theological Coll. m: Dorothy Virtue Millard. Clerk in Holy Orders. n.a: Ed S. Raphael Quarterly 1935—36. Publ: Pastors' Progress; Pastors' Psychology; Mysticism Old & New; Comfort & Sure Confidence; Be Merry; Hope; The Gate of Life; The Seven Sacraments. Ctr: Various. s.s: Mysticism, Pastoralia, Life & Works of William Law & of Thomas Traherne. Rec: Bonfires, fishing. a: 2 Abbott's Quay, Wareham, Dorset. T: Wareham 209.

HOPKINSON, Austin, J.P. b: Manchester 1879. e: Dulwich Coll. Engineer, Ind M.P. Mossley Division of Lancs 1918—29 & '31—45, J.P. for Lancashire. Publ: Religio Militis, Hope for the Workers. Ctr: Nineteenth Century, Fortnightly, Guardian, Eng Review, etc. s.s: Politics, Economics, Religion. c: Athenæum. w.s: 1914—16 & '39—42. a: 2 Whitehall Court, London, S.W.1. T: Whitehall 3160. ext 26.

HOPKINSON, Henry Thomas. b: Manchester 1905. e: St Edward's Oxf & Pembroke Coll Oxf. Married. d: 2. Journalist & Author. n.a: Asst Ed The Clarion 1934, Asst Ed Weekly Illustrated '34—38, Ed Picture Post '38—40, Ed '40—, & for Lilliput '41—46. Publ: A Strong Hand at the Helm (under the Pen-Name Vindicator); The Man Below; Mist in the Tagus; Collected Short Stories. Ctr: Horizon, New Writing, The Listener, etc. a: 26 Cheyne Row, Chelsea, London, S.W.3. T: Flaxman 7698.

HOPKINSON, Ven. John Henry. b: M/C 1876. e: Dulwich Col & Univ Col Oxf. m: Evelyn Mary Fountaine. s: 4. d: 1. Archdeacon of Westmorland & Diocesan Organiser Religious Educ Diocese of Carlisle. Publ: The Roman Fort at Ribchester; A Syllabus of Religious Instruction; etc. c.t: Journ of Hellenic Studies & Annual of Brit Sc at Athens. a: Christ Church Vicarage, Cockermouth. t: 107.

HOPKINSON Marie Ruan. m: Henry Lennox Hopkinson. s: 3. Publ: Anne of England; The Supreme Art of Bringing Up Children. s.s: Queen Anne's reign. c: Ladies Forum. a: 2 Hans St, S.W.1.

HOPKINSON, Martin. Publisher. a: c/o Martin Hopkinson Ltd, 23 Soho Sq, W.1.

HOPKINSON, Robert William. b: Newcastle-on-Tyne 1870. e: Armstrong's Sc Newcastle. Journalist. n.a: Consett Guardian 1888, Consett Chronicle (Reporter) '89, Newcastle Daily Journal (Reporter) '90, Sub-Ed 1905, Chief Sub-Ed '08–. a: 4 Swindon Terr, Newcastle-on-Tyne.

HOPP, Zinken. b: Ullensvang, Hardanger 1905. m: Einar Meidell Hopp. s: 1. d: 2. Publ: A Fairy Tale about Norway; The Adventures of Ole Bull; Hanna Winsnes, Poet & Cook; (poems) Ballads of a Governess; Mountain Songs; Kitchen Verses; Strange Enough; Within Four Walls; Trans, Alice in Wonderland. Ctr: Bergens Tidende, Aftenposten, etc. s.s: History, Biography. a: Chr. Michelsensgate 11, Bergen. T: 14281.

HOPPE, A. J. Dir of J. M. Dent & Sons Ltd. *a*: Aldine Hse, 10—13 Bedford St, W.C.2.

HOPPÉ, Emile Otho. *b*: Munich 1878. *e*: Vienna & Paris Univ. Officer Crown Rumania. *s*: 1. *d*: 1. Author & Photographer. *Publ*: The Russian Ballet; The Book of Fair Women; Picturesque Great Britain; This Romantic American; London; Romance of Mediæval Towns; Round the World with a Camera; In Gipsy Camp and Royal Palace; The Image of London; etc. *c.t*: Illus Lon News, Country Life, The Studio, Evening News, Windsor Mag. *s.s*: Travel, motoring, photography. *Rec*: Fly fishing, motoring. *c*: Savage, Authors'. *a*: Millais Hse, Cromwell Place, Lon, S.W.7. *t*: Kens. 5329.

HOPPE, Knut Ragnar Johan, Ph.D. *b*: Malmo 1885. *m*: Ellen Everz. Keeper of Dept of Prints & Drawings at National Museum Stockholm. *Publ*: The Painter Elias Martin; Degas & his Works in the North; The Drawings of François Boucher in the National Museum; Modern Swedish Painting; Towns & Artists. *Ctr*: Svenska Dagbladet, Social-Demokraten, Morgen-Tidningen, etc. *s.s*: French Art of the 19th Century, Modern Swedish Art. *c*: P.E.N. *a*: Ostermalmsgatan 6, Stockholm, Sweden. *T*: 203330.

HOPPER, Edward Allen. *b*: Blackheath 1891. Reporter. *a*: Oakhurst, Linden Av, Herne Bay. *t*: 411.

HOPPS, Marie, L.G.S.M., A.T.C.L. *b*: Glas 1906. *e*: Priv Sc, Glas High Sc & Berlin. Princ Newcastle Sc of Dramat Art. Lecturer in Eloc, Publ Speaking & German to Munic Col of Comm Newcastle-on-Tyne '32—34. *Publ*: The Spoken Word; Good Diction in School. *s.s*: Dramat Art, Eloc, Publ Speaking & German. *Rec*: Dancing & Bridge. *c*: Ladies, Newcastle-on-Tyne & Overseas. *a*: 86 Osborne Rd, Jesmond, Newcastle-on-Tyne. *t*: 766.

HOPWOOD, Adml. Ronald A., C.B. *Publ*: The Old Way; The Secret of Ships; The New Navy; (Naval Poems). *s.s*: Naval hist. *c*: United Service. *a*: 7 Sloane Gardens, S.W.1.

HORD, Percy. *b*: Thirsk. *e*: Ruskin Coll Oxf. *m*: Minnie Gunther. *s*: 1. *d*: 1. Parl Sub-Ed Dly Telegraph. *n.a*: Sub-Ed Western Daily Mercury 1907—08, Chief Sub-Ed Sheffield Independent '08—09, Sub-Ed Dly Sketch & Leader Writer Manch Ev Chron '09—10, Asst-Ed Sunday Chron '10—11, Leader Writer Dly Dispatch '12—16, Ed Manch Ev Chron '17—18, Ed Sunday Chron '19—25, Lit Ed Ev Standard '23. *a*: 13 Priory Ave, Bedford Pk, London, W.4. *T*: Chiswick 0764.

HORDER, 1st Baron, of Ashford (Sir Thomas Jeeves Horder, G.C.V.O.). *b*: Shaftesbury 1871. *e*: Priv, Lond Univ, St Bart's Hosp. *m*: Geraldine Rose Deggett. *s*: 1. *d*: 2. *Publ*: Clinical Pathology in Practice; Cerebro Spinal Fever; Essentials of Medical Diagnosis; Health & a Day; Obscurantism; The Philosophy of Jesus (with Dr. Harry Roberts). *Rec*: Gardening. *c*: Garrick, Athenæum. *a*: 32 Devonshire Pl, London, W.1. *T*: Welbeck 2200.

HORE, Harry. *b*: Truro 1891. *e*: Truro Wesleyan. *m*: Adeline Brokensha. *s*: 1. *d*: 1. Journalist, Hon Sec Cornwall Branch N.U.J., Official Shorthand Writer to Ct of Cornwall Quarter Sessions, Official Shorthand Writer to Traffic Commiss for Western Traf Area (Cornwall), Official Shorthand Writer Truro Bankruptcy Court. *n.a*: Royal Cornwall Gazette, Truro, 1906—18, Chief Reporter, West Briton, Truro, '18. *s.s*: Sport, Court & Local Government Work. *Rec*: Cricket, football & bowls. *a*: 33 Woodville Terr, Daniell Rd, Truro. *T*: 2266.

HORGAN, James Bowring, M.B., B.A.O., M.Ch., D.L.O., R.C.S. *b*: Cork 1883. *e*: Clongowes Wood Coll, Roy Univ of Ireland, Univs of Vienna, Berlin & London. *m*: Margaret Wallace. *d*: 2. *n.a*: Mem Ed-Ctte Journ of Laryngology & Otology. *Ctr*: Journ of Laryngology, Rhinology & Otology, Brit Journ of Children's Diseases, B.M.J., The Practitioner, etc. *s.s*: Laryngology & Otology. *Rec*: Fishing. *a*: 11 Sidney Pl, Cork, & Clanloughlin, Cork. *T*: Cork 762.

HORGAN, John Joseph. *b*: Cork 1881. *e*: Clongowes Wood Col Co Kildare & Queen's Col. Cork. *m*: (1) Mary Windle; (2) Mary Brind. *s*: 3 *d*: 2. Solicitor. Coroner for Cork County 1914–. Chm Cork Harbour Commssrs '24—25. Chm I.F.S. Liquor Commssn '25—28. Mem Counc Inc Law Soc of Ireland '21—33. *Publ*: Great Catholic Laymen '08; Home Rule—A Critical Consideration; The Complete Grammar of Anarchy; The Cork City Management Act—Its Origin, Provisions, & Applications '29. *c.t*: Studies, Round Table, Irish Statesman, Listener. *s.s*: Legal, & econ, polit matters. Held Inquest on Lusitania victims at Kinsale, Co Cork 10 May '15. Gold Medallist Inc Law Soc of Ireland. *a*: Lacaduv, Cork, I.F.S. *t*: 1520.

HORGAN, Paul. *b*: Buffalo, N.Y. 1903. *e*: Nardin Acad Buffalo, Publ Schs Albuquerque New Mexico & New Mexico Mil Inst. Writer, Educator. *n.a*: Reporter-Critic Albuquerque Morning Journal 1921—22. *Publ*: The Common Heart; Far from Cibola; No Quarter Given; Main Line West; A Lamp on the Plains; The Return of the Weed (Lingering Walls); The Faults of Angels; Figures in a Landscape; New Mexico's Own Chronicle (with M. G. Fulton); etc. *Ctr*: Atlantic, New Yorker, Harpers, Sat Rev of Lit, Cosmopolitan, Good Housekeeping, Sat Ev Post, etc. *s.s*: U.S. South-west History. *Rec*: Pictures, music, tennis. *w.s*: World War II Chief Army Inf Branch (Lt-Col). *a*: Roswell, New Mexico, U.S.A.

HORI, TSUNEO: professor (univ.) of Economics; b. Hakodate, Hokkaido, Apr., 1896; s. Takujiro and Yaeko (Takao) H.; educ. Midc'e Sch. in Higher Normal Sch., Hiroshima; 3rd l 'ch Sch., Kyoto; Imperial Univ., Kyoto; DEGREES: Doctor of Economics (Kyoto), 1929; m. Hisako Ono, Sept., 1922. AUTHOR (in Japanese): Economy and Liberty, 1923; Ricardian Socialism, 1928; Ricardo's Theory of Value and the History of its Criticism, 1929; A History of Economics, Vol. I, 1931; Japanese translations: David Ricardo, Principles of Political Economy and Taxation, 1921; L. Pohle, Kapitalismus und Sozialismus, 1922; James Bonar, Malthus and His Work, 1930. Contributor to Keizai Ronso (Kyoto) and a few other magazines on economics. Relig. denom., Christian. CLUBS: Fellow of Royal Economic Society, Fellow of Economic History Society (England). OFFICE: Tohoku Imperial University, Sendai, Japan. HOME: 50 Nakasugiyama-dori Sendai, Miyagi Prefecture, Japan.

HORLER, Sydney. *b*: Leytonstone 1888. *e*: Colston Sch Bristol. *m*: Rose Ellen Piper. Novelist. *n.a*: Spec Corr Hulton Newspapers March 1911, Staff Dly Mail, Dly News, Dly Citizen '12—13. *Publ*: Over 100 novels. *s.s*: Mystery Fiction, Crime, Humour. *Rec*: Collecting pipes, bowls. *c*: R.A.C. *w.s*: Air Intelligence '14—18. *a*: Penrock, Bude, Cornwall. *T*: Bude 330.

HORN, David Bayne, M.A., D.Litt. *b*: Liberton 1901. *e*: Edinburgh Inst & Univ. *m*: Barbara Mary Scott. Univ Lect. Organiser, Edin W.E.A. *Publ*: Sir Charles Hanbury Williams & European Diplomacy 1747–58; A History of Europe 1789–1930; Part Author of a History of Europe 1648–1815; Part Author of the Edinburgh Source Book of British History 1603–1707. *c.t*: Eng Hist Review, Bulletin of the Inst of Hist Research. *s.s*: European diplomacy and British foreign policy in 18th, 19th and 20th cent, Spanish hist. *Rec*: Swimming, golfing. *a*: 67 Ladysmith Rd, Edinburgh. *t*: 41728.

HORN, Helen Primrose. *b*: Lon 1912. *e*: Priv. Author. *Publ*: Summer Cynics. *s.s*: Poetry, film criticism. *Rec*: Dancing, amateur dramatics. *a*: 25 Kilburn Priory, N.W.6.

HORN, Holloway. *b*: Goring-on-Thames 1886. Author. *Publ*: Old Desire; Harlequinade; Tyranny; George; Elusive Lady; Purple Claw; Jade Monkey. *Ctr*: Punch, Dly Mail, Ev Standard, Good Housekeeping, Tatler, Bystander, Passing Show, etc. *Rec*: Politics. *c*: Author's. *a*: Dalhousie, Buckhurst Rd, Bexhill-on-Sea. *T*: 1221.

HORNBORG, Birger Harald, M.A. *b*: Helsingfors 1890. *m*: Anna Irene Wiitanen. *s*: 1. *d*: 1. Author. *Publ*: Herr von Loewenecks kamp; Martin Türkheimer och huset Sonnenburgs hemligheter; Madame d'Ébère; Patron Illbergs ungdomsdarskap; Hakenskiölds pa Illerstad; Greve Alexejs son. *s.s*: History of families and individuals. War Service. 2nd Dir, Holger Schildts Forlagsaktiebolag (publishers). Knight of the Finnish Libertycross IV class, White Rose of Finland II class. Commander of Dannebrogsorden II class. Knight of the Prussian Iron Cross II class. *c*: P.E.N. *a*: 4 Sandviksgatan, Helsingfors, Finland. *t*: Helsingfors 26.288.

HORNBY, Montague Leyland, C.B., C.M.G., D.S.O. *b*: nr Shrewsbury, Shropshire 1870. *e*: Shrewsbury Sch, Roy Mil Coll Sandhurst. *m*: Harriet M. Corbett-Winder. *d*: 4. Soldier 1889—1927 (Ret Pay), Farmer. *Publ*: Canada's Steps Towards Immigration; Canada & Post-War Immigration; The Case for Organised Empire Migration; Canada & British Immigration; The Empire Builders; A Plan for British Community Settlements in Canada. *s.s*: Brit Empire Settlement & Development, Brit Immigration to Canada. *Rec*: Reading & writing. *c*: Army & Navy. *w.s*: Waziristan, N.W. Frontier, Gubaland, Nandi Expeds, Somaliland, World War I. *a*: The Hornby Farmes, Lethbridge, Alberta, Canada.

HORNE, Alderson Burrell. *b*: London 1863. *e*: Westminster & Pembroke Coll Oxf. *m*: Maud Porter. *s*: 1. *d*: 1. Actor, Manager, Built Westminster Theatre 1931. *Ctr*: Globe, Anti-Jacobin, Madras Times, Sat Rev, Nat Observer, Nineteenth Century, Morning Post. *s.s*: Tennis. *c*: Garrick, Beefsteak, M.C.C., Hurlingham, Queens, etc. *a*: K.2, Albany, Piccadilly, London, W.1.

HORNE, Rev. Edward Hastings, M.A.(Oxon). *b*: India 1862. *e*: Clifton Col & Trinity Col Oxf. *Publ*: Divine Clues to Sacred Prophecy (1901); The Meaning of the Apocalypse; The Meaning of Daniel's Visions ('30); etc. *a*: 64 Alum Chine Rd, Bournemouth, Hants.

HORNE, Jean. See Stephen, Jessie.

HORNE, John Greig. *b*: Kirkcaldy, Fife 1872. *e*: West Sch Kirkcaldy, Maray House Training Coll, Edin Univ. *m*: Annie H. Hunter. *s*: 3. *d*: 2. Motor Engineer. *Publ*: A Lan'wart Loon; The Flooer o' the Ling; Both of Them; Our Lallan Leid. *s.s*: Scots Lit generally. *Rec*: Cricket, music, gardening. *a*: Aberdalgie Cottage, Aberdalgie, Perth.

HORNE, Robert John Maule, M.A., B.Sc., M.B., Ch.B., D.P.H. *b*: Edin 1877. *e*: Daniel Stewart's Col, Edin Univ. *m*: Laura Katherine Davies. M.B., Ch.B. M.O.H. Formerly Dept of Physiology Edin Univ. *Publ*: Annual Reports on Health of Borough of Poole, Dorset 1921—34. *c.t*: Med & Scientific Journals. *s.s*: Preventive medicine, bacteriology, physiology. Col T.A. '27. Fel M.O.H. Soc & Roy San Inst; S. African & Gt War. *Rec*: Music. *a*: Grange, Mount Rd, Parkstone, Dorset. *t*: Parkstone 188.

HORNE, Walter Jobson, M.A., M.D., B.Ch., M.R.C.P., F.R.S.M. *b*: London. *e*: Tonbridge Sch, Clare Coll Camb, St. Bart's Hosp & Berlin Univ. Senior Cons Surgeon to Metropolitan Ear, Nose & Throat Hosp. *n.a*: Hon Ed Trans of Otological Soc of U.K. 1903—07. *Publ*: British Congress for the Prevention of Tuberculosis; Sixth International Otological Congress London & Compiler & Ed of Descriptive Catalogues of their Museums. *Ctr*: B.M.J., Lancet, Ency Medica, Times, etc. *s.s*: Diseases of the Ear, Nose & Throat. *Rec*: Bygones. *a*: Mereworth, nr Maidstone, Kent.

HORNECK, Augustus. *b*: Cashel, Co Tipperary, 1885. *e*: Grammar Sc Tipperary. Married. *s*: 3. *d*: 2. Jnlst. *n.a*: Ed Irish Peasant. Ed Waitara Times (Taranaki N.Z.). Dist Reporter Leinster Leader. Founder & Owner The National Phonographer. *c.t*: Meath's Roll of Honour & History of Trim, Weekly Independent, Leinster Leader, Meath Chron. *s.s*: Sporting. *Rec*: Motoring. *a*: Sea Mont Cottage, Laytown; & Brews Hill, Navan, Co Meath.

HORNER, Arnold. *b*: Halifax. Ed. *n.a*: Leeds Dly News (now Yorks Ev Post) 1897—1900, Yorks Ev Post 1900—05, Yorks Post '05—26, Sub-Ed '26—32, Chief Sub-Ed '32— Lanc Dly Post. *a*: Ed Lancs Daily Post, 127 Fishergate, Preston. *T*: 4841.

HORNER, Rev. B., M.A. *a*: Priory of the Resurrection, 77 Westbourne Terr W.2.

HORNER, Norman Gerald. M.A., M.D., F.R.C.P., F.R.C.S. *b*: 1882. *e*: Tonbridge Sch, Camb Univ & St. Bart's Hosp. *m*: Grace Malleson Fearon. *s*: 1. Ed B.M.J. 1928—46. *n.a*: Ed New York Hosp Journ '06 —07, Asst-Ed The Hospital '08—10, Asst-Ed The Lancet '11—15, Asst-Ed B.M.J. '17—28. *c*: Savile. *a*: B.M.A. Hse, Tavistock Sq, London, W.C.1.

HORNIBLOW, Barry. *e*: Sth America & Wallasey Gr Sch, Torquay Coll. Ed Yorkshire Ev Post 1946—. *n.a*: Formerly Staff Birmingham Gazette, Dly Mail, Dly Express, P.A., Dly Mirror (Production Ed), Sunday Chron (Chief Sub), Sunday Graphic (Asst-Ed), Ev News (Asst-Ed). *Publ*: Romance of Warwickshire; etc. *a*: 435 Otley Rd, Leeds. *T*: 73584.

HORNIBLOW, Edmund Charles Thomas, Hons.B.Sc. (Econ), F.R.G.S. *e*: St Olave's Gr Sch, Lond Univ & Lond Sch of Economics. Married. *d*: 1. Headmaster & Author. *Publ*: Lands & Life series of Human Geographies; Teaching of Geography in Junior Schools; Read, Laugh & Learn—Easy Senior Readers; (pt-author) The "March of Time" Histories. *Ctr*: Educational journs. *s.s*: Education, Geography, History & English. *a*: 11 Phillimore Gdns, Willesden, London, N.W.10. *T*: Willesden 2623.

HORNIMAN, Benjamin Guy. *b*: Dovercourt 1873. *e*: Portsmouth Gr Sch & Queen's Service House. Journalist & Author. *n.a*: Asst-Ed Statesman Calcutta 1906—12, Ed Bombay Chron '13—19, Indian National Herald '26 & Bombay Sentinel '33—45. *Publ*: Amritsar & Our Duty to India; The Agony of Amritsar (with Helena Normanton); Fifty Years of Journalism. *Ctr*: Various English & Indian journs. *a*: Bombay.

HORNSBY, Hazel Marie, M.A.(Oxon), Ph.D.(Dublin). *b*: Dublin 1900. *e*: Alexandra Sch & Coll Dublin, Margaret Hall Oxf. Library Asst. *Publ*: A Gelii Noctium Atticarum Liber 1. *Ctr*: Hermathena. *Rec*: Language study, cycling, sketching. *a*: 81 Wellington Rd, Dublin, Eire.

HORNSBY-WRIGHT, Lt.-Col. Guy Jeffreys, D.S.O., T.D. *Publ*: Alumni Felstediansess. *a*: 55 St Andrews St, Cam. *t*: 39.

HORODEZKY, Samuel Aba. b: Malin, Russia 1871. e: Univs of Berlin, Zurich & Berne. m: Marie Magasanik. Writer. n.a: Hagoren, Organ of Jewish Science 1897—1931. Publ: Le Korat ha Rabbanur; Ha-Chassidut weha-Chassidim; Torat R. Nachman Mi-Brazlaw; Torat Ha-Magid Mi-Meziritsh; Torat Ha-Kabbala Schel R.Moshe Cordovera; Ha-Mistorin Be-Israel; Shlosh Meot Shanah Shel-Jahdut Polen; Jahdut Ha-Sechel W-Jahdut Ha-Regesh. Ctr: Hameliz, Hazefirah, Doar, Dawar, Haolam, Ency Judaica, etc. s.s: Jewish Mysticism (Kabbala & Hassidism). a: Tel-Aviv, Rechov Hashoftim 8, Palestine.

HOROWITZ, Jacob, Ph.D. b: Kalusz 1901. e: Univ of Vienna. m: Etshi Stern. d: 1. Lit Ed Haaretz, Hebrew Daily, Ed Staff Ktubim '27, Turim '33. Publ: Or Zarua; Shaarei Tumea; Ad Dacca, Mizmor Hankama; Gilgulo Shel Eshen Hataliyan. Ctr: Haaretz, etc. s.s: Mediæval Hist. c: P.E.N. a: c/o Haaretz, Daily Newspaper, Tel-Aviv, P.O.B. 233, Palestine.

HOROWITZ, Phineas, B.Sc. (M/c). e: Public Sc & Univ. Editor & Director. n.a: Ed Mthly Pioneer '28—32, British Fur Trade '29—, World Jewry '34. Publ: The Jewish Question & Zionism. c.t: Encyclopedia of Psychology. s.s: Science. a: 100c Queen Victoria St, London, E.C.4. t: City 4911.

HORRABIN, James Francis. e: Peterborough Gr Sch, Sheffield Sch of Art. Artist & Journalist. n.a: Art Ed Yorks Telegraph & Star 1908—11, Staff Artist Star & News Chron Lond '11—, Television News Map Series '46—47. Publ: Atlas of Current Affairs; Atlas of European History; Atlas of Post-War Problems; Atlas of U.S.S.R.; Outline of Political Geography; Short History of British Empire; How Empires Grow; Japhet & Happy Annuals; etc. Ctr: Star, News Chron, etc. s.s: Geog, Internat Affairs. a: 16 Endersleigh Gdns, Hendon, London, N.W.4. T: Hendon 8936.

HORRABIN, Winifred, see (**Wynne, Freda.**) b: Sheffield. e: Elem & Sec Schs, Sheffield Sch of Art. m: J. F. Horrabin. Writer, Film & Dramatic Criticism. N.U.J. s.s: Women's & Labour Movements. Rec: Painting. c: Women's Press. a: 92 St John's Ct, Finchley Rd, London. N.W.3. T: Maida Vale 3643.

HORROCKS, John, B.Sc. b: Hindley, nr Wigan 1898. e: Glossop G.S. & Victoria Univ M/C. Bookkeeper, Hairdress & Hairdressers' Mang. c.t: Hairdressers Wkly Journ, Relay Mag, Dog World, People's Friend. s.s: Hairdressing, retail trading & bookkeeping, & popular science. a: 18 Salisbury St, Hadfield, M/C.

HORROCKS, Sir William Heaton, K.C.M.G., C.B.(Military), M.B.(Lon), B.Sc(L on & Vic). b: Bolton 1859. e: Owen's Col & Victoria Univ. Widower. s: 1. d: 1. Colonel (ret). n.a: Ex R.A.M.C. Journal 1908–. Publ: Bacteriological Examination of Water; etc. c.t: Proc B. Roy Soc, etc. s.s: Hygiene & bacteriology of water supplies. Ex-Hon Surg to H.M. the King. Chm Anti-Gas Cmt during War. Ex-Dir of Hygiene & Chm Army Hygiene Cmt. Mem Army Med Adv Bd, War Office 15 y. Rec: Golf, motoring. Hon Fell Soc of M.O.H.'s. Fell Roy San I. a: Birch Mead, Walton-on-Thames. t: 32.

HORROX, Lewis. b: Cheadle Hulme 1898. e: Gonville & Caius Col Cam. m: Gladys Maud Cawston. d: 1. Prof of Eng Lit. s.s: Eng & Greek poetry. Rec: Walking. a: The Cedars, Denmark Rd, Exeter. t: 4358.

HORSBURGH, Percy Gilbert, M.R.C.S., L.R.C.P. D.P.H. c.t: Various N/ps & Periodicals. a: Ravelston, Nuneaton, Warwicks, & Council Hse, Nuneaton Warwicks. t: 71 & 601.

HORSEFIELD, CANON FREDERIC JOHN: clergyman; b. Manchester, Eng., Aug., 1859; s. Thomas Stanley and Caroline Emma (Gardiner) H.; educ. Accrington Acad., St. Aidan's Coll., Birkenhead, (Eng.); DEGREE: D.D. (Intercollegiate); m. Ethel Mary Wilkins, 1900. AUTHOR: Life in a Cornish Village, 1893; Devotional Meditations on the Epistle of Ephesians, 1899; The Return of the King, 1917; Parables of the Second Coming, 1924; The Church and the Coming King, 1926; Life Radiant, 1927; The Voice of Prophecy, 1928; The Life of Service, 1930. Editor (1901-09): The Church of England Endeavourer. Contributor to The Life of Faith, Christian Herald, The Christian, Geueral character of writing, religious, prophetical. Curate (Lancashire charges), 1883-7; rector Albert Memorial Ch., Manchester, 1887-95; vicar, St. Silas, Bristol, 1895-1922; rector, High Roding, Essex, 1922-5; Hon. Canon Bristol Cathedral, 1919. Nat. pres. Brit. Union of Christian Endeavour, 1912. Fellow Ph. Soc. (England). Relig. denom., Church of England. HOME: 16 Windsor Road, St. Andrew's Park, Bristol, Eng.

HORSEFIELD, Leslie Graham, A.C.I.I. (" Systemat ", " Organiser ".) b: Bristol 1907. e: Monkton G.S. m: D. Rosamond Lippiatt. d: 1. Insurance. Publ: Practical Methods in Industrial Assurance. c.t: Insurance Mail, Agents Journ, Business. s.s: Insurance & staff training, efficiency. Rec: Tennis, photography. a: 7 Theresa Ave, Bishopston, Bristol.

HORSEY, Margaret Kennedy. e: Roedean & Girton. n.a: Asst Ed The Human Factor '28—s.s: Industrial psychology, philosophy. a: 4 Lansdowne Place. W.C.1. t: Terminus 6577.

HORSFALL, Alfred Herbert, D.S.O., T.D., M.B., B.S. b: Melbourne. e: Scotch Col. Melbourne & Melbourne Univ. m: Gertrude Emily Stokes. s: 1. d: 1. Surg, Electro-Therapy. c.t: Times, Daily Telegraph, Yorkshire Post, Sydney Morning Herald, Melbourne Herald, etc., & American & Canadian papers. s.s: Migration & land settlement in the Dominions; electro-therapy & light treatment of disease. Surg, in S. African War (Des), D.S.O. Served as Surg. Specialist & Officer i/c Surgical Div Base Hosp's, Gt War (Des). Fell Roy Empire Soc. Mem Roy Inst of Internat Affairs. Rec: Travel, motoring, gardening, music. a: Red Hse, Bexley Heath, Kent. t: 221.

HORSFALL, Magdalene. Publ: (for children) Fairy Latchkey (1900); Twins of Tumbledown Dreary; (historical) Maid Marvellous: Jeanne d'Arc; (travel) Vagabond Fortunes or Wayfaring in Provence (miscellaneous) London Again Again ('25). a: 38 Redcliffe Gdns, S.W.10. t: Flaxman 9962.

HORSFIELD, Hon. Mrs. A. E., M.A., Litt.D. b: London 1885. e: Newnham Coll Camb. m: George Horsfield. Historian, Mem Inst of Historical Research. Publ: The Children's Book of Art; A Ride through the Balkans; Henry VIII's Relations with Scotland & Ireland; Quarterly of the Dept of Antiquities in Palestine. Ctr: Ency Brit. s.s: History & Archæology. c: Curzon House. a: Allington Castle. Maidstone. Kent. T: 4080.

HORSFORD, Cyril Arthur Bennett, M.D., F.R.C.S., HonR.C.M. c.t: Med Journs. a: 24 Harley St, W.1. t: Langham 1384.

HORSLEY, Terence. b: West Hartlepool 1904. e: Rugby. m: Judith Rhoda Cartmell Ridley. s: 2. d: 1. Author-Journalist. n.a: Ed Sunday Empire News. Publ: Soaring Flight; Fishing for Trout & Salmon; Flying & Fishing; Sporting Pageant; The Long Flight; Find, Fix & Strike; Round England in an L8 Car; The Odyssey of an Out of Work; (pt-author) Norway

Invaded. *s.s*: Gliding, Fishing, Wildfowling. *w.s*: Pilot Fleet Air Arm '40—45. *c*: Roy Aero. *a*: Southwold, Hale, Cheshire. *T*: Altrincham 2010.

HORSNELL, Horace. *b*: St Leonards 1883. Author. *n.a*: Dramatic Critic Observer 1923. *Publ*: The Bankrupt ('13); The Talking Woman ('23); The Tyro's Vademecum ('32); The Horoscope ('34). *c.t*: Oberver (Dramatic Criticism). Pt Author with Herbert Farjeon of—Advertising April (Criterion 1922), & Pursuit of Adonis ('33). War Service '14—19. *a*: 6 Robert St. Adelphi. W.C.2.

HORSTMANN, Francis Cecil, A.R.C.A., A.T.D., F.I.B.D., F.R.S.A. *b*: Weston-super-Mare 1906. *e*: Weston-super-Mare Sch of Art, Roy Coll of Art South Kensington. *m*: Enid Beaumont Marcroft. *s*: 1. Head of Art Dept Brixton L.C.C. School of Building. *Publ*: Painting & Decorating & Paperhanging. *Ctr*: Journal of Decorative Art. *s.s*: Lettering Decoration & other Art subjects. *Rec*: Tennis, gardening, sketching. *a*: Uphill Cott, 77 Hayes Lane, Beckenham, Kent. *T*: Beckenham 5933.

HORSWELL, Horace. *b*: St Leonards 1883. Author & Dramatic Critic. *Publ*: The Talking Woman; The Bankrupt; The Tyro's Vade Mecum; The Horoscope; Man Alone; Castle Cottage; The Cool of the Evening; The Album; The Queen's Pleasure; (plays) Advertising April (with Herbert Farjeon) & Pursuit of Adonis. *a*: 7 Stone Bldgs, Lincoln's Inn, London, W.C.2.

HORT, Sir Arthur Fenton, Bt., M.A., V.M.H. (Horticultural). *b*: Cheltenham 1864. *e*: Marlboro' Col & Trinity Col Cam. *m*: Helen Frances Bell. *s*: 2. *d*: 1. Asst Master Harrow 1888-1922. *Publ*: Life & Letters of F.J.A. Hort (2 vols); The Unconventional Garden; St Mark in Greek; etc. *c.t*: Various. *Rec*: Gardening, fishing. *c*: Savile. *a*: Hurstbourne Tarrant, Andover, Hants. *t*: Hurstbourne Tarrant 44.

HORTH, Arthur Cawdron, F.R.S.A. *b*: Dorset 1874. *e*: Chandos Sc Hereford. *n.a*: Ed Practical Education & School Crafts 1923–, The Jun Craftsman '23, Advisory Ed Newnes Popular Home Book. *Publ*: 101 Things for a Boy to Make; Constructive & Decorative Woodwork; Design & Handicraft; Allied Arts & Crafts (with J. Littlejohns); etc. *c.t*: Harmsworth's Household Ency, Harmsworth's Business Ency. *s.s*: Arts & crafts. *Rec*: Sketching. *a*: 18 Leyland Rd, Lee, S.E.12. *t*: Lee Green 1418.

HORTON, Albert Edward. *b*: Coventry, 1881. *e*: Coventry Technical Institute, Saltley Training Col. *m*: Laura Elizabeth Mattocks. *s*: 1. *d*: 1. Head teacher Coventry Education Cmt. *Publ*: When I Became a Man. *Rec*: Football, tennis. War Service '16—19. *c*: Coventry Head Teachers' Assoc. *a*: 23 Melville Rd, Coventry, Warwicks.

HORTON, Douglas, D.D., Litt.D. *b*: Brooklyn, N.Y. 1891. *e*: New Coll Edin, Mansfield Coll Oxf, Univ of Tuebingen Germany, Lawrence Coll Chicago Theol Sem, Princeton Univ. *m*: (1) Carol Scudder Williams (dec'd), (2) Mildred Helen McAfee. *s*: 1. *d*: 3. Clergyman, Lect in Congregational Polity Union Theol Sem '43—. *Publ*: Out into Life; A Legend of the Grail; Taking a City; The Art of Living Today; Christian Vocation (in collab); The Basic Formula for Church Union (Ed); The Word of God & the Word of Man (Trans). *a*: 287 Fourth Ave, New York 10, N.Y., & Randolph, New Hampshire. *T*: Gramercy 5-2121.

HORTON, J. Sec E. Sussex Br N.U.J. *a*: Brentwood, The Greys, Eastbourne.

HORTON, Joseph Arthur, A.T.C.L., M.J.I. *b*: Handsworth 1899. *e*: Handsworth Gr Sch. *m*: Eva Marion Cotterill. Freelance Journalist & Official Shorthand Writer Ct of Appeal & M.O.T. *Ctr*: Times Trade Supp, Hardware Trade Journ, Confectionery Journ, Iron & Coal Trades Review, Express & Star W'hampton, Steel (Cleveland U.S.A.), Metal Bulletin. *Rec*: Music. *a*: 5 Beacon Rd, Sutton Coldfield, nr Birmingham. *T*: Sutton 2486.

HORTON, ROBERT FORMAN: clergyman; *b*. London, Eng., Sept. 15, 1855; *s*. Thomas Gallard and Sarah Ellen (Forman) H.; educ. Tettenhall Coll., Shrewsbury Sch., New College (Oxford); DEGREES: M.A. (Oxford), D.D. (Yale, U.S.A.); *m*. Isabel Violet Basden, Apr. 4, 1918. AUTHOR: History of the Romans, 1884; Inspiration of the Bible, 1887; Verbum Dei, 1891; Revelation and the Bible, 1893; John Howe, 1895; The Teaching of Jesus, 1897; The Commandments of Jesus, 1898; Oliver Cromwell, 1899; My Belief, 1902; Great Issues, 1904; Life of Tennyson, 1905; The Springs of Jay, 1915; Reconstruction, 1916; Autobiography, 1917; The Mystical Quest of Christ, 1924; The Capacity for God, 1926. General character of writing: religious, historical. Incumbent of Lyndhurst Rd. Congregational Church (Hampstead) since leaving Oxford. Chmn. Cong. Union of Eng. and Wales, 1903; pres. Free Church Council, 1905. Relig. denom., Congregationalist. HOME: Chesils, Christ Church Road, Hampstead, London, N.W.3, Eng.

HORTON, Robert J. Author. *Publ*: Rival Ranges; Rainbow Range; Bullets in the Sun; Riders of Paradise; Prairie's End; Bannister of Marble Range; etc. *a*: c/o Collins & Co Ltd. 48 Pall Mall. S.W.1.

HORTON, Ronald. Author & Publishers' Reader, Member of the Soc of Authors & Inst of Journalists. *Publ*: Dad Morgan (thriller series). *Ctr*: Answers, Weekly Telegraph, Blighty, Modern Reading, The Writer, etc & schoolboy adventure stories for the juvenile press. *a*: The Rectory, Pinxton, Nottingham. *T*: Pinxton 78.

HORTON, Rev. Samuel, F.R.S.A. *b*: Prees 1857. *e*: Prees National Sch & Sunderland Coll. *m*: Annie Harrison. *s*: 3. *d*: 5. Methodist Minister. *n.a*: Assoc-Ed Methodist Times 1917—31, Pres Primitive Meth Ch, Pres Met Free Ch Counc, Sec United Army Board '14—21. *Publ*: The Wentworth Books; The Rum Runner; The Diary of a Sky Pilot; Mrs. Marjorum's Money; The Invisible Shield; Another Parable Please; The Road to Rome; The Big Three; For King or Parliament; The Chapel on the Hill; Rainbow Farm; The Broken Wing; etc. *Ctr*: Holborn Rev, Free Ch Chronicle, Meth Times, Bapt Times, Young Methodism, etc. *Rec*: Trav. *c*: Nat Lib. *a*: 51 The Mall, London N.14. *T*: Palmers Green 2664.

HORTON, Victor Patrick Oswald, M.J.I. *b*: Brit Guiana 1905. *e*: Queenstown, Moravian Sec Sc & Queen's Col Brit Guiana. *m*: Valentine V. V. Nelson. *s*: 1. *d*: 1. Ed Prop The Outlook. *n.a*: Ed Staff Daily Gleaner, New Daily Chronicle Brit Guiana '26—30, Trinidad Guardian '30—32, Asst Ed Daily Mirror Trinidad '32—33. News Ed Nassau Guardian, Bahamas. Pres Berbice Shorthand Writers' Assoc Brit Guiana 2 y. *Rec*: Cricket, philately. *a*: 148—156 Harbour St, Kingston, Jamaica, B.W.I.

HORTON, Walter Marshall, M.A., B.D., Ph.D. *b*: Somerville, Mass 1895. *e*: Harvard Coll, Union Theol Semin & Univ of Columb. *m*: Lidie Loring Holt. Fairchild Prof of Theology Graduate Sch of Theol Oberlin College, Mem Amer Theol Soc. *Publ*: Theology in Transition; Can Christianity Save Civilization?; The Growth of Religion (collab); Theism & The Modern

Mood; Theism & The Scientific Spirit; Contemporary Continental Theology; Our Eternal Contemporary; etc. *Ctr*: Christian Century, Christendom, Religion in Life, Student World, etc. *s.s*: Theology, Philosophy, Religion. *Rec*: Music, travel. *a*: 248 Oak St, Oberlin, Ohio, U.S.A. *T*: Oberlin 738.

HORTON-SMITH, Lionel Graham Horton, M.A., F.S.A. (Scot). *b*: London 1871. *e*: Marlborough Coll & St John's Coll Camb. *m*: Nora Blanche Dorrington. *s*: 2. *d*: 2. Barrister. *n.a*: Jt-Ed Lond Scottish Regimental Gazette 1897—1901. *Publ*: Sophocles & Shakespeare (Latin); Oscan Word " Ansasaket "; Origin of Gerund & Gerundive; Establishment & Extension of Law of Thurneysen & Havet; Passing Thoughts; The Passing of the Great Fleet; The True " Truth " about the Navy; Keep the Flag Flying; The Declaration of London, National Starvation in War & The Paralysis of Britain's Power & Rights at Sea: Britain's Imminent Danger; The Fiery Fray; Perils of The Sea; How We Kept The Flag Flying; & numerous articles upon the Navy, National & Imperial Defence, etc. The Landlord & Tenant Act & many explanatory articles on same; Jamaica of 100 years Ago & Reminiscences of the Napoleonic Wars; Francis Baily, The Astronomer 1774—1844; Many articles & pamphlets on Family Historiology. *Ctr*: Principal Poets of the World, Poetry Quarterly, The Spring Anthology, etc, Daily & Periodical Press, Legal, Naval & Nautical, Genealogical & Antiquarian periodicals. *s.s*: The Law of Landlord & Tenant, Genealogical & Antiquarian matters. *Rec*: The Classics, Philology, poetry. *c*: Athenæum. *a*: 26 Rivercourt Rd, Ravenscroft Park, London, W.6, & 4 Paper Buildings, Temple, London, E.C.4. *T*: Riverside 2536 & Central 0192.

HORWILL, Herbert William, M.A. *b*: Sandown, I.O.W. 1864. *e*: Victoria Coll Jersey, Bible Chr Coll Shebbear, Wadham Coll Oxf. *m*: Kate Florence Bourne. Journalist. *n.a*: Asst-Ed Forum (N.Y.) & Reviewing Staff Nation (N.Y.) 1901—05, Lond Corr New York Ev Post '11—20, & Nation (N.Y.) '18—20, Lond Corr N.Y. Times Book Review '24—43. *Publ*: The Old Gospel in the New Era; The Usages of the American Constitution; Dictionary of Modern American Usage; American Variations; An Anglo-American Interpreter. *Ctr*: Atlantic Monthly, Contemp Rev, Fortnightly Rev, Times Lit Supp, Manch Guardian, etc. *s.s*: American Affairs. *a*: Grosvenor Hse, Grosvenor Gdns, St Leonards-on-Sea.

HORWOOD, Arthur Reginald, F.L.S. ("A. R. H.," " Robin Hood "). *b*: Leicester 1879. *e*: St John's Foundation Sc, Leatherhead. *m*: (1) Alice Maude Hencher; (2) Adelaide Elizabeth Phoebe Bridge. *s*: 12 (8 dec). Biologist & Geologist, Keeper Leicester City Museum & Art Gallery 1902—22, Botanist Kew '24—. *n.a*: Ed Hinckley Guardian & Gas, Light, Fuel '22. *Publ*: Plant Life in British Isles (3 vols '14—16); Practical Field Botany ('14); A New British Flora; The Outdoor Botanist; The Flora of Leicestershire & Rutland (with the late (3rd) Earl of Gainsborough); etc. Ed the Wood Plant (by the late Dr. J. B. Hurry '30); etc. *c.t*: All leading London & Prov N/ps & Magazines. Sport, Athletics, Army, Farm, Garden, Nature & Technical Trade Journs, etc. *s.s*: Sport & outdoor life. *Rec*: Field Sports. Extensive research work aided by grants from Brit Assoc & Roy Soc. War Service. *a*: Prospect Hse, 67 Boston Manor Rd, Brentford, Middx.

HOSE, H. F., M.A. *Publ*: Dulwich Latin Exercises; Articles in " Greece & Rome." *a*: Dulwich Col, S.E.21.

HOSIE (Lady) **Dorothea,** M.A.(Cantab). F.R.G.S. *b*: China 1885. *e*: Newnham Coll Camb & Bedford Coll Lond. *m*: Sir Alexander Hosie (dec'd). *s*: 1 (stepson). Vice-Princ Brampton Down School 1939—46, Lecturer & Freelance, Mem Roy Asiatic Soc. *n.a*: Observer, S. Times, Glas Herald, D Mail, D Express, Ev News, Roy Asiatic Journ, etc. *Publ*: Two Gentlemen of China; Portrait of a Chinese Lady; Brave New China; Pool of Ch'ien Lung; Jesus & Woman. *s.s*: China. *Rec*: Travel. *c*: Forum. *a*: Appletree Cottage, Redlynch, nr Salisbury, Wilts.

HOSKEN, Alice Cecil Seymour (" Coralie Stanton & Heath Hosken "). *b*: Lon. *e*: Paris & Heidelberg. *m*: Ernest Charles Heath Hosken. Author. *Publ*: Chance the Juggler (1903); The Forbidden Man; A Widow by Choice; The Sinners' Syndicate; The Love That Kills; The Tears of Desire; Thistles; Ironmouth; The Baggage of Fortune; The Buried Torch; The Oldest Land; The Man From the Bush ('33); etc. *c.t*: Princ mags & n/p's in Eng & U.S.A. *s.s*: Fiction. *a*: c/o Messrs A. P. Watt & Son, Hastings Hse, Norfolk St, Strand, W.C.2.

HOSKEN, CLIFFORD (pen name: Richard Keverne): author, journalist; b. Norwich, Eng., Aug. 29, 1882; s. John Jabez and Anne Elizabeth (Nash) H.; educ. privately for the British Navy; m. Emma Harris Foster, Aug. 12, 1911. AUTHOR: Cartaret's Cure (novel), 1926. Contributor to leading British newspapers; formerly on staff of London Daily Mail and for seventeen years a member of staff of London Daily Mirror. General character of writing: fiction, travel and antiquarian subjects, particularly medieval stained glass and Old English Inns. CLUBS: Savage (London), Dabchick Sailing (Oxford). HOME: 18 Argyle Mansions, Chelsea, and The Church House, Orford, Suffolk, Eng.

HOSKEN, ERNEST CHARLES HEATH (nom de plume: Pierre Costello): author; b. Norwich, Norfolk, Eug., Jan., 1875; s. James and Anne Elizabeth (Nash) H.; m. Alice Cecil Seymour Keay, 1901. AUTHOR: A Living Clue (play, in collab. with Armiger Harvey), 1 9 0 3. (All of the following in collab. with Coralie Stanton): Chance the Juggler, 1904; The Forbidden Man, 1905; Miriam Lemaire, Moneylender (pub. in U.S.A. under title: The Adventuress), 1906; A Widow by Choice, 1906; Zoe, 1906; All that a Man Hath, 1907; The Second Best, 1907; Sinners' Syndicate, 1907; Man Made Law, 1908; The Love That Kills, 1908; Tears of Desire, 1909; Plumage, 1910; A Sinner in Israel (under nom de plume of Pierre Costello), 1910; The Muzzled Ox, 1911; Swelling of Jordan, 1912; The Money Master, 1912; Tainted Lives (under the nom de plume of Pierre Costello), 1912; Dog Star, 1912; Called to Judgment, 1913; Raven, V. C., 1913; Thistles, 1914; Out of Her Depth, 1915; Ironmouth, 1916; The Baggage of Fortune, 1916; The Stranglehold, 1918; The Book of Ethel, 1918; The Buried Torch, 1920; **Confessions of a Rich Wife, 1921;** The May Fly, 1923; The White Horseman, 1925; The Oldest Land, 1927. Editor (fiction) London Daily Mail, Amalgamated Press and Pictorial Newspapers, Ltd., between 1905-1920. Contributor to many mags. and daily papers. General character of writing: novels, plays, essays, poems. Relig. denom., Church of England. CLUBS: Cocoa Tree, Savage (both London). OFFICE: A. P. Watt and Son, Hastings House, Norfolk St., Strand, London, W. C. HOME: Savage Club, Adelphi, London, W. C. 2, Eng.

HOSKIN, John Collins. *b*: Wadebridge 1891. *e*: Mutley Gr Sch Plymouth. *m*: Edith Runnalls. *s*: 1. *d*: 2. Journalist. *n.a*: Cornish Guardian Bodmin 1906—12, Mon Labour News '12, Cornish Leader '12—14, Cornish Times '19. *s.s*: Local Govt Politics. *Rec*: Gardening, chess. *a*: 2 Manley Terr, Liskeard, Cornwall. *T*: 2242.

HOSKINS, Halford Lancaster, M.A., Ph.D. *b*: Indiana 1891. *e*: Earlham Coll & Univ of Penna, Harvard & Chicago. *m*: Edna Alice Charles. *s*: 1. *d*: 1. Historian, Educational Administrator. *n.a*: Chm Ed-Bd Middle East Journ 1947—. *Publ*: British Routes to India;

European Imperialism in Africa; The Near East (jt-author). *Ctr*: Middle East Journ, Amer Political Sc & Historical Revs, Journ of Modern Hist, Amer Geog Journ, etc. *s.s*: European Colonial Enterprise in Near & Middle East, Africa, etc. *a*: 2500 Que St, N.W., Washington, D.C., & Peterborough, New Hampshire, U.S.A.

HOSKINS, Percy. *b*: Bridport, Dorset 1904. *e*: Weymouth & Sherbourne. Journalist. *n.a*: Ev Standard '24—38, D Express '38—. *Publ*: They Almost Escaped; Great Unsolved Crimes; Studies in Murder; Script for B.B.C. Series—It's Your Money They're After. *s.s*: Criminology. *c*: Press & Albany. *a*: 55 Park Lane, London, W.1. *T*: Grosvenor 1902.

HOSKINS, Roy Graham, M.A., M.D., Ph.D. *b*: Nevinville, Iowa 1880. *e*: Kansas State, Harvard & Johns Hopkins Univs. *m*: Gertrude Austin Pavey. *s*: 1. *d*: 1. Scientific Investigator. *n.a*: Ed-in-Chief Endocrinology 1917—40, Mang-Ed Journ of Endocrinology '40—42. *Publ*: Tides of Life; Endocrinology; Biology of Schizophrenia. *Ctr*: Numerous tech journs. *s.s*: Endocrinology, Psychiatry, Gerontology. *Rec*: Travel. *a*: 86 Varwick Rd, Waban, Massachusetts, U.S.A. *T*: Las. 5512.

HOSKINS, William George. *e*: Hele's Sch Exeter, Univ Coll Exeter. Univ Teacher. *Publ*: Industry, Trade & People in Exeter 1688—1800; The Heritage of Leicestershire. *Ctr*: Countryman, Economic Hist Review, etc. *s.s*: English Local Hist, Agrarian Hist. *a*: 39 Stoneygate Rd, Leicester. *T*: 77481.

HOSKYNS, Rev. Sir Edwyn Clement, M.C. *b*: Lon 1884. *e*: Haileybury & Jesus Co. Cam. *m*: Mary Trym Budden. *s*: 4. Fell Corpus Christi Cam. *Publ*: The Riddle of the New Testament; Eng Trans of Karl Barth's Epistle to the Romans; Essays in Mysterium Christi & Essays Catholic & Critical. *c*: Oxf & Cam. *a*: 43 Grange Rd, Cam. *t*: 1322.

HOSTER, Constance, F.I.S.A., F.I.L., F.I.P.S. *b*: Lon 1864. *m*: Albert Hoster (dec). Proprietress of Typewriting, Shorthand & Translation Offices & Secretarial Training Col for Educated Girls & Women. *Publ*: Style & Title (with Ellen, Countess of Desart). *c*: Ladies' Carlton, Overseas, Cowdray, Music, Musicians. *Rec*: Music. *a*: 1 Linden Gdns, Flat 5, Bayswater, W.2. *t*: Bayswater 2366.

HOSTETTER, Helen Pansy, B.A., M.S. *b*: Douglas, Nebraska 1895. *e*: Kansas State Coll, Univs of Nebraska & North-western. Educator & Free-lance Writer. *n.a*: Ed Journ of Home Economics 1941—46. *Ctr*: Kansas City Star, Christian Sc Monitor, etc. *s.s*: Foods, Nutrition, Child Care & Family Relations. *Rec*: Hiking, golf, bird study, music, theatre. *a*: Kansas State College, Manhattan, Kansas, U.S.A. *T*: 3547.

HOTCHKISS, George Burton, M.A. *b*: Naugatuck, Connecticut 1884. *e*: Naugatuck Hgh Sch, Yale Univ. *m*: Margaret Woodbary. *s*: 2. *d*: 4. Educator, Writer. *n.a*: Ed Watch Hill Life 1904—06, Rep N.Y. Ev. Sun '09—10, Mang-Ed Journ of Accountancy '11. *Publ*: Advertising Copy; An Outline of Advertising; Milestones of Marketing; Wheeler's Treatise of Commerce; The Birthright; Business Correspondence; etc. *Ctr*: Printer's Ink, Journ of Marketing, Sales Management, Journ of Retailing. *s.s*: Advertising, Business Writing, Hist of Market Distribution. *Rec*: Golf, chess. *c*: Authors (Lond), Marshall Chess (N.Y.). *a*: 149-33 Hawthorn Ave, Flushing, New York.

HOTINE, Rev. John. *b*: Aldershot 1891. *e*: King's Col Lon. Rector of Holcott. *Publ*: Mysteria Christi; The Precious Blood. *s.s*: Liturgy & Meditation. War Service 1914-18. Chaplain R.N. '25-27. *Rec*: Tennis, swimming. *a*: Holcott Rectory, Northampton. *t*: Walgrave 22.

HOTINE, Major Martin. *b*: Lon 1898. *e*: Southend H.S., R.M.A. Woolwich Magdalen Col Cam. *m*: Kate Pearson. *d*: 2. Army Officer. *Publ*: Simple Methods of Surveying from Air Photographs ('27); Celebration of Surveying Cameras, H.M.S.O.; The Fourcade Stereogoniometer, H.M.S.O.; Surveying from Air Photographs ('31); etc. *c.t*: Ency Brit, Empire Survey Review, Geog Journ. *s.s*: Air Survey. Research Officer Air Survey Cmt '25-30. I/c Geoderic Triangulation of the 30th Meridian in Tanganyika & Rhodesia '31-33. *c*: Jnr Army & Navy. *a*: 62 Shaftesbury Av, Southampton. *t*: 74783.

HOUGH, Eleanor M., M.A., Ph.D. *b*: Washington, D.C. 1892. *e*: Wellesley Coll & George Washington Univ. Sub-Ed Mem P.E.N. *n.a*: Sub-Ed The Aryan Path & The Indian P.E.N. *Publ*: The Co-operative Movement in India, Its Relation to a Sound National Economy. *Ctr*: Poetry Rev, Poetry of To-day, Illus Weekly, The Hindu, Bombay Chron, To-morrow, etc. *s.s*: Theosophy, The Co-operative Movement, Indian Literatures, Social Work. *a*: 22 Narayen Dabholkar Rd, Bombay 6, India. *T*: 42500.

HOUGH, Walter. *b*: Chorley 1871. *e*: St Georges Elem Sc & Chorley Tech Sc. *m*: Elizabeth Holmes. *s*: 2. Teacher & Consultant on Cotton Fabrics. Compiler of Fabric Section, Skinners Cotton Trade Directory, Technical Adviser to Sir Thomas Skinner & Co Publs. *Publ*: Encyclopedia of Cotton Fabrics (5 ed). *s.s*: Cotton fabrics. Founded the Sc of Cotton Fabrics '21. Mem of Brit Assoc of Mangs. Mem of Textile Teachers Assoc. *Rec*: Bowls. *a*: 41 Faulkner St, M/C & Charnock, Portland Rd, Swinton, M/C. *t*: City 8371.

HOUGHAM, ARTHUR: artisan, author; b. Birmingham, Eng., Apr. 6, 1889; s. Richard and Julia Ann (Rollerson) H.; educated in schools of Birmingham; m. Maggie Rodway, Mar. 31, 1918. AUTHOR: Gabriel Quelford, 1923; Hammer Marks, 1924; The Street of Velvet, 1925. Contributor to numerous newspapers and publications. General character of writing: novels. HOME: 82 Abbottsford Road, Birmingham, Eng.

HOUGHTON, A. V. Sec English Assoc. *a*: 4 Buckingham Gate, S.W.1. *t*: Victoria 4471.

HOUGHTON, Alfred Thomas, M.A., L.Th. *b*: Stafford 1896. *e*: Vict Coll Bath, Clarence Sch Weston-super-Mare, Lond Coll of Divinity, Univ Coll Durham. *m*: Coralie Mary Green. *s*: 2. *d*: 4. Gen Sec Bible Churchmen's Miss Soc, Asst Bish Designate Rangoon (1940—44), Asst Sec Inter-Varsity Fellowship Evangical Unions ('44—45). *Publ*: Dense Jungle Green; Tailum Jan; & 4 booklets. *Ctr*: World Dominion, The Churchman, The Record, etc. *s.s*: Burma; History of Missions, Missionary Principles, Methods & Strategy. *a*: 9 Ascott Ave, Ealing, London, W.5. *T*: Ealing 5761.

HOUGHTON, CLAUDE (pen name); (Claude Houghton Oldfield): chartered accountant, civil servant, writer; b. Sevenoaks, Kent, Eng.; s. George Sargent and Elizabeth Harriet (Thomas) O.; educ. Dulwich Coll.; DEGREES: A.C.A. (chartered accountant); m. Dulcie Helliwell (stage name: Dulcie Benson), 1920. AUTHOR: The Phantom Host, 1917; The Tavern of Dreams, 1919; Judas, 1922; In the House of the High Priest, 1923; The Kingdoms of the Spirit, 1924; Neighbours, 1926; The Riddle of Helena, 1927; Crisis, 1929; I am Jonathan Scrivener, 1930; A Hair Divides. Numerous Short stories. Contributor to Woman's Jnl.; Daily Mail; Sunday Pictorial; Scotsman, Britannia, Cape Argus, Montreal Star, and others. CLUBS: Savage (London). ADDRESS: Savage Club, Adelphi Terrace, London, Eng.

HOUGHTON, Rev. Frank, B.A. *b*: Stafford 1894. *e*: Grosvenor Sch Bath, Clarence Sch Weston-super-Mare, Lond Univ, Lond Sch of Divinity. *m*: Dorothy Hope

Cassels. Ed-Sec China Inland Mission 1928—, Gen Dir '40—, Bishop of Eastern Szechwan '37—40. *Publ*: George King, Medical Evangelist ; The Two Hundred ; China Calling. *s.s*: Missns in China. *a*: China Inland Mssn, 1351 Sinza Rd, Shanghai.

HOUGHTON, George William, O.B.E. *b*: Perth, Scotland 1905. *e*: Dronfield Gr Sch. Journalist & Artist, Dir Information Services Germany & Austria '45—46, Group Man Geo Newnes Ltd since '47. *n.a*: Continental Life 1926—27, Ed Nice Times '27, D Mail (Paris) '28 —38. *Publ*: Here's Looking at You, (caricatures) ; Adventures of a Gadabout ; Parade of Violence ; They Flew through Sand ; etc. *s.s*: Travel. *c*: Nat Lib. *w.s*: Group Capt R.A.F. '40—45 (despatches). *a*: Geo Newnes Ltd, Tower Hse, Strand, London, W.C.2.

HOUGHTON, Rev. Thomas. *b*: Cork 1859. *e*: Owens College Manchester. *m*: Elizabeth Ann Moseley. *s*: 4. *d*: 4. Clerk in Holy Orders. *n.a*: Ed The Gospel Mag 1916—. *Publ*: Liberal Evangelicism Criticised ; The Oxford Movement ; The Holy Spirit, His Deity, Personality & Operations. *Ctr*: English Churchman. *Rec*: Walking. *a*: Whitington Vicarage, Stoke Ferry, King's Lynn, Norfolk.

HOULT, Norah. *b*: Dublin. Author & Journalist. *Publ*: Poor Women ; Time Gentlemen Time ; Apartments to Let ; Youth Can't Be Served ; Holy Ireland ; Coming From the Fair ; Smiling on the Vine ; Augusta Steps Out ; There Were No Windows ; House Under Mars. *Ctr*: John o'London's Wkly, etc. *s.s*: Topical Articles, Book Reviewing, Short Stories. *Rec*: Walking. *a*: 56 Princes Sq, London, W.2.

HOUNSFIELD, Thirza M. *b*: Sheffield. *e*: Convent de la Retraite, Quimper, Finistere. F.L. Journalist, Writer. *n.a*: Drawing & Design 1921. *c.t*: Colour, Dispatch, Royal Mag, Tatler, Occult Review, Lon Forum, etc. *s.s*: Psychology, art, metaphysics. Pt Assoc Soc of Women Artists, Lon. Past Membre de la Société des Femmes Peintres, Paris. Past Mem N. Brit Artists. Formerly Landscape Painter, showed at Paris Salon & princ Lon Shows. *Rec*: Drawing, reading. *c*: Writers' & Pioneer, Writers' Circle. *a*: 63 St George's Sq. S.W.1.

HOUSDEN, Leslie George, O.B.E. *b*: Sydenham 1894. *e*: King's Sch Canterbury & Guy's Hosp. *m*: Esther Mary Josephine Boyt. *s*: 1. *d*: 3. Hon Med Adviser Save the Children Fund. *Publ*: Mothercraft ; The Breast-Fed Baby in General Practice ; Art of Mothercraft ; The Parent's Responsibility ; Home Life & The Community ; Handbook of Parentcraft. *s.s*: Parentcraft & Family Life, Study of Infants in health & disease. *a*: Mulberry Hill, Baughurst, Hants. *T*: Heath End 339.

HOUSE, Arthur Humphry. *b*: Sevenoaks, Kent 1908. *e*: Repton & Hertford Coll Oxf. *m*: Madeline Edith Church. *s*: 1. *d*: 2. Writer & Broadcaster, Lect Eng Calcutta Univ '37, William Noble Fell L'pool Univ '40 (resumed '45—46). *Publ*: Note Books & Papers of Gerard Manley Hopkins ; The Dickens World. *Ctr*: New Statesman & Nation, Manch Guardian, Listener, Spectator, Times Litt Supp, Lond Mercury. *s.s*: 19th-Cent Eng Literature & Social Hist. *w.s*: Roy Arm Cps Trooper 1940, invalided Major '45. *a*: 61 Bateman St, Cambridge. *T*: 56300.

HOUSE, Charles Frederick, F.J.I. *b*: Idle 1894. *e*: Beaminster Gr Sch Dorset. *m*: Ellen Ethel Bristow. *s*: 1. Ed Erith Observer & Kentish Times. *n.a*: Poultry World Sub-Ed 1919, Asst-Ed '22—25, Acting Ed Health & Strength '22—, Asst-Ed Bazaar, Exchange & Mart '26—28. *s.s*: Football, Cricket, Tennis, Hockey, Bowls. *c*: Erith Rotary. *w.s*: 1914—18 & '39—45. *a*: Frenella, 9 Wellington Rd, Belvedere, Kent. *T*: Erith 2630.

HOUSE, Evan E., J.P. Editor. *a*: Southern Times & Dorset County Chronicle, Weymouth.

HOUSE, Francis. *Publ*: What is the Kingdom of Heaven? (with Rev. C. Grant). *a*: c/o Methuen & Co Ltd, 36 Sussex St, W.C.2.

HOUSE, Rev. William Joseph. *b*: Abingdon 1870. *e*: City of Lon Sc & Wadham Col Oxf. *m*: Gertrude Mellor. *s*: 2. Rector of Copford. Hon Canon Chelmsford. *Publ*: History of Dunmow Parish Church. *c*: Commonwealth. *a*: Copford Rectory, Colchester.

HOUSEHOLD, Horace West, M.A. *b*: King's Lynn 1870. *e*: Shrewsbury, Christ Ch Oxf & Gray's Inn. *m*: Lucy Beatrice Noton. *s*: 2. Sec for Educ to Glos County Counc. *Publ*: Parts of Speech & their Uses 1901; Anson's Voyage round the World; Our Sea Power; Fighting for Sea Power in the Days of Sail; Our Guardian Fleets in 1805; Hellas the Forerunner (Vol 1 & 2). *c.t*: Contemporary Review, English Review, Poetry Review, etc. Formerly Asst Master at Clifton Col & Jr Insp under Board of Educ. *c*: Eng Speaking Union. *a*: Marybone, Tivoli Circus, Cheltenham & Shire Hall, Gloucester.

HOUSEMAN, John Wade, M.A., F.R.Hist.S. Headmaster Hipperholme Gr Sch Halifax. *n.a*: Ed Yorks Archæological Journ 1934—. *Ctr*: Yorks Arch Journ, papers Halifax Antiquarian Soc. *s.s*: Local Govt 1750—1850. *a*: Hipperholme Grammar School, Halifax.

HOUSMAN, Alfred Edward, M.A. *e*: Bromsgrove & St John's Col Oxf. Professor & Poet. *Publ*: A Shropshire Lad; Last Poems; etc. Prof of Latin Cam Univ. Mem Counc Soc of Authors. *a*: Trin Col, Cambridge.

HOUSMAN, Laurence. *b*: Bromsgrove 1865. *e*: Bromsgrove Sch, Nat Art Training Sch South Kensington. Author & Playwright. *n.a*: Art Critic to the Manch Guardian 1898—1907. *Publ*: Little Plays of St Francis ; Victoria Regina ; The Sheepfold ; Trimblering ; What Next ? ; Cornered Poets ; Palestine Plays ; Collected Poems. *Ctr*: Peace News, Time & Tide ; Hibbert Journal. *s.s*: Historical Plays. *Rec*: Reading. *a*: Longmeadow, Street, Somerset.

HOUSTON, Mary Galway. *b*: Co Derry 1871. *e*: Coleraine Academical Inst, Dublin Sc of Art, Royal Col of Art. Teacher of Drawing & Dress Designing Camberwell Sc of Arts & Crafts, also lecturer on Hist of Costume, *Publ*: Ancient Egyptian Costume; Ancient Greek & Byzantine Costume. *s.s*: Methods of teaching History of costume. Royal Exhibition Dublin Sc of Art, triple gold medallist for Figure Design Royal Col of Art. *a*: 20 The Quadrangle, Herne Hill, S.E.24.

HOUSTON, N. Roy, M.D., C.M., F.R.C.S.(Edin). Physician & Surg. *c.t*: Edin Med Journ. *a*: Lyons, 21 East St, Tonbridge, Kent.

HOUSTON, Robert Alexander, M.A., D.Sc., Ph.D., F.Inst.P. *b*: Glasgow 1883. *e*: Hilhead H Sch Glas & Glas, Gottingen & Camb Univs. Univ Lect. *Publ*: Studies in Light Production; An Introduction to Mathematical Physics ; A Treatise on Light ; Intermediate Physics ; Vision & Colour Vision ; etc. *Ctr*: Proc Roy Socs & Scientific journs. *s.s*: Light Maths,, Physics. *a*: University Glasgow.

HOUSTOUN, Robert Alexander, M.A., D.Sc, PhD., F.InstP. *b*: Glas 1883. *e*: Hillhead H.S. Glas & Glas, Göttingen & Cam Univs. Univ Lect. *Publ*: Studies in Light Production (1912); An Introduction to Mathematical Physics ('12); Intermediate Physics ('30); Vision & Colour Vision ('32); etc. *c.t*: Proc Roy Scos & scientific journals. *s.s*: Light, math physics. *a*: Univ, Glas.

HOVENDEN, G. S. *a*: Glebeholme, 99 Church Rd, Barnes, S.W.13.

HOVIS, William Forney, M.A., D.D., S.T.B. *b*: Wesley, Penna 1872. *e*: Allegheny Coll, Meadville & Garrett Biblical Inst, North-western Univ. *m*: (1) Aimee Parry (dec'd), (2) Ina Mosiman. *s*: 2. Methodist Minister (ret), Author & Editor. *n.a*: Ed & Author Cornelius Publs 1934—37 & Ken Mosiman Publs '37—. *Publ*: Quality Folks; Heart Sonnets; My Words; Consolation; Poetic Sermons; etc. *s.s*: Homely Philosophy, Short Stories, Classic Poetry Digests. *Rec*: Golf & travel. *c*: Rotary, etc. *a*: 4001 N. Prospect Ave, Milwaukee 11, Wisconsin, U.S.A. *T*: Edgewood 1425.

HOW, Most Rev. John Charles Halland, Hon.D.D.(Glas). *b*: London 1881. *e*: Christ Ch Cath Choir Sch Oxf, Pocklington Sch Yorks, St John's Coll Camb, Ely Theo Coll. *m*: (1) Naomi Reynolds (dec'd). *s*: 1. *d*: 1. (2) Barbara Collcutt. Bishop of Glasgow & Galloway, Primus of the Scott Episcopal Church, Chap H.M. King 1933—38, Lect St John's & Trin Colls Camb '07—24. *Publ*: Joel & Amos; Personal Discipleship; Christian & Churchman; The Sung Eucharist. *Ctr*: New Commentary. *s.s*: Theology. *Rec*: Walking. *a*: Bishop's Hse, 14 Cleveden Cresc, Glasgow, W.2. *T*: Western 554.

HOWARD, Sir Albert, C.I.E. Hon Sec Brit Sci Guild. Jt Hon Sec Parliamentary Sci Cmt. *Publ*: Crop-production in India ('24); The Development of Indian Agriculture; The Application of Science to Crop-production; The Waste products of Agriculture ('31). *c.t*: Journ of Agricultural Sci, Agricultural Journ of India, Memoirs of the Dept of Agriculture in India, etc. *a*: Brit Sci Guild, 6 John St, Adelphi, W.C.2. *t*: Temple Bar 2789.

HOWARD, Alexander. *b*: Sibiu 1900. *e*: Univ of Vienna & Lond Sch of Econ. Editor, Mem Soc of Editors. *n.a*: Jt-Ed The City Observer. *Publ*: Pictorial History of Russia; The Menacing Rise of Japan; Ten Men who made Russia; (all with Ernest Newman). *Ctr*: Various. *s.s*: International Affairs. *c*: Press. *a*: 95 Ivor Ct, Regent's Park, London, N.W.1. *T*: Paddington 6812.

HOWARD, Basil Alvin, M.A., B.A. *b*: Southampton 1895. *e*: Taunton's Sc Southampton & Sidney Sussex Col Cam. Schoolmaster. *Publ*: First Ideas of Trigonometry; School Trigonometry; The Mixed School, a Study of Co-Education; The Proper Study of Mankind. *c.t*: New Era, Journ of Educ. *s.s*: Mathematics, Co-Education. Headmaster Addey & Stanhope Sc, Ch Exam in Mathematics, Univ of Lon, etc. *a*: 75 Coleraine Rd, Blackheath S.E.3. *t*: Greenwich 1773.

HOWARD, Frederick James. *b*: London 1904. *m*: Margaret Gipps. Author & Journalist. *n.a*: Ed Stead's Review (Aust) '29—32, Spec Writer Melbourne Herald '32—39, Leader Writer '46—47. *Publ*: The Negroes Begin at Calais; The Immigrant; Leave Us the Glory; Return Ticket. *s.s*: Fiction, Australian Affairs, Military Hist. *Rec*: Reading. *c*: Navy, Army & Air Force (Victoria). *w.s*: '39—44. *a*: Upwey, Victoria, Australia.

HOWARD, Mrs. Geoffrey ("Joyce Colmer"). *b*: Lon 1892. *e*: Notting Hill H.S. & St Mary's Col Lancaster Gate. *m*: (1) Graham Colmer; (2) Geoffrey Howard. *d*: 1. Journalist. *n.a*: Ed Welldon's Lady's Journal 1923;

Ed Nursing Mirror, Nursery World '24 Ed Nursing Mirror. *c.t*: Lon & prov press. *s.s*: All nursing or nursery matters. *Rec*: Bridge. *a*: 6 Holland Pk Mansions, Holland Pk, W.14. *t*: Park 0337.

HOWARD, George Wren, M.A., M.C. *e*: Marlborough & Trinity Col, Cam. Managing Director Jonathan Cape Ltd. Hon Treas Publishers Assoc G.B. & I. *a*: 30 Bedford Sq, W.C.1.

HOWARD, Sir H. F. *a*: Traverston, 9 West Rd, Cambridge.

HOWARD, Harry Nicholas, M.A.(Miss), Ph.D.(Calif). *b*: Excelsior Springs, Missouri 1902. *m*: Virginia Faye Brubaker. *s*: 2. Historian Dept of State Washington D.C. & Chief Near East Branch Div of Research for Near East & Africa. *n.a*: Ed-Bd Journ of Modern Hist '42—45. *Publ*: The Partition of Turkey '13—23; The Balkan Conferences & The Balkan Entente; Military Government in the Panama Canal Zone; The Problem of the Turkish Straits. *Ctr*: Foreign Affairs, Middle East Journ, Americana, Nat Ency, etc. *s.s*: Modern & Recent Diplomatic History, esp S Eastern Europe & the Near East. *Rec*: Swimming & walking. *a*: 729 North Edison St, Arlington, Virginia, U.S.A. *T*: Glebe 3327.

HOWARD, James H. *n.a*: Ed Worksop Guardian. *s.s*: Sherwood Forest, The Dukeries. *a*: 22 Sherwood Rd, Worksop, Notts. *t*: 2 & 467.

HOWARD, Jean. *b*: London 1913. *e*: Public Sch. *m*: James Macgibbon. *s*: 2. *d*: 1. *Publ*: When the Weather's Changing. *Ctr*: Folios of New Writing, Penguin New Writing, Orion, English Story. *a*: 30 St Ann's Terr, London, N.W.8. *T*: Primrose 4398.

HOWARD, John Cyril. *b*: Oldham 1885. *e*: Stonyhurst Col, M/C Univ & Abroad. Schoolmaster & Journalist. *Publ*: Porter's Knot. *c.t*: Daily Mail, Evening Standard, Saturday Evening Post, Evening News, Windsor, Grand, Novel, Quiver, etc. *s.s*: French lit, fiction. War Service 1914-20. *Rec*: Shooting, deep-sea fishing, dog training. *c*: Soc of Authors. *a*: c/o Cam Lit Ag, 8 Henrietta St W.C.2. & Atlantic Hotel, Ostend, Belgium.

HOWARD, Louise Ernestine. *b*: London 1880. *e*: South Hampstead Hgh Sch & Newnham Coll Camb. *m*: Sir Albert Howard, C.I.E. *Publ*: The Earth's Green Carpet; Labour in Agriculture; Studies in Greek Tragedy; Germany in Revolution. *Ctr*: Classical journs & those dealing with internat affairs. *c*: Farmers'. *a*: 14 Liskeard Gdns, London, S.E.3.

HOWARD, Richard Christopher, F.R.S.M. *b*: London 1900. *e*: Sherborne, Paris, St George's Hosp. *m*: Elizabeth Hollister Fish. *s*: 1. *d*: 1. *Publ*: After Consulting Hours; Bedside Manners; Physic & Fancy; Paris Prelude. *Ctr*: Lancet. *s.s*: Medicine. *w.s*: R.A.F. 1918—19, '41—45. *a*: 26 Harley St, London, W.1; *T*: Langham 2809.

HOWARD, Rev. Robert Wilmot. *b*: Combe Down, Bath 1887. *e*: Weymouth Coll, Trin Coll Camb. *m*: Nora Katharine Carr. *s*: 1. *d*: 4. Master St Peter's Hall Oxf, Ex-Vice-Prin St Aidan's Theo Coll Birkenhead & Asst Master Eton Coll, Ex-Headmaster L'pool Coll. *n.a*: Ed Ch Missny Review 1922. *Publ*: Workers Together; A Merry Mountaineer (Life of Clifford Harris of Persia); Talks in Preparation for Confirmation. *Ctr*: Inner Life, C.E. Newsps, Internat National Review of Missions, etc. *s.s*: Foreign Missns Educ. *Rec*: Tennis, golf. *w.s*: C.F. 21st Div R.F.A. (World War I). *a*: St Peter's Hall, Oxford. *T*: Oxford 3063.

HOWARD, Sidney. b: Hornsey 1892. m: Eileen Maud Bickerton (dec). Journalist. n.a: Asst Lit Ed & Sub-Ed Daily Mail 1918—20, Lit Ed Daily Graphic '20—21, Mag Ed Sunday Illustrated '21—22, Film Crit Sunday Illustrated '22—23, Sub-Ed Daily News '24, Sub-Ed Westminster Gazette '24—28, Sub-Ed Daily Chronicle '28—30, Sub-Ed Sunday Dispatch '33, Sub-Ed The Star '34. Publ: Thames to Tahiti '33; Isles of Escape '34. c.t: Princ Nat Dailies & Weekly Periodicals. s.s: South Seas, foreign trav, humorous fiction, short stories. War Service '15—17, wounded. Sailed own yacht with one companion from Dover to Tahiti across Atlantic & Pacific Oceans '31—32. Rec: Sailing. c: Benfleet Yacht, N.U.J. a: 19 Regina Rd, Tollington Park, N.4. t: Archway 3535.

HOWARD, Stanford, F.R.C.S.(Eng). b: Ballarat 1898. e: Prince Alfred Col Adelaide, Ch Ch Oxf Lon Hosp. m: Thelma Lee. s: 1. d: 1. Cons Surg. Publ: Co-Author of new edition of Russell Howard's Practice of Surgery. c.t: Lancet, B.M.J. s.s: Surgery of the chest and genito-urinary organs. Rec: Tennis, golf. c: Oxf & Cam. a: 8 Harley St, W.1. & Denby, Gordon Ave, Stanmore. t: Stanmore 380.

HOWARD, Rev. Stanley Arthur, M.A. b: Norwich 1877. e: King Edward VI Sch Norwich & St Edmund Hall Oxf. Clerk in Holy Orders, Chapl Lichfield Theol Coll 1929—30 (Vice-Prin '30—31), Vicar of Wednesfield '32—42, Rector Stoke-on-Trent '42—45. n.a: '02—14 Eastern Daily Press. Publ: Instructions for Confirmation; Instructions on Holy Communion. Ctr: Eastern Daily Press, Wolverhampton Express & Star, The Sign. s.s: Religion. w.s: Imp Vols Sth Africa 1900—01, R.E's. '14—18. a: 38 New Hall St, Cannock, Staffs.

HOWARD, Thomas. F/L. c.t: Various trade papers. s.s: Advertising. a: 14 Clovelly Rd, Chorlton-cum-Hardy, Manchester.

HOWARD, Wilbert Francis, M.A.(Manch), B.D., D.D. (Lond), Hon. D.D.(St And & Manch). b: Gloucester 1880. e: K.E. Sch Birm & Didsbury Coll Manch. m: Winifred Worsleu Bedale. s: 2. d: 2. Princ & Lamplough Prof of New Testament Lang & Lit Handsworth Coll Birm. Publ: Critical Essay on Acts in the Study Bible; The Fourth Gospel in Recent Criticism & Interpretation; Christianity according to St John. Ctr: Lond Quarterly Review, Hibbert Journ, Expository Times, Religion in Life (N.Y), Journ of Theo Studies. a: Oakfield, Friary Rd, Handsworth Wood, Birmingham 20. T: Northern 0948.

HOWARD-BURY, Col. Charles Kenneth, D.S.O., J.P., D.L. Ret. Publ: Mount Everest—the Reconnaissance (1921). c.t: Journ of Roy Geog Soc & Journ Central Asian Soc. a: 94 Mount St, Lon & Belvedere Hse. Mullingar, Ire. t: Gros 2180.

HOWARD-JONES, John, M.D., D.Sc. b: Llanwrda 1866. e: Normal Coll Swansea, Univ of Edinburgh. m: Mildred L. Lang. s: 1. d: 3. M.O.H. Borough & Port of Newport Mon 1895—1932 (ret). Publ: Lectures on Marine Hygiene. Ctr: Journ of R.S.I., Public Health, etc. s.s: Marine Hygiene, etc. Rec: Fishing, golf, etc. c: Newport Golf. w.s: Lt-Col R.A.M.C.T., T.D. a: 45 Caerau Rd, Newport, Mon. T: 3880.

HOWARD-JONES, Norman, O.B.E., M.R.C.S., L.R.C.P. b: England 1909. e: St Paul's Sch Lond, St Bart's Hosp Med Coll. m: Ruth Fontes. s: 2. d: 1. n.a: Ed Brit Med Bulletin 1943—, Dir B.M.A. Brit Med Information Service '40—41. Ctr: Les Médecins Célèbres, B.M.J., Brit Med Bulletin, Britain To-Day, Monthly Science News, Pharmaceutical Journ, etc. s.s: Hist of Med, Drugs, New Med Discoveries & Achievements. Rec: Med hist, mod langs, travel. c: Savile. a: c/o National Provincial Bank, 250 Regent St, London, W.1.

HOWARD-WATSON, Julian Arthur, F.R.G.S., F.R.Hist.S., F.R.S.L. b: Marseilles 1880. e: Merchant Taylors Sch & Liverpool Univ. m: Lilian Agnes Ellison. s: 1. d: 1. Solicitor of Supreme Court & Notary Public, Mem Law Soc. Publ: Criminal Evidence (with N. W. Sibley). Ctr: Law Journ, Liverpool Post & E. Echo, etc. s.s: History & Legal subjects. Rec: Cricket, football, model ships. c: R.A.S.C., Conservative. w.s: World War I R.A.S.C. (Capt). a: Bella-Vista, Blundellsands, Liverpool. T: Central 3974 & Great Crosby 4473.

HOWARD-WILLIAMS, Ernest Leslie, M.C., M.A., A.F.R.Ae.S., F.R.G.S., F.Z.S. b: London 1895. e: Buxton Coll, Univ Coll Oxf, Jesus Coll Camb, Imperial Coll Lond, R.A.F. Staff Coll. m: Diana Bamber. s: 2. Author & Lecturer, R.A.F. 1915—42 (Air Commodore (ret)). n.a: Air Corr Dly Telegraph '42—44, Founder-Ed Air Mail '43—45, Off The Record '46—47. Publ: Something New Out of Africa; Air Over Eden; Immortal Memory; By Order of the Shah; The Air is the Future Career; Now Or Never; The Gen Book; What's the Gen?; Sh' Gremlins. Ctr: Dly Telegraph, Weekly Times, Dly Graphic, Illus Lond News, Air Mail, Sun Graphic, News of the World. s.s: Air, War, Travel, Yachting. Rec: Sailing, tennis, cricket. c: Roy Aero, R.A.F. Yacht. a: 27 Craven Terr, London, W.2. T: Paddington 0284.

HOWARTH, Harry. Printer & Publisher, C.C. (Lancs). n.a: The Padiham Advertiser, Burnley Labour Standard, East Lancs Sentinel. Publ: Big Money. s.s: Electricity, Finance. a: 216 Burnley Rd, Padiham, Lancs. T: 81.

HOWARTH, Henry, B.A. Publ: The Specific Euclid; Romance of Cotton. a: Oakleigh, Ribbleton Av, Preston. t: 2415.

HOWARTH, Herbert Lomax, M.A.(Oxon). n.a: Sheffield Independent, Westminster Gazette, Asst Mang Nottingham Journal Ltd 1924—28, Mang Ed & Dir ('33), Swindon Press Ltd '28—34, Gen Mang & Dir Northern Press Ltd (Shields Gazette, Shields News, Blyth News, Ashington Post, Alnwick and County Gazette '34—. Mem Town Counc, Vice-Chm Educ Cmt Swindon '31—34. a: Northern Press Ltd, South Shields. t: 896; Lyndhurst, Benton, Northumberland. t: 61439.

HOWARTH, James, F.J.I. b: Bolton 1866. e: Rivington G.S. Journalist. n.a: Official Reporter Hse of Commons (38 y). Publ: Parl Gazette. a: 21 Elmfield Mans, S.W.17.

HOWARTH, Osbert John Radclyffe, O.B.E., Hon.Ph.D. (Leeds). b: London 1877. e: Westminster & Ch Ch Oxf. m: Eleanor Katherine Paget. s: 2. d: 1. Curator, Darwin Memorial (Down House) Brit Assoc for Advancement of Science. Publ: The British Association, a Retrospect; The Scenic Heritage of England & Wales; Geography of the World (with W. Bridewell); & other geog text-books. s.s: Geography. Rec: Gardening, fishing. c: Athenæum. a: Down Hse, Downe, Farnborough, Kent. T: Farnborough 6.

HOWARTH, Robert. b: Prest Lancs. e: G.S. & Harris Inst Preston. m: Lettice Davies. Journalist. n.a: Preston Guardian 1885, & Lancs Evening Post, Daily Leader Swansea '88, Pembrokes Guardian, Bristol Mercury, Evening Express Exeter 1901, in '08 launched wkly in Northern Pem. In charge of S David's & S. Dogwell's Dist for Pembrokeshire Telegraph '25—. a: Fishguard, Pembrokeshire. t: 31.

HOWARTH, Walter Goldie. Aural Surg. n.a: Ed Journ of Laryngology & Otology '28—. c.t: Various med journs & periodicals. a: 149 Harley St, W.1. t: Welbeck 4444.

HOWAT, Reginald Douglas, L.R.C.P., L.R.C.S., L.R.F.P.& S. *b*: East Kilbride, Renfrewshire 1892. *e*: Kelvinside Acad, Glasgow Univ, London Hosp, Inst of Radiology, St Mary's & Charing Cross Hosps, Mem B.M.A. *n.a*: Adv & Reviewer Health & Efficiency 1922, Abstract-Ed, Butterworth's Med Pubs '37—. *Publ*: The Threshold of Motherhood ; Elements of Chromotherapy. *Ctr*: B.M.J., The Medical World, Brit Journ of Physical Medicine, etc. *s.s*: Electrotherapy & Gen Med subjects, Soc Problems, First Aid, Lyrics. *Rec*: Photography & music. *w.s*: 1916 B.R.C. & '41—46 R.A.M.C. (Capt). *a*: No 1 Beckwith Rd, Herne Hill, London, S.E.24. *T*: Brixton 5188.

HOWDEN, Charles R. A., M.A.(Edin), F.S.A. (Scot). *b*: Edin 1862. *e*: Edin Acad & Edin Univ. *m*: L. M. Hill. Advocate Sheriff Substitute of Inverness, Elgin & Nairn. *n.a*: Lect on Private Internat Law, Edin Univ 1909-17. *Publ*: Trusts, Trustees & the Trust Acts in Scotland; The Honours of Scotland (Scot Hist Soc); Contributions to Ency of Scots Law. *Rec*: Shooting, golf, chess. *c*: Univ Edin & Elgin. *a*: Mayne, Elgin. *t*: 271.

HOWE, Eric Graham, M.B.B.S., D.P.M. *b*: London 1897. *e*: Dulwich Coll, St Thomas's Hosp. *m*: Nora Blaxill. *s*: 1. *d*: 2. *Publ*: Motives & Mechanisms of the Mind ; Time & the Child ; I & Me ; The Open Way ; The Triumphant Spirit ; Invisible Anatomy. *Ctr*: Lancet, Journ of Brit Psychological Soc, Child Educ. *s.s*: Psychological Med, Educ. *a*: 146 Harley St, London, W.1, & Rosary Cottage, Coleshill, Bucks. *T*: Welbeck 2378 & Amersham 1265.

HOWE, George William Osborn, D.Sc.(Durham), Hon. D.Sc.(Adelaide), Hon.LL.D.(Glas), M.I.E.E. *b*: Charlton, Kent 1875. *e*: Roan Sch Greenwich, Woolwich Poly, Armstrong Coll Newcastle-on-Tyne. Prof Electrical Engineering. *n.a*: Tech Ed Wireless Engineer 1926—. *Publ*: Electrical Engineering by Thomälen (trans) ; Exercises in Electrical Engineering (with T. Mather). *Ctr*: Wireless Eng, Electrician, Journ Inst Elec Eng, Procs Phys Soc. *s.s*: Electrical Engineering, Radio. *Rec*: Music, travel. *c*: Savile. *a*: Lismore Hse, Kelvin Drive. Glasgow, N.W. *T*: Maryhill 1128.

HOWE, Harrison E. *n.a*: Ed Industrial & Engineering Chemistry. *Publ*: Chemistry in the World's Work ; Industrial Chemical Monographs (with Dr. Lee Lewis). *a*: c/o Chapman & Hall Ltd, Henrietta St, W.C.2.

HOWE, John Allen, O.B.E., B.Sc., F.G.S., M.I.M.M. *b*: Matlock, Bath 1869. *e*: Priv & Roy Coll of Science. *m*: Isabel S. Bickley. *s*: 1. Geologist (ret), former Asst-Dir Geological Survey England & Wales 1920—31. *Publ*: The Geology of Building Stones ; Stones & Quarries ; Stones of London ; Handbook to the Collection of Kaolin, China Clay & Chinastone ; Attrition Tests of Road-making Stones (with E. J. Lovegrove & J. S. Flett). *Ctr*: Ency Brit, Times, Mining Journ, The Quarry, Nature, British Clay Worker, etc. *s.s*: Economic Geology, Geology of Building Stones & Ore Deposits. *a*: Haling, Ashley Rd, Epsom, Surrey. *T*: Epsom 1046.

HOWE, Russell Warren, M.J.I. *b*: London 1925. *e*: City of London Freemen's Sch, Trin Hall Camb, Sorbonne. *m*: Lesley Louise Summerfield. Author & Journalist. *n.a*: Surrey County Herald series 1942—43, Middle East United Press '47. *Ctr*: Sketch Mag, Ev Standard, Manch Guardian, Shepherd Publs. *s.s*: Short Stories, Theatre, Cinema, Books, French Trans. *Rec*: Swimming, rowing. *c*: Internat, Old Freemen, Sutton Rugby. *a*: 125 Blvd St Michel, Paris, V. *T*: Odeon .

HOWE. Sonia E. *b*: St Petersburg 1871. *m*: Rev. S. W. Howe. *Publ*: A Thousand Years of Russian History ; Some Russian Heroes, Saints & Sinners ; The False Dimitri ; Real Russians ; Old Patterns in the Weaving ; Les Heros du Sahara ; Lyautey du Maroc ; L'Europe et Madagascar ; Les Grands Navigateurs ; In Search of Spices ; etc. *s.s*: Hist. *Rec*: Travel. *a*: c/o Christy & Moore, Ltd, Gerrards Cross, Bucks.

HOWE, Rev. William Norton, M.A. *b*: Castleton 1870. *e*: Macclesfield G.S. & Exeter Col Oxf. *m*: Dora Finchett. *d*: 1. Vicar of Sleaford, Rural Dean of S. Lafford. *Publ*: Animal Life in Italian Painting; The Eye of Erasmus. *c.t*: Ch Times, Guardian, Treasury, Architectural papers, etc. *s.s*: Architecture, hist. *Rec*: Painting, photog. *c*: Lincolns Artists' Soc. *a*: The Vic, Sleaford, Lincs.

HOWELL, Dr. J., C.B.E., F.R.C.S.(Eng). *a*: 7 Imperial Sq, Cheltenham.

HOWELL, Nancy Gwendoline. *b*: Llanelly 1901. *e*: Univ Col & Hosp Lon. Dep M.O.H. Acton. *c.t*: M.A.B. Annual Report 1928-29, L.C.C. Annual Report '31 & '32, Proc Roy Soc Med. Asst M.O. N.E. Hosp '27-32. Mem B.M.A., Soc M.O.H.'s. *a*: Munic Offices, Acton, W.3. *t*: Perivale 3142.

HOWELL, Trevor Henry, M.R.C.P.(Edin), F.R.S.M. *b*: Barnsley, Yorks 1908. *e*: Bradfield Coll, St Bart's Hosp & Univ of Edin. *m*: Margaret Greig Bannochie. *s*: 2. *d*: 2. Physician Geriatric Unit St John's Hosp London S.W.11. *Publ*: Old Age, Some Practical Points in Geriatrics. *Ctr*: Lancet, B.M.J., Geriatrics, Gerontology & other med journs. *s.s*: Old Age including Geriatrics & Gerontology. *Rec*: Swimming. *w.s*: R.A.M.C. (Major). *a*: 44 Highfield Rd, Purley, Surrey, & St John's Hospital, Battersea, London, S.W.11. *T*: Uplands 7855 & Battersea 1823.

HOWELLS, Rev. George, B.A.(Lon), M.A.(Cantab), B.Litt(Oxon), PhD.(Tübingen), D.D.(St And, Wales & Serampore). *b*: Cwm 1871. *e*: Pengam G.S., Regent's Pk & U.C.L., Mansfield & Jesus Cols Oxf, Christ's Col Cam & Tübingen Univ. *m*: Beebee Mary Sophia Phillips. *s*: 1. *d*: 1. *Publ*: Trans into Oriya, The Soul of India; An Introduction to the Study of Hinduism (Angus Lects); etc. Princ Emeritus of Serampore Col Bengal & Hon Lect in Comparative Religion, Univ Col Cardiff. Lect in O.T. Lit Rawdon Col Leeds. Originated a movement for the reorganisation of Serampore Col on the Univs Lines laid down by its founders Carey, Marshman & Ward 1900. Fell Univ of Calcutta 1913-29. Mem Bengal Legis Counc '18. Dean of Faculty of Arts '26-. *Rec*: Gardening. *a*: 19 Furnival St, E.C., & Serampore, Castleton, Cardiff.

HOWELLS, Rev. Thomas Benjamin. *b*: Knaresboro. *e*: Lon Univ & New Col Lon. *m*: Florence Millicent Bauckham. *Publ*: Roman & Anglican Claims, A Free Church View. *s.s*: Hist. *a*: Thele Hse, Stanstead Abbotts, Ware, Herts.

HOWELLS-JONES, W. *b*: Llangendeirne, Carm 1882. *e*: Llangendeirne & Llanelly Sec Schs. *m*: Janet Edith Dougall. *s*: 1. *d*: 2. News Ed & Review Ed Western Mail, Mem N.U.J. 1909—, Hon Sec Sth Wales & Mon Area Newsp Press Fund (18 yrs). *n.a*: Ed. charge Nth Wales Pioneer (8 yrs), Sub-Ed & Gallery Reporter Morning Post (6 yrs). *Publ*: Life of late Walter Whitehead, F.R.C.S., Pres B.M.A. *Ctr*: Princ newsps & periodicals. *s.s*: Book Reviewing. *Rec*: Golf, angling. *a*: 153 Cathedral Rd, Cardiff, Sth Wales. *T*: Cardiff 1730.

HOWES, Edith Annie, M.B.E. *b*: London. Teacher. *Publ*: The Sun's Babies ; The Cradle Ship ; The Long Bright Land ; Fairy Rings ; Rainbow Children ; Dream Girl's Garden ; Silver Island ; Drums of the Sea. *Ctr*: Many New Zealand Dailies & Mags. *s.s*: Nature & Fairy Tales for Children. *Rec*: Gardening. *a*: 11 Motu St St Clair, Dunedin, New Zealand.

HOWES, Frank Norman, D.Sc. *b*: Richmond, Sth Africa 1901. *e*: Durban Hgh Sch, Univ of Sth Africa, Univ of Lond. *m*: Marjorie Hepher. *s*: 1. Frm Scientific Officer Roy Botanic Gdns Kew, Botanical & Agricultural Work in Sth Africa, Gold Coast, Malaya, Java, Siam & other Eastern countries. *Publ*: Plants & Beekeeping; Vegetable Gums & Resins. *Ctr*: Kew Bulletin & various botanical & horticultural journs. *s.s*: Applied Botany, Agriculture. *Rec*: Tennis, gardening, beekeeping. *a*: Royal Botanic Gdns, Kew, Surrey. *T*: Richmond 1171 Ext 21.

HOWGRAVE-GRAHAM, Alan Herbert, M.C. *b*: London 1875. *e*: Highgate Gr Sch. Major on Retired List Union of S.A. Defence Force. *Publ*: Cold Feet (by Terence Mahon); The Verdict (by Tertium Quid); Mine Unbelief (by A. H. H. G.); School Music; The Dead Companions. *Ctr*: Light, Psychic Science, Psychic Observer. *s.s*: Psychical Research, Training of Children's Voices. *c*: Pretoria, New (Jo'burg), Authors. *w.s*: 1st World War. *a*: 116 Johnston St, Pretoria, Sth Africa. *T*: 2/0372.

HOWIE, Ian Alexander. *b*: Eastbourne 1914. *e*: Shrewsbury Sch. *m*: Barbara Purdey Allen. *s*: 1. Red Currant Wine & Cider Maker. *n.a*: Trends 1946. *Publ*: Supplement to Handbook of West African Gold Mines. *Ctr*: Gold Mining Record, Soundings, Trends. *s.s*: Stock Market Graphs & Chart Reading. *Rec*: Ski-ing, tennis, gardening, reading. *c*: Ski of Gt Brit. *w.s*: 1941—45 Armd Corps (Despatches). *a*: Horam Manor, Horam, Sussex. *T*: Horam Road 256.

HOWIE, Dr. J. E. Psychiatrist. Mem Roy Medico Psychol Assoc. *a*: Wood Villas, Clifton Rd, Prestwich, Manchester.

HOWIE, James William, M.D. *b*: Oldmeldrum, Aberdeenshire 1907. *e*: Robert Gordon's Coll Aberdeen, Univ of Aberdeen. *m*: Isabella Winifred Mitchell. *s*: 2. *d*: 1. Head of Pathology Div Rowett Research Inst Aberdeen 1946—. *n.a*: Asst-Ed Journ of Pathology & Bacteriology 1947—, Ed Army Med Dept Bulletin '43—45. *Ctr*: Glasgow Ev Times, Med & Scientific journs. *s.s*: Bacteriology, Nutrition & Infection. *Rec*: Golf & cricket. *w.s*: R.A.M.C. 1941—45. *a*: 8 Devonshire Rd, Aberdeen. *T*: 2680.

HOWITT, Dr. A. B., C.V.O., M.P. *a*: 15 Chesham St, Belgrave Sq, S.W.1.

HOWITT, Edith, A.R.C.M. *b*: Lon 1902. *e*: Priv & Roy Col of Music. Widow. Journalist. *n.a*: Ed Egyptian Mail '29—32, Corr Egypt for Daily Express & Interviews '30—32, Reporter News Chronicle. *s.s*: Egypt, French lang & lit. *Rec*: Music. *a*: Drellingore, Bexley, Kent. *t*: Bexley Heath 1236.

HOWITT, Frank Dutch, C.V.O., M.D., F.R.C.P. *b*: Nottingham 1894. *e*: Uppingham & Trinity Coll Camb. *m*: Violet Norris Leverton. Physician i/c Physical Medicine Mddx Hosp, Phys B.R.C. Clinic for Rheumatism. *Ctr*: Lancet, B.M.J., Practitioner. *s.s*: Rheumatism, Rehabilitation. *Rec*: Shooting, fishing, golf. *c*: Bath, Garrick. *a*: 87 Harley St, London, W.1. *T*: Welbeck 9020.

HOWLETT, Martin, Rt. Rev. Monsignor. *b*: Ireland 1863. *e*: Downside, Seminario Pontificio Romano Rome & Academia Ecclesiastica Rome. Administrator Westminster Cathedral & Canon Theologian of Arch-diocese of Westminster. *n.a*: Ed Westminster Cathedral Chronicle 1907—18. *Publ*: Rome and the Pre-Reformation Church; Catholic Emancipation; Vatican Policy. *c.t*: Times, Yorks Herald, Catholic Press. *s.s*: Hist, theology, etc. *a*: Westminster Cathedral, Clergy Hse, Francis St, S.W.1. *t*: Victoria 1959.

HOWSON, Ven. G. J. *Publ*: Overton in Days Gone By. *a*: 3 Gambier Terrace, Liverpool.

HOY, Hugh Cleland. *b*: Belfast 1886. *e*: Chr Bros. *m*: Lily Philpott. Journalist. *n.a*: Allied N/ps '20, Racing Ed Cape Times, Cape Town. *Publ*: 40 OB or How the War Was Won. *c.t*: Sunday Sun & Sunday Chron. *s.s*: Racing. Hansard Staff, Hse of Assembly, Cape Town, Priv Sec Earl of Denbigh, K.C.V.O. Confidential Asst to Dir Naval Int during War. *Rec*: Tennis, billiards. *a*: 17 Gainsborough Gdns, Golders Green, N.W.11. *t*: Speedwell 5344.

HOYER, Dr. Galina von ("Rachmanowa Alya"). *b*: Russia 1898. *e*: Univ. *m*: Dr. Arnulf von Hoyer. *s*: 1. Authoress. *Publ*: Geheimnisse un Tataren und Gotzen (1932); Studenten, Liebe, Tscheka und Tod (trans 12 lang's); Ehen im rotem Sturm; Milchfrau in Ottakring '33 (trans several lang's). *s.s*: Psych of woman. *a*: Salzburg, Itzling Blücherstrasse 5.

HOYLAND, Geoffrey. *b*: Birmingham 1889. *e*: King Edward's Sch Birm'ham, Univ of Birm'ham, St John's Coll Camb. *m*: E. Dorothea Cadbury. *s*: 1. Schoolmaster (ret). *Publ*: The Great Outlaw; Religion & the Family; The Man Who Made a School; Sermons in Schools; The Tyranny of Mathematics; The Resurrection Pattern; Pan's Wood. *s.s*: Educ, Religion & Science, Children's Stories, Hist, Archæol & Architect. *Rec*: Photography & archæology. *a*: Tocknells Hse, Painswick, Gloucester. *T*: 3258.

HOYLAND, John Somervell, M.A., F.R.Hist.Soc. *b*: Birmingham 1887. *e*: King Edward Sch Birm & Camb Univ. Married. *s*: 4. *d*: 1. Lecturer, Educ Missny in India 1922—28, Kaiser-i-Hind Gold Medal for public service. *Publ*: Book of Prayers for an Indian College; Indian Dawn; The Divine Companionship; Brief History of Civilization; The Cross Moves East; Simon the Zealot; Christ & the Saving of Civilization; Federate or Perish; Christ & National Reconstruction. *Ctr*: Contemp Rev, The Friend. *a*: Woodbrooke, Selly Oak, Birmingham.

HOYLE, Harry. Advertising Manager & Editor. *n.a*: Halifax & Dist Advertiser '31—35. Halifax Rugby League Programme '33—35. *s.s*: Advertising, sports. *a*: York Chambers, Wards End, Halifax. *t*: 4849.

HOYLE, Dr. J. C. Physician. *Publ*: Revision Whitla's Materia Medica 1933. *c.t*: Quarterly Journ of Med, Lancet, B.M.J., Journ of Physiology, Pract. *Rec*: Golf. *a*: 6 Queen Anne St, W.1. & Brierley, Kingsmead Av, Worcs Pk. *t*: Malden 1995.

HSIUNG, Shih.I., B.A., Ph.D. *b*: Nanchang, China 1902. *e*: Teachers' Coll Peking Nat Univ. *m*: Dymia Tsai. *s*: 3. *d*: 3. Mang-Dir Pantheon Theatre Shanghai '27—29, Mem P.E.N. *Publ*: Lady Precious Stream; The Romance of Western Chamber; The Professor from Peking; The Bridge of Heaven; The Life of Chiang Kai-Shek. *Ctr*: Leading Chinese & English periodicals. *s.s*: Drama, Chinese History. *Rec*: Theatre-going, calligraphy & painting. *a*: Iffley Turn House, Oxford. *T*: 7110.

HSU, Leonard Shih-Lien, B.A.(Stanford), M.A., Ph.D.(Iowa). *b*: Siangtan, Hunan, China, 1901. *e*: Stanford & Iowa Univs. *m*: Ruth Ruby Schmidt. *d*: 2. Univ teacher. *n.a*: In Chinese—Ed Sociological World, '27—, Ed Chinese Sociological Review, '29—, Man Ed The Chinese Economic Year Book, '33—, English Ed People's Tribune (Daily bi-lingual), '25—27, Assoc Ed Jnl of Sociology and Social Research, '28—. *Publ*: In English—Political Philosophy of Confucianism: Sun Yat-Sen, His

Social and Political Ideals; Outlines in Political Science; The Chinese Labour Laws, An English Translation; The Study of a Typical Chinese Town; in Chinese—Chinese Population Problems; Principles of Population; etc. *c.t*: American Jnl of Sociology, Sociology & Social Research, China Critic, Chinese Social & Political Science Review, Chinese Sociological Review, Central Daily, Eastern Miscellaneous. *s.s*: Social & political theory. *Rec*: Tennis, swimming, hiking, the theatre. Assisting Nat Govt of China in rural reconstruction. Sen Councillor to Ministry of Industries, Nat Govt of China, & Vice-Dir of Bureau of Rural Reconstruction, Nat Economic Council in China. Made special study of social & political conditions in England, France, Germany, U.S.S.R. '30—31. *c*: Inst of Sociology (London). Corr Mem Italian Cmt for Population Studies (Rome), American Sociological Soc, American Social Research Soc. *a*: Yenching University, Peiping, (Peking), China & Ministry of Industries, Nanking, China. *t*: 21674.

HUBBACK, Eva Marian. *b*: London 1886. *c*: Newnham Coll Camb. *m*: F. W. Hubback (dec'd). *s*: 1. *d*: 2. Princ Morley Coll for Working Men & Women. Mem Ed Bd Univs Quarterly. *Publ*: The Population of Britain; Population Facts and Policies. *Ctr*: Woman's Leader, Manch Guardian, Yorks Post. *a*: 19 Wellgarth Rd, London, N.W.11. *T*: Speedwell 1294.

HUBBACK, John Henry. *b*: London, 1844. *e*: Royal Naval Sc, New Cross. *m*: Mary Page Ingram (dec). *s*: 2. *d*: 5. *Publ*: Jane Austen's Sailor Brothers (with Mrs Francis Brown); Russian Realities; The Cotton Growing Countries, Present and Potential; Corn Trade Memories, Recent and Remote (with G. S. Broomhall); Cross Currents in a Long Life. *c.t*: Economics Journ, Nineteenth Century, The Times, Observer, Pioneer (India), Encyclopædia Britannica, Cornhill. *s.s*: Family history, travel, agricultural research. *Rec*: Chess. Great nephew of Jane Austen. Tech Adviser International Inst of Agriculture Rome '16—26. Mem Mersey Docks & Harbour Board 1888—'92, Pres Liverpool Corn Trade Assoc, 1886—'87. *a*: Audlem Vicarage, Nantwich. *t*: Audlem 332.

HUBBARD, Arthur John, M.D., L.R.C.P., M.R.C.S., L.S.A. *Publ*: Neolithic Dewponds & Cattleways (with Mr George Hubbard, F.S.A.); The Fate of Empires; The Ultimate Epoch ('28). *c.t*: Cornhill, Theology, Eng Review, etc. *a*: Little Dean, Glos.

HUBBARD, Cortlandt Van Dyke. *b*: Newton Centre, Mass 1912. *e*: Phillips Exeter Acad, Harvard Coll & Law Sch. *m*: Margaret Douglas Gribbel. *s*: 1. *a*: 2. Author & Illustrative Photographer. *Publ*: Practical Book of Garden Structures and Design (with H. D. Eberlein); Colonial Interiors; Portrait of a Colonial City; Historic Houses of the Hudson Valley; History of St Peter's Church-in-the-Great-Valley. *Ctr*: House & Garden, Country Life, Architectural Forum, etc. *Rec*: Golf. *c*: Pylon (Norristown), Penn, etc. *w.s*: 2nd World War Lt-Cdr U.S.N.R. *a*: 714 Hendren St, Roxborough, Phila, U.S.A.

HUBBARD, GEORGE: architect; b. Market Bosworth, Leicestershire, Eng., March, 1859; s. John Waddington and Emma (Evans) H.; educ. London Univ. Sch. DEGREES: F.S.A.: Fellow of Inst. British Architects; m. Sarah Eleonora Bouquette, 1892 (died). AUTHOR: Neolithic Dew Ponds and Cattleways (jointly with Dr. A. J. Hubbard), 1905; The Site of the Globe Playhouse of Shakespeare, 1923. Contributor to London Times, Pall Mall Gazette, Globe, Calendar of Royal Inst. of British Architects. General character of writing: archaeological, historical. Designer of numerous War Memorials, including County Memorials in Cambridgeshire, Montgomeryshire and Shropshire; also many public buildings. CLUB: Arts. (Hon.). HOME: 27 West Park, Eltham, London, S. E. 9, Eng.

HUBBARD, Harry Lovett, M.A.(Cantab). *b*: Lon 1890. *e*: Lancing, Selwyn Col Cam. *m*: Sybil May Hardy. *d*: 3. Vicar of All Saints' Margate. Six Preacher in Canterbury Cath. *Publ*: Bethlehem & Olives (verse); The Dreamland of Reality; Self-Training in Mysticism; A Golden Bowl; etc. *c.t*: Quest, Ch Times, Education. *s.s*: Chr mysticism. *a*: All Saints' Vicarage, Margate. *t*: 785.

HUBBARD, Hesketh, V.P., R.B.A., R.O.I., F.S.A. *b*: London 1892. *e*: Felsted. Painter, Lecturer, Writer. *Publ*: Materia Pictoria; Some Victorian Draughtsmen; How to Distinguish Prints; Outline History of the Royal Society of British Artists; Colour Block Print Making; Architectural Painting in Oils; etc. *Ctr*: Connoisseur, Studio, Apollo. *s.s*: Art. *Rec*: Chess. *c*: Athenæum, Arts, Burlington Fine Arts. *a*: E.4 Albany, Piccadilly, London, W.1. *T*: Regent 4939.

HUBBARD, William Woodbridge. *b*: Burton, N.B., Canada 1866. *e*: Sunbury County Gr Sch & Ontario Agric Coll. *m*: Anna Livinia Gregory. *s*: 1. Farmer, Fruit Grower & Journalist. *n.a*: Pt Proprietor & Ed Co-operative Farmer & Maritime Dairyman 1895—1901, Ed Maritime Homestead '01—02. *Ctr*: Family Herald & Weekly Star, Canadian Grower. *s.s*: General Farming, Live stock & Fruit Growing. *Rec*: Farm life and wintering in Florida. *a*: Burton Hill Orchards, R.R.1. Oromocto, N.B., Canada. *T*: Fredericton 5600—14.

HUBBLE, Edwin Powell, B.Sc., Ph.D., B.A. *b*: Marshfield, Miss 1889. *e*: Univs of Chicago & Oxford. *m*: Grace Burke. Scientific Research. *Publ*: The Realm of the Nebulæ; The Observational Approach to Cosmology. *Ctr*: U.S.A. Scientific Journs. *s.s*: Nebular astronomy & Cosmology. *Rec*: Fly-fishing & camping. *w.s*: World War I A.E.F. (Major) & World War II Ballistician Army Ordnance. *a*: 1340 Woodstock Drive, San Marino 5, California, U.S.A. *T*: Sycamore 3-7731.

HUBEL, EDUARD: see under pen name Metsanurk, Mait.

HUBENY, Maxmilian John, M.D. *n.a*: Ed Radiology. *a*: c/o W. Heinemann (Medical Books) Ltd, 99 Gt Russell St, W.C.1.

HUBER, Miriam Blanton, A.M., B.S., Ph.D.(Columb). *b*: Lynchburg, Tenn, U.S.A. *m*: (1) Victor H. Huber, (2) Frank S. Salisbury. *d*: 1. Author & Educator. *n.a*: Ed Macmillan Coy 1928—29, American Book Coy '29—32. *Publ*: Story and Verse for Children; Work-Play Books; The Wonder-Story Books; Care-Vocabulary Readers; The Poetry Book; The Uncle Remus Book; Children's Interests in Poetry; etc. *Ctr*: Various Educ journs. *s.s*: Children's Lit. *Rec*: Theatre, music, gardening. *c*: P.E.N. *a*: 1356 La Solana Drive, Altadena, Calif., U.S.A.

HUBI-NEWCOMBE, Georgeanne. *b*: Lon 1843. *e*: Priv. *m*: John Newcombe. *s*: 3. *d*: 1. Prof voice production, music & elocution. *Publ*: Lyric Poems; Writing Lyrics for Musical Setting; Guide to Song Writing; Janet; Dreamland-Wonderland (libretto & music); The Cost of Living; Eureka; The Shrew; Cross Purposes; Miss Penelope's Will; Whisper & I Shall Hear (song). *c.t*: Home & Abroad, Quarterly Mag, all monthly mags. *s.s*: Poems & humorous sketches. *Rec*: Motoring. *a*: Overbury-Furze Lne, Purley, Surrey. *t*: 676.

HUBREGTSE, Maria Eva, B.A.(Grey, O.F.S.). *b*: Bethlehem, Orange Free State 1886. High Sch Mistress, Writer, Translator in English, Afrikaans, Latin. *n.a*: Ed-Staff Die Boerevron 1924—25. *Publ*: (Afrikaans)

Loneliness; Four Friends; Vacation Times; School Readers & Anthologies. *Ctr*: Cape Town Weekly. Pretoria Daily, S.A. Railway Mag, etc. *s.s*: Travel Tales, *Rec*: Walking, climbing, travelling. *a*: 1 Goring Ave, Auckland Park, Johannesburg, South Africa. *T*: 31-1508.

HUCH, RICARDA: author; *b*. Braunschweig, Germany, July, 1864; *d*. Richard and Emelie (Hähn) Huch; DEGREE: Ph.D.; *m* Ermanno Ceconi, M.D. AUTHOR: Eronnerungen von Ludolf Ursleu (fiction), 1894; Blütezeit und Verfall der Romantik, 1899; Aus der Triumphgasse, 1900; Michdel Unger (fiction), 1902; von den Königen und der Krone (fiction), 1903; Die Geschichten von Garibaldi (historical novel), 1905; Aus dem Zeitalter des Risorgimento; Das Lieben des Federigo Gonpalonieri, 1907; Der letzte Sommer (novel), 1907; Der Grosse Krieg in Deutschland, 1914; Der Fall Deruga (fiction), 1914; Luthers Glaube, 1916; Der Sinn der heiligen Schrift, 1918; Michael Bakunin, 1920; Der Wiederkehrende Christus; Aus dom Alten Reich. Staedtebilder, 1926; Alte und neue Götter, 1930. Religion: Protestant. HOME: Uhlandstrasse 194. Charlottenburg, Germany.

HUCK, Sheriff. *b*: Berwick-on-Tweed 1909. *e*: Kindergarten Berwick, Barnard Castle Sc, Edin Univ. *m*: Adelaide Veronica Cairney. Journalist. *n.a*: Reporter & Ed S.E. Essex Advertiser '31, Reporter N. Ayrshire & Cumbrae Courier, Ed Scot Hosiery Trade Journ '32. *c.t*: Scottish Schools Echo, Amusement World, Broadcaster, Shoe & Leather News & many other trade journs. *s.s*: Adventurous fiction, yachting. *c*: Roy Largs Yacht, Northumberland Yacht, A.A. *a*: 22 Park Gdns, Corstorphine, Edin.

HUCKLE, Arthur James. *b*: St Neots 1869. *e*: Boro' Rd Col Isleworth. *m*: Annie Plomer Roles. *n.a*: Dir (Chm) Tavistock Printing Coy. *Publ*: Official Guide to Maidenhead. *c.t*: Western Morning News, Tavistock Gazette. *s.s*: Religious hist. *a*: Rockview, Tavistock, Devon.

HUDDLESTON, George, C.I.E., V.D. *b*: Calcutta 1862. *e*: Bedford Sc. *m*: Agnes Ellen O'Reilly. *s*: 1. Mang Dir Assam-Bengal Rly (Lon Bd). *Publ*: History of the East Indian Railway; Tales for the Train (India); The White Fakir (Lon); etc. *c.t*: Englishman (Calcutta), Rly Mag (Lon), G.I.P. Rly Mag (Bombay), etc. *s.s*: India, Rly Transport. E. Indian Rly Traffic Dept. Dir & Mang Dir Assam Bengal Rly Coy 1910–. Rly Transport Officer '14–17. E. Indian Rly Volunteer Rifle Corps. Private to Hon Lt-Col V.D. 1880–1910, etc. *Rec*: Painting, writing. *c*: Oriental, Brit Legion (Northwood Br). *a*: Newlands, Newferry Hill, Northwood, Middx. *t*: 659.

HUDDLESTON, Sisley. *b*: Barrow-in-Furness 1883. *m*: Jeanne Poirier. Author, Journalist, Lecturer. *n.a*: European Edit Corr Christian Science Monitor 1919–38, Staff Dly Mail (Paris) '14–18, Paris Corr Lond Times '21–24, Paris Corr Westminster Gazette, Observer, Dly Mirror, Sketch, John o' London's Wkly, etc. *Publ*: France; Literary & Bohemian Life in Paris; War Unless—; Between the River & the Hills; Normandy; In & About Paris; The Captain's Table; Louis XIV in Love & in War; Poincaré; France & the French; Back to Montparnasse; Le Livre de Saint Pierre; Lettres a un Ami Francais; Le Mythe de la Liberté; Cities & Men; In My Time; etc. *Ctr*: N.Y. Times, Atlantic Mthly, New Republic, Dly Mail, Dly Mirror, News Chronicle, etc. *s.s*: Internat Politics, Continental Life, Hist, Criticism & Personalities. *c*: Authors. *a*: St Pierre d'Autils par Vernon, France. *T*: St Pierre d'Autils 4.

HUDDY, G. P. B., M.S.(Lon), F.R.C.S.(Eng), Surgeon Dudley Rd, Hosp Birm (ret). *Publ*: Duodenal Diverticula; Carotid Cavernous Sinus Aneurysm; Family Histories in Upper Abdominal Lesions; etc. *c.t*: Brit Journal of Surgery, Lancet, Clinical Journal. Late Capt R.A.M.C.

HUDIG, FERRAND WHALEY: professor; *b*. Rotterdam, Holland, June, 1883; *s*. Jan and Johanna (Quarles van Ufford) H.; *educ*. Gymnasium, Rotterdam, Universities Berlin and Zürich; DEGREES: Ph.D.; *m*. Margareta Frey, 1920. AUTHOR: Engelsch Aardewerk en Porcelein, 1922; Das Glas, 1923; Kunstgeschiedenis als deel der Beschavingsgeschiedenis, 1924; Essay on Dutch Glass Engravers, 1926; Frederik Hendrik en de Kunst van zijn Tyd, 1928; Delfter Fayence, 1929. Editor of Oud-Holland. Contributor to Oud-Holland, Onze Kunst, Oudheidkundig Jaarboek, Elseviers Maandblad, Tydschrift voor Geschiedenis, Op de Hoogte, Old Furniture, Art and Archaeology, Parnassus, Antiques. General character of writing: history of arts. Assistant director of Ryksmuseum, Amsterdam, 1918-1928; appointed professor of history of arts of the middle ages and modern times, University of Amsterdam, 1928. ADDRESS: Zuidlaan 1, Aerdenhout. Holland.

HUDIG-FREY, MARGARETA: writer; *b*. Zürich, Switzerland, January, 1894; *d*. Emile Frey and Josephine (Zumbuehl) Frey; *educ*. Gymnasium (Zürich); Univs. of Roma, Munich and Berlin. DEGREES: Ph.D. (Berlin); *m*. Ferrand Whaley Hudig, 1920. AUTHOR: Dia aelteste Illustration der Eneide des Heinrich von Veldeke, 1920. Contributes to: Ondheidkundig Jaarboek, Die Garbe (Basel), Tijdschrift voor Geschiedenis. General character of writing: history of arts. Member of International Federation of University Women. Religion, Roman Catholic. HOME: Zuidlaan 1, Aerdenhont, Holland.

HUDLESTON, Christophe Roy. *b*: Stroud, Glos 1905. *e*: Wycliffe Coll Glos. *m*: (1) Winifred Hawkins, (2) Patricia Sealey, (3) Joyce Hodson. *d*: 1. Ed Mang Penrith Observer. *n.a*: Bristol Times & Mirror '23–32, Lit Ed Bristol Ev Post '32—41, Forestry Work '41—45, Ed-Mang Penrith Observer since '45. *Publ*: How to See Bristol; Our Native City; Registers of Bristol Cathedral; History of Clutterbuck Family (in collab). *Ctr*: Notes & Queries, Archæolog Journ. *s.s*: Genealogy, Local History. *Rec*: Writing, reading, gardening, amateur theatricals. *a*: Laurel Bank, Penrith, Cumberland. *T*: 2482.

HUDSON, Arthur, M.A., K.C. *b*: Wisbech 1861. *e*: Balliol Col, Oxf. *m*: Mary Rose McBarnet. *s*: 1. Colonial Judge (ret). *Publ*: The Call of the Nation; A French Grammar; etc. *c.t*: Lon daily n/p's. Dis Commssr Sierra Leone 1896. Solicitor Gen '98. Attorney Gen 1901. Puisne Judge '03-08. Attorney Gen Gold Coast '08–12. *Rec*: Travel. *c*: St James, Authors, Un. *a*: 2 Vicarage Gdns, Kensington. *t*: Bayswater 2746.

HUDSON, C. H. *n.a*: Sub-Ed Oxford Times. *a*: 542 Banbury Rd, Oxford.

HUDSON, Rev. Canon Cyril Edward. *b*: Bury 1888. *e*: St. Bess' Sch, Queen's Coll Oxf, Bishop's Colls Cheshunt. Canon Residentiary St Albans. *Publ*: Nations as Neighbours; Preface to a Christian Sociology; The Church & the World (with M. B. Reckitt); A Manual of Pastoral Psychology (with L. Dewar); An Introduction to Pastoral Theology (with H. Balmforth & others). *Ctr*: Prospect for Christendom (ed M. B. Reckitt), Christendom, Theology, Internat Affairs, New Eng Weekly. *c*: United Univ. *a*: Hillingdon, St Albans, Herts. *T*: St Albans 707.

HUDSON, Derek, M.A. *b*: London 1911. *e*: Shrewsbury Sch, Merton Coll Oxf. *m*: Yvonne Patricia O'Neill. *d*: 1. Author & Journalist. *n.a*: Ed Staff Birmingham Post '37, Times '39. *Publ*: A Poet in Parliament; Thomas Barnes of the Times; Charles Keene; Norman O'Neill, A Life of Music; British Journalists & Newspapers; On the Sland (play, with A. Goldsmith). *Ctr*: Cornhill Mag, National Review, Spectator, etc. *s.s*: 18th- & 19th-Cent Hist, Hist of Journalism. *Rec*: Tennis, cricket, walking. *c*: Nat Lib. *a*: 37 Overstrand Mans, Prince of Wales Drive, London, S.W.11. *T*: Macaulay 3103.

HUDSON, Edward. Ed Country Life 1897—. *a*: 20 Tavistock St, Covent Garden. *t*: Temple Bar 7351.

HUDSON, Rev. Egbert Claud, M.A., F.S.A., Canon of York. *b*: Dulwich 1881. *e*: Trin Coll Camb & Univ Coll Lond. *m*: Annie M. P. Dunn. *s*: 1. *d*: 1. Rector of Gilling & Prebendary of Weighton in York Minster, Select Preacher Camb Univ 1942, Gov Arch Holgate's Gr Sch, Dir York Dispensary. *Publ*: A Central African Parish; The Registers of Gilling York; Picidian Antioch & the Xenou Tekmoreioi; A Yorkshire Country Parish. *Ctr*: Theology, The Guardian, Yorkshire Herald, Yorks Arch Journ. *s.s*: Antiquities & Early History of Asia Minor, Zanzibar & Tanganyika. *w.s*: C.F. Macedonia & Asia Minor '17—19. *a*: Gilling Rectory, York. *T*: Ampleforth 254.

HUDSON, Frederick John. *b*: Bicester 1889. *m*: Evelyn R. Pearce. *d*: 4 (1 dec). Sub-Ed & Chief Reporter. *n.a*: Reporter, Bicester Advertiser 1903—12, Rugby Advertiser '12—, Mem N.U.J. '17, Sec Rugby Dickens Fellowship. Chairman Coventry & Warwickshire N.U.J. '22—23 (approx), Chrm Birm & Midland I.J. '26—27. *c*: Rugby Conservative. *a*: 17 Westgate Rd, Hillmorton Paddox, Rugby. *t*: 740.

HUDSON, Gilbert, L.R.A.M., M.R.S.T. Prof of Elocution in Trin Col of Music Lon. *a*: Elm Croft, Berkhamsted.

HUDSON, Harald Hazard. *b*: Middlesboro' 1885. *e*: Wesleyan Ch Sc. *m*: Helena Blanche Easton. *s*: 1. *d*: 1. Chief Rep & Leader Note Writer Newcastle Daily Journal. *n.a*: N.E. Daily Gazette, Winnepeg Telegraph, Winnepeg Tribune, N. Mail, Evening Mail, (all between 1900 & '19), Newcastle Daily Journ 1919—. *s.s*: Stage, cinema, art. *Rec*: Golf, swimming, cycling. *a*: Parkdale, Jesmond Park West, Newcastle-on-Tyne.

HUDSON, Rev. Henry Arnold, M.A. *b*: M/C 1863. *e*: Oxf. Retired. *n.a*: Ed Trans of Lancs & Cheshire Antiquarian Soc 1923–. *Publ*: Mediæval Woodwork of Manchester Cathedral; Memorials of the Old Church of Manchester; Churches of Holland; Ed Recollections of the Old Church of Manchester; etc. *c.t*: Trans Lancs & Cheshire Antiq Soc & Hist Soc, M/C Guardian, The Sign, etc. *s.s*: Ecclesiology. Fell Soc of Antiq's (Lon). Mem Dio Adv Cmt M/C & Coventry, etc. *Rec*: Art, archæ. *a*: 19 Adelaide Rd, Leamington Spa.

HUDSON, Rev. Herbert Kynaston. M.A. *b*: London 1864. *e*: St Paul's Sch, Christ's Hosp, Wadham Coll Oxf. *m*: *s*: 3. *d*: 4. Vicar of Berden Essex 1899—1938. *Publ*: Ed: The Simple Psalter; Fire Protection. *Ctr*: Sentinel, Faith Press Quarterly, Bath Chron, etc. *s.s*: Church Music. *Rec*: Photography, sketching. *c*: Old Pauline, Christ's Hosp. *a*: Wadham, West Mersea, Colchester.

HUDSON, Rev. James T., B.A., B.D. *c.t*: Expository Times, Meth Recorder. *a*: Manse, Tredegar, Mon.

HUDSON, Jay William, A.M., Ph.D. *b*: Cleveland, Ohio 1874. *e*: Hiram Coll, Oberlin Coll & Univs of Calif & Harvard. *m*: Germaine Sansot. Visiting Prof Stephens Coll. *Publ*: Abbé Pierre; The College & New America; The Truths We Live By; The Eternal Circle; Nowhere Else in the World; Abbé Pierre's People; The Old Faiths Perish; Why Democracy?; The Treatment of Personality by Locke, Berkeley & Hume; America's International Ideals; Morning in Gascony. *Ctr*: Internat Journ of Ethics, Philos Rev, Journ of Philos, etc. *s.s*: Ethics, Political Science, Metaphysics. *Rec*: Billiards, walking, music. *w.s*: 1918 Amer Red Cross (Capt). *a*: University of Missouri, & 216 Edgewood Ave, Columbia, Missouri, U.S.A. *T*: 6708.

HUDSON, John C. *b*: N. Bucks. *e*: Priv Scs. Widower. *n.a*: Ed The Salisbury Times 1900—. Mayor of Salisbury '26—27 & Alderman of City Counc. *a*: Strathavon, Mill Rd, Salisbury, Wilts.

HUDSON, Stephen. *Publ*: A True Story; Tony; Richard, Myrtle & I; Myrtle. *a*: c/o Constable & Co, 10—12 Orange St, Leicester Sq, W.C.2.

HUDSON, Wilfred Frank Flexmore. *b*: Charters Towers, Queensland 1913. *e*: Adelaide Hgh Sch, Teachers' Coll & Univ. *m*: Myrle Desmond. Author & Editor, Fell Fellowship Australian Writers. *n.a*: Ed Poetry '41—, Austral Lit Corr Briarcliff Lit Quarterly (New York) '45—. *Publ*: As Iron Hills; In the Wind's Teeth; Indelible Voices; With the First Soft Rain; Ashes & Sparks; The Child Discovers Poetry. - *Ctr*: Poetry, Albion, Briarcliff Quarterly, Meanjin Papers, Jindyworobak Annual, Anthology, etc. *s.s*: Modern & French Poetry, Aesthetics, Hist of Australia & Pacific Islands. *Rec*: Riding, swimming, boxing, rowing, Fr & Ital languages, philosophy. *a*: 22 Nist St, Glen Iris, SE 6, Victoria, Australia. *T*: U9496.

HUDSON-WILLIAMS, Thomas, M.A., D.Litt. *b*: Cærnarvon 1873. *e*: Bd Sch Cærnarvon, Friars Sch, Bangor Univ Coll, Nth Wales & Greifswald Univ. *m*: Gwladys Prichard Williams. *s*: 2. *d*: 1. Emeritus Prof Greek Univ Coll Wales. *Publ*: The Elegies of Theognis; Early Greek Elegy; Introduction to the study of Comparative Grammar; A Grammar of Old Persian; Y Groegiaid Gynt; Welsh Translations of Russian Classics. *Ctr*: Classical Quarterly, Classical Review, Journ of Hellenic Studies, Amer Journ of Philology, Russian Studies, numerous Welsh periodicals. *s.s*: Early Gk Elegy, Compar Gram, Trans Russian into Welsh. *Rec*: Gardening. *a*: Cooldaragh, Bangor, Nth Wales. *T*: 507.

HUDSPETH, Maj. Henry Moore, D.S.O., M.C., M.Sc, M.I.M.E. Mining Engineer *c.t*: Colliery Guardian, Iron & Coal Trades Review, Transactions Institution Mining Engineers. *a*: 24 Av Rd, Doncaster. *t*: 252.

HUEBNER, Solomon Stephen, M.L., Sc.D., Ph.D. *b*: Manitowoc, Wis, 1882. *e*: Univs of Penn & Wisconsin. *m*: Ethel E. Mudie. *s*: 1. *d*: 3. Prof of Insurance Univ of Penn. *Publ*: Life Insurance; Property Insurance; Economics of Life Insurance; Life Insurance as Investment; Marine Insurance; The Stock Market; & various Govt Reports. *Ctr*: Ency Brit Year Book, American Year Book, & many insurance trade journs. *s.s*: Insurance. *Rec*: Minerology. *a*: 697 South Highland Ave, Merion, Pa, U.S.A. *T*: Evergreen 6-0100.

HUESTIS, Charles Herbert, M.A., D.D., LL.D. *b*: Jacksonville N.B. Canada 1863. *e*: Public Schs of Nova Scotia & Mt Allison Univ Sackville. *m*: Jessis Brown Ackman. *s*: 3. *d*: 1. *n.a*: Columnist Daily Star 1933—. *Publ*: Influence of Sunlight on White Men in Western Canada; The Indian Problem in Alberta; Relativity: A New View of the Universe; Sunday in the Home; Sunday in the Making. *Ctr*: Various. *s.s*: Internat Affairs, Politics & Econs. *Rec*: Motoring & walking. *c*: Edmonton. *a*: 11337, 123 St, Edmonton, Canada. *T*: 81110.

HUGGENVIK, Theodore, M.A., Th.D. *b*: Mandal, Norway 1889. *e*: St Olaf Coll, Univ of Chicago & Princeton Theol Semin, Augustana Coll. *m*: Dora Nielsen. *s*: 1. *d*: 2. Teacher, Chm Dept of Religion & Philos St Olaf Coll Northfield Minn, Mem Evangelical Lutheran Church. *Publ*: Your Key to the Bible; An Outline of Church History; Fourteen Men Who Knew Christ; The Approach to Jesus; Search the Scriptures (collab); Lessons in the Life of Our Saviour. *Ctr*: Book News Letter. *s.s*: Religion. *a*: 1218 St Olaf Ave, Northfield, Minnesota, U.S.A. *T*: 763 J.

HUGGETT, A. St George, M.B., B.Sc, PhD., M.R.C.S., L.R.C.P. Director. Ex-Sec Physiology & Reader in Pharmacology, Leeds Univ. *c.t:* Med journs. *a:* Stoneycroft, Hollins Gdns, Headingley, Leeds.

HUGGILL, Sydney Charles. *b:* Lon 1891. *a:* Fleetway Hse, Farringdon St, E.C.4.

HUGH, Charles Henry. *b:* Fowey 1893. *e:* County Sc Bodmin. Journalist. *n.a:* Reporter Cornish Guardian, Bath Herald & Surrey Advertiser 1912–, i/c Woking Dis Surrey Advertiser '22–, Snr Reporter Head Office '34–. *a:* Surrey Advertiser & County Times, Guildford. *t:* 9.

HUGH, Philip. *b:* Hitchin 1886. *e:* Hitchin G.S. Novelist. Capt R.A.F. (during War). *Publ:* Together; A Man of Manners; Night Girl; My Strange Wife. *c.t:* Daily Mirror, Evening News, Chron, Daily Dispatch, Woman. *s.s:* Antique furniture, old picture, textiles, etc. *Rec:* Golf, travel. *c:* Arts Theatre. *a:* Sollershott Hall, Letchworth. *t:* 71.

HUGHES, A. R. *b:* Llandudno 1869. *e:* Bd Sc Llangollen. *m:* (1) Elizabeth Morris; (2) Lizzie Foulkes Griffiths. *s:* 2. *n.a:* Llandudno Advertiser 1903–. *c.t:* Various. *Rec:* Bowls. *a:* Morfen, Hill Terr, Llandudno. *t:* 6650.

HUGHES, Alfred. Professor (ret). *Publ:* Practical Geography. *a:* 22 Watford Rd, King's Langley. *t:* 7565.

HUGHES, (Dom) Anselm, O.S.B., M.A. *e:* Westminster Sch & Oxf. *n.a:* Mem Ed Bd New Oxford Hist of Music, Publ Dir Faith Press Ltd 1916—20. *Publ:* Worcester Mediæval Harmony; Anglo-French Sequelæ; The House of my Pilgrimage; Latin Hymnody. *Ctr:* Times Litt Supp, Grove's Dict of Music, Music & Letters, etc. *s.s:* English Harmony to 1550. *a:* Nashdom Abbey, Burnham, Bucks. *T:* 176.

HUGHES, Archibald Cecil, C.B.E., T.D., B.Sc., M.Inst.C.E. *b:* Horsham 1886. *e:* Ascombe House Sch, Weymouth Coll, Lond Univ. *m:* Florence Isobel Hughes. *d:* 1. County Surveyor Hants. *Publ:* Tar Roads; Asphalt Roads. *Ctr:* Surveyor & other tech journs. *s.s:* Civil Engineering (road & bridge design). *Rec:* Golf, ornithology, astronomy. *c:* R.A.C., Hampshire County. *w.s:* 1914—18 & '39—45. *a:* 40 Cheriton Rd, Winchester. *T:* 4006.

HUGHES, Arthur George, B.Sc, PhD.(Lon). *b:* Shrewsbury 1890. *e:* Wrekin Col, Borough Rd Col. *m:* Ethel Wilson. *s:* 2. Inspector of Scs. *Publ:* Elementary General Science—a Book For Teachers; Elementary General Science Book (in coll with J. H. Panton). *c.t:* Brit Journ Psych, Brit Journ Educ Psych, Forum of Educ, etc. *s.s:* Educ Psych. Sec Train Coll Delegacy Univ of Lon, Chrm Educ Sec, Brit Psych Soc. *a:* 45 Harvard Rd, Isleworth, Middx.

HUGHES, Arthur Montague Durban. *b:* Worthing 1873. *e:* St Edmund's Sch Canterbury, St John's Coll Oxf. *m:* Wilhelmina Langenheim. *d:* 1. Emeritus Prof Eng Lit B'ham Univ. *Publ:* The Nascent Mind of Shelley; Carlyle's Past & Present (edited with intro & notes); Tennyson, Poems—1842 (edited with notes); Editions in the Clarendon English Series of selections from Burke, Cobbett, Shelley. *s.s:* Lit of the Romantic Revival. *Rec:* Walking. *a:* 42 Weoley Hill, Selly Oak, Birmingham. *T:* Selly Oak 0371.

HUGHES, Rev. Arthur Price. Methodist Minister. *Publ:* A Warrior on Wings; Christian View of Life; The Ministry of Revelation. *Ctr:* Christian World Pulpit, Meth Recorder & Joyful News, etc. *a:* 13 Sudbroke Rd, Balham, London, S.W.12.

HUGHES, Major Basil, D.S.O., M.A., M.B., B.Sc., B.Ch, F.R.C.S. Cons Surg. *Publ:* War Surgery, from Firing Line to Base (with Capt Stanley Banks). *c.t:* Med publ's. *a:* Moorlands, Bradford. *t:* 4512 & 1119.

HUGHES, Rev. C. E. *b:* Maidstone 1867. *e:* Kings Sc Canterbury & Keble Col Oxf. *m:* Frances Margaret Pennethorne *s:* 1. *Publ:* The Parish Register of Maltby (York) 1597-1812. *Rec:* Chess. *a:* 10a Dane Rd. St Leonards-on-Sea. *t:* 2756.

HUGHES, C. Garland, F.R.S.A., L.G.S.M. Civil Service. *c.t:* Brighton Press Syndicate, Lon Press, etc. *a:* 36 Shakespeare Cres, E.12.

HUGHES, Charles, M.B.E. *b:* Huntingdon 1881. *e:* Priv. *m:* Elsie M. Searjeant. *s:* 4. *n.a:* Gen Mang Peterboro' Advertiser 1930, Dir Peterboro' Advert Coy Ltd '30, Dir Bury St Edmunds Print & Publ Co '30. *s.s:* Politics, agriculture. 15 yrs on Lit Staff Peterboro' Advert. Hon Sec Belgium Refugee Cmt Peterboro' '15—18. 15 yrs Org East Count Liberal Federation. 2 yrs unpaid Sec to Sir R. Winfrey M.P., Parl Sec Board of Agriculture '17—18. *a:* Advertiser, Peterboro', *t:* Peterboro' 3232.

HUGHES, Charles Frank, A.B. *b:* New York 1891. *e:* Fordham Univ. *m:* Kathleen Saunders. Journalist. *n.a:* Rep Ev Sun (N.Y.) 1911, Daily Trade Record '12—13, N.Y. Times '14—17 & '19—22, Business Ed N.Y. World '22—27, N.Y. Times '27—. *Ctr:* N.Y. Times, Nations Business. *s.s:* Business. *a:* Shorefront Park, South Norwalk, Conn. *T:* Norwalk 6-7147.

HUGHES, Miss D. W., M.J.I. Journalist. *n.a:* Ed Journ of Careers 1922—. *Publ:* Careers for our Sons. *c.t:* Good Housekeeping, Times of India, etc. *s.s:* Career, education, travel, women's topics. *Rec:* Travel, art. *c:* Forum, Overseas. *a:* 61 Conduit St, W.1. *t:* Regent 0301.

HUGHES, E. Elliss, M.J.I. *b:* Aberystwyth 1872. *e:* Jasper Hse G.S. Aberystwyth. *m:* M. A. Rees. *s:* 3. *d:* 2. Journalist. *n.a:* Carmarthen Journal, Western Mail (Cardiff) '99, Chief Reporter at Cardiff (20 y). *s.s:* Welsh national affairs. *a:* 23 Tydfil Pl, Roath Pk, Cardiff.

HUGHES, Edward, M.A., F.R.Hist.S. *b:* Betley, Staffs 1899. *e:* Orme Boy's Sch Newcastle-under-Lyme & Univ of Manchester. *m:* Sarah Hughes. *s:* 2. *d:* 1. Prof of Modern History Durham Univ. *Publ:* Studies in Administration & Finance. *Ctr:* Eng Hist Rev, History, Manch Guardian, Econ Journ, Scottish Hist Rev. *s.s:* Modern British History. *w.s:* 1917—18 R.N.V.R. *a:* Manor House, Shincliffe, Durham.

HUGHES, Emrys. *n.a:* Ed Forward. *Publ:* Keir Hardie's Writings & Speeches. *a:* 26 Civic St, Port Dundas, Glas, & Lochnorris, Cumnock, Ayrs. *t:* Douglas 1360 & Cumnock 34.

HUGHES, Eric Vincent. *e:* Queen Elizabeth's Sch Barnet. *n.a:* Chief Rep, Southern Post Series 1929—. *a:* Bognor Regis Post, 190 London Rd, Bognor Regis,

HUGHES, Rev. Ernest Richard, M.A. *b:* London. *e:* City of Lond Sch & Oxf Univ. *m:* Katherine Lloyd. *s:* 2. *d:* 1. Reader in Chinese Philos & Religion Oxford Univ. *Publ:* The Invasion of China by the Western World; Chinese Philosophy in Classical Times; The Mean-in-Action & the Great Learning; The Spirit of Chinese Philosophy. *s.s*: Chinese Philosophy. *Rec*: Tennis & gardening. *a*: c/o Lincoln College, Oxford.

HUGHES, Felicity. *b*: Lon 1913. Secretary. *e*: Francis Holland C. of E. Sc. St Georges Sc, Ascot & King's Col. Gen Sec, Poetry Soc (Inc), 1934—. *Rec*: Riding, tennis, ski-ing. *a*: 17 Wimpole St, W.1. *t*: Langham 3370.

HUGHES, Frank Mainwaring, M.D., M.R.C.S., L.R.C.P.(Lon). *b*: Assam 1888. *e*: Leys Sc Cam, Lon Hosp. Physician. County Surg S.J.A.B. *Publ*: M.O.H. Publications (Yearly 1920-33). *c.t*: Lancet, B.M.J., etc. *s.s*: Children. Chev Légion d'Honneur '17. *Rec*: Golf. *c*: Old Leysian Un, Athenæum, Lon Hosp Clubs Un. *a*: Winton, Walmer, Kent. *t*: Deal 172.

HUGHES, Fred. A.S.A. *e*: Private & H.S. T.U. Sec. *n.a*: The Clerk '15—. The Socialist Christian '29—. *Publ*: Socialism & The Human Soul; Pamphlets:—Story of the Slums; Old Law & New Prophets. *c.t*: Socialist Review, Optimist. *a*: 87 Herongate Rd, E.12.

HUGHES, G. Bernard, F.R.S.A. Editor of Welfare Review. *Publ*: inc Old English Table Glass; Collectors' Treasury; Modern Industrial Lighting; etc. *a*: Mochras, Grassy Lne, Sevenoaks, Kent.

HUGHES, G. Bernard. *b*: Wolverhampton 1896. *e*: Wolverhampton G.S. Ed in Chf The Queen. *c.t*: Leading Eng & Amer women's journs. *s.s*: Art & antiques. *a*: Gainsboro', Wulfruna Gdns, Wolverhampton.

HUGHES, Gerald Stephen, M.B., B.S., F.R.C.S. *b*: Maidstone 1878. *e*: Maidstone. Cons Surg York County Hosp & Ampleforth College, Chief Med Officer Yorks Insurance Co, J.P. City of York. *Publ*: Abdominal Surgery at an Advanced Operating Centre; Wounds of the Chest as seen at an Advanced Operating Centre. *Ctr*: B.M.J., Lancet. *s.s*: Juvenile Courts & Delinquency. *Rec*: Golf. *c*: Bath, Yorkshire, United Sports. R.A.C. *a*: 6 St Leonards, York. *T*: York 3155.

HUGHES, Glenn (Arthur), M.A. *b*: Gozad, Nebraska 1894. *e*: Long Beach Calif, Polytech H Sch, Stanford Univ, Washington Univ. *m*: Babette Plechner. *d*: 1. Univ Prof, Writer, Translator & Ed. *Publ*: The Story of the Theatre; Imagism and the Imagist; The Penthouse Theatre; New Plays for Mummers; Author of 27 published full-length plays, etc. *s.s*: Drama & Poetry. *Rec*: Tennis. *c*: Rainier, Tennis, Washington Athletic. *a*: Univ of Washington, Seattle 5, Wash. *T*: Melrose 0630.

HUGHES, H. H. *a*: Northern Echo, Darlington.

HUGHES, Hector, K.C. (Eng & Ire). *b*: Dublin 1887. *e*: T.C.D. *Publ*: National Sovereignty & Judicial Autonomy in the British Commonwealth of Nations; The Law of Betting; Registration of Title; etc. *c.t*: Various. *Rec*: Riding & travel. *c*: Devonshire. *a*: 4 Paper Bldgs, Temple, E.C.4. *t*: Cen 0192.

HUGHES, Henry Harold, M.A., F.S.A., R.C.A., A.R.I.B.A. Dio Archt. *n.a*: Ed Archæologia Cambrensis 1926-. *Publ*: Old Cottages of Snowdonia (with H. L. North); Old Churches of Snowdonia (with H. L. North); Memorials of Old North Wales (Pt Author). *c.t*: Archæ Journs. *a*: Yr Aelwyd, Bangor. *t*: 286.

HUGHES, Rev. Henry Maldwyn, B.A., D.D., HonM.A. *Publ*: The Ethics of Jewish Apocryphal Literature; The Theology of Experience; Faith & Progress; The Kingdom of Heaven; What is the Atonement?; Christian Foundations. *c.t*: Ency of Rel & Ethics, etc. *a*: Wesley Lodge, Cambridge. *t*: 1609.

HUGHES, Herbert. *b*: Belfast 1882. *e*: Roy Col of Mus. *m*: Suzanne McKernan. *d*: 2. Critic & Composer. Memb of Counc of Critic Circle. *n.a*: The New Age 1907, The Morning Post 1910, Staff of The Daily Telegraph under Le Sage '11, Music Ed '31, Resigned '32, The Sat Review '32. Ed—Songs of Uladh '04: Irish Country Songs (3 vols 1909, '15, '35); Old Irish Melodies ('32); etc. *Publ*: The Joyce Book '33. *c.t*: Ulster Journ of Archæology, Mus Times, Radio Times, World Radio, News-Chronicle. *s.s*: Irish Ballads. Wrote incidental music for And So To Bed, Within the Gates, The Rivals. *Rec*: Swimming. A found of the Irish Folk Song Soc (1904). Intelligence Staff, Egyptian Expedit Force under Allenby, promoted Chief Military Censor in the Sudan (G.S.O. 2). *c*: Savile. *a*: 125 Church St, Chelsea. S.W.3. *t*: Flax 0540.

HUGHES, Herbert Delauney, M.P., B.A. *b*: Swindon Wilts 1914. *e*: Oxford. *m*: Beryl Parker. M.P. for Wolverhampton West, Parl Priv Sec to Ellen Wilkinson Min of Educ '45—47. *n.a*: Ed Fabian Quarterly '39—42. *Publ*: Towards a Classless Society; Advance in Education; Czechoslovakia, Six Studies on Reconstruction; Anderson's Prisoners; Democratic Sweden. *Ctr*: Tribune, New Statesman, Times Educ Suppl. *s.s*: Social & Political Education. *Rec*: Walking, cycling, travel. *c*: Nat Trade Union. *w.s*: R.A. 1942 —45. *a*: 12c Compton Terr, London, N.1. *T*: Canonbury 5677.

HUGHES, Irene. *b*: Swansea. *e*: Priv & Swansea Col. *m*: Rev. L. Gethin Hughes, M.B.E. F/L Journalist. *c.t*: Daily Telegraph, L'pool Echo, L'pool Post, Birm Post, Glas Evening Times, Weekly Scotsman, Yorkshire Post, etc. *s.s*: All matters pertaining to Egypt & the Soudan, Palestine & Syria. Extensive travel Middle & Nr East. *Rec*: Travel, tennis. *a*: Zetland Hse, Richmond, Yorks.

HUGHES, John Benjamin. *b*: Carmarthen 1905. *e*: Burnley G.S. *m*: Elsie F. Ratcliffe. Reporter. *n.a*: Burnley News 1922-24, Chester Chron '24-27, Doncaster Gazette & Yorks Evening News '27-28, Allied N/p M/C '28-33, Dramatic Critic Evening Chron '30-33, Allied N/p Lon '33—. *c.t*: Allied N/ps. *s.s*: Theatre, cricket, assoc football. *Rec*: Cricket. *c*: Mem N.U.J. *a*: 45 Narcissus Rd, West Hampstead, N.W.6.

HUGHES, John David Ivor. Prof of Law, Univ of Leeds. *Publ*: Transport by Rail. *c.t*: Legal Journs. *a*: The Univ, Leeds. *t*: 52303.

HUGHES, John Philip Wyndham, M.R.C.S., L.R.C.P., M.D., B.S., D.P.H. *b*: Blackwood, Mon 1914. *e*: Highgate Sch, U.C.L. & U.C.H. *m*: Christine Inee Jolley. *s*: 1. *d*: 1. Medical Research. *Ctr*: Collins Publs, Med Press. *s.s*: Medical & Medico-Social & Physiology, Children's Stories. *Rec*: Sport, gardening, etc. *a*: The Old Rectory, Balscote, Banbury, Oxon. *T*: Wroxton St Mary 64.

HUGHES, John Scott. Married. *s*: 1. *n.a*: The Times, Country Life. *Publ*: Famous Yachts; Ordeal by Air; Little Ships; Told in the Watch Below. *s.s*: The Merchant Service, yachting. *a*: 169 Gloucester Terr, W.2. *t*: Paddington 0964.

HUGHES, Rev. John Wesley. *b*: Menai Bridge 1870. *e*: Collegiate Sc Deganwy, Richmond Col Sy. *m*: Lily Jones. *s*: 1. Meth Minister. *n.a*: Ed Connexional Year Bk, Welsh Meth Chr 1900-10. *Publ*:

Hymn and Tune Bk for Wales Churches of S. Africa. Joint Ed Several Short Stories; Hist Articles. *c.t*: Meth Recorder, Times & Leader, Meth Chr Record; National Bulletin, Eurgrawn Weslеaidd. *s.s*: Meth hist, Welsh hist. Adjudicator National Eisteddfod of Wales '07. Chm Kent Meth Synod up to '31. Govn of Kent Col Canterbury, Dir Kent Col Folkestone. Journalistic Work for period 30 yrs. Winner of Chief Essay Prize Provincial Eisteddfod Corwen 1899. *a*: Brenley, Lache Pk Ave, Chester. *t*: 1995.

HUGHES, Langston, Hon.Litt.D. *b*: Joplin, Missouri 1902. *e*: Lincoln Univ. Author. *n.a*: Madrid Corr Baltimore Afro-American '37, Adv Ed-Bd Common Ground, Columnist, Chicago Defender '47—. *Publ*: (Poems) The Weary Blues; Fine Clothes to the Jew; The Dream Keeper; Shakespeare in Harlem; Fields of Wonder; (Novel) Not Without Laughter; The Ways of White Folks; The Big Sea. *s.s*: Negro-White relations in U.S.A., Negro in Amer Lit & Theatre. *Rec*: Theatre & travel. *c*: Author's & Dramatist's Guilds, etc. *a*: c/o Alfred A. Knopf Inc, 501 Madison Ave, New York 22, N.Y., U.S.A.

HUGHES, Leslie Ernest Charles, B.Sc., Ph.D., A.C.G.I., D.I.C. *e*: City & Guilds Coll. Consultant, Pres Inst of Electronics, Assoc-Ed Chambers's Technical Dictionary. *Publ*: Engineering Acoustics. *Ctr*: Nature, Electrician. *s.s*: Acoustics & Sound Recording. *a*: 15 Avenue Hse, Allitsen Rd, N.W.8. *T*: Primrose 3269.

HUGHES, Mary Elizabeth Josephine (Mary Winter Were). *b*: Edgbaston. *e*: Priv. *d*: 1. *Publ*: The Angel in the garden; Things Worth While; The Night He Came; His Roses and other Legends of the Christ Child; etc. *c.t*: Bookman, Catholic Gazette, Poetry Review, The Green Quarterly, London Forum, etc. *s.s*: Verses for motto cards, Christmas cards, lyrics for musical setting, etc. Gold Medal for Eloc, Inc Lon A.Mus. *c*: Soc of Women Journ, Poetry Soc. *a*: 42 Scott's Lane, Shortlands, Kent. *t*: Bec 2063.

HUGHES, Mary Vivian, B.A. *b*: Epping Forest 1866. *e*: North Lond Coll Sch, Cambridge Training Coll. *m*: Arthur Hughes (dec'd). *s*: 3. *d*: 1 (dec'd). Inspector of Schools for Univ of Lond. *Publ*: A London Family 1870—1900; Vivians; A London Family Between the Wars 1920—40; London at Home; America's England; Scripture Teaching To-day; About England; The City Saints; Hidden Interests in the Bible & Sundry Text-Books. *a*: Fronwen, Cuffley, Herts. *T*: Cuffley 2026.

HUGHES, Maud Grace. Editress. *n.a*: Hulton's Manch & Lond, Ed Picture Show, Picture Show Annual & Picture Show Who's Who on the Screen. *Ctr*: Lond & Prov. *s.s*: Women's Subjects, Cinema. *c*: P.E.N., Critics Circle, Film Sect Woman's Press. *a*: 24 Parkanour Ave, Thorpe Bay, Essex.

HUGHES, Merritt Yerkes, M.A., Ph.D. *b*: Philadelphia, Penn 1893. *e*: Univs of Boston, Edin & Harvard. *m*: Grace J. Dedman. *s*: 1. *d*: 1. Prof of English Lit Univ of Wisconsin. *Publ*: Virgil & Spenser; Ed: Paradise Lost; Paradise Regained; the Minor Poems & Samson Agonistes; Milton Prose Selection. *Ctr*: Studies in Philosophy, New Republic, Sewanee Review, etc. *c.s*: English Lit 1500—1675. *Rec*: Travel, gardening. *c*: Tudor & Stewart. *w.s*: Sgt A.E.F. 1918—19, Lt-Col '43—46. *a*: 150 North Prospect Ave, Madison 5, Wisconsin, U.S.A. *T*: Badger 5714.

HUGHES, Percy George. M.J.I. *b*: Oxf. *e*: Nixon's G.S. Ed East Sussex News. Dir of Lewes Building Soc. *n.a*: Oxford Times. Chief Reporter Norwood News & Norwood Review, Sub-Ed Sussex Daily News. Chm Lewes Fanciers' Assoc. Pres Lewes Flying Club. Chm Sussex Dis of Inst of Journalists. V-Chm Sussex Dis N/p Press Fund. *Publ*: A Rambler's Guide to Eastbourne & District. *s.s*: Sport, drama. *Rec* Bowls. *c*: Sussex Masonic, Brighton; South Saxon Masonic, Lewes; Lewes Constitutional. *a*: Ferndale, St John's Hill, Lewes.

HUGHES, Philip, (See **PHILLIPS, Hugh**). *Publ*: Together; A Man of Manners; Night Girl; My Strange Wife; Wild Honey; Ragged Robin; Adventure in Mayfair; Georgian Town; Coronet. *a*: Sollershott Hall, Letchworth, Herts. *T*: 565.

HUGHES, Phillida. *b*: Lon 1895. *e*: Convent of Notre Dame. *m*: Nathaniel Gubbins. *d*: 2. Journalist. *n.a*: Daily Mirror 1918—32, Sunday Dispatch Editress Women's Page & Special Writer '33. *s.s*: Fashion, beauty, cookery. *Rec* Riding, swimming, entertaining. *a*: Mavis Croft, Chipstead, Surrey. *t*: Downland 392.

HUGHES, Ray Osgood, A.M., L.H.D. *b*: Saxtons River, Vermont 1879. *e*: Vermont Acad, Univs of Brown & Pittsburgh. *m*: Helene W. Hopkins. Author & Educator. *Publ* Community Civics; Building Citizenship; The Making of Today's World; Today's Problems; Elementary Community Civics; The Making of Our United States; Fundamentals of Economics; Workbooks & Teachers' Manuals for Various Texts. *Ctr*: Social Education, American Hist Rev, Yearbook, Nat Counc for the Social Studies 1936. *s.s*: Social Studies, esp History & Government. *Rec*: Baseball. *a*: 5517 Beverly Pl, Pittsburgh 6, Pennsylvania, U.S.A. *T*: MO. 3956.

HUGHES, Richard, O.B.E., B.A. *b*: 1900. *e*: Charterhouse & Oxf. *m*: Frances Bazley. *s*: 2. *d*: 3. Author & Dramatist. *Publ*: Gipsy-Night & other Poems; The Sisters' Tragedy & other Plays; A Moment of Time; A High Wind in Jamaica; The Spider's Palace (Stories for Children); Confessio Juvenis; In Hazard; Don't Blame Me; etc. *Ctr*: Various. *c*: Pratts, Un Univ, Roy Welch Yacht. *a*: c/o Chatto & Windus, 40-42 William IV St, London, W.C.2.

HUGHES, Rupert, M.A., Litt.D. *b*: Lancaster, Mo 1872. *e*: Adelbert Coll Western Reserve Minn & Yale Univ. *Publ*: Biography of George Washington; What will People Say?; Within these Walls; Stately Tinker; The Old Nest; etc. *Ctr*: Various. *w.s*: World War I Major Mil Int, Lieut-Col U.S.A. Reserve, Colonel World War II. *a*: 4751 Los Feliz, Boulevard Los Angeles 27, California.

HUGHES, Thomas. Clerk Monmouth Cnty Counc. *Publ*: Law Relating to Welsh Intermediate Schools. *a*: Llandevaud Ct, nr Newport, Mon.

HUGHES, Rev. Thomas Hywel, M.A., D.Litt, D.D. *b*: Penclawdd 1875. *e*: New Col Lon & U.C.L. *m*: Nina Owen. Princ of Scot Cong Col. *Publ*: The New Psychology & Religious Experience. *c.t*: Expository Times, Modern Churchman, Church Quarterly Review, Brit Weekly, etc. *s.s*: Psych of religion. *Rec*: Golf. *a*: 29 Hope Terr, Edin. *t*: 51807.

HUGHES, Rt. Hon. William Morris, P.C., C.H., K.C., LL.D.(Glas, Edin, Cardiff, Birm), D.C.L., F.Z.S. M.P., *b*: London. *e*: Gr Sch Llandudno, St Stephen's Westminster. *m*: Mary Edith Campbell. *s*: 2. *d*: 3. Barrister, Prime Minister of Australia 1915—23. *Publ*: The Splendid Adventure; Australia & War Today; Case for Labour; Crusts & Crusades. *Ctr*: Sydney Dly Telegraph (Weekly article for 4½ years). *Rec*: Golf. *a*: 43 Nelson Rd, Lindfield, N.S.W., Australia. *T*: IX 3529.

HUGHES-STANTON, Barbara. Author. *Publ*: Nurse; Family Affairs. *a*: c/o Martin Secker Ltd, 5 John St, W.C.2.

HUGHES WILLIAMS, Gertrude Anne, F.L.A. b: Pontypridd 1878. e: Pontypridd Elem, Pontypridd Pupil Teachers Centre. m: Philip Williams. Former Librarian. Publ: Early History of St Catherines Church; History of Miners Libraries, etc. c.t: South Wales Echo, Library Assoc Record. s.s: Local hist. Mem Juv Advisory Cmt, Industrial Supervision Cmt for Ministry of Labour, Sec Lifeboat Instit, etc. a: Bryn-yr-Haul, Pontypridd, Glam.

HUGON, Gabriel Raphael. b: Lon 1849. e: Lon & Paris. m: Ellen Donnet. s: 1. d: 4. Mang Dir. a: Thornfield, Mitford Rd, Fallowfield, M/C. 14. t: Rusholme 1552.

HUHNER, Leon, A.M., LL.B. b: Berlin, Germany 1871. e: Coll of City of New York, Univ of Columbia. Lawyer, Historian & Poet. Publ: Jonah Touro, a biography. Ctr: Numerous articles on early American, Colonial & Revolutionary Hist. s.s: Hist & Poetry. Rec: Golf. a: 291 Broadway, Borough of Manhattan, City of New York. T: Cortlandt 7-7226.

HULBERT, Henry Harper, M.A.(Oxon), M.R.C.S., L.R.C.P. b: Corsham 1863. e: Bath Col, Magdalen Oxf & St Thomas's Hosp Lon. Married. s: 2 (Jack & Claude). d: 1. Doctor. Publ: Exercise for Health; Breathing for Voice; Voice Training in Speech & Song; Rhythm in Speaking; Rhythm in Feeling; etc. s.s: Speech training. Lect on Voice to Theol Cols. Ex-Lect on Voice to L.C.C. Training Centres, Lon Univ, etc. a: 48 Hurlingham Ct, S.W.6.

HULIN, C. Sec & Treas Lon N. Br N.U.J. a: 24 Berkshire Gdns, Palmers Green, N.13.

HULL, Albert. b: Loughborough Leics 1889. m: Mabel A. Kendall. s: 2. Ed Warrington Guardian Series. n.a: 1909 Nott'm Guardian, '11 Leicester Mail, '13 Congleton Times, '15 Cheshire Observer, '22 Warrington Guardian, Chief Rep '26, Sub Ed, '34 Ed. Rec Garden & bowls. a: Cestria, 11 Capesthorne Rd, Orford, Warrington. t: 52.

HULL, Bernard Oliver Francis, Suffragan Bishop of. Publ: About the Lambeth Conference; The Bible Day by Day; etc. c.t: Various n/ps & periodicals. a: 72 Lairgate, Beverley.

HULL, Eleanor H, HonD.Litt(NatU.I.). b: Eng 1860. e: Alexandra Col Dublin, Roy Col of Science Dublin & Brussels. Author & Critic. n.a: Formerly on Staff of Lit World. Hon Sec Irish Texts Soc, Mem Counc Folklore Soc. Publ: Pagan Ireland (1904); Early Christian Ireland ('04); The Poem-book of the Gael ('12); Folklore of the British Isles ('28); A History of Ireland Vol II from the Stuart Period to Modern Times ('31); Introduction to C. Yonges Dove in the Eagle's Nest; etc. c.t: The Times Lit Sup, Ency Italiana Roma, Folklore, Saga book of the Viking Soc, Fortnightly, Trans Victoria Inst, etc. s.s: Folklore, Irish hist. Rec Music. a: 3 Camp View, Wimbledon Common, S.W.19.

HULL, Ernest Reginald, S.J. b: 1863. R.C. Priest. n.a: Ed Bombay Catholic Examiner 1903—22, Ed Stella Maris Mag Osterley '35—. Publ: Bombay Mission-History & the Padroado Question; British Anglo-Saxon Church; William I to Henry II; John to Henry VII; Formation of Character; A Practical Philosophy of Life; Why Should I Be Moral; Our Modern Chaos & the Way Out; Civilization & Culture; Galileo & his Condemnation; etc. Ctr: Catholic Journs, etc. s.s: Theology, Philosophy, Ecclesiastical Hist, Controversial Apologetics. a: Manresa Hse, Roehampton, London, S.W.15.

HULL, Dr. G. R. Clinical Asst Roy Waterloo Hosp. Div Inspector British Red Cross Soc. Hon Surg-Lieut R.N. a: 510 Streatham High Rd, S.W.16.

HULL, Helen Rose, Ph.B. b: Albion, Mich. e: Mich State Coll & Univs of Mich & Chicago. Author, Prof at Columb Univ, Mem P.E.N. & Authors' League, etc. Publ: Hawk's Flight; Heat Lightning; etc. Ctr: Harper's, Sat Ev Post, Good Housekeeping, McCall's, Story, etc. s.s: Short Stories, Novelettes, etc. Rec: Painting, sailing, gardening, cooking. a: 878 West End Ave, New York 25, N.Y., U.S.A. T: Academy 2-1702.

HULLAH, Rev. Albert Swales, M.C. Publ: The Presence; The Heart of the Eternal; The Unseen Fellowship; The Attraction of Jesus. a: Wesley Manse, Watford, Herts. t: 2003.

HULLINGER, Edwin Ware, A.B. b: Chicago, Ill 1893. e: Univs of Kansas & Columb. m: Helen Jean Sawyer. d: 4. Writer, Film Producer & Director. n.a: United Press Mich State Manager 1917 & Foreign Corr '18—23. Publ: The Reforging of Russia; The New Fascist State; Ploughing Through; Flesh Alley (collab). Ctr: Scribner's Mag, Nation's Business, N American Rev, The Outlook, Independent, N.Y. Times, etc. s.s: Internat Affairs, Labour, Agriculture, Motion Pictures, Industrial. Rec: Swimming, piano. a: 5200 Klingle St, N.W., Washington 16, D.C., U.S.A. T: Woodley 9487.

HULME, Harold, A.B., Ph.D., F.R.Hist.S. b: Cleveland, Ohio 1898. e: Univs of Western Reserve & Cornell. m: Harriet R. Hall. s: 2. Assoc-Prof of History N.Y. Univ. n.a: Editor Journ of Modern History 1946—. Ctr: Eng Hist Rev, Can Miscellany, Amer Bar Assoc Journ, etc. s.s: Tudor & Early Stuart period. a: 25 Addison St, Larchmont, N.Y., & History Dept, Washington Sq, College of New York University, New York 3, N.Y., U.S.A. T: Larchmont 2-1284.

HULME, Rev. Thomas Ferrier, M.A., LL.D. b: Torquay 1856. e: Kingswood Sc Bath, Headingley Col Leeds, T.C.D., Bristol Univ. m: Lucy Moore Alcock. d: 2. Chm Bristol & Bath Synod, Wes Meth Ch 1907–32. Pres Wes Meth Conf '23-24. Publ: John Wesley & His Horse ('33); etc. Rep of Brit Meth to S. African Meth Conf '25, & to Gen Conf of Meth Epis Ch U.S.A. '28. a: 16 Blenheim Rd, Redland, Bristol 6. t: 34731.

HULTON, Edward George Warris. b: Harrogate 1906. e: Harrow & B.N.C. Oxf. m: Princess Nika Yourievitsch. s: 1. d: 1. Newspaper Proprietor, Writer, Called to Bar, Practised on S.E. Circuit, Man-Dir Hulton Press Ltd '38, Ed World '40. Publ: The New Age. s.s: Politics, History. Rec: Reading. c: St James's, Travellers. a: Puttenham Priory, Guildford, Surrey.

HULUGALLE, H. n.a: Ed, Ceylon Daily News. a: Lake Hse, Colombo, Ceylon.

HUM, Jack. b: London 1910. e: Secondary Sch. Editor, Mem Radio Soc of Great Brit, N.U.J. n.a: Asst-Ed Wireless Trader '28—33, Asst-Ed Murphy News '33—39, Ed Murphy News (Staff Edition, Magazine Edition, Export Edition) since '45. Ctr: Short-Wave Mag, Wireless World, Wireless Trader, The Gramophone. s.s: Radio, Gramophone Records & Reviewing Music. Rec: Radio amateur transmission, recorded music circles. w.s: R.A.F. '39—45. a: Wyldes, Bulls Green, Knebworth. T: Tewin 275.

HUMBERSTONE, Thomas Lloyd, B.Sc(Lon), A.R.C.Sc. b: Coventry 1876. e: Henry VIII Scs Coventry, Roy Col of Science Lon & Lon Sc of Economics. Publ: University Reform in London (1926); Short History of National Education ('08); An Experiment in Industrial Research; Ed New

Buildings for the University of London ('33); etc. *c.t*: Times Ed Sup, Quarterly Review, Nature, Journal of Education, etc. *s.s*: Educ, scientific research. *a*: 15 Gower St, W.C.1. *t*: Museum 0267.

HUMBLE, Benjamin Hutchison. *b*: Dumbarton. *e*: Dumbarton Acad & Glas H Sch. *n.a*: Ed Quarterly Mag, Open Air in Scotland. *Publ*: On Scottish Hills; Wayfaring Around Scotland; Tramping in Skye; The Songs of Skye. *Ctr*: The Field, Country Life, Geog Mag, Spectator, John o' London's Weekly, C.S. Monitor, Glas Herald, etc. *s.s*: Scottish Guide Books & Material, Illustrated articles on Tramping, Camping, Rock & Mountain Climbing in Scotland, Isle of Skye & Highlands. *a*: 91 Berkeley St, Glasgow C.3. *T*: Douglas 6113.

HUME, Charles Westley, M.C., B.Sc.(Lond). *b*: Wimbledon 1886. *e*: Birkbeck Coll. Formerly Sen Examiner H.M. Patent Office, Chm of Univ Fed for Animal Welfare. *n.a*: Ed to Physical Soc 1920—39. *Publ*: Various Pamphlets for UFAW. *Ctr*: Nature, Spectator, Everybody's, etc. *s.s*: Protection of Animals, Reform of Patent System, Statistical Analysis. *a*: 284 Regent's Park Rd, Finchley, London, N.3. *T*: Finchley 1079.

HUME, Dr. G. O. Ophthalmic Surgeon. *c.t*: Scientific journs. *a*: 5 Harley St, W.1.

HUME, Dr. J. B. Asst Surgeon St Bartholomew's Hosp. *Publ*: Congenital Diaphragmatic Hernia, 1931. *a*: 86 Harley St, W.1.

HUME, William Fraser, D.Sc., F.R.S.E. *b*: Cheltenham 1867. *e*: Private, Lausanne, Roy Coll of Science, Roy Sch of Mines. *m*: Ethel Gladys Williams. *s*: 1. *d*: 1. Geological Survey of Egypt 1897—1940 Dir from 1910 & later its Technical Counsellor, Mem Geological Soc, Roy Geog Soc of Lond. *Publ*: Geology of Egypt; Topography & Geology of Eastern Egypt (in collab); Topography & Geology of Eastern Sinai; Report on Oilfield Region of Egypt; Notes on Russian Geology; Cretaceous Strata of County Antrim. *Ctr*: Geographical Mag, Nature, Quarterly Journal Geological Soc, Cavio Scientific Journal, etc. *s.s*: Geology. *Rec*: Reading. *a*: The Laurels, Ash Lane, Rustington, Sussex. *T*: 233.

HUME-ROTHERY, William, F.R.S., M.A.(Oxon), Ph.D. (Lond), Sc.D.(Oxon). *b*: Worcester Park 1899. *e*: Cheltenham Coll, R.M.A. Woolwich, Magdalen Coll Oxf, Roy Sch of Mines. *m*: Elizabeth Alice Fea. *d*: 1. Roy Soc Warren Research Fell, Oxf Univ Lect Metallurgy Magdalen Coll, Senior Demyship 1925—28, Roy Soc Armourers' & Brasiers' Research Fell '29—32, Magdalen Coll Fell '38—43. *Publ*: The Metallic State; The Structure of Metals & Alloys; Atomic Theory for Students of Metallurgy. *Ctr*: Philosophical Transactions & Procs of the Roy Soc, Journ Inst of Metals, etc. *s.s*: Metallography, Physics of Metals. *Rec*: Painting & fishing. *a*: 54 Sandfield Rd, Headington, Oxford. *T*: 6694.

HUMILIS, Clement. See **Plowden-Wardlaw, James Tait.**

HUMMEL, Arthur W., M.A., Ph.D. *b*: Warrenton, Missouri 1884. *m*: Ruth Bookwalter. *s*: 2. *d*: 1. Chief Division of Orientalia Library of Congress 1927—. *Publ*: An Autobiography of a Chinese Historian; Ed, Eminent Chinese of the Ch'ing Period. *Ctr*: Various Learned Journs. *s.s*: Chinese Hist & Bibliography. *Rec*: Walking. *a*: Library of Congress, Washington 25, D.C. *T*: NA 2722 Br. 477.

HUMMEL, George Frederick, M.A., Ph.D. *b*: Southold N.Y. 1882. *e*: Williams Coll & Columbia Univ. *m*: Lillie Conrad Busch. Author. *Publ*: After All; Subsoil; A Good Man; Lazy Isle; Summer Lightning; Heritage;

Tradition; Interlude; The World Waits (play); etc. *Ctr*: Short Stories to various journs & newspapers. *Rec*: Yachting, golf, water sports in general. *c*: Williams Coll. *a*: Southold, L.I., New York.

HUMPHREY, Arthur Wilfrid. *b*: Weymouth 1888. *e*: County Sec Sch & Ruskin Coll Oxf. *m*: Harriet Benson. *s*: 1. Journalist & Author. N.U.J. *n.a*: Sub-Ed The Times 1945—, Dep Indust Corr Dly Herald '37—41, Former Indust Sub-Ed Dly Herald, Sub-Ed Dly News & Birmingham Gaz. *Publ*: International Socialism & the War; A History of Labour Representation; Robert Applegarth, Trade Unionist, Educationist, Reformer; The Modern Case for Socialism; The Worker's Share, A Study in Wages & Poverty. *Ctr*: Leading Newsps, Weekly & Monthly Revs, Labour & Co-op Journs, etc. *s.s*: Industrial. *Rec*: Gardening, reading. *a*: 162 Lynmouth Ave, Morden, Surrey. *T*: Derwent 5278.

HUMPHREY, Douglas, B.Sc(Lon). *b*: Lon 1880. *e*: Merchant Taylors' Sc, E.C. & Sidney Sussex Col Cam. *m*: Dorothy Clarke. Dir of Educ Polytech, Regent St, W.1. *Publ*: Intermediate Mechanics; Advanced Mathematics for Students of Physics & Engineering. *s.s*: Maths, mechanics. Snr Sci Master Macclesfield G.S. 1907—14. War Service '14-19. Head of Dept of Maths & Phys, Polytech '19-32. *a*: 6b High St, Hampstead, N.W.3. *t*: 5300.

HUMPHREY, Edward Frank, A.M., Ph.D. *b*: Winnebago, Minnesota 1878. *e*: Winnebago Hgh Sch, Univs of Columbia & Paris. *m*: Gertrude Warnock. *s*: 1. *d*: 3. Coll Prof & Historian. *Publ*: Nationalism & Religion in America; An Economic History of the United States; Politics & Religion in the Days of Augustine. *Ctr*: Dict of Amer Biography, Handbook of U.S. Diplomacy, Guide to Hist Lit, Hartford Courant, Nation, Hartford Times, New York Her Tri, Amer Hist Rev, etc. *s.s*: U.S. Hist. *a*: 31 N. Whitney St, Hartford, Conn. *T*: 3-5110.

HUMPHREY, F. G. *n.a*: Daily News (Old Northern edn), Lit Critic & Asst to Ed Sheffield Independent, Ideas, Ed Southern Reporter Selkirk, Birm Mail. War Service Palestine & France. Vice-Pres N.U.J. '35—36. Terr Mem N.E.C. Midlands Area. *Rec*: Motoring, angling, cinematography. *a*: 89 Sandon Rd, Edgbaston, Birm. *t*: Bearwood 1551.

HUMPHREY, William Gerald. *b*: Birmingham 1904. *e*: King Edward VII Sch Sheffield, Queen's Coll Oxf & Harvard Univ U.S.A. *m*: Margaret Swift. *s*: 1. Headmaster. *Publ*: The Christian & Education. *Ctr*: Spectator. *s.s*: Education. *a*: The Leys School, Cambridge. *T*: 55426.

HUMPHREY-DAVY, Francis Herbert Mountjoy Nelson, O.B.E. *b*: Sheffield. *e*: Priv, Univ Tutorial Coll Lond, Undergrad Lond Univ. Journalist, Sec to Hon. Esmond Harmsworth. *n.a*: Sub-Ed Lond News Ag 1908—14, Times Ed Staff '14—22, Sec to late Viscount Northcliffe '15—22, Asst Social Ed Times '23, Polit Sec to Hon Esmond Harmsworth '24—29, Daily Mail Ed Staff '24—. *Publ*: Pamphlet: How to Solve the Education Question. *Ctr*: Times, Dly Mail, Ev News, Sun Dispatch, Daily Mirror, etc. *s.s*: Genealogy, Peerage. *a*: Red Hse, Alumhurst Rd, Bournemouth, W. *T*: Westbourne 61697.

HUMPHREYS, Rev. Arthur James, B.A., B.D. *b*: Birmingham 1881. *e*: Lond Univ. *m*:. *s*: 1. *d*: 6. Tutor St Aidan's Coll Birkenhead, Lect William Temple Coll Hawarden, Hon Canon of Chester. *Publ*: Christian Morals. *Ctr*: Modern Churchman, Record. *s.s*: Ethics & Philosophy of Religion. *a*: Shotwick Vicarage, Chester.

HUMPHREYS, Christmas, M.A., LL.B. *b*: London 1901. *e*: Malvern & Trin Hall Camb. *m*: Aileen Maude

Faulkner. Barrister, Pres Buddhist Soc Lond. *Publ*: The Great Pearl Robbery of 1913; What is Buddhism?; Concentration & Meditation; Karma & Rebirth; Studies in the Middle Way; Via Tokyo. *Ctr*: The Middle Way. *s.s*: Comparative Religion & Art. *Rec*: Music, ballet, entertaining, eastern philosophy, Chinese art. *c*: Garrick. *a*: 58 Marlborough Pl, London, N.W.8. *T*: Maida Vale 4987.

HUMPHREYS, ELIZA M. Y.: see "Rita".

HUMPHREYS, Emyr Owen. *b*: Prestatyn, Flintshire 1919. *e*: U.C.W. & U.C.N.W. *m*: Elinor Myfanwy Jones. *s*: 1. Teacher & Author. *Publ*: The Little Kingdom; Michael Edwards. *Ctr*: Wales, Spectator, Good Housekeeping, etc. *s.s*: Poetry, Broadcast Features, Reviews of Lit & Sociological subjects Italy, Wales Ancient & Modern. *Rec*: Life in general. *a*: Ty Libanus, Bontnewyod, Cærnarvonshire, Wales.

HUMPHREYS, Dr. F. R. Major R.A.M.C.T. (ret)), Flight Lieut (Hon Sq Leader) R.A.F., Officer Order of St John of Jerusalem. Ex-Pres & Orator Hunterian Med Soc. *Publ*: Protection of Civil Population in Chemical Warfare (Manual issued to St J.A.A.). *a*: 15 Denton Rd, Wokingham, Berks.

HUMPHREYS, Sir G. W., K.B.E. Cons Eng. *Publ*: Contrib to Inst of Civil Engineers. *a*: 11 Queen Anne's Gate, S.W.1.

HUMPHREYS, Humphrey Francis, O.B.E., M.C., T.D., D.L., F.S.A. *b*: Bromsgrove 1885. *e*: K.E.S. Bromsgrove, Univ B'ham, Harvard Univ U.S.A. *m*: Constance Hudson. *s*: 2. Prof Dental Surgery. *Publ*: Text-Book of Surgery for Dental Students; Notes on Operative Dental Surgery. *Ctr*: British Medical Jour, British Dental Jour, Eugenics Review, Birmingham Poetry, etc. *s.s*: Dental Pathology; Dental Education. *Rec*: Hunting, gardening, archæology. *c*: Savile, Union (B'ham). *a*: Church Farm, Hampton-in-Arden, Warwickshire. *T*: 7.

HUMPHREYS, Rachel, F.R.G.S., F.R.S.A. *Publ*: Algiers, the Sahara, the Nile; Travels East of Suez; World Wide Wanderings. *c.t*: Daily Mail, Car Illus, Country Life, Englishman (Calcutta), Peoples of all Nations. *s.s*: Travel, lect War Office educ scheme. Broadcast travel talks. *Rec*: Travel. *c*: Lyceum, Forum, Overseas League. *a*: Swan Hill Court, Shrewsbury.

HUMPHREYS, Robert Arthur, O.B.E. *b*: Lincoln 1907. *e*: Lincoln Sch, Peterhouse Camb & Univ of Michigan. *m*: Elisabeth Pares. Prof of Latin American History Univ of London. *Publ*: British Consular Reports on the Trade & Politics of Latin America; The Evolution of Modern Latin America; Latin America, a Bibliography. *s.s*: Latin American History. *Rec*: Music, travel. *c*: United Univ. *a*: University College, Gower St, London, W.C.1.

HUMPHRIES, Sir Albert Edward, Kt, Hon LL.D. *b*: Bath 1864. *e*: Priv. *m*: (1) Ellen Vincent (dec). (2) Sylvia B. Burton. *s*: 1. *d*: 2. Miller *Publ*: Series of Reports on English Wheats (1906—); Several Reports to Indian Government on Wheats. *c.t*: Ency Brit, etc. *s.s*: Wheat, flour. Pres Nat Assoc of Millers '06—07, '17—18, '18—19. Chrm & Vice Chm Alternately of Nat Joint Industrial Counc Flour Milling Industry '19—. Mem Roy Comm on Wheat Supplies & Flour Mills Control '17—21. Chm Exec Cmt Nat Inst Agricultural Botany Cam '23—. *c*: Union Farmers. *a*: 43 Brondesbury Park, N.W.6. *t*: Willesden 6740.

HUMPHRIES, Rev. Albert Lewis, M.A. *b*: Bristol 1865. *e*: Elem Scs, L'pool Collegiate Sc, St John's Col Cam. *m*: May Bowen. *s*: 1. *d*: 1. Meth Min & Tutor in Systematic Theo & N.T. Greek Hartley Col M/C. *n.a*: Holborn Review, Co-Ed 1929—31. *Publ*: The Holy Spirit in Faith & Experience; St John & Other New Testament Writers; etc. *c.t*: Meth publs. *s.s*: Theo, Bibl problems. Pres P.M. Conf '26. Chm since Meth Un of M/C 2nd Dis. *Rec*: Golf. *a*: Ventnor, Kensington Gdns, Hale, Cheshire. *t*: Altrincham 1438.

HUMPHRIES, Arthur. Ed Staff Dly Graphic. *n.a*: Former Rep Reading Observer, Dly Citizen, Central News, Westminster Gazette, Sub-Ed Ev Standard, Dly Mail. *a*: Duck's Hill, Northwood, Middlesex.

HUMPHRIS Edith Mary. *b*: Cheltenham. *e*: Eng & Aust. *Publ*: Adam Lindsay Gordon & His Friends in England & Australia (in collab Douglas Sladen); The V.C. & D.S.O. (3 vols ed with Sir O. Moore Creagh, V.C., G.C.B., G.C.S.I.); The Life of Fred Archer; At Cheltenham Spa, or Georgians in a Georgian Town (collab Capt E. E. Willoughby); The Life of Mathew Dawson; The Life of Adam Lindsay Gordon; etc. *c.t*: Town Topics, Sunday Chron, Rugby Advertiser, R.M.A. Mag, Sporting & Dramatic, The Sydney Bulletin Co's Lone Hand Magazine, The Cheltenham Chronicle, Berrow's Worcester Journ, etc. *s.s*: Georgian hist, racing, steeplechasing. *a*: 13 Gloucester Rd, S.W.7.

HUMPHRIS, Maj. Francis Howard, D.M.R.E. (Cantab), M.R.C.S.(Eng), L.R.C.P.(Lon), L.M. R.A.M.C. (ret). *b*: Croydon 1866. *e*: Highgate G.S., Priv, Edinburgh Univ, U.C.L., Brussels Univ. *m*: Ethel Marion Hesketh. Consulting Physician. *n.a*: Ed American Archives of Physical Therapy, X-Ray Radium. *Publ*: Electro-therapeutics for Practitioners (2nd edn 1921), Artif Sunlight and its Therapeutic Uses; Physiotherapy, its Principles and Practice (with R. E. Stuart-Webb '30). *c.t*: Med Press & Circ, Journ of Phys Therapy, B.M.J., etc. *s.s*: Radiology, mild radium therapy, electro-therapy. *Rec*: Golf. Ex-Officer in charge X-Ray & Electrotherapeutic Dept 3rd Lon Gen Hosp. Consulting X-Ray Phys Christ's Hosp, Guildhall Sc of M & London Clinic & Inst of Phys Med. Com St John of Jerusalem, Chevalier of Order of Leopold. Freedom of City of Lon. *c*: Savage, Pilgrims. *a*: 4 Great Stanhope St, Park Lane, Lon. *t*: Grosvenor 1124 & 1646.

t. **Rev. Joseph Wellington,** O.B.E., M.C. (with bar), D.D. *b*: Truro 1887. *e*: Truro Sch, The Leys Camb, Gonville & Caius Colls Camb. *m*: Ruth Christobel Brew. *s*: 2. *d*: 3. Bishop of Truro, formerly Fellow, Dean & Tutor of Gonville & Caius Colls Camb, Senior Proctor 1925—26, Chaplain to H.M. the King from '26—35, Rector of Rugby & Archdeacon of Coventry '27—35. *Publ*: Is it Reasonable to Believe?; The Gospel for To-morrow; The Spirit of Man & the Spirit of God; Palestine in General History; Commentary on I & II Maccabees; Episcopal Ordination & Confirmation; Towards a Better England; Trees & Shrubs for Cornwall. *Ctr*: The Guardian, The C. of E. Newspaper, The Journal of the Roy Hort Soc. *s.s*: Theology. *Rec*: Gardening. *a*: Lis Escop, Truro. *T*: Truro 2183.

HUNOT, Peter. *b*: Winchester 1914. *e*: King's Sch Canterbury, Guy's Hosp Lond. *m*: Jean Garside. *s*: 1. Ed, Author, Organiser, Sociology Student & Public Relations. *n.a*: Ed A.R.P. & N.F.S. Rev 1940—44, Trade & Tech Dept Current Affairs Ltd '44, Asst-Ed Manufacturing Chemist, Paint Manufacture, Fibres, Synthetics & By-Products '44—46, Adv-Ed Trade Recorder '46, Ed International Observer '47. *Publ*: Man About the House. *Ctr*: Pilot Papers, Trade Recorder, etc. *s.s*: Scientific, Industrial, Sociological. *Rec*: Propagation of the idea of a world government, working on cttees. *a*: 112 Fitzjohns Ave, Hampstead, London, N.W.3. *T*: Hampstead 2456.

HUNT, Agnes Gwendoline, D.B.E., R.R.C. *Publ*: Orthopædic Nursing; The Story of Baschurch. *a*: Boreatton Farm Cottage, Baschurch, Shropshire. *t*: 7.

HUNT, Rev. Alfred Leedes. *b*: Ipswich 1853. *e*: Q. Elizabeth's G.S. Ipswich, St John's Col Cam. *m*: Mary Jane Ayshford (dec). *s*: 1. *d*: 2. Chap Addenbrooke's Hosp Cam. *n.a*: Home Visitor '96–97. *Publ*: David Simpson & The Evangelical Revival; Ruth the Moabitess ('94); Evangelical By-paths ('27); etc. Rural Dean of Walsingham '13–17. *s.s*: Theo & church history. *Rec*: Aquatic & football. *c*: Cam Univ Union Soc, Johnian (Cam) Soc. *a*: 2 Hinton Ave, Camb & Chaplain, Addenbrooke's Hosp Cam. *t*: Cam 23.

HUNT, Arthur John. *b*: Warwick 1910. *e*: Warwick Sc. Reporter. *n.a*: Surrey Advertiser & County Times '31–, Warwick Advertiser. *c.t*: Stage, Children's N/s, Birm Weekly Post. *s.s*: Dramatic & musical criticism. *Rec*: Swimming, rambling. *a*: 12 Agraria Rd, Guildford.

HUNT, Arthur Surridge. *b*: Romford 1871. *e*: Cranbrook Sc, Eastbourne Col & Queen's Col Oxf. *m*: Lucy Ellen Bradshaw. Prof of Papyrology Oxf Univ & Fell Queen's Col Oxf. *Publ*: Oxyrhynchus Papyri (17 vols); Tebtunis Papyri; New Sayings of Jesus & Fragment of a Lost Gospel; Two Theocritus Papyri; etc. *c.t*: Journ of Egyptian Archæ, Class Review, etc. *s.s*: Papyrology. War Service 1915–19. *Rec*: Travel, shooting. *a*: 6 Chadlington Rd, Oxf. *t*: 5549.

HUNT, Cecil. *b*: London 1902. *e*: Southgate County & King's Coll Lond. *m*: Kathleen Dykes. *s*: 2. Lit Agent, Author, Editor & Freelance, Broadcast & Televised frequently. *n.a*: Ad & Pub Man Ernest Benn Ltd, Fiction Ed Dly Mail & Ev News, Lit Ed Dly Mail. *Publ*: Over 40 books inc standard works on Journalism & Short Story Writing; The Howler books; Lit Reminiscences, etc; Humorous books (with Heath Robinson, Edmund Blampied, etc.) *s.s*: Journalism & Authorship, Literary Subjects, Schoolboy Howlers, Epitaphs, Quiz Material, etc. *Rec*: Writing. *a*: 11 Poultry, London, E.C.2. *T*: Central 4716.

HUNT, Dorothy Alice. *b*: Reading 1896. *e*: Hemdean House Caversham Heights. Author, Mem P.E.N. *Publ*: Unfettered; Meet Madame Mazova; Vagabonds All; Watching Eyes; Reflection; etc. *Ctr*: Various novels translated & serialized, Czecho-Slovakia, Illus Journ Sweden, Eastern Telegraph, etc. *s.s*: Romantic Novels with travel background, Short Stories, Poems, Recitations. *a*: 187 Pitshanger Lane, Ealing, London, W.5.

HUNT, Dr. E. R. *a*: 18 Palmeira Ave, Hove, Sussex.

HUNT, Eugene A. *b*: Highgate 1907. *e*: Stoke Newington G.S. & Univ Col Lon. *m*: Elizabeth Herries. Journalist. *n.a*: Reporter City Press (Lon) '24–29, Evening Sentinel (Stoke-on-Trent) '29–30, Sub-Ed Bucks Free Press '30–34. *c.t*: All Lon & prov dailies & nat periodicals. *c*: Mem N.U.J. *a*: Collingbourne, 254 Hughenden Rd, High Wycombe, Bucks.

HUNT, Francis George Geoffrey. *b*: Caversham 1910. *e*: Reading Sc. Bookseller's Asst. *n.a*: Reading & Dist Local Corr to Universe '33. *Publ*: Catholic Times, Catholic Fireside, Winner, Publisher's Circular, Lending Library. *s.s*: Catholicism. *Rec*: Swimming, boating. *a*: 9 Washington Road, Caversham, Reading.

HUNT, Frank Albert de Vine, F.R.G.S., F.R.S.A. *b*: Saltash, Cornwall 1900. *e*: Cannock House Sch Eltham Kent. *m*: Aenid Asken Ballin. *s*: 1. Geographer, Map Compiler, Social Worker. *Publ*: A Map, Dunkirk to Berlin—June '40—July '45 (journeys undertaken by the Rt Hon Winston S. Churchill, O.M., C.H., F.R.S., M.P.); A Time Zone Circle (prepared during the War for Mr. Churchill). *Ctr*: News Review of the Central Counc for the Care of Cripples. *s.s*: Map Design. *Rec*: Walking, swimming, travel, child welfare. *c*: R.N.V.R. *w.s*: Merchant Navy '15—19, World War II Admiralty (Lt-Cmdr). *a*: 26 John Adam St, Adelphi, London, W.C.2. *T*: Temple Bar 0865.

HUNT, Isabel Violet. *b*: Durham. *Publ*: The Maiden's Progress (1894); A Hard Woman; Unkist Unkind; Affairs of the Heart; The Cat; The Last Ditch; The Tiger Skin; The Flurried Years (1926); The Wife of Rossetti ('32); etc. *c.t*: Spectator, Saturday Review, English Review, New Statesman, Fortnightly Review, T.P.'s Weekly, etc.

HUNT, John. *b*: Leyland 1866. *e*: Hutton G.S. *m*: Mary E. Mitchell. *d*: 1. F.L. Jnlst. *c.t*: Various. *Rec*: Bowls. *c*: Leyland Cons & Leyland Cricket & Bowling. *a*: The Hollies, Crawford Av, Leyland. *t*: 81002.

HUNT, John Robert Rintoul. *e*: King's Col, Univ of Lon, Lon Sc of Economics. Journalist. *n.a*: Asst Ed North Star '21—2. Editorial staff Times '22—9. Ed Yorkshire Wkly Post. *c.t*: Numerous dlys, weeklys & mags. *a*: 1 Springwood Grove, Leeds 8. *t*: 66779.

HUNT, Joseph Wray Angus. *b*: Stone 1899. *e*: King William's Col, St Catherine's Soc Oxf. *m*: Marie Regina Adams. *s*: 1. *d*: 1. Author, Tutor. *Publ*: Growth and Development of an English Town; Growth and Development of an English Parish; Mediæval Studies; Behind the Mountains; etc. *s.s*: History, criminology. War Service 1917–22. *Rec*: Chess. *a*: 34 Alumhurst Rd, Westbourne, Bournemouth.

HUNT, K. P. *b*: M/C 1896. F/L Journalist. *c.t*: Sunday Sun Newcastle (Weekly radio features), Pearson's Weekly, The Guide for Competitors, The Daily Mirror, Daily Dispatch, etc. Trained as engineer, Joined Army as wireless operator. Became instructor at Military Wireless Sc Farnborough. Later graduated as flying officer & saw service as Flight Lieutenant with fighting squadron in France. Has travelled extensively on Continent & America. Has been free-lancing for last twelve years with exception of 3 years during which time he was manager to Jack Hylton & Assoc bands. *s.s*: Radio. *Rec*: Hiking, radio. *a*: 4 & 5 Warwick Ct, Gray's Inn, W.C.1.

HUNT, Leslie Bernard, Ph.D., M.Sc., A.M.I.A.E. *e*: Imperial Col, London. Metallurgical Engineer. *n.a*: Ed Metal Industry '35—. *a*: 22 Henrietta St, W.C.2. *t*: Temple Bar 5771.

HUNT, Rev. Richard James, F.R.A.I. *b*: Wisboro' Green 1874. *e*: Village Sc, Harley Missny T.C. *m*: Amy Jane Holloway. *s*: 2. *n.a*: S. American Missny Soc's Mag 1929–33. *Publ*: The Livingstone of South America; Trans (Lengua & Mataco dialects of the Gran Chaco); The Gospels & Acts; Prayer Book; Hymns; El Vejoz, Grammar & Dictionary; El Choroti, Grammar & Dict; etc. *c.t*: Bible in the World, The East & the West. S. Amer Missny Soc 1894–. Greatest authority on aboriginal dialects of S. Amer. *a*: The Rectory, Hardington Mandeville, Yeovil. *t*: W. Coker 13.

Who Was Who Among English and European Authors

HUNT, Major Rowland, J.P., D.L. *b*: Stoke Albany 1858. *e*: Eton & Cam. *m*: (1) Veronica Davidson; (2) Harriette Evelyn Hunt. *s*: 2. *d*: 1. *Publ*: Pamphlets: Socialism or Protection; Commercial Defence of Our People & Country; Free Trade or Freedom: Which?; S. African & European Wars. *Rec*: Hunting, fishing, shooting. *c*: Overseas League. *a*: Linley Green, Broseley, Salop. *t*: Bridgnorth 315.

HUNT, Thomas Cecil, M.D., M.R.C.P., B.A. *b*: Guildford 1901. *e*: Magdalen Col Oxf & St Mary's Hosp. *m*: Barbara Egerton. *d*: 1. Cons Phys. *Publ*: A Review of the Effects of Alcohol on Man (Pt Author, 1930); Chronic Indigestion ('33). *c.t*: Med Journ's. *s.s*: Medicine. Phys to Out-patients St Mary's Hosp, W.2. *Rec*: Golf, cricket. *a*: 12 Q. Anne St, W.1. *t*: Langham 4141.

HUNT, Miss U. D., M.A. Doctor of Univ Paris. *Publ*: Les Métamorphoses d'Ovide. Headmistress. *a*: Clapton County Sec Sc, Laura Place, E.5.

HUNTER, Rev. Adam Mitchell, M.A., D.Litt, F.R.S.E. *b*: Edin 1871. *e*: Watson's Col Edin & Univs of Edin & Marburg. *m*: Jessie Carslaw. *s*: 2. *d*: 1. Librarian of New Col Edin. *Publ*: The Age of Daniel & the Exile (1904); The Teaching of Calvin ('20). *c.t*: The Boy's Own Paper, The Expository Times, Life & Work, etc. *s.s*: Theology & astronomy. Ex-Pres of Edin Astronomical Ass. Pres of Edin Internat Club. *Rec*: Golf & tennis. *a*: 3 Suffolk Rd, Edin. *t*: 41494.

HUNTER, Allan Armstrong, M.A., D.D. *b*: Toronto, Canada 1893. *e*: Univs of Princeton & Columbia, Union Theol Sem New York. *m*: Elizabeth Sterling Walker. *s*: 1. *d*: 1. Min Mt Hollywood Congregational Church. *n.a*: Ctr Ed Pulpit Preaching 1947—. *Publ*: Say Yes to the Light; White Corpuscles in Europe ; Out of the Far East; Three Trumpets Sound ; Secretly Armed ; Youth's Adventure ; Social Perplexities ; Heroes of Good Will. *Ctr*: Christian Century, Motive, Pilgrim Highroad, etc. *s.s*: Religion, World Peace. *Rec*: Tennis, swimming, birds. *a*: 4609 Prospect Ave, Los Angeles 27, Calif, U.S.A. *T*: Mo 12004.

HUNTER, Andrew, M.A., B.Sc, M.B., F.R.S.E. *b*: Edin 1876. *e*: Geo Heriot's Sc, Univs of Edin, Berlin & Heidelberg. *m*: Janet Denholm Arthur. Prof of Physiological Chem Univ of Glas. *n.a*: Ex Asst Ed Chemical Abstracts. *Publ*: Creatine & Creatinine (Monographs on Biochem) 1928. *c.t*: Journ of Physiology, Journ of Biological Chem, Zeitschrift für Physiologische Chemie, Biochem Journ, etc. *s.s*: Biochem. *a*: Univ of Glas.

HUNTER, Bluebell Matilda. *b*: Lon. *e*: Lon & Abroad. *m*: H. S. Hunter. *s*: 1. *d*: 3. Novelist. *Publ*: Death Dams The Tide; Big Ben Looks On (John Guildford). *c.t*: Sunday Pict, A.P., Hulton Ltd. Thomson's Publs (Boris M. Hunter). *s.s*: Stories of love, adventure, crime. *Rec*: Gardening, travel. *c*: P.E. Authors' Group, Anti-War League. *a*: 55 Ladbroke Rd, W.11. *t*: Pk 8610.

HUNTER, Boris M. See **Hunter, Bluebell Matilda.**

HUNTER, Rev. Charles Frederick, B.A.(Lon). *b*: Queenstown, Cape Colony 1873. *e*: Kingswood Sc Bath & Headingley Col Leeds. *m*: Laura Lilian Scotts. *s*: 1. *d*: 1. *Publ*: What a Christian Believes & Why; Lesson Helps on the New Catechism; An Introduction to Sunday-School Work; etc. *s.s*: Sunday Sc teaching. *a*: 13 Parsonage Rd, Heaton Moor, Stockport. *t*: Heaton Moor 2503.

HUNTER. Clare Margaret. *b*: Michaelchurch, Eskley, Hereford 1900. *m*: Capt M. J. Hunter, B.A., M.P. *s*: 1. *d*: 3. Dir of The Unicorn Press, Ltd. John Heritage Publishers. *c*: Ladies Carlton. *a*: Stoke Hall, Calver, Derbyshire. *t*: Grindleford 29.

HUNTER, Dard. Litt.D., L.H.D. *b*: Steubenville, Ohio 1883. *e*: Ohio State Univ, Vienna & London. *m*: Helen Edith Cornell. *s*: 2. Writer & Publisher. *Publ*: Old Papermaking ; The Literature of Papermaking 1390—1800; Primitive Papermaking ; Papermaking through Eighteen Centuries ; Old Papermaking in China & Japan ; A Papermaking Pilgrimage to Japan, Korea & China ; Chinese Ceremonial Paper ; Papermaking in Siam ; Papermaking by Hand in India ; etc. *Ctr* : Various. *s.s*: Papermaking, Watermarking, Printing, Typefounding, etc. *a*: Massachusetts Institute of Technology, Cambridge 39, Mass, U.S.A., & Chillicothe, Ohio, U.S.A.

HUNTER, David Stevenson Taylor, F.J.I. *n.a*: Ed Financial Times. *a*: 25 Tierney Rd, S.W.2. *t*: Streatham 5408.

HUNTER, E. E. Sec Parliamentary Br N.U.J. *a*: The Firs, Green Lane, Chesham Bois, Bucks.

HUNTER, E. Kenneth. *n.a*: Ed Printer's Plant & Kentek Tech Library. *s.s*: Printing, photomechanical processes. *a*: 12 Mornington Mans, New Church Rd, Hove 3, Sussex. *t*: Portslade 9155.

HUNTER, Rev. Edward Thomas Gurney. *b*: Wensley 1880. *e*: St Paul's Sch, Trin Coll Oxf, Oxf Hse Bethnal Green, Bishop's Hostel Liverpool. *m*:. *s*: 2. Rector of S. Perrott 1940—45, Rector of Upper S. Leonards '26—40. *Publ*: Thoughts on the Invisible. *Ctr* : Sussex Ev Argus, Goodwill, For Health & Healing. *Rec*: Cricket, tennis, golf, fishing, hockey. *a*: The Old House, Baltonsborough, Glastonbury, Som. *T* : Baltonsborough 284.

HUNTER, George William, A.M., Ph.D. *b* : N.Y. City 1873. *e* : William's Coll & Univ of N.Y. *m* : Emily Isabel Jobbins. *s*: 3. College Professor. *n.a* : Assoc-Ed Science Education since foundation. *Publ* : A Civic Biology ; Life Science ; Problems in Biology ; Everyday Biology ; (collab) Civic Science Series ; March of Science ; Doorways to Science ; etc. *Ctr* : Various so journs. *s.s* : Science, Education. *Rec* : Fishing. *c* : Univ. *a* : 466 W. 10th St, Claremont, California, U.S.A. *T* : 7191.

HUNTER, Dr. J. W. *c.t*: Lancet, Medical Officer. Chief Asst M.O.H. *a*: Health Dept, Guildhall, Portsmouth.

HUNTER, James. *b*: Newcastle 1899. *e*: Elementary & secondary scs. *m*: Lillian Stookes. *s*: 1. Journalist. *n.a*: Newcastle Jnl, '19. Newcastle Chronicle '28. Newcastle Staff Daily Express, '34—. *s.s*: Labour, industrial matters. *Rec*: Golf, swimming. *a*: 165 Two Ball Lonnen, Fenham, Newcastle-on-Tyne. *t*: 34106.

HUNTER, James Alexander. *n.a*: Ed The Mercantile Guardian. *a*: 52 Bishopsgate, E.C.2.

HUNTER, John Bowman, C.B.E., M.C. *b*: London 1890. *e*: Bedford, St John's Coll Camb, U.C.H. Lond. *m*: Hilda Whitfield. *s*: 1. *d*: 1. *Publ*: Jt-Ed Rose & Carless's Manual of Surgery. *Rec*: Golf. *c*: Savile. *a*: 39 Devonshire Pl, London, W.1. *T*: Welbeck 6561.

HUNTER, Rt. Rev. Leslie Stannard, M.A., Hon.D.C.L. (Durham). b : 1890. e : Kelvinside Acad, New Coll Oxf. m : Grace Marion McAulay. Bishop of Sheffield, Residential Canon of Newcastle-on-Tyne 1922—26, Vicar of Barking '26—30, Archdeacon of Northumberland & Canon of Newcastle '31—39, Chaplain to the King '36—39, Chrm of Sheffield Hospitals Council. Publ : The Artist & Religion ; John Hunter, D.D.; A Life ; On Keeping Sunday ; A Parson's Job ; A Church Militant ; Planning Ahead ; Let Us Go Forward. s.s : Religion. Rec : Lawn tennis, music, walking. c : Athenæum. a : Ranmoor Grange, Sheffield 10. T : 32170.

HUNTER, Mrs. M., M.A.(Oxon). Priv Tutor in Classics Oxf Univ. Residential Prep for Oxford & Camb Women's Cols. a: 68 Banbury Rd, Oxford.

HUNTER, Michael John, B.A. e : Rugby, Clare Col Camb. Publisher & M.P. Chm Unicorn Press Ltd. & John Heritage. a : Stoke Hall, Calver, Derbyshire. t : Grindleford 29.

HUNTER, Norman. b : Lon 1899. e : Beckenham County Sc. m : Sylvia Marie Rangel. s : 1. d : 2. Author & Journalist. Publ : The Incredible Adventures of Professor Branestawm ; Jingle Tales ; Advertising Through the Press ; Simplified Conjuring ; The Bad Barons of Crashbania ; etc. c.t : Sunday Graphic, Evening News, Daily Express, Homes & Gardens, Modern Woman, Nursery World, Red Letter, etc. ; also B.B.C. & American, N.Z. & Aus papers. s.s : Children's stories & verse, Advertg, conjuring. Children's stories fourth in the list of favourites voted for by listeners in B.B.C. Request Week. Rec : Gardening, cinematography. a : The Haven, The Marina, Boscombe. t : Boscombe 1959.

HUNTER, Stewart. b : Glasgow 1915. e : Allan Glen's Sch Glasgow. m : Mary Lakin. d : 2. Publ : Revenant ; This Good Company ; etc. Rec : Reading, music, watching birds, badminton, etc. a : c/o Nicholson & Watson. 26 Manchester Sq, London, W.1.

HUNTER, Lieut.-Colonel T., C.I.E., I.M.S. (ret). a: Brand Hse, Ludlow, Salop.

HUNTER, Thomas. Rt Hon Lord Provost of City & Roy Burgh Perth. n.a : Ed Perthshire Constitutional & Journ. Publ: History of St John's Church ; Guide to Perth. a: Nimrod, 142 Glasgow Rd, Perth.

HUNTER, Thomas. b: Paisley 1878. e: Paisley G.S. & Glas Univ. m: Helen Nicolson. d: 1. Solicitor. n.a: Proprietor Paisley & Renfrewshire Gazette, Barrhead News, Pollokshaws News. s.s: Lit, local hist, econ. Rec: Bowls. c: Lib, Paisley. a: 35 High St, Paisley, & House Duncomb, Stanley Drive, Paisley. t: 2549 & 2531.

HUNTER, W., Jun. Cons Obstetrician & Gynæcologist. a: 245 Chester Rd, Sunderland.

HUNTER, Walter King, M.D., D.Sc. b: Glas 1867. e: Glas Acad, Glas Univ, Paris & Lon. Publ: Recent Advances in Hæmatology. c.t: Lancet, B.M.J., Brain. s.s: Hæmatology, diseases of the nervous system. Phys Glas Roy Inf. Muirhead Prof of Med Univ of Glas. Rec: Golf. c: Art, & Western (Glas), F.R.F.P. & S. Glas. a: 7 Woodside Pl, Glas, C.3. t: Douglas 1533.

HUNTER, William, M.D., B.S., M.R.C.O.G. b : Sunderland, Co Durham 1906. e : Durham Sch, Univ of Durham. m : Nellie Trainer Walton. d : 3. Ctr : B.M.J., Newcastle Med Journ, Clinical Journ, Journ of Obstetrics & Gynæcology of Brit Empire. s.s : Obstetrics & Gynæcology. Rec : Miniature cine photography. a : 10 Granville Rd, Newcastle-on-Tyne 2. T : Jesmond 2332.

HUNTER BLAIR, Rt. Rev. Sir David, 5th Baronet of Dunskey, B.A., M.A. b: Portpatrick. e: Eton, Magd Col Oxf. Cath Priest & Abbot of Benedictine Order. Formerly Capt Prince Regent's Ayr & Wigtown Militia. Publ: A Medley of Memories; Memories & Musings; John Marquess of Bute—A Memoir; Flying Leaves; Belleshiem's Hist of the Catholic Church of Scotland (Trans from German with Notes & Additions); The Holy Rule of St Benedict (Trans with Explanatory Notes); etc. c.t: Dublin Review, Month, Universe, Outlook, Field, Times, Notes & Queries, Tablet, etc. s.s : Hist, geneal, archæ, biog. Master of St Bénet's Hall Oxf Univ 10 ys. Successively Bursar, Headmaster of Abbey Sc Sub-prior, Prior & Lord Abbot of Fort Augustus Abbey, now (Titular) Abbot of Dunfermline. Chamberlain of Honour to H.H. Pope Pius IX & H.H. Pope Leo XIII. Rec: Music. c: Caledonian, New Edin & Oxf Union. a: St Benedict's Abbey, Fort Augustus, Scot.

HUNTER-COE, Katherine, F.R.S.A. b Indiana. e: Indiana Scs, Priv & Cincinnati Training Sc. m: Dr Oliver Parker Coe. Writer, Author, Editor. n.a: Poetry Ed Home & Abroad (Eng Illustrated Review Lon & Paris 1930), Co-Ed Poetry Studies (Lon '33), Asst Ed The Poets' Forum U.S.A. '28. Edited 2 Anthologies Poems of America & Poems of all Nations. Publ: The Loom of Life; Sundial Shadows (in prep). c.t: Poets' Scroll, Poets' Parchment, The Poet's Forum, Cincinnati Times-Star, Cincinnati Enquirer, Cincinnati Post, Springfield Republican, Indianapolis Star, Buckeye, Fine Arts, To-Day's Housewife, Troubadour, Columbus Dispatch, Twilight Mag, etc. s.s: Poetry, articles & short stories. c : Empire Poetry League, Woman's Press, Ohio Newspaper Woman's Assoc, Ohio Poetry Soc, American Lit Assoc, League of American Pen Woman, Société Académique d'Historie Internat. a: Apt A6, 132 W. McMillan St, Cincinnati, Ohio, U.S.A. t: Main 4638.

HUNTINGDON, 15th Earl of, Francis John Clarence Westensa Plantagenet Hastings, B.A. b : London 1901. e : Eton, Christ Ch Oxf. m : Margaret Lane. d : 3. Artist (mural painter) & Author, Pupil of Diego Rivera, formerly Parl Sec Min of Agric & Fisheries. Publ: The Golden Octopus ; Commonsense about India. Ctr : Architectural Review. Rec: Sailing, river-fishing. c : Garrick, Travellers, Artworkers Guild. a : Forston Hse, Dorchester, Dorset.

HUNTLEY, Allen. L.R.A.M. Schoolmaster A.M.A., Teacher. Publ: English Composition: Processes & Essentials. a: 60 Stratford Ave, Sunderland.

HUNTLEY, Arthur Geoffrey. Acoustical Engineer. c.t: Building Trade Journs. a: 31 Sutton Ct Rd. Sutton. t: 1949.

HURD, Sir Archibald, A.I.N.A. Mem Journ Inst. n.a : Chm & Mang-Ed The Shipping World Co. a : The Shaw, Brasted Chart, Kent. T : Brasted 63.

HURD, Sir Percy Angier. n.a : Ed-in-Chief Canada's Weekly London. Publ : The Empire ; A Family Affair ; etc. Ctr : Various Publs on Empire & Agricultural subjects. a : Hillside, Jackson's Lane, London, N.6. T : Mountview 1920.

HURD, William Burton, O.B.E.(Mil), M.A., F.R.S.C. b : Brockville, Ontario 1894. e : Univs of Man & Queen's Coll Oxf. m : Ruth Winifred Winkler. s : 1. Prof of

Econ 1935 & Head of Dept of Econ '47— McMaster Univ. *n.a*: Ed-Bd Canadian Journ of Econ & Political Sc '42—. *Publ*: Origin, Birthplace, Nationality & Language of the Canadian People; Agriculture, Climate & Population of the Prairie Provinces of Canada; Racial Origins & Nativity of the Canadian People; Demographic Trends in Relation to the Agricultural Development of Canada. *Ctr*: Queen's Quarterly, Can Banker, MacLean's Can Forum, etc. *s.s*: Population & General Economics. *Rec*: Hunting, fishing, camping. *a*: McMaster University, & 66 Oak Knoll Drive, Hamilton, Ontario, Canada. *T*: 3-1112, & 2-0919.

HURLEY, Alfred James, J.P. *b*: Chelsea 1874. Married. *s*: 2. *d*: 1. Newspaper Prop, Retired in 1945 after 40 yrs as Alderman on Wansworth Boro Counc. *n.a*: Mang-Ed Tooting & Balham Gazette 1907—. *Publ*: Days that are Gone. *Ctr*: The Star. *s.s*: Gen News. *Rec*: Farming. *a*: Warren Farm, Epsom, Surrey. *T*: Burgh Heath 1140.

HURRELL, Francis Gordon. *b*: Kenninghall 1885. Journalist. *n.a*: Night Ed Continental Daily Mail 1932—, *Publ*: A Dreamer Under Arms ('16); The Lantern Show of Paris; Married Men ('34); John Lillibud. *c.t*: Spectator. *s.s*: France, French life. *c*: I.J. *a*: 4 Rue Gerbillon, Paris VI. *t*: Littre 17—17.

HURREN, Bernard John. *b*: Lincoln 1907. *e*: Dulwich Col. *m*: Evelyn Muriel de Garston. *Publ*: Stand Easy! *s.s*: R.A.F., naval & military manœuvres, Italian politics, etc. *Rec*: Cricket, rugby football, sailing. *a*: 137a High St, Kensington, W.8. *t*: Western 3830.

HURRY, JAMIESON BOYD: author, s. Rev. Nicholas and Anne Shaw Jamieson (Boyd) H.; educ. City of London School; St. John's Coll. (Cambridge); St. Bartholomew's Hospital (London); DEGREES: M.A., M.D., D.P.H.; m. Gertrude Louisa Hill, Feb. 16, 1892. AUTHOR: District Nursing on a Providentt Basis, 1898; A History of Reading Abbey, 1901; The Rise and Fall of Reading Abbey, 1906; A History of the Reading Pathological Society, 1909; The Ideals and Organization of a Medical Society, 1913; Sumer is Icumen in (2nd edit.), 1914; The Vicious Circles of Neurasthenia, 1915; Vicious Circles in Sociology, 1915; Vicious Circles in Disease (3rd edit.), 1919, (French edit. 1913, Spanish edit. 1924, Italian edit. 1925, Japanese edit. 1929); The Trial by Combat of Henry de Essex and Robert de Montfort at Reading Abbey, 1919; King Henry Beauclerk and Reading Abbey, 1917; Poverty and its Vicious Circles (2nd edit.), 1921, (Japanese edit. 1922, French edit. 1924, Italian edit. 1925, Chinese edit. 1927; The Octocentenary of Reading Abbey, 1921; Imhotep, the Egyptian Deity of Medicine (2nd edit), 1928. Contributor to The Times, Lancet, British Medical Jnl. and many others. Founder of the Michael Foster Research Studentship at Cambridge. HOME: Hinton Firs, 9 Manor Road, Bournemouth, Eng.

HURST, Albert Edward, F.R.S.A., F.I.B.I. *b*: Stockport 1905. *e*: Elem Sch Stockport, Manch Sch of Art. *m*: Rachel Barker. *d*: 2. Interior Decorator, For 6 yrs Teacher of Painting & Decorating, Blackburn Tech Coll, Mem Painting Craft Teacher's Assoc. *Publ*: Painting & Decorating. *Ctr*: Journal of Decorative Art. *s.s*: Water colour drawings in Perspective, Technique of Painting & Decorating. *Rec*: Outdoor sketching, listening to music. *a*: 48 Earnsdale Rd, Darwen, Lancs. *T*: 662.

HURST, C. L., F.R.S.A., F.A.L.P.A., A.I.A.A., A.I.A.S. Incorp Architect, Surveyor & Estate Mang. *s.s*: Housing, town planning, surveying, estate management. Counc of M/C Branch of Incorp Assoc of Architects & Surveyors 1928. *a*: Estate Office, off 573 St Helen's Rd, Bolton.

HURST, Charles Chamberlain, Sc.D., Ph.D., F.L.S., T.D., D.L., J.P. *b*: Burbage, Leics 1870. *e*: Hinckley Gr Sch, Wes Coll Sheffield, Trin Coll Camb. *m*: Roana Hurst. *s*: 1. Biologist & Geneticist (Plants, Animals & Man). *Publ*: Experiments in Genetics; The Mechanism of Creative Evolution; Heredity & the Ascent of Man; The Orchid Stud Book; The Genetics of the Rose; The Inheritance of Eye-Colour in Man; The Inheritance of Intelligence in Man. *Ctr*: Journ Roy Hort Soc, Orchid Review, Times, Nature, etc. *s.s*: Genetics, Evolution, Agriculture, Biology, Botany, etc. *Rec*: Chess, reading, music. *w.s*: Major R.E. Signals World War I, R.O.C. & A.A.O. Civil Defence Control 1942—45. *a*: Broomhurst, Worthing Rd, Horsham, Sussex. *T*: Horsham 941.

HURST, Edward Weston, M.D., D.Sc. *b*: Birmingham 1900. *e*: King Edward's Sch Birm'ham, Univ of Birm'ham. *m*: (1) Phyllis Edith Pickett, (2) Barbara Ternent Cooke. *s*: 1. *d*: 4. *n.a*: Med Ed Bd Australian Journ of Experimental Biology & Medical Science 1937—43. *Ctr*: Ency Brit, various pathological, bacteriological, neurological journs, etc. *s.s*: Neuropathology, Virus Diseases. *a*: Biological Dept, Imperial Chems Ltd, Hexagon Hse, Blackley, Manchester. *T*: Cheetham Hill 1460.

HURST, Fannie, A.B. *b*: Hamilton, Ohio. *e*: Univs of Wash & Columb. *m*: Jacques S. Danielson. *Publ*: Hands of Veronica; Hallelujah; Lonely Parade; Great Laughter: Anitta's Dance; Imitation of Life; Back Street; Five & Ten; A President is Born; Appassionata; Lummox; Stardust; We Are Ten; Procession; Song of Life; The Vertical City; Humoresque; Gaslight Sonatas; Every Soul Hath Its Song (all trans into 14 languages); No Food with My Meals; Back Pay; Land of The Free; It Is To Laugh; Imitation of Life; Symphony of Six Million; etc. *a*: 1 West 67th St, New York, U.S.A.

HURST, His Honour Sir Gerald Berkeley, K.C., M.A., B.C.L. *b*: Bradford 1877. *e*: Bradford Gr Sch, Lincoln Coll Oxf. *m*: Margaret Alice Hopkinson. *d*: 5. Judge of County Courts 1937—, Lincoln's Inn Bencher '24, Treasurer '44, M.P. (Cons) for Manch Moss Side Div '18—23, '24—35. *Publ*: Closed Chapters; Short History of Lincoln's Inn. *Ctr*: Eng Hist Rev, & most monthlies. *s.s*: Legal History. *c*: Athenæum. *a*: 15 Church Row, Chislehurst, Kent. *T*: Imp 3618.

HURST, James Edgar. *b*: Hadfield 1893. *e*: Glossop G.S. *m*: Margery Whiteley. *s*: 1. *d*: 1. Tech Dir of Coys. *n.a*: Ed Foundry Trades Journ 1918-20. *Publ*: Metallurgy of Cast Iron ('26); Melting Iron in the Cupola. *s.s*: Ferrous metallurgy. Vice-Pres Inst of Brit Foundrymen, Oliver Stubbs Gold Medal Inst of Brit Foundrymen. Mem of the Counc of the Brit Cast Iron Research Assoc, etc. *Rec*: Golf, motoring. *c*: Constitutional. *a*: The Beeches, Green Lane, Dronfield, nr Sheffield. *T*: Dronfield 122.

HURSTON, Zora Neale, B.A. *b*: Eatonville, Florida 1903. *e*: Barnard Coll. Anthropologist & Writer. *Publ*: Mules & Men; Folklore of the United States; Tell My Horse; Study of Haitian Voodoo & Jamaica; Their Eyes Were Watching God; Jonah's Gourd Vine; Moses, Man of the Mountain. *Ctr*: Sat Ev Post, Chicago Dly News, Amer Mercury, Sat Rev of Lit, The World Tomorrow, New York Her-Tri, New York World Telegram, etc. *s.s*: Fiction & Folklore. *Rec*: Boating, golf, croquet, bridge, black jack. *a*: c/o Charles Scribner's Sons, 597 Fifth Ave, New York, 17, N.Y.

HURT, Herbert John Bellamy. *b*: Mansfield Woodhouse 1891. Reporter. *n.a*: Press Assoc Law Courts Staff. *a*: Ambergate, 18 Carrington Rd, Dartford, Kent.

HURT, Huber William, S.B., A.M., LL.D., Ph.D. *b*: Princeton, Mo 1883. *e*: Iowa Wesleyan Coll, Univs of Columbia, Chicago & Berlin. *m*: Harriet H. Hibbs. *s*: 1. *d*: 2. Author, Lecturer, Research & Publ Relations Consultant. *Publ*: Socratic Geometry; College Standards in the U.S.; Mechanics of Human Relations; College Blue Book 1924, '28, '34, '39; The Child & His Home; The Den Chief's Denbook; The Cubmaster's Pack Book; Goals; Life of Knute Rockne; The Influencing of Character; Adventuring for Sea Scouts; Scouting for Rural Boys; Respects & Courtesies in Scouting; National Survey of Aviation; Air Scout Manual; Hints to Squadron Leaders; Aeronautics; Airplane Structure; Aerodynamics; etc. *Rec:* Hunting, gardening, tennis, etc. *a:* 17th Floor, 2 Park Ave, New York 16, N.Y., & Lake Florida Creative School, R.I., Deland, Florida, U.S.A.

HURT, Jack. Salesman. *c.t:* Nott'm Journ, Daily Express. *a:* 33 Rutland Rd, W. Bridgford, Nott'm.

HURT, William George, M.J.I. *b:* Lon 1894. *e:* Stationers' Coy Sc & Sheffield Univ. Journalist. *n.a:* Daily Mail 1924, Times '25, Ed The Advertising World '27, British Roads '29. *c.t:* World's Press News, Yorkshire Evening Post, Times, Daily Mail, Flight, etc. *s.s:* Aviation, travel. Publicity Officer B.I.F. '26, & Sir Alan Cobham's Air Tour '32. Gen Mang Brit Hosp's Air Pageants '33. *Rec:* Flying, motoring, cruising. *c:* Press, Lon. *a:* Cobham Way, E. Horsley, Surrey. *t:* 146.

HUSAIN, Iqbal, M.A., B.L., Ph.D. *b:* Patna 1905. *e:* G.B.B. Coll Patna, Law Colls Patna. *m:* Fakhsunnisa. *s:* 3. Senior Prof of Persian Patna Coll. *n.a:* Mem Ed Bd Patna Univ Journ. *Publ:* The Tuhfa I Sami; The Early Persian Poets of India; Qasaid I Urfi. *Ctr:* Hindustan Review, Islamic Culture, Searchlight, etc. *s.s:* Persian Poetry of India. *Rec:* Radio & gardening. *a:* Patna Coll, P.O. Bankipore, Patna. *T:* 555.

HUSE, Howard Russell, Ph.D.(Chicago). *b:* Omaha, Nebraska 1890. *e:* Univs of Chicago & Dijon. *m:* Charlotte Jeanne Vulliémoz. *s:* 1. *d:* 1. Prof of Romance languages, Univ of North Carolina. *Publ:* Essentials of Written and Spoken French; The Psychology of Foreign Language Study; Contes et Récits; The Illiteracy of the Literate. *s.s:* Language learning, psychology of language. *c:* Modern Lang Assoc, American Assoc of Univ Profs. *a:* Chapel Hill, North Carolina, U.S.A.

HUSEY, Ernest Wynniatt. *s.s:* Finance. *c:* Carlton. *a:* 2 Tokenhouse Bldgs, E.C.2. *t:* Metropolitan 8541.

HUSKINSON, Edward. *b:* 1878. *e:* Oakham. *n.a:* Ed The Tatler. Dir Illustrated N/ps Ltd. *c:* Bath. *a:* 27a Charles St, W.1. *t:* Grosvenor 1208.

HUSSAIN, Badshah. *b:* Hyderabad, Deccan 1910. *e:* Nizam's Coll. *m:* Sheher Bano Razvi. *s:* 1. *d:* 1. H.E.H. the Nizam's Govt Servant Hyderabad-Dn India. *Publ:* (In Urdu lang) History of Urdu Drama; Compilation of Poetical Works of Taban; Living Celebrities of India; Book of Knowledge in India; Collection of Short Stories; Trans of the Autobiography of Mussolini. *Ctr:* Alamgir, Nigar, Saqi, Subras, Shahab, Ajkal, Khayyam, Adabi, Duniya, etc. *s.s:* Short Stories, Dramas, Film Stories, Hist of Urdu Lit. *c:* P.E.N. *a:* Noorkhan Bazar, Hyderabad-Dn, India, & Temp Secretariat Bldgs, Saifabad, Hyderabad-Deccan, India. *T:* 2789.

HUSSERL, Helmuth, M.D.(Vienna). *b:* Bruenn 1895. *e:* Univ of Vienna. *m:* Dr. Hedwig. Dir Vienna Clinic (Pty) Cape Town. *Publ:* The Epidemics of Naples; The Physics of the Divining Rod. *Ctr:* Forum (S.A.), various medical papers. *s.s:* Cancer Research, Cosmic & Earth Rays, Racial Questions, Biology. *Rec:* Gardening. *a:* Union Hse, Queen Victoria St, Cape Town, South Africa. *T:* 3-1112 & 39-8139.

HUSSEY, Christopher Edward Clive, M.A., F.S.A., Hon.A.R.I.B.A. *b:* 1899. *e:* Eton, Christ Church Ox. *m:* Elizabeth Maud Kerr Smiley. Architectural Consultant of Country Life. *n.a:* Joined Staff of Country Life 1921, Ed '33—40. *Publ:* Eton College; Petworth House; Garden Ornament (in collab) in The Picturesque; The Architecture of Vanburgh & his school (in collab); Tait McKenzie, Sculptor of Youth; Architecture of Sir Robert Lorimer; etc. *Rec:* Country life. *c:* Garrick, Beefsteak, Burlington Fine Arts. *a:* 2-10 Tavistock St, London, W.C.2.

HUTCHEN, Frank, F.R.G.S., F.J.I. *b:* Kettering 1870. *e:* Wellingborough G.S. *m:* Carrie M. Smith. *s:* 2. *d:* 1. Journalist. *n.a:* Asst Mang Northamptonshire Printing & Publishing Co Ltd 1894. Mang Ed Northamptonshire Evening Telegraph & Kettering Leader Series 1901. *Publ:* Under the Southern Cross. *c.t:* Lon & Prov. *s.s:* Travel, sport. *Rec:* Motoring. *c:* R.A.C. *a:* Dryden House, Kettering. *t:* 347.

HUTCHEON, William, F.J.I. *b:* Inverurie 1866. *e:* G.S. & Aber Univ. *m:* Ada M. Finer, M.B.E. J.P. *s:* 1. Journalist & Author. *n.a:* Mem Ed Staff Aberdeen Free Press 1886, Bradford Observer '87, Manchester Guardian '94, Morning Post (Night Ed) 1904—25, Dir L. Hutcheon Ltd, Advertising Agents '27. *Publ:* Disraeli on Whigs and Whiggism; Gentlemen of the Press; Memories & Friendships of Forty Years (Illus by James McRey '33); etc. *c.t:* Numerous. *Rec:* Reading. *a:* 124 Pepys Rd, Wimbledon, S.W.20. *t:* 2025.

HUTCHINGS, Monica Mary. *b:* Cardiff, Glam 1917. *e:* Marlborough Road Girl's Sch, Trowbridge H Sch, N Lond Collegiate Sch for Girls, Ilminster Girls Gr Sch. *m:* H. L. R. Hutchings, M.P.S. *Publ:* Romany Cottage, Silverlake; Hundredfold; The Chronicles of Church Farm; Rural Reflections. *Ctr:* Farmer & Stockbreeder, West Countryman, Farmer's Weekly, Countrygoer, Country, Country Review, etc. *s.s:* English Countryside (Partic Somerset & Dorset), Rural Conditions of Living. *Rec:* Visiting museums, reading. *a:* Church Farm, South Barrow, Yeovil, Som. *T:* North Cadbury 306.

HUTCHINSON, Alexander. *b:* Glasgow 1910. *e:* Whitehill Publ Sch. *m:* Margaret Livingstone Beattie Paterson. Deputy M.O.H. City of Leicester. *Ctr:* B.M.J., Lancet, Glas Med Journ, The Med Officer. *s.s:* Public Health, Mercantile Marine Social Conditions, Care of the Aged. *Rec:* Swimming, rugby football, Badminton, boxing. *a:* 10 Fosse Rd Central, Leicester. *T:* 60411.

HUTCHINSON, Arthur. O.B.E., F.R.S. Master of Pembroke. *a:* The Lodge, Pembroke Col, Cam. *t:* 670.

HUTCHINSON, Arthur Stuart-Menteth. *b:* Gorakpur 1879. *e:* St Lawrence Coll. *m:* Una Rosamond Bristow-Gapper. *s:* 2. Novelist. *n.a:* Ed Daily Graphic 1915—16. *Publ:* Once Aboard the Lugger; If Winter Comes; This Freedom; One Increasing Purpose; The Uncertain Trumpet; The Soft Spot; He Looked for a City; It Happened Like This. *a:* c/o J. B. Pinker & Son, Arundel St, London, W.C.2.

HUTCHINSON, E. H. J. *b:* Notts 1916. *e:* Priv. Writer. *s.s:* Short stories. *Rec:* Chess. *c:* Notts Writers. *a:* 295 Radford Boulevard, Notts. *t:* 76549.

HUTCHINSON, Erik. *b:* Nottingham 1916. *e:* Priv. Playwright & Journalist. *Publ:* Play :—But Now I am Returned. *Rec:* Playgoing. *a:* 295 Radford Boulevard, Notts.

HUTCHINSON, Rev. Francis Ernest, M.A., D.Litt.(Oxon), F.B.A. *b*: Forton, Hants 1871. *e*: Lancing & Trin Coll Oxf, formerly Fell of All Souls' Camb. *m*: Julia Margaret Crawford. *s*: 1. *d*: 1. Canon of Worcs 1934—43, formerly interested W.E.A. *n.a*: Ed Camb Rev '06—07. *Publ*: Works of George Herbert (ed); Henry Vaughan: A Life and Interpretation; Milton & the English Mind; Christian Freedom (Hulsean Lects); Chapters in Vols IV, VII and XII Camb Hist of Eng Lit. *s.s*: 17th Cent Eng Lit. *a*: 3 Church Walk, Oxford. *T*: 3930.

HUTCHINSON, Rev. Franklin Isaac, B.Ph., D.Litt., F.R.G.S., F.R.A.S., F.R.S.A., M.R.S.L. *b*: Co Wexford 1887. Priest Established Church. *Publ*: On Broken Pinion; A Distillation of Rumour; The Wise Thrush; Out of the Past; The Sacrament of Adultery. *s.s*: Art, Geology, Astronomy, Music, Science, Greek & Roman Literature, World Religious Systems. *Rec*: Gardening, photography, ornithology. *c*: Roy Socs & Roy Empire. *a*: Saint Francis Cote, 24 Norman Rd, Bury St Edmunds, Suffolk. *T*: 1207.

HUTCHINSON, George Thomas, M.C. *b*: Tynemouth 1880. *e*: Marlboro' & Magdalen Col Ox. *m*: Evelyn Lloyd Thomas. *s*: 1. *d*: 1. Treas Christ Church Oxf. *Publ*: From the Cape to the Zambesi; Frank Rhodes—a Memoir; Edward Fitzgerald Law (jt ed with Sir Theodore Morison). *c.t*: Quarterly Review & Times. *s.s*: Agriculture. *Rec*: Sport & travel. Barrister-at-Law 1906, Asst Sec Duchy of Cornwall '07-10. War Service '14-18. *c*: Travellers'. *a*: Christ Church, Oxford.

HUTCHINSON, HENRY NEVILLE, B.A., F.G.S.: clergyman, author; b. Chester, Eng., Mar. 27, 1856; s. Thomas Neville and Sarah (Turner) H.; educ. Grammar Sch., Rugby, Cambridge; DE-GREE: B.A., 1878; m. Bertha Hasluch, Jan. 22, 1903. AUTHOR: The Story of the Hills, 1891; Prehistoric Man and Beast, 1896; Marriage Customs in Many Lands, 1897; Primeval Scenes, 1899; The Living Race of Mankind, 1900; The Living Rulers of Mankind, 1902; Extinct Monsters and Creatures of Other Days, 1911. Contributor to many newspapers. Taught at Clifton College; ordained by Bishop of Gloucester; lecturer. CLUBS: Royal Societies; Authors'. Relig. denom., Church of England. (*)

HUTCHINSON, Hugh Lester, Dès.L.(Neuchâtel). *b*: Bury, Lancs 1904. *e*: Bootham & Univs of Neuchâtel, Genoa & Edinburgh. Schoolmaster. *Publ*: The Empire of the Nabobs; Conspiracy at Meerut; Rise of Capitalism. *s.s*: Foreign Affairs. *Rec*: Travel. *a*: 8 Ladybarn Cresc, Fallowfield, Manchester. *T*: Rusholme 3495.

HUTCHINSON, Isobel Wylie, F.R.(Scot.), G.S., J.P. *b*: West Lothian 1889. *e*: Rothesay House Sch Edin & Studely Coll Warwick. Author, Traveller & Explorer, Arctic Alaska, Aleutian Islands 1933—45. *Publ*: Stepping Stones from Alaska to Asia; Lyrics from West Lothian; How Joy was Found; Original Companions; On Greenland's Closed Shores; The Northern Gate (verse); North to the Rime-Ringed Sun; Arctic Nights Entertainments. *Ctr*: Blackwood's Mag, Scotsman, U.S. Nat Geog Mag, etc. *s.s*: Botany. *Rec*: Sketching. *a*: Carlowrie, Kirkliston, West Lothian. *T*: Kirkliston 9.

HUTCHINSON, John, LL.D., F.R.S., F.L.S. *b*: Wark-on-Tyne, Northumberland 1884. *e*: Wark Sch, Rutherford Coll Newcastle. *m*: Lilian Florence Cook. *s*: 2. *d*: 3. Botanist, late Keeper of Museums Kew. *Publ*: Families of Flowering Plants; Flora of West Tropical Africa; A Botanist in Southern Africa; The Story of Plants and Their Use to Man (with Dr R. Melville); The Evolution & Classification of British Flowering Plants; Common Wild Flowers; More Common Wild Flowers. *Ctr*: Gardeners' Chron & various Botanical Journs. *s.s*: Botany. *Rec*: Motoring, botanical exploration. *c*: Authors. *a*: 3 Holmesdale Rd, Kew, Surrey. *T*: Richmond 0486.

HUTCHINSON, John Kenvyn. *b*: Pontnewydd, Sth Wales 1920. *e*: Gr & Publ Schs. *m*: Lilian Heywood. Journalist, N.U.J. *n.a*: Macclesfield Advertiser '37, Yorks E. News Doncaster '47—. *Rec*: Cricket, motoring. *w.s*: '40—46. *a*: Wesley Manse, Rawmarsh, Rotherham, Yorks. *T*: Rawmarsh 210.

HUTCHINSON, Dr. L. *a*: Blacklow Hse, Huyton, nr L'pool.

HUTCHINSON, Ray Coryton, M.A. *b*: Finchley 1907. *e*: Monkton Combe Sch, Oriel Coll Oxf. *m*: Margaret Owen Jones. *s*: 2. *d*: 2. *Publ*: Testament; Shining Scabbard; The Unforgotten Prisoner; The Fire & the Wood; One Light Burning; The Answering Glory; Interim. *Ctr*: Eng Rev, Punch. *Rec*: Motoring, Church work, rough labouring. *c*: Garrick. *w.s*: Army, Persia & Iraq Command 1940—45. *a*: Triggs, Crondall, Farnham, Surrey.

HUTCHINSON, Richard Wyatt, F.S.A., F.R.A.I. Archæologist. *Publ*: A Century of Exploration at Nineveh (jt). *c.t*: Archæologia, Journ of Hellenic Studies, Iraq, etc. R. Arch Inst. *a*: The Orchard, Harston, Cambs.

HUTCHINSON, Robert Hare. *b*: U.S.A. 1887. *e*: St Mark's Sc, Mass & Harvard. *m*: Hesper Le Galliene. *Publ*: The Fourth Challenge; Spectral Evidence ("Robert Hare"); The Doctor's First Murder ("Robert Hare"). *c.t*: Harper's Mag. *a*: Spelmonden, Goudhurst, Kent. *t*: 72.

HUTCHINSON, W., M.A. Chairman of Hutchinson & Co., (publishers) Ltd, & subsidiary coys. *Publ*: Ed of History of Nations; Wonders of the World, etc. Chairman of Hutchinson's Printing Trust, Ltd. *a*: 34—36, Paternoster Row, E.C.4.

HUTCHINSON, Wilfrid Harvey. *b*: Louth, Lincs 1887. *e*: Grimsby Mun Col & Priv. *m*: Ethel A. Lumb. *s*: 1. *d*: 2. Journalist. *n.a*: Ex Sub Ed Sheffield Daily Telegraph. News Ed 1933—. Formerly on Staff of Yorkshire Observer, & Mang Ed of Series of Wkly papers at Harrogate, Ilkley & Otley. W.S. *c*: Hon Sec Sheffield Dist I.J. *a*: 35 Linden Ave, Sheffield 8. *t*: 45493.

HUTCHISON, Graham Seton, D.S.O., M.C., F.R.G.S. Lt-Col (ret). *b*: Lon 1890. *e*: Bradfield Col, R.M.A. Woolwich. *m*: Emilie Beatrice Durham. *s*: 2. *d*: 1. Author & Journalist. *n.a*: Founded The National Worker 1933. *Publ*: Challenge; Footslogger (illus); Warrior (illus); The W Plan; The Governor of Kattowitz; Colonel Grant's To-morrow; Eye for An Eye; Silesia Revisited; Meteor (illus); Blood Money; Minos Magnificent; Arya; Life Without End; Universe; The Viper of Luxor; etc. *c.t*: Lon & Prov Press & Foreign Press. *s.s*: Politics, India, mil hist, phys culture, international affairs, modern Germany. Staff Officer to Durbar Cmt '11. Personal Asst to Commandant General, Rhodesia 1913—14. Gt War '14—Armistice W. Front. Sec & A.D.C. Brit Commssr Silesian Plebiscite '20—21. Genoa Conf '22. Chm Brit & Imp Trade Exhib Cmt Wembley '25. Mem Lord Mayor & Sheriffs' Cmt Lon '29. Princ Shri Shivaji Mil Sc India '32. Exhib R.O.I. & other Art Exhibs. Travelled in every continent. *Rec*: Sketching, mountaineering, travel. *c*: Devonshire, N.U.J., Authors' Soc. *a*: Ickford Hse, Ickford, Bucks. *t*: 20.

HUTCHISON, Isobel Wylie. F.R.(Scot)G.S. b: West Lothian 1889. e: Rothesay House Sc Edin. Studley Hortlc Col Warwick. Publ: Lyrics From West Lothian; How Joy Was Found; Original Companions; On Greenland's Closed Shore; The Northern Gate (Verse); North to the Rime-Ringed Sun; Arctic Nights Entertainments. c.t: Blackwood's Mag, Amer-Scandinavian Review, Scotsman, Daily Mail, etc. s.s: Botany, ethnology. Rec Sketching. Travelled in Greenland 1927 & '28—29. Explored Arctic Alaska collecting plants for Kew '33—34. a: Carlowrie, Kirkliston, West Lothian. t: Kirkliston 9.

HUTCHISON, John Henderson. e: Heriot's Edinburgh, Edin Univ. Cinema Mang. n.a: Kine Weekly, Cinema Management. Publ: So This is War; The Complete Kine Manager. Ctr: Sunday Sun, Britannia & Eve, etc. s.s: Films, Cinemas & Advertising. a: 5 Cheyne Close, Hendon, London, N.W.4. T: Hendon 6640.

HUTCHISON, Sir Robert, Bt., LL.D.(Edin & B'ham), Hon. D.Sc.(Oxon). b: Kirkliston, West Lothian 1871. e: Collegiate Sch Edin, Edin & Strasbourg Univs. m: Lætitia Nora Ede. s: 2. d: 1. Publ: Food & the Principles of Dietetics; Clinical Methods; Lectures on Diseases of Children; Elements of Medical Treatment; Lectures on Dyspepsia; For & Against Doctors (author). s.s: Medical. c: Athenæum. a: Thurle Grange, Streatley-on-Thames. T: Goring-on-Thames 228.

HUTCHISON, W. Innes. b: Edin 1866. e: Primary & Priv Scs. m: Ada Florence Davis. s: 3. d: 1. Journalist. n.a: Reporter Leicester Mercury '83–89, Nott'm Guardian '89–92, Sheffield Independent & Sheffield Telegraph '92–1902, York Herald (Chief Reporter) '02–04, Daily Dispatch (Chief of L'pool Office) '04–12, L'pool Echo (Sub Ed) '12–18, L'pool Post (Night News Ed) '18–28, L'pool Corr Times '28–. c.t: L'pool Echo. s.s: Eccles matters. Rec: Coarse angling. c: L'pool Press, L'pool Caledonian Assoc, Dio Bd of Press & Publicity (Bishop of L'pool's nominee). a: 21 Lancaster Av, Sefton Pk, L'pool.

HUTCHISON, William Bruce. b: Prescott, Canada 1901. m: Dorothy Kidd McDiarmid. s: 1. d: 1. Newspaperman, Assoc Ed Winnipeg Free Press, formerly Polit Corr Vancouver Sun in Ottawa, & of Vancouver Times, Vancouver World, Vancouver Star. Publ: The Unknown Country, Canada & Its People; The Hollow Men. Ctr: Sat Ev Post, Collier's, Cosmoplitan, Liberty, Fortune, American Mercury, Strand, Nat Geog Mag, etc. s.s: Canadian Political & Econ Affairs. Rec: Gardening, fishing. a: R.M.D. 3 Victoria, B.C., Canada & The Free Press, Winnipeg. T: Albion 18r.

HUTHWAITE, Olga Pauline. b: Radcliffe-on-Trent 1901. e: Broadgate Sc Nott'm. Priv Sec. Publ: Fantasia ('28). c.t: Sunday Times, Best Poems of 1932, Hampshire Telegraph, etc. Rec: Acting. a: Foston, Grantham.

HUTT, Arthur Cyril. b: Enfield, Middlesex 1885. e: Merchant Taylor's Sch, King's Coll Lond. m: s: 1. Engineer. Publ: Combine Harvesting & Grain Drying; The Efficient Use of Fuel; Producer Gas Plant for Industrial Purposes (in collab). Ctr: Assoc Newspapers Ltd, The Builder, Architect & Building News. s.s: Fuels, Matters, Appliances & Economy of. Rec: Golf, gardening. w.s: 1914—19. a: 27 West Hill Ave, Epsom, Surrey. T: Epsom 9075.

HUTT, Cecil William, M.A., M.D.(Cam), M.R.C.P. (Lon), D.P.H. (Oxon). b: Lon. e: St Paul's Sc Hammersmith & Cam, & Lon & Manchester Univs. m: Jennie Marie Hesse. s: 3. d: 1. Med Practitioner. M.O.H. Holborn, Lecturer on Public Health Charing Cross Hosp Med Sc & Roy Inst of Public Health. Publ: Hygiene for Health Visitors, Sc Nurses & Social Workers ('13); Future of the Disabled Soldier; Internation Hygiene; Chap in the Teaching of Hygiene (The Teachers' Guide) '31; etc. c.t: Lancet, B.M.J., Journ of Roy San Inst, Vet Journ, L'Hygiéne Scolaire, Daily Express, etc. s.s: Roy Inst of Public Health. F.Roy Soc. Tropical Med & Mem B.M.A. Rec: Sailing, motor-boating. c: Tamesis Sailing. a: 35 Ennerdale Rd, Kew Gdns, Surrey. t: Richmond 3814.

HUTT, Horace Frederick. b: Cam 1902. e: Cam & County H.S. Cam. m: Edna Orton Hodges. s: 1. d: 1. Journalist. n.a: Cambridge Daily News '20, Sussex County Herald '25, Buxton Advertiser & High Peak News '27, Western Daily Press '29. Mem N.U.J. '20–. Vice-Chm Bristol Br N.U.J. c.t: Bristol Corr Central News. s.s: Rugby football, county cricket. Rec: Tennis, billiards. a: 51 Belluton Rd, Knowle, Bristol 4. t: 76392.

HUTTEN, Baroness Von. Author. Publ: Pam; Pam's Own Story; Our Lady of the Beeches; Mice for Amusement; etc. a: c/o Messrs A. P. Watt & Son, Hastings Hse, Norfolk St, Strand, W.C.2.

HUTTON, Edward. b: London 1875. e: Blundell's Sch Tiverton. m: Charlotte Miles. s: 1. n.a: Late Ed Anglo-Italian Review, Mem Counc Brit Inst Florence. Publ: Cities of Umbria; Sigismondo Malatesta; In Unknown Tuscany; Venice & Venetia; Ravenna; Cities of Sicily; Boccaccio—a biographical study; Pietro Aretino; Highways & Byways in Somerset, Wilts & Gloucester 1912—1932; Ed Crowe & Cavalcaselle's History of Italian Art (3 vols '08—09); Catholicism & English Literature; etc. Ctr: Nineteenth Century. s.s: Italian Art & Lit, Byzantine Art. Rec: Travel. a: 114 Clifton Hill, St John's Wood, London, N.W.8. T: Maida Vale 1747.

HUTTON, F. M. N/p Reporter. n.a: Newark Herald 1928, Spalding Guardian '31, Boston Guardian '32. a: 105 W. St, Boston.

HUTTON, Henry Thomas, J.P. b: Dublin 1874. e: Priv & Publ Sc. m: Mary Isabel Patton. d: 1. Landowner. Publ: The True Story of Greyfriars Bobby (1st & 2nd edns); Quoted by, & referred to in The Bunch Book by James Douglas, as " the most wonderful dog story in the world." s.s: Engineering, hortic. Inventor & patentee of the 1st foot-operated tyre-pump, now known as the "Wood-Milne". Rec: Forestry, music, photography, heraldry. a: Erin Lodge, Donaghadee, Co Down.

HUTTON, J. A. Publ: Articles on the life-history of salmon and the development of cotton-growing in the British Empire. a: Woodlands, Alderley-Edge.

HUTTON, Rev. John Alexander, D.D. b: 1868. e: Glasgow. Editor, Minister & Author. n.a: Ed British Weekly. Publ: The Authority and Person of Our Lord; The Winds of God; etc. a: British Weekly, 20 Warwick Sq, E.C.4. t: City 3704.

HUTTON, John Ernest, J.P., A.I.E.E., A.I.A.E. b: Northallerton 1877. e: Eton & Trin Hall, Cam. m: Ursula Ferrier. Engineer. Gen Sales Mang Vickers Ltd (ret). Publ: Cars & How to Drive Them; Welfare & Housing; Fishing Ways & Fishing Days; etc. c.t: Tech & sporting periodicals. s.s: Angling. Rec: Shooting, travel, photography. Pioneer motorist & motor racer. c: Oxf & Cam. a: 71 Pall Mall, S.W.1.

HUTTON, John Henry, C.I.E., D.Sc. b: 1885. e: Chigwell Sch, Worcester Coll Oxf. m: (1) Stella Eleanora Hewat (dec'd), (2) Maureen Margaret O'Reilly. s: 2. d: 1. Prof Social Anthropology. Publ: Caste in India; Report on the Census of India; The Sema

Nagas; The Angami Nagas. *Ctr*: Man, Nature. *s.s*: Ethnology. *a*: St Catharine's College, Cambridge. *T*: 56022.

HUTTON, Laura Frances. *b*: London 1889. *e*: Westfield Coll, Univ of Lond, Lond Sch of Med for Women, Charing Cross Hosp. *s*: 1 (Adopt). Psychiatrist Child Guidance Clinics (Berks), Fell Brit Psychological Soc. *Publ*: The Single Woman & Her Emotional Problems. *s.s*: Psychology of Childhood & Adolescence, Psychological Problems of Unmarried Woman. *Rec*: Reading. *a*: Sprid Cottage, Peppard, Oxon. *T*: Rotherfield Greys 335.

HUTTON, Rev. Reginald Ernest. *b*: Sompting 1859. *e*: L'pool Col, France, & Chichester Theo Col. *Publ*: The Soul Here & Hereafter ('98); The Crown of Christ; The Soul in the Unseen World; The Life Beyond (1916); etc. *c.t*: Times, Church Times, Guardian, etc. *s.s*: Eschatology. *Rec*: Travel, photography. *a*: St Margaret's Lodge, E. Grinstead.

HUTTON, Robert Salmon, D.Sc, M.A. Prof of Metallurgy Cam Univ. *c.t*: Journs of Learned Socs. *a*: 1 Chaucer Rd, Cam. *t*: 3126.

HUTTON, Samuel King. *b*: Kilkeel, Co Down 1877. *e*: Fulneck Sch, Manch Gr Sch, Manch Univ. *m*: Mary Lintott. *Publ*: Among the Eskimos of Labrador; Health Conditions & Disease Incidence Among the Eskimos of Labrador; By Patience & the Word; A Shepherd in the Snow; An Eskimo Village; By Dog-Sled & Kayak. *s.s*: The Eskimos of Northern Labrador. *Rec*: Music, photography, gardening. *c*: Rotary. *a*: The Beeches, 56 Mayfield Ave, Orpington. *T*: 1294.

HUTTON, Thomas Winter. *b*: Kirkiang, China 1887. *e*: King Edward's Sch B'ham, Merton Coll Oxf. *m*: K. M. Thornbery. *s*: 1. *d*: 1. Journalist, Ed B'ham Post, Asst Ed B'ham Gaz 1910, Leader Writer Dly Dispatch Manch, Asst Ed L'pool Courier '12, Asst Ed B'ham Post '13. *c*: Union (B'ham), Old Edwardians' Assoc. *a*: 11 St Augustine's Rd, Edgbaston, Birmingham. *T*: Edgbaston 2713.

HUTTON, WILLIAM HOLDEN: priest; b. Lincolnshire, Eng., May, 1860; s. Rev. George Thomas and Caroline (Holden) H.; educ. Magdalen Coll. (Oxford); DEGREES: M.A., D.D. (Oxford); Hon. D.C.L. (Durham); Hon. Fellow of St. John's Coll. (Oxford); chaplain of the order of St. John of Jerusalem. AUTHOR: The Political Disturbances which accompanied the Early Period of the Reformation in Germany, 1881; St. John Baptist College, in, The Colleges of Oxford, their History and Traditions, 1891; The Marquess Wellesley, 1893; King and Baronage (1135-1327), 1895; Sir Thomas More, 1895 (2nd edit. 1900); Philip Augustus, 1896; Hampton Court, 1896; The Church of the Sixth Century, 1897; A History of St. John Baptist Coll., Oxford, 1898; The English Reformation, 1899; History of the English Church, 1625-1714, 1903; Burford Papers, 1905; The Church and the Barbarians, 1906; William Stubbs, 1906; The Age of Revolution, 1908; The English Saints (2nd edit.), 1908; By Thames and Cotswold (2nd edit.), 1908; Short History of the Church in Great Britain (3rd edit.), 1909; Thomas Becket, 1910 (2nd edit. 1926); A Disciple's Religion, 1911; Highways and Byways in Shakespeare's Country, 1913; William Laud (4th edit.), 1913; Elementary Church History of Great Britain (6th edit.), 1917; The Hope of Man, 1920; John Bunyan, 1928. Contributor to Quarterly and Edinburgh reviews, Nineteenth Century and Cornhill magazines; Times, Times Literary Supplement, Spectator, and others. Fellow, tutor and recantor of St. John's Coll., Oxford, many years; obtained a first class in Modern History and university prize, Oxford; former lecturer at Trinity Coll., Oxford; selected reader at Oxford, Cambridge and Dublin. Relig. denom., Church of England. (*)

HUXLEY, Aldous Leonard, B.A. *b*: Godalming 1894. *e*: Eton & Oxf Univ. *m*: Maria Nys. *s*: 1. Writer. *n.a*: Athenæum, Vogue, Dramatic Critic Westminster Gazette. *Publ*: Crome Yellow; Antic Hay; Those Barren Leaves; Point Counter Point; Brief Candles; Brave New World; Ends & Means; After Many a Summer; Grey Eminence; Time Must Have a Stop; The Perennial Philosophy. *Ctr*: Numerous in Eng & America. *Rec*: Painting. *a*: Athenæum, Pall Mall, London, S.W.1.

HUXLEY, Elspeth Josceline, J.P. *b*: London 1907. *e*: Government Sch Nairobi Kenya, Univs of Reading & Cornell U.S.A. *m*: Gervas Huxley. *s*: 1. Writer. *n.a*: Asst Press Officer Empire Marketing Board '29—32, News Talks Asst B.B.C. '42—43. *Publ*: White Man's Country; Lord Delamere & the Making of Kenya; Red Strangers; Murder at Government House; Murder on Safari; Death of an Aryan Race & Politics in Kenya (in Collab). *Ctr*: Times, Time & Tide, B.B.C. *s.s*: Colonial Affairs, Agriculture & Soil Conservation. *Rec*: Photography, Country Life. *c*: Landsowne. *a*: Woodfolds, Oaksey, Malmesbury, Wilts. *T*: Crudwell 252.

HUXLEY, Julian Sorell, F.R S., M.A., D.Sc. Biological Editor Ency Brit (14th Ed). *Publ*: inc On Living in a Revolution; Evolutionary Ethics; Democracy Marches; The Uniqueness of Man; The Living Thoughts of Darwin; At the Zoo; etc. *a*: 31 Pond St, Hampstead, London, N.W.3.

HUXLEY, Michael Heathorn. Editor of the Geographical Magazine. *a*: Longmore, Bosham, Sussex.

HUXTABLE, Francis Richard. *b*: Challacombe, N Devon, 1876. *e*: Rock Hill, Chumleigh. *m*: Mary L. Wigley. *d*: 2. Asst Ed & agricultural corr Yorkshire Post. *n.a*: Exeter Gazette (Barnstaple), 1892—'98. Rochdale Observer, 1898—1901. Yorkshire Observer, (Bradford), '01—04. Yorks Post (Leeds), '04—. *s.s*: Agriculture. *c*: Mem Press Fund Counc. *a*: 1 Hilton Pl, Leeds. *t*: 42115.

HUXTABLE, Marjorie ("Simon Dare"). *b*: Bristol 1897. *e*: Mortimer Hse Clifton. Divorced her Husband 1931. *d*: 2. *Publ*: The Gradual Furnace; The Little Upstart ('27); A' Beggar Man Came; If the Tree Fall; The Jagged Rim; The Unrisen Moon; The Cloth is Woven ('32); Blind Madonna ('33); April Whirlwind ('34); Frost Stays the Waves; Wife; Cardboard Husband ('34); Forgotten Winds ('35); etc. *c.t*: Sunday Dispatch, Sunday Graphic, Tatler, Everywoman's, Daily Sketch, etc. *c*: Wanderers' Clifton. *a*: c/o Hutchinson & Co Ltd, 34 Paternoster Row, E.C.4.

HVASS, Hans, M.A. *b*: Copenhagen 1902. *e*: Univ of Copenhagen. *m*: Else Hvass. *s*: 1. *d*: 4. Lecturer, Zoological Author. *Publ*: The Animals in our Woods; The Animals Out There; The Amphibians & Reptiles of Denmark; Inside the Cages; The Collector of Nature; Danish Birds; Rare Danish Birds. *Ctr*: Berlingske Tidende. *s.s*: Amphibians & Reptiles. *Rec*: Danish

HYAM, Sydney. Journalist. *n.a*: Ed Parliamentary News Services, Ed The Parliamentary Bulletin for Excutives. *s.s*: Parliamentary & Political Affairs, Economics. *a*: 48 Park Ave, Hounslow, Middlesex. *T*: Hounslow 1663.

HYAMS, Ralph, M.J.I. *b*: Lon 1882. *e*: City of Lon Sc & France. *m*: Muriel Teare. *d*: 1. Journalist. *n.a*: Surveyor 1900, Education '03. *s.s*: Education. *Rec*: Golf. *c*: R.A.C. *a*: Berry Hse, Bletchingly, Surrey.

HYAMSON, Albert Montefiore, O.B.E., F.R.Hist.S. *b*: London 1875. *e*: Oxf High Sch, Swansea Gr Sch & Priv. *m*: Marie Lavey. *d*: 2. Civil Servant (ret), formerly Dir Dept of Immigration Govt of Palestine, Pres Jewish Hist Soc of Eng, Hon Treas Palestine Exploration Fund, etc. *Publ*: A History of the Jews in England; Palestine: A Policy; A Dictionary of Universal Biography; A Dictionary of English Phrases; A Dictionary of International Affairs; The British Consulate in Jersusalem; David Salomons; Palestine, Old & New; Vallentine's Jewish Ency (Jt Ed). *Ctr*: Internat Affairs, Jewish Chron, Quarterly Rev, Palestine Post, etc. *s.s*: Jewish Hist, Palestine. *a*: 12A Faraday Mansions, Queen's Club Gardens, London, W.14. *T*: Fulham 0294.

HYAMSON, Moses, B.A., LL.D. *b*: Russian Poland 1862. *e*: Jews' Coll London & U.C.L. *m*: Sara Gordon. Emeritus Prof of Jewish Codes. *Publ*: The Oral Law & Other Sermons; Sabbath & Festival Addresses; The Jewish Concept of Wine & Its Use; Jewish Method of Slaughtering Cattle for Food; Proposed Reform of the Calendar; etc. *Ctr*: Ethics, Defence of the Sabbath & Jewish Institutions. *Rec*: Trans of Jewish Classics, Study of Hebrew Text of the Bible. *a*: 65 East 96 St,, New York 28, N.Y., U.S.A. *T*: Atwater 9-0836.

HYDE, Francis Austin, M.A. *b*: Driffield 1889. *e*: Bridlington Sch & Leeds Univ. *m*: Jessie Gilchrist Anderson. Headmaster Lady Lumley's G.S. *Publ*: (One Act Plays):—Wireless & Such Like; The Ship Comes In; First Aid; The Tyrant; Honest Folk; Safe Custody; etc. After Marston Moor; Maker of Highways; Four White Socks; Spanish Wine. *Ctr*: Yorks Evening Post, Yorks Wkly Post, News Chronicle. *s.s*: Hist, Dialect. *Rec*: Golf, Tennis. *a*: The Grove, Pickering, Yorks.

HYDE, Francis Edwin, F.R.Hist.S. *b*: Wolverton, Bucks 1908. *e*: Univs of Liverpool, London & Harvard. *m*: Marian Rosa Welton. *d*: 1. University Lecturer. *Publ*: Mr Gladstone at the Board of Trade; Import Trade of the Port of Liverpool; History of Wolverton; History of Stony Stratford. *Ctr*: Economist, Chambers's Ency, Dict of Amer Biog, Econ Hist Rev. *s.s*: Econ & 19th Century History, Economics. *Rec*: Cricket, rock climbing. *a*: 8 Ludlow Drive, West Kirby, Cheshire. *T*: Hoylake 1529.

HYDE, Frederick. *b*: M/C 1870. *e*: Priv. *m*: Maud Deeley. *s*: 1. *d*: 2. Mang Dir Midland Bank Ltd. *s.s*: Banking. Ex-Pres Inst of Bankers. Ex-Pres M/C & Dis Bankers' Inst. *c*: Roy Inst of G.B. *a*: 30 Bracknell Gdns, N.W.3. *t*: Hampstead 2973.

HYDE, George Frederick. *b*: Scarboro' 1894. *e*: Scarbro Munic Sec Sc. *m*: Margaret Kathleen Boothby. Journalist. *n.a*: Chief Reporter Scarborough Evening News & Daily Post. *c.t*: Various. *s.s*: Municipal affairs, cricket, tennis. *Rec*: Golf, tennis, wireless. *c*: Scarborough Masonic. *a*: Fraisthorpe, Stepney Drive, Scarborough. *t*: 806.

HYDE, Grant M. *Publ*: Newspaper Reporting & Correspondence; Newspaper Editing; Handbook for Newspaper Workers; Journalistic Writing, Newspaper Handbook. *a*: c/o D. Appleton & Co, 34 Bedford St, London, W.C.

HYDE, Lt.-Col. Harford Montgomery, M.A.(Oxon), D.Litt.(Belfast), F.R.Hist.S., M.R.I.A. *b*: Belfast 1907. *e*: Sedbergh, Queen's Univ Belfast, Magdalen Coll Oxf. *m*: Dorothy M. B. Crofts. Barrister, Priv Sec Marquess of Londonderry '35—39. *Publ*: Mexican Empire (Macmillan Centenary Award); The Rise of Castlereagh; Judge Jeffreys; Princess Lieven; John Law; The Empress Catherine & Princess Dashkov; The Trials of Oscar Wilde; The Russian Journals of Martha & Catherine Wilmot; More Letters from Martha Wilmot; Londonderry House & its Pictures; Air Defence & the Civil Population; A Victorian Historian; The Congress of Vienna; Law Reports: Complete Current Digest '46. *s.s*: Europe Hist in 19th Cent, Comparative Law. *Rec*: Mozart's Music. *c*: Garrick, Oxf & Camb. *a*: 4 Brick Court, Temple, London, E.C.4. *T*: Central 2725.

HYDE, Lawrence, B.A.(Oxon). *b*: Birmingham 1894. *e*: Perse Gmr Sch Camb & Oxf Univ. *m*: Lorna Agnes Helen Fraser. *s*: 1. Author. *Publ*: Isis & Osiris; The Learned Knife; The Prospects of Humanism. *Ctr*: The Occult Review, Transformation, British Thought 1947. *s.s*: Philosophy, Religion, Psychology, Esotericism. *w.s*: R.A.F. 1st World War. *Rec*: Conversation, gardening. *a*: Chestnut Cottage, Reigate, Surrey, *T*: Reigate 3830.

HYDE, Robert Robertson, M.V.O. *b*: Lon 1878. *e*: King's Col Lon. *m*: Eileen Ruth Parker. *s*: 1. *d*: 1. Dir Indust Welfare Soc. *Publ*: Boy in Industry; The Camp Book. *c.t*: Various. *s.s*: Indust Ralationships. *Rec*: Fishing, gardening. *c*: Reform. *a*: Strabane, Limpsfield, Sy, & 14 Hobart Place, S.W.1. *t*: Sloane 6182.

HYDE, Stacey William. *b*: Kensington 1897. *e*: Beckenham Sec Sc. Engineering Draughtsman. *Publ*: Shop Mates (short stories); Simple Annals; The Blank Wall; The Blackleg. *c.t*: Draughtsman. *a*: Thorness, 25 Blackfen Rd, Sidcup, Kent.

HYDE, Rev. Thomas Arnold, M.A. *b*: Sheffield 1864. *e*: Oxf. *Publ*: The Kingdom of the Lovers of God. *a*: The Grove, Avonwick, South Brent, Devon. *t*: Brent 79.

HYDE, Victor, M.C. *n.a*: Ex-Ed Fish Trades Gazette, Founder-Ed Hotel & Catering Weekly. *Publ*: Freelance Journalism; Writing for L.S.D. *c.t*: Daily & Weekly n/ps & trade journs. *s.s*: Advtg, motoring, the home, the battlefields of the gt war *a*: 6 St Mark's Cres, Regent's Pk, N.W.1. *t*: Gulliver 5284.

HYDE, Walter Woodburn, A.M., Ph.D., Litt.D. *b*: Ithaca, N.Y. 1870. *e*: Univs of Cornell, Halle, Athens & Rome. Emeritus Prof of Greek & Ancient History. *Publ*: De Olympionicarum Statuis; Thessaly & the Vale of Tempe; Monastries of Meteora & Green Monasticism; The Mountains of Greece; Olympic Victor Monuments & Greek Athletic Art; Paganism & Christianity in the Roman Empire; Ancient Greek Mariners; etc. *Ctr*: Various. *s.s*: Greek Lang, Lit & Hist. *Rec*: Mountain climbing; walking. *a*: 3950 Pine St, Philadelphia 4, Pa

HYDE EDWARDS, Mrs. Patricia. *b*: Lon 1897. *e*: Kensington Park H.S. *m*: Leslie Hyde Edwards. Journalist & Editor. *n.a*: Asst Ed The Lady's Pictorial 1916–18, Ed The Lady's Pictorial '18–22, Asst Ed, Eve '22–23. *Publ*: Guide Books to The Shakespeare Country. *c.t*: The Daily Chronicle, The Daily Mirror, The Sunday Pictorial, The Morning Post, The Daily Herald, etc. *s.s*: Furnishing, decoration & needlework. *Rec*: Trav, swimming. *a*: Olney, Palace Rd, E. Molesey, Surrey. *t*: 260.

HYDER, Alan. *Publ*: Black Girl, White Lady; Prelude to Blue Mountains; Lofty; Vampires Overhead. *c.t*: Assoc N/ps, Evening News. *a*: 30 Albert Palace Mansions, S.W.11.

HYETT, Sir Francis Adams. *b*: Painswick 1844. *e*: Eton, Trin Hall, Cam. *m*: Ellen Maria Carpenter (dec). *d*: 4. Barrister. *n.a*: Glos Countryside 1933—35. *Publ*: Painswick Annual Register 1890—99; Florence, Her History & Art (1903); Gloucester in National

History ('07, 3rd edn '24); Manual of Gloucestershire Literature (with Litt Supp, 5 vols, '15—16); Glimpses of the History of Painswick ('28); Gloucester & Her Governor in the Great Civil War (1891); etc. *c.t*: Bristol & Glos Soc Trans, etc. Chm Educ Cmt 1908—19. Chm Glos Quart Sess '04—29. Chm Barnwood Hse Hosp for the Insane 1895—. *Rec*: Lit. *a*: Painswick Hse, Stroud, Glos.

HYETT, James Henry. *b*: Gloucester 1888. Free-lance Journalist. *n.a*: Rep Cheltenham Examiner 1912, Citizen Gloucester '16—25, Ed Gloucester & County Chamber of Commerce Journ, Gloucester Elector. *Ctr*: Lond & Prov press. *s.s*: Rugby, Courts & Trade Reviews. *Rec*: Motoring. *a*: 10 Clarence St, Gloucester. *T*: 3430.

HYKA, Jan Václav. *b*: Klater 1889. *m*: Mina Lindhorst. Czechoslovak Diplomatic Servant. *n.a*: Various Czech n/ps 1905—. *c.t*: Various Brit & Amer n/ps & reviews, etc. *s.s*: Econ, polit. Order of Orange; Order of the Rumanian Crown; Order of St Sava. *c*: Nat Lib, Foreign Press Assoc. *a*: Prague, Czechoslovakia, Bubenec, Zelena 4. *t*: 742—93.

HYMANS, PAUL: Minister of State; b. Brussels, Belgium; s. Louis and Louise (de l'Escaille) H.; educ. Univ. of Brussels. DEGREE: J.D.; m. Therese Goldschmidt. AUTHOR: Bruxelles Moderne (in collaboration with Henri Hymans, forming the third vol. of Bruxelles à travers les ages, by Louis Hymans), 1889: Histoire Parlement de la Belgique (in collaboration with M. Delacroix, finished work begun by Louis Hymans), 1884-1900; Frère Orban (vol. I—La formation du parti libéral belge (1812-1857), 1905, (vol. II—La Belgique et le second Empire), 1910; Portraits, essais et Discours, 1914. Contributor: Grande Revue, The Outlook, L'Opinion, Everyman, Le Flambeau, La Société des Nations, Le Times, La Vie, La Patrie Belge, and others. General character of writing: political, historical. Was Belgian envoy extraordinary and plenipotentiary to the Court of St. James from 1915 to 1917; Minister of State, Minister of Foreign Affairs, from 1918 to 1920, from 1924 to 1925, and from 1927 to 1929; Minister of Justice from 1926 to 1927; Honorary President of Brussels Univ.; Belgian Delegate to the Council of the League of Nations from 1920 to 1926; President of the first Assembly of the League of Nations; signed the Kellogg Pact for Belgium in August, 1928. Relig. denom., Protestant. ADDRESS: 15 rue Ducale, Brussels, Belgium.

HYND, John. Asst F.L. Journalist with T. H. Donald, Dunfermline. *a*: 127 Brucefield Av, Dunfermline. *t*: 738.

HYNE, Charles J. Cutcliffe, M.A. *b*: 1866. *e*: Bradford G.S. & Clare Col Cam. Author. *Publ*: Adventures of Captain Kettle; Further Adventures of Captain Kettle; The Filibusters; Thompson's Progress; Atoms of Empire; Captain Kettle, K.C.B.; My Joyful Life; etc. Travelled in W. & N. Africa, N. America, Brazil, Mexico, etc. *a*: Heaton Lodge, Bradford.

HYNES, Samuel Gordon, M.J.I., F.G.I. *b*: Glas 1876. Journalist. *n.a*: Special Commissioner Grocer's Gazette, 1921—. *c.t*: Grocer's Gazette ("Alan Gordon" & "Anon Luker"). *s.s*: Org & publicity. Creator of slogan "Unite to Serve!" widely adopted in association movement of retail grocery trade org. *a*: 3 Woodside Drive, Hyde, nr M/C *t*: Hyde 553.

HYPHER, Dr. N. C. Med Practitioner & Radiologist. *c.t*: B.M.J., Practitioner, Brit Journ Radiology, Metallurgia. M.O. to Nobel Chemicals Ltd. Radiologist to Bucks C.C. & High Duty Alloys Ltd. *a*: Pinwell, Mackenzie St, Slough, Bucks.

HYSLOP, J. R. Middlesex County Times, Ealing.

IBOTSON, Dr. E. C. B., F.R.S.M., etc. Publ: Partnerships & Antagonisms in Disease (1929); First Aid Charts, etc. Ex-Capt R.A.M.C. Ex-surgeon Union Castle Line. Clinical Asst Roy Westminster Ophthalmic Hosp. Fell Hunterian Soc. a: 11 Waverley Place, Jersey, C.I.

IBRAHIM, JUSSUF: professor of pediatrics; b. Cairo, Egypt, May 28, 1877; s. Dr. Ibrahim Pacha Hassan and Agnes (Herzfeld) I; educ. Max Gymnasium and Univ. of Munich. DEGREES: M.D. (Munich), Professor of Pediatrics and Director of Children's Hospital at Jena; unmarried. Has made contributions to several medical text books and number of papers published in scientific medical journals. Is interested in disease of digestive and nervous system of children. Formerly professor at the Univs. of Heidelberg and Munich, and professor of pediatrics at the Univ. of Würzburg. Relig. denom., Evangelical. OFFICE: Children's Clinic. HOME: Kasernenstrasse 10, Jena, Thüringen, Germany.

ICHENHAEUSER, ELIZA: author; b. Jassy, Roumania, May 12, 1869; d. A. Rozenthal and Bertha (Frieser) Rozenthal; educ. schools in Jassy, Roumania; m. Dr. Justus Ichenhaeuser, Jan. 22, 1890. AUTHOR: Der gegenwärtige Stand der Frauenfrage, 1894; Zur Frauenfrage I, 1896; Die Ausnahmestellung Deutschlands in Sachen des Frauenstudiums, 1897; Erwerbsmöglichkeiten für Frauen, 1897; Die politische Gleichberechtigung der Frau, 1898; Zur Frauenfrage, 1899; Die Dienstbotenfrage und ihre Reform, 1900; Die Journalistik als Frauenberuf, 1904; Das Frauenwahlrecht, 1906; Zur Ehereform, 1909; Frauenziele, 1913. Edited: Bilder vom Internationalen Frauen Kongress, 1904; Was die Frau von Berlin wissen muss, 1914. Contributor to Vossische Zeitung (Berlin), Hannoverscher Courier (Dresden), Neueste Nachrichten (Munich), Augsburger Abendzeitung, Kölnische Zeitung, Neues Wiener Journal, Weltbühne, Frau und Gegenwart, and others. General character of writing: sociological. Organized first international women's congress at Berlin, 1896 and 1904; lecturer on social and franchise questions; received red cross for social work during World War. CLUBS: Committee of the German Lyceum Club; President of the Verein Krankenhaus weiblicher Ärzte. Religion, Protestant. ADDRESS: Kaiserallee 41, Berlin-Wilmersdorf. Germany.

ICHIKAWA, SANKI: professor of English Language and Literature; b. Tokyo, Japan, Feb., 1886; s. Sanken and Koto (Yoshida) I; educ. Tokyo Prefectural First Middle Sch., 1898-1903; First High Sch., 1903-1906; Tokyo Imperial Univ., 1906-1909; studied in England and America, 1912-1915. DEGREES: Litt.D., Hon. Fellow of Royal Soc. of Literature (London); m. Haruko Hozumi, 1916. AUTHOR: Studies in English Grammar (Japanese), 1912; An English Pronouncing Dictionary, 1923; English Influence on the Japanese, 1928; Beginners' Latin and Greek (Japanese), 1930. Edited (with Introduction and Notes): Chaucer's Canterbury Tales; Shakespeare's Plays; Sheridan's Plays; Synge's Play; Dickens's Christmas Carol; Gissing's Ryecroft; Stevenson's Treasure Island, etc. Editor: The Kenkyusha English Classics; Studies in English Literature. Contributor to The Rising Generation (a bi-monthly mag. devoted to English). Serves on the Comm. of Examination for license of Secondary and High Sch. teachers. Pres. of English Literary oc. of Japan and of the hakespeare Assoc. of Japan. OFFICE: Imperial University of Tokyo. HOME: 25 Kitayamabushicho, Ushigome, Tokyo, Japan.

IDLE BEN. See Crossley, William Tetley.

"IFANO": see Jones, Ifano.

IFFERT, AUGUST: vocal teacher; b. Braunschweig, Germany, May 31, 1859; s. Carl and Caroline Iffert. DEGREE: Professor (k.k.); married. AUTHOR: Allgemeine Gesangschule (theoretical and practical part); Etwas vom Gesange. General character of writing: scientific, musical. Vocal teacher in the conservatories of Cologne, Dresden and Vienna. ADDRESS: Grenzstrasse 38, Dresden-Kötzschenbroda, Germany.

IGERSHEIMER, JOSEF: professor; b. Frankfurt a. Main, Germany, Sept. 3, 1879; s. Leopold and Jenny (Fraenkel) I. DEGREES: M.D., Professor (oculist); m. Alice Heinemann, 1914. AUTHOR: Syphilis and Auge, 1918 (2nd edit. 1928). General character of writing: scientific, diseases of the eye, tuberculosis, toxicology. ADDRESS: Brentanostrasse 1, Frankfurt a. Main, Germany.

IGGLESDEN, C. H. b: Ashford 1886. e: Tonbridge Sch. m: Agnes M. B. Leary. s: 1. d: 1. Journalist, F.J.I. n.a: Asst-Ed Kentish Express. s.s: Cricket. Rec: Outdoor sport. c: Press, etc. a: Trees, North Rd, Hythe, Kent.

IGGLESDEN, Sir Charles, D.L., J.P., F.S.A., F.J.I., O.St.J. b: Ashford, Kent 1861. e: Priv. m: Nellie Swatman. s: 4. Journalist & Author, Chm Publicity Cmt Safety First Assoc, etc. n.a: Ed Kentish Express 51 y. Ald Kent C.C. Publ: Saunter Through Kent with Pen & Pencil (29 vols); The Demon Eleven & Other Cricket Stories; Out There (impressions at the Front, 1915); A Mere Englishman in America; Those Superstitions; Sixty-six Years' Memories of Kent Cricket; Novels—A Flutter With Fate; Crimson Glow; etc. Ctr: London Press & many mags. Rec: Golf, fishing. c: Authors', Press. a: Heathfield, Ashford, Kent. T: 23.

"IGNOTUS" (pen name): see Adams, Henry Joseph.

IGNOTUS, Paul. b: Budapest, Hungary 1901. e: Gymnasium Budapest. Writer, Journalist, Press Attaché Hungarian Legation London. n.a: Founder & Ed Szép Szó '35—39, Leader Writer Esti Kurir '23—38, Magyar Hirlap '36—37, London Representative Nepszava, '39—47, Broadcaster B.B.C. '40—47. Publ: A Horogkersztes Hadjarat. Ctr: Manch Guardian, New Statesman & Nation, Haladas (Budapest), etc. s.s: Hungary, Politics & Literature. Rec: Swimming, walking. a: 625 Chelsea Cloisters, London, S.W.3. T: Kensington 3968.

IHNE, EGON: professor; b. Rheinbach, Germany, June 3, 1859. DEGREES: Ph.D., Dr. Engineer, Professor. AUTHOR: Geschichte der pflanzenphaenologischen Beobachtungen in Europa, 1884; Phaenologische Karte des Frühlingseinzugs in Mitteleuropa (in: Petermanns Geographischen Mitteilungen), 1905; Phaenologische Karte des Frühlingseinzigs im Grossherzogtum Hessen (in vol. 9 der Arbeiten der Landwirtschaftskammer für das Grossherzogtum Hessen, 2nd edit.), 1911; Phaehologische Karte des Frühlingseinzugs auf den Britischen Inseln (in Petermanns Geographischen Mitteilungen), 1916; Phaenologische Mitteilungen, 1929. (These series of publications cover a space of 38 years). General character of writing: scientific, nature books, chiefly about plant-phaenology. ADDRESS: Darmstadt, Hessen, Germany.

IKIN, Rutherford Graham, M.A. b: Kettering 1903. e: Norwich Sch, King's Coll Camb. Senior Hist Master St Bees, now Headmaster Trent Coll. Publ: The Modern Age; A Pageant of History; The King's Sch Ely. a: School Hse, Long Eaton, Nr Nottingham. T: 146.

ILBERG, K. TH. H. JOHANNES: professor; b. Magdeburg, Prussia, July 10, 1860; s. Fr. Th. Hugo and Clara (Weisswange) I.; educ. Univs. of Leipzig, Bonn and Berlin; m. Johanna M. C. Devrient, July 17, 1891. AUTHOR: Studia Pseudhippocratea, 1883; Fr. Th. H. Ilberg, 1885;

Hippokrates-Glossar des Erotianos, 1893; Prolegomena critica in Hippocratis opesum reversion em novam, 1894; Die Sphinx in der griechischen Kunst und Sage, 1896; Aus Galens Praxis, 1905; A. Cornelius Celsus und die Medizin in Rom, 1907; Die Überlieferung der Gynakologie des Soranos von Ephesos, 1910; Corpus Medicorum Graecorum (4th vol.), 1927. Editor: Neue Jahrbücher für Wissenschaft und Jugendbildung. General character of writing: scientific, historical, medical. ASSOCIATIONS: Ordentliches Mitglied der Sächsischen Akademie der Wissenschaften; Ordentliches Mitglied des Deutschen Archäologischen Instituts. Relig. denom., Evangelical-Lutheran. ADDRESS: Arndtstrasse 53. Leipzig S 3, Germany.

ILCHESTER, Earl of, Giles Stephen Holland Fox-Strangways, O.B.E., F.S.A. *b*: 1874. *m*: Lady Helen Stewart. *s*: 2. *d*: 2. Trustee Nat Portrait Gallery, Chairman 1941—, Trustee Brit Museum '31—, Chm Roy Comm on Historical Buildings '43, Pres Roy Literary Fund '41—, Pres London Library '40—. *Publ*: Ed Life & Letters of Lady Sarah Lennox (with Countess of Ilchester); Further Memoirs of the Whig Party 1807—21 by 3rd Lord Holland; Ed The Journals of Elizabeth, Lady Holland; Henry Fox, 1st Lord Holland; (with Lady Holland; Henry Fox, 1st Lord Holland; Ed The Journ of Hon Henry Edward Fox 1818—30, Catherine the Great, & The Life of Sir Charles Hanbury-Williams (with Mrs Langford-Brooke). The Home of the Hollands 1605—1820, Chronicles of Holland House 1820—1900; Letters of Lady Holland to her Son. *a*: Melbury Hse, Dorchester, & 14 Montagu Sq, London, W.1.

ILES, John Henry, O.B.E., M.J.I. *b*: Bristol. *e*: Ashville Coll Harrogate. *m*: Eleanor Marion Bird. *s*: 3. *d*: 1. Founder Brit Band Festival Crystal Palace 1900. *n.a*: Ed in Chief British Bandsman 1900—. *s.s*: Culture & Development of Brass Bands, Welfare of Working Men Musicans. *a*: Aurora, Cliff Rd, Birchington, Kent. *T*: 273.

ILES, Margaret, L.R.A.M. *b*: Southend-on-Sea 1903. *e*: Private Scs, Southend High Sc, Convent, Evening Inst. Brighton Training Col. School teacher. *Publ*: Season Ticket. *Rec*: Walking, golf, gardening. *a*: Midrise, Plumberow Ave, Hockley, Essex. *t*: 141.

ILIFFE, Lord, C.B.E. *b*: 1877. N/p Proprietor. Chairman Iliffe & Sons Ltd, Dir A.P., Allied N/ps, etc. One of Proprietors Daily Telegraph. *a*: 24 Carlton House Terr, S.W.1. *t*: Whitehall 4211.

ILIFFE, W. Coker. Dir Iliffe & Sons Ltd. *n.a*: Dir Midland Daily Telegraph. *a*: 16 Buckingham St, W.C.2.

ILLING, FRIEDRICH WILHELM: author; b. Aussig, a. d. Elbe, Cechoslovakia. Sept. 24, 1899; s. Dr. Friedrich and Rosa (Reichenbach) I.; educ. Gymnasium of Vienna; Univ. of Vienna. DEGREES: Jurisprudence and Philosophy; m. Elsie Böhm, June 15, 1929 AUTHOR: Erste Versuche (novels), 1918; Magedin, 1923. Contributor to Die Literatur (Berlin); Deutsche Pressekorrespondenz (Hannover); Tagblatt; Volkszeitung (Vienna); correspondent of: Der Deutsche Rundfunk (Berlin); Funkpost (Berlin); Europafunk (Munich); Radioliltteren (Copenhagen). General character of writing: novels, essays, poems, scientific literature, historical; broadcasting correspondence; critic. CLUBS: Deutscher Schriftsteller Verband; Landesgruppe Oesterreich. ADDRESS: Baumgartenstrasse 81, Vienna XIII., Vienna, Austria.

ILLINGWORTH, Charles Frederick William, C.B.E., M.D., Ch.M., F.R.C.S.(Edin), F.R.F.P.S.(Glas). *b*: Halifax, Yorks 1899. *e*: Halifax Gr Sch, Edin Univ. *m*: Eleanor Mary Bennett. *s*: 4. Regius Prof Surgery Glas Univ. *Publ*: Text Book of Surgical Pathology (jointly); Short Text Book of Surgery; Text Book of Surgical Treatment. *a*: 23 Kirklee Rd, Glasgow, W.2. *T*: West 7623.

ILLINGWORTH, Percy Parker. *b*: Skipton 1906. *e*: Ermysted's G.S. Skipton. *m*: Edna Wing. *s*: 1. News Ed W. Yorks Pioneer, Skipton. *n.a*: W. Yorks Pioneer '21—. *c.t*: Country papers. *c*: Vice-Pres Skipton & Dis Br L.N.U. & of Skipton Br League of Young Liberals. *a*: 6 Brooklands Terr, Skipton-in-Craven. *t*: Skipton 89.

ILLINGWORTH, Mrs John Richardson, (Agnes Louisa). *b*: Falmouth 1860. *m*: Rev John Richardson Illingworth, M.A., D.D. *Publ*: Sursum Corda (with Bishop W. H. Frere); Life & Letters of J. R. Illingworth; The Resurrection & the Life, Readings for Easter; Christmas Faith & Fact, Readings for Christmas. *a*: St Faith, Osney Lne, Oxford. *t*: 2935.

IMBERT-TERRY, Sir Henry M. *b*: Lon 1854. *e*: Charterhouse. *m*: Lydia M. S. Roberts (dec). *s*: 2. Author. *Publ*: Misjudged Monarch Charles 2nd; Constitutional King George 1st (1926); In Spacious Times; Acid; Nightshade; Weeds. *c.t*: Empire Review, Transaction of Roy Soc of Lit, etc. *s.s*: Hist, biog, genealogy. *Rec*: Shooting, forestry. Was Chm of the Nat Union of Conservatives '22—23, Junior Imperial League '06—28. 50 y F.R.S. Lit, Hon Treas '33. Mem of the Counc of Roy Patriotic Fund. Baronet Knight of Grace of St John. *c*: Carlton, Jun Athenæum. *a*: 4 Donn St, Mayfair. *t*: 1066 Grosvenor.

IMMISCH, OTTO: professor; b. Wartha, Germany, June 18, 1862; s. Otto and Pauline (Wiedemann) I.; educ. Kreuz-Gymnasium (Dresden), Univ. of Leipzig. DEGREES: Ph.D.; m. Elisabeth Zenker, 1891. AUTHOR: De glossis lexici Hesychiani Italicis, 1885; Klaros, 1889; Philologische Studien zu Plato, 1896 (2nd edit. 1903); Die innere Entwicklung des griechischen Epos, 1904; Wie studiert man klassische Philologie, 1909 (2nd edit. 1920); Das Echo der Alten, 1910; Der erste platonische Brief, 1913; Das alte Gymnasium und die neue Gegenwart, 1916; Das Nachleben der Antike, 1919; Aga tharchidea, 1919; Zur Frage der Plantinischen Cantica, 1923; Academia, 1924. Edited: Aristotelis Politica, 1909 (2nd edit. 1929); Theophrasti Chavacteros, 1923; Gergiae Helena, 1927. Editor of the series: Das Erbe der Alten, 1910 squ. Pavis, 1925. Contributor to German philological, historical, linguistic magazines and reviews. General character of writing: scientific, text books, historical. Relig. denom., Evangelical. ADDRESS: Zasiusstrasse 107, Freiburg im Breisgau, Baden, Germany.

IMMS, Augustus Daniel, M.A., D.Sc., F.R.S. *b*: Moseley, Worcs 1880. *e*: Univ of Camb, Mason Coll & B'ham Univ. *m*: Georgina Mary French. *d*: 2. Late Reader in Entomology Cambridge, Sometime Professor of Zoology Allahabad India, Foreign Mem American Acad Arts & Sciences, Late Pres Roy Entomological Soc London, Hon Mem Entomol Socs Finland, Holland & India. *Publ*: General Textbook of Entomology; Outlines of Entomology; Recent Advances in Entomology; Social Behaviour in Insects; Insect Natural History. *Ctr*: Nature. *s.s*: Zoology, particularly Entomology. *Rec*: Gardening, travel. *a*: Faldonside, Tipton St John, nr Sidmouth, Devon. *T*: Ottery St Mary 58.

INCE, Edward Lindsay, F.R.S.E., F.R.A.S. *b*: Amblecote 1891. *e*: Perth Acad, Edin Univ, Trinity Coll Camb & Paris. *m*: Phyliss Fry. *d*: 2. Univ Lecturer, former Prof of Pure Maths Egyptian Univ Cairo 1926—31. *Publ*: A Course in Descriptive Geometry; Cycles of Reduced Ideals in Quadratic Fields; etc. *Ctr*: Various. *s.s*: Science, Education. *Rec*: Books, gardens. *c*: Author's. *a*: 6 Rutland Gardens, Ealing, London, W.13.

INCE, Rev. George James. *b*: Blackheath 1884. *e*: Roan Sch Greenwich & King's Coll Lond. Clerk in Holy Orders. *Publ*: A Year's Course in Definite Church Teaching; A Year's Course on the Creed; A Year's Course on Holy Communion; A Short Concise Preparation for Confirmation. *s.s*: Religion. *Rec*: Golf, tennis. *a*: Rookhaye, Bowerchalke, Salisbury, Wilts. *T*: Broadchalke 210.

INCE, Richard, Basil, M.A. *b*: London 1881. *e*: Univ Coll Lond, Peterhouse Camb. *m*: Audrey Jowitt. *s*: 1. *Publ*: Franz Anton Mesmer; Joan of Arc; At the Sign of Sagittarius; When Joan Was Pope; Shadow Show; Calverley & Some Cambridge Wits; England's High Chancellor; A Dictionary of Religion; Theology & Ecclesiastical Terms; Talking Beast; The Eternal Carrot. *Ctr*: Various. *s.s*: Tudor & Stuart Hist & Lit. *a*: Marley Common, Haslemere, Surrey. *T*: 278.

INCHFAWN, Fay (Mrs. Atkinson Ward). *e*: Priv. *m*: Atkinson Ward. *d* 1. : *Publ*: Verse Book of a Homely Woman; Homely Verses of a Home Lover; Through the Windows of a Little House; Songs of the Ups & Downs; Silver Trumpets; Sweet Water & Bitter; A Book of Remembrance; The Journal of a Tent Dweller; Verse Book of a Garden; The Beautiful Presence; Verses from a Chimney Corner; The Little Donkey; Who Goes to the Wood; Who Goes to the Garden; Living in a Village; Salute to the Village; etc. *a*: Innisfree, Freshford. nr Bath.

IND, Charles Francis, M.D., M.B.B.S., F.R.S.M. *b*: Lon 1905. *e*: Taunton Sc, Taunton, Som. *m*: Kathleen Probert. *s*: 1. Physician. *c.t*: Practitioner, etc. *s.s*: Infectious diseases. Med Supt Keycol Hill Infect Hosp, Sittingbourne, Kent. *a*: 14 Park Rd, Sittingbourne. *t*: 100.

INFELD, Leopold, Ph.D., F.R.S.C. *b*: Cracow, Poland 1898. *e*: Univ of Cracow. *m*: Helen Schlauch. *s*: 1. *d*: 1. Prof of Mathematics Univ of Toronto. *Publ*: The Evolution of Physics (with A. Einstein); Whom The Gods Love; New World of Science; Quest. *Ctr*: Discovery, & many scientific journs. *Rec*: Writing. *a*: 87 Lyndhurst Ave, Toronto 10. *T*: K. I. 1945.

INFIELD, Henrik F., Ph.D. *b*: Cracow, Poland 1901. *e*: Univs of Vienna, Berlin, Heidelberg. *m*: Shulasmith Freier. *d*: 1. Exec Dir of the Rural Settlement Inst. *n.a*: Ctr Ed Sociometry, Chief Ed Die Wohnkultur (Prague) '29—30, Ed Gedezet (Basel) '30—31, Chief Ed Popular Scientific Press Service (Vienna) '32—33, Ed Kol-Noa (Tel-Aviv) '33—35. *Publ*: Co-operative Living in Palestine; Co-operative Communities at Work. *Ctr*: Yearbook of Agric & many other journs. *s.s*: Sociology of Co-operation, Research in Sociology, Co-operative Farming. *Rec*: Classical music, theatre, fiction, golf, tennis. *a*: Van Wagner Rd, R.F.D.I, Poughkeepsie, N.Y. *T*: 6060-1.

INFIELD, I. Henson, J.P. Journalist. *n.a*: Ed Sussex Daily News. *a*: 130 North St, Brighton. *t*: Brighton 2052.

INFIELD, Louis, B.A.(Cantab), O.B.E. *b*: 1888. *e*: Owen's Sch, Univ Coll Sch, Queen's Coll Camb, Univ of Gottingen. *m*: Georgina R. Namdamm. *s*: 2. *d*: 1. Civil Servant. *Publ*: Money; Lectures on Ethics; The World in Modern Science (translations). *s.s*: Science, Economics, Local Government, Folk Songs. *Rec*: Walking, children, philately, collecting of etchings. *c*: Authors. *a*: 89 Clarence Gate Gdns, London, N.W.1. *T*: Paddington 9493.

INGAMELLS, H. *b*: Boston 1863. *e*: Priv & Sec Sc. *m*: Alice Margaret Bond. *s*: 3. Journalist (ret). *n.a*: Boston Independent 1879-1900, Boston Post '00—04, Ed Staff Grimsby Evening Telegraph '05—32. *c.t*: Various. *s.s*: Athletics, cycling. Mem N.U.J. *c*: Nat Cyclists Un. *a*: The Ings, Little Coates Rd, Grimsby.

INGAMELLS, Reginald Charles, B.A. *b*: Ororoo, Sth Australia 1913. *e*: Adelaide Univ. *m*: Eileen Eva Spensley. *s*: 3. Publishers Educational Rep. *n.a*: Ed Jindyworobak Anthology 1938—41 & '47. *Publ*: Selected Poems; Gumtops; Forgotten People; Sun-Freedom; Memory of Hills; At a Boundary; News of the Sun; Unknown Lady. *Ctr*: The Bulletin, The Home, The Mail (Adelaide), Poetry, Chronicle, etc. *s.s*: Australian Aborigines, History & Lit, Educ. *c*: Jindyworobak. *a*: 431 Bourke St, Melbourne, Australia. *T*: W.M. 3721.

INGE, Very Rev. William Ralph, K.C.V.O., D.D. *b*: 1860. *e*: Eton & King's Coll Camb. Theologian & Author, Fell King's Coll Camb, Fell & Tutor Hertford Coll Oxf, Vicar of All Saints' Knightsbridge, Lady Margaret Prof of Divinity & Fell Jesus Coll Camb, etc, Trustee Nat Portrait Gallery, Former Dean of St Paul's. *Publ*: Faith & Knowledge; Studies of English Mystics; The Philosophy of Plotinus; Outspoken Essays; The Idea of Progress (Romanes Lecture); The Victorian Age (Rade Lecture); The Platonic Tradition; Lay Thoughts of a Dean; The Church in the World; Assessments & Anticipations; Things New & Old; God & the Astronomers; Vale; etc.

INGERSOLL, Ralph McAllister, B.S. *b*: New Haven, Conn 1900. *e*: Hotchkiss Sch Lakeville, Yale & Harvard Univs. *m*: Elaine Brown Keiffer. *s*: 1. Author, Lecturer. *n.a*: Rep N.Y. American '23—24, New Yorker '25, Mang-Ed '25—30, Assoc-Ed Fortune '30 & Mang-Ed '30—35, V-Pres & Gen-Man Time, Inc sponsoring Radio & Cinema The March of Time '35—38, Publisher Time Mag, Founder & Ed '40—46 PM. *Publ*: Top Secret; The Battle is the Pay-Off; Action on All Fronts; America is Worth Fighting For; Report on England; In & Under Mexico. *Ctr*: Various. *w.s*: 1940—45. *a*: Shadow Rock Farm, Lakeville, Connecticut. *T*: Lakeville 459.

INGHAM, Rev. Harry, D.D. *Publ*: The Divine Urge. *c.t*: Christian World, N.Y. Christian Advocate, Zion's Herald (Boston), etc. *a*: 17 Shepherds Hill, Highgate, N.6. *t*: Mountview 1836.

INGHAM, Jack Charles Walton, Journalist. *n.a*: The Star. *s.s*: Radio & Theatre Corr. *a*: 4 North View, Wimbledon Common, London, S.W.19. *T*: Wimbledon 6146 & Central 5000.

INGLE, Herbert, B.Sc, F.C.S., F.I.C. *b*: Leeds 1861. *e*: Leeds Univ. *m*: Alice F. W. Roddis. *s*: 1. *d*: 2. *n.a*: Lect on Agric Chem Yorks Col '96-1902, Chief Chem Transvaal Dept of Agric '02—07, Advisory & Cons Chem '09-33. *Publ*: (Jtly) The Chemistry of Fire & Fire Prevention ('00); Elementary Agricultural Chemistry ('08; 3rd edn '20); A Manual of Agricultural Chemistry; etc. *c.t*: Journ of Chem Soc, Brit Assoc Reports, Transvaal Agric Journ, etc. *s.s*: Agric, dairy & tech chem. *Rec*: Fishing. *a*: Clift Cottage, Cliff Rd, Headingley, Leeds. *t*: 51219.

INGLIS, A. E. J., M.A. *a*: Lanesborough Preparatory School, Cranley Rd, Guildford, Surrey.

INGLIS, Alex. *s.s*: Drama *a*: c/o 30 Codrington Cres, Haverton Hill, Middlesbrough.

INGLIS, James Gall, F.R.S.Edin. *b*: Edin 1864. *e*: Edin Collegiate & Craigmount Scs & Edin Univ. *m*: Charlotte Hill Kinmont. *s*: 1. Publisher & Ed. *Publ*: Ideal Ready Reckoners & other Commercial tables; Gell's Easy Guide to the Constellations, enlarged & remodelled; Norton's Star Atlas (drafting the larger portion of the preliminary letterpress). *c.t*: Mountaineering Club Journ, Scottish Mountaineering Club Guide Book, etc. *s.s*: Comm tables, popular astronomical works, revising & ed & drafting for authors. *Rec*: Golf, mountaineering. *c*: Roy Scottish Automobile, Scottish Mountaineering, Roy Scottish Geographical Soc, etc. *a*: 36 Blacket Place, Ebinburgh. *t*: 41150.

INGLIS, T. P. *n.a*: Ed Glasgow Ev Times. *a*: 65 Buchanan St, Glasgow.

INGLIS JONES, Elizabeth. *b*: Lon. *Publ*: Starved Fields (1929); Crumbling Pageant ('32). *Rec*: Reading, fishing. *a*: Derry-Ormond, Lampeter, Cardigans.

INGLIS KER, James, J.P., F.S.A., F.R.G.S., F.R.S.A. *e*: Dunfermline H.S. & Edin Univ. Ed of S.M.T. Mag. Vice Pres of the Scottish Dist Nursing Assoc. *Publ*: Scotland for the Motorist; The Spirit of the Lake; Islay's Shrine & The Land of Scott. *c.t*: Autocar, Scotsman, Glas Herald, Daily Express, etc. *s.s*: Old & new roads, Scottish romance & places of historic interest. War Work. Hon Organising Sec Scottish Red Cross Soc. Queen Alexandra Memorial. Asst in Promotion of Craigmillar Pageant, Scottish Women's Hosp, Belgian Relief Fund, Serbian Relief Fund. *c*: Scottish Arts, Roy Auto, etc. *a*: 41 George St, Edin. *t*: 31021.

INGOLD, Christopher Kelk, D.Sc.(Lond), F.R.S. *b*: Ilford 1893. *e*: Univ Coll Southampton & Imp Coll of Sc & Tech Sth Kensington. *m*: Edith Hilda Usherwood. *s*: 1. *d*: 2. Prof Org Chem Univ of Leeds 1924—30, Prof of Chem Univ of Lond '30—. *Publ*: Vat Dyes (with J. F. Thorpe). *Ctr*: Journ of Chem Soc, Journ of Soc of Chem Ind, Nature, Recueil Travaux Chimiques des Pays-Bas, Journ of Indian Chem Soc. *s.s*: Chem. *Rec*: Climbing, fives. *a*: 12 Handel Close, Canons Pk, Edgware, Middlesex. *T*: 1307.

INGPEN, Roger. *b*: Lon. *m*: Ada de la Mare. *d*: 1. *Publ*: Glory of Belgium (1914); Shelley in England; Ed Leigh Hunt's Autobiography; Ed Boswell's Life of Johnson; Shelley's Letters; etc. *c.t*: Outlook, Bookman, etc. *c*: Savage, Johnson. *a*: 28 Queen Anne's Gve, Bedford Pk, W. *t*: Chiswick 4378.

INGRAM, A. F. Winnington, D.D. Lord Bishop of London. *Publ*: Many Theological Works; What the Cross Means to Me; Has the Kingdom of God Arrived?; etc. *a*: Fulham Palace, S.W.6.

INGRAM, Bruce, Capt., O.B.E., M.C. *b*: 1877. *e*: Wincs & Trin Col Oxf. *m*: Amy Foy. *d*: 1. Editor. *n.a*: Illus Lon News 1900—; Ed Sketch '05, Dir Illus Lon News & Sketch Ltd, Illus Sporting & Dramatic News, Illus N/ps Ltd. *Rec*: Fishing, shooting, golf. *c*: Athenæum, Burlington, Fine Arts, Bath. *a*: Inveresk Hse, Strand, W.C.2.

INGRAM, George. *b*: London 1892. Author. *Publ*: Hell's Kitchen (with T. DeWitt Mackenzie); "Stir"; "Stir" Train; Cockney Cavalcade; The Muffled Man; Welded Lives. *s.s*: Crime, Cockney & Low Life. *Rec*: Travel. *a*: 49 Asquith Rd, Wigmore, Rainham, Kent. *T*: Park 4037.

INGRAM, H. Vernon, M.B., B.S.(Durham), D.O.M.S., R.C.P.&S.(Lon), M.R.C.S.(Eng), L.R.C.P. (Lon). Ophthalmic Surg. *n.a*: Ed Newcastle-on-Tyne & Northern Counties Med Journ. *s.s*: Ophthalmology. *c*: Mem Br. M.Assoc N. of Eng Ophthalm Soc, etc. *a*: 66 Jesmond Rd, Newcastle-on-Tyne, 2. *t*: Jesmond 67.

INGRAM, Kenneth. *b*: London 1882. *e*: Charterhouse. Barrister. *n.a*: Ed The Green Quarterly. *Publ*: The Sunworshipper; Why I Believe; The Modern Attitude to the Sex Problem; The Church of To-morrow; Death Comes at Night; Midsummer Sanity; Modern Thought on Trial; The Ambart Trial; Sex Morality To-morrow; Return of Yesterday; The Premier tells the Truth; Guide to the New Age; Years of Crisis, International History 1919—45; Communist Challenge. *a*: 97 Cheyne Walk, London, S.W.10. *T*: Flaxman 8783.

INGRAM, William Wilson, M.C., M.D., F.R.A.C.P. *b*: Scotland 1888. *e*: Aberdeen Univ. *m*: Dorothy Edith King. Dir Kolling Inst Med Res Sydney, Sen Hon Phys Roy North Shore Hosp Sydney, Cons Phys Hornsby & Dist Hosp Sydney. *Publ*: The Diagnosis & Treatment of Diabetes; Diabetic Diets. *Ctr*: Various Med Journs. *s.s*: Diabetes Mellitus. *w.s*: 1914—18 Capt R.A.M.C. (Dispatches & M.C.), '39—45 Lieut-Col A.A.M.C. *Rec*: Golf, fishing, sailing. *c*: Univ & Elanora Country Sydney. *a*: 185 Macquarie St, Sydney, N.S.W., Australia. *T*: B.1934.

INGRAM-BARRISH, Joanne Rutgers, B.A. *b*: Cape-Town 1911. *e*: Helpmekaar Hgh Sch Jo'burg, Potchefstroom Univ Coll. *m*: Reginald Winnington Ingram. *s*: 1. Princ of Elsie Van Huysteen Nursery Sch. *Publ*: Die Hoepie Se Lied; Marja Die Kwaai Beerin; Die Onderstebo Vlermuisie; Rrasetlako-Die Vader van Die Skoen. *Ctr*: Die Brandwag, Die Maweek, Die Jongspan, etc. *s.s*: Legends & Myths, Archæology, Dramatic Art. *Rec*: Drama, music, fishing. *a*: Box 171, Potchefstroom, Transvaal, Sth Africa. *T*: Potchefstroom 12.

INGRAMS, William Harold, O.B.E., M.R.G.S. *b*: Shrewsbury 1897. *e*: Shrewsbury Sc. *m*: Doreen Shortt. Colonial Admin Service. *n.a*: Ed Zanzibar Gazette 1924-27. *Publ*: Zanzibar: an Account of its People, Industries & History ('24); Dialects of the Zanzibar Sultanate; Zanzibar, Its History & Its People; School History of Mauritius; School Geography of Mauritius; Abu Nuwas in Life & in Legend, ('33); various pamphlets, articles & reports. *c.t*: Times. E. African & Mauritius papers, etc. *s.s*: Arab & E. African hist, ethnol & folklore. War Service, wounded. Asst Dist Commsnr Zanzibar '19. Asst Sec Zanzibar '25. Acting Asst Chief Sec Zanzibar '26. Asst Colonial Sec Mauritius '27. Acting Receiver-Gen '32. Acting Colonial Sec '32—33. Polit Officer Aden Protectorate '34, etc. Order Brilliant Star of Zanzibar. *Rec*: Nat hist, anthrop. *c*: Savile, Roy Asiatic Soc, Roy Anthrop Inst, etc. *a*: Aden, Arabia.

INGREM, Rev. C. *Publ*: Forty Years in Wimbledon; etc. *c.t*: Baptist Times, L.B.A. Quarterly, etc. *a*: Rosthorne, Stanley Rd, Wimbledon, S.W. *t*: Lib 2966.

INGSTAD, Helge. *b*: Meraker 1899. *m*: Anne Stine Moe. *d*: 1. Barrister, Author. *Publ*: Pelsjegerliv Blandt Nord-Kanadas Indianerne; Ost for Den Store Bre; Apache-Indianerne; Klondyke Bill; Siste Bat (Play). *Ctr*: Aftenposten, Norway, Goteborgs Handels och Sjofartstidning, Sweden, Berlinske Tidende, Denmark. *s.s*: Arctic Questions. *c*: Explorers'. *a*: Vettakollen, Oslo, Norway. *T*: 69. 76. 22.

INKPEN, A. E. *n.a*: Ed West Cumberland Times. *a*: 42 Brigham Rd, Cockermouth.

INKSTER, Dr. J. *c.t*: Lancet. *a*: 8 The Crescent, Linthorpe, Middlesbrough.

INKSTER, Leonard (see FETHALAND, John). *b*: Sheffield 1885. *e*: Rugby Sch, Balliol Coll Oxf & Middlesex Hosp London. *m*: Jean Donaldson. Author & Musician. *n.a*: Music Critic, New Statesman 1914, London Music, Dramatic & Art Critic, Sheffield Daily Telegraph '11—. *Publ*: The Emancipation (play); Wales (verse); etc. *Ctr*: Westminster Gaz, New Statesman, Athenæum, Manch Guardian, etc. *Rec*: Swimming, cricket & rugby football. *c*: Authors'. *a*: Norton, Newton St Cyres, nr Exeter, Devon.

INMAN, 1st Baron, Philip Albert Inman, J.P. *Publ*: inc The Human Touch; The Golden Cup; (Novel) Straight Runs Harley Street; etc. *a*: Knaresborough Hse, Warninglid, Haywards Heath, Sussex.

INMAN, Samuel Guy, M.A., LL.D. *b*: Trinity, Texas 1877. *e*: Columb & Texas Univs. *m*: Bessie Cox. *s*: 2. *d*: 3. Specialist in Latin-American Affairs, Writer, Lecturer, Univ Professor. *n.a*: Founder La Nueva

Democracia. *Publ*: Latin America, its place in World Life; What South America Thinks of Us (collab); History of Latin America; What the Informed Citizen Needs to Know (collab). *Ctr*: Philadelphia Ledger, Mexican Herald, N.Y. Times, New Republic, The Nation, La Prensa. *a*: Pondfield Ct, New York, U.S.A. *T*: Br. 2-2336.

INNES, Arthur Donald, M.A. *b*: Simla, India 1863. *e*: Marlboro' & Oriel Oxf. *m*: Helen Pittis. *s*: 1. Author & Coach. *Publ*: Seers & Singers: A Study of Five XIXth Century Poets ('92); England Under the Tudors; Class-Book of the British Commonwealth; Class-Book of Mediæval & Modern European History; Leading Figures in English History Tudor & Stewart Period; Maritime & Colonial Expansion Under the Stuarts (1932); etc. *c.t*: Harmsworth's History of the World, New Popular Educ, Concise Ency, etc. *s.s*: Modern Eng & Indian hist. Lect in Indian Hist at Sc of Oriental Studies '19–22. *c*: Univ of Lon. *a*: The Orchard, Uplyme, Lyme Regis, Dorset. *t*: 104Y.

INNES, Fred G. *e*: St Andrews Univ. *n.a*: Ed Fife Herald, St Andrew's Citizen. *Publ*: Free at Last. War Service. *a*: Fife Herald Office, Cupar, Fife. *t*: Cupar 6.

INNES, Guy Edward Mitchell, F.J.I. *b*: Ballarat 1882. *e*: Ballarat Coll, etc. *m*: Frances Blanche Gray. *s*: 1. Dep Ed Aus Newspaper Cable Service, Foundation Mem Aust Journalists' Assoc, Author of The Journalists' Code (verse). *n.a*: Reporter Melbourne Argus 1900, Chief Sub-Ed '10—11, News Ed Melbourne Herald '11 —18, Ed-in-Chief '18—21, Special Rep Melbourne Herald & Sydney Sun, Lond Mang Melbourne Herald Cable Service '23—26. *Ctr*: Eng & Aust newspapers. *s.s*: Aust Lit & Poetry, Spec American Div M.O.I. *c*: Authors'. *a*: Sloane Ave Mans, London, S.W.3. *T*: Kensington 7020.

INNES, J. R., C.M.G. Ret Judge of Supreme Ct, Brit Malaya. *Publ*: Registration of Land Titles, F.M.S. *c.t*: Law Quart Review. *a*: Montrose, Branksome Wood Rd, Bournemouth.

INNES, Kathleen Elizabeth, B.A.(Hons) (Lon). *e*: Lon Univ. *Publ*: The Prevention of War; The Bible as Literature; also various small books on the League of Nations, etc. *s.s*: International affairs & literature. *a*: 29 High Oaks Rd, Welwyn Garden City.

INNES, Maxwell Campbell, B.A. *n.a*: Sub-Ed The Architect & Building News. *s.s*: Furniture, travel, langs. *a*: 25a High St, St John's Wood, N.W.8.

INNES, ROBERT T. A.: astronomer; *b*. Edinburgh, Scotland, Nov. 1861. DEGREE: D.Sc. (Univ. Leyden); married. AUTHOR: A Reference Catalogue of South Double Stars, 1899; A Catalogue of Southern Double Stars, 1926. Contributor of scientific papers and memoirs to various technical journals. General character of writing: mathematical astronomy. CLUB: Scientific and Technical. HOME: Yeoville, Johannesburg, S. Africa.

INNES, OF LEARNEY, Sir Thomas, K.C.V.O., K.St.J., F.S.A.(Scot), Baron of Learney, Kinnairdy & Yeuchrie Lord Lyon King of Arms, Member Royal Company of Archers (King's Bodyguard for Scotland). *b*: Aberdeen 1893. *e*: Ecole Nationale Neuchâtel Switzerland, Torphins H.S. Sch, Edin Acad & Univ. *m*: Lady Lucy Buchan. *s*: 3. *d*: 1. Advocate Scots Bar 1922, Carrick Pursuivant of Arms '26, Albany Herald '35, Lord Lyon King of Arms & Secretary of Order of The Thistle '45—, Mem National Building Records Scottish Council '41—, Councils of Scottish History, Record & Ecclesiological Societies. *Publ*: Scots Heraldry; Tartans of the Clans & Families of Scotland; Law of Succession in Ensigns Armorial; Scottish Clans & Their Tartans; many articles on Scots Heraldry, History & Peerage Law. *Ctr*: Juridical Review, Scots Year Book, Procs of Soc Ant Scot, Scots Law Times, etc. *s.s*: Heraldry, Peerage Law, Scottish Genealogy, Agriculture & Forestry, Scottish Architecture. *c*: New Edin, Roy Coy Archers. *a*: Learney, Torphins, Aberdeenshire. *T*: Torphins 28. Kinnairdy Castle, Bridge of Marnoch, Banffshire. 35 Inverleith Row, Edinburgh. *T*: 84924.

INSCH, J., F.R.M.S. *b*: Fochabers 1876. East India Merchant. *Rec*: Microscopy, gardening. *c*: Oriental Lon & Bengal Calcutta. *a*: 149 Leadenhall St, E.C.3.

INSH, George Pratt, C.B.E., D.Litt. *b*: Cathcart, Glasgow 1883. *e*: Glas Univ. *m*: Alice Louisa Dummer. *s*: 1. *d*: 1. Historian. *Publ*: The Company of Scotland Trading to Africa & The Indies; Scottish Colonial Schemes; Scotland & The Modern World; The Darien Scheme; Historian's Odyssey; The Clyde, the Elusive River; Darien Shipping Papers; School Life in Old Scotland. *s.s*: Scottish History. *w.s*: (Regimental & Staff) 1914—19 & '39—44. *Rec*: Walking, travel, hist research. *c*: Nat Lib, Scottish Lib, P.E.N. *a*: Ardenvohr, Bothwell, Lanarkshire. *T*: Bothwell 2132.

INSKIP, Constance Elizabeth Hamilton, A.R.C.M. *b*: Bournemouth 1905. *e*: Cheltenham Ladies' Col & Roy Col of Music. *Publ*: The Ravelled Sleeve; Step to a Drum. *c.t*: Evening News, etc. *a*: The Walnuts, Walthamstow, E.17. *t*: 1570.

INSKIP, Very Rev. James Theodore. *b*: 1868. *e* Clifton Col, Corpus Christi Col & Ridley Hall Cam. *m*: Lilian Hamilton Ker. *s*: 1. *d*: 3. Vicar of St Paul's Penzance '94–1900, Leyton '00—07, Jesmond Newcastle-on-Tyne '07—16 & Ch Ch Southport '16-19. Bishop of Barking '19–. Special Lecturer in Pastoral Theology K.C.L. '04—05, Gower Lecturer '32—33. Hon Canon of Newcastle '14—16 & L'pool '16-19. Exam Chap Bishop of Chelmsford '14—19. Proc in Con of York '18—19. *Publ*: The Pastoral Idea ('05); The Harvest of the River ('30); Evangelical Influence in English Life ('33); The One Foundation ('33). *c.t*: C. of E. N/p, Record, Ch Quart Review. *a*: The Walnuts, Walthamstow, E.17. *t*: 1570.

"INTELLIGENCE OFFICER, THE" (pen name): see James, Lionel.

INVERARITY, Robert Bruce, B.A., F.R.S.A. *b*: Seattle, Washington 1909. *e*: Univs of Washington & Fremont. Artist, Writer & Teacher. *n.a*: Art Columnist Seattle Dly Times '30. *Publ*: Masks & Movable Figures of the North Pacific Coast Indians; Manual of Puppetry; North-west Coast Indian Art; Playable Puppet Plays; Block Printing & Stencilling; 12 Photographs by R. B. Inverarity, F.R.S.A.; The Rainbow Book. *Ctr*: Various. *s.s*: Art, Primitive Art, Northwest Coast Indians, Puppetry, Photography. *a*: 2510 West Seventh St, Los Angeles 5, Calif, U.S.A. *T*: Fairfax 2288.

INWARDS, Richard, F.R.A.S., F.R.MetSoc. *b*: Houghton Regis 1840. *e*: Foulbury, Bucks. Eng (ret). *Publ*: Weather-Lore; Temple of the Andes; Life & Work of W. S. Stanley. *c.t*: Sci Journ's. *s.s* Astronomy. Reported on or studied Engineering matters all over the world. *Rec*: Chess. *c*: Microscopic. *a*: 6 Croftdown Rd, N.W.5.

INWOOD, Frederick Max, M.J.I. *n.a*: Lon Mang Ed Starmer N/ps. *a*: 117 Bishop's Mns, Fulham, S.W.6. *t*: Putney 5542.

IONIDES, Basil, L.R.I.B.A. *b*: Kensington 1884. *e*: Priv & Tonbridge. Married. Architect. *n.a*: Homes & Gardens (Amer) & Country Life, etc.

Publ: Colour & Interior Decoration; Colour in ordinary Homes. *s.s*: Decoration. Architectural Works: Claridges Restaurant, Savoy Theatre, etc. *Rec*: Gardening, collecting china. *c*: R.I.B.A. & R.S.A. *a*: 47 Berkeley St, W.1. & Buxted Park Sx. *t*: Grosvenor 2434 & Buxted 5.

IRELAND, ARTHUR J(OSEPH): author, journalist, lecturer; b. Lime Park, Co. Galway, Ireland, May 6, 1874; s. Arthur Joseph (Staffsurg. R. N.), and Susanna Jane (Stanley) I.; educ. Royal Naval Sch. (New Cross, London), Fir Lodge Coll. (Sydenham, Eng.); DEGREES: M.A., L.L.B.; m. Agnes Maud Dearlove (died), Aug. 10, 1908. AUTHOR: Hours of Leisure, 1895; Mademoiselle Sophie, 1897; The Arabian Nights (edited), 1899; Dormitory Nights Entertainments; Episodes in the History of England, 1926. The following in preparation: Short Biographical Sketches; Men and Women of Mark; Sets of Six; Legends and Stories of London; Dawn and Dusk; Peeps into the Past. Editor and Founder of Swiss-Anglo-Saxon Mag., English editor La Gazette des Etrangers de Lausanne; editor Universal Press Service (London); fiction and asst. literary editor London Daily Mirror and lit. editor National News; chief Daily Mail War News; founder press Photographic Bureau (London); mem. edit. staff James Henderson and Sons and of Amalgamated Press; spec. correspondent Daily Graphic. Contributor to "Wonderful Britain" and to Harmsworth's Univ. Hist. of World; to many Eng. Revs., mags., papers. General character of writing: fiction, juveniles, historical and factual prose. Asst. Master Forest Hill House Sch. (London); senior Eng. Master Institut Lemania and at Ecole Hotelière, Lausanne (Switzerland); Prof. Eng. lang. and lit. Académie de Lausanne. War service in Royal Navy. Relig. denom., Church of England. (*)

IRELAND, Denis. *b*: Belfast 1894. Journalist. *Publ*: Ulster To-Day & To-Morrow (pamphlet). *c.t*: New Eng Weekly, Adelphi. *s.s*: Irish politics & economics. *c*: Arts' Belfast. *a*: 90 Eglantine Av, Belfast.

IREMONGER, F(REDERIC) A(THELWOLD): clergyman, editor; b. Longparish, Hants, Eng., July 8, 1878; s. William Henry and Mary Sophia (Lloyd) I.; educ. Clifton Coll., Keble Coll. (Oxford); DEGREE: M.A. (Oxford); unmarried. AUTHOR: A Sunday Evening Service, 1916; Before the Morning Watch, 1917; Men and Movements in the Church, 1928. Editor: The Guardian, 1922-27. Contributor to Observer, Evening News, Guardian. General character of writing: reviewing; religious. Chaplain to H. M. King George V.; Honorary Chaplain to Archbishop (Temple) of York. Relig. denom., Church of England. CLUBS: Arthur's, M.C.C. OFFICE: Vernham Dean Vicarage, Andover, Hants, Eng.

IRISH, J. S. *n.a*: Guernsey Evening Press. *a*: 8 Smith St, Guernsey, C.I.

IRON, JOHN (pen name): see Carlile, John Charles.

IRONS, Miss C. M. *a*: Tall Oak, Church Ave, Ruislip, Middx.

IRONS, Evelyn Graham, M.A.(Oxon). *b*: Glasgow 1900. *e*: St Bride's Sch Helensburgh & Somerville Coll Oxf. Journalist. *n.a*: Ed Dly Mail Women's Page '30—35 & Ev Standard Home Page '35—40, Reporter '40—44—. *Rec*: Riding, swimming. *w.s*: War Corr (French Army) '44—45, Croix de Guerre. *a*: Lodge Hill Cottage, Medmenham, Marlow, Bucks, & 172 Clifford's Inn, Fleet St, London, E.C.4. *T*: Hurley 275 & Holborn 8434.

IRONSIDE, Henry Allan, Litt.D., D.D. *b*: Toronto 1876. *e*: Wheston Coll, Bobdone Coll. *m*: Helen Georgia Schofield. *s*: 2. *d*: 1. Pastor Moody Memorial Church Chicago 1930—. *n.a*: Ed Moody Church News '30—, Spec Writer Sunday Sch Times '35—. *Publ*: Notes on—Ezra, Nehemiah & Esther, Minor Prophets, Jeremiah, Exposition of Romans, Proverbs, Ezekiel, Holiness, the False & the True; Except Ye Repent; Divine Priorities; The Way of Peace; Mysteries of God; Things Seen & Heard in Bible Lands. *Ctr*: Various. *s.s*: Bible Exposition & Christian Doctrine. *Rec*: Stamp Collecting. *a*: Plaza Hotel, 1553 N. Clark St, Chicago 10, Ill. *T*: Superior 2680.

IRONSIDE, John. See Tait, Euphemia Margaret.

IRONSIDE, Margaret. *b*: Banstead. *e*: Sutton Hgh Sch, privately & Abroad. Author. *Publ*: (Plays) The Black Sheep of Rexborough 3-act play; & The Bucket Shop (thriller); Many books for Children; & The Tale Tellers' Club; Young Diana; Jane Emerges; Lung Chung; etc. *Rec*: Motoring. *c*: Forum. *a*: 14 Tennyson Mans, Queen's Club Gdns, Kensington, London, W.14. *T*: Fulham 6118.

IRVIN, W. F/L. *n.a*: Daily Herald, Glasgow, Scotsman, Daily Express. *Publ*: Ed: Book of Glasgow. *s.s*: Shipbuilding, shipping, etc. *a*: Daily Herald, Glasgow.

IRVINE, Andrew Leicester, M.A. Schoolmaster. *Publ*: Ktema Es Aei; The Loves of Dido and Æneas; Cicero's Correspondence. *c.t*: Times, London Mercury. *a*: Pageites, Charterhouse, Godalming.

IRVINE, Amy Mary. *b*: Coleraine 1866. *e*: Sandwell Hall. Author. *Publ*: The Specialist; Roger Dinwiddie; The Probationer; The Dreams of Orlow; The School Enemy; A School Conspiracy; The Girl Who Was Expelled; Nora the Girl Guide; Adventurous Jean; Quiet Margaret; etc. *s.s*: Sch Stories, Dream Psych. *w.s*: World War I V.A.D. *Rec*: Music, painting. *a*: 78 West St, Deal.

IRVINE, Edward David, M.D., M.R.C.S., L.R.C.P., D.P.H. *b*: Liverpool 1904. *e*: St Edward's Coll L'pool, Univ of L'pool. *m*: Kathleen Robertson. *d*: 3. M.O.H. Dewsbury. *Ctr*: B.M.J., Journ of Hygiene, Journ Roy Sanitary Inst, Public Health, Medical Officer, Mother & Child, Journ of Physical Educ, Journ of Radiology, etc. *s.s*: Social Med, Care of the Aged, Health of Children. *Rec*: Reading. *a*: Ravens Lodge, Dewsbury. *T*: 172.

IRVINE, Sir James Colquhoun, C.B.E., LL.D., ScD., D.C.L., F.R.S. *b*: Glas 1877. *e*: Allan Glen's Sc Glas, Roy Tech Col Glas & St And & Leipzig Univs. *m*: Mabel Violet Williams. *s*: 1. *d*: 2. Princ & Vice-Chancellor Univ of St Andrews. *c.t*: Sci periodicals. *s.s*: Chem Research on carbohydrates. Ex-Prof of Chem & Dir of Chem Research Lab's, Utd Col Univ of St Andrews. *Rec*: Golf, tennis. *c*: Athenæum, Roy & Ancient. *a*: The Univ Hse, St Andrews, Fife. *t*: 117.

IRVINE, Lyn, M.A.(Aberdeen). *b*: Berwick-on-Tweed 1901. *e*: Aberdeen Univ & Girton Col Cantab. *m*: M. H. A. Newman. Writer. *n.a*: Ed Monologue, '34—35. *Publ*: Ten Letter Writers. *c.t*: New Statesman & Nation, Spectator, Listener, Observer, Everyman. *a*: 12a Lowndes St, S.W.1. *t*: Sloane 5910.

IRVINE, Kenneth Neville. *b*: Birkenhead 1906. *e*: Shrewsbury Sch, Magdalen Coll Oxf, St Thomas's Hosp Lond, Bellevue Hosp N.Y. City. *m*: Phyllis Josephine Chanter. *s*: 2. *d*: 2. Med Supt S. Oxon Isolation Hosp, Hon Phys Henley War Memorial Hosp. *Publ*: The B.C.G. Vaccine. *Ctr*: Brit Journ of Tuberculosis, Med Press, Health Horizon, Nature, Practitioner, Annals of

Trop Med & Parasitology, Quarterly Journ of Experimental Physiology, etc. *s.s*: The B.C.G. Vaccine, Malaria, Mepacrine. *Rec*: Rowing, alpine climbing, ski-ing, squash racquets. *c*: Alpine, Leander, Phyllis Court. *a*: Carlesgill, Henley-on-Thames, Oxon. *T*: 369.

IRVINE, William Fergusson, M.A., F.S.A. *b*: Birkenhead 1869. *e*: Birkenhead Sc. *m*: Lilian Davies-Colley. *s*: 5. *d*: 1. High Sheriff Merionethshire 1933–34. *Publ*: Notes on the History of Bidston (1894); Notes on the Churches of Wirral ('96); Liverpool in the Reign of Charles II ('99); The Hollands of Mobberley (1902); The Colleys of Churton-Heath Co Cest ('31); etc. *c.t*: Times, Manchester Guardian, Liverpool Daily Post, Athenæum, Ency Britannica. *s.s*: Archæology, hist of Cheshire & N. Wales. Gen Ed Record Soc of Lancs & Cheshire 1895–1909. Hon Sec Local Hist Sc L'pool Univ '03–10. Local Sec Cheshire for Soc of Antiquaries '09– & N. Wales '30–. *a*: Brynllwyn Hall, nr Corwen, N. Wales. *t*: Corwen 53.

IRVING, CHRISTOPHER (pen name): see Johnston, Reginald Fleming.

IRVING, George William, B.A., LL.B.(Melbourne). *b*: Heckmondwike, Yorks 1887. *e*: Wheelwright Sc, Dewsbury, Borough Rd Training Col, Isleworth & Univ of Melbourne. *m*: Mary Cecilia Butler. *s*: 1. *d*: 1. Barrister at Law. Teacher. *Publ*: Man & his Wants; An Introduction to English & Australian Economic History. *c.t*: Melbourne Argus, Melbourne Age. *s.s*: Economics. Senior master in Economics, Scotch Col, Melbourne. *Rec*: Motoring. *c*: Hawthorn. *a*: 17 Fairmount Ave, Hawthorn East, Melbourne, Victoria. *t*: Hawthorn 3676.

IRVING, John Christopher, B.A. *b*: Crowthorne. *e*: Trent Col & Cam (St John's Col). *m*: Mabel Clare Curtis. Journalist. *n.a*: Editorial Staff Lincolnshire Echo. War Service 1916–19. *Rec*: Gardening. *a*: Pottergate Lodge, Lincoln.

IRVING, REGINALD (pen name): see Johnston, Reginald Fleming.

IRVING, William Fergusson, M.A., F.S.A. *b*: Claughton, Cheshire 1869. *m*: Lilian Davies-Colley. *s*: 4. *d*: 1. Landowner. *Publ*: Liverpool in the Reign of Charles II; History of Rivington Co. Lanc; The Hollands of Mobberley; The Colleys of Churton Heath; Notes on the Old Halls of Wirral; Notes on the Churches of Wirral. *Ctr*: Ency Brit, Times, Manch Guardian, L'pool Dly Post. *s.s*: Local History, Archæology of Cheshire & N Wales. *c*: Old Hall (L'pool). *a*: Brynllwyn Hall, Corwen, North Wales. *T*: Corwen 53.

IRWIN, Geoffrey. See **Tyson, Geoffrey William.**

IRWIN, Rev. Geo. Freeman, M.A., B.D. *n.a*: Ed The Churchman & The Church Gazette. *a*: 7 Wine Office Ct, Fleet St, E.C.4.

IRWIN, Inez Haynes. *b*: Rio Janeiro 1873. *e*: Boston Radcliffe Col. Married. Author. *n.a*: Corr Metropolitan Mag during Gt War 1916–17. *Publ*: June Jeopardy ('08); The Lady of Kingdoms; The Happy Years; Maida's Little House; Gertrude Haviland's Divorce; Family Circle; Youth Must Laugh; Angels & Amazons; Strange Harvest ('34); etc. *c.t*: Amer Mag, Atlantic Monthly, Blue Book, Century Mag, Delineator, Good Housekeeping, Ladies Home Journ, Nation, Pictorial Review, Red Book, Sunset Mag, etc. *s.s*: Feminism & the Brontës. Founder, with Maud Wood Park, of Nat Col Equal Suffrage League. Winner O. Henry Meml Prize for best Amer sh st of '24. Pres Authors' League of Amer '31–33. Pres Authors Guild '26–29. Mem Nat Counc of Nat Women's Party. Mem Prix Femina Cmt '31–33. *Rec*: Swimming, gardening. *c*: Cosmopolitan, N.Y.C., Authors' League of Amer. *a*: 240 W. 11th St, New York & Scituate, Mass, U.S.A. *t*: Watkins 9–8921.

IRWIN, Margaret. *m*: J. R. Monsell. *Publ*: Still She Wished for Company; These Mortals; Knock Four Times; Fire Down Below; None So Pretty; Royal Flush; The Proud Servant; The Stranger Prince; The Bride; The Gay Galliard; Young Bess; & 2 short stories. *a*: c/o Chatto & Windus, 40-42 William IV St, London, W.C.2.

IRWIN, Will, B.A. *b*: Oneida, N.Y. 1873. *e*: Leadville & Denver Colorado & Stanford Univ. *m*: (1) Harriet S. Hyde, (2) Inez Haynes Gillmore. *s*: 1. Author & Journalist, Mem P.E.N. & Soc of Amer Historians. *n.a*: Corr London Times, N.Y. Tribune 1914—15 & Sat Ev Post '16—20. *Publ*: Youth Rides West; The Next War; The Red Button; Propaganda & The News; The Picaroons (collab); Herbert Hoover; The Latin at War; The Making of a Reporter. *Ctr*: Collier's, Century, Liberty, Everybody's, Pict Rev, etc. *s.s*: National Politics, Philosophy of Journalism, Light General Articles. *Rec*: Clubs & conversation. *c*: Dutch Treat, Player's, Bohemian, etc. *a*: 240 West 11th St, New York City 14, U.S.A. *T*: Watkins 9-8921.

IRWIN, William Knox, M.D., F.R.C.S.E. *b*: Drumquin, Co Tyrone. *e*: Roy Sch Dungannon, Aberdeen Univ, Edin, Berlin. *m*: Edith Isabel Mary Collins. *s*: 1. Hon Surg St Paul's Hosp for Genito-Urinary Diseases, Hon Cons Urological Surg Eltham & Mottingham Hosp. *Publ*: Surgical Urology; Urinary Surgery. *Ctr*: Brit Journ of Surgery, Lancet, B.M.J., Brit Journ of Urology, Med Press & Circular, Urologic & Cutaneous Review. *s.s*: Diseases of the Urinary Organs. *Rec*: Riding, gardening, travel. *c*: Aberdeen Univ. *a*: 132 Harley St, London, W.1., & Croft Hse, Watford Heath, Herts. *T*: Welbeck 2296.

IRWIN-CARRUTHERS, G., M.A.(Oxon). Schoolmaster. *n.a*: Reviewer M/C Guardian, Greece & Rome. *c.t*: Poetry Review, Poems of To-day. *c*: Hellenic Soc, Classical Assoc. *a*: City of London School, Victoria Embankment, E.C.4.

ISAAC, C. L. T.D. Cons Surg. *c.t*: B.M.J., Clinical, Journ. *a*: 5 St James' Cres, Swansea. *t*: 2372.

ISAAC, Rev. Evan. Meth Min. *Publ*: Prif Emynwyr Cymru; Humphrey Jones a Dinygiad 1859–. *c.t*: Yr Eurqrawn, Y Beirniad, The Ocean & Nat Mag. *a*: Talifsin, Cards.

ISAACS, George Alfred, J.P. *b*: Lon 1883. Trade Union Sec. *n.a*: Ed Natsopa Journ. *Publ*: Story of the Newspaper Printing Press; With the Pressmen & Assistants in North America. *s.s*: N/p printing presses. Mayor of Southwark 1919–21. M.P. Gravesend '23–24, N. Southwark '29. Parl Priv Sec to Dominions Sec, & Leader of Opposition. *Rec*: Swimming, golf. *c*: Nat Lab; Liveryman Stationers' Coy Lon. *a*: Caxton Hse, 13–16 Borough Rd, S.E.1. *t*: Hop 0493-4.

ISAACS, J., M.A.(Oxon). *b*: London 1896. *e*: Exeter Coll Oxf. *m*: . *d*: 2. Lecturer in Eng Lang & Lit King's Coll Lond Univ, Professor Eng Lit Univ of Jerusalem 1942–45. *Publ*: Shakespeare as Man of the Theatre; Production & Stage Management at Blackfriars Theatre; Contemporary Movements in European Literature (jt-ed); Shakespeare Scholarship & Criticism; 16th Century Translations & Authorised Version of Bible; etc. *Ctr*: Ency Brit, Times, Spectator, Sun Express, 19th Century, Listener, etc. *s.s*: Shakespeare, Eng Lit, Film Criticism, Theatrical & Art History. *Rec*: Travel & collecting books & pictures. *a*: 44 Fitzjohns Ave, London, N.W.3. *T*: Hampstead 2609.

ISAACS, Raphael, A.M., M.D. *b* : Cincinnati, Ohio 1891. *e* : Univ of Cincinnati, Harvard Med Sch. *m* : Agnes Wolfstein. *s* : 1. Med Research. *n.a* : Ed Bd Hebrew Med Journ, Folia Hæmatologica. *Publ* : Manual of Clinical & Laboratory Technic ; Diseases of the Blood (all in collab). *Ctr* : Various med journs. *s.s* : Hematology, Hebrew Lore. *a* : 104 South Michigan Ave, Chicago 3, Ill, U.S.A. *T* : Randolph 7370.

ISAACS, Susan Sutherland, C.B.E., M.A., D.Sc.(Vict), Hon.D.Sc.(Adelaide). *b* : Bolton, Lancs 1885. *e* : Univs of Manchester & Cambridge. *m* : Nathan Isaacs. Formerly Head of Dept Child Development University of Lond, Fell Brit Psycholog Soc. *n.a* : Ed Contribution to Modern Education, Ed Bd Brit Journs Psychology, Medical Psychology & Educational Psychology. *Publ* : Intellectual Growth in Young Children ; Social Development of Young Children ; The Nursery Years ; The Children We Teach ; An Introduction to Psychology. *Ctr* : Nature, New Era, Spectator, Internat Journ of Psycho-Analysis, etc. *s.s* : Psycho-Analysis & Child Psychology. *Rec* : Walking & gardening. *a* : 30a Primrose Hill Rd, London, N.W.3. *T* : Primrose 2861.

ISAACS, Rev. Wilfrid Henry. *b* : Malvern 1866. *e* : Rugby & King's Col Cam. *m* : Rosa Sarah Lloyd. *s* : 1. Rector of Hemingby. *Publ* : New Testament Epistles in English Prose for the General Reader— The 2nd Epistle to the Corinthians, & The Epistle to the Hebrews. *s.s* : St Paul's epistles. *a* : Hemingby Rectory, Horncastle.

ISAY, RUDOLPH: writer: b. Trier, Jan. 1, 1886; s. Adolf and Jenny (Michaels) I.; educ. Univs. of Heidelberg, Strassburg, Berlin and Bonn. DEGREE: Dr. Jur.; m. Isabella Trimborn, Nov. 23, 1918. AUTHOR: Recht am Unternehmen, 1910; Kommentar zum Preuss. Allgem. Berggesetz (with Hermann Isay; 2 vols.), 1919, 1920; Kommentar zum deutschen Kohlenwirtschaftsgesetz, 1920; Studien im privaten und öffentlichen, Kartellrecht, 1922; Kommentar zur Kartellverordnung (with S. Tschierschky), 1925; Reform des Kartellrechts (with Nipperdey), 1928; Rechtsvergleichendes Bergrecht, 1929. Contributor of many essays to various law journals. Relig. denom., Evangelical. OFFICE: Bülowstr. 103, Berlin W. 57. HOME: Koserstr. 2, Berlin-Dahlem, Germany.

ISENDAHL, WALTHER: consulting engineer; b. Frankenstein, Germany, Jan. 31, 1877; s. Theodor and Wilhelmine (Bütow) I.; educ. Realgymnasium Neisse and later at Charlottenburg; Technische Hochschule at Charlottenburg and die Friedrich-Wilhelm Universität at Berlin; m. Emmy Müller, Nov. 16, 1905. AUTHOR: Der Explosionmotor, 1901; Technisches Taschenwörterbuch (in 3 Sprachen, Deutsch, Französisch, English), 1902; Construktion und Fabrikation von Automobilmotoren (with Lehmbeck) Vol. 1, 1908; Automobil-Sport-Kalender, 1906; Automobil und Automobilsport (2 vols.), 1908; Flugmotoren, Bau und Behandlung (vol. 1), 1913; Bericht über die National-Flugspende, 1913; Bootsmotoren, Konstruktion, Einbau und Behandlung, 1915; Der Verbrennungsmotor (Lehrbücher für den Automobilbau Band 1), translated and collaborated from the Gasoline Motor of P. M. Heldt); Motor-Yachten (Vol. 1), 1917; Die Kunst, gut zu Fahren! 1931. Chief editor of Auto und Wirtschaft (Berlin). Contributor to The Motor; Dienst am Auto; The Yacht; Adac-Motor Welt; Allg. Automobil-Zeitung; Stoewer Mag.; Allgemeine technische Correspondenz; B. Z. am Mittag; Auto und Wirtschaft and others. General character of writing: popular technical, concerning all questions regarding automobilism, motorboating, flying. Collaborator of the first German automotive magazine, The Motorwagen, since 1898; a well-known motorboatman, winner of many trophies in Germany, since 1907; occupied in aviation industry, 1910-12; chief editor of Allgemeine Automobil-Zeitung, Berlin, 1904-12; then chief editor of The Motor; chief engineer of Kaiserlichen Motorboot-Korps, during Great War. Relig. denom., Protestant. CLUBS: Bund Deutscher Civil-Ingenieure, (B.D.C.-J.); V e r e i n Deutsche Sportpresse; Allgemeiner Schnaaferl-Club A. S. C.; Motor-Yacht-Club von Deutschland; Verband der Automobilbesitzer Deutschlands E. V. ADDRESS: Kaiser-Allee 191, Berlin-Wilmersdorf, Germany.

ISHERWOOD, Christopher. *b* : Cheshire 1904. *e*: St Edmund's Sc Hindhead, Repton & Corpus Christi Col Camb. Teacher of English Abroad. *Publ* : All the Conspirators; The Memorial. Work on dialogue for Gaumont British Film Little Friend 1933–4. *a* : 19 Pembroke Gdns, W.8. *t* : Western 0509.

ISHERWOOD, Christopher William Bradshaw. *Publ* : inc (Fiction) Prater Violet ; Goodbye to Berlin ; (Plays) On the Frontier ; Ascent of F.6 (both with W. H. Auden) ; (Autobiog) Lions & Shadows ; (Travel) Journey to a War (also with W. H. Auden). *a* : 1946 Ivar Ave, Hollywood 28, California, U.S.A.

ISHERWOOD, William. *b* : Kilnhurst. Married. *s* : 1. *d* : 3. F.L. Journalist. *n.a* : Sheffield Independent, Durham Chronicle, Sunderland Daily Post, Northern Daily Mail, Evening World. *c.t* : All Nat dailies. *s.s* : Assoc football, drama. War Service R.G.A. India. *Rec* : Golf. *a* : Manora, Caledonian Rd, W. Hartlepool. *t* : 2889 & 3068.

ISLES, Keith Sidney George, M.A., M.Sc. *b* : Bothwell, Tasmania 1902. *e* : Adelaide, Camb Univ. *m* : Irene Frances Clayton. *s* : 1. *d* : 2. Prof of Economics Queen's Univ Belfast Nth Ireland. *Publ* : Wages Policy & Price Level ; Money & Trade ; Compulsory Savings ; Wages Policy in War Time. *Ctr* : Various economic journs. *s.s* : Economics. *a* : 56 Rugby Rd, Belfast, Nth Ireland. *T* : 25516.

ISRAEL, Madeleine. *b* : Paris. *m* : Andre Berry. Author. *Publ* : Jules Romains, sa vie, son oeuvre ; L'amour pour l'amour ; Poemes ; Le Triomphe de Mr Frite ; Don Juan aux Enfers. *a* : 24 rue Tournefort, Paris 5e. *T* : Por 24-39.

ISRAELS, Martin C. G., M.Sc., M.D., M.R.C.P. *b* : Manchester 1906. *e* : Manchester Gr Sch & Univ. *m* : Ivy D. Livesley. *d* : 1. *Publ* : Progress in Clinical Medicine. *Ctr* : Lancet, Practitioner & other med journs. *s.s* : Medical. *Rec* : Gardening, photography. *w.s* : R.A.F.V.R. Medical Branch Wing-Cdr. *a* : 242 Brooklands Rd, Baguley, Altrincham, Cheshire. *T* : Sale 4599.

IVENS, Rev. H. John. *Publ* : John Wesley (5 act play). *a* : Ivy Bank, Windhill, Shipley.

IVENS, RICHARD: journalist; b. Great Alne, Warwickshire, Eng., Aug. 18, 1849; s. William and Sophia (Williams) L.; educ. private sch. in Birmingham; m. (1) Elizabeth Jukes Wright, (2) Betsy Ann Reid. Editor Nottingham Guardian, 1887-1925; formerly editor Leamington Courier. Contributor to most English newspapers, including London Times. General character of writing: factual prose along lines of economics and politics. Relig. denom., Church of England. HOME: Whatton-in-the-Vale, Nottingham, Eng.

IVENS, Rev. Walter George, M.A.(N.Z.), D.Litt (N.Z.), LittD.(Melb). *b* : N.Z. 1871. *e* : Christ's Col Christchurch, N.Z. & Canterbury Col N.Z. Univ. *m* : Eleanore Barrett. *Publ* : Trans of the New Testament into three lang's of Solomon Islands ; Grammars of nine lang's of Solomon Islands ; The Island Builders of the Pacific ; etc. *c.t* : Roy Anthrop Journ, etc. *s.s* : Melanesian langs & anthropology. Research Fell of Univ of Melbourne 1924-28. *c* : Fell Roy Anthrop Inst. *a* : Melanesian Missn, Church Hse, Westminster, S.W.1.

IVENS-KNOWLES, Mrs. F., C.B.E., M.S.(Lon), F.C.O.G. *Publ*: Gynæ obstet papers & monograph. Chevalier Legion d'Honneur, Croix de Guerre avec palme. *a*: Killagorden, Truro, Cornwall.

IVES, Doris Violet, B.A., M.A. F.R.S.A. *b*: Forest Gate 1905. *e*: Holmwood Col Westcliff, Southend-on-Sea H.S., Westfield Col, Lon. Literary Research, Lect. *c.t*: Modern Lang Review. *s.s*: Eng & Latin mediæval lit. *Rec*: Swimming, riding, singing, elocution, piano. *a*: The Briars, Hall Park Av, Westcliff-on-Sea, Essex. *t*: Leigh-on-Sea 76557.

IVES, Rev. E. J. *Publ*: Ever Present Christ; Message of Thomas à Kempis; Ed Eleven Christians. *a*: 94 Wembley Hill, Wembley. *t*: 1426.

IVES, GEORGE CECIL: author; b. 1867; s. G. M. Ives; educ. private tutors, Cambridge and London Univs.; DEGREE: M.A. (Cambridge); unmarried. AUTHOR: Book of Chains (poems), 1897; Eros Throne (poems), 1900; History of Penal Methods, 1914; Extra-Organic Habits of Animals, 1918; The Continued Extension of the Criminal Laws, 1922; The Graeco-Roman View of Youth, 1926. Contributor (formerly) to Saturday Rev. General character of writing: historical, collecting and indexing facts. Actively interested in criminology; formerly a Prison Visitor; lectures on criminology, Venemous Snakes, Pre-Historic Man.; member various learned socs. HOME: Royal Societies Club, London, Eng.

IYENGAR, K. R. Srinivasa, M.A., D.Litt. *b*: Sattur 1908. *e*: Hindu Coll Tinnevelly, St Xavier's Coll Palmacottah, Madras Univ. *m*: Padmasani. *s*: 1. *d*: 1. Univ Prof of English & Head of English Dept Andhra Univ Waltair. *Publ*: Lytton Strachey, a Critical Study; Sri Aurobindo, a Biographical Study; Indian Contribution to English ' Literature; Indo-Anglian Literature; Literature & Authorship in India; Life of S. Srinivasa Iyengar; Gerard Manley Hopkins, the Man & the Poet; On Beauty. *Ctr*: The New Review, The Aryan Path, Times of India, Advent, Human Affairs, Hindoosthan, etc. *s.s*: Lit Criticism, Indian Affairs. *Rec*: Walking, reading. *c*: P.E.N. *a*: Andhra Univ, Waltair, India.

IYER, Ulloor S. Parameswara, M.A., B.L. *b*: Changanacherry, N. Travancore 1877. *e*: H.H. The Maharaja's Coll Trivandrum. *m*: Sri Subbalakshmi Ammal. *s*: 5. *d*: 4. Literary Work, Dean Faculty of Oriental Studies & Fine Arts Travancore Univ, Many distinctions & awards for Prose & Verse, formerly Dewan Peishkar and District Magistrate, Pres All Kerala Lit Acad & Ed-in-Chief 1934—45. *Publ*: Umakeralam; Amba; Karnabhushanam; Pingala; Bhakti deepika; Peacock Messenger; Vijnnadeepika; History of Champu Kavyas in Malayalam. *Ctr*: Hindu, Indian Review, all Malayalam newsps & periodicals. *s.s*: Annal & Antiquities of Kerala. *Rec*: Walking. *a*: Sarada Nikeethan, Jagathy, Trivandrum, Travancore State, S India.

J. A. B. (pseudonym): see Beringer, Joseph August.

J. G. T. (pseudonym): see Grein, Jack (James) Thomas.

"J. H. H." (pseudonym): see Harley, John Hunter.

JABAVU, DAVIDSON DON TENGO: lecturer in languages; b. King William's Town, South Africa, Oct., 1885; s. John Tengo and Elida (Sakuba) J.; educ. Morija (Basutoland, South Africa), Lovedale, Cape Province, Univ. Coll. (London), Univ. Birmingham (Eng.); DEGREE: B.A. (London); m. Florence Tandisua Nakiwanem, July, 1916. AUTHOR: The Black Problem, 1920; Bantu Literature, 1921; The Life of John Tengo Jabavu, 1922; Incwadi Yaba Limi (on Agriculture), 1923; Uhambelo E. Jerusalem, 1928; The Segregation Fallacy, 1928. Contributor to Internat.. Rev. of Missions (London). General character of writing: essays and text books on matters of South African import. Organized the Cape African Teachers' Assn., South African Federation of Native Teachers, Native Farmers' Assn., Cape Native Voters' Assn. Relig. denom., Wesleyan Methodist. OFFICE: South African Native College, Fort Hare, Alice, C. P., South Africa.

JACHMANN, GUENTHER: univ. professor; b. Gumbinsen, Germany, May. 20, 1887; s. Bernhard and Margarete (Tiessen) J.; educ. Joachimsthal'sches Gymnasium (Berlin); Univs. of Göttingen and Bonn. DEGREES: Ph.D., Ord. Professor; m. Gertrude Neuels, April 7, 1921. AUTHOR: Die Geschichte des Terenztextes im Altertum, 1924; Die Originalität der römischen Literatur, 1926; A. von Hildebrands Briefwechsel (with Conrad Fiedler), 1927; Terenti codex Vaticanus, 1929. Contributed several essays on classical philology to mags. General character of writing: scientific-historical. Religion, Protestant. ADDRESS: Wolfgang Müller Strasse 24, Cologne-Marienburg, Germany.

JACK, A. A., M.A., L.L.M., LL.D. b: 1868. e: Fettes & Glas & Cam Univs. m: Lucy Nichol. Prof Eng Lit Aberdeen Univ. Publ: Thackeray (a study); Essays on the Novel; The Prince (a play); Shelley (an essay); Mathilde (a play); Poetry and Prose, being essays on Modern Eng Poetry; etc. c: Athenæum. a: 22 Queen's Rd, Aberdeen.

JACK, Daniel Thompson, M.A. b: Glasgow 1901. e: Bellahouston Acad & Glas Univ. m: Nan F. G. Dall. Professor Economics Univ of Durham, King's Coll Newcastle-on-Tyne '35—. Publ: The Economics of the Gold Standard; The Restoration of Foreign Currencies; Currency & Banking; International Trade; The Crisis of '31; Studies in Economic Warfare. s.s: Currencies & Banking, International Trade, Industrial Relations. c: Nat Lib (Lond). a: 10 Mitchell Ave, Jesmond, Newcastle-on-Tyne 2. T: Jesmond 1835.

JACK, Brig. E. M., C.B., C.M.G., D.S.O. Publ: On the Congo Frontier. a: 26 Winn Rd, Southampton.

JACK, Rev. James William, J.P., M.A., Lit.A., D.D.(Edin). b: Carlisle 1866. e: Duns Acad Berwickshire & Edin Univ. n.a: Rev of Biblical Archæology (Quarterly) to Expository Times 1930—, Rev of Books on Near Eastern Archæ (Egypt, Palestine, Mesopotamia, etc) to Expository Times, Scotsman, etc. Publ: Daybreak in Livingstonia ('01); After His Likeness or Thoughts on the Christian Ideal; Manual of French Pronunciation and Diction; Samaria in Ahab's Time; The Date of The Exodus In The Light of External Evidence; The Historic Christ—an Examination of Dr Robert Eisler's Theory; Poems—French & English; Scott's View from The Wicks of Baiglie ('33); The Ras Shamra Tablets and the Old Testament; etc. c.t: Expository Times, Scotsman, Glas Herald Rev. de l'hist. des Relig., etc. s.s: Near Eastern archæ, Old Testament history & criticism, French language & literature. Rec: Golf, tennis. a: The Manse, Glenfarg, Perthshire.

"JACK-ALL-ALONE" (pen name): see Cowper, Frank.

JACKH, ERNST: Vice-Pres. of the German League of Nations Union; b. Urach, Germany, February, 1875; s. Ludwig and Karoline (Borst) J.; educ. Univs. of Munich, Geneva and Heidelberg. DEGREES: Ph.D. (Heidelberg), Professor of the Berlin Univ.; m. Marta Ruben, 1925. AUTHOR: Friedrich Nietzsche und David Friedrich Strauss, 1908; Der aufsteigende Halbmond, 1909; Friedrich List als Orientprophet, 1910; Im türkischen Hauptquartier durch Albanien, 1911; Deutschland im Orient nach dem Balkankrieg, 1912; Deutschland und die Türkei, 1915; Werkbund und Mitteleuropa, 1916; Deutsche Völkerbundspolitik, 1919; Zur Gründung der Deutschen Hochschule für Politik, 1920; Politik und Wirtschaft-Wissen und Wille, 1922; Kiderlen-Wächter, der Staatsmann und Mensch, 1924; Kiderlen-Wächter intime d'aprèsses notes et sa Correspondance. Traduit de l'Allemand, 1924; Germany and the League, 1926; The New Germany, 1927; Deutschland, das Herz Europas, 1928; Der Völkerbundgedanke in Deutschland Während des Weltkriegs. 1929. Editor: Der Deutsche Krieg, 1914-1918; Deutsche Orientbücherei, 1915-1917; Weltkultur und Weltpolitik, 1916-1918; Deutsch Politik, 1913-1922. Contributor to all prominent German newspapers and mags. General character of writing: political. President of the German Sch. of Politics; General Manager of the International exhibition "The New Area". Member of the German delegations in Versailles, Locarno, Geneva, etc. Organizer of international relations for World Peace. Founder of the German Sch. of Politics, of the German League of Nations Union. Mem. of Executive Comm. of Liberal Party. Dissenter. Member of many German clubs. HOME: Wuthenowstrasse 2, Berlin Steglitz, Germany.

JACKMAN, Augustus Norman. Married. s: 2. d: 1. Financial Journalist & Statistician. s.s: Mining. a: 72 Coleman St, Lon E.C.2. t: Met 3304.

JACKMAN, William T. b: Kilsyth, Ontario 1871. e: Univs of Toronto, Pennsylvania, Harvard & Lond. m: Vera M. Tryon. Univ Prof (ret). Publ: Economics of Transportation; Economic Principles of Transportation; Economic Problems of Transportation; Development of Transportation in Modern England; Critical Analysis of the Canadian Railway Problem. s.s: Transportation & Industrial Traffic Management. Rec: Gardening, golf. c: Toronto Railway. a: 171 St Leonards Ave, Toronto 12, Ontario, Canada. T: Mohawk 2156.

JACKS, Lawrence Pearsall, M.A., Hon.LL.D., Hon.D.Litt., Hon.D.D. b: Nottingham 1860. e: Univs of Nott'm, London, Oxford, Gottingen & Harvard. m: Olive Cecilia Brooke. s: 5. d: 1. Prof of Philos (ret). n.a: Ed Hibbert Journ 1902—47. Publ: Mad Shepherds & Other Human Studies; The Alchemy of Thought; Among the Idolmakers; All Men are Ghosts; From the Human End; The Country Air; Religious Perplexities; Philosophers in Trouble; Legends of Smokeover; A Living Universe; The Challenge of Life; Realities & Shams; Responsibility & Culture; The Faith of a Worker; Heroes of Smokeover; Constructive Citizenship; My Neighbour the Universe; The Inner Sentinel; Education of the Whole Man; Education through Recreation; My American Friends; Elemental Religion; Revolt against Mechanism; Co-operation of Coercion; The Stolen Sword; Last Legend of Smokeover; Construction Now; Confession of an Octogenarian. Ctr: Eng & Amer Reviews. a: Far Outlook, Headington, Oxford. T: Oxford 6983.

JACKS, Maurice Leonard, M.A. *b*: Liverpool 1894. *e*: Dragon Sch Oxford, Bradfield Coll Berks, Balliol Coll Oxf. *m*: Emily Russell Greg. Dir Oxford Univ Dept of Educ, Head Master Mill Hill Sch 1922—27 & '43—44. *Publ*: Total Education; God in Education; Education as a Social Factor; Physical Education. *n.a*: Ed Oxf Mag '19—21. *Ctr*: Journ of Education, Times Educ Sup, Spectator, etc. *s.s*: Education. *Rec*: Gardening, walking, riding. *w.s*: K.R.R.C. 1914—19. *a*: Windrush, Shotover Hill, Headington, Oxford. *T*: 2174.

JACKSON, Lady Ankaret Cecilia Carolyn. *b*: London 1900. *m*: William Jackson. *s*: 1. *d*: 1. *Publ*: Portrait of Maud. *c.t*: Daily Mail, Daily Sketch, Daily Telegraph, Evening Standard, Evening News, 2 Amer periodicals. Barrister-at-Law. *Rec*: Gardening. *a*: High Dyke, Cockermouth, Cumberland.

JACKSON, B. Leslie, A.R.C.A.(Lon), R.D.S., F.R.S.A. *b*: Staffs 1866. *e*: Brampton Col, Roy Col Art. *m*: Sophie Adelaide Blakemore. *s*: 1. *d*: 1. Princ of Techinical & Art Sc. *Publ*: Course of Freehand Drawing. *s.s*: Art & languages. Mem of Notts C.C. Consult Cmt for Educ. *Rec*: Golf, bowls, billiards. *a*: Croft Lodge, The Park, Newark-on-Trent.

JACKSON, Sir Barry Vincent, Kt., Hon.M.A. (B'ham), Hon.LL.D.(St Andrews). *b*: Birmingham 1879. *e*: Priv in England & abroad. Theatre Director & Dramatic Author, Founder & Dir Birmingham Rep Theatre which he opened in 1913, Dir of Shakespeare Festival Co Stratford-upon-Avon '46 & Dir Shakespeare Memorial Theatre Stratford-upon-Avon '47 & '48, Directed Malvern Summer Festivals '29—37. *Publ & Plays*: Fifinella (with Basil Dean); Ser Taldo's Bride (with John Drinkwater); The Christmas Party; The Marvellous History of St Bernard (trans); The Marriage of Figaro (new adapt); He Who gets Slapped (from the Russian with Gertrude Schurhoff); Demos, King & Slave (adapt); The Swiss Family Robinson (with R. H. Baptist); Backward & Forward (with John Ellison). *Rec*: Painting & travelling. *a*: Repertory Theatre, Birmingham.

JACKSON, Rev. Bernard Cecil. *b*: Norwich 1880. *e*: King Edward VI Gr Sch Norwich, Christ's Coll & Ridley Hall Camb. *m*: Mary Harriet Worthington. *d*: 1. Clerk in Holy Orders, Rural Dean of Ottery. *Publ*: Devotional Commentary of St Matthew's Gospel (with late Rev S. C. Lowry); Short Commentary on The 39 Articles; Conscience; The World Problem & The Cross. *Ctr*: Lond Dioc Mag, C.M.S. Rev & local press. *s.s*: Prayer & The Devotional Life. *Rec*: Walking, motoring. *a*: The Vicar's Hse, Ottery St Mary, Devon. *T*: 62.

JACKSON, D. E. Sec Nott'm Br N.U.J. *a*: 23 Patrick Rd, W. Bridgford, Nott'm.

JACKSON, David James. B.A., M.D., Ch.B. *b*: Co Armagh 1883. *e*: Kelvin House, Queen's Coll Belfast. *m*: Margaret Cathcart-Smith. *s*: 4. Med Referee Min of Pensions, Motor Un & other Ins Coys, Anæsthetist Brit Dental Hosp. *Publ*: Leucocytosis in Different Forms of Mental Disease. *Ctr*: Sunday Dispatch, Journ of Mental Science. *Rec*: Bridge, fishing. *c*: Foxgrove Golf, Catford Stadium. *w.s*: Temp Lieut R.A.M.C. 1916—17. *a*: Coverdale, Spencer Rd, Bromley, Kent. *T*: Ravensbourne 2408.

JACKSON, Dugald, Hon.D.Sc. *b*: Kennett Square, Pa 1865. *e*: Hill Sch, Pa State Coll, Cornell Univ. *m*: Mabel A. Foss. *s*: 1. *d*: 1. *Publ*: Textbook on Electricity & Magnetism & Construction of Dynamos; Electricity & Magnetism; Alternating Currents & Alternating Current Machinery; Engineering's Part in the Development of Civilization; Present Status & Trends of Engineering Education in the United States; etc. *Ctr*: Proc Amer Philos Soc, Science, Journ of Engineering Educ, Electrical Engineering, Mechanical Engineering. *s.s*: Engineering Education. *a*: 5 Mercer Circle, Cambridge 38, Mass. *T*: Kirkland 5418.

JACKSON, Emilie. *e*: Geneva. *m*: Wilfrid Scarborough Jackson. *Publ*: Translations of works of Anatole France, Guy de Maupassant, etc (with Wilfrid Scarborough Jackson). *c.t*: Lon Mag, Passing Show & Lon Opinion. *s.s*: Trans from French. *Rec*: Travel. *c*: Albemarle & Translators' Guild. *a*: Albemarle Club, Dover St, W.1.

JACKSON, Rev. Frank Hilton, M.A.(Camb), D.Sc.(Camb). *b*: Hollingwood, Lancs 1870. *e*: Gr Sch Hull, Peterhouse Coll Camb. *m*: Elizabeth Lucy Bernarda Mulhern. Hon Canon of Durham, J.P. Co Durham, Chap & Naval Inst R.N. 1898—1906 (ret). *Ctr*: Proc Roys Soc Lond & Edin, Quarterly Journ Maths, Messenger of Maths, Renduonte Mat di Palermo, American Journ of Maths, etc. *s.s*: Pure Mathematics. *Rec*: Walking, nature study. *a*: Dronmore, 35 Osborne Rd, Eastbourne.

JACKSON, Maj. Frederick George. *e*: Denstone Col & Edin Univ. *m*: Marguerite Fisher. H.M Army, Discoverer & Explorer. *Publ*: The Great Frozen Land; A Thousand Days in the Arctic; (A Paper before the Royal Society Lon) An Experimental Inquiry into Scurvy (in collab with Vaughan Harley M.D.). *c.t*: Journs & n/ps Eng & Abroad. *s.s*: The Polar regions, Africa, Aust, Southern States of North Amer & Gulf of Mexico. 3 y spent in the bush in Queensland with Exploratory Exped. Shooting Exped to Florida & Gulf of Mexico. Exped on a Whaler up the E. Greenland Coast. Exploratory Exped to Waigatz & the Kara Sea & the Bolshaia Zemelskija Tundra. Command of the Jackson-Harmsworth Polar Exped. Comm of Mounted Infantry in the S. African War. Comm of Infantry in France & Belgium 1914. Exped across Central Africa from East to West. *Rec*: Big-game hunting, fishing, polo, golf. *a*: 63 St James's St, S.W.

JACKSON, Rev. George, B.A., HonD.D. Meth Minister. *Publ*: First Things First; Table Talk of Jesus; The Preacher & the Modern Mind; The Fact of Conversion; Studies in the Old Testament; Collier of M/C; etc. *c.t*: M/C Guardian, Meth Recorder. *a*: Rowanbrae, Grasmere, Westmorland. *t*: Grasmere 28.

JACKSON, Harvey. Consulting Surgeon. *a*: 11 Upper Wimpole St, W.1. *t*: Welbeck 1124.

JACKSON, Henry, M.A.(Cantab), B.Sc(Lon), M.B.(Edin), M.P. *b*: Heywood 1875. *e*: Univs of Cam, Lon, Edin. Married. Med Pract. *s.s*: Proc Roy Soc, Trans Chem Soc, Times. *s.s*: Transport & local govt. Fell Cam Philos Soc. Chm Lon & Home Counties Traffic Adv Cmt. Chm Standing Cmt on Mineral Transport. *a*: 19 Putney Hill, S.W.15. *t*: Putney 1105.

JACKSON, Henry Robert. *b*: London 1912. *e*: Nautical Coll. Journalist. *n.a*: Islington & Holloway Press '30, Sub-Ed Daily Mail. *Ctr*: Various. *c*: Press, R.N.V.R. *a*: 16 Ellesmere Ave, Mill Hill, London, N.W.7. *T*: Mill Hill 4148.

JACKSON, Holbrook. *b*: Liverpool 1874. Married. *d*: 1. Author & Editor. *n.a*: Ed: New Age, T.P's Weekly, T.P's Magazine, Idler, To-Day 1910—23, Ed Dir Nat Trade Press Ltd '17—46. *Publ*: Bernard Shaw; William Morris; The Eighteen-Nineties; Occasions; The Anatomy of Bibliomania; The Fear of Books; The Printing of Books; Bookman's Holiday; The Reading of Books; Dreamers of Dreams. *s.s*: English Literature, Reading, Writing & Printing. *Rec*: Reading. *a*: 1 Winterstoke Gdns, Mill Hill, London, N.W.7. *T*: Mill Hill 1177.

JACKSON, J. Hampden. *e*: Christ Church Oxf. *m*: Kathleen Baile. *s*: 2. *d*: 3. Staff Tutor Camb Univ Extra Mural Bd. *Publ*: History of England (with C. E. Carrington); England Since the Industrial Revolution;

The Between-War World; Finland; Estonia; Jean Jaurès; Clemenceau & The Third Republic. *s.s*: European Hist (esp Baltic States & France) & International Relations. *a*: The Rookery, Waterbeach, Cambridge. *T*: Waterbeach 352.

JACKSON, Lawrence Nelson, M.C., M.D. *b*: Liverpool 1898. *e*: St Paul's Sch, Balliol Coll Oxf & Lond Hosp. *m*: Margaret Constance Noel Hadley. *s*: 2. *d*: 1. Mem B.M.A., Exeter Medico-Chir Soc, Major R.A.M.C.(T) (ret). *Publ*: Some Sports & Pastimes of the English; etc. *Ctr*: Punch, Humourist, Time & Tide, Dly Express, Lancet, etc. *Rec*: Cricket, shooting, fox-hunting, fishing. *c*: Devon County Cricket. *a*: Mt Jocelyn, Crediton, Devon. *T*: 55.

JACKSON, Leonard Edward. *b*: Dover 1906. *e*: Durham Johnston Sc. *m*: Marena Liddell. Journalist. *n.a*: Reporting Staff Northern Echo & Assoc N/ps. *s.s*: Local government. *Rec*: Reading. *a*: Dunelm, Briar Walk, Blackwell, Darlington. *t*: 2770.

JACKSON, Noel Joseph, M.B., B.S., (See THE MAESTRO). *b*: Dartford, Kent 1917. *m*: Jean Dove. *d*: 2. *Publ*: Surgeon Pilot. *Ctr*: B.M.J., Flight, Motor-cycle, Autocar, Scarboro' News. *s.s*: Aviation, Medicine, Hotel Management & Catering, Writing Short Stories. *Rec*: Swimming, flying, hockey, politics. *c*: Roy Aero, A.A. *a*: 127 Queens Parade, Scarborough. *T*: 490.

JACKSON, Rev. Robert Wyse, M.A., LL.D., Litt.D., M.R.I.A. *b*: Tullamare, Eire 1908. *e*: Abbey Sch Tipperary, Bishop Foy Sch Waterford, T.C.D., Middle Temple. *m*: Margaretta Nolan MacDonald. *s*: 1. *d*: 1. Dean of Cashel. *n.a*: Lit Leader Writer Ch of Ireland Gaz '46—. *Publ*: Jonathan Swift, Dean & Pastor; Swift & his Circle; Scenes from Irish Clerical Life in 17th & 18th Centuries. *Ctr*: Church Times, Irish Independent, Irish Press, John o' London, etc. *s.s*: Jonathan Swift, Irish Humour, Anglo-Irish Lit 1600—1900, Ch Hist 1600—1800. *Rec*: Archæology, history, painting, gardening. *c*: Univ of Dublin, Irish Water Colour Soc. *a*: The Deanery, Cashel, Eire.

JACKSON, Stuart. *b*: Gt Ayton 1906. Journalist. *n.a*: Feature Writer Drama & Film Critic Northcliffe N/ps 3 y, Feature Writer Film Weekly '32, Film Critic L'pool Evening Express, Ed-Dir Star Features Ltd '33—35, Film Critic Sunday Chronicle. *c.t*: Daily Mail & Evening News, Daily Sketch, Film Pictorial, Picturegoer, Answers, Ideas, etc. *s.s*: Fiction, films. Started Fleet St when n/p slump at its worst. Took desk tiny office packed with F/L. Turned 10s. capital into £2000 in less than year. *a*: Star Features Ltd, 53 Fleet St, E.C.4. *t*: Cen 8386.

JACKSTAFF. See **Bennett, John Joseph.**

JACOB, Alaric. *b*: Edin 1909. *e*: King's Sc Canterbury. Journalist (Diplomatic Corr Reuters). *n.a*: 1926–28 Western Morning News (Reporter & Sub Ed), '29– Reuters. Mem N.U.J. '34. *Publ*: Seventeen (Sc Novel). *c.t*: Daily Express, Daily Mail, Daily Mirror, Theatre World, Daily Telegraph. *s.s*: Foreign affairs, the theatre. *Rec*: Writing plays, squash. *a*: 29 Abercorn Pl, St John's Wood. *t*: Maida Vale 6023.

JACOB, BRUNO: political economist; b. Kassel, Germany, Oct. 4, 1881; s. Julius and Agathe (Trömmer) J.; educ. Realgymnasium of Kassel, Univ. of Jena. DEGREES: Volkswirt R.V.D.; m. Hedwig Schmidt. AUTHOR: Kalender für Kurhessen, 1907 (2nd edit. 1909); Ein freies Hessen, 1919; Der Föderalismus (2nd edit.), 1924; Fritzlar, 1925; Krieg und Kaiserkrone, 1926; Geschichte des Dorfes Bettenhausen, 1927; Geschichte des Dorfes Eschenstruth, 1927; Festschrift der Verkehrsvereins Kassel, 1929. Edited Der Niedersachse from 1919 to 1922. Contributes to Neue Blätter aus Hessen; Allgemeine Rundschau, Munich; Hessenland, Kassel; Der Bund, Frankfurt a. Main; Zeitschrift für Binnenschiffahrt, Berlin, and others. General character of writing: scientific, historical, economical, political, travels. Relig. denom., Reformed Church. ADDRESS: Salzmannstrasse 2, Kassel-B, Germany.

JACOB, Charles Theodore, F.R.S.A. *b*: Calcutta 1881. *e*: Bedford Gr Sch, Dulwich Coll. *m*: Dorothy Steel. Experimental Scientific Research. *Publ*: Electric Sonometer; The Vibronome; (for priv publ): Elastic & Impact Phenomena; String & Soundboard Mechanism; Pipe Tones; Production & Propagation of Sound. *Ctr*: Hinrichsen's Musical Year Book & various musical & scientific journs. *s.s*: Elasticity, Acoustics, Astronomy, Light. *Rec*: Music, handicraft. *a*: The Red Hse, Wheathampstead, Herts. *T*: 2139.

JACOB, Ernest Fraser, M.A., D.Phil., F.B.A., F.S.A., F.R.Hist.S. *b*: Horsforth nr Leeds 1894. *e*: Winchester & New Coll Oxf. Prof Mediæval Hist Univ of Manch 1929–44, Fell All Souls' Coll Oxf, Vice-Pres Hist Assoc. Mem Hist MSS. Commission. *Publ*: Studies in the Period of Baronial Reform & Rebellion; The Legacy of the Middle Ages; Illus to the Life of St Alban; The Register of Henry Chichele; etc. *Ctr*: Eng Hist Rev, History, Manch Guardian, etc. *c*: Athenæum. *a*: All Souls' College & 205 Woodstock Rd, Oxford.

JACOB, Dr. F. H. *a*: 32 Regent Street, Nottingham.

JACOB, Gordon, D.Mus., F.R.C.M., Hon.R.A.M. *b*: London 1895. *e*: Dulwich Coll & Roy Coll of Music. *m*: Sidney Gray. Prof of Composition etc R.C. Music, Exam in Music to Univs of London & Wales. *n.a*: Ed Penguin Miniature Scores. *Publ*: Orchestral Technique, a Manual for Students; How to Read a Score; Part-author Musicianship for Students; Appendix to Widor's Modern Orchestra; also many musical comps. *Rec*: Gardening. *a*: The Spinney, 19 Beech Walk, Ewell, Surrey. *T*: 1314.

JACOB, H. *b*: Berlin 1909. *e*: Sec Sch. *m*: E. M. Spillane. Typographer. *n.a*: Ed Progreso (Swiss Quarterly on Linguistics). *Publ*: On the Choice of a Common Language; A Planned Auxiliary Language; Esperanto-Ido Dictionary; etc. *Ctr*: British Printer, Printing Review, Art in Industry. *s.s*: Linguistics, Typography, Design (Industrial). *a*: 3 Spareleaze Hill, Loughton, Essex. *T*: 3547.

JACOB, Rev. H. T. *Publ*: Poetry; Biography of Dr W. H. Rees, China. Ex-Pres Union of Welsh Independents. *a*: Min-y-ceunant, Fishguard.

JACOB, HANS: writer, translator; b. Berlin, Germany, November, 1896; s. Nathan and Else (Caro) J.; educ. Franzoesisches Gymnasium (Berlin); Univs. of Berlin, Paris. AUTHOR: Biography of Rimbaud, 1921; Christina (novel), 1929; Ueber Nacht (novel), 1930. Translator of works by Paul Morand, Anatole France, Thrysmans, Colette, Balzac, Zola, Diderot, Pirandello, and many others, between 1920 and 1927. Since 1927 has been official interpreter of the German Government, especially for German foreign office and the German delegation for the League of Nations. Contributor to 8 Uhr Obendblatt, Berliner Tageblatt, Vossische Zeitung (all of Berlin); Nouvelles Litteraires (Paris), Revue de Geneve (Geneva). CLUB: P. E. N. Religion, Israelitic. HOME: Sachsenplatz 14, Berlin-Charlottenburg 9, Germany.

JACOB, Naomi. *b*: Ripon, Yorks 1889. *e*: Middlesbrough Hgh Sch. Novelist & Journalist. *Publ*: Roots; Private Gollantz; Four Generations; Honour's a Mistress; And the "Me" Autobiographies; Jacob

Ussher; Honour Come Back; Susan Crowther. *s.s*: Italian Music & Art, Furniture & China, Cookery. *c*: Sesame, P.E.N., etc. *a*: Casa Micki, Fasano, Lago di Garda, Italy, & Sesame Club, 49 Grosvenor St, London, W.1.

JACOBI, FRANZ ERNST: actor at Bavarian state theatre; b. Lichtenfels, Germany, Dec. 27, 1864; s. Herman and Marie (Müller) J.; educ. elementary school of Weimar, teachers' college of Weimer; m. Emmy Hesse, May 28, 1878. AUTHOR: Kultur der Aussprache. General character of writing: scientific, text book. CLUBS: Professor of Academy of Musical Art. ADDRESS: Staatstheater, Nederlingerstrasse 4, Munich 39, Bavaria, Germany.

JACOBI, JOHANN CARL: professor; b. Hamburg, Germany, Sept. 12, 1857; s. Friedrich Wilhelm and Anna Weber, d. physiologist E. H. Weber, Leipzig, 1795-1878) J.; educ. gymnasium. DEGREES: M.D., Prussian privi Medical Counselor, Imperial Regierungsrat (retired); m. Helene Distel, 1889. AUTHOR: Die Pharmakologie, eine biologische Wissenschaft, 1908; Antrittsrede in Tübingen; Occultismus und Medicinische Wissenschaft, 1912; Die Flechten Deutschlands als Nähr- und Futtermaterial (3 edits.), 1915, 1916; Die Alkoholfrage vom Med. Standpunkt, 1926; Das pharmak. Institut und seine Einrichtungen, 1927; Also: Entwurf zu Pharmakologie. Einleitung des deutschen Bäderbuchs als Manuskript, 1906. Co-editor des Archivs für exp. Path. und Pharmakologie. Contributor to: Archiv für exp. Path. und Pharmakologie; Deutsche Medizinische Wochenschrift; Münchener Med. Wochenschrift; Methods and Problems of Medical Education; The Rockefeller Foundation, New York. General character of writing: scientific, medical, physiological and pharmacological. CLUBS: Kaiserl. Leop. Carol. Deutsche Akademie zu Halle; Strassburger Wissenschaftliche Gesellschaft zu Frankfurt a. Main. ADDRESS: Eugenstrasse 5, Tübingen, Württemberg, Germany.

JACOBS, Helen Hull. *Publ*: Modern Tennis. *a*: c/o G. Allen & Unwin Ltd, Museum St, W.C.1.

JACOBS, Margaret Flint (see **FLINT, Margaret**). *b*: Orono, Maine 1891. *e*: Univ of Maine. *m*: Lester Warner Jacobs (dec'd). Novelist. *s.s*: Maine Rural Scene & Characters. *a*: West Baldwin, Maine. *T*: Cornish 44.

JACOBS, Michel, F.R.S.A. *b*: Montreal, Canada 1877. *e*: New York Public Schs, Ecole des Beaux Arts Paris, Nat Acad of Design N.Y., Julian Acad Paris. Artist, Author, Sculptor, Lecturer. *n.a*: Cosmopolitan Montreal 1930, Dly Star '13, Studio Mag '16. *Publ*: Study of Colour; Art of Colour; Art of Composition; Portrait Painting; Memoires; 31,000 Colour Combinations. *Ctr*: Internat Studio, Art Digest, Amer Art Student, Women's Wear. *s.s*: Portrait Painting & Art Books. *Rec*: Cookery, gardening, swimming. *c*: Military & Naval, Nat Press, etc. *a*: Lennox Ave, Farmley Pk, Rumson, New Jersey. *T*: Rumson 1-0599.

JACOBS, MONTY: editor; b. Stettin, Germany, Jan. 5, 1875; s. Henry and Lohra (Salomon) J.; educ. Gymnasiums of Stettin and Berlin; Univs. of Munich, Berlin and Heidelberg. DEGREES: Ph.D.; m. Dora Leopohn. AUTHOR: Gersterbergs Ugolino, 1898; Maeterlink, 1901; Achim von Arnim, 1908; Deutsche Schauspielkunst, 1913; Ilsens Bühnentechnik, 1920; Paul Wegener, 1920. Contributor to: Vossiche Zeitung; Feulletonchef and Theaterkritiker. General character of writing: historical, literature. CLUBS: Vexir Berliner P r e s s e; Schutzverband Deutscher Schriftsteller. OFFICE: Kochstrasse 22-26. HOME: Normannenstrasse 11, Nikolassee, Berlin, Germany.

JACOBS, T. C. H. Author. *Publ*: The 13th Chime; Sinister Quest; Scorpion's Trail; The Kestrel House Mystery; The Terror of Torlands; Identity Unknown;

The Broken Knife; The Bronkhorst Case; Silent Terror; Appointment with the Hangman; Traitor Spy; Brother Spy; Reward for Treason; The Black Boy; The Curse of Khatra; etc; also B.B.C. Serial The Grensen Murder Case. *s.s*: Medical Jurisprudence. *c*: Press, Studio. *a*: c/o S. Paul & Co Ltd, Paternoster Hse, London, E.C.4.

JACOBS, William Wymark. *b*: Lon 1863. *e*: Private. *m*: Agnes Eleanor Williams. *s*: 2. *d*: 3. Author. *Publ*: Many Cargoes; The Skipper's Wooing; Light Freights; Sea Urchins; A Master of Craft; At Sunwich Post; The Lady of the Barge; Dialstone Lane; Salthaven; Short Cruises; Night Watches; The Castaways; Deep Waters; Sea Whispers; etc. Plays—The Monkey's Paw; The Warming Pan; Beauty & the Barge; etc. *c.t*: Strand, etc. *s.s*: Humorous fiction. Civil Servant till 1899. *c*: Garrick, Omar Khayyam, Mem Counc Soc of Authors. *a*: 8 St James's Terr, Albert Rd, N.W.8. *t*: Primrose 0330.

JACOBSOHN, PAUL: physician; b. Berlin, Germany, Sept. 30, 1868; s. Heinrich and Doris (Marcuse) J.; educ. Sophien Gymnasium of Berlin; Univs. of Berlin and Freiburg. DEGREES: M.D.: Member of the Board of Health; m. Cora Kalisky, 1900. AUTHOR: Die vornehme Kunst Kranke zu pflegen (transl. from Hawkins-Ambler), 1898; Über den theoretischen Unterricht in Krankenpflegerschulen, 1898; Handbuch der Krankenversorgung und Krankenpflege (with G. Liebe and George Meyer, 2 vols.), 1898-1902. Fürsorge auf den Gebieten des Krankenkomforts der Krankenwartung und des Krankenpflege-Unterrichts. Editor Deutsche Krankenpflege-Zeitung from 1898-1908; Zeitschrift für Krankenpflege from 1908-1915; published numerous contributions in these magazines and in German medical periodicals. General character of writing: scientific, medical. Was nominated honorary president of the German nursing organisation, 1899; Supervisor of central nursing of Berlin and vicinity, 1902; Custodian of the state nursing collection at the Kaiser Friedrich House, 1906. CLUBS: Docent of the Humboldt Academy (medical and nursing section). Religion: Jew. ADDRESS: Landshuberstr. 11-12, Berlin W. 30, Germany.

JACOBSON, Sydney, M.C. *b*: Transvaal, Sth Africa 1908. *e*: Strand Sch & Univ of London. *m*: Phylis June Buck. *s*: 2. *d*: 1. Journalist, N.U.J. *n.a*: Rep & Sub-Ed Dly Sketch 1929—, Sub-Ed News-Ed & Asst-Ed The Statesman India '29—37, Asst-Ed Lilliput '38—40, Staff Writer Picture Post '45. *s.s*: Politics, Economics, Current Foreign Affairs. *Rec*: Riding, cricket, reading. *c*: Press. *w.s*: '40—45. *a*: 50 Meadway, Barnet, Herts. *T*: Barnet 6491.

JACOBSTHAL, WALTHER: professor; b. Strassburg, Elsass, Feb. 18, 1876; s. Prof. Dr. Gustav Jacobstahl; educ. Gymnasium and Univ. of Strassburg (Elsass); m. Elisabeth Bruns. AUTHOR: Forsyth, Lehrbuch der Differentialgleichungen. (Deutsche Ausgabe mit eigenen Zusätzen des Herausgebers), 1913; Sphärik und Sphärische Trigonometrie vom gruppen-theoretischen Standpunkt. (appeared in vol. 2 of Weber and Wellstein, Encyklopädie of elementary mathematics), 1915; Mondphasen, Osterrechnung und ewiger Kalender, 1917. Contributed to Math. Annalen 56; Das Lyceum. General character of writing: scientific, mathematics. CLUBS: Deutsche Mathematicvereinigung; Berliner Mathematische Gesellschaft. Relig. denom.; Evangelical. ADDRESS: Yorckstrasse 89, Berlin SW 61, Germany.

JACOBY, MARTIN: biochemist; b. Jan. 28, 1872; s. Gustav and Betty (Neumann) J.; educ. Gymnasium (Berlin), Univs. of Freiburg and Berlin. DEGREES: M.D., Professor; m. Margarete Orgler, May 22, 1882. AUTHOR: Immunität und Disposition und ihre experimentellen Grundlagen, 1906; Einführung in die experimentelle Therapie, 1919. Contributor to Biochemical magazines. General character of writing: medical, scientific. Especially interested in enzymes. Religion, Jewish. OFFICE: Krankenhaus Moabit. HOME: Dorfflingerstrasse 19, Berlin W. 35, Germany.

JACOMB, Charles Ernest. *b*: Godalming 1888. *e*: Harrow. *m*: Dorothy Plant. *s*: 2. Author & Journalist. *n.a*: Ed Staff Financial News 1920—22, City Office Daily Mail '26—32, Asst City Ed Daily Mirror '32—33, City Ed Sunday Referee '34. *Publ*: God's Own Country; Torment; Violin Harmonics; And a New Earth. *s.s*: Financial journalism. *Rec*: Violin. *c*: Roy Socs. *a*: Farncombe Hall Godalming, Surrey.

JACOMB, Edward. L.M.S.S.A., B.A.(Oxon). *b*: Bombay 1881. *e*: Charterhouse, Magdalen Col Oxf, Paris. Univ (Licencié en droit). Barrister-at-Law. Inner Temple. *Publ*: France & England in the New Hebrides (1914); And If You Don't!; The Banana Skin; The Joy Court ('29); etc. One of H.M.'s Dep Commssrs for the Western Pacific '07—11. Acting Native Advocate to Anglo-French Condominium '11. Lieut R.N.V.R. '18. *c*: E. India Un Service. *a*: Le Clos du Hurel, St Brelade, Jersey, C.I. *t*: St Aubin 380.

JACOT, Bernard Louis. *b*: Worcs 1899. *e*: St John's Col, Oxford, King Edward's Sc, B'ham. Barrister-at-Law. *n.a*: Sub-Ed & special writer Times '23—27. Production Ed News-Chron '34. Editorial with Odham's Press '34—. Special Corr Chicago Tribune, C.S. Monitor, L.A. Herald '28—33. *Publ*: Trust Wesley; Frogs Don't Grow Feathers; Winslow Moult; The Longer Shadow; Marconi (with D.M.B. Collier), etc. *c.t*: Collier's, Liberty, American Mag, Redbook, New York Herald Tribune, etc. *s.s*: Short stories, aviation, motoring. Made films in Hollywood for M.G.M. '29—32 out of stories published in U.S. in Collier's. *Rec*: Golf, flying. *c*: New Univ Club. *a*: 2 Tanfield Court, Inner Temple, E.C.4. *t*: Central 4612.

JACOT, Michael. *b*: London 1924. *e*: France, Switzerland, Wellington Sch & St John's Col Oxf. *m*: Wendy Lennox. Journalist. *n.a*: Lit-Ed Frederick Warne & Co, P.R. Officer. *Ctr*: B.B.C., Ev Standard, Seven Mag, etc. *s.s*: Short Stories, Europe & Far East. *Rec*: Golf, swimming, theatre. *w.s*: R.A.F. *a*: 15 Heathcote Rd, Streatham, London, S.W.16. *T*: Pollards 3328.

JACQUES, Hubert. *b*: Sutton 1888. *e*: Sutton H.S. & County Sc. *m*: Elsie Violet Howick. *s*: 2. Journalist. *n.a*: Surrey County Herald 1904-09, Special Corr in Ceylon N.Y. Herald '12, Sub Ed Lon & Paris Offices N.Y. Herald '13-14, Ed Mentone & Monte Carlo News '14-19, Surrey County Herald '19—, Ed '30—, etc. *c.t*: Lon & prov press. Chm Exec Cmt I.J. '33-34, '34-35. Rep Inst in Internat Gatherings. Mem Comité de Direction de l'Union Internationale des Associations de Presse. War Service '14-19. *c*: Liveryman, Stationers' & N/p Makers' Coy. *a*: Tall Trees, Banstead Rd S, Sutton, Surrey. *t*: 1692.

JACQUES, NORBERT: author; *b*. Luxemburg, June 6, 1880; educ. Luxemburg, Univ. of Bonn. AUTHOR (novels): Funchal, 1909; Der Hafen 10; Piraths Insel, 1917; Landmann Hal, 1919; H. I. Lant, 1920; Frau Von Afrika, 1921; Dr. Mabuse, 1922; Die Pulvermühle, 1923; Ingenieur Mars, 1923; Der Kauffherr Von Shanghai, 1925; Der Feuerafe, 1926; Das Tigerschiff, 1929; (travel books): Heisse Städte, 1911; Südsee, 1922; Auf dem Chinesischen Fluss, 1922; Neue Brasilien Reise, 1925; Reise nach Sumatra, 1926; Auf dem Sturmbock durch den Stillen Ozean, 1926; Andenland, 1929. CLUB: P. E. N. Religion, Catholic. HOME: Schlachters-Lindau, Germany.

JADASSOHN, JOSEF: professor, doctor; b. Liegnitz, Germany, Sept. 10, 1863; s. Meyer and Eliese (Kohn) J.; educ. Gymnasium (Liegnitz), Univs. of Göttingen, Leipzig, Heidelberg, Breslau. DEGREES: M.D., Professor; m. Marga Kern, Dec. 20, 1896. AUTHOR: Die venerischen Krankheiten und Krankheiten des Penis nebst Harnröhre, die Hodens, Nebenhodens Samenstrangs, die Samenblase, die Prostrata (in Ebstein-Schwalbe's Handbuch der praktischen Medizin), 1900 (2nd edit. 1905); Krankheiten der Haut (in collaboration with Neisser, vol. 3 of Ebstein-Schwalbe's Handbuch der praktischen Medizin), 1901; Hautkrankheiten und Stoffwechselanomalien, 1904; Lupus erythematodes (vol. 3 of Handbuch der Krankheiten, by Mracek), 1904; Die Tuberkulose der Haut (vol. 4 of Handb. d. Krankh., by Mracek), 1907; Venerische Krankheiten (in Lehrbuch der Greisen by Schwalbe), 1909; Allgemeine Aetiologie, Pathologie, Diagnose und Therapie der Gonorrhoe (vol. 1 of Handb. d. Geschlechtskrankheiten, by Finger, Jadassahn, and others), 1910; Hautkrankheiten, Über Pyodermien (vol. 1, No. 2 of Sammlung zwangloser Abhandlungen an der Gebiete der Dermatologie), 1912; Lepra (in Handb. d. pathogenen Mikroorganismen, by Kolle-Wassermann, 2nd edit.), 1913 (3rd edit. 1928). Editor: Lehrbuch der Haut- und Geschlechtskrankh. (by Lesser, vol. 2), 1927; Handbuch der Haut- und Geschlechtskrankheiten Archiv für Dermatologie und Syphilis; Zentralblatt für Haut- und Geschlechtskrankheiten; Sammlung zwangloser Abhandlung aus dem Gebiet der Dermatologie und Syphilologie. Contributor to medical archives and journals. General character of writing: medical. Pupil of A. Neisser. Professor and Director of Dermatological clinics in Bern (Switzerland) and Breslau; President of the German Association Against Venereal Diseases. Religion, Protestant. ADDRESS: Leerbeutelstrasse 1, Breslau, Germany.

JAEGER, Muriel, M.A.(Oxon). *b*: Barnsley. *e*: Sheffield H.S. & Somerville. *Publ*: The Question Mark; The Man with Six Senses; Sisyphus. The Limits of Psychology; Experimental Lives; Hermes Speaks, The Sanderson Soviet (play). *s.s*: Lit, dramatic. *c*: Soc of Authors. *a*: 18 Offington Gdns, Worthing.

JAEGER, Werner Wilhelm. Ph.D., Hon.Litt.D. *b*: Lobberich, Rhineland 1888. *e*: Univs of Marburg & Berlin. *m*: Ruth Heinitz. *s*: 2. *d*: 2. Univ Prof Harvard 1939—, formerly St Andrews, Basle, Berlin, etc. *Publ*: Aristotle; Paideia; Demosthenes; Gregorius Nyssenus; Nemesius from Emesa; Theology of the Early Greek Philosophers; Humanism & Theology. *Ctr*: Hermes, Die Antike, etc. *s.s*: Histories of Greek Philosophy & Literature, Theology & Patristics, Classical Humanism. *a*: 43 Bailey Rd, Watertown, Massachusetts, U.S.A.

JAFFÉ, FRANZ: writer; b. Berlin, Germany, Sept. 5, 1855; s. Franz and Auguste (Hase) J.; educ. Kaiser Wilhelms Real-Gymnasium, Technical College, Bau-Akademie, Kunst-Akademie (all Berlin). DEGREES: Königl. Regierungsbaumeister, 1886; Königl. Baurat, 1902; m. (1) Amely Honrath, 1894 (died); (2) Helene Müller, 1923. AUTHOR: Die Architektur der Columbischen Welt-Ausstellung zu Chicago, 1895; Ausstellungsbauten (in Handbuch der Architektur, part 4, vol. 6, No. 4, 2nd edit.), 1906; Die Bischöfliche Klosterkirche zur Curten de Arges in Roumanien, 1912. Contributor to: Berliner Lokal-Anzeiger, Westermanns Monatshefte, Deutsche Bauzeitung, Bauwelt. General character of writing: architectural. Member of the Imperial German Commission of the International Exhibitions of Melbourne in 1888. and of Chicago in 1893. Occupied leading position as chief architect at expositions in Paris and Liège and about twenty expositions in Berlin. Studied decorative art in Berlin and made paintings of articles of historic interest for exhibitions and congresses. Member of some twenty clubs. Relig. denom., Evangelical. ADDRESS: Neue Winterfeldtstrasse 28, Berlin W. 30, Germany.

JAFFE, Dr. H. Hon Asst Surgeon Macclesfield Gen Inf; Mem Cheshire Panel Cmt; Hon Sec Macclesfield & Dist Med Soc. *a*: 20 Cumberland St, Macclesfield.

JAFFE, Dr. H. N. *c.t*: B.M.J. Physician i/c Notts Health Dept. Med Supt Children's Convalescent Home. *a*: The Hollies, Derby Rd, Notts.

JAFFE, Peter, M.A. *b*: London 1914. *e*: Rugby Sch, King's Coll Camb. *n.a*: The Economist, Business World '46—47, M.O.I. '40—45. *Publ*: British Shipping for Britain & Her Exports. *s.s*: Financial & Popular Scientific & Constitutional Questions, Projection of Britain through Industrial Achievements. *Rec*: Chess. *a*: 59, Putney Hill, London, S.W.15. *T*: Putney 6050.

JAFFRAY, Rev. William Stevenson, C.M.G., C.B.E., D.D.(Edin). *b*: Devonport 1867. *e*: Edin Univ. *m*: Ethel Annie Duncan. Princ C.F. (R.P.). Chap Commandant R.A. Ch Dept. Hon Chap to The King. *c.t*: various mags & periodicals. *s.s*: Hist, travel. S. African War 1899-1901 (des), received special promotion; medal & 6 clasps. European War '14-18. Order of St Sava 2nd Cl (Serbia); 1914 Star; Brit & Victory Medals. *Rec*: Golf. *a*: Messrs Glyn, Mills, & Co (Holts Br), Kirkland Hse, Whitehall, S.W.1.

JAGANNATHAN, K. V. *b*: Krishnarayapuram 1906. Ed Kalamiagal-Tamil Monthly. *Publ*: Tamil Karyas; Kalaignan Zyagam; Neelamani; Aruntha Thanti; Kaurijamun Cviyamun; Malligai Malai; Cru San Vayiru; etc. *Ctr*: Dhinamani, Kalamiagal, etc. *s.s*: Tamil Lit & Folk-songs. *a*: 15 St Maryis Rd, Mylapore, Sth India.

JAGGARD, Capt. William. *b*: Theale, Berks. *e*: Leamington Sc & Cam Univ. *m*: Emma Frances Cook. *s*: 3. *d*: 1. Author & Lect. *n.a*: Ed Book Queries 1804-1912. Ex-Mem Stratford Rural Counc & Bd of Guardians, Gov Shakespeare Mem'l Theatre & Mem Avon Navigation Cmt. *Publ*: First General Index to Book Prices Current ('01); Liverpool Literature, a Bibliography; Shakespeare's First Play; Birth of Printing; Second General Index to Book Prices Current ('09); First General Index to Book Auction Records; Shakespeare Mem'l Theatre, 50 years' Retrospect ('26); Dyes & Dyeing: 300 secret recipes; Shakespeare & The Tudor Jaggards; Shakespeare once a Printer & a Bookman ('34); etc. *c.t*: The Times, Morning Post, Daily Mail, Stratford-on-Avon Herald, etc. *s.s*: Shakespeare, old books. Freeman of Lon City. Liveryman Stationers & Paper Makers Coys. Life Mem Authors' Soc. Founder Avon Lit Club, Shakespeare Glee Club & Stratford Amateur Operatic Soc. War Service '14-20. *c*: Authors', Bibliographical Soc. *a*: Rose Bank, Tiddington Rd, Stratford-on-Avon.

JAGGER, C. S., M.C., A.R.A., F.R.B.S. *Publ*: Modelling & Sculpture in the Making. Sculptor Roy Artillery Mem at Hyde Pk Cnr etc. *a*: Anhalt Studio, Anhalt Rd, Battersea. S.W.11.

JAGIDAR, R. V. (" Shriranga "), M.A.(Lond). *b*: Agarkhed, Bijapur 1904. *e*: Univs of Bombay & London. *m*: Sharadadevi Chan Drachud. *s*: 1. *d*: 2. Prof Bombay Educ Service, Prof of Sanskrit Karnatak Coll Dharwar, India. *n.a*: Ed Bd Jayanti & Narasinha, Chrm Rangamanga Prakashana Publishers. *Publ*: Gita Ganbhirya; Drama in Sanskrit Literature; On Laughter & Theory of Humour; Purushartha (novel based on Gandhian movement). *Ctr*: Bombay Univ Journ, Free Press Journ & many humorous essays to various Kannada monthlies. *s.s*: Drama, Culture & Social Reform. *Rec*: Idling whenever possible, reading crime fiction. *c*: Karnetak Bch Progressive Writers Assoc (Pres). *a*: Karnatak College, Dharwar, Bombay Province, India.

JAGO, Maurice Edwin MacDowall, M.D., B.S. Med Pract. *c.t*: Lancet, etc. *a*: Stafford Hse, Church Rd, Sutton, Surrey. *t*: 50.

JAGO, WILLIAM: chemist, barrister-at-law; *b*. Marazion, Cornwall, Eng., Feb., 1854; *s*. William and Elizabeth (Harry) J.; *educ.* privately and Royal School of Mines, Royal Coll. of Chemistry (both London); *m*. Elizabeth Mary Culshaw (died), July 23, 1879. AUTHOR: Elementary Inorganic Chemistry, 1881; A Confidential Report on Wheat and Flour Supply of the United Kingdom, 1884; Chemistry of Wheat, Flour and Bread and Technology of Breadmaking, 1886 (3 subsequent edits., 1895, 1911, 1921; 4th edit. in prep.); Introduction to the Principles of Breadmaking, 1889; Advanced Inorganic Chemistry, 1890; Forensic Chemistry and Chemical Evidence, 1909; Bread Shop Practice, 1923; Cantor Lectures on Breadmaking; Cantor Lectures on Confectionery. General character of writing: technical, text books, scientific. Fellow Chemical Soc.; Fellow Institute of Chemistry. Late Examiner to City and Guilds of London Institute for Advancement of Technical Education; Cantor Lecturer on breadmaking and confectionery to Royal Soc. of Arts, London; has specialized in food chemistry, especially wheatflour; Juror for Brit. Govt., at Internat. Expositions at Paris (1900), Brussels (1910), Turin (1911). Called to Bar, 1904. Relig. denom., Church of England. HOME: 17 Wilbury Avenue, Hove, Sussex, Eng.

JAGTIANI, Lachland A., B.A.(Bombay). *b*: Hyderabad 1885. *m*: Hejibai Gidwani. *d*: 1. Teacher & Journalist. *n.a*: Co-Ed Gulistan 1939— & Mehran '46—. *Publ*: Sada Gulaba (poems); Choth-Jo-Chand (novel); Sha Ha No Shah (poetry); (plays) Umar-ain-Marui; Lakhadadha-Khe. *s.s*: Essay Writing, Short Stories. *Rec*: Hiking. *a*: Khemchand Shah Rd, Karachi.

JAIDKA, Dr. K. C., F.R.C.S.E. *Publ*: Professional articles. Hon Surg Peterborough Mem Hosp. *a*: 1 North Street, Peterborough.

JAISINGHANI, Amrita H. *b*: Taib 1903. *e*: Priv. *m*: Kirpa Khilnani. Landlord. *n.a*: Ed News Age 3 y & of Akbar Ashram Tracts. *Publ*: Talks with Eeyaa; Dialogues in an Ashram; Vision of Life; Spiritual Life; If Truth At Last Be Told; Early Offering (in Sindhi); The Model Village; etc. *c.t*: New Dawn, The Theosophist (Adyar), Sind Observer, etc. *s.s*: Philos & religion. Org Sec Akbar Ashram Karachi. Extensive travel. Believer in the ideal of Human Unity & the Unity of Religion. A supporter of the movement of Inter-Communal Marriage. *a*: Jaising Lodge, Garden Rd, Karachi, India.

JAKOB, MAX: civil engineeer and technical physicist; *b*. Ludwigshafen a. Rhein, Germany, 1879; *s*. Heinrich and Ernestine (Schloss) J.; *educ.* elementary school, humanistisches gymnasium and technical college of Munich. DEGREES: Dipl. Ing.; Technical Physicist; Dr. Professor; *m*. Anna Wassertrüdinger, April 3, 1913. AUTHOR: Osc. Knoblauch und M. Jakob, Über die Abhängigkeit der spezifischen Wärme cp des Wasserdampfes von Druck und Temperatur (Forschungsarbeiten, vols. 35 and 36), 1906; M. Jakob, Technisch-physikalische Untersuchungen von Aluminium-Elektrolytzellen (Sammlung elektrotechnischer Vorträge, 9th vol.), 1906; L. Holborn and M. Jakob, Die spezifische Wärme cp der Luft bei 600 C and 1 bis 300 at (Forschungsarbeiten, vols. 187 and 188), 1916; M. Jakob, Thermodynamische Drosselgleichung und Zustandsgleichung der Luft von weiten Gültigkeitsbereich (Forschungsarbeiten, v o l. 202), 1917; M. Jakob and S. Erk, Der Druckabfall in glatten Rohren und die Durchflussziffer von Normaldüsen (Forschungsarbeiten, vol. 267), 1924; M. Jakob, Die Verdampfungswärme des Wassers und das spezifische Volumen von Sattdampf für Temperaturen bis 210c ; M. Jakob and S. Erk, Der Wärmeübergang beim Kondensieren von Heiss- und Sattdampf. (Forschungsarbeiten, vol. 310), 1928; M. Jakob and Fr. Kretzschmer, Die Durchflusszahlen von Normaldüsen und Normalstaurändern für Rohrdurchmesser von 100 bis 1000 mm. (Forschungsarbeiten, vol. 311), 1928. Editor: Technische Mechanik und Thermodynamik. Monatliche Beihefte zur VDF-Zeitschrift. Contributor to VDD-Zeitschrift; VDF-Nachrichten; Technische Mechanik und Thermodynamik. Monatliche Beihefte zur VDF-Zeitschrift; Archiv für Wärmewirtschaft und Dampfkesselwesen; Archiv für Elektrotechnik; Die Naturwissenschaften; Gesundheitsingenieur; Zeitschrift für die gesamte Kälteindustrie; Zeitschrift für technische Physik; Zeitschrift für Physik; Annalen der Physik; Technische Physik (Wärme, Hydro- und Aerodynamics, Elektrotechnik). General character of writing: scientific, technical. Member of the Government board. CLUBS: Verein deutscher Ingenieure; Deutsche Physikalische Gesellschaft; Deutsche Gesellschaft für technische Physik; Gesellschaft für angewandte Mathematik. Religion, Mosaic. OFFICE: Physikalische-Technische Reichsanstalt. HOME: Kastanienallee 27, Berlin-Charlottenburg, Germany.

JAKSCH, FRIEDRICH: director of library; b. Budweis, Germany, April, 1894; s. Dr. Anton and Anna (Seewald) J.; educ. Gymnasium (law and philosophy), Fakultät der deutschen Universität (Prague); m. Käthe Palme, 1920. AUTHOR: Gedichte, 1914; Das heilige Feuer (drama), 1915; Eltern (tragedy), 1916; Wellen und Wogen, 1917; Märchen der Liebe (novel), 1918; Hartherz der Zwerg (drama), 1919; Sklavin (tragedy), 1920; Eros Licht (fiction), 1921; Der enthauptete Heiland (romance), 1922; Die bildstilistischen Turbulenzerscheinungen in Friedrich Hebbels Werken, 1923; Der Ritt eines Knaben in den Frühling, 1924; Bühnenkunst und Bühnendekoration der Zunkunft, 1925; Das Haus Mit den Steinfiguren, 1926; Kathrein, 1927; Lexikon sudetendeutscher Schriftsteller, 1928; Das Christkindspiel des Böhmerwaldes, 1929; Krispinus Krausenhaar, der Roman eines lachenden Lebens, 1930. Editor: Der Neue Roman, ein Halbjahr Neuester Prosa; Mitteilungen der Bücherei der Deutschen, Nationalbibliothek der Deutschen in der Tschechoslowakei; Die Bühne, dramaturgische Blätter des Reichenberg Stadtheaters. CLUBS: Verband Deutscher Bühnenschriftsteller; Verein deutscher Erzähler (both Berlin). HOME: Schanzberg 14, Reichenberg, Czechoslovakia.

JALLAND, Rev. Trevor Gervase, D.D. b: Horncastle, Lincs 1896. e: Oundle & Magdalen Coll Oxf, St Stephen's Hse Oxf. m: Beatrice Mary Hamilton Thompson. Lecturer in Theology Univ Coll of the S.W. Exeter 1945—, Proctor in the Convocation of Canterbury & Men of the Ch Assembly '44—, Vice-Prin St Stephen's Hse Oxf '22—25. Publ: The Church & the Papacy; St Leo The Great; The Bible, The Church & South India; This Our Sacrifice. Ctr: Priesthood; The Priest as Student; The Apostolic Ministry. s.s: Church Hist. Rec: Sailing. c: Athenæum. a: 2 Pennsylvania Park & University College, Exeter. T: 2568.

JAMALI, Mohammad Fadhel, M.A., Ph.D. b: Kadhimain, Baghdad 1903. e: Amer Univ of Beirut & Teachers' Coll Columbia Univ. m: Sarah Hayden Powell. s: 3. Minister of Foreign Affairs Iraq, formerly Supervisor Gen, Dir Gen & Insp Gen of Educ, Signed U.N.O. Charter for Iraq 1945. Publ: Modern Iraq, its Problem of Bedouin Education; Books on Education, Arab Unity, etc, in Arabic. Ctr: Various newsps & periodicals in Arabic language. s.s: Education, Arab Unity, Palestine. Rec: Swimming, sculling. a: Abu Nowas St, Baghdad, Iraq. T: 3711.

JAMBUNATHAN, M. R. b: Manakkal 1896. e: Priv. m: Shanti Balambal. d: 2. Journalist, ex. Publ: Atharva Vedam; Yajur Vedam; Samavedam; Yoga, A Sanas; Mazzini; Shraddanandaji; Dayananda Sarasvathi; Katharatham; etc. s.s: Ancient Vedic Literature, Ancient & Modern Tamil. Rec: Social service to Harijans. a: Radha-Nivas, Khar, Bombay 21, India.

JAMES, Rev. A. Gordon. b: Lon 1885. e: Richmond Col Lon. m: Annie Wilson. d: 2. Publ: Jesus & the Other World; Personal Immortality; The Unseen Reality; Jesus & His Friends; etc. c.t: Meth Recorder, Meth Times, etc. s.s: Theo. Rec: Golf. a: Polwarth Gve, Edin. t: 62705.

JAMES, Alfred Procter, M.A.(Oxon), Ph.D.(Chicago). b: Fox Hill, Va 1886. m: Mabel Elizabeth Williams. s: 1. Prof of History, Univ of Pittsburgh. n.a: Ed W. Penna Hist Mag 1922—27 & Ed-Bd '22—, Ed-Bd The Historian '30—. Publ: Writings of General John Forbes; The Renaissance, An Outline. Ctr: N.Y. Times, School & Society, Pittsburgh Press, American Oxonian & various hist journs. s.s: U.S. History, esp Civil War 1860—65 & of Pennsylvania. Rec: Golf, fishing, contract, chess. a: 101 Gladstone Rd, Pittsburgh, Pa, & University of Pittsburgh, Pittsburgh, Pa, U.S.A. T: Mayflower 6447.

JAMES, Arthur Leslie. b: Walsall 1906. e: Kingswood Sch Bath. Journalist. n.a: Sub-Ed Northern Echo Darlington. Rec: Rugby, cricket, tennis. a: Rothbury, Sylvan Gro, Darlington.

JAMES, C. See Clayton, Cyril James.

JAMES, Dr. C. H., C.I.E. Publ: Plague Reports Punjab, Vaccination Manual for Punjab. c.t: Indian Medical Gazette. Lt-Colonel, Late I.M.S. a: Donyngs Pl, Redhill, Surrey.

JAMES, Edward, J.P. Glam. b: Porthcawl 1885. e: Porthcawl, Bridgend County Sch. Chm Parliamentary Press Gallery & Lobby, Alderman Holborn Council Bard of the Gorsedod of Wales & the Isles of Britain, Barrister. n.a: London Ed Western Mail 1913—. Publ: Stirring Deeds in France & Flanders. s.s: Politics & World Affairs. Rec: Motoring & playgoing. a: 176 Fleet St, E.C.4. T: Central 4691.

JAMES, Edward John B.S. b: Chagford, Devon 1906. e: Scaitcliffe Prep Sch & Priv. R. Catholic Priest, Founder of the Virgil Soc. Publ: The One Thing Necessary; The Scale of the Cloisters. Ctr: The Tablet, The Month, Catholic Herald, Blackfriars, Cathedral Chron. s.s: Mystical & Ascetical Theology, Classical Lit of Greece & Rome. Rec: Wild-fowling, game shooting, Labrador retriever training. a: Stiffkey Old Hall, Wells-next-the-Sea, Norfolk. T: Binham 220.

JAMES, Prof. Edwin Oliver, D.Litt.(Oxon), Hon.D.D.(St Andrews), Ph.D.(Lond), F.S.A. b: London 1888. e: Univ Coll Sch Lond & Exeter Coll Oxf. m: Clarise Augusta. s: 1. Prof of the Philosophy of Religion Lond Univ 1945, Fell Univ Coll Lond '46. Publ: Origins of Sacrifice; Comparative Religion; Social Function of Religion; Christian Myth & Ritual; Old Testament in the Light of Anthropology; Primitive Ritual & Belief; Section-Ed Chambers Encylo; Sect-Ed United Universities Library; Ed Folk Lore '32—. Ctr: Encyclo of Religion & Ethics, Man, Journ of Theol Studies, Sociological Rev, The New Commentary, Amer Anthropologist, etc. s.s: Anthropology, Comparative Religion. Rec: Golf, foreign travel, motoring. c: Athenæum. a: Newlands, Crawley Ridge, Camberley, Surrey & The Nook, Kennington, Oxford. T: Camberley 278.

JAMES, Eric John Francis, M.A., B.Sc., D.Phil. b: Derby 1909. e: Taunton's Sch Southampton, Queen's Coll Oxf. m: Cordelia Wintour. s: 1. High Master Manch Gr Sch. Publ: Science & Education (in part); Elements of Physical Chemistry (in part). Ctr: Scientific & educational journals. s.s: Education. a: 143 Old Hall Lane, Manchester 14.

JAMES, F. a: 17 Leigham Court Road, S.W.16.

JAMES, Frank Cyril. b: London 1903. e: Oldfield Road Sch, Hackney Downs Sch, Lond Sch of Econs, Penna Univ. m: Irene Lilian Violet Leeper. Princ & Vice-Chancellor McGill Univ. Publ: Economics of Money, Credit & Banking; The Growth of Chicago Banks; England Today: A Summary of Her Economic Situation; The Road to Revival. Ctr: Various. s.s: Economics, Monetary Theory, History, Internat Affairs. Rec: Walking, gardening, reading. c: Athenæum, Nat Lib, etc. a: McGill Univ, Montreal, Canada. T: Marquette 9181.

JAMES, George William ("C. Radford-Evans", "Alan West", Columnist), M.I.P.S., M.B.T. b: Enfield 1905. e: Margate Col & King's Col Rochester. Journalist, Editor. n.a: Ed Shorthand Typist, Monthly Mag '33—34, The Lancs Observer & The Swinton Gazette '34—. c.t: Daily Express, Evening News M/C, Motor Cycle, etc. Princ Monton Col of Commerce 5 y. Pres Eccles Shorthand Writers' Assoc '33. Founder Croydon Motor Club. Author of Well-known feature Between You & Me. Rec: Golf. a: 11 Highfield Drive, Monton, Eccles, M/C.

JAMES, Godfrey Warden, M.A.(Oxon). b: London. e: St Paul's Sch Lond & Oriel Coll Oxf. Married. s: 1. Barrister; on staff Geoffrey Bles Ltd 1928—, Harper Bros (Lond Office) '30—31, Res Magistrate C.C.G. B.A.O.R., Talks Producer B.B.C. '43—46. Publ: ("Adam Broome") The Porro Palaver; The Island of Death; The Queen's Hall Murder; The Crocodile Club; Snakes & Ladders; Flame of the Forest; Dream Murder; etc. Ctr: Times. s.s: Mystery Novels. Rec: Acting, cello playing. c: Roy Emp Soc. w.s: Regional Off C.D. '39—42. a: Hollybushes, West End, Woking, Surrey. T: Brookwood 3101.

JAMES, Ven. John Daniel, M.A., B.D.(Cantab.) b: Newcastle Emlyn 1862. e: Ch Ch, Brecon & Magdalene Col Cam. m: Mary Hewlett. s: 1. Archdeacon of Llandaff. Publ: The Pastoral Epistles. s.s: New Testament criticism. a: St Andrew's, Llandaff, Cardiff. t: 506.

JAMES, Rev. John Williams, M.A., D.D. b: Rhondda Valley, Glam 1889. e: St Chad's Coll Durham. m: Dorothy Smith. s: 1. Vicar of Aberdovey & Chancellor Bangor Cathedral. Publ: A Church History of Wales. s.s: Welsh Ecclesiastical History. a: The Vicarage, Aberdovey, North Wales.

JAMES, L. D. ("David Llewellyn"). a: 14 Steele's Road, Hampstead, N.W.

JAMES, Lionel. b: Lon 1868. e: Westminster & Chr Ch Oxf. m: Ethel de Pearsall Clabburn. s: 3. d: 2. Schoolmaster. Publ: Plautus Aululuria (Ed for acting); Terence Andria (with Eng version); Aristophanes Frogs (with Eng version); Aristophanes Wasps; Jubilate Deo; Hints on Running; Ariadne—Hints on Latin Prose; Jubilate Deo; also ed Mary Wollstonecraft, a Sketch by H. R. James; etc. Sixth Form Master St Peter's Col Radley '92-1906. Headmaster Mon G.S. '06-27. Rec: Cycling, canoeing. c: Elizabethan, Class Assoc. a: Moyses, Five Ashes, Sussex. t: Mayfield 75.

JAMES, Lionel, C.B.E., D.S.O. b: Teignmouth 1871. e: Cranleigh Sch. m: Hilda Mary Arning. s: 1. d: 2. Chevalier Crown of Italy. n.a: Special Corr Reuter's Agency 1895—99, Englishman Calcutta & Times of India Bombay '95—99, Staff of Times '99—1913, Ed The Democrat 1920—21. Publ: With the Chitral Relief Force 1895; The Indian Frontier War; The Yellow War; A Study of the Russo-Japanese War; A Subaltern of Horse; History of King Edward's Horse; High Pressure; Times of Stress; (anon) On the Heels of DeWet; Green Envelopes; etc. Ctr: Times, Manch Guardian, Ev Standard, Chambers's Journal, etc. s.s: Foreign News, Sport, Horses. c: Cavalry, S. Berks. a: Fieldridge, Shefford Woodlands, Newbury. T: Great Shefford 44.

JAMES, Marquis. b: Springfield, Missouri 1891. m: Bessie Williams Rowland. d: 1. Writer. n.a: Various western & southern newspa 1909—17, American Legion Mag '22—32, The New Yorker '25—26. Publ: Life of Andrew Jackson; The Raven: a Life of Sam Houston; The Cherokee Strip; Life of W. R. Grace; Alfred I duPont: The Family Rebel; They Had Their Hour; The Metropolitan Life: A Study in Business Growth; Biography of a Business. Ctr: Various. s.s: American Hist. w.s: U.S. Army 1917—19. a: Rye, New York, U.S.A. T: Rye 7-2739.

JAMES, MONTAGUE RHODES: provost of Eton; b. Goodnestone, Kent, Eng., Aug., 1862; s. Herbert and Mary Emily (Horton) J.; educ. Temple Grove (Eastsheen, Eng.), Eton Coll., King's Coll. (Cambridge); DEGREES: B.A., M.A., Litt.D. (all Cambridge); (Hon.) D.C.L. (Oxford), (Hon.) D.Litt. (Dublin), (Hon.) L.L.D. (St. Andrews); unmarried. AUTHOR: Psalms of Solomon (with Prof. Ryle), 1891; Testament of Abraham, 1892; Revelation of Peter, 1892; Apocrypha Anecdota (1), 1893, (2), 1897; Fourth Book of Esdras, 1895; Catalogue of MSS. in the Fitzwilliam Museum and at Eton, King's, Jesus, and Sydney Sussex Colleges, 1895; Sculptures of the Lady Chapel at Eton, 1895; Two Essays on the Abbey of St. Edmund at Bury, 1895; Life and Miracles of St. William of Norwich (with Dr. Jessopp), 1895; Sources of Archbishop Parker's Collection of MSS., 1898; Catalogue of MSS. at Peterhouse, 1899; at Trinity (vol. I), 1900; (vol. II), 1901; (vol. III), 1902; (vol. IV), 1905; at Emmanuel Coll., 1905; at Pembroke, Clare, Christ's and Queen's, 1905; at Gonville and Caius Coll. (vol. I, 1907; vol. II, 1908); Trinity Hall, 1907; Magdalene Coll., 1909; Corpus Christi Coll., 1909-13 (7 parts); at St. John's Coll., 1913; in collection of J. Pierpont Morgan, 1907; in McClean collection (Fitzwilliam Museum), 1912; at Westminster Abbey (with the Dean of Westminster), 1909; MSS. in the Library of Lambeth Palace, 1900; Verses in the windows of Canterbury Cathedral, 1902; Western MSS. in the Rylands Library, 1921; Ancient Libraries of Canterbury and Dover, 1903; Ghost Stories of an Antiquary, 1905; Frescoes at Eton, 1907; More Ghost Stories, 1911; The Sculptures in the Bauvhin Chapel, Norwich Cathedral, 1908; in the Cloisters of Norwich Cathedral, 1911; The Austin Friars Library, York (in Fasciculus J. W. Clark, Dictatus), 1909; Introduction to the Trinity College Apocalypse (Roxburghe Club), 1909; to De Officiis Regun (Roxburghe Club), 1913; A Graeco-Latin Lexicon of the XIII Century in Melanges Chatelain, 1910; Chapters in Cambridge Modern History (vol. I), Cambridge History of Modern Literature (vol. I), and Mediaeval France; Old Testament Legends, 1913; Ps-Ovid di mirabilibus mundi. In Essays presented to W. Ridgeway, 1913; The Library of the Cathedral Church, Norwich (with Dean Beeching), 1914; The Chaundler MSS. (Roxburghe Club), 1916; Lives of St. Ethelbert, in English Historical Review, 1917; Biblical Antiquities of Philo, 1917; Gregorius de mirabilibus Romae, 1917; Lives of St. Walstan, 1918; Henry VI, Blacman's Memoir of, 1919; Wanderings and Homes of MSS., 1919; A Thin Ghost and Others, 1919; Lost Apocrypha of the Old Testament, 1920; L'Estoire de St. Edward (Roxburghe), 1920; List of Dr. Dee's MSS. (Biographical Society), 1921; A Petersborough Psalter and Bestiary (Roxburghe); Genesis (Edgerton MSS. 1894), 1921; Twelve Medieval Ghost Stories, 1922; The Five Jars, 1922; The Douce Apocalypse (Roxburghe), 1922; Translation of Map de Nugis Curialium (Cymmrodorion Soc.), 1923; Catalogue of Medieval MSS. in Pepys Library, 1923; an English Bible Picture-Book (Holkham MSS 660), Walpole Society, 1923; Madame Crowl's Ghost and Other Tales by Le Fanu (edited), 1923; The Apocryphal New Testament, 1924; Life of St. Alban (illustration of the Dublin MSS), 1924; Westminster Abbey (Introduction to Inventory, Comm. of Hist. Monuments), 1924; Catalogue of MSS. St. Catherine's College, Cambridge; Abbeys on the G.W.R. System; an English Medieval Sketch Book (Walpole Society); Bromholm Psalter (Roxburghe Club); Horman Vulgaria Puerorum (Roxburghe Club); The Poem Castrianus (Etoniana), 1925;

A Warning to the Curious; Lists of MSS. formerly in Peterborough Abbey Library (Bibliog. Soc.); Bury St. Edmunds MSS.; Introduction to Ghosts and Marvels and to Uncle Silas (World's Classics); Drawings by Matthew Paris (Walpole Soc.); The Apocalypse in Latin (Perrins MSS.); The Carew MSS (English Hist. Review), 1927; Eton and King's, 1875-1925; Illustration of the Old Testament (Roxburghe); Speculum Salvationis; Latin Infancy Gospels. General character of writing: antiquarian commentaries, learned essays, historical memoirs. Vice-chancellor Cambridge Univ., 1913-15; mem. many Royal Commissions; Trustee Brit. Museum; Gold Medallist Bibliographical Soc.; Officier de l' Instruction Publique, 1911; Fellow Soc. Antiquaries, Brit. Acad.; Hon. mem. Royal Irish Acad. Relig. denom., Church of England. CLUB: National. ADDRESS: The Lodge, Eton College, Bucks, Eng.

JAMES, Norah C. Author, Free-lance Journalist. *Publ*: Sleeveless Errand; Straphangers; Jealously; Hospital; Wanton Ways; The Return; Mighty City; The Gentlewoman; Two Selfish People; The Father; There is always Tomorrow; Penny Trumpet; Brittle Glory. *w.s*: A.T.S. World War II. *a*: Villa Pont Marquet, St Brelade, Jersey, C.I.

JAMES, Rev. Father ("O'Mahony"), O.M. Cap, Ph.D., D.Litt, M.A. *b*: Mitchelstown, Co Cork 1897. *e*: Chr Bros Mitchelstown, Capuchin Franciscan Col Rochestown, Cork Univ Col, Gregorian Univ Rome & Louvain Catholic Univ, Capuchin Franciscan Priest. *Publ*: The Desire of God in the Philosophy of St Thomas; Where is Thy God?; The Franciscans; The Romanticism of Holiness; The Challenge of Christ; etc. *c.t*: Irish Way, Clergy Review, Capuchin Annual, Melbourne Advocate, etc. *s.s*: Empirical psychology, metaphysics & logic of science. Pres St Bonaventure's 1928. Lecturer in Religion Cork Univ Col '32—33. Acting Prof of Philos '32—33. Lect at Cam Summer Sc & Aquinas Soc Lon. Mem Gov Body Univ Col Cork '35. Agrégé en Philosophie a l'Université Catholique de Louvain. *c*: N.U.I. *a*: St Bonaventure's, Cork Ireland.

JAMES, Robert Rutson. *b*: Burwarton, Salop 1881. *e*: Winchester, St George's Hosp Lond. *m*: Margaret Newson. *d*: 1. Cons Ophthalmic Surg St George's Hosp Lond. *n.a*: Sub-Ed 1923—29, Sen-Ed '29— Brit Journ of Ophthalmology. *Publ*: Studies in the History of Ophthalmology in England prior to 1800 A.D. *s.s*: Hist of Med. *a*: Bryn, 8 Moorfield Rd, Woodbridge, Suffolk.

JAMES, Rev. Thomas Esger. *b*: Pantglas 1869. *e*: Parkyfelvet Acad, Presbyterian Col Carmarthen. *m*: Mary Anne Cleaver. *s*: 3. *d*: 2. *Publ*: The Biography of Rev. W. Jones, Pentretygwyn; Temperance Steps; The Modern Diana. *c.t*: Tivy Side, Tyst, Celt, etc. *s.s*: Astron, agric. *a*: Maeshyfryd, Cardigan.

JAMES, Walter Culver, T.D., M.D., F.R.C.S.E. *b*: London. *e*: King's Col, Aberdeen Univ, Guys Hosp, W. Lond Hosp. Physician Surgeon Colonel Hon Art Co. *Publ*: England's Future. *c.t*: Lancet, W. Lond Med Journ, Brit Empire Review. Officer of the Roy Order of the Redeemer of Greece. Consult Physician of Westminster Gen Dispensary. Mem of the Harveian Soc & West Lond Med Chirurg Soc. Late Pres Med Bd Queen Alexandra Military Hosp Millbank. W. S. Desp. Phy Hosp for Women & Children Vincent Sq. *c*: Brit Emp, Brit Emp League. Late Gd Master Soc of S George. *a*: Cadmore End, High Wycombe Bucks. *t*: Lane End 20.

JAMES, Admiral Sir William Milbourne. *b*: Farnborough 1881. *e*: Trin Coll, Glenalmond & H.M.S. Britannia. *m*: Dorothy Alexandra Duff. *s*: 1. C.O.S. Atlantic & Meditn Fleets 1931—32, Vice-Admiral Commanding Battle Cruiser Squadron '33, Dep-Chief Naval Staff '35—38, C-in-C Portsmouth '39, Chief of Naval Information '43—44, M.P. North Portsmouth '42—44. *Publ*: British Navy in Adversity; New Battleship Organisations; Blue Water & Green Fields; Admiral Sir William Fisher; The Portsmouth Letters; The British Navies in the Second World War; The Order of Release. *c*: United Service. *a*: Road Farm, Churt. *T*: Headley Down 2239.

JAMES, William Warwick, O.B.E., F.R.C.S. *b*: Wellingboro' 1874. *e*: Wellingboro' Sc, Middx Hosp, Roy Dental Hosp. *m*: Ada Louisa Mary Froude. *s*: 6. *d*: 1. Dental Surg. *Publ*: Mouthbreathing & Nasal Obstruction (with Somerville Hastings 1932); Simple Gingivitis ('33). *c.t*: R.D.H. Gazette, Roy Soc Med, etc. Snr Dental Surg Middx Hosp. Ex-Dental Surg Hosp for Children Gt Ormond St Ex-Lect & Dental Surg Roy Dental Hosp. F.R.S.M., F.Z.S. John Lornes Prize. *Rec*: Mountaineering, golf, music. *c*. Alpine. *a*: 2 Park Cres, Portland Pl, W.1. & The Malthouse, Hurley, Berks. *t*: Welbeck 1248.

JAMES, Winifred Lewellin. *b*: Victoria, Aus. *e*: Priv. *m*: Henry De Jan. Author, Journalist, Domestic Econ & Lecturer. *Publ*: Bachelor Betty (1908); Saturday's Children; Letters to My Son; Letters of a Spinster; The Mulberry Tree; A Man for England; London Is My Lute; etc. *c.t*: Yorkshire Post, Evening Standard, Express, etc. *s.s*: Home planning. Worked among negroes in Central America for Red X during War. *Rec*: Travel. *c*: Lyceum & Soc of Authors. *a*: St Ermin's, Westminster, W.1. *t*: Victoria 3441.

JAMESON, ANNIE EDITH: see Buckrose, J. E.

JAMESON, John Gordon, B.A.(Oxon), LL.B.(Edin). *b*: Edinburgh 1878. *e*: Edin Acad, Edin Univ, Balliol Coll Oxf. *m*: Margaret Smith. *d*: 2. Advocate, Retired Sheriff-Subst of Lothian. *Publ*: The Good News (What is it?); The Bringer of the Good News; The Way of Happiness. *s.s*: Evangelism, Federal Union. *Rec*: Fencing. *c*: New, Edinburgh. *a*: 34 Gt King St, Edinburgh.

JAMESON, Margaret Storm, M.A., Hon.D.Litt. *b*: Whitby. *e*: Leeds Univ. *m*: Guy Patterson Chapman. *s*: 1. Writer. *Publ*: The Lovely Ship; The Voyage Home; Farewell to Youth; A Richer Dust; That was Yesterday; A Day Off; No Time Like the Present; Company Parade; Love in Winter; None Turn Back; The Fort; Cousin Honore; Farewell Night, Welcome Day; Europe to Let; Cloudless May; Journal of Mary Hervey Russell; The Other Side; Before the Crossing. Black Laurel. *a*: c/o Macmillan & Co Ltd, St Martin's St, London, W.C.2.

JAMIESON, Rev. Andrew Burns, M.A. *b*: Larbert 1906. *e*: K.E. VI's G.S. Birm. Presbyt Min. *Publ*: Burns & Religion ('31). Author of several plays, sketches & a musical farce. *Rec*: Tennis, amateur dramatics. *a*: The Manse, Walker, Newcastle-on-Tyne.

JAMIESON, Edward Bald, M.D. Lecturer in Anatomy (ret). *Publ*: Illustrations of Regional Anatomy; Illustrations of Anatomy for Nurses; Companion to Manuals of Practical Anatomy; Human Osteology (with Prof Dixon); Birmingham Anatomical Nomenclature (with Profs Dixon & Johnston); Surface Anatomy (with Prof Robinson); etc. ; Co-Ed Cunningham's Text Book of Anatomy & Manuals of Practical Anatomy. *a*: University, Teviot Place, Edinburgh 8.

JAMIESON, Dr. J. A., M.D.(Edin). *a*: Holyrood, Heaton Park, Manchester.

JAMIESON, Melvill Allan. *b*: Edin 1881. *e*: Edin Acad & Repton. European Mang Montreal Star & Allied n/ps. *n.a*: Staff of Montreal Star 1903, European Mang '09. Consul Gen for Republic of San Marino '22–. War Service S. Africa War & Gt War, Comm of Order of St John of Jerusalem, Grand Officer Order of San Marino, Officer Order of Crown of Italy, Officer de l'Instruction Publique France, Albert Medal of Belgium, etc. *c*: R.A.C. *a*: 42 Pall Mall, Lon, S.W.1, & Thatch End, Newnham, Baldock, Herts. *t*: Whitehall 8212.

JAMIESON, Dr. R. H., M.D., F.R.C.S. Edin. Medical Practitioner. *c.t*: B.M.J. & Lancet. Freeland Barbour Fell for Research & Ettles Schol Edin Univ 1907. *a*: Stalheim, Mulgrave Rd, Sutton, Surrey.

JAMIESON, Stewart, M.A. *b*: Sydney 1903. *e*: King's Sch & Sydney Univ, Balliol Coll Oxf. *m*: Katherine Mary Garvan. *d*: 1. Australian Diplomatic Service 1945–. *n.a*: Speciality Writer Sydney Ev News '29, Leader Writer, Sydney Morning Herald '39–40 & Spec Corr Europe & Russia '38, Hon Ed Aust & New Zealand Ski Year Book '30–40. *Ctr*: Various Australian publs. *s.s*: Australian External & Political Affairs, Films & Film Industry, Ski-ing & Rowing. *Rec*: Ski-ing, surfing. *w.s*: 1940–46 R.A.A.F. *a*: Official Secretary, Office of Australian High Commissioner, Ottawa, Canada. *T*: Ottawa 3-3458.

JANDEL, Olof Ragnar. *b*: Jamjo 1895. *Publ*: Under varstjarnor; Havets klockor; Det stilla aret; Den tranga porten, Vagledare; Kampande tro; Malort; Valda dikter; etc. *c.t*: Social Demokraten, Stockholm, etc. *c*: P.E.N. *s*: Olme, Sweden.

JANECKE, ERNST GUSTAV GEORG: chemist; b. Alt-Warmbüchen, near Hannover, Germany, March 4, 1875; s. William and Johanne (Warnecke) J.; educ. Realgymnasium (Hannover), 1882-1894; Tech. High Sch. (Hannover), 1894-1895; Univs. of Göttingen, Munich, Berlin. DEGREES: Ph.D. (Berlin), Privatdozent, 1905; Professor (Hannover Tech. High Sch.), 1912; m. (1) Hedwig Smend, 1909 (died 1920); (2) Liesel Velde, 1921. AUTHOR: Gesättigte Salzlössungen vom Standpunkt der Phasenlehre, 1908; Summary of Alloys, 1909; Kurze Übersicht über sämtliche Legierungen, 1910; Die Enstehung der deutschen Kalisalzlager, 1915 (2nd edit. 1923); Zur Konstitution des Portland-Cementes, Zusammenfassung der Vorträge (with Wetzel and Glasenapp), 1912, 1913 (2nd edit. 1921). Contributor to about 120 papers in: Zeitschrift für Physikalische Chemie, Zeitschrift für Elektrochemie, Centralblatt für Mineralogie, Internationale Zeitschrift für Metallogr., Jahrbuch d. Halleschen Verbandes, Zeitschrift für Math. and Naturw. Unterrichts, Zeitschrift Zement, and many others. Writings for the press consist principally of papers on physical chemistry, especially on Phase rule topics, on salt deposits of oceanic origin, alloys, cement, heterogeneous chemical equilibria, etc. CLUBS: Bunsengesellschaft, Verein Deutscher Chemiker, Ver. Deutscher Naturforscher u. Ärzte, Gesellschaft für Metallkunde, Chem. Gesellschaft Heidelberg, Verein Deutscher, Berg- und Hüttenleute, Iron and Steel Institute (London). Relig. denom., Evangelical. OFFICE: J. G. Farbenindustrie Akt. Ges., Ludwigshafen am Rhein. HOME: Landfriedstrasse Nr. 10, Heidelberg, Baden, Germany.

JANES, Albert William. *b*: Luton, Beds 1901. *m*: Doris E. H. Spicer. *s*: 1. *d*: 1. Newspaper Ed. *n.a*: Luton News '16–22, Bedfordshire Times Ed Staff '23, Ed '39. *Rec*: Amateur photography. *a*: 2 Ellis Rd. Bedford. *T*: 4742.

JANSEN, BERNHARD: professor of philosophy; b. Apr. 10, 1877; s. Anton and Gertrud (Münstermann) J.; educ. Gymnasium (Telgte, Westphalia), in the Colleges of German Jesuits (humanistics, philosophy, theology); Univs. of Strassburg, Bonn, and at the Vatican Library (philosophy). DEGREE: Doctor of Theology (Univ. of Freiburg, Baden), unmarried. AUTHOR: Leibnitz erkenntnistheoretischer Realist. Grundlinien seiner Erkenntnislehre, 1920; Die Erkenntnislehre Olivis. Auf Grund der Quellen dargestellt und gewürdigt, 1921; Petrus Johannis Olivi Quaestiones in Secundum librum Sententiarum. Primum ad fidem Codicum Manuscriptorum edidit. (3 vols.), 1922, 1924, 1926; Wege der Weltweisheit, 1924; Der Kritizismus Kants, 1925; Die Religionsphilosophie Kants, Geschichtlich dargestellt und kritisch-systematisch gewürdigt, 1929. Contributes to Stimmen der Zeit (Freiburg), Zeitschrift für katholische Theologie (Innsbruck), Franziskanische Studien (Münster), Philosophisches Jahrbuch (Fulda in Hessin), Gregorianum (Rome). Has taught philosophy at the Colleges of Jesuits, Valkenburg nr. Mastricht, Holland, and at Berchmanskolleg Pullach, nr. Munich, since 1907; gives the exercises of St. Ignace and holds conferences of religious and scientific nature. Became a Jesuit at 16½ years of age. SOCIETY: Priester des Jesuitenordens. ADDRESS: Berchmanskolleg, Pullach nr. Munich, Germany.

JANSSEN, ALBRECHT: author; b. Bingum, Germany, Jan. 8, 1886; s. Lurtjen and Elske (Voogd) J.; educ. Volkschule, Lehrerbildungsanstalten, Univ.; m. Gertrud Röhr, April 4, 1890. AUTHOR: Als der Weltbrand lohte (anthology), 1915; Die Frauen rings um Hebbel, 1918; Borkumer Kinder, 1919; Almuth Folkerts (drama), 1920; Der Diekrichter (drama), 1922; Der Deichgraf, 1922; Der Wundervogel, 1922; Niederdeutsches Balladenbuch (anthology), 1925; Hausbuch Niederdeutscher Lyrik (anthology), 1926; Die Nordseeinseln, 1925; Hermann Bossdorf (biography), 1927; Das einsame Land (novel), 1924. Editor: Zeitschrift des Schimmelreiter, Das Niedersachsenbuch, Der schükings. General character of writing: novels, plays and poems. Relig. denom., Lutheran. ADDRESS: Eppendorfer Weg III, Hamburg 19, Germany.

JANSSEN, Carl Emil Luplau, Hon.M.S. *b*: Frederiksberg, Denmark 1889. *e*: Univs of Copenhagen & Lund. *m*: Aase Luplau Janssen. *d*: 1. Owner & Leader Urania Observatory & Librarian of Univ Copenhagen. *n.a*: 1916–19 Ed Nordisk Astronomisk Tidskrift & Ed Urania '43–. *Publ*: The Stellar Universe & its Marvels; Astronomy & Astrophysics; Mars, The Red Planet; The Stars; also many scientific papers. *Ctr*: Politiken, Landet, etc. *s.s*: Astronomy, Double Stars, Great Planets, New Stars, Roman Languages. *a*: Urania Observatory, Dronning Olgas Vej 25, Copenhagen, Denmark. *T*: Godthaab 2366.

JANSSEN, JOHANN THEODOR: engineer; b. Oldenburg, Germany, Jan. 31, 1853; s. Eggerich and Maria (Weyers) J.; educ. Gymnasium, Tech. High School. DEGREES: Professor, Dr. Ing., h.c.; m. Else Schlitte, Dec. 14, 1905. AUTHOR: Submissionswesen und Tiefbaugewerbe, 1909; Der Bauingenieur in der Praxis, 1913 (2nd edit. 1927); Die Grundlage des technischen Denkens, 1917; Gründung der Brücken, 1920; Technische Wirtschaftslehre, 1925. General character of writing: technical. CLUBS: Architekten und Ingenieur Verein (Berlin), Deutsch Gesellschaft für Bauingenieurwesen (Berlin). Relig. denom., Evangelical. HOME: Hohenzollerndamm 183, Berlin-Wilmersdorf, Germany.

JANTZEN, HANS: univ. professor; b. Hamburg, Germany, April 24, 1881; s. Rudolf and Alwine (Lage) J.; educ. Gymnasium. DEGREE: Ph.D.; m. Marie Karnstaedt. AUTHOR: Das Niederländische Architekturbild, 1910; Niederländische Malerei im 17. Jahrhundert, 1912; Leitfaden für den Kunstgeschichtlichen Unterricht, 1912; Rembrandt, 1923; Deutsche Bildhauer des 13 Jahrhunderts, 1925; Das Münster zu Freiburg, 1929. Contributor to Zeitschrift für Aesthetik und Allgemeinen Kunstwissenschaft; Repetitorium für Kunstwissenschaft, Kunst und Künstler. General character of writing: history of art.

CLUBS: Deutsche Akademie. Relig. denom., Evangelical. ADDRESS: Burgunderstrasse 30, Freiburg, 1-Br., Germany.

JANTZEN, HERMANN: inspector of secondary schools; b. Breslau, Germany, February, 1874; s. Paul and Emma (Silz) J.; educ. College of St. Maria Magdalena, Univs. of Breslau and Berlin. DEGREES: Ph.D., M.A.; m. Else Holdefleiss, January, 1881. AUTHOR: Geschichte des deutschen Streitgedichts, 1896; Gotische Sprachdenmäler, 1898 (6th edit., 1929); Saxo Grammaticus, die ersten neun Bücher der dänischen Geschichte übersetzt und erläutert, 1900; Deutsche Romantik, 1912; Ein altschlesisches Osterspiel, 1925. Editor: Grammatik der Neuhochdeutschen Sprache (by Engelien, 5th edit.), 1902; Sappho (by Grillparzer), 1903; Lord Byron's ausgewählte Dichtungen, 1905; Meisterwerke englischer Dichtung, 1906; Wissenschaftliche Frauenarbeiten, 1906-07; Egmont (by (Goethe), 1914; Nibelungen (by Hebbel), 1917; Agnes Bernauer (by Hebbel), 1919; Literaturdenmäler des 14.|15. Jahrhunderts (3rd edit.), 1919; Taugenichts (by Eichendorff), 1922; Wolfram von Eschenbach, 1925; Hartmann von Aue und Gottfried von Strassburg, 1925; Deutsches Lesebuch (by Kippenberg), 1926; U.S.A. Poetry and Prose, 1923 (2nd edit., 1928); Walther von der Vogelweide, 1929; Zeitschrift für französischen und englischen Unterricht, from 1922-29. Contributor to Schlesische Zeitung. General character of writing: critical, historical. Interested in Germanic and English philology, and in German literary history. CLUBS: Schlesische Gesellschaft für Volkskunde, Gesellschaft für deutsche Bildung, Deutscher Sprachverein. Religion, Protestant. ADDRESS: Brandenburgerstrasse 52, Breslau, Germany.

JAPHA, ARNOLD: univ. professor; b. Koenigsberg, Prussia, Sept., 1877; s. Walter and Margarethe Japha; educ. Wilhelmgymnasium (Koenigsburg), Univ. of Freiburg and Koenigsberg. DEGREES: M. D., Ph.D.; m. Kaethe Eckleben, Aug. 4, 1913. Has made numerous contributions to scientific periodicals, and written on medical subjects. CLUBS: Deutsche Zoologische Gesellschaft; Gesellschaft für Physische Anthropologie. Relig. denom., Evangelical. OFFICE: Zoological Inst. of University. HOME: Schwuchtstr. 17, Halle a.S., Germany.

JAPHET, Ludwig. b: Hoopstad, O.F.S., Sth Africa 1890. e: Hamburg, Brussels, London, Johannesburg. s: 1. d: 1. Solicitor. Publ: What Every Motorist Ought to Know About the Law; Over Coffee & Liqueurs. Ctr: Sth African Broadcasting Corpn, Fight, South African press in general. s.s: Laws of Motoring, Internat Finance & Econs, Articles on Boxing Promotion, Epigrams & Short Stories. Rec: Golf, dancing. c: Transvaal Nat Sporting, Transvaal Auto, etc. a: 504 Mackay Mans, Rissick St, Johannesburg. T: 33-6668.

JAPHET, Raymond. Rep Islington & Holloway Press Lond 1926—29, Rep Clacton Times & East Essex Gazette Series '29—34, Dep Chief Sub (at times Acting Chief Sub-Ed) '34—39, Sub-Ed East Anglian Dly Times '39—45, Sub-Ed Dly Express (Manch) '45—46, Sub-Ed Dly Express July '46—. w.s: C.D. (N.F.S.) 1941—45. a: 22 Hamilton Rd, Dollis Hill, London, N.W.10.

JAPP, Sir Henry, M.InstC.E., M.AmSocC.E., K.B.E. b: Montrose 1869. e: Montrose Acad, Univ Col Dundee, affiliated with St And Univ, Finsbury Tech Col. m: (1) Lizzie N. Hodge; (2) Kathie M. Sutherland. s: 2 (1 dec). d: 2. Civil Eng. n.a: Chr Sci Monitor 1919-20, Gen Reporting Mexico & Boston etc. '20-22, Lon News Ed. c.t: Leading Amer sci journs. Civil Eng Supervising the construction of Publ works, Gt N. & City Tube Rly Lon, the Four East River Tunnels for Pennsylvania Railroad N.Y. & King George V Graving Dock Southampton, etc. Rec: Golf, motoring. c: Caledonian, Caledonian Soc, Eng-Speaking Un, Mem Brit Assoc. a: 10 The Orchard, Bedford Pk, W.4. t: Chiswick 2360.

JAQUES, Florence Page, A.B. b: Illinois 1890. e: Mil & Columb Univs. m: Francis Lee Jaques. Writer. Publ: Canadian Spring; Canoe Country; Snowshoe Country; Birds cross the Sky; The Geese Fly High. Ctr: Natural History, Audubon Mag, American Girl, Child Life. s.s: Nature, Birds. Rec: Canoeing, travel, camping. a: 610 West 116th St, New York 27, N.Y., U.S.A. T: University 4-6570.

JAQUES, Harry Edwin. b: Danville, Iowa 1880. e: Danville Hgh Sch, Drake Univ, Wesleyan Coll, Univ of Iowa, Ohio State Univ. m: (1) Ethel Benedict, (2) Clara B. Morohart. s: 1. d: 4. Author, Editor, Teacher. n.a: Ed Pictured-Key Nature Books 1945. Publ: How to Know the Insects; How to Know the Land Birds; Living Things—How to Know Them; How to Know the Trees; Plant Families—How to Know Them; Plants We Eat & Wear; 1,250 Common Beetles. Ctr: Various scientific journs, etc. s.s: Entomology, Identification of Plants & Animals, Nature Study. Rec: Travel, photography. a: 709 Nth Main St, Mt Pleasant, Iowa, U.S.A. T: 188 Black.

JAQUES, Robert Harold Whetham. b: Wentbridge 1875. e: Lower Sc Uppingham & Eton. m: Bertha Mary Julia Hibbert (dec). Landed Proprietor. Has been Cow-puncher in Colorado, Saloon Keeper B.C., Music Hall Proprietor B.C., Actor, Train Driver in San Francisco, Sailor before the Mast, Big-Game Hunter Manitoba & Saskatchewan, Conductor S. Pacific Rly Dining Cars, etc. Served S. African War, European War '14-17. Rec: Hunting, motoring. c: Alpine Sports, R.A.C.(Lon). Mem French, Monaco, Spanish & Italian Auto Clubs. a: Easby Abbey, Richmond. Yorks. t: 304.

JAQUIN, Noel. b: Lon 1894. e: Vermont Col, City of Lon Col. Psychologist, Diagnostician & Author. Publ: Scientific Palmistry; The Hand & Disease; The Hand of Man; etc. c.t: Pearson's Mag, Cassell's Mag, Answers, Woman's Own, Tit Bits Year Book, Swedish Press. s.s: Diagnosis of disease from the markings of the hand, psychological analysis. War Service. At close of war adopted palmistic psychology & diagnosis of disease as career. Possesses a unique collection of the imprints of the hands of famous people. Rec: Lit, bacteriology. a: 37b Green Lanes, Palmer's Green, N.13. t: Bowes Park 3109.

JARCHE, James, F.R.P.S., F.I.B.P. b: Wood Green London 1890. e: St Olave's Gr Sch. m: Elsie Gladys Jezzard. d: 1. Chief Photographer Odham's Press. Publ: People I Have Shot. s.s: Miniature Camera Photography. Rec: Golf. c: Savage. a: 96 Chiltern Ct, Baker St, London, N.W.1. T: Welbeck 5544.

JARDINE, Evelyne. See White, Evelyne.

JARMAN, Sydney Gardnor, J.P. b: Tiverton, Devon 1856. m: Mary Hooper. s: 5. Editor & Journalist. n.a: Ed North Wales Guardian 1895—. Publ: History of Bridgwater. c: Exchange (Wrexham). a: Oakdene, Wrexham.

JARMAN, Thomas Leckie, M.A., B.Litt. b: London 1907. e: Bedales Sch, New Coll Oxf, Harvard Univ. Lecturer in Education Univ of Bristol. Publ: William Marshal, First Earl of Pembroke & Regent of England; Through Soviet Russia; Turkey; etc. Ctr: Journ of Adult Educ. s.s: Hist, Educ. Rec: Travel. w.s: Army Educ Corps. a: 52 Brean Down Ave, Weston-super-Mare, Som.

JARVIE, John Gibson. b: Carluke 1883. m: Ethel Mary Patricia Rowland. s: 1. d: 3. Coy Chm & Mang Dir. Publ: Various Pamphlets on Economics. a: 9 Hyde Park Gate, S.W.7, & Gedding Hall, nr Bury St Edmund's, Suffolk. t: Western 1107 & Rattlesden 53.

JARVIE, John Ramage. *b:* Scotland. Journalist. *n.a:* Ex-Ed John Bull, etc. *c.t:* Press Assoc, etc.

JARVIS, Col. Sir Alexander Weston, C.M.G., M.V.O. *b:* King's Lynn 1855. *e:* Harrow. *m:* Diana Follett. *Publ:* Jottings From an Active Life. Served in Matabele Rebellion, Boer War, European War. *Rec:* Fishing. *c:* Carlton, Marlboro'. Ex-Chm Counc Roy Emp Soc. *a:* 1 Hobart Pl, S.W. *t:* Sloane 5632.

JARVIS, Major Claude Scudamore, C.M.G., O.B.E. Gov Libyan Oases 1920—22, Sinai '22—36. *Publ:* Three Deserts; Yesterday & To-day in Sinai; The Back Garden of Allah; Oriental Spotlight; Desert & Delta; Heresies & Humours. *Ctr:* Country Life. *s.s:* Mid-East & Sport. *Rec:* Fishing & shooting. *c:* Naval & Military. *a:* Chele Orchard, Ringwood, Hants.

JARVIS, Rupert Charles, F.S.A., F.R.Hist.S. *b:* Sudbury, Suffolk 1899. *e:* Sudbury Sch. *m:* Marjorie Wilson Hare. *s:* 2. *d:* 1. Librarian & Keeper, H.M. Customs & Excise. *Publ:* The Rebellion of 1745 from Contemporary News Sheets; Whitehaven Port Records & The '45; Cope's March North; Cope's Forces, August 1745; The Death of Walpole; Some Records of the Port of Lancaster; Lancashire Ports & Illicit Trade; Appointment of Ports in Cumberland & Westmorland; Reform in Highway Administration 1662—1837; etc. *Ctr:* Eng Hist Rev, History, Public Administration, Mod Lang Rev, etc. *s.s:* History of the Jacobite Movement, Records & History of Ports, Fiscal History. *Rec:* Mountaineering, fell walking, archæology, Shakespeare & the microscope. *a:* Shelley, Station Rd, Hockley, Essex.

JARVIS, Stanley. *b:* Leeds 1906. *e:* Bournemouth Munic Col. *m:* Lilian May Wheeler. Journalist. *n.a:* Bournemouth Daily Echo, Bournemouth Guardian, Hornsey Journal, N. Eastern Daily Gazette. *c.t:* Various. *Rec:* Golf, tennis, swimming. *a:* 18 Hall Drive, Acklam, Middlesbrough.

JAST, Louis Stanley, HonM.A.(M/C). *b:* Halifax 1868. *e:* Priv Scs & King's Col Lon. *m:* Millicent Murby. Ex-Chief Librarian, M/C. *Publ:* The Child as Reader; The Lover & the Dead Woman: & Other Plays in Verse; Libraries & Living; Shah Japan (play). *c.t:* Manchester Guardian & various prof journals, etc. *s.s:* Librarianship. Ex-Pres Unnamed Soc, M/C. Ex-Pres Library Assoc. *a:* The Cedars, Beckington, nr Bath.

JASZI, Oscar, Ph.D. *b:* Nagy Karoly, Hungary. *e:* Gymnasium Nagy Karoly, Univ of Budapest. *m:* Recha Wollmann-Rundt. *s:* 2. Prof Emeritus Oberlin Coll, former Head of Dept of Political Science. *Publ:* Dissolution of the Hapsburg Monarchy; Evolution of the Nation States; Der Zusammenbruch des Dualismus; Revolution & Counter-Revolution in Hungary; (co-author) Propaganda & Dictatorship; Refugees; The City of Man; etc; (co-ed) La Hongrie Contemporaine. *Ctr:* Ency of Soc Sci, For Affairs, Nation, New Leader, Yale Rev, Public Opinion Quarterly, etc. *s.s:* Danubian Countries. *a:* 131 Forest St, Oberlin, Ohio. *T:* 4592.

JAUNCEY, Rev. Ernest, M.A., D.D. *b:* Acton, Middlesex 1881. *e:* Elem & Priv, Durham Univ. *m:* (1) Edith Binns. *s:* 1. (2) Gwendoline C. M. C. Jauncey. *s:* 1. *d:* 2. Priest in Charge St Ninian's Episc Ch Prestwick. *Publ:* The Doctrine of Grace; History of the Parish of Brotherton. *Rec:* Walking, gardening. *a:* St Ninian's Rectory, Prestwick, Ayrshire. *T:* Prestwick 7108.

"JAVALI" (pen name): see Beadnell, Charles Marsh.

JAW-YUANRENN: see Chao, Y. R.

JAY, ARTHUR OSBORNE MONTGOMERY: clerk in Holy Orders; *b.* Landojr, India, Apr. 14, 1858; *s.* William Jay and Harriet (Osborne) J.; educ. Eton Coll.; DEGREE: M.A. (Cambridge); unmarried. AUTHOR: Life in Darkest London, 1890; Social Problems, 1891; Story of Shoreditch, 1892; Sermons, 1900. Contributor to many papers and mags. General character of writing: sociological subjects. Vicar of Holy Trinity, Shoreditch, 1886-1921; Fellow Sion Coll. (London), Magdalen Coll. (Oxford). Relig. denom., Church of England. CLUB: Junior Carlton (London). HOME: Thornburn, Malvern, Worcestershire, Eng.

JAY, Douglas Patrick Thomas, M.P. *b:* London 1907. *e:* Winchester, New Coll Oxf. *m:* Margaret Garnett. *s:* 2. *d:* 2. Journalist, M.P.(Lab) Nth Battersea '46—. *n.a:* The Times '19—33, Economist '33—37, Dly Herald '37—40. *Publ:* The Socialist Case. *s.s:* Economics. *a:* 12 Well Rd, Hampstead, London, N.W.3. *T:* Hampstead 3192.

JAY, HARRIET: author, dramatist; *b.* Grays, Essex, Eng., Sept. 2, 1853; *d.* Richard and Ann (Webb) J.; educ. Bexhill (London), Etretat (Normandy); unmarried. AUTHOR (novels): Queen of Connaught; Dark Colleen; Madge Dunraven; Priest's Blessing, 1881; My Connaught Cousins, 1883; Marriage of Convenience; Two Men and a Maid; Through the Stage Door; Strange Adventures of Miss Brown; Life of Robert Buchanan; (plays): Alone in London; Blue Bells of Scotland; When Knights Were Bold; Strange Adventures of Miss Brown (dramatized form). General character of writing: novels and plays. Relig. denom., Church of England. CLUB: Writers' (London). HOME: The Cottage, 20 Seymour Gardens, Ilford, Essex, Eng.

JAY, T. Nat Mem N.U.J. *a:* Invergarry, Redcliffe Bay, Portishead.

JAYE, Stella Constance. Bookseller. *Publ:* Shadows & Reflections. *Ctr:* Various. *s.s:* Verse & Sketches. *a:* The Old Hse, High St, Ryde, I.O.W. *T:* 2045.

JEAN, R. C. *b:* Plymouth 1893. *e:* Mutley G.S. *m:* Daisy E. James. *s:* 2. *d:* 1. Journalist. *n.a:* Western Morning News 1920-34, Personal staff H.R.H. Prince of Wales Canadian Tour '19. *c.t:* Exchange Telegraph Co, Evening Standard, Western Mail, etc. *Rec:* Gardening. *a:* 49 Lisson Grove, Plymouth. *t:* 2220.

JEAN-AUBRY, G. *b:* Paris 1882. *e:* Havre. Author & Lecturer, Chev Legion d'Honneur, Commandeur de l'order d'Isabelle (Spain), Officier Polonia Restituta (Poland), Chev de l'Ordre de Leopold (Belgium). *Publ:* La Musique Française d'aujourd'hui; Introduction to French Music; Joseph Conrad; Life & Letters; La Musique et les Nations; Vie de Conrad; Mallarne Complete Works; etc. *Ctr:* La Prensa (Buenos Aires), Revue de Paris, Mercure de France. *s.s:* Music, French & Eng Lit. *a:* 2 rue Abbi Gillet, Paris XVI. *T:* Aut 0551.

JEANS, Allan, J.P. *b:* L'pool 1877. *e:* Birkenhead Sc & Rossall. Journalist. *n.a:* Mang Dir Liverpool Daily Post & Echo Ltd. Chm C. Tinling & Co Ltd. Ex-Pres Newspaper Soc. Ex-Chm Press Assoc. *c:* Exchange, Univ Press, L'pool & Press, Lon. *a:* Delavor Noctorum, Birkenhead. *t:* 6.

JEANS, H. Chm Industrial N/ps Ltd. *a:* 49 Wellington St, W.C.2.

JEANS, Huntly Ronald. *b:* Glastonbury, Som 1908. *e:* Shrewsbury Sc, France, Germany. Journalist, Film Critic. *n.a:* West Middx

Gazette (Ealing) '29. Hornsey Journ '30. Huddersfield Dly Examiner '32. *c.t*: Many national & provincial papers. *s.s*: Cinema. *Rec*: Golf, fishing. *c*: N.U.J., Inst of Journalists. *a*: Flat 4, 54 Fitzwilliam St, Huddersfield, Yorks. *t*: 1140.

JEANS, Sir James H. *b*: 1877. *e*: Merchant Taylors Sc, Trin Col Cam. Scientist. Prof of Astronomy Royal Institution. *Publ*: The Universe Around Us; The Mysterious Universe; The Stars in Their Courses; The New Background of Science; Astronomy & Cosmogony; Through Space and Time. *s.s*: Science. *a*: Cleveland Lodge, Dorking.

JEANS, Surg. Rear-Adml. Thomas Tendron, R.N., C.M.G. Retired. *Publ*: Ed Naval Brigades South African War (1899); A Naval Venture; Gunboat & Gun Runner; The Gun Runners; Reminiscences of a Naval Surgeon; etc. *a*: c/o District Bank, 75 Cornhill, E.C.3.

JEBB, Richard. *b*: Ellesmere 1874. *e*: Marlborough & New Col Oxf. *m*: Margaret Ethel Lewthwaite. *s*: 2. *d*: 1. Landowner. *n a*: Leader Writer & Special Contrib Morning Post 1905—11. *Publ*: Studies in Colonial Nationalism; The Imperial Conference (2 vols); The Britannic Question; The Empire in Eclipse. *c.t*: Various. *s.s*: Polit future of the Empire. War Service '14—18. *Rec*: Carpentry, fishing, shooting. *c*: Roy Empire Soc, Overseas, Constitutional, County (Shrewsbury). *a*: The Lyth, Ellesmere, Shropshire. *t*: 39.

JEBENS, E. Henrietta, M.B., F.R.C.S. Cons Surg. *c.t*: Various journs. *a*: 50 Wimpole St, W.1. *t*: Welbeck 5824.

JEDLICKA, Benjamin, Ph.D. *b*: Novy Bydzov 1897. *e*: Univs of Prague & Paris. *m*: Ivana Grygarova. *d*: 1. Chief of Lit Sec Min of Ed & Culture. *n.a*: Lidove Noviny 1923—46, Rude Pravo '45—. *Publ*: Belles Lettres: Panenka z zurnalu; Smrt v srcadle; Pariz; Scientific Writings: Dobrovskeho Dejiny ve vyvoji ceske literarni historie. *c*: P.E.N. *a*: Praha XIX, Verdunska 25, Czechoslovakia. *T*: 70343.

JEFFCOATE, Thomas Norman Arthur, M.D., F.R.C.S.(Edin.), M.C.O.G. Medical. *c.t*: Lancet, B.M.J., etc. *a*: 38 Rodney St, L'pool 1. *t*: Royal 2090.

JEFFERIES, Cyril Robert. *b*: Colchester. *e*: Roy Gr Sch Colchester. *m*: Catharine Spencer Bloice. *s*: 1. *Publ*: Garrison Rhymes & Other Verses; Authors' Journalists' & Speakers' Ideas Chart; In A Moment System of Writing Newspaper Advertisements. *Ctr*: Various newsps & periodicals. *a*: Inglenook, Greenstead Rd, Colchester. *T*: 3890.

JEFFERIES, Herbert Cyril. *b*: Cirencester 1880. *e*: Cirencester G.S. *n.a*: Ed, Ross Gazette, '20—. *Rec*: Golf. R.A.F. in War. *a*: Mervyn Lodge, Ross-on-Wye, Herefordshire. *t*: 7.

JEFFERIES, Robert Frederick. *e*: Colchester Roy Gr Sch. *n.a*: Reporter Essex County Standard 1938—41 & '45—. *w.s*: 1941—45 R.N. *a*: c/o 24 High St, Halstead, Essex. *T*: 368.

JEFFERIES, Rev. W. H. *b*: Rodboro' 1863. *e*: Brit Sc. *m*: Helena Louisa Lydeard. *Publ*: The Age of Gold. *Rec*: Gardening. *c*: Pres Stroud F.C.C. *a*: The Gastrels, Rodboro', Stroud, Glos.

JEFFERSON, Horace, (Harold Philip Clunn). *b*: Southport 1879. *Publ*: The Face of London; The Face of Paris; London Rebuilt: Famous South Coast Resorts; An Analysis of Life; The Diary of a Governing Director. *c.t*: Times Literary Supplement, Brighton & Hove Herald. *s.s*: Topography. *Rec*: Cycling, walking. *c*: R.A.C. *a*: 69 Fleet St, E.C.4.

JEFFERSON, Rev. Selby. *b*: Gosforth 1866. *m*: Edith Evans. *s*: 1. *d*: 3. *Publ*: Some Churches and Churchmen in the Enchanted Isles; Adventure for Christ on Labrador; etc. *c.t*: New Outlook, Utd Chman. *a*: 49 Walmsley Blvd, Toronto, Ont. Canada.

JEFFERY, Clement, M.A. *b*: Edinburgh 1891. *e*: Leith Acad & Edin Univ. Manipulative Specialist. *Publ*: Achieving Fitness; Fit After Forty; Rheumatism: Its Causes, Prevention & Treatment. *Rec*: Walking. *a*: 12 Portman St, London, W.1, & Lyme Croft, Stoneygate Rd, Leicester. *T*: Welbeck 2661.

JEFFERY, Jeffery E. See Marston, Jeffery Eardley.

JEFFERY, Reginald Frank. *b*: Cambridge 1910. *e*: Cen Sch Camb. *s*: 1. *d*: 1. Rep staff specialising Sport '27—33, Camb Daily News & Weekly News Series, Newmarket Rep '33—44, Mang-Ed Newmarket Journal '45. *c*: Marlboro', Masonic, Newmarket. *a*: Bryony, Park Lane, Newmarket. *T*: 2426.

JEFFERY, Sydney. *b*: Warrington. *e*: Boteler Gr Sch. *m*: Blanche Ardern. *s*: 1. *d*: 2. Journalist, Dir Pharos Books Ltd. *n.a*: Warrington Examiner series of newsps (Asst-Ed) 1914—26, L'pool Dly Post & Echo '26. *Publ*: Desires & Adorations; various works on Merseyside history & literature. *w.s*: 1915—19. *a*: 46 Addingham Rd, Liverpool 18. *T*: Childwall 2526.

JEFFERYS, William Hamilton, A.B., A.M., M.D. *b*: Philadelphia 1871. *e*: Pennsylvania Univ, Greenwich Hosp, Lon Sc of Trop Med, etc. *m*: Ann Eliza Prophet. *s*: 1. *d*: 3. Surg, Author, Missny. *n.a*: Ed China Med Journ 1902—11. *Publ*: Hospital Dialogue in Shanghai & Pekinese Mandarin; The Diseases of China; Mystical Companionship of Jesus; Shuffling Coolie & Other Plays; The City Mission Idea; How Can We Know the Way?; Reasonable Faith; The Key to the Door of Divine Reality; etc. *c.t*: Med journ & Ch papers. *s.s*: Trop diseases, Chr mysticism. *Rec*: Music, fishing. Pres Amer Assoc of China. Hon Fell China Med Soc. Fell Col of Phys, Phila. *c*: Authors', Lon, Shanghai, Philadelphia, Art Alliance. *a*: Little Cranstoun, 1419 County Line Rd, Rosemount, Penn. *t*: Bryn Mawr 1302.

JEFFREY, George Rutherford, M.D., F.R.C.P.E., F.R.S.E. *b*: Jedburgh 1876. *e*: Edinburgh Acad, Univs of Glasgow, Edin & Vienna. *m*: Doris May Miskin. *s*: 1. Former Med Supt Bootham Park York. *Publ*: Common Symptoms of an Unsound Mind. *Ctr*: Various med journs. *s.s*: Nervous & Mental Diseases. *w.s*: 1914—18 R.A.M.C. (Capt). *a*: 20 Arden Rd, Finchley, London, N.3. *T*: Finchley 1057.

JEFFREY, Janet. *b*: Edin 1872. *e*: Priv Scs Edin & Paris, & Edin Univ. *Publ*: Two Little Frogs (illus colour, 1909); The Fame-Seeker & Other Poems; Martyrdom of Power (Mystic Allegory, '27, illus black & white). *c.t*: Glas Herald, Country Life. *Rec*: Music, lang. *c*: Scot Women's, Edin & Scot P.E.N. *a*: Glenairthrey, Upper Glen Rd, Bridge-of-Allan, Stirlingshire. *t*: 71.

JEFFREY, Rev. Russell Henry, M.A. *b*: Cheltenham 1867. *e*: Jesus Coll Oxford. Clerk in Holy Orders, Rector of Holdgate with Tugford. *Publ*: Village Sermons on Uncommon Texts; Village Sermons on some Strange Texts. *Rec*: Motoring. *a*: Holdgate Rectory, Much Wenlock, Salop. *T*: Ditton Priors 211.

JEFFREY, W., M.A. *e*: Glas Univ. *m*: Margaret W. J. Graham. *d*: 1. Journalist & Author. *n.a*: Ed Staff Glasgow Herald. *Publ*: Fantasia Written in an Industrial Town; Eagle of Coruisk; The Golden Stag; Mountain Songs; The Doom of Atlas; The Wise Men Come to Town; etc. *c.t*: Dublin Mag, Modern Scot, Adelphi, etc. War Service R.G.A. *Rec*: Mountaineering. *a*: 64 Terreglas Av, Glasgow.

JEFFREY-WADDELL, John, I.A., F.S.A. (Scot). *b*: Glasgow 1876. *e*: H.S. & Art Sc Glasgow. *m*: Jean Leadbetter Swan. *d*: 2. Architect. *Publ*: By Bothwell Banks; Rambles through Lanarkshire; " Greek " Thomson; Castles of Scotland; etc. *c.t*: Glas Herald, Scots Observer, Hamilton Advertiser & Architectural Press. *s.s*: Mediæval Archæology. *Rec* Sketching, etching. *c*: Automobile & Athenæum. *a*: 95 Bath St, Glasgow, & Caldergrove Hse, Hallside, Lanarks. *t*: Blantyre 80.

JEFFREYS, Harold, M.A.(Cantab), D.Sc.(Durham), F.R.S. *b*: Fatfield, Co Durham 1891. *e*: Rutherford Coll & Armstrong Coll Newcastle, St John's Coll Camb. *m*: Bertha Swirles. Plumian Prof of Astronomy. *Publ*: Methods of Mathematical Physics (with Mrs Jeffreys); The Earth; Theory of Probability; Earthquakes & Mountains; Scientific Influence; Operational Methods in Mathematical Physics. *Ctr*: Procs Royal Soc, Philosophical Mag. *s.s*: Astronomy & Geophysics. *a*: St John's Coll, Cambridge; 160 Huntingdon Rd, Cambridge. *T*: 56153.

JEFFREYS, Montagu Vaughan Castelman. M.A. *b*: Lon 1900. *e*: Wellington Col Berks, Hertford Col Oxf. Lect & Tutor Lon Univ Inst of Educ Southampton Row W.C.1. *Publ*: Play Production for Amateurs & Scs (with R. W. Stopford). *c.t*: Modern Churchman. *a*: 76 Westwood Rd, Southampton, & Aban Ct Hotel, Harrington Gdns, S.W.7. *t*: Kensington 2491.

JEFFREYS, S., F.C.A. *a*: 56 Carlton Hill, St John's Wood, N.W.8.

JEFFREYS, Dr. W. M. *a*: 8 Brookvale Rd, Southampton.

JEFFRIES, Leslie Gideon, F.R.S.A. *b*: Westcliffe 1906. *e*: Sec & Hgh Sch Dundee, External Univ & Coll. Cost Accountant & Industrial Administrator. *Ctr*: The Factory Manager, Machine Shop Mag, The Accountant. *s.s*: Cost Accountancy, Office & Factory Management & Administration. *Rec*: Sport, lit, music. *a*: 76 Clarendon Gdns, Wembley, Middlesex. *T*: Arnold 1747.

JEFFRIES, Norman Seckerson. *b*: Beckenham 1906. *e*: Malvern Coll. Journalist. *n.a*: Asst Picture-Ed Ev Standard 1929—34, Asst Picture-Ed '34 & Picture-Ed '35 Evening News. *a*: 12 Little Court, West Wickham, Kent.

JEFFRIES, Zay, B.Sc., D.Sc. *b*: Willow Lake, Sth Dakota 1888. *e*: Sth Dakota Sch of Mines, Harvard Univ. *m*: Frances Schrader. *d*: 2. Vice-Pres General Electric Co, Metallurgist & Gen-Mang Chemical Dept. *Publ*: In Collab : The Science of Metals; The Aluminium Industry; Business Ideals, Principles & Policies. *Ctr*: Kent's Mech Engineers Handbook, Ency Brit, Met & Chem Eng, Metals & Alloys, Wall Street Journ & other metallurgical journs. *s.s*: Metals. *Rec*: Golf. *a*: General Electric Co, 1 Plastics Ave, Pittsfield, Mass. *T*: 8223 Ext 289.

JEFFS, Harry. *b*: Warwick 1860. *e*: Elem Sc. *m*: Ada M. Fletcher. *s*: 2. *d*: 4. Journalist & Author. *n.a*: Ed Express & Star Wolverhampton '83–85, The Echo (Lon) Ed Staff '86–87, Christian World Ed Staff '87–1926, Ed Christian World Pulpit '87–1926. *Publ*: The Good New Times; The Art of Sermon Illustration; The Art of Exposition; Concerning Conscience (studies in Practical Ethics); Progressive Lay Preaching; Press, Preachers & Politicians (Reminiscences 1874–1932). *c.t*: Eng & Amer religious press. *s.s*: Lang (nine). Chevalier of Legion of Honour, France. *Rec*: Gardening. *a*: Sandhurst, Farningham, Kent. *t*: 176.

JEKYLL, Agnes, D.B.E., J.P. *b*: Largs. *e*: Priv. *m*: Sir Herbert Jekyll (dec). *s*: 1. *d*: 2. *Publ*: Kitchen Essays. *c.t*: Vogue, etc. Trav extensively. Lady of Justice Order of St John of Jerusalem. *a*: Munshead Hse, Godalming, Surrey. *t*: 4.

JEKYLL, GERTRUDE: garden designer, author; b. London, Eng., Nov., 1843; d. Capt. E. J. H. and Julia (Hammersley) J.; educ. privately; unmarried. AUTHOR: Wood and Garden, 1899; Home and Garden, 1900; Wall and Water Gardens, 1901; Lilies for English Gardens, 1901; Roses for English Gardens, 1902; Old West Surrey, 1904; Flower Decorations in the House, 1907; Color in the Flower Garden, 1908; Children and Gardens, 1908; Annuals and Biennials, 1918; Garden Ornament, 1918; Gardens for Small Country Houses (with Sir Lawrence Weaver); Old English Household Life, 1927. Contributor to many horticultural mags. and others. General character of writing: scientific horticulture. Trained for Art career for years in Paris, Italy, London; was for some yrs. an interior decorator, meantime studying floriculture and garden landscaping. Awarded Victoria Medal by Royal Hort. Soc.; also Veitchian Medal by same Soc.; also the George Robert White Medal of Honour by the Massachusetts Horticultural Soc. Relig. denom., Church of England. CLUB: Garden. HOME: Munstead Wood, Godaloning, Surrey, Eng.

JELF, C. R. *a*: Trapstile, Lustleigh, S. Devon.

JELF, Sir Ernest Arthur, Kt. *b*: London 1868. *e*: Haileybury & New Coll Oxf. *m*: Rose Frances Reeves. *s*: 2. *d*: 1. Retired Senior Master of Supreme Court & King's Remembrancer. *n.a*: Ed 3rd Edtn Ency of Laws of England 1938. *Publ*: The Wonderful Pagoda & other Children's Ballet Plays; Jill's Magic Island; Pope Pacificus; Where to find your Law. *Ctr*: Hibbert Journ, Cornhill Mag, Chambers's Journ, Law Times, Law Journ. *s.s*: Ballet Plays for Children. *Rec*: Arranging for production of the ballet plays. *c*: Athenæum. *a*: St Mary's Cottage, Waxwell Lane, Pinner, Middlesex. *T*: Pinner 431.

JELLETT, Henry. *b*: Aghinagh, Co. Cork, Ireland, 1872. *e*: Trinity Col Dublin. *m*: Mary Leader. *s*: 1. *d*: 1. Doctor of medicine. *Publ*: Short Practice of Midwifery; Short Practice of Gynæcology; Manual of Midwifery; Practice of Gynæcology; Causes & Prevention of Maternal Mortality. *c.t*: medical jnls. *s.s*: Gynæcology and obstetrics. *Rec*: Fishing, shooting. War Service '14—17. Consulting obstetrician to Health Dept of New Zealand. External examiner in midwifery and gynæcology to Royal Univ of Ireland, Manchester Univ, Univ of New Zealand. Ordre de la Couronne de la Belgique, Croix de Guerre Française. *c*: Univ Club, Dublin. *a*: Rosnalee, Fendalton Rd, Christchurch, New Zealand.

JELLEY, Harold. *b*: Wandsworth 1905. Asst Tech Ed. *n.a*: Tech staff Sir Isaac Pitman & Sons Ltd 1929 & Asst Tech Ed '33. *Publ*: Book of the Morris Minor; Book of the B.S.A. Three Wheeler; etc. *s.s* Motor & motor cycle instruction books *Rec*: Swimming, tennis. *a*: 29 Dalebury Rd, Wandsworth Common, S.W.17. *t*: Batt 1682.

Who Was Who Among English and European Authors

JELLICOE, Earl John Rushworth, G.C.B., O.M., G.C.V.O., LL.D., D.C.L. *b*: Southampton 1859. *e*: Prep Sc Rottingdean & H.M.S. Britannia. *m*: Florence Gwendoline Cayzer. *s*: 1. *d*: 5. R.N. Adml of the Fleet. *Publ*: The Grand Fleet 1914–16; The Crisis of the Naval War. *a*: 19 Princes Gdns, S.W.7, & St Laurence Hall, Ventnor, I.O.W. *t*: 143.

JELLICOE, Geoffrey Alan, F.R.I.B.A., M.T.P.I. *b*: London 1900. *e*: Cheltenham Coll. Architect. *Publ*: Italian Gardens of the Renaissance; Baroque Gardens of Austria; Garden Design & Decoration. *Ctr*: Archt Press. *s.s*: Gardens & Landscape Architecture. *a*: 12 Gower St, London, W.C.1. *T*: Museum 1783.

JELLINEK, Frank. *b*: London 1908. *e*: Repton & Oriel Coll Oxf. Writer. *Publ*: (Trans): November (by Gustave Flaubert); The Paris Commune; The Civil War in Spain; Outline of Mexican Music (trans). *s.s*: French, German & Spanish Trans, History of France in 19th Century, Latin-American & Spanish Politics & Economics. *a*: 96 Carlton Hill, London, N.W.8. *T*: Maida Vale 7853.

JENKINS, Arthur George, M.J.I. *b*: Lon 1902. *m*: Vera Winifred Mayes. Journalist. *n.a*: S. American Journ (Asst Ed 1927), Morning Post, Financial Sub Ed '28–, City Ed Saturday Review. *s.s*: Finance. *Rec*: Rugby. *a*: Palmerston Hse, Old Broad St, E.C.2.

JENKINS, Charles Evans, M.R.C.S., L.R.C.P. *b*: Dowlais, Glam 1890. *e*: Univ Coll Cardiff, London Hosp. Married. *s*: 1. *d*: 1. Pathologist to Manchester N. Hosp, formerly Pathological Asst Lond Hosp. *Ctr*: Journ Experimental Pathology, Journ Pathol & Bacteriol, Journ Hygiene, B.M.J., Brit Journ of Dermatology. *s.s*: Immunology. *a*: 8 St John St, Manchester 3. *T*: Bla 0444.

JENKINS, Rev. Claude, M.A., D.D., F.S.A. *Publ*: inc Cranmer's Collectiones de Divortio in Dibdin & Healey's English Church Law; (Ed) Index to Lambeth Act Books 1916–37; The Monastic Chronicler; Sir Thomas More; F. D. Maurice & the New Reformation; etc. *a*: Christ Church, Oxford.

JENKINS, Rev. David Erwyd, M.A., LittD. Secondary Schoolmaster (ret). *n.a*: Local mag 1896–1912, deciphering MSS '11–15. *Publ*: Bedd Gelert: Its Facts, Faeries & Folklore; Life of Thomas Charles of Bala (3 vols); Calvinistic Methodists Holy Orders; The Place of Humour in Practical Religion; The Life of John Calvin (in Welsh); etc. *c.t*: Various n/ps & periodicals. *a*: Gladstone Villas, Denbigh.

JENKINS, E. F. Hon Sec I.J. *a*: Park Hotel, Hof St, Cape Town, S.A.

JENKINS, Edwin A. *b*: Wallingford. *e*: County G.S. Berks & Priv. *m*: Edith S. Greenwood. Author & Journalist. *n.a*: Political Corr Daily Mirror 1904–32, Political Corr Sun Pictorial since inception. Chrm Parliamentary Lobby Journalists '29–30. *Publ*: From Foundry to Foreign Office (the Authoritative Biog of the Right Hon. Arthur Henderson, M.P., the Chrm of the World Disarmament Conference, '33). *c.t*: Lon & Prov Daily & Weekly n/ps. *s.s*: Politics. *Rec*: Theatre. *c*: Nat Lib. *a*: 61 Thornlaw Rd, W. Norwood, S.E.27. *t*: Streatham 0882.

JENKINS, George Henry, F.R.Econ.S. *b*: Birkenhead 1903. *m*: Jean Stoneham. Journalist, F.J.I. *n.a*: Night-Ed Trinidad Guardian '38–, formerly Asst-Ed Lever Bros Tech Journ '19–25, Freelance '25–26, Singapore Free Press Reporter & Sub-Ed '26–30, Bristol Ev Times '31, L'pool Chamber of Commerce '32 & Freelance '32–38. *Ctr*: Chemist & Druggist, Motor Transport, Dly Mail, N.Y. Times, etc. *s.s*: Shipping, Motor Transport, West Indies. *Rec*: Tennis.

a: c/o Trinidad Guardian, 22 St Vincent St, Port of Spain, Trinidad, B.W.I. *T*: Port of Spain, Trinidad 8871 or 6802.

JENKINS, Gilbert. *b*: Guildford 1913. *e*: Roy G.S. Guildford. Reporter. *n.a*: Surrey Times 1930–. *a*: 3 Cheselden Rd, Guildford.

JENKINS, Hugh Charles. *b*: Forest Gate, Essex 1891. *e*: Whitehall Sch Lond, Victoria Univ Coll N.Z. *m*: Olive Martin. *s*: 2. Journalist. *n.a*: N.Z. Corr Christian Sci Monitor, Meat Trades Journ Lond, Ed Mercantile Gazette of N.Z. 1919–21, Founder N.Z. Law Journ '25. Ed-Man '27, Ldr Writer Dominion '28, Ed Wanganui Chronicle '29–. *Publ*: Shipping Competition in the Pacific. *Ctr*: Bankers' Mag, Christian Sci Monitor, Insurance & Banking Record. *s.s*: Banking, commerce, Public Finance, Internat Politics. *Rec*: Golf, painting. *a*: 18 Campbell St, Wanganui, New Zealand.

JENKINS, Rev. Hywel Oliver, D.Phil.(Oxon)., D.Sc. (Wales). *b*: Nelson, Glam 1906. *e*: Univ Coll Aberystwyth, Jesus Coll Oxf, California Inst Tech Pasadena U.S.A., St Michæl's Theol Coll Llandaff. *m*: Mary Patricia Cheetham. *s*: 1. Vicar of Bradley Bilston Staffs. *Ctr*: Journ of Chem Soc, Journ of American Chem Soc, Trans of Faraday Soc, Nature, The Guardian. *s.s*: Chemistry, Physics, Theology, Philosophy. *Rec*: Cricket, tennis. *a*: St Martin's Vicarage, Bradley Bilston, Staffs. *T*: Bilston 42160.

JENKINS, Rev. Joseph. *b*: Pontrhydygroes 1887. *e*: Ammanford Gr Sch, Handsworth Coll Birm. *m*: May Williams. *s*: 1. *d*: 1. Ed of Y Winllan. *Publ*: Robin Y Pysgotwr; Straeon Athro; Bechgyn Y Bryniau; Melys A Chwerw; Cyflog Pechod; Dal Y Lleidr; Dai Y Dderwen; Ianto; Antur Gwas Y Wern; Helynt Coed Y Berw; Antur Ben a Phil; Meic. *Ctr*: Y Brython, Y Cymro, Yr Eurgrawn. *Rec*: Writing, angling. *a*: Llys Myfyr, Cardiff Rd, Pwlhelli.

JENKINS, Rev. Wilfrid John, M.A. *b*: Chester 1897. *e*: City & County Chester, Didsbury Coll Manch & Manch Univ, Bristol Univ (Research). *m*: Margaret Watson. *s*: 1. *d*: 1. Meth Min, Bath City Councillor, Lect on Social Internat Subjects. *n.a*: Ed Our Hospital. *Publ*: William Wilberforce, a Champion of Freedom; Bath's Proprietary Chapels; *Ctr*: Religious periodicals, etc. *s.s*: Biog & Homiletics. *Rec*: Reading. *w.s*: World War I R.N. *a*: Westmead, 35 Englishcombe Lane, Bath. *T*: 4527.

JENKINSON, Rev. Edward James. *b*: Workington 1895. *e*: Workington Sec & Didsbury Col M/C. *m*: Ruth Earl Merrill, M.A. Meth Min. *Publ*: Unwritten Sayings of Jesus; The Gates of Doom; Boys of the Brigade; Holding the Frontier; etc. *c.t*: Lon Quart Review, Meth Times, Statesman (Calcutta), Methodist, etc. *s.s*: Agrapha, papyrology, juvenile stories, etc. Learned to fly at Hendon 1914 on Wright Biplane. Missionary in India. War Service '15—18. *Rec*: Boys' Brigade, Girls' Life Brigade, photography. *a*: Astlea, Cheviot View, Ponteland, Newcastle-on-Tyne.

JENKS, Edward. *b*: Stockwell 1861. *e*: Dulwich Col, King's Col Cam. *m*: Dorothy Mary Forwood. *s*: 2. *d*: 1. Writer & Examiner. *n.a*: Press Ed Cam Review 1884–1905, Ed Independent Review '03–05. *Publ*: History of the Australasian Colonies ('12 3rd edn); Outline of English Local Government (7th edn); Law & Politics in the Middle Ages (3rd edn); Short History of Politics (1897), re-issued as The State & The Nation; Digest of English Civil Law (ed & pt author, '21 2nd edn); Husband & Wife in the Law; The Book of English Law (3rd edn); The New Jurisprudence ('33). *c.t*: Contemp, Quart Review, Hibbert Journ, Law Quart Review, Journ of Comparative Legislation, etc. *s.s*: Hist, jurisprudence & pol sci. Professorial Chrs at Melbourne, L'pool &

Lon Univs & Oxf. Chf Educ Officer of Law Soc 22 y. Part founder (Pres '19-20) Soc of Public Teachers of Law. Lecturer on Imp Constitutional Law at Imp Defence Col '27-29. Doct of Paris Univ. *Rec*: Music, chess. *c*: Roy Soc, Eng Speaking Union, etc. *a*: Bishop's Tawton, Barnstaple, N. Devon. *t*: 9301.

JENNER, Katharine Lee. *b*: Hayle. *e*: Priv. *m*: Henry Jenner. *d*: 1. Novelist, Writer on Art, Reviewer, Poet. *Publ*: A Western Wildflower (1882); An Imperfect Gentleman ('88); Love or Money ('91); When Fortune Frowns ('95); etc (all novels); Our Lady in Art (1907); Christian Symbolism ('10); etc. Poetry—Songs of the Stars & the Sea ('26). *c.t*: St James's Gazette, The Queen, Black & White, etc. *s.s*: Religious art. Made a Bard at Eisteddfod, Rhyle '04. *Rec*: Painting, gardening. *a*: Bospowes, Hayle, Cornwall.

JENNINGS, Miss Audrey. Author. *Publ*: Storied Urn. Asst Sec Soc of Genealogists. *a*: 40 Nottingham Pl, W.1.

JENNINGS, Elsie Winifred. *b*: Lon 1901. *e*: Clapham County Sec Sc. *m*: Ferdinand Erricker Grenfell. *d*: 1. Editor. *n. a*: Sub Ed Lady's Companion '23—25, Ed '25—. Ed Lady's Companion Knitting Series, & Household Series. Leach's New Cookery Series, Leach's Wonder Value Book of Mothercraft, Married Life & Motherhood. *s.s*: Knitting, mothercraft. *Rec*: Gardening yachting. *c*: I.J., Arts Theatre. *a*: 28 Priory Court, Mazenod Ave, N.W.6. *t*: Maida Vale 4420.

JENNINGS, Francis James Hugh. *n.a*: Man Ed Middlesex Chronicle. *a*: 136 High Sf, Hounslow. *T*: 0016.

JENNINGS, Rev. Frank Leonard. *b*: Grays, Essex 1890. *e*: Palmers Sc Grays, Paton Col Nott'm & St John's Hall, Lon. *m*: Georgina Sewell. *Publ*: In London's Shadows; Tramping With Tramps; The Traveller's Way. *c.t*: Lon dailies, John Bull, Answers, Everybody's Weekly, Sunday Companion, etc. *s.s*: Tramp life, casual wards. *Rec*: Bowls. *a*: The Manse, Derngate, Northampton.

JENNINGS, Gertrude. Dramatist. *Publ*: (plays) The Young Person in Pink; Isabel Edward & Anne; Love Among the Paint Pots; Between the Soup & the Savoury; The Rest Cure; Waiting for the Bus; Five Birds in a Cage; Family Affairs; Happy as a King; In the Fog; etc; (Pantomimes) Whiskers & Co; Sleeping Beauty; Aladdin's Cave. *Rec*: Gardening.

JENNINGS, Harry. *b*: Bradford. *m*: Mary Alice Northrop. *s*: 1. Sporting Journalist & Boxing Referee. *n.a*: F/L Sporting Journalist 22 y. *c.t*: Sun Express, Daily Herald, Sporting Life, Sporting Chronicle, Leeds Mercury. *s.s*: Boxing, Rugby Union football & athletics. Amateur athlete runner & walker. Leading boxing referee. *a*: 7 Legrams Av, Bradford, Yorks. *t*: 7578.

JENNINGS, Herbert Spencer, B.S.(Michigan), A.M., Ph.D.(Harvard), Hon.LL.D.(Clark), Hon.D.Sc.(Michigan, Pennsylvania, Oberlin Col). *b*: Tonica, Illinois, 1868. *e*: Univs of Michigan, Harvard & Jena. *m*: Mary Louise Burridge. *s*: 1. Prof of zoology, Johns Hopkins Univ. *n.a*: Mem Ed Board, Jnl of Experimental Zoology, Genetics, Biological Bulletin, Human Biology. *Publ*: Anatomy of the Cat (with Jacob Righard); Behaviour of the Lower Organisms; Life and Death, Heredity and Evolution in Unicellular Organisms; Prometheus, or Biology and the Advancement of Man; Genetics of the Protozoa; The Biological Basis of Human Nature; The Universe and Life. *c.t*: American Naturalist, Jnl of Experimental Zoology, Genetics, Biological Bulletin, Forum, Yale Review. *s.s*: Biology, heredity, variation and evolution, animal behaviour. Visiting prof at Keio Univ, Tokyo, Japan, '31—32. *c*: National Academy of Sciences, American Philosophical Soc, Trustee of Marine Biological Laboratory at Woods Hole, U.S.A. *a*: Johns Hopkins University, Baltimore, Md., U.S.A., and 505 Hawthorne Rd, Baltimore, Md., U.S.A. *t*: University 1258.

JENNINGS, Dr. J. F. *a*: 13 John St, Berkeley Sq, W.1.

JENNINGS, William Ivor, M.A., LL.B., Litt.D.(Cantab), LL.D.(Lond). *b*: Bristol 1903. *e*: Queen Elizabeth's Hosp, Bristol Gr Sch, St Catherine's Coll Camb. *m*: Helena Konsalik. *d*: 2. Vice-Chanc University of Ceylon. *n.a*: Ed Local Government Chronicle '30—40. *Publ*: Cabinet Government; Parliament; British Constitution; The Law & The Constitution; Principles of Local Government; A Federation for Western Europe; Constitutional Laws of the British Empire; etc. *Ctr*: Manch Guardian, Dly Telegraph, Ceylon Dly News, Learned periodicals. *s.s*: British Constitution, British Empire, Higher Education in Colonies, Ceylon. *Rec*: Books. *a*: University of Ceylon, Colombo, Ceylon. *T*: 8349.

JENSEN, Aage Martin Jacob Charles. *b*: Copenhagen 1897. *e*: Univ of Copenhagen. Ch Librarian Pub Lib of Christianshavn. *Publ*: Rococo Cabale; Frierleg; Borgmesteren Myrdet. *Ctr*: Okonomi og Politik, Ekstrabladet, Bogens Verden. *s.s*: Modern History & Politics After 1914. *a*: Dronningensgade 55, Copenhagen K, Denmark. *T*: Su 4136.

JENSEN, Harold Rupert, B.Sc, M.Sc, F.I.C. Industrial Sci Research. *Publ*: Evans Analytical Notes (1910-14) & Chemistry Manufacture of Cocoa & Chocolate Confectionery. *c.t*: Analyst, Pharm Journ, Chem & Druggist, New Photog, etc. *Rec*: Cycling. *a*: 27 North Drive, Wallasey, Cheshire.

JENSEN, Ove Jorgen Riisberg. *b*: Sindal, Denmark 1911. *e*: Copenhagen Tech Inst. *m*: Jytte Gram. *d*: 1. Manager. *Publ*: Nattesange; Arks; Hjertegroes; etc. *s.s*: Lyrical Poetry. *c*: Danish Authors. *a*: Store Vildmose, Pr Sulsted St, Denmark. *T*: Nr Halne 15.

JEPHCOTT, H. E. Sec Wolverhampton Br N.U.J. *a*: The Dingle, 19 Birches Barn Av, Wolverhampton.

JEPSON, Edgar, B.A. *e*: Balliol Col Oxf. Author. *Publ*: The Admirable Tinker; The Lady Noggs; Pollyooly; The Lady Noggs Assists; The House on the Mall; etc. Mem Counc Soc of Authors.

JEPSON, Rowland Walter. *b*: Shrewsbury 1888. *e*: Shrewsbury Sch & Magdalene Coll Camb. *m*: Margaret Brace. *s*: 2. *d*: 2. Headmaster Mercers' Sch 1929—46 & Gresham Prof of Rhetoric '46—47. *Publ*: English Exercises; Morris's Life & Death of Jason (ed); The Writer's Craft; First Steps in Writing English; Further Steps in Writing English; New Guide to Précis Writing; Clear Thinking; How to Think Clearly; Teach Yourself to Think; Teach Yourself to Express Yourself. *s.s*: English Language & Literature. *Rec*: Gardening. *a*: The Elms, Iron Bridge, Shropshire. *T*: Iron Bridge 2152.

JEPSON, Selwyn. *Publ*: inc Man Running; Keep Murder Quiet; The Qualified Adventurer; etc; as well as many screen plays. *a*: Cedar Hse, Liss, Hants.

JEPSON, Stanley. Hon Sec I.J. *a*: c/o Times of India, Bombay, India.

JERABEK, Castmir, LL.D. *b*: Litomysl 1893. *e*: Univ of Prague. *m*: Zdenka J. *s*: 1. *d*: 1. Municipal Official at Brno. *Publ*: World in Flames; Diabolic Paradise; Legend of Lost Ages (3 vols); Double Testimony; In the Fangs of Antichrist; The Green Twig; Annals of Czech Soul (2 vols); European Interlude. *Rec*: Tourism. *c*: P.E.N. (Prague). *a*: Brno, Botanicka 5, Czechoslovakia.

JEROME, Helen Susan. *b*: London 1886. *e*: Private. *m*: Frederick James Jerome. *s*: 1. Domestic Science Teacher, Polytechnic, Regent St. *Publ*: Sweetmaking for All; Concerning Cakemaking. *c.t*: The Schoolwoman. Yorks Evening Post. *s.s*: Cookery & dietetics. First Class Diplomas Domestic Science, Lon, Cordon Bleu, Institut de Cuisine, Paris. *Rec*: Gardening. *c*: Overseas League, mem Cookery Assoc, Assoc Teachers Domestic Science, etc. *a*: Longfield, London Rd, Knebworth, Herts.
JERROLD, Douglas. *b*: 1893. *e*: Westminster & New Col Oxf. *m*: Eleanor Arnold. Author. *n.a*: Ed English Review & Dir Eyre & Spottiswoode Ltd & English Review (1911) Ltd. *Publ*: The Royal Naval Division; The Truth about Quex (novel); Storm over Europe (novel); The Lie about the War; England; etc. *c.t*: English Review, Criterion, Sphere & daily press, etc. *s.s*: Polit, lit, hist. *c*: Athenæum, Carlton. *a*: Blanchard Hse, Chislehurst. *t*: 518.

JERRIM, E. R. *a*: The Nook, Hindon, Salisbury, Wilts.

JERROLD, Ianthe. *b*: London 1897. *m*: George Menges. Novelist. *Publ*: Young Richard Mast; Hangingstone Farm; Uncle Sabine; The Studio Crime; Dead Man's Quarry; Summer's Day; Seaside Comedy; The Dogs do Bark; Life Begins Early; Rainbows in the Morning; The Stones Await Us; (by "Geraldine Bridgman") Let Him Lie. *Rec*: Gardening, museums. *a*: 3 Pitt St, London, W.8. *T*: Western 7069.

JERSEY, Dowager Countess of (Margaret Elizabeth), D.B.E., S.P. *b*: Stoneleigh Abbey 1849. *e*: Priv. *m*: 7th Earl of Jersey. *s*: 2. *d*: 4. *Publ*: Hymns for Little Children; John Alexander & the Little Man; Fifty-one Years of Victorian Life; etc. *c.t*: Nineteenth Century, Nat Review. Pres Ladies Grand Counc Primrose League. Vice-Pres Victoria League. Mem Govg Body Charterhouse Sc. *c*: Ladies' Empire. *a*: 18 Montagu Sq, W.1.

JERVIS, Charles Eliot. *b*: L'pool 1907. *e*: Bd Sc L'pool. *m*: Ethel Braithwaite. Dramatic Critic. *n.a*: Croydon Times Dramatic Critic 1929, formerly on editorial staffs of Westmorland Gazette '24-29 & L'pool Courier '22-24. *s.s*: Dram crit. *Rec*: golf, tennis. Lect on drama to local socs, sometimes adjudicator for drama festivals. *c*: Croydon Constitutional, M.I.J. *a*: 10 Glen Gardens, Duppas Hill Rd, Croydon, Sy.

JERVOISE, Edwyn, A.M.I.C.E. *b*: Weymouth, Dorset 1884. *e*: Priv & U.C.L. *m*: Lettice Mary Williams. Eng. *n.a*: Sec for Bridges to the Soc for the Protection of Ancient Bldgs. *Publ*: Ancient Bridges of the South of England (1930); Ancient Bridges of the North of England; Ancient Bridges of Mid & Eastern England ('32). *c.t*: Architects Journs, Architectural Design & Construction, etc. Has made a survey of ancient bridges of Eng & Wales on behalf of S.P.A.B. *c*: Assoc Mem I.C.E. *a*: 100a Philbeach Gdns, S.W.5. *t*: Frobisher 1710.

JERWOOD, Bernard Ellery, M.A., M.D., B.Ch, M.R.C.S., L.R.C.P. *c.t*: B.M.J. *a*: 18 Bromley Rd, St Anne's-on-Sea. *t*: 751.

JESPERSEN, JENS OTTO HARRY: university professor; b. Randers, Denmark, July 16, 1860; s. Jens Bloch and Sophie Caroline (Bentzien) J.; educ. Frederiksborg (Danmark), Univ. of Copenhagen. DEGREES: Ph.D. (Copenhagen), (Hon.) Litt.D. (Columbia, U.S. A.), LL.D. (St. Andrews, Scotland), Ph.D. (Sorbonne, Paris); m. Ane Marie Djoerup, Apr. 13, 1897. AUTHOR: Articulations of Speech Sounds, 1889; Studies over engelske Kasus, 1891; Progress in Language, 1894; Fonetik (in Danish), 1897 (German edits. 1904 and later); How to Teach a Foreign Language, 1903; Growth and Structure of the English Language, 1905; Modern English Grammar on Historical Principles, vol. I 1909, vol. II 1914, vol. III, 1928; Language, its Nature, Development and Origin, 1922; The Philosophy of Grammar, 1924; Mankind, Nation and Individual, 1925; An International Language, 1928; Novial Lexike, 1930. General character of writing: scientific, text books. Corr. Fellow Brit. Academy; mem. of the Academies of Copenhagen, Oslo, Lund, Helsingfors, Ghent, Prague, Amsterdam. HOME: 119 Ermelund, Gentofte, Copenhagen, Denmark.

JESSE, F. Tennyson, F.R.S.L. (See Mrs. Harwood, H. M.) Journalist & Author, F.R.Lit.S. *Publ*: Tom Fool; Many Latitudes; Moonraker; Secret Bread; The White Riband; The Lacquer Lady; A Pin to See the Peepshow; The Saga of the Sam Demetrio; Story of Burma; etc. *Ctr*: Times Lit Supp, Eng Rev, Manch Guardian, etc. *a*: c/o A. M. Heath & Co, Ltd, Princes Hse, 39 Jermyn St, London, W.1.

JESSE, Florence Louise. *b*: Cardiff 1877. Teaching. *Publ*: Motherland; Babyland Abroad; Trips Abroad; Literary Readers I & II; Lilts & Lyrics for the Little Ones (7 series); Individual Reading Scheme; Nature Stories; etc. *s.s*: Music. *a*: 26 Westbourne Rd, Penarth, Glam. *t*: 113.

JESSE, WILLIAM: educationalist; b. Ingatestone, Essex, Eng., Sept. 7, 1870; s. William and Florence Emily Sophia (Prescott) J.; educ. Hereford Cathedral Sch. (Eng.) and Selwyn College, Cambridge. DEGREE: M.A.; m. Grace Grant Cameron, Aug. 28, 1894. AUTHOR: List of Birds of Lucknow Civil Division (pub. in "Ibis"). Contributor to Contemporary Rev., Round Table and other mags.; Corr. Times (Bombay, India) and of Indian Daily Telegraph. General character of writing: ornithological, political. Relig. denom., Church of England. CLUBS: Athenaeum (London), Wheler (Meerut, Ind.), Chuttar Munzil (Lucknow, Ind.), Rift Valley Sports (Nakuru, Kenya). OFFICE: Kenton College, Kijabe, Kenya. HOME: Greycote, Nakuru, Kenya, East Africa.

JESSOP, C. H. *a*: Eng Dept, Boots' Pure Drug Store, Island St, Nottingham.

JESSOP, Charles Percy Vincent. *b*: Lincoln 1907. *e*: Lincoln Munic Tech Sc. Reporter. *n.a*: Lincolnshire Forward '25-28, Lincolnshire Chronicle & Leader '28-31, Derbyshire Times '32. *c.t*: News & Trade Publ's. *a*: 15 Oakfield St, Lincoln.

JESSOP, Joseph Chasser, M.A., Ph.D., F.R.Hist.S. *b*: Perth 1892. *e*: Montrose Acad & St Andrews Univ. *m*: Ida Hallsey Bates. *d*: 2. Headmaster. *Publ*: Education in Angus From Original & Contemporary Sources; Idiomatic Expressions in English. *Ctr*: Newspapers & Educ Journs. *s.s*: Eng Lit & Hist. *Rec*: Golf. *c*: Moray Golf, Montrose Victoria Golf, etc. *a*: Seaholme, Lossiemouth. *T*: 3029.

JESSOP, Thomas Edmund, O.B.E., M.C., M.A., B.Litt. *b*: Huddersfield 1896. *e*: Leeds & Oxf Univ. *m*: Dora Anne Nugent Stewart. Prof Philosophy & Psychology, Fell Brit Psychol Soc, Dir S.C.M. Press. *Publ*: The Works of George Berkeley; Bibliography of George Berkeley; Bibliography of David Hume & of Scottish

Philosophy; The Treaty of Versailles; Science & the Spiritual; Law & Love; Effective Religion; Education & Evangelism; The Individual in Society; Reasonable Living. *Ctr*: Mind, Philosophy, Proceedings of the Aristotleian Society. *s.s*: Philosophy, Psychology, Religion, Internat Affairs. *Rec*: Gardening, travel. *w.s*: World War I (twice wounded). *a*: University College, Hull. *T*: 7753.

JESSOP, William John Edward, M.D., M.Sc., D.P.H., F.R.I.C., F.R.C.P.I. *b*: Ireland 1902. *e*: Mountjoy Sch Dublin, Trin Coll Dublin. *m*: Kathleen Anna Condill. *s*: 1. *d*: 3. Prof of Physiology Roy Coll of Surgs in Ireland. *Ctr*: B.M.J., Irish Journ of Med Science, Irish Hosp Year Book, Irish Dental Journ. *s.s*: Physiology & Biochemistry. *Rec*: Tennis, gardening. *c*: Univ (Dublin), Dublin Biological, etc. *a*: 1 Hillside Drive, Castle Park, Rathfarnham, Dublin. Eire. *T*: Dublin 95685.

JEVONS, Herbert Stanley. *b*: Manchester 1875. *e*: Giggleswick Sch, Univ Coll Lond, Trinity Coll Camb, Heidelberg Univ. *m*: Alice Beardsell. *s*: 1. *d*: 1. Adviser to Ethiopian Legation in Lond, formerly Prof Econ Cardiff, Allahabad & Rangoon. *Publ*: Economic Equality in the Co-operative Commonwealth; British Coal Trade; Essays in Economics; etc. *c*: United Univ. *a*: 95 Raglan Court, Wembley, Middlesex. *T*: Wembley 4527.

JEWELL, Norman Parsons, O.B.E., M.C. *b*: Larne, Co Antrim 1885. *e*: St Andrew's Coll Dublin, Trin Coll Dublin. *m*: Sydney E. Auchinleck. *s*: 2. *d*: 2. Surgeon to Harrow Hosp. *Publ*: Handbook of Tropical Fevers. *Ctr*: B.M.J., Journ of Trop Med, Kenya Med Journ. *s.s*: Surgery. *Rec*: Tennis, photography. *w.s*: 1914—18. *a*: Norrington, Pinner Rd, Pinner. *T*: 1528.

JEWESBURY, Reginald C., M.A., D.M.(Oxon), F.R.C.P.(Lon). Cons Physician. *Publ*: Mothercraft— Antenatal & Postnatal. *c.t*: Med Press. *a*: 5 Wimpole St, Cavendish Sq, W.1. *t*: Langham 4160.

JEWSBURY, David Philip Haydon. F.R.S.A., A.R.P.S. *b*: Solihull 1913. *e*: Priv. Pictorial Photographer & Internat Exhibitor (Amat). *Publ*: The Story of Solihull Church. *s.s*: Photography, Collecting Old Historical Books, Maps, etc esp of Warwickshire. *c*: Photographic Soc of America, Club Internat de Photographie. *a*: 44 George Rd, Solihull, Birmingham. *T*: Solihull 0566.

JEX-BLAKE, Miss H., M.A. Headmistress 10 y, Princ Lady Margaret Hall, Oxf, 12 y. *a*: 4 Airlie Gdns, Campden Hill Rd, W.8.

JEZIC, Slavko (Edward). *b*: Dubrava, Croatia 1895. *e*: Univ of Vienna, & Paris. *m*: Vishnya Petricevic. *s*: 2. Professor (Modern Languages). *Publ*: Brak Male Ra; Somnia Vitae; History of French Literature until the end of the Classical Period; Life and works of F. K. Frankopan (A study of Croatian Literature); Anthology & Documents of the Croatian Illyrian Movement; First Croatian Novelists after the Illyrian Movement; Choice of French Poets with introduction and Notes; Critical Editions of Croatian Writers; Novak, Senoa, etc. *c.t*: Vijenac, Savremenik, Hrvatska Revija, Obzor, Revue de Litterature Comparée. Ed Knjizevni Zivot (The Literary Life). *s.s*: Literature, essays. *Rec*: Travelling, bibliophily, translations of French, German & Italian into Croatian. *c*: P.E.N., Zagreb. *a*: Marulicev Trg 2/III, Zagreb, Yugoslavia.

JHA, Amaranatha, M.A., Hon.D.Litt., F.R.S.L. *b*: Darbhanga 1897. *e*: Govt Hgh Sch & Muir Central Coll Allahabad. *m*: Satyabhama(dec'd). V-Chanc Allahabad Univ 1938—47, Pres All-India Educ Fed & Adult Educ Assoc, etc, Mem Prep Sect U.N.E.S.C.O. *n.a*: Ed Allahabad Univ Mag '17—38. *Publ*: Shakespearean Comedy; Literary Studies; Ocasional Essays & Addresses; Selected Essays of Frederic Harrison; Selections from the Writings of John Morley; Padga Parang; etc. *Ctr*: English & Sanskrit Literature, Modern Hindi, Urdu & Bengali Poetry, Military Training. *Rec*: Golf & tennis. *c*: Poetry (Allahabad), Allahabad Gymkana, Calcutta South. *a*: Maya, Georgetown, Allahabad, India. *T*: 275.

JHAVERI, Mansukhlal Maganlal, M.A. *b*: Jamnagar 1907. *e*: Bombay Univ. *m*: Hasmukhgauri. *s*: 1. *d*: 4. Asst Prof of Gujarati St Xavier's Coll Bombay. *n.a*: Ed Sanskar & Madhvi Annuals '46—47. *Publ*: (Poems) Aradhana; Abhisar; Phooldol. Thoda Vivechanlekho; Abhijnana Shakuntala of Kalidas (trans). *Ctr*: Sanskriti, Manasi, etc. *s.s*: Modern Gujarati Poetry, Principles of Criticism. *Rec*: Reading, walking. *a*: 1/7 Samant Block, Cama Rd, Andheri, Bombay, India.

JILLA, Ardeshir Dadabhei. Med Pract. *c.t*: B.M.J., Bombay Parsee, etc. *a*: 9 Norton Folgate, E.1.

JILLETT, John William Leslie, B.A. *b*: Lower Hutt, New Zealand 1902. *e*: New Plymouth Boys' Hgh Sch, Auckland Univ Coll. *m*: Eva Amelia Barton. *s*: 1. *d*: 1. Journalist. *a*: Ed Ev Star Dunedin N.Z. '47—, Taranaki Dly News N.Z. '20—26, New Zealand Herald, Auckland '26—35, Argus Melbourne '35—38, Sydney Morning Herald '38—40 & '45—47, Courier-Mail Brisbane '40—42. *Publ*: Moresby's Few. *Rec*: Tennis. *c*: Univ & Otago Officers Dunedin. *w.s*: R.A.A.F. 1942—45. *a*: c/o Evening Star, Dunedin, N.Z. *T*: 11745.

JIRKO, Milos, D.Phil. *b*: Nemetice 1900. *m*: Karia Kohnova. *s*: 1. Deputy-Man Central Lib City of Prague. *Publ*: Vezen u okna; a prece; Zraje reva Cesta; Znici svet; K stare vlajce; Duben (Lyrics) Vylloupene milovani; Vrazdici pianola (novels). Travels, Essays, etc. *Ctr*: Svobodne slovo, Svobodne noviny. *Rec*: Gardening, travelling. *c*: Narodne & Umelecka beseda Prague, P.E.N. *w.s*: Czech War Cross; Mil Med 1st Class. *a*: Praha XVI, Havlickova 1. *T*: 46148.

JOACHIM, Harold Henry, F.B.A., HonLL.D.(St And). *b*: Lon 1868. *e*: Elstree, Harrow & Balliol. *m*: Elisabeth Joachim. *s*: 1. *d*: 2. Wykeham Prof of Logic in Oxf Univ. Hon Fell Merton Col Oxf. *Publ*: A Study of the Ethics of Spinoza (1901); The Nature of Truth ('06); Aristotle on Coming-to-be & Passing-away; etc. *c.t*: Journal of Philology, Mind, Philosophical Review, etc. *s.s*: Hist, philos. Fell New Col '19—. *Rec*: Violin, gardening. *a*: 11 Rawlinson Rd, Oxf.

JOAD, Cyril Edwin Mitchinson, M.A. *b*: Burnham 1891. *e*: Blundell's Sch & Balliol Coll Oxf. Hd of Dept of of Philos Birkbeck Coll, London 1930—. *Publ*: Introduction to Modern Philosophy; Philosophical Aspects of Modern Science; Guide to Modern Thought; Counter-Attack from the East; The Present & Future of Religion; A Rambler's Charter or the Future of the Countryside; Liberty To-day; Return to Philosophy; God & Evil; Guide to the Philosophy of Morals & Politics; Philosophy; The Adventures of the Young Soldier in Search of the Better World; The Untutored Townman's Invasion of the Country; Decadence; Philosophical Enquiry; etc. *Ctr*: New Statesman, etc. *s.s*: Philosophy, Psychical Research. *Rec*: Hockey, tennis, riding. *c*: Reform. *a*: 4 East Heath Rd, Hampstead, London, N.W.3. *T*: 6128, & Oakshott Farm, Hawkley, Liss, Hants.

JOAG, Ramachandra Shripad, M.A. *b*: Gadj,-Hinglaj Kolhapur State 1903. *e*: Bombay Univ. *m*: Maina Oka. *s*: 1. *d*: 3. Prof of Marathi & Sanskrit Fergusson Coll Poona, Exec Mem Maharashtra Lit Conf. *n.a*: Ed Maharashtra Sahitya Patrika '43—47. *Publ*:

A Book on Poetics; Æsthetics Applied to Literary Criticism; History of Modern Marathi Poetry; Keshavasuta, Kavyadarshana (study of a Modern Poet); Short Survey of Classical Sanskrit Poetry. *Ctr*: Sameekshaka, Abhiruchi, Satyakatha, etc. *s.s*: Criticism, esp Poetry. *Rec*: Tennis, swimming. *a*: Joag Bungalow, Municipal Colony, Poona 4, Bombay Province, India.

JOBSON, ALEX(ANDER) Brigadier General: Actuary and Chartered Accountant, financial critic; b. Clunes, Victoria, N.S.W., April, 1875; s. Christopher and Elizabeth (Cameron) J.; educ. public and private schls.; m. Madaline Ruth McFarland, Sept., 1905. AUTHOR: Jobson's Digest Year Book of Public Companies. Editor: Jobson's Investment Digest of Australia and New Zealand. Contributor to Daily Mail (Brisbane). General character of writing: financial. Served with Australian Imperial Forces, 1916-17; commanded 9th Inf. Brigade, A.I.F.; awarded D.S.O. Relig. denom., Presbyterian. CLUBS: Union, Royal Sydney Golf. OFFICE: 19 O'Connell St. HOME: 353 New South Head Road, Double Bay, Sydney, N. S. W.

JOBSON, Alexander Jeffreys. *b*: Sydney, N.S.W. 1906. *e*: Cranbrook Sc Sydney. *m*: Muriel Brenda Mummery. Publ Acc. *n.a*: Business Mang Jobson's Publs Ltd 1932, Mang Dir & Chm '33, Asst Ed Jobson's Investment Digest of Australia & N.Z. & of The Digest Yr Book of Publ Coys of Australia & N.Z. '32, Ed both publs '33. *c.t*: N.Z. Financial Times & prov papers. *s.s*: Co finance criticism. On Staff Economist Lon '30–31. Australian Garrison Artillery (Militia) '24–. Lieut '28–. Now on Reserve of Officers. *Rec*: Golf, tennis, surfing. *a*: 19 O'Connell St, Sydney, N.S.W. *t*: BW 1211.

JOBSON, John. *n.a*: Lon Ed Yorkshire Post 1930–. *a*: 171 Fleet St, E.C.4. *t*: Central 9693.

JOELSON, Annette. *b*: Cape Province 1903. *e*: Good Hope Seminary, Cape Town Univ. *Publ*: The Dancing Girl of Gilead; Raw Clay; Desire Within; Field Mouse Stories; How the Ostrich Got Its Name; etc. *c.t*: Argus n/ps, Cape Times, Evening News, Daily Mail, The Lady, etc. Teacher '24–26. *Rec*: Tennis, riding. *a*: Eindelik, Main Rd, Green Point, Cape Town, S. Africa. *t*: Sea Point 4-1736.

JOELSON, F. Stephen, M.J.I. *b*: 1893. Ed. *n.a*: Found & Ed of Lon Wkly N/p " E. Africa ", Chm 1933 & '34 of E. African Group of Overseas League, Mem Overseas Cmt Inst of Journalists. *Publ*: Tanganyika Territory ('20); Settlement in E. Africa (Compiler & Ed '27); Eastern Africa To-day (Compiler & Ed '28). *c.t*: Leading Journs. *s.s*: E. Africa. *a*: 91 Gt Titchfield St, Lon, W.1. *t*: Museum 7370.

JOERGENSEN, (Jens) Johannes. *b*: Denmark 1866. *e*: Svenbog & Copenhagen. Writer. *Publ*: Lourdes; Saint Francis of Assisi; The War Pilgrim, Huysmans (Autobiog); Mit Livs Legende I–VII; Don Bosco (1929); Som en Kaerte ('31); etc. *c.t*: Berlingse Tidende. *a*: Via Santa Maria Rose, Assisi (Perugia), Italy.

JOHANN, FISCHER: college professor; b. June 26, 1881; educ. Gymnasium and Lyceum of Dillingen a.S.; Univs. of Munich and Berlin. DEGREES: Ph.D.; unmarried. AUTHOR: Die Propheten Obadja, Joel Amos, Hosea (nach dem hebräischen Urtext übersetzt,) 1909; Isaias 40-55 und die Perikopen vom Gottesknecht, 1916; Wer ist der Ebed in den Perikopen Ts 42, 1-7; 49, 1-9a; 50, 4-9; 52, 13-53, 12? 1922; Das Alphabet der LXX-Vorlage im Pentateuch, 1924; Zur Septuaginta-Vorlage im Pentateuch, 1926. General character of writing: scientific, Old Testament. Religion, Catholic. ADDRESS: Lyceum, Luisenstrasse 20, Bamberg, Germany.

JOHANNSEN, Ernst. *b*: Hamburg 1898. *m*: R. Blanck. *s*: 2. Electrical Engineer. *Publ*: Four Infantrymen; Allo Ici, Central de Brigade; Station 3; Sturm uber Santa Rock; Sechs auf einer Insel; etc. *Ctr*: Die Zeitung, Lond, etc. *Rec*: Chess. *a*: 7 Devonshire Mews (South), London, W.1.

JOHN, Evan. *b*: London 1901. *e*: Winchester & Oxf. *m*: Dorothy Holmes-Gore. *s*: 1. *a*: 1. Writer. *Publ*: Crippled Splendour; Time in the East: King Charles I; King's Masque. *s.s*: History of the Theatre, History of War—Swordmanship, Archery, etc. *Rec*: Fencing, carpentry. *w.s*: R.A. 1939—41, Intell Corps '41—44. *c*: Garrick, Reunion Theatre Assoc. *a*: Neal's Farm, Wyfold, nr Reading.

JOHN, Gwen. *b*: Chesterfield. Writer, Actress. *Publ*: Play, Biography & Verse. *Ctr*: Varicus mags & newsps. *Rec*: Painting, fresh air. *c*: P.E.N. *a*: 9 Old Sq, Lincoln's Inn, London, W.C.2. *T*: Chancery 6023, Ashthall, Burford, Oxford.

JOHN, William Mestrezat. *b*: Trinidad, Colorado 1888. *e*: Mercersburg Acad, Princeton Univ. *m*: Alice Margaret Schleter. *d*: 1. Author. *n.a*: Rep Denver Times 1912. *Publ*: Seven Women; Every Wise Woman; Mingled Yarn; Circumstance. *Ctr*: Century, Scribner's, etc. *s.s*: Fiction. *Rec*: Travel. *c*: Denver Country, etc. *a*: 1219 Security Building, Denver 2, Colorado. *T*: Tabor 8775.

JOHN O' LONDON. See Whitten, Wilfred.

JOHNS, Charles Rowland. *b*: Holyhead 1882. *e*: Park & L'pool Coll. *m*: Jessie Harvey. *s*: 1. *d*: 1. Dir Nat Canine Defence League. *n.a*: Co-Ed Dogs Bulletin. *Publ*: Aberdeen Mac; Dogs You'd like to Meet; Let Dogs Delight; Puppies; Our Friend, The Dog Series; Let's Talk of Dogs; So You Like Dogs; Every Dog Its Day; Questions Answered about Dogs; Dog Owner's Treasury. *Ctr*: Various. *s.s*: Dog Breeding. *Rec*: Gardening. *a*: Marlowe, Ashcombe Rd, Dorking, Surrey. *T*: Dorking 2852.

JOHNS, Miss E. L., M.A. Ex-Co-Princ Queenwood Sc Eastbourne. *a*: Tudor Croft, Baslow Rd, Eastbourne, Sussex.

JOHNS, FREDERIC: officer state civil service; b. Houghton, Mich. (U.S.A.), March 22, 1868; s. Ezekiel and Sarah Ann (Uren) J.; educ. Trevelyan House Sch., West Cornwall (Eng.); m. Florence Renfrey, Mar. 14, 1894, (died May 1, 1896. AUTHOR: Johns's Notable Australians, 1906 (2nd edit. 1908); A Journalist's Jottings, 1922; Who's Who in Australia (7 edits.), 1927; Australian Biographical Dictionary (in preparation). Contributor to leading Australian papers. General character of writing: biographical. Fellow Inst. Journalists (London); on staff Adelaide (Australia) Advertiser, 1885, and Register, 1885-1914; since 1914 chief of "Hansard" staff, So. Aus. Parliament. Hon. secy. Adelaide br. Royal Soc. of St. George. Electer Member of Soc. of Authors (Eng.); Hon. Secy. of Matthew Flinders National Statue for the City of Adelaide; of the Burnside District Fallen Soldiers' Memorial (Great War), and the Princess Mary Wedding Gift Fund in So. Australia. Relig. denom., Congregationalist. OFFICE: Parliament House. HOME: Houghton Lodge, Rose Park, Adelaide, South Australia.

JOHNS, Roberts S. *Publ*: Newport Directory; Newport Tide Table; Monmouthshire Masonic Calendar; Pictures by Engraving, Etching, Mezzotint, etc. *a*: Messrs R. H. Johns Ltd, Newport, Mon.

JOHNS, W. E. *b*: Hertford 1893. Author & Journalist, Cavalry & R.A.F. 1912—30 (Capt). *Publ*: " Biggles " & " Worrals " Series of Advanced Juvenile Fiction. *Rec*: Fishing, shooting, travel. *a*: Pitchrey Lodge, Grantown on Spey, Scotland. *T*: Ballindalloch 208.

JOHNSON, Alfred. b: Lower Walton 1899. e: People's Coll Warrington. Journalist. n.a: Edit-Mang Warrington Guardian Series. Publ: Ancient Inns of Warrington & District; History of Warrington Elementary Schools. a: Wistaria, 28 Oxford Green, Warrington. T: 1290.

JOHNSON, Miss Alice N. V. c.t: Lancet & Dublin Review. a: 10a Berkeley Pl, Wimbledon, S.W.19.

JOHNSON, Anna Dorothy Philippa. b: York 1880. e: Cheltenham Ladies Coll. Publ: Doris; To Meet Mr. Stanley; Death of a Spinster; Private Inquiries; Giuliano the Innocent. Ctr: Lond Mercury, Manch Guardian, Adelphi, Eng Rev, etc. a: Burnham Close, Ripon. T: 154.

JOHNSON, Arthur, M.Sc., F.T.I., F.R.S.A. b: Keighley 1905. e: Elem & Univ. m: Sara Bower Johnson. s: 1. Use-Research Officer Courtaulds Ltd, in practice as Textile Designer 4 yrs & Spinning & W'ving Sects Textile Indus 10 yrs, Lect Textiles Nottingham Univ Coll 3 yrs & Weaving Leeds Univ 6 yrs. Ctr: Journs of Textile Industry & Soc of Dyers & Colourists, Textile Manufacture, Textile World (U.S.A.), Textile Weekly, Silk & Rayon, etc. s.s: Textiles Design, Researches on Fabric Structure & Uses for New Synthetic Fibres. Rec: Oil & water-colour painting. a: 70 Castle Grove Ave, Headingley, Leeds 6. T: 55547.

JOHNSON, Arthur Tysilio. Author & Journalist, Photographer of Flower Studies for Press Reproduction. n.a: Garden Column Writer Sunday Times. Publ: A Garden in Wales; Plant Names Simplified; Hardy Heaths; A Woodland Garden; The Garden To-day; The Mill Garden; etc. Ctr: Country Life, Times, Spectator, Gardener's Chron, My Garden, Gardening Illustrated. s.s: Gardening, Photography. Rec: Fishing, travel. a: Bulkeley Mill, Tynygroes, Conway, Nth Wales.

JOHNSON, Miss B. e: Cam (Classical Tripos). School Mistress, St Felix Sc Southwold. Publ: The Book of the Blackheath High School (Jt). a: Bermondsey, Revdon, Southwold, Suffolk

JOHNSON, Bernard, B.A., MusB.(Cantab), F.R.C.O. b: N. Pickenham 1868. e: Selwyn Col Cam. City Organist, Nott'm (ret). Publ: Cantata Ecce Homo; Organ Sonata; Vocal Music, etc. c.t: Nott'm Guardian, Nott'm Journ, Methodist Times. s.s: Lecturing in music (popular). Pres Inc Soc of Musicians ('32–). Rec: Yachting, fishing, gardening. c: Authors. a: The Loke, Horning, Norwich.

JOHNSON, Burges, A.B., Litt.D. b: Rutland, Vermont 1877. e: Amherst Coll. m: Constance F. Wheeler. s: 1 & 2. Teacher (ret), Lecturer & Writer, Prof of Eng & Dir of Public Relations Syracuse Univ 1926–34, Founder Author's League of America. Publ: Rhymes of Little Boys; As I Was Saying; Essaying the Essay; A Little Book of Necessary Nonsense; New Rhyming Dictionary & Poet's Handbook; Sonnets from the Pekinese; Professor at Bay; Rubaiyat of Omar Ky-Yi; The Art of Fiction (collab); Ladder to the Moon; As Much as I Dare; Campus versus Classroom. Ctr: Various. s.s: Education, Craftsmanship in Writing, New England & The South-west. Rec: Whittling, riding. c: Players, Dutch Treat, etc. a: 1101 Oxford Pl, Schenectady, New York, U.S.A. T: 6-4822.

JOHNSON, C. H. Med Pract. c.t: Journ of Laryngology. a: 470 Hornsey Rd, N.19, & 217 Isledon Rd, N.7. t: Archway 1818 & North 1359.

JOHNSON, Charles, M.A., F.B.A. b: Newcastle-upon-Tyne 1870. e: Newcastle Gr Sch, Giggleswick Sch, Trin Coll Oxf. m: Mabel Catherine Rudd (dec'd). Assist Keeper Public Record (ret), Mem Soc of Antiquaries, Roy Hist Soc. n.a: Joint Ed Helps for Students of History (S.P.C.K.). Publ: Dialogus de Scaccario (ed. with A. Hughes & C. G. Crump); Medieval Latin Word-list (with J. H. Baxter & Phyllis Abrahams); English Court Hand A.D. 1066–1500 (with H. Jenkinson); The Care of Documents; The Mechanical Processes of the Historian; Royal Power & Administration (in The Legacy of the Middle Ages. Ed C. G. Crump & E. F. Jacob); Registrum Hamonis Hethe (Rochester diocese) 1914––. Ctr: Eng Hist Rev. s.s: Charters of Henry I, Medieval Latin. c: Athenæum. a: 13a Downshire Hill, London, N.W.3. T: Hampstead 2648.

JOHNSON, Charles Herbert Victor. b: Sheffield 1907. m: Violet Lawrence. s: 1. Jnlst. n.a: Reporter Bristol Evening World. Formerly on Ed staff Sheffield Telegraph & Yorks Telegraph & Star. s.s: N/p articles, topical, historical sport, travel. Rec: Swimming, tennis, sailing, foreign travel. c: M.J.I. a: Hill Barton, Wembdon, Bridgwater, Somerset. t: 459.

JOHNSON, Charles Plumptre, J.P. b: Lon 1853. e: Marlboro' Col. Solicitor (ret). Chm of Govs Sevenoaks Sc. Publ: Hints to Collectors of 1st Editions Thackeray's Works ('85); Hints to Collectors of 1st Editions of Charles Dickens' Works; Early Writings of W. M. Thackeray; Ed of the Victoria Edn of the Pickwick Papers ('87); etc. c.t: Athenæum. Rec: Collection of water-colours & 1st edns. c: Athenæum, First Edition, R.Y.S. Cowes, etc. a: Park Grange, Sevenoaks, Kent. t: 232.

JOHNSON, Charles Willes. n.a: Sub-Ed M/C News Chron. s.s: Mountaineering (especially British rock climbing). Honours degree in law, Cam 1925. Rec: Rock climbing. a: M/C News Chron. M/C.

JOHNSON, Charles William Heaton. b: Cam 1896. e: King's Col Choir Sc Cam & Priv. Official Lecturer Nat Gallery Lond. Publ: English Painting; A Short Account of British Painting. Rec: Walking, cycling, swimming & drawing. a: 1 Millington Rd, Cambridge. t: 2417.

JOHNSON, Christopher George Alexander Yate, F.R.S.A. b: Edinburgh 1903. e: Edin Acad. m: Barbara Snell. s: 2. Publ: St Christopher, The Patron Saint of Travellers. Ctr: Various. s.s: Trade Marks, Industrial Designs & Copyright. Rec: Gardening, golf. a: White Gates, 4 Craigleith View, Ravelston, Edinburgh 4. T: 61911.

JOHNSON, Claudius O., M.A., Ph.D. b: Greenville, Virginia 1894. e: Univs of Chicago & Richmond. m: Mary Wilson Maxwell. Coll Prof. Publ: Government in the United States; American National Government; Borah of Idaho; Carter H. Harrison I: Political Leader. Ctr: American Polit Science Rev, Pacific N-W Quarterly, Oregon Hist Quarterly, Washington Law Rev, etc. s.s: Political Biography & Processes. a: 1809 B St, Pullman, Washington, U.S.A. T: 8381.

JOHNSON, D. G. n.a: Editor-in-Chief Health & Strength, Health & Efficiency, Superman. a: Link Hse, 4 Greville St, Holborn, E.C.1. t: Chancery 8601.

JOHNSON, Edgar Augustus Jerome, S.B., A.M., PhD. b: Illinois 1900. e: Illinois & Harvard Univs. m: Virginia Gravel. s: 1. Col Professor. Asst Prof of Econ Oklahoma Univ '24-26. Instructor in Econ & Tutor in Hist, Govt & Econ Harvard Univ '26-29. Asst Prof of Econ Cornell Univ '31-. Publ: American Economic Thought in the Seventeenth Century. c.t: Journ, Sociolog Review, New Eng Quart, Amer Econ Revue, Revue d'histoire économique et social, etc. s.s: Econ hist & hist of econ thought. Fell Social Sci Research Counc '29-30. a: Cornell Univ, Ithaca, N.Y., U.S.A.

JOHNSON, Mrs. Ellen Gertrude. Ed Children's Columns. *s.s*: Poetry, articles & s. stories. *c*: Nott'm Writers. *a*: 4 Brooklands Rd, Sneinton Hill, Nott'm.

JOHNSON, Emory Richard, B.Litt., Ph.D., Hon.Sc.D. *b*: Waupun, Wisconsin 1864. *e*: Univs of Wis & Penna. *m*: (1) Orra L. March (dec'd), (2) Hedwig A. Schroder. Prof Emeritus of Transportation & Commerce Univ of Penna. *Publ*: American Railway Transportation; Ocean & Inland Water Transportation; Elements of Transportation; Railroad Traffic & Rates (collab); Panama Canal & Commerce; etc. *s.s*: Transportation & Commerce. *a*: University of Pennsylvania, Philadelphia, Penna, U.S.A. *T*: Evergreen 6-5200.

JOHNSON, Frank Lawrence. *b*: Surbiton 1890. *e*: Priv. Dir & Ed in Chief Northern Press Ltd (Shields Gaz & Assoc Newspapers) South Shields. *n.a*: Mang-Ed Leicester Mail 1920—31, Chief Sub-Ed North Mail Newcastle-on-Tyne '20—22, Sub-Ed Dly Mail Lond '22—25. News Ed Newcastle Chron '25—27, Asst Ed N.E. Gaze '27—30. *Ctr*: Harmsworth Hist of Gt War I, & various newsps. *a*: Northside, Sunderland Rd, Harton, Sth Shields. *T*: 448.

JOHNSON, Geoffrey, B.A. *b*: Cradley Heath, Staffs 1893. *e*: Wolverhampton Gr Sch. *m*: Agnes Johnson. Schoolmaster. *n.a*: Brit Ed Lyric Virginia 1937, European Ed Poetry Chapbook New York '47, Lond Publisher's Reader '39. *Publ*: The Quest Unending; Changing Horizons; Mother to Son; The Scholar; The New Road; The Timeless Land; The Mountain; The Ninth Wave. *Ctr*: England :—Spectator, Observer, New English Review, Fortnightly, etc. American :— Poetry (Chicago), Voices (N.Y.), Atlantic Monthly (Boston) etc. *s.s*: Poetry & Belles Lettres, Translations, from Latin, French, Italian, German, Educ. *Rec*: Gardening, walking, cycling, foreign travel. *a*: Lodore, 11 Orchard Estate, Ely, Cambs.

JOHNSON, George Frederic. *b*: Wordsley 1877. *e*: King Edward VI Gr Sch Stourbridge, August Abrahamsons Stifelse Sweden, Liverpool Univ. *m*: Edith Stanway. *s*: 1. *d*: 1. Inspector of Schools (ret), Mem Nat Ch Assembly. *Publ*: Handwork & Mathematics (4 vols); Bookbinding & Bookcrafts for Schools (2 vols); Course of Bookbinding for Schools (2 vols); Modern School Woodwork; Toys & Toymaking; Rural Handicrafts; Preparatory Course of Handwork. *Ctr*: The New Teaching, The Book of School Handwork. *Rec*: Practical Education. *Rec*: Golf, photography. *a*: Naas, Tanat Drive, Liverpool 18. *T*: Allerton 1502.

JOHNSON, Harold Cottam, F.R.Hist.S. *b*: Wakefield 1903. *e*: Wakefield Gr Sch & Univ Coll Oxf. *m*: Esme Lane. *s*: 1. *d*: 1. Asst Keeper Public Records. *n.a*: Sec British Acad Cttee to Prepare Dictionary of Mediæval Latin '35—, Mem Publ Sect Cttee British Record Assoc. *Publ*: Ed (with S. C. Ratcliff) Warwick County Records, vols I to VII & (with E. F. Jacob) Register of Henry Chichele, Archbishop of Canterbury, vol II; Surrey Taxation Returns, pt II. *Ctr*: History, Eng Hist Rev, Bulletins Inst Hist Research. *s.s*: Administrative History & Archives. *a*: 10 Ranelagh Ave, Barnes, London, S.W.13. *T*: Prospect 4976.

JOHNSON, Harold Roland. *b*: Branford, Conn 1898. *e*: High Sc, United Press Syndicate Col of Journalism. *m*: E. Rheunnette Alley. Bookseller, writer & publisher. *n.a*: Contributing Ed Industrial Worker '19, Assoc & Poetry Ed The Crucible '18—24, Ed '24—26, Staff Writer Federated Press '22—30. *Publ*: Poems in :—Anthology of Revolutionary Poetry; Poets and Poetry of 1931; Contemporary American Lyricists; Poems of America; Songs of the Workers; Marine Workers Victory Songs; Anthology of Skeptical Poems (in prep). *s.s*: Poetry, economics. Have won various prizes & contests in prose & verse. *Rec*: Walking, reading, writing. *c*: American Secular Union, Loyal Order of Moose. *a*: P.O. Box 46, Station A, New York City.

JOHNSON, Rev. Henry Harrold, B.A. *Publ*: The Roadmaker & other Poems (1903); The Bridgebuilders & other Poems; The House of Life: Interpretations of the Symbolical Pictures of G. F. Watts ('11); A Short Life of Jesus ('33); etc. *c.t*: Contemp Review, Internat Journ of Ethics, etc. *a*: Iona, Wye Grove, Buxton, Derbys.

JOHNSON, Very Rev. Hewlett, M.A., B.Sc., D.D., Th.D., Ass. M.C.E. *b*: Manchester 1874. *e*: Macclesfield Gr Sch, Victorian Univ Manch, Oxf Univ. *m*: Nowell Mary Edwards. *d*: 2. Dean of Canterbury since 1931. *n.a*: Ed the Interpreter, on Board of Dly Worker. *Publ*· The Socialist Sixth of the World; Soviet Strength; Soviet Success. *Ctr*: Various. *s.s*: Russia. *Rec*: Foreign travel. *a*: The Deanery, Canterbury.

JOHNSON, J. H. *a*: 13 K. Edward Av, Chelmsford, Essex.

JOHNSON, J. R., F.S.A.A. *b*: Bedlington 1889. *e*: Allan's Endowed Sc Newcastle-on-Tyne. *m*: Edith Elsie Büsst. *s*: 1. City Treasurer B'ham. *Publ*: Loans of Local Authorities (2nd edn). *s.s*: Loc govt finance. Capt R.A.S.C. *Rec*: Golf. *c*: Jr Constitutional. *a*: The Grange, Copt Heath, Knowle. *t*: 100.

JOHNSON, John Edward. *b*: Hereford 1896. *e*: Ryelands Col Sc Hereford & Lon Univ. *m*: Olive May Taylor. *d*: 1. Journalist. *n.a*: Sub Ed Yorks Observer (1922), Bradford Telegraph & Argus ('27). *c.t*: Bradford Telegraph & Argus, Yorks Observer. *s.s*: Dramatic criticism, book reviewing. *Rec*: Golf, swimming. *a*: 25 Guy's Cliffe, Undercliffe Lane, Bradford, Yorks.

JOHNSON, John Kennedy. *b*: Willington Quay-on-Tyne. *e*: Bede Col Sc Sunderland. News Ed Northcliffe n/ps. *n.a*: Sunderland Echo, Newcastle Chronicle & allied n/ps. *Rec*: Motoring. *a*: 6 Bedford Pl, W.C.1. *t*: Museum 2567.

JOHNSON, Rev. Joseph. *b*: Staveley 1860. *e*: Nat Sc, Sci & Art Classes & Hartley Col M/C. *m*: (1) Annie E. Ogram; (2) Jennie Paull. Meth Min (ret 1929). *Publ*: Freemasonry; The Vision & Call. *c t*: Masonic Record, Meth Recorder, Meth Times & Leader. *s.s*: Freemasonry. 46 y Meth Min. Head of Meth Pubg Hse Holborn Hall, E.C. '15-20. Pres Lon F.C. Fed '19. Prominent Freemason '03-. Freeman & Liveryman City of Lon. *Rec*: Philanthropic activities. *c*: Nat Lib, Authors. *a*: 7 Trinity Av, Westcliff-on-Sea, Essex. *t*: Southend 2591.

JOHNSON, Josephine Winslow. *b*: Kirkwood, Miss 1910. *e*: Washington Univ St Louis, Mo. *m*: Grant G. Cannon. *s*: 1. *d*: 1. Writer. *Publ*: Now in November; Jordanstown; Winter Orchard; Years End; Wildwood. *Ctr*: Atlantic Monthly, Harper's Bazaar, Virginia Quarterly. *a*: Box 15 R5, Kirkwood, Missouri, U.S.A.

JOHNSON, Rev. Lewis Alexander Goold. Cong Min. *Publ*: The Legends of Israel; Hilda Johnson: A Memoir; Recreations in Verse. *a*: Field Hse, St Andrew's Rd, Bristol, 6.

JOHNSON, M. L. *b*: London 1909. *e*: Waverley Road Sch B'ham, B'ham Univ. *m*: Michael Abercrombie. *s*: 1. *n.a*: Ed New Biology (Peguin Books Ltd) '45—. *Ctr*: Various Scientific journs. *s.s*: Biology. *a*: Flat C, 17 Chesterford Gardens, London, N.W.3.

JOHNSON, Mabel Mary. *b*: Southend, Essex 1894. *e*: Vancouver. *m*: John Lowe Johnson. *s*: 1. *d*: 1. *n.a*: News Ed The Vernon News July 1942—Dec '46,

Columnist from '37—Dec '46, Vernon Representative for CKOV Kelowna. *Ctr*: Vancouver Dly Province, Country Life, B.C. Digest, etc. *s.s*: Newspaper Features. *Rec*: Reading, homelife & housekeeping, gardening. *a*: 312-7th St South, Vernon, British Columbia. *T*: 880.

JOHNSON, Marjorie Thelma. *s.s*: Gypsy & fairy lore & children's verse. *c*: Nott'm Writers & Gypsy Lore Soc. *a*: 4 Brooklands Rd, Sneinton Hill, Nott'm.

JOHNSON, Martin Christopher, M.A., D.Sc. *b*: 1896. *e*: Perse Sch & St John's Coll Camb. *m*: Jessie Faulkner. Lecturer in Physics B'ham Univ. *Publ*: Art & Scientific Thought; Time, Knowledge & the Nebulæ; Science & the Meanings of Truth. *Ctr*: Proc of the Royal Soc & other journals. *s.s*: Philosophy of Science, Astronomical Physics. *a*: 130 Witherford Way, Selly Oak, Birmingham 29. *T*: Selly Oak 0035.

JOHNSON, Nunnally Hunter. *b*: Columbus, Georgia 1897. *e*: Columbus, Georgia H Sch. *m*: Dorris Bowden. *d*: 4. Writer-Producer. *n.a*: Rep Savannah (Ga) Press 1916, New York Trib '18, Brooklyn D Eagle '19, New York Her Trib '25, New York Ev Post '26—29. *Publ*: There Ought to be a Law; & many screenplays, including, The House of Rothschild; Bulldog Drummond Strikes Back; Cardinal Richelieu; Moulin Rouge; The Country Doctor; Rose of Washington Square; Jesse James; Grapes of Wrath; Tobacco Road; The Moon is Down; etc. *Ctr*: Sat Ev Post, P.M. *w.s*: 1916—18 U.S. Army. *a*: 625, Mountain Drive, Beverly Hills, California. *T*: Crestview 5-6335.

JOHNSON, Olof Eyvind Verner. *b*: Boden 1900. *m*: Cilla Frankenhaeuser. *s*: 2. *d*: 1. Author. *n.a*: Ed Handslag '41—45. *Publ*: Strandernas svall; Romanen om Olof; Krilon; Sju liv; Kommentar till ett Stjarnfall; Nattovning; Stad i morker; Soldatens aterkomst. *a*: Bannier Publishing Hse, Stockholm, Sweden.

JOHNSON, Osa Helen. D.Sc. *b*: Chanute, Kansas 1894. *m*: Martin Johnson (dec'd) Writer, Lecturer Motion Picture Producer. *Publ*: I Married Adventure; Four Years in Paradise; Bride in the Solomons; Jungle Babies; Jungle Pets; Jungle Friends; Pantaloons; Snowball; Tarnish. *Ctr*: Nat Geographic, World's Work, Asia Mag, Collier's, Good Housekeeping, Reader's Digest, etc. *s.s*: Recording Wild Animal & Native Life for posterity. *Rec*: Fishing, hunting, golfing. *c*: Explorers, Adventurers, Business & Professional Women's Internat. *a*: 400 Park Ave, New York, N.Y., U.S.A. *T*: Plaza 5-6992.

JOHNSON, Philip. *b*: 1900. Playwright. *Publ*: Afternoon; The Cage; The Good & The Bad; Legend; The Lovely Miracle; Out Goes She; The Respectable Façade; Russian Salad; Sad About Europe; Saturday Night; Send Her Victorious; Shame the Devil; The Sister Who Walked in Silence; To-day of All Days; World Without Men; Heaven on Earth; Far, Far Away; April Shower; Four Plays; Queer Cattle; Lover's Leap; Lovely to Look At; Lark Brown; Orange Blossom; Everlasting Flowers; An Immortelle; Master Dudley; etc. *Rec*: Reading, walking, music. *a*: The Owl Pen, West Hill, Ottery St Mary, Devon.

JOHNSON, Robert William, F.J.I. *b*: Middlesbro' 1863. *e*: Newcastle Comm Acad. *m*: Jessie Harbottle. Journalist. *n.a*: Comm Ed Newcastle Daily Leader 1887-1904, Newcastle Daily Journ '04-18, Founder & Ed Compendium Lon '18, Ed staff Shipping World '30-. *Publ*: The Making of the Tyne: A Record of Fifty Years' Progress; Jt Ed River Tyne Official Handbook. *c.t*: Journ of Commerce, Shipping World, Times Trade Supp, Financial Times, etc. *s.s*: Coal, shipping, shipbuilding. *Rec*: Poetry, gardening. *a*: Tynecote, 16 Pine Walk, Woodmansterne, Banstead, Surrey.

JOHNSON, Stephen Keynor. *b*: Cam 1899. *e*: Kings Col Cam. *m*: Ida Margaret Brown. Prof of Classics Univ Col Swansea 1927-33. *Publ*: Editor of the Oxford Text of Livy. *c.t*: Classical Quart & Classical Review. Browne Medallist. *a*: Armstrong Col, Newcastle-on-Tyne.

JOHNSON, Stowers, B.A. *b*: Brentwood. *e*: Brentwood Sch, Coll of St Mark & St. John Chelsea, Queen Mary Coll Lond, Sch of Slavonic & East European Studies Lond. Headmaster. *Publ*: London Saga; The Mundane Tree; Branches Green & Branches Black; Mountains & No Mules. *s.s*: Poetry, London, Russian Literature. *Rec*: Angling, ornithology, travel. *a*: 26 Cresthill Ave, Grays, Essex.

JOHNSON, Mrs. Sybil. *b*: Worsley 1878. *e*: Priv. *m*: Harold M. Johnson. *s*: 1. *d*: 1. Mang Dir Ramsden Wood Print Works Ltd, Walsden, nr Todmorden *Rec*: Gardening, photography, etc. Magistrate County Counc Cheshire. *c*: F.R.H. Soc, F.R.S.A., Sesame, Ladies' Army & Navy. *a*: The Old Tannery, Lymm, Cheshire. *t*: Lymm, 2.

JOHNSON, Thomas Frank, O.B.E.(Mil). *b*: Baldock, Herts. *e*: Regent St Polytechnic, France & Germany. *m*: Evelyn (Rona) Lee. *s*: 1. European Publicity Officer B.B.C. Personal Sec to Dr Nansen 1921—23, League of Nations Asst High Commissioner '23—31, Sec-General L. of N. Internat Office for Refugees '31—36, Cmmdr of St Stanislaus, Officer of St Vladimir & of Star of Roumania. *Publ*: International Tramps; etc. *Ctr*: Numerous leading newspsp. & Mags *s.s*: Internat Affairs & Relations. *w.s*: 1914—18 & '39—45 service on all European fronts. *Rec*: Golf, tennis, cricket. *c*: Press. *a*: 59 Fitzjohns Ave, Hampstead, London, N.W.3. *T*: Hampstead 4430, 4464, 7464.

JOHNSON, Thomas Marvin, B.A. *b*: Buffalo, N.Y. 1889. *e*: Hobart Coll Geneva N.Y. Writer. *n.a*: Ed Staff New York Sun 1914—21, Military Writer N.E.A. Service '39—46. *Publ*: Without Censor; Our Secret War; The Lost Battalion (with Fletcher Pratt); What You should Know About Spies & Saboteurs (with Will Irwin); Unlocking Adventure; Red War (with Judson P. Philips). *Ctr*: Reader's Digest, Sat Ev Post, Colliers Wkly, Liberty, Amer Mercury, etc. *s.s*: Military, diplomatic, Internat Relations, etc. *c*: Overseas Press. *a*: 420 West 116th St, New York City 27, U.S.A. *T*: University 4-2700.

JOHNSON, Dr. W., M.C., M.D., F.R.C.P. *m*: Margery Denbigh. *s*: 1. *d*: 3. Con Physician Roy L'pool United Hosp & Roy L'pool Children's Hosp. *Publ*: Neuroses in France; War Official Med Hist. *Ctr*: B.M.J., Lancet, Quart Journ of Med, Guy's Hosp Reports. *a*: 26 Rodney St, Liverpool.

JOHNSON, Dr. W. M. C. Physician. *c.t*: M.M.J., Lancet, Quart Journ of Med, Guy's Hosp Reports. *Publ*: Neuroses in France; War Office Official Med Hist. Physician & Neurologist Roy Southern Hosp L'pool; Asst Physician Roy L'pool Children's Hosp. *a*: 26 Rodney St, L'pool.

JOHNSON, William Branch. *b*: Lon 1893. *e*: St Olave's G.S. & Priv. *m*: Winifred Helen Clark. *s*: 1. Author. *n.a*: Northampton Mercury 1912—14, Daily News '19—21, Westminster Gazette '21—23. *Publ*: Among French Folk ('22); Folktales of Brittany; Fire Fighting; Wolves of the Channel; The Age of Arsenic; Lucifer's Lieutenant ('34); etc. *c*: Many periodicals. *s.s*: French hist, folklore, short stories. *Rec*: Acting, golf. *c*: Authors. *a*: 95 Handside Lane, Welwyn Garden City, Herts. *t*: 221.

JOHNSON, Wm. Harold, M.A. *b*: Birmingham 1890. *e*: King Edward's Sch & Univ B'ham. *m*: Mary E. Barrett. *s*: 1. *d*: 1. Editor & Journalist. *n.a*:

Motor Ed Country Life 1919—30, Ed-Owner Motor Boating World & Aux Yachting '31, Mgr Sci & Tech Publications Dpt, Hutchinson & Co. *Ctr*: Autocar, Country Life, Overseas D Mail, Yachting journs, etc. *s.s*: Motoring, Foreign Touring, Yachting, Aircraft Engineering. *Rec*: Sailing. *c*: Roy Socs. *a*: Bewdley, Newhaw, Weybridge, Surrey. *T*: Byfleet 547.

JOHNSON, Rt. Rev. William Herbert, B.A., Th.D. *b*: Brighton, Sth Australia 1889. *e*: St Peter's Coll Adelaide & Univ, St John's Coll Melbourne. *m*: Frances Dymphna de Chair. *d*: 3. Bishop of Ballarat 1936—, Dean of Newcastle, N.S.W. '28—36. *n.a*: Ed Ballarat Church Chron. *Publ*: Memoirs of George Merrick Long. *Ctr*: Ballarat Courier. *w.s*: C.F., A.I.F. '17—19. *a*: Bishopscourt, Ballarat, Victoria, Australia. *T*: Ballarat 330.

JOHNSON, Winifred Ruth. *b*: London. *e*: Ursuline Convent, Belgium. *m*: Harold Arthur Cann. Editress. *n.a*: Joined A.P. Ltd 1912, Ed Women's Wkly, Woman & Home, My Home. *a*: 22 Ravenscourt Park, London, W.6.

JOHNSTON, Alexander. *b*: Buckie, 1876. Ed-reporter. *n.a*: Banffshire Advertiser. *Rec*: Bowls. *a*: Advertiser Office, Buckie. *t*: 65.

JOHNSTON, ALFRED WINTLE: writer; b. Orkney, Scotland, Sept., 1859; s. James and Margaret (Oman) J.; educ. Dollar Acad. (Scotland), Collegiate Sch. and Dr. Begbie's Private Sch. (Edinburgh); m. Kathleen Ivy Dodds, 1928. Editor: Saga Book (proceedings of the Viking Soc. for Northern Research); Year Book; Old Old-Lore Series (Orkney and Shetland). Contributor to Proceedings of Soc. of Antiquaries of Scotland (19028); Notes on the Earl's Bu and on the remains of the Round Church of Orphir, Orkney; Law Mag. and Rev., Westminster Rev., Reliquary and Illustrated Archaeologist, Scottish Historical Rev., and other papers. General character of writing: historical, archaeological. Founder Viking Soc. for Northern Research, London (founded, 1892, as Orkney, Shetland and Northern Soc. or Viking Club); F.S.A. (Scotland); F. S. (North A.) of Copenhagen); Knight 1st Class, Order of St. Olaf (Norway); Knight of the Order of the Icelandic Falcon. Church and public building architect. Relig. denom., Church of England. CLUBS: Albany, Den Norske Klub (both London). ADDRESS: 29 Ashburnham Mansions, Chelsea, London, S. W. 10. Eng.

JOHNSTON, Charles Hope. *b*: Dunoon, Argyll 1906. *e*: Dunoon Gr Sch & Glasgow Univ. Lond Ed Journ of Commerce & Shipping Telegraph '47—. *n.a*: Rep Grennock Herald '30—31, Ed Rep North Down Herald '31—35, Rep Belfast News Letter '36—41, Found & Ed Admiralty News-Sheet, Shipyard & Engineering Spotlight '42—45. *Ctr*: Sea Breezes. *s.s*: Ships & Shipping. *a*: 50 Andover Rd, Orpington, Kent.

JOHNSTON, Christopher. *b*: Liverpool. *m*: E. Carr. *s*: 1. Journalist, Chm Preston N.U.J., 1943 elected Life Member on Retirement '46. *n.a*: E. Hulton & Co., Allied Newsps, Kemsley Newsps '10—46. *Ctr*: D Dispatch, Manch Eve Chron Sun Chron, Sun Times, Sun Graphic, etc. *s.s*: Sports, Spec Corr 8 Pilgrimages Lancs to Lourdes. *Rec*: Chess, golf. *c*: Vice-Pres Preston Chess. *a*: 3 Osborne St, Preston. *T*: 4252.

JOHNSTON, Denis William, O.B.E., M.A., LL.M. *b*: Dublin 1901. *e*: St Andrew's Coll Dublin, Merchiston Castle Edin, Christ's Coll Camb, Harvard. *m*: (1) Shelah Richards, (2) Betty Chancellor. *s*: 3. *d*: 1. Barrister, Television Programme Dir '46—47, Dir Dublin Gate Theatre '32—. *Publ*: Plays: The Moon in the Yellow River; The Old Lady Says "No"; Storm Song; A Bride for the Unicorn; Blind Man's Buff; The Golden Cuckoo; Weep for the Cyclops; etc. *c*: Roy Irish Yacht. *w.s*: B.B.C. War Corr 1942—45. *a*: Glen Ellyn, Wise Lane, Mill Hill, London, N.W.7. *T*: Mill Hill 2566.

JOHNSTON, Edward. Calligrapher. *Publ*: Writing & Illuminating, & Lettering; Manuscript & Inscription Letters; various articles. Pres Arts & Crafts Exhib Soc. *a*: Cleves, Ditchling, Sussex.

JOHNSTON, Frank Norman Howard. *b*: Wolverhampton 1900. *e*: L.C.C. *m*: Kathleen Florence Trussler. Author, Journalist & Publisher. *n.a*: Ed Racing Specialist '36—. *Publ*: Highway Robber's Derby; The Fellowship of Five; Turf Racketeers; Disqualified; Li Kwang's Dagger; Easy Money; Ed The Football Encyclopedia; etc. *Ctr*: News of the World, Sun Times, Dly Express, Sun Express, Sporting Life. *s.s*: Horse-racing, Football. *Rec*: Golf, tennis. *c*: Paternosters, Roy Eastbourne & Racing. *w.s*: R.N.V.R. 1918—19. *a*: Milnthorpe Rd, Eastbourne. *T*: 3458.

JOHNSTON, Frederick, J.P. *b*: Falkirk 1859. *e*: Falkirk Classical, Stirling H.S. & Blairlodge. *m*: Mary MacGlashan (dec). Journalist & N/p Mang Ed. *n.a*: Falkirk Herald 1882—, Linlithgowshire Gazette '91—. Chm Stirlingshire Licensing Ct 1923—. *s.s*: Politics, local govt. Chm Relief, Recruiting, Prisoners of War & War Pensions Orgs '14—19. Chm E. Dis of Stirlingshire Agric Assoc '28—29, P.C.C., R.N.L.I., etc. Pres Scot N/ps Proprietors' Assoc '21—24. *Rec*: Music, gardening. *a*: Woodville, Falkirk. *t*: 18 & 570.

JOHNSTON, George Alexander, M.A., D.Phil. *b*: Jamaica 1888. *e*: Univ of Glas. *m*: Pauline Violet Roche. *s*: 1. *d*: 1. Asst Dir Gen Internat Labour Office. *Publ*: The Development of Berkeley's Philosophy; Berkeley's Commonplace Book; Citizenship in the Industrial World; International Social Progress; An Introduction to Ethics. *Ctr*: Atlantic Monthly, Quarterly Rev, Internat Journ of Ethics, Internat Labour Rev. *a*: 3450 Drummond St, Montreal. *T*: Pl 7801.

JOHNSTON, Lt.-Col. George Richard, F.R.Hist.S., F.R.S.A., F.R.E.S. *b*: Newbury 1895. *e*: Clifton Coll, Roy Mil Acad. *m*: Unity Ussher Quicke. *d*: 3. Historian. *Ctr*: Army Quarterly, Journ of Roy Artillery, etc. *s.s*: European Langs, Military Hist. *Rec*: Hunting show jumping. *c*: R.A.C. *w.s*: Regular Officer R.A. 1914—46. *a*: 285 Goldhawk Rd, London, W.12. *T*: Riverside 5253.

JOHNSTON, Rev. Henry Aloysius, S.J., M.A. *b*: Downpatrick, Ireland 1888. *e*: Mungret Coll Limerick & U.C.D. Rector of Provincial Seminary of Victoria 1930—47. *Publ*: Plain Talks on the Catholic Religion; A Critic Looks at the Catholic Church; etc. *Ctr*: The Advocate, The Australian Catholic Record. *s.s*: Religions. *a*: Corpus Christi College, Werribee, Victoria, Australia. *T*: Central 1211.

JOHNSTON, HENRY HALCRO: army officer (Colonel, retired); b. Orphir House, Orphir, Orkney, Scotland, Sept. 13, 1856; s. James and Margaret Omand (Robertson) J.; educ. Dollar Inst. and Collegiate Sch. (Edinburgh), Army Medical Sch., Netley (Eng.). DEGREES: M.B., C.M. (1880), M.D., B.Sc. (1893), D.Sc. (1894), all Univ. of Edinburgh; unmarried. AUTHOR: Report on the Relation between Malarial Fever among Her Majesty's Troops at Port Louis, Mauritius, and the Meteorological Elements of Temperature, Rainfall and Relative Humidity, for the year, 1889 (with a preliminary sketch of the Medical Topography of the Island and the Epidemic of Malarial Fever in 1866-67, 1894); Report on the Efficiency of Certain Filters for Removing Micro-organisms from Water, with Special reference to the Nordtmeyer-Berkefeld and Pasteur-Chamberland Filters, 1894. Contributor to Journ. of Botany, Trans. of the Botanical Soc. of Edinburgh; Annals of Scottish Nat. Hist., Reports of the Botanical Soc. and Exchange Club of British Isles, Brit. Med.

Journ., Journ. Royal Med. Corps., Additions to the Flora of Orkney (11th, 12th, 13th and 14th papers); Additions to the Flora of Shetland 2nd, 3rd and 4th papers). General character of writing: scientific and botanical. C.B. (1912), C. B. E. (1919); Medal with clasp and Khedive's Star (Suakin Exped., 1885); Medal with clasp, dispatches (Malakand and Buner Exped., 1897-98); 2 Medals with 3 clasps, despatches twice, C. B. (So. Africa Campaign, 1899-1902); Medal, C.B.E., Great War, 1914-19. Societies: F.R.S.E.; F.L.S.; Fellow Royal Soc. Edinburgh; Fellow Bot. Soc., Edinburgh; Fellow Edinburgh Nat. Hist. Soc.; Mem. Bot. Soc. and Exchange Club of the British Isles; Orkney Nat. Hist. Soc. (past pres.); Hon. Foreign mem. la Société Française d' Hygiène (Paris); Viking Soc. for Northern Research (London). HOME: Orphir House, Orphir, Kirkwall, Orkney, Scotland.

JOHNSTON, Rev. Hugh Liddon, M.C. *b*: Oxford 1889. *e*: Radley Coll & Magdalen Coll Oxf. *m*: Elaine Fowler. *s*: 1. *d*: 1. Rector of Cranleigh. *n.a*: Asst Ed The Challenge 1922—23, St Martin's Review '23—31. *Publ*: This Day; The Meaning & The Means. *s.s*: Practical Christianity. *a*: The Rectory, Cranleigh, Surrey. *T*: 125.

JOHNSTON, Rev. James Brown, M.A., B.D. *b*: Edinburgh 1862. *m*: Catherine E. McMichael. *s*: 2. *d*: 2. Minister Church of Scotland, St Andrew's & Falkirk 1888—1928, Reader of Proofs for New Scottish Dictionary, Hon Pres Falkirk Nat Hist Soc, F.R.Hist.Soc. *Publ*: Place Names of Scotland; Place Names of England & Wales; The Scottish Macs; Place Names of Stirlingshire; Place Names of Berwickshire. *Ctr*: Scotsman, Glas Herald, Contemp Rev, Chamber's Journ. *s.s*: Place Names of Scotland & England. *Rec*: Bowls, crosswords, walking. *a*: 63 Cluny Gardens, Edinburgh, 10.

JOHNSTON, Joseph. *b*: Dungannon, Co Tyrone 1890. *e*: Roy Sch Dungannon, Trin Coll Dublin, Lincoln Coll Oxf. *m*: Clara Jane Wilson. *s*: 1. *d*: 1. Senior Fellow T.C.D., Prof of Applied Economics Dublin Univ. *Publ*: A.K. Fellow Report; A Groundwork of Economics; The Nemesis of Economic Nationalism; *Ctr*: Economic Journ, Economist, Studies. *s.s*: Agricultural Economics. *Rec*: Golf, motoring, etc. *c*: Univ (Dublin). *a*: 36 Trinity College, Dublin & Shrubs Hse, Raheny, Co Dublin. *T*: 35787.

JOHNSTON, Lennox Matthew. *b*: Loanhead, Midlothian 1899. *e*: Ayr Acad, Glas Univ. *m*: Frieda Smith. *s*: 1. *d*: 2. *Ctr*: Lancet, Brit Med Journ, Medical World. *s.s*: Tobacco Addiction. *Rec*: Golf, bridge. *a*: 104 Mount Pleasant Rd, Wallasey, Cheshire. *T*: 769.

JOHNSTON, Mary. *Publ*: The Old Dominion; Hunting Shirt; Miss Delicia Allen; By Order of the Company; etc. *a*: Princes Hse, Jermyn St, London, S.W.1.

JOHNSTON, Myrtle. *b*: Dublin 1909. *Publ*: Hanging Johnny; Relentless; The Maiden; Laleen; The Rising; Amiel. *s.s*: Novels & Short Stories. *Rec*: Playgoing & reading. *a*: The Myrtles, Canford Cliffs, Bournemouth. *T*: Canford Cliffs 1032.

JOHNSTON, Philip Mainwaring, F.S.A., F.R.I.B.A. *b*: Brixton 1865. *e*: King's Col Sc & King's Col Lon. *m*: Florence Anna Wynne. *d*: 1. Archt. Surveyor to Dean & Chapter of Chichester 1927–. *n.a*: Ed Methuen's Little Guides to Kent, Surrey, Hants, Essex, etc. *Publ*: Old Camberwell; A Schedule of Antiquities in the County of Surrey; Articles in the Victoria County Histories of Surrey & Sussex; etc. *c.t*: Antiquaries Journ, Archæ Journ, Journ of Brit Archæ, Surrey Archæ Soc Assoc Collections, Dorset Antiqu Soc, Country Life, Lon & Middx Archæ Trans, etc. *s.s*: Ancient eccles archt, preservation of stained glass & wall-paintings. Excavated Tortington Priory Sussex, Prittlewell Priory Essex, St Helen's Nunnery Bishopsgate, E.C., etc. Built 24 War Memls, etc. Vice-Pres Brit Archæ Assoc. Vice-Pres Surrey Archæ Soc. *Rec*: Photography, gardening. *c*: Adv Cmt Dios of Southwark, Guildford, Chichester. Hon Cons Archt Shakespeare Trustees, Stratford-on-Avon, etc. *a*: Sussex Lodge, Champion Hill, S.E.5. *t*: Brixton 5331.

JOHNSTON, Priscilla. *b*: Lon 1910. *e*: Roedean, St George's Sc, Harpenden & Brighton Mun Sc of Art. *Publ*: The Narrow World; Green Girl; That Summer. *a*: Lon. *t*: Riverside 2250.

JOHNSTON, Sir Reginald Fleming, J.P., M.A. (Oxon), HonLL.D. (Hong Kong), K.C.M.G., C.B.E. *b*: Edin 1874. *e*: Priv & Magdalen Col Oxf. Prof of Chinese, Lon Univ. Asst Colonial Sec Hong Kong. J.P., Commssr of Weihaiwei, China. *Publ*: Poems (1904); A Chinese Appeal to Christendom; Buddhist China; The Chinese Drama; Confucianism & Modern China ('34); Twilight in the Forbidden City ('34); etc. *c.t*: Nineteenth Century & After, Nat Review, Eng Review, Saturday Review, Journ Roy Asiatic Soc, News-Chron, etc. *s.s*: China, Far East, Buddhism. Was Eng Tutor & Adv to last of the Manchu Emperors of China in the Forbidden City. Comptroller of the Summer Palace, Peking. Lewis Fry Meml Lect Bristol Univ '33–34. *Rec*: Travel, mountains. *c*: Athenæum, Peking & Tientsin, etc. *a*: 18 Mortlake Rd, Kew Gdns, Surrey.

JOHNSTON, Right Hon. Thomas, P.C. *b*: Dumbartonshire 1882. *e*: Lairdsland Publ Sch Kirkintilloch & Lenzie Acad, Glas Univ. Married. *d*: 2. Forestry Commissioner 1945—, Journalist, Chm North of Scotland Electric Board, M.P.(Lab) West Stirlingshire '22—24, Dundee '24—29, West Stirlingshire '29—31 & '35—45, Parl Under-Secretary Scotland '29—31, Lord Privy Seal '31, Sec of State for Scotland '41—45 (ret). *Publ*: History of the Working Classes in Scotland; The Finances & The Nation; Old Kirkintilloch; Our Noble Families. *Ctr*: Sunday Times. *s.s*: Scotland. *w.s*: Reg Comm for Scottish Civil Defence Region 1939—41. *a*: Holm Cottage, Fintry, Stirlingshire. *T*: Fintry 44.

JOHNSTON, Rev. Thomas James, M.A. *b*: Ballymacward, Co Galway 1901. *e*: Trin Coll Dublin. *m*: Violet Sarah McGrath. *s*: 2. *d*: 1. Clergyman, Rector of St Catherine's Dublin '39, Rural Dean of Newcastle Diocese of Dublin. *n.a*: Ed Church of Ireland Monthly. Mag. *Publ*: St Columbia. *Ctr*: Looking at Ireland. *Rec*: Walking, cycling, golf. *c*: Univ (Dublin), *a*: St Catherine's Rectory, South-Circular Rd, Dublin. *T*: 51935.

JOHNSTON, Walter Henry. *b*: Ealing 1895. *e*: St Paul's Sc, Trinity Col Cam. Translator. *Publ*: (Trans)—Scien of Logic, Hegel; Science of Character, Klages; The Structure of Thought, Fischer; Rudenderff, Tschuppik; The League on Trial, Beer; etc. *Rec*: Yachting. *c*: Roy Corinthian Yacht. *a*: 24 Belsize Grove, London. *t*: Primrose 6723.

JOHNSTON, William Allen. *b*: New York 1876. *e*: Union Col Univ of Michigan. Writer. *m*: Dorothy Ovens. *d*: 1. *n.a*: Hamptons Magazine, '07. New York Herald, '10. Ed Motion Picture News '13—29. Peoples Home Journal Ed '24—26. *Publ*: Deeds of Doing and Daring. *c.t*: Saturday Evening Post, New York Herald—Tribune, Century, Harpers. *s.s*: Fiction, Motion Picture Scenarios. *a*: Beverly Hills, California. *t*: Oxford 1501.

JOHNSTON-SAINT, Peter. M.A., F.R.S.E., F.Z.S., *b*: Aberdeen 1886. *e*: Rossall, St John's Coll Camb. *m*: Clare Isabel Mansell-MacCulloch. *d*: 2. Scientific

Research Worker, C.St.J., Off Legion of Hon. *Publ*: Jassamine Flowers & Green Leaves; Poems trans from Persian; Green Hills & Golden Sands; Castanets & Carnations. *Ctr*: Illust Lond News, Medical Press, Journ Roy Soc Arts, Aesculap—Paris, various Scientific journals. *s.s*: Travel, History of Medicine, Faith Healing. *Rec*: Riding, sailing, travelling. *w.s*: World War I. *c*: Roy Thames Yacht, Junior United Service, Pilgrims, Cercle Intervallié Paris. *a*: 34 Bryanston Court, London, W.1. *T*: Paddington 6146.

JOHNSTONE, Hilda, Litt.D.(Manch). *b*: Stockport 1882. *e*: Manch Hgh Sch for Girls & Univ of Manch. Hon Archivist to Bishop of Chichester, Asst-Lect Hist Univ of Manch 1906—13, Reader in Hist King's Coll Lond '13—22, Univ Prof Hist Roy Holloway Coll '22—42. *Publ*: Letters of Edward, Prince of Wales 1304—05; Edward of Carnarvon; The Queen's Household (The English Government at Work 1327—36); & Other Books on Mediæval Subjects. *Ctr*: Eng Hist Rev, History, Church Quarterly, Speculum, Oxford Mag. *s.s*: 13th & 14th Century History. *a*: 20 St Martins Sq, Chichester.

JOHNSTONE, J. Terr Mem N.U.J. *a*: 76 Teignmouth Rd, N.W.2.

JOHNSTONE, J. Alfred. *b*: 1861. *e*: T.C.D. *m*: E. C. R. Beamish, dau of the late Archdeacon Beamish & niece of the late Field-Marshal Lord Roberts. Writer. *Publ*: The Art of Teaching Pianoforte Playing; Dreams That Were Not All Dreams; Modern Tendencies & Old Standards in Musical Art; Rubato; Optimism, or Everybody's Guide to Happiness; Elementary Phrasing; Individuality in Piano Touch; etc. *c.t*: Various music journs & papers. *s.s*: Music, lit. Ex-Mem Registration Bd of Music Teachers apptd by the Govt of Victoria. For some time music critic of the Melbourne Argus. Hon F.T.C.L. *Rec*: Motoring, travel. *a*: Warrnambool, Salcombe Hill, Sidmouth, Devon.

JOHNSTONE, James William, M.B., C.M. Med Pract. *Publ*: There Is no After-Life Except Through Your Children. *a*: Hurst View, Bodenham, Hereford. *t*: 23.

JOHNSTONE, Mary Anderson, B.Sc(Lond), F.L.S. *b*: Dumfries; *e*: Edin & M/C Univ. *Publ*: Etruria, Past & Present; Physical Education of Girls; Elements of Geology; The Poet and the Flowers; etc. *c.t*: Morning Post, Scotsman, Armchair Sci, Naturalist, Annals of Archeology, Studi Etruschi (Florence), Glas Herald, etc. *s.s*: Botany, Geol, Physiology, Etruscology. *Rec*: Travel, gardening. *a*: 9 Victoria Avenue, Cheadle Hulme, Cheshire.

JOHNSTONE, Rev. Verney Lovett. *b*: Southbourne 1905. *e*: Cheltenham Col, Worcester Col Oxf & Cuddesdon Col Oxf. *m*: Joan Harward. *Publ*: A Hospital Prayer Book ('33). *c.t*: Ch Times, English Catholic, St Raphael Quart. *s.s*: Ch hist. Tutor of Keble Col Oxf '28—32. Examining Chap to the Bishop of Newcastle '32—. *Rec*: Tennis. *a*: St Gabriel's Vic, Newcastle-on-Tyne. *t*: 55843.

JOINT, Edgar James, C.M.G., O.B.E., F.R.G.S. *b*: Bristol 1902. *e*: London Sch of Economics, Caius Coll Camb. *m*: Holly Morgan. *s*: 3. H.M. Foreign Service, Commercial Counsellor to Brit Embassy Brussels. *Publ*: Official Economic Reports. *s.s*: Econs, Public Finance, International Trade. *Rec*: Poetry, Trans of Latin-American poetry. *a*: c/o Foreign Office, London, S.W.1.

JOLIVET, ALFRED: professor in Univ. of Paris; *b*. Arcay, France, 1885; *s*. Jean Baptiste and Fanny (Gaudrat) J.; educ. Lycée de Bourges, Lycée Lakanal, Ecoleé normale superieure (Paris), Universite de Berlin. DEGREE: Litt.D.; *m*. Marie Madeleine Perronneau, Sept. 2, 1922. AUTHOR: Else, conte de Noel, de Kielland; traduit du Norvegien avec une étude sur l'auteur, 1920; Wilhelm Heinse, Sa vie et son oeuvre jusqu en 1787, 1922; Les Tentatious de Nils Brosme de Kinck, traduit dusnorwegien avec une étude sur l'anteur, 1926; Le theatre de Strindberg, 1931. Contributes to Revue des Cours et Conferences (Paris), Litteris (Lund-Suede). General character of writing: literary history. Religion, Roman Catholic. HOME: 9 Avenue Beauséjour, Bourg-la-Reine (Seine), France.

JOLLIFFE, John Edward Austin. *b*: Southampton 1891. *e*: Weymouth Coll, Keble Coll Oxf. Fell & Sub-Warden Keble Coll Oxf. *Publ*: A Constitutional History of Medieval England; Pre-Feudal England; The Jutes. *Ctr*: Eng Hist Rev, Econ Hist Rev. *s.s*: English Mediæval History. *a*: 287 Woodstock Rd, Oxford. *T*: 58984.

JOLLY, Miss E. B., B.A. Principal The Laurels School, Rugby, Warwicks.

JOLLYE, Anne. *b*: London. Literary agent. with Gilbert F. Wright, literary agent, 3 y. *a*: West Residence, British Museum, W.C.1. & 8 Garrick St, W.C.2. (office). *t*: Temple Bar 3212.

JOLOWICZ, Herbert Felix, M.A., LL.D. *b*: London 1890. *e*: St Paul's Sch & Trin Coll Camb. *m*: Ruby Wagner *s*: 2. *d*: 1. Prof Roman Law Lond Univ, Barrister, Major, late Intelligence Corps. *n.a*: Ed Journal Soc of Publ Teachers of Law 1924—. *Publ*: Historical Introduction to the Study of Roman Law; Digest XLVII De Furtis with Introduction, Translation & Notes, Camb U.P. *Ctr*: Law Quarterly Rev. *s.s*: Roman Law, Jurisprudence. *a*: 9 Ferncroft Ave, London, N.W.3. *T*: Hampstead 5529.

JOLY de LOTBINIERE, Alain, B.A., Ph.B., B.Sc., F.R.S.A. *b*: Quebec, Canada 1886. *e*: Univs of Bishop's Coll & Toronto. *m*: Agnes Slayden. *s*: 1. *d*: 3. Administrator Seigniory of Lotbiniere, Director of Canadian Forestry Assoc. *Publ*: A National Forestry Policy; A Canadian Flag for Canadians; A Seigneur's Planned Economy; Lumberg in Lotbiniere; Identity; Municipal Education; Sir Henri de Lotbiniere's Black Walnuts; etc. *s.s*: Forestry. *Rec*: Fishing. *a*: Pointe Platon, Co. Lotbiniere, P.Q., Canada. *T*: Lotbiniere 39.

JONES, Dr. A. Roby. *Publ*: The Four Human Blood Groups (in conj with late Prof E. E. Glynn). *a*: 37 Church St, Southport.

JONES, Abel John, O.B.E., M.A.(Cantab), B.Sc.(Wales), Ph.D.(Jena). *b*: Rhymney, Mon 1878. *e*: Univ Coll of Wales, Clare Coll Camb, Univ of Jena (Germany). *m*: R. M. Williams. *s*: 3. H.M. Inspector of Schools (ret). *Publ*: In Search of Truth; Abbrevia Shortwriting; Character in the Making; Rudolf Eucken; I Was Privileged; From an Inspector's Bag; John Morgan M.A.; Heriaf fy Hen Syniadau. *Ctr*: Various Eng & Welsh periodicals. *s.s*: Education & Philosophy. Lit Adj Welsh Nat Eisteddfod. *Rec*: Walking, literature. *c*: Cambridge Union. *a*: Heddannedd, 291 New Rd, Porthcawl, Glam. *T*: 259.

JONES, Alcwyn Arnold, F.R.S.A. *b*: Dudley, Worcs 1881. *e*: Dudley Gr Sch. *m*:. *d*: 1. Heating & Ventilating Engineer. *n.a*: Ed Domestic Engineering 1918—32, Ed Journ of Inst of Heating & Ventilating Engineers '33. *Publ*: Modern Heating & Ventilating. *Ctr*: Heating & Ventilating Engineer, Ironmonger, Building, Domestic Engineering. *s.s*: Heating & Ventilating, Book Reviews. *a*: Gwent, 107 Carlton Ave, Preston Rd, Wembley, Middlesex. *T*: Arnold 4173.

JONES, Arnold Hugh Martin. Professor of Ancient History at University College, London, since 1946. *Publ*: inc The Cities of the Eastern Roman Provinces; The Herods of Judea; The Greek City from Alexander to Justinian; etc. *a*: 29 Chepstow Villas, London, W.11.

JONES, Aubrey, B.Sc.(Econ). *b*: Merthyr Tydfil, Glam 1911. *e*: Cyfarthfa Castle Sec Sch Merthyr Tydfil, Lond Sch Economics. Journalist. *n.a*: Western Mail (Editorial Staff & Leader-Writer) '36—37, The Times (For Editorial Staff & For Corr in Paris, Berlin, Balkans) '37—39, The Sun Times (Diplomatic Corr) '46—47, Publ: The Pendulum of Politics; Right & Left. *Ctr*: Nineteenth Century & After, Soundings, Everybody's. *s.s*: Conservatism, Conservative Policy, Political Thought, International Affairs, The Empire. *Rec*: Squash. *w.s*: Gen Staff (Military Intell) War Office, Eighth Army & Allied Forces H.Q. *a*: Flat 580, Kensington Close, Wright's Lane, London, W.8. *T*: Western 8170.

JONES, Benjamin Caradoc. *b*: Merioneth. *e*: Brit Sc Bala. *m*: Eleanor Harriet Davies. Journalist. *n.a*: Chief Reporter Colwyn Bay Weekly News 1917–. *Rec*: Bowls. *a*: Haulfre, Minydon Pk, Old Colwyn. *t*: 5310.

JONES, BENNETT MELVILL: professor of aeronautics; b. Liverpool, Eng., Jan. 28, 1887; m. Benedict and Henrietta (Melvill) J.; educ. Birkenhead Sch., Emmanuel Coll. (Cambridge). DEGREE: First Class Honors, Mechanical Science Tripos; m. Dorothy Laxton Jotham. AUTHOR: Aerial Surveying by Rapid Methods (with Maj. J. C. Griffiths); Various reports of the Aeronautical Research Committee. General character of writing: technical, aeronautics. Held research scholarship from Imperial Coll. (London). Wer service: Royal Aircraft Establishment, 1914-16; Arwamen Experimental Station Orfordness, 1916-18; Technical Dept. Air Ministry, 1918-19. Rank: Lieut.-Col.; qualified as pilot and served for a time as observer in 48th Squadron. Member Aeronautical Research Committee. OFFICE: Engineering Laboratory, Cambridge Univ. HOME: 7 Harvey Road, Cambridge, Eng.

JONES, Bernard E. Ed The Practical Woodworker; Work; The New Amateur Mechanic. *a*: c/o The Waverley Book Co, 96-7 Farringdon St, E.C.4.

JONES, Bernard Marston Ellis. *b*: Port Talbot 1910. *e*: Port Talbot Cnty Sc. Journalist. *n.a*: Apprentice to S. Wales Evening Post at Port Talbot '29, Pembrokeshire Rep S. Wales Evening Post '32, Asst Sec to Port Talbot Chamber of Trade. *Rec*: Cricket & billiards. *a*: Somerset Hse, Dark St, Haverfordwest, Pembs. *t*: H'west 221.

JONES, Bertram H. Physician. *c.t*: Lancet, B.M.J. *a*: 47 Queen Anne St, W.1. *t*: Welbeck 1035.

JONES, Brinley Richard. *b*: Llanelly, 1872. Journalist. *n.a*: Founder, Ed & Promoter Llanelly Star, Ed & J. Promoter Cardigan Advertiser. *a*: Treforgan, Cardigan. *t*: Llanelly 309, Cardigan 28.

JONES, C. B., M.B.E.(Mil). *b*: 1898. *m*: Margaret Winifred Williams. *s*: 2. *d*: 1. *n.a*: Director, Evening Post Swansea. *Ctr*: Various Articles on Rugby Football. *s.s*: Rugby Football. *Rec*: Golf, walking. *w.s*: 1914—18, Raised & Commanded 113 Rocket A.A. Bty (104 Glam H.G.) '42—45. *a*: 143 Glanmor Rd, Swansea. *T*: 88158 & 4410.

JONES, Rev. Charles. *b*: Llangollen 1878. *e*: Glyndyfrdwy Bd Sc, Menai Bridge G.S. & Didsbury Theo Col M/C. *m*: M. E. Jones. *s*: 1. *d*: 1. *Publ*: (In Welsh) Llên a Dysgeidiaeth Israel Hyd Gwymp Samaria. *c.t*: Yr Eurgrawn, Y Gwyliedydd Newydd. *s.s*: Prayer & the modern mind. *a*: 24 Halkyn Rd, Chester.

JONES, Sir Clement Wakefield, Kt., C.B., M.A. *b*: Burneside, Westmorland 1880. *e*: Haileybury, Trin Coll Camb. *m*: Enid Griffith-Boscawen. *s*: 2. *d*: 1. Chmn Commonwealth Shipping Cttee, Mem Board Brit Overseas Aviation Corp, Asst-Sec War Cabinet 1916—19, Sec Brit Empire Delegation Peace Conference Paris '19, Vice-Chmn Counc Roy Inst International Affairs Chatham Hse. *Publ*: British Merchant Shipping; Pioneer Shipowners Vols I & II; Sea Trading & Sea Training. *Ctr*: Various. *s.s*: Shipping. *Rec*: Walking, riding. *c*: Athenæum. *a*: 415 Rodney House, Dolphin Sq, London, S.W.1.

JONES, Clifford Merton, M.Sc. *b*: Cutwood Nr Wakefield 1902. *e*: Queen Elizabeth's G.S. Wakefield, Leeds Univ. *m*: Winifred May Lawrence. *d*: 2. Scmaster. *Publ*: A Beginner's Chemistry (John Murray). *s.s*: Chemistry. *a*: 3 Camden Terr, West Park St, Dewsbury.

JONES, Very Rev. D. J. *a*: The Deanery, Llandaff, Cardiff.

JONES, Daniel, M.A. *b*: London 1881. *e*: Radley Coll, Univ Coll Sch, King's Coll Camb. *m*: Cyrille Motte. *s*: 1. *d*: 1. Prof Phonetics Univ Coll Lond, Barrister, Hon Dr Phil (Zurich) 1936, Ed Le Maître Phonetique since '07. *Publ*: The Pronunciation of English; Outline of English Phonetics; Colloquial French (in coll with E. M. Stephan); Fundamentos de Escritura Fonetica (with I. Dahl); A Sechuana Reader (with S. T Plaatje); The Tones of Sechuana Nouns; A Cantonese Phonetic Reader (with Kwing Tong Woo). *s.s*: Phonetics, Pronunciations of Languages, Spelling Reform. *Rec*: Music, unorthodox theosophy. *a*: 3 Marsham Way, Gerrards Cross, Bucks. *T*: Gerrards Cross 3490.

JONES, Canon David Ambrose, M.A. *b*: Cilcennin, Cards 1866. *e*: Aberystwyth Coll, Corpus Christi Coll Oxf. *m*: Camilla Grace Lloyd. *d*: 2. Canon of St David's Cathedral (ret). *Publ*: Philosophic Thought & Religion; Life & Times of Griffith Jones; History of the Church of England. *a*: Somerville, Sketty Green, Swansea.

JONES, Rev. David Daven, B.A. *b*: Glynneath 1856. *e*: Col Sc Swansea, St David's Col Lampeter. *m*: Margaret Robinson Taylor. *Publ*: History of Kidwelly; Hints on the Compilation of a Parish History; Arwyddluniau Eglwysig; Hymnan ar Amsir Rhyfel a Therfysgau; etc. *a*: 6 Westbourne Rd, Penarth, Glam.

JONES, David Gwynfryn, Ald. *b*: Bryncrug Towyn 1869. *m*: Christiana Lloyd. *s*: 2 (1 dec). *n.a*: Mang Ed New Watchman (official weekly n/p of Welsh Methodism). *Publ*: Memoir of Rev John Hughes, D.D. *c.t*: Numerous Welsh periodicals. Mem of Ct of Univ of Wales. Sec 20 y. Fed of Free Ch's of Wales. *a*: Gwylfa, Flint Mountain, Flint.

JONES, Dudley William Carmalt, M.A., M.D.(Oxon), F.R.C.P., F.R.A.C.P. *b*: London 1874. *e*: Uppingham, Corpus Christi Coll Oxf & St Mary's Hosp London. *m*: Mabel Gertrude Tottenham. *s*: 1. *d*: 1. Emeritus Prof of Systematic Medicine Univ. of Otago N.Z. *Publ*: History of Univ of Otago Medical School; Elementary Medicine in Terms of Physiology; Organic Substances; Sera & Vaccines in Physiological Therapeutics; Introduction to Therapeutic Innoculation; Diversions of a Professor in New Zealand. *Ctr*: B.M.J., Lancet, Brain,

Practitioner, etc. *Rec*: Sketching. *c*: Athenæum, Univ Sydney & Dunedin. *a*: c/o Medical School, Dunedin, New Zealand.

JONES, E., M.Sc., M.B., Ch.B., D.P.H. *m*: Rhiannon Morris-Jones. M.O. Cardiganshire. *Publ*: Chemistry for Rural Schools. *Ctr*: Various Eng and Welsh journs, formerly Lect in Public Health Lab Manch Univ. *a*: Isallt, St David's Rd, Aberystwyth.

JONES, Rev. E. B. *b*: Llanllechid 1866. *e*: Menai Bridge, Bala, Bangor Col. *m*: Twice. *d*: 1. *Publ*: Origin of Congregationalism in Anglesey. *a*: Gwalchmai, Anglesey.

JONES, E. B. C. Coursolles. See **Lucas, Emily Beatrix**

JONES, E. P. Sec Chester Br N.U.J. *a*: The Hollies, Granville Rd, Chester.

JONES, Dr. E. W. *c.t*: Various med journs. *a*: 9 Wyndcote Rd, Mossley Hill, L'pool.

JONES, Sir Edgar Rees, K.B.E., M.A. Barrister-at-Law. *Publ*: The Art of the Orator; Selected English Speeches; Selected English Essays. *a*: 12 Whitehall, Lon.

JONES, E(DWARD) ALFRED: connoisseur, author; b. Llanfyllin, N. Wales, July, 1872; s. Thomas Jones; educated privately. DEGREES: (Hon.) M.A. (Univ. of Wales and Rutgers Univ. (U.S.A.). AUTHOR: The Church Plate of the Diocese of Bangor, 1906; The Old Church Plate of the Isle of Man, 1907; The Old Silver Sacramental Vessels of the Foreign Protestant Churches of England, 1907; Old English Gold Plate, 1907; Catalogue of the Leopold de Rothschild Plate, 1907; Illustrated Catalogues (2) of the J. Pierpont Morgan collections of Old Plate, 1908; The Old Royal Plate in the Tower of London, 1908; The Old English Plate of the Emperor of Russia, 1909; The Old Plate of the Cambridge Colleges, 1910; The Gold and Silver of Windsor Castle, 1911; The Gold and Silver and Limoges Enamels of the Baroness James de Rothschild, 1912. Editor of the Memorials of Old North Wales, 1913; The Old Silver of the American Churches, 1913; The Journal of Alexander Chesney, 1921; Catalogue of the Farrer Collection of Old Plate, 1924; Old Silver, European and American, 1928; The Loyalists of New Jersey, 1928; The Loyalists of Massachusetts, 1929. Contributor to London Times, Burlington Mag., Connoisseur, Country Life, Old Furniture, International Studio. General character of writing: historical, arts and crafts, technical. Fellow Commoner Clare Coll. (Cambridge); Fel. Roy. Hist. Soc.; Fellow Society of Antiquaries. CLUBS: Oxford and Cambridge, Royal Societies (both London). HOME: Oxford and Cambridge Club, London, S. W. 1. Eng.

JONES, Edward Vernon. *b*: Merthyr Tydfil 1911. *e*: Pentre Sec Sc Rhondda. Journalist. *n.a*: Chief Reporter Carmarthen Journ '30. *a*: 43 Francis Terr, Carmarthen.

JONES, Elwyn. *b*: Cwmaman, Glamorgan 1923. *e*: Cwmaman Boys' Sch, Aberdare Boys' County Sch & London Sch of Econ. Journalist, Mem Critics' Circle. *n.a*: Reporter '44 & Dep-Ed '46— News Review. *Ctr*: Tribune, What's On In London, Empire Life, *s.s*: Theatre, Music, Radio, Films, Books. *Rec*: Arguing. *a*: 210 Westbourne Gr, London, W.11.

JONES, Rev. Emrys, B.A., B.D., B.Litt. Prof of Theology. *a*: Hafdre, St Non's Av, Carmarthen, S. Wales.

JONES, Lady Enid. *m*: Sir Roderick Jones. *s*: 3. *d*: 1. *Publ*: A Diary Without Dates ; The Happy Foreigner ; Sailing Ships (poems); Alice & Thomas & Jane; National Velvet; Serena Blandish: or the Difficulty of Getting Married; The Squire; (Plays) Lottie Dundass; National Velvet; Poor Judas. *a*: 29 Hyde Park Gate, London, S.W.7, & North End Hse, Rottingdean, Sussex. *T*: Western 0245 & Rottingdean 9337.

JONES, Rev. Enoch. *b*: Treorchy, Glam 1887. *e*: Ystrad Meurig Gr Sch & St David's Coll Lampeter. *m*: Elizabeth Muriel Rees. *d*: 2. Clerk in Holy Orders. *n.a*: Ed Y Cyfaill Eglwysig 1924—. *Publ*: Odlau Isylog. *T*: Y Llan, Yr Haul. *s.s*: Welsh Grammar. *Rec*: Walking. *a*: 123 Croxted Rd, Dulwich, London, S.E.21. *T*: Gipsy Hill 2812.

JONES, Ernest, M.D., B.S., F.R.C.P., D.P.H. *b*: Gower, Glam 1879. *e*: Llandovery Coll, Univ Coll Sth Wales & Lond, Paris & Munich. *m*: Katherine Jokl. *s*: 2. *d*: 1. Founder & for 20 years Ed Internat Journ of Psycho-Analysis, Ed Internat Library of Psycho-Analysis, Co-Ed Internat Zeitschrift f. Psychoanalyse. *Publ*: Papers on Psycho-Analysis ; Essays in Applied Psycho-Analysis ; The Problem of Hamlet & the Oedipus Complex ; On the Nightmare ; Social Aspects of Psycho-Analysis ; Psycho-Analysis ; How the Mind Works (with Cyril Burt) ; Psycho-Analysis of the Christian Religion. *Ctr*: 230 Monographs in scientific periodicals, New Statesman. *s.s*: Psycho-Analysis, Sociology, Anthropology. *Rec*: Chess, figure-skating. *c*: Athenæum, Savile, Roy Soc of Medicine. *a*: The Plat, Elsted, nr Midhurst, Sussex. *T*: Harting 61.

JONES, Evan John, M.A., D.Litt., F.S.A *b*: Ferndale 1892. *e*: Sec Sch Ferndale, Pupil Teachers' Centre Porth, Univ Coll Cardiff. Prof of Education Univ Coll Swansea. *Publ*: Medieval Heraldry; History of Education in Wales; Buchedd Sant Martin: Gramadegau'r Pencerddiaid (with Prof G. F. Williams); Llyfr Dysgu Lladin. *s.s*: Educational. *a*: Derlwyn, Graig Terr, Ferndale, Glamorgan. *T*: Ferndale 41.

JONES, Frank, B.A.(Lond). *b*: Birmingham 1873. *e*: King Edward's Sch Aston & Mason Coll B'ham. Retired Schoolmaster, 2nd Master King Edward's Sch Aston 1896—1936, Lecturer in Lit & Anglo-Saxon Midland Inst B'ham. *Publ*: First & Second Latin Course; A First English Course; A New English Course; Brummagem English; Everyday Grammar & Similes; Ed Golden & Silver Books of Verse. *Ctr*: Sun Times, B'ham Post, B'ham Mail, John o' London's Weekly. *s.s*: Education, Phonetics, English Language, Lect City of Lond Vacation Course in Education. *Rec*: Rugby football, golf, amateur dramatics *c*: B'ham Press, Cosmopolitan. *a*: 16 Livingstone Rd, Birmingham 20. *T*: Birchfield 4355.

JONES, Frank Newling, J.P., F.J.I. *b*: Spalding 1869. *e*: Spalding G.S. *m*: Bertha Newling. *s*: 2. Ed Surrey Comet 1920–. *n.a*: Apprentice to Spalding Free Press, reporting Staff Surrey Comet, Ed Staff Western Morning News 1895-1901, Ed Staff South Wales News & Echo '01-20. *c.t*: The Daily Mail (25 y). *Rec*: Golf. *a*: Surrey Comet, Kingston-on-Thames. *t*: 1890.

JONES, Frederick Elwyn, M.P. *b*: Llanelly 1909. *e*: Llanelly County Sch, U.C.W. Aberystwyth, Gonville & Caius Coll Camb. *m*: Pearl Binder. *s*: 1. *d*: 2. Barrister, M.P. Plaistow Div (West Ham) '45—, Mem Brit War Crimes Exec Nuremberg '45—46, Pres Camb Union, Parl Priv Sec H.M. Attorney General. *Publ*: The Battle for Peace; The Attack from Within; Hitler's Drive to the East. *Ctr*: Fortnightly Rev, Spectator, Picture Post, Reynolds News. *s.s*: Foreign Affairs. *Rec*: Travelling. *w.s*: R.A. 1943—45, Deputy Judge Advocate in C.M.F. *a*: Stansfield Hse, Cranford, Middlesex. *T*: Hayes 1035.

JONES, Frederick Theophilus. *b*: Cardiff 1881. *m*: *s*: 1. *d*: 1. *n.a*: Ed-Mang Newark Herald 1906—. *Publ*: Official Guide to Newark. *Rec*: Golf. *a*: 20 Wellington Rd, Newark, Notts. *T*: Notts 555 & 64.

JONES, G. Leonard Douglas, B.A. *b*: L'pool 1891. *e*: Holt Sc L'pool & Univ of L'pool. *m*: Marie Eugenie Suzanne Tesseyre. Journalist. *n.a*: Sub-Ed-reporter China Mail Hong Kong 1915, Buenos Aires Herald '16–18 (Ed '17–18), Jt Ed Times of Brazil, Rio de Janeiro & Sao Paulo, Work at Rio for the Associated Press. Sub Ed Daily Mail, Lon, Paris & Atlantic Editions '21–28, Sub Ed Manchester Evening News '28–33, Sub Ed Daily Herald Manchester '33–. Published Special 189 page issues Buenos Aires Herald. *s.s*: Argentine, Brazil. *a*: 5 Hazel Av, Whalley Range, Manchester 16.

JONES, Gareth Richard Vaughan. *b*: Barry 1905. *e*: Barry Cnty Sc, U.C.W. Aberystwyth, Strasbourg Univ & Trin Col Cam. Journalist. *n.a*: Western Mail '33–. *c.t*: Times, Financial News, Western Mail, News-Chronicle, Star, Daily Express, Evening Standard, etc. *s.s*: Foreign affairs. *Rec*: Walking. *c*: Reform, Roy Inst Internat Affairs, Overseas League. *a*: Eryl, Barry, Glam.

JONES, George Frederick, A.M.I.W.T., I.E.E. *e*: K. Edward VII Sc Sheffield & Sheffield Univ. Married. *s*: 1. *d*: 1. *e*: Elec Eng. *Publ*: Sound Film Reproduction. *c.t*: Sheffield Independent, Elec Review, Practical Wireless, Kinematograph Weekly, Weekly Telegraph, etc. *s.s*: Radio & sound films. Instructor to Sheffield & Rotherham Educ Cmts. *Rec*: Sea travel. *a*: 139 Abbeydale Rd S., Sheffield 7.

JONES, George M. Edwardes, K.C. Barrister. *n.a*: Ed Blunt's Book of Ch Law 1892–1921, Asst Ed & Contributor Lord Halsbury's Encyc of Laws '10. *a*: 8 Fig Tree Court, Temple, E.C.4. *t*: Central 1218.

JONES, Rev. Griffith Hartwell, D.D., D.Litt, F.S.A. *Publ*: Dawn of European Civilisation; Celtic Britain & the Pilgrim Movement; Early Celtic Missionaries; The Royal Commission on Ancient Monuments & the Antiquities of Glamorganshire & Monmouthshire. *a*: Nutfield Rec, Surrey.

JONES, Gwenan. *b*: Bala, Merioneth, 1889. *e*: Univ Coll of Wales, Aberystwyth, Bryn Mawr Coll & Univ of Minnesota U.S.A. Sen Woman Lect in Education U.C.W. Aberystwyth. *Publ*: Three Welsh Religious Plays; Yr Ysgol Sul a'r Plant; Addysg yng Nghymru: Cymru a'i Chymdogion; Antur Fawr yr Apostol Paul; Ysgolion y Cymry; Ed Yr Efrydydd. *Ctr*: Bulletin of Celtic Studies & other lit, soc & educ periodicals. *s.s*: Education, Religious Education, Medieval Studies, Politics. *Rec*: Walking, travel. *a*: Llysnewydd, Llandre, Cardiganshire. *T*: Bow Street 39.

JONES, Gwilym Peredur, M.A., Litt.D., F.R.Hist.S. *b*: Birkenhead 1892. *e*: L'pool Univ. *m*: Winifred Agnes Riley. *d*: 2. Reader Econ Hist Univ of Sheffield. Assistance Bd Area Advisory Cttee. *Publ*: The Extent of Chirkland; Workers Abroad; (with Prof D. Knoop) the Mediæval Mason; A Short History of Freemasonry; (with Prof D. Knoop & D. Hamer) The Two Earliest Masonic MSS; The Early Masonic Catechisms; Early Masonic Pamphlets; (with Dr. A. G. Pool) 100 Years of Economic Development. *Ctr*: Trans Anglesey Antiquarian Soc, Hunter Arch Soc, Archæologia Cambrensis, Bulletin Bd Celtic Studies, Econ Hist Rev. *s.s*: Econ Hist, Welsh Hist, Lit & Philology, Political Theory. *Rec*: Fishing, walking. *a*: The University, Sheffield.

JONES, Gwilym Richard. *b*: Tal-y-sarn 1903. *e*: Tal-y-sarn Counc & Caernarvon Central Schs. *m*: Myfanwy Parry Jones. *s*: 2. *d*: 1. Editor, Mem N.U.J., Silver Crown 1935, Oak Chair '38 & Gold Medal '41, Nat Eisteddfod of Wales (Poetry & Prose), Mem Nat Party Exec Nat Eistedd Counc Development Assoc Cttee, etc. *n.a*: Ed Herald Mon '29–31, Y Brython '31–39, Nth Wales Times '39–45, Y Faner '45— & Ed-Mang Gee's Press '46—. *Publ*: Y Purdan; Clychau Buddugoliaeth (play); Several Plays, Poems & Books for Children. *Ctr*: Modern Story, Welsh periodicals & papers, various national papers. *s.s*: Literature, Drama, Welsh Features, Special Articles & Reviews, Welsh Nationalism, Eisteddfod, etc. *Rec*: Gardening, painting. *a*: 11 Bryn Teg, Denbigh, Nth Wales. *T*: Denbigh 219.

JONES, H. Parry, M.A. Mem Advisory Counc for Educ Wales & Counc Univ Coll Nth Wales (Bangor), late Headmaster Gr Sch Llanrwst (ret 1946), Mem Classical Assoc Cambrian Archæolog Soc. *n.a*: Formerly Ed Welsh Sec Scs Review. *Publ*: Hills & Valleys of Nth Wales. Verse Trans from Latin and English into Welsh. *a*: Hendre. Llanrwst. Denbigh. Wales.

JONES, Dr. H. S. *a*: Bassett Lodge, Bassett Av, Southampton.

JONES, Harold Spencer, M.A., ScD.(Cantab), F.R.S., F.R.A.S., F.R.MetS. *b*: Lon 1890. *e*: Latymer Sc Hammersmith & Jesus Col Cam. *m*: Gladys Mary Owers. *s*: 2. Astronomer Royal. *n.a*: Ed The Observatory 1914–23. *Publ*: General Astronomy. *c.t*: Nature, Science Progress, etc. *s.s*: Optics, astronomy. H.M. Astronomer at the Cape '23–33. Hon Fell Jesus Col Cam. *a*: Flamstead House, Greenwich Park, S.E.10. *t*: Greenwich 1238.

JONES, HENRY CHAPMAN: Lecturer on Chemistry and Photography at the Imperial College of Science and Technology (now retired); author; b. London, Eng., June, 1854; s. Charles James and Frances Caroline (Chapman) J.; educ. Private Sch., Birkbeck Inst., Royal Sch of Mines, Royal Coll. of Chemistry; m. Phoebe Simmons Morley, July 9, 1884. AUTHOR: Practical Organic Chemistry, 1881 (many subsequent edits.); Abridgements of Photography Specifications, Part 3a, 1885; Science and Practice of Photography, 1888; Science and Practice of Qualitative Analysis, 1898-9, and four subsequent editions; Practical Advanced Chemistry, 1898; Elementary Experiments in Inorganic Chemistry, 1897 (4th edit., enlarged, 1904); Photography of Today, 1913 (2nd edit., 1923). English Editor: Camera Obscura, 1899-1901. Contributor to more than 50 journs., mags and papers. General character of writing:: scientific, text books, technical. Results of researches have been published in many scientific soc. records. Fellow Inst. of Chemistry; Hon. Fellow Royal Photographic Soc. of Gt. Britain. Relig. denom., Congregationalist. HOME: Birnam, 67 Shakespeare Road, Hanwell, London, W. 7, Eng.

JONES, Rt. Rev. Herbert Gresford, D.D.(Cantab). *b*: Westmorland 1870. *e*: Haileybury & Trin Col Cam. *m*: Elisabeth Hodgkin. *s*: 1. Bishop of Warrington & Rector of Winwich. *Publ*: Uganda in Transformation; Friends in Pencil. *s.s*: Missny work, temp. Vicar of Bradford 1906-12. Archdeacon of Sheffield '12-20. *Rec*: Sketching, travel. *c*: Univ (L'pool). *a*: Winwich Rectory, Warrington. *t*: 866.

JONES, Heyland Beaufort. *b*: Rock Ferry, Cheshire. 1905. *e*: Birkenhead Sc, Reporter and salesman. *n.a*: Reuters, 1931. *s.s*: Wheat, maize and oil seeds. *Rec*: Golf, squash racquets. Asst Man in Karachi, India, for Patrick & Co (London & India). Lieut Indian Army Reserve of Officers '28–30. *c*: Sind Club, Karachi. *a*: 310 Earls Court Rd, S.W.5. & The Baltic Shipping & Mercantile Exchange, St Mary Axe, E.C.3. *t*: Flaxman 4773.

JONES, I. G. Sec Carnarvonshire Br N.U.J. *a*: Awelfryn, Dinorwic St, Carnarvon.

JONES, Ifano, M.A.(Honoris Causa Univ Wales). *b*: Aberdare 1865. *e*: Priv & at Elem Sch. *m*: Jessie Mary Charles. *n.a*: Ed Y Golofn Gymreig 1905—28, Lit A judicator Nat Eisteddfods since '01, Prov Eisteddfods ince 1894, Lect on Literary & Historical subjects. *Publ*: A History of Printing & Printers in Wales & Monmouthshire; A Classified Catalogue of the Cardiff Welsh Library; The Bible in Wales (jointly); Sir Matthew Cradock & some of his Contemporaries; Rhys ap Tewdwr Mawr; Llenyddiæth Hanner Olaf Ddeunawfed Ganrif; Dan Isaac Davies & the Bilingual Movement; W. T. Samuel: ei fywyd a'i Lafur (a biography); The Early Nonconformists of Cardiff & District; Compiler of Quarterly Bibliography of Wales. *Ctr*: Many Welsh & English periodicals. *s.s*: Bibliography, History, Lit. *Rec*: Walking & gardening. *a*: Y Weirlod, Penarth, Glam, Sth Wales.

JONES, Ira, D.S.O., M.C., D.F.C.(& Bar), M.M. *b*: St Clears 1896. *e*: Queen Elizabeth's Gr Sch Carmarthen. *m*: Olive G. Edmunds-Davies. Wing-Commander R.A.F. (ret), Medal of St George (Russia). *Publ*: King of Air Fighters; An Air Fighter's Scrap Book. *Ctr*: Sun Dispatch, Sun Pict, News of the World. *s.s*: Aviation & Rugby Football. *Rec*: Golf, tennis. *a*: Wolston Hse, St Clears, Carmarthen.

JONES, Irfon Austin Tweedie. *b*: Builth Wells 1898. *e*: Llanganten C. Sch & Builth Wells County Secondary. Journalist. *n.a*: Brecon & Radnor Express & Radnor Express 1915—'37, now in charge of Llandrindod Wells & Dist for Wellington Journ & Shrewsbury News. *Ctr*: P.A., B.B.C., Central News Ltd, Exchange Telegraph Co Ltd & all Lond & Prov dailies. *s.s*: Agricultural & General Reporting. *w.s*: World War 1 Western Front, Ireland & Egypt (wounded). *Rec*: Reading. *a*: Pantawel, Llanganten, nr Builth Wells, Brecons, & Caxton Hse, Llandrindod Wells, Rads. *T*: 2107.

JONES, James Gaymer, M.C. *b*: Upper Norwood 1891. *e*: Priv & Guy's Hosp. *m*: Nora Annie Crane. *s*: 1. *d*: 1. Medicine. *n.a*: Asst Hse Surg Guy's Hosp 1916, Out Patient Officer '20, Hse Surg '20, Surg Registrar, Tutor & Asst '20—26, Consult Surg Eden War Mem Hosp '25—26, Pres appts, Surg K. Edward VII Hosp Windsor, Maidenhead Hosp, Staines Hosp, etc. *c.t*: Med journs. *s.s*: Surgery. War Service. *Rec*: Tennis, gardening. *a*: Thornbury Hse, Windsor. *t*: 487.

JONES, John, F.R.S.A. *s.s*: Philos law & economics. Silver Medallist, R.S.A. & Exam in Rly Economics for Corp of Certified Secs. *a*: 22 Crewe St, Derby.

JONES, John Alun. *b*: Penygroes 1900. *m*: Phyllis King. Journalist. *n.a*: Western Mail & Sth Wales Echo, Ed Rep Aberdare Valley. *s.s*: Industrial, Football. *a*: 24 Glannant St, Aberdare.

JONES, John Arthur. *b*: Ruthin 1876. *e*: Ruthin G.S. *m*: Charlotte Twiddy. *s*: 2. *d*: 1. F/L. Journ. *n.a*: Denbighshire Free Press '92—95, Rep Pembrokeshire County Guardian '95—98, Lon Press Service '98—1900, Rep Sub-Ed Lon Daily News '00—06, Sub-Ed M/C Daily Dispatch '06—12, Sub-Ed & Rep Western Daily Mail '12—14 & after War until '30. *c.t*: National Press & Trade Journs & Periodicals. *s.s*: Trade & indust news. *Rec*: Bowls, S. Wales bowls. Correspondent Daily Herald, W.S. *a*: Kilcrecgan, Ty-wern Ave, Rhiwbina, Cardiff.

JONES, JOHN DANIEL: clergyman; *b*. Ruthin, Wales, April, 1865; *s*. Joseph David and Catherine (Daniel) J.; *educ*. Chorley Grammar Sch., Owens Coll. and Lancashire Independent Coll. (both Manchester). DEGREES: M.A. (Victoria), D.D. (St. Andrews); *m*. Emily Cunliffe (died), July, 1898. AUTHOR: The Model Prayer, 1899; The Glorious Company of the Apostles, 1901; The Gospel of Grace, 1907; The Hope of the Gospel, 1911; Devotional Commentary on St. Mark, 1913-21; The Gospel of the Sovereignty, 1914; If a Man Die, 1918; The Lord of Life and Death, 1920; The King of Love, 1924; The Greatest of These, 1925; Watching the Cross, 1926; The Inevitable Christ, 1928. General character of writing: religious. Chmn. Congregational Union, Eng. and Wales, 1909-10, 1925-26; made "Companion of Honor to the King", 1927; Moderator International Congregational Council, 1930—. Relig. denom., Congregationalist. CLUBS: Reform, National Liberal (both London). HOME: The Manse, St. Stephen's Road, Bournemouth, Eng.

JONES, John Harry. Prof Leeds Univ. *Publ*: The Tinplate Industry; Social Economics; The Economics of Private Enterprise; The Federal Reserve System; The Economics of Saving. *c.t*: Accountant & Bldg Socs Gazette. *a*: Highfield Hse, Headingley Lane, Leeds 6. *t*: 52559.

JONES, John Morwel. *b*: Brynhoffnant 1911. *e*: Elem & Sec Scs. N/p Reporter. *n.a*: W. Wales Guardian, '29. *a*: 12 Victoria Av, Fishguard, Pem.

JONES, John Ormsby. *b*: Wrexham 1908. *m*: Dorothy Jones. Journalist. *n.a*: Chief Reptr Nth Wales Guardian '28—30, Evesham Standard '30, Sth Cheshire Rep Cheshire Observer '30—36, Dist Mgr Nantwich Guardian '36—47, Nantwich Rep to Chester Chron '47. *s.s*: Sport, Agric. *Rec*: Bowls. *a*: 14 Mill St, Nantwich, Cheshire. *T*: 5698.

JONES, John Share, M.D. (Vet. H.C. Berne), D.V.Sc., M.Sc., M.R.C.V.S., F.R.C.V.S. *b*: Cefn. *e*: Univ Coll, King's Coll & Roy Vet Coll Lond, L'pool Univ & Paris. *m*: Mary S. Jones, M.D., Ch.B., LL.B., B.A. Prof Emeritus, formerly Dir of Vet Sc L'pool Univ & Prof of Vet Anatcmy, Chm of Wrexham & East Denbigh Live Stock Joint Cttee, Chrm Land Settlement & Training Assoc for Rural Development, etc, Pres R.C.V.S. *n.a*: Formerly Ed of Vet Student, Ed-in-Chf of The Vet News. *Publ*: Higher Agricultural Education in Wales; The Surgical Anatomy of the Horse (4 vols); etc. *Ctr*: Times, L'pool Dly Post, Ency Brit, Vet Record, etc. *s.s*: Education, Anatomy, Rural Industries, Food Production & Agricultural Educ. *Rec*: Sports. *c*: L'pool Univ. *a*: Fentrebychan Hall, nr Wrexham, & L'pool Univ. *T*: Rhos (Wrexham) 40, & L'pool Royal 5460.

JONES, John Tudor. *b*: Anglesey 1903. *e*: G.S. Llangefni, & Univs of Wales(Aberys) & Oxf (Jesus Col). Mang Ed to Messrs Hugh & Son, Publishers, Wrexham & Cardiff & Ed Y Cymro '31—34, Asst Ed Times of Ceylon '34—. Sub Ed Daily Mail '29—31, Ed Times of Mesopotamia (daily) '27—29, Western Mail, Cardiff '24—27. Acted as Times & Reuter Corr in Middle East, Chm Lit Cmt Roy Nat Eisteddfod of Wales '33. *a*: Times of Ceylon, Colombo.

JONES, Joseph, C.B.E., J.P. *b*: St Helens 1890. *e*: Nat, Tech Col & Sheffield Univ. *m*: Edith Hannah Morritt. *s*: 1. *d*: 6. Trades Un Sec, H.M. Coal Mines Re-Org & Commssr Yorks Miners' Assoc. *n.a*: Rother Valley Labour Journ 1920, Barnsley Counsellor '33. *Publ*: Organise for Victory; Why I Am in the Labour Party; Miners' Epic Struggle. *c.t*: Yorks Post, Sheffield Daily Indep, Clarion, Barnsley Chron, etc. *s.s*: Ind & local govt. Vice-Pres Miners' Fed of G.B. Chm Workers' Temp League. *Rec*: Golf, bowls, tennis. *c*: Nat Lab. *a*: Hillcrest, 15 Huddersfield Rd, Barnsley. *t*: 926.

JONES, Kenneth Cadwaladr. *b*: Carms 1907. *e*: Queen Elizabeth G.S. Carm. Journalist. *n.a*: Apprenticed Carm Journ '27—31, Tivy Side Advtr Cardigan '31—. *c.t*: Western Mail, Evening Post, Daily Express, News-Chronicle, etc. *s.s*: Sport. '34-35 Vice Pres W. Wales Branch N.U.J. *Rec*: Golf, cricket, billiards. *a*: The Glen Hotel, Cardigan, S. Wales. *t*: Cardigan 13.

JONES, L. R., F.R.G.S., B.Sc, PhD. Univ Prof. *Publ:* North England; North America; London River. *c.t:* Eng & Amer Geog Journs. *a:* Lon Sc of Econ, Houghton St, Aldwych, W.C.2.

JONES, Lawrence Evelyn, M.C., T.D. *b:* London 1885. *e:* Eton, Balliol. *m:* Lady Evelyn Alice Grey. *d:* 3. Investment banker (ret). *Publ:* You & the Peace (with G. B. Shirlaw); (Plays) Miss Fitznewton; The Dove & the Carpenter. *Rec:* Golf, shooting. *a:* 13 Wellington Ct, London, N.W.8. *T:* Primrose 3061.

JONES, Leslie Gordon Richard. *b:* Oxford 1898. *e:* Bedford House Sc Oxford. *m:* Margaret Ellen Cross. *s:* 3. *d:* 1. Ed. *n.a:* Reporter, Oxford Times, '12—14. Chief Reporter, Hastings Observer, '20—27. Ed, Kent Evening Echo, '27—29. Ed, Folkestone Herald, '29—. *Rec:* Walking, philately. *c:* Mem Folkestone Educational Cmt. *a:* St Francis, Ashley Ave, Cheriton, Folkestone. *t:* Cheriton 85316.

JONES, Rev. Maurice, D.D. *b:* Trawsfynydd, Merioneth 1863. *e:* Ch Coll Brecon, Jesus Coll Oxf. *m:* Jennie Bell Smith. *s:* 4. *d:* 2. Clergyman, Canon of St Davids, Treasurer Counc Welsh Nat Eisteddfod, formerly Princ St David's Coll Lampeter 1923—38, Fell Jesus Coll Oxf. *Publ:* The New Testament in the Twentieth Century; The Epistle to the Philippians; The Four Gospels; The Epistle to the Colossians; St Paul the Orator. *Ctr:* The Expositor, Expository Times, Church Quarterly Rev, etc. *s.s:* The New Testament. *c:* Nat Lib. *a:* 18 Spencer Rd, Chiswick, London, W.4. *T:* Chiswick 1023.

JONES, Max. *b:* London 1917. *e:* Polytechnic Sch. *m:* Betty Jones. *d:* 1. Jazz Critic & Lecturer. *n.a:* Feature Writer Melody Maker '44—, Ed Jazz Music Mag '41—, Broadcaster on Jazz & Negro Folk-Music, etc. *Publ:* Jazz Photo Album, with notes; Folk, Review of People's Music (ed). *Ctr:* Challenge Weekly, Record Changer (Amer), P.L. Jazz Yearbook, etc. *s.s:* American Jazz Music & Negro Folk-Song. *Rec:* Motoring, cricket. *a:* 26 Primrose Hill Rd, Hampstead, London, N.W.3. *T:* Primrose 7363.

JONES, Morgan Glyn Dwr. *b:* Merthyr Tydfil, Glam 1905. *e:* Merthyr Gr Sch, St Paul's Cheltenham. Married. Schoolmaster. *Publ:* (Short Stories) The Water Music; The Blue Bed; Poems. *Ctr:* Adelphi, Welsh Rev, Life & Letters To-day, Poetry, etc. *s.s:* The Short Story. *Rec:* Table tennis. *a:* 158 Manor Way, Whitchurch, Glamorgan.

JONES, Ossie Garfield, B.S., PhD. *b:* Ohio 1884. *e:* Ohio Wesleyan & Cornell Univs, Ohio State U.S.S., Chicago U.S.S., Univs of Wisconsin & Calif. *m:* Nellie Clara Nixon. Prof of Polit Sci Univ of Toledo Ohio. Head of Dept of Polit Sci, Univ of the City of Toledo Ohio 1919—. *Publ:* Parliamentary Procedure at a Glance ('33); Junior & Senior Manuals for Leadership with Lessons ('34). *c.t:* N.Y. Outlook, Review of Reviews, Current History, Asia, American Review, National Municipal Review, etc. *s.s:* Parl Procedure, Colonial Govt, Citizenship Educ. Author of Effective Citizenship course at Toledo Univ. War Service. *Rec:* Golf, tennis, contract bridge, gardening. *c:* Amer Polit Sci Assoc, Nat Munic League, etc. *a:* 2701 Rathbun Drive, Toledo, Lucas County, Ohio. *t:* Laundale 6988.

JONES, Paul John, M.A., Ph.D. *b:* Philadelphia 1897. *e:* Univ of Penn, Univ of Toulouse. *m:* . *s:* 2. *d:* 2. Writer & Journalist. *n.a:* Ed Columnist Ev Bulletin Phila 1939—. *Publ:* An Alphabet of Aviation. *Ctr:* Sat Ev Post, Colliers, Liberty, Strand, Mademoiselle, This Week, Nth Amer Rev, Women's Home Companion, etc. *s.s:* Latin American Affairs. *Rec:* Theatre, golf, walking, travel. *c:* Players, Nat Press, etc. *a:* 15 Hekamore Rd, Bala-Cynwyd, Penn, & Ev Bulletin, Phila, 5. *T:* Cynwyd 4679.

JONES, Philip Edmund, LL.B., F.R.Hist.S. *e:* Dartford Gr Sch & U.C.L. Deputy Keeper of Records, City & Corporation of London. *Publ:* The Poulters of London. *Ctr:* Many articles on Livery Companies, Local Government, London Courts of Law, etc. *s.s:* Historial & Economic matters relating to City of London. *a:* Innisfree, 18 Wansunt Rd, Bexley. *T:* Clerkenwell 2011.

JONES, Rev. Rhys. Welsh Meth Min. *Publ:* Life of St Paul. *c.t:* Y Winllan, Yr Eurgrawn, Y Gwyliedydd Newydd. *a:* 18 St Edmund's Rd, Bootle, L'pool.

JONES, Rev. Richard, B.A. Meth Min. *Publ:* Llawlyfa ar y Bedwand Efengyl; etc. *c.t:* Y Genedl, Y Gugludyd Newyd, Y Winllan, etc. *a:* Epworth Villa, Chapel St, Llandudno.

JONES, Robert Edmond. *b:* Milton, New Hampshire 1887. *e:* Harvard Univ. *m:* Margaret Carrington. Stage Designer & Director, Mem Nat Inst of Arts & Letters. *Publ:* The Dramatic Imagination; Drawings for the Theatre; Continental Stagecraft (with K. Macgowan). *s.s:* The Theatre. *c:* Harvard, Century, Players. *a:* Harvard Club, New York, U.S.A.

JONES, Robert Ivor. *b:* Bethesda Caerns 1906. *e:* Bethesda Cnty Sc. *n.a:* Sub-Ed The World's Fair, Oldham. Ex Sub-Ed Craenarvon Herald series. *c.t:* Welsh n/ps. *s.s:* Economics, foreign politics. *Rec:* Fishing, music. *a:* 23 Fern St, Oldham, Lancs.

JONES, Robert Walter. *b:* London 1890. *e:* Haberdashers' Sch. *m:* Muriel Joyce. *s:* 2. Mem Counc Inst of Bankers, Educ Ed Bankers' Magazine. *Publ:* Bankers & the Property Statutes; Studies in Practical Banking; Joint Ed of Chitty on Contracts; Dictionary of Banking. *Ctr:* Banker's Mag, Journ Institute of Bankers, The Banker. *s.s:* Banking Economics, Law of Property. *Rec:* Golf. *c:* Savage. *a:* 99 Wood Vale, Forest Hill, London, S.E.23. *T:* Forest Hill 5035.

JONES, Robert William, M.A., F.R.Hist.S. *b:* Penygroes 1899. *e:* Penygroes Gr Sch, U.C.W. & Univ of Liverpool. *m:* Gwendolen Jones. Headmaster Welshpool Primary School. *Publ:* Bywyd Cymdeithasol Cymru. *Ctr:* Montgomeryshire Express & Collections, Y Cymro, Allwedd y Tannau, Y Ford Gron, Journ of Gypsy Lore Soc. *s.s:* Welsh Social History, Music & Literature. *Rec:* Reading, book collecting. *a:* Atallon, Welshpool, Montgomeryshire. *T:* 287.

JONES, Sir Roderick, K.B.E. *m:* Enid Bagnold. *s:* 3. *d:* 1. Former Princ Proprietor Reuters, Council Mem Roy Inst of Internat Affairs, Legion of Honour, Order of the Saviour (Greece) & Order of the Brilliant Jade (China), Order of The Crown (Italy). *Ctr:* Articles in Reviews & the Press, International News, etc. *Rec:* Hunting & horses. *c:* Marlborough-Windham, Brooks, Traveller's. *a:* 29 Hyde Park Gate, London, S.W., & Rottingdean, Sussex.

JONES, Rev. Spencer John, M.A.(Oxon). *b:* Croydon 1857. *e:* Chatham Hse Ramsgate, Worcester Col Oxf & Wells Theo Col. *m:* Elizabeth Barbara Coxwell (dec). *s:* 1. *d:* 1. *n.a:* Rector of Batsford with Moreton in Marsh '87-1932 (ret). *Publ:* The Clergy & the Catechism (7th Edn 1895); England and the Holy See (Intro to late Lord Halifax); The Counter

Reformation (3rd Edn); Catholic Reunion; Our Lord & His Lessons (1907); etc. *c.t*: Reunion & The Pilot. *c*: Authors. *a*: Moreton Hse, Sidford, Sidmouth.

JONES, T. C. D. *a*: 6 Clarendon Pl, Plymouth, Devon.

JONES, Dr. T. J. *a*: 133 Thingwall Road, Wavertree, Liverpool 15.

JONES, T. W., B.Sc., F.C.S., F.S.S. *n.a*: Ed Industrial Chemist; Retail Chemist; Food. *a*: 33 Tothill St, S.W.

JONES, Thomas, C.H., LL.D. *b*: Rhymney 1870. *e*: Univ Coll of Wales Aberystwyth & Glas Univ. *m*: Eirene T. Lloyd. *s*: 1. *d*: 1. President U.C.W. Aberystwyth, Sec (1930—45) & Trustee Pilgrims Trust. *n.a*: Trustee Observer. *Publ*: Rhymney Memories; Leeks & Daffodils; The Native never Returns. *Ctr*: Observer, Manch Guardian. *s.s*: Politics, Education. *c*: Athenæum. *a*: Brynhir, Penglais, Aberystwyth. *T*: 7346.

JONES, Sir Thomas George, K.B.E. *b*: Pontnewydd 1881. *m*: Mary Matthews. *a*: 3. Newspaper Proprietor, Chief Div Food Officer, Wales, Midland & N.W., M.O.F. until 1945. *n.a*: Founder Forthcawl News 1910. *Publ*: The Unbroken Front (British M.O.F. 1916—44). *Ctr*: Western Mail, Sth Wales Argus, Cheshire Chronicle & Observer, Sth Wales Post, etc. *s.s*: Food Control & Distribution. *a*: Beachside, Porthcawl, Glamorganshire. *T*: 25.

JONES, Thomas Gwynn, M.A.(Wales). *b*: Betws-Yn-Rhos 1871. *e*: Scs & Priv (Classics & Modern Lang's). *m*: Margaret Jane Davies. *s*: 2. *d*: 1. Univ Prof, Author, Publ Lect. *n.a*: Ed & other Journalistic work in Wales, Eng & Egypt 1892-1909. *Publ*: Dante & Beatrice (play, jtly with Daniel Rees '03); Cofiant Thomas Gee (biog); Dychweledigion (trans of Ibsen's "Gjengängere"); Welsh Folklore & Folk-Custom ('30); etc. *c.t*: Revue Celtique, Literaturo, Y Cymmrodor, Y Llenor, Welsh Outlook, etc. *s.s*: Celtic lang & lit. *Rec*: Gardening. *c*: Mem Brit Folk-lore Soc, Irish Folklore Soc, etc. *a*: Hafan, Bow St, Cards.

JONES, Rev. Thomas Llechid, B.A. *b*: Llanllechid 1867. *e*: Univ Col of N. Wales, St David's Col Lampeter. *m*: Elizabeth Dolben Jones. *d*: 2. *Publ*: History of Welsh Roman Catholics in the 17th Century (1931); History of the City of Bangor ('16). *c.t*: Notes & Queries, N. Wales n/ps & periodicals, etc. *s.s*: N. Wales antiquities & local hist. Mem Hon Soc of Cymmrodorion 27 y. Hon Sec Carns to Cambrian Archæ Assoc 30 y, etc. Chief awards for Hist Essays in Welsh Nat Eisteddfod four times. *Rec*: Bookcollecting. *a*: Llysfaen Rectory, Colwyn Bay.

JONES, Tudor Jenkyn, Sc.D., M.D., F.R.S.E. *b*: Ipswich, Suffolk 1887. *e*: Christ Coll Blackheath, Univ of Glas. *m*: Gladys Mary Thurlow Williams. *s*: 1. *d*: 3. Lecturer in Embryology Univ of Liverpool 1927—. *n.a*: Ed Staff Dly News 1906, Ed Social Creditor '38—. *Publ*: (Part Author) Elements of Social Credit. *Ctr*: North Mail, Glas Herald, Nature, & various scientific journs. *s.s*: Organic Neurology, Biology, Educ, Social Credit, Politics, Philosophy of Society. *Rec*: Social Credit. *c*: Univ (London). *a*: 49 Prince Alfred Rd, Liverpool 15. *T*: Sefton Park 435.

JONES, Mrs Whitefield, B.A. *a*: High School, Howard Gdns, Cardiff.

JONES, William Alfred. *b*: Ryde, I.O.W. 1908. *e*: County Sch Sandown. *m*: Olive Gladys Bacon. Journalist. *n.a*: Isle of Wight Chron 1924—25, Portsmouth Ev News '25—28, Surrey Advertiser '28—, Woking Corr The Times. *Rec*: Photography, gardening. *a*: Mill End, Horsell Birch, Woking, Surrey. *T*: 1716 & 63.

JONES, WILLIAM GARMON: librarian, professor of History; b. Birkenhead, Eng., Nov., 1884; s. William and Jane Jones; educ. King William's Coll. (Isle of Man). DEGREE: M.A.; m. Eluned Clunes Lloyd, 1923. AUTHOR: York and Lancaster, 1914. Contributor to Eng. Hist. Rev., Bulletin of Celtic Studies, Welsh Outlook, Encyclopedia Brit. (13th edit.), Wonderful Britain, y Brython., Trans. Hon. Soc. of Cymmrodorion, Liverpool Daily Post and other papers. General character of writing: historical, literary reviews, poetry. Fellow Royal Hist. Soc.; Deputy-chrmn. Higher Educ. Com., borough of Birkenhead. CLUBS: Sandon Studios, Athenaeum (London), University (Liverpool). OFFICE: University of Liverpool. HOME: 40 Park Road West, Birkenhead, Cheshire, Eng.

JONES, Rev. William Handley. *b*: Birm 1884. *e*: Didsbury Col M/C. *m*: Florence E. Farmer. *s*: 1. *d*: 3. *Publ*: Eleven Christians. *c.t*: Poetry Review, Lon Quarterly Review, Methodist Recorder. *s.s*: Poetry, essays. Entered Wesleyan Min 1909. *a*: 8 Albert Ave, Anlaby Rd, Hull. *t*: Cen 16306.

JONES, William Henry Samuel, Litt.D., F.B.A. *b*: Birmingham 1876. *e*: King Edward VI Sch B'ham, Selwyn Coll Camb. *m*: Norah Mary Kathleen Elliott (dec'd). *d*: 1. University Officer (ret), Hon Fell & Late Pres St Catherine's Coll Camb. *Publ*: (a) Pausanias (Loeb); (b) Hippocrates (Loeb); (a) Malaria & Greek History; (b) Dea Febris; History of St Catherine's Coll; The Doctor's Oath; Disciplina; Via Nova; (a) How We Learn; (b) Scientific Method in Schools; (a) Philosophy & Medicine in Ancient Greece; (b) Anonymus Londinensis. *Ctr*: Classical Rev, Guardian. *s.s*: Ancient Medicine. *a*: 28 Millington Rd, Cambridge. *T*: 4061.

JONES, William Hickling. *b*: Walsall 1888. *e*: Northampton Gr Sch. *m*: Ruth Lester. *d*: 1. Journalist, N.U.J. *n.a*: Burton Dly Mail 1913, Lancs Dly Post '15, Tottenham Herald '21, Leicester Ev Mail '29, Hornsey Journ '31, The Cinema & To-Day's Cinema '42. *Ctr*: Various. *s.s*: Crime, Police Courts, Film Industry (Tech) & Reviews. *Rec*: Philately. *a*: 103 Pemberton Rd, Harringay, London, N.4. *T*: Mountview 1424.

JONES, William Jacob. *b*: Melbourne, Aus 1886. *e*: Univs of Wales, M/C & Leipzig. *m*: Agnes May Jones. *s*: 2. *d*: 2. Prof of Chem. *c.t*: Journal of Chem Soc. *s.s*: Chem. *a*: Chem Dept, Univ Col, Cardiff.

JONES, William John. Journalist. *n.a*: Dist Repres Evening Post Swansea. *a*: Iscoed, Ammanford, S. Wales. *t*: 92.

JONES, William Marchant. *n.a*: Formerly Ed N. Som Independent. *Publ*: Discovering Somerset; Jarge Balsh goes to Lunnon; Somerset Songs & Verse; etc. *c.t*: Bristol, Bath & local press. *s.s*: Dialect & humour. *a*: The Crossways Hse, Coleford, Bath. *t*: Wells 34.

JONES, William Morris, M.A., M.Sc, F.InstP. Dir of Educ. *c.t*: Philos mags, etc. *a*: Counc Offices, Pentre, Rhondda, & Garreg-Wen, Ystrad Rhondda, *t*: Pentre 43.

JONES, William Neilson. *b*: Lon 1883. *e*: King's Col Sc Lon & Emmanuel Col Cam. *m*: Mabel Cheveley Rayner. Hildred Carlisle Prof of Botany, Lon Univ. *Publ*: A Textbook of Plant Biology (in collab); Plant Chimæras & Graft Hybrids. *c.t*: Sci periodicals. *s.s*:

Plant physiology & genetics. *Rec*: Ski-ing, tennis. *c*: Univ of Lon. *a*: Bedford Col, Regents Pk, N.W.1. *t*: Welbeck 5743.

JONES, William Powell, A.B.(Emory, Georgia), A.M., Ph.D.(Harvard). *b* : Cochran, Georgia, U.S.A. *e* : Emory & Harvard Univs. *m* : Marian Root Ginn. *s* : 1. Prof of English & Dean of Adelbert Coll Western Reserve Univ Cleveland Ohio. *Publ* : The Pastourelle ; Thomas Gray, Scholar ; Practical Word Study. *Ctr* : Modern Philology, Speculum, Harvard Studies & Notes, P.M.L.A. *s.s* : Comparative Mediæval Literature, Eighteenth Cent English Literature. *a* : Gates Mills, Ohio, U.S.A.

JONES, William Richard, D.Sc. *b* : 1880. *e* : Roy Coll Science & Roy Sch Mines London. Married. *s* : 1. Prof Mining Geology, Pres Institution of Mining & Metallurgy, Dean of the Roy Sch of Mines. *Publ* : Tinfields of the World ; German-English Geological Terminology ; Minerals in Industry ; several scientific publications. *s.s* : Mining Geology. *c* : Athenæum. *a* : Imperial College of Science & Technology, London, S.W.7. *T* : Kensington 4861.

JONES, William Richard. *b* : Wrexham 1907. *e* : Tenby G.S. Reporter. *n.a* : Tenby Observer '23–26, Pembs Telegraph '26–27, W. Wales Guardian '28, Surrey Advertiser '29–31, News Chronicle '31. *s.s* : Courts-martial & manœuvres. *a* : The Lawn, Cargate Hill, Aldershot. *t* : 318.

JONES, Rev. William Sidney Handley. *b* : Birmingham 1884. *e* : Didsbury Coll Manch. *m* : Florence E. Farmer. *s* : 1. *d* : 3. *Publ* : John Henry Newman ; The Unveiling & Other Poems ; It Crossed My Mind ; Humanism ; Salvation. *Ctr* : Poetry Review, London Quarterly Rev, Methodist Recorder. *s.s* : Poetry, Essays, Book Reviewing. *a* : 18 Dorville Rd, Lee, London, S.E.12. *T* : Lee Green 5222.

JONES, Rev. William Tudor, M.A., D.Phil. *b* : Strata Florida 1865. *e* : Univs of Wales & Jena (Germany). *m* : Helen Clarke. Unitarian Min. *Publ* : Trans from the German of Eucken's Truth of Religion, Knowledge & Life; The Nature of Religion, & others; The Philosophy of Rudolf Eucken in the series Philosophies Ancient & Modern; The Spiritual Ascent of Man; The Training of Mind & Will; The Making of Personality; The Reality of the Idea of God; Contemporary Thought of Germany (vols i & ii); Metaphysics of Life & Death; Ed the Library of Philos & Religion; The Status & Destiny of Man in the Cosmos; etc. *c.t*: Bookman, Christian World, Christian Life, Western Daily Press, etc. *s.s*: Biology, philos, religion. Lect & preached in Aus & N.Z. 1906–10. Read papers at the Internat Congresses of Religions in Paris & Berlin. Special Lect Army, Navy, Aerodromes, Munition Factories in Britain, France & Belgium '15–19. Special Commssr '20 to inquire into the religious situation in Transylvania. *Rec*: Walking. *a*: 3 Marsworth Hse, Vane Hill, Torquay.

JONES, William Unite, F.J.I. *b*: Birm. *e*: K. E. Sc Birm. Married. *d*: 2. Journalist. *n.a*: Ed Midland Athletic Star 1882, Lit Staff Birm Dly Mail '89, Ex-Ed The Owl, Sport & Play, Sporting Ed Midland Express, Birm Evening Despatch, Ed Sports Argus, Searchlight, Ironmonger's Weekly '09, Rotaria '18–, Business Man '18–. *Publ*: The Button Industry. *c.t*: Athletic News 35 y, etc. *s.s*: Sport, trade, politics. Pres Birm Press Club 7 y. Hon Sec Birm Business Club. *Rec*: Cricket, golf, chess. *a*: Room 22, 6 Livery St, Birm. *t*: Cen 1016.

JONSSON, Thorsten Georg, B.A. *b* : Nordmaling 1910. *e* : Stockholm Univ. *m* : Maria Dahlberg. *d* : 1. Author. *n.a* : Dagens Nyheter (N.Y. Corr) 1943—46. *Publ* : Konvoj ; Fly till vatten och Morgon ; Som det brukar Vara ; Sidor av Amerika ; Six Amerikaner. *s.s* : American & English Literature. *a* : Bjorngardsgatan 3, Stockholm. *T* : 44-65-01.

JOPE-SLADE, Christine. *b*: Lon 1893. *e*: Ursuline Convent, Thildonck, Belgium. *m*: Leslie K. Clark (dec). *s*: 2. *d*: 1. *Publ*: The Madonna of the Clutching Hands; Life is Such a Rush; Britannia of Billingsgate (play & film). *c.t*: Time & Tide, Nash's Mag, Woman's Journal, etc. *a*: 37 Hanover Hse, St John's Wood, N.W.8. *t*: Primrose 0832.

JOPLING, LOUISE (Mrs. George William Rowe): artist; b. Manchester, Eng., Nov., 1843; d. Thomas Smith and Frances (Pinker) Goode; educ. Newman's School of Art, M. Chaplin's Sch. (Paris, France); m. (1) Frank Romer; (2) Joseph Middleton; (3) George William Rowe. AUTHOR: Hints to Students and Amateurs; Tete-a-tete Bridge (poems); Twenty Years of my Life (reminiscences), 1925. Contributor to Magazine of Art and other publications. General character of writing: text books, plays, poetry, biography. Exhibited for many yrs. in Royal Academy, London; mem. Pastel Soc. of Royal Brit. Artists, Ladies' Art Soc. CLUBS: Ladies' Imperial, Woman's Institute. HOME: Manor Farm, Chesham Bois, Buckinghamshire, Eng.

JOPORKOFF, THEODOR: physician; b. Bacou, U.SS.R., March 24, 1887; widower. Editor: Medical Survey of Lower Volga. Contributes to Modern Medicine. General character of writing: epidemiology and clinical treatment of infectious diseases. CLUBS: Trade Union of Medical Workmen. OFFICE: Astrachan Malarial Station. HOME: Jchschoff's Street, 50, Astrachan, U.SS.R.

JORDAN, Alfred Charles, C.B.E., M.D., D.M.R.E. (Camb), M.R.C.P.(Lon). *b*: Hale 1872. *e*: M/C G.S., Sidney Sussex Col Cam, St Bart's Hosp Lon & Berlin. *m*: Christina Brumleu. *s*: 2. *d*: 1. Physician; X-ray Specialist. *Publ*: Chronic Intestinal Stasis; A Radiological Study. *c.t*: New Health, Sunlight, Health & Efficiency, etc. *s.s*: X-rays, Dietetics. Corr Foreign Mem Belgian Roy Acad of Med. *Rec*: Music, lawn tennis, figure skating. Mem Roy Skating Club. Mem Counc & a Founder, New Health Soc. Hon Sec & Founder Men's Dress Reform Party. *a*: 82z Portland Pl, W.1. Welbeck 7370.

JORDAN, Anson Robertson, M.D., F.R.C.S. *c.t*: Lancet & B.M.J. *a*: 6 Effingham Cres, Dover. *t*: 51.

JORDAN, Arthur. *b* : Winton, Lancs 1908. *e* : County Hgh Sch for Boys Altrincham, Harvey Gr Sch Folkestone, St Bart's Hosp. *m* : Georgina Ellen Anderson. *s* : 1. Biochemist. *Publ* : Contribution a L'Etude des Forces de Dissolution ; (Trans of) Spectrophotometry in Medicine (with T. L. Tippell). *Ctr* : Lancet, B.M.J., etc. *s.s* : Biochemistry, Chem Pathology. *Rec* : Mathematics, statistics. *w.s* : R.A.M.C. 1942—46. *a* : 34 Bristol Rd, Sheffield 11.

JORDAN, Hon. Sir Frederick Richard, K.C.M.G., B.A., LL.B. *b* : London 1881. *e* : Sydney Hgh Sch & Univ. *m* : Bertha Maud Clay. Lieutenant-Governor & Chief Justice of New South Wales. *Publ* : Equity in New South Wales ; General Principles of the Administration of Justice ; Admiralty Jurisdictions in New South Wales. *Rec* : Fencing, swimming, travel. *c* : Australian & Univ (Sydney), Roy Sydney Golf. *a* : 25 Gilliver Ave, Vaucluse, Sydney, N.S.W. *T* : FU 7695.

JORDAN, Rev. George Jefferis, M.A., Litt.D., D.D., F.R.Hist.S. *b* : Boston Spa, Yorks 1890. *e* : Archbishop Holgate's Gr Sch York Leeds Univ & Clergy Sch. *m* : Edith Nicholson. *s* : 2. *d* : 2. Canon of Sheffield & Vicar of Ecclesall. *Publ* : The Reunion of the Churches ; The Inner History of the Great Schism of the West ; A short Psychology of Religion ; An Everyman Psychology ; Story of Holy Trinity Parish Church, Hull ; etc. *Ctr*

Expository Times, Cong Quarterly. *s.s*: Church History, Sociology & Psychology. *Rec*: Fishing & old churches. *a*: Ecclesall Vicarage, Sheffield 11. *T*: 70084.

JORDAN, Gerald Ray, A.M., D.D. *b*: Kinston, North Carolina 1896. *e*: Duke Univ, Emory Univ, Harvard. *m*: Caroline Moody. *s*: 2. Clergyman Meth Episcopal Church, Prof of Homiletics Emory Univ. *Publ*: What is Yours?; The Intolerance of Christianity; Faith that Propels; We Face Calvary—& Life; Adventures in Radiant Living; Why the Cross?; Look at the Stars; We Believe: A Creed that Sings; The Supreme Possession; The Emerging Revival. *Ctr*: Christian Century, Church Management, Christian Advocate, Upper Room, etc. *Rec*: Golf, football. *a*: 1039 East Clifton Rd, N.E., Altanta, Georgia, U.S.A. *T*: Dearborn 2674.

JORDAN, Herbert William, F.I.S.A. *b*: 1874. *e*: Stationers Coy Sc. Coy Registration Agent. Vice-Pres Inc Secs Assoc. Liveryman Stationers' Coy. *s.s*: Coy Law & Practice & Assoc subjects. *c*: Lon Rotary & Constitutional. *a*: 116 Chancery Lane, W.C.2., & 23 Arlington Rd, Eastbourne. *t*: Holborn 0434.

JORDAN, PHILIP (FURNEAUX), (pen name: Victor France): author, publisher; b. Birmingham, Eng., Aug., 1902; s. John Furneaux and Mildred (Player) J.; educ. Royal College (Naval), Osborne, Dartmouth; m. Ruth Castberg, Nov. 10, 1927. AUTHOR: The Lease of Paradise, 1924; The Thing Ungained, 1925; The Grey Algrim, 1926; (under pen name of Victor France): The Carved Emerald, 1926; The Naked Five, 1927. Editor to Alfred A. Knopf, Ltd., of London. Contributor to many English mags. General character of writing: fiction. On staff (formerly) Paris Daily Mail; edited (formerly) Riviera edition of Chicago Tribune (published at Nice, France). OFFICE: 37 Bedford Square. HOME: Monmouth House, Chelsea, London, Eng.

JORDAN, Dr. L. R., F.R.C.S.(Eng), M.B., ChB.(Bris). Surgeon. *c.t*: B.M.J., B.M. Chirurgical Journ. *a*: 3 Kenilworth Rd, Redland, Bristol.

JOSEPH, MORRIS: emeritus minister of religion; b. London, Eng., May, 1848; s. David and Amelia (Levi) J; educ. Westminster Jews' Free Sch., Jews' College (both London); m. Frances Amelia Henry, 1872. AUTHOR: The Ideal in Judaism, 1893; Judaism as Creed and Life, 1903 (5th edit. 1925); Lectures on the Prayer Book, 1905; The Message of Judaism, 1906; The Spirit of Judaism, 1930. Contributor to Hasting's Encyclop. of Relig. and Ethics, Jewish Quarterly Rev., Jewish Chronicle, Jewish Guardian and many other publications. General character of writing: religious. Relig. denom., Jewish. CLUB: Maccabeans. (*)

JORDAN, Vivian Thomas Searle. *b*: Falmouth 1913. *e*: Falmouth G.S. Journalist. Falmouth Packet '30 & 29-33 Sept, Peterboro' Standard (Peterboro' Press Ltd) Sept '33, Western Morn News Torquay Dec '33. *s.s*: Assoc football, yacht racing. *a*: Wood Burn, Ash Hill Road, Torquay, Devon. *t*: Torquay 2700.

JORDAN, W. T. *b*: 1898. Dis Rep for Mont & Merionethshire County Times, Welshpool. *c.t*: Assoc n/p's, M/C Guardian, Daily Dispatch, Western Mail. Mem N.U.J. *a*: London Hse, Machynlleth, Mont.

JORDAN, Wilbur Kitchener, M.A., L.H.D., Ph.D. *b*: Lynnville, Indiana 1902. *e*: Oakland City Coll & Harvard Univ. *m*: Frances Ruml. Educator, Historian, Pres Radcliffe Coll & Prof of History Harvard Univ. *Publ*: The Development of Religious Toleration in England, From the Beginning of the Reformation to the Restoration (3 vols) & the Attainment of the Theory (1 vol); Men of Substance. *s.s*: History of England 16th & 17th Centuries. *a*: Radcliffe College, 10 Garden St, & 78 Brattle St, Cambridge 38, Mass, U.S.A. *T*: Kirkland 4600 & 0555.

JORDAN-LLOYD, Dorothy, M.A.(Cantab), D.Sc (Lon). *b*: Birm 1889. *e*: K.E. H.S. Birm & Newnham Col Cam. Dir Brit Leather Mnfr's Research Assoc. *Publ*: The Chemistry of the Proteins. *c.t*: Biochem Journ, Journ of the Faraday Soc, etc. *s.s*: Biochem, leather chem. *Rec*: Climbing, riding. *c*: Internat Sportsman's, Ladies' Alpine, Fell Chem Soc, Biochem Soc, Faraday Soc, etc. *a*: 20 St Thomas St. S.E.1.

JORDAN-SMITH, Paul, B.A., B.D. *b*: Virginia 1885. *e*: Chattanooga Univ & Lombard Col. *m*: Sarah Bixby. *s*: 2. *d*: 1. Writer. *n.a*: Lit Ed Los Angeles Times 1933—. *Publ*: The Soul of Woman (Essays '16); Cables of Cobweb (novel '23); Nomad (Novel); Bibliographia Burtoniana; For the Love of Books; Edited (with Floyd Dell) Burton's Anatomy of Melancholy ('27 1st all-Eng ed); On Strange Altars (Essays); Rabelaisian Fancies (Satire); Trans of Robert Burton's Philosophaster; etc. *c.t*: To-morrow Mag, New Justice & Los Angeles Times. *s.s*: 17th cent Eng lit. *Rec*: Book collecting & chess. *c*: Authors' & Authors' League (N.Y.), etc. *a*: 170 S. Canyon View Drive, Brentwood Hgts, Los Angeles, Calif. *t*: West Los Angeles 34858.

JORGENSEN, Niels Emil. *b*: Copenhagen 1915. *e*: Univ of Copenhagen. *m*: Britt Bahnson Rosenborg. *s*: 1. *d*: 1. Chief Editor. *n.a*: Nationaltidende 1938—, Chief Ed '45—. *Publ*: In the German Slave Market; The Northern Countries & the War; Our Danish Heritage; etc. *s.s*: Politics, Danish Resistance during German Occupation. *a*: 32 Rahbeksalle Copenhagen V, Denmark. *T*: Eva 4870.

JORGENSON, Dr. George Ellington. *b*: Chicago Ill 1898. Married. *n.a*: Assoc Ed & Consulting Pathologist to scientific periodical 1924-26. *Publ*: The Circle of Vengeance; Pottery; Puppet of the Forest. *c.t*: Physical Culture, Modern Thinker, Liberty Mag, etc. *s.s*: Health articles & fiction. *Rec*: Gardening, fishing, travel. *c*: Mason, Roy Arch Mason. *a*: Clermont, Iowa. U.S.A.

JORGENSON, Nora. *b*: Clermont, Iowa. *e*: Oberlin Col Ohio, Chicago Mus Col. *m*: Dr. G. E. Jorgenson. Pianist, Music Teacher, Editor, & Writer. *n.a*: Ed & publisher Musical Notes. *Publ*: (with Dr G. E. Jorgenson) The Circle of Vengeance; Pottery & Puppets of the Forest. *c.t*: Grace Notes, Étude Mag, Mus Courier. *s.s*: Concert pianist, radio entertainment. Guest concert pianist for Radio Station Los Angles 1927–. Composer of musical sketches. *c*: Order of Eastern Star, Sisterhood of P.E.O., Iowa Fed of Music Clubs Business & Professional Women's. *Rec*: Coll graduate work, travel, keeping house. *a*: Clermont, Iowa.

JORLUND, Anders. *b*: Jorlunde 1893. *e*: Copenhagen. *m*: Margrethe Ostergaard. Cinema Proprietor. *n.a*: Italian Mail Florence. *Publ*: Glimt af Skaebner; Vi levende Skygger. *Ctr*: Various. *s.s*: Radio Plays. *c*: Danish Author's. *a*: Strandvejen 47, Copenhagen. *T*: Ryvang 5628.

JOSCELYN, Archie Lynn. *b*: Great Falls, Montana 1899. *e*: Public Schs Armington & Belt, Intermountain Union Coll Helena. *m*: Hazel E. Peterson. *s*: 2. *d*: 1. Author. *Publ*: Bitter Creek; Empty Saddles; Guns of Lost Valley; King of Thunder Valley; The Law Man of Lonesome River; The Golden Bowl;

Powdersmoke Pass; Gunsight Ranch, etc. *Ctr*: Youth's Companion, Western Story Mag, Girls Companion, Writer's Monthly, North West Stories, Toronto Star Weekly, Boys World, Cowboy Stories, etc. *s.s*: Hist Type Western Novels. *Rec*: Gardening, fishing. *a*: 1806 South Tenth St, West, Missoula, Montana. *T*: 5290.

JOSEPH, George William Neild, M.B., ChB. *b*: Oxf 1880. *e*: Calday Grange Sc W. Kirby, L'pool Univ. *m*: Dorothy Joule Reeve. *s*: 1. *d*: 1. M.O.H. *Publ*: Section of Local Government Law & Administration in England & Wales. (Ed-in-chief Rt Hon Lord Macmillan); Handbook for Home Teachers of Blind. *c.t*: Public Health, B.M.J., Medical Officer. *s.s*: Public Health. Chm Med Cmt Northern Counties Assoc for the Blind 1932–34. *Rec*: Fishing, shooting. *c*: B.M.A., Foll of Soc of M.O.H's, Fell Roy Inst of Public Health. *a*: Sandford, Grappenhall, Warrington. *t*: 17.

JOSEPH, Dr. H. M., M.C. Ophthalmic Surg. *c.t*: Lancet, B.M.J., Proc Roy Soc of Med, Transactions Ophth Soc. *a*: 90a Harley St, W.1. *t*: Welbeck 3993.

JOSEPH, Horace William Brindley, F.B.A. *b*: Chatham 1867. *e*: Wimborne G.S., Honiton G.S., Winchester Col, New Col Oxf. *m*: Margaret Bridges (dec). Ex Fell Tutor & Lect New Col, & Lect in Philos in Univ of Oxf. *Publ*: An Introduction of Logic; The Labour Theory of Value in Karl Marx; Some Problems in Ethics. *c.t*: Mind, Hibbert Journal, Philosophy. *a*: 33 Northmoor Rd, Oxf.

JOSEPH, Michael. *b*: London 1897. *e*: City of Lond Sch & Lond Univ. *m*: Edna Victoria Nellie Frost. *s*: 2. *d*: 1. Author & Journalist. *Publ*: Short Story Writing for Profit; Journalism for Profit; The Commercial Side of Literature; How to Write a Short Story; How to Write Serial Fiction (with Marten Cumberland); The Magazine Story; Complete Writing for Profit; Cat's Company; Puss in Books (with Elizabeth Drew); This Writing Business; Heads or Tails (with Selwyn Jepson); Discovery (Play); The Sword & the Scabbard; Charles, the Story of a Friendship. *Ctr*: Various. *s.s*: Cats, Journalism, Commercial Side of Lit, Short Story Writing, Publishing. *Rec*: Cats. *c*: Savage. *a*: The Garden Hse, Stanford Dingley, nr Reading.

JOSEPH, Pothan (Syr. for Philip), B.A.(Madras). Ll.B.(Bombay). *b*: Travancore 1893. *e*: C.M.S. Col Kottayam, Madras & Bombay Univs. *m*: Anna Mammen. *s*: 1. *d*: 2. Ed The Hindustan Times, Delhi. *n.a*: Sub-Ed Bombay Chron 1917–18, Asst Ed '18–20, Asst Ed Capital, Calcutta '20–24, Jt Ed Bombay Chron '26, Ed Indian Daily Mail '31. *s.s*: Indian polit, comm intelligence. Mem Bombay Munic Corp '26–29. Officer Publicity Br Indian Rlys '28–31. 1st Pres S. Indian Assoc Bombay '26. Pres Malabar Chr Assoc '27–30. Pres Delhi Journalists Assoc '31–. *Rec*: Walking. *a*: Burn Bastion Rd, Delhi, India. *t*: 5746.

JOSHI, Pranshanker Someshwar. *b*: Jetpur, India 1897. *e*: Bombay Univ. *m*: Vallabhkunvar Joshi. *s*: 1. *d*: 3. Journalist & Author. *n.a*: Special Rep in South Africa Bombay Chron, Searchlight Patna, Forward Calcutta, Hindu Herald Lahore 1925–36, Indian Express & Forum Bombay '46—. *Publ*: The Tyranny of Colour; The Struggle for Equality; (Gujarati) Rangdwesh-No Durga; Dakshin Africa-Ni Rangbhoomi; British Shahivad-Ni Janjiro; Guirarati trans of India in World Politics; The Sleeper Awakened; The Claim for Independence; Krishna's Flute. *s.s*: Indian Politics & Culture, Colour Problem in South Africa. *Rec*: Walking. *a*: 40 Bree St, Johannesburg, South Africa.

JOSLIN, Ivy Collin, B.Sc. *b*: London 1900. *e*: Skinners' Company's Sch Lond, Univ Coll Lond. Headmistress. *Publ*: General Science; Everyday Domestic Science (Joslin & Taylor). *Rec*: Walking, tennis. *c*: University Women's. *a*: Francis Holland Sch, Clarence Gate, London, N.W.1. *T*: Paddington 0176.

JOSYER, G. Ramanuja, M.A., M.R.S.L. *b*: Mysore 1891. *e*: Maharaja's Col & Madras Univ. *m*: Sri Singaramira Tatachar. *s*: 2. *d*: 1. Author & Publicist. *n.a*: Ed Mysore Social Review 1916, Ed Guardian Bangalore '24, Corr Times of India, etc. Pres Journalist's Assoc Mysore, Mysore Dt Auto Assoc & Mysore Merchants Chamber, Mem Mysore State Repres Assembly. *Publ*: Sociology or the Progress of Mankind & their Institutions; Economics of Caste; Spiritual Regeneration; History of Mysore; 4 Works in the Kanada Language, etc. *c.t*: Times, Mod Review Calcutta, Times of India Bombay, Forum, etc. *s.s*: Sociology, Sanskrit, Canares lit & Mysore hist. Organised 1st Mysore Civic & Social Conf '16, Founded Mysore State Congress '28, Organised 1st Mysore Reforms' Conf '23, Hon Mem Inst Historique & Héraldique de France. *Rec*: Walking. *c*: Cosmopolitan Mysore. *a*: Mysore, India.

JOTUNI, Marie. *b*: Kuopio, Finland 1880. *e*: Univ in Helsinki. *m*: V. Tarkiainen. *s*: 2. Author. *Publ*: I am guilty (drama); Everyday Life-story: The Rib of the Man (comedy); The Girl in the Garden of Roses; Love; When you have feelings—short stories; Wanderer & The Open Box; The Wife of the hen-pecked Man (comedy). *c*: P.E.N. *a*: Helsinki (Finland), Cygraeuksenkatu 8.A. *t*: 41347.

JOUGLET, René. *b*: France. Homme de Lettres, Sec Gen de la Confederation Internationale des Soc d'Auteurs et Compositeurs, Chev de la Legion d'Honneur. *Publ*: L'Enfant Abandonne; Freres; Le Jardinier d'Argenteuil; Soleil-Levant; Le Feu aux Poudres; Valparaiso; Nouvelles de l'Estaminet; Le Capitaine de Hong Kong; Le Masque et la Visage; Au cœur sauvage des Philippines; etc. *Ctr*: Various. *s.s*: Extreme Orient. *Rec*: Golf. *c*: P.E.N. *a*: 31 Avenue d'Eylau, Paris. *T*: Passy 90-96.

JOULES, Horace, M.D., F.R.C.P. *b*: Woodseaves, Stafford 1902. *e*: Newport Gr Sch, Univs of Cardiff & Lond. *m*: Mary Sparrow. *s*: 2. *d*: 1. Sen Phys 1935, Med Dir '39 Central Middlx Hosp, Resident Phys Selly Oak Hosp Birmingham '30. *Publ*: (Ed) The Doctor's View of War. *Ctr*: Lancet, B.M.J., Nursing Times, etc, & daily press. *s.s*: Diseases of Chest & Heart, Medico-Political. *Rec*: Gardening, Ornithology. *a*: Central Middlx Hosp, Park Royal, London, N.W.10. *T*: Elgar 5733.

JOURDAIN, Rev. Francis C. R., M.A.(Oxon). *b*: 1865. *e*: Magdalen Col Oxf. *m*: Frances Emmeline Smith (dec). *s*: 1. *d*: 1. *n.a*: Asst Ed British Birds 1909—, Ed Bulletin Brit Oolog Assoc '23—. Regional Asst Ed Ibis '30—. *Publ*: Victoria History of County of Derby Vol. I, Natural History (Zoology); The British Bird Book (4 vols, with F. B. Kirkman & Others); The Eggs of European Birds (pts I—IV); Trans Kleinschmidt's The Formenkreis Theory; etc. *c.t*: Ibis, Oologist's Record, Proc Zoo Soc, Ornithological Jahrbuch, L'Oiseau, etc. *s.s*: Ornithology, oology. Elected Hou Fell Amer Ornith Un '21; Corr Fell '18. Hon Mem Société Ornithologique de France '25. Corr Mem Ornith Soc of Holland '25. Hon Mem Ornith Soc of Germany '28, Club of Dutch Ornith '34. Leader of 1st Oxf Univ Exped to Spitsbergen '21. Vice-Pres Brit Ornith Un '34—. Pres Brit Oolog Assoc '32—. Hon Sec Internat Ornith Congress '34. *a*: Whitekirk, Belle Vue Rd, Southbourne, Bournemouth, & Clifton, Ashbourne. Derbys. *t*: Southbourne 912.

JOURDAIN, Lt.-Col. Henry Francis Newdigate, C.M.G., O.St.J., F.R.G.S., F.R.S.A.I. *b*: Audenshaw Lodge, Lancs 1872. *e*: Derby Sch & R.M.C. Sandhurst. *m*: (1) Molly O'Farrell (dec'd), (2) M. Maclennan. Lt-Col Connaught Rangers (ret). *Publ*: History of The Connaught Rangers (3 Vols); Ranging Memories; History of the Mess Plate of the 88th Connaught Rangers; Medals & Decorations of the 88th & 94th; Historical Record of the 5th Service Btn, The Connaught Rangers; etc. *Ctr*: Army Hist Research Journ. *s.s*: Military Tradition, etc. *Rec*: Tennis, gardening. *c*: Army & Navy. *w.s*: 1899—1902, 1914—18. *a*: Fyfield Lodge, Fyfield Rd, Oxford. *T*: 2789.

JOWETT, Ronald Edward. *b*: Halifax, Yorks. *e*: Leeds Univ, Paris. *m*: Lilian Waring. *s*: 2. *Publ*: (In Collab) The Injured Workman. *Ctr*: B.M.J., Journ of Laryngology, Journ of Mental Science, Med Press & Circular. *s.s*: Ear, Nose & Throat Disease. *Rec*: Photography, mountaineering, music. *a*: 15 Grange Cresc, Sunderland, Co Durham. *T*: 2923.

JOWITT, Harold, C.M.G., B.A., M.Ed. *b*: Huddersfield 1893. *e*: Univ Coll Southampton. *m*: Minnie H. Barrett. *d*: 2. Dir of Educ Bechuanaland Protectorate. *Publ*: Principles of Education for African Teachers; Suggested Methods for the African School; Suggested Organisation for the African School; Common Culture or Chaos. *s.s*: African Education, Adult Education, Race Relations, Colonial Administration. *Rec*: Writing, photography. *c*: Salisbury, Southern Rhodesia, Mafeking. *a*: Imperial Reserve, Mafeking, C.P., South Africa.

JOY, James Richard, A.M., Hon.Litt.D. *b*: Groton, Mass 1863. *e*: Yale. *m*: Emma McGee Joy. *d*: 3. Editor, Librarian. *n.a*: Ed Christian Advocate N.Y. 1915—36. *Publ*: John Wesley's Awakening; The Teachers of Drew; (Ed) Thomas Joy & His Descendants; Ten Englishmen of the XIXth Century. *Ctr*: Christian Advocate, Chautauquan, Life. *s.s*: History, Genealogy, Meth Hist. *Rec*: Photography. *a*: 29 Perry St, New York City 14, N.Y. *T*: Chelsea 3-7766.

JOY, Norman Humbert. *b*: Barrow-in-Furness, Lancs 1874. *e*: Aldenham Sch Herts, St Barts Hosp Lond. Married. *s*: 1. *d*: 2. *Publ*: A Practical Handbook of British Beetles; How to Know British Birds; British Beetles, Their Homes & Habits. *Ctr*: British Birds. *s.s*: The Migration of British Birds. *a*: Red House Hotel, Selsey, Suxxes.

JOYCE, Archibald. *b*: 1873. *e*: Paddington. *Publ*: Mus Comedies Toto & Gabrielle; Waltzes:—Dreaming; Passing of Salome; Songe d'Automne, etc. 1st composition played by Lieut Dan Godfrey. 1st English Waltz Composer to have compositions publ'd on the Continent, being styled the English Waltz King. One of 1st Mem's Performing Rights Soc. *a*: Kya, Langley Park Rd, Sutton, Surrey.

JOYCE, George Hayward, M.A. Prof of Theology. *Publ*: Catholic Doctrine of Grace; Principles of Logic; Principles of Natural Theology; Christian Marriage. *a*: Heythrop College, Chipping Norton, Oxon.

JOYCE, Henry Stanley. *b*: White Mill, Dorset 1882. *e*: Wimborne Gr Sch. *m*: Elizabeth Ruby Sanders. *s*: 1. *d*: 1. *Publ*: By Field & Stream; Holiday Trout Fishing; I Was Born in the Country; A Countryman's Notebook; A Trout Angler's Notebook; etc. *Ctr*: Game & Gun, Angling, Country Sportsman, Field Sports, etc. *s.s*: British Fresh Water Fishing, Rough Shooting, Natural History & Country Life, Scouting for Boys. *Rec*: Fishing, shooting, bird watching, sketching, choral singing, amateur acting & producing, swimming. *a*: Innisfree, Roundswell, nr Barnstaple, Nth Devon. *T*: Barnstaple 2426.

JOYCE, James. *b*: Dublin 1882. Author. *Publ*: A Portrait of the Artist as a Young Man; Dubliners; Exiles (Play); Ulysses, etc. *a*: c/o Jonathan Cape, Bedford Sq. W.C.1.

JOYCE, P. W., LL.D., M.R.I.A. *Publ*: A Short History of Gaelic Ireland; A Social History of Ancient Ireland; The Story of Ancient Irish Civilization; An Illustrated History of Ireland; A Concise History of Ireland; Outlines of the History of Ireland; The Origin & History of Irish Names of Places, etc. *a*: c/o Talbot Press Ltd, 89 Talbot St, Dublin.

JUBB, Dr. A. A., M.D., D.Sc, Brevet-Major R.A.M.C.T. *c.t*: Med journs. *a*: Ministry of Health, Whitehall, S.W.1.

JUBILEE. See **Nicholas, Joseph William.**

JUDA, Hans Peter. *b*: Trier, Germany 1904 *e*: P. S. Darmstadt, Univs of Paris, Frankfürt, Munich & Freiburg. *m*: Elsbeth Goldstein. Ed. *n.a*: Formerly Financial Ed, Berliner Tageblatt (Berlin). Ed, Internat Textiles. *Publ*: Wirtschaft wird Zeitung. *c.t*: Various N/ps & periodicals all over world. *s.s*: Finance, textiles & political economy. *a*: 113 Princess Court, Queens Rd, W.2. *t*: Bayswater 0671.

JUDD, ALFRED: author; b. Winsford, Somerset, Eng.; s. John Breay and Emily (Baker) J.; educ. Privately and at various schls.; unmarriad. AUTHOR: The Boys of Gunn Island, 1919; Jim from Jimbaloo, 1922; Toddy Scores Again, 1923; The Luck of the Lennites, 1924; The Secret of Marsh Haven, 1924; The Quest of Peril, 1924; The Mystery of Meldon School, 1924; The Conquest of the Poles, 1924 (history of Modern Polar Exploration); The Young Treasure Hunters, 1924; Derry of Dunn's House, 1925; Stirring Tales for Boys, 1925; The Raiders of the Pool, 1925; The Mystery of the Towers, 1925; The Secret of the Snows, 1925; Forrester's Fag, 1926; The Land of the Firestone, 1926; The School of the Steep, 1926; Pals at Allingham, 1926; Wrens to the Rescue, 1926; The Track of Danger, 1927; Wrens on the Trail, 1927; The Riddle of Randley School, 1927; Toddy Nott, Schoolboy, 1927; At School on the Ocean, 1928; Toddy's Progress, 1928; The Isle of Adventure, 1928; Five in a Secret, 1929; Yarns by the Fireside, 1929. Under the nom de plume, "John Winsford," have appeared, "The Trials of the Twins", 1924, and "The Secret of Samson's Farm", 1926. Contributor to Captain, Chums, Scout, Boys' Own Paper, Little Folks, Story Teller, Grand, Pearson's, Sat. Journal, Novel, Toby, Pictures, T. P.'s Weekly, and various annuals. General character of writing: juvenile fiction for boys, especially. CLUB: Motofoto. HOME: 48 Sheen Park, Richmond, Surrey, Eng.

JUDD, Rev. Francis Arthur, M.A. *b*: Lon 1882. *e*: St Paul's & Selwyn Col Cam. Parish Priest. *Publ*: Under the Swedish Colours; Monarch of the Fenland & other poems; The Rose of India. *s.s*: Verse. *Rec*: Oil painting. *a*: Holy Trinity Vicarage, Reading: *t*: Reading 2650.

JUDD, Percy, B.Mus(Lon), L.R.A.M., A.R.C.M. *b*: Southend-on-Sea 1892. *e*: R.C.M. *m*: Marcelle Bellet. *s*: 1. Singing Teacher, Singer, Composer & Lecturer. *Publ*: Singing Technique: A Guide for Students. *c.t*: Musical Times. War Service. *Rec*: Gardening, swimming. *a*: 12 Westminster Drive, Westcliff-on-Sea.

JUDGE, Arthur William, A.R.C.Sc., D.I.C., A.M.I.A.E. *b*: London 1887. *e*: Sir Joseph Williamson's Rochester, Roy Coll Science Lond. *m*: Daisy Mary Newton. *s*: 1. *d*: 3. Tech Journ Ed & Cons Eng Asst Nat Phys Lab

Teddington, I/c Air Min Instrument & Navigation Sect & Aerial Photography Sect Biggin Hill & Farnboro' Experimental Stations. *n.a*: Ed Eng Mechanics & World of Science 1922—46. *Publ*: High Speed Diesel Engines; Aircraft Engines; Modern Gas Turbines; Engineering Precision Measurements; Testing H.S. Engines; Motor Manuals; Stereoscopic Photography; Modern Motor Cars; etc. *Ctr*: Auto Eng, Times Eng Supp, Autocar, Aeroplane, Amateur Photographer, Motor Cycle, etc. *s.s*: Motor Eng, Diesel Engines, Gas Turbines, Workshop Practice, Automobile Maintenance, Mech Eng, Photography. *Rec*: Tennis, swimming. *w.s*: Tech Officer Air Min, C.F.R. & R.A.F. *a*: Moor Cottage, Old Compton Lne, Farnham, Surrey. *T*: 5587.

JUDGE, J. J. *a*: 2 Apsley Road, Plymouth.

JUDGES, Athur Valentine, F.R.Hist.S., F.R.Econ.S. *b*: Boughton-under-Blean, Kent 1898. *e*: King's Coll Lond. *m*: Rose Kathleen Mitchell. *d*: 2. Lecturer Lond Sch of Econ. *Publ*: The Elizabethan Underworld. *Ctr*: Econ Hist Review, History, Economica. *s.s*: Econ & Social Hist. *w.s*: World War I. *a*: 28 Woburn Sq, London, W.C.1. *T*: Museum 2489.

JUDSON, Clara Ingram. *b*: Logansport, Indiana 1879. *e*: Public Schs & Girl's Classical Sch Indianapolis. *m*: James McIntosh Judson. *d*: 2. Writer, Lecturer & Broadcaster. *n.a*: Children's Ed Indianapolis Star 1913—20. *Publ*: They Came From Series (1) France, (2) Sweden, (3) Scotland; Petar's Treasure; Michael's Victory; The Lost Violin. (Biogs) Fulton, Boat Builder; Railway Engineer, Stephenson, Gorgas, Soldier Doctor; etc, & 19 Mary Jane Books, 4 Billy Robin Books; etc, *s.s*: Biography, History, Economics applied to the Home. *Rec*: Reading, fine needlework, motoring, gardening. *a*: Georgian Hotel, Evanston, Illinois, U.S.A. *T*: Greenleaf 2066 & 4100.

JUDSON, Rev. William Douglas. *b*: Chorley 1857. *e*: P.M. Theo Col, Yorkshire Col Leeds. *m*: (1) Frances Annie Durnford; (2) Elizabeth Bothwick Rivett-Wallace. *c.t*: Holborn Quarterly Review, Blackpool Times, Lytham Standard, etc. Hon Sec Fylde Dis Counc L.N.U. *Rec*: Bowls. *a*: 10 Riley Av, St Annes-on-Sea, Lancs.

JUDY. See Fearon, Percy Hutton.

JUKES, Rev. Worthington, M.A. *Publ*: Jt Ed of Bible in Pashto. *c.t*: Moslem World & several n/ps. *a*: 2 Execliff, Exmouth. *t*: Exmouth 465.

"JULIA VIRGINIA" (pen name): see Laengsdorff, Julia Virginia.

JULIUS, MORITZ (pen name): see Bonn, M(oritz) J(ulius).

JULYAN, Lt.-Col. William Leopold, J.P., M.A.(Oxon). *b*: St Austell 1888. *e*: Univ Coll Oxf. *m*: Marie Eileen Phyllis Bennett (L.R.A.M., M.R.S.T.). Warden Lord Wandsworth Agric Coll 1922—45. *Ctr*: African World, Farmer's Weekly, Field, Country Life, Ed Suppl Times, etc. *s.s*: Agriculture, Old Crafts. *Rec*: Book collecting. *w.s*: D.C.L.I. World Wars I & II. *a*: Tyrells Croft Hse, Andover, Hampshire.

JUNG, Carl Gustav, D.Sc. *b*: Kesswyl, Switzerland 1875. *e*: Univs of Basel, Zurich & Paris. *m*: Emma Rauschenbach. *s*: 1. *d*: 4. Prof of Psychopathology (ret). *Publ*: Psychological Types; Psychology of the Unconscious; Psychology & Religion; Psychology & Alchemy; The Secret of the Golden Flower (with R. Wilhelm); Modern Man in Search of a Soul. *s.s*: Research Work in Comparative Psychology (Hist & Ethnological). *Rec*: Sailing, gardening. *a*: Seestrasse 228, Kusnacht-Zurich, Switzerland. *T*: 911, 809.

JUNIUS. See Thorp, Joseph Peter.

JUNNER, Gordon Mackenzie, F.R.S.A., M.I.Mech.E., M.I.R.T.E., M.Inst.Met. *b*: Dumfries 1892. *e*: St John's Coll Westcliff, Southend Tech Coll, Battersea Poly. *n.a*: The Commercial Motor Sub Ed 1912—14, Asst Ed '19—29, Ed '29—. *Publ*: (Co-Author) Vital to the Life of Industry. *Rec*: Motoring, skating. *c*: R.A.C., Albany. *a*: c/o Temple Press Ltd, Bowling Green Lane, London, E.C.1. *T*: Terminus 3636.

JUSTNIELSEN, Adda. *b*: Copenhagen 1912. Assoc Ed. *Publ*: Naar man ikke kan blive andet; Sig noget morsomt; Saadan bruger vi det her; Der er ikke no'et at le a. *Ctr*: Politiken, Berlingske Tidende, Nationaltidende, Social Demokraten, etc. *s.s*: Humour. *a*: Blidahpark 44, Hellerup, Danmark. *T*: Hellerup 5622.

"JUVENIO" see Cawston, Frederick Gordon.

JUVKAM, Lizze. *b*: Dramwick 1893. *m*: Olav Juvkam. Writer. *Publ*: Virgin's Way; The Bookkeeper, Johannes. *Ctr*: Aplinposten, Oslo, etc. *s.s*: Theatre Criticism, Beauty in Everyday Life, etc. *Rec*: Ski-ing, gardening, art (music), travel. *c*: Author's & Artist's. *a*: Ljan, Norway. *T*: 686178.

JYNGE, Andreas Grimelund. *b*: Skien, Norway 1870. *m*: Ester Lind. *s*: 1. *d*: 1. Acting Manager Norwegian State Railways. *Publ*: (Poems) Viser og Vers; Edegne Veie; (Short Stories) Hester i Fjellet. *Ctr*: Various. *s.s*: Horses, Literary & Artistic Themes. *Rec*: Travel. *a*: Roa, Hadeland, Norway. *T*: Lunner 213.

KABI, Kavichandra Kaliprasanna. *b*: Seraikella 1896. *m*: Srimati Sashimuki Debya. Literary. *n.a*: Ed Seraikella State Gazette 1940—. *Publ*: Surer Res; Hata Bhago; Kaka Babu; Asrudhara; Mahatras; etc. *Ctr*: Bansari, Sahakar, Nabin, Banabina, etc. *s.s*: Short Stories & Drama. *Rec*: Music & literary culture *a*: P.O. Seraikella, Kabi-Kutir, Seraikella State, E.S.A.

KAEMMERER, LUDWIG: director of art collections; b. Danzig, Germany, Oct. 11, 1862; s. Rudolf and Marie (Loche) K.; educ. Gymnasium of Danzig; Univs. of Berlin, Munich and Leipzig. DEGREES: Dr., Professor; m. Martha Schwartz, 1913. AUTHOR: Die Landschaft in der deutschen Kunst, 1886; Daniel Chodowiecki, 1897; Hubert und van Eyck, 1898; Hans. Memling, 1899; Max Liebermann, 1900; Abnenreihen auf dem Stammbaum des portugiesischen Königshauses, 1903; Baudenkmäler der Prinz Posen, 1909; Käthe Kollwitz, 1920. Contributor to: Jahrbuch der preussischen Kunstsammlungen; Münchener Jahrbuch für bildende Kunst; Zeitschrift für bildende Kunst. General character of writing: science, art, biography. CLUBS: Internationaler Verband der Museumbeamten. OFFICE: Director der Kunstsammlungen der Veste Coburg. ADDRESS: Coburg Veste, Coburg i.B., Germany.

KAFKA, GUSTAV: univ. professor; b. Vienna, Austria, July, 1883; educ. Schottengymnasium of Vienna, Univs. of Vienna, Göttingen, Leipzig and Munich. DEGREES: Ph.D.; m. Mathilde Trache, July 23, 1925. AUTHOR: Über das Ansteigen der Tonerregung, 1906; Versuch einer kritschen Darstellung der neueren Anschauungen über das Ichproblem, 1910; Einführung in die Tierpsychologie auf experimenteller und ethologischer Grundlage (1st vol.), 1914; Die Vorsokratiker, 1921; Platon, Sokrates und der Sokratische Kreis, 1921; Tierpsychologie, 1923; Aristoteles, 1923; Der Ausklang der Antiken Philosophie und das Erwachen einer neuen Zeit (with H. Eibl), 1928. Editor: Handbuch der vergleichenden Psychologie (3 vols.), 1923; Geschichte der Philosophie in Einzeldarstellungen (to be 40 vols.), since 1920. CLUBS: Deutsche Gesellschaft für Psychologie; Deutsche philosophische Gesellschaft. Religion, Catholic. OFFICE: Technische Hochschule, Dresden. HOME: Walderseeplatz 2, Dresden A 16, Germany.

KAHLA, Edna Agnes. *b*: Levenshulme. *c.t*: Poetry Rev, G.K.'s Weekly. Travelled in France, Italy, Egypt & Syria. *a*: Fairlie, Catherine Rd, Bowdon, Altrincham, Cheshire. *t*: 296.

KAHLE, PAUL E.: Orientalist, professor; b. Hohenstein, Ostpr., Germany, January, 1875; s. Ernst and Bertha (Schmidt) K.; educ. Univs. of Marburg, Halle, Berlin. DEGREES: Ph.D (Halle), 1898; Lic. Theol. (Halle), 1902; Dr. Theol. h. c. (Giessen), 1922; m. Marie Gisevius, 1917. AUTHOR: Textkrit. u. lexikalische Bemerkungen zum samaritanischen Pentateuchtargum, 1898; Der Masoretische Text des A. T. nach der Überlieferung der babylonischen Juden., 1902; Die Arabischen Bibelübersetzungen, 1904; Neuarabische Volksdichtung aus Ägypten, 1900; Masoreten des Ostens, 1913; Das Krokodilspiel, ein Ägyptisches Schattenspiel, 1915 (2nd edit. 1921); Volkserzählungen aus Palästina Zusammen (with Hans Schmidt), 1918 (vol. II, 1930); Beitrag zu Bauer-Leander: Historische Grammatik des Hebräischen, 1923; Der Totenklage im heutigen Ägypten, 1923; Piri Re Is Bahrīje. Das türkische Segelhandbuch für das Mitteländische Meer vom Jahre 1521. Herausgegeben, ubersetzt u. erklärt (3 vols.), 1926; Masoreten des Westens, 1927; Die hebräischen Bibelhandschriften aus Babylonien, 1928; Biblia Hebraica. Edidit Rud. Kittel, textum Masoreticum Quaravit P. Kahle: Liber Jesaiae, 1929. Liber Genesis, 1929; Masoreten des Westens, vol. II, 1930; Der Leuchtturm von Alexandria ein Arabisches Schattenspiel aus Ägypten (translation), 1930. Contributor of many scientific articles to learned journals, year books, to volume of Oriental Studies, Mags. on Assyriology in volumes on Egypt, etc. Counselor to students at the Univ. of Halle, 1909; Professor at the Univ. of Giessen, 1914; Professor at the Univ. of Bonn, 1923. Religion, Protestant. OFFICE: Orientalisches Seminar. HOME: Rottenburgstrasse 5, Bonn a. Rhein, Germany.

KAHLER, Hugh MacNair, B.A. *b*: Philadelphia 1883. *e*: Princeton Univ. *m*: Louise Kingsley. *d*: 1. Writer & Editor, *n.a*: Fiction Ed Ladies Home Journ Phila 1943—. *Publ*: The Six Best Cellars (with H. Hall); Babel; The East Wind; Father Means Well; Hills Were Higher Then; The Big Pink; Bright Danger *Ctr*: Sat Ev Post, Ladies, Home Journ, Colliers', American, Country Gentleman, Red Book, etc. *s.s*: Fiction. *Rec*: Archery, chess, golf. *c*: Coffee House (N.Y.), Cap & Gown, Franklin Inn, etc. *a*: Princetown, New Jersey.

KAHN, Leo, LL.D. *b*: Cologne 1909. *e*: Cologne Gr Sch, Univs of Cologne & Berlin. *m*: Feodore K. Joseph. *s*: 1. *d*: 1. Mang Ed Godfrey & Stephens Ltd. Publishers. *Publ*: Obliging Fellows. *Ctr*: News Chron, World Digest. *Rec*: Tennis. *a*: 66 Danes Court, Wembley Park, Middlesex. *T*: Wembley 4361.

KAHRSTEDT, ULRICH: professor of history; b. Neisse, Germany, Apr. 27, 1888; s. Otto and Mathilde (Plüddemann) K.; educ. Grammar School (Neisse); Univs. of Edinburgh, Strassburg, Berlin. DEGREES: Ph.D. (Berlin); m. Margarete Plüddemann, April 15, 1916. AUTHOR: Forschungen zur Geschichte des 5. and 4. Jahrhunderts, 1910; Geschichte der Karthager, 1913; Annalistik des Livius, 1913; Pax Americana, 1919; Griechisches Staatsrecht, 1922; Syrische Territorien, 1926. Contributor to: Eiserne Blätter; Deutsche Tageszeitung. General character of writing: historical, foreign politics. Religion, Protestant. ADDRESS: Hainholzweg 32, Göttingen, Germany.

KAISENBERG, GEORG JOHANN HEINRICH WILHELM: State Councilor of Home Office; b. Nördingen, May 4, 1883; s. Heinrich and Frieda (Weber) K.; educ. Max Gymnasium of Munich and St. Stephan of Augsburg, Ludwigsgymnasium of Munich; Univs. of Munich and Berlin. DEGREES: Referendar, 1906, Dr. Jur., 1907, Assessor, 1909; m. Maja Eysser, Nov. 27, 1916. AUTHOR: Entwürfe der Reichs-, Wahlund Abstimmungsgesetze, 1920; Reichswahlgesetz (with Hans Freiherr von Welser, 1920; Wahl des Reichspräsidenten, 1920 (2nd edit. 1925); Kleingarter-und Kleinpachtlandordnung, Kommentar, 1920 2nd edit. als Handbuch des deutschen Kleingartenrechts, 1924); Volksentscheid und Volksbegehren, 1922 (2nd edit. 1926); Die Wahl zum Reichstag, 1924 (3rd edit. 1928); Wahl zum Preussischen Landtag (with Dr. Erwin Schütze), 1924 (2nd edit. 1928); Weg der Volksgesetzgebung, 1926; Kleingartenrecht (with Otto Albrecht), 1926. Co-editor: Reichsverwaltungsblatt von Deutsche Verwaltungspartei. Contributor to: Reichsverwaltungsblatt; Verwaltungsarchiv; Deutsche Juristenzeitung; Zeitschrift für öffentliches Recht; Zeitschrift für Staatswissenschaft; Kleingartenwacht; Berliner Tageblatt; Kölnische Zeitung; Frankfurter Zeitung; Germania; 8 Uhr-Abendblatt, and others. General character of writing: scientific, politics. Co-worker on Politisches Handwörterbuch; Staatslexikon; Handwörterbuch der Rechtswissenschaft; Nipperdey; Grundrechte und Grundpflichten der Reichsverfassung; Handbuch des deutschen Staatsrechts. Is councilor in the ministry of the Home Office. CLUBS: Deutsche Gesellschaft 1914; Berliner Demokratischer Club. Religion, Roman Catholic. OFFICE: Platz der Republik 6, Berlin NW. 40. HOME: Marienbaderstr. 1, Berlin-Schmargendorf, Germany.

KAISER, F. W. ERICH: univ. professor; b. Essen, Germany, 1871; s. Dr. Wilhelm and Erna (Ehrhardt) K.; educ. Realgymnasium of Elberfeld, Univs. of Marburg, Munich and Bonn.

DEGREES: Ph.D. (Bonn) and D.Sc.h.c. (Capetown); m. Marie Rauff, 1901. AUTHOR: Die Diamantenwueste Südwestafrikas (The diamondiferous desert of S. W. Africa) (2 vols.), 1926. Editor: neues Jahrbuch für Mineralogy, Geology und Palaentology, Stuttgart. Contributor to Neus Jahrbuch für Mineraleogie, etc., Stuttgart; Zeitschrift der Deutschen geologischen Gesellschaft, Berlin; Chemie der Erde, Jena; Transactions of the Geological Society of South Africa, and others. General character of writing: scientific, text books. Followed geological and petrographical studies in Norway, Spain, Portugal, Central Asia, South and South-West Africa, where a great strip of the desert was geographically and geologically surveyed. Studies weather conditions and sedimentation in today's surface of the earth, to secure better knowledge of the older formations. ADDRESS: Neuhauserstrasse 51, Munich, Bavaria, Germany.

KAISER, Grace Lytle Edwards. b: Cincinnati, Ohio, U.S.A. 1881. e: Public Schs of Latonia, Kentucky, Davis Sch of Music. m: Oliver B. Kaiser. d: 2. Vocalist, Teacher of Voice Production, Musical Director, Composer, Author, Chautauqua Artist. Publ: Pageant—The Torch of Progress; Songs—People of All Nations; Prayer for Peace; Processional Hymn of Peace; And the Lord God Planted a Garden; Sing, Let Us Sing; Carry on the Work; Why Fear the Foe; Give Flowers of Love To-day; Hurry, Let's Go to the Fair; Fair Ohio; etc; Poem—Life's Mirror. Ctr: The Poet's Forum, Poetry Studies, The Revivalist, The Union Signal, The Ohio Messenger, The Cincinnati Post, The Cincinnati Times-Star, etc. s.s: Sacred, patriotic, Classic Verse & Music. Rec: Motoring, cruising, composing. a: Drake Rd, Rt. 10, Cincinnati 27, Ohio, U.S.A. T: Locust 7543.

KAISER, JOHAN WILLEM: writer; b. Hoorn, Holland, Feb., 1897; s. Dr. K. F. L. and Maria (Stooter) K.; educ. Elementary and Secondary Schools in Holland; unmarried. AUTHOR: Introduction into the Study and Interpretation of Drama, 1929. Contributor to Internationale Zeitschrift für Individualpsychologie (Vienna). General character of writing: psychological interpretation of works of art, especially of dramatic art. Written portraits of artists drawn from their works by psychological interpretation. Member of Internationaler Verein für Individualpsychologie (Dutch Branch). ADDRESS: Hendrik Jacobszstraat 12, Amsterdam, Holland.

KAISER, LOUISE: lector; b. Medemblik, Holland, Oct., 1891; d. Lodewyk and Maria (Stooter K.; DEGREES: M.D.; unmarried. AUTHOR: De Segmentale Innervatie van de Huid by de Duif, 1924; Proefondervindelyk Onderzoek van Betrekkingsklanken, 1926. Contributor to Archives Nèerlandaises de Phonètique Experimentale and Arch. Nèerl. de Physiologie, Nederlandsch Tydschrift voor Geneeskunde, Proceedings Koninklyke Akademie v. Wetenschappen. General character of writing: scientific. Lecturer upon experimental phonetics; the only doctor in Holland treating exclusively diseases of voice and speech. OFFICE: Rapenburgerstraat 136, Amsterdam. HOME: Prinsengracht 642, Amsterdam, Holland.

KAISER, SHUMSHER JUNG BAHADUR RANA: Indian prince and potentate; b. Thapathaly, India, Jan. 8, 1892; s. H. H. Maharaja Chandra Shumsher and Loka Bhakta Laxmi Devi; educ. Home schools at Thapathaly at Shingha Durbar; Durbar High School. Translated Kalidas's Vikramorvashi (Sanscrit drama) in Nepali language (Parbatia), 1925. H. H. Lieut.-Gen. Comdg. Mahendra Dal Brigade, Nepalese Army; accompanied father on State visit to Europe, 1908; in charge of reception on King George's visit to Nepal, 1911; led second contingent to India, 1915-16, British war medal; president of Prince of Wales' Nepal Visit Comm. and in charge of Shikar arrangements 1921; chief of official tour of Provincial inspection (Saptari), 1922-23; dir.-gen. dept. of commerce; chmn. of municipality; Rotary Judge Supreme Court of Appeal; received 1st class of Most Refulgent Order of the Star of Nepal, 1920; Hon. Knight Commander of the Most Excellent Order of the British Empire, 1924; m. H. R. H. the princess Royal, d. of H. M. Maharajahiraja Prithvi Vira Vikrama Shah Deva, King of Nepal. Religion, Orthodox Hindu. OFFICE: Jinsi Adda, Shingha, Durbar. HOME: Kaiser Mahal, Kathmandu, Nepal, India.

KAJI, Hiralal. M.A., B.Sc. b: Surat 1886. e: Bombay. m: Vasant B. Sheth. s: 4. d: 2. Prof Geog & Statistics Sydenham Coll Commerce & Econ Bombay, Advocate High Court & Justice of the Peace, latterly Princ & Prof Econ Gujarat Coll Ahmedabad. Publ: Co-operation in India; Co-operation in Bombay; Principles of General Geography; Lands Beyond the Border; Great Mystery of Life Beyond Death. s.s: Geography, Co-operation, Economics, Life Insurance, Women's Education. Rec: Chess, lawn tennis. c: P.E.N. (Bombay). a: 40a Ridge Rd, Malabar Hill, Bombay 6, India. T: Bombay 45798.

KALACHNE, ALFRED: college professor; b. Berlin, Dec. 17, 1874; s. Hermann and Marie (Hoffmann) K.; educ. Sophien-Gymnasium of Berlin, Univ. of Berlin. DEGREES: Ph.D.; m. Anni Schäfer, June 1, 1906. AUTHOR: Die neueren Forschungen auf dem Gebiet der Elektrizität und ihre Anwendungen, 1908; Grundzüge der mathematisch-physikalischen Akustik, 1910 (2nd vol. 1913); Schallerzeugung mit mechanischen Mitteln: (in vol. 8 of (Akustic) des "Handbuch der Physik"), 1927; Gliederung des Tonbereichs (Musikinstrumente Beiträge in Müller-Pouillet, Lehrbuch der Physik, 11th edit., vol. 1, part 3 (Akustik), 1929. Contributor to: Annalen der Physik; Physikalische Zeitschrift; Zeitschrift für technische Physik; Zeitschrift für wissenschaftliche Photographie; Verhandlungen der deutschen physikalischen Gesellschaft, and others. Political articles in Deutsche Zeitung. General character of writing: scientific, text books and nature books. CLUBS: Deutsche physikalische Gesellschaft; Deutsche Gesellschaft für technische Physik; Gesellschaft deutscher Naturforscher und Ärzte, Aero-Club, and others. Religion: Evangelical. OFFICE: Technical College, Danzig. HOME: Jahnstrasse 8, Danzig-Oliva, Germany.

KALACHINE, PRINCE d HOLM duc de: see Holm, Lieut.-Gen. Frits.

KALAHNE, ANNI: writer; b. Jena, Germany, June 10, 1878; d. Dietrich and Wilhelmine (Theobald) Schäfer; educ. elementary schools and private instruction at home; m. Professor Dr. Alfred Kalähne, June 1, 1906. Contributes political articles concerning the movement for women's rights; to Die deutsche Frau; Hausfrauenzeitschriften; Die Hanseatin; The New Times; Deutscher Offizierbund; Neulandblatt; Verein für das Deutschtum im Ausland; and many articles in different German newspapers. Founder of the national movement for women's rights in the German Ostmark. Delegate of the Danzig meetings since 1919; Leader of the German national women of West Prussia and Danzig since 1918. CLUBS: Deutscher Flottenbund; Alldeutscher Verband; V.D.A.; Evangelischer Frauenbund; Hausfrauen-Verein. Relig. Evangelical. ADDRESS: Jahnstrasse 8, Danzig-Oliva, Freie Stadt, Germany.

KALBFLEISCH, KARL REINHOLD: univ. professor; b. Selnhausen, Hessen-Nassau, Germany, Nov. 3, 1868; s. Konrad and Emilie (Janda) K.; educ. Gymnasium Hanau, Univs. of Leipzig and Berlin. DEGREES: Ph.D., M.D. (honoris causa); m. Hermine Hedwig Hübner, Dec. 22, 1922. AUTHOR: In Galeni de placitis Hippocratis et Platonis libros observationes criticae, 1892; Die neuplatonische Schrift Pros Gauron, 1895; Galeni Institutio logica, 1896; Über Galens Einleitung in die Logik, 1897; Galeni De victu attenuante liber, 1898; Papyri Argentoratenses Graecae, 1901; Papyri Graecae musei Britannici et musei Barolinensis, 1902; Galeni De causis continentibus libellus, 1904; Berliner Klassikertexte vol. III (with H. Schöne), 1905; Simplicii in Aristotelis Categorias commentarium, 1907; Papyri Tandanae I-IV (cum discipulis), 1912, 1913; Die Demokratie im Urteil griechescher Denker, 1920; Griechische Familienpapiere aus Ägypten, 1926. Editor: Papyri Jandanae. General character of writing: philological. In interested in classical philology, papyrology, and the history of medicine. HOME: Süd-Anlage 4, Giessen (Hesse), Germany.

KALEDIN, Victor Konstantine. *b* Rostoff on Don, Russia 1887. *e*: Imperial Lyceum cf Moscow. War Academy. *m*: Former Mrs Bruce Kemp. Author. *Publ*: F-L-A-S-H D13; K14—G.M.C.C.; High Treason. *c.t*: Asia, Medical Review of Reviews (U.S.A). *s.s*: Secret Service. *Rec*: Walking, shooting, fishing. War Service. *a*: Rosemary Cottage, West Down, N. Devon. *t*: 1.

KALELKAR, Dattatreya. *b*: Satara 1885. *e*: Bombay Univ. *m*: Laxmibai. *s*: 2. Educationist & Author. *n.a*: Asst-Ed Navajivan & Harijan. *Publ*: Travels in the Himalayas; Rivers of India; Ideal Social Virtues; Village Construction; Reminiscences of Jail Life, Boyhood, etc, & Several Essays on Art, Literature, Travel, etc. *Ctr*: Various Marathi, Gujarati & Hindi Journs. *s.s*: Education, Literature, Astronomy. *Rec*: Travel. *a*: Kakawadi, Warda, C.P., India.

KALLAS, Madame Aino Julia Maria. *b*: Viipuri, Finland. *m*: Dr Oskar Kallas, Formerly Estonian Min to Ct of St James's. *s*: 2. *d*: 2. Author. *Publ*: The White Ship; Eros the Slayer; The Wolf's Bride (1930); etc. *c.t*: Trans from Finnish into Eng, French, German, Italian, Swedish, Hungarian, Dutch & Estonian. Has lect in G.B., U.S.A., Canada, Holland. Hungary, Finland & Estonia. *Rec*: Travel, theatre. *a*: Tallinn, Estonia.

KALLAS, Dr. Oskar Philipp. *b*: Estonia 1868. *m*: Aino Julia Maria Krohn. *s*: 2. *d*: 2. Estonian Min Plenipotentiary to the Ct of St James & the Hague. *n.a*: Sec to Estonian daily n/p Postimees 1903-18. *Publ*: Works & articles on ethnography & folklore, publ mostly in Estonian; also German, Finnish & Eng. *Rec*: Walking. Candidatus Philologiæ of the Tartu Univ. Dr Philosophiæ of Helsinki Univ. *a*: 167 Queen's Gate, S.W.7. *t*: Kensington 5473.

KAMAL-UD-DIN, Khwaja, B.A., LL.B. *b*: Lahore. *e*: Central Model Sc Lahore, Forman Christian Col, Lahore, Punjab Univ, Lahore, Muslim Missionary. *m*: Mehtab Begum. *s*: 4. *d*: 2. *n.a*: Ed Islamic Review. *Publ*: The House Divided; India in the Balance; Towards Islam; The Secret of Existence; The Threshold of Truth; Reincarnation of Souls; Gospel of Action; Muslim Prayer; etc. *s.s*: Islam, comparative study of religions. Advocate, Chief Court, Punjab, India. Practised at the Bar until '12. Founded The Woking Muslim Mission. Travelled throughout the Muslim World. *a*: The Mosque, Woking, Surrey & Azeez Manzil, Brandreth Rd, Lahore, India. *t*: Woking 679. Lahore 2686.

KAMBE, MASAO: univ. professor; Member of Imperial Academy; b. Ichinomiya, Japan, Apr., 1877; s. Nushimasa and Wai Kambe; educ. in several schools, graduating from Tokyo Imperial Univ. DEGREES: Hogakushi (Tokyo Imperial Univ.), Hogaku-hakushi (Kyoto Univ.); m. Sumiko, June, 1902. AUTHOR (in Japanese): Progressive Taxation, 1901; Lecture on Public Finance, 1902; Socialism and Social Movements, 1903; Premium Savings Systems, 1904; Commercial Economic History, 1904; Redemption of Public Debt, 1908; Lecture on Political Economy, 1909; Custom Duty on Corn, 1909; Outline of Finance, 1910; Public Debt, 1910; Agricultural Emigration to Korea, 1910; Modern Investment, 1911; Economic Policy of Japan, 1911; Essays on Economics (4 vols.), 1912; Taxation, 1912; Tax on Increment Value of Land, 1912; Investment, 1912; Economic Situation of Japan, 1916; Studies on Taxation,I, 1919; Financial, Economical and Social Series (5 vols.), 1920, 1921; Studies on Taxation, II, 1920; Home Life and Financial Questions, 1920; Studies on Taxation, III, 1922; Recent Economic and Social Questions, 1922; International Relation of Japanese Economy, 1922; Daily Economical Questions (from Sept., 1922, till Dec., 1929); Studies on Taxation, IV, 1923; Manual of Political Economy, 1923; Outline of Political Economy, 1924; Studies on Taxation, V, 1924; Lecture on Public Finance, 1924, 1925; Manual of Public Finance, 1925; Studies on Taxation, VI, 1925; Studies on Taxation, VII, 1926; Lectures on Public Finance, 1927; Studies on Taxation, VIII, 1927; Public Finance, 1928; Studies on Taxation, IX, 1928; System of Public Finance, 1929; Taxation, 1929; Studies on Taxation, X, 1930; (in German Language): Der Russich-Japanische Krieg und Japanische Volkswirtschaft, 1905; Die Entwicklung der Japanischen Volkswirtschaft in der Gegenwart, 1916; Grundüge des Japanischen Steuersystems der Gegenwart, 1926. Contributor to the Kyoto Univ. Economic Review. General character of writing: economic. OFFICE: Imperial Univ. of Kyoto. HOME: Jo-dozi-Nishidamchi, Kyoto, Japan.

KAMDAR, Chhotalal Mansing, B.A. *b*: Mota Devalia 1898. *e*: Bombay Univ. *m*: Suryakumari. *d*: 1. School Teacher. *Publ*: Vishwadarshan; Jagatman Janva Jevun; Harindranan Natko; Reminiscences of G. K. Gokhle; Solarium of Jamnagar; Reminiscences of a Saint; Mahatma Gandhi; Raman Maharshi; Booker T. Washington; Strange But True Stories. *Ctr*: Sharda, Yuvak, Pratima, Kumar, Kanak, Gandiv, Kismet, Pratap, Janeta, Padmini, Jeevan, etc. *s.s*: Figures & Reference Books. *Rec*: Reading, writing, walking, bridge. *c*: Indian P.E.N. *a*: P.O. Vankaner, (Dist Kathiawar), India.

KAMM, Josephine Mary. *b*: London 1906. *e*: P.N.E.U. Sch Burgess Hill Sussex. *m*: George Kamm. *s*: 1. Novelist & Journalist. *Publ*: African Challenge; Progress Towards Self-Government in the British Colonies; Peace, Perfect Peace; Nettles to My Head; All quiet at Home; Disorderly Caravan. *Ctr*: Overseas, English Speaking World, Origins & Purposes. *s.s*: British Colonies. *c*: Women's Press. *w.s*: '39—46 M.O.I. *a*: 35 Argyll Mansions, Chelsea, London, S.W.3. *T*: Flaxman 1376.

KAMMERER, OTTO: univ. professor; b. Miesbach, Germany, 1865; s. Anton and Helene (Otto) K.; educ. Realgymnasium of Munich, Technical Univs. of Munich and Berlin. DEGREES: Dr. Engineer; m. Alice Spandau. AUTHOR: Technische Lastenförderung einst und jetzt, 1907. Contributes to Zeitschrift des Vereins Deutscher Ingenieure. General character of writing: scientific, technical. Constructed electrical cranes from 1889 to 1896; engaged in construction of machines for slewing rail tracks from 1910 to 1930. Religion: Catholic. ADDRESS: Lyck Allee 12, Berlin-Charlottenburg, Germany.

KANAAR, Adrian Charles, M.D., M.R.C.P., F.R.C.S. *b*: Beckenham 1911. *e*: Dulwich Coll, London & Edinburgh Univs. *m*: Mary Stephenson Forster. *s*: 1. Surgeon Birmingham Accident Hosp, Mem B.M.A. *Publ*: Ethiopia at the Cross Roads. *Ctr*: Everybody's, World Rev, Nineteenth Century & After, Dly Mirror, Sun Chron, Birmingham Post, etc. *s.s*: Social Aspects of Medicine, Menace of Communism, Britain's Future, Anglo-American & Anglo-Soviet

Relations. *Rec*: Swimming, lecturing. *c*: National. *w.s*: 39—45 R.A.M.C. *a*: Silverdale, 52 Anderton Park Rd, Moseley, Birmingham 13. *T*: South 3014.

KANE, Rev. John Herbert Wesley, M.A. *b*: Co Armagh 1865. *e*: Roy Sc Armagh & T.C.D. *c.t*: Historical articles to various mags & periodicals. *Rec*: Riding, cycling, cricket. *a*: The Vicarage, 2 Woolstone Rd, S.E.23. *t*: Sydenham 6355.

KANE, Pandurang Vaman, M.A., LL.M. *b*: Parsharam 1880. *e*: Bombay Univ. *m*:. *s*: 2. *d*: 3. Advocate Hgh Court Bombay 1911—47, formerly Prof in Sanskrit '04—11, Prof of Law Bombay Govt Law Coll '17—23, V-Pres Bombay Roy Asiatic Soc, etc. *Publ*: History of Sanskrit Poetics; History of Dharmasastra; etc. *Ctr*: Indian Antiquary, etc. *s.s*: Sanskrit Poetics & Classical Dharmasastra. *Rec*: Travel, long walks, Indian music. *c*: Indian P.E.N. *a*: Angres Wair, Girgaoh, Bombay 4, India.

KANEKAR, Anant, B.A., LL.B. *b*: Bombay 1905. *e*: Univ of Bombay. *m*: (1) Rekha (dec'd), (2) Kamal. *s*: 2. *d*: 2. *n.a*: Co-Ed Chitra 35—38, Co-Ed Asha '38—40. *Publ*: Chandrat ; Pikli Pane ; Tutlele Tare ; Jagtya Chhaya ; Divyavarti Andher ; Hirve Kandil ; Khetle Nikhare ; Dhoor. *Ctr*: Navyug, Sahitya, Kirloskar. *Rec*: Travel. *a*: Shanti-Kunj, 5th Lane, Hindu Colony, Dadar, Bombay 14.

KANNER, HEINRICH: author; b. Galati, 1864; educ. public schools, gymnasium and univ., all of Vienna, Austria. DEGREES: Juris utriusque Doctor; m. Ottilie Mathilde Rosenberg, 1887. AUTHOR: Die neuesten Geschichtslügen, 1921; Kaiserliche Katastrophenpolitik. Ein Stück zeitgenössischer Geschichte, 1922; Wilhelms II. Abschiedsbrief an das deutsche Volk (Anonym. 2nd vol.), 1922; Der Rechtsweg zur Revision des Friedensvertrags, 1922; Das Weltstrafgericht. Ein neuer Vorschlag zur Verhinderung von Kriegen, 1924; Der mitteleuropäische Staatenbund. Ein Vorschlag zum Frieden, 1925; Der Schlüssel zur Kriegsschuldfrage. Ein verheimlichtes Kapitel der Vorkriegsgeschichte, 1926. Contributor to: Der Krieg (Berlin); various pacifistic weeklies in Germany; Neues Wiener Journal (Austria); Prager Presse (Czechoslovakia); Journal des Débats (Paris); Contemporary Review (London); Current History (New York), and others. General character of writing: political-historical. Was member of the editorial staff of the Frankfurter Zeitung from 1890 to 1900; Chief editor of the political and literary weekly "Die Zeit", Vienna, from 1894 to 1903; Chief editor of the daily newspaper "Die Zeit", Vienna, from 1902 to 1917; Chief editor of the political monthly "Der Krieg", Berlin, since 1928. ADDRESS: Wasagasse 52, Vienna IX., Austria.

KANTOROWICZ, HERMANN: professor; b. Posen, Germany, Nov. 18, 1877; s. Wilhelm and Rosa (Gieldzinska) K.; educ. Gymnasium (Berlin); Univs. of Berlin, Geneva and Munich. DEGREES: LL.D. (Heidelberg); m. (1) Dorothea Rosenstack, 1904 (died); (2) Hildegard Kalin, 1923. AUTHOR: Goblers Karolinenkommentar, 1904; Der Kampf um die Rechtswissenschaft, 1906; Albertus Gandinus und das Strafrecht der Scholastik, 1907 (2nd edit. 1926); Zur Lehre vom richtigen Recht, 1909; Entstehung der Digestenvulgata, 1910; Was ist uns Savigny? 1912; Der Offiziershass im Deutschen Heer, 1919; Thomas Diplovatatius (1st vol.), 1919; Deutschlands Interesse am Völkerbund, 1920; Einführung in die Text-Kritik, 1921; Bismarcks Schatten, 1921; Verteidigung des Völkerbundes, 1922; Germany and the League of Nations, 1924; Aus der Vorgeschichte der Freirechtsl., 1925; Der Geist der englischen Politik und das Gespenst der Einkreisung Deutschlands, 1929. Contributor to: Frankfurter Zeitung; Vossische Zeitung; Berliner Tageblatt; Kontemporary Reisen; Columbia Law Review; Zeitschrift der Savigny Zeitschrift; Zeitschrift für die gesamte Strafrechtswissenschaft; Historische Zeitschrift, and many others. General character of writing: scientific, historical, political. Historical expert of the German Reichstag on the origin of the war. CLUBS: Deutsche Sociologische Gesellschaft; Republikanischer Klub, Kiel. Religion, Protestant. ADDRESS: The University, Feldstrasse 138, Kiel, Germany.

KAPADIA, Shaporji Aspaniarji, M.D., L.R.C.P., etc. *n.a*: Oriental Ed & Jnt Founder of The Wisdom of the East Series 1904. *Publ*: Teachings of Zoroaster & The Philosophy of the Parsi Religion. *a*: 22 Redcliffe Gdns, S. Kensington, S.W.10. *t*: Flaxman 7242.

KAPITZA, Peter, PhD., F.InstP., F.R.S. *b*: Kronstadt, Russia 1894. *e*: Sec Sc Kronstadt, Petrograd Polytech Inst (Faculty of Elec Eng). *m*: Anna Kryloff. *s*: 2. Roy Soc Messel Research Prof, Dir Roy Soc Mond Lab, Cam. *n.a*: Gen Ed International series of Monographs on Physics. *s.s*: Physics. *Rec*: Chess. *a*: 173 Huntingdon Rd. Cam. *t*: 2045.

KAPLAN. Dr. B. *Publ*: Surgical Anatomy of Fractures below Elbow Joint; A Case of Veronal Poisoning. *a*: 569 Gale St, Dagenham, Essex.

KAPP, Reginald Otto. *b*: Brentwood, Essex 1885. *e*: Germany & Univ of Birmingham. *m*: Dorothy Wilkins. *s*: 1. *d*: 1. Prof of Electrical Eng Univ Coll Lond. *Publ*: Science Versus Materialism; (Ed) Electrical Transmission & Distribution; Revision of: Transformers. *Ctr*: Various Scientific & Engineering periodicals. *s.s*: Philosophy, Electrical Eng. *Rec*: Music, gardening. *a*: Gardole, Stanhope Rd, Croydon, Surrey. *T*: 6711.

KAPPIS, MAX: professor; b. Tübingen, Germany, Oct. 6, 1881; educ. Gymnasium Tübingen and Univs. of Tübingen and Berlin. DEGREES: M.D. and Professor; m. Berta Paris, 1911. AUTHOR: Chirurgische Diagnostik, 1924; Organisation und Betrieb des chirurgischen Operationssaales, 1927. Contributor to Deutsche Wochen- und Zeitschriften (of medical and surgical character). General character of writing: scientific, text books, medical. Professor of surgery in State Hospital of Hanover, Germany. CLUBS: Deutsche Gesellschaft für Chirurgie; honorary member of Amerikanische Gesellschaft für regionäre Anästhesie. Religion, Evangelical. ADDRESS: State Hospital, Dept. of Surgery, Hanover, Germany.

KARAKA, Dosoo F., B.A.(Oxon & Bombay). *b*: Bombay 1911. *n.a*: Special Corres Bombay Chron. *Publ*: The Pulse of Oxford ; Oh ! You English ; I Go West ; Out of Dust ; Just Flesh ; There Lay the City ; Chungking Diary ; With the 14th Army ; I've Shed My Tears ; We Never Die ; This India ; No Stars, No Stripes. *s.s*: Indian Questions, Leading Articles. *Rec*: Racing. *a*: Bombay Chronicle, Bombay, India.

KARANTH, K.S. *b*: Kota 1902. *m*: Leela. *s*: 1. *d*: 1. Journalist & Author. *n.a*: Owner-Ed Vasantha '24—28. *Publ*: Back to the Soil ; Life is Light, or What I Believe ; Nine Operettas, numerous Plays & Playlets, etc. *Ctr*: Asia, Illus Weekly of India, Orient, Bombay Chron, etc. *s.s*: Indian Culture, Dance, Theatre, Photography. *Rec*: Walking & hiking. *a*: Puttur, S.K., India.

KARK, Norman. *b*: Hendelberg, Transvaal, Sth Africa 1898. *e*: King Edward VII's Sch, Johannesburg Coll. Editor. *n.a*: Ed Courier 1937—, To-day '44—, Band Wagon '45—. *s.s*: Emigration, Foreign Politics, Empire, U.S. & African Negro Affairs. *c*: Norwegian, Sth African, etc. *w.s*: '14—17 & War Corr '44—45. *a*: 607—622 Grand Buildings, Trafalgar Sq, London, W.C.2. *T*: Whitehall 4248-9.

KARN, Frederick James, MusBac(Cantab), Mus Doc. *m*: (1) Laura Marion Caddel, (2) Zena Geninazzi. *s*: 2. *d*: 4. Principal of the Lon Col of Music. *Publ*: Many Text books for Students in Music. *a*: 4 Park Village West, N.W.1. *t*: Museum 1782.

KARNEY, Rt. Rev. Arthur Baillie Lumsdaine, D.D. *b*: Isle of Wight. *e*: Haileybury Coll & Trinity Coll Camb. *m*: Georgina Fielding. *s*: 3. *d*: 4. Bishop C. of E., Bishop of Johannesburg 1922—33, Bishop of Southampton '33—43, Chaplain Missions to Seaman San Francisco 1899—1903 & Buenos Aires 1903—14. *Publ*: The Father & His Sons; An Ambassador in Chains; Studies in the Character of Christ; The Divine Gardener; Christ's Treasure House; Saying Better Prayers; God in the Bible. *Ctr*: Church Times. *w.s*: Chaplain R.N. '14—17 (p.o.w. '18), Chaplain Army '18—19. *c*: United Univs. *a*: Blendworth Rectory, Horndean, Hants. *T*: Horndean 2174.

KARNI, Yehuda. *b*: Pinsk, Poland 1884. *e*: Self taught. Poet & Journalist. *n.a*: Ed-Staff Haaretz. *Publ*: (Hebrew Poetry) Gates; In Thy Gates, Fatherland; Jerusalem Poems; Songs & Tears; Trans of Mark Twain, Pushkin, etc. *a*: Tel-Aviv, 49 Melchett St, Palestine.

KAROLIDES, PAUL: see under Carolides.

KARVE, Dattatreya Gopal, M.A.(Bombay). *b*: Poona 1898. *e*: Bombay Univ. *m*: Sumatibai Khare. *s*: 4. *d*: 1. Prof of Economics & Princ of College of Commerce Poona, Fellow Bombay Univ. *Publ*: Poverty & Population in India; Federations, a Study in Comparative Politics; Ranade, Prophet of Liberated adia; & other books on Politics & Economics. *s.s*: Economic & Constitutional Questions. *Rec*: Light lit, detective fiction, walking. *c*: Maharashtra, P.Y.C. Hindu Gymkhana Poona. *a*: B.M. College of Commerce, Poona 4, India. *T*: Poona 1443.

KÄSTNER, Dr. Erich. *b*: Dresden 1899. *e*: Sc in Dresden, Rostock, Leipzig & Berlin. Writer. *Publ*: Herz auf Taille (Poems); Ein Mann gibt Auskunft (Poems); Emil und die Detektive (Children's novel); Punktchen und Anton (Children's novel); Das fliegende Klassenzimmer (Children's novel); Fabian, die Geschichte eines Moralisten (Novel); Radio play—Leben in dieser Zeit; etc. *c*: Pen (Berlin), Verband Deutscher Buhnenschriftsteller und Komponisten. *a*: 4 Roscherstr. 16, Berlin-Charlottenburg. *t*: Bleibtreu 0490.

KATHRENS, William Harold Vaughan. *b*: Barry, Glam 1905. *e*: Barry County Sc. *m*: Agnes Anderson. *d*: 1. Journalist. *n.a*: Barry Herald '22, Salford City Reporter '25, Batley News Series '27, Evening World Bristol '30, Daily Independent, Sheffield '31, Chief Sub-Ed '33—. *s.s*: N/p Make-up, criminology. *Rec*: Golf, swimming. *a*: Porthkerry, Hartington Rd, Millhouses, Sheffield.

KATIC, Dr. Ernest Ivo Miho. *b*: Dubrovnik 1883. *e*: Classical Hgh Sch Dubrovnik & Univ of Graz Austria. *m*: Delphina Luxardo. *Publ*: (Plays) Jakobenja; Antun Serge Cvijeta Zuzzeri; Outside the Fence of Living & Dead; Petka; (Novels) Under Petka. *c*: P.E.N., etc. *a*: Dubrovnik, Yugoslavia.

KATIN, Louis. Journalist. *n.a*: Ed Welwyn Times 1929-33. Mem N.U.J. '28—. *Publ*: Cont to Symposium, Worker's Point of View. *c.t*: Printing Review, Palestine Post, Jerusalem, Light on Health, etc. *s.s*: Printing, Palestine, nature cure. *a*: 8 Melbourne Ct, Welwyn Garden City, Herts.

KATO, GENCHI: associate Professor of the Shinto Religion at Tokyo Imperial University; b. Tokyo, Japan, June 17, 1873; s. Gencho and Takako Kato; educ., graduated from Tokyo Imperial Univ. DEGREES: D.Litt.; m. Setsuko, 1901. AUTHOR: A Study of Shinto, the religion of the Japanese Nation, 1926; The Kogoshui or Gleanings from Ancient Stories (with H. Hoshino, both books in English). Translations of the Zaidan Hojin Meiji Seitoku Kinen Gakkai (Meiji Japan Soc.). HOME: 11 Maruyamacho, Koishikawa, Tokyo, Japan.

KATRAK, Sorab K. H. *b*: Karachi, India 1892. *e*: Bombay Univ. *m*: Dina Madan. *s*: 2. *d*: 3. Merchant. *Publ*: Through Amanullah's Afghanistan. *Ctr*: Times Illus (Bombay), Dly Gazette & Sind Observer (Karachi). *s.s*: Sexology, Anthropology, Philosophy. *Rec*: Tennis, cricket, swimming. *c*: Karachi. *a*: 245 Staff Lines, Karachi, India. *T*: 2622 & 5257.

KATRE, Sumitra Mangesh, M.A., Ph.D. *b*: Honnavar, Nth Kanara 1906. *m*: Radha. Director & Prof of Indo-European Philology, Deccan College Post-graduate & Research Institute Poona. *n.a*: Founder-Ed Oriental Literary Digest 1937—, New Indian Antiquary '38—. *Publ*: Introduction to Indian Textual Criticism; Formation of Konkani; Some Problems of Historical Linguistics in Indo-Aryan; Prakrit Languages & Their Contribution to Indian Culture. *Ctr*: Oriental Journ (Calcutta), Poona Orientalist, Indian Culture, Archiv Orientalni, etc. *s.s*: Linguistics, Philology, Ancient Indian Culture. *a*: Deccan College Post-Graduate & Research Institute, 10 Connaught Rd, Poona 1, India. *T*: 9-145.

KATSUMOTO, MASAAKIRA: professor of civil law; b. Tokyo, Japan, May, 1895; s. Kanzaburō and Tazuko (Niwa) K.; educ. Third High Sch. (Kyoto); Tokyo Imperial Univ. DEGREES: Hōgakushi; Hōgakuhakuski; m. Sadako Wakabayashi, 1918. AUTHOR: Glausula rebus sic stantibus in civil law, 1926; Law and Literature, 1929; Treatise on the Law of Obligation (Pt. I), 1930; Law Episodes, 1931; The Theory and Policy of Criminal Law, by Dr. Kanzaburo Katsumoto (treatises, collected and arranged by M. Katsumoto. Relig. denom., Buddhist. OFFICE: Tōhoku Imperial University, Japan. HOME: 58 Katahira-CHŌ, Sendai, Japan.

KAUFFMAN, Reginald Wright. Author. *n.a*: Ed Staff Washington Post, Boston Transcript, N.Y. Her Tribune. *Publ*: Daughters of Ishmael; Broken Pitchers; A Man of Little Faith; Front Porch; Jim Trent; The Free Lovers; The House of Bondage; Blood of Kings. *a*: Rocky Top, Sebasco, via R.F.D. Bath, Maine, U.S.A.

KAUFMAN, Louis, O.B.E. *b*: Hungary 1881. *e*: Priv. Mang Dir Truth. *s.s*: Selling & advertising. *Rec*: Golf. *c*: Constit. *a*: 10 Carteret St, S.W.1. *t*: Victoria 0205.

KAUFMANN, Helen L., B.A. *b*: New York City 1887. *e*: Barnard College. *m*: M. J. Kaufmann. *s*: 2. *d*: 1. Writer. *Publ*: Minute Sketches of Great Composers; Artists in Music of To-day; From Jehova to Jazz; You can enjoy Music; The Home Book of Music Appreciation; The Story of 100 Great Composers; Little Dictionary of Musical Terms. *Ctr*: Parent's Mag, Independent Woman, Musical American. *s.s*: Music & Musicians. *a*: Box 576, Hampton, N.J., or 59 West 12th St, New York, U.S.A. *T*: Gr 3-7264.

KAUFMANN, Ruth Hammitt. *b*: New York City. *e*: Bryn Mawr Coll & France. *m*: R. W. Kaufmann. *s*: 1. *d*: 2. Journalist, Novelist. *Publ*: Dancing Dollars; Spun Gold; Stars for Sale; His Mother's House; Street Barred; Latter Day Saints (with R. W. Kaufmann). *Ctr*: Phila Record, N.Y. Tribune, Boston

Who Was Who Among English and European Authors

Transcript, Bohemian Mag, Hampton's Mag, etc. *Rec*: Walking, riding. *c*: Shakespeare, Bryn Mawr, etc. *a*: Rockytop, Sebasco Estates, via Bath, Maine, U.S.A.

KAULITZ-NIEDECK, R. (pen name); (Rosa Anderson); author; b. Niedeck, Provinz Hannover, Germany, March 10, 1881; d. Georg and Wilhelmine (Teuteberg) Kaulitz; *educ*. Girls' College of Frankeschen Stiftungen zu Halle A. S.; Schwertfegers Institut of Göttingen; m. Ernst Anderson (editor). AUTHOR: Das Urbild von Goethes Werther, 1908; Goethe und Jerusalem, 1908; Der alte Bonner Friedhof und die berühmten Gräber, 1910; Frau Grotsnut, 1912; Wie können sich die Frauen im Kriege nützlich machen, 1914; Die Geele Rose, Goethes Erlebnisse in Trier, 1924; Das Dichtergrab auf Oesel, 1926; Die Mara, das Leben einer berühmten Sängerin, 1929. General character of writing: novels, essays, scientific, historical, technical; biographies and literary history. Relig. denom., Lutheran. ADDRESS: Liederstrasse 4, Haapsain, Estonia.

KAUS, Gina. *Publ*: To-morrow We Part; Luxury Liner; Catherine the Great. *a*: c/o European Books Ltd, 314/324 Regent St, W.1.

KAUTSKY, KARL: writer; b. Prague, Bohemia, Oct., 1854; s. Johann and Wilhelmine Eleanore (Jaïch) K.; *educ*. Latin school and university; m. Luise Tonsperger, 1890. AUTHOR: Einfluss der Volksvermehrung auf den Fortschritt der Gesellschaft, 1880; Karl Marx Oekonomische Lehern, 1887; Thomas More und Seine Utopie, 1888; Die Klassengegensaetze von 1789, 1889; Das Erfurter Programm, 1892; Der Parlamentarismus, 1893; Vorlaeufer des Sozialismus, 1894; Communism in Central Europe in the Time of the Reformation, 1897; Die Agrarfrage, 1899; Bernstein und das Sozialdemokratische Programm, 1899; Die Soziale Revolution, 1902; Ethik und Materialistische Geschichtsauffassung, 1906; Der Ursprung des Christentums, 1908; Der Weg zur Macht, 1909; Vermehrung und Entwicklung in Natur und Gesellschaft, 1910; Rasse und Judetum, 1914; Die Diktatur des Proletariats, 1918; Terrorismus und Kommunismus, 1919; [Terrorism and Communism, 1919]; Wie der Weltkrieg Entstand, 1919; [The Guilt of William Hohenzollern, 1919]; Von der Demokratie zur Staatssklaverei, 1921; Die Proletarische Revolution, 1922; [The Labor Revolution, 1925]; The Economic Doctrines of Karl Marx, 1925; Are the Jews a Race? 1926; Thomas More and His Utopia, 1927; Die Materialistische Geschichtsauffassung, 1927. Contributor to Gesellschaft, Vorwaertz, Kampf, The Labor Magazine, Le Vie Socialiste, La Nouvell Revue Socialiste. General character of writing: on the theory and practical application of Marxian socialism. Allied himself early with social democratic parties of Germany and Austria; from 1883 to 1917 published "Die Neue Zeit", a leading socialistic organ; made acquaintance of Marx and Engels in 1882; joined opposition to German government at outbreak of war and entered the revolutionary government in 1918; collected and published documents of German Foreign Office relating to outbreak of war, 1919; since then devoting to scientific work. ADDRESS: Haizingergasse 47, Vienna XVIII, Austria.

KAVAN, Anna. *Publ*: Asylum Piece; I am Lazarus; The House of Sleep. *Ctr*: Horizon, Cornhill, Harpers, New Yorker, etc. *a*: 8 Kensington Ct, London, W.8.

KAVANAGH, James Paul. *b*: Auckland 1888. *e*: St Patrick's Sc Masterton, St Patrick's Col Wellington N.Z., Auckland Col, Univ of N.Z. *m*: Winifred Mary Baylan. Barrister. *n.a*: Asst Ed The Month Auckland 1923–27, Ed N.Z. Law Journ Fortnightly '31, Asst Ed Official N.Z. Law Reports '33. Hon Ed Catholic Scs Journ '33. *Publ*: New Zealand's Greatest Woman; Sales-tax Legislation, etc. *c.t*: Universe, Osservatore Romano, La Croix (Paris), Catholic World N.Z., Law Journ (Lon), etc. *s.s*: Law, N.Z. hist. *a*: 40 St Mary's Rd, Auckland, N.Z. *t*: 26–864.

KAY, Barnet, F.J.I. *b*: Derby 1876. *e*: Priv & Saltaire Col Yorks. *m*: Edyth Mary Hallas. *s*: 2. *d*: 1. F.L. Journalist & Official Shorthand Writer. *n.a*: Reporter on Yorkshire Observer 1900–05, Manchester Evening Chronicle & Empire News '05–07, F.L. '07–08, Sheffield Daily Telegraph '08–11, Now Official Shorthand Writer under Board of Trade to Nottingham, Chesterfield & Burton-on-Trent Bankruptcy Courts, under Court of Criminal Appeal to Derby Quarter Sessions, and to sittings under Road Traffic Comm, etc. *c.t*: Various N/ps & Mags. *a*: Sunny Bank, Clarence Rd, Chesterfield. *t*: 2324.

KAY, Charles Wallace. *b*: Lucknow 1884. *e*: Cheltenham Col, Edin Univ, Bristol Univ, Charing Cross & Paris. *m*: Hamilton Marjorie Bruce Kidston *s*: 1. *d*: 1. Physician. *c*: St James', M.C.C., Lymington Yacht, Cmt Hants C.C.C. *a*: Bellevue Hse, Lymington, Hants. *t*: 41.

KAY, Freda. *b*: Gateshead-on-Tyne 1908. *e*: High Pavement Sec Sc Notts. *c.t*: Allied N/ps etc. *s.s*: Poetry, fiction. Certified Hebrew Teacher Jew's Col Lon. *Rec*: Hockey. *c*: N. Writers. *a*: 12 Belgrave Sq, Notts. *t*: 42840.

KAY, W. W., M.Sc, M.B., A.I.C. Lecturer Chemical Pathology Univ M/C. *c.t*: Various Scientific Papers. *a*: 133 Lee Lane, Horwich, Bolton, Lancs.

KAY-NEWMAN, Frank. *b*: Marlborough, Wilts. *m*: Beatrice Atkinson. *s*: 1. *d*: 1. Journalist & Short Story Writer. *n.a*: Reporter Newcastle Chron '29—33, Ed Tynedale Mirror '34, Asst Ed Tamworth News '34—. *c.t*: N/ps, mags & national dailies. *s.s*: Children's features & stories, touring & topographical articles, model railways. Writes under Pen names:—Children's Features—"Uncle Kay"; Touring, etc.—"Cayenne"; Stories—"Francis Kay." *Rec*: Motor cycling, model railways. *c*: N.U.J. *a*: Hazelwood, Comberford, nr Tamworth, Staffs. *t*: Tamworth 319.

KAYE, G. W. C. Supt Physics Dept, Nat Physical Lab. *Publ*: X-Rays; Practical Applications of X-Rays; Physical & Chemical Constants (Jt). *c.t*: Nature, Lancet, etc. *a*: 13 Waldegrave Pk, Strawberry Hill, Middlesex. *t*: Popesgrove 2281.

KAYE, Michael, M.A., B.A., Ph.D. *b*: Lon 1899. *e*: King's Col Lon. *m*: Elizabeth Wasserman. *s*: 1. Lect on Educ at Goldsmith's Col Lon. *Publ*: Human Welfare—The Social & Educational Essentials. *c.t*: Hibbert Journ, Philosophy, etc. *s.s*: Educ, philosophy. *Rec*: Music, rowing. *a*: 105 Tyrwhitt Rd, Brockley, Lon, S.E.4. *t*: Lee Green 4897.

KAYE, Walter Jenkinson, M.A., F.S.A. *e*: Ackworth & Ilkley Col & Durham & Brussels Univs. *m*: Barbara Harvey. Gov Official. *n.a*: Special Corr Paris Daily Mail, Cannes '13–14. *Publ*: Brief History of Gosberton, Co Lincoln (1897); Chapter on Brasses in Fox-Davies's Art of Heraldry (1903); Grasse (Riviera) & its Vicinity ('12); Roman Triple Vases ('14); Records of Harrogate ('22); Parish Registers; etc. *c.t*: The Antiquary, Daily Mail, etc. *s.s*: Monumental brasses, parish registers. Hon Sec Yorks Parish Register Soc. Mem Counc Yorks Archæological Soc. Mem Surtees Soc, Brit Records Assocs, etc. *a*: 6 Middle Temple Lane, Lon, E.C.4. *t*: Central 7245.

KAYE-SMITH, Sheila (Mrs. Fry). Authoress. *Publ*: The Tramping Methodist ; Starbrace ; Spell-land ; Isle of Thorns ; Three Against the World ; Sussex Gorse ; Little England ; Tamarisk Town ; Green Apple Harvest ; Joanna Godden ; The End of the House of Alard ; The George and the Crown ; Iron and Smoke ; The Village Doctor ; Susan Spray ; The Children's Summer ; The Ploughman's Progress ; Superstition Corner ; Gallybird ; Selina is Older ; Rose Deeprose ; The Valiant Woman ; Ember Lane ; The Hidden Son ; Tambourine ; Trumpet & Drum. *a*: Little Doucegrove, Northiam, Sussex.

KAYNE, George Gregory, M.D., M.R.C.P.(Lon), F.R.S.M., M.B.M.A. *b*: 1901. *e*: Germany, Belgium & Eng, Leeds Univ & St Bartholomew's Hosp Lon. Physician. Dorothy Temple Cross Research Fellow in Tuberculosis (Med Research Counc Lon) '33. *c.t*: Lancet, B.M.J., Practitioner, Nursing Mirror, Nursing Times, etc. *s.s*: Tuberculosis. Late R.M.O. Worcester Roy Infirmary, Hosp for Nervous Diseases, N. Wales & Ladywell Sanatoria & St Charles' Hosp (L.C.C.). *Rec*: Tennis, dancing, music. *c*: Hunterian Soc. *a*: c/o Westminster Bank Ltd, 240 Kensington High St, W.8.

KAYSER, Jacques. *b*: Paris 1900. Journalist. *Publ*: Vie de Lafayette; La Paix en peril; The Dreyfus Affair; etc. *c.t*: L'Œuvre, La Republique, Marianne, etc. *s.s*: Internat polit. *a*: 106 Avenue du Roule, Neuilly-sur-Seine.

KEABLE, Gladys, B.A. *e*: Somerville Coll Oxon. Organising Secretary & Adult Education Tutor. *Publ*: Towns of To-morrow ; Town & Country Planning for the Local Community. *s.s*: Town & Country Planning (non-technical) & Christian Sociology. *a*: Lower Halstow Vicarage, nr Sittingbourne, Kent. *T*: Newington 129.

KEALY, EDWARD HERBERT: Indian civil service; *b*. Alverstoke, Hampshire, Eng., June, 1873; *s*. John Robert and Charlotte Maria (Butcher) K.; *educ*. Felsted Sch.; Univ. Coll. (Oxford). DEGREES: M.A. (Oxford); *m*. Florence Tempe Bayley, Dec., 1905. AUTHOR: Report on the Census of 1911 in Rajputana and Ajmer-Merwara, India (3 vols.), 1913. Relig. denom., Church of England. CLUBS: United Service Club (Simla); Overseas Club (London). ADDRESS: care of Erindlay and Co., Agents, 54 Parliment St., London, Eng.

KEANE, E. T. *b*: Listowel 1867. *e*: St Michael's Col Listowel. N/p Proprietor & Editor. *n.a*: Proprietor & Ed Kilkenny People 1893–. *a*: James's St, Kilkenny. *t*: 15.

KEANE, Lt.-Col. Sir John, D.S.O. *c.t*: Various. Senator I.F.S. Dir Bank of Ireland. *a*: 46 Hamilton Terr, N.W.8.

KEANS, Lena Alberta, M.A. *b*: Nova Scotia 1894. *e*: Prov Normal Coll Nova Scotia & Missionary. *n.a*: Ed Baptist Missionary Rev 1929—33, Ed India Christian Endeavour '34—. *Ctr*: Educ Rev, Christian Endeavour World. *s.s*: Psychology. *Rec*: Tennis, botany, hiking. *a*: Narasarayupit, Guntur District, India.

KEARNEY, Elfric Wells Chalmers, M.I.Struct.E. *b*: Victoria, Australia 1881. *e*: Priv. *m*: Dorothy Leigh. Civil & Structural Eng. *Publ*: High-Speed Railways ; Rapid Transit in the Future ; Erone ; etc. *Ctr*: Eng & Aust Press. *s.s*: Traffic Problems, Railways, Tunnels. *Rec*: Travel. *a*: Wendouree, Burgh Heath, Surrey. *T*: 3622.

KEARSEY, Ernest Martin. *b*: Lon 1896. *e*: G.S. & Priv. *m*: Dorothy May White. *d*: 1. Journalist.

n.a: Sub Ed & Ed Staff J. Burrow & Co Ltd 1924. *c.t*: A.P., Periodicals, Blackie's Annuals, Motoring & Touring Journs, etc. *s.s*: Topog works, nat hist, nature stories. *Rec*: Rambling. *a*: 329 High St, Cheltenham, Glos. *t*: 2071.

KEARTON, Cherry. Author. *Publ*: In the Land of the Lion ; My Animal Friendships ; My Dog Simba ; My Friend Toto ; My Friends Toto & Simba ; My Happy Family ; Shifting Sands of Algeria ; The Island of Penguins ; The Lions Roar ; The Animals came to Drink ; Wild life across the World. *a*: The Jungle, Kenley, Surrey.

KEATE, E. Murray, M.B.E. *b*: Lausanne. Historian, Novelist & Temporary Civil Servant. Hist Asst to Authors of Official Naval Hist of the War Comm of Imperial Defence (5 vols) & Editors of British Documents on the Origins of the War (Foreign Office), etc. *Publ*: Novels—A Garden of the Gods '14 ; A Wild Cat Scheme ; The Jachanapes Jacket ; The Mimic ; New Official Guide to Hampton Court Palace ; The Mystery of Nelson's Coat ; etc. *c.t*: History, Pearson's Mag, Nash's Mag, Country Life, The Pharm Journ, English Review, Windsor Mag, etc. *s.s*: Hist & archæology. Employed before War by the Victoria County Hist & as Editorial Asst by Roy Commission on Hist Monuments. *Rec*: Garden & reading. *c*: Roy Empire Soc, Mem of Soc of Authors. Mem of Hist Assoc, etc. *a*: 17 Craven Hill, W.2. *t*: Paddington 9822.

KEATING, Joseph. *b*: Mountain Ash 1871. *e*: Mountain Ash. *m*: Catherine Annie Herbert. Author & Dramatist. *Publ*: (Novels): Son of Judith (1901); Queen of Swords ('06); Great Appeal; The Marriage Contract; Struggle for Life (autobiography); Flower of the Dark ('17); Exploited Woman ('23); Trans, Nana, by (Zola), etc. *Rec*: Chess, politics, music. *a*: Mountain Ash, S. Wales.

KEATING, Rev. Joseph Ignatius, S.J., B.A. *b*: Dundee 1865. *e*: Stonyhurst Col Blackburn, Lon Univ & St Beuno's Col N. Wales. *n.a*: Staff of The Month 1907 & Ed '12–. *s.s*: Sociology & lit. Entered Soc of Jesus 1883 & Ordained Priest '99. *c*: Breakspeare. *a*: 31 Farm St, Berkeley Sq, W.1. *t*: Grosvenor 1608.

KEATINGE, Gerald FitzMaurice, M.A., M.D., B.Ch., B.A.O., M.R.C.O.G. *b*: Dublin 1898. *e*: Denstone Coll Staffs & T.C.D. *m*: Margaret Evelyn Piper. *d*: 1. Hon Cons Surgeon Derbyshire Hosp for Women. *Publ*: Industrial Health (Hazards of Coal Mining). *Ctr*: Personnel Management & Welfare, Health Horizon, Brit Journ of Industrial Medicine, Hospital & Nursing Home Management, Lancet, B.M.J., etc. *s.s*: Medical & Medico-Social Matters. *Rec*: Travel, gardening, fell walking. *w.s*: 1914—18 R.N.V.R. (Surg Sub-Lt). *a*: Waingroves Hall, Codnor, Derbyshire. *T*: Ripley 107.

KEEBLE, Sir Frederick William Kt., C.B.E., Sc.D., F.R.S.L., F.R.S. *b*: London 1870. *e*: Alleyns Sch & Caius Coll Camb. *m*: (1) Marie Cecile Marechal, (2) Lillah McCarthy. *d*: 1. Former Sherardian Prof of Botany Oxf Univ. *Publ*: Plant Animals ; Pollie & Freddie ; Science Lends a Hand in the Garden ; Practical Plant Physiology ; Hardy Fruit Growing ; Fertilisers & Food Production. *s.s*: Biology, Horticulture, Agriculture. *Rec*: Yachting, golf, gardening. *c*: Athenæum. *a*: Cranley Mans, Brechin Pl, London, S.W.7.

KEEL, James Frederick. *s.s*: Folk-song & folk-lore. *a*: 207 Castelnau, Barnes, S.W.13.

KEELE, Kenneth David, M.D., M.R.C.P., F.R.S.M. (see **CASSILS, Peter).** *b* : London 1909. *e* : Epsom Coll & St Bart's Hosp. *m* : Mary Deborah Thrussell. *d* : 1. Casualty Phys, St Bart's Hosp '37—42, Phys Ashford County Hosp Mddx, Mem B.M.A. *s.s* : Medical & Nursing. *Rec* : Piano playing, reading walking. *a* : Littlecote, Chertsey Lane, Staines, Mddx. *T* : Staines 2763.

KEELER, Harry Stephen. *b* : Chicago, Ill 1894. *e* : Armour Inst of Technology Chicago. *m* : Hazel Goodwin Keeler. Novelist. *n.a* : Ed Chicago Ledger 1919—23, Ed America's Humor '26—28. *Publ* : Sing Sing Nights ; The Blue Spectacle ; The Voice of the 7 Sparrows ; The Peacock Fan ; The Vanishing Gold Truck ; The Monocled Monster ; By Third Degree ; The Chameleon ; & 32 other books. *s.s* : Plot-Construction & Theories as to Drama. *Rec* : The theatre. *a* : 3530 North Fremont St, Chicago 13, Illinois, U.S.A.

KEELEY, Golden, F.R.S.A., A.M.Inst.B.E., M.Coll.H. *b* : Chipping Campden, Glos 1898. *m* : Amelia Morris. Lecturer. *Publ* : Metalwork for Craftsmen ; Beaten Metalcraft. *s.s* : Woodwork, Metalwork & Silversmithing, Light Crafts. *a* : Wimpole Park Training College, nr Cambridge. *T* : Arrington 287.

KEELEY, Robert, F.R.S.A., F.R.San.I. *b* : Co Durham 1874. *e* : Nat Schs Durham, Tech Colls Durham, Armstrong Coll of Science Newcastle-on-Tyne & Univ of Lond. *m* : Jane P. Niel. County Sanitary Officer Lancashire (ret). *n.a* : Municipal Engineering & Sanitary Record 1925—28. *Publ* : Applied Sanitary Science. *Ctr* : The Sanitarian, Journ of Roy San Inst, Science Forum, Plumber & Decorator. *s.s* : Applied Sanitary Science. *Rec* : Gardening, motoring, violin, study of languages. *a* : 42 Albert Ave, Prestwich, Manchester.

KEELING, Edward Herbert, M.C., M.A. *b* : Bradford. *e* : Bradford G.S. & Univ Col Oxf. *m* : Martha Ann Dougherty. *s* : 1. Barrister-at-Law. *Publ* : Adventures in Turkey & Russia. *c.t* : Fortnightly Review, Geog Journ, etc. *s.s* : Middle East. Hon Sec-Gen Internat Exhib of Persian Art, R.A. 1931. *c* : Utd Univ. *a* : 20 Wilton St, S.W.1. *t* : Sloane 1937.

KEEN, Bernard Augustus, F.R.S., D.Sc. *b* : London 1890. *e* : Univ Coll of Lond(Fell). *m* : Elsie Isabelle Cowley. *s* : 2. Dir East African Agric & Forestry Research Organisation, Agric & Gardening Broadcasts to Schs 1928—42. *n.a* : Ed Journ Agric Science 1930—& Ed Bd Empire Journ Experimental Agric 1933—. *Publ* : The Agricultural Development of the Middle East ; The Physical Properties of the Soil. *Ctr* : Numerous Agric & Agric journs. *s.s* : Agriculture, its scientific, technical & administrative problems with spec reference to Peasant Agriculture. *c* : Pres Roy Met Soc '38—39, Farmer's, Savile. *a* : Governor's Conference, P.O. Box 601, Nairobi, Kenya.

KEEN, E. L. Vice-Pres Utd Press of Amer. *a*: 2 Rue des Italiens, Paris.

KEEN, Frank Noel, LL.B., A.C.A. *b* : London 1869. *e* : City of London Sch. *m* : Rosalie Muirhead. *s* : 1. *d* : 1. Barrister. *Publ* : Crossing the Rubicon ; A Better League of Nations ; Towards International Justice ; The World in Alliance ; Local Legislation 1909—11, 1912 & 1913 ; The Law Relating to Public Service Undertakings. *Ctr* : Various legal journs. *s.s* : Law, Internat Affairs. *Rec* : Golf, walking. *c* : St Stephen's. *a* : 4 Paper Bldgs, Temple, London, E.C.4. *T* : Central 5476.

KEEN, William Patrick. *b* : Lon 1911. *e* : Lon & Cardiff. Journalist & Shorthand Writer. *n.a* : Architect's Journ '28—34. *s.s* : Architecture, building. *a* : 9 Queen Anne's Gate, S.W.1. *t* : Victoria 9212.

KEENE, Mary Frances Lucas, M.B., B.S. Prof of Anatomy Lon Univ. *Publ* : Practical Anatomy by Six Teachers (Part Author). *c.t* : Sci & Med Press. *a* : Homestead Farm, Ripple, nr Dover, & 8 Hunter St, W.C.1.

KEENE, Peter. *b* : London 1920. *m* : " Vicky " Florence May Edgell. Journalist. *n.a* : Sub-Ed Chambers's Encyclopaedia 1946—. *Rec* : Swimming, sailing, fishing. *w.s* : R.N.V.R. World War II. *a* : 8 Church Street, London, S.E.5.

KEENLEYSIDE, Hugh Llewellyn, M.A., LL.D., Ph.D. *b* : 1898. *e* : Langara Sch & Public Schs Vancouver, Univ of Brit Columbia & Clark Univ. *m* : Katherine Hall Pillsbury. *s* : 1. *d* : 3. Canadian Ambassador to Mexico, Canadian First Sec to Tokyo 1929—36. *Publ* : Canada & the United States ; History of Japanese Education (with A. F. Thomas). *Ctr* : Various mags. *Rec* : Reading, outdoor sports, cooking, poker. *w.s* : Canadian Tank Corps 1918—19. *a* : Dept of External Affairs, Ottawa, Canada. *T* : 2-8211, Local 2991.

KEERS, Robert Young, M.D., Ch.B., F.R.F.P.S., M.R.C.P.E., J.P. *b* : Ballymoney, Co Antrim 1908. *e* : Campbell Coll Belfast, Edin Univ. *m* : Jessie Cameron Lockie. Med Dir Red Cross Sanatoria of Scotland, former Asst Med Supt Brit Sanatorium Montana Switzerland. *Publ* : Pulmonary Tuberculosis. *Ctr* : Brit Journ of Tuberculosis, Edin Med Journ, etc. *s.s* : Tuberculosis & Diseases of the Chest. *Rec* : The theatre, fishing. *c* : Scot Cons, Roy Soc. *a* : Red Cross Sanatoria of Scotland, Tor-Na-Dee, Milltimber, Aberdeenshire. *T* : Cults 107.

KEETON, George Williams, (M.A., LL.D. *b* : Sheffield 1902. *e* : Gonville & Caius Coll Camb & Gray's Inn. Married. *s* : 2. Barrister, Prof Law, Co-Ed World Affairs, Reader in Law & Politics Hong Kong Univ 1924—27. *Publ* : China, The Far East & the Future ; Russia & her Western Neighbours (with Dr. R. Schleinger) ; Making International Law Work (with D. G. Schwerzenberg) ; The Development of extraterritoriality in China ; The Law of Trusts ; An Introduction to Equity ; The Elementary Principles of Jurisprudence ; Shakespeare & his Legal Problems. *Ctr* : World Affairs, Fortnightly Rev, Contemp Rev. *s.s* : Internat Affairs, Far East, Law. *a* : Picts Close, Picts Lane, Princes Risborough, Bucks. *T* : Princes Risborough 94.

KEFALAS, Andrew, M.A., M.B., D.I.H. F.S.S., A.I.Mech.E. *b* : Liverpool 1896. *e* : L'pool Univ. *m* : Edna G. K. Cazes. *d* : 1. Medical Supt Wear Shipbuilders' Assoc, former Med Examiner Shipping Federation Liverpool. *Publ* : What of the Child ; Juvenile Sex Instruction. *Ctr* : Various medical & scientific journs, Parents. *s.s* : Psychology & Medicine as applied to Industry. *Rec* : Fly-fishing, rowing, fencing. *a* : Midland Bank Chmbrs, St Thomas St, Sunderland. *T* : 56463/4.

KEIGHTLEY, RIDEAL ERIC: physical chemist; b. London, Eng., Apr., 1890; s. Samuel Prideal and Elizabeth (Keightley) P.; educ. Farnham Grammar Sch.; Oundle Sch.; Cambridge and Bonn universities. DEGREES: M.A. (cantab.), Ph.D. (Bonn); D.Sc. (London); F.I.C.; F.R.S. m. Margaret Atlee Jackson, 1921. AUTHOR: Electrometallurgy, 1918; Catalysis in Theory and Practice (with H. S. Taylor), 1919 (2nd edit. 1916); Ozone, 1919; Chemical Disinfection and Sterilization (with S. Ridal; 2nd edit. 1930), 1921; Surface Chemistry, 1926. General character of writing: scientific. Contributor to various scientific jnls. on subjects pertaining to physical chemistry. Relig. denom., Church of England. CLUBS: Savile; Chemical Industry. OFFICE: Laboratory of Physical Chemistry, Cambridge, Eng. HOME: Thorndyke, Huntingdon Rd., Cambridge, Eng.

KEIGHTLEY, SAMUEL ROBERT: philosopher, novelist; b. Belfast, Ireland, Jan., 1859; s. Samuel and Katherine (Branagh) K.; educ. Belfast Academical Instit.; Queen's Coll. (Belfast); Trinity Coll. (Dublin). DEGREES: B.L., LL.D.; m. Gertrude Emily Smith, 1892. AUTHOR: A King's Daughter (poems), 1879; The Crimson Sign, 1893; The Cavaliers, 1894; The Last Recruit of Clare's, 1897; The Silver Cross, 1898; Heronford, 1899; A Man of Millions, 1900; The Pikeman, 1903; Barnaby's Bridal, 1906; A Beggar on Horseback, 1906. General character of writing: romance. HOME: The Drum House, Drumbeg, Ireland.

KEILHAU, Wilhelm, Ph.D. b: Oslo 1888. e: Oslo Univ, Vienna, Paris, Berlin & Kiel. m: Rita Steensrud. s: 1. d: 1. Prof of Econ & Econ History Oslo Univ, Pres Norwegian P.E.N. 1938—, Norwegian Econ Soc '37—, V-Pres World Federation of United Nations Assocs '46—, etc. Publ: Life & History of the Norwegian People 1814—1930 (4 vols); Norway in World History; Norway & The World War; Transition to New Monetary Unit; Die Wertungslehre; Gleams of Light upon Marx; The Comedy of Evil; Norwegian Voice from London; Bretton Woods. Ctr: Verdens Gang, Dagbladet, Statsokananisk Tidsskrift Econ Journ, Samtiden. s.s: Modern Norweigan History, Theory of Value & Money, Foreign Politics. Rec: Travel, ski-ing, mountain touring, theatre, bridge. c: Norwegian Round Table, Allied Circle, Academic, etc. a: 34 Winchester Ct, London, W.8. T: Western 3182; & Pilestredet 94, Oslo. T: Oslo 46-1705.

KEILIN, Dr. Anna. Medical practitioner. Publ: Etude Embryologique d'un Monstre Double; Historie des Monstruosités et Etude Embryologique d'un Monstre Double. a: Norman Cross, 175 Hills Rd, Cambridge.

KEIR, DAVID E(DWIN), M.A.: political lecturer, poet, journalist; b. Lauder, Scotland, Mar., 1906; s. Rev. Thomas and Lily Jane (Cross) K.; educ. Dumfries Acad.; Univ. of Edinburgh. DEGREES: M.A. (Edinburgh); M.A.; unmarried. AUTHOR: Poems, 1928; Our Tounis College, 1928. Editor: The Student (Edinburgh Univ. mag.), 1897. Contributor to Edinburgh Evening News, Country Life, The Student (Edinburgh), Gallovidian. Pres. of Edinburgh Univ. Union, 1928; pres. of Edinburgh Univ. Students' Representative Council; pres. of Edinburgh Univ. Liberal Assn.; delegate from Scottish universities to Internat. Confederation of Students' Conference at Budapest; fought two Parliamentary elections in North Midlothian for Liberal Party, 1929. Relig. denom., Church of Scotland. CLUBS: Scottish Liberal; Eighty Club (London); University Union (Edinburgh). OFFICE: 149 Strand, London, W. C. 2, Eng. HOME: 26 Craigmiller Park, Edinburgh, Scotland.

KEIR, Sir David Lindsay, Kt., Hon.LL.D. b: Co Durham 1895. e: Glasgow Univ, New Coll Oxf. m: Anna Clunie Dale. s: 1. d: 1. Pres & Vice-Chancellor Queen's Univ Belfast, Fell Univ Coll Oxf 1921, Exchange Tutor Harvard Univ '23—24. Publ: The Constitutional History of Modern Britain; Cases in Constitutional Law (with F. H. Lawson). Ctr: English Historical Rev, Law Quarterly Rev, History, Oxf Magazine. s.s: Constitutional History. Rec: Sailing. a: The Vice-Chancellor's Lodge, Lennoxvale, Belfast. T: Belfast 65370.

KEIR, Robert. b: Saline 1867. e: Elem Sc & Acad Perth. m: Blanche Mary Beasley. s: 3 (1 dec). d: 3. Journalist. n.a: Rep Dundee Courier 1883—86, Scot News Edin '86, L'pool Daily Post '87, entered Press Gallery House Comm '88, Chief of Daily Post Parl Staff 1908, Lon Ed '11, ret '34. Mem Counc N/p Press Fund '11—, Chm '22—23, Apptd Treas '31. 1st Chm N/p Conf establ '19, etc. Rec: Golf, bowls. c: Press. a: 42 Langdale Rd, Hove, Sussex.

KEIRSTEAD, Burton Seely, F.R.S.C. b: Woodstock, N.B., Canada 1907. e: Fredericton Gr Sch, Univ of New Brunswick, Exeter Coll Oxf. m: Marjorie Stella Brewer. s: 1. d: 1. Dow Prof of Political Economy & Chm Dept McGill Univ. n.a: Co-Ed Canadian Journ of Econ & Polit Sci 1944—, Spec Commentator Canadian Broadcasting Corpn '46—. Publ: The Essentials of Price Theory; The Economic Effects of the War on the Maritime Provinces of Canada; Tariff Policy & the Canadian Pulp & Paper Industry (with J. P. Day). Ctr: Culture, Canadian Journ of Econ & Polit Sci, Canadian Hist Review, etc. s.s: Econ Theory. Rec: Country life. a: 622 Grosvenor Ave, Montreal 6, P.Q., Canada. T: WA 3290.

KEISER, Albert, A.M., Ph.D. b: Neufirrel, Germany 1887. e: Wartburg Coll Ia, Univs of Illinois, Montana & Harvard. m: Lena V. McGukin. s: 1. Prof of English & Speech Lenoir Rhyne Coll Hickory N.C. Publ: The Indian in American Literature; Parliamentary Law for College Students; Lutheran Mission Work Among The American Indians; The Influence of Christianity on the Vocabulary of Old English Poetry. Ctr: Various lit journs. s.s: American Lit (especially Indian). Rec: Swimming, mountain-climbing, gardening. a: 1540 Grove St, Hickory, North Carolina. U.S.A.

KEITH, ALEXANDER: journalist; b. Kintore, Scotland. Aug., 1895; s. Alfred George and Janet Greig (Wishart) K.; educ. Kintore, Strichen Secondary; King's Coll. (Aberdeen). DEGREES: M.A. (honours in English language and literature, Aberdeen); m. Agnes Roberts MacDougall, May 8, 1922. AUTHOR: Burns and Folksong, 1922; Mine Honourable Friends, 1922; Last Leaves of Aberdeenshire Ballads and Ballad Airs, 1925. Contributor to Aberdeen Press and Journal; Aberdeen Weekly Jnl.; Scots Mag. General character of writing: essays and criticism, chiefly on matters relating to folksong and Scotland. OFFICE: 20 Broad St. HOME: 30 Victoria St., Aberdeen, Scotland.

KEITH, Sir Arthur, M.D., LL.D., F.R.S., F.R.C.S. Publ: New Discoveries Relating to the Antiquity of Man; The Antiquity of Man; The Engines of the Human Body; The Place of Prejudice in Modern Civilization; Human Embryology & Morphology; Essays in Human Evolution; The Stone Age of Mount Carmel (with T. McCown). a: c/o Williams & Norgate Ltd, 28-30 Little Russell St, London, W.C.1.

KEITH, Arthur Berriedale, D.C.L.(Oxon), D.Litt (Edin). b: Edin 1879. e: Roy H.S. Edin, Edin Univ, Balliol Col Oxf. m: Margaret Balfour Allan (dec). Barrister-at-Law Inner Temple; Advocate of Scot Bar; Regius Prof Sanskrit & Comparative Philol & Lect on Constitution of Brit Emp, Edin Univ. Publ: Sanskrit Drama; Classical Sanskrit Literature; The Religion & Philosophy of the Vedas; Indian Logic & Atomism; Buddhist Philosophy; Catalogues of the Sanskrit & Prakrit MSS in the Bodleian & India Office Libraries; State Succession in International Law; The Belgian Congo & the Berlin Act; 6th Edn Wheaton'- International Law; The War Government of the British Dominions; The Sovereignty of the British Dominions; British Constitutional Law; 6th Edn Ridge's Constitutional Law of England; 5th edn Dicey's Conflict of Laws; etc. c.t: Journ of Comparative Legislation & Internat Law, Indian Hist Quarterly, Eng Hist Review, etc. s.s: Sanskrit, Indian philos & hist, internat law. Mem Lord Crewe's Cmt on Home Admin of Indian Affairs 1919. c: Crown Mem Govg Body of Lon Sc of Oriental Studies. a: 4 Crawford Rd, Edin 9.

KEITH, Joseph Joel. b: Pennsylvania 1908. Writer, Publicist, Book Reviewer. n.a: Reviewer of Prose & Poetry Dly News (Los Angeles). Publ: The Hearth Lit; The Long Nights; The Proud People; I Sing of a Maiden; The Music Makers; Songs from American Hearts; This is My America; Drink from the Rock. Ctr: Argosy, Adam International Review, Woman's Pictorial.

Poetry, Comment, Canadian Poetry Mag, The Saturday Review of Literature, Free World, New York Times Book Review, Poetry, Saturday Eve Post, Christian Science Monitor, B'nai B'rith Messenger, Prairie Schooner, World in Books, Wings, etc. *s.s*: Poetry. *Rec*: Swimming. *c*: P.E.N., California Writers' Guild, Catholic Poetry Soc of America. *a*: 3845 Ingraham St, Los Angeles 5, California, U.S.A. *T*: Exposition 3051.

KEITH-FALCONER, Adrian Wentworth. *b*: London 1888. *e*: Eton, New Coll Oxf. *m*: Phyllis Messervy. British Armistice Commission 1919, Personal Private Sec to Marquess Curzon of Kedleston '21—23. *Publ*: The Oxfordshire Hussars in the Great War. *c*: Carlton, Turf, R.U.S.I. *w.s*: Major Oxfordshire Hussars 1914—19. *a*: Inglismaldie Castle, Laurencekirk, Kincardineshire.

KEITH MORRIS, Elizabeth. *b*: Warwicks. *e*: Harrogate & Casterlow. *m*: Charles Keith Morris (dec). *s*: 1. Author & Journalist. *Publ*: An Englishwoman in the Canadian West; Hungary: The Land of Enchantment; Black Eagle. *c.t*: Daily Mail, Lon Finan Times, Occult Review, Montreal Finan Times, etc. *s.s*: Canada. 1st short story publ when 14 y old. Lect on Canada throughout Eng; travel talks B.B.C. *Rec*: Tennis, music. *c*: Lyceum. *a*: 34 Leigham Av, Streatham, S.W.16. *t*: 2299.

KELLEHER, William Howlett, M.D., D.P.H., F.R.S.M. *b*: Macroom, Ireland 1896. *e*: St Vincent's Col Dublin, Univ Col Cork, U.C.L. Med Practitioner. *c*: B.M.J., Annual Report of M.A.B., etc. *s.s*: Publ Health. *Rec*: Fishing, shooting, golf. *c*: Fell Soc of M.O.H.'s, Fell Inst of Publ Health, Mem B.M.A. *a*: S. Eastern Hosp, Avonley Rd, S.E.14. *t*: New X 0245-6.

KELLER, Adolphe, Hon.D.Theol., Hon.D.D., Hon. LL.D. *b*: Rudlingen, Schaffhausen 1872. *e*: Univs of Basel, Geneva & Berlin. *m*: Tina Jenny. *s*: 2. *d*: 3. Professor, Mem Internat P.E.N., etc. *n.a*: Ed-in-Chief Stockholm, Ed Hands across The Sea. *Publ*: Church & State on the European Continent; Karl Barth & Christian Unity; Christian Europe To-day; Amerikenisches Christentum-Heute; Von Geist und Liebe; Five Minutes to Twelve; Zeitwende; Vom unbekannten Gott. *Ctr*: Neue Zurcher Zeitung, Der Bund, Basler Nachrichten, Neue Schweizer Rundschau, Christian Century, Christendom, Religion & Life, etc. *s.s*: Ecumenical Movement, Internat Relations, Education, Peace & Reconstruction Psychology. *Rec*: Travel, music. *c*: Psychological (Zurich), etc. *a*: 1 Avenue de la Grenade, Geneva, Switzerland. *T*: 47-994.

KELLER, Helen Adams. *Publ*: inc The Story of My Life; The World I Live In; Out of the Dark; My Religion; Helen Keller's Journal; Let Us Have Faith; etc. *a*: Arcan Ridge, Westport, Conn., U.S.A.

KELLETT, Charles Ernest. Phys. *c.t*: Med Journs. *a*: 45 Eldon Place, Newcastle-on-Tyne 2. *t*: Newcastle 20389.

KELLETT, Ernest Edward. *e*: Wadham Col Oxf. *m*: Josephine Laidler. *d*: 1. Schoolmaster (ret). *Publ*: Carmina Ephemera; The Story of Myths; The Whirligig of Taste; A Short History of the Jews; The Conflict—A Saga of the Seventh Century; etc. *c.t*: News-Chron, Chr Sci Monitor, Observer, etc. *s.s*: Religious hist. *c*: Nat Lib. *a*: 3 Park Hall, Crooms Hill, S.E.10. *t*: Greenwich 0906.

KELLEY, James J. *b*: Belfast 1911. *e*: Christian Bros, Belfast. Special Rep Belfast. *n.a*: Irish News, Belfast 1929, Irish Press Dublin '31, Irish Independent, Dublin '34. *c.t*: M/C Guardian. *Rec*: Tennis, sketching. *c*: I.J., N. Ireland Press Gallery. *a*: 510 Donegall Rd, Belfast. *t*: 3542.

KELLEY, John Douglas, B.A. *b*: Toronto. *e*: Toronto Univ. Married. *s*: 1. *d*: 1. Journalist. Ed Naft Mag. *n.a*: Mail & Empire, Toronto, Pre-War, Financial News, Lon 1920-21. *s.s*: Oil *c*: Jnr Army & Navy. *a*: 35 Rossetti Gdns Mansions, Chelsea, S.W.3. *t*: Flaxman 4813.

KELLEY, Truman Lee, Ph.D. *b*: Muskegon, Michigan 1884. *e*: Columbia Univ. *m*: Grace Winifred Cookney. *s*: 2. Teacher. *Publ*: Fundamental of Statistics; Statistical Method; Essential Traits of Mental Life; Crossroads in the Mind of Man; Scientific Method; Kelley Statistical Tables; Interpretation of Educational Measurements; Educational Guidance; Mental Aspects of Delinquency; Stanford Achievement Tests (in collab). *Ctr*: Psychological, statistical & educ journs. *s.s*: Mental Analysis, Statistical Method, Experimental & Guidance Procedure, etc. *Rec*: Outdoor sports, chess, maths, etc. *a*: 40 Quincey St, Cambridge 38, Mass, U.S.A.

KELLOGG, Charlotte, Ph.B. *e*: Univ of California. *m*: Vernon Kellogg (dec'd). *d*: 1. *Publ*: Jadwiga, Queen of Poland; Pacific Light; Pierre Curie; Jadwiga, Poland's Great Queen; The Girl Who Ruled a Kingdom; Mercier, the Fighting Cardinal; Bobbins of Belgium; Women of Belgium. *Ctr*: Atlantic Monthly, Sat Ev Post, etc. *s.s*: Biography. *Rec*: Mountaineering, horseback riding, study of shells & coastal forms. *a*: 2305 Bancroft Pl, N.W., Washington 8, D.C.

KELLY, Rev. Alfred Davenport. *b*: Ashton-under-Lyne. *e*: Manch Gr Sch, New Coll Oxf, Cuddesdon Theol Coll. Clerk in Holy Orders. *Publ*: Values of Christian Life; Rational Necessity of Theism; Faith in Fiction; Cultus of the Sacramental Presence; Claims of Spiritualism. *s.s*: Theology, Philosophy. *Rec*: Lawn tennis, rock-climbing. *a*: Kelham, Newark, Notts.

KELLY, Austin Bernard, F.I.S.A. *b*: Trim, Ireland 1890. *e*: Trim & St Finian's Col Mullingar. Acct & Incorporated Sec. *Publ*: Manual of Book-keeping; Business Methods & Everyday Office Work; Sterling Book of Tots; New Model Tot Book. *c.t*: Teacher's Work. *a*: 21 Belgrave Rd, Clontarf, Co Dublin.

KELLY, Rev. Bernard William, F.R.Hist.S. *b*: Rotherhithe, London 1872. *e*: St George's Coll Woburn Park Weybridge, St John's Seminary Wonersh. Rector Corpus Christi Church (Catholic) Brixton Hill. *Publ*: Life of Cardinal York; The Conqueror of Culloden; The Fighting Frasers; Short History of the English Bar; Some Famous Advocates & Their Speeches; Supplement to Butler's Lives of the Saints; Short Survey of Church History; The Children of the Mist. *Ctr*: Chambers's Journ, Irish Eccles Record, Clergy Review, Household Brigade Mag. *s.s*: Last Stuarts & The Jacobite Movement, 18th Century, Biography, Legal History. *Rec*: Walking, reading, fishing. *a*: 14 Trent Rd, Brixton Hill, London, S.W.2. *T*: Brixton 4625.

KELLY, Eleanor Mercein. *b*: Milwaukee, Wisconsin 1880. *e*: Convent of the Visitation, Washington. *m*: Robert Morrow Kelly, Jnr. Writer. *Publ*: Toya the Unlike; Kildares of Storm; The Mansion House; Why Joan; Spanish Holiday; Sea Change; Arabesque. *c.t*: Lippincott, Ainslie, Munsey, Century, Harpers, Pictorial Review, Cosmopolitan. *s.s*: Ethnographic fiction. *Rec*: Motoring, music, travel, wrestling, horse-racing. *c*: Cosmopolitan Club, New York, Louisville Arts Club, Colonial Dames of America. *a*: Edgehill Rd, Louisville Kentucky U.S.A.

KELLY, George Lombard, M.D., A.B., B.S. *b*: Augusta, Georgia 1890. *e*: Public Schs, Hgh Sch Augusta, Univ of Georgia, Univ of Georgia Sch of Med. *m*: (1) Adeline Mina Weatherly (dec'd), (2) Ina Melle Todd. *s*: 1. *d*: 1. Prof of Anatomy & Dean of Univ Georgia Sch of Med.

n.a: Rep Asheville (N.C) Citizen, & Times 1918. *Publ:* Sex Manual, For Those Married or About to Be; Sexual Feeling in Woman. *Ctr:* Various scientific periodicals *s s:* Scientific books & articles on Physiology or Reproduction, Endocrinology & Sexology. *Rec:* Hunting, fishing. *a:* 2131 Gardner St, Augusta, G.A., U.S.A. *T:* 3-7881.

KELLY, Rev. Herbert Hamilton, M.A. *b:* Manchester 1860. *e:* Manch Gr Sch, R.M.A. Woolwich, Queen's Coll Oxf. Priest, Mem Soc Sacred Mission, Tutor Kelham Theo Coll Newark since 1919. *Publ:* History of the Church of Christ; England & the Church; The Church & Religious Unity; The Gospel of God; Catholicity. *Ctr:* Theology, Journ Theo Studies, Church Quarterly Rev, Constructive Quarterly Rev, East & West. *a:* House of the Sacred Mission, Kelham, Newark, Notts. *T:* Newark 350.

KELLY, Jack Arthur. Journalist. *n.a:* Cheshire Observer, Chester Courant, Chester Chronicle, Widnes & Runcorn Chronicle, Daily Dispatch, Manchester Evening Chronicle, Bournemouth Daily Echo, Portsmouth Evening News. Mem N.U.J. 1919. *c.t:* Daily Mail, Daily Express, Evening News, Sunday Dispatch, Sunday Express. *s.s:* Light topical specials, aviation. *a:* 22 Alhambra Rd, Southsea, Hants. *t:* Portsmouth 2211 & 4097.

KELLY. Rev. John. *b:* Wrexham 1868. *e:* Penygelli Bd Sc, Deganwy G.S., Richmond Meth Col Welsh Univ Bangor. *m:* Sarah Jane Roberts. *s:* 1 *Publ:* Commentary on The Gospel According to St Luke. *c.t:* Eurgrawn Wesleaidd, Y Gwyliedydd Newydd, Y Traethodydd, etc. *s.s:* Psych, hist. One of leaders in the Campaign for the Disestablishment of the Welsh Ch. *a:* 77 Oak Drive, Acton Pk, Wrexham.

KELLY, Raymond, A. B. *b:* Chicago 1882. *e:* Chicago Univ. *m:* (1) Bessie Mae Case; (2) Olga A. Rehner. *s:* 4. *d:* 1. Teacher of Dramatics Kelly H.S. Chicago. *n.a:* Feature Writer Chicago Tribune 1923-26. *Publ:* Me & Andy; Ogo The Beaver; Scrambled Education (Operetta). *c.t:* Chicago Daily News, Chicago Tribune, Child Life, Junior Home, Country Gentleman. *s.s:* Juvenile stories & verse. *Rec:* Golf, fishing, motoring, shooting. *c:* Staff, Pen & Brush. *a:* 3923 W. 64th St Chicago, Ill, U.S.A. *t:* Hemlock 0906.

KELLY, RICHARD J.: barrister, King's counsel, Chevalier Red Cross Roumania; b. Tuam, Connaught, Ireland; s. Jasper and Delia (Daly) K.; educ. Christian Brothers Sch., Blackrock Coll., Queen's Coll. (Galway); m. Edith Mackay. AUTHOR: History of Tuam in School Form (appearing in Tuam Herald); Lives of Pope Pius X and Benedict V; Life of Charles Kickham; Law of Newspaper Libel; Law of Adulteration; Law of Registration of Land; Nolar and Lane Land Acts (edited and brought up to date); Old Age Pension Act; Workmen's Compensation Act of 1906; Representation of the People Act, 1918; Agriculture and Technical Instruction Act; Selections of Patriotic and Popular Poems, Irish (9 vols.); St. Jarlath; Effects and Evils of Emigration; Aran Islands; Galway as a Trans-Atlantic Port; Memoirs of the Owsley Family; Memoir of Lord Morris; Old Dublin Printing; The Irish Railway Problem, 1921. Editor and managing director (30 yrs.) Tuam (Connaught) Herald; mm. British Journalists since founding; of Soc. Brit. and Internat. Journalists. Religion, Roman Catholic. Consul in Irish Free State for the Kingdom of Roumania, and Republics of Bolivia and Estonia. CLUBS: Overseas (London); Royal Dublin Soc. (Dublin); Chamber of Commerce (Dublin). HOME: Hymany, 7, Arlesbury Road, Dublin, Ireland.

KELLY, Thomas Howard. B.S., B.Litt. *b:* Fernandina, Florida 1896. *e:* Springhill Coll, Mobile Ala. *m:* Mercedes S. Peine. *d:* 1. Author, Editor, Public Relations. *n.a:* Assoc-Ed Smart Set Mags 1928—29, Sunday Mirror Mag '33, Hearst Mags Inc '36—37 & Exec-Ed Drug World & American Druggist. *Publ:* What Outfit, Buddy?; The Unknown Soldier: Dream Lights; Hunted Lovers; (Films) His Buddy's Wife; Lover's Island; etc. *Ctr:* Reader's Digest, Cosmopolitan, Blue Book, McClure's, Esquire, Liberty, etc. *s.s:* War, Adventure, Sport. *Rec:* Swimming, hunting, fishing, tennis, golf. *c:* Sleepy Hollow, N.Y. Athlete's, etc. *a:* 333 N. Michigan Ave, Chicago 1, Illinois, U.S.A.

KELMAN, JOHN: author, clergyman; b. Scotland, June, 1864; s. of Rev. John (D.D.) and Margaret Harper (Urquhart) K.; educ. Leath High Sch.; Royal High Sch. of Edinburgh. DEGREES: M.A. (Edinburgh), D.D. (Edinburgh), Yale and Princeton), D. Litt. (Lafayette); m. Ellin R. Bell, May 18, 1892. AUTHOR: The Holy Land; The Faith of Robert Louis Stevenson; Honour Toward God; The Light That Saves; From Damascus to Palmyra; The Courts of the Temple; Ephemera Eternitatis; The Road —A Study of John Bunyan's Pilgrim's Progress (2 volumes); Among Famous Books; Salted with Fire; A Volume of Sermons Connected with the War; The War and Preaching; Some Aspects of International Christianity; The Foundations of Faith; Prophets of Yesterday and their Message for Today; A Study of Hellenism and Hebraism as represented by Thomas Carlyle, Mathew Arnold and Robert Browning. General character of writing, religious prose. CLUBS: Edinburgh University Union. (*)

KELSON, William Henry, M.D., B.S.(Lon), F.R.C.S.Eng, D.P.H.(Cantab). *b:* Lon 1862. *e:* Gresham G.S. Holt, Lon Univ, Lon Hosp, Paris. *m:* Hilda Frances Lane. Surgeon (ret). *Publ:* Handbook of Diseases of Throat, Nose & Ear; Diseases of Upper Respiratory Tract in Relation to Life Assurance; etc. *s.s:* Diseases of Throat, Nose & Ear. Cons Surg to Golden Square Throat, Nose & Ear Hosp. Lethby Prize. *Rec:* Golf. *c:* R.A.C., F.Z.S., Mem Ct of Soc of Apothecaries, etc. *a:* 4 Kent Gdns, Ealing, W.13.

KELVEY, Rev. Henry Frederick. Meth Min. *Publ:* Music & Its Influence on Life & Character; Bright Thoughts for Dark Hours. *c.t:* Meth Recorder, Meth Mag, etc. *a:* 76 Oval Rd, Erdington, Birm.

KELWAY, Clifton, F.R.G.S., F.R.HistS., F.J.I. *b:* Milford Haven 1865. *e:* Priv. Sec of Incorp Ch Building Soc. *n.a:* Ch in the West '89–90, Sub Ed Western Daily Mercury '90-97, Ed Sun '97-98, Ch Review '99-1903. *Publ:* A Franciscan Revival; Memorials of Old Essex; Story of the Catholic Revival; etc. *c.t:* Ch Times, Guardian, Ch of E. N/p. *s.s:* Ch reform & hist. Mem of Ch Assem, Chm of Gregorian Assoc, etc. *a:* 57 Warwick Sq, S.W.1. *t:* Victoria 1710.

KELWAY, Phyllis. *b:* Langport 1906. *e:* Cheltenham Ladies Col. Author. *Publ:* Widow Hedgehog; Feathered Playmates at Home; Wild Flowers in Sunny Fields; Furry Creatures of Wood and River. *c.t:* Game & Gun, My Garden, Scottish Country Life, etc. *s.s:* Nat hist, Brit wild life. Illus own work, chiefly pen & ink & photographs. *Rec:* Riding, gardening. *c:* Fell Roy Hortic Soc. *a:* Thongsbridge Hse, nr Huddersfield.

KELYNACK, Theo Nicholas. M.D., M.R.C.P., J.P. *b:* Wells. *e:* U.C.Sc & M/C Univ. *m:* Violet McLaren, M.B., ChB. *d:* 1. Cons Physician. *n.a:* Ed Brit Journ Tuberculosis 1907-34, Brit Journ Inebr '03-34. Hon Sec R.I.P.H. Hon Sec Study of Ineb & Drug Addiction. *Publ:* Renal Growths (1898); The Sanatorium Treatment of Consumption (1904); etc; Ed Tuberculosis in Infancy & Childhood ('08); Nat Health Manuals ('10-14); etc. *s.s:* Tuberculosis & affections of children. Cons Phys & Hon Gov Mt Vernon Hosp. Gen Med Adv N.C.H.O. Med Adv Shaftesbury Soc, etc. *Rec:* Travel. *a:* 19 Park Cres, Portland Pl, W.1. *t:* Welbeck 2713.

KELYNACK, Rev. William Sydney, M.A.(Cantab). *b*: Lon 1879. *e*: M/C G.S. & St John's Col Cam. *m*: Annie Lilian Hayman. *s*: 1. *Publ*: Making Melody; Moses for the Children; etc. *c.t*: Meth Recorder, Brentford & Chiswick Times, Meth Times, Chr World Pulpit, etc. *s.s*: Hymnology. *Rec*: Photography. *a*: The Manse, Sutton Ct Rd, Chiswick, W.4. *t*: 1360.

KEM, Kimon Evan (Marengo), B.A. (Oxon) *b*: Egypt 1906. *e*: Ecoles des Sciences Politiques Paris & Exeter Coll Oxf. Political Cartoonist & Journalist. *n.a*: Ed Maalesh (Egypt) 1924—30 & Anglo-Egyptian Rev Lond '24—35, Official Cartoonist M.O.I. '39—45. *Publ*: Toy Titans; Lines of Attack; (French) Alexandrie Reine de la Mediterranee; Owa Riglak; Gare les Pattes; (Arabic) Adolf & his Donkey, Benito. *Ctr*: Le Petit Parisien, Paris, La Bourse Egyptienne, New York Times, Ken (Chicago), John Bull, Gt Britain & The East, etc. *s.s*: Political Cartoons. *Rec*: Swimming, riding. *a*: 63 Hamilton Terr, St John's Wood, London, N.W.8. *T*: Cunningham 8435.

KEMBALL COOK, Hartley Trevor, M.J.I. *b*: Brighton 1878. *e*: Stanmore Park, Felsted. *m*: Ethel West. Author & Journalist. *n.a*: Ed The Seafarer 1934—38. *Publ*: The Twisted Skein; Ambrose Terring; In the Watch Below; The Birth of Flight; Those Happy Days; Over the Hills & Far Away; The Free & Independent. *Ctr*: Many newspapers & periodicals. *s.s*: Polits, Polit Hist, Cricket, Fiction. *a*: 10 Knollys Hse, Tavistock Pl, London, W.C.1. *T*: Euston 2470.

KEMBLE, James, M.B., Ch.M., F.R.C.S.(Eng & Edin). *e*: St Andrew's Coll, Sydney Univ, St Bart's Hosp (Lond). *m*: Dorothy Eleanor Wright. *s*: 2. Surg to Battersea Gen Hosp, Chief Asst Urological Dept West Lond Hosp, Surg Lond Lock Hosp, Mem B.M.A., Soc of Authors, Surg E.M.S. 1939—46. *n.a*: Ed West Lond Med Journ. *Publ*: Idols & Invalids; Hero Dust. *Ctr*: B.M.J., Proc Roy Soc Med, West Lond Med Journ, Quarterly Rev, Annals of Med Hist (N.Y.), Year Book of Urology, various journs & newsps. *s.s*: Surgery, Med Hist & Biography. *Rec*: Tennis, golf, shooting. *c*: Savage. *a*: 150 Harley St, London, W.1. *T*: Welbeck 3474.

KEMP, Reginald William, M.J.I. Rep-Sub-Editor. *n.a*: Surrey Herald Chertsey 1924—41, Middlesex Chron Staines '47—.

KEMP, Thomas, J.P. *b*: Dalkeith. *e*: Dalkeith Acad & Heriot-Watt Col Edin. Widower. *d*: 1. F.L. Journalist. *n.a*: Midlothian Rep for Chief n/ps. *Rec*: Horse-riding, golf. *c*: Chm Cong Un of Scot (Edin Dis). Ex-Chm I.J. Edin & E. of Scot Dis. *a*: Elm Lodge, Dalkeith. *t*: 6.

KEMP, William Rous, B.A. Medical. *c.t*: Fishing Gazette, B.M.J., Daily Mirror, etc. *a*: S. Lodge, Brook Rd, Cricklewood, N.W.2. *t*: Gladstone 2301.

KEMPLING, William Bailey, F.R.S.L. *b*: Hull 1869. *m*: Elizabeth Watts. Journalist. *n.a*: Daily Chronicle, 24 y service (14 y as Asst Lit Ed). *Publ*: Anthologies of Verse (5 vols, 1902–08); Shakespeare Memorials of London ('23). *c.t*: Stratford-on-Avon Herald. *s.s*: Shakespeare. *a*: 41 Playfield Cres, E. Dulwich, S.E.22.

KEMPNER, LYDIA RABINOWITSCH (pen name: Lydia Rabinowitsch): bacteriologist; *b*. Kowno, Russia, 1871; *d*. Leo and Michel (Werblunsky) Rabinowitsch; educ. Kowno, Switzerland, Univs. of Zürich and Berlin. DEGREES: Ph.D., Professor (Berlin); *m*. Dr. Walter Kempner, 1898. WRITER: Beiträge zur Entwicklungsgeschichte der Fruchtkörper einiger Gastromyceten (Allgemeine Botanische Zeitschrift), 1894; Zur Frage des Vorkommens von Tuberkelbazillen in der Marktbutter (Deutsche Medizinische Wochenschrift), 1897; Zur Frage der Infectosität der Milch tuberkulöser Kühe sowie über den Nutzen der Tuberkulinimpfung, (gemeinschaftlich mit Kempner, Deutsche medizinische Wochenschrift), 1899; Ueber den Wert der Courmont'schen Serumreaction für die Frühdiagnose der Tuberkulose (with Beck), Deutsche medizinische Wochenschrift, 1900; Über desinficierende Wandanstriche mit besonderer Berücksichtigung der Tuberkulose (Zeitschrift für Hygiene, vol. 40), 1902; Die Infektiosität der Mich tuberkulöser Kühe im Lichte der neueren Forschungen (Zeitschrift für Tiermedizin, vol. 8), 1904; Die spontane Affentuberkulose, ein Beitrag zur Tuberkulosefrage (Dt. med. Wochenschrift, No. 22), 1906; Zum gegenwärtigen Stand der Tuberkuloseforschung (Wiener med. Wochenschrift, No. 38), 1907; Experimentelle Untersuchungen über die Virulenz latenter tuberkulöser Herde (Zeitschrift für Tuberkulose, vol. 15), 1909; Die Beteiligung der Frau and der Tuberkuloseläbekämpfung. (Referat gehalten auf dem Internationalen Tuberkulose-Kongress in Rom 1912 (Wiener med. Wochenschrift No. 25), 1912; Das Friedmann'sche Tuberkulosemittel in der Behandlung der Lungentuberkulose. (Deutsche med. Wochenschrift No. 49), 1919; Zur Serodiagnostik der Tuberkulose mit dem Extrakt Besredka. (Deutsche med. Wochenschrift No. 12), 1922; Über neueste Streptokokkenuntersuchungen. (Fortschr. der Medizin No. 1), 1926; Zur Frage der Filtrierbarkeit des Tuberkulose-Virus. (Zeitschrift f. Tuberkulose. Sonderdruck a.B.52), 1928; La Tuberculosa spontanée chez les animaux de Laboratoire. (Annales de Medicine. Extrait. Tome XXV, No. 4), 1929, and numerous other articles. Editor of the Zeitschrift für Tuberkulose. General character of writing: scientific, medical. Is the only woman pupil of the great Robert Koch. OFFICE: Städtisches Krankenhaus Moabit, Turmstrasse 20, Berlin. ADDRESS: Potsdamerstrasse 58a, Berlin-Lichterfelde, Germany.

KEMPSON, E. W. E. *a*: Roy Naval Col, Dartmouth.

KEMPSTER, Christopher R. *b*: London 1869. *e*: King's Coll Lond, Cavendish Coll Camb, Westminster Hosp, King's Coll Hosp Lond. *m*: Hilda Oakes. *Publ*: Dental Radiology. *Ctr*: Lancet, B.M.J., Practitioner, Med World. *s.s*: Radiology. *Rec*: Foreign Travel. *c*: City of London Livery. *a*: 46 Portland Ct, London, W.1. *T*: Museum 9660.

KEMPSTER, John Westbeech, D.L. *b*: Birm 1864. *e*: Dulwich Col & Germany & City & Guilds Inst Lon. *m*: Eleanor Mabel Meredith-Jones. *d*: 2. Shipbuilder & Eng. *Publ*: Britain's Financial Plight; Banking Credit & the Crisis. *s.s*: Economics. Ex-Dir Harland & Wolff Ltd; Pres Clyde Shipbuilders Assoc; Pres Greenock Provident Bank; Ex-Pres Greenock Chamber of Commerce. *c*: Reform, & R.S.A.C. *Rec*: Fishing. *a*: Chalk Hill, Guildown, Guildford. *t*: Guildford 1664.

KEMPTHORNE, RT. REV. JOHN AUGUSTINE: Bishop of Lichfield; *b*. London, Eng., May, 1864; *s*. John and Eliza Gertrude (Thompson) K.; educ. Haileybury Coll., Trinity Coll. (Cambridge). DEGREE: D.D.; *m*. Hester Mary Peile, Aug., 1890. AUTHOR: Pastoral Life and Work Today, 1919. General character of writing: factual prose. Relig. denom., Church of England. HOME: Bishop's Hostel, Lichfield, Eng.

KEMPTHORNE, Rev. John Ley. *b*: Clerkenwell 1892. *e*: City of Lond Sch & King's Coll Lond. *Publ*: Falmouth Parish Church. *Ctr*: Commonwealth. *a*: St Enoder Rectory, Summercourt, Cornwall. *T*: Fraddon 39.

KEMSLEY, 1st Viscount of Dropmore, Sir James Gomer Berry, 1st Bt., LL.D., K.St.J., J.P. *b*: 1883. *m*: (1) Mary Lilian Holmes (dec'd). *s*: 5. *d*: 1. (2) Edith Dresselhuys.

Chmn Kemsley Newspapers Ltd, Daily Graphic & Sunday Graphic Ltd, etc., Grand Cross George I (Greece), Officer Legion of Honour, J.P. for Bucks. *n.a*: Ed-in-Chief & Ctr Sunday Times. *c*: R.Y.S., Carlton, Turf, Athenæum. *w.s*: R.A.S.C. (Hon Col). *a*: Dropmore, Bucks. *T*: Bourne End 880; & Chandos Hse, Queen Anne St, London, W.1. *T*: Langham 1388.

KENDALL, Alice R. *b*: New York City. *e*: Horace Mann Sch N.Y., St Trinnean's Sch Edin, Edin Coll of Art. Artist & Writer. *Publ*: Funny Fishes. *Ctr*: Punch, Art & Design, Scottish Zoo & Wild Life, Somerset Countryman, Strand Mag, Kiddies Mag. *s.s*: Art & Educ Books for children. *Rec*: Music, crossword puzzles. *a*: 19a Edith Grove, London, S.W.10. *T*: Flaxman 8425.

KENDALL, Guy. *b*: Bush Hall, Hatfield 1876. *e*: Eton Coll, Magdalen Coll Oxf. *m*: Ada Sampson. *s*: 1. *d*: 1. Formerly Headmaster Univ Coll Sch, Author & Lecturer, Newcastle Medallist Eton. Lit. Hum. Theology *Publ*: A Headmaster Remembers; Charles Kingsley & His Ideas; Robert Raikes (biography); A Modern Introduction to the New Testament; Essay Writing; The New Schoolmaster; The Sunlit Way & other poems; The Call & other poems. *Ctr*: Nearly all current London dailies, Cornhill Mag, etc. *s.s*: Biography, Christianity, Philosophy of Religion, Poetry, Politics. *Rec*: Sketching. *a*: Little Hanger, Wormley Hill, Godalming, Surrey. *T*: Wormley 17.

KENDALL, J. T. *b*: Nott'm. *e*: People's Col Nott'm. *m*: Miss Allen. *d*: 2. *c.t*: Various. P.A. Corr. *a*: Lancashire Daily Post, 127 Fishergate, Preston.

KENDALL, James Pickering, M.A., D.Sc., F.R.S., F.R.S.E. *b*: Chobham, Surrey 1889. *e*: Farnham Gr Sch, Edin Univ, Nobel Inst Stockholm. *m*: Alice Tyldesley. *s*: 1. *d*: 2. Prof Chemistry Columbia Univ New York Univ 1913—25, Dean Graduate Sch N.Y. Univ '27—28, Mem Edin Univ Court '43. *Publ*: At Home among the Atoms; Breathe Freely; Young Chemists & Great Discoveries; Revisions of chemistry text-books of Alexander Smith. *Ctr*: Endeavour. *s.s*: Chemistry. *Rec*: Cycling, bridge. *w.s*: World War I Liaison Off with Allied Gov on Naval Chem Warfare. *c*: Century, Chemists (New York), University (Edin). *a*: Chemistry Dept, The University, King's Bldgs, Edinburgh 9.

KENDALL, John Kaye. *b*: London 1869. *e*: Portsmouth, Roy Mil Acad. *m*: Katherine Githa Sowerby. *d*: 1. Writer. *Publ*: Odd Numbers; Fool's Paradise; Rhymes of the East; In the Hills; At Odd Moments; Says He; Short Doses; Oh, Helicon; The Crackling of Thorns; Odd Creatures; Dum-Dum, His Book of Beasts; Dum-Dum, His Selected Verse; etc; (Plays) Bingo; Dad; Mrs. Bill; Laughter in Court; Fond of Peter. *Ctr*: Punch, etc. *s.s*: Light Verse. *Rec*: Golf. *c*: Garrick. *a*: 32 Chelsea Pk Gdns, London, S.W.3. *T*: Flaxman 9344.

KENDALL, John Smith, M.A. *b*: Ocean Springs, Mississippi 1874. *e*: Priv & Tulane Univ. *m*: Isoline Rodd. *s*: 1. *d*: 1. Journalist, College Teacher, Emerits Prof of Spanish Tulane Univ 1939—. *n.a*: Ed Bd Picayune New Orleans 1891—1914, Louisiana Hist Quarterly 1925—. *Publ*: History of New Orleans; Recollections of a Confederate Officer; Old New Orleans Houses; Blood on the Banquette. *Ctr*: Leading American mags. *s.s*: Hist of the city of New Orleans. *c*: California Writers. *a*: c/o Tulane Univ, New Orleans, Louisiana, U.S.A.

KENDALL, OSWALD: author; b. Manchester, Eng.; s. John and Agnes (Murray) Kendall; m. Kate Orton, 1910. AUTHOR: Captain Protheroe's Fortune, 1913; The Romance of Martin Connor, 1915; The Stormy Petrel, 1926; Simmonds, 1927; The Missing Island, 1927. Contributor to Youth's Companion (American) and many English magazines. General character of writing: fiction of adventure theme. HOME: 101 Star Street, London, W. 2, Eng.

KENDALL, Prof. P. F. *a*: Briar Wood, Frinton-on-Sea, Essex.

KENDREW, Alfred, M.A., D.M.(Oxon). *b*: Devizes 1893. *e*: City of Oxf Sc, Chr Ch Oxf, Univ Col Hosp Lon & Bonn Univ. *m*: Marie Claire Renaut. Doctor of Medicine. *Publ*: A New View of the Intrathoracic & Intrapericardial Pressures in Man. *c.t*: Heart. *s.s*: Cardiac physiology & pathology. *Rec*: Lawn tennis, nat hist. *a*: Weald Ridge, Ticehurst, Sussex. *t*: 56.

KENDRICK, Harold. *b*: Wolverhampton 1894. *e*: Brewood & Walhouse (Cannock). Journalist (Sports). *n.a*: Birmingham Gazette (Editorial 1912—19. less dur of war), '19—24 Shields Daily Gazette (Sports Ed), '24—31 Dly Herald (Sports Staff & Sports Ed), '32 Daily Express (Sports Staff). *s.s*: Football, cricket. War Service '14—18. *Rec*: Gardening, golf. *a*: 6 Thurlby Rd, Wembley, Middx.

KENDRICK, Thomas Downing. Asst Keeper Brit Antiquities in the Brit Museum. *Publ*: The Druids; Archæology of the Channel Islands; A History of the Vikings; Archæology of England & Wales 1914-31 (in collab). *s.s*: Art & archæ of N.W. Europe. *c*: Savile. *a*: Brit Museum, & 8 Albert Pl, W.8.

KENEALY, Arabella, L.R.C.P.(Dublin). *b*: Portslade-by-Sea. *e*: Priv & L.S.M.W. *Publ*: Dr Janet of Harley Street (1892); Woman and the Shadow; Memoirs of Edward Vaughan Kenealy, LL.D.; The Failure of Vivisection & the Future of Medical Research (Prize Essay); Feminism & Sex Extinction ('20), etc. *s.s*: Evolution. Practised in Lon & Watford 1888—94, ret thro' ill-health. *Rec*: Reading. *a*: 21 Cleveland Gdns, Hyde Pk, W.2.

KENNARD, Lady Dorothy Katherine. *e*: Private. Dir R. Cobden Sanderson Ltd. Publishers. *Publ*: Career. A Roumanian Diary. *c.t*: N. American Review. Harpers. London Mercury. *a*: 16 Airlie Gdns, Campden Hill, W.8. *t*: Park 8014.

KENNARD, Col. Henry Gerard Hegan, C.M.G. (Mil). *b*: Lon 1871. *e*: Eton & Sandhurst. *m*: Annie Poyser. *d*: 2. Journalist. *n.a*: Christian Science Monitor 1922—, Asst to European Rep of Chr Science Pubg Soc. *s.s*: Radio. Fifth Dragoon Guards 1890—1911. Commanded 5 D.G. '07-11. During War commanded Dublin Garrison '15—18. *Rec*: Golf. *c*: Utd Service. *a*: 54b Warrington Cres, W.9. *t*: Abercorn 4696.

KENNARD DAVIS, Rushworth. *b*: London 1883. *e*: Rugby & Balliol Coll Oxf. *m*: Maude Agnes Mack. *s*: 2. *d*: 2. Schoolmaster (ret), Headmaster Woodbridge Sch 1914—21, Headmaster Birkenhead Sch '21—30, Headmaster Magdalen Coll Oxf '30—44. *Publ*: Translations from Catullus; Aeschylus Agamemnon (trans); Peleus & Thetis (poem); Diagnosis (poem). *Ctr*: Punch, Oxford Magazine. *a*: On-The-Hill, Pilton, Shepton Mallet. *T*: Pilton 41.

KENNAUGH, Alan. *b*: Workington 1908. Journalist. *n.a*: Workington Star & Cumberland Ev Mail 1922—29, Nth Echo Darlington '29. *s.s*: Dramatic Criticism *Rec*: Theatricals, Youth welfare. *a*: 25 Avondale Terr, Chester-le-Street, Durham. *T*: 2301.

KENNEDY, A. L., M.C. *b*: Brighton 1885. *e*: Harrow & Magdalen Coll Oxf. *m*: Sylvia Meysey-Thompson. *d*: 3. Publicist. *n.a*: The Times 1910—42, Asst Foreign Ed '23, B.B.C. European Service '42—45. *Publ*: Old Diplomacy & New (from Salisbury to Lloyd George);

Britain Faces Germany. *s.s*: Foreign Affairs. *c*: Traveller's. *w.s*: 1914—19. *a*: Westridge, Aspley Guise, nr Bletchley.

KENNEDY, Agnes O'D. Med Pract. *c.t*: B.M.J., Lancet. *a*: 38 Mecklenburgh Square, W.C.1. *t*: Terminus 3946.

KENNEDY, Alexander, M.D., B.S., M.R.C.P., M.R.C.S., D.P.M., F.R.S.M. (See **ALEXANDER, Kenneth.**) *b*: 1909. *e*: City of London Sch & London Univ, Johns Hopkins Univ U.S.A. *m*: Joanna Birkett. *s*: 4. Professor of Psychological Medicine Durham Univ, Dir of Dept of Psychoe Med Victoria Royal Infirmary Newcastle-on-Tyne. *Ctr*: Lancet, B.M.J., Journ of Mental Science, Journ of Neurology & Psychiatry, etc, also B.B.C. Talks on Psychological Subjects. *s.s*: Psychology, Fsychiatry Psychological Medicine, Psychological Aspects of Crime including Juvenile Delinquency. *Rec*: Travel, farming. *c*: Special Forces, etc. *w.s*: R.A.M.C. (Hon Lt-Col). *a*: 19 Gunter Grove, Chelsea, London, S.W.10; & Medical School, King's College, University of Durham, Newcastle-upon-Tyne. *T*: Newcastle 21601.

KENNEDY, Alexander Mills, M.D., F.R.C.P. *e*: Allan Glen's Sch & Univ of Glas. Prof of Med Univ of Wales Senior Hon Phys Cardiff Royal Infirmary. *Publ*: Cerebro-Spinal Fever; Parasitology; Medical Case-taking. *Ctr*: Lancet, B.M.J., Quarterly Journ of Med, Heart, Glas Med Journ, Journ of Obstetrics & Gynæcology, etc. *s.s*: Diseases of the Heart & Blood, Food Allergy. *w.s*: 1914—18. *a*: Medical Unit, Royal Infirmary, Cardiff. *T*: 5472.

KENNEDY, Alfred Ravenscroft, K.C. *b*: L'pool 1879. *e*: Eton & King's Col Cam. *m*: Daisy Chapman. *Publ*: C.I.F. Contracts; Ed of Kennedy on Salvage; etc. *c.t*: Halsbury's Laws of England. Legal Adv at Foreign Office during War. Bencher of Lincolns Inn 1922. M.P. (Cons) for Preston 1924-39. County Ct Judge '29. Commssr of Assize '33 & '34. *a*: Ablington Old Hse, Bibury, Glos & 3 Brick Ct, Temple. *t*: Bibury 17.

KENNEDY, Charles Rann. *b*: Derby, Eng 1871. *e*: Saltley Coll Sch Birmingham. *m*: Edith Wynne Matthison. Dramatist, Actor & Producer, formerly Trustee & Hd of Drama Dept (with wife)) of Bennett Sch of Liberal & Applied Arts N.Y. (ret). *Publ*: Plays:— The Winterfeast; The Servant in the House; The Idol-Breaker; The Army with Banners; The Chastening; Old Nobody; Crumbs; Flaming Ministers; The Seventh Trumpet; Face of God; Beggars Gift; Isles of the Blest; The Terrible Meek; etc. *s.s*: Greek Classics, Shakespeare Modern Drama. *Rec*: Gardening & Building Greek Theatres. *c*: Players Club, N.Y *a*: 10678 Rochester Ave, Los Angeles 24, California.

KENNEDY, Dr. J., M.B., F.R.C.S.I. *c.t*: B.M.J. *a*: 13 Belsize Park, N.W.3.

KENNEDY, Capt. James Russell, M.C., R.A., P.S.C. *b*: Port Patrick, Wigtowns 1895. *e*: Roy Mil Academy & Staff Col Camberley. *m*: Sofia Chernikova. *s*: 1. Ed Army, Navy & Air Force Gazette. *Publ*: Five Tactical Schemes, Series 1; Tactical Schemes, Series 2 (both these in collaboration with Major S. W. Kirby, M.C., R.E.). *c.t*: Nineteenth Century & After, Daily Express, Times & Daily Telegraph. *s.s*: Imperial defence & army organisation (reviews of books on these subjects). *Rec*: Golf & gardening. *c*: Army & Navy. *a*: Harrock, Oakleigh Av, Lon, N.20. *t*: Hillside 3202.

KENNEDY, Joan. *m*: J. H. Morrison. Novelist & Journalist, Mem Soc of Authors, Soc of Women Jnlsts. *Publ*: Novels :—Dusty Measure; Punchinello; Splendid Snare; According to Judy; Ragged Orchid; Deep Furrows; Miss Lavender of London; Green Harvest; Bonfires; Bird of Brass; Earthenware; Mimosa Dust; To-morrow Comes; Time's Fool; Yesterday's Roses; Community House; A Torch on Woman; This Marriage Business; Short Stories :— Piccalilli. Also various Nature books. *s.s*: Love & Marriage, Short Stories, Serial Stories. *Rec*: Gardening, foreign travel, motoring. *a*: La Vieille Maison, St Aubin, Jersey, C.I.

KENNEDY, John, F.J.I. *n.a*: Press Assoc M/C. Hon Vice-Pres I.J. *a*: Guardian Bldg, Pall Mall, M/C 2.

KENNEDY, Margaret. *b*: London. *e*: Cheltenham Ladies' Coll, Somerville Coll Oxf. *m*: David Davies, K.C. *s*: 1. *d*: 2. Writer. *Publ*: Novels :—Ladies of Lyndon; Constant Nymph; Red Sky at Morning; Return I Dare Not; A Long Time Ago; Together & Apart; The Midas Touch; The Mechanised Muse; etc; Plays—The Constant Nymph (with Basil Dean); Escape Me Never; Autumn. *Ctr*: Nash's, Good Housekeeping, English Review, Strand Mag, etc. *a*: c/o Curtis Brown, 6 Henrietta St, Covent Garden, London, W.C.2.

KENNEDY, Margaret, M.A. *b*: Perth. *e*: Perth Acad & Edin, Grenoble, Nancy, Geneva & Berlin Univs. Princ of Hutchesons' Girl's Gr Sch Glas. *Publ*: French Composition Book; French Grammar, Three Years' Course; French Grammar, Fourth & Fifth Years' Course. *s.s*: Modern Langs. *c*: Glas Lit. *a*: 28 Crown Mansions, Glasgow W.1. & Hutcheson's Girls' Gr Sch, Glasgow. *T*: Western 4965 & Queens Park 306.

KENNEDY, Mary Olivia, B.A.(Dublin). *b*: Dublin. *e*: Loreto & Univ Col Dublin. Jnlst. *n.a*: Reporting staff The Times, '17—. *Publ*: 3 Women's Sections of The Times History of the War, History of France (1789—1815); Histories of England & Ireland; Editions of French & English poetry for Univ & Intermediate exams. *c.t*: Good Housekeeping, Harper's Bazaar, Nash's etc. *s.s*: Fashions, hist, humour, fiction, film scenarios. *Rec*: Reading, the Theatre, travel. *a*: Flat L, 63 York Terrace. N.W.1. *t*: Welbeck 3042.

KENNEDY, Rev. R. *e*: Didsbury Col M/C. *m*: Ruth Norah Gibbs. *Publ*: The Redeemer, an Easter Message (poem); The Rose, The Dew Drop & The Bee; March Winds; Wizard Twilight; etc. *s.s*: Nat hist, philosophy. Won Stead Prize for Essay on Last Supper. *Rec*: Cricket, billiards. *a*: 80 Chalkwell Av, Westcliff-on-Sea, Essex.

KENNEDY, Ralph W. *n.a*: Ed Electrical Contractor. *Publ*: Electrical Housecraft. *a*: 6 Augustus Rd, London, S.W.19. *T*: Putney 5121.

KENNEDY, William Paul McClure, M.A., LL.D., Litt.D., F.R.S.C. *b*: Ireland 1879. *e*: Priv, Paris, Vienna, Trin Coll Dublin. *m*: Pauline Simpson. *s*: 2. *d*: 2. Prof of Law & Dean of the Faculty of Law Univ of Toronto. *n.a*: Legal Corr South African Law Times 1932—37, Foreign Corr Arbitration Law Journ '46—. *Publ*: The Elizabethan Interpretations—a Study in English Administrative Law; Studies in Tudor History; The Law of the Canadian Constitution; Documents of Canadian Constitutional Law 1713—1926; Visitation Articles & Injunctions Under Tudor Law 1535—1575; Elizabethan Administration—a Study In Law & Politics; etc. *Ctr*: Various including: Law Quarterly Rev, Juridical Rev, Scots Law Times, Cambridge Law Journ, English Hist Rev, Contemp Rev, etc. *s.s*: Law, Legal Hist. *Rec*: Fly-fishing, billiards. *a*: 77 Spadina Rd, Toronto 4, Ont & Narrow Waters, Beaver Lake, Kearney, Ont. *T*: Kingsdale 6978, Midway 6611.

Who Was Who Among English and European Authors

KENNEDY-BELL, Rev. D. F. K., M.A.(T.C.D.), B.D.(Durham). *Publ*: The Unforgiveable Sin. Vicar of St John with St Paul, Battersea. *a*: St John's Vicarage, North Side, Wandsworth Common.

KENNEDY-COOKE, Brian, M.C. *b*: Wendover, Bucks 1894. *e*: St Edward's Sch & Worcester Coll Oxf. *m*: Annette Rae Cooke. *s*: 2. *d*: 1.. Controller, Arts & Science Div The British Council, Order of The Nile (Egypt), Legion of Merit (U.S.A.), Sudan Political Service 1920—43, Governor Kassala Province Sudan '35—42. *Publ*: King Arthur of Britain; A Note on the Trees of Kassala Province, Sudan. *Ctr*: Britain To-day, Sudan Notes & Records, various Film & other Journs. *s.s*: Documentary Films, Sudanese Affairs, Italian Colonies, U.N.E.S.C.O. *w.s*: 1914—18, 39—45 (Bgdr). *a*: c/o The British Council, 3 Hanover St. London. W.1. *T*: Mayfair 9448.

KENNEDY-COX, Sir Reginald Kennedy. *b*: Weston-super-Mare 1881. *e*: Temple Gve, Malvern, Hertford Col Oxf. Founder & Hon Warden of all Dockland Settlements. *Publ*: Reginald Kennedy-Cox, An Autobiography; The Happiest Man; etc. *s.s*: Social work & juvenile crime. War Service '14—19; Despatches. Pres Crippled Children's Hosp at Plaistow, E. Chm Juvenile Ct at Barking. Chm Employment Cmt Canning Town Visiting Justice to Wandsworth Prison (Borstal Sec), also Feltham B.I. *Rec*: Theatre, travel. *c*: Un Soc, Oxf & Garrick, R.A.C. *a*: Boveney Ct, Boveney, Bucks & Dockland Settlement, Lon Docks, E.16. *t*: Windsor 371.

KENNETT, ROBERT HATCH, Rev.: canon of Ely, Regius Professor of Hebrew; b. St. Laurence, Kent, Eng., Sept. 9, 1864; s. John and Jane (Hatch) K.; educ. Merchant Taylor's Sch., London. DEGREES: M.A., D.D.; m. Emily Augusta Scott, June 12, 1889. AUTHOR: The Hebrew Tenses, 1901; In Our Tongues, 1907; The Composition of the Book of Isaiah (Schweich Lectures), 1909; Cambridge Biblical Essays, 1909; Hebrew Conceptions of Righteousness and Sin (the first article in Early Ideals of Righteousness), 1910; The Servant of the Lord, 1911; Deuteronomy and the Decalogue, 1920; The Last Supper, 1921; Old Testament Essays, 1928. Contributor to Hasting's Encyclopedia of Relig. and Ethics; Encyclop. Brit., Dummelow's Commentary, Peake's Commentary, and to Journ. Theol. Studies, The Interpreter and the Hibbert Journ. General character of writing: religious, critical study of the Bible. Relig. denom., Church of England. CLUB: Overseas. OFFICE: Queens' Coll., Cambridge. HOME: The Priory, The College, Ely, Cambridge, Eng.

KENNEY, Rowland. *b*: Sheldersdow 1882. Journalist, Civil Servant, F.O. 1920—38, Press Min Oslo '39—40, Foreign Div M.O.I. '40—41, Adviser to Roy Norwegian Govt in Lond '41—45, Couns Brit Embassy Oslo '45—46. *n.a*: Ed Daily Herald 1912, Reuter's Corr Oslo '17—18. *Publ*: Men & Rails; A Pedlar's Pack; Westering; The Northern Tangle; Works from German & Scandinavian Langs. *Ctr*: Times, Observer, Eng Review, etc. *s.s*: Politics, Economics. *Rec*: Reading & Writing. *c*: Savage. *a*: Savage Club, I Carlton Hse, Terr, London, S.W.1.

KENNINGTON, Alan. *b*: Tonbridge 1906. *e*: Lancing, Merton Coll Oxf & Hanover. *Publ*: Fritzi; See How They Run; Death of a Shrew; It Walks the Woods; She Died Young; The Night has Eyes; A Runaway Romance; Love on the Set; No Rope for Rats; Flying Visitor; Pastures New; Spring in My Heart; To Love & to Cherish; Wanted on Voyage, etc. Plays :—Spring Harvest; High Tension; Like the Hour; Corn in Egypt, etc. Films :—The Night Has Eyes; She Died Young. Short Stories. *Ctr*: Dly Mail, Dly Express, Sketch, News Chronicle, Everybody's. *s.s*: English Hist, Germany. *Rec*: Tennis, travel. *a*: Laurel Lodge, Lancing, Sussex. *T*: 2282.

KENNION, Roger Lloyd, C.I.E. (Russian).. *b*: Cumberland 1866. *e*: Repton, R.M.C. Sandhurst. *m*: Alice Marion Kenyon-Stow. *s*: 1. *d*: 1. Indian Army & Indian Foreign & Polit Dept (ret). *Publ*: Sport & Life in the Further Himalayas; By Mountain, Lake & Plain; etc. *c.t*: XIXth Century, Times, Field, etc. *s.s*: Sport, travel, India. St. Vladimir with Swords & St Anne with Swords. *c*: Roy Cent Asian Soc, etc. *a*: Tullecombe, Rogate, Petersfield. *t*: Rogate 11.

KENNY, Alice Annie. *b*: Ngaruawahia, N.Z. 1875. *e*: Private. Librarian. *Publ*: The Rebel; The Elsmlie Mystery; Wild Horse Gulch; The Magic Rings; The Witch's Daughter; The Good Goblin; Four Adventure Stories for Girls; Four Adventure Stories for Boys. *Ctr*: New Zealand Herald, Auckland Star, Christchurch Sun, Tasmanian Mail, Mirror, Sydney Bulletin, Punch, etc. *s.s*: Verse, Adventure, Stories for Boys & Girls, Fairy Tales for Young Children. *Rec*: Gardening, reading. *c*: P.E.N., N.Z., S.P.C.A. *a*: 599 Manukau Rd, Epsom, Auckland, New Zealand.

KENNY, Ernest James. *b*: Lon 1872. *e*: Sir Walter St John's Sc Battersea, Battersea Train Col. *m*: Olive Helena Hall. *s*: 1. Schoolmaster, Head Master L.C.C. Sc. Lect on English to the L.C.C., the Nat Union of Teachers, etc. *Publ*: Memory Work & Appreciation; Vocabulary Work; A New Course in English Composition; The Westminster Readers (7 vols in collab with Dr J. H. Jagger). *s.s*: English & Scripture. *a*: 2 Alleyn Rd, Dulwich, S.E.21. *t*: Syd 2477.

KENNY, T. J. Warren. *b*: Cork. *e*: Cork, Dublin & M/C. *m*: Louie McGuinness. *s*: 3. *d*: 4. Journalist. *n.a*: Founder, Ed & Mang Dir Connacht Tribune & Connacht Sentinel. *Publ*: A Tourist Guide to Connacht; The Goeltacht Problem; etc. *c.t*: Daily Mail, Daily Express, News Chron, Princ Irish n/ps, Press Assoc. *s.s*: Life in W. Ireland, humorous verse. Org Irish Art Club Carnival in the West. Led deputation to German Transport Min which got German trans-oceanic lines to reopen Galway port. Opened Irish Tourist Offices N.Y. '32. Pres Irish Tourist Assoc 5 y, twice Pres Galway Ch of Comm. *Rec*: Golf, aerial photography. *a*: The Crescent, Galway, & The Connacht Tribune, Galway. *t*: 21.

KENSHOLE, Dr. H. H. Dental Surgeon. Capt R.A.M.C. (T.A.). *Publ*: Papers on dental subjects. *a*: 57 Station Road, Sidcup, Kent.

KENSIT, John Alfred. *b*: London 1881. *e*: Christ's Hosp. *m*: May Dodman. *s*: 2. Secretary Protestant Truth Soc. *n.a*: Ed Churchman's Mag 1902—. *Publ*: Rome Behind the Great War; What I Saw in Rome; My Pilgrimage to Lourdes; etc. *Ctr*: English Churchman, Christian, Life of Faith, etc. *s.s*: Controversial Religious Questions. *a*: 184 Fleet St, London, E.C.4. *T*: Holborn 4960.

KENT, Charles Weller. *b*: Frant, Sussex 1864. *e*: Grove House Tunbridge Wells. *m*: Winifred Edwards (dec'd). *n.a*: Parliamentary Summary Writer, Press Assoc 1890—1904, Parl Staff Times 1904—14 *Publ*: A Splendid Inheritance; Happiness Haven; Pathway to Happiness; Make Friends of the Wise. *Ctr*: Various. *Rec*: Reading. *c*: Roy Eastbourne Golf. *a*: 34 Milnthorpe Rd, Eastbourne.

KENT, Frank R. *b*: Baltimore 1877. *e*: Priv & Johns Hopkins Univ. *m*: Elizabeth Thomas Kent. *s*: 1. Journalist. *n.a*: Sun 1900—, Rep Political Rep, Washington & London Corres, Mang-Ed, Vice-Pres. *Publ*: The Great Game of Politics; History of Maryland Politics; History of the Democratic Party; Without Gloves; Without Grease. *Ctr*: Sat Ev Post, Atlantic Monthly, Collier's, Amer Mag, etc. *s.s*: National Politics & Public Affairs. *Rec*: Golf bridge, backgammon. *a*: Lombardy Apartment, Baltimore, Maryland, U.S.A. *T*: University 0711.

KENT, Herbert Vaughan, C.B. b: Hersham 1863. e: Clifton Col & R.M.A. Woolwich. m: Helen Chauncey Tiffany. s: 1. d: 2. Engineer. Publ: Dancing on Skates; Combined Figures & Ice-Valsing; My Racing Log. c.t: Field, Yachtsman, Skating Times. s.s: Yacht racing, skating. Rec: All aquatic sports, squash, etc. c: Jnr Un Service & Bembridge Sailing. a: J.U.S. Club, Charles St, S.W.1.

KENT, John Leo. b: Wangaratta, Victoria, Australia 1902. e: St Patrick's Coll & Univ of Melbourne. Journalist. n.a: Reporter Sth China Sunday Star Hong Kong 1931—33, Ed & Prop Chop Sticks Monthly Rev & D.X. Radio Monthly '32—34, Assoc-Ed Laundry Record '34—38, Mang-Ed Power Laundry '40—45. s.s: Travel, Laundry, Technical, Education. Rec: Reading, golf, swimming. c: Press. a: 7 Churston Mansions, Gray's Inn Rd, London, W.C.1. T: Terminus 3581.

KENT, Madeleine Jane. b: London. e: London Univ. Married. Author & Lecturer. Publ: I Married a German; Island of the Innocent. Ctr: Manch Guardian, Nat Rev, Cent European Observer, etc. s.s: Foreign Affairs (Germany, Denmark, Finland, Czechoslovakia). Rec: Travel, music. c: P.E.N. a: c/o Messrs George Allen & Unwin Ltd, 40 Museum St, London, W.C.1.

KENT, Nora. b: Lewes 1899. e: Priv. Publ: Peter Thurstan; The Vintage; Barren Lands; Endless Furrows; Starveacres; Fire Among Thorns; Rainbow at Night; Pennycooks in Paradise; Cornish Excursion; The Armoured Virgin; Unto us a Child; Fear No More; The Fingerpost; Creeping Jenny. Ctr: Premier Mag; Woman's Kingdom, Twenty Story Mag, etc. Rec: Tennis, swimming. a: c/o Christy & Moore Ltd, Gerrards Cross, Bucks. T: Lewes 729.

KENT, Percy Horace Braund, O.B.E., M.C., M.A. b: Old Charlton, Kent 1876. e: Rugby & Corpus Christi Coll Oxf. m: Anna Mary Simcox. s: 2. d: 1. Barrister, Mem of Bar H.B.M.'s Supreme Court for China 1901—41, formerly Legal Adv Pekin to Ministries of Finance, Communications, Agric & Commmerce. Publ: The Twentieth Century in the Far East; Railway Enterprise in China; The Passing of the Manchus. Ctr: Economist, Eng Review, etc. s.s: China. w.s: 1914—18 Scots Gds (Capt). Rec: Golf & skating. c: Guards, Thatched House, Nat Lib. a: Clavering, Cooden Sea Rd, Bexhill, Sussex. T: Cooden 607.

KENT, Roland Grubb, A.M., B.L., Ph.D. b: Wilmington, Delaware 1877. e: Swarthmore Coll, Univ of Penn, Berlin, Munich, Athens. m: Gertrude Freeman Hall. Classical Philologist & Comparative Linguist, Chevalier de la Legion d'Honneur. n.a: Business Mang, Publs of Linguistic Soc of America 1925—40. Publ: The Sounds of Latin; The Forms of Latin; The Textual Criticism of Inscriptions; Language & Philology; (Ed) The Cipher of Roger Bacon. Ctr: Language, Classical Rev, Journ of Near Eastern Studies etc. s.s: Latin, Oscan-Umbrian, Greek, Old Persian, Comparative Linguistics. a: 324 Aubrey Rd, Wynnewood, Pa, U.S.A. T: Ardmore 6211.

KENT, W. T. Reporter. a: 20 Sandown Avenue, Dagenham, Essex.

KENT, William Richard Gladstone. b: Kennington 1884. e: Bd Sch & King's Coll. m: Edith Bryon. s: 2. d: 1. Con Lond Rambles for "Everyman" 1929—38, Lect H.M. Prisons '20—23. Publ: With Dickens in the Borough; London for Everyman; London for Heretics; The George Inn, Southwark; London for Shakespeare Lovers; Dickens & Religion; London for Dickens Lovers; Ency of London (ed); London Worthies; The Testament of a Victorian Youth; The Lost Treasures of London. s.s: Lond, Lit, etc. Rec: Cricket, antiquarianism. c: Surrey C.C., Lond. a: 71 Union Rd, Clapham, London, S.W.4. T: Macaulay 2007.

KENT HUGHES, Wilfred Selwyn, M.V.O., O.B.E., M.C. b: East Melbourne 1895. e: Melbourne Gr Sch & Christ Church Oxf. m: Edith Kerr. d: 3. Printer. Publ: Modern Crusaders; Slaves of the Samurai. s.s: Politics. c: Navy, Army & Air Force. w.s: 1914—19 & '39—46. a: 129 King St, Melbourne, C.1, Australia. T: M.B.2018.

KENT-JONES, Douglas William. b: London 1891, e: Mercers Sch Holborn, King's Coll Lond. m: Beatrice Harris. Analytical & Consultant Chemist. Publ: Modern Cereal Chemistry; Practice & Science of Bread-making. Ctr: Thorpe's Dict of Applied Chem. s.s: Cereals, Bread & Nutrition. Rec: Golf. a: 88 Madeley Rd, Ealing, London, W.5. T: Perivale 6466.

KENWOOD, HENRY RICHARD: professor of hygiene; b. Bexhill, Eng., Dec., 1862; s. John and Isabel Mary (Kenwood; educated. Tunbridge Wells Collegiate Sch., Edinburgh Univ. DEGREES: M.B. (Mast. Surg. Edinburgh), L. R. C. P. (London); m. Rose Joscelyne, 1908. AUTHOR: Public Health Laboratory Work (8th edit.), 1927; Hygiene and Public Health (8th edit.), 1929. Contributor to Public Health (Journal of the Soc. of Med. Officers of Health), Journ. Royal Sanitary Inst., Lancet, British Med. Journ. General character of writing: technical, medical, hygiene and public health. Med. officer of Health for County of Bedfordshire; emeritus prof. Hygiene Univ. of London; late pres. and Soc. Medical Officers of Health; mem. Army Hygiene Advisory Bd.; Companion Order St. Michael and St. Gorge; Fellow Royal Soc. of Edinburgh. Relig. denom., Church of England. OFFICE: University of London. HOME: Wadhurst, 126 Queen's Road, London, N. 4, Eng.

KENWORTHY, Hugh. See Walker, Rowland.

KENYON, A. Terr Mem N.U.J. a: Roeburn, Leadhall Av, Harrogate.

KENYON, Alice Amelia. b: Manchester 1883. e: Hulme G.S., Oldham Stockwell Training Col, Lond. Teacher. c.t: Woman Teacher, Oldham Chron, M/c Guardian, Oldham Standard. Daily Dispatch. s.s: Education. J.P. for County Boro' of Oldham. Suffragette. Rec: Gardening, rambling. c: Nat Pres of N.U.W.T., Workers Educ Assoc, Lab Party & Theosophical Soc. a: 177 Grange Ave, Werneth, Oldham.

KENYON, Major Gen. Edward Ranulph C.B., C.M.G. b: Lon 1854. e: Winchester Col & R.M.A. Woolwich. m: Katharine Mary McCrea De Butts (dec). s: 3 (2 dec). d: 4. Roy Eng. Publ: Notes on Land & Coast Fortification; Gibraltar Under Moor, Spaniard & Briton. c: Un Service Mag, Roy Eng Journal. War Service '14—18; 5 times des; wounded; C.R.E. 20th Div; Chief Eng IV Corps; Chief Eng 3rd Army; Major-Gen; Dep Controller Chem Warfare Dept. Vice-Pres Ch Missny Soc. Ex-Chm Ch of Eng Zenana Missy Soc. Commander Crown of Italy. a: Pradoe, Oswestry, Salop. t: Queenshead 18.

KENYON, Ethel St. Clair. b: Swinton, Yorks 1881. e: Private. Teacher. c.t: Fairyland Tales, Red Letter, Morning Rays (Church of Scotland Mag for Children). s.s: Children's stories & poems, Committee Work. Works extensively amongst deaf children. Rec: Badminton, tennis, country dancing, golf, painting, drawing, crafts. c: Soroptimist, Dundee, Sociological, Dundee, Scottish Country Dancing. a: Dudhope Bank, Lochee Rd, Dundee, Angus. t: 3951.

KENYON, Sir Frederick George, G.B.E., K.C.B., T.D., F.B.A., F.S.A., F.R.S.L., D.Litt., Litt.D., LL.D. *b*: London 1863. *e*: Winchester & New Coll Oxf. *m*: Amy Hunt. *d*: 2. Dir & Princ Librarian Brit Mus (ret). *Publ*: Aristotle on the Constitution of Athens; Poems of Bacchylides; Chester Beatty Biblical Papyri; Our Bible & the Ancient MSS; Letters of E. B. Browning; The Bible & Archæology; The Text of the Greek Bible; The Story of the Bible; The Reading of the Bible. *s.s*: Greek Papyri. *Rec*: Reading & walking. *a*: Kirkstead, Godstone, Surrey. *T*: Godstone 335.

KENYON, Kathleen Mary, M.A., F.S.A. *b*: London 1906. *e*: St Paul's Girls' Sch, Somerville Coll Oxf. Assist on Excavation Zimbabwe Sth Rhodesia 1929, St Albans '30—35, Samaria '30—35, Dir Excavations at Jewry Wall, Leics '36—39, Wrekin '39, Southwark '45—47, Breedon-on-the-Hill Leics '46. *Publ*: Samaria—Sebaste I (joint Author). *Ctr*: Archæologia, Archæolog Journ, etc. *s.s*: Archæology. *Rec*: Riding, tennis, golf. *a*: Kirkstead, Godstone, Surrey, & Institute of Archæology, Inner Circle, Regents Park, London, N.W.1. *T*: Godstone 335 & Welbeck 1697.

KENYON, ROBERT LLOYD: barrister; *b*. London, Eng., Jan. 13, 1848; *s*. John Robert and Mary Eliza (Hawkins) .; *educ*. Winchester Coll., Christ Church (Oxford). DEGREE: M.A.; *m*. Ellen Frances How, 1886. AUTHOR: Gold Coins of England, 1884; History of Parishes of Ruyton and West Felton, Shropshire (in trans. Shropshire Archaeological Soc.), 1891-1902; Shropshire Quarter Sessions Orders 1638 to 1889, 1916. Editor: 2nd and 3rd edits. Hawkins' "Silver Coins of England", 1876, 1887; Shropshire Charities for Elementary Education, 1906. Contributor to trans. Shropshire Archael. Soc., Numismatic Chronicle and other publicns. General character of writing: scientific, archaeological, numismatic. Vinerian Law Scholar (Oxford), 1872; Shropshire county alderman, 1889-1928; Recorder of Oswestry, 1896-1927; deputy chmn. Shropshire Quarter Sessions, 1889-1914; chmn., 1914-1927. Relig. denom., Church of England. HOME: Pradoe, Oswestry, Shropshire, Eng.

KENYON, Theta. *e*: Packer Coll Inst. Writer. *Publ*: Jeanne; Witches Still Live; Certain Ladies; Scarlet Anne; Pendulum; Golden Feather; Dark Root; That Skipper from Stonington. *Ctr*: Various in U.S. & England. *s.s*: American & English Hist. *a*: 42 E. Williston Ave, East Williston, L.I., N.Y., U.S.A.

KEOGAN, Barry. Jt Founder, late Co-Editor Prospect. *Publ*: (Ed) The Heart of England. *Ctr*: Birm Wkly Post, Writers of Tomorrow, B.B.C., etc. *a*: 18 Lyncourt Grove, Quinton, Birmingham 32.

KEOWN, Anna Gordon. *b*: Lon 1899. *e*: Cheltenham Ladies Col, Dresden & Ireland. Novelist. *Publ*: The Cat Who Saw God; Mr Thompson in the Attic. *c.t*: Good Housekeeping. *s.s*: Cats. Extensive travel in Canada, U.S.A. & Europe. *Rec*: Music. *a*: 4 The Village, North End, Hampstead. *t*: Speedwell 6895.

KEOWN, Eric Oliver Dilworth. *b*: London 1904. *e*: Highgate Sch, Pembroke Coll Camb & Grenoble Univ. *m*: Cicely Ritchie. *s*: 1. *d*: 1. Writer. *n.a*: Ed Staff Punch 1928—33, (pt dramatic critic) '32—40, Parliamentary Corres '33—40, Dramatic Critic '45—, Punch Table '39. *Publ*: The Dog's Dudgeon. *Ctr*: Punch as "Eric" & Book Revs as E.O.D.K. *Rec*: Fishing. *w.s*: 1940—45 R.A.F.V.R. *c*: R.A.C. *a*: Stringers Barn, Worplesdon, Surrey. *T*: Guildford 3912.

KER, Margaret Louise, B.A. *b*: Birkenhead 1892. *e*: Birkenhead H.S., Liverpool Univ & Bedford Col Lon. Teacher. *Publ*: Stories to Tell from English Literature (1931). *s.s*: Teaching of English in scs. Ex-Women's Suffrage Worker. Worked in War Office during War. *Rec*: Theatre-going. *c*: Theosophical Soc & The Women's Intern League for Peace & Freedom. *a*: 58 Denman Drive, N.W.11. *t*: Speedwell 6059.

KERAMOPULLOS, ANTONIOS D.: professor; *b*. Blatsi, Macedonia, Mar., 1870; *s*. Demetrius Ch. and Despoina K.; *educ*. Saloniki Gymnasium; Univ. of Athens, Greece; Univ. of Munich; universities of Vienna and Paris as a visitor; studied in all European Museums (archaeological). DEGREES: Diploma of Univ. of Athens; Ph.D. ibid; *m*. Aikaterina, Oct. 4, 1909. AUTHOR: A Guide to the ruins of Delphi (in Greek and French), 1908-09; Topography of Delphi (in Greek, 1912-17); Thebaika (General work on my discoveries and finds at Thebes), 1917; Apotymbanismos (A Study of the Penal Laws of Ancient Greece), 1923. Contributor to Ephemeris Archeologiki, Deltion Archaeologikon, Athena, Athenische Mitteilungen des Deutsches Archaeol. Institute (all Athens); Klio (Berlin); and others. Excavated in many parts of Greece, particularly at Macedonia, 1930-31, and Thebes, 1905-1930, where, among other important discoveries, he brought to light the Palace of the mythical Kadmos. Relig. denom., Greek Orthodox. CLUBS: Archaeological Society, Greek Academy (Athens); Society of Promotion of Hellenic Studies (London); German Archaeological Institute (Berlin); Austrian Archaeological Institute (Vienna), and others. OFFICE: University of Athens. HOME: Zaimi 23 A., Athens, Greece.

KERBY, Bernard Hesley. *b*: St Petersburg, Russia 1916. *e*: Priv & Highgate Sch. *m*: Agnete Egge. Press & Public Relations Officer, Mem N.U.J. *n.a*: Press & Public Relations Officer The Chloride Electrical Storage Co Ltd, formerly Sub-Ed Illustrated Newspapers, Revise Sub-Ed Sunday Graphic, Sen Ed Todd Publ Co Ltd. *s.s*: Motoring, Storage Batteries. *Rec*: Music, motoring, swimming, tennis, travel. *w.s*: 1941—44. *a*: Little Orchard, West End Lne, Pinner, Middlx. *T*: Pinner 2963.

KERBY, Susan Alice. *b*: Cairo, Egypt. Advertising Consultant. *Publ*: Cling to Her, Waiting; Fortnight in Frascati; Many Strange Birds; Gone to Grass; Fortune's Gift. *Ctr*: Various. *Rec*: Music, gardening. *a*: 23 Abbey Rd, St John's Wood, N.W.8.

KERLEY, Peter James. M.D., B.Ch, D.M.R.E. Radiologist. Ed X-Ray Sect Cancer Review 1926—32. *Publ*: Recent Advances in Radiology. *c.t*: Lancet, B.M.J., etc. *a*: 29 Weymouth St, Lon W.1. *t*: Langham 4007.

KERMACK, Stuart G., M.A., L.L.B. *b*: Edinburgh 1888. *e*: Edin Acad, Fettes Coll, Edin Univ. *m*: Nell White. *s*: 2. *d*: 1. Advocate, Sheriff Substitute of Lanarkshire at Glasgow, Judicial Office in Sudan & Palestine 1918—30. *Publ*: Law of Scotland; Handbook of Criminal Procedure in Palestine. *Ctr*: Jurisprudence & Philosophy of Law in Vol I of Publications of the Stair Soc. *s.s*: Jurisprudence, Sociology of Law, Comparative Law. *c*: Glasgow Art. *a*: Conylea, 41a Westbourne Gardens, Glasgow, W.2. *T*: West 4808.

KERMACK, William Ogilvy, M.A., D.Sc, F.R.S.E. Research Chem. *c.t*: Sci Journs. *a*: Wayside, Craiglockhart Grove, Edin. *t*: 63287.

KERMODE, Canon Robert Daniel, M.A. *b*: Douglas 1868. *e*: Caius & Jesus Col Cam. *m*: Bertha Harrison Clucas. *d*: 1. *n.a*: Ed Manx Ch Mag 1924—34. *c*: Ellan Vannin, Douglas & Raven, Ramsey. *a*: Lezayre Vicarage, Ramsey, I.o.M. *t*: 112.

KERNAHAN, Coulson. *b*: Ilfracombe 1858. *e*: St Alban's Sc & Priv. *m*: Jean Gwynne. *d*: 1. Writer. *n.a*: Ed & Lit Adv to Messrs Ward, Lock & Coy '89—1905. *Publ*: Six Famous Living Poets; In Good Company (Recollections of Swinburne, Oscar Wilde etc); A Dog & His Master; The Sunshine in the Room; The Garden of God; A World Without the Christ ('34); etc. *c.t*: Fortnightly Review, Army Quarterly, Strand Mag, Chambers's Journ, Punch, Morning Post, etc. *s.s*: Nature study, poetry, nat defence. Vice-Pres Dickens Fellowship. *Rec*: Riding, shooting. *c*: Savage, Whitefriars. *a*: Frognal, Fairlight, Hastings. *t*: Pett 127.

KERNAHAN, Jean Gwynne Coulson. *b*: Audley. *e*: Univ Col Lon. *m*: (1) George Thomas Bettany; (2) Coulson Kernahan. *s*: 1. *d*: 1. *Publ*: The Woman Who Understood; Ashes of Passion; A Village Mystery; The Thirteenth Man; An Artist's Model; The Vagrant Bride; etc. *c.t*: Daily Express, Sussex Daily News (serials). *Rec*: Study of wild birds. *a*: Frognal, Fairlight, Hastings. *t*: Pett 127.

KERNAHAN, S. P. *n.a*: Ed Paint Manufacture, Ed Food Industries. *s.s*: Food production, Ind chem, refrigeration, oil engines, paints & lacquers. *a*: 59 Aberdare Gdns. N.W.6. *t*: Maida Vale 6229.

KERNER, Robert Joseph, M.A., Ph.D. *b*: Chicago, Ill 1887. *e*: Chicago & Harvard. *m*: Frances Dorsey Kerner. *d*: 2. Prof of History Univ of Calif Berkeley. *n.a*: Ctr-Ed Slavonic Review London 1924—40, Ed-Bd Journ of Modern History '28—32 & American Slavic Rev '40—. *Publ*: The Urge to the Sea (Russia); Czechoslovakia (Ed & Co-author); Bohemia in the 18th Century; Balkan Conferences & Balkan Entente (collab); North Eastern Asia; Slavic Europe. *Ctr*: Foreign Affairs, Journ of Modern History, Calif Monthly, etc. *s.s*: History & Internat Relations of Eastern Europe (Slavic Countries, Russia, etc). *Rec*: Hiking. *c*: Bohemian. *a*: 1320 Arch St, Berkeley 8, California, U.S.A. *T*: Ashberry 7878.

KERNICK, Waterhouse. *b*: St Ives 1869. *e*: Bristol Trade Sc & Cam Univ. *m*: Jeane Alan Maitland. *s*: 2. (1 dec). *d*: 1. Capt Church Army. *n.a*: Longford Independent, Armagh Independent, Bray & S. Dublin Herald, Prescot Reporter, Free Lance. *c.t*: Daily Mail, Daily Express, News Chronicle, Manchester Guardian, Bolton Evening News, The Star, etc. *Rec*: Reading, walking. *a*: 50 South Av, Prescot, Lancs.

KERR, Alfred. *b*: Breslau 1867. *e*: Univs of Berlin, Breslau & Halle. *m*: Julia Weismann. *s*: 1. *d*: 1. Writer, Poet, Critic. *Publ*: Die Welt im Drama; Das Neue Drama; Der Ewigkeitszug; Die Sucher und Die Seligen; Eintagsfliegen; Das Mimenreich; Die Welt in Licht; Verweile Doch; Du Bist So Schon; Newyork und London; O Spanien; etc. Poetry :—Die Harfe; Caprichos; Melodien, etc. *Rec*: Music. *a*: Lytton Hall, Lytton Grove, London, S.W.15. *T*: Putney 4074.

KERR, Archibald William Montgomerie, M.A., LL.D.(Queen's U.), B.A., B.Sc(Lon), M.I.J. *b*: Belfast 1873. *e*: Belfast Royal Academy, Queen's Univer Belfast, Univ Lon. Journ. *n.a*: Belfast Telegraph & allied papers, 1904. Vice-Pres Church of Ireland Y.M.Soc Belfast. Mem of Standing Cmt of Convocation Queen's Univ Belfast. *Publ*: An Ironside of Ireland (historical biography); By the Pool of Garmoyle; The Shadow of Drumcarnett (historical romance). *c.t*: Irish Press. *s.s*: History & economics. *Rec*: Boating, bowls. Bank Clerk, Museum Assist & Solicitor's Clerk before entering Journalism. *c*: Univ of Lon, etc. *a*: 23 Waterloo Gardens, Antrim Rd, Belfast. *t*: 7550.

KERR, Barbara Anne, B.S.(Lond), M.R.S.C., L.R.C.P. *b*: Highgate 1906. *e*: Roedean Sch, Roy Free Hosp (Lond Sch of Medicine), Lond Univ. *m*: Dr Eric J. Kerr. Late Anæsthetist & Casualty House Surgeon at General Hosp B'ham, Late Resident Med Officer Victoria & Dist Hospital Woking. *n.a*: Sub-Ed Roy Free Hosp Mag 1928—30, Author Birth Control Supplement, The Household Physician, Late Asst Ed Brit Encyclo of Med Practice. *s.s*: Anæsthetics. *Rec*: Riding, swimming. *c*: British Med Assoc. *a*: Huntly, Richmond Rd, Worthing, Sussex. *T*: Worthing 533.

KERR, Douglas James Acworth, M.D., F.R.S.E., F.R.C.P.E., D.P.H. *b*: Bradford, Yorks 1894. *e*: St Paul's Sch London & Edinburgh Univ. *m*: Phyllis MacGregor. *s*: 2. *d*: 1. Lecturer, Forensic Medicine Sch of Med Edinburgh, Mem G.M.C. *Publ*: Forensic Medicine. *Ctr*: Various Med Journs. *s.s*: Forensic Medicine. *c*: Caledonian United Services. *a*: 7 Gordon Terr, Edinburgh. *T*: 43366.

KERR, Frank Robison, D.S.O. *b*: Melbourne 1889. *e*: Camberwell Gr Sch, Wesley Coll, Queen's Coll Melbourne Univ, Univ Coll Oxf. *m*: Myrtle Constance McMeekin. *s*: 2. *d*: 1. Commonwealth Medical Officer Melbourne, Commonwealth Dept of Health, Victorian Rhodes Scholar 1913, Mem Roy Soc of Australia, Mem B.M.A. *Publ*: Days after Tomorrow; Foundations; Inquiry into the Health of Workers in Gasmaking Plants; Inquiry into Morbidity Statistics of Victorian State School Teachers. *Ctr*: Arts in Med Journs of Aust. *Rec*: Hiking, mountaineering, sport, poetry & music. *c*: Melbourne Cricket Club. *a*: 28 Wimba Ave, Kew, Melbourne, Victoria, Australia. *T*: Hawthorn 2104.

KERR, Hamilton William. *b*: Long Island, U.S.A. 1903. *e*: Eton & Balliol Coll Oxf. Journalist 1926—30, M.P. (C) Oldham '31—45, Parl Priv Sec to Rt Hon Duff Cooper when Sec of State for War & First Lord '36—38 & Parl Sec Min of Health '45. *n.a*: Dly Mail 1928—29, Dly Telegraph '29—30. *Ctr*: Spectator, 19th Century. Country Life, Everybody's, etc. *s.s*: Foreign Affairs, Current Politics. Art. *w.s*: Aux A.F. 1939—45. *Rec*: Tennis, painting. *c*: Carlton, Athenæum, Queens. *a*: 71 Westminister Gardens, Marsham St, London, S.W.1, *T*: Victoria 8362.

KERR, Hugh Alexander. *b*: Govan 1886. *e*: Kinning Park Publ Sc. *m*: Günda Marie Strömberg. *s*: 3. *d*: 1. Clerk. *c.t*: Two Worlds, Scot Co-operator, Evening Times, etc. *s.s*: Rationalist propaganda. Hon Local Sec Rationalist Press Assoc Ltd Lon & Hon Sec Rationalist Press Assoc Glas Dist, Bd of Management Glas Roy Inf, etc. *Rec*: Bowls, chess. *a*: 18 Kingshill Drive, King's Pk, Glas, S.4. *t*: Langside 2793.

KERR, Dr. J. A. Medical Officer, Public Health 1927—29. *a*: Public Health Dept, Counc Hse, Birm.

KERR, J. Bruce. *n.a*: Ed Amateur Athletic Assoc Handbook. *a*: 15 East Heath Rd, Hampstead, N.W.3. *t*: Hampstead 3004

KERR, James, M.A., M.D., D.P.H. *Publ*: School Hygiene; School Vision & the Myopic Scholar; The Air We Breathe; The Fundamentals of School Health; Public Health in "After War Problems." *c.t*: Med, Scientific Journs. *a*: 9 Regent Terr, Edin. *t*: 30701.

KERR, James Lennox. *b*: Paisley 1893. *e*: Paisley Counc Sch. *m*: Elizabeth Lamorna Birch. *s*: 1. *Publ*: Backdoor Guest; Old Ship; Glenshiels; Ice; The Young Steamship Officer; Anthology of Sea Stories; Woman of Glenshiels; The Eager Years. *Rec*: Sea travel. *w.s*: R.N.V.R. 1915—19 & '39—45. *a*: Flagstaff Cottage, Lamorna, Nr Penzance. *T*: Mousehole 228.

KERR, James Rutherford. *c.t*: Lancet, B.M.J., Practitioner, & Engineering. *a*: 70 Scarisbrick New Rd, Southport. *t*: 3821.

KERR, Sir John Graham, Kt., Hon.LL.D., Hon Fell Christ's Coll, F.R.S. (V.P. 1937—38), M.P. *b*: Arkley, Hertfordshire 1869. *e*: Roy High Sch, Edin, Camb & Edin Univ. *m*: Isobel Dunn Macindoe. *s*: 2. *d*: 1. Prof Emeritus of Zoology Glas Univ, Scottish Univ M.P. 1935 & '45. *Publ*: Vertebrate Embryology; Evolution; Zoology for Medical Students; A Naturalist in the Gran Chaco; Author of Original Memorandum in War Camouflage 1914. *s.s*: Zoology, Embryology, Evolution, Politics. *c*: Athenæum, Univ (Edin), Conservative (Glas). *a*: Dalny Veed, Barley, Royston, Herts. *T*: Barkway 243.

KERR, John Martin Munro, M.D., F.C.O.G. *b*: Glas 1868. *e*: Glas Acad, Univs of Glas & Berlin. *m*: Emelia Androina Elisabeth Johanson. *s*: 1. *d*: 3. *Publ*: Operative Midwifery (3rd ed); Clinical & Operative Gynæcology (1922); Maternal Mortality & Morbidity ('33); etc. *c.t*: Current med journals. *s.s*: Obstetrics & gynæcology. Regina Prof of Midwifery Univ of Glas. Pres Roy Faculty of Phys & Surg Glas. Hon Fell Roy Acad of Med Ireland. Obstet & Gynæc Soc Edin. American Gynæc Soc. *c*: Western & Auto, Glas & Cons, Lon. *a*: 7 Grosvenor Cres, Glasgow. *t*: Western 5590.

KERR, Mark Edward Frederic, C.B., M.V.O. *b*: Hampton Court Palace 1864. *e*: Stubbington Hse, Fareham, H.M.S. Brittania. Training Ship of Royal Navy. *m*: Rose Margaret Gough. *d*: 2. Admiral R.N. (Ret). *Publ*: Land, Sea & Air, Sailor's Nelson; Prince Louis of Battenberg; The Navy in My Time: Poetry:—The Destroyer and a Cargo of Notions; The Rubaiyat of Kram Rerk. *c.t*: Times, Sunday Times, Morning Post, Saturday Review, National Review, Army, Navy, & Air Force Gazette, Daily Mail, Daily Telegraph, 19th Century, Outlook, etc. *s.s*: Navy, air, telepathy, Far East. A.D.C. to the King '12—'3, Vice-Admiral in Command of R. Grecian Navy '13—15, Comd. British Adriatic Squadron '16—17, V.P. United Service Corps, Dep Chief of Air Staff '18. Royal Humane Society Medal. *Rec*: Formerly:—Polo, cricket, lawn tennis, flying, shooting, hunting, race riding. *c*: Veterans, Veterans Assoc, White's. *a*: 19 Draycott Ave, S.W.3. *t*: Kensington 7396.

KERR, R(ODERICK) WATSON: journalist; *b*. Easterhouse, Lanarkshire, Scotland, Jan., 1895; *s*. Roderick and Margaret (Watson) K.; educ. Provincial Training Coll. for Teachers (Edinburgh); Univ. of Edinburgh. DEGREES: M.A.; *m*. Joan Cameron Macpherson, June 8, 1927. AUTHOR: Lyrics of a Soul, 1913; War Daubs, 1919; Annus Mirabilis, 1924; The Polite Educator (political satires), 1925. Asst. editor: Liverpool Daily Post; joint-founder of The Porpoise Press, Edinburgh, 1923; sub-editor, leader writer, reviewer, The Scotsman, Edinburgh, 1923-26. Schoolmaster, 1914-15; tank-commander in Great War, 1916-19; severely wounded in last tank engagement; awarded Military Cross. Relig. denom., Presbyterian. OFFICE: Liverpool Daily Post. HOME: 8 Buckingham Ave., Sefton Park, Liverpool, Eng.

KERR, Wilfred Brenton. *b*: Seaforth, Ontario 1896. *e*: Univ Coll Toronto, Hertford Coll Oxf, Univ of Toronto. *m*: Sara Ada Melvina Brett. *s*: 1. *d*: 2. Assoc Prof Univ of Buffalo N.Y., Mem Canadian & Ottawa Hist Socs. *Publ*: Reign of Terror; Bermuda & American Revolution; Maritime Provinces of British North America & American Revolution; etc. *Ctr*: Hist Rev, Can Defence Quarterly, Dalhousie Rev, Penn Mag of Hist & Biog, etc. *s.s*: French Revolution, Loyal Colonies in American Revolution, Military Hist of England & Canada. *w.s*: 1914—16. *a*: 282 Stillwell Ave, Kenmore, N.Y. *T*: Bedford 5907.

KERR, Rt. Rev. William Shaw, D.D. (See **DOWN & DROMORE, Bishop of.**) *b*: 1873. *e*: Dublin Univ. *m*: Amy Smith. *s*: 1. *d*: 3. Bishop of Down & Dromore. *Publ*: Independence of the Celtic Church in Ireland; Memoir of Andrew Boyd; History of Banbridge (Ed). *s.s*: Church History. *c*: Ulster (Belfast), Univ (Dublin). *a*: 32 Knocdene Park, Belfast.

KERRELL-VAUGHAN, D. P. A., F.Inst.Hsg. *b*: Cardiff 1904. P.R.O. National Housing & Town Planning Council. *n.a*: Ed Housing & Planning News Bulletin. *Publ*: The Government of the English Village; History of Thame. *Ctr*: Local Govt Chron, Fire, etc. *a*: 42 Devonshire St, London, W.1. *T*: Welbeck 8440.

KERRUISH, Jessie Douglas. *Publ*: Miss Haroun Al-Raschid; Babylonian Nights Entertainments; etc. *s.s*: Archæology. *a*: c/o C. Campbell Thomson Ltd, 12 Henrietta St, London, W.C.2.

KERSH, Gerald. *Publ*: inc Clean, Bright & Slightly Oiled; Neither Man nor Dog; Jews Without Jehovah; They Die With Their Boots Clean; The Dead Look On; Brain & Ten Fingers; The Weak & the Strong; etc. *a*: c/o Westminster Bank, 34 Sloane Sq, London, S.W.1.

KERSHAW, Rev. John Frederick, M.A. *b*: Ormskirk 1853. *e*: Harrow Sc & Trin Col Cam. *Publ*: The Re-union of Christendom. Rural Dean of Kidderminster; Rural Dean of W. Worcs. *Rec*: Golf. *a*: Chacewater, Barbourn, Worcester.

KERSHAW, Sir Leonard W. Barrister. Master of the Crown Office, K.B.D. Registrar Court of Criminal Appeal 1912—33. *Publ*: Russell on Crimes & Misdemeanurs; Wise on Riots; Wigram's Justices Note Book. *a*: Walton, Gerrards Cross, Bucks.

KERSHAW, Samuel, F.T.I. *b*: Bradford 1883. *e*: Usher Street Counc Sch Bradford & Tech Coll Bradford. *m*: Ann Machan. *s*: 3. *d*: 1. Head of Tex Dept Tech Coll Halifax (ret), Examnr City & Guilds of Lond Inst. *Publ*: Worsted; Carbonising Processes (with J. Dumville); Worsted Cone Drawing; Wool; Worsted Open Drawing; etc. *Ctr*: Textile Manufacturer, Textile Recorder, Textile Mercury, Wool Record, Journ of Tex Inst. *s.s*: Wool Manufacture. *a*: 72 Briarwood Drive, Wibsey.

KERSLEY, George Durant, M.D., F.R.C.P. *b*: Bath 1906. *e*: Malvern, Caius Coll Camb, St Barts Hosp. Married. *s*: 1. *d*: 1. *n.a*: Jt Ed Annals of Rheumatic Diseases, Ed Cttee Journ of Physical Med. *Publ*: The Chronic Rheumatic Diseases; Outlines of Physical Medicine. *Ctr*: Various Med Journs. *s.s*: Rheumatic Diseases. *a*: 6 The Circus, Bath. *T*: 2665.

KERWIN, Mrs. Madeleine. *b*: N.Y. 1887. *e*: Convent of the Sacred Heart. *m*: Andrew Joseph Kerwin, Jnr. *Publ*: How to Bid Contract Bridge; Kerwin on Contract: The One Over One for Everyone; Partnership Contract; etc. *Ctr*: Vanity Fair; Contract Bridge Mag, Golf, etc. *s.s*: Whist, auction & contract bridge. Lecturer throughout the U.S. *Rec*: Reading. *a*: 27 West 55th St, New York, U.S.A. *t*: Circle-7 2653.

KESSLER, David Francis. *b*: Pretoria, Sth Africa 1906. *e*: Leighton Park Sch, Clare Coll Camb. *m*: Mary Matilda Bray. *d*: 2. Publisher. *n.a*: Mang Dir Jewish Chron 1937. *Ctr*: Times, Sphere, B.B.C. *s.s*: Middle East Subjects. *w.s*: R.A. 1940—45. *a*: Bridge Farm, Stoke Hammond, Bletchley, Bucks. *T*: Soulbury 10.

KESTEVEN, William Henry, M.R.C.S., L.S.A. *Publ*: Work & Worry; Health & Hurry. *c.t*: St Bartholomew's Hosp Reports, Lancet, B.M J. *a*: Yorkletts Farm Hse, nr Faversham, Kent.

KETCHUM, Capt. Carleton J., M.C. *b*: Ottawa 1896. *e*: Pub & Mil Scs. War & Special Corr. *n.a*: Southam N/ps Canada 1920-21, Lon Daily Express '21-33, Pearson's Mag '33-34. War Service 2 y. Special Corr from most of countries of world. On '28 East African Tour of Prince of Wales & Duke of Gloucester. *Rec*: Riding, swimming, golf. *c*: R.A.C., Brit I.J., etc. *a*: Harewood Court, Hanover Sq, W.1. *t*: Mayfair 0441.

KETELBEY, D. M., F.R.Hist.S. *b*: Birmingham. *e*: King Edward's Sch Birmingham, Univ of B'ham, Somerville Coll Oxf. Writer & Lecturer in Hist. *Publ*: Readings from the Great Historian; A History of Modern Times; History Stories to Tell; Short History of Europe in the 19th Century. *s.s*: History. *c*: P.E.N., Forum, etc. *a*: The Soc of Authors, 84 Drayton Gdns, London, S.W.10.

KETTLEDRUM. See Standring, Willie.

KETTLEWELL, Rev. Robert, M.A. *b*: 1901. *e*: Oriel Coll Oxford. Clerk in Holy Orders. *Publ*: Cleveland Village, A Study of the Churchwarden's Accounts of Great Ayton in Cleveland 1734-1844. *a*: c/o Over-Seas Hse, Overseas League, St James, London.

KETTON-CREMER, Robert Wyndham, M.A., F.S.A. *b*: 1906. *e*: Harrow, Balliol Coll Oxf. *Publ*: Horace Walpole; Norfolk Portraits; Thomas Gray; The Early Life & Diaries of William Windham. *a*: Felbrigg Hall, Norwich.

KEVERNE, Richard. *b*: Norfolk 1882. *e*: Priv. *m*: Emma Foster. Author & Journalist. *Publ*: Carteret's Cure; William Cook, Antique Dealer; The Havering Plot; The Sanfield Scandal; The Fleet Hall Inheritance; The Man in the Red Hat; At the Blue Gates; Menace; Artifex Intervenes; He Laughed at Murder; Crook Stuff; More Crook Stuff; Crooks or Vagabonds; White Gas; Open Verdict; The Black Cripple; The Lady in No 4. *Ctr*: Various. *Rec*: Shooting, fishing. *c*: Savage. *a*: 6 Cumberland St, Woodbridge, Suffolk. *T*: Woodbridge 186.

KEY, Rev. Samuel Whittell, M.A. *b*: Bilborough, Yorks 1874. *e*: Westminster & St Catherine's Coll Camb. *m*: Katherine Hilda Browne. *s*: 2. *d*: 1. Clerk in Holy Orders, Hon C.F. *Publ*: The Material in support of the Spiritual; The Solace of the Soul; The Broken Fang; Yellow Death. *Ctr*: London, Pictorial & Pearson's Mags, etc. *Rec*: Painting & making art novelties. *a*: Fulford Vicarage, York. *T*: York 77261.

KEYNES, Geoffrey Langdon, M.D., F.R.C.S. *b*: Cambridge 1887. *e*: Rugby Sch, Pembroke Coll Camb. *m*: Margaret Elizabeth Darwin. *s*: 4. Emeritus Surg St Bart's Hosp. *Publ*: (Bibliographies) William Blake; Sir Thomas Browne; John Donne; William Harvey; etc; Blood Tranfusions; (Ed) Poetical Works of Rupert Brooke; Writings of William Blake & Sir Thomas Browne. *Ctr*: Various med journs. *s.s*: Bibliography. *w.s*: Air Vice Marshal R.A.F.V.R. 1939—45 (Sen Cons Surg to R.A.F.). *a*: 11 Arkwright Rd, Hampstead, London, N.W.3. *T*: Hampstead 3923.

KEYNES, John Maynard, C.B., M.A. *b*: 1883. *e*: Eton & King's Col Cam. Economist & Author. *Publ*: A Tract on Monetary Reform; The End of Laissez-Faire; Essays in Biography; etc. *a*: 46 Gordon Sq, W.C.1. *t*: Museum 3875.

KEYSERLING, Count Hermann, Ph.D. *b*: 1880. Author. *Publ*: The Travel Diary of a Philosopher; The Book of Marriage; The World in the Making; Europe; Creative Understanding; The Recovery of Truth; America Set Free; South American Meditations; Problems of Personal Life; La Révolution Mondiale et la Responsabilité de l'Esprit; Das Gefuege der Welt; Unsterblichkeit Philosophie als Kunst; Politik; Wirtschaft, Weisheit; Prolegomena für Naturphilosophie. Pres Sc of Wisdom, Darmstadt. *a*: Darmstadt, Prinz Christiansweg 4. *t*: 2042.

KEYTE, John Charles. *b*: Manchester. *e*: M/c G.S., M/c Univ, Oxford Univ. Writer. *n.a*: Asst Ed Statesman, Calcutta & Delhi '30—34. *Publ*: The Passing of the Dragon; A Daughter of Cathay; Minsan; The Emperor's Behest; Andrew Young; In China Now. *s.s*: Chinese history, philosophy & political changes. *Rec*: Travel. *c*: Authors' Club. *a*: Pathways, Tadworth, Surrey. *t*: Burgh Heath 1358.

KHABARDAR, Ardeshir Framji. *b*: Daman 1881. *m*: Piroja M. Patel. *s*: 2. *d*: 2. Poet & Author. *Publ*: (English Poems) The Silken Tassel; (Gujarati Devotional Songs, Patriotic Poems, etc) The Philosophy of Life; The Bird; Heaven's Abode; The Soul's Welfare; The Call of India; Songs of the Realm; etc. *Ctr*: Rev of Reviews, East & West, The Gujarati, Indian Rev, Jame-Jamshed & many Gujarati journs. *s.s*: Poetry, Eastern Astrology, Zoroastrian & Hindu Religions Literature. *a*: 788, Jame Jamshed Rd, Parsi Colony, Dadar, Bombay 14, India.

KHADDURI, Majid, B.A., Ph.D. *b*: Mosul 1909. *e*: American Univ of Beirut, Lebanon, Univ of Chicago. *m*: Majdia. *s*: 1. Professor, Iraq Delegate to the 14th P.E.N. Conf in Buenos Aires 1936, Adviser to Iraq Delegation at San Francisco Conference '45, Sec P.E.N. Club Baghdad. *Publ*: Law of War & Peace in Islam; The Government of Iraq; etc. *Ctr*: Amer Journ of Internat Law, Amer Political Sc Review, Al-Bilad (Baghdad). *s.s*: Near East Hist & Politics. *Rec*: Swimming. *a*: Higher Teachers' College, Baghdad, Iraq.

KHAN, Muhammad Fathulla. *b*: Secunderabad-Deccan 1906. *e*: Sir Rabindranath Tagore's Univ Bengal. Journalist. *n.a*: Chief Asst & Ed Hyderabad Bulletin, Ed Saqi. *Publ*: A Constitutional History of Hyderabad State; The Ships & Boats of the Ajanta Frescoes; The Cobbler & Other Short Stories; Musk Dust. *Ctr*: Illust Wkly of India (Bombay), Orient Illust Wkly (Calcutta), Hindu (Madras), Bombay Chronicle (Bombay), Sunday Statesman (Calcutta), Mysindia (Bangalore), Outlook (Bombay), Clarion (Hyderabad), Indian P.E.N. (Bombay) *s.s*: Art, Archæology, History. *Rec*: Hiking, chess. *a*: 956 King Koti Rd, Hyderabad-Deccan, India.

KHAN, Nawab Abdullah. *b*: Kasmandi 1886. *m*: Nawab Rafiqunnisa Begum. *s*: 5. *d*: 2. Lord of the towns of Kasmandi, Sirgamao, Chatari Khera. Journalist. *n.a*: Ed Orient Lucknow (Eng), Dir & Prop Urdu Daily Akhwat, Lucknow. Jt Ed Advocate of India (Bombay), Chief Ed Islamic Daily Mail (Bombay), Prop Daily Hamdam of Lucknow. *Publ*: The Usman & Mariam; The Nigaristan; The Fanoos Khiyal; etc. *c.t*: Lon Daily Mail, Westminster Gazette, Times of India (Bombay), The Orient (Lucknow), The I.D.T. (Lucknow), Hindustan Times (Delhi), etc. *s.s*: Muslim politics, rural uplift & agric problems. Press reporter on staffs of Prince of Wales, H.M. the Amir of Kabul, H.I.M. The King, Crown Prince of Germany, Duke of Connaught. Acknowledged to be the Premier Urdu writer in N.W. India. *Rec*: Shikar. *a*: Rafiq Manzil, Victoria Rd, Lucknow, U.P. India. *t*: 175.

KHAN OF TORU, The Nawabzada Muhammad Azim. *b*: Toru 1909. *e*: Magdalen Coll Sch & Queen's Coll Oxford. *m*: 2nd daughter of K. B. Sher. Dil. Khan. *s*: 1.

Who Was Who Among English and European Authors

Zamindar. *n.a*: Dir The Eastern Times Lahore. *Publ*: The Federation of India; India as I see It; The Frontier of India; India as a Continent. *Ctr*: Civil & Mil Gazette, Eastern Times, Pakistan Times. *s.s*: Political. *Rec*: Cricket, hockey, football, tennis, riding, shooting. *a*: N.W.F.P., India.

KHANNA, Balmukund, M.A., LL.B., F.R.S.A. *b*: Allahabad, India 1899. *e*: Govt Hgh Sch Cawnpore, Muir Cent Coll Allahabad. *m*: Shanti Tandon. *s*: 1. Former Lect in Econ Univ of Rangoon. *Ctr*: Rangoon Times, Rangoon Gazette, Rangoon Dly Mail, Pratap. *s.s*: Labour in Factories, Sugar Industry, Cotton Industry of India, Potteries in Burma. *Rec*: Hockey, tennis, swimming. *a*: Cotton Exchange, Karachi. *T*: 2355, Residence 7571.

KIBE, Madhav V., M.A., Wazir-ud-Bowlah, Rao Bahadur & Sardar. *b*: Indore 1877. *m*: Kamalabai Kibe. *s*: 2. *d*: 2. Deputy Prime Minister Holkar State Indore. *Publ*: The Indian States & the League of Nations; Currencies in Indian States; British Sea Customs Duty & Indian States. *Ctr*: Pioneer, Hindustan, Modern, Indian & Mysore Revs, Journ East Indian Assoc Lond. *Rec*: Reading & writing. *a*: Saraswati-Niketan, Indore, C.I.

KIDD, Beatrice Ethel. *b*: Bangor, Isycoed 1867. *e*: Brighton & Germany. *Publ*: The Cassowary (Novel "Mark Winterton"); Hadwen of Gloucester (with M. E. Richards). *Ctr*: Nineteenth Century & After, U.C.H. Mag & daily & weekly papers. *s.s*: Anti-vivisection. *Rec*: Reading. *a*: Hoe Cottage, Peaslake, Surrey. *T*: Abinger 187.

KIDD, Rev. Beresford James, D.D. *b*: Birm 1864. *e*: Chirst's Hosp & Keble Col Oxf. *m*: Agnes Walker. Warden Keble Col Oxf. Hon Canon of Ch. Ch. *Publ*: The Later Mediæval Doctrine of the Holy Eucharist ('98); History of the Church to A.D. 461 (3 vols); The Churches of Eastern Christendom; The Counter-Reformation (1933); etc. *a*: Keble Col, Oxford. *t*: 3157.

KIDD, Charles David ("Grid Leak" of the Daily Sketch & "David Hertzian"). *b*: M/C 1881. *e*: M/C G.S. & Col of Tech, & Owen's Col, Victoria. Radio Eng & Journalist. *n.a*: Radio Ed Daily Sketch. *c.t*: Allied N/ps Ltd, Northcliffe N/ps Ltd, Bristol Evening World, Technical Radio Mags, Music Trades Review. *s.s*: Wireless 1st regular corr on wireless to the daily press. Operates experimental radio trans station G5KI. Answered over 100,000 letters from wireless fans & manufrs seeking advice on radio problems. Commenced experiments in wireless 1902. *Rec*: Cricket, golf. *a*: 88 Grays Inn Rd, W.C.1. *t*: Museum 9841.

KIDD, FRANCIS SEYMOUR: see Kidd, Frank.

KIDD, FRANK (pen name): (Francis Seymour Kidd): consulting surgeon; b. Charlton, Kent, Eng., Mar., 1878; s. Joseph and Frances Octavia (Rouse) K.; educ. Winchester Coll.; Cambridge Univ.; London Hospital Medical Sch. DEGREES: M.B., M.A., MCh. (cantab.); m. Stella Cecelia Mary Williams, July 24, 1909. AUTHOR: Urinary Surgery, 1910; Common Diseases of the Male Uretha, 1917; Common Infections of the Female Uretha, 1924. Editor (with H. P. Winsbury White): British Jnl. of Urology. CLUBS: International Sportsmen's, Princes (London). ADDRESS: 55 Harley St., London, W. 1, Eng.

KIDD, Franklin. *b*: Weston-Super-Mare 1890. *e*: Tonbridge Sc & St John's Col Cam. *m*: Mary N. Owen. Scientific Research. *n.a*: Director Low Temperature Research Station Cam. *c.t*: Scientific Journs. *s.s*: Botany, food storage, transport, etc. Travelled extensively. *c*: Athenæum. *a*: Westwood, Woodlands Rd, Gt Shelford. *t*: 138.

KIDD, Percy Marmaduke, M.A., M.D.(Oxon), F.R.C.P. *b*: Greenwich 1851. *e*: Uppingham & Balliol Col Oxf. *m*: Gertrude Elinor Harrison. *s*: 3 (2 Dec). Physician. Consulting Physician to Lon Hosp & Brompton Hosp for Consumption & Chest Diseases. *c.t*: Med Press. *Rec*: Golf, fishing, music. *a*: 22 Montagu St, W.1.

KIDDY, Arthur William. *b*: Belper 1868. *e*: York Hse Southampton & Coll Sch Belper. *m*: Annie Clapham (dec'd). Financial Journalist. *n.a*: Asst City Ed Daily News 1891—99, City Ed Standard 1899—1914, City Ed Morning Post '15—37, Ed The Bankers Mag 1894—1945. Assoc City Ed Dly Telegraph 1937—46. *Ctr*: Spectator. *Rec*: Photography, billiards. *a*: Green Acre, Hadley Highstone, Barnet, Herts. *T*: Barnet 5412.

KIEK, Rev. Edward Sidney, M.A., B.D. *b*: London 1885. *e*: Central Foundation Sch, Wadham & Mansfield Colls Oxf. *m*: Winifred Jackson. *s*: 2. *d*: 1. Princ Parkin Coll Adelaide, Pres Cong Union of Aust & N.Z. 1946—48, V-Pres World Counc of Churches Aust '47— & Aust Social Soc '45—. *Publ*: The Modern Religious Situation; An Apostle in Australia; The Battle of Faith; Sin & Forgiveness; Fundamentalism & Modernism; The Christian Ethics of Sex; Group Psychology & the Contemporary Movement; The New Psychology & the Old Faith; The International Jungle & the Way Out. *Ctr*: The Advertiser, Australian Christian World. *s.s*: Church Hist, New Testament Criticism, Psychology, Political Science. *Rec*: Motoring. *a*: Parkin College, Kent Town, Adelaide, South Australia. *T*: Adelaide F 3443.

KIEK, Winifred, M.A., B.D. *b*: Manchester 1884. *e*: Urmston Higher Grade Sch & Victoria Univ Manch & Adelaide Univ. *m*: Rev. E. S. Kiek, M.A., B.D. *s*: 2. *d*: 1. *Publ*: Child Nature & Child Nurture. *s.s*: Religion & Education, Sociology, Industrial Relations. *Rec*: Handicrafts, pioneer of puppetry in Sth Australia *a*: Parkin College, Kent Town, Adelaide, South Australia. *T*: F 3443.

KIELY, Anthony Philip, M.J.I., F.R.Econ.S. *b*: Pinner, Mddx. *e*: Westminster Cathedral Choir Sch & Priv. *m*: Helen Jeger. *d*: 1. Journalist, Broadcaster & Critic. *n.a*: Music Corr West Indian Rev Jamaica. *Ctr*: Numerous econ & lit reviews at home & abroad, B.B.C. *s.s*: Foreign Commerce, Music, Switzerland, British Colonial Empire, etc. *Rec*: Recorder-playing, concert & drama, alpine climbing, etc. *c*: West Indian. *a*: 15 Fitzjohns Hse, Hampstead, London, N.W.3. *T*: Hampstead 2548.

KIELY, Benedict. *b*: Dromore, Co Tyrone 1919. *e*: Christian Bros Schs Omagh Co Tyrone. *m*: Maureen O'Connell. *d*: 2. Journalist. *n.a*: Feature-Writer & Film Critic The Standard 1941—46, now Leader Writer Irish Independent. *Publ*: Land Without Stars; Poor Scholar; Countries of Contention. *Ctr*: The Irish, Bookman & other mags in Ireland, Britain, U.S.A. & Australia. *Rec*: Walking, watching football. *a*: 61 Collymount Ave, Clontare, Dublin.

KIERNAN, Reginald Hugh, B.A.(Leeds), M.A. (Birm). *b*: Leeds 1900. *e*: Jesuit Col Leeds, Leeds & Birm Univs. *m*: Florence Watson. *s*: 1. Schoolmaster. *Publ*: Little Brother Goes Soldiering; Captain Albert Ball, V.C.; The First War in the Air. *c.t*: Birm Post, Yorks Evening Post. *s.s*: Hist, lit, aviation. War Service '17–18. *a*: Green Fields, Queen's Park Rd, Birm.

KIERNAN, Thomas, J., M.A., Ph.D. Director of Broadcasting. *Publ:* History of the Financial Administration of Ireland; A Study in National Finance; British War Finances. *c.t:* Economic Journal, etc. *s.s:* Economics. *a:* Broadcasting Studio, Dublin. *t:* 22381.

KILBOURNE, Fannie. *b:* Minneapolis, Minnesota 1890. *e:* Minneapolis Public Schs. *m:* (1) Charles Gatchell (dec'd), (2) Henry Allen Schubart. *s:* 1. *d:* 1. Writer. *Publ:* Dot & Will series; But Never be Denied. *Ctr:* Sat Ev Post, Ladies' Home Journ, Cosmopolitan, Amer Mag, Red Book, etc. *a:* 1 University Pl, New York 3, N.Y. *T:* Gramercy 7-6805.

KILGOUR, Rev. Robert, M.A., B.D., D.D. *b:* Glas 1867. *e:* Glas Univ. *m:* Agnes Elizabeth Horn. *s:* 2. Chaplain, Scots Guards. *n.a:* Ed Supt British & Foreign Bible Soc 1909–32. *Publ:* Gospel in Many Tongues; Gospel in Many Years; Nepali Dictionary. *c.t:* Times, Glasgow Herald, Scotsman, British Weekly, etc. *s.s:* Missions, languages. *Rec:* Golf. *c:* Overseas. *a:* 3 Stanway Gardens, Acton, W.3. *t:* Acorn 1224.

KILIE, Herbert William. *b:* Washford 1886. *m:* Evelyn Foy. Journalist, Mem Archæological & Record Socs, Mem N.U.J. *n.a:* West Som Free Press 1905—08, Ed Staff Kirby & Sons, Walsall Trade Paper Publishers 1908—11, Lond Rep '11—14, West Som Free Press '19—. *Ctr:* Som Archæological Soc Proc, Som Year Book, etc. *s.s:* West Country Folklore. *a:* Binnorie, Millbridge Rd, Minehead, Somerset. *T:* 315.

KILKELLY, Dr. E. R. Asst Sc M.O. & Certifying Officer. *a:* Education Offices, North St, Wolverhampton.

KILLANIN, 3rd Baron, Michael Morris (Michael Killanin), M.B.E., M.A., F.R.S.A.I., F.R.S.A. *b:* London 1914. *e:* Eton, Sorbonne (Paris), Magdalene Coll Camb. *m:* Mary Sheila Cathcart Dunlop. *s:* 1. *n.a:* Dly Express 1935—36, Dly Mail & Sun Dispatch '36—39, Dly Mail War Corr China-Japan War, 37—38. *Publ:* Sir Godfrey Knoller; Four Days; A Bunch of Blue Ribbons; Over & others (poems, priv). *Ctr:* English Rev, French & U.S. press, B.B.C. & leading English & Irish weekly & dly papers. *s.s:* Art & Archæology. *w.s:* Major K.R.R.C. 1939—45. *c:* Garrick, Beefsteak, Press, Univ (Dublin). *a:* Spiddal Hse, Co Galway, Ireland. *T:* Spiddal 3.

KILLE, Herbert William. *b:* Washford 1886. *e:* Priv. *m:* Evelyn Foy. Journalist. *n.a:* W. Som Free Press 1905–08, Ed Staff Messrs Kirby & Sons, Walsall, Trade Paper Publishers '08–11, Lon Rep '11–14, W. Som Free Press '19–. Hon Ed. The Somerset Countryman. *c.t:* Som Archæological Soc Proc, Som Year Book, Som Countryman, etc. *s.s:* West Country Folklore. Mem Som Archæological & Record Socs. War Service. Mem N.U.J. '11. Sec Minehead Chamber of Trade '20—. *a:* Binnorie Millbridge Rd, Minehead, Som. *t:* 315.

KILLER, Rev. Francis William. *c.t:* Nott'm Journ, Notts Guardian, C. of E. N/p, Symbol Mag, Derbys Times. *a:* St Cyprian's Vicarage, Marston Rd, Nott'm. *t:* Carlton 58502.

KILNER, Cyril. *b:* Wombwell 1910. *e:* Mexborough Sec Sc. Journalist. *n.a:* Barnsley Indep '27–. *c.t:* Daily Independent, Sheffield Daily Tel, Doncaster Gaz, Yorks Evening News, etc. *s.s:* Sport. *Rec:* Rugby, billiards. *a:* 2 Pickhills Av, Doncaster Rd, Goldthorpe, via Rotherham.

KILNER, Thomas Pomfret, C.B.E., M.A.(Oxon), F.R.C.S., M.B., Ch.B.(Manch), M.B.B.S.(Lond), M.R.C.S., L.R.C.P. *b:* Blackburn 1890. *e:* Queen Elizabeth's Gr Sch B'burn, Manch & Lond Univs. *m:* (1) Olive Mary Brown, (2) Florence Mary O'Neill. *s:* 3. *Publ:* Wounds of the Face & Jaws, Bailey's Surg of Mod Warfare; Plastic Surgery, Maingot's Post-Graduate Surgery; Plastic Surgery, Hare Lip & Cleft Palate; Oglivie's Recent Advances Surgery; Hare Lip & Cleft Palate, Parsons & Barling's Diseases of Infancy & Childhood. *s.s:* Plastic & Reconstructive Surgery. *Rec:* Golf, tennis, photography. *a:* White Lodge, Manor Rd, Old Headington, Oxford. *T:* 6878.

KILPATRICK, Florence Antoinette. *b:* Peterborough. *e:* Priv & France & Germany. *m:* James A. Kilpatrick. *d:* 2. *Publ:* Red Dust, Rift Valley; Getting George Married; Paradise Limited; Illicit; The Eldest Miss Grimmett; Six Marriages; Within Four Walls; Seven "Elizabeth" Books; (Plays) Wild-Cat Hetty & Virginia's Husband (also filmed); Murder without Tears; Uneasy Living; Short plays for B.B.C. *Rec:* Travel. *a:* 7 Lytton Grove, Putney Hill, London, S.W.15. *T:* Putney 3826.

KILPATRICK, James Alexander. *b:* Glasgow. *e:* Dunoon Acad & Glas Univ. *m:* Florence Antoinette Calvert. *d:* 2. Journalist. *n.a:* Former Staff Glas Ev News, Manch Dly Dispatch, Asst-Ed Yorks Post, Ed Ev Standard 1912—14, Chief Sub-Ed Lond Ev News '14—18. *Publ:* Literary Landmarks of Glasgow; Atkins at War; etc. *Ctr:* Various journs. *s.s:* Art & Statistics. *Rec:* Travel & playgoing. *a:* Croft Hse, Strawberry Hill, Middlx. *T:* Popesgrove 1657.

KILPATRICK, William Heard, M.A., Ph.D., Hon.LL.D., Hon.Litt.D. *b:* White Plains, Georgia 1871. *e:* Mercer, Johns Hopkins & Columb Univs. *m:* (1) Marie Guyton (dec'd), (2) Margaret M. Pinckney (dec'd), (3) Marion Y. Ostrander. *s:* 1. *d:* 1. Prof of Education (ret). *n.a:* Ed Frontiers of Democracy 1939—43, Ctr-Ed Social Frontier '37—39. *Publ:* Foundations of Method; Education for a Changing Civilization; Selfhood & Civilization; Group Work in a Democracy; Education & The Social Crisis; etc. *s.s:* Educational Problems, Philosophy of Social Aims & Methods. *Rec:* Golf. *a:* 106 Morningside Drive, New York City 27, N.Y., U.S.A. *T:* Monument 2-4800.

KILPIN, Ralph. *b:* Rondebosch, Sth Africa 1887. *e:* Diocesan Coll Rondebosch. *m:* Hilda Robinson. Clerk of the House of Assembly Union of Sth Africa. *Publ:* Parliamentary Procedure; The Romance of a Colonial Parliament; Parliamentary Government. *Ctr:* S.A. Law Journ, Cape Times, Cape Argus, South Africa. *s.s:* Parl Procedure. *Rec:* Tennis. *c:* Civil Service (Cape Town), Olympic (Rondebosch). *w.s:* 1916-17. *a:* Longfield, Kenilworth, nr Cape Town, Sth Africa. *T:* 73509.

KILROY, Peter Edmund. *b:* Dublin 1907. *e:* St Mary's, Athlone, Co Westmeath. Journalist. *n.a:* Westmeath Independent, Athlone '24, Asst Ed The Star Dublin '28, Sub Ed New Catholic Press, M/C '29, Irish Press Dublin, Reporting Staff '31. Now on Irish Press, Dublin. *a:* 4 Molesworth St, Dublin.

KIMBELL, Henry Julian. *b:* Boughton 1888. *e:* Northampton & County Sc & Abroad. Singing Teacher & Journalist. *n.a:* Music Critic Daily Telegraph, Express, News, Star & Musical Times. *s.s:* Reviews, music criticism & trans of French, German, Russian, and Italian songs. 1st Eng singer to take leading part in Russian. *Rec:* Golf, cricket. *a:* 34 Bloomsbury St, W.C.1, & Boughton, Northampton. *t:* Museum 2575.

KIMBER, William Joseph Teil, M.R.C.S., L.R.C.P., D.P.M. *b:* London 1888. *e:* Aldenham Sch. Med Dir & Supt Hill End Hosp & Clinic, St Albans. *Publ:*

Practical Psychology for Mental Nurses & Other Workers. *Ctr*: B.M.J., Journ of Mental Science, Mental Health, Volta Review (U.S.A.). *s.s*: Medical Psychology & Health, Child Guidance. *c*: Author's. *a*: Hill End, St Albans, Herts. *T*: St Albans 5555.

KIMCHE, John. *b*: St Gall, Switzerland 1909. *m*; Edith Christine Bromige. Man-Ed The Tribune. *n.a*: Act-Ed Tribune 1942—44, Military Corr Ev Standard '41—45, " Liberator "-Observer '42—46, Reuter's Spec Corr Spain, Austria, Persia & Middle East '44—46, Man-Ed Tribune '46. *s.s*: British Politics, Middle East, Military. *a*: The Tribune, 222 Strand, London, W.C.2. *T*: Central 2572; & 15 Glendale Drive, Wimbledon, London, S.W.19. *T*: Wimbledon 1237.

KIMHY, Dov. *b*: Yaslo, Poland 1889. *e*: Religious Coll Yaslo & Hebrew Teachers' Coll. *m*: Reina Leby. *s*: 1. Teacher, Editor, Writer. *n.a*: Haaritz, Moznayim, Moledet, Hadoar, Bizzaron, Daar Hayom, etc. *Publ*: (Hebrew Novels) Al Shiva Yammin ; On the Seven Seas ; Aimless Existence ; Yesterday ; Pontoons ; Book of Nostalgia ; Small Essays ; Between the Lines of the Bible ; Collected Short Stories. *Ctr*: Various Hebrew lit journs also general daily & weekly press. *s.s*: Literary Themes. *Rec*: Walking. *a*: 26 Ibn Ezra St, Rehaviah, Jerusalem, Palestine.

KIMMINS, Anthony Martin. *b*: Harrow-on-the-Hill 1901. *e*: Osborne & Dartmouth. *m*: Elizabeth Hodges. *s*: 1. *d*: 1. Dramatic Author, Scenarist, Film Director. *Publ*: (Plays) While Parents Sleep ; Night Club Queen ; Chase the Ace ; (Films) The Golden Cage ; White Ensign ; By-pass to Happiness ; A Friend like You ; Once in a New Moon ; His Majesty & Co ; Mr Faintheart ; Midshipman Easy ; Laburnum Grove ; Talk of The Devil ; Queen of Hearts ; The Show Goes On ; Keep Fit ; Trouble Brewing ; I See Ice ; It's in the Air ; Come on George ; Mine Own Executioner. *s.s*: Play & Scenario Writing, Film Producing & Directing. *c*: Garrick, Savage, R.A.C. *w.s*: R.N. 1917—23, Fleet Air Arm '23—32, Rejoined '39—46. *a*: 30 Jay Mews, London, S.W.7. *T*: Kensington 1568.

KIMMINS, C. W., M.A.(Cam), D.Sc(Lon). Ed The University Extension Library. *a*: c/o Ivor Nicholson & Watson Ltd, 44 Essex St, W.C.2.

KIMMINS, Grace T., C.B.E. *c.t*: Frequent contributor on subjects dealing with all aspects of work for cripples. *a*: Old Heritage, Chailey, Sussex.

KIN, Simon, M.D., M.R.C.P., D.P.H. *b*: Lon 1905. *e*: Sloane Sc, King's Col Hosp. Asst T.B. Officer, Stepney Boro' Counc. *c.t*: B.M.J. *s.s*: T.B. *Rec*: Tennis, gardening. *c*: Fell Soc M.O.H.'s, Mem T.B. Assoc, Mem B.M.A. *a*: 84 Park Av N., Willesden, N.W.10.

KINCAID, CHARLES AUGUSTUS: British Consul, Berne; formerly Judge of High Court, Bombay; b. Indore, India, Feb. 2, 1870; s. Gen. William and Martha (Shortt) K.; educ. Sherborne Sch.; Balliol Coll. (Oxford); m. Katherine Mary Kincaid, July 25, 1904. AUTHOR: Outlaws of Kathiawar, 1905; The Tale of a Tulsi Plant, 1907; Deccan Nursery Tales, 1914; Indian Heroes, 1915; Ishtur Phakde, 1917; A History of the Maratha People (with D. B. Parasnis), 3 vols., 1918, 1922, 1927; Tales from Indian Epics, 1919; Tales of Saints of Pandharpur, 1919; Shri Krisna and other Stories, 1922; Tales of King Vikrama, 1923; Tales of Old Sind, the Anchorite, 1923; Tales from Indian Drama, 1923; Folktales of Sind and Gujarat, 1924; Teachers of India, 1927; The Hindu Gods; Our Hindu Friends; Our Parsi Friends, 1930; The Land of Rangi Dulelp, 1931. General character of writing: historical and folklore. Has adapted old Sanskrit books to modern popular form, putting before the English and American public the life, beliefs and ideals of ancient and modern India. Relig. denom., Church of England. CLUBS: East India United Service (London). OFFICE: British Vice Consulate, Cherbourg, France. HOME: 15 Rue Victor Hugo, Cherbourg, France.

KINDERSLEY, Miss A. M., M.B.E. Dir of Observer. *a*: 12 Graham St, S.W.1.

KING, Alfred William Vernon. *b*: Sydney, Australia 1897. *e*: Sydney Hgh Sch. *m*: Agnes Marion. *s*: 1. Journalist, Jt Asst Man Ed Reuters. *na*: Sydney Morning Herald 1915—44, Lond Rep '28—31, Dep Chief Sub-Ed '32—36, Sports Ed '36—41, Lond Mang & Ed '41—44. *Ctr*: Aust, British & American newspapers & periodicals. *s.s*: Sports, Politics & all Aust & Sth Pacific subjects. *Rec*: Golf, gardening, motoring. *w.s*: Aust Artillery 1915—19. *a*: Tavistock Ct, London, W.C.1 ; & Reuters, London, E.C.4. *T*: Euston 3466 & Central 6060.

KING, Arthur Thomas, F.R.S.A., A.M.I.E.I. *b*: Luton 1904. *e*: Luton Tech Coll, Camden Training Coll. *m*: Joyce Susan Mantell. *s*: 3. Schoolmaster. *Publ*: Engineering Inspection Practice. *Ctr*: Practical Engineering. *s.s*: Eng Draughtsmanship, Inspection, Maths & Workshop Practice, Gen & Econ Hist. *Rec*: Motoring, nature study, archæology, etc. *a*: Brynhill, Maple Rd, Harpenden, Herts. *T*: 3897.

KING, Basil. Author. *Publ*: The Conquest of Fear; The Discovery of God; Faith & Success. *a*: c/o G. Allen & Unwin Ltd, 40 Museum St, W.C.1.

KING, Bolton. *b*: 1860. *e*: Eton & Balliol Col Oxf. *Publ*: History of Italian Unity; Italy of To-Day; Life of Mazzini; Schools of To-Day; Fascism in Italv. *a*: Redholme, Gt Missenden, Bucks.

KING, C. Daly, A.M., Ph.D. *b*: New York City 1895. *e*: Univs of Columbia & Yale. *m*: Mildred Georgina Sisson. *d*: 1. Author. *Publ*: Psychology of Consciousness ; Integrative Psychology ; Obelists at Sea ; Obelists en Route ; Obelists Fly High ; The Curious Mr. Tarrant ; Careless Corpse; Arrogant Alibi ; Bermuda Burial ; etc. *Ctr*: New English Weekly, Ellery Queens Mystery Mag, Yale Journ of Biology & Med, etc. *s.s*: Physiological Psychology, Mystery Novels, Egyptology. *Rec*: Tennis, chess, philately. *c*: Authors, New Haven Lawn, Yale, etc. *w.s*: A.E.F. 1918—19. *a*: 119 Woodland Ave, Summit, N.J., U.S.A. *T*: SU 6-2099.

KING, CECIL: marine and landscape painter; b. Gunnersbury, London, Eng., Aug., 1881; s. George Frederic and Alice Elizabeth (Bowker) K.; educ. Haileybury Coll., Eng.; art schools: Goldsmith's Inst., Westminster Art Sch. (London), Academie Julian, Steinlen's Class (Paris). DEGREES: R.I. (Royal Inst. of Painters in Water Color) 1924; R.B.A. (Royal Soc. of British Artists), 1910, resigned 1914; unmarried. Contributor to Yachting Monthly, Yachting World, Studio, Daily Mail, Manchester Guardian, Revue Maritime, Mariner's Mirror, Morning Post and others; light verse in Morning Post and others. General character of writing: travel and nautical subjects, especially maritime flags; occasionally light verse. Began life as engineering student; worked in black and white for Illustrated London News, occasionally for the Sphere and other publications, many years; served throughout Great War, Captain (retd.), Territorial Force; received territorial decoration (T.D.). Became official marine artist in the Baltic for the War Museum, London, 1919; designed historical ship models for Wembley Exhibition, 1924; councillor of Soc. for Nautical Research; mem. of Le Sabord, L'Association des Amis du Musée de Marine, Navy Records Soc., Anglo-Batavian Soc., the Societe des Beaux-Arts de la Mer; frequent exhibitor at the Salon, Royal Acad., and other exhibitions; an authority on flags; illustrator of several nautical books. CLUBS: Chelsea Arts (London); Royal Corinthian Yacht (Burham, Essex, Eng.). ADDRESS: Chelsea Arts Club, London, Eng.

KING, Charles Richard. *b*: Sutton-in-Ashfield, Notts 1897. *e*: Rossall & Balliol (Domus Exhibitioner). *m*: E. V. Blackburn. *s*: 1. Author. *n.a*: Ed Torchbearer 1924—25. *Publ*: Selected Poems; Cloud Messenger (trans of Sanskrit love-lyric); Mother of Claudine (trans from Colette). *Ctr*: Observer, Dublin Rev, Teachers' World, etc. *s.s*: Education, Poetry (the Eng Tradition), Classical Scholarship. *Rec*: Poetry. *c*: Old Rossallian. *a*: Underwood, Torquay.

KING, Clifford. *b*: Hay. *e*: Priv. *m*: Amoret Charlotte Ada Rastrick Hanson. *s*: 2. Author. *Publ*: The Royal Pearl & Other Poems (1894); Poems ('99); Poems (4th ed 1913); To the Ocean—To Greece (poem, '24); etc. *a*: Mozart Villa, Port Hall Rd, Brighton.

KING, David Wylie, M.J.I. *b*: Kilwinning, Ayrshire. *e*: Priv. *m*: Gertrude Parkinson. *s*: 2. *d*: 1. Financial Journalist. *n.a*: Mining Ed Financial Times 1920—, & The Diarist, Writer of Daily column "An Investor's Notebook". *c.t*: Stock Exchange Gazette, Hearst N/ps (U.S.A.). *s.s*: Mining. Trav Extensively, Gold & Tin Mines, Diamond Fields. *c*: Authors', Mining & Metallurgical. *a*: The Close, Draycott Ave, Kenton, Harrow, Mddx. *t*: Wordsworth 1810.

KING, Dorothy Amelia. *b*: Monton 1892. Author & Publisher's Reader. *Publ*: Stories of Scotland in Days of Old; Tales & Legends of Scotland; The Story of Don Quixote; Little Folk in Many Lands; Long, Long Ago; People of Bygone Days; Some Great Stories for Boys & Girls; etc. *Ctr*: Blackie's Children's Annuals, Collins's Children's Annuals. *s.s*: Hist & Legends. *Rec*: Reading, gardening. *a*: Girvan, 23 Newbury Rd, St Annes-on-Sea, Lancs.

KING, Dudley Robert, J.P. *b*: Lowestoft 1875. Married. *d*: 1. Secretary. *n.a*: Founder & 1st Ed Irish Printer. *c.t*: Printing Trade Journs. *a*: c/o Midland Master Printers' Alliance, 87–89 Edmund St, Birm. *t*: Birm Central 3931.

KING, E. G. N/p Chm & Mang Dir. *a*: 22 Henrietta St, W.C.2. *t*: Temple Bar 5771.

KING, E. H. F/L Journalist. *s.s*: Finance. *a*: 21 St Luke's Rd, Bayswater W.2.

KING, Edgar Samuel John, M.D., D.Sc., M.S., F.R.C.S., F.R.A.C.S. *b*: Mosgiel, New Zealand 1900. *e*: Melbourne Hgh Sch & Univ. *m*: Leonora Jane Shaw. *d*: 4. *n.a*: Mem Ed-Ctte Australian & New Zealand Journ of Surgery 1939—. *Publ*: Surgery of the Heart; Rarefying Diseases of Bone. *Ctr*: Brit Journ of Surg, Journ of Path & Bact, Surg, Gynæcol & Obstets, Amer Journ of Pathology. *s.s*: Pathology, Surgery. *Rec*: Photography. *a*: 231 Kooyong Rd, Toorak, Melbourne, Victoria, Australia. *T*: U.Y.5248.

KING, Sir Edwin James, K.C.B., C.M.G., C.G.St.J., A.D.C. to the King, J.P., D.L., M.A., F.R.S.A., R.H.S., R.N.S. *b*: London 1877. *e*: Cheltenham Coll & Chr Ch Oxf. *m*: (1) Mildred Ashby, (2) Genevieve Ghislaine Marthe Henry. *Publ*: The Knights Hospitallers in the Holy Land; The Official History of the British Order of the Hospital of St John of Jerusalem; History of the 7th Batt Middx Regt; The Rule Statutes & Customs of the Hospitallers; The Seals of the Order of St John of Jerusalem; Records of the Family of King. *Ctr*: United Service Mag, Times, etc. *s.s*: Mil History & History of the Mil Religious Orders. *Rec*: Numismatics, hist & biog. *w.s*: Comm 7th Batt Middx Regt 1907—19, Hon Col '25, Sth African 1900, '14—18, dispatches 3 times, '39—45 Zone Comm H.G. *c*: Athenæum, Junior Army & Navy. *a*: The Old Hse, East Finchley, London, N.2. *T*: Tudor 1336.

KING, Frank, M.B., Ch.B. *b*: Halifax 1892. *e*: Rishworth & Bradford Schs & Leeds Univ. *m*: Annie Naylor. *d*: 1. *Publ*: Terror at Staups House; The Ghoul; Greenface; The Owl; The Case of the Painted Girl; Green Gold; Mr. Balkram's Band; The House of Sleep; Night at Krumlin Castle; The Smiling Mask; Dictator of Death; The Midnight Sleep; Candidates for Murder; Enter The Dormouse; The Dormouse—Undertaker; The Dormouse has Nine Lives; The Dormouse—Peacemaker; Dough for the Dormouse; This Doll is Dangerous; They Vanish at Night; What Price Doubloons?; Crooks' Cross; Gestapo Dormouse; Sinister Light; Castastrophe Club; Operation Halter; Molly on the Spot; Cagliostro; The Last of the Sorcerers. *Ctr*: Most Brit & Amer mags & newsps. *s.s*: Thrillers, Detective Stories & Crime. *Rec*: Work. *a*: 3 Rhodes St, Halifax, Yorks. *T*: 2559.

KING, Frank Eustace, B.Sc. *b*: Thornton Heath 1877. *e*: Dulwich Col, Univ Col. Analyst. *Publ*: Wragg's Friend. War Service. *Rec*: Boys welfare, gardening. *a*: 3 Polworth Rd, Streatham, S.W.

KING, Frank Haviland, M.J.I. *n.a*: Ed Assoc Press of America. *a*: c/o Assoc Press of America, 9 Carmelite St, E.C.4. *t*: Central 6681.

KING, Frederick Charles. *b*: Little Ribston, Yorkshire 1892. Gardener. *Publ*: Gardening with Compost; The Compost Gardener; Is Digging Necessary. *Ctr*: Gardeners' Chron, Soil & Health, The Field, etc. *s.s*: Organic Gardening, Soil Management. *a*: The Gardens, Levens Hall, Kendal, Westmorland. *T*: Sedgwick 101.

KING, George J. S. Contributor to London, prov & overseas dailies, weeklies, mags & annuals on historical & statistical subjects. *a*: Beverley, Ring Rd, North Lancing, Sussex. *T*: Lancing 2336.

KING, Rt. Rev. George Lanchester. *b*: Gt Barton 1860. *e*: Bury St Edmund's G.S. & Clare Col Cam. *m*: Louisa Beatrice Bewley. Asst Bishop in Diocese of Rochester. *Publ*: God & Ourselves; What is the Church? Consecrated Bishop in Madagascar 1899; res 1919. Canon of Rochester '24. Asst Bishop '28. *a*: Prebendal Hse, Rochester. *t*: Chatham 2973.

KING, Hugh Charles. Sec Inc Assoc of Prep Scs. *c.t*: Various. *a*: Byeways, Beaconsfield, Bucks. *t*: 79.

KING, James Grieve, O.B.E., D.Sc., Ph.D., A.R.T.C., F.R.I.C., M.I.GasE. *b*: Alva, Stirlingshire 1891. *e*: Bellahouston Acad, Roy Tech Coll Glas. *m*: Marion Cameron. Dir of The Gas Research Board. *Publ*: Fuel (with J. S. Brame). *Ctr*: The Science of Petroleum, Recent Advances in Analytical Chemistry, Journ of Inst of Fuel, Journ Soc of Chem Industry, Publs of H.M. Stationery Office on Fuel, etc. *s.s*: Scientific Research—Fuel Technology, etc. *Rec*: Golf, swimming. *a*: 21 The Lawns, Blackheath, London, S.E.5. *T*: Lee Green 3001.

KING, James Steel. *b*: Glas 1880. *e*: Allan Glen's Sc & Roy Tech Col Glas. *m*: Eveline Gray. *s*: 1. *n.a*: Assoc with father in management of Glas Advertiser & Property Circular 1896–'31 (Glas Evening

News '31–). *Publ*: The Property Index (ref book, 1884). *a*: Glas Evening News, 67 Hope St, Glas. *t*: Central 9880.

KING, JOHN BARAGWANATH: artist; *b*. Hayle, Cornwall, Eng., Jan., 1864; *s*. William and Maria B. K.; *educ*. private schools; *m*. Helen Goldsithney, 1900. AUTHOR: Arthur and others in Cornwall; Musketry; The Laughing Cornishman; Legends and Quaint Events in Verse; short stories. Contributor to London Cornish Year Book, 1928. General character of writing: literary with art intent. Water colour painter. Patrons: His Late Majesty King Edward, Her Late Majesty Queen Alexandria and others of prominence. Exhibitor: Solon, Paris, all the prominent water colour societies' exhibitions in London and Provinces. Founder of the St. Austell Golf Club, 1911; pres., St. Austell Old Cornwall Soc., 1929; Elected a Bard of the Cornish Gorsedd, 1930. Relig. denom., Church of England. CLUBS: St. Austell Golf Club (life mem. and hon. sec.). HOME: Chyverton, St. Austell, Cornwall, Eng.

KING, John Charles. Westminster Police Court. *s.s*: Crime. *a*: 3f Kingwood Rd, Fulham, S.W.6.

KING, John Edward, D.Litt. *Publ*: (Jt with C. Cookson) The Principles of Sound & Inflexion as Illustrated in the Greek and Latin Languages 1888; Loeb series Cicero, Tusculan Disputations 1927; Bede Opera Historica; etc. *a*: Chilton Polden, Som.

KING, Joseph, M.A. *b*: L'pool 1860. *e*: Uppingham Sc & Oxf Univ. *m*: Helena Martins. Barrister-at-Law. M.P. N. Som 1910–18. *Publ*: The School Manager's Guide ('02); The Russian Revolution ('18); The Ruhr ('24); The German Revolution ('33); etc. *c.t*: Andover Review (Boston, U.S.A.). *s.s*: Electoral reform, foreign affairs. *Rec*: Gardening, forestry. *c*: Reform. *a*: Browholm, Tilford, Surrey. *t*: Elstead 50.

KING, Richard. *b*: Epperstone Notts 1879. *e*: Oakham Rutland. Author & Journalist. *n.a*: Lit Reviewer to the Tatler. *Publ*: With Silent Friends (1917); Passion & Pot Pourri; New Silent Friends; Folded Hands; At the Close of Day; One Quiet Evening ('27); Souls Dark Cottage ('30); etc. *c.t*: Tatler. *s.s*: Book reviews & essays. *Rec*: Motoring. *a*: Cliff Rd, Roedean, Brighton, Sx.

KING, W. J. *a*: 7 John St, Bedford Row, W.C.1.

KING, W. R. *n.a*: Ed Gas Journ, & Gas Salesman 1934. *a*: 11 Bolt Ct, Fleet St, E.C.4.

KING, Walter Gawen, C.I.E., M.B., C.M., D.P.H. *n.a*: Sectional Ed Sanitation Number, Trop Diseases Bulletin (Bureau of Hyg & Trop Dis) apptd 1914, resigned '20. *Publ*: Simple Sanitary Rules During Cholera Epidemics; The Plague Inspector; Vaccination in the Tropics. *c.t*: Indian Engineering (Calcutta), Madras Mail (Madras), Journ of Roy Inst of Public Health, Journ of East India Assoc, etc. *a*: 55 Sevington Rd, Hendon, N.W.4. *t*: 1276.

KING, Wilfred Thomas Cousins, B.Comm., Ph.D. *b*: Hornsey 1906. *m*: Nora Margaret Coupe. *s*: 1. *d*: 2. Financial & Econ Journalist & Lect. *n.a*: Money Market Ed & Leader Writer Financial News 1929—33, City Staff Dly Telegraph '33—35, Dep-Ed Financial News '35—40, Asst-Ed Economist '45—, Jt-Ed Banker '46—. *Publ*: History of the London Discount Market; The Stock Exchange. *s.s*: Public Finance, Money Market, Banking. *c*: Reform. *a*: Worthing, Sussex.

KING, WILLIAM JOSEPH HARDING: explorer; *b*. Churchill Court, Kidderminster, Eng., April, 1869; *s*. William Hartley and Louisa (Harding) K.; *educ*. Jesus Coll. (Cambridge), Middle Temple, (London). DEGREE: B.A. (Cambridge); *m*. Dorothy Marion Barnes, 1919. AUTHOR: A Search for the Masked Tawareks, 1903; Mysteries of the Lybian Desert, 1925. Contributor to Royal Geographical Journ. and other scientific publcns. General character of writing: scientific, geographical, sand dunes, and ethnological. Made expeditions into Western Sahara (1900, 1908), collecting Nat. Hist. Specimens and to study sand dunes and ethnology of district; From 1909–1912 made exploratory journeys into central Libyan Desert, then unknown territory. Discovered great central plateau and Gilf Kebir Mts., made first surveyed map of this territory and one of whole Libyan Desert, from information furnished by natives. Made archaeological expedition, 1913, with late Oric Bates (Harvard Univ.), to Marmarica; awarded Gill Memorial, 1919, by Royal Geog. Soc. CLUB: Royal Societies (London). HOME: Halsdon House, near Honiton, Devon., England.

KING, Rt. Hon. William Lyon Mackenzie, P.C., C.M.G., M.P., M.A., LL.B., Ph.D., Hon.D.C.L., Hon.F.R.I.B.A. *b*: Berlin (Kitchener), Ontario 1874. *e*: Univs of Toronto, Chicago & Harvard. Prime Minister of Canada. *n.a*: Ed-Staff Toronto Globe 1896—97. *Publ*: Industry & Humanity; The Secret of Heroism; The Message of the Carillon & Other Addresses; Canada at Britain's Side; Canada & the Fight for Freedom. *c*: Rideau & Country (Ottawa), Ontario (Toronto) & Harvard (N.Y.). *a*: Laurier Hse, Ottawa, Canada.

KING, William Wilfred, M.B., ChB., F.R.C.S., Ed F.C.O.G. *b*: Bath 1881. *e*: Stonyhurst Col Blackburn. *m*: Gertrude Mabel Goodridge. *s*: 2. *d*: 2. Gynæcological Surg. *n.a*: Mem of Abstract Staff, Journ of Obstetrics & Gynæcology of the Brit Emp 1912–; *c.t*: Lancet, Clinical Journ, Journ of Obstetrics & Gynæcology of the Brit Emp, etc. War Service R.A.M.C. '15–19. Hse Surg, Sheffield Roy Hosp 1906. Res Obstet Officer, Roy Infirmary, Bristol '07. Sen Res M.O. Jessop Hosp for Women, Sheffield '08–11 & Registrar '14–18. Surg in Charge of Venereal Clinic '17–20. Clinical Pathologist Roy Inf Sheffield '11–20. *Rec*: Fishing. Exam, Cent Midwives Bd. Obstet Surg Nether Edge Hosp, Sheffield. *a*: 432 Glossop Rd, Sheffield 10. *t*: 62726.

KING, Winifride Botterell. *e*: Private. *m*: A. Highmore King. Barrister. *c.t*: Butterworth's Statutes of England, & Author Playwright & Composer. *s.s*: Copyright. *a*: 3 Harcourt Buildings, Temple, E.C.4.

KING-HALL, Ella. Literary Agent. Head of Ella King-Hall. *a*: 16 Panton St, S.W.1. *t*: Whitehall 2903.

KING-HALL, Magdalen (Magdalen Perceval Maxwell). *b*: London. *e*: Private, St Leonards Sch, St Andrews. *m*: Patrick Perceval Maxwell. *s*: 2. *d*: 1. *Publ*: The Diary of a Young Lady of Fashion; I Think I Remember; Gay Crusader; Jehan of the Ready Fists; Maid of Honour; Lady Sarah; Sturdy Rogue; Life & Death of the Wicked Lady Skelton; How Small a Part of Time; Lord Edward; etc. *a*: Inch Lodge, Downpatrick, Co Down, Ireland. *T*: Downpatrick 47.

KING-HALL, Lady, (Olga). *b*: Windsor, Berks. *e*: Italy. *m*: Admiral Sir George King-Hall, K.C.B. *s*: 1. *d*: 2. *Publ*: Her Italian Husband; An Engagement; What the Blounts Did. *Rec*: Reading, writing. *a*: 3 Tite St. Chelsea. *t*: Flaxman 7361.

KING-HALL, Stephen. *b*: 1893. *e*: Lausanne, Osborne & Dartmouth. *m*: Kathleen Spencer. *d*: 3. Cov Dir. *Publ*: A Naval Lieutenant 1914—18; The

China of To-day; Bunga Bunga; Three Plays & a Plaything; Here & There; The Economist in the Witness Box (with N. F. Hall); Total Victory; Britain's Third Chance; Our Own Times. Plays (With Ian Hay): The Middle Watch; The Midshipmaid; Off the Record. *Ctr*: Fortnightly, Ev Standard, Dly Dispatch, etc. *s.s*: Foreign Affairs, Econ, Current Events, Social Problems. *c*: Athenæum, Un Services. *w.s*: 1914—29 R.N. (ret). *a*: Hartfield Hse, Headley, Borden, Hants *T*: Headley Down 2140.

KING-PAGE, Douglas, M.J.I. *b*: Hackney 1884. *e*: Priv. *m*: Florence Mary Strong. Journalist. *n.a*: Corr to Dly Telegraph 1922, Journ of Commerce '23, The Policy Holder '18, Shipbuilding & Shipping Record '15, Glasgow Herald '22 etc. *Publ*: Ed 5th edit Marine Ins by Wm Gow; The Institute Warranties. *Ctr*: Dly Telegraph, Journ of Commerce, Lloyd's List, Financial Times, Manch Guardian, Goteborgs Handelstidning, etc. *s.s*: Marine Insurance Lloyd's. *Rec*: Golf, swimming. *c*: Press, Blackheath Harriers, Lloyd's Swimming, etc. *a*: 68 Maberley Rd, Upper Norwood. *T*: Livingstone 2485; & 84 Leadenhall St, London. E.C.4. *T*: Avenue 3868.

KINGDON, Albert Sidney. *b*: Exeter 1905. *m*: Dorothy Ena Cotton. Journalist. Dis Rep Western Morning News. *c.t*: Western Weekly News, Field, etc. *s.s*: Yachting, rugby, golf. With Devon & Exeter Daily Gazette 1920-32. Received present appointment on amalgamation. *a*: Exon, Old Woods Hill, Torquay. *t*: 7611.

KINGDON, Rev. Henry Paul, M.A. *b*: London 1907. *e*: Winchester Coll & Corpus Christi Coll Oxf, Tübingen Univ. *m*: Joan Locke Mellanby. Clerk in Holy Orders. *n.a*: Ed The Way 1939—42, Ed The Oxford Mag '41—45. *Ctr*: Hibbert Journ, Modern Churchman, Theology, The Student Movement, etc. *s.s*: Church & State, Religion in Germany & Ancient Greece, New Testament. *w.s*: Home Guard 1940—45. *Rec*: Tennis, music. *a*: Religious Affairs Branch, Z.E.C.O., 62 H.Q. C.C.G.(B.E.), Bunde, B.A.O.R.

KINGDON WARD, Frank. *b*: M/C 1885. *e*: St Paul's Sc, Christ's Col Cam. *m*: Florinda Norman Thompson. *d*: 2. Explorer, Botanist, Writer. *Publ*: The Loom of the East; Plant Hunting on the Edge of the World; The Riddle of the Tsangpo Gorges; From China to Hkamti Long; etc. *c.t*: Gardener's Chron, Country Life, etc. *s.s*: Exploration. W.S. Indian Army 1914-19. Founders Medal, Roy Geog Soc '30; V.M.H. '32. *Rec*: Gardening. *c*: Sesame. *a*: Hatton Gore, Harlington, Middx. *t*: Hayes 612.

KINGSFORD, Percy Edward, M.J.I., N.U.J. *b*: Dover 1862. *e*: Dover Col. Journalist. *n.a*: Daily Western Times, Exeter, Northern Whig, etc. *Publ*: The Oxford Shorthand in Six Lessons ('87); The Oxford Shorthand International Phonetic Alphabet ('89) with Adaptation of Oxford Shorthand to Welsh; City Shorthand ('90); The Oxford Shorthand International Phonography (publ at frequent intervals, last ed 29th '33); Examination Certainties, embodying results of 50,000 & 100,000 word analyses as to the relative frequency of words; Antiquated Spelling; The Oxford Shorthand Typical Collection; etc. *c.t*: Numerous dailies, weeklies, monthlies. *s.s*: Shorthand. Inventor of " A Machine which Tells if you Hesitate," " The Oxford Shorthand Motor Rim-Tricer," timing movements in writing to within the 600th of a second, " The Little Sawmill," " The Mouse-Trap " (gravitational machine for same purpose), & many others. Life Mem Press Fund 1883–. Founded the Oxford Shorthand Soc, Nat Shorthand Un. Founded & always edited The Oxf Shorthand Chronicle, & The Oxonian. *Rec*: Mechanics, music. *a*: 423 Edgware Rd, W.2. *t*: Pad 5439.

KINGSLAND, Rev. John Paddon. *b*: Devizes 1856. *e*: Bradford G.S., Victoria Univ & Lancs Independent Col. *m*: Helen Priscilla Perkins. *s*: 1.

d: 1. Cong Min. *Publ*: Man & His Environment; The Man Called Jesus; Visions of God; Poems. *c.t*: Holborn Review. *s.s*: Theol. *Rec*: Painting, chess, billiards. Mem Devizes Bd of Guardians. *a*: The Waverley, Felixstowe.

KINGSLAND, William, M.I.E.E. *b*: Devizes, Wilts 1855. *e*: High Sc, Bradford, Yorks. *m*: Phoebe Edmonstone Chambers. Electrical Engineer (ret). *Publ*: Scientific Idealism; The Mystic Quest; Our Infinite Life; The Esoteric Basis of Christianity; Rational Mysticism; An Anthology of Mysticism; The Physics of the Secret Doctrine; The Art of Life; The Real H. P. Blavatsky; Christos, the Religion of the Future; The Great Pyramid in Fact and in Theory. *c.t*: Chambers's Journ, The London Forum, The Aryan Path. *s.s*: Science, philosophy, religion, mysticism. War Service. *Rec*: Tennis, motoring. *a*: Claremont, 43 Strand, Ryde. I.W.

KINGSLEY, Anna. See Hanshew, Hazel Phillips.

KINGSMILL, Hugh. *b*: Lon 1889. *e*: Harrow, New Col Oxf. *m*: Dorothy Vernon. *s*: 1. *d*: 2. Writer. *n.a*: Ed Isis 1911. *Publ*: The Will To Love; Matthew Arnold; The Return of William Shakespeare; Frank Harris; The Table of Truth; Samuel Johnson; etc. *c.t*: Eng Review, Bookman, Observer, Morning Post. *c*: Authors'. *a*: The Black Mill Ore, Hastings. *t*: 1659.

KINGSTON, Charles. See O'Mahony, Charles Kingston.

KINGSTON, Vera Christabel. *b*: St Albans 1891. *e*: St Helens, Blackheath & Geneva. Journalist. *Publ*: An Army With Banners. *c.t*: Harmsworth Encyclopedias. *Rec*: Walking, reading. *a*: Lindens, Upper Marlboro' Rd, St Albans, Herts. *t*: 69.

KINGSWOOD, Rev. George Hadlett. *Publ*: Boys of Hendersley. *c.t*: Religious Periodicals, Kingsbridge Observer. *a*: Pendeen, Salcombe, S. Devon. *t*: 140.

KINGZETT, Charles Thomas, F.I.C., F.C.S. *b*: Oxf 1852. *e*: Oxf. *m*: Adeline Ann Frogratt & Mina Lilian Briggs. *s*: 2. *d*: 2 (1 dec). Prof Scientific Chemist & Chemical Manufacturer (ret). *Publ*: The History Products & Processes of the Alkali Trade ('77); Nature's Hygiene & Sanitary Chemistry (5 edns); Chemistry for Beginners & Schools; Chemical Ency: a digest of chemistry & its industrial applications (5 edns 1919, '22, '24, '28 & '32); etc. *c.t*: Chemical News, Soc of Arts Journ, Chemical Age, Sanitary Record, Analysis, Lancet, Industrial Chemist, Iron, Quart Journ of Science, etc. Discovery of the Sanitas Products & their Manufacture resulting from personal Chemical investigations & Original Founders of the Inst of Chemistry of Gt Brit & Ire. *Rec*: Golf. *c*: Mem & Past Pres of Soc of Public Analysts, Mem of Soc of Chemical Industry, Mem of Constitutional. *a*: Newlands, Weybridge. *t*: 202.

KINLOCH, JOHN PARLANE: Chief Medical Officer, Department of Health for Scotland. Contributor of numerous articles in scientific journals. OFFICE: 121a Princes Street, Edinburgh. HOME: 15 Montpelier Park, Edinburgh, Scotland.

KINLOCH, Tom Fleming. *b*: Cardiff 1874. *e*: Priv, Glas Univ, Heidelberg, Berlin. Presbyterian Minister (ret). *Publ*: Pioneers of Religious Education; Six

English Economists; Catastrophe; The Story of Christianity; Village Sermons by a Novelist, etc. *s.s*: Relig Educ, Hymnology, English Religion in the XVIIth Century. *c*: Authors. *a*: 26 Coalway Rd, Wolverhampton. *T*: Penn 36747.

KINNAIRD, EMILY (Hon.): author; b. London, Eng., Oct. 20, 1855; d. Arthur K. (10th Lord Kinnaird) and Mary Jane Hoare (Fitzgerald) K.; educ. privately, at home; unmarried. AUTHOR: Reminiscences. Contributor to Zenana, Blue Triangle Gazette, and occasionally to newspapers. General character of writing: sociological, religious. Pioneer of organizations having to do with promoting welfare of workingmen and women, especially the latter, throughout the British Empire. Mem. Labor Party; earliest mem. first World's Y.M.C.A. committee and Vice-Pres; First Hon. Sec. London Y.W.C.A.; assisted in organization of Y. W. C. A. in India, Burma and Ceylon; prompter of federation of British, Canadian and U. S. A. Y.W.C.A.'s; finance sec. Nat. Y.W.C.A. of Gt. Britain; mem. World's Y.W.C.A. Executive Com.; vice-pres. Scottish Zenana Bible and Med. Mission, in interest of which she has spent some years in India, forming Y.W.C.A. Indian Branches, staying in many Indian homes and conducting religious meetings for the young. Relig. denom., Presbyterian. OFFICE: Y.W.C.A. of Great Britain, 17 Clifford St., London, W. 1. HOME: 4 Duke St., Manchester Square, London, Eng.

KINNEAR, John, O.B.E., T.D., M.D., M.R.C.P.E., D.L. *b*: Dundee 1896. *e*: Dundee Hgh Sch & St Andrew's Univ. *m*: Doris Winifred Beveridge. *s*: 1. *d*: 1. Phys for Diseases of the Skin Dundee Roy Infirmary & Lecturer Univ of St Andrews. *Publ*: Revision of Gardiner's Handbook of Skin Diseases. *Ctr*: Brit Journ of Dermatology, Excerpta Medica & other Med Publs. *s.s*: Dermatology. *Rec*: Motoring. *w.s*: 1917—20 R.A.M.C. (Capt) & A.D.M.S. Italy & M. East 1939—46. *a*: 39 Rosenangle, Dundee, Angus. *T*: 3879.

KINNEY, MAUD KINOOLE: musician, writer; b. Copenhagen, Denmark, Sept. 5, 1881; d. Henry Augustus and Selma S. (Schandorff) K.; educ. privately by tutors, Royal Conserv., Dresden, Germany; unmarried. AUTHOR: Between Fate and Akuas, 1925. Contributor to Paradise of the Pacific (Honolulu), various Copenhagen papers. General character of writing: fiction; press corres. HOMES: Copenhagen, and (Summer) Pension Guldborg, Molte, Denmark.

KINROSS, 3rd. Baron of Glasclune, John Patrick Douglas Balfour, B.A. (See **BALFOUR, Patrick**.) *b*: Edinburgh 1904. *e*: Winchester & Balliol Coll Oxf. Author & Journalist, Dir Publicity Section, British Embassy Cairo 1944—47. *n.a*: Ed-Staff Glasgow Herald 1926—27, Sun Dispatch '27—29, Dly Sketch '29—31, Ev Standard '33—40. *Ctr*: Various. *s.s*: Middle East. *c*: St James's. *w.s*: 1940—44 R.A.F.V.R., M.E.F. (Dispatches). *a*: St James's Club, Piccadilly, London, W.1.

KINSMAN, Delos Oscar, A.M., B.L., Ph.D. *b*: Fayette, Wisconsin 1868. *e*: Platteville Normal Coll, Univ of Wisconsin. *m*: (1) Nellie Williams, (2) Anna Barnard. *d*: 2. Teacher, Emeritus Prof. *Publ*: Economics or the Science of Business; Our Economic World; Essentials of Civics; Man in the Making. *s.s*: Taxation. *a*: 9100 Old Georgetown Rd, Bethesda, Maryland. *T*: Oliver 1015.

KINSOLVING, Sally Bruce. *b*: Richmond, Virginia 1876. *e*: Priv. *m*: Rev Arthur B. Kinsolving. *s*: 2. *d*: 5. *Publ*: Many Waters; Grey Heather; David & Bathsheba; Depths & Shallows. *Ctr*: Commonweal, Contemp Poetry, Ireland-Amer Rev, North Amer Rev, Personalist, Reviewer, etc. *s.s*: Religion, Philosophy, Poetry, Romance Languages, Painting, Music. *Rec*: Music. *a*: 3003 North Charles St, Baltimore 18, Maryland. *T*: Tuxedo 3014.

KINVER, RICHARD (pen name): see **Vogel, Harry Benjamin.**

KIPLING, Rudyard, HonD.Litt(Oxon, Cantab, Durham), LL.D. (McGill, Edinburgh, St Andrews, Paris, Strasbourg, Athens). *b*: 1865. *e*: Westward Ho! *m*: Caroline Starr Balestier. *d*: 1. A'uthor & Poet. *n.a*: Asst Ed Civil & Military Gazette Lahore. *Publ*: Poems—Departmental Ditties; Five Nations; Seven Seas; Barrack Room Ballads; etc. Novels & Stories—Plain Tales from the Hills; Soldiers Three; Life's Handicap; The Light that Failed; Many Inventions; The Jungle Book; The Second Jungle Book; Captains Courageous; The Day's Work; A Fleet in Being; Stalky & Co; Just So Stories; Traffics & Discoveries; Puck of Pook's Hill; Rewards & Fairies; Fringes of the Fleet; Sea Warfare; A Diversity of Creatures; From Sea to Sea; The Years Between; Letters of Travel; Land & Sea Tales for Scouts & Guides; Debits & Credits; A Book of Words; Limits & Renewals; Souvenirs of France; etc. Play—The Harbour Watch; History—A School History of England (with C. R. L. Fletcher); The Irish Guards in the War. Lord Rector St Andrews 1923. Gold Medal Roy Soc of Lit '26. Fell Magdalene Col Cam. Nobel Prize (lit) '07. *a*: Bateman's, Burwash, Sussex.

KIPPING, Frederic Stanley, PhD.(Munich), D.Sc (Lon), F.I.C., F.R.S. *b*: M/C 1863. *e*: M/C G.S., Lycée de Caen, Owen's Col M/C, & Munich Univ. *m*: Lily Holland. *s*: 2. *d*: 2. Prof of Chem. *Publ*: Perkin & Kipping's Organic Chemistry; Kipping & Perkin Inorganic Chemistry. *c.t*: Journ of Chem Soc. *s.s*: Chem of organic silicon compounds. Longstaff Medal awarded by Chem Soc & Davy Medal by R.S. *Rec*: Golf, billiards. *a*: 15 Pelham Cres, Nott'm, & Univ Col, Univ Pk, Nott'm. *t*: 3858.

KIRCHER, Dr. Rudolf. *b*: Karlsruhe, I.B. 1885. *e*: Heidel, Berlin, Freiburg, I.B. Univs. *m*: Dora Urspruch. *d*: 3. Journalist. *n.a*: Ed Frankfurter Zeitung 1920—30, Lon Corr & Now Ed-in-Chief. *Publ*: Englaender; Fair Play; Wie's die Englaender machen; Im Land der Widersprüche. *Rec*: Sport, travel. *a*: Berlin In den Zelten F. *t*: Flora 0235.

KIRCHNER, Bernard Joseph, C.B.E. *b*: London 1894. *e*: Imperial Coll of Science Lond. *m*: Vivienne Mary Ffrench. *d*: 2. Journalist & Newspaper Ed. *n.a*: Statesman Calcutta 1927, Mang The Englishman Calcutta 1928—30, Mang Ed The Statesman Calcutta '32, Chief Press Adv Govt of India '41—44. *Rec*: Golf, tennis. *w.s*: 1914—19. *a*: c/o The Statesman Ltd, Calcutta.

KIRK, A. Lindsay. Journalist. *a*: 11 Beaumont Rd, W.14.

KIRK, Lt.-Col. J. W. C., D.S.O. *Publ*: Grammar of The Somali Language; British Garden Flora. *a*: Gedling Hse, Gedling, Notts.

KIRK, John Henry, M.A., B.Com. *b*: Durban, South Africa 1907. *e*: Durban Hgh Sch, Natal Univ Coll, King's & Christ's Colls Camb, Univs of Nth Carolina & Chicago. Asst Sec Ministry of Agriculture. *Publ*: Native Segregation in South Africa; Agriculture & the Trade Cycle. *Ctr*: Econ Journ, Journ of Social Forces, New Statesman & Nation. *s.s*: Economics & Statistics. *Rec*: Tennis, golf, music. *a*: 139 Haverstock Hill, London, N.W.3. *T*: Primrose 3951.

KIRK, John Theodore. *b*: Barnsley 1889. *e*: Wakefield Sc Yorks. *m*: Minnie Cobb. *s*: 1. Jnlst. *c.t*: Daily Telegraph, Daily Chron,

L'pool Daily Post, Daily Sketch, Daily Independent, Sheffield Telegraph, Daily Dispatch. *s.s*: Domestic & international politics. *Rec*: Driving, walking. *c*: M.J.I. *a*: 6 Stanley Mansions, S.W.17. *t*: Battersea 1205.

KIRK, Canon K. E. *a*: Christ Church, Oxford.

KIRK, Laurence. See Simson, Eric.

KIRK, Rev. P. T. R. R., M.A. *b*: Dublin. *e*: Wesley & T.C.D. *m*: Louisa Deborah Seaver. *d*: 2. Vicar of Ch Ch Westminster, & Gen Dir of Industrial Christian Fellowship. *Publ*: The True Advent; The Movement Christwards; Nazareth Politics; The Economic Confusion in Christianity & the Crisis; etc. *c.t*: Various. *s.s*: Christianity, politics. Proc in Con for the Diocese of Lon. Hon Sec Universal Counc of Life & Work, etc. *Rec*: Riding, golf. *c*: Reform. *a*: Ch Ch Vicarage, Broadway, Westminster, S.W.1. *t*: Victoria 2782

KIRK, William, J.P. *b*; Dunfermline 1869. *e*: Dunfermline Sc. *m*: May Romanes. *s*: 1. *d*: 1. Ed & Mang Dir of Dunfermline Press. *n.a*: connected with Dunfermline Press for over 50 y. *Publ*: Jt Author of Royal Dunfermline. *Rec*: golf. *a*: 15 Park Terrace, Dunfermline. *t*: 2P5.

KIRK, William. *b*: Kilkenny 1875. *e*: St Kieran's Col Kilkenny. *m*: Nellie Sara Wilson. *s*: 3. *d*: 1. Civil Servant. *Publ*: Stories of Second Sight in a Highland Regiment. *c.t*: Star, Weekly Sun, Echo, Weekly Irish Times, Cork Exam, etc. *s.s* Ghost stories. *a*: 378 Thorold Rd, Ilford, Essex.

KIRKALDY, ADAM WILLIS: economist, historian; b. London, Eng., Dec., 1867; s. John Givens and Isabella (Willis) K.; educ. privately, Wadham College (Oxford), Univ. Paris. DEGREES: M.A., B.Litt. (Oxford), Diplomè de I'Ecole Hautes (Paris), M.Com. (Birmingham); m. Evelyn Frances Elliott, 1896. AUTHOR: Economics and Syndicalism, 1914; History and Economics of Transport (with A. Dudley Evans), 1914 (5 edits.); British Shipping: its History and Importance, 1914 (3 edits.); Wealth: a textbook of Elementary Economics, 1920; Edited British Finance Survey, 1914-20 (British Association); The Romance of Trade: a Survey Commercial and Economic, 1922 (2nd edit. 1928). Edited: Labour, 1914-20 (British Association); reports on Finance and Labour for British Association. Contributor to Economic Journ., Scotch Geog. Rev., Glasgow Herald, London Times, Guardian, Journal (both Nottingham) and other economic mags. General character of writing: scientific, text books, technical. Pioneer in work of higher commercial education in Britain; mem. council, Nottingham Chamber of Comm.; and chmn., 1925-26; Dean of Faculty of Economics and Commerce, Univ. Coll. (Nottingham) since 1919; lecturer on Economics to workingmen over period of 30 yrs. Relig. denom., Church of England. CLUBS: Borough Club (Nottingham), Union Soc. (Oxford), University (Birmingham). OFFICE: University College. HOME: 3, Clumber Crescent, South, The Park, Nottingham, Eng.

KIRKBRIDE, Ronald. *b*: Victoria, B.C., Canada 1912. *e*: St George's Sch Newport R.I., Occidental Coll Los Angeles. *m*:. *s*: 1. *d*: 1. Author, Editor. *n.a*: Ed Story Mag 1934, Sports Illus '35, Golf Illus '35, Douglas Handbooks '42. 20th Century Fox Studios '43, Paramount Studios '45. *Publ*: Winds, Blow Gently; Deep River; The Private Life of Guy De Maupassant; Still the Heart Sings; Spring is Not Gentle; River of Souls; Dark Surrender; Letters of An Unknown. (Plays) Christina; Many Loves; Battle of the Sexes. *s.s*: Radio, Plays, Editing, Novels, Film Writing, Quaker Themes & Co-operatives. *Rec*: Tennis, golf, riding, fishing. *c*: Authors (N.Y. & Lond). *a*: 1941 Kelton Ave, Los Angeles 25, California, & Authors' Club, Whitehall Court, London, W.1. *T*: Arizona 38831.

KIRKBY, Gerald Staniforth, M.J.I. *b*: Sunderland 1888. *m*: Annie Tulloch McFarlane. *s*: 2. Journalist (Shorthand Writer). *n.a*: Scotsman 1908-20 (Law Court Rep). *c.t*: Chemist & Druggist, Scottish Baptist Mag. *s.s*: Law Court Reports (Scotland). Pres Scot Baptist L.P. Assoc. *Rec*: Golf. *a*: 61 Spottiswoode Rd, Edin. *t*: 52250.

KIRKBY, John. *b*: Gainsborough. Journalist. *n.a*: Gainsborough News 1925. *s.s*: Co-operative movement, sport. *Rec*: Cricket. *a*: Carnethy, Gainsborough Rd, Retford. Notts. *t*: Gainsborough 155.

KIRKBY, William, M.Sc. *b*: M/C 1859. *e*: Sheffield. *m*: Phœbe A. Wagstaff. *s*: 2. Pharmaceutical & Consulting Chemist. *Publ*: Practical Prescribing & Dispensing for Medical Students; Arsenical Poisoning in Beer Drinkers (in collab with Dr T. N. Kelynack); etc. *c.t*: The Chemist & Druggist, Pharmaceutical Journ, etc. *s.s*: Hist of Sc. Past Pres Brit Pharmaceutical Conf, Hon Mem Amer Pharmaceutical Assoc. *Rec*: Collecting Books on the above, hist. *a*: Old Mill Hse, Darley Bridge, Matlock.

KIRKCONNEL, Watson, M.A., LL.D., Ph.D., F.R.Hist.S., F.R.S.C. *b*: Port Hope, Ontario, Canada 1895. *e*: Queen's Univ Kingston & Oxf Univ. *m*: (1) Isabel Peel (dec'd), (2) Hope Kitchener. *s*: 2. *d*: 3. Prof of English McMaster Univ, Nat-Pres Canadian Author's Assoc 1942—44 etc. *n.a*: Ed Canadian Poetry Mag 1944—46. *Publ*: The Flying Bull & Other Tales; The Eternal Quest; European Elegies; A Canadian Headmaster; The Humanities in Canada (with A. S. P. Woodhouse); The Magyar Muse; Golden Treasury of Polish Lyrics; Titus the Toad; etc. *Ctr*: Queen's Quarterly, Slavonic Rev, Baltic Rev, Ukranian Quarterly, Life & Letters To-day, Sat Night, etc. *s.s*: History of Communism in Canada, Literatures of Foreign Language Groups in Canada, Poetry of Hungary, Poland & Iceland. *a*: McMaster University, Hamilton, Ontario, Canada. *T*: 7-8531.

KIRKHAM, Rev. Philip Henry, M.A.(Oxon), F.R.S.L., F.R.S.A. *b*: M/C 1875. *e*: Bradford G.S., Trin Col Oxf & Wycliffe Hall Oxf. *m*: Laura Margaret Braithwaite. *d*: 2. *n.a*: Ed Sunrise (Karen) 1902-07. *Publ*: Manual of Confirmation in Sgau Karen; The Golden Fleece (poem). *c.t*: Bradford Weekly Telegraph, C.E. N/p, Indian Review, etc. *Rec*: Golf, lawn tennis. *a*: Beetham Vicarage, Milnthorpe, Westmorland.

KIRKLAND, Edward Chase. *b*: Bellows Falls, Vermont 1894. *e*: Dartmouth Coll, Harvard Univ. *m*: Ruth Stevens Babson. *s*: 1. Teacher. *n.a*: Mississippi Valley Hist Review 1945—, Journ of Econ Hist '41—. *Publ*: A History of American Economic Life; The Peace Makers of 1864; Brunswick's Golden Age. *Ctr*: New England Quarterly, Journ of Econ Hist, Amer Hist Review, Mississippi Valley Hist Review. *s.s*: American, Econ, Transportation, New England, Hists. *Rec*: Gardening, mountain climbing. *a*: 15 Cleveland St, Brunswick, Maine. *T*: 778-M.

KIRKLAND, J., M.B., Mast Surgery. Surgeon. *c.t*: Various surgical papers. *a*: 22 Leigham Ct Rd, Streatham Hill, S.W.16.

KIRKLAND, R. Physician. *c.t*: B.M.J., Amer Journ of Med Science, etc. Cons Physician Cheltenham Gen Hosp. Chm Med Staff Cheltenham Col & Cheltenham Ladies' Col. *a*: Nouvelle, Lansdowne, Cheltenham.

KIRKMAN, Frederick Bernulf Beever. *b*: Natal 1869. *e*: Beaumaris G.S., Lincoln Col Oxf & Univ of Paris. *m*: Kathleen Helena Willis. *s*: 2. Author, Sc Examiner. *Publ*: British Bird Book (Ed & pt author, 4 vols, 200 plates); British Birds (with F. C. R.

Jourdain); British Birds (originally one of the People's Books); Première Année de Français; etc. *c.t*: New Statesman, Country Life, Discovery, Times Educ Supp., etc. *s.s*: Schoolbooks (French, hist), birds. Formerly Asst Master Merchant Taylors Sc. Temp on Higher Staff Bd of Educ (4 y). Mem Modern Lang Assoc, Brit Psych Soc & Fabian Soc. *Rec*: Country walks, picture galleries *a*: Pilgrim's Place Hse, N.W.3. *t*: Hampstead 3546.

KIRKPATRICK, Very Rev. Alexander Francis, D.D. Dean of Ely Cath. *b*: Lewes 1849. *e*: Haileybury, Trin Col Cam. *m*: Julia Mary Bartlett. *s*: 5. *d*: 1. Regius Prof of Hebrew '82–1903. Lady Margaret Prof of Divinity '03–06, in the Univ of Cam. Master Selwyn Col 1898–1907. *Publ*: Commentary on Psalms (1890–1901); The Divine Library of the O.T.; etc. Gen Ed O.T. & Apocrypha in Cambridge Bible for Schools & Colleges 1893–1929. *c.t*: Ch Quarterly Review, Expositor. *s.s*: O.T. Mem Isle of Ely Educ Cmt '07–. Ex-Mem Counc of Haileybury & a Gov Harpur Trust, Bedford 50 y, representing the Univ of Cam. *a*: The Deanery, Ely.

KIRKPATRICK, Frederick Alex, M.A., F.R.H.S. *b*: 1861. *e*: Wellington, Trin Col Camb. *m*: Violet Herbert. Univ Ex Lecturer 1898–1919, Reader of Spanish in the Univ Camb 1919–33. *Publ*: Imperial Defence & Trade (Prize Essay of Roy Empire Soc); A History of Argentina; The Spanish Conquistadores; Latin-America, A Brief History; Annotated Editions of Some Spanish Classics. *Rec*: Walking, travel. *c*: Roy Empire Soc. *a*: Royal Empire Society, Northumberland Ave, W.C.2.

KIRKPATRICK, G. G. *b*: Maxwelltown 1893. *n.a*: Ed Lever Bros Mag Progress. *a*: Unilever Hse, Blackfriars, E.C.4. *t*: Central 7474.

KIRKPATRICK, J. B. *b*: Cam 1893. *e*: Marlboro', Jesus Col Cam. Journalist. *n.a*: Ed Journ of The Little Ship Club 1928–. *Publ*: Little Ship Wanderings ('33). *c.t*: Field, Yachting Monthly, Yachting World, Blue Peter & dailies. *s.s*: Yachting, the sea. *Rec*: Yacht cruising. *c*: Roy Cruising. *a*: 4 Mecklenburgh St, W.C.1.

KIRKPATRICK, T. Percy C., M.D., Litt.D.(Dublin), D.Litt.(N.U.I.), F.R.C.P.I., F.R.C.P.(Lond). *b*: Dublin 1869. *e*: Foyle Coll Londonderry, Trin Coll Dublin. Pres Roy Irish Acad 1946—. *Publ*: History of Dr Steeven's Hospital; History of Rotunda Hospital; Nursing Ethics. *s.s*: Medical History. *a*: 11 Fitzwilliam Pl, Dublin.

KIRKUS, Agnes Mary, M.A., F.R.Hist.S. *b*: York 1907. *e*: Sutton Hgh Sch, Sch of Librarianship, Univ Coll Lond. Librarian Reading Univ. *Publ*: Ed of The Great Roll of the Pipe for the 9th year of the Reign of King John 1207. *a*: 53 London Rd, Reading.

KIRKUS, Virginia, A.B. *b*: Meadville, Penna 1893. *e*: Hannah More Acad & Vassar Coll Poughkeepsie. *m*: Frank Glick. Prop Virginia Kirkus Bookshop Service, Lecturer on Books. *n.a*: Fashion-Ed Pictorial Rev & Style 1920–23, Back of the Book Ed McCalls Mag '23–25, Dept-Hd Boy & Girl Books Harper & Bro '25–32. *Publ*: A House for the Week Ends. *Ctr*: Various. *s.s*: Contemporary Books. *Rec*: Gardening, theatre. *a*: 38 Bank St, New York 14, N.Y., U.S.A., & Redding Bridge, Connecticut, U.S.A. *T*: Watkins 9-7997.

KIRKWOOD, David, M.P., J.P. *b*: Glasgow 1872. *e*: Parkhead Public Sch. *m*: Elizabeth Smith. *s*: 5. *d*: 2. Engineer, M.P. (Lab) Dumbarton Burghs 1922—, Chm Engineering Group House of Commons, J.P. for County City of Glasgow. *Publ*: My Life of Revolt. *Ctr*: Various. *a*: Karleen, Roman Rd, Bearsden, Dumbartonshire, Scotland. *T*: Bearsden 1358.

KIRTLAN, Rev. Ernest John Brigham, B.A., B.D., D.D. *b*: Cornwall. *e*: Kingswood Bath, Lon Univ. St Andrews Univ Scot & Richmond Meth Col. *m*: Saidee Wood. *s*: 2. Meth Min. *Publ*: Trans of Beowulf; Trans of Sir Gawain & the Green Knight; Pearl; Modernization of The Little Drama of the Crucifixion, etc. *c.t*: Lon Quart Review, Contemporary Review, Holborn Review, Clarion, Meth Recorder, Meth Times & Ch Times. *s.s*: Anglo Saxon lit, Old & Mediæval Eng lit, Eng & French poetry. Lecturer on Lit subjects, Social subjects. Mem of the S.D. F. of Fabian Soc for many . *Rec*; Golf, sailing. *a*: Bexwell Rd, Downham Market, Norfolk.

KIRTLAND, Lucian Swift, M.A. *b*: Ohio 1881. *e*: St Paul's Sc Concord & Yale Univ. *m*: Helen W. Johns. Writer. *n.a*: Minneapolis Journal 1904–05, Ed The Housekeeper Magazine '05–10, Corr for Leslie's Weekly '16 in Russia, Corr for Leslie's Weekly '16–19 France. Corr for various pubis in India & Far East '20–22. *Publ*: Samurai Trails; Finding the worth while in the Orient. *c.t*: Harper's Mthly, Asia Mag, Leslie's Wkly, Travel Mag, American Legion Wkly, N.Y. Herald Tribune Mag. *s.s*: Asiatic, exploration. 1911 Spent in S. E. Alaska. '13 Mem Exploring party which located & mapped sources of princ rivers in N.W. Canada. '14 walked 600 miles in Japan, tracing old Samurai routes to Tokyo. '28–29 Mem exploration party, Indo-China & Siam. *c*: Authors' (Vice Press '33–34), The Explorers, Yale & Town Hall. *a*: 51 Summit Av, Bronxville, N.Y. *t*: 1693.

KIRWAN, James. F/l Reporter. *c.t*: Leading dailies. *s.s*: France, foreign affairs, verbatim shorthand writer, crime reporter. Ex-Paris corres. C.N. Paris Corres 1927–28. *a*: Flat 5, 87 Guilford St, W.C.1. *t*: Terminus 6794.

KIRWAN, Hon. Sir John Waters, Kt., K.C.M.G. *b*: County Galway 1869. *m*: Teresa Gertrude Quinlan. *s*: 2. Journalist, Foundation Mem Emp Press Union, Rep West Australia Dly Press at Imperial Press Conf in Lond 1909, Delegate to I.P.C. at Ottawa '20 & Melbourne '25, Mem of House of Representatives of First Parliament of Commonwealth of Australia. *n.a*: Part Proprietor of Kalgoorlie Miner (Dly) & Western Argus (Wkly) from 1895 & Ed in Chief of both until 1926 *Publ*: An Empty Land; My Life's Adventure. *Ctr*: Times, Nineteenth Century, Empire Rev, West Australian, Overseas, etc. *s.s*: Empire & esp Australian Political Questions. *c*: Weld, Perth, Kildare Street, Dublin, etc. *a*: Weld Club, Perth, Western Australia.

KIRWAN, Lawrence Harold. *b*: Leamington Spa 1910. *e*: Leamington Central Sch. Married. *d*: 1. Day Ed Herts Advertiser St Albans '31–33, Rep Sub-Ed Chief Sub-Ed (Night) Press Assoc '33–40, Sub-Ed Reuters '46, Day Ed '47—. *s.s*: Politics. *Rec*: Swimming, photographing babies. *w.s*: R.A.F. *a*: 2 Chase Side Ave, Enfield, Middlesex. *T*: Enfield 2059.

KISCH, Sir Cecil Herman, M.A.(Oxon), K.C.I.E., C.B. *b*: Brit India 1884. *e*: Clifton Col & Trin Col Oxf. *m*: (1) Myra Adler (dec); (2) Kita Joseph. *s*: 2. *d*: 1. Asst Under Sec of State India Office. *Publ*: The Portuguese Bank Note Case (1932); Central Banks (4th ed '32, in collab with Miss W. A. Elkin). *c.t*: Press & monthly mags. *s.s*: Publ finance, econ. Priv Sec to Sec of State for India '17. Financial Sec India Office '21–33. Asst Under Sec of State India Office '33. Mem Prep Comm of Experts for Internat Monetary & Econ Conf, & of India Del to same '33. *c*: Reform. *a*: 21 Pembroke Sq, W.8. *t*: Western 3966.

KISCH, Harold Albert. *b*: Lon 1880. *e*: St Thomas's Hosp, U.C.L. & City of Lon Scs. *m*: Sybil Hyman. Surg for Diseases of Nose, Throat & Ear. Surg Nose, Throat & Ear Dept U.C.H. Senr Surg Cent Lon

Throat & Ear Hosp, etc. Vice-Pres Otological Section Roy Soc Med, etc. *c.t*: Trans Roy Soc of Med, Journ of Laryngology, Lancet, etc. *s.s*: Diseases of nose, throat & ear. *a*: 15 Wimpole St, W.1. *t*: Langham 2278.

KITCHEN, James. *a*: 179 Pearse St, Dublin.

KITCHEN, James Phillips, A.M.Inst, R.E. *b*: Dun Laoghaire 1902. *e*: Priv. *m*: Palmira Annette Chauvie. *s*: 1. Journalist. *n.a*: Ed & Founder Irish Radio Journ '23, & Irish Radio Trader '24, resigned '25 & founded the Irish Radio Review as a monthly, now Ed The Irish Radio News: a wkly journal incorporating Irish Radio Review. *c.t*: Irish Independent, Irish Times, The Wireless Teacher, etc. *s.s*: Broadcasting. Founder Mem The Wireless Soc of Ire, Hon Treas Dublin & Irish Asst Dist Inst of Journalists, '28–30, Chm Irish Radio Development Ass '32–33. *a*: 4 Charlemont Terr, Dun Laoghaire, Co Dublin. *t*: 43236.

KITCHEN, William Frederick. *b*: Edwinstowe, Notts 1890. *e*: Village School. *m*: Ethel Elizabeth Pratt. *s*: 1. *d*: 4. Farm Worker, Smallholder, Writer. *Publ*: Brother to the Ox; Life on the Land; The Farming Front; Jessie & His Friends; Settlers in England. *Ctr*: Dly Mirror, Brit Weekly, Countrygoer, Home Rev. *s.s*: Agriculture & Country Life. *Rec*: Reading, writing, gardening & nature study. *a*: Pleasant View, Moor Lane, Bolsover, Chesterfield, Derbyshire.

KITCHENER, Pamela Yvonne. *e*: St Bernard's Convent, Slough. Free-lance Journalist, N.U.J. *n.a*: Worthing Gazette 1937–38, Band Wagon, Courier, etc '46 Ev Standard '46. *Ctr*: Psychology, Sight & Sound, Home Notes, Dly Mirror. *s.s*: Films, Books, Nursing. *a*: Old Manor Hse, Bell Road, East Molesey. *T*: Molesey 3004.

KITCHENER, Sydney William. *b*: Hornsey 1887. *m*: Daisy Gertrude Lamb. *s*: 1. Reference Librarian Hornsey. *Publ*: An Eastern Maid & Other Poems; Woman the Tangible; Old Hornsey: Some Gleanings from the Past. *Ctr*: Internat Psychic Gazette, New World of Billiards, Hornsey Journ, etc. *s.s*: Hist & Topography of Nth London Lecturer. *Rec*: Astrology, Water-colour sketching. *a*: 1 Shepherd's Hill, Highgate, London, N.6.

KITCHIN, Darcy Butterworth. *b*: Henwick Grange 1863. *e*: Harrow & Trinity Cam. *Publ*: The Public Schools' Year Book (Ed '89–1903); Bergson for Beginners (2nd ed '14); etc. *Rec*: Yachting, golf, chess. *a*: Haldon, Canford Cliffs, Bournemouth. *t*: Canford Cliffs 543.

KITCHIN, Mary Kathleen Forsaith, M.Sc, M.B., B.S.(Lon). *b*: Bournemouth 1897. *e*: Wimbledon H.S., L.S.M.W., St Mary's Hosp. *m*: Derek Harcourt Kitchin. Med Pract & Med & Legal Journalist. *n.a*: Temp Asst Ed Lancet 1925, Brit Journ of Radiology '31, Maternity & Child Welfare '28. *c.t*: Lancet, B.M.J., Journ of Anatomy, Proc Zool Soc, Lon. *s.s*: Med Journalism. Gilchrist Student '18, Hon Acting Prosector Zool Soc Lon '18–19, Beit Meml Fell '21, Phys Tavistock Clinic for Functional & Nervous Disease '23, Lect in Phys Dartford Phys T.C. *Rec*: Reading, riding. *a*: 108 FitzJohn's Av, N.W.3. *t*: Hampstead 3103.

KITCHIN, SHEPHERD BRAITHWAITE, K.C.: Advocate of the Supreme Court of South Africa; *b*. Dalton-in-Furness, Lancashire, Eng.; *s*. David and Sarah (Braithwaite) K.; *educ*. Boys' High Sch., Kimberley (S. Africa), South African Coll. (Capetown), Trinity Hall (Cambridge, Eng.). DEGREES: B.A., L.L.B. (Cantab.) and (S. Africa); *m*. Jean Stark, 1914. AUTHOR: Reports of the High Court of Griquland (Vol. X), 1905-10; A History of Divorce, 1912; Reports of the Supreme Court of S. Africa (Griqualand West Local Division), 1910-17, 1928-1931. Editor (formerly): South African Law Journal, 1913-19. Contributor to The Friend (Bloemfontein, S. Africa), Diamond Fields Advertiser (Kimberley), Outspan, S. African Law Journ. and other periodicals. General character of writing: legal, historical, literary essays. Ex-Crown Prosecutor at Kimberley (Griqualand West); chmn. Kimberley Pub. Library and a trustee of South Africa Pub. Lib.; President North of England Assn.; contested Kimberley seat for Union Parliament, 1924; mem. Provincial Council, Cape Province, 1911-13. CLUB: Home. OFFICE: 6 Market St. HOME: 30 Carrington Road, Kimberley, S. Africa.

KITCHIN-KERR, George Ernest. *b*: Ballarat East, 1892. *e*: The Christian Brothers' College, East Melbourne. *m*: Enid Murphy. *s*: 3. *d*: 2. Journalist & Sales Manager. *n.a*: Editorial Staff, Sinraysia Daily, Mildura, '21—9; Ed The Citrus News, '29—. *s.s*: Organisation, Marketing. & Distribution of Primary products. *Rec*: Golf, bridge. *c*: Australian Journalists Assn; Comm Travellers, Melbourne. *a*: 14 Second Avenue, East Kew, Melbourne, Aust. *t*: Central 8895.

KITCHING, Rt. Rev. Arthur Leonard, M.A. *b*: London 1875. *e*: Highgate Sch, Emmanuel Coll & Ridley Hall Camb. *m*: (1) M. B. Lloyd. *s*: 1. (2) E. E. Dudley. *d*: 1. Assistant Bishop & Archdeacon of Portsmouth, Uganda 1901 as Missionary, subsequently Archdeacon of Bukedi, Busoga & Uganda, Bishop on Upper Nile 1926—36, Retired '36. *Publ*: On the Backwaters of the Nile; Luganda Dictionary (in collab); Outline Grammar of the Gang Language; Handbook of the Ateso Language; (Trans) The Four Gospels into Gang & The New Testament in Ateso. *s.s*: African Vernaculars. *c*: National. *a*: 6 Herbert Rd, Southsea, Hants. *T*: Portsmouth 31412.

KITCHING, Miss Elsie. *b*: Lon 1870. *e*: Priv, Inter Arts(Lon). Ed Parents' Review; Dir Parents' Un. Sc. *n.a*: Ed Parents' Review 1923–. Dir Parents' Un Sc '23–. Priv Sec to Miss Charlotte M. Mason 1893-1923, etc. *Rec*: Reading, travel. *a*: Scale How, Ambleside, Westmorland.

KITSON, Sir Albert Ernest, C.M.G., C.B.E., F.G.S., M.InstM.M., M.AustInstM.M., F.R.G.S. *m*: Elinore Almond Ramage. *s*: 2. Geologist & Mining Eng. *c.t*: Journs of Learned Socs Eng & Overseas. *s.s*: Economic aspects of geology & geography. Senior Geologist, Geological Survey, Victoria, 1900—06. Princ Mineral Survey S. Nigeria 1907—11. Dir Geological Survey Gold Coast '13—30. Discoveries of important coal, oil shale, manganese, diamond & aluminium ore fields in Nigeria & Gold Coast, & glacial & fossiliferous deposits in Victoria, Tasmania, Nigeria & Gold Coast. *Rec*: Travel, photography, nat hist. *a*: Benalta, Beaconsfield, Bucks. *t*: 646.

KITSON, Arthur. *b*: Lon 1859. *e*: Priv & King's Col Lon. Engineer. *n.a*: Proprietor & Ed Open Review 1908–10. *Publ*: A Scientific Solution of the Money Question; Industrial Depression: Its Cause & Cure; A Fraudulent Standard; Unemployment: Its Cause & a Remedy; An Open Letter to H.R.H. The Prince of Wales on the World Crisis; The Bankers' Conspiracy ('33); etc. *c.t*: London Times, Morning Post, Sunday Chron, Clarion, Fortnightly Review, English Review, New Age, etc. *s.s*: Econ, finance. Inventor of the Kitson Light & Suction Gas Produce. Pres Monetary Reform Assoc M/C. Chm of Cmt of Science & Arts of Franklin Inst. Received Medal of Merit from Franklin Inst for Inventions in artificial lighting 1900. Vice-pres Birm Business Club '20–34. *Rec*: Music, golf. *a*: 59 Farquhar Rd, Upper Norwood, S.E.19. *t*: Sydenham 1345.

KITSON, Charles Herbert, M.A. (Cantab) D.Mus (Oxon), F.R.C.O., F.R.C.M. *b*: Leyburn 1874. *e*: Ripon Sc & Selwyn Col Cam. *m*: Lucy Viccars. Prof Music, Univ of Dublin & R.C.M. Lon. *Publ*: Art of Counterpoint; Elementary Harmony; Counterpoint for Beginners; Six Lectures on Accompanied Vocal Writing; Rudiments of Music; etc. *s.s*: Harmony, counterpoint, etc. Late Prof of Music in Univ Col Dublin, Snr Prof of Theory Roy Irish Acad of Music, & Dean of Faculty of Music, Lon Univ. *a*: 5 Argyll Rd, Campden Hill, W.8. *t*: Western 5823.

KITTO, H.D.F. *b*: Westbury-on-Severn, Blos 1897. *e*: Crypt Gr Sch & St John's Coll Camb. *m*: Ann Kraft. *s*: 1. *d*: 1. Professor of Greek University of Bristol. *Publ*: Greek Tragedy; In the Mountains of Greece. *Ctr*: Classical Journs. *s.s*: Greek. *Rec*: Greek & Music. *a*: 9 Southfield Rd, Bristol 6.

KITTO, John Vivian, C.B., C.B.E. *b*: London 1875. *e*: Merchant Taylors, Glenalmond, Balliol Coll Oxf. *m* · Nettie Catherine Ryves. *s*: 1. *d*: 1. Asst Librarian House of Commons 1908—37, Librarian '37—46. *Publ*: Churchwardens' Accounts of St Martin-in-the-Fields, 1525—1603; Registers of St Martin-in-the-Fields, 1603—1630. *Ctr*: Various. *w.s*: World War I, Capt & Adjutant R.G.A. (A.A.). *a*: Mawgan, Manor Rd, St Albans, Herts. *T*: 1220.

KJAERGAARD, Peder Jensen. *b*: O. Hjermitslev, Berglum Herred 1898. *m*: Mary Korsgaard. *s*: 1. *Publ*: Goddag Igen; Modvind Og; Skarnsfolk; De Hjermitslev Bonder; De Fattiges Paradis; Ved Solfald Vinden Tuder om Borglum; Strenge Tider; Lyset Serjrer. *Ctr*: Various. *s.s*: History, Folk-lore, etc. *a*: Pile Alle 27 Kobenhaven F, Denmark.

KLAPPER, Charles F., A.M.I.T.A. *n.a*: Ed Omnibus Mag. *c.t*: Articles on Road, Rail, Traffic & Topographical Matters. *a*: 4 Wellington Rd, E.3.

KLAPPER, Paul, A.M., Ph.D. *b*: Jassy, Roumania 1885. *e*: Coll of the City of New York, Univ of New York & Wisconsin. *m*: Flora Eydenberg. *s*: 1. Pres Queens Coll. *Publ*: Contemporary Education: Its Principles & Practices; Teaching English in Elementary & Junior High Schools, A Manual of Method; The Teaching of Arithmetic; Teaching of History, With Chapter on the Teaching of Civics. *Ctr*: School & Society, Menorah Journ, Journ of Higher Educ, etc. *s.s*: Educ Administration, Teacher-Preparation. *c*: Town Hall. *a*: 144—80 Sanford Ave, Flushing, New York. *T*: Flushing 3-3631.

KLEE. Tage. *b*: Silkeborg 1878. Insurer. *Publ*: Timer og En Dag; "———" (Dash); Trods Alt!; *Ctr*: Politiken, Ekstrabladet Insurance, Special Literature. *a*: Norasvej 25, Charlottenlund, Denmark. *T*: Ordrup 2360.

KLEEHOVEN, HANS ANKWICZ von: state librarian; b. Böheimkirchen, Austria, Sept. 29, 1883; s. Dr. Johann Ankwicz von Kleehoven; educ. Univs. of Vienna and Berlin; Institute of Austrian Historical Research. DEGREE: Ph.D.; m. Alexandra von Sauer-Csaky. AUTHOR: Ferdinand Matthias Zerlacher (Österreichische Künstlermonographien, vol. 1), 1926. Editor: Oesterreichisches Jahrbuch für Exlibris und Gebrauchsgraphik (Austrian year book of Exlibris and applied graphic). Contributor to: Wiener Zeitung; Oesterreichische Bau- und Werkkunst; Der getreue Eckart; Mitteilungen des Institutes für österreichische Geschichtsforschung; Zentralblatt für Bibliothekswesen, Jahrbuch der Oesterreichischen Exlibris-Gesellschaft; Jahrbuch der preussischen Kunstsammlungen. General character of writing: scientific, historical. Articles and lectures about modern European art and art-industry, especially modern Austrian art and arts crafts; old German art, Viennese Humanism and library questions. Is director of the library of the Austrian Museum of Art and Industry at Vienna, Austria. Religion, Roman Catholic. OFFICE: Stubenring 5, Vienna I. HOME: Florianigasse 20, Vienna VIII., Austria.

KLEEMAN, Rita Halle. *b*: Chillicothe, Ohio 1885. *e*: Chillicothe Hgh Sch & Wellesley Coll. *m*: Arthur S. Kleeman. *s*: 3. *d*: 1. Writer, Mem Author's League of Amer, V-Pres, P.E.N., etc. *Publ*: Gracious Lady, The Life of Sara Delano Roosevelt; Young Franklin Roosevelt; Which College, *Ctr*: Sat. E. Post, Collier's, Woman's Home Comp, Good Housekeeping, Reader's Digest, This Week, Red Book, etc. *s.s*: General Articles, Medical Subjects & Travel. *Rec*: Travel. *a*: 277 Park Ave, New York 17, N.Y., U.S.A. *T*: Plaza 3-3533.

KLEIN, FELIX, ABBÉ: priest, professor, writer; b. Chateau-Chinon, Nièvres, France; s. Bernard Henri and Pierrette (Cloix) K.; educ. Séminaire de Meaux (Seine et Marne), Séminaire de Saint-Sulpice (Paris), Institut Catholique de Paris, Sorbonne (Paris). DEGREES: Bachelier en Theologie, Licencié es Lettres. AUTHOR: Le Cardinal Lavigerie et ses Oeuvres d'Afrique, 1890; Le Menteur, de Corneille; Extraits de Montaigne, 1892; Nouvelles tendences en Religion et en Littérature, 1893; Autour de Dilletantisme, 1895; Le Père Hecker, 1897; Le fait religieux et la manière de l'Observer, 1903 (2nd edit. 1912); Quelques motifs d'espérer, 1904; La séparation aux Etats-Unis, 1904; Au pays de la "Vie Intense", decorated by l'Académie Française (2nd edit. Transl. into English), 1905; L'Evêque de Metz. Vie de Monseigneur Dupont de Loges, decorated by l'Académie Française, 1906; Discours de Mariage et conference sur le Célibat, 1907; L'Amérique de demain, decorated by l'Académie Française, 1910; Mon filleul au Jardin d'Enfants (2 vols.), decorated by l'Académie Française and honored by a subscription of the Minister of Public Instruction, 1912 (Comment il s'instruit vol. 1, 6th edit., 1913; Comment il s'élève vol. 2, 5th edit., 1913); La Guerre vue d'une Ambulance (5th edit.), decorated by l'Académie des Sciences morales et politiques 1915; Les Douleurs qui esperent (6th edit.), decorated by l'Académie des Sciences Morales et Politiques, 1916; Dieu nous aime, 1918; En Amerique a la finde la Guerre, decorated by l'Académie Française, 1919; Noces Chrétiennes, 1920; Une expérience réligieuse: Madeleine Sémer, convertie et mystique, decorated by l'Académie Française (transl. into English, Italian, German; 25th edit.), 1923; L'Amérique et le Cartel des Gauches, 1924; Etudions les Mystères, 1926; Les Paraboles evangéliques, 1927; St. François d'Assise et les Fioretti, d'Après Azanam, 1927; Sept Comédies du Moyen Age, 1927, 1927; Histoire de Joseph et de sesonze frères, 1928; La Sainte Vièrge dans l'Evangile, 1928; L'Alphabet des Saints, 1929. Translations: L'Église et le Siècle (by Monseigneur Ireland), 1894; Opportunite (by Monseigneur Spalding), 1897. Editor: Le Menteur (by Corneille), 1890; Extraits de Montaigne, 1892; Les Fleurs et les Fruits (a series of books for young people). Contributor to Revue des Deux Mondes, Correspondant, Vie Catholique, Commonweal, Catholic World. General character of writing: religious, educational, literary. Became a priest in 1905; Professor of Philosophy at Meaux diocesan College in 1890; Professor of French Literature at the Catholic Institute of Paris in 1893; toured the United States and Canada in 1904, and again in 1907, giving lectures at several universities. During the war was chaplain of the American Ambulance at Neuilly, Paris, except in November and December, 1918, when he was sent to the United States by the French government. Religion, Catholic. OFFICE: Editions Spes, 17 rue Soufflot, Paris V. HOME: 1 Sentier de la Pointe, Meudon, Seine et Oise, France.

KLEIN, HERMAN: author, journalist, teacher of singing; b. Norwich, Eng., July 23, 1856; educ. Norwich and London schls.; studied singing under Manuel Garcia, London. AUTHOR: Thirty

Years of Musical Life in London, 1903; The Reign of Patti (authorized biography), 1920; The Bel Canto, 1923; Musicians and Mummers, 1925; Great Women-Singers of my Time, 1931. Co-editor, Manuel Garcia's "Hints on Singing", 1896; Translator of Librettos of "Carmen", "Aida", "Thais" and many other operas; also 60 Lieder by Schubert, Schumann and Brahms. Contributor to Christian Science Monitor, Radio Times (London), Gramophone and other mags. General character of writing: musical criticism and biography. For twenty yrs. Musical Critic for Sunday Times; thirteen yrs. prof. of singing, Guildhall Sch., London. Taught singing, New York City, for seven and one-half yrs. First. Pres. Nat. Assoc. Teachers of Singing, U.S.A.; trained many famous singers for opera, concert. CLUBS: Authors', Pilgrims, English-Speaking Union, Soc. of East Anglians, Musicians' (London). Fellow of the Inst. of Journalists; Past Grand Organist Eng. Freemasons. HOME: 40 Avenue Road, London, N. W. 8, Eng.

KLEIN, Sydney Turner, F.L.S., F.R.A.S., F.R.M.S., F.R.E.S., M.R.I. & C. *b*: Earlswood 1853. *e*: Haileybury Col. *m*: Miss Urwick. *s*: 2. *d*: 4. *Publ*: Science & The Infinite; The Way of Attainment; The Garden of Enchantment; etc. *c.t*: Trans of Learned Socs. *a*: Lilly's, Chelsfield, Kent. *t*: Orpington 390.

KLEIST, James Aloysius, M.A., Ph.D. *b*: Hindenburg, Germany 1873. *e*: German Gymnasium, Jesuit Normal Sch in Holland, Jesuit Theolgate St Louis, Univs of Berlin & St Louis. Prof of Classical Langs. *n.a*: Ed Classical Bulletin 1925—45. *Publ*: The Epistle of St Clement of Rome & the Letters of St Ignatius of Antioch; The Gospel of St Mark; A Short Grammar of Classical Greek; First & Advanced Lessons in Greek; Latin Prose Composition: A Practical Course in Latin Composition; The Dream of Scipio. *Ctr*: Crate Fratras, Amer Ecclesiastical Rev, Catholic Biblical Quarterly, Classical Bulletin, etc. *s.s*: The Greek New Testament, The Apostolic Fathers. *a*: St Louis Univ. 221, Nth Grand St, St Louis 3, Mo. *T*: Jefferson 8080.

KLIBANSKY, Raymond, M.A., Ph.D. *b*: Paris 1905. *e*: Odenwald Sch, Univs of Heidelberg, Kiel & Hamburg. Dir of Studies Warburg Institute, Univ of London 1947—. *n.a*: Gen-Ed Corpus Platonicum Medii Aevi, Jt-Ed Mediæval & Renaissance Studies. *Publ*: Nichoiai de Cusa Opera Omnia; The Continuity of the Plantonic Tradition; Ein Proklos-Fund und seine Bedentung; Magistri Eckardi Opera Latina; Philosophy & History Essays (Jt Ed with J. Paton); etc. *Ctr*: Enciclopedia Italiana, Revue du Moyen Age Latin, Times Litt Supp, etc, *s.s*: Philosophy of Religion & History, History of Philosophy esp Antiquity, Middle Ages, Renaissance, 17th & 18th Centuries. *Rec*: Reading ancient MSS. *a*: Oriel College, Oxford. *T*: 3135, & McGill University, Montreal, Canada.

KLICKMANN, Flora. *m*: E. Henderson-Smith. Author & Ed. *n.a*: Asst Ed Windsor Mag, Ed G.O.P. & Woman's Mag (22y), etc. *Publ*: The Flower-Patch Among the Hills (29 edns); Between the Larch-woods & the Weir; Mending Your Nerves; The Lure of the Pen; Mystery in the Windflower Wood; The Trail of the Ragged Robin; The Carillon of Scarpa; The Shining Way; Visitors at the Flower-Patch; The Path to Fame; Delicate Fuss; The Flower-Patch Garden Book; The Lady with the Crumbs; etc. *s.s*: Music, Forestry, Needlecraft. *a*: The Flower Patch, nr Tintern, Chepstow.

KLINE, Burton. *b*: Williamsport, Penna. *e*: Priv & Harvard Univ. *m*: Madeleine Messinger Kline. *d*: 1. Author, Editor. *n.a*: Mag Ed Boston Ev Transcript 1904—18, New York Herald Tribune' 18—19, Philadelphia Public Ledger '22. *Publ*: Three Novels & 5 Vols on Politics, Industry etc. *Ctr*: American & English Mags. *s.s*: Life in General. *Rec*: Figure skating, golf. *a*: Westfield, New Jersey. *T*: Westfield 2-0341.

KLINGBERG, Frank Joseph, A.M., Ph.D. *e*: Univ of Kansas Yale. *m*: Elizabeth Wyssor Klingberg. *s*: 1. Prof History Univ of California. *Publ*: The Anti-Slavery Movement in England; A Side-Light on Anglo-American Relations; Old Sherry, Portrait of a Virginia Family (collab); Anglican Humanitarianism in Colonial New York; The Morning of America; An Appraisal of the Negro in Colonial South Carolina; Main Currents in English History; The Warning Drum: The British Home Front Faces Napoleon (collab); Carolina Chronicle: The Papers of Commissary Gideon Johnston 1707—1716; A Free Church in a Free State. *Ctr*: American Historical Review, Journ of Modern History, Journ of Southern History. *s.s*: British-American Humanitarianism in the 18th & 19th Centuries. *c*: Authors (London), Lincoln (Los Angeles). *a*: University of California, Los Angeles 24, California. *T*: Arizona 34578

KLOPPER, Harry. *b*: Vienna 1920. *e*: Vienna. Journalist, A.I.L. *n.a*: Foreign Ed New Meridan, The Gate, Albion 1946—. *Ctr*: Coventry E. Telegraph & Standard, Populaire (France), Journal (Vienna), Der Tag (Vienna). *s.s*: Children's & Youth Questions, Sociology, Police & Crime reporting. *a*: Flat 6, 46 Vauxhall Bridge Rd, London, S.W.1. *T*: Victoria 1621.

KNAGGS, Dr. H. V. Cons Physician. *Publ*: Indigestion: Its Cause & Cure; Rheumatism & Allied Ailments; How to Prevent Cancer; etc. *a*: 25 Wimpole St, W.1. *t*: Langham 1160.

KNAPLUND, Paul, M.A., Ph.D. *b*: Bodo, Norway 1885. *e*: Redwing Sem Minn & Univ of Wisconsin. *m*: Dorothy King. *s*: 1. *d*: 1. Prof of History Univ of Wisc, Kt 1st Class, Order of St Olav Norway. *n.a*: Ed-Bd Journ of Modern History 1929—32 & Norwegian-Amer Hist Assoc '30—44. *Publ*: The British Empire 1815—1939; Gladstone & Britain's Imperial Policy; Gladstone's Foreign Policy; Editor, Speeches on Foreign Affairs by Sir Edward Grey 1904—14; Letters From the Berlin Embassy 1871—74 & 1810—85; etc. *Ctr*: Amer Hist & Canadian Hist Revs, Journ of Modern Hist, Historisk Tidsskrift, Victoria Hist Mag. *s.s*: British Empire History. *Rec*: Walking. *c*: University. *a*: 1850 Summit Ave, Madison 5, Wisconsin, U.S.A. *T*: Badger 975.

KNAPP, Rev. Sheldon. *b*: Houghton-on-the-Hill 1866. *e*: Crescent Acad, York & Meth Col Richmond. *m*: Florence Bestall. *s*: 5. *d*: 3. Meth Min (ret). *Publ*: Four Scientific Principles (illus by 24 Cartoons); The Three Laws of Prayer; The National Crisis; The A.B.C. of Monetary Reform; etc. *s.s*: Religious healing, monetary reform. Meth Missny Ceylon 15 y. *Rec*: Cycling. *a*: Rose Cottage, N. Curry, Taunton.

KNAPP, Valentine. *b*: Kingston-on-Thames, 1861. *e*: Christ's Hospital. *m*: (1) Annie Powell; (2) Florence Ellen Blatchford. *s*: 4 (1 decd). Journalist (retired). *n.a*: Surrey Comet, 1887—1920. *Rec*: Golf, walking. Director of Knapp, Drewett & Sons Ltd: Kingston-on-Thames. *c*: Pres Newspaper Soc '19—22, Hon Treasurer Newspaper Soc '23—34, Chm Journalism Cmt, Univ of London '22—32, Authors'. Press. *a*: Sidmouth, Devon. *t*: 349.

KNAPP-FISHER, H.C. Author. *Publ*: The World of Nature; The Modern World; The Ship of State; etc. *a*: 16 Graham Terr, London, S.W.1.

KNAPPEN, Marshall Mason, M.A., Ph.D., F.R.Hist.S. *b*: Sioux Falls, Sth Dakota 1901. *e*: Coll of Wooster, Univs of Oxf & Cornell. Prof of Hist & Polit Science Michigan State Univ. *Publ*: Tudor Puritanism; Constitutional & Legal History of England; And Call it Peace. *Ctr*: Journ of Mod Hist, Amer Hist Rev, Church Hist. *s.s*: English Puritanism, Amer Mil Govt & Foreign Policy. *Rec*: Tennis, walking. *w.s*: U.S. Army Air Corps 1942—46. *a*: Dept of Hist & Political Science, Michigan, U.S.A. *T*: 81511 Ext 340.

KNAPPETT, Rachel. *b*: Ormskirk, Lancs 1920. *Publ*: A Pullet on the Midden. *a*: Ormskirk, Lancashire.

KNARESBOROUGH, Rt. Rev. The Lord Bishop of. *Publ*: The Story of Ripon Minister; When Thou Hast Shut Thy Door; Penitence, Pardon & Progress. *a*: Methley Rectory, Leeds.

KNEEN, John Joseph, M.A., R.I.StO.O.(Norway). *b*: Douglas I.o.M. 1873. *e*: St George's, Douglas, I.o.M. *m*: (1) Margaret Ann Tasker; (2) Catherine Alice Bridson. *s*: 2. *d*: 1. Confectioner. *Publ*: Direct Method of Teaching Manx; Cregeen's Manx Dictionary (2nd Ed); Place Names of the I.o.M.; A Grammar of the Manx Language, etc. *c.t*: I.o.M. press. *s.s*: Place & personal nomenclature. *Rec*: writing dialect plays. *a*: 3 Queen's Av, Douglas, I.o.M.

KNIBB, Gwen. *b*: Lon 1906. *e*: Friern Barnet G.S. & Bedford Col. Journalist. *n.a*: Sub-Ed Master Builder '28–31, Ed Timber News '31–34. Mem N.U.J. '28–. *c.t*: Barnet Press, Muswell Hill Record, Lady, Advertising World, Machine Woodworker. *s.s*: Fashions, needlework, fiction. *Rec*: Hockey, tennis. *a*: Overstrand, 36 Bethune Av, N.11. *t*: Finchley 1805.

KNICKERBOCKER, Hubert Renfro. *b*: Texas, U.S.A. 1898. *e*: A.B. Southwestern U., Georgetown, Texas, Columbia U., N.Y. & Munich, Vienna & Berlin Univs. Journalist. *n.a*: Newark Morning Ledger, Newark, N.J. 1921–22, N.Y. Evening Post & N.Y. Sun '22, Southern Meth U., Dallas, Texas '22–23, N.Y. Evening Post & Phila Public Ledger, Berlin '24, News Service, Moscow '25–26, Berlin '27–28, Public Ledger Berlin '28–33, Roving Corr Internat News Service, Europe & Asia '33–. *Publ*: The Soviet Union's Five Year Plan; Soviet Trade & World Depression; Germany, Fascist or Soviet?; Can Europe Recover?; Will War Come?. *s.s*: Internat affairs. *a*: c/o Internat News Service, 78 Fleet St, E.C.4. *t*: Central 5641.

KNIGHT, Arthur Harold John. *b*: West Buckland, Nth Devon 1903. *e*: Marlborough Coll & Trinity Coll Camb. *m*: Ella Dutton. *s*: 1. *d*: 1. Fellow & Lecturer Trinity College, University Lecturer in German & Dir Scandinavian Studies Cambridge Univ. *Publ*: Aspects of the Life & Works of Nietzsche; Heinrich Julius, Duke of Brunswick. *Ctr*: Numerous Critical & Literary periodicals. *s.s*: German & Scandinavian Literature, History & Thought. *Rec*: Ski-ing, sailing mountaineering *a*: Trinity College, Cambridge.

KNIGHT, Capt. Charles William Robert, M.C. *b*: Sevenoaks 1884. *e*: Sevenoaks Sch. *m*: Eva Olive Margaret Bennett (dec'd). *d*: 1. Lecturer on Bird Life in Gt Britain, Amer, Canada, Ireland & Sth Africa 1920–. *Publ*: Wild life in the Tree Tops; The Book of the Golden Eagle; Aristocrats of the Air; Mr Ramshaw, My Eagle; All British Eagle. *Ctr*: Country Life, Field, Nat Geographic, Amer Nat Hist, etc. *s.s*: Bird Life. *Rec*: Falconry. *c*: Savage, etc. *a*: Quebec Cottage, Montreal Park, Sevenoaks, Kent. *T*: Sevenoaks 2960.

KNIGHT, Clara Millicent, D.Litt. Writer, Late Reader in Classics King's Coll Univ of Lond. *n.a*: Jt-Ed The Animal Year Book. *Ctr*: Eng & Am periodicals. *Rec*: Music. *a*: 6 Forres Gardens, London, N.W.11. *T*: Speedwell 1007.

KNIGHT, Clifford. *b*: Fulton, Kansas 1886. *e*: Public Schs, Washburn Coll, Univ of Michigan. *m*: Jessamine Paret. Novelist. *n.a*: Ed Staff Kansas City Star 1912, '20–30. *Publ*: The "Affair" (series) of the Voice; of the Scarlet Crab; of the Heavenly Voice; of the Ginger Lei; at Palm Springs; of the Black Sombrero; on the Painted Desert; of the Circus Queen; in Death Valley; of the Crimson Gull; of the Skiing Clown; of the Limping Sailor; of the Splintered Heart; of the Jade Monkey; of the Fainting Butler; of the Dead Stranger; of the Corpse Escort; of the Golden Buzzard; of the Sixth Button. *Ctr*: Various in serial form. *Rec*: Landscape painting. *c*: Authors (Hollywood). *a*: 1428 Pandora Ave, Los Angeles 24, Calif, U.S.A. *T*: Arizona 30035.

KNIGHT, Edward Frank. *b*: Romsey 1906. *e*: Barton Peveril, Eastleigh, Hants. Journalist. *n.a*: Andover Advertiser, & Romsey Advertiser '23–29, Bedfordshire Times '29–. *a*: 137 Coventry Rd, Bedford.

KNIGHT, Esmond. *b*: East Sheen 1906. *e*: Westminster Sch. *m*: Nora Swinburne. *d*: 1. Actor Old Vic 1925, later B'ham Rep & West End Productions. *Publ*: Seeking the Bubble. *Ctr*: Various magazines, Hutchinsons. *s.s*: The Theatre. *Rec*: Collecting toy soldiers (14th & 15th Cent), falconry. *w.s*: R.N.V.R. 1940–41. *a*: Savage, Green Room, R.N.V.R. *a*: 35 Bywater St, London, S.W.3. *T*: Kensington 1611.

KNIGHT, Geoffrey Cureton. Surgeon. *Publ*: St Bartholomew's Hosp Journ; Journ Physiology. *a*: 29 Abercorn Place, N.W.8. *t*: Maida Vale 6023.

KNIGHT, George ("G.E.O."), F.R.G.S. *b*: Lon 1885. *e*: Priv. Journalist & Ed. *n.a*: News Chronicle (Foreign Corr Helsingfors) 1926–27, Statesman of India Corr '21–22, Ed Books & Authors '31–33, Ed Anglo-German News & Views '34, Ihminen Helsingfors Ed '26–27. *Publ*: Intimate Glimpses of Mysterious Tibet; In Defence of Germany; Germany's Demand for Security; Mahatma Gandhi; The Story of a Rolling Stone; etc. *c.t*: News Chronicle, N.Y. Times, Books & Authors, Englishman of India, etc. *s.s*: Trav, politics. 1st to secure moving pictures of the city of Lhasa, capital of Tibet, went to Bolshevik Russia disguised as Beggar '26, Civil Prisoner of War '14–18, Trav Extensively. *Rec*: Amateur acting. *c*: Jr Green. *a*: Fetter Hse, Fetter Lane, E.C.4.

KNIGHT, George Wilson, M.A.(Oxon). *b*: Sutton 1897. *e*: Dulwich Coll, St Edmund Hall Oxf. Reader in English Lit Leeds Univ. *Publ*: The Christian Renaissance; The Wheel of Fire; The Imperial Theme; The Shakespearian Tempest; The Crown of Life; The Olive & the Sword; Principles of Shakespearian Production; The Burning Oracle; The Starlit Dome; Chariot of Wrath; Hiroshima; Atlantic Crossing The Dynasty of Stowe. *Ctr*: Hibbert Journ, Criterion, Dublin Rev, Times Lit Supp, etc. *s.s*: Lit interpretation. *w.s*: Mesopotamia & Nth Persia 1917—20. *a*: The University, Leeds 2.

KNIGHT, Grant Cochran. *b*: Williamsport, Penn 1893. *e*: Albright & Gettysburg Colls, Columbia Univ. *m*: Ruth M. Elliott. *d*: 2. Univ Prof. *Publ*: James Lane Allen & the Genteel Tradition; American Literature & Culture; The Novel in English; The Sealed Well; Superlatives; Ed: Readings from the American Mercury; Bookman, Sat Review of Lit, etc. *s.s*: American Lit (especially the 1890's). *Rec*: Cinema, walking, music, motoring. *w.s*: 1918—19. *a*: 723 Cooper Drive, Lexington, Kentucky, U.S.A. *T*: 3067-R.

KNIGHT, Hadden, M.J.I. *b*: Lon 1904. *e*: Whitgift, Croydon & Slade Sc. *m*: Marie Lucas. *d*: 1. Journalist—F.L. & Author. *n.a*: Conducted The Knowledge Box Feature Page & Competition in Sunday News during '30. *Ctr*: London Opinion, Evening News, The Star, Daily Mirror, Sunday Mercury, Everybody's Weekly, Answers, etc. *s.s*: Criminology, wireless, films, Victorian age. Son of Alfred E. Knight, author & art expert, grandson of W. H. Knight, Victorian genre painter. *Rec*: Music, poetry, exploring Lon by night. *a*: 105 Briar Av, S.W.16.

KNIGHT, Holford, M.P., K.C. *b*: Kensington 1877. *e*: Priv. Lon Univ & Middle Temple. *m*: Christine Logan. *Publ*: Advancing Woman (reprinted essays, 1920). *c.t*: Fortnightly Review, Contemporary Review, Manchester Guardian, Nation, etc. *s.s*: Legal Reform. Started movement to open English Bar to Women '13. Conducted Rights of Way Act '32 (The Rambler's Charter) thro' H.o.C. Introduced Divorce Reform Bills into Parl '30, '31, '32, '33. Recorder of W. Ham. *s.s*: Legal reform. *Rec*: Walking. *c*: Reform. *a*: 2 Brick Ct, Temple, E.C.4. *t*: Cent 4393.

KNIGHT, Kobold. *b*: S. Africa 1895. *e*: S.A. Col Sc Cape Town. Writer. *n.a*: F/L. *Publ*: The Monsoon Bird; The Doctor of Souls; Paradise Island (with Evelyn Knight); Nerves; Textbook on Short-story Writing. *c.t*: Chambers's Journ, Storyteller Mag, Windsor, Pearson's, C. Tribune, etc. *s.s*: Love stories, dog stories. Ran away from home. War Service. France, Palestine, N. Russia and W. Africa. Wandered round the world doing odd jobs. Life as planter, soldier, sailor, etc. Took up writing & found early success. *Rec*: Tennis, yachting. *c*: Soc of Authors. *a*: 143 Hampstead Way, N.W.11. *t*: Speedwell 1645.

KNIGHT, Dame Laura, D.B.E., R.A., R.W.S., R.W.A., R.E., Hon LL.D.(St Andrews). *b*: Long Eaton, Derbyshire. *e*: Brincliffe, Nottingham, St Quentin, Aisne France. *m*: Harold Knight. Painter. *Publ*: Oil Paint & Grease Paint. *c*: Forum, Lyceum. *a*: 16 Langford Pl, St John's Wood, London, N.W.8.

KNIGHT, Leonard A. Author. *Publ*: The Creeping Death; The Pawn; Deadman's Bay; Spring Cruise; The Creaking Tree Mystery; Redbeard; Spanish Cove; Conqueror's Road; The Dancing Stones; Judgement Rock; & (wireless plays) The Slip; Green Identity Card; etc. *a*: c/o Sampson Low Ltd, 25 Gilbert St, London, W.1.

KNIGHT, Lewis Stanley. *b*: Swansea 1886. *e*: Univ Coll of Wales Aberystwyth. Schoolmaster. *Publ*: The Welsh Grammar Schools to 1600. *Ctr*: Trans Cymrodorion, Archæologia Cambrensis, Carmarthenshire Antiquarian & Field Club Trans. *s.s*: Education (hist). *a*: Lewis School, Pengam, Mon.

KNIGHT, Maurice Rickards. *b*: Lon 1897. *m*: Eileen Smith. Publicity. *n.a*: Advertising Staff Hampstead Advertiser 1923-. *Publ*: Model Aeroplanes Simply Explained & Section in the Model Aeroplane Manual. *c.t*: Mod Eng. *s.s*: Aviation. War Service '14–19 R.N.A.S. & R.A.F. *c*: Asst Hon Sec Model Aircraft. *a*: 8 Cyprus St, E.2.

KNIGHT, Melvin Moses, A.B., Ph.D. *b*: nr Bloomington, Ill 1887. *e*: Texas Christian & Clark Univs. *m*: Eleanor Gehmann. University Professor. *Publ*: Economic History of Europe; The Americans in Santo Domingo; Morocco as a French Economic Venture; Introduction to Modern Economic History; etc. *Ctr*: Ency of Soc Sciences, etc. *s.s*: Economic History, Colonial Economy. *Rec*: Instrument making, pistol shooting, golf, reading. *w.s*: 1917–19 A.E.F., '42–44 U.S. Dept of State. *a*: 1397 La Loma Ave, Berkeley 8, California, U.S.A. *T*: Ashberry 3-6205.

KNIGHT, Rachel Theodosia ("R.T.G."). *b*: India 1869. *e*: Lon & Dresden. *m*: H. M. Knight (dec). Student of Comparative Philos, Religions & Art. *Publ*: (Trans from German), Mahayana Doctrines of Salvation (by D. St Schayer); Expressionism (by Herman Bahr); Mystic Lyrics from the Indian Middle Ages (a free trans); Mongolian Horde (by Roland Strasser), etc. *c.t*: N. China Herald, Madras Mail, etc. *s.s*: Art, langs. Lived 24 y on mountains of S. India. Extensive travel. *Rec*: Gardening, travel. *a*: Arkeden, The Bishop's Av, Finchley, N.2. *t*: Speedwell 4763.

KNIGHT, Robert Thomas. *b*: Fenny Compton 1896. *e*: Sec Sch Leamington. *m*: Margaret Emsie Choules. *s*: 1. *d*: 1. Newspaper Ed. *n.a*: Ed Royal Leamington Spa Courier 1944—, Ed Warwickshire Journ '36—. *Ctr*: Birmingham Post & Mail, Times, Church Times, Guardian, Press Assoc, News Chron. *s.s*: Agriculture & Ecclesiastical subjects. *Rec*: Motoring, etc. *a*: Redroof, St Helen's Rd, Leamington Spa, Warwickshire. *T*: 885.

KNIGHT, William Francis Jackson, F.R.S.L. *b*: Sutton, Surrey 1895. *e*: Dulwich Coll & Hertford Coll Oxf. Reader in Classical Literature Univ Coll of South West Exeter 1943—, Recorder of Folk-lore to Devon Assoc '44—. *Publ*: Vergil's Troy; Cumæan Gates; Accentual Symmetry in Vergil; Roman Vergil; A Virgilian Sociology; Poetic Inspiration—an Approach to Vergil; etc. *Ctr*: Amer Journ of Philol, Antiquity, Classical Journ, Philol, Quarterly Rev & Weekly, Erasmus, Folk-Lore, Greece & Rome, Journ of Roman Studies, etc. *s.s*: Vergil & Homer, Ancient Religion & Folk-Lore, Poetic Metre. *w.s*: 1915—19 R.E's, B.E.F. *a*: University College of the South West, Exeter. *T*: Exeter 4141.

KNIGHT. William Stanley Macbean, B.Litt (Oxon). *b*: London 1869. *e*: New Coll Oxf. *m*: Winifred Ida O'Sullivan. *s*: 1. *d*: 4. Barrister-at-Law. *Publ*: Business Ency (6 vols) 1902; Ed subsequent Edns; History of Gt European War (10 vols '14—19); Life & Works of Hugo Grotius ('25); etc. *c.t*: Law Quarterly; Journal of Comparative Legislation & International Law. *s.s*: Internat Law. Law Tutor New Coll Oxf '18—19. Mem L.C.C. '06—09. *a*: 21 Old Sq, Lincoln's Inn, W.C. *t*: Hol 5024.

KNIGHT-ADKIN, JAMES HARRY (pen name Knight Adkin): schoolmaster; *b*. Cheltenham, Eng., Nov., 1879; *s*. Harry Kenrick and Georgina Elizabeth (Knight) KA.; educ. Glyngarter (Cheltenham), Cheltenham Coll., Keble Coll. (Oxford), D E G R E E S: B.A. (History Honors), M.A., 1926 (Oxford); *m*. Grace Evelyn Garner, Aug. 16, 1923. AUTHOR: Schoolboy Verses, 1896; The Woman Stealers, 1905. Editor: Courtney Lodge Chronicle; asst.-editor (1902-05), "V.C.". Contributor to Spectator, Voice of the Century, Graphic, Cornhill Mag. General character of writing: fiction, poems. Formerly house-master, Imperial Service Coll., Windsor; asst.-master Harrow Sch., 1926-27; War service, 1914-18, Gloucestershire 4th Regt. (lieut. and captain); Territorial Decoration, 3 War Medals; wounded at Ploegsteert, 1915; much war verse has been reprinted in American anthologies. Relig. denom., Anglican. CLUB: Oxford Union. OFFICE: Courtney Lodge School, near Abingdon, Berks. HOME: 69 Alma Road, Bristol, Eng.

KNIGHT-CLARKE, Wilfrid *b*: Stoke Newington N. 1899. *e*: Worksop Col Notts. Journalist. Prop- & Mang Ed n/p Services, 185 Fleet St, E.C.4. *a*: 185 Fleet St, E.C.4. *t*: Holborn 1700.

KNIGHTLY, Percy Frank, D.S.O., A.C.I.S. *b*: Aldershot 1874. *e*: King's Col Lon. *m*: Sophia Fletcher. *d*: 1. Registrar of Public Coy. *Publ*: Practical Coy Secretary (1931). *c.t*: Financial News & Secretary. *s.s*: Coy law. War Service '14–18 Desps. *Rec*: Motor. *c*: Chartered Inst of Secs. *a*: Britannic Hse, Finsbury Circus, E.C.2.

KNITTEL, John. *b*: India 1891. *m*:. *s*: 1. *d*: 2. Novelist & Playwright. *Publ*: Aaron West; Traveller in the Night; Nile Gold; Into the Abyss: Midnight

People; Cyprus Wine; Via Mala; Doctor Ibrahim; Power for Sale; The Asp & other stories; (Plays) The Torch; High Finance; Abd-El-Kader. Writes in German & English. Works published in U.S.A., England, Germany, Switzerland, Sweden, Denmark, Norway, etc. *a*: Maieufeld Grisons, Switzerland.

KNITTERMEYER, HINRICH JOHANN: library director; b. Hamburg, Germany, Feb. 20, 1891; s. Peter Hinrich and Marie Cäcilie (Beckmann) K.; educ. Realgymnasium of the Johanneums, Hamburg, Univs. of Jena, Heidelberg and Marburg. DEGREES: Ph.D. (Marburg); m. Augustine Louise Götte, 1920. AUTHOR: Universitätsreform, 1919; Erziehung zur Politik, 1919; Der Terminus transzendental in seiner historischen Entwicklung bis zu Kant, 1920; Die Philosophie und das Christentum, 1927; Schelling und die romantische Schule, 1928. Contributor to: Die Christliche Welt; Zwischen den Zeiten; Theologische Literaturzeitung; Zeitschrift für Theologie und Kirche, and many others. General character of writing: scientific, philosophical. CLUBS: Secretary of Bremer Wissenschaftliche Gesellschaft. Relig. denom., Lutheran. OFFICE: State Library, Bremen. HOME: Schwachhauser Heerstrasse 253, Bremen, Germany.

KNOBEL, Dr. W. B. *a*: 96 Westbourne Terr, W.2.

KNOBLOCK, Edward. *b*: 1874. Playwright. *Publ*: Plays—The Faun; Kismet; Milestones (with Arnold Bennett); Tiger, Tiger; The Good Companions (with J. B. Priestley); Grand Hotel (from novel by Vicki Baum); Hatter's Castle (from novel by A. J. Cronin); The Edwardians (from novel by V. Sackville-West); Evensong (with Beverley Nichols); Films—Red Wagon (from Eleanor Smith's Novel); etc, etc *a*: 21 Ashley Place, S.W.1. *t*: Victoria 2422.

KNOOP, Douglas. *b*: Manchester 1883. *e*: Wm Hulme's Gr Sch, Owen's Coll Manch. Prof of Econ. *Publ*: Industrial Conciliation & Arbitration; The Riddle of Unemployment; (with G. P. Jones) The Mediæval Mason; The Genesis of Freemasonry; etc. *Ctr*: Econ Journ, Econ Hist, etc. *s.s*: Econ Hist of Building Industry. *c*: Sheffield. *a*: 25 The Grove, Totley, Sheffield. *T*: 72515.

KNOTT, Ernest Walter, M.I.A.E., M.S.A.E. *b*: Lon 1890. *e*: Owen's Sc & Finsbury Tech Col. Auto Eng. *n.a*: Light Car & Cyclecar 1924. *Publ*: The Carburetter Handbook; The Book of the Douglas. *c.t*: Light Car & Cyclecar, Motor Cycling, Fleetway Press, etc. *s.s*: Carburetters & engine tuning. *Rec*: Shooting, fishing. *a*: 87 Princes Park Av, N.W.11. *t*: Speedwell 1638.

KNOTT, Frank Alexander, M.D., F.R.C.P., D.P.H., A.R.C.Sc. *b*: London 1889. *e*: London Univ & Guy's Hosp. *m*: Dorothy Thomas. *d*: 2. Dir of Dept Clinical Pathology Guy's Hosp. *Publ*: Diseases of Respiratory Tract; Clinical Bacteriology. *Ctr*: Med & Public Health Journs. *s.s*: Lab Investigation. *c*: Junior Carlton, Athenæum. *a*: Guy's Hospital, London, S.E.1. *T*: Hop 1654; & Rushmere, Southside, Wimbledon Common, London, S.W.19. *T*: Wimbledon 1464.

KNOTT, John William, F.R.S.A. *b*: Undercliffe, Bradford 1906. *e*: Elem Sch & Priv. *m*: Evelyn Ince. *s*: 1. Printer, Teacher of Shorthand. *Publ*: Modern Shorthand. *s.s*: Shorthand, Modern Printing, Letterpress, Comparative Religion, Mythology, Transport. *Rec*: Reading. *a*: 1 Granville Rd, Frizinghall, Bradford, Yorks. *T*: 41789.

KNOWLES, Rev. A. *b*: 1858. *e*: Kingswood Sc, St John's Col Cam. *m*: Bertha L. Vigor. *d*: 4. *Publ*: Textbook of Anglican Service Music from Tallis to S.S. Wesley. *a*: Lilley Rectory, Luton. *t*: 732X.

KNOWLES, Archibald Campbell. D.D. *b*: Philadelphia 1865. *e*: Rugby Academy & Univ of Pennsylvania, Philadelphia. *m*: Mary Clements Stocker (dec'd). *d*: 1. Priest of the Episcopal Church U.S.A., Rector of Saint Alban's Church Olney Philadelphia. *Publ*: Lights & Shadows of the Sacred Ministry; The Practice of Religion; A Rendezvous with Destiny; Belief & Worship of the Anglican Church; Joscelyn Vernon: A story of King Charles I Time; Turning Points; **The Triumph of the Cross; Come Unto Me; The Holy Christ Child**: The Incarnation; The Life of Offering; Adventures in the Alps. *Rec*: Cricket, boating, climbing. *a*: 555 Pelham Road, Germantown, Philadelphia 19, U.S.A. *T*: GE 8-0243.

KNOWLES, Dorothy, M.A., L.R.A.M., D.èsL.(Paris). *b*: Johannesburg 1906. *e*: Univs of Leeds & Paris. Lect in French Liverpool Univ. *Publ*: La Réaction Idéaliste au Théâtre depuis 1890; The Censor, The Drama & the Film 1900—34. *s.s*: Mod French Drama. *Rec*: Fencing, operatic dancing. *a*: 14 Devonshire Rd, Liverpool 8.

KNOWLES, George Hogan. Author. *Publ*: Jungle Haunts; In the Grip of the Jungles; Terrors of the Jungle; A Jungle Cocktail. *a*: c/o Wright & Brown, 4 Farringdon Ave, E.C.4.

KNOWLES, George William. *b*: Bentham. *e*: Bentham Gr Sch, Nat Univ of Ireland. *m*: F. Lilian Pepler. Barrister. *Publ*: The Tale of the Turf; Book of Dogs. *a*: 33 Haling Park Rd, Croydon.

KNOWLES, Rev. Kenneth Davenport, M.A., D.D., H.C.F. Archdeacon of Huntingdon—Solicitor of the Supreme Court of Judicature. *Publ*: War Time Sermons; Huntingdon Children's Prayer Book; The Silent Soldier of Huntingdon; Earl Haig; Backs to the Wall; Buckden; Brampton Wood; etc. *c.t*: Ch of E N/p. *a*: White House, Buckden, Huntingdons. *t*: Buckden 15.

KNOWLES, Leonard. *b*: Gravesend 1901. Married. Reporter. *n.a*: Sports staff a Lon Sunday N/p; then with Brighton & Hove Herald; Brighton staff corr Star & News Chron '26–. *s.s*: Pre-hist. *a*: 36 Ship St, Brighton. *t*: 5000.

KNOWLES, Mabel Winifred (see **WINCHESTER, Mark**). *b*: Streatham 1875. Author. *Publ*: Henry de Navarre; Theodore; Red Fleur de Lys; Marcel of Zephyrs; Gipsy King; The Greater Covenant; Flower o' the Moor, etc. *Ctr*: Sentinel, etc. *s.s*: Hist, Novels, Girls' books. *a*: 93, Maplin Rd, Custom Hse, London, E.16. *T*: Albert Dock 2480.

KNOWLES, Rev. Michael David, Litt.D., F.B.A. *b*: Studley, Warwickshire 1896. *e*: Downside Sch, Christ's Coll Camb, Rome. R.C. Priest, Fellow of Peterhouse, Prof of Medieval Hist Camb Univ. *n.a*: Ed Downside Review 1930—34. *Publ*: The Monastic Order in England; Religious Houses of Medieval England. *Ctr*: Downside Rev, Dublin Rev, English Historical Rev, Cambridge Historical Journ. *s.s*: Medieval Religious History. *a*: Peterhouse, Cambridge. *T*: 4256.

KNOWLES, Dr. R. O. Gen Practitioner & Cert Surg. *a*: Clwyd Hse, Woodchurch Rd, Birkenhead.

KNOWLES, Susanne. *b*: Morby Hall, York. *e*: Abroad. Civil Servant. *Publ*: Birth of Venus & other Poems. *Ctr*: Time & Tide, Observer, New English Weekly, Poetry Quarterly. *s.s*: Poetry. *c*: P.E.N. *a*: 41 Lexham Gdns, London, W.8.

KNOWLES, Vernon. *b*: Adelaide, Sth Australia 1899. *e*: Pulteney Gr Sch & Univ of Western Australia. Author.

Publ: The Street of Queer Houses; Beads of Coloured Days; Silver Nutmegs; The Ladder; Pitiful Dust; Eternity in an Hour; Prince Jonathan; The Experience of Poetry; Two & Two Make Five; Love is My Enemy. *Ctr*: Cornhill Mag, Bookman, Ev News, Yorks Post, various Aust papers, etc. *s.s*: Poetry, Australia. *Rec*: Travel, golf. *a*: 79a The Chase, London, S.W.4. *T*: Macaulay 5191.

KNOWLES, William Plenderleith, M.C., M.A., D.Sc. *b*: Manchester 1891. *e*: Board Sch & Priv. *m*: Winifred Lawton. *s*: 1. *d*: 2. Author & Lecturer. *Publ*: Jim McWhirter. *s.s*: Biology, Psychology, Respiration, Dietetics, Eugenics, etc. *Rec*: Motoring, walking, swimming. *a*: 21 Thornton Way, Hampstead, London, N.W.11. *T*: Speedwell 6981.

KNOWLSON, F. P. *a*: 289 Manningham Lane, Bradford.

KNOWLSON, Thomas Sharper. *b*: Knaresbrough, Yorks 1867. *e*: Victoria Park Sch Harrogate, Richmond Coll Surrey. Author & Journalist. *n.a*: Sub-Ed London Opinion 1904—1908, Asst to Lit Ed N.Y. Ev Post '24. *Publ*: Art of Thinking; Originality; Think for Yourself; Selling your Ability; Your Mind & How To Use It; Put On Your Thinking Cap; Creating New Ideas. *Ctr*: Great Thoughts, New York Times, Dly Express, Fort: nightly. *s.s*: Psychology in its more practical issues. Wrote the Original Pelman course (1911—1936). *Rec*-Walking. *a*: Swingle Swangle, Matfield, Tonbridge, Kent. *T*: Brenchley 192.

KNOWLTON, Daniel Chauncey, A.B., Ph.D. *b*: Cazenovia, N.Y. 1876. *e*: Cazenovia Sem, Univs of Cornell & Bonn. *m*: Lou Osborne. *s*: 2. Prof of Hist. *n.a*: Asst-Ed Educ Service, Current Illus News 1927—30, Educ Staff Lit Digest '19—26, Ed Bd Hist Teachers Mag (later Social Studies). *Publ*: Motion Pictures in History Teaching; History & other Social Studies in Junior High School; Our American Way in Community Life; Making History Graphic; The Government of New Jersey; Essentials in Modern European History. *Ctr*: Education, Social Studies, Social Educ, American Hist Review, N.Y. Times, etc. *s.s*: History & Social Studies, Use of Visual Materials in Classroom. *Rec*: Book collector, philately, painting. *a*: Cazenovia, N.Y., U.S.A. *T*: 304-R.

KNOX, Anna Allnutt. *e*: Sherborne. *m*: Henry Daniell. Writer. *Publ*: The Green Bough; Flowerdown; Vallejo Kitty; Sons and Daughters; Featured on Broadway. *a*: 135 Swan Court, S.W.1.

KNOX, Collie. *b*: London. *e*: Rugby & R.M.C. Sandhurst. Married. Author & Journalist. *n.a*: Sub-Ed Rep Special Writer & Feature Ed Daily Express 1928—33, Spec Columnist & Radio Columnist Daily Mail '33—40, Spec Writer The Star, M.O.I. & Dir P.R. E.N.S.A. '40—45, rejoined Dly Mail '45—. *Publ*: It Might Have Been You; People of Quality; It Had to be Me; For Ever England; Heroes All; Atlantic Battle; The Un-beaten Track; Draw up your Chair; Collie Knox Calling; Collie Knox Re-calls; Collie Knox Again. *Ctr*: Dly Mail, Star, Newnes & Pearson Publs, The Queen Mag. *Rec*: Lawn tennis, motoring, golf, lyric writing. *c*: Marlborough, Garrick, Hurlingham, etc. *w.s*: 1st World War R.F.C. (Pilot) & Regular Army Officer until 1927. *a*: 19 Barrie Hse, Lancaster Gate, London, W.2.

KNOX, Rt. Rev. Edmund Arbuthnott, HonD.D. (Oxon & Aberd). *b*: Bangalore 1847. *e*: St Paul's Sc, & Corpus Christi, Oxf. *m*: (1) Ellen Penelope French. (2) Ethel Mary Newton. *s*: 4. *d*: 2. Bishop (ret). *Publ*: Pastors & Teachers; Sacrifice or Sacrament; Robert Leighton; etc. *c.t*: Record, Spectator, XIXth Century & After, Contemporary Review. Church-man. *s.s*: Reformation hist & lit. Archdeacon of Birm. Bishop Suffragan of Coventry. Bishop of M/C. *c*: National. *a*: 18 Beckenham Gve, Shortlands, Kent. *t*: Ravensbourne 0486.

KNOX, Edmund Valpy. *b*: Oxf 1881. *e*: Rugby, Oxf. *m*: Christina Frances Hicks. *s*: 1. *d*: 1. Author & Journalist; Ed of Punch. *n.a*: Mem staff of Punch 1920—. *Publ*: The Brazen Lyre; Parodies Regained; Fiction As She is Wrote; Gorgeous Times; Poems of Impudence; I'll Tell the World; This Other Eden; Folly Calling; Here's Misery, etc. *c.t*: Observer, Spectator, Sunday Times, Daily News, Morning Post, Radio Times, etc. War Service '14—18, wounded. Min of Labour '19—20. Ed Methuen's Library of Humour. *Rec*: Golf, fishing. *c*: Savile, Garrick, United Univs, Athenæum. *a*: 12 Clarence Terr, Regent's Pk, N.W.1. *t*: Paddington 4769.

KNOX, Howard Vicenté. *b*: Trinidad. *e*: Exeter Col Oxf, Sandhurst. *m*: Nesta Myfanwy Thomas. Army. *Publ*: The Philosophy of William James (1914); The Will to be Free; The Evolution of Truth ('30). *c.t*: Mind, Hibbert Journ, Quart Review, etc. *s.s*: Philos. War Service. *Rec*: Mountaineering, ski-ing, field ornithology. *c*: Alpine. *a*: 16 Park Terr, Oxf. *t*: 2188.

KNOX, Katharine McCook. *b*: Washington, D.C., U.S.A. *e*: Miss Spence's Sc, New York City. Married. *d*: 1. *Publ*: The Sharples: Their Portraits of George Washington and His Contemporaries. *s.s*: Early American paintings. Connected with the Frick Art Reference Library, New York City. Chm, Portrait Cmt of the George Washington Bicentennial Loan Exhibition, '32. *c*: Colony, New York City, Chevy Chase, Washington, Pittsburg Golf. *a*: 1642 21st St, Washington, D.C., U.S.A.

KNOX, Rt. Rev. Monsignor Ronald Arbuthnott. *Publ*: Some Loose Stones; Sanctions, a Frivolity; The Belief of Catholics; Essays in Satire; Caliban in Grub Street; Barchester Pilgrimage; God & the Atom; etc. *a*: Chapel Hse, Aldenham Park, Bridgnorth.

KNOX, Thomas Malcolm. *b*: Birkenhead 1900. *e*: Liverpool Institute & Pembroke Coll Oxf. *m*: Dorothy Ellen Jolly. Professor of Moral Philosophy. *Publ*: Translations, with commentary of Works by Hegel; R. G. Collingwood's posthumous papers (Ed). *s.s*: History of Philosophy, expecially Philosophy of Hegel. *a*: Craigard, The Scores, St Andrews, Fife. *T*: St Andrews 659.

KNOX, Rev. Wilfred Lawrence, M.A., D.D. *b*: Kibworth, Leics. *e*: Rugby Sch & Trinity Coll Oxf. Fellow & Chaplain Pembroke Coll Cambridge. *Publ*: St Paul & the Church of Jerusalem; St Paul & the Church of the Gentiles; Some Hellenistic Elements in Primitive Christianity. *Ctr*: Journ of Theological Studies, Theology. *s.s*: Theology. *Rec*: Fishing & gardening. *a*: Pembroke College, Cambridge.

KNUDSEN, Sven Valdemar. *b*: Copenhagen 1892. *e*: Univ of Copenhagen. *m*: Paula V. Knudsen. Pres The Directory of Boys & Girls of all Nations. *n.a*: Travelling Corres Berlingske 1921—22, Politiken U.S.A. '25—27, Dept Ed The Open Road Mag Boston '26—, Ekstrabladet Copenhagen '35—36, Illustreret Familie Journ Copenhagen '39—, Ed Verdensposten Copenhagen '42—43. *Publ*: With Sven Spejder Around the World; Boys of All Nations; My Friends Abroad; Books of Letters. *Ctr*: Illustreret Familie Journ Denmark, The Open Road Mag Boston, Allers Wkly Sweden. *s.s*: World-wide Correspondence for Youths of

14—21 years, Worldwide Interchange of Youths of 16—21 years. *c*: University, Copenhagen, Adventurers, Denmark, Authors' Denmark. *a*: 62 Vestersöhus, Copenhagen, Denmark. *T*: Pala 6686.

KNUDSON, Albert Cornelius, LL.D., Hon.D.D. *b*: Grandmeadow, Minn 1873. *e*: Univs of Minnesota, Boston, Jena & Berlin. *m*: Matilde S. Johnson. Prof & Dean Boston Univ Sch of Theology. *Publ*: The Principles of Christian Ethics; The Doctrine of God; The Doctrine of Redemption; The Religious Teaching of the Old Testament; The Philosophy of Personalism; The Philosophy of Peace & War; The Validity of Religious Experience; The Beacon Lights of Prophecy. *Ctr*: Methodist Review, Religion in Life, Journ of Religion, Personalist. *s.s*: Systematic Theology & Philosophy. *c*: Boston Authors. *a*: 18 Forest St, Cambridge, Mass, U.S.A. *T*: Kirkland 7088.

KOBER, Arthur. *b*: Brody, Austria-Hungary 1900. *e*: New York Elem Sch. *m*: Margaret Frohnknecht. *d*: 1. Writer, Theatrical Publicity. *Publ*: Having Wonderful Time (play, film & book); Thunder over the Bronx; My Dear Bella; That Man is Here Again; "Parm Me"; Pardon Me for Pointing. *Ctr*: New Yorker, Red Book, Theatre Mag, Morning Telegraph, Paris Comet, New York World, etc. *s.s*: Play & Film Writing. *a*: 1010 Fifth Ave, New York 28, N.Y.

KOBER, August Heinrich, D.Phil. *b*: Potsdam 1887. *e*: Berlin Univ. *m*: Mechtildis Vleugels. *s*: 1. Author, essayist, novelist, dramatist. *Publ*: Star Turns (1928); Circus Nights & Circus Days ('31); The Six Aquilas ('32). Travelled widely in America, Balkans, Russia, Scandinavia, etc. *c*: P.E.N. *a*: c/o Sampson Low, Marston & Co Ltd, 100 Southwark St, Lon S.E.

KOCH, Ludwig. *m*: Nellie Sylvia Herz. *s*: 1. *d*: 1. Broadcaster, Lecturer, Recorder of Nature Sounds, Dir of the Culture & Education Dept of the Odeon & Parlophone Gram Co. *Publ*: Songs of Wild Birds (with E. M. Nicholson); More Songs of Wild Birds (with E. M Nicholson); Animal Language (with Julian Huxley); Hunting by Ear (with Michael Berry & D. W. E. Brock). *Ctr*: Times, Picture Post. *s.s*: Originator of Sound-Books a combination of Text, Picture & Sound. Naturalist. *Rec*: To explore British countryside. *a*: 7 Gordon Hse, Western Ave, London, W.5. *T*: Perivale 3758.

KOCHER, Alfred Lawrence, M.A. *b*: San Jose, Calif 1885. *e*: Stanford Univ, Penna State Coll & Mass Inst of Tech. *m*: Margaret Taylor. *s*: 1. *d*: 1. Architect, Editor. *n.a*: Architectural Record Mang-Ed 1927—35 & Ed '35—39. *Publ*: Early Architecture of Pennsylvania; The Architectural Centre. *Ctr*: Architectural Rev (Lond) & Forum (N.Y.), Progressive Architecture, etc. *s.s*: 18th Century & Modern Architecture, Prefabrication. *a*: Coke Garrett Hse, Williamsburg, Virginia, U.S.A. *T*: 367.J.

KOENIG, Leo. *b*: Odessa, Russia 1889. *e*: Russia, Jerusalem, Munich, Paris. *m*: Fanny Hildebrand. *d*: 3. *n.a*: Ed Renaissance London 1920. *Publ*: Writers & Books; A Week After Life; Where Do We Stand; Ghetto or State; Art Monographs. *Ctr*: The Day (N.Y.), The Zukunft (N.Y.) *s.s*: Yiddish Lit, Jews in Art. *a*: 56 Hurstwood Rd, London, N.W.11. *T*: Speedwell 2115.

KOESTLER, Arthur. *b*: Budapest 1905. *e*: University of Vienna. Author. *Publ*: Spanish Testament; Darkness at Noon; Gladiators; Scum of the Earth; Arrival & Departure; The Yogi & the Commissar; Thieves in the Night. *Rec*: Chess: *c*: P.E.N. *a*: c/o Macmillans, Publishers, St Martin's St, London, W.C.2.

KOHN, Hans. *b*: Prague 1891. *e*: Prague Univ. *m*: Yetty Wahl. *s*: 1. Prof of Mod European Hist Smith Coll Northampton Mass. *n.a*: Corr Frankfurter Zeitung 1925—33, Neue Furcher Zeitung '26—35, Ed Adv Ency Brit '41—. *Publ*: The Idea of Nationalism; Prophets & Peoples; Force or Reason; Revolutions & Dictatorships; Not By Arms Alone; A History of Nationalism in the East; Nationalism in the Soviet Union; etc. *s.s*: Mod Hist, Middle (Near) East, Nationalism, Russia & the Slavonic World. *a*: 57 Dryads Green, Northampton, Mass, U.S.A. *T*: 1936.

KOHNSTAMM, PHILIPP ABRAHAM: prof. of education, formerly prof. of thermodynamics; b. Bonn, Holland, June, 1875; educ. Secondary School (Amsterdam), Univ. (Amsterdam). DEGREE: D.Sc. m. J. J. M. Kessler. AUTHOR: OverNatuurwetten, Wetmatigheid en Determinisme; Persoonlijkheid en Idee, 1921; Warmteleer, 1923; Bijbel en Jeugd, 1923; Parate Kennis, 1925; Sexueele Opvoeding, 1925; De nieuwe School, 1926; Thermodynamik der Gemische (from "Handbuch der Physik, vol. X", edited by Geiger and Scheel), 1926; Lehrbuch der Thermostatik I-II (2nd and 3rd edits., 1927); Schepper en Schepping I (Het Waarheidsprobleem), 1927; Schepper en Schepping II (Persoonlijkheid in Wording), 1929; (vol. III in preparation). Contributor to: Paedagogische Studiën; Volksontwikkeling; Algemeen Weekblad voor Christendom en Cultuur. General character of writing: scientific, philosophical, educational. Relig. denom., Dutch Reformed Church (Nederlandsch Hervormde Kerk). OFFICE: Heerengracht 196, Amsterdam. HOME: Ermelo, Holland.

KOHT, Halvdan, M.A., Litt.D., Ph.D. *b*: Tromsoe, Norway 1873. *e*: Gymn of Skien, Univs of Oslo & Leipzig & Coll des Hautes Etudes Paris. *m*: Karen Grude. *s*: 1. *d*: 1. Norwegian Minister of Foreign Affairs 1935—41, Prof of Hist Univ of Oslo '08—35. *n.a*: Ed Norwegian Historisk Tidesskrift 1913—27 & '32—36. *Publ*: Norsk Bondereising; Johan Sverdrup; Henrik Ibsen; The Voice of Norway (with S. Skard); Innhogg og Utsyn i Norsk Historie; Norway, Neutral & Invaded; Bismarck; Sosialdemokratie; De Amerikanske Nasjonen; Norsk Forfatter; etc. *Ctr*: Syn og Segn, Amer Historical & Scandinavian Revs, Samtiden, Den Ilde Mai, etc. *s.s*: Norwegian Hist & Lit, Mediæval, Contemporary & American History. *a*: Lysaker, Norway. *T*: Oslo 536277.

KOKKORIS, LYCURGUS: professor university of Athens; b. Sparta, Greece, Oct., 1877; educ. Athens Coll., Univ. of Athens, Univ. of Berlin (Germany). DEGREES: M.D., D.D.S., Professor Extraordinary, Member Supreme Sanitary State Board; unmarried. AUTHOR: Die Zahnorrlitchen Verhaltnisse Griechenlands, 1905; Physiologie und Hygienen der Bruckenarbeitan, 1913; The History of the Dental Science, 1918; The Diseases of the Mouth, 1927; The Extraction of the Teeth (2nd edit.), 1928. General character of writing: scientific, text-books, medical and historical. Organizer of the first University Dental Sch. of Greece. Relig. denom., Greek Orthodox Church. CLUB: General Greek Dentist's (pres.). OFFICE: Univ. of Athens. HOME: 30 Academy St., Athens, Greece.

KOLACHINE, DUKE OF: see Holm, H. H. Frits Vilhelm.

KOLLONTAY, ALEXANDRA (pen name: Schura): diplomat; b. Moscow, Russia; m. Ingenjören Vlademir Kollontay. AUTHOR: Die soziale Grundlage der Frauenfrage, 1908; Die Mutterschaft und die Gesellschaft, 1915; Wem nützt der Krieg? 1916; Die Lage der Frau in der Evolution der Wirtschaft, 1922; Wege zur Liebe (transl. into English, Spanish, Swedish, Norwegian, Dutch, Japanese, etc.), 1923. Contributor to periodicals. General character of writing: social problems. Has always been an active worker in the field of labor problems and the problem of modern women. In 1907, founded the first club for women workers. Was severely persecuted during the war for pacifistic activities. Following an exile of several years, was able to return to Russia after the October revolution. Was given a ministerial post in the Soviet cabinet, being the first woman ever to hold a cabinet position. Since 1922, has been in the diplomatic service, serving as ambassador to Mexico, Norway, and Sweden. OFFICE: U.S.S.R. Legation, Stockholm, Sweden. HOME: Foreign Office-Narkomindel, Moscow, U.S.S.R.

KOMACHIYA, SOZO: university professor; b. Nagano Ken, Japan, Jan., 1893; s. Jun and Jiu K.; educ. Tokyo Imperial Univ. (College of Law). DEGREE: Juris Doctor; married. AUTHOR: Essays on the Maritime Law (3 vols.), 1921-1931; Code de Commerce de l'Empire du Japan (with George Ripert, Prof. of College of Law, Paris), 1924; The Law relating to the influence of the inflation of money to the contract, 1926; Japanese translation of Havelin's Histoire de droit de commerce, 1930. General character of writing: technical—commercial law. OFFICE: Tohoku Imperial University, Sendai, Japan.

KOMED (pen name): see Langer, Alfons.

KOMISARJEVSKY, Theodore. b: Venice 1882 (Brit subject 1932). e: Univ, Acad of Archt, Mil Sc. s: 2. Theatre Régisseur & Designer. Publ: Myself & the Theatre; Costume of the Theatre; Settings & Costumes. c.t: Observer, Everyman, Week-end Review. Rec: Tennis, travel, music. c: Authors'. a: 11 Berkeley Gdns, W.8.

KOMROFF, Manuel. b: N.Y. City 1890. m: Odette Steele. Writer. n.a: Ed The Modern Library 1921—26, The Library of Living Classics '28, Ed & Founder Black & Gold Library '26. Publ: The Grace of Lambs; Juggler's Kiss; The Voice of Fire; Coronet; The Fool & Death; Two Thieves; A New York Tempest; I, The Tiger; Waterloo; The March of The Hundred; The Magic Bow: A Romance of Paganini; What is a Miracle?; A Christian Letter; In the Years of Our Lord; Feast of The Jesters; (Ed) Travels of Marco Polo; History of Herodotus; Tales of The Monks; Nietzsche's Zarathustra; The Apocrypha; Balzac's Physiology of Marriage; etc. Ctr: Leading mags. a: 400 East 52nd St, New York, N.Y., U.S.A.

KONISHI, SHIGENAO: univ. professor; b. Yonesawa, Japan, January, 1873; s. Kokichi Tondokoro and Take (Tomisawa) K.; educ. Middle Sch., Coll. of Sendai, Univ. of Tokyo. DEGREES: Ph.D. (Bungaku Hakushi); m. Moto Shiomi, 1901. AUTHOR: School Education, 1908; Study of Present Education, 1912; Study of Educational Thoughts, 1923; Nature of Education, 1930; Education by Doing, 1930. Honorary Pres. of the new school, Seijo, Tokyo. Religion, Buddhist. OFFICE: Imperial University of Kyoto. HOME: Yabunoshita Tonodan, Kyoto, Japan.

KONODY, PAUL GEORGE: art critic; b. Budapest, Hungary, Sept., 1872; s. Alexander Max and Louisa (Alexander) K.; educ. in Vienna (Austria); m. Alex Muriel Goodman. AUTHOR: The Art of Walter Crane, 1902; Velasquez (Connoisseur Portfolio), 1903; Filippini Lippi, 1905; Art Section Harmsworth's Self-Educator, 1906; The Brothers Van Eyck, 1907; Raphael, 1908; Chardin, 1909; National Gallery (co-author), 1909; The Iouvre (co-author), 1910; Delacroix, 1910; Through the Alps to the Apennines, 1911; Fra Filippo Lippi, 1911; The Uffizi, 1912; Modern War Paintings (by C. R. W. Nevinson), 1916; Art and War, 1919; Italian Painting (part-author), 1929. Editor: The Artist, 1900-1902. Contributor to Observer, Daily Mail, and numerous daily and weekly publcns. General character of writing: technical, on art. Religion, Roman Catholic. CLUBS: Savile, London Sketch. HOME: 26 New Cavendish St., London, Eng.

KONOVALOV, Sergey. M.A., B.Litt. b: Moscow 1899. e: Univs of Oxf, Geneva, Paris & Bonn. Prof of Russian Univ of Oxf & Fellow of New Coll Oxf. Publ: (Ed & Ctr) Anthology of Soviet Literature; Birmingham Memo & Monographs; Russo-Polish Relations; Blackwell's Russian Readers. Ctr: Ency Brit. a: New Coll, Oxford.

KONSTAM, His Honour Judge E. M., C.B.E., R.C. Publ: The Law of Income Tax (1st edn 1921, 6th edn '33); The Rating & Valuation Act; The Rating Relief Acts; The Modern Law of Rating; etc. a: 19 Chapel St. Belgrave Sq. S.W.1.

KONSTAM, Geoffrey Lawrence Samuel, M.D., B.S., M.R.C.P., M.R.C.S. Pub: Radiological Examination of the Male Urethra (with E. H. P. Cave, 1925). c.t: Lancet, Lon Hosp Gazette, Colour, etc. a: 40 Harley St, W.1. t: Langham 1011.

KONVISER, Maurice. B.A., F.R.G.S. b: Byalestock, Russia 1902. e: Jew's Coll & U.C.L. m: Rae Liptz. s: 2. d: 1. Minister of Religion. Publ: A Jubilee of Jewish Life in Sth Rhodesia; The Jubilee Volume of the Jewish Community in Salisbury, Sth Rhodesia. s.s: History & Theology. a: P.O. Box 342, Salisbury, Sth Rhodesia. T: 5353/3789.

KOO, VI KYUIN WELLINGTON: statesman and diplomat; b. Shanghai, China, Jan., 1888; s. Ching-chuen Yung Koo and Fu-an Tsiang; educ. St. John's Coll. (Shanghai); Anglo-Chinese Coll. (Shanghai); Cook Academy (Montour Falls, N. Y.); Columbia Univ. (New York City, N.Y.). DEGREES: B.A., M.A., Ph.D. (Columbia); LL.D. (Hon.) (Yale, 1916); (Columbia, 1917); (St. John's, 1922); m. Hoey Oeitiongham. AUTHOR: The Status of Aliens in China, 1912. Contributor to Ency. Britannica, Amer. Jnl. of Internat. Law, Amer. Political Science Assn. Quarterly, Chinese Political and Social Science Rev. (in English); Yale Rev., Foreign Supplement, Chicago Univ. Recorder and others. General character of writing: mostly on questions of International Law and Foreign Relations. CLUBS: Columbia University (New York); Rotary (Shanghai); International Golf (Peking). HOME: 193 Wellington Road, Tientsin, China.

KOPLEWITZ, Jacob. b: Poland 1893. e: Univs of Berlin & Rome. Translations chiefly from English. Publ: The Wanderer; The Hidden Path; Elegies; Modern Hebrew Literature since Bialik; etc. Ctr: Lyrics, Essays of Literary & Art Criticism, papers on Cultural Problems, etc to: Davar, Haaretz, Hapoel Hatzair Weekly, Moznayim Monthly & other periodicals in Palestine, U.S.A. & England. s.s: Hebrew Literature Old & New, History of Art, Judaism (Tocology, History & Philology). c: Hebrew P.E.N. a: 36 Haturim St, Jerusalem, Palestine.

KÖRBER, FRIEDRICH: professor; b. Duisburg, Germany, April, 1887; s. Otto and Elise (Wilhelm) K.; educ. Univs. of Munich and Goettingen; Polytechnic Academy, Munich. DEGREES: Dr. Phil., Dr. Ing. E.H.; m. Nora Schumacher, 1920. Editor: Mitteilungen aus dem Kaiser Wilhelm-Institut fuer Eisenforschung. Contributor to Mitteilungen aus dem Kaiser Wilhelm-Institut fuer Eisenforschung, Stahl und Eisen, Zeitschrift fuer Metallkunde, Die Naturwissenschaften, Zeitschrift fuer Technische Physik. General character of writing: scientific and technical. Director of the Kaiser Wilhelm-Institut fuer Eisenforschung and Privatdozent of metallurgy at the Polytechnic Academy of Aix-la-Chapelle. CLUBS: Verein Deutscher Eisenhuettenleute, Gesellschaft Deutscher Naturforscher und Aertze, Deutsche Gesellschaft fuer Metallkunde. Relig. denom., Evangelical. OFFICE: Kaiser Wilhelm-Institut fuer Eisenforschung. HOME: Kaiserswertherstrasse 164, Duesseldorf, Germany.

Who Was Who Among English and European Authors

KORDA, Tibor. Journalist. *n.a*: Mang Ed World's Press News, Advertising World, Photography, Packaging Design, Sign & Display Advertising, Printing. *a*: Cosmopolitan Hse, 48 Fetter Lane, E.C.4. *t*: Central 9064.

KORFF, HERMANN AUGUST: univ. professor; b. April 3, 1882; s. Wilhelm August and Agathe (Winz) K.; educ. Gymnasium. DEGREES: Ph.D., Ord. Professor; m. Maria Stein, 1909. AUTHOR: Scott und Alexis, 1909; Voltaire im literarischen Deutschland des 18. Jahrhunderts (2 vols.), 1917; Geist der Goethezeit, 1923 (2nd vol. 1927); Humanismus und Romantik, 1924; Die Lebensidee Goethes, 1926. Editor: Zeitschrift für Deutschkunde. General character of writing: scientific, modern German literature. ADDRESS: Montbé Strasse 21, Leipzig, Germany.

KORNITZER, Louis. Pearl Merchant. *Publ*: Trade Winds (The Adventures of a Dealer in Pearls). *a*: 27 Cator Rd, Beckenham, Kent. *t*: Sydenham 5253.

KORNITZER, Margaret. *b*: Monkseaton 1905. *e*: Public Sch. Secretary. *n.a*: Asst-Ed Nursing Illus 1940, Publicity Mang C.of E. Children's Soc '43, Ed Corsetry & Underwear '47. *Publ*: The Modern Woman & Herself; The Blue-Eyed Cat. *Ctr*: Good Housekeeping, Housewife, Manch Guardian, Dly Herald, Nursing papers, etc. *s.s*: Women, London Topography. *Rec*: Walking. *a*: 27 Cator Rd, London, S.E.26. *T*: Sydenham 5253.

KORSMO, EMIL (pen name: E. K.): professor in biology of weeds, Agricultural Royal Coll., and Dir. of the State's Scientific and Practical Experiments; b. Grue herred, Norway, June, 1863; s. Hans Hansen and Anne (Eriksdotter) K.; educ. Hedmark landbrukskole; Teknisk skole i Oslo; Det kgl. tegneskole i Oslo; Det kgl. Fredriks universitet. DEGREES: H. M. Konges Fortjenstmedalje i Guld (the medal for merit in golf, of H. M. the King); m. Aagot Jacobine Wiiger. AUTHOR: Ugraes i Ager og Eng, 1896; Hvad bor gjores ad offentlig Vel til Baekjempelse af Ugraes og andre Ekadeplanter i vort Land? (Foredrag ved Seldskapet f. Norges Vel's Mode i Drammen den 3die September 1901), 1901; Ugraessagen. Iagttagelser og Forsog, 1903; Ugraessagen. Nogle Iagttagelser og Erfaringer, 1907; Beretning om Landbrugsutstil lingens Ugraesavdeling (Plantekulturfelternes Afdeling B) 1907, 1908; Beretning om Ugraesforsokene 1, 1909. (Saertrykk av Landbruksdirektor ens Aarsberetning 1909), 1910; Kampen mot Ugraesset. 2. forok. utg., 1911; Ugraes fros evne till at passerer fordoielseskanalen hos husdyr uten at tape spireevnen, 1911; Ueber die Faehigkeit der Samen, den Verdauungskanal der Haustiere zu passieren, ohne ihre Keimkraft zu verlieren. (Saertryk av Nyt Magasin for Naturvidenskaberne B. 50), 1912; Ueber die Keimfaehigkeit des Queckensamens und ueber die Quecke (Triticum repens). (Saertryk av Nyt Magazin for Naturvidenskaberne B. 50), 1912; Forklaring til Ugraesplancher. (Serie 1-4. Planche I-XL), 1913 (2nd edit. 1918); Katalog V. Plantekulturfeltet ved Jubilaeumsutstillingen 1914, 1914; Beretning om Ugraessetes Bekjempelse. (Saertryk av Landbruksdirektorens Beretning for 1913, 1914; Ugraes (Saertryk av Landbruksdirektorens Beretning for 1914), 1915; Beretning om Forsok med Ugraesbekjaempelse i Aret 1915, 1916; N o g e n biologiske forhold vedrorende Rumex acetosa og en del andre ugraearter. (Saertryk av forh. ved 16. skand. naturforskermote 1916), 1916; Beretning om virksomheten i 1916. (Saertryk av Landbruksdirektorens Beretning for 1916), 1917; Om bekjempelse av ugraes i aapen aker. (Landbruksdepartementets smaaskrifter, nr. 4, 1917), 1917; Ograesen—var vaextodlings fiender, deras egenskaper och kampen foer deras utrotande. (Separat ur Lantbruksveckans handlinger), 1918; Demonstrajonsplancher 1-3. Farvelagte tegninger efter naturen i format 66 x 84 cm., 1918; Ugraesplancher 1-40, storrelse 66 x 84 cm., innbefattet 64 arter ugraes, tegnet i naturlig storrelse, efter levende planter, og farvelagte, 1918; Veiledning i anlegg, behandling og hostning av forsoksfelter ved bekjempelse av ugress i forskjellige groder under vekusttiden, 1919; Beretning om virksomheten i 1918 (Saertryk av Landbruksdirektorens Beretning for 1918), 1919; Forsok med ugressbekjempelse i voksende groeder av rotvekster og poteter 1918 ved Statens Smabrukslaererskole. (Efter Statens Smabrukslaererskoles beretning), 1918; Bekjempelse av ugresset i apenakergroder. (Saertryk av Tidsskrift for det norske Landbruk, 5. hefte 1919), 1919; Bekjempelse av Cirsium arvense. (Saertryk av Nordisk Jordbruksforskning), 1919; Ugraesbekjempelse. (Separat av landbruksdirektorens beretning. Tilleg K. 1919), 1920; Om vara besvaerligaste ograes och deras bekaempande. (Foeredrag vid sammanraede med Skaraborgs laens Hushallningssaellskap 30-4-1921), 1921; Motarbeidelse av ugresset i kulturmarken. Iakttagelser og erfaringer fra forsok og praksis, 1921; Ugressutryddelse, 1921; Forevisnings- og forsoksfelter. Undervisning og veiledning i ugressbekjempelse. (Saertryk av beretning fra Statens smabrukslaererskole 1920), 1922; Ugressforsok ved Statens smabrukslaererskole 1921. (Saertryk av Statens smabrukslaererskoles beretning 1921), 1922; Explanations to E. Korsmo's Weed Plates, 1923; Ugressforsok ved Statens smabrukslaererskole 1924, 1924; Betesograes. (Svenska Betes- och Vallfoereningens Arsskrift 1924, s. 72-77o), 1924; Ugress i nutidens jordbruk. Biologiske og praktiske undersokelser. 694 s. and 400 tekstfigurer, 1925; Ograes. Ograesarternas liv och kampen mot dem i nutidens jordbruk. 410 s. med 393 figurer og 63 tabeller., 1926; Resultater fra kombinert brakkog grodeforsok pa Ensrud i Faberg 1919-1923. (Saertrykk av Opland landbruksskoles beretning 1924-25), 1926; Rikkaruohojen vahingolliset vaikutukset mykaisessa maanviljelyksessä. (Ugressets skadevirkninger i nutidens landbruk). (Den finske beretning "Maa" 1926. s. 305-309), 1926; Kornstorrelseforsok. Forsok, undersokelser og iattagelser til belysning av sporsmaalet—storeller smakornet savare i planteproduksjonen. 76 s. Med sammendrag pa tysk og engelsk. (Saertrykk av "Meldinger fra Norges landbrukshoiskole" 1927;, 1927; Juolavehnaen haevittaeminen pelloista kasvusikana. (Bekjempelse av kveke (Triticum repens) i grodebaerende akerjord). (Den finske beretning "Maa" 1926. s. 380-383), 1926; Natriumklorat (Na Cl O3) som ugressdrepende middel. (Norsk Landmannsblad, nr. 12. 1927), 1927; Spiringsundersokelser og iakttagelser efter host- og varsaning av kulturfro. (Saertrykt av "Meldinger fra Norges landbrukshoiskole" 1927, 1927; Rikkarouhoksymya Norjassa. (Ugress-saken i Norge). Maatalous No. 6. 1928. s. 175-179, 1928; Bekeiempelse av akerugress under vekstidden. (Saertryll av Samvirke nr. 11, 1929), 1929; Bekjempelse av kyeke i groedebaerende akerjord. (Saertryck av Norsk Landmannsbladd nr. 18-19, 1929); Ugressaker-et jordbrukets dagsproblem. (Tidsskrift foer Finlands svenska Lantmaen, nr. 13, 1929), 1929. General character of writing: nature books, examinations and observations on the weeds and the combatting of same in Norway. Specializes in examination of the anatomical building of weeds, seeds and culture seeds capable of germinating the quality of different sorts of summer grain (experiment with grain sizes), and in chemical means for complete destruction of vegetation on railway lines, ways, etc.; also in physical examination affecting seeds of weeds. SOCIETIES: Chairman of "Nordiske Jordbruksforskeres Forenings norski avdeling." (The Norwegian division of the Northern Agricultural Researchser's Association); Mem. of the committee of "Det kgl. Selskap for Norges Vel." (Royal Society for Promoting the Welfare of Norway); Mem. "Det videnskabelig-biologiske Seldskap" (The Scientific-biological Society) in Oslo; Mem. Fellowship of the Norwegian Experiments with Field Growths. Religion, Protestant. OFFICE: Det kgl. Landbruksdepartement. HOME: Sorgenfrigaten 37, Oslo, Norway.

KOSOR, JOSIP: writer; b. Dalmatia, January, 1879; s. Nikola and Ana (Marin) K.; educ. Elemental Sch. (Otok), District Vinkovci, Slavonia, Czechoslavakia; m. Ivanka Wenedikter, Nov. 8, 1923. AUTHOR: Optuzba (Accusation; short stories), 1905; Crni Glasovi (Black Voices; short stories), 1906; Rasap (Ruin; novel), 1907; Radnici (Workers; novel), 1908; Cupalo (novel), 1911; Miris Zemlje i Mora (Perfume of Earth and Sea), 1925; Razvrat (Demoralizaton; novel), 1924; Atlantik om i Pacifikom (Across the Atlantic and Pacific). Plays: Pozar Strasti (Passion's Furnace), 1920; Pomirenje (Reconciliation), 1921; Zena (Woman), 1922; Nepobjediva ladja (The Invincible Ship), 1923; Cafe du Dome, 1924; Rotonda, 1925; Covjecanstvo (Humanity), 1926; Nyemak (The Dumb One), 1927; Hadziibrahimaga; (poems): Bijeli plamenovi (White Flames), 1927. Editor: Knjizara. Plays have been produced in many countries and have had many translations. General character of writing: plays, novels, stories, poems. Religion, Roman Catholic. ADDRESS: 13 Netherhall Gardens, Hampstead, London, N. W., Eng., and Villa Famariks, Lapad, Raguza 2, Czechoslovakia.

KOSSAK, Zofia. b: Poland 1890. m: Zygmunt Szatkowski. s: 1. d: 1. Writer, Knight of St Lazarus Cross, Polonia Restituta Cross, Golden Cross of Merit. Publ: Bez Oreza, trans into English, French, Spanish, etc; Krol Tredowaty, trans into English, Spanish, Danish; Zlota wolnosc; Legnickie Pole; Suknia Dejaniry, trans English; Beatum Scelus; Pozoga, trans English, French, Japanese; Klopoty Kacperka, trans into English; Szalency Bozy; Z Milosci, trans into Italian; Nieznany Kraj; Wielcy i Mali; Topsy & Lupus; Varna Amber; The Old Town on the Lake; etc. s.s: Historical & Religious problems. Rec: Gardening, ski-ing, cycling. a: 18 Manor Court Rd, London, W.7. T: Ealing 3946.

KOSTER, Jane. b: London 1900. e: St Angela's Hgh Sch for Girls Forest Gate. m: Rowland Koster. s: 1. d: 2. Mem N.U.J. Publ: (with Margaret Murray) Practical Knitting Illustrated; Complete Home Knitting Illustrated; Knitting for All; Knitted Garments for All; Modern Knitting; Practical Family Knitting; The Week-end Knitting Book; Stars in Wool Series; etc. Ctr: Dly Telegraph, Dly Herald, Dly Mirror, Irish Independent, Woman, Everywoman, Woman's Own, Woman & Beauty, Housewife, Nursery World, etc. s.s: Knitting, Crochet & Home Craft. Rec: Sailing & making pottery. a: 19 The Pryors, East Heath Rd, Hampstead, London, N.W.3. T: Hampstead 6664.

KOTENEV, Anatol Michael. b: Petrograd, Russia, 1882. e: Military Sc at Elizabethgrad, Univ of Moscow. m: Love Annan Terentiev. d: 1. Member of the Secretariat Staff of the Shanghai Municipal Council. n.a: Ed and publisher of the Russian Free Thought (Shanghai) '20—22. Publ: In Russian—The Truth of His God; in English—Shanghai: Its Mixed Court & Council; Shanghai: Its Council & the Chinese; New Lamps for Old in Modern China. c.t: North China Daily News, San Francisco Examiner, American Jnl of International Law. s.s: Far Eastern politics, international relations of China, history of Chinese legislation. Visiting lect, Univ of California, Los Angeles, '34. Formerly Capt in Imperial Russian Army. Knight of the Orders of St Voldemar, St Anna and St Stanislas. a: c/o Shanghai Municipal Council, Shanghai, China.

KOUMARIS, JOHN: professor of anthropology, University of Athens; b. Athens, Greece, Nov. 12, 1879; s. Georges and Ariadne (Panajotaras) Koumaris. AUTHOR: Has written many papers in Greek and German on chirological matters; and French, German and Greek papers on anthropology. Contributes to: Zentralblatt fuer Chirurgie; Archiv fuer Klinnische Chirurgie; L'Anthropologie; Zeitung fuer Rassenphysiologie; Anatomischer Anzeiger, etc. General character of writing: anthropology. Surgeon. Director of the Anthropological Museum since 1915: Professor of Anthropology at the School of Medicin of the University of Athens; General Permanent Secretary of the "Societe Hellénique d'Anthropologie." Religion: Greek Orthodox. OFFICE: Odos Akadémie 38. HOME: Tarella 3, Athens, Greece.

KRALL, Bertha Clara. b: London 1890. e: Lond & Strasbourg. Lect & Ed. Publ: (Ed) New Primary Stories; Stories for Beginners; Eastertide Stories; Harvest-tide Stories; The Adventure of Peace; Book of Christmas Stories; Author of Stories of Favourite Saints; Stories Jesus Heard; More Stories Jesus Heard. Ctr: Concise Guides, etc. s.s: Religious Educ. a: 40 Parkhill Rd, Hampstead, London, N.W.3. T: Gulliver 2046.

KRAMRISCH, Stella, Ph.D. b: Mikulov, Moravia. e: Univ of Vienna. m: L. Nemenyi. Prof of Indian Art Univ of Calcutta. n.a: Ed Journ of The Indian Society of Oriental Art Calcutta, Ed Indian section Artibus Asiae. Publ: Principles of Indian Art; Vishnu Dharmottara; History of Indian Art; Indian Sculpture; Asian Miniature Painting (collab); A Survey of Painting in the Deccan; The Hindu Temple; The Arts & Crafts of Travancore. Ctr: Ancient India, Modern Review, Indian Historical Qtly. s.s: Indian Art, Archæology, Ritual, Architecture, Iconography, Metaphysics. a: Univ of Calcutta, Asutosh Bldg, Calcutta.

KRASSNOFF, Peter. b: St Petersburg 1869. e: Infantry Upp Sc & Cavalry Sc for Officers, St Petersburg. m: Lydia Gruneisen. Publ: From Double Eagle to the Red Flag; Unforgiven; The Amazone of the Desert; The White Coat; The Black Mass; Yermak the Conqueror of Siberia; Kostia the Cossack; Napoleon & the Cossacks; Largo; etc. c.t: Russian Newspapers & Periodicals of Russian Emigrees, Russian Invalid, Watch Guard Paris, etc. s.s: Military questions, lit. After Service in Imperial Guards sent abroad. Russo-Jap War 1904-5. War Service. After Revolution served in two unsuccessful campaigns against Bolsheviks. Now ret. Rec: Riding, reading. a: Santeny par, Villecresnes, Seine et Oise, France.

KRAUS, Harry M., F.R.S.A. b: Brno, Czecho-Slovakia 1914. e: Univs of Masaryk (Docotor of Laws), Wales & London. m: Margaret Catherine Whitfield-McCracken. Lawyer. Publ: Czech without Fears or Tears; Treatises on Law (Czech). Ctr: Music Leader New York & Czech newsps. s.s: Languages, Law, Music. Rec: Music, horse-riding, listening to people. a: 10 Great Ormond St, London, W.C.1. T: Holborn 1526.

KRAUSE, Herbert, M.A. b: Fergus Falls, Minn 1905. e: St Olaf Coll & Iowa Univ. Writer & Teacher, Prof of English. Publ: The Thresher; Wind without Rain; The Oxcart Trail; Neighbor Boy. s.s: Folk-Lore & Historical backgrounds of Red & Minnesota River valleys. Rec: Ornitholcgy, lepidoptera, camping, fishing, swimming. c: Knife & Fork. a: 1811, 1st Ave South, & Augustana College, Sioux Falls, South Dakota, U.S.A. T: 1901.

KRAUSE, J. M. Publ: Poems, etc. c.t: Various. a: 3 Springvale Park, Ayr, Scotland.

KREBS, ELVIRA: univ. professor; b. Grevismühlen, Germany, 1869; d. Hubert and Sybilla (Bonn) K.; educ. high school for girls, univ. DEGREES: Professor; Member of Educational Council; unmarried. AUTHOR: Abrégé de l'histoire de la littérature française de Corneille à nos jours avec un appendice sur les arts. A l'usage des écoles, 1907 (8th edit. 1930); Anthology of English Poetry and Commentary to the Anthology (with A. Giese and W. E. Collinson), 1914; Praktische Anleitung zum englischen und französischen Lautkursus. General character of writing: literature and method of teaching (modern languages). CLUBS: Verband katholischer deutscher Philologinnen. ADDRESS: Bruchhausenstrasse 13a, Treves on the Moselle, Germany.

KREINER, George. *b*: Lon 1886. Journalist. *n.a*: Daily Mirror & Sunday Pictorial. *a*: Shirley Lodge, Lancaster Rd, W. Norwood, S.E.27. *t*: Streatham 7340.

KREIZMAN, Maurice. *b*: 1911. *e*: H.Scs & Priv. Coy Dir. *n.a*: Wythenshawe Gazette '31–32 & Salford City Observer '33. *c.t*: Various Journs & Mags. *s.s*: Lit, art & gen com subjects. *Rec*: Reading, writing, designing of mod furniture. *c*: Athenæum (M/C). *a*: Chorltonville, 93 Northern Grove, W. Didsbury, M/C.

KRESTIN, David. Cons Physician. *c.t*: Quarterly Journ of Medicine, Lancet, B.M.J., etc. *a*: 25 Wimpole St, W.1. *t*: Langham 1160.

KREY, Laura Lettie. *b*: Galveston, Texas 1890. *e*: Mary Baldwin, Sem Staunton Virg, Univ of Texas. *m*: Charles August Krey. *s*: 1. *d*: 1. Writer. *Publ*: And Tell of Time; On the Long Tide. *Ctr*: Craft of Novel Writing, Twentieth Century English. *s.s*: Hist, Fiction. *Rec*: Travel. *a*: 1588 Vincent St, St Paul, Minn, U.S.A. *T*: Nestor 3173.

KRICKA, Peter. *b*: Kelc, Moravia 1884. *e*: Prague Tech Univ, Inst Pasteur de Paris. *m*: Anne Malikcva. Mem of the Czech Acad, officier de la Couronne Belge. *Publ*: The Wildrose Bush; The Boy with the Bow; The Light Cloud; The Song of the Sword; The Demons; Bread & Salt; The White Shield; The Devil as Grefreiter. *a*: Prague XII, Ripska 1.

KRIMM, HANS: author; b. Wiesbaden, Germany, March 22, 1875; s. Professor Dr. Julius Krimm and (Schlumberger Edle von Goldeck) K.; educ. Abiturientenexamen Wiesbaden; Univs. of Lausanne, Munich; Kolonialinstitut of Hamburg; m. Gräfin von der Schulenburg. AUTHOR: **Südafrikanische** (novel), 1912; **Afrikafahrt West**, 1912; **Gang durch den Sand**, 1916; **Olsucher von Derala**, 1918; **Olewegen Sagen**, 1918; **Volk ohne Raum**, 1926; **Die dreizehn Briefe aus Deutsch Südwest-Afrika**, 1928; **Das deutsche Süd-westen Buch**, 1929. General character of writing: novels, essays, history, politics. ADDRESS: Klosterhaus, Lippoldsberg a.d. Weser, Germany.

KRISHNALAI, Mohan Lal Jhaveri. *b*: Broach 1868. *e*: Broach, Surat, Bhavngar, Bombay. *m*: Tulja Gavri. High Court Judges (ret), Chief Judge Small Cause Court Bombay. *Publ*: Milestones; Further Milestones; Present State of Gujarati Literature; Persian Prosody with Figures of Speech; etc. *s.s*: Literature, English, Gujarati & Persian. *Rec*: Walking, swimming, reading. *a*: Pitale Mansion, Kande Wadi, Girgaun Post, Bombay 4. India.

KRISTENSEN, Erling. *b*: Tlolle-heath-Tolstrup 1893. *e*: Public Sch. *m*: Alma Kristensen. *s*: 1. *d*: 1. Author. *Publ*: Stotten; Byen mellem to Taarne; Stodderkongen; Ler; Kvaernen maler; Drejers Hotel; Noget for enhver Smag; Menneske mellem Mennesker; London kalder danmark; Omkring en Menneskerade. *Ctr*: Politiken, Socialdemokraten. *s.s*: Farming, Middle-class Psychology. *Rec*: Hunting, fishing. *a*: Knolden -pr. Rindsholm St, Denmark.

"KRISTIAN PAGAN" (pen name): see **Sebellen, John Robert Francis.**

KRISTIANSEN, Kristian. *b*: Tromso, Norway 1909. *m*: Ellen Hedlund. *Publ*: Vi Baerer Bilde; Hvem Skal Havren Binde; Jeg er Ingen Spion; Over de Heye Fjelle; Ennu Star Dovre; Fredens O; Brev Til Stefan. *a*: Stockholm, Polhemagt 5, or Stavne, Trondheim, Norway. *T*: 53 35 61.

KRISTOFERSEN, Aase. *b*: Tromso, Norway 1889. School Mistress. *Publ*: Dragsug; Lommen Strek; Skrugard; Fisker-rim; Tonje. *Ctr*: Magasinet & other periodical & newsps. *Rec*: Motor cycle. *a*: Underhangsveren 11.A, Oslo, Norway.

KRITZINGER, Matthys Stefanus Benjamin. *b*: Carolina, Transvaal 1896. *e*: Carolina Publ Sch, Ermelo Hgh Sch, Grey Univ Coll Bloemfontein O.F.S. & Transvaal Univ Coll Pretoria. *m*: Esther Margaretha vander Spuy. *d*: 3. Prof of Afrikaans & Netherlands Lit Univ of Pretoria. *Publ*: Die Opstandsmotief by Vondel; Letterkundige Kragte; Oor Skrywers en Boeke; Studies en Kritieke; (collab) School Dictionary, Afrikaans-English & Eng-Afr; Groot Woordeboek; Afrikaanse Verklarende Woordeboek; Afrikaanse Spreekwoorde en Gesegdes. *Ctr*: Die Volkstem, Die Voorslag, Ons eie Boek, Die Ruiter. *s.s*: Afrikaans Literature, Lexicography. *Rec*: Tennis, gardening, farming. *a*: 221 Station St, Hatfield, Pretoria, Union of South Africa.

KROCK, Arthur, M.A. *b*: Glasgow, Kentucky 1886. *e*: Lewis Inst, Univ of Princeton. *m*: Martha Granger. *s*: 1. Newspaper Special Writer. *n.a*: News Dir 1915—19, Ed-in-Chief '19—23 Louisville (Ky) Courier-Journal, & Times, Asst to Publ N.Y. World '23—27, Washington Corr N.Y. Times '27—. *Publ*: The Editorials of Henry Watterson. *s.s*: Politics & Government. *Rec*: Farming, tennis. *a*: 717 Alber Bldg, Washington, D.C. *T*: National 3016.

KROHN, Helmi. *b*: Helsinki 1871. *e*: Hgh Sch. Writer, Mem Finnish P.E.N. & Chrm Finnish Spiritualist Assoc 1946—. *n.a*: Paaskynen 1907—35 & Octava '12—19. *Publ*: (Biogs) Lea; Siipirikko; Emelie Bergbom; Emmy Achte; Jack London; (Trans) Kipling; Shaw; London; Sinclair Lewis; Wilde; (from Swedish) Selma Legerlof; (Travel) In Search of England; etc. *s.s*: Biogs & Books for Young People. *a*: Toolontullinkatu 5, Helsinki.

KROKANN, Inge. *b*: Oppdal, Trondelag 1893. *e*: Folkehogskulelaerar. *m*: Gunnvor Lund Krokann. *s*: 1. *d*: 1. Author. *Publ*: Par Lagerkvist (in the periodical Fritt Ord), Det store hamskiftet i bondesamfunnet (Norsk Kulturhistorie V). *Publ*: I Dovre-sno; Gjenom Fonna 1—11; Pa Linfeksing; Under Himmelteiknet; Blodroter; Da bondene reiste seg; Dikt; Olav Aukrust. *Ctr*: Verdens Gang. *s.s*: Humanism. *a*: Guasdal, Gudbrandsdalen, Norway. *T*: 49. Oystre Gausdal.

KRONENBERGER, Louis. *b*: Cincinnati, Ohio 1904. *e*: Hughes Hgh Sch, Univ of Cincinnati. *m*: Emmy L. Plaut. *s*: 1. *d*: 1. Drama Critic & Writer. *n.a*: Co-Ed Fortune Mag 1936—8, Drama Critic Time Mag '38—, P.M. (N.Y.) '40—. *Publ*: Kings and Desperate Men, England in the 18th Century; The Grand Manner; The Pleasure of Their Company; Johnson and Boswell; Readers Companion; Light Verse. *Ctr*: Nation, New Republic, Atlantic Monthly, Life, New Yorker, etc. *a*: 16 West St, New York 24, N.Y., U.S.A. *T*: Tr-7-9558.

KROUT, John Allen, M.A., Ph.D. *b*: Tiffin, Ohio 1896. *e*: Univs of Michigan & Columbia. *m*: Marion Dorothy Good. *d*: 1. Prof of Hist, Columbia Univ 1940—. *n.a*: Mang Ed Political Science Quarterly 1936—. *Publ*: The Completion of Independence (in Collab); American History for Colleges (in Collab); Origins of Prohibition; Annals of American Sport; Outline History of the United States. *Ctr*: Amer Hist Rev, New York Hist, Outlook, Amer Mercury, N.Y. Times, etc. *s.s*: American Social Hist. *c*: Century (N.Y.) Cosmos (Washington). *a*: 39 Claremont Ave, New York 27, N.Y. *T*: University 4-2320.

KRUUSE, Jens, M.A., Ph.D. *b*: Odense, Denmark 1908. *e*: Copenhagen, U.C.L., Cambridge, Paris, Heidelberg. *m*: Annabeth Holland. *s*: 1. *d*: 1. Literary Critic & Author *n.a*: Lit Critic Jyllandsposten 1942— & Co-Ed Orbis' Litterarum 1944—. *Publ*: Det Foelscmme Drama; Dictere og Traditioner; Humorister; Danske Strøger; etc. *Ctr*: Various Danish papers. *s.s*: Literary Criticism, Comparative Literature, Theory of Humour, Art of Caricature. *a*: Askov, Vejen, Denmark. *T*: Askov 10.

KUCZYNSKI, Jurgen Peter, Ph.D., F.S.S. *b*: Elberfeld 1904. *e*: Univs of Berlin, Heidelberg & Erlangen. *m*: Marguerite K. Steinfeld. *s*: 2. *d*: 1. Chrm of Econ Hist Univ of Berlin. *n.a*: Ed Finanzpolitiszhe Korrespondenz 1929—33, Konjunkturstatiszhe Korrespondenz '34. *Publ*: Short History of Labour Conditions; Bewegung der Deutschen Wirtschaft 1800—1946; Fashions in Wage Theory; Labour Conditions in Western Europe 1820—1935; Les Antecedents d'une Revolution; The Economics of Barbarism; etc. *s.s*: Statistics, Econ Hist & Theory. *a*: Univ of Berlin, Dept of Econ, Unter den Linden, Berlin, Germany.

KUEHNELT-LEDDIHN, Erik-Maria, A.F. *b*: Tobelbad, Styria, Austria 1909. *e*: Theresianic Acad Vienna, Univs of Vienna & Budapest. *m*: Countess Christiane Goess, Ph.D. *s*: 1. *d*: 1. Writer & Editor, Former Prof U.S. Univs & Colls. *n.a*: Vienna Corres The Spectator 1926—28, Russian Corres The Magyarsag '30—31, Cent European Corres The Catholic World & Ed-in-Chief Kairos '47—. *Publ*: Moscow 1979; The Menace of the Herd; Gates of Hell; Night Over the East; Die Anderen (T. Vitezovic); etc. *Ctr*: Dublin Rev, Amer Mercury, New Scholastricum, Tomorrow, Commonwealth, etc. *s.s*: History, Sociology, Geography, Theology, Philosophy, Psychology & their co-ordination. *Rec*: Hiking, climbing, colour photography. *a*: Schloss Carlsberg, Post, Feistritz-Pulst, Kærnten, Austria. *T*: Feistritz-Pulst 1.

KUEHNEMANN, EUGEN (Dr): Univ. Professor of Philosophy, author; b. Hanover, Germany, July 28, 1868; son of Eugen and Ida (Stahr) Kühnemann; educ. Kaiser Wilhelm Gymnasium (Hanover), Univers. of Marburg, München, Berlin and Göttingen. DEGREES: Ph.D., Litt.D., h.c. (Harvard and Wisconsin, U.S.A.); Full Professor of Philosophy; m. Clara Pfeiffer, Aug. 8, 1895. AUTHOR: Die Kantischen Studien Schillers und die Komposition des Wallenstein, 1889; Herders Persönlichkeit in seiner Weltanschauung, 1893; Herders Leben, 1895 (same 2nd edition, greatly amplified; Herder, 1912, 3rd edition, 1927); Schiller, 1905 (7th edition, 1927), translated into English by Katherine Royce, 1915; Grundlehren der Philosophie, 1899; Ueber die Grundlagen der Lehres des Spinoza, 1902. Aus dem Weltreich Deutschen Geistes, 1926. Deutschland und Amerika, 1917; Gerhart Hauptmann, Aus dem Leben des Deutschen Geistes in der Gegenwart, 1922; Kant (2 vols.), 1923, 1924; Goethe (2 vols.), 1930; Charles William Eliot, President of Harvard University, 1909; Germany, America and the War, 1915. General character of writing: philosophical, historical, biographical. OFFICE: University of Breslau. HOME: Berslau, Silesia, Germany.

KUGELMASS, Isaac Newton, M.A., Sc.D., M.D., Ph.D. *b*: New York City N.Y. 1896. *e*: Coll of the City of New York, Johns Hopkins Univs & Univs of Yale, Columbia & Brussels. *m*: Ella H. Fishberg. Pediatrician Fifth Avenue Hosp 1927—35, Chief, Growth Clinic Hosp for Ruptured and Crippled '30—33. *Publ*: Growing Superior Children; Superior Children Through Modern Nutrition; Blood Disorders in Children; The Newer Nutrition in Pediatric Practice; The Story of Infancy; Clinical Nutrition in Infancy and Childhood; Co-Ed Our Children; etc. *Ctr*: Many Med Journs. *a*: 1060 Park Ave, New York, N.Y. *T*: Atwater 9-4900.

KUHE, Ernest. *b*: Brighton 1871. *e*: Brighton Col. Dramatic & Musical Critic (ret). *n.a*: Staff Daily Telegraph 1889, Special Corr, etc '95–, Music Critic 1902–32, Dramatic Critic Field '09–15, Music Critic Lady's Pictorial '12–20. *c.t*: Monthly Musical Record, Annual Register. *c*: Green Room, Hon Mem Critics' Circle. *a*: 4n Portman Mansions, W.1. *t*: Welbeck 2214.

KUHN, Ferdinand, Jr. *b*: N.Y. 1905. *e*: Mt Vernon H.S., N.Y. & Columbia Univ. *m*: Delia Wolf. *s*: 1. Journalist. *n.a*: N.Y. Times News Staff '25–28, Lon Bureau '28–. *c.t*: Economist. *s.s*: Brit politics, & econ. *a*: 18 Melbury Rd, W.14.

KUMARAPPA, Bharatan, M.A., B.D., Ph.D. *b*: Tanjore 1896. *e*: Univs of Madras, Hertford U.S.A. & Edinburgh. Author & Writer, Asst Sec All-India Village Industries Assoc 1935—45. *n.a*: Ed Gram Udyog Patrika 1937—45. *Publ*: Hindu Conception of the Deity as Culminating in Ramanuja; Capitalism, Socialism or Villagism; Principles of a Non-violent Political Order; My Student Days in America; Village Industries & Reconstruction; On Tour with Gandhiji; The Indian Literatures of To-day. *Ctr*: Numerous Indian newsps & periodicals in all languages also Aryan Path, Bombay. *s.s*: Mr Gandhi's Village Economy & Philos in General, Principles of Indian Culture, Religion & Philos. *Rec*: Walking, hiking & mountaineering. *a*: Gordon Hall, New Nagpada Rd, Byculla, Bombay 8, India. *T*: 43175.

KUMARAPPA, Jagadisan Mohandas. *b*: Madras 1886. *e*: Doveton Coll Madras, Harvard, Boston & Columbia. *m*: Ratnam Appasamy. *d*: 3. Dir & Prof of Social Economy Tata Inst of Social Sciences Bombay. *n.a*: Ed Indian Journ of Social Work 1941—. *Publ*: Can India Be United; (Ed) Our Beggar Problem; (Ed) Mobilising Social Services During Wartime; For Indians Going to America; A Guide-Book for Students. *s.s*: Social Work, Sociology, Philosophy, Educ. *c*: Rotary (Bombay). *a*: Dir, Tata Inst of Social Sciences, Bombay 8. *T*: 45468 & 43175.

KUMARAPPA, Joseph Cornelius, M.A., B.Sc., F.S.S.A. *b*: Tanjore 1892. Incorporated Accountant, Sec All-India Village Industries Assoc. *n.a*: (Ed) Gram Udyog Patrika 1945—. *Publ*: Why the Village Movement ?; Economy of Permanence; Public Finance & Our Poverty; Practice & Precepts of Jesus; Christianity—Its Economy & Way of Life; Philosophy of Work & Other Essays; Gandhian Economy & Other Essays; A Survey of Matar Taluka; A Plan for Rural Development; Clive to Keynes. *Ctr*: The Harijan. *s.s*: Economics, Public Finance, Social Reorganisation, Religion & Ethics. *a*: Maganvadi, Wardha C.P., India.

KUMMER, Frederick Arnold, C.E. *b*: Catonsville, Md U.S.A. 1873. *e*: Rensselaer Polytechnic Inst Troy N.Y. *m*: Marion J. McLean. *s*: 2. *d*: 2. Civil Engineer until 1907, Writer since. *n.a*: Asst Ed Railroad Gazette, New York 1894–96. *Publ*: Phryne; The Brute; The Earth's Story (3 vols); Ladies in Hades; Maypoles & Morals; Gentlemen in Hades; Forbidden Wine; etc. (Plays)—My Golden Girl; The Magic Melody; many film scenarios. *c.t*: Saturday Evening Post, Cosmopolitan Mag, Century, Ladies' Home Journal, Pictorial Review, Red Book, Country Gentleman, Good Housekeeping, etc. *Rec*: Swimming, riding. *c*: American Soc of Civil Engineers Authors' League of America, The American Dramatists, etc. *a*: 2 St Martin's Rd, Baltimore, Maryland, U.S.A. *t*: University 2492.

KUMRIA, Raja Ram, M.A. *b*: Lahore, West Punjab 1902. *e*: Punjab Univ. *m*: Savitri. *s*: 2. *d*: 2. Teacher. *Publ*: What Life Should Mean to an Indian; New Values for a New India; New Homes for a New India; The Indian child in Home and School; Scientific Living for India; Intelligence, Its Nature & Measurement. *Ctr*: Various. *s.s*: Educ, Traditional Mind. *a*: Training Coll, Jullundur City, East Punjab, India.

KUSSY, Nathan, LL.B. *b*: Newark, N.J. 1872. *e*: N.Y. Law Sch. *m*: Jennie L. Kussy (dec'd). *s*: 1. *d*: 2. Lawyer & Author. *Publ*: Grinmar; The Abyss; The Victor; (Playlets) The President Speaks; The Diamond Necklace; The Schemers; Crooks. *Ctr*: Univ Jewish Ency. *s.s*: Law, Novel & Play Writng. *a*: 158 South Harrison St, East Orange, New Jersey, U.S.A. *T*: Orange 5-0584.

KUWAKI, GENYOKU: professor of Philosophy, Tokyo Imperial Univ.; b. Tokyo, Japan, June, 1874; s. Aishin and Haruko K.; educ. Tokyo Imperial Univ. DEGREES: Litt. D. (Bungaku-Hakushi); mem. of the Imperial Academy, Tokyo. AUTHOR: Introduction to Philosophy, 1900; Essays concerning Philosophy, Literature, et cetera, 1905; Outlines of Philosophy, 1910; Five Great Philosophers, 1910; Kant and the Contemporary Philosophy, 1915; Elements of Ethics, 1915; (translations): Elements of Ethics, 1897; Muirhead, 1897; Lehrbuch der allgemeinen Geschichte der Philosophie, 1902. Contributor to the Proc. of 6th Internat. Congress of Philosophy. HOME: 34 Kita-machi (Kita-cho), Ushigome, Tokyo, Japan.

KVALE, Sigurd. *b*: Sogndal i Sogn 1902. *m*: Astrid Sandsmark. *s*: 1. *Publ*: Nar Det Blir Natt; Tider og ar; Siglaren; Sylen; Krefter. *Ctr*: Norsk Skuleblad, Norsk Tidend, Magasinet, etc. *a*: Lillestrom, Norge. *T*: 1303.

KYLE, Elisabeth (see **DUNLOP, Agnes M. R.**). *Publ*: The Begonia Bed; Gilbert the Page; Broken Glass; The White Lady; But We Are Exiles; The Pleasure Dome; The Skaters Waltz; Carp Country; Mally Lee; Holly Hotel; Lost Karin *a*: c/o Messrs. A. M. Heath & Co. Ltd, Princes Hse, Jermyn St, London, S.W.1.

KYLE, Dr. H. G. *a*: 31 Westbury Rd, Bristol.

KYLE, William Galloway. *b*: Aldbro', N Yorkshire. *e*: Priv. Journalist & Publisher, Knight of the Redeemer, Greece. *n.a*: Reporter North Star Darlington 1893, Sub-Ed '96, Founder & Co-editor Northern Counties Mag 1900, Mang Dir Erskine, MacDonald Ltd, Founder & Man Ed The Poetry Society (incorporated) '09. *Publ*: Collections of Topographical & Biographical Studies; Compiler of various Anthologies. *Ctr*: Special Commissioner Contributor to Yorkshire Post, Yorkshire Ev Post, Umpire, Newcastle Leader, Court Journal, Ladies Realm, etc, Short Stories & Verse. *s.s*: Lecturer on Poets & Poetry & Verse-speaking. *Rec*: Cricket, hearing poetry spoken, reading detective fiction. *a*: 33 Portman Sq, London, W.1.

KYLES, Rev. David. *a*: Drummond's Tract Depot, Stirling.

KYNASTON, June Hope. *b*: London 1900. *e*: Hgh Sch & Univ Coll Nottingham. *m*: Frank Crew. Free-Lance Journalist & Story Writer, Mem Soc of Women Journalists. *Publ*: The Mind that Works Miracles. *Ctr*: Prediction, Health & Efficiency, Naturist, Dly Mail, Nottingham Weekly Guardian, Sunday Mercury, etc. *s.s*: Travel & Personalities. *Rec*: Flying, music, travel, theatre, circus, painting, dress designing, photography. *a*: Sandy Bottom, Whiteleaf, Princes Risborough, Bucks. *T*: Princes Risborough 426.

LAACHE, Rolv. *b*: Oslo 1886. *e*: Katedralskole, Univs of Oslo & Oxford. *Publ*: Henrik Wergeland og Prokurator; Nordmenn og Svensker efter 1814; Henrik Wergeland og Hans Historielærer; Om Hellener og Barbarer og om Athens Herlijhei. *Ctr*: Eng Hist Rev, Edda, Samtiden, Historisk Tidsskrift. *s.s*: History & Literary History. *Rec*: Walking, cycling & outdoor life in general. *a*: 37 Oscar's Gate, Oslo, Norway.

LABARTHE, Andre. *b*: France 1902. *e*: Sorbonne. Journalist. *n.a*: La France Libre London, Tricolor N.Y., France-Soir Paris. *Publ*: La France Devant la Guerre; Retour Au Feu; Le Statusquo de la Peur. *Ctr*: France-Soir, Dly Express, La France Libre, & various American, English & French Papers & Reviews. *s.s*: Science. *Rec*: Painting. *a*: 15 Rue Chauveaux, Paris.

LABORDE, Edward Dalrymple, Ph.D., F.R.G.S. *b*: Kingstown 1890. *e*: Abroad & Univ of Lond. *m*: Hilda Guilding. *s*: 2. *d*: 1. Asst Master Harrow Sch. *n.a*: (Ed) Education To-day. *Publ*: A History of Spanish Literature; Choosing a Career; Tales of the Wind King; Popular Map Reading; The Cambridge School Geography Series; A Geography of Fiji; The World in Outline; A Geography of Western Europe & Australia, New Zealand & the Pacific Islands; Byrhtnoth & Maldon; Your Life's Work; etc. *Ctr*: Eng Hist Review, Geog Journ, Mod Lang Review, Journ of Educ. *s.s*: Mod Langs, Geog, Old Eng & Old Norse Lit & Philogy. *Rec*: Reading, walking, fives, boating, bridge, *a*: The Haven, Grove Hill, Harrow-on-the-Hill. *T*: Byron 1926.

LABY, THOMAS HOWELL: professor of physics; b. Creswick, Victoria, Australia, May, 1880; s. Thomas James and Jean Eudora (Lewis) L.; educ. Universities of Sydney, Australia, and Cambridge, Eng. DEGREES: M.A., Sc.D. (Cambridge); M.A. (Melbourne, Australia); F. R. S. (London); m. Beatrice Littlejohn, 1914. AUTHOR: Physical and Chemical Constants with Dr. G. W. C. Kaye), 1911; University Reform in New Zealand (with Professors Hunter and von Zedlitz), in press. Editor of the Report of the Imperial Geophysical Experimental Survey (with A. Broughton Edge). Contributor to Australian Quarterly, English scientific jnls., Australian daily newspapers. General character of writing: maily scientific. Has written on heat, x-rays, electricity; designed scientific instruments; prof. of physics in Univ. of Melbourne. CLUBS: University (Sydney, New So. Wales). OFFICE: University of Melbourne. HOME: University Grounds, Melbourne, Victoria, Australia.

LACEY, Leslie Frederick. *b*: Bedford 1912. Reporter. *n.a*: Hastings & St Leonards Observer group. *c.t*: Various. *s.s*: Sport, interviewing. *c*: Mem N.U.J. *a*: 58 Warrior Sq, St Leonards-on-Sea. *t*: Hastings 609.

LACH, ROBERT: univ. professor; b. Vienna, Austria, Jan. 29, 1874; s. Johann and Elise (Kovacevich-Sikom) L.; educ. Gymnasium of Vienna, Univ. of Vienna; m. Eleonora Tschoepe, Dec. 13, 1899. AUTHOR: Studien zur Entwicklungsgeschichte der ornamentalen Melopöie, 1913; Sebastian Sailer's "Schöpfung" in der Musik. (Denkschriften der Akademie der Wissenschaften in Vienna, philosophisch-historische Klasse, vol. 60), 1916; Vorläufiger Bericht über die Gesänge russischer Kriegsgefangener (Part 1), 1917 (Part 2), 1918; W. A. Mozard als Theoretiker (vol. 61), 1918; Zur Geschichte des Gesellschaftstanzes im 18. Jahrhundert, 1920; Eine Tiroler-Liederhandschrift aus dem 18. Jahrhundert (198. vol. 5), 1923; Zur Geschichte des musikalischen Zunftwesens (Ibid. 199, vol. 3), 1923; Die vergleichende Musikwissenschaft, ihre Methoden und Probleme. (Ibid. 200, vol. 5), 1914; Das Konstruktionsprinzip der Wiederholung in Musik, Sprache und Literatur. (Sitzungsberichte der Akad. d. Wissenschaften in Wien, 201. vol., 2 Abhdlg.), 1925; Vergleichende Kunst- und Musikwissenschaft (Ibid. 201 vol., 3. Abhdlg.), 1925; Katalog der musikalischen Handschriften (new series): "Supplementa musicalia No. 102102" of the Vienna National Library, pg. 216-219), 1925; Die Bruckneraten des Wiener Universitätsarchivs, 1926; Geschichte der Akademie für Musik und darstellende Kunst in Wien, 1926; Wotjakische, syriänische und perniakische Gesänge, 1926; Georgische Gesänge. (Voranzeige im "Anzeiger," etc., pgs. 1-3), 1926; Tscherenissische Gesänge. (Voranzeige im "Anzeiger"); Mingrelische, ubchastische, swanische und ossetische Gesänge; Mordwinische Gesänge; Georgische Gesänge (Sitzungsberichte der Akademie der Wissenschaften), 1928. Contributor to: Zeitschrift für französische Sprache und Literatur; Wiener Zeitschrift für die Kunde des Morgenlandes; Mouseion; Zeitschrift für die österreichischen Gymnasien; Österreichische Arbeit. Sänger-Zeitung; Zeitschrift für Aesthetik und allgemeine Kunstwissenschaft; Faust. Monatsschrift für Kunst, Literatur und Musik; Musikalischer Kurier, and many others. General character of writing: musical; songs, poems, fairy tales; text book to five operas; scientific musical history of music; comparative science of music; psychology and aesthetic of music. CLUBS: Academy of Sciences in Vienna, Deutsche Akademie in Munich. Religion, Roman Catholic. OFFICE: University of Vienna. HOME: Pötzleinsdorferstrasse 146-148, Vienna XVIII-3., Austria.

LACHMANN, ISMAR: editor; b. Reimersdorf, Germany, March 27, 1882; s. Georg and Rosa Goldenkranz) L. Editor: Karlshorster Lokal-Anzeiger, 1906; Deutsche Warte, Berliner Neueste Nachrichten, Das Echo, 1907-1921; Deutsche Allgemeine Zeitung, 1921-1924; Otto Stellberg Verlag, since 1924. Contributor to Breslauer Zeitung. General character of writing: dramatic criticism. CLUBS: Reichsverband der deutschen Presse, Schutzverband deutscher Schriftsteller, Verein Berliner Presse, Verband Berliner Theaterkritiker. Religion, Jewish. ADDRESS: Fahnstrasse 12, Berlin S. 59, Germany.

LACINA, Vaclav. *b*: Hluboka, Bohemia 1906. *e*: Faculty of Law of the Charles Univ Prague. *m*: Eliska Sourkova. Judge, Head of the 1st Dept in the Czechoslovak Min of Information 1945—47. *n.a*: Kulturni Politika, weekly, Rude Pravo, daily. *Publ*: Bristling Up; A Rat on the Shaft; A Cog-Window; The Brass Circus; The Snobs on the March; Architect Solness, the Mason; Idle Thoughts on Penmanship. *Ctr*: Kulturni Politika, Rude Pravo. *s.s*: Satire, Parody. *Rec*: Travel. *a*: Prague XVII, Holeckova 103.

LACK, David. *b*: London 1910. *e*: Gresham's Sch Holt, Magdalene Coll Camb. Dir Edward Greg Inst of Field Ornithology. *Publ*: The Life of the Robin; Darwin's Finches; The Birds of Cambridgeshire. *Ctr*: Scientific & Ornithological Journ. *s.s*: Birds. *a*: Edward Greg Institute of Field Ornithology, Oxford.

LACK, Harry Lambert, M.D.(Lon), F.R.C.S. Eng. *b*: Norfolk 1867. *e*: King's Col, Lon. *m*: Kathleen McNeill Rind. *s*: 3. *d*: 1. Surgeon. *Publ*: Diseases of the Nose (1906). *c.t*: Lancet & other med journals, British Birds. Cons Aural Surg Lon Hosp. *Rec*: Ornithology. *c*: Authors'. *a*: 31 Marlboro' Pl, N.W.8. *t*: Maida Vale 2219.

LACON. See **Watson, Edmund Henry Lacon.**

LACOSTE, Raymond Joseph Augustin. *b*: Paris 1898. *e*: Univ of Montpellier. Lon Corr L'Echo de Paris. *c.t*: La Revue de France, Europe Nouvelle, Vremé, Observer, L'Eclair du Midi, etc. *s.s*: Foreign affairs. Knight of St Sava (Serbia). Officer Crown of Roumania. *Rec*: Travel, books. *c*: Roy Central Asian Soc. *a*: 135 Fleet St, E.C.4. *t*: Central 4242.

LACOSTE, René. *Publ*: Lacoste on Tennis; How to Play Tennis. *a*: c/o E. J. Burrow & Co Ltd, 125 Strand, W.C.2.

LA COSTE-MESSELIERE, Pierre de. *b*: 1894. *e*: Licencié es Lettres. Membre de l'Ecole francaise d'Athenes. Docteur és Lettres. *m*: Jacqueline de

Vasselot de Regne. s: 3. d: 1. Dir à l'Ecole des Hautes Etudes (Sorbonne Paris), Membre de l'Inst de France, et de la Soc des Antiquaires de l'Ouest. *Publ*: Delphes; Au Musée de Delphes; Sculptures Grecques de Delphes. *Ctr*: Revues archeologiques, de l'Art, Historique *s.s*: Archeologie Grecque. *a*: 89 Rue de Lille, Paris VII.

LA COUR, Paul. *b*: Risley 1902. *m*: Gerd Marie La Cour. *d*: 3. Author. *Publ*: Leviatan; Regn over Verden; Kramer Bryder Op; Dette er Vort Liv; Alt Kraever Jeg; De Hundrede Somre; Meliem Svaerdene; Levende Vande. *Ctr*: Politiken, Information. *s.s*: French Literature & Poetry. Modern Painting Art, Trans from French. *a*: Hojgaards Alle 14 Bagsvaerd, Denmark. *T*: Bagsvaerd 660.

LACY, Edward Dacre. *b*: Southsea 1901. *e*: Bradfield Col. *m*: Phyllis Muriel Owens Thurston. *s*: 3. Technical Journalist. N/p Ed The Welder (Murex Welding Processes Ltd). *c.t*: Times Trade & Engineering Sup, Manchester Guardian Com, Shipbuilding & Shipping Record, Railway Gazette, Western Mail, Welding (U.S.A.), Electrical Review, etc. *s.s*: Welding & Engineering. *Rec*: Cricket & lawn tennis. *c*: Public Scs & Stoke Court Country Club. *a*: Greensted Hse, nr Ongar, Essex. *t*: Northweald 26.

LADDS, Samuel Charles. *b*: Leonora, Western Australia 1903. *e*: Swamp Oak & Tamworth (N.S.W.) Scs. *m*: Dulcie Dunlop. *s*: 1. Farmer. *Publ*: I'll Go No More A-Roving. *c.t*: The Queenslander, The Courier Mail, The Bulletin (Sydney). *s.s*: Culture & marketing of tropical fruit. *Rec*: Swimming, surfing. Travelled extensively. *a*: Sobraon, West Burleigh, Queensland, Australia.

LADELL, Robert George Macdonald, M.B., Ch.B. *b*: London 1881. *e*: Islington Hgh Sch, Leeds Univ. *m*: Mary Buckley Pounder. *s*: 1. *d*: 1. Neuro-psychiatrist to Min of Health & Min of Pensions. *Publ*: The First Five Years; The Parents Problem; The Stammerer Unmasked. *Ctr*: Psychologist, Birmingham Post, Sunday Mercury. *s.s*: Psychology, Sex Educ. *Rec*: Reading. *c*: R.A.C. *w.s*: 1914—16. *a*: Thornwick, Lapworth, Birmingham. *T*: Lapworth 256.

LADENBURG, RUDOLF: professor of physics: b. Kiel, Germany, 1882; s. Albert and Margarete (Pringsheim) L. DEGREES: Ph.D.; m. Else Uhthoff, 1911. AUTHOR: Plancks Wirkungsquantum, 1921; Experimentelle Prüfung der Quantentheorie, 1923. Contributor to Annalen der Physik, Physikalische Zeitschrift, Zeitschrift für Physik, Naturwissenschaften, Nature. General character of writing: scientific, physics, magneto- and electrooptics, atomistic. CLUBS: Deutsche Physikalische Gesellschaft, Kaiser Wilhelm Gesellschaft. Relig. denom., Evangelical. OFFICE: Kaiser Wilhelm Institut für physikalische Chemie und Elektrochemie, B e r l i n. HOME: Faradagasse 4-6, Berlin-Dahlem, Germany.

LADY DILKE: see Clifford, Ethel.

LAENGSDORFF, JULIA VIRGINIA (pen name: Julia Virginia): author; b. Frankfort a. M., Germany, April 1, 1878; d. Wilhelm A. and Ida (Bromm) Scheuermann; educ. Studium of Arts at Kassel); Art Studios of Franz von Lenbach, Munich; Lovis Corinth, Berlin; Lucien Simon, Paris; m. Richard L. Laengsdorff, Feb. 15, 1922. AUTHOR: Primitien (selected poetry), 1903; Sturm und Stern (selected poetry), 1905; Journal of Mary Bashkirtseff and her correspondence with Guy de Maupassant (transl. from the French), 1906; Anthology "Frauenlyrik unserer Zeit", 1907; Annette v. Droste-Hülshoff's poetry (edited and commented), 1910; Taras Shewtshenko's poetry (transl. from the Ukrainian language), 1911; Taras Shewtshenko's "Künstler" (autobiographical novel, transl. from the Ukrainian language), 1912; Das bunte Band (selected poetry), 1913. Contributor to: Frankfurter Zeitung; Neue Zürcher Zeitung; Deutsche Allgemeine Zeitung; Westermann Monatshefte, and others. General character of writing: poetry, art, biographies, travels. Is also a painter.

CLUBS: Gemeinschaft deutscher und österreichischer Künstlerinnen; Deutscher Schriftsteller-Verband. Relig. denom., Lutheran. ADDRESS: 71 Leerbachstrasse, Frankfort on Main, Germany.

LA FARGE, Christopher, A.B., B.Arch. *b*: New York, N.Y. 1897. *e*: Groton Sch, Harvard Penna. *m*: (1) Louisa Ruth Hoar (dec'd). (2) Violet Amery Loomis. *s*: 2. Writer. *Publ*: Hoxsie Sells His Acres; Each to the Other; Poems & Portraits; The Wilsons; East by Southwest; Mesa Verde; The Sudden Guest. *Ctr*: 1947 Mag of the Year, Harper's Mag, Atlantic Monthly, New Yorker, Amer Mag. *s.s*: Novels in Prose & Verse, Short Stories & Poems. *Rec*: Shooting, fishing, sailing, riding, tennis. *c*: Coffee House, etc. *a*: The River Farm, Saunderstown, Rhode Island, U.S.A.

LA FARGE, Oliver, M.A. *b*: New York City 1901. *e*: St Bernard's Sch New York, Groton Sch Mass, Harvard Univ. *m*: Consuelo Otille C. de Baca. *s*: 1. *d*: 1. Writer. *Publ*: Laughing Boy; Raw Material; The Enemy Gods; Santa Eulalia; Long Pennant; Sparks Fly Upward; All the Young Men; The Copper Pot. *Ctr*: Harper's Mag, Sat Ev Post, New Yorker, Esquire, Forum, Ladies Home Journ, Scribner's, etc. *s.s*: Aviation, American Southwest, Mexico & Central America. *Rec*: Riding, camping, hunting, etc. *c*: Coffee House. *w.s*: World War II. *a*: 647 College St, Santa Fe, New Mexico, U.S.A.

LAFFAN, Mary Nevill. *m*: Maj Laffan R.E. (dec). *Publ*: The Hand and the Mind (1928); Hand Reading: A Study of Character & Personality ('32). *a*: 17 Gayfere St, S.W.1.

LAFFAN, Robert George Dalrymple. *b*: Folkestone 1887. *e*: Eton, Balliol Coll Oxf. *m*: Hon Mabel Chalmers. Fell Queens' Coll Univ Lecturer, Cambridge. *Publ*: The Serbs, Guardians of the Gate; Select Historical Documents (800—1492). *Ctr*: Vol VIII Cambridge Medieval History; History of the Peace Conference (1918); Observer; Tablet; Quarterly Rev; Dublin Rev. *s.s*: History & Politics of Yugoslavia; etc. *a*: Queens' College, Cambridge. *T*: Cambridge 4425.

LAFONE, Harold Carlisle, B.A., LL.B. *e*: Harrow & Trinity Col, Cambridge. Barrister & Journalist. *n.a*: Jt-Ed Autocar. *s.s*: Motoring. *a*: Dorset Hse, Stamford St, S.E.1. *t*: Hop 3333.

LAGDEN, Sir Godfrey Yeatmen, K.C.M.G., K.B.E. *b*: Sherborne 1851. *e*: Sherborne. *m*: Frances Rebekah Bousfield. *s*: 3 (1 dec). *d*: 2. Ret from H.M.S. *n.a*: Special Corr Egyptian War '82. *Publ*: History of Basutoland; The Native Races of the British Empire. *c.t*: Several leading n/ps. *s.s*: Sport, Emp hist. *a*: Selwyn, Oatlands Chase, Weybridge. *t*: 268.

LAGERCRANTZ, Olof Gustaf Hugo, Litt.D. *b*: Stockholm 1911. *e*: Stockholm Univ, Switzerland & France. *m*: Martina Ruin. *s*: 2. Author. *n.a*: Lit Critic Dagens Nyheter 1939, Svenska Dagbladet 1940—, (Ed) Samtid & Framtid '44—45, Critic Bonniers Litterara Magasin '42—. *Publ*: Den doda fageln; Den enda sommaren; Jungfrun och demonerna; Trudi; Dikter fran mossen; Trans into Swedish Isaac Walton's The Compleat Angler. *s.s*: Lit Hist, Poetry. *c*: Swedish P.E.N. *a*: J. O. Wallins vag 3, Stockholm 60, Sweden. *T*: Stockholm 337068.

LAGERLÖF, Selma. *b*: 1858. Authoress. *Publ*: Gösta Berling's Saga; Jerusalem; Miracles of Antichrist, etc. First Swede to be awarded Nobel Prize.

LAGERKVIST, Par Fabian. *b*: Vaxjo 1891. Mem Swedish Acad, Doctor of Honour. *Publ*: The Dwarf; The Eternal Smile; Guest of Reality; The Hangman; The Man Without a Soul; The Man Who Lived His Life Again. *a*: Lidingo, Sweden.

LAHEY, Edwin A. *b*: Chicago, Ill 1902. *e*: Grade & Ev Schs, Harvard Univ. *m*: Grace Seidcheck. *d*: 2. Journalist. *n.a*: Columnist & Reporter, Knight Newsps,

Chicago Dly News, Detroit Free Press, Akron Beacon Journ, Miami Herald. *Ctr* : New Republic, Economist, Sat Ev Post, Extension Mag. *s.s* : Labour & Politics. *Rec* : Horse track. *a* : 5643 Western Ave N.W., Washington D.C., U.S.A. *T* : Emerson 2827.

LAIDLAW, William Allison, M.A., Litt.D. *b* : Dublin 1898. *e* : T.C.D. *Publ* : A History of Delos ; The Prosody of Terence. *Ctr* : Classical Rev, Classical Quarterly. *Rec* : Walking, music. *c* : Univ of Lond. *a* : Queen Mary College, Mile End Rd, London, E.1.

LAIDLER, Harry Wellington, A.B., LL.B., Ph.D. Hon.A.M. *b* : Brooklyn, N.Y. 1884. *e* : Wesleyan Univ, Brooklyn Law Sch & Columb Univ. *m* : Agnes Fuller Armington. *s* : 1. *d* : 1. Exec Dir League for Industrial Democracy. *n.a* : (Ed) Socialist Rev 1919—21, Labour Age '21—23, (Ctr-Ed) Modern Review '46—. *Publ* : Social-Economic Movements ; History of Socialist Thought ; Concentration of Control in American Industry ; Socialism in Thought & Action ; A Program for Modern America ; Socializing Out Democracy ; Boycotts & The Labour Struggle ; The Road Ahead—A Primer of Capitalism & Socialism. *Ctr* : Nation, New Republic, New Leader, Amer Econ Rev, Amer Mercury, etc. *s.s* : Socialism, Social Planning, Industrial Concentration. *Rec* : Walking, swimming, tennis. *c* : Town Hall (N.Y.). *a* : 292 Garfield Place, Brooklyn 15, New York U.S.A., & 112 East 19th St, New York 3, N.Y., U.S.A. *T* : So 8-3384.

LAIDLOW, Thomas William. *b* : Carlisle 1891. *e* : Ashley St Sc Carlisle. *m* : Mary Elizabeth Graham. *s* : 2. Reporter. *n.a* : Carlisle Journal 1911—31, Cumberland News, Carlisle '32—. *c.t* : Manchester Guardian. War Service. *Rec* : Walking, swimming. *a* : Ivy Garth, Pugin St, Carlisle.

LAINÉ, EDWARD : professor ; *b.* Saint-Mals, France, December, 1890 ; *s.* Alexandre and Cécile (Deschamps) L. ; *educ.* College de Saint-Mals, Univ. Catholique de l'ouest. DEGREE : Docteur es sciences mathematiques. AUTHOR : Précis d'Analyse mathématique (2 vols.), 1927 ; Récherches sur les équations s-f (x y z p q) intégrables par la methode de Darboux, 1928 ; Première Leçons de géométrie analytique et de géométrie vectorielle, 1929. Contributor to L'Enseignement mathématique, Bulletin des Sciences Mathematiques, Intermédiaire des Mathematiciens, Nouvelles Annales de Mathematiques, Comptes Rendus de l'Académie des Sciences, Bulletin de la Société mathématique polonaise. General character of writing : mathematics, text-books. CLUBS : Société mathématique de France, Société mathématique polonaise. Religion, Catholic. ADDRESS : 3 rue Rabelais, Angers, France.

LAING, Alexander. *b* : Great Neck, New York 1903. *e* : Dartmouth Coll. *m* : Dilys Bennett Laing. *s* : 1. Poet. *Publ* : Way for America ; Fool's Errand ; End of Roaming ; Wine and Physic ; The Sea Witch ; Dr. Scarlett ; The Methods of Dr. Scarlett ; Clipper Ship Men. *Ctr* : New Yorker, Harper's, Sat Review of Lit, Poetry (Chicago), N.Y. Her Trib, etc. *s.s* : Verse, Morals, Politics, Ships. *Rec* : Carpentry, gardening, reading. *a* : Box 612, Hanover, New Hampshire, U.S.A. *T* : Norwich 708-W.

LAING, Lucy Glanvill. *m* : W. A. Laing. *s* : 2 (1 dec). *Publ* : Three Conspirators ; Young Caravanners ; A Gift in Secret ; Tony's Broken down Gentleman ; Although he was Black. *c.t* : Daily Express, Scotsman, Kent Messenger, Scot's Observer, Brit Weekly, Chr Herald, etc. *s.s* : Children's stories & nature articles. *a* : Dalmahoy, Horsell, Woking, Surrey. *t* : 163.

LAIRD, Arthur Hill, B.A., M.B., B.Ch, B.A.O., D.M.R.E. Radiologist. *c.t* : Brit Journ of Actinotherapy, B.M.J., Brit Journ Radiology. *a* : 16 Regent St, Coventry & 6 Belvedere Rd, Coventry. *t* : Coventry 4849 & Leamington 336.

LAIRD, JOHN : professor of moral philosophy ; *b.* Durris, Scotland, May, 1887 ; *s.* David M.W.L. ; *educ.* Aberdeen Grammar Sch. ; Edinburgh Univ. ; Heidelberg ; Trinity Coll. (Cambridge). DEGREES : M.A. (Edinburgh) ; B.A., 1911 ; M.A., 1920 (Cambridge) ; *m.* Helen Ritchie Forbes, 1919. AUTHOR : Problems of the Self, 1917 ; A Study in Realism, 1920 ; The Idea of the Soul, 1924 ; Our Minds and their Bodies, 1925 ; A Study in Moral Theory, 1926 ; Modern Problems in Philosophy, 1928 ; The Idea of Value, 1929. Contributor to technical, philosophical journals. Regius prof. of Moral Philosophy, Univ. of Aberdeen. OFFICE : The University, Aberdeen. HOME : Powis Lodge, Old Aberdeen, Scotland.

LAIRD, Sydney Mander, M.D., B.Sc., F.R.F.P.S.G. *b* : Kilmacolm, Renfrewshire 1911. *e* : Allan Glen's Sch, Univs of Glas & Liverpool. *m* : Sarah Gwendoline Fee. *s* : 1. *d* : 2. *Publ* : Venereal Disease in Britain. *Ctr* : Lancet, Medical Press, Medical World, Nursing Mirror, etc. *s.s* : Venereal Diseases and Dermatology, Social Med. *Rec* : Tennis, gardening. *w.s* : R.A.M.C. 1939-45. *a* : Lyndale, 157 Henley Rd, Ipswich, Suffolk. *T* : 3889

LAISTER, Thomas Leslie. *b* : Lon 1908. *e* : Tollington. *m* : Edith Hunt. Reporter. *n.a* : Evening Standard, Thameside Mail, Press Assoc, Northcliffe N/ps & Daily Herald. *a* : 24 Bernard St, W.C.1 *t* : Terminus 4873.

LAKE, H. Coote. Hon Sec The Folklore Soc. *a* : The Folklore Soc, 52 Upper Bedford Pl, W.C.1.

LAKE, Norman Claude, M.D., M.S., D.Sc., F.R.C.S. *b* : Plymouth 1888. *e* : Charing Cross Hosp, Univ of Lond. *m* : Dorothy Rees. *d* : 1. Senior Surgeon & Dir Surgical Div'n Charing Cross Hosp, Sen Surg Bolingbroke Hosp. Late Examiner Univs Lond & Manch. *Publ* : The Foot ; Surgical Anatomy & Physiology ; Lectures to Chiropodists. *Ctr* : B.M.J., Lancet & other Med Journs. *s.s* : Medical & Surgical. *a* : 51 Welbeck St, London, W.1. *T* : Welbeck 8659.

LAKE, Robert. Racing Journalist. *n.a* : " Paddock Critic " The Winner 1946—, Press Assoc '30—36. *Ctr* : Dly Herald, Sunday Chron. *s.s* : Racing, Films. *a* : 55 Glebe Rd, Hornsey, London, N.8. *T* : Holborn 6195.

LAKE, Silva, M.A., Ph.D. *b* : New Haven, Connecticut 1898. *e* : Vermont, Harvard & Brown Univs. *m* : (1) Robert W. New. (2) Kirsopp Lake. *s* : 3. *d* : 1. Editor & Writer. *n.a* : Studies & Documents 1933— & Monumenta Musicae Byzantinae '36—. *Publ* : An Introduction to the New Testament ; Dated Greek Minuscule MSS ; Family II & The Codex Alexandrinus ; Caesarean Text of Mark ; Family 13 (Ferrar Text) in Mark ; Introduction to Textual Criticisms of New Testament. *Ctr* : Harvard Theol Rev, Journ of Biblical Studies, etc. *s.s* : New Testament Textual Criticism & Hist, Greek Paleography, Near Eastern Archæology. *Rec* : Gardening, bridge. *a* : 1825 Diamond Ave, South Pasadena, California, U.S.A. *T* : Cleveland 6-8990.

LAKER, Albert. *b* : Brighton 1875. *e* : Gr Sch Brighton. *m* : Thirga Spencer. Journalist. *n.a* : Chrm & Mang-Dir Municipal Journ & Municipal Year Book, Former Manager & Dir of The Globe, (Ed) The Referee 1921—31. *a* : 6 Dealtry Rd, London, S.W.15. *T* : Putney 0369.

LAKIN, Cyril Harry Alfred, M.A. *b* : Barry, Glam 1893. *e* : St John's Coll Oxf. *m* : Vera Savill. *d* : 1. Journalist Barrister (Inner Temple), News Commentator B.B.C. Empire & U.S. 1940—43, M.P. (Nat Un) Llandaff & Barry div of Glam '42—45. *n.a* : Asst-Ed Dly Telegraph 1927—33, Lit-Ed Sun Times & Dly Telegraph '33—37, Asst-Ed & Lit-Ed Sun Times '37—45. *c* : Athenæum, Cardiff & County. *a* : 154 Chiltern Court, London, N.W.1. *T* : Welbeck 5544.

LAKOWITZ, KONRAD: botanist; b. Danzig, Germany, June 22, 1859; s. Adolf and Mathilde L.; educ. Realgymnasium zu St. Johann (Danzig). DEGREES: Ph.D.; Professor; Educational Council; m. Jenny Off. AUTHOR: Die Oligozänflora von Mülhausen im Elsass, 1895; Die Algenflora der Danziger Bucht, 1907; Die Algenflora der gesamten Ostsee, 1929. Has contributed many articles in the reports of the West-Prussian botanical-zoological society of Danzig and the Naturforschenden Gesellschaft of Danzig. General character of writing: scientific, botanical. CLUBS: Vorsitzender des Westpreussischen botanisch-zoologischen Vereins; honorary member of Naturforschen Gesellschaft, and chairman of Armen-Unterstützungs-Verein. Relig. denom., Evangelical Reformed. ADDRESS: Danzig, Freie Stadt, Germany.

LALLY, Gwen. b: London. e: at home. Pageant & Play Producer, Directed Principal Pageants. *Publ*: The Street of Many Arches; (with Joan Conquest) Behind the Veil; Flaming Youth; (Plays) Jezebel; England's Greatness. *Ctr*: Country Life, Birm Post, Birm Weekly Post, Chambers's Encyclopædia, etc. *s.s*: Pageantry, Play Producing, the Drama, Shakespeare. *Rec*: Plays, motoring, dancing. *a*: Forge Cottage, Willesley Green, Cranbrook, Kent. *T*: Cranbrook 2130.

LALO, CHARLES: professor of philosophy; b. Périgueux, France, February, 1877; s. Paul Lalo; educ. Lycée de Bordeaux, Lycée Louis-le-Grand (Paris), Faculté des Lettres de Bordeaux. DEGREES: Licencié es Lettres, Agrégé de Philosophie, Docteur es Lettres; m. 1902. AUTHOR: Esquisse d'une Esthétique musicale scientifique, 1908; L'Esthétique de Fechner (augmented edition: L'Esthétique, experimentale contemporaine), 1908; Les Sentiments esthétiques (transl. into Spanish), 1910; Introduction a l'Esthétique (transl. into Russian), 1912; L'Art et la Vie Sociale, 1921; Aristote, 1922; L'Art et la Morale, 1922; La Beauté et l'Instinct sexuel (transl. into Czech), 1922; (the last two are part of the Memoire which in 1929 obtained the Prix du Budget de l'Academie des Sciences morales, upon the report of M. E. Selliere); (with Mme. Lalo): La Faillité de la Beaute, 1923; Esthétique, sciences du langage, sociologie, logique formelle, 1925; Notions d'Esthétique, 1925. Contributor to Revue Philosphique, Journal de Psychologie, Mercure de France, Revue Bleue, and others. General character of writing: aesthetics. Was awarded the Prix d'honneur de discours Français at the concours generale of 1894. Received the Prix Lévêque of l'Academie des Sciences morales in 1913. Professor of Philosophy at the Lycées of Bayonne, Limoges, Bordeaux, Versailles, Rollin and Voltaire. Is interested in synthesizing varied scientific researches, so that together they may increase appreciation of the aesthetics of nature and art. CLUBS: Société française de Psychologie (Paris). OFFICE: Lycée Voltaire, Paris. HOME: 22 Avenue de Picardie, Versailles, France.

LAMB, Lieut.-Col., D. P. Asst Works Mang. *a*: 26 Essex Rd, Gravesend, Kent.

LAMB, David Ritchie. Mem Inst of Transport, (Ed) Modern Transport. *Publ*: Several, relating to Transport. *a*: 9 Northwick Ave, Harrow. *T*: Wordsworth 1041.

LAMB, Francis W. b: Dublin 1874. *e*: T.C.D. *m*: s: 2. *Publ*: Human Experimental Physiology. *a*: Woodfield, Clara, Offaly, Eire.

LAMB, Harold Albert. b: Alpine, New Jersey 1892. *e*: Friend's Sem New York & Columbia Univ. *m*: Ruth Barbour. s: 1. d: 1. Writer. *Publ*: The Crusades; The Garden to the Eastward; The March of Muscovy; Alexander of Macedon; The March of the Barbarians; Tamerlane; Genghis Khan; Omar Khayyam. *Ctr*: Various. *s.s*: Medieval Hist of Central Asia & Eastern Europe, Migration Exploration, Inner Asia. *Rec*: Chess, travel, book collecting. *w.s*: U.S. Infantry 1917—18 & '43—45. *a*: 10048 Cielo Drive, Beverley Hills, California, U.S.A. *T*: Crestview 6-0684.

LAMB, Herbert Arthur John, A.R.I.B.A. *b*: Worting. *e*: Tonbridge Sc & Archit Assoc. Journalist. *n.a*: Ed Building Times 1934—. *c.t*: Windsor Mag, Field, Daily Mail, Evening Standard, Morning Post, Popular Flying, M/C Guardian, etc. *s.s*: Archit, photog. Changed from Archit to full-time Journalism '32. F/L. War Service, Gallipoli & Mesopotamia, France. Gassed. *a*: 80 Richmond Hill Ct, Richmond, Surrey. *t*: Richmond 0475.

LAMB, Sir Horace, ScD., F.R.S. *b*: Stockport 1849. *e*: Stockport G.S., Owen's Col & Trin Col Cam. *m*: Elizabeth Foot (dec). s: 3. d: 4. Formerly Prof of Maths Adelaide & M/C. *Publ*: Hydrodynamics (6th ed 1933); Higher Mechanics; Dynamical Theory of Sound; etc. *s.s*: Mathematical physics. Hon Fell Trinity Col Cam. Pres Brit Assoc '25. *a*: 6 Selwyn Gdns, Cam. *t*: 1617.

LAMB, Rev. John William, M.A. *b*: Derby 1896. *e*: T.C.D. & Leeds Univ. *m*: Margaret Elizabeth Tunstall. s: 1. d: 4. Rector of Bridlington, Canon & Prebendary of Ampleforth in York Minster, Rural Dean of Bridlington. *Publ*: St. Wulstan, Prelate & Patriot; Lectures on Confirmation. *Ctr*: The Record. *a*: The Rectory, Bridlington. *T*: Bridlington 2221.

LAMB, Norman Ernest, A.I.M.T.A. Incorporated & Municipal Accountant. *n.a*: Jt Financial Ed Local Govt Chronicle. *Publ*: Income Tax as Affecting Local Authorities, Education Finance; etc. *Ctr*: Various Accounting Journals *a*: Barclays Bank Chambers, Newport, Mon. *T*: 2789.

LAMB, Sybil Gwendolen ("Sybil Spottiswoode"). b: Lon. *m*: (1) Capt John Spottiswoode; (2) Brig-Gen A. E. Aitken; (3) Francis M. Lamb. s: 2. *Publ*: Marcia in Germany; Chronicles of a German Town; Her Husband's Country; The Test; The Wheel in Turning. *a*: 2 Sion Hill Pl, Bath. *t*: 3520.

LAMB, Walter Alfred. *b*: Surbiton 1896. *m*: Ethel Champion. s: 1. Journalist. *n.a*: Feature writer C.B. News Service 1944, Camberley News '44—. *Ctr*: All leading journals. *s.s*: Angling, Boxing, Naval & Military subjects. *Rec*: Angling. *c*: Rotary. *a*: Camberley News, 80 Park St, Camberley, Surrey. *T*: Camberley 937.

LAMB, Sir Walter Rangeley Maitland, K.C.V.O., M.A. *b*: Adelaide, Sth Australia 1882. *e*: Manch Gr Sch, Trinity Coll Camb. *m*: Rose Brooks. Sec Royal Acad of Arts London since 1913, Ed Camb Rev '05—06, Fellow Trin Coll '07—13, Asst Master Clifton Coll '07—09, Sec Camb Philogical Soc '10—13, Examiner for about 30 years Oxford & Cambridge Examination Board, Belgian Medal of King Albert '20. *Publ*: Clio Enthroned; The Discourses of Sir Joshua Reynolds; The Royal Academy; Translations of Plato's Dialogues & Lysias' Orations. *Rec*: Reading history & memoirs, cycling, carpentry. *a*: The Red Cottage, Eastbury Ave, Northwood, Middx. *T*: 1189.

LAMB, Winifred, D.Sc., M.A., F.S.A. *b*: London. *e*: Newnham Coll Camb. Archæologist, Keeper of Greek & Roman Dept Fitzwilliam Museum. *Publ*: Excavations at Thermi in Lesbos; Greek & Roman Bronzes; Corpus Vasorum Antiquorum Cambridge I & II. *Ctr*: Annual of Brit Sch at Athens, Archæologia, Journ of Hellenic Studies, etc. *s.s*: Prehistoric Turkey, Archæology. *Rec*: Gardening. *c*: Women's Univ. *a*: Borden Wood, Liphook, Hants.

LAMBACH, WALTHER: author; b. Rheinland, Germany, 1885; s. Wilhelm and Adelina (Koch) L.; educ. elementary schools and high schools; m. Julia Lindenberg. AUTHOR: Diktator Rathenau, 1918; Ursachen des Zusammenbruchs, 1919; Sozialisierung, 1919; Herrschaft der 500, 1926; "Politische Trasis 1926, 1927", 1926, 1927. Contributor to: Deutsche Handels Wacht, Hamburg; Deutscher Kaufmann im Auslande, Hamburg; Politische Wochenschrift, Berlin. General character of writing: political. Member of the Reichstag, 1920-1931; member of the Direction of Deutschnationale Handlungsgehilfen-Verband. CLUBS: Deutschnationale Handlungsgehilfen Verband (D.H.V.); Nationaler Klub, Berlin; Volksdeutscher Klub, Berlin. Relig. denom., Evangelical. OFFICE: Holstenwall 4, Hamburg. HOME: Paulsenstrasse 40c, Berlin-Steglitz, Germany.

LAMBART, J. H. L., M.A. Asst Master. a: Godolphin Hse, Eton Col, Windsor, Berks.

LAMBERT, Alice Dorothea ("Dorothy Lambert"). b: Mallow 1884. e: Priv. m: Eric Tom Lambert. d: 1. Publ: Redferne M.F.H.; Elizabeth Who Wouldn't; Aunts in Arcady; Moons and Magpies; Rescuing Anne; Invitation; Independence; Travelling Light, Nothing to Forgive; etc. c.t: Windsor Mag. s.s: Novels about Ireland, light comedies for amateur prod. a: Sheepsclose, Shepherdswell, Dover, Kent.

LAMBERT, Sir Arthur, Kt, M.C., D.L., J.P. Publ: Northumbria's Spacious Year 1929. s.s: Travel, Northumbrian hist. Lord Mayor of Newcastle '27 & '29, Kt of St Olaf, 1st Cl (Norway). a: 10 Kensington Terr, Newcastle-on-Tyne.

LAMBERT, Audrey. Author. Publ: Simon's Wife; Breakaway. a: c/o Eldon Press Ltd, 66 Curzon St, W.1.

LAMBERT, Charles Edmund. b: Sheen, Staffs 1872. e: Newcastle-under-Lyme H.S., Christ's Col Cam. m: Helen Mary Ellison. s: 2. Rector of St James's Piccadilly, Archdeacon of Hampstead. Publ: Ed Jeaffreson Letters. Rec: Golf. c: Athenæum. a: St James's Rectory, Piccadilly, W.1. t: Regent 5244.

LAMBERT, Constant. b: London 1905. e: Christ's Hosp, Roy Coll of Music. Composer, Conductor & Critic. Publ: Music Ho!; A Study of Music in Decline. Ctr: Radio Times, New Statesman, Figaro (Paris). s.s: Cats & Ballet. a: 197 Albany St, London, N.W.1.

LAMBERT, Eileen Marion Audrey. Author. Publ: Simon's Wife; Breakaway. a: Sheepsclose, Shepherdswell, nr Dover, Kent.

LAMBERT, Rev. Francis John, Ph.D., M.Th., B.D. b: Liverpool 1898. e: Univ of Lond. m:. s: 1. Vicar of Holy Trinity Sheerness. Publ: Divine Dynamite. s.s: Theology, History. w.s: 1914—18 Inf Comm Balkan front, '39—45 Flt-Lt R.A.F. C/O A.T.C. Squad. a: The Vicarage, Sheerness. T: 244.

LAMBERT, Sir Henry, C.M., K.C.M.G., C.B. b: Lon 1868. e: Eton & New Col Oxf. m: Aileen Arthur. s: 1. d: 3. Ex-Civil Servant. Publ: History of Banstead in Surrey (Vol I 1912 & Vol II '31); The Nature of History. c.t: Surrey Archæol Soc's Collections & to English Hist Review. Formerly in Colonial office & Sec to Imp Conf, subsequently Sr Crown Agent for the Colonies. c: Athenæum, Fellow of Antiquaries & Roy Hist Soc. a: Larklands, Banstead.

LAMBERT, Rev. Leonard. b: Birmingham 1900. e: Kelham Theol Coll. m: Madge Shwalbe. s: 1. d: 1. Vicar of Stoke Golding cum Dadlington. Publ: Guinea Legends; Verses on the Way. Ctr: Grantham Journal, Hinckley Times & Guardian, Guiana Diocesan Mag, etc. Folklore of the Aborigines of Guiana. a: Stoke Golding Vicarage, Nuneaton.

LAMBERT, Richard Stanton, M.A. b: Kingston-on-Thames 1894. e: Repton Sch & Wadham Coll Oxf. m: (1) Kate Elinor Klein, (2) Edith Margaret Joyce Morgan. s: 1. d: 1. Supervisor of Educational Broadcasts Canadian Broadcasting Corp. n.a: Ed The Listener 1928—39. Publ: Modern Imperialism; The Prince of Pickpockets; The Railway King; When Justice Faltered; The Innocence of Edmund Galley; The Universal Provider; Propaganda; The Cobbett of the West; Ariel & All His Quality; Old Country Mail; For the Time is at Hand; The Adventure of Canadian Printing; etc. Ctr: New Statesman & Nation, Listener, Countryman, To-morrow (N.Y.), Sat Night (Toronto), etc. s.s: Biography, Social History, Crime, Radio & Film, Art. Rec: Fishing, gardening. a: Apt 615, 2904 Yonge St, Toronto, Canada. T: Hyland 2714.

LAMBORN, Edmund Arnold Greening, M.A.(Oxon). b: Oxford 1877. e: Public Primary Schs. Schoolmaster (ret), late Lecturer in Education Oxford Univ Training Coll, in English War Office Sch of Education, Co-ed World's Manuals 1922. Publ: The Story of Architecture in Oxford Stone; The Rudiments of Criticism; Shakespeare, the Man & his Stage; Towns & Town Planning; Poetic Values, a companion to the Study of the Golden Treasury; Reason in Arithmetic; Expression in Speech & Writing; The English Parish Church. Ctr: Notes & Queries, Oxford, Country Life, Berkshire Arch Jnl, Medium Aevum, Jnl of the Monumental Brass Soc, Jnl of the Soc of Master Glass-Painters, Records of Bucks, Medieval England. s.s: Heraldry, Painted Glass, Genealogy, Medieval Architecture. Rec: Local history & topography, bird song. a: Littlemore, Oxford.

LAMBOTTE, PAUL, K.B.E.: Director Général des Beaux-Arts; b. Brussels, Belgium, August, 1862; s. Alfred and Marie Katherine (Doucet) L.; educ. Univ. of Brussels. DEGREE: Docteur en Droit; m. May Story. AUTHOR: Henri Evenepoel, 1908; Les Peintres de Portraits (of 19th Century), 1913; L'Art Flamand, 1928; La Peinture Anglais, 1929. Contributor to Apollo, The Studio, The Connoisseur, Revue de l'Art Ancien et Moderne, and numerous Belgian, French and foreign mags. and papers. General character of writing: art history and art criticism. Has organized many art expositions in nearly every capital in Europe. Religion, Catholic. OFFICE: Ministere des Sciences et des Arts, Brussels. HOME: 15 rue Egmont, Brussels, Belgium.

LAMBOURNE, John. b: Bury 1893. e: Bury G.S. & M/C Univ. m: Doris Joan Cooke. s: 1. Publ: The White Kaffir; Trooper Fault; Strong Waters; The Kingdom that Was; The Second Leopard; The Unmeasured Place; Inky Wooing; etc. c.t: Cornhill, Field, Country Life. s.s: Nat hist, Africa & China. Rhodesian Mounted Police 6 y, travel in interior of China for 12 y. Rec: Shooting, fishing, wild animal photog. c: Authors'. a: Colston Hse, Buckfastleigh, Devon.

LAMBTON, Arthur. b: Lon 1869. e: Westminster Sc & Jesus Col Cam. m: Marion Edith Egan Desmond. d: 1. Author. Publ: The Man with the Green Eyes (with Sir Max Pemberton); The Maternal Instinct (with the Hon Symon Ormsby-Gore); Thou Shalt do no Murder; Echoes of Causes Célèbres; The Galanty Show (1933); etc. c.t: The Daily Mail, The Sunday Dispatch, The Evening News, The Tatler, The Saturday Review, The Evening Standard, etc. s.s: Criminology & sport. Largely respons for passing of Legitimacy Bill '26 (after Sir George Bowyer) & with Mr Ingleby Oddie founded The Crimes Club, the famous criminological dining club. War Service, Special Branch, Scotland Yard (Spy Dept). c: Wellington, Reform & M.C.C. a: 7 Orslow Pl, S.W.7.

LAMBURN, Richmal Crompton, B.A. (see **CROMPTON,** Richmal). b: Bury 1890. e: St Elphin's Sch Darley Dale Matlock & Holloway Coll Lond. c: Lyceum. a: The Glebe, Oakley Rd, Bromley Common, Kent. T: Hurstway 1158.

LAMDAN, Izchak. *b*: Mlynow 1899. *e*: Sec Sch. *m*: Annie Ballheimer. *d*: 1. Ed Lit Monthly Gilyonoth. *Publ*: Massadah; Be Maaleh Akrabim; Be Ritman Meshuleshet; Sefer Hajamin; Machnajim. *Ctr*: Gilionoth, Moznajim, & various lit papers in Palestine & abroad. *s.s*: Poetry, Criticism. *Rec*: Swimming. *c*: P.E.N. *a*: P.O.B. 4017, Tel-Aviv, Palestine.

LAMERT, Sidney Streatfeild. *b*: India 1875. *e*: Loretto Sc. *m*: Elizabeth Sheepshanks. *d*: 3. Chm Thomas De La Rue & Coy Ltd. *n.a*: Ed Sun '96–1907, War Corr S. Africa 1899–1900, Ed Money Market Review. *c.t*: Investor's Chronicle. *s.s*: Economics, finance. Sth African War Medal. *Rec*: Golf, garden. *c*: Union. *a*: 18 Gloucester Sq, Hyde Park, W.2. & Harleigh Green, Five Ashes, Sussex. *t*: Padd 5309.

LAMMEYER, JOSEPH: univ. professor; b. Fulda, Prussia, March 30, 1870; s. Konrad and Josephine (Mollenhauer) L.; educ. Gymnasium, studied theology at Fulda; Univs. of Würzburg, Münster, Bonn and Freiburg. DEGREES: Dr. Theol.; Dr. Jur. Utr.; Ph.D.; Dr. Phil. of Univ. of Bonn on Rhine (Egyptology, Semitic Philosophy, Philosophy); Dr. Theol., Univ. of Freiburg; Dr. Jur. Utr., Erlangen, Bavaria. AUTHOR: Siegesdenkmal des Königs Scheschonk I. zu Karnak, 1907; Die sogenannten Gnomen des Konzils von Nicaea, 1912; Geschichte der syrischen Kirche; Syriscaharabische Sprachforschung, 1912; Geschichtliche Entwicklung der Ehe, 1930. Contributor to Wiener Reichspost, Augsburger Postzeitung, Kölnische Volkszeitung, Archiv für katholisches Kirchenrecht, Levantezeitung, Hamburg; Post für Holland. General character of writing: scientific, historical. ADDRESS: Triererstrasse 21, Cologne, Germany.

LAMONT, Corliss, A.B., Ph.D. *b*: Englewood, New Jersey 1902. *e*: Phillips Exeter Acad, New Coll Oxf & Columb Univ. *m*: Margaret H. Irish. *s*: 1. *d*: 3. Author & Teacher Columbia Sch of General Studies 1947—. *Publ*: The Illusion of Immortality; You might like Socialism; The Peoples of the Soviet Union; Issue of Immortality; A Humanist Funeral Service; (Ed) Man Answers Death; An Anthology of Poetry. *Ctr*: Journ of Philos, Humanist, Soviet Russia To-day. *s.s*: Philosophy, Civil Liberties, Soviet Union, Socialism. *c*: Columb Faculty, Harvard, etc. *a*: 450 Riverside Drive, New York 27, N.Y., U.S.A. *T*: University 4-5476.

LAMONT, William Dawson, M.A., D.Ph. *b*: Prince Edward Island, Canada 1901. *e*: Glasgow Univ & Balliol Coll Oxf. *m*: Ann Fraser Christie. Principal Makerere College Kampala Uganda 1946—, V-Chrm Cairo Group Roy Inst of Internat Affairs '44. *Publ*: Principles of Moral Judgement; Introduction to Green's Moral Philosophy. *Ctr*: Mind, Philosophy, Procs of Aristotelian & Roy Philos Socs. *s.s*: Philosophy, Ethics & Political Theory. *Rec*: Walking, sailing. *w.s*: 1939–42 Clyde River Patrol & Naval Intelligence. *a*: Makerere College, Kampala, Uganda, East Africa. *T*: Kampala 550.

LA MONTE, John L., M.A., Ph.D. *b*: Columbus, Ohio 1902. *e*: Ohio State Univ, Harvard *m*: Katherine Richardson. *s*: 1. H. C. Lea Prof of Medieval Hist Univ of Penna. *Publ*: Feudal Monarchy in the Latin Kingdom of Jerusalem; (with M. J. Hubert) Wars of Frederick II in Syria & Cyprus; Crusade of Richard Lion-Heart. *Ctr*: Byzantion, Speculum, Amer Hist Review, Renaissance, Syria, etc. *s.s*: Crusades, Medieval Syria & Cyprus. *a*: 4014 Pine St, Philadelphia 4, Penn. *T*: Ev-6-2268.

LAMPE, KARL HEINRICH: member of educational council; b. Berlin, Germany, Dec. 13, 1886; s. August and Alma (Helmke) L.; educ. Sophien-Realgymnasium of Berlin, Univs. of Berlin and Jena; m. Helene Reckling, April 3, 1885. AUTHOR: Familie Lampe, 1910; Die bäuerlichen Ministerialen des Erzstifts Magdeburg, 1911; Der Versailler Vertrag und die Ergebnisse der folgenden Verhandlungen, 1922; Die Reichsverfassung und die preussische Verfassung als Einführung in die Staatsbürgerkunde, 1922; Geschichtliche Stammtafeln, 1922; Die Bewohner der Altmark in Sitte und Brauch, 1923; Die Geschichte der Bäcker-Innung zu Neuruppin, 1927; Quellen und Literatur des Kreises Ruppin, 1928. Editor: Aus Danzigs schweren Tagen (diary from 1813), 1920; Urkundenbuch der Deutschordensballei Thüringen (1st vol.), 1930. Contributor to: Historische Vierteljahrsschrift; Mitteilungen aus der historischen Literatur; Archiv für Sippenforschung; Familiengeschichtliche Blätter; and many others. General character of writing: historical, geneology, criticisms. CLUBS: Historische Gesellschaft, and other historical and geneological societies and clubs. Relig. denom., Evangelical. ADDRESS: Möhringstrasse 1, Neurippin, Germany.

LAMPEN, Rev. Charles Dudley. *Publ*: The Dead Prior (1896); The Queen of the Extinct Volcano; Mirango the Maneater; The Stranding of the White Rose; Barcali the Mutineer; O'Callaghan the Slave-Trader; The Frozen Treasure; etc. *c.t*: Cassell's Mag, Church Times, Nassau Guardian, etc. *a*: Newchurch Rectory, New Romney, Kent. *t*: Newchurch 2.

LAMPERT, Evgueny, D.Ph., F.R.S.L. *b*: Russia 1914. *e*: Russia, Germany, France & England. *m*: Katherine Ridley. *s*: 2. Lecturer. *Publ*: The Apocalypse of History; The Divine Realm; Nicolas Berdyaev & The New Middle Ages. *s.s*: Philosophy of Religion, Theology, Russian Religions, Social & Political Thought. *a*: 7 Copse Lane, Marston, Oxford.

LAMPL, FRITZ: writer; b. Vienna, Austria, September, 1892; s. Ludwig and Rosa (Redlick) L.; educ. Gymnasium; m. Hilda Berger, 1895. AUTHOR: Gedichte (poems), 1920); Flucht (comedy), 1920; Skalven der Freiheit (novel), 1925) Cupido oder die Comodianten (play), 1926. Editor: Der Neue Daimon (mag.), 1919. Contributes to Prager Presse, Bohemia, Berliner Tageblatt (Berlin), Die Neue Rundschau (Berlin), Das Kunstblatt (Berlin), Der Brenner (Innsbruck), Deutsche Kunst und Dekoration (Darmstadt), etc. Art Director of Bimini Workshops, Society of Applied Arts, Vienna. SOCLIETY: Schutzverband Deutscher Schriftsteller in Oesterreich. Religion, Jewish. ADDRESS: Döblergasse 2, Vienna, Austria.

LAMPREY, Louise. *b*: Alexandria, New Hampshire. *e*: Concord N.H. Hgh Sch & Mount Holyoke Coll. Writer. *Publ*: In the Days of the Guild & Masters of the Guild; All the Ways of Building; Great Days in American History; The Tomahawk Trail; Children of the Ancient World; Wonder Tales of Architecture; Building an Empire; Story of Weaving; Story of Cookery; Building a Republic; (collab) The Alo Man; Natalia & Nikolai. *Ctr*: Junr Britt, Amer Mercury, Amer Affairs. *s.s*: History. *Rec*: Teaching handicrafts. *a*: Hotel Albert, 65 University Place, New York 3, & Limerick, Maine, U.S.A. *T*: Grammercy 3, N.Y.

LAMSLEY, Arthur Thomas, M.J.I. *b*: Portsmouth 1888. *e*: Esplanade Hse Sc Southsea & Portsmouth Municipal Col. *m*: Elizabeth Maria Uys. *s*: 1. Journalist & Lecturer. *n.a*: Sunday Express, Special Corr Daily Mail (Yachting), Gen Special Corr various journs British, Dominion, U.S.A. *Publ*: (Edited) Towards Industrial Statesmanship by Marquess of Londonderry K.G. (1932). *c.t*: British Dominion & American n/p's, Good Housekeeping, Windsor, Premier, Spur, Yachting, Sportsman (U.S.A.), Yachting Monthly, Yachting World & Yachtsman, Armchair Science, etc. *s.s*: Economics, yachting, football. *Rec*: Tramping, politics. *c*: Society of Authors & Individualist Luncheon. *a*: Klip Kopje, 2 Sussex Terr, Southsea.

LANCASTER, Bruce, B.A. *b*: Worcester, Mass 1896. *e*: Harvard. *m*: Jessie Bancroft Payne. Author. *Publ*: The Scarlet Patch; Guns of Burgoyne; For Us, The

Living; Trumpet to Arms; Bright to the Wanderer; (in collab) Bride of A Thousand Cedars; The Wide Sleeve of Kwannon. *Ctr*: Atlantic Monthly. *s.s*: Historical Fiction (Military Angle). *c*: St Botolph (Boston), Kobe (Japan). *w.s*: 1917—19. *a*: c/o The Atlantic Monthly Press, 8 Arlington St, Boston, Mass, U.S.A.

LANCASTER, Rev. George Harold, M.A., F.R.A.S. *b*: London 1882. *e*: Fretherne Hse Sch W.1, Mercers Sch & Univ Coll Durham. *m*: Dora Janet Kingsley Jay. Chaplain to the Forces (T.A.), formerly Sen C.F. 47th (2nd Lond) Div. *Publ*: Prophecy, the War & the Near East; Old Testament Studies; New Testament Studies; The Early Britons & the British Church: etc. *Ctr*: Religious Press & Daily Mail. *s.s*: Nat Hist, Science. *Rec*: Climbing, astron. *c*: Athenæum, Alpine. *a*: The Vicarage, Winchmore Hill, London, N.21. *T*: Palmers Green 3545.

LANCASTER, Vicky. *Publ*: The Sunset Hour; So Many Worlds; They Loved in Donegal; Sweet Shipwreck; Fixed as the Stars; Three Roads to Heaven; etc. *a*: c/o Messrs Hale, Publishers, 18 Bedford Sq, London, W.1.

LANCE, Thomas Marmaduke Constable. *b*: Battersea Pk 1901. *e*: Alleyn's Sc & Dulwich Col & E. Lon Col. Elec Research Eng. Development Eng Baird Television Coy. *Publ*: Photo Electric Cell Applications (with R. C. Walker). *c.t*: Various tech journs, etc. Radio designer to Telephone Manfg Coy '22-25. Sci Staff Research Labs of Gen Elec Coy, Wembley '25-33. Mem Counc Television Soc '29-. Assoc Mem Inst Radio Engs. *Rec*: Amateur theatricals, modelling. *a*: 1 Kingsmead Rd, Tulse Hill, S.W.2.

LANCELOT, Rev. John Bennett. *b*: Gresford 1864.. *e*: King's Sc Chester & Jesus Col Oxf. *m*: Agnes Heathcote. *s*: 1. *d*: 2. *Publ*: Francis James Chavasse; Guidance & Rule; The Religion of the Collects; Essentials of Faith & Prayer. Asst Master M/C G.S Headmaster King's Sc Rochester. Princ L'pool Col. *a*: St James's Vicarage, Birkdale, Southport. *t*: 66255.

LANCHESTER, Frederick William. Cons Engineer. *Publ*: Aerial Flight (vols 1 & 2); Aircraft in Warfare; The Flying Machine from an Engineering Standpoint. *a*: Dyott End, Oxf Rd, Moseley, Birm. *t*: South 1282.

LANCHESTER, Henry Craven Ord. *b*: Newmarket 1877. *e*: Highgate Sc, Pembroke Col Cam. *m*: Grace M. Kerslake. *s*: 2. Rector. Ex-Fell & Dean of Pembroke. *Publ*: The Old Testament; Obadiah-Jonah; etc. *c.t*: Hastings' Dictionary of Religion & Ethics. *a*: Framlingham Rectory, Suffolk. *t*: Framlingham 53.

LANCHESTER, Henry Vaughan. F.R.I.B.A., Litt.D. (Leeds). *b*: London 1863. *e*: Priv & Roy Acad Sch. *m*: Anne Gilchrist Martin. *s*: 1. Architect. *d*: Ed. The Builder 1910—12. *Publ*: The Art of Town Planning; Fischer von Erlach; Talks on Town Planning; Outline of Studies in Town Planning; Town Planning in Madras; Town Planning in Zanzibar. *Ctr*: The Builder & other architectural journs. *s.s*: Architecture, Building, Town & Country Planning, Social Conditions in the East, Education. *c*: Athenæum, Roy India Soc. *a*: 10 Woburn Sq, London, W.C.1. *T*: Museum 0846; & Overmead, Weybridge, Surrey. *T*: 2454.

LANCTOT, Gustave. B.Litt, LL.M., D.Litt. *b*: St Constant 1883. *e*: Montreal Col Montreal & Oxf Univ. *m*: Marie Chauvin. Chf French Archivist Canada. *n.a*: Le Canada 1901, La Patrie '09. *Publ*: Le Dernier effort de la France au Canada ('18); François Xavier Garneau; Les Archives du Canada; L'Administration de la Nouvelle France; (Ed with Dr Kennedy) Reports on the Laws of Quebec; (with Dr Doughty) Cheadle's Journal of Trip across Canada ('31); etc. *c.t*: Cam Univ Hist of Brit Emp, Ency of Social Scis, Journ of Amer Folklore, Canadian Historical Review, La Revue Moderne, etc. *s.s*: Canadian hist & French regime. *Socs*: Pres of Canadian Folklore Soc, Société Historique d'Ottawa, & Soc of Authors, Ottawa, Jt Sec & Ed Canadian Hist Soc, Fellow Roy Soc of Canada, Roy Hist Soc Eng, France-Amerique & Alliance Française, etc. Mem Canadian Special Mission to France '17, Asst Dir War Trophies '18, Canadian Delegate Internat Congress Rio de Janeiro '22 & Brussels '23, Jt Sec Fed Prov Conf Ottawa '27, Canada's Delegate to Colonial Historical Exhib Paris '29. *Rec*: Golf, tennis. *c*: Canadian, etc. *a*: 185 Daly, Ottawa.

LANCUM, F. Howard, M.B.E., F.L.S., F.Z.S. *Publ*: A Sportsman's Medley; Memoirs of a Field Naturalist; Sport & Agriculture; Press Officer Please. *Ctr*: Various Outdoor & Country Mags. *a*: 55 Whitehall, London, S.W.1. *T*: Whitehall 3400.

LANDA, Myer Jack. *b*: Leeds. *m*: Gertrude Gordon. *d*: 1. Journalist. *n.a*: Began on Sheffield Daily Telegraph 1896; subsequently on Birmingham Gazette, which sent him to Lon in 1900 as Lon Ed; later on Daily Mail, Daily News (14 y) & Westminster Gazette (Parl sketch writer). Now Parl sketch writer for Starmer Group. Was mem Mil Tribunal in E. Lon during War. *Publ*: The Alien Problem ('11); The Jew in Drama ('26); Palestine As It Is ('32); Jacob across Jabbok (novel, '33); Kitty Villareal (novel, '34; last 2 in collab with Mrs Landa). *c.t*: Fortnightly Review, Hibbert Journal, Cornhill Mag, etc. *s.s*: Drama, Jewish subjects, politics. *c*: Nat Lib. *a*: 60 Bedford Ct Mansions, W.C.1. *t*: Mus 0587.

LANDAU, M. Elsie, M.D.(Lon), F.R.C.S.(Eng). Senr Asst Surgeon Elizabeth Garrett Anderson Hosp. *a*: 14 Harley St, W.1.

LANDAU, Rom. Author & Sculptor. *Publ*: Minos the Incorruptible; Pilsudski; Paderewski; God is my Adventure; Seven; Thy Kingdom Come; Search for Tomorrow; Love for a Country; Of No Importance; We have seen Evil; Hitler's Paradise; The Fool's Progress; Islam To-day; Letter to Andrew; The Brother Vane; The Wing; Sex, Lifes Faith; The Merry Oasis; Odysseus. *s.s*: Philosophy, Religion, Sex, Middle East Affairs, Fiction. *Rec*: Countryside. *w.s*: World War II R.A.F. *a*: The Manor, Stoughton, Chichester, Sussex. *T*: Compton 18.

ANDAUER, SAMUEL: Oriental languages; b. Krumbach, Germany, February, 1846; s. Meier and Jeanette Landauer; educ. Univs. of Munich, Leipzig, Strassburg (Germany). DEGREES: Hon. Professor of Univ. (Strassburg); m. Anna Rödelheimer. AUTHOR: Die Psychology des Ibn Sina ("zeitschrift der Deutsch-Morgenländischen Gesellschaft", vol. 29), 1875; Kitab al-Amanat von Saadia al- Fajjûmi, 1880; Katalog der Orientalischen Handschriften der Univ- und Landesbibliothek Strassburg, 1881; Ferdusii leber regum, qui inscribitur Schahname (3 vols.), 1884; Separat-Abdruck aus der Zeitschrift für Assyr. (3 vols.), 1888; Die Orientalischen Handschriften der Gross-herzoglich-Badischen Bibliothek in Karlsruhe, 1892; Die Masorah zum Onkelos, 1896; Themistii in libros Aristotelis de Cavlo paragraphis, 1902; Themistii in Aristotelis Metaphysicorum librum paraphrasis, 1903; Das Elif als mater lectionis im Jüdisch-Aramaischen (Festscrift für A. Berliner), 1903; Zum Targum der Klagelieder (Festschrift für Theodor Nöldeke), 1906; Ein interessantes Fragment des Pseudo-Jonathan (Festschrift für A. Harkavy), 1908. Has contributed many articles to sicentific journs. Specializes in Oriental languages and literature; beside the Arabian and Persian literature, especially the post-Biblical literature in its different Semitic dialects; has made special study of the text and language of the "Targumin". A voluminous work about the "Targum" of the "Prophetae Majores" is in preparation. SOCIETY: Member of Scientific Society of Strassburg. Religion, Jewish. HOME: 34, Volkstrasse, Augsbury, Germany.

LANDER, Cecil Howard, C.B.E., D.Sc. *b*: Stockport 1881. *e*: Priv Schs & Manch Univ. *m*: Beatrice Whalley. *d*: 2. Chrtd Civil & Mech Eng, Dean of Military Coll of Sci, Govt Dir Fuel Research 1924—31, Mem Brit Nat Cttee World Power Conf, etc. *Publ*: Low Temperature Carbonisation; Ventilation & Humidity in Textile Mills & Factories. *Ctr*: Sci Journs. *s.s*: Power & Fuel Utilisation. *Rec*: Music, motor-boating. *a*: Military College of Science, Shrivenham, nr Swindon, Wilts. *T*: Swindon Trunks 17.

LANDER, Pinhas Aharon. *b*: Ropczyce, Poland 1905. *e*: Teecher Coll. *m*: Wardah. *s*: 1. *d*: 1. Journalist, Staff of Haaretz. *n.a*: Staff of Moznaiim, Gazitu, & Haduar. *Publ*: Al-Eretz-Zo; Shadmoth Moladti; Jessie Sempter Poems; etc. *s.s*: Poetry, Translations, Newspaper Reporting. *Rec*: Touring. *c*: P.E.N. *a*: 6 Lessing St, Tel Aviv, Palestine. *T*: 6313.

LANDERSDORFER, SIMON: priest; *b.* Oct. 2, 1880; *s.* Lorenz and Elisabeth (Haberthaler) L.; educ. Gymnasium (Scheyern and Freising), High Sch. (Eichstatt), Univ. of Munich. DEGREES: D.D., Ph.D. AUTHOR: Altbabylonische Privatbriefe, 1908; Die Bibel u. d. südarab. Altertumsforschung, 1910; Arabien und seine Kultur, 1911; Eine babyl. Quelle für das Buch Job, 1911; Ausgewählte Schriften der syrischen Dichter cyrillomas, Balaeus, Isaak von Antiochien und Jakob von Sarug, 1912; Die Kultur der Babylonier und Assyrer, 1913; Die Götterliste des Mar Jakob von Sarug in seiner Homilie über den Fall der Götzenbilder, 1914; Sumerisches Sprachgut im Alten Testament, 1916; Fortsetzung der Bücherliste; Die Sumerischen Parallelen zur biblischen Urgeschichte, 1917; Die Sumerische Frage und die Bibel, 1917; Der Baal tetramophos und die Kerube des Ezechiel, 1918; Die Psalmen, 1922; Studien zum bibl. Ver-söhnungstag, 1924; Die Bücher der Könige, 1927. SOCIETY: O. S. B. Religion, Catholic. ADDRESS: Abtei Scheyern, Bayern, Germany.

LANDI, Elissa. *b*: Venice 1904. *e*: Priv, Eng & Europe. *m*: J. C. Lawrence. Actress, author. *Publ*: Neilsou 1926; The Helmers; House for Sale; The Ancestor (1st book of a trilogy, The New Monarchy) 1934. Made debut on Lon stage in Storm by C. K. Munro, 1924. Left for New York in '30 to play in A Farewell to Arms. Subsequently entered motion pictures. *Rec*: Riding, gardening, music. *a*: 1515 Amalfi Drive, Pacific Palisades, S. Calif, U.S.A.

LANDIS, Paul H., A.M., Ph.D. *b*: Cuba Ill, 1901. *e*: Univs of Iowa, Mich & Minn. *m*: Bessie Edith Banks. *s*: 1. *d*: 2. Prof of Sociol State Coll of Washington. *n.a*: Asst-Ed Amer Social Rev 1947— & Co-op-Ed Social & Social Research '47—.. *Publ*: Social Policies in the Making; Rural Life in Process; Adolescence & Youth; Social Control; Population Problems; Your Marriage & Family Living; Social Living (collab); etc. *Ctr*: Journ Farm Economics, Educational Digest, School & Society Commonweal, National Digest, The Churchman & many other scientific & popular journs. *s.s*: Sociology, Education, Sports. *Rec*: Hunting, fishing, gardening, etc. *a*: Harvey Rd, & 318 New Science Bldg, State College of Washington, Pullman, Washington, U.S.A. *T*: 5413 & 7063.

LANDMAN, Julian, M.D. *b*: 1882. *e*: Leeds Univ & Paris. *m*: Lily Lightman. *s*: 1. *d*: 1. Physician. *n.a*: Lon Corr N.Y. Med Journ. *c.t*: Lancet, Med Times, etc. *s.s*: Diseases of chest & lungs. *Rec*: Travel, econ. *c*: F.R.EconSoc. *a*: 62 Queen Anne St, W.1. *t*: Welbeck 8286.

LANDON, Fred, M.A., F.R.S.C. *b*: London, Ontario 1880. *e*: London & Univ of Western Ontario. *m*: Margaret Smith. *s*: 1. *d*: 1. Librarian Univ of Western Ontario 1923—47, V-Pres & Dean of Graduate Studies '47—. *n.a*: Parliamentary Corres, Ottawa Press Gallery 1907—08 & '12—14. *Publ*: Western Ontario & the American Frontier; Lake Huron. *Ctr*: Can Hist Rev, Journ of Negro Hist, Mich Hist Mag, London Free Press, etc. *s.s*: Canadian-American relations prior to 1900, The Negro in Canada before Civil War, Great Lakes Hist & Shipping. *Rec*: Country life & Great Lake shipping pictures. *a*: 846 Hellmuth Ave, London, Ontario, Canada.

LANDON, Philip Aislabie, M.C., M.A. *b*: Exeter 1888. *e*: Kelly Col, Brasenose Col Oxf. Fellow of T.C. Oxf. *Publ*: Stephen's Commentaries on Laws of England (17th & 18th edns); Pease & Landon, Law of Contract (1925). *c.t*: Legal periodicals. *c*: United Univ. *a*: T.C. Oxf & 2 Harcourt Bldgs, Temple, E.C.4. *t*: Oxf 3116.

LANDQUIST, John, Ph.D. *b*: Stockholm 1881. *e*: Upsala Univ. *m*: Solveig Bohlin. *d*: 1. Prof in Psychology & Pedagogy at Lunds Univ 1936—46. *n.a*: Lit Critic Dagens Nyheter 1910—17, Aftonbladet '24—35 Lit. Critic Aftonbladet & Stockholms-Tidningen '47—. *Publ*: The Will, a psychological study; Gustaf Freding (Swedish Poet); Knut Hamsun, a romantic poet; Knowledge of Man; Erik Gustaf Geijer, His life & work; Henri Bergson; Modern Swedish Literature in Finland; Psychology; History of Pedagogy. *Ctr*: Bonniers Litterara Mag, Svensk Litteraturtidskift, Samtid och framtid, etc. *c*: P.E.N. *a*: Villavagen 19, Stocksund.

LANDRY, Robert John. *b*: East Haddam, Conn 1903. *m*: Marcia Landry. Author, Editor, Radio Network Official. *n.a*: Mang Chicago Office Variety 1930—31, Hollywood Office '31—32, Ed (Radio & Music) Variety New York '33—42. *Publ*: Who, What, Why in Radio; This Fascinating Radio Business; The Making of the Columbia Workshop. *Ctr*: Ladies Home Journ, Reader's Digest, Atlantic, New Republic, Esquire, Scribner's, etc. *s.s*: Broadcasting. *a*: 18 West 70 St, New York City 23.

LANDSBERG, Leonore Julia. *b*: Germany. *e*: Art in Germany, Italy. Art Ed, Mem N.U.J. *n.a*: Art Ed Der Deutsche Rundfunk Berlin, & Ed Funk Post 1927—36, Asst Art Ed Harpers Bazaar & Good Housekeeping Mag '41—46, at present Free-lance & Art Ed with high class export mags. *Ctr*: Wine & Food. *s.s*: Art Editing of Mags & Books. *Rec*: Music, cocking, reading. *a*: 7 Courtfield Gdns, London, S.W.5. *T*: Frobisher 2578.

LANE, Allen. *b*: Bristol 1902. *e*: Bristol G.S. Publisher. *a*: The Bodley Head, Vigo St, W.1. *t*: Regent 5025.

LANE, Lt.-Col. Clayton, M.D., M.R.C.S., L.R.C.P. *n.a*: Ed Trans Roy Soc Trop Med & Hyg 1925—30, Sectional Ed, Trop Diseases Bulletin, Malaria '21—29, Helminthiasis '29—. *Publ*: Hookworm Infection. *c.t*: Indian Journ Med Res, Indian Med Gazette, Lancet, B.M.J., Trans Roy Soc Trop Med & Hyg, Annals Trop Med & Parasit, etc. *a*: Heathfield, 1 Castle Bar Pk, Ealing, W.5. *t*: Perivale 1984.

LANE, Edward Valentine, M.R.S.T., B.A., M.A. *b*: Birkenhead 1896. *e*: Birkenhead Inst, L'pool Univ. *m*: Mildred Blythe Storey. *s*: 1. *d*: 1. Head of Geog Dept Bec Sc, Lon S.W.17. *Publ*: South America (1931); North & Central America; Asia ('34). *c.t*: Times Educ Supp, Sheffield Daily Telegraph, etc. *s.s*: Geog, regional survey, ind hist. Broadcast series of lectures on ind development of Sheffield & on Sir Henry Bessemer in '26. War Service 15—19. *Rec*: Tennis, photog. *c*: Mem Geog Assoc. *a*: 66 Tybenham Rd, Merton Pk, S.W.19.

LANE, Frederic Chapin, M.A., Ph.D. *b* Lansing, Michigan 1900. *e*: Tufts Coll, Univs of Cornell, Harvard & Bordeaux. *m*: Harriet W. Mirick. *s*: 2. *d*: 1. Prof of Hist The Johns Hopkins Univ Baltimore. *n.a*: Ed Journ of Econ Hist 1943—. *Publ*: Venetian Ships & Shipbuilders of the Renaissance; Andrea Barbarigo, Merchant of Venice 1418—1449; (in collab) The World's History. *Ctr*: Journ of Econ & Business Hist. Hist

Rev, Mariner's Mirror, Journ of Econ Hist, etc. *s.s*: Econ Hist, Venice. *Rec*: Tennis. *c*: Cosmos, Hamilton Street. *a*: 4725 Keswick Rd, Baltimore 10, Maryland, U.S.A. *T*: Hopkins 0900.

LANE, H. G. Editor. *a*: The Freemason, 73–75 Minories, E.C.4.

LANE, Kenneth Westmacott (see **WEST, Keith**). *b*: 1893. *e*: Rugby, Balliol Coll Oxf. *Ctr*: Graphic, Sunday Pictorial, Ev Standard, Dly Mail, Cosmopolitan (N.Y.), Best Short Stories of 1932, etc. *s.s*: Novels & Short Stories, mainly Chinese Hist. *a*: c/o Christy & Moore Ltd Gerrards Cross, Bucks. *T*: 2387.

LANE, Margaret. *Publ*: inc The Tale of Beatrix Potter; Where Helen Lies; Faith, Hope, No Charity; Edgar Wallace: The Biography of a Phenomenon; etc. *a*: Forston Hse, Dorchester, Dorset.

LANE, Major-Gen. Sir R. B., K.C.B., K.C.V.O., J.P., D.L.(Suffolk). *b*: Lichfield 1847. *e*: Wimbledon Sc. Married. *s*: 1 (dec). Commanding Garrison Alexandria 1878—1901, Infantry Battn '01—03, Mil Sec W.O. '03—04. *c*: Army & Navy. *a*: Carlton Hall. Saxmundham.

LANE, Dr. R. E., M.R.C.P. *Publ*: The Rôle of Punctate Basophilia in Industrial Plumbism; Punctate Basophilia in the Diagnosis of Plumbism. Physician to Chloride Elec Storage, etc. Mem Advisory Med Comm Ind Welfare Soc. *a*: 31 Moorland Rd, Didsbury, M/C.

LANE, Temple, M.A., Ph.D. *b*: Co Tipperary. *e*: Sherborne Sch for Girls & T.C.D. Novelist & Lecturer, Mem P.E.N. *Publ*: The Bands of Orion; The Little Wood; Blind Wedding; Sinner Anthony; April Gift (Jean Herbert); Fisherman's Wake; various novels of Irish life, etc. *Ctr*: Bystander, The Quiver, My Home, Woman & Home, Irish Times, Dublin Mag, Woman's Pictorial. *s.s*: English & French Lit & Poetry, Irish Life & Customs. *c*: Women Writer's. *a*: Innislonagh, Greenfield Park, Ballsbridge, Dublin, Eire. *T*: Dublin 92963.

LANE, Sir William Arbuthnot, Bt., M.S., F.R.C.S., C.B. *b*: Fort George, N.B. *e*: Stanley Hse, Bridge of Allan & Lon Univ. Married. *s*: 1. *d*: 3. Surg (ret). Cons Surg to Guy's Hosp, to Hosp for Sick Children Gt Ormond St, to French Hosp, Pres New Health Soc. *Publ*: Manual of Operative Surgery (1886); Cleft palate & adenoids, etc ('97); Cleft palate & hare lip (1905); The first & last kink in chronic intestinal stasis ('11); etc. *c.t*: Journals in Eng & abroad. *Rec* Fishing. *c*: Athenæum. *a*: 29 Portland Pl, W. & Glendalough Hse, Reeess, Co Galway. *t*: Langham 2712.

LANE-CLAYPON, Janet. (See **FORBER, Lady Janet Elizabeth**). *Publ*: The Hygiene of Women & Children; Milk & its Hygienic Relation; The Child Welfare Movement. *a*: Flat 3, Ravenhurst, St John's Rd, Eastbourne.

LANE-JACKSON, NICHOLAS (pen name: Creston): journalist, writer; *b*. Devonshire, Eng., Nov. 1, 1849; *s*. Nicholas and Mary (Pryor) L.; educ. Clapham Grammar Sch.; coached for army, but took commission in Volunteer Engineers; m. Marianne Williams, Jan. 20, 1869; now widower. AUTHOR: and editor of The Pastime Lawn-Tennis Handbook; The Cricket Handbook; The Rugby Union Football Handbook; The Association Football Handbook; The Rowing Handbook; The Swimming Handbook; The Hockey Handbook; The Lacrosse Handbook; The Athletic Handbook; The Athletic Guide: Association Football, 1928; all others from 1883 to 1927. Owner and editor of Football, Pastime, The Cricket Field, The Athlete. Contributor to Fortnightly and Saturday reviews, Cassell's Mag., The Field, Times, Country Life, and nearly all London daily papers. General character of writing: sports and pastimes. Founded the Corinthian Football Club, London Football Assn; Lawn-Tennis Assn.; Stoke-Poges Club; all sport at Le Touquet Golf and Sports Club; the Cabourg Golf and Sports Club; the Berks, and Oxon Golf Union; associated in forming many other sports clubs. Relig. denom., Church of England. CLUBS: Stoke-Poges; Royal Automobile, and many sporting clubs. HOME: Farnham Common, Buckinghamshire, Eng.

LANE-ROBERTS, Cedric Sydney, C.V.O., M.S., F.R.C.S., F.R.C.O.G. *b*: Aberdeen 1888. *e*: Cheltenham Coll & Guy's Hosp London. *m*: Ellen Miles-Sharp. *Publ*: (Jt-Author) Sterility & Impaired Fertility; Royal Northern Operative Surgery; Queen Charlotte's Practice of Obstetrics. *Ctr*: Various med journs. *s.s*: Diseases of Women, Obstetrics & Gynæcology. *Rec*: Rugby. *c*: Burlington, Fine Arts. *w.s*: 1915—19 R.A.M.C. (Capt). *a*: 64 Harley St, London, W.1. *T*: Langham 3663; & Mill Hse, Tewin, Herts.

LANG, AUGUST: univ. professor; *b*. Huppichteroth i. Rheinland, Germany; *s*. Wilhelm and Amalie (Sohn) L.; educ. Gymnasium of Dillenburg in Nassau, Univs. of Bonn and Berlin. DEGREES: Lic. Theol. of Bonn; D.D. (honoris causa), Univs. of Halle, Wittenberg, Geneva and Debrecen (Hungary); m. Elisabeth Calaminus, 1904. AUTHOR: Die Bekehrung Johannes Calvino, 1897; Der Evangelien-Kommentar Martin Butzers und die Grundzüge seiner Theologie, 1900; Der Heidelberger Katechismus und vier verwandte Katechismen, 1907; Johannes Calvin, ein Lebensbild, 1909; Die Reformation und das Naturrecht, 1909; (English transl. in Princeton Review, 1909); Die Domkirche und die Domgemeinde, 1912; Zwingli und Calvin, Monographie zur Weltgeschichte, 1913; Der Heidelberger Katechismus. (Zu seinem 350 jährigen Gedächtnis), 1913; Bekenntnis und Katechismus in der englischen Kirche unter Heinrich VIII., 1917; Die Reformation, 1917; Reformation und Gegenwart (gesammelte Aufsätze), 1918; Kirchen und Sekten in den Vereinigten Staaten, 1926; Die Weltkonferenz in Lausanne, 1927; Der kongregationalistische Kirchenbegriff, in "Die Frage nach der Kirche", 1927. Contributor to: Reformierte Kirchenzeitung; Barmen, and other church periodicals; The Evangelical Quarterly (edited by Mackay and MacLean). General character of writing: religious, church history. Is moderator of the Reformed Alliance for Germany; member of the Presbyterian Alliance; member of the Continuation Committee for Faith and Order since 1920; member of the Subjects Committee of this movement from 1920 to 1927. Research work is of the Swiss Reformation and of the history of the Reformed and Presbyterian Church. Relig. denom., Reformed. ADDRESS: Domplatz 3, Halle on S., Germany.

LANG, Cosmo Gordon, D.D., D.C.L., LL.D., D.Litt. *b*: 1864. *e*: Glas Univ & Balliol Oxf. Archbishop of Canterbury. Vicar of St Mary Oxf '94—96, Vicar of Portsea '96—1901, Bishop of Stepney & Canon of St Paul's Cath '01—08, Archbishop of York '08—28. *Publ*: The Miracles of Jesus (1900); The Parables of Jesus ('06); The Opportunity of the Church of England ('06); Roy Victorian Chain '23. *c*: Athenæum. *a*: Lambeth Palace, S.E.1. & Old Palace, Canterbury. *t*: Hop 6598 & Canterbury 303.

LANG, Elsie M. Author. *Publ*: British Women in the Twentieth Century; Oxford Colleges; Literary London; Old English Towns (with William Andrews). *a*: c/o T. Werner Laurie Ltd, 24 Water Lane, E.C.4.

LANG, F. E. *a*: Mason Lang Ltd, 33 Norfolk St, W.C.2.

LANG, Rev. Gordon, M.P. *b*: Monmouth 1893. *e*: Monmouth Gr Sch & Chestnut Coll. *m*: Emily Anne Evans *s*; 1, *d*: 1. M.P. (L) Stalybridge & Hyde 1945—. *Publ*: Laughter in Court; Consider Your Verdict; Mr Justice Avory. *Ctr*: Cornhill, Nineteenth Century, Tit-Bits, Dly Herald, Everybody's, Manch Guardian, Dly Express, People, etc. *s.s*: Criminology, Prison Conditions, Religion. *c*: Nat Lib. *a*: Wyecliffe, Chepstow, Mon. *T*: 462.

LANG, Rev. Lewis Wyatt, M.A. (Oxf). *b*: London 1881. *e*: Christ's Hosp & Oxf Univ. *m*: Elsie Mary Lang. *s*: 2. *d*: 1. *Publ*: A Study of Conversion; Christ's Psychology of The Kingdom. *s.s*: Psychology. *Rec*: Gardening. *a*: Frinsted Rectory, Sittingbourne, Kent. *T*: Wormshill 219.

LANG, Very Rev. Marshall Buchanan, M.A., D.D.(Glas), T.D., F.S.A.(Scot), O.St.J. *b*: Glasgow 1868. *e*: Glasgow Acad & University, Univs of Gottingen & Leipzig. *m*: Mary Eleanor Farquharson. *s*: 1. *d*: 3. Clergyman, Moderator of General Assembly of Church of Scotland 1935. *Publ*: The Seven Ages of an East Lothian Parish; The Story of a Parish. *Ctr*: Life & Work Mag, Church Service Soc Annuals, Trans Scottish Eccles & East Lothian Antiquarian (Jt-Ed) Socs. *s.s*: History & Antiquities. *Rec*: Reflection. *a*: Innisfree, Gifford, East Lothian. *T*: Gifford 239.

LANG, Robert Turnbull, J.P., F.R.G.S. *b*: Glasgow 1870. *e*: Newcastle. *m*: (1) Linda Tilley (dec'd), (2) Annie L. Nelson. *s*: 2. *Publ*: (Ed) The Hutchinson Road Books & Lang's Guides; C.T.C. Road Books. *Ctr*: Country Life. *s.s*: Roads & Local Hist. *Rec*: Books, cycling. *c*: Devonshire. *a*: 184 Strand, London, W.C.2,; Applegarth, Hayton, Carlisle. *T*: Temple Bar 2044 & Hayton 232.

LANG, William Dickson, ScD., M.A. Keeper of Geology Brit Museum. *Publ*: Catalogue of the Fossil Bryozoa (Polyzoa); A Handbook of British Mosquitoes. *c.t*: Proc Geog Assoc, Annals & Mag of Nat Hist, Quarterly Journ of Geol Soc, Entomologist, Nat Hist Mag, etc. *a*: Brit Museum (Nat Hist), Cromwell Rd, S.W.7. & 22 Daisy Lane, Fulham, S.W.6.

LANGA-LANGA. See **Hermon-Hodge, Harry Baldwin.**

LANGBRIDGE, Rosamond Grant. *b*: Glenalla, Co Donegal. *e*: Privately. *m*: J. S. Fletcher. *s*: 1. Writer. *Publ*: The Psychology of Charlotte Bronte; The Flame & the Flood; The Simple Eye; The Green Banks of Shannon; The Land of the Ever Young (Poems); The White Moth; (Play) The Spell. *Ctr*: Manch Gdn, Sat Westminster, etc. *Rec*: Motoring, travel, garden, philosophies. *a*: Castle Hill Hse, Dundee. *T*: 3403.

LANGDON, John. *b*: Ealing 1906. Publisher. *n.a*: Ed "Signs" ('27), Dir Blandford Press Ltd ('33). *a*: 43 Blandford St, W.1.

LANGDON, Stephen Herbert. *b*: Michigan, U.S.A. 1876. *e*: Univs of Michigan, Columbia, Un Theo Seminary, N.Y.C., Paris & Leipzig. *m*: May Adelaide Gregory. Prof of Assyriology Oxf. *n.a*: Assoc Ed Babyloniaca 1910–, Ed Oxf Cuneiform Texts '25–, Dir of Oxf Field Museum Exped in Mesopotamia '23–33. Schweich Lect for Brit Acad '33. *Publ*: Neu-Babylonische Königsinschriften; Sumerian Grammar; Semitic Mythology; Tammuz & Ishtar; Sumerian & Babylonian Psalms; etc. *c.t*: Cam Ancient Hist, Ency of Religion & Ethics, Journ of Roy Asiatic Soc, Revue d'Assyriologie, Times, Daily Telegraph, etc. *s.s*: Babylonian, Sumerian. Fell Brit Acad. Corr Mem Institut de France. O.B.K. of B. Rec: Golf. *c*: Mem Counc & Vice-Pres Roy Asiatic Soc '18–32. *a*: Jesus Col, Oxf & 16 Lathbury Rd. *t*: 5796.

LANGDON-DAVIES, Bernard Noel, M.A. *b*: Anerley 1876. *e*: St Paul's Sch, Pembroke Coll Camb, Lincoln's Inn. *m*: Ethel May. *s*: 1. *d*: 1. Bookseller, Pres Cambridge Union, Univ Lect & Examiner, Man Dir Labour Pub Co 1920–33. *Publ*: Young England; Democracy & the Press. *Ctr*: Manch Gdn, Dly Herald, Dly Express, John o' London, etc. *s.s*: Politics & Political History, Education. *Rec*: Reading, discussions. *a*: 61 Valley Rd, Welwyn Garden City, Herts. *T*: Welwyn Garden 966.

LANGDON-DAVIES, John, M.B.E. *Publ*: inc Achievement in the Act of Healing; American Close Up; Fifth Column; Man & His Universe; Short History of Women; Behind the Spanish Barricades; Nerves Versus Nazis; etc. *a*: 4 Redlands View, North Holmwood, Surrey.

LANGE, CARL GUSTAV ALBERT: (pen name: "Penklub"); author; b. Schöneberg, Germany, Jan. 27, 1885; s. Carl and Mathilde (Riede) L.; educ. Wilhelmgymnasium, Körner Realschule, Oberrealschule, Military Technical Academy; m. Maria Ruyter, Oct. 29, 1919. AUTHOR: Verse, 1912; Meinen Kameraden (poems), 1914; Borkumer Kriegszeitung (edited), 1916-1917; Auswahlband (edited), 1917; Strom aus der Tiefe, 1919; Der Kronprinz und sein wahres Gesicht, 1920; Almanach der Ostdeutschen Monatshefte (edited), 1924, 1925, 1926; Deutscher Geist im Osten (edited), 1927; Harzbuch; Die Zoppoter Waldoper (edited), 1926 (2nd edit. 1927; 3rd edit.); Danziger Bote (edited), 1926-1928; Festschrift zum 25. jährigen Jubiläum der Stadt Zoppot (edited), 1927; Abreisskalender Danziger Bote für das Jahr, 1927, 1928, 1929 und 1930 (edited); Festschrift 750 Jahre Oliva (edited), 1928; Die Freie Stadt Danzig (edited, with Fritz Braun), 1929. Editor: Ostdeutsche Monatshefte, also contributor to same. General character of writing: essays, poems. Major (retired). CLUBS: Penklub; Reichsverband der deutschen Presse; Verband der Danziger Presse; Schutzverband deutscher Schriftsteller; Kogge, Vereinigung nieders. Dichter; chairman of the East-German Tennis-Turnier-Alliance. Religion, Protestant. ADDRESS: Schefflerstrasse 2, Freistadt Danzig-Oliva, Germany.

LANGE, EDMUND BERNHARD: univ. librarian (retired); b. Altenburg, Thüringen, Germany, April 27, 1855; s. Schulrat Eduard and Antonie (Besser) L.; educ. elementary school and Gymnasium at Altenburg; Univs. of Jena, Munich, Berlin and Halle. DEGREE: Ph.D. (Halle); m. Anna Marie Wilhelmine Mecklenburg, Oct. 21, 1899. AUTHOR: Quid cum de ingenio et titeris, tum de poetris Græcovum Cicero sensevit. (Dissertation), 1880; Kleon by Thukydides. Gymnasial-Progr., 1886; Thukydides und sein Geschichtswerk, 1893; Franz Grillparzer. Sein Leben, Dichten und Denken, 1894; Thukydides in Auswahl (edited), 1895 (2nd and 3rd edits.); Erklärungen, 1896; Die Greifswalder Sammlung Vitae Pomeranovum alphab.vers, 1898 (Ergänzungen, 1905); Xenophon, 1900; Sokrates, 1906; Paul Schütze, Theodor Storm (edited, 2nd edit., 1907; 3rd edit., 1911; 4th edit., 1925). General character of writing: historical. Relig. denom. Evangelical. ADDRESS: Wilhelmshöherstrasse 22, Berlin-Friedenau, Germany.

LANGE, RUDOLF KARL OTTO: member of the goverment board; b. Berlin, Germany, July 12, 1850; s. Adolf and Auguste (Büchner) L.; educ. Gymnasium (Berlin). DEGREES: Ph.D., Professor; Privy Member of Government Board; m. Else Streckfuss, Oct. 4, 1883 (died June 24, 1913). AUTHOR: Altjapanische Frühlingsgegend, 1884; Einführung in die japanische Schrift (vol. 15 of text book of Orient. Sem. for study of Japanese writings, vol. 19, 2.A.09), 1896; Text book of Japanese Language (Engl. transl. by Noss, vol. 1. of text book of Orient. Se. 1, 2.A.I. "text book of religious history" e. P. D. Chantepie de la Saussaye, 3. A. 1905 "Die Japaner; Aufs. i. d. Mitt. d. Orient. Sem.), 1906; Das Onna daigaku (position of the woman in Japan during the feudal age), 1898; Lange und Senga Geschichte Japans, 1889-1899; Lied a. d. Japanische Volksschule, 1900; Japanisches Kinderlied, 1900; Über japanische Frauennamen; Alphabetisches Verzeichnis japanischer Frauennamen, 1902; Japanische Wappen, 1903; Über einige Besonderheiten der Schreibweise der chinesischen Zeichen in Japan, 1909; Die Zahl der japanischen Lehnsfürsten im Jahre 69, 1911; Der Lehnsfürst nach der Schlacht am Sekigahara, 1912; Thesaurus Japonisus Lex. die in der japanischen Sprache üblichen chinesischen Zeichen (vol. I 13, vol. II 19, vol. III 20), 1913. General character of writing: scientific, teaching Oriental languages. Was teacher in graue Kloster gymnasium, 1874; teacher in med. school at Tokyo, 1874-1881; teacher in Kaiser Wilhelm Realgymnasium, Berlin, 1883-1885; in Sem. f. ord. Spr. of Univ. of Berlin, 1887-1920; at Kriegsakademie from 1906 to 1914. Relig. denom., Evangelical. ADDRESS: Kurfürstenstrasse 4, Berlin-Steglitz, Germany.

LANGE, WALTER WILHELM MAX: museum curator; b. Leipzig, Germany, Jan. 6, 1886; s. Wilhelm Max and Lina (Ronneberger) L.; educ. Univs. of Leipzig and Tübingen. DEGREES: Ph.D. AUTHOR: Sonnenwende (poems); Richard Wagner's Leben und Werk (historical); Richard Wagner's Universale Bedeutung; Richard Wagner und seine Vaterstadt Leipzig (historical); Heinrich Laubes Aufstieg. Ein deutsches Künstlerleben im papiernen Leipzig (historical); Der Rauchwarenhandel und seine Beziehungen zu Leipzig (scientific); Friedrich der Grosse. Eine Prüfung (poems), Mein Nachtbuch, Erste Vigilie (novel); Das tausendjährige Leipzig, Werden und Wesen einer deutschen Grossstadt (film); Leipziger Messe, Ihre Entwicklung und Bedeutung für die Weltwirtschaft (film); Erstes Halbjahrtausend der Leipziger Kürschnerinnung 1423-1923 (historical); Lipsia triumphans (historical); Durch Befreiung und Einigung zur modernen Grosstadt (historical); Von der Senfte zur Kraftdroschke (Beitrag zur Geschichte des Leipziger Verkehrs, 1703-1927 (historical); Cantatefeier in Biedermeier. Ein Quodlibet in Prosa (novel); Das 1000 jährige Leipzig, Die Stadt der Mitte (historical); Der König am Scheidewege (novel), 1930. Contributor to Leipziger Neueste Nachrichten, Leipziger Abendpost, Neues Wiener Journal, Reclams Universum, Leipzig, Illustrierte Zeitung, Neue Zeitschrift für Musik, and others. General character of writing: historical, novels, poems. CLUBS: Leipziger Kunstverein, Verein für die Geschichte Leipzigs, Societe Union Musicologique, Fürstliches Institut für musikwissenschaftliche Forschung Bückeburg, Fraternität der Notarien und Literaten in Leipzig, and others. Relig. denom., Evangelical. OFFICE: Stadtgeschichtliches Museum, Altes Rathaus. HOME: Christianerstrasse 27, Leipzig, Germany.

LANGER, ALFONS (pen names: Paul Schultze; "Komed"): chemist, b. Breslau, Germany, 1859; s. Joseph and Luise Langer; educ. Univ. of Berlin. DEGREES: Ph.D., Apothecary; m. Martha Therese Bludau, July 3, 1890. AUTHOR: Im Kampf ums Dasein (play), 1896; Bunsen (biography), 1910; Mirowitsch (tragedy), 1911; Liebig (biography), 1913; Aus der Billionenzeit (comedy), 1923. Contributor to Posener Zeitung, Berliner Tageblatt, Schlesische Zeitung, Germania, Deutschlands Jugend, Goldener Garten, Phaomazeutische Zeitung, Apothekerzeitung, Chemiker Zeitung, Kazett. General character of writing: plays, nature books, scientific. Religion: Roman Catholic. ADDRESS: Anklamerstrasse 38, Berlin, 31, Germany.

LANGER, FELIX: author; b. June 18, 1889; s. Abraham and Antonie (Schwarz) L.; educ. Gymnasium (Brünn), Univ. of Vienna. DEGREE: LL.D. AUTHOR (plays): Der böse Schicksal, 1912; Lore Ley, 1913; Der Obrist, 1916; Das goldene Schloss, 1918; Banknotten, 1919; Zweikampf, 1920; Krisis der Weiblichkeit, 1922; Ebbe und Flut, 1923; Der Kümmerer, 1924; Weltklamauk und Liebe, 1925; Die Verführung des Heiligen, 1927; Schabernak oder Was tun Sie, wenn..? 1929; (short stories) Magelon; Münchhausens Verwandlung; (novels)

Erotische Passion; Die Maschine. Editor: Deutscher Bühnen-Klub. Contributor to Berliner Tageblatt, 8 Uhr Abendblatt, Berlin, Bohemia, Prag, N. W. Journal, and others. Works have been translated into English, Danish, and Tscheck. CLUBS: Der Deutsche Bühnen Klub. Religion, Mosaic. ADDRESS: Halensee Kurfürstendamm 134, Berlin, Germany.

LANGER, Dr. Frantisek, M.D.(Prague). b: Prague 1888. e: Gymnasium Prague & Charles Univ. m: Anna Ludmila. s: 1. d: 1. General Czechoclovak Army & Writer, Czech Acad Sc of Art, Roy Soc of Med Gt Britain, etc. Publ: (Plays) The Camel goes Through the Needle's Eye; Periphery; Cavalry Patrol; The Conversion of Ferdys Pistora; Angels among Us; Number 72; etc; Suburban Stories; Miracle in the Family; Brotherhood of the White Key; Children & The Dagger; etc. s.s: Film Librettos, Radio Plays, Short Stories, etc. Rec: Photography, bibliophily, gardening, mineralogy. a: Prague, Czechoslovakia, Smichov 2213. T: 46534.

LANGER, William Leonard, LL.D. b: Boston, Mass 1896. e: Boston Latin Sch & Univs of Harvard & Vienna. m: Rowena Morse. s: 5. d: 1. Prof Harvard Univ. Publ: The Franco-Russian Alliance; European Alliances & Alignments; Foreign Affairs Bibliography (collab); The Diplomacy of Imperialism; Encyclopedia of World History; Our Vichy Gamble. Ctr: N.Y. Herald Tribune, Amer Hist Rev, Journ of Mod Hist, Polit Sci Quart. s.s: European Hist since 1815, History of Diplomacy, Internat Relations. Rec: Golf, tennis, swimming. c: Harvard, Metropolitan. a: 1 Berkeley St, Cambridge, Massachusetts, U.S.A. T: Kirkland 0444.

LANGFELD, Herbert Sidney, Ph.D. b: Philadelphia 1879. e: Haverford Coll & Univ of Berlin. Emeritus Prof of Psychology. n.a: Ed Psychological Review 1934—47. Publ: The Aesthetic Attitude; (Jt-Author & Ed) Psychology; Manual of Psychological Experiments; Introduction to Psychology; (Jt-Ed) Psychology for the Fighting Max; etc. Ctr: Various Scientific journs. s.s: Psychology & Aesthetics. Rec: Golf, fishing. c: Harvard & Princeton Hassan. a: Elm Rd, Princeton, New Jersey, U.S.A. T: 1304.

LÄNGIN, THEODORE: librarian; b. Karlsruhe, i.-B., Germany, May, 1867; s. Georg and Eugenie (Bilharz) L.; educ. Gymnasium (Karlsruhe), Univs. of Heidelberg, Berlin, Bonn and Freiburg. DEGREES: Ph.D., Professor; m. Ella von Sallwürk, March, 1902. AUTHOR: Sprache des jungen Herder, 1891; Deutsche Handschriften der Badische Hof und Landesbibliothek, 1894; Georg Längin, 10. Todestag, 1907; Kindergärten in Karlsruhe, 1911. Editor: Christus der Geschichte (by G. Langin), vol. 2, 1897; Hermann Albrechts Erzählungen I-III, 1910-21; J. P. Hebel, Biblische Geschichte, 1921; Buch der Märterer, Karlsruher Bruchstücke, 1921. General character of writing: technical. CLUBS: Verein deutsche Bibliothekar, Verein für den Deutschtum in Ausland. Religion, Protestant. OFFICE: Badische Landesbibliothek. HOME: Karlstrasse 89, Karlsruhe, Germany.

LANGLEY, Arthur Swainson, F.R.Hist.S. b: Manchester 1874. e: Ardwick Higher Grade Sch, Manch Baptist Coll & Victoria Univ of Manch. m: Alice Maude Kinsey. s: 1. d: 1. n.a: British Corres to Western Recorder Louisville Kentucky since 1898, The American Baptist since 1928. Publ: Birmingham Baptists, Past & Present; Faith, Heritage & Mission of Baptists; Memos on Social Conditions, etc. Ctr: The Collegian, The Baptist, Baptist Times, Sunday Sch Times, Manch Guardian, etc. s.s: Free Church History, Social Conditions, Education. a: 327 Golf Estate, Wednesbury, Staffs.

LANGLEY, Bruce. b: Kirton 1906. e: Kirton & Donington G.Sc. m: Marjorie M. Tyler d: 1. Reporter. n.a: Jnr Reporter (Head Office) Lincs Standard '23, 2nd to Chief Rep '27, joined Aldershot Command News, Ed '28—34, Evening Standard '34—. s.s: Boxing, football, cricket. a: Atte Feld, York Cres, Aldershot, Hants. t: 244.

LANGLEY, Edwin. *b*: Yarmouth 1862. *m*: Sarah Ann Kidd. *s*: 2. *d*: 3. Printer. Press N.W. Alliance of Fed of Master Printers. *s.s*: Printing. *Rec*: Collecting books, showing progress of the craft & gardening. *a*: Woodlands, 16 Victoria Av, Barrow-in-Furness. *t*: 94.

LANGLEY, Ernest Felix. *b*: Toronto, Canada 1874. Married. *d*: 3. *Publ*: The Poetry of Giacomo da Lentino; Beaumarchais, Le Mariage de Figaro; Romantic Figures in Pen & Color; etc. *c*: Romantic Review, etc. *s.s*: Romance Langs & Lit. *c*: Harvard Faculty. *a*: 2 Potter Pk, Cambridge 38, Mass. *T*: Kir 5417.

LANGLEY, F. O., M.C., LL.B., B.A. *b*: Wolverhampton 1883. *e*: Uppingham & Cam. *m*: Muriel Lewis. *s*: 1. *d*: 1. Metro Magis & Chancellor of Dioceses Lichfield & Ripon. *c.t*: Punch, etc. *s.s*: Light verse & letters. *c*: Brooks's. *a*: Old St Police Ct, E.C.1, & Alderton, Woodbridge, Suffolk. *t*: Central 3980.

LANGLEY, Noel A., B.A. *b*: Durban 1911. *e*: Natal Univ Coll. *m*: Naomi Legate. *s*: 3. *d*: 2. Novelist, Playwright. *Publ*: Cage me a Peacock; There's a Porpoise Close Behind Us; Hocus Pocus; The Music of the Heart; The Cabbage Patch; The Land of Greenginger; Desbarollda the Waltzing Mouse; Maytime; Wizard of Oz; Florian; They Made Me a Fugitive; (Play, with Robert Morley) Edward, My Son. *Ctr*: Sat Ev Post. *s.s*: Screen Plays. *a*: c/o Pearn, Pollinger & Higham Ltd, 39 Bedford St, London, W.C.2.

LANGLEY MOORE, Doris. *m*: R. S. Moore. *d*: 1. Author. *Publ*: Anacreon, 29 Odes rendered into English Verse; The Technique of the Love Affair; A Winter's Passion (novel); The Bride's Book (with June Langley Moore); The Pleasure of Your Company (with June Langley Moore); The Unknown Eros (novel); etc. *c.t*: N/ps & periodicals here & abroad. *s.s*: The influence of fashion. *Rec*: Collecting Victoriana. *c*: Forum, etc. *a*: 92 Duchy Rd, Harrogate. *t*: 4308.

LANGMEAD, Frederick Samuel, M.D., F.R.C.P. *e*: Cranleigh Sch, St Mary's Hosp. Prof of Med St Mary's Hosp. *n.a*: Corr Lancet, B.M.J., Med Press & Circular 1912—20. *Publ*: Dictionary of Practical Medicine (in collab). *Ctr*: Various med journs. *s.s*: Gen Med & Pediatrics. *a*: Quilters, West Chiltington, Pulborough. *T*: West Chiltington 49.

LANGSAM, Walter Consuelto, A.M., Ph.D., B.S. *b*: Vienna, Austria 1906. *e*: Immanuel Luthesan Acad, City Coll of New York, Columbia Univ. *m*: Julia Elizabeth Stubblefield. *s*: 2. Coll President & Historian. *n.a*: Hist Ed J. B. Lippincott Co Chicago 1934—, Mem Bd of Eds Journ of Mod Hist '40—47. *Publ*: The World since 1914; Documents & Readings in the History of Europe since 1918; The Napoleonic Wars & German Nationalism in Austria; The Quest for Empire; The Problem of Colonies; Major European & Asiatic Developments since 1935; Since 1939 : 'a Narrative of War'; (contributor to) War in the Twentieth Century; War as a Social Institution. *Ctr*: Amer Hist Rev, Journ of Mod Hist, etc. *s.s*: Hist, Internat Relations, World Politics. *Rec*: Book collecting, handball. *c*: Rotary, Town Hall, etc. *a*: Wagner Coll, Staten Island 1, New York. *T*: Gibraltar 7-7880.

LANGSFORD, Dorothy Mary. *b*: Mintard, Sth Aust 1896. *e*: Priv & Methodist Ladies Coll Wayville Sth Aust. *m*: Thomas Henry Edwards. *n.a*: Ed Kindergarten & Primary Mag Sth Aust 1937—47. *Publ*: The Outlaw; Sun-Chased Shadows; Dan of The Ridge; Cooee of Glenowie. *Ctr*: The Chron Sth Aust. *Rec*: Motoring, gardening, cycling, sketching. *a*: 24 Sherbourne Rd, Medindie Gdns, Sth Australia.

LANGSTAFF, Gilbert Walter. *b*: King's Lynn 1895. Journalist, Chm Deal Chamber of Trade. *n.a*: Sub-Ed Boston Guardian (Lincs) 1919—26, Ed Sleaford Standard (Lincs) '26—29, Asst Ed Barnsley Chron '29—31, Ed & Mang Barnsley Chron '31—45, Ed & Mang Deal, Walmer, Sandwich & East Kent Mercury '45—. *a*: 35 Leas Rd, Deal, Kent. *T*: 280.

LANGSTON, Earle Legh, M.A. *b*: London 1879. *e*: Framlingham Coll, Lond Coll of Div, Univ Coll Durham Univ. *m*: Alice Carr. *s*: 2. *d*: 2. *Publ*: How God is Working to a Plan; Balaavis Prophecies; Ominous Days; The Biography of the late Bishop Taylor-Smith; God & Modern Problems; Glad Tidings; The Pathway to the Fulness of Blessing. *Ctr*: The Record, C. of E. Newspaper, The Christian, Life of Faith. *s.s*: Exposition of Scripture. *Rec*: Golf, swimming, mountain climbing (Switzerland). *c*: National. *a*: Gleneden, 8 Newstead Rd, Southbourne, Bournemouth. *T*: Southbourne 937.

LANGTON, Rev. Edward, D.D., F.R.Hist.S., F.R.A.S. *b*: Nr Tarpley 1886. *e*: Handsworth Coll Birmingham, London Univ. *m*: Helen Mary Willis. *s*: 2. Methodist Minister. *Publ*: Good & Evil Spirits; Satan, A Portrait; Essentials of Demonology; Supernatural; The Ministries of the Angelic Powers; The Teaching of the New Testament. *Ctr*: Hibbert Journ, British Weekly, etc. *s.s*: Doctrine of Spirits, Church History, Theology. *Rec*: Motoring, reading. *a*: 11 Henry St, Brighouse, Yorks. *T*: 725.

LANGTON, Joseph L., M.Sc., M.I.E.E. *b*: Roumania 1877. *e*: Manchester Gr Sch, Victoria Univ of Manch. *m*: Lilian Carr. *s*: 1. Formerly Senior Lect Univ of Manch in High Voltage Eng 1903—44. *Publ*: Electric Arc Lamps; Electricity in the Textile Industries; Technological German Readers (with Classen); Overhead Power Transmission. *Ctr*: Inst of Elec Engineers, Times. *s.s*: Porcelain Line Insulators, Insultation, High Voltage Phenomena & Troubles. *Rec*: Bridge. *a*: 4 Longton Ave, Withington, Manchester 20. *T*: Didsbury 2133.

LANGTON, P. S. B. *a*: Roy Earlswood Int, Redhill, Surrey.

LANHAM, H. J. Sec Yeovil Br N.U.J. *a*: 125 St Michael's Av, Yeovil.

LANKARD, Frank Glenn, M.A., B.D., LL.D., Ph.D. *b*: Anderson County, Kansas 1892. *m*: Myrtle Etna Denlinger. Prof of Biblical Literature & Dean of Brothers Coll of Drew Univ Madison N.J. *Publ*: A History of the American Sunday School Curriculum; Difficulties in Religious Thinking; The Bible & the Life & Ideals of the English Speaking People; The Wanted Generation; The Bible Speaks to Our Generation; etc. *Ctr*: Various. *s.s*: Religion & Religious Education. *Rec*: Gardening, Philately, Epitaphs. *c*: Monday (N.Y.). *a*: 11 Academy Rd, Madison, New Jersey, U.S.A. *T*: Madison 6-1080.

LANKS, Herbert Charles, A.M. *b*: Houtzdale, Pennsylvania 1899. *e*: Pennsylvania State Coll, Univ of Pennsylvania & Mexico. *m*: Gladys Crisman. *d*: 2. Writer, Photographer, Lecturer. *Publ*: By Pan-American Highway Through South America; Highway to Alaska; Pan-American Highway from Rio Grande to Canal Zone; Adventures in Central America; Nancy Goes to Mexico. *Ctr*: N.Y. Times, Christian Science Monitor, This Week Mag, Sat Ev Post, Life Mag, etc. *s.s*: Hemispheric Highways. *Rec*: Hunting, camping, fishing, photography. *a*: 320 Greenwood Ave, Jenkintown, Pennsylvania. *T*: Ogontz 2522W.

LANSBURY, George, M.P. *Publ*: Your Part in Poverty; My England; My Life; etc. *a*: 39 Bow Rd, E.3. *t*: East 3247.

LANSDALE-RUTHVEN, Hugh Peter. *b*: Malta 1897. *e*: Bedford. *m*: Edwina Ann Mears. Barrister-at-Law. *Publ*: The Law of Libel for Journalists; Common Law Ed of Wharton's Law Lexicon (14th edn); Radio plays—1935 and Before That; Only a Lowbrow; etc. *c.t*: D. Telegraph, D. Herald, Birm Post, Star, Bristol World, Punch, Chambers's Journ, etc. *s.s*: Polit, secret service. Regular broadcaster Midland Regional Children's Hour. *Rec*: Fishing. *c*: Fabian Soc. *a*: 102 Colmore Row, Birm. *t*: Central 3711.

LANSING, Marion F., M.A. *b*: Waverley, Mass. *e*: Mount Holyoke, Radcliffe. Writer. *Publ*: Magic Gold, A Story of Roger Bacon; Life in the Greenwood; Page, Esquire & Knight; Makers of the Americas; Liberators & Heroes of South America; Liberators & Heroes of Mexico & Central America; Calling South America; Against All Odds—Pioneers of South America; Great Moments (Series); in Science; in Exploration; in Freedom. *s.s*: History, Biography—for Younger Readers. *c*: Pen & Brush, Boston Authors. *a*: 147 Lexington Ave, Cambridge, Mass.

LANSON, GUSTAVE: honorary professor in the faculty of letters; b. Orléans, France, Aug. 5, 1857; educ. Lycée d'Orléans, Lycée Charlemagne (Paris), Ecole Normal Supérieure (Paris). DEGREE: Licencié es Lettres, Fellow in Letters, Doctorat d'État; m. Alice de Gondre. AUTHOR: Conseils en Part d'ecrire, 1887; La Chaussée la Chaussée de la Comédie Larmoyante, 1887; Bossuet, 1891; Boileau, 1892; Histoire de la littérature française, 1894; Corneille, 1898; Voltaire, 1906; Esquisse d'un histoire de la tragédie française, 1920 (2nd edit. 1928). Editor: Édition critiques d'ouvrages de Voltaire, 1909; Édition critique d'ouvrages de Lamartine, 1917. Contributor to Revue de Deux Mondes, Revue de Paris, Revue d'Histoire littéraire de la France, Grande Revue, Revue du mois, and others. General character of writing: literary history. CLUBS: Club de la Rennaissance (Paris), and others. ADDRESS: 282 Boulevard Raspail, Paris, France.

LANYON, Carla. *b*: Comber, Co. Down 1906. *m*: Major E. S. Hacker. *s*: 2. *d*: 1. Poet. *Publ*: The Wanderer & Other Songs; The Second Voyage; Far Country. *c.t*: Observer, Poetry, U.S.A. Flower painter. Exhibited Paris Salon & own exhibition London '34. *c*: Pioneer & writers. *a*: The Pioneer & Writers Club, 12 Cavendish Pl, Cavendish Square, W.

LANYON, Ronald Albert. *b*: Penzance 1907. *e*: Penzance Sec Sc. *m*: Georgina Bruce. Reporter. *n.a*: Cornishman '22–29, Western Morning News '29. *c.t*: Western Weekly News. *s.s*: Ships, Cornish folklore. C'wall Chm N.U.J. '34. *Rec*: Swimming. *a*: 11 Tencreek Av. Penzance. *t*: 399.

LANZA, Conrad H. *b*: New York 1878. *e*: George Washington Univ, General Staff Coll. *m*: Renee Nazareth. *d*: 1. Colonel, U.S. Army (ret), *n.a*: Field Artillery Journ 1925—, Life '42–45, Chicago Tribune & Syndicated Papers '41–45. *Publ*: Forts Henry & Donelson; The Peninsular Campaign (McClellan in 1862); Jena Campaign; Marengo Campaign; Marne Campaign 1918; Franco-Prussian War 1870; Napoleon's Maxims. *Ctr*: Field Artillery Journ. *s.s*: Strategy & Hist. *w.s*: 1917–18 & '41–42. *a*: 1911 Elm St, Manchester, New Hampshire, U.S.A. *T*: 74-17.

LAPAGE, Charles Paget, M.D., F.R.C.P. *b*: Nantwich 1879. *e*: Epsom Col & M/C Univ. *m*: Hilda MacDonald. *s*: 3. *d*: 1. Physician to Children. *n.a*: Senr Phys M/C Children's Hosp, Phys to Children St Mary's Hosp M/C, Lect Diseases of Children M/C Univ. *Publ*: Feeblemindedness in Children of School Age; etc. *c.t*: Med Journals. *s.s*: Diseases of children. War Service. Major R.A.M.C. Despatches. *Rec*: Mountaineering, golf. *c*: Un, M/C. *a*: Barton Hse, 11 Didsbury Pk, Manchester & 20 St John St, Manchester. *t*: Blackfriars 2524 & Didsbury 3318.

LAPAGE, Geoffrey, M.A., M.Sc., M.D., F.Z.S. *b*: Nantwich, Cheshire 1888. *e*: Bradfield Coll, Ellesmere Coll, Manch Univ. *m*: Enid Oldham. *s*: 1. *d*: 1. Parasitologist Inst of Animal Pathology Univ of Camb. *Publ*: Parasites; Nematodes Parasitic in Animals; Shoes for the Gosling (Verse); Pursuit (Verse); Bedtime Rhymes. *Ctr*: Lancet, B.M.J., New Statesman, Westminster Gazette, Yorkshire Post, Cornhill Mag, Manch Guardian, etc. *s.s*: Biology, Med, Parasitology of Farm Animals & Man. Poetry, Essays, Short Stories. *Rec*: Canoeing, cycling, writing poetry. *a*: 3 Barton Close, Cambridge.

LAPORTE, Rene. *b*: Toulouse 1905. *e*: Lycee de Toulouse, Faculte de Droit Toulouse. *m*: Renee Lamon. *n.a*: Dir Revue les Capices Libres 1926–35, Revue de Paris '33–37. *Publ*: L'An Quarante; Les Chasses de Novembre; Le Cheval Volant; Les Passagees d'Europe; Federigo; etc. *Ctr*: Opera, La Monde Illustri, Revue de Paris, Radio diffusion francaise. *a*: 12 Rue Lavoiner, Paris. *T*: Dupon 12-67.

LAPRADE, William Thomas, A.B., F.R.Hist.S., Ph.D. *b*: Franklin County, Va 1883. *e*: Wash Christian Coll, The John Hopkins Univ. *m*: Nancy Hamilton Calfee. *d*: 1. Prof of Hist Duke Univ. *n.a*: Ed South Atlantic Quarterly 1945—. *Publ*: Public Opinion & Politics in 18th Century England; British History for American Students; England & the French Revolution; etc. *Ctr*: American & English Hist Revs, Journ of Modern Hist, etc. *s.s*: English Hist & Politics, The Hist of the Press & Public Opinion. *a*: 1108 Monmouth. Ave, Durham, North Carolina, U.S.A. *T*: J1081.

LAPWORTH, Arthur, LL.D.(St And & Birm), M.Sc(M/C), F.R.S. *b*: Galashiels 1872. *e*: Univ of Birm, Cent Tech Col S. Kensington. *m*: Kathleen Holland. Sir Samuel Hall Prof of Chem & Dir Chem Lab's M/C. *c.t*: Journal Chemical Soc, Memoirs of M/C, Lit & Philos Soc, Nature. *s.s*: Chem. Davy Medal Roy Soc '1931. *Rec*: Music, fishing, golf. *a*: Victoria Univ, Manchester.

LARG, David. Author. *Publ*: Garibaldi; Ruskin; Trial by Virgins. *a*: c/o Peter Davies Ltd, 30 Henrietta St, W.C.2.

LARGE, Dorothy Mabel. *b*: Tullamore 1891. *e*: Dr Williams Sc, Dolgelley & Braunschweig, N. Germany. *m*: John W. Large. *Publ*: Cloonagh; Irish Airs; The Open Arms; An Irish Medley; The Cloney Carol (verse). *c.t*: Punch, Irish Times, Chambers's Journ, Christian Science Monitor, etc. *s.s*: Irish country life, animals & birds. *Rec*: Golf. *c*: Women Writers', Dublin. *a*: Glenview Cottage, Shankill, Co Dublin.

LARKE, Sir W. J., K.B.E. Eng Dir Brit Iron & Steel Fed. *c.t*: Various. *a*: Cray Hill, Sidcup, Kent. *t*: 369.

LARKINS, Viola. *b*: India 1866. *e*: Kensington Hgh Sch. *Publ*: Tomorrow Fair; The Glory & the Dream; etc. *s.s*: English Lit. *Rec*: Painting, art, needlework. *a*: The Match Box, Albury, Surrey. *T*: Shere 7.

LARMINIE, Margaret Rivers. See Tragett, Margaret Rivers.

L'ARNEAU, Arnold H. Lever. b: Bournemouth 1909. e: Blackpool H.S. & the Polytech. w: F.L. Journalist. c.t: Radio Mag, Hairdressers' Weekly Journ, Birm Mail, Magazine Programme, etc. s.s: Hairdressing, beauty culture, interviews with stage, screen & radio stars. Entered the premier hairdressing firm in Oxford St, W. Rec: Swimming, rowing. c: Interval. a: 3 Holly Mansions, Hampstead, N.W.6. t: 3312.

LARRETT, Walter Denham, M.A., M.R.S.T. b: Colchester 1900. e: Watford G.S. & Christ's Col Cam. m: Evelyn Pullen. s: 1. Snr Math Master King's Sc, Peterboro. Publ: A Junior Algebra; A Senior Algebra; A Junior Practical Geometry (Jt Author with F. F. Potter); Graphs & their Applications; A Revision Course in Mathematics for Matriculation; etc. s.s: Educ. Rec: Lawn tennis. c: Math Assoc & Legal Sub Cmt Incorp Assoc Asst Masters. a: Dunkeld, Cobden Av, Peterboro.

LARSEN, Aage Emil. b: Roskilde 1900. e: Methodist Theol Sch Copenhagen. m: Lucy Lund. s: 3. d: 1. Pastor Bethel Church Tingvej. n.a: Ed Morgenstjernen since 1946. Publ: (Poems) Jorden Lykkelige ... Orkenen blomstrer; Sang og Glæde; Kristendom og Ungdom; Ydre Former—Indre Liv; Hils Danmark; Dagens stills Stund (Andagtsbog); Havstedfiskerne aendrer Kurs; Kjeld fra Hedebjerg. Ctr: Kirkeklokken, Kristelig Pressebureau; Morhenstjennen. a: Forhaabningsholms Alle 11, Copenhagen V, Denmark. T: VEster 55.

LARSEN, Esper Signius, B.S., Ph.D. b: Astoria, Oregon. m: Eva Audrey Smith. s: 2 Prof of Petrography Harvard Univ. n.a: Assoc-Ed The American Mineralogist 1920—. Publ: (In collab) Microscopic Determination of the Nonopaque Minerals; Geology of the San Mountains of Southwestern Colorado; Igneous Rocks of the Highwood Mountains, Montana. Ctr: Amer Journ of Science, etc. s.s: Geology, Petrography. Rec: Gardening. a: 59 Orchard St, Belmont, Mass, U.S.A. T: Belmont 0817.

LARSEN, Gunnar Otterbech. b: Oslo 1900. m: (1) Minda Juell L'Orange, (2) Bergliot Marie Langaard. s: 1. d: 2. Lawyer. n.a: Ed Dagbladet Oslo. Publ: Last Summer; Two Suspicious Subjects; Weekend in the Eternity; Bull; Henry Morton Stanley; Trans, etc. s.s: Lyrics, Theatre. a: Holmenkrollen, Oslo, Norway. T: 416890 & 699357.

LARSEN, Oscar. b: Norway 1885. e: H.S. m: Jenny Gundersen. s: 2. Editor. n.a: Tromso's 1923–. a: Tromso, Norway. t: 386.

LARSON Anker Johannes. b: Langeland 1877. m: s: 2. Actor, Producer, Censor Royal Theatre (ret). Publ: Martha & Mary; With the Door Open; etc. (Dramatic Works) Son of Zeus; Magdalene, etc. a: Vinkelvej 6, Farum, Denmark.

LA RUE, Mabel Guinnip. b: Nr Honesdale Pa. e: Pa, Teachers Coll, Syracuse Univ. m: Daniel W. La Rue. s: 2. Writer of Juvenile Books. Publ: The F-U-N Book; Under the Story Tree; Little Indians; Hoot-Owl; Dicky & the Indians; Zip the Toy Mule; In Animal Land; The Tooseys; Cats for the Tooseys; The Billy Bang Book. Ctr: Story Parade. s.s: Stone Age Civilization background (Indians). Rec: Gardening. a: East Stroudsburg, Pennsylvania, U.S.A. T: 1029-R.

LASCELLES, Charles, F.R.H.S. b: London 1890. e: Rugby. Former Actor & Water-colourist. Publ: Madame Benoit's Secret. a: Fairstead, Shaldon, Teignmouth, South Devon. T: Shaldon 257.

LASCELLES, Edward Charles Ponsonby, O.B.E. b: Lon 1884. e: Winchester & abroad. Barrister. Chm Trade Bds. Chm Metro Ct of Referees. Mem Roy Commssn on Unemployment Ins 1930. Publ: Granville Sharp (biog, '28); In Collab:—Unemployment in East London; Poverty: A Survey; etc. a: 38 Argyle Rd, Campden Hill, W.8. t: Western 5521.

LASH, Rt. Rev. William Quinlan, M.A. (See **BOMBAY**, Bishop of.) b: York 1905. e: Tonbridge Sch, Emmanuel Coll Camb, Westcott House. Bishop of Bombay. n.a: Ed The Ashram Review 1937—. Publ: Approach to Christian Mysticism. Ctr: Times of India. s.s: Lit, Religion, Christianity in India. a: Bishop's Office, The Cathedral, Churchgate St, Bombay Fort.

LASKI, Harold J. Publ: inc Faith, Reason & Civilization; Parliamentary Government in England; The State in Theory & Practice; The Problem of Sovereignty; Liberty in the Modern State; also Edited the Letters of Burke & an autobiography of J. S. Mill. a: Devon Lodge, Addison Bridge Pl, London, W.14.

LASKI, Marghanita, B.A. (See **RUSSELL, Sarah.**) b: London 1915. e: Ladybarn House Sch Manchester, Somerville Coll Oxf. m: John Howard. s: 1. d: 1. Journalist. Publ: Love on the Super-Tax; The Patchwork Book; Stories of Adventure; Victorian Stories for Girls; Tory Heaven. Ctr: Vogue, Time & Tide, Woman & Beauty, etc. Rec: Travel. c: Women's Press. a: The Abbot's House, Abbot's Langley, Hertfordshire. T: King's Langley 3049.

LASKI, Neville Jonas, M.A., K.C. b: Manchester 1890. e: Manch Gr Sch, Clifton Coll & Corpus Christi Coll Oxf. m: Phina Emily Gaster. s: 2. d: 2. Recorder Burnley 1935—, Bencher Inner Temple '38, Pres Lond Cttee Deputies of British Jews '33—40. Publ: Jewish Rights & Jewish Wrongs. w.s: 1st World War Gallipoli, France, 6th Lancs Fus (Capt). Rec: Walking. a: 1 Hare Court, Temple, London, E.C.4. T: Central 2925.

LASSEN, Carl Christian. b: Hellebaek 1883. e: Mod Sch Helsingor & Semin Copenhagen. m: Nico Johannessen. Teacher & Librarian, Mem Danish Author's Assoc. Publ: Viggo Stuckenberg; Vaar og Sol; Daemring; Fremad; Gustaf Froding; Hans Liv og Digtning; Sommer og Sol; Otte Nordiske Kvinder; Disse Bakker—Disse Dale. Rec: Reading novels & lyric poetry. a: Jyllandsgade 2, Ringsted, Denmark. T: 270.

LASSEN, Tyge. b: Denmark 1899. e: Copenhagen Univ. Ed in Chief & Jt Publisher Aalborg Amtstidende Denmark, Knight of the Order of Danebrog. c: R.A.C., Kongelig Dansk Automobilklub Copenhagen, Aalborg Rotary, Klubben Enigheden Aalborg. a: Aalborg Amtstidende, Denmark. T: 904 & Stat 23.

LAST, A. W. a: Melbourne Hse, Aldwych, W.C.

LAST, Hugh Macilwain, M.A., Hon.LL.D. Camden Professor of Ancient History & Fellow of Brasenose Coll Oxford. a: Brasenose College, Oxford.

LATHAM, Alan Thomas, J.P. b: Collingwood 1883. e: Univ Hgh Sch Melbourne. m: Minnie Estelle Delbridge. s: 3. d: 2. Sec Hist Soc of Victoria 1918—. Publ: Save Australia. Rec: Motoring, tennis. a: 147 New Ave, Middle Brighton, Victoria, Australia. T: XB 5362.

LATHAM, ALBERT GEORGE: Emeritus professor of modern languages, Univ. of Durham; b. Wakefield, Eng., Mar. 31, 1864; s. Edward and Mary (Button) L.; educ. Wakefield Lancasterian, Borough Road Training Coll. (London); Univ. of Bonn; studied in Caen, Paris, Florence. DEGREES: B.A. (London) (1st class honours in modern languages); M.A. (London and

Dunelm); m. Katharine Wright Murray, Dec. 28, 1897. Translated Goethe's Faust, in J. M. Dent and Sons Temple Classics, Pt. I, 1902, Pt. II, 1905; Treasury of French Literature, Vol. I, 1915; translated Schiller's Wilhelm Tell (Temple Classics, 1904); (Old Tyneside, 1913); Arias from the Operas of G. F. Handel, lyrics and commentaries (with Dr. W. G. Whittaker, musical editor); many lyrics, translated and original in Oxford Choral Songs from the Old Masters; lyrics, translated and original, in Clarendon Song Books, since 1927. Contributor to Longman's Mag., Cornhill Mag., Westminster Gazette, Punch Almanac, North Mail, Evening Mail, Sunday Sun. General character of writing: varied, but inclined toward essay, verse in lighter vein and for music. An educator from elementary through to university training. Former prof. of modern languages, Armstrong Coll. (Durham), Newcastle-upon-Tyne; an examiner in modern languages to various universities and others. Relig. denom., Free Church. HOME: Charnwood, Holywell Ave., Monkseaton, Northumberland, Eng.

LATHAM, Alison. (See **LATHAM, Murray.**) *b*: Monkseaton, Northumberland. *e*: Central Newcastle Hgh Sch, King Edward VII Sch of Art, Municipal Sch of Art Birmingham. Novelist. *Rec*: Camping, travel, landscape painting. *a*: 214 Gilesgate, Durham.

LATHAM, Esther, (See **LATHAM, Murray**). *b*: Monkseaton, Northumberland. *e*: Monkseaton Hgh Sch, Univs of Durham & Göttingen. Novelist. *Rec*: Camping, travel, translation. *a*: 214 Gilesgate, Durham.

LATHAM, Rev. Henry Guy Dampier, M.A. (Cantab). *b*: Torquay. *e*: Rugby, Univ Col Sc & Caius Col Cam. *m*: Florence Gertrude Latham. *Publ*: An Apostle's Correspondence; Pioneer Clubs for Working Men; The Gibbous Moon & Other Verses; etc. *c.t*: Cornhill Mag. *a*: The Old Rectory, Offord Cluny, Huntingdon.

LATHAM, Rt. Hon. Sir John Greig, P.C., G.C.M.G., M.A., LL.M., K.C. *b*: Ascot Vale, Victoria 1877. *e*: State Sch, Scotch Coll, Univ of Melbourne. *m*: Eleanor Mary Tobin. *s*: 1. *d*: 1. Chief Justice of Australia, Minister to Japan 1940—41, Chanc Univ of Melbourne '30—41. *Publ*: Australian & The British Commonwealth of Nations. *Ctr*: Various articles on legal, political & internat subjects. *Rec*: Tennis & fly-fishing. *c*: Melbourne & Australian, etc. *a*: High Court of Australia, Law Courts Pl, Melbourne, & 239 Domain Rd, South Yarra, Victoria, Australia. *T*: Windsor 6162.

LATHAM, Katharine Wright. *b*: Newcastle-on-Tyne. *e*: Gateshead H.S. *m*: Prof Albert G. Latham. *s*: 1. *d*: 3. *Publ*: Christabel (1909); Christabel in France ('10); Little French Plays for Little English Children ('13); The Young Crofters; Those Two & the Queer Folk ('28); Where All Roads Led ('31); etc. *c.t*: Blackie's Children's Annual, Cassell's Wonder Book, Little Folks, Newcastle Evening Mail, Newcastle Sunday Sun, etc. Broadcasting at Newcastle B.B.C. '23—26, part of time as Dir of Women's & Children's Hours. *Rec*: Cycling, gardening. *a*: Charnwood, Holywell Av, Monkseaton, Northumberland.

LATHAM, Leslie John, F.R.S.A., F.R.G.S., F.G.S. F.R.A.S. *b*: St Pancras 1913. *e*: Little Clacton, King's Coll Lond, Gray's Inn of Court. *m*: Joan Heslop. *d*: 1. Naturalist. *Publ*: A History of Southern Arabia. *Ctr*: Numismatic Chron, Essex Review, Aden Argus, East Essex Gazette, etc. *s.s*: Archæology, Hist, Horticulture, Polit Sci, Numismatics, Radiethesia. *Rec*: Welfare Case Work, Oriental Langs. *a*: 72 West Cromwell Rd, Kensington, London, S.W.5. *T*: Western 3232.

LATHAM, Murray. (See **LATHAM, Alison & Esther.**) *Publ*: Enjoy Such Liberty; River in the Dark; Even From the Law. *a*: 214 Gilesgate, Durham.

LATHBURY, Lt.-Col. Ernest Browning, O.B.E. *b*: Derby 1882. *e*: Epsom Col & Bart's Hosp. *m*: Rhoda Matilda Fyson. *s*: 1. *d*: 1. R.A.M.C. Regular Army (ret). *c.t*: Field. *s.s*: Med practice (ins work). Inventor & Patentee " Improvements in Night Shooting Apparatus ". War Service India & N. Russia. Mons Star & bar, Victory Medal. *Rec*: Shooting, fishing. *c*: Fell Roy Emp Soc, Fell Hunterian Soc, Mem B.M.A., Jnr Army & Navy. *a*: Revenue Hse, 7 Poultry, E.C.2. *t*: City 3344.

LATIF, Syed Abdul, B.A., Ph.D. *b*: Alampur 1891. *e*: Madras Christian Coll, Univ of London. *m*: Ahamad-Un-Nisa (dec'd). Former Prof of Eng Osmania Univ India. *n.a*: Ed Research Journ Osmania Univ 1933—36, Founder-Ed The Clarion, Hyderabad-Deccan, '46—. *Publ*: The Influence of English Literature on Urdu Literature; Ghalib; Concept of Society in Islam; Muslim Culture in India; Muslim Problem in India; Cultural Basis of a Lasting Civilisation; Islamic Cultural Studies. *s.s*: Lit Criticism, Social Science. *a*: Khurshid Manzil, Kachiguda, Hyderabad-Deccan, India.

LATOURETTE, Rev. Kenneth Scott, M.A., B.S., D.D., LL.D., Litt.D., Ph.D. *b*: Oregan 1884. *e*: Linfield & Yale. Clergyman & Teacher. *Publ*: A History of the Expansion of Christianity; The Chinese, Their History & Culture; A History of Christian Missions in China; A Short History of the Far East; Development of China; Development of Japan; The History of the Early Relations Between the United States & China 1784—1844; The Christian Outlook. *Ctr*: Amer Hist Rev, Atlantic Monthly, Christendom, Religion in Life, Pacific Affairs, etc. *s.s*: History of Christianity, Christian Missions, Far Eastern History. *Rec*: Gardening, hiking, geology. *c*: Century, Authors. *a*: 409 Prospect St, New Haven, Connecticut, U.S.A. *T*: 73131-460-3.

LATTA, Gorden Cuthbertson. *b*: London 1904. *e*: Rugby Sch, Corpus Christi Coll Oxf. *m*: Nina Bucknall. Author. Barrister. *Publ*: Arnholt Makes His Bow; Re-enter Arnholt; Exit Arnholt; (Trans) The Heart Line (Play). *Ctr*: Windsor Mag, Bystander, etc. *s.s*: Adventure Novels. *Rec*: Lawn Tennis. *c*: Guards, Boodle's. *a*: 78 New Cavendish St, London, W.1. *T*: Langham 4278.

LATTER, Oswald Hawkins. *Publ*: Natural History of Some Common Animals; Elementary Zoology; Bees & Wasps; etc. *Ctr*: Nature, School Science Review. *a*: The Elms, Charterhouse Rd, Godalming, Surrey.

LATTEY, Cuthbert Charles. *b*: Kensington 1877. *e*: Beaumont Coll, Old Windsor, Oxford. Lecturer Theological Coll of the Eng Province of the Soc of Jesus (Jesuits) at Heythrop since 1911, Doctor in Philosophy & Theology (papal). *Publ*: First Notions of Holy Writ; Paul; Back to Christ; Back to the Bible; Readings in 1st Corinthians; Thy Love & Thy Grace; Ed of the Westminster Version of the Sacred Scriptures; Ed of the Lecture Books of the Camb Summer Sch of Cath Studies. *Ctr*: The Month, Clergy Rev, Cath Biblical Quarterly; Journ of Theolog Studies, Hibbert Journ. *s.s*: Holy Scripture esp St Paul & the Doctrine of Biblical Inspiration. *a*: Heythrop College, Chipping Norton, Oxford. *T*: Enstone 38.

LATTIMORE, Owen. *b*: Washington, D.C. 1900. *e*: St Bees Sch Cumberland, Grad Sch, Harvard Univ. *m*: Eleanor Holgate. *s*: 1. University Professor. *n.a*: Peking & Tienstin Times 1920—21, Ed Pacific Affairs '34—41. *Publ*: The Desert Road to Turkestan; High Tartary; Manchuria, Cradle of Conflict; Mongols of Manchuria; Inner Asian Frontiers of China; Mongol Journeys; America & Asia; Solution in Asia; China (with Eleanor Lattimore). *Ctr*: Atlantic Monthly, Nat Geographic, Geographic Journ, Geographic Review, Foreign Affairs. *s.s*: Far East, Hist, Geography, Politics, Manchuria, Mongolia, Sinkiang. *a*: Page School of International Relations, John Hopkins University, Baltimore, Maryland, U.S.A., & Ruxton, Maryland, U.S.A.

LAUBACH, Frank Charles, A.M., Ph.D. *b*: Benton, Pennsylvania 1884. *e*: Union Theol Sem, Univs of Princeton & Columbia. *m*: Effa Seely. *s*: 1. Missionary, Educator. *Publ*: Teaching the World to Read; The Silent Billion Speak; Prayer, the Mightiest Force in the World; Letters of a Modern Mystic; Streamlined English Lessons; Story of Jesus; You Are My Friends; India Shall Be Literate; Toward a Literate World; Rizal, Man & Martyr; Seven Thousand Emeralds; People of the Philippines; Why There Are Vagrants; etc. *Ctr*: Nea Journ, Clear Horizons, Upper Room Publs. *s.s*: Literacy, Prayer. *a*: Committee on World Literacy 156, Fifth Ave, New York 10, N.Y., U.S.A. *T*: CH-2-3230.

LAUDER, Sir Harry. *Publ*: Roamin' in the Gloamin'; Wee Drappies. *a*: c/o Charles Lavell, 13 Serjeants' Inn, E.C.4.

LAUDET, FERNAND CHARLES (pen name: "Film"): author; *b*. Paris, France, March 3, 1860; *s*. Julien and Anna (Seitivant) L.; educ. College des Jésuits Vangirard, Ecole des sciences politiques, Ecole de droit. DEGREES: Bachelier es Lettres, Licencié en droit; *m*. Adrienne Arban, April 22, 1914. AUTHOR: Souvenirs d'hier-Rome, Gascogne; Ombres et lumières, La vie qui palle; Les Semeurs; Paris pendant la Guerre; Quelques aspects de la France en Guerre; Histoire populaire de Jésus; L'Enfant chérie du monde Ste. Therese de Lisieux; L'Institutens des instituteurs St. Jean Baptiste de la Salle; En Armagnac il y a un Siecle; La Vie d'un aieul. Contributor to Revue Hebdomadaire, Correspondent, Revue Bleue, Opinion, La Vie Catholique, Figaro, Journal des Debate, L'Echo de Paris, France Amérique. General character of writing: essays, religious and moral. Former editor of la Revue Hebdomadaire. SOCIETIES: Cercle Interalliée, Membre de l'Institut de France (Académie des Sciences morales et politiques). Religion, Catholic. ADDRESS: 2 rue de Gribeauval, Paris, France.

LAUGHLIN, Clara Elizabeth. *b*: N.Y. City 1873. *e*: Chicago Publ Scs. Author, Editor, Lecturer, Travel Agent. *n.a*: Lit Ed The Interior (leading Presbyt weekly) '92-, Special Writer for Chicago Evening American 1917-18, Founded new mag "So You're Going" News (travel monthly) '31-. *Publ*: The Evolution of a Girl's Ideal; The Death of Lincoln; Children of To-morrow; The Keys of Heaven; Foch, the Man; So You're Going to Paris!; So You're Going to England!; So You're Going to Spain!; So You're Going to Rome!; etc. *c.t*: Princ Amer n/ps & periodicals. *s.s*: Travel. 1st Woman to own & operate an internat group of Travel Offices. *Rec*: Theatre, reading. *c*: The Cordon, Midland Authors, Arts Club of Chicago, P.E.N., etc. Chevalier Legion of Honor, etc. *a*: 2238 Lincoln Pk W, Chicago, & 410 S. Michigan Av, Chicago. *t*: Harrison 0021.

LAUGHLIN, George Ashton. *b*: Wheeling, W. Va, U.S.A. 1862. *m*: Anna Boettger Bruning. *n.a*: Publr Wheeling Daily Intelligencer 1902--08, Ed & Publr Wheeling Telegraph '13--25. *Publ*: Six Trips as Made & Described by George A. Laughlin; Australia & Around the World ('23); South Africa & Around the World ('26); Europe ('30); etc. West Virginia Legislature '01 & '31. Del to Republican Nat Convention in Chicago '08, Kansas City '25. Ex Pres Wheeling Bd of Trade. *c*: Fort Henry Country Wheeling, Duquesne Pittsburgh, Union Cleveland, Nat Press Washington, Nat Arts N.Y.C. & Arts of Washington. *a*: 201 Intelligencer Bldg, Wheeling, W. Va, U.S.A. *t*: Wheeling 282.

LAUGHTON, F. *n.a*: Sub-Ed Leicester Evening Mail. *a*: 43 Severn St, Leicester.

LAUGHTON, Freda. *b*: Bristol 1907. *e*: Bristol. *m*: (1) L.E.G. Laughton. *s*: 1. *d*: 1. (2) John Midgley. Poet. *Publ*: (Poems) A Transitory House. *Ctr*: Irish Times, The Bell. *s.s*: Illustration of Books. *Rec*: Writing children's stories & illustrating them, gardening, Jungian psychology. *a*: The Hill Farm, Echlinville, Rubane, Kircubbin, Ards Peninsula, Northern Ireland.

LAUNDER, Frank. President The Screenwriters Association. *Publ*: (Screenplays) A Girl Must Live; Two Thousand Women; (with Sidney Gilliat) The Lady Vanishes; Night Train to Munich; The Young Mr Pitt; Millions Like Us; The Rake's Progress; (with Wolfgang Wilhelm) Captain Boycott; The Blue Lagoon. *a*: Empire House, 117 Regent St, London, W.1.

LAURENT, L. J. M., B.S.(Lond), M.D., M.R.C.P.(Lond). *b*: Mauritius 1894. *e*: Roy Coll Mauritius, U.C.L., U.C.H. *m*: Dorothy Mary Lewin. *s*: 1. *d*: 1. Deputy Med Supt Park Hosp Hither Green London S.E.13. *Publ*: Diphtheria Toxoid; Diphtheria Complications; Measles & Purpura; Worms & Meningism. *Ctr*: Brit Journ of Child Diseases, Clinical Journal *s.s*: Infectious Diseases & Pediatrics. *a*: Woodside, Epsom Rd, Sutton, Surrey. *T*: 1686.

LAURENT, Louis Philippe Eugène, M.D.(Lon), M.R.C.P.(Lon), F.R.S.M. *b*: Mauritius 1906. *e*: Epsom Col, U.C.L., U.C.H. Physician. *c.t*: Proc Roy Soc Med, Lancet, Clinical Journ. *a*: U.C.H., Gower St, W.C.

LAURIE, Rev. Albert Ernest, M.C., D.D., F.R.S.E., J.P., S.C.F. *b*: Edin 1866. *e*: Bonnington Acad, Edin Univ, Edin Theo Col. Rector of Old St Paul's Edin. Canon & Chancellor of Edin Cath. *s.s*: Educ. *c*: New (Edin). *a*: Lauder Hse, Jeffrey St, Edin. *t*: 26532.

LAURIE, Maxwell. *b*: Edin 1868. *e*: Edin & Cam Univs. M.V.O. *m*: Marjorie Thirkell White. *s*: 2. I.C.S. (ret). *Publ*: The Black Blanket; The Shameless Innocent; A Young Man at Sea.

LAURIE, ROBERT DOUGLAS: professor of zoology; *b*. Birkenhead, Eng., Oct. 27, 1874; *s*. Robert and Eleanor (Ord) L.; educ. Birkenhead Sch., Univ. Liverpool, Univ. Oxford. DEGREES: B.A., Zoology Hons. M.A. (both Oxon); *m*. Elinor Beatrice Ord, July, 1912. Editor: Marine and Fresh Water Investigations. (Dept. of Zoology, Univ. Coll. of Wales, Aberystwyth). Contributor to many scientific periodicals. General character of writing: technical, marine zoology. A founder and first pres. of Ass'n. of University Teachers of Eng. and Wales; Hon.-gen. secy. same from 1920 to present. CLUBS: 1917, Oxford Union. OFFICE: University College of Wales. HOME: Willow Lawn, Caradoc Road, Aberystwyth, Wales.

LAURIE, Thomas Werner. *e*: George Watson's Col, Edinburgh. Publisher. *a*: 24--26 Water Lne, E.C.4. *t*: City 6240.

LAURIE-LONG, Ernest. *b*: London 1886. *e*: City of Lond Sch. *Publ*: On Schedule; As They Rise; Flynn of the Martagon; Port of Destination. *s.s*: Sea. *Rec*: Photography. *a*: 87 Lake Rise, Romford, Essex. *T*: Romford 3544.

LAURITSEN, P. *b*: Aalborg 1878. *e*: Publ & Commercial Sch. *m*: Karen Nielsen. *s*: 3. *d*: 2. Aalberg Bank 1895—1935, Member Danish Authors Assoc. *Publ*: (Novels) Den Storste Dag; En Ungdoms Historie; Erkebiskoppens Ungdomskaerlighed; Da Solen Sank; Under Julens StJerner; Hvor Kampen staar; etc. (Poetry) Vort Faedreland; Danske Strenge; Ranker og Runer; Stjernelys; Lykkens

Hemmelighed; 1 Nattens Moerke og Dagens Sol. (Biog) A. D. Joergensen; H. P. Hanssen; Danske Mand. (Drama) Mirakler. *Ctr:* Various. *s.s:* History of South Jutland. *Rec:* Cycling. *a:* Ejderstedgade 30, Copenhagen, Denmark. *T:* Vester 2367v.

LAUTERPACHT, Hersch. *b:* Zolkiew 1897. *e:* Vienna & London Univs. *m:* Rachel Steinberg. *s:* 1. Whewell Prof of International Law Univ of Camb, Fellow of Trinity Coll Camb. *Publ:* Private Law & Analogies of International Law; Function of Law in the International Community; Recognition in International Law; International Bill of the Rights of Man; Development of International Law by the Permanent Court of International Justice. *Ctr:* Brit Year Bk of Int Law, Camb Law Journ, Modern Law Rev, American Journ of Int Law, Harvard Law Rev, Yale Law Journ, Columbia Law Rev. *n.a:* Ed Ann Digest & Reports of Int Law Cases, Ed Oppenheim's Int law. *Rec:* Gardening, walking. *a:* 6 Cranmer Rd, Cambridge. *T:* Cambridge 54622.

LAVARRE, William, F.R.G.S. *b:* Richmond, Va 1898. *e:* Harvard Univ. *m:* Alice L. Elliott. *d:* 1. Explorer, Journalist, Govt Official, Spec Corres Nth American Newsp Alliance 1935—39, Dir Amer Foreign Service Counce '44—. *Publ:* Up the Mazaruni for Diamonds; Johnny Round the World; Gold, Diamonds & Orchids; Dry Guillotine; Southward Ho. *Ctr:* Various. *s.s:* Mexico, Argentine & Chilian Geog Resources, Politics, History, etc. *Rec:* Photography. *c:* Harvard (N.Y.), Univ (Wash). *a:* 1135 Sixteenth St, N.W., Washington, D.C., U.S.A.

LAVELL, Edward Joseph. Journalist. *n.a:* Bolton Evening Chron, Kent Argus, Anglo-Scottish Press, L'pool Evening Express (Sub-Ed 1929—). *Publ:* Treasure Trove & Other Stories; The Vision Beautiful; The Blue Danube; Mr Povy, a Seventeenth Century Panorama. *s.s:* Italy, music drama. *Rec:* Travel. *a:* Monticello, Rufford Rd, Crossens, Southport.

LAVER, James, F.R.S.A., F.R.S.L., Hon.R.E. *b:* Liverpool 1899. *e:* L'pool Inst & New Coll Oxf. *m:* Veronica Turleigh. *s:* 1. *d:* 1. Keeper Vic & Alb Museum. *Publ:* Nymph Errant; Background for Venus; Whistler; Wesley; History of British & American Fashion; Nostradamus, Taste & Fashion; etc. *Ctr:* Times, News Chron, Sphere, Dly Telegraph, Studio, Burlington Mag, Ev Standard, etc. *s.s:* Hist of Costume & Stage Design, Etching, Painting, Social History. *a:* 11 Wellington Sq, London, S.W.3. *T:* Sloane 3177.

LAVIN, Mary, M.A. *b:* East Walpole, Mass, U.S.A. 1912. *e:* Loreto Convent Dublin; Nat Univ of Ireland Dublin. *m:* William Walsh. *d:* 2. *Publ:* Tales from Bective Bridge; The Long Ago; The House in Clewe Street; The Becker Wives; At Sally-Gap. *Ctr:* Dublin Mag, Atlantic Monthly, Harpers Bazaar, English Story, Kenyon Review, To-morrow, Yale Review, The Bell, Good Housekeeping, etc. *s.s:* Short Stories. *a:* Bective Hse, Co Meath, Eire. *T:* Kilcarn 4.

LA VIOLETTE, Wesley. *b:* St James, Minn 1894. *e:* Lewis & Clark Hgh Sch, Northwestern Univ, Chicago Musical Coll. *m:* Harriet M. Lewis. Composer, Conductor, Author, Poet, Lecturer. *n.a:* Music Critic Kenosha E. News 1918—23, Music Ed De Paul Univ Press 1937—. *Publ:* Music & Its Makers; The New Bhagavada Gita; The Creative Light; A Secret of Bach's Technique. *Ctr:* Christian Century Mag, various poetry mags, etc. *s.s:* Poetry, Music, Fine Arts, Philos. *Rec:* Hiking, travel. *c:* Los Angeles, Athletic, etc. *w.s:* 1918 A.E.F. *a:* 181 South Sycamore Ave, Los Angeles, 36 California, U.S.A. *T:* York 6794.

LAVRIN, Janko. *b:* Yugoslavia 1887. *e:* Austria & Russian, Scandinavian & French Univs. *m:* Nora Fry. *s:* 2. Prof Russian Lang & Lit, Mem P.E.N. *n.a:* Co-Ed European Quarterly. *Publ:* Dostoevsky; Nietzsche; Tolstoy; Russian Literature; Gogol; Studies in European Literature; Aspects of Modernism; Introduction to the Russian Novel; Pushkin & Russian Literature. *Ctr:* New English Weekly, Life & Letters, Slavonic Rev, etc. *s.s:* Art, Philos. *Rec:* Mountaineering. *a:* University College, Nottingham.

LAW, Alice, F.R.HistS., F.R.S.L. *b:* Padiham. *e:* Girton Col Cam. Author. *Publ:* Songs of the Uplands (1908); Wild Lyrics; Patrick Branwell Brontë, Victoria County History; etc. *c.t:* Fortnightly Review, Dictionary of Polit Econ, Athenæum, Econ Journ, Scot Hist Review, etc. *s.s:* Hist. *Rec:* Fishing. *c:* Lyceum, London. *a:* 135 Queen's Rd, Blackburn.

LAW, Arthur James, M.A. *b:* Beualla, Victoria, Aust 1885. *e:* Melbourne Teachers Coll & Univ. *m:* Lillie L. Chapman. *s:* 3. *d:* 3. Princ Teachers Coll, Inspector of Schs 1922—34. *n.a:* Prop Herald, Tallangutta Vic. *Publ:* Modern Teaching. *Ctr:* Herald Tallangutta, Age Melbourne. *s.s:* Education. *Rec:* Cricket, football, tennis. *a:* Teachers Coll Univ, Melbourne, Victoria. *T:* FJ 2912.

LAW, Frank William, M.A., M.D., B.Chir., F.R.C.S. *b:* Isleworth 1898. *e:* St Paul's Sch Camb & Middls Hosp. *m:* Brenda Marjorie Thomas. *s:* 1. *d:* 1. Surg Moorfields Eye Hosp, Ophth Surg Guy's Hosp, Mem B.M.A., F.R.S.M. *Publ:* Ultra-Violet Therapy in Eye Diseases. *Ctr:* Brit Journ of Ophth, B.M.J., Lancet. *s.s:* Ophth. *Rec:* Music, fishing. *c:* Leander. *a:* 36 Devonshire Pl, London, W.1. *T:* Welbeck 1055.

LAW, Frederick Houk, M.A., Ph.D. *b:* N.Y. City 1871. *e:* Amherst Coll, Univs of Columb & New York. *m:* (1) Mary Kenniston Thorp (dec'd). (2) Carrie Ramsey Shields. *s:* 3. *d:* 2. *n.a:* Ed Educational Dept Reader's Digest. *Publ:* English for Immediate Use; Modern Great Americans; Our Class Visits South America; Civilization Builders; He Got The Job; Our American Series etc. *Ctr:* Various. *s.s:* English, Technology & Science. *Rec:* Travel. *c:* Adventurer's (NY.). *a:* 472 Argyle Rd, Brooklyn 18, New York, U.S.A. *T:* Buckminster 2-1602.

LAW, Hugh Alexander. *b:* Dublin 1872. *e:* Rugby & Oxf. *m:* Charlotte Stuart. *s:* 1. *d:* 3. Barrister-at-Law, Mem of Dail (I.F.S) 1927-32. *Publ:* Contributions to History of Ireland—Nations of To-day series; Anglo-Irish Literature. *c.t:* Daily Telegraph, M/C Guardian, Fortnightly Review, Dublin Review, Irish Independent, Irish Statesman, etc. *s.s:* Irish hist, biography, French lit. Knight of Malta (Sovereign & Military Order of St John of Jerusalem). *Rec:* Riding, fishing, golf. *c:* Stephen's Green, Dublin. *a:* Marble Hill, Ballymore, Lifford, Co Donegal.

LAWFORD, Florence. Author. *Publ:* Bogey Lane; Red Thimbles; October Snow; Merryheart. *a:* c/o S. Paul & Co Ltd, Paternoster Hse, E.C.4.

LAWL, Dr. Jag Mohan, M.B., ChB. *Publ:* Sankhaya; The Man's Place in the Nation; The Unseen Rainbow (1921). *a:* 276 Camden Rd, N.W.1. *t:* Gulliver 3839.

LAWLOR, Pat. *b:* New Zealand 1895. *e:* St Patricks Col, Wellington. *m:* Amy Martha Lambert. *s:* 1. *d:* 3. Journalist & Publishers' Rep. *n.a:* Ed N.Z. Artists' Annual, N.Z. Rep Sydney Bulletin, & Newspaper News. *Publ:* Poetry of Dick Harries; Confessions of a Journalist; Maori Tales; More Maori Tales & stories in Anthology N.Z. *c.t:*

The Bulletin, & Australian & N.Z. Jnls. *s.s*: Book reviewing, short stories. Founder of N.Z. Edition of Aussie & N.Z. Artists' Annual. *Rec*: Book collecting. *c*: N.Z. Ex Libris Society, & N.Z. Centre of the P.E.N. *a*: 14 Panama St, Wellington, New Zealand. *t*: 45—913.

LAWRENCE, Anthony. *b*: London 1912. *e*: King's Coll Sch Wimbledon. Reporter & Free-Lance Journalist, N.U.J. *s.s*: Roads, Road Building. *a*: 60 Kenton Rd, Kenton, Middlesex. *T*: Wembley 2816 & Wimbledon 5100.

LAWRENCE C(HARLES) E(DWARD): writer and editor; b. Thurlstone, Yorkshire, Eng., Dec. 24, 1870; educ. privately. AUTHOR: Pilgrimage, 1907; The Wisdom of the Apocrypha, 1918; **Mrs. Bente**, 1918; Youth went Riding, 1918; Such Stuff as Dreams, 1919; **The God in the Thicket**, 1920; The Iron Bell, 1921; Mr. Ambrose, 1922; Lass of the Sword, 1923; The Gentle Art of Authorship, 1924; William Purdie Treloar, 1925; The Old Man's Wife, 1926; The Hour of Prospero: A Play, 1927; Cockadoodle, 1927; Swift and Stella: A Play, 1928; Underneath, 1928; Spikenard: A Play, 1930. Joint editor of Quarterly Review. Contributor to Quarterly Review, Cornhill Mag., Bookman and others. CLUBS: Savage. OFFICE: 50 Albemarle St., London, W. 1, Eng.

LAWRENCE, Charles Judge. *e*: William Ellis Sc, Gospel Oak, N.W. Circulation Manager. *n.a*: Circulation Mang Daily Express, Northern Ed'n Jan 1934, London Ed'n June '35. *a*: 14 Hocroft Court, Hendon Way, N.W.4. *t*: Hampstead 1836.

LAWRENCE, Edwin Gordon. *b*: Philadelphia, Penn., U.S.A. 1859. *e*: Philadelphia & N.Y. *m*: Sadie Secord (div). *s*: 1. *d*: 3. Educator, Author. *n.a*: Ed Writer Miami, Florida Herald 1921, Assoc Ed Palm Beach, Florida Times '23—, Special Feature Writer Fairchild Pubs N.Y. '15-19. *Publ*: The Power of Speech ('09); How to Master the Spoken Word; How to Improve the Memory; Sidelights on Shakespeare; Rudiments of Speech; Homespun Verse (poems '32); etc. *c.t*: Los Angeles Times, El Paso Times, Athol Transcript, etc. *s.s*: Nat & world topics & poems. *Rec*: Riding. *a*: 125 South St, Concord, New Hampshire, U.S.A.

LAWRENCE, F. W. *n.a*: Shipping Ed Lloyd's List, Lloyd's Shipping Index—Loading List—Weekly Casualty Reports—Book of Ports & Shipping Places. *a*: Lloyd's, London, E.C.3. *T*: Avenue 7644.

LAWRENCE, George Clarke, M.A.(Edin). *b*: Edin 1892. *e*: Watson's Coll Edin & Edin Univ. *m*: Agnes Mary Cunningham. *n.a*: Scotsman (Sub-Ed & Reviewer) 1919, Gen Ed Industrial Information 1919, Ed Current Opinion '22, Asst Dir Publicity Brit Empire Exhib Wembley '23—25, Dir Publicity Land & Nation League '25—27, Dir Publicity Empire Exhib Scotland '38, Adviser on Publicity to Nat Fed of Building Trades Employers & London Master Builders Assoc '40 to date. *Ctr*: Numerous newsps & periodicals. *s.s*: Industrial. *a*: 13 Henrietta St, London, W.C.2. *T*: Temple Bar 0130.

LAWRENCE, James Stephen. *b*: London 1892. *e*: City of Lond Sch. Art Dir Daily Mail, formerly Ed & Foreign Ed. *n.a*: Dly Mail, Dly Dispatch Manch, People, Ev Standard. *a*: The Daily Mail, Northcliffe Hse, London, E.C.4. *T*: Central 6000.

LAWRENCE, Dr. L. A., F.R.C.S., F.S.A. *c.t*: Numismatic Chron, Brit Numismatic Journ. *a*: 44 Belsize Sq, N.W.3.

LAWRENCE, Margery. *b*: Wolverhampton. *m*: Arthur E. Towle. Novelist. *Publ*: Miss Brandt: Adventures; Red Heels; Bohemian Glass; The Madonna of Seven Moons; Terraces of Night; Silken Sarah; Drums of Youth; Snapdragon; Nights of the Round Table; Madame Holle; The Crooked Smile; etc. *Ctr*: Dly Mail, Sun Express, Sun Chron, Sun Dispatch, Tatler, Nash's, etc. *s.s*: Art, Fiction. *Rec*: Travel, music, sailing, reading, dogs, collecting antiques, golf, fishing. *c*: Forum, Embassy. *a*: 25 Princess Ct, Bryanston Pl, London, W.1. *T*: Paddington 0582.

LAWRENCE, Robert Daniel, M.A., M.D., F.R.C.P. *b*: Aberdeen 1892. *e*: Aber Gr Sch & Univ also Germany & France. *m*: Anne Batson. *s*: 3. *Publ*: The Diabetic Life, trans into French Dutch, German, Italian, (13th edn 1945); Happiness & Our Instincts. *Ctr*: Sci & Med journals. *s.s*: Diabetes. *Rec*: Music, fishing, tennis. *c*: R.A.C., Savile, Fly-Fishers. *w.s*: Capt R.A.M.C. (S.R.) 1914—19. *a*: 149 Harley St, London, W.1. *T*: Welbeck 4444.

LAWRENCE, Sydney Boyle. Author & Journalist. *n.a*: Late Special Correspondent & Leader Writer Standard, Ev Standard, late Asst Ed & Dramatic Critic Dly Express, late Dramatic Critic Dly Mail, Ev News. *Publ*: (Plays) Her Own Rival; A Promise; A Man of His Word; The First Kiss; The Heel of Achilles (with Louis N. Parker); The Popinjay (with Frederick Mouillot); De Cameron Nights (with Robert McLaughlin); Celebrities of the Stage. *Ctr*: Beecham Opera Books. *c*: Savage, Roy Automobile. *a*: Bowling Green Cottage, Plaistow Lane, Bromley, Kent. *T*: Ravensbourne 3165.

LAWRENCE, Capt. Vincent Augustus, M.C. *b*: London 1895. *e*: Ongar Gr Sch. *m*: Elsie Collins. Journalist & Theatrical Press Rep. *n.a*: Fiction & Feature Dept Allied Newspapers 1933—, Ev News Dramatic Critic 2 yrs, Asst Ed Sun Chron. *Ctr*: Dly Chron, Dly Sketch, Star, Ev Standard, Empire News, Sun Graphic, theatre & film trade papers. *s.s*: Theatres, Films, Military Matters. *Rec*: Fishing. *c*: Press & Stage. *w.s*: 1914—18. *a*: 10 Duke St, Adelphi, London, W.C.2. *T*: Temple Bar 7133.

LAWRENCE, Sir Walter Roper, Bt., G.C.I.E., G.C.V.O., C.B. *b*: Moreton Ct, nr Hereford. *e*: Cheltenham & Balliol Oxf. *m*: Lilian Gertrude James (dec). *s*: 2. *Publ*: The Valley of Kashmir; The India we Served. *c*: Garrick & Air Force. *a*: 94 Eaton Sq, S.W 1.

LAWRENCE, William Edward Beaumont. *b*: Tamworth. Married. *s*: 4. Lon Mang L'pool Daily Post & Echo. *c*: Aldwych. *a*: Mersey Hse, 132-4 Fleet St, E.C.4. & 69 Chadwick Rd, Westcliff-on-Sea. *t*: Cen 7656 & Southend-on-Sea 3093.

LAWRENCE, William John, HonD.Litt(Q.U.B.). *b*: Belfast 1862. *e*: Meth Col Belfast. *m*: Florence Fanny Bradley. F.L. Journalist. *Publ*: The Life of Gustavus Vaughan Brooke, Tragedian ('92); The Elizabethan Public Playhouse (1927); Shakespeare's Workshop ('28); etc. *c.t*: Life & Letters, Review of English Studies, Music Quarterly (N.Y.), Times Lit Supp, Daily Telegraph, Stage, Dictionary of National Biography, etc. *s.s*: Theatrical hist. Lect on Elizabethan theatre & drama in eight American Univs. *a*: 12 Jasper Rd, Upper Norwood, S.E.19.

LAWREY, William, F.R.S.A., F.C.I. *b*: Cornwall 1879. *e*: Priv. *m*: Miss Bassett. *c.t*: L'pool Echo. *s.s*: Mathematics, numerology. *a*: 9 Warwick Rd, Upton Wirral, Ches.

LAWRIE, H. H. Journalist & Research Worker. Polit & Trade Union Org. Ex-M.P. Stalybridge & Hyde. *a*: 41 Plumstead Rd, S.E.18.

LAWRIE, J. F. *n.a*: Sub-Ed The Bulletin, Glasgow & Northcliffe N/ps London. *a*: c/o Daily Express, M/C.

LAWRIE, James Pickett. *b*: London 1902. *e*: Millfields London. *m*: Lilian Agnes Loughnane. Analytical Chemist. *Publ*: The Home Cinema. *c.t*: Evening Press, Express Sunday, Hampshire Chronicle, Kinematograph Weekly, Cinema, nearly every photographic paper in Eng & the U.S.A. *s.s*: Amateur cinematography, photography. Lieut R.A. (T.) Rtd. Many Years Chemist to Photographic & Cinema Firm. *Rec*: Films, plays. *c*: F.R.S.A., etc. *a*: 66 Boundary Rd, St John's Wood, N.W.8.

LAWS, Bernard Courtney, D.Sc, D.èsSc., A.R.C.Sc, M.I.C.E., M.I.N.A. *b*: Portsmouth. *e*: Priv, H.M. Dockyard Portsmouth & Roy Col of Sci. *m*: Eugénie Miller Watson. *s*: 2. Cons Naval Archt & Eng. *Publ*: Answers to Questions in Naval Architecture; Stability & Equilibrium of Floating Bodies (trans into Russian by order of Imp Acad, St Petersburg). *c.t*: Cassiers Mag, Philos Mag, Engineering, Journ of Comm, Trans Inst of Naval Archts, etc. *s.s*: Physics, education, research in materials & structures, strength & vibration in ships' structures under sea-going conditions. Holds George Stephenson Gold Medal of Inst C.E. Many y Exam in Shipbuilding subjects to the City & Glds of Lon Inst. *Rec*: Cricket, tennis. *a*: Claverton, Cheam Rd, Sutton, Surrey, & 70 Victoria St, S.W.1. *t*: Sutton 2133. Victoria 6053.

LAWS, Betty. *b*: London. *e*: The Old Grange Sch Hampton-on-Thames. *Publ*: Ariel's Friend; Pam & the Fearless Fourth; The Girls of Stornham Central; Kidnappers at Elmhurst School; etc. *Ctr*: Brit Girls' Annual, Girls' Budget, Every Girl's Annual, etc. *s.s*: Girls' Stories. *Rec*: Theatre. *a*: Holly Lodge, Werter Rd, Putney, London, S.W.15.

LAWS, Frederick. *b*: Stockton-on-Tees 1911. *e*: Stockton Sec Sch, King's Coll Camb. *m*: Elizabeth Virginia Molteno. *d*: 2. Journalist. *n.a*: Art Critic News Chron 1938—39, Radio Critic News Chron '42—47, Personal Problems Feature (" John Aubrey ") News Chron '45—46. *Publ*: Made for Millions; Randolph Caldecott; Radio & the Public. *Ctr*: News Chron, New Statesman, Contact, John o' London's. *s.s*: Radio, Art, Psychology, Educ. *a*: 7 Reynolds Close, London, N.W.11. *T*: Speedwell 9121.

LAWS, Rev. Robert, C.M.G., D.D., LL.D., F.R.G.S., F.R.S.G.S. *b*: Aberdeen 1851. *e*: King's & Marischall Col's, Univ of Aberdeen, Univ of Glas, Anderson's Univ, Glas & Un Presbyterian Ch Theo Hall Edin. *m*: Margaret Troup Gray. *d*: 1. Med Missny (ret). *n.a*: Ed The Livingstonian News till 1927. *Publ*: Trans of New Testament into the Nyanja Language; Reminiscences of the Livingstonian Mission; English-Nyanja Dictionary. *a*: 69 Merchiston Cres, Edin.

LAWSON, Rev. Anthony Clifford, D.D.(Oxon). *b*: Kirkburton, Huddersfield 1888. *e*: Bradford Gr Sch & Jesus Coll Oxf. *m*: Violet Clunas Goodeve. *s*: 5. *d*: 1. Vicar of St Michael, Shrewsbury & Rural Dean of Shrewsbury. *Publ*: The Sources of the De Ecclesiasticis Officiis of S. Isidore of Seville; etc. *Ctr*: La Revue Benedictine, Journ of Theological Studies, Laudate. *s.s*: Patrology, S. Isidore of Seville. *Rec*: Gardening. *w.s*: France-Belgium 1916—19. *a*: St Michael's Vic, Shrewsbury. *T*: 3771.

LAWSON, Cecil, C. P. *b*: London. *e*: Charterhouse. Military artist. *Publ*: Naval Ballads & Sea Songs. *s.s*: Naval & military hist. *c*: Soc of Hist Research, Société de la Sabre Tache, Paris. *a*: 21 Warwick Cres, W.2.

LAWSON, Col. Hon. Edward Frederick, D.S.O., M.C. *b*: 1890. *e*: Eton & Balliol Col Oxf. Journalist. *n.a*: Gen Mang Daily Telegraph. *a*: Hall Barn, Beaconsfield, Bucks.

LAWSON, Frederick Arthur. *b*: Smethwick, Staffs, 1892. *e*: University Col London, London Sc of Economics. *m*: Winsome Hendley Ellis. *s*: 1. Journalist. *n.a*: Sec to late Sir Sidney Lee '23, Special writer, parliamentary and general reporter, The Cape Times, '23—26, Reporter, Press Assoc, '26—27, Personal staff Otto H. Kahn, banker New York, '27—28, Associate, Ivy Lee, New York, '28—32, Press publicity, British Industries Fair, '32—34, Leader writer, The Star, '34—. *c.t*: Clarion, Cape Times, Financial News, Yorkshire Post, Spectator, The Star, The Times, American publications. *Rec*: Walking, cricket, tennis, swimming, bridge. War Service. Military Medal. *a*: 26 Old Bldgs, Lincolns Inn, W.C.2, *t*: Holborn 2170.

LAWSON. G. Murray. *n.a*: Sports Ed, Ed Sports Dispatch, Edin. *a*: Edinburgh Evening Dispatch, Edin.

LAWSON, John Cuthbert, O.B.E., M.A. *b*: Weston-in-Gordano 1874. *e*: Bradfield Col & Pembroke Col Cam. *m*: Dorothy Frances Holden. *s*: 2. *d*: 2. Fell & Tutor Pembroke Col Cam & Univ Lect in Classics. *Publ*: Modern Greek Folklore & Ancient Greek Religion; The Litany of the Elves; Æschylus, Agamemnon; etc. *c.t*: Class Review, Greek Quarterly. *s.s*: Greek Lit & Philos. War Service 1916—19. Lt-Commdr R.N.V.R. & Commdr Roy Hellenic Navy, as Intelligence Officer of Brit Naval Missn to Greece '17—19. Order of the Redeemer (Greek). *Rec*: Tennis. *a*: Foxton Hall, Royston, Herts. *t*: Harston, Cambs 204.

LAWSON, John Howard. *b*: New York 1894. *e*: Cutler Sch New York, Williams Coll Williamstown Mass. *m*: (1) Kathryn Drain, (2) Susan Edmond. *s*: 2. *d*: 1. Author. *n.a*: Mem Ed Bd Hollywood Quarterly 1945 —46. *Publ*: Theory & Technique of Playwriting; (Plays) Roger Bloomer; Processional; Loudspeaker; The International; Success Story; With a Reckless Preface; Marching Song. *Ctr*: Mainstream, Hollywood Quarterly, New Masses. *s.s*: Screenwriting, Playwriting *a*: 9354 Burnet Ave, San Fernando, California, U.S.A

LAWSON, Rt. Hon. John James, P.C., D.C.L., M.P. *b*: Whitehaven 1881. *e*: Elem & Ruskin Coll Oxf. *m*: Isobella Scott. *d*: 3. Sec of State for War 1945—46, Financial Sec to War Office '24, Parl Sec Min of Labour '29—31, M.P. (Lab) Chester-le-Street Div Co Durham since '19. *Publ*: A Man's Life; Man in the Cap. *Ctr*: Dly Herald, British Weekly. *s.s*: Industrial & Social. *a*: House of Commons, London, S.W.1.

LAWSON, John Minnikin. *b*: Birtley 1872. *m*: Martha Milburn. *d*: 1. Registrar of Births, Deaths & Marriages. *c.t*: Meth Recorder. *s.s*: Nat hist, music. Band of Hope Pres. Local Preacher & Class Leader, S.S. Teacher. *a*: Holly Hse, Birtley.

LAWSON, M. Journalist. *n.a*: Ed Empire News. *a*: Withy Grove, Manchester. *t*: Blackfriars 1234.

LAWSON, Robert Neale, C.B. *b*: Weston-in-Gordano, Som 1873. *e*: H.M.S. Britannia. *m*: Malvina Nathalia Felton. *s*: 2. *d*: 4. Rear Admiral R.N. (ret). *Publ*: Beloved Shipmates; Happy Anchorage (novels); Monograph on European Air Service. *s.s*: European air police. Flag Capt Neptune & Iron Duke (Fleet Flagships) 1913—15. Capt of Chester, Battle of Jutland '16; Despatches. *Rec*: Gardening, camping. *a*: Hillside, Northam, N. Devon.

LAWSON, Will. b: Gateshead, Durham, England 1876. e: Public Schs in Brisbane Queensland, Brisbane Gr Sch. m: Vera Wills. Author, former Journalist. n.a: Former Staff Ev News Sydney, N.Z. Herald, Smith's Weekly N.Z., Dly Guardian Sydney, etc. Publ: The Lady of the Heather; Pacific Steamers; When Cobb & Co was King; Three Kings & other Verses; Old Man Murray; Harpoons Ahoy; In Ben Boyd's Day; The Laughing Buccaneer; Black Diamonds; Paddlewheels Away. Ctr: Sydney Bulletin, Smith's Weekly Sydney, Weekly Times Melbourne. s.s: Sea-life, Railway Stories, Hist Romances. Rec: Golf, bush-hiking, swimming, studying bird life. a: 14a Martin-place, Sydney, N.S.W., Australia. T: B 3001 B 2186.

LAWSON-REECE, Clifford. b: B'ham 1911. e: King Edward's Sc B'ham, Barcelona & Dresden. Dir of Brit. Educational Film Guild, etc. c.t: Various n/p. s.s: Modern languages, education & cooking. Rec: Poetry, music, chess. c: Inst Linguists, R.S.A.(Fellow), etc. a: Little Pitfold, Hindhead, Surrey. t: Hindhead 497.

LAWTON, Annie, L.R.A.M., A.R.C.M., A.T.C.L. b: Newcastle-on-Tyne 1885. e: Quaker Boarding School, Ackworth, Yorks. Teacher of Music. Publ: Foundations of Practical Ear Training. Jt Ed Folk-song Sight Singing Series. a: Scottish National Academy of Music, Glasgow C.2.

LAWTON, Charles Louis, M.Sc.(Econ), F.I.B. b: Hessle, East Yorks 1904. e: St Peter's Sch York, Lond Sch of Econs. m: (1) Nellie Elizabeth Bowyer (dec'd), (2) Charlotte Marthe Petit. s: 1. d: 1. Barrister, Jt Chief Actuary York County Savings Bank. Ctr: Accountancy, Law Journ, Bankers Mag, Law Notes. s.s: Banking & Currency, Commercial Law, Law of Trusts. a: Meadow Lodge, 15 Wetherby Rd, York. T: 78737.

LAWTON, Harold. M.J.I. b: Darlington. e: St Francis Xavier's Col L'pool. m: Hilda Strauss. Journalist. n.a: Night Ed The Tribune 1906-08, Mang Ed Mons Evening & Weekly Post '08-12, Ed Staff Daily Mail '12-19, News Ed Sunday Times '19-20, Ed Daily Graphic '20-22, Night Ed Australian Press Assoc '23-. Publ: Wit & Wisdom of Lord Tredegar; etc. s.s: Politics, sociology. a: 25 Belsize Cres, Hampstead, N.W.3. t: 4458

LAX, Rev. William Henry. b: M/C 1868. e: Didsbury Theo Col. m: Minnie Browell. Publ: Lax of Poplar; Let's Go To Poplar; Adventure in Poplar. c.t: Meth Recorder, Meth Times, Sunday Circle, etc. Ald Poplar Boro' Counc. Mayor of Poplar 1918-19. 32 y Supt of Poplar & Bow Meth Missn. a: 1 Woodstock Rd, Poplar, E.14. t: East 1009.

LAY, Cecil Howard, F.R.I.B.A. b: Aldringham. e: Queen Elizabeth's Sch Ipswich & Archt Assoc Lond. m: Joan Chadburn. Author, Artist, Archt, Pze Win Daily Mail Village Sign Comp. Publ: Sparrows & Other Poems; Grotesques & Arabesques; Seven Poems; April's Foal; Ha & He; etc. Ctr: Dly Mail, Eng Rev, Studio, Dly Telegraph, etc. s.s: Poetry about Birds & Animals, Rural Paintings. a: Arch Hse, Aldringham, Leiston, Suffolk.

LAYTON, Frank George, M.R.C.S., L.R.C.P., J.P. b: Hounslow 1872. e: King's Col & St Thomas's Hosp. m: Dorothea Yonge. s: 3. d: 2. Panel Doctor. n.a: Assoc Ed Birm Medical Review, Snr Physician Walsall General Hosp. Publ: The Serpent & the Cross; Sable & Motley; The Parish Pump; The Black Sheep (play); The Invalid (play); The Little Doctor ('33); Psychology in Court ('33); etc. c.t: Various. s.s: Psychology. Rec: Reading. a: 35 Birmingham Rd, Walsall, Staffs. t: 2424.

LAYTON, Gilbert Clemens. b: Chelsea 1888. e: City of Lond. m: s: 1. d: 1. Dir of The Economist Bookshop. n.a: The Economist, Ed Staff 1911, Asst Ed '16, Mang '28. Rec: Golf. a: 22 Ryder St, London, S.W.1.

LAYTON, Thomas Arthur. b: London 1910. e: Bradfield Coll. m: E. E. de Peyster Marshall. s: 1. Wine Merchant, Writer. Publ: Choose Your Wine; Table for Two; Restaurant Roundabout. Ctr: Time & Tide, Vogue, Strand Mag. s.s: Wine. a: Grindfield Farm, Furners Green, nr Uckfield, Sussex.

LAYTON, Thomas Bramley, D.S.O., M.S., F.R.C.S. b: Sth Hampstead 1882. e: Bradfield Coll, Guy's Hosp. m: Edney Eleanor Layton. s: 1. d: 1. Consulting Surgeon (Throat & Ear) to Guy's Hosp. Publ: An Industry of Health; etc. Ctr: Lancet, Procs of Roy Soc of Med, Guy's Hosp Gazette. s.s: Social Medicine. Rec: Literature. c: Athenæum. a: The Shaws, Newchapel Rd, Lingfield, Surrey. T: Lingfield 338.

LAYTON, 1st Baron of Danehill, Walter Thomas Layton, C.H., Kt., LL.D. b: London 1884. e: King's Coll Sch, Westminster City Sch, Univ Coll Lond, Trin Coll Camb. m: Eleanor Dorothea Osmaston. s: 3. d: 4. Journalist, Chm News Chronicle Ltd, Star Newspaper Ltd, Vice-Chm Dly News, Dir of Reuters, Dir Gen of Programmes M.o.S. 1940—42, Chief Adv (Programmes & Planning) Min of Prod '42—43. n.a: Ed The Economist 1922—38, now Chm. Publ: Relations of Capital & Labour; An Introduction to the Study of Prices. Ctr: Economist, News Chron, Foreign Affairs (American), etc. s.s: Econs, Adviser Ind Statutory Commis. Rec: Golf, music. c: Nat Lib, R.A.C. a: Twitten Hse, Furners Green, Uckfield, Sussex & 57 Marsham Ct, London, S.W.1. T: Victoria 8181.

LAZARUS, Nathaniel. b: Smolevitcht, Russia 1884. e: Whitechapel Foundation Sc Lon & King's Col Lon. m: Kate Cohen. s: 2. Journalist. n.a: Jewish Chronicle 1907, Jewish Morning Journal N.Y. '08, Doar Hayom, Jerusalem '33. c.t: Daily Telegraph, Harmsworth Children's Ency, Jewish Times, Lon, Moment, Warsaw, Davar, Tel-Aviv. s.s: Jewish news & foreign politics. Rec: Debating. a: 65 Cazenove Rd, Stamford Hill, N.16. t: Clissold 4030.

LAZARUS-BARLOW, Walter Sydney, B.A., M.D., F.R.C.P. Prof Experimental Pathology (ret). Publ: General or Experimental Pathology; Text Book of Pathological Anatomy. c.t: B.M.J., Lancet & other Brit & Foreign Med Journs. a: Smith's Hall, W. Mersea, Essex. t: 38.

LAZENBY, Frank Stanley. b: L'pool 1901. m: Doris Hoare. d: 3. Ed Amal Press Publ, Sports Cartoonist Westminster Gazette '26, Evening Standard '29—34. a: Green Gates, Coombe Wood Hill, Purley, Surrey. t: 2806.

LAZENBY, A. Secretary the Press Club Ltd. a: 7 St Bride's Hse, Salisbury Sq, E.C.4. t: Cen 2644.

LEA, Charles, N.U.J. b: Birm. e: K.E. G.S. Aston, m: Doris Rose Bailey. s: 1. F.L. Journalist. Sec Midlands Br Master Sign Makers Assoc. c.t: Trade journals & tech press. s.s: Ind hist. Rec: Cycling. c: Midland Inst, Birm. a: 176 Kingstanding Rd, Erdington, Birm.

LEA, Frank Alfred, B.A. b: Manchester 1915; e: Charterhouse & Trinity Hall Camb. Editor, formerly Headmaster Burgess Hill Sch Hampstead & Mem of Nat Peace Council, Pacifist since 1937. n.a: Asst Ed Adelphi, Ed of Peace News since 1946. Publ: Carlyle—

Prophet of To-day; Shelley & the Romantic Revolution; The Wild Knight of Battersea; The Bookworm's Nightmare & other plays for children. *Ctr*: Adelphi, Phœnix Quarterly, The Aryan Path, Reconciliation, Geological Mag. *s.s*: The Romantic Poets, Philosophers, History of the Early Church. *Rec*: Squash, skating, sketching. *a*: 1 Belsize Gr, London, N.W.3. *T*: Primrose 5706.

LEA, Frederick Charles, O.B.E., D.Sc. *b*: Crewe 1871. *e*: Church Sch, Univ of Manch, Roy Coll of Science London. *m*: (1) Alice Sunman. *s*: 1. *d*: 2. (2) Elizabeth M. Taylor. Prof of Eng & Dean of the Faculty of Eng Univ of Sheffield 1924—36, Pres Eng Sec Brit Assoc '29' Prof of Civil Eng Univ of Birmingham '13—24. *Publ*: Hydraulics; Elementary Hydraulics; Hardness of Metals; Cutting Tools for Metal Machining (with Max Kurrein); Sir Joseph Whitworth—a pioneer of Mech Eng; The Machining of Steel (with Eric Simons). *s.s*: Science & Engineering. *a*: Wayside Dore, Sheffield. *T*: 70383 Sheffield.

LEA, John, M.A. *b*: Staffordshire 1871. *e*: Gonville & Caius Coll Camb, Heidelberg, London Hosp. *m*: Elsie Ida Gifford. Biologist, Lecturer & Educational Administrator. *Publ*: Romance of Bird Life & other Books on Nat Hist. *Ctr*: Globe, Times, Birm Dly Post, Animal World. *s.s*: Education, Field Nat Hist, Art, Short Stories, Verse. *Rec*: Handicrafts, field nat hist. *a*: Mangalore, Llandrindod-Wells; Athenæum, London, S.W.1.

LEA, Leslie Mervyn ("Michael Lamont"). *b*: Nairobi, E. Africa 1914. *e*: Wellington Sc Som & Univ Col Sc Frognal, Lon. *n.a*: Reporter Hastings & St Leonard's Observer. *c.t*: Periodicals & agencies. Travelled extensively. *Rec*: Rugby, swimming, tennis, chess, shooting. *a*: 24 Holmesdale Rd, Bexhill, Sussex. *t*: 1629.

LEA, Thomas Simcox, B.D., D.D. *b*: Lon 1857. *e*: Haileybury Col Hertford Col Oxf. *m*: Mary Gay. *s*: 1. *Publ*: The Apostolic Gnosis (Parts I & II with F. B. Bond, 1919—22). *s.s*: Greek Gematria of the Early Chr Ch, illus from New Testament, the Early Greek Fathers & the Coptic Gnostic Books. Served Roy Soc Exped to Fernando de Noronha under H. N. Ridley 1887. Subsequently put a collec of Brit plants into Kidderminster Museum. *Rec*: Botany, lepidoptera. *a*: Hespera, Cyprus Rd, Exmouth.

LEACH, Henry, F.R.G.S. *b*: Chorley, Lancs 1874. *e*: Priv. Writer. *n.a*: Invited by Lord Northcliffe (Alfred Harmsworth) from the provs to Lon '98 & for 20 yrs held many important appointments in Fleet St & subsequently in Spain & N. Africa. *Publ*: The Spirit of the Links; Fleet Street from Within; The Happy Golfer. *c.t*: Various n/ps. *s.s*: Spanish & N. African affairs. 1st Brit Sub to go through the Riff with Spanish mil escort. *Rec*: Motoring, golf, scientific photog. *c*: Savage & Spanish & R.A.C. *a*: 5 Queen Anne Row, Walmer, Kent. *t*: Dea 393.

LEACH, Nathaniel. *b*: Darwen 1849. Widower. *s*: 1. Printer & publisher. *n.a*: Owner, Darwen Advertiser. *Rec*: Walking, gardening, motoring. *a*: Advertiser Office, Darwen. *t*: 29.

LEACHMAN, Rev. Edgecombe Walter. *b*: Lewisham 1870. *e*: Priv & King's Col Lon. *m*: Martha Ashburner. *d*: 1. *n.a*: Ed The Depositor 1931—32. *Publ*: The Church's Object Lessons; Diverting Stories of Clerical Life; etc. 30 y on Govg Body Nat Deposit Fr endly Soc. *Rec*: Motoring. *a*: 19 Holmesdale Gdns, Hastings, Sussex. *t*: 86.

LEACOCK, Stephen Butler, B.A., PhD., LL.D., etc. *b*: 1869. *e*: Canada & U.S.A. Professor & Author. *Publ*: Literary Lapses; Nonsense Novels; Behind the Beyond; Arcadian Adventures with the Idle Rich; Winsome Winnie, Frenzied Fiction; Life of Charles Dickens; Mark Twain; Lincoln Frees the Slaves; Humor: its Theory & Technique; etc. Political Economy Prof McGill University, Montreal. *a*: 3869 Côte des Neiges Rd, Montreal Canada.

LEADBETTER, Rev. William George. *Publ*: Like Unto Leaven; Spring Blossoms; At the Sign of the Shoe; The Red Ambassador; A Russet Robe. *c.t*: Meth Leader, Bromsgrove Messenger, etc. *a*: The Coppice, Lickey, Bromsgrove.

LEADER, Dr. H. *a*: 279 Glossop Rd, Sheffield.

LEAHY, Michael Patrick, F.R.S.M., B.A., M.B., B.Ch, B.A.O.(Dublin). *b*: Newcastle, W. Ireland 1882. *e*: Clongowes Wood Col Kildare & T.C.D. *m*: Adeline Kate Pomeroy. *d*: 2. Doctor. *c.t*: Spiritual Healing, B.M.J. 1925, Aetiology of Alcoholism, & Psychical Impotence, Trans Roy Soc Med '28, An article on Fear, Amer Med Journ '28. *Publ*: The Mind in Disease ('26). *s.s*: Hypnotism, Psychotherapy, special ref to treatment by suggestion. Ex-Heavyweight Boxing Champion Ireland '08—09. Ex-Light-Heavyweight Army Champion '13. War Service, France; Wounded; prisoner (10 mths); leg amputated. Boxing & rowing again '16. Ret Major R.A.M.C. *c*: Bath & Bucks, etc. *a*: 45 Clarges St, W.1. *t*: Grosvenor 1369.

LEAK, Walter Norman, M.D., M.R.C.S., L.R.C.P. *b*: Winsford, Cheshire 1891. *e*: Berkhampstead Sch, Trin Coll Camb, St Georg's Hosp Lond, Lond Sch of Tropical Med. *m*: Bessie Hamlett Williams. *s*: 2. *d*: 1. *Publ* Islam & Its Needs. *Ctr*: Nature, Medical Press, Times, Economist, Spectator, Times Lit Supp, etc. *Rec*: Photography. *a*: Dingle Hse, Winsford, Cheshire. *T*: Winsford 2339.

LEAKE, Percy Dewe. *m*: Desiree Mary Image (dec'd). Founder & Senior Partner P. D. Leake & Co, Fellow of the Zoological Soc, Fellow Inst of Chart Accountants, Member of the Board of Trustees of Albany. *Publ*: Depreciation & Wasting Assets; Commercial Goodwill; Leake's Register of Industrial Plant; Balance Sheet Values; The Use & Misuse of the Sinking Fund. *Ctr*: Times, Economist, Accountant, & many articles & lectures on economic subjects & on the science of industrial accounting. *s.s*: Efforts to advance the practice of industrial accounting to the rank of an exact science, Periodical Measurement of Ind' Profit & Loss, Govt Finance. *Rec*: Walking, shooting, fishing, rowing, bicycling, squash, mountaineering, travel & reading. *a*: K1 Albany, Piccadilly, London, W.1; & 1 Cornhill, London, E.C.3. *T*: Regent 1443, & Mansion House 5801.

LEAKEY, James. *b*: Lon 1849. *e*: Lycée Louis-le-Grand, Paris. *m*: Mary Emily Smith. *s*: 2. *d*: 2. Shipbroker, Wine Merchant, Trav (ret). *Publ*: Leakey's Introduction to Esperanto; Outward Houl *c.t*: English & Foreign Press. *s.s*: Languages, Esperanto, emigration. *Rec*: Travel. *a*: Greybole, Hatfield, Herts. *t*: 73.

LEAKEY, Louis Seymour Bazett, M.A., Ph.D., F.G.S., F.R.A.I. *b*: Kabete, Kenya 1903. *e*: Weymouth Coll, St John's Coll Camb. *m*: (1) Wifrida Avern, (2) Mary D. Nicol. *s*: 3. *d*: 1. Prehistoric Archæologist, Curator of Coryndon Memorial Museum Nairobi 1945—. *Publ*: Stone Age Cultures of Kenya; Stone Age Races of Kenya; Stone Age Africa; Adams Ancestors; Kenya Contrasts & Problems; White African. *Ctr*: Times, Man, Illus Lond News, Science Progress, Scientia,

Ency Brit, etc. *s.s*: Prehistoric Archæology, Social Authropology, Kikuyu Lang, Handwriting in Criminology. *Rec*: Reading. *a*: Box 658, Nairobi, Kenya. *T*: Nairobi 2008.

LEALE, Enid Alison Wilkins, L.L.A. *b*: Guernsey 1882. *e*: Guernsey Ladies Col. *Publ*: Peeps at Historical Songs; Tony's Desert Island. *c.t*: Schoolmistress, Glasgow Herald, Fairyland Tales, Christian Science Monitor, Sheffield Telegraph, etc. *a*: Rue a L'Or, St Saviours, Guernsey.

LEAN, Edward Tangye. *b*: Merstham, Surrey 1911. *e*: Leighton Park & Univ Coll Oxf. *m*: Doreen Myra Way. *s*: 2. B.B.C. *n.a*: Leader Writer News Chronicle 1934, Book Reviews News Chron '37, Editor B.B.C. French Service for Europe '43, West European Services Director '45, Asst Controller (Output) European Div B.B.C. '46. *Publ*: Voices in the Darkness; Undergraduate Novels. *Ctr*: Horizon, News Chron, London Mercury. *s.s*: Lit Criticism, French & German Lit, Hist, Broadcasting. *Rec*: Foreign travel, guide books, English countryside. *a*: 13 Ivor Pl, London, N.W.1. *T*: Paddington 9571.

LEAN, Rev. Leslie Victor George Fiddian. *b*: Lon 1898. *e*: Burlington Hse Sc Richmond, Surrey, St Michael's Col Kensington & King's Col Lon. Assoc of King's Col Lon Asst Priest St Mary's Ch, Paddington Green, W.2. *Publ*: The Voice of Undivided Christendom; The Drama of the Holy Mass; What Think Ye?; etc. *s.s*: Ch doctrine & hist. *Rec*: Music & coin collecting. *a*: Rosmead Lodge, 79 Lansdowne Rd, Holland Pk, W.11.

LEAPER, William Joseph. *b*: Wynberg, Sth Africa. *e*: Birkbeck Coll Lond, Inner Temple E.C.4. *n.a*: Chief Rep Halifax Guardian, Rep Yorkshire Post, & Observer Huddersfield Examiner, Art Ed Newcastle Ev Chron, Assoc Ed Advertisers Weekly, Ed Sales Management & Marketing Policy, Journ of the Advertising Assoc. *Ctr*: The World Book (Hist of Brit Empire, Labour Party, etc.), Geography & Man, etc. *s.s*: Law, Market Research, History, Economics. *w.s*: R.E. & R.A.F. *a*: 1 Cedar Close, East Molesey, Surrey.

LEARMONTH, David. *b*: Lon 1899. *e*: Eton & Shrewsbury. *m*: Doña Anita Josefina Del Rey de la Fuente. Author, Journalist. *n.a*: Racing & hunting Ed Illus Sporting & Dramatic News, Circulation Mang Sat Review. *Publ*: Galloping Gold; Tainted Turf; Red Mammon; Tic-Tac; The Empty Glass; After The Battle. *c.t*: Various n/ps & periodicals. *s.s*: Racing, cricket, satirical verse. War Service. *Rec*: Shooting, hunting, tennis. *c*: Bachelors. *a*: 8 Stanley Mansions, Park Walk, S.W.3. *t*: Flaxman 0324.

LEARY, B.A. (Miss), M.A. *a*: County Sc for Girls, Ashford, Kent.

LEARY, Rev. Lewis Gaston, M.A., B.Sc., D.D., Ph.D. *b*: Elizabeth, New Jersey 1877. *e*: Union Theol Sem, Rutgers, New York & Vermont Univs. *m*: Beatrice Emily Knight. *s*: 3. *d*: 2. Pastor of West Milford (N.J.) Presbyterian Church. *Publ*: The Christmas City; The Real Palestine; Andorra, The Hidden Republic; Syria the Land of Lebanon; Problems of Protestantism; (Compiler of) The Bible When You Want it; For Them That Mourn; The Service Book of Scripture & Prayer. *Ctr*: Various. *s.s*: Middle East, Adolescent Psychology. *Rec*: Gardening. *a*: West Milford, New Jersey, U.S.A. *T*: West Milford 7371.

LEASK, GEORGE ALFRED: author, journalist; *b*. London, Eng., May 29, 1878; *s*. George and Jane (Davidson) L.; *educ*. Regent St., Polytechnic Sch .(London), Robert Sardon Coll. (Aberdeen, Scotland); DEGREE: M.A., Honors Aberdeen Univ.); unmarried. AUTHOR: Nineteenth Century Hymn Writers, 1902; Life of Porter Thompson, 1905; The Story of Our Hymns, 1910; Stories of Famous Hymns, 1911; A Little Book of Success, 1912; V. C. Heroes of the War, 1915; Hymns in Time of War, 1915; Life of Field-Marshal Sir William Robertson, 1916; Golden Deeds of Heroism, 1918; A Drawing Room Drama (4-act play), 1922; The Circus of Europe, 1924; Queen Mab (a 4-act play), 1924; The Boys of Felton, 1929. (Founded and) Edited, The World Scout (formerly). Contributor to Christian Endeavor Times, Sunday Companion, Good Words, Christian Herald and many Brit. popular wklys. General character of writing: juveniles, religious, historical, plays. Assoc. for yrs. with Scout Movement in Britain; has lectured extensively on Hymnology. On editorial staff Amalgamated Press since 1903. Relig. denom., Presbyterian. CLUBS: National Liberal, Junior Liberal (both London). OFFICE: Amalgamated Press, London, Eng.

LEATHER, Charles Henry, E.A. *b*: Aston 1888. *e*: Queen's Coll Oxf. Teacher. *Publ*: Common Errors in French; Common Errors in German; German Oral Practice; English Oral Practice; Lisons et Parlons; Livre des Petits; Essential French Idioms. *Ctr*: Modern Languages. *a*: 12 Gourock Rd, Eltham, London, S.E.9.

LEATHER, John Walter, PhD. *b*: Rainhill 1860. *e*: Priv, Univ of Bonn, Germany. *m*: Annie Lyon *d*: 3. Chemist. Indian Agric Service, Govt of India. *c.t*: Various. *s.s*: Agricultural Chemistry. War Service 1915-18. *c*: Fell Inst of Chem G.B. & I, Fell Chem Soc. *a*: Ridgeway Hse, Ridgeway Cross, Malvern. *t*: Ridgeway Cross 8.

LEATHERLAND, Charles Edward, M.S.M., J.P., F.R.Econ.S., N.U.J. *b*: Birmingham 1898. *e*: Elem Sch & Univ Ext Courses. *m*: Mary Morgan. *s*: 1. *d*: 1. *n.a*: News Ed Daily Herald. *Publ*: (Pt-Author) Book of the Labour Party; many political pamphlets. *Ctr*: Labour Mag & periodicals on political subjects. *Rec*: Hunting, riding. *a*: The Old Rectory, Dunton, Essex. *T*: Laindon 164.

LEATHES, John Beresford. F.R.S., Hon.D.Sc.(Sheff & Manch). *b*: London 1864. *e*: Winchester & New Coll Oxf, Univs of Berne & Strasbourg. *m*: Sonia Muronova. *d*: 1. Retired Prof of Physiology. *n.a*: Ed Journ of Physiology 1926—37. *Publ*: Problems in Animal Metabolism; Biochemical Monograph; etc. *Ctr*: Various sci journs. *s.s*: Chemistry in Biology. *Rec*: Painting in pastels. *c*: Mem Phys & Biochemical Socs & Fell Chem Soc. *a*: Burley, Silver St, Lyme Regis, Dorset. *T*: Lyme Regis 370.

LEATHES, Sir Stanley, K.C.B., M.A. *b*: 1861. *e*: Eton & Trin Col Cam. Mem Counc Soc of Authors.

LEATHLEY, Rev. S. A., D.D., LL.B., M.A. *Publ*: Hist of Marriage and Divorce; The Roman Family. *a*: Belgrave Col, Promenade, Lytham, Lancs.

LEATHLEY, William John. *b*: Sudbury 1906. *e*: Sudbury G.S. *m*: V. M. King. *s*: 1. *d*: 1. Journalist (Dis Rep E. Anglian Daily Times Ltd). *n.a*: Joined Staff of E. Anglian Daily Times '25, Beccles Rep '29. Younger son of late W. L. Leathley, 30 y Sudbury Rep E. Anglian Daily Times. 1st Hon Sec Suffolk County A.A.A. (res '29). *Rec*: Football, cricket, swimming, yachting, golf. *a*: 21 London Rd, Beccles, Suffolk. *t*: 163.

LEAVER, Nelson. *b*: Maidstone 1884. *e*: Priv. *m*: Elsie Lilian Beckley. *s*: 4. *d*: 2. Journalist. *n.a*: Chief Sub-Ed & Night Ed Daily Sketch, News Ed 1925—. *Rec*: Tennis. *c*: N.U.J. *a*: 50 King's Hall Rd, Beckenham. *t*: Sydenham 2083.

LEAVIS, Frank Raymond. *e*: Elem Sch, Gr Sch, Emmanuel Coll Camb. Univ Teacher, Fell Downing Coll. *n.a*: Co-Ed Scrutiny. *Publ*: New Bearings in English Poetry; For Continuity; Mass Civilization & Minority Culture; Culture & Environment (with Denys Thompson); Revaluation; Tradition & Development in English Poetry; Education & the University; The Great Tradition. *a*: Downing College, Cambridge.

LEAVITT, Ezekiel, M.R.S.A. *b*: Russia 1880. *e*: Odessa Univ, Columbia Univ N.Y. Author, Rabbi, Professor, Lecturer. *Publ*: Sipurim v' Ziyurim (Hebrew 1896); Money, Money Above Everything (Russian 1900); Russian Poems; Fables & Poems; Songs of Grief & Gladness; The Pleasures of the Czar; Hebrew Poems ('20, trans into Hungarian by Josef Patai); Parrot Gods; The Higher Love; When Love Runs Wild 34); etc. *c.t*: Eng, Hebrew, Russian, Yiddish publs. *s.s*: Philos, poetry, drama, theo & criticism. Hon Mem Luther Burbank Soc, etc. *a*: 435 Sutter Ave, Brooklyn, N.Y., U.S.A.

LEBLANC, Felix Raoul. *b*: Mauritius 1892. *e*: Roy Coll Paris, Guy's Hosp. *m*: Maud Emma Murray. Hse Surg at Guy's Hosp 1916, Pathologist to Brit Army '17 —18, Clin Asst Skin Dept Evelina Hosp. *Publ*: Venereal Disease & its Prevention. *s.s*: Diseases of Women. *Rec*: Farming, ski-ing, punting. *w.s*: V.D. Co. No. 5 V.D. Hosp 1939—45. *a*: 11 Welbeck St, London, W.1, & Wood Farm, Henley, Ipswich. *T*: Welbeck 7069, & Witnesham 279.

LEBLANC, Maurice. *Publ*: Arsene Lupin (creator of Arsene Lupin character); Wanton Venus; Man of Miracles, etc. *a*: c/o A. M. Heath & Co Ltd, 188 Piccadilly, W.1.

LE BLOND, Elizabeth Alice Frances. *b*: Dublin 1860. *e*: Priv. *m*: Aubrey Le Blond. *s*: 1. Officier de l'Instruction Publique. Chevalier de la Legion d'Honneur. *Publ*: The High Alps in Winter; Cities & Sights of Spain; True Tales of Mountain Adventure; Day in, Day out (autobiography); The Old Gardens of Italy; The Dunkelgraf Mystery (with O. V. Maecker); etc. *c.t*: Times, Daily Telegraph, Nineteenth Century, etc. *s.s*: Mountaineering, Italian gardens, hist. Hon Sec Anglo-French Luncheon Club, Pres Ladies Alpine Club 1934 (1st Pres '07). *Rec*: Writing, publ speaking, promotion of Anglo-French Entente. *c*: Ladies Alpine & Forum. *a*: St Ermins, S.W.1. *t*: Victoria 3441.

LEBRETON, Jules Marie. *b*: Tours 1873. Prof of Hist of Christian Origins, Faculty of Catholic Theology Paris. *Publ*: La Vie Chrétienne au Premier Siècle; La Vie et L'enseignement de Jésus Christ (2 vols); Le Dieu Vivant; Le Père Leonce de Grandmaison; etc. *c.t*: Études, Recherches de Science Religieuse. *s.s*: History of Christian origins. Docteur és lettres. *a*: 15 rue Monsieur Paris VII. *t*: Ségur 74—77.

LE BROCQ, Walter. *b*: Jersey 1876. *m*: Edith Alice Evans. *d*: 4. Journalist. *n.a*: Press Assoc 1908–. *s.s*: Roy ct reporting, cattle shows. War Service. *Rec*: Cricket, billiards. *c*: Brit Legion. *a*: Lewis St, Jersey. *t*: St Helier Cent 27.

LE CHAMPION, Loftus Claude Gerald (" Streamline "). *b*: Lon 1895. *e*: Eton & Sandhurst. *Publ*: Foretold. *c.t*: Motor, Garage Monthly, Collins' Motor Annual, Cage Birds, etc. *s.s*: Flying, motor-racing, psych research. Served R.N.A.S. & R.F.C. Rubber Planter (Malaya). Driver Brooklands 1922–25, Winner Gold Cup '24, etc. *Rec*: Photography, music. *a*: 169 Clifton Rd, Rugby. *t*: 749.

LECHE, Dr. A. V., M.O.H. *a*: Elmcroft, Axbridge, Somerset.

LECKIE, Joseph Hanney, D.D., B.Sc(Agr). *b*: Isle of Cumbrae. *e*: Glas Univ, Edin Theo Col. *m*: Belle Primrose Miller. *s*: 2. *d*: 2. Doctor. *Publ*: World to Come & Final Destiny; Authority in Religion; Life of Fergus Ferguson, D.D.; Vocation of the Church. *c.t*: Expositor, Expository Times. *s.s*: Eschatology. *Rec*: Sailing. *c*: Authors'. *a*: 86 Craighouse Rd, Edin. *t*: 62490.

LECKY, Capt. Halton Stirling, C.B., A.M., R.N. *b*: Portrush, Co Derry 1878. *e*: Eastmans, Stubbington & H.M.S. Britannia, Dartmouth. *m*: Agnes Close. *s*: 2. *d*: 6. Naval Officer (ret). *Publ*: The King's Ships (3 vols); Wrinkles in Practical Navigation; etc. *s.s*: Naval hist, horticulture. Chevalier of Legion of Honour (France). Officer of Roy Order of the Saviour (Greece). Silver Medal of Roy Humane Soc. Lloyds Silver Medal for Saving Life at Sea. S. African & European War (1914–19). *Rec*: Boat-sailing. Mem Authors Soc, Un Service Club, Soc for Nautical Research (Ex-Counc), Nat Rose Soc (Vice-Pres & Counc), Roy Un Service Inst, etc. *a*: 7 Tudor Rd, Upper Norwood, S.E.19. *t*: Livingstone 1023.

LECLAIRE, Gordon, B.A., Litt.D., F.R.S.A. *b*: Quebec, Canada 1905. *e*: MacDonald Coll, McGill Univ, Irvine Studio for the Theatre. *m*: Zita Harris. English Specialist, Poet-Lecturer, Metaphysician. *n.a*: Canadian Ed Avon & Poetry Caravan, Assoc Ed The Crucible. *Publ*: More Life in Living; Though Quick Souls Bleed; Star-Haunted; Sonnets to the Stars; Intimate Moments. *Ctr*: N.Y. Times, N.Y. Herald-Tribune, Sat Rev of Lit, Montreal Gaz & Daily Star, Washington Star, etc. *s.s*: Poetry, Metaphysics, English Lang & Lit. *Rec*: Motoring, tennis, badminton, swimming, theatre. *a*: 1490 Fort St, Apt 104, Montreal, Quebec, Canada. *T*: Wi 3757.

LECLER, Anthony Rene, B.A. *b*: 1914. *e*: Sorbonne Paris. Journalist. *n.a*: Foreign Affairs Staff News Review 1946—. *Ctr*: World Review, Everybody's London Forum & various French publications, etc. *s.s*: Foreign Affairs, Travel & Geog. *a*: 8 Clarendon Lodge, 56 Clarendon Rd, Kensington, London, W.11. *T*: Park 4544.

LECOMTE, GEORGES: author; b. Macon, France, July, 1867; s. Jules Lecomte. DEGREES: Bachelier es Lettres, Licencié en droit; married. AUTHOR: La Meule (play in 6 acts), 1891; L'Art Impressionist, 1892; Mirages (drama in 5 acts), 1893; Espagne, 1895; Des Valets (novel), 1879; Suzeraine (novel), 1898; La Maisonen Fleurs (novel), 1898; Les Cartons Verts (novel), 1900; Le Veau d'Or (novel), 1902; Les Hannetons de Paris, 1903; L'Espoir (novel), 1908; Les Allemandes Chez eux, 1909; Pour celles qui pleurent, pour ceux qui souffrent, 1915; Les Lettres au service de la Patrie, 1917; Clemenceau, 1918; Bouffoneries dans la tempête (novel), 1919; Jours de Batailles et de Victoire, 1919; Auguste Delacherche, 1920; Camille Pissarro, 1921; Guillaumin, 1922; La Lumière retrouvée (novel), 1923; Albert Besnard, 1924; Louis Charlot, 1925; Le Mort saisit le vif (novel), 1926; J. F. Rafaelli, 1926; La Vie Amoreuse de Danton, 1927; Lamartine, 1928; La Vie Heroïque et glorieuse de Carpenna, 1928; Au chant de la Marseillaise, 1929; Les Prouesses du Bailli de Suffren, 1929. General character of writing: historical novels, criticism of art. SOCIETIES: Académie Français, Société des Gens de Lettres de France (Honorary President). Religion, Catholic. ADDRESS: 18 Boulevard Auguste Blanqui (13e), Paris, France.

LE COUTEUR, Frank. *b*: Jersey. *e*: Victoria Coll Jersey. *m*: (1) Hilda May Campbell (dec'd), (2) Ellen Sylvia Pearson. *d*: 2. Journalist. *n.a*: Rep, Sub-Ed, Chief Sub-Ed & Art Ed Ev News 1905—22, Dly Express '22—24, Ed The Graphic '24—26, Asst Ed Sun Express '27—28, Dly Express '29—. *Ctr*: Punch, etc. *a*: 46 Fitzjohns Ave, London, N.W.3. *T*: Hampstead 6687.

LEDBROOKE, Archibald William. *b*: Woking. *e*: Leamington Col. *m*: Eileen Burridge. *d*: 1. Journalist. Sports Ed M/C Evening News. *n.a*: Reporter Times & Mirror, Bristol 1928, M/C Evening News '29, Sports Ed M/C Evening News '30–. *a*: Alderhurst, Wardle Rd, Sale, Cheshire.

LEDBURY, Capt. Francis Harris. *b*: Bathwick 1901. *e*: K.E. VI Sch & Tech Coll Bath. *m*: Jean Margaret Stratton Fergusson. *s*: 1. *d*: 1. Hon Sec Bath Branch N.U.J. 1926—36 & Chm '37, Dir South-Western Regional News Service '46—. *n.a*: Bath Herald 1919—23, Western Dly Press '23—39. *Ctr*: Various London & Bristol Dailies & B.B.C. *s.s*: Sport, Crime, Country Articles. *Rec*: Motoring, drama, tennis. *w.s*: Army Welfare Officer World War II. *a*: 8 Pulteney Gdns, Bath, Somerset. *T*: 3139.

LEDERER, Josie Peppina. *b*: Lon. *e*: Browns Wood Col & Priv. F.L. Journalist. *n.a*: Ed Asst & Assoc Ed Picturegoer (Odhams Press) 1920-25, Film Corr Woman's Pictorial, Women's Page Film Weekly, Film Corr Hairdressing Fashions, etc. *c.t*: Film Weekly, Home Notes, Woman's Friend, and General Press. *s.s*: Screen stage interviews & articles, woman's page articles, & fashion & design. Visited film studios in France, N.Y. & Hollywood '30. Asst Answers Man in Picturegoer 5 y. *Rec*: Travel, theatre, reading, films, meeting celebrities, trying to write plays. *a*: 67 Hodford Rd, N.W.11.

LEDGER, Arthur Thomas. *n.a*: Ed Surrey Herald Series. *Ctr*: Numerous London papers. *a*: The Cedars, Chertsey, Surrey. *T*: 2234.

LEDINGHAM, Alex. *a*: The Studio, Grantown-on-Spey.

LEE, Rev. Albert ("Lindon Romaine"), M.V.O., PhB., F.R.G.S. *b*: Bristol 1858. *e*: Bristol, Westminster, Illinois Univ. *m*: (1) Emily Hanney Webster; (2) Minnie Annie Thompson. *d*: 2 (dec). *n.a*: The Recorder of the King's Archives. *Publ*: The Frown of Majesty; The Baronet of Corduroy; A King's Treachery; The Maid of the Mayflower; Daydawn; 'Twixt Love & Duty; The Queen's Displeasure; etc. *s.s*: Mil hist. *a*: 2 Claremont Rd, Windsor.

LEE, Rev. Alexander Greenhow, B.A. *b*: Birkenhead 1884. *e*: B'head Inst, L'pool Univ & Wycliffe Hall Oxf. *m*: Gladys Evangel Gill. *s*: 2. *d*: 1. Vicar of Rawtenstall 1935, Rural Dean of Rossendale '42, Proctor in Convocation '45, Vicar of Hunmanby Yorks '46, Missny in China 17 years. *Publ*: A Soul with a Sword. *Ctr*: Chinese Recorder, L'pool Rev. *s.s*: Propagation of Christianity. *a*: Hunmanby Vicarage, Yorks. *T*: Hunmanby 294.

LEE, Rev. Alfred Allen. Cong Min. *Publ*: Making the Sabbath a Delight; Something We Once Knew (broadcast addresses); etc. *c.t*: Brit Weekly, Christian World, etc. *a*: Brooklands, Chadwick Rd, Westcliff-on-Sea. *t*: Southend 3514.

LEE, Alfred McClung, M.A., Ph.D. *b*: Oakmont, Pennsylvania 1906. *e*: Oakmont Public Hgh Sch, Yale & Pittsburgh Univs. *m*: Elizabeth Briant Lee. *s*: 4. Social Scientist, Author, Public Opinion Analyst. *Publ*: The Daily Newspaper in America; Outline of the Principles of Sociology (Ed & Co-Author); (in collab) The Fine Art of Propaganda; Race Riot. *Ctr*: Sat Review of Lit, Amer Sociological Rev, Public Opinion Quarterly, Ed & Pub Library Journ, etc. *s.s*: Public Opinion, Propaganda, Public Relations, Sociological Theory, Mass Communications. *Rec*: Mountain climbing, trout fishing, hiking, farming. *c*: Yale (N.Y.), Exchange (Northville), etc. *a*: 164 East Cady St, Northville, Michigan, U.S.A. *T*: Northville 140-W.

LEE, Alfred Morgan. *b*: Sheffield 1901. *e*: Huddersfield Col. *m*: Nellie Brierley. *s*: 1. *d*: 1. Journalist. *n.a*: Sports Ed Huddersfield Examiner '29–. Mem N.U.J. '23–. *s.s*: Sport. *Rec*: Chess. *a*: 90 Heaton Rd, Huddersfield. *t*: 2720.

LEE, Annabel. Author. *Publ*: Lumberjack Jill; Beyond the Veldt; Windlestraw Island; Cinderella Wife; A Quixote Against His Will; Love Came to Veronica; To Ride in a Coach; Choose What is Best; Stolen Eden; Life is for Living; The Daughter of Eve. *c.t*: Woman & Beauty, Home Chat, A.P. Publs, etc. *s.s*: Serials, light fiction. *a*: c/o Messrs Curtis Brown, 6 Henrietta St, W.C.2.

LEE, Anne. *b*: Southwell. Free-Lance Journalist. *n.a*: Southwell Area Corres Nottingham Guardian, Ev Post, Nottinghamshire Weekly Guardian, Newark Advertiser. *Publ*: Truant Train; Cautionary Tales; Tale of Billy Boy; The Litter Fairies; Thomas Grey; Birds Nests; The Fire Engine; Forgetful Jane; Flora The Fish; Saucepan Alfie; etc. *Ctr*: Nottinghamshire Countryside, Notts Weekly Guardian, C. of E. Newsp, Child Education, Teachers World, etc. *s.s*: Child Psychology, Nature Study, Birds, etc, Gardening, Bees, Arch of Churches, River Lore, Aigres etc, Local History. *Rec*: Study of birds, music, cycling. *a*: 5 Westgate, Southwell, Notts. *T*: 2109.

LEE, Atkinson, M.A. *b*: Driffield 1880. *e*: St Peter's Col Cam. *m*: Frances Juan Evans, B.A. Lect in M/C Univ & Tutor Hartley Col M/C. *Publ*: Sociality: The Art of Living Together. *c.t*: Lon Quarterly & Holborn Review. *s.s*: Religious educ. Mem Brit Inst of Philos. *Rec*: Golf, music. *a*: Invergowrie, King's Rd, M/C, S.W.16.

LEE, Auriol. Stage Director. *e*: Classical. *a*: 4 Adam Street, Adelphi, W.C.2. *t*: Temple Bar 3794.

LEE, Bert. *b*: Yorks 1880. *e*: Wheelwright G.S. Dewsbury. *m*: Marlie Longmire. Author. *Publ*: Part Author (Musical Comedies, Reviews): The Peep Show; Brighter London; Round in Fifty; Leap Year; Pot Luck; The Girl Friend; Hit the Deck; Virginia; Lucky Girl; Hold Everything; Little Tommy Tucker; Song of the Drum; Tell Her the Truth; He Wanted Adventure; Give Me a Ring; Yes Madam. Has written & composed over 2000 songs. *Rec*: Golf. *c*: Savage, Stage & Golf. *a*: 32 Riverview Gdns, Barnes, S.W.13. *t*: Riverside 2273.

LEE, Cecile Margaret Kerslake, M.J.I. *b*: London. *m*: Charles Edward Lee. Asst Ed Aviation Year Book. *a*: 2 Dukes Rd, Tavistock Sq, London, W.C.1. *T*: Euston 1319.

LEE, Charles Edward, F.R.S.A., F.R.G.S., C.I.Mar.E., M.J.I., A.M.Inst.T., F.P.W.I. *b*: London. *m*: Cecile Margaret Kerslake Lee. Tech Journalist. *n.a*: Travel-

By-Road Guide 1921—22, F.L. '22—25, The Railway Gazette, Asst Ed Ship-building & Shipping Record & The Marine Engineer '28—32, Asst Ed The Railway Gazette & The Railway Mag '33—35, Assoc Ed Railway Gaz & Railway Mag '35—, V-Pres The Omnibus Soc, V-Pres Railway Club, Ed Aviation Year Book. *Publ*: The Blue Riband of the Atlantic ; The World's First Public Railway ; Father Tooth, a biographical memoir ; The Evolution of Railways ; Early Railways in Surrey ; The First Passenger Railway ; Passenger Class Distinctions ; Narrow Gauge Railways in North Wales. *Ctr* : Daily, trade & tech press. *s.s* : Transport. *a* : 2 Dukes Rd, Tavistock Sq, London, W.C.1. *T* : Euston 1319.

LEE, Donovan Henry, B.Sc., M.I.C.E., M.I.Mech.E. *b* : London 1900. *e* : Switzerland, Woodford Coll & King's Coll. *m* : *s* : 1. Civ Eng, Cons Eng to Brit Iron & Steel Fed, etc, Tech Dir Aston Const Co & Chief Eng Christiani & Nielson Ltd Reinf Conc Eng & Contractors 1931—38. *Publ* : Steelwork in Buildings under the L.C.C. Code ; Sheet Piling, Cofferdams & Caissons. *Ctr* : Structural Eng. *s.s* : Reinforced Concrete, Structural Steelwork. *a* : 66 Victoria St, London, S.W.1. *T* : Victoria 4288.

LEE, Dorcas. *b* : Croydon 1904. *m* : Alexander Patterson. *d* : 1. *Publ* : The Offending Adam. *Ctr* : Ev News, Answers, The Aeroplane, The Writer. *Rec* : Books & the theatre. *a* : 9 Morshead Mans, Maida Vale, London, W.9. *T* : Cunningham 1292.

LEE, Dwight Erwin, A.M., Ph.D. *b* : Newark, New York 1898. *e* : Univs of Rochester & Harvard. *m* : Margaret Shipley. *d* : 1. Prof of Mod European Hist Clark Univ. *n.a* : Spec Ed Writer Worcester Telegram & Gazette 1928—30, Mem Ed Bd Journ of Mod Hist '43—46, Internat Organisation '46—. *Publ* : Ten Years : the World on the Way to War ; Great Britain & the Cyprus Convention Policy of 1878. *Ctr* : Journ of Mod Hist, American Hist Review, Polit Science Quarterly, etc. *s.s* : European Diplomatic Hist since 1871, Contemporary European Internat Relations. *a* : 3 Woodman Rd, Worcester, Massachusetts, U.S.A. *T* : 3-4827.

LEE, Rev. Edward Henry Hoare, B.A., M.A. *b* : Co Antrim 1865. *e* : Kensington G.S., St Paul's Sc, Christ's Col Cam. *m* : Fanny Rooke. *s* : 1. *d* : 2. Canon of Salisbury with the Prebend of Bedminster & Redclyffe, annexed 1932. Vice-Chm Bridport R.D.C. '33. *Publ* : The Plan of Caiaphas ; History of Whitechurch Canonicorum, Dorset ; History of Hilton, Dorset. *c.t* : Various n/ps & periodicals. *s.s* : Theo, hist. *a* : Whitchurch Canonicorum Vicarage, Bridport.

LEE, Elsie Marion. *b* : Lon 1884. *e* : Southlands Col. *m* : Frank Harold Lee. *d* : 3. Teacher. *Publ* : The Lure of the Sea ; The Children's Hiawatha ; The Children's London ; Folk Tales of all Nations ; The Children's England ; The Children's Gulliver ; etc. *s.s* : Folk lore, children's books. *a* : 6 Hollybank, Muswell Hill, N.10. *t* : Tudor 3543.

LEE, Ernest Markham, M.A., Mus.D., F.R.C.O. Author, Lecturer, Composer. *Publ* : Brahms, The Man & his Music ; On Listening to Music ; Brahms's Symphonic Works ; & several musical text books. *Ctr* : Various musical papers. *s.s* : Composition, etc. *a* : c/o Midland Bank Ltd, Bideford, Devon.

LEE, Helen. See Wilford, Dorothea Louise.

LEE, Herbert. Mem Counc J.I. *n.a* : Ch Repres Hull Yorkshire Post. *a* : 147 Park Av, Hull.

LEE, J. L. *b* : Dundee 1876. *e* : Dundee Sch, Slade Sch of Art. *m* : Dorothy Havercroft Barrie, A.R.A.M. Journalist & Artist. *n.a* : Dundee Courier 1904—06, Dundee Advertiser '09—14, Dly Chron & News Chron '19—46. *Publ* : Ballads of Battle ; Work-a-Day Warriors ; A Captive at Carlsruhe ; Tales o' Our Town ; Fra Lippo Lippi. *Ctr* : Spectator, Nation, Manch Guardian, etc. *s.s* : Art, Theatre, Scot Subjects, Poetry, etc. *w.s* : 1914—19. *a* : 4 Argyle Pl, Thomson St, Dundee.

LEE, Jennie, M.A., LL.B., M.P. *b* : Lochgelly, Fife 1904. *e* : Cowdenbeath & Edin Univ. *m* : Rt Hon Aneurin Bevan, M.P. (Lab) Cannock Div Staffs 1945—. Journalist & Lecturer, Crossed America 5 times & Soviet Russia 3 times also many visits to France & Austria. *n.a* : Director of Tribune 1945—. *Publ* : To-morrow is a New Day ; This Great Journey ; Our Ally Russia. *Ctr* : Tribune. *a* : 23 Cliveden Pl, London, S.W.1.

LEE, John Alexander, D.C.M. *b* : Dunedin, N.Z. 1891. *e* : Public Sch. *m* : Marie Ethel Guy. *s* : 3. Publisher, Publicist. *n.a* : Prop-Mang John A. Lee's Weekly 1940 —47, Assoc Ed Protestant New York '36—. *Publ* : Children of the Poor ; Socialism in New Zealand ; Civilian into Soldier ; Shining with the Shiner ; The Hunted ; The Yanks are Coming ; I Fight for New Zealand ; etc. *s.s* : Sociology, Politics, Life in New Zealand, Anti-Clericalism. *Rec* : Gardening, writing, dancing, rugby league football. *c* : P.E.N. *a* : Box 51, Newton, Auckland, New Zealand. *T* : 81799.

LEE, John Robert, O.B.E. Consulting Surg. *c.t* : Australian Med Journ, B.M.J. *a* : 8 Harley St, W.1. *t* : Langham 4360.

LEE, KATHARINE (pen name) : see Jenner, Katharine Lee.

LEE, Laurie. *b* : Stroud, Glos 1914. *e* : Slade Council & Stroud Central Sch. Script Writer, Crown Film Unit 1941—43, Green Park Film Unit '46—47. *n.a* : Ed Publ Division M.of I. *Publ* : The Sun My Monument ; The Bloom of Candles (Poems) ; Land at War ; Official Story of British Farming ; etc. *Ctr* : Horizon, Penguin New Writing, New Writing & Daylight, Orion, The Listener, Geog Magazine, New Statesman & Nation. *Rec* : Music, woodcutting, drawing. *c* : P.E.N. *a* : c/o John Lehmann Ltd, 31 Egerton Cresc, London, S.W.3.

LEE, Norman. *b* : South Norwood 1900. *m* : Bobbie Hunter. *s* : 3. Author, Film Director, Mem Screen Writers Assoc. *Publ* : A Film is Born ; Landlubbers Log ; My Personal Log ; Action on the Rolling Road ; The Hoodoo Ship ; The Terrified Village ; Amateur Theatre ; Deputy Wife ; I Want to go to Sea ; etc. *Ctr* : Theatre & Cinema, The Screen Writer (U.S.A.). *s.s* : Thrillers & Adventure Stories. *Rec* : Writing, films, theatre, travel. *c* : Rotary. *a* : c/o Jasmine Chatterton, 20 Princes Gate, Kensington, London, S.W.7.

LEE, Robert. *b* : Middlesborough 1872. *e* : Elem & Priv Sch. *m* : Elizabeth Taylor. Sec & Gen Supt Manch City Missn, Sec Manch Keswick. *Publ* : The Outlined Bible (14th edn trans into Japanese, Russian & German) ; The Outlined John ; The Outlined Acts ; The Outlined Romans ; The Outlined Galatians ; The Outlined Hebrews ; Handfuls on Purpose (Vol. XI & XII) ; The Mildmay Bible Study Book (6 Vols) ; etc. *s.s* : Witness, Bible Student (India), etc. *s.s* : Devotional Books. *Rec* : Gardening. *a* : 3 St Ann's Churchyard, Manchester 2. *T* : Blackfriars 4057.

LEE, Walter. *b* : Todmorden 1883. *e* : Newport (I.W.) G.S., Merchant Venturers Bristol & Hartley Col Southampton. *m* : Gwladys Mary Duggan. *s* : 1. Journalist. *n.a* : Todmorden Advertiser 1905—14, Industrial Information Lon '19—23, Eastern Daily Press '23—. War Service '14—19 (Des). *Rec* : Lawn tennis. *a* : Langfield, Sprowston, Norwich.

LEE HOLLAND, Hetty, M.A.(Dub). *b*: Highgate 1878. *e*: N. Ldn Collegiate Sch & Newnham Col Cam. *m*: Richard Holland, C.B.E. Organiser in Religious Teaching to National Society. *n.a*: Sub-Ed School Guardian, Ed Child Life. *Publ*: Present Day Problems in Religious Teaching; Half Hours in Old Testament Library Lessons on Life of Our Lord; The Sunday Kindergarten; New Stories in Sunday Kindergarten. *c.t*: School Guardian, New Chronicle. *s.s*: Religious education. Examiner etc to Nat Froebel Union. *Rec*: Music & painting. *a*: 21 St Peter St, S.W.1. & Park Corner Heathfield, Sussex.

LEE-WOLF, Rev. Bertram, M.A., B.Sc., B.D., Ph.D. *b*: Bradford Yorks. *e*: United Coll Bradford, Univs of Edinburgh, Halle, Marburg & Berlin. *m*: Margaret Alice Jones. *s*: 2. *d*: 1. Univ Extension Lect London & Oxford 1932—. *Publ*: The Authority of Jesus; The Background of the Gospel; Introduction to the New Testament for Teachers; (Translations from German), Lietzmann's, Beginnings of the Christian Church, Founding of the Church Universal, From Constantine to Julian, & Dibelius's From Tradition to Gospel. *s.s*: Theology, Ancient History, Reformation Period. *c*: Nat Lib. *a*: Edge Wood, Woodside Rd, Beaconsfield, Buckinghamshire.

LEECH, Lt.-Col. Arthur Graves, B.A., LL.B., LL.D.(T.C.D.), D.S.O. *b*: Dublin 1877. *e*: St Columba's Col Rathfarnham. Army (ret). *Publ*: The Laws & Usages of War on Land (1906). *c.t*: Service Journ's. *s.s*: Internat law. *Rec*: Riding, golf. *a*: Brightmere, Kelsale, Saxmundham. *t*: Yoxford 20.

LEECH, Ernest Bosdin, M.A., M.D., F.R.C.P. *b*: Stretford 1875. *e*: Cheltenham Coll, Christ's Coll Camb & Victoria Univ Manch. *m*: Mary Barker. *d*: 2. Hon Physician Manch Roy Infirmary. *Publ*: Early Medicine & Quackery in Lancashire; Medicine in the Provinces in England; Surnames in Lancashire; A Note on Early Liverpool Doctors & Ship's Surgeons; Picturesque Episodes of Manchester Medical History; Parish Registers of Lancashire; Some Impressions of the Continent, Medical & Otherwise; The Leech Family in Ashton-under-Lyne. *a*: Chadlington Hse, Daisy Bank Rd, Victoria Pk, Manchester 14. *T*: Rusholme 1059.

LEECH, George William, R.I. *b*: London 1894. *e*: Emanuel Sc, Wandsworth Common, Putney & Lambeth Scs of Art. *m*: Helen Priestley. *s*: 2. Painter, designer. *n.a*: Art Ed, Strand Mag '30—. *s.s*: Figure & landscape. Exhibitor, R.A. Instructor, Heatherley's Sc of Fine Art. *c*: Savage, London Sketch. *a*: 6 New Court, Carey St, W.C.2. *t*: Holborn 3839.

LEECH, Joseph. *b*: Wigan 1882. *e*: New Jerusalem, Wigan. *m*: Maude Willgoose. Newsp Editor. *n.a*: Wigan Examiner 1903—, Ed '29—, Mem N.U.J., Belgian Croix de Guerre. *Publ*: History of Wigan Rugby Football Club (Cherry & White); Fifty Years of Association Football in Wigan. *c.t*: Dly Mail, Lancs Dly Post, Kemsley Newsps, L'pool Echo, Yorks Ev News, etc. *s.s*: Rugby Football, Dramatic Criticism. *w.s*: 4 yrs. *Rec*: Golf, bridge. *a*: 20 Milton Grove, Wigan. *T*: 3574.

LEEN, Rev. Edward, M.A., D.D. *b*: Abbeyfeale, Co Limerick 1885. *e*: Rockwell Col Cashel. Royal & Nat Univs Ireland, Gregorian Univ Rome. Prof of Philosophy. *c.t*: Irish Indep, Irish Ecclesiastical Record, etc. *s.s*: Education. *a*: Blackrock College, Dublin. *t*: Blackrock 27.

LEENEY, Osmond Harold, F.R.S.A. *b*: Hove 1874. *e*: Brighton G.S. *m*: Florence Henrietta Stringer. Lect & Bookseller. *c.t*: Daily Mail, Chambers's Journ, Sussex Archæ Soc Coll, Brighton Herald, etc. *s.s*: Archt, Mediæval Art. Extensive travel. War Service 1918/19. *Rec*: Pedal cycling, archæ. *a*: Ivydene, Church Lane, Southwick, Sussex.

LEES, Charles Herbert, D.Sc(M/C), F.R.S., F.InstPhy. *b*: Oldham 1864. *e*: Priv Sc & Univs of M/C, Lon & Strasburg. *m*: Evelyn May Savidge. *s*: 3. *d*: 2. Prof Emeritus of Physics Lon Univ. *Publ*: Intermediate Practical Physics; Exercises in Practical Physics. *c t*: Manchester Guardian, Nature, Philosophical Mag, etc. *s.s*: Heat, elec. On Govt Cmts Air Inventions Cmt 1917-20. Food Investigation Bd Eng Cmt '18–. Safety in Mines Research Bd '23-33. Road Research Bd '33–. Pres Phys Soc '18–20. Vice-Princ E. Lon Col, Univ of Lon '17–30. Asst Dir Phys Lab's Univ of M/C '00–06. *Rec*: Handicrafts, gardening. *a*: Greenacres, Dry Hill Rd, Tonbridge, Kent.

LEES, DAVID: surgeon; *b*. Tarbolton, Scotland, Feb., 1881; *s*. Robert (M.R.C.V.S.) and Agnes (Drennan) L.; educ. Ayr (Scotland) Acad., Edinburgh Univ. DEGREES: M.A., M.B., ChB., F.R.C.S., M.R.C.P., F.R.C.P., D.P.H.; *m*. Effie Laurie Brechin, 1919. AUTHOR: Vaccine Therapy in Gonorrhoea, 1920; Keratodermia, 1922; Clinical Chapters on Gonorrhoea (with Dr. D. Thomson), 1922; Intolerance to Arsenobenzol and its Derivatives, 1923; The Diagnosis and Treatment of Venereal Diseases, for Students and Practitioners, 1927 (2nd edit.), 1931; Chapters on Gonorrhoea (Walton's Surgical Diagnosis), 1929. Contributor to Edinburgh Med. Journ., British Med. Journ., Brit. Journ. of Venereal Diseases. General character of writing: scientific, medical. Army service in Great War, 1915-19; awarded D.S.O., 1917; Mentioned in dispatches, 1918; Fellow Edinburgh Obstetrical Soc.; Fellow Edinburgh Pathological Club; mem. Edinburgh Medico-Chirurgical Soc.; Pres. Med. Soc. for Study of Venereal Diseases; Surg. in chg. Venereal Diseases, Royal Infirmary, Edinburgh; Lctrer. on Venereal Diseases, Univ. Edinburgh; Dir. V. D. dept. Edinburgh Corp. Pub. Health Serv.; chmn. Med. Advisory Bd., Brit. Social Hygiene Council. Relig. denom., Presbyterian. CLUBS: Edinburgh University Union, Caledonian United Service. OFFICE: 21 Coates Gardens, Edinburgh, Scotland.

LEES, Iain C. See Carvel, John Lees.

LEES, John Morton. See Middleton, Ellis.

LEES-SMITH, Hastings Bertrand, M.A.(Oxon), D.Sc(Lon), P.C. *b*: India 1878. *e*: Aldenham, R.M.C. Woolwich, Queen's Col Oxf. *m*: Joyce Eleanor Holman. *s*: 2. Reader, Lon Univ. *n.a*: Ex-Asst Ed Economic Journ. *Publ*: India & the Tariff Problem; Studies in Indian Economics; The Insurance Act; Guide to Parliamentary Papers; Second Chambers in Theory & Practice. *c.t*: Econ Journ, Spectator, Current History. *s.s*: Publ admin. *a*: 77 Corringham Rd, N.W.11. *t*: Speedwell 1000.

LEES, William. *e*: Greenacres G.S. & M/C Univ. *n.a*: Fiction Feature Series Ed Allied N/p's Ltd 1923—. Fiction Ed E. Hulton & Co Ltd '15—23. *s.s*: Fiction, biography travel books, anything that will serialise successfully in a n/p. *a*: Allied N/p's, Ltd, 200 Grays Inn Rd, W.C. *t*: Museum 9841.

LEESON, Albert Edward, B.Sc (Eng). *b*: Coventry. *e*: King's Col Lon. Schoolmaster. *Publ*: The Principles of Educational Craftwork in Wood & Metal (1931). *s.s*: Art & crafts. *Rec*: Agricultural pursuits. *a*: 68 Clifton Rd, Rugby.

LEESON, Harold Howard, M.C. *b*: Brighton, Sussex 1881. *e*: St Paul's Sch London, St George's Hosp. *m*: Mary Mabel Thompson-Grey. *s*: 1. Lt-Col R.A.M.C. (ret). *Publ*: Your Doctor of the Future; State Medicine or What; Medicine in the Melting Pot; The Experiences of a Locum. *Ctr* : Lancet, Medical World, Times. *s.s* : Development of the Nat Health Services, Conditions of General Practice in England. *Rec* : Sailing, tennis, golf. *c* : R.A.C. *w.s* : R.A.M.C. World Wars I & II. *a* : 50 Alexandra Rd, Worthing, Sussex. *T* : Worthing 2627.

LEETE, Frederick Deland, L.H.D., LL.D. *b* : Avon, N.Y. 1866. *e* : Syracuse Univ. *m* : Jeanette G. Fuller. *s* : 1. *d* : 2. Bishop of the Methodist Church. *Publ* : Christianity in Science ; Christian Brotherhoods ; Palestine, Peoples & Scenery ; Palestine, Land of the Light ; New Testament Windows ; The De Land Family in America ; Adventures of a Travelling Preacher ; Skyward—A Book of Horizons. *Ctr* : Various religious papers & mags. *s.s* : Religion, Science, Hist, Poetry. *a* : 366 East 45th St, Indianapolis, Indiana, U.S.A.

LE FANU, Thomas Philip, C.B. *b* : Dublin 1858. *e* : Haileybury & Trin Col Cam. *m* : Florence Mabel Sullivan. *s* : 1. *d* : 1. Ex-Commssr of Publ Works in Ireland. *Publ* : Registers of the French Nonconformist Churches of Dublin; Register of the French Church of Portarlington; Memoir of the Le Fanu Family. *c.t* : Proc Huguenot Soc, Proc R.I.A., Journ Roy Soc of Antiquaries of Ireland, etc. *s.s* : The Huguenots in Ireland. *c* : Savile. *a* : Abington, Bray, Ireland.

LEFCOPARIDIS, Xeno. *b* : Constantinople 1898. Editor. *Publ* : Yassoumis ; Jeunesse ; Horizons. *n.a* : Dirige revue mensuelle, Les Balkans et maison d'éditions Flamma. *c* : P.E.N. *a* : P.E.N. Club, Centre d'Athènes.

Le FEVRE, FELICITÉ (pen name) : see **Smith-Masters, Margaret.**

LEFEVRE, Laura Zenobia (see **BIRD, Zenobia**). *b* : Strasburg, Pennsylvania. *e* : Public Schs & Priv. Writer. *n.a* : Sunday School Times, Correspondence Ed 1921—45, Review Ed '25—45. *Ctr* : Sunday Sch Times, etc. *s.s* : Fiction Writing, Book Reviewing. *Rec* : Reading, travel. *a* : 120 Nevin St, Lancaster, Pennsylvania, U.S.A. *T* : Lancaster 2-0780.

LE FLEMING, Ernest Kaye, M.A., M.B., B.C. (Cantab), M.D., M.R.C.S., L.R.C.P. *b* : Tonbridge 1872. *e* : Tonbridge Sc, Cam Univ, St George's Hosp & T.C.D. *m* : Florence Murton Beeching. *s* : 2. *c.t* : B.M.J., Lancet, Med Annual. *s.s* : Medico-polit. Mem (direct election) Gen Med Counc. Mem Counc B.M.A. Chm Repres Body B.M.A. 1931—34. Chm Nutrition Cmt B.M.A. report of '34. *Rec* : Golf. *c* : Roy Socs, Oxf & Cam Golfing, etc. *a* : St Margarets, Wimborne, Dorset. *t* : 33.

LEFRANC, Abel Jules Maurice. *b* : Elincourt Ste Marguerite, Oise, France 1863. *e* : Petit Seminaire de Noyon, Ecole des Chastes, Ecole Pratique des Hautes Etudes. *m* : Jeanne Vauthier. *s* : 2. *d* : 2. Prof French Language & Lit Coll de France, Prof Ecole des Hautes Etudes Sorbonne, Comm de la Legion d'honneur, Off de l'Ordre de Leopold Belgique. *Publ* : Oeuvres de Francois Rabelais ; Les Navigations de Pantagruel ; La Jeunesse de Calvin ; Les Dernieres Poemes de Marguerite de Navarre ; Histoire du College de France ; Maurice de Guerin ; Sous le Masque de William Shakespeare ; etc. *s.s* : Histoire de la Renaissance en France 6me Siecle, Religious Hist of 16th Cent, Shakespearean Theatre & Queries. *Rec* : Walking, ancient books. *a* : Rue Denfert-Rochereau 38 bis, Paris V. *T* : Odeon 04-53.

LEFROY, Walter John Magrath. *b* : Guernsey 1870. *e* : R.N., Giggleswick & Queen's Oxf. *m* : Ella Christina Michell. Journalist. *n.a* : Founded & Ed Brit Columbia Review '97, Founded & Ed Canada, Canada To-day & Canadian Trade Journals. *Rec* : Fishing, shooting. *c* : Savage, Brit Empire. *a* : 3 Tregunter Rd, The Boltons, S.W.10 & 9 Northumberland Av, W.C.2.

LEFTWICH, Bertram Ralph, M.B.E., F.S.A., F.R.Hist.S. *b* : London 1879. *e* : City of Lond Sch. *m* : Elsie Smith. *s* : 4. *d* : 2. Librarian H.M. Board of Customs & Excise (ret). *Publ* : A History of the Excise ; Pageant of Tower Hill (with Rev P. B. Clayton) ; Tower Hill Regained ; Short History & Guide to St Swithin, London Stone ; Short History & Guide to St Ethelburga Bishopgate ; The Church & Parish of St Nicholas, Deptford ; Burns & The Excise ; Later History & Administration of the Customs Revenue in England (1671—1814). *Ctr* : Times, Ency Brit. *s.s* : Mediæval History of England, particularly London area. *Rec* : Historical & antiquarian research. *a* : 1 The Avenue, High Barnet, Herts. *T* : Barnet 3455.

LEFTWICH, Joseph. *b* : Zutphen, Holland 1892. *e* : Elem Sch Lond. *m* : Sala Bochenek. *d* : 1. Author & Journalist. *n.a* : South African Jewish Times 1939—, Yediot Achranot Palestine '45—, Ed Jewish Telegraphic Agency '21—36. *Publ* : Visroel ; What will happen to the Jews ; Yiddish Language & Literature (with Prof Birnbaum) ; The Tragedy of Antisemitism (with A. K. Chesterton) ; (Poetry) Along the Years ; Golden Peacock. *Ctr* : Chambers's Ency, Valentine's Jewish Ency. *s.s* : Jewish. *a* : 2 Winchester Pl, Highgate, London, N.6. *T* : Mountview 6580.

LE GALLIENNE, Richard. *Publ* : inc From a Paris Garret ; The Beautiful Lie of Rome ; Painted Shadows ; Pieces of Eight ; The Romantic 90's ; etc.

LEGARD, Brig.-Gen. D'Arcy, C.M.G., D.S.O. Cavalry Officer. *Publ*: Cavalry on Service, trans from German of General von Pelet-Narbonne. *a* : Maes Ct, Tenbury, Worc. *t* : Newnham Bridge 3.

LEGGE, Mary Dominica, M.A., B.Litt., F.R.Hist.S. *b* : London 1905. *e* : L'pool Coll Huyton, Somerville Coll Oxf. Lect in French Univ of Edin. *n.a* : Ed Selden Society. *Publ* : Anglo-Norman Letters & Petitions ; The Year Book of 10 Edward II (with Sir William Holdsworth) ; Le Roman de Balain. *Ctr* : Mod Language Rev, Medium Aevum, History, Eng His Rev, Arthuriana, French Studies. *s.s* : Anglo-Norman (esp Law-French), Old French Languages & Lit. *Rec* : Walking, fencing, music. *c* : Univ Women's, Overseas, Eng Speaking Union. *a* : University of Edinburgh.

LEGGE, Rev. Robert George. *b* : London 1887. *e* : Priv & King's Coll London. *m* : Elsie Violet Smith. *s* : 2. *d* : 3. Mem Brit Inst Philos, Council Philos Soc of Eng, Council of Personalist Group, Exec of Nat Trade Union Club. *Publ* : Builders' Accounts & Costs ; Christian Theism in Contemporary Thought ; Seer, Scribe & Sage. *Ctr* : The Builder. *s.s* : Philos, Judaism. *a* : St George's Vicarage, Brentford, Middlesex. *T* : Ealing 2940.

LEGGETT, Bernard John, M.R.C.S., L.R.C.P., M.I.E.E., F.R.S.M. *b* : London 1890. *e* : West Ham Tech Coll, Lond Hosp Med Coll & Berlin. *m* : Amy Emilie Bessie Clarke. *s* : 1. *d* : 2. Radiological Consultant (Medical). *Publ* : Wireless Telegraphy ; Theory & Practice of Radiology. *Ctr* : Journ Inst Elect Engs & other med & elect journs. *s.s* : Radiology (medical, physical, engineering & historical). *w.s* : Lieut R.E. (ret) & O i/c 1st Wireless Corps B.E.F. 1916. *Rec* : Collecting books on radiology, shooting. *a* : 353 Romford Rd, Forest Gate, London, E.7. *T* : Maryland 3460.

LEGGETT, Harry W. *b* : London 1888. Editor. *n.a* : Sub-Ed Financial Times 1912—20, Leader Writer Investors Chronicle '20—21, Ed Grand Magazine '27—39 & Ironmongers Weekly '45—. *Publ* : The Idea in Fiction ; Under Suspicion ; Joan Peterson. *s.s* : Economic & Technical Questions, Magazine Fiction. *Rec* : Yachting. *a* : Flat D, 119 Cromwell Rd, London, S.W.7. *T* : Frobisher 0148.

LE GRAND, Ernest Gabriel. *b*: France 1881. *e*: College d'Airanche, Université de Rennes. *m*: Alice Robin. *s*: 3. *d*: 1. Senr Mod Langs Master. *Publ*: Le Français Rendu Plus Facile; The Certificate Unseen Translation; Grammar Composition; etc. *s.s*: Modern French. Lecturer. Officier d'Académie Officier d'Instruction Publique. *a*: Bradfield Col, Berks.

LEHMANN. Beatrix Alice. *b*: Bourne End 1903. *e*: Priv. Actress & Authoress. *Publ*: But Wisdom Lingers ('32); Rumour of Heaven ('34). 10 y Stage Work. *Rec*: Swimming, riding. *c*: Brit Actor's Equity Assoc. *a*: 26 St Georges Sq, S.W.1. *t*: Victoria 1549.

LEHMANN, John. *b*: Bourne End 1907. *e*: Eton (K.S.), Trinity Col Cam. *Publ*: A Garden Revisited & Other Poems ('31); The Noise of History ('34); Jt-Ed The Year's Poetry. *c.t*: Listener, New Statesman & Nation, New Stories, etc. *s.s*: Poetry. *Rec*: Prose. *a*: Fieldhead, Bourne End, Bucks.

LEHMANN, John Frederick. *b*: Bourne End, Bucks 1907. *e*: Eton & Trinity Coll Camb. Author, Publisher & Editor. *n.a*: Founder & Ed New Writing, Adv-Ed Geographical Mag 1941—45, Partner & Gen Man The Hogarth Press '38—46, Chrm & Mang Dir John Lehmann Ltd '46—. *Publ*: (Poetry) A Garden Revisited; The Noise of History; Forty Poems; The Sphere of Glass; (Travel) Prometheus & the Bolsheviks; Down River; (Novel) Evil was Abroad; (Crit) New-Writing in Europe; (Anthologies) Poems from New Writing; Shelley in Italy. *Rec*: Aquatic & literary. *c*: Athenæum, Bath, Allies, Eton Viking. *a*: 31 Egerton Cresc, London, S.W.3.

LEHMANN, Lotte. *b*: Perleberg, Germany. Singer (Concert, Opera, Radio). *Publ*: More than Singing; Midway in My Song; Eternal Flight. *s.s*: Interpretation of Song & Opera. *Rec*: Painting, etching, pottery. *a*: Hope Ranch, Santa Barbara, California, U.S.A.

LEHMANN, Rosamond Nina. *b*: Bourne End. *e*: Priv & Girton Coll Camb. *m*: Wogan Philipps. *s*: 1. *d*: 1. *Publ*: Dusty Answer; A Note in Music; Invitation to the Waltz; The Weather in the Streets; The Ballad & The Source; The Gypsy's Baby; Hogarth Letters Series; A Letter to a Sister. *c*: Inc Soc Authors, Playwrights & Composers. *a*: Manor Hse, Little Wittenham, Abingdon, Berks. *T*: Clifton Hampden 8.

LEHMKLHL, H. K. *b*: Bergen 1887. *e*: Univ Leipzig. *m*: Ellen Meier. *s*: 1. Journalist. *n.a*: Lon Corr Aftenposten (Oslo), Dir Bergenske (Lon), B & N Line Roy Mail Ltd. *Rec*: Ski-ing. *c*: Savile & Press. *a*: Bergen Hse, 22/25 St Mary Axe, E.C.2.

LEHRBURGER, Egon (see **LARSEN, Egon** & **HELBURNE, Roger G.**). *b*: Munich 1904. *e*: Sec Sch Munich. *m*: Ursula Burschell-Lippmann. *s*: 1. Writer & Author, Screenwriter, Journalist. *s.s*: Films, Popular Science. *Rec*: Tennis, sailing. *c*: P.E.N. *a*: 4 Stirling Mans, Canfield Gdns, London, N.W.6. *T*: Maida Vale 4448.

LEIGH, Gertrude Anne. *b*: Tettenhall, Staffs. Writer. *Publ*: Tasso and Eleonora (drama with hist notes, 1912); New Light on the Youth of Dante; The Passing of Beatrice; A Study in the Heterodoxy of Dante; The Story of Winchelsea Church (privately publ & now in 7th edn). *c.t*: Quart Review, Ch Quart Review. *s.s*: Life & works of Dante Alighieri, the hist & religious problems of the 13th & 14th centuries. *a*: Attewall, Winchelsea, Sussex.

LEIGH, James. Journalist. *n.a*: Ed Prediction. *Publ*: Manual & Who's Who of Spiritualism & Psychical Research; Fortune-Telling. *s.s*: The Ocult. *a*: 24 Store St, London, W.C.1. *T*: Museum 9792.

LEIGH, Thomas Egerton. *b*: Abergele 1910. *e*: Abergele Gr Sch. *m*: S. A. Fell. *s*: 1. *d*: 1. Journalist, Mem N.U.J. *n.a*: Former Staff Rep Abergele Times, Staff Rep Cheshire Observer & Chester Courant 1946—. *Publ*: North Wales Football Annual (Founder & Ed). *Ctr*: Several national daily, weekly, newspapers & periodicals. *s.s*: Nth Wales Soccer & Cricket. *Rec*: Philately, local government, soccer. *a*: Clifton, Clwyd Ave, Abergele, Nth Wales; & c/o Cheshire Observer & Chester Courant, The Cross, Chester. *T*: Chester 31, Abergele 70.

LEIGH, Ursula. See Gwynn, Ursula Grace.

LEIGH, W. RYE (pen name): see Riley, Willie.

LEIGHTON, Clare. *e*: Priv & Slade Sch. Wood Engraver & Author, Fellow Roy Soc of Painters, Architects & Engravers. *Publ*: The Farmer's Year; Woodcuts & Wood Engraving; The Wood that Came Back; The Musical Box; Four Hedges; Country Matters; Sometime, Never; Southern Harvest. *s.s*: Country, Children's Books, Engraving. *a*: 37 Belsize Pk Gdns, London. N.W.3.

LEIGHTON, George Ross. *b*: Methol, N.Y. 1902. *e*: Phillips Exeter Acad, Harvard Coll. *m*: Josephine Gund. *s*: 1. Writer & Editor. *n.a*: Staff, Asst Ed, Assoc Ed Harper's Mag 1932—44. *Publ*: Five Cities; The Wind That Swept Mexico (in collab). *Ctr*: New Yorker, American Mercury, Atlantic Monthly, New York Times Mag, Harper's. *a*: 354 East 51 St, New York City, U.S.A. *T*: Plaza 3-0468.

LEIGHTON, Gerald Bowley, O.B.E. *b*: Bispham 1868. *e*: Nelson Coll N.Z., Manch Gr Sch, Edinburgh Univ. *m*: Clara Gordon. *d*: 1. Prof of Pathology, Roy (Dick) Vet Coll Edinburgh 1903—13, Med Off Dept of Health for Scotland '13—33, Insp of Food Contracts to H.M. Admiralty & War Office '13—19, wrote the official report of the Loch Maree Tragedy (deaths from Botulism). *Publ*: Principle & Practice of Meat Inspection; The Meat Industry & Meat Inspection; Botulism; British Serpents; British Lizards; Huxley—his life & work; Embryology; The Greatest Life. *Ctr*: Harmsworth Self-Educator. *s.s*: Public Health Administration (Foods), Biology. *Rec*: Gardening. *w.s*: Lt-Col R.A.S.C. 1913—19. *a*: Sharston, Port Lefaigue, Maughold, Isle of Man.

LEIGHTON, Joseph Alexander, B.A., LL.D., B.D., Ph.D. *b*: Caledon, Ontario, Canada 1870. *e*: Trin Coll Toronto, Episcopal Theol Sch Harvard, Univs of Cornell, Tuebingen, Berlin & Erlangen. *m*: (1) Victoria Paul, (2) Helan Gager Brown. *s*: 2. Prof & Head of Dept of Philosophy Ohio State Univ. *Publ*: Man & the Cosmos; Social Philosophies in Conflict; The Field of Philosophy; The Individual & the Social Order; Religion & the Mind of To-Day; Typical Modern Conceptions of God; Jesus Christ & the Civilization of To-Day; (in collab) Contemporary American Philosophy; Contemporary Idealism in America. *Ctr*: Various Scholarly Publs. *s.s*: Philosophy, Ethics & Sociology, Religion, Cultural Hist. *Rec*: Poetry, hist, travel, golf, fishing. *a*: 817 Oxford St, Worthington, Ohio, U.S.A. *T*: Columbus FR-2-5118.

LEIGHTON, Margaret, A.B. *b*: Oberlin, Ohio, U.S.A. *e*: Public Schs Cambridge Massachusetts, Priv Schs in Paris, Lucerne & Lausanne, Radcliffe Coll Camb Mass. *m*: James Herbert Leighton. *s*: 2. *d*: 2. Writer. *Publ*: The Singing Cave; Twelve Bright Trumpets; The Secret of the Old House; The Secret of the Closed

Gate. *Ctr*: American Girl, Child Life, Classmate, etc. *s.s*: Books for Boys & Girls. *c*: P.E.N., Santa Monica Authors. *a*: 226 Palisades Ave, Santa Monica, California, U.S.A. *T*: Santa Monica 56243.

LEIGHTON, MARIE CONNOR: author; *b*. Clifton, Gloucestershire, Eng.; *d*. Capt. James Nenon Connor, 87th Foot) and Elizabeth (Trelawney) Connor; *educ*. in France and at Tunbridge Wells (Eng.); *m*. Robert Leighton. AUTHOR: A Morganatic Marriage; Husband and Wife; The Heart's Awakening; The Harvest of Sin (new edition, 1931); Convict 99 (Daily Mail); Michael Dred, Detective; In God's Good Time; A Napoleon of the Press; Hush Money, 1901; Vengeance is Mine, 1902; Was She Worth It? 1903; The Amazing Verdict, 1904; Sealed Lips, 1907; An Eye for an Eye, 1907; Her Ladyship's Silence, 1907; Money, 1909; Convict 413 L, 1910; Joan Mar, 1910; Her Convict Husband, 1911; Greed, 1911; Builders of Ships, 1911; Justice, 1911; The Triangle, 1911; The Missing Miss Randolph, 1912; Black Silence, 1913; Under the Broad Arroe, 1914; The Fires of Love, 1915; The Man Who Knew All; Boy of My Heart (autobiographical war book, pub. anonymously), 1916; Human Nature; The Story of a Great Sin; Dark Peril; The Mystery of the Three Fingers; The Shame of Silence, 1917; The Baked Bread, 1917; (published anonymously): The Letters of an Expectant Grandmother, 1918; (published anonymously): The Stolen Honeymoon, 1920; The Crooked Cat; Lady Highmoor's Daughter. Contributor to many newspapers and mags. General character of writing: fiction. CLUB: After Dinner Club of 1920. HOME: The Garth, Hockerrill Park, Bishop's Stortford, Herts, Eng.

LEIPER, Robert Thomson, M.D., D.Sc, F.R.S. Prof of Helminthology in the Univ Lon. *n.a*: Founder & Ed Journ of Helminthology & Helminthological Abstracts. *Publ*: Researches on Egyptian Bilharziases. *c.t*: Various. *a*: Lon Sc of Hygiene & Tropical Medicine, Keppel St, Lon, W.C. *t*: Museum 3041.

LEIPOLDT, Christian Frederic Louis, F.R.C.S., Hon D.Lit (Witwatersrand). *b*: Cape Colony S.A. 1880. *e*: Priv & Graz Univ. *s*: 1 (adop). Medical Practitioner. *n.a*: Ed S.A. News Cape Town 1900—02, Hosp Lon '04—11, Transvaal Med Journ '17—26, Co-Ed Sc Hygiene, Die Volkstem, Ed S.A. Med J. '26. Asst Sc M.O. L.C.C. Chief Med Inspt Transvaal '14—22. Org Med Insp Cape Province '19. Surg Gen Botha's staff '14—15 (des). *Publ*: Commonsense Dietetics ('11); School Nurse; Oom Gert Vertel (8th edn, '32); 3 vols verse (7th ed '34); 7 novels & vols of essays 8th ed '34) etc. *c.t*: M/C Guardian, Chicago Record, Petit Blue, etc. *s.s*: Children, dietetics, malaria. *Rec*: Billiards, tennis, bridge. One of the pioneers of Afrikaans. Is lect on diseases of children at the Univ Cape Town. Visiting pediatric phys to New Somerset Hosp Cape Town. Local sec Pen Club. *c*: Civil Service, etc. *a*: Arbury, Ascot Rd, Kenilworth, Cape Town. *t*: Wynberg 604.

LEITCH, Charlotte Cecilia Pitcairn. F/L. *n.a*: All Principal Publications in G.B. & U.S.A. '10—. *Publ*: Golf; Golf Simplified; Golf for Girls. *s.s*: Golf. *a*: 1 Tenby Mansions, Nottingham St, W.1. *t*: Welbeck 8652.

LEITCH, John Neil, M.D., M.R.C.P.(Lon), D.P.H., D.T.M. & H.(Eng). *b*: Lon 1897. *e*: Highgate Sc, Lon Univ, St Bart's & Lon Sc of Hyg & Trop Med. Married. Pathologist & Physician. *Publ*: Standard Treatments (1928); Beriberi; Sierra Leone Government; First Steps in Dietetics; Native Remedies & Poisons of West Africa ('34); etc. *s.s*: Dietetics. *a*: 20-22 Chenies St, W.C.1. *t*: Museum 3262.

LEITCH. Mary Sinton. *b*: New York City 1876. *e*: Miss Dana's Sch, Ossining Sch, Smith Coll, Columbia Univ. *m*: John David Leitch. *s*: 1. *d*: 2. Writer. *Publ*: The Coming of the Cross; Love Letters of Bismark (trans); Verse: Spider Architect; From Invisible Mountains; The Waggon & the Star; The Unrisen Morrow; The Unseen Kingdom. *Ctr*: Harper's Monthly, Cornhill, Ladies Home Journ, North American Review, Catholic World, etc. *s.s*: Verse. *Rec*: Swimming, motor trips. *c*: Norfolk Poetry, etc. *a*: Wycherley, Lynnhauen, Virginia, U.S.A. *T*: Norfolk 44838.

LEJEUNE, C. A. *b*: Manchester. *e*: Manch Univ. *m*: M. E. Roffe Thompson. *s*: 1. *n.a*: Film Critic The Observer, The Sketch. *Publ*: Cinema; Chestnuts in Her Lap. *a*: 22 Tudor St, London, E.C.4.

LELEAN, PERCY SAMUEL: professor of hygiene; *b*. Ontario, Can., July, 1871; *s*. William Cox and Annie (Furse) L.; *educ*. Hart House (Cornwall, Eng.), St. Mary's Hospital (London). DEGREES: F.R.C.S., L.R.C.P., D.P.H.; *m*. Mary Ellen Gillam, June 18, 1902. AUTHOR: Sanitation in War, 1915. General character of writing: medical. Late Brevet-Col. Royal Army, M.C.; late Prof. Military Hygiene, London, Univ. Relig. faith, Protestant. CLUB: University. OFFICE: Edinburgh University. HOME: 2 Barnton Loan, Edinburgh, Scotland.

LE LIEVRE, Abraham. *b*: Jersey 1865. *e*: Oxenford Hse Sc Jersey. *m*: Amy Jane Harding. *s*: 1. *d*: 3. Journalist. *Publ*: Protestant's Treasury (1911). *c.t*: Princ n/ps. *s.s*: Protestantism. *a*: 151 Ilford Lane, Ilford.

LEMAY, Alan, Ph.B. *b*: Indianapolis, Indiana 1899. *e*: Univ of Chicago. *m*: (1) Esther Skinner, (2) Arlene Hoffman. *s*: 2. *d*: 2. Writer. *Publ*: Old Father of Waters; Pelican Coast; Painted Ponies; Bug Eye; Cattle Kingdom; Useless Cowboy; Empire for a Lady; Winter Range. *Ctr*: Colliers, Sat Ev Post, Cosmopolitan, True, etc. *s.s*: Americana. *Rec*: Flying, polo. *a*: 12735 Hanover St, Los Angeles 24, California, U.S.A. *T*: Arizona 3-5722.

LE MESURIER, Lt.-Col. Herbert Grenville, C.I.E. *Publ*: English Ancestors of Epes Sargent; Pattern & Patchwork; (in press) C.O.D. & P.O.D. *s.s*: Lexicography & crosswords. *a*: 4 Barnfield Av, Exmouth.

LE MESURIER, Lilian, O.B.E. *b*: Dublin 1873. *e*: Lond Sch of Econ. *m*: Major Eugene Le Mesurier (dec'd). *s*: 1. Author, formerly worked for the Home Office (Prisons Commr) in Boys Prisons. *Publ*: Common Sense Economics; Boys in Trouble; The Open Way (with James Howe); God's Carpet; A Book of Verse; The Socialist Woman's Guide to Intelligence; Handbook of Probation. *Ctr*: Observer, Westminster Gaz, The (Indian) Pioneer, The (Indian) Statesman, The (Indian) N & M Gaz, Challenge, Kotlabos, etc. *s.s*: Sociology, Philosophy, Religion & Psychology. *Rec*: Reading, writing, travelling. *a*: 210 Coleherne Ct, Redcliffe Gdns, London, S.W.5 *T*: Frobisher 6064.

LE MESSURIER, Rev. Ralph Huie. *b*: St John's, Newfoundland 1898. *e*: Bishop Feild Coll St John's, McGill Univ Montreal Canada & Keble Coll Oxf. *m*: Jean McCallum Austin Stevenson. *s*: 1. *d*: 1. Clerk in Holy Orders (ret). *Publ*: The Choice; The Absent Christ; The Inner Circle; The Hidden Life; The Priest & His Servers; Mysterious Motherhood; The Hope of Glory. *Ctr*: Theology, Peace News, New Vision, Reconciliation. *Rec*: Gardening formerly ice hockey, rugby, rowing. *w.s*: Roy Newfoundland Regt 1916—19. *a*: Pentillie, Mevagissey, Cornwall. *T*: Mevagissey 221

LEMON, Robert James. b: Mylor Bridge, Cornwall. m: Alice Rachel Easton. n.a: North Devon Herald 30 y (Chief Reporter). c.t: Lon & prov n/p's & periodicals. Hon Sec Barnstaple & N. Devon Br N.U.J. 19 y. Mem Nat Press Fund & Bristol & W. of England Press Fund. a: 4 Ladysmith Villas, Barnstaple, Devon. t: 6.

LENANTON, Carola Mary A., F.R.S.L., F.R.Hist.S. (see OMAN, Carola). e: Wychwood Sch Oxf. Writer. a: Bride Hall, Welwyn, Hertfordshire. T: Wheathampstead 3160.

LENDON, ALFRED AUSTIN: medical practitioner (retired); b. Maidstone, Kent, Eng., Sept. 23, 1856; s. Edwin and Isabella Ann (Harding) L.; educ. Maidstone Grammar Sch., King's College Sch., University Coll. (London). DEGREES: M.D. (London and Adelaide); m. Lucy Isabel Rymill, O.B.E., 1889 (died). AUTHOR: Clinical Lectures on Hydated Disease of the Lungs, 1902; Nodal Fever, 1905. Contributor to various medical journals; to local newspapers (South Australia). General character of writing: medical. Has researched extensively into the early history, medical especially, of South Australia. Relig. denom., Church of England. CLUBS: Adelaide (South Australia), Authors' (London). HOME: 66 Brougham Place, North Adelaide, South Australia.

LENDRUM, Gwendollyn May. b: Denend, Kirkcaldy 1893. e: Southbank Girl's Sch Kirkcaldy. Writer. n.a: Ed Fife and Angus Annual 1934—35. Ctr: Country Life, Chambers's Jnl, S.M.T. Mag, Scots Mag, Weekly Scotsman, etc. s.s: History, Biography, Short Stories, Character Sketches. Rec: Philately, walking, drama, Old china & antiques of all kinds. w.s: A.T.S. 1939—41, Censorship '42—45, S.S.A.F.A. '45—47. a: Overseas League, Overseas Hse St James', London, S.W.1; or 34 Earlscourt Gdns, London, S.W.5. T: Frobisher 0789.

LENEHAN, John Christopher. b: Longford. e: Marlboro' Training Col Dublin. m: Linda Fletcher. s: 1. Schoolmaster. Publ: The Marked Pistol; The Tunnel Mystery; The Silecroft Case; The Mansfield Mystery; The Masked Blackmailer; Death Dances Thrice; Carnival of Death; etc. c.t: Various. s.s: Criminology, education. Knight of St Columba. c: Nott'm Writers', Long Eaton Cons. a: 49 Acton Rd, Long Eaton, Nott'm.

LE NEVE FOSTER, Peter A., B.A'.(Cantab), A.R.P.S. b: Wilmslow 1903. e: Shrewsbury Sc, Magdalene Col Cam. c.t: Amateur Cine World, Picturegoer, Photographic Journ, etc. s.s: Motion pictures. Visited U.S.A. & U.S.S.R. to study motion-picture production. Rec: Keeping Abyssinian cats, travel. c: Roy Photo Soc, Brit Film Inst, Lon & Amateur Cinema League Inc, N.Y. a: 1 Raynham Av, Didsbury, M/C. t: 2104.

LENEY, Miss L. A. Ophthalmic Surg. a: 5 Duchess St, Portland Pl, W.1.

LENGLEN, Suzanne. e: Inst Massena. Publ: Lawn Tennis for Girls; The Love Game, etc. c.t: Paris Soir, Le Journal Intransigeant. s.s: Tennis. a: 4 Square Jean-Paul Laurens, Paris. t: Aut 7468.

LENGYEL, Emil. b: Budapest 1895. e: Budapest Univ (Doc Juris). m: Livia Dalej. s: 1. Author & University Professor. n.a: Vienna Centres Budapest Newsps 1919—21, U.S. Corres Cent European newsps '21—25, Spec Corres N.Y. Times '25—41, Asst Prof Education N.Y. Univ Sch of Education '42—47 & Assoc Prof '47—. Publ: Millions of Dictators; Hitler; The Danube; Siberia; America's Role in World Affairs; Turkey; Dakar; The Cauldron Boils; Cattle Car Express; New Deal in Europe; etc. Ctr: N.Y. Her Trib, Nation (N.Y.), Sat Rev of Lit, Annals of Polit & Soc Sciences. s.s: Political & Economic Conditions of E. & S.E. European Countries. c: P.E.N., Overseas Press, etc. a: 76-15 35 Ave, Jackson Heights, New York. T: Newtown 9-5688.

LENNARD, Reginald Vivian. b: Lightcliffe 1885. e: New Coll. Reader in Econ Hist Univ of Oxf, formerly Sub-Warden Wadham Coll. Publ: Economic Notes on English Agricultural Wages; Rural Northamptonshire under the Commonwealth; (Ed & pt author) Englishmen at Rest & Play; Some Phases of English Leisure 1558 —1714; Democracy: The Threatened Foundations (1941, Germ trans 1946); etc. Ctr: Economic Journal, Eng Hist Rev, History, Journ of Political Economy (Chicago), Edin Review, Contemp Rev, Music & Letters, etc. s.s: Econ Hist. a: Paine's Close, Lower Heyford, nr Oxford, & Wadham College, Oxford.

LENNARD-JONES, Sir John (Edward), K.B.E., F.R.S. Sc.D.(Cantab), D.Sc.(Manch). b: Laigh 1894. e: Manch Univ & Trin Coll Camb. m: Kathleen Mary Lennard. s: 1. d: 1. Prof Theological Chem Camb Univ, Chmn Sci Advisory Counc Min of Supply. Ctr: Procs Roy Soc, Procs Physical Soc, Trans Faraday Soc, etc. s.s: Math Physics, Theoretical Chem. Rec: Golf, tennis. w.s: Dir-Gen Sci Research Min of Supply 1939—46. a: Middlefield, Huntingdon Rd, Cambridge, & Corpus Christi College, Cambridge. T: 76234.

LENNIE, Robert Aim, T.D., M.D., F.R.F.P.S.G., F.R.C.O.G. b: Cambuslang, Lanarks 1889. e: Glasgow Hgh Sch & University. m: Mary Kirk Jeffrey. Regius Professor of Midwifery University of Glasgow. Publ: A Glasgow Manual of Midwifery (pt-author). Ctr: Various medical journals. s.s: Obstetrics & Gynæcology. Rec: Golf, shooting. c: Conservative & Roy Scot Automobile Glasgow. w.s: 1914—18 1st Lowland Field Amb (despatches), '39—41 Col late R.A.M.C. a: 13 Park Circus, Glasgow, C.3. T: Douglas 0123.

LENNOX, Laura Geraldine. b: Bantry, Co Cork 1883. e: Trinity Church Sc Cork. Secretary. n.a: 'Staff of Votes for Women. Sub Ed The Suffragette '12. Publ: Pamphlet—The Suffragette Spirit. c.t: Several N/ps. s.s: Women's status. Rec: Social work. c: Mem Cmt of Management of Women's Pioneer Housing Assoc, Hon Sec The Douglas-Pennant League, Late Custodian Suffragette Fellowship, etc. a: 12 St George's Mansions, Vauxhall Bridge Rd, S.W.1. t: Victoria 6096.

LENOX, A. b: Stamford 1892. e: Bluecoat Sc, Stamford. m: I.B. Hughes. Sub-Editor. n.a: Stamford Mercury 1913-. Mem N.U.J. '13-. Sec Peterboro' Br N.U.J. Sec Home Counties Dis Counc N.U.J. War Service. a: 16 St Peter's St, Stamford, Lincs.

"LENS" (pen name): see Saleeby, Caleb Williams.

LENSKI, Lois. B.S. b: Springfield, Ohio 1893. e: Ohio State Univ, Art Students League N.Y., Westminster Sch of Art Lond. m: Arthur S. Covey. s: 1. Author & Illustrator of Children's Books. Publ: Indian Captive; Strawberry Girl; Bayou Suzette; Blue Ridge Billy; Judy's Journey; Phebe Fairchild, Her Book; Ocean-Born Mary; Puritan Adventures; Blueberry Corners; A Going to the Westward; & several Picture Books for very young children. s.s: Books for Children of all Ages. a: Greenacres, R.F.D. No. 2, Torrington, Connecticut, U.S.A.

LENTON ROMAINE (pen name): see Lee, Albert.

LEON, Derrick Lewis. *b*: Lon 1908. *e*: St Paul's Sc. Interior Decorator. *Publ*: Livingstones ('33); Wilderness ('35). *a*: 3 The Clock Tower, Heath St. Hampstead.

LEON, Esther Phoebe. *e*: Queen's Coll & Univ Coll. Vice-Pres Shakespeare Reading Soc. *Publ*: A Browning Primer. *s.s*: Browning, Elocution, Shakespeare. *a*; 45 Leinster Gdns, London, W.2. *T*: Paddington 7278.

LEON, Mariette Eileen, M.B.E. *b*: Norwich 1889. *e*: Norwich H.S., Hanover & Girton, Sorbonne. *m*: Philip Leon, M.A. *d*: 2. Univ Lecturer. *n.a*: Mod Lang Staff, Harraps 1922, French Lectureship Leicester Univ Col '23, Visiting German Mistress Girl's Collegiate Sc Leicester '29, German Lectureship, Leicester Univ Col '33. *Publ*: La Formation Philosophique d'Ernest Renan; Three German Plays; English Translation: Sur Les Traces Du Bouddha; Short Stories by Maupassant; Lots Fin Du Monde Antique (with P. Leon). *s.s*: German & French lit. Decoder at Admiralty '19. Sec Naval Intelligence Dept. Paris Peace Conf '20. *Rec*: Music, Drama. *c*: Brit Fed of Univ Women & Mod Lang Assoc. *a*: Arden, Stoughton Rd, Leicester. *t*: 77701.

LEON, Paul. *b*: Rueil Seine-et-Oise 1874. *e*: Normal Superieure Sch. *m*: Madeleine Alexandre. *s*: 2. Hon Dir Gen Beaux Arts, Grand Cross of the Legion of Honour. *Publ*: Fleuves, Canaux, Chemins de fer; Les Monuments Historiques; La Renaissance de Ruines; Art et Artistes; L'art francais; Eaux et Fontaines de Paris; Paris; Histoire de la Rue. *Ctr*: Revue des Deux Mondes, Revue de Paris, Art et Artistes. *s.s*: Monumental History. *a*: 15 Rue De La Pompe, Paris XVI, France. *T*: TR0.23.42.

LEONARD, Irving Albert, M.A., Ph.D. *b*: New Haven, Connecticut 1896. *e*: Univs of California & Yale. *m*: Dorothea Taggart Leonard. *s*: 1. *d*: 1. Univ Prof *n.a*: Assoc Ed Revista Moderna Hispanica 1940—,. Revista de Filologia Hispanica '40—, Handbook of Latin American Studies '35—. *Publ*: Don Carlos de Siguenza, A Mexican Savant of the XVII Century; Romances of Chivalry in the Spanish Indies; (in collab) Spanish in Review; Outline History of Spanish American Literature; An Anthology of Spanish American Literature; (Trans) The Mercurio Volante of Siguenza y Gongora; The Spanish Approach to Pensacola; etc. *Ctr*: Hispania, Hispanic Review, etc. *s.s*: Spanish & Spanish American Lit. *Rec*: Walking, cycling, hist research. *a*: Univ of Michigan, Ann Arbor, Michigan, U.S.A.

LEON, Philip, M.A. *b*: Vaslui 1895. *e*: Manchester Gr Sch & New Coll Oxf. *m*: (1) Mariette Soman, (2) Elizabeth Palmer Elliott. *d*: 2. Lecturer in Classics Univ Coll Leicester 1923—, Mem Classical Assoc. *Publ*: The Ethics of Power; The Philosophy of Courage; Plato; Body, Mind & Spirit; (Trans to English) de Maupassant & Lot's Fin du Monde Antique (with M. Leon). *Ctr*: Mind, Philosophy, Hibbert, Classical Quarterly, Time & Tide, Nation. *s.s*: Philosophy, Latin & Greek Literature. *Rec*: Tennis, swimming, climbing, walking & cycling. *a*: Arden, 42 Stoughton Rd, Leicester. *T*: 77701.

LEONARD, Very Rev. Martin Patrick Grainge, D.S.O., M.A. *b*: Torpenhow Cumberland 1889. *e*: Rossall Sch, Oriel Coll Oxf. *m*: Kathleen Knights-Smith. *s*: 2. *d*: 2. Provost of St Mary's Cathedral Glasgow, formerly Administrative Padre of Toc H now a Vice-Pres of Toc H, Deputy Camp Chief of Boy Scouts Assoc. *Publ*: Scouts Owns. *Rec*: Mountains & hills, philately. *a*: 16 Bute Gdns, Glasgow, W.2. *T*: Western 1106.

LEONID. See Bosworth, Willan G.

LE PATOUREL, John Herbert, M.A., D.Phil.(Oxon). *b*: Guernsey, C.I. 1909 *e*: Elizabeth Coll Guernsey. Jesus Coll Oxf. *m*: Hilda Elizabeth Jean Bird. *s*: 2. Professor of Medieval History Univ of Leeds, Lect in History Univ Coll Lond 1933—43, Reader in Medieval History Univ Coll London '43—45, Archivist to the Royal Court of Guernsey '46—. *Publ*: The Medieval Administration of the Channel Islands 1199—1399. *Ctr*: English Historical Rev, History, Transactions of La Soc Guernesieise. *s.s*: Medieval History, History of the Channel Islands. *a*: 15 Moor Pk Ave, Leeds 6, & The University, Leeds 2. *T*: Leeds 54405.

LE PLA, Frieda. Writer. *Publ*: Nature's Wonderland; Francesca's Robber Guest; etc. *s.s*: Nature stories for Children. Blind & Deaf. *a*: St Endas', Beaconsfield, Bucks.

LE PLA, Lillie. *b*: London 1894. *e*: Priv. *Publ*: The Call of the Dawn; The Secret of Desborough House; Tangletrees; The Treasure of Monks Burn; The Secret of the Wood; Round the Corner; The Secret Shore; In All Things Charity; etc. *Ctr*: Chatterbox, Kiddies Mag. *s.s*: Juvenile Lit, & Poetry. *a*: St.Enda's, Beaconsfield, Bucks.

LEROI, David. Journalist. *n.a*: Asst Ed New Universal Encyclopedia. *Ctr*: Service & Science magazines. *s.s*: Service, Science, Tech. *w.s*: R.A.F.V.R. 1939—45. *a*: 24 Liverpool Rd, Thornton Heath, Surrey. *T*: Central 8080 Ext 333.

LE ROSSIGNOL, James Edward, A.B., LL.D., Ph.D. *b*: Quebec, Canada 1866. *e*: McGill Coll Montreal, Denver, Leipzig & McGill Univs. *m*: Jessie Katherine Ross. *s*: 1. *d*: 1. Univ Teacher. *Publ*: From Marx to Stalin; First Economics; Economics for Everyman; What is Socialism; State Socialism in New Zealand; Orthodox Socialism; Monopolies, Past & Present; (Fiction) The Habitant-Merchant; The Flying Canoe; The Beauport Road; Jean Baptiste; Little Stories of Quebec. *Ctr*: Journ of Polit Econ, Amer Econ Review, Canadian Mag, Outdoor America, etc. *s.s*: Socialism, Fiction, French Canada. *Rec*: Trout fishing, chess. *c*: Rotary, Round Table, etc. *a*: 1801 Pepper Ave, Lincoln 2, Nebraska, U.S.A. *T*: 3-4317.

LERRY, George Geoffrey, M.B.E. *b*: Oswestry 1883. *e*: Oswestry Sch. *m*: Bertha Schreiber. Journalist. Dir Principality Press. *n.a*: Ed Wrexham Leader. *Publ*: Story of Football in Wales; Biography of Alfred George Edwards, Archbishop of Wales; The Collieries of Denbighshire: Past & Present. *s.s*: Assoc Football. *Rec*: Walking, lawn tennis. *a*: 16 Gerald St, Wrexham.

LERT-BAUM, VICKI: see Baum, Vicki.

LESCARBOURA, Austin C., D.Litt. *b*: New York 1891. *e*: N.Y. Public Schs, Hgh Sch of Commerce, Harlem Tech Coll. *m*: Miriam Jennings. *s*: 1. *d*: 1. Journalist & Author, Prop Austin C. Lescarboura & Staff. *n.a*: Ed Modern Electrics & Mechanics 1909—11, Assoc Ed Dun's Review '11—13, Ed The World's Advance '13—15, Mang Ed Scientific American '15—24. *Publ*: Radio for Everybody; Behind the Motion Picture Screen; The Cinema Handbook; Scientific American Home Owner's Handbook; This Thing Called Broadcasting (in collab). *Ctr*: Collier's, N.Y. Times, Rotarian, Radio News, etc. *s.s*: Popular Science, Industry, Business, Radio, Photography. *Rec*: Photography-motoring travel. *c*: Advertising (N.Y.), Rotary (N.Y.), *a*: 64 Lexington, Drive, Croton-on-Hudson, N.Y., U.S.A. *T*: Croton 3444.

LE SIDANER, Louis. *b*: Etaples (Pas de Calais) 1898. *e*: L'Ecole Libre des Sciences Politique Licenciet en Droit. *m*: Simone Vogt. *s*: 2. *d*: 1. Homme de Lettres. *Publ*: Amour Couleur de Paris; Le Pharmacien de Bornicres; Hydrogene et Cosmetique; Monsieur Narcel; Le Coeur Humain; Le Commencement de la Fin. (Essais) La Condition de l'Ecrivairin; Les Machines qui parlent. (Etudes Critiques) Maurice Maeterlinck; Gustave Flaubert; Eugene Dabit. *Ctr*: Midi, L'Age Nouveau, Afrique, Le Mondial, L'homme et La Vie. *s.s*: Roman Psychologeques, Essais, Critiques. *a*: 60 Ave de New York, Paris 16. *T*: Trocadero 55-20.

LESLIE, Desmond. *b*: 1921. *e*: Ampleforth, Trin Coll Dublin. *m*: Agnes Bernelle. *Publ*: Careless Lives; Pardon My Return; Angels Weep. *s.s*: Theatrical & film technique. *Rec*: Inventing. *w.s*: R.A.F. Fighter Pilot 313 & 131 Sqdns. *a*: 36 South Lodge, Grove End Rd, London, N.W.8.

LESLIE, Doris. *b*: London. *m*: Dr W. Fergusson Hannay. *Publ*: (Novels) The Starling; Fools in Mortar; The Echoing Green; Terminus; Puppets Parade; Full Flavour; Fair Company; Concord in Jeopardy; Another Cynthia; House in the Dust; Folly's End; The Peverills; (Biog Studies) Royal William; Polonaise; Wreath for Arabella. *Ctr*: Dly Express, News Chron, Ev News, Dly Sketch, Britannia & Eve. *s.s*: History. *Rec*: Reading, riding. *c*: United Hunts. *a*: c/o A. P. Watt & Son, 10 Norfolk St, Strand, W.C.2.

LESLIE, Dudley Gordon. *b*: London. *e*: Haileybury & Oriel Coll Oxf. *m*: Audrey Erskine-Lindop. *d*: 1. Playwright, Film Writer & Director. *n.a*: Former Rep Dly Mail, Film & Dramatic Critic Sun Dispatch 1930—32. *Ctr*: Britannia & Eve, etc. *s.s*: Film Scripts, Short Stories, Plays. *Rec*: Bull Terriers, travel *w.s*: R.N. World War 11. *a*: 34 Barkston Gardens, London, S.W.5. *T*: Frobisher 2105.

LESLIE, Henrietta. *d.o*: Arthur Raphael (dec). *m*: Dr. H. Schütze. *n.a*: Daily Herald (3 y). *Publ*: Fiction—A Mouse with Wings; Conflict; Dedication; Hirelle; The Road to Damascus; After Eight O'clock; Mrs Fischer's War; Naomi's Child; Mother of Five; etc. Travel—Where East is West, Life in Bulgaria; also many short stories, articles, etc. *Ints*: Music, languages. *Rec*: Travel, motoring. *c*: P.E.N. Pioneer and Writers'. *a*: Glebe Hse, Glebe Pl, Chelsea, S.W.3. *t*: Flaxman 5477.

LESLIE, Rev. James Blennerhassett, M.A., D.Lit., M.R.I.A. *b*: Clouncannon, Co Kerry Eire 1865. *e*: Pococke Sch Kilkenny & T.C.D. *m*: Mary Bulfin. *d*: 2. Clerk in Holy Orders, Rector of Kilsaran Co Louth, Rural Dean of Atherdee & Drogheda 1934—. *n.a*: Ed Irish Clergy List 1909—18 & Irish Church Directory '28—40. *Publ*: Armagh Clergy & Parishes; Ferns Clergy & Parishes; Derry Clergy & Parishes; Ardfert Clergy & Parishes; Raphoe Clergy & Parishes; Irish Churchwardens Handbook. *Ctr*: Louth Archæol Journ, Church of Ireland Gazette. *s.s*: Clerical Biog, Parish & Church Hist, Church Laws. *Rec*: Detective stories. *a*: Kilsaran Rectory, Castlebellingham, Co Louth, Eire.

LESLIE, James Campbell, M.A., B.Sc. *b*: Drumlithie, N.B. 1896. *e*: Stonehaven Mackie Acad & Aber Univ. *m*: Jessie Birkett. *d*: 1. Princ of East Anglian Inst of Agric. Org of Agric Educ, Cambs 1927-30, & of Lindsey, Lincs '24-27. Lect in Agric Leeds Univ '22-24. Teacher, Annan Acad Dumfriesshire '22. *c.t*: Journal of University of Agric, Essex Farmers' Journal, Agric Trades Journals, Agric Progress, etc. War Service '15-19. *Rec*: Golf, badminton, tennis. *c*: Farmers', A.A., A.E.A. *a*: E. Anglian Inst of Agric, Chelmsford. *t*: 124.

LESLIE, John. See Howitt, Capt. J. Leslie, Despard.

LESLIE, Lt.-Col. John Henry, D.L.(Yorks). *b*: Lon 1858. *e*: Elstree, Shrewsbury, R.M.A. Woolwich. *m*: Alice Maud Graham (dec). *s*: 2. *d*: 3. Army ret. *n.a*: Hon Ed of Journ of Soc for Army Hist Research 1921-33. *Publ*: History of Langaurd Fort in Suffolk ('98); History of No 18 Coy Eastern Division R.A. ('97). *c.t*: Journ of Roy Artillery, Journ of Soc for Army Historical Research. *s.s*: Hist of regts. Gov of Roy Sc Offs' Daughters, Boy Scouts, County Commissioner Yorks West Riding. *c*: Army & Navy. *a*: Gunnersholme, Palmerston Rd, Sheffield 10.

LESLIE, Lionel Alistair David, F.R.G.S. *b*: Lon 1900. *e*: Eton & Sandhurst. Sculptor. *Publ*: Wilderness Trails in Three Continents. *s.s*: Trav. Lt Cameron Highlanders '22-26. Explorer Labrador '28, R.G.S. Exped. Big Game Hunter. Artist. Sculp admitted Paris Salon '34. *Rec*: Boxing. *a*: Glaslough, Monaghan, Ireland.

LESLIE, MARION (pen name): see Tooley, Sarah A(nne).

LESLIE, Shane, M.A. *b*: London 1885. *e*: Eton & Camb. *m*: Marjorie Ide. *s*: 2. *d*: 1. Writer, Lect Univs of Pennsylvania & Notre Dame U.S.A. *n.a*: Ed Dublin Review, Sat Review. *Publ*: Cardinal Manning; End of a Chapter; Doomsland; Epic of Jutland; The Passing Chapter; Mrs Fitzherbert; George IV; The Cantab; Masquerades; Film of Memory; Irish Tangle; Sublime Failures. *s.s*: Biog, Celtic. *Rec*: Rowing, forestry. *a*: Glaslough, Co Monaghan, Ireland.

LESLIE-ROBERTS, Hugh, M.D. *b*: M/C, 1860. *e*: M/C, Edin, Lon, Hamburg, Vienna, Paris. *m*: Katie Parker. *d*: 2. *n.a*: Sub-Ed Brit Journ of Dermatology '88-89. *Publ*: Study of the Mould Fungi Parasite in Man ('93). *c.t*: Sci journ's. *s.s*: Dermatology. Foreign Mem Dermatological Soc of France. Mem Danish Dermatological Soc. *Rec*: Golf, water-colour painting. *a*: 31 Rodney St, L'pool. *t*: Royal 4670.

LESSORE, Major F. Sculptor & Art Dealer. Mem Art Workers Gld. *a*: 7 Bruton Pl, W.1.

LESTER, Rev. John Michael Fyvie. *b*: Stoney Stratford 1882. *e*: Haileybury Col Keble Col Oxf & Wells Theol Col. *Publ*: Dear St. Catharine's Nottingham, a Pilgrimage & a History (1929); Confirmation Instructions for Young Boys ('31). *a*: Greens Norton, Towcester.

LESTER, Muriel. *b*: Leytonstone 1883. *e*: St Leonard Sch, St Andrews Scotland, Travelling Sec Internat Fellowship Reconciliation 1938, Lecturer, Mem Fellowship of Reconciliation, Women's International League. *Publ*: Ways of Praying; Entertaining Gandhi; Why Worship?; My Host the Hindu; It Occurred to Me; Dare You Face the Facts?; It So Happened. *Ctr*: Hindustani Times, Christian Century. *s.s*: Pacifism. *Rec*: Music, drama. *a*: Kingsley Cottage, Loughton, Essex. *T*: Loughton 457.

LESTER, Reginald Mounstephens, F.R.Met.S., F.J.I., F.A.L.P.A. *b*: Hawkhurst, Kent 1896. *e*: St Paul's Sch, Lond Univ. *m*: Marjorie Hermon. Author & Journalist, Chm Free-lance Sect & Mem Counc of Inst of Journalists since 1944, Chem Lond Dist '45, Vice-Pres London Writers Circle. *n.a*: Ev Standard & Financial Times 1946—, Woman's Mag '44—, Ed All England Homefinder '45—. *Publ*: Weather Prediction; Property Investment; Practical Astronomy for the Forces; Air Training Courses; Meteorology; Everybody's Weather Book; Estate Agent's Reference Book. *Ctr*: Country Life, Everybody's Illustrated,

Picture Post, etc. *s.s*: Housing, Meteorology. *Rec*: Rifle shooting. *w.s*: 1914—18 & '39—45 Lt-Col Middlx Regt. *a*: 5 New Court, Lincoln's Inn, London, W.C.2. *T*: Chancery 5229.

LESTER, Wilfred. *b*: Lon 1905. *e*: Lon Hosp. *m*: Ulrica Scurr. Phys & Surg. *c.t*: Brit Journ Venereal Diseases. *s.s*: Venereal diseases. *Rec*: Reading. *c*: Mem Soc for Study of Venereal Diseases. *a*: 26 Queen Anne's Pl, Bush Hill Pk, Edmonton. *t*: Enfield 2880.

LESTER-GARLAND, Lester Vallis. *b*: Swanage 1860. *e*: Sherborne & Magdalen Col Oxf. *Publ*: Memoir of Hugo Daniel Harper; Flora of the Island of Jersey; Religious Philosophy of Baron F. von Hügel. *c.t*: Hibbert Journ, Theology. Princ Victoria Col Jersey '96-1911. Ex-Fell St John's Col Oxf. *c*: Fell Linn Soc. *a*: Bathford Hse, Bathford, nr Bath.

LESTER SMITH, William Owen, C.B.E. *b*: Llanbrynmair, Wales 1888. *e*: King's Sch Chester, Merton Coll Oxf. *m*: Rose Lloyd Evans. Chief Education Officer Manchester, Mem Central Advisory Counc for Educ (Eng). *Publ*: To Whom do Schools Belong; Short History of Europe. *Ctr*: Ency Brit, & various educ journs. *s.s*: Education. *a*: Education Office, Deansgate, Manchester.

L'ESTRANGE, Guy. Mang Dir Central Press Agency Ltd, Dir Central Press Photos Ltd. *c.t*: Provinc Press, Daily Graphic (Leader writer), Lon Ed L'pool Courier. Ex-Political Sec late Earl Spencer. *Rec*: Golf. *c*: Constitutional, Royal Wimbledon, Worplesdon. *a*: 80 Fleet St, E.C.4. *t*: Central 1307.

LE STRANGE, Viola. *b*: Norfolk 1905. *e*: Winceby House Sc Shelford & Burchet House Dorking. Journalist. *Publ*: Brambles & Other Poems; Out of the Jaws of Women; Will o' the Whispers, children's operetta; Things that go Bump in the Night; Fairy Gold; The Forest Fire; (plays); etc. *c.t*: Windsor Mag, Observer, Morning Post, Cork Weekly Examiner, Woman's Life, Bournemouth Weekly Post, Guide, Music Teacher, etc. *s.s*: Short stories, one-act plays. V.A.D. '24—33. Nursery governess & chauffeuse '29—31. *Rec*: Golf, tennis, swimming, dress designing. *c*: Inc Soc Authors, Playwrights & Composers, League of British Dramatists. *a*: The Homemead, Heacham, Norfolk. *t*: 52.

L'ESTRANGE MALONE, Cecil John, F.R.Ae.S. *b*: Dalton Holme, Yorks. *e*: Priv Schs, R.N. & R.N. Coll Greenwich. *m*: Leah Kay. *d*: 1. Journalist, M.P. East Leyton 1918—22, M.P. Northampton '28—31, Parl Priv Sec Min of Pensions '31. *n.a*: Lond Corr Nya Daglict Allehanda (Stockholm) 1919—20, Spec Corr Abo Underrattelser (Finland) '27—28, Repres Orient Press Service Geneva '30—, Repres Orient Press Service at World Economic Con '33. *Publ*: The Russian Republic; New China; Manchoukuo Jewel of Asia. *Ctr*: Oriental newspapers. *s.s*: Politics, Orient, Aviation. *Rec*: Mountaineering, squash. *c*: Roy Aero, Alpin Francais. *w.s*: 1914—18 (Des twice), '39—45 Staff Officer C.D. Westminster, Admiralty Small Vessels Pool (Des twice). *a*: Flat 6, 36 Buckingham Gate, London, S.W.1. *T*: Victoria 7406.

L'ESTRANGE MALONE, Leah, Hon.M.A. (Oxon). *e*: Oxford Univ. Mem L.C.C. *Publ*: The Great Infanta. *c.t*: Various N/ps. *s.s*: Public assistance, history. *a*: 6 Phene St, Chelsea, S.W.3. *t*: Flaxman 7765.

LETHBRIDGE, Mabel Florence, O.B.E. *b*: Porlock 1900. *e*: St Angela's Convent & Rochelle Coll Cork. Free-lance Journalist. *m*: Noel Eric Kalenberg. *d*: 1. *Publ*: Fortune Grass ; Against the Tide. *Ctr*: Picture Post, Allied newspapers, etc. *s.s*: Women's Feature Articles. *Rec*: Swimming, gardening. *a*: 55 Oakley St, Chelsea, S.W.3. *T*: Flaxman 5645.

LETHBRIDGE, Olive. Writer, Novelist & Dramatist. Chm Drama Bd & Lyceum Club Stage Soc 1933—. *Publ*: As a Lioness that Sleeps ('32) ; The Dancer of El Touran ; Where Caravans Pass By ('35) ; Plays produced— April & The Mother; etc. *c.t*: Lon, Grand, Story Teller, Premier, McCall's Mag, Novel, Odham's Press, etc. *s.s*: Africa. *Rec*: Tennis, bridge, singing. *c*: Lyceum. *a*: c/o Lyceum Club, 9 Chesterfield Gdns, W.1.

LETHBRIDGE, Sybil Campbell. Author. *Publ*: The Crime of Jane Dacre; Common to All; The Long Day's Task; The Wild Feather. *a*: c/o Methuen & Co Ltd, 36 Essex St W.C.2.

LETHBRIDGE, Sir Wroth Periam Christopher. *b*: Brighton 1863. *e*: Eton. *m*: Hilda Mary Blundell. *s*: 1. *d*: 2. Late Capt Grenadier Guards. *c.t*: Service mags. *s.s*: Military & gen lit. *a*: 29 Cheyne Walk, S.W.3, & La Mancha Hall, Halsall, Ormskirk. *t*: Flaxman 5406.

LETT, Hugh, C.B.E., F.R.C.S. *c.t*: Various Med Journs. *a*: 8 Lower Berkeley St, Portman Sq, W.1. *t*: Welbeck 6212.

LETT, Stafford Charles. *b*: London 1884. *e*: Christ Ch & Pelman Inst. *m*: Lilian Stevens. *d*: 2. Financial jnlst. *n.a*: Investors' Chron. Now with Financial News (since '25). *s.s*: Commercial & industrial companies. *Rec*: Gardening & table tennis. War Service '16—19. *c*: N.U.J. *a*: 8 Wellesley Rd, East Croydon, Surrey. *t*: Croydon 1391.

LETTERS, Francis Joseph Henry, M.A., LL.B. *b*: Gympic, Queensland, Australia 1897. *e*: Christian Bros Coll Waverley Sydney, Sydney Univ. *m*: Kathleen Mary Logue. *d*: 4. Sen Lect in Classics & English New England Univ Coll Armidale N.S.W. *Publ*: Virgil ; The Great Attainder; An Introduction to Thomas Mann ; J. K. Huysman : A Study. *s.s*: The Classics & Comparative Lit, General Essays, Verse. *Rec*: Walking. *a*: 32 Mossman St, Armidale, N.S.W., Australia. *T*: Armidale 224.

LETTS, C. F. C. *a*: Oakley Hall, Cirencester.

LETTS, Malcolm, F.S.A., F.R.HistS., F.R.G.S. *b*: Lon 1882. *e*: Priv & abroad. *m*: Alice Mary Wilson. Solicitor *Publ*: Bruges & Its Past; True History of Hans Staden; Diary of Jorg von Ehingen; A Wayfarer on the Rhine; A Wayfarer in Central Germany; etc. *c.t*: The Times, Times Lit Supp, Cornhill, Contemporary Review. *s.s*: Mediæval hist, law & travel. Corr Mem Roy Belgian Acad. *Rec*: Tennis, motoring. *a*: 27 W. Heath Drive, N.W.11. *t*: Speedwell 3921.

LETTS, Winifred M. *e*: St Anne's Abbots Bromley, Alexandra Coll Dublin. *m*: W. H. F. Verschoyle. Masseuse in Wartime. *Publ*: Songs from Leinster, Hallow E'en ; Diana Dethroned ; Knockmaroon ; Naughty Sophia ; St Patrick the Travelling Man ; Pomona's Island ; Pomona & Co ; etc. *Ctr*: Cornhill, Punch, Country Life, Yale Review & Commonwealth (American). *s.s*: Stories for Children's Hour B.B.C. *Rec*: Gardening. *c*: P.E.N. *a*: Old Vicarage, Faversham, Kent.

Who Was Who Among English and European Authors

LEUNBACH, Jonathan, M.D. *b*: Lidemark, Denmark, 1884. *Publ*: Birth Control Abortion & Sterilization. *s.s*: Birth control, sex reform. Co-Pres of the World League for Sex Reform. *a*: Stockholmsgade 39, Copenhagen. *t*: Obro 5586.

LE VAY, David, M.S., F.R.C.S. *b*: London 1915. *e*: Haberdasher's Aske's Hampstead Sch, Univ Coll & Univ Coll Hosp Lond. *m*: Marjorie Le Vay. *s*: 2. *Publ*: A Synopsis of Orthopædic Surgery; A Guide to the National Health Service; Anatomy; Physiology. *Ctr*: Lancet. *s.s*: Medicine, Surgery, Orthopædic Surg, Nat Health Service. *Rec*: Reading, cooking. *a*: 35 Alleyn Park, London, S.E.21, & 10 Harley St, London, W.1. *T*: Gipsy Hill 0678 & Langham 4280.

LEVENTHAL, Abraham Jacob, M.A., Ph.D. *b*: Dublin 1896. *e*: Wesley Coll Dublin, & T.C.D. *m*: Gertrude Zlotover. *d*: 1. Univ Lecturer, Hon Sec P.E.N. (Dublin Centre). *n.a*: Asst Ed Hermathena 1937—, Dramatic Critic Dublin Magazine '43—. *Ctr*: Irish Times, Dublin Mag, Irish Art, Hermathena. *s.s*: Modern French Literature, Drama, Art. *Rec*: Table talk. *a*: 51 Leeson Park, Dublin. *T*: 63640.

LEVETUS, Amelia Sarah. *b*: Birm 1853. *e*: K.E. Birm, Midland Inst Birm, Cam T.C., Vienna Univ. Writer. *n.a*: Ed Reconstruction 1920—23. Lect in Eng at People's Univ, (Volksheim). Pres John Ruskin Club. *Publ*: Imperial Vienna; Frank Brangwyn, Etcher (in German); The Art Revival in Austria; Peasant Art in Austria & Hungary; etc. *c.t*: Studio, Archt Review, Moderne Bauformen, Christian Sci Mon, Display, & Austrian & Hungarian n/ps. *s.s*: Modern art, peasant art, art ind training, etc. Extensive travel. *Rec*: Music, reading. *a*: 27 Peter Jordanstrasse, Vienna XIX, Austria. *t*: A. 13828.

LEVER, Sir Tresham (Joseph Philip), Bt., M.A. *b*: Leicester 1900. *e*: Harrow & Univ Coll Oxf. *m*: Frances Parker. *s*: 1. Barrister 1925. *Publ*: Profit & Loss; The Life & Times of Sir Robert Peel; The House of Pitt. *Ctr*: Nat Press. *Rec*: Shooting. *c*: Carlton, St James's. *a*: Ryemead House, Winkfield, Windsor, Berkshire.

LEVERTOFF, Beatrice Adelaide. *Publ*: Prisoners of Hope; Panorama of Jerusalem in the Time of Christ. *Ctr*: English & Foreign mags. *a*: 5 Mansfield Rd, Ilford, Essex. *T*: Ilford 2366.

LEVERTOFF, Denise. *Publ*: The Double Image (Verse). *Ctr*: English & U.S. mags. *a*: 5 Mansfield Rd, Essex. *T*: Ilford 2366.

LEVERTOFF, Olga. *Publ*: The Wailing Wall; The Jews in a Christian Social Order; Glory in the Face; Rage of Days (poems); etc. *a*: 5 Mansfield Rd, Ilford, Essex *T*: Ilford 2366.

LEVERTOFF, Rev. Paul Philip, D.D. *b*: Orscha 1878. *e*: Continental Univs. *m*: Beatrice Adelaide Spooner-Jones. *d*: 2. Clerk in Holy Orders. *n.a*: Ed Church & Jews. *Publ*: Commentary on St Matthew (with Canon Goudge); The Life of Christ; The Christian Doctrine of God; A Hebrew-Christian Liturgy; (Trans) Zohar on Exodus; Orte und Wege Jesu; Paulus unter den Juden; & several books on Religion & Philosophy, etc. *Ctr*: Internat Biblical Ency, Mind, Teacher's Commentary, Midrash Sifre; Life of St Paul; Hebrew trans of St Augustin's Confessions; etc. *s.s*: Hebrew & Aramaic, Jewish & Christian Mysticism, Hebrew, Russian & German Lit. *Rec*: Reviewing novels & plays. *a*: 5 Mansfield Rd, Ilford, Essex. *T*: Ilford 2366.

LEVESON, Lionel. *b*: Johannesburg 1891. *m*: Margaret Victoria Glisson. *s*: 1. *d*: 1. Solicitor, Ex Mayor of Johannesburg. *Publ*: The Law of Collisions in Sth Africa (with Adv I. Isaacs). *Ctr*: Star, Sunday Times, Insurance Banking & Finance, Municipal Mag, Municipal Affairs, etc. *Rec*: Golf, tennis. *c*: New, Glendower. *a*: Sanlam Buildings, Loveday St, Johannesburg, Sth Africa. *T*: 33. 3291.

LEVESON GOWER, Sir George Granville, K.B.E., M.A. *b*: London 1858. *e*: Cheam, Eton, Balliol Coll Oxf. *m*: The Hon Cicely Violet Adelaide Monson. *d*: 1. Pri Sec Mr Gladstone 1880—85, M.P. for Stoke on Trent '90—95, Comptroller of Household '92—95, Commissioner of Woods & Forests (Crown Lands), Chairman Lilleshall Co. *Publ*: Years of Content; Years of Endeavour; (Ed) Memoirs of Capt Elers. *Ctr*: Westminster Gaz,· & others. *Rec*: Tennis, Golf shooting, cards. *c*: Athenæum, M.C.C. *a*: 18 York Ho, Kensington Church St, London, W.8. *T*: Western 8846.

LEVESON-GOWER, Henry Dudley Gresham. *e*: Winchester Coll, Magdalen Coll Oxf. Pres Surrey County Cricket Club 1929—40, Vice-Pres '41. *Publ*: Cricket Personalities. *Ctr*: Wisden's Cricket Almanacks. *a*: 30 St Mary Abbotts Court, London, W.14. *T*: Western 1339.

LEVESON-GOWER, Margaret Rosemary. *b*: 1903. *Publ*: Chuckles; The Fighting Six; The Good Detectives. *s.s*: Children's books. *a*: 16 Thurloe Pl, S.W.7. *t*: Kensington 1337.

LEVI, Dr. David, M.B., M.S., L.R.C.P., F.R.C.S. *Publ*: Infection Treatment in Medical Practice. *c.t*: Lancet, B.M.J., Brit Journ of Surgery. *a*: 15 Harley St, W.1. *t*: Langham 1700.

LEVI, Joseph. *b*: Lon. Married. *s*: 1. *d*: 2. Lon Mang Southern N/ps. War Service. *Rec*: Sport, gardening. *c*: P.A.M.A. *a*: 69 Fleet St, E.C.4. *t*: Cen 4352.

LEVI, Thomas Arthur, LL.B., M.A., B.C.L. *b*: Swansea 1874. *e*: Ardwyn Sch Aberystwyth, Univ Coll of Wales, Lincoln Coll Oxf, Inner Temple. Barrister, Prof English Law Univ Coll of Wales. *Publ*: Collection of the Poems of Wales; The Opportunity of a Faculty of Law. *Ctr*: Western Mail, Law Journ, Law Times. *s.s*: English Law, British Constitutional Law. *Rec*: Rowing. *a*: Arfron, St Davids Rd, Aberystwyth, Wales.

LEVICK, Claude Blaxland, M.B., ChM., F.R.C.P., F.R.S.M. Physician. *c.t*: Scientific Journs, etc. *a*: 22 Harley St, W.

LEVICK, George Murray, F.G.S., F.Z.S. *b*: Newcastle-on-Tyne 1876. *e*: St Pauls Sch, St Barts Hosp. *m*: Edith Audrey Beeton. *s*: 1. Surg Cmdr R.N. (ret), with Capt Scott last South Pole Exp 1910—13, Founded Public Schs Exploring Soc, Founded R.N. Rugby Union, Cttees Lucas Tooth Boys Training Fund, Grenfell Assoc, Physical Education Lond Univ, Mem Council Roy Empire Soc. *Publ*: The Social Habits of Antarctic Penguins; A Monograph on Adelie Penguins; Young Pioneers in Northern Finland; various medical works. *s.s*: Exploration. *Rec*: Golf. *a*: White Barn, Old Oxted, Surrey. *T*: Oxted 590.

LEVICK, Harry Driffield. Surgeon. *Publ*: Hunting Trips in the Caucasus (Jt Ed). *c.t*: B.M.J. *Rec*: Fishing, alpine sports. *a*: Willerby Cam Rd,, Middlesbro'. *t*: Linthorpe 8736.

LEVIEN, John Mewburn, Hon.R.A.M. *b*: London 1863. *e*: Birkenhead Sch, Chatham House Ramsgate, St John's Coll Camb. Prof of Singing, Writer & Lecturer, Mem Court of Authority of the Worshipful Co of Musicians, Mem Counc Lond Soc, formerly Hon Treas & Hon Sec Roy Philharmonic Soc, Prof of Singing Guildhall Sch of Music & Trinity Coll of Music, Hon Treas Concerts at the Front 1914. *Publ*: Beethoven & the Royal Philharmonic Society; Sir Charles Santley; The Garcia Family; Some Notes for Singers; Impressions of W. T. Best; The Singing of John Braham. *Ctr*: D.N.B., Grove's Dict of Music, Modern Dict of Music. *s.s*: Authentic old Italian Sch of Singing, the Instruments of the Human Voice, the Organ—specially Sch of W. T. Best. *Rec*: Economics & political history. *c*: Athenæum, Savage. *a*: 57 Rosslyn Hill, London, N.W.3. *T*: Hampstead 6800.

LEVINGER, Lee J., Ph.D. *b*: Burke, Idaho, U.S.A. 1890. *e*: Hebrew Union Coll, Univs of Chicago & Penn. *m*: Elma Ehrlich. *s*: 1. *d*: 1. Rabbi, Educator. *Publ*: History of the Jews in the U.S.; The Story of the Jews (in collab); Anti-Semitism Yesterday & Tomorrow; A Jewish Chaplain in France. *Ctr*: Nat Jewish Monthly, Jewish Social Studies. *s.s*: Jewish Hist (U.S.). *Rec*: Travel. *w.s*: Chaplain U.S. Army World War 1. *a*: 25 Taylor St, San Francisco, California, U.S.A.

LEVINE, Israel, M.A., D.Litt. Univ Lecturer. *Publ*: The Unconscious, A Study in Freudian Psychology; Reason and Morals; etc. *a*: Univ Col, Exeter, Devon. *t*: 3341.

LEVINSON, Maurice. *b*: Russia. *e*: Elem Sch. *m*: Rachel Anne Tobert. *s*: 1. *d*: 1. London Taxi-Driver. *Publ*: The Trouble With Yesterday. *Ctr*: New Statesman & Nation. *s.s*: Boxing, East End Life & Orphanage Upbringing. *Rec*: Painting. *a*: 63 Preston Hill, Kenton, Harrow, Middlx. *T*: Wordsword 5317.

LEVINSON, Dr. R. *Publ*: Expression of Neuroses; Mental Hygiene. Hon Consulting Psychologist West End Hosp. Psychiatrist East Lon Child Guidance Clinic. *a*: West Ham Mental Hosp, Goodmayes, Essex.

LE VIREGE, L. F/L. Mem I.J. *a*: 5 Orford Rd, South Woodford, E.18.

LEVISON, Sir Leon, K.B. *b*: Calcutta 1881. *e*: Abroad, Edin Univ, New Col. *m*: Kate Barnes. *s*: 3. *d*: 1. Author & Editor. *n.a*: Ed Hebrew Christian Quarterly 1928. *Publ*: Life of St Paul; Jew in History; Zionism—Racial or Religious; Heroes of the Old Testament; Passover & Its Relation to the Lord's Supper; The Jew & the World War; etc. *c.t*: Christian, Record, Life of Faith, etc. *s.s*: Philos, econ. Knighted for important services during the War. Raised £200,000 towards the Russian Jews Relief & other funds. Dir of Messrs Marshall, Morgan & Scott Ltd. Kt of Cross & Star, Imp Order of Russia. *Rec*: Chess, billiards. *c*: Pres Internat Hebrew-Chr Alliance, etc. *a*: 9 Albert Terr, Edin. *t*: 52888.

LEVITT, Walter Montague, M.D., M.R.C.P. Radiologist. *n.a*: Ex-Mem Ed Committee Brit Journ of Radiologists. *Publ*: Deep X-Ray Therapy & Malignant Disease; etc. *c.t*: B.M.J., Proc Roy Soc Med. etc. *a*: 40 Harley St, W.1. *t*: Langham 1011.

LEVONIAN, LOOTFY: professor, author; *b*. Aintab, Asia Minor, May 18, 1881; *s*. Ohannes and

LEVY, A. Harold, B.A., M.D., C.M., F.R.C.S. Ophth Surg. *n.a*: Ed Cmt Brit Journ of Ophth. *c.t*: Sci Journs. *a*: 149 Harley St, W.1. *t*: Welbeck 4444.

LEVY, Aaron, M.R.S.T., F.R.S.A., F.I.C. *b*: Lon 1881. *e*: King's Col, Univ Col & Paris Univ. *m*: S. Schoub. *s*: 1. Princ Col of Swiss Mercantile Soc Ltd. *Publ*: Warp & Woof of Modern English. *s.s*: Eng, French & economics. Ex-Snr French Master Walworth Sc Lon. *Rec*: Manual work. *a*: 31 Craven Walk, Stamford Hill, N.16. *t*: Clissold 8025.

LEVY, Arnold. *e*: Priv. *m*: Lena Esther Jacobs. Rubber Manufacturer. *Publ*: This I Recall; Inside Britain To-day. *s.s*: Industrial Problems. *Rec*: Walking, riding, reading. *a*: Roy Auto. *a*: Horwood Cottage, Hindhead, Surrey, & 4 Clarence Gate Gardens, London, N.W.1. *T*: Hindhead 230 & Paddington 8548.

LEVY, Benn W. *b*: 1900. *e*: Repton & Univ Coll Oxf. Dramatist, M.P. (L.) Eton & Slough. *Publ*: Art & Mrs Bottle; The Devil; Springtime for Henry; This Woman Business; Mud & Treacle; Man with Red Hair; Mrs Moonlight; Hollywood Holiday (collab); The Poets Heart; The Jealous God; Clutterbuck. *c*: Garrick, Queen's. *a*: c/o William Heinemann Ltd, 99 Gt Russell St, London, W.C.1.

LEVY, Frederick David, M.A. *b*: Manningham, Bradford 1890. *e*: Clifton & St John's Coll Oxf. *m*: Ena Norgen. Barrister. *n.a*: Co-Ed Oxford Fortnightly 1910—13. *Ctr*: Various newspapers. *s.s*: Criminal Law & Rating. *c*: R.A.F., Constitutional, Press. *w.s*: World War I. *a*: 4 Pump Court, Temple, London, E.C.4.

LEVY, Hermann (Joachim), Dr., ner pol *b*: Berlin 1881. *e*: Berlin, Univ of Munich. *m*: Margarete Schlegel. *s*: 1. Writer, Lecturer, Research Economist, Guest Lecturer King's Coll Camb Univ 1934, Sydney Ball Lecture in Oxford '35, Addressed the Brit Assoc in '37. *Publ*: Large & Small Holdings; Monopolies Cartels & Trusts in British Industry; Economic Liberalism; The New Industrial System; Industrial Germany; Retail Trade Assocs; Nat Health Ins; The Shops of Britain; and (in collaboration with the late Sir Arnold Wilson) Industrial Assurance; Burial Reform & Funeral Costs; Workmen's Compensation. *Ctr*: Times, Manch Gdn, New Statesman & Nation, Spectator, Fortnightly Rev, Contemporary Rev, The New English Rev, Economist, Banker, Britain To-day. *s.s*: Industrial Organisation, Retail Distribution, Social Insurance, Rehabilitation & Resettlement of the Physically Handicapped, Textile Industry & Trade, Sociology of the Middle Classes, Economic History from 1600 to 1750. *Rec*: Music, novel writing. *a*: 149 Lichfield Court, Richmond, Surrey. *T*: Richmond 4420.

LEVY, Hyman, M.A., D.Sc., FR.S.E. *e*: Univs of Edin, Oxf & Göttingen. Prof Univ of Lond. *Publ*: Philosophy for a Modern Man; Universe of Science; Social Thinking; Modern Science; Elements of Probability; Elements of Statistics; etc. *s.s*: Maths. *Rec*: Scientific Journalism. *a*: Imperial Coll of Science, London, S.W.7. *T*: Kensington 4861.

LEVY, Ivan Moltke. *b*: Melbourne 1877. *e*: Brisbane G.S. *m*: Maude Mary Jessie Corrigan. *s*: 1. *d*: 1. Ed & Trade Reporter. *n.a*: Reporter Brisbane Telegraph '93-95, F/L. '95-98, Sub-Ed Australian Cyclist Melbourne 1900-02, Reporter, Dramatic Critic, etc, The N.Z. Times (daily) Wellington '02-23, Reporter The Dominion Wellington '23-30. *Publ*: Plugger Bill's Biography ('02). *c.t*: Bulletin (Sydney), Lone Hand (Sydney), Pals (Melbourne), N.Z. Observer (Auckland), Weekly Press (Christchurch), etc. *s.s*: Short stories. Extensive travel. Won Christchurch Sun's National Xmas Short Story Comp '20. Has written a number of short plays for vaudeville. Author of the sensational adventure hoax story " Cornered by a Moa ". Christchurch Weekly Press '19. Wrote an extensive survey of radio conditions in N.Z. for Eng trade interests. Eng Sec to Japanese Trade Commissioner in N.Z. *Rec*: Swimming, snooker, radio. *a*: Ed, N.Z. Worker, Marion St, Wellington, N.Z. & 20 McFarlane St, Wellington, N.Z. *t*: 50–250,

LEVY, Joseph, B.Sc., F.R.S.A. F.R.I.C. *b*: Gibraltar 1891. *e*: King's Coll, Univ of London. Analytical & Consulting Chemist & Assayer. *n.a*: Ed Bulletin of The British Legion Lima (Peru), Bulletin of The British Commonwealth Soc of Peru. *Ctr*: Bulletin of The Chem Soc of Peru. *s.s*: Chemistry. *Rec*: Music, tennis *a*: Casilla 301, Lima, Peru. *T*: 31225.

LEVY, Muriel. *b*: London 1905. *e*: Liverpool Coll for Girls. *m*: Rudolph Fayer-Taylor (dec'd). Radio Artist & Journalist, Organiser B.B.C. Children's Hour Liverpool (5 yrs). *n.a*: Ed Children's Page Liverpool Echo 1929—. *Publ*: Author of Children's Books, Plays, Songs, etc, & Radio Scripts notably Dramatisation of John Galsworthy's "Forsyte Saga". *a*: 84 Queens Drive, Mossley Hill, Liverpool, 18. *T*: Sefton Park 3005.

LEVY, Roger Goodman. *b*: Bookham, Surrey 1910. *e*: Cheam & Shrewsbury Schs. *m*: Gwendolen Irene Evans. Journalist. *n.a*: Asst Poetry Review 1928—29, John O' London's Weekly '29 —31, Asst-Ed '81—47, Ed '47—, Rotary Service. *Ctr*: Various. *s.s*: Music. *Rec*: Music, theatre, tennis, cricket. *a*: 61 Parliament Hill Mansions, Lissenden Gardens, London, N.W.5.

LEVY-SCHNEIDER, LION: professor at Univ. of Lyon; b. Lyon, France, May, 1867; s. Telir and Elie (Myria) L.; educ. Lycée of Lyon, Lycée Louis le Grand (Paris), University of Paris. DEGREE: Fellow, Dr. of History; m. Sophie Schneider, Oct. 30, 1893. AUTHOR (essays): La Conventions et l'Armée, L'Oeuvre Sociale de la Revolution, 1903; L'Application du Concordat par un prélat d'Ancien Regime, Monseigneur Champion de lier Archevêque d'Aix et d'Arles 1802-1870, 1927; Histoire contemporaine jusqu'au milieu du XIXe Siecle (with Rouland), 1928; and others. Contributor to Revue des Universités du Midi, Bulletin de la Société d'histoire du protestantisme français, Revue d'histoire de l'Englise de France, La Revolution française, La Revolution de 1848, Revue d'histoire modernes et contemporaine, and others. General character of writing: historical. Specializes in the history of the French Revolution and the Empire, and in the history of Lyon. Is a Chevalier of the Legion d'Honneur. Religion, Jew. OFFICE: Faculté des Lettres, 7C Quai Claude Bernard, Lyon, France.

LEWCOCK, Francis James. A.C.I.S., A.I.B., F.R.EconS. *b*: Holborn. *e*: Stationers' Coy Sc Lon. Married. *s*: 4. *d*: 1. Journalist. *n.a*: Ed & Founder Branch Banking 1933. *Publ*: The Securities Clerk in a Branch Bank; Organization & Management of a Branch Bank; etc. *c.t*: Princ n/ps. *s.s*: Banking & all branches of finance. On staff Barclay's Bank '13–33. Top place in U.K. & Silver Medallist in Advanced Banking of R.S.A. Special Prizeman in Stock Exchange Law & Practice of the Lon Ch of Comm. Vice-Pres W. Yorks Br Chrtd Inst of Secs. Chm Leeds Br Bank Officers Gld '31–32. Ex-Sec No 14 (Lon) Br & Mem Lon Area Counc, etc. Ex-Mem Cmt of Leeds Inst of Bankers. *a*: 24 Essex St, W.C.2. *t*: Central 1138.

LEWER, Ethel Harriet. *b*: India. *e*: Priv. *m*: S. H. Lewer. *d*: 2. Ed Feathered World. *Rec*: Gardening. *c*: Aldeburgh Golf. *a*: 9 Arundel St Strand, W.C. *t*: Tem 2323.

LEWES, Evelyn. *b*: Woolwich. *e*: Private. F/1. *Publ*: Out with the Cambrians; Life & Work of Dafydd Ab Gwilym; Dream Folk & Fancies; The New Guide to Aberayson. *c.t*: Western Mail, Family Herald, Bookman, Land & Water, Queen, Western Home Mnthly (Canada), & over 40 others. *s.s*: History, literature & antiquities of Wales. Mem Ct of Governors of Univ of **Wales. Mem Counc for** Preservation of Rural Wales. Counc Mem of Cambrian Archæological Assoc. Vice-Pres Cardiganshire **Antiquarian Soc.** *Rec*: Reading, concerts, motoring. *c*: Lon Lyceum. Mem Hon Soc of Cymmrodorion. *a*: Eithinfa, Cliff Terr. Aberystwyth, Wales. *t*: 278.

LEWIN, Everest. *b*: Darjeeling, India 1878. *e*: Cheltenham Col. *m*: T. M. Macdonald. *s*: 2. *d*: 2. *Publ*: Poems. *c.t*: London Mercury. *Rec*: Cinematography, photography, violin playing, black & white drawing. *c*: Mem Royal Soc of Literature. *a*: Barguillean, Taynuilt, Argyll, Scotland. *t*: 24.

LEWIN, Percy Evans, M.B.E., F.R.HistS., F.L.A. *b*: Boston, Lincs 1876. *m*: Léontine Berthe Dorman (dec). *d*: 3. Librarian Roy Emp Soc. *Publ*: Catalogue of Port Elizabeth Library; The Germans & Africa; Resources of the Empire; Catalogue of the Library of the Royal Empire Society; etc. *c.t*: 19th Century, Quarterly Review, Yale Review, Foreign Affairs, Atlantic Monthly, etc. *s.s*: Hist of the Brit Emp. Membre de l'Institut Colonial Internat. *a*: 218 Coombe Lane, Wimbledon, S.W.20. *t*: 1588.

LEWIS, Dr. A. J. *a*: 22 Trafalgar Rd, Birkdale, Southport.

LEWIS, Miss A. K., M.A., G.P.D.S.T. Headmistress. *a*: Blackheath H.S., Wemyss Rd, S.E.3.

LEWIS, Rev. Arthur, M.A. *b*: Bristol 1854. *e*: Bristol Gr Sch & Queens Coll Oxf. *m*: *d*: 1. Clerk in Holy Orders, Chaplain Kangra District Punjab. *Publ*: Biography of George Maxwell Gordon; Biography of Edmund Peck; Bilochi Stories; A Dream of Adolf Hitler; The Seed of the Church; Brakers Ahead. *Ctr*: Cassell's Magazine. *a*: Downgate, Portishead, Bristol, Gloucestershire.

LEWIS, Arthur William. *b*: Merthy Vale, Glam 1905. *e*: Univ Coll of Wales Aberystwyth. *m*: Susanna Helen Tompkins. *d*: 1. Lecturer, Mem Coll of Handicraft, Judd Research Award. *n a*: Book-Reviews Western Morning News 1936—38. *Publ*: Wood Decoration with V-Tool & Gouge; (Pt-Author) Woodwork for the Handyman; Gifts You Can Make Yourself; More Gifts to Make; Games, Puzzles & Hobbies; Wooden Toymaking. *Ctr*: The Woodworker. *s.s*: Woodwork—Cabinet & Joinery, Bookbinding & Bookcrafts, Toymaking, Party Games. *Rec*: Athletics, hockey, tennis, cricket. *a*: 43 Fairmount Drive, Loughborough, Leicestershire. *T*: 3791.

LEWIS, B. Roland, M.A., M.Sc., D.Litt. *b*: St Marys, Ohio 1884. *e*: Ohio Northern, Chicago & Harvard Univs. *m*: Bessie Blanche Collins. *d*: 2. Prof of English Univ of Utah Salt Lake City. *n.a*: Cons-Ed Webster's New Internat Dictionary 1935. *Publ*: The Shakespeare Documents; Creative Poetry; The Technique of the One-Act Play; Contemporary One-Act Plays; Creative Writing; University of Utah Plays; etc. *Ctr*: Times Lit Supp (Lond), N.Y. Times, Shakespeare Assoc Bulletin. *s.s*: William Shakespeare & the Elizabethan Drama. *Rec*: Motoring, fishing. *c*: Timpanogos, Harvard of Utah. *a*: 1271 East Fifth South St, Salt Lake City, Utah, U.S.A., & The Shakespeare Laboratory, Univ of Utah, Salt Lake City, U.S.A. *T*: Dial 4-0283.

Who Was Who Among English and European Authors

LEWIS, Dr. C. J. *Publ*: Public Health & Preventive Medicine; Natality and Fecundity. Asst Prof of Public Health, Birm Univ. *a*: Univ, 10 Great Charles St, Birm.

LEWIS, Cecil Day. F.R.S.L. *b*: Ballintubber, Ireland 1904. *e*: Sherborne Sch & Wadham Coll Oxf. *m*: Constance Mary King. *s*: 2. Schoolmaster 1927—35, Min of Inf '41—45, Clark Lecturer at Camb Univ '46. *Publ*: A Hope for Poetry; A Time to Dance; Collected Poems; Word Over All; Poetry for You; The Poetic Image; Overtures to Death; The Georgics of Virgil (trans): etc. *c*: Savile. *a*: Musbury, Axminster, Devon.

LEWIS, Charles Lee. A.M., B.S. *b*: Doyle, Tennessee 1886. *e*: Burritt Coll, Tennessee & Columbia Univs. *m*: Flora Louise Quarles. *s*: 1. *d*: 1. Teacher 1916—, Prof '35—, Dept of English & Hist U.S. Naval Acad. *Publ*: David Glasgow Farragut: Admiral in the Making; David Glasgow Farragut: Our First Admiral; Admiral De Grasse & American Independance; Books of the Sea: An Introduction to Nautical Literature; The Romantic Decatur; Famous Old-World Sea Fighters; Matthew Fontaine Maury: Pathfinder of the Seas; Famous American Naval Officers; etc. *Ctr*: Dicts of Amer Biog, Amer Hist, World Book Ency, Amer Hist Rev, Baltimore Sun, Maryland Hist Rev, etc. *s.s*: Naval Hist & Biog. *Rec*: Gardening, motoring. *c*: Naval Acad Officers, etc. *a*: 41 Southgate Ave, Annapolis, Maryland. *T*: 2177.

LEWIS, Clarence Irving. *b*: Stoneham, Mass, U.S.A. 1883. *e*: Harvard Univ. *m*: Mabel Maxwell Graves. *s*: 2. Prof of Philosophy Harvard Univ. *Publ*: Survey of Symbolic Logic; Mind & the World-Order; Symbolic Logic (with C. H. Langford); An Analysis of Knowledge & Valuation. *Ctr*: Journ of Philosophy, Philosophical Review, Mind, The Monist. *s.s*: Philosophy, Logic. *c*: American Philosophical Assoc, American Academy of Arts & Sciences. *a*: 23 Oakland St, Lexington, Mass, U.S.A.

LEWIS, Clive Staples, Hon.D.D.(St Andrews). *b*: Belfast 1898. *e*: Malvern Coll & Priv. Fellow of Magdalen Coll Oxford, Lecturer Ballard Matthew Bangor 1941, Riddell Durham '44, Clarke Trinity Camb '45. *Publ*: Pilgrim's Regress; Allegory of Love; Out of the Silent Planet; Problem of Pain; Screwtape Letters; Perelandra; Abolition of Man; That Hideous Strength; Miracles. *Ctr*: Time & Tide, Spectator, Times Litt Supp, Punch. *s.s*: Popularised Theology, English Literary History, Fantastic Fiction. *w.s*: 1918—19 Som Light Inf. *Rec*: Walking. *a*: Magdalen College, Oxford.

LEWIS, D.T. *c.t*: Merthyr Express & Western Mail. Sec Nelson Chr of Trade. *a*: Tydfil Hse, Nelson, Glam.

LEWIS, David. *b*: London 1913. *e*: Haberdashers' Sch Hampstead. Journalist. *n.a*: Cavalcade 1938—. *Ctr*: Nat Dailies, Everybody's, Courier, Bandwaggon. *s.s*: Inside Political News Reporting, Political & Social Gossip Features, Profiles, Dramatic Criticism. *a*: 112 Beaufort Park, London, N.W.1. *T*: Speedwell 9541.

LEWIS, David Emrys. *b*: Machynlleth, Mont 1887. *e*: Machynlleth Counc & Inter Scs. *m*: Margaret Roberts. *s*: 2. Journalist. *n.a*: Montgomery County Times, Cambria Daily Leader, Western Mail. *c.t*: Welsh Outlook, Daily News, Y Cymro. *s.s*: Welsh. *Rec*: Bowls. *a*: Bodlondeb, Middle Rd, Fforestfach, Swansea. *t*: 55885.

LEWIS, Dominic Bevan Wyndham, F.R.S.L. Author & Journalist. *n.a*: Daily Express ("Beachcomber") 1919—24, Daily Mail ("At the Sign of the Blue Moon") 25—30, Sunday Referee ("Mustard & Cress") '31—33,

Daily Mail ("Crazy News Reel") '33—34, News Chronicle ("Timothy Shy") '34—. *Publ*: Francois Villon, A Documented Biog; Emperor of the West (Charles V); Barbey d'Aureuilley; The Anatomy of Dandyism (trans); Welcome to All This; The London Spectacle (with Felix Topolski); Ronsard; The Hooded Hawk; etc. *Ctr*: Bystander, Radio Times, New Yorker, Strand Mag, Lilliput, etc. *s.s*: 15th Cent Hist, Lit, especially French. *Rec*: Music, golf. *a*: c/o A. D. Peters, Adelphi, W.C.2.

LEWIS, Edmund Oliver, M.A., D.Sc., M.R.C.S., L.R.C.P. *b*: Rhondda 1882. *e*: Univ Coll of Wales Aberystwyth, St John's Coll Camb, Univ of Jena. *m*: Maude Mary Jones. *Publ*: Report on the Incidence of Mental Deficiency. *Ctr*: Brit Journ of Psychology, Journ of Mental Science, etc. *s.s*: Mental Deficiency. *c*: Nat Lib. *a*: 12 Dorset Sq, London, N.W.1. *T*: Paddington 6769.

LEWIS, Edwin, A.B., D.D., Th.D. *b*: Newbury. England 1881. *e*: Mt Allison Univ Sackville N.B., N.Y. State Teachers Coll, Drew Theol Sem, Dickinson Coll. *m*: Louise Newhook Frost. *s*: 3. *d*: 2. Prof of Systematic Theol & Philos of Religion Drew Theol Sem. *n.a*: Jt-Ed Abingdon Bible Commentary 1926—29. *Publ*: Jesus Christ & the Human Quest; God & Ourselves; A Philosophy of the Christian Revelation; The Creator & the Adversary; A Christian Manifesto; A New Heaven & a New Earth; The Faith We Declare; A Manual of Christian Beliefs; etc. *Ctr*: Religion & Life, Canadian Journ of Religion, Methodist Review, Christian Advocate, etc. *s.s*: Theology, Philosophy of Religion, Biblical Interpretation, Religion, Hist & Lit. *Rec*: Gardening, planting & care of trees, Handwork. *a*: Drew Univ, Madison, New Jersey, U.S.A. *T*: MAD 6-1314.

LEWIS, Edwin John Godfrey. *b*: Acton 1903. *e*: Ealing County Sc, Tech Col for Radio N. Lon. *m*: Derothy Edith Burt. *s*: 1. *d*: 1. Radio Engineer, Head of Tech Section, E.M.I. Service Ltd Hayes Middx. *Publ*: Radio Receiver Servicing & Maintenance. *c.t*: World Radio, Popular Wireless, English Mechanics. For several years on radio investigation work in Eng, Scot & Wales. *Rec*: Reading, cinemas. *c*: Assoc Brit Radio Inst. *a*: 40 Grange Pk, Ealing, W.5.

LEWIS, Eiluned. *m*: Graeme Hendrey. *d*: 1. Writer. *n.a*: Editorial Staff of Sunday Times 1931—36. *Publ*: Dew on the Grass; The Captain's Wife; The Land of Wales (with Peter Lewis); December Apples; Morning Songs. *Ctr*: Country Life, etc. *Rec*: Walking, riding. *c*: Arts Theatre. *a*: 20 Edwardes Sq, London, W.8; & Rabbits Heath Cottage, Blechingley, Surrey.

LEWIS, Elizabeth Foreman. *b*: Baltimore, Maryland 1892. *e*: Baltimore Grade Schs, Maryland Inst of Fine Arts, Tome Inst, Biblical Sem of N.Y. *m*: John Abraham Lewis (dec'd). *s*: 1. Writer. *Publ*: Young Fu of the Upper Yangtze; Ho Ming, Girl of New China; When the Typhoon Blows; Portraits From a Chinese Scroll; etc & several Young peoples books. *Ctr*: Chris Sci Mon, Everywoman's, Classmate, Target, Portal, & English & Scandinavian newspapers. *s.s*: China. *Rec*: Natural hist, poetry, dogs, music. *a*: Briar, Cliff-on-Severn, Arnold, Maryland, U.S.A. *T*: Annapolis 2943.

LEWIS, Ervin Gibson, B.A. *b*: Ramona, Oklahoma 1910. *e*: Knox Coll Galesburg Ill, Univ of Oklahoma. *m*: Ruth Wilkin. *s*: 1. Radio Ed-Broadcaster. *n.a*: News Ed Radio Station KTUL Tulsa Oklahoma 1934—38, Assoc News Ed Radio Station WLS Chicago '38—. *Ctr*: Prairie Farmer, Chicago. *Rec*: Golf, photography. *a*: 6208 Nth Hoyne Ave, Chicago 45, Illinois, U.S.A. *T*: Briargate 4152.

LEWIS, Rev. F. Warburton, M.A.(Cantab), B.A. (Lon). *b*: Broseley, Salop 1871. *e*: K.E. Sc Birm, Lon Univ, Mansfield Col Oxf & Trin Col Cam. *m*: Julia C. Middleton. *d*: 2. Meth Min. *Publ*: Disarrangements in the Fourth Gospel; Jesus of Galilee; Jesus, Saviour of Men; etc. *c.t*: Expository Times. *s.s*: The Bible. *Rec*: Lawn tennis, walking. *a*: Woodleigh, Northwood, Middx. *t*: 1196.

LEWIS, Frank. Publisher. *Publ*: Floral Art-Decoration & Design; The British Empire Panels designed for the House of Lords by Frank Brangwyn R.A.; A History of British Carpets; English Decorative Fabrics; A Survey of British Industrial Arts; Carpet Designs & Designing; English Chintz—From The Earliest Times until the Present Day; etc. *s.s*: Applied Decorative arts. *a*: P.O. Box 3, Benfleet, Essex. *t*: Hadleigh, 58127.

LEWIS, Harry Llewelyn. *b*: Carmarthen 1894. *m*: Gertrude Annie Baskerville. *s*: 1. *d*: 1. Editor. *n.a*: Ed The Welshman Carmarthen. *a*: 10 Lime Grove Ave, Carmathen. *T*: 7359.

LEWIS. Helen Prothero. *b*: Llandilo. *m*: James J. G. Pugh. Writer. *Publ*: As God Made Her; Hooks of Steel; The Fire Opal; Tobias & the Angel; The Peepshow; Henrietta; Love in the Whirlwind; etc. *c.t*: Royal Mag, Novel, Quiver, Ideas, etc. *s.s*: Fiction, adventure. *Rec*: Travel, music. *c*: P.E.N., After-Dinner, Bookman Lit Circle, Richmond Athenæum. *a*: Cefngoleu, Llandilo, Carms. *t*: 76.

LEWIS, Henry. *b*: Clydach 1889. *e*: Ynystawe Bd Sch, Ystalyfera County Sch, Univ Coll Cardiff. *m*: Gwladys Thomas. *d*: 2. Prof of Welsh Lang & Lit Univ Coll Swansea. *Publ*: Iolo Goch ac Eraill; Delwy Byd; Datblygiad Yr Iaith Gymraeg; Hen Gerddi Crefyddol; Brut Dingestow; Llawlyfr Llydaweg Canol; Llawlyfr Cernyweg Canol; Concise Comparative Celtic Grammar (with H. Pedersen). *Ctr*: Y Cymmrodor, Bulletin of Bd of Celtic Studies, Zeitschrift fur celtische Philologie, etc. *s.s*: Welsh. *a*: Y Gilfach Glyd 332 Gower Rd, Swansea, Sth Wales.

LEWIS, Rev. James. *b*: Cregrina 1864. *e*: Ebbw Vale Inst & Wesleyan Col Richmond Surrey. *m*: Margaret Mary Richards. *s*: 2. Methodist Minister in India & Eng. *Publ*: Life of William Goudie; Life of Francis Asbury, Bishop of Methodist Episcopal Church. *c.t*: Methodist Recorder, Methodist Times, etc. *s.s*: Biblical linguistics, Indian history. Cost Clerk in Steel, Iron & Coal Offices. Tanul Missionary. Superintendent Minister Cam, Lon, Edin, etc. Delegate to Ecumenical Conf Toronto 1911. Moved first resolution for Meth Union '12. Weslyan Conf (Pastoral Session). Chm Cardiff & Swansea Dist. *a*: 7 Queen's Road, Chelmsford.

LEWIS, Janet, Ph.B. *b*: Chicago, Ill 1899. *e*: Lewis Inst Chicago, Univ of Chicago. *m*: Yvor Winters. *s*: 1. *d*: 1. *Publ*: The Invasion; The Wife of Martin Guerre; Against a Darkening Sky; Good-bye Son; The Trial of Soren Quist; The Earth-Bound. *Ctr*: Poetry, New Yorker, Bookman, McCalls Mag, etc. *a*: Box 625, R2, Los Altos, California, U.S.A. *T*: Los Altos 4579.

LEWIS, John. *b*: Selkirk 1861. *e*: George Watson's Col Edin & Edin Univ. Journalist. *n.a*: Ed Southern Reporter Falkirk '86-95, Local Corr for Scotsman '86-95, Mem Ed Staff Tariff Reform League, Founder Internat Psychic Gazette Lon 1912 & Sole Ed '34. *s.s*: Spiritualism & psychical research. *a*: 69 High Holborn, W.C.1.

LEWIS, John David. *b*: Carmarthen 1911. *e*: Q. Elizabeth G.S. Sub Ed & Reporter. *n.a*: The Welshman, Carmarthen. *c.t*: Farmer & Stock-Breeder & Sport Papers. *Rec*: Football & billiards. *a*: Market Villa, Carmarthen.

LEWIS, John F. *b*: London 1909. *e*: Pub Sec Sch. Journalist, Mem N.U.J. *n.a*: Tech Pubs (Vehicles) Min of Supply 1940—44, Odhams Press Ltd Book Dept '44—. *s.s*: Internal Combustion Engine, Car Maintenance, Electrical & Handyman Subjects. *Rec*: Motoring, amateur dramatics, interior decoration. *a*: 46 Old Lodge Lne, Purley, Surrey. *T*: Uplands 2203.

LEWIS, Joseph. *b*: Montgomery, Alabama 1889. *e*: Public Schs. Married. *d*: 1. Author-Lecturer. *n.a*: Ed The Freethinker. *Publ*: The Ten Commandments; The Bible Unmasked; Thomas Paine, Author of the Declaration of Independence; Voltaire, The Incomparable; Burbank, The Infidel; Spain, A Land Blighted by Religion; In Humanity's Name; & several Pamphlets. *s.s*: American Hist & Religion. *c*: Lotos, Advertising (N.Y.), Town Hall. *a*: Purdys, New York, & 370 West 35th St, New York 1, N.Y. *T*: Croton Falls 635 & PE-6-9248.

LEWIS, Leslie. *b*: Grantham 1903. *e*: Kingswood Sch Bath. Editor & Journalist. *n.a*: Ed Advertiser's Weekly, Furnishing Trades' Organiser, Furnishing World, Furniture Manufacturer, Furnishing Dir Ideal Home. *s.s*: Furnishing. *Rec*: Sailing, rugby. *a*: 7 Tadcaster Court, Richmond, Surrey. *T*: 6210.

LEWIS, Rev. Lionel Richards, M.A. *b*: Highbury, London 1888. *e*: Merchant Taylor's Sch, St Johns' Coll Oxf, Ely Theological Coll, Priest C. of E., formerly Mem of Canadian Railway Mission, Rector of Inverary Argyll & Holy Trinity Bath, Mem of the Classical Assoc. *Publ*: Meditations for the Months; Boys' Camps, & How to Run Them. *s.s*: Devotional Works, Boy's Camps. *a*: Poughill Rectory, Crediton, Devon. *T*: Cheriton Fitzpaine 36.

LEWIS, Rev. Lionel Smithett, M.A. *b*: Margate 1867. *e*: Oundle & Queen's Coll Camb. *m*: Lilian Isolda Vereker. Vicar of Glastonbury since 1922, 5 yrs Priest in West Lond, 1 yr in Chapter Bristol, 22 yrs Priest in East London. *Publ*: St Joseph of Arimathea at Glastonbury; Glastonbury, the Mother of Saints; Her Saints A.D. 37—1549. *s.s*: History, Anti-Vivisection, Anti-Vaccination, Kindness to Animals. *Rec*: Motoring, cycling, gardening, antiquarianism, genealogy, heraldry, poetry. *c*: Eaton Square. *a*: The Vicarage, Glastonbury, Somerset.

LEWIS, Lionel William Pelling, M.A.(Cam), F.R.AstronS., M.R.S.T. *b*: Lon 1871. *e*: Univ Col Sc, Bedford G.S. & K. Edward VI Birm. Ret Schoolmaster. *n.a*: Snr Class Master Bishops Stortford, Newport & Bradford. *Publ*: Practical Hints on the Teaching of Latin (1919); Foundations for Latin Prose Composition (collab with E. H. Goddard); Foundations for Greek Prose Comp (in collab with L. M. Styler, '34); etc. *s.s*: Classical hist. Trav extensively. *Rec*: Golf. *a*: Solva Mawgan Porth, St Columb Minor, Cornwall. *t*: St Mawgan 26.

LEWIS, M. M., M.C., M.A., LL.B. *c.t*: Law Quarterly Review, Brit Year Book of Internat Law. *a*: 57 Pembroke Rd, Clifton, Bristol. *t*: 34746.

LEWIS, Michael Arthur. *b*: Freeland 1890. *e*: Uppingham Sch & Trinity Coll Camb. *m*: Muriel Doris Cruikshank. *s*: 1. *d*: 1. Prof of History & English R.N. Coll Greenwich. *Publ*: Afloat & Ashore; Fleeting Follies; Beg of the Upland; The Brand of the Beast; The Island of Disaster; Roman Gold; The Three Amateurs; The Crime of Herbert Wratislaus; When

First We Practise; England's Sea-Officers; British Ships & British Seamen; Armada Guns; The Ships & Seamen of Britain; The Navy of Britain. *Ctr*: Punch, Mariner's Mirror, Seafarer, Listener. *s.s*: Naval Hist & Nautical Research. *Rec*: Fishing, walking. *a*: 36 Dartmouth Row, London, S.E.10. *T*: Tideway 3517.

LEWIS, Mortimer Harman, B.Sc., F.Inst.F. *b*: Wolverhampton 1897. *e*: Forest Sch Walthamstow & London Univ. *m*: Doris Beatrice Edgington. *s*: 1. Cons Engineer. *n.a*: Ed Engineering & Boilerhouse Review 1931—39. *Ctr*: Fuel Economist, Iron & Coal Trades Review, Combustion (America), etc & Tech Papers to Eng Assocs. *s.s*: Investigations, into Use of Various Coals in Gt Brit & Abroad, & into Heat Absorption & Transfer in Large Water Tube Boiler Units. *Rec*: Motoring, motor engineering. *a*: 39 Arundel Ave, Ewell, Surrey. *T*: 1266.

LEWIS, Oscar. *b*: San Francisco, California 1893. *e*: Californian Schs. *m*: Betty L. Mooney. Writer. *Publ*: The Big Four; Bonanza Inn (with C. D. Hall); I Remember Christine; The Uncertain Journey; The Silver Kings; Hearn & His Biographers; A History of San Francisco; Lola Montez in California. *Ctr*: Atlantic Monthly, Harper's Monthly, Amer Mercury, N.Y. Times, Kansas City Star, N.Y. Her Trib, etc. *s.s*: Biography, Hist & Fiction (especially San Francisco). *a*: 549 Market St, San Francisco 5, California, U.S.A.

LEWIS, P. G., M.D., M.R.C.S., L.S.A. *Publ*: Principles & Practice of Nursing; Delicate Children; Spinal Curvature; Manual of Medical Exercises. *c.t*: Med papers. *a*: 22 Manor Rd, Folkestone. *t*: 3475.

LEWIS, P. J. *n.a*: Reporter Surrey Mirror Series. *a*: 11 Jubilee Terr, Dorking.

LEWIS, Paul. *b*: Lon 1873. *e*: Bedford G.S. & K. Edward H.S. Birm. *m*: Agnes Ottilia Valborg. *Publ*: The Romance of Water Power. *s.s*: Swedish-Eng trans. *a*: Hillside, Manaton, Newton Abbot.

LEWIS, Richard. *e*: Manchester G.S. *n.a*: Northern News Ed Sunday Dispatch. *a*: 19 Avonlea Rd, Sale, Cheshire. *t*: Sale 2341.

LEWIS, Robert Thomas, B.A., A.K.C. *b*: Blackpool 1893. *e*: Blackpool Gr Sch, King's Coll & London Univ. *m*: Lucy Rostrom. *s*: 1. Mang Ed. *n.a*: Asst Art Ed Dly Chronicle 1924, Cartoonist & Special Writer Sun Pictorial & Northcliffe Newsps '28, Mang Ed Bristol Ev World '31, Mang Ed & Dir Dly Mail Manch '37, Dir of Development Assoc Newsps '44, Chm Press Assoc '47—. *Publ*: Romulus or the Future of the Child; Composition Through Writing; New Outline Grammar of Function (collab); Business & Colloquial English for Foreign Students (collab); etc. *s.s*: Child Psychology & Humourous Cartooning. *a*: c/o Daily Mail, Northcliffe Hse, London, E.C.4.

LEWIS, Saunders, M.A.(L'pool). *b*: Wallasey 1893. *e*: Priv & Univ of L'pool. *m*: Margaret Gilchrist. *d*: 1. Pres Welsh Nat Party 1926—39. *Publ*: Books of Literary Criticism & History in Welsh; Volumes of Poems & Poetic Drama; Essays on Welsh Economic & Political Matters. *Ctr*: Welsh Monthlies & Lit. Quarterlies *s.s*: Welsh Lit & Polit (Nationalism). *a*: Llanfarian, Aberystwyth, Wales.

LEWIS, Sinclair. *Publ*: inc Our Mr Wrenn; Main Street; Babbitt; Martin Arrowsmith; Elmer Gantry; The Man Who Knew Coolidge; Dodsworth; Ann Vickers; Gideon Planish; Cass Timberlane; etc. c/o Random Hse, 457 Madison Ave, New York 22.

LEWIS, Thomas. M.A., B.D *b*: Conwil Elvet 1869. *e*: Univ Col Bangor, M/C & Marburg. *m*: Augusta Flora Williams. *s*: 3. *d*: 3. Princ of Theology Col. *Publ*: Commentary on Book of Amos; The Literature & Theology of the Prophets; The Old Testament: Its Contents & Message. *s.s*: Hebrew, Old Testament & Talmud. *a*: Memorial Col. Brecon. *t*: 179.

LEWIS, Rev. Thomas Frederick. *Publ*: Poems of Calm and Stress. *a*: 81 Newsham Drive, Newsham Park, L'pool.

LEWIS, Thos. H., O.B.E., M.B.E., F.R.G.S. ("Pat Riot," "Martin Sewell," "Theo Wiseman"). *e*: St Thomas Charterhouse, Lon. Journalist. *n.a*: Founder & 1st Ed The Service S. Africa, Founder & 1st Ed South African Chemist & Druggist, Formerly Asst Ed Farm & Home & Gardening Illus, Ed Sales Management 1921–. Org P.A.T.A. of S. Africa '13. Chm S. Ealing Traders' Assoc '28–29. Chm The Brit Sales Promotion Assoc '33. *Publ*: Women of South Africa; Children of South Africa; A Short Retail Selling Course. *c.t*: Business Ency & Journals throughout the world (400); wrote Salesmanship section of Retailers' Compendium. *s.s*: Salesmanship & business management. War Service, despatches. Exam in Shop Management & Retail Selling, Nat Pharm Un. Mem Faculty I.C.S. *Rec*: Song writing. *a*: 20 Bride Lane, E.C.4. *t*: Cent 7010.

LEWIS, Victor Alexander, M.J.I. *b*: Lon 1904. *e*: Bishop's Stortford & Lon Univ. *m*: Adelaide Maysie MacKay. *d*: 1. Journalist. *n.a*: Special Corr North Eastern Daily Gazette '26–27, F/L. '25–28 in North of Eng later in Lon, Jnd Reporting Staff Guernsey Star '28, Asst Ed '30, Ed Football Star '30, Acting Ed Guernsey Star '33, Ed '34, Mang Ed Channel Islands News Service '32, Times Corr '33. Mem Advertising Comm Guernsey Chamber of Comm, Press Publicity Officer States Comm for Advertising & Island, Sec Guernsey Business Hse Assoc, Pres Guernsey Branch L.N.U. (youth group), Press Censor Chamber of Comm. *Publ*: History of Channel Islands College Cricket ('29); Cricket Without Tears; Atlantic: A History of Atlantic Flights (in prep, '34); etc. *c.t*: Times, Observer, Sun Times, Daily Telegraph, Daily Mirror, Daily Express, News-Chronicle, Evening Standard, Cricketer, Aeroplane, Brit & Eve, Motor, Punch, etc. *s.s*: Aircraft & cricket. Mem Worshipful Coy of N/p Makers & Stationers. *Rec*: Cricket, rollerskating, hockey. *a*: 1 Arcade Ct, Guernsey, C.I. *t*: 1714.

LEWIS, W. F/L. *a*: 68 Makenade Avenue, Faversham, Kent.

LEWIS, William Charles. Journalist. *n.a*: Surrey Times, West Cumberland Times 1922–23, Carlisle Journ '24–. *a*: 4 Trevor St, Summer Hill, Lon Rd, Carlisle.

LEWIS, William Dodge, A.M., Ph.D. *b*: Russell, N.Y. 1870. *e*: Syracuse Univ. *m*: Louise Graff. *s*: 1. *d*: 1. Former Princ of Gr & Hgh Schs. *Publ*: Democracy's High School; The Silent Readers; (Co-Author) Practical English for High Schools; English for Grades Three to Eight; Grammar to Use; & Ed of various Text Books. *Ctr*: Outlook, Sat Ev Post, Ladies Home Journ, etc. *s.s*: English Composition & Lit. *Rec*: Music, bridge. *a*: 38 East Greenwood Ave, Lansdowne, Pennsylvania, U.S.A. *T*: Madison 2614.

LEWIS, Wilmarth Sheldon, M.A., Litt.D. *b*: Alameda, California 1895. *e*: Thatcher Sch, Yale, Brown & Rochester Univ. *m*: Annie Burr Auchincloss. Editor. *Publ*: The Yale Edition of Horace Walpole's Correspondence; Three Tours Through London in the

Years 1748, 1776, 1797; The Yale Collections, Tutor's Lane; (Ed) Private Charity in England 1747—57. *Ctr*: Atlantic Monthly, Yale Review. *s.s*: Horace Walpole & the English 18th Century. *Rec*: Tennis, croquet. *c*: Elizabethan. *w.s*: U.S. Army 1917—19. *a*: Farmington, Connecticut, U.S.A. *T*: Farmington 61.

LEWIS, Winifred. *b*: Woodford, Essex 1905. *e*: Loughton Hgh Sch. *m*: Richard Sheppard Kay. Journalist. *n.a*: Sub Ed Womans Pictorial 1926, Woman's Journ '27, Woman's Feature Writer '32, Woman Ed Britannia & Eve, Fashion Ed Illustrated Newsps Group '46—. *Ctr*: Various English & American periodicals (Women's), & newsps. *s.s*: Women's Interests (Fashions). *a*: 1 New Oxford St, London, W.C.1. *T*: Holborn 6955.

LEWIS, Winifred Agnes. *b*: Hafod 1865. *e*: St Winifred's Convent, Swansea. Woman Corr. *n.a*: S. Wales Daily Post 1902-. *a*: 1363 Neath Rd, Hafod.

LEWIS, Wyndham. Artist & Author of several volumes inc The Hitler Cult; The Mysterious Mr Bull; The Art of Being Ruled; Paleface; Filibusters in Barbary; Blasting & Bombardiering; etc.

LEWIS-BOWEN, Kathleen Mary. (See **PARR, Cooper.**) *b*: Poona, India 1910. *e*: Lourdes Mount Sth Ealing. *m*: Lt-Col J. W. Lewis-Bowen. *s*: 1. *d*: 4. *Ctr*: Illustrated Weekly of India, Onlooker (India). *s.s*: Fiction, Child Welfare, Blind Welfare. *Rec*: Bridge, tennis. *a*: Clynfiew, Boncath, Pembrokeshire, Wales.

LEWIS COX, Euphrasia. *b*: Penarth. *e*: Priv. *m*: William Charles Lewis Cox. *d*: 1. Novelist. *Publ*: King's Yellow; Mists That Blind; Jonathan; The Finest Thing; Arab; The Sea Gypsy; Strange Heaven; Hey, Mister; Honeymoon; Sandboy; Little Urchin; Love's Melody; Wildflower; Love Pirate. *c.t*: Bystander. *s.s*: Novels. *Rec*: Riding, travel. *c*: Pioneers, Writers. *a*: 36 Eresby Hse, Rutland Gate. S.W.8. *t*: Kens 3845.

LEWIS-DALE, Henry Angley, M.B.E., M.Inst. C.E., M.I.Mech.E. *b*: Weaverham 1876. *e*: Owens College, Manchester. Dep Dir of Works, Air Ministry. *Publ*: Aviation and the Aerodrome. *c.t*: Scientific & Technical Societies. *s.s*: Aerodrome Construction. Twice awarded Telford Premium for Papers on aerodrome Construction. *a*: 13 Keyes Rd, Cricklewood, N.W.2.

LEWISOHN, Ludwig, M.A. *b*: Berlin, Germany 1883. *e*: Charleston Hgh Sch & Coll, Columbia Univ. *m*: Louise Wolk. *s*: 1. Writer & Editor. *n.a*: Assoc Ed New York Nation 1918—24, Ed The New Palestine '43—47, Ed American Zionist Review '47—. *Publ*: An Altar in the Fields; The Defeated; Lost Days of Shylock; The Case of Mr Crump; The Island Within (British Title: The Defeated); Expression in America; Trumpet of Jubilee; Renegade; Breathe Upon These; Anniversary; etc. *Ctr*: Harper's Atlantic, Esquire, etc. *s.s*: Jewish History & Literature, Zionism, Goethe, Am Literature, Fiction. *a*: 57 Montgomery Pl, Brooklyn 15, N.Y. U.S.A., & Zionist Organisation of America, 41 East 42nd St, N.Y., U.S.A. *T*: Main 2-1668.

LEWITT, Ernest Henry. *b*: Nott'm 1891. *e*: Univ Col Nott'm. Married. *s*: 1. *d*: 1. Univ Lect in Eng. *Publ*: Hydraulics; The Rigid Airship; Thermodynamics Applied to Heat Engines. *s.s*: Mech, civil & aero eng. *c*: Inst Mech Engs. *a*: Imp Col of Science & Tech. S. Kensington.

LEX. (See **SANDERS, John Herne** & **ANDERSON, John.**) *Publ*: India at the Cross Roads. *a*: The Waldrons, Beechwood Ave, Weybridge. *T*: Walton 536.

LEWSEN, S. C. Physician. *c.t*: Lancet, B.M.J., etc. *a*: 25 College Cres, N.W.3. *t*: Primrose 6300.

LEY. A. S. R., F.R.I.B.A. *a*: Montague Hse, Sidcup, Kent.

LEY, Henry Ernest. *b*: Bristol 1902. *m*: Beatrice Eden. *s*: 1. Dis Staff Reporter. *n.a*: L'pool Post & Echo. *a*: 65 Norwood Cres, Southport. *t*: 8228.

LEY, Henry George, M.A., Mus.D., F.R.C.M., F.R.C.O. *b*: Chagford 1887. *e*: Uppingham & Keble Coll Oxf. *m*: Evelyn Mary Heurtley. Pres R.C.O., Precentor & Director of Music Eton Coll, Prof Roy Coll of Music. *Publ*: 4 Vols of Songs; Organ Music; The Church Anthem Book (with Sir Walford Davies); Church Music; Oxford Psalter & Chant Book (Jt-Ed). *Rec*: Golf, chess. *a*: Combewater Cottage, Metcombe, Ottery St Mary, Devon. *T*: Ottery St Mary 54.

LEY, James William Thomas. *b*: Bristol 1879. *e*: Bristol G.S. *m*: Florence Madeleine Westcott. *s*: 1. Journalist. *n.a*: Asst Ed Monmouthshire Evening Post; Leader Note Writer S. Wales Evening Express; now Ed Rep Western Mail & South Wales Echo. *Publ*: The Trial of John Jasper for the Murder of Edwin Drood (1914); The Dickens Circle: A Narrative of the Novelist's Friendships ('18); Annotated Edition of John Forster's Life of Charles Dickens ('28). *c.t*: The Dickensian (founder). *s.s*: Life & works of Charles Dickens. Founded Bristol & Clifton Dickens Soc '02 (first in Eng). Hon Gen Sec Dickens Fellowship '04—09. Vice-Pres Dickens Fellowship '19—. Chm S. Wales Br N.U.J. '15 & '33. Mem Nat Exec Counc '22—23. *Rec*: Books. *a*: Hatherleigh, 2 Allt-yr-Yn Rd, Newport, Mon. *t*: 3676.

LEYBOURNE-WHITE, Grace Gwendoline, M.A., B.Sc., Ph.D. *b*: Cardiff 1908. *e*: Howard Gardens Sch Cardiff, Univs of Cardiff, Liverpool & Chicago. *m*: Kenneth White (dec'd). Social Scientist & Psychologist. *Publ*: Education & the Birth Rate (with Kenneth White); Capacity & Opportunity for University Education; Children for Britain (with K. White); etc. *Ctr*: Pilot Papers, Sociolog Rev, Eugenics Rev, Philosoph Mag, etc. *s.s*: Psychology, Educ, Population Problem, Social Statistics. *Rec*: Walking, reading, music, art, theatre. *a*: 6 Scotsdale Close, Cheam, Surrey. *T*: Vigilant 3277.

LEYDS, WILLEM JOHANNES: writer; b. Magelang, Java, May 1, 1859; s. Willem Johannes and Nine Van Beuningen (Van Helsdingen) L.; educ. State School for Teachers (Haarlem), Amsterdam Univ. DEGREE: J. D. (cum laude); m. Anna Castens, 1910. AUTHOR: Derechtsgrond der schadevergoeding voor preventieve hechtenis, 1884; The First Annexation of the Transvaal (transl. into Dutch and German); Herinneringen aan President Krüger, 1918; Eenige Correspondentie uit 1899, 1919; The Transvaal Surrounded (transl. into Dutch) 1919. General character of writing: historical. Attorney-General South African Republic (Transvaal), 1884-1889; Justice of Peace for whole Republic, 1889; State Secretary, 1889-1898; Minister Plenipotentiary, 1898-1902. CLUBS: New Literary Club. Relig. denom., Protestant. HOME: 337 Frankenslag, The Hague, Holland.

LEYEL, Hilda Winifred. *b*: London. *e*: Halliwick Manor & France. *m*: C. F. Leyel (dec'd). *s*: 2. Chm & Mang Dir Soc Herbalist, French Palme Academique, Founded Soc Herbalists also Culpeper Shops. *Publ*: The Magic of Herbs; The Lure of Cookery; Herbal Delights; Compassionate Herbs; Elixirs of Life; Heartsease; The Truth about Herbs; Ed, Mrs Grieve's Modern Herbal. *s.s*: Herbs, Medicine & Cookery. *a*: 20 Old Square, Lincoln's Inn, London, W.C., & Shripney Manor, Shripney, Sussex.

LEYS, Norman Maclean, M.B., D.P.H. *Publ*: Kenya; A Last Chance in Kenya; etc. *c.t*: New Statesman, M/C Guardian, etc. *a*: Brailsford, nr Derby. *t*: 28.

LEYSMITH, Walter Farquharson. *b*: Burton-on-Trent 1886. *e*: Burton G.S. & Derby Tech Col. *m*: Daisy Compton Nunn. Engineer & Journalist. Gen Eng England, Canada, N.Z., Aust. C.P.R. Surveys W. Canada 1907-08. Otira Tunnel N.Z. '08-09. *n.a*: Ed The Motor in Australia '10-'11, Motoring, Aviation & Gen Staff Corr Sydney Morning Herald '11-14, Served Egypt, Sinai, France until Oct '17, Rep Daily Mail '17-21, Night News Ed Daily Express '21-22, Staff Corr Aust N/ps Cable Service '22-29, Foreign Corr Staff N.Y. Times '29-. *s.s*: Engineering, golf. Is believed to be the 1st rep to receive an assignment by wireless telephony at Hampstead Heath, July 23, '20, when an experimental portable set built by Marconi was used. *Rec*: Travel. *c*: Roehampton. *a*: 40 Clarelawn Av, E. Sheen, S.W.14. *t*: Prospect 4115.

LEYTON, Mrs H. G., M.D. Med Research. *Publ*: Septic Foci in Normal Labour; etc. *a*: Hinksey Hill, nr Oxford.

LEYTON, Otto. *b*: Lon 1873. *e*: Trin Col Cam. *m*: Doris Catherine McPhail. *s*: 1. *d*: 1. Physician. *Publ*: Diagnosis & Treatment of Diabetes Mellitus. *c.t*: Med Journals, & Price's Textbook of Medicine, Prognosis. *s.s*: Metabolic diseases & diseases of the internal secreting glands. *Rec*: Lawn tennis. *a*: 92 Portland Pl, W.1, & Monks Corner, Marlow. *t*: Welbeck 2299.

LHOYD-OWEN, Cmdr. John Hugh, F.R.Hist.S., R.N. *b*: Penisarwaen, Wales 1895. *e*: The Elms Colwall & Rossall Sch. Naval Historian. *Publ*: Co-Author 1914—18, Author '39— of the Confidential Admiralty Staff Hist of Naval Operations. *Rec*: Cricket, carpentry, amateur stage management. *w.s*: World War I. *a*: Gallions Reach, Romany Rise, Crofton, Orpington, Kent. *T*: Orpington 1026.

LIAS, Godfrey. *e*: St Lawrence Col Ramsgate & King's Col Cam. *m*: Una Rosamond Money. *d*: 2. Journalist. *n.a*: Diplomatic Corr Christian Science Monitor 1921-. *c.t*: News-Chron, Morning Post, Sunday Times, Punch, Week-end Review, etc. *s.s*: Foreign affairs, travel. Frequently broadcast on current events, etc. *c*: Oxf & Cam, Roy Inst of Internat Affairs. *a*: 109 Lonsdale Rd, S.W.13. *t*: Riverside 0711.

LIBERTY, Rev. Dr Stephen, D.D.(Oxon). *b*: West Brompton 1871. *e*: Westminster Sch & Christ Ch Oxf. *m*: Mary Pearson. Vice-Princ Lichfield Theological Coll 1899—1901, Sub-Warden St Deiniol's Library Hawarden '05—10, Examining Chaplain to Bishop of Gloucester '29—46, Benefices Held in Furness (Lancs), Westmorland & Gloucestershire, Retired from Parish Work in '46. *Publ*: The Political Relations of Christ's Ministry; Religion in Wordsworth; The Father of Warren Hastings. *Ctr*: XIX Century & After, Journ of Theological Studies, Ch Quarterly Review, etc. *s.s*: New Testament Scholarship & First Century History, Study of Wordsworth. *a*: The Old Smithy, Filkins, Lechlade, Glos.

LICHFIELD, Lord Bishop of (John Augustine Kempthorne). *Publ*: Pastoral Life and Work To-day. *a*: The Palace, Lichfield, Staffs.

LICHNOWSKY, PRINCESS MECHTILDE: writer; *b*. Castle Schönburg (Germany); *d*. Conut Maximilian and Baroness Olga (Werther) Arco; educ. in a convent from 1892-1896; *m*. Prince Carlmax Lichnowsky, Aug. 22, 1904 (died 1928; was German Ambassador in London from 1912-1914). AUTHOR: Götter Könige und Tiere in Aegypten, 1912; Der Stimmer, 1914; Gott betet, 1914; Ein Spiel vom Tod, 1915; Der Kinderfreund, 1916; Geburt, 1918; Der Kamp mit dem Fachmann, 1923; Das Rendez-vous in Zoo, 1926; An der Leine, 1930. Contributes to Berliner Tageblatt, Frankfurter Z e i t u n g, Deutsche Rundschau, Schlesiche Blätter, Der Querschnitt. General character of writing: fiction, essays, plays, poems. Religion: Catholic. ADDRESS Villa des Fleurs, Cap d'Ail, A. M., France.

LIDDELL HART, Basil Henry. Military Correspondent & Author of The Revolution in Warfare; Why Don't We Learn from History? The Strategy of Indirect Approach; Dynamic Defence; and many other works on military tactics, defence & history. *a*: Tilford Hse, Tilford.

LIDDIARD, Mabel, S,R.N., S.C.M., Cert.M.T.S. Formerly Nursing Dir Mothercraft Training Soc. *Publ*: Mothercraft Manual; Red Cross Infant Welfare Manual. *a*: 9a Bisham Gardens, Highgate, London, N.6. *T*: Mountview 9295.

LIDGETT, Albert. *b*: Longton 1876. *e*: Longton Endowed Sc. *m*: L. Newman. N/p Prop. *n.a*: Staffs Daily Sentinel '94, Staffs Evening Post '95, Stafford Chronicle '96, Oldham Daily Standard '97, Ed Croydon Chronicle '99, Prop Ed Petroleum Times 1901-. *Publ*: Petroleum. *s.s*: Petroleum. During War (in conj with Mr Charles Watney late Ed Daily Mail) organised Russian Red Cross Days throughout Eng, whilst also conducting his wkly journ in Lon. Raised over £300,000. After the Russian Revolution organised Italian Red Cross Days & later St Dunstan's Flag Day in Lon raising £66,000 for the late Sir Arthur Pearson. Mem Coy of Needlemakers. *a*: 4 Broad St Pl, E.C.2, & Edelweiss, Purley, Surrey.

LIDGETT, John Scott, C.H., M.A., D.D., LL.D. *b*: Lewisham 1854. *e*: Blackheath Proprietary & Univ Coll London. *m*: Emmaline Martha Davies. *s*: 1. *d*: 1. Meth Min & Warden Bermondsey Settlement. *n.a*: Ed Methodist Times 1907—18, Jt Ed Contemporary Review '11—. *Publ*: The Spiritual Principle of the Atonement; The Fatherhood of God in Christian Life & Truth; God, Christ & the Church; The Victorian Transformation of Theology; etc. *Ctr*: Contemporary Review, etc. *Rec*: Music. *a*: Bermondsey Settlement, Farncombe St, London, S.E.16. *T*: Bermondsey 2127.

LIDSEY, J. A. Journalist. *a*: 8 Debenham Rd, Yardley, Birmingham.

LIDSTONE, George Henry. *b*: Pembroke 1911. Journalist. *n.a*: Ed Staff North Devon Herald 1925-29, Dist Reporter Western Morning News '29-33, Guernsey Star '34, Chief Reporter Torquay Times & Torquay Directory '34-. *a*: Ivanhoe, 25 Lower Shirburn Rd, Torquay.

LIDSTONE, George James, LL.D(Edin). F.I.A., F.F.A., F.A.S. *b*: London 1870. *e*: Private Sc Lond. *m*: Florence Mary Gay. Retired. *c.t*: Journal of Inst Actuaries; Trans of Faculty of Actuaries; Mathematical Gazette; Proc Edin Math Soc. *s.s*: Actuarial Science. Finite Differences. Presented 1929 by Insti Actuaries & Faculty of Actuaries in Scotland, with Gold Medal specially designed by Gilbert Bayes, R.S.B.S. in recognition of Services to Actuarial Science. *Rec*: Music, lawn tennis, travel; *c*: Junior Carlton; City of London University (Edin). *a*: Hermiston House, Hermiston, Midlothian. *t*: Currie 22.

LIE, Haakon. *b*: Fyresdal, Norway. *m*: Hjordis Dorthea Smevig Dahl. *s*: 3. Master of Forestry (Norwegian Govt). *Publ*: Mold og Makter; Dagen og Draumen; Nord i Elvelendet; Gjester pa Jordi; Ekorngutten; (poems) Solspelet; Floyta og Fela; Det Skugger over Hei; etc. *Ctr*: Tidens Tegn, Morgenbladet, Norsk Tidend, Syn og Segn, etc. *s.s*: Poetry, Life of Peasants & Hunters, Norwegian Animal Wild Life, etc. *Rec*: Gardening, walking tours in the mountains. *a*: Lillehammer, Norway. *T*: 50242.

LIEBENBERG, Schalk Willem Jacobus. *b*: Piketberg 1905. *e*: Edin, Stellenbosch Univ. *m*: Henrietta Christiene Smith. *s*: 2. *d*: 1. Mang Dir S.C.A. Coy of Sth Afria & of Univ Publishers & Booksellers Ltd. *n.a*: Co-Ed Dir Oorvloedige Lewe 1945—. *Publ*: Kaptein Yan sy Skool; Onder n Vraagteken; Die Dromer en Ander Verhale; Hanhou Wen; Oorwinnende Genade; Gideon Scheepers. *Ctr*: Die Wekroep, etc. *s.s*: Religious, Devotional. *Rec*: Golf. *a*: P.O. Box 25, Stellenbosche, Cape, Sth Africa. *T*: 814.

LIEBESCHUTZ, Hans, M.A., D.Phil.(Heidelberg). *b*: Hamburg 1893. *e*: Johanneum Hamburg, Univ of Berlin, Marburg, Heidelberg. *m*: Rahel Plant. *s*: 2. *d*: 1. Univ Lect in Medieval History, History Master Lichtwark Schule Hamburg 1929—34, Lecturer for Medieval Latin Hamburg Univ '29—34, Lect for Medieval Hist Jewish Coll Berlin '36—39, Liverpool Univ since '46. *Publ*: Das Weltbild der Neiligen Hildegard; Fulgentius Metaforalis. *Ctr*: Bibliography of the survival of the Classics, The British Journ of Educational Psychology, etc. *s.s*: Hist of Medieval Thought. *c*: Univ L'pool. *a*: The Mount, 6 Westhill Ave, Epsom Surrey.

LIED, Jonas, F.R.G.S. *b*: Veoey, Norway 1881. *e*: State Sch. Farmer. *Publ*: Return to Happiness; Sidelights on the Economic Situation in Russia; Prospector in Siberia; Over De Hoye Fjelle. *Ctr*: Times, Russian & Siberian Newsps. *s.s*: Russian & Siberia. *Rec*: Skiing, fishing. *c*: Junior Carlton (Lond). *a*: Nesjestranda, Norway.

LIEF, Stanley. *e*: Johannesburg & Chicago. Osteopath. *n.a*: Ed Health for All. *Publ*: Diet-Reform Simplified; How to Feed Children. *c.t*: Various N/ps. *s.s* Nature cure. *a*: Dell Pond, Champneys, Tring, Herts. *t*: Berkhamsted 406.

LIEFERANT, Henry. *b*: 1892. *e*: Sec Sch. *m*: Sylvia B. Lieferant. Writer. *n.a*: Ed 1928—42, Supervising Ed '42—46 Macfadden Publs. *Publ*: Grass on the Mountain; Seven Daughters; United They Stand; They Always Come Home; Doctors Wives; One Enduring Purpose; Charity Patient; Teacher's Husband; Hospital—Quiet Please; Heavenly Harmony; Fields White to Harvest. *Ctr*: U.S., British & Canadian Mags. *a*: 54 Riverside Drive, New York 24, N.Y., U.S.A. *T*: Endicott 2-8031.

LIEN-TEH, WU: physician, naturalist; b. Penang, Malaya, China, March, 1879; s. Wu Hsuch Chi and Lin Choi-fan; educ. Penang Free Sch. (Malaya); Emmanuel Coll. (Cambridge, Eng.); St. Mary's Hospital (London); Johns Hopkins Univ. Sch. of Hygiene (Baltimore, U.S.A.); DEGREES: M.A., M.D. (Cambridge); LL.D. (Hongkong); C.P.H., M.D. (Tokyo); Litt. D. (Peking); Sc.D. (Shanghai); m. Huang-Shu Chiung, 1905. AUTHOR: Medical Education in China, 1913; A Treatise on Pneumonic Plague, 1926; Health Preservation in China, 1929; History of Chinese Medicine, (Dr. K. C. Wong), 1929. Editor of National Medical Jnl. of China, 15 yrs. Contributor to American Jnl. of Hygiene, British Jnl. of Hygiene, National Medical Jnl. of China, Japan Medical World, Centralblatt für Bakteriologie; China Medical Jnl., Lancet (Eng.), and others. General character of writing: mostly medical and scientific, sometimes on social subjects. Leader of modern medicine in China; founder of National Medical Jnl.; pres. of National Med. Assn. of China, 1915-20; physician extraordinary to successive presidents of China, 1911-26; government delegate to scientific, medical and opium conferences all over world. Interested in all philanthropic and humanitarian undertakings. Relig. denom., Free Thinker. CLUBS: Union, Shanghai, and others. ADDRESS: Plague Prevention Service, Harbin, China.

LIGHT, Donald Alfred. *b*: 1894. *e*: Our Lady Immaculate's Everton & Priv. *m*: Ellen McConnell. *s*: 2. *d*: 1. Journalist. *n.a*: Shipping Ed Journ of Commerce & Shipping Telegraph 1919—. *s.s*: Shipping. *Rec*: Gardening. *w.s*: 1914—18. *a*: 23 Allangate Rd, Liverpool 19. *T*: Central 7601.

LIGHTBURN, J. G. *n.a*: Sub-Ed Westmorland Gazette. *a*: Park Av, Kendal.

LIGHTFOOT, George Cecil, B.A., M.A. *b*: Lancaster 1903. *e*: Lancaster Roy G.S., Downing Col Cam. Schoolmaster. *Publ*: Progressive Latin Reader; Progressive Latin Exercises; Lucretius V; Modern English Grammar; etc. *s.s*: Classics. *Rec*: Football, swimming, philately. *c*: I.A.A.M. Lon Branch Official. *a*: 4 Ravenna Rd, Putney, S.W.15.

LIGHTHALL, William Doruv. K.C., LL.D., F.R.S.L., F.R.S.C. *Publ*: inc The Law of Cosmic Evolutionary Adaptation; The Diffusion Controversy; Astronomy Decides It; The Beginnings of British Settlement in the Province of Quebec; & many historical & literary works. *a*: Westmount, Montreal, Canada.

LIGHTLEY, Rev. John William, M.A., D.Lit. (Q.U.B.), B.D.(Paris). *b*: Simonside 1867. *e*: Didsbury Col M/C, Paris Protestant Faculty of Theo & Sorbonne, Leipzig Univ. Princ Wesley Col Leeds. *Publ*: Les Scribes; Jewish Sects & Parties in the Time of Christ. *s.s*: Old Testament. Pres Wes Conf 1928-29. *Rec*: Golf. *a*: Col Hse, Wesley Col, Headingley, Leeds 6. *t*: 51256.

LIGHTWOOD, James Thomas. *b*: Leeds 1856. *e*: Kingswood Sc Bath. *n.a*: Ed The Choir 1910—. *Publ*: Hymn Tunes and their Story; Romance of Cycling; Charles Dickens and Music; Music & Literature. *c.t*: Methodist Mag. *s.s*: Music. *Rec*: Cycling. *c*: Authors. *a*: 14 West Beach, Lytham, Lytham St Annes Lancs.

LILLEY, Rev. Alfred Leslie. *b*: Co Armagh 1860. *e*: Roy Sch Armagh & Trin Coll Dublin. *m*: Mary Leslie Blackburn. *d*: 2. *Publ*: Adventus Regni; The Soul of St Paul; The Religion of Life; The Nation in Judgment; Prayer in Christian Theology; Modernism—A Record & Review; Worship; Sacraments; Religion & Revelation (Paddock Lectures for '31); etc. *Ctr*: Speaker, Contemporary Review, Guardian, Independent Review, Hibbert Journ, Church Quarterly Review, Theology, etc. *a*: 25 Norham Rd, Oxford.

LILLIE, John Adam, M.A., LL.B., K.C.(Scot). Barrister-at-Law Middle Temple. Lect on Mercantile Law Edin Univ. *Publ*: The Mercantile Law of Scotland (with A. McNeill). *c.t*: Green's Ency of Scots Law. *a*: 85 Gt King St, Edin. *t*: 25858.

LIM, BOON KENG: (L. M. Wen Ching); physician, president University of Amoy; b. Singapore, Straits Settlements, Oct., 1869; s. Lim Tian Giao and So Ching Tien; educ. Raffles Institution (Singapore), Univ. Edinburgh, Univ. Cambridge). DEGREES: M.B., C.M. (First

Class Honors), LL.D. (Hong Kong Univ.); m. Grace Pekha Yin, April 4, 1907. AUTHOR: Chinese Crisis From Within, 1901; The Great War from the Confucian Point of View,, 1919; Tragedies of Eastern Life, 1927; Translation of the Li Sao, 1929; The New China, 1929. Editor (acting): Malaya Tribune. Contributor to Straits Chinese Mag., Malaya Tribune, Edinburgh Med. Journ., Journ. of Straits Branch, Brit. Med Assn., Tropical Hygiene and Medicine. General character of writing: Medical, historical, fiction, poems, essays. Queen's Scholar, Straits Settlements, 1887; librarian and pres.-elect Royal Med. Soc. (Edinburgh), 1892; mem. Legislative Council, S. S., 1895; J. P., Singapore. Started New Confucian restoration; introduced the Mandarin Study in Malaysian for public services; O.B.E.; represented China at Internat. Hygiene Exhibition, Dresden; 2nd Class Chia Ho and 2nd Class Wen Hu decorations of Chinese Republic. Pres. Amoy Univ. since 1921. Relig. faith, Confucian. CLUB: Garden (Singapore). OFFICE: President's Office, University, Amoy. HOME: Pit-Kay-San, Kulangsu, Amoy, Fukien Province, China.

LILLINGSTON, Rev. Canon A. B. G. Canon & Sub-Dean Durham Cathedral. *Publ*: Thoughts on Evangelism. *a*: The Col, Durham. *t*: 44.

LIMA, Amoroso Alceu (see **ATHAYDE, Tristao de**). *b*: Federal District 1893. *e*: Law Sch. *m*: Maria Thereza de Faria. *s*: 4. *d*: 3. Prof of Brazilian Lit in the Univ of Brazil (Rio de Janiero) Mem of the Brazilian Acad of Letters. *s.s*: Lit Criticism, Sociology. *Rec*: Symphonic concerts, cinema. *a*: 149 Rua Dona Mariana, Rio de Janiero, Brazil. *T*: 26. 1304.

LIMNELIUS, George. See **Robinson, Lewis George.**

LINAKER, Percy, F.I.J. *e*: Preston G.S. *m*: G. M. Attenborough. Journalist. *n.a*: Ed Leamington Chronicle & Oxf Chronicle 1903-28. *c.t*: Times Lit Supp, Glas Herald, Oxf Times, etc. *s.s*: French lit. *Rec*: Travel. *c*: Oxf Union. *a*: 2 Black Hall Rd, Oxf. *t*: 3870.

LINCOLN, ARTHUR (pen name): see **Haydon, Arthur**.

LINCOLN, E. R. W. Ed Cage Birds 1922—. *a*: 1 Dorset Hse, Stamford St, London, S.E.1.

LINCOLN. Eric. See **Waldron, Eric.**

LINCOLN, Cmdr. Fredman Ashe, K.C., M.A., B.C.L., R.N.V.R. *b*: Plymouth 1907. *e*: Hoe Gr Sch Plymouth, Paterson Hgh Sch New Jersey U.S.A., Haberdashers Askes Sch & Exeter Coll Oxf. *m*: Eileen Sybil Cohen. Barrister, Mem Roy Inst of Internat Affairs. *Publ*: Statesmanship & other Essays; Legal Background to the Starra; Is Orthodoxy Worth While; The Starra. *Ctr*: Law Quarterly Review. *s.s*: Polit Sci, Legal Hist. *Rec*: Riding, tennis, philately. *c*: Roy Auto, Roy Corinthian Yacht. *a*: Armitage Hse, 4 Armitage Rd, Golder's Green, London, N.W.11. *T*: Speedwell 3841.

LINCOLN, Rt. Rev. the Bishop of. *Publ*: The Fullness of Sacrifice. *a*: The Old Palace, Lincoln.

LIND, Walter Peterson, M.C. *b*: Lon 1876. *e*: Eng, Lausanne, Gottingen & Bergen, Norway. *m*: Randi de Lange. *s*: 2. Coffee Planter. *c*: Lon Philatelist, Collectors Club Philatelist (N.Y.), etc. *s.s*: Stamps of Guatemala. War Service. *Rec*: Golf, fishing. *c*: F.R.S.A., City Carlton, M.R.P.S.L., Norwegian (Lon). *a*: The Copse Hse, Surbiton, Surrey. *t*: Elmbridge 2200.

LINDE, Per Johan Ebbe Fredrik. *b*: Kolmarden 1897. *e*: Univs of Stockholm & Gothenburg. *m*: *s*: 1. *d*: 3. Teacher on Electrochemistry at Chalmers Polytech Inst Gothenburg. *Publ*: (Poems) I-III ; (Plays) The Outlook; Bride's Spur; The Mustard Grain; The Ice-Light; Gilgamesh; (Essays) Crime & Punishment. *Ctr*: Bonniers Litterara Mag, Expressen, Ny Tid, etc. *s.s*: Theatre, Psychology. *Rec*: Canoeing, swimming, cycling, travel. *a*: Ljungatten 4 A, Gothenburg (summers Kolmarden) Sweden. *T*: Goteborg 13 74 99.

LINDEGREEN, Johan Erik. *b*: Lulea, Sweden 1910. *e*: Stockholms Hogskola. *m*: *d*: 1. *Publ*: Mannen Utan Vag; Sviter. *Ctr*: B.L.M. Stockholms Tidn, VI. *s.s*: Modern Poetry. *Rec*: Tennis. *c*: P.E.N. *a*: Oregrundsgatan 8, Stockholm, Sweden. *T*: 673621.

LINDEMAN, Eduard Christian, LL.D., B.S. *b*: St Clair, Michigan 1885. *e*: Michigan State Coll. *m*: Hazel Charlotte Taft. *d*: 4. Teacher & Writer. *n.a*: Ctr Ed New Republic 1924—47, Adv Ed Rural America, Youth Leaders, Ctr Ed Journ of Social Forces. *Publ*: The Community; Social Discovery; The Meaning of Adult Education; Urbak Sociology; Dynamic Social Research; Social Education; Wealth & Culture; Leisure: A National Issue; (Ed) Emerson, The Basic Writings of. *Ctr*: New Republic, Survey, Atlantic Monthly, etc. *s.s*: Sociology, Educ (Adult), Philosophy. *Rec*: Tennis, ornithology. *a*: 235 East 22nd St, New York 10, N.Y., U.S.A. *T*: Murray Hill 6-8947.

LINDEMANN, Edward Kelvin. *b*: Kainsk 1911. *m*: Elena Martens. *d*: 2. Writer. *Publ*: The House with the Green Tree; Den Kan Vel Frihed Baere. *Ctr*: Various Scandinavian periodicals. *s.s*: Scandinavian Hist & Politics, Gold Coast Hist, Film Plays. *Rec*: Fishing & horse-riding. *c*: Adventurers' (Copenhagen). *a*: Hunters Cott, Fredensborg, Denmark. *T*: Fredensborg 1580.

LINDESAY, Lt.-Col. V. E. H., I.M.S.(ret). *c,t*: Lancet, B.M.J., etc. *a*: Bisterne Croft, Burley, Hants. *t*: 69.

LINDLEY, Sir M. Frank, C.B., LL.D., B.Sc. *b*: Burgess Hill, Sussex 1881. *e*: Brighton Science Sch & U.C.L. *m*: Razel Elizabeth Hargreaves. *s*: 1. *d*: 1. Comptroller-Gen of Patents Designs & Trade Marks & Comptroller of the Industrial Property Dept of the Bd of Trade 1932—44, Scientific Adv to Appointments Dept Min of Lab & Nat Service '44—45, Barrister, Mem Enemy Debts & Trade Marks & Internat Copyright Cttees. *Publ*: The Acquisition & Government of Backward Territory in International Law (a treatise on the law & practice relating to colonial expansion). *Rec*: The countryside. *a*: Hestia, Woodland Way, Kingswood, Surrey. *T*: Mogador 2538.

LINDRUM, Walter. *Publ*: Billiards. *a*: c/o Methuen & Co Ltd, 36 Essex St, W.C.2.

LINDSAY, Anna Robertson Brown, M.A., Ph.D. *b*: Washington D.C. 1864. *e*: Wellesley Coll, Oxf Univ, Univ of Penna. *m*: Samuel Lindsay. *s*: 1. *d*: 2. Author. *Publ*: What is Worth While; The Victory of Our Faith; Culture & Reform; Giving What We Have; What Good Does Wishing Do; The Warriors; The Spiritual Care of a Child; Working With Giant Power; etc. *s.s*: Lit, Religious Educ. *c*: Wellesley (N.Y.), Town Hall (N.Y.). *a*: 29 Claremont Ave, New York 27, N.Y. *T*: Un 4-6866.

LINDSAY, David Kenneth Llewelyn, M.A., M.D., D.T.M., F.R.G.S. *b*: Paraguay 1904. *e*: Southport Col, Edin, Prague, L'pool & London Univs. *m*: Muriel Buckenham. Physician.

Capt I.M.S. *c.t*: Med & geog journs. *s.s*: Tropical medicine. Extensive travel. *c*: Overseas. *a*: BM/CNPJ, W.C.1.

LINDSAY, Douglas. See **Palmer, W. T.**

LINDSAY, E. C., C.B.E., F.R.C.S., M.B., B.S.(Lon). *Publ*: Intussusception; Post-operative Gastric Acidity; etc. *a*: 33 Wimpole Street, W.1.

LINDSAY, Howard. *b*: Waterford, New York 1889. *e*: Boston Latin Sch. *m*: Dorothy Stickney. Dramatist. *Publ*: Plays—(with B. Robinson) Tommy; Your Uncle Dudley; Oh Promise Me; (with R. Crouse) Anything Goes; Red Hot & Blue; Hooray for What; Life With Father; Strip for Action; State of the Union; (with Damon Runyon) A Slight Case of Murder; (from Novel by E. Hope) She Loves Me Not. *a*: 13 East 94th St, New York City, N.Y.

LINDSAY, Jack. *b*: Melbourne 1900. Author. *Publ*: I am a Roman; Rome for Sale; Mediæval Latin Poets; Caesar is Dead; The Romans; Last Days With Cleopatra; Storm at Sea; Lost Birthright; Hannibal Takes a Land; Stormy Violence; Barriers Are Down; Beyond Terror; Time to Live; The Subtle Knot; Men of 48; Song of a Falling World; (Ed) New Development Series. *a*: c/o Andrew Dakers Ltd, 39 Store St, London, W.C.1.

LINDSAY, Jean Olivia, M.A., Ph.D. *b*: Bangalore, India 1910. *e*: Queen's Coll Harley Street Lond, Girton Coll Camb. *m*: H. D. R. P. Lindsay. Lecturer in Modern History Camb Univ. *Publ*: Trade & Peace with Old Spain. *Ctr*: Camb Hist Journ, English Hist Review, Political Quarterly. *s.s*: Mod European Hist, Political Science, Economic Hist. *Rec*: Local government, Sunday sch teaching, international historical congresses. *w.s*: Served with the F.A.N.Y. 1943—45, North Africa, Italy, Egypt & Greece. *a*: Girton College, Cambridge. *T*: Cambridge 76219.

LINDSAY, John Maurice. *b*: Glasgow 1918. *e*: Glasgow Academy, Roy Scottish Nat Academy of Music. Scottish Poet, Author, Journalist, Broadcaster, Rockfeller Atlantic Award 1947. *Publ*: The Enemies of Love; Selected Scots Poems; Hurlygush. *n.a*: Music Critic Bulletin & Scots Pictorial 1947—, Music & Drama Critic Scottish Dly Mail '46, Ed Con Brio, Ed Modern Scottish Poetry, Poetry Scotland Nos 1—4, No Scottish Twilight (with Fred Urquhart). *Ctr*: Life & Letters, Scottish Art & Letters, The Voice of Scotland, Music & Letters, The Scots Rev, Contemp Poetry (U.S.A.), Poetry Australia, Poetry London, Poetry Quarterly, Irish Times. *s.s*: Scottish Literature, Scots Poetry, Scots Language, 18th-Cent Music. *Rec*: Walking, advancing the cause of Scottish home rule and debunking the English. *a*: 13 Southpark Ave, London, W.2. *T*: Kelvin 1442.

LINDSAY, Kathleen. Author. *Publ*: The Mystery at Greystones; It Happened at the Cape; 'Neath the Southern Cross; Green Domino; Wind of Desire; Harvest of Deceit. *a*: 113 Churchgate, Hesketh Pk, Southport.

LINDSAY, Kenneth Martin, M.P. *b*: London 1897. *e*: St Olave's Gr Sch & Worcester Coll Oxf. M.P. (Ind) Combined Eng Univs, Parl Sec Bd of Educ 1937—40, Pres Oxf Univ. *Publ*: Social Progress & Educational Waste; English Education. *Ctr*: Spectator, Observer, Manch Guardian, etc. *s.s*: Educational Questions, European Politics & Parl Institutions. *Rec*: Cricket, tennis, climbing. *c*: Athenæum. *a*: 39 Hill St, London, W. *T*: Grosvenor 3484.

LINDSAY, Sir Lionel Arthur, Kt. Author of several works on Art inc Addled Art; Charles Keene The Artist's Artist; A Book of Woodcuts; A. J. Munnings, R.A.; etc. *a*: 7 Burns Rd, Wahroonga, Sydney, Aust.

LINDSAY, Martin Alexander, D.S.O., M.P. *b*: London 1905. *e*. Wellington Coll Sandhurst. *m*: Joyce Lindsay. *s*: 2. *d*: 1. Soldier, Explorer: Brit Arctic Air-Route Expd 1930—31, Leader Brit Trans-Greenland Expd '34. *Publ*: Those Greenland Days; The Epic of Captain Scott (Great Occasions); Sledge, the British Trans-Greenland Expd; So Few got Through; Three Got Through; The House of Commons; Shall We Reform the Lords? *s.s*: Politics, Travel, War. *w.s*: World War II (Des). *a*: House of Commons, London, S.W.1.

LINDSAY, Philip, F.S.A.(Scot). Author of many historic novels inc Panama is Burning; London Bridge is Falling; Pudding Lane; Kings of Merry England; Crowned Kings of England; etc. *a*: c/o Curtis Brown Ltd, 6 Henrietta St, Covent Gdn, W.C.2.

LINDSAY, Samuel McCune, LL.D., Ph.D. *b*: Pittsburgh, Pa 1869. *e*: Univs of Pennsylvania, Halle, Berlin, Vienna, Rome & Paris. Prof Emeritus of Social Legislation Columbia Univ 1939—. *Publ*: Price Movements of the Precious Metals; Social Aspects Philadelphia Relief Work; Railway Labor in the U.S.; Reports on Education in Porto Rico; Financial Administration of Great Britain (in collab); Social Insurance; etc. *Ctr*: Polit Sci Quarterly, Ency Brit, etc. *s.s*: Social Legislation, Econs (Labor), Sociology. *Rec*: Golf, tennis. *c*: Century, Town Hall (N.Y.), etc. *a*: 29 Claremont Ave, New York 27, N.Y. *T*: Un 4-6866.

LINDSAY, Thomas, M.D., F.R.C.S.E., D.P.M. Supt Caterham Mental Hosp. *c.t*: B.M.J., Journ of Mental Science. *a*: The Pines, Caterham. *t*: 116.

LINDSAY, Thomas Fanshawe. *b*: Bhagalpur, India 1910. *e*: Seaford, Charterhouse & Corpus Christi Coll Oxf. Asst Dir Dept of Information Services Conservative Central Office 1947—. *n.a*: Ed The Isis & attached Ed Staff News Chron 1932—35, Asst Ed The Tablet '36—37, Asst Press Officer British Council '38, Asst Dir Press Div '40, Production Div '45. *Publ*: Psychoanalytical Method & the Doctrine of Freud (from the French of R. Dalbiez); The Holy Rule for Laymen. *s.s*: Modern Medical Psychology, Benedictine Monasticism. *Rec*: Hunting, bridge, chess. *c*: Oriental. *a*: 9 Beaufort Gdns, London, S.W.3. *T*: Kensington 7658; & The Cott, Wellesbourne, Warwick. *T*: Wellesbourne 221.

LINDSAY, T(HOMAS) S(OMERVILLE): Archdeacon (retired); b. Cork, Ireland, Nov., 1854; *s*. Joseph Woodley and Anna Somerville (Reeves) L.; educ. Trinity Coll. (Dublin); DEGREES: M.A., B.D. (Dublin); m. Sara Elizabeth Twigg. AUTHOR: Healthy, Wealthy and Wise, 1900; St. Doulagh's Church, 1906; The Church's Song, 1920; Plant Names, 1925; Sunlit Hours, 1927; Some Archbishops of Dublin, 1928; A Shortened Psalter, 1930. Relig. denom., Church of Ireland. CLUBS: University. HOME: Malahide, Dublin, Ireland.

LINDSAY, Dr. W. J., M.B.E. Ophthalmic Surg. *Publ*: Papers on medical subjects. *a*: 79 Wimpole St, W.1.

LINDSAY, Lilian, C.B.E., LL.D., M.D.S., H.D.D. (see **MURRAY, Lilian**). *b*: London 1871. *e*: Camden & Nth Lond Schs for Girls, Edin Dental Sch. *m*: Robert Lindsay (dec'd). Pres B.D.A. 1946—47, B.S.S.O.'38—. *n.a*: Sub-Ed British Dental Journ. *Ctr*: Brit Dental Journal, Proc Roy Soc Med, Journ of American Dental Assoc, etc. *s.s*: Hist of Dentistry. *a*: 13 Hill St, Berkeley Sq, London, W.1. *T*: Grosvenor 1592.

LINDSELL, Lieut-General Sir Wilfrid Gordon, G.B.E., K.C.B., D.S.O., M.C., LL.D. *b*: Portsmouth 1884. *e*: Birkenhead Sch, Victoria Coll Jersey & Roy Mil Acad Woolwich. *m*: Marjorie Ellis Holland. *d*: 2. Major-General i/c Administration Southern Cmmd 1938—39, Q.M.G. B.E.F., Lt-Gen i/c Administration Middle East '42—43, Princ Admin Officer Indian Cmmd '43—45. *Publ*: Military Organisation & Administration; A & Q or Military Administration in War. *Ctr*: Journs of Roy United Service Inst & Roy Artillery, Army Quarterly. *s.s*: Military subjects, mainly administration. *c*: Army & Navy. *a*: The Heymersh, Britford, Salisbury. *T*: Salisbury 3093.

LINDSEY, Arthur Ward, A.B., M.S., Sc.D., Ph.D. *b*: Council Bluffs, Iowa 1894. *e*: Morningside Coll Sioux City, State Univ of Iowa. *m*: Winifred Irene Wood. Coll Prof. *n.a*: Asst Mang Ed 1940—42, Mang Ed '45—47, Entomological Soc of America Annals. *Publ*: Textbook of Evolution & Genetics; The Problems of Evolution; Textbook of Genetics; The Science of Animal Life. *Ctr*: Various scientific journs. *s.s*: Entomology, Biology (Organic Evolution), Biology of Man. *Rec*: Angling, gardening, landscape painting. *a*: Denison Univ, Granville, Ohio, U.S.A.

LINDSEY, John. See Muriel, John St. Clair.

LINDSEY, R. N. Sec Edin & Dis Br N.U.J. *a*: 58 Hillview Rd, Corstorphine, Edin.

LINDSEY-REA, Robert, B.Sc., M.D., M.Ch., F.R.C.S., F.C.S.M. *b*: Belfast 1881. *e*: Model Sch & Tech Sch & Queens Univ Belfast, Middx Hosp & Univ de Paris. *m*: Mary Eleanor Waddell. *s*: 2. *d*: 2. Ophthalmic Surg to West End Hosp for Nervouse Diseases & Brit Hosp for, Mental Disorders & Nervous Diseases, Cons Surg to Western Ophthalmic Hosp, Senr Demonstrator of Anatomy Queen's Univ Belfast. *Publ*: Affections of the Eye in General Practice; Interstitial Keratitis; Neuro-Ophthalmology; etc. *Ctr*: Med press, etc. *s.s*: Ophthalmology. *Rec*: Golf. *c*: Sunningdale & Moor Pk. *a*: 101 Harley St, London, W.1. *T*: Welbeck 2356.

LINDT, August Rodolphe. *b*: Berne 1905. *e*: Geneva & Berne Univs. *m*: Susan Margaret Dunsterville. *d*: 1. Journalist & Author, Dr L. *n.a*: Special Corr in Manchuria '32 for Journ de Geneve & Deutsche Allgemeine Zeitung, Special Corr in Palestine & Transjordan '33 for Journ de Geneve. *Publ*: Special Correspondent—with Bandit and General in Manchuria ('32). *c.t*: Spectator, Journ de Geneve, Deutsche Allgemeine Zeitung, Koralle Berlin, etc. *s.s*: Asiatic & Far Eastern questions *Rec*: Swimming, riding, ski-ing. *c*: Roy Cent Asian Soc. *a*: c/o Union de Banques Suisses, Berne, Switzerland.

LINE, Cecil Richmond. *b*: Newport Pagnell 1874. *e*: Newport Pagnell C. of E. Sc. & Trinity Sc Stratford. Married. *s*: 1. *d*: 1. Ed & Mang Partner Bucks Standard. For 30 yrs amateur vocalist (baritone) Oratorio, Gilbert & Sullivan operas, concerts, etc. *a*: Carlton Villa, Newport Pagnell, Bucks. *t*: 20.

LINE, E. J. *a*: St John's Road, Isleworth.

LINE, Edward Dexter. *b*: Chiswick 1893. Married. *s*: 2. Journalist. *n.a*: Chief Reporter Grimsby News 1918; Rep Staff Grimsby Evening Telegraph '20; Asst Ed Saturday Telegraph '29. *s.s*: Sport. *a*: 141 Legsby Av, Grimsby. *t*: 6610.

LINFORD, Madeline. *b*: Kilmacolm. *e*: St Catherine's Bramley. Journalist. *n.a*: Ed Women's Page & Illus Ed M/C Guardian. *Publ*: Out of the Window; The Roadside Fire; Broken Bridges; etc (novels); Life of Mary Wollstonecraft; etc. *c.t*: Good Housekeeping, Radio Times, World Radio, Sphere, etc. Mem N.U.J. *a*: 95 Claude Rd, Chorlton-cum-Hardy, M/C. *t*: Chorlton 1158.

LING, Princess Der. Author. *Publ*: Old Buddha; Kowtow. *a*: c/o Chapman & Hall Ltd, Henrietta St, W.C.2.

LING, Thomas Mortimer, M.D., M.R.C.P. *b*: London 1903. *e*: Downside, New Coll Oxf & St Thomas's Hosp. *m*: Sylvia Margaret Burne. *s*: 2. *d*: 1. *Publ*: Recent Advances in Industrial Hygiene & Medicine; Psychology in General Practice (collab). *Ctr*: Lancet, Brit Med Journ, Industrial Welfare, Times, Journ of Occupational Medicine (U.S.A.). *s.s*: Social & Industrial Psychiatry. *Rec*: Gardening, travel. *a*: Roffey Park Rehabilitation Centre, Horsham, Sussex. *T*: Faygate 204.

LINGARD, William Edward. *b*: Wednesbury, Staffs 1876. *m*: Edith Agnes Wall. *s*: 2. *d*: 4. Gen man Newcastle Morning Herald (Australia). *n.a*: Queensland Times 29 y, Newcastle Morning Herald 6 y. *a*: 28 Bolton St, Newcastle, N.S.W., Australia.

LINGENGELTER, Mary Rebecca, M.S. *b*: Philipsburg, Pennsylvania 1893. *e*: Drexel Inst Library Sch, Univ of Penna, Columbia Univ Sch of Library Service, Library Sch Univ of Chicago. Writer & Librarian. *Publ*: Vocations in Fiction; Books on Wheels; Wartime Jobs for Girls; (in collab) Vocation for Girls; Vocation for Boys; Manners Now & Then. *Ctr*: Classmate, Pilgrim Youth, & various educ & religious journs. *s.s*: Guidance, Visual Educ, Library Science, Bibliography. *Rec*: Tennis, swimming, gardening. *a*: Chester Rd, R.D., 3 West Chester, Pa, U.S.A. *T*: West Chester 1519-R3.

LINKE, Lilo. *b*: Berlin 1906. Writer, Journalist, Social Worker, Consultant of UNESCO on Latin American Literature. *Publ*: Restless Flags; Allah Dethroned; Andean Adventure. *Ctr*: Fortnightly, Times Educ Supp, World Rev, etc. *s.s*: Latin America, Education, Travel, Social Surveys, Short Stories. *Rec*: Travelling. *c*: P.E.N. Lond Centre, Casa de la Cultura Quito Ecuador. *a*: 1 Vincent Ct, Green Lane, London, N.W.4. *T*: Hendon 3054.

LINKLATER, Eric, M.A., LL.D. *b*: 1899. *e*: Aberdeen Gr Sch, Aberdeen Univ. *m*: Marjorie Macintyre. *s*: 2. *d*: 2. Commonwealth Fellow in U.S.A. 1928—30, Rector of Aberdeen Univ '45. *Publ*: (Novels & Stories) Whitemaa's Saga; Poet's Pub; Juan in America; The Men of Ness; Magnus Merriman; Ripeness is All; Juan in China; The Sailor's Holiday; The Impregnable Warren; Judas; Private Angelo; The Wind on the Moon; God Likes Them Plain; Sealskin Trousers; (Plays) The Devil's in the News; Crisis in Heaven; (for radio) The Cornerstones; The Raft and Socrates Ask Why; The Great Ship *and* Rabelais Replies; (Biography) Ben Jonson & King James; Mary Queen of Scots; Robert the Bruce; (Autobiography) The Man on my Back; (Essays) The Lion & the Unicorn; The Art of Adventure; (Verse) A Dragon Laughed. *c*: Savile, Univ (Edin). *a*: Pitcalzean Hse, Nigg, Ross-shire. *T*: Nigg 33; c/o Jonathan Cape, 30 Bedford Sq, W.C.1.

LINNELL, John Wycliffe, B.A., M.D.(Cantab), F.R.C.P. (Lond), F.R.S.M. *b*: Burton-on-Trent 1878. *e*: Bedford Modern Sch, St John's Coll Camb & London Hosp E.1. Served on Staffs of several Hospitals. *Publ*: Old Oak. *Ctr*: Various medical journs. *w.s*: World War I R.A.M.C. (Mjr) M.C. & despatches. *Rec*: Tramping. *a*: 41 Devonshire St, London, W.1. *T*: Welbeck 8407.

LINNELL, Wilfred Herbert, PhD., M.Sc, F.I.C., PhC. *b*: Sandbach 1894. *e*: Stockport G.S., Halifax, New Sc, Armstrong Col Durham Univ & Lincoln Col Oxf. *m*: Margery Louisa Jane Hughes. *s*: 1. Reader in Pharmaceutical Chem Lon Univ. Examiner Pharmaceutical Soc of G.B. *n.a*: Mem Editorial Cmt Quarterly Journ of Pharmacy & Pharmacology 1928-. *Publ*: Organic Pharmaceutical Chemistry; Inorganic and Analytical Pharmaceutical Chemistry. *c.t*: Journ Chem Soc, Journ Soc of Chem Industry, Nature, etc. *s.s*: Chemotherapy. *Rec*: Music, tennis. *a*: Sun Patch, West End Lane, Pinner & 17 Bloomsbury Sq, W.C.1. *t*: Holborn 8171.

LINNEY, Albert Gravely. *b*: Ackworth. *e*: Ackworth Friends Sc, Bootham Sc York. *m*: Constance Helen Cooper (dec). *s*: 1. *d*: 1. Journalist & Publisher. *n.a*: Ed White Star Mag 1923, P.L.A. Monthly '25. *Publ*: Peepshow of the Port of London; Lure & Lore of London's River; Pocket Guide to the Docks of London. *c.t*: Times, Observer, Sphere, Lloyd's List. *s.s*: Port of Lon. Mem Stationers & N/s Makers Co. Freeman City of London. Man Dir D. C. Benson Ltd. *c*: Press. *a*: 110 Strand, Lon, W.C.2. *t*: Tem Bar 7081, 7082.

LINNEY, Edward John. *b*: Lon 1870. *e*: Priv & Sec. *m*: Florence Maude Preece. *d*: 2. *n.a*: Co-Ed Bowling 1910, Ed '21-23, Ed Bowling World '33, Asst Ed Cycle Referee 1897, Special Commssr The Cycle '93, Advt Repres Photography 1900. *Publ*: History of Game of Bowls ('33). *c.t*: Princ daily & Sunday Lon & prov n/ps. *s.s*: Bowls, curling. Asst Hon Sec Polytech Cycling Club. Ed Poly C.C. Gazette. S. Africa & Rhodesia with 1st Brit Bowling Team '21. Winning rink Herts Champ'ship '33. *a*: 16 Water Lane, E.C.4. *t*: Central 1392.

LINSTEAD, Hugh Nicholas, O.B.E. *b*: Brighton 1901. *e*: City of Lond Sch, Pharmaceutical Soc Sch, Birkbeck Coll Lond. *m*: Alice Winifred Freke. *d*: 2. Barrister, Secretary & Registrar Pharmaceutical Soc of Gt Brit 1926, M.P. (C) for Putney Div of Wandsworth '42, Mem Poisons Board (Home Office) & Vice-Chm Hansard Soc, Cttee of Research Defence Soc. *Publ*: Poisons Law; Patent Medicines. *Ctr*: Scientific & other publications. *s.s*: Parliamentary Aspects of Education & Health. *Rec*: Mountains, hills, rivers, sea. *a*: 17 Bloomsbury Sq, London, W.C.1. *T*: Holborn 8967.

LINTERN, Bernard Francis. *b*: 1908. *e*: Chigwell, Univ of Lond. Ed Illustrated Carpenter & Builder 1934—. *n.a*: Sub-Ed various trade & tech journs 1929—32, Ed Discovery & Assoc Ed Television '32—34, Assoc Ed. Industria Britannica '34. *w.s*: R.N. 1940—42, F.A.A. '42—46. *a*: 7 Ormond Rd, Richmond, Surrey. *T*: Richmond 1284.

LINTON, David Leslie. *b*: London 1906. *e*: Haberdashers' Sch, Univ of Lond, King's Coll. *m*: Vera Cicely Tebbs. *s*: 3. *d*: 1. Prof of Geography Univ of Sheffield. *n.a*: Hon Ed Geography 1947. *Publ*: Structure Surface & Drainage in South-East England (with S. W. Wooldridge). *Ctr*: Geographical Journ, Scottish Geographical Mag, etc. *s.s*: Physical Geography, Geomorphology. *Rec*: Music, sketching. *w.s*: S/Ldr R.A.F. Photographic Intelligence 1940—45. *a*: University of Sheffield, & 8 Sale Hill, Sheffield 10. *T*: 60994.

LINTON, Rt. Rev. James Henry, B.A., D.D. *b*: Hawick, Scotland 1879. *e*: Church Missionary Coll Lond & St John's Coll Durham. *m*: Alicia Pears Aldous. *s*: 4. *d*: 1. Asst Bishop of Birmingham & Rector of Handsworth. *Publ*: Persian Sketches; Jesus Christus Heiland und herr. *Ctr*: Various Church papers. *s.s*: Training in Evangelism. *Rec*: Tennis, mountain climbing. *a*: Handsworth Rectory, Birmingham 20. *T*: Northern 3407.

LINTON, Ralph, M.A., Ph.D. *b*: Philadelphia, Pennsylvania 1893. *e*: Swarthmore, Univs of Penna & Harvard. *m*: Adelin Briggs Hohlfeld. *s*: 1. Sterling Prof of Anthropology Yale. *n.a*: Ed American Anthropologist 1938—43, Viking Fund Anthropological Papers '45—. *Publ*: The Study of Man, An Introduction; The Cultural Background of Personality; The Tanala, A Madagascar Hill Tribe; The Material Culture of the Marquesas Islands; (Ed) Acculturation in Seven American Indian Tribes; The Science of Man in the World Crisis; etc. *Ctr*: Atlantic Monthly, American Mercury, Amer Anthropologist, Amer Antiquity, etc. *s.s*: (Gen Anthrop, Personality & Culture, Primitive Arts. *Rec*: Reading. *c*: Cosmos (Wash). *a*: 346 Willow St, New Haven, Connecticut, U.S.A. *T*: N.H. 5-9948.

LINTON, Robert George, Ph.D.(Edin), M.R.C.V.S. *b*: Corsham 1882. *e*: Roy Vet Coll Edin. *m*: Anne Gwendoline Baird. *s*: 2. Prof of Hygiene Roy Vet Coll Edin (ret). *Publ*: Veterinary Hygiene; Animal Nutrition. *Ctr*: Numerous Scientific Journs. *s.s*: Animal Welfare. *Rec*: Gardening, fishing. *a*: Fairlaw Farmhouse, Reston, Berwickshire. *T*: Reston 242.

LINTON, Lt.-Col. S. F., R.A.M.C., M.Sc, M.D., D.P.H., T.D. *c.t*: Lancet, etc. *a*: The Old Mill, Gloughton, nr Scarborough. *t*: 21.

LINTOTT, Frederick Stacey. Jnlst. *c.t*: Daily Mirror. *s.s*: Football, cricket, golf. *a*: Rhodes Hse Farm, Middleton, Lancs.

LINTOTT, J. N. T., B.Sc(Lon). *c.t*: Daily Express, Daily Mail, Daily Telegraph, Evening Standard, Birm Mail, Answers, Ideas, Good Housekeeping, Woman's Life, Mod Woman, Armchair Sci, etc *s.s*: Sci fiction. *a*: 6 Milford Rd, Southall, Middx.

LINVALD, Axel, F.R.Hist.S. *b*: Copenhagen 1886. *e*: Copenhagen & Uppsala Univs & Sorbonne. *m*: Adda Hannover. *s*: 2. *d*: 1. Chief Dir of the Nat Record Office 1934—. *n.a*: Historiske Meddelelser om Copenhagen 1923—34, Dansk hist Tidsskrift '32—43. *Publ*: Kronprins Frederik og hans Regering 1797—1807; Christian VIII Den unge Prins; Kong Christian VIII's Dagbogger og Optegnelser 1799—1814; Dansk Arkivvaesen. *Ctr*: Politiken, & Danish & foreign reviews. *s.s*: Hist of Denmark in the 18th & 19th Centuries, Hist of Sleswig. *Rec*: Farming. *a*: Norgesmindevej 20, Copenhagen, Hellerup. *T*: Hellerup 5325.

LIPPINCOTT, Horace Mather, M.A., Ph.B. *b*: Philadelphia, Pa 1877. *e*: Germantown Acad, Univ of Penna. *m*: Sarah S. Jenkins. *s*: 1. *n.a*: Ed Graduate publs Univ of Penna 1902—45. *Publ*: The Colonial Homes of Philadelphia & its Neighbourhood; Early Philadelphia, Its People, Life & Progress; Philadelphia; Portraiture of the People Called Quakers; George Washington & the Univ of Penna; etc. *s.s*: Local Hist. *c*: Univ (Penna). *a*: East Lane, Chestnut Hill, Philadelphia, Pa., U.S.A. *T*: Whitemarsh 8.0317.

LIPPINCOTT, Joseph Wharton, B.S. *b*: Philadelphia, Pa 1887. *e*: Germantown Acad, Episcopal Acad Coll, Wharton of Univ of Penna. *m*: (1) Elizabeth Schuyler Mills (dec'd), (2) Virginia Jones. *s*: 2. *d*: 3. Publisher (J. B. Lippincott Co). *Publ*: Wilderness Champion; Animal Neighbours of the Countryside; Chisel Tooth the Beaver; The Red Roan Pony; The Wolf King; Long Horn Leader of the Deer; Persimmon Jim the Possum; Striped Coat the Beaver; & other animal stories. *Ctr*: Nature Mag, Bird-Lore, Guide to Nature, The Spur, Publisher's Weekly, Country Life, etc. *s.s*: Nature, Stories for Children. *Rec*: Hunting, fishing. *c*: Explorers, Philadelphia, Downtown, etc. *a*: Oak Hill, Bethayres, Montgomery County, Pennsylvania, U.S.A.

LIPPMAN, Walter. *Publ*: inc The Good Society; U.S. Foreign Policy; Shield of the Republic; The Political Scene; A Preface to Morals; The New Imperative; etc. *a*: 230 West 41st St, New York, U.S.A.

LIPS, Eva Elizabeth. *b*: Leipzig, Germany 1906. *e*: Univs of Leipzig, Paris, Cologne & Columbia. *m*: Dr Julius E. Lips. Writer, Lecturer. *Publ*: Savage Symphony; What Hitler Did to Us; Rebirth in Liberty; Das Rad Von Monte-Carlo. *Ctr*: Various American periodicals. *s.s*: Non-Fiction Books (Cultures of Civilized & Primitive Socs). *Rec*: Book illustrating, silk embroidery. *c*: P.E.N. (N.Y.). *a*: 640 Riverside Drive, New York 31, N.Y., U.S.A. *T*: Wadsworth 6-0876.

LIPSCOMB, William Percy, M.C. *b*: Merton. Married. *d*: 1. Journalist, Author, Playwright. *Publ*: Staff Tales; Educating Peter; Clive of India (play, Pt Author); Stella Breaks it Gently. Screen plays— I Was a Spy; Good Companions; Man from Toronto; Faithful Heart; Loyalties; Speckled Band. Scenarios —Jack's the Boy; There Goes the Bride; etc. Dir & scenario of Colonel Blood. Original story & scenario Channel Crossing. *c*: Savage. *a*: 3 Adelphi Terr, W.C.2. *t*: Temple Bar 3741.

LIPSON, Ephraim. *b*: Sheffield 1888. *e*: T. C. Cam & New Col Oxf. Author. *Publ*: The Economic History of England (Vol I, The Middle Ages 1915); Vols II & III, The Age of Mercantilism '31; History of the English Woollen Industries ('21); Increased Production ('21); etc. *c.t*: London Times, Sunday Observer, Fortnightly Review, etc, Ed The Economic History Review. *s.s*: Eng econ hist. Reader in Econ Hist in Oxf Univ '21–31. Lowell Lect Boston, U.S.A. '32. Trav round world '33. *Rec*: Travel. *c*: Authors. *a*: New Col Oxf.

LIPSON, Mordecai. *b*: Poland 1885. Writer & Journalist. *n.a*: Ed Hotzofe Tel-Aviv 1938—44, Hadoar New York '21—22, Bustnai Tel Aviv '31—33. *Publ*: Midor Dor; Die Well Dirzelt; Mold; (trans) Pan Knut Hamsun; The Seventh Cross; Teatchers; Poland. *Ctr*: Davar, Hauretz-Tel-Aviv. *s.s*: Folklore, Translation, Fiction. *a*: 106 Adhad Haam St, Tel Aviv, Palestine.

LIPSON, Solomon. *b*: Swansea 1909. *e*: King's Col Lon. Jnlst. *n.a*: Founded Varsity Press Agency '33. Prop Lon General Reporters '35. *c.t*: Nat & provincial N/ps. *s.s*: English lit, economics, hist, sport. *Rec*: Reading, sport. *a*: 145 Fleet St, E.C.4. *t*: Central 7345.

LIPTON, Marcus, M.A. *b*: Sunderland 1900. *e*: Merton Col Oxf. Writer. *n.a*: Asst Ed Isis '21—22. *Publ*: The Jewish Question in Anglo-Swiss Diplomacy; Francis Francia the Jacobite Jew; Jewish Poverty in East London. *c.t*: Jewish Chron. *s.s*: Jewish questions & Zionism. Mem P.A.C. for City of Lon, Stepney & Poplar. *Rec*: Rowing, garden. *a*: 21 Gresham Rd, S.W.9. *t*: Brixton 2836, Bishopsgate 5868.

LISSAUER, ERNST: author; b. Berlin, Germany, Dec. 10, 1882; s. Hugo and Zerline (Friedeberger) L.; educ. Friedrich-Werdersches Gymnasium (Berlin), Univs. of Leipzig and Munich; m. Margarete Langner, Aug. 29, 1929. AUTHOR: Der Acker, 1907; Der Strom, 1912; 1813, 1913; Bach, 1916; Die Ewigen Pfingsten, 1919; Der Tuwendige Weg, 1920; Gloria Anton Bruckners, 1921; Eckermann, 1921; Yorck, 1921; Von der Sendung des Dichters, 1922; Gestlicher Werktag, 1922; Deutsche Balladen, 1923; Flammen und Winde, 1923; Gewalt, 1924; Das Kinderland, 1924; Glück in Oesterreich, 1925; Der Heilige Alltag, 1926; Die dritte Tafel, 1927; Das Weib des Jephta, 1928; Luther und Thomas Münzer, 1929; Die Deutsche Lyrik des 18. Jahrhunderts, 1930. Contributor to Die Literatur, Vossische Zeitung, Deutsche Allgemeine Zeitung, Börsenzeitung, Börsenkurier, Munchner neueste Nachrichtung, Hannover Courier, Veehagen und Klasings Monatshefte, and others. General character of writing: novels, plays, poems, and essays. CLUBS: Pen Club, Schutverband deutscher Schriftsteller, Verband deutscher Bühnenschriftsteller, Concordia, and others. Relig. denom., Jew. ADDRESS: Armbrustergasse 10 I, Vienna, Austria.

LISSENDEN, George Bertie, M.Inst.T. *b*: Whitstable 1879. *m*: Elizabeth Gibbs. *s*: 1. *d*: 2. Former Dock & Traffic Controller Messrs Lever Bros Ltd (ret). *Publ*: Industrial Traffic Management; Railway Passengers & Their Luggage; Export Shipping; The Seeress; The Revolt; A Woman's Prerogative; From Cabin Boy to Traffic Controller. *s.s*: Transport Law & Practice, Commercial Law. *Rec*: Golf. *a*: Rosedale, Spital Rd, Bromboro', Cheshire.

LISTER, SIR FREDERICK SPENCER, Kt.: medical (research); b. Nottinghamshire, Eng., April, 1876; s. Frederick and Sarah Elizabeth (Spencer) L.; educ. Barton Sch. (Wisbech, Eng.); St. Bartholomew's Hospital (London): DEGREES: M.R.C.S. (Eng.); L.R.C.P. (London); LL.D. (Hon.) (Cape Town Univ.); F.R.S.S.Af. (Fellow of the Royal Society of South Africa); m. (1) Alice Jeanette Baker, 1912;; (2) Ruby May Johnstone, 1921. AUTHOR: Specific Serological Reactions with Pneumococci from different sources, 1913; An Experimental Study of Prophylactic Inoculation against Pneumococcal Infection in the Rabbit and in the Man, 1916; Lysed Bacterial Serum; Further Observations on Pianticiation; A Note on Phagocytosis in the Absence of Serum (with A. R. Friel, M.D.), 1917; Prophylactic Inoculation of Man against Pneumoccocal Infections and more particularly against Lobar Pneumonia, 1917; Observations and Experimental Investigations in Epidemic Influenza (with E. Taylor, M.D.), 1919; Tropical Ulcer in Native Mine Labourers on the Witwatersrand (with H. Q. F. Thompson, M.R.C.S., L.R.C.P.), 1921; The Laboratory Aspect of Meningococcal Meningitis with a Brief Review of Infection and Immunity, 1921; A Filter-passing Micro-organism associated with Epidemic Influenza, 1922; The Use of Pneumococcal Vaccine, 1924; The Work of the Laboratory in Relation to the Practice of Medicine, 1925; An Electrical Thermometer for rapidly recording the Temperature of Groups of People, 1929; A Note on the Aetiology of Epidemic Influenza and Secondary Pneumonia, 1929. Editor of the series of publications of the S. African Institut. for Medical Research. Contributor to the Transvaal Medical Jnl., 1911. Dir. of S. African Inst. for Medical Research; Hon. prof. of Pathology and Bacteriology in Univ. of Witwatersrand; mem. of S. African Medical Council and of following Govt. advisory bodies: Union Council of Public Health; The Leoprosy Advisory Board; The Research Grant Board; mem. of Federal Council of the Medical Assn. of S. Africa. Relig. denom., Church of England. CLUBS: Country Club (Johannesburg). OFFICE: South African Institute for Medical Research. HOME: Director's House, South African Institute for Medical Research, Johannesburg, Transvaal, South Africa.

LISTER, Leonard Binns. Lon Mang Eastern Daily Press, Eastern Evening News, & Allied papers. *a*: 151 Fleet St, E.C.4.

LISTER, Dr W. A. *a*: 7 The Crescent, Plymouth.

LITCHFIELD, FREDERICK: art expert (retired since 1903); b. London, Eng., Sept., 1850; s. Samuel and Catherine (Collins) L.; educ. South Kensington Art School; m. Emily Mary Tasker, Apr. 22, 1873. AUTHOR: Pottery and Porcelain, a Guide to Collection, 1879 (revised edit. 1927); Illustrated History of Furniture, 1892 (now in 7th edit.); Antiques, Genuine and Spurious, 1925. Editor of Chaffers' Marks and Monograms on Pottery and Porcelain since 1893. Contributor to Connoisseur (London); Women (London); House Beautiful (Boston, U.S.A.); Harmsworth's Ency. (London); Antiques (Boston). General character of writing: technical information in popular form. Lectures on Pottery and Porcelain, and furniture of different countries and periods. Served in the Artists' Rifles, 1880-1894; Chief Officer of Volunteer Fire Brigade for Esker and the Ditton, Surrey, Eng., 1900-06; war service mem. of Tribunal, 1915-8. Relig. denom., Church of England. CLUBS: Junior Carlton; Roehampton. (*)

LITTLE, A. n.a: Reporter Shields News, N. Shields. a: 11 Windsor Gardens, North Shields.

LITTLE, Alex. n.a: Night Editor Daily Mirror, London. a: 2 The Meadway, Chelsfield, Kent.

LITTLE, SIR ERNEST GRAHAM: Knight-Bachelor, Cr. 1931; physician; b. Bengal, India, Feb. 1867; s. Michael Little and Anna (English) G.; educ. South African Coll. (Capetown), Univ. London. DEGREES: M.D. (London), B.A. (Capetown), F.R.C.P. (London), M.R.C.S. (Eng.); m. Sarah Helen Kendall, 1911; Contributor to Wright's Medical Annual, Lancet, British Med. Journ., Brit. Journ. Dermatology, XIX Century, Contemporary Rev., Edinburgh Rev., Empire Rev., London Times, Telegraph and other papers. General character of writing: scientific, medical, political. M. P. for London Univ. since 1924; mem. Senate of London Univ. since 1906; Phys. in chg. Skin Dept., St. Mary's Hosp.; lecturer on Dermatology, Med. Sch. London Univ., since 1902; Consulting phys., E. London Hosp. for children; corr. mem. Amer. Derm. Assn., and of Derm. Socs. of France, Germany, Denmark, Berlin; hon. mem. Derm Soc. Italy and of Royal Acad., Rome; Fellow of the Royal Soc. of Physicians, Budapest; hon. mem. Norwegian Med. Soc. Relig. denom., Church of England. CLUB: Athenaeum. OFFICE: 40 Wimpole St. and House of Commons, London, Eng.

LITTLE, Eric. b: London 1891. m: Yvonne George. Journalist. n.a: Assoc Ed Music Trades Review '34. Publ: 4 Standard Musical Educational Works, Ed of several others. c.t: Melody maker 1926—30, Music Trades Review '31, Tune Times '33—, Rhythm '35. s.s: Music. Originator & Ed The Drummer '28—33, Originator & Ed Percussion. Rec: Music, walking. a: 48 Fitzroy St, W.1. t: Museum 2738.

LITTLE, James Stanley. b: Lon. e: King's Col Sc, King's Col Lon. m: Countess Fanny Maride Thérèse de La Blache. s: 1. d: 1. Author. n.a: Ed African Review, 1895—97, & 1901—02. Art critic Public Opinion, London, West Sussex Gazette, Bournemouth Daily Echo. Publ: South Africa; What is Art?; My Royal Father; Doubt; The Life & Work of W. Q. Orchardsons R.A.; The British Empire in the XIXth Century; The Doom of Western Civilization; At the Sign of the Half Moon. c.t: The Times, Morning Post, Daily Mail, Daily Express, Artist, Art Journ, Studio, Natal Mercury, Cape Times, etc. s.s: Art, World & Imperial politics. Rec: Walking, genealogical research. With J. J. Robinson organised Shelley Centenary Celebrations at Horsham (1897 & 1927). c: Hon Sec Shelley Soc, Vice-Pres British Empire Union, 1st Executive Sec Soc of Authors (1888—90). a: Chichele, Parkstone, Dorset.

LITTLE, Rev. Richard Ernest. b: Castleford 1866. e: Pomfret Priory & Wes Col, Richmond, Surrey. m: Minnie Watson. Meth Min. Publ: A Nation on Fire; Personal Impressions of the World Disarmament Conference (written to, accepted & acknowledged by, His Most Gracious Majesty The King); etc. c.t: Meth Times & Leader, Brit Weekly, John o' London's, etc. s.s: Peace & Disarmament. Rep the religious men at The Signing of the Paris Peace Pact, Naval Conf, Round Table (Indian) Conf, World Disarmament Conf. Sometime Custodian of Wesley Museum. Rec: Angling. c: West Hist Soc. a: Woodlands, Yarm Lane, Stockton-on-Tees, Co Durham. t: 66683.

LITTLE, William Buller. b: Bristol 1888. e: Wrekin Coll, Bristol Univ. Publ: Science in the Home; Science in the City; Science for Junior Schools; Nature all Around; Classroom Science (3 vols); English for Senior Schs (3 vols); Junior Health Reader; Science & Health; English for the Young Citizen; More English for the Young Citizen; etc. Ctr: Schoolmaster, Teachers' World. s.s: Educational Bks. a: 6 Glebe Ave, Enfield, Middlx. T: Enfield 4276.

LITTLE LADY OF THE STARS, THE (pen name): see Proctor, Mary.

LITTLEJOHNS, IDALIA BLANCHE: author, artist; b. Worcestershire, Eng., Nov., 1892; m. John Littlejohns, R.B.A., R.B.C., F.R.S.A. AUTHOR (text-books): Ornamental Homecrafts, 1926; Prints and Patterns, 1929; Gesso, 1929; Beadcraft, 1929; Printed Fabrics, 1930. Contributes to the Schoolmistress and other educational publications. General character of writing: artistic craftsmanship from an education standpoint. Painter and exhibitor, artist-craftsman, writer, lecturer to teachers in London schools. CLUBS: Women's International Art Club. HOME: 4 Brook Green Studios, W. 14, London, Eng.

LITTLEJOHNS, John, R.I., R.B.A., F.R.S.A. m: Ida Blanche Littlejohns. d: 1. Author, artist, lecturer, illustrator. Publ: Technique of Water Colour Painting; How to Enjoy Pictures; Art in Schools; Landscape Sketching & Composition; Art for All Drawing & Painting (22 books). c.t: Radio Times, Times Educational Supplement, Teachers World, Schoolmaster, Practical Education. s.s: Art—theory, practice & education. c: Arts. a: 2 Orchard Studios, Brook Green, W.6. t: Riverside 5415.

LITTLEJOHNS, John. B.Litt. b: Gunnislake. e: Aberaman Brit, Worcester H.S., Trin Col Chicago. m: Genevra Hodge. s: 3. d: 2. Schoolmaster, Lect Hist Assoc, etc. n.a: Glam Times '95, Western Mail 1901—20, Daily Express, Kentish Mercury '21—32. Instr in Oratory '11—17. Mem L.C.C. for E. Lewisham '25—28. Publ: The Flowing Tide; England Against the World; Lovat Fraser; The Tory Ideal; etc. c.t: Glam Times, Merthyr Express, Western Mail, Morning Post, etc. s.s: Hist, oratory. Vice-Pres Internat Faculty of Science. a: High Sc, Burnt Ash Hill, Lee, S.E.12. t: 4937.

LITTLEWOOD, John. b: Tankersley 1906. e: Mexboro' Sec Sc. m: Doris May Beeson. Sports Ed. n.a: S. Elmsall Times '23, Mexboro' & Swinton Times Reporter, Sports Ed's Asst '24—27, Doncaster Gazette, Yorks Evening News '27—28, Express & Star '29, Ed Sporting Star '30. s.s: Football, racing. One of youngest Sports Eds in Eng. Youngest Ed Sporting Star. Rec: Tennis, cricket. a: Castlecroft Rd, Finchfield, Wolverhampton. t: 22233.

LITTLEWOOD, John Edenson, F.R.S., HonD.Sc. Prof Mathematics Cam. *Publ:* The Elements of the Theory of Real Functions. *c.t:* Various. *a:* Trin Col, Cambridge. *t:* 580.

LITTLEWOOD, Miss K. D. B., M.A.(Oxon). Ex School of Lady Margaret Hall. Member of the Executive of the Assocn of Head Mistresses. Head Mistress of Bromley H.S. (G.P.D.S.T.). *a:* 23 Cromwell Avenue, Bromley, Kent.

LITTLEWOOD, Samuel Robinson, F.J.I. *b:* Bath 1875. *e:* Merchant Taylors, Dover Coll, St Pauls. *m:* Phœbe Stella Hayes. *s:* 1. *d:* 3. Journalist. *n.a:* Ed, The Stage 1943—, Dramatic Critic Pall Mall Gazette '15—23, Morning Post '27—37, B.B.C. '35. *Publ:* Dramatic Criticism ; The Story of Pierrot ; Perrault's Fairy Tales ; The Story of Santa Claus ; The Fairies— Here & Now ; The Child of the Sea ; Valentine & Orson ; Elizabeth Inchbald & Her Circle. *Ctr:* Various. *s.s:* Drama. *Rec:* Playgoing. *c:* Savage, etc. *a:* 220 Worple Rd, Wimbledon, S.W. *T:* 1957.

LITVINOFF, Emanuel. *b:* London 1915. *e:* Wood Close Sch Lond. *m:* Irene Maud Pearson. *s:* 1. *d:* 1. Author. *Publ:* (poems) A Crown for Cain ; The Untried Soldier. *Ctr:* Tribune, Time & Tide, Modern Reading, New Writing & Daylight, World Digest, Poetry (London), Writing Today, etc. *s.s:* Cinema, Radio, Social Hist (Vagrancy & Slums), Metaphysics, Contemporary Verse, Occult Philosophy. *Rec:* Cinema, radio Experimental Drama. *w.s:* World War II. *a:* 85 Fitzjohn's Ave, Hampstead, London, N.W.3. *T:* Hampstead 7980.

LIU, HERMAN CHAN EN: educator; b. Hupeh, China, Dec. 12, 1896; s. Wei Feng and Feng Ching (Lo) L.; educ. Soochow Univ., China, Univ. of Chicago (U.S.A.), Columbia Univ. (New York City, U.S.A.); DEGREES: B.S., M.A., Ph.D., LL.D.; m. Frances Wang, Sept. 5, 1922. AUTHOR: Non-Verhal Tests for Use in China, 1922; Vocational Guidance, 1923; Citizenship Training Projects, 1924; How to be a Good Citizen, 1925; Problem of Peace, 1926; Citizenship Songs, 1926; Problem of Clean Living, 1927. Founder of Citizenship Training Movement in China; Father of Vocational Guidance Movement in China; pres. of University of Shanghai; research dir. of Natl. Vocational Education Assn. of China; Natl. Educational Sec. of Y.M.C.A. in China. Relig. denom., Baptist. OFFICE: University of Shanghai, Shanghai, China.

LIU, SHIH-SHUN: diplomat, legistor and professor; b. Hsianghsiang, Honan, China, July, 1900; s. Tien-Chu and I-Hsiu (Tsou) L.; educ. Tsing Hua Coll. (Peking) and Johns Hopkins, Harvard, Michigan, Columbia Univs. (All U. S. A.). DEGREES: A.B. (Johns Hopkins, 1921); A.M. (Harvard, 1923); Ph.D. (Columbia, 1925); m. Chi Fu-Chu, 1920. AUTHOR: Extraterritoriality: Its Rise and Its Decline, 1925. General character of writing: historical. Member, Legislative Yuan, National Government, Republic of China. Counsellor, Ministry of Interior, 1930—. Counsellor, Ministry Foreign Affairs; concurrently, Senior mem. Treaty Comm. same, 1927-1930. Professor Internat. Law, Nat. Central Univ., Nanking (China). Fellow Internat. Law, Carnegie Endowment for Internat. Peace, 1923-24; Prof. Internat. Relations, Tsing Hua Univ. (Peking, China), 1925-29; Legal adviser to Commr. Foreign Affairs, Hupeh (China); govt. examiner for Diplomatic and Consular Serv. and mem. publication comm., Ministry of Foreign Affrs.; 1928. Mem. Amer. Soc. Internat. Law and Chinese Social and Polit. Science Assn. OFFICE: Legislative Yuan, Nanking. HOME: Ifeng, Kiangsi, China.

LIVEING, Edward George Downing, M.A. *b:* 1895. *e:* Bradfield Coll & St John's Coll Oxf. *m:* Gladys Constance Baker. *d:* 1. Author, Jt Sec Educational Interchange Counc, B.B.C. North Reginal Director 1928—37. *n.a:* Ed Discovery 1921—23. *Publ:* Attack ; Motoring in Denmark. *Ctr:* Blackwood's Mag, Fortnightly Rev, etc. *Rec:* Travel, walking, motoring. *c:* Savile. *w.s:* 1914—18 Lond Regt France & Palestine, '42—43 B.B.C. Liaison Middle East. *a:* By-the-Stream, Chideock, Dorset. *T:* Chideock 309.

LIVENS, William Howard, D.S.O., M.C., M.A. *b:* Lincoln 1889. *e:* Oundle Sch & Ch Call Camb. *m:* (1) Elizabeth Price (dec'd), (2) Arron Perry. *d:* 3. *n.a:* Asst Ed Country Life 1913—14. *Ctr:* Times, Sketch, Graphic, Dly Graphic, Morning Post, etc. *s.s:* Eng, Chem Warfare. *Rec:* Sailing. *c:* R.T.Y.C. *w.s:* World Wars I & II (Des). *a:* 32 Howitt Rd, Hampstead, London, N.W.3. *T:* Primrose 4177.

LIVERSIDGE, Alfred. *n.a:* South Yorkshire Times and allied papers. Organist. *a:* Altrude, Stump Cross Road, Wath-on-Dearne, Nr Rotherham.

LIVERSIDGE, Henry Douglas. *b:* Swinton, Yorks 1913. Journalist. *n.a:* Junr Reporter Sth Yorks Times & Assoc Newsps, Subsequently Ed Staff Yorks Post (Lond), Sun Chron (News Ed), Dly Mail, Dly Express etc, Feature Writer P.A.-Reuter Features 1945—. *Ctr:* Various European, Empire & Nth American Newsps & mags. *Rec:* Horse-riding, music, art. *c:* Press & screenwriters. *a:* 1 Hawthorn Drive, Willowbank, Uxbridge, Mddx.

LIVETT, Rev. Greville Mairis, B.A., F.S.A. *b:* Wells, Somerset 1859. *e:* King's Sch Peterborough, St John's Camb. Canon Emeritus of Rochester. *Publ* Southwell Minster: An Account of the Collegiate & Cathedral Church of Southwell ; Foundations of the Saxon Cathedral Church at Rochester. *a:* Stoneleigh, Old Dover Rd, Canterbury, Kent. *T:* Canterbury 2908.

LIVINGSTON, Marjorie. *b:* Lon. *e:* Priv. Married. *Publ:* The Elements of Heaven ; The New Nuctemeron ; The Harmony of the Spheres ; An Outline of Existence. *c.t:* Light, Survival, Beyond, etc. *s.s:* Occultism. *Rec:* Athletic sport. *c:* British Col, Psychic Sci Lon Spiritualist Alliance, etc. *a:* 18 Collingham Gdns, S.W.5.

LIVINGSTONE, Florence Bingham. *b:* Vermont. *e:* Public & Priv Scs & Columbia Univ. Writer, Lecturer. *Publ:* The Custard Cup (1921, filmed) ; Under a Thousand Eyes ; This Man & This Woman. *c.t:* The American, Country Gentleman, Good Housekeeping, Sunset Mag, McCall's Mag, etc. *s.s:* Human-interest fiction, articles & talks on social subjects, hist research. Has joined bread lines, been in a strike, worked in shops, orchards, berry fields & canneries. *Rec:* Gardening, walking, motoring. *c:* P.E.N., 20th Cent, Berkeley. *a:* 3006 Claremont Av, Berkeley, Calif. *t:* 4011.

LIVINGSTONE, Sir Richard Winn, Kt., M.A., Hon.D.Litt., Hon. LL.D. *b:* 1880. *e:* Winchester & New Coll Oxf. *m:* Cecile Maryon-Wilson. *s:* 1. *d:* 2. Vice-Chanc Oxf Univ 1944—47, Pres Corpus Christi Coll Oxf '34—, Pres Educational Sect of Brit Assoc '36, Hellenic Soc '31—38, Classical Assoc '40—41. *n.a:* Ed (with J. T. Sheppard) Classical Review 1920—22, Gen Ed & Originator of method Employed in The Clarendon Series of Greek & Latin Authors. *Publ:* The Greek Genius & Its Meaning to Us ; A Defence of Classical Education ; (with C. E. Freeman) Caesars Gallic War (Books IV, V, VI & VII) ; Ed & Ctr, The Legacy of Greece ; Pageant of Greece ; Mission of Greece ; Greek Ideals & Modern

Life; Portrait of Socrates; Selections from Plato; The Future in Education; Education for a World Adrift; Some Tasks for Education; Thucydides; Plato & Modern Education; Essays, various articles etc. *a*: Athenæum. *a*: Corpus Christi College, Oxford.

LJUNGQUIST, Tvar Adolf. *b*: Kristdala, Sweden 1892. *e*: Sec Sch. *m*: Dagmar Karlsson. Journalist, Mem Nat Inst of Swedish Journalists. *n.a*: Staff Dagans Nyhater Stockholm 1919, Local News Ed '19—23, Chief Exec Ed '23—47. *Publ*: In Darkest Smaland; Struggle of Life; Nils Dacke; Garden Plot of Our Lord; Son of Smaland, Thank You. *c*: P.E.N. *a*: Norr Malarstrand 72, Stockholm. *T*: Stockholm 535759.

LLEWELLIN, Rev. Frederick George, B.D. (Durham), D.Lit, F.R.HistS. *b*: L'pool 1879. *e*: T.C.D. & D'ham Univ. *m*: Elinor Annie Williams. *n.a*: Ed the English Churchman 1929. *Publ*: Lectures on Sunday School Teaching ('10); Reformers & the Reformation; Lucerna Dei, a Book of Evangelical Theology; The Lighter Side of a Parson's Life; Friendly Talks on Vital Topics ('34); etc. *c.t*: The Record, Churchman's Mag, English Churchman. *s.s*: Reformation hist & lit. Chaplain of Lancaster Castle Prison '10—13. *a*: Kidsgrove Vicarage, Stoke-on-Trent.

LLEWELLYN, Alun. *e*: Alleyn's Sch Dulwich, St John's Coll Camb. Barrister, Lincoln's Inn, Author, Sec Central Valuation Board Coal Nationalisation 1947, Legal Translator Geneva Secretariat League of Nations '37—39. *Publ*: Confound Their Politics; The Deacon; The Strange Invaders; Soul of Cezar Azan; Jubilee John. International Politics. *a*: 93 Wood Vale, S.E.23. *T*: Forest Hill 2453.

LLEWELLYN, Fewlass. Actor and film artist, also broadcaster, teacher of dramatics and eloc. *a*: 15 Atney Road, S.W.15.

LLEWELLYN-AMOS, William (Mervyn Thompson), F.R.G.S., F.R.H.S., F.Z.S. *b*: Shoreham 1894. *e*: Before the mast. *Publ*: The Camera Book (1926); over 100 short stories. *c.t*: Leading n/ps & journs, Britain, Amer, Continent & Japan. *s.s*: Aerial navigation, ballooning, jewellery, goldsmithing, silversmithing, photography & the science of homœopathy. Prominently associated with agitation which resulted in a more efficient Post Office & Telephone Service ('31—32). Originated the movement known as The Gold Rush, when £14,000,000 was raised for the country during a time of nat difficulty, by the sale on the part of the public of old gold trinkets & hoarded sovereigns. Personal adv to His Grace the Duke of Atholl during his famous campaign undertaken to compel a change in the Lottery Laws of Eng. Originator of many Charity schemes, including Royal Snapshot Exhibition ('30); Jewels of Empire Ball ('30). Representatives maintained in many towns in Gt Britain & abroad. War Service, Commissions in R.N.A.S. & R.A.F. Admrlty '17—20. *a*: 38 Parliament St, Whitehall, S.W.1. *t*: Whitehall 4606 & 16 Greenhalgh Walk, N.2. *t*: Speedwell 5914.

LLEWELLYN-JONES, Frederick. B.A.(Wales & Lon), LL.B.(Lon). Dr Sc Pol (hons causa) Univ Pécs (Hungary), F.R.Econ Soc. *b*: Glanogwen, Caerns 1866. *e*: Friars Sc Bangor, Bala Col, & Univ Col of Wales, Aberystwyth. *m*: Elizabeth Roberts. *s*: 3. *d*: 2. Solicitor, H.M. Coroner & M.P. for Flints. Associated with Education & Health administration in Wales. *Pub*: Road Traffic Law; The League of Nations & the Health of Nations; The International Control of Dangerous Drugs; Plebiscites; Nationality of Married Women; National Minorities in British Empire. *c.t*: Trans of Grotius Soc., Medico-Legal Soc., Manchester Guardian, etc. *s.s*: Comparative Law, Internat Law, L.o.N., Publ Health, Constitutional Law, Local Govt, Social Services. *c*: Nat Lib, Overseas, Roy Inst of Internat Relations. *a*: Isfryn, Mold. Flints. *t*: 99.

LLEWELLYN THOMAS, Beatrice ("F. H. Dorset"). *b*: Swanage 1890. *e*: Godolphin Sc Salisbury, Chelsea Art Sc. *m*: Hugh Llewellyn Thomas. *s*: 3. *d*: 1. Author. *Publ*: Jehu Poole; Surging Tide specially recomm Broadcast Michael Sadlier, 1931); Silent Meadows (recomm Book Soc); Window of the World; Beggarman's Fortune; The Marching Cloud. *c.t*: Cornhill Mag, Daily Herald, Windsor Mag, etc. *s.s*: English life between 1860 & 1900, novels of humour & adventure. *Rec*: Gardening. *c*: Exiles. *a*: 18 Park Rd, Haywards Heath, Sussex.

LLEWELYN-EVANS, A. Hon Sec Mon Br N.U.J. *a*: 37 Harrow Rd, Newport, Mon.

LLOYD, Albert John. *b*: Radnors. *m*: Mabel H. Porter. *s*: 1. *d*: 1. Journalist. *n.a*: Rep at Taunton & Nott'm, Sub-Ed Nott'm Daily Guardian, Ed Mansfield & N. Notts Advertiser, Ed & pt Prop Glam Advertiser, Ed & Dir Shrewsbury Circular. *Publ*: Newstead & Byron. *s.s*: Astronomy, local hist. *Rec*: Golf. *a*: Shrewsbury Circular, Shrewsbury.

LLOYD, Albert Lancaster. *b*: London 1908. *e*: Lond Elem Schs. *m*: Charlotte Marie Adam. *s*: 1. *d*: 1. *n.a*: Script writer Drama & Features Dept B.B.C. 1938—40, Mem Ed Staff Picture Post '40—42 & '46—, Lond Ed Britansky Soyuznik (Moscow) '44—45. *Publ*: The Singing Englishman; Lament for the Death of a Bullfighter; Corn on the Cob; Shadow of the Swastika; etc. *Ctr*: Picture Post, Leader, Lilliput, Our Time, Radio Times, Listener, etc. *s.s*: Social & Industrial, Whaling, Folk Music & Folklore, Social Hist (U.S.A. & Australia). *a*: 2 St Albans Villas, London, N.W.5. *T*: Gulliver 5208.

LLOYD, Rev. Alfred Manby, L.Div. *b*: Lon 1868. *e*: Priv. *Publ*: American Shrines in England. *c.t*: Leamington Spa Courier, Western Mail. *s.s*: Philos, ethics, travel. Ex-Vicar of Rock Creek, B.C. Late Rector of Dewsall, Hereford. *Rec* Violin & Viola. *a*: Dolobran, 151 Leam Terr, Leamington Spa.

LLOYD ARMITAGE, J. Sec Huddersfield Br N.U.J. *a*: Huddersfield Examiner, Huddersfield.

LLOYD, Charles Mostyn, M.A. *b*: Lon 1878. *e*: Merchant Taylors Sc & Oxf Univ. *m*: Theodosia Rowson. *s*: 2. *d*: 1. Journalist & Univ Lect. *n.a*: Special Corr Manchester Guardian, Paris Peace Conf 1919: Leader Writer & Asst Ed New Statesman '20—29. Acting Ed '30; Foreign Ed New Statesman & Nation '31—. *Publ*: Trade Unionism; Russian Notes; The Intelligent Man's Way to Prevent War (section on "The Problem of Russia"). *c.t*: New Statesman & Nation, London Mercury, Political Quarterly, etc. *s.s*: Internat affairs, politics, social economics. Barrister-at-Law Inner Temple '07. Org Sec Nat Cmt for Prevention of Destitution '10—14. War Service '15—18. Head Dept of Social Science, Lon Sc of Econ. *c*: Savile. *a*: 21 Ladbroke Gve, W.11. *t*: Park 3059.

LLOYD, Christopher. *b*: Bangalore 1906. *e*: Marlborough Coll, Lincoln Coll Oxf. *m*: K. B. Sturge. *s*: 1. *d*: 1. Lect Roy Naval Coll Greenwich. *Publ*: Lord Cochrane; Pacific Horizons; Captain Marryat; Fanny Burney; The Englishman & the Sea; Democracy & its Rivals. *s.s*: Naval & Maritime Hist, Hist Geog. *c*: Un Univ. *a*: 17 Dartmouth Row, Greenwich, London, S.E.10. *T*: Tideway 2830.

LLOYD, Ellis. *b*: Newport, Mon. Barrister-at-Law. *Publ*: Novels—Scarlet Nest; A Master of Dreams. M.P. (Labour) for Llandaff & Barry 1929–31. *a*: Dryburgh, Cowbridge Rd, Bridgend, Glamorgan. *t*: 243.

LLOYD, J. F. P. Journalist. *n.a*: Literary Ed Daily Express. *a*: Fleet St, E.C.4. *t*: Central 8000.

LLOYD JAMES, Arthur. *b*: Ystrad 1884. *e*: Llanelly, Cardiff Univ Col & Trin Col Cam. *m*: Elsie Owen. *s*: 1. Univ Prof of Phonetics; Broadcast English I, II, III, IV; Phonetic Ed of Linguaphone European & Oriental Language Courses; Talking Films on King's English. *c.t*: Ency Brit, Radio Times, Listener, Amer Speech Journ, Bulletin of Sc of Oriental Studies. *s.s*: Phonetics, linguistics. Linguistic adviser to B.B.C. Lecturer in Phonetics at U.C.L. 1920. *Rec*: Tennis, music, etc. *c*: Nat Lib. *a*: Egdon Hse, Prince Arthur Rd, N.W.3. *t*: Hampstead 1348.

LLOYD, John A. T., B.A., LL.B. *b*: Brighton 1870. *e*: Rugby & T.C.D. *m*: J. M. O. de Testenoire. Author & Journalist. *n.a*: Toronto Week 1891–93, Academy 1902–03, T.P.'s Weekly '03–08. *Publ*: A Great Russian Realist; Sappho; The Murder of Edgar Allan Poe; Prestige; Eros; The Staircase; The Uprooters; Two Russian Reformers; The Three Destinies; The Real Canadian; Quis? The Atheist; Leila Braddock; The Skein; Good-Better-Best; Proximity; Ivan Turgenev; Fyodor Dostoevsky; various Trans from the French; *Ctr*: Times Lit Supp, Daily Telegraph, Morning Post, Nash's Mag, John O'London, Bookman, etc. *s.s*: Fiction & Critical Biog. *c*: Authors' *a*: 20 Lansdowne Pl, Hove, Sussex. *T*: 1875.

LLOYD, Sir John Edward, Knt, M.A., D.Litt (Oxon), Hon D.Litt (Wales), F.B.A., F.S.A., F.R.HistS. *b*: L'pool 1861. *e*: Univ Col of Wales, Aberystwyth & Lincoln Coll Oxf. *m*: Clementina Miller. *s*: 1. *d*: 1. Emeritus Prof of Univ Col of N. Wales Bangor. *n.a*: Ed The Bulletin of the Board of Celtic Studies of Univ of Wales 1921—. *Publ*: A History of Wales to the Edwardian Conquest (2 vols '12); A History of Wales ('30); etc. *c.t*: Dictionary of Nat Biography, Cam Mediæval Hist, Ency Britannica (14th ed), Archæologia Cambrensis, Cymmrodorion Soc's Publ's, English Hist Review. *s.s*: Hist of Wales. Mem staff Bangor Col 1892—1930 (Prof Hist '99—). *a*: Gwaen Deg, Bangor, N. Wales. *t*: 233.

LLOYD, Llewelyn Cyril. F.L.S. *b*: Nottingham. *m*: Phyllis M. Perry. Hon Curator of Zoology Shrewsbury Museum. *n.a*: Mang Dir & Ed Shrewsbury Circular, Radio Corres The Spectator. *Publ*: The Inns of Shrewsbury; The Book Trade in Shropshire; Paper Making in Shropshire; etc. *s.s*: Natural Hist, Local Hist & Music. *Rec*: Music & photography. *a*: c/o Shrewsbury Circular, Shrewsbury, Shropshire. *T*: 2113.

LLOYD, Llewelyn Southworth, C.B.(Civil). *b*: Cheadle Hulme 1876. *e*: King William's Coll I.O.M., Christ's Coll Camb. *m*: Margaret Christine Parker. *d*: 1. H.M. Inspector of Schools 1905—16, Asst Sec Dept of Scientific & Industrial Research '17—43. *Publ*: Music & Sound; The Musical Ear. *Ctr*: Various musical & scientific periodicals. *s.s*: Musical Acoustics. *a*: Sandiway, Milton Ave, Gerrards Cross, Bucks. *T*: Gerrards Cross 2791.

LLOYD, (Maria) Teresa. *b*: Lon 1890. *e*: Notre Dame Training Col, Dowanhill, Glas. Teacher. *Publ*: Jesus: For Little Folk; A Child's Life of St Thomas Aquinas; A Child's Life of Anthony of Padua; A Child's Life of Blessed Thomas More; A Child's Life of Philippine Duchesne. *c.t*: Rosary, Catholic Fireside, Franciscan Monthly, etc. *s.s*: Eng Lit, Biog & Hist. Lon Univ Diploma in Lit with distinction, Gilchrist Medal for Lit, Churton Collins Prize for Lit 1933, Trainer's N.F.U. Diploma '33. *c*: L.T.A. & N.U.T. *a*: 11 Cheniston Gdns, W.8. *t*: Western 0153.

LLOYD, Mollie. *b*: London 1914. *e*: Dulwich Hgh Sch, Oakfield Sch West Dulwich. *m*: Oswald Lloyd. *s*: 1. *d*: 1. Mem Inst of Women Journalists. *Ctr*: Mother, Home Review, The Doctor, B.B.C. Kitchen Front (Series). *s.s*: Cookery & Women's Features. *Rec*: Reading. *a*: 34 Lensfield Rd, Cambridge. *T*: 2519.

LLOYD, Dr. N. L. *a*: 60 Oakley St, Chelsea, S.W.3.

LLOYD, RICHARD ERNEST: physician, biologist; b. London, Eng., Sept., 1875; s. John and Elizabeth Green (Rideal) L.; educ. Dulwich Coll., Univ. Coll. (London). DEGREES: M.B., D.Sc. (both London Univ.); m. Edith Alice Dakin, Feb., 1902. AUTHOR: Introduction to Biology for Students in India, 1908; The Growth of Groups in the Animal Kingdom, 1910; What is Adaptation? 1912; Life and Word, 1924. General character of writing: scientific, philosophical. In Indian Med. Service, 1902-20; sometime Prof. of Biology, Medical Coll., Calcutta; at present engaged in agricul. experiment work in Africa. Relig. denom., Church of England. HOME: Kaombi Farm, Serenje, Northern Rhodesia, Africa.

LLOYD, Richard Maurice George. *b*: Belfast 1897. *e*: Highgate & New Col Oxf. *m*: (1) Dorothy Kynoch (who obtained divorce); (2) Ruby Clayton-Collier. *s*: 2. *d*: 1. Journalist & Specialist Organiser. *n.a*: Daily News 1919-20, Soc of Archs Journ '20–21, The Structural Eng (Ed) '21–28, Cape Argus '29, Nat Press Agency '32–33, N. Rhodesian Gazette (Ed) '29. *Publ*: The Devil's Dagger ('28); Killing No Murder; Stonewall Steevens Investigates; The Jade Hatpin; The Orange Ray ('34); etc. *c.t*: Various n/ps. *s.s*: Aviation, sports, educ. *Rec*: Cricket, golf & shooting. *a*: c/o Curtis Brown Ltd, 6 Henrietta St, W.C.2.

LLOYD, Capt. Robin Wynell Mayow, D.S.O. *b*: Market Drayton 1884. *e*: Bedford & H.M.S. Britannia. *m*: Amy Gladys Painter. *s*: 1. *d*: 1. Roy Navy (ret) *Publ*: Navigation of Han River (China) 1914 in Yangtse Sailing Directions. *c.t*: Engineering, Graphic, etc. *s.s*: Travel, pilotage & navigation. R.N. 1898–1922. Asst Schoolmaster Pinewood Farnborough '23–24. Mang Dir McGruers Hollow Spar Co '24-25. Organising Sec (Midlands) Roy Nat Lifeboat Inst '25–26. Yacht Organisation & Commands '26–33. Mount Everest Climbing Expedition '24. *Rec*: Motoring, yachting & walking. *c*: United Service & Roy Navy, etc. *a*: Ricochet, Lee-on-Solent, Hants. *t*: Portsmouth 79270.

LLOYD, Rev. Roger Bradshaigh. *b*: 1901. *e*: Shrewsbury Sc & St John's Col Cam. *Publ*: The Stricken Lute; A Biog of Abelard; The Religious Crisis. *s.s*: Mediæval hist & theo. *a*: The Vicarage, Gt Harwood, Blackburn.

LLOYD, T. S. *n.a*: Ed Oldham Ev Chron. *a*: Union St, Oldham, Lancashire.

LLOYD, Thomas Alwyn, J.P., F.R.I.B.A. *b*: Liverpool 1881. *e*: Liverpool Coll & University. *m*: C Ethel Robarts M.A. Architect & Town Planner. *Publ*:

Planning in Town & Country; Brighter Welsh Villages; South Wales Plan (for the Minsister of Town & Country Planning 1948). *Ctr*: Wales Quarterly, T.P.I. Journ, R.I.B.A. Journ, Western Mail. *s.s*: Town & Country Planning, Architecture. *Rec*: Rambling, studying Buildings, " Preserving the Countryside ". *a*: 6 Cathedral Rd, Cardiff. *T*: Cardiff 54.

LLOYD, William, F.R.C.S., L.R.C.P., L.S.A. (Lon), F.F.Sc, F.R.S.M. *b*: Carmarthens. *e*: Aberys, Wales Col & Lon Hosp E. Nose, Ear & Throat Surgeon. Hon Aural & Laryngeal Surg to Music Hall Artistes Benevolent Home. Late Senior Clinical Asst Nose & Throat Dept London Hosp. Late Hon Aural & Laryngeal Surg to Kensington & Fulham Gen Hosp & St Pancras & Gt Northern Disp, Hse Surg Lon Throat Hosp, etc. *Publ*: Hay Fever; Hay Asthma (3rd edn, 1931); etc. *c.t*: Daily Mail, Med Journs, etc. *Rec*: Ornithology, travel. *c*: R.A.C. *a*: 58 Brook St, Grosvenor Sq, W.1. *t*: Mayfair 3085.

LLOYD, Wyndham Edward Buckley, M.A., F.R.A.S., M.R.C.S., L.R.C.P. *b*: London 1901. *e*: Winchester Coll, Caius Coll Camb, St Bart's Hosp. *Publ*: A Hundred Years of Medicine. *Ctr*: Lancet, Times, *s.s*: Medicine, Astronomy. *Rec*: Field Botany. *c*: Athenæum, Reform. *a*: 3 Red Cliff, Chelston Rd, Torquay. *T*: 65595.

LLOYD-JONES, Charles. *b*: Shrewsbury 1897. *e*: Shrewsbury Sc. *m*: Mary Elizabeth Brindley. Author. *Pub'*: The House of Cand (1926); Gemini; The Matriarch; Irene Says—; Laughter in Heaven; Sea-Change ('34); Village Wooing ('35). *c.t*: Cornhill. *s.s*: Fiction. *Rec*: Sailing. *a*: Oaklands Cottage, Kingsdown, Sevenoaks.

LLOYD-JONES, Major William, D.S.O. *b*: Lon 1888. *e*: Stuffington Hse, Cheltenham Col, Sandhurst. *m*: Norah Leila Jefferd. *s:1*. Capt of Invalids. *n.a*: Staff Britannia 1926. *Publ*: Havash! *c.t*: Cornhill, Chambers's Journ. *s.s*: Cent Africa. Severely wounded L. Rudolf (Abyssinian Border), amputation of leg. *Rec*: Deep sea fishing. *a*: Roy Hosp, Chelsea. *t*: Sloane 4770.

LLOYD THOMAS, Richard Garwyn. *b*: Nottingham 1905. *e*: Sidcot Sc, Somerset. *m*: Myfanwy Lewis. *s*: 1. Journalist. *n.a*: Warwick Advertiser 1920. Westminster Gazette 1924. Special Corres Observer 1925. B'ham Corres Observer 1926. Australian Corres Dly Herald 1929—. *c.t*: Morning Post, West Australian, Melbourne Age, Western Mail Cardiff, etc. *s.s*: Aviation, Empire trade & migration. *Rec*: Motoring, cricket. *a*: Box 95 P.O., Newcastle, New South Wales, Australia. *t*: Newcastle 1622.

LO, R(EN) Y(EN): university professor, welfare worker, author; b. Kiukiang, China, Oct., 1890; educ. William Nast Coll. (Kiukiang), Baldwin-Wallace Coll. (Berea, Ohio), Syracuse Univ. (N.Y.), Michigan Univ. (last three U.S.A.). DEGREES: A.B., A.M., Ph.D.; m. Helen Y. Lo, June 15, 1916. AUTHOR: The Social Teaching of Confucius, 1914; Illustrations for Preachers, 1923; Christianity and New China, 1924; What is Democracy? 1926; Around the World in Four Months, 1928; The Opium Problem in China, 1929; China's Revolution From the Inside, 1931. Contributor to many Chinese and foreign dailies and periodicals. Editor: Chinese Christian Advocate; Young Peoples' Friend. Prof. Social Science, William Nast Coll.; lecturer at Comparative Law Sch., Soochow Univ.; adviser on foreign affairs to Kangsi Provincial govt.; Delegate to Rehabilitation Congress called by Nat. Govt., 1924; Delegate to Jerusalem Conf. and Methodist Gen. Conf. (Kansas City, U.S.A.), 1928; Delegate to Nat. Opium Suppression Conf., 1928; Member of the Opium Suppression Commission of the Chinese Nat. Govt.; chmn. Nat. anti-opium Assn.; vice-chmn. Nat. Child Welfare Assn.; vice- chmn. Executive Gen. Bd. of Methodist East Asia Conf.; vice-chmn. China National Christian Council. Relig. denom., Methodist Episcopal. OFFICE: 23 Yuen Ming Yuen Rd., Shanghai. HOME: 49 Feng-lo Terrace, N. Szechuen Road, Shanghai, China.

LOANE, George Green. *b*: Cork 1865. *e*: Middleton Col Co Cork, Roy Sc Armagh, T.C.D. & Trin Col Cam. *m*: Edith Armitage. *d*: 4. Late Master St Paul's Sc. *Publ*: A Thousand & One Notes on: A New English Dictionary; A Short Handbook of Literary Terms. *c.t*: Times. *s.s*: Oxf Eng dictionary. *Rec*: Gardening, music. *c*: Classical Assoc Philological Soc, Rationalist P.A. *a*: Woodthorpe, Thrupp, nr Stroud, Glos. *t*: Brinscombe 116.

LOBB, Frances. *b*: London. *e*: France, Germany & Italy. Writer. *Publ*: Handsome Johnnie; The Strangers; etc. *s.s*: Translation from French, German & Italian. *Rec*: Entertaining. *a*: 63 Frognal, London, N.W.3. *T*: Hampstead 2524.

LOBLEY, Edward Percival. *b*: Batley 1878. *e*: Elem & Wheelwright G.S. *m*: Edith Fawcett. Printer. *n.a*: Heavy Woollen District Free Press. *a*: 27 Bradford Rd, Dewsbury. *t*: 1111.

LOBLEY, John Hodgson, F.R.S.A., R.B.A. *b*: Huddersfield 1878. *e*: Huddersfield Tech Coll, Roy Coll of Art, Slade Sch, Roy Acad Schs. *m*: Olive Lillie Hargreaves. *s*: 1. Painter, Exhibitor R.A. & Principal British Galleries & at the Salon. *Ctr*: Various Provincial newsps including Huddersfield Examiner, The Porcupine, Poole & Bournemouth newsps. *s.s*: Articles on Art & General Descriptive Writing. *Rec*: Reading, principally history. *a*: 12 Poole Hill, Bournemouth. *T*: Canford Cliffs 538.

LOBINGIER, Charles Sumner, M.A., LL.M., Ph.D., D.C.L. *b*: Lanark, Illinois. *e*: Nebraska State Univ. *m*: Ellen Hunker. Internat & Comparative Jurist, Legal Educator, Author. *Publ*: The People's Law; Evolution of Roman Law; Philippine Practice; Beginnings of Law; Las Siete Partidas; History of the Supreme Council; Ancient & Accepted Scottish Rite. *Ctr*: N.Y. Times, North Amer Rev, Ency Brit, etc. *s.s*: Comparative Law & Hist Jurisprudence. *Rec*: Travel. *a*: Usamgik Dept of Justice, Seoul, Korea (c/o P.M., S.F., Cal, APO. 235-2). *T*: 217.

LOCHHEAD, Daniel C. *n.a*: Ed Paisley Daily Express. *a*: 20 New St, Paisley.

LOCHHEAD, Marion Cleland, M.A. *b*: Wishaw. *e*: Glas Univ. *Publ*: Poems; Painted Thing & Other Poems; Anne Dalrymple; Cloaked in Scarlet; The Dancing Flower; Feast of Candlemas; Highland Scene; Tintock Tap; The Scots Household. *Ctr*: Glasgow Herald, Bulletin, Scotland's Magazine, Scottish Field, Time & Tide, Blackfriars. *Rec*: Music, book collecting. *c*: P.E.N. *a*: The Beeches, Wishaw, Scotland. *T*: 103.

LOCHNER, Louis P., A.B., Litt.D. *b*: Springfield, Illinois 1887. *e*: Univ of Wisconsin. *m*: Hilde Steinberger. *s*: 1. *d*: 2. Author, Foreign Corres, Lect Radio Commentator. *n.a*: A.P. Corres Berlin 1924—42, A.P. War Corres Europe '44—46 Nth. American Newsp Alliance Corr Germany '46, Pacific Coast News Commentator Nat Broadcasting Co '43—44. *Publ*: What About Germany; America's Don Quixote; The Goebbels Diaries; etc. *Ctr*: A.P., Nth American

Newsp Alliance, Modern Industry, Argosy Mag. *s.s*: Germany (Nazi & Post-War Period). *Rec*: Music, swimming, hiking. *c*: Overseas Press. *a*: 325 East 41st St, New York 17, N.Y. *T*: Murray Hill 4-5469.

LOCK, Charles John. *b*: Marylebone 1861. *e*: Birbeck Col, City of Lon Col & Priv. *m*: Annie Cluett. *s*: 1. *d*: 4. *n.a*: Asst Ed Draper's Record, Ed Cigar & Tobacco World, Asst Ed Furniture Record, Lon Repres Hardwareman & Saddlery & Harness. *Publ*: Marquetry ('94). *c.t*: Nelson's Ency, etc. Exam in Shorthand Col of Preceptors. Sec & Asst Ed Roy Microscopical Soc 1918-27. *Rec*: Gym, sculling, cycling. *c*: F.J.I., N/p Press Fund. *a*: 78 Sinclair Rd, W. Kensington, W.14.

LOCK, Henry Osmond. Solicitor. *Publ*: With the British Army in the Holy Land, 1917—18; Conquerors of Palestine through Forty Centuries; Dorset; History of Dorsetshire Regiment in the Great War; Advice to a Young Solictor. *a*: York Hse, Dorchester, Dorset. *T*: 115 & 500.

LOCK, Nan K. *b*: Wilmslow 1906. Journalist & Artist. *n.a*: Jt Ed & Art Ed South African Lady's Pictorial, Cape Town '31-32. *c.t*: Numerous Brit & S. African mags & periodicals. *s.s*: Hist drawings in line & wash, aviation. *a*: BM/NKL, Lon. W.C.1.

LOCK, W(ALTER), Rev.: (formerly canon of Christ Church Cathedral; Lady Margaret professor of divinity, Oxford; b. Dorchester, Dorset, Eng., July, 1846; s. Henry and Susan Ware (May) L.; educ. Dorchester Grammar Sch., Marlborough Coll., (scholar) Corpus Christi Coll. (Oxford). Hertford Scholar, 1867; Craven Scholar, 1869; Fellow of Magdalen, 1869;; Professor Emeritus, 1928. DEGREES: M.A., D.D. (Oxford); m. Jane Cecil Campion, Sept. 28, 1892. AUTHOR: Sermons (in Keble College Sermons), 1877-79; essay on "The Church" in Lux Mundi, 1890; John Keble: a biography, 1892; (edited with notes and introduction) Keble's "The Christian Year", 1895, and Lyra Innocentium, 1899); St. Paul: the Master Builder, 1899; The Bible and Christian Life, 1905; The Ephesians in Westminster Commentaire, 1929, on St. John's Gospel in New Commentary on the Bible (5th edit., 1920). Editor, Westminster Commentaries on the Bible. Contributor to Church Quarterly Rev., Journ. of Theol. Studies, Theology, Guardian, Dictionary of Christian Biography, Hasting's Dict. of the Bible. General character of writing: religious commentary and scholarly research. Teacher at Keble Coll., Oxford, 1930; Warden, 1897; Dean and Professor of Exegesis, 1895; Select Preacher at Oxford and Cambridge; Exam. Chaplain to the Bishop of York. Relig. denom., Church of England. HOME: 13 Rawlinson Road, Oxford, Eng.

LOCKE, Arthur H. *b*: Woking 1910. *e*: Woking County Sc. *m*: Aileen Gale-Brown. Journalist. *n.a*: Woking Herald. *s.s*: Music, motor & motor cycle racing, football. *Rec*: Tennis, fishing. *c*: Woking Round Table. Mem N.U.J. *a*: Braeside, Saunders Lane, Mayford.

LOCKE, Dorothy Mary. *b*: Hove. *e*: Ireland. Novelist. *Publ*: Cast Not a Stone; Open Till Sunset; Some Women Shouldn't Marry; Winds of Winter; Night in November; Two Ways Meet; Saints & Salamander; etc. *s.s*: Philos & Sci. *Rec*: Swimming. *a*: Da's Gardens, Felpham, Sussex. *T*: Bognor Regis 305.

LOCKE, Rev. Herbert John, C.F. *b*: Sudbury 1883. *e*: G.S. & Cliff Col. *m*: Ethel May Taylor. Cong Min. *Publ*: Cruel as the Grave; Stronger Than Death; Paul Ruskin's Vow; A Crushed Lily. *c.t*: Sunday Companion, Chr Herald, etc. *s.s*: Hist, romance. Chaplain R.A.F. & Publ Asst Inst, Epping '30-. *Rec*: Travel, tennis, bowls. *c*: L.N.U., B.&F.B.S. *a*: Oakridge, Epping.

LOCKE, S. E. *Publ*: The Littlest House & Ann. Mem Irish Literary Society. *a*: 2 Frewin Rd, Wandsworth Common, S.W.18.

LOCKER-LAMPSON, Godfrey Lampson Tennyson, P.C., M.P. for Wood Green. *Publ*: Consideration of the State of Ireland in the 19th Cent; On Freedom; Financial Procedure in the House of Commons; Oratory British & Irish—The Great Age: Thoughts in Middle Life; A Tale in Everything; A Soldier's Book of Love Poems; The Country Gentleman; etc. *a*: 14 Southwick Cres, Hyde Park.

LOCKETT, Richard Cyril, J.P., F.S.A., F.R.N.S. *b*: L'pool 1873. *m*. *s*: 2. *d*: 1. Merchant (ret). Ctr Numismatic Chron, Brit Numismatic Journ. *s.s*: Numismatics. *c*: Carlton. *a*: 58 Cadogan Place, London, S.W.1.

LOCKETT-FORD, Ven. Abraham, M.A. *b*: Newry 1853. *e*: Roy Inst Sc L'pool. *m*: Hilda Fleming. *s*: 3. *d*: 1. Archdeacon of Armagh. *c.t*: Official Diocesan Corr of Irish Ch Gazette, Ed Report of 1st Ch of Ireland Conference. *Publ*: For Ever, Manual for Communicants; Ad Clerum; Advent Sermons on Lord's Prayer; Tales Told by a Trooper. *c.t*: Irish Ch Gazette, Clergyman's Mag, The Churchman. *s.s*: Liturgical studies. *c*: Dublin Univ. *a*: Rectory, Ardee, Co Louth. *t*: 20.

LOCKHART, Rev. Douglas David Alexander, M.A. *b*: Malaga, Spain 1898. *e*: Wellington Coll, Roy Mil Coll, Trin Coll Oxf, Ely Theol Coll. Rector of Old St Paul's Church Edin. *Publ*: God's Family at Worship; Five Qualities of the Kingdom; Seeds of War; Ceremonial of the Scottish Liturgy. *s.s*: Religious. *Rec*: Walking. *w.s*: 1st Gordon Highlanders World War I. *a*: Lauder Hse, Jeffrey St, Edinburgh. *T*: 26532.

LOCKHART, J. G. Dir. *Publ*: The Feet of the Young Men; Mysteries of the Sea; The Peacemakers; Cecil Rhodes; etc. *a*: 20 Ashley Gardens, S.W.1.

LOCKHART, John Gilbert. *b*: Wimbledon 1891. *e*: Marlboro' & Trin Col Oxf. Publisher. *Publ*: Mysteries of the Sea; A Great Sea Mystery; East All the Way; Pulpits and Personalities; The Peacemakers; Cecil Rhodes. *c.t*: Church Times. *s.s*: Biog, hist & nautical subjects. War Service 1914-18. Sec Carriage & Wagon Works Nott'm '19-22. Dir Philip Allan & Co Ltd (Publishers) '24-31. Lit Adviser & later Dir of Geoffrey Bles Ltd (Publishers) '31-34. *Rec*: Tennis, golf. *c*: Windham, The Sette of Odd Volumes, etc. *a*: 208 Ashley Gdns, S.W.1. *t*: Victoria 4795.

LOCKHART-MUMMERY, John Percy, M.A., B.C., F.R.C.S. *e*: Public Sch & Camb. *Publ*: After Us; Nothing New Under the Sun; Diseases of the Rectum & Colon; The Cause of Cancer. *Ctr*: Lancet & various other med journs. *s.s*: Rectal & Colon Diseases. *a*: Southease, Barrowfield Drive, Hove, Sussex.

LOCKHART, Sir Robert Hamilton Bruce, K.C.M.G. *b*: Anstruther 1887. *e*: Fettes, Berlin & Paris. Author, H.M. Consular & Comm Diplomatic Services 1911—23, Brit Representative to Prov Czechoslovak Govt '40—41, Deputy Under Sec of State in Foreign Office & Dir-Gen of Political Warfare '42—45. *n.a*: Ed Staff of Ev Standard 1929—37. *Publ*: Memoirs of a British Agent; Retreat from Glory; Return to Malaya; My Scottish Youth; Guns or Butter; Comes the Reckoning; etc. *s.s*: Foreign Affairs. *Rec*: Fishing. *a*: St James's Club, Piccadilly, London, W.1.

LOCKITT, Charles Henry, M.A., B.Sc(Lon), F.R.HistS. *b*: Lon 1877. *e*: Whitgift Sc & U.C.L. *m*: Helen Stanton. *s*: 1. Headmaster Bungay G.S. *Publ*: The Relations of French & English Society 1763—1793 (1920); etc. *s.s*: Hist. Chm E. Anglian Br Classical Assoc '33. Supp Lect Cam Extra-Mural Bd '30. *Rec*. Cricket, tennis, golf. *c*: Authors'. Mem Counc Inc Assoc of Headmasters '25—29. *a*: The Tower Mill, Bungay Suffolk.

LOCKLEY, Fred. *b*: Leavenworth, Kansas 1871. *e*: Willamette Univ, Salem Kansas. *m*: (1) Hope Gans (dec'd), (2) Laura Simpson (dec'd). *s*: 1. Mem Faculty N.Y. Univ. *n.a*: Part Owner & Ed Writer East Oregonian Pendleton, Mang & Ed Northwest Livestock Journ, Gen Mang Pacific Monthly Portland. *Publ*: History of the Columbia River Valley; Oregon Folks; Oregon's Yesterday; Oregon Trail Blazers; Sol Tetherow Wagon Train Master; Across the Plains by Prairie Schooner; Vigilante Days in Virginia City; etc. *Ctr*: Oregon Journ, Colliers, Oregon Hist Quarterly, etc. *s.s*: Hist Writing & Interviews. *Rec*: Collecting Rare Western Books on Overland Travel & Biogs. *w.s*: War Corres World War I. *a*: 4227 S.E. Stark St, *T*: East 6566.

LOCKLEY, Ronald Mathias. Writer & Author. *Publ*: Dream Island Days; The Sea's A Thief; I Know an Island; The Way to An Island; Shearwaters; Inland Farm; The Island Farmers; Early Morning Island; Birds of the Sea; Islands Round Britain; Letters from Skokholm; etc. *s.s*: Country life. *Rec*: Ornithology, yachting. *a*: Dinas Cross, Pembrokeshire. *T*: Dinas Cross 17.

LOCKMILLER, David Alexander, M.A., LL.B., Ph.D. *b*: Athens, Tennessee 1906. *e*: Emory Univ, Univs of Cumberland & North Carolina. *m*: Alma Russell. *s*: 1. *d*: 1. Pres Univ of Chattanooga. *Publ*: Sir William Blackstone; Mangoon in Cuba; History of the North Carolina State College (1889—1939); The Consolidation of the University of North Carolina. *Ctr*: Hist & Educ Journs. *s.s*: Hist (American), Law (Legal Biog), Educ. *Rec*: Travel. *c*: Methodist, Rotary. *a*: Univ of Chattanooga, Chattanooga, Tennessee, U.S.A. *T*: 6-7363.

LOCKWOOD, Ernest. *b*: Linthwaite 1879. Reporter. *n.a*: Colne Valley Guardian 1903-13, Huddersfield Exam '13–. *a*: 50 New St, Milnsbridge, Huddersfield.

LOCKWOOD, J. F., M.A. Univ Lecturer. *Publ*: Smith's Smaller Latin-English Dict (3rd ed). *c.t*: Various periodicals. *a*: University College, Gower St, W.C.

LOCKWOOD, Vera Irene. *b*: London 1906. *e*: Priv Sch. Authoress. *Publ*: Ramazan the Rajah; Claws of Africa; London Lights; A Persian Carpet; Dancer of India; Marry the Caid; Pride in Egypt; Flaming Lanterns; Affairs in Eden; Passionate Pilgrimage; Veiled Wife; etc. *s.s*: Eastern Romances *Rec*: Rowing, tennis, painting, gardening. *a*: Goldstone Lodge, Lloyd Rd, Hove, Sussex.

LOCKYER, Cuthbert Jones, M.D., B.S., F.R.C.P., F.R.C.S., F.R.C.O.G. *b*: Evergreech, Somerset 1867. *e*: King's Sch Bruton, St Thomas & Charing Cross Hosps, Vienna, Bonn, etc. *m*: (1) Minnie Coombs, (2) Violet Gwendonline Morton. *s*: 2. *d*: 1 Gynaecologist (ret). *Publ*: Gynaecology, A Textbook for Students; A System of Gynaecology; (Ed) Fibroids & Allied Tumours; (Ed & Trans) Vagino-Peritonal Operations; etc. *s.s*: Gynaecology. *Rec*: Etching, gardening. *a*: Alverton Cott, Penzance, Cornwall. *T*: 3266.

LODER, JOHN DE VERE: author; b. London, Eng., Feb. 5, 1895; s. Gerald Walter Erskine and Louise de Vere (Beauclerk) L.; educ. Eton Coll.; m. Margaret Tennant, June 3, 1920. AUTHOR: The Truth About Mesopotamia, Palestine and Syria, 1923; Industry and the State, 1927; Red October: A Picture of Soviet Russia, 1931. Contributor to Saturday Rev., Edinburgh Rev., Fortnightly Rev., Contemporary Rev., Das Neue Europa. General character of writing: historical, political, informational survey. Service in Great War, 1914-19; Dardanelles, Egypt, Palestine campaigns; Capt. Royal Sussex Regt. and Staff Capt., Intelligence Corps; mentioned in dispatches; employed in Foreign Office, London, 1919-21; M.P. (Conservative), for Leicester (East), 1924-29. Hon. treas., Brit. Inst. of Adult Education, 1923; has travelled extensively in Europe, Near and Middle East, N. Africa, S. America, Australia. Relig. denom., Church of England. CLUBS: Athenaeum, Travellers, Carlton. HOME: Jacques Hall, Manningtree, Essex, Eng.

LODER, Vernon. See Vahey, John George Haslette.

LODGE, Alfred, M.A.(Oxon). *b*: 1854. *e*: Horncastle G.S. & Magdalen Col Oxford. *m*: Winifred Derriman. *s*: 3. *d*: 3. *Publ*: Mensuration and Elementary Differential and Integral Calculus; Compiled Tables Bessel and other Functions; etc. Formerly Prof of Maths at Roy Ind Eng Col. *a*: 330 Banbury Road, Oxford.

LODGE, Eleanor Constance, C.B.E., M.A., D.Litt(Oxon), Litt.D., F.R.HistS. *b*: Hanley 1869. *e*: Lady Margaret Hall Oxf. Princ Westfield Col (ret). *Publ*: End of the Middle Age (1909); Social & Economic History of Berkshire; Gascony under English Rule ('26); Account Book of an English Estate ('27); Sully, Colbert & Turgot ('31); English Constitutional Documents 1307—1485 (jt); etc. *c.t*: Eng Hist Review, etc. *s.s*: Mediæval hist. Librarian & Teacher of Hist Lady Margaret Hall 1895, Hist Tutor '99—1921, Vice-Princ '06—21, Princ Westfield Col '21—31, Exam in Hist Lon Univ '22—31. Hon Fell Lady Margaret Hall & Westfield Col. *Rec*: Gardening. *a*: 5 Fyfield Rd, Oxf.

LODGE, John, M.A. *b*: Feltham 1890. *e*: Palmer's Sch, Grays, Christ's Hosp Horsham & King's Coll Univ of Lond. *m*: Winifred Tier. *s*: 1. Headmaster. *Publ*: Songs from Camp & College (with A. A. Cock). *s.s*: Lit & Drama. *Rec*: Amateur acting & play producing. *a*: Nantwich & Acton Grammar School, Nantwich, Cheshire. *T*: 5264.

LODGE, Margaret Beatrice. *b*: Oxford. *Publ*: Seven Plays of Fairy Days; Other Plays of Fairy Days; A Fairy to Stay; The Wishing Wood; Felicity at Fairliholm; Sir Richard Lodge (biog). *a*: Lane End, Harpenden, Hertfordshire. *T*: Harpenden 87.

LODGE, Sir Oliver, F.R.S. *b*: 1851. *e*: Univ Col Lon. Scientist & Author. *Publ*: Man & the Universe; The Survival of Man; Reason and Belief; Modern Problems; Raymond, or Life & Death; Science and Human Progress; Pioneers of Science; Ether and Reality; Making of Man; Evolution and Creation; etc. Many years Princ Birm Univ. Pres British Assoc 1913. *s.s*: Wireless telegraphy, psychical research. *a*: Normanton Hse, Lake, nr Salisbury.

LODGE, Sir Richard, HonLittD.(M/C), HonLL.D. (Glas & Edin). *b*: Penkhull 1855. *e*: Christ's Hosp & Balliol Oxf. *m*: Annie Gwendoline Morgan. *s*: 1. *d*: 3. *n.a*: Prof of Hist in Glas Univ '98-99 & Edin Univ '04-1925. *Publ*: Students' Modern Europe; Richelieu; Studies in Eighteenth Century Diplomacy; Private Correspondence of Chesterfield & Newcastle (Ed); Private Correspondence of Sir Benjamin Keene (Ed); etc. *c.t*: Trans Roy Hist Soc, English Hist Review, History. *s.s*: European hist in 18th century. Pres Roy Hist Soc '29-32. *c*: Athenæum. *a*: Lane End, Harpenden, Herts. *t*: 87.

LODGE, Rupert Clenden, M.A., F.R.S.C. *b*: Rusholme, England 1886. *e*: Manch Gr Sch, Brasenose Coll Oxf, Univ of Manch, Marburg & Berlin. *m*: Edith Warren Melcher. *d*: 1. Univ Prof of Philosophy. Author. *Publ*: Plato's Theory of Ethics; Plato's Theory of Education; Philosophy of Business; Philosophy of Education; The Questioning Mind; Introduction to Modern Logic; Locke's Simple Modes; Varisco's Great Problems; Manitoba Essays. *Ctr*: Journ of Philosophy, Mind, Queens' Quarterly, etc. *s.s*: Philosophy. *Rec*: Yachting, piano. *a*: 132 Earl St, Kingston, Ontario, Canada.

LODGE, Thomas, C.B. *b*: Newport, Mon 1882. *e*: L'pool Inst & Trinity Coll Camb. *m*: Isobel Scott. *d*: 3. *Publ*: Dictatorship in Newfoundland. *Ctr*: Spectator. *c*: Reform. *a*: Blunham Grange, Bedford. *T*: Blunham 220.

LODGE PATCH, Charles James, M.C. *b*: Madras 1887. *e*: Edin Univ & Roy Coll of Surgeons. *m*: Edith Jeffrey. *s*: 1. *d*: 2. Lt-Col Indian Medical Service (ret), Sen Govt Psychiatrist in India. *Publ*: A Manual of Mental Diseases; A Critical Review of Mental Hospitals in the Punjab. *Ctr*: Indian Medical Gazette, B.M.J., Journ of Mental Science, Student, etc. *s.s*: Psychiatry, Psychotherapy, Hist of Mental Diseases. *Rec*: Sport. *a*: 88 Harley St, London, W.1. *T*: Langham 2757.

LODS, FRANÇOIS PAUL ADOLPHE: professor in Sorbonne; *b*. Courbevoie (Seine), France, 1867; *s*. Eduard and Marie (Denonvilliers) L.; educ. Lycée Condorcet, Faculté des Lettres (Sorbonne), Faculté de Théologie Protestante de Paris, Univs. of Berlin and Marburg. DEGREES: Licencié en Théologie, Docteur és Lettres; *m*. Marie Jackson, 1893. AUTHOR: L'Ecclésiaste et la Philosophie Grecque, 1890; Le Livre D'Hénoch, Fragments Découverts à Akhmim (Haute Egypte), Publiés Avec les variantes du Texte Éthiopen (translated, with notes), 1892; Evangelii Secundum Petrum et Petri Apocalypseos quae Supersunt, 1872; L'Évangile et l'Apocalypse de Pierre, 1893; Mémoires Publiés par la Mission Argheologeuse Française au Gaire, IX, 3, 1893; Les Sourges des Récits du 1st Livre de Samuel sur l'Institution de la Royauté Israelite (in Etudes de Theologie et d'Histoire, 1901; La Groyance à la vie Future et le Culte des Morts (in L'Antiquité Israelite, 2 vols.), 1906; La Morale des Prophètes, 1909; La Sainte Bible (new transl. after the better texts with introduction and notes), 1913; l'Ange de Yahve et l'Ame Extérieure (in Wellhausen's Festschrift), 1914; Jean Astruc et la Critique Biblique au XVIIIe, Siècle (with biographical notes by Paul Alphandéry), 1924; Congrès International d'Histoire des Religions tenu à Paris en Octobre, 1923, 1925; Les Idées des Israelites sur la Maladie, ses Causes et ses Remédes (in Marti's Festschrift), 1925; Quiques Remarques sur l'Histoire de Samson (ibidem); Rites et Sacrifices (in Dieux et Religions), 1926; Le Rôle des Idées Magiques dans la Mantalité Israelite (in Old Testament Essays), 1927; La Chute des Anges, Origine et Portée de Cette Spéculation (in Congrès d'Histoire du Christianisme Jubilé Alfred Loisy), 1928. Contributes to Annales de Bibliographie Theologique, Revue Chretienne, Revue de l'Histoire des Religions, Revue d'Histoire et de Philosophie Religieuses, Revue critique d'Histoire et de litterature Journal de Psychologie, etc. General character of writing: history of religion. Conducted course in theology, 1891-1906: Professor of Literature at Univ. of Paris, 1906—. SOCIETIES: Société Ernest Renan, Société Biblique Protestante de Paris. Relig. denom., Lutheran. HOME: 129 Boulevard Rospail, Paris (6e), France.

LODWICK, Edith Mary. *b*: Carmarthen. *e*: Girls' Cty Sch Carmarthen & Univ of Sth Wales Cardiff. *m*: J. M. Lodwick. *s*: 1. Art Mistress at Withington Girls' High Sch Manchester 1927—29, Journalist & Artist. *Ctr*: Manchester Ev News, Manchester Guardian, East Anglian Dly Times, Dly Mail, etc. *s.s*: Black & White Book Illustration, Book Reviews, Women & Children's Features, etc. *a*: 34 King Street, Carmarthen.

LODWICK, Jasper Malcolm. *b*: Carmarthen 1899. *e*: Carmarthen Sch of Art, Swansea Tech Coll. *m*: Edith Mary Lloyd. *s*: 1. Mem N.U.J. *n.a*: Sub-Ed Cmyric Times 1922—28, Nottingham Journ '29, Manch Guardian '30—32, Manch Ev News '32—33, News Ed Cymric Times '34—. *Ctr*: Various. *s.s*: Short Stories, Humour ("Harlequin"), Book Illus & Review, Cartoons, *Rec*: Rifle shooting, swimming. *a*: 34 King St, Carmarthen. *T*: 7147.

LODWICK, Rupert Randolph. *b*: Carmarthen 1910. *e*: Queen Elizabeth Gr Sch. Journalist, Mem N.U.J. *n.a*: Cymric Times 1926—28, Beds Times & Independent '28—29, Sussex & Surrey Courier '29—35. *s.s*: Book Reviews, Short Stories, etc. *Rec*: Rifle shooting, bowls. *a*: 1 Hereward Rd, Peterborough, Northants.

LOEB, Leonard Benedict, B.S., Ph.D. *b*: Zurich, Switzerland 1891. *e*: Univs of California, Columbia, Chicago, Manch. *m*: Charlotte Pearson. *d*: 4. Prof of Physics. *Publ*: Kinetic Theory of Gases; Fundamental Processes, Electrical Discharge in Gases; Atomic Structure; Fundamentals—Electricity & Magnetism; Nature of a Gas; Laboratory Manual of Electricity & Magnetism; etc. *Ctr*: Physical Rev, Philosophical Mag, Journ of Applied Physics, Ency Brit, etc. *s.s*: Atomic Physics, Electricity & Magnetism, Internat Affairs, Naval Strategy. *Rec*: Swimming, fishing, gardening, reading hist, biog, music. *c*: Cosmos (Wash), Bohemian (San Francisco). *w.s*: A.E.F. 1918—19 & Capt U.S.N.R. World War II. *a*: 2615 Etna St, Berkeley 4, California, U.S.A. *T*: Bexb 0417 W.

LOEWEL, Pierre. *b*: Paris 1890. *m*: Paulette Cavaillon. Author, Advocate, Chevalier Legion d'Honneur, Diplome de l'ecole des Hautes Etudes Sociales. *Publ*: Tableau du Palais; Inventaire; Le canal de Panama. *Ctr*: L'Aurore, L'Ordre. Aux Ecoutes, France. *s.s*: Literary & Theatre Critic. *a*: 4 rue Edouard, Fournier, Paris. *T*: Tro 14-40.

LOEWENSTEIN, F. E., Ph.D. *b*: Berlin 1901. *e*: University. *m*: Agnes. *d*: 3. Bibliographer, Founder of the Shaw Soc; *Publ*: History of An Unsocial Socialist; The Sketches of the Japanese Woodcut-Masters. *s.s*: Bibliography, Bernard Shaw. *Rec*: Collecting Shaw & Shaviana. *a*: Shaw's Corner, Ayot, St Lawrence, Welwyn, Herts. *T*: Codicote 218.

LOEWY, Frederic Ernest, M.D.(Vienna), M.R.C.P. (Lon), M.R.C.S., F.R.S.M.(Eng). *b*: Vienna 1895. *e*: Vienna Univ, Middx Hosp. Physician. *c.t*: Klinische Wochenschrift, Wiener Klinische Wochenschrift, Lancet. *c*: Anglo-German, B.M.A., etc. *a*: 13 Welbeck St, W.1. *t*: Welbeck 8052.

LOFARGUE, René. *b*: Thann, Haut Rhin, 1894. *e*: Cols of Thann, Forbach, Sasbach, Mulhause, Fribourg-en-Brisgau. *m*: Paulette Erichson. Doctor of Medicine. *n.a*: Ex director of L'Evolution Psychanalylogue. Director of La Revue française de Psychanalyse. *publ*: La Psychanalyse et les Névroses (with René Allendy); Des Processus d'Auto Punition (with Hesnard); L'Echec de Baudelaire; Libido Angst und Zivilisation; Misère de l'Homme. *c.t*: Progrès Médical, Revue Française de Psychanalyse, Zeitschrift für die gesammte Neurologie und Psychiatrie, Internationale Zeitschrift für Psychoanalyse, Jnl of Psycho-analysis. Prof at the Inst of Psychoanalysis, Paris. *c*: Founder and Ex-Pres of La Société Psychanalylogue de Paris. *a*: 1 Rue Miguet, Paris, 16e.

LOFSTEDT, Annie. *b*: Stockholm 1896. *e*: Lund Univ. *m*: Einar Lofstedt. *s*: 1. *d*: 1. Lit Critic, Lit Adviser to the publ house Natur och Kultur Stockholm 1946—. *Publ*: En Kvimna oun Bocker; Figurer mot Mork Botten. *Ctr*: Sydsvenska Dagbladet 1922—23, Goteborgs Haudelstidring. *c*: P.E.N. *a*: Gyllenkroks Alle 3, Lund, Sweden.

LOFTHOUSE, Rev. William Frederick, D.D. *b*: S. Norwood 1871. *e*: City of Lon Sc & T.C. Oxf. Princ Handsworth Col. *Publ*: Ethics & Atonement; Ethics & the Family; Jeremiah; Altar, Cross & Community; Israel after the Exile; etc. *a*: Handsworth Col. Birm. *t*: 1035.

LOFTING, Hugh. Author. *Publ*: The Story of Dr Dolittle; The Voyages of Dr Dolittle; Dr Dolittle's Post Office; Dr Dolittle's Circus; Dr Dolittle's Zoo; etc. *a*: c/o Jonathan Cape Ltd, 30 Bedford Sq, W.C.2.

LOFTS, E. Allan. Terr Mem N.U.J. *a*: 138 Henley Rd, Caversham.

LOFTS, George Ernest. *e*: Lincoln Tech Col. Engineer & Journalist. *n.a*: Ed Electric Vehicles & Batteries '33. Ed Crushing, Grinding, Mining & Quarrying Journ '34. Ed Rural Electrification & Electro-farming '34. Jt-Ed Electric Power '35. *c*: Founder Mem Inst of Fuel, mem Jnr Institution of Engineers (Incorp). *a*: 13—16 Fisher St, W.C.1. *t*: Holborn 5171.

LOFTS, Norah. *b*: Shipdham 1904. *m*: Geoffrey Lofts. *s*: 1. *Publ*: Jassy; To See a Fine Lady; Out of this Nettle; Road to Revelation; Blossom Like the Rose; Hester Roon; Requiem for Idols; White Hell of Pity; I Met a Gypsy; Here was a Man; Michael & All Angels. *a*: 98 Henley Rd, Ipswich, Suffolk. *T*: Ipswich 2347.

LOFTUS, Col. Ernest Achey, O.B.E., T.D., D.L.(Essex), M.A.(T.C.D.), B.Sc.Econ(Lond), L.C.P., F.R.G.S. *b*: Hull 1884. *e*: Archbishop Holgate's Gr Sch York, Trin Coll Dublin & Lond. *m*: Elsie Cole. *s*: 2. Headmaster of Barking Abbey Sch since 1922. *Publ*: Education & the Citizen; History of a Branch of the Cole Family; (Pt Author) Barking Pageant (8 scenes) &[Essex Pageant (1 scene). *Ctr*: Feature article in Lond dailies & wkly papers & periodicals & educ journs. *s.s*: Education, History. *Rec*: Genealogy, walking. *c*: Jnr Army & Navy. *a*: Polwicks, West Tilbury, Essex, & Barking Abbey School, Essex. *T*: Tilbury 32, & Rippleway 2005.

LOFTUS, Pierse Creagh, J.P. *b*: Mt Loftus, Kilkenny, Ireland. *e*: Oratory Sch. *m*: (1) Dorothy Reynolds, (2) Eileen Elkington. *s*: 2. Dir Brewery & Hotel Co, J.P. (Suffolk), M.P. (Nat Cons) Lowestoft Div 1934—45, High Steward Borough Southwold '45—. *Publ*: The Creed of a Tory; A Main Cause of Unemployment; The Conservative Party & The Future. *Ctr*: New English Rev, Nineteenth Century & After, World Rev, New Eng Weekly, Eastern Dly Press, East Anglian Dly Times. *s.s*: Economics & Monetary Reform, Politics, Agriculture. *w.s*: Pietermaritzburg Defence Force 1899, B.E.F. (Capt 5th Suffolks) 1914—19 (Despatches). *a*: Reydon Covert, Southwold, Suffolk. *T*: 3141; & 12 Montpelier Sq, London, S.W.7. *T*: Kensington 3112.

LOGAN, Agnes. See Adams, Agnes Louise Logan.

LOGAN, James, M.A. *b*: Co Antrim 1880. *e*: T.C.D. *m*: Marguerite Reade Milnes. *s*: 1. *d*: 2. Princ Bedford Col Belfast. *Publ*: School & Examination Bookkeeping (1902); English Composition Simplified; Talks to Boys; Ulster in the X-Rays; Verses Grave & Gladsome; The Bright Side of School Life ('26); Four One-Act Comedies ('31); etc. *s.s*: Essays, verse, school humour & howlers, parodies. *Rec*: Golf. *a*: 42 Ravenhill Pk, Belfast. *t*: 7239.

LOGAN, Mrs. Jennie B. *e*: Glasgow, Edinburgh & Paris. *m*: J. Gordon Logan. *n.a*: Ed The Scottish Triangle '28—. *Publ*: The Jewel of Life in an Eastern Setting; Various pamphlets. Hon Sec Fellowship of Faith for the Moslems. *a*: St Brigids, West Kilbride, Ayrshire. *t*: West Kilbride 150.

LOGAN, Phyllis Duncan. *e*: Cheltenham Ladies Col. *m*: Hugh Logan. *d*: 1. *Publ*: No Retreat; How Faultless the Nymph!; William Looks On. *c*: Forum. *a*: 83 Vincent Sq. S.W.1. *t*: Victoria 6150.

LOGGINS, Vernon, A.M., Ph.D. *b*: Hempstead, Texas 1893. *e*: Univs of Texas, Chicago & Columbia. *Publ*: The Negro Author; Two Romantics; American Literature; etc. *Ctr*: Story, Sat Review of Lit, & various other mags & periodicals. *Rec*: Music. *c*: Authors (N.Y.), etc. *a*: 400 West 119th St, New York 27, N.Y. *T*: University 4-0200.

LOHR, Miss M. Actress. 8 Devonport St, Hyde Pk, W.2.

LO-JOHANSSON, Karl Ivar. *b*: Osmo, Sormland, Sweden 1901. *e*: Public Sch. Author & Novelist. *Publ*: (Novels) Mana is Dead; Goodnight Earth; The King's Street; Only a Mother; The Tractor; (Stories) The Staters; The Proletarians of the Earth. *Ctr*: Lantarbetaren. *a*: Badstugatan 21, Stockholm, Sweden. *T*: 40 24 31.

LOKANATHAN, Palamadai Samu. *b*: Madras 1894. *e*: Univs of Madras & London. *m*: Janaki. *s*: 2. *d*: 4. Dir U.N.O. Lake Success. *n.a*: Ed Eastern Economist (New Delhi) 1943—47. *Publ*: Industrial Organization in India; Economic Planning in India; India's Economic Reconstruction & Its International Aspects; Industrial Welfare in India. *Ctr*: India Quarterly, Foreign Affairs (U.S.A.). *s.s*: Currency & Banking Industry, Planning Trade. *a*: Executive Secretary, Economic Commission for Asia & Far East, Shanghai, China.

LOM, Stanislav. *b*: Prague 1883. *e*: Prague Univ. *m*: Maria Vopalkova. Mem Civil Service, Mem Acad of Arts & Science Prague. *Publ*: Charles IV Odysseus; Cagliostro; The Rocky Gardener; The Death Friend; Venus doing penance; The Overthrow; The Leader. *s.s*: Dramatics. *a*: Prague XIX Baba 1783/1. *T*: 71222.

LOMAS, JOHN (ERNEST WILLS): business executive, author; b. London, Eng., Nov., 1896; s. of John Ernest Howarth and S. F. (Wills)

Lomas; educ. Repton Coll. (Derbyshire); Brasenose Coll. (Oxford). DEGREES: B.A., Barrister-at-Law; m. M. E. Faulkner, Apr. 30, 1927. AUTHOR: The Man With the Scar, 1926. General character of writng: novels. CLUBS: Cavendish (London). OFFICE: 24 Wallbrock, London, E.C.4. HOME: Birches Farm, Isfield, Sussex, Eng.

LOMAX, Alfred, F.I.B.D., F.R.S.A. Decorator *a*: Glenart, Church Drive, Rhos-on-Sea, N. Wales.

LOMAX, Cecil Chadwick. *b*: Lon 1898. *e*: Eton & Sandhurst. Publisher. *n.a*: Chm Lomax, Erskine & Coy Ltd. *Rec*: Hunting. *c*: Cavalry, Bucks. *a*: 29a Chapel St, S.W.1. & 16 New St Sq, W.C.2. *t*: Cent 8445.

LOMAX, John A., M.A. *b*: Goodman, Mississippi 1867. *e*: Univ of Harvard. *m*: *s*: 2. Registrar. *Publ*: Cowboy Songs & other Frontier Ballads; The Book of Texas; Songs of the Cowcamps & Cattle Trail; American Ballads & Folk Songs; Our Singing Country; The Hundred & Fifteen Best American Ballads; etc. *Ctr*: N.Y. Times, Herald-Tribune, Atlantic Monthly, etc. *s.s*: Folk Songs. *a*: 8170 San Benito Way, Dallas, Texas. *T*: F2-1438.

LONDON, Lord Bishop of (see WAND, Rt. Rev. & Rt. Hon. J. W. C., P.C., M.A., Hon.D.D.(Oxon).)
LONDON, Hugh Stanford, M.A., F.S.A. *b*: Rhyl, Nth Wales 1884. *e*: Eton & Oxford. *m*: King's Sch Canterbury, Dulwich Coll & Clare Coll Camb. *m*: Edith Madeleine Wilkins. Brit Foreign Service (ret). *n.a*: Asst Ed New Dict of Brit Arms. *Ctr*: Archives Heraldiques Suisses, Miscellanea Genealogica et Heraldica, Notes & Queries, Revue Francaise D'Heraldique, etc. *s.s*: Heraldry, Biog of English Heralds. *Rec*: Heraldic research. *c*: Athenæum. *a*: Coldharbour, Buxted, Sussex.

LONDONDERRY, Marchioness of, D.B.E. *Publ*: Henry Chaplin, a Memoir; The Magic Inkpot; Character & Tradition, an Essay; Retrospect; Fleet of the Future; The Land of Hearts Desire (priv); Ed (with Mr Hyde) Russian Diaries of Catherine Martha Wilmot. *a*: Londonderry Hse, Park Lane, London, W. *T*: Grosvenor 1616; & Mount Stewart, Newtownards, Co Down. *T*: 3270.

LONDONDERRY, Marquess of, Charles Stewart Henry Vane-Tempest Stewart, K.C., P.C., M.V.O. *b*: London 1878. *e*: Eton & Oxford. *m*: Hon Edith Chaplin. *s*: 1. *d*: 4. Chancellor Queen's Univ Belfast 1923— & Durham Univ '31—, Ld Lieutenant Co Durham, H.M. Lieutenant Co Down, Hon Air Commodore 502 Squadron. *Publ*: Wings of Destiny; Ourselves & Germany. *c*: Carlton & Roy Yacht Sq. *a*: Londonderry Hse, Park Lane, London, W.1. *T*: Grosvenor 1616.

LONEY, Sidney Luxton. *Publ*: Various text books on Statics, Dynamics, Hydrostatics, Trigonometry & Co-ordinate Geometry; etc. *a*: Parkside, 172 Kew Rd, Richmond, Surrey. *t*: 0080.

LONG, Brandon James, M.J.I. *b*: Tralee, Co Kerry 1868. *e*: Nat & Chr Brothers Sc. *m*: Winifred Mary Chapman. *s*: 2. *d*: 1. Ed The Nationalist Clonmel. *n.a*: Dis Rep Eng Dailies & News Ag's & Irish Dailies. Chm Munster Br Inst of Journalists. *Publ*: Tipperary's Annual. Over 43 y on The Nationalist. *Rec*: Gardening, swimming. *a*: 8 Gordon Pl, Clonmel, Co Tipperary. *t*: 17.

LONG, Edward Ernest, C.B.E., F.J.I. *e*: Sutton Valence Sch & Abroad. Journalist. *n.a*: Singapore Free Press 1901, Ed Rangoon Times '05, Ed Indian Dly Telegraph '07, The Times (corresp Nth India) '09. *Publ*: The King Emperor's Activities in War-Time; The Anarchist (one-act Play). *Ctr*: Illus Lond News, Ency Brit. *s.s*: Eastern Lands. *a*: 4 Ruskin Mans, Queen's Club Gdns, London, W.14. *T*: Fulham 0924.

LONG, GABRIELLE MARGARET: (pen name: Marjorie Bowen); author; b. Hampshire, Eng., Nov., 1886; d. Vere Douglas and Josephine Lizbeth (Bowen-Ellis) Campbell; educ. privately; studied Art at Slade Sch. (London) and in Paris; m. Arthur Leonard Long, Dec. 4, 1917. AUTHOR (historical novels): I Will Maintain; God and the King; Defender of the Faith; The Viper of Milan; The Glen o' Weeping; The Sword Decides; Black Magic; The Governor of England; A Knight of Spain; The Quest of Glory; Because of these Things; The Carnival of Florence; Prince and Heretic; The Third Estate; A Soldier from Virginia (Mr. Washington); Kings at Arms; The Leopard and the Lily; William, by the Grace of God; The Burning Glass; Mr. Misfortunate; The Cheats; The Haunted Vintage; Roccoco; The Jest; Nell Gwynn; Boundless Water; Winged Trees; Two Carnations; The Golden Roof; Dickson; (modern novels): Five Winds; Stinging Nettles; The Presence and the Power; Five People; The Pagoda; The Countess Fanny; (volumes of short stories): God's Playthings; Shadows of Yesterday; Brave Employments; English Paragon; Curious Happenings; Crimes of Old London; The Pleasant Husband; Seeing Life; Dark Ann; The Gorgeous Lovers; Exits and Farewells; Old Patche's Medley; Grace Latouche and the Warringtons; Sheep's Head and Babylon; (other works: The Netherlands Displayed; The Temple; The State of England at the Peace of Ryswick; Sundry Great Gentlemen; Holland; Prince of Orange, 1650-1673; The Third Mary Stuart (Mary II of England); Prince of Orange, 1674-1688 (in prep.); (3-act plays): Chosen Cakes; Safety; Interruptions; (1-act plays): The Family Comedy, 1840 (also adapted for Wireless); The Question. Contributor to nearly all British and to many Amer. mags. and papers. General character of writing: fiction, films, historical, plays, essays; first hist. novel written at age of 17; many of her books trans. into Dutch, Scandinavian, Italian. Fellow Royal Soc. Lit.; F. R. Hist. Soc.; Hon. Fellow Utrecht Soc. of Arts and Learning; Hon. Fellow Lit. Soc. Leyden. CLUB: Albemarle (London). HOMES: 37a Craven Terrace, W. 2, London; and Aspley Hill, Woburn Sands, Bedfordshire, Eng.

LONG, Gavin Merrick, B.A. *b*: Foster, Victoria 1901. *e*: All Saints Coll Bathurst, St Paul's Coll, Univ of Sydney. *m*: Mary Jocelyn Britten. *s*: 1. *d*: 1. Journalist. *n.a*: Argus Melbourne 1926—31, Sydney Morning Herald '31—35 (Chief Cable Sub-Ed, Lond Office, War Corres), Gen Ed Australian Official War History '43—. *Ctr*: Various. *s.s*: Military Affairs. *w.s*: War Corres '39—42. *a*: 1 Mugga Way, Canberra, A.C.T. *T*: F601.

LONG, George, J.P., F.R.G.S. Author & Journalist. *Publ*: The Folklore Calendar; The Mills of Man; Churches With a Story; English Inns & Roadhouses; Sport & the English Countryside; etc. *Ctr*: Many British, American & foreign newsps & mags. *s*: Hist, Folklore, Travel at Home & Abroad. *a*: Clifton Hse, Whitchurch, Hants. *T*: 89.

LONG, H. W. Shirley. *b*: London 1905. *m*: Gladys Mann. *s*: 2. Manager Rich & Cowan publishers. *n.a*: B.B.C. European Service, Sun Pictorial, Amalgamated Press Ltd. *a*: 19 Cumberland Mans, Hampstead, London, N.W.6.

LONG, Harold Cecil, I.S.O., B.Sc.(Agric. Edin). *b*: Potters Bar 1876. *e*: Hartley Coll Southampton, Edinburgh Univ. *m*: (1) Annette Shapland Killick, (2) Nellie Pridmore. *s*: 2. *d*: 1. Ret Civil Servant. *n.a*: Gen Ed Crosby Lockwood's Agric & Hort Series, Ed Journ of the Ministry of Agriculture & in charge of Publ Branch of the Ministry 1914—38. *Publ*: Common Weeds of the Farm & Garden, 1910; Plants Poisonous to Live Stock;

Poisonous Plants on the Farm; Weeds of Grass Land; Weeds of Arable Land; Suppression of Weeds by Fertilizers & Chemicals, 1934, new Ed with Dr Winifred Brenchley, 1946; also ed Farmer & Stock Breeder Handbooks. *c.t*: Yorkshire Post, Dly Telegraph, Milk Industry, Far & Stock Breeder, Farmers Weekly, Harmsworth's Self Educator, Encyclopædia Britannica, Journ of Bath & West of Eng Agric Soc, Journ Roy Agric Soc, Trans Highland Agric Soc, Bibby's Annual & Hearth & Farm, etc. *s.s*: Agriculture. *Rec*: Gardening. *a*: Mead Lodge, 63 Manor Rd North, Esher, Surrey. *T*: Emberbrook 1233.

LONG, John Cuthbert, A.B. *b*: Babylon, N.Y. 1892. *e*: Amherst Coll, Harvard Univ. *m*: Mary Catherine Parsons. *s*: 1. *d*: 1. Writer. *n.a*: Ed Staff Writer New Yorker 1927—30. *Publ*: Mr Pitt, & America's Birthright; Lord Jeffery Amherst, A Soldier of the King; Bryan, the Great Commoner; Long's Bible Quiz; Motor Camping (collab); The Liberal Tradition; Public Relations. *Ctr*: Reader's Digest, Sat Rev Lit N.Y. Her-Trib, Colliers, Christ Sci Mon. *s.s*: 18th-Century Hist, American Polit Hist, Biography. *Rec*: Tennis, play writing, golf. *c*: Century, Nat Arts, etc. *a*: Route 2, Bethlehem, Pennsylvania, U.S.A. *T*: 7-4024.

LONG, Justin A. G. *b*: Streatham 1912. *e*: Manor Hse Sc Clapham & King's Col Lon. Author & jnlst. *n.a*: Amalgamated Press Ltd 31—. *c.t*: N/ps & periodicals. *s.s*: Popular fiction, real life stories & sport. *Rec*: Cricket & motoring. *a*: 12 Canford Rd, S.W.11. *t*: Battersea 4328.

LONG, Mason, M.A., Litt.D. *b*: Bellegrove Penna 1892. *e*: Lebanon Valley Coll, Penna State Coll, Yale Univ, Cornell. *m*: Esther K. Moyer, Prof of Lit Penna State Coll. *Publ*: The New College Grammar; Poetry & its Forms; A College Grammar; The Bible & English Literature; Handbook of English Grammar. *Ctr*: Education, Christian Leader, etc. *s.s*: Eng Gram, Influence of the Bible upon Eng & Amer Lit, Victorian Lit. *Rec*: Hiking. *a*: 255, West Park Ave, State Coll, Pennsylvania, U.S.A. *T*: 2525.

LONG, Major S. H. *Publ*: In The Blue. *a*: Doannee, Bray, Berks.

LONG, Sydney Herbert, M.D.(Cantab), F.Z.S., M.B.O.U. *b*: Wells 1870. *e*: Epsom Col, Cam Univ, Paris, Univ Col Hosp Lon. *m*: Grace Violet Christie. *d*: 1. Consulting Physician. *n.a*: Ed Trans of the Norfolk & Norwich Naturalists Soc 1912-32. *Publ*: The Autobiography of Sir Peter Eade ('16). *c.t*: Trans of the Norfolk & Norwich Natur Soc. *s.s*: Medicine, natural hist. Senior Physician Norfolk & Norwich Hosp & Jenny Lind Hosp for Children, Norwich. Hon Sec Norfolk & Norwich Natur Soc '12. Ex-Hon Sec & Treas Norfolk Natur Soc. *a*: 31 Surrey St, Norwich. *t*: 607.

LONGAKER, John Mark, B.A.(Lenoir), Ph.D. (Univ of Pennsylvania). *b*: Newport, Kentucky 1900. *e*: Lenoir & Pennsylvania Univs. *m*: Lenuschka Magava-Dasu. *s*: 1. Asst prof of English language & literature, Univ of Pennsylvania. *Publ*: The Della Cruscans and William Gifford; English Biography in the XVIIIth Century, Contemporary Biography. *s.s*: Biographical writing, XVIIIth Century literature. *Rec*: Fishing, boating, European travel, archæology. *a*: 3425 Powelton Ave, Sunderland Court, Philadelphia, Pennsylvania, U.S.A. *t*: Evergreen 1391.

LONGDEN, Major Alfred Appleby, D.S.O., O.B.E. *b*: Sunderland. *e*: Durham Sch, Art Sch Sunderland, Roy Coll of Art. *m*: Betty Marie Ahlberg. *d*: 1. Dir Fine Art Dept Brit Council, Officer of Legion of Honour. *Publ*: British Cartoon & Caricature; Literature & Art of the Empire (collab). *Ctr*: Studio Magazine, Art & Industry, etc. *s.s*: Painting, Watercolours, Prints (old & modern), Caricature. *Rec*: Sketching, fly-fishing. *c*: Arts. *a*: 7 Sion Hill Pl, Bath, Somerset.

LONGDEN, Fred, M.P. *b*: Ashton-under-Lyne. *e*: W.E.A., Owen's & Ruskin Colls. *m*: Alice Sherlock. *d*: 1. F.L. Lect & Writer, M.P. for Deritend. *Publ*: Essentials of Public Speaking; Co-operative Politics inside Capitalist Society; The Proletarian Heritage; Co-operation & the New Orientation; Shekels & Talents; Apprenticeship in English & Belgian Iron-Founding; Why This Unemployment? *s.s*: Modern Econ & Political Problems, Ind & Const Hist. *Rec*: Gardening, reading. *a*: 58 Ansell Rd, Birmingham 24. *T*: Erdington 0411.

LONGDEN, G. A., F.G.S., F.R.G.S. *a*: Draycott Lodge, Nr Derby.

LONGDEN, Rev. Henry Isham, M.A., HonC.F., F.S.A., F.R.HistS., F.S.G. *b*: Lamport 1859. *e*: Wellington Col Berks, Keble Col Oxf. Rector Heyford, Northampton. *Publ*: Some Notes on Sir Euseby Isham and his Virginian Descendants ('99); The Hist of the Washington Family (1927); The Parish Churches and Religious Houses of Northamptonshire, their Dedications, Altars, Images and Lights by the Rev R. M. Serjeantson M.A. F.S.A. and the Rev H. Isham Longden M.A. *c.t*: The Genealogist's Mag. *s.s*: Genealogy. *Rec*: Cricket, hunting. *a*: Heyford Rectory, Northampton.

LONGDEN, Reginald Thelwall, F.R.I.B.A., F.R.S.A., M.T.P.I. *b*: Burslem 1879. *e*: Orme Scs Newcastle. *m*: H. A. James. *s*: 2. *d*: 1. Archt, Town Planner (Secondary). *Publ*: Proposals in Reference to the Panel System as Applied to the Archtl Amenities of the Country (known as "Longden" Panel Scheme) 1929. *c.t*: Builder, Brick Builder, etc. *s.s*: Preservation of countryside. Founded N. Staffs Archt Assoc '26. Hon Sec R.I.B.A. Small Hse Panel Cmt '29-31. Hon Sec '34 & Mem R.I.B.A. Housing & Town Planning Cmt. *Rec*: Golf. *c*: Archt. *a*: The High Barn, Ladydale, Leek, Staffs. *t*: 256.

LONGFORD, Rev. William Wingfield, D.D., F.S.A., F.R.S.L. *b*: Birmingham 1882. *e*: King Edward's Sch B'ham & Ch Ch Oxf. *m*: Georgina McIntosh. *s*: 1. *d*: 3. Rector of Sefton Lancs, Ex Proctor York & Canterbury Convocations. *n.a*: Ed Trans Hist Soc. Lancs & Cheshire 1934—38. *Publ*: Music & Religion; The Problem of Re-Union. *Ctr*: Nineteenth Century, Modern Churchman. *s.s*: History. *w.s*: Senr Chap XXI Army Corps Palestine & Senr C.F. Egypt (des 1918). *Rec*: Fly fishing. *a*: Sefton Rectory, Liverpool 23. *T*: Maghull 94.

LONGHURST, Henry Carpenter. *b*: Bedford 1909. *e*: Charterhouse & Clare Coll Camb. Journalist, M.P. Acton 1943—45, Cttee English Golf Unions. *n.a*: Golf Corr Evening Standard 1933, Sun Times & Tatler. *Publ*: Golf; It was good while it lasted; I wouldn't have missed it. *s.s*: Golf. *a*: 10 Markham Sq, London, S.W.3. *T*: Kensington 3784.

LONGHURST, Percy William. *b*: London 1874. *e*: Lond Univ. *m*: Rose Carr. *d*: 1. Author, Hon Sec & Treas Internat Amateur Wrestling Fed 1920—33, Official at every Olympic Games Mtg '03—32, Mem Lond A.C., Soc of Authors. *Publ*: Wrestling; Jujitsu & Self Defence; Handbook of Boxing; Wrestling All Styles; Various Boys' Books; etc. *Ctr*: Dly Mail, Observer, Health & Strength, Scout, Windsor Mag, Chambers's Ency, Ency of Sports, etc. *s.s*: Wrestling, Self-Defence, Athletic & Phys Training. *c*: A.W.A. (Brit), Internat A.W. Fed. Life. *a*: Gairloch, Wallington, Surrey.

LONGLEY, Ronald Stewart, A.M., Ph.D. *b*: Paradise, Nova Scotia 1896. *e*: Acadia Univ Wolfville, Harvard Univ. *m*: Vera Harris Eaton. Alumni Prof of Hist Acadia Univ Wolfville N.S. *Publ*: Sir Francis Hincks; Acadia Univ 1838—1938. *Ctr*: Can Hist Rev, Proc Can Hist Assoc, New England Quarterly, etc. *s.s*: Canadian Hist. *Rec*: Tennis, fishing, curling. *a*: 9 Acadia St, Wolfville, Nova Scotia, Canada. *T*: Wolfville 414.

LONGMAN, Heber Albert, F.L.S., C.M.Z.S. *b*: Wiltshire, England 1880. *e*: English Schs *m*: Irene Bayley Biologist (ret), Dir Queensland Museum 1918—45. *Publ*: Religion of a Naturalist. *Ctr*: Memoirs of the Queensland Museum; various Aust Sci journs, etc. *s.s*: Vertebrate Palæontology & Nat Hist. *Rec*: Gardening, reading, bridge. *a*: Cotley, River Terr, Chelmer, Brisbane, Queensland, Australia. *T*: U7824.

LONGMAN, R. G. *a*: Longmans, Green & Co Ltd, 39 Paternoster Row, E.C.4.

LONGMAN, William. *b*: Lon 1882. *e*: Harrow & Oxf. *m*: K. E. Stuart. Publisher. Chm Croquet Assoc 1924—26. Capt Eng Croquet Team *v* Aus '15. Pres Pub's Assoc '30. *Rec*: Numismatics & croquet. *c*: United Univ, Fell Brit Numismatic Soc. *a*: 23 Glebe Pl, S.W.3. *t*: Flaxman 8977.

LONGRAIS, Frederic Jouon des. *b*: Rennes 1892. *e*: Univ of Paris. *m*: Yolande de la Taille Tretinville. Dir of Foreign History Sorbonne Univ, Advocate Court of Appeal Paris, Conservator Seine Tribunal Library. *Publ*: La conception anglaise de la saisine du XII ou XIV siecle; Etudes d'institutions anglaises; Deux tracts caracteristiques de la Coutume de Bretagne; etc. *s.s*: History composed of Law & Institutions of France, England & Asia. *Rec*: Travel. *a*: 4 Rue de la Terrasse, Paris VI mem arr.

LONGRIDGE, Rev. George. *b*: Lon 1857. *e*: Eton & B.N.C. Oxf. *Publ*: History of the Oxford Mission to Calcutta; Spiritualism & Christianity; A Preparation for Marriage. *a*: Hse of the Resurrection, Mirfield, Yorks.

LONGSTAFF, Doris Sybil. *b*: Brighton 1929. *e*: Priv & County Hgh Sch. Journalist, Mem N.U.J. *n.a*: Western Telegraph 1946—, Hon Press Officer Haverfordwest Dist Young Conservatives. *Rec*: Reading, tennis, fashions, riding. *a*: Glengariff, 7 New Rd, Haverfordwest, Pembrokeshire.

LONGSTAFF, Tom George, M.A., D.M.(Oxon). *b*: Summergangs Hall, E. Yorks 1875. *e*: Eton, Ch Ch Oxf & St Thomas's Hosp. *m*: Dora Mary Hamilton Scott. Vice-Pres Alpine Club. Hon Sec R. Geog Soc. Pres Climbers' Club & Arctic Club. *c.t*: Alpine Journ, Geog Journ, British Birds, Times, etc. *s.s*: Mountaineering, nat hist, ornithology. War Service 1914—18. *Rec*: Shooting. *c*: Athenæum. *a*: Picket Hill, Ringwood, Hants.

LONGSTREET, Helen Dortch, A.B. *b*: Franklin County, Georgia. *e*: Brenau Coll, Notre Dame Convent. *m*: Gen James Longstreet. Journalist, Author, Lecturer. *Publ*: Lee & Longstreet at High Tide; Sure Road to World Peace; & many Short Stories. *Ctr*: Various mags in U.S.A. *s.s*: Rights of American Citizenship for the Negro, Strategy of Gen Lee's Gettysburg Campaign. *Rec*: Tennis, horseback riding, hiking. *a*: Savannah Beach, Georgia, U.S.A.

LONGSTRETH, T. Morris. *b*: Philadelphia, Pennsylvania 1886. *e*: Westtown Sch, Haverford Coll. Writer. *Publ*: Tad Lincoln; Two Rivers Meet in Concord; In Scarlet & Plain Clothes; Hideout; Sons of the Mounted Police; The Catskills; Knowing the Weather; etc. *Ctr*: Chris Sci Mon, Colliers Weekly, etc. *s.s*: Boys, the Weather, Henry D. Thoreau. *Rec*: Ski-ing, bicycling. *a*: Concord, Massachusetts, U.S.A. *T*: Concord 1230M.

LONGWORTH, Frank. Ll.B. *b*: Lancashire 1891. *e*: Bolton Sc. Manchester Univ. *m*: Ellen Noblet. *s*: 1. Free Lance Journalist. *c.t*: Evening News, Daily Mail, Evening Standard, Star, News of the World, John Bull, Leader, Birmingham Mail, Nottingham Daily Post, etc. *s.s*: Law, local government, prison reform. *Rec*: Motoring. *a*: 3 Amen Corner, E.C.4. *t*: City 7587.

LONSDALE, Frederick. *b*: 1881. Dramatist. *Publ*: The King of Cadonia; The Balkan Princess; Maid of the Mountains; Spring Cleaning; The Last of Mrs Cheyney; Canaries Sometimes Sing; The Fake; The Street Singer; On Approval; The High Road; Aren't We All?; Another Love Story; But for the Grace of God. *a*: c/o Methuen & Co, 36 Essex St, London, W.C.2.

LOOKER, Samuel Joseph. *b*: London 1888. Writer & Publisher's Reader. *Publ*: Travel Old & New; On the Green; The Chase; Cricket; Green Branches; Float & Fly; One Plum More; Race-Course & Hunting Field; Cock-fighting & Gamefowl; Superman; Satires; Jefferies' England; Jefferies' Countryside; Richard Jefferies London; Jefferies' Notebooks; The Spring of the Year ' Richard Jefferies, A Tribute; W. H. Hudson, A Tribute; Richard Jefferies' Companion; Six vols of verse. *Ctr*: Prose Fiction to Vol 3 Camb Bibliography of Eng Lit: Field, Nineteenth Century, Times Lit Supp, etc. *s.s* Nature Lore, Politics, Films. *a*: The Book Nook, South Green, Billericay, Essex.

LOOMES, Frank Henry Heath. *b*: Whittlesey, Cambs 1862. *e*: City of Lon Sc & private *m*: Agnes Marshall Pettit. *d*: 2. *n.a*: Ed, Peterborough Advertiser, 1897—. *Publ*: Compiler & ed local guide books & directories. *Rec* Cycling, gardening, archæology. Jt founder & builder of first Voluntary Infant Welfare Centre in England. *c*: Chm Northants, Hunts & Beds dist Inst of Jnlsts, 1902. *a*: 44 Fletton Ave, Peterborough. *t*: 3232.

LOOMIS, Alfred F. *b*: Brooklyn 1890. *e*: Gr Sc, Mount Pleasant Acad (Mil). *m*: Priscilla Lockwood. *s*: 2. *d*: 1. Writer. *n.a*: Asst Ed Country Life in America 1907-12, Assoc Ed Motor Boating '13-17. *Publ*: The Cruise of the Hippocampus ('22); The Bascom Chest; Walt Henley, Skipper; Fair Winds in the Far Baltic; Troubled Waters; Hotspur's Cruise in the Ægean; Tracks Across the Sea; Paradise Cove; Millions for Defense (in coll with Herbert L. Stone). *c.t*: Atlantic Monthly, Harper's Mag, Yachting, Sportsman. *s.s*: Sea stories for boys, ocean racing. Served with 110 foot U.S. Submarine Chasers in Corfu Greece during World War. Commissioned Ensign U.S.N.R.F. ('18–). *a*: 122 East 76th St, N.Y.C.

LOOMIS, Frederick Moris, A.B., M.D. *b*: Ann Arbor, Michigan 1877. *e*: Michigan Staff Univ Hosp. *m*: Evalyn Feigenberg. *d*: 2. Prospector, Assayer, Miner, Alaska 1902—08, Pres California Writers' Club. *Publ*: Consultation Room; The Bond Between Us. *Ctr*: Reader's Digest, Pageant, Coronet, etc. *s.s*: Medical Fiction & Reminiscences. *Rec*: Travel. *c*: Claremont Country. *a*: 516 Park Way, Piedmont, California. *T*: Piedmont 1880.

LOOMIS, Louise Ropes, A.M., Ph.D. *b*: Yokohama, Japan 1874. *e*: Newton Hgh Sch, Wellesley Coll, Columbia Univ Coll. Teacher of Hist (ret), Adv Ed

Classics Club New York 1943—. *Publ*: See of Peter (collab); Medieval Hellenism; Book of the Popes: (Ed) Plato on Man & His Universe; Aristotle; Iliad, Homer; etc. *Ctr*: Amer Hist Rev, Church Hist Mag. *s.s*: Medieval Hist, Hist of Ideas. *Rec*: Reading, gardening, motoring. *a*: 92 Livingston St, New Haven 11, Connecticut, U.S.A. *T*: 57170.

LOOS, Anita. Author. *Publ*: Gentlemen Prefer Blondes; etc. *a*: c/o Jonathan Cape Ltd, 30 Bedford Sq, W.C.

LOOS, Cécile Ines. *b*: Basel 1883. *e*: Bern, France, Eng, Italy. *Publ*: Matka Boska; Die Rätsel der Turandot; Leise Leidenschaften; Das Königreich Manteuffel. *c.t*: Neue Zürcher Zeitung, Corona, Literatur Berlin, Berliner Morgenpost, etc. *s.s*: Poetry, novels. *a*: St Alban Rheinweg 150, Basel, Switzerland. *t*: 30.971.

LOOSE, Ernest Edward. *b*: Macclesfield 1885. *e*: St Paul's Macclesfield. *m*: Bertha A. Knowles. Journalist. *n.a*: Ed Staff Advertiser series, & Ches Daily Echo, Stockport 1902. Sec Alderley Edge & Wilmslow Horti & Rose Soc. Vice-Pres Alderley Edge & Wilmslow Footpaths Preservation Soc. *a*: Orchard Grn, Alderley Edge, Cheshire. *t*: 294.

LOOSLEY, Rev. Ernest George, B.D.(Lon). *b*: Maidenhead 1878. *e*: E. Anglian, Bury St Edmunds, Marlowe G.S. & Wesleyan Col Richmond. *m*: Florence Ethel Edwards. Meth Min. *Publ*: Through the Eyes of His Enemies (1928). *c.t*: Preacher's Mag, etc. *s.s*: Gospels. Asst Tutor Richmond Col '04–06. *c*: Barrow Educ Comm. *a*: 111 Abbey Rd, Barrow-in-Furness.

LORAINE, Winifred. *n.a*: Daily Express. *a*: Fleet St, E.C.4.

LORANT, Michael. *b*: Hungary 1891. *e*: Univ of Technique Budapest. *m*: Piroska Ver. Journalist & Caricaturist. *Publ*: The Hero of the Ocean; The Stamp. *Ctr*: Various illustrated mags. *Rec*: Philately, golf. *a*: 99a Addison Rd, London, W.14. *T*: Park 8172.

LORANT, Stefan. *b*: Budapest, Hungary 1901. *e*: Evangelical Gymnasium, Acad of Econs. Author & Editor. *n.a*: Ed Munchner Illus Presse Munich 1927—33, Ed Lilliput Lond '37—40, Ed Picture Post '38—40. *Publ*: I Was Hitler's Prisoner; Lincoln, his life in Photographs; The New World. *Ctr*: Sat Ev Post, Life Mag. *s.s*: American Hist. *a*: Lenox, Massachusetts, U.S.A. *T*: Lenox 363 W.

LORD, Carey. Ed Clitheroe Advertiser & Times 1904–. Started First Eng Daily in Baghdad (Baghdad Times). *a*: 6 Market Pl, Clitheroe.

LORD, Charles Fletcher. *b*: Shaw 1895. *e*: High Crompton C. of E. Sc. *m*: Eva Richardson. Journalist. *n.a*: Reporter Oldham Chronicle, Special Cotton Trade Writer for M/C Guardian & M/C Guardian Commercial 1919–30, Ed Crompton & Royton Guardian 29–31, Ed Spalding Guardian '31–. *s.s*: Cotton trade, Fenland flower trade. War Service '15–19. *Rec*: Photography. *c*: I.J. *a*: 20 Station St, Spalding, Lincs. *t*: 40.

LORD, Daniel A., A.M., Lit.D. *b*: Chicago 1888. *e*: St Ignatius Hgh Sch Chicago, Loyala Univ, Boston Coll, St Louis Univ. Catholic Priest. *n.a*: Ed, Now 1947. *Publ*: The Glorious Ten Commandments; My Mother;

Our Lady in the Modern World; Some Notes on the Guidance of Youth; Some Notes on the Guidance of Parents; etc. *Ctr*: Various. *s.s*: Religion, Social Problems for Young People, Criticism, Modern Pictures. *Rec*: Music, etc. *a*: 3115, S. Grand Bowl, St Louis 18, Missouri, U.S.A. *T*: Sidney 3434.

LORD, Rev. F. T., D.D., B.A. *b*: Burnley 1893. *e*: Rawdon Col M/C & Lon Univ. *m*: S. A. Entwisle. *s*: 1. *d*: 1. *n.a*: Jt Ed Baptist Quarterly. *Publ*: Unity of Body & Soul; The Master & His Men; The Acts of the Apostles; Man & His Character; Christ on the Road; Man in the Dark Room. *c.t*: Chr World, Bapt Times, Sunday at Home, Evening News, Sunday Companion, etc. *s.s*: Psych, theo. *Rec*: Tennis. *a*: Bloomsbury Cent Ch, Shaftesbury Av, W.C.2.

LORD, L. C., M.A. *a*: 11 Barton Crescent, Mannamead, Plymouth, Devon.

LORD, Fred Townley, D.D. *e*: London Univ. Vice Pres The Baptist World Alliance. *n.a*: Ed The Baptist Times 1941—. *a*: 4 Southampton Row, London, W.C.1. *T*: Holborn 5516.

LORD, John, M.A. *b*: Birm 1899. *e*: Hulme G.S. M/C & Christ's Col Cam. *m*: Margery Nicholson. Schoolmaster. *n.a*: Hist Master L'pool Collegiate Sc 1922–25, Hulme G.S. '25–32, Headmaster Audenshaw G.S., Lancs '32–, Lecturer to W.E.A. '24–32. *Publ*: Capital & Steam Power 1750–1800; Progressive History of Britain; Edited Macaulay's Essays on Clive & Warren Hastings ('31); Life & Work, an Introduction to Economics ('32). *s.s*: Hist & economics. *c*: Incorp Assoc Headmasters, Hist Assoc, Workers' Educ Assoc. *a*: The Hollies, Denton, nr M/C. *t*: 2315.

LORD, JOHN ROBERT: psychiatrist; *b*. Blackburn, Eng., Aug., 1874; *s*. Samuel and Agnes (Barrow) L.; educ. Blackburn Grammar and Higher Studies Schls., Owen Coll. (Univ. Manchester), Edinburgh Univ., Guy's Hospital (London). DEGREES: M.B., C.M., M.D., M.R.C. P.E., F.R.C.P.E.; *m*. Dr. Ruby Thornton Carr, March 21, 1931. AUTHOR: The Story of the Horton War Hospital, 1920; Social Workers and the Insane, 1923; The Clinical Study of Medical Disorders, 1926; Mental Hospitals and the Public: the need for closer cooperation, 1926. Edited: The Mott Memorial, (1929); The Mott Memorial Volume, 1929, and Proceedings of the Westminster Conferences on Mental Health, 1929 and 1931. Contributor to Psychiatry, Neurology, Sociology. General character of writing: scientific, sociological. In Great War, Lieut.-Col. Royal Army Med. Corps, 1915-1920; twice mentioned in despatches; created C.B.E., Mil. Div.; organized and commanded Horton War Hosp.; Editor: Journal of Mental Sience since 1911; Member General Nursing Council for England and Wales; Hon. secy. Nat. Council Mental Hygiene; lctrer. on clinical psychiatry, London Sch. of Med. for Women; mem. governing body same; supt. Horton Mental Hosp.; President, 1926-27; and chmn. Research and Clinical com. Royal Medico-psychological Assn.; mem. International. Comm. for Mental Hygiene; Fellow Royal Soc. Med., Med. Soc. of London; Mem. Brit. Med. Assn., Associe de la Societe de Med. Ment. de Belgique; Mem. American Acad. Political and Social Science; Associe de la Socite Medico-Psychologique de Paris. Relig. denom., Church of England. CLUB: Royal Automobile. OFFICE: Horton Mental Hospital. HOME: Horton House, Epsom, Surrey, Eng.

LORD, Louis E., A.M., L.H.D., Ph.D. *b*: Ravenna, Ohio 1875. *e*: Oberlin Coll, Harvard, Yale, Univ of Berlin. *m*: Frances M. Partridge. *d*: 1. Teacher. *n.a*: Ed Oberlin Alumni Mag 1904—15. *Publ*: Thucydides & the World War; History of the American School of Classical Studies at Athens; Seven Orations of Cicero;

Politian's Orfeo & Tasso's Aminta ; The Odes of Anacreon (Ed) ; Third Year Latin Book (collab) ; The Roman Historians. *Ctr* : Amer Journ of Archaeology, Hesperia, Journ of Roman Studies. *s.s* : Ancient Classics & Archæology. *Rec* : Travel. *a* : Scripps Coll, Claremont, California, U.S.A. *T* : Claremont 3386.

LORD, Russell, B.Sc. *b* : Baltimore, Maryland 1895. *e* : Agricultural Hgh Sch Sparks Maryland, Univs of Cornell & California. *m* : Helen Kate Kalkman. Writer & Editor. *n.a* : Ctr Ed The Country Home 1929—36, Progressive Farmer & Country Gentleman, Founder Ed The Land '41—. *Publ* : The Wallaces of Iowa ; The Agrarian Revival ; Behold Our Land ; Men of Earth ; (Ed) Voices From the Fields ; Democracy Reborn ; etc. *Ctr* : New Yorker, New Republic, Cosmopolitan, Reader's Digest, Agricultural Journs, etc. *s.s* : Agriculture & Conversation. *c* : Cosmos (Wash). *a* : The Landmark, Bel Air, Harford County, Maryland, U.S.A. *T* : Bel Air 10.

LORD, William. *n.a* : Ed Barrow Guardian & Series. *c.t* : Many daily papers. *s.s* : Iron, shipbuilding, etc. *a* : 47 Croslands Park, Barrow-in-Furness.

LORIMER, Lt-Col. David Lockhart Robertson, C.I.E. *b* : Dundee 1876. *e* : High Sch Dundee, Univ Coll Dundee, R.M.C. Sandhurst. *m* : Emily M. Overend. Indian Army (ret), served in Foreign & Political Dept Govt of India. *Publ* : The Burushaski Language ; The Syntax of Colloquial Pashtu ; Persian Tales (with E. O. Lorimer) ; The Phonology of the Bakhtiari Badakhshani & Madaglashti Dialects of Modern Persian ; The Dumaki Language. *c* : Jnl Roy Asiatic Soc, Bulletin of Sch of Oriental & African Studies, Folklore. *s.s* : Languages of N.W. India & Persian Dialects. *a* : 32 Parkway, Welwyn Garden City, Herts. *T* : Welwyn Garden 696.

LORIMER, Emily Overend, O.B.E., M.A. *b* : Dublin 1881. *e* : Alexandra Sch & Coll Dublin, Somerville Coll Oxf, France & Germany. *m* : D. L. R. Lorimer. *d* : 1. Reviewer, Translator, Tutor Germanic Philology Som Coll Oxf 1907—10. *n.a* : Times Corres in Kashmir 1934—35. *Publ* : Persian Tales (with D. L. R. Lorimer) ; What Hitler Wants (Penguin Special) ; Language Hunting in the Karakoram ; What the German Needs ; (Trans from German & French, various including) Twilight in Vienna ; Christian IX of Denmark ; Wilhelm Filchner : A Scientist in Tartary ; Jerome Carcopino ; Daily Life in Rome at the Zenith of the Empire. *Ctr* : Times Lit Supp, Time & Tide, John o' London's. *c* : Univ Women's. *a* : 32 Park Way, Welwyn Garden City, Hertfordshire. *T* : Welwyn Garden 696.

LORIMER, George Horace. *b* : Kentucky 1868. *e* : Mosely H.S. Chicago, Colby & Yale. *m* : Alma Viola Lorimer. *s* : 2. Ed of Sat Evening Post, Chm of Curtis Publ Co. *Publ* : Letters from a Self-Made Merchant to his Son ; Old Gorgon Graham ; The False Gods ; Jack Spurlock—Prodigal. LittD., LL.D., Chevalier de la Legion d'Honneur Commander Order of Crown of Italy. *Rec* : Gardening, farming. *c* : Huntingdon Valley Hunt, Huntingdon Valley Country, Yale (Phila), Nat Press. *a* : Church Rd. Wyncote, Pa, & The Curtis Publ Co, Independence Sq, Philadelphia. *t* : Ogontz 208 & Lombard 6500.

LORIMER, Miss H. L., M.A. *b* : Edin. *e* : Univ Col Dundee, Girton Cam. Fell & Tutor Somerville. & Univ Lect Oxf. *c.t* : Journ of Hellenic Studies. L'pool Annals of Art & Archæ. *a* : Somerville Col, Oxf.

LORIMER, Norma. *b* : Perthshire. *e* : Hgh Sch I.O.M. (Castletown). Author. *Publ* : By the Waters of Egypt ; By the Waters of Sicily ; The Mediterranean & Beyond ; A Wife out of Egypt ; The Gods' Carnival ; False Value ; Millstones ; Story of Isobel Lennox ; etc. *s.s* : Egypt & Sicily. *Rec* : Travel. *c* : Overseas League. *a* : 7 Pitcullen Terr, Perth, Scotland.

LORING, Elisabeth Ann. *b* : 1908. Novelist. *n.a* : Beauty Editress Sunday Dispatch, Radio Pictorial. *Publ* : Ladies Paradise ('33) ; Elisabeth Ann's Book of Beauty ('33). *c.t* : Sunday Dispatch, Modern Weekly, Modern Home, Woman's Journal, Miss Modern, etc. *s.s* : Beauty. Recorded " Elisabeth Ann Slenderising " '34. *c* : Arts Theatre. *a* : c/o Charles Lavell, 13 Serjeant's Inn, Fleet St, E.C.4.

LORING, Emilie. Author. *Publ* : Hilltops Clear ; Come on, Fortune! ; Fair To-morrow. *a* : c/o S. Paul & Co Ltd, Paternoster Hse, E.C.4.

LORWIN, Lewis L., Ph.D. *b* : 1883. *e* : Public & Sec Schs, Columbia Univ. Economist & Author. Adv to U.S. Rep on Econ & Social Counc of United Nations 1946—48. *n.a* : Spec Edit & Feature Writer New York World 1919—20, Spec Corres (Moscow) Chicago Dly News '21—22. *Publ* : Time for Planning ; Economic Consequences of the Second World War ; Post-War Plans of the United Nations ; Labor & Internationalism ; The American Federation of Labor ; The Labor Movement in France ; etc. *Ctr* : N.Y. Times, New Republic, Atlantic Monthly, Ency Brit, etc. *s.s* : Internat Relations, Labor. *c* : Cosmos (Wash). *a* : 3000 39th St, N.W., Washington, D.C., U.S.A.

LOSEBY, Henry Victor, M.A. *b* : Otley ,Yorks 1897. *e* : Bradford Gr Sch & Univ Leeds. *m* : Isobel Skirrow. *d* : 3. Schoolmaser. *Publ* : Advanced Latin Prose. *s.s* : Classics, Education, Greek Games. *Rec* : Cricket, rambling, naturism. *a* : Ling Moor, Marriner's Drive, Heaton, Bradford, Yorkshire.

LOT, Ferdinand, Litt.D. *b* : Paris 1866. *e* : Univ of Paris. *m* : Myrrha Borodine. *d* : 3. French Historian, Officer of Legion of Honour. *Publ* : Les Invasions Germaniques ; Le Regne de Charles le Chauve ; Le regne de Hugues Capet ; La France, des origines a la guerre de cent ans ; L'Armee et l'art militaire au Moyen Age en Europe et dans le proche Orient ; Le Lancelot en prose, etc. *s.s* : History. *a* : 53 rue Boucicaut, Fontenay-aux Roses, France.

LOTHAR, RUDOLPH: author; b. Budapest, Hungary, Feb. 23, 1865; s. Albert and Louise (Adler) L.; educ. Gymnasium Vienna, Univs. of Vienna, Rostock, Jena, Heidelberg. DEGREE: Ph.D.; m. Margarethe Cassel, Oct. 24, 1922. AUTHOR: King Harlekin, 1900; Biography of Henrik Ibsen, 1904; (novels): Septett, 1905); A Trip into the Unknown, 1908; Life Says So, 1910; Kurfürstendamm, 1910; The Master of Berlin, 1910; The Fascination of the World, 1918; (plays, mostly comedies): The Great Congregation (with Leopold Lipshütz), 1906; The Girl in Black, 1907; The Royal Box, 1918; Casanova's Son, 1920; The Javanese Doll (with Bachwitz), 1921; Maitre Cog (with Lucien Besnard), 1921; The Werwolf, 1921; The Critical Year, 1921; The Lady with the Mask, 1922; The Black Mess, 1923; The Beautiful Melusina (Anna), 1925; The Duchess of Elba (with Ritter-Winterstein), 1926; The Ghostship (with Ritter), 1926; Command to Love (with Fritz Gottwald), 1926; The Night of the Three Women (with W. Lichtenberg), 1926; Author-Author, 1927; Love Among the Chickens (with Wodehouse), 1927; Divorce, 1927; Is That so Important? 1929; Type 31 (with Gottwald), 1929; (travel books): The Soul of Spain, 1915; Between Three Worlds, 1927; (essays): The German Drama of the Present Day, 1905; The Art of Seduction, 1925; (operas): The Lowlands (with d'Albert), 1904; Izeyl (with d'Albert), 1910; Li Tai Be (with Franckenstein), 1921. Translated from the French and the English: The Front Page; The Royal Family; The Trial of Mary Dugan; Machinal; Park Lane 77, etc. At one time member of staff of the Neue Freie Presse (Vienna) as feuilletonist and critic; later wrote feuilletons to the Lokalanzeiger (Berlin). Began writing for the Viennese papers when a schoolboy. Now contributes to 8 Uhr Abendblatt (Berlin), Neues Wiener Journal (Vienna). Began to write for stage at early age; first great international success was the play "King Harlekin", at first forbidden in all monarchistic lands owing to its anti-royalistic tendencies, but finally produced despite censorship and translated into 16 languages, receiving the Bauernfeld prize. Among other plays "The Werwolf" was played 600 times in Berlin, and many thousand times all over the world; "Casanova's Son" had 500 performances in Berlin, and others have had similar success. In America the plays "The Werwolf", "The Command to Love", "The Duchess of Elba" and "Anna" have been produced. Films have been made of "King Harlekin" and "The Command to Love". SOCIETY: Société des Auteurs et Compositeurs. CLUBS: P. E. N., Verband Deutscher Bühnenschriftsteller, Automobil Club von Deutschland, Real Automobil Club d'Italia, Real Automobil Club d'Espana. HOME: Sponholzstr. 51-52, Berlin-Friedenau, Germany.

LOW, David Morrice. *b*: Northwood 1890. *e*: Westminster Sch, Oriel Coll Oxford. *m*: Heather Belle Hancocks. Lecturer in Classics & Sub Dean of Arts Faculty Univ of London, King's Coll, Temp Senior Asst Foreign Office 1943—45. *Publ*: Edward Gibbon; Gibbon's Journ to 28th Jan 1763; Twice Shy; This Sweet Work. *Ctr*: Times, Times Lit Supplt, Glasgow Herald, Geographical Mag, Spectator, Classical Rev, Rev of English Studies. *s.s*: Edward Gibbon the Historian, Classics, Travel in Mediterranean Lands. *a*: 10 Craven Hill, London, W.2. *T*: Paddington 4467.

LOW, GEORGE CARMICHAEL: Consulting Physician in tropical diseases; b. Monifieth, Scotland, Oct., 1872; s. Samuel Miller and Grace (Lyell) L. DEGREES: M.A., M.B., C.M., M.D., F.R.C.P. (London); m. Edith Nash, Dec. 1, 1906. AUTHOR: Tropical Section in A Text Book of the Practice of Medicine, 1920; Literature of the Charadriiformes from 1894 to 1924, 1924; List of the Birds in the Zoological Gardens 1828-1927, 1929. Contributions to many med. journals. General character of writing: Tropical Medicines and scientific ornithology. Senior Physician Hospital for Tropical Diseases; Seamen's Hosp., Royal Albert Docks and Tilbury Hosp.; Pres. Royal Soc. of Tropical Medicine and Hygiene. OFFICE: 86 Brook St., Grosvenor Square, W. 1. HOME: 7 Kent House, Kensington Court, London, W. 8, Eng.

LOW, Sir Francis, Kt. *b*: Aberdeenshire, Scotland 1893. *e*: Robert Gordon's Coll. *m*: Margaret Helen Adams. *s*: 2. *d*: 1. Ed The Times of India. *n.a*: Aberdeen Free Press 1910, Chief Rep Aberdeen Free Press '20, Chief Sub-Ed Times of India '22, Ed Ev News of India '23, Asst Ed Times of India '27, Ed '32—. *s.s*: Indian Politics. *Rec*: Walking, golf. *w.s*: 1914—18, Mesopotamian Expeditionary Force, Special Service Officer G.H.Q. Baghdad '19—20. *c*: Roy Bombay Yacht. *a*: c/o The Times of India, Hornby Rd, Fort, Bombay. *T*: 30971.

LOW, Robert Cranston, M.B., Ch.B., M.D., F.R.C.P.E., F.R.S.E. *b*: Edinburgh 1879. *e*: Merchiston Castle Sch Edinburgh, Univs Breslau, Hamburg, Vienna, Paris. *m*: Alice A. Grant. *s*: 1. Formerly Lecturer on Dermatology Edin Univ, Consulting Physician Skin Dept Edin Roy Infirmary. *Publ*: Anaphylaxis & Sensitisation; The Common Diseases of the Skin; Carbonic Acid Snow as a Therapeutic Agent in the Treatment of Diseases of the Skin; Atlas of Bacteriology. *Ctr*: Numerous articles in med & scientific journs on Dermatology & Bacteriology. *s.s*: Dermatology & Bacteriology. *Rec*: Golf, gardening, water-colour painting. *a*: 37 Oxgangs Rd, Fairmilehead, Edinburgh 10. *T*: Edinburgh 71360.

LOW, Sir Stephen Philpot, Kt. *b*: London 1883. *e*: Dragon Sch Oxf, Winchester Coll & Magdalen Coll Oxf. *m*: Bertie Faith Crosse. *s*: 3. Solicitor to Bd of Trade & Min of Fuel & Power. Barrister, Asst Solictor Min of Labour 1925—34. *Publ*: Unemployment & Insurance (collab with St V. F. Coules). *c*: Oxf & Camb. *a*: 26 Pembridge Gardens, London, W.2. *T*: Park 6645.

LOTHROP, Samuel Kirkland, A.B., Ph.D. *b*: Milton, Mass 1892. *e*: Groton Sch Harvard. Archaeologist. *Publ*: Cocle: An Archaeological Study of Central Panama; Tulum; Atitlan; Zacualpa; Pottery of Costa Rica & Nicaragua; Indians of Tierra del Fuego; Indians of the Parana Delta, Argentina; Inca Treasure. *Ctr*: Various Tech Publs. *s.s*: Latin American Archaeol. *Rec*: Fishing. *a*: 1061 Madison Ave, New York City, N.Y. *T*: Bu 8-4530.

LOUDAN, Jack. *b*: 'Armagh, Nth Ireland. Journalist & Playwright, Compiler of featured programmes & Author of many Plays for B.B.C. 1934—39. *n.a*: Feature Writer Daily Express 1934—36, Staff Radio & Drama Critic, Belfast News Letter '36—39. *Publ*: In Search of Water; (Plays) The Ball Turns Once; Story for To-day; Henry Joy McCracken. *a*: Mellstock, Finaghy Rd North, Belfast. *T*: Dunmurry 3213.

LOUGEE, Francis Claude. *b*: Apperley Bridge 1876. *e*: Bradford G.S. Married twice. *s*: 1. *n.a*: Staff Daily Argus Bradford '92, Yorks Evening Argus, Ed 15 yrs Football Argus & Cricket Argus, Sub-Ed Telegraph & Argus 1926. *s.s*: Football, cricket, golf. Found Mem N.U.J. Pres West Riding br N/p Press Fund '30. *Rec*: Golf. *a*: 17 Springfield Place, Bradford.

LOUGHBOROUGH, Dr. G. T. Consulting Radiologist. *a*: 41 Devonshire Street.

LOUGHEED, William James. *b*: Forest, Ontario 1875. *e*: Forest Public & Hgh Schs, Hamilton Coll, Toronto Univ. Prof Emeritus of Maths Ontario Coll, Toronto Univ. *Publ*: (In collab) Geometry for High Schools; Modern Geometry for High Schools; General Mathematics; Rapid Calculation; Drills in Rapid Calculation. *s.s*: Methods in Maths. *Rec*: Bowling, gardening. *c*: Empire (Toronto). *a*: 286 Runnymede Rd, Toronto, Ontario. *T*: Ly 1793.

LOUIS, Edward. Literary. *n.a*: Chief of Lit Dept with T. B. Browne Ltd (Advtg Agents) 1910—15. *Publ*: His Lordship the Crook; The Love Cruise (musical play); Don't be Jealous (revue); His Fiancee (farce); etc. *Ctr*: Passing Show, Punch, etc. *s.s*: Publicity Lit. *a*: 14 Hubbard Rd, London, S.E.27. *T*: Gipsy Hill 1401.

LOUIS, HENRY: consulting mining and metallurgical engineer; b. London, Eng., Dec., 1855; s. Sigmund and Julia (Lipmann) L.; educ. City of London Sch., Royal Sch. of Mines. DEGREES: M.A., D.Sc. (Hon. Dunelm); m. Rosalie James, 1895. AUTHOR: A Handbook of Gold Milling, 1893 (2nd and 3rd edits. 1899, 1902); The Production of Tin, 1896; Treatise on Ore Deposits (jointly with Phillips), 1896; Schnabel's Hand book of Metallurgy (trans.), 1898; Goldfields of Australasia, by Schmeiser and Vogelsand (trans.), 1898; Traverse Tables (jointly with Caunt), 1900 (2nd edit. 1906); Electricity in Mining, 1901; Shaft Sinking, in practical Coal Mining, 1907; Dressing of Minerals, 1909; Metallurgy of Tin, 1911; Traverse Tables (jointly with Caunt), 1919; Mineral Valuation, 1923; The Preparation of Coal for the Market, 1928. Editor, Benn's Mining Series. Contributor to Journ. and Trans. of Inst. of Mining Engineers, Iron and Steel Inst., Soc. Chemical Industry, Inst. Civil Enginrs., Journs. and Trans. of Inst. of Mining and Metallurgy, Inst. of Metals, Amer. Inst. of Mining and Metallurgical Enginrs., Mineralogical Soc., Mining Journ., Yorkshire Post, Newcastle Chronicle, Singapore Free Press, Mineral Industry, Fuel Economy Rev., Iron and Coal Trades Rev., Colliery Engineering. General character of writing: technical, text books, scientific. Emeritus prof. mining; past-pres. Soc. Chemical Industry; past-pres. Iron and Steel Inst., past-pres. Inst. Mining Engineers; past vice-pres., Memb. Council, Inst. Min. Met.; late Wm. Cochrane lectrer. on Metallurgy at Armstrong Coll., Univ. Durham, James Forrest lectrer. Instn. Civil Engrs., 1908. CLUBS: Royal Societies, Chemical Industry. HOME: 4 Osborne Terrace, Newcastle-on-Tyne, Eng.

LOURENCO-FILHO, Manoel Bergstrom, B.Sc. *b*: Sao Paulo 1807. *e*: Primary, Secondary, Normal Sch Faculdade de Direito de Sao Paulo. *m*: Aida Carvalho Lourenco. *s*: 2. Prof of Educational Psychology Univ of Brasil, Dir of Nat Inst of Pedagogical Studies Min of Educ 1939—46, Gen Dir of Dept of Nat Educ '47—. *n.a*: Escola Nova 1930—31, Revista Brasileira de Estudos Pedagogicos '44—. *Publ*: Joaseiro do Padre Cicero; Tendencias da Educacao Brasileira; Cartilha do Povo; La Pensee de Ribot dans la Psychologie Sud-Americaine; etc. *Ctr*: Ency of Modern Educ, O Estado de Sao Paulo. etc. *s.s*: Educational, Psychology, Administration & Organisation. *a*: Rua Pedro Guedes, 56, Rio de Janeiro, Brazil.

LOVAT FRASER, Grace, F.R.S.A. *b*: Paris. *e*: Paris, Milan, Rome, Munich. *m*: C. Lovat Fraser (dec'd). *d*: 1. Industrial Design Consultant & Journalist. *n.a*: Design Ed & Asst Ed Town & Country Homes, Assoc Ed Art & Industry 1940—41. *Publ*: Plastics & Industrial Design (collab); (trans) The Liar; Modern Publicity in War (collab). *Ctr*: Sun Times, Sun Chron, Fashions & Fabrics, Ideal Home, Everywoman, Ev News, etc. *s.s*: Textiles, Plastics, Interior Decoration, Packaging. *Rec*: Swimming, riding, collecting toys. *a*: 26 Ashley Pl, Westminster, London, S.W.1. *T*: Victoria 9952.

LOVE, Robert John McNeill, M.S., F.R.C.S., F.P.C.S. *b*: Plymouth 1891. *e*: Taunton Sch & Lond Hosp. *m*: Dorothy Ida Borland. *s*: 1. *d*: 1. Mem of Counc Roy Coll of Surgeons. *Publ*: Short Practice of Surgery (collab); Surgery for Nurses (collab); Minor Surgery; Guide to the Surgical Paper; The Appendix. *Ctr*: Brit Journ of Surgery, B.M.J., Lancet, etc. *s.s*: General Surgery Thyroid & Gall Bladder. *Rec*: Shooting, golf, philately. *c*: Eccentric, Highgate Golf. *a*: 142 Harley St, London, W.1., & 12 Stormont Rd, London, N.6. *T*: Welbeck 3562 & Mountview 3846.

LOVEDAY, Alexander, M.A. *b*: Cameron, Fife 1888. *e*: Shrewsbury Sc Peterhouse Cam. *m*: Natalie Tarnoschi. *s*: 2. Dir of Financial Sect & Econ Intelligence Serv of L. of N. *Publ*: History & Economics of Indian Famines (1914); Britain & World Trade; Quo Vadimus & other Economic Essays. *c.t*: Economic & Statistical Journ. *s.s*: Economics, finance. Fell of Internät Statis Soc. Hon Mem Swedish Roy Acad of Science. Hon Mem Hungarian Statis Soc. *c*: Reform. *a*: 164 Route de Malagnou, Geneva, Switzerland.

LOVEDAY, Arthur Frederic, O.B.E., Kt Cmdr Spanish Order of Merit, Cmdr of Chilean Order of Merit. *b*: Wardington 1878. *e*: Haileybury Coll. *m*: Mary C. Backus. *s*: 2. *d*: 2. Merchant (ret). *Publ*: World War in Spain. *n.a*: Times 1913—20, Morning Post '25—33. *Ctr*: Quarterly Rev, National Rev, New English Rev, Tablet, Catholic Herald, Weekly Rev. *s.s*: Spain, South America. *a*: Travellers Club, London, S.W.1.

LOVEGROVE, E(DWIN) W(ILLIAM): formerly headmaster Ruthin School; *b*. Nottingham, Eng., June, 1865; s. Rev. Edwin and Rosa Cecilia (Young) L.; educ. Colegio de Santo Tomas (Barcelona, Spain); Merchant Taylors', Crosby (Liverpool); New Coll. (Oxford) (Scholar 1st class honours). DEGREES: M.A. (Oxon.); F.S.A.; F.R. Hist. S.; m. Septima Jane Roberts ,Aug. 16, 1899 (died). Contributor to Archaeologia Cambrensis, Archaeological Jnl.; Jnl. of the British Archaeological Assn.; Inventory for Pembrokeshire of the Royal Comm. on Historic Monuments. General character of writing: mediaeval architecture and archaeology. Mem. Royal Irish Acad.; Fellow Royal Soc. of Antiquaries of Ireland; Foreign correspondent, Société Nationale des Antiquaires de France; mem. Société Française d'Archéologie. Relig. denom., Church of England. CLUBS: Royal Societies (London). HOME: Ynys, St. Asaph, N. Wales, Great Britain.

LOVELACE, Delos Wheeler. *b*: Brainerd, Minn 1894. *e*: Univs of Minn & Camb (England). *m*: Maud Hart. *d*: 1. Writer. *n.a*: Minneapolis Tribune 1916—17 & '19—21, New York Dly News '21—23, Staff New York Sun '28—. *Publ*: Rockne of Notre Dame; General Ike Eisenhower; The Golden Wedge; One Stayed at Welcome (Collab); Gentlemen from England (Collab). *Ctr*: Sat Ev Post, Country Gentleman, American, Ladies Home Journ. *s.s*: Biog. *w.s*: A.E.F. 1917—19. *a*: 63 Wyatt Rd, Garden City, New York. *T*: Garden City 4847.

LOVELACE, Mary Countess of. Landowner. *Publ*: Zelinda & the Monster; Ralph, Earl of Lovelace—a Memoir. *a*: Ockham Pk, Ripley, Surrey.

LOVELACE, Maud Hart. *b*: Mankato, Minn 1892. *e*: Univ of Minnesota. *m*: Delos Wheeler Lovelace. *d*: 1. Writer. *Publ*: Betsy-Tacy; Betsy-Tacy & Tib; Over the Big Hill; Downtown; Heaven to Betsy; Betsy in Spite of Herself; Betsy Was a Junior; The Black Angels; Early Candlelight; One Stayed at Welcome (Collab); Gentlemen From England (Collab); The Golden Wedge (Collab). *s.s*: Americana, Books for Children. *a*: 63 Wyatt Rd, Garden City, New York. *T*: Garden City 4847.

LOVELESS, Ralph Edgar. *b*: Farnham 1890. *e*: Farnham Gr Sch. *m*: Olive Hawgood. Journalist. *n.a*: London Ed Yorkshire Post from 1947, Farnham Herald Series '07—15, Globe Lond '19—20, Yorkshire Observer (London) '20—26, Chief Rep Yorkshire Post (London) '30—46. *s.s*: Caravanning, swimming. *w.s*: 1915—19. *a*: 10 Randolph Cres, London, W.9. *T*: Cunningham 3627.

LOVELL, HENRY TASMAN: professor of psychology; *b*. Kempsey, N. S. Wales, Jan., 1878; *s*. James Haines and Elizabeth (Sheppard) L.; educ. State School, Fernmount; Frt Street Model Training Sch., Sydney. DEGREES: M.A. (Sydney); Ph.D. (Jena); *m*. Alice Eleanor Arnold. AUTHOR: Der Utilitarismus in der Erziehung, Inaugural Dissertation, 1909; Dreams (Monograph Series No. 2), 1923. Editor of Australasian Jnl. of Psychology and Philosophy of Sydney. Contributor to Records of the Education Soc., No. 20, 1914; to Art in Australia, Sydney Morning Herald, Sydney Sunday Sun. General character of writing: psychological. Tutor for Workers' Educational Assn.; pres. of Bd. of Social Study and Training; rep. of Carnegie Corp. for the establishment in Australia of an inst. of Educational Service and Research. Relig. denom., Anglican. CLUBS: University. OFFICE: University of Sydney, Australia. HOME: 1 Honda Road, Neutral Bay, Sydney, New South Wales, Australia.

LOVELL BURGESS, Marjorie Agnes, M.J.I. Articled Pupil on Staff of Eastbourne Gaz & Sx County Herald, Asst-Ed British Red Cross Socs Publs 1939—43, Editorial & Public Relations Brit Waterworks Assoc '44—46, Ed Brit Gas Gazette '46—. *Publ*: Great Possessions; Provincial Interlude; The Amateur Cine Movement. *s.s*: Public Utilities, Documentary Films. *a*: 72 Queens Rd, Wimbledon, London S.W.19.

LOVETT, Sir Verney, K.C.S.I. *b*: Exeter 1864. *e*: Sherborne Sc & Balliol Oxf. Married. *d*: 1. I.C.S. (ret). *Publ*: History of the Indian Nationalist Movement; 10 Chap C. Mod Hist Ind; etc. *s.s*: Indian hist Served 35 y in I.C.S. & 12 y Reader in Indian Hist at Oxf Univ. K.-I.-H. Medal. *a*: 11 Linton Rd, Oxf.

LOVIBOND, Frances Elizabeth, J.P., F.R.S.A. F.R.M.S. *b*: Mere Down. *e*: Priv. *m*: Joseph Locke Lovibond. *Publ*: The Beauty & Usefulness of Colour; Colour Permanence; Pastilles & Their Colours; etc. *s.s*: Heraldry, Welfare Work. Hon Mention for War Work. 5 y Local Sec Q. Mary's Needlework Guild. Sec Local Belgium Refugee Clothing Cmt, etc. *Rec*: Sketching, painting. *a*: Windover Hse, Salisbury, Wilts. *t*: 629.

LOVRICH, Bozo. *b*: Split, Dalmatia, Yugoslavia 1881. *e*: Gymnasium, Split Yugoslavia, Univ, Zagreb. *m*: Tina Kroupova. *s*: 1. Author & journalist. *n.a*: Centralnada Europa, Prague. *Publ*: More (the Sea) novel; Ver Sacrum (poems); Plays: Sin (the son); Osudjen Ni zu Sto, Apostata, etc. *c.t*: Obzor, Novosti, Morgenblatt, Zivot i Rad, Prager Presse, etc. *Rec*: Water sports. *c*: Pen, Zagreb, Association of Czechoslovak Newspapermen, Prague, etc. *a*: Prague XIII, Ursovice, Palackeho 2, Czechoslovakia.

LOW, A. Regius Prof Anatomy Aberdeen Univ. *c.t*: Scientific papers. *a*: 144 Blenheim Place, Aberdeen.

LOW, Archibald Montgomery, D.Sc., Ph.D., A.C.G.I., M.I.A.E., F.C.S., F.R.G.S., F.I.Arb. F.B.I.R.E. *b*: Purley 1888. *e*: St Paul's Skerry's Glas & Cent Tech Coll of Imp Science Lond. *m*: Amy Woods. *s*: 2. Cons Eng & Prof of Physics, Inventor & Designer, Chmn A.C.U., Pre Inst of Patentees, Designed Radio Robot 1916, Infra Red Photography for Internal Combustion Engines '19, Invented Oscillographic Indicator & Audiometer Television '14. *n.a*: Armchair Science 1932, Ed Order of Road Journ '31, Hon Tech Cons Sun Chron '29, Hon Tech Adv The Motor '19. *Publ*: The Two Stroke Engine; The Wonderbook of Invention; Tendencies of Modern Science; On My Travels; Our Wonderful World of To-morrow; Science in Wonderland; Prof Low's Book of Home Experiments; Science in the Home; Conquering Space & Time; Popular Scientific Recreations; Recent Inventions; Life & Its Story; What New Wonders; Modern Armament; The Way It Works; Musket to Machine Gun; Your World To-morrow; Science in Industry; The Submarine at War; Facts & Fancies; Parachutes in Peace & War; Benefits of War. *s.s*: Acoustics, the Future Internal Combustion Engines. *Rec*: Research. *w.s*: Commanded R.F.C. Experimental Works 1916, Major Roy Pioneer Corps World War II. *c*: R.A.C., A.C.U. J.C.C., B.A.R.C. *a*: 1 Woodstock Rd, London, W.4, & 207 Abbey Hse, Westminster, London, S.W.1. *T*: Whitehall 1616.

LOW, Bevis Brunel, M.A., A.M.I.MechE., A.M.I. A.E. *b*: Lon 1896. *e*: Bancrofts Sc Woodford & St John's Col Cam. *m*: Isabel C. Shanks. *s*: 3. Lect Mech Eng, Mil Col of Sci Woolwich. *Publ*: Mathematics. *s.s*: Eng, maths. *a*: 16 Baldwyns Pk, Bexley, Kent.

LOW, David. *b*: Dunedin, New Zealand 1891. *e*: Boys Hgh Sch Christchurch N.Z., & Priv. *m*: Madeline Grieve Kenning. *d*: 2. Cartoonist & Caricaturist. *n.a*: N.Z. & Australian papers, Star 1919, Ev Standard '27. *Publ*: Caricatures; Lions & Lambs; The Best of Low; Low & Terry; The Modern Rake's Progress; Portfolio of Caricatures; Ye Madde Designer ;Political Parade; Low Again; Cartoon History of Our Time; Europe Since Versailles; Europe at War; The World at War ;Low's War Cartoons; Low on the War (U.S.A.); British Cartoonists & Caricaturists; C'est la Guerre; Valka Zacala Mnichovem; Years of Wrath; etc. *Ctr*: Various newsps & periodicals. *s.s*: Personal Portrait Caricature, Independant Politics. *Rec*: Cinema, golf. *c*: Nat Lib, Savile. *a*: Rodborough Rd, London, N.W.11.

LOW, David Allan, M.I.MechE. *b*: Dundee 1857. *e*: Dundee H.S., Owen's Col M/C & Glas Univ. *m*: E. J. Millar. *s*: 1. *d*: 3. Emeritus Prof of Civil & Mech Eng E. Lon Col. *Publ*: Practical Solid Geometry in Two Parts; A Manual of Machine Drawing & Design (with A. W. Bevis); Heat Engines; A Pocket-Book for Mechanical Engineers; etc. *Rec*: Travel, music. *c*: Authors'. *a*: E. Lon Col, Mile End Rd, Lon.

LOW, David Halyburton, M.A.(Edin). *b*: Aberdeen 1877. *e*: Edin Univ, The Sorbonne & College de France, Paris & Marburg Univ. *m*: Mara Yovitchitch. *s*: 1. *d*: 2. Schoolmaster. *n.a*: Belgrade Corr Daily Mail 1907-10. *Publ*: The Ballads of Marko Kraljević ('22). *c.t*: Glas Herald, Slavonic Review, Blackie's Boys' Annual, etc. *c*: Glas Ballad, Scot P.E.N. *a*: 20 Sutherland St, Glas, W.2. *t*: Western 4677.

LOWBURY, Edward Joseph Lister. *b*: London 1913. *e*: St Paul's Sch, Oxford Univ, Lond Univ. *n.a*: Co-Founder & Ed of Equator (East Africa) 1944—46. *Publ*: Crossing the Line. *Ctr*: Penguin New Writing, Time & Tide, New Eng Rev; New Eng Weekly. *s.s*: Poetry. *Rec*: Music. *w.s*: Army 3 yrs East Africa. *a*: 21 Menehk Rd, London, N.W.2. *T*: Hampstead 3634.

LOWDE, Miss E., B.A. *a*: Girls' County High Sc, Petersfield.

LOWE, Rev. Alfred Hardwick, B.D.(Lon). *b*: L'pool. *e*: Elem & Didsbury Col M/C. *m*: N. M. Simonson. *Publ*: Manner of the Master or Studies in Teaching of Jesus; Sunlit Fields, or Cricket & Life. *s.s*: Greek Testament. *Rec*: Cricket, tennis. *a*: 80 Pepys Rd, Wimbledon.

LOWE, Boutelle Ellsworth, A.B., A.M., Ph.D. *b*: Marion, N.Y. 1890. *e*: Denison, Rochester & Columbia Univs. *m*: Louise Alberta Caroline Klein. Authorship & Educ, Pres of Lang Inst of N.Y. City 1918—35, Nat Educ Assoc & Nat Geog Soc, etc. *Publ*: Representative Industry & Trade Unionism of an American City; Internationalism Aspects of the Labour Problem; Historical Survey of International Action Affecting Labour (jointly); International Education for Peace; International Protection of Labour—International Labour Organisation History & Law; etc. *Ctr*: N.Y. Sun School & Soc, Town & Country Review, etc. *s.s*: Labour Problems & Internat Relations. *Rec*: Trav. *a*: 125 Lawrence Ave, Hasbrouck Heights, N.J. *T*: Hasbrouck 8-0374.

LOWE, C. Egerton, F.T.C.L. *b*: Lon 1860. *e*: Leipzig. *m*: Constance M. Küster. *d*: 1. Examiner for Trinity Col of Music. *Publ*: Primer on Harmonics; Hints to Young Violinists; Cyclopædic Handbook of Elocution; Viva Voce; Candidate's Guide; Form in Pianoforte Music; Beethoven's Sonatas; Art of Pianoforte Practising; Word-Phrases to Bach's "48"; Teacher's Vade Mecum; Chronological

History of Music & Musicians; etc. *s.s*: Pianoforte & violin. Travelled all over Empire examining & lecturing. Adjudicator Brit & S. African Mus Festivals. *a*: 158 Portsdown Rd, W.9. *t*: Maida Vale 1863.

LOWE, Charles Edward Berkeley, D.S.O., M.C. Stockbroker Lon Stock Exchange. *Publ*: Siege Battery 94 during the Great War. *a*: Raddery, Blackheath, nr Guildford, Surrey. *t*: Shalford 121.

LOWE, David. *a*: 157 Crofthill Road, Croftfoot, Cathcart.

LOWE, Edward Cronin, M.B.E. *b*: Dunedin, N.Z. 1880. *e*: Wellington Col N.Z. & Guy's Hosp Lon. *m*: Helena Maud Fruen. *d*: 3. *c.t*: Lancet, B.M.J., Journ of Radiology, Practitioner. *s.s*: Biochem, cancer. Capt N.Z.M.C. 1916–19. Pathologist Southport Infirmary, Eye & Ear Inf, L'pool & to Hahnemann Hosp L'pool. *Rec*: Tennis, caravaning. *c*: Univ (L'pool), Roy Socs (Lon), L'pool Med Inst, B.M.A. *a*: 31 Church St, Southport. *t*: 5447.

LOWE, Elias Avery, Ph.D. *b*: 1879. *e*: Cornell Univ, Halle, Munich. *m*: Helen Tracy Porter. *d*: 3. Palæographer. *Publ*: Die ältesten Kalendarien aus Monte Cassino (1908); The Bobbio Missal ; Codices Lugdunenses Antiquissimi; " Handwriting " in Legacy of the Middle Ages; Scriptura Beneventana ('29); Codices Latini Antiquiores, Pt I ('34); etc. *c.t*: Class Review, Journ Theo Studies, Eng Hist Review, etc. *s.s*: Latin palæ. *Rec*: Fishing, golf. *a*: Corpus Christi Col, Oxf, & Littlehouse, Oriel St, Oxf. *t*: 4056.

LOWE, Sir F. Gordon. *b*: Edgbaston 1884. *e*: Charterhouse & Clare Coll Camb. *m*: *s*: 1. *d*: 1. Proprietor Gordon Lowe, Sports Journalist. *Publ*: Gordon Lowe on Lawn Tennis ; The Lawn Tennis Guide ; Lawn Tennis Made Easy ; Ed, Lowe's Lawn Tennis Annual. *Ctr*: Star, Scotsman, News of the World, Yorks Post, etc. *s.s*: Lawn Tennis. *a*: 97 Ember Lane, Esher, Surrey. *T*: Emberbrook 1301.

LOWE, Hubert Frank. *b*: Beeston 1881. *e*: Elem & Hr Educ. Married. *d*: 2. *c.t*: Nott'm Guardian, Times, Daily Express, Mail, Herald, etc. *Rec*: Tennis. *a*: West Gate, Long Eaton, Notts. *t*: 140.

LOWE, JAMES HENRY: (formerly Loewe): Hebrew Classics; *b*. Brighton, Eng., Aug., 1852; s. Louis and Emma (Siberstein) Loewe; educ. Brighton Sch. (Eng), Friedrichs Gymnasium (Breslau, Ger.); *m*. Emma Immerwahr, 1881. AUTHOR: Tutorial Preparation for Misnoh and Gemoro, 1926; Rashi on Genesis, 1929. Translator: Ethnology (by Haberlandt), 1900-1920; Civilization of the East (by Hommel), 1900; Primitive Man (by Hoernes), 1900. Contributor to Stock Exchange Gazette, Financial Times, Jewish Guardian, Jewish Chronicle. General character of writing: Classical, Religion, Jew. OFFICE: 33 Berner St., London, E. 1, Eng.

LOWE, Joyce Egerton, M.A. *b*: London 1892. *e*: Nth Lond Collegiate Sch for Girls, Bedford Coll for Women (Lond Univ). Lect in Classics, Asst in Latin Univ Coll Lond. *Publ*: Church Latin for Beginners ; Folia Latina ; Magic in Greek & Latin Literature ; Ecclesiastical Greek for Beginners ; The Key of the Door (Trans) ; Select Odes of Catullus, X Ovid, Metamorphoses XIV. *c*: Univ Women's. *a*: Flat 3, 158 Randolph Ave, London, W.9. *T*: Cunningham 8962.

LOWE, P. Bruce, M.J.I. *b*: Hale 1906. *e*: Cath Sc Shanghai, Bowdon Col Cheshire, St George's Harpenden, Neuchatel & Lon Sc of Econ. Journalist. Clerk '25–29. *n.a*: Ed Clare Market Review '30–31, Huddersfield Examiner, Asst Leader-Writer & Sub-Ed '31. *c.t*: Forward View. *s.s*: Politics, econ. *Rec*: Ornithology, fencing. *c*: Hon Sec Huddersfield Br N.U.J., Round Table, Huddersfield. *a*: Flat 7, 54 Fitzwilliam St, Huddersfield. *t*: 1140.

LOWE, Percy Roycroft, O.B.E., B.A., M.B., B.C. *b*: Stamford 1870. *e*: Priv & Jesus Coll Camb. *m*: Harriet Dorothy Meade-Waldo. *d*: 1. Head of Ornithological Dept Brit Museum. *Publ*: A Naturalist on Desert Islands ; Our Common Sea Birds. *Ctr*: Nature, Proc Zoological Soc, etc. *Rec*: Golf, shooting. *c*: Athenæum. *w.s*: World War 1 (In Charge Hosp Team). *a*: 2 Hugo Hse, 178 Sloane St, London, S.W.1. *T*: Sloane 1887.

LOWE, Robson, F.R.S.A. *b*: London 1905. *e*: Fulham Central Sch. *m*: Winifred Marie Denne. *d*: 2. Philatelist. *n.a*: Ed The Philatelist 1934—, Ed The White Cross '46—47. *Publ*: The Regent Catalogue of Empire Postage Stamps ; The Handstruck Postage Stamps of the Empire ; The Regent Encyclopædia of Empire Postage Stamps ; The Birth of the Adhesive Postage Stamp ; Masterpieces of Engraving on Postage Stamps ; The Postage Stamps of Great Britain ; The First Colonial Postage Stamps ; Indian Post Offices Abroad. *Ctr*: Numerous Philatelic Journs. *s.s*: Philately, Postal Hist. *Rec*: Philately & postal hist. *a*: 50 Pall Mall, London, S.W.1, & 1320 Widener Building, Philadelphia, Pa, U.S.A. *T*: Abbey 4034.

LOWE, Lt.-Col. T. A., D.S.O., M.C. (See "**TALLOW.**") Army (ret). *n.a*: Ed The Services Territorial Magazine. *Ctr*: Star, Truth, Fighting Forces, Picture Show, Picturegoer, Times of India (Bombay), Statesman (Calcutta), Men Only, Strand, Field, Tit-Bits, Kemsley Newsps. *c*: Savage. *a*: Twin Sisters, Iden, Sussex.

LOWE-PORTER, Helen Tracy. *b*: U.S.A. 1876. *e*: Wells Col, etc. *m*: Dr E. A. Lowe. *d*: 3. Trans of Dr Thomas Mann. *a*: 6 Oriel St, Oxf. *t*: 4056.

LOWELL, Juliet. *b*: New York City 1901. *e*: Calhoun Sch, Vassar Coll. *m*: Ben Lowell. *s*: 1. *d*: 1. Author. *Publ*: Dumb-Belles Lettres ; Dear Sir ; Dear Sir or Madam ; Coming Our Dear Mr Congressman. *Ctr*: Ency Brit, Warner Bros, Fox & R.K.O. Picture Companies (Shorts), etc. *s.s*: Humour. *Rec*: Tennis, horseback riding, swimming, mountain climbing, camping. *c*: Woman's Press. *a*: 606 Nth Alpine Drive, Beverly Hills, California, U.S.A. *T*: Crestview 65123.

LOWENBACH, Jan, LL.D. *b*: Rychnov n.K. 1880. *e*: Gymnasium Rychnov & Czech Univ Prague. *m*: Vilma Zucker. *d*: 2. Lawyer, Expert on Music & Copyright. *n.a*: Ed Hudebni Revue 1908—18 & Soutez a Ivorba '24—88, Music Corre Lidove Noviny '08—18, Musical Courier '45—. *Publ*: Gluck & Bohemia ; Copyright ; New Copyright Law ; Soldier & Dancer ; The White Lord ; Czech-Russian Music Relations ; etc. *Ctr*: Svobodne Noviny, Svobodny Litrek, Musical Courier & Musical Quarterly (New York). *s.s*: Music & Copyright, Chemistry of Education. *Rec*: Hiking, ski-ing. *a*: Prague 12, Rimska 36, Czechoslavakia.

LOWENFIELD, Margaret Frances Jane, M.R.C.S. (Eng), L.R.C.P.(Eng). *b*: Lon. *e*: Cheltenham Col, Roy Free Hosp. Cons Phys. *Publ*: A Study of the Variations in the Chemical Composition of Normal Human Colostrum & Early Milk (with Miss Widdows, M. Bond & E. Taylor); Researches in Lactation (with S. T. Widdows); A Study of the

Composition of Human Milk: The Influence of the Method of Extraction on the Fat Percentage (with S. T. Widdows); A New Approach to the Problem of Psychoneurosis in Childhood (Brit Journ of Med Psych Vol XI, pt III, 1931); etc. *c.t*: The New Era. *s.s*: Psych, folklore, lang. Founder & Co-Dir Inst of Child Psych. *Rec*: Gardening, travel. *c*: Eng Speaking Un. *a*: 21 Devonshire Pl, W.1. *t*: Welbeck 8223.

LOWIE, Robert H., B.A., Sc.D., Ph.D. *b*: Vienna, Austria 1883. *e*: Coll of the City of New York, Columbia Univ. *m*: Winifred Cole. Anthropologist. *n.a*: Ed American Anthropology 1924—33. *Publ*: Primitive Society; The Crow Indians; History of Ethnological Theory; Primitive Religion; The Origin of the State; The German People; etc. *Ctr*: New Republic, American Mercury, Tomorrow, Freeman, etc. *s.s*: Anthropology. *Rec*: Travel, walking, swimming. *c*: Faculty, Berkeley. *a*: 2521 Benvenue Ave, Berkeley, California, U.S.A. *T*: Ashberry 3-3417.

LOWINSKY, Ruth. *b*: London 1892. *e*: Private. *m*: Thomas Lowinsky. *s*: 2. *d*: 2. *Publ*: Lovely Food; More Lovely Food; What's Cooking. *s.s*: Cooking. *Rec*: Golf, bridge. *a*: The Old Rectory, Aldbourne, Wilts. *T*: 36.

LOWIS, Cecil Champain. *b*: Bengal 1866. *e*: Newton Coll Devon, Germany & Corpus Christi Coll Camb. *m*: Sarah Josselyn Man. *d*: 3. I.C.S. (ret). *Publ*: (Novels) Fascination; Four Blind Mice; The Grass Spinister; Green Sandals; In the Hags Hands; The Dripping Tamarinds; The Penal Settlement; The Green Tunnel; Prodigal's Portion; etc. *w.s*: World War I. *a*: Elm Hse, Marshall Rd, Godalming, Surrey. *T*: 180.

LOWIS, Rev. Douglas William, D.D.(Lon), B.A.(Lon). *b*: Loughborough 1882. *e*: Hr Grade Derby. Handsworth Meth Col. *m*: Alice Mary Heath. *d*: 2. Meth Minister. Examiner in Church History and Church Doctrine, Headingley Meth Col. *Publ*: History of Church in France 950–1000; etc. *c.t*: London Quarterly Review, Methodist Recorder, etc. *s.s*: Church history. *a*: 77 Balmoral Rd, Morecambe.

LOWNDES, Marie Adelaide Belloc. *m*: Frederic Sawrey Lowndes. Novelist. *Publ*: The Heart of Penelope; The End of Her Honeymoon; Love and Hatred; What Timmy Did; Bread of Deceit; The Lodger; Letty Lynton; Another Man's Wife; What Really Happened; The Chianti Flask; etc. *Plays*: The Key: With All John's Love. *Rec*: Reading. *a*: 9 Barton St, W.C.1. *t*: Whitehall 6673.

LOWNDES-YATES, Christobel. *e*: Priv & Wimbledon Art Coll. Journalist & Novelist, Hon Sec Lyceum Stage Soc (Lond), Ex Ed Wayfarer Gazette, Hon Sec Sac of Women Journalists. *Publ*: Robbers in Purple; Gods Must be Fed. *Ctr*: Dly Mail, Dly Mirror, Strand Mag, Stage Era, Tatler, Amer Short Story Mag, etc. *s.s*: Short Dramatic Stories, Agriculture Articles, Womens Articles. *Rec*: Collecting antiques, politics. *w.s*: Civil Defence, Commandant Brit Red Cross World War II. *c*: Forum. *a*: 88 Beaufort Mansions, Chelsea, London, S.W.3. *T*: Flaxman 9588.

LOWRIE, Walter. *b*: Philadelphia, Pennsylvania 1868. *e*: Princetown Theol Sem, Univs of Princetown, Greifswald & Berlin, American Acad Rome. *m*: Barbara Armour. Clergyman. *Publ*: Jesus According to St Mark; The Short Story of Jesus; Art in the Early Church; Essential Action in the Liturgy; S.S. Peter & Paul in Rome; Religion of a Scientist; Kierkegaard; etc. *s.s*: Early Christian Art, New Testament Interpretations, Hist of Early Church, Christian Liturgy. *Rec*: Mountain climbing. *a*: 83 Stockton St, Princeton, New Jersey, U.S.A. *T*: Princeton 1866.

LOWRISON, George C. Science Tutor. *Pnbl*: Articles on science. *a*: The Limes, 157 Burnt Ash Hill, S.E.12.

LOWRY, Fesington Carlyle, M.A., LL.B., B.S. *b*: McMinnville, Tennessee 1885. *e*: Alfred Holbrook Normal Univ, Univ of Tennessee, Chattanooga Coll of Law, George Peabody Coll for Teachers. *m*: Margaret Frances Gillespie. *s*: 2. *d*: 3. Educator & Editor, Administrative Sec & Dir of Univ Extension of the Univ of Tennessee, Mem U.S. Nat Film Cttee for the United Nations 1947—. *Publ*: Extension of Federal Power; Appropriations for Elementary Schools in Tennessee; Correspondence Courses for College Credit; The Man in the Street Looks at the Peace; The Obligations of Extension in This New Order. *a*: 950 Temple Ave, Knoxville 16, Tennessee, U.S.A. *T*: 2-5078.

LOWRY, Thomas Martin, C.B.E., HonM.A. (Cantab), F.R.S., HonLL.D.(Dublin), D.Sc(Lon). *b*: Bradford 1874. *e*: Kingswood Sc Bath & Cent Tech Col S. Kensington. *m*: Eliza Wood. *s*: 2. *d*: 1. Prof of Phys Chem Cam Univ. *Publ*: Historical Introduction to Chemistry; A Class Book of Physical Chemistry (with Sugden); Inorganic Chemistry; etc. *c.t*: Journ Chem Soc, Proc Roy Soc, Nature, Chemistry & Industry, etc. *s.s*: Phys chem. *Rec*: Camping. *a*: 54 Bateman St, Cam. *t*: 2702.

LOWTHER, Lady Alice. *b*: Paris 1873. *e*: Private. *m*: The Rt Hon Sir Gerard A. Lowther Bt, P.C., G.C.M.G., C.B. *d*: 3. *Publ*: Land of the Gold Mohur. *c.t*: Nat Review, Morocco, Letter Guild Journ. *s.s*: Travel sketches. Lived 3 y in Morocco, 5 y in Turkey. Awarded Turkish Grand Cordon of the Order of Mercy, Silver Medal (Coronation) of Their Majesties of Great Britain, Bronze Medal of H.M. Queen Elizabeth of the Belgians, Silver Medal of the Italian Red Cross. *c*: Vice-Pres St George's Hospital. Jt Hon Sec American Women's War Relief, Pres Belgian Prisoners War Relief, Pres Lady Lowther's (Turkish) War Relief Fund, etc. etc. *a*: 23 Belgrave Sq, S.W.1. *t*: Sloane 9495.

LOWTHER, MAJOR GEN. SIR CECIL, K.C.M.A., C.B., R.V.O., D.S.O.: Army (retired); *b*. Ampthill Park, Bedfordsmire, Eng., June 27, 1869; *s*. William and Charlotte (Alice) L.; *educ*. private Sch. at Brighton, 1880-2; Charterhouse, 1882-87; R.M.C. Sandhurst, 1887-90; married. AUTHOR: Pillar to Post, 1911. Edited Charterhouse Mag., Guards Brigade Mag. Secretary of the Army Football Assn. for 2 years. CLUBS: Turf, Beefsteak, Bath, Wentworth Virginia Water, Coombehill Golf. Relig. denom., Church of England. HOME: 19 Queen St., Mayfair, W. 1, London, Eng.

LOYD, Rt. Rev. Philip Henry. M.A. (See **St Albans, Bishop of**.) *b*: Northampton 1884. *e*: Eton & King's Coll Camb. *Publ*: The Way According to St Mark; The Life According to St John; Doers of the Word; The Treasure of the Heart of Jesus; By Faith with Thanksgiving; Teach Me Thy Statutes. *c*: Oxf & Camb Univ. *a*: Abbeygate Hse, St Albans, Hertfordshire. *T*: St Albans 305.

LUARD, William Blaine, O.B.E. *b*: Falmouth 1897. *e*: Naval. *m*: May Gladys Hayes. Cdr R.N. (ret), Inventor of Yachtman's Course & Bearing Corrector & Channel Tidograph, also Luard's Patent Parallel Rule. *n.a*: Assoc Ed Sail. *Publ*: A Celtic Hurly Burly; All Hands; Yachtman's Modern Navigation &

Practical Pilotage; Conquering Seas; A.B.C. of Blue Water Navigation; Wild Goose Chase; Northern Deeps; Changing Horizons; Where the Tides Meet. *Ctr*: Blackwoods, Times, Blue Peter, Chambers's Journ, Field, etc, & Yachting papers. *Rec*: Yachting, ocean racing. *c*: Jnr United, Roy Cruising, Royal Ocean Racing, Overseas, etc. *a*: Trelour, Mawnan Smith, Nr Falmouth, Cornwall. *T*: Mawnan Smith 328.

LUBBOCK, Basil. M.C. *b*: Barnet 1876. *e*: Eton. *m*: Dorothy Mary Thynne. Author & Critic. *Publ*: Round the Horn before the Mast; Jack Derringer; The China Clippers; The Log of the Cutty Sark; Sail (2 vol); The Last of the Windjammers (2 vol); The Nitrate Clippers ('32); Bully Hayes, South Sea Pirate ('32); The Opium Clipper's ('33); Deep Sea Warriors; The Colonial Clippers; The Blackwall Frigates; The Western Ocean Packets; The Down Easters; Barlow's Journal (2 vols '34); etc. *c.t*: Blue Peter, Country Life, etc. *s.s*: Naval hist, nat hist of sea. War Service Boer War (Desps), Gt War '14—19, India & France. *Rec*: Yachting. *c*: Roy Y. Squadron & R.A.C. *a*: Monks Orchard, Seaford, Sx. *t*: 484.

LUBBOCK, Percy. Author. *Publ*: Roman Pictures; The Craft of Fiction; Earlham; Shades of Eton; *a*: c/o Jonathan Cape Ltd, 30 Bedford Sq, W.C.

LUBBOCK, S. G., M.A. *a*: Farnborough School, Hants.

LUBER, JET (pen name); (Henrietta C. A. Meulenbelt-Luber): author; b. Bussum, Netherlands, June, 1889; d. Jan Wynand and Antje (Zunderdorp) Luber; educ. University (medicines); m. H. H. Meulenbelt, Jr., July 26, 1918. AUTHOR: De Drie Levens Van Nina Vesper (The Three Lives of Nina Vesper), 1927; Mr. Jeanne Jacquelline, 1928; Het Gezin (The Family), 1929. Contributor to Elsevier's Geillustreerd Maandschrift; Groot-Nederland, De Vrouw en haar Huis, De Groene Amsterdammer, Democratic and Vrye Arbeid, Nova, Panorama, Wereldkroniek, Nederland; newspaper de Telegraaf. "The Family" was awarded a prize by the World's Library on occasion of a competition amongst Dutch writers. General character of writing: fiction, essays, educational articles. HOME: Rynlaan 164 bis, Utrecht, Netherlands.

LUBIN, Isador. *b*: Worcester, Massachusetts 1896. *e*: Clark, Missouri & Michigan Univs. *d*: 2. Economist. *n.a*: Publisher Monthly Labor Review 1933—40 *Publ*: The British Coal Dilemma; The Absorption of the Unemployed By American Industry (Collab); Government Control of Prices During the War; Miners Wages & the Cost of Coal; The British Attack on Unemployment. *Ctr*: Various econ & statistical journs. *s.s*: Labour, Internat Econ Problems. *Rec*: Horseback riding, camping, swimming, gardening. *c*: Cosmos (Wash), Lotos (N.Y.). *a*: 983 Park Ave, New York City 28, N.Y. *T*: Regent 7-3476.

LUCAS, Donald William. *b*: London 1905. *e*: Rugby & King's. *m*: Mary Irene Cohen. Fellow King's College. *Publ*: Trans Bacchæ of Euripides. *Ctr*: Classical Rev, Classical Quarterly. *s.s*: Classics. *Rec*: Travel. *a*: King's Coll, Cambridge. *T*: 1152.

LUCAS, Edward Verrall, C.H. *b*: 1868. Publisher & Essayist. *Publ*: The Open Road; Wisdom while you Wait (with C. L. Graves); Highways & Byways in Sussex; A Wanderer in Holland; A Wanderer in London; Landmarks; Mr. Ingleside; Old Lamps for New; Over Bemerton's; Vermeer of Delft; Genevra's Money; Encounters and Diversions; The Joy of Life; A Wanderer in Rome; The Fronded Isle; The More I See of Men; A Rover I would be; Windfalls Eve; Down the Sky; French Leaves; etc. *c.t*: Punch, etc. *s.s*: Charles Lamb. Chm Methuen & Co, 1924. Mem Counc Soc of Authors'. *a*: 36 Essex St. W.C.

LUCAS, Emily Beatrix Coursolles (E. B. C. Jones). *b*: Lon 1893. Novelist & Critic. *n.a*: Asst Ed Woman's Leader 1918—19. *Publ*: Quiet Interior; Singing Captives; Wedgewood Medallion; Helen & Felicia; Morning & Cloud; etc. *c.t*: New Statesman, Adelphi. *s.s*: Fiction. Mem Counc Civil Liberties. *Rec*: Poetry. *a*: Craston's Orchard, Yattendon, Berks.

LUCAS, Frank Archibald William, K.C. *b*: Pietermaritzburg 1881. *e*: Marist Brothers' Sch Jo'burg & S.A. Coll Capetown, Worcester Coll Oxf. *m*: Caroline Robertson Whittingham. *d*: 1. *Publ*: South Africa as She Might Be. *Ctr*: Chr Sc Monitor, Forum, Star, Common Sense, Outspan, The Free People. *s.s*: Poverty, Cause & Remedy. *Rec*: Golf. *c*: Pretoria. *a*: 14 Campbell Rd, Parktown West, Johannesburg. *T*: 44. 2318.

LUCAS, Frank Laurence, O.B.E., M.A., F.R.S.L. *b*: Hipperholme 1894. *e*: Rugby & Camb Univ. *m*: (1) Emily Beatrix Coursolles Jones, (2) Prudence Dalzell Wilkinson, (3) Elna Kallenberg. *Publ*: Seneca & Elizabethan Tragedy; Euripides & His Influence; Authors Dead & Living; Works of John Webster; Tragedy; Art of Dying (collab); Studies French & English; From Olympus to the Styx (collab); Mount Peacock (from French of Marie Mauron); Decline & Fall of the Romantic Ideal; Delights of Dictatorship; Journal under the Terror; Ten Victorian Poets; Critical Thoughts in Critical Days; Tennyson; The River Flows; Cécile ;The Woman Clothed with the Sun; Dr Dido; Time & Memory; Ariadne; Poems 1935; (Plays) The Bear Dances, Four Plays; Greek Anthology; Vigil of Venus; Hymn to Aphrodite (Anthologies etc); A Greek Garland. *Ctr*: Times Litt Supp. *s.s*: Eng Lit. *w.s*: World War I, F.O. 1939—45. *Rec*: Travel. *a*: King's College, 20 West Rd, Cambridge. *T*: 2730.

LUCAS, Ian. *b*: Walmer 1902. *e*: Lancing Coll. *m*: Sheelah Bennett. Journalist. *n.a*: Ed Staff Daily Mail 1922—23, Reuters '23—. *Publ*: The Royal Embassy: An Account of the Duke & Duchess of York's Tour to Australia. Reuters Special Corr with Duke & Duchess of York to Australia 1927, with Prince of Wales to Sth & East Africa '30, & with Prince of Wales & Prince George to Sth Amer '31. *Rec*: Golf. *c*: Sandy Lodge. *a*: Benluce Copthorne Rd, Rickmansworth, Herts. *T*: 2753.

LUCAS, St. John (Welles), M.A. *b*: Rugby 1879. *e*: Haileybury, Univ Col Oxf & Middle Temple. Author, Barrister-at-Law (ret). *Publ*: Poems & New Poems; Saints, Sinners & the Usual People; Certain Persons; The Oxford Book of Italian Verse; Ronsard; etc. *c.t*: Blackwood's Mag Fortnightly Review, Spectator. *s.s*: French & Italian. War Service 1915–19. War Medal, Victory Medal '19. *c*: Athenæum. *a*: 5 Pump Ct, Temple, E.C.4.

LUCAS, Stanley Bennett, B.A. Schoolmaster. *n.a*: Ed A.M.A. 1923—. *c.t*: Various educational journs. *a*: 20 Stanhope Gdns, Highgate, N.6. *t*: Mountview 6023.

LUCAS, Van Norman. *b*: Lon 1900. *e*: Fitzroy Col. *m*: Lillian Phillips. *d*: 1. Journalist & Business Mang. *n.a*: G.K.'s Weekly, Ltd, music critic '27, Mang '29, Sec '33–. *c.t*: Christian Science Monitor, The Sackbut, Melody Maker, etc. *s.s*: Music, politics. *a*: 5 Ormonde Terr, Regent's Pk, N.W.8. *t*: Primrose Hill 0412.

LUCAS, William Robert. b: Birm 1884. e: Counc Sc. m: Mary Thomson. s: 1. d: 2. Naturopath. n.a: Ed Health Philosopher '31. Publ: Physical Culture Simplified; How to Conquer Constipation; How to Adjust Your Weight; How to Cure Rupture; etc. c.t: Health for All, Health & Strength, Superman, Mod Salesmanship, etc. s.s: Nature cure, physical culture. Rec: Gardening, swimming. a: Langholme, 73 Sutton Rd, Heston, Mdx. t: Houslow 2581.

LUCATO, Constantine Rasi. b: Lon 1892. e: St And Col, Streatham & Priv. Journalist. n.a: Motorcycling 1920, Motor '21, Ed The Morris Owner '27–. Publ: The Art of Driving a Motorcycle. c.t: Most dailies, all motor journals. s.s: Motoring, humorous, continental travel, financial & money market articles. War Service. Rec: Golf, tennis, sailing. a: The Limes, Dorchester, Oxf. t: Warborough 46.

LUCE, Arthur Aston, M.C., Litt.D., D.D. b: Gloucester 1882. e: Eastbourne Coll, Trin Coll Dublin. m: Lilian Mary Thompson (dec'd). s: 2. d: 1. Fell Trin Coll Dublin, Prof of Moral Philosophy, Chancellor St Patricks Cathedral Dublin. Publ: Berkeley & Malebranche; Berkeley's Philosophical Commentaries; Berkeley's Immaterialism; etc. s.s: Philosophy. Rec: Fishing, shooting, chess. w.s: R.I. Rifles 1915—18. a: Ryslaw, Bushby Park Rd, Dublin. T: 95572.

LUCE, Clare Boothe. b: New York City 1903. e: St Mary's Sch Long Island, Miss Mason's Sch New York. m: Henry R. Luce. Playwright, Author & Lecturer, Mem of Congress. n.a: Assoc Ed 1931, Mang Ed 1933 Vanity Fair. Publ: Stuffed Shirts; Europe in the Spring; (Plays) The Women; Kiss the Boys Goodbye; Margin for Error. Ctr: Life, Sat Ev Post, McCalls, Vogue, etc. c: P.E.N., Overseas Press. a: Limestone Rd, Ridgefield, Connecticut, U.S.A. T: Ridgefield 1140.

LUCE, Rev. Edmund. b: Amersham 1854. e: Oundle Sc, St John's Col Cam. m: Margaret Eleanor Goodhart. s: 2. Priv Tutor. Publ: Help to Latin Translation at Sight; etc. s.s: Latin, Greek, Eng, hist, divinity. Chaplain Roedean Sc 1897—1902. Asst Class Tutor Eton 1908—24. Rec: Golf. a: 43 Banbury Rd, Oxf.

LUCE, MORTON: author; b. High Wycombe, Bucks, Eng., May 7, 1849; s. Rev. Edmond Jones Luce; educ. Oundle, London Univ. AUTHOR: Guide to Parsing and Analysis, 1882; New Studies in Tennyson, 1892; A Handbook to the Works of Tennyson, 1895; Shakespeare's Tempest (Arden Edit.), 1902; Primer of Tennyson, 1901; A Handbook to the Works of Shakespeare, 1905; Shakespeare's Twelfth Night (Arden Edit.), 1905; Thysia, an Elegy, 1908; Rich's Apolonius and Silla (in Shakespeare Classics), 1910; Thysia (Amer. edit.), 1910; Threnodies, Sketches and Other Poems (enlarged), 1910; Idyllia, 1911; Shakespeare, the Man and His Work, 1913; Enlarged Handbook to Tennyson, 1914; The Tempest and Twelfth Night (rev. and enlarged edit.), 1918; New Idyllia; Sketches of a Stream, 1923; Reviews and Essays; Idyllia, New Series, 1927; The Tempest, 3rd edit. (Arden Series), 1926. Wrote Introduction to Tennyson (Temple Primers), 1902. Contributes to XIXth Century, Angler, Fortnightly Rev., Contemporary Rev., Hibbert Journal, etc. Formerly Lecturer, Bristol University. HOME: 6, Walliscote Rd. South, Weston-Super-Mare, Eng.

LUCHAIRE, Julien. b: Bordeaux 1876. e: Ecole Normale Superieure. m: Antonina Vallentin. s: 2. d: 1. Dramatic Writer & Novelist, Off Legion d'honneur, Grand Croix de l'ordre de Roumanie. Publ: L'Evolution intellectuelle de l'Italie de 1815—1830; Les Democrates Italiennes; Confession d'un Francais moyen; Chateau gay La Ceinture Rose; Altitude 3200; Berenice; Boccace Conte 19. s.s: Romans, Nouvelles Scenarios et Dialogues de Films. c: P.E.N. a: 96 Avenue de Ternes, Paris XVIIe. T: Etoile 4725.

LUCK, Peter. Author. Publ: Infallible Witness; Two Shots; The Killing of Ezra Burgoyne; etc. a: c/o Herbert Jenkins Ltd, 3 York St, S.W.1.

LUCKER, Sydney Charles. b: London 1897. m: Florence Hardy. d: 1. Gen Man & Ed National Sunday School Union Business Dept 1939—. n.a: Ed Sunday School Chron 1930—, Ed Graded Teacher Series '39—, Chief European Corres Religious New Service U.S.A. '38—. Publ: Answers to Life's Questions. Ctr: Religious Press generally. s.s: Religious News & Education. Rec: Photography. c: Nat Lib & Roy Empire Soc. a: 22 Winchester Ct, London, W.8. T: Western 3182.

LUCKETT, F. W. Journalist. s.s: Football, greyhounds. a: 38 Highmoor Rd, Caversham, Reading. t: 71892.

LUCY, Geoff. b: Hale, Cheshire 1914. e: Altrincham Gr Sch. m: Irene Roberta Rees. Journalist, Mem N.U.J. n.a: Rep Southport Journ 1933, Daily Mail Manch '37, Dept Ed News Review '38, News Ed '47. Rec: Sailing. a: 32 Parkview Ct, London, S.W.6. T: Putney 1705.

LUDDY, Rev. Ailbe John. b: Cloghean 1885. e: Mount Melleray Seminary. Prof Mental Philos at Mount Melleray Seminary. n.a: Ed Mount Melleray Col Mag 1912–. Publ: Translation of the Works of St Bernard (6 vols); Life of St Malachy; The Story of Mount Melleray; The Cistercian Nuns; The Coming of St Patrick and the Second Spring (oratorio); etc. c.t: Irish Catholic, Tablet, etc. s.s: Mental philos, hist. a: Mount Melleray Abbey, Cappoquin, Co Waterford, I.F.S.

LUDGATER, Alfred. b: Tolleshunt D'Arcy 1858. e: Colchester Nat Sc. m: Annie Samms. s: 2. d: 4. Journalist. n.a: People's News '86–, Essex Chronicle '88–99, Essex Wkly News '99–1921, E. Anglian Daily Times '87. Publ: Mistress of Broadmarsh ('24). c.t: Times, Daily Telegraph, Standard, Daily Sketch. s.s: Archæology. a: The Market Pl, Braintree, Essex. t: 35.

LUDLAM, Henry Edward Burdett. b: Leicester 1891. Typographer. n.a: Founder & Ed Social Yoga, The Age of Plenty. Publ: Money, Power & Progress; Industrial Democracy & the Printing Industry; History of Trades Unionism in the Printing Industry. s.s: Social Philosophy, Econ, Sociology. Rec: Walking. a: 12 Grantham St, Coventry, Warwickshire.

LUDLOW, Brig.-Gen. Walter Robert, C.B. (Civil & Mil). b: Erdington 1857. e: Solihull G.S. & Malvern Col. m: Helen Florence Hart. s: 1. d: 4. Land Agent, Surveyor & Valuer. Publ: Zululand & Cetewayo. c.t: Birm Daily Post, Warwick County News, Ypres Times, etc. s.s: Military, sport. Commanding 184th Inf Brig 1915–16. Area Commandant, B.E.F. Flanders '17–18. D.L. County of Warwick. J.P. Warwick & City of Birm. V.D., T.D., Hon Brig-Gen Army. F.S.I. Rec: Beagling, otter hunting, fishing. c: Union, Cons, Birm. a: Lovelace Hill, Solihull. Warwicks. t: 0029.

LUDOVICI, Anthony M. b: London 1882. e: Priv. Author. Publ: Woman; A Vindication; Enemies of Women; Who is to be Master of the World; Nietzsche.

His Life & Works; A Defence of Aristocracy; Reminiscences of Auguste Rodin; Man: An Indictment; The Sanctity of Private Property; The Secret of Laughter; Violence, Sacrifice & War The Choice of a Mate; The Four Pillars of Health; (Novels) Mansel Fellowes; Catherine Doyle; Too Old for Dolls; etc. *s.s:* Sexology & Politics. *Rec:* Painting. *a:* The Homestead, Rishangles, Eye, Suffolk.

LUDWIG, ALBERT: writer; *b.* Berlin, Germany, Dec. 24, 1875; *s.* Wilhelm and Lina (Goldstein) L.; *educ.* Falk Real Gymnasium (Berlin), Univ. of Berlin. DEGREE: Ph.D.; *m.* Charlotte Bittmann, July 15, 1901. AUTHOR: Lope de Végas Dramen aus dem karolingischen Sagenkreis, 1898; Das Urteil über Schiller im 19. Jahrhundert, 1905; Schiller und die deutsche Nachwelt, 1909; Schiller, sein Leben und Schaffen, 1911; Die dramatische Dichtung, 1923; Von Gottsched bis zur Romantik (in: Das deutsch Drama), 1925; Britain and the British, Kulturkundliches Lesebuch (with H. Gade), 1929. Co-editor: Zeitschrift für deutschkunde; Das Drama (new edit. of Busse, vols. II-IV), 1919-1922. Contributes to Die Literatur, Archiv für das Studium der Neueren Sprachen, Germanisch Romanische Monatsschrift, Vossische Zeitung, Shakespeare Jahrbuch. General character of writing: history of literature, book reviewing. SOCIETIES: Gesellschaft für das Studium der Neueren Sprachen, Gesellschaft für deutsche Literatur, Shakespeare Gesellschaft. Religion, Protestant. ADDRESS: Park-ave. 12, Berlin-Lichtenberg, Germany.

LUDWIG, Emil. Author. *Publ:* Napoleon; Bismark; Masaryk; 1914, Leaders of Europe; The Son of Man; William II; Lincoln; Beethoven; Bolivar; Freud; Goethe; The Practical Wisdom of Goethe; Hindenburg; Mackenzie King; Talks with Mussolini; Stalin; etc. *a:* Ascona, Switzerland.

LUETKENS, Charlotte, Ph.D. *b:* Erfurt 1896. *e:* Univ of Berlin & Heidelberg. *m:* G. O. Luetkens. *s:* 1. Visiting Lecturer Bedford College Sociology 1944—45. *n.a:* Corr Frankfurter Zeitung in Sofia 1924, New York '25—27. *Publ:* Women & a New Society; Staat und Gesellschaft in Amerika; Die Deutsche Jugendbewegung; Wandlungen des liberalen England durch die Kriegswirtschaft; German Trans of Beveridge Full Employment in a Free Society. *Ctr:* Ciba Review, Ciba Symposium. *s.s:* Sociology, Social & Economic Hist. *a:* 39 Gloucester Ave, Regent's Pk, London, N.W.1. *T:* Gulliver 1548.

LUGARD, The Rt. Hon. Lord, P.C., G.C.M.G., C.B., D.S.O., HonD.C.L.(Oxon & Durham), Hon LL.D.(Cantab, Glas & Hong Kong). *b:* Fort St George, Madras 1858. *e:* Rossall & R.M.C. Sandhurst. *m:* Flora Louise Shaw (dec). Army & Colonial Admin. *Publ:* Our East African Empire ('93); The Dual Mandate (1922). *c.t:* The Time's & leading journals. *s.s:* African administration. High Commiss N. Nigeria '00–06. Gov Hong Kong '07-12. Gov N. & S. Nigeria '12-13 & Gov-Gen Nigeria '14-19. British Mem Permanent Mandates' Commission of L.o.N. '23-. Chm Exec Counc Internat Inst African Languages & Cultures '26-. *c:* Athenæum, R.G.S. (Hon), Roy Empire Soc (Hon). *a:* Little Parkhurst, Abinger Common, Surrey. *t:* Abinger 79.

LUKE, Claude F. *b:* Chelmsford 1905. *e:* Rutlish Sch: Merton. *m:* Rose Anne Harvey. *d:* 1. Free-lance Journalist, Feature Writer, Dir Public Relations R.A.F. Cinema Corpn 1947. *n.a:* Public Relations Cons. N.A.A.F.I., Founder Ed N.A.A.F.I. News & Ad Astra. *Publ:* History of the N.A.A.F.I. at War; etc. *Ctr:* Leading British newsps & mags. *c:* Press, Savage. *a:* The Rise, East Horsley, Surrey. *T:* East Horsley 2506.

LUKE, H. T. *b:* Taunton 1893. *e:* Wellington, Somerset. *m:* Edith M. Punchard. Dis Reporter. *n.a:* Wellington Weekly News 1908-25, Western Times Co Ltd '19-. War Service. Chm S. Devon Branch N.U.J. *c:* Newton Abbot Rotary. *a:* 7 Lime Tree Walk, Newton Abbot.

LUKE, Sir Harry Charles, K.C.M.G., D.Litt., LL.D. Lieut-Governor of Malta, Gov of Fiji & High Commsr Western Pacific 1938—42, Chief Rep (Brit Council) Carribbean '43—46. *Publ:* The Fringe of the East; The City of Dancing Dervishes; Cyprus under the Turks; Mosul & its Minorities; Prophets, Priests & Patriarchs; In the Margin of History; An Eastern Chequerboard; More Moves on an Eastern Chequerboard; The Making of Modern Turkey; From a South Seas Diary; Britain & the South Seas; etc. *Ctr:* Times, Quarterly Review, Blackwood's, Fortnightly, Nineteenth Century, etc. *a:* St James's & Athenæum Clubs, London, W.1.

LUKER, Charles. *b:* Faringdon 1876. *e:* Faringdon. Widower. *s:* 2. *n.a:* Proprietor & Publ of Henley & S. Oxon weekly paper, J.P. Henley Boro', Ald & Ex-Mayor Henley T. Counc. *Rec:* Golf. *a:* Caxton Works Henley-on-Thames. *t:* 76.

LUKER, Marion Joss. *e:* Gravesend County Sc, Goldsmiths Col. Bank Clerk. *c.t:* Various periodicals. *s.s:* Psychology, education, income tax. Certificated Teacher. *a:* The Orchard, 57, Riverview Grove, Chiswick, W.4

LUMB, Rev. T. W. *a:* Merchant Taylors' School, Sandy Lodge, Middx.

LUMB, William. *b:* Burnley 1886. *e:* St John's Col Cam & Université de Clermont-Ferrand. Married. Schmaster. *Publ:* Les Affaires; An Introduction to Report Writing. *s.s:* Educ'l books with comm bias. Continent business experience 7 yrs. *a:* 55 Birchfield Rd, Birm 19.

LUMBY, Rev. Edward, F.R.S.A., F.G.S., M.R.S.T. *b:* Sidcup, Kent. *e:* St Paul's Sch, Lond Univ & Clifton Theol Coll. Chaplain, 22 yrs Missionary work in Tropics. *n.a:* Ed Hoi eleutheroi 1937—39. *Publ:* The Church & The People; Coal Mining in a Christian Country. *s.s:* Religion. *Rec:* Tennis, rowing, swimming. *a:* 8 Mildenhall Rd, Stoke Poges Lane, Slough, Bucks.

LUMGAIR, Jessie Yates. *b:* Birkenhead 1883. *e:* Hr Tranmere H.S., Birkenhead. *m:* David Lumgair. *s:* 3. *c.t:* Queen, Children's Own Mag, Answers, Amateur Gardener, Brit Weekly, etc. *s.s:* Children's articles, stories, verse, playwriting. *Rec:* Amateur dramatics, music, gardening. *a:* Woodcot, Lustleigh, S. Devon.

LUMLEY, Gascoigne, I.S.O. *b:* Gateshead 1873. *e:* Priv & Durham Col of Sci. *m:* Mary Pickering. *Publ:* Ju-ju & Justice in Nigeria; Journal of a Jackaroo; Glimpses into Infinity (all with F. Hines). *s.s:* Travel. 22 y service Nigeria 1898—1920. *Rec:* Golf. *c:* Sports. *a:* Glenholme, Jesmond, Newcastle-on-Tyne.

LUMSDEN, James C. *b:* Glas 1906. *e:* Glas Univ. Journalist. *n.a:* Motor-cycling Corr Glasgow Evening News, Scottish Daily Express, etc. *c.t:* Glasgow Evening News, Scottish Daily Express, Hardware Trade Journal, Electrical Industries, World's Press News, Tobacco, etc. *s.s:* Trade in Glas & W. Scotland. Jt Founder & Gen Sec Glasgow Speedway Club. *Rec:* Motor-cycling, physical culture, etc. *c:* Glasgow Unity, Glasgow Rhythm. *a:* 3 Cleland St, Glas, C.5.

LUMSDEN, Sir John, K.B.E., M.D., F.R.A.M. *b*: Drogheda 1869. *e*: Dublin Univ. *m*: Caro F. Kingscote. *s*: 1. *d*: 5. *Publ*: Infant Feeding; Research & Report on Workmen's Conditions of Living & Diets. *c.t*: B.M.J., Lancet, Medical Press. Commissioner St John's Ambulance Brigade Irish District. Chm Order of St John & Bros., I.F.S. Knight of Justice Order of St John. Formerly Senior Visiting Physician Mercer's Hosp, Chief Med Officer Guiness's Brewery. Organised Red X Fever Hosps in Southern Ireland 1914-18. War Service '17-18. *Rec*: Golf, fishing. *c*: Friendly Brothers'. *a*: 4 Fitzwilliam Pl, Dublin, & Earlscliff, Baily, Co Dublin. *t*: Dublin 61354 & Sutton 119.

LUMSDEN, Dame Louisa Innes, D.B.E., M.A. (Cantab), HonLL.D.(St And). *b*: Aberdeen 1840. *e*: Priv, Brussels & Lon. Formerly Res Tutor, Girton College; First Headmistress, St Leonard's Sc; First Warden, Univ Hall, St Andrews. *Publ*: Lessons in German; Yellow Leaves, Memories of a Long Life. *c.t*: London Evening News, Time & Tide, Scotsman, Blackwood's Mag, Chambers's Journ, etc. Ed Our Fellow Mortals. *s.s*: Scottish hist & interests, animals, Women's rights. Rec degrees of B.A. and M.A. in 1928, was only student of Girton & Newnham who gained them 55 y before. *Rec*: Formerly riding, cycling, etc, now chiefly reading, etc. *a*: 1 Doune Terr, Edinburgh.

LUNAN, John. Publisher & Editor. *n.a*: Alyth Gazette & Guardian. *a*: 2 St Andrew St, Alyth, Perthshire. *t*: 30.

LUND, Capt. T. *b*: Bergen 1886. *e*: Oslo Univ & Berlin. Officer with Canadian Exped Forces & R.A.F. (ret '28). Author. *Pub*: Weston of the Royal N.W. Mounted Police; Up North; The Murder of Dave Brandon; In the Snow; Robbery at Portage Bend; Steele Bey's Revenge. *a*: Hawkesbury, Ontario, Canada.

LUND, Torben. *b*: Aarhus, Denmark 1902. *m*: Ella Stochholm. *d*: 2. Prof Univ of Aarhus Denmark. *Publ*: The Fine Arts & the Law; The Danish Law of Copyright; On the Droit Moral; The Protection of the Art Industry Abroad. *s.s*: Copyright. *a*: Univ of Aarhus, Denmark.

LUNDGREN, Hjalmar. *b*: Norrkoping 1880. *e*: Uppsala Univ. *m*: Nora von Samson-Hismmelstierua. *d*: 1. Writer. *Publ*: Syrinx; Llegi Och Epigram; De Gula husen; Kuhlmans; Under ornems Klc; etc. *Ctr*: Various. *Rec*: Travel, books. *c*: P.E.N. *a*: Norrkoping. *T*: 20772.

LUNDH, Nils Wilhelm. *b*: Malmo 1879. *e*: Malmo Hgh Sch. *m*: Hetty Bryant-Meisner. *d*: 2. Author. *Publ*: Vita kyekans; Mars, Martini, Stranden, Ljunghuset; Bleik; Fran Etna och Vesuvius; Pa Vulkanisk Mark; etc. *c*: P.E.N. *a*: Langholmsgat 11, Stockholm, Sweden.

LUNDQUIST, Harold L., LL.B., D.D. *b*: Minneapolis, Minnesota 1894. *e*: Univ of Minnesota, Princeton Theol Sem, Wheaton Coll. *m*: Beatrice Elizabeth Anderson. *s*: 1. *d*: 2. Clergyman & Educator. *n.a*: Lit Ed Christian Life & Times 1947—. *Publ*: Can America be Saved; Why Study Prophecy, An Appraisal of its Dangers & an Appreciation of its Blessing; Dynamic Christian Living; Leadership for Christ; etc. *Ctr*: Moody Monthly & various newsps & journs. *s.s*: Religion—Devotional & Practical Theory. *a*: 2443 Wilson Ave, Chicago 25, Illinois, U.S.A.

LUNDSFORD, Hugh (see BUCK, Charles Neville). *Publ*: The Law of Hemlock Mountain; Flying Heels.

LUNN, Arnold. Editor British Ski Year Book. *Publ*: inc The Third Day; Switzerland & the English; Mountain Jubilee; The Englishman n the Alps; Ski-ing for Beginners; The Complete Ski-runner; The Italian Lakes & Lakeland Cities; etc.

LUNN, Brian Holdsworth. *b*: Bloomsbury 1893. *e*: Westminster Sc & Christ Ch. *m*: Betty Duncan (from whom divorced). Author & Translator. *Publ*: Trans from German—House of Rothschild, by Corti; The Woman with a Thousand Children, by Clara Viebig; Trans from French—Pictures of France, by Paul Valery; From Serfdom to Bolshevism, by Baron Wrangel; etc. Author—The Memoirs of Satan (with William Gerhardi); Martin Luther. *c.t*: The Caterer. *s.s*: Theo, hist. Ex-Mang Dir of Sir Henry Lunn's Tours. *Rec*: Swimming, ski-ing. *c*: Alpine Ski. *a*: 26 Edmund Rd, Clive Vale, Hastings. *t*: 2502.

LUNN, Rev. George Henry, M.A. *b*: Boston Spa, Yorks 1870. *e*: Wharfdale Coll, St Aidans Theo Coll & Durham Univ. *m*: Blanche Edith Maude Spicer. *s*: 1. *d*: 2. Clerk in Holy Orders, Rector of Blisworth. *Publ*: Under the Shadow; In the School of Christ; Ideals of Socialism; The Church & the Second Advent; Youth & the Bible; etc. *Ctr*: The Christian, The Life & Faith, English Churchman & various religious publications. *s.s*: Bible Expositions & Evangelical & Protestant Propaganda. *a*: Blisworth Rectory, Northampton. *T*: Blisworth 83.

LUNN, Henry Fletcher, B.Sc., M.B., B.S., F.R.C.S. *b*: Shrewsbury 1916. *e*: Berkhamsted Sch, Guy's Hosp & Lond Univ. *m*: Agnes Rosalind Wright. *s*: 1. *d*: 2. Anatomical Curator & Sir Halley Stewart Research Fellow of the Coll of Surg (Eng). *n.a*: Ed Guy's Hosp Gazette 1939—40. *Ctr*: Guy's Hosp Gazette, Brit Med Journ, Parasitology, Journ of R.A.M.C., Journ of Anatomy, Brit Journ of Surgery, Annals of Roy Coll of Surgeons of England. *s.s*: Anatomy & Surgery. *a*: C.M.S. Hospital, Old Cairo, Egypt.

LUNN, Sir Henry Simpson, M.A., M.D. *b*: Horncastle 1859. *e*: Horncastle G.S. & T.C.D. *m*: Ethel Moore. *s*: 3. *n.a*: Ed of Review of the Churches '91-1930, J.P., Vice-Pres L.N.U. *Publ*: Chapters from My Life; Round the World with a Dictaphone; Nearing Harbour. *Rec*: Reading, writing. *c*: Reform, Authors', Eighty. *a*: 79 Eccleston Sq, S.W.1. *t*: Victoria 7803.

LUNT, Ronald Geoffrey, M.C. *b*: Wimbledon 1913. *e*: Eton Coll, Queen's Coll Oxf, Westcott Hse Camb. *m*: Veslemoy Sopp Foss. Schoolmaster in Holy Orders, Headmaster Liverpool College. *Publ*: Editions of Marlowe's Dr Faustus & Edward II. *Ctr*: Theology, Convoy. *s.s*: Philosophy, Theology, English Literature, Education, Middle East. *Rec*: Gardening, mountaineering & travel. *w.s*: Chaplain in the Army 1940—45, attached Commandos, Coldstream Gds, S.A.S. *a*: Liverpool College, Liverpool 18. *T*: Allerton 1765.

LUNT, Rev. T. R. W. *b*: Birm 1878. *e*: Merchant Taylors', Haileybury & Univ Col Oxf. *m*: Isabel Ethel Glass. *n.a*: Sen Ed United Counc of Missny Educ. *Publ*: The Story of Islam; The Quest of Nations; Talks on Africa; Talks on India; Talks on China; Talks on David Livingstone; Talks on Races to be Won. *c.t*: The Times, Contemporary Review. *s.s*: Education, religion, science. *Rec*: Fishing. *c*: Authors'. *a*: Worfield Vicarage, Bridgnorth. *t*: Worfield 25.

LUNT, William Edward, A.B., Hon.L.H.D., Ph.D. *b*: Lisbon, Maine 1882. *e*: Bowdoin & Harvard. *m*: Elizabeth Elliott Atkinson. *s*: 1. Prof of Hist Haverford Coll. *n.a*: Adv Ed Speculum 1932—35, Assoc Ed American Hist Review '41—46. *Publ*: Financial Relations of the Papacy with England to 1327; The Valuation of Norwich; Papal Revenues in the Middle Ages; History of England. *Ctr*: Eng Hist Review, Amer Hist Review, Quarterly Journ of Econs, etc. *s.s*: Hist of Eng & the Papacy in the Middle Ages. *a*: Haverford, Pennsylvania.

LUNTZ, George Richard William Neal, M.R.C.S., L.R.C.P. *b*: Johannesburg, Sth Africa 1915. *e*: Parktown Hgh Sch Johannesburg, Univ of Witwatersrand, Guy's Hosp Med Sch Lond. *n.a*: Amateur Boxing Corres R.D. Mail Jo'burg 1937—38, Dly Express, Jo'burg '37—38, Med Corr Diabetic Journ Lond '46—47, the Physiotherapist Lond '47. *Publ*: Medicine. *Ctr*: Guy's Hosp Gazette, Medical Press, The Physiotherapist, etc. *s.s*: Med Educ, Diabetes, Tuberculosis. *Rec*: Boxing, swimming, classical music. *a*: Preston Hall Hosp, Maidstone, Kent. *T*: Aylesford 7262.

LUPINO, Stanley. *Publ*: Crazy Days; From the Stocks to the Stars Autobiography. *a*: c/o H. Jenkins Ltd, 3 York St, S.W.1. *t*: Streatham 2900.

LUPTON, Miss A. M., M.B.E. *Publ*: The Phœnix; A Journal of Housing. Dir of The Housing Centre. Hon Sec Fulham Housing Assoc. *a*: 7 Mallord Street, Chelsea, S.W.3.

LUPTON, Dilworth, D.D. *b*: Cincinnati, Ohio 1883. *e*: Shadyside Acad, Scheffield Scientific Sch of Yale, Meadville Theol Sch. *m*: Elisabeth Beamish Hall Lewis. *d*: 1. Minister, formerly Steel Salesman, Lecturer & Newsp Columnist. *n.a*: Columnist Cleveland Press 1942—47. *Publ*: Religion Says You Can. *Ctr*: Christian Register, Christian Century, Christian Leader. *s.s*: Liberal Religion, Social & Racial Problems. *a*: 100 Summit St, Waltham 54, Massachusetts. *T*: Waltham 2395R.

LUPTON, Samuel, O.B.E., F.J.I. *b*: M/C 1873. *e*: M/C G.S. & Priv. *n.a*: Ed Daily Gazette, Karachi 1916—21, Sind War Journ '17—19, Sind Sachai '19—21, Karachi Handbook, Buenos Aires Daily Herald '22—23, Daily Argosy (B. Guiana) '23—30, previously held important appts in S. Africa & Aus, & in Lon. *c.t*: Numerous n/ps & periodicals at home & abroad. *s.s*: Indian affairs, trop agric, cotton ind. Only passenger in 1st Air Mail in the East, Karachi to Bombay, Feb '20. Indian War Badge & Desp '19. *Rec* Travel, bridge. *a*: 7 Kingsgate Mansions, Red Lion Sq, W.C.1. *t*: Holborn 6256.

LUSCOMBE, J. T., LL.B.(Lon). Barrister-at-Law Inner Temple. *a*: Breams Bldgs, Fetter Lane, E.C.4.

LUSCOMBE, W. J. Journalist. *a*: 56 Woodville Rd, Torquay.

LUSHINGTON, Franklin (see **SEVERN, Mark**). *b*: Switzerland 1892. *e*: Eton, R.M.A. Woolwich. *m*: Bridget Howard. *s*: 1. Lt-Col (ret), C.C.G. Germany 1947—. *Ctr*: Nat Review, Army Quarterly, Blackwoods. *Rec*: Cricket, gardening. *c*: Un Service. *w s*: 1939—45. *a*: Pigeon Hoo, Tenterden, Kent. *T*: Tenterden 65.

LUSHINGTON, Franklyn de Winton. *b*: Madras 1868. *e*: Clare Col, Camb. *m*: Monica Sydney Sanderson. *d*: 1. *Publ*: Sermons to Young Boys; On Personal Service; The Character of the Saint; Addresses on the Beatitudes; Possibilities in a Country Parish; Christ's Way and Modern Problems; etc. *s.s*: Religious educ of young people. Archdeacon of Malta, resigned owing to wife's illness. Headmaster of Elstree Sch 8 y. Chaplain to the Forces in France. Invalided out of Service H.C.F. Played cricket for I Zingari and Free Foresters, Rugby Football for Harlequins and Kent County. *Rec*: Poetry, foreign languages.

Authors', Mem of the Coun of the Poetry Soc, etc. *a*: The Rectory, Weston-under-Lizard, Shropshire. *t*: Weston 25.

LUSTY, Robert Frith. Publisher. Served on Kent Messenger then Publishing Hse of Hutchinson. Ed Booklover & Manager Assoc Co of Selwyn & Blount. *a*: 14a Torrington Pl, W.C.1. *t*: Museum 9349.

LUTOSLAWSKI, Wincety, M.A., Ph.D. *b*: Warsaw 1863 *e*: Riga Politecnicum Univs of Dorpat, Livonia Coll de France. *m*: Wanda Peszynski. *s*: 1. *d*: 5. Prof of Philosophy. *Publ*: The origin & growth of Plato's Logic; The Polish Nation; Volonte et Liberte; Bolshevism & Poland; The Knowledge of Reality; The World of Souls; etc. *Ctr*: Mind, Hibbert Journ, Internat Journ of Ethics, Current Thought, Defender (Melbourne) & many other foreign mags. *s.s*: Metaphysics, Logic, Philos of Hist, Polish Philosophy. *Rec*: Reading, writing, travel, lecturing. *a*: Szwedzka 10, Debniki, Krakow, Poland.

LUTS, OSKAR (HINDREKU poeg): author; *b*. Palamusel, Dec. 26, 1886; s. Hindrek and Leena Luts; educ. Realschule in Dorpat, Farmazeutische Abteilung zu Universitat Tartu; m. Valentina Krdertzkaga. AUTHOR: Kevade; Suvi; Tootsi pulm; Äripäev; Soo; Kirjad Maariale; Karavan; Harald tegutseb; Inderlin; Nukitsamees; Vähkmann ja Ko; Tulilill; Andresse elukäik; Kirjanapp; Iiling; Olga Nukrus; Ants Lintner; Opilane Valter; Vana Kübar; Pett ja Parbu; Udu; Pankrot; Vanad; Talvised teed; Läbi tuule ja vee. Plays: Laul Onnest (drama); Paunvere; Kapsapää; Arimehed; Pärijad; Mahäjaetud maja; Kalevi kojutulek; Soo-tuluke; Ulemiste teekond; Sinihallik; Viinne pidu; Onu paremad päevad; Arusaamata lugu; Skoudid; Valimised; Harald teotseb; Tootsi lood. General character of writing: novels, juveniles, plays. CLUBS: Eesti Kirjanikkude lisdu lüge. Relig. denom.: Lutheran. OFFICE: Noor-Eesti. HOME: Mäe 26, Tartu, Estonia.

LUYTEN, Willem Jacob, B.A., Ph.D. *b*: Semarang, E. Indies 1899. *e*: Amsterdam & Leiden Univs. *m*: Willemina Miedema. *d*: 1. Professor of Astronomy. *Publ*: The Pageant of the Stars. *c.t*: De Telegraaf (Amsterdam), Boston Globe, N.Y. Times, The Johannesburg Star, Bloemfontein Friend, Cape Argus, St Nicholas. *s.s*: Gen science, travel. *Rec*: Travel. *a*: University of Minnesota, Minneapolis, Minn, U.S.A.

LUTYENS, Mary. *b*: Lon 1908. *e*: Queen's Col Lon. *m*: Anthony Sewell. *Publ*: Forthcoming Marriages. *c.t*: Spectator. *a*: 54 Rutland Gate, S.W.7.

LUTYENS, Rev. William Enderby, M.A. *b*: London 1872. *e*: Sherborne & Camb. *m*: Muriel Langslow Chapman. Canon Emeritus Rochester. *Publ*: The Servant; The Dying Thief; Notes for Meditation; The Will to Love; Sons of God; God's way with a Soul; Walking with Christ; The Divine Guest; After His Likeness. *s.s*: Verse & Books of Devotional Life. *Rec*: Golf. *a*: Butlers Wood, Awbridge, Romsey, Hants.

LUTZ, Ralph Haswell, A.B., LL.D., Ph.D. *b*: Circleville, Ohio 1886. *e*: Stanford, Univs of Washington, Heidelberg, Southern California. *m*: Margaret Longyear. *d*: 3. Prof of History. *Publ*: Fall of the German Empire (2 Vols); The Organization of American Relief in Europe (collab); The Treaty of St Germain (collab); The German Revolution 1918—1919; etc. *Ctr*: Journ of Mod Hist, Amer Hist Review, etc. *s.s*: Modern Europe, World Wars I & II, Germany since 1914, Internat Relations. *a*: Arenas Rayandas, Comino de Oro, Twenty-nine Palms, California.

LUXFORD, John Hector. b : Palmerston North, New Zealand 1890. e : Primary State Sch, Wanganui Collegiate Sch, N.Z. Univ. m : Laura Dagmar Otton. s : 2. Barrister, Principal Stipendiary Magistrate Auckland. n.a : Cons Ed Magistrates Courts Decisions 1939—. Publ : With the Machine Gunners in France & Palestine ; Liquor Laws of New Zealand ; Police Law in New Zealand ; Real Estate Agency in New Zealand ; Commercial Law in New Zealand. s.s : Legal. Rec : Golf, bowls. w.s : Major N.Z.E.F. World War I (des). c : Northern Auckland. a : 35 Orakei Rd, Remuera, Auckland, New Zealand. T : 20404.

LVOFF, Mark. b : Russia 1867. e : Univ of St Petersburg. Engineer. Publ : The Eng Tech Dictionary (French-English & English-French). s.s : Tech trans. a : 88 Farringdon St, Lon, E.C.4.

LYALL, Archibald Laurence. B.A.(Oxon). b : Lon 1904. e : Winchester Col & New Col Oxf. Author. n.a : Asst Ed The Geographical Mag. Foreign Ed The Bridge Mag. Publ : The Balkan Road ('30) ; It Isn't Done ('30) ; A Guide to the Languages of Europe ; Envoy Extraordinary ; Russian Roundabout ('33) ; etc. c.t : News Chronicle, Spectator, Evening Standard, Daily Sketch, Listener, Architectural Review, etc. s.s : Europe. c : Oxf & Cam. a : 9 Queen's Gate Gdns, S.W.7. t : Western 4983.

LYALL, Leonard Arthur. b : Lon 1867. e : Bloxham. Mem Permanent Central Opium Bd Geneva. Publ : Sayings of Confucius (trans); Mencius (trans); China (The Modern World). s.s : China & Chinese lit. Mem Chinese Customs Service 1886–1927. c : Roy Inst of Internat Affairs. a : Queen Anne's Mansions, Flat 5 Centre, S.W.1. t : Victoria 5510.

LYBURN, Eric Frederick St. John, M.D., B.A. b : Dublin 1930 e : Trinity Coll Dublin. m : Margaret Heddon. Publ : Dr Futuer ; The Fighting Irish Doctor. s.s : Medical, Biog & Novels. Rec : Boxing, politics. a : Lyburn Clinic, Tunbridge Wells, Kent. T : 1706.

LYBYER, Albert Howe, A.M., Ph.D. b : Putnamville, Indiana 1876. e : Hgh Sch Brazil Indiana, Univs of Princeton & Harvard. m : Clara Sidney Andrews. Prof of Hist (Educator). n.a : Annual of World Book Ency 1933–46. Publ : The Government of the Ottoman Empire in the Time of Suleiman the Magnificent. s.s : Hist of Near East, Far East, Recent Internat Relations. Rec : Motoring, hiking, farm work. c : Harvard (East Illinois), etc. a : 808 South Lincoln Ave, Urbana, Illinois, U.S.A. T : 7-3743.

LYDALL, Cecil Wykeham French, M.A.(Cantab). b : Birmingham 1901. e : King Edward's Sch B'ham & Trinity Hall Camb. Schoolmaster. Publ : Practical Latin Grammar. s.s : Classics. a : 2 Carlton Rd, South Croydon, Surrey.

LYDE, Lionel William. b : Wigton 1863. e : Sedbergh Sc & Queen's Col Oxf. m : Elizabeth Gildea. s : 2. Teacher. Publ : Atlas of Economic Geography; Peninsular Europe; Continent of Europe; Continent of Asia; Patchwork from Pindar; etc. c.t : Times, Cornhill, Journal of Roy Geog Soc, Scot Geog Mag. etc. s.s : Geography. Headmaster Bolton G.S. Prof of Econ Geog in Univ Col Lon 1903–28. Emeritus Prof of Geog in Lon Univ. Hon Fell Roy Hungarian Acad of Science. a : Yew Garth, Sandhurst, Berks. t : Yateley 53.

LYDENBERG, Harry Miller, A.B., Litt.D., L.H.D. b : Dayton, Ohio 1874. e : Harvard Coll Cambridge Mass, New York Public Library, Columbia Univ, Yale. m :

Madeliene Rogers Day. s : 1. d : 1. Librarian, Mem N.Y. Hist Soc. Publ : History of the New York Public Library ; Life of John Shaw Billings ; The Care & Repair of Books (collab) ; (Ed) Archibald Robertson, Lieut Gen, Royal Engineers ; (Trans) On the Origin of Paper ; On the Origin of Printing & Engraving. s.s : Library & Bibliographical Periodicals, Library Hist & Book Art. Rec : Library work, gardening, walking. a : 118 East Avondale, Greensboro', North Carolina, U.S.A. T : Greensboro 3-4754.

LYELL, David. b : Angus 1866. e : Arbroath H.S. & Edin Univ. m : K. C. M. Briggs. s : 2. Civil Engineer & Coy Dir. c.t : Ency Brit. s.s : Mech science. War Service S. African & European. Rec Shooting. c : Authors', St Stephen's. a : Waterdale Hse, Garston, Herts. t : Garston (Watford) 101.

LYELL, Denis David. b : Calcutta 1871. e : Priv & Taunton Col. m : Marion Brown. Publ : Hunting Trips in Northern Rhodesia (1910) ; Wild Life in Central Africa ('13) ; Memories of an African Hunter ('23) ; The Hunting & Spoor of Central African Game ('29) ; African Adventure (Letters from Famous Big-Game Hunters) ; etc. c.t : Scotsman, Field, Game & Gun, East Africa. s.s : Nat history, sport at home & abroad. Medals for Boer & Gt Wars. Rec : Shooting, fishing. c : Shikar, Mem Brit Field Sports Soc. & Order of the Road. a : Rossdhal, Comrie, Perthshire. t : 1.

LYELL, James Patrick Ronaldson, J.P., B.Litt (Oxon). b : Hampstead 1871. e Merchant Taylors' Sc. Univ Col Lon & New Col Oxf. Solicitor. Publ : Cardinal Ximenes ; Early Book Illustration in Spain ; Mrs Piozzi & Isaac Watts ; A Fifteenth Century Bibliography ; etc. c.t : Literary World, Library, etc. s.s : Early Spanish lit & printing. Mem Hampstead Bench of Magistrates 25 y, Chm 12 y. Mem Cent Unemployed Body for Lon 23 y, Chm 1909. Chm Stoke Newington House Hosp for Women. Legal Adv to Presbyt C. of E. Pres Oxford Bibliographical Soc '35. Rec : Bibliography, fishing, golf. c : Savage, Sette of Odd Volumes, Mem Lon Bibliographical Soc, etc. a : Falkland, Boars Hill, Oxf. t : Boars Hill 3.

LYLE, Herbert Willoughby, M.D., B.S., F.R.C.S., F.Z.S., F.K.C. b : London 1870. e : King's Coll Sch, King's Coll Lond. m : Grace Kime. s : 2. d : 3. Cons Ophthalmic Surg to King's Coll Hosp. n.a : Ed The Practitioner 1906–09. Publ : Manual of Physiology (with D. de Scuza) ; King's & Some King's Men. Ctr : Practitioner's Ency, Med Times, etc. s.s : Med Educ. Rec : Lawn tennis, gardening. a : Fircliff, Portishead, Somerset. T : Portishead 3243.

LYLE, Thomas Keith, M.A., M.D., M.Chir.(Cantab). F.R.C.S.(Eng), M.R.C.P.(Lond), L.M.S.S.A.(Lond). b : Bromley 1903. e : Dulwich Coll, Sidney Sussex Coll Camb & King's Coll Hosp Lond. Ophth Surg King's Coll Hosp & Nat Hosp Queen Sq, Mem " Livery " of the Soc of Apothecaries of Lond. n.a : Treas King's Coll Hosp Gazette 1927–29. Publ : Practical Orthoptics, Ctr : Med Press & Circular, Annals of Surgery, B.M.J. etc. s.s : Ophth, Neurology. c : R.A.C., R.A.F., Bath. Rec : Tennis, squash. w.s : R.A.F.V.R. (Air Commodore). a : 42 Charles St, Berkeley Sq, London, W.1, & Fircliff, Portishead, Som. T : Grosvenor 2481.

LYLE, Watson. b : Scot. e : Priv & Public Sc. Author & Journalist. n.a : Music Crit Musical Standard 1917–32, Review of Reviews '21–22, Great Thoughts '32, Theatre World '30, etc. Publ : Camille Saint-Saëns: His Life and Art; Pastoral Moods and Impressions;

Singing Made Easy. *c.t*: Theatre World, Bookman, Nash's Mag, Homes & Gardens, Sunday Times, Daily Express, Exchange & Mart, etc. *s.s*: Contemp biog, music criticism, book reviews. Work in music analyses & criticism has been commended by Rachmaninoff, Pouishnoff, Myra Hess, Joseph Szigeti, Sir Granville Bantock, M. Arthur de Greef, etc. *Rec*: Pianoforte playing, gardening. *c*: Incorp Soc of Authors, Playwrights & Composers. *a*: The White Hse, Navestock, Brentwood.

LYMAN, George D., A.B. *b*: Virginia, Nevada 1882. *e*: Univs of Columbia & Stanford, Coll of Phys & Surgs. *m*: Dorothy L. Van Sicklen. *d*: 2. *Publ*: Care & Feeding of the Infant; John March: Pioneer; Saga at the Comstack; Ralston's Ring; The Book & the Doctor; Forward: A Doctor Comes to California; etc. *Rec*: Californiara. *c*: Bohemian, P.E.N. *a*: 3673 Jackson Street.

LYMBEY, Alf. F/L Sports Writer. *a*: Fairbourne, Alexandra Park, Nottingham.

LYMINGTON, Viscount G. V. W. *Publ*: Ich Dien; The Tory Path; Horn Hoof & Corn. *a*: 5a Dean's Yd, S.W.1.

LYNAM, Edward William O'Flaherty. D.Litt., M.R.I.A., F.S.A. *b*: London. *e*: Clongowes, & Queen's Coll (Cork), Roy Univ of Ireland & Lond Univ. *m*: s: 1. *d*: 1. Superintendent of Map Room & Asst Keeper Brit Museum. *n.a*: Mem of Edit Board The American Neptune. *Publ*: The First Engraved Atlas of the World; British Maps & Map Makers; Period Ornament Writing & Symbols on Maps 1250—1500; The Map of the British Isles of 1546; The Character of England in Maps; Richard Hakluyt & his Successors; etc. *Ctr*: Times, Times Lit Supp, Observer, Spectator, Tablet, Geog Journ, Geog Magazine, Library, Cornhill, etc *s.s*: Historical Geog, Scandinavian Lit & Langs, Hist of Exploration. *w.s*: Capt R.I. Regt 1914—19, Home Guard '41—43. *a*: 62 Shepherd's Hill, Highgate, London, N.6. *t*: Mountview 6904.

LYNCH, Albert John, J.P. *b*: Enfield 1872. *e*: Westminster Col. *m*: Jessie Dora Kale. *s*: 2. Headmaster. *Publ*: Individual Work & the Dalton Plan; The Rise & Progress of the Dalton Plan, Part Author:—The Case for Nursery Schools; The Next Step in Education. *c.t*: Schoolmaster, Schoolmistress, Teachers World, The New Era, The Sentinel Newspaper. *s.s*: Educ, social studies. Lect on Educ in U.K., France, Germany, Scandinavia, Holland, Poland, Finland, Estonia & S. Africa. *Rec*: Reading, music. *a*: 104 Downhills Pk Rd, N.17. *t*: Bowes Park 2867.

LYNCH, Patricia. *b*: Cork 1898. *e*: Convent Schs Ireland, England & Belgium. *m*: Richard Michael Fox. Writer, Mem of P.E.N. (Dublin). *Publ*: The Turf Cutters Donkey; Donkey Goes Visiting; The Cobbler's Apprentice; The Green Dragon; A Storyteller's Childhood; Knights of God; King of the Tinkers; The Grey Goose of Kilnevin; Strangers at the Fair; Fiddlers Quest; Long Ears; etc. *Rec*: Reading, travel, gardening. *c*: Irish Women Writers. *a*: 39 The Rise, Griffith Ave, Dublin.

LYNCH, Stanislaus. *b*: Ballyjamesduff, Co Cavan. *e*: Castleknock Coll Dublin. Writer. *Publ*: Rhymes of an Irish Huntsman; Echoes of the Hunting Horn; Life Sketch of an Irish Hunter. *Ctr*: Field, Riding, Horse & Hound, Country Life, Field Sports, Town & Country, Irish Field, etc. *s.s*: Hunting, Riding, Show Jumping, Fox-Hounds. *Rec*: Hunting & everything connected with it. *c*: P.E.N., Soc of Authors, Sth County Dublin Harriers Hunt. *a*: Dunedin, 9 St Helen's Rd, Booterstown, Co Dublin, Ireland.

LYND, Robert W. *b*: Belfast 1879. *e*: Roy Acad Inst & Queen's Col Belfast. *m*: Sylvia Dryhurst. *d*: 2. Journalist & Author. *n.a*: Lit Ed News Chron. *Publ*: The Pleasures of Ignorance; The Blue Lion; Books & Authors; Ireland a Nation; The Cockleshell; The Art of Letters. *c.t*: New Statesman, John o' London's. *a*: 5 Keats Gve, N.W.3.

LYND, Sylvia. *b*: Hampstead. *e*: King Alfred's Sch. *m*: Robert Lynd. *d*: 2. Writer. *Publ*: The Chorus; The Thrush & the Jay; The Goldfinches (Poems); The Swallow Dive; The Mulberry Bush; The Yellow Placard (Poems); The Enemies; English Children (Britain in Pictures Series); Collected Poems. *Ctr*: News Chron, Sun Times, Observer, Nation & New Statesman, Time & Tide, etc. *s.s*: Books. *a*: 5 Keat's Grove, Hampstead, London, N.W.3. *T*: 0850.

LYNDE, Carleton John, B.A., Ph.D. *b*: Mitchell, Ontario, Canada 1872. *e*: Univs of Toronto, Chicago, Berlin & Heidelberg. *m*: (1) Helen Eldred Storke (dec'd), (2) Katharine Koon Truxell. *s*: 1. Prof of Physics. *Publ*: Science Experiments with—Home Equipment; Ten Cent Store Equipment; Inexpensive Equipment; Physics of the Household; Everyday Physics; Glass Blowing for Boys; Hydraulic & Pneumatic Engineering for Boys; Light Experiments for Boys. *s.s*: Books on Science. *c*: Men's Faculty (Columbia). *a*: 114 Morningside Drive, New York 27, N.Y., U.S.A. *T*: Cathedral 8-8280.

LYNDOE, Edward. *c.t*: The People. *a*: 93 Long Acre, W.C.2, & BM/Lyndoe, Lon, W.C.1.

LYNDON, Barre. *b*: Lon 1896. Author & Journalist. *Publ*: Speed Fever (1930); Combat; Circuit Dust ('34). *c.t*: Leading Brit & Amer Mags. *s.s*: Motor Racing. *Rec*: Boxing. *c*: Brooklands Auto Racing. *a*: 13 Old Sq, Lincoln's Inn, W.C.2. *t*: Holborn 1648.

LYNDON, Rev. Edwin Israel. *b*: Wednesbury 1865. *e*: Wesleyan Day School & Richmond Col. *m*: Edith Ellen Hugill. *Publ*: Prophetic Spokesmen, or Studies in the Twelve Minor Prophets; The Ministry of the Mountains, & other Sketches (Nature Studies); The Foundations of Sapphires and Other Addresses. *c.t*: Meth & other n/ps & mags. *s.s*: Nature & foreign travel. Foreign Missny Sec in Newcastle-on-Tyne Wes Dis. Pres F.C.C. Derby '26—27. *Rec*: Walking. *a*: Mayfield, Marlboro', Wilts.

LYNE, Peter. *b*: Faversham 1905. *e*: Aldenham Sc & Clare Col Cam. *m*: Heather Braithwaite. *s*: 1. *d*: 2. *n.a*: Lon Staff Corr Christian Science Monitor '29. *Rec*: Golf, squash, gardening. *c*: Thames Hse, Assoc of American Corr's in Lon, Roy St David's Golf. *a*: 71 Dunstan Rd, Golder's Green, N.W.11. *t*: Speedwell 6911.

LYNE, Robert Nunez, F.L.S., F.R.G.S. *b*: Paignton, Devon 1864. *e*: Bloxham & Univ of New Zealand. *m*: Hilda Bailey. *s*: 1. Late Dir Agriculture Zanzibar services lent by British Govt. *n.a*: Ed Zanzibar, Gazette 1912—15 & Tropical Agriculturist '12—17. *Publ*: Zanzibar in Contemporary Times; An Apostle of Empire; Mozambique, its Agricultural Development; Four Bishops; The Church of St Peter-in-the-East, Oxford. *Ctr*: Empire Rev, Journ of Roy African Soc. *s.s*: Tropical Agriculture, Travel, Biography, Religion, Science. *Rec*: Astronomy, chess, writing, boat-sailing. *a*: 5 Beaufort East, Bath.

LYNE, Rear-Adm. Sir Thomas John Spence, K.C.V.O., C.B., D.S.O. *b*: 1870. *e*: Beers Sch Devon. *m*: Ethel Louise Stobbart. *d*: 1. R.N. (ret), Entered Navy as boy 1885, First ranker in modern times to reach rank of Captain (1918), Commanded Central Reserves & Impregnable Boys Training Establishment, Rear-Adm (ret) '31. *Publ*: Something about a Sailor ; Notes on the Navigation of the Han Kiang, China. *Ctr*: Various, *a*: Hamilton Hse. Wolverstone, Ipswich, Suffolk.

LYNHAM, JOHN E. A.: physician, radiologist; *b*. 1882; *s.* Prof. J. I. Lynham (M.D.); *educ*. Queen's Colleges, Galway, Belfast; St. Bartholemew's Hosp., Middlesex Hosp. (both London). DEGREES: B.A., M.B., B.Ch., B.A.O., R.U.I., M.D. (all Belfast), M.R.C.P. (London), D.M.R.E. (Cambridge); *m*. Harriet Maud Hopkins, Dec. 1912. Contributor to many Medical Journals, chiefly on Radiological aspects of Tuberculosis, treatment of Cancer and other diseases by Radium and X-Rays. General character of writing: medical. Past-pres. Electro-Therapeutic section, Roy. Soc. of Med. OFFICE: 14A Upper Wimpole St., London, W. 1, Eng.

LYNN, Escott. *m*: Alice Lilian Pope. *s*: 1. *d*: 4. *Publ*: Blair of Balaclava ; When Lion Heart was King ; Under the Red Rose ; For Bonnie Prince Charlie ; Oliver Hastings, V.C.; Knights of the Air ; Lads of the Lothians ; Comrades Ever ; Stirring Days in Old Virginia ; Three Dashing Subalterns ; Fortune's Vassal ; Under the Golden Dragon ; The Red Spears of Honan ; etc. *Ctr*: Mags & Service Papers, etc. *s.s*: Brit Regimental Hist. *Rec*: Tennis, golf. *a*: 25 Rosemont Rd, London, W.3.

"L Y N X" (pseudonym): see Angermayer, Fred Antoine.

LYON, C. *a*: Craiglea, 6 Tanat Drive, Mossley Hill, Liverpool, 18.

LYON, David Murray, M.D., D.Sc, F.R.C.P.E. Prof of Clinical Med & Therapeutics. *c.t*: Med Journals. *a*: Univ. Edin.

LYON, E. Wilson, B.A., LL.D., Litt.B., Ph.D. *b*: Heidelberg, Mississippi 1904. *e*: Mississippi, Chicago & Colgate Univs, St John's Coll Oxf. *m*: Carolyn Bartel Lyon. *s*: 1. *d*: 1. College Pres. *n.a*: Bd Eds, Journ of Mod Hist 1943—46, Adv Bd Pacific Spectator '46—. *Publ*: Louisiana in French Diplomacy 1759—1804 ; The Men Who Sold Louisiana ; The Life of François Barbe Marbois. *Ctr*: Journ of Mod Hist, Amer Hist Rev. *s.s*: Higher Educ, Hist of Franco-American Relations, Modern French Hist. *Rec*: Gardening. *c*: California, Univ (Los Angeles). *a*: 345, College Ave, Claremont, California, U.S.A. *T*: Claremont 3061.

LYON, Francis Hamilton, M.B.E. *b*: Laleham 1885. *e*: Winchester & Oxf. *m*: Cecilia Margerison. *s*: 1. *d*: 2. Journalist & Writer. *n.a*: Staff Morning Post 1908—15 & '19—24, Spec Corr in Northern Europe '19 —24, Financial News Sub-Ed '29—33 & '37—39, Financial Times News Ed '33—36. *Publ*: Translations from German, Swedish, Danish, French & Russian. *Ctr*: Times, etc. *s.s*: Entomology, Shipping. *c*: Athenæum, M.C.C. *w.s*: 1915—19 (des) & '40—47. *a*: c/o Westminster Bank, 263 Strand, London, W.C.2.

LYON, Leverett Samuel. *b*: Sollitt, Illinois 1885. *e*: Chicago-Kent Coll, Univ of Chicago. *m*: Lucille Norton. *s*: 2. Chief Exec Officer Chicago Assoc of Commerce & Industry. *Publ*: The National Recovery Administration ; Government & Economic Life ; Making a Living ; Our Economic Organisation ; Hand to Mouth Buying ; Education for Business ; Salesmen in Marketing Strategy ; Economics of Our Price Systems ; The Economics of Free Deals ; Advertising Allowances ; Elements of Debating ; Vocational Readings ; etc. *Ctr*: American Econ Rev, Journ of Polit Econ, etc. *c*: Chevy Chase (Wash), etc. *a*: Chicago Assoc of Commerce & Industry, 1 North La Salle St, Chicago 2, Illinois, U.S.A. *T*: Franklin 7700.

LYON, M. D. *Publ*: Cricket. *a*: c/o Eyre & Spottiswoode Ltd, 6 Gt New St, E.C.4.

LYON, Percy Hugh Beverley, M.C. *b*: Darjeeling, India 1893. *e*: Rugby & Oriel Coll Oxf. *m*: Nancy Elinor Richardson. *d*: 3. Schoolmaster. *Publ*: Songs of Youth & War ; Turn Fortune ; The Discovery of Poetry ; (Ed) The Shorter Herodotus ; The Merchant of Venice. *c*: United Univs. *a*: Wester Ogil, Headington Hill, Oxford. *T*: Oxford 6910.

LYON, Thomas Matthew, F.J.I. *m*: Nan Banks. *n.a*: Ed Kilmarnock Standard. *Publ*: In Kilt & Khaki ; More Adventures in Kilt & Khaki. *s.s*: Dogs. *a*: Deanbank, Beansburn, Kilmarnock. *T*: 796.

LYONS, Henry George, F.R.S. *b*: Lon 1864. *e*: Wellington Coll & R.M.A. Woolwich. *m*: Helen Julia Hardwick. *s*: 1. *d*: 1. *Publ*: The Island & Temples of Philce; The Physiography of the Nile Basin; The Cadastral Surveys of Egypt; etc. *c*: Athenæum. Gov Imperial Coll of Science & Industry. *a*: 3 York Terr, Regent's Pk, N.W.1. *t*: Welbeck 4776.

LYONS, Ronald Samuel. *b*: London 1904. Publicity Manager Newnes-Pearson Publs. *n.a*: Asst-Ed The Scout 1924—25, Sub-Ed Pearson's Weekly '25—29, Comp-Ed C. Arthur Pearson Ltd. '30—32. *Publ*: Several Juvenile Books for Boys & Girls. *s.s*: Juvenile Fiction, Motoring & Sports Topics. *w.s*: P.R.O. to R.A.F. (Italy) World War II. *a*: Two Meadway, Gidea Pk, Essex. *T*: Romford 1777.

LYSTER, Robert Arthur, M.D., Ch.B., B.Sc., D.P.H. *b*: Aston Manor. *e*: King Edward's Gr Sch, Queen's Coll Birmingham, Birmingham Univ, London Univ, St Bart's Hosp. *Publ*: First Stage Hygiene ; Second Stage Hygiene ; School Hygiene ; School Reader on Hygiene. *Ctr*: Various articles on Public Health, Venereal Disease Prevention, etc. *s.s*: Public Health, Sanitary Science, Venereal Disease Prevention, School Hygiene, Health Administration, Legal Medicine. *Rec*: Travelling. *a*: 33 Methuen Rd, Bournemouth, Hants. *T*: Boscombe 64.

LYTTELTON, The Hon. Mrs. Alfred (Edith), G.B.E. *m*: Rt Hon Alfred Lyttelton (dec'd). *s*: 1. *d*: 1. *Publ*: The Faculty of Communion ; Our Superconscious Mind ; Some Cases of Prediction ; Memoir of Alfred Lyttelton ; Literary & Travel Articles, Plays, etc. *Ctr*: Times, Nat Rev, etc. *s.s*: Internat Politics. *Rec*: Reading, travel. *a*: 18 Great College St, Westminster, London, S.W.1.

LYTTELTON, Rev. Edward, Hon Canon of Norwich, M.A., D.D., D.C.L. *b*: Lon 1855. *e*: Eton, Trin Col Cam. *m*: Caroline Amy West. *d*: 2. *Publ*: Mothers & Sons; Memories & Hopes; Whither; etc. *c.t*: Hibbert Journ, Contemporary Review, Quarterly Review, Edinburgh Review, etc. *s.s*: Religious educ, cricket. Headmaster Haileybury '90–1905. Headmaster Eton '05-16. Dean Whiteland's Col '20-28. *Rec*: Music. *a*: Grange Gornan, Overstrand, Cromer. *t*: Overstrand 40.

LYTTON, Earl of (Victor Alexander George Robert), K.G., P.C., G.C.S.I., G.C.I.E. *b*: Simla 1876. *e*: Eton & Trinity Col Cam. *m*: Pamela Chichele-Plowden. *s*: 1. *d*: 2. *Publ*: The Life of Edward Bulwer 1st Lord Lytton. *s.s*: Education & psychology. Priv Sec to Rt Hon George Wyndham in Ireland; Civil Lord of the Admiralty; Under-Sec of State for India; Gov of Bengal; Viceroy & Acting Gov-Gen of India, Del 7th, 8th & 11th Assemblies League of Nations Commission of Enquiry in Far East. *c*: Athenæum & Carlton. *a*: Knebworth House, Knebworth, Herts, & 10 Buckingham St, S.W.1 *t*: Knebworth 10 & Victoria 4020.

LYTTON, Sir Henry. Knight. Actor. *Publ*: Secrets of a Savoyard; Wandering Minstrel; Knights of the Road; 60 short stories & articles. *a*: 54 Barkston Gardens, S.W.5. *t*: Frobisher 0985.

LYTTON SELLS, Arthur. *b*: Edgbaston 1895. *e*: Univs of Camb & Paris. *m*: Iris Esther Robertson. *s*: 1. Prof Durham Univ. *Publ*: Les Sources Francaises de Goldsmith; The Early Life of J. J. Rousseau; Earth of the Tarentines. *Ctr*: Mod Lang Review, French Studies, Durham Univ Journ, etc. *s.s*: French, English, Greek & Italian Lit, Comparative Lit. *Rec*: Travel, nat hist. *c*: Overseas. *a*: Dunster Hse Durham. *T*: 525.

"**M. A. C.**" (pen name): see Macfadden, Dugald.

M. H. S. (pen name): see Spielmann, Marion Harry.

MA, YIN CH'U: teaching and banking; b. Chehkiang, 1882; s. Ching Ch'ang Ma and Chiu Nien (Wang) M.; educ. Anglo-Chinese Coll. (Shanghai); Pei-Yang Univ.; Yale and Columbia universities; DEGREES: B.A. (Yale); Ph.D. (Columbia); m. Mary Chang. AUTHOR: The Finances of the City of New York, 1914; Economic Lectures (vol. 1), 1924; vol. 2, 1925, vol. 3, 1926, vol. 4, 1928; A Treatise on Chinese Banking, 1929. Contributor to Peking Morning Post, Shanghai China Times, The Sun Pao in Shanghai; magazines: Eastern Miscellany, Commercial World (Shanghai), Bankers' Mag. (Peking and Shanghai); Chinese Economic Monthly; Chinese Weekly Economic Bulletin. General character of writing: popular lectures; scientific books. Former lecturer at schools, universities, business associations, government dept., and others on current economic topics; mem. legislative Yuan. OFFICE: Legislative Yuan, Nanking, or Economics Department, Central University, Nanking. HOME: KaiB Kai-Yuan Road, Hangchow, China.

MAAS, William Harold. *m*: Winifred Mary Bridger. *d*: 1. Journalist. *n.a*: Served under Lord Northcliffe, C. Arthur Pearson Ltd, Dly Express, Ed Black & White Budget, Dly Chronicle 1906, Fiction Ed, Feature Ed, Lit Ed, Asst Ed, Ed The Winner '31—, London Ed Provincial Newsps '37. *Ctr*: Punch, etc. *a*: c/o Barclay's Bank Ltd, Piccadilly Circus, London, W.1.

MABANE, William, M.A. *b*: Leeds 1895. *e*: Woodhouse Grove & Caius Coll Camb. *Journ*, Politician, Company Director, Dir Kemsley Newspapers Ltd. *n.a*: Political Correspondence Sun Ref 1932, Warden of Univ Settlement L'pool '20—23, M.P. (L) Huddersfield '31—45, Asst Post Master Gen '39, Parl Sec Min of Home Security '39—42, Parl Sec Min of Food '42—45, Min of State Foreign Office since '45. *Ctr*: Sun Ref, Yorkshire Post, Sydney Sun, Week-end Review, etc. *s.s*: Eonomics, Politics, History. *Rec*: Travel. *c*: Nat Liberal. *a*: South Hill, South Ridge, St George's Hill, Weybridge. *T*: Weybridge 3168; & 36 Lands Lane, Leeds. *T*: 30181.

MABERLY, Alan, M.A., M.B., B.Ch., M.R.C.S., L.R.C.P. Author of Commonsense & Psychology & contributor of articles on Psychology to the medical press. *a*: 3 Devonshire Pl, London, W.1. *T*: Welbeck 3637.

MABY, Joseph Cecil, B.Sc.(London), A.R.C.S., F.R.A.S, *b*: Maritzburg, Natal, S.A. 1902. *e*: Priory Sch Gt Malvern, Cheltenham Coll, Imperial Coll of Science, London Univ. *m*: Adelaide Louise Brownlie. *s*: 2. Author, Artist & Scientist, Demonstrator Sch of Forestry Oxford & Research Asst Forest Products Research Laboratory D.S.I.R. 1926—30, Technical Adviser to Natural Therapy Inst London '34, Mem Royal Astronomical Soc, Soc for Psychical Research, Investigation Ctte Brit Soc Dowsers '36—46, Counc Inst Exper Metaphysics Lond '45—. *Publ*: Walls of Jericho; By Stygian Waters; The Physics of the Divining Rod. *Ctr*: Allen's Commercial Organic Analysis, The Gloucestershire Echo, The Analyst, Oxford Univ Forestry Jnl, Oxford Mail, The Listener, Antiquity, Jnl of British Astronomical Assoc. *s.s*: Wood Identification, Photo-micrography, Electrical Apparatus for Bio-Physical Research. *Rec*: Music, painting, gardening.

MACADAM, Elizabeth, M.A. *b*: Scotland 1871. *e*: Canada & Dresden. Writer on social questions. *n.a*: Jt Ed Woman's Leader 1921—31. *Publ*: The Equipment of the Social Worker. *a*: 50 Romney St, S.W.1. *t*: Victoria 9550.

MACADAM, John. *n.a*: Chief Sports Columnist Daily Express. *Publ*: The Reluctant Erk; Minus the Man from Cooks; Air Aces (with Gordon Anthony). *a*: Daily Express, Fleet St, London, E.C.4. *T*: Central 8000.

MACAFEE, Charles Horner Greer, M.B., B.Ch., F.R.C.S. F.R.C.O.G. *b*: Omagh, Co Tyrone 1898. *e*: Omagh Acad, Foyle Coll Londonderry, Queen's Univ Belfast. *m*: Margaret Crymble Lowry. *s*: 2. *d*: 1. Prof of Midwifery & Gynæcology Queen's Univ Belfast, Surg Roy Maternity Hosp Belfast 1945—. *Ctr*: Ulster Med Journ, Journ of Obstetrics & Gynæcology, Whitla's Dict of Treatment & various newsps & periodicals. *s.s*: Midwifery & Gynæcology. *Rec*: Golf & yachting. *c*: Union (Belfast), Roy Belfast Golf, etc. *a*: 18 University Sq. Belfast. *T*: 23024.

MACALISTER, Robert Alexander Stewart, Litt.D., F.S.A. *b*: Dublin 1870. *e*: Rathmines Sch Dublin, private study in Germany, Camb Univ. Prof (ret) of Celtic Archæology Univ Coll Dublin. *Publ*: The Excavation of Gezer; The Philistines, their History & Civilisation; A Century of Excavation in Palestine; Report on the Excavation of the Hill of Ophal, Jerusalem; The Language Smiths of Palestine; The Archæology of Ireland; etc. *a*: Barrmore, Lady Margaret Rd, Cambridge. *T*: Cambridge 2512.

MACALISTER-BREW, Josephine, M.A., LL.D. *e*: Univs Wales, Lond & Heidelberg. Lecturer & Broadcaster. *Publ*: In the Service of Youth; Informal Information; To Start You Talking (pt author); Young People in Public Houses; etc. *Ctr*: Times Educ Supp, Further Educ, Journ of Educ, New Era, Star, S. Express, etc. *s.s*: Adolescence, Juvenile Delinquency, Informal Educ. *Rec*: Sewing, film & theatre. *a*: 5 Grafton Chmbrs, Churchway, London, N.W.1. *T*: Euston 3124.

MACALISTER of TARBERT, Lady Edith F. B. Former J.P., Medaille de la Reine Elizabeth (Belgium). *Publ*: Uncle Hal; Fairy Ground; Misdeeds of Maria; Life of Sir Donald Macalister of Tarbert. *Ctr*: Glasgow Dly Record & Mail. *a*: Barrmore, Cambridge. *T*: Cambridge 2512.

MACALPINE, James Barlow, D.Sc., F.R.C.S. *b*: Accrington 1882. *e*: Mill Hill Sch, Vic Univ Manch, Lond Hosp & Vienna. *m*: Doris Agnes Jones. *s*: 2. *d*: 2. *Publ*: Cystoscopy & Urography. *Ctr*: Surgery of Modern Warfare, Textbook of Genito Urinary Surgery, Brit Surg Practice, Brit Journ of Surg, Brit Journ of Urology, Brit Med Journ, Lancet, Practitioner, Post Graduate Med Journ. *s.s*: Urological Surgery. *Rec*: Golf, billiards, music. *c*: Union & Clarendon (Manch). *a*: Michael's Nook, Grasmere, Westmorland. *T*: Grasmere 135.

MACAN, Reginald Walter, D.Litt(Oxon), Hon LittD.(Dublin), F.R.S.L. *Publ*: The Resurrection of Jesus Christ; The Fourth, Fifth and Sixth Books of Herodotus (2 vols); The Seventh, Eighth and Ninth Books of Herodotus (3 vols); etc. *a*: Broom Hill Hse, nr Oxford.

"**MacAOIDH**" (pen name): see Mackie, Albert David.

MACARDLE, Donald Frederick. *b*: Dundalk, Eire. *e*: Cheltenham Coll (Preparatory), Oratory Sch (Edgbaston). *m*: Enid Valnette Morgan. Scenario Ed Brit & Dominions Film Corp 1931—32. *Publ*: Thursday's Child (filmed 1942) Tansy. *Ctr*: Brittania & Eve, Woman's Mag, Woman's Own, Woman's Sphere, etc. *a*: 1 Airlie Gdns, Kensington, London, W.8. *T*: Park 6543.

MACARDLE, Dorothea Marguerita Callan, B.A. *b*: Dundalk, Ireland 1889. *e*: Alexandra Coll Dublin & Nat Univ of Ireland. Writer & Broadcaster. *Publ*:

The Irish Republic; Uneasy Freehold; The Seed was Kind; Fantastic Summer. Plays, Abbey & Dublin Gate Theatres. *Ctr*: The Irish Press, Theatre Arts Monthly, etc. *Rec*: Travel, motoring, playing with children. *w.s*: Broadcasts on Children of Europe, Lect Save the Children Fund 1947. *a*: Creevagh, Dundrum Rd, Dublin. *T*: 97045; 16 Bedford Gdns Hse, London, W.8.

MACARTHUR, Bessie J. B., L.R.A.M. *b*: Duns 1889. *e*: Charlotte Sq Inst, St George's Edin. *m*: J. C. C. MacArthur. *s*: 3. *d*: 1. *Publ*: Clan of Lochlann; The Starry Venture; Scots Poems; Last Leave; etc. *Ctr*: Various newspapers & periodicals. *Rec*: Music, Gaelic. *c*: P.E.N. *a*: Nunnerie, Elvanfoot,, Lanarks. *T*: 24.

MACARTHUR, David Wilson, M.A. *b*: Glasgow 1903. *e*: Ayr Acad, Glas Univ. *m*: Joan Payton. *Publ* (Travel); The River Windrush; The River Fowey; The Road to Benghazi; Auto Nomad in Sweden; Auto Nomad in Barbary; Auto Nomad in East Africa; Hudson's Bay Adventure; (Novels) Yellow Stockings; Lola of the Isles; Mystery of the David M; Landfall; Quest of the Stormalong; They Sailed for Senegal; Convict Captain; (other books) The Royal Navy; North Patrol; Carlyle in Old Age; East India Adventure; The Young Chevalier; also over 500 short stories. *Ctr*: Nearly 2,000 newspaper & magazine articles. *s.s*: North, East & South Africa, Canada, Faroe Islands, Naval, Archery, etc. *Rec*: Unorthodox travel, study of big game & wild life generally. *a*: c/o Nat Bank of Scotland, Gourock, Renfrewshire,; c/o Standard Bank of Sth Africa, Durban, Natal.

MACARTNEY, Carlile Aylmer, M.A., Foreign Mem Hungarian Acad of Science. *e*: Winchester, Trin Coll Camb. *m*: Nedella Mamarchev. Fell All Souls Coll Oxf, For Off Research Dept 1939—46. *Publ*: The Social Revolution in Austria; The Magyars in the IXth Century; Hungary (Modern World Series); Nat States & National Minorities; Hungary & her Successors; Problems of the Danube Basin; Studies in the Earliest Hungarian sources. *Ctr*: Ency Brit, Chambers's Ency, various Brit & Cent European periodicals. *s.s*: History & Conditions of Central Europe, Problems of Nationality & National Minorities. *Rec*: Travel. *w.s*: World War I 1914—19. *a*: Hornbeams, Boar's Hill, nr Oxford. *T*: Ox 35224; All Souls' Coll Oxf.

MACARTNEY, Frederick Thomas Bennett. *b*: Melbourne, Australia 1887. *e*: State Sch. Poet & Critic. *n.a*: Ed Birth 1919—20. *Publ*: (Poetry) Something for Tokens; A Sweep of Lutestrings; Hard Light; Ode of Our Time; Gaily the Troubadour; Tripod for Homeward Incense. *Ctr*: Sydney Bulletin, Meanjin, Southerly, etc. *s.s*: Australian Lit. *Rec*: Music, handcrafts. *c*: P.E.N. *a*: 66 Stanley St, Black Rock, Victoria, Australia. *T*: XW2183.

MACARTNEY, James Edward. *b*: Kalgoorlie 1911. *e*: Hale Sch Perth. *m*: Margaret Bessell-Brown. *s*: 1. *d*: 3. Journalist. *n.a*: Rep Staff West Australian 1929, Ed Broadcaster '34, Mang Ed Dly News '36. *a*: c/o Daily News, Perth, Western Australia. *T*: B5178.

MACASKIE, George Keith Cunningham. *b*: Harrogate 1900. *e*: Shrewsbury Sc. N/p Proprietor. *c*: Jun Carlton. *a*: The Hereford Times Ltd, Hereford. *t*: 2551.

MACASKIE, John Arthur. *b*: York 1909. *e*: Warwick Sch Warwick. Journalist, Mem of N.U.J. *n.a*: Rep Yorks Ev News Leeds 1927, Dep Chief Rep Yorks Ev News '34, Dist News Ed Yorks Ev News '46. *s.s*: Railways. *Rec*: Golf, walking. *c*: Old Warwickian. *a*: Primrose Ville, Horsforth, Leeds. *T*: 702-2578.

MACASKIE, N. L., K.C. Recorder of York *a*: 5 Paper Buildings, Temple, E.C.4, & Maylord Street, Hereford.

MACAULAY, Rev. Alexander Beith, D.D. *b*: Irvine, Ayrshire 1871. *e*: Univs of Edinburgh, Frieburgh, Berlin, New Coll Edin. *m*: Mary Elizabeth Howden. *s*: 2. *d*: 6. Prof (ret) of Theology Trin Coll Glas. *Publ*: The Death of Jesus; The Word of The Cross; Up Against It; The Vulgate Psalter; Jt Trans of the Works of Ritschl & Schliermacher. *s.s*: Dogmatic Theology. *Rec*: Golf, fishing. *a*: 3 Corrennie Drive, Edinburgh 10. *T*: 53676.

MACAULAY, Frederick Robertson, M.A., LL.B., Ph.D. *b*: Montreal, Canada 1882. *m*: Beulah Ines Stearns. *d*: 2. Economist. *Publ*: Some Theoretical Problems; The Smoothing of Time (series). *Ctr*: Numerous. *s.s*: Forecasting of Business Conditions & Security Prices. *a*: 11 Clover Drive, Great Neck, N.Y.

MACAULAY, Francis Sowerby, M.A., D.Sc, F.R.S. *s.s*: Algebra, geometry. *a*: 7 Cranmer Rd, Cam.

MACAULAY, Dr. H. M. C. Middlesex Guildhall, Westminster, S.W.1.

MACAULAY, Rose. Author of many novels inc Life Among the English; They Went to Portugal; The Writings of E. M. Forster; Keeping Up Appearances; Staying With Relations; Some Religious Elements in English Literature; Crewe Train; etc. *a*: 20 Hinde Hse, Hinde St, London, W.1.

MACAULAY, W. H. *a*: Walton House, Clent, Stourbridge.

MACAULEY (Edward), Thurston (Bancroft). *b*: Ohio, U.S.A. 1901. *e*: Asheville, N.C., U.S.A. & Trin Col Hartford U.S.A. *m*: Francie Marion Berry. *d*: 1. Journalist & Author. *n.a*: Editorial Staffs, Yonkers Statesman Yonkers N.Y. U.S.A. '22, Baltimore Sun Maryland U.S.A. '23, N.Y. Evening Sun '23–24, N.Y. Herald, Paris '27–28, N.Y. Times '28–29, N.Y. Times Lon Staff '29–. Theatrical press rep & F/L. writer N.Y. '25–26. *Publ*: Donn Byrne: Bard of Armagh ('29); The Festive Board ('31). *c.t*: N.Y. Times, Forum, N. American Review, New Republic, Nation, Living Age, U.S.A. Aviation, sea. *Rec*: Trav, theatres, tennis. *a*: 78 Church St, Chelsea, S.W.3. *t*: Flaxman 9094.

MACBEATH, Rev. John, M.A. *b*: Edin. *e*: Warrender Pk Sc, Heriot-Watt Col Edin, Glas Univ. *m*: Margaret Mackenzie. Clergyman. *Publ*: The Hills of God; The Face of Christ; The Circle of Time; What is His Name?; Roadmakers & Roadmenders; Lamps & Lamplighters; etc. *a*: Various. Lecturer in Homiletics & Pastoral Theology, Scottish Baptist Theo Col, Glas. Pres Baptist Union of Scotland 1934–35. *a*: 24 Lilybank Gdns, Glas, W.2. *t*: W 4016.

MACBRIDE, Ernest William. M.A., D.Sc, LL.D., F.R.S. Prof of Zoology Univ Lon. *Publ*: Textbook of Invertebrate Embryology; Life of Huxley; etc. *c.t*: Nature, Discovery, etc. *a*: West Bank, Alton, Hants. *t*: 97.

MACBRIDE, Henry John. *b*: Glas 1893. *e*: Glas H.S. & Glas Univ. *m*: Jean Alexandra Orr. Physician. *n.a*: Revue Neurologique Lon Corr 1923–27. *c.t*: Journ of Neurol & Psycho-pathology. *s.s*: Neurology. Hon Sec of Students Union Glas Univ. *Rec*: Golf. *a*: 79 Harley St, W.1. *t*: Welbeck 74761.

MACBRIDE, Lionel Murray. *b*: Lon 1902. *e*: St Paul's Sc. *m*: Kathleen Mary Hogg. *d*: 1. Journalist. *n.a*: Reporter Daily Express '21, Asst News Ed '27, News Ed Daily Herald '30, Foreign Ed '31–. *a*: Daily Herald Offices, 12 Wilson St, Long Acre, W.C.2. *t*: Temple Bar 7788.

MacCABE, Frederick Faber. b: Waterford 1868. e: Downside & Univ of Dublin. m: Mary Pauline Sheehy. s: 2. d: 1. n.a: Founded & Edited for some years Irish Field & Irish Horse (1934). Publ: Human Life; War with Disease; Horse Mastership; A Living Machine. Ctr: Various. s.s: Preventive Medicine for Man & Animals. Rec: Racing, lawn tennis, natural history. w.s: Served in Sth African War, Brevet Lt-Col R.A.M.C. 1914—18. a: Oreen Sandycove, Co Dublin, Ireland. T: Dublin 81374.

MACCALL, Seamus (Farry Owen). M.C., F.R.S.A. b: 1892. e: Ireland & England, Univ, America. m: Catherine Morris. s: 2 d: 1. Writer. n.a: Ass Ed Eire '23. Ed Garda Review '28—31. Art Ed Irish Press '31. Irish Commentator to Sunday Dispatch '32. Publ: And So Began the Irish Nation; Gods in Motley (novel); The Story of Our Nation; The Perjury of Kings (historical fantasy); Melody Moore (biography). c.t: Sunday Independent, Dly Express (Irish Edition), Sunday Dispatch, Irish Times, Irish Press. s.s: Cultural commentaries, Celtology & allied subjects, modern political affairs in Ireland. Broadcast from Dublin Studios for 3 ys. Widely travelled. Took part in ethnological survey in several Latin American countries. Served British Expeditionary Forces '14—18. Did archæological research work in South West Europe, North Africa & Aegean Islands. Rec: Music, badminton. c: Geographical Soc of Ireland, Dublin P.E.N. Roy Soc of Antiquaries. a: Dun Daire, Dalkey, Co Dublin. t: Dalkey 198.

MacCALLAN, Arthur Ferguson, C.B.E., M.D., F.R.C.S. b: New Basford, Notts 1872. e: Charterhouse, Christ's Coll Camb, St Mary's Hosp Lond. m: Hester Boyd Carpenter. s: 2. d: 1. Publ: Trachoma in Egypt; Macallan's Trachoma. s.s: Diseases of Conjunctiva. c: Un Univ. a: The Downs, Hertford Heath, Hertford.

MAC CALLUM, MUNGO WILLIAM: university teacher and administrator; b. Glasgow, Scotland, Feb., 1854; s. Mungo and Isabella (Renton) M.; educ. Glasgow High Sch.; Glasgow Univ.; postgrad. study in Germany; DEGREES: M.A. (Glasgow, 1876); LL.D. (honorary) (Glasgow, 1906); D.Litt. (honorary) (Oxford, 1925); m. Dorette Margaret Peters, 1882. AUTHOR: Studies in Low German and High German Literature, 1884; George Meredith, poet and novelist, 1892; Tennyson's Idylls and Arthurian Story, 1894; Authorship of the Lost Hamlet, 1901; Shakespeare's Roman Plays, 1910 (2nd edit. 1925); A. B. Weigall, 1913; The Cawdor Problem, 1916; Browning after a Generation, 1923; Dramatic Monologue in the Victorian Period, 1925; The Literary Study of Literature, 1929; Hamlet, 1930; Virgil in the Middle Ages, 1930 (published in celebration of the two-thousandth anniversary of Virgil's Birth (Sydney); Jezebel, a Dramatized Dialogue, 1930. General character of writing: literary history and criticism. Luke Fellow, Glasgow Univ., 1876; prof. of English Literature and History, Univ. Coll., Aberystwyth, 1879-86; prof. of Modern Literature, Sydney Univ., 1887-1920; prof. Emeritus and Hon. prof. of Eng. Literature from 1921; Wharton lecturer for British Academy, 1925; Order, K.C.M. G., 1926. Administrative positions: Dean of the Faculty of Arts, Sydney Univ., 1898-1914, 1916-1920; Fellow of Sydney Univ. Senate, 1898-1914, 1916 until present time; acting warden and warden, 1923-4; v. chancellor, 1914-17; deputy chancellor, 1928-31. Life pres. of Australian English Assn. since 1923; chmn. of Sydney Grammar Sch., 1929. Relig. denom.: Church of England. CLUBS: University; Australian. OFFICE: University, Sydney, N. S. Wales. HOME: 227 N. South Head Road, Darlingpoint, Sydney, N. S. Wales, Australia.

MACCALMAN, Douglas Robert, M.D., Ch.B., F.B.Ps.S. b: Dunoon, Argyll 1903. e: Glas Acad, Univs of Glas & Harvard. m: Helen Grego Dawson. d: 1. Prof of Mental Health. Publ: Sections in: Textbook of Medical Treatment; Psychology in General Practice; Diseases of Sick Children; etc. Ctr: Journ of Mental Sci, Practitioner, New Era, Child Life, Mental Educ Journ, Ev Express, Aberdeen Press & Journ, etc. s.s: Med Educ, Child Psychology, Delinquency, Educ. Rec: Fishing, photography, ornithology. c: Roy Northern (Aberdeen). a: Dept of Mental Health, The Univ, Aberdeen. T: 7955.

MacCANN, Rev. Gerald, O.F.M. b: Belfast 1910. e: Rochestown Coll, Nat Univ of Ireland. Catholic Priest. n.a: Ed Father Mathew Record. Ctr: Various periodicals. a: P.O. Box 105, Capuchin Friary, Church St, Dublin. T: 74121.

MACCARTHY, Desmond, LL.D., F.R.S.L. b: Plymouth 1877. e: Eton & Trin Coll Camb. m: Mary Warre Cornish. s: 2. d: 1. Author & Journalist, Pres English P.E.N. 1944—. Publ: The Court Theatre; Life of Lady John Russell; Remnants; Portraits; Criticism; Experience; Drama; Essay on Leslie Stephen. Ctr: Sun Times (Lit Criticism), New Statesman (Dramatic Criticism). c: Beefsteak, Athenæum, R.A.C. a: Garricks Villa, Hampton-on-Thames, Middlx.

MACCARTHY, John Bernard. b: Crosshaven, Co Cork 1888. e: Priv. m: Brigid Walsh. s: 1. d: 1. Author. n.a: Formerly Ed of Lit Review & Press Corr. Publ: (Novels) Covert; Possessions; Ezile's Bread; (Plays) The Valley Farm; The Men in Possession; The Down Express; The Able Dealer; The Sea Call; The Supplanter; When a Man Marries; etc; (Poems) The Shadow of the Rose. s.s: Playwriting. a: Swanarus, Monkstown, Co Cork, Ireland.

MacCAUGHLEY, Vaughan. b: Huron, Sth Dakota 1887. e: San Francisco State Coll, Cornell & Chicago Univs. m: Janet H. Brooker. s: 2. d: 4. Teacher, Lecturer, Editor. n.a: Founder Ed Hawaii Educ Review, Ed Sierra Educ News 1923—, Publ: The Natural History of Chantauqua. Ctr: School & Society, American Naturalist, Cornell Countryman, The Friend (Honolulu), etc. s.s: Educ. Rec: Gardening, hiking. a: Ed, Sierra Educ News, Californian Teachers, Assoc. 391 Sutton St. San Francisco 8, California, U.S.A. T: Garfield 1-0175.

MACCHIORO, VITTORIO D.: professor; b. Trieste, November, 1880; s. Davide and Noemi (Lenghi) M.; educ. Gymnasium (Trieste), University (Bologna); m. Rosita Parsa, 1909. AUTHOR: Il Contenuto Oltremondano Della Ceramica Italiota, 1911; Gli Elementi Etrusco-Italici Nella Civilta Italiota, 1914; Un Ditiramdo di Jon, 1915; Zagreus, Studi Sull'orfismo, 1920; Theoria Generale Della Religione come Esperienza, 1922; Christianesimo ed Ebraismo, 1922; Orfismo e Paolinismo, 1922; Eraclito, Nuovi Studi Sull'orfismo, 1922; L'Evangelio, 1922; Euripide, le Baccanti, con Introduzione e Note, 1925; Lutero, 1925; Zagreus (2nd edit., reviewed and enlarged), 1929; Roma Capta, Saggio sulla Religione Romana, 1929; Orfeo, Tragedia Mitica, 1929. Contrbutes to reviews and magazines as follows: (Italy): Rivista Istorica, 1908; Rivista Archeologica, 1908; Ausonia, 1909; Klio, 1909; Rivista Filosofia, 1912; Rivista Indo-Grecoitaliana, 1918; Gnosis, 1920; Nuova Cultura, 1921; Rivista D'Italia, 1928; (English): The Methodist Review, 1924; Journal of Religion, 1928; Austral. Journal of Exp. Psychology, 1925; Classical Philology; (German): Oesterreich Jahrbuch, 1909 and 1910; Politishanthrop. Revue, 1908; Kultur, 1911; Proceedings of academies and societies: Academy of Naples, 1912; Archeological Academy of Naples, 1919; Academy of Sciences of Turin, 1920. OFFICE: National Museum. ADDRESS: 8 via Domenico Cirillo, Naples, Italy.

MACCO, HERMANN FRIEDRICH: writer; b. Aachen, Germany, July 13, 1864; s. Ferdinand and Elise (Mappes) M.; educ. Gymnasium, Univ.; m. (1) Lina Sachs, May 7, 1893 (died);

(2) Amy Müller, Aug. 23, 1927. AUTHOR: Beiträge zur Geschichte und Genealogie rheinischen Adelsfamilien, 1884 (vol. 2); Beiträge zur Geschichte und Genealogie Rheinischen Adels- und Patrizierfamilien, 1887; (vol. 3, 1901; vol. 4, 1906); Die Reformatorischen Bewegungen des 16. Jahrhunderts in Aachen, 1900; Schloss Kalkofen bei Aachen, 1904; Aachner Emigranten des 16. Jahrhunderts, 1906; Aachner Wappenbuch, 1906; Aachner Wappen und Genealogien, 1907 (vol. 2, 1908); Zur Reformationsgeschichte Aachens, 1907; Königin Luise von Preussen gemalt 1800 von Alexander Macco, 1908; Die Bedeutung des königlichen Staatsarchivs zu Wetzlar für die deutsche Geschichte und die historischen Hilfsgenossenschaften, 1909; Beiträge zur Geschichte der Familie Wassermann (vol. VI), 1911; Bringt materielles oder sociales Aufsteigen den Geschlechtern in Rassehygienischen Beziehungen Gefahren? 1912; Genealogie und Heraldik in der Kriminalistik, 1913; Zur Familiengeschichte Clouth, 1916; Stammtafel der Familien von Marcken an Marcken gen. Merckens, 1923; (other works): Auswanderung der Scweizen zur Pfalz im 17. und 18. Jahrhundert; Geschichte und Genealogie des Geschlechts Huber in der Schweiz und Pfalz und sein Auswanderung nach Amerika; Geschichte und Genealogie der verschiedenen Geschlechten Standt, Stande in Deutschland und Amerika. General character of writing: genealogical. CLUBS: Verein für Heraldik und Genealogie (honorary member), Herold, Nederlandsche Leenn im Haag, corresponding member of many scientific clubs in other countries. Relig. denom., Evangelical. ADDRESS: Humboldtstrasse 2, Berlin-Steglitz, Germany.

MACCOLL, Dugald Sutherland, M.A., LL.D., D.Litt., Fell Univ Coll Lond. *b*: Glasgow 1859. *e*: Glas Acad, Univ Coll Sch & Coll Lond, Lincoln Coll Oxf (Scholar & Newdigate prizeman). *m*: Andree Zabe (dec'd). *s*: 2. Writer & Painter, Hon Mem Eng & Scott Watercolour Soc, R.I.B.A. & N.E.A.C., Initiator & Part-ed Oxford Mag 1894, Art Critic Spectator, Saturday Rev from '90, Ed Architectural Rev & of Artwork 1929, former Keeper of Tate Gallery & Wallace Collection. *Publ*: Greek Vase Paintings (with Jane Harrison); Maladministration of the Chantrey Bequest; Nineteenth Century Art; Confession of a Keeper, Reprinted as Penguin What is Art; Poems; Life Works & Setting of P. W. Steer. *Ctr*: Times, Manch Guardian, Nat Rev, etc. *s.s*: Designing of Bookbindings. *Rec*: Swimming. *c*: Athenæum. *a*: 1 Hampstead Way, London, N.W.11. *T*: Speedwell 1988.

MACCORMAC, H., C.B.E. Physician. *Publ*: Jacobi's Atlas of Dermochromes. *a*: 23 Wimpole St, W.1. *t*: Langham 1817.

MacCORMACK, Gilson (Brian Setanta). *b*: Dover 1899. *e*: Simon Langton Sc Canterbury. *m*: Alice Story. *s*: 1. Prine Literary Service. *n.a*: Special Repres Paris Dancing Times 1924—32. *Publ*: Memoirs of the Chevalier de Biron; Felicia: or My Youthful Follies; The Alcoves of Prince & Prelate; Courtisan Princesses & Escapades of Casanova (trans from French). *s.s*: Choreography, theatrical biog, French lit, etc. Founded Setanta Lit Service for specialising in preparation Speeches, Lectures & Propaganda '34. *c*: Soc of Authors. *a*: 10 Poplar Grove, W.6.

MacCRINDLE, Ada Mary, M.A. *b*: Ireland 1878. *e*: Penzance Ch of Eng High Sc, London Univ. *m*: Lieut-Col J. G. MacCrindle. *Publ*: Ice in Egypt. *a*: Mount Howe, Topsham, Devon.

MacCULLOCH, Donald Brown, A.M.I.N.A. *b*: Gourock 1898. *e*: Banavie Elem Sc & Fort William H.S. Archt. *Publ*: The Island of Staffa (1927); 2nd edn entirely re-written & greatly enlarged, & title altered to The Wondrous Isle of Staffa ('34) the only book publ devoted wholly to Staffa. *c.t*: Scot Field, Oban Times, Daily Record (Glas). *s.s*: Illus descriptions of W. Scot. War Service R.N.V.R. *Rec*: Golf. *a*: 1 Fairlie Park Drive, Partick, Glas.

MACCULLOCH, Canon John Arnott, Hon.D.D. (St And). *b*: Edin 1868. *e*: Merch Coy's Sch Edin, Theo Coll of Episcopal Ch Edin. *m*: Mary Julia Crawford. *s*: 2. *d*: 2. Clerk-in-Holy Orders, formerly Exam Chap to Bishop of St And & former Rector of St Saviour's Bridge of Allan. *n.a*: Ed The Scottish Churchman 1933—46. *Publ*: Comparative Theology; The Misty Isle of Skye; Early Christian Visions of the Other World; Celtic Mythology; Eddic Mythology; Mediæval Faith & Fable; The Religion of the Ancient Celts; Religion, Its Origin & Forms; The Childhood of Fiction; A Study of Folk-Tales & Primitive Thought; R. L. Stevenson & The Bridge of Allan; The Harrowing of Hell. *s.s*: Anthropology, Folk Lore. *a*: 19 Merchiston Ave, Edinburgh 10. *T*: 54688.

MACCURDY, Edward Alexander Coles. *b*: Nottingham 1871. *e*: Loughboro' & Balliol Oxf. *m*: Sylvia Winifred Annette Stebbing. *s*: 2. *d*: 4. *Publ*: Roses of Paestum; Leonardo da Vinci (Great Masters Series); Essays in Fresco; A Literary Enigma (The Canadian Boat Song); The Note Books of Leonardo da Vinci (2 vols); Raphael Santi; Lays of a Limpet; Poems; The Mind of Leonardo da Vinci, The Artist; etc. *Ctr*: Quarterly Review, Nineteenth Century & After. *a*: Oakdene, Ashtead, Surrey. *T*: Ashtead 484.

MacCURDY, J. T. *a*: Corpus Christi College, Cambridge.

MACDERMOT, Major Dermot. *n.a*: Paris Corr Western Mail & S. Wales News. Hon Vice-Pres I.J. *a*: 12 Rue Angelique Veriens, Neuilly-sur-Seine, France.

MACDERMOTT, Ven. George Martius, L.Th, B.A., M.A. *b*: Lon 1863. *e*: Barnsbury Hall & Durham Univ. Widower. *s*: 1. Archdeacon of Norwich. *n.a*: Ed Norwich Diocesan Gazette, & Norwich Diocesan Calendar 1911. *Publ*: Commentaries on St Matthew, St Mark St Luke & St John; Evolution & the Resurrection; etc. *s.s*: Evolution. *Rec*: Tennis. *a*: 11 W. Parade, Norwich.

MACDERMOTT, Rev. Kenneth Holland, L.Th, A.R.C.M., H.C.F. *b*: Lon 1867. *e*: Clewer Hse Sc Windsor & Durham Univ. *m*: Elizabeth Jane Lewin. *s*: 3. *d*: 1. Rector of Buxted 1925–. *Publ*: Bosham Church: Its History & Antiquities ('11); Sussex Church Music in the Past; Buxted the Beautiful; The Simple Guide for Communicants; etc. *c.t*: Sussex County Mag, etc. *s.s*: Archæology. *Rec*: Boating, music, lawn tennis. *a*: Buxted Rectory, Sussex.

MACDIARMID, D. S., B.A., LL.B.(Glas), J.P. Lanarks & Dumbartonshire). *b*: Glas 1873. *e*: Leys Sc & King's Coll Cam, Glas Univ. *m*: Ruby Constance Grinson. *d*: 2. Advocate. Sheriff-Subt of Lanarks at Glas. *Publ*: Life of General Sir J. M. Grinson, K.C.B. *c.t*: Various n/ps & Periodicals. Legal Sec Lord Advocate for Scot 1910–12. County Adjutant Dumbartonshire Volunteer Regt '15–18. *Rec*: Walking, lawn tennis. *c*: Western, Glas. *a*: 1 Kirklee Circus, Glas, W. *t*: Western 4158.

MacDONAGH, Donagh, M.A. *b*: Dublin 1912. *e*: Belvedere Coll S.J., Univ Coll Dublin, King's Inn Dublin. *w*: (1) Maura Smyth. (2) Nuala Smyth. *s*: 2, *d*: 1. Barrister, Justice of the District Court of Ireland. *Publ*: Twenty Poems; Veterans & Other Poems; Happy as Larry; The Hungry Grass & Other Poems; Poems from Ireland—An Anthology. *Ctr*: Criterion, To-morrow, Horizon, New Writing, Irish Writing,

Poetry, The Bell, Dublin Mag, etc. *s.s*: Poetry, Short Stories. *a*: 141 Strand Rd, Sandymount, Dublin. *T*: 63204.

MACDONAGH, George. *b*: Limerick 1872. *e*: Christian Bros, Leamy's Sec Sc & Civil Service Sc. *m*: Florence McDonnell. *s*: 1. *d*: 1. Chief Reporter Irish Independent Dublin. *n.a*: Ed Limerick Leader, 1901—05. *a*: 2 Upper Columba Rd, Drumcondra, Dublin. *t*: Drumcondra 152.

MACDONAGH, Michael, F.J.I. *b*: Limerick 1860. *e*: Christian Bros Limerick, Univ Col Dublin. *m*: Mary Josephine Govan (dec). *s*: 1. Journalist & Author. *n.a*: Munster N/s (Limerick), Freeman's Journ (Dublin), Times, Observer (Lon). *Publ*: Irish Life & Character; The Reporter's Gallery; Parliament: Its Romance, Comedy & Pathos; The Home Rule Movement; William O'Brien, Irish Nationalist; Life of Daniel O' Connell; The English King; The Pageant of Parliament; etc. *s.s*: Parliament, Ireland. Entered the Reporter's Gallery Hse of Parliament in '87. *Rec*: Nature study. *c*: Nat Lib. *a*: 139 Worple Rd, S.W.20. *t*: Wimbledon 1748.

MACDONALD, Rev. Alan John, D.D., Commdr Star of Roumania. *b*: London 1887. *e*: Priv Sch, Trin Coll Camb. *m*: Gertrude Meredyth Lowe. Rector St Dunstan-in-The-West. *Publ*: Trade, Politics & Christianity in Africa & the East; Lanfranc, His Life, Work & Writings; Berengar & Sacramental Doctrine; Evangelical Doctrine of Holy Communion; Hildebrand (Gregory VII); Authority & Reason in Early Middle Ages; God, Creation & Revelation; The Interpreter Spirit. *Ctr*: Guardian, Church Times, C. of E. Newspaper, Record, Journ of Theolog Studies. *s.s*: Church History, Theology. *Rec*: Walking, tennis. *c*, Athenæum. *a*: St Dunstan's Vestry, Fleet St, London: E.C.4. *T*: Chancery 6027.

MACDONALD, Alexander, F.R.G.S., F.R.Scot G.S. *b*: Stirling Scot 1878. *m*: Naomi Hingston. *s*: 1. *d*: 1. Author, Film Producer, Mining Engineer & Explorer. Mang Dir Mammoth Copper Mine Ltd, N. Queensland, Chm Mount Wandoo Gold Ltd & Epic Films Ltd. *Publ*: In Search of Eldorado; The Lost Explorers; The Pearl Seekers; The Invisible Island; The White Trail; The Quest of the Black Opals; The Island Traders; etc. *s.s*: Exploration. *a*: Savage Club, Lon & Australian Club, Sydney, N.S.W.

MACDONALD, Allan. *n.a*: Ed Greenock Telegraph. *a*: 12—16 Charles St, Greenock.

MACDONALD, Anne. *b*: Aberdeen. *e*: Aberdeen, Edin, Germany. Headmistress & Founder St Helen's Sch Bridge of Allan. *Publ*: (Juvenile Stories) Bud & Adventure; Dorty Speaking; Dimity Dand; Briony, Called Squibs; Jill's Curmudgeon; Lilt from the Laurels; (Children's Verse) Dormer Windows; Through the Green Door; A Pocketful of Silver; Sung By the Sea; (Lyrics) In Life's Garden; Echoes of Song; Spindrift; (Novel) The Deceiving Mirror. *Ctr*: Chambers's Journ, Good Housekeeping, Colour. *Rec*: Music, writing, motoring. *c*: P.E.N., Overseas. *a*: Hamewith, Marihhall Rd, Edinburgh.

MACDONALD, Charles Baird, M.A., Ch.B., M.D. *b*: Montrose, Angus 1885. *e*: St Andrews Univ Fife. *m*: Sophia Jane Wilkie. *s*: 2. *d*: 1. *Ctr*: Lancet, Brit Med Journ, Med World, The Prescriber. *s.s*: The Treatment of Toxic Goitre. *Rec*: Tennis, golf, contract bridge, music. *w.s*: Gallipoli & France Capt R.A.M.C. 1915—19. *c*: St Andrews Racquet, Royal &

Ancient Golf. *a*: 1 Allerton Rd, Liverpool 18, & 63 Rodney St, Liverpool. *T*: Sefton Park 216 & Royal 2996.

MACDONALD, Ernest Kenneth, O.B.E., M.D., B.S., M.R.C.S., L.R.C.P. *b*: London 1896. *e*: Monkton Combe Sch Bath, St Thomas's Hosp Lond. *m*: Vera Grace Orpwood. *d*: 3. Med Officer of Health City of Leicester. *Publ*: First Aid at the Incident. *Ctr*: Public Health, Medical Officer, etc. *s.s*: Public Health. *a*: 57 Stoneygate Rd, Leicester. *T*: 77307.

MACDONALD, Dr. F. G. *a*: c/o Messrs Macdonald & Stacey, 2 Norfolk Street, Strand, W.C.2.

MACDONALD, Mrs. Frances Margaret, L.L.A. *b*: Inverness 1875. *e*: H.S. Inverness & St Georges Train Col for Teachers Edin. *m*: Allan MacDonald. *d*: 1. *Publ*: The Death of the Brahan Seer (one act play). *s.s*: Highlands. Mem Ross & Cromarty Educ Authority. Pres Fortrose & Rosemarkie Lit Soc. *Rec*: Bowls, bridge. *a*: Bank of Scotland Hse, Fortrose, Ross-shire.

MACDONALD, Rev. Frederick Charles, M.A., O.B.E. *e*: Oriel Col Oxf. Hon Canon Durham Cath. *Publ*: Handley Moule (Biog, Pt II); Bishop Stirling of the Falkland Islands; Lightfoot of Durham (Jt Ed). *a*: Purleigh Rectory, Chelmsford. *t*: Purleigh 32.

MACDONALD, Sir George, K.C.B., D.Litt, LL.D., F.B.A. *b*: Elgin 1862. *e*: Ayr Acad, Edin Univ, Balliol Col Oxf. *m*: Margaret Tannahill Younger. *s*: 1. Civil Servant (ret). *Publ*: Catalogue of Greek Coins in the Hunterian Collection; The Evolution of Coinage; The Roman Wall in Scotland; Ed Haverfield's Romanization of Roman Britain & Roman Occupation of Britain; Coll in 2nd Ed of Head's Historia Nummorum. *c.t*: Numismatic Chron, Hellenic Journ, Archæologia, Proceedings of Brit Acad, Zeitschrift Für Numismatik. *s.s*: Numismatics, ancient hist. Schoolmaster '87—92. Lect in Univ of Glas '92—1904. Asst Sec of Scottish Educ Dept '04—22, Sec '22—28. *c*: Chm Roy Comm on Ancient Monuments (Scot), Vice-Chm of Ancient Monuments Board (Scot). Mem Roy Fine Arts Comm (Scot), etc. *a*: 17 Learmonth Gdns, Edin. *t*: 23868.

MACDONALD, Hugh, Hon.M.A.(Oxon). *b*: Marlborough 1885. *e*: Repton. *m*: Charlotte R. D. Young. *d*: 1. *Publ*: John Dryden, A Bibliography of Early Editions & Drydeniana; Portraits in Prose; Observations Upon A Late Libel; On Foot; A Journal From Parnassus; Arden of Feversham; Poems of Richard Leigh; Englands Helicon; The Phoenix Nest. *Ctr*: Rev of English Studies, Essays of the English Assoc. *s.s*: Seventeenth Cent Lit & Bibliography. *Rec*: Walking on Mountains. *a*: Fairholme, Princes Risborough, Buckinghamshire. *T*: Princes Risborough 505.

MACDONALD, Rt. Hon. J. Ramsay, M.P., P.C. *b*: 1866. Politician & Author. *Publ*: The Awakening of India; American Speeches; etc. Ex-Prime Minister. Elder Brother Trinity Hse. Mem Counc Soc of Authors. *a*: Upper Frognal Lodge, Hampstead, N.W.3.

MACDONALD, James Leslie Auld, B.Sc, D.Sc, D.S.O. *b*: Lon 1887. *e*: Rugby Sc & St Andrew's Univ. *m*: Gladys M. MacEvoy. *s*: 1. *d*: 1. Scientist, in charge Tech Lab. *c.t*: Trans Chem Soc (Lon), Proc of Tech Section of Papermakers Assoc, Paper Trade Press, etc. *s.s*: Chemistry & technology of cellulose. War Service 1914—19, Major Roy Scots. *c*: Roy Soc, Roy & Ancient. *Rec*: Golf, fishing, gardening. *a*: Cadham, Markinch, Fife. *t*: Markinch 42.

MACDONALD, Lucy Maud, F.R.S.A.L. *b*: Clifton, P.E. Island 1874. *e*: Prince of Wales Col. *m*: Rev Ewan Macdonald. *s*: 2. Novelist. *Publ*: Anne of Green Gables; Anne of The Island; Anne's House of Dreams; Kilmeny of The Orchard; The Story Girl; The Golden Road; Magic for Marigold; Anne of Avonlea; Rainbow Valley; Rilla of Ingleside; The Blue Castle; Pat of Silver Bush; Emily of New Moon; etc. *Rec*: Reading, walking. *c*: Canadian Women's Press, etc. *a*: Norval, Ont, Canada.

MACDONALD, Murray. Author. *Publ*: The Lake (with Dorothy Massingham); Mrs Nobby Clark (jt). *a*: c/o Samuel French Ltd, 26 Southampton St, W.C.2.

MACDONALD, Norman, M.A., Ph.D. *b*: Invernesshire 1887. *e*: Edin Univ & Harvard. *m*: Anna Esslemont. Prof of History. *Publ*: Canada 1763—1841: Immigration & Settlement; The Barton Lodge 1795—1945. *Ctr*: Various reviews & periodicals. *s.s*: Immigration & Colonisation. *c*: Rotary. *a*: McMaster Univ, Hamilton, Canada. *T*: 2.8174.

MACDONALD, Norman Pemberton ("Pertinent"). Political & General Speaker. *Publ*: Britain's Future (1933). *s.s*: Fascism, polit, econ, post-war history. *a*: 1 Devonshire Rd, Sutton, Surrey.

MACDONALD, Philip. Author. *Publ*: The Rasp; The Noose; The Link; The White Cow; Death on My Left; The Wraith; Moonfisher; Rope to Spare; Murder Gone Mad; The Polferry Mystery; The Rynox Mystery; Harbour; etc. *a*: c/o A.M. Heath & Co., Ltd, Princes Hse, Jermyn St, London, S.W.1.

MACDONALD, Lt.-Col. Reginald James, D.S.O. *b*: Victoria B.C. 1867. *e*: Priv & R.M.C. Kingston, Canada. *m*: Mary Schofield. *s*: 1. *d*: 1. Army (ret). *Publ*: The History of the Dress of the Royal Artillery. *c.t*: Army Soc for Hist Research Jnl. *s.s*: Mil hist. *Rec*: Golf & painting. War Service 1914—19. Victory Medal, Despatches, etc. *c*: Army & Navy, Roy Utd Service Inst. *a*: Aird, Inverness, & The Army & Navy Club, Pall Mall, S.W.1.

MACDONALD, William James (Cormac Simpson). *b*: Aberdeen 1886. Married. Schoolmaster. *Publ*: Plays:—Ayont the Hill; The Flower in the Vase; Scobie Betters Himself. *c.t*: Various periodicals. Plays performed by The Scottish National Players, stage & wireless. *a*: 54 Wernbrook St, Plumstead Common, S.E.18.

MACDONALD, Yvonne. *b*: Argentine 1906. *e*: Holy Child Convent Mayfield Sussex & Neuilly Paris. *m*: Gerard Ankerman. *s*: 1. *d*: 1. *n.a*: Ed Staff Vogue 1932—33. *Publ*: Red Tape Not Withstanding. *w.s*: Comd Mech Trans Corps, France 1939—40. *a*: Lower Fullbrook, Elstead, Surrey. *T*: Elstead 3163.

MACDONALD CLARK, Mary E., M.A., Ph.D., F.R.S.A. *b*: Edinburgh 1879. *e*: Hgh Sch & Edin Univ. Teacher & Coach in Modern Languages, Mem of P.E.N. *Publ*: Maurice Maeterlinck, Poet & Philosopher; A Child's French Poetry Book; L'Ame Francaise (collab). *Ctr*: Chambers's Journ, Journ of Educ. *s.s*: Modern Languages. *Rec*: Reading, working for Red Cross. *a*: 24 Murrayfield Ave, Edinburgh 12. *T*: 63159.

MACDONAUGH, Michael, F.I.J. *b*: Limerick 1860. *e*: Christian Bros Limerick, Univ Col Dublin. *m*: Mary Josephine Govan (dec). *s*: 1. Journalist & Author. *n.a*: Munster N/s (Limerick), Freeman's Journ (Dublin), Times, Observer (Lon). *Publ*: Irish Life & Character; The Reporter's Gallery; Parliament: Its Romance, Comedy & Pathos; The Home Rule Movement; William O'Brien, Irish Nationalist; Life of Daniel O'Connell; The English King; The Pageant of Parliament; etc. *c.t*: Fortnightly Review, Contemporary Review, Nat Dict of Biog, Ency, etc. *s.s*: Parliament, Ireland. Entered the Reporter's Gallery Hse of Parliament in '87. *Rec*: Nature study. *a*: National Liberal Club, S.W.1. *t*: Whitehall 9871.

MACDONELL, A. G. Author. *Publ*: England, Their England; Napoleon and His Marshals; How Like an Angel; A Visit to America. *a*: c/o Hascombe Court, Godalming, Surrey.

MACDONELL, Oliver Stephen, A.M.I.C.E. *b*: Lon 1878. *e*: Priv, Clifton Hall Derby & Lon Univ. *m*: Annie Rachel Harris. *s*: 1. Civil Eng (ret). *Publ*: George Ashbury. *c.t*: Spectator, Rangoon Gazette. *s.s*: Railways. *Rec*: Tennis, mountain walking. *a*: Greenbank, Cockermouth, Cumb'ld. *t*: Cockermouth 132.

MacDONOGH, Patrick. *b*: Dublin 1902. *e*: Avoca Sch & Dublin Univ. *m*: Ellen May Connell. *d*: 1. *Publ*: Over The Water; The Vestal Fire; A Leaf in the Wind. *Ctr*: Dublin Mag, Irish Times, Irish Press. *s.s*: Poetry & Criticism. *Rec*: Gardening, fishing, golf, walking. *a*: Cintra, Malahide, Co Dublin. *T*: Portmarnock 28.

MACDOUGALL, Margaret ("Margaret Armour"). *b*: W. Lothian. *e*: Edin, Munich & Paris. *m*: W. B. MacDougall. Poet & Novelist. *Publ*: Home & Early Haunts of Stevenson (1895); Songs of Love & Death ('96); Fall of the Nibelungs (from mediæval German, '97); The Shadow of Love (poems, '98); Verse trans in 3 vols from Heine; Trans of Wagner's Ring (2 vols); Agnes of Edinburgh (novel, 1910); Gudrun (from mediæval German, '28); etc. *s.s*: Northern lit. *Rec*: Sailing & caravan tours. *a*: The Cottage, Debden Green, Loughton, Essex.

MACDOWELL, Maeve Cavanagh. *b*: Dublin 1878. *e*: Central Model Sch & Priv. *m*: Cecil Grange MacDowell. Milliner, Mem of P.E.N. *Publ*: A Flame from the Whins; Sheaves of Revolt; A Voice of Insurgency; Passion Flowers; Soul & Clay; Songs of the Months; (Plays) In the Time of the Tans; The Test. *Ctr*: America, Monitor, Catholic Bulletin. *Rec*: Music, reading, walking. *c*: Women Writer's. *a*: 53 Larkfield Grove, Harold's Cross, Dublin, Ireland.

MACE, Herbert George. *b*: London 1882. *e*: Priv. *m*: Anne Louise Slack. *d*: 1. Lawyers Clerk, Accountant, Paper Merchant, Small Holder, Author. *n.a*: Ed Beekeeping Annual 1928—. *Publ*: A Book about The Bee; Adventures Among Bees; Some Other Bees; Modern Beekeeping; Bee Matters & Beemasters; Bee Farming in Britain; Storing, Preserving & Pickling. *Ctr*: Various newsps & mags. *s.s*: Bees & Beekeeping, Entomology, Botany & Rural Topics in General. *w.s*: B.S.F. 1916—19. *Rec*: Gardening, natural history, amat theatricals. *a*: Faircotes, Harlow, Essex.

MacEACHRAN, John Malcolm, M.A., Ph.D., LL.D. *b*: Glencoe, Ontario 1877. *e*: Glencoe Public & Hgh Sch, Queens, Berlin, Leipzic & Sorbonne Univs. *m*: Elizabeth J. Russell. Emeritus Prof Univ of Alberta. *Publ*: Pragmatismus, Eine Neue Richlung; Der Philisophie; Some Present Day Tendencies in Philosophy; Twenty Five Years of Philosophical Speculation; John Watson. *s.s*: Philosophy & Psychology. *Rec*: Golf. *a*: 11619 Saskatchewan Drive, Edmonton, Alberta, Canada. *T*: 32641.

MACEK, Josef. *b*: Krumpach, Moravia 1887. *e*: Gym Zabreh, Czech Univ Prague, Univ Berlin. *m*: Bela Krizkova. *s*: 2. Prof Econ Univ of Prague. *n.a*: Ed monthly review Nase Doba 1923—. *Publ*: Principles of Social Policy; Price Problems in Socialism; Moral Ideas of Adam Smith; The Struggle with Error & Poverty; Gold Standard & State Notes; Social Economics; Socialism; Work, Money & Politics; The Way out of Crisis; Ways of Self Education; etc. *s.s*: Narodoni Osvobozeni, Novy Den, Dnesek, etc. *s.s*: Theory of Money, Methods of Social Policy, Principles of Politics. *c*: P.E.N. *a*: Prague XV, Hodkovicky 111. *T*: 041.146.

MACENTEE, S. *Publ*: Poems. Minister for Fin Saorstat Eireann, Mem Roy Dub Soc, etc. Elec Eng. *a*: Herbert Park, Ballsbridge, Dublin.

MACER-WRIGHT, Philip. *b*: Sheerness-on-Sea, Isle of Sheppey. Author & Journalist. *n.a*: Special Corr Evening Westminster Gazette, Asst-Ed Dramatic Critic & Art Critic Morning Westminster Gazette, Asst-Ed Daily Chron, Asst Features Ed News-Chron, Press Dir Travel Assoc of Gt Britain & Ireland 1934—. *Publ*: The Square Peg; Knee Deep in Daisies; Purple Hours (with intro by G. K. Chesterton). *c.t*: Many Periodicals. 1st to broadcast eye-witness account of hist events in Lon. *c*: Authors'. *a*: Park Hse, Kew, Surrey. *t*: Richmond 1988.

MACEVOY, H. J., B.A.(Douai), M.A., B.Sc(Lon). *b*: Lon 1863. *e*: Beauvais Col & Lon & Paris. Physician. *c.t*: Journ of Mental Science, Concours Medical, B.M.J. *s.s*: French lit. *a*: 19 Mowbray Rd, Brondesbury, N.W.6. *t*: Willesden 0625.

MACEWAN, Desiree. F.R.A.M. Pianist & Professor R.A.M. *Publ*: The First Two Years of Piano Study; First Adventures in Music-land. *a*: 98 Elmbourne Rd, S.W.17. *t*: Streatham 6128.

MacEWAN, Gerald Thomson, F.R.Econ.S. *b*: London 1891. *e*: Highgate Sch. *m*: Winifred Matilda. *d*: 1. Overseas Trade Cons, Dir of Export & Import Coys. *Publ*: Overseas Trade & Export Practice. *Ctr*: Times, Times Trade & Engineering, etc. *s.s*: Overseas Trade & Econs Generally. *a*: Northgate Hse, 20-24 Moorgate, London, E.C.2. *T*: Monarch 8787.

MACEWEN, Sir A. M., B.L. *b*: Calcutta 1875. *e*: Edin Univ. *m*: Mary Beatrice Henderson. *s*: 3. *d*: 2. *Publ*: The Thistle & The Rose. *c.t*: Spectator, Scots Independent, etc. *s.s*: Scotland. Provost of Inverness '1925–31. Chairman Scot Nat Party '34. *a*: Lethington, Inverness. *t*: 330.

MACEWEN, Dr. H. A. *Publ*: Food Inspection; The Public Milk Supply. Sen M. O. Min Health. *c*: Savage. *a*: Ministry of Health, Whitehall, S.W.1.

MACEWEN, John A. C. Surgeon. *Publ*: Surgical Anatomy; Fractures, Compound Fractures, Dislocations, Artificial Limbs; Text Book of Surgery. *c.t*: Professional Journs. *a*: 3 Woodside Cresc, Glas, & Garrachty, Kingarth, I.O.B. *t*: Douglas 5194 & Kilchattan Bay 31.

MACEWEN, Pearl Forbes ("Kathleen Forbes"). *b*: Glas. *e*: Shawlands Acad & Glas Sc of Art. Illustrator & Writer. *c.t*: Glas Herald, Glas Evening News, Bulletin (Glas), Scottish Country Life, etc. *s.s*: Woman's page articles, childrens stories & poems & book illus. *a*: 551 Sauchiehall St Glas. *t*: Douglas 4948.

MACEY, Alan. *b*: Lon 1897. *e*: Priv. Bookseller. *Publ*: The Romance of the Derby Stakes (2nd edn 1932); Hypnotism Explained (2nd edn '33); Your Hidden Powers (2nd edn '34); The Crime Syndicate; Checkmated. *c.t*: Daily Express, Evening News, Allied N/ps, prov papers, etc. *s.s*: Sport, psych, fiction. Interned Ruhleben. Served W.O. Postal Censorship. *Rec*: Cycling, tennis, theatre. *a*: 19 Rowlands Rd, Worthing.

MACFADYEN, Dugald. M.A.(Oxon). F.R.HistS. *b*: Manchester 1867. *e*: M/C G.S., Merton Col Oxf, Mansfield Col Oxf & Berlin. *m*: Edith Barnett Bates. *s*: 2 (1 dec). *d*: 2. Cong Min (ret). Now Publicist & Author. *Publ*: Alfred of Wessex, King of the English; The Pilot; Life's Compass; Life of Alexander Mackennal; Remarkable Story of Andrew Swan. Sir Ebenezer Howard, Author Town Planning Movement; etc. *c.t*: Contemporary Review, Manchester Guardian, Times, Christian World, British Weekly, etc. *s.s*: Hist, garden cities. War Service. *Rec*: Golf, sailing, travel. *c*: Nat Lib, Eng Speaking Un, Rotary, etc. *a*: Bramble Bank, Alington Lane, Letchworth, Herts. *t*: 186.

MACFALL, John Edward Whitley, M.D.L'pool, M.B., B.S.Vict, D.P.H., F.R.T.P.H., PhD. Widower. *s*: 1. *d*: 2. Medico-Legal Expert. Prof of Forensic Medicine L'pool Univer, Examiner in Forensic Medicine for Law & Medical Students Univers of Glas, Aberdeen, B'ham, E'burgh, Sheffield & M/C. *Publ*: Text Book of Forensic Medicine; Dental Jurisprudence; Aspects of Legal Live Birth; Experiences of a Medico-Legal Investigator; etc. *c.t*: Odontological Journ, Police Journ. *s.s*: Medico-legal. War Service 1914–18. Medals 1914 T, General & Durbar. *Rec*: Riding, swimming, tennis, revolver shooting. *a*: Rose Brae, 15 Green Lane, Stoneycroft, Liverpool 13. *t*: Old Swan 531.

MACFARLAND, Charles Stedman, B.D., Ph.D.(Yale), LL.D.(Elon), D.D.(Geneva, Paris, Ursinus Coll). *b*: Boston, Mass 1866. *e*: Yale. *m*: (1) Mary Perley Merrill, (2) Genevieve Dayton. *s*: 2. *d*: 1. Clergyman, Author, Lecturer, Boy Scouts Commissioner America, Officer Legion of Honour France, Officer Order of Leopold I Belgium, Officer Order of Leopold II Belgium, Officer Order of Phoenix Greece, Chevalier Holy Sepulchre Jerusalem. *n.a*: Congregationalist 1894—1900, Reformed Church Messenger '35. *Publ*: Christian Unity in Practice & Prophecy; Chaos in Mexico; The Infinite Affection; International Christian Movements; Christian Service & the Modern World; etc. *Ctr*: Lit Digest, Rev of Reviews, etc. *s.s*: Religious Internat & Social Affairs. *w.s*: France & Belgium 1918. *c*: Yale, New York. *a*: 297 4th Ave, New York, & Mountain Lakes, N.J.

MACFARLANE, C. B. Golf Corr Evening News. *a*: Carmelite Hse, E.C.4. *t*: Central 6000.

MACFARLANE RAE, Priscilla, M.J.I. *b*: Shalford 1908. *e*: West View, Ispwich, Brighton & Hove H.S. Reporter. *n.a*: Reporter Eastbourne Gazette & Herald. *s.s*: Women's features, cinema. *a*: Rindge, 39 Tisbury Rd, Hove, Sussex. *t*: 5065.

MACGARVIE, William Kenneth. *n.a*: Advt Mang East Ham Echo. *s.s*: Advertising. *a*: 11 Rattray Road, Brixton, S.W.2.

MACGEORGE, Ethel Luxmoore. *b*: S. Aus. *Publ*: The Spirit of Cannes; Le Cannet Old & New; The Story of Two Ancient Towns (Winchelsea & Rye); The Life & Reminiscences of Jessie Bond; etc. *c.t*: Aus papers & Tatler. *s.s*: Trav, biog. 2 y France with Y.M.C.A. as Librarian during War *a*: Winchelsea Beach, Sussex.

MacGIBBON, Duncan Alexander, M.A., LL.D., Ph.D., F.R.S.C. *b*: Lochaber Bay, Quebec, Canada 1882. *e*: McMaster & Chicago Univs. *m*: Dorothy Delamere Curry. *s*: 2. Commissioner Bd of Grain Cmmsrs for Canada, former Lect & Prof. *Publ*: Railway Rates & the Canadian Railway Commission; An Introduction to Economics for Canadian Readers; The Canadian Grain Trade; Population Policies; etc. *w.s*: 1st Canadian Tank Regiment (Lieut) 1918. *a*: 190 Elm St, Winnipeg, Manitoba, Canada.

MACGILL, Patrick. *Publ*: inc Gleaning from a Navvy's Scrapbook; Lanty Hanlon; Tulliver's Mill; The House at the World's End; etc.

McGILLICUDDY, Owen Ernest. *b*: Ontario 1887. *e*: Goderich Publ & H.Scs, Ottawa Col Inst. *m*: Blanche Dunham. *s*: 2. Journalist. *n.a*: Toronto Daily Star 1911–28, The Mail & Empire, Toronto '28–. *Publ*: The Little Marshal & Other Poems ('18); The Making of a Premier: Life of Rt Hon W. L. Mackenzie King, C.M.G. *c.t*: N. Amer Review, Amer Review of Reviews, Current History, Chambers's Journ, Empire Review Lon, etc. *s.s*: Biog, short verse. *c*: Canadian Authors Assoc, Toronto Writers. *a*: 4 Algonquin Av, Toronto, Canada.

MACGILLIVRAY, Evan James. *b*: 1873. *e*: Edin Acad & Trin Col Cam. Barrister. Mem Counc Soc of Authors. *a*: 3 Temple Gdns, E.C.4. *t*: Central 3484.

MACGILLIVRAY, Rev. George John. *b*: Edin 1876. *e*: Edin Acad, Edin Univ & Trin Col Cam. Catholic Priest. *Publ*: Father Vernon and his Critics; Through the East to Rome; The Life of Our Lord for Catholic Schools; The Christian Virtues. *c.t*: Month, Catholic Gazette, Clergy Review. *s.s*: Theo. Ordained in C.o.E. 1900, curacies at Portsmouth & Croydon, Archbishop's Assyrian Missn in Kurdistan 4 y, then Dundee, Received into Catholic Ch 1919, ordained priest '22. *a*: Grove Hse, Week St, Maidstone. *t*: 2603.

MACGILLIVRAY, JAMES PITTENDRIGH: (pen name: "P. M." or Peter Maitland); sculptor; b. near Inverurie, Aberdeenshire, Scotland, May, 1856; s. William and Margaret (Pittendrigh) M.; educ. various, including art school. DEGREES: R.S.A. (mem. of Royal Scottish Acad.); LL.D. (Aberdeen) His Majesty's sculptor for Scotland; H.I.A.S. (Hon. Fellow of the Incorporation of Architects in Scotland); mem. of Royal Fine Art Comm. Scotland; m. Frieda Rettig, 1886. AUTHOR: Pro Patria, 1915; Bog-Myrtle and Peat Reek, 1922; many papers and addresses, mainly on art subjects; also short stories. Principal works in sculpture: Burn's Statute, Irvine; Dean Montgomery Memorial, St. Mary's Cathedral, Edinburgh; John Knox Memorial, St. Giles Cathedral, Edinburgh; Scottish National Memorial to the Right Honourable William E. Gladstone, St. Andrew's Square, Edinburgh; Byron Statue, Aberdeen; Statue of the late Marquis of Bute, Cardiff; Robert Fergusson (poet) Memorial in St. Giles Cathedral, Edinburgh. ADDRESS: Ravelston Elms, Murrayfield Road, Edinburgh, Scotland.

MACGOWAN, Gault, F.J.I. *b*: England 1894. *e*: Manch Gr Sch. *m*: Wendy Corley-Smith. *s*: 1. Del Imp Press Conf 1930, Shared with Sir Percival Phillips the Gordon Selfridge Prize for Foreign Correspondence '33. *n.a*: Mang Ed Trinidad Guardian 1929—35, previously with N/p Features Ltd, Dly Express & Lond Times, Ed Trov N.Y. Sun '34, War Correspondent N.Y. Sun '39—45, European Manager N.Y. Sun '45. *Ctr*: New York Times, Manch Guardian, Dly Mail, Pioneer, Times of Ceylon, Wide World, Chicagoan, etc. *s.s*: Travel, Comparative Philosophy & Psychology. *c*: Authors, Press. *w.s*: 1914—20, Belgium, France & Italy. *a*: New York Sun, London Bureau, 15 Carlton Hse Terr, London, S.W.1. *T*: Whitehall 0242.

MACGOWAN, Kenneth, B.Sc. *b*: Winthrop, Massachusetts 1888. *e*: Harvard. *m*: Edna Behre. *s*: 1. *d*: 1. Teacher. *n.a*: Ed Bd Hollywood Quarterly. *Publ*: Theatre of Tomorrow; Continental Stagecraft; Footlights Across America; Masks & Demons; What is Wrong with Marriage (collab); Sleuths. *Ctr*: Hollywood Quarterly, N.Y. Times, N.Y. Her Trib, New Republic, Century, etc. *s.s*: Theatre, Screen, Anthropology. *Rec*: Golf. *a*: Univ of California, Los Angeles 24, California, U.S.A.

MACGREGOR, Alasdair Alpin. *b*: 1899. *e*: Geo Watson's Coll Edin & Edin Univ. Author. *Publ*: Behold the Hebrides; Summer Days Among the Western Isles; A Last Voyage to St Kilda; The Haunted Isles; Life in the Hebrides; Searching the Hebrides with a Camera; Over the Sea to Skye; Wild Drumalbain; The Road to Meggernie & Glen Coe; Hebridean Sea Pieces (poems); Somewhere in Scotland; The Peatfire Flame; Folktales & Traditions of the Highlands & Islands; The Goat Wife; Portrait of a Village; Vanished Waters; Portrait of a Highland Childhood; Auld Reekie; Portrait of a Lowland Boyhood; The Turbulent Years: A Portrait of Youth in Auld Reekie; The Buried Barony; The Western Isles; etc. *Ctr*: Times, Chambers's Journ, Country Life, Field, Quarterly Rev, etc. *s.s*: The Highlands & Islands of Scotland, Edinburgh & the Lothians. *Rec*: Swimming, photography, music, cruising. *a*: One Acre, Bracknell, Berkshire. *T*: 223.

MACGREGOR, David Hutchison, M.C., Hon.LL.D. *e*: Trin Coll Camb. Emeritus Prof of Econs. *n.a*: Jt-Ed Econ Journ 1924—36. *Publ*: Enterprise, Purpose & Profit; Industrial Combination; Evolution of Industry; Public Aspects of Finance; Lord Macaulay; The Thane of Cawdor. *Ctr*: Various. *s.s*: Econs. *a*: All Souls College. Oxford. *T*: 2606.

MACGREGOR. Rev. George Hogarth Carnaby, M.A., B.D.(Cantab), D.Litt.(Glas), D.D.(Edin). *b*: Aberdeen 1892. *e*: Eastbourne Coll, Gonville & Caius Coll Camb, New Coll Edin. *m*: Christine Elizabeth Goold. *s*: 2. *d*: 2. Prof of Biblical Criticism Univ of Glas. *Publ*: The Gospel of John; Eucharistic Origins; Jew & Greek; Tutors unto Christ; The New Testament Basis of Pacifism; The Relevance of the Impossible. *Ctr*: Expository Times, Journ of Biblical Lit, etc. *s.s*: New Testament Language & Literature, Hellenistic Studies. *Rec*: Golf. *c*: Roy Philos Soc of Glas, Un Soc Camb. *a*: Muskoka, Milnagavie, Glasgow. *T*: Milnagavie 1344.

MACGREGOR, J. V. Physician. *c.t*: Lancet. *a*: 99 Finchley Rd, Hampstead, N.W.3. *t*: Primrose 6603.

MacGREGOR, Jock. *b*: Gibraltar 1914. *e*: Brighton Coll. Journalist-Publicist, Lond Mang Showmen's Trade Review New York City. *n.a*: Asst Publicity Mang Garrett Klement Pictures Ltd 1935, Film Critic New Review, Publicity Mang Embassy Cinema Tottenham Court Road '39. *s.s*: Film Corres & Critic for trade & lay press, Technical & Hollywood articles. *Rec*: Cinema, fishing, shooting. *w.s*: Army 1940—46. *a*: 16 Leinster Mews, London, W.2. *T*: Ambassador 3601.

MACGREGOR, JOHN (pen name: "Ralph"): Colonel Indian Medical Service (retired); b. Stornoway, Lewis. Scotland, Feb., 1848; s. John and Janet (MacDonald) M.; educ. Free Church Sch., Stornoway; Glasgow Univ.; Army Medical Sch., Netley, and others; DEGREES: M.B., C.M., M.D., I.M.S.; married. AUTHOR: The Girdle of the Globe, 1890; Toil and Travel, 1892; Through the Buffer State, 1896; Luinneagh Luaineach (Random Lyrics in Gaelic), 1897; Through Death to Victory, 1922; The Legend of Alompra, 1924; Echoes out of Camp and Jungle; The Epic of Glenfruin; Mystery of Angkor Wat. Contributor to Chambers's Jnl., and various other periodicals. General character of writing: descriptive and imaginary. Has written extensively in Gaelic and on Gaelic phraseology; composed many Gaelic songs. First Bard of the

Clan Gregor since the revival of the name of MacGregor by Act of Parliament in 1774, after a proscription lasting nearly 200 yrs. Has held various government appointments. One time prof. of Medicine and surgeon to European General Hospital, Bombay; civil surgeon and supt. of Aden paol; has seen service in India, Arabia, Beluchistan, Siam, Burma and other countries; Sr. officer with Frontier Brigade at Bhamo, on remote borders of China; with Mougog Expedition and various flying columns. One of the widest of travellers, through parts of Borneo, Siam, Cambodia, over regions never before visited by Europeans. Freemason from Fortrose Lodge of Stornoway, Isle of Lewis; worshipful master of Masonia Lodge at Aden, afterwards Grand Master of Ceremonies of all Scottish Freemasonary in India. Relig. denom., Presbyterian. ADDRESS: care of Bank of Scotland, The Mound, Edinburgh, Scotland.

MACGREGOR, William Malcolm. *b*: Glas 1861. *e*: Dundee H.S., Edin Univ, Trin Col Glas & Erlangen. *m*: Amy Stevenson. *s*: 2. *d*: 2. Prof New Testament Lit & Theol, & Princ in Trinity (Theol) Col Glas. *Publ*: Jesus Christ the Son of God (1907); Some of God's Ministries; Christian Freedom: the Baird Lecture for 1913; Repentance Unto Life; For Christ & the Kingdom ('32). *a*: 51 Hamilton Drive, Glas, W.2. *t*: Western 4760.

MACGREGOR-MORRIS, John Turner. Prof of Elec Engineering. *a*: 3 Lyndhurst Rd, Hampstead, N.W.3.

MACH, FELIX: agricultural chemist; *b*. Tilsit, Germany, November, 1868; *s*. Adolph and Johanna (Morgen) M.; educ. Realgymnasium (Tilsit), Univs. of Königsberg and Berlin. DEGREES: Ph.D., Professor; *m*. Elise Gerlach. AUTHOR: Stallmist und seine Behandlung, 1911; Ruhenhilfe für rationelle Dringung, 1921. Editor: Jahresbericht für Agrikultur Chemie. Contributor to Chemiker-Zeitung, Zeitschrift für analytische Chemie, Landwirtschaftliche Versuchsstation, Deutscher Landwirtschaftliche Presse, and others. General character of writing: scientific. Experiments in the chemistry of agriculture and winds, also in analytical chemistry. CLUBS: Verein deutscher Chemiker, and others. Relig. denom., Evangelical. ADDRESS: Augustenberg Post Grötzingen, Baden, Germany.

MACHEN, Arthur. Author. *Publ*: Hieroglyphics; The Secret Glory; The Hill of Dreams; Far Off Things; Things Far & Near; The London Adventure; The Shining Pyramid; The Chronicle of Clemendy; Dreads & Drolls; The Three Impostors; The Great God Pan; etc. *a*: c/o Martin Secker Ltd, 5 John St, W.C.2.

MACHIN, Frank. *b*: Wellington Salop 1901. *e*: Elem Sch. *m*: Ada Johnson. *d*: 1. Journalist, Northern Ed Daily Herald. *n.a*: Formerly Northern Indust Corres Dly Herald, Rep Ev News Lond, Manch Ev News, Blackpool Gazette & Herald. *s.s*: Industrial (Lancs Cotton Indust). *a*: 32 Dunollie Rd, Sale, Cheshire. *T*: Sale 2707.

MACHIN, Robert Ernest, M.Sc., F.C.S., M.R.S.T., M.S.M.A. *b*: Brimington 1884. *e*: Lond Univ. Schoolmaster, Examiner in Chem to N. Univs, Lond Univ, L.C.C. & Civil Service Commsn. *Publ*: Science in a Coalfield. *s.s*: Chem. *a*: South View, Grosvenor Ave, Carshalton, Surrey.

MACHRAY, Robert. *b*: Scotland 1857. *e*: St John's Col Sc, St John's Col, Univ of Manitoba, Sidney Sussex Col, & Cam Univ (Schol). Author & Journalist. *n.a*: War Ed Daily Mail 1904—05. *Publ*: Life of Archbishop Machray;

Poland '14—31; The Night Side of London; etc. Novels—A Blow Over The Heart; etc. *s.s*: Foreign affairs. *Rec*: Travel. *a*: Authors' Club, 2 Whitehall Ct, S.W. *t*: Western 0991.

MAC ILWAINE, JOHN BEDELL STANFORD: landscape painter; *b*. Dublin, Ireland, April, 1857; *s*. John Stanford and Rachel (Jesson) M.; educ. Dublin High School, Royal Hibernian Acad. DEGREE: Academician (Royal Hibernian); unmarried. AUTHOR: Practical Poultry Keeping for Women; How England Played the Game; Sketching from Nature with Oil Colors. Contributor to Lady of the House, Field, Agricultural Gazette, Irish News, Northern Whig, Irish Times, Dog World, Orbit, British Numismatist's Journ. General character of writing: technical, nature books, political. Identified with Dublin Art movements; exhibits in R. Acad. (London) and in Municipal Gallery (Dublin). Relig. denom., Church of Ireland. CLUB: Imperial Three Arts (Dublin). HOME: Anaghroe House, Caledon, Tyrone, Ulster, Ireland.

MACINNES, Charles Malcolm. *b*: Calgary, Alberta, Canada 1891. *e*: Dalhousie Univ N.S. Canada, Balliol Coll Oxf. *m*: Violet Ethel Peake. *s*: 1. Prof of Imperial Hist Univ of Bristol. *n.a*: Ed Universities Review 1925—47. *Publ*: A Gateway of Empire; In the Shadow of the Rockies; England & Slavery; etc. *Ctr*: Various newsps & periodicals. *s.s*: British Imperial Hist, English Social Hist. *Rec*: Riding, rowing. *c*: Savile, Bristol Savages. *a*: The University, Bristol 8. *T*: 20993 & 36174.

MacINNES, Helen. *b*: Glasgow. *e*: Univs of Glas & Lond. *m*: Gilbert Highet. *s*: 1. Writer. *Publ*: Above Suspicion; Assignment in Brittany; The Unconquerable (While Still We Live, in U.S.A.); Horizon; Friends & Lovers. *Ctr*: Sat Ev Post, Ladies Home Journ, Cosmopolitan. *Rec*: Music, travel. *a*: 535 Park Ave, New York, U.S.A.

MACINNES, Malcolm, M.A.(Edin), LL.B.(Cape of Good Hope). *b*: Drumfearn 1871. *e*: Portree Sc Skye & Raining Sc Inverness. *Publ*: Massacre of Glencoe; Mary Queen of Scots; Songs of the Isle of Skye; Ishabel of the Shealing (a play in Gaelic & Eng verse); etc. *s.s*: Gaelic voc & pipe music. *a*: Ostaig, Sleat, Skye, Scot.

MACINNES, William Alexander. Prof of French Univ Col Hull. *Publ*: L'Œuvre Française de Swinburne; La Fortune Littéraire de Thomas Gray en France; Ed Swinburne's Borderland Ballads. *c.t*: French Revs. *a*: 48 Newland Pk, Hull. *t*: 7859.

MACINTOSH, Robert Reynolds, M.A., M.D., F.R.C.S., D.A. *e*: New Zealand & Guy's Hosp Lond. Prof of Anæsthetics Univ of Oxf, Anæsthetist Radcliffe Infirmary Oxf. *Publ*: (in collab) Essentials of General Anæsthesia; Local Anæsthesia; Brachial Plexus; Physics for the Anæsthetist. *Ctr*: Various Med journs. *a*: Pembroke College, Oxford. *T*: 2271.

MAC INTYRE, JOHN: see Bandane, John.

MACINTYRE, Robert, F.J.I. Journalist. *n.a*: Asst Ed Fairplay 1919—. *c*: Press. Vice-Pres N/p Press Fund. *a*: 113 Bute Rd, Wallington, Surrey.

MacIVER, Robert Morrison, Hon.Litt.D. *b*: Stornoway, Scotland 1882. *e*: Nicolson Inst Stornoway, Edin Univ, Oriel Coll Oxf. *m*: Ethel Marion Peterkin. *s*: 2. *d*: 1. Prof at Columbia Univ. *Publ*: The Web of Government; Community; Social Causation; Towards an Abiding Peace; Society; Leviathan & the People; The Modern State; Elements of Social Science. *Ctr*: N.Y. Times

Book Review, etc. *s.s*: Theory of Govt Analysis of Social Insts & Social Changes. *Rec*: Golf, bridge, mycology. *c*: Harvard (N.Y.). *a*: Palisades, New York, U.S.A. *T*: Piermont N.Y. 864.

MACK, Edward C., M.A., Ph.D. *b*: Cincinnati, Ohio 1904. *e*: Princeton & Columbia Univs. *m*: Ruth P. Mack. *s*: 1. *d*: 1. Asst Prof English Coll of City of New York. *Publ*: Public Schools & British Opinion 1780—1860; Public Schools & British Opinion 1860—1939. *s.s*: 19th-Cent Literature. *a*: 430 West 116th St, New York 27. *T*: Mo 2-5664.

MACKAIL, Denis George. *b*: Kensington 1892. *e*: St Paul's Sch, Balliol Coll Oxf. *m*: Diana Granet. *d*: 2. Author. *Publ*: Greenery Street; Romance to the Rescue; The Flower Show; Ian & Felicity; Another Part of the Wood; David's Day; The Square Circle; The Wedding; Our Hero; Huddleston House; The Story of J.M.B. *Ctr*: Strand, Pearson's, Nash's, London, Royal, Windsor, Cosmopolitan, etc. *c*: Athenæum, Garrick. *a*: c/o A. P. Watt & Son, 10 Norfolk St, London, W.C.2.

MACKANESS, George. O.B.E., M.A., D.Litt., F.R.A.H.S. *b*: Sydney, N.S.W. 1882. *e*: Hgh Sch Drummoyne & Univ of Sydney. *m*: Alice M. Simmons. *d*: 1. Senior Lecturer Sydney Teachers' Coll & Univ of Sydney. *Publ*: The Life of Vice-Admiral William Bligh; The Life of Admiral Arthur Phillips, First Governor of Australia; Sir Joseph Banks: His Relations with Australia; Robert Louis Stevenson: His Associations with Australia; Inspirational Teaching; Bligh's Explorations & Discoveries in Van Diemans Land; Some Fictitious Voyages to Australia; etc. *Ctr*: Sydney Morning Herald, Sydney Bulletin, The Forum of Education. *s.s*: Australian Hist & Lit, The Teaching of English. *Rec*: Australiana, amateur play prod. *a*: 39 Collingwood St, Drummoyne, Sydney, N.S.W., Australia. *T*: W.A. 2268.

MACKAY, Alexander Leslie Gordon, D.C.M., M.A., M.Econ., M.Litt. *b*: Sydney, Australia 1892. *e*: All Saints Coll Bathurst, Univ of Sydney, Trin Coll Camb. *m*: Jean Margaret Owen Harris. *s*: 1. *d*: 1. Lect & Tutor, Delegacy of Extra Mural Studies Oxf in Internat Affairs, Econs & Psychology, Lect in Economics Adelaide Univ 1925—28, Rockefeller Research Fell Trinity Coll Camb '29—30, Prof of Econs Rangoon Univ '31—36. *Publ*: The Australian Banking & Credit System; Experiments in Educational Self-Government; Economics: the Study of Wealth; Business Organisation & Commerce. *Ctr*: Econ Journ, Sth Australian Register, News (Sth Aust) Gazette (Rangoon), Public Administration. *s.s*: Credit & Government, Internat Affairs. *Rec*: Rugby football, boxing, tennis, swimming. *a*: 62 Park Town, Oxford.

MACKAY, Colin Neil. *b*: Glasgow 1912. *e*: Glasgow Univ. Journalist. *n.a*: Film & Dramatic Ed Daily Express. *s.s*: Screen, stage, Scottish amateur drama. Lecturer on Dramatic Art & Production. *a*: 28 Glen Rd, Glasgow. *t*: Bell 1300.

MACKAY, David. *b*: Kilmarnock 1906. Journalist. *n.a*: Corr Ilkeston & Heanor Dis Derby Ev Telegraph & Ilkeston Gazette 1945, South Notts Echo, Nottingham Advertiser. *a*: c/o 53 Redland Gr, Carlton, Nottingham.

MACKAY, Dorothy Mary, B.A., B.Sc. *b*: Croydon. *e*: Univ Col, Lond. *m*: Ernest John Henry Mackay. *s*: 1. Joint Ed Ancient Egypt and the East. *Publ*: Ancient Cities of Iraq. *e.t*: Sphere, Daily Telegraph, C.S. Monitor, Asia (U.S.A.), Report of Smithsonian Institution, etc. *s.s*: Archæology, Near & Middle Eastern travel. *Rec*: Gardening. *a*: Whiteleaf, Monks Risborough, Bucks. *t*: Princes Risborough 240.

MACKAY, Eneas. Publisher. *s.s*: Scottish Books. *a*: 44 Craigs, Stirling. *t*: 222.

MACKAY, Ernest John Henry. M.A., D.Litt., F.S.A. *b*: Bristol 1880. *e*: Bristol G.Sc, Univ of Bristol. *m*: Dorothy Mary Simmons. *s*: 1. Archæologist. Excavations in Egypt, Palestine, Iraq, Bahrein Is., Indus Valley. *Publ*: "A" Cemetery at Kish; A Sumerian Palace; Excavations at Jemdet Nasr; The Indus Civilization; Further Excavations at Mohenjo-daro; Collaborated in Hebron; Le Haram al-Khalil and in Mohenjo-daro and the Indus Civilization. *c.t*: Archæological & anthropological journals. *Rec*: Archæology. *a*: Whiteleaf, Monks Risborough, Bucks. *t*: Princes Risborough 240.

MACKAY, Dr. Helen M. M. *a*: 28 John Street, Bedford Row, W.C.1.

MACKAY, Rev. Henry Falconar Barclay, M.A. *b*: Milford Haven 1864. *e*: Merton Col Oxf & Cuddesdon. *Publ*: The Religion of an Englishman; The Message of Francis of Assisi; Assistants at the Passion; Studies in the Ministry of Our Lord (1st series); Followers in the Way; etc. Prebendary of St Paul's Cath '20. *Rec*: Reading. *a*: All Saints Vicarage, 7 Margaret St, W.1.

MACKAY, Hugh. *b*: Glas 1879. *m*: Margaret Jane Alexander Inglis. *d*: 1. Gen Mang. *n.a*: John Leng & Co Dundee 1912—19, George Outram & Co Glas '19—20, A.P. '20—23. Liverpool Daily Post & Echo '23—. *c*: L'pool Press, Lon Press, L'pool Univ, L'pool Exchange, Formby Golf. *a*: Reay, Freshfield, Lancs.

MACKAY, Ian. *b*: Wick, Scotland 1898. *e*: Wick Academy & Hgh Sch, Lond Univ. Journalist. *n.a*: Columnist Northern Ensign & John o' Groat Journ 1918—21, Lond & Political Corr Western Morning News (Plymouth) '22—33, Industrial Corr & Columnist News Chronicle '33—. *s.s*: Industry, Politics, Econ & Lit *c*: Press. *a*: News Chronicle, Bouverie St, London, E.C.4. *T*: Central 5000.

MACKAY, JESSIE: journalist, author; b. Canterbury, N. Z., Dec., 1864; d. Robert and Elizabeth (Bemiston) MacK.; educ. Christchurch (N. Z.) Normal Sch.; unmarried. AUTHOR: The Spirit of the Ransatira, 1889; The Sitter on the Rail, 1891; Land of the Morning, 1909; Poems, 1910; The Bride of the Rivers, 1926. Editor (formerly), Lady's Page of Canterbury Times (Christchurch, N. Z.); associate-editor (formerly), White Ribbon (N. Z. organ of W.C.T.U.). Contributor to Aukland Star, Dunedin Star, Christchurch Times, Star; Sydney Bulletin, Artists Annual, Art in New Zealand, Time and Tide (London), and many other publcns. General character of writing: poems, literary criticism, text books, historical, juvenile. Relig. denom., Presbyterian. HOME: Cashmere Hills, Christchurch, N. Z.

MACKAY, John Robertson, M.A. *b*: Strathy 1865. *e*: Strathy Publ Sc, Aber Old G.S., St And Univ, & New Col Edin. *m*: Georgina Graham Grant. *s*: 1. Prof of New Testament Exegesis, Free Ch Col Edin. *n.a*: It Ed Evang Quarterly, 1929. *Publ*: The Inquisition, The Reformation & the Counter-Reformation; Trans of Edourd Naville's La Haute Critique dans le Pentateuque ('23). *c.t*: Princeton Theo Review. Moderator of Assembly of F.C. of Scot '29. Rec Fishing. *a*: 5 Rochester Terr, Edin.

MACKAY, Margaret. B.A. *b*: Oxford, Nebr, U.S.A. 1907. *e*: Univ of Cal. *m*: Cpt A. H. Mackay (killed in action 1942). Author. *Publ*: Mrs Dale of Peking; Valiant Dust; Lady with Jade; Homeward the Heart; Like Water Flowing; For all men Born; etc. *Ctr*: Vogue, New Yorker, Cosmopolitan, Ladies' Home Journ, etc. *s.s*: Late Victorian Period (1880—1900) in China inc Boxer Rebellion & in Hawaii. *Rec*: Collecting Chinese blue porcellaneous figurines, swimming, gardening. *c*: Query, New York City. *a*: c/o Hutchinson & Co Ltd (Publishers), London, & c/o John Day Co (Publishers), New York.

MACKAY, Norman Douglas, M.D., B.Sc., D.P.H. *b*: Aberfeldy 1882. *e*: Breadalbane Academy Aberfeldy, Edin Univ, Lond Sch of Medicine. *m*: Gladys Dorothy Elizabeth Cutts. *d*: 1. *n.a*: Asst Ed Caledonian Med Journ. *Publ*: Two Years After; A Holiday in Germany, Denmark & Sweden; Iceland, Spitsbergen, Norway, Diary of a Summer Cruise (Published Privately); etc. *Ctr*: Numerous Med journs. *s.s*: Medicine. *Rec*: Travel, writing, photography. *a*: Dall-Avon, Aberfeldy, Perthshire. *T*: Aberfeldy 11.

MACKAY, Ronald William Gordon, M.A., LL.B. *b*: Australia 1902. *e*: Sydney Gr Sch, Univ of Sydney. *m*: Doreen Armstrong. Solicitor, Lect in Econs Univ of Sydney. *Publ*: Federal Europe; Coupon or Free; Some Aspects of Primary & Secondary Education. *Ctr*: Manch Guardian. *s.s*: Foreign Policy, Federation of Europe, Proportional Representation. *Rec*: Golf, walking. *a*: 12 Gordon Mans, Torrington Pl, London, W.C.1. *T*: Museum 1180.

MACKAY. W. K. *c.t*: Various. Former Dir E. Hulton & Co Ltd & John Heywood Ltd Publishers. *a*: Sherwood, St Werburghs Rd N. Chorlton, M/C.

MACKAY, William. *b*: Glenlivet, Banffshire. Widower. *s*: 1 (dec). *d*: 2. Journalist. *n.a*: Ed N. Brit Agriculturist & Farming News 1919-. Ex-Agric Ed Aberdeen Free Press; On Staff of Elgin Courant & Courier, Ross-shire Journ, etc. *c.t*: Trans of Highland & Agric Soc of Scot, etc. *s.s*: Agric. Reported every show of the Highland & Agric Soc 1889-without break. *Rec*: Golf, bridge. *a*: 23 Morningside Pk, Edin.

MACKEAN, Very Rev. William Herbert, D.D., Res Canon of Rochester Cath. *b*: Dunnington 1877. *e*: Bristol G.S., Corpus Christi Col Oxf. *m*: (1) Beatrix Margaret Irene Graham; (2) Hilda Gifford. *d*: 5. *Publ*: Christian Monasticism in Egypt; Eucharistic Doctrine of the Oxford Movement; etc. Vicar of St John's, Notting Hill 1916-25. Rural Dean Kensington '24-25. Proctor of Convocation '29-. Select Preacher Oxf '30-32. *c*: Un & Athenæum. *a*: The Precinct, Rochester, Kent.

MacKEITH, Ronald Charles, M.A., D.M., M.R.C.P. *b*: Southampton 1908. *e*: K.E. VI Sch S'hampton, Queen's Coll Oxf, St Mary's Hosp Lond & Bellevue Hosp New York. *m*: Elizabeth M. Bartrum. *s*: 1. *d*: 1. *c.t*: The Scientific Film, Norway, Lancet, B.M.J., & many other med journs, Discovery, News Rev, B.B.C. *s.s*: Medical, Infancy & Childhood. *Rec*: Travel, sailing. *w.s*: R.N. 1941-46. *a*: 5 Hanover Terr Mews, Regents Park, London, N.W.1. *T*: Hop 3500.

MACKENNA, Robert Merttins Bird, M.A., M.D., B.Ch., F.R.C.P. *b*: Liverpool 1903. *e*: Roy Naval Colls Osborne & Dartmouth, Camb & St Thomas's Hosp. *m*: (1) Helen Dora Todrick, (2) Margaret Hopkins *s*: 1. *d*: 2. Cons in Dermatology to the British Army, Phys in Charge Skin Dept St Bart's Hosp Lond. *Publ*: Diseases of the Skin; Aids to Dermatology; Modern Trends in Dermatology; etc. *Ctr*: Numerous med journs. *s.s*: Dermatology. *Rec*: Reading, motoring. *c*: Garrick, Univ (L'pool). *a*: 5 Mansfield St, London, W.1. *T*: Langham 1548.

MACKENNAL, Rev. William Leavers. *b*: Bowdon, Cheshire 1881. *e*: Rugby, Trin Col Cam, Farnham Theo Col. *m*: Gladys Hope Whitworth. *Publ*: Life of Major John Haworth Whitworth. *c.t*: Interpreter, Optimist, Commonwealth. *Rec*: Golf, travel. *a*: The Vicarage, Kirkby Lonsdale.

MACKENZIE, Agnes Mure, C.B.E., M.A., D.Litt. *b*: Stornoway. *e*: Aberdeen Univ. *Publ*: History of Scotland (Six Vols); Foundation of Scotland; Robert Bruce King of Scots; The Rise of the Stewarts; The Scotland of Queen Mary & the Religious Wars; The Passing of the Stewarts—Scotland in Modern Times; The Kingdom of Scotland; A History of Britain & Europe for Scottish Schs; Scottish Pageant 81—1513 & 1513—1625 (two Vols); Keith of Kinnellan; Cyprus in Moonlight; Between Sun & Moon; Single Combat; etc. *s.s*: Scot Hist & Affairs. *a*: 15 Langbourne Mansions, Highgate, London, N.6.

MACKENZIE, Alexander William Noble. *b*: Kirkwall 1890. *e*: Inverness Roy Acad. *m*: Helen Johnstone Jardine. *s*: 2. Org Sec. *n a*: Tech Adv to Messrs Brown, Son & Ferguson Ltd, Publs, Glas 1922–. *Publ*: Games for Scouts; Games for Guides; Surveying & Mapping Simplified; First Aid for Girl Guides; Wolf Cub Tests; etc. *c.t*: Scot & Amer n/ps. *s.s*: Cover designs & book illus (drawing pseudonym " Mac "). Qualified as Civil Eng. War Service, severely wounded. *Rec*: Scouting, chess, philately. *a*: 25 Danes Drive, Glas, W.4. *t*: Glas Central 5698.

MACKENZIE, Charles Fraser, C.I.E. *b*: Simla, India 1880. *e*: Malvern Coll, Roy Mil Acad. *m*: Nelly J. Martinet. *d*: 1. Author & Director of Companies. *Publ*: Cancer is Curable, Citizens Versus Doctors; A Citizen's Chamber of Health; Food for Health & Thought; The Miracle of Homoeopathy; Vitality From Within; A Jackal in Persia; Common Sense About Cancer. *s.s*: Nature Laws, Food Reform, Natural Nutrition. *Rec*: Golf, curling, bridge. *c*: St James. *a*: 18 Curzon St, W.1.

MACKENZIE, Compton, O.B.E., B.A., LL.D. *b*: West Hartlepool 1883. *e*: St Paul's Sch, Magdalen Coll Oxf. *m*: Faith Stone. Author. *n.a*: Lit Critic Dly Mail 1931—, Gramophone Critic Sun Pictorial '25—30, Ed The Gramophone '22—. Rector Glasgow Univ '31—34. *Publ*: Poems; Carnival; Sinister Street; Sylvia Scarlett; The Vanity Girl; The Seven Ages of Women; The Old Men of the Sea; Coral; Rogues & Vagabonds; Extraordinary Women; Gallipoli Memories; April Fools; Prince Charlie; Reaped & Bound; The Four Winds of Love. (Plays) The Lost Cause; Carnival; Columbine; etc. *Ctr*: Times, Morning Post, Ev Standard, Ev News, etc. *s.s*: Novels, Plays, Lit & Musical Criticism. *c*: Savile, Highland Yacht, Edin Arts, Authors. *w.s*: 1915—18. *a*: Denchworth Manor, Wantage, Berks.

MACKENZIE, Donald Alexander, M.C., M.A. *e*: Manch Univ. *m*: Winifred M. Pinniger. *s*: 1. *d*: 1. Principal, Educ Div G.B. Instruct Films. *n.a*: Asst Ed & Feature Writer The Teachers World 1924—44, Spec Feature Writer Newnes-Pearson Publications '44—45. *Ctr*: Strand Mag, John O'London's Weekly, Dly Mail, John Bull, Sight & Sound & other film journs. *s.s*: Literary Criticism, Visual Educ. *Rec*: Walking, climbing & travel. *c*: Author's, Press. *a*: The Grove, Greville Park Ave, Ashtead, Surrey.

MACKENZIE (EDWARD MONTAGUE) COMPTON: author and editor; b. West Hartlepool, Eng., Jan. 17, 1883; s. Edward Compton and Virginia Frances (Bateman) M.; educ. St. Paul's Sch. (London), Magdalen Coll. (Oxford). DEGREE: B.A. (Oxford); m. Faith Nona Stone, Nov. 30. 1905. AUTHOR: Poems, 1907; **The Passionate Elopement,** 1911; Carnival, 1912; Kensington Rhymes, 1912; Sinister Street (2 vols.), 1913-14; Guy and Pauline, 1915; Sylvia Scarlett, 1918; Sylvia and Michael, 1919; Poor Relations, 1919; The Vanity Girl, 1920; Rich Relatives, 1921; The Altar Steps, 1922; **The Seven Ages of Woman,** 1922; **The Parson's Progress,** 1923; Gramophone Nights (with Archibald Marshall), 1923; **The Heavenly Ladder,** 1924; Santa Claus in Summer, 1924; **The Old Men of the Sea,** 1924; Coral, 1925; Fairy Gold, 1926; Rogues and Vagabonds, 1927; **Vestal Fire,** 1927; Extremes Meet, 1928; Extraordinary Women, 1929; The Three Couriers, 1929; Gallipoli

Memories, 1929; April Fools, 1930; Told, 1930; First Athenian Memories, 1931; Buttercups and Daisies, 1931; Our Street, 1931; (plays): The Gentleman in Gray, 1906; Carnival, 1912; Columbine, 1920. Editor: The Gramophone (a monthly review of recorded music), founder and sole editor. Editor (during undergraduate days): The Oxford Point of View. Contributor to many mags. and papers in Britain and America. General character of writing: fiction, juveniles, poems, plays, historical. Service in Great War as Capt. in Royal Marines; with Royal Naval Div. at Gallipoli; invalided, 1915; mil. control officer, Athens, 1916: dir. Aegean Intelligence Service, 1917. Decorations: O.B.E., 1919; Chevalier Legion d'Honneur; Chev. of the Redeemer (Greece); Officer White Eagle with swords (Serbia). Relig. denom., Catholic. CLUBS: Savile, Royal Highland Yacht, Oxford and Cambridge Musical, Authors', Savage (London); Edinburgh Arts, Dublin Arts, Royal Channel Islands Yacht. HOME: Isle of Jethou, Channel Isles, Great Britain; Eilean Aigas, Beauly, Invernessshire, Scotland.

MACKENZIE, FREDERICK ARTHUR: author, journalist; b. Quebec, Canada, Sept., 1869; s. John Mill and Priscilla Mackenzie; educ. private schls.; m. Kathleen Willett, Apr. 30, 1901. AUTHOR: Sober by Act of Parliament, 1894; From Tokio to Tiflis, 1905; Tragedy of Korea, 1908; The Unveiled East, 1909; Through the Hindenburg Line, 1919; Russia Before Dawn, 1926; World Famous Crimes, 1927; The Thaw Case, 1928; Landru, 1929; The Clash of Cymbals, 1929; King George—In His Own Words, 1929. Editor: Weekly Edition London Times, 1910-14. Contributor to innumerable papers and to Nineteenth Century, Spectator, London Daily News and many other mags. General character of writing: historical, sociological. War corres. London Daily Mail, 1901-10; corres. (staff), Chicago Daily News, Russia, 1921-24; Northern Europe, 1925-26; European corres., Japan Daily News Jiji Shimpo, since 1926. Has lectured extensively, U.S.A. and Britain. Excluded from Russia (Soviet) because of advocacy in the cause of political exiles. Has travelled extensively in Central Asia. Relig. denom., Episcopal. CLUBS: Savage, Whitefriars. HOME: Mayfield, Hillcrest Road, Sydenham, London, S. E. 26, Eng.

MACKENZIE, George, F.R.G.S. Journalist. n.a: Ed Northern Chronicle. s.s: Econs, Travel, Hist, Archæology. a: The Sutors, 28 Broadstone Park, Inverness. T: 717.

MACKENZIE, Rev. H. W. a: 25 Winchester Rd, Oxford.

MACKENZIE, Col. Harry Malcolm, C.I.E., M.B., ChB.(Edin), D.P.H.(Cantab). b: Helensburgh. e: Roy H.S., Edin Univ & Cam. m: Elfreda Hudson. s: 1. d: 1. I.M.S. (ret). c.t: B.M.J., Lancet. Rec: Golf, shooting. c: Army Golfing Soc, Roy Dornoch Golf. a: c/o Lloyds Bank, 6 Pall Mall, S.W.1.

MACKENZIE, Hettie Millicent, M.A. b: Clifton 1863. e: Priv Scs Clifton & Switzerland, Univ Col Bristol & Cam Training Col. m: Prof John Stuart Mackenzie. Prof of Educ (Cardiff) till 1915. Publ: Training of Teachers in U.S.A., Hegel's Theory & Practice of Education; Freedom in Education. s.s: Educ. Lect Tours in India, Burma & U.S.A. Rec: Reading, travel. c: Crosby Hall. a: Upfield Cottage, Brockweir, Mon.

MACKENZIE, Iain Fraser, M.D., Ch.B., D.P.H b: Inverness-shire 1907. e: Dunoon & Edinburgh. m: Jean Cameron. s: 2. d: 1. Deputy County M.O.H. Cumberland. Publ: Social Health & Morals. c.t: B.M.J., Med Officer. s.s: Medical Subjects of Broad Social Interest. Rec: Cycling & Hill-climbing. a: County Health Dept, 11 Portland Sq, Carlisle.

MACKENZIE, Ian. b: Dingwall, Scotland 1916. e: Dingwall Acad, Keil Sch Dumbarton. Journalist. n.a: North Star Dingwall 1935, Dundee Courier '36—37, People's Journ Glasgow '38, Birmingham Gazette '39, Liverpool Dly Post '46, News Chron '46—47, Assoc Press '47. Rec: Travel, collecting fine wines, motoring. c: Lond Pres. a: 38 Castelnau, Barnes, London, S.W.13. T: Riverside 2988.

MACKENZIE, Joan Noble, LL.A. b: Dumfries. e: Priv, Mem Scot P.E.N. Publ: The Homeward Tide; The Deadly Game; Linda Walked Alone; All for the Apple. Ctr: Weekly Scotsman, Glasgow Herald, Scot Country Life, Chambers's Journ, People's Friend, Life & Work. Rec: Gardening, walking. a: 12 Queen's Cresc, Edinburgh. T: 44228.

MACKENZIE, John. b: Rothesay 1887. e: Rothesay Acad. m: Helen M. Donaldson. s: 1. d: 2. Ed & Publisher. n.a: Calgary Albertan (Canada) 1909, Strathmore Standard (Canada) '10—25, U.F.A. (Calgary) '26. Ctr: Outram Publs (Glas). Rec: Golf. a: Strathmore, Montford, Rothesay, Scotland. T: 219.

MACKENZIE, John. b: Invermoriston 1898. e, Public Sch. m: Martha Welsh Walker. Reporter: n.a: Dist Corr The Scotsman, Scottish Dly Express. Dly Herald, Edin Ev Dispatch, B.B.C., Rep West Lothian Courier 1937. Ctr: Scottish Field. s.s: Angling, Gardening. Rec: Angling, gardening, bowling. a: 59 High St, Linlithgow. T: 92.

MACKENZIE, John Maurice Kerr. b: Calcutta 1877. e: Stockwell Orphanage, Lon. m: May Allan (dec). F.L. Journalist. n.a: Ed Indian Daily Telegraph, Lucknow 1915-21; Asst Ed Rangoon Gazette '22-29. Publ: Verses (1897). c.t: Times, News Chronicle, Times of India Illus Weekly, Calcutta Gazette, etc. s.s: Lit & Reviewing, short stories, verses, articles on India & Burma. Appointed by Lord Meston to U.P. Publ Cmt at Lucknow '15-18. Press Rep at Delhi Coronation Durbar '11. Travelled extensively. Rec: Walking. a: Chesney, Selsea Av, Herne Bay, Kent. t: 268.

MACKENZIE, John Stuart, LittD.(Cam), LL.D. (Glas). b: Glas 1860. e: Glas H.S. & Univ & Trin Col Cam. m: H. Millicent Hughes. Prof of Philos (ret). Publ: Introduction to Social Philosophy; Manual of Ethics; Arrows of Desire; Cosmic Problems; Elements of Metaphysics, etc. c.t: Mind, Philosophy, Internat Journ of Ethics. s.s: Philos. Lect tours in India, Burmah & U.S.A. Rec: Reading. a: Upfield Cottage, Brockweir, Mon.

MACKENZIE, Rt. Rev. Kenneth Donald, M.A. b: Surbiton, Surrey 1876. e: Radley, Hertford Coll Oxf, Wells Theological Coll. Fell Dean & Chap Pembroke Coll Oxf 1905—10, Canon of Salisbury '34—45, Bishop of Brechin '35—43. m: Elizabeth Janet Forbes. Publ: Confusion of the Churches; The Way of the Church; The Faith of the Church; The Case for Episcopacy; The Catholic Rule of Life; The Fruit of the Spirit; Christ The King; The Meaning of Churchmanship. a: 15 Wimborne Rd, Bournemouth, Hants. T: 3720.

MACKENZIE, Sir Leslie., LL.D. Crown Nominee for Scot on Gen Med Counc. Publ: Health & Disease; Medical Inspection of School Children; Health of School Children; Child at School. c.t: Med papers, etc. a: 14 Belgrave Pl, Edin. t: 20554.

MACKENZIE, Margaret. b: Malta. e: The English Convent, Bruges. Publ: The Station Platform & other Poems; The Child Who Had Never Heard of Christmas; The Seeker & Other Poems; Satan Among the Saints. Ctr: Catholic World, Thought, etc. a: St Lucy's, Rye, Sussex. T: Rye 3232.

MACKENZIE, Marion Ellen, M.B., Ch.B.(Edin). *b*: Yorks 1873. *e*: Germany & Edinburgh Univ. *m*: Dr James McManus. *s*: 1. *d*: 1. Journalist, Asst Med Officer of Health City of Denbigh 1916—18, Med Asst Leeds Public Health Dept (Maternity & Child Welfare) '18—27. *Ctr*: Yorkshire Evening Post, Allied Newspapers, New Health, Chambers's Journ, Time & Tide, Manch Ev News, Sun Chron, Girls Own Paper. *s.s*: Psychology of Children, Infant Welfare, Psychology. *c*: Outlook, Leeds. *a*: 4 Cumberland Rd, Leeds 6. *T*: Leeds 51462.

MACKENZIE, Murdo, M.D., M.R.C.P. *b*: Inverness 1895. *e*: Edin Academy & Guy's Hosp Lond. *m*: Norah C. Carter. Lecturer in Psychology Extra-Mural Dept, Univs of Lond & Oxf. *Publ*: The Human Mind; When Temperaments Clash. *Ctr*: Brit Journ of Psychology, Journ of Clinical Research & other med journs. *s.s*: Psychology. *Rec*: Walking. *c*: Authors Reform. *a*: 141 Harley St, London, W.1. *T*: Welbeck 8682.

MACKENZIE, Nicol Finlayson, M.I.C.E., F.R.G.S. *b*: Nairn 1857. *e*: Edin Inst, Edin Univ, Roy Indian Eng Col Coopers Hill. *m*: Isobel Lamb (dec). *s*: 1. Civil Engineer. *Publ*: Methods of Surveying; Notes on Irrigation Works; Report on the Investigation of Rivers (jt author); *c.t*: Various tech papers. *s.s*: Irrigation & surveying. 24 y Indian Irrigation Dept, ret '02. Under Sec for Irrigation to Indian Govt. Sanitary Engineer to United Prov Govt India. Sr Instructor in Surveying R.I.E. Col Coopers Hill. Instructor in Surveying to Scs of Engineering, Forestry & Geog Oxf Univ. Special Lecturer on Irrigation to Graduates King's Col Lon. During War Insp under Min of Muns. *Rec*: Fishing, golf. *a*: 185 Woodstock Rd, Oxf. *t*: Summertown 5712.

MACKENZIE, Norman Archibald MacRae, C.M.G., M.M., K.C., B.A., L.L.M., D.C.L., F.R.S.C. *b*: Pugwash, Nova Scotia 1894. *e*: Pictou Acad, Univs of Dalhousie, Harvard, New Brunswick, Toronto, St John's Coll Camb. *m*: Margaret Thomas. *s*: 1. *d*: 2. Pres The Univ of British Columbia. *Publ*: Legal Status of Aliens in Pacific Countries; Canada & the Law of Nations (collab); Canada in World Affairs (collab). *Ctr*: Canadian Bar Review, etc. *s.s*: Internat Law. *Rec*: Golf, fishing, hunting. *c*: Vancouver. *a*: 4 Acadia Camp, The Univ of British Columbia, Vancouver, B.C., Canada. *T*: Alma 1191.

MACKENZIE, Norman Ian, B.Sc.(Econ). *b*: London 1921. *e*: Haberdasher Aske's, Hatcham, Lond Sch of Econs. *m*: Jeanne Sampson. Journalist & Author, Occasional Broadcsats on Political Topics. *n.a*: Ed. Staff New Statesman & Nation '43—47. *Publ*: Argentina. *Ctr*: New Statesman & Nation, Political Quarterly, Toronto Star Weekly, etc. *s.s*: British Political & Social Questions, Film Criticism, Internat Affairs, Labour & Socialist Book Criticism, History, Nth & Sth American Politics. *Rec*: Chess, book collecting, films. *a*: 87 Fitzjohn's Ave, Hampstead, London, N.W.3. *T*: Hampstead 0225.

MACKENZIE, Orgill, M.A. *b*: Stranraer. *e*: Edin Univ. *m*: Alister MacKenzie. *Publ*: Poems & Stories (1930); The Crooked Laburnum ('32). *a*: Claysemore, Iwerne Minster, Dorset. *t*: Childe Okeford 52.

MACKENZIE, W. J. M., B.A., LL.B. *a*: Magdalen Col, Oxf.

MACKENZIE, William Cook, F.S.A. *b*: 1862. *m*: Gertrude Mary Anderson (dec'd). Author. *Publ*: The Shirra; A Tale of the Isles; The Races of Ireland & Scotland; The War Diary of a London Scot; The Book of the Lews; The Life & Time of John Maitland, Duke of Lauderdale 1616—1682; Scottish Place Names; The Western Isles: Their History, Traditions & Place Names; Lovat of the Forty-Five; The Highland & Isles of Scotland; etc. *Rec*: Golf. *a*: 14 St Georges Rd, St Margarets, Middlx.

MACKENZIE, William Mackay, M.A., D.Litt. *b*: Cromarty 1871. *e*: Cromarty Public Sch, Edin Univ. Married. Late Sec Roy Comm on Ancient & Historic Monuments of Scotland, Prof Antiquities Roy Scott Acad. *Publ*: Hugh Miller; Battle of Bannockburn; Outline of Scottish History; Pompeii; Barbour's Bruce; Book of Arran; The Secret of Flodden; Bannockburn Myth; Poems of William Dunbar; The King's Quair; etc. *Ctr*: Scotsman, Glasgow Herald. *a*: Calrossie, 4 Barkly St, Cromarty, Scotland.

MACKENZIE-BELL, E. A., M.J.I. *b*: London. *e*: Monkton Combe & Univ Col. F/L Author & Journalist. *n.a*: Financial Ed Chicago Tribune Paris, News Ed Madras Mail, Ed Businness, Lect L.C.C., etc. *c.t*: Various. *s.s*: Finance, literary, travel. *Rec*: Golf. *c*: Eng Assoc, etc. *a*: Glebeside, Harrington Rd, Brighton, Sussex. *t*: Preston 2640.

MACKERETH, James Allan. *b*: Ambleside 1871. *e*: St Bees Sch. *m*: Emily Hilda Bell. *d*: 2. *Publ*: In Grasmere Vale; The Cry on the Mountain; A Son of Cain; On the face of a Star; The Red, Red Dawn; Storm Wrack; Earth, Dear Earth; Hands; To a Great City; A King's Sacrifice; Jungle; etc. *s.s*: Poetry. *Rec*: Gardening. *a*: Stocka Hse, Cottingley, Bingley, Yorks.

MACKESY, Leonora Dorothy Rivers. (See **STARR, Leonora.**) *b*: Aberdeen 1902. *e*: Priv. *m*: Maj Gen P. J. Mackesy, C.B., D.S.O., M.C. *s*: 2. Novelist. *Ctr*: Various mags. *Rec*: Breeding Cairn terriers, country life (Scotland). *a*: Lane End, Southwold, Suffolk. *T*: Southwold 2273.

MACKEWN, Allen Raymond. *e*: Guildford G.S., West Australia. Master Mariner. *c.t*: Grand Mag, Wide World, Everyman, Overseas, Orient Observer, Nautical Magazine, etc. *s.s*: Flying, sea travel. *a*: 15 Palace Court, W.2. *t*: Bayswater 0558.

MACKIE, Albert David, M.A. *b*: Edinburgh 1904. *e*: Broughton Sec & Edin Univ. *m*: Isabella Kerray. *s*: 1. *d*: 2. Editor Ev Dispatch, Edin Scots Poet. *n.a*: Reporter Dly Record 1928, News Ed Jamaica Dly Gleaner '28, Sub-Ed The Scotsman '30, Leader Writer Scotsman '32, Leader Writer Glas Ev News '35, Spec Writer Scottish Sun Express '41. *Publ*: Poems in Two Tongues; Sing a Sang o Scotland. *a*: 27 Blachford Ave, Edinburgh 9. *T*: 43227.

MACKIE, David (David Mackie Jr.). *b*: Tarbolton 1891. *e*: Tarbolton Publ Sch & Ayr Acad. *m*: (1) Ethel L. Cameron (dec'd), (2) Peggy Hogarth. *d*: 2. Journalist. *n.a*: Ed Southern Reporter & Southern' Annual, previously on Staffs Kilmarnock Standard, Carlisle Journ, Buchan Observer, etc. *Publ*: The Shirra o' the Forest; Songs of an Ayrshire Yeoman; Bandolier & Bandages; Selkirk's Finest Hour. *Ctr*: Scot & Eng newspsp, Marine Mag, Scots Observer, etc. *s.s*: Agriculture, Rural Indus, Scots Hist. *w.s*: World War I, Home Guard World War II. *a*: 18 Scott Cresc, Selkirk, Scotland.

MACKIE, J. Watt. *b*: Falkirk 1901. *e*: Falkirk H.S. Married. *s*: 1. *d*: 1. Mang Ed Lincolns Echo. *n.a*: From Falkirk Mail '15 via Glas Herald, Daily Record Glas, Sunday Mail Glas & Lon Office of Sun Mail, Press Assoc Lon, Allied N/ps Lon Office, Sun Sentinel, Northcliffe N/ps, Evening Telegraph Derby to pres position in Lincoln '33—. *Rec*: Walking. *a*: 40 Mount St, Lincoln, & Lincolns Echo, Lincoln. *t*: 1510 (priv).

MACKIE, John. Bronze & Silver Medallist of City & Guilds of Lond Inst (cloth construction & designing). *Publ*: Dialect Poems & A Play; How To Make a Woollen

Mill Pay; The Wooing of Widow Wallington (one act dialect play), etc. *Ctr*: Somerset County Herald & Somerset Year Book. *s.s*: Dialect & Cloth Structure *a*: 87 Corringham Rd, Golders Green, N.W.11. *T*: Speedwell 3896.

MACKIE, John. *b*: Stirling. *e*: Stirling H.S., Stanley Hse Bridge of Allan & Priv. Writer. *Publ*: The Devil's Playground; The Prodigal's Brother; They that Sit in Darkness; Black Man's Rock; The Great Antarctic; The Treasure Hunters; etc. *c.t*: Daily Mail, Chums, Pearson's, Boys' Own Paper, Wide World Mag, etc. *s.s*: Exploration, adventure, anthropology. Roy N.W. Mounted Police, Canada. Exploration & Pioneering in Aus. Extensive travel. Gold Medallist Highland & Agric Soc of Scot & S. African War Medal (five clasps). *Rec*: Reading, fishing, shooting, flying. *a*: Arlington Hse, Lexham Gdns, S. Kensington, W.8.

MACKIE, John Duncan, C.B.E., M.C. *b*: Edinburgh 1887. *e*: Middlesborough Hgh Sch, Jesus Coll Oxf *m*: Cicely Jean Paterson. *s*: 2. *d*: 1. Prof of Scottish History & Lit Univ of Glas, O.St.J., Chev Legion' d'Honneur. *Publ*: Cavalier & Puritan; Vol II (16th Century) Hist of the Brit People; Negotiations Between James VI & I & Ferdinand I of Tuscany; Thomas Thomson's Memorial on Old Extent; Estate of the Burgesses in the Scots Parliament (with Dr G. S. Pryde); Andrew Lang & the House of Stuart. *Ctr*: English Hist Review, Scottish History Review, History, Scotsman, Glas Herald, Manch Guardian. *s.s*: Scottish Hist, Hist of 16th Century. *Rec*: Golf, tennis. *c*: Royal & Ancient Golf of St Andrews. *w.s*: 1914—18 Argyll & Sutherlands. *a*: 9 The Univ, Glasgow, W.2. *T*: Glasgow West 3068.

MACKIE, Robert Laird, M.A., B.Litt. *e*: Dundee Hgh Sch, St Andrews Univ. Lecturer in English & Hist. *Publ*: Short History of Scotland; Short Social & Political History of Britain; A Book of Scottish Verse (Ed). *Ctr*: Scots Mag, Scotland, Scotsman. *s.s*: Scots Hist & Lit. *a*: Abercraig, West Newport, Dundee. *T*: Newport 3340.

MACKIE, Thomas. Journalist. *n.a*: Ed & Proprietor Falkirk Mail. *c*: Rotary (Past Pres), Edin Press. *a*: Falkirk Mail Buildings, Falkirk. *T*: 780 & 731.

MACKIE, Thomas Jones, C.B.E., M.D., LL.D., D.P.H., F.R.S.E. *b*: Hamilton 1888. *e*: Hamilton Academy, Glasgow Univ. Prof of Bacteriology Edinburgh Univ. *Publ*: Manual of Bacteriology (jointly); Handbook of Practical Bacteriology (jointly) *Ctr*: Several books on Bacteriology, Immunology & Medicine, author of various papers in medical & scientific journals & periodicals. *s.s*: Bacteriology & Immunology. *a*: 22 Mortonhall Rd, Edinburgh. *T*: 42566.

MACKIE, William Soutar, M.A. *b*: Aberdeenshire, Scotland 1885. *e*: Aberdeen & Oxf Univs. *m*: Elizabeth Mary Chudleigh. Univ Prof. *Publ*: The Exeter Book; A Book of English Verse for South African Readers. *Ctr*: Modern Language Rev, Journ of Germanic Philology, etc. *s.s*: Eng Language. *Rec*: Chess, bowls. *c*: Civil Service, Owl (Cape Town). *a*: Drumoak, Greenfield Rd, Kenilworth, Cape Town, Sth Africa. *T*: 72910.

MACKIM, T. B. *n.a*: Mang Ed & Dir Hull Dly Mail & associated newspapers, President Yorkshire Newspaper Soc 1947—48. *a*: Hull Daily Mail, Jameson St, Hull. *T*: Hull 15100.

MACKINDER, Dorothy. *e*: Convent Sch. *Publ*: The Violent Take It By Storm; Captain Cerise; Brief Was the Laurel; Silver Fountains. *Rec*: Gardening, cooking. *a*: Thimblepen, Box, Stroud, Glos.

MACKINDER, RT. HON. SIR HALFORD JOHN: privy councillor; b. Gainsborough, Eng., Feb., 1861; s. Draper M. and Fanny Anne (Hewitt) M.; educ. Epsom Coll., Christ Church (Oxford). DEGREE: M.A. AUTHOR: Britain and the British Seas, 1902 (2nd edit. 1907); The Rhine: its Valley and History, 1908; Eight Lectures on India, 1910; Democratic Ideals and Reality, 1919; Chapter I, The Sub-Continent of India (in Cambridge Hist. of India), 1922; Elementary Studies in Geography and History, in 8 vols. (17th edit.), 1927. Editor: Great Britain section of Encyclo. Americana, 1907; A Chart of Human Progress (in Times Historians' History of the World), 1907. Contributor to Geographical Journ., Nat. Rev. and many other mags. General character of writing: text books, educational, historical. Chmn. Imperial Shipping and Economics Comms.; formerly Reader in Geography, Univ. Oxford; prof. of Geog., Univ. London; prin. Univ. Coll., Reading; Student (Fellow) Christ Church (Oxford). Led expedition to summit of Mt. Kenya, E. Africa, 1899; M.P. 1910-1922; Brit. High Comm. for South Russia, 1919-20; Knighted, 1920; sworn of H. M. Privy Council, 1926. CLUBS: Athenaeum, Carlton, Alpine. HOME: 27 Grosvenor Place, London, S. W. 1, Eng.

MACKINLAY, Caroline Mary Cranston, M.A. *b*: Glasgow. *e*: Cheltenham Ladies' Coll & St Andrews Univ. *n.a*: Sub-Ed Amalgamated Press, Woman's Illustrated 1941—42, Copywriter Overseas Propaganda Min of Inf '42—44, Asst Ed Le Messager de la Liberte, L'arc en Ciel, Political Intelligence Dept Foreign Office '44—45, Asst Ed Envoy Mag for Belgium Min of Inf '45—46, Visualiser Future '46—. *s.s*: Hist, Fashion. *Rec*: Reading, riding. *a*: 3 Grape St, London, W.C.2. *T*: Temple Bar 6132.

MACKINLAY, Leila S. (" Brenda Grey "). *b*: London 1910. *e*: Priv. Novelist, Lecturer Regent St Polytech & Y.W.C.A., Festival Adjudicator. *n.a*: Play Pictorial (2 yrs), Dancing Times (5 yrs). *Publ*: Little Mountebank; Fame's Fetters; Madame Juno; An Exotic Young Lady; Willed to Wed; The Pro's Daughter; Modern Micawbers; Shadow Lawn; Into the Net; Love Goes South; Young Man's Slave; Night Bell; Doubting Heart; Apron Strings; Theme Song; Caretaker Within; Reluctant Bride; Only Her Husband; Woman at the Wheel; Man Always Pays; None Better Loved; Ridin' High; Time on Her Hands; The Brave Live On; Green Limelight; Lady of the Torch; Two Walk Together; Piper's Pool; Piccadilly Inn; Blue Shutters; Peacock Hill; Echo of Applause. *s.s*: Music, Drama, Amateur Stage Criticism & Drama Adjudications. *a*: 41 Portman Mans, Baker St. London, W.1. *T*: Welbeck 2640.

MACKINLAY, Malcolm Sterling, M.A. *b*: London 1876. *e*: Eton & Oxf (Trin Coll). *m*: Dagny Hansen (dec'd) *d*: 1. Teacher & Writer, Inc Soc of Authors, Roy Soc of Musicians, Adjudicated for Nat Competition in Operatic Art, Drama Festivals & Musical Festivals. *Publ*: Origin & Development of Light Opera; Garcia the Centenarian (biography); Antoinette Sterling & Other Celebrities; The Singing Voice & its Training; Light Opera (Art & Technique); English Diction for Foreign Students; (Novels) Reparation; The Enemy Agent. *Ctr*: Strand Mag, Dly Telegraph, Play Pictorial, Musical News, Tatler, etc. *s.s*: Singing, Elocution, Light Opera & Musical Plays. *Rec*: Reading. *a*: 41 Portman Mans, Chiltern St, London, W.1. *T*: Welbeck 2640.

MACKINNON, James, M.A., PhD., D.D., D.Th, L.L.D., F.R.S.E. *b*: Turriff 1860. *e*: Parish Sc, Univs of Edin, Bonn & Heidelberg. *m*: Pauline Klein. *s*: 1. Regius Prof of Ecclesiastical Hist Edin Univ. *Publ*: Culture in Early Scotland (1892); History of Edward III; A History of Modern Liberty (1906-08); Constitutional History of Scotland; Luther and The Reformation; The Historic Jesus; The Gospel in the Early Church ('33); etc. *c.t*: Ency Brit, Glas Herald, Kölnische Zeitung, Aberdeen Free Press, etc. *s.s*: Hist. Mem Counc Roy Soc of Edin. *Rec*: Golf, gardening. *a*: 12 Lygon Rd, Edin. *t*: 42437.

MACKINNON, James A. R., M.A., LL.B. Mem Scottish Bar, Sheriff-Substitute of Forfars. *Publ*: (in collab with father, Prof James Mackinnon) The Constitutional History of Scotland (1924). *a*: Thornlea, Forfar, Angus. *t*: 219.

MACKINNON, Lachlan (Jr), D.S.O., T.D. *e*: Gordon's Coll & Aberdeen Univ. Advocate in Aberdeen, Lecturer in International Law Aberdeen Univ, Brevet Colonel T.A. (ret), Croix de Guerre. *Publ*: Leading Cases in the International Private Law of Scotland; Company Law & Conveyancing, Manual of (collab). *a*: Ardbeck Milltimber, Aberdeenshire. *T*: Cutler 2269.

MACKINNON. Mervyn Alexander, M.C. *b*: 1889. *e*: Bundell's Sc & Abroad. Legal Adviser to Publ Firms. *Publ*: Libel for Laymen (with J. Alan Bell); Pratt's Industrial & Provident Societies (15th edn). *c.t*: Halsbury's Laws of Eng, Eng & Colonial Periodicals, etc. *s.s*: Law of libel. War Service (des & wounded). *a*: 13 Alfred Pl, S.W.7. *t*: Kensington 0435.

MACKINTOSH, Sir Alexander. Parl Corr Liverpool Post (ret). *Publ*: Joseph Chamberlain: An Honest Biography; From Gladstone to Lloyd George; Echoes of Big Ben. *Ctr*: Brit Weekly. *s.s*: Politics. *Rec*: Golf, walking. *c*: Nat Lib. *a*: 57 Union Rd, London, S.W.4. *T*: Macaulay 4047.

MACKINTOSH, Hugh Ross, D.Phil(Edin), D.D. (Edin & Oxon), ThD.(Marburg). *b*: Paisley 1870. *e*: Neilson Inst Paisley, Roy Acad Tain, Geo Watson's Col Edin, Univs of Edin, Freiburg, Halle, Marburg, & New Col Edin. *m*: Jessie Air. *s*: 1. *d*: 3. Prof of Theol New Col Edin. *Publ*: Jt Trans & Ed of Ritschl's Justification & Reconciliation (1900); Doctrine of the Person of Jesus Christ ('12, 7th ed '31); The Christian Experience of Forgiveness ('27, 4th ed '34); Jt Trans & Ed Schleiermacher's The Christian Faith ('28); The Christian Apprehension of God ('28); The Highway of God ('31); etc. *c.t*: Expository Times, Ch Quarterly Review, Theol Literatur Zeitung, American Journ of Theology, etc. *s.s*: Theology. Moderator Ch of Scot '32. *Rec*: Golf. *a*: 81 Colinton Rd, Edin. *t*: 61649.

MACKINTOSH, J., K.C., LL.D. Advocate. *Publ*: Roman Law of Sale (2nd edn 1906); Roman Law in Modern Practice (Tagore Law Lects Calcutta Univ '33). Prof of Cost Law, Dean of Faculty of Law Edin Univ, Sheriff of Ross '12, etc. *a*: 6 Clarendon Cres, Edin.

MACKINTOSH. Norman. *b*: Torosay, Isle of Mull. *e*: George Watson's Col Edin, Heriot-Watt Col Edin, Edin Univ & Edin Sc of Art. *m*: Agnes Rhoda Angus. Journalist. Press Repres C.P.R. Lon. *n.a*: Sub-Ed & Mag Ed D. C. Thomson & Co Publs Dundee 1904—10, Rep on Evening Telegram Toronto '10, Rep Optimist prince Rupert B.C. '10—12, Ed Prince Rupert Daily News '12, Marine Ed Vancouver Sun '13, Surburban Ed Toronto Telegram '14; Ed Prince Rupert Empire '14—16, Assoc Ed Maclean Publs Montreal & Toronto '16—18, Features Ed Toronto Telegram '18—27, Press Repres C.P. Lon '27—. *Publ*: Special articles on Northern B.C. & short-story series " Skipper Joe " under pen-name " Norman Scott " (in Vancouver Sunset); serial & short stories to Ryerson Press Publs Toronto " Two Boys in B.C. ", " The Boy Pre-Emptors", etc. *c.t*: Various n/ps & periodicals. *s.s*: Canada, travel, cruising. *Rec*. Golf, photography, sketching. *c*: Press (Lon), British Empire, Studio, & C.N.A.P. club. Mem N/p Press Fund, etc. *a*: 62—56 Charing X, S.W.1. *t*: Whitehall 5100.

MACKMURDO, Arthur Heygate. *b*: Edmonton 1851. *e*: Felsted Sc & Oxf Univ. *m*: Eliza Carte. Architect. *Publ*: Pressing Questions; Profit Sharing; The Human Hive, its Life & Law; A People's Charter; Plain Handicrafts; etc. *s.s*: Sociology. *a*: Wickham Bishops, Essex.

MACKNESS, Constance, B.A. *b*: Tuena, N.S.W. 1882. *e*: High Sc, Sydney & Univ of Sydney. Headmistress Presbyterian Girls Col, Warwick. *Publ*: Miss Pickle; The Young Beachcombers; Growing Up; The Blossom Children; Gem of the Flat; Miss Billy; Di-Double Di; The Glad School. *c.t*: Table Talk, Australian Jnl, Queenslander, Australian Woman's Mirror, New Nation. *s.s*: Children's fiction, short stories, light verse, educational articles. *Rec*: Gardening, bridge. Lecturer on literary subjects. *a*: Presbyterian Girls Col, Warwick, Queensland, Australia. *t*: Warwick 83.

MAC KOWSKY, HANS: professor of art; b. Berlin, Germany, Nov., 1879; s. Ludwig and Bessie (Schaff) Mac K.; educ. French College (Berlin), DEGREES: Professor, Dr. Phil.; m. Else Altmann, 1906. AUTHOR: Verrocchio, 1901; Michelangelo, 1908 (4th edit. 1925); Rauch, 1917; Alt-Berlin, 1921; Schinkel, 1921; Menzel, 1924; J. G. Schadow, 1927. Contributes to Frankfurter Zeitung, Berlin Tageblatt, Burlington Mag., Kunst und Kunstler, etc. General character of writing: art. CLUBS: P.E.N. Religion, Protestant. ADDRESS: Schinkelplatz 6, Berlin, Germany.

MACKY, S. Ophthalmic Surg. *Publ*: John Black; The Trap (plays). *c.t*: B.M.J., Proc Roy Soc Med. *a*: 126 Harley St, W.1. *t*: Wel 5632.

MACLACHLAN, Rev. Lewis, M.A. *b*: Blackford 1804. *e*: Crieff & Glas Univ, Westminster Coll Camb. *m*: Mary Hally. *s*: 2. *d*: 1. Min of Presbyt Ch of Eng. *n.a*: Ed Reconciliation. *Publ*: Religion for the Non-Religious; The Faith of Friendship; Intelligent Prayer; Defeat Triumphant. *Ctr*: Presbyterian Messenger, Christian World, etc. *s.s*: Theo, Peace, China & the Far East. *a*: 11 Montenotte Rd, London, N.8. *T*: Mountview 7819.

MACLACHLAN, T. Kay, M.A., M.B., B.Ch, F.R.F.P.S. Cons Physician. *c.t*: Brain, B.M.J., Quarterly Journ of Med, Clin Journ, etc. *a*: 3 Woodside Pl, Glas, C.3. *t*: Douglas 1498.

MACLAGAN, Sir Edward Douglas, K.C.S.I., K.C.I.E. *e*: Winchester, New Coll Oxf. Indian Civil Service (ret). *Publ*: The Jesuits & the Great Mogul. *a*: 39 Egerton Terr, Kensington. *T*: Kensington 4075.

MACLAGAN, Rev. Patrick Johnston, M.A., D.Phil, D.D. *b*: Berwick-on-Tweed, 1865. *e*: Edin Univ. United Presbyt Theo Hall, Edin. *m*: Emily Elizabeth Gauld. *s*: 2. *d*: 3. Presbyt Minister; Foreign Missions Sec of Presbyt Church of England. *Publ*: The Gospel View of Things, 1906; The Gospel & its Working '21; Chinese Religious Ideas '26. Missionary at Swatow, S. China 1888-1914. Moderator of Presbyt Church of England '29. *a*: 15 Russell Sq, W.C.1.

MACLAREN, James. *e*: Shawlands Acad. Publisher & Bookseller. *Publ*: Gaelic Self Taught; Ed Island of Mull; Skye Iochdar Trotternish, etc. *s.s*: Scots gaelic. *a*: 7 Denholm Drive, Giffnock, Glasgow.

MACLEAN, Angus, B.Sc(Glas & Lon). *b*: Kilcalmonell 1863. *e*: Glas Univ. *m*: Maud M. L. Pagan. *s*: 1 (dec). *d*: 1. Princ of Paisley Tech Col (ret).

n.a: Ed Handbook of Ind's of Glas & W. of Scotland, prepared for the Brit Assoc Mtg held in Glas 1901. Acting Sec & Ed of Proc of Roy Philos Soc of Glas '01. *Publ*: Text Book of Practical Physics ('12). *s.s*: Experimental Physics. Pres Paisley Philos Inst 3 y. Convener of the Coats' Observatory Cmt, Paisley 3 y. *Rec*: Mineralogy, boating. *a*: Brecklarach, Tarbert, Argyll.

MACLEAN, Right Rev. Arthur John, D.D.(Cam & Glas). *b*: Bath 1858. *e*: Eton & King's Col Cam. *m*: Eva MacLean. *Publ*: Grammar of Vernacular Syriac; Dictionary of Vernacular Syriac; Trans E. Syrian Daily Offices ('94); etc. *c.t*: Hastings' Ency of Religion & Ethics, Ency Britannica. *c*: Scott Conservative, Edin. *a*: Eden Ct, Inverness.

MACLEAN, Catherine Macdonald, F.R.S.L. *b*: Muir of Ord. *e*: Muir of Ord & Dingwall Acad, Edin Univ, Cherwell Hall Oxf, Univ Coll Lond. Writer & Lecturer, Lect Univ of Wales 1921—37. *Publ*: Born Under Saturn (a Biography of William Hazlitt); Dorothy Wordsworth: the Early Years; Dorothy & William Wordsworth; Seven for Cordelia; The Tharrus Three; Farewell to Tharrus; Alexander Scott, Montgomerie, & Drummond of Hawthornden as Lyric Poets. *Ctr*: Times Lit Supp, Observer, Scotsman, Glasgow Herald, English Review, Chambers's Journ, Mod Lang Review, etc. *s.s*: English Lit. *Rec*: Walking, gardening. *a*: 10 Melbourne Mans, Queen's Club Gdns, London, W.14.

MACLEAN, F. J., B.A.(Oxon). Author & Journalist. *Publ*: The Human Side of Insurance (1931); Henry Moore, R.A. ('10); Belgium. L.C.C. Lecturer, Art of writing. *a*: Sollas, Long Lane, Hillingdon, Mdx.

MacLEAN, Hugh, M.D., D.Sc. *b*: 1879. *e*: Aberdeen, London & Berlin Univs. *m*: Ida Smedley (dec'd). *s*: 1. *d*: 1. Formerly Prof of Chemical Pathology Univ of Lond, St Thomas's Hosp, Prof of Med Univ of Lond & Dir of the Medicinal Clinic St Thomas's Hosp, Hon Consulting Physician to the Min of Pensions & St Thomas's Hosp. *Publ*: Lecithin & Allied Substances; Albuminuria & War Nephritis in British Troops in France; Modern Methods in the Diagnosis & Treatment of Renal Disease; Modern Views on Gastric Diseases; etc. *Rec*: Fishing, shooting, golf. *a*: Summerfold, High Drive, Woldingham, Surrey.

MACLEAN, Ida Smedly, D.Sc, F.I.C. *b*: Handsworth 1877. *e*: K. Edward's H.S. Birm, Newnham Col Cam. Married. *s*: 1. *d*: 1. Research Chem, Mem Staff Lister Inst of Preventive Med. *c.t*: Biochem Journ, Lancet, Journ of Chem Soc. *s.s* Pres Brit Fed of Univ Women. *a*: 2 Elm Pk, Gdns S.W.10. *t*: Flaxman 6382.

MACLEAN, John Bayne, LL.D. *b*: Crieff, Ontario, Canada 1862. *e*: Toronto Public & Normal Schs, Roy Sch of Artillery Kingston Ont. *m*: Anna Perkins Slade. *s*: 1. Company Founder, Chm & Pres The Maclean Hunter Pub. Co Ltd. *n.a*: Former Rep Toronto World, Commercial Ed The Mail, Financial Ed The Empire, Founder The Canadian Grocer, etc. *s.s*: Commerce, Indust, Finance, Politics. *c*: Canadian Officers. *a*: 7 Austin Terr, Toronto 10, Ontario, Canada. *T*: Mi 2244.

MACLEAN, Magnus, M.I.E.E., F.R.S.E., M.A., D.Sc, LL.D., J.P. *b*: Glendale 1857. *e*: Colbost Sc, Free Ch Train Col & Glas Univ. *m*: Joanna Murchison. *s*: 4. *d*: 2. Prof of Elec Engineering. First Lect on Physics Glas Univ '92-99. *Publ*: Model Solutions; Physical Units; Literature of the Celts; Literature of the Highlands; etc. *c.t*: Herald, Scotsman, Oban Times, Inverness Chron, etc. *s.s*: Celtic literature. Prof of Elec Eng Roy Tech '99-1923. Founded Glas Gaelic Soc 1887. One of Three Founded Highland Assoc '91. *a*: 108 University Av, Glasgow, W.2.

MACLEAN, Rev. Norman, M.A. (St And), D.D. (Edin). *b*: Portree 1869. *e*: Raining's Sc Inverness, St And & Edin Univs. *m*: Hon Iona, only d. of Lord Macdonald. *d*: 4. Min St Cuthbert's Parish, Edin. Ex Mod Gen Assembly 1927. Chap to the King '26. *Publ*: Dwellers in the Mist; Hills of Home; The Burnt Offering; Stand up Ye Dead; Life of Sir James Cameron Lees; The Future Life; Death Cannot Sever; How Shall We Escape? *c*: Univ (Edin). *a*: 6 Grosvenor Gdns, Edin. *t*: 61790.

MAC LEAN-WATT, LAUCHLAN: clergyman, littérateur; b. Scotland, Oct., 1877; s. Andrew and Margaret Gilanders (MacLean) W.; educ. Edinburgh Univ. DEGREES: M.A., B.D., D.D., F.R.S.E.; m. Jennie Hall Reid, 1897. AUTHOR: God's Altar Stairs, 1899; In Love's Garden (poems), 1901 (3rd edit. 1929); The Grey Mother and Songs of Empire, 1903; The Communion Table, 1903; By Still Waters (a book of prayer), 1906 (5th edit.), 1927; The Tryst:a Book of the Soul (poem), 1907; Edragil (novel), 1907; Attic and Elizabethan Tragedy, 1908; Moran of Kildally (novel), 1909; In Poet's Corner (poem), 1910; Carlyle (Nations Library), 1912; Literature and Life (Guild Library), 1912; History of Britain, George I to George V, 1912; Scottish Life and Poetry, 1912; The House of Sands (novel), 1913; Burns: a Life and Criticism, 1913; Hills of Home and Essays of R.L.S., 1915; Gates of Prayer, 1915; History of Seaforth Highlanders, 1915; In the Land of War, 1916; The Soldier's Friend, 1916; In France and Flanders with the Fighting Man, 1917; The Heart of a Soldier, 1918; The Land of Memory (poems), 1918; Gawain Douglas and his Aeneid, 1919; Oscar (novel), 1919; Life and Religion, 1923; Cameron Highlanders, 1923; Black Watch Highlanders, 1923; Argyle and Sutherland Highlanders, 1923; Gordon Highlanders, 1 9 2 3; (plays): Bonnie Prince Charlie; Ashes, or Isaac the Jew; The Wind that Shakes the Barley; Hoolachan, etc. Edited: Smithes "Summer in Skye"; Mrs. Stowe's "Dred"; Scott's Poetical Works. Contributes to the Spectator, Everyman and various mags. and the press. General character of writing: novels, essays, religious, plays, poems, text books, historical and criticism. CLUBS: Authors' (London), Arts (Edinburgh), Western (Glasgow). Relig. denom., Church of Scotland. ADDRESS: The Cathedral, Glasgow, Scotland.

MACLEAY, John Thomson. *b*: Inverness. *e*: Inverness Roy Acad & Edin Univ. *m*: Agnes Steyne Philip. *s*: 1. *d*: 1. Ed Liverpool Daily Post & Mercury. *n.a*: Scottish Leader (Edin), Dundee Advertiser, Nottingham Guardian, Liverpool Courier, Liverpool Daily Post & Mercury. *a*: 11 Percy St, Liverpool. *t*: Roy 453.

MACLEHOSE, James, M.A., LL.D., F.S.A., F.S.A.Scot. *b*: Glas 1857. *e*: Univ of Glas. *m*: Mary Macmillan. *s*: 1. *d*: 2. Chm & a Mang Dir Robert MacLehose & Co Ltd. *n.a*: Ed Scot Hist Review 1903—28. *Publ*: The Glasgow University Press 1638—1931. Pres Fed of Master Printers & Allied Trades of G.B. 1921—22. Chm Jt Ind Counc of Printing & Allied Trades of G.B. '21—22. Mem King's Bodyguard for Scot, Roy Coy of Archers. Trustee of Nat Library of Scot. Ed several vols on Scot Hist & Archæ. *c*: Athenæum, Beefsteak, New (Edin), Western (Glas). *a*: The Old Parsonage, Lamington, Lanarks, & St John's Hse, 30 Smith Sq, Westminster, S.W.1. *t*: Victoria 0177.

MacLEISH, Norman, M.A., B.Phil. *b*: Angus, Scotland 1898. *e*: Harris Acad Dundee, Univ of St Andrew's, New Coll Edin. *m*: Gladys Margaret Burnett. *s*: 3. Prof of Theology. *Publ*: The Nature of Religious Knowledge; Ideal Manhood: An Essay on the Sinlessness of Jesus. *Ctr*: Reformed Theol Review, The Messenger (Melbourne). *s.s*: Philosophy of Religion. *w.s*: B.E.F. World War I. *a*: 2 Ormond Coll, Univ of Melbourne, Carlton, N.3, Melbourne, Australia. *T*: FJ 2085.

MACLENNAN, Alexander. *b*: Glas 1872. *e*: Glas H.S. *m*: Helen Adamson. Surgeon. *Publ*: Abdominal Manipulation in Pregnancy; Surgical Materials & Their Uses. *c.t*: Glas Med Journ, Practitioner, Clin Journ, etc. *s.s*: Surgery of Children & Orthopædics. *Rec*: Fishing *a*: 6 Woodside Terr, Glas, C.3. *t*: Douglas 4309.

MACLENNAN, Hugh, M.A., Ph.D. *b*: Glace Bay, Nova Scotia 1907. *e*: Halifax Acad, Univs of Dalhousie, Oxford, Princeton. *m*: Dorothy Duncan. Novelist. *Publ*: Two Solitudes; Barometer Rising; Oxyrhynchus: an Economic & Social Study. *Ctr*: Sat Rev of Lit, MacLeans Mag, Vogue. *s.s*: Canadian Subjects & Problems, Novel Writing. *Rec*: Tennis, walking, gardening. *c*: North Hatley, Montreal Indoor Tennis. *a*: North Hatley, Quebec, Canada. *T*: 48.

MACLEOD, Alexander Cameron, M.B., B.S., F.R.C.S. *Publ*: Some Radium Cases at the Middlesex Hospital, a Photographic Record. *a*: 18 Harley St, W.1, & Trellis Cottage, Grove Pl, N.W.3. *t*: Langham 1626 & Hampstead 5611.

MACLEOD, Frederick Thomas, F.S.A.(Scot). *e*: Hgh Sch Inverness & Edin Univ. *m*: Anna Prince. *s*: 2. Solicitor, Hon Sec Scottish Gaelic Texts Soc. *Publ*: Eilean a Cheo (The Isle of Mist); Joint Ed of the Book of the Feill; The MacCrimmons of Skye; Hereditary Pipers to the MacLeods of Dunvegan. *Ctr*: Proc of Soc of Antiquaries of Scotland, Trans Inverness Scientific Soc & Field Club, Gealic Soc of Inverness. *s.s*: Lect on Celtic & Highland Subjects, Highland Antiquities. *Rec*: Golf. *c*: Lib Edin, Mortonhall Golf Edin. *a*: 55 Grange Rd, Edinburgh. *T*: 41849.

MACLEOD, Sir James MacIver. K.B.E., C.M.G., Chevalier Legion of Honour. *b*: Glas 1866. *e*: Cardross, N.B. & Dollar, N.B. *m*: Elizabeth Agnes Brown (dec). *d*: 2. Consul-Gen (ret). *n.a*: Special Corr in Morocco Glasgow Herald '91—96 & Reuter's Telegraph Agency '93—96. *Publ*: Grammar—Arabic—Vulgar of Morocco (Eng edn of Lerchundi's (Spanish) work). *c.t*: Journ Roy Geog Soc, Journ African Soc. *s.s*: Morocco, Tunisia. Brit Consular Rep at Fez, Morocco '92—1917. Foreign Office '17—19. Consul-Gen in Chile '19—23. Consul-Gen Tunis '23—30. *c*: Roy Socs, Lon, Roy Geog Soc, Lon, African Soc, Lon & Roy Inst of Internat Affairs, Lon. *a*: 56a The Ridgway, Wimbledon, S.W.19. *t*: 3848.

MACLEOD, John James Richard, F.R.S., F.R.C.P. *b*: Dunkeld 1876. *e*: Aberdeen G.S. & Univ. *m*: Mary W. McWalter. Regius Prof of Physiology. *n.a*: Jt Ed Nutrition Abstracts & Reviews 1930–. *Publ*: Diabetes ('11); Carbohydrate Metabolism & Insulin ('26); Physiology & Biochemistry in Modern Medicine (6th ed '30). *c.t*: Journals of Physiology & Biochem. *s.s*: Physiology & Biochem. Nobel Prize in Physiology & Medicine '23. Was Prof of Physiology in Cleveland, U.S.A. '03–18 & Toronto, Canada '18–28. *Rec*: Golf. *c*: Authors, Lon & Univ Aberdeen. *a*: Craigievar, Bieldside, Aberdeenshire. *t*: Cults 211.

MACLEOD, John MacLeod Hendrie, M.A., M.D., F.R.C.P. *b*: Galston, Ayrshire 1870. *e*: St Andrews & Aberdeen Univs. *m*: Eva J. Ruston. *s*: 1. *d*: 1. Cons Phys for Skin Diseases & Vice-Pres Charing Cross Hosp. *n.a*: Late Ed British Journ of Dermatology. *Publ*: The Diseases of the Skin; Histopathology of the Skin; Burns & Their Treatment. *Ctr*: Ency Brit & various med journs & dicts, etc. *s.s*: Diseases of the Skin. *Rec*: Fishing, shooting, sailing. *c*: Athenæum, Bath. *a*: Pannells, Lower Bourne, Farnham, Surrey. *T*: Frensham 479.

MacLEOD, John Nicolson. *b*: Kilmuir 1880. *e*: Kilmuir Public Sch & Un F.C. Training Coll Aberdeen. Married. *s*: 1. Schoolmaster. *Publ*: Reiteach Moraig; Posadh Moraig; Dain Spioradail le Calum Mac Neacail; Litrichean Alasdair Mhoir. *Ctr*: Highland News, North Star, People's Journ, etc. *c*: An Comunn Gaidhealach Gaelic Soc of Inverness. *a*: Breacleit, Ferry Rd, Beauly, Scotland. *T*: 298.

MACLEOD, Joseph Todd Gordon, M.A. *b*: Middlesex 1903. *e*: Rugby Sch, Balliol Coll Oxf, Inner Temple Lond. *m*: Kit Macgregor Davis. Mang Dir Scottish Nat Film Studio Glasgow 1946—47, Announcer & News Reader B.B.C. '38—45. *Publ*: The New Soviet Theatre; Actors Across the Volga; A Job at the B.B.C.; The Ecliptic (Poem) / Foray of Centaurs (Poem); Overture to Cambridge; Beauty & the Beast. *Ctr*: John Bull, Chambers's Ency, Spectator, Our Time, Today & Tomorrow, & English & Scots dailies. *s.s*: Soviet Theatre, Theatre Hist, Scotland. *Rec*: Music, bird-watching. *c*: Literary (Glas). *a*: 86 Regency Lodge, Swiss Cott, London, N.W.3. *T*: Primrose 2655.

MACLEOD, Malcolm, D.S.O., M.C., Colonel. *c.t*: Military & Tech Journs, etc. *a*: Fleet, Hants.

MACLEOD, Robert Duncan. *b*: Greenock. Librarian & Editor. *n.a*: Ed Library Review. *Publ*: County Rural Libraries; Rural Libraries & Rural Education; Modern Scottish Literature; A Guide Book Catalogue. *s.s*: Bibliog & Hist of Publishing Houses. *c*: Art (Glas). P.E.N., Lond Press. *a*: Bonawe, Malcolm St. Dunfermline.

MACLEOD, Rev. William Brash. *b*: Argyllshire. *e*: Glas Univ & Trin Col Glas. *m*: Lydia Comrie. *s*: 2. *Publ*: The Afflictions of the Righteous; Christ & the Churches; Frederick Tennyson, the Man & his Poetry. *c.t*: Scotsman, Life & Work, Presbyterian, etc. *s.s*: Theol, poetry. *Rec*: Golf. *a*: 29 Gordon Rd, Edin 12. *t*: 86188.

MacLIAMMOIR, Micheal. *b*: Cork, Ireland 1899. *e*: Priv. Theatrical Dir, Actor & Designer. *Publ*: All for Hecuba; Darmuid agus Grainne; Oiche Bheaitaine; Oicheanna Sidhe; La agus Oiche. *Ctr*: The Bell, Dublin Mag, Irish Statesman, Irish Times, etc. *s.s*: Theatre, French & Spanish Painting, Irish Folklore & Literature. *Rec*: Travel, ballet. *a*: Gate Theatre, Dublin, & Beann Eadair, Co Dublin, Ireland. *T*: Dublin City 28553.

MacMAHON, Ella. *b*: Dublin *e*: Priv. Novelist, Writer & Broadcaster, Granted Civil List Pension for Literary Work. *Publ*: About 25 novels & 2 vols short stories. *Ctr*: Fortnightly Rev, Blackwood's Mag, English Rev, Nat Rev & leading daily newspapers, etc. *s.s*: Topographical, Historical & Archæological, Social & Literary. *c*: Lyceum. *a*: The Elms, Welwyn, Herts. *T*: Welwyn 27.

MACMANUS, Emily Elvira Primrose, C.B.E. *b*: London 1886. *e*: Priv. Trained Nurse, Matron Guy's Hosp 1927—47. *Publ*: Hospital Administration for Women; Nursing in Time of War (in collab). *Ctr*: Nursing Times, Nursing Mirror, Odhams Press, etc. *s.s*: Nursing Schs & Hospital Administration. *Rec*: Reading, writing, fishing, gardening. *c*: Cowdray, United Arts (Dublin). *w.s*: 1915—18 (Des). *a*: Carrickbarrett Lodge, Bofeenaun, Ballina, Co Mayo. Eire.

MACMANUS, J. T., M.D., D.P.H. *Publ*: Modern Methods in the Diagnosis & Treatment of Phthisis with special Reference to Tuberculin. *a*: 268 Walworth Rd, S.E.17. *t*: Rodney 3677.

MACMANUS, P. J. Francis, B.A.(Univ of Ireland). *b*: Kilkenny City, 1909. *e*: Christian Brothers Kilkenny & Nat Univ of Ireland.

Teacher. *n.a*: Assoc Ed, Outlook (Dublin) to '32. *Publ*: Stand & Give Challenge; Toirthneach Luimnighe (pla... Storm-Rock (play). *c.t*: Capuchin Annual, Father Mathew Record, Irish Press, Irish Monthly. *s.s*: Gaelic lit, Catholic sociology. *Rec*: Walking, cycling. Lecturer & lit critic. *a*: 18 Lower Fitzwilliam St, Dublin. *t*: 22686.

MACMANUS, T. J. Sec Dublin Br N.U.J. *a*: 90 Lindsay Rd, Glasnevin, Dublin.

MACMASTER, A. B. *Publ*: Articles on Outbreak of Para-Typhoid Fever; Local Government and Medicine. M.O.H. Town and Port of Dover. Officer Order of St John of Jerusalem. *a*: St Stephen's, Godwyne Road, Dover.

MACMASTER, Joseph. *b*: Hamilton 1912. *e*: Glasgow Univ. Jnlst. *n.a*: Periodical Sub-Ed. *c.t*: Glasgow Evening News, Edinburgh Evening Dispatch, Daily Mail, Daily Herald, Daily Record, Daily Express, all English & Scottish Sunday N/ps, etc. *s.s*: Industry, local govt, sport & economics. *c*: N.U.J. *a*: Kia-Ora, Kethers St, Motherwell. *t*: 244.

MACMICHAEL, Sir Harold Alfred, Kt., G.C.M.G. D.S.O. *b*: Winster 1882. *e*: King's Lynn, Bedford, Magdalene Coll Camb. *m*: Agnes De Sivras Edith Stephens. *d*: 2. Governor of Tanganyika 1936—38. High Comm for Palestine & Transjordan '38—44, Special Rep of H.M.G. to Malaya '45, Constitutional Comm Malta '46. *Publ*: A History of the Arabs in the Sudan; The Anglo-Egyptian Sudan; The Tribes of Northern & Central Kordafan. *s.s*: Sudan & Middle East. *c*: Athenæum, Conservative. *a*: Nouds Teynham, Kent. *T*: 232.

MACMILLAN, Arthur Tarleton. *b*: London 1880. *e*: Priv & Balliol Coll Oxf. *m*: Margaret McLarty Macmillan. Barrister. *Publ*: What is Christian Marriage?; Marriage, Divorce & the Church. *c*: Athenæum. *a*: 118 Oakwood Ct, London, W.14.

MACMILLAN, Douglas (see **CARY, D. M.**). *b*: Castle Cary 1884. *e*: Sexey's Bruton & Sidcot, Winscombe. *m*: Margaret Fielding Miller. Civil Servant (ret). *n.a*: Ed The Better Quest 1911, Word Lore '26—28, Somerset Year Book '21—31, The Journal of Cancer '13—22, Cancer Relief Bulletin since '33. *a*: Walden, Knoll Rd, Sidcup, Kent. *T*: Footscray 1791.

MACMILLAN, Sir Frederick, C.V.O. *b*: 1851. *e*: Uppingham. Publisher. Chm Macmillan & Co. Ex-pres Publishers Assoc. Chm Bd of Nat Hosp for Paralysis & Epilepsy. *a*: 22 Devonshire Pl, W.1. *t*: Welbeck 7674.

MACMILLAN, G. A. Hon D.Litt(Oxon), Fell Lincoln Col Oxford. *b*: 1855. Director Macmillan & Co. *Publ*: Articles in Blackwood's Magazine, Macmillan's Magazine. *s.s*: Travels in Greece, the Hellenic Soc, the Soc of Dilettanti, etc. On Council Roy Col Music 1898, Hon Sec 1919—34. J.P. Lon and N.R. Yorkshire. *a*: 27 Queen's Gate Gardens, S.W.7.

MacMILLAN, Georgina (Ena) Fitzgerald. (**E. Fitzgerald Macmillan.**) *b*: Isle of Wight. *e*: Priv. Widow of J. A. MacMillan, F.C.W.A. Journalist, Novelist, Special Correspondent, Hon Sec I.o.J., Hon Mem Theatre Civic Arts Leeds. *n.a*: Yorks Corres Drapers' Record, Men's Wear 1935—48, Dancing Times '37—, Corres New Theatre Mag '46—. *Publ*: Patcola; The Witch Queen of Khem; And the Stars Fought. *Ctr*: John Bull, Reynolds News, British Weekly, Everywoman, British Textiles, Yorks Observer, Yorks Even News, etc. *s.s*: Textiles, Clothing Manufacture (Men's & Women's), All Theatrical Subjects esp mod developments & technique. *Rec*: Talking with friends, languages, reading, travel, needlework & creating new designs. *a*: 48 Headingley Ave, Leeds 6. *T*: Leeds 53671.

MACMILLAN, Norman, M.C., A.F.C., F.R.S.A., A.F.R.Ae.S. *b*: Glasgow 1892. *e*: Allan Glen's Sch & Roy Tech Coll. *m*: G. M. Peterkin Mitchell. Chief Test Pilot Fairey Aviation Co 1924—30, Founder Mem Warden Guild of Air Pilots 1929 & Dep Master '34—35, Chief Consultant Test Pilot Armstrong Siddeley Aero Co '31—33, Pres Nat League of Airmen '35—38. *n.a*: Spec Aviation & Air Corresp Dly Mail 1936—39. *Publ*: The Art of Flying; Into The Blue; The Air Traveller's Guide to Europe; An Hour of Aviation; The Romance of Flight, Sefton Brancker; The Romance of Modern Exploration & Discovery; Freelance Pilot; The Chosen Instrument; How to Pilot an Aeroplane; The Pilots' Book on Advanced Flying; The Royal Air Force in the World War; How We Fly; Best Flying Stories. *s.s*: Air History & Mil Air Strategy. *c*: Roy Aero. *a*: Cadgwith, Helston, Cornwall.

MACMILLAN-BROWN, John, LL.D. *b*: Irvine 1846. *e*: Irvine Acad, Glasgow & Edinburgh Univs, Balliol Col Oxon. *m*: Helen Connor (decd). *d*: 2. Chancellor, Univ of N.Z. '23—. *Publ*: A Manual of English literature (1750—1850); Maori & Polynesian; The Dutch East; The Riddle of the Pacific: Peoples and Problems of the Pacific; etc. *c.t*: N.Z. newspapers, The Sydney Morning Herald. *s.s*: Anthropology. *Rec*: Reading, travel. 21 y travel in Pacific Islands, Central America & Malay Archipelago. *a*: Holmbank, Cashmere Hills, Christchurch, New Zealand.

MACMORRAN, Kenneth Mead, K.C., M.A., LL.B. *b*: London 1883. *e*: Westminster, King's Coll Camb. *m*: Freda Mary Knight. Bencher Middle Temple, Chanc of Dioceses of Chichester, Lincoln, Ely, St Albans, Newcastle & Guildford. *Publ*: Halsbury's Law of England (Hailsham Edition), Titles: Burial, Ecclesiastical Law; Cripps' Law of Church & Clergy; Handbook for Churchwardens & Parochial Church Councillors. *s.s*: Ecclesiastical Law. *c*: Athenæum, National. *a*: New Court, Temple, London, E.C.4. *T*: Central 4480; & Melfort, Ashwood Rd, Woking, Surrey. *T*: Woking 1978.

MACMULLAN, C(HARLES) K(IRKPATRICK): see Munro, C. K.

MACMUNN, Lt.-Gen. Sir George Fletcher, K.C.B., K.C.S.I., D.S.O. *b*: Chelsea 1869. *e*: Kensington Sch, *m*: (1) Alice Emily Watson, (2) Kathleen Maude Woods. *s*: 1. *d*: 1. Warden Sackville Coll. *Publ*: Armies of India; Behind the Scenes in Many Wars; Religions & Hidden Cults of India; The Indian Underworld; Kipling's Women; Black Velvet; The Living India; Lure of the Indus; Turmoil & Tragedy in India; 1914 & After; Rudyard Kipling, Craftsman; Indian Mutiny in Perspective; Crimea in Perspective; American War of Independence in Perspective. *c*: Sackville. *a*: Sackville College, East Grinstead, Sussex. *T*: 436.

MACMURRAY, John, M.C., M.A. *b*: Maxwelton, Kircudbright 1891. *e*: Gr Sch, Robert Gordon's Coll Aberdeen, Glas Univ, Balliol Coll Oxf. *m*: Elizabeth Hyde Campbell. Prof Moral Philosophy Univ Edin. *Publ*: Freedom in the Modern World; Reason & Emotion; The Clue to History; Interpreting the Universe; The Structure of Religious Experience; The Boundaries of Science. *Ctr*: New Statesman, World Review, Future Books, etc. *s.s*: All Philosophical subjects especially Social & Political Philosophy & Philosophy of Religion. *Rec*: Music & golf. *c*: Edinburgh New. *a*: Bright's Cresc, Edinburgh 10. *T*: Edinburgh 42330.

MACNAB, Iain. *b*: Iloilo, Phillippine Islands 1890. *e*: Merchiston. *m*: Helen Mary Tench. Painter & Engraver, Joint Dir of Art Studies Heatherley Sch of Art 1946.

Publ: Figure Drawing; Wood Engraving. *Ctr*: The Studio, Architectural Design, The Artist, etc. *s.s*: All Forms of Pictorial Expression. *c*: Savage. *w.s*: B.E.F. 1914—16 & R.A.F. '41—45. *a*: 33 Warwick Sq, London, S.W.1. *T*: Victoria 5933 & 5492.

MACNAB, W. *Publ*: Trans of Berthelot's Sur La Force des Matières Explosives; ed Tech Records of Dept Explosive Supply. *c.t*: Various n/ps & tech journs. *a*: 10 Cromwell Crescent, S.W.6.

MACNAGHTEN, Lettice. *b*: London. *Publ*: Pistol v Poleaxe; A Handbook on Human Slaughter. *Ctr*: Nineteenth Century, Edin Review, Scottish Country Life, Estate Mag. *s.s*: Slaughter Reform, Highland Hist & Legends, Gaelic Langs. *Rec*: Gardening, walking, reading. *a*: Nairne Lodge, Edinburgh 8.

MACNAIR, Robert. *b*: Alnwick 1894. *e*: George Watson's Coll, Edin Univ. *m*: Isobel Cunningham. *s*: 2. *Publ*: Real Human Needs. *s.s*: Sexology, Ornithology. *Rec*: Riding, swimming, golf. *a*: 146 Ferry Rd, Edinburgh 6, Scotland. *T*: Leith 35058.

MacNALTY, Arthur Salusbury, M.A. *e*: Priv & Oxf. Author. *Publ*: A Book of Crimes; The Mystery of Captain Burnaby; etc. *s.s*: Biog, Fiction. *c*: Athenæum. *a*: Athenæum Club, Pall Mall, London, S.W.1.

MACNAMARA, Brinsley. *b*: Delvin 1890. *e*: Priv. Mem Irish Acad of Letters. *Publ*: Novels—The Valley of the Squinting Windows (1918); In Clay & Bronze; The Mirror in the Dusk; Return to Ebon Theever ('30); etc. Plays—The Glorious Uncertainty; The Master; Margaret Gillan ('34); etc. *a*: 47 Waterloo Rd, Dublin. *t*: Ballsbridge 836.

MACNAMARA, Rachel Swete. *b*: Ennis, Ireland. *e*: Priv. *Publ*: The Trance; The Fringe of the Desert; Lover's Battle; Torn Veils; The Dragon Tree; Let Them Say; Duet for a Trio; White Witch; Strange Encounter; etc. *c*: Forum. *a*: Cloonagh, New Milton, Hants.

MACNAUGHTON, Donald Allan, M.A. *b*: Kenmore, Perthshire 1875. *e*: Parish Sch, George Watson's Coll, Edin & Camb Univs. *m*: Ethel Sing. *s*: 3. Classical Master Oundle & Tounbridge, H.M. Inspector of Schools (ret). *Publ*: Position of Greek & Latin in grant-aided Secondary Schools of England; The Mirror of History (collab). *Ctr*: Times, Spectator, Yorkshire Post, etc. *s.s*: Lit (Ancient & English Classics), Educ. *Rec*: Fishing, shooting. *a*: Remony, Leyburn, Yorkshire. *T*: Leyburn 3135.

MACNAUGHTON, Duncan, M.A., LL.B., W.S., F.R.S.E. *b*: Edinburgh 1892. *e*: Edin Acad, Edin & McGill Univs. *Publ*: A Scheme of Babylonian Chronology. *s.s*: Astron, Archæ & Anthrop. *Rec*: Tennis, golf, skating. *c*: Scottish Cons. *a*: 11e Claremont St, Edinburgh. *T*: 20737.

MacNEICE, Louis. *Publ*: inc The Dark Tower; The Poetry of W. B. Yeats; The Earth Compels; Autumn Journal; Springboard; etc. *a*: Tilty Hill Hse, Duton Hill, nr Dunmow, Essex.

MacNEIL, Neil. B.A., LL.D. *b*: Boston Massachusetts 1891. *e*: St Francis Xaviers Univ Nova Scotia. *m*: Elizabeth Quinn. *s*: 1. *d*: 2. Journalist, Mem of P.E.N. *n.a*: Former Staff Dly Mail (Montreal), The Gazette (Montreal), Asst Mang Ed New York Times 1930—. *Publ*: An American Peace; The Highland Heart in Nova Scotia; Without Fear or Favor; How to be a Newspaperman. *Ctr*: N.Y. Times Mag, Sat Ev Post, The Sign, etc. *s.s*: Foreign Affairs, Journalism. *Rec*: Walking, fishing, golf. *c*: N.Y. Athletic, Players. *a*: The New York Times, New York, U.S.A. *T*: Lackawanna 4-1000.

MACNICOL, Nicol, M.A., D.Litt, D.D. *b*: Lochranza 1870. *e*: Glas H.S., Glas Univ, Un Free Ch Col Glas. *m*: Margaret Brodie. *d*: 2. Missny of Ch of Scot in India. *n.a*: Ed Indian Interpreter (Quarterly) till 1919, & Nat Chr Counc Review (India) '26-29. *Publ*: Indian Theism; The Making of Modern India; The Living Religions of the Indian People; etc. *s.s*: Indian religion. *a*: 7 Roseburn Cliff, Edin.

MACNUTT, Rev. Canon F. B., M.A., H.C.F., F.R.Hist.S. Canon Emeritus of Canterbury, Chaplain to the King, late Provost of Leicester, Archdeacon of Leics. *Publ*: The Inevitable Christ; Advent Certainties; The Reproach of War; From Chaos to God; Early Diocese of Leicester; Theodore, Bishop of Winchester (collab); A War Primer of Prayers; Four Freedoms; Atlantic & Christian; (Ed) The Church in the Furnace; Classics of the Inner Life. *a*: Fircroft, Tower Hill, Horsham, Sussex. *T*: Horsham 222.

MACOWAN, Norman. *b*: St Andrews 1877. *e*: Edinburgh. *m*: Violet Stephenson. *s*: 2. *d*: 1. Actor & Dramatist. *Publ*: The Infinite Shoeblack; Glorious Morning; (Plays) Lord o' Creation; Jacob's Ladder; The Infinite Shoeblack; The Blue Lagoon (jtly); The Demagogue; The Chalk Line; The New Tenant; Glorious Morning. *c*: Green Room, Soc of Authors, etc. *a*: 31 Avonmore Rd, London, W.14. *T*: Fulham 2573.

MACPHEE, G. Graham, M.A., M.D., L.D.S., R.F.P.S.G. *b*: Glasgow. *e*: Kelvinside Acad, Glas Univ, Vienna. *m*: Jean Craigie. *s*: 2. *d*: 2. *Publ*: Studies in the Aetiology of Dental Caries; Ben Nevis—Scottish Mountaineering Club Guide. *Ctr*: Brit Dental Journ, Brit Journ of Dental Sci, B.M.J., Dental Record, Journ of Dental Research, Alpine Journ, Liverpool Dly Post, etc. *s.s*: Dentistry, Mountaineering. *Rec*: Mountaineering, motoring, swimming, music. *c*: Alpine, Athenæum, Roy Scot Auto, etc. *w.s*: World War I. *a*: The Old Hse, Grassendale Pk, Liverpool 19, & 76 Mount Pleasant, Liverpool 3. *T*: Garston 553, & Royal 2221.

MACPHERSON, Arthur Holte, B.C.L., M.A. (Oxon). *c.t*: Nat hist journs. *s.s*: Birds. *a*: 21 Campden Hill Square, Kensington, W.

MACPHERSON, Charles James Ian Douglas. *b*: Lon 1907. *e*: Haberdasher's Aske's Hampstead Sc & Priv. Journalist & Musical Critic. *n.a*: Manitoba Free Press, Winnipeg '29—30, Daily Express M/C '30, Willesden Chron & Kilburn Times '30—35. *c.t*: Various. *s.s*: Music, plays, descriptive work. Mem N.U.J. *a*: 17 The Paddocks, Wembley Pk, Middx.

MACPHERSON, Rev. Hector, M.A., Ph.D. *b*: Edinburgh 1888. *e*: Edin Univ, New Coll Edin. *m*: Catherine Anne Chisholm. *s*: 2. *d*: 2. Minister Church of Scotland, Elder Lecturer on Astronomy Roy Tech Coll Glas 1923 —32, '38—39, '45—46. *Publ*: Modern Astronomy: Its Rise & Progress; Modern Cosmologies; Makers of Astronomy; Astronomers of To-day; Herschel; Guide to the Stars; The Church & Science; The Covenanters under Persecution. *s.s*: Astronomy, Science-&-Theology, History (Political, Ecclesiastical). *Rec*: Golf, motoring. *a*: 7 Wardie Cresc, Edinburgh. *T*: Edinburgh 83770.

MACPHERSON, Ian. Author. *Publ*: Shepherd's Calendar; Land of Our Fathers. *a*: c/o Jonathan Cape Ltd, 30 Bedford Sq, W.C.

Who Was Who Among English and European Authors

MACPHERSON, William Charles, C.S.I., J.P. *b*: Blairgowrie 1855. *e*: Winchester Col & Wren's, Lon. *m*: Isabella Mary Kinloch. *s*: 2. *d*: 3. I.C.S. (ret). *Publ*: Soldiering in India 1763 to 1787. *s.s*: Clan Chattan hist & genealogy. I.C.S. 33 y. Dir of Dept of Land Records & Agric. Comm of a Div. Chief Sec & Mem Bd of Revenue & Mem Legislative Counc in Bengal. Ret 1911. C.C. for Perthshire '13–29. *a*: The Newton of Blairgowrie. Perthshire. *t*: 97.

MACPIKE, Eugene Fairfield. *b*: Illinois 1870. *e*: Lincoln Sc & Rockford Business Col. *m*: (1) Ada Florence Denton (dec); (2) Mary J. W. Dillingham. *d*: 2. Supt, Perishable Freight Service. *n.a*: Official Deleg of U.S. Govt & Railroad Refrigerator Service Assoc, U.S., to 2nd Internat Congress of Refrigeration Vienna 1910. Mem Refrigeration Cmt. *Publ*: (Ed) Correspondence & Papers of Edmond Halley; etc. *c.t*: Notes & Queries (Lon), Mag of Hist (N.Y.). Dir of Amer Inst of Refrigeration, Mem Oxf Hist Soc, Soc of Genealogists of Lon, Inst of Transport (Lon), Amer Hist Assoc, Amer Library Assoc, etc. *Rec*: Original hist research. *a*: 135 E. Eleventh Pl, Chicago, Illinois, U.S.A. *t*: Calumet 4811.

MacQUEEN, Ian Alexis Gordon, M.A., M.B., Ch.B., D.P.H. *b*: Kirknewton 1909. *e*: George Watson's Coll & Univs of Edin & Lond. *m*: Elizabeth U. Bryant. M.O. Mansfield 1943—47, Pres Mansfield & Dist Br N.A.L.G.O. '45—47. *n.a*: Ed The Student '36. *Publ*: From Drains to Genetics (collab). *Ctr*: The Med Officer, B.M.J. *s.s*: Public Health. *Rec*: Bridge, Dramatic Art. *a*: 62 Paisley Cresc, Edinburgh 8. *T*: 76485.

MACRAE, Angus. Psychologist. *Publ*: Talents and Temperaments; The Case for Vocational Guidance. *c.t*: Various. *a*: 68 Corringham Rd, N.W.11. *t*: Speedwell 6925.

MACRAE, Robert Stuart ("Stuart Macrae"), M.J.I. *b*: Whitley Bay 1900. *e*: City of Lon. *m*: Geraldine Mary Perpetua Wynter. *s*: 2. Journalist & Editor. *n.a*: Motoring Corr News of the World, Ed Roy Mag '29—31, Pres Post on Editorial staff of The Motor. *c.t*: Daily Mail, Daily Express, Evening Standard, Mod Woman, Home Notes, Roy Mag, 20 Story Mag, etc. *s.s*: Short stories, semi-technical articles. Engineering Apprentice Westinghouse Brake Co Ltd '16. Asst Designer Central Aircraft Co Ltd '18. Publicity Mang T. B. Andre Ltd '27. Tech Dir Satelite Neon Signs Ltd '32. *Rec*: Golf. *c*: Arts Theatre & Column. *a*: 211*b* Adelaide Rd, N.W.3. *t*: Primrose 5209.

MACRO, Herbert Charles. *m*: Lillian Joyce White. *s*: 2. Mang Dir The Westminster Press. *n.a*: Ed Mang Dir The Fleet (Journ of Brit Navy), Former Ed Printing Trades Journ. *a*: 260 All Souls' Ave, London, N.W 10. *T*: Willesden 3064.

MACROBERT, Thomas Murray. *b*: Dreghorn 1884. *e*: Glas Univ, Trin Coll Camb. *m*: Janet McGillivray Violet McIlreaith. *s*: 2. *d*: 1. Prof of Maths Glas Univ. *Publ*: Functions of a Complex Variable; Spherical Harmonics; Bessel Functions (in collab); Trigonometry (in collab). *a*: 10 The University, Glasgow, W.2. *T*: Western 5799.

MACSWEENEY, Edward Francis. *b*: Ilford 1909. *e*: St Bonaventure's W. Ham, Lon & Glasthule, Ireland. Journalist. *n.a*: Reporter Irish Times 1931–. *c.t*: Flight, Popular Aviation (Chicago), Irish Motor News, Chemical Age, etc. *s.s*: Aviation & ind development. Mem Ed Bd Irish Auto-Sport. *Rec*: Riding, shooting. *c*: Irish Aero, Nat Aero, I.F.S. *a*: Beach Hse, Dun Laoghaire, Co Dublin.

MACSWINEY, Constance Patricia. *e*: K. Edwards H.S. Birm. Classical Mistress, Roedean Sc Brighton. *a*: Roedean Sc, Brighton.

MACSYMON, John. *b*: 1876. *e*: Col Prep Sc Greenock & L'pool Col. *m*: Isabel Margaret Watt. *d*: 1. Writer on Art & Photography Painter in Oils & Water Colour. *n.a*: Ed The Camera. *c.t*: The Photographic Press Eng & America. *s.s*: Composition, feeling, colour, constructive criticism. Pres "The Northern". Pres Liverpool Amateur Photo Assoc. Vice-Pres L'pool Sketching Club. Judged nearly all the more important photo exhib's in U.K. *c*: R.P.S. & L.A.P.A. *a*: 4 Arno Rd, Birkenhead. *t*: 2361.

MACTAGGART, Morna. *b*: Rangoon 1907. *e*: Bedales Sc & U.C.L. *m*: Alan Staniland. *Publ*: Turn Single; Broken Music. *a*: Sands, Ideford Coombe, Devon.

MACVICAR, Angus, M.A. *b*: Duror 1908. *e*: Glas Unvi *m*: Jean S. McKerral. *s*: 1. Author & Journalist. *n.a*: Asst Ed Campbeltown Courier 1932—34. *Publ*: The Purple Rock; Death by the Mistletoe; The Screaming Gull; Ten Green Brothers; Crimes Masquerader; Eleven for Danger; The Crooked Finger; The Singing Spider; Strangers from the Sea; The Crouching Spy; The Cavern; Death on the Machar; Greybreek; The Crocodile Men; Flowering Death. *Ctr*: John Bull, Illustrated, People's Journ, etc. *s.s*: Serials, Radio Features. *Rec*: Golf, photography, reading thrillers. *w.s*: 1939—45. *a*: Southend, Argyll.

MACWATT, John, M.B., C.M., J.P. *Publ*: Primulas of Europe. *c.t*: Various. *a*: Morelands, Duns. *t*: 16.

MACWILLIAM, John Alexander, M.D., LL.D., F.R.S. Prof of Physiology (ret). *c.t*: Proc Roy Soc, Journ of Physiology, B.M.J. *a*: Inverdee, Cults, Aberdeen. *t*: 106.

MADAN, Falconer. *Publ*: Oxford Books 1468–680: Two Family Histories (Gresley, Madan); etc. *s.s*: Oxf lit & bibliog. Hon Fellow Brasenose Col, Oxf. *a*: 94 Banbury Rd, Oxf.

MADAN, Indar Nath, M.A., Ph.D. *b*: Panjab 1910. *e*: Panjab Univ. Prof of English & Hindi, Mem of P.E.N. *Publ*: Modern Hindi Literature; Prem Chand; Saratchandra Chatterjee; Hindi Kala Kar; Hindi Kavya Vicechna. *Ctr*: Essays & Studies, Triveni, The Tribune, Saraswati, The Behar Gazette, Northern India Observer. *s.s*: Indian Literature, Hindi Literature. *Rec*: Bibliography. *a*: Dyal Singh College, Lahore, India. *T*: 2905.

MADARIAGA, Don Salvador de, M.A., *Publ* inc The Heart of Jade; The Sacred Giraffe; Anarchy or Hierarchy; The World's Design; etc. & many essays on Spanish & English Poetry. *a*: Atenen, Madrid.

MADDEN, Mabel Sarah. *b*: Cork. *e*: Bedford H.S. *n.a*: Continental Daily Mail 1923—, N.Y. Herald, Ed Alpine Post '21—, Reuter's Corr. *Publ*: Fitzgerald Family; Sir Guyon the Interloper; Sir Guyon in Snowland. *s.s*: Winter sports, children's stories. *a*: Private Hotel, St Moritz, Switzerland & c/o Rev. Canon Madden, Castle Haven Rectory, Skibbereen, Co Cork.

MADDOCK, James Gerard, M.J.I. *b*: Rosslare, 1908. *e*: Mount St Joseph's, Wexford. Journalist. *n.a*: Irish Press 1931, Independent Newspapers '32, Press Assoc '33, Cork Examiner '33, Daily Mail '33, Daily Express & Irish Times '35. *c.t*: Leading N/ps. *s.s*: Marine & travel articles. Local corres Rosslare Harbour & South East Wexford. Travelled extensively. *Rec*: Yachting, swimming, tennis. *c*: Rosslare G.C. *a*: Oak Dale, Rosslare Harbour, Co Wexford. I.F.S. *t*: Rosslare Harbour 4.

MADELEY, Helen Mortimer. b: Handsworth. e: Edgbaston High Sch, Cheltenham Ladies Coll, St Hilda's Coll Oxford. *Publ*: History as a School of Citizenship; Time Charts; Why & When Histories; History in the Making. *s.s*: Education, History. *c*: Univ Women's. *a*: 14 The Butts, Warwick.

MADELOVA, Sister Mary, M.A., Ph.D. b: Cumberland, Wisconsin 1887. e: Univs of Wisconsin, Notre Dame, California, Manhattan Coll N.Y., Mount Mary Coll Wisconsin. Teacher & Prof of English. *Publ*: Knights Errant & other Poems; Chaucer's Nuns & other Essays; The Pearl: a Study in Spiritual Dryness; Penelope & other Poems; A Question of Lovers & other Poems; Gates & other Poems; Christmas Eve & other Poems; Four Girls; Addressed to Youth; etc. *Ctr*: America, American Mercury, Bookman, Catholic World, New Republic, N.Y. Times, Sat Rev of Lit, etc. *a*: St Mary's Coll, Notre Dame, Holy Cross, Indiana, U.S.A.

MADELUNG, Aage. b: Sweden 1872. e: Birkerod Coll Denmark, Roy Agric Coll Copenhagen. m: Elisabeth Rafn. s: 2. d: 2. Free-lance Writer, Author. *Publ*: Jagt paa Dyr og Mennesker; Elsker Hverandre; Forvandlinger; I Dyreham; Med Stav i Haand; Paa en Sten Under Himlen; Pigen de Sogte; Forforelse; etc. *Ctr*: Various European newsps & periodicals, etc. *s.s*: Fiction. *Rec*: Horseback riding, hunting. *a*: Godthaabsvej 132, Copenhagen F., Denmark.

MADGE, Inez, B.A. (see **LAKE, Elizabeth**). b: London 1913. e: Convents in France & England, Somerville Coll Oxf. m: Charles Madge. s: 1. d: 1. *a*: 2 Regents Pk Terr, London, N.W.1. *T*: Gulliver 4657.

MADGE, Sidney Joseph, D.Sc., F.S.A. b: West Hartlepool 1874. e: Northampton Sch of Science, Oxf Centra Sch, St Paul's Coll Cheltenham, Lond Sch of Econs & Polit Science. m: s: 2. d: 2. Hon Asst Keeper Dept of Printed Books, Brit Museum. *n.a*: Hon Ed Lond & Middx Archæolog Soc Transactions 1921—23. *Publ*: The Domesday of Crown Lands; England Under Stuart Rule; Hornsey Records; Borzoi County Histories; Gloucestershire Inquisitions; London Inquisitions; The Place Names of Middlesex. *Ctr*: Archæologia, Clare Market Review, Notes & Queries, Times Lit Supp & various journs & newsps. *s.s*: Econs, Social & Ind Hist, Topography. *Rec*: Travel, historical research. *c*: Athenæum. *a*: Harbledown, 23 Russell Hill Rd, Purley, Surrey. *T*: Uplands 7978.

MADOL, Hans Roger. b: Berlin 1903. e: Berlin. *Publ*: The Shadow King (Lious XVII foreign edns '30); Ferdinand of Bulgaria; Godoy; The Last of Ancient Spain, Spanish German & Danish edns ('34); Gedichte (poems); La Perruque de M. Schlegel; Les Princes du Prochre Orient et la Guerre ('34). *c.t*: Berliner Tageblatt, L'Illustration (Paris), Vu, Neue, Freie Presse (Vienne) Excelsior Paris, etc. s.s: Biog, hist, etc. Travelled widely. *Rec*: Trav, billard japonais. *c*: P.E.N. *a*: Castle Avernaes Pr, Ebberup, Danemark, & 9 Rue de Mézières, Paris 6me. *t*: Littré 63–14.

MADSEN, Arthur Wilhelm, B.Sc. b: Edinburgh 1880. e: Roy Hgh Sch Edin, Edin Univ & Marburg. m: Lilian Rattray. Journalist. *n.a*: Ed Land & Liberty since 1933. *Publ*: Land Value Rating; House Famine & the Land Blockade; State as Manufacturer & Trader; Why Rents & Rates are High. *s.s*: Land Value Taxation & Free Trade. *a*: 1 Parkfield Ave, East Sheen, London, S.W.14. *T*: Prospect 1655, Abbey 6665.

MADSEN, THORVALD: physician; b. Copenhagen, Denmark, Feb. 18, 1870; s. V. H. O. and Albertine (Peterson) M.; educ. High Sch.; Univ. (both Copenhagen). DEGREES: Doctor Medicine (Copenhagen), Doctor Juris honoris causa (Glasgow), Dr. Med. honoris causa Frankfurt, Germany); m. Emelie Gad, Feb. 1, 1906. Contributor of numerous articles on Immunology and Epidemiology to medical journals.

Edited: Communications de l'Inst. serologique de l Etat Ianois. President Health Comm., League of Nations. President Permanent Standard Commission, League of Nations. Dir. state Serum Inst. (Copenhagen). OFFICE: Statens Serum Institute, Copenhagen, Denmark.

MAEGRAITH, Brian, M.A., M.D., B.Sc., B.S., D.Phil. b: Adelaide, Sth Aust, 1907. e: St Peter's & St Mark's Colls Adelaide, Adelaide Univ, Magdalen & Exeter Colls Oxf. m: Lorna Langley. s: 1. Prof of Trop Med, Dean Sch of Trop Med. *n.a*: Ed Annals of Trop Med & Parasitology. *Publ*: Pathological Processes in Malaria & Blackwater Fever; etc. *Ctr*: Lancet, B.M.J., Practitioner, Geog Mag, Annals of Trop Med, Trop Diseases Bulletin, etc, Manual of Malariology. *s.s*: Trop Med, Physiology, Pathology, Anthropology, Astronomy, Short Stories. *Rec*: Music. *c*: Liver, Univ (Liverpool). *a*: 23 Eaton Rd, Cressington Pk, Liverpool 19. *T*: Garston 1133.

MAEGRAITH, Kerwin. b: Adelaide, Sth Australia 1903. e: Collegiate Sch of St Peter Adelaide. m: Nellie Dean. s: 1. Cartoonist, Journalist, Company Director. *n.a*: Adelaide Advertiser —1933, Sydney Dly Mirror '41—43. *Publ*: Celebrites in Caricature; Who's Who in Adelaide; Wigs & Wags; Our 'Arbourosities; Who's Zoo; Maegraith's Annual. *Ctr*: Sydney Morning Herald, The Bystander, Sketch, Sporting & Dramatic News, Dly Herald. *s.s*: Sporting Cartoons, Deep Sea Angling. *Rec*: Golf, tennis, surf-riding. *w.s*: World War II. *c*: Savage, Good Companions, Swordfish. *a*: 1 Patterson St, Double Bay, Sydney, Australia. *T*: F.M.2519.

MAETERLINCK, Count Maurice. b: 1862. Dramatist & Essayist. *Publ*: Pelleas and Melisande; Alladine and Palomides; Interior; The Death of Tintagiles; The Treasure of the Humble; Monna Vanna; The Blue Bird; Mary Magdalene; The Burgomaster of Stilemonde; etc. Nobel Prize 1911. *a*: Nice, France.

MAETSCHKE, ERNST: professor of history and geography; b. Crainsdorf (County of Glatz), Germany, April 18, 1860; s. Ernst and Emma (Kirschte) M.; educ. St. Elizabeth's College (Breslau), Breslau Univ. DEGREES: Ph.D. AUTHOR: Geschichte der Grafschaft Glatz, 1888; Geschichte des Realgymnasiums zum Heiligen Geist, 1899. Editor: Schlesische Flurnammensammler. Contributor to Geschichte des Vereins für die Geschichte Schlesiens, Heimatkunde des Kreises Landeshut, Heimatkunde der Grafschaft Glatz, Zeitschrift für die Geschichte Schlesiens. General character of writing: historical, also essays. CLUBS: Verein für die Geschichte Schlesiens (honorary member), Historische Commission für Schlesien. Relig. denom., Lutheran. HOME: Lutherstrasse 2, Breslau, Germany.

MAGEE, Hugh Edward, D.Sc., M.B., Ch.B. b: Dromore Co Down, Ireland 1893. e: The Acad Banbridge Co Down, Queens Univ Belfast, Univ of Aberdeen. m: Catherine Teresa Savage. s: 1. d: 2. Adv in Nutrition M.O.H. *Ctr*: Many Papers dealing with Physiology, Biochemistery & Public Health. *s.s*: Physiology, Nutrition, Public Health. *Rec*: Farming, golf, shooting. *a*: 19 York Mans, Prince of Wales Drive, S.W.11. *T*: Macaulay 1712.

MAGENNIS, Edward, M.D., B.A.O., R.U.I., L.R.C.S.E., L.R.C.P.E., L.A.H., D.P.H. e: Queen's Col Belfast, Roy Lon Col. m: Mary M. H. Grew. s: 2. d: 1. *Publ*: Physical Deterioration in the Schoolroom; Eye Symptoms as Aids in Diagnosis, etc. *s.s*: Ophthalmology. Fellow of the Roy Inst of Public Health, Examiner for Incorporated Inst Hygiene, etc. *Rec*: Golf. *c*: Ex Portmarnock & Milltown Golf, Kilcroney Golf & County Sports Club. Mem The General Medical Council. Mem The Medical Registration Council (I.F.S). *a*: 86 Harcourt St, Dublin. *t*: 51301.

MAGENNIS, Most Rev. Peter Elias, O.Carm, D.Th. b: Tandragee, Co Armagh 1868. e: Chr Bros Belfast, Carmelite Col Terenure, Royal Dublin & Gregorian Rome Univs. n.a: Asst Gen Carmelite Order 1908 & Gen '19-. Publ: Life & Times of Elias The Prophet of Carmel; For Old Times' Sake; Life of Simon Stock, First English Carmelite General; Corn & Cockle; Stories of Several Lands; Origin, History & Legislation of All Scapulars; Privilegium Sabbatinum, etc. c.t: Various n/ps & periodicals. s.s: Hist, liturgy, hagiology. Prof in Ire 1887–94. Missny in Aus '96–1906, in Carmelite Curia, Rome 1908–15. Amer Missn '15–19. Superior General of Carmelite Order '19–31 (Rome). a: White Friars St, Dublin, Ireland.

MAGIAN, Anthony John Capper, M.D., B.S., F.R.G.S., F.L.Hist.S., F.R.I.P.H., F.S.A.(Scot), F.R.S., F.Z.S. b: London 1878. e: Lond, Manch, Paris. m: Margery Ainley. s: 2. d: 1. Author, Dramatist, O.St.J., Pres of the Cancer Soc, Lecturer post-graduate clinics. n.a Ed Cancer Journal. Publ: Several works on Cancer Diseases of Women, Sex Disorders; Several novels & plays. s.s: Cancer, Public Health, Gold Medal for Cancer Research. a: 136 Harley St, London, W.1. T: Welbeck 4280.

MAGILL, Ethel Mary, O.B.E., M.B., B.S., D.P.H., D.M.R.E. e: Salt Scs, Shipley, Yorks & Lon Sc of Med for Women. Physician. Publ: Notes on Galvanism & Faradism. c.t: Lady, Yachtsman, Austin Mag, Evening Standard, Morning Post. s.s: Radiology & electrotherapeutics. Med Practice in Canada & Calif. M.O. i/c X-ray Dept Mil Hosp '15–19. Govt Radiologist Gold Coast Colony '21–24. Radiologist to S. Lon Hosp for Women '26–. Rec: Sailing, swimming. c: Brit Inst of Radiology, Med Women's Fed, Brit Fed of Univ Women, Motor Boat Assoc (Mem Counc), Roy Yacht Club de Belgique. a: 35 Woburn Sq, W.C.1. t: Museum 9121.

MAGILL, Marcus. See **Hill, Brian.**

MAGNUS, LAURIE: author; b. London, Eng., Aug., 1872; s. Sir Philip Magnus, Baronet, and Katie, d. of Ald. Emanuel, J.P. of Portsmouth; educ. St. Paul's Sch. (London), Magdalen Coll. (Oxford. DEGREE: M.A. (Oxford); m. Dora, d.q Sir Isidore Spielman, C.M.C., July 22, 1903. AUTHOR: A Primer of Wordsworth, 1897; Prayers from the Poets, 1899; Introduction to Poetry (several edits.), 1901; How to Read English Literature, 1906; English Literature in the XIXth Century, 1909; The Third Great War in Relation to Modern History, 1914; A General Sketch of European Literature, 1918; Jubilee Book of the Girls' Public Day Schools Trust, 1923; Dictionary of European Literature, 1926 (2nd edit. 1927); English Literature in its Foreign Relations, 1927; The Jews in the Christian Era, 1929. Editor: School, 1904-5. Contributor to Quarterly Rev., Hibbert Journ., Cornhill Mag., Sunday Times, Berlin Corres. of the Morning Post, 1896-99; German Corres. of "Literature" (Times Literary Supplement), 1897. Was youngest contributor to Blackwood's Mag., while Oxford undergraduate, 1895. General character of writing: literary history and criticism, especially European literature. Chairman of Council Girls Public Day School Trust; Stood for Parliament, Bristol, 1910; Major Royal Defense Corps. CLUBS: Athenaeum, Carlton (both London). Religion: Judaism. HOME: 34 Cambridge Square, London, W. 2, Eng.

MAGNUS, Sir Philip, Bt. b: London 1906. e: Westminster Sch, Wadham Coll Oxf. m: Jewell Allcroft. Civil Servant. Publ: Life of Edmund Burke. Ctr: Sun Times, Spectator, Quart Rev, Cornhill. s.s: History & Letters. Rec: Tennis, climbing. w.s: Intell Corps (Major) 1939—45, & Cont Commsn Italy. c: Athenæum, Carlton. a: 2 Culross St, London, W.1. T: Mayfair 2452.

MAGOR, Nancy. m: Major Philip Magor. Publ: Life Marches On. Ctr: The Modern Mystic, Mthly Sc Rev, Occult Rev, Mid Sx Times, etc. s.s: Occultism, Federal Union. Rec: Music, yachting. a: White House Cott, Wimbledon Common, London, S.W.19.

MAGUINNESS, William Stuart. Publ: Ed Racine's Bérénice. c.t: Class Review, Class Quarterly, etc. a: The Univ, Sheffield.

MAGUIRE, John MacArthur. b: Denver, Colorado 1888. e: Cutler Acad, Colorado Coll, Harvard Law Sch. m: Mary Ballantine Hume. d: 2. Prof of Law. Publ: Maguire's Edition of Thayer's Cases on Evidence; Morgan & Maguire Cases on Evidence; Evidence: Common Sense & Common Law; The Lance of Justice; Magill & Maguire Cases on Taxation. Ctr: Harvard Law Review, Ency Brit, Ency of Social Sciences, etc. s.s: Evidence, Taxation. Rec: Photography, fly fishing, mountain climbing. c: Harvard Faculty, Harvard (Boston). a: Harvard Law School, Cambridge, Massachusetts, U.S.A. T: Kirkland 7600, line 320.

MAHADESHWAR, D. R. b: Bombay 1904. e: Wilson Col, St Xavier Col Bombay, Bombay Univ. Ed Indian Daily Telegraph & Author. n.a: Assoc Ed, Excelsior, India '23–25, Jt Ed Himalayan Times '26, Ed Indian Daily Telegraph '27–33. c.t: Times of India, Indian Daily Mail, Statesman, Calcutta, Pioneer, Daily Herald, Lahore, Daily Chronicle, Delhi. s.s: Politics & philos. Rec: Tennis. c: Maharashtra, Lucknow, Three Arts Circle Bombay, etc. a: Saith Ramjas Rd, Lucknow, India.

MAHADESHWAR, M. R. b: Bombay 1900. e: Wilson Col & Grant Med Col Bombay. Journalist. n.a: Mang Ed Indian Daily Telegraph, Lucknow '27–33. c.t: Illus Weekly of India Bombay, Three Arts Bombay Himalayan Times, Dehradun, etc. Rec: Tennis, ping-pong. c: Y.M.C.A. Lucknow, Three Arts Circle Bombay. a: Saith Ramjas Rd, Lucknow, India.

MAHAFFY, Robert Pentland. b: Dublin 1871. e: Marlborough, King's Col Cambridge. m: Evelina Dillon. s: 2. Barrister-at-Law. n.a: Leader Writer Morning Post 1894–1908. Lon Corr Dub Daily Exp 1899–1901. Publ: Sev vols of Calendar of State Papers 1897–1914; Life of Emperor Francis Joseph 1908; The Road Traffic Act '30; The Statute of Westminster '32; Road & Rail Traffic Law '34. War Service, wounded '16. Judge, Blue Nile & Kordofan Prov '17–19. Asst Legal Adviser Rhineland High Commiss '19–20. Legal Adviser to Gov of Malta '21–29. s.s: Modern history. c: United University, Leander. Rec: Golf. a: Greatash, Chislehurst, & New Court, Temple, E.C.4. t: Cent 4480.

MAHAPATRA, Chakradhar. b: Sasan, Narsingpur, E.S.A., India 1905. e: Indian Colls. m: Srimati Kanaka Manjari Devi. s: 5. d: 2. In State Service. Publ: Gobar Gotei; Apurna Prema; Sunajhia; Balangi; Ranamadhuri; Extracts of Oriya Folk Songs; Oriya Folk Songs; etc. Ctr: D. Samaj, Sahakan, Chano, Nabeen, Modern Reviewer, Geog Mag (America), etc. s.s: Oriya Folk Songs. a: C.D. Mahapatra, P.O. Narsingpur, Cuttack, Orissa, India.

MAHAPATRA, Lakshmi Kanta, B.A. b: Cuttack 1888. e: Calcutta Univ. m: Lavanga Lata Das. s: 2. Writer, Mem of P.E.N. n.a: Ed Dagaro 1936—37 & '42—44 & Dir '44—. Publ: Jivan Sangit; Kallol; Dunduvi; Kaliya Dalan; Parikshyar Phala; Sikshanabis Premika; Kumari. Ctr: Mukur, Utkal Sahitya, Sahakar, Asha, Current Affairs, Moyurbhanj Chronicle, Observer. s.s: Writing Humourous Skits & Sarcastic Poems, Composing Songs. Rec: Music, crossword puzzles. a: P.O. Bhadrak, Orissa, India.

MAHESH, Maheshwari Sinha, M.A. *b*: Bhagalpur 1913. *e*: Zila Sch, T.N.J. Coll Bhagalpur, Calcutta Univ. *m*: Tara Devi. *s*: 1. Prof of Hindu & Maithili. *n.a*: Asst Ed She Navayuga (Calcutta) 1935, The Vishwamitra (Calcutta) 1936, Ed The Biswin Sadi (Bhagalpur) '38. *Publ*: Suhag; Yugavani; Anal Vina; Saral Rajniti Vijnan. *Ctr*: Calcutta: Lokmanya, Vishwamitra, Vishal Bharat, Vina (Indore), Balak (Patna), Samaj (Benares), etc. *s.s*: Poetry, Criticism, Biog. *a*: T.N.J. Coll, Bhagalpur, Bihar India. *T*: Bhagalpur 73.

MAHEUX, Arthur (Joseph Thomas), O.B.E. *b*: St Julie de Megantic, Quebec 1884. *e*: Laval Univ, Sorbonne Paris. Prof, Lecturer, Archivist, Head of Dept of Hist & Geog Laval Univ. *n.a*: Ed L'Enseignement Secondaire au Canada 1918—31, Le Canada francais '38—43, Hebdo Plage St Laurent '45—. *Publ*: Propos sur L'Education; Ton Histoire est une Epopee; French Canada, A New Interpretation; Pourquoi sommes-nous divises; What keeps us Apart?; Problems of Canadian Unity. *Ctr*: The Financial Post, The Monetary Times, etc. *s.s*: Canadian Hist. *Rec*: Gardening. *a*: University Laval, Quebec City, Canada. *T*: 2-2379.

MAHINDRA, Kailash Chandra, M.A.(Punjab), B.A.(Cantab). *b*: Lahore 1894. *e*: Punjab & Cam Univs. Widower. *s*: 1. *n.a*: Ed Hindustan Review 1921—26, Martin Burn Hse Mag '27—32 & India Monthly Mag '34—. *Publ*: Indian Currency & Exchange ('22); India's Wagon Industry; Rajendranath Mookerjee (Biog) '32. *c.t*: Various n/ps. *s.s*: Finance, commerce. *c*: Calcutta, Lake & South. *a*: 6/1 Queen's Pk, Calcutta. *t*: Park 1509.

MAHON, Alfred Ernest, D.S.O. *b*: Scarborough 1878. *e*: Priv. *m*: Frances Amelia Fleming. Colonel Indian Army (ret). *Ctr*: The Field, Morning Post, Truth, The Yachtsman, Un Services Mag, Empire Review, Orient Observer, Illus Weekly of India, etc. *s.s*: Military, Sport, Humourous, Art, Archæology. *c*: Un Services. *w.s*: 1914—18, France, Belgium Mohmand Blockade & Waziristan Exped. *a*: Manali, Kulu, Punjab, India.

MAHR, Adolf, M.R.I.A., F.R.S.A.I. *b*: Italy 1887. *e*: Vienna Univ. *m*: Maria van Bemmelen. *s*: 1. *d*: 3. Keeper of Irish Antiquities. *Publ*: Christian Art in Ancient Ireland 1932. *c.t*: Irish Naturalists' Journal, L'Anthropologie (Paris), Irish Daily Press, etc. *s.s*: Archæology and anthropology. Formerly Asst Keeper Vienna Museum. Hon Corres mem Roy Archæ Inst Gt Brit & Ire. *a*: National Museum, Dublin.

MAHR, August Carl, Ph.D. *b*: Frankfurt-am-Main 1886 *e*: Lessing Gymnasium, Univs of Heidelberg, London Freiburg, Frankfurt. *m*: Elizabeth Hastings Transeau. *s*: 2. *d*: 2. Prof of German Lit Ohio State Univ. *n.a*: Ed-in-Chief Die Tide 1919—21. *Publ*: Die Hexe; Agnes; Trauerspiel von L. Braunfels; Dramatische Situationsbilder undbildtypen; The Visit of the " Rurik " to San Francisco in 1816; Origin of the Greek Tragic Form; Relations of Passion Plays to St Ephrem the Syrian. *Ctr*: Germanic Review, Journ of Ger & Eng Philology, Frankfurter Zeitung, etc. *s.s*: Hist & Aesthetics of the Drama. *w.s*: German Field Artillery 1915 —18. *a*: 2079, West Fifth Ave, Colombus 12, Ohio, U.S.A. *T*: Kingswood 4628.

MAIER, HANS WOLFGANG: professor of psychiatry; b. July 26, 1882; s. Gustav and Regina (Friedlander) M.; educ. College at Zürich, Univs. of Zürich, Vienna, Strasbourg, Munich. DEGREES: M.D.; m. Elena Schauffele, 1919. AUTHOR: Die Nordamerikanischen Gesetze gegen die Vererbung von Verbrechen und Geistesstörung und deren Anwendung, 1911; Der Cocainismus, 1926. Contributor of numerous articles on psychiatry, forensic psychiatry, psychopathology and child problems in psychiatric mags,, also to: Zeitschrift für die gesamte Neurologie und Psychiatrie; Archiv für Neurologie und Psychiatrie; Monatsschrift für Kriminalpsychologie und Strafrechtsreform. Has been working since 1925 in psychiatric clinic at Zürich with Eugen Bleuler; since 1927 director of the psychiatric clinic and policlinic, also professor in the Univ. of Zürich. HOME: Burghölzli, Zürich 8, Switzerland.

MAIER, HERMANN NICOLAUS: statesman; b. Stuttgart, Germany, May 14, 1877; s. Prof. Friedrich and Anna (Adam) M.; educ. Realgymnasium (Stuttgart), studied mathematics and natural sciences, 1895-1902. DEGREES: Sc.D., Oberregierunsrat; m. Alice Lambrecht, Aug. 8, 1906. AUTHOR: Versuch einer Darstellung der craniocerebralen Topographie in steographischer Darstellung, 1897; Über den feineren Bau der Wimperapparate der Infusorien, 1902; Altersbestimmung bei Fischen, 1906; Über das Hörvermögen der Fische, 1907; Der Karpfenteichwirt, 1907; Leitfaden der Vergleichenden Anatomie der Wirbeltiere, 1909; Praktische Anweisung für Anfänger in der Karpfenteichwirtschaft, 1909; Handbuch der Binnenfischerei Mitteleuropas (with Demoll and others), 1922; Entwicklung der Schwimmblase und ihrer Verbindung mit Schädel und Cloake bei Clupeiden (with Scheuring), 1923; Grundzüge der Karpfenteichwirtschaft (with Hofmann), 1931; Fischereilexikon (with Wundsch), 1931. Editor: Allgemeine Fischereizeitung, Handbuch der Binnenfischerei Mitteleuropas, Fischereilexikon. Contributor to Wissenschaftlich und Wirtschaftlich für Fischerei. General character of writing: scientific and technical. From 1902-1904, Assistant for international sea research at Helgoland; from 1904-1906, first assistant at the zoological institute of the Univ. of Tübingen; from 1906-1909, traveling teacher for fisheries in upper Bavaria. Since 1909, has been councillor of fisheries in the Bavarian ministry of the interior; since 1914, director of the school of fisheries in Starnberg. From 1916 to 1919 was commissioner of fish preservation. Since 1919 has been president of the German Fisheries Club; since 1920, member of the council of state; since 1921, lecturer on the breeding of fish at the technical college in Wilhelmstephan; since 1922, member of the government railroad board. Religion, Protestant. OFFICE: Ministry of the Interior. HOME: Lautererstrasse 18, Munich 51, Germany.

MAIER, Norman Raymond F., A.B., M.A. PhD.(Mech). *b*: Michigan 1900. *e*: Wayne Univ, Mich Univ, & Berlin Univ. *m*: Ayesha Ali. *s*: 1. Faculty of Mich Univ. *Publ*: A Psychological Approach to Literary Criticism (with Reninger). *c.t*: Amer Journ Psych, Journ Comparative Psych, Psycho Review, Journ Genetic Psych, Brit Journ Psych, etc. Nat Research Counc Fell 1929—31. *Rec*: Tennis. *c*: Sigma Xi, Amer Psych Assoc. *a*: 1677 Broadway, Ann Arbor, Michigan, U.S.A. *t*: 4459.

MAIER, Walter Arthur, A.M., LL.D., Ph.D., D.D. *b*: Boston, Massachusetts 1893. *e*: Concordia Coll Inst, Univs of Boston & Harvard, Concordia Sem. *m*: Hulda Augusta Eickhoff. *s*: 2. Clergyman, Prof in Concordia Sem, Radio Speaker. *n.a*: Ed Walther League Messenger 1920—45. *Publ*: For Better, Not For Worse; The Lutheran Hour; Christ for Every Crisis; Christ for the Nation; The Cross From Coast to Coast; Victory Through Christ; America Turns to Christ; Rebuilding With Jesus; Let Us Return Unto the Lord. *Ctr*: Concordia Theol Monthly, Augusta Quarterly, etc. *s.s*: Old Testament Exegesis. *Rec*: Collecting old books, swimming, fishing. *a*: 11 Seminary Terr North, Saint Louis 5, Missouri, U.S.A. *T*: Parkview 3131.

MAIGNON, FRANÇOIS: professor of physiology; b. Lyon, France, November, 1877; s. Ferdinand and Christine (Colombier) M.; educ. Faculté des Sciences de Lyon, École Vétérinaire de Lyon. DEGREES: Docteur es Sciences naturelles, Docteur Vétérinaire; m. May 25, 1909. AUTHOR: Récherches sur le role des graisses dans l'utilisation des albuminoides, 1919. Contributor to Académie des Sciences de Paris, La Société de Biologie de Paris, Journal de Physiologie et de Pathologie générale, Archives Internationales de

Physiologie, Annales de Médecine, and others. General character of writing: scientific. Is interested in physiology and the problem of nutrition. Also does research work on the treatment of diabetes. CLUBS: Académie Vétérinaire de France. Religion, Catholic. OFFICE: École Vétérinaire, d'Alfort, Seine. HOME: 3 Square Robiac, Paris VII, France.

MAILLART, Ella (Kini). b: Geneva 1903. Writer. n.a: Special Corr Petit Parisien 1934—37. Publ: Oasis Interdites (Forbidden Journey); Des Monts Celestes aux Sables Rouges (Turkestan Solo); Gypsy Afloat; The Cruel Way; Cruises & Caravans; Parmi la Jeunesse Russe. Ctr: Various illustrated periodicals. s.s: Sailing, Ski-ing, Asiatic Journeys & Customs. Rec: Hockey, travels or dreaming. c: R.G.S., Kandahar Ski-Club, etc. a: 10 av. Vallette, Geneva, Switzerland. T: 504.19; & c/o Pearn, Pollinger & Higham, 39 Bedford St, Strand, London.

MAIN, Rev. Archibald, M.A. b: Glas 1876. e: Glas Univ & Balliol Col Oxf. m: May Jardine Giffen. d: 1. Prof of Eccles Hist, Glas Univ 1922–. Chap-in-Ordinary to H.M. in Scot '25–. Publ: The Emperor Sigismund ('03). c.t: Glas Herald, Hastings' Dictionaries, etc. s.s: Ch Hist & Polit Philos. Rec: Curling, golf. c: Roy & Ancient Golf, St Andrews. a: 8 The Univ, Glas. t: Western 2560.

MAIN, Dr. David Duncan. Med Missny. n.a: N. China Daily News Corr in Hangchow, China, many yrs. Publ: Hangchow; Biography Dr Apricot of Heaven Below. a: 2 W. Coates, Edin. t: 61386.

MAIN, Ernest, M.A. b: Truro. e: G.S. & Aberdeen Univ. m: Barbara Wallace Farquharson. d: 1. Journalist. n.a: Sub Ed Daily Mail 1919—20. Chief For Sub Westminster Gazette '21—25, Daily Express '25—29, Assoc Ed Scottish Edn, Mang Ed Times of Mesopotamia & acting Ed Bagdad Times '29—33, Daily Mail Special Corr in Iraq, Turkey & the Balkans '33, Corr in Iraq for Times, Daily Mail, Reuter's, Chicago Tribune '29—33. Managing Ed, Dorset County Chron, Sunday Times, & Sherborne Post. Publ: In & Around Bagdad; Iraq From Mandate to Independence. s.s: Foreign polit, etc. F.R.C.A.S. c: St Andrews, E. India Utd Services. a: St Andrew's Club, 2 Whitehall Ct, S.W.1.

MAINE, Rev. Basil Stephen, M.A. b: Norwich 1894. e: City of Norwich Sch & Queen's Coll Camb, Rector of Warham, Norfolk, Author, Critic, Broadcaster. n.a: Broadcast Critic Sun Times till 1939, Music Critic Dly Telegraph 1921—27, Morning Post '27—33, Lond Music Critic Yorks Post '33—39, Ed Music Bulletin '26—29, Lond Corr Musica America '30—38. Publ: Receive It So; Reflected Music (essays); Rondo; Plummer's Cut; The King's First Ambassador (Biog Study of the Prince of Wales); The Best of Me (Autobiog); Life of Franklin Roosevelt; New Paths in Music; Maine on Music; etc. s.s: Music, Biography, Essays & Broadcasting. a: Warham Rectory, Wells, Norfolk.

MAINGOT, Rodney, F.R.C.S. b: Trinidad, B.W.I. 1893. e: Yshaw Coll Durham & St Bart's Hosp. m: Rosalind Smeaton. Senr Surg Southend Gen Hosp, Surg Roy Free Hosp. Publ: The Management of Abdominal Operations; Post-Graduate Surgery; Abdominal Operation; Technique of Gasfric Operations; War Wounds & Injuries (Pt-Ed); The Treatment of Varicose Veins; Haemorrhoids & Other Conditions. s.s: Abdominal Surgery. Rec: Golf, cricket. a: 12 Wimpole St London, W.1. T: Langham 3341.

MAINWARING, James, M.A., D.Litt., F.B.Ps.S., F.R.Hist.S. b: Kidsgrove, Staffs 1892. e: Adam's Gr Sch Newport Salop, Univs of Liverpool & Birmingham.

m: Gladys Irene Moyle. Lecturer Training Coll Dudley Worcs. Publ: Man & His World; Introduction to the Study of Map Projection. Ctr: Brit Journ of Psychology, Brit Journ of Educ Psychology, History. s.s: Psychology (Aesthetics), Music, Hist. Rec: Bridge, painting. a: Lingwood, St James Rd, Dudley, Worcs. T: Dudley 2061.

MAIR, George Brown, M.D., Ch.B., F.R.S.C.E. F.R.F.P.S.G. b: Troon 1914. e: Kilmarnock Acad, Glas Univ. m: Geertruida Van Der Poest Clement. Publ: The Surgery of Abdominal Hernia. Ctr: B.M.J., Lancet, Brit Journ of Surgery, American Journ of Surgery, Glas Med Journ, Kilmarnock Standard, etc. s.s: Surgery (Hernia). Rec: Foreign travel, oil painting, mountain climbing, dogs, opera, ballet. a: Hazlehead Hse, Carluke, Lanarkshire, Scotland. T: Carluke 3377.

MAIR, L. P., M.A., PhD. Lect in Colonial Administration Lon Sc of Econ. Publ: The Protection of Minorities; An African People in the 20th Century. a: c/o London School of Econs, Houghton St, W.C.2.

MAIR, Dr. W. c.t: Journ of Pathol & Bacter, Biochem Journ, etc. a: 17 Sunningfields Road, Hendon, N.W.4.

MAIR, William, F.R.S.E., F.C.S., F.R.S.G.S. b: Dundee 1868. e: Univ Coll Dundee. Married. s: 1. d: 1. Manufacturing Chemist (ret). Publ: Historic Morningside; Indigenous Drugs of India; An Index of Modern Remedies (Series 1-4). Ctr: Chem & Druggist, Pharmaceutical Journ. Rec Continental travel. a: 32 Braid Hills Rd, Edinburgh. T: 51473.

MAIRE, RENÉ CHARLES JOSEPH ERNEST: professor of botany; b. Lons-le-Saunier, France, May 29, 1878; s. Pierre Jean Jacques Charles Ernest and Delphine Lucie (Thirion) M.; educ. College de Gray, Univs. of Dijon and Nancy. DEGREES: D.Sc., M.D.; m. Simone Henrietta Anna Ferron, Nov. 4, 1926. AUTHOR: Flore Grayloise ou Catalogue des Plantes de l'Arrondissement de Gray, 1894; Carte phytogéographique de l'Algérie et de la Tunisie (with notes), 1925. Contributor to Bulletin de la Société Mycologique de France; de la Société Bolanique de France; de la Société d'Histoire Naturelle de l'Afrique du Nord; de la Société des Sciences Naturelles du Maroc; Comptes-Rendus de l'Académie des Sciences de Paris, Annales Mycologici; Bulletin de la Société des Sciences de Nancy, etc. General character of writing: botany, mycology, photo-geography, flora of the Orient and of North Africa. SOCIETIES: Corres. de l'Académie des Sciences de Paris, de l'Académie d'Agriculture de Torino, de la Société Biologie (Paris); Foreign Mem. of the Linnaean Society of London. OFFICE: University of Alger. HOME: 3, rue de Linne, Alger, Algeria, No. Africa.

MAIRET, Ethel, R.D.I. b: Barnstaple, Devon 1872. e: Local Lond, Bonn Univ, Germany, India, Handloom Weaver & Designer for Industry. Publ: Vegetable Dyes; Hand Weaving To-Day; Hand Weaving & Education. s.s: Textiles. a: Gospels, Ditchling, Sussex. T: Hassocks 174.

MAIS, Stuart Petre Brodie, M.A. b: 1885. e: Ch Ch Oxf. Married. d: 3. Lecturer, Author & Broadcaster. Publ: Isles of the Island; This Unknown Island; Delight in Books; Some Books I like; The High Lands of Britain; S.O.S.; These I Have Loved; Week-Ends in England; A Modern Columbus; Round about England; Walking at Week-Ends; The Character of England; England's Pleasance; The Writing of English; History of English Literature; & twenty novels. Rec: Walking, cricket. c: Achilles. a: Tansley, Shoreham-on-Sea, Sussex. t: 312.

Who Was Who Among English and European Authors

MAITLAND, Francis Anthony Hereward. *b*: Hampstead 1897. *e*: Priv. *m*: Lucy Mary Randall. *s*: 1. Journalist. *n.a*: Ed American's Shakespeare N.Y. 1928; Sundry Publicity Appointments N.Y. & Hollywood. *Publ*: Marigolds & Men ('32); Hussar ('34). *c.t*: American Press. *s.s*: Country lore, military subjects, American craft & gangdom. *Rec*: Riding, cricket, hockey. Prisoner of War Apr '18 escaped Oct '18. *a*: Mount Pleasant, Great Billington, Leighton Buzzard, Beds.

MAITLAND, Hugh Bethune. *b*: Canada 1895. *e*. Univ of Toronto. *m*: Mary Logan Cowan, B.A., M.B. *d*: 1. Prof of Bacteriology. *c.t*: Scientific Journals. *a*: 34 Denison Rd, Victoria Pk, M/C 14. *t*: Rusholme 4823.

MAITLAND, Patrick Francis. *b*: 1911. *m*: Stanka Losanitch. *s*: 1. Editor The Fleet Street Letter Service 1945—, formerly Spec Corres The Times (Warsaw & The Balkans); War Corres (U.S.A. Forces) in the Pacific. *Publ*: European Dateline. *a*: Cottage Walk, Sloane St, London, S.W.1.

MAITLAND, PETER (pen name): see MacGillivray, James Pittendrigh.

MAITLAND, THOMAS GWYNNE: physician; educ. Univ. College Sch., London, and privately; Univs. of Edinburgh, Manchester, Paris. DEGREES: M.A., B.Sc., M.D., B.S., Ph.D. AUTHOR: Examination of the Basis of Personality; Hysteria, a Psychological Study. Co-editor: Midland Medical Review; former editor: Manchester Medical Gazette. Lecturer on Psychology at Univ. of Wales, Manchester, Birmingham. Demonstrator of Psychology at Manchester. Lecturer on Psychology at Midland Lnst. Served as Lieut.-Col. in Serbian Army. ADDRESS: Cunard Buildings, Liverpool; Brackens, Kingsley, Cheshire, Eng.

MAITLAND DAVIDSON, Margery Dora. *b*: Tiptree Essex. *m*: Rowland Bower Jackson. Author & Novelist. *Publ*: Painted Blind; The Music Goes Round; Ladies in the Sun; Town Mice; Full Board Pin Dust. *Ctr*: Various newsps & periodicals. *Rec* Golf, gardening, reading, travel. *c*: Berks Golf. *a* Beggar's Roost, Warfield, Bracknell, Berks. *T* Winkfield Row 3200.

MAIZELS, Dr. Montague, M.D.(Lon) M.R.C.P. (Lon). Clinical Pathologist Univ Col Hosp. Ed Guy's Hosp Gazette, 1920. *a*: 79 Mount Pleasant Rd, Brondesbury Park, N.W.10.

MAJDALANY, Fred, M.C. *b*: Manchester 1913. *e*: King William's Coll, Isle of Man. Author & Journalist. *n.a*: Dramatic Critic Sun Referee 1937—39, Film Critic Dly Mail '46—. *Publ*: The Monastery. *Ctr*: Various. *s.s*: Films, Drama. *Rec*: Swimming, walking. *w.s*: Major Lancs Fusiliers World War II. *a*: 3 Grays Inn Pl, London, W.C.1. *T*: Holborn 2838.

MAJOR, Frederick Stanley Wells. *b*: Skegness 1902. *e*: Magdalen Col Sc Wainfleet & Lincoln Tech Inst. *m*: Mabel Abbott. *s*: 2. Journalist. *n.a*: Skegness News '21—, News Ed '26—2. *c.t*: Various prov daily & weekly journs. *s.s*: Munic & gen Eng, dramatic & film criticism. Press Stwd Skegness Motor Races '25-31. Official handicapper & course surveyor Skegness & E. Lincs Aero Club '32-33. *Rec*: Yachting, cave exploration. *c*: Avenue, Skegness. *a*: Rothesay, Albert Av, Skegness, Lincs. *t*: 108.

MAJOR, Rev. Henry Dewsbury Alves, M.A., D.D. *b*: 1871. *e*: St John's Coll & Univ Coll N.Z., Exeter Coll Oxf. *m*: Mary Elizabeth McMillan. *s*: 1. *d*: 1. Clerk in Holy Orders, Princ Ripon Hall, Vicar of Merton Bicester, Canon of Birm. *n.a*: Founder & Ed Modern Churchman 1911. *Publ*: Nobel Lectures, Religion & Civilisation; The Gospel of Freedom; The Mission & Message of Jesus; A Resurrection of Relics; Jesus by an Eye-Witness, etc. *Ctr*: Hastings Dict of Rel & Ethics, Hibbert Journal, Modern Churchman, etc. *s.s*: English Archæology, Ecclesiastical History. *c*: Author's. *a*: Merton Vicarage, Oxon.

MAJOR, Ralph Hermon, M.D. *b*: Liberty, Missouri 1884. *e*: William Jewell, Johns Hopkins Colls & Univs of Chicago, Leipzig, Heidelberg & Munich. *m*: Margaret Jackson. *s*: 2. *d*: 1. *Publ*: Classic Descriptions of Disease; Physical Diagnosis; Fatal Partners: War & Disease; Faiths That Healed; Disease & Destiny; The Doctor Explains. *Ctr*: Various med journs. *s.s*: Internal Med, Hist of Med. *a*: 6105 High Drive, Kansas City, Missouri, U.S.A. *T*: GI 5329.

MAJOR, Stephen. *b*: Wigan 1901. *m*: Alice Mawdesley. *s*: 1. *d*: 1. Editor. *n.a*: Ed Textile Recorder '33, Textile Recorder Year Book '33, Silk Journ & Rayon World '33, Ex Ed Boxmaker's Journ & Packaging Review. *a*: Danesway, Wigan.

MAJUMDAR, Jatindra Kumar, M.A., B.L., Ph.D. *b*: Calcutta 1896. *e*: Calcutta, Univ Coll Lond. *m*: Leela. *s*: 4. *d*: 1. Advocate High Court Calcutta. *Publ*: Life & Achievements of Raja Rammohun Roy; Indian Speeches & Documents on British Rule; The Sankhya Conception of Personality. *Ctr*: Philos Review, Monist, Open Court, Mod Review, Aryan Path, Indian Review, The New Era, etc. *s.s*: Philos, Hist, Law. *Rec*: Travel, music. *c*: P.E.N. *a*: " Bhagirathi Sadan " (Block 21), 237 Cadell Rd, Bombay 28, India.

MAKEPEACE, Gordon, B.A. *b*: Egremont, Cumberland 1903. *e*: Jeppe Hgh Sch Johannesburg & Univ of the Witwatersrand. *m*: Ethel Agnes Wilson. Journalist. *n.a*: Various Sth African newsps 1920—39, Ed The Outspan '47. *Publ*: Safari Sam; Cape Town to Stockholm. *Rec*: Bowls, golf, music. *c*: Bloemfontein. *a*: The Outspan, P.O. Box 245, Bloemfontein, Orange Free State, South Africa. *T*: Bloemfontein 1070.

MAKEPEACE, Walter, J.P., F.J.I. *b*: Coventry 1859. *e*: Saltley Col & Birkbeck Inst. *m*: Ray Pitt. *s*: 1 *d*: 2. Journalist. *n.a*: Singapore Free Press '87-1926, Ed '16-26, Ed Utusan Malaya (Malay Herald), Daily Chron, Reuter's Singapore Corr '05-26. *Publ*: One Hundred Years of Singapore ('19, 2 vols); Handbook of Singapore ('07). Malayan Delegate Imp Press Conf Ottawa '20. Ex-pres Malayan Br Roy Asiatic Soc. Ret Major Commanding Singapore Volunteer Artillery. *c*: F.R.E.S. *a*: 22 Holmes Gve, Henleaze, Bristol. *t*: 67223.

MAKIN, William James. *b*: Manchester 1894. *m*: Norline Maye Boon. *d*: 2. Editor. *n.a*: Manchester Guardian 1916—18, Pioneer (Allahabad) 18—20, Daily Mail '21. Cape Argus (S. Africa) '21—26, Pearson's & Screen Pictorial '26—34. *Publ*: Novels—The Price of Exile; Syncopated Love; Murder at Convent Garden; The Four Brains; etc. Travel—Across the Kalahari Desert; Red Sea Nights; African Parade; Swinging the Equator; etc. Accompanied Prince of Wales & Duke of Gloucester on overseas tours. *c*: Savage. *a*: 51 Linden Lea, Hampstead Garden Suburb, N.W.2. *t*: Speedwell 4911.

MAKINS, GEORGE HENRY: surgeon; b. Surbiton, Eng., Nov., 1853; s. George Hogarth and Sarah (Ellis) M.; educ. Gloucester, St. Thomas' Hosp. (Vienna). DEGREES: F.R.C.S., LL.D. (Cambridge and Aberdeen), G.C.M.G., C.B.; m. Margaret Augusta Kirkland. AUTHOR: Surgical Experiences in South Africa, 1900; Gun

Shot Injuries to the Blood Vessels, 1919. Contributes numerous articles to medical press, and to Systems of Surgery. Has had wide experience in Military Surgery. Past. pres. Royal Coll. of Surgeons of England; late senior Consulting Surgeon Army Med. Department; Hon. Major Gen.; late Dean of Med. School of St. Thomas' Hosp., London. CLUBS: Athenaeum, Alpine. Religion, Protestant. HOME: 33 Wilton Place, London. S. W. 1. Eng.

MAKOWER, Walter, M.A.(Cantab), D.Sc(Lon), F.InstP., O.B.E. *b*: Lon 1879. *e*: Univ Col Sc, U.C.L., & Trin Col Cam. *m*: Dorothy Lois Drey. *s*: 1. *d*: 2. Prof of Science R.M.A. Woolwich. *Publ*: The Radioactive Substances (1908); Practical Measurements in Radioactivity (with H. Geiger '12). *c.t*: Proc of Roy Soc, Phys Soc, Phil Mag, etc. Fell U.C.L. *c*: Oxf & Cam Musical, etc. *a*: 153 Eglinton Hill, S.E.18. *t*: Woolwich 1049.

MALACRIDA, MARCHESE (pen name: Piermarini): writer; b. Milan, Italy, March, 1890; s. Marchese Gretano Malacrida and Countess Marazzi M.; educ. Classic Pub. Sch. (Milan), Bologna Univ., Cambridge Univ. DEGREE: Doctor Oriental Languages; m. Madya Green, 1922. AUTHOR: Ireland, 1912; What I Saw in Berlin, 1915; Life Begins Today, 1923; Footprints on the Sand, 1925. Contributes to Daily Mail, Evening News (both London). General character of writing: topical and political. Religion, Roman Catholic. HOME: 53 Grosvenor Street, London, Eng.

MALAN, RT. HON. FRANCOIS STEPHANUS, P. C.: Senator; b. Wellington, South Australia, March, 1871; s. Daniël Gerhardus and Elizabeth Johanna (Malan) M.; educ. Paarl, Stellenbosch Coll., Cambridge Univ. DEGREES: B.A. L.L.B., LL.D.; m. Anna Elizabeth Brummer. AUTHOR: Wynboerseun in Franse Wyngaarde, 1895; Marie Koopmans-DeWet, 1924; 'N Ideale Huwelik, 1928. Editor: Ons Land, 1895-1908. Has contributed to development of Dutch press in So. Africa. General character of writing: political, biographical. Member Parliament for Malmesbury for 24 years; Senator since 1927; Minister of Education, 1910-1920; Minister of Mines and Industries, 1912-1924. Holds policy of broad nationalism; mem. of National Convention that brought about Union of So. Africa. CLUB: City. Relig. denom., Dutch Reformed. OFFICE: Houses of Parliament. HOME: Oranjezicht, Cape Town, South Africa.

MALCOLM, Charles Alexander, M.A., PhD. *b*: Edin. *e*: Geo Watson's Col & Edin Univ. Librarian. *Publ*: The Piper in Peace & War (1927); Gardens of the Castle in Book of Old Edinburgh (vol XIV); Cordiners of Canongate—Book of Old Edinburgh Club (vol XVIII); etc. *c.t*: Scottish Law Review, Chambers's Journal, Scotsman, Observer, Glasgow Herald, etc. *s.s*: Scottish Hist. *Rec*: Bowls, golf. *a*: 74 Marchmont Cres, Edin.

MALCOLM, Sir Dougal Orme, K.C.M.G., M.A., Fell All Souls Coll Oxf. *b*: Poetallock, Kilmartin, Argyll 1877. *e*: Eton, New Coll Oxf. *m*: Lady Evelyn Farquhar. Pres The Brit South Africa Co, Chm & Dir of Various Coy's, Hon Treas Children's Country Holidays Fund since 1934, Vice-Chm Court of Gov Lond Sch Economics & Political Science. *Publ*: Nuces Relictae; The British South Africa Co 1889-1939. *Ctr*: Time Lit Supp, Observer, Sun Times, Quart Rev, etc. *s.s*: Classical Lit, Sth African Hist & Lit. *a*: 53 Bedford Gardens, London, W.8. *T*: Park 8784.

MALCOLM, G. W. *a*: 31 Curling Wale, Onslow Village, Guildford, Surrey.

MALCOLM, Sir Ian, K.C.M.G., D.L., J.P., F.R.G.S., F.R.Z.S. *b*: Quebec 1868. *e*: Eton & N.C. Oxf. *m*: Jeanne Marie Langtry. *s*: 3.

d: 1. Dir of Suez Canal Coy. *Publ*: Indian Pictures & Problems; War Pictures behind the Lines; Trodden Ways; Vacant Thrones; Lord Balfour—a Memory; etc. *s.s*: Biog. M.P. for Stowmarket Div of Suffolk '95—1906, M.P. for Croydon '10—1919, Asst Priv Sec Marquess of Salisbury 1895—1900, Priv Sec Rt Hon George Wyndham M.P. 1900—03, Priv Sec to Rt Hon A. J. Balfour '16—19, Grand Cordon of the Nile, Comm of Legion of Honour. *c*: Carlton, M.C.C., Roy Bodyguard Scot, etc. *a*: 57 Onslow Sq, S.W.7 & Poltalloch, Kilmartin, Argyll. *t*: Ken 7538.

MALCOLM, John D, F.R.C.S. *c.t*: B.M.J., Lancet, etc. *a*: Sheet House, Petersfield. *t*: Petersfield 326.

MALCOLMSON, V. A., M.A.(Cantab), J.P. *Publ*: The place of Agriculture in The Life of a Nation; Seven Lean Kine; Rural Housing; etc. *s.s*: Agric econ. *a*: Aston Bury, Stevenage, Herts.

MALDEN, Very Rev. Richard Henry. *b*: London 1879. *e*: Eton, King's Coll Camb. *m*: Etheldred Theodora MacNaughton. *Publ*: Foreign Missions; The Temptation of the Son of Man; Watchman What of the Night; Problems of the New Testament; This Church & Realm; The Roman Catholic Church & The Church of England; etc. *c*: Athenæum. *a*: The Deanery, Wells, Somerset.

MALDEN, Walter James. *b*: Cardington. *e*: Bedford. *m*: Lillian Waldron. *d*: 1. Land Agent, Agric Expert, Writer. *n.a*: Staff Farmer & Stockbreeder 35 y, etc. *Publ*: Actual Farming (3 vols, 1926); Grassland Farming; Technical Training in Farm Work; Physical Culture in Farm Work; Tillage & Implements; Evolution of the British Breeds of Pig ('35); etc. *c.t*: Bayly's Mag, Game & Gun, XIXth Century, Fortnightly, etc. *s.s*: Grassland Culture, livestock breeding, plant production. *c*: Farmers. *a*: 1 The Mount, Caversham Heights, Reading.

MALE, Emile. *b*: Commentry (Allier) 1862. *e*: Ecole Normale Superieure. *m*: Marguerite Granier. *s*: 1. *d*: 1. Prof Hon de l'Ecole francaise d'archiologie de Rome, Grand Off Leg d'honneur, Mem Acad francaise, l'Acad des Inscriptions et Belles Lettres. *Publ*: L'art religieux du XIIIe Siecle en France; L'art religieux de la fin du moyen age en France; L'art religieux du XIIe Siecle en France; L'art religieux apres le Concile de Trente; Art et Artistes du moyen age; Rome et ses ieillves eglises; Pages choisies de l'oeuvre de l'auteur. *a*: Paris (V) II rue de Navarre, Paris, France. *T*: Jo 78-20.

MALET, LUCAS (pen name): (Mary St. Leger Harrison): novelist, dramatist; b. Everley, Hants, June 4, 1852; y. d. Charles Kingsley (poet, novelist, preacher and social worker); Rector of Eversley and Canon of Westminster) and Frances Elija (Grenfell) Kingsley; educ. at home and Slade Sch., Univ. College (London); m. William Harrison, 1876 (died). AUTHOR: Mr. Lorimer, 1880; Colonel Enderly's Wife, 1881; A Counsel of Perfection-Little Peter; The Wages of Sin, 1890; The Carissima, 1893; The Gateless Barrier, 1899; The History of Sir Richard Calmady, 1901; (from 1906 to 1925): The Far Horizon; The Loss of the Golden Galleon; Adrian Savage; Damaris; The Survivors; The Dogs of Wants. Also author of two volumes of short stories. Contributes articles on various subjects to mags. and newspapers. Religion, Roman Catholic. ADDRESS: Care A. P. Watt and Son, London, Eng. HOME: Montreaux, Switzerland.

MALET, Oriel. *b*: London 1923. *e*: Priv. *Publ*: Trust in the Springtime; My Bird Sings; Marjory Fleming (Biog). *Ctr*: Homes & Gardens. *s.s*: Children.

929

Rec: Sailing, theatre. *a*: Portnal Lea, Virginia Water, Surrey. *T*: Wentworth 3197.

MALIK, Ghulam Farid, B.A. *b*: Kunjah 1898. *e*: Punjab Univ. *m*: Nawab Begam. *s*: 5. *d*: 1. Journalist. *n.a*: Ed The Sunrise, 1928—31; The Review of Religions '32—. *Publ*: Islam the Religion of Humanity. *c.t*: Times, Observer, Spectator, Outlook, India & Near East. *s.s*: Comparative Hist of Religions. *Rec*: Cricket, walking. *a*: Qadian, India.

MALIM, Barbara. *e*: Brussels. Literary Agent. *Publ*: Death by Misadventure; To this End; Missing from Monte Carlo. *a*: 40 Craven Hill Gardens, W.2. *t*: Paddington 5836.

MALIN, Brendan Thomas. *b*: Tara, Co Meath 1914. *e*: Local National Sch & Caffreys Intermediate Coll Dublin. *m*: Joan Corcoran. *s*: 2. *d*: 1. Journalist, Mem of N.U.J., Internat Organisation of Journalists. *n.a*: Dist Rep Meath Chronicle 1930—32, Mayo News '32—33, Staff Rep Irish Press '33—45, Political Corr & Deputy News Ed Irish Press '45—. *Ctr*: Reynolds News, The Standard (Dublin), Irish Travel (Dublin). *s.s*: Politics, National Econs, Trade Union Development. *Rec*: Walking, cycling, tennis. *a*: 8 Ardpatrick Rd, Dublin, Ireland. *T*: 75709.

MALINOWSKI, Bronislaw, PhD., D.Sc. *b*: Poland 1884. *e*: King John Sobieski Publ Sc Cracow, & Cracow, Leipzig & Lon Univs (Lon Sc of Econ). *m*: Elsie Rosaline Masson. *d*: 3. Prof of Anthopology Lon Univ. Corr Mem Polish Acad of Science; Foreign Corr Anthropological Soc of Vienna; Mem R.A.S. of Netherlands. *Publ*: The Family Among the Australian Aborigines (1913); Argonauts of the Western Pacific ('22); Myth in Primitive Psychology ('26); Crime & Custom in Savage Society ('26); Sex & Repression in Savage Society ('27); The Sexual Life of Savages in N.W Melanesia ('29); etc. *c.t*: Nature, Man, Journ of the R. Anthro Inst, Zeitschr für Völkerpsychologie und Soziologie, Africa. *s.s*: Anthropology. Messenger Lect at Cornell Univ '33. *a*: 6 Oppidans Rd, N.W.3. *t*: Primrose 3052.

MALKANI, Mangharem Udharam, B.A. *b*: Hyderabad, Sind 1896. *e*: Univ of Bombay. *s*: 2. *d*: 1. Prof of Eng & Sindhi Sind Coll Karachi. *n.a*: Ed The Indus 1934—36. *Publ*: Kismet; Ekta Jo Alap; Khina Ji Khata; Anarkali; Pangati Parda; Preet Ja Geet; Gitanjali; etc. *Ctr*: Sind Observer, Asha, Sindhu, Mehran (Karachi), etc. *s.s*: Mod Eng Drama ,Development of Sindhi Prose. *Rec*: Photography. *a*: Supt, Metheram Hostel, D.J. Sind Coll, Karachi, Sind, Pakistan.

MALKANI, Naraindas R., M.A., LL.B. *b*: Hyderabad, Sind 1890. *e*: Bombay & Calcutta Univs. *m*: Rukmani Malkani. *s*: 1. *d*: 2. Congress Writer. *n.a*: Various Indian & English Newsps. *Publ*: Gothani Chahr; Anar Dana; Sind Ja Hunar; Kashmir Ja Sair; Gujerat; etc. *Ctr*: Sind Observer, Dly Gazette, Hindustan Times, Free Press Journ. *s.s*: Econ, Political & Social Conditions of Sind. *Rec*: Writing in Sindhi. *a*: 35 Amil Colony, Hyderabad, Sind, India.

MALLALIEU, Joseph Perival William, M.P. *b*: Delph, Yorks 1908. *e*: Dragon Sch Oxf, Cheltenham Coll, Trinity Coll Oxf, Univ of Chicago. *m*: Harriet Rita Riddle Tinn. *s*: 1. *d*: 1. M.P. (Lab) Huddersfield, Journalist, Pres Oxf Union 1931, Commonwealth Fell '30—32, N.U.J. *n.a*: Rep Lexington Herald Kentucky 1932, American Ed & Lobby Corres Financial News '33—35, Asst City Ed Ev Standard '35—36, Asst-City Ed Dly Express '37—39, Sub-Ed Dly Express '39—42. *Publ*: Very Ordinary Seaman; Passed to You, Please; Rats; *Ctr*: Tribune, Spectator, Everybody's, Lilliput, Leader. *Rec*: Walking, gardening, Assoc football. *c*: Press. *a*: The Ship Hse, Liphook, Hants. *T*: Liphook 3160, & 124 Sloan Court, London, S.W.3. *T*: Flaxman 4458.

MALLESON, Constance (Collette O'Niel). *b*: Castle Wellan, Nth Ireland 1889. *e*: Dresden, Paris, R.A.D.A. *m*: Miles Malleson. Author, formerly Actress, Played in many West End productions & various Repertory Theatres, Toured Sth Africa, Rhodesia, Egypt, Palestine (with Sybil Thorndike). *Publ*: After Ten Years; The Coming Back; Fear in the Heart; In the North. *a*: Sundborn, Sweden.

MALLESON, William Miles, B.A. *b*: Croydon 1888. *e*: Brighton Coll, Emmanuel Coll Camb. Married. *s*: 2. Dramatist & Actor. *Publ*: (Plays) Six Men of Dorset; Merriles Wise; (Comedy) Youth; The Fanatics; Conflict; Four People; Yours Unfaithfully; (For Children) The Little White Thought; Paddly Pools; Maurice Own Idea; " D " Co; Black 'Ell; Four Short Plays (1 vol); etc. *a*: 60 Wigmore St, London, W.1. *T*: Welbeck 3021.

MALLET, Sir Charles E. M.P. Plymouth 1906—10. *b*: Lon 1862. *e*: Harrow & Balliol Col Oxf. *m*: Margaret Roscoe. *s*: 2. Politics & Letters. Financial Sec W.O. '10. *Publ*: A History of the University of Oxford (3 vols '24—27); Mr Lloyd George: A Study ('30); Lord Cave: A Memoir; Herbert Gladstone: A Memoir; etc. *s.s*: Hist, biography. *c*: Athenæum. *a*: Millbrook Hse, Guildford. *t*: Guildford 693.

MALLETT, Cecil Finer. *b*: Bradford 1891. *m*: Elsie Stansfield. *s*: 2. *d*: 2. Jnlst. *n.a*: Partner in Mallett & Co, Journalists (sport & wool trade) & Shorthand Writers. Ed & Prop (with W. H. Sawyer) Weekly Wool Chart, Bradford. *s.s*: Wool trade, sport. *c*: Mem Wool Statistics Advisory Sub-Cmt Imperial Econ Cmt, Royal Statistical Soc, Royal Econ Soc, Assoc of Professional Shorthand Writers. *a*: Commerce Hse, Cheapside, Bradford, Yorks. *t*: 7112.

MALLETT, Edward, D.Sc., M.I.E.E., M.Inst.C.E, F.Inst.P. Princ Woolwich Polytechnic. *Publ*: Telegraphy & Telephony; Vectors for Electrical Engineers; Foundation of Technical Electricity (with T. B. Vinycomb). *Ctr*: Tech Press. *a*: King's Court, Writtle, Essex. *T*: Roxwell 234.

MALLETT, Josiah Reddie Martin. *b*: Lon 1864 *e*: Priv Scs, Mill Hill Sc, Leipzig & Stuttgart Conservatoriums. *m*: Clara Thomas. *d*: 2. Writer. *Publ* Preventable Suffering; Too Much Doctoring; Nature's Way; The Cure of Cancer by " Nature's Way " Poems from Beyond & other Verse, etc. *s.s*: Nat treatment of disease. *Rec*: Boating. *a*: Dunsford Hill, Exeter.

MALLETT, Richard. *b*: West Norwood 1910. *e*: Lowestoft Sec Sch. Journalist. *n.a*: Ed Staff Ev News Lond 1931—34, Ed Staff Punch '37—, Film Critic '38—, Mem Punch " Table " *Publ*: Doggerel's Dictionary. *c*: Authors, Press. *a*: 103 Cliffords Inn, London, E.C.4.

MALLIK, Gurdial. *b*: Dera Ismail Khan 1896. *e*: Bombay Univ. Schoolmaster. *n.a*: Leader Writer Baluchistan Gaz Quetta 1921—35, The Servant of Sind Karachi '36—37, Asst Ed Sind Herald Karachi '27—29, Asst Ed The Young Builder Karachi '33—36. *Publ*: Short Stories of Premchand; The Peace Ideal; Davaram Gidumal; J. Krishnamurti; Jamshed Nusserwanji, *Ctr*: Dly Gazette (Karachi), Sind Observer, Hindustan Standard, etc. *Rec*: Tennis, reading, social service. *c*: P.E.N. *a*: c/o Shri M.C. Setalvad, Mirant, Juhu, Bombay 23, India. *T*: 86077.

MALLING, Anders Christopher. *b*: Randers, Denmark 1896. *m*: Johanne Henckel Bachmann. *d*: 3. *Publ*: Lovsang; Fra Kaerlighedens Kongerige; Danmarks Kirke; Mellem salige Kyster; Syngende Naetter; Gudsfulde Rustning; En Konge dor. *Ctr*: Kristeligt

Dagblad, Kirken og Folket, Kirken, Kirken og Tiden. *s.s*: Hymnology. *c*: Danish Authors. *a*: Brons, Denmark. *T*: Brons 14.

MALLINSON, Rev. Thomas Harold. B.A.(Lon), *b*: Linthwaite 1875. *e*: Almondbury G.S., Harrogate Col. *m*: Gertrude des Ormeaux Taylor. *d*: 1. *Publ*: Lift Up Your Hearts. *c.t*: Meth Times, Experience, etc. *s.s*: Liturgiology. *a*: The Moorings, Shavington Av. Newton, Chester.

MALLISON, Eric Mallie Ling. B.Sc. *b*: Chelsea 1905. *e*: Clifton Col de Normandie, France, Lille Univ, Peterhse, Cam. Barrister at Law. *Publ*: Law Relating to Women ('30); Law Relating to Advertising ('31). *Rec*: Swimming. *c*: Leics. *a*: 5 Elm Ct, Temple, E.C.4., 27 Friar Lane, Leicester & 57 Prom des Anglais, Nice. *t*: Leicester 59796 & Central 6634/5.

MALLOCH, George Reston. *b*: Elderslie 1875. *e*: Paisley Gr Sch & Privately. *m*: (1) Ethel Josephine Victoria Oliver, M.B.E., (2) Amy Cecilia Felton. Author. *Publ*: 5 vols Verse; (Plays) Soutarness Water; The Coasts of India; etc; also many short plays. *Ctr*: Short Stories principal mags & journals, England, America, Dominions, also European journals. *c*: Authors' *a*: 2 Suffolk Rd, S.W.13. *T*: Riverside 5655.

MALLON, J. J. *a*: Toynbee Hall, 28 Commercial St, E.1.

MALLON, Paul Raymond, Hon.Des.L., LL.D. *b*: Matton, Illinois 1901. *e*: Notre Dame & Louisville Univs. *m*: Viola Jane Wingreene. Columnist. *n.a*: Former Staff Louisville Courier-Journal, Herald Post, Post (Louisville), South Bend Indiana News-Time, Washington Column " News Behind The News " 1932. *Publ*: The Ease Era; Practical Idealism. *Ctr*: Various mags & newsps. *s.s*: Econs, Political, Nat & Internat Affairs. *Rec*: Growing roses & camelias. *c*: Nat Press, Belle Haven Country. *a*: 15 Fort Drive, Belle Haven, Alexandria, Virginia, U.S.A. *T*: District 8181.

MALLORY, Walter Hampton. *b*: Newburgh, New York 1892. *e*: Columbia Univ. *m*: Alice Caroline Evans. *s*: 1. Executive Director Council on Foreign Affairs, President China Institute in America 1943—, Mem Allied Mission to observe the Elections in Greece (rank of U.S. Min) '46. *Publ*: Ed Annual, Political Handbook of the World; China: Land of Famine. *Ctr*: Foreign Affairs, N.Y. Times, N.Y. Herald-Tribune, Current History, Quarterly Journ of Econs. *s.s*: International Relations (China & the Far East). *Rec*: Golf. *c*: Century, Cosmos, St Andrews Golf. *a*: 58 East 68th St, New York 21, N.Y., U.S.A. *T*: Butterfield 8-6750.

MALM, Johan Einar Fredrik, Ph.D. *b*: Norsborg, Sweden 1900. *e*: Univ of Upsala. *m*: Vera Lund. *s*: 1. Author & Translator. *Publ*: (Poems) Ditten 1920—32; Ur Askan i Elden; Stormvarning; An flyga svanarna; Pejlingar; Valda dikter; Ankargrund; Roslagsvisor; Nagot att forlora; (Prose) Siouxindianernas sista strid; Sitting Bull och kampen om Vilda Vastern; & several other Trans. *Rec*: Nature. *a*: Aspholmen, Spillersboda, Sweden. *T*: Spillersboda 28.

MALMBERG, Bertil Frans Harald. *b*: Hernosand 1889. *e*: Univs of Upsala & Lund. *m*: Greta de Brun. Poet, critic. *Publ*: Atlantis; Orfika; Slojan; Vinden; Illusionernas Trad; Ake och hans Varld. *c.t*: Ord och bild, Bonnier's Literary Mag. *c*: P.E.N. *a*: Klostergatan 4, Mariefred, Sverige. *t*: Mariefred 43.

MALMESBURY, Lord Bishop Suffragan. *n.a*: Dir Bristol Evening Post 1932, Ed Bristol Diocesan Review '19—27. *a*: Brinkworth Rectory, Chippenham, Wilts.

MALONE, Andrew E.. (Laurence Patrick Byrne). *b*: Dublin 1890. *e*: Dublin. *m*: Elizabeth Purcell. *s*: 1. *d*: 1. Author & jnlst. *n.a*: New Ireland '15—21; Irish Opinion '18; Dublin Magazine '25; Irish Tribune '26. Irish Corr New York Herald-Tribune & B'ham Post. *Publ*: The Irish Drama: 1899—1928; Twentyone Years of the I.A.W.S.; Co-operation in Ireland; Donn Byrne: An Irish Realist. *c.t*: Yale Review, 19th Century, Fortnightly, etc. *s.s*: Drama, the theatre, films, politics, economics. *Rec*: Reading, the theatre. *c*: Mem Acad of Political Science, M.J.I., Hon Sec Irish P.E.N. *a*: 23 Ranelagh Rd, Dublin, I.F.S. *t*: Rathmines 809.

MALONE, Henry L'Estrange. *b*: Cowes, I.O.W. 1872 *e*: Private. *m*: Ethel Gertrude Vincent. *s*: 1. *d*: 1. Company Director. *Publ*: Nipping Bear; Shaggy the Great; Lost Fairy Tales; Winfred; The Red King; Adventures of Anne; The Wizard's Spell; etc. *s.s*: Fairy Tales. *Rec*: Fruit farming. *a*: 59b Kensington Gardens Sq, London, W.2. *T*: Bayswater 5524.

MALTBY, H. F. Author & Playwright. *Publ*: Bees & Honey; The Laughter of Fools; Mr Budd of Kensington S.E.; The New Religion; The Right Age to Marry; The Rotters; Three Birds; What Might Happen; For the Love of Mike; Jack o'Diamonds; The Shadow; Maggie; A Temporary Gentleman; The Age of Youth; Many Grand Guignol Plays, is Author or Part Author of over seventy films. *Ctr*: Various. *a*: 62 Langdale Gdns, Hove, Sussex. *T*: 3485.

MALTBY, S. E., M.A. Schoolmaster. *Publ*: Manchester & National Elementary Education; Education; Handbook of European History. *a*: Friends' Sc, Penketh, nr Warrington *t*: 31.

MALTBY, Thomas Flower. *b*: Dover, Kent 1912. *e*: Dover Coll. *m*: Betty Margaret Lambert Oatridge. Journalist, Mem N.U.J. *n.a*: Rep Gravesend & Dartford Reporter 1929—35, Asst Ed Tothill Street Press '35—40, News Ed The Recorder '46. *s.s*: Shipping, Shipbuilding Indust, Aviation & Econs, Naval Affairs. *Rec*: Fishing, motor boating, swimming. *c*: Press, Colne Yacht, R.N.V.R. *w.s*: 1941—46, Stoker to Lieut Cmdr. *a*: 30 Lydhurst Ave, Streatham Hill, London, S.W.2, & The Plaice, 87 Beach St, Deal ,Kent. *T*: 769.

MALTBY, Rev. William Russell, D.D.(Glas). *b*: Selby 1866. *e*: Kingswood Sch Bath. *m*: Catherine Russell Barrowclough. *s*: 2. *d*: 2. Pres Wes Conf 1926—27. *n.a*: Ed Manuals of Fellowship 1915—29. *Publ*: The Significance of Jesus; Christ & His Cross. *a*: St Fillans, Grove Rd, Ilkley. *T*: 1380.

MALTHOUSE, Gordon Spencer. *b*: Twickenham 1909. *e*: Hampton Gr Sch. Journalist & Editor. *n.a*: Ed Amateur Cine World, Miniature Camera World, Sun Bathing Rev, Book Ed Link Hse Publs. *Publ*: Modern Encyclopedia of Photography (Assoc Ed). *s.s*: Photography, Films. *a*: Link Hse, 24 Store St, London, W.C.1. *T*: Museum 9792.

MALTWOOD, Katharine E., F.R.S.A. *b*: Nr London, England 1878. *e*: Moira House Eastbourne, The Sla de Lond Univ Coll. *m*: John Maltwood. Sculptor & Writer. *Publ*: A Guide to Glastonbury's Temple of the Stars; Air View Supplement to the Temple of the Stars; The Enchantment of Britain; King Arthur's Round Table of the Zodiac; Itinerary of the Somerset Giants. *Ctr*: Journ of Roy Astrono Soc of Canada, Canadian Theosophist. *s.s*: Discovery of Traditional Zodiac Nr Glastonbury (King Arthur's Round Table). *Rec*: Travel in search of art & antiquity. *a*: The Thatch, Royal Oak, Vancouver Island, B.C., Canada.

MALTZ, Albert, A.B. *b*: Brooklyn, N.Y. 1908. *e*: Public Schs, Columbia Coll & Yale Univ. *m*: Margaret Larkin. *s*: 1. *d*: 1. Author. *Publ*: The Cross & the Arrow; The Underground Stream; The Way Things Are; Black Pit; Peace on Earth. *Ctr*: New Yorker, Harpers, N.Y. Times, New Masses, Scholastic, P.M., Southern Rev, Equality. *s.s*: Novels, Short Stories, Films. *Rec*: Baseball, chess, tennis. *c*: Authors. *a*: c/o Little Brown & Co, 34 Beacon Street, Boston 6, Massachusetts, U.S.A.

MALWALD, Sangappa Sanganabasappa, M.A. *b*: India 1910. *e*: Bombay Univ. *m*: Shantaden. *Publ*: (Ed) Kannata Gadyamale; Probhendeva Regale; Haribaram Rajelegabi; etc. *Ctr*: Various Indian hist newsps & periodicals. *s.s*: Kannata Lang & Lit, Criticism, Indian Politics. *a*: Karnatak Coll, Dharwar, Bombay Presidency, India.

MAMMEN MAPPILLAI, K.C., B.A. *b*: Niranum, Tiruvalla 1872. *e*: C.M.S. Col, Kottayam, Maharaja's Col, Trivandrum, Madras Christian Col. Married. *s*: 8. *d*: 1. *n.a*: Chief Ed Malayala N/p. *s.s*: Journalism, banking, commerce. Pres Travancore National Bank Ltd, Mang Dir Malayala Manorama Co. Ltd. Mang Dir The Guardian of India Insurance Co. Ltd. Formerly Head Master M.D. Seminary H.S. Returned several times as Mem of Sreemulam Assembly & The Legislative Council. *a*: Malayala Manorama, Kottayam, Travancore, S. India.

MANAS Y BONVI, JOSÉ: industrial engineer; b. Vinaroz, Spain, September, 1885; s. Juan Manas Lara and Primitiva Bonvi Carcases; educ. Grammar School (Vinaroz), Antonio Segura's School, High School, Instituto de Cartelton, School of Industrial Engineers (Barcelona); studied aviation, Escuela de Nautica (Barcelona). DEGREES: Bachelor, Industrial Engineer, Professor; m. Luisa Redo Forner, 1917 AUTHOR: Quimica General inorganica y Organica, 1911; Experimentos y Practicas de Quimica (with A. F. Ribas), 1913; Optica Aplicada 1914; Electroquimica; Quimica aplicada a los oficios y bellas artes, 1918; Experimentos y practica de Quimica (with A. F. Ribas), 1919; Elementos de Fisica y Geologia (with A. Inclan), 1924; Experimentos y Practicas de Quimica, 1927; Curso de Quimica (with A. F. Ribas), 1926; Compendio de las Lecciones de Quimica General, 1928; Problemas de Fisica, 1929. Contributor to Technica de la Asociacion de Ingenieros de Barcelona; El Progreso Fotografico; Iberica, Revista General de Artes y Ciencias. Graduated as Optician Engineer from the "Institute d'Optique" in Paris, 1924. Sent by Spanish Government to France. Professor of Physics and Chemistry; engaged in finding methods for various uses of artificial light. CLUBS: Asociacion Ingenieros Industriales; Asociacion para el Progreso de las Ciencias; Club de Natacion. Religion: Roman Catholic. OFFICE: School of Engineers. HOME: Muntaner, 98, 4o. 2a., Barcelona, Spain.

MANCE, Elizabeth Hope. *Publ*: My Lady's Bargain. *a*: Hill Top, Frith Hill, Godalming. *t*: 526.

MANCE, Sir Harry Osborne. K.B.E., C.B., C.M.G., D.S.O., M.Inst.T. *b*: Karachi 1875. *e*: Bedford Sch, Roy Mil Acad, Sch Mil Eng, Chatham. *m*: Elizebeth Hope Stenhouse. *s*: 2. *d*: 1. Brit Rep Central Rhine Commiss, Transport & Communications Commiss of United Nations, Dir of Railways War Off 1916—20, Trans Adviser Brit Del Paris Con '18—19, Pres Commun Section Supreme Economic Counc '18—20, Dir Canals Min of War Trans '41—44. *Publ*: The Road & Rail Transport Problem; International Telecommunication; International Air Transport; International River & Canal Transport; International Sea Transport; International Road Transport, Power, Electricity & Miscellaneous Questions; Frontiers, Peace Treaties & International Organisation. *Ctr*: Times, Modern Transport, Rly Gazette. *s.s*: Inter Trade & Transport. *Rec*: Fishing. *c*: Army & Navy. *a*: Hill Top, Frith Hill, Godalming. *T*: 526.

MANDEL, HERMANN: professor; b. Dec. 13, 1882; s. Heinrich and Wilhelmine (Schulte) M.; educ. Gymnasium (Mörs), Univs. of Halle, Königsberg und Greifswald. DEGREES: Lic. Theol., Professor, Dr. Theol. (honoris causa); m. Margarete Stursberg, Aug. 29, 1912. AUTHOR: Erkenntnis des Übersinnlichen (vol. 1, Genetische Religionspsychologie; vol. 2, System der Ethik als Grundlegung der Religion), 1912; Christliche Versöhnungslehre, 1916; Das Gotteserlebnis der Reformation, 1917. Editor: Theologia deutsch, 1912. Relig. denom., Protestant. ADDRESS: Niemannsweg 53, Kiel, Germany.

MANDER, Sir Frederick, Kt., M.A., B.Sc., Hon.F.E.S.I. *b*: Luton 1883. *e*: Luton Higher Grade Sch, Westminster Training Coll. *m*: Hilda Irene Sargent. *s*: 2. *d*: 1. Dir of Newnes Educational Publ Co, Gen Sec N.U.T. 1931—47, Mem Teachers Registration Counc. *n.a*: Sec Schoolmaster Publg Co Ltd '31—47. *Ctr*: Schoolmaster & Woman Teacher's Chron, Scottish Educ Journ. *s.s*: Education. *Rec*: Fishing, walking, field botany. *a*: 24 Stockwood Crescent, Luton. Bedfordshire.

MANDER, Lady, M.A. (R. Glynn Grylls). *b*: 1905. *e*: Queen's Coll Lond, Lady Margaret Hall Oxf. *m*: Geoffrey Le Mander. *s*: 1. *d*: 1. *Publ*: Mary Shelley; Claire Clairmont. *a*: 604 St Ermins, London, S.W.1.

MANDER, Miles. *b*: 1891. *e*: Harrow & Loretto. *m*: Kathleen Bernadette French. *s*: 1. Author, Actor & Film Dir. *Publ*: Oasis; Gentleman by Birth: To My Son in Confidence; (Plays) Its a pity about Humanity; Santa Maria; etc. *a*: Bath, Nash's, Fabian Soc. *a*: 108 Park St, W.1. *t*: May 1678.

MANDEVILLE, Ernest Wyckoff. B.Sc. *b*: N.Y. 1896. *e*: Union Col Schenectady, Columbia Univ. *m*: Ruth Elizabeth Turner. *s*: 3. Publicist, Ed & Clergyman. *n.a*: Ed Chesterfieldian 1919—20, News Ed Churchman, '23—, Ed Writer Outlook, Christian Century. *Publ*: The Story of Middletown ('27). *c.t*: Forum, Outlook, Chr Advocate, etc. *s.s*: Econ & soc welf. Rector of oldest Episcopal Ch in New Jersey. *a*: 6 E. 45th St, N.Y. & Chr Ch Rectory, Middletown, N.J. *t*: Murray Hill 2—3900.

MANDINIAM, Dr. M. M. *Publ*: Phlebite Precace Dans la Fievre Typhoid (Geneva 1908). *a*: 32 Edith Rd, W.14. *t*: Park 2134.

MANEK, Karssandas. *b*: Karachi 1901. *e*: Univ of Bombay. *m*: Radhabai. *s*: 1. *d*: 1. Journalism, Writing Film Dialogues. *Pub*: Albel; Mahobatnemandve; Malini; Kalio ane Kusumo; Vaishampayani-vani; Aho Rayaji Sunie; Kalyana-yatri etc. *Ctr*: Janmabhoomi Group of papers. *Rec*: Reading of the Classics. *a*: "Janmabhoomi," Meadows St, Fort, Bombay. *T*: 22057.

MANGER, Itzik. *b*: Cernauti, Roumania 1901. Writer. *n.a*: Ed Lit Weekly, Measured Words, Krakow 1929—33, Co-Ed Lit Weekly Forward Warsaw '27—29. *Publ*: Stars on the Roof; Lantern in the Wind; Biblical Songs; Twilight in the Mirror; Book of Esther's Song; The Book of Paradise; Clouds Over the Roof; Hotsmach Play (A Goldfaden Dream). *Ctr*: Future, Lit Almanack, Jewish Fighter, etc. *Rec*: Reading. *c*: P.E.N. *a*: 15 Lyncroft Gdns, Hampstead, London, N.W.6, England. *T*: Primrose 2585.

MANGOLD, ERNST: professor of physiology; b. Berlin, Germany, Feb. 5, 1879; s. Dr. Wilhelm Mangold and Anna (Hoffman) M.; educ. Askanisches Gymnasium (Berlin), Univs. of Jena, Leipzig, and Giessen. DEGREES: M.D. (Jena), 1903; Ph.D. (Jena), 1905; Approb. Arzt (Jena), 1903; Professor (Freiburg), 1912; m. Susanne Peter, May 5, 1910. AUTHOR: Unsere Sinnesorgane und ihre Funktion, 1909 (2nd edit. 1919); Das Verhalten der Niederen Organssmen, 1910; Tierisches Licht in der Tiefsee, 1910; Hypnose und Katalepsie bei Tieren, 1914; Die Erregungsleitung im Wirbeltierherzen, 1914; Bewegung und Innervation des Wiederkauermagens, 1914; Våra sinnesorgan och deras funktioner, 1918; Tierphysiologisches Praktikum, 1928; Schlaf und Schlafähnliche Zustände bei Menschen und Tieren, 1929; (in Handbooks): Vergleichenden Physiologie; Normalen u. patholog. Physiologie; Hals-, Nasen-, Ohrenkrankheiten; Ernährung und des Stoffwechsels der landwirtschaftlichen Nutztiere (4 vols., edited), 1929. Editor: Archiv für Wissenschaftliche Landwirtschaft. Has contributed more than 200 articles on medicine, biology, etc., to mags. and the press. SOCIETIES: Deutsche Physiologische, Berliner Physiologische, Berliner Medizinische, Leopoldinisch-Carolinische Akademie der Naturforscher (Halle a.S.). Relig. denom., Evangelical. OFFICE: Direktor des Tierphysiologischen Instituts der Landwirtschaftlichen Hochschule, Invalidenstr. 42, Berlin N. 4. HOME: Flensburgerstr. 8, Berlin, Germany.

MANGOLD, FRITZ: professor in Univ. of Basel; b. Basel, Switzerland, March, 1871; s. R. Mangold and M. (Hoffner) M. DEGREE: Ph.D.; m. Gertrud Müller, 1902. AUTHOR: Die Basler Mittwoch und Samstag Zeitung, 1899; Johann Jakob Speiser, 1904; Die Bank in Basel, 1909; Die Industriegesellschaft für Schappe, 1924. Editor: Zeitschrift für Schweizerische Statistik und Volkswirtschaft. Contributor to Zeitschrift für Schweiz; Statistik und Volkswirtschaft. General character of writing: economic. Has made great number of scientific researches. CLUBS: International Statistic Institute. Religion, Protestant. OFFICE: Schweizerische Wirtschaftsarchiv. HOME: Mittlere Strasse 159, Basel, Switzerland.

MANHATTAN, Avro. *b*: Milan 1910. *e*: Studied Philosophy & Social Science, Author. *Publ*: The Catholic Church Against the Twentieth Century; Towards the New Italy; The Rumbling of the Apocalypse (In Italian); L'Homme a la Vitre (in French); The U.S.A. & the Vatican; Spain & the Vatican; The Vatican in Asia; Religion in Russia; etc. *s.s*: Religion. *Rec*: Painting, writing poetry, astronomy, walking, swimming. *a*: 12 Woodside Hse, Wimbledon, London, S.W.19. Wimbledon 4341.

MANHIRE, Wilson, L.R.A.M., A.R.C.M., F.T.C.L., L.G.S.M. *b*: Bugle, Cornwall 1887. *Publ*: Land of the Midnight Sun (Piano Suite); First Principles of Music; Elementary Music Manual; School Manual for Violin; Guide to Piano Scale-playing; etc. *s.s*: Educ music, text books, training manuals, sc music & classics. *a*: Molinnis, Bugle, Cornwall.

MANHOOD, Harold Alfred. *Publ*: Nightseed; Gay Agony; Apples by Night; Crack of Whips; Fierce & Gentle; Sunday Bugles; Lunatic Broth. *a*: Holmbush, nr Henfield, Sussex.

MANIGK, ALFRED: univ. professor; b. Angerburg, East Prussia, Germany, Sept. 10, 1873; s. Otto and Elise (Schulze) M.; educ. Friedrich Wilhelm-Gymnasium (Posen). DEGREES: Dr. Jur. Utr.; m. Frida Seidelmann, July 14, 1900. AUTHOR: Hat der nachstehende Pfandgläubiger das Recht des Verkaufs der Pfandsache? 1897; Das Verhältnis der Begriffe Rechtsgeschäft und Willenserklärung, 1900; Anwendungsgebiet der Vorschriften für die Rechtsgeschäfte, 1901; Pfandrechtliche Untersuchungen I. Zur Geschichte der römischen Hypothek, 1904; Rechtswirkungen und juristische Tatsachen, 1904; Fiducia, 1906; Willenserklärung und Willensgeschäft, ein System der juristischen Handlungen, 1907; Assyrisch-babylonische Rechtsurkunden, 1907; Gräko-ägyptisches Pfandrecht, 1909; Antichvetische Grundstückhaftung im Gräko-ägyptischen Recht, 1910; Gläubigerbefriedigung durch Nutzung, ein Institut der antiken Rechte, 1910; Hypotheca. Hyperocha, 1913; Savigny und der Modernismus, 1914; Irrtum und Auslegung, 1918; Das Wesen des Vertragsschlusses in der neueren Rechtsprechung, Beiträge zu den Begriffen des Consenses und Dissenses, 1925; Die Idee des Naturrechts, 1926; Wie stehen wir heute zum Naturrecht? 1926; Formalismus und Freirechtsschule, 1927; Unwirksamkeit und Ungültigkeit, 1929; Revisibilität der Auslegung von Willenserklärungen; mit Beiträgen zur Methodik der Rechts- und Tatfrage, 1929. General character of writing: scientific, Roman, Greek and German law, law philosophy. CLUB: Member of University Club. OFFICE: University. HOME: Renthof 8b, Marburg, a.L., Germany.

MANLEY, Francis Hardwicke. *b*: Jubblepoore 1852. *e*: Blundell's Sc Tiverton & Exeter Col Oxf. *m*: Catharine Ann Evans (dec). Rector Gt Somerford, Wilts '87–. Hon Canon of Bristol Cath 1916–. *c.t*: Wilts Archæ Mag. *s.s*: Local antiquarian hist. Temp Master at Winchester Col. Master at Felstead Sc. Vicar of Little Dunmow, Essex. *a*: Gt Somerford Rectory, Chippenham.

MANLEY, Rev. George Thomas, M.A.(Camb). *b*: Hull 1872. *e*: Wakefield Gr Sch & Christ's Coll Camb. *m*: Christabel Ashby. Retired. *Publ*: It is Written; Missionary Study Principle; Christian Unity; (Ed) Search the Scriptures & New Bible Handbook. *s.s*: Biblical Literature. *a*: 37 Ravensdale Ave, North Finchley, London, N.12. *T*: Hillside 1715.

MANN, A. H. *a*: Yorks Post, Leeds.

MANN, Charlton. *Publ*: Plays—(Jtly), The Blue Lagoon; Author of The Knave of Diamonds; The Moneymoon; Beau Geste. Theatrical Manager. For 16 years mang Adelphi Theatre; Also in partnership with Herbert Jay & Mrs T. C. Dugnall & others. *a*: 12 Park Road, Wallington, Surrey.

MANN, Edward. *b*: Alford, Lincs 1876. *e*: St Augustine's Norwich. *m*: Alice Millicent Miles. *s*: 1. *d*: 1. F.L. Journalist. *n.a*: Norfolk papers '91–1913, Ed St Pancras Chronicle '13–16, Ed City of London Observer '17–18, Press Assoc '18–31. Mem N.U.J. '21–. Sec E. Ham South Cons Assoc '32–33. *c.t*: All principal Lon papers. *s.s*: Agric. *Rec*: Politics, gardening. *c*: Stowmarket Constitutional. *a*: Pound Cottage, Wetherden, Stowmarket, Suffolk. *t*: Elmswell 64.

MANN, Francis Oscar, O.B.E. *b*: Lon 1885. *e*: U.C.L., Balliol Col Oxf. *m*: Marjorie Ellen Turner. *s*: 3. H.M. Div Insp of Scs. *Publ*: Works of Thomas Deloney; The Sisters (verse); Albert Grope; The Old Woman Talks; Three the Drive; Young George; etc. *s.s*: Educ. Apptd by Egyptian Govt to report on Egyptian System of Educ 1929. *c*: Savile, Bd of Educ S.W.1. *a*: 4 College Gdns, Dulwich Village, S.E.21.

MANN, FRITZ KARL: univ. professor; b. Berlin, Germany, Dec. 10, 1883; s. Louis and Anna (Behrens) M.; educ. Joachimsthalsches Gymnasium (Berlin); Univs. of Freiburg, Munich, Berlin, London, Paris, and of Göttingen. DEGREES: Dr. Jur., Ph.D.; m. Ingeborg Papendieck, June 3, 1899. AUTHOR: Der Marschall Vauban und die Volkswirtschaftslehre des Absolutismus. Eine Kritik des Markantilsystems, 1914; Kregswirtschaft in Rumänien, 1918 (transl. into Rumanian); Ostdeutsche Wirtschaftsforschung, 1926; Deutsche Finanzwirtschaft, 1929. Editor: Sozialwissenschaftliche Bausteins (Jena). General chararcter of writing: political economy. Jurist (Kammergerichtsreferendar) until 1907; changed to political economy; served in the war, 1914 to 1918; delegate to the peace negotiations at Bukarest, Roumania. CLUBS: Herdergesellschaft in Riga; Deutsche Soziologische Gesellschaft; Königsberger Gelehrte Gesellschaft. Relig. denom., Evangelical. ADDRESS: Bayentalgürtel 10, Cologne, Germany.

MANN, Gladys. *b*: Yorks. *m*: H. W. Shirley Long. *d*: 1. *n.a*: Amalgamated Press, '23—26. Dietetics & cookery expert & editorial publicist for Eat More Fish campaign, Saward Baker & Co Ltd, '30. *c.t*: Daily Express, Daily Mirror, Household Encyclopedia, Woman's Life, **Miss Modern**, Woman's Fair. *s.s*: Cookery & domestic science. *a*: 71 Fortune Green Rd, N.W.6. *t*: Hampstead 6149.

MANN, Harold Hart, D.Sc(Leeds), M.Sc (M/C), F.I.C. *b*: York 1872. *e*: Elmfield Sc York, Univ of Leeds & Pasteur Inst Paris. *m*: Katharine Collie. Asst Dir Woburn Experimental Station (Lawes Agric Trust). *Publ*: The Pests & Blights of the Tea Plant (with Sir G. Watt, 1903); Tea Soils of North East India; Tea Cultivation & Its Development in Tanganyika & Nyasaland ('33); etc. *s.s*: Tea Culture & Manfr in India, Africa & Russia; Indian Agric & Village Conditions. Chem Asst for Research to Roy Agric Soc 1895–1900. Scientific Officer to Indian Tea Assoc '00–07. Princ Agric Col, Poona & Agric Chemist to Govt of Bombay '07–18. Dir of Agric, Bombay Pres '18–20 & '21–27. Agric Adv to Nizam's Govt '28 & '30. Tech Adv to Russian Govt on Tea Developments '30–33. K.I.H. 1st Cl India. *c*: Calcutta & Bombay. *a*: Woburn Experimental Station, Aspley Guise, Bletchley. *t*: Ridgmont 30.

MANN, HEINRICH: author; b. Lübeck, Germany, March 27, 1871; s. Thomas Johann Heinrich und Julia (da Silva Bruhns) M.; educ. Gymnasium of Lübeck, Univ. of Berlin; m. Maria Kahn. AUTHOR: Berlin (novel), 1900; Im Schlaraffenland; Die Göttinnen; Die Jagd nach Liebe; Professor Unrat; Zwischen den Rassen; Die kleine Stadt; Der Untertan; Die Armen; The Patrioteer (novel), 1914; Der Kopf; Liliane und Paul; Mutter Marie (novel), 1926; Das Wunderbare; Flöten und Dolche; Stürmische Morgen; Das Herz; Die Rückkehr vom Hades; Variete; Die Schauspielerin; Die grosse Liebe; Madame Legros; Brabach; Der Weg zur Macht; Das gastliche Haus; Gustave Flaubert; Macht und Mensch. General character of writing: novels, essays, plays. ADDRESS: Leopoldstrasse 59, Munich, Bavaria, Germany.

MANN, Ida. M.A., D.Sc.(Lond), M.B., B.S., F.R.C.S. *b*: London 1893. *e*: Lond Univ. *Publ*: The Development of the Human Eye; Developmental Anomalies of the Human Eye; The Science of Seeing. *Ctr*: Journ of Anatomy, Brit Journ of Ophthalmology, Amer Journ of Ophthalmology, Lancet, Trans of Opth Soc, etc. *s.s*: Ophthalmology, Embryology, Comparative Anatomy. *Rec*: Travel. *a*: 87 Harley St, W.1. *T*: Welbeck 6233.

MANN, Miss J. De L., M.A. *Publ*: The Cotton Trade & Industrial Lancashire (with A. P. Wadsworth). *a*: St Hilda's Col, Oxf.

MANN, James Gow. *b*: Lon 1897. *e*: Winchester, New Col Oxf. *m*: Mary Cooke. *d*: 1. Reader in Hist of Art, Lon Univ. Asst Keeper Ashmolean Mus 1921–24; Snr Asst to Keeper Wallace Collection '24–32. Dep Dir Courtauld Inst of Art '32. *Publ*: The Armoury of the Castle of Churburg (with Count Trapp); Catalogue of the Sculpture, Bronzes, etc, in the Wallace Collection. *c.t*: Archæologia, Antiquaries Journ, Connoisseur, etc. *s.s*: Armour & Arms, Ch monuments. *Rec*: European travel. *c*: Athenæum, Burlington Fine Arts, F.S.A. *a*: 4 Upper George St, W.1., & Courtauld Inst of Art, W.1.

MANN, Jean, J.P., M.P. *b*: Glasgow 1889. *e*: Secondary. *m*: Wm Lawrence Mann. *s*: 3. *d*: 2. Ed Scots Town & County Councillor, Mem Town & Country Planning Assoc, Vice-Pres Scott Housing & Town Planning Counc. *Publ*: Re-planning Scotland; Guide to Rent Acts. *Ctr*: Town & Country Planning periodicals, Dly Herald, Forward, etc. *s.s*: Local Government, Housing & Town Planning, Domestic Politics. *Rec*: Caravanning, reading, chess. *a*: 9 Victoria Park Corner, Glasgow, W.4. *T*: Scotstoun 1190.

MANN, Sir John, K.B.E., J.P., M.A. *b*: Glas 1863. *e*: Glas Univ. *m*: Margaret Henderson. *s*: 2. *d*: 3. Chrtd Acct. *c.t*: Ency of Accounting, Roy Philos Soc of Glas, Times, etc. *s.s*: Acctncy, housing. Controller of Contracts, Min of Munitions '15–19. *c*: Reform, City of Lon. *a*: 8 Fredericks Pl, Old Jewry, E.C.2. *t*: Metro 5401.

MANN, KLAUS: author; b. Nov. 18, 1906; s. Thomas and Katja (Pringsheim) M.; educ. Wilhelmsgymnasium of Munich; unmarried. AUTHOR: Vor dem Leben, 1925; Anja und Esther, 1925; Der fromme Tanz, 1925; Kindernovelle, 1926; Revue zu Vieren, 1926; Heute und Morgen, 1927; Rundherum, 1929; Alexander, 1929; Abenteuer, 1929; Gegenüber von China, 1929. General character of writing: novels, essays. ADDRESS: Poschingerstrasse 1, Munich, Bavaria, Germany.

MANN, Leonard. LL.B. *b*: Melbourne, Australia 1895. *e*: State Schs, Wesley Coll & Univ of Melbourne. *m*: Florence Eileen Mann. *s*: 1. *d*: 1. Writer. *Publ*: The Go-Getter; Mountain Flat; A Murder in Sydney; Flesh in Armour; Human Drift; (Verse) The Delectable Mountains; Poems from the Mask; The Plumed Voice. *Ctr*: Meanjin Papers, Poetry (Australia). *w.s*: 1st A.I.F. France 1914—18, Commonwealth Dept Aircraft Production Ind & Staff Mgr '40—47. *a*: 27 Ferncroft Ave, East Malvern, Melbourne, S.E.5., Australia. *T*: UL 410A.

MANN, Ludovic MacLellan, F.S.A.(Scot). *e*: Scotland & Continent. Organised Prehistoric Relics Exhb Glasgow 1911 & Italian Old Stone Age Relics Lond '34. *Publ*: The Barochan Cross; Archaic Sculpturings; Queen Mary of Scots; A Lost Civilization; Craftsmen's Measures in Prehistoric Times; Earliest Glasgow; Ancient Measures, Their Origin & Meaning; Appeal, The Druid Temple Glasgow; The Druid Temple Explained. *Ctr*: Special articles to various journs. *Rec*: Large collection Prehistoric, mediæval & neo-archaic relics. *c*: Roy Socs, Rotary, Conservative, Art, Glasgow. *a*: 113 Kingsway, London, W.C.2, & 183 West George St, Glasgow.

MANN, Thomas. *Publ*: inc Three Essays; Children & Fools; Sketch of My Life; Young Joseph; Joseph in Egypt; The Coming Victory of Democracy; etc. *a*: 1550 San Remo Drive, Pacific Palisades, California.

MANN, Tom. *b*: Coventry 1856. *e*: Elem Sc. Married. *s*: 3. *d*: 5. Engineer. *n.a*: Ed Socialist Melbourne, Aus 1907—09, Ed Militant Trade Unionist, Lon '33—. *Publ*: From Single Tax to Syndicalism ('13); Tom **Mann's** Memoirs ('23). *c.t*: Daily Worker, Lon, Gudok (Rlyman's paper, Moscow). *s.s*: Ind Unionism, communism. Pres Dockers Un Lon 1889—92. Mem Roy Comm on Labour '92—93. Gen Sec Amal Eng's '19—21. *a*: Homelands, Sunningvale Av, Biggin Hill, Kent.

MANN, William Thomson, M.A., M.J.I. *b*: Lumsden 1909. *e*: Aberdeen G.S. & Univ. Asst Ed Shaw Standard Reference Series '33—. *c.t*: Sunday Express, etc. *s.s*: Golf. *Rec*: Golf. *a*: 9 Balcombe St, N,W.1. *t*: Paddington 9145.

MANNHARDT, WOLF: Judge of the Court of Appeal; b. Hamburg, Germany, Jan. 22, 1864; s. Dr. Julius Mannhardt and Mathilde (Vollmer) M.; educ. Florence Swiss school, Hanerau boarding school, Eutin public school; Univs. of Freiburg, Leipzig, Munich and Berlin. DEGREE: LL.D.; m. Hedwig Klöpper, Sept. 30, 1899. AUTHOR: Zur Frage einer amtlichen Vertretung des Kleinhandelsstandes (The Question of an Official Representation of the Retail Trade), 1899; Aus dem englischen und schottischen Rechtsleben (Sketches of the English and Scottish Law-Life), 1907; Summarisches Strafverfahren in England und Schottland (Summary Procedure in England and Criminal Procedure in Scotland), 1908; Auswahlausgabe aus Alfred Lichtwarks Schriften (a selection of Alfred Lichtwarks' Works), 1917. Contributor to: Grenzboten; Lotse; Jurist; Wochenschrift; Deutsche Juristenzeitung; Das Recht; Hamburger Nachrichten, and others. General character of writing: scientific, jurisprudence, political economy, essays. CLUBS: Member Nationalklub of 1919. Religion, Lutheran. HOME: Blumenstrasse 17, Hamburg, Germany.

MANNHEIM, Hermann. b: Libau 1889. e: Univs Munich, Freiburg, Strasbourg & Koenigsberg. m: Mona Mark. Reader in Criminology Univ Lond (Sch Econ), Mem Execut Comm Howard League for Penal Reform, Mem Counc Instit Scientific Treatment of Delinquency. Publ: Criminal Justice & Social Reconstruction; Social Aspects of Crime in England Between the Wars; The Dilemma of Penal Reform; Young Offenders (with A. M. Carr-Saunders & E. C. Rhodes); War & Crime; Juvenile Delinquency in an English Middle-town; Pressrecht; Revision im Strafverfahren. Ctr: Modern Law Rev, Times, Howard Journ, Fortnightly, World's Children, etc. s.s: Criminology & Criminal Law. Rec: Music & gardening. a: London School of Economics, Houghton St, Aldwych, London, W.C.2, & 20 Goddington Lne, Orpington, Kent. T: Orpington 1463.

MANNHEIMER, ERNST: writer; b. Waidhofen, Austria, Sept. 20, 1893; s. Theodor and Caroline (Färber) M.; educ. High School, College and Univ. of Vienna. DEGREES: Ph.D.; unmarried. AUTHOR: Die Nächte um Gina, 1923; Eros, 1926. Contributor to: Zeitschrift für Parapsychologie; Reclames Universum; Das Orchester; Zeitschrift für Geisteskultur. General character of writing: poems, essays. Religion, Mosaic. ADDRESS: Josefstädterstrasse 33, Vienna VIII., Austria.

MANNIN, Ethel Edith. b: London 1900. e: Bd Sch & Comm Training Coll. m: (1) John Alexander Porteous. d: 1. (2) Reginald Reynolds. Novelist, Writer of Travel & Educ Books Publ: Confessions & Impressions; Privileged Spectator; The Dark Forest Late Have I Loved Thee; The Blossoming Bough; No More Mimosa; Proud Heaven; Bread & Roses (A Survey of a Blueprint for Utopia); Lucifer & the Child; Rose & Sylvie; Comrade O Comrade; etc. s.s: Child Psychology, Educ. Rec: Gardening, walking. a: c/o Jarrolds Ltd, 55 Pont St, London, S.W.7.

MANNIN, Phyllis Caroline. b: London 1908. e: Holy Cross Convent, Wimbledon & Switzerland. m: J. Wallace Walker. d: 1. Editor & Journalist. n.a: Ed Asst & Sec The Outline 1927, Asst Sub Ed Modern Home '28, Home Notes' 29, Sub Ed Modern Home '30, Ed Miss Modern '32—35. Publ: Several Romantic Novels. Ctr: Women's & Fiction mags, daily newsps. s.s: Romantic Fiction. Rec: Music. a: Kerin, Clandon Close, Stoneleigh, Epsom, Surrey. T: Ewell 5580.

MANNING, B. L. Fell Jesus Col Cam. Publ: The People's Faith in the Time of Wyclif; The Making of Modern English Religion. c.t: Cam Mediæval Hist. a: Jesus Col, Cam.

MANNING, L. V. b: Bristol 1887. e: St Marks, Bristol. n.a: Sports Ed Daily Sketch & Sunday Graphic 1919-. a: 25 Cranbourne Gdns, Temple Fortune, N.11. t: Speedwell 7595.

MANNING FOSTER, Alfred Edge, F.R.S.L. b: Lon. e: U.C.S. & U.C.L. m: Olga Bijou Dina Curtis. s: 1. Author & Journalist. n.a: Ed & Proprietor Bridge Mag, formerly Ed & Proprietor "The County Gentleman" & "Land & Water", Bridge Corr The Times, Observer & Field. Publ: Auction Bridge for All; Contract Bridge for All; English Contract Bridge; Auction Bridge Dialogues; London Restaurants; Dining & Wining; Through the Wine List; etc. s.s: Bridge, food & wine. c: Portland, Conservative, Royal Thames Yacht, Savage, Soc of Authors, I.J., Freeman of City of Lon, N/ps Proprietors & Stationers Coy. a: 1 Washington Hse, Basil St, S.W.3. t: Kensington 8670.

MANNING-SANDERS, George. b: Liskeard 1894. e: Priv. m: Ruth Manning. s: 1. d: 1. Publ: Drum & Monkey! The Burnt Man, Little Comfort. c.t: M/C Guardian, Eng Review, John O' Lon, News Chron, Everyman, Daily Herald, etc. s.s: Folk tales. a: Esthers Field, Sennen, Cornwall.

MANNING-SANDERS, Ruth Vernon. b: Swansea 1895. e: Channing Hse Sc Highgate & Owen's Col M/C. m: George Manning-Sanders. s: 1. d: 1. Author. Publ: Prose—Twelve Saints; Waste Corner; The Crochet Woman; She Was Sophia; Run Away; etc; Verse—The Pedlar, Martha Wish-You-Ill; The City; etc. c.t: London Mercury, Time & Tide, Good Housekeeping, Nation & Athenæum, Sphere, Poetry, American Bookman, etc. a: Esther's Field, Sennen, Cornwall.

MANNION, John Patrick. Jnlst. General Publicity Agent. n.a: Ed Irish News Echo, Special Correspondent Thinkers Jnl. c.t: Irish Press Local & Provincial Papers. a: 15 Cambridge St, Wigan.

MANNIX, James William. b: Macclesfield 1874. e: Sec Sc. Journalist. n.a: Chief Sub Ed Irish Weekly & Sunday Independents 1922—. a: 44 Windsor Av, Fairview, Dublin. t: 21306.

MANNOCK, Patrick Lucius. b: London. e: Latymer Foundation Sch Hammersmith. m: Laura Whetter. d: 2. Dramatic & Film Critic Dly Herald, Pres Critics Circle 1943—44. n.a: Odhams Press 1922, Ed Picturegoer '27—30. Ctr: Dly Mail, Referee, John Bull, Everywoman, Passing Show, etc. s.s: Films, Drama. Rec: Music. c: Savage, Green Room. a: 88 Teignmouth Rd, London, N.W.2. T: Gladstone 9327.

MANNOURY, GERRIT: ordinary professor of mathematics in University of Amsterdam; b. Wormerveer, Holland, May 17, 1867; s. Gerrit and Anna (van Beek) M.; educ. "Hoogere Burgerschool met vijfjarige cursus" (Middle school) at Amsterdam; Autodidact; m. Elisabeth Maria Berkelbach van der Sprenkel, Aug. 8, 1907. AUTHOR: Methodologisches und Philosophisches zur Elementarmathematik, 1909; Wiskunst, Filosofie u Socialisme, 1924; Mathesis u Mystick (an essay on significance of Communist standpoint), 1924. General character of writing: Communist philosophy. HOME: Corantijnstraat 7, Amsterdam, Holland.

MANOCK, Thomas. b: Heywood 1887. m: Ethel Mary Todd. d: 1. Editor & Mang Dir Rugby Advertiser. n.a: Heywood News (Weekly), Rochdale Times (Biweekly), Halifax Guardian, Leicester Ev Mail. Rec: Golf. a: 118 Dunchurch Rd, Rugby. T: 2700.

MANSBRIDGE, Albert, C.H., Hon.M.A., Hon.LL.D., F.L.A. b: Gloucester 1876. e: Elem Sch, Sir Walter St John's Middle Sch, Battersea Gr Sch. m: Frances Jane Pringle. s: 1. Building Soc Pres, Founded W.E.A.

Publ: The Older Universities of England ; An Adventure in Working Class Education ; University Tutorial Classes ; The Trodden Road ; Talbot & Gore ; Margaret McMillan ; The Kingdom of the Mind. *Ctr* : Various. *s.s* : Education, Religion. *Rec* : Walking. *a* : Windways, 296 Dartmouth Rd, Paignton, S. Devon. *T* : Churston 81265.

MANSEL, COURTENAY: barrister-at-law; *b*. Maesycrugian, Eng., Feb. 25, 1880; *s*. Richard Mansel and Maude Margaretha (Jones) M.; *educ*. Harrow School; *m*. Mary Phillipa Agnes **Germaine Littlewood**, Oct., 1906. AUTHOR (poems): Masque of King Charles VI, 1913; South Wind, 1923. Member of Parliament, Pennryn and Falmouth Div. of Cornwall, 1923-24; Justice of Peace of Cormathen and Cardigan on Council of English Arborcultural Soc. CLUB: Athenaeum (London). Relig. denom., Church of England. HOME: Maesycruquian Manor, Maesycruquian, Carmarthenshire, Eng.

MANSEL-PLEYDELL, Rev. John Colvile Morton, M.A. *b* : Kimmeridge, Dorset, 1851. *e*: Eton & Trin Col Cam. Prebendary of Salisbury. *m* : Beatrice Maud Smith. *s* : 4 (3 dec). *d* : 2. *Publ* : Ed Rabin Hill's Poems in the Dorset Dialect. *c.t* : Wright's Dialectic Dictionary. *s.s* : Antiquarian. Formerly Hon Treas Dorset Field Club. *c* : Athenæum. *a* : 19 Moore St, S.W.3. *t* : Kensington 3343.

MANSELL, Harry Edward. *b* : Hastings 1901. *e*: Malvern Col, Pembroke Col Oxf. *n.a*: Ed St George's Hospital Gazette '27 & '28. *c.t*: Lancet, Brompton Hosp Reports, St George's Hosp Gazette. *s.s*: Cardiology, T.B. *Rec*: Music, travel, squash. *c*: Overseas, Osler (Co-founder). *a*: Lambeth Hosp, Brook St, S.E.11. *t*: Reliance 2211.

MANSELL-MOULLIN, Charles William, C.B.E., D.M.(Oxon), F.R.C.S. *b*: Guernsey 1851. *e*: Private, Pembroke Col Oxf (Fellow). *m*: Edith Ruth Thomas. *s*: 1. Consulting Surgeon. *n.a*: Redcliffe Travelling Fell Oxf 1878, Vice-Pres R.C.S. 1912-13, Pres Rontgen Soc 1889, Hunterian Prof R.C.S., Examiner in Surgery, Univs Oxf, Cam & Glas. *Publ*: Enlargement of Prostate, 2nd Edit; When to Operate in Inflammation of Appendix, 2nd Edit; Biology of Tumours (Bradshaw Lecture R.C.S.); etc. *c.t*: Lancet, B.M.J.; scientific societies. *s.s*: Surgery. *Rec*: Shooting, fishing, archæology. *a*: 28 Victoria Rd, Kensington, W.8. *t*: Reliance 1118.

MANSERGH, Nicholas, O.B.E., M.A., B.Litt., D.Phil. *b* : Tipperary 1910. *e*: Coll of St Columba Co Dublin, Pembroke Coll Oxf. *m* : Diana Mary Keeton. *s* : 2. *d* : 1. Abe Bailey Prof of Brit Commonwealth Relations, Roy Inst of Internat Affairs. *Publ* : Britain & Ireland ; The Irish Free State, Its Government & Politics ; The Government of Northern Ireland ; Ireland in the Age of Reform & Revolution ; Jt Ed Advisory Bodies a Study of their Uses in Relation to the Central Government. *Ctr* : Politica, Round Table, Internat Affairs. *s.s* : Commonwealth Affairs, Politics & Mod Hist. *Rec* : Tennis, gardening. *c* : Un Univ & Univ (Dublin). *a* : Little Paddock, Oxted, Surrey. *T* : Oxted 927.

MANSFIELD, Frederick John. *b*: Folkestone 1872. *e*: Priv. *m*: Julia Venables. *s*: 3. *d*: 1. Journalist. *n.a*: Chatham News 1886—91, African Review '91—93, Western Morning News '93—1903, Standard '09—14, Times '14—34. Lect & Exam in Practical Journalism, Lon Univ '25—34. Pres N.U.J. '18—19; now a Trustee. *Publ*: Sub-Editing. *s.s*: Hist & technique of journalism, reviewing. L.P. in Wes Ch '98—. Sec Times Pension Fund '21—33. *a*: Kynance, Noak Hill Rd, Romford, Essex. *t*: Ingrebourne 120.

MANSFIELD, Dr. O. A., MusDoc(Toronto), F.R.C.O., F.A.G.O., L.Mus, L.C.M., L.MusT.C.L., etc. *Publ*: The Student's Harmony (17th edn); Rudiments of Music. *a*: Sirsa Hse, Cheltenham, Glos.

MANSFIELD, Purcell James, HonR.C.M., F.R.C.O., A.R.C.M., L.MusT.C.L. Musical Composer. *Publ*: Opera—The Duke's Dilemma; Choral Arrangements of Scot Airs & Negro Spirituals. *a*: 84 Mosspark Oval, Glasgow.

MANSI, Ronald Lewis, M.R.C.S., L.R.C.P. *b* : London 1908. *e* : Salesian Coll Lond, St Barts Hosp Med Sch Lond. *m* : Violet Elizabeth Ferry. *s* : 1. *d* : 1. Radiologist to the Miller Gen Hosp, Prince of Wales Gen Hosp, Woolwich Memorial Hosp Lond. *Ctr* : Electronic Engineering, Brit Journ of Radiology, B.M.J. *s.s* : Med Radiology, Electronic Engineering. *Rec* : Model Engineering, motoring, music. *w.s* : Major R.A.M.C. 1941—46. *a* : 41 Pinewood Drive, Orpington, Kent. *T* : Farnborough (Kent) 3120.

MANSON, JAMES BOLIVAR: author, artist; *b*. London, Eng., June, 1879; *s*. James Alexander and Margaret Emily (Deering) M.; *educ*. Alleyn's School (Dulwich), Heatherly Sch. of Art, Lambeth Sch. of Art, Academie Julian (Paris) under Jean-Paul Laurens; *m*. Lilian Laugher, Aug., 1904. AUTHOR: Rembrandt, 1924; Hours in the Tate Gallery, 1924; Introduction to Works of J. S. Sargent, 1927; Degas, 1927. Translated: Cezanne (by Tristan), 1924; Bibliography of Works for Life of John S. Sargent (by Hon. Evan Charteris), 1927; The Tate Gallery, 1930; English Oil-Colour Painters, 1930. Contributed article: Modern Painting, to Encyclopedia Britannica (14th edit.). Contributes to The Studio, Apollo, Illustration, Saturday Review, Burlington Mag. General character of writing: critical essays. Art Critic, successively, of the Outlook, Daily Herald; One-man exhibitions at Leicester Galleries (London), and Galerie Balzac (Paris). Has pictures in permanent collections of Aberdeen, Manchester, Birmingham, Brussels National Gallery, Millbank (London). Assistant Keeper of Tate Gallery since 1912; Director since 1930. CLUBS: Burlington Fine Arts, Chelsea, New English Art, Eccentric. Religion, Swedenborgian. OFFICE: National Gallery, Millbank. HOME: 98 Hampstead Way, London, Eng.

MANSON, Thomas Walter, M.A., D.D., D.Litt., F.B.A. *b* : Tynemouth 1893. *e* : Tynemouth High Sch, Glas Univ, Christ's Coll, Westminster Coll Camb. *m* : Nora Wallace. Rylands Prof Biblical Criticism & Exegesis in Univ Manch, Grinfield Lecturer Oxf 1943—45. *Publ*: The Teaching of Jesus ; The Mission & Message of Jesus ; (with H. D. A. Major & C. J. Wright); God & the Nations ; (Ed) A Companion to the Bible. *Ctr* : Jour of Theo Studies, Classical Rev, etc. *s.s* : New Testament, Later Judaism, Early Church Hist. *Rec* : Music, painting, fishing. *w.s* : Operations Off N.W. Reg & Capt 61st Bn Lancs H.G. *a* : 1 Woodneys, Mersey Rd, Heaton Mersey, Stockport. *T* : Heaton Moor 3847.

MANSON, Rev. William, Hon.D.D. *b* : Cambuslang 1882. *e* : Univs of Glas & Oxf. *m* : Mary D. Ferguson. Prof of Biblical Criticism in the Univ of Edin. *Publ* : Jesus & Messiah ; The Gospel According to St Luke; The Incarnate Glory ; Christ's View of the Kingdom of God. *s.s* : New Testament Theology, Worship, Ecumenical Relations. *a* : 37 Gilmour Rd, Edinburgh 9.

MANSON-BAHR, Sir Philip Henry, C.M.G., D.S.O. *b* : Liverpool 1881. *e* : Rugby Sch, Trin Coll Camb, Lond Hosp, Lond Sch Tropical Medicine. *m* : Edith Margaret Manson. *s* : 1. *d* : 3. Ed Manson's Tropical Diseases, Late Lecturer Lond Sch Hygiene & Tropical Medicine, Dir Clinical Div, Cons Physician Hosp for Tropical Diseases & Albert Dock London. *Publ* : Mansons Tropical Diseases ; Dysenteric Disorders ; Synopsis of Tropical Medicine ; Life & Work of Sir Patrick Manson. *Ctr* : Tropical Disease Bulletin, Lancet, Practitioner, Encyl Brit, etc. *s.s* : Tropical Medicine, Ornithology. *Rec* : Bird watching, painting, riding. *c* : Devonshire. *a* : 149 Harley St, London, W.1. *T* : Welbeck 4444.

MANSOORUDDIN, M., M.A. *b* : Eastern Bengal 1904. *e* : Calcutta Univ. *m* : Sharifa Khatoon. *s* : 3. *d* : 4. Prof of Bengali, Govt Coll Dacca Univ Eastern Pakistan,

India. *Publ*: Haramani; Shirni; Dhaner Manjari; Aurangajel; Kavya Samput; Poyla July; etc. *Ctr*: Probash, Kallol, Mahammadi, Saogat, Azad, etc. *s.s*: Folklore of Bengal, Islamic Culture & Hist. *Rec*: Gardening. *a*: P.O. Khaljilpur, Dist Pabna, Eastern Pakistan, India.

MANTEUFFEL-ZOEGE-KATDANGEN, B A R O N CARL von: author; *b*. Gaiken, in Kurland, Germany, July 20, 1872; *s*. Baron Carl von and Baroness Alice (von Foelkersam) M.-Z.-K.; *educ*. Gymnasium, Univs. of Bonn and Halle. DEGREES: Ph.D. and Kreismarschall (retired); unmarried. A U T H O R: Socialaristocratische Ideen, 1896; Deutschland und der Osten, 1926. Different poems published in different newspapers and magazines. Contributor to Deutsche Zeitung, Mitausche Zeitung, and others. General character of writing: political and social, political essays. Participated in Russian-Japanese war; was elected prefect of the district of Kurland in 1905; founder and chairman of the German Verein in Kurland. At the outbreak of the World War was exiled to Wjatka by the Russian government, but escaped in 1917 to Germany. As member of the Kurland Landtag was sent to offer the Dukal crown of Kurland to Wilhelm I. in 1918; joined the army. Religion, Protestant. ADDRESS: Potsdamer Privatstrasse 121 H, Berlin W. 35, Germany.

MANTRIPP, Rev. J. C. *n.a*: Ed Primitive Methodist Church 1926–31. *Publ*: The Faith of a Christian. *c.t*: Hibbert Journ, Holborn Review, Cong Quarterly, Meth Recorder, etc. *a*: 6 Clarendon Terr, St Ives, Hunts.

MANUEL, Herschel Thurman, A.M., Ph.D. *b*: Indiana 1887. *e*: Univs of De Pauw, Chicago, Illinois. *m*: Dorothy Broad Beaird. *s*: 1. *d*: 2. Prof of Educ Psychology, Univs of Texas. *n.a*: Ed Research Bulletins of Texas, Commission on Co-ordination in Educ 1936—. *Publ*: Education of Mexican & Spanish-Speaking Children in Texas. *Ctr*: Various. *s.s*: Educ measurement & psychology. *a*: 1202 West 22½ St, Austin 21, Texas, U.S.A. *T*: 2-3784.

MANUEL-LELIS, Jean. *b*: Paris 1897. Secretaire de la Cinematheque et de la Bibliotheque de Commissariat General au Tourisme. *n.a*: L'Humanite, Regards, Vendredi, Russie d'Aujourd'hui, Europe, Commune. *Ctr*: La Marseillaise, Le Monde Illustre. *s.s*: Critiques Theatricales & Litteraires, Recits de Voyages. *c*: P.E.N. *a*: 32 rue Mederic, Paris 17e. *T*: Carnot 43-31.

MANVELL, Arnold Roger, D.Ph. *b*: Leicester 1909. *e*: Lond Univ. *m*: Margaret Manvell. Sec-Gen British Film Acad, Executive Ed Penguin Film Review, Research Worker for the Cinema, Editor, Journalist, Lecturer & Broadcaster & Televisor. *Publ*: Film; Twenty Years of British Film; Experiment on the Film; History of the British Film, Vol I ; (last three co-author) ; Ed of series on the International Cinema. *Ctr*: Tribune, Sight & Sound, Times Educ Supp, Hollywood Quart, etc. *s.s*: Films, Literature & Drama. *Rec*: Travel & talking. *c*: Brit Film Inst. *a*: 54 Lancaster Gate, London, W.2. *T*: Ambassador 1369.

MANWARING, Rev. Alfred. *b*: 1855. Missionary in India 1879—1910, Rector of Leire, Leics 1910—21. *Publ*: Marathi Proverbs. *Ctr*: Times of India. *a*: 81a Beaufort Rd, St Leonard's-on-Sea, Sussex. *T*: Hastings 2263.

MANWARING, George Ernest, F.R.HistS. *b*: Lon 1882. *m*: Lilian Gilbert. *s*: 3. Asst-Librarian Lon Library, St James's Sq, S.W.1. *n.a*: Asst-Ed Mariner's Mirror 1922—25, Gen Ed Seafarer's Library '28—29. *Publ*: Life & Works of Sir Henry Mainwaring; Bibliography of British Naval History; My Friend the Admiral ('31); The Floating Republic (with Bonamy Dobrée '35); etc. *s.s*: Naval Hist, Eng lit. *a*: 38 Sarsfeld Rd, S.W.12.

MAQUARIE, Arthur, B.A. *b*: Dubbo, N.S.W. 1874. *e*: Sydney Univ. *m*: Mary Campbell Lintner. Formerly Hon Foreign Sec & Mem Counc Roy Soc of Lit, Hon Org Sec of Brit Cmt for Promoting an Intellectual Entente 1914—19. *Publ*: The Dance of Olives; The Voice in the Cliff; The Wheel of Life; The Happy Kingdom; A Rhapsody for Lovers; The Meaning of Love; Fioralisa; The Days of the Magnificent; etc. *s.s*: Art & Archt. *a*: Hurst Hse, Molesey, Surrey. *T*: 508.

MARCEL, Gabriel Honore. Chev de la Legion d'Honneur. *b*: Paris 1887. *e*: Paris, Lycee Carnot, Sorbonne. *m*: Jacqueline Boegner. *s*: 1. Critique dramatique, Dir de Collection. *Publ*: Journal Metaphysique; Etre et Avoir; Du Refus a l'Invocation; Homo Viator; (Theatre) Un Homme de Dieu; Le Monde Casse; Le Chemin de Crete; Le Dard; La Soif; etc. *Ctr*: Nouvelle Litt, Revue Theatrale, Times Litt Sup, Theatre Arts (New York), etc. *s.s*: Philosophy, Theatre, Lit Criticism. *a*: 21 rue de Tournon, Paris 6. *T*: Danton 29-28.

MARCH, (Miss) Norah Helena, B.Sc, F.R.SanI. *b*: Sunderland. *e*: Durham Univ. Ed Mother & Child, Sec Health & Cleanliness Counc, Sec Nat Baby Week Counc. *n.a*: Home Page Adv to Evening Standard '32–. *Publ*: Towards Racial Health; Sex Knowledge. *c.t*: Evening Standard, Allied N/ps Ltd, etc. *s.s*: Eugenics & educ for parenthood. *c*: Forum. *a*: 5 Tavistock Sq, W.C.1. *t*: Euston 1820.

MARCH, Wilfrid Laws. *b*: Norton-on-Tees 1912. *e*: St Mary's Col Middlesbro'. Journalist. *n.a*: Pocklington Weekly News, Darlington & Stockton Times, Yorkshire Gazette, Northern Echo. *Rec*: Music, reading. *a*: c/o South Holme, Coatham Rd, Redcar, Yorks. *t*: 408.

MARCHANT, Bessie. *b*: Petham, Kent. *e*: Priv. *m*: Rev J. A. Comfort. *d*: 1. Author. *Publ*: More than 150 books for young people. *a*: Gothic Hse, Charlbury, Oxon.

MARCHANT, Edgar Cardew. Sub-rector of Lincoln Col Oxf. *Publ*: Xenophon, Opera Omnia (5 vols); Xenophon, Scripta Minora (2 vols); etc. *c.t*: Classical Review. *a*: Rosedale, Iffley, Oxf. *t*: Cowley 7020.

MARCHANT, Edgar Walford. *b*: Sevenoaks 1876. *e*: Private, Univ Sch, Hastings Central Tech Coll. *m*: Mary Ethel Brooker. *s*: 4. Ret Prof of Elect Engineering Univ of L'pool, Pres of Inst Elect Engnrs 1933—34, Pres of L'pool Engineering Soc '15, Fellow of City & Guilds Coll. *Publ*: Introduction to Electrical Engineering; Radio Telegraphy; Modern Electric Practice; Dictionary of Applied Physics; Examples in Electrical Engineering; International Electrotechnical Vocabulary. *Ctr*: Electrician, Electrical Review, L'pool Dly Post, Nineteenth Century, Philosophical Mag, etc. *s.s*: Radio Telegraphy & Electrical Engineering. *Rec*: Golf, fishing, lawn tennis, motoring. *c*: University. *a*: Rostrevor, Harthill Rd, Liverpool 18. *T*: Allerton 2597.

MARCHESI, Blanche Elisabeth, Baroness Anzon Caccamisi. *b*: Paris 1863. *e*: Vienna, Frankfort, Paris. *m*: (1) Baron de Poohràgy, (2) Baron Anzon Caccamisi. *s*: 4. Lyric Opera Singer & Singing Tea. *Publ*: Singer's Pilgrimage; Singer's Catechism & Creed. *s.s*: Singers' careers. Has been declared by the greatest critics of Eng, Amer, etc, as the greatest living interpreter of song. Has sung at the greatest Orch Socs under Hans Richter, Thomas Beecham, Sir Henry Wood, Sir Alexander Mackenzie, Sir Frederic Cowen, etc. Queen Victoria's Diamond Jubilee Medal; Belgian Order of Elisabeth, etc. *a*: 8 Rue du Bois de Boulogne, 16th Paris. *t*: Passy 55.82.

MARCKS, ERICH: univ. professor; *b*. Magdeburg, Germany, Nov. 17, 1861; *s*. Albert and Therese (Coqui) M.; *educ*. Paedagogium des Klosters Unserer Lieben Frauen, Magdeburg; Univs. of Strassburg, Bonn, Berlin, Strassburg. D E-

GREES: Ph.D., Strassburg, 1883-1884; m. Friederike von Sellin, 1889. AUTHOR: Bundesgenossen Krieg 91-89 V. Chr., 1884; De alis, 1886; Zusammenkunft von Bayonne, das französische Staatsleben und Spanien, 1889; G. von Coligny I, 1892; H. Baumgarten, 1894; Kaiser Wilhelm I, 1897 (8th edit. 1918); Königin Elisabeth von England und ihre Zeit, 1897 (2nd edit. 1896); Zu Bismarcks Gedächtnis (with Schmoller and Lenz), 1899; Bismarcks Gedanken und Erinnerungen, 1899; Deutschland und England, 1900; Ludwig Häusser, 1903; Die Universität Heidelberg, 1903; Die imperialistische Idee, 1903; H. von Tritschke, 1906 Bismarck, (vol. I); Bismarcks Jugend, 1909 (17th edit. 1915); Einheitlichkeit der englischen Auslandspolitik, 1910; Männer und Zeiten, Aufsätze und Reden (2 vols.), 1911 (6th edit. 1922); Historische und akademische Eindrücke aus Nordamerika, 1913; Alfred Lichtwark, 1914; Wo stehen wir? 1914; Otto von Bismarck, ein Lebensbild, 1915 (23rd edit. 1924); Many single writings, 1914-1921 (printed later in "Männer und Zeiten"); England und Frankreich, 1923; Geschichte und Gegenwart, 1925; Auf- und Niedergang im deutschen Schicksal, 1927; Karl August von Weimar, 1928; Die Gegenreformation in Westeuropa 1555-1610, in der Propyläenweltgeschichte (vol. 5), 1929. Edited: Leipziger Studien, 1895-1902; Heidelberger Abhandlungen, 1902-1908; Forschungen zur Geschichte, 1929; Das Bismarckjahr, 1904-1915; Erinnerungen an Bismarck, 1915; Lebensfragen des Britischen Weltreichs, 1921; Meister der Politik, 1922 and 1923 (2nd and 3rd ed.); Carl August-Werk, I-IV, 1915-1923; Deutsche Geschichte (Sammelwerk) (vol. 2), 1927-1930. General character of writing: historical. Engaged in scientific work at Paris and London, 1885-1886; Professor in University of Berlin, 1887-1893; O. Professor at Freiburg i. B., 1893; Leipzig, 1894; Heidelberg, 1901; Hamburg (scientific history), 1907; Munich, 1913; Berlin, 1922; guest professor at Cornell, 1913; member of the Munich Historical Commission (president 1922); member of the Academy of Munich, Leipzig and Berlin. Religion, Protestant. ADDRESS: Kurlaender Allee 13, Berlin-Charlottenburg 9, Germany.

MARCONI, Marchese, G.C.V.O., LL.D., D.Sc. *Publ*: Various lectures & political speeches. *c.t*: Various n/ps. Nobel Prize for Physics. *a*: 11 Via Condotti, Rome, Italy.

MARCOSSON, Isaac Frederick. *b*: Louisville, Kentucky 1876. *e*: Public Schs. *m*: Ellen Pitts. Author & Journalist. *n.a*: City Ed Louisville Times, Assoc Ed The Worlds Work, Chief Foreign Corr Sat Ev Post. *Publ*: Adventures in Interviewing; Turbulent Years; The Black Golconda; Caravans of Commerce; The Business of War. *s.s*: Personalities, World Econs, Polit Conditions. *Rec*: Golf, walking. *a*: 7 Gracie Sq, New York 28, N.Y., U.S.A.

MARCUS, Michael, B.L. *b*: 1896. *e*: George Heriot's Sc & Edin Univ. *m*: Bessie Morris. Formerly Solicitor in Edin. *Publ*: Legal Aspects of Trade Unionism. *c.t*: Star, Scotsman, Edin Even News, etc. *s.s*: Politics, literature, law. M.P. (Labour, Dundee 1929-31), Mem Edin Town Council 1926-9. *Rec*: Tennis. *a*: 14 Gloucester Gdns, Golders Green, N.W.11. *t*: Speedwell 3731.

MARENGO, Kimon Evan, B.A. (See KEM). *b*: Egypt 1906. *e*: Ecole des Sciences Politiques Paris, Exeter Coll Oxf. Political Cartoonist & Journalist. *n.a*: Ed & Illus Maalesh, Alexandria, 1924—30, Ed Anglo-Egyptian Review Lond '34—36. *Ctr*: Carrefour (Paris), N.Y. Times, John Bull, Dly Herald, Dly Telegraph, Bystander, etc. *s.s*: Political Cartoons, Hist 1760—1832. *Rec*: Swimming, riding. *a*: 63 Hamilton Terr, St John's Wood, London, N.W.8. *T*: Cunningham 8435.

MARETT, Robert Ranulph, M.A., D.Sc(Oxon), Hon LLD.(St And), F.B.A. *b*: Jersey 1866. *e*: Victoria Col Jersey & Balliol Oxf. *m*: Nora Kirk. *s*: 2. *d*: 2. Rector of Exeter Col Oxf. *Publ*: The Threshold of Religion (1909); Faith, Hope & Charity in Primitive Religion ('32); Sacraments of Simple Folk ('33); etc. *c.t*: Ency Britannica, Hastings' Dictionary of Religion & Ethics. *s.s*: Social anthropology. *a*: Rector's Lodgings, Exeter Col, Oxf, & La Haule Manor, Jersey.

MARGARET ELIZABETH: see Countess of Jersey.

MARGERISON, Frances Ida, B.A.(Lon). *n.a*: Asst Ed Nursing Times. *a*: 47 Abbey Rd Mansions, St Johns Wood, N.W.8.

MARGETSON, A. *a*: 25 Claremont Drive, Headingly, Leeds.

MARGETSON, A, J, *a*: c/o Board of Education, Whitehall, S.W.1.

MARGETSON, Elisabeth Bertram. *b*: Waterford 1900. *e*: Ireland, England & Germany. Jnlst. *n.a*: 1925—35: New York American (N.Y.); Melbourne Herald (Australia); Youth; Daily Chron; Sunday Chron; Sunday Graphic; now with Sunday Express. *c.t*: Short stories to many English & Amer mags & N/ps. *s.s*: Descriptive writing & special interviews. Travelled all over the world. *Rec*: Swimming, motoring, racing driving. *a*: Malvern Hse, Nassau St, W.C.1. *t*: Museum 6379.

MARGISON, W. F/L Journalist. Taynuilt, Oxford Street, Rotherham.

MARGOLIOUTH, David Samuel, F.B.A. Laudian Prof of Arabic Oxf. *Publ*: Mohammed & the Rise of Islam; Mohammedanism; Eclipse of the Abbasid Caliphate. *c.t*: Journ of Roy Asiatic Soc, Eng Historical Review, Islamica (German), Islamic Culture; Ch of Eng N/p & Moslem World. *a*: Romney, Boar's Hill, Oxf. *t*: 166.

MARGOLIOUTH, Herschel Maurice, M.A. *b*: Greenwich 1887. *e*: Rugby & Oxf. *m*: Maude Lilian Ogden. Fellow of Oriel. *n.a*: Ed Oxford Mag. *Publ*: Marvell; Wells of English. *Ctr*: The Guardian, Rev of English Studies. *s.s*: Wordsworth, Marvell, Blake. *w.s*: World War I. *a*: 14 Bradmore Rd, Oxford.

MARGRIE, William. *b*: London. *e*: Elem. Founder & Pres Lond Explorers, Life Mem Soc of Authors. *Publ*: Diary of a London Explorer; A Camberwell Man; Rosemary Street; The Invincible Smile; The Story of a Great Experiment; A Cockney's Pilgrimage; The Mighty Heart; The New Town Hall; Pickwicks of Peckham. *Ctr*: The New Age, local newsps. *s.s*: Modern London. *Rec*: Rambling. *c*: London Immortals. *a*: 24 Nigel Rd, Peckham Rye, London, S.E.15.

MARGULIES, Leo J. *b*: Brooklyn N.Y. 1900. Editor. *n.a*: Ed Dir Thrilling Love, Thrilling Adventures, Sky Fighters, The Phantom Detective, etc. *a*: 112 East Norwalk, Connecticut.

MARIE LOUISE, Princess. *Publ*: A Choice of Carols. *a*: c/o Methuen & Co Ltd, 36 Essex St, W.C.2.

MARILLIER, Henry Currie. *b*: Grahamstown, Sth Africa 1865. *e*: Christ's Hosp & Camb Tech. Adviser to Ministry of Works, Pall Mall Gazette 1890—1892. *Publ*: Dante Gabriel Rossetti—a memoir; Work of Aubrey Beardsley; History of Christie's; The Liverpool School of Painters; Handbook to the Teniers Tapestries; Handbook to 18th century English Tapestries;

University Magazines & their Makers. *s.s*: Tapestry-Weaving, The Morris Art Movement. *Rec*: Gardening. *a*: Westbrook House, Upperton, Petworth, Sussex. *T*: Petworth 2185.

MARIN, Bego. *b*: Split, Yugoslavia 1881. *e*: Univs, Zagreb & Vienna. *m*: Ljerka Tomie. *s*: 2. Lawyer. *Publ*: In Expectation; Eternal Illusion; Novels; Down our Coast; Eve; From the Sea. *c.t*: Novi List, Balkan Trieste, Narodni List, Novo Doba, Zivot, Savremenik. *s.s*: Fiction. Order Saint Sava III el Yugoslav Crown IV. *Rec*: Yachting. *c*: Local Cmt Yugoslav Action, Pres & Mem of B. of D. *a*: Sokolska ulica 4, Split, Yugoslavia.

MARISCHKA, Franz. *b*: Vienna 1918. *e*: Vienna Theresianum Acad, Max Rinehardt's Acad of Dramatic Art. Actor & Screenwriter. *Written* (in collab) Escape from Fear (from the novel " Happy Now I Go "); & several screen plays & adaptations. *w.s*: Army Intell Corps 6 yrs. *a*: Flat 117, 20 Abbey Rd, London, N.W.8.

MARITAIN, Jacques. *b*: Paris 1882. Prof at the Catholic Inst Paris. *Publ*: Art et Scolastique; Le Docteur Angélique; Religion et Culture; Du Régime Temporel et de la Liberté; Trois Reformateurs; Primanté du Spirituel; De la vie d'oraison, with Raissa Maritain; etc. (All trans into English). *c.t*: Études Carmélitaines, etc. *s.s*: Philosophy. *c*: Académie Romaine de Saint-Thomas. *a*: 10 rue du Parc, Meudon, Seine et Oise, France.

MARK-WARDLAW, William Penrose, D.S.O. *b*: Sutton, Surrey 1887. *e*: Foster's Sch Stubbington, H.M.S. Britannia Dartmouth. *m*: *d*: 2. Rear-Admiral (ret). *Publ*: At Sea with Nelson. *Ctr*: Several short articles. *Rec*: Fishing, riding. *c*: United Service, Roy Yacht Squad, Roy Singapore Yacht. *a*: Alyscroft, Crowthorne, Berks.

MARKHAM, Frederick. See Wheldon, J. D.

MARKHAM, Sydney Frank. B.Litt., M.A., Dip Econ. *b*: Stony Stratford. *e*: Wadham Coll Oxf. *m*: Frances Lawman. *s*: 1. *d*: 1. M.P. Rochester & Chatham 1929—31, Parl Priv Sec to Rt Hon James Ramsay MacDonald '31, M.P. Nottingham Sth '35—45, Pres Museums Assoc '39—42. *Publ*: History of Socialism; Life of King Edward VII; Surveys of Museums & Art Galleries of Canada, Australia, N.Z.; Climate & the Energy of Nations; etc. *Ctr*: Museums Journ, Times, Listener. *s.s*: Politics. *Rec*: Hockey, travel. *a*: 1 Calverton Rd, Stony Stratford. *T*: 3125.

MARKHAM, Violet Rosa, C.H., LL.D.(Edin), D.Litt. (Sheff), F.R.Hist.S., F.R.G.S., J.P. *b*: Chesterfield. *Publ*: South Africa, Past & Present; The New Era in South Africa; The South African Scene; A Woman's Watch on the Rhine; Romanesque France; Paxton & the Bachelor Duke. *s.s*: Social Questions. *c*: Ladies Empire. *a*: 8 Gower St, London, W.C.1. *T*: Museum 0799.

MARKHAM, Virgil, M.A. *b*: Oakland, California 1899. *e*: Columbia Coll & California Univ. Teacher & Writer, Chrm Dept of English, Wagner Coll Staten Is N.Y. since 1942. *Publ*: The Scamp; Death in the Dusk; The Devil Drives; Inspector Rusby's Finale; The Dead are Prowling; Snatch; Red Warning; The Deadly Jest. *a*: 92 Waters Avenue, Staten Island 2, New York.

MARKLAND, Russell, PhilB. *b*: Wilmslow 1892. *n.a*: Jt Ed Staffs Poets 1928. *Publ*: The Amethyst Scarab, & Other Poems; The Poetry of H. Rex Freston; Ultimate Light; Poems, etc. *c*: Roy Lytham & St Anne's Golf, Johnson Soc, Lancs Authors' Assoc. *a*: Ingersley, Links Gate, St Anne's-on-Sea. *t*: 40.

MARKS, A. D. *b*: Alfreton 1877. *e*: Bury St Edmunds G.S. *m*: Amy Basnett. *d*: 1. Publisher. Mang Dir to T. Fisher Unwin Ltd till 1926. Mang Dir Ernest Benn Ltd '26—29. Mang Dir Philip Allan & Coy Ltd '30—. *c*: Nat Lib, & The Paternosters. *a*: 35 Kenilworth Av, Wimbledon, S.W.19. *t*: Wimbledon 2840.

MARKS, Lord George Croydon, 1st Baron of Woolwich, C.B.E., J.P., K.B., M.I.MechE., A.M.I.C.E. *b*: Eltham 1858. *e*: Roy Arsenal Sc Woolwich & King's Coll Lon. *m*: Margaret Maynard. Cons Eng. *n.a*: Ed Practical Engineer & Engineers Gazette 1895-1905. *Publ*: Hydraulic Machinery; British & Foreign Patent Laws; Industries & Inventions; Working of British Patents; etc. M.P. N.E. C'wall 1905-24. Mem Roy Comm's on Decim Coinage, & the Bestowment of Polit Honours. Created Peer '29. *c*: Reform. *a*: 58 Lincolns Inn Fields, W.C.2. & Oak Hse, The Avenue, Bournemouth, W. *t*: Holborn 1302.

MARKS, Gertrude Catharine. *b*: Cardiff. *e*: Priv. Journalist & Sec. *n.a*: Reporter to B.M.J. & Nursing Journals. *Publ*: The Maternity Nurse's Daily Guide; The Maternity Nurse's Charts. *s.s*: Midwifery. Formerly Artist & Exhib at Publ Exhibs. Sec to Hammersmith & W. Kensington Synagogue, 1918-. *a*: 10 Matheson Rd, W. Kensington.

MARKS, Percy Leman. *b*: Ealing 1867. *e*: Gt Ealing Sc, Archt, Surveyor & Journalist. *n.a*: Sub Ed, Art Critic & Book Reviewer The Architect, Acting Ed The Illus Carpenter & Builder. *Publ*: Principles of Architectural Design (o.p.); Thermometric Conversion Chart; The Merging of Ronald Letheredge; Principles of Planning Buildings; etc. *c.t*: Architect, Illus Carpenter & Builder, etc. *s.s*: Archt, indexing books & journals. *a*: 10 Matheson Rd, W. Kensington. W.14.

MARKS, Thomas Edward, J.P., A.S.I. *b*: Keighley 1876. *e*: Keighley G.S. *m*: Annie Ambler. *s*: 1. *d*: 1. Barrister-at-Law. *Publ*: The Land & the Commonwealth; The Life of Angelica Patience Fraser. *c.t*: Several n/ps & periodicals. *s.s*: Law, econ, banking, investments, finance, etc. Chm & one of Founders of The Religious Film Soc & The Guilds of Light to encourage production of religious educ & cultural films. Chm other bodies concerned with Child Welfare. Law Exam to Prof Inst in Law of Fixtures, Dilapidations, Easements & Riparian Rights for some yrs. Mem Lincoln's Inn. *Rec*: Gardening, walking. *c*: Nat Lib. *a*: 30 Wimborne Gdns, Ealing, W.13. *t*: Perivale 1234.

MARLE, RAIMOND van: art historian; b. The Hague, Holland, June, 1887; s. Martin van Marle; educ. private schs. in Holland; Ecole des Charts, Ecole du Louvre, Ecole des Hautes Studes, Faculty of Lettres of Univ. of Paris (all Paris). DEGREE: Doctor of Faculty of Letters of the Univ. of Paris; m. Charlotte Murdoch Birmie. AUTHOR (in Dutch): Historical Bibliography of The Hague, 1908; The Mystical Teaching of Master Eckehart, 1916; (in French): The Country of Holland under Philip the Good, 1908; The Town of Hoorn in the Middle Ages, 1910; A Chancelor of France under Charles VI, 1910; Simone Martini and the Painters of His School, 1920; Researches of the Iconography of Grotto and Duccio, 1920; Roman Painting in the Middle Ages, 1921; Iconography of Profane Art in the Middle Ages and during the Renaissance, 1931; (in English): The Development of the Italian Schools of Painting (complete in 18 vols.), of which the 13th has just appeared. Work is conceded to be the most extensive history of Italian painting, or any other school of painting, ever written. An Italian translation is intended), vol. XIII, 1931. Religion, Protestant. HOME: San Marco, Perugia, Italy.

MARLIN, Thomas. Physician. *Publ*: Manipulative Treatment for the Medical Practitioner. *c.t*: Lancet, B.M.J., Practitioner, etc. *a*: 10 Park Cres, Portland Pl, W.1. *t*: Welbeck 6346.

MARLING, Col. Sir Percival Scrope (Bt.), V.C., C.B., J.P., D.L. *b*: King's Stanley 1861. *e*: Harrow & R.M.C. Sandhurst. *m*: Beatrice C. Beaumont. Chm Chancery Lane Safe Deposit Co Ltd & Coy Dir. *Publ*: Rifleman & Hussar (foreword by Field-Marshal Viscount Plumer). *c.t*: National Review, Jnl of the African Soc, etc. *Rec*: Shooting & gardening. *c*: Carlton, Cavalry & Bath. Commanded 18th Q. Mary's Own Roy Hussars, Hon Col 5th Btn Glo'ster Reg. *a*: Stanley Park, Stroud. *t*: 35.

MARLOW, Frederick William, M.D., C.M., M.R.C.S., L.R.C.P., F.R.C.S. Surg. *n.a*: Snr Attending Gynæcologist, Toronto Gen Hosp, Assoc Prof of Gynæcology, Toronto Univ. *c.t*: Med Press. *s.s*: Abdominal surg & gynæcology. *c*: Granite (Toronto) & Canada Med Assoc, etc. *a*: 417 Bloor St W., Toronto, Canada. *t*: Kingsdale 8789.

MARLOW, Louis. See Wilkinson, Louis Umfreville.

MARLOWE, CHARLES (pen name): see Jay, Harriet.

MARLOWE, Mabel. *b*: Kensington 1887. Married. *s*: 2. F/l Writer. *Publ*: Barney Blue Eyes; The Copper Gnomes; Wotta-Woppa; Stories for Little People; Tramping Troubadour; Broody; Singing Fever; Princess Dimple; Zipalong; Clop—the Runaway Donkey; The Wiggly Weasel; Lazy Lob; Trouble in the Upper Third; etc. *c.t*: Daily News, Chron, Star, Standard, American Childhood, Melbourne Argus, Cape Argus. *s.s*: Child-psychology. Stories broadcast throughout the world, also used as Readers & Examination Tests in Australia, New Zealand & U.S.A. Translations used in European periodicals. *Rec* Music. *a*: 40 Wallingford Ave, Kensington, W.10. *t*: Park 9347.

MARMUR, Jacland. *b*: Sosnowiec, Poland 1901. *e*: Public Schs of Brooklyn, Brooklyn Boys Hgh Sch. *m*: Vernita Alyce Pellow. Author. *Publ*: Wind Driven; The Golden Medallion; The Sea & the Shore; Ecola; Three Went Armed; Sea Duty; Andromeda; etc. *Ctr*: Blue Peter, Strand, Pearson's, Britannia, etc, Sat Ev Post, Collier's Blue Book, etc. *s.s*: Sea Stories. *Rec*: Gardening, fishing. *c*: P.E.N. *a*: c/o Sydney A. Saunders, Esq., 522 Fifth Ave, New York City, U.S.A.

MARNOCH, Sir John, M.A., M.B., C.M., LL.D., D.L., K.C.V.O. Surgeon. *c.t*: Surgical Periodicals. *a*: 28 Albyn Pl, Aberdeen. *t*: 326.

MAROCHETTI, Baron George, B.A. *b*: Vaux s/Seine 1894. *e*: Priv & Oxf. Retired Army Off & Dir of Ccys, On New York Times 1929—32. *Publ*: Rich in Range— (Autobiog). *c*: N. Y. Times, Dly Telegraph, Sun Ex, & Wine Trade papers. *s.s*: Modern History, International Affairs, Food & Wines. *Rec*: Good food & fishing. *c*: Naval & Military, Roehampton. *w.s*: 11th Hussars 1915—18 World War II '40—45. *a*: 9 Brompton Sq, London, S.W.3.

MARPLES, Arthur Frederick, F.Z.S. Editor. *n.a*: Ed Our Dogs. *Publ*: Part-author Show Dogs: How to Choose a Dog; Great Danes. *s.s*: Dogs. *a*: 14 Scarisbrick Rd, Levenshulme, Manchester. *t*: Rusholme 1613.

MARPLES, George, A.R.C.A. *b*: Derby 1868. *e*: Col Sc Derby, Ecole des Beaux Arts Paris, Roy Col of Art, Lon. *m*: Anne Harrison. *s*: 2. Art Master & Lect. Associate Roy Soc of Painter Etchers. *Publ*: Sea-Terns or Sea-Swallows. *c.t*: Times, Country Life, Liverpool Daily Post, British Birds, etc. *s.s*: Ornithology, etching, archt. Princ L'pool City Sc of Art. Princ Hull City Sc of Art. Mem Brit Ornithological Union. Mem Chicago Soc of Etchers. Mem Print Makers Assoc, California. *Rec*: Camping. *a*: Lower Mead, Sway, Hants.

MARPLES, Morris, M.A., F.R.G.S. *b*: Huddersfield 1901. *e*: St Bees Sch & Exeter Coll Oxf. *m*: Olive Singleton. *d*: 1. Headmaster Wolstanton Newcastle-u-Lyme Gr Sch, Mem Staffs County Educ & Newcastle-u-Lyme Ed Cttees, Inc Assoc Hdmasters, Classical Assoc. *Publ*: Public School Slang; Sarn Helen; A Roman Road in Wales; History of Bideford Grammar School; etc. *Ctr*: Times Educ Supp, Journ of Educ, Greece & Rome, Scots Mag, etc. *s.s*: Education, Philology esp Slang, Archæology. *Rec*: Walking, camping, reading, travel. *a*: Bar Hill Cottage, Madeley, nr Crewe, Cheshire. *T*: Madeley 273.

MARQUAND, Hilary Adair, M.A., E.Sc., M.H. *b*: Cardiff 1901. *e*: Hgh Sch & Univ Coll Cardiff. *m*: Rachel Eluned Rees. *s*: 2. *d*: 1. Formerly Prof of Industrial Relations Univ Coll Cardiff, Sect for Overseas Trade 1945—47, Paymaster-General 1947—, M.P.(Lab). for Cardiff East. *Publ*: Dynamics of Industrial Combination; Industrial Survey of South Wales (collab); Industial Relations in the U.S.A.; South Wales Needs a Plan; etc. *Ctr*: Times, Manch Guardian, Politicia Quarterly, Week-end Rev, Western Mail. *Rec*: Travels. *c*: Nat Trade Union. *a*: Cabinet Offices, Great George St, London, S.W.1.

MARQUARD OTZEN, Joern. *b*: Sorœ 1921. Author, Editor, Translator, Journalist. *n.a*: Ed Poliom 1946—. *Publ*: Kun en Mikrobe; Foto-Mikkel; Sejren; Kammerater; Jeg vil ikke lyve; Droemme-Lars. *Ctr*: Berlingske Aviser, Nationaltidende, Motor, Poliom, Aalborg Stiftstidende. *c*: Danish Authors. *a*: Nordrehoejalle 14, Kastrup, Copenhagen, Denmark. *T*: Kastrup 969.

MARQUIS, Don. *a*: Messrs. Faber & Faber, 24 Russell Square, W.C.1.

MARR, Rev. George Simpson, M.A., M.B., Ch.B., B.D. D.Litt. *Publ*: The Periodical Essayist of the Eighteenth Century; A Faith for To-day; Christianity & the Cure of Disease; Happy Youth; Sex in Religion. *c*: Edin Univ Union. *a*: 222 Colinton Mains Rd, Edinburgh. *T*: 87919.

MARRIAGE, Herbert James, M.B., B.S., F.R.C.S. Aural Surg. *c.t*: Lancet, Proc Roy Soc Mec, etc. *a*: 109 Harley St, W.1. *t*: Welbeck 3602.

MARRIAN, Pauline. *b*: London. *e*: Wycombe Abbey Sc & Lon Univ. Voluntary worker, St Pancras Sc for Mothers '23— & mem of Executive Cmt. *Publ*: Under This Tree; Destruction's Reach. *Rec*: The theatre, walking, swimming, breeding blue persians. *c*: Arts Theatre. *a*: 21 Teignmouth Rd, Brondesbury, N.W.2. *t*: Gladstone 5902.

MARRINER, Margaret. *b*: Denmark. Holds medical degree Edinburgh. *Publ*: First Aid to Marriage. *c.t*: Women's papers. *s.s*: Preventive medicine and literature. *a*: Pond Close, Langton Green, Kent.

MARRIOTT, Anne. *b*: Victoria, Canada 1913. *e*: Priv Norfolk House Sch. Writer. *n.a*: Asst Ed Canadian Poetry Mag 1946—, Documentary Film Script & Commentary Writer Nat Film Bd 1945—47. *Publ*: Calling Adventures; The Wind Our Enemy; Sandstone & other Poems; Salt Marsh & other Poems. *Ctr*: Canadian Poetry Mag, Saturday Night, Sat Ev Post, Montreal Standard, Winnipeg Free Press, Chamber's Journ, N.Y. Times, etc. *s.s*: Documentary Dramas. *Rec*: Music, walking. *a*: 310 Iruing Rd, Victoria, B.C., Canada. *T*: G 2073.

MARRIOTT, Rev. George Leicester. *Publ*: Macarii Anecdota. *a*: Cautley Vicarage, Sedbergh, Yorks. *t*: 1.

MARRIOTT, Rev. Horace, M.A., D.D., B.Mus. *b*: Blackburn 1885. *e*: Keble Coll Oxf. *m*: Amy Barbara McClenaghan. *s*: 2. Clerk in Holy Orders. *Publ*: The Sermon on the Mount. *a*: Geldeston Rectory, Beccles. *T*: 2255.

MARRIOTT, Ida (Ida Lee). *b*: Kelso, Bathurst, N.S.W. 1865. *e*: Springfield Col, Sydney, N.S.W. *m*: C. J. Bruce Marriott. *s*: 1. *Publ*: The Coming of the British to Australia; Commodore (afterwards Sir John) Haye's Life & Voyage; The Logbooks of the Lady Nelson; Captain Bligh's Second Voyage to the South Sea; Early Explorers in Australia; The Voyage of the Caroline. *c.t*: Geographical Jnl, Empire Review, Sydney Mail, Tasmanian Mail, Western Mail (W. Australia). *s.s*: Geography, history. Hon Fel R.A. Hist Soc. Corres Mem Soc Women Geographers, Washington, U.S.A. *a*: The Dower House, Sizewell, Leiston, Suffolk. *t*: 43.

MARRIOTT, Sir J. A. R. *b*: Bowdon, Cheshire. *e*: Repton & Oxf Univ. *m*; Henrietta Robinson. *d*: 1. Historian. *Publ*: A History of Europe; Economics & Ethics; The Mechanism of the Modern State; English Political Institutions; The Eastern Question; The European Commonwealth; The Evolution of Prussia; The Makers of Modern Italy; The English in India; Europe & Beyond. M.P Oxf 1917—22, York '23—29. *a*: Carlton Club, Pall Mall, S.W.1.

MARRIOTT, James William. *b*: Codnor 1884. *e*: Sevenoaks Sc. *m*: Margaret Waters. *d*: 2. Lect, F/L. Journalist. *n.a*: Weekly Reviews of books for Teachers World & Ed vols of plays for Messrs G. G. Harrap & Co Ltd. *Publ*: The Soul of a Teacher; The Theatre; The Art & Craft of Writing; Great Modern British Plays; One-Act Plays of To-day (6 vols); Exercises in Thinking & Expressing; Short Stories of Today; etc. *c.t*: Evening News, Humorist, Schoolmaster, Atlantic Monthly, Strand, London Opinion, etc. *s.s*: Educ, child psych. Specialist in Eng teaching until 1929. Now writing books on Eng, lecturing to teachers & doing work for exam bodies. *a*: 5 Montpelier Rise, N.W.11. *t*: Speedwell 4081.

MARRIOTT, R. B. Asst Drama Critic. *Publ*: Sale's History; History on the Borders; Three Plays; short stories. *s.s*: Drama, interviewing, book reviewing, film notes. *a*: The Era, 11 Soho Sq, W.1.

MARRIS, Rev. Cyril Cathay. Meth Min. *Publ*: The Methodist Cavalcade (with Rev. J. S. B. Phippen), etc. *a*: Manse, Corringham Rd, Stanford-le-Hope, Essex.

MARROW, N. *a*: The Grammar School, Watford, Herts.

MARSCHALL, Phyllis. *b*: Hampton, Iowa, U.S.A. 1907. *e*: Emerson Col & Yale Univ. *m*: J. de M. C. Crane. Dramatic dir & author. *Publ*: The Dauntless Liberator (jt); George Washington Plays; Plays About Lincoln; Christmas Plays. *c.t*: Pax Mag. *s.s*: Play writing, directing plays for blind. 3 yrs dir of Light House Players (totally blind). Teacher of Eng. *Rec*: Horse riding. *c*: Amer Woman's Assoc. *a*: c/o Malcolm H. Frost, 72 Wall St. N.Y.C. & c/o D. Appleton Century Co, 33W—32nd St, N.Y. City, U.S.A. *t*: Hanover 2—7951.

MARSDEN, Antony. Novelist & Journalist. *Publ*: The Man in the Sandhills; Salter's Folly; The Moonstone Mystery; Thieves Justice; Death on the Downs; The Six Hour Mystery; Swooning Venus; The Mercenary; Death Strikes from the Rear; etc. *a*: c/o F. R. Steele & Son, Haymarket Ct, 32 Haymarket, London, S.W.1.

MARSDEN, Kenneth Elgar. *b*: Leeds 1907. *e*: St James' Church Sch Leeds, Leeds Boys Mod Sch, Ilkley Gr Sch, Leeds Tech Coll, Bradford Tech Coll, Leeds Univ. *m*: Ellen Farrar. *s*: 1. *d*: 1. Technical Dyer, Assoc Inst of Journalists, Mem Brit Amateur Press Assoc. *Publ*: Careers in Textile Dyeing & Finishing Trades; Specialised Journalism; There's Money in the Written Word. *Ctr*: Textile trade press, etc. *s.s*: Textiles, Popular Science, Industry, Economics, Management. *a*: Tregenna, 65 Copgrove Rd, Leeds 8, Yorks. *T*: Leeds 44373.

MARSDEN, Monica. *e*: Public Sch & Univ. Author. *Publ*: Night Adventure; Secrets of the Treasure Box; Sabotage; Friends of Freedom; Enemy Agent; Abbey Ruins; To Save the King; Spanish Treasure; Stolen Goods; Lighthouse Adventure; Secret Eye; Hidden River; Script for Adventure; Behind the Dragon's Teeth; Broken Chime; Under Cover of Fog; Black Light; Necklet of Buddha; Double Crescent; Mystery at Dale House; Jan the Dachshund; Adventures of Sooty; Tales about Tails; Lost Valley; Lost, Stolen or Strayed; Nursery Rhyme Stories; Rainbow that Wouldn't Curve; Cobbler, Cobbler; Stories of the Nursery Toys; Eleven Companion Volumes; etc. *Ctr*: Amalgamated Press, Kemsley Press, Odhams Press, B.B.C., etc. *s.s*: Juvenile Literature. *a*: Kenilworth Court, London, S.W.15. *T*: Putney 1872.

MARSDEN, W. Murray. *Publ*: The Wine Drop. *c.t*: Music & Letters, S.M.T., etc. *Rec*: Music, natural history, fishing. Officier d'Académie Française. *a*: Cedar Ct, Castle Hill, Farnham, Surrey.

MARSH, A. *n.a*: Sub-Ed Wilts County Mirror, Salisbury & Andover Advertiser. Late official shorthand writer at Andover Quarter Sessions. *a*: 3 Wolverdene Road, Andover.

MARSH, Sir Edward Howard. K.C.V.O., C.B., C.M.G., M.A. *b*: London 1872. *e*: Westminster & Trin Coll Camb. Civil Servant (ret), Chm Contemporary Art Soc, Vice-Pres R.S.L. *Publ*: Memoir of Rupert Brooke; La Fontaine's Fables (verse trans); Odes of Horace (verse trans); A Number of People (memoir); Georgian Poetry, 5 Vols (Ed). *Rec*: Play-going & picture-collecting. *c*: Brooks's, Burlington Fine Arts. *a*: 86 Walton St, London, S.W.3. *T*: Kensington 0944.

MARSH, Eileen. *b*: Aldington, Kent 1900. *m*: Jack Heming. *s*: 3. *d*: 2. Novelist. *Publ*: We Lived in London; I Had a Son; A Walled Garden; Eight Over Essen; Barbed Wire; So Built We. *s.s*: Adventure & Sunday School Books for Children. *Rec*: Music, motoring, camping. *a*: Preswylfa, Cranbrook, Kent. *T*: Cranbrook 2156.

MARSH, Rev. Fred Shipley. *b*: Gainsborough 1886. *e*: Gainsboro' Gr Sch, Selwyn Coll Camb. Fell Selwyn Coll & Lady Margaret Prof of Divinity Univ of Camb. *n.a*

Cttee Journ of Theol Studies 1932—. *Publ*: The Book of the Holy Hierotheos; etc. *Ctr*: Journ of Theol Studies, Hasting's Dict, Ency Brit, etc. *s.s*: Theology & Semetic Langs. *a*: Selwyn Coll. Cambridge.

MARSH, James Ernest, M.A.(Oxon), F.R.S. *b*: St Helens 1860. *e*: Rugby, Balliol, Bonn, Paris. *m*: Lavinia Paintin. *d*: 5. *Publ*: The Origins & the Growth of Chemical Science; Stone-Decay & Its Prevention. *c.t*: Roy Soc, Chem Soc, etc. *s.s*: Chem. *Rec*: Sailing. *a*: 2 Davenant Rd, Oxf.

MARSH, Jean. *b*: Pershore, Worcs 1898. *e*: Malesowen Gr Sch. *m*: Gerald E. Marshall. *s*: 1. *d*: 1. Author & Broadcaster. *Publ*: Death Stalks the Bride; Murder Next Door; Shore House Mystery; Mystery at Castle Rock Zoo; Judith & the Dolls. *Ctr*: Dly Express, Birmingham Mail, etc. *s.s*: Children's Plays & Stories, Domestic Serials & Short Stories. *Rec*: Golf, cinema, cooking. *a*: The Firs, Drews Holloway, Cradley, Staffs. *T*: Cradley Heath 69187.

MARSH, John. *b*: Halifax 1907. *e*: Giggleswick Sch Yorks. Author. *Publ*: Maiden Armour; Lonely Pathway; Return They Must; Body Made Alive; Many Parts; Two Mrs Farrells; etc. (Ed) Poppy Annual. *a*: The Press Club, Salisbury Sq, London, E.C.4. *T*: Central 2644.

MARSH, John Henry. *b*: Cape Town 1914. *e*: Sea Point Boys Hgh Sch. *m*: Leona Thom. *d*: 2. Journalist, Former Publicity Officer, Broadcaster & Free-lance. *n.a*: Shipping Ed 1933—, Air Ed '43—, Cape Argus, Cape Town. *Publ*: Skeleton Coast; South Africa & the War at Sea. *Ctr*: World's leading Shipping Journs. *s.s*: Shipping, Aeronautics, Publicity & Photography. *c*: P.E.N., Scribbler's. *a*: Bellerive, Strathmore Rd, Camps Bay, Cape Town, Sth Africa. *T*: 3-9647.

MARSH, Ngaio. *b*: Christchurch, New Zealand 1899. *e*: St Margaret's Coll & Canterbury Coll Sch of Arts N.Z. Novelist & Theatrical Producer. *Publ*: Final Curtain; Died in the Wool; Colour Scheme; Death & the Dancing Footman; Surfeit of Lampreys; Overture to Death; Death at the Bar; etc. *Ctr*: Sat Ev Post, New Theatre, & various other publs. *s.s*: Detective Fiction, Drama. *Rec*: Reading, theatre, gardening, travel. *a*: 25 Valley Rd, Cashmere Hills, Christchurch, New Zealand. *T*: 37-300.

MARSH, Richard Oglesby, D.Sc. *b*: Washington, D.C. 1883. *e*: Massachusetts Institute of Technology, Univ of Lausanne. *m*: Helen Louise Cleveland. *s*: 1. *d*: 3. Civil Engineer, scientist. *Publ*: White Indians of Darien; Lost Colony of Greenland Norsemen; Sandiro—Patriot of Nicaragua; Revival of the Indian in Latin America (in press). *c.t*: Time, Literary Digest, Science Service. *s.s*: Ethnology, Latin America, China, Japan, Philippines, Morocco, Greenland. Formerly in U.S. Diplomatic Service. Credited with discovery of White Indians in Darien. Rank Major U.S.A. Service, Rank of General Latin-America. *Rec*: Tennis, shooting, fishing, boating, gardening. *c*: Boston City, University, Washington, D.C. *a*: 105 Leland St, Chevy Chase, Maryland, U.S.A. *t*: Wisconsin 4612.

MARSH, Rev. Robert Alban. *Publ*: The New Outlook & the Old Message. *s.s*: Theology. *a*: St Mary's Rectory, Wavertree, L'pool. *t*: 1061.

MARSH, Lt.-Col. William Lockwood, O.B.E., M.A., L.I.B., F.R.Ae.S., M.S.A.E. *b*: Sheffield 1886. *e*: Uppingham, Pembroke Col Cam. *m*: Diana Powell-Jones. *s*: 2. Editor. *n.a*: Aircraft Engineering 1928. *Publ*: Aeronautical Prints & Drawings; The A.B.C. of Flying; Flying. *c.t*: Tech Periodicals & Wkly & Daily N/ps. *s.s*: Aeronautics. Chm Brit Standard Aircraft Nomenclature Comm, Gen Sec Internat Air Congress '23. *Rec*: Tennis. *c*: United Univ. *a*: 112 Bunhill Row, E.C.1. *t*: National 5432.

MARSH, William Thomas, M.A. Headmaster St Albans Sc. *a*: Sc Hse, St Albans, Herts. *t*: 156.

MARSHALL, Alan John, B.Sc. *b*: Sydney 1911. *e*: Univs of Sydney & Oxford. Zoologist. *Publ*: The Black Musketeers; The Men & Birds of Paradise; Australia Limited. *Ctr*: The Australian Rationalist, Sydney Dly Telegraph, Times (London), Listener, Geog Mag, etc. *Rec*: Walking, talking, drinking. *a*: Dept of Zoology, University Museum, Oxford. *T*: Oxford 47726.

MARSHALL, Albert James. *e*: Secondary Sch. Mem N.E.C., Chmn East Sussex Branch N.U.J. *n.a*: Sub-Ed. Hastings & St Leonards Observer 1943—. *s.s*: Drama, Lawn Tennis. *a*: 53 Wykeham Rd, Hastings, Sussex. *T*: Hastings 3055.

MARSHALL, Archibald, LittD.(Yale). *b*: Lon 1866. *e*: Highgate Sc, Trin Col Cam. *m*: Helen May Banks. *d*: 1. Author. *n.a*: Ed Daily Mail Books Supp 1906-09, Special Corr Daily Mail '09-11, Paris Corr Daily News '16-17. *Publ*: Peter Binney, Undergraduate (1899); The House of Merrilees (1905); 4 Clinton of Kencote Novels ('09-14); 3 Anthony Dare Novels ('21-24); many other novels; Claimants ('33); Nothing Hid ('34); A Spring Walk in Provence ('19); Simple Stories; The Birdikin Family; Out & About (Reminiscences, '33); etc. *c.t*: Punch, London Mercury, Strand Mag, Windsor Mag, etc. *a*: c/o T. B. Pinker & Son, Talbot Hse, Arundel St, W.C.2.

MARSHALL, Arthur. *b*: London 1873. *e*: Univ Coll Sch, Cen Tech Coll. *m*: Ada Watts. Chemist, For 20 years Chemical Adviser to Indian Ordnance Dept. *Publ*: Explosives (3 Vols); Dictionary of Explosives; Short Account of Explosives. *Ctr*: Journ of Chemical Soc, Analyst, Nature, etc. *s.s*: Explosives. *c*: Athenæum. *a*: 10 Aubrey Walk, London, W.8. *T*: Park 7957.

MARSHALL, Bruce. *b*: Edinburgh 1899. *e*: Edin Academy, Glenalmond, St Andrew's & Edin Univs. *m*: Mary Pearson Clark. *d*: 1. Novelist. *Publ*: Father Malachy's Miracle; Yellow Tapers for Paris; All Glorious Within; George Brown's Schooldays; The Red Danube, *a*: c/o Pearn, Pollinger & Higham, 39-40 Bedford St, London, W.C.2.

MARSHALL, C. Jennings, M.S., M.D., F.R.C.S., M.B. *Publ*: Text Book Surgical Pathology; The Surgeon; Text Book Surgical Anatomy & Physiology (with N. C. Lake). *c.t*: B.M.J., Lancet, Brit Journ of Surg, etc. *a*: 121 Harley St, W.1. *t*: Wel 6818.

MARSHALL, Chapman Frederick Dendy, M.A. *b*: Acton 1872. *e*: Hurstpierpoint & Trin Col Cam. *m*: Adela Rose Clarke. *n.a*: Mang Ministry of Munitions Journ. *Publ*: The Resistance of Express Trains (1925); The British Post Office from its Beginnings to End of '25; Centenary History of the L'pool & M/C Rly; The Motion of Rly Vehicles on a Curved Line ('32). *c.t*: Eng, Rly Eng, etc. *s.s*: Rly science & Post Office history. Tech Exam to Munitions Inventions Dept during Gt War for engines of all kinds, & during part of the time for Aeronautics. Awarded gold medal, plaque, 3 bronze medals & Geo Stephenson Research Prize for books, formed two important collections, one relating to rly hist, the other to Brit Post Office. *Rec*: Lawn Tennis. *c*: Mem Inst of Loc Eng, Roy Aero Soc, Vice Pres Newcomen Soc, Roy Philatelic Soc, R.A.C., etc. *a*: Chinthurst Lodge, Wonersh, Guildford. *t*: Shalford 14.

MARSHALL, Charles Frederic, M.D., M.Sc, F.R.C.S.(Eng). *b*: Birm 1864. *e*: Owen's Col M/C & Bart's Hosp Lon. *m*: Blanche Emmett. *s*: 1. Surgeon. *Publ*: A New Theory of Cancer (1932); Syphilis & Venereal Diseases (4th edn '21); Trans—(Fr) Saboraud's Regional Dermatology ('06); etc.—(Ger) Strümpel's Practice of Medicine ('32). *c.t*: B.M.J., Lancet, Med Press & Circular, Practitioner, Medizinische Klinik. *s.s*: Cancer, skin diseases, syphilis. Ex-Surg Hosp for Diseases of Skin, Lon. *Rec*: Lawn tennis. *c*: Hon Sec New Cancer Soc, Fell Med Soc of Lon, etc. *a*: 68 Crowstone Rd, Westcliff-on-Sea, Essex. *t*: Southend 4602.

MARSHALL, Dorothy. *b*: Morecambe 1900. *e*: Park Sch Preston, Girton Coll Camb, Lect Univ Coll of South Wales & Monmouthshire 1936—. *Publ*: The English Poor in the Eighteenth Century; The Rise of George Canning. *Ctr*: Articles on Econ Hist in various periodicals. *s.s*: Econ Hist (English Eighteenth Century). *Rec*: Travel, country life. *a*: 9 Warwick Hse, Castle Court, Cardiff.

MARSHALL, Edison, M.A. *b*: Rennselaer, Indiana 1894. *e*: Univ of Oregon. *m*: Agnes Sharp Flythe. *s*: 1. *d*: 1. Author. *Publ*: Yankee Pasha; Great Smith; Benjamin Blake (Film, Son of Fury); The Upstart; Shikar & Safari. *Ctr*: Cosmopolitan, Good Housekeeping, American, Sat Ev Post, Liberty, Reader's Digest, True, etc. *s.s*: Hist Novel. *Rec*: Big Game Hunting. *a*: Breetholm, Augusta, Georgia, U.S.A.

MARSHALL, Evelyn May. *b*: Shipley 1898. *e*: St Brandon's, Clifton, Bristol & Sheffield Univ. Married. *s*: 1. Editor & Author. *n.a*: Ed Barry & Dis News Woman's Page, Ed New Empire Annual & Schoolboys' Annual, & Asst Ed Sunday at Home & Boys' Own Paper 1933—. *s.s*: Children's fiction. *a*: English Speaking Un, Charles St, W. *t*: Cent 8428.

MARSHALL, Francis Hugh Adam, C.B.E., Sc.D.(Camb), D.Sc.(Edin), Hon.D.Sc.(Manch), Hon.LL.D.(Edin), F.R.S F.R.S.E. Fell Christ's Coll, Reader in Agricultural Physiology (ret), formerly Dean & Vice-Master of Christ's Coll, Jt-Ed Journ Agricultural Science; & Journ Endocrinology. *Publ*: The Physiology of Reproduction; Physiology of Farm Animals. *Ctr*: Many scientific journals. *s.s*: Physiology of Breeding. *Rec*: Ornithology. *c*: Athenæum. *a*: Christ's Coll, Cambridge.

MARSHALL, Frederick Henry. *b*: Hampstead 1878. *e*: Merchant Taylors Sch, Emmanuel Coll Camb. *m*: Priscilla Mary O'Meara. Asst Dept of Greek & Roman Antiquaries Brit Museum 1901—12, Lect at Emmanuel Coll Camb '12—19, Lect & Reader in Classics Birkbeck Coll '19—26, Prof of Byzantine Mod Greek Kings Coll London '26—43, Served in Uncommon Language Dept of the Postal Censorship War Office '15—19 & '39—40. *Publ*: The Second Athenian Confederation; Catalogues of Ancient Rings & Jewellery; Ancient Greek Inscriptions Brit Museum; Discovery in Greek Lands; Old Testament Legends; Siege of Vienna in 1683; (in collab) Three Cretan Plays. *Ctr*: Journal of Hellenic Studies, Church Quarterly Review, The Christian East, The Link, etc. *s.s*: Ancient Byzantine & Modern Greek, Classical Archæology. *a*: 20 Somali Rd, London, N.W.2.

MARSHALL, Harold. Publisher. *a*: 1—2—11 & 12 Paternoster Bldgs, E.C.4. *t*: City 6021.

MARSHALL, Henry Salmon, F.R.S.A., A.M.I.S.E., L.R.I.B.A., M.I.H.E.(London). *m*: Annie McNabb. *s*: 1. Architectural engineer. *Publ*: All About Brighton Resort. *c.t*: Indian Engineering, Mayurbhanj Gazette, Action, Englishman Daily. *s.s*: Architecture, engineering, surveying, building, photography, drawing, valueing, designing, economic housing problems. *Rec*: Walking, boating, sketching. Expert advisor, surveyor and valuer to the Crown. Awarded First Prize at All India Calcutta Art Exhibition. Architect, promoter and director of Brighton Resort scheme on the east coast of India. Government Art Sc Diploma for drawing teacher, etc. *c*: Ex Mem Calcutta Golf and Rotary Club, Ex Master Mason of Dist Grand Lodge, Bengal. *a*: 1 Rawdon St, Calcutta, India. *t*: Park 96.

MARSHALL, Rev. Henry Stirling, M.A.(Bristol), A.K.C. *b*: Southampton 1885. *e*: Priv & King's Coll Lond. Clerk in Holy Orders. *Publ*: The Witness of the Church; Understanding Christianity; Pastoralia for Women (Ed); Why are Infants Baptised? *Ctr*: Expository Times, Theology, Teaching, Church Review. *s.s*: Theology. *Rec*: Gardening. *a*: 10 Longton Ave, London, S.E.26. *T*: Sydenham 7113.

MARSHALL, Howard. Journalist & Author. *n.a*: Sports Staff Daily Telegraph. *a*: c/o Daily Telegraph, Fleet St, E.C.4.

MARSHALL, Janet Sophia, M.B.E. *b*: Penkridge, Staffs. *e*: Brighton & Oxf. *m*: Charles Marshall. *s*: 3. Journalist. *Publ*: How to Cook; 365 Dishes for Little Cooks; Savouries & Supper Dishes; Handbook of Cookery; Culinary Portion of Harmsworth Household Ency; etc. *c.t*: Manchester Guardian, News-Chron, Nursing Times, Lady, Homes & Gardens, Daily Mail, etc. *s.s*: Cookery. Late Dietitian to War Office. Expert on Food & Cookery, all questions of dietary. Gold & Silver Medallist Food & Cookery Exhib. *Rec*: Bridge. *c*: Soc of Women Journalists, Writers, Pioneer. *a*: 18 Hampton Gve, Beeston, Nott'm.

MARSHALL, HON. MR. JUSTICE JOHN EDWIN: Judge (retired); b. West Hartlepool, Eng., Mar. 3, 1864; s. William and Elizabeth (Raine) M.; educ. Durham Sch. DEGREE: Barrister-at-law; m. Elizabeth Best. AUTHOR: The Egyptian Enigma, 1928. Contributor to Quarterly Rev., Nineteenth Century and After; National Rev., English Rev., L'Egypte Contemporaire, The Times, Egyptian Gazette. General character of writing: political, critical, historical, legal. Called to Bar, Middle Temple, 1889; mem. and treas of Bar Council of International Courts in Egypt; Judge in Egyptian Court of First Instance, 1897, Court of Appeal, 1905; retired, 1923. Grand Officer of the Order of the Nile. Commander of the Mejedieh; Hereditary Freeman of City of Durham. CLUB: Savile (London). Relig. denom., Church of England. HOME: Bellaria, Tour de Peilz, Vaud, Switzerland.

MARSHALL, John Frederick, M.A.(Cantab). *b*: Lon 1874. *e*: Rugby Sc & King's Col Cam. *m*: Blanche Gray. *d*: 1. Founder & Dir Brit Mosquito Control Inst, Hayling Island. *Publ*: Principles & Practice of Mosquito Control; The Organization of Mosquito Control Work. *c.t*: Sci journ's. Winner M.C.C. Gold Tennis Prize 1914. Barrister-at-Law. *Rec*: Tennis. *c*: Athenæum, Prince's Tennis, Roy Auto. *a*: Seacourt, Hayling Island, Hants. *t*: 77851.

MARSHALL, Sir John Hubert, Kt., C.I.E., M.A., Litt.D., F.S.A., A.R.I.B.A. *b*: 1876. *e*: Dulwich Coll & King's Coll Camb, Dir-General of Archæology in India 1902—31. *Publ*: Mohenjo-Daro & the Indus Civilization; Taxila; etc. *a*: Avondale, Sydney Rd, Guildford, Surrey. *T*: 62511.

MARSHALL, Joseph Warnock. *b*: Whitby. Dis Reporter. *n.a*: N.E. Daily Gazette, Middlesbro' 1903, N. Mail & Chron, Newcastle '27. *a*: 58 Wansbeck Gdns, W. Hartlepool. *t*: 2832 & 2866.

MARSHALL, Lenore G., A.B. *b*: New York 1897. *e*: Barnard Coll. *m*: James Marshall. *s*: 1. *d*: 1. Writer. *n.a*: Poetry Ed American Mercury Mag 1938. *Publ*: No Boundary; Hall of Mirrors; Only the Fear. *Ctr*: Sat Review of Lit, Poetry Mag, New Yorker, American Mercury, New Republic, Scribners, etc. *s.s*: Fiction, Poetry. *Rec*: Farming, gardening, cooking, travel. *a*: 30 West 54th St, New York City. *T*: Circle 7-7200.

MARSHALL, Marion Alice. *b*: Hastings. *e*: St Hugh's Col Oxon. F/L. Jnlst. *c.t*: Hospital, Commonwealth, Week-end Review, New Statesman, Spectator, etc. *s.s*: Hospital reform. *Rec*: Rifle shooting, rowing. Gave written evidence before Lancet Commission on Nursing. Studied sociology at Liverpool, Oxford & Lon. *c*: Univ Women's Club. *a*: The University Women's Club, 2 Audley Sq, South Audley St, W.1. *t*: Grosvenor 2268.

MARSHALL, Mary Vera. *b*: Huddersfield 1904. *e*: Cheltenham Ladies Col. *n.a*: Sub Ed The Guide '28, Ed '30-. *Publ*: The Quest of the Sleuth Patrol; Tracks to Adventure. *Rec*: Physical exercises, country dancing. *a*: Drake Hse, Cheltenham, & Nutford Hse, Nutford Pl, W.1. *t*: Cheltenham 2205.

MARSHALL, May. *n.a*: Assoc Ed Nursing Mirror. *Publ*: 5 Novels & 4 Children's Books. *c*: Founder Mem Women's Press Lond. *a*: Dorset Hse, Stamford St, London, S.E.1. *T*: Waterloo 3333.

MARSHALL, Percival, C.I.Mech.E. *b*: London 1870. *e*: Cent Foundation Sch, Finsbury Tech Coll, Victoria Univ Manch. Chm Percival Marshall & Co Ltd, Vice Pres Periodical Trade Press & Weekly Newsp Props Assoc, Dir Electrical Press Ltd, Engineering Review Publishing Co. *n.a*: Founder & Ed The Model Engineer, The Model Railway News & Ship Models. *Publ*: Practical Lessons in Metal Turning & Screw-cutting; Metal Working Tools & Their Uses; Mechanics in Miniature. *s.s*: Engineering, Model Making, Experimental Mechanics, Tech Educ. *c*: Press, Wimbledon Park Golf. *a*: 23 Great Queen St, London, W.C.2. *T*: Chancery 6681.

MARSHALL, Robert, N.U.J. *b*: Market Drayton 1878. *e*: Alleynes' G.S. Stone, Staffs. *m*: Ethel Annie Ball. *s*: 1. Ed Newport & Market Drayton Advert, formerly Sub-Ed Wellington Journ & Shrewsbury News. *Rec*: Motoring. *a*: 26 Avenue Road, Newport, Salop.

MARSHALL, Robert Lyons, M.A., LL.D., F.R.Hist.S. *b*: Drumragh, Co Tyrone 1887. *e*: Sixmilecross P.E.S., Roy Sch Dungannon, Queen's Coll Galway, Assembly's Coll Belfast. *m*: Isobel Marion Scott Portrush. *s*: 1. Prof of English & History Magee Univ Coll Londonderry. *Publ*: The Historical Criticism of Documents; (penname Tullyneil): The Heart of Tyrone; At Home in Tyrone; Rhymes of Tyrone. *Ctr*: Expositor, Expository Times, Studies, Belfast Ev Telegraph, Fishing Gaz, etc. *s.s*: History, Eng Litt, Angling, Tyrone Dialect. *Rec*: Fishing, shooting. *a*: 1 College Ave, Magee University College, Londonderry, N.I.

MARSHALL, Roy Langley. *b*: Wimbledon. *e*: Prep Elem & Public Sch, Rutlish, Merton. *m*: Winifred Mary Mathews. *s*: 2. Reporter, Mem N.U.J. *n.a*: Wimbledon Advertiser 1929, Freelance '34, Founder of R. L. Marshall '35 Ltd & later Middlesex News Service, Served since '39 on Women's Wear News, Dly Herald & Fashion Trade Weekly. *Publ*: (In collab) Various books on travel, tennis, etc. *s.s*: Clothing Industry & Retail Trade. *Rec*: Gardening, motoring, music. *c*: Arts. *a*: 78 Marryat Rd, Wimbledon, S.W.19. *T*: Wimbledon 6057.

MARSON, Rev. Gerald Francis, B.A.(Lond). *b*: Higham Hall nr Nuneaton. *e*: Stanmore Park & Leamington Coll. *m*: Margaret Monica Robinson. *s*: 2. *d*: 1. Vicar of Granby & Rector of Elton. *Publ*: Ghosts, Ghouls & Gallows; Jerusalem & Bethany, A Passion Play; St Christopher (play); The Power of the Cross. *s.s*: Fiction, Religious Drama. *Rec*: Gardening. *w.s*: 1914—18 C.F. 11th Inf Div & 13th Inf Div. *a*: Granby Vicarage, Notts. *T*: Whatton 280.

MARSON, Harvey, M.J.I., N.U.J. *b*: Worcester 1877. *e*: Dean Close Sc, Cheltenham. *m*: Alys Beatrice Owen. *s*: 1. *d*: 1. *n.a*: 12 y Worcester Echo, Sub-Ed Yorks Evening News, Leeds, Leicester Mail, L'pool Courier, Bournemouth Echo, Ed n/ps Channel Isles, Nice S. France, Shrewsbury & Sleaford. Composer of a number of songs, dances, musical monologues, etc. *Rec*: Music, stamp-collecting. *a*: Merillyn, London Rd, Sleaford, Lincs & Gazette Office, Sleaford. *t*: 27 & 52.

MARSON, Thomas Bertrand, M.B.E. *b*: Higham-on-the-Hill, Leics 1880. *e*: Lindley Lodge, Nuneaton, Oakham Sc, Rutland. *m*: Ellen Gertrude Atkins. *s*: 1. *d*: 1. Wing-Cmdr R.A.F. *Publ*: Scarlet & Khaki; 'Twixt Grass & Plough; The Duke of Buccleuch's Hunt. A Reminiscence of the Season '26—27. *s.s*: Fox hunting, agriculture, Roy Air Force. S. African War 1899—1900, Gt War '14—18, Egypt, Gallipoli, France, special aviation mission U.S.A. & France. Priv Sec to Lord Trenchard, Chief of Air Staff, Air Ministry, Lon '19—26. *Rec*: Hunting, cricket, flying. *a*: Home Park, Aberdour, Fife.

MARSTON, Sir Charles, Kt., J.P., F.S.A. *b*: Wolverhampton 1867. *e*: Wolverhampton G.S. & Birm Univ. Married. *d*: 2. Manufr. *Publ*: The Christian Faith & Industry; New Knowledge About the Old Testament; New Bible Evidence. *c.t*: Times, Morning Post, Daily Mail, Observer, N.Y. Times, etc. *s.s*: Bibl archæ. 45 y a large Employer of Labour, intimately assoc with U.S.A. & with Brit politics. A J.P. for Wolverhampton 1924—. Assoc with numerous excavations in Bible lands. *Rec*: Fishing. *c*: Carlton, Nat & R.A.C. *a*: 4 Camden Pk, Tunbridge Wells, Kent.

MARSTON, David. *b*: Nuneaton 1875. *e*: Nuneaton. *m*: Rose Ellen Bass. *s*: 2. *d*: 2. *n.a*: Ed Rep Coalville Times '96. Mem N.U.J. Sec Coalville Times Charity Cricket Cup Compet, etc. *c.t*: Lon & Prov N/ps. Apprenticeship Nuneaton Observer '95—96, Dist Rep Brentwood & Chelmsford for Essex Times, Ex Pres Leics branch N.U.J. *Rec*: Bowls. *a*: The Cottage, Meadow Lane, Coalville, Leicester. *t*: 175.

MARSTON, Edward Walton. *b*: Croydon 1884. *e*: Dulwich Coll. *m*: Helen Elvery Lucy Panchaud. *s*: 2. Publisher. *n.a*: Ed The Publishers Circular & Booksellers Record 1928, Jt-Ed The Fishing Gazette. *Publ*: English Catalogue of Books; etc. *c*: Fly Fishers. *a*: 171 High St, Beckenham, Kent. *T*: Beckenham 5350.

MARSTON, Robert Leslie. *b*: Richmond 1891. *e*: Dulwich. *m*: Adela Frances Hobson. *d*: 2. Journalist. *n.a*: Jt Ed The Fishing Gazette 1927. *Ctr*: Weekly Sketch, News of the World, Dly Mail, Yorks Post, etc. *Rec*: Fishing. *c*: Fly Fishers, etc. *a*: 30 Purley Bury Close, Purley.

MARSTON, Walton. *b*: Croydon 1884. *e*: Dulwich Col. *m*: Helen Elvery Lucy Panchaud. *s*: 2 (1 dec). Publisher. *n.a*: Ed The Publisher's Circular & the Publisher & Bookseller 1928, Jt Ed The Fishing Gazette. *Publ*: English Catalogue of Books; etc. *c*: Fly Fishers. *a*: 56—8 Whitcomb St, Leicester Sq, W.C.2. *t*: Whitehall 1196.

MARTEL, Sir Giffard, K.C.B., K.B.E., D.S.O., M.C., M.I.Mech.E. *b*: Southampton 1889. *e*: Wellington Coll, R.M.A. Woolwich. *m*: Maud Mackenzie. *s*: 1. Army Officer (ret). *Publ*: In the Wake of the Tank; The Problem of Security; Our Armoured Forces; The Russian Outlook. *Ctr*: Ev Standard, Dly Mail. *s.s*: Military Subjects, Sports & Games (Boxing), Big Game Shooting. *Rec*: Hunting & shooting. *c*: Army & Navy, R.A.C. *w.s*: Comm 50th Northumberland Div 1939—40, Comm Roy Armoured Corps '40—42, Head of Brit Military Mission to Russia '43. *a*: Bulford Lodge, Heatherside, Camberley.

MARTELL, Edward Drewett, M.J.I. *b*: Luton 1909. *e*: St George's Sc Harpenden. *m*: Ethel Maud Beverley. *s*: 1. Journalist. *n.a*: World's Press News '29–31, Gen Mang Saturday Review '31–32, Ed Shaw's Standard Reference Series '33–. *Publ*: The Devil's Camera (with R. G. Burnett); Young Man's Medley; The Last Line; The Author's & Writer's Who's Who (ed); etc. *c.t*: Everyman's Encyclopædia, Times, Daily Telegraph, Saturday Review, etc. *s.s*: Reference books, short stories, Rugby football. *Rec*: Rugby football, cricket, tennis. *a*: 96 Malvern Av, S. Harrow. *t*: Byron 1288 & Central 9891.

MARTELL, Ethel. *Publ*: From One Mother to Another; etc. *a*: 1 Park Av, Bedford. *t*: 2207.

MARTELLI, George Ansley. *b*: London 1903. *e*: R.N. Coll Dartmouth. *m*: Ann Farrell. *s*: 3. Parliamentary Agent, Coy Dir & Farmer. *n.a*: Morning Post 1928—37, Brit & For News Service '38—39, Man Ed, News Chron '37, Special Corr. *Publ*: Italy Against the World; Whose Sea; From Such a Seed; Snotty. *Ctr*: Dly Telegraph, Tribune, Sphere, Cornhill, etc. *s.s*: Foreign Affairs, Farming, Fiction. *w.s*: Political Intell Dept For Off 1939—43, R.N. '43—46. *a*: Rads End Farm, Eversholt, Beds. *T*: Ridgmont 57.

MARTENS, Paul. *Publ*: Death Rocks the Cradle; The Truth about My Father. *a*: c/o Messrs. Wm. Collins, 48 Pall Mall, S.W.

MARTIN, Alec Edmund, M.D., D.P.H. *b*: Oldham 1912. *e*: Coalbrookdale Hgh Sch & Manch Univ. *Publ*: Serological Studies in Influenza; Child Neglect; A Problem of Social Administration. *Ctr*: Various Med journs. *s.s*: Public Health & Social Problems. *a*: Oak Cott, Coalbrookdale, Shropshire, & 13 Riverview Gdns, London, S.W.13. *T*: Riverside 2361.

MARTIN, Rev. Alexander, D.D., LL.D. *b*: Panbride 1857. *e*: George Watson's Col Edin, Edin Univ, New Col Edin. *m*: Jane Thorburn Addis. *s*: 2. *d*: 1. Princ New Col Edin. *Publ*: The Finality of Jesus for Faith; Winning the Soul; Church Union in Scotland. Princ of New Col 1919–. Moderator Gen Assembly Utd F. C. of Scot '20 & '29. Chaplain in Ordinary to H.M. the King. *c*: Univ Edin. *a*: 17 Grange Terr, Edin. *t*: 43107.

MARTIN, Rev. Arthur Davis, A.T.S. *b*: Brockley, Lon 1869. *e*: Aske's Sc, Hatcham & Hackney & New Col Lon. *m*: Nellie Gertrude Carter. *s*: 1. *d*: 2. *Publ*: Aspects of the Way; Doctor Vanderkemp; Una Breakspear: A Tale of the 17th Century; etc. *s.s*: Bibl scholarship. *a*: Little Baddow, nr Chelmsford, Essex. *t*: Danbury 81.

MARTIN, Basil Kingsley. *b*: Hereford 1897. *e*: Hereford & Mill Hill, Camb Univ. Editor & Author. *n.a*: Manch Guardian 1927—31, Ed New Statesman & Nation '31—. *Publ*: The Triumph of Lord Palmerston; The British Public & the General Strike; Low's Russian Sketch Book; Magic of Monarchy; Propaganda's Harvest; The Press the Public Wants; etc. *a*: New Statesman & Nation, 10 Great Turnstile, London, W.C.1. *T*: Holborn 8471-6.

MARTIN, Bernard. *b*: Southampton 1897. *e*: George Watson's Col Edin. *m*: Grace E. Powell. *s*: 1. Author. *Publ*: Strange Vigour: a Biography of Sun Yat-Sen; Red Treasure; William the Silent; The Pagoda Plot; Over My Shoulder. *s.s*: Biog, China & the Far East. *a*: Dellwood, Danbury, Essex. *T*: Danbury 236.

MARTIN, Rev. Cecil Henry, M.A.(Cantab). *b*: Bickley 1867. *e*: Pembroke Col Cam. Rector of Blendworth. *Publ*: Allnutt of Delhi, a Memoir (1922); etc. *s.s*: Hist, foreign missny work. *Rec*: Pen & ink drawing & photography. *a*: Blendworth Rectory, Horndean, Portsmouth.

MARTIN, Cecil Percy, M.A., M.B., Ch.B., D.Sc., M.R.I.A. *b*: Dublin Ireland 1892. *e*: Trin Coll Dublin. *m*: Kathleen Humphreys. *s*: 2. *d*: 2. Prof of Anatomy McGill Univ, Montreal Canada. *Publ*: The Decline of Religion; Prehistoric Man in Ireland. *a*: 570 Milton St, Montreal, Canada. *T*: LA 2736.

MARTIN, Clara. *b*: Cwmavon. *e*: Highfield. Authoress. *Publ*: A Little Aversion; The Spanish Dress; Love in Absence; Honey-Pot; Susan Jane; Doctor's Day; A Day Like Another; Bearing Gifts. *Ctr*: Cornhill, Chambers's Journ. *s.s*: Novels, Short Stories. *c*: Overseas. *a*: BM/BHB2, London, W.C.1.

MARTIN, David. *b*: Budapest 1915. *m*: Elizabeth Richenda Powell. *s*: 1. Author, Mem N.U.J. *n.a*: Editorial Dly Express (Glas) 1941—42, European Service of B.B.C. '41—45 (Features & Editorial), Lit Ed Reynolds News '45. *Publ*: The Shoes Men Walk In; The Shepherd & the Hunter; Tiger Bay; Battlefields; The Burning River; Rhyme & Reason. *Ctr*: Argosy, Chamber's, Lilliput, News Theatre, Tribune, New Life, Nat Newsps, etc. *s.s*: Lit Criticism, Jewish Arab Relations, Stories for Children. *Rec*: Discussion. *a*: 4 Heath Hurst Rd, London, N.W.3. *T*: Hampstead 6548.

MARTIN, E. K., M.S., F.R.C.S. *c.t*: Med Journs. *a*: 40 Wimpole St, W.1. *t*: Euston 2122.

MARTIN, Edgar Stanley. *b*: Gorham, N.Y. 1873. *e*: Kenka Col N.Y. State Col for Teachers & Cent Univ. *m*: Gertrude Bishop. *s*: 1. *d*: 2. Teacher, Author & Ed. *n.a*: Ed Scoutmastership Notes, Scouting 1926–, in charge of all pubsl of Boy Scouts of Amer Handbooks, Merit Badge Library, Service Library. *c.t*: Various n/ps & periodicals. Citation for work in Gt Flood of 1913 by Pres Wilson, Horniday Medal for service to Wild Life in Amer. *Rec*: Camping, fishing, hunting. *c*: Nat Arts, N.Y. Mason, Swiss Alpine. *a*: 158 Harrison St, E. Orange, N.J. *t*: 2-2894.

MARTIN, Edward Alfred, F.G.S. *b*: Brighton. Civil Servant. Vice-Chm Pub Libraries Cmt Croydon. Formerly Hon Curator Grangewood Museum Norwood. Hon Sec S.E. Un of Scientific Soc's. *Publ*: Bibliography of Gilbert White of Selborne; Life in a Sussex Windmill; Sussex Geology; Natural History & Antiquities of Croydon; etc. *c.t*: Geological Mag, Geographical Mag, Journal of the Board of Agriculture, Nature, etc. *s.s*: Dew-ponds, coal, chalk. *Rec*: Music. *a*: 14 High View Close, Norwood, S.E.19. *t*: Liv 3252.

MARTIN, Rev. Edward Osborn, M.C., H.C.F. *Publ*: The Gods of India. *c.t*: Various. *a*: 16 Waterloo Cres, Dover.

MARTIN, Eric. *n.a*: Cricket Corr Daily Herald. *a*: 67 Long Acre, W.C.2.

MARTIN, Ernest Walter. *b*: Devon 1914. *e*: Shebbear Coll & Seale Hayne Coll & Priv. *m* Elisabeth-Editha Frances Mallendaine. Author, Critic, Editor. *n.a*:

English Ed Semaphore. *Publ*: Heritage of the West; Parade of Time; In Search of Faith; The New Spirit; Country Miscellany. *Ctr*: Mod Reading, Transformation, John o' Londons, etc. *s.s*: Criticism, Philosophy, Broadcasting. *a*: Editha Cott, Black Torrington, Beaworthy, Devon.

MARTIN, Francis Harold. Reporter. *a*: Evening Post, Bristol.

MARTIN, Geoffrey. *b*: Leicester 1914. *e*: Barnsley G.S. Journalist. *n.a*: Barnsley Chron '31–. *s.s*: Dramatic criticism, humour. *Rec*: Angling, tennis. *a*: 21 Walton St, Barnsley.

MARTIN, Rev. George Currie, M.A. B.D.(Edin). *b*: Edin 1865. *e*: George Watson's Edin, Knox Inst Haddington, Edin Univ & N.C.L. *m*: (1) Mary A. Leslie; (2) Evelyn Archer. *d*: 1. Cong Min, Prof & Lecturer. *Publ*: The Church & the Hymn Writers; The Story of the Adult School Movement, etc. *c.t*: Dictionary of the Bible, Expository Times, Bookman, Christian World, etc. *s.s*: Greek Testament, Dante & China. Hon Sec of R.L.S. Club (Lon), Mem Counc of China Soc, Lecturer to Adult Sc Union 1912–32. *Rec*: Trav, music & microscope. *c*: P.E.N. & Y.M.C.A. Nat Comms. *a*: 30 Ambrose Av, N.W.11. *t*: Speedwell 6101.

MARTIN, Harry Brownlow. *b*: Salem Illinois 1878. *e*: Vincennes Univ. *m*: Susie F. Flanders. *s*: 1. *d*: 1. Artist & Writer. *n.a*: N.Y. American 1903, Ev Globe '16, Ed & Publisher The Metropolitan Golfer '23–30. *Publ*: Fifty Years of American Golf; Golf Yarns; Pictorial Golf; What's Wrong With Your Game; Great Golfers in the Making; How to Play Golf; Golf Made Easy; Tips on Golf. *Ctr*: N.Y. American, N.Y. World, N.Y. Globe, N.Y. Times. *s.s*: Golf, Trees. *Rec*: Golf, chess, bridge, sketching, trees. *a*: 143 East 39th St, New York, N.Y., U.S.A.

MARTIN, Henry Charles. *b*: Gravesend. Journalist. *c.t*: Princ Lon & Provincial n/ps. *s.s*: Local gov, ecclesiastical, gen research statistics. Took an active part in securing for E. Ham a Charter of Inc as a County Borough. Mem of Gen Advisory Cmt, Chm of the Charter Fin Cmmt. Mem of the Charter Legal Cmt, etc. *a*: Elm View, Woodford Green, Essex. *t*: Buckhurst 2308.

MARTIN, Herbert Henry. *b*: Norwich 1881. Secretary. *n.a*: Ed Lord's Day Mag. Ed Happy Greetings. *Publ*: The Royal Way; Shall Britain Copy the Continental Sunday?; Key to Happiness; The Happy Man, etc. *c.t*: Daily Express, Tit-Bits, Free Churchman, Sentinel, etc. *s.s*: Church Attendance campaign. *a*: 22 Red Lion Sq, W.C.1. *t*: Chancery 7588.

MARTIN, Hubert, C.B.E. *b*: Lon 1879. *e*: Priv & King's Col Lon. Chief Passport Officer, Foreign Office. *Publ*: Scouting in Other Lands; Adventures in the Wide World of Scouting. *c.t*: Various. *s.s*: Scouts, travel. International Comm Boy Scouts Assoc '17–. Hon Dir Boy Scouts Internat Bureau 1920–. *Rec*: Camping. *c*: St James's, Anglo-Belgian Union, Anglo-Danish Soc, Anglo-Batavian Soc, Anglo-Baltic Soc. *a*: 21 Down St, W.1. *t*: Mayfair 5880.

MARTIN, Rev. Hugh, M.A., Hon.D.D. *b*: Glasgow 1890. *e*: Glas Acad, Roy Tech Coll Glas, Glas Univ, Glas Baptist Coll, Trin Coll Glas. *m*: Dorothy Greenwood. *s*: 2. Baptist Minister, Man Dir & Ed S.C.M. Press Ltd, Chrm Nat Exec C.O.P.E.C. 1920–24, Hon Treas World's Student Christian Fed '28–35, Min of Inform (Dir Religious Div) '39–43, Chrm Administrative Comm Brit Counc of Churches. *Publ*: Christian Reunion; The Parables of the Gospels; The Meanings of the Old Testament; Christ & Money; The Kingdom without Frontiers; Morality on Trial; Great Christian Books. *s.s*: Christian Reunion & Inter-Church Relationships. *Rec*: Gardening. *c*: Athenæum. *a*: 56 Bloomsbury St, London, W.C.1. *T*: Museum 3841.

MARTIN, Lt.-Col. Hugh Gray, D.S.O., O.B.E., F.R.G.S. *b*: Dumbartonshire 1887. *e*: Marlboro' Col & R.M.A. Staff Col. *m*: Lorna Ffrench-Mullen. *d*: 1. Army Officer. *c.t*: Blackwood's Mag, Cornhill, Chambers's Journ, etc. *s.s*: Fiction. *Rec*: Fishing, hunting. *c*: Army & Navy, Roy Geog Soc, Roy Cent Asia Soc, Himalayan Club. *a*: Ladysmith Hse, Longmoor, Liss, Hants. *t*: Blackmoor 22.

MARTIN, J. P., M.A., M.D., F.R.C.P.(Lon). *c.t*: Med Journs. Phys Nat Hosp for Nervous Diseases, etc. *a*: 9 Harley St, W.1.

MARTIN, James Sackville. M.D., M.R.C.S. *b*: Portlaw, Co Waterford, Ireland 1874. *e*: Sheffield Gr Sch, Edin Univ. *m*: Florence Amy Lorne Gladwell. Mem B.M.A. & Soc of Authors. *Publ*: Cupid and the Styx (Play); Idle Hours; Adventure (Play); A Garnered Sheaf. *Ctr*: Cornhill, Temple Bar, Sketch, Strand, Graphic, etc. *Rec*: Golf. *w.s*: R.A.M.C. 1914–16. *a*: Imtarfa, 73 Hillsboro Rd, Bognor Regis.

MARTIN, John Hanbury. *b*: Ledbury 1892. *e*: Oxford. M.P. Central Southwark (L) since 1940. *n.a*: Ed Challenge 1920–22. *Publ*: Corner of England, Peace Adventure. *Ctr*: Survey of Life & Labour in London 1931–35, Fortnightly Review, Contemporary Review, Week-End Review, etc. *s.s*: Social Conditions esp in poorer London, Housing, Foreign Questions. *w.s*: 1914–19. *a*: 24 Chester St, London, S.W.1.

MARTIN, John Middleton, M.D. *b*: Exeter 1870. *e*: Exeter Sc, Peterhouse Cam & U.C. Hosp Lon. *m*: Louisa Margaret Rolfe. *d*: 1. M.O.H. Glos. *c.t*: Prof papers. *s.s*: Publ health. *a*: Shire Hall, Glos. *t*: 2848.

MARTIN, Joseph Bryan. *b*: Grantham 1873. *m*: Florence B. Moore. Journalist. *n.a*: Nott'm Guardian, Scarboro' '94, connected with Scarboro' Post (defunct), Scarboro' Evening News & other local papers; now F.L. rep P.A. Daily Express, Daily Telegraph. Shorthand writer for Bankruptcy Ct. Fell M.J.I. *c*: Masonic & Const, Scarboro'. *a*: Oakdene, Manor Av, Scarboro'. *t*: 1674.

MARTIN, Lawrence, A.M., Ph.D. *b*: Stockbridge, Mass 1880. *e*: Cornell & Harvard Univs. *m*: Laura Hatch Martins. *d*: 3. Geographer. *n.a*: Ctr Ed Geog Review 1922–48, Assoc Ed Bulletin Amer Geog Soc '10–15, Assoc Ed Journ of Geog '09–16. *Publ*: Alaska Glacier Studies; College Physiography; Physical Geography of Wisconsin; Antarctica Discovered by a Connecticut Yankee; U.S. Constitution Sesquicentennial Maps; Disturnell's Map; etc. *Ctr*: Chic Trib, Colliers, Lit Digest, Rev of Reviews, etc. *s.s*: Geog Maps, Glacial Geology, Internat Boundary. *a*: 3126 38th St, N.W., Washington 16, D.C., U.S.A. *T*: Ordway 4606.

MARTIN, Leonard Cyril, B.Litt., M.A. *b*: Leyton 1886. *e*: Chigwell & Keble Coll Oxf. *m*: Dorothy Mary Martin. Prof of Eng Lit L'pool Univ. *Publ*: The Works of Henry Vaughan; The Poems of Richard Crashaw; Marlowe's Poems; etc. *c*: Univ (L'pool). *a*: The University, Liverpool. *T*: Royal 6301.

MARTIN, Mary Ellen Rodd. *b*: Dawlish 1857. *e*: Malvern Wells. *Publ*: A King's Worker in Burma; Trans of La Femme dans l'Inde Antique (by Mlle Clarisse Bader). *c.t*: Asiatic Review, Indian Mag & Review, etc. Nat Counc of Women. *a*: 2a Schubert Rd, Putney, S.W.15.

MARTIN, Percival William. *b*: Lon 1893. *e*: Aske's (Haberdasher's) Sc, Columbia Univ. Married. I.L.O. Official. *Publ*: The Flaw in the Price System; The Limited Market; Unemployment & Purchasing Power; The Problem of Maintaining Purchasing Power. *s.s*: Monetary, lab & internat questions. *a*: 12 Rue Carteret, Geneva, Switzerland. *t*: 24927.

MARTIN, Percy F., F.R.G.S. *b*: Lon 1861. *e*: Lon Univ. Journalist & Author. *n.a*: Special Corr (S. Africa) Financial Times '90, Glas Herald (Aust) '96, Financial News (Amer) '06, Special Comm of The Engineer (S. & C. Amer) '09—12, The Times (Mexico & India) '07—08, Special Corr The Pall Mall Gazette (nr East) '11—12, Special Comm of The Times (Lyons Fair) '19, Ed of S. American Page of Financial Times '18—20, Reuter's Corr '22—33, Corr of the Times (Spain) '24, Special Corr The Journ of Commerce (N.Y.) '24—33. *Publ*: Through Five Republics of South America ('05); Mexico of the XXth Century ('08); Greece of the XXth Century; Maximilian in Mexico; The Sudan in Evolution; Egypt Old & New ('23); etc. *s.s*: Commerce, Latin Amer commerce. Ret from active work '33. *Rec*: Trav. *a*: c/o Coutts & Co, 440 Strand, W.C.

MARTIN, Philippa, M.S., F.R.C.S. Ophthalmic Surg. *c.t*: Med Journs. *a*: 40 Wimpole St, W.1. *t*: Euston 2122.

MARTIN, Thomas, M.Sc. *b*: Norwood 1893. *e*: Alleyns Sch, Univ Coll Lond. *m*: Dorothy Sylvia Vernon. *s*: 2. Gen Sec Roy Inst since 1929, Chmn Film Sub Commsn Unesco Commsn on Tech needs '47. *n.a*: Ed Journ of Scientific Instruments 1928—29. *Publ*: Faraday; Ed Faraday's Diary. *Ctr*: Various Scientific journs. *c*: Athenæum & Savile. *w.s*: R.A. 1914—19, '39—45. *a*: Royal Institution, 21 Albemarle St, London, W.1.

MARTIN, Rev. Thomas Johns. *b*: Eskdale 1875. *m*: Mary E. Murray. *s*: 1. *d*: 2. Meth Min. *s.s*: Internat affairs & science. *a*: 14 Yarburgh St, Whalley Range, M/C 16.

MARTIN, Thomas Muirhead, M.D., M.B., C.M., L.R.C.P. & S.E., L.F.P.S.G., F.R.S.M. *b*: Lanarks. *e*: Hamilton Acad, George Watson's Col Edin & Edin Univ. *m*: Margaret Munro Ramsay. *s*: 2. *n.a*: Neurologist Min of Pensions, Phys Board of Control '31 (Mental Deficiency Act). *Publ*: Pocket Notes on Nerves; Infantile Diarrhœa. *c.t*: Med papers. *s.s*: Neurology & psychology. Late Maj R.A.M.C. *Rec*: Golf. *a*: Northolme, Upper Clapton, N. & 51 Harley St, W.1. *t*: Clissold 1354 & Langham 2551.

MARTIN, Timothy Stuart, F.R.S.A., M.R.S.T., F.C.I.A.D. *b*: Bolsover, Derbyshire 1908. *e*: Chesterfield Sch of Art, Chesterfield Tech Coll, Univ Coll, Coll of Art Nottingham. *m*: Ann Johnson. *s*: 1. *d*: 1. Arts & Crafts Master Queen Elizabeth's Boys' Gr Sch Mansfield. *n.a*: Ed Boys Practical Aid 1937—. *Ctr*: English Mechanics, The Parthenon, Illustrated Carpenter & Builder, The Householder, Building Times, Nottingham Journ, Derbyshire Times, Western Morning News, Derbyshire Countryside. *s.s*: Woodwork, Metalwork, Illustrated Archæological Articles. *Rec*: Philately, typography layout & design. *c*: Constitutional. *a*: Westwood, Chesterfield Rd South, Mansfield, Notts.

MARTIN, W. *a*: 1037 Middleton Road, Oldham.

MARTIN, W. A. Gibson, F.R.G.S. Author, Journalist, Lecturer, Traveller, Commissioned to Lecture by Brit Admlty in Middle East & Brit Council in Europe. *n.a*: Motoring Corresp, Furnishing & Decorating Corresp to Tech Publs. *Publ*: Ship Furnishing & Decoration; Furnishing Handbook; Narrow Fabrics; Venetian Blinds; Ships; Hangings & Carpets; Book of the Rover, Hillman Minx, Wolseley; etc. *Ctr*: Times, Manch Guardian, Journ of Commerce, The Pianomaker, etc. *s.s*: Decoration, Plastics, Engineering, Colonial Developments. *Rec*: Golf, music, philately. *c*: Roy Empire, Lyceum L'pool. *a*: Whinmoor Ct, Sandfield Pk, Liverpool 12. *T*: Stoneycroft 1136.

MARTIN, WILHELM: director Royal Picture Gallery (The Hague), extraordinary professor at Leyden Univ.; b. Quakenbruck, June 20, 1876; educ. Lower Sch. and Gymnasium, Univ. of Leyden. DEGREES: Litt. D., Professor; m. Maria Cornelia Visser, Aug. 9, 1906. AUTHOR: Het Leven en de Werken van G. Dou, 1901; Gerard Dou, 1902; Gerard Dou, Klassiker der Kunst, 1902; Oudeschilderkunst in Nederland the Hague (2 vols.), 1910, 1911; Alt holländische Malerei (2 vols.), 1910, 1911; Albert Neuhuys, 1914; Catalogue raisonné du Musee Royal de Tableaux a' la traye, the Hague, 1914 (2nd edit. 1931); Alt Holländische Bilder, 1917 (2nd edit. 1921); Johannes Bosboom, the Hague (with G. Marius), 1917; Jan Steen, 1924, and many others. In preparation: first volume of a history of Dutch painting in the 17th Century. General character of writing: historical. As museum director chief work is in buying pictures, making catalogues, etc. As university professor, teaches the history of Christian art (painting, sculpture, architecture). Has taken part in arranging of many exhibitions of old Dutch art and in that of Burlington House, 1929. Has lectured on Dutch art in England, U. S. A. (at Harvard Univ.), Germany, Belgium, Ireland, Sweden, Denmark, etc. SOCIETIES: Member of Nieuwe Literaire Societeit, The Hague; Hon. Mem. Pulchri Studio, The Hague; hon. mem. Burlington Fine Arts Club (London). Religion, Protestant. OFFICE: Mauritshuis, The Hague. HOME: Wilhelminaplein 4, Wassenaar near The Hague, Holland.

MARTIN, William. B.Sc.(Otago), F.R.G.S. *b*: Fairfield, Otago, N.Z., 1886. *e*: Fairfield and Albany Scs, Dunedin Training Col and Otago Univ. *m*: Jeanie Calder Miller. *s*: 6. *d*: 1. School teacher. *n.a*: Ed of nature study and elementary science section of Nation Education '30—. *Publ*: Native Plants of Dunedin; The New Zealand Nature Book (Vols I & II); Vegetation of Marlborough, N.Z. *c.t*: Otago Daily Times, Marlborough Express. *s.s*: Botany and natural history, agriculture. *Rec*: Mountaineering, bowls. *c*: Hon Sec 1st N.Z. Inst Science Congress '19, Past Pres Otago Inst, Pres Blenheim Rotary Club, Pres Marlborough Branch N.Z. Educational Inst, Past Master Mason, Pres Dunedin Naturalists' Field Club. *a*: George St, Blenheim, New Zealand. *t*: 1541.

MARTIN, William Ernest Russell. *b*: Devonport 1867. *e*: Col Hse Saltash, & Cheveley Hall, Mannamead, Plymouth. *m*: Annie Josephine Langworthy Baker. *s*: 1 (dec). R.N. '83—1922. *n.a*: Special Corr for Daily Mail during Volcanic Eruptions at St Vincent & St Pierre, Martinque 1892, also during Trinidad Riots; Ed the Italian Mail (Florence) '26—29. *Publ*: Adventures of a Naval Paymaster ('24). *c.t*: Times, Western Morning News, Ypres Times, Sphere, etc. *s.s*: Photography, sketching. Brit Fascist, Pres Plymouth Br, Fell of Freedom & Reform. *Rec*: Sailing, golf. *a*: Mabruk, 4 Essa Rd, Saltash, Cornwall.

MARTIN, William Keble, M.A. *b*: Radley. *e*: Marlborough Col, Chr Ch Oxf. *m*: Violet Chaworth-Musters. *s*: 1. *d*: 2. Vicar of Torrington. *Publ*: A History of the Ancient Parish of Wath-on-Dearne. *s.s*: Archæ, botany. C.F. 1918. *a*: The Vicarage, Torrington. *t*: 107.

MARTIN-HURST, William, M.A., F.R.G.S. *b*: Manningham 1876. *e*: Marlboro', Giggleswick, France, Germany & Canada. *m*: Eda Mary Forrest. *s*: 2.

d: 2. Journalist. *n.a*: Reporter Montreal Herald '96, Special Writer Montreal Star '96-98, Ed Staff Daily Mail '98-1902, Trav Corr Bulgaria, Serbia, Greece, Russia, Turkey; Mang Ed Exclusive News Ag '04-. *Publ*: Book of Famille Rose ('25), with Dr G. C. Williamson. *c.t*: Nat Press, Brit & Foreign Geog & Educ Works & Ency's. *s.s*: Geog, foreign travel, Oriental ceramics. Writer on Oriental Ceramics of the Yung Cheng & Chi'en Lung Periods. Trav extensively in every European country, Nr East, N. Africa & N. America. *Rec*: Collecting rare porcelain, gastronomy. *c*: Authors'. *a*: The End Hse, Roehampton, S.W.15. *t*: Putnev 0363.

MARTIN-LEAKE, Hugh, Sc.D., O.N. *b*: Hadley, Middx 1878. *e*: Dulwich Coll, Christ Coll Camb. *m*: Millicent Frieda Bloxam. *s*: 2. Retired Indian Agriculture Service, Tech Advisor to the Egyptian Gov 1919, Tech Advisor to the Sudan Gov '23—24, Principal The Imperial Coll of Tech Agric '24—27. *n.a*: Agric Ed Internat Sugar Journ since 1945. *Publ*: Unity National & Imperial; Recent Advances in Agricultural Plant-Breeding; Land Tenure & Agricultural Production in the Tropics; The Foundation of Indian Agriculture; Studies in Tropical Land Tenure. *Ctr*: Numerous Arts in Scientific & Tech Journs. *s.s*: Economics, Practice of Agriculture (Tropical). *c*: Roy Empire. *a*: 10 Queen Ediths Way, Cambridge. *T*: 87371.

MARTINDALE, Rev. Cyril Charlie, M.A., S.J. *b*: London 1879. *e*: Harrow, Stonyhurst, Campion Hall Oxf. *Publ*: Lives of R. H. Benson; Fr Bernard Vaughan; Fr C. D. Plater; The Risen Sun; The Faith of the Roman Church; Vocation of Aloysius Gonzaga; The Mind of the Missal; African Angelus; Athens, Argentine, Australia; What Are Saints; Broadcast Sermons; The Words of the Missal. *s.s*: Hist of Religions, etc. *c*: Un Univ. *a*: 114 Mount St, London, W.1. *T*: Grosvenor 1608.

MARTINDALE, Hilda, C.B.E. *b*: London 1875. *e*: Brighton Hgh Sch for Girls, Roy Holloway Coll Englefield Green, Bedford Coll for Women. Retired Civil Servant, Tech Advis to Brit Gov Del to the Internat Lab Conferences Geneva. *Publ*: From One Generation to Another; Women Servants of the State. *s.s*: The Civil Service, Industrial & Social Questions, Care of the Homeless Child. *Rec*: Travelling, needlework. *c*: Univ Woman's. *a*: 44 Cleherne Ct, London, S.W.5. *T*: Frobisher 6796.

MARTINDALE, Louisa, C.B.E., J.P., M.D., B.S. (Lon), F.C.O.G., F.R.S.M. *e*: Roy Holloway Col, & L.S.M.W. Gynæ Surgeon. Hon Snr Surg New Sussex Hosp Brighton. Hon Surg Marie Curie Hosp Lon. *Publ*: The Woman Doctor & Her Future; Under the Surface. *c.t*: Lancet, B.M.J., Enyc Medica, Edin Med Journ, etc. *s.s*: Abdominal surgery. *c*: Ex-Pres Med Women's Fed, Vice-Pres Med Women's Internat Assoc. *a*: 25 Manchester Sq, W.1. & Little Rystwood, Forest Row, Sussex. *t*: Welbeck 1518.

MARTINEK, Frank Victor. *b*: Chicago, Ill 1895. *e*: Healy Sch, Fort Dearborn Business Coll, Institute of Fine Arts Chicago. *m*: Clara Gault Powell. Asst Vice Pres Standard Oil Coy of Indiana, Creator of Don Winslow of the Navy newsp adventure strip. *Publ*: Gasoline Tax Evasion & Other Rackets in the Oil Business; Don Winslow in Ceylon; Don Winslow Secret Code Book; Know Your Man; Don Winslow of the Navy; Don Winslow Face to Face with the Scorpion; Don Winslow Breaks the Spy Net; Don Winslow Saves the Secret Formula; Don Winslow & the Scorpion's Stronghold; Series of Don Winslow Big Little Books. *Ctr*: Numerous papers in U.S.A. & foreign countries; *s.s*: Criminology, Scientific Crime Detection. *Rec*. Golf. *c*: South Shore Country, Westerners (Chicago). *a*: 4940 East End Ave, Chicago 15, Illinois, U.S.A. *T*: Harrison 9200.

MARTINEZ, VARGAS ANDRES: Professor of Diseases of Children in Univ. of Barcelona; *b*. Barbastro, Huesca, Spain, Oct. 27, 1861; *s*. of Andres Martinez Burrel and Carlota Vargas La-torre; educ. College of Medicine (Barcelona); Hospital of the Red Cross (Barcelona); Director and Professor of the Nurses. DEGREE: M.D.; *m*. Angela Mariana Frau (died). AUTHOR: Tratado de Pediatria, 1914; Mi Visita al Frente Francés, 1918; Manual de las Damas Enfemeras de la Cruz Roja; La Salud del Nino. Has published many articles and pamphlets. Editor and owner: La Medicina de Los Ninos, founded in 1900. Contributes to different magazines in Spain and foreign countries, also to some newspapers. General character of writing: medical, technical, social. Former Dean of Faculty of Medicine, and former Rector of the Univ. of Barcelona; Ex-Senator of the Kingdom of Spain; former President of Royal Academy of Medicine; founder of Instituto Nipiologice Martinez Vargas of Barbastro, 1916; founder of the School of Puericultura; Pres. of Society of Spanish Pediatrics; dir. Hospital of the Red Cross; professor of the nurses of the Red Cross. CLUBS: Circulo Ecuestre, Centro Cultural del Ejército y Armada. Religion: Roman Catholic. HOME: Travesera, 96—98, Hotel, Barcelona, Spain.

MARTINEZ-DELGADO, Luis. *b*: Bogota, Colombia 1896. *e*: Coll of the Jesuits Bachillerato Bogota, London & Paris. *m*: Alina Delgado de Martinez Delgado. Writer. *Publ*: Historia Politica de Colombia; Geografia de Colombia; Apuntes Historico-biograficos; Hacia Berruecos; Historia del Minasterio de Carmelitas Descalzas de Bogota 1609—1947; etc. *Ctr*: El Siglo, Revista Literaria, El Tiempo, etc. *s.s*: History, Political Writings. *a*: Apartado (Box) 505, Carrera 16 A.No.46-21-Bogota, Republic de Colombia, S.A. *T*: 16-83 Chap.

MARTINO, PIERRE: professor of French Literature in Univ. at Alger; *b*. Clermont-Ferrand, France, June, 1880. AUTHOR: L'Orient dans la littérature française au XVIIe et au XVIIe siècles, 1906; Etudes sur Fromentin, 1910-1914; Le roman réaliste sous le second empire, 1913; Stendhal, 1914; Jules Lemaître à Alger, 1919; Le Naturalisme française, 1923; Le Second Empire dans l'Histoire de la littérature français illustrée de J. Bédier et P. Hazard, 1924; Verlaine, 1924; Parnasse et Symbolisme, 1925. Editor: Racine and Shakespeare (by Stendhal), with Introduction and Notes, 1925, 1928; La Pratique du Theatre (by L'Abbé d'Aubignac), with Introduction and Notes, 1927; La Chartreuse de Parme (by Stendhal), with Introduction and Notes, 1928; Le Theatre de Clara Gazul (by Mérimée), with Introduction and Notes, 1929. Collaborator on: A la Revue de littérature Comparée; A la Revue Critique; A la Revue d'Histoire littéraire de la France, etc. HOME: 131 rue Michelet, Alger, Algeria, No. Africa.

MARTINSEN, Aamodt M. *b*: Norway 1893. Married. *s*: 1. *d*: 1. Lon Corr The Norwegian Journ of Commerce & Shipping, Oslo. *n.a*: Nya Dagligt Allehanda, Stockholm, etc. *c.t*: Eng & foreign press. *a*: 5 Clarence Rd, N.W.6. & Norway Hse, Trafalgar Sq, S.W. *t*: Maida Vale 5675.

MARTINSON, Helga Maria. *b*: Vardnas 1890. *s*: 5. Author. *Publ*: Kvinnor och Appeltrad; Ragvakt; Mor Giffer jig; Kurkbrollop; Kungens rosor; Motsols; Armin vid Horisonten; etc. *Ctr*: Fib, Vi, Workers Press. *c*: P.E.N. *a*: Osmo, Sweden.

MARTYN, Oliver. *Publ*: The Body in the Pound. *a*: c/o A. M. Heath & Co Ltd, Princes Hse, Jermyn St, London, S.W.1.

MARTYN, Wyndham. Author. *Publ*: Death by the Lake; Anthony Trent, Master Criminal; Christopher Bond; Adventurer; The Great Ling Plot; Scarlet, Murder; The Social Storming; The Trent Trail; etc. *a*: c/o H. Jenkins Ltd, 3 York St, James's St, S.W.1.

MARVELL, Holt. See **Maschwitz, Eric.**

MARVIN, Francis Sydney, M.A., F.R.HistS. *b*: Lon 1863. *e*: Merchant Taylors' Sc & St John's Col Oxf. *m*: Edith Mary Deverell. *s*: 2. Late Staff Insp (Bd of Educ). Prof Modern Hist, Univ of Egypt 1929–30. *Publ*: The Living Past; The Modern World; The Nation at School ('33); etc. *c.t*: Contemporary Review, Hibbert Journ, M/C Guardian, etc. *s.s*: Hist, educ. Extensive travel as lect. *Rec*: Tennis, music. *c*: Nat Lib. *a*: Guessens Ct, Welwyn Garden City. *t*: 379.

MARWICK, Hugh, O.B.E., M.A., D.Litt.(Edin). *b*: Rousay, Orkney 1881. *e*: Edin Univ. *m*: Jane Barritt. Dir of Educ for Orkney (ret), Chevalier (1st Class) of Norwegian Order of St Olaf. *Publ*: The Orkney Norn; Merchant Lairds of Long Ago; The Place-Names of Rousay. *Ctr*: Proc of Orkney Antiquarian Soc. *s.s*: Orkney Dialect & Place-Names. *a*: Alton, Kirkwall, Orkney. *T*: Kirkwall 61.

MARYON, Herbert. *b*: London 1874. *e*: Lower Sch of John Lyon, Harrow. *m*: Muriel D. Wood. *s*: 1. *d*: 2. Master of Sculpture & Lecturer in the Hist of Art King's Coll (Dur Univ) (ret). *Publ*: Metalwork & Enamelling; Modern Sculpture. *Ctr*: Journ Soc of Antiquaries, Tech Studies in the Fine Arts, Yale, Goldsmiths Journ, etc. *s.s*: Metalworking, Technical Methods of workers of all ages & countries, History of Sculpture. *Rec*: Archæology, travel. *a*: British Museum, London, W.C.1.

MARYON-WILSON, The Rev. Sir (George) Percy (Maryon), 12th Baronet of East Borne. *b*: London 1898. *e*: Eton Coll, Magdalen Coll Oxf. Priest, Rector of Christ Church St Leonards-on-Sea, Vice-Pres St Pancras Housing Soc Ltd, formerly Military aide-de-camp to the Gov-Gen of Sth Africa. *Publ*: Whom the Lord hath redeemed; Some Common Obstacles to Faith; Caritas Christi; In Whose Heart are Thy Ways; Advent to Easter. *Ctr*: Dict of Nat Biography, Westminster Gaz. *s.s*: Religion. *Rec*: Squash racquets. *a*: Christ Church Rectory, St Leonards-on-Sea, & Reform Club, London, S.W.1. *T*: Hastings 2513.

MASANI, Minoo, B.A., LL.B. *b*: Bombay 1905. *e*: Bombay & London. *m*: Shakuntala Srivastava. Secretary Public Relations Dept Tata Sons Ltd, Barrister, Mayor of Bombay 1943—44. *n.a*: Asst Ed Dly Sun 1934. *Publ*: Our India; Picture of a Plan; Your Food; Socialism Reconsidered; India's Constitution at Work (collab). *s.s*: Econs, Politics, Internat Affairs, Socialism, Communism & India. *a*: Bombay Hse, Bruce St, Bombay 1, India. *T*: 45107.

MASCALL, Rev. Eric Lionel, M.A., D.D., B.Sc. *b*: Sydenham, Kent 1905. *e*: Latymer Upper Sch H'smith, Pembroke Coll Camb, Theo Coll Ely. Clerk in Holy Orders, Student & Tutor of Christ Church, Ed Sec Central Soc of Sacred Study 1945—, formerly Ed of Sobornost, formerly Scholar of Pembroke Coll Camb '24—28, Wrangler in Mathematical Tripos '27, Sub-warden of Scholæ Cancellarii Lincoln '37—45. *Publ*: He Who Is: A Study in Traditional Theism; Christ the Christian & the Church; A Guide to Mount Carmel; Man, his Origin & Destiny; The God-Man; The Church of God; An Anglo-Russian Symposium (Ed). *Ctr*: Times Lit Supp, Theology, Jour of Theo Studies, etc. *s.s*: Theology & Philosophy. *a*: Christ Church, Oxford. *T*: 2745.

MASCALL, William Neville, M.A.(Cantab), M.R.C.S., L.R.C.P. *b*: Middlesbro' 1902. *e*: Wycliffe Col, Stonehouse, Glos & Pembroke Coll, Cam. M.O., L.C.C. *c.t*: B.M.J., Lancet, etc. *s.s*: Venereology. Asst M.O. County Boro' of Rotherham. Chief Asst L.C.C. Whitechapel Clinic. *a*: 43 Q. Anne St, W.1. *t*: Welbeck 6988.

MASCARO, Juan, M.A., M.R.S.L. *b*: Majorca. *e*: Priv, Palma, Camb Univ. V-Princ Paramesvara Coll Ceylon, Dir English Studies Barcelona Univ 1933—37. *Publ*: Himalayas of the Soul: trans from the Sanskrit of several Upanishads. *Ctr*: Camb Rev, Ind Art & Letters. *s.s*: Literary Trans from the Sanskrit. *Rec*: Walking & watching nature. *a*: The Retreat, Comberton, Cambridge.

MASCHWITZ, Eric, O.B.E. *b*: Birmingham 1901. *e*: Repton Sch, Gonville & Caius Coll Camb. *m*: (1) Hermione Gingold, (2) Phyllis Gordon. B.B.C. 1926—37. *Publ*: (Plays) Gay Hussar; Balalaika; Magyar Melody; Waltz Without End; Good Night Vienna; (Revues) New Faces; Between Ourselves; (Films) Good Night Vienna; Balalaika; Goodbye Mr Chips; The True Glory; (Songs) These Foolish Things; A Nightingale Sang in Berkeley Square; Room 504. *Rec*: Music, lawn tennis, theatre-going. *c*: Savile, Camb Univ. *w.s*: Lt-Col Intelligence Corps, Chief Broadcasting Officer 21 A.G. World War II. *a*: 69 Brook St, London, W.1.

MASEFIELD, John. O.M., Hon.D.Litt(Oxon). *b*: Ledbury 1878. *e*: King's Sch Warwick & Training Ship Conway. Sailor, Poet, Playwright, Novelist, Poet Laureate since 1930. *Publ*: The Everlasting Mercy; Dauber; The Conway; St George & the Dragon; The Old Front Line; Gallipoli; Recent Prose; A Mainsail Haul; A Tarpaulin Muster; Multitude & Solitude; The Widow in the Bye-Street; Daffodil Fields; Lollingdon Downs; Reynard the Fox; Sard Harker; Odtaa; The Midnight Folk; Philip the King; The Tragedy of Pompey the Great; The Tragedy of Nan; Captain Margaret; Salt Water Ballads; Melloney Hotspur; The Wanderer of Liverpool; Thanks Before Going; New Chum; In the Mill; Dead Ned; Live & Kicking Ned; Eggs & Baker; The Country Scene; etc; (Plays) The Tragedy of Pompey the Great; The Tragedy of Nan; etc. *a*: Abingdon, Berks.

MASEFIELD, Peter Gordon, M.A., F.R.Ae.S., M.I.Ae.S., G.I.Mech.E. *b*: Trentham, Staffs 1914. *e*: Westminster Sch, Chillon Coll Switzerland, Jesus Coll Camb. *m*: Patricia Doreen Rooney. *s*: 2. *d*: 1. Aeronautical Eng, Dir Gen of Long Term Planning Min of Civil Aviation 1946—. *n.a*: Asst Tech Ed The Aeroplane 1937—39, Tech Ed '39—43, Air Corr Sun Times '40—43, Founder & Ed The Aeroplane Spotter & The Official Journ on Aircraft Recognition '41—43, Aviation Commentator B.B.C. & Newsweek (U.S.A.) '42—43, Air Corr North American Newsp Alliance '41—43. *Ctr*: Aeroplane, Sun Times, N.A.N.A. (New York), Aeroplane Spotter, Newsweek (New York). *s.s*: Aeronautics. *Rec*: Flying, motoring, swimming, squash racquets. *c*: Roy Aero, R.A.C., Aero Club of Washington D.C. *a*: Warley Lodge, Denton Rd, Eastbourne, Sussex. *T*: 1650.

MASH, A. E. *b*: London 1908. P.R.O. Rootes Securities. *n.a*: Dly Express, Dir of Public Relations, Min of Aircraft Production. *a*: 10 Roehampton Gate, London, S.W.15. *T*: Prospect 1449.

MASKE. John. *b*: Hove. *e*: Priv. Novelist. *Publ*: The Dinard Mystery; The Saint-Malo Mystery; The Cherbourg Mystery; Ghost of a Cardinal. *a*: c/o Messrs Curtis Brown Ltd, 6 Henrietta St, Covent Gdn. W.C.2.

MASKELL, Henry Parr. *b*: Lon 1865. *e*: Merchant Taylors' & Cranbrook Scs, & London Univ. Journalist. *n.a*: Various Tech Journals, on Ed Staff C. A. Pearson Ltd 1915—34. *Publ*: New Wheels in Old Ruts (1896); Hints on Building a Church; The Soul of Picardy; The Signs & the Planets (1931); The Human Wireless ('34); etc. *c.t*: Tech & religious publs. *s.s*: Photography, inns. *Rec*: Gardening, wayfaring. *a*: 19 Berriedale Drive, Sompting, Sussex.

MAS MARI, Ramon. *b*: Tortosa, Spain 1894. *e*: Barcelona Spain. *m*: Joan Morgan. *s*: 2. Mycologist, Acting Consul General for Spain. *Publ*: Mushroom Growing, Insects & Diseases. *s.s*: Mycology. *Rec*: Travelling, reading, nat hist. *a*: 35 Rosedale Rd, Gordon, N.S.W., Australia. *T*: J.X. 4419 & B. 2575.

MASON, Alfred E. W. Hon Fell Trin Coll Oxf. *Publ*: A Romance of Wastdale; The Courtship of Morrice Buckler; The Philanderers; Parson Kelly (collab); Lawrence Clavering; The Watchers; Clementina; Ensign Knightley; Colonel Smith; The Four Feathers; The Truants; Running Water; The Broken Road; Miranda of the Balcony; The House of the Arrow; No Other Tiger; The Prisoner in the Opal; The Dean's Elbow; The Witness for the Defence; Open Windows; At the Villa Rose; The Turnstile; The Four Corners of the World; The Summons; The Winding Stair; The Three Gentlemen; The Sapphire; The Life of Sir George Alexander; Dilemmas (short stories); They Wouldn't be Chessmen; Fire over England; The Drum (film); Konigsmark; The Life of Francis Drake;. Musk & Amber; The House in Lordship Lane; etc *a*: 51 South St, London, W.1. *T*: Mayfair 2812.

MASON, Arthur. *b*: Strangford, Co Down, Ireland 1876. *e*: Rural Sch. *d*: 1. Retired Sea Captain & Writer. *Publ*: The Wee Men of Ballywooden; From the Horn of the Moon; The Flying Bo'sun; Wide Seas & Many Lands; Come Easy Go Easy; Swansea Dan; The Roving Lobster; The Cook & the Captain Bold; The Fossil Fountain. *Ctr*: Atlantic Monthly, American, Red Book. *s.s*: Sailing Ship Stories, Fantasy, Children's Stories, Personal Adventure, Gold Hunting in Nevada. *a*: Oak Ridge Rd, Mt Kisco, N.Y., U.S.A. *T*: Mt Kisco 6263.

MASON, Bernard Sterling, A.B., Ph.D. *b*: Warren, Michigan 1896. *e*: Ohio State & Michigan Univs. Writer, Camp Dir. *n.a* = Ed The Camping Mag 1935—42. *Publ*: Woodcraft; The Junior Book of Camping & Woodcraft; The Book for Junior Woodsmen; The Book of Indian-Crafts & Costumes; Dances & Stories of the American Indians; Cabins, Cottages & Summer Homes; Camping & Education; (Collab) The Theory of Play; Active Games & Contests; Social Games for Recreation; etc. *Ctr*: Various. *s.s*: Woodcraft, Campcraft, Games & Recreations, Indian Dancing & Lore, Cowboy Skills. *Rec*: Camping. *a*: 2530 Salem Ave, Cincinnati, Ohio, U.S.A. *T*: East 2133.

MASON, Cecil. Chief Reporter. *s.s*: Amateur drama, rugby league football. *a*: Wigan Examiner, Public Hall, King St, Wigan.

MASON, D. M., M.P., A.I.B. *b*: Campsie 1865. *e*: Scotland, Germany. *m*: Mary Crouse. *s*: 2. *d*: 5. *Publ*: Six Yrs of Politics, Monetary Policy 1914—28. *s.s*: Finance, currency. Reported to French Govn on Stabilization of Franc, etc. *Rec*: Shooting, fishing, golf. *c*: Reform. Bath. *a*: 34 Queen's Gate Gdns, S.W.7. *t*: Western 0099.

MASON, F. Van Wyck, B.S. *b*: Boston, Mass 1901. *e*: Berkshire Sch & Harvard Coll. *m*: Dorothy Louise Macready. *s*: 2. Novelist. *Publ*: Three Harbours; Stars on the Sea; Rivers of Glory; Eagle in the Sky; Fighting Americans; etc. *Ctr*: Writer Mag. *s.s*: Early American & British History. *Rec*: Shooting, polo, fishing, sailing. *c*: Harvard (N.Y.), Maryland(Baltimore), Army & Navy (Washington, D.C.). *a*: Gunner's Ridge, Riderwood, Maryland. U.S.A.

MASON, Harvey Hope. *b*: India 1866. *e*: Priv. *m*: Marion May Thorp. *s*: 1. *d*: 4. Journalist & Publisher. *c.t*: Various trade & tech journs Eng, Aust, & Amer, Nature & Health Monthly Mag. *s.s*: Fruit, flowers & vegetables. Mem of Legion of Frontiersmen. *Rec*: Horticulture & music. *a*: 1 Mitre Ct, Temple, E.C.4. *t*: Central 1862.

MASON, Hugh Churchill. *b*: Truro, 1873. *e*: Scs and cols in South Africa. Retired civil engineer. *n.a*: Ed, Burghersdorp Albert Times, 1900—01. *Publ*: The Golden Mean; The Inner Court; The Devil's Christmas Box; Adventures in Religion. *c.t*: South African papers and jnls, proceedings of scientific socs, Jnl of Astonomical Soc of S.A., Proceedings of S.A. Soc of Civil Engineers, Proc of the S.A. Assoc for Advancement of Science. *s.s*: Religious philosophy, astronomy, civil engineering, socialism. *Rec*: Walking, travelling. Boer War service. 26 y as civil engineer to Durban & Cape Town municipality. Travelled in Africa, the Near East and the Soviet Union '33. *c*: Hon Treas Hundred New Towns Assoc (London). *a*: c/o Standard Bank of South Africa, 10 Clements Lne, Lombard St, E.C.4.

MASON, J. Alden, A.B., Ph.D. *b*: Philadelphia, Penn 1885. *e*: Central Hgh Sch Phila, Univs of Pennsylvania & Calif. *m*: Florence Roberts. *s*: 1. Anthropologist, Curator, American Sect Univ Museum Univ of Penna, Phila, U.S.A. *n.a*: Ed American Anthropologist 1945—, Ed Panamericanismo '44—. *Ctr*: American Anthropologist, Amer Antiquity, Journ of Amer Folklore, Nat Geog Mag, Nat Hist, Scientific American, Geog Review, etc. *s.s*: Anthropology of America & Hispano-America. *Rec*: Gardening, tennis. *a*: Conestoga Rd, Berwyn, Pennsylvania, U.S.A. *T*: Berwyn 0246.

MASON, John. *b*: Lon 1867. *e*: Elem Sc & Priv. *m*: Jane Foster. *d*: 2. *n.a*: Mem of Official Rep Staff of House of Commons for 20 yrs. *s.s*: Labour politics. *Rec*: Walking. *a*: 148 Wightman Rd, Hornsey N.8.

MASON, Kenneth, M.C., F.R.G.S. *b*: Sutton, Surrey 1887. *e*: Cheltenham Coll, Roy Mil Acad Woolwich. *m*: Dorothy Helen Robinson. *s*: 2. *d*: 1. Lt-Col R.E. (ret), Prof of Geography Univ of Oxf, Mem of Expeditions of Exploration & Survey, Chinese Pamirs, Headwaters of Yaskand River. *n.a*: Founder & Hon Ed Himalayan Journal 1929—42. *Publ*: Several on Survey of India, Admiralty Geographical Handbook. *Ctr*: Himalayan Mag, Alpine Journ, Himalayan Journ. *s.s*: Geographical subjects, Travel. *c*: Alpine, Himalayan. *a*: 1 Belbroughton Rd, Oxford. *T*: Oxford 58158.

MASON, L. R. Mang Machinery. *a*: High Holborn Hse, 52–54 High Holborn, W.C.1.

MASON, Madeline. *b*: New York 1915. *e*: Priv New York, England & France. *m*: Malcolm Forbes McKesson. Drug Manufacturer. *n.a*: Authorised for N.A.N.A. 1932—33. *Publ*: Hill Fragments; Riding for Texas; Le Prophete. *Ctr*: N.Y. Times, N.Y. Her Trib, N.Y. Sun, Wash Post, Sat Rev of Lit, Ladies Home Journ, Coronet, Liberty. *s.s*: Americana, Literary Criticism. *Rec*: Music, tennis, swimming, mountaineering. *c*: Authors League. *a*: 77 Park Ave, New York 16, N.Y., U.S.A. *T*: Caledonia 5-95-11.

MASON, Michael Henry (Cameron Blake), F.Z.S. *b*: Carnbee, Fife 1900. *e*: Eton & R.M.C., Sandhurst. *m*: Hon Annette Baird. Landed Proprietor. *Publ*: The Arctic Forests; Deserts Idle; Trivial Adventures in the Spanish Highlands; Where Tempests Blow; Where the River runs Dry; The Paradise of Fools; Novels under name of Cameron Blake:—Set Stormy; Only Men on Board. *Ctr*: Field, Times, Country Life. *s.s*: Natural History. *Rec*: Natural history, sailing. *c*: Carlton, Beefsteak, Roy Yacht Squadron, etc. *a*: Scott's Hse, Evnsham Pk, Witney, Oxon. *T*: Freeland 283.

MASON, Philip, C.I.E., O.B.E. (See **WOODRUFF, Philip.**) *b*: London 1906. *e*: Sedbergh & Balliol Coll Oxf. *m*: Eileen Mary Hayes. *s*: 1. *d*: 2. Indian Civil Service. Joint Sec to the Government of India Defence Dept 1944—47. *Rec*: Walking, riding, sailing, fishing. *a*: Greenlands Farm, Morcombelake, Bridport, Dorset.

MASON, Reginald H., M.A., F.I.B.P., F.R.P.S. *b*: Buxton 1911. *e*: Downside Sch, Sidney Sussex, Camb. Commercial Photographer, Dir Gilchrist Studios Ltd,

Pres Inst of Brit Photographers 1946—47. *n.a*: Cons Art Ed Amateur Photographer '45—. *Publ*: To be a Professional Photographer; Manual of Photography; The Complete Photographer. *Ctr*: Amateur Photographer, Photography, Imperial Rev, Record. *s.s*: Photography. *Rec*: Golf, squash. *c*: Constitutional, Camera. *a*: 10 Elsworthy Rd, London, N.W.3. *T*: Primrose 6658.

MASON, Robert. *b*: Glasgow, 1905. *e*: Glasgow Academy, Morrison's, Crieff. Journalist. *n.a*: Dundee Evening Telegraph; Sunday Post, Glasgow, 1923—9. Publicity work 1930—. *Publ*: The Slaying Squad; Murder to Measure. *Rec*: Golf. *c*: Press. *a*: 236 Castellain Mansions, W.9. *t*: Abercorn 4661.

MASON, Ronald Allison Kells. *b*: Auckland, New Zealand 1905. *e*: Auckland Gr Sch, Univ Coll. Editor. *n.a*: Ed Phœnix 1933, In Print '41, Challenge '43. *Publ*: This Dark Will Lighten; No New Thing; Squire Speaks (Radio Play); The Beggar; Frontiers Forsaken; An Outline History of the Cook Islands; End of Day; International Brigade. *Ctr*: Labour Periodicals. *s.s*: Polynesian Hist & Polit Sci. *Rec*: Walking, riding, acting. *a*: Crown Hill, Milford, New Zealand. *T*: Auckland 78-512.

MASON, Sidney John. *b*: London 1900. *m*: Elizabeth Rose Bacon. *s*: 1. *d*: 1. Journalist, Chief News Editor Reuters. *n.a*: Chicago Tribune 1923—25, Central News '25—37, Chief Foreign Sub-Ed, Night Ed, Chief Sub-Ed Financial Times '37—40, Chief Foreign Sub-Ed B.U.P. '40—42, Night Ed, News Ed Reuters '43—, Night Ed, Chief News Ed. *s.s*: Foreign News. *c*: Press. *a*: 54 West Ave, Finchley, London .N.3. *T*: Finchley 1812.

MASSEY, Arthur, M.D., D.P.H.(Leeds), D.P.A. (Lon). *b*: Keighley, Yorks 1894. *m*: Dorothy B. I. Cleife. *d*: 1. Doctor. M.O.H. for City of Coventry. *Publ*: Epidemiology in Relation to Air Travel (1933). *c.t*: Quarterly Review, various Med Journals. *s.s*: Publ health, social admin. Formerly Lieut R.A. & Capt R.A.M.C.(T.A.). *Rec*: Motoring, travel. *a*: Monkswood, Woodland Av, Coventry. *t*: 3271.

MASSEY, Gertrude. *b*: London 1868. *e*: Priv. *m*: Henry G. Massey. *d*: 1. Artist. *Publ*: Kings, Commoners & Me. *Rec*: Painting, bridge. *a*: Heatherleys, 33 Warwick Sq, Westminster, London, S.W.1. *T*: Victoria 6077.

MASSEY, Harrie Stewart, F.R.S., B.A., M.Sc.(Melb), Ph.D.(Cantab). *b*: Melbourne, Australia 1908. *e*: Melbourne Univ, Cavendish Lab Camb. *m*: Jessie Bruce. *d*: 1. Prof of Mathematics Univ Coll Lond, Dep Chief Scientist Mine Design Dept Admiralty 1941—43, Dep Leader '43 & Leader since '45 Brit Scientific Group, Atomic Bomb Research, Berkeley Calif U.S.A. *Publ*: Theory of Atomic Energy; Negative Ions. *Ctr*: Scientific Journs, World Affairs. *s.s*: Atomic Energy & other scientific questions. *Rec*: Cricket, tennis, billiards, travel. *c*: Univ of Lond. *a*: 36 Grove Way, Esher, Surrey. *T*: Emberbrook 1891.

MASSEY, John Stuart. *b*: Stretford 1900. *e*: Erith County Sc. Journalist. *n.a*: Luton News '24—26, Herts & Beds Pictorial '26—30, N. Kent Argus '30—32, Kentish Times. *Rec*: Amateur dramatic production. *c*: Erith Rotary. *a*: 2 Lesney Pk, Erith, Kent.

MASSEY, Rt. Hon. Vincent, C. H. *b*: Toronto, Canada 1887. *e*: Toronto Univ, Balliol Coll Oxf. *m*: Alice Stuart Parkin. *s*: 2. Chancellor Univ of Toronto 1947—, formerly H.M. Canadian Minister to U.S.A. & High Commissioner for Canada in U.K. *Publ*: Good Neighbourhood & other Addresses; The Sword of Lionheart & other War-time Speeches. *c*: Athenæum, Brooks', Beefsteak. *a*: Batterwood Hse, nr Port Hope, Ontario, Canada.

MASSIE, Alice. *b*: London. *Publ*: Unresting Year; Crossing; The Shadow on the Road; The Cotswold Chronicle; etc. *a*: Ivy Mount, Lichfield Rd, Four Oaks, Warwickshire.

MASSINGHAM, Harold John. *b*: London 1888. *e*: Westminster & Queen's Coll Oxf. *m*: Anne Penelope Webbe. Author. *n.a*: Lit Ed Athenæum 1912—13, Lit Staff of Nation '17—24, '38 onwards Field. *Publ*: People & Things; Untrodden Ways; In Praise of England; Birds of the Seashore; Wold Without End; Golden Treasury of the 17th Century Verse; Poems about Birds; E. J. Trelawny—A Biography; Dogs, Birds & Others; The Natural Order; Cotswold Country; Shepherd's Country; A Countryman's Journal; Chiltern Country; Men of Earth; This Plot of Earth; (Ed with Hugh Massingham) The Great Victorians; etc. *s.s*: Anthropology, Nat Hist & Birds. *Rec*: Gardening. *c*: Overseas. *a*: Reddings, Long Crendon, Thame, Oxon.

MASSON, FLORA: writer; b. London, Eng., e. d. of David and Emily Rosaline (Orme) M. Edited: Memories of London in the Forties, 1908; Memories of Two Cities, Edinburgh and Aberdeen, 1911 (both by David Masson); The Brontës, 1912; Charles Lamb, 1913; Life of Robert Boyle, 1914. Contributor to Blackwood, Cornhill, Scotsman, etc. General character of writing: biographies, general literature. R.R.C. (1st Class), 1919. Relig. denom., Episcopalian. HOME: 20 Ann St., Edinburgh, Scotland.

MASSON, Rosaline. *b*: Edin. Author. *Publ*: A Better Man; Leslie Farquhar; Nina; Life of Robert Louis Stevenson; Life of Wordsworth; Edinburgh; Poets, Patriots, & Lovers (1933); Scotland: The Nation ('34); Ed Shakespeare Personally, by late Prof David Masson; Ed I Can Remember Robert Louis Stevenson; Use & Abuse of English (Text-Book). *s.s*: Scot hist. *a*: 20 Ann St, Edin. *t*: 26942.

MASTERMAN, Ernest Wm Gurney, M.D., F.R.C.S., D.P.H., F.R.G.S. *b*: Sussex 1867. *e*: Clifton Col & Monkton Combe Sc, St John's Col, Cam & St Bart's Hosp (Schol & Gold Medallist). *m*: Johanna Zeller. *s*: 1. *d*: 6. Ex-Med Supt St Giles' Hosp Lon. *Publ*: Studies in Galilee; Hygiene & Disease in Palestine in Modern & in Biblical Times; The Deliverance of Jerusalem. *c.t*: Chambers's Ency. Geog Journ, Sunday at Home, Near East, M/C Guardian, Lancet, B.M.J., etc. *s.s*: Palestine. Hon Sec Palestine Exploration Fund 1920—. 20 y in Palestine & Syria. *Rec*: Travel. *a*: 2 De Crespigny Pk, S.E.5. *t*: Rodney 2437.

MASTERMAN, John Cecil, O.B.E. *b*: Kingston-Hill, Surrey 1891. *e*: R.N. Coll Osborne & Dartmouth. Provost of Worcester Coll Oxf, Student & Tutor of Christ Church Oxf 1919—46, Fell Eton Coll. *Publ*: An Oxford Tragedy; Fate Cannot Harm Me; Marshal Ney. *Rec*: Cricket & other games. *c*: United University. *a*: Provost's Lodgings, Worcester Coll, Oxford. *T*: Oxford 47777.

MASTERMAN, BISHOP JOHN HOWARD BERTRAM: Bishop of Plymouth; b. Tunbridge Wells, Eng., Dec., 1867; s. Thomas William and Margaret Hanson (Gurney) M.; educ. Weymouth Coll.; University College Sch. DEGREES: M.A., D.D. (Cambridge), Hon. M.A. (Birmingham); m. Margarethe Matilda, Therese Bodemer, 1893. AUTHOR: The Age of Milton, 1897; Introduction and Notes to First Epistle of St. Peter, 1900; Was Jesus Christ Divine? 1904; I Believe in the Holy Ghost, 1906; The House of Commons: its place in National History, 1908; The Dawn of Mediaeval Europe, 1909; Parliament and the People, 1909. A History of the British Constitution, 1910; The Challenge of Christ, 1913; Studies in the Book of Revelation, 1918; Aspects of Christian Character, 1921; The Christianity of Tomorrow, 1929. Relig. denom., Church of England. HOME: Rectory, Devonport, Plymouth, Eng.

MASTERMAN, Lucy Blanche. *b*: Gibraltar 1884. *e*: Private, France. *m*: Rt Hon Charles Masterman (dec). *s*: 1. *d*: 2. *n.a*: Lit Ed Outlook, '17—18. *Publ*: Mary Gladstone, Diary & Letters ; Poems ; A Book of Wild Things ; Lives of the Wives of Prime Ministers (jtly). *s.s*: Politics, unemployment, housing, poetry, English lit, child psychology. Liberal candidate for Salisbury, '29 & '31. *c*: Chm Liberal Women's Unemployment Enquiry Group, Chm Battersea Housing Assoc. *a*: 26 Prince of Wales Mansions, Battersea Pk, S.W.11. *t*: Macaulay 2624.

MASTERMAN, Margaret Mary. *b*: London 1910. *e*: Hamilton Ho, Tunbridge Wells, Institut Britannique, Paris & Newnham Coll Camb. *m*: Richard Bevan Braithwaite. *s*: 1. *d*: 1. Founder & Prop Barn Theatre Shere 1932—35, Hon Sec Camb Refugee Cttee '38—39. *Publ*: Gentlemen's Daughters ; The Grandmother ; Death of a Friend ; Stage prod Libretto to Music for Light Opera by Gardiner ; Through the Looking Glass ; part author of Death in Vienna. *Ctr*: Ev News, Lond Mercury. *a*: 11 Millington Rd, Cambridge. *T*: 4822.

MASTERS, David. Author. *Publ*: Romance of Excavation ; Wonders of Salvage ; Conquest of Disease ; How to Conquer Consumption ; New Cancer Facts ; Perilous Days ; Glory of Britain ; When Ships Go Down ; S.O.S. ; On the Wing ; Deep-Sea Diving ; I.D., Tales of the Submarine War ; Divers in Deep Seas ; So Few, The Immortal Record of the Royal Air Force ; Up Periscope ; With Pennants Flying, The Immortal Deeds of the Royal Armoured Corps ; Miracle Drug, The Inner History of Penicillin. *a*: c/o Eyre & Spottiswoode Ltd, 15 Bedford St, London, W.C.2.

MASTERS, John William. *b*: South Petherton, Som. *m*: Elizabeth Lane England. *s*: 2. Journalist. *n.a*: Chief Reporter of Huddersfield Examiner. Formerly on staff of Western Chron (Yeovil), Sussex Dly News, Ilford Guardian, Bradford (afterwards Yorkshire) Observer (Chief Reporter 6ys), Ed Bradford Evening Argus. Chm of West Riding branch of N/ps Press Fund '34—35. *a*: Petherton Hse, Huddersfield Rd, Brighouse. *t*: Brighouse 84.

MASTERS, Rev. William Walter. *b*: Yeovil 1894. *c*: Kelham Hall. *Publ*: Airways (1927) ; Eleven ; Murder in the Mirror (1931). Mem the Society of Authors. *a*: 54 Gold-Croft, Yeovil, Som.

MASTIN, John, M.A., ScD., PhD., F.S.A.Scot, F.L.S., F.C.S., F.R.A.S., F.R.M.S., F B.A. *Publ*: Through the Sun in an Airship; The Stolen Planet; The Immortal Light. *a*: c/o C. Griffin & Co, 42 Drury Lane, W.C.2.

MATEJCEK, Antonin. *b*: Budapest 1889. *e*: Univs of Prague, Paris, Vienna. Prof of the Hist of Art, Univ Charles IV Prague. *Publ*: History of Art ; Modern & Contemporary Czech Art ; Work of J. Manes ; History of Illustration ; Gothic Painting in Bohemia ; Bible of Welislaus ; etc. *s.s*: Hist of Art. *a*: Prague XVI, Dienzenhoferovy Sady 2.

MATHER, Frank Jewett (Jr.), A.B., Ph.D., D.H.L. *b*: Deep River, Connecticut 1868. *e*: Williams Coll, John Hopkins Univ. *m*: Ellen Suydam Mills. *s*: 1. *d*: 1. Dir Univ Museum Princetown 1922—47. *n.a*: N.Y. Ev Post, Ed Writer 1900—06, Art Critic '03, '04, '10, Asst Ed The Nation 1900—06, American Ed Burlington Mag '03—05, Act Ed Art in America '14—17, Jt Ed Art Studies '17—20. *Ctr*: Atlantic Monthly, Forum, Scribner's, Century Mag, Nation, Art Bulletin, etc. *Rec*: Fly-fishing. *w.s*: U.S.N.R.F. 1917—18. *a*: 3 Evelyn Pl, Princeton, New Jersey, U.S.A.

MATHER, John Sidney. *b*: London 1913. *e*: Davenant Foundation Sch, Univ Coll Lond, Inst of Education. Journalist, Mem Press, N.U.J. *n.a*: Columnist Dly Mirror 1937, Art Ed Reynolds News '38—40, Dly Express '41—, Features Ed '46, Re-write Ed '46—. *a*: 24 Arran Hse, London, N.16. *T*: Stamford Hill 2714.

MATHER, Joyce. *e*: Hull Hgh Sch for Girls, Bruntsfield, I. of W., Bedford Coll, Univ of Lond. *m*: F. W. Schofield (dec'd). *d*: 2. Journalist. *n.a*: Leeds Mercury 1925—, Yorkshire Post '39—. *a*: 1 Ridge Mount, Hyde Pk, Leeds 6. *T*: 53697.

MATHER, Kirtley F. Sc.D., Litt.D., Ph.D., L.H.D. *b*: Chicago, Illinois 1888. *e*: Colby Coll & Univs of Denison & Chicago. *m*: Marie Porter. *d*: 3. Prof of Geology Harvard Univ. *n.a*: Chm Ed Board Scientific Book Club 1930—46, Mem Board of Judges Non-fiction Book Club '46—, Book Rev Ed American Scientist '42—, Chm Publs Cttee American Assoc for the Advancement of Science '46—. *Publ*: Enough & To Spare ; Sons of the Earth ; Old Mother Earth ; Science in Search of God ; Source Book of Geology (collab). *Ctr*: Atlantic Monthly, Science, Scientific Monthly, etc. *s.s*: Geology, Science & Religion, Educ for Democracy, Adult Educ. *Rec*: Swimming, motion picture photography. *c*: Boston Authors. *a*: 155 Homer St, Newton Centre, 59, Massachusetts, U.S.A. *T*: Lasell 7-4158.

MATHER, T. M.I.E.E., F.R.S. Emeritus Prof of Elec Engineering (City of Guilds Eng Col). *Publ*: Exercises in Electrical Engineering (with Prof Howe —3 edn) ; Practical Electricity (with Prof Ayston— 2 edn & 3 reprints). *a*: 51 Wyatt Park Rd, Streatham Hill, S.W.2.

MATHER, Virginia. B.Sc. *b*: Great Falls, Montana 1900. *e*: Grade & Hgh Sch Great Falls, Montana, Univ of Minnesota. *m*: R. E. Liebeler. *s*: 1. *d*: 2. Teacher Univ of Minnesota, Pres The Writer's Workshop in Minneapolis 1944—45, Pres The Novel Workshop '43—46. *n.a*: Blue Cross Ed of Hospital Management, having Edited The Bulletin of the Minnesota Assoc for Crippled Children, Ed for 5 years Blue Cross News. *Publ*: You, The Jury. *Ctr*: Hospital Management, The Modern Hospital, The Granger. *s.s*: (Hospitalization) articles, Biographical Sketches, Fiction. *Rec*: Swimming, fishing, hunting, bridge, contesting. *a*: 4431 Dupont Ave South, Minneapolis 9, Minnesota, U.S.A. *T*: Regent 5826.

MATHERS, Edward Powys, B.A. *b*: Lon 1892. *e*: Loretto & Trinity Col Oxf. *m*: Rosamond Crowdy. Author. *n.a*: Staff of The Observer. *Publ*: Coloured Stars ; Black Marigolds ; The Garden of Bright Waters ; The Thousand Nights & One Night ; Procreant Hymn ; Eastern Love ; Salambo ; Amores of Ovid (1932) ; Torquemada Puzzle Book. *s.s*: Trans. crossword puzzles. *c*: Oxf Union Soc & New Theatre Arts. *a*: 48 Upper Mall, W.6. *t*: Riverside 2635.

MATHESON, Charles. *b*: Elgin 1896. Jnlst. *s.s*: Sport. *a*: 24 Chestnut Avenue, Derby. *t*: Derby 2296.

MATHESON, Cyril, M.A. *Publ*: A Catalogue of the publications of Scottish Historical Clubs; The Life of Henry Dundas, Viscount Melville. *a*: 5 The Butts, Harrow-on-the-Hill. *t*: Byron 2601.

MATHESON, Hilda. *n.a*: Radio Critic The Observer. *Publ*: Broadcasting. *a*: 22 Tudor St, E.C.4.

MATHESON, M. C. Lecturer. *Publ*: Women's Work & Wages (jt); Domestic Training in Switzerland; Citizenship; Indian Industry—Yesterday, Today & To-morrow; etc. *c.t*: Various. *a*: 19 Elsworthy Rd, N.W.3. *t*: Primrose 2049.

MATHESON, Marie Cecile. *b*: London 1874. *e*: Priv & Bedford Coll Lond. Formerly Warden Birmingham Settlement, formerly University Extension Lecturer for Oxf & Camb Univs. *Publ*: Teaching of Domestic Science in Switzerland; Domestic Training of Girls in Germany & Austria; Women's Work & Wages; (with E. Cadbury & G. Shann); Citizenship (Introductory Handbook); Indian Industry; Economic Status of Women (International Council of Women). *Ctr*: Many articles in various periodicals & papers. *s.s*: Civic & Industrial. *a*: 14 Moreland Ct, London, N.W.2. *T*: Hampstead 3561.

MATHESON, Percy Ewing, M.B.E. *b*: Nott'm 1859. *e*: Nott'm H.S., City of Lon Sc & Balliol Oxf. *m*: Hon Elizabeth Fox Bruce. Ex-Tutor & Dean New Col. *Publ*: Life of Hastings Rashdall, Dean of Carlisle; Anton Reiser, by C. P. Moritz (trans & ed); Trans Epictetus; The Growth of Rome, in World's Classics; Taylorian Lecture (German Visitors in England 1770–95) ('30); Edns of Demosthenes (with Evelyn Abbott). *c.t*: Fortnightly, Cornhill, Nat Review, etc. Mem Roy Commssn on Civil Service '12–15, Statutory Commssn on Univ of Oxf '23, of Sec Scs Exam Counc '17–24, Del O.U.P. '07–32. Fell New Col, Fell Winchester Col. *Rec*: Walking. *c*: Athenæum. *a*: 3 Brookside, Headington, Oxf. *t*: 6942.

MATHEW, Rev. David, M.A., LittD.(T.C.D.), F.R.HistS. *b*: Lyme Regis 1902. *e*: R.N.C. Osborn & Dartmouth & Balliol Col, Oxf. Chap to R.C. Lon Univ '34. Asst priest at St David's Cathedral, Cardiff & Chap to R.Cs. at Univ Col, Cardiff '30–34. *Publ*: The Celtic Peoples & Renaissance Europe ('33); The Reformation & the Contemplative Life ('34 with Gervase Mathew). *c.t*: Eng Hist Review, Dublin Review, Blackfriars, etc. *s.s*: 16th & 17th cent hist. *c*: Athenæum. *a*: 1 Woburn Sq, W.C.1. *t*: Museum 5687.

MATHEWMAN, Phyllis. *b*: Leeds. *e*: Leeds Girls Hgh Sch. *m*: Sydney Matthewman. Author. *Publ*: A New Role for Natasha; Pat at the Helm; Because of Vivian; Timber Girl; Set to Partners; Utility Wedding; Stable Companion; etc. *Ctr*: Girls Own Weekly, Woman's Weekly. *s.s*: Stories for Girls, Romantic Fiction, Youth Club Work, Drama (Production etc). *Rec*: Youth work, motoring, play prod. *a*: Gervase Cottage, Merstham, Surrey. *T*: Merstham 203.

MATHEWMAN, Sydney, F.Z.S. *b*: Leeds. *e*: Leeds Modern Sch, Leeds Univ. *m*: Phyllis Matthewman. Literary Agent. *n.a*: Yorks Ed Poetry Review 1921, Ed Yorkshire Poetry '21–24, Assoc Ed The Decachord '23–29, Ed The Bookmart '46–47. *Publ*: (Verse) Poetry; Gabriel's Hounds; Christmas; Shaping Fantasies; (Prose) The Crystal Casket; Sketches in Sunshine; The High House Press: An Appreciation. *Ctr*: Yorks Post, Yorks Observer, Sphere, Poetry, Caxton, Church Times, etc. *s.s*: Poetry, Plays, Pantomimes, Lit Criticism & Review, Typography, Youth Work, Nat Hist, Bibliography & Books in General. *Rec*: Cruising, motoring, youth work. *a*: Gervase Cottage, Merstham, Surrey. *T*: Merstham 203.

MATHEWS, A. S. *b*: Leamington Spa 1889. *e*: Market Harboro' G.S. & Warwick Sc. *m*: Janetta Chater. *s*: 3. Chief Reporter. *n.a*: Bath & Wilts Daily Chron & Herald, & Allied papers. *c.t*: Various n/ps & periodicals. *Rec*: Motoring. *c*: Pres Bath & W. of Eng Motor Club, Counc Som Football Assoc. *a*: Wharfedale, Pulteney Rd, Bath. *t*: 3312.

MATHEWS, Basil Joseph. *b*: Oxford 1879. *e*: Oxf Hgh Sch & Univ. *m*: Winifred Wilson. Author. *n.a*: Lit Staff Christian World 1904–10, Ed Sec Lond Missny Soc '10–19, Chmn & Sec Lit Cttee of Min of Inf '17–18, Prof Chr World Relations Boston Univ & Andover-Newton Theo Inst Mass U.S.A. '32–44, Professor Union Coll Vancouver B.C. '44—. *Publ*: The Splendid Quest; John Williams the Ship-builder; Three Years of War for Peace; The Ships of Peace; Life of Jesus; World Tides in the Far East; John R. Mott; The Jew & the World Ferment; The Clash of Colour; Consider Africa; There Go the Ships; India Reveals Herself; United We Stand; Booker T. Washington. *c*: Athenæum. *a*: Union College, Vancouver, B.C., Canada.

MATHEWS, Godfrey William, F.S.A., F.R.HistS. *b*: L'pool 1878. *e*: Marlboro' Col. *m*: Grace Dorothy Elias. Cotton Industry. *Publ*: The Search for Pan, & Other Poems; The Chester Mystery Plays; The Poetry of John Drinkwater; Pirandello: A Study in the Psychology of the Modern Stage; The Madonna of Montmartre; Hathor; Mon Baiser Reste; Walt Whitman—a Study; William Roscoe; More Things in Heaven and Earth; Horatio; etc. *c.t*: Notes & Queries, Open Air, Dawn. *s.s*: The drama, antiquarian research. *c*: Athenæum, Lyceum. *a*: Monkswood, Spital, Cheshire.

MATHEWS, Gregory Macalister, C.B.E., F.R.S.E. *b*: Biamble, N.S.W. 1876. *e*: King's Sch Parramatta N.S.W. *m*: Marian White (dec'd). *s*: 1. Ornithologist. *n.a*: Ed Austral Avian Record 1912—27, Assoc Ed Ibis '31—41. *Publ*: Birds of Australia; Manual of Birds of Australia; Birds of Norfolk & Lord Howe Islands; Systema Avium Australasianarum; etc. *Ctr*: Auk, Ibis, Emu, British Birds, Avicultural Mag, Victorian Naturalist, S. Australian Ornithologist, etc. *s.s*: Australian, New Zealand & South Pole Birds. *Rec*: Shooting, travel. *a*: Meadway, Saint Cross, Winchester, Hants. *T*: 4198.

MATHIAS, Eileen. *b*: Brecon. *e*: Taskers Hgh Sch Haverfordwest, Normal Coll Bagnor Nth Wales. *m*: John D. Morris. *s*: 1. *d*: 1. Teacher Surrey Educ Authority. *Publ*: The Teller of Tales; The Teller of Tales Returns; The Island of Doom; Tales From the Christmas Tree. *Ctr*: Child Educ. *s.s*: Childrens Books. *Rec*: Caravanning. *a*: 68 Mayfield Rd, Sanderstead, Surrey.

MATHIESON, William Law, HonLL.D.(Aberd). *b*: Edin 1868. *e*: Edin Acad & Edin Univ. *m*: Christian Mary Shaw. Historian. *Publ*: Politics & Religion in Scotland, 1550–1695 (1902); The Awakening of Scotland, 1747–1797; Great Britain & the Slave Trade, 1839–1865; British Slave Emancipation 1838–1849 ('32); etc. *c.t*: Athenæum, Scotsman. *s.s*: Scot & Brit hist. *Rec*: Rowing. *c*: Scot Arts, Edin. *a*: 9 Wardie Av, Edin.

MATKIN, T. D. *b*: Liverpool 1907. P.R.O. Retail Fruit Trade Federation. *n.a*: Ed Fruit Trade Review. *Publ*: Retailers Guide to Fruit Marketing. *Ctr*: Fruit Trades Journal, Fruit Grower, Times Trade Supp. *a*: 252 Russell Court, Woburn Pl, London, W.C.1. *T*: Terminus 2656.

MATSON, Geoffrey James. *b*: Yiewsley, Middx 1903. *e*: G.S., Faversham. *m*: Rita Scotney. Free-Lance Journalist (full-time). *c.t*: Over 200 n/ps & mags. *s.s*: Radio, films, theatre. *a*: 36 Orchard Ave. Cambridge. *t*: 2445.

MATTERN, Johannes, PhD. *b*: Germany 1882. *e*: Gymnasium Cleve, Univ Munster & Bonn, Johns Hopkins Univ 1917–22. *m*: Carola Glaser. *s*: 2. Asst Librarian & Lect Pol Science. *Publ*: The Plebiscite in the Employment of Sovereignty; Bavaria & the Reich; Concepts of State Sovereignty & International Law; Principles of the Constitutional Jurisprudence of the German National Republic. *c.t*: The Commonweal, etc. *s.s*: Government, politics, internat relations. Asst The Library of Congress Washington D.C. '09–10. Reorganiser of Library of Bureau of Statistics of Department of Commerce & Labour Washington D.C. Asst Librarian Johns Hopkins Univ '11. Lecturer Pol Science, Johns Hopkins Univ '24–25, '32. *c*: Johns Hopkins &

Who Was Who Among English and European Authors

Learned Assocs in field of Pol Science & Internat Law. *a*: 606 Evesham Ave, Baltimore, Md., U.S.A. *t*: Tux 1449 W.

MATTERS, Leonard Warburton. *b*: Adelaide, Australia 1881. *e*: State Schs. *m*: Romana Kryszek. Journalist. *n.a*: Lond Ed The Hindu (Madras) 1933—48, Ed Review of South America '24—30, Mang Ed Buenos Aires Herald '14—21. *Publ*: Through the Kara Sea; The Mystery of Jack the Ripper; India. *Ctr*: Times, Dly Mail, Star. *s.s*: India, Latin-America, Journalism. *Rec*: Golf, gardening. *c*: Press (Lond). *a*: Fiddler's Brook, Much Hadham, Herts, England. *T*: Central 7800.

MATTHAY, TOBIAS: musician; *b*. Clapham, London, Eng., Feb., 1858; *s*. Tobias and Dorothea (Wittich) M.; educ. Royal Academy of Music. DEGREES. F.R.A.M., F.R.C.M.; *m*. Jessie Kennedy, 1893. AUTHOR: The Act of Touch, 1903; First Principles of Pianoforte Playing, 1905; Relaxation Studies, 1908; Some Commentaries on Piano Technique, 1910; Musical Interpretation, 1912; The Child's First Steps in Piano Playing, 1912; The Forearm Rotation Principle, 1912; The Problems of Agility, 1918; The Pianist's First Music Making (3 vols.), 1918; On Method in Teaching, 1920; On Memorizing, 1926; The Slur or Couplet of Notes, 1927; The Visible and Invisible in Piano Technique (in press). Has contributed to Musical Times, Music Teacher, Daily Telegraph, The Etude, etc. Has written great quantity of pianoforte music, both for concert use and for students, and compositions for piano and violin, piano and strings, concerts for piano and orchestra. Works on musical interpretation and technique generally conceded to have revolutioned piano teaching. Founder and principal of the Tobias Matthay Pianoforte School, London, which has between 300 and 400 students. OFFICE: 96 Wimpole St., London, W. HOME: High Marley, Haslemere, Surrey, Eng.

MATTHES, Francois Emile, B.S., LL.D. *b*: Amsterdam, Holland 1874. *e*: Univ of Calif, Harvard Univ, Inst of Technology Mass. *m*: Edith Lovell Coyle. Geologist & Glaciologist. *Ctr*: Geologic History of the Yosemite Valley, Glacial Sculpture of the Bighorn Mountains, The Alps of Montana & to Geographical Rev, Sierra Club Bulletin, Mazama, The Mountaineer. *s.s*: Geomorphology, Glaciology, Glacial Geology. *Rec*: Canoeing, mountaineering. *c*: Sierra, Alpine. *a*: 858 Gelston Pl, El Cerrito, California, U.S.A.

MATTHEW, Dr. David, M.C. Psycho-Analyst. *Publ*: Anxiety Hysteria (with C. H. L. Rixon). *a*: 59 Holland Park, W.11. & 17 Queen Anne St, W.1. *t*: Park 9009.

MATTHEWMAN, SYDNEY: author, journalist; *b*. Leeds, Eng., Jan., 1902; *s*. John and Matilda (Wardman) M.; educ. Leeds Modern Sch., Univ. of Leeds; *m*. Phyllis Barton, 1930. AUTHOR: The Gardens of Meditation, 1921; The Lute of Darkness, 1922; The Way to Araby, 1923; The Harlequin (play), 1923; Poems of the Road, 1924; The Crystal Casket (prose fantasy), 1924; Sketches in Sunshine (essays), 1925; The Vision of Richard (prose fantasy), 1926; Collected Poems, 1927; Brother Theodosius (prose fantasy), 1928; Interlude, 1929; Epigrams of Theokritos, 1930. Translations (in preparation): Plum Blossom and Nightingales (from the Japanese); The Ruba'iyat of Sarmad (with B. Ahmad Hashmi); Complete Poems of Meleager. Associate Editor: Poetry Review, 1921-23; Asst. Editor: the Decachord, from 1924. Founder and editor of Yorkshire Poetry, 1922-24. Contributes to the Chap Book, Highway, London Mercury, Poetry Rev., Poetry and the Play, The Sphere, etc.; newspapers: Yorkshire Post, Yorkshire Observer, Western Morning News. General character of writing: leaders, essays, reviews, poems, criticism (drama and literary). Has served as secretary to various scientific societies.

Joined Leeds Civic Playhouse, 1927, taking part of Channon in first Eng. prod. of The Dybbuk, also other important parts. CLUBS: Leeds Art, Leeds Motor, Royal Society of Literature. Religion: Buddhist. OFFICE: Swas Press, Leeds. HOME: BM-FPC 6, London, W. C. 1, Eng.

MATTHEWS, Sir Alfred (Herbert) Henry, K.B. *b*: Church Handborough 1870. *e*: Col Hse, Edmonton. *m*: Ada Buckler Mace. Dir of Coys. *Publ*: Fifty Years of Agric Politics (Hist of Cent Chamb of Agric 1865-1915). *c.t*: Times, Morning Post, Daily Telegraph, Land & Water. *s.s*: Agric, development of the Overseas Empire. Twice round the world visiting Dominions. 27 y Sec Cent Chamb Agric. Mem Mr Jos Chamberlain's Tariff Comm 1906-16. Mem numerous Cmt's & Inquiries on Agric matters. *Rec*: Gardening, travel *c*: Farmers. *a*: 9 Alwyn Av, Chiswick, W.4.

MATTHEWS, Bache. *b*: Birm 1876. *e*: Priv. *Publ*: A History of the Birmingham Repertory Theatre (1924). *c.t*: Birm n/ps. *s.s*: Theatrical hist. Ex-Asst Dir Birm Rep Theatre. *Rec*: Books. *c*: Mem Bibl Soc & Malone Soc. *a*: 7 Tavistock Pl, W.C.1. *t*: Terminus 4874.

MATTHEWS, CHANNING (pen name): see Channing-Renton, Ernest Matthews.

MATTHEWS, Rev. Canon Charles Henry Selfe. *b*: Wellington Coll Berks. *e*: Leeds Gr Sch, Kings Coll Camb, Wells Theological Coll. *m*: Gertrude Ethelwyn Malkin. *s*: 3. Clerk in Holy Orders, Canon Emeritus of Coventry Cathedral, Sometime Vicar of St Peters-in-Thanet, Chaplain of Marlborough Coll 1930—38, Vicar of Kenilworth, Rector of Fenny Compton, Hon Canon of Coventry '46, Canon Emeritus '47. *Publ*: A Parson in the Australian Bush; Bill, A Bushman; The Roots of Religion & the Old Testament; A Religion of Your Own; Dick Sheppard—A Man of Peace. *Ctr*: Morning Post, St Martins Review, Coventry E. Telegraph, Leamington Courier, etc. *s.s*: Religious Education, Church Reform. *Rec*: Painting, golf, carpentry. *a*: The White Cottage, Wilcot-Marlborough, Wilts. *T*: Pewsey 2186.

MATTHEWS, Cyril Edwin. *b*: Essex. *e*: Dulwich. Journalist. *a*: 10 Alleyn Park, West Dulwich, S.E.21. *t*: Sydenham 6589.

MATTHEWS, Dorothy, B.A. *b*: Wood Green 1890. *e*: Wd. Green Coll, W. Ham Hgh Sch, Girton Coll Camb & Lond Univ. Writer, Teacher of Eng & Foreign Langs 1909—19, Lecturer on Educ & Lit Subjects & Organiser for various Socs '20—30. *Publ*: The Winding Way (poems); Poetry in the Making; The Open Gates (poems); The Growth of the Writer; Out of the Darkness (poems). *s.s*: Oral Expression, Psychology. *Rec*: Walking. *a*: 32 Primrose Hill Rd, London, N.W.3. *T*: Primrose 5686.

MATTHEWS, SIR HERBERT: Secretary Central and Associated Chambers of Agriculture of Great Britain from 1901 to 1927; *b*. Oxfordshire, Eng., July, 1870; *s*. Alfred Thomas and Elizabeth Matthews; educ. College House, Edmonton, Middlesex, Eng.; *m*. Ada Buckler, 1900. AUTHOR: Fifty Years of Agricultural Politics, 1915. Contributor of articles dealing with agricultural problems to the Times, Morning Post, Daily Telegraph, Land and Water, etc. Was secretary of the Central and Associated Chambers of Agriculture of Great Britain for 27 years; and in the writing of his book summarized the activities of this body not only for fifty years (1865-1915), but also earlier legislation affecting agriculture. CLUBS: The Farmer's. Relig. denom., Church of England. OFFICE: 28 Westminster Palace Gardens, Artillery Row, S. W. 1. HOME: 9 Wyn Ave., Chiswick, London, W. 4, Eng.

954

MATTHEWS, Right Rev. James Edmund, M.A. b: Earlstown 1871. e: Ampleforth Col, St Benet's Hall Oxf. Abbot of Ampleforth. Headmaster of Ampleforth 1903–24, Abbot '24–. c.t: Ampleforth Journ. s.s: Catholic educ. a: Ampleforth Abbey, York.

MATTHEWS, Mrs. Publ: Addresses on the Lord's Prayer. a: The White House, Wooton-under-Edge, Glos.

MATTHEWS, T. W. n.a: London Ed Sunday Mail. a: 200 Gray's Inn Rd, W.C.1.

MATTHEWS, Thomas Soady. Civil Service. Publ: Channing: A Study; The Brontës: A Study; Studies of a Reviewer. a: 2 Napier Terr, Plymouth, Devon.

MATTHEWS, Very Rev. Sir Walter Robert, K.C.V.O., M.A., D.Litt., Hon.D.D., S.T.D. b: London 1881. e: Wilson's Gr Sch, King's Coll London. m: Margaret Alice Bryan. s: 2. d: 1. Dean of St Paul's since 1934, Hon Bencher of Gray's Inn, Mem Senate Univ of Lond, Dean of King's Coll Lond '18–31, Chaplain to H.M. the King '23–31, Fell King's Coll Lond. Publ: Studies in Christian Philosophy; The Gospel & the Modern Mind; Dogma in History & Thought; Seven Words; God in Chistian Thought & Experience; Essays in Construction; etc. s.s: Ethics & General Philos. c: Athenæum. a: The Deanery, St Paul's, London, E.C.4.

MATTINGLY, C. H. a: 18 Henrietta St, W.C.2. t: Temple Bar 3521.

MATTINGLY, Garrett, A.B., Ph.D. b: Washington, D.C. 1900. e: Harvard Coll, Harvard Univ. m: Gertrude L. McCollum. Teacher of History. n.a: Assoc Ed Journ of Mod Hist 1946—. Publ: Further Supp to State Papers (Spanish); Catherine of Aragon: A Biography. Ctr: Eng Hist Review, American Hist Review, Speculum, Journ of Mod Hist, Atlantic Monthly, etc. s.s: History, XVI Century. c: Harvard (N.Y). w.s: 1918–19 U.S. Inf, '42–45 Lt Cmdr U.S. Naval Reserve. a: 135 West 79th St, New York 24, N.Y. T: Schuyler 4-6210.

MATTINGLY, Harold, F.B.A., F.S.A. b: Sudbury, Suffolk 1884. e: Leys Sch Camb, Gonville & Caius Coll Camb. m: Marion Grahame Melkeham. s: 3. d: 1. Civil Servant. Publ: British Museum Catalogue of Roman Coins: I–IV; Roman Coins; History of the Ancient World; The Man in the Roman Street. Ctr: Journ of Roman Studies, Numismatic Chronicle. s.s, Roman Numismatics, Roman History, Art, Religion. a: Little Prestons, 13 Mountfield Rd, C.E. Finchley, London, N.3. T: Fin 5301.

MATURIN, Rev. Merrick Persse, M.A. b: Rathmullan, Ireland 1862. e: Foyle Col Derry, T.C.D. m: Elizabeth Knox Warke. Publ: Ich Dien; The Golden Stair; The Mind & Art of Dante; etc. c.t: Religious press, etc. s.s: Homiletic lit. a: Edgar Hotel, Bath.

MAUD, J. P. Bishop of Kensington. Publ: Life in Fellowship. a: c/o Nisbet & Co Ltd, 22 Berners St, W.1.

MAUD, Sir John Primatt Redcliffe, K.C.B., C.B.E. b: Bristol 1906. e: Eton, New Coll Oxf, Harvard Coll U.S.A. m: Jean Hamilton. s: 1. d: 2. Permanent Sec Min of Educ, Master Birkbeck Coll Lond Univ 1939–43, Dep Sec ,later Second Sec Min of Food '41–44, Second Sec Office of Min of Reconstruction '44–45, Sec Office of Lord Pres of the Council '45, Mem of Archbishops' Commission on Training of the Ministry '36, Chm of Economics Section of Oxf Conference on Church Community & State '37. Publ: English Local Government; City Government: The Johannesburg Experiment; Chapter in Oxford & the Groups; Chapter in Personal Ethics; Johannesburg & the Art of Self-Government. s.s: Government, Education. c: Savile. a: 3 Regents Park Terr, London, N.W.1. T: Gulliver 2337.

MAUDE, Colonel Alan Hamer, C.M.G., D.S.O., T.D., D.L. b: Highgate, Middx 1885. e: Oriel Coll Oxf m: Dorothy Maude Upton. s: 1. Journalist, Hon Colonel 56th (London) Armoured Divisional Column R.A.S.C. n.a: Ed The Isis (Oxf) 1907–08, Sub-Ed Dly Chronicle '12–14, Ed Staff The Times '20–47, as Sub-Ed '20–36, Ed Special Numbers '36–39, Chief Sub-Ed (Home Dept) '45–47. Publ: Ed War History of The 47th (London) Division (1914–18). Rec: Gardening, photography, genealogy, rifle-shooting. c: Junior Army & Navy. w.s: 1915–19, '39–45. a: Daintrey Hse, Petworth, Sussex. T: Petworth 2205.

MAUDE, Aylmer. b: Ipswich 1858. e: Christ's Hosp Lon & Lyceum, Moscow. m: Louise Shanks. s: 4. Author & Ed O.U.P. edns of Tolstoy's works. Mem Cmt of Management Soc of Authors 21 y & Treas 12 y. Publ: Life of Tolstoy (2 vols); Marie Stopes, Her Work & Play: A Peculiar People, the Doukhobors, etc. s.s: Russia, birth control movement. Dir Russian Carpet Co Moscow 1892–97. Arranged with Canadian Govt for migration of 7363 Russian peasants from the Caucasus to Assiniboia. Publ the Life of Tolstoy 1908 & '10 (the year of his death). Undertook the Centenary Edn of his works '28. Mem Sc of Russian Studies. c: Nat Lib. a: Gt Baddow, Chelmsford. t: Gt Baddow 59.

MAUDE, Cyril. b: London 1862. e: Charterhouse. m: Winifred Emery. s: 1. d: 2. Actor Manager. Publ: Behind the Scenes with Cyril Maude; The Haymarket Theatre; The Actor in Room 13. c: Garrick, Roy Torbay Yacht. a: Dundrum, Torquay. T: 3300.

MAUDUIT, George Vicomte de. b: Villeblevin France 1893. e: Priv Eng, France, U.S.A. Publ: Private Views; The Vicomte in the Kitchen; The Vicomte in the Pantry; Mimie & Shah; The Vicomte in the Kitchenette; etc. Ed Good Cookery Magazine. c.t: Lon & prov dailies & weeklies. s.s: Children's stories, cookery. Airman, Inventor (Inst Patentees Dip), World Traveller, Linguist & Art Connoisseur. Ex-Eng The Thomson-Houston Coy. Rec: Cookery, yachting, shooting, " petit-point " tapestry. a: 68 Fleet St, E.C.4.

MAUGHAM, Reginald Charles Fulke, C.B.E., F.R.G.S., F.Z.S. b: Ashton upon Ribble, Lancs 1866. e: Priv. m: Hilda Wollaston Greene. One of H.M. Consuls General (ret). Publ: Portuguese East Africa; Zambezia; Wild Game in Zambezia; The Republic of Liberia; Africa as I Have Known It; Nyasaland in the 'Nineties; A Handbook of the Chi-Makua Language; The Island of Jersey To-day; Jersey Under the Jack Boot. Ctr: Times, Empire Review, United Empire, Crown Colonist, African World, West African Review. s.s: South, Central, East & West Africa. Rec: Shooting, yachting, motoring, tennis. c: St James's. a: Spring Bank, Vallee des Vaux, Jersey, Channel Islands. T: Central 815.

MAUGHAM, William Somerset, F.R.S.L., M.R.C.S., L.R.C.P., Commandeur Leg of Honneur. b: 1874. e: King's Sch Canterbury, Heidelberg & St Thomas's Hosp. m: Syrie Barnardo. d: 1. Medical, Playwright & Author, Mem Counc Soc of Authors. Publ: Liza of Lambeth; Mrs Craddock; The Merry Go Round; The Bishop's Apron; The Explorer; The Magician; Of Human Bondage; The Moon & Sixpence; The Trembling of a Leaf; On a Chinese Screen; The Painted Veil; The Casuarina Tree; Ashenden; The Gentleman in the Parlour; Cakes & Ale; First Person Singular;

The Narrow Corner; Ah King; The Razors Edge; Then & Now; Creatures of Circumstance; (Plays) A Man of Honour; Lady Frederick; Jack Straw; Mrs Dot; The Explorer; Penelope; Smith; Grace; Loaves & Fishes; The Land of Promise; Caroline; Cæsar's Wife; East of Suez; Our Betters; The Constant Wife; The Sacred Flame; Sheppey, etc. *w.s*: 1914—18. *a*: Villa Mauresque, Cap Ferrat, France.

MAUGHAN, Rev. Herbert Hamilton, M.A. *b*: Chiddingstone 1884. *e*: King's Sc Canterbury & Keble Col Oxf. *m*: Gertrude Margery Bowles. *d*: 1. Author, Journalist. *Publ*: The Leslie Dialogues; The Liturgy of the Eastern Orthodox Church; Some Brighton Churches; Stunt Religion, or Churchgoing Without Tears (A Satire '33); etc. *c.t*: Various n/ps & periodicals. *s.s*: Hist, liturgiology, archt. Master '14 & Housemaster '15 Ellesmere Col. Master '16 Cranleigh Sc. *Rec*: Reading, music. *c*: Authors'. *a*: Authors' Club, Lon, & Flat 2, 6 Clermont Rd, Preston, Brighton.

MAUGHAN, James, M.D., M.B., M.R.C.S., L.R.C.P. Anæsthetist. *n.a*: Ed Nat Dental Hosp Gazette 1906-14, Gen Anæsthesia for Dental Operations (Glassington's Dental Materia Medica 1896). *c.t*: B.M.J. *a*: 56 Albany St, N.W.1. *t*: Museum 6526.

MAUNDER, Annie Scott Dill, F.R.A.S. *b*: Co Tyrone, Strabane. *e*: Girton Coll Camb. *m*: Edward Walter Maunder. Astronomer. Computer at the Roy Observatory Greenwich 1891—95 & '15—20, Ed Journ Brit Astronomical Assoc 1894—96, 1917—'30 Vice-Pres B.A.A. 1896—99, 1900—03, '42. *Publ*: Catalogue of Recurrent Groups of Sunspots; Astronomical Allusions in the Sacred Books of the East; Early Hindu Astronomy; Astronomy & Meteorology of the Rigveda Hymns; Iranian Migrations Before History; Origin of the Planetary Symbols; Origin of the Constellations; Astronomical Appendix to the Travels of Peter Mundy, Vol V 1650—1667 Hakluyt Soc, also various researches in Astronomy published with her husband in the Proc Roy Soc Lond, etc. *Ctr*: Many astronomical mags & papers. *a*: 52 Elm Cresc, Clapham Park, London, S.W.4.

MAURAULT, Jean Leon Olivier, C.M.G., LL.D., D.Litt., D.C.L., F.R.S.C. *b*: Sorel, P.Q., Canada 1886. *e*: Montreal, Paris. Rector of the Univ of Montreal. *Publ*: Marges D'Histoire; La Paroisse; Centenaire de Notre-Dame; Moisson De Ville-Marie; Le Mexique de Mes Souvenirs; Propos et Portraits; Par Voies et Par Chemins de L'Air; French Canadian Backgrounds (collab). *Ctr*: Groliers Ency, Le Cahier Des Dix; Le Monde Francais, etc. *s.s*: Hist, Lit, Educ Topics, Lecturing. *Rec*: Travel, music. *c*: Cercle Universitaire. *a*: 5221 Louis-Colin Ave, Montreal 26, P.Q., Canada. *T*: AT 9877.

MAURICE, Albert Jafa, L.D.S., R.C.S.Ed. *b*: Lon 1864. *e*: King's Sc Chester & Univ Col L'pool. *m*: Matilda Sykes. *s*: 1. Dental Surg. *n.a*: Ed The Dental Surgeon 1926-32. *Publ*: On the Use of Anæsthetics in Dental Surgery; Prize Essay on the Uselessness & Cruelty of Experiments on the Teeth of Animals, & the Best Means of Preventing Dental Decay in Man. *c.t*: Numerous ed articles & notes over many yrs. Lt-Col Terr Army. War Service France & Salonika. Hon Cons Dent Surg to St Pancras Disp. Ex-Hon Dent Surg Belgrave Hosp for Children & to Lon Lock Hosp. Mem Brit Dental Assoc, etc. *Rec*: Archæology, croquet. *a*: 10 Portman St, Marble Arch, W.1. & 21 College Cres, Swiss Cottage, N.W.3. *t*: Mayfair 6470 & Primrose 2700.

MAURICE, Major-Gen. Sir Frederick, K.C.M.G. C.B., LL.D. Author. *Publ*: Forty Days in 1914; Robert E. Lee The Soldier; British Strategy; The 16th Foot. *a*: c/o Constable & Co Ltd, 10 Orange St, W.C.2.

MAURICE, FURNLEY (pen name): see Wilmot, Frank Leslie.

MAURICE, Michael. See Skinner, Rev. Conrad Arthur.

MAUROIS, Andre, Hon.K.B.E., D.C.M. *b*: 1885. *e*: Lycee de Rouen. Author, Commandeur Legion de Honneur. *Publ*: The Silences of Colonel Bramble; Ariel, or the Life of Shelley; Life of Disraeli; Essay on Dickens; Aspects of Biography; Byron; Voltaire; Edward VII; The Family Circle; Englishwomen & Others; Lyautey; Dickens; A History of England; Chateaubriand; The Art of Living; Battle of France; Tragedy in France; I Remember, I Remember (autobiog); Woman Without Love; etc. *a*: Neuilly-Sur-Seine, France.

MAVOR, OSBORNE HENRY: see Bridie, James.

MAVROGORDATO, John Nicolas. *b*: Lon 1882. *e*: Eton, Exeter Col Oxf. Married. *s*: 2. *n.a*: Literary Ed English Review 1911-12, reader & literary adviser to various publishers. *Publ*: Cassandra in Troy; The World in Chains (a socialist looks at the War); The Erotokritos (a Greek romantic epic of 1645); Three Cretan Plays (with Prof F. H. Marshall). *c.t*: Times, Edin Review, New Statesman, Classical Quarterly, etc. *s.s*: Modern English literature, modern Greek hist & literature, etc. *c*: Savile, Garrick. *a*: 11 Redington Rd, Hampstead, N.W.3.

MAWER, Allen, F.B.A. *b*: Lon 1879. *e*: Coopers' Coy's G.S., Univ Col Lon & Gonville & Caius Col Cam. *m*: Lettice M. K. Heath. *d*: 4. Provost Univ Col Lon. *Publ*: The Vikings; Place Names of Northumb & Durham; Problems of Place-name Study. *c.t*: Mod Lang Review, Review of Eng Studies, etc. *s.s*: Hist of Viking period, place names. *c*: Athenæum. *a*: 12 Dawson Pl, W.2. *t*: Bayswater 2170.

MAWER, Irene Rose. *b*: London 1893. *e*: Putney Hgh Sch, Cen Sch of Speech Training & Dramatic Art. *m*: Mark Edward Perugini. Dir Ginner Mawer Training Coll & Theatre Co, Actress, Producer of Mime, Trainer of Teachers & Stage Artists, Mem of Assoc of Teachers of Speech & Drama, Pres Inst of Mime. *Publ*: The Art of Mime; Twelve Mime Plays; The Dance of Words. *s.s*: Mime, Its Hist, Technique & Mod Development, Hist of Theatre & Drama. *Rec*: Walking, swimming. *a*: 9 Montpellier Spa Rd, Cheltenham.

MAWSON, SIR DOUGLAS: univ. professor; *b*. Bradford, Eng., May, 1882; *s*. Robert Ellis and Margaret Anne (Moore) M.; educ. Univ. of Sydney. DEGREES: B.E., D.Sc.; *m*. Francisca Adriana Delprat, 1914. AUTHOR: The House of the Blizzard, 1914. CLUBS: Royal Societies, Royal Thames Yacht (both London); Sydney Univ. (Australia). Relig. denom. Church of England. OFFICE: University, Adelaide, Australia.

MAWSON, E. Prentice, F.R.I.B.A., M.T.P.I., P.I.L.A. *Publ*: Dudley, A Study in Development; Art & Craft of Garden Making, 5th Ed (Jt); etc. Liveryman of the Gardeners' Co. Order of King George of Greece. Brit Rep on Internat Commn for Replanning Salonika. *a*: High St. Hse, Lancaster.

MAX. See Whitehead-Smith, Sidney.

MAXFIELD, Rev. Thomas Harold William. *b*: Annesley Woodhouse, Notts 1897. *e*: St Edmund's Sch Canterbury. Clerk in Holy Orders, Rector of Meonstoke & Rural Dean of Bishop's Waltham, Chaplain to the Bishop of Portsmouth 1947. *n.a*: B'ham Correspondent of Church of England Newsp 1928—34. *Publ*: The Words of Institution. *Ctr*: Ch of Eng Newsp, Mod Churchman. *s.s*: Theology. *Rec*: Gardening, travel. *a*: Meonstoke Rectory, Southampton. *T*: Droxford 99.

MAXTON, George Scrimgeour, M.A., Ph.D. *b*: Perth. *e*: Perth Acad & Edin Univ. Gen Ed & Dir McDougall's Educational Co Ltd. *Publ*: The Economics of Commerce ; From Earliest Times to Present Day ; etc. *Ctr*: Eductnl & Gen Press. *s.s*: Educational. *Rec*: Fishing, golf. *a*: Falcon Bank, Liberton, Edinburgh. *T*: Edin 79354.

MAXTONE, GRAHAM, Joyce. (See **STRUTHER, Jan.**) *b*: London 1901. *e*: Private. *m*: Anthony Maxtone Graham. *s*: 2. *d*: 1. Writer. *a* 17 Alexander Pl, London, S.W.7. *T*: Kensington 0296.

MAXWELL, Arthur Stanley. *b*: London 1896. *e*: Brighton Sec Sc & Stanboro' Col. *m*: Rachel E. Joyce. *s*: 4. *d*: 1. Ed of The Present Truth. *Publ*: Great Issues; Protestantism Imperilled ; After Many Days ; Uncle Arthur's Bedtime Stories (three & a half million copies sold); This Mighty Hour ; Back to God ; Our Wonderful Bible; Discovering London; etc. Ed of Present Truth 1920—. Gen Mang of the Stanboro' Press Ltd '25—32. *a*: Glencairn, Sheepcote Lane, Watford. *t*: 5004 Watford.

MAXWELL, Constantia, M.A., Litt.D. *b*: Dublin 1885. *e*: St Leonards Sch, St Andrews Fife & Trin Coll Dublin. Lecky Prof of Modern History Trin Coll Dublin. *Publ*: Irish History from Contemporary Sources; County & Towns in Ireland under the Georges ; Dublin under the Georges; The History of Trinity College Dublin ; The English Traveller in France ; The Wisdom of Dr Johnson ; Ed of Arthur Young's Travels in France; Arthur Young's Tour in Ireland. *Ctr*: English Hist Rev, History; Sewanee Rev, etc. *s.s*: Social & Economic History, France & Ireland in the 18th Century. *a*: Trinity College, Dublin.

MAXWELL, C. Bede. (See **MAXWELL, Violet.**) *Publ*: Cold Nose of the Law ; Wooden Hookers. *a*: 15 Hardy St, Ashfield, Sydney, Australia. *T*: UA 1289.

MAXWELL, Donald. *b*: Clapham 1877. *e*: Manor Hse Sc, Clapham Common & Slade Sc, Univ Col. *m*: Evelyne Morgan. *d*: 2. Artist & Author. *n.a*: Naval & Travel Artist Corr Graphic 1906-26, Official Artist to Admrlty '18. Made sketches in Palestine & Mesopotamia & for Imp War Museum. With Prince of Wales in *Renown* & thro' India to make colour sketches of the tour. *Publ*: The Enchanted Road; A Detective in Kent, Surrey, Sussex, Essex; A Painter in Palestine; The New Lights o' London; The Landscape of Thomas Hardy; Excursions in Colour; A Pilgrimage of the Thames, etc. *s.s*: Eng topography. *Rec*: Small-boat cruising. *a*: E. Farleigh Hse, nr Maidstone. *t*: Barming 86234.

MAXWELL, Sir George, K.B.E., C.M.G. *b*: Malacca 1871. *e*: Clifton Col. *m*: Florence Evelyn Stevenson. *s*: 2. Colonial Civil Servant (ret). *Publ*: In Malay Forests. Brit Rep Slavery Cmt L.N. *a*: Sunning Wood, Boars Hill, Oxf. *t*: Boars Hill 139.

MAXWELL, Sir Herbert Eustace, Bart., P.C., F.R.S., K.T., LL.D., D.C.L. *b*: Edinburgh 1845. *e*: Eton & Ch Ch Oxf. *m*: Mary Campbell. *s*: 2 (dec). *d*: 3. Landowner. *Publ*: Life of the Rt Hon W. H. Smith; Sixty Years a Queen '97; The House of Douglas; A Century of Empire; The Place-names of Galloway; Flowers: a Garden Note Book; Meridiana: Noontide Essays; Evening Memories; etc. *s.s*: Archæology, botany, nat hist. M.P. Wigtowns '80–95. Lord of the Treasury '86–92, Lord Lieut of Wigtowns 1903–34, Chm Roy Comm on Tuberculosis '97–98 & of Roy Comm on Ancient Monuments (Scotland) 1907–34, Pres of Soc of Antiquaries '00–13. *Rec*: Horticulture, angling. *a*: Monreith, Whauphill, Wigtownshire. *t*: Port William 18.

MAXWELL, James, M.D., F.R.C.P. *b*: Rutherglen, Scotland 1901. *e*: Highgate Sch, St Barts Hosp. *Publ*: Introduction to Diseases of the Chest ; The Care of Tuberculosis in the Home. *Ctr*: Med Journs. *s.s*: Med (Diseases of the Chest). *c*: R.A.C. *a*: 17 Harley St, London, W.1. *T*: Langham 3930.

MAXWELL, James Laidlaw, C.B.E., M.D., B.S.(Lond). *b*: Birmingham 1873. *e*: Univ Coll Sch Lond, St Bart's Hosp Med Sch. *m*: Millicent Bertha Saunders. *d*: 3. Head Dept of Field Research Henry Lester Institute of Med Research Shanghai 1929—36, Dir Institute of Hosp Technology Hankow '37—40, Sec Internat Red Cross for Central China '37—40. *n.a*: Ed China Med Journ 1925—31, Assoc Ed Internat Journ of Leprosy '31—. *Publ*: Diseases of China; Leprosy: A Practical Textbook for Use in China. *s.s*: Leprosy. *Rec*: Gardening. *w.s*: Major R.A.M.C. 1915. *a*: 52 Kings Rd, Flitwick. Bedford. *T*: Flitwick 289.

MAXWELL, Sir John, K.B., C.M.G. *b*: Maxwelltown 1875. *e*: Dumfries Acad & Glas Univ. Chm N. Area Traffic Comm. *Publ*: Handbook Gold Coast Colony. Colonial Service 27 y. *Rec*: Shooting, golf. *c*: Roy Socs, Lon, Scot Cons, Edin, & Union, Newcastle/Tyne. *a*: 41 Grey St, Newcastle-on-Tyne, Westfield Hse, Gosforth, Northumberland, & Tarquah, Dumfries.

MAXWELL, Rev. John Lowry. *b*: Lurgan, Co Armagh, Ireland 1880. *e*: Lurgan Coll. *m*: Ellen R. Steadman. *d*: 2. Clergyman (C. of E.). *Publ*: Nigeria: The Land The People & Christian Progress ; An Old Testament History (In Hausa) ; A Version of Bunyan's Holy War (in Ha[u]sa); etc. *Ctr*: The Lightbearer. *s.s*: Nigerian Langs. *a*: Pigeon Hse Farm, Walberton, Sussex. *T*: Yapton 289.

MAXWELL, Joseph, V.C., M.C., D.C.M. *b*: Sydney, Australia 1898. *e*: Gilluston Public Sch N.S.W. Journalist. *n.a*: On Staff Sydney Metropolitan Newsps. *Publ*: Hells Bells & Mademoiselles. *s.s*: Topical Events. *Rec*: Swimming, watching cricket, football & boxing. *a*: 8 Fanlight St, Manly, N.S.W., Australia.

MAXWELL, Maclean, F.J.I. *b*: Rothesay, Buteshire 1879. *m*: Margaret MacPherson. *s*: 1. *d*: 1. Journalist. *n.a*: Ed & Manager Greenock Herald & West Coast Courier, Ed & Proprietor Bridge of Weir Advertiser. *Ctr*: Various. *s.s*: Politics, Industry, Photography, etc. *Rec*: Music, cinema, theatre, chess, travelling. *c*: Ardgowan Bowls. *a*: Press News Agency, Greenock, Scotland, & Ardgowan Sq, Greenock.

MAXWELL, R. C., O.B.E., LL.D. Barrister. *Publ*: Various Municipal & Local Govt & Legal Publs. *a*: 2 Elm Court Gdns, E.C.4. *t*: Central 6634.

MAXWELL, S., LL.B.(Cantab), M.A., F.R.A.S. *Publ*: Poetry for Boys. *s.s*: Educ, Astron. *a*: Manor Hse Sc, Clapham Common, S.W.4.

MAXWELL, Struthers Burt. *b*: Baltimore 1882. *e*: Priv Sc Philadelphia, Princeton Univ & Merton Col Oxf. *m*: Katharine Newlin. *s*: 1. *d*: 1. Author. *n.a*: Reporter The Philadelphia Times (2 y). *Publ*: Three books of verse; Chance Encounters; The Diary of a Dude Wrangler; The Delectable Mountains; They Could Not Sleep; The Other Side (1929); Festival (English Book Society choice '32); Entertaining The Islanders ('33); etc. *c.t*: Scribner's Mag, Harper's Magazine, The Forum, The Saturday Evening Post, Chicago Tribune, North American Review. *s.s*: Fiction. Rancher, Wyoming 1908. U.S.A. Air Service '18. Fellow Nat Inst Arts & Letters. *c*: Coffee Hse, Franklin Inn. *a*: Three River Ranch, Moran, Wyoming, & Hibernia, Southern Pines, N. Carolina.

MAXWELL, Violet. (See **MAXWELL, C. Bede.**) *b*: Sydney, Australia 1901. *e*: Sydney Girls Hgh Sch. *m*: C. Bede Maxwell. *s*: 1. *d*: 1. Writer. *Ctr* Kennel Review. *s.s*: Australiana, Sea Hist of Australia, Australian Surf Lifesaving, Dogs (Gun). *Rec*: Dog-Breeding. *a*: 15 Hardy St, Ashfield, Sydney, Australia. *T*: UA 1289.

MAXWELL, William Babington. *m*: Sydney Constance Brabazon Moore. *s*: 1. *d*: 1. Chm Soc of Authors. Chm Nat Book Counc. *Publ*: The Guarded Flame; Mrs Thompson; The Devil's Garden; Spinster of this Parish; We Forget Because We Must; The Concave Mirror; And Mr Wyke Bond; etc. *c.t*: Evening Standard. War Service '14—18. *Rec*: Riding, golf. *c*: Carlton, Beefsteak. *a*: 11 Ashley Gdns, S.W.1. *t*: Victoria 8693.

MAXWELL, William (Keepers). M.A. *b*: Lincoln, Illinois 1908. *e*: Public Schs Lincoln, Chicago, Illinois, Univs of Illinois, Harvard. *m*: Emily Gilman Noyes. Writer & Editor. *n.a*: Ed Staff The New Yorker 1936—47. *Publ*: The Folded Leaf; They Came Like Swallows; Bright Centre of Heaven; The Heavenly Tenants. *Ctr*: New Yorker, Harper's Bazaar, Atlantic Monthly, Horizon Time & Tide, Life & Letters To-day, La Nouvelle Revue Francaise, Sat Review, etc. *s.s*: Fiction. *c*: Harvard, P.E.N. *a*: Baptist Church Rd, Yorktown Heights, N.Y.

MAXWELL-LYTE, Sir Henry Churchill, K.C.B., M.A., HonD.Litt, F.B.A., F.S.A., F.R.Hist.S. *b*: Lon 1848. *e*: Eton & Ch Ch Oxf. *m*: Frances Fownes Somerville. *s*: 3. *d*: 3. Dep Keeper of Records 1886–1926. *n.a*: A Mem Roy Comm on Historical MSS '86–1934. *Publ*: History of Eton College (1877); History of the University of Oxford ('86); Some Somerset Manors ('31); etc. *c.t*: Proc Somerset Archæological Soc, Somerset & Dorset Notes & Queries. *s.s*: Local hist. Before '86 an insp of Hist MSS. *Rec*: Photography. *c*: Athenæum. *a*: 61 Warwick Sq, S.W.1. *t*: Victoria 7422.

MAY, Allan. *b*: E. Bridgford. Librarian to late Lady Tennyson for some y. *Publ*: Thoughts & Dreams of Quiet Hours. *c.t*: Answers, Sign, People's Friend, I.W. County Press. *s.s*: Poetry, song lyrics. Won the 1st prize in Answers £50 prize lyric competition. Has had four songs published. *Rec*: Tennis, swimming. *a*: Bridgford, Freshwater Bay, I.O.W.

MAY, Arthur Victor. *b*: Highgate, London 1898. *e*: Priv, Guildhall Sch of Music, Tech Coll, Northampton Inst. *m*: May Martin. *s*: 1. *d*: 1. Writer. *n.a*: Ed House Organs for Lever Brothers 1922—26, Copy-Chief American & English Advertising Agencies '26—32, Leader Writer Nat Trade Press '43—45, Ed Textile Mag for Home & Overseas '45—47. *Publ*: The Story of Wool; Coal, Steel & Textiles; The Jaeger Legend. *Ctr*: Nat Press, etc. *s.s*: Historic Background to Industries & Commodities, Textiles, Horology, Art, Music, Advertising. *Rec*: Pianoforte, riding, swimming. *a*: Thanage, Parkgate Cresc, Hadley Wood, Barnet, Hertfordshire.

MAY, BERNICE (pen name): see **Cross, Zora Bernice May.**

MAY, Major-Gen Edward Sinclair, K.C.B., C.M.G., D.L., J.P. *b*: Dublin 1856. *e*: Rugby Sc & R.M.A. Woolwich. *m*: (1) Evelyn Kekewich; (2) Charlotte Dorothea Stirling. *s*: 1 (dec). *d*: 6. Army Officer (ret). *Publ*: Achievements of Field Artillery (1893); Imperial Defence; Introduction to Military Geography; Changes & Chances of a Soldier's Life (1925); etc. *c.t*: Proc R.A. Inst, Un Service Inst, Mil Soc of Ireland, etc. Commanded 8th Lucknow Div '14–18. Des 4 times in S. African War. Des Gt War in India. Kt Legion of Honour & of St John of Jerusalem. Mem Terr Cmt of Devon. County Commssr Boy Scouts for Devon '19–32. *Rec*: Fishing. *c*: Athenæum. *a*: Rockbeare Ct, Rockbeare, Devon. *t*: Whimple 215.

MAY, Fred. M.B.E. *b*: Wallasey. *e*: Wallasey, Reading Univ. *m*: Amy Kidger. *s*: 1. *d*: 1. Artist & Caricaturist. *n.a*: Tatler, Graphic & Weekly Sketch 1915—47, formerly Artist & Cartoonist Liverpool Dly Post & Echo, Sheffield Telegraph, Hultons (Manch), Dly Gazette (Middlesbrough). *s.s*: Cartoons, Humorous Drawings & Caricatures. *a*: Rokeby, Allcroft Rd, Reading, Berks. *T*: 81008.

MAY, Rev. George Lacey. *b*: Birch, Nr Colchester 1872. *e*: Felsted Sch, Pembroke Coll Camb, Ely Theological Coll. *m*: Dorothy De Denne. *s*: 3. *d*: 3. Priest. *Publ*: Some Eighteenth Century Churchmen; English Religious Verse; The Book Luminous; Fellowship of the Prayer; He Spake in Parables; The Saving Christ; The Heavenly Ladder. *a*: 28 Edgar Rd, Winchester.

MAY, Herbert Richard Dudfield, M.C., M.A., LL.D. *b*: Hendon 1878. *e*: Charterhouse, St John Coll Camb. *m*: Mabel Sturdy. Barrister. *Publ*: Edward Racedale's Will; Nancy's Heart; Preparation; The Gold Touch. *a*: The Green Hall, Ashbourne.

MAY, James Lewis. *b*: 1873. *e*: Univ Coll Sch & France. *m*: Elizabeth Hyde. *s*: 1. *d*: 1. Author, Chev Legion of Honour. *n.a*: Jt-Ed with Henry D. Davray of The Anglo-French Review 1919—22. *Publ*: Anatole France: The Man & His Work; Cardinal Newman: A Study; The Path Through the Wood; Father Tyrrell & the Modernist Movement; The Oxford Movement; Charles Lamb: A Study; An English Treasury of Religious Prose; Memories of John Lane & The Bodley Head; The Unchanging Witness; Thorn & Flower; Fenelon: A Study; etc. *Ctr*: Dict of National Biography. *a*: 2 Winterstoke Gdns, Mill Hill, London, N.W.7. *T*: Mill Hill 2077.

MAY, Surg Capt Percival Marshall, R.N. *b*: Allington, Bridport, Dorset 1869. Exeter Sch, Roy Devon & Exeter Hosp, Guy's Hosp. *m*: Evelyn Beryl Stephens. *s*: 1. *d*: 2. *Publ*: Active Immunization Against Diphtheria (with Surg Rear-Adm Sir Sheldon Dudley, R.N. & Surg-Capt J. A. O'Flynn, R.N.); Observations on the Immunity & Disability caused by Vaccinia (with Surg Rear-Adm Sir Sheldon Dudley, R.N.). *Ctr*: B.M.J. *Rec*: Cricket, lawn tennis, cycling, motoring, golf. *a*: Brynsworthy, Hosey Hill, Westerham, Kent. *T*: 116.

MAY, Percy. D.Sc(Lon), F.I.C. *b*: Lon 1886. *e*: Tollington Pk Col Lon & U.C.L. Cons Chem. *Publ*: The Chemistry of Synthetic Drugs. *c.t*: Lancet, Science Progress, Chem & Ind, etc. *s.s*: Chem patents. *Rec*: Golf, music. *c*: Chemical. *a*: 1 The Riding, N.W.11, & 70 Chancery Lane, W.C.2. *t*: Speedwell 2317 & Holborn 0437.

MAY, Richard William. *b*: Lon 1853. *e*: Stockwell G.S. & Kelvedon Sc. Chm of Grant & May, Salmon & Fish Factors. Common Counc City of Lon, Billingsgate Ward 1915–. *Rec*: Cycling. 1 Gresham Rd, Brixton S.W.9, & 5 Billingsgate Market, E.C.3. *t*: Brixton 0805 & Royal 1199.

MAY, THOMAS HENRY: priest; b. London, Eng., Feb. 26, 1851; s. Thomas Henry and Elizabeth (Bradley) M.; educ. privately, Haverfordwest Grammar Sch. DEGREES: S.G.L., M.A., D.D. (Oxford); m. Caroline Nelson, Apr. 10, 1883. AUTHOR: The Place and Work of the Prophets in the Catholic Church, 1914; Laying on of Hands, 1926; Requiem, 1927; Hymn for Airmen, 1928; Ordained Deacon, 1874; Priest, 1875; Curate of Bramley, 1874-78; Preston, 1878; S. Margaret, Ilkley, 1879; Leeds Parish Church, 1879-1881; Senior Curate and Clerk in Orders,

Leeds, 1881-1889; Rector of Heswall, 1890-1921; Rural Dean of Wirral, 1897-1916; Hon. Canon of Chester, 1914; Proctor in Convocation, 1916-1923; Librarian of Chester Cathedral, 1923-1929. Relig. denom., Church of England. HOME: 41 Esplanade Road, Scarborough, Eng.

MAY, Rev. William John, D.Litt (U.S.A.). Meth Minister. *Publ*: Alphabet of Stories; Sunday Morning Stories; John Bunyan, Pilgrim Preacher; According to Mary, Martha, etc. *c.t*: Teachers & Taught, Young Meth, Meth Recorder, Meth Times & Leader, etc. *a*: 74 Victoria Rd, Fulwood, Preston.

MAYCOCK, Alan Lawson, M.C., M.A. *b*: Hove 1898. *e*: Marlborough Coll, Clare Coll Camb. *m*: Edith Nathan. *d*: 1. Asst Sec Univ of Camb Appts Board. *Publ*: An Oxford Notebook; Things Seen in Cambridge; Nicholas Ferrar of Little Gidding; The Apocalypse. *s.s*: History, Archt. *Rec*: Water-colour painting. *a*: Elton Lodge, Great Shelford, Cambridge.

MAYER, Joseph, M.A., Ph.D., LT.D. *b*: San Antonio, Texas 1887. *e*: Univs of Texas, Columbia, Harvard Southwestern. *m*: Helen O'Neill. Economist & Sociologist. *n.a*: Mem Advisory Cttee Scientific Book Club Inc 1929—, Ctr Ed Social Science '30—, Spec Foreign Corr Washington Post '37. *Publ*: The Seven Seals of Science; Postwar National Income; Metric VS. English System of Weights & Measures; Profit Sharing in American Industry; Bigger Men in Better Jobs; The Income & Wealth of the American People. *Ctr*: Scientific Monthly, Social Science, American Econ Rev, Isis, The American Journ of Sociology. *s.s*: Science, Technology, Postwar Reconstruction, Econ & Social Theory. *Rec*: Legerdemain, swimming. *a*: 722 Jackson Pl, N.W., Washington 6, D.C., U.S.A. *T*: National 8940.

MAYER, Sir Robert, Kt., F.R.C.M. *b*: Mannheim 1879. *e*: Abroad. *m*: Dorothy Moulton Piper. *s*: 2. *d*: 1. Financier, Philanthropist, Founder of the Robert Mayer Concerts for Children, Chm Brit Amer Corp, Chm Elizabeth Fry Centenary Fund, Hon Treas Internat Student Service, Gov Chaigeley Sch for Maladjusted Children, Hon Sec Transatlantic Foundation, Hon Treas Childrens Theatre. *Publ*: Young People in Trouble. *Ctr*: Educational & musical periodicals. *s.s*: Education, Pioneer Work in the Social Field, Particularly Affecting the Young. *Rec*: Music & riding. *c*: Athenæum. *a*: 7 Gloucester Sq, London, W.2. *T*: Paddington 6659.

MAYER, Sylvain, K.C., B.A., Ph.D. *b*: Paris 1863. *e*: Univ Coll Sch, Univ Coll, Heidelberg Univ. *m*: (1) Lilian Mary Blakeway (dec'd). *s*: 1. *d*: 3. (2) Gladys Marion Millicent Cooper. *Publ*: Law of Rating & Procedure on Appeal (3 editions); Law of Compensation; Law of Agricultural Holdings (6 editions); Representation of the People Act; The French Commercial Code of Commerce; Reminiscences of a K.C. (theatrical & legal); Captured in Court (a novel with Anthony Guest); Translation of the Oration of Pericles from Thucydides; Papa's Honeymoon, (a Comedy with W. K. Tarpey); A Gay Widower, a Comedy. *Rec*: Golf, chess. *c*: Savage. *a*: 18 Lexham Gdns, Kensington, London, W.8. *T*: West 9206.

MAYES, Harold. *b*: Thrapston 1915. *e*: Kimbolton. *m*: Journalist, formerly Reuter War Corresp. *n.a*: Sports Ed Sunday Empire News. *Rec*: Billiards, golf. *c*: Press. *a*: 1 Cresc Rd, Crouch End, London, N.8. *T*: Mount View 5620.

MAYHEW, L. Mary. *b*: London. *e*: Priv. Journalist *n.a*: Ed Newnes, Sub Ed for Benn Bros, Sub Ed for Sir Chas Higham, Ed for the Citizen & for Feminine Life. *Publ*: Miracle Healing. *Ctr*: Dly Telegraph, Dly Mail. Dly Sketch, Dly Dispatch, Sheffield Telegraph, Birmingham Post, Ev News, Standard, Star, Everyman, Ency, Woman's Ency, etc. *s.s*: Child Welfare, Med Journalism. *Rec*: Theatre, reading. *a*: Chevington, 129 Leylands Rd, Burgess Hill, Sussex.

MAYNARD, Major–Gen. Sir Charles Clarkson Martin, K.C.B., C.M.G., D.S.O. *b*: Rangoon 1870. *e*: St Paul's Sc & R.M.C. Sandhurst. *m*: Dorothy Agnes Davidson. *s*: 1. *d*: 1. Major Gen (ret). Col of Devon Regt. *Publ*: The Murmansk Venture. Grand Gordon St Anne of Russia. Legion of Honour, France. White Eagle, Serbia. *Rec*: Fishing, golf. *a*: Glassenbury Cottage, Bexhill-on-Sea, Sussex. *t*: 991.

MAYNARD, Constance Louisa, M.A. *b*: Lon 1849. *e*: Priv, Girton Cam. 1st Princ of Westfield Col Lon '82–1913. *Publ*: Life of Dora Greenwell; Progressive Creation; A Threefold Revelation; Take With You Words; We Women; etc. *c.t*: Hibbert Journ, Christian, etc. *s.s*: Religion. Extensive Travel. *c*: New Alliance. *a*: The Sundial, Gerrard's Cross, Bucks.

MAYNARD, John Albert, M.A., Ph.D., L.L.M., Pd.M. *b*: France 1884. *e*: Univs of Paris, Chicago, New York. Teacher. *Publ*: Les tendances apocalyptiques chez Ezechiel; Studies in Religious Texts from Assur; A Survey of Hebrew Education; The Living Religion of the World; Seven Years of Old Testament Study; The Birth of Judaism; The Huguenot Church of New York; Les livres de Samuel. *s.s*: History, Archæology, Philology. *Rec*: Travel. *a*: 111 East 60th St, New York, N.Y., U.S.A. *T*: Regent H 0010.

MAYNARD Ralph Shields. *b*: East Maitland, N.S.W. Aust 1881. *e*: Sydney Gr Sch. *m*: Margaret Harvey Armour. *s*: 1. *d*: 1. Writer. *n.a*: Ed Live Stock Bulletin 1911— Advertising Fractioner, 1911—. *Publ*: Australian Dairymans Handbook; His Was the Vision; A Life of C. D. Meares; Successful Gardening. *s.s*: Cattle Breeding, Economics. *a*: 39 Park St, Sydney, Australia *T*: M.A. 3721.

MAYNARD, Theodore, M.A., Ph.D. *b*: Madras, India 1890. *e*: Priv, Fordham & Georgetown Univs, Catholic Univ of America. *m*: (1) Sara Casey, (2) Kathleen Sheehan. *s*: 4. *d*: 3. Author, formerly Univ Prof. *Publ*: Story of American Catholicism; Collected Poems; The World I Saw; The Reed & the Rock; Queen Elizabeth; Humanist as Hero, the Life of Sir Thomas More; Orestes Brownson; etc. *Ctr*: Yale Rev, Sun Times, Sat Review of Lit, London Mercury, American Mercury, Catholic World, Atlantic Monthly, etc. *s.s*: Tudor Hist, American Catholic. *a*: 44 Murray Ave, Port Washington, N.Y., U.S.A. *T*: Port Washington 2667J.

MAYNE, Arthur Brinley. *b*: Swansea 1893. *e*: Llandovery & Balliol Coll Oxf. *m*: Dorothy Watson. *s*: 2. Headmaster Camb County High Sch for Boys 1922—45, Mem of Comm of Headmasters' Conference '33, Examiner in Mathematics for various Examinations. *Publ*: Essentials of School Geometry; Essentials of School Algebra; Essentials of School Arithmetic. *s.s*: Mathematics. *Rec*: Various. *a*: 10 Eversley Rd Sketty, Swansea.

MAYNE, Ethel Colburn. *b*: Johnstown Ireland. *e*: Priv. Biographer, Novelist. *Publ*: Life of Byron; Life & Letters of Lady Byron; Novels: The Fourth Ship; One of Our Grandmothers; etc. *c.t*: Yorkshire Post, New Statesman, Week-End Review, etc. *s.s*: Byron. *a*: 23 Ellerker Gdns, Richmond-on-Thames.

MAYNE, Rev. William Cyril, M.A. *b*: Glos 1877. *e*: Westminster Sc & Trin Col Cam. *m*: Mary Onslow. Clerk in Holy Orders. *Publ*: Verse Trans of Pindar's Olympian Odes; Ed Educ Books. Asst Master Rugby Sc 1907–12. Princ Bishop's Col Cheshunt '20–25. Exam Chap Bishops of Lon & St Albans. Boyle Lect '29–31. *c*: Leander. *a*: Chiswick Vicarage, W.4. *t*: Chiswick 5855.

MAYO, The Rt. Hon. The Earl of. *Publ*: The Bridgewater Gallery (with the late Sir Lionel Cust); The Thames Valley; Oxfordshire: A Survey. (Both jtly with Profs S. D. Adshead & Patrick Abercromby). *a*: Maidenhead, Berks.

MAYO, Eileen. *b*: Norwich. *e*: Clifton Hgh Sch Bristol, Slade Sch London. *m*: R. Gainsborough. Artist & Author. *Publ*: The Story of Living Things; Shells & How They Live; Little Animals of the Countryside; etc. *Ctr*: Sphere, Countrygoer, etc. *s.s*: Drawing & Painting on Natural Hist. *Rec*: Painting. *a*: Fletching, nr Uckfield, Sussex, & 33 Royal Ave, London, S.W.3. *T*: Newick 6.

MAYO, Katherine. *e*: Boston Mass. Critic & Essayist. *Publ*: The Standard Bearers; Mounted Justice; Mother India; Slaves of the Gods; Soldiers; What Next; etc. *a*: New York, U.S.A.

MAYO-ROBSON, SIR ARTHUR (WILLIAM): consulting surgeon, Col. A. M. S. (retired); b. Filey, Yorkshire, Eng., Apr. 17, 1853; s. John Binnington and Mary Susannah (Mayo) Robson; educ. privately, and at Wesley College (Sheffield), Yorkshire Coll., Victoria Univ.; Leeds Univ.; as post graduate: London, and Paris. DEGREES: F.R.C.S., D.Sc., K.B.E., C.B., C.V.O., Kt. Bach., Knight of grace, Order of St. John of Jerusalem, Chevalier Legion d'Honneur; m. Florence Walker, Sept. 5, 1883 (died July 24, 1930). AUTHOR: A Guide to the Instruments and appliances Required in Various Operations, 1889, 1891; Diseases of the Gall Bladder and Bile Ducts, 1897 (2nd edit. 1900; 3rd edit., assisted by J. F. Dobson, F.R.C.S., 1903); On Gall Stones and Their Treatment, 1892; Gall Stones, Their Complications and Treatment (with Cammidge), 1909; Diseases of the Stomach and Their Surgical Treatment with Moynihan), 1901 (2nd edit. 1904; Diseases of the Pancreas and Their Surgical Treatment (with Moynihan), 1903; Cancer and Its Treatment, 1905; The Pancreas: Its Surgery and Pathology (with Cammidge); Operations upon the Bile Passages and the Pancreas (in "A System of Operative Surgery" edited by F. F. Burghard), 1909; Surgery of the Stomach (in "Surgery, its Principles and Practice", edited by W. W. Keen), 1908; Cancer of the Stomach, 1907; Sections on Diseases and Affections of the Stomach and Duodenum; of the Gall Bladder and Bile Ducts: and of the Pancreas (in Vol. II of "A System of Treatment", edited by A. Latham and T. Crisp English), 1912. Contributor to Vol. XLVII of the Proc. of the Royal Society, "Observations on the Secretion of Bile"; Articles on Diseases of the Gall Bladder and Bile Ducts to Clifford Albert's System of Medicine; Numerous Articles in The Lancet, Brit. Med. Journ., Annals of Surgery, Medical Annual, Brit. Gynaecological Journ., etc. Joint editor: Surgery, Medicine and Gynaecology. Hon. Surgeon General Infirmary, Leeds, 1887; Hon. Consulting Surgeon since 1902; Hon. Consulting Surgeon King Edward VII Memorial Hosp., Windsor; Mem. Council Royal Coll. of Surgeons, 1893-1909; V.P.R.C.S., 1902-3 and 1904-5; Hunterian Prof. R.C.S. 1897, 1900 and 1909; Bradshaw Lecturer R.C.S. 1905; Hon. Cons. Surg. Dreadnought Hosp., 1906; Hon. Fellow Amer. Surgical Soc.; Hon. Fellow Southern Surgical Assn.; Hon. Associé Soc. de Chir., Paris; Hon. Mem. Royal Soc. de Medic., Ghent; Prof. Surgery York Coll., 1890-99; Emeritus Prof., 1899; and Leeds Univ. since 1900; rep. of Senate on Council of York Coll., 1898; Pres. Brit. Gynaecology Soc. 1897, and of Leeds and W. R. Med. Chir. Soc., 1896; Hon. Pres. Internat. Congress, Lisbon, 1906; V. P. Fellowship of Med. and Post Grad. Assn., Governor Imperial Service Coll., Windsor; V. P. Brit. Science Guild; Served during Great War as Consulting Surgeon on Gallipoli, Egypt, France and Southern Command, 1914-1920 (Despatches twice); Consulting Surg. Croix Rouge Francais; Mem. Consultants, Counter-War Office, during war, and Inspector Orthopaedic Hospitals. CLUBS: Athenaeum, Bath Club, Royal Societies Club. Relig. denom., Church of England. HOME: Broadoak, Seale, Surrey, Eng.

MAYOL, Lurline Bowles. *b*: Franconia, New Hampshire, U.S.A. 1889. *e*: Dow Academy Franconia & New Hampshire Normal Sc, Plymouth, N.H. *m*: Frank E. Mayol. Writer. *Publ*: Jiji Lou; The Talking Totem Pole; The Big Canoe. *s.s*: History, primitive civilisations. *Rec*: Gardening, walking. *a*: Box 683, Route 7, Seattle, Washington, U.S.A.

MAYOR, Beatrice. *b*: London. *e*: Les Marroniers Paris. *m*: R. J. G. Mayor, C.B. *s*: 1. *d*: 2. Writer. *Publ*: (Plays) The Pleasure Garden; Thirty Minutes in a Street; Little Earthquake; Voices From the Crowd; Poems; Four Plays for Children; (Novels) The Stream; The Story Without an End. *a*: 26 Addison Ave, London, W.11. *T*: Park 4148.

MAYOR, Fred. *e*: Hutton Gr Sch (Public). Princ Lytham St Anne's Press Service. *n.a*: Chief Reporter Halifax Gdn 1897, Special Commissioner Cotton Factory Times 1900, Asst Ed Papermaker '01, Ed Textile Journal '01, Ed Lytham Standard '02—13, Ed Lytham Times '29—46. *Ctr*: American Journs. *s.s*: Textile, Sport. *a*: 2a Pleasant St, Lytham. *T*: 406 & 6403.

MAYOU, Marmaduke Stephen, F.R.C.S. *b*: Monmouth 1876. *e*: Hereford, King's Col, Lon Hosp. *m*: Daphne England. *d*: 3. Ophth Surg. Surg to Cent Lon Ophth & Bolingbroke Hosps. *Publ*: Diseases of the Eye; Bacteriology & Pathology of the Eye; Operations on the Eye. Hunterian Prof & Jacksonian Prizeman R.C.S. *Rec*: Golf, sailing. *c*: Athenæum, Savile. *a*: 59 Harley St, W.1. *t*: Museum 3366.

MAZE, Paul Lucien, D.C.M., M.M. *b*: Havre 1887. *e*: France. *m*: Mrs Thomas Nelson. *s*: 1. *d*: 1. Painter. Awarded Bar to M.M. & Croix de Guerre. *Publ*: A Frenchman in Khaki. *Ctr*: Various. *a*: Rock Cottage, Harting, Petersfield, Hants. *T*: Harting 65.

McALIECE, W. J. Journalist. *n.a*: Sports Ed The Observer. *a*: 22 Tudor St, E.C.4. *t*: Central 2943.

McALLISTER, Alister, B.A., (Anthony Wharton, Lynn Brock). *b*: Dublin 1877. *e*: Clongowis Wood Col, Nat Univ of Ireland, Trinity Col Dublin. *m*: Cicely Neville Blagg. Author, dramatist. *Publ*: Plays, Under pseudonym Anthony Wharton—Irene Wycherley; At the Barn; 3 Simon Street; Benvenuto Cellini; Nocturne; etc; books, under pseudonym Anthony Wharton—The Man on the Hill; Joan of Over Barrow; Evil Communications; under pseudonym Lynn Brock—The Deductions of Colonel Gore; The Kink; Colonel Gore's Second Case; The Slip Carriage; The Dagwort Coombe Mystery; Q.E.D.; Nightmare; etc. *c.t*: Saturday Evening Post, (Pa U.S.A.), most Eng mags. *s.s*: Short stories. War Service '15—19. *Rec*: Golf, skating. *a*: 9 Upper Belgrave Rd, Clifton, Bristol.

McALLISTER, Elizabeth May, M.A. *b*: Glasgow 1912. *e*: Glas Univ. *m*: Gilbert McAllister. *s*: 2. *n.a*: Ed Town & Country Planning 1942—47. *Publ*: Town & Country Planning (with G. McAllister); Homes, Towns & Countryside (with G. McAllister); Houses & Towns After the War. *Ctr*: Ideal Home, Modern Woman, John o' London's Weekly, etc. *s.s*: Housing, Town Planning, Women's Interest Features. *a*: 17 Park Sq East, Regents Pk, London, N.W.1. *T*: Welbeck 3633.

McALLISTER, Gilbert, M.A., M.P. *b*: Cambusnethan 1906. *e*: Wishaw High Sch, Glas Univ. *m*: Elizabeth Glen. *s*: 2. Journalist, Dir of E. Walter George Ltd. *n.a*: Glas Bulletin, Glas Dly Record, Glas Ev News, United Press Assoc of America, Ed Town & Country

Planning. *Publ*: Homes, Towns & Countryside ; Town & Country Planning (with Elizabeth Glen McAllister) ; James Maxton—the Portrait of a Rebel ; Houses as Homes ; The Book Crisis (with J. B. Priestley & others). *Ctr*: Dly Herald, The Fortnightly, Ency Brit, etc. *a*: 17 Park Sq East, Regents Pk, London, N.W.1. *T*: Welbeck 3633 ; 55 Kenilworth Ave, Wishaw, Lanarkshire. *T*: Wishaw 270.

McALLISTER, Isabel G., M.J.I. *Publ*: Two Biographies. *c.t*: Many periodicals (F/L). *a*: 32 Abingdon Villas, Kensington, W.8.

M'CALLUM, Andrew. *b*: Giffnock 1870. *e*: Elem Scs. *m*: Agnes G. W. Cameron. Journalist. *Publ*: Brochures—Christopher North & the Parish of Mearns (for private circulation); Pollokshaws Village & Burgh, 1600–1912; Graham of Fintry—Patron of Robert Burns (with J. C. Ewing); Alexander Cunningham—Friend of Burns (with J. C. Ewing). *c.t*: Various daily & weekly n/ps. *s.s*: Robert Burns, curling. Was Mem County Counc of Renfrewshire 15 y. On Exec Cmt Burns Fed 25 y. Extensive travel. *Rec*: Golf, cycling. *a*: Gowanbrae, 33 Hillside Rd, Mansewood, Pollokshaws, Glas, S.3. *t*: Langside 118.

McANALLY, Arthur Patrick, B.A. *b*: London 1909. *e*: Charterhouse & Ch Ch Oxf, Lond. *m*: Basil Hamilton Stuart Knight. *s*: 1. *d*: 1. Market Research Director, Founder of Organisation & Methods Branch Admiralty. *Publ*: Modern Business Principles & Practice. *Ctr*: Oxford Mag, Journ Advertising Assoc, Week End Review, Journ of Education, O.M. Bulletin, etc. *s.s*: Scientific Management, Marketing, Education, Distribution, Civil-Service Organisation & Publicity. *c*: Oxf & Camb Univ, Inst of Indust Adminst, Market Research Soc. *a*: 20 Clare Lawn Ave, East Sheen, London, S.W.14. *T*: Prospect 5617.

McARTHUR, Donald Neil, D.Sc., PhD., F.I.C., F.R.S.E. *b*: Glas 1892. *e*: Allan Glen's Sc Glas & Univ of Glas. *m*: A. V. Brough. *s*: 1. Prof of Agricl Chem. *a*: Dept of Chem, W. of Scotland Agric Col, Glas, C.2. *t*: Douglas 2240.

McATEE, Waldo Lee, A.M. *b*: Jalapa, Indiana 1883. *e*: Indiana Univ. *m*: Fannie E. Lawson. *s*: 1. *d*: 1. Biologist. *n.a*: Ed Journ of Wild Life Management 1937—42, Wildlife Review '35—47. *Ctr*: Nature & Sci articles to many periodicals inc the Auk (N.Y.), Nature Mag (Wash), etc. *s.s*: Names of Birds & Plants in the Past, Feed Habits of Birds, Classification of Hemiptera. *Rec*: Reading, writing, country excursions. *c*: Washington Biologists Field. *a*: 6342 Ellis Ave, Chicago, Illinois, U.S.A.

McAULEY, ALEXANDER: professor of mathematics; b. Luton, Eng., Dec., 1863; s. Samuel and Jane Anne (Sowerby) McA.; educ. New Kingswood Sch. (Bath, Eng.). DEGREES B.A. (Cantab., Australia), M.A. (Melbourne, Australia); m. Ida Mary Butler. AUTHOR: Utility of Quaternions in Physics, 1893; Octonions, 1898; Five Figure Logarithms, 1909. Contributes to Philosophical Mag, Messenger of Mathematics, Nature (letters); communication to the Royal Societies and other associations. General character of writing: pure and applied mathematics. OFFICE: University of Tasmania. HOME: Gare Lock, Lower Sandy Bay, Hobart, Tasmania, Australia.

McBAIN, James William, M.A., D.Sc., Ph.D., F.R.S.A. *b*: Chatham, New Brunswick 1882. *e*: Toronto, Leipzig, Heidelberg, Bristol, Brown Univ. *m*: Mary Evelyn Laing. *s*: 1. *d*: 1. Prof of Chemistry. *Publ*: Sorption of Gases & Vapours by Solids. *Ctr*: Numerous to Scientific Journs. *s.s*: Chemistry. *Rec*: Ski-ing, boating, gardening. *a*: 571 Foothill Rd, Stanford Univ. California, U.S.A. *T*: Palo Alto 8334.

MacBEATH, Alexander. *b*: Applecross, Ross-shire 1888. *e*: Applecross Pub Sch, Hutchison's Sch Glas, Glas Univ. *m*: Grace Ann Stewart. *s*: 3. *d*: 1. Prof of Logic & Metaphysics Queen's Univ Belfast since 1925, Sec Glas Soc for Social Service '19—20, Lecturer Glas Univ '20—25. *Publ*: The Moral Self ; The Elements of Logic. *s.s*: Philosophy. *a*: Balmoral Ave, Belfast. *T*: Belfast 65458.

McBRIDE, Jack. *c.t*: Sunday Mercury, Larne Times, Ballymena Observer. *s.s*: Antrim coast, sea-faring subjects. Formerly in Merchant Navy, now writer. *a*: Grey Rock, Garronpoint, Co Antrim.

McBRIDE, Peter, M.D., F.R.C.P.E., F.R.S.E. *b*: Hamburg 1854. *e*: Clifton Col, Edin Univ. Vienna. *Publ*: Diseases of the Throat, Nose and Ear ; The Philosophy of Sport : The Riddle of Personality ; Doctors and Patients ; etc. *c.t*: Medical journs, etc. *Rec* Bridge. *c*: Union, Univ Club, Edinburgh, etc. *a*: 3 St Peter's Grove. York.

McCABE, Joseph. Author of numerous works inc A History of the Popes ; The Papacy in Politics Today ; Modern Rationalism ; Life & Letters of George & Jacob Holyoake ; The Decay of the Church of Rome ; The Principles of Evolution ; The Influence of the Church on Marriage & Divorce ; The Marvels of Modern Physics ; The Hundred Men Who Moved the World ; Key to Love & Sex ; The Splendour of Moorish Spain ; etc. *a*: 22 St George's Rd, Golders Green, London. N.W.

McCAIG, Norman Alexander. *b*: Edinburgh 1910. *e*: Edin Univ. *m*: Isabel I. R. Munro. *s*: 1. *d*: 1. School Teacher. *n.a*: Edit Board Scottish Periodical. *Publ*: The Inward Eye ; Far Cry. *Ctr*: Various. *Rec*: Trout fishing. *a*: 7 Leamington Terr, Edinburgh 10.

McCALEB, Walter Flavius, M.A., B.Lit., Ph.D. *b*: Benton, Texas 1873. *e*: Univs of Texas & Chicago. *m*: Marie Idealie McCaleb. *s*: 1. *d*: 3. Banker, Writer. *n.a*: Assoc Ed Public Ledger (Philadelphia) 1904, Reviewer N.Y. Times '03—04, Amer Hist Rev. *Publ*: The Aaron Burr Conspiracy ; Present & Past Banking in Mexico ; The Public Finances of Mexico ; Theodore Roosevelt (Biog) ; History of the Brotherhood of Railroad Trainmen ; The Conquest of the West. *s.s*: Banking, Finance, Hist. *Rec*: Golf, fishing, sailing, gardening. *a*: Bloxom, Virginia, U.S.A.

McCALL, Annie, M.D. *a*: 165 Clapham Rd, S.W.9.

McCALL, Oswald Walter Samuel, Litt.D., D.D. *b*: Melbourne, Australia. *e*: Univ of Melbourne. *m*: Florence May Jones. *d*: 3. Clergyman. *Publ*: The Hand of God ; In Such a Night as This ; The Uses of Literature in the Pulpit ; Christ's Shining Way ; The Stringing of the Bow ; The Gods of Men ; Cardinals of Faith ; The Fulfillment. *Ctr*: Religion & Life, United Church Observer, Advance, Christian Advocate, Pulpit, etc. *s.s*: Religious Thought & Practice. *Rec*: Boating, writing. *c*: Canadian. *a*: 6530 Marine Cresc, Vancouver, B.C., Canada. *T*: Kerrisdale 1893L

McCALLISTER, William J., B.A.(R.U.I.), M.A.(Q.U.B.), BSc, PhD.(Lon). *b*: Co Down 1882. *e*: Roy Queen's & Lon Univs. Prof Educ Queen's Univ Belfast. *Publ*: The Growth of Freedom in Educ. *c.t*: Journ of Educ Psychology, Teacher's World, Journ of Educ. *s.s*: Philosophy, psychology. Princ Stranmillis Train Col 1927–31. Exam in Educ Univs of Birm & Leeds. *a*: Haslemere, Myrtlefield Pk, Belfast. *t*: Malone 30.

McCALLUM, Alexander, F.J.I. *b*: Helensburgh 1861. *e*: Elem & Priv. Widower. *s*: 2 (1 dec). *d*: 1. Journalist. *n.a*: Glas Herald, & various trade papers.

c.t: Glas Herald, Rly Gazette, Transport World, etc. *s.s*: Rlys & tramways. *Rec*: Reading. *a*: 91 Kirkstall Rd, Streatham Hill, S.W.2. *t*: Tulse Hill 6184.

McCALLUM, James Ramsay. *b*: Birmingham 1901. *e*: King Edward's Sch B'ham & Balliol Coll Oxf. *n.a*: Ed Chelmsford Clergy Directory & Year Book 1943. *Publ*: Abelard's Ethics; A Short Method for Pulpit & Services; Colchester's Port, The Hythe & its Church. *Ctr*: Modern Churchman, Guardian, local journs. *s.s*: Mediæval Philosophy, Local Church History. *Rec*: Touring, cycling. *a*: Alresford Rectory, Colchester, Essex. *T*: Wivenhoe 288.

McCANCE, Robert Alexander, M.A., M.D., PhD., M.R.C.P. *Publ*: The Carbohydrate Content of Foods; The Chemistry of Flesh Foods & Their Losses on Cooking. *c.t*: Biochem Journ, Brain, Lancet, B.M.J., Quarterly Journ of Med, Physiological Review, etc. *a*: 109 College Rd, Dulwich, S.E.21. *t*: Sydenham 4669.

McCANN, Frederick John. Surgeon. *Publ*: Cancer of the Womb; etc. *c.t*: Lancet, Practitioner, etc. *a*: 86 Portland Pl, W.1. *t*: Welbeck 5734.

McCANN, Rev. Philip Justin. Master St Benet's Hall Oxf. *Publ*: The Cloud of Unknowing: The Spirit of Catholicism; The Life of Father Augustine Baker; etc. *a*: St Benet's Hall, Oxf. *t*: 4422.

McCARDLE, Kenneth J., B.A. *b*: Grandforks, B.C. 1905. *e*: Public Scs & Mont St Louis & Loyola Colls. *m*: Mary I. McCrea. *d*: 3. *Publ* Mang Ed of Canadian Business. *n.a*: Ed & Publ The Arvidian, Arvida, Ed & Advertising Staff The Financial Times, Montreal. *c.t*: Nation's Business. *s.s*: Trade, commerce, finance. *Rec*: Golf, swimming, hunting. *c*: Advertising (Montreal), etc. *a*: Canadian Business, 530 Board of Trade Bldg, Montreal, Canada. *t*: Marquette 6591.

McCARRISON, Sir Robert, Kt., C.I.E., M.A., M.D., D.Sc., LL.D., F.R.C.P., F.C.P. *b*: Portadown, Nth Ireland 1878. *e*: Queen's Coll Belfast. *m*: Helen S. Johnston. Indian Medical Service 1901—35, Hon Physician to H.M. The King '28—35. *Publ*: Studies in Deficiency Disease; Food; Nutrition & National Health; The Thyroid Gland; The Simple Goitres; Scientific Memoirs; Rice in Relation to Beri-Beri; etc. *Ctr*: India Journal of Medical Research & other Mediacl journals. *s.s*: Nutrition, Goitre & Cretinism. *a*: 18 Linton Rd, Oxford. *T*: Oxford 58229.

McCARROLL, James Joseph. *b*: Augher, Ireland 1889. *e*: Nat Sc & Christian Brothers, Armagh. *m*: Mary J. Coghlan. *s*: 2. Journalist, Dir & Farmer. *n.a*: Western Gazette 1907, Derry People '08, Belfast Telegraph '10, Derry Journal '11. M.P. N. Ireland, Foyle Div '29–. *Rec*: Golf, gardening. *c*: Derry Catholic, Nat Belfast. *a*: Derryowen, Coshquin, Londonderry. *t*: Brookhall 15.

McCARTHY, Denis Francis. B.Sc., M.D., B.Ch., B.A.O., D.P.H., L.M. *b*: Innishannon, Co Cork 1903. *e*: Clongowes Wood Coll, Univ Coll Cork & Univs of Camb & Birmingham. *m*: Lois Doreen Wainright-Barker, *s*: 1. *d*: 2. County Medical Officer Co Mayo. *Publ*: Juvenile Rheumatism. *Ctr*: Brit Med Journ, Lancet, The Medical Officer, Journ of the Med Assoc of Eire. *s.s*: Tuberculosis & Diseases of the Chest, Infectious Diseases, Nutrition. *Rec*: Swimming, reading. *a*: Trentlea, Castlebar, Mayo, & Public Health Dept, Castlebar, Mayo. *T*: 43.

McCARTHY, Justin Huntly. *b*: 1861. *e*: Univ Col. Historian, Dramatist, Author. *Publ*: The Dryad; The Illustrious O'Hagan; Seraphica; A Health Unto His Majesty; Calling the Tune; Fool of April; etc; History—England under Gladstone; Ireland Since the Union; The French Revolution; Sport History of the United States; etc; Plays—If I were King; Cæsar Borgia; The O'Flynn; The Duke's Motto; etc.

McCARTHY, Lillah, O.B.E. *b*: Cheltenham. *e*: Priv. *m*: Sir Frederick Keeble, C.B.E., F.R.S. Actress-Mang'ess. *Publ*: Myself & My Friends. *s.s*: Recitals. *Rec*: Golf. *a*: Hamels, Boar's Hill, Oxf. *t*: Boar's Hill 30.

McCARTHY, Michael. *b*: Addingham 1885. *e*: Ermysted's Gr Sch Skipton-in-Craven. *m*: Anne Hopkins. *s*: 1. Journalist, Mem N.U.J. & Newspaper Press Fund (West Riding Dist Cttee). *n.a*: On staff Yorks Observer, Telegraph & Argus & Yorks Sports 1920—. *Ctr*: Various periodicals. *s.s*: Book Reviews & Sociology *Rec*: Bowls. *a*: The Gables, Wakefield Rd, Dewsbury, Yorks. *T*: 477.

McCARTHY, Roy ("Robert Crawley"). *b*: London 1907. *e*: Holyhead County Sch & Bangor Univ. *m*: Margery Colman. Journalist. *n.a*: Ed Camping & Outdoor Life 1947, Ed Canoe & Small Boat '36—40, Pres Sec Boy Scouts Assoc '32—35, Assist Ed The Ruc-Sac '31—32. *Publ*: Camping, Canoeing. *Ctr*: Dly Mirror. *s.s*: Camping, Canoeing, Rambling, Cycling, Youth Hostels, Countryside. *Rec*: Camping, gardening. *c*: Camping. *a*: Wells Cottage, Cores End, Bourne End, Bucks.

McCARTNEY, Alexander Campbell. Ed Birm N/ps. *a*: 290 Alceston Rd, Moseley. *t*: Midland 0472.

McCARTNEY, James Elvins, M.D., D.Sc, M.B., Edin. Dir of Research & Path Services L.C.C. *Publ*: An Introduction to Practical Bacteriology by T. J. Mackie & J. C. McCartney (4th edn, 1934). *c.t*: Sci Journs. *a*: 147 Burnt Ash Hill, Lee, S.E.12. *t*: Lee Green 3138.

McCASKIE, Harry Bertram. *b*: Great Ouseburn, Yorks 1877. *e*: Westminster Sch, Caius Coll Camb & St George's Hosp. Doctor of Medicine (ret). *n.a*: Ed St George's Hosp Gaz 1903—05. *Publ*: The Poems of Francois Villion (trans). *Ctr*: The Field. *w.s*: Cpt R.A.M.C. 1916—19. *Rec*: Trout fishing. *c*: Flyfishers. *a*: 32 Queen's Gate Terr London, S.W.7. *T*: Western 3769.

McCAUSLAND, Dominick Eckley, K.C., M.A., LL.B. *b*: Herefordshire, England 1879. *e*: Hereford & Brasenose Coll Oxf. *m*: *s*: 1. *d*: 1. Editor. *n.a*: Ed Cape Argus 1938——, Ed British Africa Monthly. *Rec*: Reading, Ornithology, golf. *c*: Civil Service & Royal Cape (Cape Town). *a*: c/o Standard Bank of Sth Africa, Adderley St, Cape Town, Sth Africa.

McCAUSLAND, Nora Kennedy. *Publ*: The Cunning Chemist. *s.s*: Poetry. *a*: 16 Dalmeny Rd, Southbourne-on-Sea, Hants.

McCLEAN, Douglas, M.B., B.S., M.R.C.S., L.R.C.P. *c.t*: New Statesman & Nation, various scientific journs. *a*: c/o The Westminster Bank, Lower Sloane St, S.W.1.

McCLEAN, William Newsam. A.M.I.C.E., M.I.Mech.E., M.I.W.E., F.R.A.S., M.A.(Cantab), F.R.Met.S., F.R.G.S. *b*: London 1874. *e*: Rugby & Camb Univ. *m*: Agnes Maude Whipham. *s*: 3. *d*: 2. Civil Engineer, Chm & Mang Dir Cannock Chase Colliery etc. *n.a*: Chrm Cannock Chase Colry Coy Ltd 1912—. *Publ*: Records of Rivers Dee, Ness, Garry, Moriston & Lochy 1929—44. *Ctr*: Proc of Inst Water Engineers, Roy Geog Soc, Inst of Civ Engrs, Roy Met Soc, etc. *s.s*: River Flow Measurements & Records. *Rec*: Old tennis, etc. *c*: St Stephen's, New Univ & Queen's. *a*: 39 Phillimore Gardens, London, W.8. *T*: Western 6193.

McCLEARY, Dorothy, A.B. *b*: Washington, D.C. 1894. *e*: George Washington Univ. *m*: Harry M. Hamilton. *s*: 1. Author. *n.a*: Ed Marriage Stories 1922—24. *Publ*: A Primer of Cooking; Creative Fiction Writing; (Novels) Not for Heaven; Naked to Laughter; Paved with Good Intentions. *Ctr*: Story Mag, Harper's Bazaar, Woman's Home Companion, New Yorker, Writer's Digest, Life, etc. *s.s*: Technique of Writing. *Rec*: Gardening, walking, cycling, theatre. *a*: 239 East 109th St, New York 29, N.Y., U.S.A.

McCLEARY, George Frederick, B.A., M.D., D.P.H. *b*: Manchester 1867. *e*: Roy Coll Music, Trin Hall Camb, Middlesex Hosp. *m*: Hilda Cox. *s*: 1. *d*: 2. Dep Sen Med Officer of Health (ret). *n.a*: Ed of Public Health 1908—12. *Publ*: Race Suicide; Population To-day's Question; The Menace of British Depopulation; The Maternity & Child Welfare Movement; The Early History of the Infant Welfare Movement; National Health Insurance; Infantile Mortality; The Development of British Maternity & Child Welfare Services. *Ctr*: The Fortnightly, Nat Rev, Contemp Rev, Hibbert Journ, Spectator, Time & Tide, Lancet. *s.s*: Population, Maternity & Child Welfare, Health Insurance, Music, Cricket, Mountaineering, Golf. *Rec*: Music, Mountaineering, golf. *a*: 80 Corringham Rd, London, N.W.11.

McCLEARY, His Hon. Judge Robert, B.A. (Cantab). *b*: Chorlton 1869. *e*: Priv & Trin Hall, Cam. *m*: Ottilie Flora Frankel. *d*: 2. County Ct Judge. *Publ*: McCleary's County Court Precedents of Claims; McCleary's County Court Precedents After Claims; The County Courts Consolidation Act 1934. *s.s*: Law & practice of County Cts. *Rec*: Golf, bridge. *c*: Oxf & Cam. *a*: Langdale, Highfield, Sale. Cheshire. *t*: 3455.

McCLELLAND, Rev. Henry Simpson, B.A., B.D. *b*: Belfast 1882. *e*: Ulster Prov Sch, New Coll Lond & Lond Univ. *m*: Ruby Shuttleworth Frew-Gaff. Journalist. *Ctr*: Nash's, Windsor, Glas Herald, Sun Chronicle, Dly Sketch, Assoc Scottish Newsps, Christian World Pulpit, etc. *s.s*: Social Problems. *w.s*: C.F. 1917—19. *a*: Trinity Church, Claremont St, Glasgow.

McCLELLAND, William Wither, C.B.E., M.A., B.Sc., B.Ed., F.R.S.E. *b*: Newton-Stewart 1889. *e*: Leith Academy, Edin Univ. Executive Off Nat Comm for the Training of Teachers, formerly Prof of Education St Andrews Univ, Chm Advisory Council on Education in Scotland. *Publ*: Selection for Secondary Education. *Ctr*: Brit Journ of Psychology, Year Book of Education, etc. *s.s*: Education & Psychology. *c*: Scottish Liberal. *a*: 4 Castlelaw Rd, Colinton, Edinburgh. *T*: 87802.

McCLEMENTS, Samuel. *b*: Ireland 1900. *e*: Banbridge Acad, Stanboro' Col Watford & King's Col Lon. *m*: Doris Alice Cumming. *d*: 1. Med Pract. *c.t*: B.M.J. Mem L.C.C. '34–. *Rec*: Cycling, shooting, travel. *a*: 15 West Horne Av, Eltham, S.E.9. *t*: 1613.

McCLENDON, Mrs. Sidney S., Jnr (Marie Millicent). *b*: Houston, Texas, U.S.A. 1900. *e*: Priv Sc Houston, Hannah More Acad Baltimore. Stetson Univ Deland, Salem Col Winston-Salem, Massey Business Col Houston. *m*: Sidney S. McClendon Jnr. *s*: 1. Writer. *Publ*: Mystery Camp; Secrets Inside. *Rec*: Swimming, riding. *c*: Jnr Current Lit, Tuesday Musical, etc. *a*: 5318 Crawford St, Southmore, Houston, Texas, U.S.A. *t*: Lehigh 9243.

McCLURE, Robert Baird, M.D., F.R.C.S.E. *b*: Portland, Oregon 1900. *e*: Priv & Public Schs in China & America, Univ of Toronto. *m*: Amy Louise Hislop. *s*: 1. *d*: 3. *Publ*: Tales From the Burma Road; Tales From Free China; Over the Burma Road. *Ctr*: Reader's Digest, Maclean's Mag, etc. *s.s*: China—Social Changes & Changes in Modern Thought. *Rec*: Flying, swimming, travel. *a*: 108 Strathallan Blvd, Toronto 12, Canada, & c/o Union Hosp, Hankow, China. *T*: Mayfair 5698.

McCLURE, Wallace, A.M., LL.B., Ph.D. *b*: Knoxville, Tennessee 1890. *e*: Baker-Heimel Sch, Univs of Tennessee & Columbia. *m*: *s*: 2. Official of the Dept of State of the United States 1920—. *Publ*: World Prosperity; International Executive Agreements; A New American Commericial Policy; State Constitution Making. *Ctr*: Amer Journ of Internat Law, Washington Post, Knoxville Sentinel, Knoxville Journ, etc. *s.s*: U.S. Constitutional Law as it Affects Internat Relations, World Affairs, Econs in its Internat Aspects. *Rec*: Attending, & critizing motion pictures, travel. *c*: Cosmos & Un Nations (Wash). *a*: 949 Temple Ave, Knoxville, Tennessee, U.S.A. *T*: National 0302.

McCLURE-SMITH, Hugh Alexander. *b*: Melbourne Australia 1902. *e*: Melb Gr Sch & Balliol Coll Oxf. *m*: Margaret Vincent Buddy. *d*: 1. Ed-in-Chief Sydney Morning Herald 1938—, Spec Corres S.M.H. America & Ottawa Conf '32, Corres Times New York & Washington '33—35, Ed Staff Times '36, Assoc Ed S.M.H. '37. *Ctr*: Reviews on newsps in Britain & America. *s.s*: Internat Politics & Economics. *c*: Junior Carlton Lond & Union Sydney. *a*: 77 Drumalbyn Rd, Bellevue Hill, Sydney, Australia.

McCOLVIN, Lionel Roy, F.L.A. *b*: Newcastle-on-Tyne 1896. *m*: Mary Carter. *s*: 2. *d*: 2. Chief Librarian Westminster Public Libs, Hon Sec of the Lib Assoc. *Publ*: Music in Public Libraries; The Theory of Book Selection; To Kill the Queen; How to Use Books; How to Find Out; How to Enjoy the Drama; How to Enjoy Music; Libraries & The Public; Library Staffs; The Public Library System of Gt Britain; British Libraries (collab); Public Libraries in Australia; etc. *Ctr*: Radio Times, Listener, Library World, Musical Times, Sackbut, etc. *s.s*: Music, Libraries, Drama. *Rec*: Play-going. *a*: 12 Sarre Rd, London, N.W.2. *T*: Hampstead 6813.

McCONKEY, B. Fel Inst Journalists. Formerly Mang Ed Dublin Daily Express. Until recently Publicity Agent Canadian Govt. *a*: The Briars, Groombridge, Sussex.

McCONNELL, Adams Andrew, B.A., M.B., B.Ch, B.A.O.(Dublin), F.R.C.S.I. *b*: Belfast 1884. *e*: Acad Inst Belfast & T.C.D. *m*: Nora Gwendoline Boyd. Surgeon. Snr Surg Richmond Hosp Dublin. Mem & Rep in Ireland Société International de Chirurgie. Mem Soc of Brit Neurological Surgs. Mem Assoc of Surgs of G.B. & I. Mem Counc R.C.S.I. *Publ*: The Decompression Operation for Cerebellar Tumour (1912); Ventriculography; Neurological Surgery in America; Chordotomy for Pain ('30); Some Lesions in the Region of the Pituitary Body ('32); Fields of Vision in Connection with Intracranial Lesions ('33); Treatment of Tumours of the Bladder with the High Frequency Current; Vesical Pain; Cyst of the Common Bile Duct; etc. *c.t*: B.M.J., Practitioner, Irish Journal of Medical Science, British Journal of Surgery, Medical Press & Circular, Lancet. *s.s*: Neurological surgery (brain), genito-urinary & abdominal surgery. Lect in Applied Anatomy, T.C.D. '19–28. Prof of Surgery R.C.S.I. '27–30. *Rec*: Golf, motoring. *c*: Roy Socs, Lon & Univ Dublin. *a*: 75 Merrion Sq, Dublin, & Conna, Shankill, Co Dublin. *t*: 61771.

McCONNELL, Albert Joseph, M.A., D.Sc.(Dublin), F.T.C.D. *b*: Ballymena, Ntn Ireland 1903. *e*: Ballymena Acad, Trinity Coll Dublin & Univ of Rome. *m*: Hilda Evelyn May McGuire. Prof Applied Maths Univ of Dublin. *Publ*: Applications of the Absolute Differential Calculus; Collected Works of Sir W. R. Hamilton. *s.s*: Mathematics & Mathematical Physics. *a*: Trinity College, Dublin.

McCORD, David, A.M. *b*: New York City 1897. *e*: Priv & Public Schs, Harvard. Author, Editor, Univ Administration. *n.a*: Drama & Music Staff Boston Ev Transcript 1923—28, Assoc Ed '23—25, Ed '40—46, Ed Chm '46—, Harvard Alumni Bulletin, Lit Agent for Coward, McCann Inc Publishers 1928—. *Publ*: Stirabout; The Crows; Bay Window Ballads; Notes on the Harvard Tercentenary; And What's More; On Occasion; What Cheer(Ed); The Pocket Book of Humourous Verse(Ed). *Ctr*: New Yorker, Sat Review of Lit, Atlantic Monthly, Yale Review, etc. *s.s*: Poetry, Light Verse, Essays, Book Reviews. *Rec*: Watercolour landscapes, fly-fishing. *c*: Faculty (Camb), St Botolph, etc. *a*: 310 Commonwealth Ave, Boston, Massachusetts, U.S.A.

McCORKINDALE, Isabel. *b*: Rutherglen, Scotland. *e*: Brisbane Queensland Australia. Writer & Lecturer. *n.a*: Ed White Ribbon Signal 1939—46. *Publ*: Frances Willard Centenary Book; Pioneer Pathways; Temperance & Life; Adventure of Life; Youth Book of Citizenship Service; Youth to the Rescue. *Ctr*: Australian Women's Digest, White Ribbon Signal. *s.s*: Women's Affairs in Australia, Social Service, Scientific Temperance. *Rec*: Golfing & motoring. *c*: Business & Professional Women's Club of Melbourne. *a*: Willard Hall, Wakefield St, Adelaide, Australia.

McCORMICK, George Donald King. *b*: Rhyl 1911. *e*: Oswestry Sc. Journalist. *n.a*: Westminster Record '30, West Sussex County Times '31, Brighton & Hove Herald '34. Shoreham & Dist Press Corr for Press Assoc. *Publ*: The Talkative Muse (Essays in dialogue form). *s.s*: Art & lit criticism, politics. *Rec*: Plays & films. *a*: The Firs, Buckingham Rd, Shoreham, Sussex. *t*: Shoreham 160.

McCORMICK, Kenneth Dale. *b*: Madison, N.J. 1906. *e*: Willamette Univ Oregon. *m*: Elizabeth Tibbette McCormick. *d*: 1. Ed-in-Ch Doubleday & Co. *a*: 136 East 64th St, New York City, N.Y., U.S.A. *T*: Regent 7-1795.

McCORMICK, Thomas Carson, M.A., Ph.D. *b*: Tuscaloosa, Alabama 1892. *e*: Peabody Coll, Univs of Alabama & Chicago. *m*: Lillie Anderson Griffith. *d*: 3. Prof of Sociology Univ of Wisconsin 1935—. *Publ*: Agriculture for Rural Teachers; Rural Relief & Non-Relief Households; Elementary Social Statistics; Radio in the Classroom (Ed with Barr & Ewbank); Problems of the Postwar World (Ed). *Ctr*: Amer Journ of Sociology, Social Forces, Sociology & Social Research, Journ of the American Statistical Assoc, etc. *s.s*: Sociology, Social Statistics, Social Psychology, Population. *Rec*: Bull terrier breeder, travel, drawing, genealogy. *c*: West End (Madison). *a*: 4202 Wanetah Trail, Madison, Wisconsin, U.S.A. *T*: Badger 2143.

McCRACKEN, Elizabeth A. M., ("L. A. M. Priestly"). *b*: Co Down. *e*: H.S. Londonderry & Richmond Lodge Lon. *m*: George McCracken. *s*: 3. F/L. Journalist & Author. *Publ*: The Love Stories of Some Eminent Women; The Feminine in Fiction; The Story of Co Down. *c.t*: T.P.'s Weekly, Great Thoughts, The Lady, John o' London's, Tit-Bits, etc. *a*: Seafield House, Bangor, Co Down. *t*: 138.

McCRACKEN, Esther Helen. *e*: Central Newcastle Hgh Sch. Playwright. *Publ*: Quiet Wedding; Quiet Weekend; Living Room; No Medals; The Willing Spirit; etc. *a*: High Seat, Heddon-on-the-Wall, Northumberland. *T*: Wylam 374.

McCRAITH, Sir Douglas. *b*: Nottingham 1878. *e*: Harrow & Trin Coll Camb. *m*: Phyllis Marguerite Lynam. *s*: 2. Solicitor. *Publ*: By Dancing Streams; Dancing Streams in Many Lands; More Dancing Streams. *Ctr*: Field, Times, Fishing Gaz & Shooting Times. *s.s*: Angling Reminiscences. *Rec*: Angling & golf. *c*: Flyfishers. *a*: Normanton Grange, Plumtree, Notts. *T*: Plumtree 28.

McCREA, Rev. Alexander, M.A., D.D. *b*: Gorcnagullion, Co Fermanagh. *e*: Public Elem Sch, Methodist Coll Belfast, Queen's Univ Belfast. *m*: Kate Wolfe. *s*: 2. *d*: 2. Minister of Methodist Church Ireland, Tutor in Edgehill Theolog Coll 1920 & Princ '31, Chaplain to Paris of Nth Ireland. *Publ*: Why This Waste; A Defence of Christian Missions; The Mind of Christ; Irish Methodism in the Twentieth Century: A Symposium; The Work of Jesus in Christian Thought. *a*: 22 Wellington Park, Belfast. *T*: 65542.

McCREA, William Hunter, M.A., Ph.D., B.Sc., F.R.S.E.. *b*: Dublin 1904. *e*: Chesterfield Gr Sch, Trin Coll Camb, Gottingen Univ. *m*: Marian Nicol Core Webster. *d*: 2. Prof Mathematics Univ Lond, Co-Ed Observatory 1935—37, Co-Ed Monthly Notices, Roy Astronom Soc '46—. *Publ*: Relativity Physics; Analytical Geometry of Three Dimensions. *Ctr*: Various scientific Journs & Ency-Brit. *s.s*: Mathematics & Astronomy. *Rec*: Walking. *c*: Sec Roy Astronom Soc. *w.s*: R.A.F.V.R. (Training Branch) 1941—45, Temp Principal Experimental Off Admiralty '43—45. *a*: Holmwood, Sunninghill, Ascot. Berks. *T*: Ascot 327.

McCRONE, Guy Fulton, B.A. *b*: Birkenhead 1898. *e*: Glasgow Academy & Pembroke Coll Camb. *m*: Sylvia Louise Shanks. Novelist, Mem of P.E.N. *Publ*: Wax Fruit; The Striped Umbrella; Duet for Two Merklands; (Plays) Alec Went to Amberley; Sunstroke; The Government Inspector. *Ctr*: Glasgow Herald, English Digest, etc. *s.s*: Adaptations of French & German Plays. *Rec*: Music, reading, hill-climbing. *a*: 13 Huntly Gardens, Glasgow, W.2., Scotland. *T*: Western 4884.

McCULLAGH, L. Joseph. *b*: Dublin 1906. *e*: O'Brien Inst, Fairview, Dublin. *m*: Mary Josephine O'Duffy. *s*: 1. *d*: 2. Journalist & Author. *n.a*: Asst Ed Our Boys '26—30, Ed-in-Chief Kingdom Press Ltd '30—33. *c.t*: Sunday Dispatch (Irish), & Amer Publs. *s.s*: Stranger-than-fiction strips. Known as "The Irish Ripley." *Rec*: Cinema, theatre. *a*: 195 Mt Prospect Av, Dollymount, Dublin.

McCULLEY, Johnston. *b*: Ottawa, Illinois 1883. *e*: Public Schs & Priv. *m*: Louris Munsey Powers. *d*: 1. Author, Fictionist, Dramatist. *Pub l*: The Mark of Zorro; The Crimson Clown; The Spider's Den; The Caballero; Captain Fly-by-Night; A White Man's Chances; The Avenging Twins; Rose of the Rio Grande; etc. *Ctr*: Various. *s.s*: Hist Romances, Crime-mystery Fiction, Western Fiction, Psychological Drama. *Rec*: Motoring, fishing. *w.s*: Intelligence Officer World War I. *a*: Twin Peaks, California, U.S.A.

McCULLOCH, David. *n.a*: Agric Ed Press & Journ, Aberdeen. *a*: 11 Richmond Hill Rd, Aberdeen.

McCULLOCH, Derek, O.B.E. *b*: Plymouth 1897. *e*: Croydon Hgh Sch & Plymouth. *m*: Eileen Hilda Barry. *d*: 2. Joined Staff B.B.C. 1926, Childrens Hour Dir '38. *Publ*: Nonsericks; Gardening Guyed; Travellers Three; Hank; Cornish Adventure; Ed Children's Hour Annual. *Ctr*: Radio Times, Listener, Dly Telegraph, Dly Mail, Sun Dispatch, Book Reviews. etc. *Rec*: Fishing, cinematography, travel. *c*: Devonshire. *a*: The Beacon Corner, Banstead, Surrey.

McCULLOCH, John, O.B.E., F.J.I. *b*: Scotland 1885. *e*: Meoul Sch Wigtownshire. *m*: M. L. Mackinnon. *s*: 1. *d*: 1. *n.a*: Exchange Telegraph Coy Ltd London 1906—18, First Press Officer Min of Labour London '19—22, Northern Ireland Publicity '22—27, B.U.P. '27, Ed Galloway Advertiser '27—35, Allied Newsps '36, Chief Press Officer War Office '37—, Ed The Highway, Ulster Bulletin, Dulwich & Peckham Echo. *Publ*: Guide to Ruins of Galloway; His French Bride; Politics—Red, White & Blue; Short Stories. *s.s*: Politics, Agriculture. *Rec*: Shooting, golf. *c*: Authors'. *a*: 12 Oaks Ave, Gipsy Hill, London, S.E.19. *T*: Gipsy 2690.

McCULLOCH, Rev. Joseph. *b*: Liverpool *e*: L'pool Collegiate Sch, Exeter Coll Oxf. *m*: Betty Gillingham. *s*: 1. *d*: 2. Rector of Chatham, Regular Broadcasts on Religion since 1935. *Publ*: Limping Sway; A Parson in Revolt; The Divine Drama; The Faith that Must Offend; We Have Our Orders; The Trumpet Shall Sound; Medway Adventure. *Ctr*: Church Times, The Guardian, C.of E. Newspaper. *s.s*: Current Church Affairs, Psychology of Religion. *Rec*: Walking & talking. *a*: 20 Prospect Row, Old Brompton, Chatham. *T*: 2088.

McCULLOUGH, William Donald Hamilton, M.A.(Edin), A.I.P.A. *Publ*: (With Fougasse) Aces Made Easy; You Have Been Warned; How To Run a Brains Trust. *a*: Park House, Old Hunstanton, Norfolk. *T*: Hunstanton 400.

McCUNN, James, M.R.C.S., L.R.C.P. *e*: Brunts Sch, Roy Vet Coll, Lond Hosp. Prof of Anatomy Roy Vet Coll. *n.a*: Jt-Ed Veterinary Journ, Mem Ed Cttee Vet Rec. *s.s*: Anatomy & Surgery. *a*: Larks Hall Farm, Chingford, Essex. *T*: Silverthorn 1069.

McCURDY, Charles Albert. P.C., K.C., B.A. *b*: Nott'm 1870. *e*: Loughboro' G.S. & Cam Univ. *m*: Louise Parker. King's Counsel. *n.a*: Chm Utd N/ps Ltd 1923—27, Dir Lon Express N/p Coy Ltd. '30—. Jt 1st Lord of the Treasury. Min of Food. *Publ*: Free Trade or Common Sense; Empire Free Trade. *s.s*: Politics, econ. *c*: Bath, Reform, Ranelagh. *a*: 31 Hamilton Terr, N.W.8. & 2 Brick Ct, Temple, E.C.4. *t*: Cent 3794.

McCURRICH, Hugh James, M.S., F.R.C.S. *b*: Clifton, Bristol 1890. *e*: Clifton Coll, Univ of Bristol, St Bartholomews Hosp, Vienna, Bonn, Paris, Stockholm & U.S.A. *m*: Beltine Ellis. *s*: 2. *d*: 1. *Publ*: The Treatment of the Sick Poor in this Country & the Preservation of the Health of the Poor in this Country. *Ctr*: Brit Journ of Surgery, Brit Med Journ & various other medical journs, The Times. *s.s*: Surgery & Gynæcology, Medical Administration & Planning. *Rec*: Yachting, golf, tennis, lawn tennis, squash racquets. *w.s*: Middx Regt & R.A.M.C. World War I. *c*: Parkstone Yacht & Sussex Yacht. *a*: 19 Palmeira Ave, Hove 3, Sussex. *T*: 1688.

McCUTCHEON, John Tinney, F.R.G.S. *b*: Indiana 1870. *e*: Purdue Univ, Indiana. Married. *s*: 3. Cartoonist, Chicago Tribune. *n.a*: Chicago Record '89-1903, Artist, Cartoonist, war corr Spanish, American, Filipino, Boer, Mexican & Gt War Chicago Tribune '03-34. *Publ*: Stories of Filipino Warfare; Congressman Pumphrey, the People's Friend; Cartoons by McCutcheon; The Mysterious Stranger and other Cartoons; The Restless Age; An Heir at Large; etc. *c.t*: Sat Evening Post, Cent Mag, Collier's. *s.s*: Contemporary hist and polit. Extensive travels in Cent Asia, Cent Africa, Far East & S. America. Pres of the Zool Soc and Park. *c*: Univ N.Y. & Chicago, etc. *a*: Tribune Tower, Chicago, U.S.A. *t*: Superior 0100.

McDANNALD, Alexander H., LL.B. *b*: Warm Springs, Virginia 1877. *e*: Public & Priv Schs, Univ of Virginia. *m*: Irene Elizabeth Drake. *s*: 1. Editor, Author. *n.a*: Rep Baltimore News 1906—09, Polit Ed Baltimore Ev Sun 1910—19. *Publ*: Across Germany; Costs of the World War (I); The Storied Hudson. Ed Ency Americana 1919—48; Modern Ency; Concise Ency; etc. *Ctr*: Morning Telegraph (N.Y.), Enquirer (Cincinnati), etc. *s.s*: Hist, Biog, Geog, Lit. *Rec*: Motoring, fishing, hunting. *c*: Engineers. *a*: 40 West 45th St, New York 19, U.S.A. *T*: Murray Hill 2-4390.

McDAVID, Hugh. *b*: 1902. *m*: *d*: 3. Journalist *Ctr*: Leading British daily & weekly newsps. *a*: Castle Douglas, Kirkcudbrightshire. *T*: Kirkcudbright 121.

McDERMOTT, Capt. F., F.R.G.S. *b*: London 1896. *e*: City of London Sc. *m*: Margaret Frances Young. *s*: 1. *Publ*: How to to Happy in Switzerland—Winter Sports; Curling in Switzerland (in collab with A. Noel Mobbs, O.B.E); William Penn, Thomas Gray & Stoke Poges; The Amazing Amazon; Through Atlantic Clouds—The History of Atlantic Flight (in collab with Clifford Collinson). *c.t*: Daily Express, Evening News, Sphere, Queen, Lady, R.A.F. Qtly, Aero & Airways, Public Speaker, British Journ of Photography, etc. *s.s*: Travel, aviation, winter sports, psychical research. Ret Indian Army Officer. War Service. Broadcasts to scs & lectures in British Isles. *Rec*: Tennis. *c*: Overseas. *a*: Devereux Bldgs, Devereux Ct, Strand, W.C.2. *t*: Central 5914.

McDIARMID, HUGH, (pen name): (Christopher Murray Grieve): journalist, author; b. Langholm, Scotland, Aug., 1892; s. James and Elizabeth (Graham) Grieve; educ. Langholm Acad., Broughton Junior Student, Centre Sch. (Edinburgh); m. Margaret Cunningham Thompson Skinner, June 13, 1918. AUTHOR: Annals of the Five Senses, 1920; Sangschaw, 1925; Penny Wheep, 1926; A Drunk Man Looks at the Thistle, 1926; Contemporary Scottish Studies, 1926; Albyn; or Scotland and Her Future, 1927; The Present Condition of Scottish Music, 1927. Editor (formerly): The Scottish Nation (weekly); The Scottish Chapbook (monthly); The Northern Review (monthly). Contributor to New Age (London), Irish Statesman (Dublin), Scottish Educational Journ., Scottish Independent, Les Nouvelles, Litteraires and many other publications. A leader of the Scottish Nationalist movement and well-known opponent of Burns cult; writes under Gaelic name of Gillechrisiosd Mac a Ghreid hit. Most of writing is done not in English, but in Synthetic Scots in an effort to standarize Scots dialect into modern literary medium; critic (European literature) for London New Age, for several yrs.; transl. (from Spanish of Ramon Maria) Tenvievo; has also transl. poems of Alexander Blok, Stefan Georg and others. Most of his Scottish poems have been transl. into French and many have been set to music. CLUB: P.E.N. (London and Scottish centres). HOME: 16 Links Avenue, Montrose, Scotland.

McDONAGH, James Eustace Radclyffe. *b*: London 1881. *e*: Bedford Grm Sch, St Bart's Hosp & Vienna. *s*: 1. *Publ*: Venereal Diseases; The Nature of Disease (vols 6); The Common Cold & Influenza; The Universe Through Medicine; The Nature of Disease Up to Date; The Universe in the Making; The Nature of Disease Institute's Annual Reports. *Rec*: Horticulture. *c*: Pratts. *a*: 42 Wimpole St, London, W.1. *T*: Welbeck 6847-8.

McDONALD, Edward, F.R.S.A., F.I.A.A., F.R.S.A.I. *b*: Lon 1884. *e*: Kensington & various Tech Cols. *m*: Margaret Hicks. Chrtd Archt. *c.t*: Numerous Articles on Archæ, Archt, etc. *c*: Mem Brit Archæ Assoc. *a*: 262 Rainsford Rd, Chelmsford, Essex.

McDONALD, J. V. *a*: Darlington & Stockton Times, Darlington.

McDONNELL, Sir Michael Francis Joseph, Kt. *b*: London 1882. *e*: St Paul's Sch, St John's Coll Camb. *m*: Muriel Coddington Harvey. Barrister, C.St.J., Chief Justice of Palestine 1927—37, Ex-officio Presiding Judge of H.B.M.'s Full Court of Appeal of Egypt '30—37, Chmn of Appellate Tribunal for Conscientious Objectors since '40. *Publ*: Ireland & the Home Rule Movement; A History of St Paul's Sch; The Laws of Sierra Leone; Law Reports of Sierra Leone; Law Reports of Palestine. *c*: Athenæum. *a*: 6 Mulberry Walk, Chelsea, London, S.W.3. *T*: Flaxman 9551.

McDONNELL, Randal William, B.A. *b*: Dublin 1870. *e*: Armagh Roy Sc T.C.D. *m*: Mary Kathleen Gertrude Hamilton. *s*: 1. Local Govt Ins. *Publ*: Kathleen Mavourneen; Ardnaree; How the Steam-engine Works; How to become a Locomotive Engineer; Songs of Seaside Places; etc. Asst, Locomotive Dept Gt S. Rly Ireland, Lit Reviewer Dublin Freemans Journ, Asst Librarian Marsh's Library Dublin. *a*: 5 Longford Terr, Monkstown, Co Dublin.

McDOUGALL, Archibald Purvis, M.J.I. *b*: Venezuela 1894. *m*: Vera Hirtzel Foster. *n.a*: Reporter Daily Express 1925, Sub Ed '26, Scot Ed '28, Northern Ed Daily Herald '30. *c.t*: Conservative Review (leader-writing & lit criticisms). War Service '14—19. *Rec*: Motoring. *c*: Union, M/C, Roy Scot Auto. *a*: 25 Anson Rd, Victoria Pk, M/C. *t*: Rusholme 1608.

McDOUGALL, Lady (Ellen Mary). *e*: Laleham. *Publ*: Songs of the Church ; Beginning of History ; Mothers in Council. *a*: Appleton-le-Moors, Yorks.

McDOUGALL, Frank Lidgett, C.M.G. Econ Adviser Australian Gov in Lon. *Publ*: Sheltered Markets. *a*: Australia Hse, Strand, W.C.2. *t*: Tem Bar 1567.

McDOUGALL, William, M.B., F.R.S. Prof Psychology Duke Univ. Author. *Publ*: An Introduction to Social Psychology; Body & Mind; National Welfare & National Decay; An Outline of Psychology; An Outline of Abnormal Psychology; The Energies of Men; Character & The Conduct of Life; Ethics & Some Modern World Problems; etc. *a*: c/o Methuen & Co Ltd, 36 Essex St, W.C.2.

McDOWALL, ARTHUR (SYDNEY): author, critic; *b*. London. Eng., Oct. 23, 1877; *s*. Rev. Charles McDowall, D.D., and Georgiana (Osborne) McDowall; *educ*. Marlborough College; Oxford University. DEGREES: M.A.; *m*. Mary Creighton, 1914. AUTHOR: Realism, 1918; Nature and Men, 1923; Ruminations, 1925; Thomas Hardy: A Critical Study, 1931. Contributor to London Times Literary Supplement, London Mercury and other publcns. General character of writing: essays, critical and speculative studies. HOME: Woolstone, Faringdon, Berks, Eng.

McDOWALL, Robert John Stewart, M.D. *e*: Watsons Coll Edin. *m*: Jessie Mary Elizabeth Macbeth. *d*: 2. Prof Physiology Kings Coll Lond Univ, Vice Pres Medical Advisory Comm Asthma Research Counc, Dep Assist Dir Medical Services G.H.Q., E.E.F., Dean Faculty of Medicine King's Coll Lond Univ. *Publ*: The Control of the Circulation of the Blood ; The Handbook of Physiology ; The Science of Signs & Symptoms ; Sane Psychology ; Anatomy & Physiology for Students of Physiotherapy (with Smouth) ; Clinical Physiology ; The Mind by various Authors (Ed) ; Chambers's Ency (Ed Anatomy & Physiology Section). *Ctr*: Journ Physiology, Lancet, Brain & other medical journals. *s.s*: Physiology & Psychology. *Rec*: Golf, chess, swimming. *a*: 34 Park Drive, London, N.W.11. *T*: Speedwell 2858.

McDOWALL, Rev. Stewart Andrew, M.A., B.D. *b*: Bedford 1882. *e*: Colet Court, St Paul's, T.C.C. *m*: Hilda Margaret Wallis. *s*: 3. Chap Sr Science Master Winchester Col. *n.a*: Select Preacher Oxf & Cam, Hulsean Lecturer Cam. *Publ*: A Laboratory Note Book of Physics; Evolution & the Need of Atonement (2nd edn 1914); Evolution & the Doctrine of the Trinity; Beauty & the Beast; Creative Personality & Evolution; Biology & Mankind; Is Sin our Fault? ('32); etc. *c.t*: Spectator, Nineteenth Cent, Nature, etc. *s.s*: Biological educ. Temporary Prof of Zoology Christian Col, Madras '05. *Rec*: Fishing, painting. *c*: Roy Numismatic Soc, Cam Philos Soc, Phys Soc of Lon, etc. *a*: 5 Kingsgate St, Winchester. *t*: 932.

McDOWELL, Rachel Kollock. *b*: Newark, New Jersey, U.S.A. 1880. *e*: Priv & Public Schs Newark N.J. Journalist. *n.a*: Rep Newark Ev News 1902—08, Religious News Ed N.Y. Herald '08—20, N.Y. Times '20—. *Publ*: My Audience with the Holy Father; Witnessing ; Reasons for My Faith ; One Woman's Views ; Pacific Presbyterianism as I Saw It ; etc. *Ctr*: The Press Woman, The Presbyterian, etc. *s.s*: Religion. *Rec*: Collecting prayers, travelling to religious shrines, crusading against blasphemy & profanity. *a*: Times Sq Hotel (Room 1431), Corner Eighth Ave & West Forty-Third St, N.Y. 18, N.Y. *T*: Lackawanna 4-6900.

McEACHERN, Alistair Campbell, M.B., B.S. (Adelaide), F.R.C.S.(Edin). *b*: Aus 1904. *e*: Univs of Adelaide, Edin & Lon. *m*: Margaret McAnaney, M.B., B.S. Med Pract. *c.t*: B.M.J. *s.s*: Surgery. *c*: Mem B.M.A. *a*: c/o Nat Bank of Australasia, Ltd, 7 Lothbury, E.C.2.

MC ELDERRY, ROBERT KNOX: professor of Greek; *b*. Ballymoney, No. Ireland, July 1869; *s*. John and Matilda (Knox) McE., *educ*. Coleraine Academical Instit., Queen's Coll. (Belfast), St. John's Coll. (Cambridge). DEGREES: M.A. (Royal Univ. of Ireland); M.A. (Cambridge); *m*. Margaret Clarke, 1909. Contributes articles on Ancient History to Journal of Roman Studies, and to Classical Review. Fellow of St. John's Coll. Cambridge, and of Royal Univ. of Ireland; Senior Classical Master, Campbell Coll., Belfast, 1896-1902; Prof. of Greek, Queen's Coll., Galway, Ire., 1902-1916; Prof. of Ancient Classics, 1916-1924; Prof. of Greek Queen's Univ., Belfast, since 1924. Sometime Mem. of Council of Society for Promotion of Roman Studies: Dean of Faculty of Arts, Queen's Univ., Belfast, 1926-1929; Dean of Faculty of Theology since 1927. External Examiner in Classics to the Univ. of Glasgow. Relig. denom., Presbyterian. OFFICE: Queen's University. HOME: Glenside, 34, Sans Souci Park, Belfast, Ireland.

McELLIGOTT, Maurice Gerald, F.R.C.S.I. *b*: Listowel 1868. *e*: St Michael's Listowel, St Bede's Coll, Manch Univ, Colls of Blackrock & Dublin. *m*: Eleanor M. Malins. *s*: 1. *n.a*: Ed The Catholic Guardian 1929—39. *Publ*: Spanish-English Medical Dictionary. *Ctr*: Lancet, B.M.J., Times, The Cork Examiner. *s.s*: Spain, Irish Archæology & Genealogy. *Rec*: Fishing, cycle-touring. *w.s*: World War I. *a*: Heathwood, Bushey Heath, Hertfordshire, & Listowel, Co Kerry, Eire. *T*: Bushey Heath 1405.

McELROY, Margaret Julia, A.B. *b*: Newton, Iowa 1889. *e*: Iowa State Coll, Cornell Univ. Author, Mem American Library Assoc. *Publ*: Adventures of Johnny T. Bear ; A Child's First Book in Reading ; Teacher's Manual in Reading ; The Squirrel Tree (collab) ; Tatters ; Toby Chipmunk (collab). *a*: Doylestown, Pennsylvania, U.S.A.

McELROY, Robert McNutt, B.A.(Princeton), M.A., PhD., LL.D.(St John's, China), D.Litt (Oxon), F.R.HistS. *b*: Kentucky 1872. *m*: Louise Robinson Booker. *d*: 2. Harmsworth Prof of American Hist in Oxf Univ 1925—. *n.a*: Assoc of N.Y. Times Current Hist Mag '24—'25. *Publ*: Kentucky in the Nation's History (1909) ; The Winning of the Far West ; The Representative Idea in History ; Grover Cleveland, the Man & the Statesman (2 vols. '23) ; Phelps Historical Atlas (Putnam's Hist Atlas in America, Co Ed '27) ; The Pathway of Peace; Levi Parsons Morton, Banker, Statesman & Diplomat ('30) ; etc. *c.t*: Cyclop of American Govt, Harmsworth's Univ Hist, N.Y. Times, London Times, The Independent, Japan Advertiser, etc. *s.s*: American hist. Edwards Prof of Amer Hist Princeton Univ 1909—25. Trustee Wells College. Fell Queen's Col Oxf '25. 1st American Exchange Prof to China '16—17. *Rec*: Golf, fishing. *c*: Athenæum. *a*: 78 Banbury Rd, Oxf.

McELWEE, Patience Arden. b: Ben Rhydding, Yorks 1910. e: Priv. m: William McElwee. d: 1. Publ: Roman Holiday; Love or Money. Rec: Antique furniture. a: Vancouver Lodge, Dadford, Buckingham. T: Buckingham 2212.

McEVOY, Rev. Cuthbert, M.A. b: Birm 1870. e: King Edward's (Birm), Perse Camb, Christ's Col Cam. m: Margaret Kate Ulph. s: 2. d: 1. Schmaster. Publ: The Great Embassy; Latin for To-day, Part I; Lives of Ion Keith Falconer, Mary Slessor, Sir Wilfred Grenfell; etc. c.t: The Expositor, Greece & Rome. Rec: Tennis, gardening. Minister of Cricklewood Cong Ch '98–1920. a: Alesia, 35 Parkside Drive, Watford, Herts.

McEWEN, Capt. John Helias F., M.A., J.P., D.L., M.P. b: Edin 1894. e: Eton & Trin Col Cam. m: Bridget Lindley. s: 3. d: 1. Publ: Poems (1920); History of 5th Battalion Q.O. Cameron Highlanders 1914–1919; J. R. D. McEwen: A Memoir. c.t: Monthly reviews. War Service. H.M. Diplomatic Service (2nd Sec) '20–27. c: New, Edin & Marlboro'. a: Marchmont, Berwicks. t: Greenlaw 21.

McFADDEN, Gertrude Violet. b: Southampton. e: Priv. Author. Publ: The Honest Lawyer; His Grace of Grub Street; The Preventive Man; Narcissus in the Way; So Speed We; The Bride's Groom; A Bridport Dagger; etc. Ctr: Dorset Year Book. s.s: Provincial Life in early 19th Century. Rec: Gardening. a: Durlston, Paisley Rd, Bournemouth.

McFADDEN, Roy. b: Belfast 1921. e: Belfast Univ. Lawyer, Co-Ed Lagan, & Ulster Voices. Publ: The Heart's Townland; Flowers for a Lady; Swords & Ploughshares; 3 New Poets. Ctr: Life & Letters, Irish Times, The Bell, Dublin Magazine. a: Lisburn, Co Antrim.

MCFADYEAN, Sir A. Publ: Reparation Reviewed. a: 73 New Cavendish Street, W.1.

McFADYEN, JOHN (EDGAR): professor of Old Testament Language, Literature and Theology; b. Glasgow, Scotland, July, 1870; s. James Hemphill and Jane (McKee) McF.; educ. Hutcheson's Gram. Sch., 1882–1886; Univ. of Glasgow, 1886–1890; Univ. of Oxford, 1890–1894; Glasgow Free Church College, 1894–1898; Univ. of Marburg (Germany), 1896. DEGREES: M.A. (Glasgow), B.A. (Oxford), D.D. (Halifax, N. S., Canada), D.D. (Glasgow); m. Marienne Sophie Wilhelmine Emilie Caroline Marie Scheffer, Sept. 1, 1898. AUTHOR: Messages of the Prophetic and Priestly Historians, 1901; The Divine Pursuit, 1901; Thoughts for Silent Hours, 1902; Old Testament Criticism and the Christian Church, 1903; Messages of the Psalmists,' 1904; Introduction to the Old Testament, 1905; Prayers of the Bible, 1905; Ten Studies in the Psalms, 1907 (2nd edit. 1916); Commentary on the Epistles to the Corinthians and Galatians, 1909 (2nd edit. 1911); The City with Foundations, 1909; The Way of Prayer, 1910; Commentary on Isaiah in Bible for Home and School Series, 1910; Historical Narrative of the Old Testament, 1912; A Cry for Justice (a Study in Amos), 1912; Revision of A. B. Davidson's Hebrew Grammar, 1914; Psalms in Modern Speech, 1916; The Wisdom Books in Modern Speech, 1917; Problem of Pain, 1917; Isaiah in Modern Speech, 1918; Jeremiah in Modern Speech, 1919; Use of the Old Testament, 1922; Interest of the Bible, 1922; Key to Hebrew Grammar, 1924; Approach to the Old Testament, 1926; Guide to the Understanding of the Old Testament, 1927; Old Testament Scenes and Characters, 1928; The Message of Israel, 1931. Contributed The Psalms in The Study Bible, 1926; Articles in Peake's One Volume Commentary, and The Abingdon Commentary, 1929. Joint-editor: The Humanism of the Bible series; and The Living Church series. Contributor to Hibbert Journal, Expositor, Expository Times, Biblical World, Homiletic Review, Pilgrim Teacher, Contemporary Review, Glasgow Herald. Snell Exhibitioner, Balliol Coll., Oxford, 1890–1894; Professor of Old Testament Literature and Exegesis, Knox Coll., Toronto Ont., Canada, 1898–1910; Visiting professor (Old Testament Dept.) at Univ. of Chicago, 1927. CLUB: Liberal. Relig. denom., Presbyterian. OFFICE: Trinity College, Glasgow. HOME: 4 Bruce Road, Polloskshields, Glasgow, Scotland.

McFARLANE, Charles Leslie. b: Ontario 1902. e: Haileybury Public & H. Scs. m: Amy Ashmore Arnold. s: 1. d: 2. Author. News Ed Sudbury Star '21–24, Ed Madison (N.J.) Eagle '26, Special Writer Springfield Republican '26. Publ: Streets of Shadow; The Murder Tree. c.t: MacLean's Mag (Canada), Real Detective Tales, Adventure, etc. s.s: Mystery, adventure, humorous & sport fiction. Author of more than 200 publ short stories & novelettes, also 30 volumes of juvenile fiction. Rec: Fishing, hunting, bowls. a: Haileybury, Ontario, Canada.

McFARLANE, Nora. b: Dublin. n.a: Ed founder & proprietor, The Londoner. s.s: Present & past history of London. a: 62 Lifford Rd, London, S.W.18. t: Battersea 0240.

McFARLANE, Peter N. Ex-Director The Graphic, Bystander, Cassell & Co Ltd, Simpkin, Marshall Ltd. Past President City Livery Club, Farringdon Ward Club, Burns Club of London, Caledonian Society of London. Chairman 1932—34 Livery Committee Worshipful Company of Stationers & Newspaper Makers. Knight Treasurer-Knights of The Round Table Club (A.D. 1720). Director of the Technical Press Ltd. 5 Ave Maria Lane, London, E.C.4.

McFEE, William, A.M.I.Mech.E. b: England 1881. e: Culford Sch Bury St Edmunds Suffolk. m: (1) Pauline Khondoff, (2) Beatrice Allender. Publ: Letterf from an Ocean Tramp; Command; Harbours os Memory; The Harbour Master North of Suez; No Castle in Spain; Sailor's Wisdom; The Beachcomber; Derelicts; Watch Below; Spenlove in Arcady; Ship to Shore; In the First Watch; Family Trouble. Ctr: N.Y. Sun, Harper's Mag, Atlantic Monthly. s.s: Fiction, Sea Life. a: P.O. Box 95, Roxbury, Connecticut, U.S.A.

McGARRISON, James, F.I.J. b: Lisburn. m: Margaret Frazer. Journalist. n.a: Ed Lisburn Herald 1892–. Governor Lisburn & Hillsborough Dist Hosp. Chm & Vice-Chm Ulster Dist I.J. a: 4 Bachelors Walk, Lisburn, N. Ireland. t: Lisburn Herald 42.

McGARRY, Frederick Bartholomew Francis. b: Sligo 1908. e: De La Salle Sc Limerick. Reporter. n.a: Western Gazette '25–, Poole & East Dorset Rep '28–. c.t: Universe, Irish Papers, English Folk Press. s.s: Walking, descriptive articles. Rec: Walking, hockey, scouting. Mem N.U.J. a: 151 Fernside Rd, Poole, Dorset.

McGOWN, Chester Charlton, B.A., Ph.D., D.D. b: Orion, Illinois 1877. e: DePauw, Chicago, Berlin & Heidelberg Univs. m: Harriet Doney. s: 2. d: 1. Teacher, Archæologist. Publ: Genesis of the Social Gospel; The Search for the Real Jesus; The Ladder of Progress in Palestine; Excavations at Tellen-Nasbeth; The Promise of His Coming; The Testament of Solomon. Ctr: Journ of Biblical Lit, Journ of Religion, Religion in Life, etc. s.s: New Testament Lang & Interpretation, Archæology, Palestinian & Hellenistic. Rec: Photography, carpentry. a: 1611 Scenic Ave, Berkeley 9, California. T: Ashberry 3-1036.

McGRADY, S. H., M.A. *b*: 1885. *e*: St Albans Sch, St John's Coll Camb. *Publ*: Drifting Leaves; The Surrender of Helen; A Digest of British History; A Note Book of European History; A Note Book of Modern European History 1789—1945; (Ed) Legends & Myths of Greece & Rome; etc. *s.s*: Fiction & History. *w.s*: 1915—19. *a*: Windows, Keston, Kent.

McGRANE, Reginald Charles, M.A., Ph.D. *b*: Cincinnati, Ohio 1889. *e*: Univ of Cincinnati & Chicago. *m*: Lenore R. Foote. Prof of American Hist & Fell in Graduate Sch. *n.a*: Ed Bd Mississippi Valley Hist Review 1925. *Publ*: Foreign Bondholders & American State Debts; Panic of 1837; Economic Development of the American Nation; Life of William Allen; etc. *Ctr*: Amer Hist Rev, Nation, School & Society, Mississippi Valley Hist Rev, etc. *s.s*: Amer Econ Hist. *a*: 860 Clifton Hills Terr, Cincinnati, Ohio, U.S.A. *T*: Wo 8437.

McGRATH, JOAN ROSITA: see Forbes, Rosita.

McGRATH, Raymond, B.Arch., F.R.I.B.A. *b*: Sydney, Australia 1903. *e*: Fort St Sch Sydney, Univs of Sydney & Cambridge. *m*: Mary Catherine Crozier. *s*: 1. Architect. *Publ*: Twentieth Century Houses; Glass in Architecture & Decoration; Seven Songs of Meadow Lane; The Labyrinth. *Ctr*: English & Continental Architectural & Art journs. *s.s*: Architecture. *a*: Monkstown Hse, Monkstown, Co Dublin, Eire. *T*: 81249.

McGRATH, Dr. T. N., M.B. *n.a*: Mang & Secretary Cork Examiner 1931–. *a*: 95 Patrick St, Cork, I.F.S. *t*: Blackrock 3.

MCGREGOR, D. H., M.C. *Publ*: Industrial Combination; The Evolution of Industry; Enterprise, Purpose & Profit. *a*: 9 Adelphi Terrace, W.C.2.

McGREGOR, Reginald James. *b*: Bristol 1887. *e*: Bristol Cathedral Sch, St Paul's Coll Cheltenham & Bristol Univ. *m*: Alice May Brooks. *s*: 3. *d*: 2. Schoolmaster. *Publ*: Many books, plays & radio stories for young people. *Ctr*: Teachers' World, Pearson's Weekly, The Bookman. *s.s*: Plays for Children, Books for Boys. *Rec*: Reading, writing & seeing plays. *w.s*: 1914—18. *a*: 28 Cotham Rd, Bristol. *T*: 25145.

McGUFFIE, Duncan John. *b*: Whaley Bridge, Cheshire 1913. *e*: Oundle Northants. Market Garden Coy Dir. *Publ*: Spring Onions; Cabbages & Committees. *Ctr*: B'ham Post, Farmers Weekly, Countryman, Farmer & Stockbreeder, Ministry's Journ of Agriculture. *s.s*: Farming, Country-side. *Rec*: Hunting, golf. *c*: Farmers. *a*: Kings Coughton, Alcester, Warwickshire. *T*: Alcester 137.

McGUINNESS, Charles John. *b*: Londonderry 1893. *e*: Irish National Sc. Master Mariner. *n.a*: Asst Ed Ay t Eyreazzae All Irish Weekly '34—35. *Publ*: Nomad; Viva Irlanda. *c.t*: Irish Independent. *s.s*: Adventure, travel, Antarctic & Arctic Exploration. *Rec*: Boating, swimming. *c*: Adventurers, New York Adventurers of the World, Los Angeles, Cal. *a*: 9 Cavendish Row, Dublin.

McGUIRE, Dominic Paul. *b*: Peterborough, Sth Australia 1903. *e*: Christian Brothers Coll Adelaide & Univ of Adelaide. *m*: Frances Margaret Cheadle. Author. *n.a*: Overseas Ed The Argus & Australasian of Melbourne 1945—46. *Publ*: Westward the Course; Australian Journey; Price of Admiralty (collab); The Two Men & Other Poems; The Spanish Steps; Burial Service; W.1.; The Poetry of Gerard Manley Hopkins; etc. *Ctr*: Various. *s.s*: Pacific Problems, Australia, Social Movements. *c*: Savile, Navy, Army & Air (Melbourne). *w.s*: Royal Australian Navy World War II. *a*: c/o Banks of Adelaide, 11 Leadenhall St, London, E.C.3.

McGUIRE, Ollie Roscoe, A.M., LL.D., S.J.D. *b*: Cyclone, Monroe, Co Kentucky. *e*: Kentucky State Normal Sch, Louisiana State & George Washington Univs. *m*: Ava Hale. *s*: 1. *d*: 1. Lawyer, Farmer & Writer. *Publ*: Americans on Guard; May it Please the Court (Ed); Notable Virginia Bar Addresses (Ed); Our Wonderland of Bureaucracy; Vanishing Rights of the States. *Ctr*: Illinois Law Rev, Texas Rev, N.Y. Times & other Law reviews. *s.s*: Internat & Constitutional Law. *Rec*: Stockraising, farming. *c*: Nat Press & Metropolitan. *a*: 1703 North Highland St, Arlington, Virginia, U.S.A. *T*: Chestnut 7004.

McGUIRE, Paul. Author. *Publ*: Death Fugue; Murder in Haste; There Sits Death; etc. *a*: c/o Skeffington & Sons Ltd, 55 Pont St, London, S.W.1. *T*: Kensington 0166.

McILRAITH, C. H., M.D. *c.t*: Lancet, British Medical Journal, Journal Laryng, Rhinol & Otol, Medical Press etc. Late 1st Asst Throat Dept King's Col Hosp. Aural Surgeon to the 4th London Gen Hosp. Aural Asst London Hosp. *a*: Springfield, 44 Half Moon Lne, Herne Hill, S.E.24.

McILROY, Dame Anne Louise, D.B.E., LL.D., M.D., D.Sc., F.R.C.O.G., F.R.C.P. *b*: Lavin House, Co Antrim 1877. *e*: Glasgow, London, Berlin, Vienna & Paris. Consultant Surgeon to Marie Curie & Bermondsey Medical Mission Hosps Lond & Cons Obstetrician to Boroughs of Walthamstow, Holborn & Finsbury, Croix de Guerre. *Publ*: From a Balcony on the Bosphorus; The Toxeamias of Pregnancy. *Ctr*: Clinical & Research, & numerous other Med journs. *s.s*: Obstetrics & Gynæcology. *Rec*: Fishing. *c*: Forum. *w.s*: 1915—19 in France, Salonica & Serbia. *a*: 115a Harley St, London, W.1. *T*: Welbeck 9883.

McINERNEY, Michael. *b*: Limerick 1906. *e*: Nat & Sec Schs Limerick, Lond & Holland. *m*: Nancy Goedheer. *d*: 1. Journalist, Mem N.U.J. *n.a*: Ed Irish Democrat 1939—41, Indust Corres Irish Times '46. *Ctr*: Irish Times, Times Pictorial, Irish Review & Annual, & other weekly & monthly periodicals. *s.s*: Econs, Trade Union Labour Movement, Irish Polit Affairs, Irish Indust Development. *Rec*: Rugby football, swimming, music, lit. *c*: Irish Times. *a*: 130 Rock Rd, Booters Town, Co Dublin, Ireland. *T*: 76555.

McINNES, Donald James Lindsay. *b*: Portsmouth 1911. *e*: Portsmouth Jnr Tech Sc. N/p Reporter. *n.a*: Staff Portsmouth N/ps Ltd 1927, Newport, I.o.W. & Cowes Rep Evening News Portsmouth. *a*: 123 Medina Av, Newport, I.O.W. *t*: 180.

McINNES, James Ewart, F.J.I. *n.a*: Ed The Times Weekly Edition. *a*: c/o Times Office, Printing Hse Sq, E.C.4.

McINNES, Robert Clapham, F.J.I. *b*: Wakefield 1873. *e*: Wakefield G.S. F.L. Journalist & Shorthand Writer. Mem Assoc Professional Shorthand Writers. *a*: 11 Wood St, Wakefield. *t*: 2947.

McINTOSH, Katherin. *b*: Leamington 1911. *e*: Westcliff Sc, Weston-super-Mare, Som. *m*: Keith Jackson. *Publ*: Darkness Appeas'd; Lions Marked Different. *c.t*: Punch, John o' London's, Glos Countryside, etc. *s.s*: Eng countryside, hist, biog, poetry. Broadcasts own stories for Children's Hour. *a*: 46 Pulteney St, Bath, Som. *t*: 4240.

McINTOSH, PROFESSOR (pen name): see McIntosh, William Carmichael.

McINTOSH, WILLIAM CARMICHAEL (pen name: Professor McIntosh): psychiatrist and professor of Natural History, Univ. of St. Andrews; b. St. Andrews, Glasgow; s. John and Eliza Rymer (Mitchell) McI.; educ. Infant School in Madras Coll. (St. Andrews), Univ. of Edinburgh. DEGREES: M.D. (Oxford and Dunham), LL.D. (St. Andrews and Edinburgh); unmarried. AUTHOR: Monograph of the British Marine Annelids (Vol. I), 1873-1874; The Marine Invertebrates and Fisher of St. Andrews; Report on the Annelider collected by H. M. Ship "Challenger", 1872-76; Monograph of the British Marine Annelids (Vol. II), 1898; (Vol. III, 1908; Vol. IV, 1910; Vol. V, 1915; Vol. VI, 1916); The Resources of the Sea, 1899;. Is author of many works. In Memoriam: an extensive list of Zoological Memoirs and Papers; Medical papers on the Ears of the Insane; The Subcutaneous Injection of Morphia in Insanity; Notes on Asylums and the Insane in France and Belgium; On Morbid Impulse; On the Diagnosis and Treatment of Morbid Impulse, etc. In preparation: British Food Fishes (2nd edit). In the press: Additions to the Marine Fauna of St. Andrews since 1874. Contributor to Medical Times and Gazette, Journ. Mental Science, Med. Critic and Psychol. Journ., Edin. Med. Journ., The Scotsman, Perthshire Journ., Journ of Anat. and Phys., Proc. Linn. Soc. Seventh Ann. Rep. Fishery Bd. for Scotland; Ann. Nat. Hist. and many learned publications. CLUBS: Science, Association and Rugby Football Clubs, University Harriers, Caledonian United Service. Relig. denom., Congregationalist. OFFICE: Gatty Marine Laboratory. HOME: 2 Abbotsford Crescent, St. Andrews, Fife, Scotland.

McINTYRE, DAVID MARTIN: minister of religion; b. Monikie, Forfarshire, Scotland, Jan. 2, 1859; s. Malcolmn and Mary Anne (Miller) McI.; educ. Edinburgh Univ.; Edinburgh New College; English Presbyterian Coll. (London). DEGREES: D.D. (Glasgow); m. Jane Christian Bonar, 1893. AUTHOR: The Divine Authority of the Old Testament, 1904; The Hidden Life of Prayer, 1906; The Upper Room Company, 1906; Waymarks in the Pursuit of God, 1908; The Spirit in the Word, 1908; Life in His Name, 1909; Spirit of Power, 1912; Love's Keen Flame, 1920; Faith's Title Deeds, 1924; The Prayer Life of our Lord, 1926; In His Likeness, 1927; The Rest of Faith, 1929. Contributor to many magazines and journals. Principal of the Bible Training Institute (Glasgow), and in charge of same since 1913. Relig. denom., Church of Scotland. ADDRESS: 64 Bothwell St., Glasgow 62, Scotland.

McINTYRE, Donald M.B.E., Ch.B., M.D., F.R.S.E., F.R.C.S.E., F.R.C.O.G., F.R.F.P.S.(G). b: Greenock 1891. e: Glas Univ. m: Jean Gracie Menzies. Obstetrician & Gynæcologist, Roy Samaritan Lecturer in Gynæcology Glas Univ, Senior Visiting Surgeon Roy Samaritan Hosp Glas. Publ: Combined Text Book of Obstetrics & Gynæcology; Maternal Mortality & Morbidity; Operative Obstetrics (all part author). Ctr: Lancet, Journ Pathol & Bacter, Practitioner, etc. s.s: Obstetrics &Gynæcology. Rec: Shooting, yachting, fishing, golf. c: R.S.A.C, R.C.Y.C. a: 9 Park Circus, Glasgow, C. T: Douglas 4741.

McINTYRE, JOHN E(BENEZER): clergyman; b. Largs, Ayrshire, Scotland, March, 1874; s. Rev. J. B. K. McIntyre and Elisa (Bell) McI.; educ. High School (Glasgow). DEGREE: M.A. (Glasgow Univ.); m. Catherine Campbell Morison, 1905. AUTHOR: The Idealism of Jesus, 1928. Ordained Missionary to Manchuria (No. China), 1899; lost property and health in Boxer Movement, 1900; inducted to Highta, Dumfriesshire, United Free Church, 1905; inducted to Mause Road Church, Motherwell, to begin a new congregation, 1911. Pacifist during war; inducted to St. Mary's United Free church of Scotland, Edinburgh, 1923 (name of church is now altered to Barony Church of Scotland. Relig. denom., Church of Scotland. OFFICE: Barony Church of Scotland. HOME: 11 Inverleith Place, Edinburgh, Scotland.

McIVER, Rev. Daniel. b: Greenock 1877. m: Helen Lang Munn. s: 2. d: 1 (dec). n.a: Ed Beith Supp 1921. Publ: An Old-time Fishing Town: Eyemouth; The Church's Need & the Secret of Revival. c.t: Christian News, Scot Congregationalist, Scot Endeavourer. a: 96 Broomfield Rd, Glas, N.

McKAIG, Joseph, M.J.I. b: Co Antrim 1883. Journalist. n.a: Lond Ed Belfast Telegraph 1921—, Sub-Ed Belfast Telegraph '19—21. Rec: Tennis, dancing. c: Constitutional. w.s: 1915—19. a: Belfast Telegraph, 112 Fleet St, London, E.C.4. T: Central 8358.

McKAIL, David, M.D., Ch.B., F.R.F.S.P.(G), D.P.H. (Camb). b: Glasgow 1874. e: Allan Glen's Sch & Glasgow Univ. m: Catherine Bain Clarke. s: 1. d: 2. Former Lecturer on Med Subjects. Publ: Public Health Chemistry & Bacteriology; A Public Medical Service (collab); The Household Physician. s.s: Hygiene & Public Health, School & Industrial Hygiene. Rec: Reading. a: c/o Fisher, 21 Highview, Pinner, Middlesex.

McKAY, Donald Cope, M.A., Ph.D. b: Salt Lake City, Utah 1902. e: Stanford Univ, Harvard. m: Ruth S. Capers. s: 2. d: 1. Prof of Hist Harvard Univ. Publ: The National Workshops; Makers of Modern Europe (Ed); American Foreign Policy (collab Ed); etc. Ctr: Yale Review, Amer Hist Rev, Journ of Mod Hist, Christ Sci Mon, Boston Herald, etc. s.s: Hist of France since 1815, Internat Relations. Rec: Swimming. c: Harvard Faculty, Metropolitan. a: 127 Littauer Centers, Cambridge, Massachusetts, U.S.A. T: Kirkland 7600 Ext 673.

McKAY, George Leslie, A.B.(Chicago). b: Columbus Grove, Ohio, U.S.A. 1895. e: Univs of Chicago & Paris, Library Sch of New York Public Library. m: Maxine McKillip. s: 1. Curator Grolier Club New York, Mem Amer Antiquarian Soc, Bibliographical Soc (Lond), N.Y. Hist Soc. Publ: A Bibliography of the Writings of Sir Rider Haggard; A Bibliography of Robert Bridges; American Book Auction Catalogues; A Register of Artists, Engravers, Booksellers, Bookbinders, Printers & Publishers in New York City 1633—1820; Early American Currency. s.s: Bibliography. c: Ohio Soc of New York, Bibliographical Soc of America. a: 47 East 60th St, New York City, U.S.A. T: Regent 4-3351.

McKAY, George Thomlinson. Publ: Practical Outlook Geographies. c.t: Times Educ Supp, Schoolmaster, Geography. a: Perin's Grammar Sc, Alresford, Hants.

McKAY, Herbert Couchman, F.R.P.S. b: Terre Haute, Indiana 1895. e: Indiana State Coll. m: Frances Pendleton Adams. d: 3. Research & Writing, Photography & Microscopy. n.a: Ed Zeiss Mag, Minicam Photography, Dept Ed American Photography. Publ: Principles of Stereoscopy; Motion Picture Photography for the Amateur; The Photographic Negative; Cine Titling & Editing; The Cine Camera; Handbook of Motion Picture Photography; etc. Ctr: Leading American photographic mags & several in Europe, etc. s.s: Motion Picture Photography, Stereoscopic Photography, Microscopy & Photomicrography, Popularized Optics. Rec: Rifle & pistol shooting, boating. a: Eustis, Florida, U.S.A. T: 68 Green.

McKAY, Rev. John. b: Woburn 1870. e: Oxf Hse Sc Thame & Ch Missny Col Islington. m: S. Caroline Grover. s: 1. d: 1. Exam in Yoruba to Nigerian Govt 1925-30. Pres Exam Yoruba to Univs of Oxf, Cam, Lon & Glas. Publ: Ifarapa Aisan (Yoruba Text

Book). *c.t*: West African Review. *s.s*: African lang & culture. Archdeacon of Yoruba Country, Nigeria '25-30. Rector of Swithland '32-. *Rec*: Lawn tennis, badminton. *a*: Swithland Rectory, Loughborough. *t*: Woodhouse Eaves 76.

McKAY, Robert Alexander. *b*: Macduff, Banffshire 1895. *e*: Macduff Hgh Sch & Priv. *m*: Elizabeth Scott (dec'd). *d*: 1. Journalist, Proprietor Press Photos (R. A. McKay). Elgin, Morayshire. *n.a*: Sub-Ed People's Journ 1921—28, Ed Elgin Courant '29—34, Dly Telegraph Sub-Ed '44—47, Sub-Ed Aberdeen Press Journ '47. *Ctr*: Leading National & Scottish newspapers. *s.s*: Scottish Farming, Fishing, Folklore, Distilling. *Rec*: Golf. *a*: Moray St, Elgin, Morayshire.

McKAY, Seth Shepard, M.A., Ph.D. *b*: Holland, Texas 1888. *e*: Univs of Texas & Pennsylvania. *m*: Bama Lawson Camp. *s*: 1. *d*: 1. Coll Prof (American Hist). *Publ*: The E. J. Davis Regime in Texas; Making the Texas Constitution in 1876; Debates in the Texas Constitutional Convention of 1876; Seven Decades of the Texas Constitution; W. Lee O'Daniel & Texas Politics 1938—42; Politics in the South Texas German Counties 1914—44. *Ctr*: Southwestern Hist Quarterly, West Texas Hist Assoc Year Book, Dict of Amer Biog, Dict of Amer Hist, Handbook of Texas, etc. *s.s*: Texas Political & Constitutional Hist. *Rec*: Volleyball, etc. *a*: 2909 Twentieth St, Lubbock, Texas, U.S.A. *T*: 5905.

McKAY, Thomas Allan. *b*: Lawrence, Otago, N.Z. 1887. *e*: Priv & Business Coll. *m*: Ethel R. Edwards. *s*: 3. Chm of Dirs Speciality Press Pty Ltd Melbourne, Chm Dirs Australian Digest of World Reading. *Publ*: Seeing the World Twice. *Rec*: Books, gardening, music. *c*: Athenæum. *a*: The Bent Tree, Studley Rd, Victoria, Australia.

McKAY, Thomas M. *b*: 1910. *m*: *s*: 1. *d*: 1. *n.a*: Sub-Ed Dly Express since 1939. *c*: Press, R.N.V.R. *w.s*: 1941—45 Lieut R.N.V.R. *a*: Flat 1, 16 Broadway, Westminster, S.W.1, & Windy Ridge, Chedworth, Glos. *T*: Whitehall 7680 & Fossebridge 77.

McKAY, William John Stewart. M.B., M.Ch., B.Sc. *b*: Sydney, Australia 1866. *e*: Sydney Gr Sch, Sydney Univ, London, Birmingham, Paris, Berlin, Vienna, Bonn, Heidelberg, Leipzig. *Publ*: Lawson Tait's Perineal Operations; History of Ancient Gynæcology; The Preparation & After Treatment of Section Cases; Operations Upon the Uterus, Perineum & Round Ligaments; Lawson Tait, His Life & Work, a Contribution to the History of Abdominal Surgery & Gynæcology; Just Too Late; The Evolution of the Endurance, Speed & Staying Power of the Racehorse; The Dog, Its Ailments & Diseases; Racehorses in Australia (with Dr Lang & Ken Austin); Appendicitis, When & How to Operate. *Ctr*: The Australasian, The Referee (Sydney), Dly Telegraph. *s.s*: Surgery & Gynæcology, the Influence of the Racehorse's Heart on Its Staying Power. *Rec*: Horse racing, biology. *a*: T & G Blg, Lismore, N.S.W., Australia.

McKEAG, William. Solicitor, Coy Dir. *c.t*: Various. *a*: Glenshee, Whickham, Co Durham. *t*: 87210.

McKEAN, Frank Chalmers, A.M., D.D. *b*: Evans, Colorado 1874. *e*: Lenox, Princeton Univ. *m*: Ethel Vaughn Wallace. *s*: 2. Presbyterian Minister. *Publ*: The Magnetism of Mystery; The Legacy of Great Days. *s.s*: Bible Stories for Children, Patriotic Addresses. *Rec*: Fishing, hunting, golf. *c*: Rotary. *a*: 1146 Hacienda Pl, Hollywood 46, California, U.S.A. *T*: HE 9719.

McKECHNIE, Alexander, M.A.(Oxon). *b*: London 1902. *e*: Cheltenham Col, France, Switzerland, Austria, Christ Ch, Oxford. *m*: Marjorie Connolly. *s*: 1. *d*: 1. Departmental Assistant of Federation of British Industries. *n.a*: Hon Attaché, H.M.'s Legation in Prague '24. Appointed to Overseas Dept of Federation of British Industries '26. *Publ*: Introduction to Gaelic Scotland; Translation of Casanova Loved Her. *c.t*: The Irish Press, Oban Times, Stornoway Gazette. *s.s*: Gaelic, translations from French, German, Italian, Spanish. Scottish rep on Committee of Celtic Conference '30, Initiator of the Highland League of Youth. *Rec*: Golf, fishing, hunting. *c*: Oxford & Cambridge, Royal Mid-Surrey, Gaelic Soc of Inverness, Au Comunn Gaidhealach. *a*: Sudbrook Cottage, Ham Common, Surrey. *t*: Kingston 6192.

McKECHNIE, Samuel. *b*: Glas 1899. *m*: Fanny Clarke Putnam. *d*: 1. Civil Servant. *n.a*: Founder & Late Ed 1928-31 Civil Service Arts Mag. *Publ*: Romance of the Civil Service (foreword by Viscount Snowden); Popular Entertainments through the Ages, etc. *c.t*: Daily Herald, Glas Evening Times, Pictorial Weekly, Writer, etc. *s.s*: Theatre, films, circus & working class conditions. Complimentary message from H.R.H. Prince George for publication in Civil Service Arts Mag. *Rec*: Music. *c*: Soc of Authors, Playwrights & Composers. *a*: 38 Onslow Gdns, Muswell Hill, N.10. *t*: Tudor 5948.

McKECHNIE, William Wallace, C.B., B.A. *Publ*: Edn of Baudelaire's Scarabée d'Or. *a*: 4 Hermitage Terr, Edin.

McKEE, George Kenneth. F.R.C.S., L.R.C.P. *b*: Ilford, Essex 1906. *e*: Chigwell Sch, St Bartholomew's Hosp Sch. *m*: S. B. Bird. *s*: 1. Hon Med Staff Norfolk & Norwich Hosp & Jenny Lind Hosp. *Ctr*: Brit Journ of Surg, Lancet, etc. *s.s*: Orthopædic Surgery. *Rec*: Golf, sailing, riding. *a*: 81 Newmarket Rd, Norwich, Norfolk. *T*: Norwich 23968.

McKEE, Ruth Eleanor, M.A. *b*: Bardsdale, California 1903. *e*: Univs of California & Hawaii. *s*: 1. Librarian. *n.a*: Book reviewing for Honolulu Star Bulletin & Honolulu Advertiser 1929—32. *Publ*: The Lord's Anointed; After a Hundred Years; Under One Roof; Three Daughters; Christopher Strange; Storm Point; California & Her Less Favoured Minorities; The Wartime Handling of Evacuee Property; Wartime Exile. *s.s*: Race Relations, Calif & Hawaiian Hist, 20th Cent Lit. *Rec*: Reading Gardening. *a*: 1201 M St, N.W. Apt 6. Washington 5, D.C.

McKEE, William Henry. *b*: Belfast. *e*: Meth Coll Belfast & Queen's Univ Belfast. Journalist. *n.a*: Belfast Newsletter 1904, Lond Ed '16—28, Ed '28—.

McKEEHAN, Hobart D. *b*: Mannsville, Pennsylvania. *e*: F. & M. Acad, Univs of Valparaiso & Oxf, Priv. *m*: Marie Verna Mahaffy. *s*: 1. Clergyman. *n.a*: Homiletical Ed Church Management Cleveland 1946—. *Publ*: Life's Golden Hours; What Men Need Most; The Patrimony of Life; (Ed) Great Modern Sermons; Anglo-American Preaching; etc. *Ctr*: C. of E. Newsp, Homiletical Rev, Christian Century, Expository Times, Best Sermons, American Pulpit, etc. *s.s*: Religion, Poetry, Culture. *Rec*: Gardening. *c*: Rotary. *a*: The Abbey Church, Huntingdon, Pennsylvania, & Greenshadows, Newport 2, Pennyslvania. *T*: 215-R.

McKENDRICK, Archibald, F.R.C.S.(Edin), J.P., D.P.H., F.R.S.(Edin), L.D.S. *b*: Kirkcaldy 1876. *m*: Gertrude Maud Smith. *s*: 2. *Publ*: Medico-Legal Injuries; Back Injuries; Malingering; X-Ray Atlas; Public Health Law & Vital Statistics. *a*: 12 Rothesay Pl, Edinburgh. *T*: 25852.

McKENNA, Martha. *b*: Westroosebeke, Belgium 1892. *e*: Ghent Medical Col. Writer. *Publ*: I Was a Spy; Spies I Knew; A Spy was

Born. *c.t*: Evening Standard. *s.s*: Espionage articles. Worked as nurse in Germany Military Hospital in Roulers, Belgium '15—17 & British Secret Service Agent. *Rec*: Housework, gardening. *a*: Villa Roseberry, Westroosebeke, Belgium.

McKENNA, Stephen. *b*: 1888. *e*: Westminster & Ch Ch Oxf. Author. *Publ*: Sonia; Midas & Son; Sonia Married; The Secret Victory; The Oldest God; The Shadow of Guy Denver; The Datchley Inheritance; Happy Ending; Superstition; Sole Death; While of Sound Mind; Last Confession; The Home That Jill Broke; Breasted Amazon; A Life for a Life; Mean Sensual Man; Reginald McKenna 1863—1943: A Memoir; etc. *Ctr*: Short Stories to various Mags & Newsps. *a*: Honeys, Waltham-St Lawrence, Berks.

McKENZIE, Alexander, M.A., D.Sc, Ph.D., F.R.S., F.I.C. Mem K. L. Deutsch Akad Naturf Halle. Prof of Chem. *c.t*: Journ Chem Soc, Journ Soc Chem Industry, Berichte der deutschen Chemischen Gesellschaft Biochemische Zeitschrift, Bulletin de la Société Chimique de France, etc. *a*: Univ Col, Dundee. *t*: 7112.

McKENZIE, Dan, M.D., F.R.C.S.E., F.S.A. *b*: Larkhall. *e*: Hamilton Acad, Glas H.S., Glas Univ. *m*: Dora Christine Stone. *s*: 1. *d*: 1. *n.a*: Ed Journ of Laryngology 1911—20. *Publ*: Diagnosis in Diseases of Throat, Nose & Ear; The City of Din, a Tirade Against Noise; La Paralysie Faciale; Pride o' Raploch, & other Poems; etc. *c.t*: Med Journ's. *s.s*: Folk-Medicine. Cons Surg to Cent Lon Throat & Ear Hosp. Oto-Laryngologist to French Hosp Lon. *Rec*: Writing verse, angling. *c*: Athenæum. *a*: 9 Weymouth St, W.1. *t*: Langham 1787.

McKENZIE, Very Rev. John, C.I.E., Hon.D.D. Hon.F.E.I.S. *b*: Turriff, Aberdeenshire 1883. *e*: Gordon's Coll Aberdeen, Aberdeen Univ, New Coll Edin Univ of Tubingen. *m*: Agnes Ferguson Dinnes. Prof Philosophy Wilson Coll Bombay 1908—44, Moderator of General Assembly Church of Scotland '46. *Publ*: Hindu Ethics; Ed The Christian Task in India, & Worship, Witness & Work by R. S. Simpson. *s.s*: Study of Hindu Thought. *a*: 21 Woodburn Terr, Edinburgh 10. *T*: 56234.

McKENZIE, John Grant, M.A., D.D.(Aber.) *b*: Aberdeen 1882. *e*: Gordon's Coll Aberdeen, Aber Univ & Un Theol Coll Bradford. *m*: Margaret Ann MacDonald. *s*: 1. *d*: 1. Jesse Boot Prof of Social Science & Psychology Paton Coll Nott'm, Tate Lect Manch Coll Oxf 1944 & '47. *Publ*: Achievement of Christian Personality; Teachers Allies; Souls in the Making; Personal Problems of Conduct & Religion; Psychology, Psycho-Therapy & Evangelicitism; Character & Nervous Disorders. *Ctr*: Various weeklies & monthlies, Great Thoughts, Glas E. Citizen. *s.s*: Psychology & Psycho-Therapy. *Rec*: Golf. *a*: Oakdene, 6 Southey St, Nottingham. *T*: 77280.

McKENZIE, Roderick Duncan, A.B.(Manitoba). Ph.D.(Chicago). *b*: Winnipeg, Canada, 1885. *e*: Univs of Manitoba & Chicago. *m*: Eva Irene Bissett. Univ prof. *n.a*: Advisory Ed, American Jnl of Sociology. Co Ed, Sociology & Social Research. *Publ*: The Neighborhood. A Study of the Local Life of Columbus, Ohio; L'Evolution Economique du Monde; The Metropolitan Community. *c.t*: The City, the Urban Community. Survey of American Foreign Relations. Social Attitudes, Methods in Social Science, The Jnl of American Sociology, Social Forces. *s.s*: Sociology and economics. *Rec*: Golf, swimming, walking, motoring. Delegate to the Inst of Pacific Relations, Honolulu, '27—. Leader of the Round Table, Institute of Politics, Williamstown, '28. Leader of Round Table, Inst of Race Relations, Riverside, Cal. Assoc Prof of sociology, West Virginia Univ, '19—20. Assoc Prof of sociology, Univ of Washington, '20—26. Prof of sociology and Chm of dept, Univ of Washington, '26—30. Prof of sociology and Chm of dept of sociology, Univ of Michigan '30—. Acting prof of sociology at Univs of Chicago and Stanford, summer sessions, '34. *c*: American Sociological Soc, American Statistical Soc. *a*: Univ of Michigan, Ann Arbor, Michigan, U.S.A. & 832 Oakland Ave, Ann Arbor, Michigan, U.S.A. *t*: 4694.

McKENZIE, Thomas Clyde, T.D., J.P., D.L. *b*: Birmingham 1896. *e*: B'ham Univ. *m*: Winifred Mary Fowler. *s*: 1. *d*: 2. *Publ*: Ultra Violet Light Therapy. *a*: 229 High St, Smethwick, Staffs. *T*: 0105.

McKEOWN, Keith Collingwood. *b*: Burwood, N.S.A., Australia 1892. *e*: Public Sch. *m*: Marie Julia Matthew. *s*: 1. Entomologist Australian Museum Sydney 1929—. *Publ*: Catalogue of the Cerambycidae of Australia; Australian Insects; Spider Wonders of Australia; Insect Wonders of Australia; The Land of Eyamee; Australian Wild Life or Tessa in Termitaria. in Legend & Fact; Magic Seeds *Ctr*: Sydney Morning Herald, Sydney Mail, Bulletin Sydney The Sun Sydney, Walkabout Melbourne, Man Sydney, Australian Nat Journ, etc. *s.s*: Entomology, Popular Sci, Short Stories, Children's Books. *Rec*: Reading, photography. *a*: Australian Museum, College St, Sydney, Australia.

McKERROW, James Clark, M.B., Ch.B. *b*: Workington 1887. *e*: Edin Univ. *Publ*: The Appearance of Mind; Aberrations of Life; Economics for Nicodemus; Novius Organum; Introduction to Pneumatology; Religion & History; etc. *a*: 34 Cartwright Gardens, London, W.C.1.

McKERROW, Ronald Brunlees, LittD., F.B.A. *b*: 1872. *e*: Harrow & Trin Col Cam. *n.a*: Ed Review of English Studies 1925—. *Publ*: Works of Thomas Nashe; English Writers' & Publishers' Devices; Introduction to Bibliography; Title Page Borders (with F. S. Ferguson '32). *c.t*: Library, Mod Lang Review. *s.s*: Eng bibiliog Hon Sec Bibliog Soc, Hon Lecturer in Eng Bibliog King's Col. *a*: Picket Piece, Wendover, Bucks.

McKIE, Helen Madeleine. *b*: London. *e*: Lambeth Sch of Art. Artist & Journalist, Exhibited at Paris Salon, Roy Hibernian Academy, Commissioned to paint picture of War Room Admiralty for presentation to Mr Winston Churchill. *Publ*: Travelling South in the Reigns of the Six Georges. *Ctr*: Illustrated articles in the Graphic, Autocar, Ford Times, Navy & various periodicals. *s.s*: Illustrated Articles. *Rec*: Travel. *c*: Women's Press. *a*: 53 Glebe Place, Chelsea, London, S.W.3. *T*: Flaxman 2473.

McKIE, Phyllis Violet, Ph.D., D.Sc. University Lecturer. *c.t*: Journ Chem Soc, Biochem journ. *s.s*: Chemistry. Formerly Fell Univ of Wales & Lady Margaret Hall, Oxford. *a*: Westfield College, London. *t*: Hampstead 6271.

McKINLAY, Arthur Patch, A.M., Ph.D. *b*: Missouri 1871. *e*: Sumner Acad, Univs of Oregon & Harvard. *m*: Jessie Goddard. Prof Latin Emeritus Univ of California. *Publ*: Arator the Codices; Letters of a Roman Gentleman; The Passing Show. *Ctr*: Classical Journ, Speculum, etc. *s.s*: The Drinking Problem in Ancient Times. *Rec*: Mountain climbing, tramping. *a*: 769 Gelemont Ave, Los Angeles, California, U.S.A. *T*: Arizona 35043.

McKINLEY, Mabel Burns. *b*: Ontario. *e*: Collegiate Inst, Coll of Educ Ontario. *m*: David Fuller McKinley. *s*: 1. *d*: 1. *Publ*: Canadian Heroes of Pioneer Days; Famous Men and Women of Canada; Courageous

Women ; Three Boys on the Yangtse. *s.s* : Canadian Hist Tales, Stories of China. *c* : Canadian Women's, Press. *a* : Bronte, Ontario, Canada. *T* : 93.

McKINNEY, Howard Decker. *b* : Pine Bush, New York 1889. *e* : Sec Schs New York State, Rutgers & Columbia Univs. Prof of Music Rutgers Univ. *n.a* : Ed J. Fischer & Bro Music Publishers 1940. *Publ* : (collab) Music in History ; Discovering Music ; The Challenge of Listening ; Music & Man. *s.s* : Music & Art. *Rec* : Walking, photography, travel. *c* : Univ (N.Y.). *a* : 66 Harrison Ave, New Brunswick, N.J., U.S.A. *T* : New B. 2-1327.

McKINNEY, Laurence. *b* : Albany, N.Y. 1891. *e* : Albany Acad, Harvard Coll. *m* : Betsy Marvin. *s* : 2. Pres James McKinney & Sons Inc Alban Steel Fabricators. *Publ* : People of Note ; Garden Clubs & Spades ; Lines of Least Resistance ; Social Ledger. *Ctr* : Sat Ev Post, Colliers, Life, Fortune, Harper's, Atlantic, N.Y. Her Trib, N.Y. Post, etc. *s.s* : Light Verse. *Rec* : Gardening. *a* : Loudonville, Albany, Co N.Y. *T* : 3-6308.

McKOWN, Harry Charles, M.A., B.S., Ph.D. *b* : Peoria, Illinois 1892. *e* : Knox Coll, Univs of Illinois & Columbia. *m* : Ruth Irene Hord. *s* : 2. *d* : 1. Author, Editor, Educator. *n.a* : Ed School Activities 1934—, Ed Adv McGraw-Hill Book Co Inc '33—. *Publ* : Extracurricular Activities ; School Clubs ; Home Room Guidance ; The Trend of College Entrance Requirements 1913—22 ; Character Education ; The Student Council ; Adventures in Thrift ; Fools & Foolishness ; How to Pass a Written Examination ; (collab) A Boy Grows Up ; So You Were Elected ; etc. *Ctr* : School Review, Journ of Educ, School & Society, etc. *s.s* : Educ. *Rec* : Flying, flowers. *w.s* : U.S. Air Service 1917—19. *a* : Gilson, Knox County Illinois, U.S.A.

McKOWN, Robert. *b* : London 1908. *e* : Collyer's Sch Horsham. Editorial Officer Industrial Safety Div Royal Soc for the Prevention of Accidents. *n.a* : Ed Brit Journ of Industrial Safety. *s.s* : Indust Safety, The Theatre. *a* : Robin Hill, 22 King's Stone Ave, Steyning, Sussex.

McLACHLAN, Herbert, M.A., D.D., Litt.D., F.R.Hist.S. *b* : Dulesgate 1876. *e* : H.G. Sch Bacup, Manch Univ & Unitarian Coll Manch. *m* : (1) Mary Jane Taylor (dec'd), (2) Jane McWilliam. *s* : 1. Former Princ Unitarian Coll Manch & Lect in Hellenistic Greek Manch Univ. *Publ* : St Luke, The Man & His Work ; Education Under The Test Act ; The Unitarian Movement in the Religious Life of England ; Alexander Gardens, A Biography ; The Religion of Milton, Locke & Newton ; Warrington Academy ; The Methodist Unitarian Movement ; The Unitarian College Library. *Ctr* : Hibbert Journ, Manch Guardian, etc. *s.s* : Noncomformist Hist, Biog. *Rec* : Gardening. *a* : 11 Sydenham Ave, Liverpool 17. *T* : Sefton Park 3045.

McLAGGAN, John Douglas, F.R.C.S.(Eng), F.R.C.S.(Edin), M.B., ChB., M.A., F.R.S.M. *b* : Torphins, Aberdeen 1893. *e* : Robert Gordon's Col, Aber Univ, Vienna. *m* : Elsa V. Adams, M.B., B.S. Cons Surg. *Publ* : Diseases of the Ear, Nose & Throat in General Practice. *c.t* : Lancet, B.M.J. *s.s* : Ear, nose & throat. W. S. 4th Bn Gordon Highlanders 1914—17. Physiol Medal Aber '18. *c* : B.M.A. *a* : 93 Harley St, W.1. *t* : Welbeck 7444.

McLAREN, Jack. *b* : Melbourne, Australia 1887. *e* : Scotch Coll Melbourne. *m* : Ada McKenzie Moore. Author. *Publ* : My Crowded Solitude ; Blood on the Deck ; Songs of a Fuzzy-Top ; Isle of Escape ; A Diver Went Down ; My Odyssey ; Sun Man ; Devil of the Depths ; The Marriage of Sandra ; Their Isle of Desire ; Gentlemen of the Empire ; The Crystal Skull ; Stories of the South Seas ; Stories of Fear ; New Love for Old ; etc. *a* : c/o John Farquharson, 8 Halsey Hse, Red Lion Sq, London, W.C.1.

McLAREN, Moray David Shaw. *b* : Edinburgh 1901. *e* : Merchiston & Corpus Christi Camb. *m* : Lennox Milne. Was 2nd in Command Scottish Region 1930 & Programme Dir '33 of B.B.C. *n.a* : Asst Ed Lond Mercury, Asst Ed Listener. *Publ* : Return to Scotland ; A Wayfarer in Poland ; Scottish Delight—A contribution to Scotland in Quest of Her Youth ; Escape & Return ; A Dinner with The Dead ; The Noblest Prospect (under the pseudonym Michael Murray) ; (Play) One Traveller Returns. *s.s* : Scottish Affairs, Travel. *Rec* : Trout fishing, golf. travel. *c* : Savile. *a* : Savile Club, London.

McLAREN, Robert, HonM.I.M.E. *b* : Airdrie 1856. *e* : Rawyards Sc Airdrie & Coatbridge Tech Sc. *m* : (1) Margaret Mahon; (2) Mary McAra. *s* : 1. *d* : 2. Colliery Mang. H.M. Insp of Mines. Cons Mining Eng. Pres Mining Inst of Scotland 1910-19. *c.t* : Trans Mining Inst Scot. *s.s* : Mining, theoretical & practical. Teacher in Mining & Geology Coatbridge & Glas. M.P. N. Lanark '18-22. *Rec* : Golf, bowls. Mem Lanarks Educ Authority. *a* : Colinton, 23 Bogton Pk, Muirend, Glas.

McLAUGHLIN, Francis Leo, M.D., Ph.D., D.P.M., F.R.S.M. *b* : Glas 1900. *e* : Univ Col Dublin, U.C. Hosp Lon. Physician. Asst Phys in Dept of Psych Med U.C.H. Lon. A.M.O. & Research worker L.C.C. Mental Hosp Dept. *c.t* : Lancet, Practitioner, Journ Sci, Jour Neurology & Psycho-pathology, Jour Nervous & Mental Diseases, etc. *s.s* : Neuro-pathology, biochem. *Rec* : Golf, fishing. *a* : L.C.C. Hosp, New Southgate, N.11.

McLAUGHLIN, Henry Woods, A.B., D.D. *b* : Marlington, West Virginia 1869. *e* : Hampden-Sidney Coll, Student Union Theol Sem, Washington & Lee Univs, Presbyterian Theol Sem. *m* : Nellie Brown. *s* : 6. *d* : 3. Dir Country Church Work Presbyterian Church U.S. (ret). *n.a* : Expositor 1928—35, Southern Planter '36—38. *Publ* : The New Call ; Christ & the Country People ; Religious Education in the Rural Church ; The Gospel in Action ; (collab) Youth & Sunday School Extension ; Evangelism Through Sunday School Extension ; (Ed) The Country Church & Public Affairs. *Ctr* : Christian Observer, Presbyterian Survey, Biblical Review, etc. *a* : 1302 Avondale Ave, Richmond, Virginia, U.S.A. *T* : 68729.

McLEAN, Stuart Alfred Dominic. *b* : Essex 1906. Journalist. *n.a* : Dep Chief Reporter Ilford Recorder. *a* : 117 Betchworth Rd, Seven Kings. *t* : 2505.

McLEAN, William Hannah, PhD., M.InstC.E., M.P. *b* : Dalmuir 1877. *m* : Gwendolin Donohue. *d* : 3. Civil Servant Egypt (ret). *Publ* : Regional & Town Planning; City of Alexandria Town Planning Scheme *s.s* : Economic planning. Commander of Orders Ismail & The Nile, Esquire of the Order St John of Jerusalem. Planned Khartum under direction of Lord Kitchener, Prepared protective planning scheme for Jerusalem. officially approved by Lord Allenby. *Rec* : Golf, fishing. *c* : Roy Soc. *a* : Drimard, Dunoon, Argyllshire. *t* : 118.

McLELLAN, Duncan Tait Hutchison, M.A. (Aberdeen). *b* : Brechin, Scotland, 1893. *e* : Brechin High Sc, Univ of Aberdeen. *m* Mary Howard. *s* : 1. Chaplain, Indian Ecclesiastical Establishment. *Publ* : A' Short History of the Royal Scots ; The Laird of Balfrie ; The Hanging of Captain Green ; Crown and Covenant. *s.s* : History. *Rec* : Fishing, golf, painting. War service '14—19. Prof of history, Scottish Church Col, Calcutta, '20—22. Chaplain Indian Ecclesiastical Establishment '22—. St Andrew's Church, Dalhousie Square, Calcutta, India. & The Cottage, Dollerie Terr, Crieff, Scotland.

McLELLAN, Rev. Edward. *b* : Woodley 1870. *e* : Brit Sc, Hartley Col M/C. *m* : Mary E. North. *s* : 1. *d* : 1. Meth Min. Pres P.M.

Conf '31. *Publ*: Jesus the Reformer (Hartley Lect '29); The Winning of Gloria; The Blood of the Broomes; Gungersby's Grit; Shrewsbury of the Guards; The Cruise of the Tiger; Old Glory; An Interlude in Arcady; etc. *s.s*: Serials for religious press. *a*: 27 Colwyn Rd, Northampton.

McLELLAN, Robert. *b*: Linmill, Kirkfieldbank, Lanarks 1907. *e*: Bearsden Academy, Glas Univ. *m*: Kathleen Heys. *d*: 1. Scots Dramatist & Poet. *Publ*: (Plays) Toom Byres; Torwatletie; Jamie the Saxt; Jeddart Justice; The Changeling; The Cailleach; The Carlin Moth (in verse). *Ctr*: Poetry-Scotland, Scottish Art & Letters, Chapbook. *Rec*: Fishing. *w.s*: R.A. 1940—46, *a*: High Corrie, Isle of Arran.

McLENNAN, John Cunningham, PhD.(Toronto), LL.D.(Tor & McGill), D.Sc(L'pool & M/C). *b*: Ontario 1867. *e*: Univs of Toronto & Cam. *m*: Elsie Monro Ramsay. Emeritus Prof of Physics Univ of Toronto. Fell & Vice-Pres Roy Soc Lon. *c.t*: Proc Roy Soc, Phil Mag, Nature. *s.s*: Spectroscopy, radioactivity. Mem Sub Cmt Internat Cmt of Weights & Measures. Mem Govg Body on Radium Beam Therapy Research. Mem Counc of Roy Soc Lon. *Rec*: Golf. *c*: Athenæum. *a*: Ramsay Lodge, Wentworth, Virginia Water, Surrey & 88 Prince Arthur Av, Toronto, Canada. *t*: Wentworth 168.

McLENNAN, W. Cons Phys. *Publ*: Manual of Diseases of Stomach. *c.t*: Med Journs. *a*: 4 Woodland Terr, Glas, C.3. *t*: Douglas 4782.

McLEOD, Angus. *b*: West Hartlepool 1904. *e*: Hymer's Col Hull. *m*: May Dorothy Read. Journalist. *n.a*: F/L. '27-29, Newcastle Evening World '29-32. Comm & Shipping Ed Newcastle Journ '32-. *s.s*: Shipping, commerce, football. *Rec*: Reading, sailing. *c*: N.U.J. *a*: 61 Barnesbury Rd, Newcastle-on-Tyne 4.

McLEOD, James Walter. Bacteriologist. *c.t*: Journ Pathology & Bacteriology, Lancet, Journ of Hygiene, Biochemical Journ, Quarterly Journ of Med, etc; *a*: 9 North Parade, West Park, Leeds 6. *t*: 51044

McLEOD, John Nicholson. *b*: Kilmnis 1880. *e*: Kilmnis Pub Sc & Un F.C. Training Col Aber. Married. *s*: 1. Schoolmaster. *Publ*: Reiteach Moraig (Gaelic play, 1911); Posadh Moraig (Gaelic play); Dain Spioradial le Calum Mae Neacail; Litrichear Alasdais Mhoir ('32). *c.t*: Highland News, North Star, People's Journ, An Rosarnach, Alba, etc. *c*: An Comann Gaidhealachi Gaelic Soc of Inverness. *a*: Knockain, Kirkhill, Inverness. *t*: Drumchardine 15.

McLEOD, Marjorie. *b*: Dimboola, Australia 1893. *e*: Clarendon Coll Ballarat. *m*: Norman Victor McLeod. *s*: 1. *d*: 1. Teacher Donnington Girls Sch. *Publ*: (Plays) The Enchanted Tryst; Travail; Moonshine; The Fairies Tree (collab). *Ctr*: The Star, Australasian, The Bulletin. *s.s*: Voice Production, Dramatic Art, Influence of Shakespeare on the Young. *Rec*: Reading, walking. *a*: 6 Pritchard St, Swan Hill, Victoria, Australia.

McLINTOCK, Alexander Hare, M.A., Ph.D. *b*: Gore Southland, N.Z. 1903. *e*: Otago Boys Hgh Sch, Univ of Otago, King's Coll & Lond Univ. *m*: Eva Maude Adams. *d*: 1. Historian, Dir Otago Centennial Historical Publications. *Publ*: The Establishment of Constitutional Government in Newfoundland, 1783—1832; New Zealand Art; etc. *Ctr*: Otago Dly Times. *s.s*: Colonial Hist. *Rec*: Music, etching, gardening, bowls. *c*: University (Dunedin). *a*: 59 Passmore Cresc, Maori Hill, Dunedin, New Zealand.

McLOUGHLIN, A. A. *b*: Essex 1916. P.R.O. Metropolitan Borough of Paddington, Chief Information Dept, Port of London Authority. *Ctr*: Navy Mag. *a*: 299 Harrow Rd, London, W.9. *T*: Cunningham 7391-3.

McLOUGHLIN, Cornelius Frederic. *b*: Gallan 1897. *e*: Blackrock Col Dublin & N.U.J. Journalist & Writer. *n.a*: Ed The Irish Farmer 1921-34 *Publ*: Various. *s.s*: Irish stamps, short stories. *Rec*: Gardening, golf. Deported '16 as a Capt of Irish Volunteers, twice wounded, Irish wars. Asst Gen Sec of Irish Farmers Un '21-28. Dir of Elections the Farmers' Party '27. *c*: The Utd Arts Dublin. *a*: c/o National City Bank Ltd, 10 Col Green, Dublin.

McMAHON, John Thomas. *b*: Ennis, Ireland 1893. *e*: Castleknock Coll Dublin, All Hallows Coll Dublin, Nat Univ of Ireland, Catholic Univ of America (U.S.A.). Catholic Priest. *n.a*: Ed The Record 1928—32. *Publ*: Some Methods of Teaching Religion; Building Character From Within; A Little Harvest; Ramblers From Clare; Live the Mass; Pray the Mass; etc. *Ctr*: West Australian, Catholic Educ Review, Catholic Review, etc. *s.s*: Religious Educ. *Rec*: Golf, swimming. *a*: Forrest St, South Perth, Western Australia. *T*: MU 1386.

McMICHAEL, Hugh. *b*: Edinburgh 1901. *e*: George Watson's Coll & George Heriot's Sch. *m*: Jessie B. Henderson. *d*: 1. Journalist, Hon Sec Edin Dis I.J. 1927—31, Cmt Mem Lond Dis I.J. '32—33, Mem Counc Newsp Press Fund '41—. *n.a*: Rep & Sports Writer Southern Reporter Selkirk 1921—22, Rep Dundee Courier '22—23, The Scotsman Edin '23—31, Parl Corr & Sketch Writer The Scotsman Lond '32—40, Lond Ed Scotsman '41—. *s.s*: Polit, Sport. *a*: 17 Rochester Ave, Bromley, Kent. *T*: Ravensbourne 3202.

McMICHAEL, John, M.B., ChB., M.D. Gold Medal. Lect in Human Physiology. *c.t*: Edin Med Journ, Journ of Physiology, Journ of Pathology, etc. *a*: Dept of Physiology, Univ of Edin.

McMICHAEL, Leslie, M.I.E.E., F.R.S.A. Elec & Radio Engineer. Mang Dir & Chm McMichael Radio Ltd. *c.t*: Many n/ps & periodicals. *a*: Everest, Princes Pk Av, Golder's Green, N.W.11. *t*: Speedwell 3430.

McMILLAN, Anthony Stewart. *b*: Kenilworth, Warwickshire, 1898. *e*: Rugby Sc. *m*: Hilda Mary Hutton. *s*. 1. Jnlst. *n.a*: Ed Coventry Herald 1933. *Rec*: Walking, the theatre, music. *a*: Keresley Croft, Corley, Coventry, Warwickshire. *t*: Keresley 28.

McMILLAN, MARGARET: writer, social worker; d. James and Jean (Cameron) McM.; educ. Inverness Acad., Edinburgh Acad., E Cole Secondaire de Geneva; unmarried. AUTHOR: Early Childhood, 1900; Education through the Imagination, 1904 (2nd edit. 1922); Labor and Childhood, 1907; The Child and the State, 1909; The Camp School. 1917; The Nursery School, 1919; The Life of Rachel McMillan, 1928. Pamphlets: The School Clinics—What is it? 1906; The Open Air Nursery School—What it is Not, 1907. Contributor to Morning Post, Manchester Guardian, Daily News, Labour papers and mags., Westminster Gazette, etc. General character of writing: social, educational. HOME: Rachel McMillan Training Centre, Deptford, S.E., London, Eng.

McMILLAN, William Kenneth. *b*: Sydney, Australia 1894. *e*: Haberdasher's Aske's Hampstead Sch. *m*: Elizabeth Grace Biggs. *s*: 2. *d*: 2. Mem N.U.J. *n.a*: Richmond & Twickenham Times 1912—15, Sheffield Dly Telegraph '15—16, Sporting Life '19—23, Surrey Weekly Press Guildford (Ed, Mang) '23—26, Dly Telegraph Lond '26—30, Sun Express '27—30, Rugby Critic Dly

Herald '30—45, Hon Sec Press Room M.O.I. '42—45, Ed Kent & Sussex Courier '45—46. *s.s*: Rugby Football, Cricket & all Sports. *c*: Press. *a*: 8 Carville Ave, Southborough, Tunbridge Wells. *T*: Southborough 477.

McMORDIE, Mrs. Julia, C.B.E., J.P. *b*: Hartlepool 1860. *e*: Priv & Chislehurst. *s*: 1. *d*: 1. Lady of Grace of St John of Jerusalem. Freeman of Belfast. M.P. for S. Belfast in First Ulster Parliament 1921. First women elected on Belfast Corporation. Alderman 10 y. High Sheriff Belfast '28. *c*: Overseas League, Ulster & Lon, Vice-Pres Women's Unionist Assoc, etc. *a*: Ardenza, Knock, Belfast. *t*: Knock 135.

McMULLAN, Thomas. *b*: Belfast 1897. *m*: A. S. Gault. Journalist. *n.a*: Asst Ed Belfast Telegraph. *a*: 2 Sunningdale Pk, Belfast. *T*: 46408.

McMURTRIE, Francis Edwin. *b*: London 1884. *e*: Salway Coll. *m*: Grace Eleanor Trudgett. Journalist, Assoc Inst Naval Architects. *n.a*: Naval Corr Sun Express. *Publ*: Great Pacific War (collab); Romance of Navigation; Cruise of the Bismarck. *Ctr*: Tech & Gen Press. *s.s*: Naval & Shipping Affairs. *c*: Roy Thames Yacht, Garrick, Press, Norwegian Roy United Service Inst. *a*: Mandeville, Hoddesdon, Hertfordshire. *T*: Hoddesdon 2464.

McMURTRY, Robert Gerald, B.A., LL.D. *b*: Elizabethtown, Kentucky 1906. *e*: Centre Coll of Kentucky & Iowa Wesleyan Coll. *m*: Florence Louis Koberly. *s*: 1. *d*: 3. Author, Teacher & Research Historian. *n.a*: Chief Ed Lincoln Herald. *Publ*: The Lincoln Migration from Kentucky to Indiana (1816); Let's Talk of Lincoln; The Kentucky Lincolns on Mill Creek; The Lincoln Log Cabin Almanac; Lincoln's Other Mary (collab); etc. *Ctr*: Indiana Mag of Hist, Journ of the Illinois State Hist Soc, Lincoln Herald, etc. *s.s*: Lincolniana, Civil War. *c*: Filson. *a*: Lincoln Memorial University, Harrogate, Tennessee, U.S.A. *T*: Cumberland Gap 2311.

McNAB, FRANCES (pen name): see **Fraser, Agnes Maud.**

McNABB, Surg. Rear-Admiral Sir Daniel Joseph Patrick, K.B.E.(Mil), C.B.(Civ). *b*: Greenock 1862. *e*: St Cuthbert's Col Durham; Durham Univ Col of Medicine & Lon Hosp. *m*: Kate Mayes Negus. *s*: 2. *d*: 2. Naval M.O. (ret). *c.t*: Ushaw Mag, Practitioner, Journ of Roy Inst Pub Health. *s.s*: Naval Hygiene. *Rec*: Golf & fishing. Naval Service 1886-1922. Asst to Med Dir-Gen & later Dep Dir-Gen at Admiralty (1916-19). *a*: 21 Alexandra Rd, Walmer, Kent. *t*: Deal 223.

McNAE, Leonard Cyril James. *b*: 1902. *e*: Ealing Sc. Journalist. *n.a*: Foreign Sub-Ed Irish Times, Ed Irish Jewellery News Sect of Goldsmith's Journ. Mem N.U.J. '25. Hon Treas Dublin Branch. *s.s*: Foreign politics, Jewellery trade. *a*: 27 Cremore Rd, Glasnevin, Dublin.

McNAIR, ARNOLD DUNCAN: univ. law lecturer: *b*. Mar. 4. 1885; *s*. John and Jeannie (Ballantyne) McN.; educ. Aldenham Sch., Gonville and Caius Coll. (Cambridge). DEGREES: M.A., LL. D.; *m*. Marjorie Bailhache, Mar. 28, 1912. AUTHOR: Some Legal Effects of War. 1920. Editor: Oppenheim's International Law (Vol. I), 1926; (Vol. II), 1928. Joint-editor: Annual Digest of Public International Law Cases, 1929 and 1931. Contributor to Law Quarterly Rev., Cambridge Law Journ., Brit. Year Book of Internat. Law. OFFICE: Gonville and Caius College. HOME: 9 Harvey Road, Cambridge, Eng.

McNALLY, William James, A.M. *b*: New Richmond, Wisconsin 1891. *e*: New Richmond Hgh Sch, Univ of Minnesota, Harvard. *m*: Lois Aldrich McNally. *s*: 1. Author, Editor. *n.a*: Vice Pres & Mang Minneapolis Tribune 1940-41, Pres Minnesota Tribune Coy '43—' Vice-Pres Minneapolis Star Journ & Tribune Coy '41—44, Pres Minnesota Broadcasting Coy, Ed Doughboy Publs '44—. *Publ*: Roofs of Elm Street; House of Vanished Splendor; The Barb; Prelude to Exile (Play). *Ctr*: Minneapolis Tribune, Nation, Forum. *Rec*: Music. *c*: Minneapolis. *a*: 350 Second St, New Richmond, Wisconsin, & 1806 Foshay Tower, Minneapolis, Minnesota *T*: Geneva 4320.

McNAMARA, William Henry, F.R.H.S., F.I.J. *b*: Cheshunt 1865. *e*: Nat Scs. *m*: Kate Allt. *s*: 4. *d*: 2. *n.a*: Reporter on the East Anglian Daily Times 1882, Sub-Ed & Dis Reporter Sussex Daily News '83—84, Ed Luton Reporter '85—1902. East Anglian Daily Times Lit Staff '02—11, Ed Home Rule Counc '11—12, Assoc Ed Land and Housing Counc '13, Liberal Mag '14—21, Editorial Staff of Coalition Liberals '21—23, Lit Ed East Anglian Daily Times '17—. *s.s*: Hist, music. *a*: 29 Campbell Rd, E.17.

McNAUGHT, William, B.A.(Oxon). *b*: Lon 1883. *e*: U.C.S. & Worcester Col Oxf. Journalist. *n.a*: Morning Post Music Critic 1908—14 & '19—26, Glas Herald, Lon Music Critic '30—, Evening News Music Critic '33—, Asst Ed Music Times '08—. *s.s*: Music. *c*: Inc Soc of Musicians, Alpine. *a*: 168 Norbiton Hall, London Rd, Kingston.

McNAUGHT, William George. *b*: Ealing 1912. *n.a*: Acting Ed Hardware Trade Journal. *a*: Bouverie Hse, 154-160 Fleet St, E.C.4.

McNEE, John William, D.S.O., M.D., D.Sc., F.R.C.P. (Lond). *b*: Mount Vernon, Lanarkshire 1887. *e*: Univ of Glas, Freiburg, John Hopkins (U.S.A.). *m*: Geraldine Z. L. Le Bas. Regius Prof of Med Univ of Glas. *n.a*: Sen Ed Quarterly Journal of Medicine. *Publ*: (in collab) Diseases of the Liver, Gall-bladder, & Bile Ducts; Text-Book of Medical Treatment. *Ctr*: Numerous in Medical & Scientific journals. *s.s*: Diseases of the Liver, Spleen & Gastro-Intestinal Tract. *Rec*: Gardening, golf, fishing. *c*: Athenæum, Fly Fishers, Western (Glas). *a*: Gardiner Institute of Medicine, Univ of Glas, 50 Church St, Glasgow, W.1. *T*: Western 2800.

McNEIL, Allan, J.P., M.A. *b*: Govan 1864. *e*: Renfrew G.S. & Glas Univ. Married. *s*: 1. *d*: 4. Writer to Signet Edin. *n.a*: Lecturer in Banking Edin Univ. *Publ*: Banking Law (7th edn); Mercantile Law of Scotland; Company Law in Scotland & Bills of Exchange, Cheques & Promissory Notes. *c.t*: Banker's Mag, Glas Herald, Scotsman, etc. *s.s*: Banking, commerce & economics. Mem Roy Order of Scot, Exam in Law, Banker's Inst of Scot. *Rec*: Bowls, golf & yachting. *c*: Constit, Conserv, Glas & Scottish Conserv (Edin). *a*: 19 Young St, Edin & Cedarbrook, Hermitage Drive, Edin. *t*: 22607 & 52860.

McNEILL - MOSS, Geoffrey ("Geoffrey Moss"). *b*: Lon 1886. *e*: Rugby & Sandhurst. *m* Esther McNeill. *s*: 1. Maj Grenadier Guards (ret). *Publ*: Sweet Pepper; Whipped Cream; New Wine; Modern Melody; Little Green Apples; Thursby; I Face the Stars; etc. *a*: Ford Pl, Ford, Sussex. *t*: Yapton 235.

McNERNEY, Joshua William, F.J.I. *b*: Dublin 1872. *e*: Catholic Univ Sc Dublin. *m*: Eileen Mary Sherlock. *s*: 1. Journalist. *n.a*: Dublin Evening Mail '91, Daily Express (Dublin) '92, Irish Daily Independent (now Irish Indep) '97—, Lon Office Staff 1902—, Lon Ed '05—. *s.s*: Politics & law. Barrister-at-Law. Lobby Journalist '06—. Mem N.U.J. *c*: Nat Lib. *a*: Eastlea, 56 Rodenhurst Rd, Clapham Park, S.W.4. *t*: Tulse Hill 5185.

McNICOL, John. b: Hanover, Ontario 1869. e: Knox Coll Toronto, Univ of Toronto. m: Louisa Maud Burpe. Minister & Teacher. Publ: The Christian Evangel; Thinking Through the Bible; The Bible's Philosophy of History. Ctr: Biblical Review, Evangelical Quarterly, etc. s.s: Biblical Lit & Church Hist. a: 16 Spadina Rd, Toronto. Ontario. T: KL 4531.

McPEAKE, Alan Young. b: Dublin 1899. e: Highgate Sch. m: Agatha Watson. Dir Nat Mag Co. n.a: Westminster Gazette 1919, Nash's Mag & Good Housekeeping '23, Pall Mall Mag '26, Harper's Bazaar '30. c: Savage & Moor Park. a: Short Hills, Sandy Lodge Rd, Moor Pk, Herts. T: Rickmansworth 2331.

McPHAIL, Rev. Peter. b: N. Shields 1860. e: Hartley Theo Col M/C. m: Jane Cort. s: 3. d: 1. c.t: Springtime, Christian Messenger, Aldersgate, Holborn Review. s.s: Theo & points of religion. Conductor Springtime, Chr Endeavour Reading Un 25 y, with 5 study circles, a Bibl, a Missny, a Philos, a Lit & a Social. 20 y Exam Hartley Theo Col M/C. 30 y Exam of Mins on Probation & 5 y Sec. a: 19 Portland St, Lancaster.

McPHEE, John, M.A. b: Neilston 1881. e: Paisley Gr Sch, Glas Univ, Morbihan France. m: Olive Campbell. s: 1. d: 1. Former Teacher of Mod Langs Glas Hgh Sch, Headmaster Hamilton Crescent (Glas) Jun Sec Sch, Headmaster Woodside (Glas) Sen Sec Sch, Lec in French Paisley Tech Coll. Publ: (In collab with R. M. Jack) Primary French; Higher French; Intensive French Readers; Standard Tests in French; Lower Grade Leaving Certificate Papers in French & in German; Higher Grade Leaving Certificate Papers in French & German; Progressive German; etc. Ctr: Scot Sec Sch Journ. s.s: French & German. a: 42 Deanwood Ave, Muirend, Glasgow S.4.

McPHERSON, Kenneth Roderick. b: Simla 1885. e: Bedford Sc. m: Ellen Rosetta Griffin. s: 2. d: 1. Egyptian Civil Service (ret). Publ: The A to Z of Contract Bridge. c.t: Bridge Mag & Brit Bridge World. Rec: Bridge, gardening & amateur conjuring. a: Hazelbrae, St Saviour's Rd, St Leonard's-on-Sea, Sussex. t: Hastings 1468.

McPHERSON, Marjorie Carson. b: Towerpoint. e: Greenock H.S., Greenock Acad & Glas Col. Editor. n.a: Helensburgh News 1926, Corr, Ed Greenock Herald '27, Partner & Ed W. Coast Courier & Helensburgh Courier '28. Rec: Tennis, golf, music. a: 40 Cathcart St, Greenock, & 34 Grosvenor Terr, Greenock. t: 796.

McQUAID, Edward. b: Wishaw 1895. e: Glas Univ. m: Jean Clyde. Organiser Odeon Cinema Clubs for Children. n.a: Sunday Referee as "Beaumains II," "Mustard & Cress" Feature 1934—, Cavalcade, Column "Touchstone". Ctr: People's Journ, Red Letter, Smart Novels, My Weekly, T.P.'s Weekly, B.B.C. (Plays), etc. s.s: Humour, One-Act Plays, Short Stories. Rec: Golf, bridge. w.s: Roy Scots Fusiliers 1914—20. a: 16 Neale Close, London, N.2. T: Tudor 6983.

McQUEEN, Rev. David. n.a: Ed Scots Observer 1930—32, "Clericus" Glas News '24—. c.t: Glas News, Daily Record, Sunday Mail, Sunday Dispatch (Over the Coffee Cups feature). s.s: Church, religions, social, Scottish. a: Sherwood Manse, 15 Greenlaw Drive Paisley. t: 3057.

McQUILLAND, Louis. b: Donegal. e: St Malachy's Coll Belfast. n.a: Ev News, Dly Graphic, Lit Ed Dly Express & Sun Express, Lond Ed Cork Examiner. Publ: The Tragedian's Last Supper (collab); The King at Ease; Song of the Open Road; A Little Book of Irish Verse. Ctr: T.P.'s Weekly, The Bookman, The Passing Show, The Ideal Home, The New Witness. s.s: Book Reviewing, Film Criticism. a: 6 Lawrence Mans, Lordship Pl, Cheyne Row, Chelsea, London, S.W.3.

McREATH, Dugald Stuart. b: Whitchurch Hants 1906. e: Osborne Hse Romsey. m: Eva Marjorie Pope. Journalist. n.a: Ed Romsey Advertiser '22, Dunstable Borough Gazette '32. a: 145 Chiltern Rd, Dunstable. t: 155.

McSORLEY, Joseph, M.A., D.Litt., S.T.L. b: Brooklyn, N.Y. 1874. e: St John's Coll Brooklyn, Catholic Coll of America. Priest, Roman Catholic Church. n.a: Ctr Ed Catholic World 1932—. Publ: Outline History of the Church, from St Peter to Pius XII; Think & Pray; A Primer of Prayer; The Sacrament of Duty; Be of Good Heart; Italian Confessions; (Collab) Spanish Confessions; Short History of the Catholic Church. Ctr: Catholic World, Ecclesiastical Review, Information, etc. s.s: Religion—Apologetics, Spiritual Works, Hist. a: 415 West 59 St, New York 19, N.Y., U.S.A. T: Columbus 5-3210.

McTAGGART, Maxwell-Fielding, D.S.O. & Bar. b: Aldershot 1874. e: Harrow & Sandhurst. m: Winifred Grace Law. Army Officer (ret). Publ: Hints on Horsemanship; From Colonel to Subaltern; Stable & Saddle; A Handbook for Horseowners; etc. c.t: Morning Post, Country Life, 19th Century, Sportsman (U.S.A.), etc. s.s: Horsemanship. c: Cavalry. a: 5 Herbert Mansions, Hans Cres, S.W.1. t: Sloane 5030.

McWATERS, Matthew Robert Cecil, M.B., F.R.C.S. b: Bath 1878. e: King Edward VI Sch Bath, King's Coll London. m: Nona Conway Richards. d: 1. Lt-Col Indian Medical Service (ret). Publ: Principles of Surgical Dressing. Ctr: Lancet, Indian Med Gazette, B.M.J., Geog Mag. s.s: Kashmir & Ladak, Surgery. Rec: Travel, photography. w.s: 1914—16 & R.A.M.C. '41—46. a: c/o Standard Bank of South Africa, Cape Town.

McWEENEY, Cecil Brazil. b: Dublin 1896. e: Belvedere Col Dublin & R.C.S.I. m: Violet Reid. n.a: Ed Irish Tatler & Sketch 1932. Asst Dis Officer Political & Admin Service, Nigeria. War Service '15—19. Rec: Swimming, mountaineering. c: R.A.F. & Utd Arts, Dublin. a: 1 Toberna Terr, Monkstown, Co Dublin, & Commercial Bldgs, Dublin, C.3. t: 22551.

McWHINNIE, Hugh George Willet. n.a: Ed North Devon Journal-Herald. a: West Country Hse, High St, Barnstaple. T: 2218-9.

MEABY, Kenneth Tweedale, C.B.E., D.L. b: 1883. e: St Bees Sch, Cumberland. Clerk of the Peace & of the County Counc Nottinghamshire & Clerk of the Lieutenancy since 1920, Legal Adviser to Midland Agricultural Coll, Clerk of War Zone Court for North Midland Region, Late Pres Law Society for Nottingham, Flag Officer R.N.V.R. (ret). Publ: Conservation of Water Supplies; Survey of County Government in Nottinghamshire during 50 years; Nottinghamshire County Records during the 18th Century. Rec: Yachting, golf. c: Roy Cruising, Roy Southern Yacht, Roy Western Yacht. a: Burgage Court, Southwell, Notts. T: Southwell 2261.

MEACHEN, George Norman, M.D., B.S., M.R.C.P., F.R.S.M. b: Beccles 1876. e: Priv & Guy's Hosp, (Univ Lond.) m: Mabel Ethel Reis. d: 1. n.a: "Medicus" of Southend Standard 1920—32, Sub-Ed Medical Press & Circular '02—12. Publ: Short History of Tuberculosis; First Course in Human Physiology; Skin Diseases, their Nursing & General Management. Ctr: Professional Journs. s.s: Tuberculosis & Skin

Diseases. *Rec*: Music, organ playing. *a*: Petherton Cottage, Ashley Heath, Ringwood, Hants. *T*: Ringwood 450.

MEAD, GEORGE ROBERT STOW: editor, author, lecturer; b. Mar. 22, 1863; s. Robert Mead, Colonel H. M. Ordnance, and Mary Mead; educ. The King's Sch. (Rochester, Eng.), St. John's Coll. (Cambridge—Scholar), Univ. of Claremont (France). DEGREE: M.A. (Class Tripos, 1884); m. Laura May, d. of Frederick Cooper, C.B., I.C.S., 1899 (died 1924). AUTHOR: Simon Magus, 1892; Orpheus, 1896; The Upanishads (2 vols), 1896; Fragments of a Faith Forgotten, 1900 (2nd edit. 1906; 3rd edit. 1930); Pisti's Sophia: A Gnostic Miscellany, 1921; Apolionius of Tyana, 1901; The Gospels and the Gospel, 1902; The Jesus Talmud Stories and Toldoth Jeschu, 1903; Thrice Greatest Hermes (3 vols.), 1906; Echoes from the Gnosis, 1907; The World Mystery, 1908; Some Mystical Adventures, 1910; Quests Old and New, 1913; The Subtle Body in Western Tradition, 1919; The Gnostic John the Baptizer, 1924; The Sacred Dance in Christendom, 1926. Editor: The Quest, Quarterly Review (now ceased publication), The Quest Series. Relig. denom., Church of England. OFFICE: 21 Cecil Court, London, W. C. 2, Eng.

MEAD, Guy Roper. *b*: Hove 1911. *e*: Willaston Sc Cheshire. *m*: Florence Louisa Sangster. Journalist. *n.a*: Dis Rep West Sussex Gazette '29-30, Times & Guardian series, Hendon '30-34. M.J.I. '30-. *a*: 9 Grove Av, Church End, Finchley, N.3. *t*: Finchley 2156.

MEAD, Frank S., A.B., B.D. *b*: Chatham, N.J., U.S.A. 1898. *e*: Univ of Denver, Union Theol Seminary. *m*: Judy Duryee. *s*: 1. *d*: 1. Writer, Editor. *n.a*: Exec Ed Christian Herald. *Publ*: The March of Eleven Men; See These Banners Go; The Twelve Decisive Battles of Christianity; Right Here at Home; Who's Who's in the Bible; Tales From Latin America; On Our Own Doorstep. *Ctr*: Various. *s.s*: Religion, History, Missions. *Rec*: Golf. *a*: Christian Herald, 27 East 39th St, New York 16, N.Y., U.S.A. *T*: Caledonia 5-1210.

MEAD, Thomas Francis. *b*: Sidney, N.S.W. 1918. *e*: Marist Bros Coll Randwick. *m*: Vaila Pender. Journalist-Author. *n.a*: National Advocate 1937-39, Dly News Sydney '39-41, Dly Mirror Sydney '41-47, Courier-Mail Brisbane '47—. *Publ*: Man is Never Free. *Ctr*: Man, Cavalcade. *s.s*: Australian Hist & Federal Politics, Music. *Rec*: Cricket, fishing, music. *a*: 283 Main St, Kangaroo Point, Brisbane, Australia.

MEADER, Stephen Warren, B.A. *b*: Providence, Rhode Island 1892. *e*: Pub Schs Rochester, Moses Brown Sch Providence, Haverford Coll. *m*: Elizabeth White Hoyt. *s*: 2. *d*: 2. Advertiser, Assoc Copy Dir N.W. Ayer & Son Inc Philadelphia. *n.a*: Assoc Ed The Country Gentleman 1920—21. *Publ*: The Black Buccaneer; Down the Big River; Longshanks; Away to Sea; King of the Hills; The Will to Win; Shadow in the Pines; Behind the Ranges; etc. *Ctr*: Boy's Life, American Boy, Open Road for Boys, Ladies' Home Journ. *s.s*: Fiction for teen-age Boys. *Rec*: Canoeing, painting, nature study. *a*: 17 Colonial Ave, Moorestown, New Jersey, U.S.A. *T*: Moorestown 9-0906.

MEADOWS, Ken. *b*: Southport 1912. *e*: K. George Sc Southport. N/p Reporter. *n.a*: Southport Guardian '29-33, Warrington Guardian '33, Southport Guardian '33-. *s.s*: Sport, music, drama. *a*: 61 Hawkshead St, Southport, Lancs. *t*: 4867.

MEAGHER, Maude. *b*: Boston, U.S.A. *e*: Calif Univ. Author & Journalist. *n.a*: Lon Corr San Francisco Chron. *Publ*: White Jade; Fantastic Traveller; The Green Scamander (1934). Extensive travel. *Rec*: Archæ, hist. *c*: Lyceum. *a*: c/o A. M. Heath & Co Ltd, 188 Piccadilly, W.1.

MEAKIN, Annette M. B. *b*: Clifton, Bristol. *e*: England & Germany, Stern Conservatoire Berlin. Author. *Publ*: Goethe & Schiller; Hannah More; Galicia: the Switzerland of Spain; In Turkestan; A Ribbon of Iron; Enlistment or Conscription; Nausikaa. *Ctr*: Various. *Rec*: Reading, music. c/o National Provincial Bank, 69 Baker St, London, W.1.

MEAKIN, Walter. Sec N/p Press Fund. *n.a*: Leamington Chron 1904—05, Yorks Observer '05—12, M/C Guardian '12—17, Daily News '17—30. *a*: 11 Garrick St, W.C.2. *t*: Tem Bar 7288, Amersham 687.

MEALAND, Richard Lewis. Ed Nash's Mag. *a*: 153 Q. Victoria St. E.C.4.

MEANS, Florence C. *b*: Baldwinsville, New York 1891. *e*: Kansas City Hgh Sch, East Denver Hgh Sch, Read Sch of Art, Central Baptist Theol Sem, Univ of Denver. *m*: Carleton Bell Means. *d*: 1. Author. *Publ*: A Candle in the Mist; Shuttered Windows; The Moved-Outers; Great Day in the Morning; Tangled Waters; Whispering Girl; The End of Nowhere; Dusky Day; Teresita of the Valley; Ranch & Ring; A Bowlful of Stars; The Singing Wood; Adella Mary in Old Mexico; Shadow Over Wide Ruin; Penny for Luck; etc. *Ctr*: Various. *s.s*: Minority Groups of the U.S.A. *Rec*: Travel, painting. *c*: Denver Woman's Press, Pen & Brush (N.Y.), Bookfellows. *a*: 595 Baseline Rd, Boulder, Colrado, U.S.A. & Palmer Lake, Colorado. *T*: Palmer Lake 2422.

MEANS, Gardiner Coit, M.A., Ph.D. *b*: Windham, Connecticut 1896. *e*: Harvard Coll & Harvard Univ. *m*: Caroline F. Ware. Economist. *Publ*: The Modern Corporation & Private Property; The Structure of The American Economy; The Modern Economy in Action; The Holding Company. *Ctr*: American Econ Rev, Quarterly Journ of Econs. *s.s*: Econs. *Rec*: Farming. *a*: R.F.D. Route 1, Box 58, Vienna, Virginia, U.S.A. *T*: Vienna 169 WX.

MEARES, John Willoughby, C.I.E., M.InstC.E., M.ConsE., M.I.E.E., F.R.A.S. *b*: Barnet 1871. *e*: Winchester Col & Univ Col Lon. *m*: (1) Frances Helen Curteis; (2) Margaret Helen Lane. *s*: 2. Cons Eng. Elec Adv Govt of India. Chief Eng Hydro-Elec Survey of India. *Publ*: The Law Relating to Electrical Energy in India; Electrical Engineering Practice (with R. E. Neale, 4th ed); Hydro-Electric Developments. *c.t*: N/ps & periodicals. *s.s*: Electricity, water power. *a*: 14 Cawley Rd, Chichester, Sussex. *t*: 345.

MEARES, Raymond. *b*: Bradford. *e*: Hulme G.S. M/C & Wallasey G.S. Journalist. *n.a*: Reporter Bootle Times, Birkenhead Advertiser, Crewe & Nantwich Observer, & Staffordshire Evening Sentinel. *c.t*: Various. *s.s*: Football, boxing. *a*: 257 Nantwich Rd, Crewe, Cheshire. *t*: 2498.

MEARNS, Alexander Gow, M.D., D.P.H., F.R.S(Ed). *b*: 1902. *e*: Hgh Sch & Univ of Glasgow. *m*: Agnes Russell. Senior Lecturer & Examiner in Hygiene Univ of Glasgow, Med Adviser Scottish Counc for Health Educ. *Publ*: (With J. R. Currie) Text Book of Hygiene; Manual of Laboratory Practice; etc. *Ctr*: Med Jurisprudence, Health Educ Journ, Lancet, B.M.J. *s.s*: Hygiene, Health Educ, Med Educ. *Rec*: Travel, music. *c*: Glasgow Univ. *a*: 43 Verona Ave, Glasgow, W.4. *T*: Scotstoun 2834.

MEARNS, Hughes. *b*: Philedelphia, Pennsylvania 1875. *e*: Univs of Pennsylvania & Harvard. *m*: Mabel Fagley. *d*: 1. Writer, Educator. *Publ*: The Creative Adult; Creative Power; Creative Youth; I Ride in My Coach; The Vinegar Saint; Lions in My Way; Richard Richard. *Ctr*: Sat Ev Post, Ladies Home Journ, American Mag, Woman's Home Companion,

Colliers, N.Y. Herald Tribune, etc. *s.s:* Creative Educ. *Rec:* Travel, citrus farming, viewing & collecting pictures & objects of art, writing light verse. *c:* Franklin Inn (Phila). *w.s:* Captain World War I. *a:* Bearsville, Ulster County, New York, U.S.A. *T:* Woodstock, N.Y. 89F4.

MEARS, Rev. Edward, M.A. *b:* W. Hartlepool 1864. *e:* Queen's Col Oxf. *m:* Mary Florence de Quincey. *s:* 5. Anglican Rector. Warden of the Brotherhood of St Paul. Scholar of Queen's Col Oxf. *Publ:* The Gospel of St John (1930). *a:* Little Bardfield Rectory, Braintree, Essex. *t:* Gt Bardfield 44.

MEARS, Louisa Wilhelmina, A.M., B.Ed. *b:* Beatrice, Nebraska 1874. *e:* Nebraska State Teachers' Coll Univs of Nebraska, Chicago, Minnesota, Wisconsin, Clark. Writer, former Teacher of Geography. *Publ:* Life & Times of a Midwest Educator: Carroll Gardner Pearse; Hills of Peru; Geography of Wisconsin; America's Fairyland: The Hawaiian Islands; etc. *Ctr:* Instructor Mag, State Educ Mags & various daily newsps. *s.s:* Geography, Pioneer History. *Rec:* Travel. *a:* Box 67 State Hse Station, Lincoln 9, Nebraska, U.S.A.

MEARSON, Lyon. *b:* Montreal, Canada 1888. *e:* Hgh Sch, New York Law Sch. *m:* Rose Mary Cone. *s:* 2. Writer & Editor. *n.a:* Ed Metropolitan Mag 1922, Art Critic N.Y. Ev Mail '14—18. *Publ:* The Whisper on the Stair; Footsteps in the Dark; Phantom Fingers; The French They Are A Funny Race; (Co-Author, Plays) People Don't Do Such Things; Our Wife; Love Costs Money; Murder by Appointment; Class Reunion; The Vulture in the Parlor. *Ctr:* American & Brit mags. *s.s:* Art & Music. *Rec:* Chess, poker. *w.s:* World War I. *a:* 1115 Jerome Ave, New York 52, N.Y. *T:* Jerome 8-1798.

MECKLIN, John Moffatt, L.J.D., Ph.D. *b:* Poplar Creek, Mississippi 1871. *e:* Southwestern Coll, Union Seminary, Princeton Seminary, Leipzig Univ. *m:* (1) Laurie W. Babcock (dec'd), (2) Hope Davis. *s:* 1. *d:* 1. Prof of Sociology. *Publ:* (Autobiography): My Quest for Freedom; Introduction to Social Ethics; The Story of American Dissent; The Passing of the Saint: A Study of a Cultural Type; The Survival Value of Christianity; etc. *Ctr:* Various. *s.s:* Religion, Social Ethics, Social Philosophy. *Rec:* Fly fishing. *a:* Dartmouth College, Hanover, New Hampshire, U.S.A. *T:* 197J Hanover.

MECREDY, Eric J., M.C. *b:* Bray, Co Wicklow 1896. *e:* Portora, Enniskillen & Bristol Univ. *m:* Aileen F. Barnard. *s:* 1. *d:* 1. Journalist. *n.a:* Dir Wheelman Printing & Pubg Co, Ltd (Sackville Press), Ed Irish Motor News. *c.t:* Various. *s.s:* Motoring. War Service, Croix de Guerre avec Palme. *c:* Roy Irish Auto. *a:* Tigeen, Gordon Av, Foxrock, Co Dublin.

"MEDARDO" (pen name): see Nibbi, Guio.

MEDD, Mrs. Anna Maude Seaton ("A. K. B."), M.D. *Publ:* Psalms of Solitude. *a:* c/o Lloyd's Bank Streatham, S.W.

MEDD, William Thomas. *b:* Scarboro' 1881. *e:* Scarboro' Cent & Scarboro' G.S. Married. *s:* 1. *d:* 1. Journalist. *n.a* Chief Reporter Scarboro' Evening Post 1909-20, Sub-Ed Scarboro' Evening News & Post '20-. *c:* Lon Press, Scarboro' Masonic & Scarboro' Const. *a:* Boa Vista, 59 Manor Rd, Scarboro'. *t:* 441.

MEDE, JOSEPH (pen name): see Garland, David John.

MEDLEY, C. P., A.M.I.MechE., F.R.S.A. Chrtd Mech Engineer. *a:* 103 Worship St, E.C.2. *t:* Bishopsgate 1834.

MEDLEY, Dudley Julius, M.A., LL.D. *e:* Keble Coll Oxf. Emeritus Prof of Hist Univ of Glasgow. *Publ:* Students Manual of English Constitutional History; Original Illustrations of English Constitutional History. *a:* Ashby, Pydehams, Newbury. *T:* 533.

MEDLEY, Robert P., M.A. *a:* Felsted School, Chelmsford, Essex

MEDLICOTT, William Norton, M.A., F.R.Hist.S. *b:* Lond 1900. *e:* Haberdasher's Aske's Sch, Univ Coll, Institute of Historical Research Lond. *m:* Dorothy Kathleen Coveney. Prof of Hist Univ Coll Exeter, Prof of Mod Hist Univ of Texas U.S.A. 1931—32, Hon Sec Hist Assoc '43—46, Princ Officer Board of Trade '41-42, Official Historian to Min of Econ Warfare since '42, Chm Publications Cttee Hist, Assoc since '46, Mem Inst of Internat Affairs, Mem of Eng Speaking Union. *Publ:* The Congress of Berlin & After; British Foreign Policy since Versailles; Origins of the Second Great War. *Ctr:* Eng Hist Review, History, Quarterly Review, Slavonic & East European Review, etc. *s.s:* 19th & 20th Century Diplomatic Hist & Internat Affairs. *a:* Woodlands, Topsham, Devon. *T:* Topsham 8509.

MEE, Arthur. *b:* 1875. Journalist & Author. *n.a:* Ex Ed Black & White, Literary Ed Daily Mail, Ed The Children's Newspaper. *Publ:* Arthur Mee's Gift Book; One Thousand Beautiful Things; Arthur Mee's Story Book, etc.; Edited, Harmsworth History of the World; The Children's Encyclopædia, etc. *a:* Eynsford Hill, Eynsford, Kent.

MEE, Herbert Fletcher. *b:* Stapleford 1881. *e:* Bd Sc. *m:* Jane Bingham. *s:* 1. *d:* 1. Sub-Ed Nott'm Evening Post. *a:* Park Rd, Daybrook, Nott'm.

MEECHAM, Henry George, B.A (Lon), M.A., B.D., PhD. (M/C). *b:* M/C 1886. *e:* Hartley Col & Univ M/C. *m:* Gladys Lee Gerrard. *s:* 2. Tutor in Meth Theo Col. *Publ:* Light from Ancient Letters (1923); The Oldest Version of the Bible: "Aristeas" on its Traditional Origin ('32). *c.t:* Meth Denominat Mags, Meth Recorder, Expository Times, etc. *s.s:* Hellenistic Greek. Entered Meth Ministry '11, Prof Hartley Col, M/C '30, Hartley Lect 32, Examiner in N.T. Lang & Lit for students & probationers of Meth Ch. *Rec:* Golf. *c:* Mem Federal Counc of Free Ch of Eng. *a:* Auldyn, 43 Spring Bridge Rd, Alexandra Pk, Manchester 16. *t:* Chorlton 1471.

MEEDS, Walter. *b:* Sheffield 1889. *e:* Pyebank & Ellesmere Rd, & Sheffield Tech Sc. *m:* Marjorie Geary. Sporting Journalist. *n.a:* Sheffield Daily Telegraph & Star 1910-23, Sporting Life '23-. *s.s:* Racing, athletics. *c:* Press. *a:* 154 Park Rd, Hendon, N.W.4. *t:* 1665.

MEEK, ALEXANDER: professor of Zoology; b. Broughty Ferry, Eng., April, 1865; educ. Univ. of St. Andrews (Scotland), Univ. of Freiburg (Germany). DEGREES: B.Sc. (St. Andrews), Hon. D.Sc. (Univ. of Durham); m. Christine Agnes Fowler, 1893. AUTHOR: The Migrations of Fish, 1916; Essentials of Zoology, 1922; The Progress of Life, 1930. Editor: Annual Reports Dove Marine Laboratory, Cullercoats. CLUBS: Northumberland Yacht. OFFICE: Armstrong College. HOME: 19 Eslington Terrace, Newcastle-upon-Tyne, Eng.

MEEK, Charles Kingsley, D.Sc. *b:* Larne, Nth Ireland 1885. *e:* Rothesay Acad, Bedford Sch, Glas Univ, Brasenose Coll Oxf. *m:* Helen Marjorie Hopkins.

s: 2. Lecturer in Social Anthropology Oxford. *Publ*: Northern Tribes of Nigeria; Tribal Studies in Nth Nigeria; A Sudanese Kingdom; Law & Authority in a Nigerian Tribe; Land Law & Custom in the Colonies. *s.s*: Social Anthropology. *c*: Roy Socs. *a*: Green Tye, Churt, Surrey. *T*: Headley Down 2122.

MEEK, Sterner St Paul, Sc.A.(Chicago), B.S.(Alabama), (Col S. P. Meek). *b*: Chicago, Ill, U.S.A. 1894. *e*: Univs of Chicago, Alabama & Wisconsin, The Massachusetts Instit of Technology. *m*: Edna Brundage Noble. *s*: 1. Colonel U. S. Army (ret), Ballistician Hawaiian Criminology Laboratory 1931—35. *n.a*: Feature Writer Press Reporting Syndicate 1928—. *Publ*: Jerry: The Adventures of an Army Dog; Frog: The Horse that Knew No Master; Gypsy Lad: The Story of a Champion Setter; The Monkeys Have No Tails in Zamboanga; Island Born; Franz: A Dog of the Police; Gustav: A Son of Franz; Dignity: A Springer Spaniel; Rusty: A Cocker Spaniel; Inspection of Ordnance Material; So You're Going to Get a Puppy; Pat: The Story of a Seeing Eye Dog. *Ctr*: American, British & Canadian publications. *s.s*: Military & Animal Stories. *Rec*: Hunting, fishing, outdoor sports, judging field trials & dog shows. *c*: Army Ordnance Assoc, Reynolds, Pacific Saltfish, Press. *a*: c/o Jacques Chambrun Inc, 745 Fifth Ave, New York City, U.S.A.

MEEK, Theophile James, B.A., Ph.D., B.D. *b*: Port Stanley, Ontario 1881. *e*: Univs of Toronto, Marburg, Berlin, Chicago, Sch of Oriental Research Jerusalem, McCormick Theol Sem. *m*: Susan Dorothea Carrier. *s*: 1. *d*: 1. Prof of Oriental Languages Univ of Toronto. *n.a*: Assoc Ed American Journ of Semitic Languages 1931—41. *Publ*: Old Akkadian, Sumerian & Cappadocian Texts from Nuzi; Hebrew Origins; The Song of Songs: An American Translation; Some Explanatory Lists & Grammatical Texts; Ancient Oriental Seals in the Royal Ontario Museum; etc. *Ctr*: Ency Brit, Amer Journ of Semitic Languages, Journ of Near Eastern Studies, Antiquity, Rev d'Assyriologie, Asia, Canadian Geog Journ, Journ of Religion, etc. *s.s*: Assyriology (the cuneiform languages), The Old Testament (languages, literature & history). *Rec*: Tennis. *c*: Faculty. *a*: 52 Elgin Ave, Toronto 5, Canada. *T*: Kingsdale 0930.

MEEKER, Arthur, Jr. *b*: Chicago, Illinois 1902. *e*: Chicago Latin Sc, Princeton & Harvard Univs. Novelist. *Publ*: Vestal Virgin; Strange Capers; American Beauty. *c.t*: American N/ps & periodicals. Dir Soc of Midlands Authors '30 (Elected vice-Pres for Illinois '34). Sec & Charter Mem Exec Cmt of Chicago Chapter of P.E.N., Mem Board of Dirs of Chicago Grand Opera Co. *Rec*: Music, walking. *c*: Arts, (Chicago). *a*: 1100 Lake Shore Drive, Chicago, Illinois, U.S.A. *t*: Superior 3030.

MEES, C. E. Kenneth, D.Sc., F.R.S. *b*: Wellingborough, England 1882. *e*: Kingswood Sch Bath, St Dunstan's Coll Catford, Univ Coll Lond. *m*: Alice Crisp. *s*: 1. *d*: 1. Vice Pres in Charge of Research Eastman Kodak Co. *Publ*: The Theory of the Photographic Process; The Path of Science; Photography; Organisation of Industrial Scientific Research; Photography of Colored Objects; The Fundamentals of Photography. *s.s*: Industrial & Photographic Research. *Rec*: Golf. *c*: Athenæum, Nat Lib. *a*: Eastman Kodak Co, Rochester 4, N.Y., U.S.A.

MEES, James Henry. Dir & Coy Mang. *Publ*: Handbook of Wesleyan Methodist Church Stourbridge Circuit. *a*: 129 King William St, Amblecote, Stourbridge. *t*: Brierley Hill 7061.

MEGAW, Arthur Stanley, B.A. ("Arthur Stanley"). *b*: Holywood, Co Down, Ireland. *e*: Sullivan Upper Sch Holywood, Queen's Univ Belfast. *m*: Bertha Smith. *s*: 3. Writer & Solicitor (ret), Hon Sec Belfast Lit Soc 1928—. *Publ*: The Bedside Book; The Out-of-Doors Book; The Testament of Man; The Seven Stars of Peace; The House of Tranquility; The Bedside Bible; Madame De Sevigne; The Bedside Bunyan. *Ctr*: Times, Times Lit Supp, Blackwood's, Army Quarterly, etc. *s.s*: Anthology. *a*: Arden, Fortwilliam Drive, Belfast. *T*: Belfast 46063.

MEGGY, Gordon. *b*: Chelmsford 1878. *e*: Felsted Sc. Journalist. *n.a*: Staff Essex Chron '96-1901, Daily Mail staff & Ed Sunday Dispatch ('03-05), free-lance '05-14. *c.t*: Daily Mail, Daily Express, Evening News, Strand Mag, Punch, The Tatler, etc. *Rec*: Golf, fishing. War Service '14-19. Founded Premier Sc of Journl. *a*: 4 Adam St, Adelphi, W.C.2. *t*: Temple Bar 2188.

MEGHNAD, SAHA: professor of Physics ;*b*. Dacca, Province Bengal, India; *s*. Jagannath and Bhubaneshwari Meghnad; *educ*. Dacca Coll., Presidency Coll. (Calcutta). DEGREES: M.S.C. (Calcutta), D.Sc. (Calcutta); married. AUTHOR: Theories of Thermal Ionisation: Selective Radiation Pressure. Has written large number of original papers in the Proc. Royal Soc. (London), Philosophical Mag., Zeitschrift fur Physik and other scientific journs. Translator of number of papers on Theories of Relativity from German into English. Contributor to Modern Review (Calcutta). General character of writing: scientific. ADDRESS: The University, Allahabad, India.

MEGROZ, Rodolphe Louis. *b*: London 1891. *e*: Eng & Geneva, Lond Univ. Writer. *n.a*: 1st Dly Herald Gossip Ed, Rep to Islington Dly Gazette, Sun Express, Dly Express & Dly Herald, former Asst Ed World Digest, Sub-Ed B.B.C. European News 1942—45. *Publ*: (Verse) Personal Poems; Story of Ruth; Script of Eros; (Prose) Walter de la Mare; The Three Sitwells; For Fathers: a Book of Domestic Letters; Letters of Women in Love; Dante Gabriel Rossetti; Francis Thompson; Joseph Conrad; Modern English Poetry; Five Novelist-Poets of To-day; English Poetry for Children; The Lear Omnibus; The Dream World; The Real Robinson Crusoe; Come Out of Doors (" C. D. Dimsdale "); Profile Art Through the Ages; 31 Bedside Essays; etc. *Ctr*: Various newsps & periodicals. *s.s*: Psychology of Dreams, Popular Nat Hist, Nonsense in Lit & Art. *c*: Press. *a*: 116 Tufnell Park Rd, London, N.7.

MEHROTRA, Kewal Krishna, M.A., B.Litt. *b*: Saharanpur 1905. *e*: Allahabad Univ, St Catherine's Oxf. *c.t*: Lecturer in English, Univ of Allahabad. *n.a*: Asst Ed Allahabad Univ Mag '28, Assoc Ed '33. *Publ*: Horace Walpole and the English Novel '34. *s.s*: Eng lit. Tennis Capt Allahabad Univ '27, winning the singles championship of that year. *Rec*: Tennis. *c*: Union Soc Oxf, Friday Club of Allahabad Univ. *a*: 10 Old Survey Rd, Dehra Dun, India.

MEHTA, Chandravadan Chimanlal, M.A. *b*: Surat 1901. *e*: Government Hgh Sch, Elphinstone Coll Bombay. Programme Executive All India Radio Bombay. *n.a*: Conducted Congress Bulletins 1930—32, Once Ed of " Gndib " a weekly from Surat. *Publ*: Aggadi; Akho; Prem Nu Moti; Shikharin; Dhara Gurjari; Narmad, several short stories, etc. *Ctr*: Kumar, Prasthan. Gujarat, Kaumudi, Gujarati, Navchetan, Chronicle, Jame Jamshed. *s.s*: Drama. *Rec*: Mountaineering. *c*: P.E.N. *a*: 101 Queens Rd, Bombay. *T*: 31031.

MEHTA, Sir Chunilal Bhaichand, Kt. *b*: Bhavnager, India 1888. *e*: Bombay. *m*: Tapibai. *s*: 1. *d*: 2. Merchant, Sheriff of Bombay 1935—36, Visited New York in '44 as Leader of the Indian Delegation to the International Business Conference. *n.a*: Ed The Financial News since 1932. *s.s*: Finance, Gold & Foreign Exchange. *Rec*: Travelling. *c*: Rotary, Bombay, Roy Western India Turf, etc. *a*: 52 Ridge Rd, Malabar Hill, Bombay 6, India. *T*: 42383.

MEHTA, Sir Homi, Kt., K.C.I.E., K.B.E., J.P. *b*: Gandevi 1871. *e*: Bombay. *m*: Goolbai Umrigar. *s*: 3. *d*: 2. Mill-owner & Merchant, Apptd Delegate League of Nations 1933, Dir Reserve Bank of India '34, Employers' Delegate World's Labour Conference at Geneva '36. *Publ* : Financial Control during this war & the last war ; The Future of Cotton ; Possible Effects of Post-war Currency Plans on India. *Ctr* : Times of India. *Rec* : Cricket, boxing, golf, billiards. *c* : National Liberal, Royal Automobiles, Willingdon Sports, Roshanara (Delhi), Western India Turf. *a* : Mehta Hse, Apollo St, Fort Bombay. *T* : 20364 & 40719.

MEHTA, Nanalal Chamanlal. *b* : Ahmedabad, India 1892. *e* : Saurashtra Hgh Sch, Wilson Coll Bombay, Fitzwilliam House Camb, Sch of Econs Lond, Gray's Inn Lond. *m* : Shanta Mehta. *s* : 2. *d* : 2. I.C.S. (ret), Barrister, Prime Minister Holkar State Indore. *Publ* : Studies in Indian Painting ; Gujerati Painting in the 15th Century ; Bharatiya Chitra Kala ; Contribution of Islam to Indian Culture. *Ctr* : Various. *s.s* : Indian Art, Literary subjects, including Indian History. *Rec* : Tennis, riding, swimming. *a* : Prime Minister's Residence, Indore, Central India. *T* : 22.

MEIER-GRAEFE, Alfred Julius. *b* : Resitza 1867. *e*: Munchen, Zurich, Berlin, Paris. *m*: (1) Annemarie Epstein; (2) Helen Lienhart. *s* : 1. Author. *n.a*: Ed Marées-Gesellschaft. *Publ*: Entwicklungsgeschichte der modernen Kunst (3 vols); Hans von Marées (3 vols); Eugene Delacroix; Corot; Renoir; Vincent van Gogh (Eng trans); Der Vater (novel); Die reine Farbe (drama); Geschichten neben der Kunst (stories); etc. *c.t*: Frankfurter Zeitung. War Service, Russian front 1914. Travelled extensively. *a*: St Cyr-sur-Mer, France.

MEIGS, Charles Hardy. *b* : Albany, New York 1867. *e*: Albany H.S. *m* : Ida Brown. *s* : 1 (dec). *d* : 3. Writer. *n.a*: Special Stenographic Reporter New Haven Register, etc. *Publ*: Old Ezra ; The Prisoner of Alcatraz ; The Man of Uz. Free Lance writer on international politics with headquarters at Berlin 1900—14. *a*: 17 Bow St, Forest Hills, Long Island, New York, U.S.A. *t*: Boulevard 8—1692.

MEIKLE, Henry William, C.B.E., M.A., D.Litt., Hon.LL.D., Hon.R.S.A. *b* : Edinburgh 1880. *e*: Daniel Stewart's Coll, Edin Univ. *m* : Jessie Mollison McLetchie. H.M. Historiographer in Scotland, Lect d'Anglais Univ Lyons 1904—05, Lect in Scottish Hist Univ of Edin '08—16, Sec & Librarian Inst of Hist Research Univ of Lond '23—27, Keeper of MSS '27—31 & Librarian '31—46 Nat Lib of Scot, David Murray Lect Univ of Glas '47. *Publ* : Scotland & the French Revolution ; Works of William Fowler ; Correspondence of the Scots Commissioners in London 1644—1646 ; Calendar of State Papers Relating to Scotland ; Scotland. *Ctr* : Scottish Historical Review, Scotsman, Times Litt Supplement, English Historical Review. *s.s* : Scottish History. *c* : Univ, Internat Hse Edin. *a* : 23 Riselaw Rd, Edinburgh 10. *T* : 52451.

MEIKLE, John. *b*: Glasgow 1889. *e* : Glas Hgh Sch. *m*: Marguerite Celestine Zimmerman. *s* : 1. *d* : 3. Parl Sketch & Lond Letter Writer, Mem N.U.J. 1920—. *Ctr* : Wall Street News U.S.A. & Financial Times. *s.s* : Econ & Politics. *a* : 261 Whitehorse Lane, Sth Norwood, S.E.25. *T* : Livingstone 4568.

MEIKLEJOHN, Sir R. S., K.B.E., C.B., M.A First Civil Service Commr since 1928. *a*: Brook's Club, St James's St, S.W.1.

MEINERTZHAGEN, Col. Richard, D.S.O. *b* : London 1878. *e*: Aysgarth & Harrow. *m* : Anne Constance Jackson (dec). *s* : 1. *d* : 1. Scientist. *Publ* : Birds of Egypt; Life of a Boy. *Ctr* : The Ibis, Journ Roy Geog Soc, Proc Zoological Soc. *s.s* : Ornithology. *Rec* : Travel for scientific research. *a* : 17 Kensington Pk Gdns, London, W.11.

MEISSNER, Rev. John Ludwig Gough, M.A. *b* : Belfast 1884. *e* : R.A.I. Belfast, Q.U.B., T.C.D. *m* : Anne Hill. *s* : 1. *d* : 1. Mem R.I.A., former Rector Altedesert (Pomeroy) Diocese of Armagh, Barrister, Rector of Carlingford & Curate in Charge of Omeath Diocese of Armagh. *Publ* : The Celtic Church in England After the Synod of Whitby ; History of the Church of Ireland from the Earliest Times to the Present Day ; Vol I, The Celtic Church (the whole vol except Chapters I, IV & Appen dix M) ; Earliest Times to Present Day. *Ctr* : Proc R.I.A., Report of Church of Ireland Conf, etc. *s.s* : Hist of Celtic Christianity from earliest period to time of Danish invasions. *Rec* : Music, rose-growing. *c* : Dinner. *w.s* : 1914—19. *a* : The Rectory, Carlingford, Co Louth, Eire.

MELCHETT, 2nd Baron, Henry Mond. *b*: London 1898. *e* : Winchester. *m* : Amy Gwen Wilson. *s* : 1. *d* : 1. Coy Dir, M.P. (L) Isle of Ely 1923—24, (C) East Toxteth Div Liverpool '29—30. *Publ* : Why the Crisis ; Modern Money ; Thy Neighbour. *c* : Carlton. *a* : 50 Grosvenor Sq, London, W.1. *T* : Grosvenor 4377.

MELCHIOR-BONNET, Christian. *b*: Marseille 1903. *e*: Bethune Coll Versailles, Ecole de Droit, Ecole du Louvre Faculte. *m* : Bernardine Paul-Doubois-Taine. *s* : 2. *d* : 1. Writer. *n.a* : Director de collection chez Flammarion, Director of Revue Historia, Ed in Chief Oeuvres Libres. *Publ*. Scenes et portraits de Chateaubriand historien ; Les Memoires du Cardinal de Retz ; Le comte de Tilly page, de Marie Antoinette. *s.s* : Histoire. *a* : 69bis Boulevard de Courcelles Paris VIII. *T* : Carnot 57-38.

MELDON, Lt. Col. Philip Albert, D.S.O., M.A. *e* : Beaumont Coll & Dublin Univ. Chm & Mang Dir of Burns, Oates & Washbourne Ltd. *a* : 43/45 Newgate St, E.C.1. *t* : City 4971.

MELDRUM, D. S. *Publ*: Rembrandt's Paintings, Novels; etc. *a* : 15 St George's Rd, St Margarets-on-Thames.

MELDRUM, Helen Myers. *b* : Kilmuir Easter 1876. *e*: Kilmuir Easter Sc, Ch of Scot T.C. Aberdeen. *m*: James Alexander Scott, M.A. *d* : 1. *Publ*: Songs from a City Garden. *c.t*: Edin Evening News, Glas Herald, etc. *s.s*: Scot hist. *c*: Many y on Exec Cmt Equal Citizenship Soc; Mem Cmt Scot Br Nat Vigilance Soc. *a*: 24 Dudley Gdns, Edin 6.

MELFORD, Austin Alfred. *b*: Alverstoke 1884. *e* : Portsmouth Gr Sch. *m* : Jessie Winter. *s* : 2. Actor, Author, Producer. *Publ* : Pt Author Musical Comedies : Battling Butler ; Patricia ; Ladies Night ; etc ; (Author) It's a boy ; Night of the Garter ; Oh Daddy ; etc. *s.s* : Farce, Musical Comedy, Film Scenarios. *Rec* : Golf. *c* : Green Room. *a* : 3 The Close, Marlboro' Pl, St John's Wood, N.W.8. *T* : Primrose 6119.

MELHUISH, Charles William. *b*: Cardiff 1860. *e*: Canton Cardiff Nat & Sci & Art Scs. *m*: Jane Watts. *d* : 3. Builder & Contractor (ret). Ald Cardiff City Counc, Lord Mayor 1931-32. *c*: Riverside Conservative etc. *a*: 1 Clare Gdns, Cardiff.

MELLANBY, E., F.R.S., F.R.C.P., M.A., M.D. *b*: W. Hartlepool 1884. *e*: Barnard Castle Sc, Emmanuel Col Cam, St Thomas's Hosp. *m*: May Tweedy. Sec of Med Research Counc. *Publ*: Experimental Rickets (1921, No 61); Experimental Rickets ('25, No 93); etc. *c.t*: Phys Proc, B.M.J., Brain, Lancet, etc. *a*: 109 Ashdell Rd, Sheffield.

MELLANBY, Mrs. M., HonD.Sc. Investigator for Med Research Counc. *Publ*: Diet & the Teeth, an Experimental Study (Pt I 1929, No 140); Pt II ('30, No 153); Pt III ('34, No 191). *c.t*: B.D.J., Phys Rev, Amer Dent Ass, B.M.J. *a*: 109 Ashdell Rd, Sheffield.

MELLAND, C. H., M.D., F.R.C.P. *c.t*: Med Journs. *a*: 96 Mosley St, M/C.

MELLAND, Frank Hulme, B.A. *b*: Heaton Mersey 1879. *e*: Shrewsbury & Oxf Univ. *m*: Evelyn Cassandra Scroggs. *s*: 1. *d*: 3. Journalist. *n.a*: Ed Staff East Africa, Special Corr Bristol Empire Review. Civil Service N. Rhodesia '01—27. N. Rhodesia Rep in Lon '29—32. *Publ*: Through the Heart of Africa (1912); In Witchbound Africa ('23). *c.t*: The Times, Telegraph, Spectator, Listener, Time & Tide, Chambers, etc. *s.s*: Witchcraft, nat hist, anthropology. Traversed Africa from S. to N. *Rec*: Gardening, photography. *c*: Un Univ. *a*: The Hill, Caterham Valley, Surrey.

MELLARD, Louis. *b*: Nott'm. *e*: Priv & Bedford. Widower. *d*: 1. Author & Journalist. *n.a*: Now mainly F.L. Writer, usually under own name, but for certain n/p work under " Anoni " or " Drallem." *Publ*: Lost Romances of the Midlands; Tramp-Artist in Derbyshire & Devon; An Historical Survey of Derbyshire; Benastro's Daughters; Lady Witch of Woolpack Lane; Mysterious Mr. Riddell of Redhill; etc. *c.t*: Chambers's Journal, Windsor Mag, Weekly Telegraph, Nottinghamshire Guardian, Nottingham Journal, etc. *s.s*: Dramatic Adventure & hist fiction. Originally trained for Stock Exchange career, but lit & artistic interests prevailed. Has been a tramp-artist, general-utility & play producer, commercial trav, lit coach, lect, book-editor, etc. *Rec*: Travel. *a*: 3 Low Pavement, Nott'm.

MELLEN, Ida M. *b*: New York City 1877. *e*: Normal Sch, Marine Univ, Eugenics Research Assoc. Biologist & Author. *Publ*: Fishes in the Home; The Young Folks Book of Fishes; Roof Gardening; 1,001 Questions Answered About Your Aquarium; A Practical Cat Book; The Science & the Mystery of the Cat; The Mellen Tribe in America; Twenty Little Fishes; etc. *Ctr*: Nat Geog Mag, Nature Mag, Zoonos, N.Y. Zoological Soc, Journ of Heredity, Science, etc. *s.s*: Gen Biology & Eugenics. *a*: 547 East 4th St, Brooklyn 18, N.Y., U.S.A.

MELLONE, Sydney Herbert. *Publ*: inc Review of Modern French Thought; Bearings of Psychology on Religion; Studies in Philosophical Criticism & Construction; The Apocrypha: Its Story & Message; The Dawn of Modern Thought; etc. *a*: 6 Springbank Pl, Manningham, Bradford.

MELLOR, Allan Starkie. *b*: Oldham 1888. *e*: Gr Sch, Art Sch Manchester. Cartoonist, Sporting Artist, Freelance Journalist, Mem N.U.J. *n.a*: Manch Ev News 25 yrs, Cartoonist Oldham Chron 10 yrs. *Ctr*: Manch Ev Chron, My Garden, Captain, Hobbies, Yorks Post, Sun Chron. *s.s*: Sports, Cartoons, Nature Articles, Illus Articles on Sport. *c*: Manch Sketch, Manch Press. *a*: Manchester Press Exchange, 336 Corn Exchange Bldg, Manchester. *T*: DEA 2922.

MELLOR, Capt. Francis Horace, F.R.G.S. *b*: Lytham, Lancs 1897. *e*: King William's Col, Isle of Man. Author & Lecturer. *Publ*: Sword & Spear; Quest Romantic; The Papal Forces. *c.t*: Morning Post, The Listener, Kodak Mag, Times Weekly. *s.s*: Travel, history, politics, Africa. West Yorkshire Regt. & Indian Army 2/128th Pioneers 1915—23. Served France & Flanders 1916—18. Served in Turkey (Army of Black Sea) 1920—21—22, British South African Police 1923—24. A/Commissioner Northern Nigeria Police 1924—30, Captain West Yorkshire Regt (R.A.R.O.). *Rec*: Fly fishing, golf, travel. *a*: 112. Mayfield Rd, Sanderstead, Surrey. *t*: 1233.

MELLOR, William, B.A. *b*: Crewe 1888. *e*: Elem Scs & Willaston Sc Nantwich, & Oxf Univ. *m*: Edna Thomson. *s*: 1. Journalist. *n.a*: Entered journalism in 1903 as Sub-Ed Daily Herald, & after War became Industrial Corr, News Ed & in '26 Ed. Ed Daily Herald '26—30. Asst Mang Ed '30— Odhams Press Ltd. *Publ*: Direct Action ('20); Meaning of Industrial Freedom (with G. D. H. Cole). *s.s*: Econ & politics, with special ref to the working-class movement. Mem Nat Counc of Socialist League. Vice-Pres Univ Labour Fed. Parl Labour Candidate for Enfield. *a*: 63 Prince of Wales Mansions, Battersea Pk, S.W.11. *t*: Macaulay 4648.

MELLOWS, William Thomas, M.B.E., LL.B., F.S.A. F.R.Hist.S. *b*: Peterborough 1882. *e*: Bishop's Stortford Coll & Lond Univ. *m*: Beatrice Edith Pitt. *s*: 2. Solicitor, former Town Clerk of Peterboro', Archivist of Peterboro' Cathedral. *Publ*: Chronicle of Hugh Candidus, a monk of Peterborough; Ed, Book of Fees of Henry of Pytchley; Peterborough Parochial Government before the Reformation; The Last Days of Peterborough Monastery; etc. *s.s*: Annual Reports of Peterboro' Natural Hist, Scientific & Archæological Soc. *s.s*: Hist of Peterboro' & Northamptonshire, Monastic & Church Hist, Development of Local Government Insts. *Rec*: Entomology, photography, fishing. *a*: The Vineyard, Minster Precincts, Peterborough, Northamptonshire. *T*: 2619.

MELLUISH, T. W., M.A. *c.t*: Greece & Rome. *a*: 32 Poplar Walk, S.E.24.

MELVILLE, C. F. *b*: Lon 1896. *e*: St Ignatius Col Lon. *m* Gabriella Talvy. *s*: 1. Journalist. *n.a*: Diplomatic Corr Westminster Gazette 1925—28, Sunday Referee '25—32, Starmer Group '28—29, Mang Ed World Press Features Ltd (Ag), & Diplomatic Corr Sheffield Daily Telegraph. *Publ*: The Russian Face of Germany; The Truth About the New Party. *c.t*: Fortnightly Review, etc. *s.s*: Internat relations, foreign affairs, etc. with special reference to Central Europe & Balkans. *Rec*: Travel, music. *c*: Nat Lib. *a*: Elmside, Bridge Rd, Chertsey, Surrey. *t*: Chertsey 2228.

MELVILLE, Fred J., M.J.I. *b*: Edin 1882. Journalist & Author. *n.a*: Harmsworth Bros Ltd (A.P.) 1897—1909, Daily Telegraph, Philatelic Ed '10—30, Ex-Ed Cosy Corner, Good Words, etc., Ed The Postage Stamp '09—29, Ed Stamp Lover '08—. Stamp Collector's Fortnightly '22—, Ed The British Philatelist. *Publ*: The A.B.C. of Stamp Collecting; The Complete Philatelist; Phantom Philately; The Tapling Collection at the British Museum; Postage Stamps of Great Britain; Postage Stamps of the United States; Rare Stamps; How to Recognise Them; etc. *s.s*: Philately & postal hist of all countries. Founder & Pres the Jnr Philatelic Soc 1899. Pres & Chief Org Lon Internat Stamp Exhib's of 1912 & '23. Org Dir Lon Internat Air Post Exhib '34. Rep G.B. as Judge at many Internat Exhib's in Europe & America. Has Lectured & Broadcast on Stamps. *c*: N/p Press Fund. *a*: 10a Ardbeg Rd Herne Hill, S.E.24. *t*: Brixton 2179.

MELVILLE, LEWIS (pen name): see Benjamin, Lewis Saul.

MELZER, Shimshon. *b*: Tluste, Poland 1909. *e*: Hgh Sch of Teaching Lwow. *m*: Miriam Shechter. *s*: 3. Writer & Redacteur. *n.a*: Davar (Palestine Labour Daily) 1935—47, Am Oved Publishing House '45—47. *Publ*: Seven Strings; Ten Gates; Tales From Childhood. *Ctr*: Various Periodicals in Palestine. *s.s*: Ballads about Jewish Mysticism (Hassids). *a*: Tel-Aviv, Kiriat Meir 10, Palestine.

MEMBER FOR TREORKY (pen name): see Bowen-Rowlands, Ernest Bowen Brown.

MEMBRE, Henri Constant Victor, Leg d'Honneur, Croix de guerre. *b*: Valenciennes 1890. *e*: Facultes des Lettres et de Droit des Universites de Lille et de Paris. *m*: Germaine Prailly. *s*: 1. *d*: 1. Writer, Sec Gen (Hon) du Centre francais P.E.N., Sec Gen (Hon) de la Maison Internationale des P.E.N. Clubs, A etabli les plans & execute les premiers films d'une Historie de l'Art par le cinema. *Publ*: Petit-Bourgeois ; Non-lieu ; Un occidental en U.R.S.S.; Le Poete et le Peuple; etc. *Ctr*: Lettres francaises, Une Semaine dans le Monde, etc. *s.s*: Litteratures etrangeres (articles de critique—Et Direction d'une collection de traductions). *a*: 66 rue Pierre Charron, Paris VIII & La Croix Blanche, St Leger en Yvelines (S. & O.). *T*: Elysees 59-03.

MEMORY, Frederic William. *b*: Willesden 1883. *e*: Kilgrimol, Lancs. *m*: Isobel Louise Wilson. *s*: 1. Newspaper man. *n.a*: Chief Reporter Daily Mail. *Publ*: Memory's (The Adventures of a Newspaper-man). *c.t*: Princ n/ps & periodicals. *s.s*: Near East, crime. War Service. *Rec*: Shooting, fishing, golf. *c*: Press. *a*: Greengate, Moss Lane, Pinner, Middx. *t*: 150.

MENAI, Huw. See **Williams, Hugh Menai.**

MENARDOS, TIMOS: univ. professor; b. Mytitene, Sesbos; s. George Menardos and Augusta (Frangendis) M. DEGREES: Ph.D., LL.D. (Athens), Hon. M.A. (Oxford); m. Helen Pascal Constantinides. AUTHOR: The Place Names of Cyprus, 1905; The Value of Byzantine and Modern Greek in Hellenic Studies (an Inaugural Lecture before the University of Oxford), 1908; Three Lectures (Athens), 1921; Stephanos, 1924; The Monastery of Machaira in Cyprus (2nd edit.), 1929. Editor: Stephanos, an Anthology of ancient Greek poems, transl. into modern Greek. Contributor to: Athena, Philological Mags.; Journal of Hellenic Studios (London); Annual of the National University (Greece); Nea Hestia (Athens); The Poetry Review (London), 1928. General character of writing: essays, scientific, poems, historical. Lecturer in the University of Oxford, 1908-14; Professor of Greek in the National University at Athens (since 1911); Rector of the National University at Athens, 1924-25; General Secretary to the Greek Academy (since its foundation, 1926); poet and author, professor and conferencier. CLUBS: Literary Society "Parnassus". OFFICE: Academy (Athens). HOME: Thiras 19, Athens, Greece.

MENCKEN, H. L. *b*: Baltimore 1880. *e*: Baltimore Polytechnic. *m*: Sara Powell Haardt (dec'd). Author & Editor. *n.a*: Baltimore Herald 1899—1906, Baltimore Sun '06—41, Ed The Smart Set '14—23, Ed American Mercury '24—33. *Publ*: The American Language ; Treatise on the Gods ; Prejudices (six vols) ; Notes on Democracy ; Happy Days ; Newspaper Days ; Heathen Days. *a*: c/o Jonathan Cape Ltd, 30 Bedford Sq, W,C.

MENDELSSOHN, Felix. *c.t*: Various. *s.s*: Music, producing plays, etc. *a*: 14 Hoop Lne, Golder's Green, N.W.

MENDL, Gladys. See **Leslie, Henrietta.**

MENDL, Robert William Sigismund, M.A. (Oxon). *b*: Lon 1892. *e*: Harrow & Univ Col Oxf. *m*: Dorothy Williams Burnett. *s*: 1. Shell-Mex & B.P. Ltd. *Publ*: From a Music-Lover's Armchair; The Appeal of Jazz. *c.t*: Quarterly Review, Eng Review, Musical Opinion, Musical Times, Daily Telegraph, Music Teacher, Radio Times, etc. *s.s*: Musical criticism. War Service. Barrister-at-Law Inner Temple. *Rec*: Reading, swimming. *a*: 34 Ordnance Rd, St John's Wood, N.W.8. *t*: Primrose 3260.

MENEFEE, Selden C., M.A. *b*: The Dalles, Oregon U.S.A. 1909. *e*: Univ of Washington. *m*: Audrey Granneberg. *s*: 1. *d*: 3. Writer. *n.a*: Columnist Wash Post 1942—46, Spec Corr Christian Science Monitor '42—46, War Corr '43—46. *Publ*: Assignment : U.S.A.; The Pecan Shellers of San Antonio (collab); Mexican Migratory Workers of South Texas ; Vocational Training & Employment of Youth ; Industrial Conflict : A Psychological Interpretation / etc. *Ctr*: N.Y. Times, Liberty, Look, The Nation, New Republic, Amer Sociol Rev, Amer Journ of Sociol. *s.s*: Far Eastern Affairs, Propaganda, U.S. Public Opinion. *Rec*: Travel, tennis. *c*: Nat Press (Washington). *a*: 2720 Daniel Rd, Chevy Chase, Maryland, U.S.A. *T*: Wisconsin 7976.

MENG, John J., M.A., Ph.D. *b*: Cleveland, Ohio 1906. *e*: Catholic Univ of America, Ecole Libre des Sciences Politiques Paris. *m*: Marjorie Brunini. *s*: 3. *d*: 2. Chm Dept of Political Science Queens Coll. *n.a*: Adv Ed Catholic Hist Review 1938—43, Reviewing Staff America '47, Book Survey '47. *Publ*: Despatches & Instructions of Conrad Alexandre Gerard ; Libraries & Archives of Paris ; The Comte de Vergennes : European Phase of His American Diplomacy 1774—1780. *Ctr*: American Hist Review, Sign, America, Unity, Review of Politics, Catholic Hist Review, etc. *s.s*: Diplomatic Hist of the U.S., American Catholic Church Hist, Political Theory. *a*: The Loch, Roslyn, N.Y., U.S.A.

MENNE, Bernhard H. *b*: Fredeburg, Germany 1901. *m*: Elfriede Kupke. Writer. *n.a*: Ed Arbeiter Zeitung 1925—28, Ed Prager Mittag '37—38. *Publ*: Krupp, The Lords of Essen ; German Industry on the Warpath ; the Case of Dr Bruening ; Armistice & German Food Supply. *s.s*: Contemporary Hist, German Econ Hist, Armaments Hist. *a*: 111 Grove Hall Ct, St John's Wood, London, N.W.8. *T*: Cunningham 3800.

MENNELL, J. B. *Publ*: Physical Treatment; Backache; Treatment of Fractures by Mobilisation & Massage. *a*: 17 Park Cres, Portland Pl, W.1.

MENNELL, Dr. Z., M.B., M.R.C.S., L.R.C.P. Snr Anæsthetist St Thomas's Hosp & Nat Hosp, Queen Sq. Ex-Pres Anæsth Sect R.S.M. Treas Anæsth Assoc. *c.t*: Trans Med Soc, Proc Roy Soc, Amer Journ of Surg, etc. *a*: 149 Harley St, W.1. *t*: Welbeck 4444.

MENNICKEN, PETER: professor; b. Aix-la-Chapelle, Germany, April, 1894; s. Theodor and Sophie (Kueppers) M. DEGREES: Ph.D. AUTHOR: Die Seele des Aachener Muensters, 1923; Antiford, 1924; Die Philosophie des Nicholas Malebranche, 1927. General character of writing: scientific. ADDRESS: Lousbergstrasse 2, Aix-la-Chapelle, Germany.

MENON, Mrs. A. Velayndha, B.A., L.T. *b*: Tripunithwra, Cochin State, India 1896. *e*: Presidency Coll Madras, Lady Willingdon Training Coll Madras. *m*: A. Velayndha Menon. *s*: 1. *d*: 1. Headmistress Girls Hgh Sch Ernaklnam. *Publ*: Sharangaviharam, etc in Malayalam; etc. *Ctr*: Various Malayalam periodicals. *s.s*: Education, Kerala Culture, Translation of Books from English into Malayalam & vice versa. *Rec*: Women's movements, social welfare of women. *a*: Vijayavilas, Convent Rd, Ernakulam, Cochin State, India.

MENON, Chillay Narayana, D.Litt., Ph.D. *b*: Cochin State 1901. *e*: Univ of Madras. *m*: Lakshmi Menon. *s*: 2. Prof of English Benares Hindu Univ. *n.a*: Ed Benares Hindu Univ Journ. *Publ*: Shakespeare Criticism : an Essay in Synthesis ; An Approach to Ramayana ; The Spiritual Foundations of Economics ; On Kalidasas Kumarasambhava. *Ctr*: Aryan Path, The Argus, Indian Journ of Psychology, Indian Journ of Polit Sci, Indian Journ of Educ, East & West, Indian Finance, Hindustan Review, etc. *s.s*: Educ Psychology, Lit Criticism & Linguistic Research. *Rec*: Painting. *a*: Benares Univ, India.

MENON, Kappana Krishna. b : Tellicherry 1896. e : Madras Univ. m : Narayani-Kuttimalu. s : 4. d : 1. Lawyer. Publ : Keralavarma-Pazzazzi Raja ; Cheraman-Perumal ; Kairali. Ctr : Mathrubhumi Weekly, Short Story Mag, All India Radio. s.s : Old·History of Malabar. Rec : Tennis, shooting. c : P E.N. a : Convent Rd, Calicut, India.

MENON, Nalapat Narayana. b : Punnayurkulam, Malabar, Sth India 1887. e : Sanskrit Studies. m : Kalipurayat Balamaniamma. Publ : Teardrops ; The Horizon ; The Thrills ; The Kingdom of Venus ; The Pouranic Heroine ; The World ; (Trans) Les Miserables ; The Light of Asia. Ctr : Mathrubhumi. s.s : Philosophy. a : Punnayurkluman, Malabar, Sth India.

MENON, T. K. Krishna, B.A. b : Mathanchery, Cochin, India 1869. e : Maharaja's Coll Ernakulam, Presidency Coll Madras. m : T. C. Kalyani Amma. s : 2. d : 1. Lawyer. n.a : Ed Bulletin of the Research Inst of the Cochin State, & several others. Publ : Dravidian Culture & its Diffusion ; The Vanchi Problem ; History of Malayalam Literature ; etc. Ctr : Various. s.s : Malayalam Literature, Archæology. Rec : Walking. a : Kamaralayam, Diwan's Rd, Ernakulam, Cochin State, India.

MENZIES, A. G. a : 97 Heythorpe St, Southfield, S.W.18.

MENZIES, Sir Frederick Norton Kay, K.B.E., M.D., L.L.D., F.R.S.M., F.R.C.P., F.R.S.E. b : Carnarvon 1875. e : Edin, Vienna, Berlin. m : Harriet May Lloyd. s : 2. d : 1. Chief M.O. L.C.C. Numerous Reports on Publ Health & Hosp Services to L.C.C. Reports on the Voluntary Hosp's of G.B. 1924 & '25, etc. s.s : Publ Health & Hosp Admin. Kt of Grace, Order St John of Jerusalem. Rec : Shooting. Fell Soc of M.O.H.'s. F.R.San.I. a : 29 Egerton Gdns, S.W.3. t : Ken 6188.

MENZIES, George Kenneth, C.B.E., M.A. b : London 1869. e : St Andrews Univ & Balliol Coll Oxford. m : Mary Strathearn Gordon Burnet. Late Sec Roy Soc Arts 1917—35. Publ : Provincial Sketches & Other Verses ; The Story of The Royal Society of Arts. Ctr : Punch, Dly Chronicle, Manch Guardian, Pall Mall Gazette, etc. c : Savage. a : Upland Cottage, Marley Heights, Haslemere. T : Haslemere 318.

MENZIES, James J. W., F.R.S.A. Life Governor Lon Hosp. b : Lon 1895. e : Univ Col Sc, Roy Acad Arts Lon. Publicist. n.a : Staff Daily Telegraph 1929-30. c.t : Architectural Journs. s.s : Theosophy, architecture, philosophy, psychology. Rec : Golf. a : 124 Adelaide Rd, Hampstead, N.W.3.

MENZIES, W. J. M., F.R.S.E. b : Walton/Thames 1889. e : H.S. of Stirling & Priv. m : Joyce Isobel Munro. d : 1. Insp of Salmon Fisheries of Scot. Publ : The Salmon—Its Life Story. c.t : Observer, Scotsman, Field, Times. s.s : Freshwater fish & fishing. Rec : Golf, gardening. c : Caledonian Utd Service. a : Fishery Bd for Scot, Edin.

MERBER, Sadie. b : Johannesburg, Sth Africa. e : Univ & Coll. Writer for Radio, etc. Publ : Die Seefee en ander Verhale ; Floetels en die Maan en ander Verhale ; Elsie en die Kat en ander Verhale ; Prinses Perel en ander Verhale ; Helde van die Weterskap ; etc. Ctr : Brandwag, Jongspan, Star, Rand Dly Mail, Sun Times, etc. s.s : Children's Stories & Plays, Dramatising for Radio, Native Stories. Rec : Theatre, music, motoring. a : 491 Marshall St, Belgravia, Johannesburg, Transvaal, Sth Africa. T : 24-3906.

MERCER, Major Cecil William. (See YATES, Dornford.) a : Cockade, Eaux Bonnes, France (B.P.)

MERCER, Frank Alfred, F.R.S.A. b : Tunbridge Wells 1889. e : King Charles T. Wells. Married. d : 1. Mem Counc of the Roy Soc of Arts, Mem Publisher's Circle, Rep Mem Lond Chamber of Commerce & the American Chamber of Commerce in London, Mang Dir The Studio Ltd Lond, Ed Royal London & other Studio books, First Pres The Studio Publ's Inc N.Y. n.a : Ed Art & Industry 1926 & since '39, Modern Publicity, Gardens & Gardening. Publ : The Industrial Design Consultant : Who he is, What he does. a : 8 Ashley Pk, Tunbridge Wells. Kent.

MERCER, Rev. Samuel Alfred Browne, B.A., Ph.D. b : Bristol, England 1880. e : Field Coll St John's Newfoundland, Harvard, Munich & Nashotah House. m : Genevieve Magee. d : 1. Priest of the Church of England, Prof of Semetic Langs & Egyptology Trin Coll Univ of Toronto. n.a : Ed Anglican Theol Review 1918—24, Egyptian Religion '33—36, Biblical & Oriental Series '19—21. Publ : The Tell el-Amarna Tablets ; Sumero-Babylonia Sign-List ; Horus, Royal God of Egypt ; Etudes sur les Origines de la Religion de l'Egypte ; Ethiopic Liturgy ; Ethiopic Text of the Book of Ecclesiastes ; Egyptian Grammar ; Assyrian Grammar ; Ethiopic Grammar ; etc. Ctr : Various encys, dicts & religious journs. s.s : Egyptology, Cuneiform & Ethiopic. Rec : Walking. a : Trinity College, Toronto, Ontario, Canada.

MERCER, Thomas Stanley. A.M.Inst.Mech.Engs., M.T.S.Ing.Auto. b : Liverpool 1883. e : Dean Close Cheltenham & Regent Street Poly Lond. m : Kate Hyam. d : 1. Journalist. n.a : Asst Ed Automobile Engineer 1919—. s.s : Auto Eng, Aircraft Eng. Rec : Book Collecting. w.s : Tech Officer Air Min World War I. a : 15 Speer Rd, Thames Ditton, Surrey. T : Emberbrook 2482.

MERCER, Thomas William. b : Nutfield 1884. e : Elem Sc, Glas Univ. Journalist. n.a : Ed Co-op Official 1920—, Co-op Review '26—27, People's Weekly '28-31, Publ Ed Co-op Un M/C '21—27, Lon Rep Co-op News '27—, Dramatic Critic Reynolds's Illus Weekly News '32—. Publ : The Adult School Movement (with E. F. Hobley, '10) ; Sixty Years of Co-operative Printing ; etc. c.t : Co-op News, Reynolds's Illus Weekly News, Millgate, etc. s.s : Co-operative movement. Jt Hon Sec Nat Co-op Men's Guild '22—, Mem Nat Cmt Co-op Party '22—. Has served on several cmts of Co-op Un. c : Co-op Secs Assoc, N.U.J. a : 23 Grendon Gdns, Wembley Pk, Middx.

MERCER, Walter, M.B., Ch.B., F.R.C.S., F.R.S. b : Stow 1890. e : George Watson's Coll, Edin Univ. m : Helen May Margaret Lunan. s : 1. Publ : Orthopædic Surgery. Ctr : Edin Med Journ, B.M.J., Brit Journ of Surg, Journ of Bone & Joint Surg, Journ of Massage, Lancet & many other medical publs. s.s : Surgery, Orthopædic & Chest. Rec : Golf, curling, tennis, photography, postal history. c : Golfers (London). a : 12 Rothesay Terr, Edinburgh. T : 20889.

MERCER-WILSON, Rev. Richard, B.A., M.A. b : Cork 1887. e : St Patrick's Cath Sc & T.C.D. m : Rhoda Hanna. s : 3. d : 1. Gen Sec Irish Ch Missn 1922. Prof of Ch Hist Wycliffe Col Toronto '28. Gen Sec Religious Tract Soc Lon. n.a : Ed Lutterworth Press '32. Publ : Before the Reformation ; Vital Themes ; Fourfold Aspect ; etc c.t : Record, etc. s.s : Devotional lit, biography. Carson Bibl Prize, Downes' Prize, Archbishop King's Prize, Gold Medal, Logics & Ethics. Vice-Pres Guilds of Light (Religious Film Soc). Mem Counc World's Evang Alliance. Rec : Tennis, swimming. c : Authors' a : 15 Spencer Rd, S. Croydon, Surrey. t : Fairfield 5846.

MERCIER, Louis Joseph Alexandre, A.B., A.M.(Chicago), D.Litt.(Loyola Univ. Chicago). b : Le Mans, France 1880. e : St Ignatius Col & Loyola Univ Chicago. m : Zoé Lassague. s : 2. d : 5. Associate prof of French & educ, Harvard Univ. n.a : Associate Ed, French

Review, '28—30. *Publ*: Junior French; French Pronunciation and Diction; Mes Premiéres Lectures; College French; Critical essays—Le Mouvement Humaniste aux Etats-Unis; The Challenge of Humanism. *c.t*: North American Review, American Review, Forum, Education, French Review, L'Education Nouvelle, La Revue Hebdomadaire, La Revue Bleue, La Revue Mondiale, La Nouvelle Revue etc. *s.s*: Teaching of French, French literature, dualistic humanism (American school), comparative philosophy, literature. Interpreter, B.E.F., '14—17. Instructor, Harvard O.T.C., '18. *c*: Pres New England Mod Lang Assoc '28, Pres American Assoc of Teachers of French '33—, Fell in Romance langs Chicago and Columbia Univs, Laureate of the Académie Française, Kt of the Legion of Honour. *a*: 134 Brattle St, Cambridge, Mass., U.S.A.

MEREDITH, Hubert Angelo. O.B.E. *b*: London 1884. *e*: St Paul's Sch. *n.a*: Financial Ed in Chief Assoc Newsps Ltd (Dly Mail, Continental Dly Mail, Ev News, Northcliffe Newsps 1931—35), also City Ed Daily Mirror '25—& Sun Pictorial '26—. *Publ*: The Drama of Money Making. *s.s*: Finance. *c*: Marlborough-Wyndham, R.A.C. *a*: The Old Star Hse, Star Hill, Dunton Green, Kent.

MEREDITH, James Creed. LittD., M.R.I.A., K.C. *b*: Dublin 1875. *e*: T.C.D. *m*: Lorraine Percy. *d*: 2. High Court Judge I.F.S. Vice-Pres Saar Supreme Plebiscite Tribunal 1st Sept '34—1st March 35. *Publ*: Kant's Critique of Aesthetic Judgment; Kant's Critique of Teleological Judgment; Proportional Representation in Ireland. *c.t*: New Ire Review. *s.s*: Philos. Ex Quarter Mile Champion of Eng & Ire, 100 yds, 220 yds & Quarter Mile Champion of Ire, Formerly Pres of the Supreme Ct of Irish Republican Cts '20—23. *Rec*: Garden. *c*: Univ Dublin & Roy Irish Yacht. *a*: Hopeton, Rathgar, Dublin. *t*: Terenure 301.

MEREDITH, William Campbell James, K.C. *b*: Montreal 1904. *e*: Wellington Coll England, Trin Coll Camb. *m*: Francoise Martin Harwood. *s*: 1. Barrister, Mem Canadian Bar Assoc. *Publ*: Civil Law on Automobile Accidents; Insanity as a Criminal Defence. *Ctr*: Canadian Bar Revue, Canadian Med Assoc Journ, Quebec Bar Revue. *s.s*: Legal. *Rec*: Tennis, fishing, amateur radio. *c*: Univ of Montreal, Montreal Indoor Tennis. *a*: 1461 Mountain St, Montreal, Canada. *T*: Lancaster 9171, & Plateau 3325.

MEREDITH, William Richmond. *b*: Lon 1872. *e*: Sec Scs. Proof reader. *n.a*: Times, Recorder, San Francisco, U.S.A., Buenos Aires Herald, Paris Daily Mail, Ency Brit & News of the World. *s.s*: Humour. Composer of an Operetta "The Magic Mirror" & Songs. *Rec*: French, Spanish. *a*: 10 Ipswich Rd, S.W.17.

MEREWETHER, Lt.-Col. John Walter Beresford, C.I.E. *b*: Karachi 1867. *e*: Marlboro' Col & R.M.C. Sandhurst. *m*: Lylie Evelyn Aitchison. Lt.-Col (ret). *Publ*: The Indian Corps in France (semi-official), in collab with late Earl of Birkenhead. *c.t*: Princ Eng & Indian papers. *s.s*: India. Mil & Polit Appts in India, Africa & Arabia. War Service, Somaliland 1901, Aden '03—04, Gt War '15—18. *Rec*: Riding, golf. *c*: Naval & Mil. *a*: 47 Abbey Lodge, Hanover Gate, Regents Pk, N.W.8. *t*: Ambassador 1817.

MERGET, Robert M. F. *b*: Brussels 1907. Married. *s*: 1. *d*: 1. Journalist. *n.a*: Dir La Revue Nationale (founder). *Publ*: La Gueule Cassee; L'Esprit de la Race; Le Sonneur; Le Manifeste des Jeunes Ecrivains nationaux; La Tragedie de 1839; Henry Carton De Wiart et Notre Histoire. *Ctr*: Le Soir, Midi, Journ Des Combattants, L'action Nationale, La Rev Nationale, Tribune, etc. *s.s*: Hist & Hist Criticism. *a*: 35 Avenue Van Goolen, Brussels, Belgium. *T*: 33.77.50.

MERIAM, Richard Stockton, A.B., Ph.D. *b*: Salem, Massachusetts 1893. *e*: Harvard Univ. *m*: Alice Godfrey O'Brien. *s*: 3. *d*: 1. Economist, Prof of Business Economics, Cons Standard Oil Co (N.J.) 1938—; *Publ*: (Ed in collab) Current Economic Policies; Chapters in : Economics, Sociology & the Modern World ; Exploration in Economics. *Ctr*: Quarterly Journ of Econs, Review of Econ Statistics, American Econ Review, Harvard Business Review. *s.s*: Public Relationships & Responsibilities, Administrative Policy. *c*: Univ (N.Y.). *a*: Baker Bridge Rd, South Lincoln, Massachusetts, U.S.A.

MERILLAT, Louis Adolph. *b*: Wooster, Ohio 1868. *e*: Univ of Toronto Sch of Veterinary Med, McKillip Vet Coll. *m*: Mary Smith. *s*: 1. Veterinarian. *n.a*: Ed in Chief Journ of the American Vet Med Assoc & the American Journ of Vet Research 1938, Ed Nth American Veterinarian '25—30, Veterinary Med '21—25. *Publ*: Veterinary Military History; Principles of Veterinary Surgery; Veterinary Surgical Operations; Animal Dentistry & Stomatology; Antiseptic Treatment of Wounds; Style Book of the American Veterinary Medical Association; etc. *Ctr*: Bulletin de l'Academie Veterinaire de France, American Legion Mag, Cornell Veterinarian, Vet Med, Vet Record, etc. *s.s*: Anatomy, Surg & Therapeutics of Domestic Animals, Application of Vet Sci in the Public Interest. *Rec*: Fishing, farming. *w.s*: Chief Vet First Army A.E.F. 1918—19. *a*: 453 East 87th Pl, Chicago 19, Illinois, U.S.A. *T*: Triangle 8006.

MERIVALE, Bernard. B.A., LL.B., O.B.E. *b*: Newcastle-on-Tyne 1882. *e*: Sedbergh Sc & St John's Col Cam. *m*: Cicely Leila Stuckey. *d*: 1. Dramatic Author. *Publ*: The Night Hawk; Fancy Dress; Marriage by Instalments; Mr Peter; A Unique Opportunity; The Wrecker; The Flying Fool; Tattenham Corner; None But the Brave; The Command to Love: The Unguarded Hour; etc. *Rec*: Modern lang. *c*: Savile & Savage. *a*: 21 Bedford Gdns, Kensington, W.8.

MERKEL, Andrew Doane. *b*: Morley, New York 1884. *e*: Priv & Univ of King's Coll Windsor N.S. *m*: Florence Elizabeth Sutherland. *s*: 1. *d*: 2. Journalist (ret). *n.a*: News Ed St John Standard 1908, Ed Halifax Dly Echo '10—17, Supt Canadian Press Halifax '18—46. *Publ*: The Order of Good Cheer; Tallahassee. *Ctr*: Various. *s.s*: History. *Rec*: Swimming. *a*: Lower Granville, Annapolis County, Nova Scotia, Canada. *T*: Annapolis 207-21.

MERLIN, S. P. J., B.L. *b*: Dolgelley 1873. *e*: Priv & City of London Sch. *m*: Lillie Rebecca Buckland. *s*: 2. Barrister, Chm Hampstead Rent Tribunal. *Publ*: Landlord & Tenant Act; Law of Interpleader; Landlord & Tenant (War Damage). *Ctr*: Various. *Rec*: Tennis, fly-fishing. *a*: Goldsmith Bldg, Temple, London, E.C.4. *T*: Central 8450.

MERRETT, Charles Henry. *b*: Leicester 1898. *e*: Burton-on-Trent G.S. & K. Edward VII Sc Sheffield. *m*: Clare Chapman. Officer, Customs & Excise. *Publ*: Hidden Lives. *c.t*: Nott'm Journ, Nott'm Guardian, Derby Evening Telegraph, Customs & Excise Journ. *s.s*: Plays. Nott'm Playgoers Club Prize Play Award 1931 & '33. War Service '16—18, p.o.w. '18—19. *Rec*: Gardening, producing plays. *c*: Chm Nott'm Writers'. *a*: 22 Eton Gve, Wollaton Pk, Nott'm.

MERRETT, Cyril Vincent, M.A.(Oxon), F.I.L. *b*: Torquay 1902. *e*: Cheltenham Gr Sch, Pembroke Coll Oxf, Lyon Univ. Schoolmaster: Classics & Mod Languages Queen Mary's Sch Walsall, Mem Classical Assoc. *Publ*: Verse Trans of Vergil's Aeneid Bk VI; Verse Trans of Vergil's Aeneid Bk IV. *s.s*: Latin, Greek, French & Spanish. *Rec*: Foreign travel, country walking. *a*: Brooklands, Arboretum Rd, Walsall, Staffs. *T*: Walsall 2679.

MERRIAM, Charles Edward, LL.D. *b*: Hopkinton, Iowa 1874. *e*: State Univ Iowa, Univs of Columbia & Berlin. *m*: Elizabeth Hilda Doyle. *s*: 3. *d*: 1. Prof Emeritus of Political Science, *Publ*: Systematic Politics; History American Political Theory; Chicago: a More Intimate View of Urban Politics; The New Democracy; The American Party System; The Role of Politics in Social Change; Public & Private Government; etc. *Ctr*: Reviews in Social Science. *s.s*: Political Theory & Parties, Urbanism. *Rec*: Bowling. *a*: 6041 University Ave, Chicago, Illinois, U.S.A. *T*: Hyde Park 4643.

MERRICK, Elliott T., A.B. *b*: Montclair, N.J., U.S.A. 1905. *e*: Yale Univ. *m*: Kate I. Austen. *s*: 2. *d*: 1. *n.a*: Rep Passaic Dly News 1928—29, Ed U.S. Forest Service '46—. *Publ*: True North; From This Hill Look Down; Frost & Fire; Ever the Winds Blow; Northern Nurse; Passing By. *Ctr*: Scribners Mag, Readers Digest, Amer Mercury, New Yorker, London Dly Mail, etc. *a*: Craftsbury Common, Vermont, U.S.A.

MERRICK, Leonard. *b*: 1864. *e*: Brighton Col & private scs. Author. Widower. *d*: 1. *Publ*: A Chair on the Boulevard; Conrad in Quest of his Youth; While Paris Laughed; The House of Lynch; The Quaint Companions; When Love flies out of the Window; The Man Who was Good; Cynthia; The Actor-Manager; One Man's View; To Tell You the Truth; The Man Who Understood Women; The Little Dog Laughed; The Worldlings; The position of Peggy Harper: A Collection of his work with introductions by famous writers issued '18. Plays with late Michael Morton, G. R. Sims & F. C. Philips, etc. *a*: Savage Club, Adelphi, W.C.

MERRINGTON, Ernest Northcroft, M.A., Ph.D., F.R.G.S. *b*: Newcastle, N.S.W., Aust 1876. *e*: Sydney Hgh Sch, St Andrew's Coll Sydney, Univs of Sydney, Edin & Harvard. *m*: Flora Livingston. *s*: 1. *d*: 2. Presbyterian Minister & Master of Knox Coll Dunedin till Retirement 1941. *Publ*: The Problems of Personality in the light of Recent Thought; The Possibility of a Science of Casuistry; etc. *Ctr*: Otago Dly Times, Journ of Psychology & Philosophy, Christian World Pulpit, The Digger, Ev Star (Dunedin), Ev Post (Wellington), etc. *s.s*: Internat Affairs, N.Z. Early Hist, Philosophy, Exploration in the Pacific in 17th & 18th Centuries. *Rec*: Bowls, chess. *a*: 4 Papawai Terr, Wellington, S.I., New Zealand. *T*: 56-631.

MERRITT, Abraham. *b*: Beverley, N.J. 1884. *e*: Philadelphia H.S., Univ of Pennsylvania. *m*: Eleanor Humphrey. *d*: 1. Editor & Author. *n.a*: City Ed Philadelphia Inquirer '08, Asst Ed American Weekly '10—. *Publ*: Burn Witch Burn; Creep Shadow; Dwellers in the Mirage; The Ship of Ishtar; The Moon Pool; The Face in the Abyss. *c.t*: Cosmopolitan Argosy, Weird Tales, Colliers, Red Book. *s.s*: Witchcraft & sorcery, comparative religions, archæology, botany, general science. *Rec*: Bee keeping, floriculture, music. *c*: The Players, New York, New York Academy of Sciences, The Author's League. *a*: Clover Hill Rd, Hollis, Long Island, New York, U.S.A.

MERRITT-HAWKES, Onèra Amelia, B.Sc(Lon), M.Sc(B'ham). *b*: N.Y. 1887. *e*: Malvern Hse Reading & B'ham & Lon Univs. *m*: R. J. J. Hawkes (divorced him). *s*: 2. *d*: 1. Journalist & Writer. Mem N.U.J. 1930. *Publ*: The Cottage by the Common ('24). *c.t*: Spectator, Strand, Tatler, English Review, B'ham Post, American Journ of Heredity, Scottish Country Life, M/C Guardian, Eugenics Review, etc. *s.s*: Heredity, genre studies, travel in France, Bulgaria, Russia, Persia, U.S.A. Has trav all Europe except Finland & Roumania. Has done much lecturing on Heredity & Russia. *Rec*: Gardening, fencing. *c*: English Speaking Union. *a*: 1 Metchley Lane, Harborne, B'ham. *t*: 1724.

MERRY. Ralph Vickers, B.A., M.A.(McGill), Ed.M., Ed.D.(Harvard). *b*: Magog, Quebec 1903. *e*: McGill & Harvard Univs. *m*: Frieda Annetta Kiefer. Prof & head of dept of secondary education, Morris Harvey Col. *Publ*: Problems in the Education of Visually Handicapped Children. *c.t*: Jnl of Abnormal & Social Psychology, Jnl of Applied Psychology, Jnl of Genetic Psychology, Valta Review, Teachers Forum for Instructors of the Blind, Social Work Year Book of the Russell Sage Foundation, Der Blindenfreund. *s.s*: Psychology & education of visually handicapped children. *Rec*: Reading, radio. *c*: American Psychological Assoc. *a*: Morris Harvey College, Barboursville, W. Virginia, U.S.A.

MERRY, Wilfred Osburn. *b*: Wardington, Oxon. *e*: Brighton. *m*: Elizabeth Ethel Taylor. *d*: 1. *n.a*: Chief Sub-Ed Hereford Journ & Hereford Mercury 1918 —21, Sub-Ed Ev Dispatch (B'ham) '21—27, Features Ed & Ldr Writer The Star (Sheffield) '27—47, Dep-Ed The Weekly Telegraph (Sheffield). *a*: 11 Bristol Rd, Sheffield 11, Yorkshire. *T*: Sheffield 60567.

MERRY ANDREW. See **Freeman, John Henry Gordon.**

MERSEY, 2nd Viscount, Charles Clive Brigham. *Publ*: inc Alexander of Macedon; A Picture of Life 1872— 1940; A Year in China; The Kings of England; The Chief Ministers of England; etc. *a*: 22 Eaton Pl, London, S.W.1.

MERSON, Alick James, M.A., F.E.I.S. *b*: Buckie 1885. *e*: Aber Univ. *m*: Jessie May Jack, M.A. *s*: 1. *d*: 1. Headmaster. *Publ*: (Ed) A Book of Classical Stories; Sea Stories of Adventure; A Book of Notable Escapes; etc; (au) Reading & Compositions; Junior Test Papers in English; Senior Test Papers in English; etc. *c.t*: Scot Educ Journ. *Rec*: Golf, bridge. *a*: Lentran, Maybole, Ayrs.

MERTINS, Louis, Hon.LL.D. *b*: Jackson County, Mo 1885. *e*: William Jewell Coll Liberty Mo. *m*: (1) Lena Lee Holman, (2) Esther Erickson. *s*: 1. *d*: 3. Poet. *n.a*: Ed Writer Long Beach California Sun 1926—30. *Publ*: The Intervals of Robert Frost (collab); The Wishing Gate; The Sumac Trail; The Covered Wagon; The Baratarians; The Mail Cart Man; The Voices Crying in the Wilderness; This Way Out; Chaucer: His Further Pilgrim. *Ctr*: Colliers, Kansas City Star, Farm & Fireside, Youth's World, Boy's Life, etc. *s.s*: Robert Frost. *Rec*: Gardening. *a*: Far Hills, 554 Terracina Boulevard, Redlands, California, U.S.A. *T*: Redlands 5495.

MESS, Henry Adolphus, B.A., PhD. *b*: Lon 1884. *e*: Bancroft's Sc & Univ of Lon. *m*: Sofie Cathrine Hansen. *s*: 2. *d*: 1. Social Worker. *Publ*: Casual Labour at the Docks; The Facts of Poverty; Factory Legislation & Its Administration; Industrial Tyneside; etc. *c.t*: Times, Lancet, Nation, etc. *s.s*: Social sciences. Carried out a social survey of thirteen Tyneside towns 1925-28. *a*: 53 Grosvenor Pl, Newcastle-on-Tyne.

MESSEL, Oliver. *b*: London 1904. *e*: Eton, Slade Sch of Art. Artist, Scenic Designer & Decor. *Publ*: Stage Designs & Costumes, Romeo & Juliet. *a*: 17 Pelham Pl, London, S.W.1, *T*: Kensington 0728.

MESSER, Mona. *b*: Thornton Heath Surrey. *e*: Sidcot Sc, Roy Holloway Col. *m*: H. R. Messer. *s*: 1. *d*: 2. Novelist. *s.s*: Hist. *Rec*: Motoring, gardening. *a*: Gibraltar, Tunbridge Wells. *t*: 2089.

MESTON, 2nd Baron of Agra & Dunottar, Dougall Meston. *b*: Budaun United Provinces, India 1894. *e*: Charterhouse, Roy Mil Acad Woolwich. *m*: Diana Mary Came Doll. Barrister. *Publ*: Law of Money Lenders ; Law of Nuisances ; Town & Country Planning ; Powers of the Police ; Law Affecting Builders ; several works on War Damage, Local Government, Highways, Public Health, Housing Acts. *s.s*: Town & Country Planning, War Damage, Housing. *c*: Reform. *a*: Hurst Pl, Cookham Dean, Berkshire. *T*: Bourne End (Bucks) 162.

METCALF, Henry Ernest, M.I.Mech.E., M.I.N.A. *b*: Bradford 1868. *e*: Priv & Finsbury Tech Coll. *m*: Edith Mary Crosland. *s*: 3. Mechanical Engineer & Naval Architect (ret). *Publ*: On Britain's Business ; Russia's Great Opportunity ; India's Glorious Future ; Our Indebtedness to China. *Ctr*: Manch Guardian. *s.s*: Japan, China, India, Russia, Poland, Germany, etc. *c*: Junior Carlton. *a*: 16 Victoria Mansions, Eastbourne Sussex. *T*: 2730.

METCALF, Rev. T. *n.a*: Ed Old Chariot 1929–. *Publ*: Hypnotism; Mental Healing. *c.t*: Methodist Times, Leader, etc. *a*: Joseph Terr, Chopwell, Co Durham.

METCALF, William Day. *c.t*: M/C Guardian, Yorkshire Post, Yorkshire Evening Post, etc. *a*: The Old Vicarage, Church Fenton, Leeds.

METCALFE, Maj. T. Washington. *b*: London 1884. *e*: Cranleigh Sch, R.M.C. Sandhurst & Freiburg Breisgau Univ. Author. *Publ*: The Prince ; One Night in Santa Anna ; Aloysius O'Callaghan ; Fare You Well my Shining City ; A Sea Lover's Memories ; Port of Heaven ; Captain Viaud & Madame Laconture ; Memorials of the Military Life ; Quis Separabit ; Leviathan's Day ; A Country Bloke's Chronicle ; etc. *Ctr*: Military Articles, Untd Services Rev, etc. *s.s*: Music & Boxing. *Rec*: Sailing, motoring, billiards. *c*: Som County, Authors. *w.s*: R.A.F. Mons Star World War I, Lt Col Home Guard World War II. *a*: c/o Christy & Moore Ltd, 22 Strand, London W.C.2, & Fathoms, Hordle Cliff, Milford on Sea, Hants. *T*: Milford on Sea 421.

METHUEN, Baron P. A. Painter. *Publ*: Scientific papers in proc Zool Soc & other journs. *a*: 12 Medway St, S.W.1.

METSANURK, MAIT (pen name); (own name: Eduard Hubel): author; b. Tartu, Estonia, Nov. 19, 1879; s. Jaan and Loviisa (Veltmann) Hubel; educ. Elementary Sch., Junior High Sch. *m*. Vanda Reichenbach, Feb. 2, 1895. AUTHOR: Isamaa Oilmed (Homeland Blossoms; novel), 1908; Vahesaare Villem (novel), 1910; Jumala Lapsed (God's Children; tales), 1911; Orjad (Slaves), (novel), 1913; Toho-oja Anton (tales), 1918; Ecce Nomo! (novel), 1919; Vagade elu (The Life of Saints; drama), 1920; Jumulata (Without God; tale), 1921; Jaavet Soovere elu ja surm (Life and Death of Jaavet Soovere; novel), 1922; Kindrali poeg (General's Son; drama), 1925; Valge pilv (The White Cloud; novel), 1926; Punane tuul (Red Wind; novel), 1928; Talupoja poeg (Peasant's Son; drama), 1929; Arraste ja Pojad (novel), 1930; Elu murral Sisse (Life Penetrates; tales), 1931; Mässuvaim (The Spirit of Revolt; drama), 1931. Editor: Tallinna Teataja (daily newspaper), 1911-1925. Contributes to Looming Mag., Eesti Kirjandus; newspapers: Paevaleht, Postimees, Vabamaa. General character of writing: critical essays, novels, plays. Engaged as journalist from 1905 to 1917. Emphasizes the realist reaction to present-day conditions since the World War, and the fact that Estonia, during the last decade, has shown very little of Anglo-Saxon influence, being impressed mainly by German and French literature and mode of thought. CLUBS: Pen, Fry Masons, Eesti Kirjanikkude Lüt (League of National Authors). Is president of last named. Relig. denom., Lutheran. OFFICE: Päevaleht. HOME: Vaestekooli tan, 6-a, Tallinna, Estonia.

MEULENBELT-LUBER, HENRIETTA C. A.: see Luber, Jet.

MEURIG-DAVIES, Rev. T. E., M.A. *c.t*: Welsh periodicals, etc. Vicar & Rural Dean of Winchcombe. *a*: The Vicarage, Winchcombe, Glos.

MEYENDORFF, Baron Alexander, Hon.L.C.L.(Durham Univ). *b*: Baden-Baden 1869. *e*: Weimar Gymnasium & Stuttgart, St Petersburg Univ. Reader Lond Univ (ret), Mem Russian Duma 1907—17. *Publ*: Background of the Russian Revolution ; Correspondence Diplomatique du Baron de Staal, Paris, Marcel Riviere. *Ctr*: The Slavonic & East European Rev. *s.s*: Land Problem in Russia, Psychology of Law. *a*: c/o Midland Bank Ltd, 237 Tottenham Court Rd, London, W.1. *T*: Paignton 54-97.

MEYER, Ernst Hermann, D.Ph., Mus.D. *b*: Berlin-Schoeneberg 1905. *e*: Classical Sch, Univs of Heidelberg & Berlin, State Acad of Music. Musicologist & Composer, Lecturer on Music. *Publ*: English Chamber Music ; Die Mehrstimmige Spielmusik in Mittel—und Nordeuropa ; Eine unbekannte Bluteperiode der niederlandischen Instrumentalmusik. *Ctr*: Music & Letters, Music Rev, Musical Times, Keynote, Listener, Radio Times, The Times. *s.s*: 16th & 17th Century Instrumental Music, Music in Relation to General Social & Political Hist, Music in Films. *Rec*: Playing chamber music. *a*: Flat 2, 41 England's Lane, London, N.W.3.

MEYER, T. *b*: 1913. *m*: B. Ejrias Tullund. *d*: 1. Author. *Publ*: Guds Palet ; Ester Regn ; etc. *Ctr*: Various. *a*: Englandreig, 368 Taarnby, Kastrup, Denmark.

MEYER, William Charles Bernard, B.A., M.B., ChB., F.R.C.S. *c.t*: Lancet, Brit Journ of Surgery. *a*: 137 Harley St, W.1. *t*: Welbeck 3956.

MEYERSTEIN, Edward Harry William, M.A., F.R.S.L. *b*: Hampstead 1889. *e*: Harrow, Magdalen Coll Oxf. *Publ*: (Verse) Wade's Boat ; Voyage of Ass ; Eclogues ; Division ; (Prose) The Trireme ; Terence Duke ; Joshua Slade ; A Life of Thomas Chatterton ; Coxere ; Adventures by Sea (Ed). *Ctr*: Times Lit Supp, English, Music Review. *Rec*: Music. *a*: 3 Gray's Inn Pl, London, W.C.1.

MEYNELL, Esther Hallam. *b*: Yorks. *e*: Private. *m*: Gerard Meynell. *d*: 2. *Publ*: Sussex (County Books), (Novels) Grave Fairytale ; Quintet ; Times Door ; Lucy & Amades ; English Spinster ; (Biographies) Sussex Cottage ; Building a Cottage ; A Woman Talking ; Country Ways ; Cottage Tale ; Little Chronicle of Magdalena Bach ; Bach ; The Young Lincoln. *Ctr*: Observer, Everybody's Wkly. *s.s*: Country Life, Architecture. *Rec*: Living in the country. *a*: Conds Cott, Ditchling, Sussex.

MEYNELL, Francis. *b*: Lon 1891. *e*: Downside & T.C.D. Publisher. *n.a*: Assoc Ed Daily Herald 1918. *Publ*: Typography of Newspaper Advertisements ; Eyes of Youth (Jt) ; Manifesto (Jt) ; etc. *Rec*: Cricket, tennis, bridge. *a*: 37 Gordon Sq, W.C. *t*: Mus 0695.

MEYNELL, Laurence Walter. (See **ETON, Robert.**) *b*: Wolverhampton 1899. *e*: Old Hall Green. *m*: Shirley Darbyshire. *d*: 1. Author, Broadcaster, Lecturer. *Publ*: Bluefeather, The Evil Hour ; Strange Landing ; The Dandy ; The House in the Hills ; The Bright Face of Danger ; etc. *s.s*: Dr Johnson. *Rec*:

Walking, canoeing, tree-felling, tennis. *w.s*: 1914—18 H.A.C., '39—45 R.A.F. (despatches). *a*: Lime Tree Cottage, Great Kingshill, High Wycombe. *T*: Holmer Green 3152.

MEYNELL, Viola. Author. *Publ*: A Girl Adoring; Follow the Fair Sun; First Love. *a*: 47 Palace Court, London, W.2. *T*: Bayswater 2847.

MEYNELL, Wilfrid, C.B.E. (See **OLDCASTLE, John.**) *a*: 47 Palace Court, London, W.2.

MEYRICK, Rev. Frederick James. *b*: Blickling 1871. *e*: Felsted & New Col Oxf. *m*: Helen Richmond. *d*: 4. Canon of Chichester. *Publ*: Fifteenth Century Glass; Round About Norfolk & Suffolk; Hove & the Parish Church. *c.t*: Eastern Daily Press, Star, Guardian, Church Newspaper, etc. *s.s*: Archæology, fishing. *Rec*: Gardening. *c*: Ch Imp. *a*: Vicarage, Hove. *t*: 4683.

MIALL, Agnes M. *b*: Lon. F.L. Journalist. *n.a*: Ed Woman's Life 1929-30. *Publ*: Loose Covers & Simple Upholstery ('31); Home Dressmaking; Complete Needlecraft ('33). *c.t*: Daily Express, Home Notes, Modern Home, Woman's Life, Woman's Mag, Lady s Companion, Wife & Home, etc. *s.s*: Needlework, fortune telling, psychology. *Rec*: Swimming, palmistry, patchwork. *c*: Central. *a*: Flat 26, 26 Charing X Rd, W.C.2. *t*: Temple Bar 8575.

MIALL, Bernard. *b*: Lon 1876. *m*: Margaret Salter. Publisher's Reader, Translator, Editor. *Publ*: Nocturnes & Pastorals, Pierre Garat; also some 60 trans of Aulard, Barrès, Anatole France, Maeterlinck, Bismarck, Wassermann, Hans Andersen, Saudet, Portigliotti, etc. *s.s*: Trans of verse, psychology, biology, medicine, fiction. *a*: Lower Longclose, Combe Martin, Devon.

MIALL, Stephen, LL.D., B.Sc. *e*: Yorkshire Coll Leeds, Ed Chemistry & Industry 1923—45. *Publ*: History of British Chemical Industry; Poets at Play. *s.s*: Chemistry. *a*: 28 Clifton Hill, London, N.W.8. *T*: Maida Vale 1345.

MIAN, Bashir Ahmad, B.A. *b*: Lahore, India 1893. *e*: Oxf Univ. *m*: Geti Ara Begum. *s*: 1. *d*: 2. Barrister, Mem Legislative Assembly Punjab. *n.a*: Prop & Ed Humayun Lahore. *Publ*: Talism-i-Zindegi; Musalmanon Ka Mazi Hal Aur Mustaqbil. *s.s*: Hist (Islamic), Lang Question in India & Pakistan. *Rec*: Walking. *a*: 32 Lawrence Rd, Lahore, Pakistan.

MICHAEL, Constantinidis. Dean of the Greek Cathedral. *Publ*: Life & Work in the Diocese of Athens (1928); The Orthodox Church London; The Priest—Alexandria; The Imitation of Christ; A Brief Sketch of the Anglican Church; etc. *c.t*: Exkleissia (Athens), Pantaenos (Alexandria). *a*: St Sophia's Presbytery, Moscow Rd, Bayswater, W.2. *t*: 4643.

MICHAEL, Edward. *b*: Tynemouth 1853. *e*: King's Col Lon. *n.a*: Mang Ed The Morning '92 (1st halfpenny Lon daily), Drama Critic Weekly Dispatch. *Publ*: The Tramps of a Scamp. *c.t*: Various n/ps & periodicals. Establ'd the 1st Lon halfpenny daily n/p. *c*: Savage. *a*: Savage Club, Adelphi, W.C.2.

MICHAEL, Emlyn. *b*: Clydach Vale 1898. *m*: Lillian Evans. *s*: 1. *d*: 2. F/L Journalist. *n.a*: Western Mail & Evening Express 1924. *c.t*: All n/ps & periodicals. *s.s*: Rugby football, boxing & music. One of Founders Welsh Board of Boxing Control '27-28. Promoted musical & educ movements in the Rhondda. Prominent Charity Organiser in S. Wales. Frequently broadcasts eye-witness accounts of boxing events on W. Regional. *Rec*: Golf, bowls. *a*: Tonypandy, Glam. *t*: 70.

MICHAELES, Karin. *b*: Randers, Denmark 1872. Authoress. *Publ*: Dangerous Age; Andrea; Ulla Faugel; Don Juan after Death; Mette Trap; Seven Sisters; The Sunhild Books, a Series of five Tours; The Bibi Books, series of five (translated in 21 languages). *c.t*: Berliner Tageblatt, Neue Freie Presse, Pester Lloyd, Politiken, Dagens Nyheter etc. Has travelled extensively. *a*: Thurö, Denmark.

MICHELL, Humfrey, F.R.S.C. *b*: London 1883. *e*: Dulwich, Queens Coll Oxf, Univ of Heidelberg. *m*: Dorothea Edwards. *s*: 1. *d*: 1. Univ Prof. *Publ*: Elementary Economics; Outlines of Economic History; Economics of Ancient Greece. *Ctr*: Various. *s.s*: Political Economy, Econ Hist. *Rec*: Gardening. *a*: McMaster University, Hamilton, Ontario, Canada.

MICHIE, Allan Andrew, A.B. *b*: Aberdeen, Scotland 1915. *e*: Ripon Coll Wisconsin, Univ of Chicago Law Sch. *m*: Barbara Mary Townsend. *d*: 1. Journalist. *n.a*: Foreign News Ed Time Mag 1937—39, Lond Corres Fortune Mag '39—40, Lond News Ed Life & Fortune '40—41, Roving Corres Reader's Digest '42—. *Publ*: Retreat to Victory; The Air Offensive Against Germany; Their Finest Hour; Keep the Peace Through Air Power; Dixie Demagogues; Lights of Freedom; Every Man to His Post; Honour For All. *Ctr*: Atlantic Monthly, Harper's, New Republic, Nation, Courier, Toronto Star Weekly, Maclean's Mag, Skyways, Coronet, etc. *s.s*: European Affairs. *Rec*: Golf, book-collecting. *w.s*: War Corres 1941—45. *a*: 5 Brompton Sq, London, S.W.3. *T*: Kensington 0639.

MICKLE, Alan Durward. *b*: Melbourne 1882. *e*: Queen's Coll St Kilda, Melbourne Church of England Gr. *m*: Ida Jeanette Cameron. Author. *Publ*: Apartment in Brussels; Of Many Things; The Trio from Rio; Suzanne & I; Six Plays of Eugene O'Neill; The Questing Mind; The Pilgrimage of Peer; The Great City. *Ctr*: Times, Sun Observe., Melbourne Herald, Argus, Age, Sydney Morning Herald, Sydney Bulletin, etc. *Rec*: Reading, troutfishing, painting. *c*: Bread & Cheese Melbourne. *a*: 27 Brighton Rd, St Kilda, Australia. *T*: LA 2853.

MICKLEM, Edward Romilly. *b*: Brondesbury 1892. *e*: Rugby, New & Mansfield Coll Oxf. *m*: Phyllis Winifred Benham. *s*: 2. Chap, Tutor, Lect Mansfield Coll Oxf 1921—38, Minister Congregational Church Gerrards Cross. *Publ*: Miracles and the New Psychology; Our Approach to God; A Book on the Bible for Everyman; Heart in Pilgrimage; The World's Ransom. *a*: The Manse, Gerrards Cross, Buckinghamshire. *T*: 2551.

MICKLEM, Rev. Nathaniel, M.A.(Oxon), D.D. (Glasgow), D.D., LL.D.(Queen's Univ Canada). *b*: London 1888. *e*: Rugby, New & Mansfield Colls Oxf. *m*: Agatha Frances Silcock. *s*: 3. Princ & Prof of Dogmatic Theo Mansfield Coll, formerly Min Highbury Chapel Bristol, Prof of Old Testament Lit & Theol to Selly Oak Colls Birm, Prof of New Testament Literature at Queen's Theol Coll Canada. *Publ*: National Socialism of the Roman Catholic Church; The Theology of Politics; The Labyrinth; The Doctrine of Our Redemption; *a*: Principals Lodgings, Mansfield Coll, Oxford. *T*: 2340.

MICKLEM, Rev. Philip Arthur, D.D.(Oxon). *b*: Waltham-St Lawrence, Berks 1876. *e*: Harrow Sch, Hertford Coll, Oxf Univ. *m*: Evelyn Auriac. Clerk in Holy Orders, Provost of Derby 1937—47. *Publ*: St Matthew; Westminster Commentary; Principles of Church Organisation; Values of the Incarnation; The Secular & the Sacred. *c*: Oxford & Cambridge. *a*: Marigolds, Staplecross, Nr Robertsbridge.

MICKLEWRIGHT, Frederick Henry Amphlett, M.A., F.R.S.A.I., F.S.A.(Scot), F.R.Hist.S. *b*: Chipstead 1908. *e*: Dulwich Coll, St Peters Hall Oxford. *m*: Irene Isobel Burnett. Minister & Lecturer, Manch Univ Extension Lect from 1943, Manch City Councillor from

'45, Minister Cross St Chapel Manch from '43. *Publ*: Religion To-Morrow ; Rationalism & Culture ; The New Orthodoxy ; Catholic Schools & Democratic Rights. *Ctr*: Notes & Queries, Inquirer, Vistas, Manch Ev Chron. *s.s*: Historical & Antiquarian, Liberal Religious, Political & Social. *Rec*: Hiking & exploring Gr Britain. *c*: International Manch. *a*: 25 Albert Rd, Whalley Range, Manchester 16.

MICKS, Robert Henry, M.D., F.R.C.P.I. *b*: Killiney, Co Dublin 1895. *e*: St Stephens Green School, Dublin University. *m*: Fanny Geraldine Townsend MacFetridge. Physician. *Publ*: Essentials of Materia Medica Pharmacology & Therapeutics. *Ctr*: Numerous medical journals. *a*: 18 Fitzwilliam Pl, Dublin.

MIDDLE WALLOP. See **Sprake, Leslie**.

MIDDLEMISS, James Ernest, F.R.F.P.S.G. *b*: Bradford, Yorkshire 1879. *e*: Salt Sch Shipley, Univ of Leeds. *m*: Ruby Ogston Clubb. *d*: 1. Formerly Asst Med Officer Gartloch Mental Hosp. *Ctr*: Medical Press & Circular, B.M.J., Edin Med Journ, Journ of Mental Science, Lancet, etc. *s.s*: Mental Deficency & Psychotherapy. *Rec*: Golf, music, lit. *a*: The Crest, 660 Scott Hall Rd, Leeds 7. *T*: 62504.

MIDDLEMIST, F., M.A. Headmaster All Hallow's Sc, Honiton, Devon, 1901–31. *a*: Broadhayes, Honiton, Devon.

MIDDLETON, A. Safroni. *Publ*: inc Ragged Romance ; Tropic Shadows ; Rhymes from the Bush, the Sea & Mountain ; Stars that Pass in the Night ; Under Many Names ; (Essay) Subconcious Philosophy ; & several poems. *a*: c/o Boosey & Co, 295 Regent St, London, W.1.

MIDDLETON, Edgar C. Author. *Publ*: Potiphar's Wife ; Banned by the Censor ; Tin Gods. *a*: c/o T. Werner Laurie Ltd, 24 Water Lane, E.C.4.

MIDDLETON, Ellis, L.R.I.B.A., A.M.Inst.C.E. *b*: Preston 1884. *e*: Blackpool Gr Sch. *m*: Florence Stella Carpenter. Novelist, Architect, Civil Eng. *Publ*: The Road of Destiny ; Chance—& the Woman ; The King's Pleasure ; Vaulting Ambition ; Morella the Gypsy ; High Water ; Fine Raiment (" John Morton Lees ") ; Sylvia, Elizabeth & Anne ; etc. *s.s*: Hist Romance. *Rec*: Gardening. *a*: Fylde Lees, Wootton Rd, Gaywood, King's Lynn. *T*: 4130.

MIDDLETON, George. *b*: Paterson, N.J. 1880. *e*: Columbia Univ, Sorbonne. *m*: Fola La Follette. Dramatist. *Publ*: These Things Are Mine ; (Author or Co-Author : Plays) That Was Balzac ; Polly With a Past ; Adam & Eva ; Hiss, Boom, Blah ; The Big Pond ; Hit-the-Trail-Holliday ; The Road Together ; The Cavalier ; Nowadays ; The Cave Girl ; The Sinner ; Blood Money ; Accused (From the French of Brieux) ; A Wife's Strategy ; The Other Rose (From the French of Bourdet) ; The Light of the World ; The Prodigal Judge (From the Novel) ; The House of a Thousand Candles (from the Novel) ; The Bride ; Madame Carpet (from the French) ; (One-Act Plays) Embers ; Possession ; Masks ; Tradition ; Back of the Ballot ; Criminals ; The Unknown Lady. *a*: The Players, 16 Gramercy Park, New York City, U.S.A.

MIDDLETON, Horace Stanley. *b*: Leicester 1909. *e*: Wyggeston Sch, Leicester. Dist Mang Sale & Stretford Guardian. *n.a*: Reporter Leicester Mercury 1926—29, E. Sentinel Stoke on Trent '29—32, Shrewsbury Chronicle '32—33, Warrington Guardian '33. *a*: 6 Delauney Rd, Sale, Cheshire.

MIDDLETON, Leslie Rupert, M.A., B.Sc., F.R.S.A. *b*: Tamworth, Staffs 1908. *e*: Queen Elizabeth's Gr Sch Tamworth & Downing Coll Camb. *m*: Dorothy Nicoll. *d*: 2. Senior Physics Master City of Lond Sch. *Publ*: A Text Book of Light ; School Certificate Exercises in Physics. *s.s*: Physics. *Rec*: Tennis, swimming, reading. *a*: 1 Whitton Drive, Greenford, Middlesex. *T*: Wembley 5053.

MIDDLETON, Robert Dudley. *e*: St John's Coll Oxf. *Publ*: Magdalen Studies ; Dr Routh ; Newman & Bloxam, an Oxford Friendship. *w.s*: World War I (des). *a*: St Margarets Vicarage, Oxford.

MIDDLETON, Samuel H., Hon.D.D. *b*: Burton-on-Trent, England 1884. *e*: Kingston Coll Nottingham. *m*: Kathleen Underwood. *s*: 1. *d*: 2. Rector of St Paul's Church, All Saints' Church Waterton Park, Princ St Paul's Res Sch. *Publ*: History of the Sun Dance ; History & Legends of Blood Indians ; Blackfoot Confederacy ; Origin of Waterton Lakes ; Lives of Indian Chiefs ; etc. *Ctr*: Church & Circular Press. *s.s*: Indian Lore & Anthropology. *Rec*: Touring, mountaineering, lecturing. *c*: Rotary, Gardston, Explorers' (N.Y.). *a*: St Paul's Residential School, Diocese of Calgary Gardston, Alta. Canada. *T*: X1610.

MIDDLETON, Thomas George. *m*: Alice Allott. *s*: 1. *d*: 1. Journalist, author. *n.a*: Dir National News Agency. *s.s*: Royalty, science. health. Former News Ed Pall Mall Gazette. Hulton Group & Allied Newspapers Group. *a*: 41 Cromwell Rd, S. Kensington. *t*: Kensington 3138.

MIDFORTH, Godfrey Norman. *b*: Glos 1908. *e*: Sir Thomas Rich's Sc. Journalist. *n.a*: Gloucester Echo, Cheltenham 5 y, Chief Glos Reporter 2 y, Bristol Evening Times & Echo, Original mem Bristol Evening Post Staff. Chm Bristol Br N.U.J. '33. *c.t*: Various. *s.s*: Film & dramatic criticism. *Rec*: Angling. *c*: Glos Cons, Bristol Motor Cycle & Light Car. *a*: 83 Woodland Rd, Bristol. *t*: 21721.

MIDGLEY, Cyril, B.Sc, M.Sc. *b*: Hull 1897. *e*: Sheffield & Birm Univ. *m*: Frances Mary Lear. *d*: 2. Editor. *n.a*: A. Wheaton & Co Ltd, Exeter. *Publ*: Wheatons Sketch Map Geographies ; Wheaton's Individual Geographies ; The Elementary Teaching Atlas ; The Picture Atlas of the World We Live In ; Wall Maps of World Climates ; etc. *s.s*: Trav. War Service 1917–19. *a*: The Mount, Portland Av, Exmouth. *t*: 636.

MIDGLEY, David Rhodes, LL.B. *b*: Leighton Buzzard 1911. *e*: King's Coll Lond. Barrister. *n.a*: Mang Ed Leighton Buzzard Observer & North Bucks Times. *a*: Beaufort Hse, Wing Rd, Leighton Buzzard. *T*: 3136.

MIDGLEY, Eber. *b*: Shipley 1874. *e*: Shipley Tech Sc & Leeds Univ. Prof of Textile Industries, Bradford Tech Col. *Publ*: Analysis of Woven Fabrics ; Finishing of Woven Fabrics ; Technical Terms in the Textile Trade. *c.t*: Textile journs. *s.s*: Industrial textile research. Vice-Pres Textile Inst. *Rec*: Golf, hortic. *a*: Haworth Rd, Heaton, Bradford, Yorkshire. *t*: Bradford 4736.

MIDGLEY, Wilson. *b*: Bingley, Yorks 1887. *e*: Keighley Gr Sch, Leeds Univ. *m*: Helen Bamford. Editor. *n.a*: American Corr Lond Dly News, Dep Ed The Star (Lond), Ed John O' London's Weekly. *Publ*: Possible Presidents ; From My Corner Bed ; The Terrible Turk. *s.s*: Books. *Rec*: Broadcasting. *c*: Authors, P.E.N. *a*: John O' London's Weekly, Tower Hse, Southampton St, London, W.C.2. *T*: Temple Bar 4363.

MIDLETON, Earl of. *a*: Midleton, Co Cork, Ireland.

MIERS, SIR HENRY ALEXANDER: Trustee of British Museum; b. Rio de Janeiro, May 25, 1858; s. Francis Charles and Susan Mary (Fry) M.; educ. Eton College; Oxford Univ. DEGREES: M. A., D.Sc. (Oxford); LL.D. (Michigan, Liverpool); D.Sc. (Manchester, Sheffield); unmarried. AUTHOR: The Soil in Relation to Health (with R. Crosskey), 1893; Mineralogy, 1902 (2nd edit. 1929); Report on the Public Museums of the British Isles to the Carnegie United Kingdom Trustees, 1928. Editor of Mineralogical Mag. (1891-1900). General character of writing: scientific and educational. Asst. in British Museum (Natural history), 1882-95; Prof. of Mineralogy, Univ. of Oxford, 1895-1908; Prin. of Univ. of London, 1908-1915; Vice-chancellor, Univ. of Manchester, 1915-26. Relig. denom., Church of England. CLUBS: Athenaeum (London); University of London. HOME: 18 Aberdare Gardens, N. W. 6, London, Eng.

MIGEOD, Frederick William Hugh, F.R.G.S., F.R.A.I. *b* : Chislehurst 1872. *e* : Folkestone. *m* : Madeleine Banks (dec'd). Colonial Civil Servant (ret). *Publ* : Mende Language ; Languages of West Africa (2 vols) ; Mende Natural History Vocabulary ; Grammar of the Hausa Language ; Earliest Man ; Across Equatorial Africa ; Through Nigeria to Lake Chad ; Through British Cameroons ; A View of Sierra Leone ; Aspects of Evolution ; Worthing—Survey of Times Past & Present. *s.s* : Trop Africa. *a* : 46 Christ Church Rd, Worthing, Sussex.

MIKES, George. *b* : Siklos, Hungary 1912. *e* : Budapest Univ. *m* : Lea Hanak. *s* : 1. Writer, Programme Asst Hungarian Sect B.B.C. *Publ* : How to Be An Alien ; We Were There to Escape ; The Epic of Lofoten ; How To Scrape Skies (with N. Bentley). *Ctr* : A Reggel, various Lond mags & periodicals. *Rec* : Tennis, bridge. *a* : 28 Bronwen Court, Grove End Rd, London, N.W.8. *T* : Cunningham 3706.

MIKKELSEN, Borge. *b* : Lokken, Denmark 1906. *e* : Public Sch. *m* : Marie Brynildsen. *s* : 2. *d* : 1. When Copenhagen Harbour Police. *Publ* : Somandssange, gamle og nye ; Jorn Havbo gaar tis Sos ; Jorn Havbo Atter paa Farten ; Jorn Havbo blandt Smuglere ; Jorn Havbo i Kystpolitiet ; Jorn Havbo vender hjem ; Tre Slags Folk ; Jeg vil gore alt for dig ; Pigen fra Piraeus. *s.s* : Ships, Seamen & their Lives. *Rec* : Sport & fishing. *c* : Adventurer's (Denmark). *a* : Halfdansgade 19, 1 Copenhagen, Denmark. *T* : Sundby 2491 Ydun.

MILBURN, C(HARLES) H(ENRY): surgeon; b. Sheffield, Eng., 1860; s. Rev. Joseph and Eliza (Wilkinson) M.; educ. Coll. of Science (Newcastle-on-Tyne); Univ. of Durham, Coll. of Medicine (Newcastle-on-Tyne); London Univ. DEGREES: Bachelor of Medicine, Master of Surgery (Durham); m. Edith Gleadow, 1890. Contributor to British Medical Jnl. General character of writing: current medical topics. Relig. denom., Church of England. CLUBS: Harrogate Literary. ADDRESS: 19 Park View, Harrogate, Yorkshire, Eng.

MILBURN, Rev. Robert Gordon. *b* : Tulse Hill 1870. *e* : Tonbridge Trinity Coll Oxf. *m* : Mary Agnes Myers. Clergyman & Educational Missionary (India) (ret). *Publ* : The Theology of the Real ; The Logic of Religious Thought ; The Religious Mysticism of the Upanishads ; The International Commonwealth. *s.s* : The Philosophy of Religion. *a* : Durris, Stubbs Wood, Chesham Bois, Bucks.

MILDMAY, Rev. Aubrey Neville St John, M.A. *b* : Long Marston 1865. *e* : New Coll Oxf, Wells Theol Coll. *m* : Louisa J. Maunder. *s* : 1. *d* : 1. Priest, C. of E., Ed & Founder Trinity Servant (1883—84). Writer & Univ Tutor. *n.a* : Mus Critic, Ldr Writer 25 yrs with Vancouver News Advertiser, Sun & other dailies & weeklies. *Publ* : Horae Mediterraneae ; In the Waiting—Time of War ; Sea Room ; Vignettes & Brown Studies (Autremonde) ; Laureates of the Cross. *Ctr* : Nat Rev, Spectator, Sun Times, Brit Weekly, Classical Mag, etc. *s.s* : Manuscripts of Sidonius Apollinaris. *a* : Little Manor, Ringmer, Lewes, Sussex. *T* : Ringmer 56.

MILES, Alexander. LL.D., M.D., F.R.C.S. *b* : Leith, Scotland 1864. *e* : George Watson's Coll Edin Univ. *m* : Helen Greig. *s* : 1. *d* : 1. *n.a* : Formerly Ed Edinburgh Medical Journal, Univ of Edin Journal. *Publ* : Manual of Surgery ; Operative Surgery ; Surgical Ward Work ; The Edinburgh School of Surgery Before Lister. *s.s* : Surgery. *a* : 6 Blackford Rd, Edinburgh. *T* : 52447.

MILES, Cecil Arthur. *n.a* : Ed Mansfield Advertiser 1925—. *a* : 23 Meadow Ave, Mansfield.

MILES, Constance. *b* : Kelso 1881. *e* : Priv. *m* : Major E. Miles. *s* : 2. *Publ* : (with brother) Lord Richard in the Pantry ; Cupid Goes North ; Dream Child Come True (novel) ; The Unwilling Schoolgirl ; Lady Richard in the Larder ; Coffee, Please !; etc. *c.t* : Brit Weekly, Good Housekeeping, C.E. N/p, etc. *s.s* : Light novels, serials, children's books. *Rec* : Travel. *c* : Soc of Authors. *a* : Spring Field, Shere, Guildford.

MILES, Eustace, M.A. *b* : London 1868. *e* : Eastbourne Coll Marlborough, King's Coll Camb. *m* : Hallie Killick. *Publ* : Muscle, Brain & Diet ; Training of the Body ; Daily Health ; Prevention & Cure ; What Foods Feed Us ; The Cricket of Abel, Hirst & Shrewsbury ; Tennis Racquets & Squash ; Self-Health as a Habit ; Quickness ; How to Remember, Without Memory Systems & With Them ; Life After Life ; A History of Rome ; 150 " Milestones " or Booklets of Health & Well-Being ; etc. *Ctr* : Dly Express, Dly Mail, Mirror, Sketch, Dly Graphic, Windsor Mag, Pearsons, Nat Review, etc. *s.s* : Grammar of Langs, Games, Diet, Breathing, Self-Health, Mental Training, New Testament Greek, Physiology. *Rec* : Patience, Puns. *c* : Bath. *a* : 66 York Mansions, London, S.W.11. *T* : Macaulay 3600.

MILES, Mrs. Eustace. *b* : Erchfont. *e* : Priv. *m* : Eustace Miles, M.A. Author. *Publ* : Life's Orchestra ; Life's Colour ; The Animals' Sunday Rest ; The Ideal Home ; Pilgrimage of the Cross ; Story of the Coronation of King Edward VII ; Untold Tales of War-time London ; Health without Meat ; etc. *Ctr* : Dly Express, Dly Sketch, Dly Mirror, Ev News, Leader, etc. *s.s* : Home Life, Cookery, description of beauty spots & general interests. *Rec* : Home life, sketching, writing. *c* : Soc of Women Journalists. *a* : 66 York Mansions, London, S.W.11. *T* : Macaulay 3600.

MILES, Lady Favell. *Publ* : Red Flame ; Stony Ground ; Lorna Neale ; This Flower ; Tread Softly ; The Fanatic ; etc. *a* : Walton-in-Gordano, Clevedon, Somerset.

MILES, Rev. Frederic James, D.S.O., O.B.E., V.D. Th.D., Litt.D., D.D. *b* : London 1869. *m* : Isabella Killick. *s* : 2. Internat Sec Russian Missn Soc, Missn to Ceylon 1892—1900, Australia 1900—14. *n.a* : Ed The Friend of Russians 1930. *Publ* : The Miracle of Miracles ; The World's Best Seller & Why ; Triumph for the Troops ; His Life on Earth & Ours ; Christ The Coming & the Comforter ; The Greatest Unused Power in the World ; Prophecy Past, Present & Prospective ; Russia & Palestine in Prophecy ; The Debt We Owe to the Jew ; Understandest Thou ; The Horsemen are Riding. *Ctr* : The Christian, The Life of Faith, The British Weekly Revelation, The Pilot, Moody Monthly. *s.s* : Russia & Biblical Exposition. *Rec* : Tennis, golf, bowls. *c* : Authors. *a* : 13 Vowler St, London, S.E.17. *T* : Rodney 3512.

MILES, Hamish. *b* : Edin 1894. *e* : Edin Acad, Balliol Col Oxf. *n.a* : Ed Life & Letters 1933, New Stories '34, Cmt Translators' Gld '33, Lit Ed Jonathan Cape Ltd. *Publ* : The Oxford Circus ('22) ; Fair Perthshire ; A War Museum ('32) ; Trans works by André Maurois, Paul Morand & Jacques Bainville, etc. *c.t* : New Statesman, Spectator, Criterion, Fortnightly Review, etc. *a* : Long Hoyle, Heyshott, Sussex. *t* : Graffham 9.

Who Was Who Among English and European Authors

MILES, Sir John Charles, M.A., B.C.L.(Oxon), F.S.A. *m*: Marion Frances Charlotte Langley. *Publ*: Cases Illustrating Law of Torts (with F. R. Y. Radcliffe, K.C.); Torts in Jenks's Digest of English Civil Law; Cases in the Law of Contract (with Prof J. L. Brierly, D.C.L.); Jt Ed with Prof J. L. Brierly of Anson's Contract. *c.t*: Legal periodicals. *c*: Union. *a*: Merton Col, Oxf, & 22 Merton St, Oxf. *t*: 2861.

MILES, T. *n.a*: Didcot Advertiser, Didcot, Berks.

MILFORD, Sir Humphrey Sumner, Kt., Hon.D.Litt. (Oxon). *b*: East Knoyle 1877. *e*: Winchester, New Coll Oxf. *m*: (1) Marion Smith (dec'd), (2) Rose Wilson. *s*: 2. *d*: 1. Former Publisher to Oxf Univ. *Publ*: Ed The Oxford Cowper, Ed The Oxford Leigh Hunt, etc. *c*: Athenæum. *a*: The White Hse, Drayton St Leonard, Oxford. *T*: Stadhampton 68.

MILFORD, Rev. Lionel Sumner. *b*: Farnham Castle 1855. *e*: Haileybury & Pembroke Col Oxf. *m*: Mary Frances Lowe. *d*: 1. *Publ*: Ed Four edns of the Haileybury College Register; Author Haileybury College (o.p.). Asst Master Haileybury for nearly 40 y & for 7 y Rector of Widford, Herts. Resident at Easington '25-, has the permission of the Bishop of Oxf to take Clerical Work in the Dio. *a*: The Dower Hse, Easington, Watlington, Oxf.

MILL, Hugh Robert, D.Sc., LL.D. *b*: Thurso, Caithness 1861. *e*: Priv & Edin Univ. *m*: (1) Frances MacDonald (dec'd), (2) Alfreda Dransfield, Geographer & Rainfall Expert, Pres Roy Met Soc 1907. Pres Geog Assoc '32. *Publ*: Siege of the South Pole; Realm of Nature; Life of Sir Ernest Shackleton; Record of Royal Geographical Society. *Ctr*: Times, Manch Guardian, Quarterly Rev, Edin Rev, Nature, etc. *s.s*: Polar Regions, Meteorology, Geography, Travel. *Rec*: Travel, reading. *a*: Hill Crest, Dormans Park, East Grinstead, Sussex. *T*: Dormans Park 219.

MILL, William Allin, M.S.(Lon), F.R.C.S.(Eng). Surgeon. *c.t*: Med Press. *a*: 28 Devonshire Place, W.1. *t*: Langham 1923.

MILLAIS, JOHN GUILLE: author, artist; b. London, Eng., March, 1865; s. Sir Everett (P. R. A.) and Euphemia Chalmers (Gray) M.; educ. Marlborough Coll.; Trinity Coll. (Cambridge); m. Fanny Margaret Skipwith, Oct. 31, 1894. AUTHOR: Game Birds and Shooting Sketches, 1892; A Breath from the Veldt, 1895; British Deer and their Horns, 1897; Life and Letters of Sir John Everett Millais, P.R.A., 1899; The Wildfowler in Scotland, 1901; The National History of British Surface-feeding Ducks, 1902; The Mammals of Great Britain and Ireland, Vol. 1, 1904; Vol. 2, 1905; Vol. 3, 1906; Newfoundland and its Untrodden Ways, 1907; The Natural History of British Game Birds, 1909; British Diving Ducks, 2 vols., 1913; Deer and Deer Stalking, 1913; European Big Game (The Gun at Home and Abroad), 1914; American Big Game (The Gun at Home and Abroad), 1915; Rhododendrons and their Hybrids, 1917; The Life of Capt. F. C. Selous, D.S.O., 1918; Wanderings and Memories, 1919; Rhododendrons and their Hybrids (2nd series), 1919; Far Away up the Nile, 1924; Magnolias, 1927; at present engaged in animal sculpture and a large work on the courtship of birds. Contributor to Field, Country Life, Times, Pearson's Mag., and others. General character of writing: scientific, sporting, biography, travel, zoology. Served in Somerset Light Infantry, 3 yrs.; 1st Seaforth Highlanders, 7 yrs.; Lieut. Commander of Royal Volunteer Naval Reserve during European War, 4 yrs.; (Victory and Allies medals); an extensive traveller of Europe, Africa, North America, Arctic Regions; explored the whole of the center of Newfoundland and mapped same; naturalist and big game hunter; gold medal of honour R.H.S., 1927. (*)

MILLAN, F. W. Journalist. *n.a*: Day Ed Morning Advertiser. *a*: 18 St Andrew St, E.C.4.

MILLAR, Eric George, M.A., D.Litt(Oxon), F.S.A. *b*: London 1887. *e*: Charterhouse, Corpus Christi Coll Oxf. Keeper of Manuscripts & Egerton Librarian British Museum 1944—47. *Publ*: The Lindisfarne Gospels; English Illuminated Manuscripts from the 10th to the 13th Century; English Illuminated Manuscripts of the 14th & 15th Centuries; The Library of A. Chester Beatty, A Descriptive Catalogue of the Western MSS (Vols I & II); The Luttrell Psalter; The Rutland Psalter. *s.s*: Illuminated Manuscripts. *Rec*: Collecting MSS, books and drawings, gramophone, troutfishing, gardening. *c*: Athenæum. *a*: 28 Holland Park Rd, Kensington, London, W.14, & The Summer Hse, Dinton, Salisbury.

MILLAR, George Reid. *b*: Baldernock, Scotland 1910. *e*: Loretto & St John's Cambridge. *m*: Isabel Beatriz Paske-Smith. Author. *n.a*: Dly Telegraph (Reporter) 1936—37, Dly Express (Reporter) '38—39, Dly Express (Paris Correspondent) '39—40. *Publ*: Maquis; Horned Pigeon; My Past was an Evil River; Isobel and the Sea. *a*: The Gate' Hse, Bingham's Melcombe, Dorset.

MILLAR, James Primrose Malcolm. *b*: Edinburgh 1893. *e*: Musselburgh Gr Sch, Roy Hgh Sch, Cent Labour Coll. *m*: Christine Davidson Hastie. *s*: 1. *d*: 1. Gen Sec. Lect, Ed, Gen Sec Nat Counc Lab Colls. *n.a*: Ed Plebs etc, Mang Ed Publ Soc. *Publ*: More Production—More Poverty; The Trained Mind—Trained for What? *Ctr*: Forward, Railway Review, etc. *s.s*: Adult Educ. Econ. *a*: Tillicoultry, Scotland. *T*: 248

MILLAR, John Alexander Stevenson, M.V.O. *b*: Paisley 1854. *e*: Paisley G.S., Madras Col, St And & Edin Univs. *m*: Dora Shillinglaw (dec). *s*: 3 (1 dec). *d*: 3. Writer to H.M. Signet. *c.t*: Scotsman, Glas Herald, Chambers's Journ, etc. *s.s*: Conveyancing, ch law. *Rec*: Golf, fishing, shooting. *c*: Scot Cons, Hon Coy of Edin Golfers. *a*: 41 Coates Gdns, Edin. *t*: 62419.

MILLAR, Ruddick. *b*: Belfast 1907. *e*: Pub Elem Sch. *m*: Henrietta Wolsey. *s*: 1. *d*: 1. Journalist, Mem of P.E.N. *n.a*: Rep Northern Whig 1929—80, Irish News '30—36, Sub-Ed Belfast News Letter '36—. *Publ*: Stirabout From An Ulster Pot; More Stirabout; Collected Poems; Plus Fours & No Breakfast; Four Irish Pictures; (Three Act Plays) A Yank From Ulster; The Land Girl; Johnny Comes Marching Home; etc. *Ctr*: The Observer, Manch Guardian, Sun Chronicle, etc. *s.s*: Radio Drama & Features. *Rec*: Watching sport. *a*: 1 Upper Castle Park, Belfast, Ireland. *T*: 46868.

MILLARD, Allen Douglas. *e*: Caterham. Publisher & literary adviser. *c.t*: Periodicals & n/ps. *a*: 47 Park Mans, S.W.8. & 7 Racquet Court, Fleet St, E.C.4. *t*: Reliance 3754 & Central 1797.

MILLARD, D. K., M.D., D.Sc. *Publ*: Population & Birth Control; The Vaccination Question: Euthanasia. M.O.H. City of Leicester. *a*: The Gilross, Groy Road, Leicester.

MILLARD, Ernest James. *b*: Cardiff 1899. *e*: Gladstone, Allensbank & Blogg's Scs Cardiff. *m*: Betty Cuell. *s*: 2. *d*: 1. *n.a*: S. Wales Echo, S. Wales News 1919, Western Mail & Echo '28. *s.s*: Football, golf, cricket. War Service. *Rec*: Gardening, tennis. *a*: 51 Clare St, Manselton, Swansea, Glam. *t*: 5373.

MILLARD, Rev. Frederick Luke Holland, M.A. (Oxon & Durham). *b*: W.I. 1865. *e*: L'pool Col & St Edmund Hall Oxf. *m*: Margaret Josephine Ferguson s: 3. *Publ*: Early Church History for Schools Commentary on S. Mark for Teachers; etc. *s.s*: Sociology. C.F. France, Egypt, Palestine. Travelled India, S. Africa, Canada, U.S. *Rec*: Golf. *a*: St John's Vicarage, 49 Wiltshire Rd, S.W.9. *t*: Brixton 5066.

MILLARD, Winifred, B.A. *b*: Bournemouth 1905. *e*: Bournemouth H.S. & Oxf Univ. Teaching. *Publ*: Poems ('33) *s.s*: Nature & mythology. *a*: Brooklands, Longham, Wimborne, Dorset.

MILLEN, A. E. *b*: Croydon 1887. *e*: Whitgift M.S. & Workers Educ Assoc. *m*: C. Howell. *s*: 3. *d*: 3. Journalist (ch Sub Ed). *n.a*: Croydon Advtr, P.A. 1915-18, Daily Sketch '26-32, Sun Graphic '26-32, Sun Evening Telegram '18-24. *s.s*: Educ. *Rec*: Walking. *a*: Reynolds's Illustrated News, 8 Temple Av, E.C.4. *t*: Central 9191.

MILLER, Amy. *b*: Bristol. *n.a*: Ed Smart Fiction 1919-24. *Ctr*: Shurey, Thomson, Newnes & Other Publs. *s.s*: Astrology. *Rec*: Travel, theatre. *a*: 6 Grove Hse, & 99 Larkhill Rise, S.W.4.

MILLER, Arthur Hallowes, M.D.(Cantab), M.R.C.P. (Lond). *b*: Colombo 1880. *e*: Marlboro', Trin Coll Camb, Guy's Hosp & Berlin. Pathologist (ret). *Publ*: The Biological Concept of Man. *Ctr*: Times & med periodicals. *s.s*: Pathology. *Rec*: Golf. *a*: Branksea Tower, Osborne Rd, Parkstone, Dorset.

MILLER, Betty. *b*: 1910. *e*: Cork, France & Notting Hill H.S. *m*: Dr. Emanuel Miller. *Publ*: The Mere Living (B. Bergson Spiro); Sunday. *c.t*: Adelphi & J. o' London's Wkly. *Rec*: Cinema. *a*: 23 Park Cres, W.1. *t*: Welbeck 8875.

MILLER, Douglas, A.M. *b*: Fayetee, Iowa 1892. *e*: Univs of Denver & Oxf. *m*: Elizabeth von Rieben. Former Commercial Attache U.S. Embassy Berlin. *Publ*: You Can't Do Business With Hitler; Via Diplomatic Pouch. *Ctr*: Atlantic Monthly, Readers Digest, N.Y. Times, Life. *s.s*: Internat Relations, Economics. *a*: 4028 Arkansas Ave, N.W. Washington 11, D.C., U.S.A. *T*: Taylor 8990.

MILLER, Edmund Morris, M.A., Litt.D., F.B.Ps.S. *b*: Pietermaritzburg, Natal, Sth Africa 1881. *e*: Wesley Coll Melbourne, Univs of Melbourne & Edin. *m*: Catherine Mackinnon Carson. *d*: 1. Prof of Psychology. *Publ*: Australian Literature: A Descriptive & Bibliographical Survey; Moral Law & the Highest Good; Basis of Freedom; Brain Capacity & Intelligence; Libraries & Education; Some Phases of Preference in Imperial Policy; etc. *Ctr*: Psychological & Philosophical journs in Australia. *s.s*: Australian Lit, Kantian & Post-Kantian Philosophy. *Rec*: Bowls. *a*: University of Tasmania, Hobart, Tasmania.

MILLER, Emanuel, M.A., M.R.C.S., F.R.C.P., D.P.M. *b*: London 1893. *e*: City of Lond Sch, St John's Coll Camb & Lond Hosp Med Sch. *m*: Betty Spiro. *s*: 1. Physician in Child Psychiatry St George's Hosp, Senior Physician in Psychotherapy Maudsley Hosp, Co Dir Inst Scientific Treatment of Delinquency, Hons Cons Psychiatrist West End Hosp. *Publ*: Types of Mind & Body; Modern Psychotherapy; Science & To-Day (collab); How the Mind Works (collab); Neurosis in War; Growing Child & Its Problems; Insomnia & other Disorders of Sleep. *Ctr*: Brain, Journ of Psychopathology, Brit Journ Med Psych, Journ Mental Sci, etc. *s.s*: Mental Diseases, Psych of Childhood, Educ. *Rec*: Painting, modelling. *w.s*: Late Lt-Col R.A.M.C. *a*: 13 Harley St, London, W. *T*: Langham 2664.

MILLER, Ernest Sharpe, F.J.I. *b*: Millom. *m*: Elizabeth Craighill. *s*: 1. *d*: 1. Night Ed News Chronicle, Northern Ed Manch. *n.a*: Rep Workington News, Surrey Mirror (Redhill), Surrey Times (Weybridge), Chief Rep & Sub-Ed Aldershot News, Chief Sub-Ed Northern Echo (Darlington), Daily News 1909, Copy Taster Lond Office '21—28. *Rec*: Bird-watching, golf. *a*: 353 Wilmslow Rd, Didsbury, Manchester. *T*: Didsbury 2138.

MILLER, Ethel Hull. *b*: Hartford, Ohio 1889. *e*: Hartford, Ohio Sem, Hiram, Ohio Coll. *m*: Messenger Miller. *s*: 2. *d*: 2. Writer. *Publ*: White Saddle; Out of the Roaring Loom. *Ctr*: Holiday Mag, Klaus und Klare, The Argus (Melbourne), Buffalo Ev News, Erie Dispatch Herald, Lexington Herald Leader, Pittsburgh Press, Chicago Herald Examiner, etc. *s.s*: Travel Features; Nonfiction Stories of the Woods & Wildlife, Outdoor Stories for Children. *Rec*: Travel, motion pictures, wildlife study. *a*: Quailwood, Poland, Ohio.

MILLER, FLORENCE FENWICK, (pen name: Filomena): writing and lecturing; b. London, Eng., Nov. 5, 1854; d. John and Eleanor (Fenwick) M.; educ. private schools; The Ladies' Medical Coll. (London); m. Frederick Alfred Ford. AUTHOR: Simple Lessons in Health, 1877; The House of Life: Human Physiology in its Application to Health, 1878; An Atlas of Anatomy, 1879; Physiology for Schools, 1881; Readings in Social Economy, 1883; Natural History for the Standards; Life of Harriet Martineau (in the Eminent Women Series), 1884; In Ladies' Company (Biographies of Women), 1892. Editor of Outward Bound (a quarterly periodical of general literature), for 18 yrs.; of the Woman's Signal, 1895-99. Contributor of a ladies' page for the Illustrated London News weekly for 33 yrs., 1886-1918; to leading London and provincial newspapers and magazines, including The Fortnightly Review, The English Review, The National Review, The Strand Magazine, etc. Three yrs. on the staff of the London Daily News, The Sunday Sun, etc. General character of writing: the interests and progress of women, both in the home and in the wider world. Her principal life work has been journalism. Was one of the pioneers of the woman's movement in England. Was elected when 22 yrs. old, by a vote of 15,000 electors, to be mem. of Sch. Bd. for London. HOME: 23 Brunswick Road, Hove, Brighton, Sussex, Eng.

MILLER, Frederick A. *b*: South Bend 1868. *e*: Pub Scs. *m*: Flora Dunn. Journalist. *n.a*: Pres & Ed S. Bend Tribune. *Rec*: Gardening. *c*: Mem Nat Pr, American Soc of N/p Ed, Indiana Republican Ed Assoc. *a*: 1307 E. Jefferson Boulevard, South Bend, Ind, & Tribune Building, 225 W. Colfax Ave. *t*: Res 3-6767, Office 3-6161.

MILLER, Helen Topping. *b*: Fenton, Michigan 1885. *e*: Michigan State Col. *m*: Roger Miller. *s*: 1. Writer. *Publ*: Sharon; The Flaming Gahagans; Blue Marigolds. *c.t*: McCalls, Pictorial Review, Good Housekeeping, Saturday Evening Post, Liberty. *s.s*: fiction. *Rec*: Fishing, swimming. *a*: Skyland, North Carolina, U.S.A.

MILLER, Henry Arthur, A.M.I.E.E., F.R.S.A. *b*: Liverpool 1910. *e*: L'pool Inst Hgh Sch for Boys, L'pool Tech Coll. *m*: Hilda Eleanor Miller. *s*: 2. Tech Author, Admiralty Dept of Scientific Research & Experiment 1940—45. Mem Authors Soc. *Publ*: Luminous Tube Lighting; High Voltage Fluorescent Lighting; Electronic Devices. *Ctr*: Electrical Engineer, Electrical Review, Electrical Times, Signs, London Opinion. *s.s*: Electronics. *Rec*: Portraits in Pastel. *a*: 8 Linnet Hse, Ullet Rd, Liverpool 8. *T*: Lark Lane 1780.

MILLER, Herbert Adolphus, A.M., PhD. *b*: New Hants 1875. *e*: Dartmouth Col. Harvard. *m*: Bessie Cravath. *s*: 1. *d*: 1. Prof of Sociology. *Publ*: The School & the Immigrant; Old World Traits Transplanted (Jt Author); Races, Nations & Classes

(1924); The Beginnings of To-morrow ('33). *c.t*: The Survey, New York Times, American Journal of Sociology, The Nation (New York), Annals of the American Academy, The American Scholar, World Unity, etc. *s.s*: Nationality, immigration, social psychology. Organiser & Dir of Mid-European Union; Chrm Ohio Assoc on Penal Affairs; Chrm Philadelphia International Inst, etc. *Rec*: Golf, bridge, travel. *c*: Mem Exec Comm Amer Sociolog Soc. *a*: Bryn Mawr Col, Bryn Mawr, Pa, U.S.A. *t*: 1849 J.

MILLER, J. Corson. *b*: Buffalo, N.Y., U.S.A. 1883 *e*: St Agnes Parochial Sch, Academic Dept Canisius Coll Buffalo N.Y. *m*: Ottilia Schneider. *d*: 1. Staff of Municipal Civil Service Commission Buffalo N.Y., Mem Poetry Soc of America. *Publ*: (Verse) Veils of Samite; A Horn From Cærleon; Cup of the Years; Finger at the Crossroads. *Ctr*: Nation, Vanity Fair, Catholic World, Commonweal, America, N.Y. Sun, Times, etc. *s.s*: Writing of Verse. Book Reviews & Essays in Lit Criticism. *Rec*: Reading contemporary verse. *a*: 310 Ideal St, Buffalo 6, N.Y., U.S.A. *T*: Hu 7950.

MILLER, James, M.D., D.Sc., F.R.C.P., F.R.S.C. *b*: Edinburgh 1875. *e*: Edin Acad & Univs of Edin & Freiburg. *m*: Margaret Elizabeth Clare. *s*: 1. *d*: 3. Univ Prof (ret). *Publ*: Practical Pathology. *Ctr*: Journ of Pathology & Bacteriology, Edin Med Journ, Lancet, Canadian Med Assoc Journ, Dalhousie Rev. *s.s*: Pathology & Public Health. *Rec*: Walking, fishing. *c*: Authors. *w.s*: Capt R.A.M.C. 1914—19. *a*: The Old Pound, Balscote, Banbury, Oxfordshire. *T*: Wroxton 49.

MILLER, John Anderson, Ph.B. *b*: N.J. 1895. *e*: Yale Univ. *m*: Frances Elizabeth Daggett. Awarded Wellington Prize by Amer Soc Civil Engineers 1927. *n.a*: Asst Ed Transit Journ 1923, Assoc Ed '24—28, & Mang Ed '29—30, *Publ*: Master Builders of Sixty Centuries; Fares Please; Men & Volts at War. *Ctr*: World's Work, Amer Year Book, Nat Real Estate Journ, Mil Eng, American City Mag, Public Utilities Fortnightly, Ency Brit, Business Week, Eng News, etc. *s.s*: Transportation Engineering. *w.s*: U.S. Army 1916—19. *a*: 27 Front St, Schenectady, N.Y., U.S.A. *T*: 2-2640.

MILLER, Very Rev. John Harry, M.A.(Glas), D.D.(Edin), C.B.E., T.D. *b*: Glas 1869. *e*: Albany Acad, Glas Univ, Glas F.C. Col. *m*: Marie S. de Joannis. *d*: 5. Principal of St Mary's Col '35—. *Publ*: The Rapture of the Forward View; God & My Soul. Warden of New Col Settlement Edinburgh 1908—35. Moderator of Ch Assembly 1928—29. *Rec*: Swimming, golf. *c*: Eng Speaking Union. *a*: St Mary's College, St Andrews, Fife. *t*: 170.

MILLER, Sir John Ontario, K.C.S.I., Hon LL.D. (Aber). Indian Civil Service (ret). *Publ*: (pamphlets) High Prices & the Quantity Theory (published 1920); Politicians, Financiers & Currency ('31). *c.t*: Fortnightly Review, etc. *a*: 6 Sx Pl, W.2. *t*: Pad 3410.

MILLER, Joseph H., A.M., LL.D., Litt.D., Ph.D. *b*: Virginia, U.S.A. 1899. *e*: Univs of Richmond, Virginia, Columbia, Keaka Coll & Alfred Univ. *m*: Nell C. Critzer. *s*: 2. Assoc Commissioner of Educ New York State. *Publ*: Colleges at War & After; Veterans Challenge the Colleges; The Practice of Public Prayer. *Ctr*: N.Y. Times, N.Y. Herald Tribune, Educ Record, Commonweal, Sch & Society, etc. *s.s*: Educ, Youth Problems, Religion & Educ, Philosophy, Professional Educ. *Rec*: Golf, fishing, hunting, sailing. *c*: University. *a*: 128 Adams Pl, Delmar, N.Y., U.S.A. *T*: 9-2676 Albany (Office).

MILLER, Laurence, B.Sc(Lon, Econ). *b*: 1909. Playwright & Novelist. *Publ*: Head-on Crash ('33); Gloomy Romeo ('35). *a*: 4 De Parys Av, Bedford.

MILLER, Margaret Stevenson, M.A., B.Com. (Edin), Ph.D.(Econ Lond). *Publ*: Economic Development of Russia; The New Russia (Jt Author), Financial Democracy (Jt Author). *a*: 101 Ellison Rd, S.W.16.

MILLER, Mary Britton. *b*: New London, Connecticut 1883. *e*: Priv. *Publ*: Do I Wake or Sleep; The Crucifixion; In the Days of Thy Youth; Without Sanctuary; Songs of Infancy; Intrepid Bird; Menagerie. *Ctr*: New Yorker, Harper's Bazaar, Nat Bd of Review Mag. *a*: 81 Barrow St, New York City, U.S.A. *T*: Walker 5-8427.

MILLER, Nellie Burget, B.S., Litt.D. *b*: Fayette, Iowa. *e*: Upper Iowa Univ & Univ of Colorado. *m*: Lucas A. Miller. *s*: 1. *d*: 2. Writer, Poet Laureate Colorado. *n.a*: Ed Board of Several Poetry Mags. *Publ*: In Earthern Bowls; The Living Drama; The Flame of God; Pictures from the Plains & Other Poems; The Sun Drops Red; Land Where the Good Dreams Grow; Once in a Blue Moon; Verses for Victory. *Ctr*: American Home, Mind Digest, Clear Horizons, Nautilus, etc. *s.s*: Poetry & Metaphysics. *Rec*: Gardening. *a*: 20 West Washington, Colorado Springs, Colorado, U.S.A. *T*: Main 879.

MILLER, Osborn Maitland, M.C., F.R.G.S. *b*: Perth, Scotland 1897. *e*: Trin Coll Glenalmond, Roy Mil Acad Woolwich. Geographer. *n.a*: Staff American Geog Soc 1922—. *Publ*: World Maps & Globes (collab); Sections to: Manual of Photogrammetry; Problems of Polar Research; Northernmost Labrador Mapped From the Air; The Fiord Region of East Greenland. *Ctr*: Geog Review, Journ of Optical Soc of America, etc. *s.s*: Cartography, Map Projections, Mapping From Air Photographs. *Rec*: Golf, bridge, music, problems of transportation. *a*: 300 West 105th St, New York City, N.Y., U.S.A.

MILLER, Park Hays, M.A., D.D. *b*: Pittsburgh 1879. *e*: Pittsburgh Univ & Western Theol Sem. *m*: Bessie P. Crider. *s*: 1. *d*: 1. Religious Editor. *n.a*: Assoc Ed Board of Christian Educ 1923—30, Assoc Ed Supervisor Educational Materials '30—37, Ed '37—42. *Publ*: Christian Doctrine for Sunday School Teachers; The New Testament, Its Teaching & Its Scriptures; Our Reasonable Faith; Some Cross Sections of Old Testament Literature; etc. *Ctr*: Pioneer, Forward, etc. *s.s*: Sunday School Lesson Material. *a*: 904 Lindale Ave, Drexel Hill, Pennsylvania, U.S.A. *T*: Sunset 1987.

MILLER, Patrick. Author. *Publ*: Port Polli; The Magic Circle; The Natural Man; etc. *a*: c/o Hamish Hamilton, 90 Gt Russell St, W.C.1. & Sandhurst. Author & Journalist. *n.a*: Reporter Daily Mail 1920 & Sunday Dispatch '21—22. *Publ*: From Piccadilly to Devil's Island (travel); The Blue Spider; Black Royalty; Live Bait; etc. *c.t*: Daily Mail, Daily Telegraph, Daily Express, etc. *s.s*: Little known countries. Severely wounded La Bassée '14. Only known Brit Journalist to get Inside Prison at St Laurent du Maroni, French Guiana. *Rec*: Golf, gardening. *c*: Garrick. *a*: Stables Cottage, Hurst Wickham, Hassocks. *t*: Hurstpierpoint 188.

MILLER, Rex. *b*: Newton, Kansas 1894. *e*: Univs of Kansas & Oxf. *m*: Sonya Mitchell Miller. Radio News Commentator & Author. *n.a*: Foreign Corres & Ed Christian Science Monitor 1929—40. *Publ*: I, John; I, Paul. *Ctr*: N.Y. Times, N.Y. Herald Tribune, This Week Mag. *s.s*: Internat Relations, American Politics. *Rec*: Gardening, fishing. *a*: Mutual-Don Lee Broadcasting System, Hollywood, California, U.S.A. *T*: HO 8111.

MILLER, Walter, Litt.D., LL.D. *b*: Ashland Co, Ohio 1867. *e*: Univs of Michigan, Leipzig, Amer Sch of Classical Studies Athens. *m*: Jennie Emerson. *d*: 2.

Teacher & Administrator. *n.a*: Assoc Ed The Classical Journ 1905—33, Ed in Chief & Bus Mang '33—35, Ed in Chief The Standard American Ency '36—37. *Publ*: Greece & the Greeks; Xenophon's Cyropædia; A History of the Akropolis of Athens; etc. *Ctr*: Amer Journ of Archæology, Southern Educ Rev, Atlantis, etc. *s.s*: Greek, Latin, Classical Archæology, Sanskrit. *Rec*: Gardening. *a*: 1516 Wilson Ave, Columbia, Missouri, U.S.A. *T*: 5983.

MILLER, Warren Hastings. *b*: Honesdale, Pennsylvania 1876. *e*: Pingry Sch, Stevens Inst of Technology. *m*: (1) Susan Barse, (2) Elizabeth White. *s*: 4. *d*: 2. Mech Eng, Editor, Author. *n.a*: Ed Field & Stream 1910—18. *Publ*: Home Builders; Lone Woodsman; Tiger Bridge; Sahara Sands; Tiger Trails in Burma; Ape-Man of Sumatra; Across Borneo; In Darkest New Guinea; Red Mesa; Black Panther of the Navaho; White Buffalo; Ring-necked Grizzly; Sea Fighters; Castaways of Banda Sea; Under the Admiral's Stars; etc. *Ctr*: Blue Book, Red Book, Adventure, Field & Stream, Everybody's, Esquire, McClure's, Outdoor Life, Country Life, House & Garden, Youth's Companion, etc. *s.s*: Outdoor Adventure, Sea Stories, Country Life. *Rec*: Yachting, hunting, fishing, camping out. *w.s*: Lieut U.S.N.R. 1918—19. *a*: Grapevine Rd, Gloucester, Massachusetts, U.S.A. *T*: 1812-M.

MILLER, Webb. *b*: Michigan, U.S.A. 1893. *e*: America. *m*: Marie Alston. *s*: 1. Gen European News Mang of United Press of Amer. *n.a*: Staff of Chicago n/ps 1913-16, United Press Corr Mexican Border '16-17, Lon Bureau United Press '17-, War Corr at American front in France '18, Lon Bureau '19, Mang Paris Bureau '20-25, European News Mang United Press in Lon '25-. *s.s*: Foreign political & economic affairs. Covered news for United Press in 29 countries in Europe, Africa, Asia & America. Covered wars in Mexico, Morocco & France. Made 16,000 mile airplane flight to India & return on Gandhi story. Covered most of the European Internat Conf since War. Only Corr to fly in an airplane over the Armistice Lines at end of War & cover retreat of German army from the air. *a*. United Press of Amer; 30 Bouverie St. *t*: Central 22-82.

MILLER, WILLIAM: author, journalist; b. Wigton, Eng., Dec. 8, 1864; s. William and Fanny (Perry) M.; educ. at Rugby. **DEGREES: M.A. (Oxford) 1st class classical moderations, 1st class finals**; Hon. LL.D. (Athens); m. Ada Mary Wright, 1895. AUTHOR: The Balkans, 1896 (3rd edit. 1922); Travels and Politics in the Near East, 1898; Greek Life in Town and Country, 1905; The Latins in the Levant, 1908; The Latin Orient, 1920; Essays on the Latin Orient, 1922; A History of the Greek People, 1922; The Turkish Restoration in Greece, 1922; Trebizond: The Last Greek Empire, 1926; Greece (The Modern World Series), 1928; The Ottoman Empire and Its Successors (3rd edit.), 1927; The Early Years of Modern Athens, 1926; The English in Athens before 1821, 1926; the chapters on the Balkans in the last volume of The Cambridge Modern History, and on the Balkans and medieval Greece in the Cambridge Medieval History, Vol. IV, 1911-23; The Historical sections of The Peace Handbooks (used at the Paris Conference) on Greece, Macedonia, Serbia; numerous articles on Greece in present and last editions of Ency. Britannica, 1926-29. Contributor to Foreign Affairs; Quarterly, Historical, Contemporary Reviews; History, Jnl. of Hellenic Studies, Byzantinische Zeitschrift, Byzantinisch. Nevgriechische Jahrbücher, Morning Post, Cambridge Historical Jnl.; Annual of the British School at Athens; Jnl. of Modern History (Chicago), and others. General character of writing: history and politics of the Near East, especially medieval and modern Greece. An honorary student of the British Archaeol. Sch. at Athens; Hon. mem. various Greek historical societies, and of the Academia de buenas letras of Madrid; Fellow of Royal Historical Soc. Relig. denom., Protestant. CLUBS: Athenian. HOME: British Archaeological School, Athens, Greece.

MILLER, William Christopher. *b*: Nyasaland, Bri East Africa. *e*: Colchester Roy Gr Sch, Royal (Dick) Vet Coll Edin, Univ of Edin. *m*: Margaret Alice Munro. *s*: 2. Dir Equine Research Station Vet Education Trust, Held Posts in Royal (Dick) Vet Coll, Animal Breeding Research Inst Edin, Roy Vet Coll Lond. *Publ*: Black's Veterinary Dictionary; Practical Animal Husbandry; Parasites of British Sheep; Animal Husbandry & Veterinary Services—Trinidad & Tobago & British Guiana; Animal Health & Husbandry in the Gold Coast. *Ctr*: Various scientific journals. *s.s*: Animal Husbandry & Veterinary Science. *Rec*: Shooting, fishing. *a*: Lanwades Park, Moulton, Newmarket, Suffolk. *T*: Kentford 215.

MILLER, William John. B.S., Sc.D., Ph.D. *b*: Red Bluff, California 1880. *e*: Coll of the Pacific, Stanford Univ, Johns Hopkins Univ. *m*: Pearl Breniman. *s*: 1. Prof of Geology Univ of Calif 1924—. *Publ*: The Geological History of New York State; The Story of Our Earth; Elements of Geology; Cystalline Rocks of Southern California; etc. *Ctr*: Many geol & scientific publs. *s.s*: Geology, esp Research Papers on Igneous & Metamorphic Rocks, Coll Text Books, Popular Books. *Rec*: Travel. *a*: 691 Loring Ave, Los Angeles, California, U.S.A. *T*: Arizona 33621.

MILLERAND, ALEXANDRE: advocate at the court of Paris; b. Paris, France, Feb. 10, 1879; educ Lycées Michelet and Henri IV, School of Law, Paris. DEGREE: Licencié en droit. AUTHOR: Le Socialisme reformiste, 1903; Travail et travailleurs, 1908; Politique de réalisations, 1911; Pour la défense nationale, 1913; La Guerre liberatrice, 1918; Choix de plaidoyers, 1921; Le retour de l'Alsace-Lorraine a la France, 1923. General character of writing: political. Minister of Commerce from 1899-1902; of Public Works, from 1909-1910; of War, from 1912-1913, and in August, 1916; of Foreign Affairs, from January to September, 1920, being at the same time President of the Council. Was President of France from 1920 to 1924. Was Commissioner General of the Republic to Strasbourg in 1919 and 1920. Deputy of Paris from 1889-1920. CLUBS: L'Institut Français (Academie des Sciences morales et politiques). Religion, Catholic. OFFICE: 2 Avenue de Villars, Paris VII, Paris. HOME: 14 Avenue des Champs Elysees, Paris VIII, France.

MILLETT, Andrew George, A.L.C.M. *b*: Ballarat, Victoria 1892. *e*: Mt Pleasant & Alfred Cresc State Scs (N. Fitzroy Melbourne). *m*: Janet E. Burns. Journalist, Publicist, Lecturer. *n.a*: Ex Ed Gippsland Mercury, Ed Horsham Times Victoria. Ex Pres Horsham Mechanics Inst & Free Lib, Ex Sec Australian Literature Society, Ex Publicity Officer Australian Inst of Arts & Lit. *c.t*: Princ Aust n/ps. *s.s*: Advertising. Lecturer on Aust Lit & its authors. Winner of Gold Medal Victorian Government for Essay on Aust Lit in 20th Cent. *Rec*: Photog, swimming, music. *a*: Horsham, Victoria, Aust.

MILLETT, NIGEL STANSBURY Comte de Clerval, de Surcey-Beaupre: see Oke, Richard.

MILLIGAN, Cecil Davis. *b*: Londonderry 1888. *e*: Private. *m*: (1) Rebecca Walker (dec'd), (2) Kathleen Hamilton Johnston. *s*: 4. *d*: 2. Ed Londonderry Sentinel. *n.a*: Rep Derry Standard 1905—11, Rep Belfast Telegraph '11—13, Sen Rep Londonderry Sentinel '13—19, Chief Rep Londonderry Sentinel '19—32, Ed since '32, Man Ed since '44. *Publ*: The Walker Club Centenary; The Relief of Derry; The Murray Club Centenary. *Ctr*: Lond, Manch & Irish daily newspapers. *s.s*: Irish Politics & History, Football, Cricket, Sport. *Rec*: Studying ancient Ulster hist. *a*: 25 Fairman Place, Londonderry, Nth Ireland. *T*: 2418 & 2678.

MILLIGAN, Ernest Henry Marcus. *b*: Belfast 1878. *e*: Meth Coll & Campbell Coll Belfast, Q.U.B. & T.C.D. *m*: Sarah McMullan. *d*: 3. Part-time M.O. Min of Health, Fell Soc of M.O.H.'s, Mem B.M.A. *Publ*:

Up-Bye Ballads (Will Carew) ; The Ballad Singer (play) ; The Physical & Nutritional Condition of Children in War Time. *Ctr* : Practitioner, Trans Ulster Med Soc, B.M.J. *s.s* : Dialect, Poetry. *Rec* : Yachting. *a* : Dinting Lodge, Glossop, Derbys. *T* : 324.

MILLIGAN, J. Lewis. *b* : Liverpool, England 1876. *e* : St John's Tue Brook, Holy Trinity Anfield Anglican. *m* : Margaret Elizabeth Quirk (dec'd). *s* : 2. *d* : 2. Journalist. *n.a* : Mail & Empire 1923, Dir of Publicity Ontario Dept of Mines '27, Stratford Beacon-Herald '35. *Publ* : Songs in Time's Despite ; The Beckoning Skyline ; Judas Iscariot (play) ; They Shall Return ; Siluria. *Ctr* : Liverpool Courier, Lond Dly Chron, Weekly Graphic, British Weekly, Nineteenth Century & After, Saturday Night, Christian Guardian, Canadian Mag, Lit Digest, Churchman, etc. *Rec* : Fishing, walking. *c* : Arts & Letters, Writers (Toronto). *a* : 1 Four Oaks Gate, Toronto 6, Canada, & 600 Bay St, Toronto, Canada. *T* : Waverly 8247.

MILLIGAN, Capt. Leo A. *b* : Co Sligo, Ireland. *e* : Priv & Avoca Sch Blackrock Dublin. Married. *s* : 2. Journalist, Mem Inst of Journ. *n.a* : Assoc Press of Gt Britain 1933—48. *Ctr* : Country Life, Riding, Geo Newnes' Publs, Field Press, The Rangoon Times, Iliffe Press, Everybody's. *s.s* : Riding, pistol shooting. *Rec* : Horse-riding & horse training, shooting. *w.s* : 1914—18 & '40—45. *T* : Central 1515.

MILLIGAN, WILLIAM: aurist and laryngologist; b. Aberdeen, Scotland, Aug., 1864; s. William and Mary Ann (Moir) M.; educ. Gymnasium (Old Aberdeen); Univ. of Aberdeen; Univ. of Vienna. DEGREES: M.B., M.Sc., M.D.; m. Bertha Warden Anderson, 1890. AUTHOR: Diseases of the Ear, 1911; Diseases of the Ear (arr. for students), 1914; Tubercular Disease of Mucous Membrane of Middle Ear, 1895; Development of Auditory Nerve in Vertebrates (J. Anat. and Physiol., Vol. 44). Contributor to Lancet, British Medical Jnl.; Jnl. of Laryngology; Practitioner; Acta Laryngologica. General character of writing: medical and scientific. Consulting Aurist and Laryngologist, Royal Infirmary, Manchester, Eng. Relig. denom., Church of England. CLUBS: Athenaeum (London); Reform (Manchester). OFFICE: 12 St. John St. HOME: Westbourne, Manchester, Eng.

MILLIGAN, William Liddell, M.D., B.Sc., Ch.B., L.R.C.P., L.R.C.S., L.R.F.P.S. *b* : Old Kilpatrick 1908. *e* : Clydebank Hgh Sch & Glasgow Univ. *m* : Elsie Gwendoline Higgs. *s* : 1. *d* : 1. Dep Dir Portsmouth Mental Health Service, Cons in Psychological Medicine to Roy P'mouth Hosp. *Publ* : The Treatment of the Depressive Psychoses ; Report of the Portsmouth Mental Health Service 1940—46. *Ctr* : Lancet, B.M.J., etc. *s.s* : Physical Therapy in Psychiatry. *Rec* : Music, sailing, walking. *w.s* : R.A.F. 1941—43. *a* : St James Hospital, Milton, Portsmouth, Hants & Belmont 18 Underwood Rd, Rutherglen, Glasgow. *T* : Portsmouth 32208 & Rutherglen 2166.

MILLIGAN, Wyndham Anstruther, M.A., M.D., C.M., F.R.C.S. *Publ* : Chronic Granular Nephritis in Child ; Pyelonephritis of Pregnancy ; Diagnosis of Early Extra-Uterine Gestation ; Crusade Against Cancer of Uterus. *a* : 9 Nth Audley St, London, W.1. *T* : Mayfair 1908.

MILLIKAN, Robert Andrews, A.B., Ph.D. *b* : Morrison, Illinois 1868. *e* : Maquoketa Hgh Sch Iowa, Oberlin Coll, Univs of Columbia, Berlin & Gottingen. *m* : Greta Irvin Blanchard. *s* : 3. Physics & Univ Administrator. *Publ* : Electrons (+ & −), Protons, Photons, Neutrons, Mesotrans & Cosmic Rays ; Cosmic Rays ; Evolution in Science & Religion ; Time, Matter & Values ; New Elementary Physics (collab) ; Mechanics, Molecular Physics, Heat & Sound (collab) ; Electricity, Sound & Light (collab) ; A First Course in Physics for Colleges (collab). *Ctr* : Physical Rev, Proc Nat Acad of Sciences, Science, Nature, Atlantic Monthly, etc. *s.s* : Physics & University Administration. *a* : 1640 Oak Grove Ave, San Marino, California, U.S.A. *T* : Sycamore 3-2706.

MILLIN, Sarah Gertrude. *m* : Mr Justice Philip Millin. Author. *Publ* : Dark River ; Middleclass ; Adam's Rest ; The Jordans ; God's Stepchildren ; Mary Glenn ; An Artist in the Family ; The Coming of the Lord ; The Fiddler ; The Sons of Mrs Aab ; What Hath A Man ; The Herr Witchdoctor ; The South Africans ; South Africa ; Rhodes (biog) ; Smuts (biog) ; The Night is Long (autobiog) ; War Diary ; World Blackout ; The Reeling Earth ; The Pit of the Abyss ; The Sound of the Trumpet ; Fire Out of Heaven ; The Seven Trumpets ; (Play) No Longer Mourn ; (Film) Rhodes of Africa. *a* : 34 Pallinghurst Rd, Westcliffe, Johannesburg, South Africa.

MILLINGTON, Edwin Charles, M.Sc., Ph.D. *b* : London 1903. *e* : Univ Coll Lond. Inspector (Further Educ) L.C.C. *Publ* : Seamen in the Making (History & Survey of Nautical Training) ; Science for Sailors. *Ctr* : Nautical Mag, Lychnos, Annals of Science. *s.s* : Nautical Educ, Maritime Hist & Science. *a* : 10 Manor Rd, Ruislip, Middlesex.

MILLIOT, LOUIS: professor in the School of Law; b. Bugeaud (Constantine), April 13, 1885; educ. Faculté de Droit d'Algiers and Ecole Coloniale de Paris. DEGREE: Agrégé des Facultés de Droit; m. Germaine Camaret, April 16, 1914. AUTHOR: La Femme Musulmane au Maghreb (Maroc, Algerie, Tunesie), 1910; L'Association Agricole chez les Musulmans du Maghreb, 1911; Démembrements du Habous (menfa'a, Zini, g'za, gudsa, istiglirag), 1918; Recueil de Jurisprudence Cherifienne, 1919-1924; Terres Collectives, études de Legislation Marocaine, 1923. Contributor to Revue Algérienne, Tunisienne et Marocain de Legislation et de Jurisprudence, Année politique français et étrangère, Hesperis, Bulletin du Comité de l'Afrique Française. General character of writing: law, language, and sociology. Secretary general of la Revue Algérienne, Tunisienne et Marocaine de Législation et de Jurisprudence. Specialist in questions of Mussulman law and customs of Northern Africa. CLUBS: Racing Universitaire d'Alger (President) and Automobile Club d'Alger. ADDRESS: 7 rue Zola, Algiers, Algeria, No. Africa.

MILLIS, Walter, A.B. *b* : Atlanta, Georgia, U.S.A. 1899. *e* : Yale Univ. *m* : (1) Norah K. Thompson, (2) Eugenia Sheppard. *s* : 1. *d* : 1. Author & Newspaperman. *n.a* : Ed & Staff Writer New York Herald-Tribune 1924—. *Publ* : The Martial Spirit ; Road to War ; This is Pearl ; Why Europe Fights ; The Last Phase. *Ctr* : Yale Review, Atlantic Monthly, New Republic, Nation, Virginia Quarterly Review, etc. *s.s* : Recent Hist, Current Comment on Internat & Political Affairs. *Rec* : Sailing. *c* : Century (N.Y.). *a* : 1 West 72nd St, New York 23, N.Y., U.S.A.

MILLMAN, F. W. *a* : Morning Advertiser, 18 St Andrew St.

MILLNER, Joy Vida. *b* : Tettenhall 1915. *e* : Wolverhampton H.S. Journalist. *n.a* : News Staff Wolverhampton Express & Star '33—, Women's Sports Corr '34—. Ed mag of Wolverhampton H.S. '31—32. *s.s* : Studied in France '32-33. Women's Sports. *Rec* : Hockey, mountaineering, music. *c* : N.U.J., Tettenhall Ladies' Hockey. *a* : Home Lea, Tettenhall, Staffs. *t* : 51562.

MILLS, Arthur. *b* : Bude 1887. *e* : Wellington & Sandhurst. Author & Journalist. *n.a* : Rep Dly Mail 1920 & Sunday Dispatch '21—22. *Publ* : From Piccadilly to Devil's Island ; The Blue Spider ; Don't Touch the Body ; Black Royalty ; Live Bait ; etc. *Ctr* : Dly Mail, Dly Telegraph, Dly Express, etc. *s.s* : Little-Known Countries. *Rec* : Golf, gardening. *a* : Holmwood Farm, Hordle, Hants. *T* : New Milton 443.

MILLS, CAPT. ARTHUR HOBART: in late Duke of Cornwall's Light Infantry; m. Dorothy Mills, 1916. AUTHOR: The Danger Game. ADDRESS: 91-A Ebury St., S. W. 1, London, Eng.

MILLS, Clarence Alonzo, A.B., Ph.D., M.D. *b*: Miami, Indiana 1891. *e*: Univs of South Dakota & Cincinnati. *m*: Edith Clarissa Parrett. *s*: 2. *d*: 1. Physician & Teacher, Prof of Experimental Medicine Univ of Cincinnati 1930—. *Publ*: Living with the Weather; Medical Climatology; Climate Makes the Man. *Ctr*: Harper's Mag, Amer Mercury, Woman, Amer Weekly, etc. *s.s*: Blood Clotting & the Control of Hæmorrhage, Climatic & Weather Influences in Health & Disease. *a*: Cincinnati General Hospital, Cincinnati 29, Ohio, U.S.A. *T*: University 3100.

MILLS, David Roy. *b*: Northwich 1915. *e*: Gr Sch. *m*: *d*: 2. Journalist, Mem N.U.J. *n.a*: Ed The Services & Territorial Mag. *Publ*: Run Your Own Show. *Ctr*: Service & specialised journals. *s.s*: Service Matters, Films Revue Production. *Rec*: Photography. *c*: Regent Advertising. *a*: 26 Coleherne Rd, London, S.W.10.

MILLS, Dorothy Anna Hayward, F.R.S.A. *b*: Frocester, Gloucs. *e*: Cheltenham Ladies' Coll Polytechnic, St John's Wood Art Sch. *Publ*: Bruges, Ghent, Ypres (with 27 wood engravings); The Log-Book of a Dream-Ship (with Illustrations & Poems); Tewkesbury (with 14 wood engravings); also illustrated Ten Polish Folk-Tales & Happy Endings. *Ctr*: Gloucs Echo, Weekly Rev. *s.s*: Poetry, Historical Stories & Articles, Black & White Illustrations & Colour. *a*: Glenview, Harp Hill, Battledown, Cheltenham.

MILLS, Lady Dorothy Rachel Melissa, F.R.G.S. *b*: Lond. Author, Explorer, Mem Geog Soc of Lisbon. *Publ*: (Travel) The Road to Timbuktu; Beyond the Bosphorus; A Different Drummer; The Country of the Orinoco; (Novels) The Dark Gods; Jungle; etc. *s.s*: Anthropology, Primitive Theo, etc. *Rec*: Travel, dancing. *c*: Roy Geog Soc, Ladies Emp.

MILLS, Frederick Cecil, M.A., LL.D., B.L., Ph.D. *b*: Santa Rosa, California 1892. *e*: Univs of California & Columbia, Lond Sch of Econs. *m*: Dorothy Katherine Clarke. *s*: 2. *d*: 1. Economist. *Publ*: The Behaviour of Prices; Economic Tendencies in the United States; Prices in Recession & Recovery; Statistical Methods; Price Quantity Interactions in Business Cycles; Contemporary Theories of Unemployment. *Ctr*: American Econ Review, etc. *s.s*: Prices, Business Cycles, Production & Productivity, Statistical Methods. *c*: Century (N.Y.), Men's Faculty (N.Y.). *w.s*: Lieut A.E.F. 1917—18. *a*: 460 Riverside Drive, New York 27, N.Y., U.S.A. *T*: CA8-3469.

MILLS, G. T. *a*: Southfield, Kenilworth.

MILLS, George Percival, M.B., B.S., L.R.C.P., F.R.C.S. Cons Surgeon. *Publ*: Surgery for Dental Students; Practical Hints on Minor Operations; etc. *c.t*: B.M.J., Lancet, etc. *a*: 20 Westfield Rd, Edgbaston, Birm.

MILLS, Henry Joseph, M.A.(Oxon), B.Sc.(Econ) (Lond), A.R.Hist.S. *b*: Norton-on-Tees, Co Durham 1906. *e*: Coatham Sch Yorks, St Edmund Hall Oxf, Lond Univ. *m*: Aileen Rowe. *s*: 2. *d*: 1. Head Master Southern Gr Sch for Boys Southsea Hants, Headmaster Okehampton Gr Sch 1941—47, Broadcasts for Australian Broadcasting Commission '33—35. *n.a*: Ed The Australian Teacher 1933—35. *Ctr*: The English Historical Review, Times Educational Supp. *s.s*: Hist & Economics, Education. *Rec*: Cricket, rugger, sailing, fishing, historical research. *a*: 144 Essex Rd, Southsea, Hants.

MILLS, James Philip, C.S.I., C.I.E. *b*: Norbury Moor, Cheshire 1890. *e*: Winchester & Corpus Christi Coll Oxf. *m*: Pamela Moira Vesey-Fitzgerald. *d*: 2. I.C.S. Hon Dir of Ethnography to the Govt of Assam. *Publ*: The Ao Nagas; The Lhota Nagas; The Rengma Nagas. *Ctr*: Man, Man India, etc. *s.s*: Anthropology. *Rec*: Fishing, shooting. *a*: c/o Lloyds Bank Ltd, 101/1 Clive St, Calcutta, India.

MILLS, Rev. James Webb, M.A. *b*: Worthing 1881. *e*: Dover Col, Clare Col Cam. Priest—formerly Solicitor. *Publ*: The Labyrinth, & other poems. *c*: Roy Empire Soc. *a*: Cardington Lodge, 65 Finchley Rd, N.W.8. *t*: Primrose 4260.

MILLS, John, M.D., Ch.B., M.R.C.S., L.R.C.P., D.P.H., F.R.I.P.H. *b*: Birkenhead 1915. *e*: Jesuit Coll Lancs, Univ of Liverpool, L'pool Sch of Art, Gray's Inn of Court Lond, Law Sch Guildford. *m*: Sheila Linphord-Graham. *d*: 2. *Publ*: Smallpox, A Clinical Survey; Forensic Medicine in a Nutshell. *Ctr*: L'pool Dly Post, L'pool Echo, Ev News, etc. *s.s*: Short Stories, Humour, Medico-Legal Subjects, Preventive Medicine, Joke Drawings. *Rec*: Golf, fishing, photography, music. *c*: I. of W. Sailing (Cowes), I. of W. Arts. *a*: Shaet Corner Cottage, Chillerton, Isle of Wight. *T*: Chillerton 14.

MILLS, John Edmund. *b*: Fremantle, W. Aus 1882. *e*: Plymouth Hr Gr Sc. *Publ*: From the Back Benches; From Czardom to Genoa. *c.t*: Daily Mail, Reynolds's News, etc. Visited Germany, Italy, Poland, Russia, Austria, Egypt, France & I.F.S. on Publ Del's. M.P. Dartford 3 times; def. *Rec*: Cricket, swimming. *c*: Engineers, Dartford Labour. *a*: 4 Lassa Rd, Eltham.

MILLS, J(OHN) SAXON: journalist, barrister, author; b. Ashton-under-lyne, Eng., s. James and Martha (Saxon) M.; educ. Manchester Grammar Sch.; The Owens Coll. (Manchester); St. John's Coll. (Cambridge); the Inner Temple; DEGREES: B.A. (Manchester); M.A. (Cambridge); barrister-at-law (Inner Temple); m. Grace Keeling, 1901. AUTHOR: Fascials Versiculorum (poetry); Landmarks of British Fiscal History, 1907; England's Foundation: Agriculture and the State, 1911; The Panama Canal, 1913; The Future of the Empire, 1918; The Question of Thrace (with M. G. Chrussachi), 1920; Life of Sir Edward Cook, 1921; The Genoa Conference, 1922; Life and Letters of Sir Edward Herkomer, 1923; Press and Communications of the Empire, 1924; David Lloyd George, War Minister, 1924; A Chapter on South-west Africa in The Empire at War, 1924. Contributor to Nineteenth Century, Contemporary Review, Fortnightly Review, Outlook and many other magazines and leading British newspapers. General character of writing: political, literary, social, musical. One time editor of Cape Times, S. Africa. Served on Council of Royal Empire Soc., 12 yrs.; closely associated with all Empire movements; had much to do with introduction of the sugar beet culture into England. Relig. denom., Congregationalist. CLUBS: Royal Empire Society (London). OFFICE: Royal Empire Society, London. HOME: Spring Wood, Oxkey, Watford, Hertsfordshire, Eng.

MILLS, M. Edward. *b*: Beckenham 1901. *e*: Dower Hse Sc Wallington. *m*: Olive Kathleen Walsh. *s*: 1. Journalist. *n.a*: Ed Pupil Islington Chron '19, Reporter, Sub-Ed & Ed S. C. Phillips & Co (Publs of The Paper Maker, etc) '20—27, Ed The Phono Record '27—28, Ed The Talking Machine & Wireless Trade News, & The Gramophone & Radio News '29—31, Working partner & Rep-Sub World News Ag, Middx Chron '32—33. Publ Cmt Staines Urban Dis Unemployment Cmt. *c.t*: Various trade, tech & nat press. *s.s*: Music, film & dramatic criticism, gramophone & radio notes. War Service. *Rec*: Tennis, boating, riding, travel. *c*: Musicians. *a*: Maybury, Wheatsheaf Lane, Staines, Middx.

MILLS, Percy George. *b*: Cheltenham 1912. *e*: Cheltenham Tech Coll. *m*: Winifred Mary Pailing. *d*: 1. Journalist. *n.a*: Glos Echo. *s.s*: Motoring, Aviation. *Rec*: Cricket, yachting, flying. *a*: The Holt, Berkeley St, Cheltenham.

MILLS, Walter Owen. *b*: Cheltenham. *e*: Cheltenham Sc. *n.a*: Ed Western Evening Herald, Plymouth 1921—. Chm Devon & Cornwall Dis N/p Press Fund. *a*: 3 Hill Crest, Plymouth *t*: 185.

MILLS, William James. *n.a:* Cycling corr News-Chron, Out o'Doors. Eng rep Irish Cyclist. *s.s:* Cycle racing. Organiser World's Cycling Champ Trial, Brooklands, '33 & '34. Track Mang W. G. Spencer's Six Days' Bicycle Races (Eng). *a:* Middlerow Pl, High Holborn, W.C.1. *t:* Holborn 3989.

MILLS YOUNG, F. E. *b:* Twickenham. *e:* Eng, Paris & S. Africa. Author. *Publ:* A Mistaken Marriage; Sam's Kid; Grit Lawless; The Purple Mists; The Art of Michael Haslett; The White Locust; The Laws of Chance; The Shadow of the Past; The Immovable Flame; The Great Unrest; Wife of Hess; The Almonds of Life; The Unlicensed Prospector; The Rich Cargo; The Romantic Tragedy; Missing; Sunshine Lane; In Command; etc. *Rec:* Gardening, croquet, billiards. *a:* Broadlands, Torquay, Devon. *t:* 7889.

MILLWARD, C. C. Public Information Officer No 1 (Welsh) Wing Air Training Corps. *n.a:* Chief Rep Western Mail & Echo. *a:* Briar Lyn, Lake Rd Nth, Roath Park, Cardiff.

MILLWARD, Edgar. *b:* Barrow-in-Furness, 1905. *e:* Barrow-in-Furness Grammar Sc. *m:* Elsie Sumpter. Reporter & journalist. *n.a:* Hull Daily Mail, Hull & Lincolnshire Times. *c.t:* Nottingham Jnl, Lincolnshire Echo, Grimsby Telegraph. *s.s:* Motoring, agriculture. *Rec:* Tennis, rugby football. *a:* Bigby Rd, Brigg, Lincs. *t:* 62.

MILMAN, Marjorie A. *e:* Priv Schs. *n.a:* Social Corres Coty Pioneer India 1903, Madras Mail '06, Bombay Gazette '07. *Ctr:* Broad Views, Queen, Light, The Two Worlds, Internat Psychic Gazette, Christian Spiritualist. *s.s:* Psychic, Religions. *a:* Lonach, Bushmead Ave, Bedford.

MILNE, Alan Alexander. *b:* 1882. *e:* Westminster & Trin Coll Camb. Journalist, Playwright, Author. *n.a:* Punch (9 y). *Publ:* The Holiday Round; Once a Week; The Sunny Side; When We Were Very Young; Winnie the Pooh; Peace with Honour; Chloe Marr; (Plays) Mr Pim Passes By; The Truth About Blayds; The Dover Road; To Have the Honour; Michael & Mary; The Ivory Door; etc. *a:* Cotchford Farm, Hartfield, Sussex. *T:* Hartfield 17.

MILNE, Alexander Taylor. M.A., F.R.Hist.S. *b:* Finchley 1906. *e:* Christ's Coll Finchley, Univ Coll Lond. Secretary & Librarian Inst of Hist Research, Univ of Lond Extension Lecturer History & Current Affairs. *Publ:* Compiler of Writings on British History, an annual bibliography; Catalogue of Bentham Manuscripts; History of Broadwindsor. *Ctr:* Hist Journs, Internat Affair, Times Litt Supp, etc. *s.s:* History, Political Thought. *Rec:* Lawn tennis, music. *c:* Roy Empire Soc. *w.s:* 1939—45 Maritime Artillery, Army Bureau of Soc. *w.s:* 1939—45 Maritime Artillery, A.B.C.A. (Sub-Ed), Research Dept Foreign Office (Head of U.S.A. Section). *a:* 14 Allison Grove, Dulwich Common, London, S.E.21. *T:* Gipsy Hill 3959.

MILNE, Charles Ewart. *b:* Dublin 1903. *e:* Christchurch Cathedral Gr Sch Dublin. Poet & Author. *Publ:* (Poems) Jubilo; Listen Mangan; Letter From Ireland; Forty North Fifty West. *Ctr:* Irish Times, New Statesman & Nation, Life & Letters To-day, Dublin Mag, Modern Reading, Poetry (Chicago), Irish Writing, Tribune, New English Weekly. *s.s:* The State of Man. *c:* P.E.N. *a:* Creeksea Hall, Burnham-on-Crouch, Essex. *T:* 2227.

MILNE, David, C.I.E., B.Sc. *b:* 1876. *e:* Aberdeen Univ. *m:* Joan Annie Cargill. Late I.A.S. *Publ:* Handbook of Field & Garden Crops of the Punjab; The Date Palm & its Cultivation in the Punjab; & many Govt Reports, Pamphlets, etc. *a:* 6 Urie Crescent, Stonehaven, Scotland.

MILNE, Edward Arthur, M.B.E., M.A., D.Sc.(Oxon), Hon.D.Sc(Amersterdam), F.R.S. *b:* Hull 1896. *e:* Elem Schs, Hymers Coll Hull, T.C. Camb. *m:* (1) Margaret Scott Campbell, (2) Beatrice Brevoort Renwick. *s:* 1. *d:* 3. Professor of Maths Oxf Univ, Pres Lond Maths Soc 1937—39, Pres R.A.S. '43—45. *Publ:* Relativity, Gravitation & World Structure. *Ctr:* Trans Roy Soc, Procs Roy Soc, Philos Mag, Nature, etc. *s.s:* Astrophysics, Cosmology. *w.s:* Lieut R.N.V.R. 1916—18. *a:* 19 Northmoor Road, Oxford & Wadham College, Oxford. *T:* 58945.

MILNE, James. *b:* Strathdon. *e:* Strathdon & Aboyne Schs, Edin Univ. Journalist & Author. *n.a:* Aberdeen Free Press, Scottish Leader (Edin), Cent News (Lond), Dly Chron (Lond), Lit-Ed Dly Chron 1903—18, Founder & Ed Book Monthly, The Graphic. *Publ:* A Window in Fleet Street; Travels in Hope; The Road to Kashmir; The Black Colonel; The Epistles of Atkins; Memoirs of a Bookman; Over the Hills & Far Away; Printer's Devil Or, How Books Happen; etc. *Ctr:* Dly Telegraph, Scotsman, etc. *s.s:* Lit Gossip, Book Reviews. *Rec:* Fishing. *a:* Caledonian Club, Halkin St, S.W.

MILNE, James Mathewson, M.A., D.Litt. *b:* Aberdeen 1883. *e:* Aberdeen Gr Sch, Aberdeen & Rennes Univs. *m:* Jane Murray Crockart. Schoolmaster & Writer. *Publ:* Intermediate Latin Tests; Junior Latin Unseens; Easy Latin Readings; Junior Latin Composition; Intermediate French Tests; Advanced French Tests; La Pomme d'Or; etc. *s.s:* French, Latin. *Rec:* Golf, fishing, motoring. *a:* Old Manse, Speymouth, Fochabers, Morayshire.

MILNE, Rev. James Napier. *b:* Peterhead 1874. *e:* Peterhead Acad, Handsworth Col Birm. *m:* Olive E. Barrow-Clough. *s:* 2. *d:* 2. *n.a:* Ed N.Z. Meth Times 1920—23. *Publ:* The Dream That Comes True (Study in the Life Beyond the Horizon); Sandy & Other Sketches; etc. *c.t:* Meth Times, Sunday at Home, etc. *s.s:* Biog. Extensive travel. *Rec:* Walking. *a:* Wesley Manse, 84 Queen's Rd, Reading, Berks. *t:* 3674.

MILNE, Rev. John James, M.A. *b:* Lancaster 1852. *e:* Lancaster G.S. & St John's Col Cam. Married. *d:* 1. Schoolmaster. *Publ:* Weekly Problem Papers; Geometrical Conics; Treatise on Cross Ratio (Anharmonic); etc. *c.t:* Mathematical Gazette. *s.s:* Geometrical conics. Prince Seafield Park Engineering Col '96-1901 (ret). *a:* Glengarry, Lee-on-the-Solent, Hants. *t:* 79222.

MILNE, Joseph Grafton, M.A., D.Litt. *e:* Manchester, Oxford, Athens. Deputy Keeper of Coins, Oxf Univ. *Publ:* History of Egypt under the Romans; Catalogue of Greek Inscriptions, Cairo Museum; Catalogue of Alexandrian Coins, Oxford; Greek & Roman Coins & the Study of History; Greek Coinage. *Ctr:* Various periodicals & encys. *s.s:* Graeco-Roman History. *a:* 23 Belsyre Ct, Oxford. *T:* 4517.

MILNE, Mary Lewis, Hon.M.A., Hon.F.R.A.I. *e:* Edinburgh, Rome, Florence. Author, Mem Roy Asiatic Soc. *Publ:* Dictionary of Palaung Lang; Grammar of Palaung Lang; The Home of an Eastern Clan; Shans at Home. *s.s:* Painting. *Rec:* Embroidery. *a:* Lloyds Bank, 39 Old Bond St, London, W.1.

MILNE, WILLIAM PROCTOR: professor of Mathematics; b. Aberdeenshire, Scotland, May 22, 1881; s. Andrew and Jessie (Proctor) M.; educ. Longside Sch.; Peterhead Acad., Aberdeen Grammar Sch. DEGREES: M.A., D.Sc. (Aberdeen); M.A. (Cambridge); m. Mary Deas Burnett, Aug. 13, 1910. AUTHOR: Homogeneous Coordinates, 1910; Projective Geometry,

1911; Higher Algebra, 1913; First Course in the Calculus (with G. J. B. Westcott), 1920. Editor of Bell's Mathematical Series for Colleges and Schools. General character of writing: scientific. Contributor to the Proceedings of the London Mathematical Soc. of papers on mathematical research and synthetic Geometry. Relig. denom., Scotch Episcopalian. OFFCE: University of Leeds, Eng. HOME: 16 Monkbridge Road, Headingly, Leeds, Eng.

MILNE-BAILEY, W. *Publ*: Trade Union Documents (1929); Trade Unions and the State ('34). *s.s*: Politics & social science. Head of Research Dept T.U.C. *a*: 8 Bigwood Ct, N.W.11.

MILNE-THOMSON, Louis Melville, M.A., F.R.A.S., F.R.S.E. *e*: Clifton Coll, Corpus Christi Camb. Prof of Maths R.N.C. Greenwich. *Publ*: Standard Table of Square Roots; The Calculus of Finite Differences; Theoretical Hydrodynamics; Theoretical Aerodynamics; etc. *Ctr*: Nature, Math Gazette, Proc Roy Soc Edin, Proc Edin Math Soc, Zentralblatt für Mathematik, etc. *s.s*: Maths. *Rec*: Sailing. *c*: Athenæum, Carlton. *a*: Royal Naval College, London, S.E.10. *T*: Greenwich 1630.

MILNER, Ashley. *b*: Manchester 1881. *m*: Lilah Hope. *Publ*: Dawn Breaking Red; And Then Comes Love; That Fool Peter; England's Part in the War (special articles comm by H.M. Min of Inf). *c.t*: The princ mags & n/ps. *Rec*: Golf, travel. *a*: Brighton Pl, Wolverhampton. *t*: Fordhouses 74.

MILNER, Rev. Gamaliel. *b*: Redhill 1880. *e*: Crypt Sc Glos, Pembroke Col Oxf. *m*: Anna Frances Horsley. Vicar of Kirkby, Fleetham. *Publ*: The Problem of Decadence; The Threshold of the Victorian Age. *c.t*: Modern Churchman, etc. *s.s*: History, politics. C.F. 1917-19. *a*: Kirkby Fleetham Vicarage, Northallerton, Yorkshire.

MILNER, Henry Brewer, M.A., D.I.C., F.G.S., F.C.S., M.InstP.T. *b*: Lon 1893. *e*: U.C.S. Lon, Trin Col Cam. *m*: Eleanor Mary Lawrence. *s*: 1. *d*: 1. Cons Geologist & Petroleum Technologist. Dir Geochem Lab's Lon. *Publ*: Methods in Practical Petrology; Sedimentary Petrography; Alluvial Prospecting. *c.t*: Nature, Mining Mag, Geological Mag, Revue de Geologie, etc. *s.s*: Petrol tech, geochem. Lect in Oil Tech, Imp Col of Sci Lon 1919-31. *Rec*: Field geology, golf. *c*: St Stephen's, Westminster. *a*: 92 Victoria St, Westminster, S.W.1. *t*: Victoria 4160.

MILNER, Viscountess. *m*: (1) Lord Edward Cecil, K.C.M.G. (dec'd), *d*: 1. (2) 1st Viscount Milner, K.G. (dec'd). Ed National Review since 1932. *a*: Great Wigsell, Bodiam, Sussex.

MILNER, Rev. Walter Metcalfe Holmes, R.G.S. *b*: Greenock 1859. *e*: Hartford Hse & Marlbro'. *m*: Laura M. J. Bainbridge. *s*: 3. Vicar (ret). *n.a*: The Messenger '86, Covenant People 1904. *Publ*: Israel's Wanderings (1880); Russia Japhet; The Royal House of Britain (copies accepted by King Edward, Queen Alexandra & Queen Mary); Russia in Ezekiel (1933). *c.t*: Brit Israel Herald, Geog Journ. *s.s*: Britain in the Bible. *c*: Roy Geog Soc, Victoria Inst, Nat Geogs Soc of Amer. *a*: The Dene, Marlow, Bucks. *t*: 260.

MILNER-WHITE, Rev. Eric. D.S.O. *b*: Southampton 1884. *e*: Harrow Sch, King's Coll Camb, Cuddesdon Theol Coll. Fell King's Coll Camb, Dean of York 1941. *Publ*: Cambridge Offices & Orisons (with Rev B. T. D. Smith); One God & Father of All (with Rev W. L. Knox); etc. *Ctr*: Theology, Church Quarterly Review, *s.s*: Eccles Art. *c*: M.C.C. *a*: The Deanery, York. *T*: 3608.

MILNES, Nora, B.Sc. *b*: London. Reader in Social Studies Univ of Edin, & Head of the Dept of Social Study, formerly Lect Social Sciences Dept Lond Sch of Econs. *Publ*: A Study of Industrial Edinburgh; Economics of Wages & Labour; Child Welfare, from the Social Point of View. *Rec*: Music. *c*: Ladies' Caledonian. *a*: 12 Nelson St., Edinburgh.

MILNES, Phyllis Spurling Clare. *e*: Alice Ottley Sch, Worcester. *m*: William Henry Goodenough Milnes. *s*: 1. *d*: 1. *Publ*: Nursery Lessons. *a*: Elizabeth College, Guernsey, C.I. *T*: 183.

MILNES. Sibyl. *b*: Suffolk 1902. Artist. *c.t*: Punch. Exhibitor Royal Academy, Paris Salon. Done work for B.B.C. Children's Hour. *Rec*: Walking, reading. *a*: 7 Gauden Rd, Clapham, S.W.4.

MILNES, Rev. William Henry Goodenough, M.C., M.A. *b*: London 1898. *e*: R.M.C. Sandhurst, Worcester Col, Oxf, Westcott House Camb. *m*: Phyllis Spurling Clare Milnes. *s*: 1. *d*: 1. Clerk in Holy Orders. Headmaster. *Publ*: A Rational History of England. *s.s*: History, Neology, Science. *Rec*: Tennis, rugby football, swimming. *w.s*: R.F.C. & R.A.F. 1916-19. *a*: Elizabeth College, Guernsey, C.I. *T*: 2084.

MILROY, Mary Elizabeth Wallace. *b*: London 1874. *e*: Queen's Col, Lond. Greylady. *Publ*: Guide to Lace-Making; Church Lace; Home Lace making. *c.t*: Harmsworths Encyclopædia, The People's Friend, Needlecraft. *s.s*: Lace making. *a*: Greyladies Col, Coventry.

MILSTED, George. *c*: Winchester & Oxford. *n.a*: Dir Gerald Duckworth & Co Ltd. *a*: 3 Henrietta St, W.C.2, & Ditchling, Sussex. *t*: Temple Bar 1634.

MILTON, Ernest. *m*: Naomi Royde-Smith. Actor. *Publ*: Christopher Marlowe: A Play; To Kiss the Crocodile (novel); Paganini (play " David Wells "). *c*: Savage. *a*: c/o Spotlight Ltd, 42 Cranbourn St, W.C.2.

MILTON, F. V. *b*: Yeovil 1873. *n.a*: Ed Hints for Holidays 1916, Southern Railway Mag '18, etc. *a*: 59 Melrose Av. S.W.19.

MILTON, Harry, B.A. *b*: Leeds 1902. *e*: Leeds Central H.Sc & Leeds Univ. Asst Master. *Publ*: Clarendon French Course. *s.s*: Modern Languages. *c*: Roy Soc of Teachers, Asst Masters' Assoc, Modern Languages Assoc. *a*: 224 Bradford Rd, Riddlesden, Keighley.

MILUM, Rev. John Parton, B.Sc, PhD.(Lon), C.F. *b*: Faversham 1882. *e*: Woodhouse Grove Sc. *m*: Annie E. Wilkins. *s*: 1. *d*: 3. Meth Min. *Publ*: Revolutionary Christianity; Art Thou a King Then?; Evolution & Spirit of Man; Evolution for Christians. *c.t*: Lon Quarterly Review & Contemporary Review. *s.s*: Evolution & anthropology. C.F. (des). *Rec*: Fossil & plant hunting. *a*: St Winifride's, New Rd, Solihull, Birm.

MILWARD, Charles Frederic, F.R.S.A. *b*: N.Y. 1860. *e*: Priv & King's Col Lon. *m*: Emily Constantia Ellis (dec). *s*: 3. *d*: 3. Manufr. Chm Redditch Indicator Coy Ltd past 30 y. *c.t*: Various n/ps & periodicals. Lt-Col of 8th Worcs Regt. V.D.D.L. J.P. County Ald. Chm Worcs C.C. 1930-. *a*: The Leys, Alvechurch, Worcs. *t*: Barnt Green 96.

MIMS, Edwin, M.A., Ph.D. *b*: Richmond, U.S.A. 1872. *e*: Webb Sch, Cornell Univ. Teacher, Lecturer, Author, Head of Dept of English, Vanderbilt Univ 1912—42. *Publ*: Adventurous American; History of Vanderbilt University; Chancellor Kirkland of Vanderbilt; etc. *Ctr*: Atlantic Monthly, Nation, World's Work, Outlook, Sat Review of Lit, N.Y. Sun, Chicago Record-Herald, etc. *s.s*: Nineteenth Century English Lit, American Lit. *Rec*: Tennis, walking. *a*: Vanderbilt Univ, Nashville, Tennessee, U.S.A.

MINCHIN, Harry Christopher. M.A.(Oxon). *b*: Gloucester 1861. *e*: Malvern Col, Wadham Col Oxf. *m*: Olivia Yorke. Journalist, Author, Private Tutor. *Publ*: The Life of Robert Browning (with W. Hall Griffin); The Arcadians; Simples from Sir Thomas Browne's Garden; Oxford (with R. Peel); Talks & Traits; Walter Savage Landor; Last Days, Letters & Conversations; A Little Gallery of English Poets; etc. *s.s*: Lit criticism & biog. *a*: Gorsedenc Cottage, Farnham, Surrey. *t*: Frensham 121.

MINGANA, Alphonse. M.R.A.S., M.A.O.S. Prof & Curator. *Publ*: Narsai Homiliæ et Carmina (2 vols 1904—05); Odes & Psalms of Solomon (2 vols, Co Ed '16—20); Book of Religion & Empire (2 vols '22—23); Catalogue of the Mingana Collection of MSS (Vol I '33); Catalogue of the Arabic MSS in The John Rylands Library ('34); Woodbrooke Studies (Early Christian Documents edited & trans 7 vols '27—34); Encyclopædia of Philosophical Natural Sciences in A.D. 817 ('35); etc. *c.t*: M/C Guardian, etc. *s.s*: Theological & Oriental studies. Made from Near & Middle East, '24—33, collection of Syriac, Arabic & other Oriental MSS (Mingana Collection), Pres M/C Egyptian & Oriental Soc '32. *a*: 168 Middleton Hall Rd, King's Norton, & Selly Oak Colleges Library, Birm. *t*: King's Norton 1732 & Selly Oak 0120.

MINNEY, Rubeigh James. *b*: Calcutta 1895. *e*: King's Coll Lond. *m*: Edith Anne Fox. *s*: 1. *d*: 1. Author, Playwright & Film Producer. *n.a*: Sub-Ed Dly Express 1923, Asst-Ed Sunday News '24—27, Ed Everybody's Weekly '24—35, Sunday Referee '35—39, Ed War Weekly '39—41, Ed Strand Mag '41—42. *Publ*: Clive; India Marches Past; The Journalist; The Road to Delhi; Across India by Air; Night Life of Calcutta; Midst Himalaya Mists; Excursions in Ink; Distant Drums; Hollywood by Starlight; A Woman of France; Nothing to Lose; How Vainly Men . . .; Talking of Films; (Plays) Clive of India; Gentle Cæsar; They Had His Number; etc. Films (produced) The Wicked Lady; Madona of the Seven Moons; A Slave of One's Own; Idol of Paris; etc. *s.s*: India. *c*: Savage. *a*: Lawford Hse, Manningtree, Essex. *T*: Manningtree 35.

MINNIGERODE, Meade. *b*: London, England. *e*: Harrow Sch, Yale Univ. *m*: Mildred R. Bright. Author. *Publ*: Aaron Burr (collab); Jefferson, Friend of France; The Son of Marie Antoinette; Marie Antoinette's Henchman; Black Forest; The Fabulous Forties; The Terror of Peru; Cordelia Chantrell. *Ctr*: Sat Ev Post, Collier's, Ladies' Home Journ. *s.s*: Biog, U.S. & French Hist. *Rec*: Philately. *c*: Rotary (Saybrook), Essex Yacht. *a*: 9 Little Point St, Essex, Connecticut, U.S.A.

MINNIKIN, George Rennison, M.P.S., F.R.S.A. *b*: Keswick 1869. *e*: Keswick & S. Lon Col of Pharmacy. *m*: Fanny Mabel Reade. Chemist. *Publ*: Straight Tips for Photographers; Hints & Wrinkles for Amateur Photographers; Guide to Windermere & Neighbourhood. *s.s*: Photography & photographic papermaking. Mang Dir Kentmere Ltd (23 y, ret 1929). *a*: Birthwaite Lodge, Windermere, Westmorland.

MINNS, Sir Ellis Hovell, Litt.D., F.B.A. *b*: London 1874. *e*: Charterhouse, Pembroke Coll Camb. *m*: Violet Nalder. *s*: 1. *d*: 1. Prof of Archæology (ret'd). *Publ*: Scythians & Greeks; The Russian Icon (Ed); The Art of the Northern Nomads. *Ctr*: Journal of Hellenic Studies, Man, Cambridge Review, Antiquaries Journal, Antiquity. *s.s*: Archæology of Russia & Northern Asia, Russian Icons, Palæography. *Rec*: Languages, architecture & topography. *c*: Athenæum. *a*: 2 Wordsworth Grove, Cambridge. *T*: 4731.

MINORSKY, Vladimir, F.B.A. *b*: Korcheva 1877. *e*: Moscow Univ (Faculty Law), Moscow (Lazarev) School of Oriental Languages, Ecole des Hautes Etudes. *m*: Tatiana Shebounine. *s*: 1. Prof Emeritus Russian Diplomatic Service 1903—19, Russian Commissioner for the delimitation of the Turco-Persian frontier '13—14, travelled extensively in Turkey, Central Asia, Persia, Hon Fellow School of Oriental Studies, membre honoraire de la Société Asiatique. *Publ*: Hudud al-Alam, a Persian Geography of A.D. 982; Marvazi on China, the Turks & India; A Manual of Safavid Administration; 110 Articles in the Encyclopedia of Islam Leyden 1925—37; Notes sur la secte des Ahlé-Haqq; Complete Bibliography published in Calcutta. *Ctr*: Journ Asiatique, Journ of the Roy Asiatique Soc. *s.s*: Oriental Studies (Middle East). *Rec*: Music. *a*: 9 Green St, Cambridge.

MINSHALL, Thomas Herbert, D.S.O., M.I.E.E. A.M.Inst.C.E. *e*: Priv & Lond Univ. Consulting Engineer. *n.a*: Cons Ed Railway Gazette, Shipbuilding Record, Crown Colonist, etc 1904—41. *Publ*: What to do with Germany; Future Germany; On Disarming Germany. *Ctr*: The Times, Internat Affairs, etc. *s.s*: Germany, Public Ownership. *a*: Wooton Hse, Isle of Wight.

MINTER, Davide C. *b*: London 1892. *e*: Eng, France & Germany. *m*: Max Ritson. *s*: 1. *d*: 1. Journalist, Dir Max Ritson Partners, Reg Practitioners in Advertising. *n.a*: Ed Book of the Home, The Practical Infant Teacher, Nature Study for Juniors, The Complete Knitting Book, Modern Needlecraft, Modern Home Crafts, etc. *Publ*: Children's Parties & How to Arrange Them; Home Dyeing & Cleaning; etc. *Ctr*: Women's Journs. *s.s*: Women, Children, Educ. *Rec*: Tennis, golf. *c*: Overseas. *a*: 77 Hillfield Ct, Belsize Ave, London, N.W.3. *T*: Primrose 1215.

MINTER, Robert Wheatley, A.I.E.E., A.I.R.E., F.R.S.A. *b*: Shortlands 1899. Cons Elec Eng & Lect. *n.a*: A.P. 1934, Snr Staff Writer for Elec Ency. *c.t*: Signal, Electrical Review, Mechanical World, Helios etc. *s.s*: Elec eng, photography, radio eng. Polytechnics & L.C.C. Lect. Org Eng & Consultant. Special Lect Chelsea Polytech on The Accumulator. *Rec*: Photography, psychological & econ geog studies of a material nature. *a*: 51 Foxbury Rd, Bromley, Kent.

MINTO, Mary, Countess of. *b*: England. *m*: 4th Earl of Minto, K.G. (dec). *s*: 1 (dec). *d*: 3. Lady-in-Waiting to H.M. Queen Mary. *Publ*: India, Minto & Motley. Crown of India, Kaisir-i-Hind, Lady of Justice, Order of St John of Jerusalem. *a*: 48 Chelsea Park Gdns, S.W.3. *t*: Flaxman 5501.

MINTY, Leonard Le Marchant, Ph.D., B.Sc., B.Comm., LL.B., A.I.B. *b*: Newport 1894. *e*: Lond Univ. Barrister S.E. Cir Surrey Sessions, Central Criminal Court. *Publ*: American Banking Methods; English Banking Methods; The Legal & Ethical Aspects of Medical Quackery; etc. *Ctr*: Journ of the Inst of Bankers, Solicitors' Journ, Law Journal, Canadian Bankers' Mag. *s.s*: Law Relating to Med, Dental & Vet Practice. *Rec*: Tennis. *w.s*: 1915—19 & '40—45. *a*: 2 Garden Ct, Temple, E.C.4. *T*: Central 4675.

MINTY, Tom. *n.a*: Manager & Ed Purley, Caterham & Oxted Gazette, '03—12. Prop Coulsdon & Purley Weekly Record '12—35. *a*: 4 Downs Road, Coulsdon. *t*: Purley 2318.

MIRZA, Youel Benjamin, M.A., PhD. *b*: Persia 1888. *e*: Johns Hopkins Univ. *m*: Althea Brown. Writer. *Publ*: Iran & the Iranians (1914); When I was a Boy in Persia; Myself When Young; Children of the Housetops; Son of the Sword ('34). *c.t*: Review of Reviews, Nation, Asia Mag. *s.s*: Persia. *a*: 1826 Ravenwood Av, Dayton, Ohio, U.S.A.

MISCHKOWSKI, Agnes Agata Maria. *b*: Finten 1907. *e*: Publ Sc Germany. Librarian. *Publ*: Yoga & Soul Culture. *c.t*: Indian n/ps. *s.s*: Comparative religion. *a*: 110 Cleveland Gdns, Hendon Way, N.W.2. *t*: Gladstone 1294.

MISHRA, Baldeo Prasad, M.A., D.Litt., LL.B. *b*: Rajnandgaon State, India 1898. *m*: Rampyari Devi. *s*: 2. *d*: 4. Principal S.B.R. Arts Coll Bilaspur India. *Publ*: Tulasi Darshan; Saket Sant; Jeevan Sangeet; Jeeva Vijnen; Mishra Smriti; Kranti; Koshal Kishore; What a Ruler Should Know. *Ctr*: Various Indian publs. *s.s*: Indian Philosophy, Hindu Religion & Culture, Hindi Literature. *Rec*: Travel. *a*: Principal S.B.R. Arts College, Bilaspur, C.P., India.

MISHRA, Jayakant, M.A. *b*: Darbhanga, India 1922. *m*: Shrimati Aparajita Devi. *s*: 1. Lecturer in English at the Univ of Allahabad 1944—. *Publ*: A Short History of Maithili Literature. *Ctr*: Aryavarth, Indian Nation, Allahabad Univ Mag, Leader (Allahabad), etc. *s.s*: Maithil's History & Mathili Literature. *Rec*: Crosswords, gardening. *a*: c/o Mahamahopadhyaya Dr Umesha Mishra, 1 Allengonj Rd, Allahabad, India.

MISHRA, Vishnu Dutt (" Tarangi "). *b*: Mandla C.P. 1912. *e*: Govt H.S. Sangor, Modern H.S. Jubbulpore, Jagannath H.S. Mandla, Anand Col Dhar & Holkar Col Indore. *m*: Parbati Bai. Journalist. *n.a*: Asst Ed Swadesh Sangor '26-28, Asst Ed Karmavir Khandwa '28-31, Asst Ed Vishwamitra Calcutta '31-32, Asst Ed Vertman Cawnpore '33–. *c.t*: Madhuri Lucknow, Saraswati Allahabad, Vishwamitra Calcutta, Bharat Allahabad, etc. *Rec*: Cinemas. *a*: Daily Vertman, Civil Lines, Cawnpore.

MISLER, L. *b*: Tonnerre 1873. *e*: France & Lon. Journalist & Editor. *n.a*: Ed La Chronique de Londres 24 y. *Publ*: French Military Book. Pres Société Sportive Française de Londres. Mem Foreign Press Assoc in Lon. Chevalier de la Légion d'Honneur. *Rec*: Sports. *a*: 15-16 Lisle St, W.C.2. *t*: Gerrard 6563.

MISSELWITZ, Henry Francis. *b*: Leavensworth, Kansas 1900. *e*: Elem & Hgh Schs, Univ of Missouri & Columbia. *m*: Carolyn Converse. Freelance Writer & Radio Commentator. *n.a*: St Louis Post-Dispatch 1922—23, Japan Advertiser Tokyo '24—27, New York Times China (Shanghai) '27—29, United Press Assocs N.Y. '30—37, Scenario Writer Metro-Goldwyn-Mayer Studios Culver City '37—38. *Publ*: The Melting Pot Boils Over; The Dragon Stirs; Japan Commits Hara-Kiri; Shanghai Romance. *Ctr*: The Quill, Living Age, Kansas City Star, Los Angeles Times, N.Y. Times, etc. *s.s*: World Affairs (Far East). *Rec*: Golf. *c*: Commonwealth, Press, China Tiffin, San Francisco. *a*: The Roost, Phelps Rd, San Carlos, California, U.S.A. *T*: San Carlos 360.

MISTRAL, Gabriela. *b*: Vicuna, Chile 1889. Writer, Consul of Chile. *Publ*: Desolacion; Ternura; Tala; Poems; Anthology; Diktar. *Ctr*: El Mercurio, La Nacion, El Tiempo, El Mundo. *s.s*: Poems. *a*: 729E Anapamu St, Santa Barbara, California, U.S.A. *T*: 4372.

MITCHELL, Charles Ainsworth, D.Sc(Oxon). *b*: Thetford 1869. *e*: K. William's Col I.O.M. & Exeter Col Oxf. *m*: Edith Frances Boyle. Cons in Forensic Chem. *n.a*: Ed Journ of Soc of Publ Analysts 1921–. *Publ*: Documents & Their Scientific Examination; Inks: Their Composition & Examination (3rd edn); Science & the Criminal; The Scientific Detective & Expert Witness (2nd edn). *c.t*: Chambers's Graphic, Strand Mag, etc. *s.s*: Criminology. *Rec*: Photography. *c*: Chem Soc, Inst of Chem. *a*: Tar Corner, Stubbs Wood, Chesham Bois, Bucks. *t*: Victoria 8363 & Amersham 461.

MITCHELL, David Motherwell. M.A. *b*: Airdrie 1901. *e*: Edin Acad, Lincoln Col Oxf. *Publ*: Sir Tristram (play in blank verse); Cri Du Coeur ('32). Asst Master St Andrew's Col Toronto, Canada '24—26. *Rec*: Tennis, play & film going. *c*: Overseas League, Unity Club, Glasgow (Pres). *a*: The Unity Club, 509 Sauchiehall St, Glasgow. *t*: Douglas 112.

MITCHELL, E. A. Dramatic Critic. *a*: Southern Daily Echo, Southampton.

MITCHELL, Frank Wyndham, M.A., B.Sc., Ph.D. *b*: Adelaide, Sth Australia 1906. *e*: St Peter's Coll Adelaide, Univs of Adelaide & Lond. *m*: Elizabeth Oakes Freeth. *s*: 2. Prof of Educ Univ of Otago. *n.a*: Assoc Ed Australian Maths Teacher (Sydney). *Publ*: The Nature of Mathematical Thinking; Student Health; The Values of Boys' Clubs. *Ctr*: Listener (N.Z.), Journ of Health & Physical Educ, Scout Leader (S. Aust), & various newsps. *s.s*: Educ, Physical Educ, Educational Broadcasting, Youth Work. *Rec*: Hiking, tennis, gardening. *c*: Univ. *a*: The University of Otago, Dunedin, New Zealand.

MITCHELL, George J., F.R.S.A., A.R.C.A.(Lon). *t.w*: Arch Design, Painting & Sculpture. *s.s*: Fine & gutter art. *a*: The Close, Norton-Sub, Ham, Som.

MITCHELL, Gladys. *b*: Cowley 1901. *e*: Green Sch Isleworth Middx, Lond Univ, Goldsmith's & Univ Colls. *Publ*: Speedy Death; Mystery of a Butcher's Shop; Longer Bodies; Saltmarsh Murders; Death at the Opera; The Devil at Saxon Wall; Death & the Maiden; Here Comes a Chopper; The Rising of the Moon; etc. *s.s*: Archæology, Architecture, Athletics. *Rec*: Reading, swimming, etc. *c*: Detection, P.E.N. *a*: Swyncombe Ave, Ealing, London, W.5.

MITCHELL, Harold Paton, M.A., F.R.G.S., M.P. *b*: Fife 1901. *e*: Eton, R.M.C. Sandhurst, Univ Col Oxf. *Publ*: Downhill Ski Racing. Elected M.P. for Brentford & Chiswick '31; Appointed Parl Priv Sec to Overseas Trade Min '31; Rep G.B. Ski-ing '29, '31, '33; Pres Scot Ski Club. *Rec*: Ski-ing, climbing. *c*: Carlton, Bath, Alpine. *a*: Tulliallan Castle, Kincardine on Forth & Riverside Hse, Strand on the Green, W.4.

MITCHELL, Henry McCormick. *b*: Castlederg, Co Tyrone 1870. *e*: Castlederg G.S., Meth Col Belfast & Aber Univ. *m*: Ethel Jane Watts. *d*: 1. B.M. & M.S. *c.t*: B.M.J., Med World, etc. *s.s*: Cancer & skin diseases. Hon Dermatologist L'pool Radium Inst & Hosp for Cancer & Skin Diseases. Dermatologist City of L'pool Hosps. *Rec*: Golf. *c*: Birkdale. *a*: 17 Sandingham Rd, Birkdale, Lancs, & 24 Rodney St, L'pool. *t*: Royal 2305 & Birkdale 66695.

MITCHELL, Isabel Mary. *b*: Melbourne, Victoria, Aust 1893. *e*: Priv. Author. *Publ*: A Warning to Wantons; One More Flame; Meat for Mammon; Dark Tapestry; Pendulum Swing; The Wood & the Trees; Servants of the Future; Decline & Fall of a British Matron; Who Pays?; Stupidity's Harvest; Viper's Progress; Simon Learns to Live; Maidens Beware. *c*: Alexandra (Melbourne). *a*: Kalorama, Victoria, Australia. *T*: Kalorama 25.

MITCHELL, John, M.A., F.R.A.S. *b*: Huddersfield 1867. *e*: Christ's Col Cam. *m*: Florence Amy Bromhead (dec). *s*: 1. Director (ret). *Publ*: Pitam of Bankura, or The Merry Leper. *c.t*: Calcutta Statesman, Meth Recorder, Indian Meth Times, etc. *s.s:* Geol & astronomy. Founder & First Principal Bankura Col Bengal. Fellow of Calcutta Univ 1907–17. Last Chm Twickenham U.D.C. 2nd Mayor of Twickenham '27–28. Travelled extensively. Lect on astron, travel, etc. *Rec:* Golf, travel. *c:* Royal Astron Soc, etc. *a:* The Croft, Bourn, Cambs.

MITCHELL, John William, F.R.S.A., M.Inst.T. *b:* New Shildon 1898. *e:* New Shildon Sch. *m:* Annie Fuller. *s:* 2. Company Dir & Transp Supt. *Publ:* The Wheels of Industry. *Ctr:* Motor Transport. *s.s:* Transport. *Rec:* Golf, shooting, scale model building. *w.s:* 1914—18. *a:* 3 Northumberland Rd. Carlisle. *T:* 2127.

MITCHELL, Janet Charlotte. B.A., L.R.A.M. *b:* Melbourne, Australia 1896. *e:* Priv, Roy Acad of Music Lond, Bedford Coll for Women, Univ of Lond. Asst Supervisor Youth Education, Australian Broadcasting Commission Victorian Branch 1941—. *n.a:* Aust Corres North China Dly News 1933. *Publ:* Spoils of Opportunity; Tempest in Paradise. *Ctr:* Sydney Morning Herald, Sydney Dly Telegraph, Melbourne Herald, The Queen (Lond), etc. *s.s:* Women in Internat Affairs. *Rec:* Reading, gardening, music. *c:* Lyceum (Melbourne). *a:* 12 Grange Rd, Kew, Melbourne, E.4, Australia. *T:* WA 2664.

MITCHELL, Mary. *Publ:* A Warning to Wantons; Pendulum-Swing. *c.t:* Harper's Bazaar, Woman's Journ, etc. *a:* c/o Christine Campbell Thomson Ltd., 12 Henrietta St, W.C.2.

MITCHELL, Rosamond Joscelyne, M.A., B.Litt., F.R.Hist.S. *b:* Harrow-on-the-Hill 1902. *e:* St Hugh's Coll Oxf. *m:* J. A. Leys. *s:* 1. *Publ:* Life & Adventure in Medieval Europe; English People of the Past (with M. J. Whicher); Ye Goode Olde Dayes (with I. L. Plunket); John Tiptoft. *Ctr:* English Hist Review, Italian Studies, etc. *s.s:* Medieval Hist. *Rec:* Gardening. *a:* Ware Lane, Lyme Regis, Dorset.

MITCHELL, Rosslyn, M.A., LL.B., J.P. Solicitor. *Publ:* Impressions; Ladies & Gentlemen. *c.t:* Daily Record, Evening News. M.P. for Paisley 1924–29. Member Town Counc Glasgow '09. *a:* 24 Drury St, Glasgow, C.2.

MITCHELL, Susanna Valentine. *b:* Philadelphia. *e:* Westover Sch Connecticut. *m:* William Gammell, Jr. *s:* 1. *d:* 3. Poet & Novelist. *Publ:* Journey Taken by a Woman; No Second Second. *Ctr:* Blue & Gold, Smoke. *Rec:* Riding, playing the piano. *a:* The Meadows, East Greenwich, Rhode Island, U.S.A. *T:* Greenwich 644.

MITCHELL, Col. Thomas John, D.S.O. *b:* Perth 1882. *e:* Perth Acad, George Watsons Coll Edin, St Andrew's Univ. *m:* Blanche Katherine Bruce. Late R.A.M.C., served France, Belgium, India, H.Q. Staff War Office & Brit Forces in Egypt. *n.a:* Joint Ed Gen Hist official Med Hist of the Great War Vol IV & Casualties & Med Statistics, Ed & Manager R.A.M.C. News 1924—28, Ed Health of the Army '24—28. *Publ:* Articles in Disease of the War Vol 1 & 2. *Ctr:* Various to R.A.M.C. Journ, Blackwood Mag. *Rec:* Golf, fishing, shooting, motoring. *c:* Bath, Army & Navy, University, Edinburgh, Royal & Ancient, St Andrews. *a:* Errogie, Dundee Rd, Perth. *T:* 136.

MITCHELL, Thomas Walker, M.D. *b:* Avoch 1869. *e:* Fortrose Acad & Univ of Edin. *m:* Henrietta Violet Kerans. Physician. *n.a:* Ed British Journ of Medical Psychology 1920–34. *Publ:* The Psychology of Medicine; Medical Psychology & Psychical Research; Problems in Psychopathology. *s.s:* Psychical research. *a:* Hope Meadow, Hadlow, Kent. *t:* 48.

MITCHELL, W. G. *b:* Lightcliffe. *e:* Crossley Sc Halifax. N/p Ed & Proprietor. *n.a:* Ed Peeblesshire Advertiser, S. Midlothian Advertiser. Pres N.U.J. 1930–31. *a:* Rosebank, Peebles, N.B. *t:* 26.

MITCHELL, Wesley Clair, A.B., Ph.D. *b:* Rushville, Illinois 1874. *e:* Univ of Chicago. *m:* Lucy Sprague. *s:* 2. *d:* 1. Economist. *Publ:* Business Cycles; The Backward Art of Spending Money & other Essays; Business Cycles: the Problem & its Setting. *Ctr:* Quarterly Journ of Econs, Journ of Political Economy, American Econ Review. *s.s:* Economics. *Rec:* Woodworking, golf. *a:* Westover Rd, Stamford, Connecticut, U.S.A. *T:* Stamford 3-3283.

MITCHELL, William, M.A.(Aber), LL.B.(Edin), K.C. *b:* Keith 1872. *m:* Kathryn Brammer. Sheriff-Sub of Selkirks. *Publ:* Burgh Government; Prince Charles Stewart & the "Forty-Five." *c.t:* Ency of Law of Scotland, Contemporary Review, Glas Herald. *a:* Abbotshill, Galashiels. *t:* 138.

MITCHELL, William Henry, M.J.I. *b:* Stainfield, Lincs 1888. *e:* Stamford Sc. *m:* F. M. Billingham. *s:* 2. Journalist. *n.a:* Stamford Guardian 2½ y, Bedford Circular, Ed Woburn Times 2 y, 2nd Reporter Beds Standard, Dis Reporter Express & Star Wolverhampton 1910–. Chm Birm & Midland Counties Dis I.J. '30–31, '31–32. *s.s:* Football. *a:* Hill Crest, Barrs Rd, Old Hill, Staffs. *t:* Cradley 6339.

MITCHELL-HEDGES, Frederick Albert. *Publ:* inc Battles with Giant Fish; Land of Wonder & Fear; Battling with Sea Monsters; etc. *a:* Canterton Manor, nr Cadnam, New Forest, Hants.

MITCHINER, Philip Henry, C.B.(Mil), C.B.E.(Mil), T.D., M.D., M.S., F.R.C.S., Hon.D.C.L.(Durham), D.L. *b:* Croydon 1888. *m:* Margaret Philpott Hon Surgeon to H.M. the King, Mem Counc R.C. of Surgeons of England, Mem Senate, Univ of Lond, Maj-Gen T.A., Knight of St Sava, C.St.J. *Publ:* Science & Practice of Surgery; Pocket Surgery; Surgical Practice & Medical Organisations in Air Raid Emergency Treatment; Nursing in War Time; Modern Treatment of Burns & Scalds. *Ctr:* Professional Journs. *s.s:* Surgical Matters. *Rec:* T.A., gardening. *c:* Athenæum. *a:* 6 Morpeth Mansions, London, S.W.1.

MITCHISON, Naomi. *b:* Edinburgh 1897. *e:* Dragon Sch Oxf. *m:* G. R. Mitchison. *s:* 3. *d:* 2. Co Councillor, Argyll, Mem Highlands & Islands Advisory Panel. *Publ:* The Conquered; Cloud Cuckoo Land; Black Sparta; The Corn King & the Spring Queen; An Outline for Boys & Girls & Their Parents; The Delicate Fire; The Home; We Have Been Warned; The Moral Basis of Politics; The Fourth Pig; The Blood of the Martyrs; The Bull Calves; etc. *Ctr:* New Statesman, Forward, Manch Guardian, etc. *a:* Carradale, Campbeltown, Argyll.

MITMAN, Maurice, M.D., F.R.C.P. Med Supt L.C.C. River Hosps Joyce Green nr Dartford. *Publ:* Clinical Practice in Infectious Diseases (with E. H. R. Harries); Section in: Diet in Health & Diseases. *Ctr:* Lancet: B.M.J., Journ of Hygiene, Practitioner, Health Educ Journ, Journ of State Med, Brit Journ of Dermatology, Brit Journ of Radiology, etc. *s.s:* Infectious Diseases, Kitchen Hygiene. *a:* Joyce Green House, Dartford, Kent. *T:* Dartford 3231.

MITRANY, David. D.Sc., Ph.D. *b:* Bucarest 1888. *e:* Bucarest, Paris, Hamburg, London. *m:* Ena Limebeer. Univ Prof, Vis Prof Harvard Univ 1931—33, Prof in Sch of Economics & Politics Inst of Advanced Study Princeton N.J. *n.a:* Ed Staff Manch Guardian 1919—22, Asst European Ed Carnegie Endowments, Economic & Social History of the World War '22—35. *Publ:* Problem of International Sanctions; The Land & the Peasant in Rumania; The Progress of International Government; The Effect of War in South-Eastern Europe; Marx v the Peasant; American Policy & Opinion; American Interpretations ; A Working Peace System. *s.s*: International Organisation. *Rec*: Walking, gardening. *a*: Lower Farm, Kingston Blount, Oxford. *T*: Kingston Blount 236.

MITTON, G. E. *b*: Bishop Auckland. *m*: Sir J. G. Scott. Author. *n.a*: Sometime Ed Who's Who Year Book, Writer's & Artist's Year Book, Englishwoman's Year Book. *Publ*: Hawk of the Desert ; The Lost Cities of Ceylon ; The Book of London ; The Judge's Daughters ; The Book of Scotland ; etc. *Ctr*: Cornhill (serials & short-stories). *s.s*: Scotland, London, Astronomy, Burma. *a*: Thereaway, Graffham. nr Petworth.

MIZON, H. J. *b*: Cambridge 1881. *e*: Cambridge. Manager. *n.a*: W. H. Smith & Son '93–. *a*: Hambleden Hse, Sheffield. *t*: 21164.

M'KINLAY, Samuel Livingstone, M.A. *b*: Glas 1907. *e*: Whitehill Sec Sc & Glas Univ. Journalist. *n.a*: Sub-Ed Glasgow Herald 1929–. *c.t*: Glasgow Bulletin, Golf Illustrated, Popular Motoring, etc. *s.s*: Golf Internat in Scot golf team '29–33. *Rec*: Fishing. *a*: 20 Eastercraigs, Glas, E.1.

M'LEAN, Jack. *b*: Glas 1911. *s.s*: Golf. Mem of Brit Walker Cup Team '34. Won Scottish & Irish Amateur Golf Championship '32 & '33. Played for Scotland *v* England, Ireland & Wales in Amateur Internats '32 & 33. *Rec*: Golf. *c*: Hayston, Western Gailes Golf. *a*: 463 King's Park Av, Glas. *t*: Cent 9880.

MOBERLY, Miss C. A. E. *b*: Winchester Col. *Publ*: Dulce Domum; An Adventure. Princ St Hugh's Col Oxf 1886–1915. *a*: 4 Norham Rd, Oxf.

MOBERLY, Brig.-Gen. Frederick James, C.B., C.S.I., D.S.O. Indian Army (ret). *Publ*: Mesopotamia Campaign 1914–18 (4 vols); Military Operations Togoland & Cameroons (1 vol). *a*: Fairlea, Bideford, Devon. *t*: 329.

MOBERLY, Rt. Rev. Robert Hamilton. (See **STEPNEY, Bishop of**). *e*: Winchester & Oxf. *Publ*: The Great Friendship. *a*: 25 Compton Terr, London, N.1. *T*: Canonbury 1135.

MOBERLY-BELL, Enid, M.A. *b*: Alexandria 1881. *e*: Francis Holland Sch & Newnham Coll Camb. Headmistress. *Publ*: Octavia Hill ; C. F. Moberly Bell ; Flora Shaw. *s.s*: Biog. *c*: Univ Women. *a*: 7 Mallord St, London, S.W.3. *T*: Flaxman 2163.

MOCATTA, Frances. *b*: Georgia, U.S.A. 1900. *e*: Lon. *m*: Cyril H. Mocatta. *s*: 3. Author. *Publ*: Thine Shall Be Mine ; Enchanted Dust ; A Lonesome Road ; Yesterday's Daughter ; etc. *s.s*: Novels. Stories published at age of ten. *Rec*: Reading. *a*: 27 Edwardes Sq Kensington, W.8. *t*: Western 3914.

MOCKFORD, Julian. *b*: Montreal, Canada 1898. *e*: South African Coll Hgh Sch Capetown, Witwatersrand Univ Johannesburg. *m*: Lettice Mary Rees. P.R.O. South African High Commissioner London, Mem I.O.J. *n.a*: Acted in capacity of Rep, Spec Corres, Mag Ed, Ed Pretoria News, Lond Corres, War Corres The Star (Johannesburg) & its group 1919—42, S.A. Gov Press Officer for Royal Visit '47, Represented Times & S.A. afternoon Newspapers on the late Duke of Kent's Tour '35. *Publ*: Here Are South Africans ; Khama King of the Bamangwato ; Union of South Africa ; South Africa To-day. *Ctr*: Numerous newspapers & periodicals in S.A., Great Britain, U.S.A., Australia, Canada. *s.s*: Union of South Africa. *Rec*: Travel. *c*: Roy Auto, Roy Empire. *a*: 152 Chiltern Ct, Baker St, London, N.W.1. *T*: Welbeck 5544.

MOEN, OLAV: professor of horticulture; *b*. Voll, Romsdal, Norway, September, 1875; *s*. Joern and Brit Moen; educ. Public Grammar School, Public High School, Agricultural School, Horticultural School, Agricultural College; married. AUTHOR: Storst mulig avl med minst mulig fro, 1918; Noko um verlaget og froavlen, 1918; Froavl av havevekster og akerrotvekster (in collaboration with J. H. Lund and G. Gulli), 1918; Litt om gronnsakdyrkning i U. S. A., 1921; Erfaringer vedrorende froavl av kjokkenurter i Norge, 1921; Kal, 1923; Mer kal uten drivbenk, 1923; Norske hagebrukskandidater (biografiske data), 1924; "3 Artikler" (gjaeret kal m. m.), 1925; "Groensakdyrkningskjama", 1926; Kalrot, 1926; Mer gronnsaker, 1926; Om akklimatisering av treagtige planter, 1926; Melding om drift av plantesskalen og gronnsakforseka (arlig), 1927; "Dobbelavling", 1927; Om vare gronnsakveksters og rotveksters foredling, 1927; En del gronnsaksorters navn, deres uttale og betydning, 1927; Om elektrisitetens utnytting til opvarming av drivbenker (in collaboration with A. H. Bremer and G. Jacobsen), 1927; Sommerbearbeidning av jorden ved gulrotdyrkning, 1927; Lonsomhetsforhold ved bruk av elektrisitet til opvarming i benk og pa friland, 1928; "100 vekstogn efter tidlig slatt" (veiledning i dobbelavling), 1918. Contributes to great number of magazines. Professor and teacher in agriculture; head of experimental stations in horticulture; chief of nursery. Relig. denom., Lutheran. HOME: Aas, Norway.

MOFFAT, Graham. *b*: Glasgow 1866. *e*: St Stephen's Sch & Rosemount Acad Glas. *m*: Maggie L. Linck. *d*: 1. Playwright & Actor. *Publ*: (Plays) Bunty Pulls the Strings ; A Scrape o' the Pen ; Susie Tangles the Strings ; Granny. *s.s*: Plays of Scottish life & character. *Rec*: Psychical research. *a*: Côte d'Azur, Camp Bay Drive, Cape Town, Sth Africa. *T*: 39624.

MOFFAT, John. *b*: 1891. Editor. *n.a*: Ed Brit Zone Rev Control Comm for Germany, Press Chief Brit Sect Berlin & Ed Der Berliner 1945—46, Ed-in-Chief Yorks Herald Newsp Coy '30—36, Ed Staff Scotsman, Glasgow Herald, Allied Newspapers, Manch Guardian, Manch Ev News, Yorks Post, etc. *a*: Capelgill, Muncaster, Yorkshire.

MOFFETT, John. *b*: 1905. *e*: Public Schs & Christ's Coll. *m*: Madge Yates. *s*: 1. *d*: 1. Journalist. *n.a*: Rep Southland Dly News Invercargill 1922—25, Rep then Sub-Ed Press Christchurch '25—29, Leader-Writer '29—46, Ed '46, Otago Dly Times Dunedin. *Publ*: Russell Clark, N.Z. Artist & Illustrator (Monograph). *Ctr*: Times Litt Supp, Various N.Z. Journs. *c*: Dunedin. *a*: Otago Dly Times, Dunedin, New Zealand.

MOGFORD, H. H. Hon Sec & Treas Leics Br N.U.J. *a*: 22 Trafford Rd, Leicester.

MOHOMED ALI, M.A., LL.B. *b*: India 1880. *e*: Govt State Col Lahore, Punjab Univ. *m*: Mehrunnissa Begum. *s*: 2. *d*: 6. Author & Leader of Ahmadiyya Soc. *n.a*: Ed Review of Religious (Qadian) 1902–07. *Publ*: English trans of the Holy Quran with commentary & Text; The Babi Movement; The Prophet of Islam; Selections from the Holy Quran, etc. *c.t*: Islamic Review, Woking, Muslim Revival, Lahore, Moslemisch Revue, Berlin. *s.s*: Islamic theol, etc. *Rec*: Morning walk. Sacrificed worldly career after passing Law at the bidding of the founder of the Ahmadiyya movement to serve the cause of Islam & the Muslims. *a*: President Ahmadiyya Anjurnan, Ishaat Islam, Ahmadiyya Bldgs, Lahore.

MOIR, Rev. Arthur Lowndes, M.A., F.R.Hist.S. *b*: Knutsford, Cheshire 1887. *e*: Haileybury Coll, Trin Coll Oxf, Wycliffe Hall Oxf. *m*: Aline Parkin. *d*: 2. Vicar of Bromfield. *Publ*: Bromfield Priory & Church ; Story of Brereton Hall, Cheshire ; Twelve Adventures of Saint Paul ; The Bells of the Old Church Tower ; The

Parish of Lilliput. *s.s*: Local Hist, Religious Educ of Children. *Rec*: Chess. *a*: Bromfield Vicarage, Ludlow, Salop. *T*: Bromfield 34.

MOIR, Charles Mitchell, M.J.I. *b*: Brechin 1881. *m*: Ethel Emily Murrell. *d*: 1. Reporter. *n.a*: Dundee Courier & Evening Post '95–1905, Chatham News '06, E. Kent Gazette '06–. *c.t*: Press Assoc. *s.s*: Football. War Service. *Rec*: Swimming, gardening. *a*: 1 Council Houses, London Rd, Milton Regis, Sittingbourne, Kent. *t*: 226.

MOIR, James Reid, F.R.A.I. Archæologist. *Publ*: The Antiquity of Man in East Anglia; Pre-Palæolithic Man; etc. *c.t*: Times, Illustrated London News, etc. *a*: Hedges, One House Lane, Ipswich. *t*: Ipswich 2159.

MOIR, John Chassar, M.D., F.R.C.S.E., M.C.O.G. *b*: Montrose 1900. *e*: Edin Univ. Gynæcologist. *c.t*: Med press. *s.s*: Obstet & gynæ. Rockefeller Fellowship '32. *a*: Univ Col Hosp, W.C.1.

MOISTER, William R. H. *b*: Fulham 1873. *e*: Walham Green Middle Cl Sc. *m*: Laura Barber. Editor. *n.a*: Masonic Journ of S. Africa 1911–, S.A. Masonic World '22, amal the two papers '31. *Publ*: Booklets—The Sixth Step: Seven Essays on Music in ts Relation to Freemasonry ('16); Music in its Relation to Worship ('06). *c.t*: Jewish Chron, Zion st Record, Trans Authors' Lodge Lon, etc. *s.s*: Freemasonry, music. Extensive travel. *Rec*: Fishing. *a*: 80 Permanent Bldgs, Johannesburg, & Roseview Mansions, Rosebank, Johannesburg. *t*: 33–7952.

MOKRY, Frantisek Viktor. *b*: Prague 1892. *e*: Univ of Charles IV, Acad of Arts & Crafts Prague. *m*: Jarmila Mokra. *d*: 1. Artist, Painter Writer, Art Teacher Univ Palacky of Olomouc, Hon Mem Art Teachers Guild Lond, Mem P.E.N. Club Prague. *Publ*: Life & Art of Jaroslava Cermaka ; Painters of South Bohemia ; Alois Moravec ; Bohumil Ullrych ; The Manual of Figural Drawing & Painting ; Realistic Czechoslovaquian Painting ; The Manual of Painting ; Clair-obscur in the Painting. *Ctr*: Various newsp, & revues of Prague. *s.s*: Art (Painting & Drawing), Art Education. *Rec*: Travelling. *a*: Trida marsala Tita 11, Prague, Czechoslovaquia. *T*: 734. 62.

MOLESWORTH, H. M., B.A., A.C.A. *a*: c/o Imp Chem Industries Ltd, Strand Rd, Calcutta.

MOLLER, Viggo F. *b*: Odense 1887. *e*: Odense Kathedralskole. *Publ*: Nerver ; Beg den graa Facade ; Halvdelen af To ; Familien Zero ; Saere og Gale ; En Sten bliver kastet paa Vandet ; Kyx ; Det Skjulte ; Forbrydere ; Det sidste Dogn ; I Kraft af mig selv ; Den excentriske Hverdag ; Menneskemagt ; Hyggelige Historier ; Venlige Vers ; etc. *s.s*: Psychology, Psycho-analysis. *a*: Under Elmene 14b, Copenhagen, S, Denmark. *T*: Sundby 792.

MOLLISON, James Allan, M.B.E., A.R.Ae.S. *b*: Glasgow 1905. *e*: Glas & Edin Acads. *m*: Phyllis Louis Verley Hussey. Aviator, Made First Solo Westward Flight North Atlantic, First Flight England to Sth America and England to the Cape by the Direct (Sahara) Route, formerly Held Australia-England, England-Cape & England-India Records. *Publ*: Death Cometh Soon or Late ; Playboy of the Air. *Ctr*: Various nat newsps. *s.s*: Aviation. *Rec*: Flying, swimming. *c*: Roy Aero. *a*: Royal Aero Club, 119 Piccadilly, London, W.1. *T*: Grosvenor 1246.

MOLLOY, Edward. *e*: Salford Sec Sch, Roy Tech Coll Salford. Editor. King's Prizeman in Applied Mechanics 1910. *n.a*: Ed Pitmans Tech Dept 1924—29, General Editor Newnes Technical Books Dept '29—. *Publ*: (Ed) " Electrical Engineer Reference Book," etc. *s.s*: Electrical Engineering. *a*: 38 The Pryors, London, N.W.3. *T*: Hampstead 5035..

MOLLOY, James R. *b*: Dublin. Journalist. *n.a*: Asst Ed Irish Farming World until 1918, Farmers' Gazette until '20, Reporter & Agric Corr Irish Times Dublin. *s.s*: Agric. *a*: 26 Charlemont Rd, Clontarf, Dublin.

MOLLOY, Robert (William). *b*: Charleston, J.C., U.S.A. 1906. *e*: High Sch. *m*: Marion Knapp Jones. *s*: 2. Author, Free-lance Reader for various publishers. *n.a*: New York Sun 1936—45, Literary Ed '43—45. *Publ*: Pride's Way ; Uneasy Spring ; (Trans) Dona Barbara. *Ctr*: N.Y. Sun, Times, Post. *Rec*: Music, tennis. *c*: Authors' Guild. *a*: 601 West 190th St, New York 33, N.Y.. U.S.A. *T*: Wadsworth 3-1072.

OLLOY, Tony. Journalist, Mem N.U.J. *n.a*: Drama Critic The Irish Press Dublin. *Publ*: The Quest of O-M ; Caught in the Callow. *Ctr*: B.B.C. & several mags. *s.s*: Writing for Children & Boys, Theatre, Irish Lang & Folklore, Celtic Subjects, Light Verse. *a*: 52 Pembroke Rd, Dublin, Ireland.

MOLNAR, Ferenc. Author. *Publ*: Angel Making Music; The Swan; Liliom. *a*: c/o Elkin Mathews & Marrot Ltd, 44 Essex St, W.C.2.

MOLONEY, Rev. Canon Brian Charles, O.B.E., T.D., M.A. *e*: Rugby, Trin Coll Camb, Headmaster, Public Sch. *Publ*: Analytical Geometry ; Numerical Trigonometry. *s.s*: Maths. *a*: Worksop College, Worksop, Notts. *T*: Worksop 2391.

MOLONY, John Chartres. *b*: Ennis, Ireland 1877. *e*: Portora Roy Sc & Dublin Univ. *m*: Frances Adams. *s*: 2. *d*: 1. I.C.S. *Publ*: Savinelli; Antony Vanroy; The Riddle of the Irish; Ireland's Tragic Comedians; A Book of South India. *c.t*: Times, Blackwood's Mag, The Hindu, etc. *s.s*: Indian & Irish Affairs. *Rec*: Cycling. *a*: 14 Northmoor Rd, Oxf. *t*: Summertown 58027.

MOLSON, Arthur Hugh Elsdale. *b*: Chelmsford 1903. *e*: R.N.C. Osborne, Dartmouth, Lancing, New Col Oxf. Barrister, M.P. Pres Oxf Un '25. Polit Sec Assoc Chambers of Comm of India & Ceylon '26–29. *Rec*: Golf, squash. *c*: Athenæum. *a*: 21 St James's Ct, Buckingham Gate, S.W.1. *t*: Victoria 2360.

MOLTENO, Percy Alport, M.A., LL.M. *b*: Edin 1861. *e*: Cape of Good Hope Univ, Trin Col Cam. *m*: Elizabeth Martin (dec). *s*: 2 (1 dec). *d*: 1. Barrister-at-Law, Shipowner. *Publ*: The Life & Times of Sir John Charles Molteno; A Federal South Africa; A Plea for Small Holdings; The Proposed Guarantee Pact. *c.t*: Times, M/C Guardian, Glas Herald, Scotsman, etc. *s.s*: Politics, agriculture. Started Vienna Emergency Relief Fund. *c*: Reform, Nat Lib, etc. *a*: 10 Palace Court, W.2, & Parklands, Shere, nr Guildford. *t*: Bays 1674 & Shere 17.

MOMBERT, ALFRED: author; b. Karlsruhe, Germany, Feb. 6, 1872; educ. Heidelberg. DEGREE: Ph.D. AUTHOR: Tag und Nacht, 1894; Der Glühende, 1896 (3rd edit. 1921); Die Schöpfung, 1897 (3rd edit. 1921); Der Denker, 1901 (2nd edit. 1920); Der Sonne-Geist, 1905 (2nd edit. 1923); Aeon der Weltgesuchte, 1907 (2nd edit. 1921); Aeon zwischen den Frauen, 1910 (2nd edit. 1921); Aeon vor Syrakus, 1911 (2nd edit. 1921); Der himmlische Zwecker, 1909 (2nd edit. 1922); Der Held der Erde, 1919; Atair, 1925; Aïglas Herabkunft, 1929. General character of writing: plays and poetry. ADDRESS: Heidelberg, Germany.

MONAHAN, Rev. William Beattie, M.A., B.D. *b*: Ballyshannon, Co Donegal 1867. *e*: Wesley Coll Dublin, Trin Coll Dublin. *m*: Hannah Louisa Piggott. *d*: 3. *Publ*: The Psychology of St Thomas Aqinas ; The Moral

Theology of St Thomas Aquinas; St Thomas Aquinas on the Sacraments; St Thomas Aquinas on the Eucharist; St Thomas Aquinas on The Life of Christ; St. Thomas Aquinas on the Incarnation; Benediction in The Church of England; The Popes & the Bible; Stations of the Cross. *s.s*: Thomistic Theology. *Rec*: Water-colour painting. *a*: St Swithun's Rectory, Worcester. *T*: 4949.

MONCK, Walter Nugent Bligh, O.B.E., F.R.A.M *b*: Welshampton 1878. *e*: Royal Institution School Liverpool, Royal Academy of Music London. Theatrical Producer, has produced all the plays of Shakespeare in Maddermarket Theatre Norwich. *Publ*: Mancroft Pageant; Norwich Pageant; Ipswich Pageant; The Blickaling Mosque; The Pilgrims Progress *s.s*: The Elizbethan Stage, The Mediæval Stage *Rec*: Travelling, music. *a*: 6 Ninhams Courts, Norwich, Norfolk. *T*: Norwich 26560.

MONDY, Dr. S. L. C. *a*: Yeddo, 18 Bruce Grove, Tottenham, N.17.

MON KTON, Ella. *b*: London 1899. *e*: Wycombe Abbey. *m*: Clifford Webb. *s*: 2. *d*: 1. *Publ*: The Gates Family; The Top of the Mountain; For the Moon The Go-to-Bed Book; August in Avilion. *a*: Dormers, Abinger Hammer, Surrey. *T*: Abinger 172.

MONCKTON, Marmaduke, B.A. *Publ*: The Saints Everlasting Rest (Ed & Prefaced). *a*: 38 Compayne Gdns, London, N.W.6 *T*: Maida Vale 4240.

MONELLI, Paolo ("Bernardo Prisco"). *b*: Fiorano di Modena (Italy) 1894. *e*: Bologna Univ. *m*: Augusta Renata Severi. Journalist. *n.a*: Special Rep Europe & Amer, Special Corr La Gazetta del Popolo. *Publ*: Le Scarpe al Sole (1920), English trans Toes Up; Io e Itedeschi ('29); Sette Battaglie; Questo Mestieraccio; L'Alfabeto di Bernardo Prisco ('32); Barbaro Dominio ('33); etc. *c.t*: Italian Press. *s.s*: Alpine sports, foreign policy, etc. War Service 4 medals—Al Valore, cross, Al Merito di Guerra, Croix de Guerre Belge. *Rec*: Yachting, climbing, etc. *a*: Via Tasso 3, Milan, Italy.

MONEY, Sir Leo Chiozza, F.S.S., F.R.G.S., F.Z.S. *b*: Genoa 1870. *e*: Priv. *m*: Gwendolen Stevenson. *d*: 1. Author & Journalist. M.P. 1905—18. Under Sec Min of Pensions '16 & of Shipping '16—18. *Publ*: Riches & Poverty; Product Money; Can War be Averted?; Sonnets of Life; etc. *s.s*: Politics, foreign affairs. Drafted the new War Pensions Warrant '16. Devised the "Rationing" Blockade policy which made the success of the blockade of Germany '15—18; Devised the Atlantic concentration strategy which helped to defeat the submarine blockade of '17—18. *c*: Roy Socs, P.E.N. *a*: Bramley, nr Guildford, Surrey. *t*: Bramley 276.

MONEY, Robert Jarratt, M.InstC.E. *b*: Deptford 1862. *e*: Haileybury Col & Crystal Palace Engineering Sc. *m*: Geraldine Isabel Lempriere. *c.t*: Minutes of Proc Inst of Civil Engineers, Journ Roy Geog Soc, Engineer, etc. *s.s*: Civil eng & contracting. *c*: Savile & S.A. *a*: North Cave, Pembroke Rd, Woking. *t*: 225.

MONEY, Rev. Canon William Taylor, M.A. *b*: Deptford 1873 *e*: Dean Close Sch Cheltenham & Emmanuel Coll Camb *m*: Agnes Dalton Clerk in Holy Orders, Canon Emeritus Southwark, Proctor in Convocation 1934—44, Life Gov Dean Close Sch, Vice-Pat Roy Mansonic Sch for Boys, also R.M. Sch for Girls *Publ*: Higher Flights for Airmen; A Shelf in the Store Room; A History of the Frederick Lodge of Unity; A History of the Frederick Chapter of Unity. *Ctr*: Church of Eng Newsp, Masonic Record, The Freemasons' Chronicle

s.s: History of Greenwich, The Antiquity of the Cross as a Symbol. *Rec*: Golf, billiards, chess. *w.s*: 1914—19 C.F., '41—45 Chap 23rd Lond Home Gd. *a*: Creselly, 40 The Drive, Sevenoaks, Kent. *T*: Sevenoaks 2655.

MONEY-KYRLE, Roger Ernie. M.A., Ph.D. *b*: Broxbourne 1898. *e*: Eton, Camb, Vienna, London. *m*: *s*: 4. *Publ*: The Meaning of Sacrifice; The Development of the Sexual Impulses; Aspasia or the Future of Amorality; Superstition & Society *s.s*: Psych & Anthrop. *w.s*: 1916—19 & '39—45. *a*: Whetham, Calne, Wilts. *T*: Bromham 44.

MONIE, Ian Whitelaw. M.B., Ch.B. *b*: Paisley, Scotland 1919. *e*: John Neilson Inst Paisley, Univ of Glasgow. *m*: Murielle McPhee Stobo. *s*: 1. *d*: 1. Asst Prof of Anatomy, Lect in Anatomy Univ of Glasgow 1942—47. *Ctr*: B.M.J., Journ of Anatomy. *s.s*: Anatomy, Embryology. *Rec*: Walking, languages, philately. *a*: c/o Dept of Anatomy, Medical College, Winnipeg, Canada. *T*: 27913.

MONK, Frank Vivian. M.R.S.T. *b*: Salisbury 1886. *e*: Bishop Wordworth's Sch Salisbury & St Mark's Coll Chelsea. *m*: Dora Kathleen Wheeler. Schoolmaster. *Publ*: (With H. T. Winter) Adventure Above the Clouds; Great Exploits in the Air; Aircraft & Flying; Blackie's Flying Series. *Ctr*: Dly Mail, Pearson's Mag, Ev News, Teachers' World. *s.s*: Nature Study, Flying, Swimming, Boxing. *Rec*: Cricket. *c*: De Havilland Flying. *a*: Whitstone Head, Holsworthy, Devon.

MONK, Rev. H. C. *n.a*: Magazine Ed 1931—34. *Publ*: Centenary Booklet, 100 Years' Work & Worship. *c.t*: Mag Monthly. *a*: The Manse, Gt. Totham, Maldon, Essex.

MONK, Sidney Gordon, M.Sc., M.I.E.E., M.J.I.E. *b*: London 1889. *e*: U.C.L. Lecturer. *Publ*: Classified Examples in Electrical Engineering; Induction Motors. *s.s*: Elec Eng. *c*: Plymouth Rotary (Pres 1938—39). Plymouth Model Engineers' Soc (Founder Pres 1946—48). *a*: Faraday, Saltash Passage, Plymouth. *T*: St Budeaux 72.

MONK, Canon William Henry. *b*: Toronto 1878. *e*: Basingstoke G.S., St George's Col Weybridge & St John's Seminary, Wonersh, Surrey. Finan Sec to Dio of Southwark. Canon of Dio (R.C.) of Southwark. *Publ*: Pilgrim's Way. *c*: A.A. *a*: Bishop's Hse, St George's Rd, Southwark, S.E.1. *t*: Hop 2967.

MONKHOUSE, Allan Noble, D.Litt(M/C). *b*: Barnard Castle 1858. *e*: Priv Scs. *m*: Elisabeth Dorothy Pearson. *s*: 2. *d*: 2. Journalist (ret), Author, Dramatist. *n.a*: Ed Staff Manchester Guardian 1902—32. *Publ*: Novels:— A Deliverance; Love in a Life; Dying Fires; Men and Ghosts; Marmaduke; Alfred the Great; Farewell Manchester; etc. Plays:—Mary Broome; Sons & Fathers; The Education of Mr Sarrage; The Haylings; Cecilia; The Grand Cham's Diamond; The Conquering Hero; etc. *c.t*: Manchester Guardian. *a*: Meadow Bank, Disley. *t*: 90.

MONKHOUSE, John Parry, F.R.C.S. *c.t*: Med Journs. *a*: 15 Upper Wimpole St, W.1. *t*: Welbeck 7384.

MONKHOUSE, Patrick James. *b*: Disley 1904. *e*: Rugby & Trin Col Oxf. *m*: Joan Leach. *s*: 1. Journalist. *n.a*: M/C Guardian Reporter '27—30, Leader Writer '30—32, News Ed '32—. *Publ*: On Foot in the Peak; On Foot in North Wales. Ed Oxford Poetry '25, Oxford Outlook

'24—26. c: M/C Press. Chm M/C br N.U.J. '32—34, Treas '35. a: 108 Birch Lane, M/C 13. t: Rusholme 3096.

MONKSWELL, Lord (Robert). b: Lon 1875. e: Eton, Cam. m: Katharine Gastrell (2nd wife). s: 1. d: 1. Publ: French Railways (1911), Railways of Great Britain; Railways ('28). c.t: Various n/p's & periodicals. s.s: Rlys. c: Athenæum. a: 28 Ashburn Pl, S.W.7. t: Frobisher 4433.

MONNINGTON, Reginald John William, M.J.I. b Leamington 1897. m: Doris May Hawkes. d: 2. Journalist. n.a: Trained Leamington Chron, Rep Northampton Echo 1918—19, Chief Rep Evesham Journ '19—26, Ed Evesham Journ '26—, Ed Tewkesbury Register '31—. s.s: Agriculture, Fruit, Vegetable Marketing. Rec: Observing wild Life. w.s: 1914—18. a: Middle Farm Hse, Ashton-under-Hill, Evesham, Worcs. T: Ashton-under-Hill 241.

MONOD, WILFRED: professor of theology; b. Paris, France, November, 1867; s. Théodore and Gertrude (Monod) M.; educ. (in France): Sorbonne (Faculty of Letters), Montauban (Faculty of Theology); (in Germany): Univ. of Berlin. DEGREES: Bachelier es lettres, Licencié en philosophie, Docteur en théologie; m. Dorina Monod, Sept. 30, 1891. AUTHOR (published sermons): Il a souffert, 1894; Il régnera, 1898; Il vit, 1898; L'Evangile du Royaume, 1900; Sur la Terre, 1902; Vers la Justice, 1903; Certitudes, 1910; Delivérances, 1913; Pour la reconstruction, 1920; Aux chercheurs, 1922; Les "Anges", 1925; Notre culte, 1926; La Tentation, 1927; Les bras étendus, 1928; (books of meditation): Le Problème de la mort, 1904; Silence et Prière, 1909; Prière et Silence, 1912; Pour communier, 1914; Vers L'Evangile sous la nuée de guerre, 2 vols., 1915; Courts sermons pour culte sans pasteur, 1922; (discussions): Aux Croyants, et aux Athées; La fin d'un Christianisme; Jésus ou Barrabas; Echos et Reflets, 1907; A Paris et ailleurs; (catechism); Ton règne vienne! 1902; "Venez a moi", 1905; Vers Dieu, 1921; "Viens et vois", 1928; (for ministers): L'Esprit du Ministère, 1906; Vademecum pastoral, 1907; (theology): L'Espérance Chrétienne (Le Royaume), 1899; L'Espérance Chrétienne (le Roi), 1901; Pour la reforme des Etudes theologiques (in collaboration), 1902; Du Protestantisme, 1928; La Nuée de témoins, 2 vols., 1929; (other works): Théologie pastorale; Que signifie: "Croire en Dieu"?; a series of about sixty pamphlets dealing with religious and moral questions, 1891-1925. Contributor to Les Veilleurs. General character of writing: religious and sociological. Is honorary president of the national union of reformed churches of France. President of the French committee of the universal alliance for the promotion of international friendship through the churches. Member of the executive committee of the directing committee of the Universal Alliance for Practical Christianity at Stockholm in 1925, and one of the vice-presidents of the European division. Member of the executive committee of the Church Council at Lausanne, 1927. Relig. denom., Presbyterian. ADDRESS: 6 Square de Port Royal, Paris XIII, France.

MONRAD-KROHN, Georg Herman, M.D. (Oslo), F.R.C.P.(Lon), M.R.C.S.(Eng). b: Bergen 1884. e: Cathedral Sc Bergen & Oslo, Berlin & Lon Univs. m: Elisabeth Nobel Nielsen. s: 2. d: 3. Prof of Med Roy Frederick Univ Oslo. Mem Ed Bd Acta Psychiatrica et Neurologica. Publ: Clinical Examination of the Nervous System (6th edn, 1933), The Neurological Aspect of Leprosy ('23); Abdominal Reflexes ('18); Fasciculus Atrio-ventricularis ('11). c.t: Journ Mental Sci, Brain, etc. s.s: Hist. Chevalier de la Légion d'Honneur. Fell Norwegian Acad of Sci. Various Hosp Appts in Norway & in Eng. Rec: Riding, ski-ing, yachting, music. c: Norwegian Med Soc, Norwegian Neurological Soc, Roy Norwegian Auto Club. a: Fritznersgate 12, Oslo. t: 46091.

MONRO, HAROLD (EDWARD): author, publisher, bookseller; b. Brussels, Belgium, Mar. 14, 1879; s. Edward William M.; educ. Radley Coll.; DEGREES: B.A. (honours in modern languages) (Cambridge). AUTHOR: Poems, 1906; Evolution of the Soul, 1907; Judas, 1907; Chronicle of a Pilgrimage, 1909; Before Dawn, 1911; Children of Love, 1914; Strange Meetings, 1917; Some Contemporary Poets, 1920; Real Property, 1922; One Day Awake (A Morality), 1922; The Earth for Sale, 1928. Founded and edited Poetry and Drama before the war and The Chapbook (which ran 40 numbers) after the war. Compiled: Twentieth Century Poetry (an Anthology of Modern British Poetry), 1929. Contributor to various magazines and newspapers. General character of writing: literary. Lecturer on the poetry of this century throughout Gt. Britain; reader and organizer of readings of poetry. CLUBS: Royal Automobile. ADDRESS: 38 Great Russell St., London, W. C. 1, Eng.

MONRO, Margaret Theodora. b: Ranaghat, Bengal 1896. e: Priv Schs, Wimbledon Hgh Sch & Girton Coll Camb. n.a: Ed Sec S.P.C.K. Arabic Br Cairo 1928—33. Publ: The Path Divides; A Story of Egypt; Breaking out of Prison: A Book for the Deaf & their Friends; Mother Forbes of Craiglockhart; Seeking for Trouble; A Book of Unlikely Saints; Enjoying the New Testament. a: 66 Croydon Rd, Beckenham, Kent.

MONRO, Thomas Kirkpatrick, M.A., M.D., LL.D. b: Arbroath 1865. e: Arbroath Hgh Sch, Glas Univ. m: Jane Christian Brand. s: 2. d: 1. Emeritus Regius Prof of Med in Glas Univ, Hon Fellow of Royal Faculty of Physicians & Surgeons Glas. Publ: Manual of Medicine; Raynaud's Disease; History of Chronic Nervous Disease. Rec: Books & reading. c: Literary Glasgow. a: 12 Somerset Pl, Glasgow, C.3. T: Douglas 2577.

MONSARRAT, Keith Waldegrave, T.D. b: Kendal 1872. e: King Williams Coll Isle of Man, Univ of Edin. Hospital Group Officer Min of Health 1939—45. Publ: Human Understanding & Its World; Human Powers & Their Relations; My Self, My Thinking, My Thoughts; Thoughts, Deeds & Human Happiness; Poems; Praise, a Tale of Knowledge; etc. s.s: Science. c: Univ (Liverpool). a: c/o Midland Bank, 43 Portman Sq, London, W.1.

MONSARRAT, Nicholas. Publ: This is the Schoolroom; H.M. Corvette; East Coast Corvette; Corvette Command; Three Corvettes; It Depends What You Mean by Love; Leave Cancelled; H.M. Frigate. Ctr: Dly Telegraph, Trident, Allied newsps. s.s: Naval Subjects. a: c/o D.C. Benson & Campbell Thomson Ltd, 6 Norfolk St, London, W.C.2.

MONSELL, John Robert. b: Ireland. m: Margaret Irwin. Publ: Balderdash Ballads; Polichinelle; The Hooded Crow; The Pink Knight. s.s: Children's books. c: Savile. a: 66 Holland Rd, W.14. t: Western 3450.

MONTAGU, Hon. Lily H., O.B.E., J.P. b: London 1874. e: Private Schs & Tutors. Hon Sec West Central Jewish Day Settlement, Chmn W.C. Girls' Club, Lay Minister of the W.C. Liberal Jewish Congregation, Hon Sec World Union for Progressive Judaism, Pres Union of Progressive Synagogues. n.a: Jewish Religious Union Monthly, World Union Bulletin. Publ: Naomi's Exodus; Thoughts on Liberal Judaism; My Club & I; The Faith of a Jewish Woman; Letters to Anne & Peter; A Little Book of Comfort. a: The Red Lodge, 51 Palace Court, London, W.2. T: Bayswater 1124.

MONTAGUE, Francis Charles. Barrister-at-Law, Univ Teacher. Publ: Limits of Individual Liberty; Life of Sir Robert Peel; Elements of English Constitutional History (1894); etc. c.t: Eng Hist Rev, History. a: 177 Woodstock Rd, Oxf.

MONTAGUE, Joseph Franklin, M.D. *b*: New York 1893. *Publ*: Pruritus of the Perineum; Taking the Doctor's Pulse; I Know Just the Thing for That; Believe It or Not; Why Bring That Up?; Nervous Stomach Trouble; etc. *Ctr*: Journ Amer Med Assoc. *c*: Rotary, New York, Columbia Yacht, Gourmets Soc, etc. *a*: 104 East 40th St, New York 16, New York, U.S.A.

MONTAGUE, Laurence, B.A. *b*: Manchester 1909. *e*: St Edward's & Balliol Oxf. *m*: Margaret Anne Bell. *s*: 2. *d*: 2. Journalist, Mem N.U.J. *n.a*: Manch Guardian 1933, Sports Ed '34—39 & '46—. *s.s*: Football. *Rec*: Golf, gardening. *c*: Manch Old Rectory. *w.s*: A.F.S. & N.F.S. 1939—43, Lt-Col Army '43—46. *a*: c/o Manchester Guardian, Cross St, Manchester. *T*: Blackfriars 2345.

MONTAGUE, Margaret Prescott. *b*: White Sulphur Springs, U.S.A. *e*: Priv. Writer. *Publ*: The Poet, Miss Kate, & I; The Sowing of Alderson Cree; In Calvert's Valley; Linda; Closed Doors; Lucky Lady; Twenty Minutes of Reality; Home to Hims Muvver; Uncle Sam of Freedom's Ridge; England to America; Up Eel River; Leaves From a Secret Journal, etc. *Ctr*: Atlantic Monthly, Harper's, etc. *s.s*: West Virginia Folklore, Deafness & Blindness, Religion. *Rec*: Swimming, gardening, bridge. *a*: Oakhurst Orchards, White Sulphur Springs, W. Va., U.S.A., & 303 North Allen Ave, Richmond, Va, U.S.A. *T*: Richmond 5-5580.

MONTAGUE, Sydney Robert. *b*: Northfleet, Kent 1904. *e*: Elem Sch & Private. *m*: Hazel Horton. Lecturer & Author. *Publ*: North to Adventure; I Lived With The Eskimos; Riders in Scarlet. *Ctr*: Readers Digest, Boys Life Magazine, Rotarian Mag, etc. *s.s*: Philosophy, Adventure, Travel. *Rec*: Fishing, flying, swimming, riding. *a*: 4449 Price St, Hollywood 27, Los Angeles, Calif. *T*: Normandy 6952.

MONTEFIORE, Claude Joseph Goldsmid, M.A.(Oxon), HonD.D.(M/C). *b*: Lon 1858. *e*: Priv & Balliol Col Oxf. *m*: (1) Therese Schorstein; (2) Florence Fyfe Brereton. *s*: 1. *Publ*: Origin & Development of the Religion of the Ancient Hebrews; The Bible for Home Reading; The Synoptic Gospels; Judaism & St Paul; Liberal Judaism & Hellenism; Rabbinic Lit & Gospel Teachings; etc. *c.t*: Hibbert Journal, etc. *s.s*: Theology. Pres of the Anglo-Jewish Assoc. 1896-1921. Pres of the Liberal Jewish Synag, etc. *c*: Athenæum. *a*: 42 Portman Sq, W.1, & Hopedene, Holmbury St Mary, Dorking. *t*: Welbeck 6122.

MONTESSORI, Dr. Maria. Evolved the Montessori method of teaching children. *Publ*: The Montessori Method; The Mass Explained to Children; etc. *a*: Rome, Italy.

MONTGOMERY, HENRY HUTCHINSON: late Bishop of Tasmania; b. Cawnpore, India, Oct., 1847; s. Robert (K.C.B., G.C.S.I.) and Ellen Jane (Lambert) M.; educ. Temple Grove, East Sheen, Surrey; Harrow Sch. (Middlesex); Trinity Coll. (Cambridge). DEGREES: D.D. (Cambridge); D.D. (Oxford); D.C.L. (Durham); K.C.M.G.; m. Maud Farrar, July 28, 1881. AUTHOR: History of Kensington, 1889; Foreign Missions, 1902; The Light of Melanesia, 1904; Mankind and the Church, 1907; The Church on the Prairie, 1908; Visions I, 1909, II, 1913, III, 1915; Service Abroad, 1910; Life's Journey, 1910; Musings, 1919; Life and Letters of Bishop G. A. Lefroy, 1920; Life of Bishop Francis Balfour, 1925; Life of Brook Deedes, 1925; Life of Bishop Corfe, 1926; Life of Bishop Scott, 1928; The Joy of the Lord. Vicar of Kennington, London, 1879-89; Bishop of Tasmania, 1889-1901; Sec. of Soc. Props. of Gospel in London, 1901-19; Prelate of the Order of St. Michael and St. George from 1906. Relig. denom., Church of England. CLUBS: Church Imperial Club (London). HOME: Newpark, Moville, Co. Donegal, Ireland.

MONTGOMERY, John. *b*: Edinburgh 1916. *e*: Brighton Coll Sussex. Publicist & Journalist. *n.a*: Asst Publicity Mang Sound City Film Studios 1934, Publicity Mang Reunion Films '36, Jack Payne & Louis Levy '37, for Variety at Radiolympia Exhibition '39, John Baxter Productions '47, Nettlefold Films Ltd '48. *Ctr*: Leader, Cavalcade, Picturegoer, Sun Express (Johannesburg), Cape Argus (Cape Town), Hutchinsons Pie Publs. *s.s*: Films & Theatre, Arab Countries. *w.s*: 1939—46. *a*: 62 Bury Walk, Chelsea, London, S.W.3. *T*: Kensington 9735.

MONTGOMERY, K. L. *b*: Dublin. *e*: Eng. *Publ*: Cardinal's Pawn; Major Weir; Ark of the Curse; Colonel Kate; etc (jt author with sister under name K. L. Montgomery); 'Ware Venice; trans Bremond's Histoire du Sentiment Religieux en France. *c.t*: Many n/p's & periodicals. *a*: 81 Iffley Rd, Oxf.

MONTGOMERY, R. Ames, A.B., LL.D., D.D. *b*: Hendricks County, U.S.A. 1870. *e*: Miami Univ, McCormick Theol Sem. *m*: Mary Frances Allhands. *d*: 4. Presbyterian Minister, Educ Administrator. *n.a*: Column Ed Othumwa Courier 1917—18. *Publ*: The Secret Race; The Triumphant Ministry; Thomas D. Foster; Preparing Preachers to Preach; Expository Preaching; Reality in Religion; Listen to the Angels Sing; etc. *s.s*: Evangelical Faith & Life. *Rec*: Fishing. *a*: The Manor School for Boys, Jonesville, Michigan, U.S.A. *T*: 241.

MONTGOMERY, Robert Mortimer, K.C., M.A. *b*: King's Sch Chester, St Catherine's Society Oxford. *Publ*: Licensing Laws; War Damage Acts; Finance Act, 1907. *s.s*: Local Government. *a*: 3 Paper Buildings, Temple, London, E.C.4. *T*: Central 4488.

MONTGOMERY OF ALAMEIN, 1st Viscount Field-Marshal Bernard Law Montgomery. *Publ*: Normandy to the Baltic.

MONTIZAMBERT, Elizabeth, B.A.(Toronto). *b*: Quebec, Canada 1875. *e*: Bishop Strachan Sch Toronto, Trinity Univ Toronto. Writer. *n.a*: The Gazette Montreal 1912—44. *Publ*: Unnoticed London; London Discoveries. Michael's London; London Adventure. *Ctr*: Montreal Star, Lancet, The World's Work, Queen, Morning Post, Sunday Times. *s.s*: History of Old Cities. *Rec*: Gardening. *c*: Ladies Empire. *a*: Ladies Empire Club, 69 Grosvenor St, London, W.1. *T*: Frobisher 3988.

MONTMORENCY: see De Montmorency.

MONTROSS, Lynn. *b*: Battle Creek, Nebraska, U.S.A. 1895. *e*: Univ of Nebraska. *m*: Lois Katherine Hartzell. *s*: 1. *d*: 2. Writer. *n.a*: Ed Chicago Saturday Blade 1919—20, Copy Desk, Chicago Daily News '20—21, Publicity Dir Illinois Agricultural Assoc '21—23, Advert Writer New York '23—24. *Publ*: Half Gods; East of Eden; (with Lois Montrose) Town & Gown; Fraternity Row; The Talk of the Town; War Through the Ages. *Ctr*: Collier's, American, McCall's, Ladies' Home Journ, Woman's Home Companion, Sat Ev Post, Coronet, Esquire, etc. *s.s*: History & Biog, Historical Novels, Short Stories with Historical Background. *Rec*: Trout fishing, golf, travel. *w.s*: A.E.F. Infantry 1917—19. *a*: c/o Gregory, Fitch & Hendricks, 366 Madison Ave, New York, 17, N.Y. *T*: Murray Hill 6-2626.

MOODIE, William, M.D., F.R.C.P., D.P.M. *b*: Arbroath, Angus 1886. *e*: Arbroath Hgh Sch, St Andrew's Univ. *m*: Mary Enid Hardy. *d*: 2. Physician Univ Coll Hosp, Dept of Psychological Med. *Publ*: The Doctor & the Difficult Child; The Doctor & the Difficult Adult; Child Guidance. *Ctr*: B.M.J., Lancet, etc. *s.s*: Med Psychology. *Rec*: Sailing, motoring, travel. *c*: Authors. *w.s*: Lieut-Col R.A.M.C. 1939—45. *a*: 52 Harley St, London, W.1. *T*: Welbeck 8070.

MOODY, Charles Harry, C.B.E., Mus.D., F.S.A., F.R.C.O., F.R.S.A., Hon.R.C.M. *b*: Stourbridge, Worcs 1874. *e*: Bangor Cathedral & Private. *m*: Mary Grindal Brayton. *s*: 1. *d*: 2. Organist & Master of the Choristers Ripon Cathedral, Lecturer on English Cathedrals & Abbeys in Canada & America. *Publ*: Selby Abbey, A Historical Survey; A Handbook to Ripon Cathedral; The Choirboy in the Making. *Ctr*: Times, Yorkshire Post, Musical Times, Cambridge Review. *s.s*: Music, Mediæval Architecture. *Rec*: Archæology. *a*: Woodbridge, Ripon, Yorkshire. *T*: Ripon 342.

MOODY, Harold Arundel, M.D., B.Sc, L.R.C.P. (Lon), M.R.C.S.(Eng). *b*: Jamaica 1882. *e*: Wolmer's Sc Kingston Jamaica, King's Col & King's Col Hosp Lon. *m*: Olive Hable. *s*: 4. *d*: 2. Med Pract. *c.t*: M/C Guardian, London Times, Christian World, W. Africa, etc. *s.s*: The race & colour problem. Founder & Pres League of Coloured Peoples. Ex-Chm Colonial Missny Soc, Dir Lon Missny Soc. *Rec*: Tennis, philately. *a*: 164 Queen's Rd, Peckham, S.E.15. *t*: New X 1834.

MOODY, Irene Helen. *b*: St. Thomas, Ontario. *e*: St. Thomas Collegiate Institute, Alma Col, St. Thomas, The Curry Sc of Expression, Boston, Mass. *m*: Dr. William H. Moody (dec). *s*: 1 (dec). Reader & lecturer. *Publ*: Wraiths (poetry); Delphine of the Eighties. *c.t*: Mags & N/ps. *s.s*: Poetry. *c*: Past Pres B.C. Mainland Branch of the Canadian Authors' Assoc, Exec Mem Pacific Northwest Academy of Arts, Mem Arts & Letters Club, Convener Vancouver Poetry Writers' Group, Twice Chm Vancouver Board of School Trustees. Past Pres B.C. School Trustees Assoc, Life Mem National Council of Women. *a*: 1927 West 17 Ave, Vancouver, B.C., Canada. *t*: Bayview 8667 Y.

MOODY, Theodore William. *b*: Belfast 1907. *e*: Roy Academical Inst Belfast, Queen's Univ Belfast, Univ of Lond. *m*: Margaret C. P. Robertson. *s*: 1. *d*: 3. Fellow of Trin Coll & Prof of Mod Hist Univ of Dublin. *n.a*: Jt Ed Irish Hist Studies 1937—; Jt Ed Studies in Irish History '44—. *Publ*: The Londonderry Plantation 1609—41: the City of London & the Plantation in Ulster; Ulster Plantation Papers; Thomas Davis 1814—45. *Ctr*: Irish Hist Studies, etc. *s.s*: Mod Irish Hist, English Colonisation in Ireland, Irish in America, Mod Irish Nationalism, Michael Davitt. *Rec*: Walking, cycling, listening to music. *a*: 14 Heatherfield Rd, Terenure, Dublin. *T*: 96738.

MOODY, William Robert, B.A., D.D. *b*: Columbus, Mississippi, U.S.A. 1900. *e*: Hampden-Sydney Coll, Univ of the South, Virginia Theol Sem. *m*: Cordie Lee Winston Moncure. *d*: 2. Bishop The Protestant Episcopal Church. *n.a*: Ed American Church School Mag 1940—45, Lexington Diocese Mag '45—. *Publ*: A Candle in the House; In the Cross of Christ I Glory; Victory Through the Cross; Understanding the Book of Revelation; Heroes of the Faith; The Moral Law in the Modern World; Vital Elements in the Gospel of Jesus. *s.s*: Religion. *Rec*: Salt-water fishing. *a*: 436 West Sixth St, Lexington 12, Kentucky, U.S.A. *T*: Lexington 914.

MOOJEN, Wilhelmina Alberta. *e*: Hgh Sch. Public Relations Officer, Journalist. *n.a*: Public Relations Directorate Min of Supply 1942—44, Asst Ed International Industry '44—45. *Ctr*: Everybody's, Sport & Country, Fashion. *s.s*: Textiles, Colonial Welfare, Fashion. *a*: 6 Stanley Mansions, Park Walk, London, S.W.10. *T*: Flaxman 8604.

MOOKERJI, RADHA KUMUD: professor of Indian History; b. Berhampore, Bengal, India, Jan., 1884; s. Gopal Chandra Mookerji and Jaganmohini (Devi) Mookerji; educ. Berhampore Collegiate Sch., Presidency Coll. (Calcutta). DEGREES: M.A., Ph.D.; m. Anasuya Devi, 1910. AUTHOR: A History of Indian Shipping, 1912; The Fundamental Unity of India, with an Introduction by the Rt. Hon. J. Ramsay MacDonald, 1914; Local Government in Ancient India, with a foreword by Lord Crewe, 1919; Nationalism in Hindu Culture (Mysore University Extension Lectures), 1919; Men and Thought in Ancient India, 1924; Harsha (Calcutta Univ. Readership Lectures), 1926; Asoka (Gaekwad Lectures and Sir Manindra Chandra Nandy Lectures, Benares Hindu University), 1928. General character of writing: historical. Relig. denom., Brahmin. OFFICE: University of Lucknow. HOME: 6 Ekdalia Road, Calcutta; Berhampore, Bengal, India.

MOON, Grace. *b*: Indianapolis, Indiana. *e*: Priv, Univ of Wisconsin, Chicago Art Inst. *m*: Carl Moon. *s*: 1. *d*: 1. Writer. *Publ*: Chi-Wee; Chi-Wee & Loki; The Runaway Papoose; Nadita; The Magic Trail; The Missing Katchina; Singing Sands; Daughter of Thunder. *Ctr*: Various. *s.s*: American Indians, Stories of Mexico. *c*: Literary. *a*: 565 No. Mentor Ave, Pasadena, California, U.S.A. *T*: Sycamore 27077.

MOON, Robert Oswald. *b*: Lon 1865. *e*: Winchester & New Col Oxf. *m*: Ethel R. G., Waddington. *s*: 1. *d*: 4. Physician. *Publ*: Relation of Medicine to Philosophy; Growth of Our Knowledge of Heart Disease; Trans of Goethe's Autobiography (The Poetry & Prose of My Life); etc. *s.s*: Diseases of the heart. *c*: Reform. *a*: 21 Wimpole St, W.1. *t*: Langham 2711.

MOOR, Rev. Charles, D.D., F.S.A., F.R.HistS. Ret. *Publ*: Hist of Gainsburgh; Knights of Edward I (5 vols); Erminois. *c.t*: Antiquarian Soc's Proc, etc. *a*: 14 Lexham Gdns, W.8. *t*: Western 4526.

MOOR, Miss M. F., M.A., B.Litt. Hon Sec Assoc of Reform of Latin Teaching. *a*: 10 Church St, Old Headington, Oxford.

MOORCROFT, W., F.R.S.A., R.C.A. Medallist. Potter to H.M. the Queen. *c.t*: Various mags. Spent greater part of life originating & developing Moorcroft pottery. Gold Medallist St Louis, Brussels, Ghent, Paris, etc. Medal of Honour Brit Emp Exhib. Diploma of Honour Milan 1933. *a*: Trentham, Staffs. *t*: 49058.

MOORE, Sir Alan Hilary, Bt. *b*: London 1882. *e*: Eton, Trin Coll Camb, St Bart's Hosp. *m*: Hilda Mary Burrows. *s*: 2. *d*: 2. Med Officer of Health (ret), Mem of the Technical Cttee that restored H.M.S. Victory 1926, Mem of the Soc for Nautical Research & Navy Records Soc. *Publ*: Last Days of Mast & Sail; Sailing Ships of War 1800—1860. *Ctr*: Mariner's Mirror, Navy Records Soc's Naval Miscellany, Times Lit Supplement 1924—38. *s.s*: Nautical Research. *Rec*: Sailing, canoeing. *c*: Oxford & Cambridge, Leander Rowing, Cambridge Univ Cruising. *w.s*: Temp Surgeon R.N. 1914—19. *a*: Hancox, Whatlington, Battle, Sussex. *T*: Sedlescombe 209.

MOORE, Alfred S., *b*: Portrush, Co Antrim 1876. *e*: Roy Academical Inst Belfast, Queen's Univ Belfast, Coll of Technology. *m*: Anna A. Stephenson. Journalist & Author. *n.a*: Ed Prop The Investor 1905—14, Textile Corres Belfast-News Letter '26—, Linens & Domestics (N.Y.) '26—. *Publ*: Linen; Linen: From Field to Factory; Life of Sir Crawford M'Cullagh of Belfast; Magic Miles in Ireland; A Straggler From Saturn; Red Guide to Northern Ireland; Belfast To-Day; Trade Cycles. *Ctr*: Numerous. *s.s*: Linen & Textiles, Local & Ulster Hist & Life. *a*: 755 Lisburn Rd, Belfast, Nth Ireland. *T*: Belfast 65096.

MOORE, Anne Carroll. *b*: Limerick, Maine, U.S.A. 1871. *e*: Gr Limerick Acad, Bradford Acad (Maine). Librarian (ret). *n.a*: The Bookman 1918—26, Ed Three Owls, Critic (Children's Books), N.Y. Herald Tribune '24—30. *Publ*: My Roads to Childhood; Nicholas; The Bold Dragoon; Nicholas & the Golden Goose; Reading Boys Like. *Ctr*: Various. *s.s*: Criticism of Children's Books. *Rec*: Theatre, travel. *a*: 35 Fifth Ave, New York 3, N.Y., U.S.A.

MOORE, Archie, M.A., F.R.C.S.(Eng). *b*: Pretoria S. Africa 1904. *e*: Lon Univ (King's Col) & Lon Hosp. Consult Surg. *c.t*: B.M.J. *s.s*: Orthopædic Surg. Mem Soc of Apothecaries, Mem Anatomical Soc of Gt Brit, Mem Brit Med Assoc. *a*: 89 Harley St, W.1. *t*: Welbeck 9344.

MOORE, Arthur, M.B.E. *b*: Glenavy, Co Antrim 1880. *e*: Campbell Coll Belfast, St John's Coll Oxf. *m*: Maude Eileen Maillet. *s*: 1. Chmn 1933—43 India Burma & Ceylon Section of Emp Press Union, Founder & Pres Indian & Eastern Newsp Soc '39—43, Mem Indian Cen Legislative Assem '26—33, Pub Rel Adviser to Supreme Allied Commdr S.E.A.C. '44—45. *n.a*: Foreign & War Corr The Times 1908—14 & '19—22, Ed The New Age '22—23, Asst Ed The Statesman (Calcutta & Delhi '24—33), Man Ed The Statesman '33—43. *Publ*: The Orient Express; This Our War; The Miracle. *Ctr*: Fortnightly, Dly Express, Atlantic Monthly, Contemporary, etc. *s.s*: Foreign & Commonwealth Affairs, Central Asia, Middle East, etc. *c*: Savile, Bengal, Imperial Delhi Gymkhana. *w.s*: 1915—19 Rifle Bde & R.A.F. *a*: Savile Club, 69 Brook St, London, W.1.

MOORE, Arthur Collin. *e*: Bradfield & Queen's Coll Oxf. Solictor (ret). *Publ*: The Eyes of Light; The Knight Punctilious; (With E. Dawson) Adrian Rome; A Comedy of Masks. *Ctr*: Yellow Book, etc. *a*: 69 Springfield Rd, London, N.W.8. *T*: Maida Vale 1690.

MOORE, Beatrice Esther. *b*: London. *e*: St John's Sch Lond. *m*: Rev Canon W. Moore J. P., R.D. (dec'd). *s*: 2. *d*: 1. Author & Journalist. *n.a*: Ed of Mother in Council '26. *Publ*: Verses & Carols; A Verse Kalendar. *Ctr*: Various. *s.s*: Literature, History, Rural Life. *a*: Cecil Lodge, Woodhall Spa, Lincs.

MOORE, Bertha, O.B.E. *b*: Brighton 1862. *e*: Brighton Sc, Roy Acad of Music, Lon. *m*: Frank Huth. *s*: 1. *d*: 1. *Publ*: Plays at Frenchs; Short Stories for Magazines. *s.s*: Music, writing, lecturing. Worked for the soldiers during war & collected £52,000 by her concerts for them. *a*: 29 Clarendon Rd, Holland Park, W.11. *t*: Park 1915.

MOORE, Bertram Percy. *b*: Birmingham 1877. *e*: St Paul's Sch & Balliol Coll Oxf. *m*: Fanny May. *d*: 1. Civil Servant (ret). *Publ*: Ovid's Art of Love (Verse trans). *c*: United Univs. *a*: 15 Elm Bank Mansions, Barnes, London, S.W.1. *T*: Prospect 3121.

MOORE, Charles. *Publ*: Advanced Thought & Spiritualism. *c.t*: Psychic Press, etc. Ed & Publ of Moore's Journ, The Unknown. *c*: Authors. *a*: 12 Holborn Viaduct, E.C.1. *t*: City 4145.

MOORE, Cyril. *n.a*: Yorkshire Evening News. *a*: 6 Wedgwood Grove, Leeds, 8. *t*: 61738.

MOORE, David Richard, A.B., Ph.D. *b*: Port Hope, Ontario 1877. *e*: Victoria Coll, Univs of Toronto & Chicago. *m*: Ethel May Hallam. *s*: 1. *d*: 2. Prof of Hist Oberlin Coll. *Publ*: A History of Latin America; Historia de la America Latina; Canada & the United States 1815—1830. *Ctr*: Various Hist Mags. *s.s*: Latin American Hist. *a*: Oberlin, Ohio, U.S.A. *T*: 1142.

MOORE, Eldon. *b*: London 1901. *e*: Lancing, Trin Coll Camb. Journalist. *n.a*: Rep Sub-Ed London, Provincial & Nat Press, Ed Eugenics Review 1927—33, Ed Bulletin of Imperial Bureau of Animal Genetics '29—30, Act Ed Everyman '33—34, Lond Press Exchange '37—40, B.B.C. (Overseas) '41—46. *Publ*: A Bibliography of Differential Fertility (Ed); Heredity—Mainly Human; The Magic Halibut. *Ctr*: Dly Mail, Dly Telegraph, Eugenics Review, Yorks Post, etc. *s.s*: Biology, Eugenics. *Rec*: Carpentry, flying. *a*: Eliot Vale Hse, Blackheath, London, S.E.3. *T*: Lee Green 3737.

MOORE, EVA (Mrs. Henry V. Esmond): actress; *b*. Brighton, Eng., Feb., 1868; *d*. Edward Henry and Emily (Strachan) Moore; educ. Brighton, privately; *m*. Henry V. Esmond (died, Paris, 1922), 1891. AUTHOR: Exits and Entrances; Eva Moore's Memories, 1924. Contributor to Woman's Journ., London Evening News and other papers. General character of writing: reminiscences. A leading actress of British stage from 1888; played with Willard, Mrs. John Wood, Ed. Terry, Charles Hawtrey, George Alexander, Beerbohm Tree and many others, appearing in My Lady Virtue, Old Heidelberg, The Bat, Sweet Kitty Bellairs, Little Lord Fauntleroy, Eliza Comes to Stay, Best People, Dangerous Age, When We Were Twenty-one, Caesar's Wife, Mary, Mary Quite Contrary, Garden of Eden, Hay Fever, Cat's Cradle, Getting Mother Married. Other plays: The Swan, A Grain of Mustard Seed. Toured Canada, 1921; played in 48 theatres; in New York, first, 1913; has done much film work, British and German companies. A founder and vice-pres. of The Stage Guild; one of the founders of Woman's Emergency Corps, which rendered outstanding service during Great War, 1914-19; received Belgian medal, Reign de Elizabeth. Relig. denom., Church of England. CLUBS: Bath, Ladies' Imperial, Pioneer, Arts Theatre. HOME: 50 Onslow Gardens, South Kensington, London, S. W. 1, Eng.

MOORE, Frederick Ernest. *b*: Blyth 1908. *e*: Blyth Sec & Priv. Journalist. *n.a*: Ed Staff Newcastle Journal 10 y as dis rep in princ mining area of Northumberland. *s.s*: Mining, road transport. *Rec*: Motoring. *a*: 146 Station Rd, Ashington, Northumberland. *t*: 55.

MOORE, Gerald. *b*: Watford 1899. *e*: Watford Gr Sch. Pianoforte Accompanist, Lecturer, has accompanied world's leading singers & instrumentalists in London, Paris, Vienna, Berlin, etc, Lectures & gives broadcast talks on music & the art of accompanying, records exclusively for H.M.V. *Publ*: The Unashamed Accompanist. *s.s*: Music. *Rec*: Golf, bridge, reading. *c*: Savage. *a*: 235 Sussex Gdns, Hyde Park, London, W.2. *T*: Paddington 7939.

MOORE, Geoffrey. *b*: Sydenham 1901. *e*: Brighton & Hove G.S. *m*: Doris Byron-Brown. Sub-Ed Kentish Independent. *n.a*: Times '15, '17 propaganda for Ferroris Della State (Italian State Rlys); '28—29 Rep Industrial Daily News, '29— Kentish Independent. *c.t*: Various n/ps & periodicals. *s.s*: Theatre, music hall, circus, films. *Rec*: Travel, philately, conjuring. *a*: 42a Tranquil Vale, Blackheath, S.E.3.

MOORE, George Edward, Litt.D., Hon.LL.D.(St Andrews), F.B.A., Fellow of Trin Coll Camb. *b*: Upper Norwood 1873. *e*: Dulwich Coll, Trin Coll Camb. *m*: Dorothy Mildred Ely. *s*: 2. Emeritus Prof of Philos, Craven Univ Scholar 1895, Visiting Prof in U.S.A. 1940—44. *n.a*: Ed "Mind" 1921—47. *Publ*: Ethics; Principia Ethica; Philosophical Studies. *Ctr*: Mind, International Journal of Ethics, Proceedings of the Aristotelian Society. *s.s*: Philosophy, Ethics, *Rec*: Gardening, singing, piano. *a*: 86 Chesterton Rd, Cambridge. *T*: 56666.

MOORE, Henderson. *b*: Seaton Delaval 1866. *e*: Priv. *m*: Isabella Davison. *s*: 3. *d*: 2. Journalist. *n.a* Newcastle Chronicle 40 y, Northcliffe n/p's 3 y.

s.s: Politics, general, trade union & labour affairs. *a*: Hillcote, Jesmond Dene Rd, Newcastle-on-Tyne. *t*: Gosforth 51919.

MOORE, Henry Francis, M.D., D.Sc., B.Ch., B.A.O., F.R.C.P.(Lond). T.R.C.P.I. *b*: Cappoquin 1887. *e*: St Brendan's Killarney & Univ Coll Dublin. *m*: Frances L. Thomas. *s*: 1. Prof of Med Univ Coll Dublin 1926—, Phys Mater Misericordia Hosp Dublin '20—, Cons Phys Nat Maternity Hosp Dublin '29—Mem Med Registration Counc of I.F.S. '28—, Mem Med Research Counc of Ireland, F.R.S.M., Roy Acad of Med Ireland. *Publ*: Ueber Anaphylaxie mit verschiedenen Fractionen von Seris, Zeitschr fur Immunitatsforshung; A Further Study of the Bactericidal Action of Ethylhydrocuprein on Pneumococci. *Ctr*: Lancet, B.M.J., Index of Therapeutic Agents; Biochem Study, & other med books. *s.s*: Internat Med. *c*: Roy Irish Yacht. *a*: 58 Fitzwilliam Sq, Dublin, & Susquehanna, Killiney, Co Dublin. *T*: 61834 & Dalkey 309.

MOORE, Rev. Henry Kingsmill, B.A., M.A., B.D., D.D.(Oxon), F.L.S., F.R.S.A.I. *b*: Dublin. *e*: Midleton Col Co Cork, K.Ed. VI Sc Bromsgrove & Balliol Oxf. *m*: Constance Turpin. *s*: 1. *d*: 1. *Publ*: Class Teaching; Irish History for Young Readers; Reminiscences & Reflections; The Centenary Book of the Church of Ireland Training College; etc. *c.t*: Ch Quarterly Review, Connoisseur, Journ of Educ, Garden, Brit Fern Gazette, etc. *s.s*: Educ & Brit ferns. Princ Ch of Ireland T.C. 1884-1927. *Rec*: Music, cycling, gardening. *a*: Cedar Mt, Dundrum, Co Dublin. *t*: 12.

MOORE, JAMES MIDDLETON: university lecturer; *b*. Lauder, Berwickshire, Scotland, Oct., 1871; *s*. William and Elsie (Swinton) M.; *educ*. Lauder Parish Sch., Edinburgh Univ. DEGREES: M.A. (1st Honors), Univ. Edinburgh, (Rhind scholar in Classical Lit.); *m*. Jessie Christina Peters, July 23, 1903. AUTHOR: An Intermediate French Course in Five Parts, 1911; Manual of French Composition (in collab. with Prof. R. L. G. Ritchie), 1914; Translation from French, 1918; French Prose from Calvin to Anatole France, 1918; French Verse from Villon to Verlaine, 1922; Junior Manual of French Composition, 1926; Illustrated edition of Colomba (Prosper Mérimée), and Lettres de Mon Moulin (Daudet), 1926; Junior Translation from French, 1928; Nelson's French Course, with Readers, 1928-30. General character of writing: text books, educational. Senior French Master, Royal High Sch., Edinburgh (formerly) and Rector Madras Coll. (St. Andrews). Relig. denom., Church of Scotland. OFFICE: The University, Edinburgh. HOME: 43 Mardale Crescent, Edinburgh, Scotland.

MOORE, John Cecil. *b*: Tewkesbury 1907. *e*: Malvern Coll. Author. *Publ*: Dixon's Cubs; Dear Lovers; Tramping Through Wales; The Book of the Fly-Rod (with Hugh Sheringham); King Carnival; The Walls Are Down; Overture Beginners; Country Men, Clouds of Glory; Countryman's England; Anglers' Week End Book (with Eric Taverner); Fleet Air Arm; Wits End; Escort Carrier; Portrait of Elmbury; Brensham Village. *a*: Orchards, Bredon, Nr Tewkesbury, Glos.

MOORE, John Robert, M.A., Ph.D. *b*: Pueblo, Colorado, U.S.A. 1890. *e*: Univs of Harvard & Missouri. *m*: Alice A. Beer. *s*: 1. *d*: 2. Prof of English & Library Cons in Augustan Literature Indiana Univ. *Publ*: Defoe in the Pillory & Other Studies; Defoe's Sources for Robert Drury's Journal; Daniel Defoe & Modern Economic Theory; Symphonies & Songs; etc. *Ctr*: Mod Lang Rev, Mod Lang Notes, Mod Philology, etc. *s.s*: The Life & Writings of Daniel Defoe, Original Poetry. *Rec*: Chess, walking, travel. *w.s*: World War I. *a*: 611 S. Jordan Ave, Bloomington, Indiana, U.S.A. *T*: 4170.

MOORE, John William. *b*: Peterborough 1929. *e*: Private, Deacon's Sch Peterborough. Journalist, Mem R.A.F. Assoc & N.U.J. *n.a*: Peterborough Standard since 1945. *Ctr*: Hunts County Mag, Evening Standard. *s.s*: Historical Subjects Relating to Huntingdonshire, Cambridgeshire, Northamptonshire, Sailing, Boating, Motoring. *Rec*: Boating, Rugby football. *c*: Authors & Writers. *a*: Glen Parva, 14 Fletton Ave, Peterborough, Northants. *T*: 3926.

MOORE, SIR JOHN WILLIAM: physician; D. Dublin, Ireland, Oct. 23, 1845; *s*. William Daniel Moore, M.D., and Catherine Mary (Montserrat) M.; *educ*. Dublin High Sch., Univ. Dublin. DEGREES: M.A., M.D., M.Ch., D.Sc. (honoris causâ, Oxon), F.R.C.P.I.; *m*. (1) Ellie Ridley (died 1878), (2) Louisa Emma Armstrong, 1881. AUTHOR: Eruptive and Continued Fevers, 1892; Meteorology: Practical and Applied, 1894 (2nd edit. 1910); Smallpox (Twentieth Century Practice of Medicine), 1898; The Climate of Ireland (in Climates and Baths of Great Britain and Ireland), 1902; Pneumonia (Clinical Section, Encyclopedia Medica, vol. IX). Editor (from 1873 to 1920): Dublin Journal of Medical Science. General character of writing: medical, text books, scientific. Physician to Meath Hosp. (Co. Dublin) Infirmary; cons. phys. to Cork St. Fever Hosp. and to Coombe Lying-in Hosp. (Dublin); rep. Royal Coll. of Physicians of Ireland on Gen. Medical Council; cons. phys., Dental Hosp. of Ireland and to Drumcondra Hosp. (Dublin); pres. Roy. Coll. of Phys. (Ireland), 1898-1900; knighted, 1900; Hon. Phys. to H. M. the King, in Ireland. Hon. Fellow Swedish Soc. Physicians; Fellow Roy. Meteorol. Soc.; pres. Roy. Acad. Med. (Ireland), 1918-21. Relig. denom., Church of Ireland (Protestant). CLUBS: University (Dublin), Oxford Medical Graduates. HOME: 40 Fitzwilliam Square, Dublin, Ireland.

MOORE, Marianne Craig, A.B. *b*: St Louis, Missouri 1887. *e*: Bryn Mawr Coll. Writer. *n.a*: Ed The Dial 1925—29. *Publ*: Nevertheless; Selected Poems. *Ctr*: N.Y. Times, Nation. *s.s*: Verse. *Rec*: Tennis, sailing. *a*: 260 Cumberland St, Brooklyn 5, New York, U.S.A.

MOORE, Martin. Daily Telegraph Staff. *a*: 28, Parliament Hill, Hampstead, N.W.3.

MOORE, Mary Fielding, B.A. *b*: Horwich, Lancs 1898. *e*: St Annes Sch Lancs, St Annes Soc Oxf. Author (Children's Books). *Publ*: The Mary Moore Series; Canadian Magic; Dorcas, The Wooden Doll; Crusading Holiday; The Lion Who Ate Tomatoes; Holidays With Herta. *Ctr*: The Christian Science Monitor, Manch Guardian, etc. *s.s*: Sch Nature Readers, Animal Stories. *Rec*: Swimming, cycling, handicrafts. *a*: 32 Chatsworth Rd, St Annes-on-Sea, Lancs. *T*: 1862.

MOORE, Mary Macleod. See Rees, Mrs. Leonard.

MOORE, Maurice, C.B. *b*: Mayo, Ireland 1854. *e*: Oscott Col & Sandhurst. *m*: Evelyn Handcock. *s*: 1. Senator I.F.S. Dublin. *Publ*: An Irish Gentleman; etc. *s.s*: Irish & Eng Finan arrangements. *c*: Un Arts Dublin. *a*: 5 Sea View Terr, Donnybrook, Dublin. *t*: Balls Bridge 748.

MOORE, Maj.-Gen. The Hon. Newton James, K.C.M.G., V.D. *b*: Australia 1870. *e*: Prince Alfred Col Adelaide S.A. *m*: Isabel Lowrie. Pres Dominion Steel & Corporation Canada. *n.a*: Dir Odhams Press 1920. *Publ*: Notes on Western Australian Timbers. *s.s*: Forestry, emigration, steel & coal. Premier of Western Australia '06-10. Min for Lands & Agriculture. Colonial Treas. 1st Pres Land Surveyors Inst. Maj-Gen A.F. '14-18. Agent-Gen for Western Aust '11-17. M.P. at Westminster '18-32. M.P. Richmond '32. Chrm Standing Orders Counc in H. of C. 11 y. *Rec*: Golf, hunting. *c*: Carlton, Constitutional, etc. *a*: 16 Northumberland Av, Lon, W.C.2, & Mayes Park, Warnham, Sussex. *t*: Whitehall 1777.

MOORE, Rev. Philip Samuel, C.S.C., A.B., Ph.D. *b*: Wabash, Indiana 1900. Head Dept of Philosophy 1942 & Dean the Graduate Sch, Univ of Notre Dame '44—. *Publ*: (Ed) The Works of Peter of Poitiers; Petri Pictaviensis Allegoriæ super Tabernaculum Moysi; Sentientiæ Petri Pictaviensis. *a*: Corby Hall, Notre Dame, Indiana, U.S.A.

MOORE, Ralph Westwood, M.A.(Oxon). *b*: Wolverhampton 1906. *e*: Wolverhampton Gr Sch, Christ Church Oxf. *m*: Elsie Barbara Tonks. *s*: 2. Head Master of Harrow, Head Master Bristol Gr Sch 1933—42. *Publ*: The Moving of the Spirit; Where God Begins; Christ the Beginning; The Roman Commonwealth; The Romans in Britain; Comparative Greek & Roman Syntax; Idea & Expression; Prose at Present. *Ctr*: Times Lit Supp, Sunday Times. *s.s*: Theology, Literary Criticism, Greek & Roman Antiquities. *c*: Athenæum. *a*: The Headmaster's, Harrow, Middlesex.

MOORE, Ramsey Bignall. *b*: Douglas 1880. *e*: Douglas Gr Sch & Sec Sch. *m*: Agnes Cannell Clague. *s*: 2. H.M. Attorney-Gen I.o.M. 1921—45, Ex-Pres I.o.M. Nat Hist & Antiquarian Soc, Mem House of Keys '19—21, Supt of Rose Mt Meth S. Sc '15—41. *Publ*: The Isle of Man & International Law; Introduction to Centenary Volume of T. E. Brown; Revised Index of Manx Statutes; etc. *s.s*: Antiquities of the I.o.M. *Rec*: Gardening, fishing. *a*: Brookdale, Cronkbourne Rd, Douglas, Isle of Man. *T*: 746.

MOORE, Raymond. *b*: Queensland 1903. *e*: Toowoomba G.S. & Queensland Univ. *m*: Florinda Luck. Journalist. *n.a*: Sci Corr Daily Express. *c.t*: Various. *s.s* Sci News & Fiction, film & theatre criticism, fiction for boys. *Rec*: Swimming, tennis, photography. *a*: 17 Churston Mansions, Grays Inn Rd, W.C.1. *t*: Museum 8485.

MOORE, Raymond Cecil, A.B., Ph.D., Sc.D. *b*: Roslyn, Wash, U.S.A. 1892. *e*: Univs of Denison & Chicago. *m*: Lilian Boggs. Geologist. *n.a*: Ed Amer Assoc Petroleum Geologist Bulletin 1920—25, Journ Palæontology '29—37, Kansas Geol Survey Publs '17—47. *Publ*: Historical Geology; Intro to Historical Geology; Early Mississippian Formations of Missouri; Pennsylvanian Rocks of Kansas; Crinoids from Pennsylvanian & Permian of Texas. *Ctr*: Journ Geology, Amer Journ Sci, Journ Palæontology. *s.s*: Geology, Palæontology, Stratigraphy. *w.s*: 1942—45. *a*: University of Kansas, Lawrence, Kansas, U.S.A.

MOORE, ROBERT: professor of Hebrew; b. County Tyrone, Ireland, June, 1863; s. Turbitt and Dorcas (Pollock) M.; educ. Sandville Academical Instn. (Londonderry, Ireland). DEGREES: B.A. (Oxon), B.D. (Edinburgh); m. Margaret Halliday, April, 1921. AUTHOR: Life of William Dobbin, 1901. Contributor of article

MOORE, ROBERT FOSTER: ophthalmic surgeon; b. Cambridge, Eng., Oct., 1878; s. Edward and Mary (Stothart) M.; educ. Christ's Coll. (Cambridge), St. Bartholomew's Hosp. (London). DEGREES: M.A., B.Ch. (Cantab), L.R.C.P., F.R.C.S. (Eng.); m. Elizabeth Atteridge, 1919. AUTHOR: Medical Ophthalmology, 1922 (2nd edit. 1925). Contributor to numerous medical books and journals. General character of writing: medical, scientific. Surg. to Moorfields Eye Hosp. (oldest and largest eye hospital in England); senior surgeon St. Bartholomew's Hosp., (founded 1123). Relig. denom., Congregationalist. HOME: 53 Harley St., London, Eng.

MOORE, Robert Thomas, A.M., F.R.G.S. *b*: Haddonfield, New Jersey 1882. *e*: Univs of Pennsylvania & Munich, Harvard. *m*: Margaret Forbes Cleaves. *s*: 3. *d*: 2. Scientist & Poet. *n.a*: Ed Cassina 1911—16. *Publ*: Eileen; Check List of the Birds of Mexico (collab). *Ctr*: The Auk, The Condor, Wilson Bulletin, Alpine Journ, Wings, etc. *c*: Explorers' (N.Y.), Orpheus (Phila). *a*: Borestone Mountain, Monson, Maine. *T*: Sylvan 0-1123.

MOORE, T. G. *n.a*: Chm Motor Sport 1929. *s.s*: Motor racing, all matters connected with sports. *a*: 39 Victoria St, S.W.1. *t*: Victoria 5218.

MOORE, T. S. Prof Chemistry, Univ Lon. *a*: Hillside, Egham, Surrey.

MOORE, T. W., C.B.E. Gen Mang Imp Merchant Service Guild, The Arcade, Lord Street, Liverpool.

MOORE, THOMAS STURGE: autnor, poet, engraver on wood; b. Hastings, Eng., March, 1870; s. Daniel and Henrietta (Sturge) M.; educ. Dulwich Coll., London City Guilds Technical Inst (Kensington); m. Marie Henrietta Leonie Appia, 1903. AUTHOR (poetry): The Vinedresser and Other Poems, 1899; Aphrodite Against Artemis, 1901; Absalom, 1903; Danae, 1903; The Little School, 1905; Poems, 1906; A Sicilian Idyll, 1911; Marianne, 1911; Judith, 1911; The Sea is Kind, 1914; The Little School (enlarged), 1917; Tragic Mothers, 1920; Judas, 1923; Roderigo of Bivar, 1925; Collected Edition of Poems, 1931; (prose): The Centaur and the Bacchante (from the French of Maurice de Guerin), 1899; The Powers of the Air, 1920; (criticism): Altdorfer, 1903; Durer, 1904; Corregio, 1906; Art and Life, 1910; Hark to These Three, 1915; Some Soldier Poets, 1919; Armour for Aphrodite, 1929. Contributor to Criterion, Life and Letters, Apollo and other mags. General character of writing: poetry, prose criticism, essays, plays. An original mem. Society of Twelve, also of Academic Com. of the Roy. Soc. of Literature. HOME: 40 Well Walk, London, N. W. 3, Eng.

MOORE-GUGGISBERG, Lady Decima, C.B.E. *b*: Brighton, Sussex. *e*: Boswell Hse Coll Brighton, Blackheath Conservatoire of Music. *m*: Brig.-Gen. Sir Gordon Guggisberg. Actress & Organiser. *Publ*: We Two in West Africa; A Black Mark. *Ctr*: Various papers. *Rec*: Ski-ing, motor-driving, golf. *a*: Overseas Hse, Park Pl, St James, London, S.W.1.

MOOREHEAD, Alan, O.B.E. *b*: Melbourne 1910. *e*: Scotch Coll Melbourne, Melbourne Univ. *m*: Lucy Milner. *s*: 1. *d*: 1. *n.a*: War Corr Dly Express 1939—45, The Observer '47—. *Publ*: African Trilogy — Mediterranean Front; A Year of Battle; The End of Africa; Eclipse; Montgomery. *Ctr*: The Observer & other publ. *c*: Garrick, Savile. *a*: Portofino, Italy.

MOORHEAD, Thomas Gillman, M.D., D.P.H., F.R.C.P.I., F.R.C.P., Hon.LL.D. *b*: Co Tyrone, Ireland 1878. *e*: Trin Coll Dublin, Vienna. *m*: (1) Mai Beatrice Quinn, (2) Sheila Gwynn. Regius Prof of Med Trin Coll Dublin. Vice-Pres Roy Irish Acad. *Publ*: Short History of Sir Patrick Dun's Hospital; Surface Anatomy; *Ctr*: Various Med Journs. *Rec*: Motoring, fishing. *c*: Roy Irish Yacht, Kildare St (Dublin). *a*: 23 Upper Fitzwilliam St. Dublin, Ireland. *T*: 61851.

MOORHOUSE, Alfred Charles. *b*: Rhos-on-Sea, Nth Wales 1910. *e*: King Edward VI Sch Birmingham & Gonville & Caius Coll Camb. University Lecturer. *Publ*: Writing & the Alphabet. *Ctr*: Classical Review, Classical Quarterly, Greece & Rome, American Journ of Philology. *s.s*: Linguistics & Philology (esp Greek & Latin), History of Writing. *Rec*: Walking, cycling, tennis. *a*: University College, Swansea.

MOORHOUSE, Herbert. *b*: Huddersfield 1908. *e*: Huddersfield Col. Journalist. *n.a*: Asst Staff, Repres of Yorks Observer Huddersfield '25—29, Wakefield Staff Rep of Yorks Observer '29—. *s.s*: Sports. *Rec*: Golf, swimming. Appnt Press & Publicity for Wakefield & W. Riding Historical Pageant produced June '33. *a*: 1 Horne St, Wakefield, Yorks. *t*: 2997.

MOORMAN, Rev. John Richard Humpidge, M.A., D.D.(Camb). *b*: Leeds 1905. *e*: Gresham's Sch Holt & Emmanuel Coll Camb. *m*: Mary Caroline Trevelyan. Prin Chichester Theological Coll & Chancellor Chichester Cathedral *Publ*: Church Life in England in the 13th Century; The Sources for the Life of St Francis; B. K. Cunningham, A Memoir; A New Fioretti. *Ctr*: Eng Hist Review, Bulletin of John Rylands Library, Ch Quart Review, Theology. *s.s*: Mediæval History. *Rec*: Music & country life. *a*: The Theological College, Chichester. *T*: 3369.

MORAES, Frank, M.A. *b*: Bombay, India 1907. *e*: Univs of Bombay & Oxf. *m*: Beryl D'Monte. *s*: 1. Ed-in-Chief The Times of Ceylon. *n.a*: War Corres (Burma & China) for Times of India, Bombay & Allied Newsps (Kemsley Group) 1942—45. *Publ*: Story of India; Introduction to India (with R. Stimson). *s.s*: Politics. *c*: Cricket of India (Bombay). *a*: Salcombe, Buller's Lane, Colombo, Ceylon. *T*: 8437.

MORAN, 1st Baron of Manton, Charles McMoran Wilson, M.C. *b*: Skipton-in-Craven, Yorks. *m*: Dorothy Dufton. *s*: 2. *Publ*: The Anatomy of Courage. *Ctr*: Various. *Rec*: Country life, golf. *w.s*: 1914—18. *a*: 129 Harley St, London, W.1. *T*: Welbeck 4647.

MORAND, Dexter. *b*: Lon. *e*: Polytech & Univ Col Lon. *Publ*: Monumental & Commercial Architecture of Great Britain; Minor Architecture of Suffolk. *c.t*: Architect & Building News, Design for To-day, Archittura Rome, Obras, Madrid, Ideal Home, etc. *s.s*: Archt, sculpture, decoration. *a*: 23 Market St, Mayfair, W.1. *t*: Grosvenor 3354.

MORAND, Paul. *b*: 1889. *e*: Paris & Oxford. Diplomatist & Author. *Publ*: New York; London; Open all Night; Closed all Night; Black Magic; Lewis & Irene; etc. *a*: 99 Gt Russell St, W.C.

MORAY WILLIAMS, Ursula. *b*: Petersfield 1911. *e*: Priv. *Publ*: Jean Pierre; For Brownies; The Autumn Sweepers; Kelpie—The Gipsies Pony; Anders and Marta ('35); all with illustrations; etc. *a*: North Stoneham Hse, nr. Eastleigh, Hants. *t*: Bassett 68317.

MORDAUNT, Elinor. Author. *Publ*: Cross Winds; Mrs Van Kleek; Traveller's Pack; Purely for Pleasure. *a*: c/o Martin Secker Ltd, 5 John St, W.C.2.

MORDEY, William, F.R.S.A., F.R.G.S., F.R.Econ.S., J.P. *b*: Bishop Auckland, Co Durham 1882. *e*: Newport Gr Sch, Friends Sch Saffron Walden, Bootham Sch York. *m*: Mary Forbes Smith Leckie. *s*: 2. *d*: 1. Shipowner & Shipbroker. *n.a*: Ed Bootham 1912—21. *Ctr*: South Wales Argus, Bootham, Economist. *s.s*: Trade & Econs, Hist & Lit. *Rec*: Walking, mountaineering, gardening. *a*: The Knoll, Clytha Park, Newport, Mon. *T*: 3441.

MORDI, Chukwuma Cyril, F.R.S.A. *b*: Asabe, Nigeria 1919. *e*: Govt Coll Umuahia, Higher Coll Yaba Nigeria, Imp Coll of Tropic Agric, Univ of Lond, Lincoln's Inn. *Ctr*: The West African Rev (Liverpool), The Nigerian Press, Trinidad Guardian Ev News. *s.s*: Law & Current Problems. *Rec*: Tennis, photography, writing. *a*: c/o 103 Gower St, London, W.C.1, & Umuaji, Asaba, Sth Nigeria, West Africa. *T*: Asaba 5 (Nigeria).

MORE, Brookes. *b*: Dayton, Ohio 1859. *e*: Publ Scs of St Louis Missouri. *m*: Bedelia Margaret Madden. *s*: 1. *d*: 1. Poet, Publisher, Printer. *Publ*: Great War Ballads (1916, republd as Sweet Maggie McGee '23); The Lover's Rosary ('18); The Beggar's Vision ('21); The Ring of Love; Bootleg Charlie; Ovid's Metamorphoses Books I—V inclusive in blank verse ('33); etc. *c.t*: Princ Poets of the World, Yr Books of the American Poetry Assoc. *s.s*: Poetry. Pres Cornhill Pubg Co '22—. Vice-Pres Jordan & More Press Boston '21—33, Pres '34—. *c*: Boston Authors, Shakespeare Assoc of Amer, Amer Poetry Assoc, New England Poetry, Boston Classical. *a*: Gt Hill, Hingham, Mass, U.S.A. *t*: 0999.

MORE, David Pennefather Thomas. *e*: St Lawrence Col Ramsgate. *m*: Gladys Stampfer. *d*: 3. Journalist. *n.a*: Essex County Standard, Colchester, Westminster Gazette, Reporter Starmer Group 1929–. Mem N.U.J. '24–. *Rec*: Walking, painting. *a*: 49 Valley Rd, Streatham, S.W.16.

MORECROFT, John Henry. *b*: Dover 1907. *e*: Dover County Sc. Journalist. *n.a*: News Ed South London Observer, Camberwell & Peckham Times. Mem N.U.J. '28–. *c.t*: All daily papers. *s.s*: Crime. *Rec*: Rowing. *a*: 80c Madeira Rd, Streatham, S.W.16. *t*: 4879.

MORELAND, John Richard. *b*: Norfolk, Virginia, U.S.A. *n.a*: Founder & 1st Ed of The Lyric, cont Ed of the Will o' the Wisp, consulting Ed of the Kaleidograph. *Publ*: Red Poppies in the Wheat; The Sea and April; Blowing Sand; Newry; The Moon Mender; etc. *c.t*: Personalist, Midland, Catholic World, Contemporary Verse, Good Housekeeping, McCalls Magazine, Modern Priscilla, Commonweal, Voices, Shadowland, Ave Maria, Harp. Lariat, etc. *s.s*: Criticism and teaching of prosody. *c*: Poetry Soc of America, Poetry Soc of Spring Hill, Alabama, Poetry Soc of Alabama. *a*: Spottswood Manor, Norfolk, Virginia. U.S.A.

MORETON, Arthur Sydney. Publisher. *a*: 12 St Mary Axe, E.C.3. *t*: Ave 9941.

MORENO, Jacob L., M.D. *b*: Bucharest, Roumania 1892. *e*: Univ of Vienna. *m*: Florence Bridge. *d*: 1. Psychiatrist, Lecturer on Sociometry, Sociatry, Psychodrama. *n.a*: Founder & Chmn Ed Bd Sociometry 1937—, Founder & Ed Society '47—. *Publ*: The Theatre for Spontaneity; Who Shall Survive; The Words of the Father; The Concept of Sociodrama. *Ctr*: American Sociological Review, etc. *s.s*: Sociometry, Psychodrama, Sociatry, Psychiatry. *a*: 259 Wolcott Ave, Beacon, New York, U.S.A.

MORETON, Rev. Canon Harold Albert Victor, B.A., F.R.Hist.S., D.ès.L. *m*: Anne D. Farrington. *s*: 2, *d*: 2. Canon Residentiary & Chancellor of Hereford Cathedral. *n.a*: Editor of Oecumenica 1934—39. *Publ*: La Réforme Anglicane; Rome et L'Eglise Primitive; (Ed) L'Anglicanisme. *s.s*: Unity of Christendom, Early Church Hist. *a*: The Close, Hereford. *T*: 2817.

MOREY, Richard Adrian, M.A.(Camb), D.Phil.(Munich), F.R.Hist.S. *b*: London 1904. *e*: St Paul's & Latymer Schs, Christ's Coll Camb & Univ of Munich. Bursar Downside Abbey & School. *Publ*: Bartholomew of Exeter, A Study in the 12th Century. *Ctr*: Downside Review, Cath Hist Review of America. *s.s*: Mediæval Hist (Eng 12th Century). *a*: Downside Abbey, Stratton-on-the-Fosse, nr Bath. *T*: Stratton-on-the-Fosse 5.

MORGAN, Alexander, O.B.E., M.A., D.Sc. *b*: Leith 1860. *e*: Old Town G.S. Aber & Edin Univ. *m*: Isabel Duthie. *s*: 2. Dir of Studies & Princ of Edin T.C. Pres Educ Inst of Scot 1911—12. Mem Ct of Univ of Edin. *Publ*: Education & Social Progress; Makers of Scottish Education; Scottish University Studies; etc. *c.t*: Edin Univ Journ, etc. *s.s*: Education. *Rec*: Golf. *c*: Scot Lib, Edin. *a*: 1 Midmar Gdns, Edin. *t*: 51817.

MORGAN, Ann Violet. *b*: Swansea. *n.a*: Gloucestershire Echo, Cheltenham Chronicle. *s.s*: Fashions, cookery, children's page, etc. *a*: c/o The Echo, Cheltenham.

MORGAN, Arthur Ernest, D.Sc., LL.D. *b*: Cincinnati, U.S.A. 1878. *e*: Hgh Sch St Cloud Minnesota. *m*: Lucy Middleton Griscom. *s*: 2. *d*: 1. Hydraulic Engineer, Educator. *n.a*: Ed Antioch Notes 1923—36. *Publ*: The Small Community; The Long Road; Edward Bellamy, A Biography; Nowhere Was Somewhere; My World; A Business of My Own; etc. *Ctr*: Atlantic Monthly, N.Y. Times, Civil Engineering, Ency Britannica, Motive, Amer Mercury. *s.s*: Hydraulic Engineering (River Control). *Rec*: Gardening. *a*: 114 E Whiteman St, Yellow Springs, Ohio, U.S.A. *T*: Yellow Springs 2161.

MORGAN, Arthur Eustace, M.A., Hon.LL.D.(MacMaster), F.R.S.C. *b*: Bristol 1886. *e*: Univ Coll Bristol, Trin Coll Dublin. *m*: Mabel Eugenie Melhuish. *d*: 4. Educ Dir British Counc since 1945, Princ & Vice-Chancellor McGill Univ Montreal '35—37, Regional Information Officer M.o.I. Newcastle-on-Tyne '39—41, Asst Sec Min of Lab & Nat Service '41—45. *Publ*: Scott & His Poetry; Tendencies of Modern English Drama; English Plays; Needs of Youths; Young Citizen; etc. *Ctr*: Various. *Rec*: Motoring. *c*: Athenæum. *w.s*: R.A. 1915—19. *a*: c/o the Athenæum Club, Pall Mall, S.W.1.

MORGAN, Betty, B.A., D.Litt. *n.a*: Spec Corres Starmer Group 1932—33, Woman's Ed Woman's Sec Farmers Weekly '34, Ed Staff B.B.C. European Service '40—46, Berlin Corres Brit Zonal Newsp '46—. *Publ*: Histoire du Journal des Scavans. *Ctr*: Dly Telegraph, News Chron, S. Times. *a*: 12 Mortimer Cresc, London, N.W.6. *T*: Maida Vale 4163.

MORGAN, C. Lloyd. *Publ*: Emergent Evolution; The Emergence of Novelty. *a*: 79 Pevensey Rd, St Leonards-on-Sea.

MORGAN, C. Naunton, F.R.C.S. *a*: 40 Harley St, W.1.

MORGAN, Charles, M.A., LL.D., F.R.S.L. *b*: Kent 1894. *e*: Roy Naval Colls Osborne & Dartmouth, B.N.C. Oxf. *m*: Hilda Vaughan. *s*: 1. *d*: 1. Novelist & Dramatist, Legion of Honour. *n.a*: Dramatic Critic The Times 1921—39, Lit Critic S. Times '45. *Publ*: The Gunroom; My Name is Legion; Portrait in a Mirror; The Fountain; Epitaph on George Moore; Sparkinbroke; The Voyage; Empty Room; The Flashing Stream (Play); Reflections in a Mirror; the Judge's Story. *Ctr*: Times, N.Y. Times, etc. *s.s* Eng 17th Century, Aesthetic Philosophy, Drama. *Rec*: Swimming, drawing. *c*: Garrick. *a*: 16 Campden Hill Sq, London, W.8.

MORGAN, Rev. Charles, M.R.S.L. *b*: St Helens. *e*: Priv, St Aidan's Coll Birkenhead. *m*: Elizabeth E. Hartley. Clerk in Holy Orders. *Publ*: Theism; Immortality. *s.s*: Philosophy of Religion. *Rec*: Reading, walking. *a*: Ebchester, Co Durham.

MORGAN, CONWY LLOYD: emeritus professor, Bristol Univ.; b. London, Eng., Feb., 1852; s. James Arthur and Mary (Anderson) M.; educ. Royal Grammar Sch. Guildford (Eng.), Royal Coll. of Science and Royal Sch. of Mines (London). DEGREES (Hon.) LL.D (Aberdeen), (Hon.) D.Sc. (Bristol and Wales), Murchison Medallist, De la Beche Medallist, Duke of Cornwall Scholar and Associate in Mining and Metallurgy (London); F.R.S.; m. Emily Charlotte Maddock, 1879. AUTHOR: Water and Its Teachings, 1882; Facts Around Us, 1884; Springs of Conduct, 1885; Animal Biology, 1887; Animal Life and Intelligence, 1890; Animal Sketches, 1891; Introduction to Comparative Psychology, 1894; Psychology for Teachers, 1895; Habit and Instinct, 1896; Animal Behaviour, 1900; Interpretation of Nature, 1905; Instinct and Experience, 1912; Eugenics and Environment, 1919; Emergent Evolution, 1923; Life, Mind and Spirit, 1926; Mind at the Crossways, 1929; The Animal Mind, 1930. Contributor to Hibbert Journ., Realist, Nature, Monist, Journ. of Philosoph. Studies. General character of writing: scientific, text books, philosophical. Letrer. in English and Physical Science, Diocesan Coll., Rondebosch (S. Africa), 1878-1883; prof. Biology and Geology, Univ. Coll. (Bristol), 1884; prin. same, 1887-1909; first vice-chancellor Univ. Bristol, 1909; since retirement has held professorship of Psychology. Relig. denom., Church of England. HOME: 79 Pevensey Road, St. Leonards-on-Sea, Eng. on Pre-existence to Hastings's Ency. of Religion and Ethics. Contributor to Free Church of Scotland Record, Evangelical Quarterly (Edinburgh and Amsterdam). General character of writing: religious, historical biographical. Relig. denom., Presbyterian. OFFICE: Free Church College, Edinburgh, Scotland. HOME: Loughnease, Strabane, County Tyrone, Northern Ireland.

MORGAN, David Derwenydd. *b*: Llansawel 1872. *e*: Llansawel G.S. & Sc of Pharm Lon. *m*: Mary Davies. Chem & Druggist. *Publ*: A Welsh Doctor; The Tavern Across the Street; etc (Eng novels); Difyrrwr y Dorf; Torrir Gadwyn; Doctor Jim; Dic Penderyn; etc. *c.t*: Cymric Times, Cambrian News. *s.s*: Welsh life. *a*: The Pharmacy, Pencader, S. Wales.

MORGAN, Rt. Rev. Edmund Robert. *b*: London 1888. *e*: Winchester, New Coll Oxf. *m*: Isabel Charlotte Jupp. *s*: 3. Suffragan Bishop of Southampton. *n.a*: Ed East & West Review 1935—45. *Publ*: The Mission of the Church. *Rec*: Fishing, gardening. *c*: Athenæum. *a*: 5 The Close, Winchester. *T*: Winchester 3535.

MORGAN, Edward Victor. *b*: Harbury 1915. *e*: Warwick Sch, Sidney Sussex Coll Camb. *m*: Margaret Elizabeth Lewis Huggins. *s*: 1. *d*: 1. Prof of Econs Univ Coll of Swansea. *Publ*: The Theory & Practice of Central Banking 1797—1913. *Ctr*: Economic Journal, Economica, Banker. *s.s*: Economics, especially Monetary & Financial Questions. *Rec*: Sailing, swimming, bridge. *a*: 42 Pinewood Rd, Uplands, Swansea. *T*: 5395.

MORGAN, Rev. George Campbell, D.D.(Chicago). *b*: Tetbury 1863. *e*: Priv & Douglas Sc Cheltenham. *m*: Annie Morgan. *s*: 4. *d*: 2. *Publ*: Crises of Christ; Teaching of Christ; The Analysed Bible; Messages of Books of Bible; The Acts; The Ministry of the Word; etc. *s.s*: The Bible. *a*: 310 St Ermin's, S.W.1. & Westminster Cong Ch, Buckingham Gate, S.W.1.

MORGAN, Gerda Myfanwy. *Publ*: The Stones & Story of Jesus Chapel, Cambridge; This Flower & This Nettle; King George the Fifth; Egypt & the Desert; The People of the Far North. *a*: 12 Cheyne Gdns, London, S.W.3.

MORGAN, Gwenllian Elizabeth Fanny, F.S.A., M.A., J.P. *Publ*: Eastnor Castle; Brecon Cathedral; Hanerd Chapel; Old Welsh Chips, etc. *c.t*: Archæological papers & mags. *s.s*: Social reform, archæology, public work. First woman Town Councillor in Wales, First lady to be elected Mayor in Wales, coronation Mayor of Brecon 1910—11, coronation medal, Gov Welsh Nat Library. *a*: Buckingham Pl, Brecon.

MORGAN, Sir Herbert E., K.B.E., F.R.S.L. Dir of Allied Newspapers 1937—39, Dir of Economists Bookshop Ltd. '47. *Publ*: The Dignity of Business; Munitions of Peace; Careers for Boys & Girls. *s.s*: Propaganda, Business & Administration. *Rec*: Punting, golf. *c*: Reform, Savage. *a*: 1 Carlton Hse Terr, London, S.W.1.

MORGAN, HILDA CAMPBELL: see Vaughan, Hilda.

MORGAN, J. H. Sec Mansfield Br N.U.J. *a:* 20 Stella St, Mansfield.

MORGAN, Rev. Canon James, M.A., D.D. *b:* Leicester 1873. *e:* Wyggeston Gr Sch, Selwyn Coll Camb, Trin Coll Dublin. Vicar of Christ Church, Blacklands, Hastings. *Publ:* The Importance of Tertullian in the Development of Christian Dogma; The Psychology of St Augustine; The Church of St Andrew the Great, Cambridge; Christ Church, Blacklands, Hastings. *s.s:* Educ. *a:* Blacklands Vicarage, Hastings. *T:* 1821.

MORGAN, John. *b:* Bath 1892. *m:* Mary Wright. *d:* 4. Farmer, jnlst. *n.a:* Agricultural Ed Daily Herald '31. *Publ:* The Scene is England; Twelve Studies of Soviet Russia. *s.s:* Agriculture, countryside topics, politics, economics. Prospective Labour Parliamentary Candidate Leicester West '35. Founder "For Farmers Only" Talks B.B.C. '33—35. *a:* Chesters, Gt Chesterford, Essex. *t:* 4.

MORGAN, John Charles. *b:* Southend-on-Sea 1923. *e:* Mid-Essex Tech Coll & Sch of Art Chelmsford. Journalist. *Rec:* All sport. *w.s:* R.A.F. 1939—45. *a:* Barrington, New Century Rd, Laindon, Essex. *T:* Laindon 2256.

MORGAN, Brig.-Gen. John Hartman, K.C., M.A., D.L., J.P. *b:* 1876. *e:* Balliol Coll Oxf. Barrister. *Publ:* The House of Lords & the Constitution; The New Irish Constitution; The German War Book; War, Its Conduct & Legal Results; Leaves From a Field Note-Book; Gentleman-at-Arms; The Present State of Germany; Viscount Morley: An Appreciation; Remedies Against the Crown; What We Are Fighting For; Assize of Arms. *Ctr:* Times, Quarterly Review, etc. *s.s:* Legal, Military, Lit. *Rec:* Walking, riding, tennis. *a:* 4 Temple Gdns, Temple, London, E.C.4. *T:* Central 8549.

MORGAN, Louise, M.A., Ph.D. *m:* (1) G. S. Fulcher, (2) O. F. Theis. *s:* 2. *d:* 1. Journalist. *n.a:* The Outlook (Lond) 1923—28, Assoc Ed Everyman '29—32, Ed '32—33, Special Corr News Chronicle '34—. *Publ:* George Wilde & the Academic Drama, MSS & Proofs Destroyed in Sack of Louvain; Writers at Work, etc. *Ctr:* Good Housekeeping, C.O.I. *a:* 10 Old Sq, Lincoln's Inn, London, W.C.2. *T:* Holborn 8316.

MORGAN, Marjorie McCallum, B.Litt., M.A., D.Phil. *b:* Shrewsbury 1915. *e:* Shrewsbury Priory County Sch, Lady Margaret Hall Oxf, Sorbonne Paris. *m:* A. C. Chibnall. *d:* 2. Lecturer in Hist, Girton Coll Camb. *Publ:* The English Lands of the Abbey of Becl *Ctr:* Eng Hist Rev, History, Journ of the Brit Archæo. Assoc, Trans of the Roy Hist Soc, Aberdeen Univ Rev. *s.s:* History. *a:* Madingley Rise, Madingley Rd, Cambridge. *T:* Cambridge 3923.

MORGAN, Montague Travers. M.C. *b:* L'pool 1889. *e:* L'pool Col & Wolverley Kidderminster. Married. *s:* 2. Civil Servant. *c.t:* Bulletin of Hygiene, etc. *s.s:* Public health. *Rec:* Golf, fishing. *a:* Ministry of Health, Whitehall, Lon. *t:* 4300.

MORGAN, Oswald Gayer, M.A., M.Ch, F.R.C.S. Ophthalmic Surg. *c.t:* Brit Journ Ophthalmology, Proc Roy Soc Med, B.M.J. *a:* 24 Harley St, W.1. *t:* Lang 2661.

MORGAN, Rev. Stuart Miles. *b:* London 1887. *Publ:* Choirs in Little Churches; Music in the Village Church. *a:* Oborne Rectory, Sherborne, Dorset.

MORGAN, Thomas Amesfield. *b:* Workington 1888. *e:* Workington Acad & Garfield Hse. *m:* May Bingham. *s:* 2. Sub-Ed Nott'm Guardian. *n.a:* Chester Courant & Cheshire Observer 1908—14, Nott'm Guardian '14—. *c.t:* Lond & Prov n/ps. *s.s:* Industrial, textile, general, football. *Rec:* Photography, reading, walking. *a:* 98 Danethorpe Vale, Sherwood, Nottingham. *t:* 68117.

MORGAN, William Thomas. *b:* Cardiff 1886. *m:* Elsie Vincent. *s:* 1. *d:* 1. *n.a:* Junior Rep Barry Dock News, Rep Devon & Exeter Gazette, Western Times, Express & Echo Exeter 1906—08, Sub-Ed Cardiff Ev Express '08—11, Sub-Ed The Star '11—21, Chief Sub-Ed '21—30, News Ed '30, Asst Ed '40—45, Dep Ed , (ret) '47. *Rec:* Tennis, gardening. *a:* Craigower, St Andrews Close, Nth Finchley, London, N.12. *T:* Hillside 3261.

MORGAN-POWELL, Samuel. *b:* London. *e:* Ellesmere, Univ of Lond. *m:* Velma Alberta Dawson. Lit & Dramatic Critic Montreal Star 1929—. *n.a:* Sub-Ed Demarara Dly Chron 1900—03, Ed Demerara Argosy '03—04, Mem Ed Staff Montreal Witness '05, Montreal Herald '06, News Ed Montreal Star '08, Asst Ed-in-Chief '29, Lit & Dramatic Critic '29—, Ed-in-Chief '40—46. *Publ:* Memories That Live; Night Thoughts; Down the Years. *s.s:* Drama & Lit Criticisms. *Rec:* Reading, motoring, play & song writing. *a:* 3493 Atwater Ave, Montreal, Quebec, Canada. *T:* Wilbank 6812.

MORGAN-WEBB. Charles Crofton, M.A. (Cantab). *b:* Yandoon, Burma, 1900. *e:* Leys Sc Cambridge, Sidney Sussex Col Cantab. *m:* Margaret Noël Holyoake. Mang ed. *n.a:* Western Times Co. Ltd., '21—25. Mang Finchley Press Ltd., '25—29; Mang Ed, '29—. *a:* Yardley, Oakhurst Ave, East Barnet, Herts. *t:* Barnet 2074.

MORI, SHO-ZABURO: professor in Tokyo Imperial Univ.; b. Shiga, Japan, March, 1887; s. Shuku and Tsuna (Kega) M.; educ. Peers' Sch., Tokyo Imperial Univ., Univ. of London, Univ. of Paris, in London and Paris, 1914-1917. DEGREES: B.A., Ph.D. (both Tokyo); m. Momoyo Mori, 1917. AUTHOR (in Japanese): Studies on Social Insurance, 1921; Health Insurance Act, 1923; Modern Insurance Problems, 1926; Essays on Social Insurance, 1928. Editor: The Life Insurance Management. Contributor to Journ. of Economics, Social Insurance (Rome, Italy). General character of writing: economic, commercial. Professor of Insurance, Faculty of economics, in Tokyo Imperial Univ., Pres. Life Insurance Management Soc., mem. of Social Insurance Commission of the Imperial Govt. CLUBS: University, Peers'. Religion, Buddhist. HOME: 30 Nakanocho, Ichigaya, Tokyo, Japan.

MORIARTY, Cecil Charles Hudson, C.B.E., L.L.D. (T.C.D.). *b:* Tralee, Eire 1877. *e:* Trinity Coll, Dublin Univ. *m:* Muriel U. Shæn Carter. *d:* 3. District Insp Royal Constabulary 1902—18, Asst Chief Constable Birm'ham '18—35, Chief Constable Birm'ham '35—41, Rugby Football Irish Int Team 1899, C.St.J. *Publ:* Police Law; Police Procedure & Administration; Emergency Police Law (with James Whiteside); Questions & Answers in Police Duties; Further Questions & Answers in Police Duties; Questions & Answers in Police Duties (Third Series). *Rec:* Gardening, fishing. *a:* Albyns, Tenbury Wells, Worcestershire.

MORING, Alexander. *e:* Univ Col Sc & Taunton Sc. Publisher. *n.a:* Sub Ed Tree Lover Mag. *Publ:* One Hundred Portraits of Famous Men & Women (Biographies). Diploma in History & Art (Lon Univ). *a:* 2a Cork St, W.1. *t:* Regent 4792.

MORISON, G. G. T. *c.t:* Proceedings Roy Soc, Journ of Agric, Science, Nature. *a:* Christ Church, Oxf.

MORISON, Rev. E. F., D.D. *Publ:* St Basil & his Rule; Rufinus on the Creed; The Lord's Prayer. *c.t:* Journ of Theo Studies, Church Quarterly Review, Expository Times. *a:* The Rectory, Fakenham, Norfolk. *t:* 102.

MORISON, Ernest, M.J.I., O.B.E. *b:* Hull 1868. *e:* Priv. *m:* Annie Irene Stoakes. *s:* 2. Journalist & Advtg Contractor. *n.a:* Apprenticed Hull Daily News, Mang Dir Morison's Advtg Ag (Hull) Ltd, Dir Publicity Hull, Wembley Exhib 1924–25. *Publ:* Publicity, A Journal for Business Men 1887–92; First Brit advtg mag with world wide circulation; Why Britain is Losing Its Dominion Markets ('26); etc. *c.t:* Eng, American, Canadian & S. & E. African papers, etc. *s.s:* Publicity, advertising. Dir Hull City A.F.C. 15 y. War Service '14–19; despatches twice. *Rec:* Travel, fly-fishing. *a:* 99 Holden Rd, N.12. *t:* Hil, 2366.

MORISON, Frank, A.I.P.A. *b:* Birm 1881. *e:* K.E. G.S. Stratford-upon-Avon, & Birm. *m:* Annie Mills. *d:* 1. *Publ:* Who Moved the Stone? a Study of the Historical Problem of the Resurrection; Sunset, a scientific phantasy; J. H. Jowett, M.A., a critical appreciation. *c.t:* Sphere. *s.s:* History & religious criticism. Photographer Roy Flying Corps. *Rec:* Astronomy, photography, travel. *c:* Assoc Inst of Practitioners in Advert. *a:* The White Cottage, Norbury Av, Lon, S.W.16.

MORISON, George Herbert. *b:* Wellington N.Z. 1888. *e:* King's Col Lon & Chelsea Polyt. *m:* Beryl Marie Kerber. Journalist. *n.a:* Repres Financial Times as Berlin Corr 10 ys until 1933, Formerly Berlin Corr Westminster Gazette, Sunday Times, Sydney Aust, North Amer N/ps Alliance. Berlin Corr Sunday Times. Mem N.U.J. '33. *Publ:* Danzig's Yesterday & To-morrow; Those Happy Days in Danzig. *c.t:* Daily Mail, Daily Express, Scientific Amer, N. American N/p Alliance, Scientific Amer, Popular Sci Monthly. etc. *s.s:* Finance & econ & popular sci & technology. 4 ys internment Germany during War. Attended Paris Peace Conf '19 special Corr of Irish Times. Lived nearly yr Free City Danzig during critical period '31 & through this & frequent trips Poland as Corr Financial Times became authority all political & econ problems Europe's Eastern frontiers. Expert French & German linguist. *Rec:* Trav. *c:* Press Assoc (Berlin). *a:* Berlin W. 35, Tirpitz Ufer 58, Germany. *t:* Berlin a2 Lützow 2000.

MORISON, John Lyle, M.A., D.Litt., LL.D. *b:* Greenock 1875. *e:* Greenock Acad & Glasgow Univ. *m:* Maud Willes. *d:* 1. Prof (Emeritus) of Hist Univ of Durham, Prof of Hist Queens Univ Kingston Canada 1907–22 & King's Coll Newcastle '22–40. *Publ:* Lawrence of Lucknow : A Life of Sir Henry Lawrence ; British Supremacy & Canadian Self-Government ; Life of the Eight Earl of Elgin ; Reginald Pecock's Book of Faith ; etc. *Ctr :* Cambridge Hist Journ, Scottish & Canadian Hist Revs, Glasgow Herald. *s.s:* Brit Imperial Hist. *Rec:* Walking, cycling. *w.s:* 1914–19. *a:* The Park, Toward, Argyll, Scotland. *T:* Toward 205.

MORISON, Lennox James. *b:* London. *e:* King's Coll Sch Lond & Pembroke Coll Oxf. Civil Servant (ret), Asst Sec Bd of Education. *Publ:* The Binding of Prometheus ; The Antigone of Sophocles. *Ctr :* Ch Quarterly Rev, Guardian, Journ of Education. *s.s:* Classical Literature, Writers of 1st & 2nd Centuries A.D. *c :* Oxf & Camb. Classical Assoc, Brit Inst of Philosophy. *a :* North End, by Henley-on-Thames, Oxon.

MORISON, Rutherford, F.R.C.S.(Edin & Eng), D.C.L., LL.D.(Edin). *b:* Co Durham 1853. *e:* Edin & Vienna. *m:* Widower. *s:* 2. *d:* 3. Surgeon. *n.a:* Ed Northumberland & Durham Medical Journ 1894–1904. *Publ:* An Introduction to Surgery; Abdominal & Pelvic Surgery for Practitioners; Aneurysm (Index of Treatment); Abscess in Connection with the Vermiform Appendix; etc. *c.t:* B.M.J., etc. Emeritus Prof of Surgery Durham Univ. Examiner in Surgery at L'pool & Birm. *Rec:* Farming. *a:* Hilton's Hill, St Boswell's, Roxburgh.

MORISON, S. *Publ:* Studies on the History of Hand-Writing, Printing & Newspapers. *a:* 43 Fetter Lane, E.C.

MORISON, Stanley. *n.a :* The Times. *Publ:* inc Introduction to Liturgical Books; Black Letter; First Principles of Typography; The English Newspaper; Type Faces & Type Design; etc. *a :* The Times, Printing House Square, London, E.C.4.

MORISON, SIR THEODORE: Principal Armstrong College, Newcastle-upon-Tyne, 1919-1929; vice-chancellor University of Durham; b. Malta, May 9, 1863; s. James Cotter and Frances (Virtue) M.; educ. Westminster Sch., Trinity Coll. (Cambridge). DEGREES: M.A. (Cambridge), (Hon.) D.C.L. (Durham); m. Margaret Cohen, 1895. AUTHOR: Imperial Rule in India, 1899; Industrial Organization of an Indian Province, 1906; Economic Development of India, 1910. General character of writing: economic and political sociology. A believer that education is the surest form of social service, his life has been divided between university work and public service, India and England. Mem. Council of India, 1907-17; served during Great War in East Africa, retiring as Lt.-Col. Relig. denom., Anglican. CLUB: United University (London). HOME: Eastwood, Bridgewater Road, Weybridge, Surrey, Eng.

MORK, RASMUS: lecturer in dairy economics; b. Ørsta, Norway, January, 1896; s. R. P. and Johanna (Steen) M.; educ. Royal Agricultural College of Norway, Univ. of Oslo. DEGREES: Cand. Agric., Cand. Oecon.; m. Hjordis Thornes, Aug. 15, 1922. AUTHOR: Korfattet Neieridriftslare. Contributor to Mildinger fra Norges Landbrukshoiskole, Norsk Neieritidende, Neieriposten. General character of writing: technical. Religion, Protestant. ADDRESS: Landbruckshoisholen i Aas, Norway.

MORLAND, Egbert Coleby. *b:* Croydon 1874. *e:* Bootham, Owen's Col & St Bart's. Med Journalist. *n.a:* Asst Ed Lancet 1915–. *c:* Athenæum, Penn. *a:* 7 Adam St, W.C.2. *t:* Temple Bar 7229.

MORLAND, Harold. *b :* Clayton-le-Moors, Lancs 1908. *e:* Gr Sch Accrington Lancs. Lect Training Coll for Teachers. *Publ:* Fables & Satires. *Ctr:* Listener, Poetry Quarterly, Poetry Folios, Life & Letters, etc. *s.s:* Poetry. *Rec:* Foreign travel. *a:* Newland Park, Chalfont St Giles, Bucks. *T:* Chalfont 393.

MORLAND, Nigel. *b:* London 1905. *e:* Private. *m:* Peggy Barwell. Publisher. *n.a:* Ed The Book Tag '31. *Publ:* The Moon Murders; The Goofus Man; Cachexia; Dawn was Theirs; People we have never Met; Abrakadabra; Mary l; The Phantom Gunman; etc. *s.s:* Books, book trade. Publicity Manager Ivor Nicholson & Watson Ltd. '32–34, Book Critic World's Press News '34, Book Consultant to Selfridge's 34–5, Mang Dir Street & Massey Ltd. *Rec:* Reading, writing. *c:* Society of Authors, League of British Dramatists. *a:* 10 Shepherd Hse, Mayfair, W.1. *t:* Grosvenor 3239.

MORLEY, Arthur, O.B.E., D.Sc., M.I.Mech.E. *b :* Cheadle Hulme 1876. *e:* Owens Coll, Univ of Manch. *m:* Catherine M. Brown. *s:* 2. *d:* 1. Civil Servant (ret). Prof of Mech Eng (Univ Coll Nottingham), H.M. Insp of Schs (Tech), Staff Insp (Eng) 1912–36. *Publ:* Strength of Materials; Theory of Structures; Mechanics for Engineers; Applied Mechanics; Elementary Applied Mechanics (with W. Inchley); Mechanical Engineering Science (with E. Hughes); Elementary Engineering Science (with E. Hughes). *Ctr:* Various Technical-scientific articles. *a:* Applegarth, Sham Castle Lne, Bath. *T:* 5943.

MORLEY, Arthur S., F.R.C.S., L.R.C.P. *b*: London 1877. *e*: Univ Coll Sch, St George's Hosp. *m*: Phœbe Harris. *s*: 1. *d*: 1. Temp Asst Surg St Mark's Hosp. *Publ*: Hæmorrhoids: Their Ætiology, Prophylaxis & Treatment by Means of Injections; Adjustment of Sickness & Accident Claims. *Ctr*: Lancet, B.M.J., etc. *s.s*: Rectal Surg, Accident Insurance Work. *Rec*: Golf. *c*: Roehampton. *a*: 13 Upper Wimpole St, London, W.1. *T*: Welbeck 6092.

MORLEY, Christopher. *Publ*: inc The Eighth Sin; The Haunted Bookshop; The Trojan Horse; Thorofare; etc; & several poems. *a*: Roslyn Heights. N.Y., U.S.A.

MORLEY, Edith Julia, Hon., M.A., Oxon Fell & Ass of King's Coll, F.R.S.L., J.P. *b*: London 1875. *e*: Priv, King's Coll, (Women's Dept) Univ Coll. Emeritus Prof Univ of Reading. *Publ*: The Life & Times of Henry Crabb Robinson; Edited :—The Correspondence of Crabb Robinson with the Wordsworth Circle; Crabb Robinson on Books & their Authors; Crabb Robinson on Blake, Coleridge & Wordsworth; Crabb Robinson In Germany 1801—05; Hurd's Letters on Chivalry & Romance; Young's Conjectures on Original Composition; Women's Work in Seven Professions. *Ctr*: Year's Work in English Studies. *c*: Forum, British Federation of University Women. *a*: 96 Kendrick Rd, Reading, Berks. *T*: 4191.

MORLEY, Henry. *n.a*: Ed & Founder Hucknall Dispatch. *c.t*: Various Jnls. *s.s*: Byron & Local subjects. *a*: Park Drive, Hucknall. *t*: 28.

MORLEY, Henry Forster, M.A., D.Sc(Lon), F.I.C. *b*: Lon 1855. *e*: Univ Col Sc, Lon Univ Col, & Bonn, Munich, Berlin & Paris Univs. *m*: Ida Rose Tayler. *s*: 1. Dir Internat Catalogue of Scientific Lit. *Publ*: Outlines of Organic Chemistry; Jt Ed: Watts's Dictionary of Chemistry; International Catalogue of Scientific Literature (238 vols). *c.t*: Chemical Soc's Journ, etc. Formerly Asst Prof of Chemistry at Lon Univ Col, Lecturer on Chemistry at Charing Cross Hosp Med Sc, Prof of Chemistry at Queen's Col Lon, & Exam at Lon Univ, etc. *a*: 5 Lyndhurst Rd, Hampstead, N.W.3. *t*: Midhurst 232 & Hampstead 5208.

MORLEY, Henry Thomas, J.P., F.R.Hist.S., F.S.A.(Scot). *b*: Reading, Berks 1861. *e*: Lancastrian Sch Reading. *m*: (1) Francis E. Barley, (2) A. Elizabeth York. *s*: 2. *d*: 2. Illuminator Designer, Hon Curator Reading Mus 18 yrs, Hon Sec of Berkshire Archæol Soc 25 yrs. *Publ*: Old & Curious Playing Cards; Monumental Brasses of Berkshire; Rides & Rambles around Reading. *s.s*: Hist of Playing Cards, Hist of Card Games, Invitation, Trade & Funeral Cards, Hist of Book Plates. *Rec*: Medieval archæol, exhibitions, collection of 20,000 original playing cards. *a*: 312 Kings Rd, Reading, Berks. *T*: 62330.

MORLEY, Iris. *b*: 1910. *m*: Alaric Jacob. *d*: 1. Writer. *n.a*: Moscow Corr of Observer & Yorkshire Post 1943—45, Ballet Critic Dly Worker '45—. *Publ*: Cry Treason; The Mighty Years; We Stood For Freedom; Soviet Ballet; Nothing but Propaganda. *s.s*: English 17th-Century Hist, Ballet. *a*: Chetwynd Hse, Hampton Ct Green, Middlesex. *T*: Molesey 3603.

MORLEY, Ralph. Schoolmaster. *c.t*: Educ & Socialist Press. *a*: 35 Radstock Rd, S'hampton.

MORLEY, Sylvanus Griswold, A.M., Ph.D. *b*: Templeton, Mass, 1878. *e*: Goddard Sem, Tufts Coll, Harvard Univ. *m*: Drusilla D. Tufts. *s*: 2. *d*: 1. Prof of Spanish, Univ of California. *Publ*: The Chronology of Lope de Vega's Comedias; Sonnets & Poems of Anthero de Quental (trans); Beside the River Sar (trans collab); History of Spanish Literature (collab); The Covered Bridges of California; Galdos Mariucha; etc. *Ctr*: Nation, Forum, Boston Transcript. *s.s*: Spanish Ballads, Classic Drama, Versification & Metrics. *c*: Commonwealth of California, Faculty (Berkeley). *a*: 2635 Etna St, Berkeley 4, California, U.S.A. *T*: BE 7-5239J.

MORLEY, Walter. Principal Asst & Deputy to W. H. Ainsworth, Ed of The People. *a*: 276 Upper Richmond Rd, S.W.14. *t*: Prospect 1298.

MORLEY-BROWN, William Smith, F.I.J. *b*: Aber 1867. *e*: Aber. *m*: Agnes Mackenzie Connon. *s*: 2. *d*: 1. Journalist. *n.a*: Aber Daily Journal, Aber Evening Express '85-1903, Chief Sub-Ed & Asst Ed Sporting Life '04-11, Sport Ed Lon Daily Chronicle & Lloyds News '11-14, Sporting Life '14, & Man. Ed '20, including The Sportsman '24-27 (ret '27). *s.s*: Sports. During Gt War was largely responsible for Sportsmen's Ambulance Fund, which raised £60,000 & sent out 100 ambulances to allied fronts. *Rec*: Golf. *a*: 88 Vineyard Hill Rd, Wimbledon Park, S.W.19. *t*: 0927.

MORLEY-WHITE, Raymond. *b*: Bristol 1889. *e*: Fairfield, Bristol. *m*: Beatrice A. Bailey. *d*: 1. Journalist. *n.a*: Rep Bristol Mercury & Echo, Birm Evening Despatch (Sub-Ed & Chief Sub-Ed) 1910, Org Ed Birm Gazette & allied papers '29, Ed-in-Chief Birm Gazette '33. *s.s*: Drama, lit. *Rec*: Reading. *c*: Birm Lib. *a*: 18 Dyott Rd, Moseley, Birm. *t*: South 2454.

MORPURGO, Jack Eric, B.A. *b*: Tottenham 1918. *e*: Christ's Hospital, Coll of William & Mary in Virginia U.S.A. *m*: Catherine Cammaerts. *s*: 2. *n.a*: Edit Board Penguin Books 1946, Ed Penguin Parade '47, Ed Falon Press History of England. *Publ*: Charles Lamb & Elia; Leigh Hunt's Autobiography (Ed). *Ctr*: Tribune, Time & Tide, Life & Letters, Windmill, B'mghm Post, Fortnightly, Books of the Month. *s.s*: American Hist & Contemporary Affairs, Mil Hist, Romantic Literature. *c*: P.E.N. *w.s*: R.A. 1939—45. *a*: 84a Philbeach Gdns, Earls Ct, London, S.W.5.

MORRAH, Dermot Michael Macgregor, M.A. *b*: Ryde 1896. *e*: Winchester & New Coll Oxf. *m*: Ruth Houselander. *d*: 2. Author & Journalist, Late Fell, All Souls Coll. *n.a*: Times Ed Staff 1931—, Ed Round Table '45—. *Publ*: The Mummy Case; The British Red Cross; Princess Elizabeth; The Royal Family in Africa; Caesar's Friend (Play, with Campbell Dixon); Chorus Angelorum (Play); & some anon works. *Ctr*: Times, Times Litt Supp, Round Table, etc. *s.s*: History, Constitutional Law, Heraldry, Imperial Affairs. Spec Corres Times Royal Tour Sth Africa 1947. *Rec*: Chess, ombre, lawn tennis. *c*: Oxf & Camb, Roy Inst Internat Affairs. *w.s*: 1st World War Lt R.E. *a*: 95 Bedford Ct Mans, London, W.C.1. *T*: Museum 8463.

MORRELL, J. W., B.A.(King's Coll Lon). Member of Classical Assocn. Chartered Accountant. *a*: 27 Mortlake Road, Kew, Surrey.

MORRELL, William Parker, M.A., D.Phil. *b*: Auckland, N.Z. 1899. *e*: Otago Boys Hgh Sch & Otago Univ, Balliol Coll Oxf. *m*: Ethel M. Evans. *s*: 1. *d*: 1. Prof of Hist Otago Univ N.Z., Mem of Counc Roy Hist Soc 1943—46. *Publ*: British Colonial Policy in the Age of Peel & Russell; The Gold Rushes; The Provincial System in New Zealand; Select Documents on British Colonial Policy (collab); Early Days in Western Australia (collab). *Ctr*: English Hist Revs, History, Internat Affairs. *s.s*: Hist of Brit Commonwealth. *Rec*: Walking, chess, music. *c*: Dunedin. *a*: 16 Skibo St, Kew, Dunedin, N. Zealand.

MORRELL MASSEY, Edward. *b*: Philadelphia 1893. *e*: Episcopal Acad, Phila, Penna Univ, Penna Acad of Fine Arts. Writer. *Publ*: New & Original Magic (1922); Left Hand Left ('32); Through the Lens; The Adventures of a Boy Magician ('34). *c.t*:

Country Gentleman, Sphinx. *s.s*: Mystery stories, magic & conjuring. *Rec*: Sleight of hand, golf. *a*: Bryn Mawr, Pa, U.S.A.

MORRICE, Dr., The Rev. J. C., M.A., B.Litt, D.Phil(Oxon). *b*: Portmadoc 1874. *e*: Univ Col Bangor & Corpus Christi Col Oxf. Late Rector Terling. *Publ*: Manual of Welsh Literature; Poetical Works of Wm Llyn; Poems of Hywel Lwrdwal; Poems of Gruffydd ab Ienan; Wales in the Seventeenth Century. *c.t*: Geninen, Essex Dio Mag, etc. *s.s*: Hist, Celtic. Exam at Oxford, Univ of Wales & St David's Col Lampeter. C.F. 1914-18. *Rec*: Gardening. *c*: Oxf Un (Life Mem). *a*: The Old Rectory, Ashton, Northants.

MORRILL, John Henry. *b*: Miller, Sth Dakota 1903. *e*: Minneapolis Pub Schs & U.S. Naval Acad, Annapolis Maryland. *m*: Dorothy M. Wilde. *s*: 2. *d*: 1. Capt United States Navy. *Publ*: South from Corregidor (with Pete Martin). *Ctr*: Sat Ev Post. *s.s*: Submarines, Small Ships, Navigation. *Rec*: Exploring. *c*: Army & Navy, Manila PI, Pearl Harbour Navy Athl Assoc, Navy Alumni Assoc. *a*: 214 West 24th St, Minneapolis, Minnesota, U.S.A. *T*: Kenwood 9152.

MORRIS, Alan William. *b*: Leicester 1909. *e*: Ald Newton's Sc Leicester. Accountant. *n.a*: Jt Ed Camyl '30-31, Dis Corr Trade Press Service '32. *c.t*: Leicester Mercury, Northern Weekly Gazette, etc. *s.s*: Acctncy, fiction for children. French lang. Founder of Leicester Writers' Club '29. *Rec*: Chess, table tennis, photography. *c*: Leicester Writers, Leicester Y.M.C.A., etc. *a*: 34 East St, London Rd, Leicester.

MORRIS, Arthur Daniel, M.D., B.S., M.R.C.S., L.R.C.P. *b*: Treorchy, Glam 1889. *e*: Taunton Sc, Univ Col Hosp, Univ of Brussels. Hon Sec Harveian Soc of Lon. *c.t*: Med Press & Circular, Medical Officer, Lancet, etc. *s.s*: Med items of popular interest. *Rec*: Tennis. *c*: Green Room. *a*: Hammersmith Hosp, Ducane Rd, W.12. *t*: Shepherds Bush 4465.

MORRIS, Charles James. *b*: Guildford 1901. Sub-Ed. *n.a*: Reporter Surrey Advtr Guildford '16-25, Reporter Burton Daily Mail '25-26, Sub-Ed Kent Evening Echo Folkestone '27-29, Sub-Ed Cumberland News & Cumberland Evening News '29-. *Rec*: Golf, badminton. Mem of Stanwix Parochial Ch Counc. *c*: Longtown Golf. *a*: 31 Etterby St, Stanwix, Carlisle, Cumberland.

MORRIS, Charles Richard. *b*: Kent 1898. *e*: Tonbridge Sc & Trinity Col Oxford. *m*: Mary de Selincourt. *s*: 3. *d*: 1. Fellow & Tutor of Balliol Col Oxford. *Publ*: A History of Political Ideas (with Mary Morris); Locke, Berkeley, Hume; Idealistic Logic. *c.t*: Proceedings of Royal Aristotelian Soc. *s.s*: Philosophy & politics. Lieut R.G.A. 1916-9. *a*: 5 Mansfield Rd, Oxford. *t*: Oxford 3097.

MORRIS, David Buchan. *b*: Stirling 1866. *e*: Stirling H.S. *m*: Ann Gibson. Town Clerk of Stirling. *Publ*: Extracts from the Records of the Merchant Gild of Stirling (1916); The Stirling Merchant Gild & Life of John Cowane; Robert Louis Stevenson & the Scottish Highlanders ('29). *s.s*: Archæology, geology, botany. Trustee of Nat Library of Scotland. *a*: 15 Gladstone Pl, Stirling. *t*: 38.

MORRIS, Edita. *b*: Orebro, Sweden. *e*: Brumerska Skolan, Stockholm. *m*: I. V. Morris. *s*: 1. Novelist & Short Story Writer. *Publ*: Birth of an Old Lady; My Darling from the Lions; Three Who Loved. *Ctr*: Harper's Mag, Atlantic Monthly, Reader's Digest, Best American Short Stories (Annual), etc. *c*: P.E.N. (N.Y.). *a*: Box 175, Manchester, Massachusetts, U.S.A.

MORRIS, Rev. Edward Arthur. *b*: Rhewl, nr Llangollen 1876. *e*: Wes Col Handsworth Birm. *m*: N. Pugh Dolgellan. *s*: 3. *n.a*: Y Berllan 1928-31, Y Gorlan '31-34. *Publ*: Welsh Dramas:—Arthur Wyn yr Hafod; Mari'r Forwyn ('25). *c.t*: Y Gwyliedydd Newydd, Y Brython, L'pool Daily Post & Mercury. *s.s*: Welsh poetry, lit. First in Connection for Eng Essay '07. *Rec*: Gardening. *a*: The Manse, Llanasa, Holywell, Flints, N.W.

MORRIS, Edward Herbert. *b*: Carharrack 1868. *e*: Bedford Modern Sc. *m* Ethel Kate Vibert. *s*: 3. *d*: 1. *Publ*: A Brief History of London; India: Past & Present; Twenty Five Years a King; etc. *c.t*: Chambers's Journal, Sphere, Autocar, Gas News, etc. *s.s*: Hist, economics, biography, advtg. Formerly Advtg Mang Austin Motor Coy Ltd & Ed Austin Advocate. Advtg Mang to Lotus Ltd of Stafford & Northampton & Ed Lotus & Delta News. *Rec*: Billiards, tennis. *a*: 9 Sandland St, Bedford Row, W.C.1. *t*: Holborn 7155.

MORRIS, Edward James McCarthy. *b*: Leap, Co Cork 1871. *e*: St Faughnan's Col Ross & Roy Col Surgeons, Edin. *Publ*: Motionism, or the World's True Religion; The Riddle of Creation & the Key. *Rec*: Walking, philos. *a*: Cedar Lodge, 41 Poynder's Rd, Clapham Pk, S.W.4. *t*: Tulse Hill 2057.

MORRIS, Ernest, F.R.Hist.S., F.R.G.S. *b*: Leicester 1889. Verger & Vestry Clerk, Vice-Pres Leicester Diocesan Guild of Bell Ringers, Hon Consultant to the Bishop's Advisory Cttee Leicester Diocese, Mem Ancient Soc of Coll Youths Lond & 25 Ringing Guilds & Socs of Gt Britain. *Publ*: History & Art of Change Ringing; History of St Margaret's Church Leicester; Transcribed Registers of all Births, Marriages and Deaths at St Margaret's Leicester 1604—1837; Legends o' the Bells; Bells of All Nations; Chronology of British Bellfounders. *Ctr*: Church Monthly, Blue Peter, Radio Pictorial, Chambers's Ency, Meccano Mag, etc. *s.s*: Bell Ringing, Chimes, Carillons. *Rec*: Genealogy. *c*: Johnson Soc. *a*: Verger's Lodge, St Margaret's Vicarage, Leicester. *T*: 65037.

MORRIS, G. Ivan (G. I. Vann). *Publ*: Various articles & series. *s.s*: Articles on Acctncy, Income Tax & Comm. Senior Fellow Internat Accts Corporation. *a*: 35 Frescati Pk, Blackrock, Dublin.

MORRIS, Guy Wilfred. *b*: London 1884. *e*: Merchant Taylor's Sch, St John's Coll Oxf. *m*: Hilda Brown. *s*: 1. *d*: 1. Late Headmaster Colfe's Gr Sch. *Publ*: Golden Fleece; Britain in the Nineteenth Century; etc. *s.s*: Hist (Modern). *Rec*: Walking. *c*: Headmasters Assoc, Hist Assoc, Roy Empire. *a*: The Green, Northmoor, Oxford. *T*: Standlake 267.

MORRIS, H. G. Chief Reporter Cambridge Daily News. *n.a*: Ex-Reporter Sussex Daily News, Reporter Gloucestershire Echo. *a*: Cambridge Daily News, Cam.

MORRIS, Harrison S. *b*: Phil 1856. *e*: Public & Priv Scs. *m*: Anna Wharton. *d*: 1. Author. *c.t*: Evening Bulletin Phila, Scribner's Century, Lit World, etc. *s s*: Art & letters. *c*: Mem Advisory Cmt on Art, Chicago & St Louis World's Fairs, Incorp Amer Acad Rome Italy. *a*: Chelten Av, York Rd, W. Phila, Pa, U.S.A. *t*: Waverley 1982.

MORRIS, Herbert Charles, M.A.(Cantab), F.R. C.O., L.R.A.M., A.R.C.M., F.T.C.L. *b*: Coventry 1872. *e*: Henry VIII G.S. Coventry, Downing Col Cam, & The Roy Col of Music Lon. Organist. *Publ*: Church & Organ Music. *s.s*: Music. Vicar Choral Organist & Master of Choristers at St David's Cathedral, Pembrokeshire S. Wales '96-22. *Rec*: Chess. *a*: Oakfield, 124 Waterloo Rd, Wolverhampton.

MORRIS, Hugh McEvoy, M.D., B.Ch., D.M.R.E. *b*: Glenarm, Co Antrim 1898. *e*: Belfast & Liverpool Univs. *m*: Helen Margaret Cateaux. *s*: 2. Hon Radiologist Salford Roy Hosp, Manch Jewish Hosp, Dist Hosp Buxton, Lect in Electrotherapy Devonshire Hosp Buxton. *Publ*: Medical Electricity for Massage Students; Physiotherapy in Medical Practice; Jones, A, Finds the Body (under pseudonym Hugh McEvoy). *Ctr*: B.M.J., Brit Journ of Radiology, Radiology, Larne Times, Q.U.B. (Belfast), *s.s*: Electrotherapy, Radiology (Diagnostic). *Rec*: Watching football, window shopping. *w.s*: R.A.M.C. World War II. *a*: Grasmere, Bentinck Rd, Altrincham, Cheshire. *T*: Altrincham 3019.

MORRIS, I. V. *b*: Chicago, Illinois 1903. *e*: Milton Acad, Univs of Harvard & Heidelberg. *m*: Edita Morris. *s*: 1. Novelist & Free-lance Writer. *Publ*: Marching Orders; Covering Two Years; Liberty Street. *Ctr*: Leading American Mags. *a*: Box 175, Manchester, Massachusetts, U.S.A.

MORRIS, Ira. *b*: Moscow 1917. *e*: Parliament Hill Sch & Paris. *m*: Robert Morris. Journalist. *n.a*: Art Ed Everywoman 1945—. *Publ*: The Glass of Fashion. *s.s*: Fashion, Design for Applied Arts. *Rec*: Books. *a*: 20 Oakeshott Ave, Highgate, London, N.6 *T*: Mountview 5731.

MORRIS, JAMES ARCHIBALD: architect; *b*. Ayr, Scotland, Jan. 14, 1857; s. Archibald and Ann (Watson) M.; educ. Ayr. Acad., Glasgow School of Art, Slade Sch. (Univ. Coll. London), Royal Acad. Schls. DEGREES: A.R.S.A., F.R.I.B.A., Royal Soc. (Edinburgh), F.S.A. (Scotland); m. Elizabeth Forgan, Jan. 11, 1883. AUTHOR: Crosraguel Abbey, 1884; Brig of Ayr, 1910; Appreciation of Robert Burns, 1912; Ayrshire White Needlework, 1916; Lister and the Lister Ward, 1917; The Auld Toon o' Ayr, 1928; The Brig o' Doon, 1929. Contributor to Hibbert Journ., Spectator, Architectural Rev., Burns Chronicle, Glasgow Herald and other papers. General character of writing: art, technical and historical. Has researched extensively in the excavation and preservation work of ancient buildings such as Crosraguel Abbey, Greenan Castle, Brig o'Ayr, etc. Lecturer on preservation of ancient buildings, application of art to industry, painting, archaeology. Relig. denom.: Presbyterian. CLUBS: Glasgow Art, Crestwick Golf. OFFICE: Wellington Chambers. HOME: Savoy Croft, Ayr, Ayrshire, Scotland.

MORRIS, John, M.A., M.Sc. *b*: Gravesend, Kent 1898. *e*: King's Coll Camb. B.B.C. Far Eastern Service Dir. B.B.C. Corres in Japan 1946. *Publ*: The Gurkhas: their Manners, Customs & Country; Living With Lepchas; Traveller From Tokyo; The Phœnix Cup; etc. *Ctr*: Listener, New Statesman & Nation, Fortnightly, *s.s*: Japan. *Rec*: Mountaineering, Eng lit, music, theatre, travel. *c*: Savile, Camb Univ Alpine, Japan Alpine. *a*: c/o Christy & Moore Ltd, Literary Agents, The Ride Annexe, Dukes Wood Ave, Gerrards Cross, Bucks.

MORRIS, John Arthur, F.R.S.A. *b*: Shrewsbury 1862. *e*: Newport, Salop G.S. Surveyor, Valuer. Counc Salop Archæ Soc. Hon Curator Shrewsbury Museum, Archæ Section. *Publ*: Guide-Books Shrewsbury; Viroconium (Wroxeter) & Excavations; Historical Accounts of many Shropshire Churches; Parish Registers & Church Accounts; Shrewsbury Castle, Town Walls, & Old Buildings; etc. *c.t*: Trans Salop Archæ Soc, Antiquarian Journs, etc. *s.s*: Archæ. *Rec*: Photography. *a*: The Priory, Port Hill, Shrewsbury. *t*: 2302.

MORRIS, Rev. Marmaduke Charles Frederick, B.C.L., M.A. *b*: Crambe 1844. *e*: Bradfield Col, New Col Oxf. Headmaster St Michael's Col Tenbury '69-74. Diocesan Insp of Scs for York Diocese '74-80. *Publ*: Yorkshire Folk-Talk; Francis Orpen Morris, A Memoir; Nunburnholme, its History & Antiquities;

The British Workman, Past & Present (1928); etc. *s.s*: Yorkshire Dialect, archæ. Hon Fell St Michael's Col Tenbury 1874). Choral Schol New Col Oxf '63-67. *Rec*: Reading. *a*: 14 Newbiggin, Beverley, Yorks.

MORRIS, May. Craftsman. *c.t*: Various Art Journals. *s.s*: Design, embroidery. Edited with Introductions 24 vols William Morris Works; lectured extensively England & U.S.A. Order of the Falcon (Iceland). *a*: Kelmscott Manor, Lechlade, Glos.

MORRIS, Mollie. *b*: Nott'm 1910. *e*: Priv. Writer. *Publ*: New Harrowing ('33). *s.s*: Psych. First publ'd story written at the age of nine. Finished writing " New Harrowing " at age of 22. *Rec*: Music, skating. *a*: Bleasby, Notts.

MORRIS, Myer. *n.a*: Ed Jewish Times. *a*: 325 Whitechapel Rd, E.1.

MORRIS, Myra Evelyn. *b*: Boort, Victoria, Australia. *e*: Brigidine Convent Rochester. Author, Mem of P.E.N. *Publ*: The Wind on the Water; Dark Tumult; White Magic; The Township. *Ctr*: Bulletin, Home, Sydney Morning Herald, etc. *Rec*: Gardening. *a*: Melbourne Rd, Frankston, Victoria, Australia. *T*: Frankston 230.

MORRIS, Noah. Physician. *Publ*: Acidosis & Alkalosis (with Dr S. Graham). *c.t*: Various. *a*: Barone, 7 West Chapelton Cres, Bearsden, Glas. *t*: 453.

MORRIS, Reginald Owen. M.A., D.Mus(Oxon), F.R.C.M. *b*: York 1886. *e*: Harrow, New Coll Oxf, Royal Coll of Music. Teaching Staff of R.C.M. *Publ*: Contrapuntal Technique in the Sixteenth Century; The Structure of Music; The Oxford Harmony (Vol I); Introduction to Counterpoint. *c*: Savile, Oxford & Cambridge. *a*: 2 Addison Gdns, London, W.14.

MORRIS, Samuel. *b*: London. Journalist. *n.a*: Founded Newspaper Press Exchange & N.P.E. Illustrations Service, '19—. *s.s*: Films, the theatre, social matters, features. *Rec*: Walking, photography. *a*: 23 Ashcroft Rd, E.3. *t*: Clissold 4959.

MORRIS, Maj. Walter Frederick, B.A., M.C. *b*: Norwich 1893. *e*: King's Sch Norwich, St Catherine's Coll Camb. *m*: Mary Lewine Corney. *s*: 1. *d*: 1. Asst Master Ealing Priory Sch. *Publ*: Bretherton; Behind the Lines; Pagan; The Hold-up; Veteran Youth; Something to His Advantage; No Turning Back; The Channel Mystery. *s.s*: Fiction with a French Setting, Mystery & Adventure. *Rec*: Tennis. *w.s*: 1914—19. *a*: 34 Waldeck Rd, Ealing, London, W.13. *T*: Perivale 7388.

MORRIS, William George. *b*: Oxford 1891. *e*: Harpur Sch Bedford. *Publ*: Round About Adelphi; The Purlieus of Soho; New Rambles in Old London; Along Cheapside; The Squares of Bloomsbury; etc. *s.s*: English Hist & Topography. *a*: 17 Prebend St, Bedford.

MORRIS-JONES, Sir Henry, Kt., D.L., J.P., M.P. *b*: Waenfawr, Caernarvonshire 1884. *e*: Menai Bridge Gr Sch, St Mungo's Coll Glas, Vienna. *m*: Leila Augusta Paget Marsland. M.P. (Lib Nat) Denbigh. *Publ*: Surgical Experiences at Wimereux 1914; Sections to: Commemorative Book of the Life of Sir O. M. Edwards. *Ctr*: Various daily newsps. *Rec*: Shooting, riding, travel. *c*: Reform. *a*: The Shrubbery, Ermine Rise, Royston, Herts. *T*: Royston 3332.

MORRISON, Arthur, F.R.S.L. b: 1863. Author. Publ: Tales of Mean Streets ('94); A Child of the Jago; To London Town; Cunning Murrell; The Dorrington Deed-box; Martin Hewitt, Investigator; Chronicles of Martin Hewitt; Adventures of Martin Hewitt; The Hole in the Wall; The Red Triangle; Divers Vanities; Green Ginger; The Painters of Japan; Fiddle o' Dreams; etc; Plays (in collab); That Brute Simmons (1904); The Dumb Cake; A Stroke of Business ('07). s.s: Oriental art. c: Savage. a: High Barn, Chalfont St Peter, Bucks. t: Chalfont St Giles 170.

MORRISON, Emmeline. b: Prestwich. e: Erfurt, Germany. Novelist. Publ: Good Grain (John Long £500 prize Novel 1921); As We Look Back, 1935, etc. a: Durban North, Natal, South Africa.

MORRISON, Henry Fontaine. b: Edinburgh. Journalist (ret), Chmn Edin & E. of Scotland Dist I.J. 1930—31, Official Shorthand Writer Law Courts Edin '09—15, F.J.I. n.a: Sub Ed Scotsman 1904—08, Edin Corr of Lond & Eng prov newsps, Rep Edin Staff Glas Herald '15—40. Rec: Golf. a: 50 Spottiswoode St, Edinburgh. T: 53386.

MORRISON, Rt. Hon. Herbert Stanley, P.C., J.P., M.P. b: London 1888. e: Elem Sch. m: Margaret Kent. d: 1. M.P. (L) East Lewisham 1945—, Lord President of the Council & Leader of the House of Commons '45—, Sec to London Labour Party, Min of Transport '29—31, Mem Cabinet '31, Leader L.C.C. '34, Mem Nat Exec of Labour Party '15—40, Min of Supply '40, Home Sec & Min of Home Security '40—45, Mem War Cabinet. Publ: Socialisation & Transport; How Greater London is Governed; Looking Ahead. Ctr: Various newsps & periodicals. s.s: Politics, Local Govt, Transport. a: 11 Downing St, London, S.W.1.

MORRISON, John Tertius, O.B.E. b: Calcutta 1888. e: Fettes Coll & Edin Univ. m: Eliza Mary Wrigley. s: 1. d: 1. Dean of the Faculty of Medicine Univ of Liverpool. Publ: Manual of War Surgery. Ctr: B.M.J., Lancet, Brit Journ of Surg. s.s: Surgery, Thoræic Surg. Rec: Fishing. w.s: Army 1914—18. a: The University, Brownlow Hill, Liverpool 1. T: Roy 4567.

MORRISON, Laurence Henry, F.R.S.A. b: Shetland 1886. e: Shetland. Master Mariner. s.s: Nautical subjects. Rec: Reading. a: Cleethorpes, St James's Rd, Gravesend.

MORRISON, Margaret. b: London 1883. Trained Nurse, S.R.N. Publ: Written for Elizabeth; Lady of Justice; The Reverse Be My Lot; Sally Strange; Angles; Flying High; Miss Domore; After Long Years; Paid To Be Safe; etc. c: Cowdray. w.s: Brit Red Cross Soc 1942, Air Transport Auxiliary '44. a: c/o Lloyds Bank Ltd, Odiham, Hants.

MORRISON, Nancy (Agnes) Brysson. b: Glas. e: Park Sc Glas & Harvington Col Lon. Publ: Breakers; Solitaire; The Gowk Storm; The Strangers. Rec: Riding. a: Alness, High Burnside, Glas.

MORRISON, NORMAN: author; b. Island of Lewis, Scotland, Oct., 1869; s. Donald and Annie (McLeod) M.; educ. Public Schls. of Shawbost, Island of Lewis. DEGREES: B.Sc., D.Sc., F.Z.S. (Scotland), F.P.C. (London); m. Elizabeth McKay, Dec. 23, 1897. AUTHOR: The Romance of the Atom; Heredity and Environment; The Utopia of the Future; The Philosophy of Life; The Fauna and Flora of the Flannan Islands; The Evolution of Language; The Romance of Druidism; The Folklore and Mythology of the Highlands; The Shawbost Freebooter, 1920; The Romance of the Damsel of Deep, 1920; A Fairy Drama, 1921; The Legend of the Water Horse, 1922; The Knight of Lochrhainbhade, 1923; The Life Story of the Adder, 1924; The Story of the Common Eel, 1926; The Rat Species, 1927; The Romance of the Beat, 1928; The Adventures and Romance of a Naturalist, 1929. Contributor to Nature, Science Progress, Fishing Gazette, Field, Naturalist, Shooting Times, Scottish Field, Glasgow Herald, Scotsman, Fishing News, Evening Citizen, Evening Times. General character of writing: fiction, essays, nature books. An authority upon the adder and the common eel; has contributed largely to sum knowledge of immunology in the animal kingdom (discovered that frogs, toads and slow worms are immune to adder poison and that the common eel hibernates during the cold season, somewhat similar to land reptiles); an authority, also, upon the ancient Gaelic tongue, folklore and history and has made valuable contributions to literature of same. Relig. faith, Protestant. HOME: Beith Place, Cambeltown, Argyllshire, Scotland.

MORRISON, Robert Livingstone Cameron. b: Glasgow, 1868. e: Kirkcleatham Sc Redcar, Normal Col Swansea, Thistleboon Sc Mumbles. m: Maud Mary Tucker. s: 1. d: 2. N/p ed. n.a: Ed Tenby Observer, 1895—. s.s: Detective stories. Rec: Walking. Winner of over 3000 prizes in N/p competitions. Has written over 200 short stories, sketches & articles. a: 3 Greenhill Ave, Tenby, Pembs. t: 48.

MORRISON, Thomas James. b: Glasgow 1906. e: Glas Hgh Sch. m: Hedy Knoblock. Novelist & Scenarist. n.a: Ed Staff Ev News (Glasgow) 1929—31, Scenario Ed Assoc Brit Picture Corp '44—46. Publ: The Truce Breaker; The Queen of Spades; They're Home Again; It's Different Abroad; The Cairn; Tony Potter; Death Comes on Derby Day. Ctr: Tatler, Sketch, Argosy, etc. s.s: Screen plays. Rec: Riding, fishing, reading. a: 244 Finchley Rd, London, N.W.3. T: Hampstead 7747.

MORRISON, Rev. William Douglas, L.L.D. (St And). m: Alice Butler. s: 1. d: 1. Rector of St Marylebone. Publ: The Jews under the Roman Empire; Crime & Its Causes; Juvenile Offenders; Ed Theo Trans Library. a: St Marlebone Rectory, 38 Devonshire Pl, W.1. & Sandbanks, Littlestone, Kent. t: Welbeck 7630.

MORRISON, Rt. Hon. William Shepherd, P.C., M.C., K.C., M.A., LL.D.(Edin & Leeds), M.P. (C) Cirencester & Tewkesbury Division of Glas since 1929, Chancellor of the Duchy of Lancaster '39—40, Minister of Food '39—40, P.M.G. '40—43. n.a: Ed The Student 1913. Ctr: Manch Guardian, English Rev, Scots Mag Saturday Rev, Week End Rev. a: 1 Tanfield Ct, Temple, E.C.4.

MORRISON-BELL, Arthur Clive. b: Darlington 1871. e: Eton & Sandhurst. m: Hon Lilah Wingfield. d: 2. Late Major Scots Guards. Publ: Tariff Walls. s.s: Politics. M.P. for E. Devon 22 y. c: Alpine, Carlton, Turf. a: 49 Montagu Sq, W.1. t: Paddington 3413.

MORRISSEY, Joseph Laurence. b: L'pool 1905. e: Wandsworth Tech Sc & St Francis Xavier's Col L'pool. m: Constance Higginson. Publ: The Double Problem ('32); High Doom (recommended by Crime Book Soc June '33). s.s: Crime, detection, fiction & popular love tales. c: Mem Soc of Authors. a: 24 Highgate, Blackpool 41153.

MORROW, E. Lloyd, M.A., B.D., Ph.D. b: Willbrook, Ontario, Canada 1884. e: Univs of Toronto, Edin & Chicago. m: Janet Thom Cringan. s: 1. d: 1. Prof (ret), Research Worker. Publ: A Bibliography of the

Ontological Argument ; Church Union in Canada : Its History, Motives, Doctrines & Government ; The Doctrinal Significance of the Church Union Movement in Canada. *Ctr* : Sociological & Theological journs. *s.s* : Orientals, Philos, Sociol, in Relation to Modern Thinking. *Rec* : Lawn bowling, music, motoring. *a* : 6 Highbourne Rd, Toronto 12, Canada. *T* : Hu 3900.

MORROW, Rev. H. W., D.D. Author. *Publ*: Under the Shadow of God; Life's Greatest Victory; Nights of Sorrow and of Song; War & Immortality. *a*: c/o J. Clarke & Co Ltd, 9 Essex St, W.C.2.

MORROW, I. F. D., B.A.(T.C.D), Ph.D.(Cantab). *e*: T.C.D., Camb & Vienna Univ. Writer. *Publ*: The Austrian Tyrol. *a*: Savile Club, 69 Brook St, W.1.

MORROW, William David. *b*: Lurgan 1910. Ed Portadown News. *c.t*: Three Irish dailies. *a*: 17 Tavanagh Av, Portadown, Co Armagh. *t*: 31.

MORROW, Very Rev. William Edward Reginald, M.A. *b*: Dublin 1869. *e*: Wesley Col & T.C.D. *m*: Lucy Matilda Watney (dec). *Publ*: Christ Magnified. *c.t*: Contemporary Review, Bristol Times & Mirror, Christian World Pulpit, etc. *s.s*: Italian art, reformation period. Rector of Chelmsford & Provost of Cathedral 1929, Proctor in Convocation '30. *Rec*: Golf, tennis. *c*: Freemasons. *a*: Provost's Hse, Guy Harlings, Chelmsford. *t*: 514.

MORROW, Winston Vaughan, A.B. *b*: Cincinnati 1887. *e*: Rollins Acad Winter Pk Florida, Kenyan Col Gambier Ohio & Univ of Cincinnati. *m*: Selma von Egloffstein. *s*: 2. Editor. *n.a*: Ed Livingston Enterprise & Post Montana 1913-15, Douglas Dispatch Arizona '15-16, Ed Furniture Manufacturer & Assoc Ed Furniture Record Grand Rapids Mich '22-28, Ed Metalcraft Mag '28-31, Assoc Ed Furniture Index & Woodworking Industries Jamestown N.Y. '28-31. *c.t*: Feedstuffs, American Baker, Food Industries, Furniture Publs, etc. *s.s*: Furniture, metal fabrication, flour milling. War Service. Capt Officers Reserve Corps since war. Assoc Dir Nat Retail Furniture Inst '28-28. *Rec*: Golf. *a*: 235 Wallace Av, Buffalo, N.Y., U.S.A. *t*: Crescent 1938-J.

MORSE, Alfred Handley Chipman, M.A., D.D., Ph.D. *b*: Bridgetown, Nova Scotia 1871. *e*: Ewing Coll, Acadia Univ, Rolgate-Rochester Divinity Sch. *m*: Ida Maud Churchill. *d*: 1. Baptist Clergyman, Lecturer on Christian Philosophy Denver Univ. *Publ*: Modernism ; The System of Indulgences ; The Voice of the Flowers ; Eternal Contrasts ; What's the Matter : A Lack, or a Leak ; A Quiver of Sunbeams ; A Handful of Nuggets ; Mirrors & Windows. *Ctr*: Various. *s.s*: Philosophy. *a* : 626 Bergen Ave, Jersey City, New Jersey, U.S.A. *T*: Del 3-1880.

MORSE, Eleanor. *b*: Brookline Massachusetts U.S.A. 1894. *e*: Brookline Scs & Lon. *m*: Arthur H. Sawyer. *s*: 1. *Publ*: The Middle Child; The Doll; She Left her Husband. *Rec*: Reading, travelling, music. *a*: Walpole, New Hampshire, U.S.A. *t*: 75.

MORSE, Glenn Tilley, B.A., B.D. *b*: Saint Louis, Missouri 1870. *e*: Smith Acad St Louis, Stowell Sch Lexington, Harvard Coll, Episcopal Theol Sch. Episcopal Clergyman (ret). *Publ*: The Ark & the Dove ; Old Newbury Initiatives ; Twenty-Five Years of All Saints ; Silhouettes by Evelyn von Maydell ; The Little Red School House. *Ctr*: Antiques Mag, Old Wedgwood Year Book, etc. *s.s*: Silhouettes, Wax Portraits, Seals, Spoons & Old Silver, Engraved Gems, Shells, American Hist. *Rec*: Painting portraits, travel, gardening. *c*: Boston Art, Harvard (Boston), etc. *a*: 186 High St, Newburyport, Massachusetts, U.S.A. *T*: Newburyport 1062.

MORSE, Richard, F.L.S. Author, Editor, Lect. *n.a*: Founder & Ed Country Side Diary 1923—, Ed Country Side '27—, Nat Hist Ed The Countryman '43—46. *Publ* : The Open Book of Wild Life ; Wild Life Through the Year ; A Book of Common Trees ; Life in Pond & Stream ; The Countryside Book ; The Book of Wildflowers ; The Book of Birds ; etc. *Ctr*: Schoolmaster, Teachers' World, Scottish Educ Journ, Pict Educ, Child Educ, Health & Strength, Health & Efficiency, Christian Science Monitor, etc. *s.s*: Biol, Nat Hist, Health, Educ. *a*: Wilbury Eaves, Letchworth, Herts.

MORSE-BOYCOTT, Rev. Desmond, L.Th. *b*: London 1892. *e*: Priv & Lichfield Theol Coll. *m*: Marguerite Harriet Sandford. *d*: 1. *n.a*: Edited Sunday Referee, Spec Anglo-Catholic Congress issue & Ch Corres Sun Referee. *Publ*: Ten Years in a London Slum ; Fields of Yesterday (Autobiog) ; The Secret Story of the Oxford Movement ; Lead Kindly Light (Biogs of Leaders of Oxf Movement) ; Mystic Glow ; When We Are Very Good ; Fear Not ; They Shine Like Stars. *Ctr*: Dly Express, Dly Sketch, Manch Ev News, Star, Sun Referee, etc. *s.s*: Theol. *Rec*: Philately, painting. *a*: St Mary-of-the-Angels Song School, Addlestone, Surrey. *T*: Weybridge 2464.

MORSHEAD, Leonard Frederick, C.S.I. *b*: Winchester 1868. *e*: Winchester, Balliol. *m*: Sybil May Hills. *s*: 2. I.C.S. *Publ*: On Firmness, by a Sojourner in India. *a*: Launceston, Cornwall.

MORSON, Albert Clifford, O.B.E., F.R.C.S. *b*: Lon. *e*: Haileybury. *m*: Adela Frances Maud Phenè. *s*: 3. Surgeon. *Publ*: Urinary Infections; A Guide to Urinary Diseases (with Abrahams). *c.t*: B.M.J., Practitioner, etc. *s.s*: Urology. *Rec*: Outdoor games. *c*: Conservative. *a*: 86 Brook St, Grosvenor Sq, W.1. *t*: Mayfair 5001.

MORT, Paul R., A.M., Ph.D. *b*: Elsie, Michigan 1894. *e*: Univs of Indiana & Columbia. *m*: Mildred Willey. *s*: 2. College Prof. *Publ*: Principles of School Administration ; Public School Finance ; A Look at Our Schools (collab) ; The Law & Public Education (collab) ; State Support for Public Education (collab) ; Adaptability of the Public School System ; etc. *Ctr*: Educ Mag. *s.s*: Educ. *c*: Cosmos (Wash). *a*: 4662 Iselin Ave, Riverdale, N.Y. City, U.S.A. *T*: Ki 6-0812.

MORTENSEN, Johan Martin, D.Litt (Lund). *b*: Sweden 1864. *e*: Lund Sweden, Sorbonne Paris. *m*: Anna Berg. *d*: 3. Lon Ed Sydsvenska Dagbladet Snällposten, Malmö, Sweden. *Publ*: Profandramat i Frankrike (1897); Fran Aftonbladet till Roda Rummet (1905, 2nd edn '13); Selma Lagerlof ('08, 2nd edn '13); London av idag; London Kaleidoskop; Strindberg som jag minnes honom ('31); etc. *c.t*: Swedish papers & mags. *s.s*: French mediæval lit, Swedish 19th cent lit. Hon Prof Lund '20. *c*: P.E.N., Foreign Press Assoc, Lon. *a*: 18 Woodstock Rd, Bedford Pk, W.4. *t*: Chiswick 2399.

MORTENSEN, Niels Th. *b*: Assens 1909. *e*: Realeksamen Studenterkursus, Copenhagen Univ. *m*: Frida Marie Christine Hansen. *s*: 1. Author. *n.a*: Kristeligt Dagblad 1931—33. *Publ*: Idealisten ; Dreng og Droem ; Præstekjolen ; Dansk Billedkunst gennem en Menneskealder ; Religioes Malerkunst i Danmark ; (Poems) Den evige Længsel ; Mellem to Kyster ; Den tunge Flugt ; Vi er af samme Sind. *s.s*: Art & Literature. *a*: Udsigten, Bredballe Strand pr Vejle, Denmark. *T*: Bredballe 108.

MORTENSEN, OLE THEODOR JENSEN: see Mortensen, Th.

MORTENSEN, TH. (pen name); (Ole Theodor Jensen Mortensen): writer; b. Hillerod, Denmark, Feb. 22, 1868; s. Johannes Gottlieb and Petra Catherine (Jensen) M.; educ. Frederiksborg,

Denmark. DEGREE: Dr. of Science; m. Valborg Nathalia Blomberg, 1901. AUTHOR: Studies of the Development and Larval forms of Echinoderms, 1921; Handbook of the Echinoderms of the British Isles, 1927. Monograph: Echinoidea. I Cidaroidea, 1929. Edited: Papers from Dr. Th. Mortensen's Pacific Expedition, 1914-1916. Contributor of numerous papers published in Scientific Periodicals in all parts of the world. General character of writing: scientific. OFFICE: Zoological Museum. HOME: Sortedams Dossering, 65 A, Copenhagen, Denmark.

MORTIMER, Alice Maud. *e*: Private. Advertising Manager. *c.t*: Daily Mirror, Time & Tide, Sunday Referee. *a*: 45 Kings Gdns, Hampstead. *t*: Maida Vale 7939.

MORTIMER, E. S. *n.a*: Est and edited Head Teachers' Review 1910-19; *Publ*: Learning to Read. Head Master, ret since 1919. Pres N.H.T.A. '10 Leeds; Pres L.T.A. '09 London. *a*: Inglemere, Capel Road East, Barnet, Herts.

MORTIMER, F. J., HonF.R.P.S. *n.a*: Ed The Amateur Photographer, Ed Photograms of the Year. *a*: c/o Iliffe & Sons, Dorset Hse, Stamford St, S.E.1.

MORTIMER, JANUARY (pen name): see Gallichan, Walter N.

MORTIMER, Raymond. Literary Editor The New Statesman & Nation. *Publ*: inc Duncan Grant; Channel Packet; etc. *a*: 6 Endsleigh Pl, London, W.C.1.

MORTIMER BATTEN, Harry. *b*: 1888. *e*: Oakham. *m*: Ivy Godfrey. *s*: 1. *d*: 2. Author & Lect. *Publ*: Habits & Characters of British Wild Animals; How to Feed & Attract the Wild Birds; Jock & Old November; 2LO Animal Stories; 2LO Bird Stories; Go Back; The Life Story of an Alsatian; etc. *Ctr*: Blackwoods, Chambers's Journ, London, Scotsman, Quiver, Times, etc. *s.s*: Nat Hist & Engineering. *Rec*: Fishing, shooting, wild nature photography. *c*: New Edin. *a*: Hartlington, Burnsall, Skipton, Yorks.

MORTLOCK, Rev. Charles Bernard, M.A., F.S.A., Hon.A.R.I.B.A., F.J.I. *b*: London 1888. *e*: Jesus Coll Camb. Clerk in Holy Orders, Author, Journalist, Hon Chaplain to the Forces, Pres Critics Circle 1946—47, Chmn Press Cttee, Press Publs Board of the Church Assembly, Mem Counc Inst Journ, Mem Ed Staff Dly Telegraph since '20, Church Times since '19, Dram Crit, Theatre Corresp Weekly Despatch '23—25, Ed the Challenge '14—16, Ed Treasury Mag '18—20 & Asst Ed Country Life, U.K., Corresp Living Church (U.S.A.) *Publ*: Some Famous London Churches; The People's Book of the Oxford Movement. *Ctr*: Various. *s.s*: Ecclesiastical, Art, Drama, Ballet, Archæology, Athenæum. *w.s*: Overseas Lect to H.M. Forces. *a*: 45 Warwick Sq, London, S.W.1. *T*: Victoria 5500 & Whitehall 4843.

MORTLOCK, Herbert James. *b*: Pimlico 1879. *e*: Holy Trinity Sc Chelsea. *m*: Ethel Ida Cissie Purkiss. *s*: 1. *d*: 2. On staff of Exchange Telegraph Coy Ltd. *s s*: Shooting. War Service '14-16. *Rec*: Motoring, billiards. *a*: Ethelbert, 10 Valleyfield Rd, Streatham, S.W.16. *t*: Str 3245.

MORTON, Eva, M.R.C.S., L.R.C.P., L.T.C.L. *Publ*: The Pneumococcus & Pneumococcal Affections (with Dr D Page). *c.t*: Lancet, Tubercle, Brit Journ Child Dis, Maternity & Child Welfare, etc. *a*: 24 Park Cres, Portland Pl, W.1. *t*: Welbeck 3674.

MORTON, George Fletcher, M.A., B.Sc., D.ès.L. *b*: Macclesfield 1882. *e*: Macclesfield Gr Sch. *m*: J. C. B. Templeton. *s*: 2. *d*: 1. Headmaster. *Publ*: Childhood's Fears; Hike & Trek; Hike & Hero; Madhouse for the Million. *Ctr*: Yorks Post, New Eng Review, Dly Mail, Yorks Even News, Yorks Even Post, etc. *s.s*: Psychology, Education, World History. *Rec*: Walking & camping. *c*: Rotary, Overseas. *a*: 14 Weetwood Ave, Headingley, Leeds 6. *T*: 51786.

MORTON, George Frederick. *b*: Lincoln 1906. *e*: Lincoln City Sch. *m*: Ruby Harrison Hayes. Reporter. *n.a*: Rep Lincolnshire Echo 1922, Chief Rep '45—. *a*: Towan Blistra, Mount St, Lincoln. *T*: 8120.

MORTON, Guy. *Publ*: The Black Robe; The Forbidden Road; The Silver Voiced Murder; etc. *a*: c/o A. M. Heath & Co, Ltd, Princes Hse, Jermyn St, London, S.W.1.

MORTON, Guy Mainwaring. B.A. ("Peter Traill"). *b*: London 1896. *e*: Rugby Sch & Univ Coll Oxf. *m*: Clare Maclean Horsley. *s*: 1. Author & Playwright, Barrister. *n.a*: Press & Censorship Div M.O.I. 1939—45. *Publ*: (Plays) Tread Softly; (with late M. Morton) Fallen Angels; By Right of Conquest; The Stranger in the House; (Books) Woman to Woman; Memory's Geese; The Divine Spark; Under the Cherry Tree; Some Take a Lover; The Life Fashionable; Great Dust; Here Lies Love; The Angel; Carry Me Home; Red, Green & Amber; Half Mast; The Sleeve of Night; Not Proven; Six of One; Golden Oriole; The Wedding of the Jackal; No Farthing Richer; The Deceiving Mirror; Under the Plane Tree; The Portly Peregrine. *Ctr*: Sat Review, Tatler, Sketch, John o' London's, Dly Express, Ev Standard. *s.s*: Plays, Novels, Sport. *Rec*: Golf, tennis. *c*: Bath, Conservative. *w.s*: World War I. *a*: 24 Cliveden Pl, London, S.W.1. *T*: Sloane 7388.

MORTON, Rev. Harold Christopherson, B.A., PhD. *b*: Bradford 1870. *e*: City of Lon Sc, Kingswood Sc, Weslyan Col Sheffield & Lon Univ. *m*: Elizabeth Thomas. *s*: 2. *d*: 1. *n.a*: Ed The Fundamentalist. *Publ*: The Bankruptcy of Evolution; Messages That Made the Revival. *c.t*: Journal of Trans Phil Soc. *s.s*: Philosophy, theology. Mem Counc Victoria Inst. *Rec*: Gardening. *a*: 7 Longdown Lane, Ewell, Surrey.

MORTON, Henry Vollam. Author & Journalist. *n.a*: Birmingham Gazette & Express 1910—12, Empire Mag, Dly Mail '13, Ev Standard '19, Dly Express, Dly Herald. *Publ*: The Heart of London; The Spell of London; The London Year; The Nights of London; London (Little Guides); The Lands of the Vikings; In Search of England; In Search of Scotland; In Search of Ireland; In Search of Wales; The Call of England; In Scotland Again; In the Steps of the Master; In the Steps of St Paul; Through Lands of the Bible; Women of the Bible; Ghosts of London; Atlantic Meeting. *Ctr*: Odhams Publs. *a*: c/o Messrs Methuen & Co, 36 Essex St, Strand, London, W.C.2.

MORTON, J. B. ("Beachcomber"). *b*: 1893. Journalist & Author. *n.a*: Daily Express. *Publ*: Penny Royal; Mr. Thake; Mr Thake Again; By the Way; Hag's Harvest; Old Man's Beard; Sobieski, King of Poland; Stuff & Nonsense; Morton's Folly; Maladetta; Skylighters; Drink up, Gentlemen; Who's Who in the Zoo; Gorgeous Poetry; Tally-Ho; The Death of the Dragon; Nineteen Thirty-Three & Still Going Wrong; Vagabond; The Adventures of Mr Thake; Enchanter's Nightshade; The Cow Jumped Over the Moon; The Barber of Putney; St Martin of Tours; Mr Thake & the Ladies; The Bastille Falls; Gallimaufry; The Dauphin; Sideways through Borneo; The New Ireland; A Diet of Thistles; The Dancing Cabman; Pyrenean; Saint-Just: A Bonfire of Weeds; I Do Not Think So; Fool's Paradise; Captain Foulenough & Company. *a*: c/o Daily Express, Fleet St, E.C.4.

MORTON, J. V. *a*: Eastcheap Buildings, E.C.3

MORTON, J. W. b: Morel 1886. e: Morel G.S., Peterboro' Sc of Art & Cam Sc of Art. m: Mildred Violet Carter. Journalist. n.a: Tech Ed Root & Potato Grower, & Journ of Market Gardening 1933–. Publ: Practical Vegetable Growing; Practical Fruit Growing; The Garden Through the Seasons; Practical Pruning; Tomato & Cucumber Growing. c.t: Farm, Field & Fireside, Amateur Gardening, Fruit, Flower & Vegetable Trades Journ's, Peterborough Advertiser. s.s: Farming, gardening, nature. Rec: Tennis, bowls. a: Inglenook, March, Cambs. t: 136.

MORTON, James Herbert. b : Newcastle-on-Tyne 1885. e : Roy Gr Sch Newcastle-on-Tyne. m: (1) Florence Anne. Walker (dec'd), (2) Beatrice Wilson. s : 1. d : 3. Chartered Accountant. Publ : National Finance. Ctr : Accountant. s.s : Taxation & Econ. c : City Livery, Guildhall, etc. a : Tudor Cottage, Gossmore, Marlow, Bucks. T : Marlow 519.

MORTON, May. b : Limerick. e : Celbridge Collegiate Sch, Kildare Place Training Coll Dublin. Vice-Princ Girls' Model Sch Belfast (ret). Publ : Dawn & Afterglow (Verse). Ctr : B.B.C. Talks & Verse, London Calling, English Digest, Cornhill Mag, Belfast Telegraph, Irish News, Irish Weekly, The Northman, Ulster Country Woman. Rec : Garden planning, needlework, cookery. c : Belfast P.E.N. (Hon Sec). a : 19 Waterloo Gdns, Belfast, Nth Ireland. T : 46698.

MORTON, Stella. b : East Sheen, Surrey. e : Richmond & Brighton. m : Edward Dover (div'd). d : 2. Novelist & Short Story Writer. Publ : Turn of Days ; Shadow of Wings ; The Convoys Pass ; Garden of Paradise ; And We Shall Build ; He Too Was a Gallant Gentleman ; Listen Beloved ; Out of Tomorrow. Ctr : Homes & Gardens, Woman & Home, Weldons Ladies Journ, The Outspan (Sth Africa), Woman's Pictorial, My Home, etc. Rec: Painting, music, reading, philosophy. a : Freshfields, High Salvington, Worthing, Sussex. T : Swandean 691.

MORTON, W. C., C.B.E., M.A., M.D. Publ: Principles of Anatomy; The Abdomen Proper; The Language of Anatomy (with Dr Robert Bridges). c.t: Articles in Med Journs. s.s: Rhythm of speech. a: 34 Headingley Lane, Leeds 6.

MORTON, William Ernest, F.T.I., M.Sc.Tech.(Manch). b : Penrith 1902. e : St Bees Sch, Manch Univ (Faculty of Tech). m : Elsie Maud Harlow. s : 2. d : 2. Prof of Textile Tech, Tech Asst to the Dir B.C.I.R.A. 1923—26, Hon Tech Adv to the Dir of Narrow Fabrics '42—45. Publ : An Introduction to the Study of Spinning. Ctr : Journal of the Textile Institute, Various Trade Journals. s.s : Textile Tech, Tech Educ. Rec : Golf, tennis. a : Solway, Hawley Drive, Hale, Cheshire. T : Ringway 4520.

MOSBACHER, Eric. b: Lon 1903. e: St Paul's Sc & Magdalene Col Cam. m: K. Gwenda David. Ed Anglo-American News 1933. a: American Chamber of Commerce, Aldwych House, Aldwych, W.C.2. t: Holborn 2327.

MOSELEY, Maboth. b : 1906. Journalist & Author. n.a. : Ad Man Milton Antiseptic Ltd 1941—47, Ed Staff Dairy Industries & Instrument Practice. Publ : Cold Surge ; This Lady Was a Gentleman ; God Created Them Apart ; War Upon Women. Ctr : Various. s.s : History, Industrial Publicity, Book Collecting, Caravanning. Rec : Book collecting, cats. a : c/o Rupert Crew Ltd, King's Mews, Gray's Inn Rd, London, W.C.1. T : Chancery 8319.

MOSELEY, Sydney Alexander. b : London 1888. Author, Journalist & Broadcaster (U.S.A.) n.a : Spec Contributor, Dly Express 1910—18, Ev News '15, Official War Corr M.E.F. for Central News & Exchange Telegraph Co. '15, Ed Egyptian Mail '13—14, Sphinx '12, Dly Herald' 30—. Publ : A Singular People ; The Truth About the Dardanelles ; Who's Who in Broadcasting ; An Amazing Seance : The Truth about a Journalist ; With Kitchener in Cairo ; From Fleet Street to Times Square ; etc. c : Press, Screen, R.A.C. Overseas Press of America. a : c/o R.A.C., Pall Mall, London.

MOSES, Belle. b : Savannah, Georgie, U.S.A. e : Home Col. Montgomery, Alabama. Author. Publ: Louisa M. Alcott; Lewis Carroll; Dickens and His Girl Heroines; Helen Ormesby; The Treasure Finders; Heroes of American Revolution ; The Master of Mount Vernon ; Franklin Delano Roosevelt, The Minute Man of '33. c.t : St Nicholas, The New York Herald, Montgomery Advertiser. s.s : Biography. Rec: Concerts, theatres, travel. a : Phipp Garden Apartments, 3819 50th St, Long Island City, New York.

MOSLEY, Leonard Oswald. b : 1911. n.a: Gossip Writer Argus, Empire News Lon, Corr Amer Wkly N.Y. Motion Picture Mag, & Movie Classic, Mem Ed Staff Daily Mirror N.Y. '30, Broadcast Commentator Los Angeles Calif '31, Mem Scenario Staff Universal Pictures Corp Universal City Hollywood '32—33. Rec: Riding. a: c/o Empire News, Withy Grove, M/C.

MOSLEY, Sir O. E., M.P. Publ: Greater Britain and many booklets and pamphlets. Member of Labour Govt 1929-30. a: 8/9 Smith Square, Westminster, S.W.1.

MOSS, Bernard. b : Wellington, New Zealand 1913. Journalist. Publ : Scoop the Pools ; Scoop the Pools Again ; Permutations for All. Ctr : Sun Empire News, S. Sun, Dly Dispatch, Ev Standard, Sporting Chron Football Up To Date Weekly. s.s : Football & Football Pools, Sporting & Competition Articles. Rec : Tennis, country rambles, boating. a : BM/12X, London, W.C.1.

MOSS, Rev. Claude Beaufort, M.A.(Oxon), D.D.(Dublin). b : Shrewsbury 1888. e : Eton Coll, Chri Ch Oxf, Cuddesdon Theol Coll. Mem Archbishop of Canterbury's Counc on Relations with Foreign Churches since 1933. Publ : The Body is One ; The Old Catholic Churches & Reunion ; The Orthodox Revival ; The Christian Faith ; The Old Catholic Movement. Ctr : Church Quarterly Rev, Empire Rev, Christian East, English Catholic, Altkatholische Kirchenzeitung, Katholik, etc. a : Appleton Manor, Abingdon, Berks. T : Cumnor 19.

MOSS, Enoch. b : Southsea, Wrexham 1892. m : C. E. Cartwright. s : 1. d : 2. Free-lance Journalist. n.a: 1st Ed Shropshire Post, Ex-Ed Wrexham Star. Ctr : Nat Daily & Sunday Newsps. s.s : Local Govt & Sport. Rec : Photography. a : Plaskynaston Lane, Cfn Mawr, nr Wrexham. T : Ruabon 2165.

MOSS, Frederick George. b: Romford 1900. e: Elem. Married. s: 4. Clerk. c.t: Romford Recorder, Weekly Dispatch, Sunday Express, Answers, Weekly Telegraph, etc. s.s: Mil hist, sport, football. c: Dagenham Lab Party, etc. a: 41 Keppel Rd, Dagenham, Essex.

MOSS, Geoffrey. See McNeill-Moss, Geoffrey.

MOSS, Kenneth Neville, O.B.E., M.Sc, F.G.S., F.InstF., A.M.I.C.E. b: Walsall 1891. e: Q. Mary's Sc Walsall & Birm Univ. m Dorothy Warington. d: 4. Prof of Mining Eng Birm Univ. Publ: Gases, Dust & Heat in Mines (1927); Historical Review of Coal Mining (Ed & Co-Author, '24). c.t: Roy Soc Proc, Trans Inst Mining Engs. s.s: Hot & deep mine problems, diet & work output of miners. War Service '15-19 (the twice). Ex-Pres Nat Assoc of Colliery Mangs. Rec: Tennis, yachting. c: Athenæum. a: 22 Vernon Rd, Edgbaston, Birm 16. t: Edgbaston 0775

MOSS, Lady Penelope. *Publ*: A Scamper Round the World; *c.t*: Various. *a*: 9 Hay Hill, Berkeley Sq. W.1. *a*: Regent 3840.

MOSS, Robert Alfred. *b*: Nuneaton 1903. *e*: Richmond House Sch Birm. Writer & Ed. *Publ*: The House of the Hundred Heads; The Amiable Mankiller; Skeletons Only Whisper. *Ctr*: Newspapers, journs, juvenile publs, B.B.C. *s.s*: Juvenile Fiction, Brit Topography. *a*: 110 Cumberland Rd, Shortlands, Bromley, Kent. *T*: Ravensbourne 0750.

MOSS, William Henry, F.C.I.S., A.S.A.A. *b*: 1905. *e*, Doncaster Gr Sch. *m*: *d*: 1. Publishing Manager British Medical Journal & other B.M.A. publications. *a*: B.M.A. Hse, Tavistock Sq, London, W.C.1. *T*: Euston 2111.

MOSS, Winnifred. See Yeomans, Peggy Winnifred.

MOSS SCOTT, Rose. *b*: Paris, Illinois 1869. *e*: Chrisman H.S., priv & Valparaiso Univ. *m*: William Thomas Scott. *s*: 1. Writer. *n.a*: Ed The Pilgrim News Letter '30—. *Publ*: Illinois State History of the Daughters of the American Revolution; Chronicles of the Moss Family; Back Home (verse). *c.t*: Chrisman Courier, State Hist Soc, Bookfellow Anthology, Home & Abroad, Amer Poetry. *s.s*: History, poetry. Chm of The Nat Old Trail Road for Illinois. For work accomplished was made a life-mem of The Great Hist Highway of Amer Assoc. State Historian of the Daughters of the Amer Revolution '27—29. Sec of State T.B. Assoc (3 y). *Rec*: Motoring. *c*: League of Amer Pen Women, Amer Lit Assoc, State Hist Soc, etc. *a*: Willrose Farm, Chrisman, Illinois. *t*: 4258.

MOSSCOCKLE, Rita Francis. *b*: Corbyn's Hall, Worcestershire. *m*: Charles Mosscockle (dec). *Publ*: Fantasias; The Golden Quest; The Four Ages; Poems; Collected Poems. *s.s*: Poetry, music. *Rec*: Singing, lit, animals esp dogs. *c*: Poetry Soc (Vice-Pres) & Dante Soc. *a*: Clewer Park, Clewer, Berks, & 26 Hertford St, Mayfair. *t*: Grosvenor 2370 & Windsor 11.

MOSSCROP, J. L. *Publ*: Articles. *a*: 3 Elm Drive, Carlton, Notts.

MOSSE, Lt.-Col. Arthur Henry Eyre, C.I.E. *b*: Jamaica 1877. *e*: King's Sc Canterbury, Bedford Sc & R.M.C. Sandhurst. *m*: Grace Maude Cruickshank. *s*: 1. *d*: 1. Indian Army (ret). *Publ*: My Somali Book (1913). *c.t*: Times, Cornhill, Journal Bombay Nat Hist Soc, Field, Game & Gun, Wide World, Times of India, etc. *s.s*: Nat hist, big game. Served 31 y Indian Polit Service (despatches '18). Officiated as Agent to Gov-Gen States of W. India '31. *Rec*: Golf, Nature study. *a*: Birdswood, 45 Birling Rd, Tunbridge Wells. *t*: 304.

MOSSOP, Irene Maude. *m*: Charles John Swatridge. Author. *Publ*: Charm's Last Chance; The Taming of Prickles; Una Wins Through; Hilary Leads the Way; Vivien of St Val's; The Fifth at Cliff House; Prunella Plays the Game; Well Played, Juliana; Theresa On Trial; The Fourth at St Faith's; The Grey Adventure; etc. *s.s*: Juv Work, Animal Welfare, Romance. *Rec*: Music, farming, gardening, etc. *a*: Oak Bank, Woking, Surrey. *T*: 1482.

MOTT, Francis John. *b*: Felsted 1901. *m*: Gwendolen Mayhew. Publisher. *Publ*: Law Emerges; Quest; Haunted Woman; Christian Economics; Moses or Hitler?. *s.s*: Religion, philosophy, science, psychic matters. *Rec*: Motoring, country life. *a*: 31a Lyndhurst Rd, Hampstead. *t*: Hampstead 3967.

MOTT, Frank Luther, A.M., Ph.D., Litt.D., L.H.D. *b*: Iowa 1886. *e*: Univs of Chicago, Columbia, Boston, Simpson Coll, Temple Univ. *m*: Vera I. Ingram. *d*: 1. Dean, Sch of Journalism Univ of Missouri. *n.a*: Ed Marengo Republican 1907—14, Ed Grand Junction Globe '14—17, Co-Ed The Midland '25—30, Ed Journalism Quarterly '30—34, Lit Ed Kiwanis Mag '44—45. *Publ*: History of American Magazines; Golden Multitudes; Rewards of Reading; The Man With the Good Face; The Literature of Pioneer Life in Iowa. *Ctr*: N.Y. Times, N.Y. Her Trib, Kansas City Star, etc. *s.s*: Hist of Magazines, Newsps & Popular Reading, Hist & Criticism of Amer Lit. *Rec*: Gardening, book collecting. *a*: 1809 Anthony St, Columbia, Missouri, U.S.A. *T*: 5637.

MOTT, Nevill Francis, M.A., F.R.S. *b*: Leeds 1905. *e*: Clifton Coll, St John's Coll Camb. *m*: Ruth Horder. *d*: 2. Univ Prof, Pres of Assc of Atomic Scientists of G.B., Hughes Medal of Roy Soc. *Publ*: Electronic Processes in Ionic Crystals (with R. W. Gurney); Theory of the Properties of Metals & Alloys (with H. Jones). *Ctr*: Various Scientific & Technical Journs. *s.s*: Physics, Atomic Physics, Quantum Theory. *a*: Stuart Hse, Royal Fort, Bristol 8. *T*: 21846.

MOTT, Rodney L., M.A., Ph.D. *b*: Pullman, Washington 1896. *e*: Stanford & Wisconsin Univs. *m*: Harriet L. Minton. *d*: 1. Political Scientist, Dir Div of Social Science Colgate Univ. *n.a*: Mang Ed State Government 1930—34. *Publ*: Due Process of Law; Constitution of the States & the United States (collab); Men, Groups, & the Community (collab); Materials Illustrative of American Government. *Ctr*: Amer Polit Sci Rev, Polit Sci Quart, Nat Municipal Rev, etc. *s.s*: Polit Sci, Courts & Administration of Justice, Military Govt, Constitutional Law. *Rec*: Music. *c*: Torch. *a*: 9 University Ave, Hamilton, New York. *T*: Hamilton 161.

MOTT, Col. T. Bentley, D.S.M., C.M.G. *b*: Virginia 1865. *e*: West Point. *m*: Georgette Saint Paul. U.S. Army (ret). *Publ*: Biography of Myron T. Herrick; Eng trans Memoirs of Marshal Foch & Marshal Joffre. *c.t*: Scribner's Mag, Harper's, Saturday Evening Post. Liaison Officer between Gen Pershing & Marshal Foch 1918-19. *Rec*: Shooting, golf. *c*: Union (N.Y. & Paris), etc. *a*: 3 Rue de Chaillot, Paris.

MOTTRAM, James Cecil. Med Profession. *Publ*: Flyfishing—Some New Arts & Mysteries; Sea Trout & Other Fishing Studies; The Care & Management of Trout Fisheries. *s.s*: Flyfishing. *a*: 43 Charing X, S.W.

MOTTRAM, Ralph Hale, J.P., F.R.S.L. *b*: Norwich 1883. *e*: Norwich & Lausanne. *m*: Margaret Allan. *s*: 2. *d*: 1. Author & Writer, Barclays Bank for 20 yrs. *Publ*: Spanish Farm; Our Mr. Dormer; The Lame Dog; The Ghost & the Maiden; Visit of the Princess; The Gentlemen of Leisure; East Anglia; Success to the Mayor; A Journey to the Western Front; Old England; John Crome; Portrait of an Unknown Victorian; Bowler Hat; Buxton the Liberator; etc. *Ctr*: Observer, Inquirer, Statesman. *s.s*: Fiction, Financial History, Local History, Biography. *Rec*: Gardening. *a*: 4 Poplar Ave, Eaton, Norwich. *T*: Eaton 235.

MOTTRAM, Vernon Henry, M.A. *e*: Caterham Sch, St Olave's Sch, Trin Coll Camb. Prof of Physiology Lond Univ (ret). *Publ*: Food & the Principles of Dietetics (collab); Physical Basis of Personality; Food & the Family; Healthy Eating; Manual of Histology. *s.s*: Nutrition. *a*: Hope Cottage, Donhead St Mary, Shaftesbury, Dorset. *T*: Donhead 396.

MOULD, George. b: Bury. e: M/C G.S. m: Anne Constance Colquhoun, News Ed. n.a: Junr Reporter Radcliffe Times 1913, Bury Times '13, Special Corr, D. C. Thompson & Co, Dundee, '14, D. C. Thomson & Co '19, rep Daily Mail '26, Nthrn News Ed, Daily Mail '30—32, Spec Corr & Asst News Ed M/C Eve News '33, News Ed Leadley News Service '33—34. c.t: Various. s.s: Theatre. War Service 4½ y. Rec: Travel. a: Annesley, Eighteen, Gibbs Green, Edgware. t: Mill Hill 2693.

MOULE, Arthur Christopher. b: Hangchow 1873. e: King's Sch Canterbury, Trin Coll Camb. Vicar of Trumpington 1918—33, Rector of Mundford '40—45, Prof of Chinese Camb '33—38, Fell Trin Coll Camb. Publ: Christians in China Before the Year 1550; Marco Polo (with the late P. Pelliot); Trumpington Church. Ctr: T'oung-pao Leiden, Journ Roy Asiatic Soc, Hist Teachers Miscellany, Trumpington Mag, etc. s.s: Sinology, Local History. a: 34 Chesterton Hall Cres, Cambridge. T: Cambridge 56624.

MOULE, Rev. George Herbert, M.A. b: Hangchow, China 1876. e: Clare Coll & Ridley Hall Camb. m: Edith Mary Bernau. Clerk in Holy Orders, Missionary to Japan. Publ: The Spirit of Japan; The Problem of Japan; Stinsford Church & Parish; Sunday Theological Books in Japanese. s.s: Japan. Rec: Gardening. a: Swallowcliffe, Southbourne Cliff Drive, Bournemouth.

MOULE, Ven. Walter Stephen, M.A. b: Ningpo, China 1864. e: Monkton Combe Sch & Corpus Christi Coll Camb, Ridley Hall Camb. m: Agnes Lucy Wright. Clerk in Holy Orders, C.M.S. Missionary in China 1888—1925, Archdeacon in Chekiang 1911, Vicar of Abbotsbury Dorset '25—42, (ret). Publ: The Offerings made like the Son of God; Holy Communion; Abbotsbury 1946; The Bible, its Contents & Message; The Christian contemplates his Bible; Behold the Man; also several works in Chinese. a: Swallowcliffe, Southbourne Cliff Drive, Bournemouth.

MOULLIN, Eric Balliol, M.A.(Cantab & Oxon), Sc.D. b: Dorset 1893. e: Priv & Downing Coll Camb. Prof of Elec Eng Camb, Fell King's Coll Camb, Vice-Pres Inst Elec Eng, Formerly Fell of Magdalen Coll Oxf, Chmn Guernsey Soc. Publ: Radio Frequency Measurements; Principles of Electromagnetism; Spontaneous Fluctuations of Voltage. Ctr: Roy Soc, Journ Inst Elec Eng, Wireless Eng, etc. s.s: Vibration Problems of Naval Archt. c: Un Univs. a: King's Coll, Cambridge.

MOULT, Bessie. m: Thomas Moult. d: 1. Writer & Lecturer. n.a: Asst Ed Voices, A Magazine of the Creative Arts, Asst Ed Best Poems of the Year. Ctr: Spectator, Manch Guardian, Athenæum, Englishwoman, Millgate, Dly Express, etc. s.s: Education, Travel, Lit Women's Interests. a: 239 Johnson St, Santa Fé, New Mexico, U.S.A. & 18 Eastside Rd, Temple Fortune, N.W.11. T: Speedwell 3379.

MOULT, Thomas. b: Mellor Hall. e: Marple & Manch. m: Bessie Boltianskye. d: 1. Author & Journalist. n.a: Ed of Voices 1919—22, Mang Ed of The Clarion '24 —25, Ed Modern Writers & Playwrights series. Publ: Snow over Elden; Down Here the Hawthorn (poems); Barrie, A Critical Biography; Sally go Round the Moon; Saturday Night; Mary Webb, Her Life & Work; The Best Poems of the Year; W. H. Davies; Bat & Ball, a New Book of Cricket; Willow Pattern; etc. s.s: Literary Crit, Football, Cricket. c: Savage. a: 239 Johnson St, Santa Fé, New Mexico, U.S.A. & 18 Eastside Rd, Temple Fortune, London, N.W.11. T: Speedwell 3379.

MOULTON, Hon. Hugh Fletcher, M.C. e: Eton, King's Coll Camb. Barrister. Publ: Without the Law; The Man in the Turkish Bath; The Unofficial Executor; The Girl He Left Behind Him; Urgent Private Affairs; A Certain Liveliness; Trial of A. C. Mason; Trial of Arthur Podmore; Life of Lord Moulton; The National Tariff Policy; etc. s.s: Patents, Trade Marks, Detection. a: 16 Argyll Rd, London, W.8. T: Western 2687.

MOUNTAIN, Julian. b: Queensland 1908. e: Australian Public Schs. Novelist. Publ: The Pioneers; Love is Vanity; Prose & Verse (with D. Cowie); Diary of a Young Married Man. a: c/o The Tantivy Press, Malvern, Worcs.

MOUNTFORD, Charles Pearcy, F.R.A.I. b: Hallett, Sth Australia 1890. e: State Sch & Univ of Adelaide. m: Bessie I. Johnstone. s: 1. d: 1. Lect, Film Dir, Ethnologist, Aust Dept of Information. Publ: The Art of the Australian Aboriginal (collab); The Art of Albert Namatjira; Brown Men & Red Sand. Ctr: Nat Geog Mag, Natural Hist, Wild Life, Walkabout, etc. s.s: Life & Customs of Australian Aborigines (primitive art). Rec: Tennis, photography. a: 25 First Ave, St Peters, Sth Australia. T: F 2773.

MOUNTFORD, James Frederick, M.A.(Oxon), D.Litt (B'ham). b: West Bromwich 1897. e: West Bromwich Gr Sch Univ of B'ham, Oriel Coll Oxf. m: Doris May Edwards. d: 3. Vice-Chancellor Univ of Liv since 1945, Prof of Classics Cornell Univ '24—27, Faraday Fell St John's Coll Oxf '24—27. Prof of Latin, Univ Coll Aberystwyth '28—32, Prof of Latin Univ of Liv '32—45. Publ: Classical Quotations in Mediæval Latin Glossaries; Edition of Kennedy's Latin Primer; Edition of Bradley's Latin Prose Composition. Ctr: Classical Quarterly, Journ of Hellenic Studies, Classical Philogy. s.s: Ancient Music, Latin Language & Lit. Rec: Music. a: The University, Liverpool. T: Liverpool Royal 6301.

MOURANT, Arthur Ernest, M.A., B.M., B.Ch., D.Phil., F.G.S. b: Jersey, Channel Islands 1904. e: Victoria Coll Jersey, Exeter Coll Oxf, St Bart's Hosp Lond. Medical Research Worker. Publ: The Earthquakes of the Channel Islands. Ctr: Nature, Lancet, Brit Journ of Experimental Pathol, Science, Quarterly Journ Geol Soc, Geol Mag, etc. s.s: Blood Groups, Geology, Hist, Archæol, Nat Hist of Channel Islands. Rec: Photography, travel. a: Lister Institute, Chelsea Bridge Rd, London, S.W.1. T: Sloane 8775.

MOUSLEY, Edward Opotiki, M.A., LL.B. b: New Zealand 1886. Barrister, Writer. Publ: The Place of International Law in Jurisprudence; An Empire View of the Empire Tangle; The Secrets of a Kuttite; Blow Bugles Blow; An English Odyssey; Mr. Salt Finds Happiness; Le Siege De Kut-El-Amara; Man or Leviathan; Federal Union. Ctr: Various. s.s: Political Science, Sociology, Internat Affairs. Rec: Riding, golf, tennis. a: Far Curlews, North Shore Rd, Hayling Island, Hants.

MOUSSU, GUSTAVE: professor, publicist; b. St. Laurent en Gatines, France, Jan. 1, 1864; educ. École de Médecine de Paris, Faculté des Sciences de Paris (Sorbonne). DEGREES: M.D., Sc.D. AUTHOR: Maladies du Mouton et de la Chèvre, 1923; Maladies du porc (2nd edit.), 1924; Maladies du gros Bétail (5th edit.), 1928; Maladies des Volailles et des Lapins (2nd edit.), 1929. General character of writing, scientific. CLUBS: L'Académie d'Agriculture de France (former President), Conteiller municipal de la commune de St. Maurice, La Société de Biologie de Paris (former Vice-President). Religion, Catholic. OFFICE: École, Nationale Veterinaire d'Alfort. HOME: Villa des Epinettes à St. Maurice, Saint Maurice (Seine), France.

MOWAT, Brig.-Gen. Magnus, C.B.E., T.D. b: Bombay 1875. e: Aberdeen G.S., Blackheath Proprietary Sc & King's Col Lon. Chrtd Civil & Mech Engineer. Sec Inst Mech Engs 1920—. n.a: Ed Inst Journ & Proceedings. c.t: Eng & educ journs. s.s: Engineering, educ. War Service. Commanding Royal Engineer of Division & Dir of Roads & Bridges '20. Rec: Shooting, gardening. Fell Roy Soc Edin F.C.I.S. Mem Inst Civil Engs, Mem Inst of Mech Engs. Hon Life Mem Inst of R.E.s, etc. c: Nat, Overseas, City Livery, etc. a: Ebor Hse, Sheen Gate Gdns, S.W.14. t: Whitehall 7476.

MOWAT, Robert Balmain. *b*: Edin 1883. *e*: George Watson's Col, Merchiston Castle Edin & Balliol Col Oxf. *m*: Mary George Loch. *s*: 5. *d*: 1. Prof of Hist Bristol Univ. *n.a*: Ed Mod States Series 1933. *Publ*: A History of Great Britain; European Diplomacy (3 vols); The Diplomacy of Napoleon; Problem of the Nations; Public & Private Morality; etc. *c.t*: Quart Review, L'Esprit Internat, Edin Review. *s.s*: Diplomatic hist, internat affairs & econs. Visited U.S.A. in '25-8-30. *Rec*: Working for L.N.U. *c*: Eng-Speaking Union. *a*: Downfield Lodge, Clifton, Bristol 8.

MOWERY, William Byron, M.A. *b*: Adelphia, Ohio, U.S.A. 1899. *e*: Illinois & Ohio State Univs. *m*: . *d*: 4. Naturalist & Novelist, Teacher. *Publ*: The Silver Hawk; The Girl from God's Mercie; Forbidden Valley; Challenge of the North; Resurrection River; The Outlaw Trail; The Valley Beyond; The Constable of Lone Sioux; also plays & poetry. *Ctr*: Red Book, Country Gentleman, Poet-Lore, Sat Ev Post, Liberty, Reader's Digest, Amer Mag, etc. *s.s*: N.W. Territory of Canada, Entomology, Mammalia of the North American Cretaceous. *Rec*: Field sciences, flying. *c*: Author's Guild of America, Cliff Dwellers. *a*: Division of General Education, New York Univ, Washington Sq East, New York City. *T*: Spring 7-2000.

MOWLE, Alfred Charles, M.A., M.B.(Cantab),M.R.C.S., L.R.C.P. *b*: Toronto, Canada 1896. *e*: Emmanuel Coll Camb, St Thomas's Hosp. Hon Surg Devizes & Dis Hosp, Chief M.O. Cyprus Mines Corp. 1927—31. *Publ*: The New Turkish. *a*: Lansdowne Hse, Devizes, Wilts.

MOWSHAY, Ben. See **Summerfield, Woolfe.**

MOXON, Frank, M.B., B.S., O.B.E. Hon Major. *b*: Hull 1879. *e*: Ockbrook Moravian Sc, Durham Univ. *m*: (1) Elsie Gilford; (2) Mrs B. P. Eykyn. *s*: 1. *d*: 1. Ophth Surg. *s.s*: Ophth. Ophth Specialist in France 1914—19, 1st & 5th Armies (des). *Rec*: Gardening. *a*: 8 Murray Rd, Wimbledon, & 4 Bentinck St, W.1. *t*: Welbeck 5021 & Wimbledon 1976.

MOXON, Canon Reginald Stewart, M.A., D.D. *b*: London 1875. *e*: Manch G.S., Gonville & Caius Coll Camb. *m*: Ina Mary Rowson. *s*: 2. *d*: 1. Hon Canon of Portsmouth, Examining Chaplain to the Bishop of Portsmouth. *Publ*: Vincent of Lerins; Doctrine of Sin; Modernism & Orthodoxy. *Ctr*: Smith's Dictionary of the Bible. *s.s*: Theology. *Rec*: Motoring & golf. *a*: Dunraven, Trinity St, Ryde, I.O.W. *T*: Ryde 2525.

MOXON, Rev. Thomas Allen. *b*: Lon 1877. *e*: M/C G.S. & St John's Col Cam. *m*: Evelyn Goodwin Stroyan. *s*: 2. *d*: 1. Headmaster Denstone Col. *n.a*: Prebendary of Lichfield 1934–. *Publ*: Chrysostom: On the Priesthood; Aristotle & Demetrius on Style; etc. *c.t*: Hastings's Dictionary of the Bible, Ch Quarterly Review, etc. *s.s*: Divinity, classics. *a*: Denstone Col, Staffs. *t*: Rocester 2.

MOY, A. G., M.J.I. *n.a*: Ed Llandudno Advertiser. *a*: Bron Wendon, Church Walks, Llandudno.

MOYES, John Scott. *b*: Plumstead 1916. *e*: Oratory Sch Lond. *m*: Nesta Moyes. *s*: 1. *d*: 1. Journalist, Mem Inst of Journ. *n.a*: Rep The Paper Container 1934—40, Rep The Outfitter '46—47, Exec Ed '47—. *Ctr*: The Star, Packaging. *s.s*: One Act Plays, Packaging, Clothing & Irish History. *Rec*: Table tennis. *w.s*: R.A.F. 1940—46. *a*: 34 Elthiron Rd, London, S.W.6. *T*: Renown 2530.

MOYES, Rt. Rev. John Stoward, M.A., D.D. (See **ARMIDALE, Bishop of).** *b*: Koolunga, Sth Australia 1884. *e*: St Peter's Coll Adelaide, Univ of Adelaide, St Barnabas Theol Coll Adelaide. *m*: Helen Margaret Butler. *s*: 4. *d*: 2. Bishop of Armidale, N.S.W. *Publ*: Australia, the Church & the Future; Marriage & Sex; American Journey; The Church & the Hour. *Ctr*: Sunday Sun, Morning Herald (Sydney). *s.s*: Christianity & Social Questions. *Rec*: Tennis, bowls, music. *c*: Univ (Sydney). *a*: Bishopscourt, Armidale, N.S.W., Australia. *T*: 355.

MOYLAN, Sir John Fitzgerald, C.B., C.B.E. Receiver Metrop Police Dis. *Publ*: Scotland Yard & The Metropolitan Police. *c.t*: Times, Dly Telegraph, Police Journ. *a*: New Scotland Yard & Byeways, Hayward's Heath, Sussex.

MOYLE, Christopher George. *b*: Leominster 1914. *e*: Leominster Gr Sch. Journalist. *n.a*: Hereford Bulletin, Dly Express, Asst Press Officer Min of Educ. *s.s*: Humour, Feature Writing, Short Stories. *Rec*: Music, theatre, literature. *a*: 11b Melrose Rd, London, S.W.18.

MOYLE, Edmund John. *b*: S. Minver. *e*: Weymouth Col. Sec Assoc Conservative Clubs. *n.a*: Ed Conservative Clubs Gazette 1902, News Ed The People '08-18. *Publ*: Humours of Politics; Five Notable Men; Club Secs' Legal Guide; etc. *s.s*: Clubs. *a*: 25 Well Walk, Hampstead, N.W.3. *t*: 6636.

MOYNE, 2nd Baron of Bury St. Edmunds. (See **GUINNESS, Bryan Walter.**) *b*: 1905. *e*: Eton, Ch Ch Oxf. Married. *s*: 4. *d*: 3. Barrister, Author & Novelist. *a*: Biddesden Hse, Andover. *T*: Ludgershall (Wilts) 37.

MOYNIHAN, Rt. Hon. Baron Berkeley George Andrew, K.C.M.G., C.B., D.C.L., LL.D., M.D., D.Sc, M.S., M.B., F.R.C.S., F.R.C.S.E. *Publ*: Abdominal Operations (5 edns); Gall Stones & Their Surgical Treatment (2 edns); Duodenal Ulcer (2 edns); Diseases of the Spleen; Pathology of the Living; etc. *c.t*: Lancet, B.M.J., etc. *a*: 11 Portland Pl, W.1. & Carr Manor, Leeds. *t*: Langham 2030.

MOYNIHAN, Rev. Senan, O.F.M. *b*: Co Kerry 1900. *e*: St Brendan's Killarney & Nat Univ of Ireland. Catholic Priest. *n.a*: Founder & Ed Capuchin Annual. *Ctr*: Various Catholic Newsps. *a*: P.O. Box 105, Capuchin Friary, Church St, Dublin. *T*: 74121.

MOYSHEH OYVED. See **Good, Edward.**

MOZLEY, Lt. Col. Edward Newman, D.S.O. *b*: Mirfield, Yorks 1875. *e*: Eton & R.M.A. Woolwich. *m*: Annie Campbell Scott. *s*: 1. *d*: 2. Army Officer, Savings Officer under the Treasury for Northern Command 1941—45, Headmaster later partner Red House Sch nr York '21—41. *Publ*: Graduated Exercises in Mathematics; Guide to the Old Testament; The Housing Question; History of the Corps of Roy Engineers in Gallipoli; Theology of Albert Schweitzer. *Ctr*: Various. *s.s*: Theology & Politics. *Rec*: Walking. *w.s*: 1914—19 Brevet Lt-Col. *a*: Lynwood, Ripon. *T*: Ripon 395.

MOZLEY, H. *b*: Aughton 1914. *e*: Woodhouse Gr Sch. Journalist. *n.a*: Rotherham Express. *a*: Howard St, Rotherham. *T*: 4434.

MOZLEY, Rev. James Frederick, D.D. *b*: Wigginton, Oxon 1887. *e*: Winchester & Exeter Coll Oxf. Clerk in Holy Orders, Former Schoolmaster. *Publ*: William Tyndale; John Foxe & his Book. *s.s*: Hist of the English Bible, The English Reformation. *a*: 52 Avenue Rd, London, N.6.

MOZLEY, Rev. John Kenneth, D.D.(Cam). *b*: Newlay 1883. *e*: Malvern Col, Leeds G.S., Pembroke Col Cam. *m*: Mary Geraldine Nutt. Canon & Chancellor of St Paul's Cathedral. *n.a*: Ed Cam Review

1909. *Publ*: The Doctrine of the Atonement; The Heart of the Gospel; The Beginnings of Christian Theology; The Gospel Sacraments; etc. *c.t*: Journ of Theol Studies & Theology *s.s*: Theology, Hist of dogma. Princ of Leeds Clergy Sc '20-25. Warden of St Augustine Hse Reading '30. *Rec*: Golf, chess. *c*: Nat Lib. *a*: 3 Amen Ct, E.C.4. *t*: City 3517.

MUCHA, Jiri George. *b*: Prague 1915. *e*: Charles Univ Prague. *m*: Geraldine Thomson. Writer, Novelist, Playwright. *n.a*: Ed Military Broadcasts B.B.C. Czech Sect 1941—43, Ed Ceskoslovensky Boj Paris '39—40, Czech Corres New Writing in Prague & l'Arche Paris in Prague '45—. *Publ*: The Problems of Lieutenant Knap; The Bridge; Fire Against Fire; Ugie; The Daughter of Lot; The Golden Age (Play). *Ctr*: New Writing, L'Arche (Paris), Svobodne Niviny (Prague), Kytice (Prague), etc. *s.s*: The War & the Life of People after it. *Rec*: Hunting, motoring, farming. *c*: Nat (Prague). *w.s*: R.A.F. & War Corres. *a*: Praha XIX, V Tisine 4, Czechoslovakia. *T*: 750-66.

MUCKLESTON, Edith Margaret. *b*: Carlisle, Pennsylvania. *e*: Wellesley Coll Massachusetts, Sorbonne, Paris, Univ of California. *m*: Harold S. Muckleston. *d*: 3. Writer. *Publ*: The Red Lantern; The Wanderer on a Thousand Hills; Jade Mountains; etc. *Ctr*: Hollywood News. *Rec*: Motoring. *a*: 400 University Circle, Claremont, California, U.S.A.

MUDGETT, Bruce D., B.A., Ph.D. *b*: Ashland, Nebraska 1884. *e*: Univs of Idaho & Pennsylvania. *m*: Mildred Dennett. *d*: 2. Prof of Economics & Statistics. *Publ*: Life Insurance (collab); Disability Provision in American Life Insurance Contracts; Statistical Tables & Graphs; Report of War Trade Board (collab). *Ctr*: Journ American Statistical Assoc, Econometrica. *s.s*: Statistics. *a*: 1417 East River Rd, Minneapolis, 14 Minnesota. *T*: Br 1720.

MUDIE, Ian Mayelston. *b*: Hawthorn, Sth Australia 1911. *e*: Scotch Coll Adelaide. *m*: Renee Dunford Doble. *s*: 2. Author & Journalist. *Publ*: Poems 1934-44; The Australian Dream; Corroboree to the Sun; This is Australia; Their Seven Stars Unseen; (Ed) Poets at War; etc. *Ctr*: Bulletin, Walkabout, Advertiser (Adelaide), Poetry, Salt, etc. *s.s*: Hist of Darling-Murray Basin, Sth Aust Hist, Austr Travel. *Rec*: Gardening. *a*: 53 Marine Pde, Seacliff, Sth Australia. *T*: X7372.

MUDIE, J. A. W. *a*: Sunday Post, 186 Fleet Street, E.C.4.

MUDIE, Rev. P. Laurence K. *b*: Hamilton 1876. *e*: Clydesdale Col, Hamilton Acad, Glas H.S., Edin Univ, New Col. *m*: Agnes Fleming. Sub Convenor of Students of Divinity Cmt for Presbytery of Ayr. *Publ*: Sir Walter Scott & the Lure of the Road; etc. *c.t*: Scots Observer, Brit Weekly, Young Scotland, The Banffshire Journ, Oban Times, etc. *s.s*: Eng lit, apologetics, polemics. *c*: Theo & Fraternal Socs of Presbytery of Ayr. *a*: Newton-on-Ayr Manse, Scotland.

MUECKE, Francis Frederick, C.B.E., F.R.C.S., M.B.B.S. Aural Surg. *c.t*: B.M.J., Lancet, Practitioner, Post-Graduate Journ. *a*: 36 Cavendish Sq, W.1. *t*: Mayfair 6126.

MUGGE, Maximilian August. *b*: 1878. Married. *s*: 1. *d*: 1. *Publ*: Friedrich Nietzsche, His Life & Work (4th ed 1915, o.p.); Eugenics & The Superman; The War Diary of a Square Peg; Kew Gardens Adventures—Fairy Tales for Grown-Ups; A New German Word-Book ('32); etc. War Service B.E.F. *c*: Authors.

MUGGERIDGE, Malcolm. *b*: Sanderstead 1903. *e*: Elem Sch, Sec Sch, Camb Univ. *m*: Katherine Dobbs. *s*: 2. Journalist, Mem N.U.J. *n.a*: Leader Writer Manch Guardian 1930—32, Internat Labour Office '33—34, Ed Staff Statesman (Calcutta & Delhi). *Publ*: Three Flats (Play); Autumnal Face (Novel); Winter in Moscow. *Ctr*: Life Tide, Fortnightly, Eng Rev, Life & Letters, Truth, Nineteenth Century. *s.s*: Russia & Far East. *Rec*: Swimming, riding, travel. *a*: 19 Grove Terrace, London, N.W.5. *T*: Gulliver 4392.

MUIR, Arthur William, D.S.O., M.C., B.Sc. *b*: L'pool 1891. *e*: Rutherford Col Newcastle-on-Tyne & Armstrong Col Durham. *m*: Madge Borradale. *s*: 1. Elec Eng. Part-time Lect in Tech writing M/C Col of Tech 1924—. *c.t*: Electrician. *s.s*: Tech book reviews. War Service 1914-19; ret Major. Metro-Vickers Elec Co '19-, research, publicity & A.C. machine design. *Rec*: Tennis, badminton. *a*: Bankfield Hse, W. Grove, Brooklands, Ches.

MUIR, Augustus. *b*: Ontario 1892. *e*: George Heriot's Edin & Edin Univ. *m*: Jean Murray Dow Walker. Author & Journalist. *n.a*: Asst Ed & later Ed The World. *Publ*: The Riddle of Garth; The Silent Partner; Beginning the Adventure; Raphael, M.D.; The Crimson Crescent; Scotland's Road of Romance; The Intimate Thoughts of John Baxter, Bookseller; Joey & the Greenwings; Heather-Track & High Road, a Book of Scottish Journeys; Scottish Portrait; Saintsbury Memorial Volume (Assoc Ed); The Man Who Stole the Crown Jewels; The Sands of Fear; The Blue Bonnet; Castles in the Air; Scottish Portrait. *s.s*: Scotland. *c*: Savage, Scots Arts (Edin). *a*: Parkhill, Stansted, Essex. *T*: Stansted 2289.

MUIR, Charles Mackenzie, B.Comm., F.R.S.A. *b*: Dalry, Scotland. *e*: Smith's Inst Public Sch Ayr, Aberdeen Univ. *m*: Jean Fyfe Smart. Marketing Executive. *Publ*: The Wonderful Cross; *Ctr*: Mar Dly Press, Marketing, Advertising, Salesmanship & Religious periodicals. *s.s*: Econ, Marketing, Packaging, Religion. *Rec*: Golf. *a*: 13 Highworth Ave, Cambridge. *T*: 55712.

MUIR, Daphne. *b*: S. Africa 1896. *Publ*: The Virtuous Woman (1929); The Lost Crusade; The Secret Bird; Barbaloot; Very Heaven ('34). *s.s*: Hist. *Rec*: Gardening. *a*: Mole End, Up Somborne, Hants.

MUIR, Dorothy Erskine. *e*: St Felix Sch Southwold, Somerville Coll Oxf. *m*: T. A. E. Muir. *s*: 1. *d*: 1. History Coach. *Publ*: A History of Milan under the Visconti; In Muffled Night; Five to Five; Machiavelli; Oliver Cromwell; Florence Nightingale. *s.s*: Italian Hist & Detective Fiction. *a*: 2 Bradmore Rd, Oxford.

MUIR, Edwin. *Publ*: inc (autobiog) The Story & the Fable; (biog) John Knox; & many poems; also (fiction) The Marionette; Poor Tom; etc. *a*: 8 Blantyre Terr, Edinburgh 10.

MUIR, Ernest, C.I.E., M.D., F.R.C.S, LL.D. *b*: Scotland 1880. *e*: George Watkin's Coll Edin, Edin Univ. *m*: Sophie Vartan. *s*: 1. *d*: 1. Research Worker Sch of Trop Med Calcutta 1920—35, Prof of Trop Med Sch of Trop Med Calcutta '33—35, Med Sec Brit Emp Leprosy Assoc '35—47, Hon Sec & Treasurer Internat Leprosy Assoc since 1935. *n.a*: Ed Leprosy Review 1936—47. *Publ*: Kala Azar; Leprosy (with Sir L. Rogers). *Ctr*: Internat Journ of Leprosy & other Med Journs. *s.s*: Leprosy. *Rec*: Gardening. *c*: Roy Empire. *a*: 29a Crawford Ave, Wembley, Middlesex. *T*: Wembley 2048.

MUIR, Jean Seaton. *e*: Univ Coll Lond, Germany, France, Belgium, Italy. Married. Hon Sec Glasgow Literary Club. *Publ*: Grizel Cochrane, Men of the Westland; Masque of the Seasons; Stone of Destiny; Privilege of Light; The Kist in the Mist; All Souls' Day; Wishing Well; Puck in a Serious Hour; Freya;

Iduna; Forget-me-Not; The Sword of Justice; The Maori Legends; etc. *Ctr*: Various. *s.s*: History, Poetry, Art. *a*: St Anne's, Barasie, Troon, Ayrshire, Scotland. *T*: Troon 134.

MUIR, John Ramsay Bryce. *b*: Otterburn 1872. *e*: Univ of L'pool & Balliol Oxf. Writer & Politician. *n.a*: Ed Weekly Westminster 1923–26. *Publ*: History of Liverpool; Peers & Bureaucrats; Short History of the British Commonwealth (2 vols); Making of British India; The Expansion of Europe; How Britain Is Governed; The Interdependent World & Its Problems; etc. *s.s*: Hist, polit theory. Prof of Modern Hist L'pool '07–13, M/C '14–21. M.P. Rochdale '23. Mem Parl Del to S. Africa '24. Chm '30 & Pres '33 Nat Lib Fed. *c*: Reform, Nat Lib. *a*: Sennen, Layter's Way, Gerrards X, Bucks. *t*: 993.

MUIR, Kenneth, B.A. *b*: London 1907. *e*: Priv & Epsom Coll, St Edmund Hall Oxf. *m*: Mary Ewen. *d*: 1. Lect in English Litt, Leeds Univ. *n.a*: Ed Leeds Weekly Citizen 1945—. *Publ*: The Voyage to Illyria (collab); The Nettle & the Flower; English Poetry; Jonah & the Whale. *Ctr*: Yorks Post, Spectator, Adelphi, New English Weekly, Leeds Weekly Citizen, Penguin New Writing. *s.s*: Shakespeare & Elizabethan Litt, Drama, 19th Century Poetry. *Rec*: Walking, swimming, acting. *a*: 28 Heathfield, Leeds 6, Yorks. *T*: 74069.

MUIR, Mary. *b*: India. *e*: Priv & St Margaret's Convent Edin. Journalist & Short story writer. *c.t*: Universe, Catholic Times, Irish Catholic & Glas Observer, Sussex Daily News, Evening Argus, Oxf Mail, etc. *s.s* Short stories, trav. Lit Prizes: Bookman 1st prize, prize winner in Sussex Mag, Cork Wkly Exam, etc. *a*: c/o Grindlay & Co, 54 Parliament St, Westminster, S.W.1.

MUIR, Sir Robert, Kt., M.A., F.R.C.P., LL.D. (Hon Edin, Glas), D.Sc.(Hon Bristol, Leeds, Dublin), D.C.L., F.R.S. *b*: Balfron, Stirlingshire. *e*: Hawick Acad, Edin Univ. *Publ*: Manual of Bacteriology; Studies on Immunity; Textbook of Pathology. *Ctr*: Various. *s.s*: Pathology, Bacteriology and Immunity. *Rec*: Reading, golf, angling. *c*: Savile, Edin Univ. *a*: 24 Eglinton Cresc, Edinburgh. *T*: Edin 62916.

MUIR, Wilhelmina Johnstone, M.A. *b*: Montrose 1890. *e*: Montrose Acad & St And Univ. *m*: Edwin Muir. *s*: 1. Author & Translator. *Publ*: Imagined Corners; Mrs Ritchie; Trans with Edwin Muir: Jew Suss; Three Cities; The Castle; Little Friend; etc. *s.s*: Trans from German, educ. *a*: 7 Downshire Hill, Hampstead, N.W.3. *t*: 1280.

MUIRHEAD, A. M., M.A. Schoolmaster. *Publ*: G. R. Osler, A Brief Memoir (1931). *s.s*: Book-collecting & bibliography, particularly works of William Cobbett. *a*: 83 The Limes Av, New Southgate, N.11.

MUIRHEAD, Findlay, M.A.(Edin). *b*: Glas. *e*: Roy H.S. Edin & Edin & Leipzig Univs. Widower. *s*: 1. Lit Ed & Journalist. *Publ*: An organizer & ed of the Blue Guides; has publ Blue Guides to England, Great Brit, Scot, Wales, Lon, Paris, Switzerland, Spain, etc. *a*: 14 Devonport St, W.2. *t*: Sloane 4384, Paddington 0245.

MUIRHEAD, Islay Burns, M.A., M.D., C.M. *Publ*: Epicurean Science & Poetry Selected from Jucretius (1895); Extra-ocular Pressure & Myopia (1916). *c.t*: The Med World, etc. *a*: 6 Editha Mans, Edith Grove, S.W.10.

MUIRHEAD, James Thorburn, B.Sc.(Edinburgh), F.R.G.S., A.M.Inst.C.E. *b*: Edinburgh 1899. *e*: Edinburgh Univ. *m*: Cecilia Brennan. Colonial Service, author, journalist. *Publ*: Brother Ceylon; Without Prejudice; Pepperpot. *c.t*: Saturday Review, Empire Review, Chambers Jnl, National Review, Scottish Field, Times of Ceylon, Shooting Times, Glasgow Weekly Herald. *s.s*: Politics, philosophy, native self-government, native customs ceremonies and festivals, big game hunting, travel, Sudan, Ceylon, West Indies. *Rec*: Squash racquets, golf, polo, swimming, big game hunting. Awarded Rugby, Football Blue at Edinburgh, '21–22–23. War Service '14–18. Served 4½ y in Sudan Civil Service, latter part in patrols in Southern Sudan. *a*: c/o Barclays Bank (Dom. Colon. & Overseas), 29 Gracechurch St, E.C.3.

MUIRHEAD, John Henry, LL.D.(Glas & Calif), F.B.A. *b*: Glas 1855. *e*: Glas Acad & Univ, & Balliol Oxf. *m*: (1) Mary Talbot Wallas; (2) Pauline Bailey. Prof of Philos Birm Univ. Ed Library of Philos. Chm Counc Brit Inst of Philos. *Publ*: Elements of Ethics (frequently revised since); The Use of Philosophy; Coleridge as Philosopher; The Platonic Traditions in Anglo-Saxon Philosophy; Rule & End in Morals (1932); etc. *c.t*: Mind, Philos. *s.s*: Ethics & metaphysics. *Rec*: Gardening. *a*: Dyke End, Rotherfield, Sussex.

MUIRHEAD, L. Russell. *b*: London 1896. *e*: Univ Coll Sch, Christ's Coll Camb. *m*: 1. Ed of Guide Books, etc. *n.a*: Ed of The Blue Guides since 1930, Ed Penguin Guides since '38, Ed Discovery '34–38, Ed the Chemical Age '39–46. *Publ*: Various volumes in the Blue Guides Series. *Ctr*: Fortnightly, Times Educ Suppl. *s.s*: Travel. *a*: 80a, Landsdowne Rd, London, W.11.

MUIRHEAD, Thorburn, F.R.G.S., A.M.I.C.E. *b*: Edinburgh 1899. *e*: Edin Univ. *m*: Cecilia Brennan. *d*: 1. Writer, Dir Industrial Facilities Corp & Other City Companies. *Publ*: Without Prejudice; Brother Ceylon; Strange to Relate; Air Attack on Cities; Out of the Ashes; Amber Light; etc. *Ctr*: Times, Dly Telegraph, Ev Standard, Clydebank Press. *s.s*: Big Game Hunting, Travel, Sudan, West Indies. *Rec*: Fly-fishing, polo, shooting. *c*: Scot Lib. *w.s*: 1914–18. *a*: Combe Manor, Wadhurst, Sussex.

MUIRSON BLAKE, Mrs., F.Ph.S. (See DELAIRE, Jean.) *b*: France 1888. *e*: Private. *m*: Capt H. W. Muirson Blake. Novelist, Essayist, Free-lance Journalist, Founded the Philos Circle of the Lyceum Club. *s.s*: Eastern Scs of Philos, Gnosticism, Modern Theosophy, Health Reform, etc. *Rec*: Driving. *a*: Mon Abri, Chorley Wood, Herts. *T*: Chorley Wood 327.

MUKAROVSKY, Jan, Ph.D. *b*: Pisek 1891. *e*: Charles Univ Prague. *m*: Zdenka Mesanyova. *d*: 1. Prof in Aesthetics Charles Univ Prague. *n.a*: Slovo a Slovesnost. *Publ*: Kapitoly z ceske poetiky; Esteticka funkce; Machuv Maj; Polakova Vznesenost prirody; Prispevek k estetice ceskeho verse; O volnem versi ceskem. *Ctr*: Travaux du Cercle Linguistique de Prague. *s.s*: Aesthetics, Philosophy, Linguistics. *a*: Prague XIX, Bubenecska 17, Czechoslovakia. *T*: 733-35.

MUKERJEA, Satya Vrata, M.A. *b*: Dinajpur, Nth Bengal 1887. *e*: Presidency Coll Calcutta, Exeter Coll Oxf. *m*: Arvuna Mukerjea. *s*: 1. *d*: 1. Senior Councillor Baroda State (ret). *Publ*: Census Reports on Baroda. *Ctr*: Calcutta Rev, Modern Rev, Indian Philos Mag, East & West, etc. *s.s*: Lit Criticism, Comparative Religion, Constitutional Reforms in States, Comparative Politics, Statistics, Census, Tribal Langs. *Rec*: Golf, badminton, squash racquets, football. *a*: Chief Minister, Tripura State, Agartala. *T*: Tripura 9.

MUKERJI, Bimala Prosad, M.A. *b*: Baraset, Bengal 1906. *e*: Mitra Inst & Presidency Coll Calcutta. *m*: Lena Banerji. *s*: 1. *d*: 1. Prof of Hist Ripon Coll Calcutta. *n.a*: Ed Lekhan Annual Anthology 1946,

Asst Ed Krishak '47. *Publ*: Byaktigata; Secondhand; Sanchari; Bharater Aitihya; Panchami; Chandrakala; Capitalist; Sankranti. *Ctr*: Amrita Bazar Patrika, Hindustan Standard, Anada Bazar Patrika, Desh, Literary Weekly (Bombay). *s.s*: Literary Reviews, Cultural & Socio-Economic Hist of India. *Rec*: Indian classical music, travel. *a*: 19 Ekdalia Rd, Ballygunge, Calcutta 19, India. *T*: Park 1649.

MUKHERJI, Balai Chand, M.B., B.S. (Bana Phal). *b*: Manihari, India 1899. *e*: Patna Univ. *m*: Lila Banerji. *s*: 2. *d*: 2. Clinical Bacteriologist. *Publ*: Trinakhanda; Mrigaya; Ratri; Kichukshan; Baitarani Tirey; Seyo Ami Nirmoke; Dwairath; Jangam; Saptarshi; Agni; Swapna Sambhat; Sri Madhusudan; Vidyasagar; Mantamugda; Stories of Banaful; Binduvisarga; Angarparni Bhuyo Darshan; Chaturdashi; Ahabaniya; Banaphuler Kabita; Kækti; Dasabhan; etc. *Ctr*: Prabasi, Sanibarer Chithi, Galpa Bharati, etc. *s.s*: Fiction, Drama, Short Stories. *Rec*: Gardening, cooking. *a*: Golekuthi, Adampur, Bhagalpur, India.

MUKHERJI, Dr. Santosh Kumar, M.B. *b*: Calcutta 1893. *e*: Med Col of Bengal Calcutta & Calcutta Univ. *m*: Pratima Bhattacharjee. *s*: 1. *d*: 2. Ed Indian Med Record, Med Practitioner & Dir Indian Med Lab, Ltd. *Publ*: (Med Books in Eng & Trans)—Infantile Cirrhosis of the Liver (1922) (Bengali & Tamil Edns); Practical Prescriptions (Bengali Edn); Modern Treatment of Disease ('35); (General) Prostitution in India ('35); Birth Control; Incompatibility in Prescriptions ('32) (Eng & Bengali Edns); Elements of Endocrinology ('35 Eng & Bengali); etc. *s.s*: Tropical diseases, diseases of internal secretions & Hindu med. Mem Exec Cmt of Indian Journalists Assoc '24—31. Mem Exec Cmt Bangiya Sahitya Parishat '20—21. Asst Sec Indian Art Sc, etc. *a*: 44 Badur Bagan St, Calcutta, India. *t*: BB 355.

MULDOON, Hugh Cornelius, D.Sc. *b*: Truxton, N.Y. *e*: Union Univ Coll of Pharmacy Albany, Valparaiso Univ. Prof of Chem Dean Sch of Pharmacy Duquesne Univ. *n.a*: Ed The Science Counsellor 1935—. *Publ*: Organic Chemistry; Pharmaceutical Latin; Laboratory Manual of Organic Chemistry. *Ctr*: Pharmaceutical Journs. *s.s*: Chem, Pharmacy, Science, Educ. *Rec*: Farming, music. *a*: Hotel William Penn, Pittsburgh, Pennsylvania, U.S.A. *T*: Grant 4635.

MULK, Raj Anand, B.A., D.Phil. *b*: Peshawar 1905. *e*: Univs of Punjab, Lond & Camb. Author. *n.a*: Ed M.A.R.G. Mag 1945—. *Publ*: Untouchable; Coolie; Two Leaves & a Bud; The Village; Across the Black Waters; The Sword & the Sickle; The Barbers' Trade Union; The Big Heart; Persian Painting; The Hindu View of Art; Indian Fairy Tales. *Ctr*: Life & Letters To-day, Fortnightly Review, Our Time, Penguin New Writing, Spectator, Tribune, etc, also major Indian newps. *s.s*: Fiction, Art & Literary Criticism. *Rec*: Mountaineering. *c*: Arts Theatre. *a*: c/o Arts Theatre Club, Little Newport St, London, W.1, & 25 Cuffe Parade, Colaba, Bombay.

MULGAN, Alan Edward, O.B.E. *b*: Katikati, New Zealand 1881. *m*: Marguerita Pickmere. *s*: 2. *d*: 1. Journalist, Sometime Lecturer in Journalism at Auckland University Coll, Talks Supervisor N.Z. Broadcasting Service 1935—46. *n.a*: Lit Ed Auckland Star. *Publ*: The English of the Line; Three Plays of New Zealand; Home: A Colonial's Adventure; Golden Wedding; Spur of Morning; First with the Sun; From Track to Highway; A Pilgrim's Way in N.Z.; The City of the Strait; Literature & Authorship in N.Z. *Ctr*: New Zealand, London Mercury. *a*: York Bay, Eastbourne, Wellington, New Zealand.

MULFORD, Clarence Edward. *b*: 1883. Author. *Publ*: Bar 20; Hopalong Cassidy; Mesquite Jenkins; The Deputy Sheriff; The Round Up; Trial Dust; etc. *a*: c/o Hodder & Stoughton, Warwick Sq, London, E.C.4.

MULLALLY, Frederic. *b*: London 1918. *m*: Suzanne Warner. Political Columnist Sunday Pict. *n.a*: Sports Ed Times of Malta 1936, Ed Sunday Standard Bombay '37—38, Sub-Ed & Spec Writer Financial News '40—43, Art Ed News Rev '44, Asst-Ed Tribune '45—46. *Publ*: Death Pays a Dividend; Fascism Inside England. *s.s*: Fascism, British Film Industry, Domestic Politics. *Rec*: Painting, reading, conjuring. *a*: 6 Melton Ct, London, S.W.7. *T*: Kensington 3811.

MULLALY, Rev. Charles J., S.J. *b*: Washington, D.C., U.S.A. 1877. *e*: Gonzaga Hgh Sch & Coll Woodstock Maryland & Tortosa Spain. Catholic Priest. *n.a*: Spanish Corres America 1909—12, Assoc Ed '17—20, Ed '20—41, The Messenger of the Sacred Heart. *Publ*: The Priest Who Failed; The Bravest of the Virginia Cavalry; Could You Explain Catholic Practices? Spiritual Reflections; etc. *Ctr*: Catholic Ency & many American & European Mags. *s.s*: Theology. *a*: Jesuit Novitiate, Wernersville, Pennsylvania, U.S.A. *T*: Sinking Spring 8032.

MULLER, Frederick. *e*: Private. Publisher. With Methuen & Co Ltd (Publishers) 1896—'33. Founder, Frederick Muller Ltd, '34. *a*: 29 Gt James St, Bedford Row, W.C.1. *t*: Holborn 6553.

MULLER, Hermann Joseph, M.A., Ph.D. *b*: New York City 1890. *e*: Columbia Univ. *m*: Dorothea Kantorowicz. *s*: 1. *d*: 1. Prof of Biology Indiana Univ 1945—. *Publ*: The Mechanism of Mendelian Heredity (collab); Out of the Night; Genetics, Medicine & Man (collab). *Ctr*: Science, Genetics, Amer Naturalist, Journ of Heredity. *s.s*: Genetics, Evolution, Biology, Eugenics, Chromosomes, Heredity. *a*: 1001 East First St, Bloomington, Indiana, U.S.A. *T*: Bloomington, Ind 7660.

MULLER, Jorgen Peter. *b*: Island of Als, Denmark 1866. *e*: Nykobing Cath Sc & Univ of Copenhagen. *m*: Maria Schonberg (dec). *s*: 2. Author. *n.a*: Sports Ed Kobenhavn 1893-1901, Ed Superman (Lon) '34. *Publ*: My System ('04); My System for Children; My Breathing System; My Sunbathing & Fresh Air System; 3 vols on Spiritualism; etc. *c.t*: Sunday Times, Daily Mail, Health & Strength, etc. *s.s*: Hygiene. Served in Roy Danish Eng's. Insp at Vejlefjord Sanatorium for Consumptives '01-05. Introduced most sports & games into Denmark. Exam to Inst of Hyg several yrs. Three degrees in Philos & Divinity. Kt'hood of Roy Danish Order of Dannebrog. *Rec*: Rowing, swimming, winter sports. *c*: R.A.C., Danish. *a*: c/o The Muller Inst, Grand Bldgs, Trafalgar Sq, London, W.C.2. *t*: Whitehall 2000.

MÜLLER, MARGARETHE M.: prof. emeritus, Wellesley College; b. Hanover, Germany, Sept. 25, 1862; d. Hermann and Emmy (Bauermeister) M.; educ. Hanover Normal Coll., Göttingen Univ.; unmarried. AUTHOR: Glück auf, 1902; Maria Stuart; Keller's Legenden; Carla Wenckebach, Pioneer, 1908; Elsbeth, 1914. Contributes to Atlantic Monthly, Churchman. HOME: 62 Kunigunden St., Munich, Germany.

MULLIGAN, James, K.C., M.A. *b*: Anaghlone, Co Down 1847. *e*: Queen's Univ Ireland. *m*: Kate Helen Starr de Wolfe. *s*: 2 (1 dec). County Ct Judge 15 yrs Norfolk Circuit. *Publ*: The Riddle of Justice; Justice in the After-Life; Overcrowding & Unemployment; Old Age & Things in General. [*a*: 29 Burlington Gdns, Chiswick. W.4.

MULLINS, Claud. *b*: 1887. *e*: Univ Coll Sch Lond, Mill Hill Sch, Abroad. *m*: Gwendolen Brandt. *s*: 1. *d*: 2. Metropolitan Police Court Magistrate 1931—47, South-Western Police Court. *Publ*: London's Story; The Leipzig Trials; In Quest of Justice; Marriage, Children & God; Wife v. Husband in the Courts; Crime & Psychology?; Why Crime. *Rec*: Reading & writing.

walking. *w.s*: Army 1915—19 served Mesopotamia & India, '17—19 Member of British Commission to War Criminal Trials at Leipzig. *c*: Savile. *a*: 14 Burgh Heath Rd, Epsom. *T*: Epsom 2122.

MULLINS, Rev. Joseph Dennis, B.A.,M.A.(Oxon), D.D.(Univ of W. Ontario & Emmanuel, Sas.). *b*: M/C 1858. *e*: Pemb Col Oxf. *n.a*: Asst Ed Sec Ch Missny Soc 1898-1902, Ed Greater Britain Messenger '02-25. *Publ*: The Wonderful Story of Uganda ('04); Jt Author The Missionary Speaker's Manual ('01). *c.t*: Record N/p. *s.s*: Foreign missns. Sec Colonial & Continental Ch Soc '02-25. *c*: Nat. *a*: 44 St John's Wood Rd, N.W.8.

MULLOWNEY, John James, M.D. *b*: Seacombe, England 1878. *e*: English Grade Schs, American Grade & Hgh Schs, Phillips Exeter Acad, Harvard Univ. *m*: Mabel Mullowney. *s*: 3. Medical Education, Administrator & Writer. *Publ*: The Power of Thought; America Gives a Chance; I Believe. *Ctr*: Various on med, religious & educ subjects. *s.s*: Spiritual or Christian Healing. *Rec*: Walking. *a*: 630 East Seminary St, Gainesville, Florida, U.S.A.

MULLOY, Patrick. *b*: Dublin 1903. *e*: Private. Civil Servant, I.F.S. *Publ*: Jackets Green. Captain Irish Free State Army (ret). *a*: c/o John Hackney, 6 John St, Adelphi, W.C.2. *t*: Temple Bar 8908.

MUMBY, C. *b*: Thoresby 1855. *e*: Wes Day Sc. *m*: Janet Moseley. *s*: 1. *d*: 2. Journalist. *n.a*: Reporter Halifax Guardian '78-99, Mang '99-1916, On Commercial Staff Amal of Halifax Courier & Halifax Guardian. *a*: 19 St Jude's St, Halifax.

MUMBY, Frank Arthur. *b*: London 1872. *m*: Mary Eleanor Brooke. *s*: 1. *d*: 1. Author & Journalist. *Publ*: Publishing & Bookselling: Letters of Literary Men; Sir Thomas More to Twentieth Century; The Fall of Mary Stuart; George 111 & the American Revolution; etc. *Ctr*: Times, Times Lit Supp. *s.s*: History. *Rec*: Gardening. *a*: 135 Foxley Lane, Purley, Surrey. *T*: Uplands 0416.

MUMFORD, Alfred Harold, B.A.(Lon), B.D. (Edin). *b*: Antigua, W.I. 1864. *e*: Fulneck Sc, Owen's Col, Edin Univ. *m*: Emilie Louise Foskett. Moravian Min, Princ Moravian Col (ret). *Publ*: Our Church's Story; Metrical Version of Job; etc. *c.t*: Moravian Messenger, Holborn Review, etc. *s.s*: Theo. Travelled extensively. *Rec*: Motoring. *a*: Pine Hill, Weston-super-Mare.

MUMFORD, Lewis, A.R.I.B.A. *b*: Flushing, Long Island 1895. *e*: Coll of the City of New York, Columbia Univ. New Sch for Social Research. *m*: Sophia Wittenberg. *s*: 1. *d*: 1. Writer. *n.a*: Acting Ed Sociological Rev 1920, Contrib Ed New Republic '29—40. *Publ*: The Condition of Man; Technics & Civilization; The Culture of Cities; Faith for Living; Green Memories; The Golden Day; The Story of Utopias. *Ctr*: The Freeman, Journ of Amer Inst of Architects, Amer Mercury, New Yorker, etc. *Rec*: Walking, swimming. *a*: Amenia, New York, U.S.A. *T*: Amenia 193-m.

MUNCASTER, Claude Grahame, R.W.S., R.B.A., S.M.A. *b*: West Chiltington 1903. *e*: Queen Elizabeth's Sch Cranbrook. *m*: Primrose Keighley Balfour. *s*: 2, Artist, Author, Lecturer, Regular Exhibitor Royal Academy 1921—. *Publ*: Rolling Round the Horn; Students Book of Water-colour Painting. *Ctr*: The Artist. *n.a*: Painting, Water-colours & Oil Painting. *Rec*: Tennis, golf, singing. *c*: Chelsea Arts, The Arts. *w.s*: R.N.V.R. 1940—44. *a*: Four Winds, Petworth, Sussex. *T*: Petworth 3214.

MUNCEY, Raymond Waterville Luke, M.A. (Cantab). *b*: Lon. *e*: Aldenham Sc & Trinity Hall Cam. Chap & Master Imp Service Col Windsor 1930-. *Publ*: The Consecration of Churches & Churchyards; The Romance of Parish Registers ('33); etc. *s.s*: Ecclesiastical hist. War Service. Asst Priest Ch Ch, Albany St, Lon '22-28. *Rec*: Cycling. *a*: Imperial Service Col, Windsor.

MÚNCK, Ebbe. *b*: Copenhagen 1905. *e*: Copenhagen Univ. *m*: Grace Mette. Journalist. Special Corr Europe, America, Asia, etc. *s.s*: Politics. Mem French Scoresby Sound Exped '26. Mem Danish Scoresby Sound Exped '27. *Rec*: Golf, travel. *a*: 136 Chiltern Ct, Baker St, N.W.1. *t*: Welbeck 7656.

MUNDAY, Arthur Wm. Ernest. F/L. Journalist. Special Corr. *a*: Woodcroft, 5 Scawfell Rd, Carlisle. *t*: 1223.

MUNDY, Talbot. Author. *Publ*: Rung Ho!; Winds of the World; Hira Singh's Tale; King, of the Kyber Rifles; Guns of the Gods; The Ivory Trail; The Eye of Zeitoon; Told in the East; The Nine Unknown; On—The Secret of Arbor Valley; Ramsden; The Bubble Reputation; Queen Cleopatra; The Woman Ayisha; Gup Bahadur; Jimgrim; W.H.; Black Light; The Marriage of Meldrum Strange; The Hundred Days; Jungle Jest; C.I.D.; When Trails were New; Caves of Terror; The Lion of Petra; The King in Check; The Gunga Sahib; Tros of Samothrace; The Mystery of Khufu's Tomb; There Was a Door; Lost Trooper; etc. *a*: c/o Hutchinson & Co, Paternoster Row, London, E.C.4.

MUNK, Frank. *b*: Kutna Hora, Czechoslovakia 1901. *e*: Prague Univ Sch of Business Admin. *m*: Nadezda Prasilova. *s*: 1. *d*: 1. Prof Reed Coll Portland Oregon. *Publ*: Legacy of Nazism; The Economics of Force; Problem of Distribution & Distribution Costs. *s.s*: World Affairs, Internat Relations & Econs. *c*: City (Portland). *a*: 3808 S.W. Mt Adams Drive, Portland 1, Oregon, U.S.A. *T*: Sunset 1112.

MUNN, Marguerite. *b*: Chippenham, Wilts 1870. *e*: Priv. *m*: P. W. Munn. *d*: 1. *Publ*: Christopher Hibbault; Anne Kempburn; Felicity Crofton; Redemption of Richard; Dear Idiot; Mrs Fuller; Shadow of a Stone; Adventures of Louis Dural; Courageous Marriage; etc. *Rec*: Gardening, Village drama. *a*: Shepherds Way, Pimperne, Blandford, Dorset. *T*: Tarranthinton 289.

MUNN, Norman Leslie, M.A., B.S., Ph.D. *b*: Adelaide, Aust 1902. *e*: Springfield Coll Mass, Clark Univ. *m*: Anna Lawlor Sullivan. *s*: 1. Prof of Psychology. *n.a*: Assoc Ed Journ of Psychology 1937—. *Publ*: Psychology: The Fundamentals of Human Adjustment; Introduction to Animal Psychology; Psychological Development; Students Manual to Accompany Psychology; Manual of General Experimental Psychology. *Ctr*: Psychological Journ. *s.s*: Psychology. *Rec*: Writing. *a*: Bowdoin College, Brunswick, Maine, U.S.A. *T*: 1271 W.

MUNN, Rev. William. *b*: Greenwich 1877. *e*: C.M. Coll Islington. *m*: Marian Frances Symonds. Clerk in Holy Orders. *Publ*: Three Men on a Chinese Houseboat; Chinese Heroes in Legend & History. *Ctr*: C.M. Rev, North China Dly News & Herald, etc. *s.s*: Chinese Literature, Christian Missions. *a*: Runham Vicarage, Gt. Yarmouth, Norfolk. *T*: Fleggburgh 40.

MUNRO, C. K. (pen name), (Charles Kirkpatrick MacMullen): civil servant, playwright; b. Ireland, 1889; s. Samuel James and Anne Marshall (Weir) MacMullan; educ Harrow, Pembroke Coll. (Cambridge). DEGREE: B.A. (Cantab); m. Mary Sumner, 1921. AUTHOR

1026

(plays): The Rumour, 1922; At. Mrs. Beam's, 1923; Storm, 1924; Progress, 1925; The Mountain, 1926; Cocks and Hens, 1927; Veronica, 1928; Mr. Eno, 1929; and plays have been produced in London; At Mrs. Beam's and Storm also in New York, and The Rumour also in Berlin and Vienna. OFFICE: Ministry of Labour, Whitehall. HOME: 89 Fitzjohn's Avenue, London, N. W. 3, Eng.

MUNRO, Dr. D. G. M. *a*: 1 Inverness Gardens, Kensington, W.8.

MUNRO, Dana Gardner, LL.D. *b*: Providence, R.I., U.S.A. 1892. *e*: Brown, Wisconsin, Munich & Pennsylvania Univs. *m*: Margaret Bennett Wiley. *s*: 1. *d*: 2. Univ Prof. *Publ*: The Five Republics of Central America; The United States & The Caribbean Area; The Latin American Republics, A History; Refugee Settlement in the Dominican Republic (Ed & Co-Author) *Ctr*: Various. *s.s*: Latin American Hist & Relations. *Rec*: Sailing. *c*: Cosmos, Nassau. *a*: 158 Springdale Rd, Princeton, New Jersey, U.S.A. *T*: 1238.

MUNRO, Air Vice-Marshall Sir David, K.C.B., C.I.E., M.A., M.B., LL.D., F.R.C.S. *b*: Elstree 1878. *e*: Privately, St Andrews & Edinburgh Univs. *m*: Isabel Cunningham. *s*: 1. *d*: 1. R.A.F. (ret), Late Rector of St Andrews Univ. *Publ*: It Passed too Quickly (autobiography). *Ctr*: Blackwoods & others (short stories), scientific articles in med journals. *Rec*: Hunting, polo, golf. *c*: The Athenæum. *a*: Crosshill, Wendover, Bucks. *T*: Wendover 3171.

MUNRO, Donald, M.A., LL.B. *b*: Aberdeen 1899. *e*: Aberdeen Univ. *m*: Violet Louise Buck. *s*: 1. *d*: 1. Book Editor Aberdeen Town Counc 1921—24, Edin Town Counc '40—43. *n.a*: Oxford Univ Press '24—34, Oliver & Boyd Pubs '35—43, Odhams Press Book Dept since '43. *s.s*: Politics Education, Economics, Local Government. *Rec*: Golf. *a*: 31 Springfield Mount, N.W.9. *T*: Temple Bar 2468.

MUNRO, Donald John, C.M.G. *b*: Glengarry. *e*: Vil Sch Roy Acd Inverness. *m*: Isobel Sandell. *d*: 2. Capt Royal Navy, joined Mercantile Marine Service 1880 & R.N. 1895, served in Burma War, & on Geological Survey of Burma 1895—91, Sierra Leone Rebellion, European War 1914—18, Inventor of Harbour Defence, Mine Sweeping by Trawlers, etc. *Publ*: Roaring Forties & After; Scapa Flow, a Naval Retrospect; Convoys, Blockages & Mystery Towers. *Ctr*: Highland News, Scotsman, Nautical Mag. *s.s*: Nautical Affairs, Highland Affairs, Loch Ness Monster, Commodore Paul Jones, father of the U.S. Navy. *c*: Junr Army & Navy. *Rec*: Fishing. *a*: Cearwell, New Galloway. *T*: 232.

MUNRO, Donald Smeaton, M.I.E.E., F.R.S.S.A. *e*: Hgh Sch & Glasgow Univ, Roy Tech Coll Glasgow. Electrical Engineer. *n.a*: Ed Scottish Electrical Engineer. *Publ*: The Practice of Electrical Wiring. *Ctr*: Engineering journs. *s.s*: Installation. *a*: 11 Randolph Pl, Edinburgh. *T*: 20356.

MUNRO, Ellison, B.Sc. *b*: Tain 1897. *e*: Edinburgh Univ. *Publ*: The Deadly Virtue; Summer Solstice; etc. *Ctr*: Various magazines & newspapers. *w.s*: 1914—18. *a*: 63 St George's Sq, London, S.W.1.

MUNRO, Harold Neville, F.I.I.A., F.R.S.A., F.S.S. *b*: London 1892. *e*: L.C.C. Sch of Engineering, Queen Mary's Coll, Univ of Lond, King's Coll Lond. *m*: Edna Grainger. *s*: 2. Secretary & Educ Officer, Jt Sec Inst Indust Admin. *n.a*: Sometime Ed Business, Sometime Book Reviewer Industry Illustrated, Sometime Dir Management Journals Ltd, Mang Country Life Book Dept 1927. *s.s*: Industrial Management, Commerical Management, Business Management, Education, Trade Education. *Rec*: Social Service. *c*: R.A., London Rotary. *w.s*: R.A.F. 1914—18. *a*: 22 Belsize Park Gdns, Hampstead, London, N.W.3. *T*: Primrose 7459.

MUNRO, Rev. Harry Clyde, A.M. *b*: Cheboygan, Co Michigan 1890. *e*: Hiram Coll, Spokane Univ, Coll of the Bible Lexington Ky. *m*: Vera Segur June. *s*: 1. *d*: 3. Minister, Dir Nat Christian Teaching Missn. *n.a*: Founder-Ed Bethany Church Sch Guide 1926—29. *Publ*: Christian Education in Your Church; The Church as a School; How to Increase Your Sunday School; The Pastor & Religious Education; Agencies for Religious Education of Adolescents; The Effective Adult Class; Why Should I Teach?; etc. *Ctr*: Religious Educ, New Century Leader, etc. *s.s*: Religious Educ, Family Life, Evangelism. *Rec*: Building, gardening, writing. *a*: 203 Nth Wabash Ave, Chicago 1, Illinois, U.S.A. *T*: Cen 4192.

MUNRO, Ion S. *b*: Gourock 1887. *e*: High Sc, Glasgow. Glasgow Univ. *m*: Elizabeth Forrester Murdoch. *s*: 1. *d*: 1. Journalist. *n.a*: Ed Scots Pictorial '12—14, Editorial Staff Glasgow Herald '19—20. Foreign Room staff Morning Post '20, Rome Corr '24. *Publ*: Through Fascism to World Power: a History of the Revolution in Italy; Beyond the Alps. *s.a*: Italy, Italian life, Italian affairs, home foreign & colonial. War Service. Commander of the Crown of Italy. *c*: I.J., Union Club, Rome. *a*: 48 Via Margutta, Rome, Italy. *t*: Rome 64608.

MUNRO, J. A. R. M.A. Rector. *a*: Lincoln Col, Oxford.

MUNRO, J. W. M.A.(Oxon), D.Sc(Edin). Prof of Zool & Applied Entomology in Lon Univ. *a*: Imp Col of Sci & Tech, S.W.7.

MUNRO, Leo ("Elmo"). Journalist, & Artist. *n.a*: Sometime Ed & Cartoonist Golfing, Rep, Cartoonist & Asst Ed The Sportsman, Rep Dly Express. *Ctr*: Various. *s.s*: Rugby football, golf. *a*: 59 Trinity Rise, Tulse Hill, S.W.2.

MUNRO, Thomas, M.A., Ph.D. *b*: Omaha, Nebraska 1897. *e*: Columbia Univ. *m*: Lucile Nadler. *s*: 1. *d*: 3. Curator Cleveland Museum of Art, Prof of Art Western Reserve Univ. *n.a*: Ed Journ of Aesthetics & Art Criticism 1945—. *Publ*: Scientific Method in Aesthetics; Great Pictures of Europe; Primitive Negro Sculpture (collab); Art in American Life & Education (collab). *Ctr*: Journ of Aesthetics, Coll Art Journ, Mag of Art, Journ of Philosophy. *s.s*: Aesthetics, Philosophy & Psychology of Art, Art Educ, Cultural Hist. *Rec*: Golf, travel, gardening. *w.s*: World War I. *a*: 2244 Harcourt Drive, Cleveland, Ohio, U.S.A. *T*: Cedar 4862.

MUNRO KERR, John Martin, M.D.(Glas), F.R.C.O.G., L.L.D.(Glas). *b*: Glasgow 1868. *e*: Glas Acad, Glas Univ., Berlin Univ. *m*: E. A. Johanson. *s*: 1. *d*: 3. Regius Prof of Midwifery Glas Univ 1927—35, Pres of Roy Faculty of Physicians & Surgeons Glas '33—34, Hon Fell Roy Soc of Med of Ireland, Hon Fell American & Gynæcological Soc Edin, Hon Fell Obstetrical & Gynæcological Soc. *Publ*: Operating Obstetrics; Combined Textbook in Obstetrics & Gynæcology (Editor & Part Author); Maternal Mortality & Morbidity. *Ctr*: Many papers in obstetrics & gynæcology. *s.s*: Obstetrics & Gynæcology. *Rec*: Golf, fishing. *c*: East Kent Canterbury. *a*: 5a Ethelbert Rd, Canterbury, Kent. *T*: 2723.

MUNSHI, Lilavati. *b*: Ahmedabad, India 1899. *m*: K. M. Munshi. Authoress, Public & Social Worker. *Publ*: Rekhachitra Ane Bija Lekho; Kumardevi; Jeevanmathi Jadeli; Rekha Chitro June Ane Nava;etc. *Ctr*: Various. *a*: 26 Ridge Rd, Bombay, India. *T*: 42317.

MUNTHE, Axel. C.V.O., M.D. *b*: Stockholm. *Publ*: Letters from A Mourning City; Red Cross & Iron Cross; Memories & Vagaries;

Who Was Who Among English and European Authors

The Story of San Michele. *c*: St James's. *a*: San Michele, Ana Capri, Bay of Naples, & St James's Club, Lon.

MUNZ, SIGMUND: writer; b. Leipnik, Moravia, May 7, 1859; s. Jacob and Hanny (Weinreb) M.; educ. Gymnasium at Olmütz and Nikolsburg (Moravia), Univs. of Vienna and Tübingen. DEGREE: Ph.D. (Univ. of Vienna); unmarried. AUTHOR: Aus dem Modernen Italien, 1889; Aus Quirinal und Vatican, 1891; F. Gregorovius und seine Briefe an Gräfin Caetani Lovatelli, 1896; Italienische Reminiscenses und Profile, 1898; Römische Reminiscenses und Profile, 1900; Moderne Staatsmänner, 1901; Von Bismarck bis Bülow, 1912; Balkan-Herrscher und Staatsmänner, 1912; Oesterreichische Profile und Reminiscenzen, 1913; Ein Appell an Präsident Masaryk in twölfter Stunde, 1919; Weltcongress und Weltgericht—ein Appell an die hohen Geister aller Völker, 1919; Fürst Bülow, der Staatsmann und der Mensch.—Aufzeichnungen und Erinnerungen, 1930. Former editor of the Neue freie Presse; now Vienna corres. of the "Nacion" of Buenos Aires. Has contributed to North American Review, Foreign Affairs, Current History Mag. (U.S.A.); English Contemporary Rev., Quarterly Rev., Fortnightly (England). General character of writing: social, political and literary. CLUB: Oesterreichischer. Religion: Jew. ADDRESS: III, Rechte Bahngasse 22, Vienna, Austria.

MURAD, Feroz Din, M.S. *b* : Sialkot City 1889. *e*: Punjab Univ Lahore. *m* : Saeeda Fazaldin. *s* : 3. *d* : 3. Prof of Physics Aligarth M. Univ (ret). *n.a* : Hon Ed (Science Sect) The Conference Gazette 1920—25. *Publ*: Neglect of Science in India ; Water in the Economy of India ; Tohfa I Science ; Badal Ke Bachche ; Sachchi Sharafat ; Urdu Translations of Sherlock Holmes. *Ctr* : Northern Indian Journs & Dly newsps. *s.s* : Radio-Telephony & Telegraphy, Nuclear Structure of the Atom, Sound Ranging & Rationalism. *Rec* : Tennis, walking. *c* : Tollinton (Sialkot City). *a* : Sialkot City, India.

MURCHIE, Guy (Junr), S.B. *b*: Boston, Mass 1907. *e*: Harvard Univ. *m*: Eleanor Forrester Parker. *s*: 2 (step). Journalist, Author, Illustrator, Lecturer. *n.a*: Chicago Tribune, Sunday Ed Dept '34–. *Publ*: Men on the Horizon. *c.t*: N.Y. Journal, N.Y. Herald Tribune Sunday Magazine, Chicago Sunday Tribune, The Sportsman, Common Sense, The Yorkville Advance. *s.s*: International relations, interviews with people of every class & occupation, travel. Rowed in Harvard Boat '27 & '28. *a*: Chicago Tribune, Chicago, Illinois, U.S.A. *t*: Superior 0100.

MURDOCH, John McIlwraith. *b*: Ayr, 1906. *e*: Higher grade. *m*: Elizabeth Campbell. Jnlst. *n.a*: Evening Dispatch (Edinburgh). Scottish Co-operator. Kilmarnock Herald. Galloway Advertiser. Greenock Herald. Sub-Ed Clydebank Press, '29—. *Publ*: Songs—My Lady of Midsummer Night; Sally's Got a Sunshine of Her Own. *c.t*: Shop Asst, Daily Express, Sunday Post (Glasgow), Sunday Mail (Glasgow), Glasgow Herald, Melody Maker. *s.s*: Music, drama, sport. *Rec* Boxing, billiards. *c*: Mem N.U.J. *a*: Clydebank Press, 6 Second Ave, Clydebank.

MURDOCH, Robert. F.L. Journalist & News Corr. *n.a*: Ed Stirling Journ & Advertiser 1924–28. *s.s*: Reports, special articles. *a*: 1 Princes St, Stirling, Scotland. *t*: 652.

MURDOCH, WALTER: university professor of English; b. Scotland, Sept., 1874; s. James and Helen (Garden) M.; educ. Scotch Coll. (Melbourne, Australia). DEGREE: M.A.; m. Violet Hughston, 1897. AUTHOR: The Struggle for Freedom; The Australian Citizen; Loose Leaves, a Book of Essays; The Making of Australia; The Oxford Book of Australian Verse; Alfred Deakin: a Sketch; Anne's Animals (verse). Contributes to the Argus (Melbourne), The West Australian (Perth). OFFICE: The University, Perth, Western Australia.

MURDOCH, William David. *b*: Bendigo, Aus 1888. *e*: Melbourne Univ, R.C.M.Lon. *m*: Antonia Dorothea Simon. *s*: 2. *d*: 2. Pianist. *Publ*: Brahms, with an Analytical Study of the complete pianoforte works; Chopin, His Life & Works (2 vols). Prof R.A.M. Mem Counc Inc Soc of Musicians. *Rec*: Golf, billiards. *c*: Savage. *a*: 35 Acacia Rd, St John's Wood, N.W.8. *t*: Primrose 1564.

MURDOCH, William Garden Blaikie. *b*: N.Z. 1880. *e*: Geo Watson's Col Edin. Writer. *n.a*: Ex-Ed Booklover's Mag. *Publ*: The Royal Stuarts in Their Connection with Art & Letters; Japanese Literature in the Era of the Japanese Print; The Art Treasures of Edinburgh; etc. *c.t*: Weekly Scotsman, Connoisseur, etc. *s.s*: Scot hist, Scot archt. Extensive Travel. *a*: 33 Dundas St, Edinburgh.

MURDOCK, George Peter. B.A., Ph.D. *b* : Meriden, Connecticut 1897. *e* : Yale Univ. *m* : Carmen Emily Swanson. *s* : 1. Prof of Anthropology Yale Univ. *Publ* : Our Primitive Contemporaries ; Studies in the Science of Society ; The Evolution of Culture. *Ctr* : Amer Anthropologist, Scientific Monthly, Amer Social Rev, etc. *s.s* : Social Organisation. *Rec* : Tennis. *w.s* : World War I & II. *c* : High Lane (Hamden, Conn), Yale (New York City). *a* : 960 Ridge Rd, Hamden 14, Connecticut, U.S.A. *T* : New Haven 2-5798.

MURDOCK, Sir Keith Arthur. Kt. *b* : Melbourne, Victoria, Australia 1886. *e* : Camberwell Gr Sch, Lond Sch of Econs. *m* : Elizabeth Greene. *s* : 1. *d* : 3. Journalist. *n.a* : Former Staff Age (Melbourne), Now Mang Dir The Herald (Melbourne), Sun News-Pictorial & Assoc publs, Chm of Dirs of Australian Newsprint Mills Pty Ltd, Dir The Advertiser & The News (Adelaide, The Courier-Mail (Brisbane). *Publ* : The Day—And After (W. M. Hughes War Speeches). *Rec*: Golf, riding. *w.s* : War Corres World War I. *a* : 39 Albany Rd, Toorak, Victoria, Australia.

MURDOCK, Kenneth Ballard, A.M., Ph.D. *b*: Boston, Mass 1895. *e* : Harvard Univ. *m* : (1) Laurette E. Potts, (2) Eleanor Eckhart. *d* : 2. Prof of English Harvard Univ. *n.a* : Ed Harvard Graduates Mag 1929—31, Publs Colonial Soc of Massachusetts '25—30, New England Quarterly '28—38 & '39—, Amer Literature '29—38 & '39—. *Publ*: Increase Mather ; The Sun at Noon ; Portraits of Increase Mather ; (Ed) The Notebooks of Henry James (collab) ; Selections from Cotton Mather ; Handkerchiefs from Paul ; A Leaf of Grass from Shady Hill ; etc. *Ctr* : Various. *s.s* : 17th Century Hist & Lit (English & American), Amer Intellectual Hist. *Rec* : Book Collecting, golf, dogs, travel. *a* : 28 Chestnut St, Boston 8, Massachusetts, U.S.A. *T* : Capital 0163.

MURDOCK, Nina. *b* : Melbourne, Victoria, Australia 1890. *e*: Girls' High Sch, Sydney N.S.W. *m*: J. D. Brown. Journalist. *n.a* : Drama Critic, Interviewer & Spec Writer Sun News Pictorial Melbourne 1922—27. *Publ* : Tyrolean June ; She Travelled Alone in Spain ; Seventh Heaven ; Vagrant in Summer ; Miss Emily ; Songs of the Open Air ; More Songs of the Open Air ; etc. *Rec* : Reading, concerts, art shows. *c* : Lyceum, P.E.N. (Melbourne). *a* : 55 Prospect Hill Rd, Camberwell, E.6, Victoria, Australia. *T* : WF 8128.

MURDOCK, Walter, C.B.E. *b* : Aberdeenshire, Scotland 1874. *e* : Scotch Coll Melbourne, Univ of Melbourne. *m* : Violet Hughston. *s* : 1. *d* : 2. Univ Prof (ret). *Publ* : Alfred Deakin (a Biography) ; Collected Essays ; Steadfast ; A Short History of Australia. *Ctr* : Sydney Morning Herald, Melbourne Herald, Adelaide Advertiser, West Australian (Perth). *s.s* : Literary Criticism, Public Affairs. *a* : Blithedale, South Perth, West Australia. *T* : MU 1372.

MURIEL, John St. Clair ("John Lindsey"). b: Hadleigh, Suffolk 1909. e: Hurstpierpoint Col & Durham Univ. m: Mary Troughton. Novelist. Publ: Molten Ember; Stricken Gods; The Bull Calf; Peacock's Feathers; Tenderness; Youth in Bondage; The Voice of One; The Lady and the Mute; Vicarage Party; etc. c.t: Daily Herald, Evening Standard, Evening News, Dly Mail, Dly Express, Bookman. s.s: Mediæval hist. Rec: Gardening, riding. a: Orchard Hse. Toppesfield, Gt Yeldham, Essex.

MURISON, Alexander Falconer, M.A., LL.D., K.C. b: Walhowe, Aberdeens 1847. e: Parish Scs, G.S. & Aber Univ. m: Elizabeth Logan (dec). s: 2. n.a: Acting Ed Weekly Dispatch '89, Ed Educational Times 1902-12, Sub-Ed St James's Gazette (1881), Prof Roman Law '83-1925, Jurisprudence '01-25, Emeritus Prof U.C.L. '25, etc. Publ: Cassell's Educational Year Book, 1879, '80, '81, '82, '85; The Globe Readers (8 vols); Sir William Wallace & King Robert Bruce (Famous Scots series); Revised & Ed Bain's English Grammar ('79); trans from French, Dutch, Danish; Verse Trans:—Horace (1931); Vergil's Bucolics & Georgics ('32); Pindar ('33); etc. s.s: Law & lit. Rec: Reading, walking. a: 26 Victoria Rd, Clapham Common, S.W.4.

MURLAND, J. R. W., B.Sc., A.M.I.C.E., A.M.I.E.E. A.M.I.I.A., A.C.G.I. Married. d: 1. Consulting Engineer. Publ: The Royal Armoured Corps; To be an Engineer. Ctr: Engineering & Allied periodicals, encycs, etc. s.s: All Aspects of Engineering, Hist of the Royal Arm'd Corps. w.s: Lt-Col R. Inniskilling Dragoon Guards. a: c/o Cecil Hunt, Literary Agent, 11 Poultry, Cheapside. E.C.2.

MURLI THAKUR. (See THAKUR, M. R.) Publ: Safu-nu-Sakhya (Poems, with Mr Bhall); Parabnau-Pani; Melo, Songs for Children; Premal-Fyot; Gujarati-nu-Adhyapan (with Prof Vakil); Fijiji, Trans from Hindi.

MURNAGHAN, Francis D., D.Sc. b: Omagh, Co Tyrone, Ireland 1893. e: Christian Bros Sch Omagh, Univ Coll Dublin, Johns Hopkins Univ. m: Ada May Kimbel. s: 1. d: 1. Prof of Applied Maths Johns Hopkins Univ. n.a: Ed American Journ of Mathematics 1927—, Co-Ed Quarterly of Applied Mathematics '43—. Publ: Theory of Group Representations; Theoretical Mechanics (collab); Vector Analysis & the Theory of Relativity; Differential & Integral Calculus; Analytic Geometry; Introduction to Applied Mathematics. s.s: Pure & Applied Maths. a: 6202 Sycamore Rd, Baltimore 12, Maryland, U.S.A.

MURPHY, Cornelius James, M.J.I. n.a: Reuter's Cable Ed. a: 19 Hemington Av, Frien Barnet, N.11.

MURPHY, Diarmuid, M.A., Ph.D. b: Ballincollig, Co Cork 1895. e: Our Lady's Mount Sec Cork, Univ Coll Cork. m: Annie Jean Wright. s: 2. d: 4. Univ Professor of English Galway, Chmn Gaelic Theatre, Play Producer. Publ: Hewn of Rock; (plays) Tabharthas an Bhais; Milleadh; etc. Ctr: Short Stories in various periodicals. s.s: Irish Peasant Life, Historical subjects. Rec: Amateur dramatics. a: Glanville Hse, Newcastle Rd, Galway, Ireland. T: Galway 264.

MURPHY, Emma Luise. b: Russia 1908. e: Sec Ventspius Latvia & Eng Inst Riga Latvia. Publ: Eng trans of Prof V. H. Bechterev's General Principles of Human Reflexology; Eng trans of L. Slancitajs Magnetic Measurements in the Baltic Sea. c.t: Pedeja Bridi (Riga, Latvia). s.s: Trans of works on philos, psychology & nat sci. Rec: Reading. c: Translator's Gld (Lon) & Panel of Expert Translators (Lon). a: Park Hse, 223 Earl's Ct Rd, S.W.5.

MURPHY, John, M.A., B.D.(Glas), D.Litt., D.D.(Glas), F.R.A.I. b: Lanark, Scotland 1876. e: Lanark Gr Sch, Univs Glas, Berlin, Heidelberg, Edinburgh Congregational Coll. m: Isabel Simpson. Congregational Minister, Prof of Comparative Religion & Theology. Publ: Primitive Man: His Essential Quest; Lamps of Anthropology. Ctr: Man, Expositor, Expository Times, Philosophy, Hibbert Journal, Christian World, Congregational Quarterly. s.s: Anthropology, Philosophy of Religion, Comparative Religion, Theology. a: 118 Davyhulme Rd, Manchester.

MURPHY, John Joseph. b: Dublin 1897. e: O'Connell Scs Dublin. Journalist. n.a: Chief Sub-Ed Evening Herald Dublin. Rep Press Assoc Lon. a: 3 Willfield Pk, Ballsbridge, Dublin. t: 21036.

MURPHY, John Thomas. b: Manchester 1888. e: Elem & Evening Continuation Sch. m: Ethel Morris. s: 1. Mem N.U.J., P.E.N. n.a: Lond Corr Pravda 1925—32. Publ: Preparing for Power; Modern Trade Unionism; New Horizons; Russia on the March; Victory Production; Stalin; Labour's Big Three—Attlee, Morrison & Bevin; Eclipse of Japanese Empire. Ctr: Picture Post, Illustrated, etc. s.s: Politics, Social, Industrial, Econs, Geog, Internat Affairs. a: 7 Broughton Gdns, Highgate, London, N.6. T: Mountview 2318.

MURPHY, Thomas William, F.J.I. b: Dublin 1872. m: Annie Jane Allen. s: 2 (1 dec). d: 3. n.a: Publ's of Mecredy, Percy & Coy Ltd '92-1931; Now F.L. Ex-Chm Dublin & Irish Assoc Dis I.J. Present Chm Dublin Dis N/p Press Fund. s.s: Sport & transport. a: 64 Brighton Sq, South, Dublin, S.1. t: Terenure 677.

MURPHY, William Lombard. n.a: Chm Independent N/p's Ltd. a: Independent Hse, Middle Abbey St, Dublin.

MURRAY, Adam George, M.A. b: Midlothian 1893. e: George Watson's Coll & Univ of Edinburgh. m: Maud Wilkinson. s: 1. d: 1. Chartered Accountant, Prof of Accounting & Business Method Edin Univ. n.a: Ed The Accountants' Mag. s.s: Taxation & Accounting. Rec: Golf. w.s: 1914—18. c: University (Edin), New Golf (North Berwick), a; 4 Roltesay Place, Edinburgh. T: 34058.

MURRAY, Albert Victor, M.A., B.Litt(Oxon), B.D.(Cantab). b: Choppington 1890. e: Choppington National Sch, Morpeth Gr Sch, Magdalen Coll Oxf, Mansfield Coll Oxf, St John's Coll Camb. m: Winifred Seares. s: 2. d: 1. President of Cheshunt Coll Camb, Vice-Pres Methodist Conference 1947—48, Travelling Fellowship in Africa '27—28, Educational Adviser to Christian Council Nigeria '31-32, Prof of Educ Univ Coll Hull '33—45, Chairman of the Trg Coll Assoc of England & Wales '40—42. Publ: The School in the Bush; Personal Experience & Historical Faith; The School & the Church. Ctr: The Friend, The Spectator, The Christian World, The Yorkshire Post, etc. s.s: Education, Africa, Religion. Rec: Sketching, walking. c: P.E.N. a: Cheshunt College Lodge, Cambridge. T: 2593.

MURRAY, ALEXANDER HENRY HALLAM: publisher (retired); b. London, Eng., April, 1854; s. John and Marion Murray; educ. Eton Coll., Gonville and Caius College (Cambridge). DEGREES: M.A., F.S.A., F.R.G.S.; m. Alice M. Du Cane, Dec., 1884. AUTHOR: The High Road of Empire (with water-color and pen-and-ink illustrations in India, Ceylon and Egypt, by the author), 1905. Illustrator of: Old Time Travel (by Alex Innes Shand), 1903; The Old Road Through France to Florence (by H. W. Nevison and M. Carmichael), 1906; The Pilgrims Way from Winchester to Canterbury (by Julia Ady), 1911. General character of writing: travel sketches. Has travelled extensively,

India, Ceylon, Egypt, N. Africa, Australia, New Zealand, and has sketched and painted in all these countries. Has exhibited at Royal Acad. and in Bond St. (London). Relig. denom., Church of England. CLUB: Athenæum. HOME: Sandling, Hythe, Kent, Eng.

MURRAY, Rev. Alfred Lefurgy, B.D., Th.D., S.T.D. *b*: Bradalbane, Prince Edward Island 1900. *e*: Temple & Boston Univs, Colgate-Rochester & Eastern Sems. *m*: Frances B. Hoar. *s*: 1. *d*: 1. Clergyman. *n.a*: Ctr Ed Pulpit Digest, Lit Ed U.S. Baptist 1940—43. *Publ*: Youth's Marital Problems; Psychology For Christian Teachers; Youth's Problem No. 1; Youth's Courtships Problem; The Evangelistic Congregation; The Supreme Test; etc. *Ctr*: Secret Place, Missions, etc. *s.s*: Religious, Psychological & Sociological. *Rec*: Writing, boating. *a*: 40 Elm St, Westerly, Rhode Island, U.S.A. *T*: 5178.

MURRAY, Lt.-Col. Hon. Arthur C., C.M.G., D.S.O. *b*: 1879. *e*: R.M.C. Sandhurst. *m*: Faith Celli Standing (dec'd). Dir Barrow Paper Mills Ltd, Wembley Stadium Ltd, Asst Mil Attaché Washington 1917—18. *Publ*: Master & Brother; At Close Quarters; The Five Sons of Bare Betty; Reflections on British Foreign Policy Between Two Wars; Decisive Battles in History; Sir Gideon Murray of Elibank & His Times 1560—1621. *Ctr*: Quarterly Rev. *s.s*: Hist, Biog. *Rec*: Fishing, gardening. *w.s*: World War I. *c*: Brooks's (Lond), New (Edin). *a*: An Cala, Isle of Seil, Argyll. *T*: Balvicar 237.

MURRAY, C. C. *n.a*: "Ben Rhydding" of Yorkshire Ev News, formerly Deputy News Editor, Pictures Ed & Features Ed Yorkshire Ev News. *a*: 23 Carrholm View, Leeds 7.

MURRAY, David Leslie. *b*: London 1888. *e*: Harrow & Balliol Oxf. *m*: Leonora Evles. Novelist & Journalist. *n.a*: On Staff Times 1920—44, Dramatic Critic Nation & Athenæum '20—23, Ed Times Literary Supplement '38—44. *Publ*: Scenes & Silhouettes; Disraeli; Stardust; The English Family Robinson; Trumpeter, Sound!; Regency; Commander of the Mists; Tale of Three Cities; Enter Three Witches; Folly Bridge; Leading Lady. *Rec*: Riding. *a*: 7 Stanford Close, Hove 4, Sussex. *T*: Preston 4750.

MURRAY, David Stark, B.Sc., M.B., Ch.B. *b*: Barrhead Scotland 1900. *e*: Glasgow Hgh Sch & Univ. *m*: Jean Stirling. *d*: 1. *n.a*: Ed.Medicine Today & Tomorrow 1937—. *Publ*: Health for All; Your Body: How it is Built & How it Works; The Future of Medicine; Now for Health; Science Fights Death; The Search for Health; Man Against Disease; Powders, Pills & Potions. *Ctr*: Reynolds News, Tribune. *s.s*: Health Med Services & Science, Social Services. *Rec*: Badminton, music. *a*: 176 Kew Rd, Richmond, Surrey. *T*: Richmond 0472.

MURRAY, E. *b*: London 1903. *e*: Priv & Slade Sch of Art. *Publ*: Comedy; The Partridge; The Gilded Cupid; June Lightning. *a*: 8 Hamilton Terr, St John's Wood, London, N.W.8. *T*: Cunningham 3570.

MURRAY, George Gilbert Aime, O.M., M.A., D.Litt., D.C.L.(Oxf), LL.D.(Glas), F.B.A., F.R.S.L. *b*: Sydney, N.S.W. 1866. *e*: Merchant Taylor's Sch Lond & St John's Coll Oxf. *m*: Lady Mary Henrietta Howard. *s*: 1. *d*: 1. Regius Professor of Greek Oxf Univ 1908—36, Charles Eliot Norton Prof of Poetry Harvard Univ '26, Trustee of Brit Mus '14, Pres Int Cttee of Int Co-operation '28—, Chmn League of Nations Union, Co-Press '23-28, 38. *Publ*: Rise of the Greek Epic; Five Stages of Greek Religion; The Classical Tradition in Literature; Aeschylus, Creator of Tragedy; Euripides & his Age; Aristophanes; Critical Texts (Greek) of Euripides (3 vols) & Aeschylus; Translations of many Greek Plays; The Ordeal of This Generation; The Policy of Sir Edward Grey; From the League to U.N. *c*: Athenæum, Nat Lib. *a*: Yatscombe, Boars Hill, Oxford. *T*: 85261.

MURRAY, George Redmayne, M.A., M.D. (Cantab), F.R.C.P., HonD.C.L.(Durham), HonM.D. (Dublin), D.L. *b*: Newcastle-on-Tyne 1865. *e*: Eton, Trin Col Cam, U.C.H., Lon, Berlin & Paris. *m*: Annie Katharine Bickersteth. *s*: 1. *d*: 1. Cons Phys, Emeritus Prof of Med, Univ of M/C. Fell U.C.L. *Publ*: Diseases of the Thyroid Gland. *c.t*: Twentieth Century Practice of Med, Quain's Dictionary of Med, Allbutt & Rolleston's System of Med, etc. *s.s*: Endocrinology. *Rec*: Fishing. *c*: Union, M/C. *a*: 13 St John St, M/C 3, & The Manor Hse, Mobberley, Cheshire. *t*: Blackfriars 2937 & Mobberley 22.

MURRAY, Gladstone. Publicity & Edit Mang B.B.C. 1924—35, Gen Man C.B.C. '36—42, Dir Gen of Broadcasting in Canada '42, Founder & Dir Responible Enterprise Movement '43—47. *Publ*: The Case for Capitalism; Things to Care About; Formula for Harmony; Twilight or Dawn; The Profit Motive. *a*: Victory Building, Toronto 1, Canada. *T*: AD 8184.

MURRAY, James. *b*: Holytown, Lanarkshire 1880. *e*: Hamilton Gr Sch. *m*: Rona Martelli Syme (dec'd). *d*: 1. Banker. *Publ*: Auditing the One Pound Note. *Ctr*: Scottish Bankers' Journ & leading Australian Metropolitan newsps & Econ journs. *s.s*: Banking & Currency. *Rec*: Gardening, motoring. *c*: Adelaide, Australian (Melbourne). *a*: Salisbury Lodge, Salisbury St, Balwyn, E.8., Victoria, Australia. *T*: W.F. 2868 (Melbourne).

MURRAY, Sir John, K.C.V.O., D.S.O. (& Bar), M.A., F.S.A., T.D. *b*: London 1884. *e*: Eton & Magdalen Coll Oxf. *m*: Lady Helen de Vere, Lt Col late Scot Horse & the Roy Scots, Croix de Guerre, Sen Partner John Murray Publishers, D.L. Co of London & High Sheriff 1914. *n.a*: Ed Quarterly Review. *Publ*: The Magdalen College Record. *Ctr*: Quarterly Review. *c*: Athenæum. *w.s*: Gallipoli, Egypt & France 1914—19. *a*: 50 Albemarle St, London, W.1. *T*: Regent 4361.

MURRAY, John Grey, M.B.E. *e*: Eton & Oxf. Partner in John Murray Publishers. *n.a*: Asst Ed Cornhill Mag. *a*: 50 Albemarle St, London, W.1.

MURRAY, JOHN HUBERT PLUNKETT: Lieutenant Governor of Papua; b. Sydney, N.S.W. Dec., 1861; s. Terence Aubrey and Agnes (Edwards) M.; educ. Sydney Grammar Sch. (Sydney, Australia), Sinzig (Germany). DEGREE: B.A. (Oxford); widower (m. Sybil Maud Jenkins—died). AUTHOR: Papua, 1912; Papua of Today, 1920. Was barrister of Inner Temple, 1886; Lieut. Colonel Commonwealth Military Forces (So. African War); at present also Judge of the Central Court of Papua. CLUB: Australian (Sydney, N.S.W.). Relig. denom., Roman Catholic. ADDRESS: Port Moresby, Papua; Sydney, N.S.W., Australia.

MURRAY, Rev. John Owen Farquhar, D.D. Hon Canon of Ely Cathedral, Hon Sec of Central Readers Bd (C. of E.). *n.a*: Mem Editorial Cmt of Lay Reader Mag '28—. *Publ*: The Goodness & Serenity of God; Du Bose as a Prophet of Unity; Studies in the Temptation of the Son of God; The Revelation of the Lamb; Asking God. *a*: 15 Selwyn Gardens, Cam. *t*: 934.

MURRAY, Joni. *b*: Washington 1906. *e*: Hgh Sch & Roy Coll of Music. *m*: John D. Murray (dec'd). *s*: 1. *d*: 1. Journalist, Mem N.U.J. *n.a*: Northcliffe Newsps 1928—29, Odhams Press '43—47, Asst Ed Everywoman Hon Ed Radar Bulletin (Radar Assoc) '46—. *Ctr*: Everywoman, Radar Bulletin. *s.s*: Women's Interests, Music. *Rec*: Music, science, reading, golf, dancing, skating, flying. *c*: Women's Press, Whydown Place Country. *a*: 6 Ladbroke Terrace, London, W.C.1.

MURRAY, Joseph Wickham, M.A. *e*: Liverpool Univ. Dep Sec Nat Union of Teachers, Editor, Sec Assoc of Teachers in Tech Insts. *n.a*: Ed Tech Journ, 1928, Ed Higher Education Journ '39—44. *Ctr*: Many scientific & educational journs. *s.s*: Philosophy, Education. *a*: Hamilton Hse, Mabledon Pl, London, W.C.1. *T*: Euston 2442.

MURRAY, Keith Anderson Hope, M.A., B.Litt(Oxon), B.Sc.(Edin), Ph.D.(Cornell). *b*: Edin 1903. *e*: Edin Acad, Edin Univ, Cornell Univ York, Oriel Coll Oxf, Rector of Lincoln Coll Oxf. *Publ*: Land & Life; The Planning of British Agriculture; Factors Affecting the Price of Livestock; Habits of Milk Consumption; Britains Food Imports. *Ctr*: Proceedings of Agricultural Econ Soc, Lloyds Bank Monthly Review. *s.s*: Agricultural Economics, Further Education. *c*: Athenæum. *a*: Lincoln College, Oxford. *T*: 2580.

MURRAY, Lilian, L.D.S.(Edinburgh). *b*: Lon 1871. *e*: Camden & N Lon Scs for Girls, Edinburgh Dental Sc. *m*: Robert Lindsay (dec). Dental surgeon. *n.a*: Sub Ed British Dental Journ. *Publ*: Short History of Dentistry. *c.t*: British Dental Journ, Proceedings of Roy Soc of Medicine, Transactions of Internat Congress of the Hist of Medicine. Transactions of 8th Int Dent Congress, Journ of Amer Dental Assoc. *s.s*: Hist of dentistry. 1st woman to take L.D.S. in G.B. Hon Librarian British Dental Assoc, '20—. Gave address at Cent of Progress Congress, Chicago, '33. *c*: Hon Mem Odonto-Chirurgical Soc of Scotland, Fel Roy Soc Med., Mem British Soc for study of Orthodontics. Pres Metro Branch of British Dental Assoc, '32—. *a*: 13 Hill St, Berkeley Sq, W.1. *t*: Grosvenor 1592.

MURRAY, M. J. *b*: Dublin 1902. Editor. *n.a*: Evening Mail, Dublin '19—24, Ed Catholic Pictorial, Irish Catholic Almanac '22—, Ed Catholic Times '29—33, Catholic Fireside '29—, Catholic Home Annual '27—. *c.t*: Nat Catholic Welfare News Service, U.S.A., etc. *s s*: Catholic ch hist. *a*: c/o Catholic Fireside, Field Hse, Bream's Bldgs, E.C.4. *t*: Holborn 0180.

MURRAY, Margaret. *b*: London 1906. *e*: Lady Holles Sch for Girls, Central Sch of Arts & Crafts. Technical Journalist, Mem N.U.J. *Publ*: Practical Knitting Illustrated; Complete Home Knitting Illustrated; Knitting for All Illustrated; Knitted Garments for All Illustrated; Modern Knitting; Practical Family Knitting; The Week-end Knitting Book; Stars in Wool (Series), etc. *Ctr*: Dly Telegraph, Dly Mirror, Dly Herald, Irish Ind. Woman, Woman's Own, etc. *s.s*: Knitting & Crochet Design, Home Crafts. *Rec*: The River, gardening. *a*: 28 The Pryors, East Heath Rd, London, N.W.3. *T*: Hampstead 0364.

MURRAY, Margaret Alice. D.Lit.(Lond). *b*: Calcutta. *e*: Priv. Egyptologist, has excavated in Egypt, Palestine Transjordan, Malta, Minorca & England. Order of St Sava of Serbia, Fellow of Univ Coll Lond. *Publ*: Osireion at Abydos; Saqqara Mastabas; Elementary Egyptian (Hieroglyphic) Grammar; Ancient Egyptian Legends; The Witch Cult in Western Europe; Egyptian Temples; The God of the Witches; Petra, The Rock of Edom. *Ctr*: Man, Journal of Royal Anthropological Institute, Antiquity, Ancient Egypt. *s.s*: Ancient Egypt, Ancient Religions, Social Conditions in Ancient World, Witches. *Rec*: Travelling, sketching. *c*: Univ of Lond. *a*: University College, London, W.C.1.

MURRAY, Lady, Mildred Octavia. *b*: Southampton 1876. *e*: Oxford Hgh Sch for Girls. *m*: Sir Oswyn Murray, G.C.B. *s*: 1. *d*: 1. *Publ*: The Making of a Civil Servant. *Rec*: Gardening, reading. *a*: Annery Cottage, Wonersh Common, nr Guildford, Surrey.

MURRAY, Pamela. *b*: Sunningdale 1906. *e*: Endcliffe, Eastbourne. *m*: E. B. C. Woodbury. *s*: 1. Journalist & Press Photographer. *c.t*: Tatler, Sketch, Bystander, Vogue & Harper's Bazaar. *s.s*: Social gossip & snapshot photog. *a*: 58 Sion Ct, N.W.8. *t*: Abercorn 1134.

MURRAY, Robert, J.P. *b*: Barrhead 1870. *e*: Elem Sch. *m*: Margaret McCallum MacKinlay. *s*: 1. *d*: 3. Dir Scottish Co-operative Wholesale Soc, Mem N.U.J., Mem Board of Trade Advisory Counc. *n.a*: Parl Corr 1922—24, Ed Scottish Co-operator '17—26. *Publ*: Land Question Solved. *Ctr*: Glas Herald, Chambers's Journ, Scots Mag, Millgate Mthly, Glas Ev Newsps, etc. *s.s*: Scottish Lit, Co-op Principles, Practice & Hist. *c*: Glasgow Ballad. *a*: Arlan Rhu, Barrhead, Scotland, Scotland. *T*: 268.

MURRAY, Rev. Robert H., M.A., Litt.D. *b*: Belfast 1879. *e*: Queen's Col Belfast & T.C.D. *m*: Mary Mildred Falkiner. *c.t*: Times Lit Supp, Birm Post, Quarterly Review, Ch Quarterly Review, etc. *s.s*: Political history. Rural Dean. Dir of Studies for Diocese of Worcester. Canon of Worcester. *a*: Pershore Vicarage, Worcester. *t*: Pershore 36.

MURRAY, Robert Kyle. *b*: Portsmouth 1878. *e*: Portsmouth G.S. *m*: Emilie Ethel Long. *s*: 3. Journalist. *n.a*: S. Daily Mail, Portsmouth 1896—99, 1903—05, Western Morning News, Plymouth '99—03, '14—, Western Daily Mercury Plymouth '05—14. *c.t*: Naval & Mil Record, etc. *s.s*: Naval & Mil. Ex-Hon Sec I.J. Portsmouth. Ex-Chm '29—. Hon Treas Plymouth & Dis Br N.U.J. *a*: 4 Sussex St, Plymouth.

MURRAY, Thomas Basil. *b*: N. Shields 1900. *e*: Tynemouth Sec Sc. *m*: Mabel Doris Kennard. Journalist. *n.a*: Dis Rep Newcastle Chron Publ's & Assoc N/p's. *s.s*: Sport. *Rec*: Tennis, golf. *c*: N.E.Dis I.J. *a*: 52 Howard St, N. Shields. *t*: 957.

MURRAY, Thomas C. *b*: Macroom, Co Cork 1873. *e*: St Patrick's Dublin. *m*: Christina Moylan. *s*: 1. *d*: 4. Headmaster (ret), Mem Irish Acad of Letters, Pres Irish Playwrights' Assoc. *Publ*: Birthright & the Pipe in the Fields; Aftermath; Autumn Fire; Michaelmas Eve; Spring Horizon; etc. *Ctr*: Irish Independent, Irish Press, Dublin Mag. *s.s*: Drama. *Rec*: Gardening, swimming. *a*: 11 Sandymount Ave, Ballsbridge, Dublin. *T*: Ballsbridge 61213.

MURRAY, Rev. William, F.Inst.P.I. *b*: Wishaw, Scotland 1876. *e*: Bd Sch, S.P.C.K. Coll, Wolsey Coll Oxf. *m*: J. A. Cummings. Clergyman. *Publ*: The Messiah. *s.s*: Gospel. *Rec*: Walking, Gospel, Open-air Preaching. *a*: Whitehall Hse, Luzley, Ashton-under-Lyne, Lancs.

MURRAY, William Ledebur. A.J.I. *n.a*: European Gen Mang Reuter's. *a*: 16 Lansdowne Ct, W.11.

MURRAY LAWES, Robert Lethbridge. *c.t*: Times, Morning Post, Dly Telegraph, etc. *a*: Old Park, nr Dover, & 38 Eaton Pl, S.W.1. *t*: Kearsney 8 & Sloane 9022.

MURRAY SMITH, James. *b*: London 1908. Journalist. *n.a*: Chief Sub Ed C. Arthur Pearson Ltd. '24—29. F/l Pearson's Wkly '30—34, Daily Herald '34. *c.t*: Daily Herald, Passing Show, John Bull, Sunday Referee, Sphere, Radio Pictorial, Ideas, etc. *s.s*: Radio, motoring, theatre. Formerly Stage Producer, Steeplejack. Lecturer, Parachutist. *c*: Press, N U.J. *a*: 83 Gower St, W.C.1. *t*: Museum 2592.

MURRY, John Middleton, O.B.E., M.A. *b*: 1889. Author & Journalist. *n.a*: Ex-Ed Athenæum, Ed The Adelphi. *Publ*: About 40 Books. *Ctr*: Times Lit Supp, etc. *a*: Thelnetham, West Suffolk. *T*: Botesdale 43.

MURSELL, WALTER ARNOLD: author, lecturer; b. London, Eng., Jan., 1870; s. Arthur and Louisa (Read) M.; educ. King Edward VI Sch. (Birmingham, Eng). DEGREES: (Hon.) M.A. (Aberdeen), (Hon.) D.D. (St. Andrews); m. Elizabeth McKinley Fraser, 1899. AUTHOR: Ideal Manhood, 1902; The Wagon and the Star, 1903; Two on a Tour, 1909; Sermons on Special Occasions, 1912; Byways in Bookland, 1914; Afterthoughts, 1914; The Bruising of Belgium, 1915; Ports in the Storm, 1919; Echoes of Strife, 1919; The Bishop's Boots, 1926; Footnotes: a Pedestrian Journal, 1926; Isles of Sunset: Impressions of the Hebrides, 1931. Contributor to Paisley (Scotland) Daily Express. General character of writing: essays, religious, poems. Minister in chg. St. Michael's Church (Coventry), 1892-1905; minister Leamington Rd. Baptist Ch. (Blackburn, Lancashire), 1895-98; minister Thomas Coats Memorial Ch. (Paisley, Scotland), 1898-1921. Lecturer, Public Reading and Speaking, Aberdeen Univ., since 1921, retired 1931. Relig. denom., Baptist. HOME: 78 Partickhill Road, Glasgow, Scotland.

MURTHY, Vasudeva. b: Bangalore. e: Bombay Univ. Govt Service Mysore Agriculture Dept. n.a: Ed Mysore Agricultural & Experimental Union 1939—. Publ: Gulistan Kathegalu ; Parsi Kavindraru. Ctr : Various Kannada journs. s.s : Interpretating Persian Lit to Kannada Lang. a : 17, 2nd Cross Rd, Shankara Duram, Bangalore City, India.

MUSKETT, Netta Rachel. b: Sevenoaks 1887. e : Kent Col Folkestone. m : Henry Wallace Muskett. s : 1. n.a : News of the World 1916—28. Publ: The Jade Spider ; The Open Window ; The Flickering Lamp ; After Rain ; The Shallow Cup ; Wings in the Dust ; Nor any Dawn ; Plaster Cast ; A Mirror for Dreams ; Painted Heaven. Teaching maths Northampton '12—14. Driving ambulance '15—16. Rec : Tennis, swimming, needlework, pottery. a : 16 Penwortham Rd. Streatham, S.W.16.

MUSPRATT, Eric. b: 1899. Author, War Correspondent to Roy Australian Navy till 1945. Publ : My South Sea Island ; Wild Oats ; The Journey Home ; Greek Seas ; Ambition ; Going Native ; Russia Plans the Future ; The Life of Unk White ; Time is a Cheat ; Fire of Youth. Ctr : Various British & Foreign. s.s : General Travel. w.s : 1914—18 & '39—45. a : " Seaforth " Oliver's Hill, Frankston, Victoria, Australia. T : Frankston 379.

MUSPRATT, Rosalie Helen. b : Formby, Lancs. e: New Hall Chelmsford, Villa Arbelyz, St Jean de Luz. M.J.I. Publ : Sinister Stories ; Tales of Terror. Ctr : Tatler, Queen, S. Mail, Cork Recorder, Home & Country, The Supernatural Omnibus, Keep on the Light, Grim Death, Weird Stories. s.s : Ghost Stories. Rec : Travel, reading, gardening. a : The Dower Hse, Forty Hill, Enfield, Middlesex. T : 3380.

MUSPRATT, William Henry. b: Bath 1878. e : Priv. m : Helena May Arnold. Journalist. n.a : Formerly Ed Norfolk Chron, now Corres London Newspapers. Ctr : Various. s.s : News, Biog Sketches. a : 21 Petersham Rd, Richmond, Surrey. T : 0610.

MUSSABINI, Nicholas George. b: Brighton 1888. e: Dulwich & Priv. m: Florence Wilson. s : 1. d : 1. n.a: Tribune 1905-07, Standard '07-10, Sporting Life '10-14, Sunday Referee '19-34. s.s : Sport. War Service '15-19, despatches. Rec: Cricket, tennis, golf, billiards. a: The Bungalow, Garratt Rd, Edgware, Middx.

MUSSELWHITE, Ralph Sydney. b: Roston 1892. e : Beverley. m : Amy Smith. s : 1. d : 2. Journalist. n.a : Beverley Guardian 1908—13. Grimsby News '13—15, Wellington Journ '19—. War Service '15—19. Rec: Cricket. a: Bygate, Wrockwardine Rd, Wellington, Salop. t : 16.

MUSSEN, Sir Gerald, Kt. b : Dunedin, New Zealand 1872. e : Southland Hgh Sch Invercargill N.Z. m: Florence Elizabeth Gordon. s : 2. d : 1. Dir ot Several Industries. n.a: Sydney Dly Telegraph 1897—1907, Founder with late J. E. Davidson Ev News Adelaide '22. Publ: Australia Tomorrow ; Family Spirit in Australian Industry ; The Humanising of Commerce & Industry. s.s: Industrial Policy in Industry, Developing New Industries. Rec: Golf. a: 185 Prospect Hill Rd, Canterbury, Melbourne, Australia.

MUSSER, John, A.M., Ph.D. b : Huntingdon, Pennsylvania 1887. e : Mercersburg Acad, Franklin & Marshall Coll, Univ of Penn. m : Grace Winter Greene. s : 1. d : 1. Dean Emeritus Graduate Sch New York Univ 1943—. Publ: Establishment of Maximilian's Empire in Mexico. Ctr : N.Y. Her Trib, Miss Valley Hist Review. Rec : Yachting. c : Seaside Park Yacht. a : 106 D. St, Seaside Park, New Jersey, U.S.A.

MUSSILMAN, Thomas Edgar, A.M., Sc.D. b : Quincy, Illinois 1887. e : Shattuck Mil Acad, Univ of Illinois, Carthage Coll. m : Mary Locke Scripps. d : 2. Executive, Instructor, Publisher & Writer. n.a : Quincy Herald-Whig, Nature Mag, Country Life in America. Publ: History of the Birds of Illinois ; One Grand Year in Nature. s.s : Ornithology, Herpetology, Mycology, Botany. Rec : Tennis. a : 124 South 24th St, Quincy, Adams Co, Illinois, U.S.A. T : 2097.

MUSSOLINI, Benito. Prime Minister of Italy. Publ: Napoleon, The Hundred Days (play). a: c/o Sidgwick & Jackson Ltd, 44 Museum St, W.C.1.

MUSTOE, Nelson Edwin, M.A., LL.B. b: Woodstock, S. Africa 1896. e: Wynberg H.S. & T.C.D. m: Edith Lake Patra. s : 1. Barrister. Publ: Law and Organisation of the British Civil Service; Vendors and Purchasers (2nd edn); Estate Agent's Commission (with J. Stevenson); Agricultural Holdings; etc. c.t: Law Journ, Estates Gazette, Builder, Incorp Auctioneers' Journ. s.s: Econ, land ownership & C.o.E. Lecturer in Law at City of Lon Col 1927-31. Exam in Agri Law Lon Univ. Rec: Tennis. c : R.EconS., Roy Emp Soc. a: Beaufort, Radlett, Herts. t: 6317.

MUTCH, Nathan, M.A., M.D.(Cantab.) F.R.C.P.(Lond). b : Rochdale 1886. e : Manch Gr Sch, Camb Univ, Guy's Hosp Lond. m : Eileen C. Arbuthnot Lane. s : 1. d : 1. Cons Phys to Guy's Hosp Lond. n.a: Ed Board Brit Journ of Pharmacology & Chemotherapy. Publ : Cocaine ; Chapters in Colyer's Dental Pathology ; Arbuthnot Lane's Intestinal Stasis, etc. Ctr : Journ of Physiology, Journ of Pharmacology & Experimental Therapeutics, B.M.J., Practitioner, Quarterly Journ of Med, Canadian Practitioner, N.Y. Med Journ, etc. s.s: Rheumatism, Pharmacology. c: R.A.C. a: Pitt-White, Uplyme, Devon, & 84 Harley St, London, W.1. T : Lyme Regis 94 & Langham 3949.

MYATT, William Arthur. b: Newcastle-under-Lyme 1897. Ed Daily Gazette Karachi. c.t: Times, Morning Post, Daily Express, Statesman, Calcutta, Times of India, etc. s.s: India, Cent Asia, humour. War Service 1914-18. Rec: Tennis, travel. c: Authors'. P.E.N., M.J.I. a: Meherbai Lodge, Beaumont Rd, Karachi, India. t: Karachi 313.

MYER, George Val, F.R.I.B.A. b: 1883. e : Univ Coll Sch & Univ Coll. m : Betty Vera Cowell. Architect. Publ: Art & Engineering ; Camouflage. s.s : Art & Architectural Criticism. Rec ; Boatbuilding & golf. w.s : R.E. 1914—18 & '39—45. c : Walton Heath (Golf), Little Ship. a : 21 Grosvenor Cresc Mews, Hyde Park Corner, London, S.W.1. T : Sloane 3028.

MYER, H. n.a: Asst Ed. a: Jewish Times, 175 Fleet Street, E.C.4.

MYER, Morris. *b*: Rumania 1878. *e*: Rumanian Liceum Bacal. *m*: Rachel Bromberg. *s*: 4. *d*: 1. *n.a*: Ed & Mang Dir of Jewish Times Ltd 1913. Vice-Pres Zionist Fed of Gt Brit & Ire, Vice-Chrm Fed of Jewish Relief Organisations. Mem Jewish Board of Deputies, etc. *Publ*: Yiddish Utopia; George Eliot; Many Trans into Yiddish. *c.t*: N/ps & Periodicals Eng & Amer. *s.s*: Hist, politics, painting, dramatic art. Brit by Naturalisation. *a*: 60 Ashbourne Av, N.W.11. *t*: Speedwell 7338.

MYER, Reginald. *b*: Hereford 1879. *e*: City of Lon Sc & Priv. *m*: Hon Elsie d. of 1st Lord Swaything. *s*: 1. *d*: 2. **Mang Dir.** *Publ*: A Gross Calculator; Chats on Old English Tobacco Jars. *c.t*: Times. *s.s*: Silver Resiste, Old Eng Pottery & Flemish Tapestries. etc. *Rec*: Skating, golf. *c*: Authors, Almacks. etc. *a*: 50 Westbourne Terr, W.2. *t*: Pad 6638.

MYERS, Rev. A. J. William, M.A., B.D., Ph.D. *b*: Prince Edward Island, Canada 1877. *e*: Prince of Wales Coll, Dalhousie Univ Halifax, Presbyterian Theol Coll Halifax, Univ of Columbia. *m*: Mae Ethel Dickenson. Clergyman & Prof, Head of Dept of Educ Hartford Seminary Foundation 1907—43, Minister Wanstead United Church Toronto '45—. *Publ*: The Old Testament in the Sunday School; Teaching Values of the Old Testament; Christian Life in the Community; What Is Religious Education; Teachers of Religion; Religion for Today; etc. *Ctr*: Religious Educ, Social Science, etc. *s.s*: Religious Educ, Religion, Worship. *Rec*: Bowls, gardening, reading. *a*: 118 Lytton Boulevard, Toronto 12, Canada. *T*: MA 8409.

MYERS, Alec Reginald, M.A., F.R.Hist.S. *b*: Huddersfield, Yorks 1912. *e*: Huddersfield Coll, Manch Univ. *m*: Christabel Ruth Owen. *d*: 1. Lect in Univ of Liverpool. *Ctr*: English Hist Review, Univ of Toronto Law Journ, Chambers's Ency, John Rylands Library Bulletin. *s.s*: Mediæval Hist. *Rec*: Tennis, badminton, gardening. *c*: Univ (L'pool). *w.s*: Royal Navy 1942—45. *a*: 12 Park Rd South, Birkenhead, Cheshire.

MYERS, Alys. *b*: M/C. *e*: M/C H.S. Journalist. *n.a*: Ed Woman's Page, Blackpool Times 1930—33. Pres Fylde Art Soc '31—32. Hon Sec (Blackpool Br) Nat League of Young Lib '29—. *c.t*: News-Chron, M/C Guardian, Sunday Mercury, Jewish Chron, M/C Evening News, etc. *s.s*: Women's interests, human news stories. 1st woman from locality to broadcast talks. Designer of book plates & black & white illus. *Rec*: Reading, swimming. *a*: 82 Osbourne Rd, S. Shore, Blackpool. *t*: 42026.

MYERS, Arthur Wallis, C.B.E. *b*: Kettering 1878. *e*: Watford & The Leys, Cam. *m*: Lilian A. Gentry. *s*: 1. *d*: 4. Journalist & Author. *n.a*: Daily Telegraph 1908—. Lawn Tennis Ed The Field '07—29, Ed of Ayres' Lawn Tennis Almanack '08—. *Publ*: Lawn Tennis at Home & Abroad; The Complete Lawn Tennis Player; Lawn Tennis: Its Principles and Practice; Captain Anthony Wilding; The Story of the Davis Cup; Fifty Years of Wimbledon (Jubilee Official Volume); On & off the Court (with A. F. Wilding); Britain Transformed; Memory's Parade; War Speeches of British Ministers (Edited). *c.t*: Daily Telegraph, The Sportsman (U.S.A.), etc. *s.s*: Lawn tennis. Founder of International Lawn Tennis Club, '24, Capt Brit Lawn Tennis Teams in S. Africa & India & on the Continent. Chevalier of Legion of Honour. *Rec*: Golf. *a*: Berrow, Epsom. *t*: Epsom 488.

MYERS, Bernard E., C.M.G. *b*: N.Z. *e*: Wellington Col, N.Z. & Edin Univ. *m*: Violet Hayman. *d*: 3. Physician. *n.a*: Hon Ed Clinical Section Proc Roy Soc Med 1929—32. *Publ*: Letters of a Professional Man; Practical Handbook on the Diseases of Children; The Care of Children; etc. *s.s*: Medicine. War Service *Rec*: Croquet. *c*: Savage, Roehampton, Edin Univ. *a*: 26 Devonshire Pl, W.1. *t*: Welbeck 6461.

MYERS, Denys P. *b*: Newton, Iowa 1884. *e*: Harvard. *m*: Ethel May Johnston. *s*: 1. Publicist. *n.a*: Boston Herald 1903—07, Boston Globe '08, Chris Sci Mon '08—10, Ed & Writer World Peace Foundation '10—42. *Publ*: Notes on Control of Foreign Relations; Industry, Governments & Labour; Origin & Conclusion of Paris Pact; The Reparation Settlement; World Disarmament—Its Problems & Prospects; Handbook of the League of Nations; Massachusetts & the First Ten Amendments to the Constitution; Process of Constitutional Amendment; The Treaty of Versailles; Annotations of the Text of the Treaty; etc. *Ctr*: N.Y. Times, Current Hist, etc. *s.s*: Internat Relations. *c*: Cosmos (Wash). *a*: 3401 Sedgwick St, N.W., Washington 8, D.C., U.S.A. *T*: Woodley 5334.

MYERS, Garry Cleveland, A.B., Ph.D. *b*: Sylvan, Pennsylvania 1884. *e*: Ursinus Coll, Columbia Univ. *m*: Caroline Elizabeth Clark. *s*: 2. *d*: 1. Psychologist, Editor, Newpaper Columnist. *n.a*: Ed-in-Chief Children's Activities 1934—46, Founder-Ed Highlights for Children '46—. *Publ*: The Modern Parent; Developing Personality in Child at School; Building Personality in the Child; Modern Family; Learning to be Likable; The Learner & His Attitude; (Collab) Books & Babies; Measuring Minds; Myers Mental Measures. *Ctr*: Many newsps in U.S. & Canada, scientific & educ journs. *s.s*: Child Development & Guidance, Family Relations, Personality & Mental Health. *Rec*: Fishing, gardening. *a*: Boyds Mill, Pennsylvania, U.S.A. *T*: Beachlake 30-R-5.

MYERS, George Norman M.D., PhD., M.Sc., B.S., B.Sc.(Hons), A.I.C., F.R.S.M. *b*: Newcastle-on-Tyne 1898. *e*: Univs of Cam & Durham. *m*: Florence Karen Danielsen. *s*: 1. *n.a*: Ed Univ of Durham Col of Med Gazette 1923—28. *Publ*: Cow's Synopsis of Pharmacology; Action of Some New Narcotic Drugs; Substitutes for Morphine & Heroin; etc. *c.t*: Journ of Hyg, B.M.J., etc. *s.s*: Therapeutics, med. Teacher in Univ of Cam (Med). Exam in Pharmacology & Therapeutics Univ of Cam. *Rec*: Riding, tennis. *c*: Mem Soc of Apothecaries, Lon. *a*: 7 Grantchester Rd. Cam. *t*: 639.

MYERS, J. E., O.B.E., D.Sc. *b*: Bolton 1890. *e*: M/C G.S. & Univ. *m*: Elsie Ingram. *s*: 1. Snr Tutor & Sec to Faculty of Sci, M/C. *Publ*: Physico-Chemical Periodicity. *c.t*: Observer. *Rec*: Gardening, Vice-Chm Jt Matric Bd. *a*: Kinder Rood, Ridge Av, Marple. *t*: 253.

MYERS, James, A.B. *b*: Owasco, N.Y. 1882. *e*: Columbia Univ, Auburn Theol Seminary. *m*: Marjorie Ripley Clapp. *s*: 3. *d*: 1. Church Official. *Publ*: Do You Know Labour?; Religion Lends a Hand; Representative Government in Industry; Prayers Personal & Social; Federal Council Churches. *s.s*: Labour Relations, Churches & Social Action, Religious Interpretation. *a*: 76 Irving Pl, New York, N.Y., U.S.A.

MYERS, Jay Arthur, M.S., M.D., Ph.D. *b*: Croton, Ohio 1888. *e*: Univs of Ohio, Cornell & Minnesota. *m*: Faithe Lavonne McCracken. *s*: 2. *d*: 2. Prof of Medicine, Public Health Univ of Minnesota Med & Graduate Schs. *n.a*: Ed Diseases of the Chest 1945—, Chmn Ed Bd, Journal-Lancet '30—. *Publ*: The Chest & the Heart; The Evolution of Tuberculosis as Observed for Twenty Years at Lymanhurst; Man's Greatest Victory over Tuberculosis; Tuberculosis Among Children & Young Adults; Diseases of the Chest; Fighters of Fate; Childhood Type Tuberculosis—Lymanhurst; etc. *Ctr*: Many med journs. *s.s*: Diseases of the Chest. *Rec*: Writing, gardening. *a*: 730 La Salle Building, Minneapolis 2, Minnesota. *T*: Ma 4749.

MYERS, Leopold Hamilton. *b*: Cam 1881. *e*: Eton & Trin Col Cam. *m*: Elsie Palmer. *d*: 2. *Publ*: The Near & the Far; Prince Jali; etc. *c*: Travellers. *a*: Leckhampton Hse, Cam.

MYERS, Maurice. *b*: Lon 1883. *e*: City of Lon Sc. *m*: Elizabeth Grœnewoud. Journalist. *n.a*: Sub-Ed Cent News Ltd 1926–, previously Lon Ed Palestine Weekly, Chief Rep Jewish Chron. Mem N.U.J. '29–. *Publ*: The Passover Haggadah (trans in prose & verse). *c.t*: Jewish Chron, Punch, Trans Jewish Hist Soc, Daily Telegraph. *s.s*: Jewish hist, biog, etc. Formerly an active worker in Jewish community. War Service R.A.F. *a*: 3 Mowbray Rd, N.W.6. *t*: Willesden 1376.

MYERS, Thora Wallis. *b*: Ashtead, Surrey 1908. *e*: Glyn House North Foreland Thanet. Journalist, Mem N.U.J. *n.a*: Mang Ed The Guider 1934—37, Ed Asst Girl's Own Paper '43—47. *Publ*: Which Career For You. *Ctr*: Dly Mail Yr Book, Chris Herald, Star, *s.s*: Careers for Women & Girls, Youth Organisations. *Rec*: Lawn tennis. *a*: Berrow, Downs Ave, Epsom, Surrey. *T*: 488.

MYERS, Tom, J.P. New Woollen & Cotton Rag Merchant. *c.t*: Local press. *a*: Thornhill Lees, Dewsbury.

MYERS, W. A. *n.a*: Chief Rep Northern Echo & Northern Dispatch Darlington since 1928. *a*: The Northern Echo, Darlington. *T*: Darlington 2230.

MYERSON, Abraham, M.D. *b*: Yanova, Russia 1881. *e*: English Hgh Sch Boston, Tufts Med Sch. *m*: Dorothy Marion Loman. *s*: 2. *d*: 1. *Publ*: The Nervous Housewife; Foundations of Personality; Inheritance of Mental Diseases; When Life Loses its Zest; Psychology of Mental Disorders; The German Jew, His Share in Modern Culture (with I. Goldberg); Social Psychology; Eugenical Sterilisation. *Ctr*: Various Med & Sci Journs. *s.s*: Neurology & Psychiatry, Mental Disease. *Rec*: Reading, writing, research. *a*: 33 Taylor Crossway, Brookline, Massachusetts.

MYLREA, Norah. *b*: London 1904. *e*: Priv. *m*: N. C. Easey. *d*: 1. *n.a*: Outside Fashion Rep 1927—31 Portsmouth Newsps Ltd. *Publ*: Lisbeth of Browndown; The Mystery of the Eagle; Browndown Again; Unwillingly to School; That Mystery Girl; Spies at Candover; etc. *Ctr*: Spectator, Woman's Pictorial. *s.s*: Children's Fiction. *Rec*: Swimming, badminton, riding. *a*: 35 Kent Rd, Southsea, Hants. *T*: Portsmouth 4628.

MYRDDIN-EVANS, Sir Guildhaume, K.C.M.G., C.B. *e*: Llandovery & Christ Church Oxf. Civil Servant. *Publ*: The Employment Exchange Service of Great Britain (with T. S. Chegwidden). *a*: 6 Chester Pl, Regent's Pk, London, N.W.1. *T*: Welbeck 5696.

MYRES, JOHN LINTON: professor of ancient history; b. Preston, Lancashire, Eng., July, 1869; s. William Miles and Jane (Linton) M.; educ. Winchester Coll. DEGREES: M.A. (Oxford), (Hon). D.Sc. (Wales), (Hon.) D. Litt. (Witwatersrand); m. Sophia Florence Ballance, July 25, 1895. AUTHOR: A Catalogue of the Cyprus Museum (with Dr. Ohnefalsch-Richter), 1899; A History of Rome, 1902; The Dawn of History, 1911; Notes and Queries in Anthropology (edited), 1912; Handbook of the Cesnola Collection of Antiquities from Cyprus, 1914; The Political Ideas of the Greeks (Bennett Lectures), 1927; Who Were the Greeks? (Sather Lectures, Univ. California), 1929. Contributor to Classical Rev., Annual of British School of Athens, Journ. of Hellenic Studies, Geographical Journ., Journ. Royal Anthropol. Inst., Scottish Geog. Mag., Folklore, Man, Eugenics Rev. and many other mags. General character of writing: historical. Relig. denom., Church of England. OFFICE: New College, Oxford. HOME: The Copse, Hincksey Hill, Oxford, Eng.